THE DOW JONES GUIDE TO THE WORLD STOCK MARKET

1996 EDITION

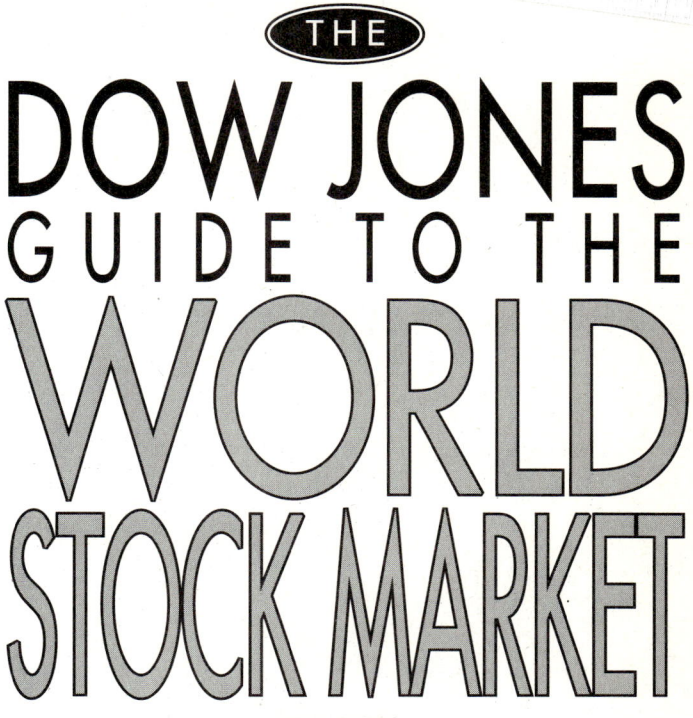

By the Editors of DOW JONES & COMPANY
In Association with MORNINGSTAR

PRENTICE HALL
Englewood Cliffs, New Jersey 07632

Prentice-Hall International (UK) Limited, *London*
Prentice-Hall of Australia Pty. Limited, *Sidney*
Prentice-Hall Canada, Inc., *Toronto*
Prentice-Hall Hispanoamericana, S.A., *Mexico*
Prentice Hall of India Private Limited, *New Delhi*
Prentice-Hall of Japan, Inc., *Tokyo*
Simon & Schuster Asia Pte. Ltd., *Singapore*
Editora Prentice-Hall do Brasil, Ltda., *Rio de Janeiro*

10 9 8 7 6 5 4 3 2 1

Library of Congress Cataloging-In-Publication Data

The Dow Jones guide to the world stock market / the editors of Dow Jones & Company, in association with Morningstar, Inc. — 1996-1997 ed.

p. cm.

Index Included

ISBN 0-13-398736-1 (alk. paper)

1. Stocks. 2. Corporations — Finance. 3. Stock exchanges.

I. Dow Jones & Co. II. Morningstar, Inc.

HG4661.D68 1995

332.63'22—dc 20 94 -43722

CIP

ISBN 0-13-398736-1

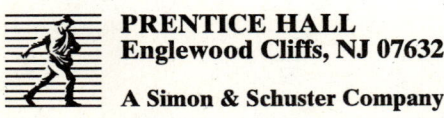

PRENTICE HALL
Englewood Cliffs, NJ 07632

A Simon & Schuster Company

Printed in the United States of America

Contents

Introduction

This is not a book intended to be read from cover to cover. It's a book to look up information when you need it, for investing or other purposes. But if you are interested in foreign stock markets, you could do no better than to read through the introductions to each country.

These are written by Dow Jones reporters stationed around the globe, on the scene in the countries they write about and familiar with the local stock markets because they cover them assiduously as business journalists. Reading through them, as I have in preparing this third volume of The Dow Jones Guide to the World Stock Markets, I was impressed anew with how thorough a grounding they provide in each country's economic and market trends.

And what are those trends? On the economic front, recovery and growth are in ascendancy throughout the world — particularly so in the Asia/Pacific region, but notably in Europe as well. The dominant influence in this regard — mentioned again and again by the writers — was the ability of the Federal Reserve to engineer a "soft landing" in the U.S. economy. In 1994, the Fed raised interest rates to decelerate growth and to head off an inflationary spiral before it got started. That move sent ripples of similar slowdowns around the globe, partly because many other countries' economies are closely tied to that of the U.S., and partly because still other countries chose to follow in the Fed's precautionary footsteps. The world's economic gears slowed, and investors collectively held their breath in apprehension of an international recession. Stock prices treaded water in some places, sank in others.

But, wonder of wonders, the U.S. economy began to show signs of renewed vigor in the second half of 1995. Jubilant investors sent U.S. stock prices soaring. The happy mood spread from country to country as their economies also strengthened but inflation remained docile. The repercussions haven't fully played out as this volume goes to press, but it's easy to conclude that one would be unwise to underestimate the influence of U.S. economic policy on the health of world business.

The U.S. wasn't alone in exercising global force over the past 12 months. In December, Mexico surprised investors by devaluing its peso. The resulting financial shock clobbered Mexico's stock market, of course, but it had repercussions for "emerging" or "developing" countries worldwide. If it can happen in Mexico, investors reasoned, it can happen anywhere. They expressed their dismay by selling stocks in most of these countries, causing slumps from which prices were still struggling back nearly a year later.

As for stock markets, the worldwide trend is thankfully toward greater openness — "transparency" is the term of choice among investors — and less tolerance for insider trading and other abuses. In several country introductions, you will read about these reforms reaching for an "international standard." There isn't any such thing officially, but unofficially the regulatory benchmark is that of the U.S. The U.S. market may have its troubles, but it is light years ahead of most others in the world in accessibility and fair play.

Another aspect of international "standards" is investors' expectations as they venture beyond their home countries. Again, the U.S. takes the lead in the form of investors demanding more and more that they be treated overseas as they are at home. And they put their money where their demands are, which in many cases isn't the home markets of the stocks they are trading. Many foreign stocks are traded in London, for example, rather than in Germany, Belgium, the Netherlands or wherever. The exchanges in the home countries are working hard to get that business back, an effort that typically includes reforms of market procedures, lower taxes and other moves to attract investors.

Of course, we understand that you bought this book primarily for the company listings. There are more of them than ever before — the total approaches 2,700, to be more specific — and three more countries than the previous edition, for a total of 29. The new countries are The Philippines, South Africa and South Korea.

For those of you who have telephoned or written to request adding certain countries, please be assured that the additions you want are on our list, too. For reasons of quality control and sheer manageability, we have chosen to build this annual volume in conjunction with the Dow Jones World Stock Index. The countries included herein are those in the index, with the exception of Taiwan; that country has been excluded from the world index because it doesn't allow individual foreign investors to buy its stocks, but this restriction is expected to be lifted, or at least modified, soon. In any event, as soon as we can add countries to the world index we will include them in this book.

The Dow Jones World Stock Index was introduced as a new benchmark of stock performance for global investors in the January 5, 1993, edition of *The Wall Street Journal.* Dow Jones & Company, which publishes the Journal, created the index to provide a comprehensive measure of stock performance worldwide as investors' interest in global markets grows rapidly. The world index is the latest addition to an expanding tool kit of market barometers from Dow Jones. The oldest and best-known tool is the Dow Jones Industrial Average, which tracks 30 blue-chip stocks of large companies that are widely followed by individual and institutional investors.

The Dow Jones World Stock Index is a global expansion of the Dow Jones Equity Market Index for the U.S., which organizes the complex U.S. market into nine economic sectors and 124 industry groups. Now, the world index stocks are placed into these same industry groups, plus a few extra to accommodate types of companies whose shares aren't traded in the U.S. (such as fishing concerns, consumer electronics and plantations).

As we were constructing the indexes, we realized that people would be curious about the companies whose stocks make up our index. That's what led us to produce this book. Far more than a simple, giant list, this book presents a miniature portrait of every company. A brief description tells about the main lines of business, sometimes a bit of history and any recent major events affecting the company. Each company's industry-group assignment is included, as are three years of sales or revenue as well as earnings. Ratios of stock prices to per-share profit and book value, plus the dividend yield, provide more readings on each company's performance. If your information appetite is larger, we give the address and phone number (for both voice and fax, when available) so you can contact the companies directly. Companies are listed by country; index in back let you search worldwide by alphabetical order and by industry group.

These corporate portraits are the work of Morningstar, Inc., a Chicago-based company best known for its mutual-fund data and analysis. Morningstar has expanded into publications about non-U.S. stocks, starting with *Morningstar Japan* in 1992 and *Morningstar ADRs* in 1994. In 1994, Morningstar purchased a U.S. equities database and software product from Marketbase, and launched *U.S. Equities OnFloppy*. In its search for basic and

Dow Jones World Stock Index Performance

Dow Jones Europe Stock Index Performance

Dow Jones Asia/Pacific Stock Index Performance

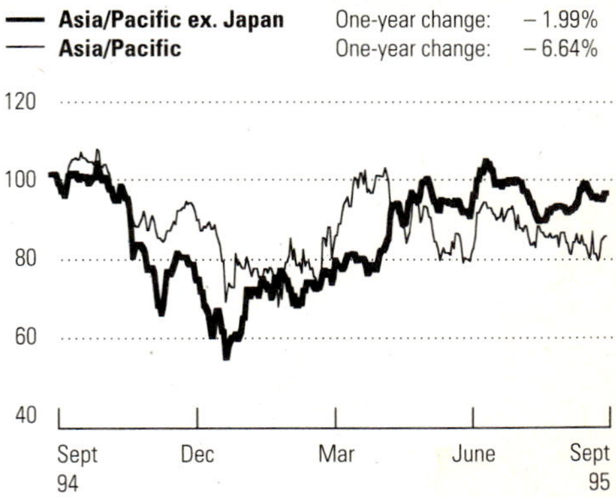

fundamental information about companies, Morningstar goes to original source documents — annual reports, filings with regulatory agencies and so on — many of which are available only in the native language of each country. The ability to translate pertinent business information into common-sense English is prized at both Morningstar and Dow Jones, and the two companies are proud to collaborate on this book.

In addition, some of the economic data for each country came from the New York office of EcoWin, a comprehensive database for Windows-based personal computers.

The Dow Jones World Stock Index offers superior measures of stock market performance by providing investors with two comparative views: geographic and industrial. Investors can assess the political, economic and financial forces affecting the global markets and measure how an individual issue has performed against its peers on a global, regional, or national basis. For example, they can look at the auto manufacturing industry just in the U.S., Europe, or the Far East, or around the world.

Countries in the world index are grouped into three geographic regions: Asia/Pacific, Europe/Africa, and the Americas. The industry groups are organized within nine broad sectors, such as basic materials, utilities, consumer, and financial. The same industry-group structure is used in every country, and the same criteria were applied in selecting stocks. That way, investors are assured of comparability when they assess one group of stocks in Japan, for example, and the same group in the U.S.

Each country's index is calculated in the country's own currency, plus the dollar. The regional and world indexes are calculated in the four "global" currencies for the convenience of investors around the world. Calculations are made in multiple currencies because the value of a stock portfolio is affected both by the prices of stocks and by the exchange rate of two currencies: the currency in which stocks trade and the one in which the portfolio is measured. When the two currencies are the same, as is the case for a U.S. investor with only U.S. stocks, exchange rates aren't an issue. But currency translations can add or subtract substantially from market performance when the stocks are in other countries.

While this book is based on a stock index, you don't have to be an investor to profit from having this volume within reach on your shelf. Nowhere else is there such a compendium of useful information about so many companies in so many countries of the world. Business people, researchers, government and non-profit organization employees—this book is for all of you whose interest and curiosity stretch beyond the horizon.

John A. Prestbo,
Editor of the
Dow Jones World Stock Index

Statistical Overview

Dow Jones World Stock Index Performance

In U.S. Dollars

Region/Country	09/30/95 Closing Index	12 Month Change%	12 Month High	12 Month Low	Weighting
Americas	**136.97**	**23.65**	**137.60**	**106.19**	**42.88**
Canada	106.17	4.44	109.86	89.01	1.71
Mexico	81.47	-52.70	175.28	47.80	0.43
U.S.	553.41	26.75	555.80	420.11	40.74
Europe/Africa	**132.44**	**14.60**	**135.89**	**111.61**	**25.70**
Austria	103.94	-1.65	113.71	95.91	0.16
Belgium	132.83	15.96	137.64	111.37	0.57
Denmark	109.73	12.91	115.10	92.02	0.34
Finland	289.60	46.63	303.04	188.52	0.37
France	114.60	4.04	127.25	104.68	2.93
Germany	135.30	12.95	142.97	115.32	3.24
Ireland	148.34	20.81	150.72	116.86	0.16
Italy	108.30	-14.28	123.75	96.93	1.02
Netherlands	157.55	19.53	161.76	129.00	2.11
Norway	133.16	18.53	140.54	110.62	0.21
South Africa	129.64	-1.45	141.97	118.90	1.34
Spain	103.54	9.43	109.95	84.41	0.84
Sweden	167.05	45.15	167.05	113.66	1.17
Switzerland	211.37	31.58	216.12	156.14	2.70
United Kingdom	121.74	14.69	124.32	102.79	8.54
Eur/Africa (ex.U.K. & S.A.)	141.22	14.56	145.44	118.86	15.83
Asia/Pacific	**114.95**	**-7.20**	**126.51**	**105.71**	**31.42**
Australia	126.06	9.18	129.71	105.85	1.54
Hong Kong	215.95	-2.37	219.09	158.31	2.04
Indonesia	177.23	-6.88	199.98	150.13	0.20
Japan	108.74	-8.28	121.55	100.71	24.66
Malaysia	226.36	-10.65	256.08	182.55	1.11
New Zealand	174.72	8.91	189.29	153.09	0.20
Philippines	113.69	-29.97	165.05	101.59	0.13
Singapore	181.09	0.01	198.39	150.60	0.78
South Korea	161.71	-6.81	183.26	138.74	0.17
Taiwan	113.69	-29.95	165.05	101.59	—†
Thailand	198.55	-11.74	234.45	168.46	0.58
Pacific (So. Asia)	198.91	-8.97	222.65	167.21	2.68
Pacific (ex. Japan)	170.56	-2.74	176.66	139.97	6.75
World	**127.96**	**9.98**	**128.89**	**109.36**	**100.00**
World (ex. U.S.)	120.57	0.54	124.00	108.24	59.26

Indexes based on 6/30/82=100 for U.S., 12/31/91=100 for World.

†Not a component of the World Stock Index.

Country Performance in U.S. Dollars

Ending 09/30/95

Country	12 Month Change%
Best Performing Countries	
Finland	46.63
Sweden	45.15
Switzerland	31.58
USA	26.75
Ireland	20.81
Worst Performing Countries	
Mexico	-52.69
Philippines	-29.97
Taiwan	-29.97
Italy	-14.28
Thailand	-11.74

Country Performance in Local Currency

Ending 09/30/95

Country	12 Month Change%
Best Performing Countries	
Sweden	34.67
Finland	27.92
USA	26.75
Ireland	21.63
Switzerland	19.43
Worst Performing Countries	
Taiwan	-27.26
Mexico	-12.10
Malaysia	-12.06
Thailand	-11.58
South Korea	-10.39

Industry Group Performance Evaluation

Industry Group	In U.S. Dollars 09/30/95 Closing Index	12 Month Change%	Weighting	P/E Ratio	P/B Ratio
Dow Jones World Stock Index	**127.96**	**9.98**	**100.00**	**19.68**	**2.12**
BASIC MATERIALS	**131.35**	**-0.66**	**7.09**	**28.55**	**2.06**
Chemicals - All	134.46	4.27	3.09	21.93	2.19
Commodity Chemicals	141.63	2.44	2.09	21.42	2.06
Specialty Chemicals	120.14	8.46	1.01	23.06	2.52
Forest Products	152.64	-5.46	0.40	14.30	1.91
Mining	144.13	3.94	0.45	21.13	2.29
Non-Ferrous Metals - All	134.34	5.62	0.74	NMF	2.03
Aluminum	147.60	14.38	0.40	28.16	2.12
Non-Ferrous Metals - Other (Exc. Aluminum)	119.01	-4.62	0.33	NMF	1.93
Paper Products	124.10	3.47	0.88	28.97	1.74
Precious Metals	146.39	-9.05	0.41	25.08	2.32
Steel	114.90	-15.54	1.12	NMF	1.87
CONSUMER CYCLICAL	**130.83**	**2.50**	**14.48**	**25.26**	**2.09**
Advertising	168.17	19.11	0.08	28.46	4.96
Airlines	107.29	3.20	0.70	43.72	2.27
Automobile Manufacturers	156.23	-0.76	2.77	17.70	1.55
Automobile Parts & Equipment	141.05	-1.77	0.99	28.01	1.98
Tires & Rubber	145.02	-2.34	0.31	27.31	2.00
Other Auto Parts	139.10	-1.50	0.68	28.37	1.97
Entertainment & Leisure- All	139.18	15.94	2.14	36.01	3.07
Casinos	214.90	2.82	0.27	65.10	3.06
Recreational Products & Services - All	128.80	17.00	1.47	39.73	3.08
Entertainment	166.42	22.16	0.24	NMF	10.45
Other Recreational Products & Services	130.38	15.60	0.95	37.24	2.63
Toy Manufacturers	99.53	17.49	0.28	27.28	2.98
Restaurants	150.24	21.34	0.41	22.20	3.06
Home Construction	139.91	1.40	0.65	19.01	1.61
Home Furnishings & Appliances	129.31	-9.62	1.11	NMF	1.44
Consumer Electronics	128.13	-12.36	0.81	NMF	1.32
Other Home Furnishings	133.45	-0.65	0.31	16.84	1.91
Lodging	118.24	-0.24	0.28	23.49	1.45
Media (Publishing & Broadcasting)	154.76	12.97	1.65	22.43	3.46
Broadcasting	165.83	8.63	0.58	41.21	4.87
Publishing	150.55	15.27	1.07	18.15	3.01
Retailers - Broadline	108.45	1.38	2.13	22.90	2.41
Retailers - Specialty - All	113.26	2.52	1.30	18.15	2.61
Apparel Retailers	84.83	4.24	0.27	18.13	2.32
Drug-based Retailers	151.99	25.72	0.22	11.68	2.92
Other Specialty Retailers	113.90	-3.10	0.80	21.35	2.65
Textiles & Apparel - All	96.39	-8.82	0.69	39.85	1.66
Footwear	110.15	19.05	0.14	21.25	2.56
Clothing & Fabrics	93.01	-13.84	0.55	50.61	1.53
CONSUMER, NON-CYCLICAL	**120.15**	**24.21**	**16.04**	**24.44**	**3.56**
Beverages - All	125.73	24.76	2.58	21.86	3.54
Distillers & Brewers	102.86	12.18	1.29	17.51	2.34
Soft Drinks	161.95	41.29	1.29	30.02	8.01
Consumer & Household Products & Svcs - All	142.52	21.34	1.13	21.07	3.70
Household Services	146.32	9.46	0.12	16.98	2.66
Household Products - All	142.30	22.75	1.01	21.76	3.90
Household Products (Durable)	94.58	2.45	0.14	20.87	2.66
Household Products (Non-Durable)	153.82	26.77	0.87	21.91	4.21

Industry Group Performance Evaluation

Industry Group	09/30/95 Closing Index (In U.S. Dollars)	12 Month Change%	Weighting	P/E Ratio	P/B Ratio
Cosmetics & Personal Care	146.60	18.59	0.55	27.81	3.98
Food	106.67	7.94	2.90	20.27	2.60
Fishing	76.59	-11.21	0.03	82.14	2.65
Other Food	107.15	8.21	2.87	20.09	2.60
Food Retailers & Wholesalers	127.82	12.63	1.14	24.64	3.44
Health Care Providers	176.20	2.48	0.35	20.35	3.19
Medical Supplies	125.71	30.72	0.62	25.47	4.06
Pharmaceuticals	114.93	38.55	5.53	22.51	4.43
Tobacco	109.98	30.73	1.25	15.95	4.05
ENERGY	**121.21**	**9.58**	**5.85**	**23.73**	**1.70**
Coal	106.50	-7.33	0.06	26.48	1.97
Oilfield Equipment & Services - All	117.13	17.13	0.35	30.39	2.49
Oil Drilling	135.44	25.31	0.04	NMF	2.14
Oilfield Equipment & Services - Other	113.55	16.03	0.30	26.89	2.55
Oil - Integrated Majors	125.55	13.74	4.06	20.77	1.60
Oil - Secondary	103.61	-4.58	1.12	47.70	1.86
Pipelines	151.19	11.56	0.27	16.22	1.94
FINANCIAL	**125.06**	**7.92**	**21.47**	**11.90**	**1.55**
Banks - All	120.62	6.20	12.97	9.27	1.69
Banks - Money Center	118.21	5.37	7.51	26.32	1.89
Banks - Regional	124.20	7.40	5.47	5.10	1.50
Banks - Central U.S.	851.85	22.70	0.75	12.96	1.99
Banks - Eastern U.S.	548.48	36.75	0.64	13.80	1.93
Banks - Southern U.S.	530.36	30.24	0.56	12.09	1.85
Banks - Western U.S.	739.06	22.70	0.23	12.78	2.05
Financial Services - Diversified	139.96	15.10	2.07	16.67	1.74
Insurance - All	134.72	19.95	3.90	20.61	1.73
Insurance - Full Line	139.71	21.42	1.80	20.55	1.39
Insurance - Life & Health	134.89	21.80	0.61	16.40	2.39
Insurance - Property & Casualty	127.63	17.28	1.49	23.44	2.03
Real-Estate Investment	112.42	-10.14	1.26	19.99	0.63
Savings & Loans (U.S. Only)	129.06	26.54	0.11	13.29	1.26
Securities Brokers	146.97	2.67	1.16	NMF	1.67
INDUSTRIAL	**117.02**	**0.21**	**10.56**	**28.14**	**2.26**
Air Freight & Couriers	161.81	13.75	0.08	15.31	2.06
Building Materials	113.32	-7.19	1.49	24.98	1.94
Containers & Packaging	105.68	1.56	0.34	58.93	1.89
Electrical Components & Equipment	129.83	0.99	1.59	29.02	2.35
Factory Equipment	98.49	-11.26	0.35	59.12	2.19
Heavy Construction	90.04	-5.06	0.98	35.91	1.72
Heavy Machinery	134.32	-4.43	0.48	28.84	2.36
Industrial & Commercial Services - All	114.75	5.23	1.47	22.65	2.73
Pollution Control, Waste Management	84.29	2.65	0.32	21.18	3.26
General Industrial & Commercial Services	128.13	5.68	1.15	23.08	2.61
Industrial - Diversified	144.31	11.97	1.61	20.90	2.53
Marine Transportation	102.48	-7.57	0.46	30.37	1.99
Railroads	119.24	6.94	1.16	56.01	3.22
Transportation Equipment - All	114.97	-6.47	0.31	20.77	1.88
Land Transportation	124.75	1.43	0.19	15.13	1.83
Shipbuilding	99.86	-16.05	0.13	31.14	1.93
Trucking	104.43	-13.85	0.25	28.69	2.01

Industry Group Performance Evaluation

Industry Group	09/30/95 Closing Index (In U.S. Dollars)	12 Month Change%	Weighting	P/E Ratio	P/B Ratio
TECHNOLOGY	**173.04**	**29.59**	**11.88**	**25.44**	**3.05**
Aerospace & Defense	188.76	42.48	0.76	27.69	2.34
Communications Technology	169.31	16.19	3.45	39.25	3.66
Communications Tech w/o AT&T (U.S. Only)	1105.46	57.04	0.76	30.36	5.67
Computers	147.17	38.18	1.86	15.03	2.66
Computers without IBM (U.S. Only)	465.93	61.38	0.91	23.07	3.20
Diversified Technology	164.56	23.35	2.32	23.22	2.17
Industrial Technology	138.94	15.36	0.24	55.13	2.78
Medical & Biotechnology - All	125.45	54.15	0.43	41.12	6.29
Biotechnology	120.52	47.15	0.19	54.29	6.58
Advanced Medical Technology	131.34	62.28	0.24	34.38	6.06
Office Equipment	151.87	7.52	0.45	29.81	2.16
Semiconductors & related	375.93	74.59	1.13	17.74	3.45
Software	201.27	43.20	1.25	43.49	6.97
UTILITIES	**114.05**	**7.61**	**8.82**	**18.90**	**1.98**
Electrical Utilities - All	109.99	9.68	3.66	16.56	1.64
Electrical Utilities - Central U.S.	104.34	18.38	0.43	13.26	1.51
Electrical Utilities - Eastern U.S.	97.38	18.70	0.49	12.89	1.20
Electrical Utilities - Southern U.S.	110.30	19.58	0.58	14.95	1.51
Electrical Utilities - Western U.S.	88.17	25.51	0.31	13.14	1.34
Gas Utilities	84.77	-4.75	0.60	23.06	1.85
Telephone Systems - All	133.31	7.61	4.26	22.07	2.61
Regional Telephone Systems (U.S. Only)	140.37	22.39	2.01	27.66	3.28
Mobile Communication Systems (U.S. Only)	198.67	3.99	0.18	NMF	3.35
Long Distance Telephone Systems (U.S. Only)	138.73	24.18	0.27	16.74	2.21
Water Utilities	118.46	7.58	0.30	12.09	1.25
INDEPENDENTS	**138.47**	**4.82**	**3.81**	**27.89**	**2.25**
Conglomerates	149.41	11.65	2.94	21.51	2.52
Overseas Trading	106.51	-13.04	0.77	NMF	1.58
Plantations	224.71	-13.87	0.10	26.23	2.36

Best Performing Industry Groups in U.S. Dollars

1 Year Ending 09/30/95

Industry Group	12 Month Change%	P/E Ratio	P/B Ratio
Semiconductors & related	74.59	17.74	3.45
Advanced Medical Technology	62.28	34.38	6.06
Medical & Biotechnology - All	54.15	41.12	6.29
Biotechnology	47.15	54.29	6.58
Software	43.20	43.49	6.97
Aerospace & Defense	42.48	27.69	2.34
Soft Drinks	41.29	30.20	8.01
Pharmaceuticals	38.55	22.51	4.43
Computers	38.18	15.03	2.66
Banks - Eastern U.S.	36.75	13.80	1.93

Worst Performing Industry Groups in U.S. Dollars

1 Year Ending 09/30/95

Industry Group	12 Month Change%	P/E Ratio	P/B Ratio
Shipbuilding	-16.05	31.14	1.93
Steel	-15.54	NMF	1.87
Plantations	-13.87	26.23	2.36
Trucking	-13.85	28.69	2.01
Clothing & Fabrics	-13.84	50.61	1.53
Overseas Trading	-13.04	NMF	1.58
Consumer Electronics	-12.36	NMF	1.32
Factory Equipment	-11.26	59.12	2.19
Fishing	-11.21	82.14	2.65
Real-Estate Investment	-10.14	19.90	0.63

World Company Rankings

Largest Companies–Market Capitalization

as of 09/30/95

Company	Mkt. Cap. (US$Mil)	Country
Nippon Telegraph and Telephone	136,521	Japan
General Electric	107,255	United States
Royal Dutch/Shell	105,013	Netherlands/UK
AT&T	104,302	United States
Exxon	89,718	United States
Coca-Cola	87,022	United States
Toyota Motor	71,063	Japan
Philip Morris	70,141	United States
Merck & Co.	69,255	United States
Industrial Bank of Japan	68,354	Japan
Fuji Bank	61,490	Japan
Sumitomo Bank	60,660	Japan
Mitsubishi Bank	57,370	Japan
Wal-Mart Stores	57,146	United States
Dai-Ichi Kangyo Bank	56,500	Japan
Sanwa Bank	54,272	Japan
IBM	53,673	United States
Microsoft	53,000	United States
Procter & Gamble	52,928	United States
Intel	49,513	United States
Johnson & Johnson	48,014	United States
Motorola	45,045	United States
Singapore Airlines	43,443	Singapore
Hewlett-Packard	42,647	United States
Glaxo Wellcome	42,277	United Kingdom
British Petroleum	41,598	United Kingdom
Nestlé	41,152	Switzerland
American International	40,306	United States
PepsiCo	40,163	United States
Allianz	40,146	Germany
Mobil	39,411	United States
BT	39,191	United Kingdom
Nomura Securities	38,297	Japan
Du Pont	38,154	United States
GTE	38,146	United States
Unilever	37,148	Netherlands/UK
Bristol-Myers Squibb	36,961	United States
Tokyo Electric Power	36,511	Japan
BellSouth	36,309	United States
Sakura Bank	36,017	Japan
Hitachi	35,708	Japan
General Motors	35,035	United States
Pfizer	33,851	United States
Abbott Laboratories	33,825	United States
SBC Communications	33,516	United States
Ford Motor	33,431	United States
Matsushita Electric Industrial	32,064	Japan
Chevron	31,702	United States
Amoco	31,481	United States
Bank of Tokyo	30,487	Japan

Largest Companies–Net Income

as of 09/30/95

Company	Income (US$Mil)	Country
Ford Motor	5,308.0	United States
Exxon	5,100.0	United States
General Motors	4,900.6	United States
General Electric	4,726.0	United States
Philip Morris	4,725.0	United States
AT&T	4,710.0	United States
Chrysler	3,713.0	United States
Citicorp	3,366.0	United States
IBM	3,021.0	United States
Merck & Co.	2,997.0	United States
Du Pont	2,727.0	United States
BT	2,721.0	United Kingdom
Wal-Mart Stores	2,681.0	United States
HSBC Holdings	2,666.0	Hong Kong
Procter & Gamble	2,645.0	United States
Coca-Cola	2,554.0	United States
GTE	2,451.0	United States
British Petroleum	2,426.2	United Kingdom
Nestlé	2,388.0	Switzerland
Intel	2,288.0	United States
Telefonos de Mexico	2,266.1	Mexico
Royal Dutch/Shell	2,248.6	Netherlands/UK
BankAmerica	2,176.0	United States
American International	2,175.5	United States
BellSouth	2,159.8	United States
FNMA	2,132.0	United States
Roche	2,101.4	Switzerland
Johnson & Johnson	2,006.0	United States
Glaxo Wellcome	1,953.5	United Kingdom
BAT Industries	1,853.8	United Kingdom
Bristol-Myers Squibb	1,842.0	United States
Barclays	1,813.8	United Kingdom
Amoco	1,789.0	United States
PepsiCo	1,752.0	United States
Volvo	1,725.6	Sweden
Chevron	1,693.0	United States
NationsBank	1,690.0	United States
NatWest	1,681.5	United Kingdom
SBC Communications	1,648.7	United States
Hanson	1,613.6	United Kingdom
Hewlett-Packard	1,599.0	United States
Motorola	1,560.0	United States
American Home Products	1,528.3	United States
Abbott Laboratories	1,516.7	United States
Sears Roebuck & Co.	1,454.0	United States
U.S. WEST	1,426.0	United States
American Express	1,413.0	United States
Ciba-Geigy	1,405.6	Switzerland
BTR	1,340.0	United Kingdom
Toyota Motor	1,337.5	Japan

Largest Companies–Revenue
(as of 09/30/95)

Company	Revenue (US$Mil)	Country
Mitsubishi	177,048	Japan
Mitsui & Co.	172,673	Japan
Itochu	168,981	Japan
Sumitomo	163,596	Japan
General Motors	154,951	United States
Marubeni	151,223	Japan
Ford Motor	128,439	United States
Exxon	112,128	United States
Nissho Iwai	101,571	Japan
Wal-Mart Stores	82,494	United States
Toyota Motor	82,317	Japan
Hitachi	76,958	Japan
AT&T	75,094	United States
Nippon Telegraph and Telephone	71,332	Japan
Matsushita Electric Industrial	70,429	Japan
Tomen	70,383	Japan
Mobil	66,757	United States
Philip Morris	65,125	United States
Daimler-Benz	64,523	Germany
IBM	64,052	United States
General Electric	60,109	United States
Nissan Motor	59,137	Japan
Nichimen	56,590	Japan
Kanematsu	56,241	Japan
Sears Roebuck & Co.	54,559	United States
Siemens	51,117	Germany
British Petroleum	50,948	United Kingdom
Tokyo Electric Power	50,707	Japan
Volkswagen	49,622	Germany
Chrysler	49,363	United States
Toshiba	48,561	Japan
Unilever	45,640	Netherlands/UK
Nestlé	41,803	Switzerland
Allianz	40,980	Germany
Fiat	40,626	Italy
Sony	40,377	Japan
VEBA	40,293	Germany
Honda Motor	40,202	Japan
Du Pont	39,333	United States
NEC	38,207	Japan
Elf Aquitaine	37,656	France
Japan Tobacco	35,502	Japan
Chevron	35,130	United States
UAP	34,971	France
Mitsubishi Motors	34,607	Japan
Royal Dutch/Shell	34,215	Netherlands/UK
Kmart	34,025	United States
Philips Electronics	33,689	The Netherlands
Procter & Gamble	33,434	United States
RWE	33,125	Germany

Largest Companies–Book Value
(as of 09/30/95)

Company	Book Value (US$Mil)	Country
Toyota Motor	58,112	Japan
Zurich Insurance	53,417	Switzerland
Nippon Telegraph and Telephone	50,019	Japan
Matsushita Electric Industrial	37,676	Japan
Exxon	37,415	United States
Hitachi	35,109	Japan
General Electric	26,387	United States
Sanwa Bank	23,528	Japan
IBM	23,413	United States
Dai-Ichi Kangyo Bank	22,987	Japan
Fuji Bank	22,973	Japan
Sumitomo Bank	22,333	Japan
Ford Motor	21,659	United States
Mitsubishi Bank	21,156	Japan
Sakura Bank	21,140	Japan
Royal Dutch/Shell	20,683	Netherlands/UK
Nomura Securities	19,830	Japan
BT	19,667	United Kingdom
BankAmerica	18,891	United States
AT&T	17,921	United States
Citicorp	17,769	United States
Union Bank of Switzerland	17,382	Switzerland
Tokyo Electric Power	17,322	Japan
British Petroleum	17,277	United Kingdom
Mobil	17,146	United States
Nissan Motor	16,540	Japan
American International	16,422	United States
Industrial Bank of Japan	16,306	Japan
Deutsche Bank	15,097	Germany
Chevron	14,596	United States
Amoco	14,382	United States
BellSouth	14,367	United States
Elf Aquitaine	14,321	France
Korea Electric Power	14,276	South Korea
Kansai Electric Power	13,929	Japan
Japan Tobacco	13,853	Japan
HSBC Holdings	13,790	Hong Kong
Mitsubishi Heavy Industries	13,636	Japan
Telecom Italia	13,328	Italy
Siemens	13,130	Germany
Daimler-Benz	13,065	Germany
Toshiba	12,949	Japan
Nestlé	12,934	Switzerland
Tokai Bank	12,885	Japan
Long-Term Credit Bank	12,844	Japan
General Motors	12,824	United States
Du Pont	12,822	United States
Philip Morris	12,786	United States
Fujitsu	12,735	Japan
Wal-Mart	12,726	United States

Glossary

ADR
American Depositary Receipt. This is a mechanism by which U.S. investors can hold ownership interest in shares of a foreign company. Each ADR represents a claim on a specific number of underlying foreign shares. The foreign shares are held by a U.S. sponsor bank on behalf of the ADR owner. The price of an ADR is denominated in U.S. dollars and fluctuates based on the change in share value, as well as any exchange-rate movements. For companies with American depositary receipts, the ADR trading symbol is listed.

Address
The address, telephone number, and fax number are those of the company's headquarters.

Book Value
The difference between a company's assets and its liabilities, usually expressed in per-share terms. Book value is also referred to as stockholders' equity and is calculated by subtracting liabilities from assets and dividing the result by the number of shares outstanding. Comparing book value to share price is one way to gauge if a company's stock is undervalued or overvalued.

CEO
Chief Executive Officer. In Australia, Hong Kong, Italy, Malaysia, New Zealand, Singapore, Spain and the United Kingdom, the CEO is sometimes titled Group Managing Director. In Germany, the CEO is also called the Chairman of the management board.

Chairman
Chairman of the board of directors. In Germany, this refers to the chairman of the supervisory board.

Consumer Prices, Consumer Price Index
The CPI is a measure of change in prices of consumer goods, and therefore a key gauge of inflation. In the U.S., the figures, released monthly by the Labor Department, are based on a list of specific goods and services as purchased in urban areas. Components include food, housing, apparel, transportation, medical care and entertainment. The change in consumer prices is usually reported in terms of a percentage increase or decrease.

Dividend
The amount paid per share to holders of stock, whether common or preferred. Payouts are generally made in quarterly installments.

Earnings per Share
The figure obtained by dividing the number of common shares outstanding into the net income left after dividends have been paid on any preferred stock. This is also called "primary" earnings per share.

Per-share earnings calculated on a "fully diluted" basis presuppose that all dilutive securities (such as warrants, options, convertible debt, etc.) have been exercised into common shares.

Exchange

The primary stock exchange on which the company's shares are listed.

AMEX	American Stock Exchange
ASE	Alberta Stock Exchange
MSE	Montreal Stock Exchange
NASDAQ	a coined word that was fashioned from National Association of Securities Dealers Automated Quotations system
NYSE	New York Stock Exchange
TSE	Toronto Stock Exchange

Gross Domestic Product (GDP)

The total value of goods and services produced by a nation inside its borders. It is considered more indicative of a nation's economy than the GNP. In the U.S., the GDP is calculated by the Commerce Department, and it is the main measure of U.S. economic output. It is expressed in current dollars or constant dollars (base date is 1987.)

Gross National Product (GNP)

The value of a nation's output of goods and services, usually measured yearly. The value of the final product is taken in consideration, not the sum of its parts. For example, the value of the automobile is counted, not the purchase of the steel used to make it. The three factors which make up the GNP are: government spending, consumer purchases and private investment, which includes investments into foreign economies, but not investments from other countries into the home nation's economy.

Group of Seven (G-7)

An organization of the seven major industrialized nations. The countries' leaders meet annually to discuss monetary and fiscal issues that affect the global economy. The G-7 countries are the U.S., Canada, Britain, France, Italy, Germany and Japan. At the 1995 meeting, in Halifax, Canada, G-7 leaders approved a plan—stimulated by the economic problems that followed the devaluation of the Mexican peso in December 1994—to push International Monetary Fund members to publish timely financial data that would alert financial markets to emerging problems and give them a chance to react before a crisis erupts. However, the meeting ended with the leaders wanting to scale back their annual summit after the 1995 meeting became as much a forum for bilateral squabbles as it was a showcase for international cooperation.

Hi-Low

The high and low share prices from 9/30/94 to 9/30/95, based on daily closing prices.

Holding Company

A company whose principal assets are the securities it owns in firms that actually provide goods and services. A holding company is typically formed to enable one corporation to control several diverse companies by holding a majority of their stock.

Industry

Dow Jones classifies each company into one of 124 industry groups. For definitions and codes, see Market Sector Codes and Definitions in the back of this book.

Inflation
A rise in prices. Inflation may be caused by an increase in the money supply; when there are more dollars available to spend, each dollar buys less. It may also be caused by rising manufacturing costs, a decrease in supply of goods, or a combination of factors.

Initial Public Offering (IPO)
The first offering of stock that a closely held company makes to the public.

Internation Monetary Fund (IMF)
IMF is a specialized agency of the United Nations established in 1945 and located in Washington, D.C. Its primary purpose is to develop monetary cooperation between countries, help countries deal with currency fluctuations, trade expansion, and deal with balance of payments difficulties.

Loss
In corporate reports, the excess of expenses over revenue during a company's fiscal period.

Market Cap
Market capitalization. This represents the company's worth based on the market price of its outstanding shares. It is calculated by multiplying the 9/30/95 share price by the number of shares outstanding on that same day. For a company with multiple classes of shares, the market capitalization is the sum of all shares that are components of the Dow Jones World Stock Index.

Mutual Fund
A fund run by an investment company that provides a way for small investors to pool their money so that together they can afford to hire a professional money manager. Though a fund is owned by its shareholders, it is usually established, managed and distributed by the fund's investment adviser and its affiliated companies.

Net Income, Profit, Earnings
As it concerns an earnings report, the amount left after a company pays taxes and all other expenses.

A portion may be committed to pay preferred dividends. Some of what remains may, at the company's discretion, be paid in dividends to holders of common stock. The rest may be invested to obtain interest revenue or spent to acquire new buildings or equipment to increase the company's ability to make a future profit.

North American Free Trade Agreement, Nafta
Nafta phases out tariffs among the U.S., Canada and Mexico over 15 years and greatly eases investment across borders. It was passed by Congress in late 1993, and took effect Jan. 1, 1994.

Operating Profit/Loss
Net income excluding income derived from sources other than the company's regular activities and before income deductions, including taxes. Also called net operating income/loss.

Organization for Economic Cooperation and Development (OECD)

The OECD is an organization of developed nations which was formed in 1961 with a twenty-four country membership, located in Paris, France. Members are committed to help developing countries, work toward economic growth and increase world trade.

President

In Canada, Sweden, Switzerland, and the United States, this title is usually given to the chief executive of the company.

Price

Share price on 9/30/95. For companies with multiple share classes, the price of the class with the largest number of shares outstanding is listed.

Price/Book Ratio

A company's share price on 9/30/95 divided by the book value per share of its most recent fiscal year-end. The P/B ratio is used by investors to gauge how a company is valued by the marketplace in relation to the book value of its assets.

Price/Earnings Ratio

A company's share price on 9/30/95 divided by the earnings per share of its most recent fiscal year-end. The P/E ratio is a standard measure in examining a company's market valuation in relation to its earnings.

Pro-Forma Earnings

A term that applies to a recently merged company's results. It is the results that the company would have achieved had it been in its combined form throughout the full period covered by a financial report.

Revenue

For banks, revenue includes interest income plus other operating income such as commissions, fees, and foreign-exchange income.

For insurance companies, revenue includes premiums, investment income, and other operating income.

For real-estate companies, revenue includes net rental income, property sales, fees, and commissions.

For securities companies, revenue includes investment income and income from asset-management activities, including fees, commissions, and other service charges.

Sales

Net sales of goods and services, or gross sales less returns, discounts, and allowances.

SEDOL No.

Stock Exchange Daily Official List number. This number is an identifier assigned to issues trading on the International Stock Exchange in London.

Soft Landing

A slowdown in economic growth to a pace that contains inflation without tipping the nation into recession.

Spinoff
The distribution to a company's shareholders of the stock in a division or subsidiary.

Ticker
The stock-exchange identifier assigned to each issue traded on U.S. or Canadian stock exchanges.

Ton(s) / Tonne(s)
A ton is 2,000 lbs. or 907.18 kilograms, also known as a short ton. A tonne is a metric ton and equivalent to 2,204.6 lbs. or 1,000 kilograms.

World Bank
An organization created to make loans primarily in developing countries, with the stipulation that the country's government must guarantee the loan. The full name is International Bank for Reconstruction and Development.

World Trade Organization
An arbitration and oversight body created by the General Agreement on Tariffs and Trade to oversee the provisions of the pact. The WTO is the successor to the GATT organization, which was created in 1947 to lower trade barriers. The new organization has a more powerful dispute-resolution system, with three-person arbitration panels. The panels have to follow strict schedules for rendering decisions; WTO members can't veto the findings, as was the case under GATT. That's a big plus for U.S. agriculture, which had won GATT rulings against European Union subsidies of soybeans and other produce, only to have the EU block the decisions. Congress approved the GATT agreement in late 1994.

Yield
The ratio of the most recent full year's dividend per share to share price on 9/30/95.

Australia

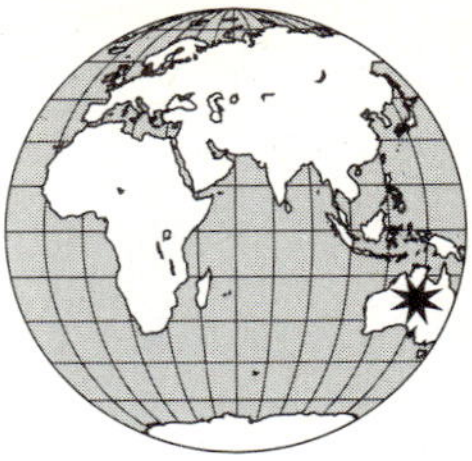

Australia

Anthony Patrick,
Sydney

Local Trading Hours	**Time Difference from New York**	**Population (Est. 3/95)**
10:00-4:00	Sydney is 14 hours ahead for most of the year and 16 hours ahead during the Australian summer	18,000,000

Australia's stock market differs from others in the Asia-Pacific region in that it has strong representation of mining and oil shares. Indeed, about 400 of the 1,130 domestic companies listed on the Australian Stock Exchange (ASX) produce or at least explore for minerals.

Mining and oil stocks account for one third of the market value of all domestic stocks, which totaled $323 billion (Australian) in August, up from A$287 billion a year earlier.

Some of Australia's mining companies are among the biggest resources concerns in the world — stocks such as Broken Hill Proprietary Co. (BHP), Western Mining Corp., CRA Ltd. and North Ltd. They produce a range of minerals, usually including gold, copper, zinc, iron ore and coal, mostly in Australia but also elsewhere. This diversity helps to smooth corporate profits as world minerals' markets soar and plunge.

Australia, one of the world's top gold producers, also has a growing selection of gold-mining companies, such as Placer Pacific Ltd., Newcrest Mining Ltd. and Plutonic Resources Ltd. A few others produce silver or diamonds.

But the biggest group of resources stocks are the small explorers, formed by geologists and their financiers to seek richs in Australia's vast Outback. A few strike it lucky and their shares rocket. Poseidon Ltd. shot to over A$200 from 20 cents when the company reported signs of a nickel discovery during a boom in the world nickel market.

Most of the explorers, though, exhaust funds raised from initial public offerings and fade away. This group should be considered highly speculative.

Foreign mining stocks will form yet another sector, if the ASX succeeds in a plan to enhance its diversity and depth in the resources area. The exchange intends to introduce depositary receipts denominated in Australian dollars to facilitate trading in foreign stocks and hopes to list a South African mining concern soon.

Dow Jones Australia Equity Market Index Performance

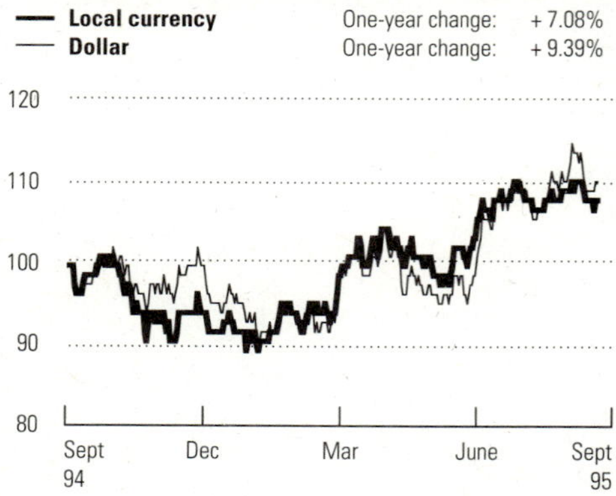

Still, the Australian market isn't all metals and energy. It includes significant groups of stocks whose businesses cover food and drinks, banking, transportation, media, building

Gross Domestic Product	Three-year Average GDP Growth (93-95)	Main Industries	Consumer Price Index	Monetary Unit	Exchange Rate (9/95)
US$340 billion (fiscal year ended June 30, 1995)	4%	Manufacturing, finance and property, retailing, construction, mining, agriculture and tourism	3.2% (in fiscal year ended June 30, 1995)	Australian dollar	A$1.32 to US$1.00

materials, retailing and manufacturing. Privatization of some big government corporations, such as Qantas Airways Ltd., Commonwealth Bank and betting concern TABCorp., has broadened the market in the past year or so.

In addition to 1,130 domestic stocks, the ASX lists nearly 50 foreign shares and wants more. The exchange has made a special effort to attract new companies from China and currently trades eight China-based stocks.

Longer trading hours are being considered as the ASX jostles with other exchanges such as Singapore to maintain, and perhaps enlarge, its share of regional trading activity.
The ASX is complemented by its derivatives arm, which trades options and warrants on shares and a world-first product named share-ratio contracts. Share ratios are based on the performance of individual stocks compared with a share-price index.

The Sydney Futures Exchange, a separate market, trades futures contracts on the All Ordinaries share price index and futures on some individual stocks.

Australian share prices, measured by the All Ordinaries Index, were flat in the fiscal year ended June 1995.

Average daily turnover slipped to A$467 million from a record A$508 million a year earlier. The market liquidity ratio, calculated by dividing the average value of domestic market capitalization of companies into the total value of equity turnover for the fiscal year, was 41%, similar to liquidity on the London market but double liquidity of the Tokyo exchange.

Ten Largest Capitalized Companies
as of 9/30/95

Stock	Market Cap. US$Mil
Broken Hill Proprietary	26,107,271.3
National Australia Bank	12,377,988.4
News Corporation	10,657,765.1
CRA	9,346,661.6
BTR Nylex	7,800,135.3
Westpac Banking	7,407,800.2
Western Mining	7,258,759.5
ANZ Banking	5,964,526.4
Amcor	4,538,835.9
Coles Myer	3,834,104.2

According to the ASX, the long-term performance of the Australian stock market has exceeded the average of other major world markets.

Brokers generally are optimistic about the market's outlook. The Australian economy has expanded in each of the past four fiscal years, after a recession in fiscal 1990-91. Corporate earnings and dividend performances have been strong.

A government target to keep the underlying inflation rate close to 2%-3% likely means interest rates won't rise to levels that battered stock prices in past economic cycles.

Australians have become more aware of the benefits of investment in stocks. For a start, they get a tax break on dividends compared with fixed-interest income. And the potential is high for greater participation in the stock market. About 21% of Australian adults own shares directly or through managed equity funds, up from 16% in 1991, but still below proportions achieved elsewhere.

Overseas investors, too, are showing more interest. The value of Australian shares bought by foreigners reached 24% of total turnover last fiscal year. Americans became the largest single foreign purchasers of Australian shares in the fourth quarter of 1994. The value of U.S. purchases in all of fiscal 1994-95 totaled A$6.5 billion, an increase of 427% in four years. Investment from the U.K. remains very significant, but British purchases rose 86% in the past four years, well below the comparable U.S. rate.

The ASX says its national computer-based trading system is well established and reliable. It boasts about a share settlement system rated the best in the world, after the U.S. Other good news: Fees charged by brokerage firms have become more flexible and a tax on share transfers was cut in 1995.

Securities regulators and the exchange have cleaned up the market's image, too, after a period in the 1980s when a handful of high-profile "entrepreneurs" ran some listed companies like private domains. But some investors believe the ASX still must insist on tougher corporate governance standards to match best overseas practice.

Foreign investors face few restrictions in Australian stocks. Only Quantas Airways and a small number of media companies have limits on foreign ownership. Profits earned by foreigners on shares generally aren't subject to Australia's capital gains tax and they are liable to pay a dividend-witholding tax only to the extent that dividends they receive aren't "franked" under a system designed to eliminate double-taxation of dividend income. Dividends are classified as "franked" if they are paid out of profits on which company tax has been paid.

The withholding tax usually is 15% for investors from countries that have signed a tax treaty with Australia.

Amcor

Industry: **Containers & Packaging**

Amcor is one of the world's 10 largest packaging companies by sales. The company manfactures paper and fiber and container-packaging materials, including beverage cans and containers for personal-care items and industrial products, and flexible packaging for food. Amcor and Kimberly-Clark U.S. jointly own Kimberly-Clark Australia, which produces and sells Kleenex, Huggies, Kotex, Wondersoft, Medesa, and Delsey goods in Australia and New Zealand. Amcor has operations in 19 countries; sales outside of Australia represent 20% of revenues.

A$ mil	06/92	06/93	06/94	US$mil 06/94				
Sales	**4,111.6**	**4,824.6**	**5,549.1**	**3,832.2**	P/E Ratio	**17.3**	Price (9/30/95)	**9.92**
Net Income	**266.5**	**314.9**	**256.6**	**177.2**	P/B Ratio	**2.2**	52 Wk Hi-Low	**10.88-8.48**
Book Value	**2,035.6**	**2,601.0**	**2,755.0**	**2,011.0**	Yield %	**3.4**	Market Cap	**US$4,538.8mil**

Address **South Gate, Twr. E., 40 City Rd.**
S. Melbourne, VIC 3205
Tel **03-694-9000**
Fax **03-686-2924**
ADR **AMCRY**
SEDOL No. **6066608**
Managing Director **Stan Wallis**
Chairman **Athol Lapthorne**

Ampolex

Industry: **Oil - Secondary**

Ampolex explores for and produces crude oil and natural gas. Its total crude-oil production averages 35,000 barrels per day, with reserves of 230 million barrels. Ampolex's annual natural-gas production is approximately 6.5 billion cubic feet, with reserves of 257 billion cubic feet. It produces more than 50% of its oil from Papua New Guinea's Lake Kutubu region, and another 40% from its Australian operations. It also has exploration and production operations in the United States, China, Thailand, Cambodia, Argentina, the Philippines, New Zealand, and Tunisia.

A$ mil	06/92	06/93	06/94	US$mil 06/94				
Sales	**174.6**	**369.2**	**365.7**	**252.5**	P/E Ratio	**15.7**	Price (9/30/95)	**2.88**
Net Income	**37.2**	**80.6**	**55.4**	**38.2**	P/B Ratio	**0.7**	52 Wk Hi-Low	**4.11-2.88**
Book Value	**652.0**	**787.8**	**1,156.8**	**844.4**	Yield %	**1.7**	Market Cap	**US$632.6mil**

Address **580 George St.**
Sydney, NSW 2000
Tel **02-364-4999**
Fax **02-364-4930**
ADR **APLXY**
SEDOL No. **6030807**
Managing Director **Peter E. Power**
Chairman **Campbell M. Anderson**

ANZ Banking

Industry: **Banks - Regional**

Australia & New Zealand Banking (ANZ) is one of Australia's four largest banks, and has the largest overseas exposure of the four. It provides services in general banking, finance, life insurance, property development, leasing, and mortgage lending. Nearly 70% of its assets are in Australia, with 10% in New Zealand. Roughly one third of its domestic loans are mortgages. ANZ's subsidiaries are active in Europe, the Americas, the Middle East, Asia/Pacific, and South Asia. It recently opened new banking offices in China, Indonesia, and Vietnam.

A$ mil	09/92	09/93	09/94	US$mil 09/94				
Revenues	**10,193.2**	**8,955.5**	**8,453.7**	**5,995.5**	P/E Ratio	**10.1**	Price (9/30/95)	**5.67**
Net Income	**-579.0**	**672.9**	**821.9**	**582.9**	P/B Ratio	**1.4**	52 Wk Hi-Low	**5.71-3.65**
Book Value	**4,542.3**	**5,089.0**	**5,455.6**	**4,041.2**	Yield %	**4.4**	Market Cap	**US$5,964.5mil**

Address **100 Queen St.**
Melbourne, VIC 3000
Tel **03-273-6141**
Fax **03-273-6142**
ADR **ANZ**
SEDOL No. **6065586**
CEO **Don Mercer**
Chairman **John Gough**

Argo Investments

Industry: **Financial Services - Diversified**

Argo Investments is a value-oriented investment firm with mutual funds invested in more than 250 companies, primarily those listed on the Australian Stock Exchange. The market value of its investments exceeds A$513 million. It has more than 23,000 shareholders, its largest being the State Government Insurance Commission, which owns more than 5% of the issued shares. Wholly owned subsidiaries include Argo Equities, Argo Group Nominees, Centurion Investments, Clipper Investments, and Stoddarts Holdings. Its affiliates include Bounty Investments and Wakefield Investments.

A$ mil	06/92	06/93	06/94	US$mil 06/94				
Revenues	**21.6**	**32.2**	**45.9**	**31.7**	P/E Ratio	**19.3**	Price (9/30/95)	**2.30**
Net Income	**21.0**	**22.9**	**27.0**	**18.6**	P/B Ratio	**0.9**	52 Wk Hi-Low	**2.69-2.30**
Book Value	**398.4**	**469.4**	**504.1**	**368.0**	Yield %	**5.2**	Market Cap	**US$335.9mil**

Address **13 Grenfell St.**
Adelaide, SA 5000
Tel **08-212-2055**
Fax **08-212-1658**
ADR
SEDOL No. **6049104**
President **R.J. Patterson**
Chairman **D.F. Wicks**

Arnotts

Industry: **Other Food**

Arnotts is the world's seventh-largest and Australia's leading cookie manufacturer and distributor, with 65% of the country's market share. The company manufactures cookies, crackers, and snacks; makes and markets packaging materials and containers; and engages in flour-milling and engineering activities. Its brand-name products include Sao crackers and Famous Biscuits. The U.S. food company Campbell Soup owns 60% of Arnotts.

A$ mil	06/92	06/93	01/94 *	US$mil 01/94				
Sales	**693.0**	**718.3**	**622.5**	**424.0**	P/E Ratio	**15.9**	Price (9/30/95)	**9.25**
Net Income	**47.1**	**47.2**	**81.1**	**55.2**	P/B Ratio	**4.2**	52 Wk Hi-Low	**9.26-8.00**
Book Value	**259.7**	**273.7**	**304.7**	**216.1**	Yield %	**3.5**	Market Cap	**US$975.6mil**

Address **11 George St.**
Homebush, NSW 2140
Tel **02-394-3555**
Fax **02-394-3500**
ADR
SEDOL No. **6050388**
Managing Director **Paul G. Bourke**
Chairman **William K. Purdy**

*Irregular period due to fiscal year change.

Ashton Mining

Industry: **Precious Metals**

Ashton Mining engages in diamond mining; it also produces silver, opals, and rare-earth oxides. The company produces roughly 40 million carats of diamonds annually, from its 40%-owned Argyle diamond mine in Australia. Ashton Mining is exploring for diamonds in Australia, China, Canada, Indonesia, Finland, and the U.S., and has claims on land in Karelia, Sweden, and Norway. It also has a 60% stake in a diamond-mining joint venture, Ashton Mining of Canada. The company sold its interest in Aurora Gold in 1993.

A$ mil	12/92	12/93	12/94	US$mil 12/94				
Sales	**287.1**	**213.9**	**186.5**	**136.9**	P/E Ratio	**15.5**	Price (9/30/95)	**1.75**
Net Income	**35.4**	**36.6**	**31.7**	**23.2**	P/B Ratio	**1.5**	52 Wk Hi-Low	**3.19-1.70**
Book Value	**310.6**	**324.5**	**331.6**	**257.1**	Yield %	**4.6**	Market Cap	**US$370.9mil**

Address	**441 St. Kilda Rd.**	Tel	**03-828-4200**	ADR	**ASHMY**	Managing Director	**R. John Robinson**
	Melbourne, VIC 3004	Fax	**03-828-4211**	SEDOL No.	**6056999**	Chairman	**Nobby Clark**

Australian Gas Light

Industry: **Gas Utilities**

Australian Gas Light Company (AGL) distributes natural gas and explores for and produces natural gas and oil. The company distributes natural gas to more than 670,000 customers throughout New South Wales and the Australian Capital Territory. AGL holds a 50% interest in Elgas, a distributor of liquefied petroleum gas that serves more than 500,000 customers throughout Australia. It also owns 50% of Industrial Pipe Systems, which manufactures pipes and pipe fittings in Australia and China. In 1994, AGL acquired a 51% interest in the Moomba-Sydney natural-gas pipeline.

A$ mil	06/93	06/94	06/95	US$mil 06/95				
Sales	**839.8**	**773.6**	**801.5**	**572.5**	P/E Ratio	**13.6**	Price (9/30/95)	**4.60**
Net Income	**70.6**	**87.2**	**94.0**	**67.1**	P/B Ratio	**1.7**	52 Wk Hi-Low	**4.70-4.10**
Book Value	**671.4**	**720.5**	**771.5**	**547.2**	Yield %	**5.7**	Market Cap	**US$966.2mil**

Address	**AGL Ctr., 111 Pacific Highway**	Tel	**02-922-0101**	ADR		Managing Director	**Leonard F. Bleasel**
	North Sydney, NSW 2060	Fax	**02-957-3671**	SEDOL No.	**6064969**	Chairman	**Richard C. Mason**

Australian National Industries

Industry: **Industrial - Diversified**

Australian National Industries (ANI) is active in manufacturing and engineering. It produces specialty-steel goods, ferrous castings, and specialty metals through its Comsteel, Bradken, and Aurora (U.K.) subsidiaries. ANI's environmental-engineering division has a joint venture with I. Kruger Engineering and an 85% stake in Germany's Holter Group, a waste-management firm. ANI holds US$1.8 billion in environmental-engineering contracts. It acquired steel-products maker Palmer Tube Mills in September 1994. ANI derives 72% of revenues in Australia.

A$ mil	06/92	06/93	06/94	US$mil 06/94				
Sales	**1,155.6**	**1,189.2**	**1,487.9**	**1,027.5**	P/E Ratio	**12.3**	Price (9/30/95)	**1.25**
Net Income	**-66.6**	**56.7**	**65.0**	**44.9**	P/B Ratio	**1.2**	52 Wk Hi-Low	**1.56-1.16**
Book Value	**602.9**	**632.1**	**662.9**	**483.8**	Yield %	**7.2**	Market Cap	**US$744.2mil**

Address	**Merlin Ctr., 235 Pyrmont St.**	Tel	**02-552-2600**	ADR	**ANNDY**	Managing Director	**H.E. Rees**
	Pyrmont, NSW 2009	Fax	**02-660-1395**	SEDOL No.	**6066103**	Chairman	**A.E. Harris**

Boral

Industry: **Building Materials**

Boral produces and distributes construction materials, manufacturing and engineering components, and energy. Its products include plasterboard, asphalt, windows, steel, bricks, scaffolding, wire products, cement, elevators, coal, retreaded tires, gas, and oil. The firm runs more than 400 gas stations in Australia. Its North American subsidiaries produce bricks, roof tiles, gypsum wallboard, and construction aggregates. Boral also operates in 21 countries in Europe and Asia. Overseas activities generate 20% of Boral's sales and 8% of operating profits.

A$ mil	06/92	06/93	06/94	US$mil 06/94				
Sales	**3,697.8**	**4,215.1**	**4,646.9**	**3,209.2**	P/E Ratio	**27.2**	Price (9/30/95)	**3.34**
Net Income	**152.0**	**228.9**	**121.8**	**84.1**	P/B Ratio	**1.3**	52 Wk Hi-Low	**3.75-3.20**
Book Value	**2,260.9**	**2,394.3**	**2,755.4**	**2,011.2**	Yield %	**6.0**	Market Cap	**US$2,785.4mil**

Address	**Norwich Hse., 6-10 O'Connell St.**	Tel	**02-232-8800**	ADR	**BORAY**	Managing Director	**Anthony R. Berg**
	Sydney, NSW 2001	Fax	**02-233-6605**	SEDOL No.	**6112200**	Chairman	**J.B. Leslie**

Bougainville Copper

Industry: **Non-Ferrous Metals - Other (Exc. Aluminum)**

Bougainville Copper mined metals in Papua New Guinea's North Solomons province until unrest and violence on the Bougainville island led to the suspension of operations in May 1989. The company has not inspected the mine, which remains closed, since then. Total available mill feed is estimated at 691 million tonnes averaging 0.40% copper and 0.47 grams per tonne gold. Bougainville Copper does not expect to be re-establishing operations before the end of 1995, a process it estimates will take 18 months to complete. The company is majority-owned by CRA Ltd.

Kina mil	12/92 P	12/93 P	12/94 P	US$mil 12/94				
Sales	**0.0**	**0.0**	**0.0**	**0.0**	P/E Ratio	**NMF**	Price (9/30/95)	**0.63**
Net Income	**-1.4**	**-2.7**	**7.8**	**7.8**	P/B Ratio	**0.6**	52 Wk Hi-Low	**1.07-0.55**
Book Value	**236.4**	**233.8**	**241.6**	**206.5**	Yield %	**0.0**	Market Cap	**US$191.4mil**

Address	**Level 33, 55 Collins St.**	Tel	**03-283-3333**	ADR	**BOCOY**	President	**W.T. Palmer**
	Melbourne, VIC 3000	Fax	**03-283-3707**	SEDOL No.	**6113913**	Chairman	**G.D. Klingner**

P=Parent company data.

Brambles Industries

Industry: **General Industrial & Commercial Services**

Brambles Industries provides specialized materials-handling services. The company's services include specialized transport, waste treatment and disposal, and industrial- and mining-equipment rental. Through a joint venture with the diversified conglomerate GKN (U.K.), Brambles runs the CHEP group of materials-handling companies throughout Australia, Europe, and the United States. In Australia and the U.S., Brambles' wholly owned Cleanaway subsidiaries collect, treat, recycle, and dispose of industrial and household waste.

A$ mil	06/92	06/93	06/94	US$mil 06/94				
Sales	**2,435.8**	**2,606.0**	**2,640.1**	**1,823.3**	P/E Ratio	**19.1**	Price (9/30/95)	**14.60**
Net Income	**180.2**	**166.1**	**-233.2**	**-161.0**	P/B Ratio	**2.3**	52 Wk Hi-Low	**14.60-11.40**
Book Value	**1,563.2**	**1,707.9**	**1,354.4**	**988.6**	Yield %	**4.1**	Market Cap	**US$2,424.3mil**

Address	**Gateway, 1 Macquarie Pl.**	Tel	**02-256-5222**	ADR		President	**John Fletcher**
	Sydney, NSW 2000	Fax	**02-256-5299**	SEDOL No.	**6120009**	Chairman	**Alan W. Coates**

Broken Hill Proprietary

Industry: **Conglomerates**

Broken Hill Proprietary (BHP) is Australia's largest company in terms of market valuation, with major operations in mining, steel, and energy in more than 20 countries worldwide. Its mining operations produce more than 40 million tons of thermal and metallurgical coal annually, as well as copper, manganese, iron ore, and gold. The steel division commands roughly 80% of the Australian steel market. BHP's petroleum division holds proven reserves of more than 1.5 billion barrels of oil equivalent.

A$ mil	05/93	05/94	05/95	US$mil 05/95				
Sales	**15,933.6**	**16,544.1**	**17,739.0**	**13,238.1**	P/E Ratio	**23.2**	Price (9/30/95)	**18.24**
Net Income	**990.6**	**1,283.8**	**1,216.0**	**907.5**	P/B Ratio	**3.0**	52 Wk Hi-Low	**19.96-16.05**
Book Value	**8,867.1**	**10,178.9**	**11,868.0**	**8,538.1**	Yield %	**2.7**	Market Cap	**US$26,107mil**

Address	**BHP Tower, 600 Bourke St.**	Tel	**03-609-3333**	ADR	**BHP**	President	**John B. Prescott**
	Melbourne, VIC 3000	Fax	**03-609-3015**	SEDOL No.	**6144690**	Chairman	**Brian T. Loton**

BTR Nylex

Industry: **Industrial - Diversified**

BTR Nylex is a diversified industrial-manufacturing conglomerate. It manufactures polymers, glass and plastic packaging, engineering and automotive products, construction and building products, quarry products, industrial minerals, and textiles. It serves the automotive, construction, aerospace, and interior-decorating industries. BTR Nylex derives 51% of sales from overseas manufacturing and marketing operations in Malaysia, Taiwan, China, the U.S., the U.K., and Eastern Europe. It holds a 50% stake in Bridge Wholesale Acceptance Corp., an Australian finance company.

A$ mil	12/92	12/93	12/94	US$mil 12/94				
Sales	**5,733.3**	**6,213.9**	**6,675.1**	**4,901.0**	P/E Ratio	**19.7**	Price (9/30/95)	**3.55**
Net Income	**362.5**	**398.6**	**474.9**	**348.7**	P/B Ratio	**2.4**	52 Wk Hi-Low	**3.58-2.22**
Book Value	**3,580.5**	**3,804.9**	**4,317.6**	**3,347.0**	Yield %	**3.4**	Market Cap	**US$7,800.1mil**

Address	**15th Fl., 390 St. Kilda Rd.**	Tel	**03-823-5700**	ADR	**BTRUY**	Managing Director	**Philip S. Aiken**
	Melbourne, VIC 3004	Fax	**03-867-4103**	SEDOL No.	**6437129**	Chairman	**Alan R. Jackson**

Burns, Philp & Co.

Industry: **Other Food**

Burns, Philp & Co. produces food, food ingredients, and health-care products in 28 countries. It holds 13% of the world's yeast market, is the world's largest vinegar producer by volume, and is the second-largest spice producer in the western world, with large shares of the North American and European spice markets. Its brand names include Fleischmann's, French's, Durkee, and Spice Island. The firm's health-care division makes antibiotics and food preservatives. In 1994, the company sold its hardware division to Australia's Howard Smith for roughly US$340 million.

A$ mil	06/92	06/93	06/94	US$mil 06/94				
Sales	**2,257.2**	**2,683.2**	**2,786.5**	**1,924.4**	P/E Ratio	**N/A**	Price (9/30/95)	**2.80**
Net Income	**92.1**	**110.1**	**123.0**	**84.9**	P/B Ratio	**1.1**	52 Wk Hi-Low	**3.55-2.64**
Book Value	**961.4**	**1,074.7**	**1,106.2**	**807.4**	Yield %	**6.8**	Market Cap	**US$972.4mil**

Address	**7 Bridge St.**	Tel	**02-259-1111**	ADR	**BPHCY**	CEO	**Ian Clack**
	Sydney, NSW 2000	Fax	**02-251-3254**	SEDOL No.	**6155733**	Chairman	**Andrew Trunbull**

Caltex Australia

Industry: **Oil - Secondary**

Caltex Australia refines, distributes, transports, and sells petroleum products. It also operates nearly 1,100 service stations, and supplies fuel to 108 distributors throughout Australia. Through its 55% interest in Bayswater Colliery in New South Wales, Caltex mines and sells coal. In December 1994, a proposal was announced to merge its down stream petroleum operations with those of Ampol Ltd., a wholly owned subsidiary of Pioneer International. Caltex Australia is 75% owned by Texas-based Caltex Petroleum which is owned by the U.S. companies Texaco and Chevron.

A$ mil	12/92	12/93	12/94	US$mil 12/94				
Sales	**1,966.6**	**1,878.6**	**1,712.8**	**1,257.6**	P/E Ratio	**14.3**	Price (9/30/95)	**4.25**
Net Income	**0.4**	**53.7**	**58.6**	**43.0**	P/B Ratio	**1.0**	52 Wk Hi-Low	**4.55-2.95**
Book Value	**728.1**	**759.6**	**792.0**	**614.0**	Yield %	**2.6**	Market Cap	**US$579.5mil**

Address	**Caltex Hse., 167-187 Kent St.**	Tel	**02-250-5000**	ADR		President	**Barry K. Murphy**
	Sydney, NSW 2000	Fax	**02-231-6427**	SEDOL No.	**6161503**	Chairman	**Barry K. Murphy**

Coca-Cola Amatil

Industry: **Soft Drinks**

Coca-Cola Amatil (CCA) operates an international network of Coca-Cola franchises. CCA holds Coca- Cola franchise rights in Austria, Hungary, and the Czech, Slovak, and Belarus republics, in addition to its operations in Australia. The company's Pacific market includes New Zealand, Papua New Guinea, Fiji, and Indonesia. CCA operates more than 40 bottling plants worldwide. Beverage brands that CCA distributes include Coca-Cola, Sprite, Fanta, Lift, Deep Spring, Mount Franklin Spring, and Fonzies.

A$ mil	12/92	12/93	12/94	US$mil 12/94				
Sales	**2,108.2**	**1,951.0**	**2,239.1**	**1,644.0**	P/E Ratio	**43.6**	Price (9/30/95)	**9.95**
Net Income	**65.9**	**329.9**	**110.8**	**81.4**	P/B Ratio	**4.2**	52 Wk Hi-Low	**9.95-7.52**
Book Value	**764.2**	**1,134.8**	**1,131.2**	**876.9**	Yield %	**1.4**	Market Cap	**US$3,667.1mil**

Address **71 Macquarie St.**
Sydney, NSW 2000
Tel **02-259-6666**
Fax **02-259-6623**
ADR **CCLAY**
SEDOL No. **6207010**
Managing Director **N.P. Cole**
Chairman **D.R. Wills**

Coles Myer

Industry: **Retailers - Broadline**

Coles Myer is the largest retailer in Australia and New Zealand, and among the top-20 retailers in the world. It is also one of the region's 10 largest companies based on market capitalization. It operates approximately 1,700 supermarkets, department stores, restaurants, and specialty stores under the names Bi-Lo, Target, Kmart, Myer, Fosseys, Liquorland, Myer Grace Bros., and Chili's. Its stores are located exclusively in Australia and New Zealand and have more than 3 million square meters of selling area. New Zealand operations account for only 1% of sales.

A$ mil	07/92	07/93	07/94	US$mil 07/94				
Revenues	**15,178.0**	**15,168.1**	**15,921.4**	**11,079.6**	P/E Ratio	**N/A**	Price (9/30/95)	**4.27**
Net Income	**370.7**	**411.8**	**424.2**	**295.2**	P/B Ratio	**1.6**	52 Wk Hi-Low	**4.55-3.85**
Book Value	**3,070.3**	**3,244.4**	**3,368.2**	**2,495.0**	Yield %	**4.7**	Market Cap	**US$3,834.1mil**

Address **800 Toorak Rd.**
Tooronga, VIC 3146
Tel **03-829-3111**
Fax **03-829-6787**
ADR **CM**
SEDOL No. **6209908**
CEO **Peter Bartels**
Chairman **Solomon Lew**

Comalco

Industry: **Aluminum**

Comalco is the 10th-largest aluminum producer in the world. It accounts for almost 10% of the world's bauxite production, at 11 million tons per annum. Most of the company's bauxite is processed through its three smelters, which produce more than 400,000 tons of aluminum annually. Finished and semifinished products include aluminum sheets, foil, extrusions, and cast wheels. The company's mines are located in Australia and Guinea, Africa. Manufacturing facilities are located in Australia, New Zealand, Italy, and the United States. Australia's CRA owns 67% of Comalco.

A$ mil	12/92	12/93	12/94	US$mil 12/94				
Sales	**2,110.5**	**2,208.3**	**2,397.9**	**1,760.6**	P/E Ratio	**25.2**	Price (9/30/95)	**6.55**
Net Income	**41.2**	**79.0**	**145.6**	**106.9**	P/B Ratio	**2.9**	52 Wk Hi-Low	**7.18-4.30**
Book Value	**1,119.3**	**1,175.3**	**1,246.6**	**966.4**	Yield %	**1.5**	Market Cap	**US$2,781.9mil**

Address **55 Collins St.**
Melbourne, VIC 3001
Tel **03-283-3000**
Fax **03-283-3707**
ADR **CLMOY**
SEDOL No. **6211419**
CEO **Terry Palmer**
Chairman **Leon Davis**

Commonwealth Bank

Industry: **Banks - Regional**

Commonwealth Bank of Australia (CBA) is the country's fourth-largest bank, and its largest retail bank, by assets. It offers personal, business, and institutional banking, and financial services. It is the largest lender in the Australian housing market, with a 21% market share. CBA's financial services division is the fifth-largest fund manager in Australia with A$14.3 billion under management. CBA owns State Bank of Victoria, the state's largest retail bank. The company has offices in Hong Kong, Singapore, and Indonesia. The Australian government owns 50.4% of CBA.

A$ mil	06/92	06/93	06/94	US$mil 06/94				
Revenues	**9,429.7**	**7,880.4**	**6,944.5**	**4,795.9**	P/E Ratio	**20.2**	Price (9/30/95)	**10.24**
Net Income	**408.8**	**443.1**	**682.1**	**471.1**	P/B Ratio	**1.6**	52 Wk Hi-Low	**10.76-7.18**
Book Value	**5,470.8**	**5,568.7**	**5,965.2**	**4,354.2**	Yield %	**5.9**	Market Cap	**US$3,580.2mil**

Address **48 Martin Pl.**
Sydney, NSW 2000
Tel **02-378-7111**
Fax **02-378-2311**
ADR
SEDOL No. **6215035**
President **David V. Murray**
Chairman **Morrish A. Besley**

CRA

Industry: **Mining**

CRA primarily mines and processes iron, coal, and aluminum. It also has significant mining and processing interests in diamonds, lead, zinc, copper, gold, silver, and salt. CRA's annual production includes roughly 48 million tons of iron ore, 28 million tons of coal, and 282,000 tons of aluminum. It operates mines and processing plants in Indonesia, New Zealand, the Netherlands, Italy, the U.S., and Chile. Its largest Australian subsidiaries include wholly-owned Hammersley Iron and the 67%-owned aluminum producer, Comalco. U.K.-based RTZ owns 48.9% of CRA.

A$ mil	12/92	12/93	12/94	US$mil 12/94				
Sales	**5,237.1**	**5,927.8**	**5,810.8**	**4,266.4**	P/E Ratio	**23.1**	Price (9/30/95)	**20.70**
Net Income	**394.8**	**826.1**	**480.5**	**352.8**	P/B Ratio	**2.8**	52 Wk Hi-Low	**22.16-16.34**
Book Value	**3,954.9**	**4,325.6**	**4,471.3**	**3,466.1**	Yield %	**2.9**	Market Cap	**US$9,346.7mil**

Address **55 Collins St.**
Melbourne, VIC 3001
Tel **03-283-3333**
Fax **03-283-3707**
ADR **CRADY**
SEDOL No. **6220103**
Managing Director **Leon A. Davis**
Chairman **John A. Uhrig**

CSR

Industry: **Building Materials**

CSR produces construction and building materials, timber products, and aluminum. The firm is also Australia's largest producer of raw and refined sugar, with seven sugar plants. Its wholly-owned CSR America is the largest U.S. producer of premixed concrete, concrete blocks, and concrete pipes. CSR's construction- and building-materials businesses also produce plasterboard, insulation, bricks, and roof tiles. CSR also operates in New Zealand, the United Kingdom, Canada, and Asia. Sales outside of Australia and New Zealand generate about 25% of total revenues.

	A$ mil 03/93	03/94	03/95	US$mil 03/95				
Sales	**4,636.0**	**5,430.2**	**6,248.4**	**4,645.7**	P/E Ratio	**10.3**	Price (9/30/95)	**4.40**
Net Income	**231.3**	**296.5**	**392.6**	**291.9**	P/B Ratio	**1.3**	52 Wk Hi-Low	**4.70-4.12**
Book Value	**2,867.1**	**3,097.7**	**3,307.9**	**2,432.3**	Yield %	**6.6**	Market Cap	**US$3,145.9mil**

Address **1 O'Connell St.**
Sydney, NSW 2000
Tel **02-235-8000**
Fax **02-235-8044**
ADR **CSRLY**
SEDOL No. **6238645**
Managing Director **Geoffrey V. Kells**
Chairman **Alan W. Coates**

Email

Industry: **Other Home Furnishings**

Email manufactures household appliances, building materials, and industrial products, and is active in metals distribution. Its household-appliances division produces Westinghouse, Kelvinator, and Frigidaire. Email also makes door- and window- security products, bathroom and kitchen fixtures, office furniture, central air conditioners, steel construction materials, and meters for water, gas, and electricity. Nearly 6% of Email's revenues come from overseas; it has operations in New Zealand, Singapore, the Philippines, Indonesia, the Middle East, and the U.S.

	A$ mil 03/93	03/94	03/95	US$mil 03/95				
Sales	**1,466.3**	**1,791.4**	**2,134.3**	**1,586.8**	P/E Ratio	**9.5**	Price (9/30/95)	**3.57**
Net Income	**60.1**	**87.8**	**100.0**	**74.3**	P/B Ratio	**1.5**	52 Wk Hi-Low	**4.20-3.27**
Book Value	**533.6**	**577.4**	**682.1**	**501.5**	Yield %	**7.0**	Market Cap	**US$752.5mil**

Address **Joynton Ave.**
Waterloo, NSW 2017
Tel **02-690-7333**
Fax **02-699-3190**
ADR **EMALY**
SEDOL No. **6313003**
Managing Director **J.M. Hanna**
Chairman **P.J.W. Cottrell**

Energy Resources

Industry: **Non-Ferrous Metals - Other (Exc. Aluminum)**

Energy Resources of Australia (ERA) mines, processes, and exports uranium. It operates the Northern Territory's Ranger uranium mine and the adjacent Jabiluka deposit. ERA's ore resources total more than 160,000 tonnes, placing ERA among the world's top-three uranium companies. It supplies 6% of the uranium required by nuclear electricity reactors. The natural-resources company North Broken Hill Peko owns 66% of ERA. Other major shareholders include a group of numerous Japanese and European uranium consumers which collectively holds 25% of ERA.

	A$ mil 06/93	06/94	06/95	US$mil 06/95				
Sales	**159.5**	**152.2**	**140.0**	**100.0**	P/E Ratio	**68.3**	Price (9/30/95)	**4.37**
Net Income	**57.7**	**26.5**	**12.4**	**8.9**	P/B Ratio	**2.8**	52 Wk Hi-Low	**4.37-1.97**
Book Value	**625.1**	**651.7**	**640.8**	**454.5**	Yield %	**57.7**	Market Cap	**US$254.5mil**

Address **1 Macquarie Pl.**
Sydney, NSW 2000
Tel **02-256-8900**
Fax **02-251-1817**
ADR
SEDOL No. **6317715**
Chief Executive **Phillip Shirvington**
Chairman **Campbell Anderson**

F.H. Faulding

Industry: **Pharmaceuticals**

F.H. Faulding & Co. develops, produces, and markets drugs. It manufactures specialized medical equipment and owns Australia's only national pharmaceutical-distribution network. Faulding manufactures health- and personal-care products such as Kapanol, a sustained-release oral morphine, as well as oral and injectible drug delivery systems. It also produces Olympus microscopes and endoscopes. Faulding's 56%-owned Purepac subsidiary (U.S.) manufactures generic drugs. The company is also the full owner of Selby Scientific. U.S. sales contribute 8% of revenues.

	A$ mil 06/92	06/93	06/94	US$mil 06/94				
Sales	**991.9**	**1,142.5**	**1,259.3**	**869.7**	P/E Ratio	**18.5**	Price (9/30/95)	**5.95**
Net Income	**23.7**	**28.5**	**32.2**	**22.2**	P/B Ratio	**2.2**	52 Wk Hi-Low	**6.65-5.23**
Book Value	**241.9**	**265.9**	**304.4**	**222.2**	Yield %	**2.6**	Market Cap	**US$500.1mil**

Address **GPO Box 1618**
Adelaide, SA 5001
Tel **08-372-1500**
Fax **08-373-3120**
ADR **FAFHY**
SEDOL No. **6332600**
CEO **E.D. Tweddell**
Chairman **Alan McGregor**

Foster's Brewing

Industry: **Distillers & Brewers**

Foster's Brewing Group is the world's fourth-largest brewer, operating 22 breweries worldwide. Its main beer brands include Foster's, Molson, and Carlton; the firm also produces Miller beers in Canada. Foster's wholly-owned Carlton and United Breweries maintain a 53% share of the Australian beer market, and 40%-owned Molson commands a 47% share of the Canadian market. It also has joint ventures with three Chinese breweries and generates 57% of its sales outside of Australasia. The company sold Courage, its U.K. brewer, to Scottish & Newcastle in 1995.

	A$ mil 06/92	06/93	06/94	US$mil 06/94				
Sales	**6,359.1**	**6,272.6**	**5,068.4**	**3,500.3**	P/E Ratio	**14.4**	Price (9/30/95)	**1.25**
Net Income	**-950.8**	**310.3**	**281.7**	**194.5**	P/B Ratio	**1.5**	52 Wk Hi-Low	**1.30-1.06**
Book Value	**1,374.5**	**2,467.2**	**2,787.2**	**2,034.5**	Yield %	**4.8**	Market Cap	**US$3,093.5mil**

Address **One Garden St.**
South Yarra, VIC 3141
Tel **03-828-2424**
Fax **03-826-9310**
ADR **FBWGY**
SEDOL No. **6307705**
CEO **Edward T. Kunkel**
Chairman **Neil R. Clark**

General Property Trust

Industry: **Real-Estate Investment**

General Property Trust is Australia's largest listed property trust by assets. Its property-investment portfolio contains 11 retail, one industrial, and three office sites. Most of its retail investments are shopping centers, including a 33% stake in Erina Fair, which is the only shopping center on New South Wales' central coast. The shopping centers' major tenants include Kmart, David Jones, Coles, Woolworths, and Target. It also owns Australia Square and MLC Centre, buildings in Sydney's central business district.

A$ mil	12/92	12/93	12/94	US$mil 12/94				
Sales	**180.7**	**174.8**	**184.8**	**135.7**	P/E Ratio	**12.3**	Price (9/30/95)	**2.29**
Net Income	**112.8**	**104.1**	**115.8**	**85.0**	P/B Ratio	**0.8**	52 Wk Hi-Low	**2.52-2.10**
Book Value	**1,552.8**	**1,591.2**	**1,801.4**	**1,396.4**	Yield %	**8.7**	Market Cap	**US$1,091.3mil**

Address **Australia Sq., George St.**
Sydney, NSW 2000
Tel **008-025-095** Fax **N/A**
ADR SEDOL No. **6365866**
Chief Executive **John Mulcahy**
Chairman **Gilles Kryger**

Gio Australia

Industry: **Insurance - Full Line**

Gio Australia Holdings is Australia's largest general insurer. Its three main areas of operation are life insurance, personal investment, and consumer lending. The company is also involved in reinsurance, mutual-fund management, asset management, and securities and bond trading. Gio operates AA-Gio Insurance, a joint venture with the New Zealand Automobile Association, which offers car, house, and contents coverage. All revenues from Gio's insurance and financial services are generated in Australia; reinsurance is the only service it provides internationally.

A$ mil	06/92	06/93	06/94	US$mil 06/94				
Revenues	**1,423.3**	**2,132.6**	**1,871.9**	**1,292.7**	P/E Ratio	**13.2**	Price (9/30/95)	**2.75**
Net Income	**117.0**	**103.1**	**126.1**	**87.1**	P/B Ratio	**1.2**	52 Wk Hi-Low	**2.85-2.47**
Book Value	**1,034.7**	**1,110.0**	**1,227.2**	**895.8**	Yield %	**5.8**	Market Cap	**US$1,156.0mil**

Address **2 Martin Pl.**
Sydney, NSW 2000
Tel **02-228-1000** Fax **02-235-3909**
ADR SEDOL No. **6359836**
Managing Director **William J. Jocelyn**
Chairman **John A. Iliffe**

Gold Mines of Kalgoorlie

Industry: **Precious Metals**

Gold Mines of Kalgoorlie (GMK) owns and operates the Jubilee gold mine. It also holds a 50% stake in Kalgoorlie Consolidated Gold Mines, which owns and operates the Super Pit (Australia's largest gold mine by production) and the nearby Mt. Charlotte mine. GMK has an annual attributable production of about 400,000 ounces of gold, and reserves of 10.8 million ounces. The Jubilee mine accounts for about 20% of the company's total gold production and 8% of its reserves. Poseidon Gold, a member of the Normandy Poseidon resource group, owns more than 17% of GMK.

A$ mil	06/92	06/93	06/94	US$mil 06/94				
Sales	**241.1**	**241.1**	**252.0**	**174.0**	P/E Ratio	**29.8**	Price (9/30/95)	**1.19**
Net Income	**38.3**	**26.6**	**28.5**	**19.7**	P/B Ratio	**2.4**	52 Wk Hi-Low	**1.37-0.81**
Book Value	**281.4**	**307.2**	**343.4**	**250.6**	Yield %	**2.5**	Market Cap	**US$860.8mil**

Address **100 Hutt St., P.O. Box 7175**
Adelaide, SA 5000
Tel **08-303-1700** Fax **08-232-0198**
ADR **GMKGY** SEDOL No. **6375661**
President **Anthony J. Palmer**
Chairman **Steven G. Dean**

Goodman Fielder

Industry: **Other Food**

Goodman Fielder is Australasia's largest food company. Its main areas of business are baking and milling, consumer foods, food ingredients for the retail market, and poultry. Goodman controls Continental Europe's largest baking company, and holds 30% of the bread market in Australia, 57% in New Zealand, 90% in Singapore, and 13% in Malaysia; it also commands a 30% share of the Australian poultry market. The firm manufactures, markets, and distributes its products in more than 20 countries. In fiscal 1993, it generated 40% of its revenues outside of Australia and New Zealand.

A$ mil	06/92	06/93	06/94	US$mil 06/94				
Sales	**3,909.2**	**3,982.9**	**3,715.3**	**2,565.8**	P/E Ratio	**14.7**	Price (9/30/95)	**1.35**
Net Income	**49.5**	**182.0**	**93.4**	**64.5**	P/B Ratio	**1.2**	52 Wk Hi-Low	**1.36-1.09**
Book Value	**1,245.5**	**1,353.3**	**1,370.8**	**1,000.6**	Yield %	**8.1**	Market Cap	**US$1,224.1mil**

Address **Grosvenor Pl., 225 George St.**
Sydney, NSW 2000
Tel **02-258-4000** Fax **02-247-2810**
ADR **GMFIY** SEDOL No. **6336549**
CEO **David Hearn**
Chairman **David Clarke**

James Hardie Industries

Industry: **Building Materials**

James Hardie Industries' main areas of business are plumbing, pipelines, irrigation, building boards, building services and technologies. The company manfactures fiber-cement goods, plumbing equipment, gypsum plaster, electronic security systems, and water-heating equipment. It also offers fire-protection, air-conditioning, and engineering services. The firm's products include Quell fire extinguishers, Lawn Genie lawn-care equipment, Rainjet irrigation systems, Hardiplank siding, Irwell bathroom-plumbing equipment, and Equibond steel-insulated wall panels.

A$ mil	03/93	03/94	03/95	US$mil 03/95				
Sales	**1,462.2**	**1,615.5**	**1,725.4**	**1,282.8**	P/E Ratio	**11.3**	Price (9/30/95)	**2.25**
Net Income	**61.0**	**48.0**	**74.6**	**55.5**	P/B Ratio	**1.3**	52 Wk Hi-Low	**2.46-1.92**
Book Value	**659.7**	**639.0**	**687.9**	**505.8**	Yield %	**5.3**	Market Cap	**US$656.9mil**

Address **James Hardie Hse., 65 York St.**
Sydney, NSW 2000
Tel **02-290-5333** Fax **02-262-4394**
ADR **JHINY** SEDOL No. **6409407**
Managing Director **Keith Barton**
Chairman **John B. Reid**

Highlands Gold

Industry: **Precious Metals**

Highlands Gold is a gold-mining concern that is 65%-owned by the Australian metals and mining company M.I.M. Holdings. It explores for and mines gold through its 25% stake in Papua New Guinea's Porgera gold mine, which suffered a fire in January 1994 and shut down for seven months. The mine has 17.9 million ounces of gold reserves. Highlands Gold owns Porgera with partners Placer Pacific, Renison Goldfields Consolidated, and the Papua New Guinea government. It also explores for copper, nickel cobalt, and chromite in Papua New Guinea and Indonesia.

Kina mil	06/91	06/92	06/93	US$mil 06/93				
Sales	**95.1**	**168.5**	**131.7**	**92.6**	P/E Ratio	**11.2**	Price (9/30/95)	**0.94**
Net Income	**29.1**	**51.9**	**26.3**	**18.5**	P/B Ratio	**0.8**	52 Wk Hi-Low	**1.63-0.83**
Book Value	**342.5**	**363.3**	**364.1**	**246.0**	Yield %	**2.4**	Market Cap	**US$402.0mil**

Address **Champion Pde., Port Moresby**
Papua New Guinea
Tel **0675-21-7633**
Fax **0675-21-7551**
ADR
SEDOL No. **6425867**
Managing Director **Ian A. Goddard**
Chairman **N. Coldham- Fussell**

Homestake Gold

Industry: **Precious Metals**

Homestake Gold of Australia explores for and mines gold. It holds a 50% stake in Kalgoorlie Consolidated Gold Mines, which owns and operates several major mines, including the Super Pit, Australia's largest-producing gold mine. The Super Pit has annual gold production of more than 600,000 ounces. Homestake Gold also operates 13 exploration properties throughout Australia, and owns a 70% stake in the Timbarra mine in New South Wales and an 86% stake in Copper Canyon mine in Queensland. The U.S.-based Homestake Mining Company owns 82% of Homestake Gold.

A$ mil	12/92	12/93	12/94	US$mil 12/94				
Sales	**168.6**	**175.6**	**184.0**	**135.1**	P/E Ratio	**33.7**	Price (9/30/95)	**1.99**
Net Income	**2.6**	**27.4**	**34.8**	**25.6**	P/B Ratio	**6.7**	52 Wk Hi-Low	**2.02-1.15**
Book Value	**113.5**	**184.0**	**176.5**	**136.8**	Yield %	**0.0**	Market Cap	**US$892.3mil**

Address **226 Great Eastern Hwy.**
Belmont, WA 6104
Tel **09-270-4111**
Fax **09-479-4845**
ADR
SEDOL No. **6434830**
Managing Director **Richard A. Tastula**
Chairman **Bryan N. Kelman**

Incitec

Industry: **Specialty Chemicals**

Incitec produces chemicals and transports hazardous materials. It produces crop-protection and home-garden products and industrial chemicals. The company consumes 60% of the natural-gas supply of Brisbane, where it serves as a feedstock for Incitec's ammonia plants. It provides 70% of Australia's ammonia, for both industry and agriculture, and is its largest producer of explosive-grade ammonium nitrate for mining. Crop Care Australasia Pty Ltd., Incitec's joint venture with ICI Australia, is the largest crop-protection marketer in Australasia.

A$ mil	09/92	09/93	09/94	US$mil 09/94				
Sales	**634.3**	**633.4**	**667.2**	**473.2**	P/E Ratio	**15.6**	Price (9/30/95)	**4.82**
Net Income	**32.1**	**31.8**	**29.6**	**21.0**	P/B Ratio	**2.9**	52 Wk Hi-Low	**5.00-3.50**
Book Value	**187.7**	**192.2**	**172.4**	**127.7**	Yield %	**4.1**	Market Cap	**US$398.2mil**

Address **Paringa Rd., Gibson Island**
Murarrie, QLD 4172
Tel **07-867-9300**
Fax **07-867-9310**
ADR
SEDOL No. **6008815**
President **J.F. Babon**
Chairman **R. J. Hunt**

Jupiters

Industry: **Lodging**

Jupiters owns and operates the Hotel Conrad and the Jupiters Casino in Broadbeach and the Hotel Conrad and Treasury Casino in Brisbane, two of only 12 licensed casinos in Australia. The company also has a strategic interest in the Breakwater Casino in northern Queensland. The company derives 74% of its revenues from casino operations. Its Broadbeach location houses two restaurants and convention facilities, and both casinos feature acts from Asian performing artists. Conrad International Investment holds a 20% interest in Jupiters.

A$ mil	06/92 R	06/93	06/94	US$mil 06/94				
Sales	**241.7**	**246.8**	**283.2**	**195.6**	P/E Ratio	**13.3**	Price (9/30/95)	**3.00**
Net Income	**31.6**	**40.3**	**49.3**	**34.0**	P/B Ratio	**1.4**	52 Wk Hi-Low	**3.60-2.84**
Book Value	**376.3**	**383.0**	**499.6**	**364.7**	Yield %	**5.7**	Market Cap	**US$548.5mil**

Address **Niecon Twr., 17 Victoria Ave.**
Broadbeach, QLD 4218
Tel **07-570-2500**
Fax **07-538-6315**
ADR
SEDOL No. **6476713**
Managing Director **Richard K. Barnes**
Chairman **Lawrence J. Willett**

R=Restated.

Leighton Holdings

Industry: **Heavy Construction**

Leighton Holdings is an engineering and construction company. It provides specialized-engineering, contract-mining, and waste- and environmental-management services. The German construction company Hochtief Ltd. owns 48% of Leighton Holdings. The company is beginning the fulfillment of new contracts in Hong Kong worth over A$330. In March 1994, Leighton Holdings led the consortium that won the bid to build Sydney's first gambling casino. The company will manage and have a 5% stake in the A$1billion casino, which is to be completed in 1997.

A$ mil	06/92	06/93	06/94	US$mil 06/94				
Sales	**1,556.4**	**1,517.3**	**1,692.5**	**1,168.9**	P/E Ratio	**44.9**	Price (9/30/95)	**3.10**
Net Income	**22.5**	**15.1**	**33.1**	**22.9**	P/B Ratio	**2.3**	52 Wk Hi-Low	**3.20-1.65**
Book Value	**244.0**	**285.8**	**302.5**	**220.8**	Yield %	**2.9**	Market Cap	**US$544.6mil**

Address **472 Pacific Highway**
St. Leonards, NSW 2065
Tel **02-925-6666**
Fax **02-925-6005**
ADR
SEDOL No. **6511227**
President **Wallace M. King**
Chairman **Morrish A. Besley**

Lend Lease

Industry: **Real-Estate Investment**

Lend Lease Corporation is a real-estate and financial-services firm. It is involved in commercial-property development and management, construction and reconstruction, asset management, life and nonlife insurance, and personal-investment services. Lend Lease has property-development operations throughout Australia, New Zealand, Malaysia, and Singapore. Financial services constitute the firm's largest division; its MLC group and Australian Eagle Life investment and insurance companies provide more than 60% of net profits.

	A$ mil 06/92	06/93	06/94	US$mil 06/94				
Sales	**1,013.2**	**1,155.9**	**1,438.8**	**993.6**	P/E Ratio	**17.0**	Price (9/30/95)	**18.70**
Net Income	**195.3**	**206.1**	**232.1**	**160.3**	P/B Ratio	**1.9**	52 Wk Hi-Low	**18.98-15.48**
Book Value	**1,768.4**	**1,853.3**	**2,079.9**	**1,518.2**	Yield %	**4.3**	Market Cap	**US$3,102.7mil**

Address **Australia Sq. Tower, George St.** **Sydney, NSW 2000**
Tel **02-236-6111** Fax **02-252-2192**
ADR SEDOL No. **6512004**
Chief Executive **John P. Morschel**
Chairman **Stuart G. Hornery**

Mayne Nickless

Industry: **General Industrial & Commercial Services**

Mayne Nickless operates transport, security, and health-care businesses. The company's transport division provides freight, courier, and distribution services. Its security activities include armored-transport and general-security services. It also operates private hospitals and holds 21% of Optus Communications, which provides telephone and cable-television services in Australia. The company has transport and security subsidiaries in North America and Europe. More than 50% of Mayne Nickless' revenues come from North America and Europe.

	A$ mil 06/93	06/94	06/95	US$mil 06/95				
Sales	**2,765.0**	**2,837.4**	**3,000.7**	**2,143.4**	P/E Ratio	**N/A**	Price (9/30/95)	**6.27**
Net Income	**58.8**	**69.5**	**79.2**	**56.6**	P/B Ratio	**1.6**	52 Wk Hi-Low	**7.36-5.45**
Book Value	**1,204.2**	**1,217.4**	**1,189.3**	**843.4**	Yield %	**0.0**	Market Cap	**US$1,459.5mil**

Address **390 St. Kilda Rd.** **Melbourne, VIC 3004**
Tel **03-868-0700** Fax **03-867-1179**
ADR **MAYNY** SEDOL No. **6574606**
Managing Director **William T. Bytheway**
Chairman **Ian E. Webber**

MIM Holdings

Industry: **Mining**

M.I.M. Holdings, Australia's second-largest mining company, explores for, mines, and refines precious metals and coal. Its main customers are located in Australia, Asia, Europe and Japan. The Mt. Isa and Hilton mining and metallurgical complexes are the company's most important bases, where it mines more than 250 million tonnes annually. It also has two smelter refineries located in the United Kingdom and Germany. M.I.M. operates an Australian national land-transport company, and it holds a 65% stake in the Australian gold-mining company Highlands Gold.

	A$ mil 06/92	06/93	06/94	US$mil 06/94				
Sales	**1,754.3**	**1,928.2**	**2,194.0**	**1,515.2**	P/E Ratio	**35.8**	Price (9/30/95)	**1.90**
Net Income	**106.3**	**74.0**	**-195.1**	**-134.7**	P/B Ratio	**1.2**	52 Wk Hi-Low	**2.93-1.70**
Book Value	**2,552.5**	**2,533.0**	**2,492.8**	**1,819.6**	Yield %	**2.6**	Market Cap	**US$2,292.2mil**

Address **MIM Plz., 410 Ann St.** **Brisbane, QLD 4000**
Tel **07-833-8000** Fax **07-832-2426**
ADR **MIMOY** SEDOL No. **6550167**
President **R. Bruce Vaughan**
Chairman **R. Bruce Vaughan**

National Australia Bank

Industry: **Banks - Money Center**

National Australia Bank (NAB) is Australia's largest and most-profitable banking group. Almost half of the bank's assets are held outside of Australia. Its overseas subsidiaries include Clydesdale Bank (U.K.), Yorkshire Bank (U.K.), National Irish Bank (Ireland), and Northern Bank (Ireland). It owns the Bank of New Zealand, that country's largest financial institution, and has also acquired Michigan National. Other services include life insurance, financial-planning services, and travel services. The group operates more than 2,000 branches worldwide.

	A$ mil 09/92	09/93	09/94	US$mil 09/94				
Revenues	**9,458.6**	**9,632.1**	**9,693.0**	**6,874.5**	P/E Ratio	**9.2**	Price (9/30/95)	**11.70**
Net Income	**675.1**	**1,128.8**	**1,708.0**	**1,211.3**	P/B Ratio	**1.6**	52 Wk Hi-Low	**12.54-10.16**
Book Value	**7,995.1**	**8,815.8**	**9,852.0**	**7,297.8**	Yield %	**6.3**	Market Cap	**US$12,378mil**

Address **500 Burke St.** **Melbourne, VIC 3000**
Tel **03-641-3171** Fax **03-641-4927**
ADR **NAB** SEDOL No. **6624608**
CEO **Donald R. Angus**
Chairman **William R.M. Irvine**

Newcrest Mining

Industry: **Precious Metals**

Newcrest Mining finds, develops, and mines gold orebodies in Australia and overseas. It holds interests in six Australian gold mines, both open-pit and underground. Its average annual gold production totals more than 730,000 ounces, with estimated gold reserves of 13.6 million ounces. Its Telfer mine in Western Australia is the country's second-largest gold producer. The company's offshore exploration programs are located in Indonesia, Chile, Argentina, Peru, Bolivia, and Greece. Newcrest sells 25,000 tonness of Telfer concentrate to Japanese smelters annually.

	A$ mil 12/92	12/93	12/94	US$mil 12/94				
Sales	**424.2**	**437.8**	**432.6**	**317.6**	P/E Ratio	**26.9**	Price (9/30/95)	**5.80**
Net Income	**0.9**	**37.5**	**50.4**	**37.0**	P/B Ratio	**N/A**	52 Wk Hi-Low	**7.21-4.23**
Book Value	**404.1**	**413.9**	**N/A**	**N/A**	Yield %	**2.1**	Market Cap	**US$1,013.5mil**

Address **9th Fl., 600 St. Kilda Rd.** **Melbourne, VIC 3004**
Tel **03-522-5333** Fax **03-525-2996**
ADR **NEW** SEDOL No. **6637101**
President **John C. Quinn**
Chairman **Sir Roderick Carnegie**

News Corporation

Industry: **Publishing**

News Corp. is a diversified media and entertainment company with operations in the Pacific Rim, the United States, and the United Kingdom. It is the largest newspaper publisher in the world. Newspaper and magazine titles include TV Guide, The New York Post, The Boston Herald, and the U.K.'s Times and Sun. Its publishing and television subsidiaries include HarperCollins and Fox Broadcasting. It also owns Twentieth Century Fox Film, which produces and distributes films and videos, and a 50% share of Ansett Airlines.

A$ mil	06/92	06/93	06/94	US$mil 06/94				
Sales	**10,189.0**	**10,685.5**	**11,621.0**	**8,025.6**	P/E Ratio	**11.3**	Price (9/30/95)	**7.36**
Net Income	**592.0**	**873.5**	**1,212.0**	**837.0**	P/B Ratio	**1.0**	52 Wk Hi-Low	**8.38-4.70**
Book Value	**10,898.8**	**12,108.7**	**13,976.0**	**10,201.5**	Yield %	**0.4**	Market Cap	**US$10,658mil**

Address **2 Holt St.**
Sydney, NSW 2010
Tel **02-288-3000**
Fax **02-228-3254**
ADR **NWS**
SEDOL No. **6886925**
President **D.F. DeVoe**
Chairman **K. Rupert Murdoch**

Normandy Mining

Industry: **Precious Metals**

Normandy Mining (formerly Normandy Poseidon) is a diversified mining group with operations in mineral exploration, mining, mineral processing, and marketing. Its wholly-owned Commercial Minerals is Australia's largest producer and marketer of industrial minerals, including magnetite, calcite, feldspar, zinc dust, and zinc oxide. Its 58%-owned Poseidon Gold produces roughly 800,000 ounces of gold per annum. Other products include copper and diamonds. It has a joint venture with South Africa's Anglo American for mineral exploration in Indonesia, Vietnam, and Laos.

A$ mil	06/92	06/93	06/94	US$mil 06/94				
Sales	**680.9**	**898.2**	**951.4**	**657.1**	P/E Ratio	**N/A**	Price (9/30/95)	**1.74**
Net Income	**33.6**	**58.2**	**85.3**	**58.9**	P/B Ratio	**1.4**	52 Wk Hi-Low	**2.63-1.44**
Book Value	**538.7**	**528.5**	**605.8**	**442.2**	Yield %	**3.4**	Market Cap	**US$647.5mil**

Address **100 Hutt St.**
Adelaide, SA 5000
Tel **08-303-1700**
Fax **08-232-0198**
ADR **NDYMY**
SEDOL No. **6645201**
Managing Director **Anthony J. Palmer**
Chairman **R.J.C. de Crespigny**

North

Industry: **Forest Products**

North (formerly North Broken Hill Peko) is active in mining, forestry, and mining-equipment production. The company produced 12.4 million tonnes of iron ore in 1993, in addition to gold and copper. North owns 66% of Energy Resources of Australia, the country's largest producer of uranium. North's Tasmania- based forestry division produces woodchips and fiber for the paper industry. North sold its paper and pulp operations in 1993. It increased its stake in Dominion Mining to 15% in 1994. Exports to North America and Europe contribute nearly 10% of North's sales.

A$ mil	06/92	06/93	06/94	US$mil 06/94				
Sales	**1,543.0**	**1,513.1**	**1,131.0**	**781.0**	P/E Ratio	**13.4**	Price (9/30/95)	**3.80**
Net Income	**84.2**	**132.4**	**185.3**	**128.0**	P/B Ratio	**1.9**	52 Wk Hi-Low	**3.97-2.77**
Book Value	**1,017.8**	**1,149.2**	**1,308.8**	**955.3**	Yield %	**3.4**	Market Cap	**US$1,956.3mil**

Address **476 St. Kilda Rd.**
Melbourne, VIC 3004
Tel **03-829-0000**
Fax **03-867-4351**
ADR **NTHLY**
SEDOL No. **6644037**
Managing Director **C.M. Anderson**
Chairman **C. Michael Deeley**

OPSM Protector

Industry: **Other Specialty Retailers**

OPSM Protector makes and distributes prescription- eyewear products, and industrial and household safety equipment. Its OPSM division is Australia's leading retailer of eyewear products and services by sales, and operates 219 retail outlets. The division also distributes ophthalmic, medical, surgical, and diagnostic instruments. Its Protector Safety division makes safety helmets, suits for bomb-disposal personnel, waterproof clothing, industrial footwear, and respirator canisters. OPSM Protector has businesses in Australia, New Zealand, and Europe.

A$ mil	06/92	06/93	06/94	US$mil 06/94				
Revenues	**322.2**	**342.9**	**381.1**	**263.2**	P/E Ratio	**14.7**	Price (9/30/95)	**2.20**
Net Income	**16.6**	**0.3**	**21.4**	**14.8**	P/B Ratio	**2.5**	52 Wk Hi-Low	**2.32-1.77**
Book Value	**129.3**	**116.1**	**125.6**	**91.7**	Yield %	**5.5**	Market Cap	**US$235.6mil**

Address **Level 4, 194 Miller St.**
North Sydney, NSW 2060
Tel **02-922-3666**
Fax **02-929-7031**
ADR
SEDOL No. **6655501**
Chief Executive **Jeff Kelly**
Chairman **Adrian J. Lane**

Orbital Engine

Industry: **Other Auto Parts**

Orbital Engine develops engine and fuel-systems technology, primarily related to its patented Orbital Combustion Process (OCP) two-stroke engine. Its OCP engine is cheaper to manufacture, 40% lighter, 60% smaller, 35% more fuel-efficient, and produces substantially lower emissions than conventional engines of equal power. Orbital has technology- licensing agreements with Fiat Auto, General Motors, and Ford Motor Company, from which it earns fees and expects to earn royalties. The company recently opened its first commercial-production factory in Michigan.

A$ mil	06/92	06/93	06/94	US$mil 06/94				
Sales	**39.7**	**16.8**	**11.4**	**7.9**	P/E Ratio	**NMF**	Price (9/30/95)	**1.50**
Net Income	**22.8**	**11.2**	**-17.0**	**-11.7**	P/B Ratio	**1.0**	52 Wk Hi-Low	**2.00-1.10**
Book Value	**455.7**	**479.7**	**463.1**	**338.1**	Yield %	**N/A**	Market Cap	**US$367.2mil**

Address **152-158 St. George's Terrace**
Perth, WA 6000
Tel **09-429-3100**
Fax **09-429-3111**
ADR **OE**
SEDOL No. **6777171**
President **Kim Schlunke**
Chairman **Russel Fynmore**

Pacific Dunlop

Industry: **Conglomerates**

Pacific Dunlop is a diversified international marketer and manufacturer of clothing, sporting goods, food, medical equipment, batteries, latex goods, tires, and plastics. The firm sells Dunlop-brand footwear, tires, and sportswear in Australia. Other brands include Champion batteries, Slazenger sporting goods, and Lifestyle condoms. The building division produces power and telecommunications cable and is also Asia's largest bedding supplier. In fiscal 1993, the firm generated 35% of sales and 43% of profits outside Australia.

	A$ mil 06/92	06/93	06/94	US$mil 06/94				
Sales	5,806.2	6,304.6	6,966.8	4,811.3	P/E Ratio	11.2	Price (9/30/95)	3.29
Net Income	220.6	269.9	308.4	213.0	P/B Ratio	1.5	52 Wk Hi-Low	4.14-2.70
Book Value	2,159.7	2,388.2	2,368.7	1,729.0	Yield %	7.0	Market Cap	US$2,709.7mil

Address **Level 41, 101 Collins St.**
Melbourne, VIC 3000
Tel **03-270-7270**
Fax **03-270-7300**
ADR **PDLPY**
SEDOL No. **6286611**
President **Philip Brass**
Chairman **John B. Gough**

Pasminco

Industry: **Non-Ferrous Metals - Other (Exc. Aluminum)**

Pasminco explores for and mines base metals, mainly zinc, lead, silver, and gold. It is Australia's only primary producer of refined zinc and lead metals, and holds 8% of the world's zinc market and 6% of the world's lead market. It has four zinc-, lead-, and silver-mining operations, and three primary smelters in Australia. Its Pasminco Europe subsidiary runs a zinc and lead smelter and zinc-processing operations in the Netherlands. Pasminco exports to more than 50 countries. Metal sales consist of 42% zinc, 30% silver, and 28% lead.

	A$ mil 06/92	06/93	06/94	US$mil 06/94				
Sales	1,318.2	1,372.1	1,193.7	824.4	P/E Ratio	NMF	Price (9/30/95)	1.55
Net Income	-140.1	-86.9	-14.4	-9.9	P/B Ratio	1.7	52 Wk Hi-Low	2.26-1.21
Book Value	759.4	665.7	739.6	539.9	Yield %	0.0	Market Cap	US$933.0mil

Address **15th Fl., 380 St. Kilda Rd.**
Melbourne, VIC 3004
Tel **03-288-0333**
Fax **03-288-0406**
ADR
SEDOL No. **6671080**
President **Peter C. Barnett**
Chairman **Mark R. Rayner**

Pioneer International

Industry: **Oil - Secondary**

Pioneer International produces, distributes, and retails construction materials and refines, distributes, and retails petroleum products. It produces premixed concrete, cement, asphalt, roof tiles, bricks, pavers, and plasterboard. Its construction-materials businesses operate in Australia, Europe, Israel, the United States, and Asia. It garners about 40% of total revenues overseas. Its wholly-owned Ampol subsidiary recently merged with Caltex, an Australian oil refining and marketing company, to form Australian Petroleum Pty Ltd.

	A$ mil 06/92	06/93	06/94	US$mil 06/94				
Sales	5,015.3	5,244.1	5,501.9	3,799.7	P/E Ratio	15.4	Price (9/30/95)	3.50
Net Income	178.7	151.6	199.8	138.0	P/B Ratio	1.6	52 Wk Hi-Low	3.62-2.96
Book Value	1,902.5	1,939.6	1,943.0	1,418.2	Yield %	4.3	Market Cap	US$2,349.1mil

Address **Level 20, 580 George St.**
Sydney, NSW 2000
Tel **02-323-4000**
Fax **02-323-4008**
ADR **PONNY**
SEDOL No. **6688701**
President **John Schubert**
Chairman **Tristan Antico**

Plutonic Resources

Industry: **Precious Metals**

Plutonic Resources is a gold-mining and -exploration company. The company operates five mines and five exploration projects in Australia. It produces an average of 332,800 ounces of gold annually, 52% of which is mined at its Plutonic Gold Mine. Plutonic has a 50% interest in the Bellvue Mine, an underground-gold-mining operation, and has begun underground mining at Plutonic and Darlot. It also holds a 62% interest in Lachlan Resources, an Australian base-metals-mining company, and a 67% interest in Peak Hill Mine, a gold-mining joint venture with North.

	A$ mil 12/92	12/93	12/94	US$mil 12/94				
Sales	84.6	208.7	193.9	142.4	P/E Ratio	32.3	Price (9/30/95)	6.85
Net Income	30.5	35.2	38.1	28.0	P/B Ratio	3.9	52 Wk Hi-Low	6.85-5.45
Book Value	145.8	295.1	319.3	247.5	Yield %	1.2	Market Cap	US$934.5mil

Address **100 Miller St.**
North Sydney, NSW 2060
Tel **02-900-5000**
Fax **02-955-9620**
ADR
SEDOL No. **6644349**
Managing Director **Ronald J. Hawkes**
Chairman **Sir Eric McClintock**

PosGold

Industry: **Precious Metals**

PosGold (formerly Poseidon Gold) is the 58%-owned gold-mining subsidiary of Normandy Mining. It has an attributable annual production of roughly 800,000 ounces of gold from reserves of more than 6 million ounces. It owns or has substantial interests in 12 mines in Australia. Its 76%-owned Mt. Leyshon Gold Mines accounts for roughly 20% of Poseidon's production. Other major interests include Gold Mines of Kalgoorlie (25%) and North Flinders Mines (50%). The company explores for gold in Australia, Turkey, and Southeast Asia.

	A$ mil 06/92	06/93	06/94	US$mil 06/94				
Sales	513.1	693.0	762.2	526.4	P/E Ratio	14.8	Price (9/30/95)	2.47
Net Income	49.2	71.5	78.0	53.9	P/B Ratio	2.3	52 Wk Hi-Low	4.05-1.86
Book Value	279.5	374.6	586.8	428.3	Yield %	4.0	Market Cap	US$1,077.3mil

Address **100 Hutt St.**
Adelaide, SA 5000
Tel **08-303-1700**
Fax **08-232-0198**
ADR **PSGLY**
SEDOL No. **6065081**
Managing Director **A.J. Palmer**
Chairman **R.J.C. de Crespigny**

Publishing & Broadcasting

Industry: **Broadcasting**

Publishing & Broadcasting operates television and radio stations in Australia and New Guinea and publishes magazines. The company was formed by a merger in third-quarter 1994 of the operations of Australian Consolidated Press, a magazine publisher, into those of Nine Network, a television broadcaster. It also has an investment unit operated by PBL Enterprises. It has a joint venture with Village Roadshow to develop and operate theme parks and entertainment centers throughout Asia. Publishing & Broadcasting is controlled by media businessman Kerry Packer.

A$ mil	06/92	06/93	06/94	US$mil 06/94				
Sales	**522.5**	**557.4**	**585.5**	**404.4**	P/E Ratio	**15.0**	Price (9/30/95)	**4.12**
Net Income	**60.5**	**70.4**	**88.3**	**61.0**	P/B Ratio	**1.8**	52 Wk Hi-Low	**4.33-3.62**
Book Value	**714.0**	**726.0**	**771.8**	**563.4**	Yield %	**3.4**	Market Cap	**US$1,024.3mil**

Address **24 Artarmon Rd.**
Willoughby, NSW 2068
Tel **N/A**
Fax **07-220-0074**
ADR
SEDOL No. **6637082**
Managing Director **Brian Packer**
Chairman **Kerry F.B. Packer**

QBE Insurance Group

Industry: **Insurance - Full Line**

QBE Insurance Group is a general-insurance and reinsurance company, with operations throughout Australia, Asia, and North America. QBE provides a range of insurance products for commercial and individual customers. Motor-vehicle coverage, its largest insurance line, contributes more than one fourth of premium income. About 42% of QBE's total gross premiums originate in Australia. QBE operates joint ventures in Vietnam, Thailand, Indonesia, and French Polynesia. Its reinsurance division, the Sydney Reinsurance Group, accounts for 36% of gross premium income.

A$ mil	06/92	06/93	06/94	US$mil 06/94				
Revenues	**1,017.6**	**1,213.0**	**1,520.3**	**1,049.9**	P/E Ratio	**17.8**	Price (9/30/95)	**5.63**
Net Income	**54.9**	**64.5**	**110.0**	**76.0**	P/B Ratio	**2.0**	52 Wk Hi-Low	**6.05-4.15**
Book Value	**457.4**	**516.8**	**597.7**	**436.3**	Yield %	**3.6**	Market Cap	**US$933.4mil**

Address **2nd Fl., 82 Pitt St.**
Sydney, NSW 2000
Tel **02-235-4444**
Fax **02-235-3166**
ADR
SEDOL No. **6715740**
President **John Cloney**
Chairman **David Burns**

QCT Resources

Industry: **Coal**

QCT Resources produces and sells coking coal for steel production and thermal coal for power generation. Through two local joint ventures, the company runs nine mines throughout Australia. Its largest mine is at South Blackwater, which produces 23% of the company's coal shipments. Japan, which is QCT's largest customer nation, consumes 24% of the company's coal output. Other major customers include the Dutch power producer GKE and Australia's BHP Steel Group. QCT also has production and sales joint ventures with Mitsubishi, BHP, AMP, and Pancontinental.

A$ mil	06/92	06/93	06/94	US$mil 06/94				
Sales	**620.4**	**698.3**	**659.9**	**455.7**	P/E Ratio	**15.9**	Price (9/30/95)	**1.65**
Net Income	**40.4**	**67.0**	**61.1**	**42.2**	P/B Ratio	**1.7**	52 Wk Hi-Low	**1.74-1.25**
Book Value	**462.1**	**492.8**	**563.7**	**411.5**	Yield %	**5.5**	Market Cap	**US$758.8mil**

Address **10th Fl., 307 Queen St.**
Brisbane, QLD 4000
Tel **07-229-9600**
Fax **07-229-7240**
ADR
SEDOL No. **6713476**
Managing Director **Christopher D. Rawlings**
Chairman **J.K. Allister McLeod**

QNI

Industry: **Non-Ferrous Metals - Other (Exc. Aluminum)**

QNI explores for and mines nickel and cobalt in Queensland. Its wholly-owned Queensland Nickel Venture subsidiary operates a nickel- and cobalt-processing facility outside Townsville in Queensland. QNI has an annual average production of almost 28,000 tonnes of nickel and 1,400 tonnes of cobalt. It is Australia's largest producer of cobalt and second-largest producer of nickel. It imports most of its nickel ore from Indonesia and New Caledonia, and also maintains exploration programs in the Philippines, Indonesia, New Caledonia, and the Solomon Islands.

A$ mil	06/92	06/93	06/94	US$mil 06/94				
Sales	**N/A**	**218.7**	**207.4**	**143.2**	P/E Ratio	**NMF**	Price (9/30/95)	**2.75**
Net Income	**N/A**	**-9.7**	**1.2**	**0.8**	P/B Ratio	**2.7**	52 Wk Hi-Low	**2.88-1.65**
Book Value	**N/A**	**301.3**	**380.1**	**277.4**	Yield %	**0.0**	Market Cap	**US$848.5mil**

Address **Waterfront Pl., 1 Eagle St.**
Brisbane, QLD 4000
Tel **07-224-3400**
Fax **07-229-2398**
ADR
SEDOL No. **6713948**
Managing Director **Wyn Davies**
Chairman **Max Roberts**

Renison Goldfields

Industry: **Precious Metals**

Renison Goldfields Consolidated (RGC) explores for and mines gold, mineral sands, coal, tin ore and concentrates, and copper ore and concentrates. It has mining interests in Australia, the Philippines, Papua New Guinea, and Indonesia, in addition to mineral-exploration programs in Bolivia, Greece, and the United States. The company holds a 25% stake in the Porgera gold-mining operation in Papua New Guinea, which produces approximately 37,000 kilograms of gold annually. RGC is 40% owned by the U.K. industrial-management company Hanson PLC.

A$ mil	06/92	06/93	06/94	US$mil 06/94				
Sales	**608.1**	**622.1**	**610.9**	**421.9**	P/E Ratio	**NMF**	Price (9/30/95)	**5.31**
Net Income	**-10.1**	**-24.4**	**2.0**	**1.4**	P/B Ratio	**2.0**	52 Wk Hi-Low	**5.65-3.99**
Book Value	**543.0**	**544.2**	**532.9**	**389.0**	Yield %	**0.0**	Market Cap	**US$806.6mil**

Address **Gold Fields Hse., 1 Alfred St.**
Sydney, NSW 2000
Tel **02-934-8888**
Fax **02-934-8555**
ADR
SEDOL No. **6732330**
Managing Director **Mark D. Bethwaite**
Chairman **Anthony R. Cotton**

Rothmans Holdings

Industry: **Tobacco**

Rothmans Holdings produces and distributes tobacco and packaging products. The company makes cigarettes, cigars, and other tobacco products sold under names such as Rothmans, Dunhill, and Winfield. Its Winfield 25 brand is the best-selling cigarette in Australia. Rothmans also produces and sells the R.J. Reynolds brand tobacco products Winston, Camel, and Salem. It runs plants in Australia, New Zealand, Indonesia, the Philippines, Papua New Guinea, Fiji, and Western Samoa. Its operations also include printing, packaging, and paper and board converting.

A$ mil	03/93	03/94	03/95	US$mil 03/95				
Sales	**1,484.7**	**1,558.0**	**1,564.2**	**1,163.0**	P/E Ratio	**7.8**	Price (9/30/95)	**5.05**
Net Income	**40.5**	**61.2**	**78.9**	**58.7**	P/B Ratio	**1.6**	52 Wk Hi-Low	**5.75-4.35**
Book Value	**411.7**	**427.7**	**393.9**	**289.6**	Yield %	**7.9**	Market Cap	**US$466.3mil**

Address **Northpoint, 100 Miller St.**
North Sydney, NSW 2060
Tel **02-956-0666**
Fax **02-956-7442**
ADR
SEDOL No. **6752134**
Chief Executive **Gerald Vessey**
Chairman **John W. Utz**

Santos

Industry: **Oil - Secondary**

Santos conducts oil and gas exploration, production, and marketing. Total production is about 36 million barrels of oil equivalent per year. The company has reserves of approximately 663 million barrels of oil equivalent. Its Cooper/Eromanga fields in South Australia account for about 70% of the company's total production and 60% of reserves. Operations in the United States account for less than 5% of production and reserves. Santos conducts exploration in Australia, the U.S., the United Kingdom, Ireland, Indonesia, Malaysia, and Papua New Guinea.

A$ mil	12/92	12/93	12/94	US$mil 12/94				
Sales	**689.0**	**680.2**	**640.0**	**469.9**	P/E Ratio	**10.2**	Price (9/30/95)	**3.70**
Net Income	**112.7**	**219.3**	**190.4**	**139.8**	P/B Ratio	**1.3**	52 Wk Hi-Low	**4.05-3.27**
Book Value	**1,231.7**	**1,380.6**	**1,532.2**	**1,187.8**	Yield %	**5.9**	Market Cap	**US$1,505.0mil**

Address **39 Grenfell St.**
Adelaide, SA 5000
Tel **08-218-5111**
Fax **08-212-5476**
ADR **STOSY**
SEDOL No. **6776703**
Managing Director **Norman Ross Adler**
Chairman **John Allan Uhrig**

Seven Networks

Industry: **Broadcasting**

Seven Network operates commercial television stations in Australia. The company holds several sports-broadcasting rights, including the exclusive rights to the Australian Football League games and exclusive rights from MGM/United Artists to broadcast their movies and television programs. The company owns 30% of Legion Telecall, an audiotext operator. Chairman Kerry Stokes is Seven Network's largest shareholder, owning almost 20% of the share capital. Other shareholders include media concern News Corporation (15%) and telecommunication company Telstra (12%).

A$ mil	06/92	06/93	06/94	US$mil 06/94				
Sales	**N/A**	**564.4**	**555.5**	**383.6**	P/E Ratio	**10.7**	Price (9/30/95)	**3.33**
Net Income	**N/A**	**-39.9**	**84.6**	**58.4**	P/B Ratio	**1.6**	52 Wk Hi-Low	**3.49-2.78**
Book Value	**N/A**	**-30.2**	**569.2**	**415.5**	Yield %	**4.8**	Market Cap	**US$698.0mil**

Address **1 Pacific Hwy.**
Sydney, NSW 2060
Tel **02-967-7777**
Fax **N/A**
ADR
SEDOL No. **6783855**
Chief Executive **Kerry Stokes**
Chairman **Kerry Stokes**

Howard Smith

Industry: **Marine Transportation**

Howard Smith is active in shipping, harbor towage, ship salvage, shipping agency, and shipbuilding in Australia. It also operates in the southwest Pacific and the United Kingdom. The company also distributes industrial supplies and metals, and is active in container terminals and engineering. It is Australia's largest designer and manufacturer of rolling railway stock. The company entered the retail hardware market with the acquisitions of BBC Hardware Group and the Campbells Hardware Group in 1994.

A$ mil	06/92	06/93	06/94	US$mil 06/94				
Sales	**783.2**	**843.1**	**981.1**	**677.5**	P/E Ratio	**16.1**	Price (9/30/95)	**6.20**
Net Income	**53.5**	**47.0**	**40.8**	**28.2**	P/B Ratio	**1.9**	52 Wk Hi-Low	**6.68-5.35**
Book Value	**416.8**	**444.5**	**548.7**	**400.5**	Yield %	**N/A**	Market Cap	**US$824.0mil**

Address **1 York St.**
Sydney, NSW 2000
Tel **02-230-1777**
Fax **02-251-1190**
ADR **SMHWY**
SEDOL No. **6816308**
Managing Director **Kenneth John Moss**
Chairman **Frank Conroy**

Southcorp

Industry: **Distillers & Brewers**

Southcorp operates 88 plants in 10 countries in the beverage, food, packaging, and appliance businesses. Its six Australian wineries produce wine under such names as Penfolds, Seppelt, and Lindemans. The firm's appliance division produces and sells Rheem water heaters, Vulcan dishwashers, and Chef stoves. Its packaging division's production includes beverage cans and cartons, aseptic film packaging, and adhesive tape. Its wholly-owned U.S. subsidiaries include Mor-Flo, a water-heater maker, and North America Packaging, plastic-packaging manufacturer.

A$ mil	06/92	06/93	06/94	US$mil 06/94				
Sales	**2,022.5**	**2,292.0**	**2,254.3**	**1,556.8**	P/E Ratio	**30.8**	Price (9/30/95)	**2.96**
Net Income	**114.2**	**119.0**	**49.8**	**34.4**	P/B Ratio	**1.4**	52 Wk Hi-Low	**3.12-2.67**
Book Value	**1,062.8**	**1,146.8**	**1,156.4**	**844.1**	Yield %	**5.6**	Market Cap	**US$1,271.4mil**

Address **State Bank Ctr., 91 King William**
Adelaide, SA 5000
Tel **08-239-7777**
Fax **08-231-0886**
ADR **STHHY**
SEDOL No. **6764689**
Managing Director **G.J. Kraehe**
Chairman **R.H. Allert**

Stockland Trust Group

Industry: **Real-Estate Investment**

Stockland Trust Group is a real-estate developer and investor that builds, manages, and sells retail, residential, and commercial properties. Its two subsidiaries, Stockland Trust and Stockland Corp., operate exclusively in Australia. Retail properties make up 56% of total assets and account for over half of the firm's total pretax profits. Stockland manages several Australian shopping centers and commercial properties meant for small- and medium-size companies. Stockland is developing Australia's first retail supercenter, a shopping center for large-volume merchandisers.

A$ mil	06/92 R	06/93	06/94	US$mil 06/94				
Sales	**66.9**	**72.8**	**100.5**	**69.4**	P/E Ratio	**58.3**	Price (9/30/95)	**3.09**
Net Income	**12.4**	**13.3**	**16.0**	**11.0**	P/B Ratio	**7.5**	52 Wk Hi-Low	**3.35-2.70**
Book Value	**98.6**	**111.3**	**123.4**	**90.1**	Yield %	**7.8**	Market Cap	**US$728.2mil**

Address **13th Fl., 181 Castlereagh St.**
Sydney, NSW 2000
Tel **02-321-1500**
Fax **02-267-1529**
ADR
SEDOL No. **6850856**
Managing Director **Peter J. Daly**
Chairman **Ervin Graf**

R=Restated.

TNT

Industry: **Air Freight & Couriers**

TNT transports freight in Australia, Asia, Europe, and the Americas. Its transport services operate by road, rail, and air, and include divisions that carry and warehouse cars, bulk goods, and frozen foods. The firm holds a 50% stake in Ansett Transport, an Australian airline operator. TNT also holds 50% of express parcel-delivery business GD Express Worldwide; the other portion is held by GD Net, a consortium composed of the post offices of Canada, France, Germany, the Netherlands, and Sweden.

A$ mil	06/93	06/94	06/95	US$mil 06/95				
Sales	**2,852.4**	**2,855.5**	**3,606.3**	**2,475.2**	P/E Ratio	**N/A**	Price (9/30/95)	**2.03**
Net Income	**-133.7**	**48.5**	**37.2**	**25.5**	P/B Ratio	**1.4**	52 Wk Hi-Low	**2.50-1.73**
Book Value	**513.4**	**706.9**	**815.5**	**578.4**	Yield %	**0.0**	Market Cap	**US$884.1mil**

Address **TNT Plz., Tower One, Lawson Sq.**
Redfern, NSW 2016
Tel **02-699-2222**
Fax **02-699-9238**
ADR **TNTMY**
SEDOL No. **6888329**
Managing Director **David A. Mortimer**
Chairman **Frederick W. Millar**

Tubemakers of Australia

Industry: **Steel**

Tubemakers of Australia manufactures and sells steel tubing, welded-steel sections, pressure pipes, ductile-iron and steel pipeline, polyethylene pipes, and exhaust systems. Its products serve the construction, automotive, manufacturing, mining, oil- and gas-production, and water-distribution industries. Its 50%-owned subsidiary, Vinidex Tubemakers, supplies pipes, plastic valves, and fittings to Australia, Hong Kong, China, Malaysia, and Indonesia. The company holds a 50% interest in Steel & Tube Holdings (New Zealand).

A$ mil	06/92	06/93	06/94	US$mil 06/94				
Sales	**1,126.0**	**1,163.2**	**1,481.7**	**1,023.3**	P/E Ratio	**15.6**	Price (9/30/95)	**3.33**
Net Income	**18.5**	**43.3**	**58.4**	**40.3**	P/B Ratio	**1.9**	52 Wk Hi-Low	**3.75-2.98**
Book Value	**451.6**	**465.8**	**485.4**	**354.3**	Yield %	**3.9**	Market Cap	**US$698.7mil**

Address **Level 23, 1 York St.**
Sydney, NSW 2000
Tel **02-239-6666**
Fax **02-251-3042**
ADR
SEDOL No. **6907008**
Managing Director **Anthony B. Daniels**
Chairman **John A.L. Hooke**

Wesfarmers

Industry: **Industrial - Diversified**

Wesfarmers manufactures and retails fertilizers, chemicals, building materials, forest products, natural gas, coal, and food. The company also provides transportation and insurance services, and retails livestock, wool, and consumer products. It operates five fertilizer plants, a gas plant, and three coal mines. Wesfarmers also operates 66 gas-appliance retail stores, 80 hardware stores, 72 insurance branches, and 34 supermarkets. Its wholly owned subsidiary, Kleenheat Gas, supplies natural gas to over 14,000 business customers and 160,000 domestic consumers.

A$ mil	06/92	06/93	06/94	US$mil 06/94				
Sales	**1,260.5**	**1,704.0**	**2,281.6**	**1,575.7**	P/E Ratio	**20.7**	Price (9/30/95)	**8.00**
Net Income	**63.0**	**74.3**	**139.5**	**96.3**	P/B Ratio	**2.6**	52 Wk Hi-Low	**9.65-7.70**
Book Value	**449.0**	**498.3**	**613.3**	**447.7**	Yield %	**5.1**	Market Cap	**US$1,335.3mil**

Address **11th Fl., 40 The Esplanade**
Perth, WA 6000
Tel **09-327-4211**
Fax **09-327-4216**
ADR
SEDOL No. **6948836**
President **Michael A. Chaney**
Chairman **C.H. Perkins**

Western Mining

Industry: **Mining**

Western Mining (WMC) is one of Australia's largest gold and nickel producers. WMC also manufactures copper, silver, uranium, petroleum, talc, and fertilizer. It produced roughly 60,000 tonnes of nickel, 900,000 ounces of gold, 71,000 tonnes of copper, and 5 million barrels of oil in fiscal 1993. WMC holds a majority stake in Central Norseman Gold, and 39% in Alcoa of Australia, the world's largest alumina producer. It has mineral-exploration interests in the Americas, Southeast Asia, Australia, and New Zealand. In fiscal 1993, 13% of WMC's sales came from exports.

A$ mil	06/92	06/93	06/94	US$mil 06/94				
Sales	**1,434.9**	**1,364.3**	**1,500.5**	**1,036.3**	P/E Ratio	**N/A**	Price (9/30/95)	**8.66**
Net Income	**-8.5**	**64.0**	**132.0**	**91.2**	P/B Ratio	**3.2**	52 Wk Hi-Low	**9.27-6.42**
Book Value	**2,859.8**	**2,881.4**	**3,026.3**	**2,209.0**	Yield %	**N/A**	Market Cap	**US$7,258.8mil**

Address **360 Collins St.**
Melbourne, VIC 3000
Tel **03-685-6000**
Fax **03-670-9591**
ADR **WMC**
SEDOL No. **6954985**
Managing Director **H.M. Morgan**
Chairman **Arvi Parbo**

Westfield Holdings

Industry: **Real-Estate Investment**

Westfield Holdings manages retail properties, including 25 Australian shopping centers with more than 1.25 million square meters of rental area. The company manages Westfield Trust, Australia's largest listed property trust whose current holdings exceed A$2.3 billion. In 1994, Westfield, with two U.S. partners, purchased CentreMark Properties Inc., adding 19 new U.S. sites and 1.6 million square meters to its property portfolio. It jointly owns several properties with Dutch investment firm Rodamco, including the Garden State Plaza shopping center in New Jersey.

A$ mil	06/92	06/93	06/94	US$mil 06/94				
Sales	**383.8**	**223.1**	**212.1**	**146.5**	P/E Ratio	**36.7**	Price (9/30/95)	**13.78**
Net Income	**31.5**	**35.7**	**46.3**	**32.0**	P/B Ratio	**2.8**	52 Wk Hi-Low	**13.80-7.80**
Book Value	**417.1**	**441.4**	**475.7**	**347.2**	Yield %	**1.5**	Market Cap	**US$1,023.2mil**

Address	**100 William St.**	Tel	**02-358-7000**	ADR		President	**David H. Lowy**
	Sydney, NSW 2011	Fax	**02-358-7077**	SEDOL No.	**6956419**	Chairman	**Frank P. Lowy**

Westfield Trust

Industry: **Real-Estate Investment**

Westfield Trust, Australia's largest listed property trust by market capitalization, owns and develops shopping centers. It is managed by Westfield Management Ltd., a wholly owned subsidiary of Westfield Holdings. Its chain of 23 Shoppingtown shopping centers are located throughout Canberra, Adelaide, Melbourne, Sydney, Brisbane, and Wollongong. Its Shoppingtown Miranda center, at 108,213 square meters, is Australia's largest shopping center. The trust maintains partnerships with Rodamco of the Netherlands and AMP Society, Australia's largest property investor.

A$ mil	12/92	12/93	12/94	US$mil 12/94				
Sales	**194.3**	**227.8**	**258.0**	**189.4**	P/E Ratio	**14.9**	Price (9/30/95)	**2.34**
Net Income	**129.0**	**140.5**	**158.6**	**116.4**	P/B Ratio	**0.9**	52 Wk Hi-Low	**2.50-2.16**
Book Value	**1,657.5**	**1,822.3**	**2,093.3**	**1,622.7**	Yield %	**8.1**	Market Cap	**US$1,444.6mil**

Address	**100 William St.**	Tel	**02-358-7466**	ADR		President	--
	Sydney, NSW 2011	Fax	**02-358-7077**	SEDOL No.	**6956312**	Chairman	**Frank P. Lowy**

Westpac Banking

Industry: **Banks - Money Center**

Westpac's businesses include banking, investment- portfolio management, unit-trust and superannuation-fund management, nominee and custodian facilities, insurance, foreign-exchange dealing, and stockbrokering. Westpac operates through more than 2,000 branches concentrated in Australia and New Zealand. The company also conducts banking operations in Papua New Guinea, Fiji, French Polynesia, and New Caledonia. Over the past two years Westpac has been selling its subsidiaries in Southeast Asia.

A$ mil	09/92	09/93	09/94	US$mil 09/94				
Revenues	**9,464.1**	**8,086.6**	**6,915.6**	**4,904.7**	P/E Ratio	**14.9**	Price (9/30/95)	**5.36**
Net Income	**-1,562.4**	**39.2**	**704.7**	**499.8**	P/B Ratio	**1.4**	52 Wk Hi-Low	**5.48-4.05**
Book Value	**6,519.2**	**6,889.7**	**7,213.7**	**5,343.5**	Yield %	**3.4**	Market Cap	**US$7,407.8mil**

Address	**60 Martin Pl.**	Tel	**02-226-3311**	ADR	**WBK**	Managing Director	**Robert L. Joss**
	Sydney, NSW 2000	Fax	**02-226-4128**	SEDOL No.	**6076146**	Chairman	**John A. Uhrig**

Woodside Petroleum

Industry: **Oil - Secondary**

Woodside Petroleum is an oil and gas exploration and production company operating in Western Australia. It operates and holds a one-sixth interest in the North West Shelf project, an offshore field in Western Australia that produces liquefied natural gas, liquefied petroleum gas, oil condensate, and crude oil. The firm also has oil- and gas-exploration interests in the region, including the Laminaria oil well, in which the company has a 50% stake (Broken Hill Proprietary and Shell Australia each hold 25%.). Shell has a 34% stake in Woodside.

A$ mil	12/92	12/93	12/94	US$mil 12/94				
Sales	**452.6**	**544.2**	**526.5**	**386.6**	P/E Ratio	**49.3**	Price (9/30/95)	**6.36**
Net Income	**63.2**	**82.3**	**85.8**	**63.0**	P/B Ratio	**3.6**	52 Wk Hi-Low	**6.65-4.45**
Book Value	**1,046.3**	**1,095.9**	**1,161.7**	**900.5**	Yield %	**1.4**	Market Cap	**US$3,212.1mil**

Address	**Level 40, 385 Bourke St.**	Tel	**03-252-2000**	ADR	**WOPEY**	Managing Director	**Charles Allen**
	Melbourne, VIC 3000	Fax	**03-602-5621**	SEDOL No.	**6979728**	Chairman	**Bill Rogers**

Woolworths

Industry: **Retailers - Broadline**

Woolworths Ltd., the second-largest retailer in Australia, operates supermarkets, general- merchandise stores, and specialty retail shops. It is one of the top 25 retailers in the world in terms of sales. Woolworths is Australia's largest food retailer with approximately 32% of the branded grocery market. The company sells general merchandise through its Big W and Variety chains, and its specialty retail shops include Rockmans and Dick Smith Electronics. It has 974 stores in Australia and New Zealand, 367 of which are located in New South Wales and 228 in Queensland.

A$ mil	06/92 R	06/93	06/94	US$mil 06/94				
Revenues	**9,183.4**	**10,489.1**	**11,482.2**	**7,929.7**	P/E Ratio	**18.1**	Price (9/30/95)	**3.10**
Net Income	**139.8**	**171.2**	**200.1**	**138.2**	P/B Ratio	**4.1**	52 Wk Hi-Low	**3.16-2.70**
Book Value	**745.5**	**617.3**	**768.9**	**561.2**	Yield %	**3.9**	Market Cap	**US$2,445.1mil**

Address	**5th Fl., 540 George St.**	Tel	**02-323-1555**	ADR		President	**Reginald J. Clairs**
	Sydney, NSW 2000	Fax	**02-261-8489**	SEDOL No.	**6981239**	Chairman	**Paul Simons**

R=Restated.

Austria

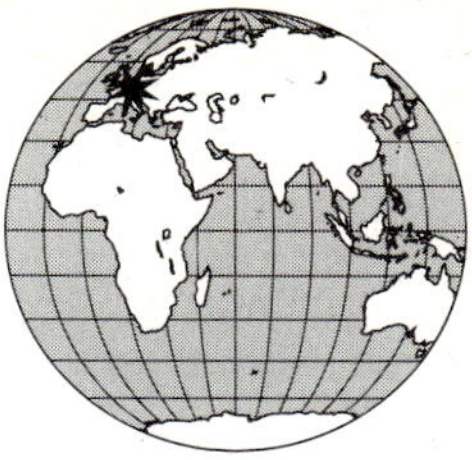

Austria

Roger Malone,
Vienna

Local Trading Hours	**Time Difference from New York**	**Population (Est. 93)**
9:30-1:30	6 hours ahead usually; 7 hours ahead for a brief period in spring and 5 hours ahead for a period in autumn	8,015,000

"Vienna is something else, that's for sure." So began one Austrian analyst's remarks on the Vienna Stock Exchange, Austria's only domestic equities market. The tiny market can one day be bullied along by international trends, only to turn inward the next day and buck the global pattern by focusing on such domestic issues as the federal budget or the next futures expiration.

With total turnover in 1994 of 408.2 billion schillings, the Vienna Stock Exchange is one of western Europe's smallest markets. Share sales hit a record in 1994, risinge almost 71% from 1993 turnover of 238.9 billion schillings. Through August 1995, turnover on the Viennese market totaled 299.2 billion schillings, up 5.3% from 284.2 billion schillings during the same period in 1994. The Vienna Stock Exchange tracks turnover using the double-count method, tallying both sales and purchases on the market.

The increase in sales was spurred by Austria's recovery from the European recession of the early 1990s. The increase in volume on the Vienna Stock Exchange was also pushed along by the state's continuing privatization program, as well as initial public offerings on the Austrian market. In 1994, the Austrian government placed a majority of engineering group VA Technologie AG on the market, the state's largest privatization to date. That same year four private companies brought out their first traded shares.

The trend has continued into 1995, when the government offered shares in specialty steel group Boehler-Uddeholm AG and steel group VA Stahl for the first time, as well as continuing the privatization of oil group OMV AG and Flughafen Wien AG, which runs the Vienna international airport. IPOs also expanded the range of stock offered in the Viennese market.

Dow Jones Austria
Equity Market Index Performance

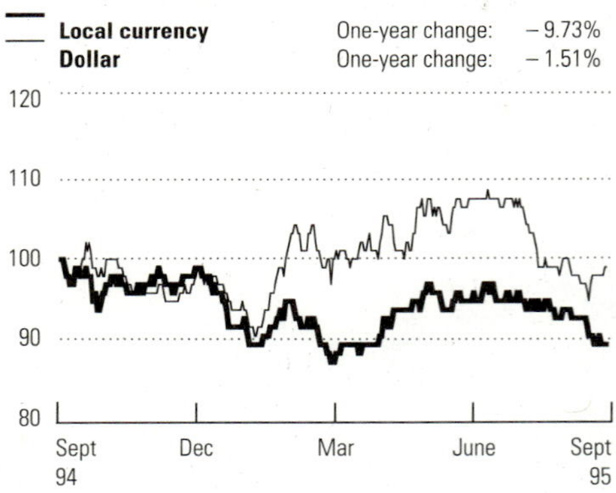

Vienna's equities market is generally dominated by large domestic institutional players, although day-to-day shifts are commonly dictated by foreign investors, particularly those based in London. Although the exchange has tried to generate interest in stock ownership among Austrians, progress has been slow. At the end of 1994, only about 4% of Austrians (up from 3% in 1993) owned corporate shares, compared with 7% of Germans and 10% of Swiss. In the U.S., Britain and Japan more than 20% of the population owns corporate stock.

Gross Domestic Product (94)	Three-Year Average GDP Growth (92-94)	Main Industries	Consumer Price Index (93-94)	Monetary Unit	Exchange Rate (9/95)
$202.2 billion	1.5%	Agriculture, machinery and engineering, electronics, chemicals, iron and metal works, automotive, stonework and ceramics, and wood processing	3%	Schilling	As10.00 to US$1.00

But the exchange hasn't been able to translate increased turnover into increased share price. In 1994, the benchmark Austrian Traded Index lost 73.54 points or 6.5% to end the year at 1,055.24 points, and by the end of August, the benchmark index had slipped another 42.71 points or 4% to 1012.53 points. The ATX is a weighted index comprising the 18 consecutively traded shares on the Vienna exchange, representing the country's 17 blue chip groups. Creditanstalt Bankverein AG has both preferred and common shares included in the ATX. In 1995 the number of companies in the ATX was cut sharply as seven companies were dropped from the index because of insufficient share turnover.

The Vienna Stock Exchange Index (WBI), which includes all domestic shares on the official market, also fell in 1994 and the first eight months of 1995. During 1994, the WBI slipped 54.03 points or 11% to close the year at 429.64 points. By the end of August, the broader-based index had fallen another 25.09 points or 5.8% to end the month at 404.55 points.

In the first half of 1994, share prices on the Austrian exchange were pressured by change in direction in key U.S. interest rates and, domestically around mid-year, by uncertainty over the outcome of a vote on entry into the European Union (E.U.). The resounding approval to E.U. helped prices strengthen until autumn, when the national election in Austria uncovered significant support for the political far right and brought the cohesion of the long-time ruling coalition of social democrats and conservatives into question. The imminent entry into the E.U. on Jan. 1, 1995, helped support prices toward the end of the year.

Ten Largest Capitalized Companies
as of 9/30/95

Stock	Market Cap. US$Mil
OMV	2,524,500.0
Verbund	2,064,940.0
Bank Austria	2,025,791.1
VA Technologie	1,735,500.0
Creditanstalt	1,549,800.0
Wienerberger	1,380,376.0
EVN	1,152,350.0
Mayr-Melnhof Karton	766,800.0
Gösser Brauerei	553,316.4
BBAG	446,688.0

The dollar's persistent weakness in the first half of 1995 kept the pressure on Austrian share prices, pushing the ATX significantly below 1000 points for the first time since 1993. In June 1994, the ATX had dipped under 1000 points in intraday trading, but always managed to close above that level. The market began recovering around midyear as Austrian blue chips reported strong recoveries following the recession, but it slid lower again in late summer as investor interest and confidence in the market faded. This was due in part to worries over the fate of the 1996 federal budget and the near collapse of Maculan Holding.

Maculan, once the darling of foreign investors and the poster child for Austria's new entrepreneurial spirit, shocked the market twice in 1995. After generally rosy company forecasts, Maculan announced unexpected problems in Austrian and German units, which it said would take a deep bite from 1994 profits. Then it said it expected a "considerable loss" in 1995 because of continued problems in its German division.

The construction group turned to its creditor banks for new, immediate lines of credit and hired an outside consultant to orchestrate an emergency restructuring. At midyear, investigations by the exchange were pending on whether the company complied with information disclosure and insider trading rules. The debacle soured many London investors' attitudes to the Austrian market generally and added to the late summer weakness.

By sopping funds from the market, the two major privatizations of 1995 — Boehler-Uddeholm and VA Stahl — contributed to the market's inability to capitalize on generally sound economic fundamentals. The Austrian National Bank, following steps by the Deutsche Bundesbank, continued to lower its key interest rates and the Gomex rate, the Austrian money market indicator. Also, with an annual rate of 2.1% in August, inflation had hit its lowest level since 1988. The weak dollar cut into Austria's expected exports proceeds in 1995, but the country's recovery from the recession was seen proceeding, with gross domestic product (GDP) seen growing by a real 2.4% after 2.7% growth in 1994 and a decline of 0.1% in 1993. The strong economic fundamentals were expected to help the Austrian market recover later in 1995.

The Vienna Stock Market lists common and preferred shares and participation certificates for 150 companies. Of these, 111 are domestic firms. In 1994, turnover in domestic shares accounted for about 93% of the sales on the Austrian market, with domestic share turnover increasing while movement in foreign shares fell. The pattern continued in the first months of 1995.

Only banks, official brokers and non-official brokers can trade on the Vienna Stock Exchange's three markets: the official market, the non-official market and the unregulated market. There are no significant restrictions that apply specifically to foreign brokers.

The strictest admission criteria are set for companies seeking a listing on the official market. Generally, these companies must have high trading volumes, nominal share value of at least 40 million schillings and a minimum value of other securities of 10 million schillings, as well as having existed and filed annual reports for at least three years.

Companies listed on the non-official market must have existed for at least one year and have a nominal share value of at least 10 million schillings. Admittance to the unregulated market requires only that the

company's shares be printed properly.
Trade of the Vienna Stock Exchange opens at 9:30 a.m. and closes at 1:30 p.m., with deals handled through an open-outcry method and helped by a computer system known as the Partly Assisted Trading System (PATS). The delayed debut of a fully automated trading system called EQOS, which would eventually replace the open-outcry system, is set for Feb. 23, 1996. In the first stage, shares companies that are also listed on the Austrian Futures and Options Exchange will be handled by the automated system, which will allow trades by participants not on the grounds of the exchange. The system will include all continuously traded shares in the second stage and all shares in the final stage. Also on Feb. 23, trading hours are set to be extended to 2 p.m.

The exchange has no plans for electronic pre- and after-market trading similar to Germany's IBIS session.

In terms of market capitalization, the Vienna Stock Exchange is dominated by the financial and energy sectors, which account for about 51% of the total market capital. Total capitalization at the end of 1994 was 321.3 billion schillings, down from 330 billion schillings a year earlier. Of the 1994 total, banks accounted for 21%; utilities, 16%; and insurers, 14%. Rounding out the top five sectors, machine, transportation and technology companies accounted for 11% and building material suppliers, 7.9%.
The pattern repeats itself in terms of share turnover, with stocks in the financial and energy groups taking seven of the top ten spots.

Agrana

Industry: **Other Food**

Agrana is Austria's largest producer of sugar and starch. It refines natural products into high-grade foods and products. Its 83%-owned Agrana Zucker sugar subsidiary sells sugar wholesale to the soft-drink, confectionery, and alcohol industries, and retails it under its own label. It also sells fodder and carbon lime fertilizer. Its 88%-owned Agrana Stärke starch subsidiary sells starch to the cereal and sausage industries, as well as wheat and milk to the baking industries. Agrana also has other subsidiaries in the Czech Republic and Hungary.

	ATS mil 09/92 P	09/93 P	09/94 P	US$mil 09/94				
Sales	**11.0**	**10.0**	**10.1**	**0.9**	P/E Ratio	**1.1**	Price (9/30/95)	**231.00**
Net Income	**168.0**	**121.0**	**127.9**	**11.0**	P/B Ratio	**0.6**	52 Wk Hi-Low	**280.00-225.00**
Book Value	**3,281.0**	**3,281.0**	**3,313.9**	**303.5**	Yield %	**56.3**	Market Cap	**US$34.7mil**

Address **Hollandstr. 2**
1020 Vienna
Tel **01-211-37-0**
Fax **01-211-37-2998**
ADR
SEDOL No. **4015088**
President --
Chairman Supv Bd **Christian Conrad**

P=Parent company data.

Austrian Airlines

Industry: **Airlines**

Austrian Airlines is Austria's largest passenger airline in terms of sales. It provides charter and cargo services and flies to more than 70 destinations in 40 countries, including New York, London, and Tokyo. Its fleet of roughly 24 aircraft carries nearly 3 million passengers and 53 tons of freight annually. Austrian Airlines subsidiaries include Touropa Austria, Austria's largest travel agency, and 43%-owned regional Austrian airline Tyrolean. Austrian Airlines has route partnerships with Swissair, Delta Airlines, British Midland, and All Nippon Airways.

	ATS mil 12/92	12/93	12/94	US$mil 12/94				
Sales	**10,507.0**	**10,344.0**	**10,353.4**	**912.0**	P/E Ratio	**NMF**	Price (9/30/95)	**1,700.00**
Net Income	**-437.0**	**-737.0**	**-200.7**	**-17.7**	P/B Ratio	**0.8**	52 Wk Hi-Low	**2,075.0-1,325.0**
Book Value	**6,967.0**	**6,400.0**	**5,469.5**	**501.3**	Yield %	**0.0**	Market Cap	**US$442.0mil**

Address **Fontanastr. 1**
1017 Vienna
Tel **01-68-35-11**
Fax **01-68-65-26**
ADR
SEDOL No. **4065793**
Chairman Exec Bd **Herbert Brammer**
Chairman Supv Bd **Rudolf Streicher**

Bank Austria

Industry: **Banks - Regional**

Bank Austria, provides retail banking, investment advice, asset management, and life insurance both domestically and internationally. It operates more than 5 million customer accounts in its 329 branch offices, of which 20 are abroad. It offers electronic-banking and bank-by-phone services. Since acquiring Austrian holding company Wiener, Bank Austria is the largest diversified company in Austria. It recently acquired U.K.-based automotive- and sports-supply company Unitech, and has a stake in Lenzing. Bank Austria is 20.4% controlled by the Republic of Austria.

	ATS mil 12/92	12/93	12/94	US$mil 12/94				
Revenues	**48,041.0**	**44,895.0**	**44,863.2**	**3,951.7**	P/E Ratio M	**36.5**	Price (9/30/95) M	**837.00**
Net Income	**1,264.0**	**1,431.0**	**1,474.5**	**129.9**	P/B Ratio M	**1.7**	52 Wk Hi-Low M	**940.00-702.00**
Book Value	**29,020.0**	**31,746.0**	**31,450.0**	**2,882.7**	Yield % M	**1.2**	Market Cap M	**US$2,025.8mil**

Address **Zollamtstr. 13**
1030 Vienna
Tel **01-711-91-0**
Fax **01-711-91-3230**
ADR **BAAGY**
SEDOL No. **4999621**
Chairman Exec Bd **René A. Haiden**
Chairman Supv Bd **Siegfried Sellitsch**

M=Multiple issues in index; reflects most active.

Bank für Ober und Salzburg

Industry: **Banks - Regional**

Bank für Oberösterreich und Salzburg (Oberbank) is one of Austria's largest commercial banks. The bank offers asset management, foreign exchange services, money market trading, investment advice, and retail and private banking. Oberbank's assets totalled more than $6.68 billion at year-end 1994. It has 88 branches located throughout Austria and a representative office in the Czech Republic. Its Oberbank Bayern subsidiary provides retail and private banking services in Germany. Creditanstalt-Bankverein holds a 31% share in Oberbank.

	ATS mil 12/92	12/93	12/94	US$mil 12/94				
Revenues	**6,000.2**	**5,537.6**	**5,176.8**	**456.0**	P/E Ratio	**34.1**	Price (9/30/95)	**587.00**
Net Income	**123.4**	**130.8**	**133.4**	**11.8**	P/B Ratio	**1.2**	52 Wk Hi-Low	**605.00-573.00**
Book Value	**3,497.7**	**3,624.1**	**3,848.8**	**352.8**	Yield %	**2.6**	Market Cap	**US$410.9mil**

Address **Hauptplatz 10-11**
4010 Linz
Tel **0732-2802-0**
Fax **N/A**
ADR
SEDOL No. **4081294**
Chairman Exec Bd **Herman Bell**
Chairman --

BBAG

Industry: **Distillers & Brewers**

Österreichische Brau-Beteiligungs (BBAG) produces and distributes beer and nonalcoholic beverages such as soft drinks, mineral water, and fruit juices. BBAG runs specialty restaurants and staff canteens and prints labels for its own and other companies' products. It also has a real-estate division. Its brand-name beverages include Kaiser beer, Gössinger mineral water, and Pago fruit juice. The company has an agreement with the Coca-Cola Company to operate Coca-Cola franchises in Linz and Innsbruck until 1998. Beer generated 76% of BBAG's revenues in 1994.

	ATS mil 12/92	12/93	12/94	US$mil 12/94				
Sales	**10,717.0**	**10,785.0**	**11,359.3**	**1,000.6**	P/E Ratio	**11.8**	Price (9/30/95)	**517.00**
Net Income	**213.0**	**332.0**	**475.8**	**41.9**	P/B Ratio	**1.4**	52 Wk Hi-Low	**632.00-485.00**
Book Value	**2,331.0**	**3,429.0**	**3,234.5**	**296.5**	Yield %	**3.1**	Market Cap	**US$446.7mil**

Address **Poschacherstr. 35**
4020 Linz
Tel **0732-69-51-0**
Fax **0732-69-51-150**
ADR
SEDOL No. **4621731**
Chairman Exec Bd **Johannes Brandl**
Chairman **Fritz Kretz**

Creditanstalt

Industry: **Banks - Regional**

Creditanstalt-Bankverein offers a full range of banking and financial services primarily in central and eastern Europe. Its activities include retail banking, financing of foreign public debt, and involvement in the currency and stock markets. Creditanstalt-Bankverein, which is controlled by the Austrian government, operates more than 450,000 personal accounts in over 200 branches throughout Austria and Central Europe. It holds majority interests in construction firm Universale-Bau and Imperial Hotels Austria.

ATS mil	12/92	12/93	12/94	US$mil 12/94				
Revenues	**52,834.0**	**51,852.0**	**55,821.2**	**4,916.9**	P/E Ratio M	**11.7**	Price (9/30/95) M	**540.00**
Net Income	**1,560.0**	**1,682.0**	**1,809.4**	**159.4**	P/B Ratio M	**0.7**	52 Wk Hi-Low M	**663.00-540.00**
Book Value	**31,111.0**	**28,809.0**	**29,614.7**	**2,714.5**	Yield % M	**1.9**	Market Cap M	**US$1,549.8mil**

Address **Schottengasse 6**, **1010 Vienna** | Tel **01-531-31-0** | Fax **01-531-31-7566** | ADR | SEDOL No. **4228916** | Chairman Exec Bd **Guido Schmidt-Chiari** | Chairman Supv Bd **Walter Fremuth**

M=Multiple issues in index; reflects most active.

EVN

Industry: **Electrical Utilities - All**

Energie-Versorgung Niederosterreich (EVN) produces and distributes electricity and natural gas. It operates 63 power stations, 52 of which are hydroelectric. The company supplies energy to 800,000 individual and industrial customers in Lower Austria. EVN transferred its stake in Rohol-Aufsuchungs to the natural-gas-procurement, -storage, and -transport company RAG Beteiligungs, in which EVN holds a 40% interest. Electricity sales represented more than two thirds of all revenues in 1994 and gas sales represented nearly 30% of the total.

ATS mil	08/92 P	08/93 P	08/94 P	US$mil 08/94				
Sales	**9,852.0**	**10,310.0**	**10,524.5**	**903.8**	P/E Ratio	**13.2**	Price (9/30/95)	**1,213.00**
Net Income	**439.0**	**538.0**	**563.6**	**48.4**	P/B Ratio	**2.1**	52 Wk Hi-Low	**1,423.0-1,184.0**
Book Value	**11,532.0**	**11,889.0**	**5,612.0**	**505.1**	Yield %	**1.9**	Market Cap	**US$1,152.4mil**

Address **Johann-Steinböck-Str. 1**, **2344 Maria Enzerdorf** | Tel **022-36200-0** | Fax **022-36200-2600** | ADR **EVNVY** | SEDOL No. **4295374** | Chairman Exec Bd **Rudolf Gruber** | Chairman Supv Bd **Siegfried Ludwig**

P=Parent company data.

Gösser Brauerei

Industry: **Distillers & Brewers**

Brau-Union Goss-Reininghaus-Osterriechische Brau (Brau-Union) is a holding company for subsidiaries involved in the production of alcoholic and nonalcoholic beer. The company's subsidiaries include its principal brewery BRAU, Adambräu, Vereinigte Kärntner, and Martfü breweries. Brau Union's other holdings include wholly-owned Steirerbrau and Brau und Getränke which produce its nonalcoholic beers. Brand-name beers include Kaiser Bier, Gösser, Starobrno, and Puntigamer. Exports generate nearly one third of the company's profits.

ATS mil	12/90 P	12/91 P	12/92 P	US$mil 12/92				
Sales	**27.2**	**27.0**	**5.0**	**0.5**	P/E Ratio	**4.8**	Price (9/30/95)	**563.00**
Net Income	**26.9**	**31.1**	**38.0**	**3.5**	P/B Ratio	**2.7**	52 Wk Hi-Low	**750.00-556.00**
Book Value	**426.0**	**629.0**	**632.0**	**57.0**	Yield %	**2.2**	Market Cap	**US$553.3mil**

Address **Poschacherstr. 35**, **4020 Linz** | Tel **03842-23646** | Fax **03842-22621** | ADR | SEDOL No. **4378383** | Chairman Exec Bd **Alfred Weitzendorf** | Chairman **Dr. Johannes Brandl**

P=Parent company data.

Lenzing

Industry: **Paper Products**

Lenzing produces plastics, synthetic fibers, and paper. Other products include plastics machinery, high-performance products, and synthetic films. The company is awaiting government confirmation of its plans to build its own waste-combustion plant. It is the world's largest producer of viscose by market share. It supplies its products to the garment, textile, tire, and printing industries. Its subsidiaries include wholly-owned U.S. firms Lenzing USA and Lenzing Fibers, and Indonesian firm P.T. South Pacific Viscose. Bank Austria owns 33% and Creditanstalt-Bankverein owns 17% of Lenzing.

ATS mil	12/92	12/93	12/94	US$mil 12/94				
Sales	**7,984.0**	**8,742.0**	**8,420.1**	**741.7**	P/E Ratio	**40.0**	Price (9/30/95)	**881.00**
Net Income	**-105.0**	**-144.0**	**93.4**	**8.2**	P/B Ratio	**1.9**	52 Wk Hi-Low	**1,225.0-770.0**
Book Value	**3,051.0**	**2,755.0**	**1,729.1**	**158.5**	Yield %	**1.1**	Market Cap	**US$323.8mil**

Address **Lenzing Aktiengesellschaft**, **4860 Lenzing** | Tel **076-72-701-0** | Fax **076-72-75-740** | ADR **LNZNY** | SEDOL No. **4512330** | CEO **Dr. Heinrich Stepniczka** | Chairman **Gerhard Randa**

Mayr-Melnhof Karton

Industry: **Paper Products**

Mayr-Melnhof Karton is a forest products and paper company. The company is Europe's largest manufacturer of cardboard by sales. It also manufactures folding boxes and has waste paper-salvaging and trading interests. The firm's subsidiaries include folding box manufacturer Walmsley of the United Kingdom and German recycling firms Holz and Loerch, which, together collect 34,000 tons of waste paper per year. Mayr-Melnof's cardboard division accounted for nearly two thirds of revenues in 1994 and its folding boxes division accounted for 21%.

ATS mil	12/92	12/93	12/94	US$mil 12/94				
Sales	**N/A**	**8,439.4**	**10,754.4**	**947.3**	P/E Ratio	**42.1**	Price (9/30/95)	**639.00**
Net Income	**N/A**	**116.5**	**182.2**	**16.0**	P/B Ratio	**1.8**	52 Wk Hi-Low	**680.00-539.00**
Book Value	**N/A**	**2,071.5**	**4,276.6**	**392.0**	Yield %	**2.2**	Market Cap	**US$766.8mil**

Address **Brahmsplatz 6**, **1040 Vienna** | Tel **01-50136** | Fax **01-50136-16** | ADR | SEDOL No. **4563640** | CEO **Michael Gröller** | Chairman --

OMV

Industry: **Oil - Secondary**

ÖMV is an energy group with interests in the chemicals and plastics businesses. It is involved in crude oil exploration, production, transit and storage. ÖMV's refineries, which generated 48% of the company's 1994 turnover, supply petroleum and distillate products and petrochemical materials. The company owns filling stations and other trading companies operating primarily in Austria and Eastern European countries. ÖMV also produces fine chemicals, nitrogen products, and plastics for the automotive, packaging, and construction industries.

	ATS mil 12/92	12/93	12/94	US$mil 12/94				
Sales	**82,792.0**	**81,926.0**	**84,014.6**	**7,400.2**	P/E Ratio	**40.9**	Price (9/30/95)	**935.00**
Net Income	**-596.0**	**-4,412.0**	**617.5**	**54.4**	P/B Ratio	**1.7**	52 Wk Hi-Low	**1,139.0-882.0**
Book Value	**17,206.0**	**12,712.0**	**15,193.8**	**1,392.6**	Yield %	**1.1**	Market Cap	**US$2,524.5mil**

Address **Otto-Wagner-Platz 5**
1091 Vienna
Tel **01-404-40**
Fax **01-404-40-909**
ADR
SEDOL No. **4651459**
Chairman Exec Bd **Dr. Richard Schenz**
Chairman Supv Bd **Dr. Oskar Grünwald**

Perlmooser

Industry: **Building Materials**

Perlmooser Zementwerke is Austria's largest manufacturer of cement by market share. It manufactures ready-mix cement, specialty cement, plaster, and heat-insulating construction materials. The company's wholly-owned Unitech and Schmidt Armaturen subsidiaries manufacture metal and plastics. Perlmooser Zementwerke has controlling interests in more than 40 Austrian companies that operate in the cement, construction, and construction-materials sectors. The company has plants at Mannersdorf, Retznei/Weissenegg, Rodaun, and Kirchbichl.

	ATS mil 12/92	12/93	12/94	US$mil 12/94				
Sales	**3,928.0**	**3,851.0**	**2,315.9**	**204.0**	P/E Ratio	**10.1**	Price (9/30/95)	**820.00**
Net Income	**249.0**	**489.0**	**394.3**	**34.7**	P/B Ratio	**1.6**	52 Wk Hi-Low	**935.00-700.00**
Book Value	**2,445.0**	**2,829.0**	**2,517.7**	**230.8**	Yield %	**2.4**	Market Cap	**US$396.9mil**

Address **Operngasse 11**
1040 Vienna
Tel **0222-58889472**
Fax **0222-58889205**
ADR
SEDOL No. **4681564**
Chairman Exec Bd **Gerhard Raffel**
Chairman Supv Bd **Gerhard Randa**

A. Porr

Industry: **Heavy Construction**

Allgemeine Baugesellschaft-Arthur Porr operates construction and civil-engineering activities. The company's construction division builds private residences, apartments, and commercial buildings. Its civil-engineering division builds roads, bridges, tunnels, and power stations. Its construction and civil engineering divisions each contribute roughly half of the company's revenues. Nearly 30% of sales are generated from foreign activities. The company recently acquired 50% of Austrian construction company Bauwesen.

	ATS mil 12/92	12/93	12/94	US$mil 12/94				
Sales	**3,650.4**	**3,825.3**	**5,856.1**	**515.8**	P/E Ratio	**17.8**	Price (9/30/95)	**1,350.00**
Net Income	**52.8**	**56.3**	**75.9**	**6.7**	P/B Ratio	**2.7**	52 Wk Hi-Low	**1,950.0-991.0**
Book Value	**540.0**	**572.2**	**1,153.9**	**105.8**	Yield %	**1.5**	Market Cap	**US$181.2mil**

Address **Rennweg 12**
1031 Vienna
Tel **0222-797-20**
Fax **0222-799-1332**
ADR
SEDOL No. **4019950**
Chairman Exec Bd **Gerhard Randa**
Chairman Supv Bd **Horst Pöchhacker**

Radex-Heraklith

Industry: **Industrial - Diversified**

Radex-Heraklith Industriebeteiligungs manufactures building materials including polystyrene board, refractories, rock wool, and roofing shingles. It also provides sintered and caustic magnesia and other mixes to the nonferrous-metal, steel, and glass industries. Veitsch-Radex, the group's majority-owned refractories subsidiary, generated 67% of sales in 1994; its 69%-owned Heraklith Baustoffe building-materials subsidiary provided 33%. In March 1995, the company agreed to terms for ownership of German refractories maker Didier-Werke, to be finalized in 1997.

	ATS mil 12/92	12/93	12/94	US$mil 12/94				
Sales	**8,511.0**	**7,845.0**	**10,625.7**	**935.9**	P/E Ratio	**8.1**	Price (9/30/95)	**334.00**
Net Income	**-114.0**	**-319.0**	**63.8**	**5.6**	P/B Ratio	**1.1**	52 Wk Hi-Low	**425.00-300.00**
Book Value	**2,515.0**	**2,049.0**	**2,095.7**	**192.1**	Yield %	**3.0**	Market Cap	**US$231.4mil**

Address **Opernring 1**
1010 Vienna
Tel **01-5877671**
Fax **01-5873380**
ADR
SEDOL No. **4719915**
Chairman Exec Bd **Dr. W. Ressler**
Chairman Supv Bd **Dr. Karl Ludwig**

RZB

Industry: **Banks - Regional**

Raiffeisen Banking Group provides a wide range of banking services internationally, including personal and commercial loans; securities brokerage; international, securities, and investment banking; and asset management. Its total year-end assets in 1994 were $73 billion. It operates 716 Raiffeisen banks with more than 1,700 branches worldwide. Through its Raiffeisen Zentralbank Österreich bank subsidiary it runs a group of regional Austrian banks, as well as its international banking operations with offices in London, New York, Hong Kong, Paris, and Singapore.

	ATS mil 12/92	12/93	12/94	US$mil 12/94				
Revenues	**16,065.0**	**15,249.0**	**18,370.6**	**1,618.1**	P/E Ratio	**2.9**	Price (9/30/95)	**458.00**
Net Income	**430.0**	**631.0**	**426.8**	**37.6**	P/B Ratio	**0.2**	52 Wk Hi-Low	**475.00-450.00**
Book Value	**10,441.0**	**11,032.0**	**11,430.1**	**1,047.7**	Yield %	**12.7**	Market Cap	**US$202.8mil**

Address **Am Stadtpark 9**
1030 Vienna
Tel **01-717-07-0**
Fax **01-71707-1715**
ADR
SEDOL No. **4369194**
Chairman Exec Bd **Dr. Klaus Liebscher**
Chairman Supv Bd **Dr. Christian Konrad**

Steyr-Daimler-Puch

Industry: **Land Transportation**

Steyr-Daimler-Puch is a manufacturer of automotive components. Its main products include components for commercial vehicles, agricultural machinery, military technology, and weapons. It also distributes, services, and repairs passenger vehicles and small trucks of the Fiat, Lancia, and Alfa brand names in Austria. Steyr-Daimler-Puch products include Steyr trucks, Puch Pinzgauer all-terrain motor vehicles, and Steyr Mannlicher hunting rifles. In 1994, more than 50% of the company's revenues came from exports generated mainly in western Europe and the U.S.

ATS mil	12/92	12/93	12/94	US$mil 12/94				
Sales	**13,940.0**	**10,415.0**	**9,119.8**	**803.3**	P/E Ratio	**12.0**	Price (9/30/95)	**195.00**
Net Income	**-139.0**	**-171.0**	**162.3**	**14.3**	P/B Ratio	**0.8**	52 Wk Hi-Low	**206.00-136.00**
Book Value	**3,316.0**	**3,160.0**	**2,517.4**	**230.7**	Yield %	**0.0**	Market Cap	**US$195.0mil**

Address **Franz-Josefs-Kai 51**
1010 Vienna
Tel **01-531-44-0**
Fax **01-535-63-83**
ADR
SEDOL No. **4846608**
Chairman Exec Bd **Dr. Rudolf Streicher**
Chairman Supv Bd **Dr. Guido Schmidt-Chiari**

Steyrermühl Papier

Industry: **Paper Products**

Steyrermühl Papierfabriks- und Verlags produces newsprint, printing paper, mechanical pulp, thermomechanical pulp, and sawn timber. The firm is Austria's largest producer of newsprint by market share. It also manufactures environment-friendly Eco-Gravure and Ecoset magazine papers. Paper production, pulp, and newsprint accounted for nearly 90% of sales in 1994. About 80% of all sales are generated abroad, with European Community countries accounting for more than 70% of exports. In 1994 its total paper output increased to approximately 440,000 tons.

ATS mil	12/92	12/93	12/94	US$mil 12/94				
Sales	**2,558.0**	**2,468.0**	**2,632.7**	**231.9**	P/E Ratio	**NMF**	Price (9/30/95)	**4,110.00**
Net Income	**-330.0**	**-327.0**	**-157.8**	**-13.9**	P/B Ratio	**2.6**	52 Wk Hi-Low	**4,210.0-4,050.0**
Book Value	**811.0**	**1,184.0**	**1,062.3**	**97.4**	Yield %	**0.0**	Market Cap	**US$277.4mil**

Address **Fabriksplatz 1**
4662 Steyrermuhl
Tel **07613-2436-0**
Fax **07613-21-74**
ADR
SEDOL No. **4846686**
Chairman Exec Bd **Walter Pillwein**
Chairman Supv Bd **Walter Flötti**

Universale Bau

Industry: **Heavy Construction**

Universale Bau is a construction company. Its activities include building, public works, and road construction. The company's public works activities include the construction of power plants, bridges, subways, and underground canals, and its building projects include residential, commercial, and industrial properties. Its foreign projects are concentrated in Germany, Hungary, the Czech Republic, and Switzerland, and account for roughly 30% of sales revenues. Universale Bau, which sold its Spanish interests in 1993, also has a Venezuelan affiliate.

ATS mil	12/91	12/92	12/93	US$mil 12/93				
Sales	**2,613.0**	**2,924.0**	**3,266.0**	**280.6**	P/E Ratio	**NMF**	Price (9/30/95)	**397.00**
Net Income	**-706.0**	**55.0**	**-607.0**	**-52.1**	P/B Ratio	**2.3**	52 Wk Hi-Low	**729.53-359.89**
Book Value	**1,395.0**	**1,450.0**	**783.0**	**64.2**	Yield %	**0.0**	Market Cap	**US$178.7mil**

Address **Renngasse 6**
1011 Vienna
Tel **01-534-61-0**
Fax **01-533-47-19**
ADR
SEDOL No. **4920900**
Chairman Exec Bd **Dr. Josef Vlcek**
Chairman **Dr. Guido Schmidt-Chiari**

VA Technologie

Industry: **Diversified Technology**

VA Technologie, Austria's largest engineering company, provides engineering and construction services. It operates in three areas: energy and environmental engineering, which generates 43% of revenues; metallurgical engineering, which generates 22% of revenues; and construction and engineering services, which generates 35% of revenues. It provides mechanical and electrical engineering, maintenance services, and system solutions to its customers. It also builds thermal and hydroelectric power plants. Nearly half of the firm's orders originate in non-European countries.

ATS mil	12/92	12/93	12/94	US$mil 12/94				
Sales	**23,591.2**	**22,451.8**	**27,896.7**	**2,457.2**	P/E Ratio	**19.4**	Price (9/30/95)	**1,157.00**
Net Income	**805.4**	**843.5**	**896.6**	**79.0**	P/B Ratio	**2.4**	52 Wk Hi-Low	**1,274.0-980.0**
Book Value	**4,957.4**	**6,651.4**	**7,288.3**	**668.0**	Yield %	**2.1**	Market Cap	**US$1,735.5mil**

Address **Lunzerstr. 64**
4031 Linz
Tel **05986-0**
Fax **05980-3414**
ADR
SEDOL No. **4921635**
Chairman Exec Bd **Othmar Pühringer**
Chairman Supv Bd **Herbert Krejci**

Veitsch-Radex

Industry: **General Industrial & Commercial Services**

Veitsch-Radex is a major manufacturer of refractories, and is the world's largest producer of magnesite refractory products by market share. The company is a partially-owned subsidiary of Radex-Heraklith Industriebeteiligungs. Veitsch-Radex's wholly-owned Societe d'Interets Magnesiens subsidiary based in the Netherlands produces sinter for the company and its subsidiaries. Iron and steel refractories generate more than 70% of revenues. Forty-one percent of sales were generated by EC member countries.

ATS mil	12/92	12/93	12/94	US$mil 12/94				
Sales	**6,393.0**	**5,585.0**	**7,096.0**	**625.0**	P/E Ratio	**15.9**	Price (9/30/95)	**232.00**
Net Income	**-235.0**	**-157.0**	**142.8**	**12.6**	P/B Ratio	**1.2**	52 Wk Hi-Low	**349.00-215.00**
Book Value	**2,584.0**	**2,270.0**	**1,850.9**	**169.7**	Yield %	**3.4**	Market Cap	**US$227.6mil**

Address **Mommsengasse 35**
1040 Vienna
Tel **01-50213-0**
Fax **01-50213-213**
ADR **VEITY**
SEDOL No. **4927688**
Chairman Exec Bd **Dr. Günter Mörtl**
Chairman Supv Bd **Hellmut Longin**

Verbund

Industry: **Electrical Utilities - All**

Verbund is the leading generator of electricity in Austria, providing more than half of the country's supply. Hydro power, generated in more than 76 hydro plants, accounts for 90% of the company's electricity. It also operates six thermal power plants bringing its total generating capacity to 8250 megawatts. Verbund is also involved in electricity distribution through its interests in STEG and KELAG companies. Customers include the provincial electricity companies, industry, and the Austrian Federal Railway. Verbund also supplies the foreign electricity market.

	ATS mil 12/92	12/93	12/94	US$mil 12/94				
Sales	**19,431.0**	**19,645.9**	**19,266.6**	**1,697.0**	P/E Ratio	**14.3**	Price (9/30/95)	**670.00**
Net Income	**500.5**	**704.4**	**1,236.0**	**108.9**	P/B Ratio	**1.3**	52 Wk Hi-Low	**745.00-565.00**
Book Value	**7,624.1**	**7,489.0**	**16,298.1**	**1,493.9**	Yield %	**2.4**	Market Cap	**US$2,064.9mil**

Address **Am Hof 6**
1010 Vienna

Tel **01-13-2630**
Fax **01-13-2694**

ADR
SEDOL No. **4661607**

Chairman Exec Bd **Hans Haider**
Chairman Supv Bd **Herbert Krejci**

Wienerberger

Industry: **Building Materials**

Wienerberger Baustoffindustrie is a building-materials company that operates in four sectors: wall, ceiling, and roofing systems; pipe systems and sewage technology; metals and alloys; and real estate. The company's products include bricks, ceilings, chimney systems, roofing tiles, clay and plastic pipes, and cement. In 1994, wall, ceiling, and roofing products accounted for 38% of its revenues; metals and alloys 32%; and pipe systems and sewage technology 26%. Wienerberger has 102 factories throughout Europe, three plants in North America, and two in Southeast Asia.

	ATS mil 12/92	12/93	12/94	US$mil 12/94				
Sales	**11,711.0**	**12,120.0**	**10,553.5**	**929.6**	P/E Ratio	**13.9**	Price (9/30/95)	**2,180.00**
Net Income	**435.0**	**626.0**	**1,188.1**	**104.6**	P/B Ratio	**1.9**	52 Wk Hi-Low	**2,686.7-2,125.0**
Book Value	**5,912.0**	**6,343.0**	**7,413.5**	**679.5**	Yield %	**1.3**	Market Cap	**US$1,380.4mil**

Address **Wienerbergerstr. 11**
1102 Vienna

Tel **01-60192-0**
Fax **01-60192-473**

ADR
SEDOL No. **4969602**

CEO **Erhard Schaschi**
Chairman **Guido Schmidt-Chiari**

Belgium

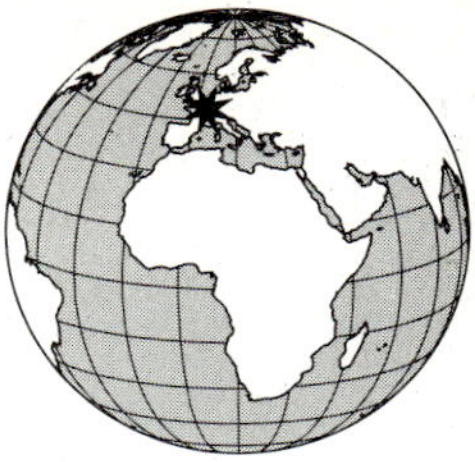

Belgium

Peter Goldstein,
Brussels

Local Trading Hours	Time difference from New York	Population (Est. 1/95)
10:00-4:30	6 hours ahead of EST	10,130,000

Officials at the Brussels Bourse seem to be taking their cues these days from the charming cherubs carved in the facade of the exchange building, depicted in earnest toil at mercantile tasks. Symbolic of the companies quoted within, the cherubs busily forge metal, distill chemicals, draught blueprints, and pore over rolls of financial documents.

Bourse authorities, while no doubt a bit older and more fully clothed, are equally busy hashing out reforms aimed at boosting the market's allure in time to meet the challenge of the European Union's investor services directive (ISD) slated for implementation in 1996.

The ISD will give European stock brokerages and banks a "single passport" to trade securities throughout the 15-nation bloc. As a result, smaller exchanges such as Brussels are taking action lest business drifts to larger, more sophisticated financial centers.

This is a tall order for the exchange first chartered by Napoleon in 1801 and credited with originating "bourse" as a word to denote stock market. Despite its advanced age, the exchange's market capitalization ranks a modest ninth among the 17 bourses tracked by the Federation of European Stock Exchanges in 1994, while neighboring Amsterdam, for example, is fifth.

Completed and proposed reforms focus on increasing independence and accountability of the Bourse's oversight body, tightening fiduciary and transparency requirements for brokerages, and boosting liquidity with various technical innovations.

These could include abolition of a tax on Bourse transactions, which stands at 1.7% up to a maximum 10,000 francs, and the annual listing tax now set at 0.42% of turnover. A government advisory body on Bourse reform also has proposed the creation of a system for trading non-quoted stocks, roughly equivalent to the Nasdaq system,

Dow Jones Belgium Equity Market Index Performance

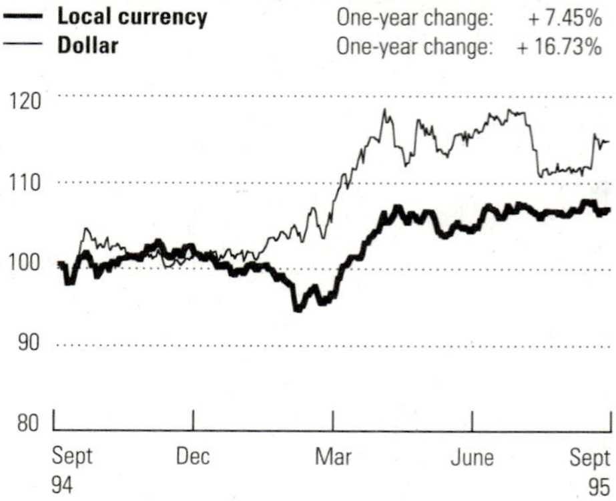

Most trading is on the so-called forward market, based on a 14-day settlement. It operates from 10 a.m. to 4:30 p.m. via a screen-based quotation system known as CATS. Cash transactions, relatively minor in scale, until recently had been conducted on an open outcry basis on the floor of the Bourse building for one hour starting at lunch time.

Gross Domestic Product (1994, constant prices)	Three-year Average GDP Growth (92-94)	Main Industries	Consumer Price Index (93-94)	Monetary Unit	Exchange Rate (9/95)
5.78 trillion Belgian francs	1.13%	Processing, manufacturing, extraction, energy, banking, insurance and retailing	2.3%	Belgian franc	BEF29.37 to US$1.00

However, the Bourse has decided to adopt a new electronic system, known as the New System of Quotation (NSQ), developed by the Paris Bourse, which will also include cash-market transactions.

Another exponent of the reform movement is that banks will now have direct access to the market, rather than being obliged to operate via a stockbroker unit. This measure builds on the Bourse's "Little Bang" of 1990, which granted banks and insurance companies the right to acquire brokerages. While the change is required under the ISD, market participants doubt it will have much practical impact at the Bourse, where banks already dominate through their brokerage units. Early in 1995, the Bourse also abolished the policy of a fixed commission of 200 Belgian francs per transaction.

The Bourse's market capitalization was 2.62 trillion Belgian francs at end-1994, down from an end-1993 record of 2.82 trillion francs. The value of Belgian stock equity trading, however, rose to 428.9 billion francs from 387.4 billion francs.

While 165 stocks trade on the exchange, about 81% of turnover is accounted for by the 20 stocks used to calculate the widely followed Bel-20 index. A single stock, electrical generation group Electrabel SA, racked up 46.2 billion francs turnover, or 11% of the total in 1994, while the top 10 stocks had a 58% share. After Electrabel, the most active list included non-ferrous metals producer Union Miniere SA, chemicals manufacturer Solvay et Cie., oil and gas company Petrofina SA, and Societe Generale de Belgique, the country's leading holding company owned by Cie. de Suez of France.

Ten Largest Capitalized Companies
as of 9/30/95

Stock	Market Cap. US$Mil
Petrofina	7,189,292.1
Générale de Belgique	4,686,018.4
Solvay	4,438,163.1
Générale de Banque	3,973,168.5
Fortis AG	3,440,117.5
Kredietbank	3,144,242.4
BBL	2,739,084.8
Electrafina	2,460,211.1
Royale Belge	2,331,638.4
Powerfin	2,280,821.2

Following the replacement of holding company Gevaert NV by steel maker Cockerill Sambre SA last December, the Bel-20 now comprises 10 industrial and extractive concerns, four holdings, two insurers, two retailers, one bank, and one utility. The Bel-20 basket is reevaluated every December, based on the past 12 months activity.

The index lost 6.22% in 1994 to close the year at 1389.64, following a 31% rise the previous year. The negative swing was attributed to unexpectedly high interest rates, which have reversed course in 1995 and so far have helped fuel a recovery, aided by robust first-half earnings. However, the predominance of a handful of internationally oriented, dollar-linked issues leaves the Bourse vulnerable to fluctuations in the foreign exchange market. The U.S. currency averaged 33.43 Belgian francs in 1994, while Belgian analysts were looking for something closer to 29 or 30 francs in 1995.

The volume of trading in foreign shares totaled 124.8 billion francs in 1994, with gold companies predominant. The foreign line-up includes a number of South African gold concerns, notably Freegold, Driefontein, and Vaal Reefs, prompting the Bourse to launch in December 1994 its own Gold Mines Index, based on those in Johannesburg and London.

The stock market is complemented by Belfox, the options and futures exchange established by the Bourse in partnership with some Belgian banks and brokerages. Here investors can find options and futures for the Bel-20 index and in Belgian government debt, as well as options in a number of leading stocks: retailers Delhaize "Le Lion" SA and GIB SA, Petrofina, Solvay, Union Miniere, insurer Fortis AG, and steel wire maker Bekaert NV. Although trading in the Bel-20 derivatives has been on the thin side, brokers note that Bel-20 basket trades linked to the derivatives have a visible impact on the course of the market.

Indeed, one goal of the recent reform drive is to heighten the interest of non-Bel-20 stocks which suffer from anemic volume under normal circumstances. One suggested solution is to "segment" the market into various categories with differing transaction requirements.

Under current rules, the value of share blocs traded must be a minimum 30 million francs on the 14-day market and 20 million francs in the cash market. Traders say the latter floor hinders activity in smaller issues, where 5 million to 10 million francs would be a relatively sizeable transaction. They also grumble about rules restricting block trades to Bourse business hours, which relegates off-market activity to other financial centers.

Another possible innovation may be the creation of a so-called "price-driven" system for large block trades, in which market makers offer shares at a range of bid and offer prices. Currently, Brussels is "order-driven," with one price for both buyers and sellers.

The Belgian government levies a 25.75% withholding tax on most company dividends, although the rate on shares issued since Jan. 1. 1994 is only 13.39%, thanks to the government's "Global Plan" to restore competitiveness and create employment. By contrast, the withholding tax on fixed-income interest is only 10%, which likely penalizes the attractiveness of stock investments in a country that survives on domestic bond issues. The Belgian government debt was 135% of gross domestic product in 1994, and the country prides itself on its ability to finance the debt domestically.

Almanij

Industry: **Financial Services - Diversified**

Algemene Maatschappij voor Nijverheidskrediet (Almanij) is a holding company with interests in the financial sector. Almanij is Belgium's largest financial-services company by market capitalization. It offers banking, financial, insurance, and asset-management services. Almanij's primary investment is a controlling interest in Kredietbank, Belgium's third-largest bank by assets. Other holdings specialize in insurance and property-related services. Almanij acquired Spaarkrediet, the Belgian domestic banking group, in 1994.

BEF mil	12/92 *	12/93	12/94	US$mil 12/94				
Revenues	**420.0**	**5,126.0**	**4,865.1**	**146.6**	P/E Ratio M	**8.8**	Price (9/30/95) M	**7,900.00**
Net Income	**3,465.0**	**5,476.0**	**5,719.1**	**172.3**	P/B Ratio M	**1.1**	52 Wk Hi-Low M	**8,190.0-7,100.0**
Book Value	**36,227.0**	**40,100.0**	**44,313.6**	**1,392.2**	Yield % M	**2.5**	Market Cap M	**US$1,481.6mil**

Address **Snyderhuis, Keizerstr. 8**
2000 Antwerp
Tel **03-234-29-97**
Fax **03-231-44-09**
ADR
SEDOL No. **4021104**
Managing Director **Ferdinand Verdonck**
Chairman **Jan Huyghebaert**

*Irregular period due to fiscal year change; M=Multiple issues in index; reflects most active.

Banque Nationale de Belgique

Industry: **Banks - Regional**

Banque Nationale de Belgique (BNB), Belgium's central bank, provides comprehensive currency and credit services. The bank is responsible for the production and destruction of bank notes and it is also responsible for putting coins into circulation, which are produced by the Belgian Royal Mint. Other operations include the provision of cash transfers to private financial institutions and financial support for the national treasury. Banque Nationale de Belgique also prints securities and acts as a repository for documentation and statistics.

BEF mil	12/92 P	12/93 P	12/94 P	US$mil 12/94				
Revenues	**38,609.0**	**39,299.0**	**28,420.3**	**856.2**	P/E Ratio	**4.0**	Price (9/30/95)	**38,625**
Net Income	**3,244.0**	**3,838.0**	**3,826.3**	**115.3**	P/B Ratio	**0.3**	52 Wk Hi-Low	**39,250.0-34,000.0**
Book Value	**40,379.0**	**43,956.0**	**46,909.0**	**1,473.7**	Yield %	**4.3**	Market Cap	**US$526.0mil**

Address **Blvd. de Berlaimont 14**
1000 Brussels
Tel **02-221-22-60**
Fax **02-221-31-00**
ADR
SEDOL No. **4076944**
Vice-Governor **William Fraeys**
Governor **Alfons Verplaetse**

P=Parent company data.

BBL

Industry: **Banks - Regional**

Banque Bruxelles Lambert (BBL) is an international bank that caters to both individual and corporate clients. It offers retail banking, life insurance, investment management, corporate finance, currency services, and travel services. The bank serves roughly 1.8 million customers through its network of 980 local branches. BBL also has 35 offices in the world's major financial centers-- most notably in Europe, the United States, and the Asia Pacific region-- and a network of about 5,000 correspondent banks worldwide. At year-end 1994 BBL had BEF2,589 billion in total assets.

BEF mil	12/92 *	12/93	12/94	US$mil 12/94				
Revenues	**212,065.0**	**225,031.0**	**193,621.6**	**5,833.0**	P/E Ratio	**12.2**	Price (9/30/95)	**4,980.00**
Net Income	**2,916.0**	**6,733.0**	**7,753.3**	**233.6**	P/B Ratio	**1.1**	52 Wk Hi-Low	**5,030.0-3,980.0**
Book Value	**62,286.0**	**67,578.0**	**71,671.3**	**2,251.7**	Yield %	**3.2**	Market Cap	**US$2,739.1mil**

Address **24 Ave. Marnix**
1050 Brussels
Tel **02-547-24-84**
Fax **02-547-38-44**
ADR
SEDOL No. **4075424**
CEO **Daniel C. de Lichtbuer**
Chairman **Jacques Moulaert**

*Irregular period due to fiscal year change.

Bekaert

Industry: **Steel**

Bekaert is a worldwide manufacturer of wire, wire products, and steel cord. Its products include steel wire and cables for rubber reinforcement, steel and metal fibers, and high-carbon steel wires. The company supplies its goods to customers in the automotive, tire, chemical, and computer industries. Sales of wire and wire products account for 60% of revenues, and steel wire and cable for rubber reinforcement account for 35%. Bekaert has 55 manufacturing facilities in 18 countries. Overseas exports, primarily to the United States, accounted for 37% of sales in 1994.

BEF mil	12/92	12/93	12/94	US$mil 12/94				
Sales	**53,194.0**	**54,333.0**	**59,337.7**	**1,787.6**	P/E Ratio	**8.0**	Price (9/30/95)	**23,200**
Net Income	**2,623.0**	**2,102.0**	**6,480.8**	**195.2**	P/B Ratio	**1.6**	52 Wk Hi-Low	**25,000.0-18,575.0**
Book Value	**25,490.0**	**27,774.0**	**32,309.8**	**1,015.1**	Yield %	**1.9**	Market Cap	**US$1,493.7mil**

Address **President Kennedypark 18**
8500 Kortrijk
Tel **05-623-05-11**
Fax **05-623-05-43**
ADR
SEDOL No. **4089481**
CEO **Rafaël Decaluwé**
Chairman **Baron Velge**

CBR

Industry: **Building Materials**

CBR Cement Works (Cimenteries CBR) produces cement, ready-mix concrete, aggregates, and building materials. The company's products have more than a 35% share of the cement market in Belgium, the Netherlands, and Rhineland-Westphalia. CBR also sells its products on the west coast of North America. Cimenteries CBR has formed a partnership with German cement manufacturer Heidelberger Zement, which controls just under half of CBR's shares. Sales in North America contributed 35% of the company's revenues in 1994.

BEF mil	12/92	12/93	12/94	US$mil 12/94				
Sales	**47,012.0**	**48,354.0**	**52,879.5**	**1,593.0**	P/E Ratio	**18.6**	Price (9/30/95)	**11,875**
Net Income	**2,778.0**	**2,730.0**	**2,882.8**	**86.8**	P/B Ratio	**1.6**	52 Wk Hi-Low	**12,275.0-11,250.0**
Book Value	**28,195.0**	**28,833.0**	**34,554.3**	**1,085.6**	Yield %	**3.3**	Market Cap	**US$1,512.6mil**

Address **Chaussée de la Hulpe 185**
1170 Brussels
Tel **02-678-32-11**
Fax **02-660-64-33**
ADR
SEDOL No. **4161408**
CEO **Donald Fallon**
Chairman **Peter Schuhmacher**

CMB

Industry: **Marine Transportation**

Compagnie Maritime Belge (CMB) is a diversified transport company that transports oil, gas, and dry cargo; operates liner and port services in Antwerp and Zeebrugge; and provides insurance and financial services. The company's BOCIMAR subsidiary conducts its bulk and crude-oil operations, while liner services are provided by its 51%-owned CMB Transport subsidiary and its 97%-owned Portuguese Transinsular subsidiary. Crude-oil and gas-transport services accounted for roughly 40% of revenues, liner services for 33%, and terminal services for 23% in 1994.

	BEF mil 12/92	12/93	12/94	US$mil 12/94				
Sales	**38,422.1**	**38,493.3**	**39,082.2**	**1,177.4**	P/E Ratio M	**15.7**	Price (9/30/95) M	**2,195.00**
Net Income	**931.2**	**458.2**	**1,052.2**	**31.7**	P/B Ratio M	**1.1**	52 Wk Hi-Low M	**2,605.0-2,050.0**
Book Value	**18,320.0**	**18,311.4**	**17,892.5**	**562.1**	Yield % M	**3.4**	Market Cap M	**US$580.3mil**

Address **De Gerlachekaai 20** Tel **03-247-59-11** ADR Managing Director **Marc Saverys**
2000 Antwerp Fax **03-248-09-06** SEDOL No. **4221948** Chairman **Etienne Davignon**

M=Multiple issues in index; reflects most active.

Cobepa

Industry: **Financial Services - Diversified**

Cie. Belge de Participations Paribas (Cobepa) is a merchant bank that has interests in a range of French financial and commercial firms. It provides assistance in the areas of stock-exchange listings mergers and acquisitions, and capital increases. French holding company Paribas owns two thirds of it. Cobepa's holdings include stakes in four financial holding and investment companies: 73% in IBEL, 50% in Fidepa, 72% in Companie Générale Mosane, and 66% in Luxembourg's CPI. It also holds a 32% interest in the Dutch electronic-engineering firm SAIT-RadioHolland.

	BEF mil 12/92	12/93	12/94	US$mil 12/94				
Revenues	**2,395.0**	**1,897.0**	**1,868.7**	**56.3**	P/E Ratio M	**15.7**	Price (9/30/95) M	**1,054.00**
Net Income	**2,722.0**	**3,750.0**	**4,577.2**	**137.9**	P/B Ratio M	**1.0**	52 Wk Hi-Low M	**1,104.0-960.0**
Book Value	**41,357.0**	**42,388.0**	**47,744.0**	**1,500.0**	Yield % M	**3.5**	Market Cap M	**US$1,298.0mil**

Address **Blvd. Emile Jacqmain 162** Tel **02-218-00-55** ADR CEO **Pierre Scohier**
1210 Brussels Fax **02-217-62-01** SEDOL No. **4207205** Chairman **François Morin**

M=Multiple issues in index; reflects most active.

Delhaize

Industry: **Food Retailers & Wholesalers**

Delhaize Brothers and Company (Delhaize Frères & Cie. Le Lion) is a food and wine retailer with roughly 1,540 outlets, including 412 in Belgium. Its majority-owned U.S. subsidiary, Food Lion, has more than 1,000 Food Lion supermarkets in 14 states, generating 70% of the group's revenues. Delhaize's subsidiary Super Discount Markets owns 13 Cub Foods discount markets in Atlanta and Georgia. Delhaize operates 12 Delvita supermarkets in Prague, 19 Alfa-Beta Vassilopoulos supermarkets in the Athens area of Greece, and 30 P.G supermarkets in France.

	BEF mil 12/92	12/93	12/94	US$mil 12/94				
Sales	**326,666.0**	**365,964.0**	**380,820.3**	**11,472.6**	P/E Ratio	**16.1**	Price (9/30/95)	**1,260.00**
Net Income	**6,383.0**	**1,003.0**	**4,017.0**	**121.0**	P/B Ratio	**2.7**	52 Wk Hi-Low	**1,378.0-1,120.0**
Book Value	**22,365.0**	**23,249.0**	**23,586.1**	**741.0**	Yield %	**1.8**	Market Cap	**US$2,200.6mil**

Address **Rue Osseghem 53** Tel **02-412-21-11** ADR Managing Director **Jacques Boël**
1080 Brussels Fax **02-412-21-94** SEDOL No. **4262118** Chairman **Gui de Vaucleroy**

Electrabel

Industry: **Electrical Utilities - All**

Electrabel is an energy, communications, and water-services company. It produces 86% of Belgium's electricity and operates cable-television systems and electricity-, natural-gas-, and water-distribution services. Electrabel distributes almost 90% of Belgium's natural gas and serves more than half of the country's cable-television customers. It is partially owned by Powerfin, a company that invests in firms that generate, transport, and distribute energy. Electrabel has an interest in the Spanish electric company Iberdrola.

	BEF mil 12/92	12/93	12/94	US$mil 12/94				
Sales	**197,260.0**	**200,945.0**	**205,190.6**	**6,181.6**	P/E Ratio	**15.3**	Price (9/30/95)	**6,540.00**
Net Income	**24,983.0**	**25,838.0**	**25,839.7**	**778.4**	P/B Ratio	**1.7**	52 Wk Hi-Low	**6,570.0-5,280.0**
Book Value	**202,112.0**	**205,749.0**	**209,836.5**	**6,592.4**	Yield %	**4.9**	Market Cap	**US$2,153.9mil**

Address **Blvd. du Régent 8** Tel **02-518-61-11** ADR CEO **Jean-Pierre Hansen**
1000 Brussels Fax **02-511-68-50** SEDOL No. **4148014** Chairman **Philippe Bodson**

Electrafina

Industry: **Oil - Secondary**

Electrafina is the holding company for a group of oil and natural-gas businesses. Its principal holdings include a 23% share of the petroleum company Petrofina and a 20% share of the diversified utility firm Tractebel. Oil-industry subsidiaries include Cometra of Canada and 66%-controlled Nimex Resources. The group also has interests in multimedia, primarily through multimedia holding company CLMM, in which the company has a 25% stake. Electrafina is 45% controlled by the Belgian holding company Groupe Bruxelles Lambert (GBL).

	BEF mil 12/92	12/93	12/94	US$mil 12/94				
Sales	**1,245.0**	**1,058.0**	**1,286.0**	**38.7**	P/E Ratio	**15.3**	Price (9/30/95)	**2,900.00**
Net Income	**2,705.0**	**4,194.0**	**5,342.0**	**160.9**	P/B Ratio	**1.1**	52 Wk Hi-Low	**3,110.0-2,530.0**
Book Value	**64,209.0**	**68,724.0**	**77,745.0**	**2,442.5**	Yield %	**3.5**	Market Cap	**US$2,460.2mil**

Address **Ave. Marnix 24** Tel **02-547-21-11** ADR CEO **Thierry de Rudder**
1050 Brussels Fax **02-542-22-73** SEDOL No. **4213075** Chairman **Albert Frère**

Fortis AG

Industry: **Insurance - Full Line**

Fortis is an insurance and banking firm, jointly owned by Fortis AG and the Dutch firm Fortis AMEV. Fortis' insurance products include life, non-life, and pension policies, and its financial services include retail banking, mortgages, and fund-management services. It also sells life insurance, health and disability insurance, and investment products in the United States, United Kingdom, France, and Spain. Insurance revenues generated 62% of income and banking the remainder. Overseas revenues, primarily in the U. S., account for nearly one third of the company's revenues.

BEF mil	12/92	12/93	12/94	US$mil 12/94				
Revenues	**8,920.0**	**9,884.0**	**11,153.0**	**336.0**	P/E Ratio	**10.5**	Price (9/30/95)	**3,150.00**
Net Income	**7,261.0**	**8,265.0**	**10,074.3**	**303.5**	P/B Ratio	**1.3**	52 Wk Hi-Low	**3,275.0-2,375.0**
Book Value	**55,725.0**	**71,790.0**	**75,675.6**	**2,377.5**	Yield %	**2.4**	Market Cap	**US$3,440.1mil**

Address **Blvd. Emile Jacqmain 53**
1000 Brussels
Tel **02-220-81-11**
Fax **02-220-81-50**
ADR
SEDOL No. **4001526**
CEO **Valère Croes**
Chairman **Maurice Lippens**

GBL

Industry: **Conglomerates**

Groupe Bruxelles Lambert (GBL) is a holding company whose main interests are in the energy,multi-media, financial services, and property businesses. GBL has a 46% interest in electricity company Electrafina, through which it holds 23% of petrochemicals producer Petrofina and 20% of utilities group Tractebel. Partially-owned subsidiaries Royale Belge and Banque Bruxelles Lambert offer insurance and universal banking services. In 1994, Compagnie Luxembourgeoise Multi Media (CLMM) was established as a vehicle for GBL's multi-media holdings.

BEF mil	12/92	12/93	12/94	US$mil 12/94				
Sales	**3,898.0**	**2,725.0**	**2,242.0**	**67.5**	P/E Ratio M	**13.8**	Price (9/30/95) M	**3,900.00**
Net Income	**6,335.0**	**6,382.0**	**6,633.0**	**199.8**	P/B Ratio M	**1.2**	52 Wk Hi-Low M	**4,040.0-3,415.0**
Book Value	**68,336.0**	**71,370.0**	**74,184.0**	**2,330.6**	Yield % M	**3.7**	Market Cap M	**US$2,022.4mil**

Address **Ave. Marnix 24**
1050 Brussels
Tel **02-547-21-11**
Fax **02-547-22-85**
ADR
SEDOL No. **4391551**
Chairman Exec Bd **Gerald Frère**
Chairman Supv Bd **Albert Frère**

M=Multiple issues in index; reflects most active.

Générale de Banque

Industry: **Banks - Money Center**

Générale de Banque, Belgium's largest bank by assets (BEF4,040 billion at year-end 1994), offers a variety of financial products and services to individual and corporate clients. Its network in Belgium consists of more than 1,100 branches and 32 regional offices that serve two million individual customers and roughly two thirds of Belgian companies. It also operates abroad through branches and representative offices. The company's subsidiaries offer private-banking, diamond- and vehicle-finance, insurance, stock-brokerage, and venture-capital services.

BEF mil	12/92	12/93	12/94	US$mil 12/94				
Revenues	**320,836.0**	**317,745.0**	**273,052.1**	**8,225.9**	P/E Ratio M	**10.9**	Price (9/30/95) M	**9,240.00**
Net Income	**10,733.0**	**11,586.0**	**12,651.3**	**381.1**	P/B Ratio M	**1.4**	52 Wk Hi-Low M	**9,470.0-7,280.0**
Book Value	**90,071.0**	**92,323.0**	**101,482.0**	**3,188.3**	Yield % M	**3.9**	Market Cap M	**US$3,973.2mil**

Address **Montagne du Parc 3**
1000 Brussels
Tel **02-516-21-11**
Fax **02-516-42-22**
ADR
SEDOL No. **4383116**
CEO **Ferdinand Chaffart**
Chairman **Paul E. Janssen**

M=Multiple issues in index; reflects most active.

Générale de Belgique

Industry: **Conglomerates**

Société Générale de Belgique is an industrial holding company with interests in eight large companies in the industrial and service sectors. It holds an 18% share of Coficem, the majority shareholder in French firm Sagem, which specializes in electronics and advanced telecommunication technology. It has a 27% stake in the energy and industrial company Tractebel, which generates 93% of the electricity consumed in Belgium. Générale de Belgique owns 29% of the insurance firm Générale de Banque and 19% of Fortis AG, co-owner of the insurance firm Fortis.

BEF mil	12/92	12/93	12/94	US$mil 12/94				
Sales	**195,874.0**	**182,391.0**	**153,306.0**	**4,618.5**	P/E Ratio	**14.0**	Price (9/30/95)	**2,190.00**
Net Income	**6,220.0**	**8,688.0**	**11,011.0**	**331.7**	P/B Ratio	**0.9**	52 Wk Hi-Low	**2,320.0-1,875.0**
Book Value	**157,862.0**	**163,519.0**	**165,769.0**	**5,207.9**	Yield %	**3.9**	Market Cap	**US$4,686.0mil**

Address **Rue Royale 30**
1000 Brussels
Tel **02-507-02-11**
Fax **02-512-18-95**
ADR
SEDOL No. **4819677**
CEO **Gérard Mestrallet**
Chairman **Etienne Davignon**

Gevaert

Industry: **Conglomerates**

Gevaert is a holding company with interests in financial institutions, transport, and chemicals in Belgium, the Netherlands, and Germany. Its major holdings are Bayer (Germany), Aegon (the Netherlands), Almanij (Belgium), and Compagnie de Navigation Mixte (France). These four companies generate nearly 60% of Gevaert's dividend income. Other holdings include Kredietbank S.A. Luxembourgeoise and Hapag-Lloyd (Germany). As of year-end 1994, Gevaert's portfolio consisted of financial-services holdings (45%), transport and shipping (28%), and chemicals (10%).

BEF mil	12/92	12/93	12/94	US$mil 12/94				
Sales	**1,817.0**	**1,903.9**	**1,692.3**	**51.0**	P/E Ratio	**9.2**	Price (9/30/95)	**1,660.00**
Net Income	**1,996.3**	**2,930.0**	**4,644.1**	**139.9**	P/B Ratio	**1.5**	52 Wk Hi-Low	**1,700.0-1,422.0**
Book Value	**24,374.1**	**25,018.8**	**28,072.4**	**881.9**	Yield %	**2.7**	Market Cap	**US$1,457.1mil**

Address **Septestraat 27**
2640 Mortsel
Tel **03-443-02-11**
Fax **03-440-04-78**
ADR **GEVAY**
SEDOL No. **4368209**
Managing Director **Marc Francken**
Chairman **André Leysen**

GIB Group

Industry: **Food Retailers & Wholesalers**

GIB Group is Belgium's largest distribution company. It operates supermarkets, hypermarkets, department stores, home-improvement stores, fast-food restaurants, and specialized retail outlets. The company's food-retail division, which accounts for approximately 60% of revenues, consists of more than 700 stores. GIB owns the home-improvement chains Brico and Handy Andy, which operate in Belgium and the United States respectively. The company also operates Quick fast-food restaurants in Belgium, France, and Luxembourg.

BEF mil	01/93	01/94	01/95	US$mil 01/95				
Sales	**227,938.0**	**232,958.0**	**232,459.9**	**7,085.2**	P/E Ratio M	**19.2**	Price (9/30/95) M	**1,238.00**
Net Income	**3,260.0**	**-3,527.0**	**2,167.3**	**66.1**	P/B Ratio M	**2.0**	52 Wk Hi-Low M	**1,438.0-1,206.0**
Book Value	**22,866.0**	**18,419.0**	**19,001.7**	**608.1**	Yield % M	**2.4**	Market Cap M	**US$1,269.1mil**

Address **Ave. des Olympiades 20**
1140 Brussels
Tel **02-729-21-11**
Fax **02-729-20-96**
ADR
SEDOL No. **4357735**
Managing Director **Diego du Monceau**
Chairman **Pierre Scohier**

M=Multiple issues in index; reflects most active.

Kredietbank

Industry: **Banks - Regional**

Kredietbank offers banking, insurance, and other financial services. The company operates approximately 740 branches in Flanders and Brussels. In addition, it operates in six other countries through branches and representative offices. Kredietbank, together with its holding company Almanij, and its associated company Fidelitas, owns Omniver and Omniver Leven, which respectively offer general insurance and life insurance. In 1994, the bank generated 57% of its operating revenue in Belgium, 19% in Luxembourg, 9% in the Netherlands, and 5% in Ireland.

BEF mil	12/92 *	12/93	12/94	US$mil 12/94				
Revenues	**179,573.0**	**220,973.0**	**192,584.0**	**5,801.8**	P/E Ratio M	**9.9**	Price (9/30/95) M	**7,120.00**
Net Income	**7,271.0**	**9,775.0**	**10,496.5**	**316.2**	P/B Ratio M	**1.3**	52 Wk Hi-Low M	**7,260.0-5,950.0**
Book Value	**66,722.0**	**73,217.0**	**80,252.2**	**2,521.3**	Yield % M	**3.0**	Market Cap M	**US$3,144.2mil**

Address **Arenbergstraat 7**
1000 Brussels
Tel **02-517-52-62**
Fax **02-517-51-95**
ADR
SEDOL No. **4497749**
President **Marcel Cockaerts**
Chairman **Marc Santens**

*Irregular period due to fiscal year change; M=Multiple issues in index; reflects most active.

Petrofina

Industry: **Oil - Integrated Majors**

Petrofina is a petroleum company that explores for and produces oil and natural gas; produces feedstocks, plastics, and paints; and operates the Fina chain of retail gas stations in Europe and the southern United States. Petrofina's activities in Norway and the southern U.S. produce natural gas and more than 119,000 barrels of oil per day. Its recently acquired Belgian subsidiary Montfina and its U.S.-based subsidiary make it the world's second-largest producer of polypropylene. Exports to North America account for 23% of sales; the remainder of sales are made in Europe.

BEF mil	12/92	12/93	12/94	US$mil 12/94				
Sales	**537,294.0**	**540,893.0**	**540,893.0**	**16,294.9**	P/E Ratio	**45.9**	Price (9/30/95)	**9,130.00**
Net Income	**4,631.0**	**7,144.0**	**7,144.0**	**215.2**	P/B Ratio	**1.7**	52 Wk Hi-Low	**9,890.0-8,150.0**
Book Value	**121,280.0**	**127,064.0**	**127,064.0**	**3,992.0**	Yield %	**3.1**	Market Cap	**US$7,189.3mil**

Address **52 rue de l'Industrie**
1040 Brussels
Tel **02-288-91-11**
Fax **02-288-34-45**
ADR **PTRFY**
SEDOL No. **4684002**
Mng Dir & CEO **François Cornelis**
Chairman **Albert Frère**

Powerfin

Industry: **Electrical Utilities - All**

Powerfin invests in international projects for electricity and steam production, as well as in the transport and distribution of electricity and natural gas. Powerfin is the major shareholder of Electrabel, which produces 93% of Belgium's total electricity and operates communication activities and public services. Powerfin is partially owned by the Tractebel energy, communications, and services company. Powerfin has interests in electricity-generation plants in the United States, Ireland, Portugal, and Oman. It also owns 25% of Argentinian gas-distribution firm Tibsa.

BEF mil	12/92	12/93	12/94	US$mil 12/94				
Sales	**853.0**	**2,596.0**	**4,137.0**	**124.6**	P/E Ratio M	**11.4**	Price (9/30/95) M	**3,285.00**
Net Income	**6,904.0**	**6,474.0**	**7,032.0**	**211.8**	P/B Ratio M	**1.3**	52 Wk Hi-Low M	**3,295.0-2,620.0**
Book Value	**56,496.0**	**58,379.0**	**61,913.0**	**1,945.1**	Yield % M	**3.0**	Market Cap M	**US$2,280.8mil**

Address **Pl. du Trône 1**
1000 Brussels
Tel **02-510-70-37**
Fax **02-510-73-30**
ADR
SEDOL No. **4699363**
President **--**
Chairman **Philippe Bodson**

M=Multiple issues in index; reflects most active.

Royale Belge

Industry: **Insurance - Full Line**

Groupe Royale Belge is an insurance company that offers a broad range of insurance and reinsurance products to corporate and private customers. The company provides property, automobile, accident, workers' compensation, and legal-protection insurance, as well as a range of life insurance products. It generates more than 70% of its income from insurance activities. The firm's subsidiaries operate in the areas of banking, real estate, commercial businesses, and finance. It offers banking services through its Banque Ippa and Royale Belge Finance subsidiaries.

BEF mil	12/92	12/93	12/94	US$mil 12/94				
Revenues	**67,866.0**	**71,509.0**	**75,123.7**	**2,263.2**	P/E Ratio M	**14.9**	Price (9/30/95) M	**5,140.00**
Net Income	**4,386.0**	**4,875.0**	**5,505.5**	**165.9**	P/B Ratio M	**1.6**	52 Wk Hi-Low M	**5,500.0-4,200.0**
Book Value	**48,661.0**	**50,052.0**	**51,696.5**	**1,624.1**	Yield % M	**3.4**	Market Cap M	**US$2,331.6mil**

Address **Blvd. du Souverain 25**
1170 Brussels
Tel **02-661-61-11**
Fax **02-661-93-40**
ADR
SEDOL No. **4756752**
Managing Director **Jean-Pierre Gerard**
Chairman **J.P. de Launoit**

M=Multiple issues in index; reflects most active.

Solvac

Industry: **Financial Services - Diversified**

Solvac is an investment holding company whose main subsidiaries operate in the chemical- manufacturing industry. The company's holdings include manufacturers of plastics, alkalis, peroxygens, polypropylene, and pharmaceuticals. Its subsidiaries export chemical products to markets in western Europe, North America, South America, and Asia. The company's principal asset is a 25% interest in Belgian industrial-chemical manufacturer Solvay, which specializes in the production of alkalis, peroxides, plastics, and health products.

BEF mil	02/93	02/94	02/95	US$mil 02/95				
Revenues	**N/A**	**1,524.9**	**1,457.5**	**45.0**	P/E Ratio M	**18.1**	Price (9/30/95) M	**1,880.00**
Net Income	**N/A**	**1,385.4**	**1,402.9**	**43.3**	P/B Ratio M	**4.9**	52 Wk Hi-Low M	**1,880.0-1,450.0**
Book Value	**N/A**	**5,785.0**	**5,187.7**	**171.9**	Yield % M	**4.1**	Market Cap M	**US$481.4mil**

Address **Rue Keyenveld 58**
1050 Brussels
Tel **N/A**
Fax **N/A**
ADR
SEDOL No. **4821036**
Managing Director **D. Janssen**
Chairman **P. de Laguiche**

M=Multiple issues in index; reflects most active.

Solvay

Industry: **Commodity Chemicals**

Solvay is the parent company of a chemical group specializing in five major areas: alkalis, peroxygens, plastics, processing, and health. Its alkalis sector supplies products to the glass, metal, textile, and paper industries. Solvay also produces high-density polyethylene, polypropylene, and polyvinyl chloride. Its plastic processing includes coating, extrusion, blow molding, and thermoforming. Solvay's health sector makes vaccines, pharmaceuticals, and enzymes. Exports, primarily to North America, accounted for one third of Solvay Group's revenues.

BEF mil	12/92	12/93	12/94	US$mil 12/94				
Sales	**254,470.0**	**244,146.0**	**262,227.0**	**7,899.8**	P/E Ratio	**17.0**	Price (9/30/95)	**15,650**
Net Income	**9,755.0**	**-7,165.0**	**7,691.0**	**231.7**	P/B Ratio	**1.4**	52 Wk Hi-Low	**16,675.0-13,550.0**
Book Value	**103,263.0**	**94,288.0**	**94,778.0**	**2,977.6**	Yield %	**3.2**	Market Cap	**US$4,438.2mil**

Address **Rue du Prince Albert 33**
1050 Brussels
Tel **02-509-61-11**
Fax **02-509-66-17**
ADR
SEDOL No. **4821100**
CEO **Daniel Janssen**
Chairman **Yves Boël**

Tractebel

Industry: **Electrical Utilities - All**

Tractebel owns and operates communication, energy, and service businesses. The firm supplies 93% of the country's electricity, and provides and transports gas through its partially-owned Electrabel and Distrigas subsidiaries. Tractebel's Coditel subsidiary engages in communication activities, which include cable-television, cellular-phone, and audiovisual operations, as well as technical installations, real estate investment, and engineering. Tractebel is 41%-controlled by industrial holding company Société Générale de Belgique.

BEF mil	12/92	12/93	12/94	US$mil 12/94				
Sales	**252,495.0**	**263,495.0**	**297,776.6**	**8,970.8**	P/E Ratio M	**13.5**	Price (9/30/95) M	**10,500**
Net Income	**9,318.0**	**9,905.0**	**10,721.2**	**323.0**	P/B Ratio M	**1.5**	52 Wk Hi-Low M	**10,975.0-8,970.0**
Book Value	**90,668.0**	**90,608.0**	**94,908.4**	**2,981.7**	Yield % M	**3.4**	Market Cap M	**US$791.2mil**

Address **Pl. du Trône 1**
1000 Brussels
Tel **02-510-71-11**
Fax **02-510-73-88**
ADR
SEDOL No. **4900300**
Managing Director **Philippe Bodson**
Chairman **Gérard Mestrallet**

M=Multiple issues in index; reflects most active.

UCB

Industry: **Specialty Chemicals**

UCB is a diversified pharmaceutical and chemical company. Its activities are divided into three areas: the Pharma Sector is involved in the research, production, and marketing of prescription pharmaceuticals; the Chemical Sector manufactures intermediate, fine, and specialty chemicals; and the Films and Packaging Sector is involved in the production and conversion of films and flexible materials for the food and medical industries. Each sector accounts for roughly one third of the company's sales. Overseas exports accounted for 22% of revenues in 1994.

BEF mil	12/92	12/93	12/94	US$mil 12/94				
Sales	**49,836.0**	**48,075.0**	**52,325.0**	**1,576.3**	P/E Ratio	**24.4**	Price (9/30/95)	**33,900**
Net Income	**2,246.0**	**2,293.0**	**2,332.0**	**70.3**	P/B Ratio	**2.6**	52 Wk Hi-Low	**34,925.0-22,925.0**
Book Value	**16,460.0**	**18,205.0**	**19,214.0**	**603.6**	Yield %	**1.4**	Market Cap	**US$1,321.6mil**

Address **Avenue Louise 326**
1050 Brussels
Tel **02-641-14-11**
Fax **02-641-16-49**
ADR
SEDOL No. **4910622**
Chairman Exec Bd **Georges Jacobs**
Chairman Supv Bd **Willy De Clercq**

Canada

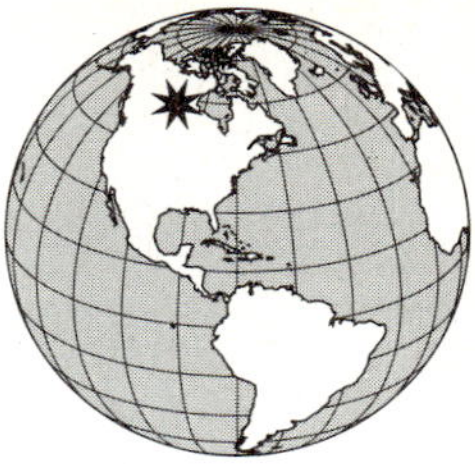

Canada

Solange De Santis, Toronto

Local Trading Hours	Time Difference from New York	Population (Est. 3/95
9:30-4:00 (Toronto and Montreal); 9:30-4:30 (Vancouver)	Toronto and Montreal same as EST; Vancouver 3 hours behind EST	29,500,000

If Canadian stock market performance were a student, its report card for the first eight months of 1995 might read thus: "Classic underachiever. Some improvement, but failed to keep up with others in class."

While the Dow Jones Industrial Average in the U.S. burst through record highs on a regular basis, the Toronto Stock Exchange (TSE) index of 300 major issues crawled higher by inches. Toward the end of September, the TSE 300 stood at the 4550 level, up about 6% from yearend 1994, when it was at the 4300 level. In the same period, the Dow Jones average soared 24% to the 4700 level, up from about 3800 at the end of 1994.

Several factors contributed to Canada's sluggish gain, said Josef Schachter, market strategist with Richardson, Greenshields of Canada Ltd., a Winnipeg-based brokerage firm.

First, the U.S. central bank, the Federal Reserve, raised interest rates to slow the economy and squeeze out inflationary pressure. A slowdown in the American economy hits Canada hard, Mr. Schachter noted.

Second, "Free trade has worked," he said. "Exports are now about 40% of Canada's gross domestic product, compared to 20% in the 1970s. Stocks started to back off as exports started slowing down." In 1994, exporters reaped the benefit of a weak Canadian dollar, but the currency strengthened slightly in 1995 and even that advantage was diluted.

In addition, the technology group was the "big juicer" in the U.S. stock market rise and that sector isn't a big factor in Canada, Mr. Schachter said.

On the political scene, a new Conservative government was elected in Ontario and most other provincial governments were dedicated to cutting spending, but several provinces continued to carry burdensome deficits.

Uncertainty surrounding the perennial question of Quebec independence was another damper on stock prices, Mr. Schachter said. A vote on sovereignty was set for October 1995 in Quebec.

Dow Jones Canada Equity Market Index Performance

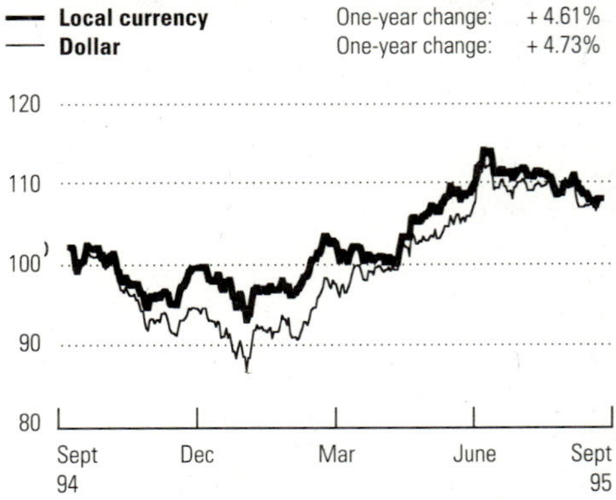

Although foreign investment in Canadian equities isn't as big a factor as it is in bonds and the currency, some market watchers believe Canada needs to improve its competitiveness as a place to invest.

Gross Domestic Product (94)	Three-year Average GDP Growth (92-94)	Main Industries	Consumer Price Index (8/94-8/95)	Monetary Unit	Exchange Rate (9/95)
C$750.1 billion	2.5%	Autos and auto parts, oil and gas, forest products, mining, agriculture, finance, communications	+2.3%	Canadian dollar	C$1.34 to US$1.00

"If I were a European looking at investing in North America, I'd obviously look to the States. There are lingering international doubts about whether we can get our fiscal situation in order and political situation in order," said Peter Wallace, chairman of Toronto investment firm Wallace, Dewan and Partners Inc.

Share volume on the Toronto Stock Exchange hit 10.3 billion for the first eight months of 1995, down from 10.8 billion shares in the year-earlier period. However, the dollar value of stocks traded was C$133.9 billion, up from C$125.1 billion. The average share price rose to C$12.94 from C$11.53.

Montreal and Vancouver posted gains also. Share volume on the Montreal exchange hit 1.8 billion from January through August, 1995, compared to 1.7 billion the year before. Total value was C$25.1 billion, up from C$22.0 billion. Average share price was C$13.64, up from C$12.84.

The Vancouver exchange attracts companies seeking venture capital, so the trading volume is high, but the share prices are low. Four billion shares changed hands in the first eight months, compared to 3.6 billion a year earlier. Dollar value was C$4.2 billion, flat from the year before. And average share price declined to C$1.03 from C$1.20.

A substantial gain in the TSE 300 index in 1996 depends upon U.S. economic performance and on political stability in Quebec, Mr. Schachter said. "If the U.S. gross national product gains 2.5%, the TSE index could go to 5000. If it grows 3.5%, it could be 5300," he said. Looking at various sectors, he believes the cyclical base metals and forest products companies should tie for the lead in stock market performance.

Ten Largest Capitalized Companies
as of 9/30/95

Stock	Market Cap. US$Mil
Seagram	18,017,800.9
Barrick Gold	12,278,426.0
Northern Telecom	12,101,378.0
BCE	10,319,977.4
Alcan Aluminum	9,773,797.5
Placer Dome	8,346,940.0
Royal Bank of Canada	6,916,098.9
Bank of Montreal	5,844,016.0
Canadian Imperial Bank	5,668,781.8
Canadian Pacific	5,484,104.5

The Toronto Stock Exchange's new president, Rowland Fleming, in office since January 1995, is supervising the exchange's plan to close its trading floor and move to electronic trading. The project has been hamstrung by technical glitches, but Mr. Fleming would like to see it completed in 1996, said TSE spokesman Steven Kee.

The Toronto exchange is also moving toward decimal trading, that is, quoting stock prices in dollars and cents instead of the traditional eighths. The move is aimed at more efficient pricing, said Mr. Kee.

He also noted that, although there is little decimal trading on U.S. exchanges, all European exchanges have a form of decimal trading. "With automation, it's a lot easier to trade," Mr. Kee said.

The Vancouver Stock Exchange got a new president, Michael Johnson, in October, 1995. Outgoing president Don Hudson, from the perspective of 14 years in the job, said Mr. Johnson's top challenge will be to continue to improve the reputation of the VSE, long criticized as a haven for scam artists as well as legitimate companies. "We believe we are making progress, but there is still a long way to go," Mr. Hudson said.

The British Columbia government moved to shore up securities regulation by giving the B.C. Securities Commission rule-making power and financial independence. The commission must also produce an annual report to the legislature.

The VSE inaugurated The Asian Board, a securities trading market exclusively for Asian companies seeking a listing in North America.

Looking toward Europe, the exchange sold its computerized trading system to Tradepoint Market Systems PLC in London, which has started an institutional investors' trading system in competition with the London Stock Exchange. Doing business with the VSE led Tradepoint to seek a listing on the exchange.

Nasdaq, the U.S. over-the-counter market, made some waves by applying to Quebec securities regulators for permission to install a trading terminal at Marleau, Lemire Inc., a Montreal broker. The Toronto Stock Exchange opposed the move on the grounds that it is not allowed to install its trading terminals in the U.S. "Reciprocity is a central issue," said TSE lawyer Philip Anisman. A decision on the Nasdaq application was expected by the end of 1995.

Industry Group Performance
1 Year Change Through 9/30/95

Industry	Change % (US$)
Best Performing	
Consumer & Household Services - Only	66.91
Software	47.80
Aerospace & Defense	39.15
Tobacco	25.80
Paper Products	25.78
Worst Performing	
Airlines	-35.67
Chemicals - All	-34.45
Broadcasting	-30.32
Steel	-27.63
Commodity Chemicals	-27.27

Abitibi-Price

Industry: **Paper Products**

Abitibi-Price specializes in the manufacture of groundwood papers and newsprint. The concern operates 10 paper mills across North America, including three joint-venture mills, and produces more than 2 million tons of paper per year. Its major markets include the newspaper, advertising, and office-supply industries. Abitibi-Price sells about two thirds of its newsprint in the United States, and has a 10.6% share of the North American newsprint market overall. The company distributes its office products through subsidiaries.

C$ mil	12/92	12/93	12/94	US$mil 12/94				
Sales	**1,600.8**	**1,869.0**	**2,111.0**	**1,542.0**	P/E Ratio	**NMF**	Price (9/30/95)	**23.38**
Net Income	**-219.3**	**-121.7**	**-55.0**	**-40.2**	P/B Ratio	**2.4**	52 Wk Hi-Low	**25.63-16.88**
Book Value	**764.8**	**729.8**	**838.0**	**598.6**	Yield %	**0.0**	Market Cap	**US$1,348.1mil**

Address	**207 Queens Quay W.**	Tel	**416-203-5089**	Exchange	**TSE**	President & CEO	**Ronald Y. Oberlander**
	Toronto, ON M5J 2P5	Fax	**416-203-5090**	Ticker	**A**	Chairman	**Bernd K. Koken**

Air Canada

Industry: **Airlines**

Air Canada, Canada's largest airline by revenues, provides scheduled and charter air transportation for passengers and cargo. Its passenger network serves 27 North American cities, while connecting carriers have 50 Canadian and six U.S. destinations. It also serves 24 cities in Europe, Asia, and the Caribbean. Cargo operations serve 51 international destinations. Air Canada owns five Canadian regional airlines, Air Canada Vacations, a Canadian tour operator, and Galileo Canada, a reservation service. It also holds a 23.8% voting interest in Continental Airlines (U.S.).

C$ mil	12/92	12/93	12/94	US$mil 12/94				
Sales	**3,501.0**	**3,598.0**	**4,024.0**	**2,939.4**	P/E Ratio	**NMF**	Price (9/30/95)	**4.90**
Net Income	**-454.0**	**-326.0**	**129.0**	**94.2**	P/B Ratio	**1.6**	52 Wk Hi-Low	**8.88-4.80**
Book Value	**316.0**	**230.0**	**365.0**	**260.7**	Yield %	**0.0**	Market Cap	**US$433.2mil**

Address	**P.O. Box 14000**	Tel	**514-422-5000**	Exchange	**TSE**	President	**Hollis L. Harris**
	Saint-Laurent, PQ H4Y 1H4	Fax	**514-422-5739**	Ticker	**AC**	Chairman	**Hollis L. Harris**

Alberta Energy

Industry: **Oil - Secondary**

Alberta Energy Company (AEC) is among Canada's top 10 oil and gas companies by reserves, production levels, and exploratory landholdings. Its reserves include 1.9 trillion cubic feet of natural gas and 310 million barrels of oil. Oil and gas exploration, production, marketing, storage, and pipeline transportation make up more than 90% of assets. An 820-mile network of three crude-oil pipeline systems makes AEC the largest intra-Alberta oil transporter. It also has forest-product operating interests over more than two million acres of Canadian timberland.

C$ mil	12/92	12/93	12/94	US$mil 12/94				
Sales	**567.5**	**626.2**	**922.9**	**674.1**	P/E Ratio	**15.0**	Price (9/30/95)	**20.38**
Net Income	**42.2**	**91.6**	**100.5**	**73.4**	P/B Ratio	**1.4**	52 Wk Hi-Low	**22.00-16.63**
Book Value	**907.1**	**979.7**	**1,061.9**	**758.5**	Yield %	**2.0**	Market Cap	**US$1,132.3mil**

Address	**421 Seventh Ave. S.W.**	Tel	**403-266-8111**	Exchange	**TSE**	President & CEO	**Gwyn Morgan**
	Calgary, AB T2P 4K9	Fax	**403-266-8154**	Ticker	**AEC**	Chairman	**David E. Mitchell**

Alcan Aluminum

Industry: **Aluminum**

Alcan Aluminum is one of the world's largest aluminum companies by production, and is North America's largest manufacturer of fabricated aluminum products. Alcan is involved in bauxite mining and aluminum refining, manufacturing, marketing, and recycling. Primary markets include the containers, packaging, electrical, and construction industries. Alcan has operations on five continents, with its primary mining and alumina-processing operations in Canada, Ireland, and Jamaica. Nonaluminum products account for roughly 16% of sales.

$ mil	12/92	12/93	12/94	US$mil 12/94				
Sales	**7,596.0**	**7,232.0**	**8,216.0**	**8,216.0**	P/E Ratio	**95.4**	Price (9/30/95)	**43.50**
Net Income	**-112.0**	**-104.0**	**96.0**	**96.0**	P/B Ratio	**1.7**	52 Wk Hi-Low	**49.38-31.75**
Book Value	**4,266.0**	**4,096.0**	**4,308.0**	**4,308.0**	Yield %	**0.5**	Market Cap	**US$7,293.9mil**

Address	**1188 Sherbrooke St. W.**	Tel	**514-848-8368**	Exchange	**TSE**	President & CEO	**Jacques Bougie**
	Montreal, PQ H3A 3G2	Fax	**514-848-8115**	Ticker	**AL**	Chairman	**John Evans**

Alliance Forest Products

Industry: **Forest Products**

Alliance Forest Products is an integrated forest-products company that produces newsprint, uncoated groundwood paper, and lumber, and engages in forest harvesting and management. It has cutting rights to 1.4 million cubic meters of wood and operates two newsprint and paper mills with an average annual paper production of 405,000 tonnes. In 1995, Alliance purchased Quebec-based lumber company Guerette Group, which operates three sawmills and one treatment plant. Alliance was formed in the spring of 1994 to acquire assets that were scheduled for disposal by Domtar.

C$ mil	12/92	12/93	12/94	US$mil 12/94				
Sales	**217.6**	**259.2**	**184.8**	**135.0**	P/E Ratio	**15.7**	Price (9/30/95)	**26.88**
Net Income	**0.7**	**26.8**	**30.4**	**22.2**	P/B Ratio	**2.1**	52 Wk Hi-Low	**29.38-22.50**
Book Value	**201.8**	**192.9**	**224.2**	**160.1**	Yield %	**0.0**	Market Cap	**US$358.0mil**

Address	**1000 de la Gauchetière W.**	Tel	**514-954-2100**	Exchange	**TSE**	President & CEO	**Pierre Monahan**
	Montreal, PQ H3B 4W5	Fax	**514-954-2167**	Ticker	**ALP**	Chairman	**Robert Despres**

Anderson Exploration

Industry: **Oil - Secondary**

Anderson Exploration explores for, extracts, and processes natural gas and crude oil in western Canada. The company produces an average of 222 million cubic feet of natural gas, 1,734 barrels of natural-gas liquids, and 6,533 barrels of crude oil daily. It has reserves of 1,378 billion cubic feet of natural gas and 43.9 million barrels of crude oil and natural-gas liquids. Its undeveloped-land inventory consists of 985,000 acres, 96% of which is in the province of Alberta. Anderson is active in exploration projects in Peace River Arch, Alberta, and areas in eastern Alberta.

C$ mil	09/92	09/93	09/94	US$mil 09/94				
Sales	**75.7**	**110.1**	**166.3**	**122.5**	P/E Ratio	**56.1**	Price (9/30/95)	**12.63**
Net Income	**3.2**	**15.0**	**24.2**	**17.8**	P/B Ratio	**3.5**	52 Wk Hi-Low	**16.00-11.75**
Book Value	**196.3**	**276.1**	**410.7**	**306.5**	Yield %	**0.0**	Market Cap	**US$1,133.0mil**

Address **2300 W. Canadian Pl., 700 9th Ave. Calgary, AB T2P 3V4** Tel **403-264-9800** Fax **403-263-3274** Exchange **TSE** Ticker **AXL** President **Larry J. Macdonald** Chairman & CEO **J.C. Anderson**

Avenor

Industry: **Paper Products**

Avenor is a diversified forest-products company that produces newsprint, pulp, white paper, and wood products. It is North America's largest supplier of recycled-content newsprint and Canada's largest exporter of market pulp. It operates four mills for both virgin- and recycled-content newsprint, three pulp mills, and one white-paper mill. It owns 51% of Canada's Pacific Forest Products, which produces softwood lumber products. 38% of the company's total revenues come from the sale of newsprint, 28% from pulp, 15% from white paper, and 16% from wood products.

C$ mil	12/92	12/93	12/94	US$mil 12/94				
Sales	**1,825.5**	**1,834.1**	**1,896.7**	**1,385.5**	P/E Ratio	**NMF**	Price (9/30/95)	**28.63**
Net Income	**-248.0**	**-285.6**	**-71.0**	**-51.9**	P/B Ratio	**2.1**	52 Wk Hi-Low	**33.25-24.88**
Book Value	**999.2**	**865.8**	**912.8**	**652.0**	Yield %	**0.0**	Market Cap	**US$1,433.0mil**

Address **1250 René-Lévesque Blvd. W. Montreal, PQ H3B 4Y3** Tel **514-846-4811** Fax **514-846-4850** Exchange **TSE** Ticker **AVR** President & CEO **Paul E. Gagné** Chairman **Michel Bélanger**

Bank of Montreal

Industry: **Banks - Money Center**

Bank of Montreal is the Canadian holding company for three firms: Bank of Montreal, which operates 1,160 branches throughout Canada; Newbitt Burns, which provides investment services; and Harris Bankcorp, which operates 120 branches in the Chicago area. The banks provide savings and checking accounts, as well as business, consumer, and real-estate loans. The company's Harris Newbitt Thomson Securities subsidiary is the only Canadian-controlled primary dealer of U.S. government paper in the United States. The company also makes loans to foreign companies.

C$ mil	10/92	10/93	10/94	US$mil 10/94				
Revenues	**8,847.0**	**8,706.0**	**9,108.0**	**6,697.1**	P/E Ratio	**10.4**	Price (9/30/95)	**29.50**
Net Income	**640.0**	**709.0**	**825.0**	**606.6**	P/B Ratio	**1.2**	52 Wk Hi-Low	**30.00-23.63**
Book Value	**5,164.0**	**5,686.0**	**6,538.0**	**4,843.0**	Yield %	**4.1**	Market Cap	**US$5,844.0mil**

Address **129, rue Saint-Jacques Montreal, PQ H2Y 3S8** Tel **416-867-6660** Fax **416-867-7193** Exchange **TSE** Ticker **BMO** President **F. Anthony Comper** Chairman **Matthew W. Barrett**

Bank of Nova Scotia

Industry: **Banks - Money Center**

Bank of Nova Scotia (Scotiabank) is the third-largest bank in Canada with $132.9 billion in assets. It offers retail-, commercial-, international-, corporate-, investment-, and private-banking services and products. Its wholly owned ScotiaMcLeod subsidiary provides brokerage and underwriting services. It has 1,236 branches and offices across Canada and more than 150 located in 44 other countries. As Canada's most internationally diverse bank, it has links to banks in South America, the Caribbean, and the Far East, including a branch opening in Guangzhou, China.

C$ mil	10/92	10/93	10/94	US$mil 10/94				
Revenues	**7,959.5**	**7,671.0**	**8,533.0**	**6,274.3**	P/E Ratio	**8.4**	Price (9/30/95)	**28.25**
Net Income	**676.2**	**714.0**	**482.0**	**354.4**	P/B Ratio	**1.0**	52 Wk Hi-Low	**30.13-24.63**
Book Value	**5,079.1**	**5,904.0**	**6,241.0**	**4,623.0**	Yield %	**4.1**	Market Cap	**US$4,801.1mil**

Address **Scotia Plz., 44 King St. W. Toronto, ON M5H 1H1** Tel **416-866-6161** Fax **416-866-3750** Exchange **TSE** Ticker **BNS** President **Peter C. Godsoe** Chairman **Cedric E. Ritchie**

Barrick Gold

Industry: **Precious Metals**

Barrick Gold, formerly American Barrick Resources, is the world's largest gold-mining company outside of South Africa. In 1994, it produced 2.3 million ounces of gold, predominantly in North America, at a cash operating cost of US$167 per ounce. As of Dec. 31, 1994, gold reserves exceeded 44 million ounces, 37.6 million in the proven and probable category. Barrick Gold operates mines in Nevada, at the Goldstrike property, at Cadillac Break in Quebec, Canada, and in Chile's El Indio Belt in South America. All together, the company operates 11 mining sites.

$ mil	12/92	12/93	12/94	US$mil 12/94				
Sales	**540.4**	**667.5**	**936.1**	**936.1**	P/E Ratio	**32.0**	Price (9/30/95)	**34.75**
Net Income	**174.9**	**213.4**	**250.5**	**250.5**	P/B Ratio	**3.5**	52 Wk Hi-Low	**37.25-28.13**
Book Value	**992.7**	**1,190.9**	**2,617.2**	**2,617.2**	Yield %	**0.2**	Market Cap	**US$9,163.0mil**

Address **Royal Bank Plz., South Twr. Toronto, ON M5J 2J3** Tel **416-861-9911** Fax **416-861-0727** Exchange **TSE** Ticker **ABX** President **Robert Smith** Chairman & CEO **Peter Munk**

BC Gas

Industry: **Gas Utilities**

BC Gas is the largest gas utility in North America by territory served. It provides natural-gas services to more than 680,000 residential, commercial, and industrial customers in 100 communities throughout mainland British Columbia. This covers over 90% of the province's natural-gas users. The company is also involved in electrical-power generation and natural-gas exploration and production. Its 46%-owned subsidiary Trans Mountain Pipe Line Company transports petroleum from Alberta to British Columbia and Washington state, and ships crude oil offshore from Vancouver.

C$ mil	12/92	12/93	12/94	US$mil 12/94				
Sales	**699.0**	**794.7**	**854.0**	**623.8**	P/E Ratio	**9.4**	Price (9/30/95)	**14.63**
Net Income	**26.2**	**55.6**	**37.3**	**27.2**	P/B Ratio	**1.2**	52 Wk Hi-Low	**14.88-13.25**
Book Value	**569.7**	**485.3**	**545.8**	**389.9**	Yield %	**6.2**	Market Cap	**US$491.9mil**

Address **1111 West Georgia St.** **Vancouver, BC V6E 4M4**
Tel **604-443-6500** Fax **604-443-6929**
Exchange **TSE** Ticker **BCG**
President **Robert E. Kadlec**
Chairman **Ronald L. Cliff**

BC Telecom

Industry: **Telephone Systems - All**

BC Telecom (formerly British Columbia Telephone Company) is a telecommunication, high-tech, and cellular-communication firm. BC TEL, its core business, is Canada's second-largest telecommunications provider. It offers local and long-distance services throughout British Columbia, including WATS lines, 800 services, and directory advertising. The BC Tel Mobility Cellular subsidiary has almost 60% of the B.C. cellular-phone market. The company's MPR Teltech subsidiary offers advanced telecommunication systems to business clients in more than 20 countries.

C$ mil	12/92	12/93	12/94	US$mil 12/94				
Sales	**2,037.2**	**2,209.6**	**2,295.4**	**1,676.7**	P/E Ratio	**12.6**	Price (9/30/95)	**23.50**
Net Income	**205.7**	**214.6**	**224.5**	**164.0**	P/B Ratio	**1.4**	52 Wk Hi-Low	**26.13-22.25**
Book Value	**1,733.1**	**1,862.1**	**1,939.8**	**1,385.6**	Yield %	**5.2**	Market Cap	**US$2,016.5mil**

Address **3777 Kingsway** **Burnaby, BC V5H 3Z7**
Tel **604-432-2413** Fax **604-434-9467**
Exchange **TSE** Ticker **BCT**
President **Brian A. Canfield**
Chairman **Brian A. Canfield**

BCE

Industry: **Telephone Systems - All**

BCE is Canada's largest telecommunication company. The firm, with its subsidiaries and affiliates, serves approximately 70% of Canada's population. BCE's Bell Canada subsidiary serves more than 7 million customers in Ontario and Quebec. Other subsidiaries include equipment manufacturer Nortel and Bell Canada International. Besides providing local and long-distance service, BCE publishes telephone directories. BCE is developing network and multimedia services together with other Canadian telephone companies and long-distance carrier MCI.

C$ mil	12/92	12/93	12/94	US$mil 12/94				
Sales	**19,572.0**	**19,827.0**	**21,670.0**	**15,829.1**	P/E Ratio	**12.7**	Price (9/30/95)	**44.88**
Net Income	**1,390.0**	**-656.0**	**1,178.0**	**860.5**	P/B Ratio	**1.4**	52 Wk Hi-Low	**48.38-41.38**
Book Value	**12,307.0**	**10,923.0**	**10,123.0**	**7,230.7**	Yield %	**6.0**	Market Cap	**US$10,320mil**

Address **1000 Gauchetière W.** **Montreal, PQ H3B 4Y7**
Tel **514-397-7114** Fax **514-397-7321**
Exchange **TSE** Ticker **B**
President & CEO **L.R. Wilson**
Chairman **L.R. Wilson**

Bombardier

Industry: **Aerospace & Defense**

Bombardier designs, manufactures, and distributes transportation equipment. Its aerospace-and-defense division produces and markets business jets (some through its Learjet subsidiary), amphibious aircraft, and airplane components. Its transportation-equipment division makes rail equipment, including subway cars, intercity trains, and trams. Bombardier also produces motorized consumer products, including Ski-Doo snowmobiles. Bombardier generates 88% of its sales outside Canada, with 43% from the United States and Mexico, and 34% from Europe.

C$ mil	01/93	01/94	01/95	US$mil 01/95				
Sales	**4,388.3**	**4,671.5**	**5,831.3**	**4,237.9**	P/E Ratio	**21.7**	Price (9/30/95)	**15.75**
Net Income	**132.8**	**175.6**	**241.9**	**175.8**	P/B Ratio	**3.2**	52 Wk Hi-Low	**18.00-10.31**
Book Value	**984.1**	**1,383.1**	**1,641.9**	**1,164.5**	Yield %	**1.0**	Market Cap	**US$2,847.4mil**

Address **800 René-Lévesque Blvd. W.** **Montreal, PQ H3B 1Y8**
Tel **514-861-9481** Fax **514-861-7053**
Exchange **TSE** Ticker **BBD.B**
President & COO **Raymond Royer**
Chairman & CEO **Laurent Beaudoin**

Brascan

Industry: **Mining**

Brascan is a holding company with stakes in companies in the natural-resources, financial-services, and utilities sectors. One of Brascan's holdings, Noranda, produces zinc, copper, nickel, gold, newsprint, pulp, oil, and natural gas. Brascan's financial services divisions offer life-insurance, merchant-banking, asset-management, and real-estate-brokerage services. The company's utilities operations are conducted through Great Lakes Power, an electricity-generating firm that serves more than 42,000 customers.

C$ mil	12/92	12/93	12/94	US$mil 12/94				
Sales	**107.7**	**442.6**	**275.6**	**201.3**	P/E Ratio	**19.0**	Price (9/30/95)	**22.25**
Net Income	**-113.4**	**109.3**	**154.3**	**112.7**	P/B Ratio	**0.9**	52 Wk Hi-Low	**23.88-17.50**
Book Value	**2,251.8**	**2,153.8**	**2,265.5**	**1,618.2**	Yield %	**4.7**	Market Cap	**US$1,457.7mil**

Address **BCE Pl., 181 Bay St.** **Toronto, ON M5J 2T3**
Tel **416-363-9491** Fax **416-363-2856**
Exchange **TSE** Ticker **BL.A**
President & CEO **Jack L. Cockwell**
Chairman **J. Trevor Eyton**

CAE Industries

Industry: **Aerospace & Defense**

CAE Industries designs and produces flight simulators, training devices, and computer-based systems for air-traffic management, space exploration, and electric-power generation and transmission. Its industrial-products, aerospace, and electronics divisions have operating subsidiaries throughout Canada, the United States, and Europe. CAE also provides maintenance and repair services for flight and tactics simulators, and produces telecommunication equipment and software for telefax and telex communications. CAE's main export destinations are the United States and Asia.

	C$ mil 03/93	03/94	03/95	US$mil 03/95				
Sales	**1,001.6**	**1,027.3**	**657.6**	**476.2**	P/E Ratio	**66.1**	Price (9/30/95)	**9.25**
Net Income	**32.2**	**-395.0**	**15.6**	**11.3**	P/B Ratio	**7.3**	52 Wk Hi-Low	**9.88-6.75**
Book Value	**599.9**	**174.6**	**138.8**	**99.1**	Yield %	**1.7**	Market Cap	**US$750.6mil**

Address	**Ste. 3060, Royal Bank Plz.**	Tel	**416-865-0070**	Exchange	**TSE**	President & CEO	**John E. Caldwell**
	Toronto, ON M5J 2J1	Fax	**416-865-0337**	Ticker	**CAE**	Chairman	**David H. Race**

Cambior

Industry: **Precious Metals**

Cambior primarily mines for gold and other various metals in North and South America. The company has interests in nine mines, numerous development projects, and more than 100 exploration properties. Cambior produced 522,077 ounces of gold in 1994, at an average cash cost of US$264 per ounce. As of 12/31/94, Cambior had proved and probable reserves of 4.4 million ounces of gold, and 609,000 ounces of possible reserves. In May 1995, Cambior announced that it had uncovered an additional 466,000 ounces of proved and probable reserves.

	C$ mil 12/92	12/93	12/94	US$mil 12/94				
Sales	**187.3**	**280.0**	**306.0**	**223.5**	P/E Ratio	**NMF**	Price (9/30/95)	**14.25**
Net Income	**-4.4**	**15.0**	**2.5**	**1.8**	P/B Ratio	**1.2**	52 Wk Hi-Low	**18.88-13.13**
Book Value	**359.7**	**570.0**	**567.7**	**405.5**	Yield %	**1.0**	Market Cap	**US$521.1mil**

Address	**1075 3rd Ave. E.**	Tel	**819-825-0211**	Exchange	**TSE**	President & CEO	**Louis P. Gignac**
	Val d'Or, PQ J9P 6M1	Fax	**819-825-9694**	Ticker	**CBJ**	Chairman	**Gilles Mercure**

Cambridge Shopping Centres

Industry: **Real-Estate Investment**

Cambridge Shopping Centres is a real-estate investment company focusing on retail properties. Its property portfolio totals 27.8 million square feet, of which Cambridge owns 15.8 million. The company owns and manages 36 regional shopping centers, and 10 downtown and community centers. It owns interests in 31 self-storage properties in western Canada under the Sentinel and Securespace names. Cambridge has a 50% interest in Donahue Schriber, which manages 8.5 million square feet of leasable space in 20 shopping centers and buildings in the southwestern U.S.

	C$ mil 03/93	03/94	03/95	US$mil 03/95				
Sales	**329.6**	**320.1**	**308.0**	**223.0**	P/E Ratio	**25.3**	Price (9/30/95)	**13.00**
Net Income	**-77.5**	**23.5**	**-27.4**	**-19.8**	P/B Ratio	**0.8**	52 Wk Hi-Low	**13.88-10.00**
Book Value	**482.7**	**751.7**	**709.0**	**506.4**	Yield %	**2.5**	Market Cap	**US$444.8mil**

Address	**Ste. 300, 95 Wellington St. W.**	Tel	**416-369-1200**	Exchange	**TSE**	President	**J. Lorne Braithwaite**
	Toronto, ON M5J 2R2	Fax	**416-369-1326**	Ticker	**CBG**	Chairman	**J. Lorne Braithwaite**

Canadian Imperial Bank

Industry: **Banks - Money Center**

Canadian Imperial Bank of Commerce (CIBC) is the the second-largest bank in Canada, with $151 billion in assets. It has two main businesses: The Personal and Commercial Bank provides financial services to six million individuals, small businesses, and farmers; and the Investment and Corporate Bank serves institutional investors and corporate clients. CIBC also offers financial services including insurance, credit cards, and mutual funds. In 1994, it acquired The Personal Insurance Company of Canada. CIBC has more than 1,500 branches in Canada and 15 other countries.

	C$ mil 10/92	10/93	10/94	US$mil 10/94				
Revenues	**11,388.0**	**10,844.0**	**11,214.0**	**8,245.6**	P/E Ratio	**NMF**	Price (9/30/95)	**35.13**
Net Income	**12.0**	**730.0**	**890.0**	**654.4**	P/B Ratio	**0.9**	52 Wk Hi-Low	**35.13-30.88**
Book Value	**6,638.0**	**7,954.0**	**8,435.0**	**6,248.1**	Yield %	**3.8**	Market Cap	**US$5,668.8mil**

Address	**Commerce Ct.**	Tel	**416-980-2211**	Exchange	**TSE**	President	**Al L. Flood**
	Toronto, ON M5L 1A2	Fax	**416-980-6442**	Ticker	**CM**	Chairman	**Al L. Flood**

Canadian Natural Resources

Industry: **Oil - Secondary**

Canadian Natural Resources explores for, acquires, and develops oil and natural-gas properties in northeast British Columbia and northern Alberta. It has drilling operations in 226 wells. Canadian Natural Resources produces an average of 237.5 million cubic feet of natural gas and about 12,820 barrels of crude oil and natural-gas liquids daily. Its daily gas-transport capacity is more than 350 million cubic feet. Canadian Natural Resources owns several million net acres of land in Alberta and Saskatchewan. Colborne Capital Group has a 20% holding in the company.

	C$ mil 12/92 R	12/93	12/94	US$mil 12/94				
Sales	**77.0**	**157.9**	**259.0**	**189.2**	P/E Ratio	**19.3**	Price (9/30/95)	**16.38**
Net Income	**13.9**	**34.3**	**54.2**	**39.6**	P/B Ratio	**3.1**	52 Wk Hi-Low	**18.63-11.25**
Book Value	**81.5**	**171.2**	**356.2**	**254.4**	Yield %	**0.0**	Market Cap	**US$900.9mil**

Address	**Ste. 2000, 425 First St. S.W.**	Tel	**403-221-2100**	Exchange	**TSE**	President	**John G. Langille**
	Calgary, AB T2P 3L8	Fax	**403-233-8941**	Ticker	**CNQ**	Chairman	**Allan P. Markin**

R=Restated.

Canadian Occidental Petroleum

Industry: **Oil - Secondary**

Canadian Occidental Petroleum explores for and produces oil and natural gas. As of December 31, 1994, proved and probable reserves totaled 209 million barrels of oil, 539 billion cubic feet of natural gas, and 147 million barrels of synthetic crude oil. CanadianOxy's reserves are found in North and South America, the North Sea, Yemen, Kazakhstan, and Vietnam. In 1994, the company produced an average of 117,600 barrels of crude oil and condensate per day, 241.4 million cubic feet of natural gas per day, and 379 long tons of sulphur per day.

C$ mil	12/92	12/93	12/94	US$mil 12/94				
Sales	519.8	625.0	1,015.2	741.5	P/E Ratio	29.6	Price (9/30/95)	42.63
Net Income	17.3	6.8	96.3	70.4	P/B Ratio	3.5	52 Wk Hi-Low	45.63-29.63
Book Value	700.0	722.0	825.0	589.3	Yield %	0.9	Market Cap	US$2,138.0mil

Address **635 8th Ave. S.W.** Tel **403-234-1932** Exchange **TSE** CEO **Bernard F. Isautier**
Calgary, AB T2P 3Z1 Fax **403-263-8673** Ticker **CXY** Chairman **Ray R. Irani**

Canadian Pacific

Industry: **Conglomerates**

Canadian Pacific competes in two main business sectors--transportation and energy. It has major holdings in real estate, hotels, communications, and waste services. Its CP Rail subsidiary operates North America's seventh-largest railway, with a 18,700-mile network. As of December 1994, the company's PanCanadian Petroleum had energy reserves equivalent to 1.1 billion barrels of oil. Canadian operations account for 76% of consolidated revenues, with the United States generating most of the remainder.

C$ mil	12/92	12/93	12/94	US$mil 12/94				
Sales	8,963.6	6,579.4	7,053.4	5,152.2	P/E Ratio	17.8	Price (9/30/95)	21.50
Net Income	-478.3	-27.6	510.7	373.0	P/B Ratio	1.1	52 Wk Hi-Low	24.63-18.88
Book Value	6,271.4	6,015.8	6,799.4	4,856.7	Yield %	1.5	Market Cap	US$5,484.1mil

Address **910 Peel St.** Tel **514-395-5797** Exchange **TSE** President **J.F. Hankinson**
Montreal, PQ H3C 3E4 Fax **514-395-7306** Ticker **CP** Chairman & CEO **W.W. Stinson**

Canadian Tire

Industry: **Other Specialty Retailers**

Canadian Tire Corporation is Canada's leading hard-goods retailer. Its merchandise business division supplies automotive products, sporting goods, housewares, lawn and garden needs, and hardware products through 423 Canadian Tire stores throughout Canada. Its petroleum division is the country's largest independent retailer of gasoline, operating 202 gasoline and convenience-products outlets. Its financial-services division manages the Canadian Tire credit-card program, operates a national emergency roadside service, and markets insurance products.

C$ mil	01/93	01/94	12/94	US$mil 12/94				
Revenues	3,221.9	3,479.9	3,599.2	2,629.1	P/E Ratio	16.7	Price (9/30/95)	15.13
Net Income	72.3	81.4	5.5	4.0	P/B Ratio	1.2	52 Wk Hi-Low	16.75-10.50
Book Value	1,155.7	1,208.3	1,152.1	822.9	Yield %	2.6	Market Cap	US$957.6mil

Address **2180 Yonge St.** Tel **416-480-3000** Exchange **TSE** President **Stephen E. Bachand**
Toronto, ON M4P 2V8 Fax **416-484-8872** Ticker **CTR** Chairman **H. Earl Joudrie**

Canadian Utilities

Industry: **Electrical Utilities - All**

Canadian Utilities is a natural-gas and electric company that markets its resources to industrial, commercial, residential, and rural customers, primarily in western Canada. Its two natural-gas subsidiaries serve 713,455 customers in Alberta, and its four electricity subsidiaries serve more than 174,000 customers, 70% of which are industrial clients. The company owns 31.2% of oil and gas company ATCOR Resources. It also has a 51% interest in U.K.-based electric-power provider Thames Power. The Canadian energy company ATCO owns 50.1% of the company's shares.

C$ mil	12/92	12/93	12/94	US$mil 12/94				
Sales	1,213.6	1,386.3	1,576.3	1,151.4	P/E Ratio	12.5	Price (9/30/95)	24.50
Net Income	175.1	180.7	183.2	133.8	P/B Ratio	0.9	52 Wk Hi-Low	25.25-21.88
Book Value	1,641.7	1,663.5	1,721.3	1,229.5	Yield %	5.9	Market Cap	US$706.1mil

Address **10035 105th St.** Tel **403-420-7757** Exchange **TSE** President **J.D. Wood**
Edmonton, AB T5J 2V6 Fax **403-420-7400** Ticker **CU** Chairman **R.D. Southern**

Canfor

Industry: **Forest Products**

Canfor Corporation is a fully integrated forest-products company. It is one of the largest lumber producers in the world in terms of yearly lumber output, and wood and wood products make up 80% of its annual sales. Its ten sawmills produce paper pulp, sack kraft paper, newsprint, lumber, and hardboard. Canfor operates lumber-remanufacturing plants in Idaho and Washington, and has paper-sales offices in Vancouver, Brussels, and Tokyo. Canfor-Weldwood Distribution, its joint venture with Vancouver lumber firm Weldwood, distributes building materials.

C$ mil	12/92	12/93	12/94	US$mil 12/94				
Sales	976.3	1,166.6	1,406.2	1,027.2	P/E Ratio	19.3	Price (9/30/95)	14.00
Net Income	-49.9	41.2	124.5	90.9	P/B Ratio	1.1	52 Wk Hi-Low	20.00-13.75
Book Value	586.1	611.0	698.2	498.7	Yield %	1.9	Market Cap	US$594.9mil

Address **Bentall Ctr., 1055 Dunsmuir St.** Tel **604-661-5241** Exchange **TSE** President **Arild S. Nielssen**
Vancouver, BC V7X 1B5 Fax **604-661-5472** Ticker **CFP** Chairman **Peter J.G. Bentley**

Cara Operations

Industry: **Restaurants**

Cara Operations is a restaurateur and office-products retailer. Cara operates two restaurant chains: the Swiss Chalet chain of 149 family-style restaurants, and the Harvey's chain of 281 fast-food hamburger restaurants. It has Harvey's outlets in the Czech Republic and Swiss Chalet outlets in Florida and New York. Cara's office-products division manages 62 office-furniture and -equipment retail outlets under the Grand & Toy name. Cara also operates flight kitchens and commissaries for domestic airlines, contract-catering services, and a wholesale food-distribution business.

C$ mil	03/93	04/94	04/95	US$mil 04/95				
Sales	**781.4**	**821.9**	**908.9**	**658.1**	P/E Ratio M	**17.5**	Price (9/30/95) M	**4.00**
Net Income	**30.5**	**30.8**	**26.8**	**19.4**	P/B Ratio M	**1.6**	52 Wk Hi-Low M	**4.65-3.00**
Book Value	**252.5**	**273.9**	**291.3**	**214.2**	Yield % M	**2.0**	Market Cap M	**US$186.7mil**

Address **230 Bloor St. W.**
Toronto, ON M5S 1T8
Tel **416-962-4571**
Fax **416-969-2547**
Exchange **TSE**
Ticker **CAO.A**
President **Gunter B. Otto**
Chairman & CEO **M. Bernard Syron**

M=Multiple issues in index; reflects most active.

Cominco

Industry: **Non-Ferrous Metals - Other (Exc. Aluminum)**

Cominco is a natural-resources company active in mining, fertilizer production, smelting, and refining. The company is one of the world's largest producers of zinc and lead concentrates, accounting for about 8% and 6%, respectively, of mine production in the Western world. Other concentrates include copper, molybdenum, and germanium. Exploration is currently being conducted in western Canada, Turkey, Peru, and Mexico. Cominco's fertilizer sector, marketed under the Elephant brand name, produces nitrogen, phosphate, and potash for farming purposes.

C$ mil	12/92	12/93	12/94	US$mil 12/94				
Sales	**1,467.4**	**982.5**	**1,097.9**	**802.0**	P/E Ratio	**16.5**	Price (9/30/95)	**26.75**
Net Income	**-30.2**	**-113.2**	**132.1**	**96.5**	P/B Ratio	**2.1**	52 Wk Hi-Low	**29.63-21.50**
Book Value	**983.1**	**871.2**	**1,011.8**	**722.7**	Yield %	**0.0**	Market Cap	**US$1,586.9mil**

Address **500-200 Burrard St.**
Vancouver, BC V6C 3L7
Tel **604-682-0611**
Fax **604-685-3019**
Exchange **TSE**
Ticker **CLT**
President & CEO **David A. Thompson**
Chairman **Norman B. Keevil**

Corel

Industry: **Software**

Corel, founded in 1985, is a software developer that deals primarily in graphics programs and small-computer interface (SCSI) software. Its best-known product is the CorelDRAW graphics software program which has received more than 90 first-place awards from software magazines. The firm's CorelSCSI software allows individual PCs to interface with a central host, and is available on DOS, Windows, and OS/2 platforms. The company also produces a CD-ROM utilities package for sound and photos. Corel distributes its products in 60 countries through more than 100 distributors.

$ mil	11/92	11/93	11/94	US$mil 11/94				
Sales	**90.1**	**140.2**	**164.3**	**164.3**	P/E Ratio	**23.6**	Price (9/30/95)	**22.13**
Net Income	**11.2**	**27.8**	**32.5**	**32.5**	P/B Ratio	**4.8**	52 Wk Hi-Low	**26.25-15.38**
Book Value	**98.8**	**148.5**	**165.0**	**165.0**	Yield %	**0.0**	Market Cap	**US$789.7mil**

Address **1600 Carling Ave.**
Ottawa, ON K1Z 8R7
Tel **613-728-3733**
Fax **613-728-9176**
Exchange **TSE**
Ticker **COS**
CEO **Michael C.J. Cowpland**
Chairman **Michael C.J. Cowpland**

Co-Steel

Industry: **Steel**

Co-Steel, with a steel-making capacity of nearly three million tonnes per year, is one of the world's largest minimill companies. Its three wholly owned subsidiaries are located in Ontario, New Jersey, and England. They produce steel, concrete-reinforcing bars and rods, and structural shapes for the construction, automotive, appliance, and machinery industries. Co-Steel owns 60% of Mayer Parry Recycling, a European scrap-processing company. Gallitin Steel, its joint venture with Canada's Dofasco, produces flat-rolled steel from a newly completed minimill in Kentucky.

C$ mil	12/92	12/93	12/94	US$mil 12/94				
Sales	**873.5**	**1,057.2**	**1,260.4**	**920.7**	P/E Ratio	**9.5**	Price (9/30/95)	**21.63**
Net Income	**3.2**	**26.4**	**68.9**	**50.3**	P/B Ratio	**1.1**	52 Wk Hi-Low	**30.63-21.63**
Book Value	**483.0**	**508.6**	**597.7**	**426.9**	Yield %	**1.6**	Market Cap	**US$490.6mil**

Address **Scotia Plz., 40 King St. W.**
Toronto, ON M5H 3Y2
Tel **416-366-4500**
Fax **416-366-4616**
Exchange **TSE**
Ticker **CEI**
President & CEO **William J. Shields**
Chairman **William J. Shields**

Delrina

Industry: **Software**

Delrina is a world leader in PC fax and forms software. The company is organized into three product/service units: business software, consumer software, and communication services. Delrina designs, develops, markets, and services mass-market software for use on personal computers. Products include software for forms processing, fax communication, and publishing products. These products are produced in five major European languages and are distributed in 29 countries.

C$ mil	06/92	06/93	06/94	US$mil 06/94				
Sales	**18.5**	**47.9**	**101.1**	**75.3**	P/E Ratio	**29.5**	Price (9/30/95)	**22.75**
Net Income	**-2.0**	**-9.7**	**16.8**	**12.5**	P/B Ratio	**5.6**	52 Wk Hi-Low	**25.50-14.63**
Book Value	**16.1**	**28.1**	**89.2**	**64.6**	Yield %	**N/A**	Market Cap	**US$365.2mil**

Address **895 Don Mills Rd.**
Toronto, ON M3C 1W3
Tel **416-441-3676**
Fax **416-441-0333**
Exchange **TSE**
Ticker **DC**
President **Mark Skapinker**
Chairman & CEO **Dennis Bennie**

Dofasco

Industry: **Steel**

Dofasco is a steel producer that makes a variety of flat-rolled steels. It has a capacity of more than 3.5 million tons of raw steel per year. Its products include cold- and hot-rolled, galvanized and Galvalume, tin-plated, prepainted, chromium-coated, and motor-laminated steels. Dofasco's steels are used in the energy, automotive, and appliance industries by machinery and equipment manufacturers; in the production of industrial and consumer containers; and in construction. Dofasco has a joint venture with Co-Steel in Kentucky to produce hot-rolled steels.

C$ mil	12/92	12/93	12/94	US$mil 12/94				
Sales	**1,952.9**	**2,102.9**	**2,261.7**	**1,652.1**	P/E Ratio	**7.0**	Price (9/30/95)	**16.25**
Net Income	**-207.1**	**138.6**	**220.9**	**161.4**	P/B Ratio	**0.8**	52 Wk Hi-Low	**23.50-16.25**
Book Value	**1,369.0**	**1,482.6**	**1,764.4**	**1,260.3**	Yield %	**1.8**	Market Cap	**US$1,031.4mil**

Address **1330 Burlington St. E.**
Hamilton, ON L8N 3J5
Tel **905-544-3761**
Fax **905-545-3236**
Exchange **TSE**
Ticker **DFS**
President & CEO **John T. Mayberry**
Chairman **Charles H. Hantho**

Domtar

Industry: **Paper Products**

Domtar is a producer and marketer of communication and specialty papers, containerboard, construction materials, and pulp. The company is North America's largest producer of decorative melamine panels and the third-largest maker of gypsum product. Its woodlands operations supply more than 5.5 million cubic meters of wood to the company's seven sawmills and six pulp-and-paper mills. Pulp-and-paper products account for more than half of the company's revenues, with packaging, construction materials, wood residues, and gypsum making up the remainder.

C$ mil	12/92	12/93	12/94	US$mil 12/94				
Sales	**1,884.0**	**1,968.0**	**2,141.0**	**1,563.9**	P/E Ratio	**54.3**	Price (9/30/95)	**12.50**
Net Income	**-159.0**	**-111.0**	**33.0**	**24.1**	P/B Ratio	**2.4**	52 Wk Hi-Low	**14.75-7.13**
Book Value	**704.0**	**595.0**	**667.0**	**476.4**	Yield %	**0.0**	Market Cap	**US$1,188.9mil**

Address **395 de Maisonneuve Blvd. W.**
Montreal, PQ H3A 1L6
Tel **514-848-5861**
Fax **514-848-5162**
Exchange **TSE**
Ticker **DTC**
President & CEO **Stephen Larson**
Chairman --

Donohue

Industry: **Forest Products**

Donohue is the largest lumber producer in eastern Canada. It operates two lumber mills, one kraft-pulp mill, and two newsprint mills. Two thirds of the company's operating earnings are derived from its lumber businesses. The company produces 317,000 tonnes of kraft pulp and 490,000 tonnes of newsprint each year. It owns 50% of Donohue Matane, a bleached chemithermomechanical pulp mill. Donohue also owns 50% of Finlay Forest Industries, a joint venture with Slocan Forest Products, which operates two sawmills and produces 200,000 tonnes of newsprint each year.

C$ mil	12/92	12/93	12/94	US$mil 12/94				
Sales	**519.9**	**574.1**	**807.4**	**589.8**	P/E Ratio	**11.2**	Price (9/30/95)	**17.75**
Net Income	**-14.7**	**16.8**	**114.2**	**83.4**	P/B Ratio	**2.6**	52 Wk Hi-Low	**21.63-15.50**
Book Value	**364.9**	**379.6**	**538.0**	**384.3**	Yield %	**1.4**	Market Cap	**US$812.1mil**

Address **801 chemin Saint-Louis**
Quebec, PQ G1S 4W3
Tel **418-684-7700**
Fax **N/A**
Exchange **TSE**
Ticker **DHC**
President & CEO **Michel Desbiens**
Chairman **Charles A. Poissant**

Echo Bay Mines

Industry: **Precious Metals**

Echo Bay Mines is a precious-metals miner that ranks among the largest gold producers in North America. In 1994, it produced 817,900 ounces of gold, at a cash cost of US$214 per ounce, and 10.4 million ounces of silver. The company extracts gold from four mines in the western United States and Canada, with silver production concentrated at the company's McCoy/Cove operation in Nevada, its largest gold and silver producer. As of Dec. 31, 1994, Echo Bay's proven and probable reserves totaled 11.3 million ounces of gold and 82.7 million ounces of silver.

$ mil	12/92	12/93	12/94	US$mil 12/94				
Sales	**312.4**	**366.5**	**377.6**	**377.6**	P/E Ratio	**NMF**	Price (9/30/95)	**14.63**
Net Income	**-27.4**	**13.6**	**17.3**	**17.3**	P/B Ratio	**2.4**	52 Wk Hi-Low	**18.63-12.13**
Book Value	**440.3**	**513.7**	**509.7**	**509.7**	Yield %	**0.4**	Market Cap	**US$1,230.1mil**

Address **10180 101st St.**
Edmonton, AB T5J 3S4
Tel **403-496-9704**
Fax **403-424-7378**
Exchange **TSE**
Ticker **ECO**
President **Richard C. Kraus**
Chairman & CEO **Robert F. Calman**

Finning

Industry: **Other Specialty Retailers**

Finning sells, finances, and services Caterpillar mobile equipment and engines and other related equipment. Finning also distributes heavy moving and lifting equipment under the Thunderbird, JLG, Wagner, and Gardner-Denver brand names to logging, construction, mining, and petroleum companies. Finning operates nearly 50 distribution and service centers in Canada, the United Kingdom, the Netherlands, and Poland. It owns Gildemeister S.A.C. in Santiago, Chile, which sells and services Caterpillar, Ingersoll-Rand, Grove, and Kenworth equipment.

C$ mil	12/92	12/93	12/94	US$mil 12/94				
Revenues	**832.7**	**1,043.0**	**1,457.5**	**1,064.6**	P/E Ratio	**13.3**	Price (9/30/95)	**21.25**
Net Income	**2.0**	**22.0**	**61.4**	**44.9**	P/B Ratio	**1.8**	52 Wk Hi-Low	**23.25-17.25**
Book Value	**308.7**	**381.4**	**448.5**	**320.4**	Yield %	**1.2**	Market Cap	**US$610.6mil**

Address **555 Great Northern Way**
Vancouver, BC V5T 1E2
Tel **604-872-4444**
Fax **604-872-2994**
Exchange **TSE**
Ticker **FTT**
President & CEO **James F. Shepard**
Chairman **W. Robert Wyman**

First Marathon

Industry: **Securities Brokers**

First Marathon is a financial-services firm that provides corporate and institutional clients with stock-trading services and real-estate financing. Its services include securities underwriting, distribution, and trading; mergers and acquisitions; securities backing; and research, execution, and clearing. Its wholly-owned First Marathon Securities subsidiary has operations in North America and Europe and provides financing to major Canadian companies. The firm also manages a First Marathon Bank in Germany to provide securities-related activities there.

	C$ mil 12/92	12/93	12/94	US$mil 12/94				
Sales	**106.1**	**187.5**	**160.5**	**117.2**	P/E Ratio	**13.6**	Price (9/30/95)	**14.00**
Net Income	**21.2**	**74.2**	**25.2**	**18.4**	P/B Ratio	**1.3**	52 Wk Hi-Low	**15.25-10.50**
Book Value	**187.6**	**254.8**	**255.3**	**182.4**	Yield %	**2.6**	Market Cap	**US$231.0mil**

Address **2 First Canadian Pl.**
Toronto, ON M5X 1J9
Tel **416-869-3707**
Fax **N/A**
Exchange **TSE**
Ticker **FMS**
President & CEO **Lawrence S. Bloomberg**
Chairman **Thomas E. Kierans**

Franco-Nevada Mining

Industry: **Precious Metals**

Franco-Nevada Mining Corporation invests in resource properties that contain reserves of gold, platinum, or hydrocarbons. Its main asset is its interest in the 2,140-acre Goldstrike Mine at Carlin Trend in northern Nevada. The mine is operated by Barrick Gold Corporation and holds 25% of the world's gold reserves outside of the former Soviet Union and South Africa. The company also receives royalties from 620 acres of the Hemlo Camp in Ontario, a 17,193-acre platinum mine in Western Bushveld, South Africa, and 1 million acres of oil and gas properties in western Canada.

	C$ mil 03/93	03/94	03/95	US$mil 03/95				
Sales	**25.5**	**48.5**	**77.2**	**55.9**	P/E Ratio	**26.0**	Price (9/30/95)	**80.50**
Net Income	**17.2**	**31.9**	**50.2**	**36.4**	P/B Ratio	**5.4**	52 Wk Hi-Low	**90.50-61.00**
Book Value	**108.1**	**206.0**	**246.9**	**176.4**	Yield %	**1.9**	Market Cap	**US$974.2mil**

Address **20 Eglinton Ave. W.**
Toronto, ON M4R 1K8
Tel **416-480-6480**
Fax **416-488-6598**
Exchange **TSE**
Ticker **FN**
President **Pierre Lassonde**
Chairman & CEO **Seymour Schulich**

GEAC Computer

Industry: **Computers**

GEAC Computer develops UNIV/RISC-based computer systems. The firm provides vertical-application software, hardware platforms, and support programs to corporate customers and libraries. Its products include GLIS and Advance Integrated Library Systems, the Advanced Financial System, the IFS 2000 asset-management system, and the Value Added Reseller. It is involved in local area networks and client/server technology. In 1995, GEAC entered into an alliance with IBM to resell IBM's point-of-sale hardware with its UltraTouch software system used by quick-service restaurants.

	C$ mil 04/93	04/94	04/95	US$mil 04/95				
Sales	**102.7**	**150.3**	**185.0**	**134.0**	P/E Ratio	**16.7**	Price (9/30/95)	**18.50**
Net Income	**4.5**	**22.9**	**32.0**	**23.2**	P/B Ratio	**4.2**	52 Wk Hi-Low	**19.00-13.25**
Book Value	**70.7**	**96.9**	**127.4**	**93.7**	Yield %	**0.0**	Market Cap	**US$397.6mil**

Address **11 Allstate Pkwy.**
Markham, ON L3R 9T8
Tel **905-475-0525**
Fax **905-475-3847**
Exchange **TSE**
Ticker **GAC**
President & CEO **Stephen J. Sadler**
Chairman **Donald C. Webster**

George Weston

Industry: **Food Retailers & Wholesalers**

George Weston is a diversified international food-processing and -distribution company. Among its subsidiaries are Weston Foods, a bakery, dairy, and confectionery processor; and Loblaw, a food-distribution chain. The company's products include Neilson and Cadbury dairy products and chocolates, President's Choice goods, and Ready Bake frozen-dough products. Loblaw manages supermarkets and wholesale clubs, including Real Canadian Superstores, Zehrs Markets, and Weston's. George Weston operates Weston Resources, a forest-products and fish-processing concern.

	C$ mil 12/92	12/93	12/94	US$mil 12/94				
Sales	**11,599.0**	**11,931.0**	**13,002.0**	**9,497.4**	P/E Ratio	**18.8**	Price (9/30/95)	**46.50**
Net Income	**48.0**	**57.0**	**117.0**	**85.5**	P/B Ratio	**1.6**	52 Wk Hi-Low	**49.00-37.50**
Book Value	**1,266.0**	**1,289.0**	**1,404.0**	**1,002.9**	Yield %	**1.5**	Market Cap	**US$1,633.1mil**

Address **22 St. Clair Ave. E.**
Toronto, ON M4T 2S7
Tel **416-922-2500**
Fax **416-922-4395**
Exchange **TSE**
Ticker **WN**
President **W. Galen Weston**
Chairman **W. Galen Weston**

Hees International

Industry: **Financial Services - Diversified**

Hees International Bancorp is a merchant bank offering financial and asset-management services. Through its four primary Canadian affiliates, the company invests in real-estate, utility, and natural-resources firms. It holds an 87% stake in Carena Developments, a real-estate firm, and 49% in Brascan, a company with interests in utilities and natural resources. Together with Brascan, it owns 56% of Trilon Financial and 98% of Great Lakes Power, which owns or has interests in 14 power-generating stations in Canada and one hydroelectric plant in the United States.

	C$ mil 12/92	12/93	12/94	US$mil 12/94				
Revenues	**405.0**	**358.7**	**449.1**	**328.0**	P/E Ratio	**12.0**	Price (9/30/95)	**13.25**
Net Income	**36.3**	**67.0**	**112.1**	**81.9**	P/B Ratio	**0.5**	52 Wk Hi-Low	**16.25-11.25**
Book Value	**2,104.5**	**2,083.8**	**2,192.9**	**1,566.4**	Yield %	**7.4**	Market Cap	**US$803.1mil**

Address **BCE Place, 181 Bay St.**
Toronto, ON M5J 2T3
Tel **416-865-0430**
Fax **416-865-1288**
Exchange **TSE**
Ticker **HIL**
President & CEO **Robert J. Harding**
Chairman **Timothy R. Price**

Hemlo Gold Mines

Industry: **Precious Metals**

Hemlo Gold Mines operates two Canadian gold mines. As of Dec. 31, 1994, the company had proven and probable gold reserves of 6 million ounces. In 1994, gold production totaled 489,000 ounces, at a cash cost of US$109 per ounce. The Golden Giant Mine in Ontario, one of the world's lowest-cost producers, is Hemlo's primary source. The company also owns 55% of the Silidor mine in Quebec. It has stakes in two development projects, the New World site (60%) and the Holloway Joint Venture (85%), which together account for 35% of Hemlo's proven and probable reserves.

C$ mil	12/92	12/93	12/94	US$mil 12/94				
Sales	**211.9**	**217.1**	**254.6**	**185.9**	P/E Ratio	**20.5**	Price (9/30/95)	**13.75**
Net Income	**41.9**	**45.7**	**64.5**	**47.1**	P/B Ratio	**3.8**	52 Wk Hi-Low	**16.50-11.63**
Book Value	**265.7**	**282.6**	**351.9**	**251.3**	Yield %	**2.5**	Market Cap	**US$993.1mil**

Address	**1 Adelaide St. E.**	Tel **416-982-7116**	Exchange **TSE**	President & CEO	**Ian D. Bayer**
	Toronto, ON M5C 2Z9	Fax **416-982-7388**	Ticker **HEM**	Chairman	**Alex G. Balogh**

Hollinger

Industry: **Publishing**

Hollinger publishes newspapers and magazines in Canada, the United Kingdom, the United States, Australia, Israel, and the Cayman Islands. As of December, 1994, its publishing interests included 135 daily newspapers and 397 nondaily newspapers. Total paid daily circulation, including The Daily Telegraph of London and the Chicago Sun-Times, is 4.6 million. Total circulaton of the nondailies, including magazines, is about 8.5 milllion. Hollinger's largest subisidiaries are The Telegraph of the United Kingdom (59%-owned) and American Publishing Company (64%-owned).

C$ mil	12/92	12/93	12/94	US$mil 12/94				
Sales	**857.0**	**873.4**	**1,271.0**	**928.4**	P/E Ratio	**5.2**	Price (9/30/95)	**11.25**
Net Income	**76.7**	**30.9**	**129.5**	**94.6**	P/B Ratio	**1.7**	52 Wk Hi-Low	**13.88-10.88**
Book Value	**217.4**	**238.9**	**358.0**	**255.7**	Yield %	**4.4**	Market Cap	**US$531.2mil**

Address	**1827 West 5th Ave.**	Tel **416-363-8721**	Exchange **TSE**	President	**F. David Radler**
	Vancouver, BC V6J 1P5	Fax **416-364-2088**	Ticker **HLG**	Chairman & CEO	**Conrad M. Black**

Hudson's Bay

Industry: **Retailers - Broadline**

Hudson's Bay Company (HBC) is Canada's largest department store retailer, accounting for 40% of department-store sales in Canada. It operates 103 Bay fashion department stores, 292 Zellers discount department stores, and nine distribution centers throughout Canada. The Zellers division accounts for 59% of the company's sales, and is Canada's largest department-store chain. HBC makes 40% of its sales in Ontario, 33% in western Canada, and 20% in Quebec. Kenneth R. Thomson, chairman of the Thomson Corporation, and his family together control 23% of the company.

C$ mil	01/93	01/94	01/95	US$mil 01/95				
Revenues	**5,152.2**	**5,441.5**	**5,829.2**	**4,236.3**	P/E Ratio	**8.0**	Price (9/30/95)	**26.00**
Net Income	**116.7**	**147.7**	**184.3**	**133.9**	P/B Ratio	**0.8**	52 Wk Hi-Low	**28.63-23.75**
Book Value	**1,315.5**	**1,614.5**	**1,772.9**	**1,257.4**	Yield %	**3.5**	Market Cap	**US$1,118.3mil**

Address	**401 Bay St.**	Tel **N/A**	Exchange **MSE**	President & CEO	**George J. Kosich**
	Toronto, ON M5H 2YA	Fax **N/A**	Ticker **HBC**	Governor	**David E. Mitchell**

Imasco

Industry: **Tobacco**

Imasco is a diversified consumer-products and -services firm. The company's business interests include tobacco, retail financial services, restaurants, drugstores, and specialty retailers. It owns Imperial Tobacco, maker of the cigarette brands Player's and du Maurier, which has a 64% market share. Imasco's other subsidiaries include CT Financial Services (with 410 branches) and Hardee's fast-food restaurants (4,496 outlets in the U.S. and Canada). Imasco owns the chain of 689 Shoppers Drug Mart/Pharmaprix stores, Canada's market leader in drugstore retailing.

C$ mil	12/92	12/93	12/94	US$mil 12/94				
Sales	**9,957.2**	**9,681.0**	**9,385.0**	**6,855.4**	P/E Ratio	**11.4**	Price (9/30/95)	**23.88**
Net Income	**380.4**	**409.0**	**506.0**	**369.6**	P/B Ratio	**1.6**	52 Wk Hi-Low	**26.63-18.50**
Book Value	**3,057.8**	**3,100.0**	**3,337.0**	**2,383.6**	Yield %	**3.3**	Market Cap	**US$4,235.1mil**

Address	**600 de Maisonneuve Blvd. W.**	Tel **514-982-9111**	Exchange **MSE**	President & CEO	**Brian M. Levitt**
	Montreal, QC H3A 3K7	Fax **514-982-9369**	Ticker **IMS**	Chairman	**Purdy Crawford**

Inco

Industry: **Non-Ferrous Metals - Other (Exc. Aluminum)**

Inco is one of the world's largest nickel-mining and -processing companies, supplying about 30% to 33% of the western world's nickel. It also mines copper, cobalt, and precious metals. The company produces high-nickel alloys used in aerospace and energy applications, and manufactures precision industrial components. Operations are centered in Canada, but Inco also produces nickel through a subsidiary in Indonesia. In 1994, Inco produced 345 million pounds of nickel. As of Dec. 31, 1994, nickel reserves at Inco's producing properties amounted to 7.57 million tons.

$ mil	12/92	12/93	12/94	US$mil 12/94				
Sales	**2,558.9**	**2,130.5**	**2,483.6**	**2,483.6**	P/E Ratio	**NMF**	Price (9/30/95)	**46.13**
Net Income	**-17.6**	**28.2**	**21.7**	**21.7**	P/B Ratio	**2.3**	52 Wk Hi-Low	**51.13-32.25**
Book Value	**1,608.1**	**1,606.7**	**1,766.7**	**1,766.7**	Yield %	**0.6**	Market Cap	**US$4,033.6mil**

Address	**Royal Trust Twr., Toronto-Domin-**	Tel **416-361-7511**	Exchange **TSE**	President	**Scott M. Hand**
	ion Ctr., Toronto, ON M5K 1N4	Fax **416-361-7781**	Ticker **N**	Chairman & CEO	**Michael D. Sopko**

IPL Energy

Industry: **Pipelines**

IPL Energy, formerly Interprovincial Pipe Line System, operates the world's longest petroleum pipeline. It transports crude oil and other liquid hydrocarbons. The system extends across North America and transports approximately three fourths of the crude oil produced in western Canada to refining centers and markets in the midwestern United States and eastern Canada. The company holds an 85% stake in Toronto-based Consumers Gas, one of Canada's largest natural-gas-distribution companies.

C$ mil	12/92	12/93	12/94	US$mil 12/94				
Sales	**392.4**	**395.2**	**570.3**	**416.6**	P/E Ratio	**28.2**	Price (9/30/95)	**30.75**
Net Income	**75.5**	**80.8**	**43.6**	**31.8**	P/B Ratio	**2.8**	52 Wk Hi-Low	**31.25-27.13**
Book Value	**458.9**	**463.2**	**446.4**	**318.9**	Yield %	**6.5**	Market Cap	**US$913.4mil**

Address **3100 Bow Valley Sq. II**
Calgary, AB T2P 2V7
Tel **403-231-3900**
Fax **403-231-3920**
Exchange **TSE**
Ticker **IPL**
President & CEO **Brian F. MacNeill**
Chairman **H. Gordon MacNeill**

IPSCO

Industry: **Steel**

IPSCO is a steelmaker with steel mills in Canada and the United States. Its subsidiary, Western Steel, operates a smaller steel mill in Calgary, Alberta. IPSCO's steelmaking capacity is more than 1 million tons per year. The company produces hot-rolled coils, which it either sells or processes into tubular products. These include plumbing pipe for water distribution, oil and gas well casing and tubing, water- and sewage- transmission pipe, and products for building and construction applications. IPSCO is currently at work on a minimill in Iowa.

C$ mil	12/92	12/93	12/94	US$mil 12/94				
Sales	**480.4**	**573.2**	**847.9**	**619.4**	P/E Ratio	**12.2**	Price (9/30/95)	**26.00**
Net Income	**15.5**	**28.7**	**57.7**	**42.1**	P/B Ratio	**1.1**	52 Wk Hi-Low	**26.75-22.00**
Book Value	**320.8**	**599.1**	**662.3**	**473.1**	Yield %	**1.8**	Market Cap	**US$525.5mil**

Address **P.O. Box 1670**
Regina, SK S4P 3C7
Tel **306-924-7700**
Fax **N/A**
Exchange **TSE**
Ticker **ISP**
Chief Executive **Roger Phillips**
Chairman **Thomas Kierans**

Kinross Gold

Industry: **Precious Metals**

Kinross Gold Corporation mines gold and silver. Its five mines produce more than 174,000 ounces of gold and almost 5.2 million ounces of silver annually. Its Hoyle Pond mine in Ontario contains gold reserves of 578,000 ounces. It operates an additional two mines in Nevada, one in Idaho, and one in British Columbia, and has interests in two mines in Zimbabwe. In a joint-venture with Canada's Teck Corporation, the company is exploring for reserves in the El Callao district of Venezuela. Kinross is also involved in exploration projects in El Salvador and Tanzania.

C$ mil	12/92	12/93	12/94	US$mil 12/94				
Sales	**11.8**	**43.8**	**131.1**	**95.8**	P/E Ratio	**42.6**	Price (9/30/95)	**11.50**
Net Income	**-1.1**	**6.7**	**24.7**	**18.0**	P/B Ratio	**4.9**	52 Wk Hi-Low	**11.88-5.75**
Book Value	**31.8**	**125.9**	**230.3**	**164.5**	Yield %	**0.0**	Market Cap	**US$709.8mil**

Address **Scotia Plz., 40 King St. W.**
Toronto, ON M5H 3Y2
Tel **416-365-5123**
Fax **416-363-6622**
Exchange **TSE**
Ticker **K**
President & CEO **Robert M. Buchan**
Chairman **Robert M. Buchan**

Laidlaw

Industry: **Pollution Control, Waste Management**

Laidlaw is a leading waste-management and transportation-services business. It is North America's third-largest solid-waste-treatment company and its biggest hazardous-waste-management company. In addition, Laidlaw is North America's leading student-transportation company. The company also offers health-care-transportation services. Laidlaw owns 23.8% of ADT, a Bermuda-based security-services firm, and recently acquired Mayflower Group, a busing company. The United States and Europe account for 85% of Laidlaw's revenues.

$ mil	08/92	08/93	08/94	US$mil 08/94				
Sales	**1,925.6**	**1,993.3**	**2,128.3**	**2,128.3**	P/E Ratio M	**26.3**	Price (9/30/95) M	**11.63**
Net Income	**132.4**	**-291.6**	**90.8**	**90.8**	P/B Ratio M	**1.5**	52 Wk Hi-Low M	**13.50-9.75**
Book Value	**1,950.4**	**1,543.7**	**1,585.9**	**1,585.9**	Yield % M	**1.0**	Market Cap M	**US$413.2mil**

Address **3221 North Service Rd.**
Burlington, ON L7R 3Y8
Tel **905-336-1800**
Fax **905-336-0670**
Exchange **TSE**
Ticker **LDM**
President & CEO **James R. Bullock**
Chairman **Peter N.T. Widdrington**

M=Multiple issues in index; reflects most active.

Loewen Group

Industry: **Household Services**

Loewen Group is the second-largest funeral-service company in North America. The company owns and operates 734 funeral homes, 159 cemeteries, 29 crematoria, and 16 advanced-planning centers throughout Canada and the United States, providing nearly 90,000 funeral services each year. Loewen also owns one funeral-services home in Mexico and two in Puerto Rico. The company offers direct services to the public and succession-planning programs to funeral-home owners. Loewen's U.S.-based operations contribute about 85% of the company's revenue.

$ mil	12/92	12/93	12/94	US$mil 12/94				
Sales	**294.3**	**397.8**	**417.5**	**417.5**	P/E Ratio	**42.7**	Price (9/30/95)	**55.50**
Net Income	**26.1**	**37.0**	**38.5**	**38.5**	P/B Ratio	**4.1**	52 Wk Hi-Low	**55.63-30.75**
Book Value	**312.3**	**430.5**	**411.1**	**411.1**	Yield %	**0.1**	Market Cap	**US$1,698.8mil**

Address **4126 Norland Ave.**
Burnaby, BC V5G 3S8
Tel **604-299-9321**
Fax **604-299-2369**
Exchange **TSE**
Ticker **LWN**
President **Tim Hogenkamp**
Chairman & CEO **Raymond L. Loewen**

MacMillan Bloedel

Industry: **Forest Products**

Macmillan Bloedel is among North America's largest forest-products companies. It produces lumber, panelboards, newsprint, printing papers, containerboard, corrugated containers, engineered wood, and SpaceKraft-brand recyclable liquid containers. The firm manages about 1.5 million hectares of timberland, two thirds of which are in British Columbia. It also has operations in the United States and continental Europe. The company's Trus Joist Macmillan joint venture with TJ International produces engineered-wood products for use in housing and bridges.

	C$ mil 12/92	12/93	12/94	US$mil 12/94				
Sales	**3,039.3**	**3,762.0**	**3,948.8**	**2,884.4**	P/E Ratio	**11.6**	Price (9/30/95)	**16.50**
Net Income	**-48.8**	**53.2**	**180.2**	**131.6**	P/B Ratio	**1.2**	52 Wk Hi-Low	**21.38-16.00**
Book Value	**1,448.6**	**1,629.9**	**1,703.0**	**1,216.4**	Yield %	**3.6**	Market Cap	**US$1,523.8mil**

Address	**925 West Georgia St.**	Tel	**604-661-8311**	Exchange	**TSE**	President & CEO	**R.B. Findlay**
	Vancouver, BC V6C 3l2	Fax	**604-681-5908**	Ticker	**MB**	Chairman	**R.V. Smith**

Magna International

Industry: **Other Auto Parts**

Magna International manufactures automotive systems, assemblies, and components. It is one of the most diversified independent auto-parts suppliers in North America. Its main products include automotive-interior systems, metal-body and exterior-appearance components, and transmission systems. It makes components for the U.S. Big Three, Toyota, and Honda. German subsidiaries supply air bags, mirrors, and steering wheels to European automakers. Magna is constructing a stamping facility in South Carolina for BMW's first North American assembly operation.

	C$ mil 07/92	07/93	07/94	US$mil 07/94				
Sales	**2,358.8**	**2,606.7**	**3,568.5**	**2,639.4**	P/E Ratio	**14.5**	Price (9/30/95)	**60.75**
Net Income	**98.0**	**140.4**	**234.4**	**173.4**	P/B Ratio	**2.8**	52 Wk Hi-Low	**65.50-43.50**
Book Value	**590.3**	**844.4**	**1,319.8**	**956.4**	Yield %	**1.3**	Market Cap	**US$2,755.4mil**

Address	**36 Apple Creek Blvd.**	Tel	**905-477-7766**	Exchange	**TSE**	CEO	**Donald Walker**
	Markham, ON L3R 4Y4	Fax	**905-475-0776**	Ticker	**MG.A**	Chairman	**Frank Stronach**

Maritime Tel & Tel

Industry: **Telephone Systems - All**

Maritime Telegraph & Telephone Company (MT&T) is a holding company for a group of telecommunication utilities. Its wholly owned subsidiary, Maritime Tel & Tel, provides telecommunication services to customers in Nova Scotia and on Prince Edward Island, with nearly 662,000 lines. Other MT&T subsidiaries include 52%-owned Island Tel, and wholly owned MT&T Mobility, and MT&T Leasing. Local services account for 48% of MT&T's total revenues and long-distance services account for 46%. Its mobile-communication network serves about 30,000 subscribers.

	C$ mil 12/92	12/93	12/94	US$mil 12/94				
Sales	**543.3**	**545.0**	**546.6**	**399.3**	P/E Ratio	**11.9**	Price (9/30/95)	**19.13**
Net Income	**64.0**	**59.8**	**48.2**	**35.2**	P/B Ratio	**1.0**	52 Wk Hi-Low	**25.13-18.75**
Book Value	**463.7**	**564.9**	**532.1**	**380.1**	Yield %	**6.7**	Market Cap	**US$400.3mil**

Address	**1505 Barrington St.**	Tel	**902-487-4311**	Exchange	**TSE**	President & CEO	**Ivan E.H. Duvar**
	Halifax, NS B3J 2W3	Fax	**902-487-4161**	Ticker	**MTT**	Chairman	**Ivan E.H. Duvar**

Methanex

Industry: **Specialty Chemicals**

Methanex is the world's largest producer of chemical-grade methanol, with a 21% share of the global market. Methanol provides more than 80% of the company's sales. Its other products are gasoline and ammonia. Derived from natural gas, methanol is used as a key ingredient in the manufacture of acetic acid, formaldehyde, and MTBE, a gasoline additive. The company's gasoline is a synthetic variety that is produced from crude methanol. Methanex has seven factories in Canada, New Zealand, and Chile, and buys production from others in Europe, Trinidad, and the U.S.

	C$ mil 12/92	12/93	12/94	US$mil 12/94				
Sales	**147.6**	**533.4**	**1,487.9**	**1,086.9**	P/E Ratio	**4.1**	Price (9/30/95)	**9.25**
Net Income	**-10.9**	**10.7**	**442.7**	**323.4**	P/B Ratio	**1.8**	52 Wk Hi-Low	**17.75-9.00**
Book Value	**105.3**	**430.0**	**1,007.7**	**719.8**	Yield %	**0.0**	Market Cap	**US$1,344.7mil**

Address	**Waterfront Ctr., 200 Burrard St.**	Tel	**604-661-2600**	Exchange	**TSE**	President & CEO	**Pierre Choquette**
	Vancouver, BC V6C 3M1	Fax	**604-661-2676**	Ticker	**MX**	Chairman	**J.E. Newall**

Midland Walwyn

Industry: **Securities Brokers**

Midland Walwyn is a full-service investment dealer. Its primary subsidiary, Midland Walwyn Capital, is one of Canada's largest investment dealers catering to individual investors, with 400,000 clients, $20.6 billion in managed assets, and 135 offices. Midland Walwyn and U.S. investment firm Piper Jaffray have a joint venture that markets a group of international mutual funds. It has alliances with Dean Witter and Laurentian Bank of Canada. It owns 70% of the Financial Concept Group, Canada's second-largest financial-planning company, serving 65,000 clients.

	C$ mil 12/92	12/93	12/94	US$mil 12/94				
Sales	**332.1**	**496.0**	**480.8**	**351.2**	P/E Ratio	**9.5**	Price (9/30/95)	**8.38**
Net Income	**27.5**	**63.0**	**29.1**	**21.3**	P/B Ratio	**1.4**	52 Wk Hi-Low	**11.13-6.50**
Book Value	**97.2**	**174.4**	**203.3**	**145.2**	Yield %	**1.4**	Market Cap	**US$207.3mil**

Address	**Ste. 400, 181 Bay St.**	Tel	**416-369-7400**	Exchange	**TSE**	President & CEO	**Robert B. Schultz**
	Toronto, ON M5J 2V8	Fax	**416-591-6250**	Ticker	**MWI**	Chairman	**John A. Rhind**

Molson Companies

Industry: **Distillers & Brewers**

The Molson Companies is a diversified firm with primary interests in brewing, cleaning and sanitizing, lumber, and retail merchandising. It owns 40% of Molson Breweries, Canada's largest brewer with a 47% market share, and the second-largest exporter of beer to the U.S. Its Diversey subsidiary is among the top-four cleaning and sanitizing companies worldwide. It makes surface cleaners and disinfectants for water-management systems. Molson also owns the Montreal Canadiens NHL franchise, and a 25% interest in the chain Home Depot Canada.

	C$ mil 03/93	03/94	03/95	US$mil 03/95				
Sales	**3,085.8**	**2,966.9**	**2,885.6**	**2,089.5**	P/E Ratio	**15.1**	Price (9/30/95)	**22.50**
Net Income	**164.7**	**125.7**	**86.8**	**62.9**	P/B Ratio	**0.9**	52 Wk Hi-Low	**24.25-18.00**
Book Value	**1,168.3**	**1,308.5**	**1,373.6**	**981.1**	Yield %	**3.2**	Market Cap	**US$725.4mil**

Address **Scotia Plz., 40 King St. W.**
Toronto, ON M5H 3Z5
Tel **416-360-1786**
Fax **416-360-4345**
Exchange **TSE**
Ticker **MOL.A**
President & CEO **Marshall Cohen**
Chairman **Eric H. Molson**

Moore

Industry: **General Industrial & Commercial Services**

Moore is a global leader in information-handling products and services. Its three primary divisions are forms, systems, and services; labels and label systems; and customer-communication services. In 1994, forms, systems, and services accounted for 79% of total revenues. Moore's primary markets are the finance, health-care, and transportation industries. Government agencies are also one of Moore's biggest markets. In August 1994, Moore purchased an 18.5% stake in JetForm, a Canadian company that produces electronic forms.

	$ mil 12/92	12/93	12/94	US$mil 12/94				
Sales	**2,433.0**	**2,328.6**	**2,401.4**	**2,401.4**	P/E Ratio	**16.7**	Price (9/30/95)	**27.25**
Net Income	**-2.3**	**-77.6**	**121.4**	**121.4**	P/B Ratio	**1.5**	52 Wk Hi-Low	**31.88-23.25**
Book Value	**1,475.5**	**1,312.9**	**1,365.2**	**1,365.2**	Yield %	**2.6**	Market Cap	**US$2,024.8mil**

Address **1 First Canadian Pl.**
Toronto, ON M5X 1G5
Tel **416-364-2600**
Fax **416-364-1667**
Exchange **TSE**
Ticker **MCL**
President & CEO **Reto Braun**
Chairman **M. Keith Goodrich**

National Bank of Canada

Industry: **Banks - Money Center**

National Bank of Canada is a banking firm catering to the Quebec business community. It offers mutual-fund and investment-fund management and is entering the trust business. The firm also offers brokerage services through its subsidiary Levesque Beaubien Geoffrion. It has 641 branches in Canada and 551 automated-teller machines. It has subsidiaries in the United States, the Bahamas, Hong Kong, Singapore, Amsterdam, and Barbados, an office in Mexico, reciprocity agreements with six European banks, and lending operations in 17 major U.S. cities.

	C$ mil 10/92	10/93	10/94	US$mil 10/94				
Revenues	**3,713.2**	**3,419.0**	**3,591.2**	**2,640.6**	P/E Ratio	**10.3**	Price (9/30/95)	**11.50**
Net Income	**1.0**	**174.6**	**217.2**	**159.7**	P/B Ratio	**0.8**	52 Wk Hi-Low	**11.50-8.63**
Book Value	**1,773.0**	**1,971.6**	**2,317.0**	**1,716.3**	Yield %	**3.5**	Market Cap	**US$1,388.0mil**

Address **600 de La Gauchetière W.**
Montreal, PQ H3B 4L2
Tel **514-394-4000**
Fax **514-394-8434**
Exchange **TSE**
Ticker **NA**
President & COO **Léon Courville**
Chairman & CEO **André Bérard**

National Trustco

Industry: **Banks - Regional**

National Trustco is a holding company for trust and loan companies. Its subsidiaries and affiliates provide retail-banking, personal-trust, investment-management, commercial-lending, and custodial services, as well as mutual funds. Its wholly owned National Trust subsidiary offers consumer loans, mortgages, and credit- and debit-card services. Its banking operations include 190 branches and more than 200 automated teller machines. Its wholly owned subsidiary, Cassels Blaikie, provides portfolio-management and retail brokerage services to trust clients.

	C$ mil 10/92	10/93	10/94	US$mil 10/94				
Revenues	**1,581.6**	**1,369.1**	**1,235.4**	**908.4**	P/E Ratio	**11.6**	Price (9/30/95)	**19.00**
Net Income	**39.3**	**47.6**	**57.7**	**42.4**	P/B Ratio	**0.9**	52 Wk Hi-Low	**22.75-18.50**
Book Value	**715.4**	**737.7**	**776.0**	**574.8**	Yield %	**4.6**	Market Cap	**US$497.3mil**

Address **1 Ontario St.**
Stratford, ON N5A 6S9
Tel **519-271-2050**
Fax **519-271-7040**
Exchange **TSE**
Ticker **NT**
President & CEO **J. Christopher Barron**
Chairman **J.C.C. Wansbrough**

Noranda

Industry: **Mining**

Noranda is a diversified mining, smelting, and refining company. It operates 18 mines, 11 metallurgical plants, and 11 fabricating facilities in North America, Norway, the Dominican Republic, Guinea, and Mexico. Noranda is one of the world's largest producers of zinc and nickel. It also mines copper, lead, gold, silver, and cobalt. Its forest-products division operates six pulp and paper mills, 13 sawmills, eight panelboard mills, and six paper plants. Noranda's oil and gas group explores for, develops, and produces natural gas, natural-gas liquids, and crude oil.

	C$ mil 12/92	12/93	12/94	US$mil 12/94				
Sales	**8,538.0**	**5,255.0**	**6,633.0**	**4,845.1**	P/E Ratio	**18.8**	Price (9/30/95)	**27.25**
Net Income	**79.0**	**-37.0**	**330.0**	**241.1**	P/B Ratio	**1.5**	52 Wk Hi-Low	**29.75-21.75**
Book Value	**4,123.0**	**3,943.0**	**4,085.0**	**2,917.9**	Yield %	**3.7**	Market Cap	**US$4,625.3mil**

Address **BCE Pl., 181 Bay St.**
Toronto, ON M5J 2T3
Tel **416-982-7111**
Fax **416-982-7423**
Exchange **TSE**
Ticker **NOR**
President **David W. Kerr**
Chairman **Alfred Powis**

Norcen

Industry: **Oil - Secondary**

Norcen Energy Resources is an oil and gas company with production operations in western Canada, the Gulf of Mexico, Venezuela, and Argentina. It is also involved in crude-oil development projects in Russia and Indonesia, and operates a pipeline-distribution system in western Canada. Its subsidiary Superior Propane is the largest retail marketer of propane in Canada and the fourth largest in North America, with a distribution network across Canada and in 10 states in the United States. Norcen's mineral-resources arm invests in iron ore, lead, and zinc mining and marketing.

C$ mil	12/92	12/93	12/94	US$mil 12/94				
Sales	**1,009.1**	**1,421.1**	**1,297.4**	**947.7**	P/E Ratio	**NMF**	Price (9/30/95)	**18.63**
Net Income	**38.9**	**24.5**	**-114.0**	**-83.3**	P/B Ratio	**1.2**	52 Wk Hi-Low	**20.88-15.38**
Book Value	**1,310.4**	**1,403.3**	**1,242.3**	**887.4**	Yield %	**3.2**	Market Cap	**US$1,148.1mil**

Address	**715 Fifth Ave. S.W.**	Tel **403-231-0111**	Exchange **TSE**	President & CEO	**Grant D. Billing**
	Calgary, AB T2P 4V4	Fax **403-231-0187**	Ticker **NCN**	Chairman	**Edward G. Battle**

Northern Telecom

Industry: **Communications Technology**

Northern Telecom, along with its subsidiaries, manufactures and sells telecommunication equipment to telephone companies, cable-television companies, corporations, governments, and universities. Products include central switching systems and cellular mobile telecom switches. The company has operations in North America (where it is the second-largest manufacturer of telecom equipment behind AT&T), South America, Asia, and Europe. Northern Telecom owns 70% of Bell-Northern Research. Bell Canada owns the remaining 30%.

$ mil	12/92	12/93	12/94	US$mil 12/94				
Sales	**8,408.9**	**8,148.0**	**8,874.0**	**8,874.0**	P/E Ratio	**22.3**	Price (9/30/95)	**47.75**
Net Income	**548.3**	**-878.0**	**408.0**	**408.0**	P/B Ratio	**2.7**	52 Wk Hi-Low	**55.88-43.88**
Book Value	**3,967.3**	**3,014.0**	**3,355.0**	**3,355.0**	Yield %	**0.6**	Market Cap	**US$9,030.9mil**

Address	**3 Robert Speck Pkwy.**	Tel **905-566-3000**	Exchange **TSE**	President & CEO	**Jean C. Monty**
	Mississauga, ON L4Z 3C8	Fax **905-275-1143**	Ticker **NTL**	Chairman	**Donald J. Schuenke**

Nova Scotia Power

Industry: **Electrical Utilities - All**

Nova Scotia Power generates and distributes electricity throughout the province. With a distribution network of more than 24,000 kilometers, it supplies 415,000 customers, or approximately 95% of the electricity requirement in Nova Scotia. 45% of the company's electricity sales are to residential customers, 31% to commercial clients, and 20% to industrial users. Nova Scotia Power operates more than 40 electricity-generating facilities including coal-fired and hydroelectric plants, and wind and gas turbines.

C$ mil	12/92 *	12/93	12/94	US$mil 12/94				
Sales	**498.2**	**709.1**	**715.6**	**522.7**	P/E Ratio	**10.6**	Price (9/30/95)	**11.63**
Net Income	**38.0**	**95.4**	**110.8**	**80.9**	P/B Ratio	**1.0**	52 Wk Hi-Low	**12.13-10.88**
Book Value	**749.1**	**973.7**	**1,005.6**	**718.3**	Yield %	**6.5**	Market Cap	**US$741.1mil**

Address	**Scotia Sq., 1894 Barrington St.**	Tel **902-428-6230**	Exchange **TSE**	President & CEO	**Louis R. Comeau**
	Halifax, NS B3J 2W5	Fax **902-428-6100**	Ticker **NSI**	Chairman	**Joseph A.F. Macdonald**

*Irregular period due to fiscal year change.

Nova

Industry: **Commodity Chemicals**

Nova of Alberta transports natural gas through its Alberta Gas Transmission Division. AGTD carries more than 15% of North America's annual gas production. Nova also markets, stores, and processes natural gas through Nova Gas Services. Novacor Chemicals, another Nova subsidiary, is North America's largest ethylene producer, its fourth-largest polystyrene producer, and its fifth-largest polyethylene producer. In addition, the company owns 24% of Methanex, the world's leading methanol producer and marketer.

C$ mil	12/92	12/93	12/94	US$mil 12/94				
Sales	**3,027.0**	**3,274.0**	**3,724.0**	**2,720.2**	P/E Ratio	**8.6**	Price (9/30/95)	**10.63**
Net Income	**164.0**	**202.0**	**575.0**	**420.0**	P/B Ratio	**1.5**	52 Wk Hi-Low	**14.88-10.50**
Book Value	**2,022.0**	**2,125.0**	**3,341.0**	**2,386.4**	Yield %	**2.3**	Market Cap	**US$3,225.0mil**

Address	**801 7th Avenue S.W.**	Tel **403-290-6000**	Exchange **TSE**	CEO	**Ted Newall**
	Calgary, AB T2P 2N6	Fax **403-290-6379**	Ticker **NVA**	Chairman	**Richard F. Haskayne**

Numac Energy

Industry: **Oil - Secondary**

Numac Energy is engaged in the exploration, development, production and marketing of crude oil, natural-gas liquids, and natural gas. The Calgary-based company produces over 20,000 barrels of crude oil and natural-gas liquid per day, and 138.7 million cubic feet of natural gas per day. Proved and probable reserves for crude oil and natural gas liquid are 68.8 million barrels, and 704 billion cubic feet for natural gas. Numac has over 1 million net acres of undeveloped land in western Canada, 317,000 of which are in northeastern British Columbia.

C$ mil	12/92	12/93	12/94	US$mil 12/94				
Sales	**126.7**	**152.9**	**228.9**	**167.2**	P/E Ratio	**23.7**	Price (9/30/95)	**6.63**
Net Income	**-126.1**	**11.5**	**26.5**	**19.4**	P/B Ratio	**1.2**	52 Wk Hi-Low	**7.75-6.00**
Book Value	**247.5**	**497.7**	**528.7**	**377.6**	Yield %	**0.0**	Market Cap	**US$458.3mil**

Address	**321 6th Ave. S.W.**	Tel **403-260-9400**	Exchange **TSE**	Chief Executive	**Stewart D. McGregor**
	Calgary, AB T2P 3H3	Fax **403-260-9457**	Ticker **NMC**	Chairman	**Stewart D. McGregor**

Oshawa Group

Industry: **Food Retailers & Wholesalers**

Oshawa Group distributes food, manages supermarkets and drugstores, provides food services, and manages real-estate holdings. It operates 111 supermarkets, including 37 Food City supermarkets and 43 IGA and 24 Price Chopper stores. The company manages franchise programs for more than 1,400 independent grocers under trade names such as IGA, Krechtel, Food Town, and Bonichoix. It manages 150 Pharma Plus and Metro Drug outlets. Other operations include produce-packing and wholesaling facilities, public cold-storage plants, uniform rental, and a dairy.

	C$ mil 01/93	01/94	01/95	US$mil 01/95				
Sales	**5,011.4**	**5,727.8**	**6,069.8**	**4,411.2**	P/E Ratio	**15.2**	Price (9/30/95)	**21.38**
Net Income	**41.8**	**50.2**	**53.2**	**38.7**	P/B Ratio	**1.1**	52 Wk Hi-Low	**22.13-17.38**
Book Value	**664.9**	**707.3**	**751.0**	**532.6**	Yield %	**2.3**	Market Cap	**US$595.1mil**

Address	**302 The East Mall**	Tel	**416-236-1971**	Exchange	**TSE**	President & COO	**Jonathan A. Wolfe**
	Etobicoke, ON M9B 6B8	Fax	**416-236-2071**	Ticker	**OSH.A**	Chairman & CEO	**Allister P. Graham**

Placer Dome

Industry: **Precious Metals**

Placer Dome is an international mining company with interests in 16 mines, 13 of them gold mines, in Australia, Canada, Chile, Papua New Guinea, the Philippines, and the United States. In 1994, gold production attributable to Placer Dome totaled 1.7 million ounces, at a cash production cost of US$197 per ounce. The company also produced 6.6 million ounces of silver, 10.4 million pounds of copper, and 13.7 million pounds of molybdenum. At the end of 1994, proven and probable gold reserves amounted to 19.8 million ounces.

	$ mil 12/92	12/93	12/94	US$mil 12/94				
Sales	**1,020.0**	**917.0**	**899.0**	**899.0**	P/E Ratio	**59.3**	Price (9/30/95)	**35.00**
Net Income	**111.0**	**107.0**	**105.0**	**105.0**	P/B Ratio	**4.1**	52 Wk Hi-Low	**39.75-25.38**
Book Value	**1,459.0**	**1,514.0**	**1,529.0**	**1,529.0**	Yield %	**0.6**	Market Cap	**US$6,229.1mil**

Address	**1600-1055 Dunsmuir St.**	Tel	**604-682-7082**	Exchange	**TSE**	President & CEO	**John M. Wilson**
	Vancouver, BC V7X 1P1	Fax	**604-682-7092**	Ticker	**PDG**	Chairman	**Robert M. Franklin**

Poco Petroleums

Industry: **Oil - Secondary**

Poco Petroleums produces, explores for, and markets natural gas and crude oil. The company's operations are concentrated in west central and northwestern Alberta and northeastern British Columbia, however it does have some activities in eastern Alberta and southeastern Saskatchewan. Its average daily production is 20,265 barrels of crude oil and natural-gas liquids and 191.5 million cubic feet of natural gas. Poco has reserves of 52 million barrels of crude oil and natural-gas liquids and 866.4 billion cubic feet of natural gas.

	C$ mil 12/92	12/93	12/94	US$mil 12/94				
Sales	**165.8**	**188.7**	**227.0**	**165.8**	P/E Ratio	**60.8**	Price (9/30/95)	**9.13**
Net Income	**-97.5**	**5.4**	**13.5**	**9.9**	P/B Ratio	**1.5**	52 Wk Hi-Low	**10.13-7.25**
Book Value	**429.8**	**455.6**	**576.9**	**412.1**	Yield %	**0.0**	Market Cap	**US$640.4mil**

Address	**250 6th Ave. S.W.**	Tel	**403-260-8000**	Exchange	**TSE**	President & CEO	**Craig W. Stewart**
	Calgary, AB T2P 3H7	Fax	**403-263-2708**	Ticker	**POC**	Chairman	**John R. Yarnell**

Potash

Industry: **Mining**

Potash Corporation of Saskatchewan (PCS) is the world's largest potash producer. It supplies 14% of global potash production. The company also has 22% of the world's production capacity, with 40% of the market's excess capacity. PCS' seven potash mines in western and eastern Canada have a production capacity of 11 million metric tons. In 1994, PCS produced 5.3 million tonnes. Ninety-five percent of this potassium product is used in fertilizer, though it also has other industrial and agricultural applications.

	C$ mil 12/92	12/93	12/94	US$mil 12/94				
Sales	**370.0**	**374.3**	**596.7**	**435.9**	P/E Ratio	**28.1**	Price (9/30/95)	**83.75**
Net Income	**58.2**	**63.1**	**128.0**	**93.5**	P/B Ratio	**2.7**	52 Wk Hi-Low	**92.75-42.75**
Book Value	**1,145.6**	**1,278.3**	**1,352.8**	**966.3**	Yield %	**1.3**	Market Cap	**US$2,686.8mil**

Address	**122 1st Ave. S.**	Tel	**306-933-8500**	Exchange	**TSE**	President & CEO	**Charles E. Childers**
	Saskatoon, SK S7K 7G3	Fax	**306-652-2699**	Ticker	**POT**	Chairman	**Charles E. Childers**

Power Corporation

Industry: **Financial Services - Diversified**

Power Corporation of Canada has interests in the financial-services and media sectors. Through a 69%-owned subsidiary, Power Financial Corporation, the firm owns controlling interests in Great-West Lifeco, an insurer, Investors Group, a mutual fund manager, and Pargesa Holding of Switzerland, a holding company. Its media division consists of wholly owned Gesca Ltee, owner of Montreal's daily newspaper, La Presse; wholly owned Power Broadcasting, operator of 17 radio and three TV stations; and an 18.7% interest in Southam, Canada's largest newspaper publisher.

	C$ mil 12/92	12/93	12/94	US$mil 12/94				
Revenues	**6,181.5**	**6,087.2**	**6,904.2**	**5,043.2**	P/E Ratio	**13.9**	Price (9/30/95)	**20.25**
Net Income	**152.3**	**150.2**	**186.4**	**136.2**	P/B Ratio	**0.9**	52 Wk Hi-Low	**22.88-17.38**
Book Value	**2,236.7**	**2,295.6**	**2,495.5**	**1,782.5**	Yield %	**3.5**	Market Cap	**US$1,711.5mil**

Address	**751 Victoria Sq.**	Tel	**514-296-7400**	Exchange	**MSE**	President & COO	**André Desmarais**
	Montreal, PQ H2Y 2J3	Fax	**514-286-7424**	Ticker	**POW**	Chairman	**Paul Desmarais**

Quebecor

Industry: **Publishing**

Quebecor is involved in printing, publishing, and paper production. Its wholly-owned Quebecor Group subsidiary publishes magazines, books, and newspapers, including Le Journal de Montreal. Its 55.7%-owned Quebecor Printing, Canada's largest commercial printer, handles the group's custom-printing activities. Quebecor's third subsidiary, 25%-owned Donohue, produces 195,000 tonnes of newsprint and 325 million board feet of lumber annually. In 1993, U.S. sales accounted for 65% of revenues; Canadian sales made up 32%; and Europe and other areas made up the remainder.

	C$ mil 12/92	12/93	12/94	US$mil 12/94				
Sales	**2,535.6**	**3,077.0**	**3,975.6**	**2,904.0**	P/E Ratio	**15.1**	Price (9/30/95)	**20.25**
Net Income	**87.3**	**74.6**	**88.6**	**64.7**	P/B Ratio	**1.6**	52 Wk Hi-Low	**21.50-15.50**
Book Value	**643.6**	**742.3**	**828.4**	**591.7**	Yield %	**1.2**	Market Cap	**US$542.9mil**

Address **612 Saint-Jacques St.** **Montreal, PQ H3C 4M8**
Tel **514-877-9777** Fax **514-877-9757**
Exchange **TSE** Ticker **QBR**
CEO **Pierre Péladeau** Chairman **Pierre Péladeau**

Ranger Oil

Industry: **Oil - Secondary**

Ranger Oil prospects for and recovers oil, natural gas liquids (NGLs), and natural gas mainly from western Canada and the Gulf of Mexico. It also explores and produces in the North Sea, Angola, Namibia, Algeria, and Peru. Canada accounts for one half of the company's production. In 1994, the firm produced 15,000 barrels of oil per day and 106.2 million cubic feet of natural gas per day. As of December 31, 1994, proven and probable reserves totaled 62 million barrels of oil and NGLs and 425 billion cubic feet of natural gas.

	$ mil 12/92	12/93	12/94	US$mil 12/94				
Sales	**153.7**	**152.6**	**158.6**	**158.6**	P/E Ratio	**97.9**	Price (9/30/95)	**7.88**
Net Income	**23.5**	**20.2**	**6.1**	**6.1**	P/B Ratio	**1.3**	52 Wk Hi-Low	**10.13-7.38**
Book Value	**447.8**	**460.2**	**458.9**	**458.9**	Yield %	**0.8**	Market Cap	**US$579.4mil**

Address **321 6th Ave. S.W.** **Calgary, AB T2P 3H3**
Tel **403-232-5200** Fax **403-263-0090**
Exchange **TSE** Ticker **RGO**
President & CEO **F.J. Dyment** Chairman **S.S. Reisman**

Renaissance Energy

Industry: **Oil - Secondary**

Renaissance Energy operates crude-oil and natural-gas businesses in Alberta's Plains region. Its activities include exploration, development, production, and marketing. The company's average daily oil production is almost 43,000 barrels, and its average daily natural-gas production is 362 million cubic feet. It has oil and liquid reserves of 247 million barrels and natural-gas reserves of more than 1.3 trillion cubic feet. Its drilling activities span 1,200 oil, natural-gas, and dry wells. The company also has interests in 6.1 million acres of undeveloped land in Canada.

	C$ mil 12/92	12/93	12/94	US$mil 12/94				
Sales	**266.1**	**381.7**	**522.4**	**381.6**	P/E Ratio	**42.6**	Price (9/30/95)	**30.25**
Net Income	**24.6**	**49.0**	**63.1**	**46.1**	P/B Ratio	**2.7**	52 Wk Hi-Low	**31.88-23.75**
Book Value	**451.1**	**713.5**	**1,048.8**	**749.1**	Yield %	**0.0**	Market Cap	**US$2,113.5mil**

Address **Ste. 3000, 425 First St. S.W.** **Calgary, AB T2P 3L8**
Tel **403-750-1400** Fax **403-750-1468**
Exchange **TSE** Ticker **RES**
President & CEO **Clayton H. Woitas** Chairman **Ronald G. Greene**

Rio Algom

Industry: **Mining**

Rio Algom mines uranium, copper, molybdenum, and coal in North and South America and distributes metals and metals products in North America, New Zealand, and Australia. In 1994, it produced 157.5 million pounds of copper, 1.2 million pounds of molybdenum, 1.8 million pounds of uranium, and 544 thousand metric tons of coal. Rio Algom's metals-distribution division is managed by its subsidiaries: Atlas Alloys, Vincent Metals, and Atlas Steels Limited. The three subsidiaries market refined metal in flat-rolled, bar, wire, and tube form.

	C$ mil 12/92	12/93	12/94	US$mil 12/94				
Sales	**1,028.2**	**955.4**	**1,212.1**	**885.4**	P/E Ratio	**18.3**	Price (9/30/95)	**27.13**
Net Income	**39.4**	**53.5**	**75.2**	**54.9**	P/B Ratio	**1.6**	52 Wk Hi-Low	**29.25-23.13**
Book Value	**632.2**	**650.6**	**902.4**	**644.6**	Yield %	**2.2**	Market Cap	**US$1,051.8mil**

Address **120 Adelaide St. W.** **Toronto, ON M5H 1W5**
Tel **416-367-4000** Fax **416-365-6870**
Exchange **TSE** Ticker **ROM**
President & CEO **Colin A. Macaulay** Chairman **Gordon C. Gray**

Rogers Communications

Industry: **Broadcasting**

Rogers Communications operates wireless-communication, telecommunication, and media businesses. Rogers Cantel Mobile Communication is Canada's largest wireless-telephone company and the sole nationwide provider of cellular services. Rogers Cablesystems provides cable television to 2.6 million customers and runs a chain of 110 video-rental outlets. Rogers Multi-Media operates 20 radio stations, 3 television stations, and 10 daily papers, including The Toronto Sun. In 1994, the company acquired Maclean Hunter, a Canadian cable-television and multimedia business.

	C$ mil 12/92	12/93	12/94	US$mil 12/94				
Sales	**1,148.7**	**1,136.5**	**2,250.2**	**1,643.7**	P/E Ratio	**NMF**	Price (9/30/95)	**13.25**
Net Income	**-180.3**	**-287.0**	**-168.0**	**-122.7**	P/B Ratio	**3.2**	52 Wk Hi-Low	**20.63-13.00**
Book Value	**1,143.9**	**1,038.3**	**1,204.6**	**860.4**	Yield %	**0.0**	Market Cap	**US$2,213.7mil**

Address **Scotia Plaza, 40 King St. W.** **Toronto, ON M5H 3Y2**
Tel **416-864-2373** Fax **416-864-2385**
Exchange **TSE** Ticker **RCI.B**
President & CEO **Edward S. Rogers** Chairman **H. Garfield Emerson**

Royal Bank of Canada

Industry: **Banks - Money Center**

Royal Bank of Canada is the country's largest financial-services entity by assets, and its leading provider of consumer loans and mortgages. The bank has more than 1,700 Canadian branches and 3,900 banking machines. Its individual, small-business, and corporate clients number more than eight million. It provides corporate and investment banking and sells Treasury products in 32 countries outside Canada, and offers retail banking in the Caribbean. Through its subsidiary Royal Trust, it is Canada's second largest mutual-fund operator with almost C$13 billion in assets.

C$ mil	10/92	10/93	10/94	US$mil 10/94				
Revenues	**12,199.0**	**11,676.0**	**13,434.0**	**9,877.9**	P/E Ratio	**9.2**	Price (9/30/95)	**29.50**
Net Income	**107.0**	**300.0**	**1,169.0**	**859.6**	P/B Ratio	**1.1**	52 Wk Hi-Low	**31.25-26.25**
Book Value	**7,506.0**	**7,930.0**	**8,589.0**	**6,362.2**	Yield %	**3.9**	Market Cap	**US$6,916.1mil**

Address **1 Pl. Ville Marie, Montreal, PQ H3C 3A9**
Tel **514-874-2110** Fax **514-874-7197**
Exchange **TSE** Ticker **RY**
President & CEO **John E. Cleghorn**
Chairman **Allan R. Taylor**

Scott's Hospitality

Industry: **Restaurants**

Scott's Hospitality operates in the food-service, transportation, and hotel industries. It specializes in fast food, owning 408 Kentucky Fried Chicken franchises in Canada. It also owns 231 Manchu Wok Chinese restaurants in the United States and Canada, and the Gino's chain and several Perfect Pizza franchises in the United Kingdom. Scott's owns interests in the Sizzler, Baskin-Robbins, and Wendy's U.S. chains. Scott's also operates the Charterways (Ontario) and Charterway National (U.S.) school-bus services, maintaining a fleet of more than 5,000 vehicles.

C$ mil	04/93	04/94	04/95	US$mil 04/95				
Sales	**785.3**	**809.6**	**845.6**	**612.3**	P/E Ratio	**16.7**	Price (9/30/95)	**8.88**
Net Income	**0.0**	**29.2**	**31.7**	**23.0**	P/B Ratio	**1.3**	52 Wk Hi-Low	**10.00-6.75**
Book Value	**370.2**	**391.1**	**409.3**	**301.0**	Yield %	**2.9**	Market Cap	**US$243.5mil**

Address **BCE Place, 181 Bay St., Toronto, ON M5J 2T3**
Tel **416-369-9050** Fax **416-369-2500**
Exchange **TSE** Ticker **SRC**
President & CEO **John S. Lacey**
Chairman **Patrick W.E. Hodgson**

Seagram

Industry: **Distillers & Brewers**

Seagram is a leading beverage producer and marketer. Its primary products are distilled spirits, wines, coolers, mixers, and fruit juices. Its brand names include Seagram Coolers, Chivas Regal, and Tropicana. The company is also the global marketer and distributor of Absolut vodka. Seagram operates in 30 countries and participates in joint ventures in Japan, South Korea, Thailand, Taiwan, and China. Seagram has established offices in China and a subsidiary in India. The company has a 14.99% stake in Time Warner and an 80% stake in MCA.

$ mil	01/93	01/94	01/95	US$mil 01/95				
Sales	**6,101.0**	**6,038.0**	**6,399.0**	**6,399.0**	P/E Ratio	**16.6**	Price (9/30/95)	**48.38**
Net Income	**472.6**	**379.0**	**811.0**	**811.0**	P/B Ratio	**2.4**	52 Wk Hi-Low	**51.88-36.25**
Book Value	**4,930.0**	**5,001.0**	**5,509.0**	**5,509.0**	Yield %	**0.9**	Market Cap	**US$13,446mil**

Address **1430 Peel St., Montreal, PQ H3A 1S9**
Tel **514-987-5209** Fax **514-987-5232**
Exchange **TSE** Ticker **VO**
President **Edgar Bronfman, Jr.**
Chairman **Edgar M. Bronfman**

Shaw Communications

Industry: **Broadcasting**

Shaw Communications is the third-largest multisystem cable-television operator in Canada. Through its network of wholly owned Shaw Cablesystems subsidiaries, the company serves approximately 900,000 cable-television subscribers in six provinces. Its radio division operates eight radio stations in British Columbia, Alberta, and Ontario. Its televisual-networks division provides cable-television-advertising services to local, regional, and national clients. The company also owns 13% of the U.S. cable-television operator International Cablecasting Technologies.

C$ mil	08/92	08/93	08/94	US$mil 08/94				
Sales	**166.0**	**233.7**	**288.4**	**212.5**	P/E Ratio	**12.3**	Price (9/30/95)	**7.25**
Net Income	**18.8**	**24.6**	**33.3**	**24.5**	P/B Ratio	**1.1**	52 Wk Hi-Low	**10.63-7.25**
Book Value	**210.6**	**223.4**	**431.2**	**314.7**	Yield %	**1.0**	Market Cap	**US$294.6mil**

Address **7605 50th St., Edmonton, AB T6B 2W9**
Tel **403-468-1230** Fax **403-466-4544**
Exchange **TSE** Ticker **SCL**
President **James R. Shaw**
Chairman **James R. Shaw**

Sherritt

Industry: **Specialty Chemicals**

Sherritt produces fertilizers, mines commodity metals, produces oil and natural gas, and develops industrial materials. The company generates 56% of its revenues through sales of nitrogen and phosphate fertilizers. Its metals unit mines nickel and cobalt, and operates coinage and rolling mills. Its mining partnership with General Nickel of Cuba began operations in December 1994. Sherritt's Canada Northwest Energy subsidiary explores for oil and natural gas in Cuba, Italy, Spain, Indonesia, and Pakistan. Sherritt also develops specialty materials for industrial applications.

C$ mil	12/92	12/93	12/94	US$mil 12/94				
Sales	**435.8**	**410.8**	**920.8**	**672.6**	P/E Ratio	**13.7**	Price (9/30/95)	**17.75**
Net Income	**2.3**	**-41.5**	**80.0**	**58.4**	P/B Ratio	**1.9**	52 Wk Hi-Low	**18.13-11.88**
Book Value	**333.3**	**296.1**	**639.1**	**456.5**	Yield %	**0.0**	Market Cap	**US$896.8mil**

Address **10101 114th St., Fort Saskatchewan, AB T8L 2P2**
Tel **403-998-6911** Fax **403-998-6568**
Exchange **TSE** Ticker **SE**
Chief Executive **Ian W. Delaney**
Chairman **Ian W. Delaney**

Slocan Forest Products

Industry: **Forest Products**

Slocan Forest Products supplies lumber, plywood, chlorine-free pulp, newsprint, specialty printing papers and oriented strand board to markets in North America and Asia. In 1994, Slocan and Donohue of Canada jointly purchased Finlay Forest Industries, a diversified lumber concern with two sawmills, a pulp mill, and a paper mill with an annual production of 165,000 tonnes of newsprint. The company also owns 80% of Fibreco, one of the world's largest suppliers of chemithermomechanical pulp with a 25% market share. Slocan has operations at 14 locations in British Columbia.

C$ mil	12/92	12/93	12/94	US$mil 12/94				
Sales	**257.3**	**466.4**	**728.3**	**532.0**	P/E Ratio	**4.9**	Price (9/30/95)	**12.63**
Net Income	**6.4**	**61.5**	**97.7**	**71.4**	P/B Ratio	**1.6**	52 Wk Hi-Low	**16.00-11.25**
Book Value	**62.1**	**204.0**	**295.1**	**210.8**	Yield %	**1.6**	Market Cap	**US$361.2mil**

Address **10451 Shellbridge Way**
Richmond, BC V6X 2W8
Tel **604-278-7311**
Fax **604-278-7316**
Exchange **TSE**
Ticker **SFF**
President & CEO **Irving K. Barber**
Chairman **Irving K. Barber**

Southam

Industry: **Publishing**

Southam publishes newspapers, provides business information, and retails books. It is Canada's largest daily-newspaper group, with an average daily circulation of 1.5 million. It publishes 17 daily newspapers, including The Vancouver Sun and The Gazette (Montreal), and 33 weekly newspapers. It publishes 37 business magazines and tabloids, and distributes business information through Infomart Online and CD-ROM services. It operates 259 bookstores under the Coles the Book People!, The Book Company, Active Minds, and World's Biggest Bookstore names.

C$ mil	12/92	12/93	12/94	US$mil 12/94				
Sales	**1,183.5**	**1,176.2**	**1,202.4**	**878.3**	P/E Ratio	**23.9**	Price (9/30/95)	**13.88**
Net Income	**-262.9**	**21.6**	**44.0**	**32.1**	P/B Ratio	**2.3**	52 Wk Hi-Low	**16.38-12.50**
Book Value	**237.7**	**433.4**	**454.8**	**324.9**	Yield %	**1.4**	Market Cap	**US$791.5mil**

Address **1450 Don Mills Rd.**
Don Mills, ON M3B 2X7
Tel **416-445-6641**
Fax **416-442-2077**
Exchange **TSE**
Ticker **STM**
President & CEO **William E. Ardell**
Chairman **Paul G. Desmarais**

Stelco

Industry: **Steel**

Stelco is a steel producer and fabricator. It is made up of two business units, Hilton Works and Lake Erie Works, and 11 wholly owned subsidiaries. Stelco supplies the automotive and construction industries with high-value steel and hot-rolled sheet products. Its subsidiaries include Stelwire, Stelco-McMaster, and Stelpipe, a producer of large-diameter oil- and gas-transmission pipes. Stelco has seven joint ventures, with activities that include prepainting of rolled-steel coils, automotive-parts production, and iron-ore mining and production in Mexico, Chile, and Peru.

C$ mil	12/92	12/93	12/94	US$mil 12/94				
Sales	**2,203.0**	**2,491.0**	**2,794.0**	**2,040.9**	P/E Ratio	**5.6**	Price (9/30/95)	**5.63**
Net Income	**-127.0**	**-36.0**	**115.0**	**84.0**	P/B Ratio	**0.5**	52 Wk Hi-Low	**9.25-5.63**
Book Value	**967.0**	**929.0**	**1,160.0**	**828.6**	Yield %	**0.0**	Market Cap	**US$443.0mil**

Address **Stelco Tower**
Hamilton, ON L8N 3T1
Tel **905-528-2511**
Fax **905-577-4575**
Exchange **TSE**
Ticker **STE**
President & COO **Robert J. Milbourne**
Chairman **Frederick H. Telmer**

Stone Consolidated

Industry: **Paper Products**

Stone-Consolidated Corporation produces newsprint, uncoated groundwood, specialty papers, and lumber. It produces 890,660 tonnes of newsprint, 486,300 tonnes of uncoated groundwood papers, and 223.2 million board feet of lumber at its five sawmills and four paper mills in Quebec. It operates its Bridgewater Paper Company subsidiary in England which produces newsprint from recycled paper for distribution in the United Kingdom and western Europe. Stone-Consolidated is a 75%-owned subsidiary of Stone Container, a U.S.-based paper and packaging firm.

C$ mil	12/92	12/93	12/94	US$mil 12/94				
Sales	**840.8**	**928.0**	**1,091.3**	**797.2**	P/E Ratio	**NMF**	Price (9/30/95)	**19.38**
Net Income	**-110.2**	**-68.7**	**-7.8**	**-5.7**	P/B Ratio	**1.0**	52 Wk Hi-Low	**22.00-16.50**
Book Value	**1,033.9**	**1,263.2**	**1,283.5**	**916.8**	Yield %	**0.0**	Market Cap	**US$939.8mil**

Address **800 René-Lévesque Blvd. W.**
Montreal, PQ H3B 1Y9
Tel **514-875-2160**
Fax **N/A**
Exchange **TSE**
Ticker **SO**
President & CEO **James Doughan**
Chairman **Roger W. Stone**

Talisman Energy

Industry: **Oil - Secondary**

Talisman Energy is an oil and gas company that produces crude oil, natural-gas liquids, and sulphur. It operates exploration and production facilities in British Columbia, Alberta, Saskatchewan, Ontario, the Netherlands, the North Sea, Algeria, Indonesia, and Cuba. It acquired Canada's Bow Valley Energy, a natural-resources company that explores for and produces oil and natural gas, in August 1994. Through the acquisition, Talisman became Canada's third-largest natural-gas producer, with an average daily output of 500 million cubic feet.

C$ mil	12/92	12/93	12/94	US$mil 12/94				
Sales	**227.2**	**336.2**	**589.8**	**430.8**	P/E Ratio	**31.9**	Price (9/30/95)	**26.13**
Net Income	**11.2**	**25.8**	**64.0**	**46.7**	P/B Ratio	**1.6**	52 Wk Hi-Low	**29.50-21.38**
Book Value	**315.1**	**614.3**	**1,580.3**	**1,128.8**	Yield %	**0.0**	Market Cap	**US$1,877.1mil**

Address **2400 855-2 Street S.W.**
Calgary, Alberta T2P 4J9
Tel **403-237-1170**
Fax **403-237-1027**
Exchange **TSE**
Ticker **TLM**
President & CEO **James W. Buckee**
Chairman **S. Keith McWalter**

Teck

Industry: **Mining**

Teck Corporation operates mining businesses. Its eleven Canadian mines produce gold, copper, zinc, lead, silver, niobium, and metallurgical coal. It owns 36% of Cominco, a Canadian mining and smelting company, 44% of goldminer Golden Knight Resources, and 10% of mineral-explorer Aur Resources. Teck also has a 29% interest in a copper mine in Chile, and is exploring for resources in Mexico, Cuba, Venezuela, Bolivia, Peru, Brazil, and West Africa. Teck's average annual production includes 67.6 million pounds of copper, 57.7 million pounds of zinc, and 344,000 ounces of gold.

C$ mil	12/92	12/93	12/94	US$mil 12/94				
Sales	**377.6**	**492.1**	**551.4**	**402.8**	P/E Ratio	**34.7**	Price (9/30/95)	**26.75**
Net Income	**25.5**	**29.2**	**69.1**	**50.5**	P/B Ratio	**2.3**	52 Wk Hi-Low	**29.00-22.38**
Book Value	**840.7**	**976.2**	**1,032.6**	**737.6**	Yield %	**0.7**	Market Cap	**US$1,712.3mil**

Address	**200 Burrard St.**	Tel	**604-687-1117**	Exchange	**TSE**	President & CEO	**Norman B. Keevil**
	Vancouver, BC V6C 3L9	Fax	**604-687-6100**	Ticker	**TEK**	Chairman	**Robert J. Wright**

Telus

Industry: **Telephone Systems - All**

Telus Corporation is a telecommunication and information-management firm. Its largest subsidiary, wholly-owned AGT Group, offers telephone, data, and video-telecommunication services. AGT Mobility is Alberta's leading supplier of mobile wireless-communication equipment, including cellular, paging, and radio systems. AGT Directory publishes the Alberta white and yellow pages, and provides direct marketing services. Telecential Communications, Telus' joint venture with U.K. cable-system operator CUC Broadcasting, operates cable-television and telephone service.

C$ mil	12/92	12/93	12/94	US$mil 12/94				
Sales	**1,176.6**	**1,262.5**	**1,360.1**	**993.5**	P/E Ratio	**10.8**	Price (9/30/95)	**16.38**
Net Income	**177.8**	**180.6**	**211.7**	**154.6**	P/B Ratio	**1.3**	52 Wk Hi-Low	**17.00-14.88**
Book Value	**1,615.6**	**1,667.3**	**1,759.5**	**1,256.8**	Yield %	**5.6**	Market Cap	**US$1,702.8mil**

Address	**10020-100 St.**	Tel	**403-498-7311**	Exchange	**ASE**	President & CEO	**George K. Petty**
	Edmonton, AB T5J 0N5	Fax	**403-498-7399**	Ticker	**AGT**	Chairman	**James Palmer**

Tembec

Industry: **Forest Products**

Tembec produces lumber, pulp, coated paperboard, kraft paper, chemicals, and newsprint. It has equipment at one of its mills in Quebec that manufactures carton board for cigarette packages, pharmaceutical boxes, and other packaging applications. Its 41%-owned Spruce Falls Acquisition subsidiary produces newsprint and groundwood paper mainly from spruce trees. It entered into a joint venture with Cascades Paperboard International to buy a mill in southwestern France that produces fluff pulp used in the manufacture of sanitary products.

C$ mil	09/92	09/93	09/94	US$mil 09/94				
Sales	**336.5**	**370.3**	**485.4**	**357.4**	P/E Ratio	**5.8**	Price (9/30/95)	**13.00**
Net Income	**-28.8**	**-48.6**	**72.7**	**53.5**	P/B Ratio	**1.2**	52 Wk Hi-Low	**16.25-12.38**
Book Value	**280.3**	**234.2**	**433.4**	**323.4**	Yield %	**0.0**	Market Cap	**US$360.3mil**

Address	**800 René-Lévesque Blvd. W.**	Tel	**514-871-0137**	Exchange	**TSE**	President & CEO	**Frank A. Dottori**
	Montreal, PQ H3B 1X9	Fax	**514-397-0896**	Ticker	**TBC.A**	Chairman	**Jacques Giasson**

Toronto Dominion Bank

Industry: **Banks - Money Center**

The Toronto Dominion Bank is Canada's fifth-largest bank by assets. It operates 975 branches and offices in Canada, for individuals and corporate clients. It also provides securities administration, estate planning, and mutual-fund services. Its two discount brokerages, Green Line Investor Services and Marathon Brokerage, control 12% of the Canadian retail-brokerage market. Its Central Guaranty Trust subsidiary offers personal and pension-trust services. The bank has operations in the United States, Australia, the United Kingdom, Japan, Hong Kong, Taiwan, and Singapore.

C$ mil	10/92	10/93	10/94	US$mil 10/94				
Revenues	**6,138.0**	**6,366.0**	**6,993.0**	**5,141.9**	P/E Ratio	**10.7**	Price (9/30/95)	**23.00**
Net Income	**376.0**	**246.0**	**683.0**	**502.2**	P/B Ratio	**1.3**	52 Wk Hi-Low	**23.00-19.75**
Book Value	**4,559.0**	**4,608.0**	**5,439.0**	**4,028.9**	Yield %	**3.4**	Market Cap	**US$5,169.9mil**

Address	**Toronto-Dominion Ctr., King St. W.**	Tel	**416-982-8222**	Exchange	**TSE**	President	**Robert W. Korthals**
	Toronto, ON M5K 1A2	Fax	**416-982-5671**	Ticker	**TD**	Chairman & CEO	**Richard M. Thomson**

Torstar

Industry: **Publishing**

Torstar is a print-communication company engaged in newspaper and book publishing and direct-mail marketing. It owns The Toronto Star, Canada's largest daily newspaper; Metroland Printing, Publishing & Distributing, publishers of community newspapers and distributors of advertising materials and commercial printers; Harlequin Enterprises, the world's largest publisher of romance fiction; direct-mail marketer Miles Kimball; and Marshall Editions, a packager of hardcover, nonfiction books. Torstar generates approximately 56% of its sales outside Canada.

C$ mil	12/92	12/93	12/94	US$mil 12/94				
Sales	**921.1**	**975.0**	**1,054.8**	**770.5**	P/E Ratio	**19.5**	Price (9/30/95)	**21.25**
Net Income	**48.8**	**-9.6**	**44.0**	**32.1**	P/B Ratio	**1.5**	52 Wk Hi-Low	**25.00-19.25**
Book Value	**608.6**	**552.9**	**574.4**	**410.3**	Yield %	**4.0**	Market Cap	**US$559.7mil**

Address	**One Yonge St.**	Tel	**416-869-4010**	Exchange	**TSE**	Chief Executive	**David A. Galloway**
	Toronto, ON M5E 1P9	Fax	**416-869-4183**	Ticker	**TS.B**	Chairman	**John Evans**

TransAlta

Industry: **Electrical Utilities - All**

TransAlta Corporation operates electricity-generation and -distribution businesses through two main subsidiaries, TransAlta Energy and TransAlta Utilities. TransAlta Energy runs two cogeneration plants in Ontario, and has a 27% interest in a hydroelectric facility in Argentina and interests in two electricity-distribution companies in New Zealand. TransAlta Utilities services 1.7 million customers through a distribution network of more than 100,000 kilometers of power lines. It supplies approximately two thirds of all electricity used by utility customers in Alberta.

	C$ mil 12/92	12/93	12/94	US$mil 12/94				
Sales	**1,101.6**	**1,208.3**	**1,261.0**	**921.1**	P/E Ratio	**12.0**	Price (9/30/95)	**14.13**
Net Income	**182.5**	**183.8**	**225.9**	**165.0**	P/B Ratio	**1.5**	52 Wk Hi-Low	**14.75-13.25**
Book Value	**1,446.0**	**1,477.6**	**1,515.0**	**1,082.1**	Yield %	**6.9**	Market Cap	**US$1,674.1mil**

Address **110 12th Ave. S.W. Calgary, AB T2P 2M1**
Tel **403-267-7301**
Fax **403-267-2559**
Exchange **TSE**
Ticker **TA**
President & CEO **Ken F. McCready**
Chairman **Harry G. Schaefer**

TransCanada Pipelines

Industry: **Pipelines**

TransCanada Pipelines is one of North America's leading natural-gas transporters. Its mainline gas-transmission system crosses four provinces. The company is affiliated with three other Canadian and U.S. pipelines, giving TransCanada access to four of North America's major gas markets. TransCanada's pipelines deliver approximately 2,100 billion cubic feet of gas each year. The firm exports more than 40% of its production. It also operates businesses in gas marketing, power generation, gas-liquids extraction, gas storage, and carbon-black production.

	C$ mil 12/92	12/93	12/94	US$mil 12/94				
Sales	**3,757.5**	**4,242.1**	**5,204.2**	**3,801.5**	P/E Ratio	**11.1**	Price (9/30/95)	**17.75**
Net Income	**328.7**	**355.6**	**358.6**	**261.9**	P/B Ratio	**1.4**	52 Wk Hi-Low	**18.75-16.75**
Book Value	**2,098.2**	**2,314.3**	**2,536.4**	**1,811.7**	Yield %	**5.3**	Market Cap	**US$2,448.1mil**

Address **111 5th Ave. S.W. Calgary, AB T2P 3Y6**
Tel **403-267-6100**
Fax **403-267-6444**
Exchange **TSE**
Ticker **TRP**
President & CEO **George W. Watson**
Chairman **Gerald J. Maier**

Trimac

Industry: **Trucking**

Trimac provides bulk trucking services, truck leasing and rentals, contract-drilling services, and environmental services to industrial customers. It also has interests in oil and gas exploration, oil-field equipment service, engineering and construction, and information technology. Trimac's core transport division manages a fleet of almost 4,000 trailers, operating from 96 terminals. It also owns Kenting, an oil- and natural-gas- drilling contractor. Trimac's 48%-owned BOVAR and wholly owned TriWaste subsidiaries operate its environmental and waste-management businesses.

	C$ mil 12/92	12/93	12/94	US$mil 12/94				
Sales	**476.1**	**618.8**	**687.2**	**502.0**	P/E Ratio	**11.2**	Price (9/30/95)	**11.38**
Net Income	**26.8**	**27.4**	**41.5**	**30.3**	P/B Ratio	**1.5**	52 Wk Hi-Low	**15.63-10.00**
Book Value	**211.1**	**277.9**	**314.1**	**224.4**	Yield %	**1.3**	Market Cap	**US$344.9mil**

Address **Ste. 2100, 800 Fifth Ave. S.W. Calgary, AB T2P 2P9**
Tel **403-298-5100**
Fax **403-298-5258**
Exchange **TSE**
Ticker **TMA**
President & CEO **Jeffrey J. McCaig**
Chairman **John R. McCaig**

United Dominion Industries

Industry: **Industrial - Diversified**

United Dominion Industries is a major industrial enterprise consisting of businesses that provide proprietary, manufactured products and engineering for customers worldwide. As of Dec. 31, 1994, the company employed 12,282 people at 55 locations in 14 countries. Its products include compacting equipment, fluid-handling equipment, cast-iron boilers, submersible water pumps, and precision components for the aerospace industry. The company manufactures Ceco and Windsor doors and door systems. In 1994, the company generated 83% of its revenues in the U.S.

	$ mil 12/92	12/93	12/94	US$mil 12/94				
Sales	**1,710.7**	**1,826.8**	**2,036.4**	**2,036.4**	P/E Ratio	**15.5**	Price (9/30/95)	**32.13**
Net Income	**25.7**	**39.8**	**62.1**	**62.1**	P/B Ratio	**1.8**	52 Wk Hi-Low	**34.00-24.50**
Book Value	**398.4**	**412.9**	**527.2**	**527.2**	Yield %	**0.5**	Market Cap	**US$945.6mil**

Address **2300 First Union Ctr., 301 S. College St., Charlotte, NC 28202**
Tel **704-347-6800**
Fax **704-347-6900**
Exchange **TSE**
Ticker **UDI**
President **Jan K. Ver Hagen**
Chairman & CEO **William R. Holland**

Videotron

Industry: **Broadcasting**

Le Groupe Vidéotron offers cable television, broadcasting, and telephone services in Canada, the United Kingdom, and the United States. Its core business is a Quebec-based cable network serving 1.1 million subscribers in Canada. Videotron Holdings, its U.K. subsidiary, maintains a fiber-optic network that provides cable television and telephone services mainly in the London area. The company purchased licenses to provide wireless cable to homes in San Francisco, Spokane, and Tampa. It owns 40% of Télé-Métropole, a French-language broadcaster in Quebec.

	C$ mil 08/92	08/93	08/94	US$mil 08/94				
Sales	**539.2**	**583.7**	**641.0**	**472.4**	P/E Ratio	**90.9**	Price (9/30/95)	**10.00**
Net Income	**12.6**	**25.1**	**20.5**	**15.1**	P/B Ratio	**2.0**	52 Wk Hi-Low	**13.00-9.75**
Book Value	**448.5**	**416.5**	**550.3**	**401.7**	Yield %	**0.6**	Market Cap	**US$397.0mil**

Address **300 Viger Ave. E. Montreal, PQ H2X 3W4**
Tel **514-281-1232**
Fax **514-985-8425**
Exchange **MSE**
Ticker **VDO**
President **Serge Guoin**
Chairman & CEO **André Chagnon**

Wascana Energy

Industry: **Oil - Secondary**

Wascana Energy is involved in crude-oil and natural-gas exploration, production, transportation, marketing, and technology development. Its daily production average is 43,600 barrels of crude oil and natural-gas liquids, and 197 million cubic feet of natural gas. Wascana has drilling activities at 33 exploration wells and 260 development wells. Other activities include waterflood recovery, steam-injection stimulation, environmental restoration, heavy crude-oil processing, and oil pipeline maintenance, transportation, and storage.

C$ mil	12/92 R	12/93	12/94	US$mil 12/94				
Sales	**389.1**	**389.3**	**437.6**	**319.6**	P/E Ratio	**19.6**	Price (9/30/95)	**12.13**
Net Income	**-39.0**	**-33.7**	**49.0**	**35.8**	P/B Ratio	**1.7**	52 Wk Hi-Low	**13.13-9.38**
Book Value	**459.5**	**522.4**	**573.9**	**409.9**	Yield %	**0.0**	Market Cap	**US$719.0mil**

Address **1777 Victoria Ave.**
Regina, SK S4P 3C4
Tel **306-781-8200**
Fax **306-781-8364**
Exchange **MSE**
Ticker **WE**
President & CEO **Frank W. Proto**
Chairman **Theodore M. Hanlon**

R=Restated.

West Fraser Timber

Industry: **Forest Products**

West Fraser Timber Company harvests forests and produces solid wood products, wood chips, linerboard, kraft paper, and newsprint. It operates six sawmills and three pulp and paper mills in British Columbia and Alberta. West Fraser is currently constructing a new sawmill on the western coast that will begin operations in early 1995. The company has a 49% interest in a plant that remanufactures shop-grade lumber from one of its sawmills into specialty wood products. It also operates 28 Revelstoke Homes Centres and three Revy Home & Garden superstores.

C$ mil	12/92	12/93	12/94	US$mil 12/94				
Sales	**677.3**	**904.0**	**1,280.5**	**935.4**	P/E Ratio	**6.1**	Price (9/30/95)	**31.88**
Net Income	**10.2**	**53.4**	**118.5**	**86.6**	P/B Ratio	**1.4**	52 Wk Hi-Low	**38.75-31.00**
Book Value	**276.0**	**393.6**	**532.2**	**380.1**	Yield %	**1.3**	Market Cap	**US$558.7mil**

Address **1000-1100 Melville St.**
Vancouver, BC V6E 4A6
Tel **604-895-2700**
Fax **604-681-6061**
Exchange **TSE**
Ticker **WFT**
President & CEO **Henry H. Ketcham III**
Chairman **Henry H. Ketcham, Jr.**

Westcoast Energy

Industry: **Pipelines**

Westcoast Energy distributes natural gas throughout Canada. Its Centra Gas, Union Gas, and Pacific Northern Gas subsidiaries distribute more than 1 trillion cubic feet of natural gas to 1.2 million customers. The company's western-pipeline division uses 3,000 miles of pipeline to transport nearly 580 billion cubic feet of natural gas throughout British Columbia and into the United States. In addition, Westcoast holds stakes in two power-generation plants in Ontario and one in British Columbia. It also operates NGX Canada, a computerized natural-gas trading exchange.

C$ mil	12/92	12/93	12/94	US$mil 12/94				
Sales	**1,780.0**	**3,627.0**	**3,712.0**	**2,711.5**	P/E Ratio	**10.9**	Price (9/30/95)	**19.88**
Net Income	**-64.3**	**158.0**	**173.0**	**126.4**	P/B Ratio	**1.2**	52 Wk Hi-Low	**23.38-19.88**
Book Value	**1,020.9**	**1,345.0**	**1,448.0**	**1,034.3**	Yield %	**4.5**	Market Cap	**US$1,265.5mil**

Address **1333 W. Georgia St.**
Vancouver, BC V6E 3K9
Tel **604-691-5500**
Fax **604-691-5702**
Exchange **TSE**
Ticker **W**
President **Arthur H. Willms**
Chairman & CEO **Michael E.J. Phelps**

WIC

Industry: **Broadcasting**

WIC Western International Communications (WIC) is a communication, broadcast, and entertainment firm offering television, pay-television, radio, and satellite-network services. It owns eight television and 11 radio stations in Canada and licenses Superchannel, MovieMax!, and Home Theatre, a pay-per-view service, in western Canada. WIC also produces films, television programs, and commercials. It owns 52.6% of Canadian Satellite Communications, and 50% of the Family Channel. It also owns the rights to CellularVision television and radio cellular-distribution technology.

C$ mil	08/92	08/93	08/94	US$mil 08/94				
Sales	**295.8**	**343.4**	**392.2**	**289.0**	P/E Ratio	**50.6**	Price (9/30/95)	**20.25**
Net Income	**3.8**	**3.0**	**9.8**	**7.2**	P/B Ratio	**1.6**	52 Wk Hi-Low	**21.63-13.38**
Book Value	**239.3**	**300.2**	**300.4**	**219.3**	Yield %	**2.7**	Market Cap	**US$352.2mil**

Address **1960-505 Burrard St.**
Vancouver, BC V7X 1M6
Tel **604-687-2844**
Fax **604-687-4118**
Exchange **TSE**
Ticker **WIC.B**
President & CEO **Douglas M. Holtby**
Chairman **Frank A. Griffiths**

Denmark

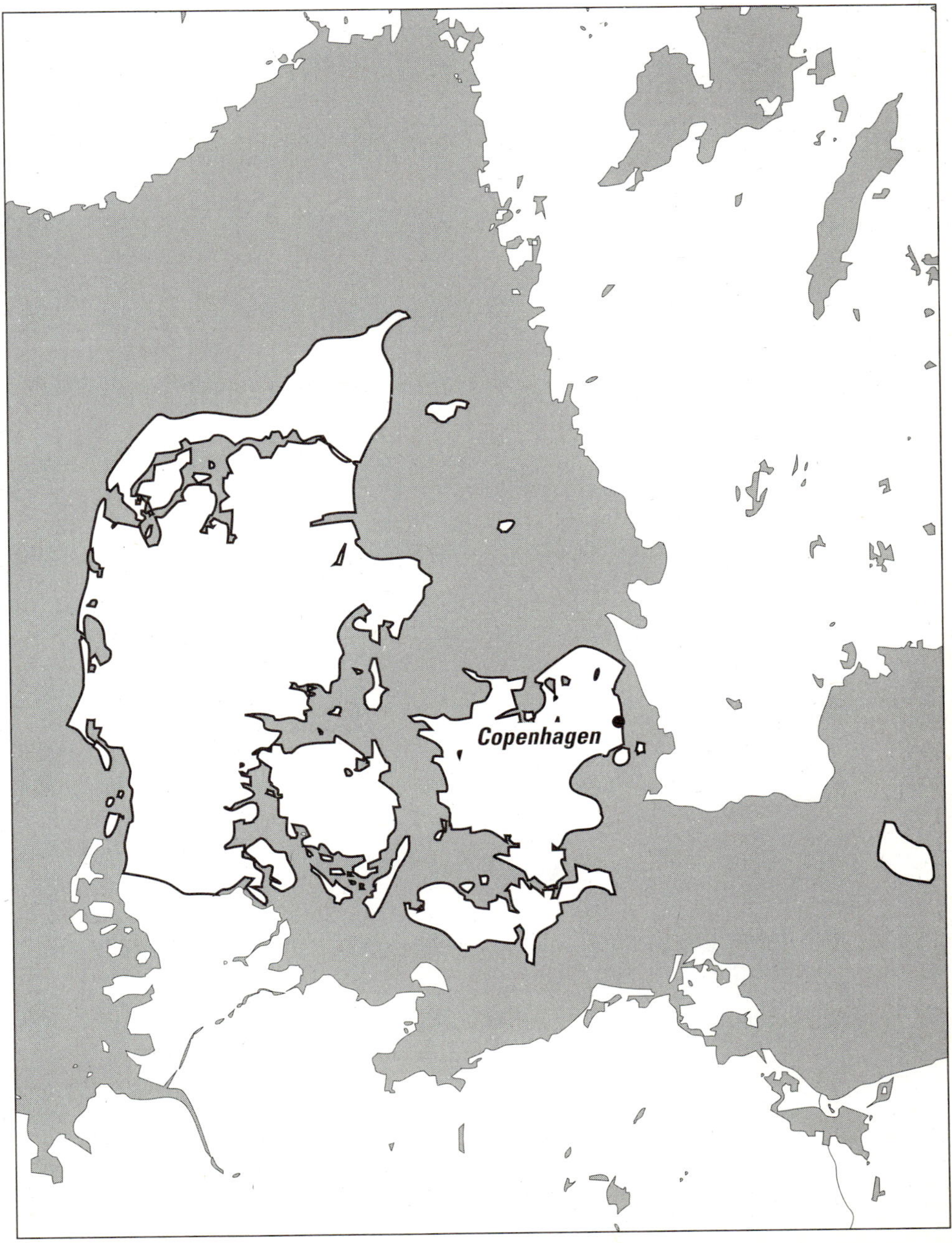

Denmark

Xueling Lin, Copenhagen

Local Trading Hours	Time Difference from New York	Population (Est. 7/95)
9:00-3:30	6 hours ahead of EST	5,227,862

The Danish stock exchange is gearing up for a major reform aimed at recapturing trade from London and opening the market to a greater number of foreign players. If these modernization efforts succeed, traders say, it will boost Copenhagen's chances of holding onto its title as a significant regional player.

Although only tenth largest in European terms, Copenhagen ranks second among the five Nordic stock exchanges, behind Sweden's. However, smaller markets such as Copenhagen have been under serious pressure in recent years because of increasing liberalization of the European financial markets.

And while Copenhagen's share turnover at market prices amounted to 174.4 billion Danish kroner in 1994, up 13% from 1993, the stock exchange says investors are already being lured away by the high-liquidity attractions of London and even neighboring Stockholm.

The reform, which will be in place by 1996, is aimed at opening up the market and making it more competitive. The stock exchange will lose its monopoly, but at the same time it will be allowed to convert to a limited liability company from its current status as a self-governing semi-official body. According to the stock exchange, this change will allow it "..greater commercial freedom, which will be a decisive factor in the tougher competition of the future."

At the same time, the stock exchange plans to upgrade its electronic trading system, Electra, which was introduced in 1987, to make trading and information facilities more flexible and cheaper. The stock exchange got rid of its trading floor back in 1987 and all trading is decentralized, taking place in stockbrokers' offices through terminals.

In fact, the stock exchange claims even with its Electra system it is technologically ahead of many other European bourses, since the system is able to handle trading in virtually every instrument, including bonds, shares, warrants, investment certificates, futures and options. Share certificates also disappeared some time ago, with the securities market going totally scripless in 1988.

Dow Jones Denmark Equity Market Index Performance

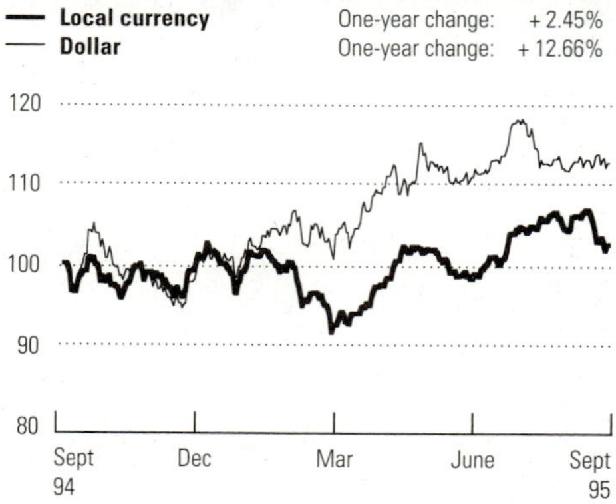

The stock exchange is also eager see more foreign participants; of the 26 stock broking companies registered as members of the Copenhagen Stock Exchange at the end of

Gross Domestic Product (94)	Three-year Average GDP Growth (92-94)	Main Industries	Consumer Price Index (93-94)	Monetary Unit	Exchange Rate (9/95)
$163.68 billion	2.2%	Shipping, manufacturing and processing, banking and insurance, food and beverages, retailing	+ 2.0%	Danish krone	DKK5.54 to US$1.00

June 1995, three are Swedish-owned, one is Dutch, one French, one British and the rest Danish.

Trading hours run from 9 a.m. to 3:30 p.m. local time, a far cry from the 17th century when the stock exchange first started and trading lasted a mere one and a half hours. However, latter-day stock brokers have been clamoring for longer trading hours and the stock exchange is considering extending its opening by half an hour in the afternoon session to bring Copenhagen in line with its Nordic counterparts, Stockholm and Oslo, which close at 4 p.m.

Although a total of 252 companies are listed on the Copenhagen stock exchange, the bulk of interest tends to center on the 20 companies in the key KFX index, which acts as a benchmark index for tracking highly capitalized, high liquidity stocks.

The index includes Denmark's two biggest banks, a leading international shipping group, a bio-engineering company, two telecommunication companies, three food and drink companies, three conglomerates, an airline holding company and an airport authority, and several industrial and service companies. Together, these twenty companies accounted for about 46% of the market's total capitalization of 345 billion Danish kroner at the end of 1994.

Topping the list in terms of size is the A.P. Moeller shipping group, more commonly known internationally as Maersk. Moeller's two companies D/S 1912 and D/S Svendborg were by far the largest companies listed on the stock exchange with market values of 24.9 billion kroner and 24.8 billion kroner respectively. However, because of their unusually high per-share price—a single share cost 167,000 kroner or about $27,800 in mid-1995—they are considered the domain of a small number of heavy-weight institutional investors.

Ten Largest Capitalized Companies
as of 9/30/95

Stock	Market Cap. US$Mil
Novo Nordisk	3,898,570.4
Den Danske Bank	3,362,743.7
Tele Danmark	3,269,926.9
Danisco	2,418,252.7
D/S Svendborg	2,186,371.8
D/S 1912	2,144,404.3
Unidanmark	2,041,056.0
Carlsberg	1,731,029.6
Codan	887,274.4
FLS Industries	690,931.4

A significant new player though entered the market in 1994, with Tele Danmark, the national telecommunications operator, making its debut in a partial privatization carried out by the Danish state.

The launch of Tele Danmark's "B" category share was the largest single share issue ever made on the Copenhagen Stock Exchange, attracting a surge of foreign investor interest. The share issue gave the telecommunication operator gross proceeds of 19.3 billion kroner and made Tele Danmark the second largest company by capitalization listed on the stock exchange, after the Moeller shipping group.

Interest in Tele Danmark was so keen the company managed to oust Novo Nordisk, a bio-engineering group, from its traditional place as the most actively traded share on the Copenhagen stock exchange in 1994.

Analysts also estimate foreign share ownership in Denmark has risen sharply on the back of high-profile new share listings such as Tele Danmark, with 10% to 15% of the market held by foreign investors in 1995 compared with 6% in 1993.

Outside the KFX companies, second-tier stocks fall into a category called "liquid and lower turnover shares." The only three notable shares for foreign investors being Bang&Olufsen, the sophisticated hi-fi and television manufacturer, Codan Forsikring, Denmark's largest insurance group and Oticon, a hearing aid manufacturer.

Finally, there is a "stock exchange 3" which is a residual category of very small, illiquid issues, which have novelty interest such as two Danish football clubs.

Recent trends indicate Denmark's strong economic recovery since 1993, with a projected growth in gross domestic product of 3.9% in 1995 and 2.9% in 1996, will keep industrial stocks strong as corporate sales continue to boom. At the same time, with bond yields heading lower in 1995, analysts also predict interest rate-sensitive shares, such as banks and insurance companies, will rally.

However, the picture looks less rosy for dollar-sensitive shares, which took a heavy bashing in the first half of 1995. Some of the blue chips that have been hardest hit by the dollar's woes: Moeller, which is dollar vulnerable because international shipping rates are quoted in the U.S. currency; Novo Nordisk, which is a big insulin supplier in the U.S.; and ISS, which is a leading U.S. cleaning services group although based in Copenhagen.

Foreign investors, though, will be pleased the value of their Danish share holdings got a lift from a sharply stronger Danish krone in the first half of 1995.

On the tax front, there is no turnover tax for foreign investors, and the capital transfer tax was abolished in 1993. There are also no currency restrictions.

Danish companies pay dividends only annually, with dividends subject to a 30% withholding tax. However, if a double taxation agreement exists between Denmark and the country in which an investor lives, the non-resident can apply for a refund of the tax.

Aalborg Portland Cement

Industry: **Building Materials**

Aalborg Portland Holding operates as a holding company with subsidiaries in the cement-manufacturing and building materials industries. It owns 50% of cement-manufacturer Aalborg Portland and 49% of calcium-carbonate producer Faxe Kal. Its wholly-owned subsidiary Dansk Eternit makes roofing materials and wall coverings. Aalborg Portland Holding owns 35% of Danish company NKT, which manufactures power-supply and telecommunication cables, electrical-installation equipment, and vacuum cleaners.

DKK mil	12/92	12/93	12/94	US$mil 12/94				
Sales	**2,658.0**	**2,691.0**	**2,534.1**	**400.7**	P/E Ratio	**8.7**	Price (9/30/95)	**530.00**
Net Income	**108.0**	**122.0**	**194.9**	**30.8**	P/B Ratio	**0.7**	52 Wk Hi-Low	**650.00-430.00**
Book Value	**2,003.0**	**2,053.0**	**2,190.3**	**359.6**	Yield %	**2.8**	Market Cap	**US$214.4mil**

Address **44 Rordalsvej**
9100 Aalborg
Tel **098-16-77-77**
Fax **098-10-11-86**
ADR
SEDOL No. **4001979**
President & CEO **Ib Christensen**
Chairman **Christian Kjær**

Bikuben

Industry: **Banks - Regional**

Sparekassen Bikuben is a savings bank that provides mortgage-financing advice and offers credit, finance, and international-banking services to its one million private and corporate customers. Bikuben has 382 branches in Denmark, branches in Frankfurt and London, and subsidiaries in Dublin. Its subsidiaries provide banking, leasing, insurance, property, and investment services. Its wholly-owned Luxembourg-based Bikuben International subsidiary offers private banking, arranges loans for Danish companies, and provides currency and securities trading.

DKK mil	12/92	12/93	12/94	US$mil 12/94				
Revenues	**10,350.0**	**10,245.0**	**7,839.0**	**1,239.4**	P/E Ratio	**NMF**	Price (9/30/95)	**187.00**
Net Income	**-1,196.0**	**177.0**	**-1,050.4**	**-166.1**	P/B Ratio	**0.9**	52 Wk Hi-Low	**203.00-165.00**
Book Value	**4,428.0**	**4,519.0**	**3,797.3**	**623.5**	Yield %	**0.0**	Market Cap	**US$647.0mil**

Address **Silkegade 8**
1113 Copenhagen
Tel **033-12-01-33**
Fax **033-12-09-33**
ADR
SEDOL No. **4833194**
CEO **Henrik Thufason**
Chairman **Aage Spang-Hanssen**

Carlsberg

Industry: **Distillers & Brewers**

Carlsberg is a brewing company that also has interests in bottling, fine-ceramics, silver, and crystal operations. Its best-selling alcohol products are Carlsberg and Tuborg beers. The company generates approximately 80% of its beer revenues outside Europe and has brewing operations in 40 countries. Carlsberg's wholly-owned subsidiary Dadeko produces Coca-Cola and Fanta beverages in Denmark. Royal Copenhagen, its industrial-arts subsidiary, manufactures ceramics, silver, and crystal for Carlsberg. The company generates half of its overall sales from exports.

DKK mil	09/92	09/93	09/94	US$mil 09/94				
Sales	**14,957.0**	**15,595.0**	**16,919.0**	**2,607.7**	P/E Ratio M	**21.8**	Price (9/30/95) M	**272.00**
Net Income	**854.0**	**910.0**	**802.0**	**123.6**	P/B Ratio M	**2.4**	52 Wk Hi-Low M	**287.00-242.00**
Book Value	**6,422.0**	**7,094.0**	**7,288.0**	**1,196.7**	Yield % M	**1.1**	Market Cap M	**US$1,731.0mil**

Address **100 Vesterfælledvej**
1799 Copenhagen
Tel **033-27-33-27**
Fax **033-27-47-11**
ADR
SEDOL No. **4169208**
President & CEO **Poul J. Svanholm**
Chairman **Poul Chr. Matthiessen**

M=Multiple issues in index; reflects most active.

Codan

Industry: **Insurance - Full Line**

Codan Insurance Group (Codan Forsikring), the largest Danish insurer based on premium income, provides life insurance and general insurance. In 1994, the company's life-insurance and general-insurance operations accounted for 23% and 44%, respectively, of gross premium income. Codan offers personal accident, motor, fire, marine, commercial, transport, and aviation insurance. It also manages pension plans and operates a bank that acts as a stockbrokerage. Its wholly-owned Fösäkringsaktiebolaget Holmia subsidiary sells personal-insurance products in Sweden.

DKK mil	12/92	12/93	12/94	US$mil 12/94				
Revenues	**2,754.0**	**12,088.0**	**8,226.0**	**1,300.6**	P/E Ratio	**NMF**	Price (9/30/95)	**725.00**
Net Income	**-74.0**	**816.0**	**2.0**	**0.3**	P/B Ratio	**1.1**	52 Wk Hi-Low	**1,130.0-700.0**
Book Value	**4,876.0**	**4,733.0**	**4,633.0**	**760.8**	Yield %	**4.1**	Market Cap	**US$887.3mil**

Address **Codanhus, 60 Gl. Kongevej**
1790 Copenhagen
Tel **031-21-21-21**
Fax **031-21-21-22**
ADR
SEDOL No. **4324858**
President **--**
Chairman **Henrik Christrup**

Danisco

Industry: **Other Food**

Danisco is the largest Danish producer and supplier of ingredients, packaging, and technology (mainly processing equipment for dairy products) for the world food industry. The company processes sugar at two plants in Germany, and produces and distributes wines, spirits, and frozen foods throughout the world. It also manufactures a range of plastic and paper packaging, and supplies industrial food technology to food-packaging companies. Sugar operations generate more than 40% of Danisco's revenues. Exports, primarily to Europe, generate nearly two thirds of its sales.

DKK mil	04/93	04/94	04/95	US$mil 04/95				
Sales	**13,027.0**	**12,844.0**	**14,192.6**	**2,343.6**	P/E Ratio	**13.2**	Price (9/30/95)	**242.00**
Net Income	**809.0**	**830.0**	**1,014.8**	**167.6**	P/B Ratio	**1.9**	52 Wk Hi-Low	**257.00-186.00**
Book Value	**6,134.0**	**6,652.0**	**7,197.3**	**1,325.5**	Yield %	**1.3**	Market Cap	**US$2,418.3mil**

Address **Langebrogade 1**
1001 Copenhagen
Tel **031-95-17-00**
Fax **031-54-36-50**
ADR
SEDOL No. **4155586**
CEO **Palle Marcus**
Chairman **Hugo Schroder**

Den Danske Bank

Industry: **Banks - Money Center**

Den Danske Bank is one of Denmark's largest banks. It offers retail and corporate banking. Its retail business serves more than 2 million customers. The bank's wholly-owned subsidiary Danske Kredit Realkreditaktieselskab provides mortgages for individuals and corporations. Den Danske Bank offers pensions and life insurance, and has a 78% stake in Denmark's largest general-insurer, Baltica, and wholly-owns nonlife insurer Danske Phonix. Den Danske Bank has operations in the United Kingdom, Germany, Luxembourg, the United States, Singapore, and Hong Kong.

DKK mil	12/92	12/93	12/94	US$mil 12/94				
Revenues	**32,619.0**	**31,197.0**	**24,972.5**	**3,948.2**	P/E Ratio	**23.5**	Price (9/30/95)	**352.00**
Net Income	**-1,584.0**	**2,402.0**	**816.1**	**129.0**	P/B Ratio	**0.9**	52 Wk Hi-Low	**389.00-296.00**
Book Value	**18,287.0**	**20,042.0**	**20,310.2**	**3,335.0**	Yield %	**3.4**	Market Cap	**US$3,362.7mil**

Address **2-12 Holmens Kanal**
1092 Copenhagen
Tel **033-44-00-00**
Fax **031-18-58-73**
ADR **DEAFY**
SEDOL No. **4262925**
President **--**
Chairman **Poul J. Svanholm**

D/S 1912

Industry: **Marine Transportation**

Dampskibsselskabet af 1912 operates a shipping, oil, and natural-gas partnership with Dampskibsselskabet Svendborg under the Maersk name. The partnership transports products such as oil, natural gas, ore, coal, grain, and timber. It operates container and supply vessels, tankers, gas carriers, and drilling rigs. The group operates 58 tankers and gas vessels and 94 container vessels. The partnership owns 39% of Dansk Undergrunds Consortium, which produced 9.2 million tons of oil and sold 4.3 billion cubic meters of natural gas in 1994.

DKK mil	12/92	12/93	12/94	US$mil 12/94				
Sales	**109.0**	**119.0**	**123.0**	**19.4**	P/E Ratio M	**127.8**	Price (9/30/95) M	**110,000**
Net Income	**165.0**	**188.0**	**186.0**	**29.4**	P/B Ratio M	**15.2**	52 Wk Hi-Low M	**121,000-96,000**
Book Value	**1,411.0**	**1,486.0**	**1,559.0**	**256.0**	Yield % M	**0.5**	Market Cap M	**US$2,144.4mil**

Address **Esplanaden 50**
1098 Copenhagen
Tel **033-14-15-14**
Fax **033-93-15-14**
ADR
SEDOL No. **4248765**
Managing Owner **A.P. Moller D/S**
Chairman **M. McKinney Moller**

M=Multiple issues in index; reflects most active.

D/S Svendborg

Industry: **Marine Transportation**

Dampskibsselskabet Svendborg is engaged in international shipping and in oil and natural-gas production. The firm operates a fleet of tankers and liners through a 50/50 partnership with Dampskibsselskabet 1912. The partnership operates container and supply vessels, tankers, and gas carriers, as well as drilling rigs. It entered into agreements with petroleum companies Shell and Texaco to transport 7 billion cubic meters of natural gas per year. It inaugurated new container routes to Central and South America and the Caribbean, and opened offices in China in 1994.

DKK mil	12/92	12/93	12/94	US$mil 12/94				
Sales	**109.0**	**119.0**	**123.0**	**19.4**	P/E Ratio M	**106.0**	Price (9/30/95) M	**161,500**
Net Income	**188.0**	**210.0**	**227.0**	**35.9**	P/B Ratio M	**12.4**	52 Wk Hi-Low M	**174,000-137,274**
Book Value	**1,731.0**	**1,829.0**	**1,944.0**	**319.2**	Yield % M	**0.5**	Market Cap M	**US$2,186.4mil**

Address **Esplanaden 50**
1098 Copenhagen
Tel **033-14-15-14**
Fax **033-93-15-14**
ADR
SEDOL No. **4253059**
Managing Owner **A.P. Moller D/S**
Chairman **M. McKinney Moller**

M=Multiple issues in index; reflects most active.

FLS Industries

Industry: **Industrial - Diversified**

FLS Industries operates as a holding company with building-materials, engineering, transportation, and manufacturing subsidiaries. Its 50%-owned subsidiary Aalborg Portland produces cement, and its wholly-owned subsidiaries F.L. Smidth and Fuller construct cement plants. FLS's DanTransport subsidiaries provide international transport and forwarding services. FLS subsidiaries also manufacture industrial packaging and perforated-metal products for the building industry, and provide aircraft-maintenance services. Roughly 40% of FLS' subsidiaries' sales are exports.

DKK mil	12/92	12/93	12/94	US$mil 12/94				
Sales	**12,080.0**	**12,143.0**	**14,477.0**	**2,288.9**	P/E Ratio	**10.7**	Price (9/30/95)	**492.00**
Net Income	**275.0**	**28.0**	**278.0**	**44.0**	P/B Ratio	**1.7**	52 Wk Hi-Low	**580.00-380.00**
Book Value	**2,161.0**	**2,472.0**	**2,632.0**	**432.2**	Yield %	**2.4**	Market Cap	**US$690.9mil**

Address **Vigerslev Allé 77**
2500 Valby
Tel **036-18-18-00**
Fax **036-30-44-41**
ADR
SEDOL No. **4816203**
President & CEO **Birger Riisager**
Chairman **Christian Arnstedt**

Great Nordic

Industry: **Communications Technology**

GN Great Nordic is a telecommunication and data-communication company. It operates international telecommunication networks and manufactures pay phones, headsets, and hearing aids. GN makes electronic measuring instruments for data-communication and telecommunication applications and has real-estate interests. It owns 36% of SONOFON, which operates Denmark's mobile-telephone network. GN owns U.S.-based Laser Precision Corp., which makes fiber-optics and test equipment. In 1994 GN generated 17% of its sales in North America and 10% in Asia.

DKK mil	12/92	12/93	12/94	US$mil 12/94				
Sales	**1,336.0**	**1,622.0**	**1,700.0**	**268.8**	P/E Ratio	**17.3**	Price (9/30/95)	**415.00**
Net Income	**33.0**	**147.0**	**150.8**	**23.8**	P/B Ratio	**1.3**	52 Wk Hi-Low	**575.00-380.00**
Book Value	**1,567.0**	**1,640.0**	**1,882.4**	**309.1**	Yield %	**2.9**	Market Cap	**US$447.1mil**

Address **Kongens Nytorv 26**
1015 Copenhagen
Tel **033-12-00-88**
Fax **033-12-03-89**
ADR
SEDOL No. **4357627**
President & CEO **Thomas F. Duer**
Chairman **Erik B. Rasmussen**

Chr. Hansen

Industry: **Other Food**

Christian Hansen's Laboratorium is a biotechnology company. Sales to the food industry of products such as enzymes, bacteria cultures, colors, and natural flavors generate more than 65% of the company's revenue. The company also manufactures growth stimulants for animal feed and biotechnical products for the agriculture market. Hansen's is also involved in the diagnosis and treatment of allergic diseases. Its ALK subsidiary manufactures Profylac for the treatment of milk allergies. Hansen's generates more than 95% of its revenues outside Denmark.

DKK mil	08/92	08/93	08/94	US$mil 08/94				
Sales	**1,118.0**	**1,496.0**	**1,588.9**	**243.2**	P/E Ratio	**18.8**	Price (9/30/95)	**525.00**
Net Income	**98.0**	**120.0**	**141.0**	**21.6**	P/B Ratio	**2.3**	52 Wk Hi-Low	**560.00-440.00**
Book Value	**766.0**	**1,071.0**	**1,149.9**	**184.9**	Yield %	**3.8**	Market Cap	**US$429.7mil**

Address	**Boge Allé 10-12**	Tel	**045-76-76-76**	ADR		President & CEO	**Poul Hansen**
	2970 Horsholm	Fax	**045-76-55-76**	SEDOL No.	**4173179**	Chairman	**Sven D. Madsen**

ISS

Industry: **General Industrial & Commercial Services**

International Service System (ISS) provides cleaning and maintenance services for commercial, retail, and industrial clients in Europe and North and Latin America. It offers linen-distribution and security services to hospitals, and provides airport and aircraft cleaning services. ISS manages catering and snack-bar services for public and private organizations, and offers landscape and grounds maintenance to golf courses, hotels, and other commercial customers. In 1994, ISS generated 43% of its revenues in North America and 24% in European countries outside of Scandinavia.

DKK mil	12/92	12/93	12/94	US$mil 12/94				
Sales	**11,356.0**	**13,307.0**	**14,232.5**	**2,250.2**	P/E Ratio M	**15.4**	Price (9/30/95) M	**151.00**
Net Income	**266.0**	**462.0**	**288.4**	**45.6**	P/B Ratio M	**2.5**	52 Wk Hi-Low M	**188.00-141.00**
Book Value	**998.0**	**1,357.0**	**1,765.9**	**290.0**	Yield % M	**1.5**	Market Cap M	**US$104.7mil**

Address	**Kongevejen 195**	Tel	**045-41-08-11**	ADR		President & MD	**Poul Andreassen**
	2840 Holte	Fax	**045-41-08-88**	SEDOL No.	**4442631**	Chairman	**Arne Madsen**

M=Multiple issues in index; reflects most active.

Jyske Bank

Industry: **Banks - Regional**

Jyske Bank offers retail and corporate banking, mortgage lending, and insurance products. The bank also offers leasing services, currency exchange, and provides investment advice. It has roughly DKK 48 billion in assets, and it generated a net profit of DKK 90 million in 1994. Its Jyske Bank subsidiary in Gibraltar provides portfolio management, foreign-currency loans, foreign-exchange, and investment services. Its subsidiaries operate in the areas of real estate, data processing, banking, and finance. Jyske Bank has subsidiary banks located throughout Europe.

DKK mil	12/92	12/93	12/94	US$mil 12/94				
Revenues	**5,424.0**	**5,702.0**	**4,491.4**	**710.1**	P/E Ratio	**38.9**	Price (9/30/95)	**347.00**
Net Income	**-924.0**	**423.0**	**80.3**	**12.7**	P/B Ratio	**1.1**	52 Wk Hi-Low	**390.93-320.67**
Book Value	**2,569.0**	**2,857.0**	**2,837.1**	**465.9**	Yield %	**1.8**	Market Cap	**US$563.7mil**

Address	**Vestergade 8-16**	Tel	**089-22-22-22**	ADR		Mng Dir & CEO	**Kaj Steenkjær**
	8600 Silkeborg	Fax	**089-22-24-96**	SEDOL No.	**4479963**	Chairman	**Leon Rasmussen**

Korn-og Foderstof

Industry: **Other Food**

Korn-og Foderstof Kompagniet(KFK) develops and manufactures feed for livestock, and sells feedstuffs, cereals, seed corn, salt, oil, and coal. Other activities include the production of compounds, arable products, and fertilizers. KFK sold nearly 3.5 million tons of seed, fertilizer, and feedstuffs in 1994. Its chain of laboratories perform roughly 200,000 tests every year on raw materials and compounds used in animal feed. KFK controls more than half of the Danish market for broiler feeds, and is its largest producer of day-old chicks for the poultry market.

DKK mil	12/92	12/93	12/94	US$mil 12/94				
Sales	**6,815.0**	**7,254.0**	**6,762.1**	**1,069.1**	P/E Ratio	**20.2**	Price (9/30/95)	**250.00**
Net Income	**169.0**	**203.0**	**150.6**	**23.8**	P/B Ratio	**1.8**	52 Wk Hi-Low	**250.00-192.00**
Book Value	**1,906.0**	**2,061.0**	**2,173.3**	**356.9**	Yield %	**1.1**	Market Cap	**US$548.1mil**

Address	**Groendalsvej 1**	Tel	**089-47-71-00**	ADR		Managing Director	**Albert Beckenkamp**
	8260 Viby	Fax	**086-14-10-85**	SEDOL No.	**4536738**	Chairman	**Trygve Refvem**

J Lauritzen

Industry: **Marine Transportation**

J. Lauritzen Holding is a holding company with interests in shipbuilding, shipping, industry, and transportation. Its wholly-owned subsidiaries include J. Lauritzen AS, which operates over 100 vessels and offshore units to transport oil, bulk cargo, and other products; DFDS, which operates Scandinavian Seaways; Danyard, which builds and repairs cargo vessels; Sabroe, which manufactures freezer and refrigeration systems for ships and industry; and Aalborg Industries, which develops, manufactures, and services boilers for marine vessels, power plants, and industry.

DKK mil	12/92	12/93	12/94	US$mil 12/94				
Sales	**13,556.0**	**13,446.0**	**14,915.8**	**2,358.2**	P/E Ratio	**NMF**	Price (9/30/95)	**920.00**
Net Income	**83.0**	**-171.0**	**-104.2**	**-16.5**	P/B Ratio	**0.8**	52 Wk Hi-Low	**1,320.0-897.8**
Book Value	**3,310.0**	**3,122.0**	**3,032.4**	**497.9**	Yield %	**0.0**	Market Cap	**US$401.9mil**

Address	**28 Sankt Annæ Plads**	Tel	**033-11-12-22**	ADR		President	**Sven D. Madsen**
	1291 Copenhagen	Fax	**033-15-00-90**	SEDOL No.	**4506582**	Chairman	**Karsten Laursen**

NKT Holding

Industry: **Electrical Components & Equipment**

NKT Holding is a holding company for a group of companies in the electrical, industrial, and telecommunication industries. Its subsidiaries manufacture power cables for the energy and construction industries, and optical-fiber cables for the telecommunication industry. Its wholly- owned LK subsidiary makes electrical-installation equipment and electricity meters, and Fisker & Nielsen manufactures vacuum cleaners and floor- maintenance equipment. Danish holding company Alborg Portland has a 35% stake in NKT. Exports outside Europe made up 13% of sales in 1994.

	DKK mil 12/92	12/93	12/94	US$mil 12/94				
Sales	**4,997.0**	**4,877.0**	**5,067.2**	**801.1**	P/E Ratio	**6.7**	Price (9/30/95)	**330.00**
Net Income	**43.0**	**68.0**	**364.8**	**57.7**	P/B Ratio	**1.0**	52 Wk Hi-Low	**372.00-283.00**
Book Value	**2,215.0**	**2,183.0**	**2,445.3**	**401.5**	Yield %	**3.6**	Market Cap	**US$446.2mil**

Address **NKT Allé 1**	Tel **043-48-20-00**	ADR	Managing Director **Gerhard Albrechtsen**
2605 Brondby	Fax **043-96-18-20**	SEDOL No. **4642464**	Chairman **Christian Kjær**

Novo Nordisk

Industry: **Pharmaceuticals**

Novo Nordisk manufactures pharmaceuticals and bioindustrial products. It provides diabetics with insulin and insulin-delivery systems, and manufactures hormone-replacement-therapy products. The firm produces industrial enzymes for customers in the detergent, starch, and textile industries. Its wholly-owned Ferrosan subsidiaries sell dietary supplements and digestive aids. The company recently won approval to market its human growth hormone Norditropin in the U.S. It generated 47% of its 1994 revenues outside Europe, primarily in Japan and North America.

	DKK mil 12/92	12/93	12/94	US$mil 12/94				
Sales	**10,699.0**	**12,163.0**	**13,524.0**	**2,138.2**	P/E Ratio	**17.6**	Price (9/30/95)	**672.00**
Net Income	**1,276.0**	**1,426.0**	**1,432.0**	**226.4**	P/B Ratio	**1.9**	52 Wk Hi-Low	**678.00-510.00**
Book Value	**10,584.0**	**11,914.0**	**13,136.0**	**2,157.0**	Yield %	**0.7**	Market Cap	**US$3,898.6mil**

Address **Nove Allé**	Tel **044-44-88-88**	ADR **NVO**	President & CEO **Mads Ovlisen**
2880 Bagsævrd	Fax **044-49-05-55**	SEDOL No. **4651910**	Chairman **Vagn Andersen**

Potagua

Industry: **Building Materials**

Potagua is a holding company with interests in the construction, engineering, packaging, and aerospace industries. The company holds 51% of FLS Industries, Denmark's largest industrial supplier. It also has a 61% stake in cement manufacturer Aalborg Portland Holding. Potagua's subsidiaries supply building services worldwide, provide aircraft engineering and support, and manufacture construction materials, telecommunication equipment, and packaging. Its European exports account for 31% of its income, exports to the Americas 18%, and the rest of the world 22%.

	DKK mil 12/92	12/93	12/94	US$mil 12/94				
Sales	**14,341.0**	**14,412.0**	**14,492.0**	**2,291.2**	P/E Ratio	**14.5**	Price (9/30/95)	**550.00**
Net Income	**170.0**	**70.0**	**150.0**	**23.7**	P/B Ratio	**1.2**	52 Wk Hi-Low	**650.00-490.00**
Book Value	**1,672.0**	**1,813.0**	**1,895.0**	**311.2**	Yield %	**2.9**	Market Cap	**US$273.6mil**

Address **Kalvebod Brygge 20**	Tel **033-91-58-00**	ADR	Managing Director **Frede Bjergvang**
1560 Copenhagen	Fax **033-91-17-50**	SEDOL No. **4698230**	Chairman **Jens Münter**

Radiometer

Industry: **Advanced Medical Technology**

Radiometer manufactures, develops, and sells measuring and monitoring instruments used primarily in medical and industrial applications. Its products include blood-analyzing instruments, patient-monitoring equipment, pH meters, and equipment used to determine bacteria levels in food. Sales of the company's medical instruments generate more than 55% of its revenues. European exports accounted for 37% of sales in 1994, while exports to non-European countries, primarily in North America and Australasia, accounted for 57% of revenues.

	DKK mil 04/92	04/93	04/94	US$mil 04/94				
Sales	**1,156.0**	**1,579.0**	**1,705.0**	**258.0**	P/E Ratio	**21.9**	Price (9/30/95)	**365.00**
Net Income	**112.0**	**171.0**	**165.0**	**25.0**	P/B Ratio	**2.3**	52 Wk Hi-Low	**365.00-264.00**
Book Value	**836.0**	**948.0**	**1,088.0**	**167.4**	Yield %	**1.4**	Market Cap	**US$387.9mil**

Address **Emdrupvej 72**	Tel **039-69-63-11**	ADR	President & CEO **Johan Schroder**
2400 Copenhagen	Fax **039-67-81-11**	SEDOL No. **4720092**	Chairman **Steen Rasborg**

Sophus Berendsen

Industry: **General Industrial & Commercial Services**

Sophus Berendsen provides business services and manufactures industrial equipment. It operates in four sectors: Rentokil Group, Textile Service, Power & Motion Control, and Electronics and Data. It derives 57% of its income from a 52% stake in U.K.-based Rentokil, which provides environmental, security, personnel, and delivery services. Sophus Berendsen also makes hydraulics, workwear, mats, and operates laundry services. Its Berendsen subsidiary distributes electronics and data products. Exports account for nearly one third of the company's income.

	DKK mil 12/92	12/93	12/94	US$mil 12/94				
Sales	**7,771.0**	**9,874.0**	**12,320.2**	**1,947.9**	P/E Ratio M	**31.2**	Price (9/30/95) M	**606.00**
Net Income	**465.0**	**1,121.0**	**464.5**	**73.4**	P/B Ratio M	**7.5**	52 Wk Hi-Low M	**625.50-456.00**
Book Value	**1,825.0**	**2,077.0**	**1,945.1**	**319.4**	Yield % M	**0.7**	Market Cap M	**US$654.5mil**

Address **Klausdalsbrovej 1**	Tel **039-69-85-00**	ADR	President & CEO **Hans Werdelin**
2860 Soborg	Fax **039-69-73-00**	SEDOL No. **4826440**	Chairman **Robert Koch-Nielsen**

M=Multiple issues in index; reflects most active.

Superfos

Industry: **Other Food**

Superfos operates through three main divisions: road construction, packaging, and chemicals. The company's road contruction division produces asphalt and broken granite, and also surfaces roads. Its U.S. construction subsidiaries, including Couch, Western Mobile, and Bullard Excavating, accounted for one third of Superfos' revenues in 1994. Its wholly-owned subsidiary Jeppsson Pac manufactures plastic and cardboard containers in Sweden and France. Superfos doubled its chemical division by acquiring Swedish chemical trade and distribution company Chematex.

	DKK mil 12/92	12/93	12/94	US$mil 12/94				
Sales	**7,422.0**	**8,005.0**	**4,310.3**	**681.5**	P/E Ratio	**18.1**	Price (9/30/95)	**490.00**
Net Income	**67.0**	**285.0**	**164.6**	**26.0**	P/B Ratio	**1.9**	52 Wk Hi-Low	**515.00-380.00**
Book Value	**1,447.0**	**1,572.0**	**1,605.7**	**263.7**	Yield %	**2.0**	Market Cap	**US$546.4mil**

Address **Frydenlundsvej 30**
2950 Vedbæk
Tel **042-89-31-11**
Fax **045-66-04-05**
ADR
SEDOL No. **4856492**
CEO **Peter Hojland**
Chairman **Poul Andreassen**

Tele Danmark

Industry: **Telephone Systems - All**

Tele Danmark, 51%-owned by the Danish state, provides telecommunication services. Domestic telephone services are its core business activity with more than 3 million lines and nearly half a million mobile-phone subscribers. It supplies and services business-telecommunication systems and data networks, operates a cable-television network with more than half a million subscribers, publishes telephone directories, and provides public-telephone services. It launched Telenordia, a joint telecommunication venture operating in Sweden, with British Telecom and Norway's Telenor.

	DKK mil 12/92	12/93	12/94	US$mil 12/94				
Sales	**15,586.0**	**16,293.0**	**17,849.0**	**2,822.0**	P/E Ratio	**14.6**	Price (9/30/95)	**286.50**
Net Income	**916.0**	**1,561.0**	**2,570.0**	**406.3**	P/B Ratio	**0.9**	52 Wk Hi-Low	**347.00-276.00**
Book Value	**7,322.0**	**8,752.0**	**23,527.0**	**3,863.2**	Yield %	**4.2**	Market Cap	**US$3,269.9mil**

Address **Kannikegade 16**
8000 Aarhus
Tel **089-33-77-77**
Fax **089-33-77-19**
ADR **TLD**
SEDOL No. **4889874**
CEO **Hans Würtzen**
Chairman **Knud Heinesen**

Topdanmark

Industry: **Financial Services - Diversified**

Topdanmark is the parent company of a financial-services group that offers life-insurance, general-insurance, reinsurance, and personal and corporate financial services. It derives 78% of its general-insurance income from its auto-, personal-, and agricultural-insurance products. The company operates a direct-marketing bank that provides a full range of banking services by telephone, telefax, or mail. Topdanmark also has property interests throughout Finland. Nonlife insurance generated more than two thirds of Topdanmark's revenues in 1994.

	DKK mil 12/92	12/93	12/94	US$mil 12/94				
Revenues	**6,406.0**	**6,841.0**	**4,368.7**	**690.7**	P/E Ratio	**NMF**	Price (9/30/95)	**663.00**
Net Income	**-53.0**	**107.0**	**427.1**	**67.5**	P/B Ratio	**0.9**	52 Wk Hi-Low	**732.42-508.00**
Book Value	**2,444.0**	**2,535.0**	**2,251.5**	**369.7**	Yield %	**0.0**	Market Cap	**US$375.3mil**

Address **Borupvang 4**
2750 Ballerup
Tel **044-68-33-11**
Fax **044-68-28-05**
ADR
SEDOL No. **4897747**
CEO **Kaj G. Schou**
Chairman **K. Bonde Larsen**

Unidanmark

Industry: **Banks - Money Center**

Unidanmark is a holding company. Its main business is conducted through its wholly-owned subsidiary Unibank, which offers retail and corporate banking through more than 400 branches. Unidanmark had assets totaling nearly DKK 222 billion in 1994. Unibank offers asset management, securities and foreign exchange, and brokerage services to its customers. Unikredit, Unibank's mortgage-banking subsidiary offers new home loans, commercial property loans, and corporate mortgage loans. Unibank has branch offices in Germany, the U.K., the U.S., Singapore, and Hong Kong.

	DKK mil 12/92	12/93	12/94	US$mil 12/94				
Revenues	**26,379.0**	**29,104.0**	**18,836.4**	**2,978.1**	P/E Ratio	**24.2**	Price (9/30/95)	**242.00**
Net Income	**-4,660.0**	**884.6**	**519.6**	**82.2**	P/B Ratio	**1.0**	52 Wk Hi-Low	**280.00-215.00**
Book Value	**15,429.0**	**10,693.0**	**13,540.3**	**2,223.4**	Yield %	**1.7**	Market Cap	**US$2,041.1mil**

Address **Torvegade 2**
1786 Copenhagen
Tel **033-33-33-33**
Fax **033-33-12-12**
ADR
SEDOL No. **4914185**
CEO **Thorleif Krarup**
Chairman **Jorgen H. Pedersen**

Jens Villadsens Fabriker

Industry: **Heavy Construction**

Jens Villadsens Fabriker is one of Europe's largest roofing-felt companies and a leader in construction and civil engineering. It manufactures building components, road materials, plastic films, and plastic pipes. Contract roofing work, and roofing products such as felt, shingles, and insulation materials, account for approximately 75% of revenues. The company also produces and lays asphalt road-surfacing materials, and manufactures carrier bags and drainage pipes. It generates 59% of its revenues in Scandinavia and 95% in Europe as a whole.

	DKK mil 12/92	12/93	12/94	US$mil 12/94				
Sales	**3,361.0**	**3,304.0**	**3,551.9**	**561.6**	P/E Ratio	**14.0**	Price (9/30/95)	**1,580.00**
Net Income	**88.0**	**188.0**	**230.6**	**36.5**	P/B Ratio	**2.3**	52 Wk Hi-Low	**1,750.0-1,500.0**
Book Value	**1,079.0**	**1,219.0**	**1,390.6**	**228.3**	Yield %	**1.6**	Market Cap	**US$584.7mil**

Address **Mileparken 38**
2730 Herlev
Tel **044-88-55-00**
Fax **044-53-55-00**
ADR
SEDOL No. **4472672**
Managing Director **Hans C. Andreasen**
Chairman **Alf Torp-Pedersen**

Finland

Finland

Local Trading Hours	Time Difference with New York	Population (Est. 94)
10:00-5:00	7 hours ahead	5,069,000

Carolina Johansson, Helsinki

When Finland entered the European Union at the start of 1995, it sent a clear signal that it now sees its future in the west. For decades, the country persisted in the shadow of its super-power communist neighbor, a hopeless situation for attracting investments. But over the past few years, Finland has managed to shake off its reputation as an isolated outpost. It has loosened up foreign ownership restrictions and opened up its borders for non-resident investors. Nowhere is the change clearer than on the stock exchange, which has has experienced a huge inflow of foreign capital over the past few years.

Boosted by foreign cash, Finland's stock exchange, located in the capital of Helsinki, outperformed most European exchanges with a 16% gain in share prices in 1994. The gain came amidst rising activity and average daily turnover shot up to a record 274 million markkaa in 1994, easily exceeding 184 million markkaa in 1993 and 40 million markkaa the year earlier.

The influx of capital from abroad came after Finland abolished foreign ownership restrictions on most assets in 1993. Since then, the share of foreign ownership has grown to about a third of the total market, although it varies widely among individual stocks. In last year's new issue activity, non-residents supplied a bulk of the fresh venture capital, but domestic investors are expected to increase their share of the market. Currently, the biggest source of new capital for the market is pension savings, which up to now has been invested mainly in corporate lending.

Finland's economy may rest on natural resources such as its vast forests and mines, but high technology dominates on the stock exchange. The global telecommunications group Nokia Oy, a leading maker of mobile phones, has grown so rapidly in recent years that it now singlehandedly sets the market's pace.

Dow Jones Finland Equity Market Index Performance

In early September, the telecommunication group's market capitalization was 97 billion markkaa, or 40% of the total market value of 241 billion markkaa. Gains in Nokia's share price thus tend to dwarf developments elsewhere on the exchange. In January-to-September, 1995, the exchange's general HEX index gained 25%, but strip away Nokia, and the index dropped 2.5%.

Gross Domestic Product (94)	Three-Year Average GDP Growth (92-94)	Main Industries	Consumer Price Index (94)	Monetary Unit	Exchange Rate (9/95)
$116.8 billion	0.8%	Metal products and machine industry, paper and graphic industry, chemical industry and wood industry	1.0%	Markka	FIM4.27 to US$1.00

On any given day, Nokia may account for about 40% of turnover, making it the most actively traded stock on the exchange. The ten most actively traded stocks make up about 76% of turnover. Trailing Nokia on the most traded list are forestry groups Repola Oy, Enso-Gutzeit Oy and Kymmene Oy. The other companies in the top 10 are banking group Unitas Ltd., industrial group Metra Oy, the partially state-owned metals and mining group Outokumpu Oy, forest sector group Metsae-Serla Oy, consumer goods group Huhtamaeki Oy and steel group Rautaruukki Oy, another state-controlled company.

Nokia's dominance on the exchange is a source of concern, although Finns tend to revel in the success story. Given the group's strong standing, market players have welcomed the addition of new companies over the past year. And more are expected to follow. Late in 1995, the country's largest company by turnover, the state-owned oil and gas group Neste Oy, was to make its debut on the exchange after a share issue that would reduce the Government's stake in the company to around 80%.

Such partial privatizations and other spin-offs have lifted the total number of companies listed on the exchange to 72 as of September, 1995, from around 60 a year earlier. The companies listed represent 93 different shares because some companies issue both ordinary and preference shares. Preference shares usually have a first claim on dividends, but usually carry less voting power. Another 25 companies are currently considering listing.

Ten Largest Capitalized Companies
as of 9/30/95

Stock	Market Cap. US$Mil
Nokia	9,105,386.4
Repola	3,431,111.9
Kymmene	2,534,894.6
Outokumpu	2,216,441.2
Merita Bank	1,268,927.9
KOP	1,090,488.7
Enso-Gutzeit	888,955.5
Sampo	886,416.9
Kesko	661,329.0
Metra	642,533.7

The increase in listing activity after a few lackluster years reflects the positive stock market trend since Finland started crawling out of its recession in the early 1990s. Dependency on the former Soviet Union for exports through the 1980s and strong gearing toward cyclical industries sent Finland deeper into recession than other European nations. Between 1990 and 1993, Finland's total output of goods and services plunged close to 15%.

The turnaround came late in 1992 and was helped by the central bank's decision to cut the markka lose from its unilateral link to the European Currency Unit. The markka depreciation boosted corporate competitiveness and helped spur an export-led economic recovery, which has now begun to spill over to the domestic sector. In 1995, gross domestic product was forecast to expand 5%, and by 4.5% in 1996.

Legal and fiscal measures, such as a lowering of capital gains taxes and the abolition of stamp duty, have also helped increase the attractiveness of stocks as an investment.

All listed companies as well as banks and brokerages active on the trading side are required to be members of the stock exchange, which operates as a cooperative following a reorganization in 1984. The exchange was founded 1912 as an informal association.

The stately Stock Exchange Building in downtown Helsinki is no longer the bustling place it once was. Floor trading ended completely in 1990 and was replaced by computer cables. Brokers now carry out their business via screens and phones from their home offices. Trading is conducted through the Helsinki Stock Exchange Automated Trading and Information System (HETI), a decentralized, fully automated order-driven system.

The trading day begins at 8:30 a.m. with a pre-trading period during which brokers feed their opening buy and sell offers into the system. Offers are matched at 9:50 a.m. to determine the opening quotations. Official trading begins at 10:00 a.m. and extends to 5:00 p.m.

Transactions are cleared on the fourth banking day following. Stock ownership is registered through computers after a reform in 1992 when the first companies switched to a completely paperless securities system based on computerized book entries. By early 1995, all but a handful of companies have joined the system.

Book entry registers are maintained by the central share register of Finland and registration of holdings is mandatory. Foreigners are, however, partially exempt from this requirement because they may register holdings in a nominee name.

Foreign investors are not taxed on capital gains or interest income earned in Finland, but they must pay a withholding tax on dividends. The rate varies and is specified in individual tax treaties. Most countries have bilateral tax treaties with Finland. In the absence of such a treaty, the withholding tax is 25%.

At the start of 1996, Finland's new Companies Act is scheduled to go into effect. The Act has been harmonized with E.U. regulations and the key amendments relate to the voting rights of different share series. The new act will reduce the number of shares carrying no voting rights, for example.

In addition to the Helsinki stock exchange, the Finnish Association of Securities Dealers maintains an over-the-counter list of 33 companies, and a so called unofficial Brokers' List, with 20 companies listed. Average daily trading volumes on these lists have risen alongside the increase in stock trading generally, but activity remains moderate. Last year, the total trading volume on the OTC list was 1.3 billion markka, while trading on the Brokers' List amounted to 1.2 billion markka. By comparison, total trading on the Helsinki Stock Exchange amounted to 68.7 billion markka.

Amer Group

Industry: **Conglomerates**

Amer Group manufactures and trades a variety of consumer products, including Wilson racquets and sports equipment and MacGregor golf equipment. Amer Group imports and sells Toyota, Lexus, Citroen, and Suzuki vehicles. It manufactures Marlboro cigarettes under a licensing agreement with Philip Morris and makes its own brands of cigarettes and tobacco products. Its Austrian sports-equipment subsidiary Atomic, manufactures downhill and cross-country skis, in-line skates, hiking boots, and clothing. Exports to North America generated 42% of sales in 1994.

FIM mil	02/93	12/93 *	12/94	US$mil 12/94				
Sales	**7,000.0**	**6,360.0**	**6,711.0**	**1,297.3**	P/E Ratio	**8.3**	Price (9/30/95)	**82.00**
Net Income	**39.0**	**101.0**	**185.0**	**35.8**	P/B Ratio	**0.7**	52 Wk Hi-Low	**112.00-69.50**
Book Value	**2,160.0**	**2,231.0**	**2,852.0**	**601.7**	Yield %	**3.7**	Market Cap	**US$416.8mil**

Address **Mäkelänkatu 91**
00610 Helsinki
Tel **0-757-71**
Fax **0-757-7200**
ADR **AGPDY**
SEDOL No. **4024006**
President & CEO **Seppo Ahonen**
Chairman **Raimo Taivalkoski**

*Irregular period due to fiscal year change.

Cultor

Industry: **Other Food**

Cultor is a food-processing firm that manufactures animal feed, health-care products, sweeteners, bakery products, and related enzymes and additives. It generates more than half of its revenues from its animal-feed business. Cultor's subsidiaries include sweetener producers Finnsugar and Xyrofin and industrial enzyme manufacturer Genencor. Cultor operates the Vaasa chain of bakeries, and has a majority stake in the Estonian bakery firm Leibur. In 1994, Cultor generated 51% of its revenues in Finland, 37% elsewhere in Europe, and 12% in the rest of the world.

FIM mil	11/92	11/93	12/94 *	US$mil 12/94				
Sales	**6,015.0**	**6,359.0**	**6,395.3**	**1,236.3**	P/E Ratio	**10.1**	Price (9/30/95)	**162.00**
Net Income	**-53.0**	**365.0**	**347.0**	**67.1**	P/B Ratio	**2.5**	52 Wk Hi-Low	**162.00-120.00**
Book Value	**761.0**	**1,140.0**	**1,500.9**	**316.6**	Yield %	**2.8**	Market Cap	**US$575.9mil**

Address **Kyllikinportti 2**
00240 Helsinki
Tel **0-134-411**
Fax **0-1344-1344**
ADR **CULTY**
SEDOL No. **4859446**
President & CEO **Björn Mattsson**
Chairman **Eero Utter**

*Irregular period due to fiscal year change.

Enso-Gutzeit

Industry: **Paper Products**

Enso-Gutzeit manufactures a wide variety of forestry goods. Its product lines include packaging board for liquids and foods, graphic boards, fine paper, publication paper, market pulp, sawn goods, and prefabricated timber-frame houses. Enso operates 30 production plants in eight countries. In 1994, the company generated 20% of its revenues in Finland, 61% in Europe, and 19% in the rest of the world. Enso-Gutzeit acquired a 35% share in state-controlled forestry company Veitsiluoto, making it one of Europe's leading producers of fine paper and newsprint.

FIM mil	12/92	12/93	12/94	US$mil 12/94				
Sales	**10,263.0**	**13,060.0**	**17,711.3**	**3,423.8**	P/E Ratio M	**5.0**	Price (9/30/95) M	**36.00**
Net Income	**61.0**	**110.0**	**412.6**	**79.8**	P/B Ratio M	**1.3**	52 Wk Hi-Low M	**45.90-31.30**
Book Value	**4,924.0**	**5,727.0**	**5,976.8**	**1,260.9**	Yield % M	**2.8**	Market Cap M	**US$889.0mil**

Address **Kanavaranta 1**
00160 Helsinki
Tel **0-162-91**
Fax **0-162-9471**
ADR
SEDOL No. **4318293**
President & CEO **Jukka Härmälä**
Chairman **Jukka Härmälä**

M=Multiple issues in index; reflects most active.

Huhtamäki

Industry: **Other Food**

Huhtamäki Oy is a pharmaceutical, food, and packaging company. Its wholly-owned Leaf subsidiary, which accounted for 60% of revenues in 1994, makes Jolly Rancher, PayDay, and Heath confectionery products. Its wholly-owned Polarcup subsidiary (29% of revenues) supplies food manufacturers with plastic and paper-based packaging. It owns the pharmaceutical firm Leiras, which makes eye medicines and hormonal contraceptives such as Norplant. In 1994, Huhtamäki generated 47% of its revenues in Europe, 32% in North America, and 6% in Asia.

FIM mil	12/92	12/93	12/94	US$mil 12/94				
Sales	**6,403.0**	**7,935.0**	**8,284.8**	**1,601.5**	P/E Ratio M	**12.1**	Price (9/30/95) M	**147.00**
Net Income	**334.0**	**372.0**	**317.9**	**61.5**	P/B Ratio M	**1.2**	52 Wk Hi-Low M	**170.00-125.00**
Book Value	**2,436.0**	**3,728.0**	**3,742.7**	**789.6**	Yield % M	**2.7**	Market Cap M	**US$585.1mil**

Address **Eteläranta 8**
00130 Helsinki
Tel **0-708-8100**
Fax **0-660-622**
ADR
SEDOL No. **4447476**
President & CEO **Timo Peltola**
Chairman **Timo Peltola**

M=Multiple issues in index; reflects most active.

Kesko

Industry: **Other Food**

Kesko, one of Finland's largest diversified retail companies, supplies a network of nearly 2,500 stores. Its commercial operations are organized into three divisions: foodstuffs, agricultural and builders' supplies, and specialty and home goods. The foodstuffs division generated 57% of revenues in 1994, and the agricultural and builders' supplies division generated 33%. Kesko's products include agricultural equipment, household goods, building supplies, clothing, and shoes. It imports and retails Volkswagen and Seat cars and operates 38 Citymarket hypermarkets in Finland.

FIM mil	12/92	12/93	12/94	US$mil 12/94				
Sales	**26,641.0**	**25,822.0**	**27,060.5**	**5,231.1**	P/E Ratio	**14.4**	Price (9/30/95)	**47.50**
Net Income	**178.0**	**357.0**	**465.5**	**90.0**	P/B Ratio	**0.6**	52 Wk Hi-Low	**59.00-41.50**
Book Value	**4,226.0**	**4,448.0**	**7,674.6**	**1,619.1**	Yield %	**2.9**	Market Cap	**US$661.3mil**

Address **Satamakatu 3**
00161 Helsinki
Tel **010-5311**
Fax **0-655-473**
ADR
SEDOL No. **4490005**
CEO **Eero Kinnunen**
Chairman **Eero Kinnunen**

Kone

Industry: **Heavy Machinery**

Kone Corporation's main business is the manufacture, installation, modernization, and maintenance of elevators and escalators. Kone has operations in 24 countries. The maintenance and modernization of elevators and escalators generated 60% of sales and the sale of new units generated 37%. In 1994, Kone acquired U.S.-based Montgomery Elevator Company, significantly increasing its presence in North America. In 1994, it generated 75% of sales in Europe, 10% in North America (not including the Montgomery acquisition), and 10% in Asia and Australia.

FIM mil	12/92	12/93	12/94	US$mil 12/94				
Sales	**11,279.0**	**10,813.0**	**7,661.7**	**1,481.1**	P/E Ratio	**11.2**	Price (9/30/95)	**475.00**
Net Income	**279.0**	**287.0**	**257.5**	**49.8**	P/B Ratio	**1.1**	52 Wk Hi-Low	**557.00-459.00**
Book Value	**2,395.0**	**2,613.0**	**2,609.7**	**550.6**	Yield %	**2.1**	Market Cap	**US$556.3mil**

Address	**Kartanontie 1**	Tel	**0-4751**	ADR		President	**Anssi Solia**
	00331 Helsinki	Fax	**0-475-4309**	SEDOL No.	**4496672**	Chairman	**Pekka Herlin**

KOP

Industry: **Banks - Regional**

Kansallis-Osake-Pankki (KOP) provides individuals and businesses with banking services. Its retail business has more than 2 million individual customers and approximately 100,000 corporate customers. Its corporate division offers treasury- and equity-investment services. Twenty-five percent of the money loaned by the bank in 1993 was loaned to foreign clients. KOP owns 98% of Nordfinanz Bank Zurich, which provides portfolio-management and treasury-investment services. In 1995, the bank merged its operations with Unitas Bank.

FIM mil	12/92	12/93	12/94	US$mil 12/94				
Revenues	**18,307.0**	**16,280.0**	**9,309.2**	**1,799.6**	P/E Ratio	**NMF**	Price (9/30/95)	**4.48**
Net Income	**-3,458.0**	**-2,255.0**	**-1,871.1**	**-361.7**	P/B Ratio	**0.6**	52 Wk Hi-Low	**7.57-3.84**
Book Value	**7,001.0**	**6,863.0**	**7,230.6**	**1,525.4**	Yield %	**0.0**	Market Cap	**US$1,090.5mil**

Address	**Aleksanterinkatu 42**	Tel	**0-1631**	ADR		CEO	**Pertti Voutilainen**
	00100 Helsinki	Fax	**0-163-3595**	SEDOL No.	**4482381**	Chairman	**Tauno Matomäki**

Kymmene

Industry: **Paper Products**

Kymmene is a forest-products company that produces pulp, paper, wood-based panels, and sawn timber in its facilities throughout Europe. In 1994 the company produced 1,729 tons of panels and sawn timber, 1,502 tons of fine paper, 1,108 tons of magazine paper, and 415 tons of newsprint. The company's wholly-owned Schauman Wood subsidiary supplies the vehicle and construction industries with plywood. Its publication and fine-paper products accounted for nearly two thirds of sales in 1994. It generated 84% of its revenues in Europe, and 10% in North America in 1994.

FIM mil	12/92	12/93	12/94	US$mil 12/94				
Sales	**13,607.0**	**16,297.0**	**18,882.6**	**3,650.2**	P/E Ratio	**NMF**	Price (9/30/95)	**132.00**
Net Income	**-257.0**	**453.0**	**-299.4**	**-57.9**	P/B Ratio	**2.1**	52 Wk Hi-Low	**145.00-104.00**
Book Value	**4,459.0**	**5,577.0**	**5,259.8**	**1,109.7**	Yield %	**1.9**	Market Cap	**US$2,534.9mil**

Address	**Mikonkatu 15 A**	Tel	**0-131-411**	ADR		CEO	**Harri Piehl**
	00101 Helsinki	Fax	**0-653-884**	SEDOL No.	**4498872**	Chairman	**Casimir Ehrnrooth**

Merita Bank

Industry: **Banks - Regional**

Merita Bank is the banking arm of Unitas, a financial-services holding company. It was formed by the merger of the Union Bank of Finland (Unitas) and Finnish bank Kansallis-Osake-Pankki. The bank offers retail and corporate banking, and asset management and investment services. It also provides portfolio management, real-estate brokerage, capital markets, and foreign-exchange services to both retail and corporate clients. The newly formed bank is the largest in the Nordic region with approximately 300 billion markkaa in assets.

FIM mil	12/92	12/93	12/94	US$mil 12/94				
Revenues	**16,963.0**	**14,141.0**	**9,847.0**	**1,903.5**	P/E Ratio M	**NMF**	Price (9/30/95) M	**13.00**
Net Income	**-2,074.0**	**-2,732.0**	**-1,369.0**	**-264.6**	P/B Ratio M	**0.8**	52 Wk Hi-Low M	**14.90-11.00**
Book Value	**8,899.0**	**8,072.0**	**7,644.0**	**1,612.7**	Yield % M	**5.4**	Market Cap M	**US$1,268.9mil**

Address	**Aleksanterinkatu 30**	Tel	**0-165-42815**	ADR		President & CEO	**Vesa Vainio**
	00100 Helsinki	Fax	**0-612-1264**	SEDOL No.	**4827175**	Chairman	**Ahti Hirvonen**

M=Multiple issues in index; reflects most active.

Metra

Industry: **Industrial - Diversified**

Metra manufactures diesel engines, security products and systems, and bathroom-ceramic products. Its Wärtsila Diesel division, which accounted for 67% of sales revenues in 1994, makes power-plant and marine engines. Other divisions include Sanitec, Europe's largest producer of bathroom ceramics, Imatra Steel, manufacturers of specialty steel, and Cimcorp, which specializes in factory automation systems. It holds 48% of Assa Abloy, the world's largest lock-technology firm. In 1994, Metra generated 47% of its revenues in Europe, 23% in Asia, and 13% in North America.

FIM mil	02/93	12/93 *	12/94	US$mil 12/94				
Sales	**10,653.0**	**9,433.0**	**10,108.4**	**1,954.1**	P/E Ratio M	**13.6**	Price (9/30/95) M	**197.00**
Net Income	**-179.0**	**61.0**	**384.5**	**74.3**	P/B Ratio M	**1.5**	52 Wk Hi-Low M	**206.00-132.00**
Book Value	**2,570.0**	**2,561.0**	**3,515.2**	**741.6**	Yield % M	**2.0**	Market Cap M	**US$642.5mil**

Address	**John Stenbergin ranta 2**	Tel	**0-70-951**	ADR		President & CEO	**Georg Ehrnrooth**
	00101 Helsinki	Fax	**0-762-278**	SEDOL No.	**4525178**	Chairman	**Robert G. Ehrnrooth**

*Irregular period due to fiscal year change; M=Multiple issues in index; reflects most active.

Metsä-Serla

Industry: **Paper Products**

Metsä-Serla is a forest-products company that processes sawn goods, pulp, paper, paperboard, corrugated board, tissue, and chemicals. It produced 310,600 tons of magazine paper, 262,300 tons of fine paper, and 215,100 tons of tissue and high-density paper in 1994. Metsä-Serla has production operations in Sweden, Denmark, the Netherlands, the U.K., Greece, and the Canary Islands. More than 70% of sales are made in Europe, and the remaining sales are made primarily in the U.S., China, and the Far East. Half of its sales are generated by paper and paperboard.

FIM mil	12/92	12/93	12/94	US$mil 12/94				
Sales	**7,752.0**	**8,239.0**	**9,476.5**	**1,831.9**	P/E Ratio M	**7.3**	Price (9/30/95) M	**165.00**
Net Income	**406.0**	**612.0**	**527.1**	**101.9**	P/B Ratio M	**0.8**	52 Wk Hi-Low M	**240.00-160.00**
Book Value	**2,418.0**	**4,119.0**	**5,748.6**	**1,212.8**	Yield % M	**3.0**	Market Cap M	**US$280.8mil**

Address **Revontulentie 6**
02100 Espoo
Tel **0-469-431**
Fax **0-469-4355**
ADR
SEDOL No. **4585514**
President & CEO **Timo Poranen**
Chairman **Juhani Ahava**

M=Multiple issues in index; reflects most active.

Nokia

Industry: **Diversified Technology**

Nokia is a telecommunication, cable, and consumer-electronics company. It supplies telecommunication systems and equipment for fixed- and mobile-phone networks, and sells its own cellular phones in 100 countries. It makes televisions, satellite receivers, computer monitors, car-audio systems, and other industrial and consumer electronics. It manufactures telecommunication and power cables, and produces and sells the machinery used to make them. Its telecommunication operations account for 64% of sales. Exports outside Europe account for nearly one third of sales.

FIM mil	12/92	12/93	12/94	US$mil 12/94				
Sales	**18,168.0**	**23,697.0**	**30,177.0**	**5,833.6**	P/E Ratio M	**27.3**	Price (9/30/95) M	**300.00**
Net Income	**-354.0**	**-1,073.0**	**3,658.0**	**707.1**	P/B Ratio M	**8.3**	52 Wk Hi-Low M	**340.00-131.25**
Book Value	**1,073.0**	**5,319.0**	**10,857.0**	**2,290.5**	Yield % M	**0.8**	Market Cap M	**US$9,105.4mil**

Address **Eteläesplanadi 12**
00101 Helsinki
Tel **0-18071**
Fax **0-656-388**
ADR **NOK.A**
SEDOL No. **4632830**
President & CEO **Jorma Ollila**
Chairman **Casimir Ehrnrooth**

M=Multiple issues in index; reflects most active.

Outokumpu

Industry: **Non-Ferrous Metals - Other (Exc. Aluminum)**

Outokumpu, 40%-owned by the Finnish government, is an integrated metals and engineering company. It mines, smelts, and refines copper, zinc, nickel, and stainless-steel, and it produces a wide range of tube, strip, and roll products. The firm manufactures stainless-steel products and equipment for industries ranging from mining to power generation. Its operations are located in Europe, North America, and Australia. In 1994, Europe accounted for 60% of sales, the U.S. 23%, and Asia 9%; and copper products generated 39% of sales, stainless-steel 23%, and base metals 21%.

FIM mil	12/92	12/93	12/94	US$mil 12/94				
Sales	**15,125.0**	**15,827.0**	**16,683.0**	**3,225.0**	P/E Ratio	**10.7**	Price (9/30/95)	**76.00**
Net Income	**-43.0**	**448.0**	**831.0**	**160.6**	P/B Ratio	**1.5**	52 Wk Hi-Low	**106.00-60.70**
Book Value	**987.0**	**2,725.0**	**6,247.0**	**1,317.9**	Yield %	**1.3**	Market Cap	**US$2,216.4mil**

Address **Länsituulentie 7A**
02101 Espoo
Tel **0-421-1**
Fax **0-421-3888**
ADR
SEDOL No. **4665148**
President & CEO **Jyrki Juusela**
Chairman **Jyrki Juusela**

Partek

Industry: **Building Materials**

Partek manufactures building products, mines and processes minerals, and makes cargo-handling equipment. Its building-products business, which accounts for 47% of revenues, produces precast-concrete elements, rock-wool-based insulation, and cement. Its wholly-owned Nordkalk subsidiary mines and processes limestone. Through its Cargotec division, Partek manufactures knuckleboom cranes and Loglift forestry cranes. It owns 25% of the Swedish Euroc group, which produces and distributes mineral-based building materials. Exports accounted for 82% of sales in 1994.

FIM mil	12/92	12/93	12/94	US$mil 12/94				
Sales	**6,628.0**	**6,610.0**	**6,166.3**	**1,192.0**	P/E Ratio	**NMF**	Price (9/30/95)	**64.00**
Net Income	**-443.0**	**-393.0**	**-193.9**	**-37.5**	P/B Ratio	**1.4**	52 Wk Hi-Low	**79.77-53.50**
Book Value	**2,016.0**	**1,601.0**	**1,790.7**	**377.8**	Yield %	**0.9**	Market Cap	**US$577.0mil**

Address **Oy Partek Ab**
21600 Pargas
Tel **021-74261**
Fax **021-742-6340**
ADR
SEDOL No. **4672632**
CEO **Christoffer Taxell**
Chairman **Carl O. Tallgren**

Repola

Industry: **Paper Products**

Repola operates through its subsidiaries United Paper Mills, Rauma, and W. Rosenlew. United Paper Mills manufactures newsprint and magazine paper, packaging materials, and mechanical woodworking products; it generated two thirds of sales in 1994. Rauma generated 30% of sales and is an engineering firm specializing in forest, pulp, and wood-based panels machinery and industrial valves. Repola also owns 75% of the plastic-packaging company W. Rosenlew, which manufactures flexible plastic packaging. Non-European exports account for 36% of sales.

FIM mil	12/92	12/93	12/94	US$mil 12/94				
Sales	**23,752.0**	**25,326.0**	**28,622.0**	**5,533.0**	P/E Ratio	**8.6**	Price (9/30/95)	**96.00**
Net Income	**-360.0**	**532.0**	**1,197.0**	**231.4**	P/B Ratio	**1.8**	52 Wk Hi-Low	**104.00-68.20**
Book Value	**5,595.0**	**6,554.0**	**7,992.0**	**1,686.1**	Yield %	**2.6**	Market Cap	**US$3,431.1mil**

Address **Snellmaninkatu 13**
00171 Helsinki
Tel **0-182-81**
Fax **0-182-8219**
ADR **RPOLY**
SEDOL No. **4733379**
President **Tauno Matomäki**
Chairman **Yrjö Niskanen**

Sampo

Industry: **Insurance - Property & Casualty**

Sampo Insurance Company offers general insurance. The company's direct-insurance activities, including fire, property, and motor insurance, have a 35% share of the Finnish insurance market. Its Kaleva Mutual Insurance subsidiary provides life and pension services for private individuals and companies. Its wholly-owned Industrial Insurance subsidiary insures large companies. Sampo's pension business, which accounted for 43% of revenues in 1994, provides pension coverage for more than 200,000 people.

FIM mil	12/92	12/93	12/94	US$mil 12/94				
Revenues	**11,149.0**	**11,848.0**	**3,986.3**	**770.6**	P/E Ratio	**27.1**	Price (9/30/95)	**250.00**
Net Income	**6.0**	**323.0**	**100.0**	**19.3**	P/B Ratio	**1.2**	52 Wk Hi-Low	**274.00-167.00**
Book Value	**2,768.0**	**3,150.0**	**3,133.5**	**661.1**	Yield %	**1.6**	Market Cap	**US$886.4mil**

Address **Yliopistonkatu 27**
20100 Turku
Tel **021-266-3311**
Fax **021-266-5811**
ADR
SEDOL No. **4773193**
Chairman Exec Bd **Jukka Härmälä**
Chairman Supv Bd **Kalevi Numminen**

Stockmann

Industry: **Retailers - Broadline**

Stockmann is a broadly diversified retail company. Its department-store division accounted for 45% of revenues in 1994, owns five department stores in Finland, and has operations in Russia and Estonia. Stockmann operates 16 Sesto supermarkets and 64 Seppälä clothing and cosmetics stores. Its nine Academic Bookstores are located in Finland's university cities. It sells Ford, Nissan, Volkswagen, Audi, and Chrysler vehicles through five retail outlets in the Helsinki area. Stockmann also owns Hobby Hall, a household and leisure products mail-order company.

FIM mil	12/92	12/93	12/94	US$mil 12/94				
Revenues	**3,233.0**	**3,659.0**	**4,507.0**	**871.3**	P/E Ratio	**19.6**	Price (9/30/95)	**251.00**
Net Income	**56.0**	**102.0**	**178.6**	**34.5**	P/B Ratio	**2.8**	52 Wk Hi-Low	**280.00-195.00**
Book Value	**1,084.0**	**1,169.0**	**1,289.4**	**272.0**	Yield %	**2.4**	Market Cap	**US$487.3mil**

Address **Aleksanterinkatu 52**
00101 Helsinki
Tel **0-1211**
Fax **0-121-3101**
ADR
SEDOL No. **4851130**
Managing Director **Ari Heiniö**
Chairman --

France

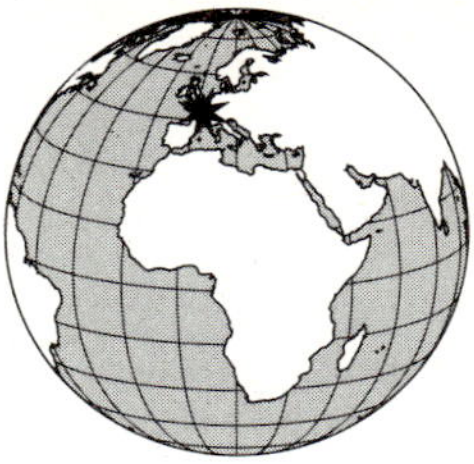

France

Max Berley,
Paris

Local Trading Hours	**Time Difference with New York**	**Population (Est. 94)**
10:00-5:00	6 hours ahead	57,840,000

The first six months of 1995 were disastrous for the Paris Bourse. While some European exchanges, such as London and Frankfurt, approached record highs, the Paris exchange languished in the doldrums. In September, Merrill Lynch placed the Paris stock exchange last in its listing of stock exchanges rated by investor interest.

Of all the largest stock exchanges, the French market has shown the worst performances since Jan. 1, 1993, with 2% growth, compared with 40% for New York, 36% for Frankfurt, 23% for London, and 7% for Tokyo. In 1994, the CAC 40 index was down 17%, while Frankfurt's DAX was down 7% and London FT 100 was down 10%.

In terms of volume, however, activity on the Paris Bourse reached an all-time record high in 1994, with 22.8 million transactions, up 19% from 19.4 million in 1993. New issues also reached a record level in 1994, with 156 billion francs in capital raised. Of that amount, 48.4 billion came from privatizations, and more than 100 billion francs were raised on the primary market.

The new government of President Jacques Chirac, elected in May 1995, has so far done little to attract investors to the Paris Bourse. The dismissal in July of Finance Minister Alain Madelin for having antagonized labor unions was read by the markets as a signal that the government could submit to union demands and could be reluctant to trim government spending. Madelin's dismissal further depressed market operators as the former finance minister was pressing for a plan to introduce pension funds to France, which would have given new dynamism to the stock market.

In addition, the market is pessimistic that the government of France will be able to reduce the budget deficit to its stated goal of 322 billion francs in 1995 and 290 billion francs in 1996.

Dow Jones France Equity Market Index Performance

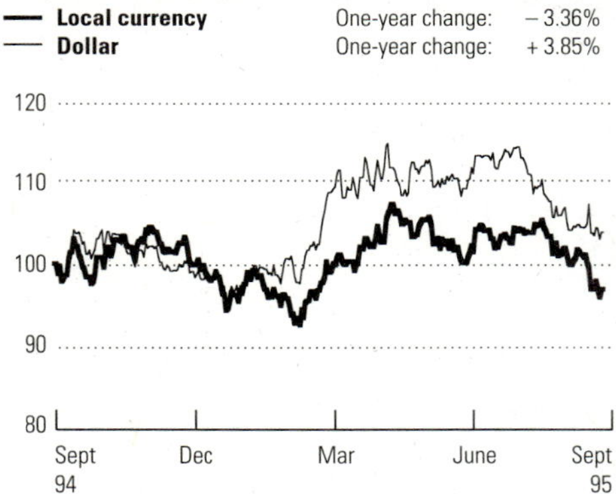

The market from late 1994 through 1995 has been marked by the privatization program initiated by French Prime Minister Edouard Balladur when he took office in April 1993. Under Balladur, Banque Nationale de Paris, chemicals and drug group Rhone-Poulenc SA, oil company Elf Aquitaine SA, Union des Assurances de Paris (UAP), and Credit Local de France have all been privatized. The

Gross Domestic Product (94)	Three-Year Average GDP Growth (92-94)	Main Industries	Consumer Price Index (8/95)	Monetary Unit	Exchange Rate (9/95)
7.376.9 trillion FRF ($1.475 trillion)	1.16%	High technology, banking and finance, consumer goods, retailing, extraction and energy, processing and manufacturing	1.9%	French franc	FFr4.92 to US$1.00

Balladur government also privatized the state tobacco monopoly Seita in February 1995.

The new Chirac administration privatized steel company Usinor Sacilor in May. In addition, the government has said that auto maker Renault SA, and aluminumn giant Pechiney are scheduled for privatization before the end of 1995. But the government has brought down its goal of 50 billion francs in privatization revenue in 1995, to only 20 billion francs.

While the privatization program was very successful in 1994, the privatization of Usinor has been something of a disappointment. Usinor shares have languished around their initial offering price of 86 francs a share.

Also, a climate of rising long-term interest rates has made financial issues less attractive. While the Bank of France has said repeatedly that it would like to bring rates lower, its policy of gradual reductions has failed to help the franc gain strength against the Deutsche mark, which has caused investors to shy away from the stock exchange.

Financial and insurance stocks, which make up 21.66% of CAC 40 stocks, were also hard hit by losses from their their sizeable real-estate portfolios, which suffered from the enduring crisis in that sector.

In addition, the weakness of the dollar in the first half of 1995 had a strong negative impact on earnings for export-oriented stocks.

In the mid-1980s, liberalization of foreign investment restrictions and installation of an advanced computer system transformed the Paris Bourse from a small, local market with intermittent manually posted quotes to a fully modernized, international market with a heavy foreign presence among brokers and investors.

Ten Largest Capitalized Companies
as of 9/30/95

Stock	Market Cap. US$Mil
Elf Aquitaine	17,803,377.7
LVMH	16,418,942.1
L'Oréal	15,684,682.9
Carrefour	15,061,481.7
Total	13,707,454.9
Alcatel Alsthom	12,334,204.2
Danone	11,274,239.8
Générale des Eaux	10,826,508.5
L'Air Liquide	10,370,790.2
Saint-Gobain	9,901,585.4

Trading moved from the ring or "Corbeille" on the floor of the Palais Brongniart, the colonnaded, 19th century bourse in the old financial district to fully automated, on-screen trading from offices around the country. Only futures and options trading, including the popular CAC 40 index derivatives, takes place on the Bourse floor through open outcry.

One-third of the 62 registered brokerages in France are foreign controlled.

At June 1995, according to the Bank of France's most recent monthly bulletin, non-residents held 34% of all publicly traded

French shares, stable from year-earlier.

The Paris Bourse is considered the third largest stock market in Europe, after London and the combined German exchanges, with a market capitalization at the end of July 1995 of 2.498 trillion francs.

The 40 most active stocks make up the CAC 40 index, which is also the focus of most of the market activity, enhanced by index futures and options. There are, however, two other indexes: The SBF 120, which has been calculated on a real-time basis since March 1994, and has helped expand interest in the non-CAC 40 "80," and the SBF 250 index that is less closely followed.

The CAC 40 comprises the following major sectors: 59.6% industrials, 18.69% services, and 21.66% financials. In a further breakdown, 11.7% are energy stocks, 11.7% agro-food, 6.9% construction and 9.0% capital goods.

The main share listing is the monthly account, essentially a forward trading system that allows a trader to take a position without paying for shares until the end-of-month settlement period. The "bourse month" ends before the calendar month. If a position is rolled over into the next month, interest is charged. As a result, most positions are liquidated each month.

There are 265 companies on the monthly account, 183 French and 82 foreign. The less actively traded Second Market lists 267 companies, of which 264 are French. The Paris Bourse lists a total of 906 companies.

Industry Group Performance
1 Year Change Through 9/30/95

Industry	Change % (US$)
Best Performing	
Recreational Products & Services - All	57.33
Other Recreational Products & Services	57.33
General Industrial & Commercial Services	48.36
Food Retailers & Wholesalers	37.09
Pharmaceuticals	33.40
Worst Performing	
Aerospace & Defense	-61.58
Oilfield Equipment & Services - Other	-42.39
Insurance - Property & Casualty	-35.47
Steel	-25.92
Advertising	-21.43

The monthly account listing comprises almost all the blue chips of the French market, including state and private sector companies. Both ordinary shares and non-voting investment certificates of state-owned companies, such as Credit Lyonnais and Pechiney, are traded.

In May 1995, the stock exchange inaugurated the mid-CAC index of 100 mid-range French stocks. For the time being, however, the index is only calculated twice a day, at the opening and the closing.

In February 1995, the Paris stock exchange administrator SBF-Paris Bourse announced the opening of a new market in 1996. Known as the Nouveau Marche, it is designed to help young, innovative companies raise equity, much like the Nasdaq Stock Market does in the U.S.

CAC 40 futures and options are traded on the Marche des Options Negotiables de Paris (MONEP) and the Marche a Terme Internationale de Paris (MATIF). Arbitrageurs trade the CAC 40 stocks in "baskets" hedged against CAC 40 futures or options contracts.

Accor

Industry: **Lodging**

Accor owns and operates hotels, restaurants, leisure facilities, and catering services. Additionally its business services division has three core activities: Service Vouchers, Institutional Catering and Travel Agencies. Accor owns more than 2,200 luxury and budget hotels, including those in the Novotel, Ibis, Sofitel, and Motel 6 chains. In March 1994, the company formed a joint venture with its travel agency subsidiary Wagonlit Travel and U.S. travel firm Carlson Travel creating Carlson Wagonlit Travel, the world's largest business travel network by sales.

FFr mil	12/92	12/93	12/94	US$mil 12/94				
Sales	**29,479.0**	**28,162.0**	**33,472.0**	**6,069.3**	P/E Ratio	**21.3**	Price (9/30/95)	**610.00**
Net Income	**802.0**	**615.0**	**711.0**	**128.9**	P/B Ratio	**0.9**	52 Wk Hi-Low	**680.00-507.00**
Book Value	**10,629.0**	**12,010.0**	**16,101.0**	**3,015.2**	Yield %	**3.0**	Market Cap	**US$3,095.3mil**

Address **2 rue de la Mare Neuve**
91021 Evry
Tel **1-60-87-43-20**
Fax **1-60-77-04-58**
ADR
SEDOL No. **4112321**
Co-Chairman **Paul Dubrule**
Co-Chairman **Gérard Pélisson**

AGF

Industry: **Insurance - Property & Casualty**

State-controlled Assurances Générales de France (AGF) is among the largest insurance companies in France. Its products include life, health, auto, transport, and fire insurance. In 1994 the group generated more than 40% of its premium income outside of France. AGF owns one third of German insurer Aachener und Münchener Beteiligungs and a partial stake in real-estate firm Groupement pour le Financement de la Construction. In early 1995, management requested that privatization be deferred until AGF's performance results could be improved.

FFr mil	12/92	12/93	12/94	US$mil 12/94				
Revenues	**82,329.0**	**90,550.0**	**90,055.0**	**16,329.1**	P/E Ratio	**10.5**	Price (9/30/95)	**134.50**
Net Income	**1,495.0**	**977.0**	**880.0**	**159.6**	P/B Ratio	**0.6**	52 Wk Hi-Low	**241.50-121.50**
Book Value	**23,574.0**	**30,344.0**	**30,299.0**	**5,674.0**	Yield %	**2.2**	Market Cap	**US$3,719.0mil**

Address **87 rue de Richelieu**
75060 Paris
Tel **1-44-86-20-00**
Fax **1-44-86-21-34**
ADR
SEDOL No. **4034737**
Managing Director **Jean-François Debrois**
Chairman **Antoine Jeancourt**

L'Air Liquide

Industry: **Specialty Chemicals**

L'Air Liquide produces gases and chemicals, and has welding, engineering, and construction operations. It also manufactures medical products such as anesthesiology equipment, operating tables, and surgical lighting systems. The firm's main products include liquid oxygen, nitrogen, carbon dioxide, and hydrogen peroxide. It manufactures welding and cutting equipment and related products, including electrodes and wires. L'Air Liquide also constructs oxygen-production units for the steel and glass industries. Overseas exports represent nearly half of its revenues.

FFr mil	12/92	12/93	12/94	US$mil 12/94				
Sales	**29,926.0**	**30,376.0**	**31,751.6**	**5,757.3**	P/E Ratio	**20.6**	Price (9/30/95)	**784.00**
Net Income	**2,221.0**	**2,225.0**	**2,452.3**	**444.7**	P/B Ratio	**2.5**	52 Wk Hi-Low	**834.00-681.00**
Book Value	**18,380.0**	**20,598.0**	**20,781.1**	**3,891.6**	Yield %	**1.8**	Market Cap	**US$10,371mil**

Address **75 Quai d'Orsay**
75321 Paris
Tel **1-40-62-55-55**
Fax **1-45-55-58-76**
ADR **AIQUY**
SEDOL No. **4011406**
CEO **Alain Joly**
Chairman **Alain Joly**

Alcatel Alsthom

Industry: **Communications Technology**

Alcatel Alsthom provides telecommunication equipment and transportation services, and generates power in more than 100 countries. Its wholly-owned Dutch telecommunication subsidiary, Alcatel, provides network systems, satellites, and fiberoptic cables. Alcatel Alsthom has a 50% stake in GEC Alsthom (Netherlands), which operates combined-cycle gas-turbine power plants, supplies high-speed railway equipment, and builds ships. Alcatel Alsthom's Cegelec subsidiary and Germany's AEG operate an industrial-controls joint venture. Exports account for nearly 30% of sales.

FFr mil	12/92	12/93	12/94	US$mil 12/94				
Sales	**161,677.0**	**156,334.0**	**167,643.0**	**30,397.6**	P/E Ratio	**16.3**	Price (9/30/95)	**414.10**
Net Income	**7,053.0**	**7,062.0**	**3,620.0**	**656.4**	P/B Ratio	**1.0**	52 Wk Hi-Low	**534.00-387.50**
Book Value	**49,895.0**	**57,884.0**	**59,784.0**	**11,195.5**	Yield %	**3.6**	Market Cap	**US$12,334mil**

Address **54 rue La Boétie**
75008 Paris
Tel **1-42-56-15-61**
Fax **1-40-76-14-00**
ADR **ALA**
SEDOL No. **4216825**
CEO **François de Laage**
Chairman **Marc Viénot**

Axa

Industry: **Insurance - Full Line**

Axa Groupe is an insurance company providing a full range of insurance and reinsurance services in Europe, North America, and Asia. Axa offers banking and real-estate services in France and the United States. Brokerage and investment-banking firm Donaldson, Lufkin & Jenrette is a wholly-owned subsidiary. In 1994, over 60% of the company's insurance-premium income was generated in Europe. Axa has a 49% stake in U.S. insurance company The Equitable and a 51% stake in National Mutual, Australia's second-largest life insurance company.

FFr mil	12/92	12/93	12/94	US$mil 12/94				
Revenues	**103,076.0**	**126,284.0**	**134,362.0**	**24,363.0**	P/E Ratio	**18.4**	Price (9/30/95)	**259.70**
Net Income	**1,546.0**	**2,038.0**	**2,268.0**	**411.2**	P/B Ratio	**1.2**	52 Wk Hi-Low	**296.80-206.40**
Book Value	**31,508.0**	**33,092.0**	**36,130.0**	**6,765.9**	Yield %	**2.1**	Market Cap	**US$8,479.9mil**

Address **23 ave. Matignon**
75008 Paris
Tel **1-40-75-57-00**
Fax **1-40-75-57-50**
ADR
SEDOL No. **4026927**
CEO **Claude Bébéar**
Chairman **Claude Bébéar**

Bail Investissement

Industry: **Real-Estate Investment**

Bail Investissement owns and manages real estate throughout France and the United Kingdom. It leases and rents warehouses, commercial and professional space, and parking lots. Its property portfolio is concentrated in Paris and London. Two of the company's main properties are an office and retail center in London, and an apartment building in France. The investment holding company Compagnie de Suez owns more than 24% of Bail Investissement, while French insurer Union des Assurances de Paris holds 16%.

FFr mil	12/92	12/93	12/94	US$mil 12/94				
Sales	**888.0**	**910.0**	**8,014.0**	**1,453.1**	P/E Ratio	**11.1**	Price (9/30/95)	**820.00**
Net Income	**274.0**	**230.0**	**226.3**	**41.0**	P/B Ratio	**2.5**	52 Wk Hi-Low	**920.00-781.00**
Book Value	**1,471.0**	**1,482.0**	**1,016.2**	**190.3**	Yield %	**8.6**	Market Cap	**US$509.0mil**

Address **Grand Ecran, 30 place d'Italie**
75628 Paris
Tel **1-40-78-52-52**
Fax **1-40-78-53-53**
ADR
SEDOL No. **4070708**
CEO **Christian Sabbe**
Chairman **Michel Hémar**

Compagnie Bancaire

Industry: **Financial Services - Diversified**

Compagnie Bancaire is a banking and financial-services company that serves individual and corporate clients. The company is responsible for human-resources development and administers its own property portfolio. Compagnie Bancaire owns UCB (which provides mortgage loans), 60% of Cardif (which provides life insurance and savings plans), 71% of UFB Locabail (which offers financing for business equipment), and 73% of Cetelem (which provides consumer loans). French holding company Compagnie Financière de Paribas has a 47% stake in Compagnie Bancaire.

FFr mil	12/92	12/93	12/94	US$mil 12/94				
Revenues	**30,871.0**	**29,594.0**	**22,968.0**	**4,164.6**	P/E Ratio	**24.0**	Price (9/30/95)	**458.90**
Net Income	**369.0**	**365.0**	**536.0**	**97.2**	P/B Ratio	**1.0**	52 Wk Hi-Low	**611.00-412.64**
Book Value	**11,933.0**	**12,297.0**	**12,536.0**	**2,347.6**	Yield %	**2.0**	Market Cap	**US$2,490.7mil**

Address **5 ave. Kléber**
75116 Paris
Tel **1-45-25-25-25**
Fax **1-40-67-38-74**
ADR
SEDOL No. **4214948**
Chairman Exec Bd **François Henrot**
Chairman Supv Bd **André Lévy-Lang**

Banque Nationale de Paris

Industry: **Banks - Money Center**

Banque Nationale de Paris (BNP), a money-center bank in France, offers retail-banking, foreign-exchange, commercial-banking, and investment-banking services to customers in Europe, North America, and Asia. The company also provides securities-trading facilities, institutional broking services, and international financing for multinational corporations. BNP owns interests in several major French companies including a 5% stake in financial services firm Compagnie de Suez and a 19% stake in insurer Union des Assurances de Paris (UAP). In turn, UAP has a 15% interest in BNP.

FFr mil	12/92	12/93	12/94	US$mil 12/94				
Revenues	**161,288.0**	**148,383.0**	**119,872.0**	**21,735.6**	P/E Ratio	**22.2**	Price (9/30/95)	**193.00**
Net Income	**2,168.0**	**1,018.0**	**1,656.0**	**300.3**	P/B Ratio	**0.8**	52 Wk Hi-Low	**272.50-193.00**
Book Value	**43,714.0**	**46,804.0**	**48,153.0**	**9,017.4**	Yield %	**1.7**	Market Cap	**US$7,455.1mil**

Address **16 Blvd. des Italiens**
75009 Paris
Tel **1-42-44-45-46**
Fax **N/A**
ADR
SEDOL No. **4133667**
Chief Executive **Michel Pebereau**
Chairman **Michel Pebereau**

Bongrain

Industry: **Other Food**

Bongrain produces dairy products and gourmet foods. The company's cheeses, which contribute two thirds of total revenues, are sold under such brand names as Caprice des Dieux, Fol Epi, and Menu Fromage. Bongrain has activities in Europe, North and South America, Australia, and Japan, and is continuing its expansion into central and eastern Europe, most notably in the former Soviet Union, Czech Republic, and Hungary. France is Bongrain's largest European market, accounting for nearly two thirds of sales, while Germany accounted for 17% of sales in 1994.

FFr mil	12/92	12/93	12/94	US$mil 12/94				
Sales	**9,706.0**	**9,591.0**	**9,672.5**	**1,753.9**	P/E Ratio	**13.9**	Price (9/30/95)	**2,647.00**
Net Income	**354.0**	**434.0**	**366.3**	**66.4**	P/B Ratio	**N/A**	52 Wk Hi-Low	**3,062.0-2,566.0**
Book Value	**2,870.0**	**3,273.0**	**3,336.5**	**624.8**	Yield %	**2.3**	Market Cap	**US$1,035.1mil**

Address **Route de Dampierre 7**
78280 Guyancourt
Tel **30-48-12-00**
Fax **30-43-37-23**
ADR
SEDOL No. **4110444**
CEO **Jean-Noël Bongrain**
Chairman **Claude Boutineau**

Bouygues

Industry: **Heavy Construction**

Bouygues is a construction, public-works, and real-estate company that also holds interests in media and food businesses. Its operations include infrastructure projects, maritime construction, waterproofing, public-utilities management and distribution, and gas exploration. Bouygues is a partner in the Channel Tunnel project, controls 34% of the French television station TF1, and owns feature-film production company Ciby 2000. In October 1994 a consortium headed by Bouygues won the licence to operate France's third mobile-telephone network.

FFr mil	12/92	12/93	12/94	US$mil 12/94				
Sales	**62,720.0**	**61,183.0**	**72,410.0**	**13,129.6**	P/E Ratio	**22.2**	Price (9/30/95)	**566.00**
Net Income	**685.0**	**469.0**	**573.0**	**103.9**	P/B Ratio	**1.4**	52 Wk Hi-Low	**634.00-505.00**
Book Value	**7,243.0**	**7,939.0**	**9,298.0**	**1,741.2**	Yield %	**0.0**	Market Cap	**US$2,568.4mil**

Address **1 ave. Eugène-Freyssinet**
78061 St.-Quentin-Yvelines
Tel **1-30-60-23-11**
Fax **1-30-60-48-61**
ADR
SEDOL No. **4115159**
Managing Director **Martin Bouygues**
Chairman **Martin Bouygues**

Canal Plus

Industry: **Broadcasting**

Canal Plus operates a pay-television station, manufactures reception equipment, and produces and distributes films and television programs. Canal Plus's sales have surpassed HBO's (U.S.), making it the leading pay-television company in the world. It has more than 3.8 million subscribers in France and more than 900,000 each in Spain and Germany. It owns and operates foreign-language channels and European Television Networks' thematic channels, including the European Sports Network. The company derives most of its income from its pay-television operations in France.

FFr mil	12/92	12/93	12/94	US$mil 12/94				
Sales	**7,937.0**	**8,675.0**	**9,566.7**	**1,734.7**	P/E Ratio	**28.3**	Price (9/30/95)	**839.00**
Net Income	**1,104.0**	**1,202.0**	**626.3**	**113.6**	P/B Ratio	**2.6**	52 Wk Hi-Low	**909.00-575.00**
Book Value	**5,321.0**	**6,413.0**	**7,029.6**	**1,316.4**	Yield %	**1.8**	Market Cap	**US$3,680.5mil**

Address	**85/89 Quai André Citroën**	Tel	**1-44-25-10-00**	ADR	**CNPLY**	CEO	**Pierre Lescure**
	75015 Paris	Fax	**1-44-25-12-34**	SEDOL No.	**4171720**	Chairman	**Pierre Lescure**

Cap Gemini Sogeti

Industry: **Software**

Cap Gemini Sogeti Group is a computer-services and consulting company. The firm provides custom-designed information-technology services and solutions. Its areas of business include consulting, project services, information-systems management, and software-package development. Its project-services division generated over 60% of its sales in 1994. Cap Gemini Sogeti owns Hoskyns, a British systems-integration and facilities-management firm. The company is active in 13 European countries and the United States.

FFr mil	12/92	12/93	12/94	US$mil 12/94				
Sales	**11,884.0**	**11,028.0**	**10,176.2**	**1,845.2**	P/E Ratio	**NMF**	Price (9/30/95)	**138.00**
Net Income	**-72.0**	**-429.0**	**-94.3**	**-17.1**	P/B Ratio	**1.2**	52 Wk Hi-Low	**198.80-127.40**
Book Value	**5,250.0**	**5,232.0**	**6,063.2**	**1,135.4**	Yield %	**0.0**	Market Cap	**US$1,488.5mil**

Address	**3 rue Malakoff**	Tel	**76-59-50-00**	ADR		CEO	**Serge Kampf**
	38005 Grenoble	Fax	**N/A**	SEDOL No.	**4163437**	Chairman	**Serge Kampf**

CarnaudMetalbox

Industry: **Containers & Packaging**

CarnaudMetalbox makes metal and plastic packaging for customers in the food, beverage, personal-care, and industrial sectors. It supplies beverage and aerosol cans, high-performance plastics, and vacuum closures to such customers as Nestlé, Kraft General Foods, Coca Cola, and Cadbury Schweppes. Its Eurosteel division, which represents its food, aerosol, and specialty packaging operations, accounts for more than half of CarnaudMetalbox's revenues. U.S. packaging firm Crown Cork & Seal has offered $5.2 billion to purchase the company.

FFr mil	12/92	12/93	12/94	US$mil 12/94				
Sales	**24,830.0**	**24,340.0**	**24,890.0**	**4,513.1**	P/E Ratio	**17.8**	Price (9/30/95)	**206.60**
Net Income	**976.0**	**835.0**	**950.0**	**172.3**	P/B Ratio	**1.4**	52 Wk Hi-Low	**219.10-167.00**
Book Value	**10,857.0**	**11,118.0**	**12,306.0**	**2,304.5**	Yield %	**2.1**	Market Cap	**US$3,455.8mil**

Address	**153 rue de Courcelles**	Tel	**1-44-15-68-00**	ADR		CEO	**B. Jürgen Hintz**
	75017 Paris	Fax	**1-40-53-03-53**	SEDOL No.	**4160568**	Chairman	**Ernest A. Seillère**

Carrefour

Industry: **Food Retailers & Wholesalers**

Carrefour is a retailer and wholesaler. Its Carrefour hypermarkets sell food, housewares, electronics, clothing, and hardware; some of its stores also sell insurance products and vacation packages. The company has more than 750 stores, including 218 Erteco discount stores and the chain of Euromarché hypermarkets. It also holds a 90% stake in the gas wholesaler Carfuel, and has a 15% stake in Office Depot (United States), an office-supplies retailer, and PriceCostco (U.S.), a discount-warehouse retailer. Overseas exports accounted for more than 21% of revenues in 1994.

FFr mil	12/92	12/93	12/94	US$mil 12/94				
Sales	**117,139.0**	**123,204.0**	**136,299.0**	**24,714.2**	P/E Ratio	**34.9**	Price (9/30/95)	**2,890.00**
Net Income	**1,335.0**	**3,010.0**	**2,124.0**	**385.1**	P/B Ratio	**5.7**	52 Wk Hi-Low	**2,952.0-2,041.0**
Book Value	**9,416.0**	**11,922.0**	**12,907.0**	**2,417.0**	Yield %	**0.9**	Market Cap	**US$15,061mil**

Address	**6 ave. Raymond Poincaré**	Tel	**1-53-70-19-00**	ADR		Chairman Exec Bd	**Daniel Bernard**
	75116 Paris	Fax	**1-53-70-86-16**	SEDOL No.	**4177546**	Chairman Supv Bd	**Jacques Fournier**

CGIP

Industry: **Financial Services - Diversified**

Compagnie Générale d'Industrie et de Participations (CGIP) is a holding company with main interests in packaging, software, health-care, abrasive pellets, and real estate.It owns 32% of packaging company CarnaudMetalbox, 5% of software-services group Sogeti, and 33% of microbiology firm BioMèrieux Alliance. Abrasive-pellets manufacturer Wheelabrator-Allevard and real-estate company Orange-Nassau are wholly-owned subsidiaries. CGIP's majority shareholder is holding company Marine-Wendel. In 1994, CGIP sold its 84% position in cement company Cedest.

FFr mil	12/92	12/93	12/94	US$mil 12/94				
Revenues	**16,724.0**	**28,445.0**	**26,274.6**	**4,764.2**	P/E Ratio	**5.9**	Price (9/30/95)	**945.00**
Net Income	**543.0**	**547.0**	**1,010.6**	**183.2**	P/B Ratio	**0.6**	52 Wk Hi-Low	**1,291.0-945.0**
Book Value	**7,161.0**	**8,081.0**	**9,187.3**	**1,720.5**	Yield %	**3.7**	Market Cap	**US$1,207.9mil**

Address	**89 rue Taitbout**	Tel	**1-42-85-30-00**	ADR		CEO	**Ernest A. Seillière**
	75009 Paris	Fax	**1-42-80-68-67**	SEDOL No.	**4162616**	Chairman	**Ernest A. Seillière**

Chargeurs

Industry: **Clothing & Fabrics**

Chargeurs is a diversified company with activities divided into three main sectors: textiles, entertainment, and transportation. The textile division processes and sells wool and fabrics for cars and clothing. The entertainment division produces and distributes television programs and films, and develops multimedia products. Its Walon transportation subsidiary is Europe's largest transporter of automobiles. Chargeurs also owns 20% of French Canalsatellite and 17% of British BSkyB satellite television companies. More than 75% of Chargeurs' sales are made outside France.

	FFr mil 12/92	12/93	12/94	US$mil 12/94				
Sales	**10,080.0**	**8,602.0**	**9,829.0**	**1,782.2**	P/E Ratio	**21.0**	Price (9/30/95)	**1,020.00**
Net Income	**724.0**	**-97.0**	**344.0**	**62.4**	P/B Ratio	**1.1**	52 Wk Hi-Low	**1,225.3-907.0**
Book Value	**7,094.0**	**6,815.0**	**7,122.0**	**1,333.7**	Yield %	**1.2**	Market Cap	**US$1,582.0mil**

Address **5 blvd. Malesherbes**
75008 Paris
Tel **1-49-24-40-00**
Fax **1-49-24-40-89**
ADR
SEDOL No. **4188441**
CEO **Jérôme Seydoux**
Chairman **Jérôme Seydoux**

Club Méditerranée

Industry: **Other Recreational Products & Services**

Club Méditerranée manages 140 resort villages in 35 countries, runs cruises, and conducts tours. Its resorts operate under the Club Med, Valtur, Club Med Affaires (which caters to business travelers), and Club Aquarius names. It owns two cruise ships, Club Med 1, which sails the Mediterranean and Caribbean, and Club Med 2, which cruises the Pacific. The company has operations in Europe, Africa, and South America. It has agreed to buy the remaining 29% share in its U.S. subsidiary Club Med, which manages North and Central American and Asian activities.

	FFr mil 10/92	10/93	10/94	US$mil 10/94				
Sales	**8,251.0**	**8,147.0**	**8,767.3**	**1,563.6**	P/E Ratio	**55.8**	Price (9/30/95)	**477.00**
Net Income	**161.0**	**-296.0**	**93.7**	**16.7**	P/B Ratio	**1.6**	52 Wk Hi-Low	**536.00-401.00**
Book Value	**3,588.0**	**3,301.0**	**3,170.0**	**614.3**	Yield %	**0.0**	Market Cap	**US$1,062.6mil**

Address **25 rue Vivienne**
75002 Paris
Tel **1-42-61-85-00**
Fax **1-40-20-91-44**
ADR **CLMDY**
SEDOL No. **4204370**
CEO **Serge Trigano**
Chairman **Serge Trigano**

Colas

Industry: **Heavy Construction**

Colas has operations in road construction, civil engineering, and building. Its activities include building-distribution systems for utilities and public services, earth moving, and dam construction. Colas is a partially owned subsidiary of Bouygues, a diversified construction, public-works, and real-estate company. Colas has operations throughout Europe, and in Africa, the Middle East, the Far East, Canada, and the United States. In 1994, about 70% of the company's revenues were generated in France.

	FFr mil 12/92	12/93	12/94	US$mil 12/94				
Sales	**12,884.0**	**16,206.0**	**16,555.0**	**3,001.8**	P/E Ratio	**16.6**	Price (9/30/95)	**880.00**
Net Income	**288.0**	**289.0**	**342.0**	**62.0**	P/B Ratio	**1.8**	52 Wk Hi-Low	**1,016.0-758.0**
Book Value	**2,294.0**	**2,459.0**	**3,234.0**	**605.6**	Yield %	**2.6**	Market Cap	**US$1,150.6mil**

Address **7 place René Clair**
92653 Boulogne-Billancourt
Tel **1-47-61-75-00**
Fax **1-47-61-76-00**
ADR
SEDOL No. **4208918**
CEO **Alain Dupont**
Chairman **Alain Dupont**

Comptoirs Modernes

Industry: **Food Retailers & Wholesalers**

Comptoirs Modernes is a holding company with subsidiaries in the food-retailing industry. It operates a network of nearly 400 Comod supermarkets, and 23 Marché Plus markets. The company also operates more than 700 Stoc discount supermarkets (of which 22 are franchised), which accounted for roughly 73% of total revenues in 1994. In addition, Comptoirs Modernes operates 10 Merca Plus supermarkets in northeastern Spain. The French retailer Carrefour runs 16 Carrefour hypermarkets in a joint venture with Comptoirs Modernes.

	FFr mil 12/92	12/93	12/94	US$mil 12/94				
Sales	**22,572.0**	**23,643.0**	**25,747.0**	**4,668.5**	P/E Ratio	**39.3**	Price (9/30/95)	**1,629.00**
Net Income	**335.0**	**370.0**	**403.3**	**73.1**	P/B Ratio	**2.6**	52 Wk Hi-Low	**1,629.0-1,258.0**
Book Value	**2,629.0**	**2,920.0**	**3,246.4**	**607.9**	Yield %	**1.2**	Market Cap	**US$1,695.2mil**

Address **1 place du Gué de Maulny**
72019 Le Mans
Tel **1-43-86-28-20**
Fax **1-43-72-32-75**
ADR
SEDOL No. **4215167**
CEO **Jean-Claude Plassart**
Chairman **Jean-Claude Plassart**

CPR

Industry: **Financial Services - Diversified**

Compagnie Parisienne de Réescompte (CPR) offers banking, proprietary-trading, asset-management, and brokerage services. Proprietary trading contributes 64% of the company's total net income, while brokerage activities contribute 25%. The company also has financing and capital-markets operations, and holds a 26% interest in Spanish securities broker SIAF. Through its 100% interest in the French bank CGM, CPR controls BBT-Dagues-Bié, France's third-largest money broker by revenues.

	FFr mil 12/92	12/93	12/94	US$mil 12/94				
Revenues	**17,806.0**	**15,304.0**	**14,955.2**	**2,711.7**	P/E Ratio	**11.2**	Price (9/30/95)	**330.00**
Net Income	**166.0**	**342.0**	**276.0**	**50.0**	P/B Ratio	**1.2**	52 Wk Hi-Low	**397.00-309.00**
Book Value	**2,095.0**	**2,434.0**	**2,615.6**	**489.8**	Yield %	**6.1**	Market Cap	**US$628.8mil**

Address **4 cité de Londres**
75312 Paris
Tel **1-45-96-20-00**
Fax **1-45-96-25-55**
ADR
SEDOL No. **4671888**
CEO **Jean-Néel Barthélémy**
Chairman **Henri Cukierman**

Crédit Commercial

Industry: **Banks - Regional**

Crédit Commercial de France (CCF) offers personal- and investment-banking services. It is involved in asset management through Framlington, its United Kingdom subsidiary, and quantitative manager CCF SAM. The firm's retail banking network contributed 35% of gross profits in 1994 and its five regional banks an additional 13%. Investment-banking services, which include a 90% stake in British merchant bank Charterhouse, accounted for a third of gross profits. CCF also operates insurance, private-banking, and equipment-leasing businesses and airport bureaux de change.

	FFr mil 12/92	12/93	12/94	US$mil 12/94				
Revenues	**44,729.0**	**58,874.0**	**53,743.3**	**9,744.9**	P/E Ratio	**12.0**	Price (9/30/95)	**217.00**
Net Income	**978.0**	**1,078.0**	**1,203.2**	**218.2**	P/B Ratio	**1.1**	52 Wk Hi-Low	**244.00-195.30**
Book Value	**10,524.0**	**10,877.0**	**13,745.8**	**2,574.1**	Yield %	**2.1**	Market Cap	**US$2,981.8mil**

Address **103 ave. des Champs-Elysées** Tel **1-40-70-70-40** ADR CEO **Charles de Croisset**
75008 Paris Fax **1-47-20-23-72** SEDOL No. **4230870** Chairman **Charles de Croisset**

Crédit Foncier

Industry: **Banks - Regional**

Crédit Foncier de France is a real-estate and mortgage firm offering a wide range of property financing to the private sector, including medium- and long-term loans, and financing for property developers. The firm maintains a relationship with the French government by providing government-subsidized loan financing and loans guaranteed by France. The government appoints the governors of the firm and is represented on its board. Crédit Foncier also offers asset-management, investment-fund, and life-insurance services.

	FFr mil 12/92	12/93	12/94	US$mil 12/94				
Revenues	**39,184.0**	**38,841.0**	**33,819.7**	**6,132.3**	P/E Ratio	**13.7**	Price (9/30/95)	**103.80**
Net Income	**411.0**	**515.0**	**274.3**	**49.7**	P/B Ratio	**0.4**	52 Wk Hi-Low	**278.00-100.00**
Book Value	**6,737.0**	**8,475.0**	**8,522.6**	**1,596.0**	Yield %	**9.0**	Market Cap	**US$767.0mil**

Address **19 rue des Capucines** Tel **1-42-44-80-00** ADR Deputy Chairman **Jean-René Bernard**
75001 Paris Fax **1-42-44-86-99** SEDOL No. **4679581** Chairman **Jean-Claude Colli**

Crédit National

Industry: **Banks - Regional**

Crédit National is a financial institution specializing in term lending. Its core areas of business are corporate lending, with an emphasis on long- and medium-term loans; equity financing; capital markets; and real-estate activities. The company has offices in Europe and the United States and partnerships with a range of financial institutions, including IKB Deutsche Industriebank (Germany), Hambros (United Kingdom), Citibank (United States), and Fujibank (Japan). In 1994 Crédit National became fully independent from state control.

	FFr mil 12/92	12/93	12/94	US$mil 12/94				
Revenues	**15,083.0**	**14,542.0**	**11,551.0**	**2,094.5**	P/E Ratio	**75.4**	Price (9/30/95)	**346.90**
Net Income	**586.0**	**330.0**	**67.0**	**12.1**	P/B Ratio	**0.6**	52 Wk Hi-Low	**455.60-321.00**
Book Value	**6,506.0**	**7,121.0**	**7,025.0**	**1,315.5**	Yield %	**3.5**	Market Cap	**US$843.1mil**

Address **45 rue Saint-Dominique** Tel **1-45-50-90-00** ADR CEO **Emmanuel Rodocanachi**
75700 Paris Fax **1-45-55-89-58** SEDOL No. **4242455** Chairman **Emmanuel Rodocanachi**

Damart

Industry: **Clothing & Fabrics**

Damart is a holding company with manufacturing, retailing, and property interests. Its retailing division, Damart International S.A. (DISA), distributes its Damart clothing line through direct marketer Serviposte and through the Belmart chain of retail outlets. Its manufacturing division includes Somfy International S.A. (SISA), which makes automatic doors and shutters for domestic, commercial, and industrial use. Damart's Brevidex and Vernier Leurent subsidiaries manage and invest in rental properties. About 53% of Damart's revenues are generated in France.

	FFr mil 12/92	06/93 *	06/94	US$mil 06/94				
Sales	**3,955.0**	**1,800.0**	**5,367.8**	**932.1**	P/E Ratio	**48.7**	Price (9/30/95)	**5,010.00**
Net Income	**-16.0**	**13.0**	**235.9**	**41.0**	P/B Ratio	**2.7**	52 Wk Hi-Low	**6,100.0-4,501.0**
Book Value	**929.0**	**923.0**	**1,144.2**	**209.6**	Yield %	**1.2**	Market Cap	**US$633.4mil**

Address **25 rue de la Fosse-aux-Chênes** Tel **20-11-45-00** ADR CEO **Paul G. Despature**
59100 Roubaix Fax **20-11-45-59** SEDOL No. **4252788** Chairman **Jules Despature**

*Irregular period due to fiscal year change.

Danone

Industry: **Other Food**

Groupe Danone produces food and beverages and makes packaging materials. Its products include Evian and Volvic mineral waters, Danone and Dannon yogurt, and San Miguel and Kronenbourg beers. Danone also owns Irish cookie maker W&R Jacob; U.S.-based Lea & Perrins, a producer of sauces and condiments; and 80% of Italian cheese producer Galbani. In 1994, Danone and Saint Louis merged their canned and frozen-food operations to create Panzalim. Exports to North and South America, Africa, and Asia account for 12% of sales; the remainder come from France and Europe.

	FFr mil 12/92	12/93	12/94	US$mil 12/94				
Sales	**70,840.0**	**70,108.0**	**76,820.0**	**13,929.3**	P/E Ratio	**15.4**	Price (9/30/95)	**796.00**
Net Income	**3,638.0**	**3,422.0**	**3,527.0**	**639.5**	P/B Ratio	**1.6**	52 Wk Hi-Low	**885.00-696.00**
Book Value	**27,778.0**	**31,914.0**	**35,068.0**	**6,567.0**	Yield %	**2.0**	Market Cap	**US$11,274mil**

Address **7 rue de Téhéran** Tel **1-44-35-20-20** ADR **GPDNY** President **Franck Riboud**
75008 Paris Fax **1-42-25-67-16** SEDOL No. **4070236** Chairman **Antoine Riboud**

Dollfus Mieg

Industry: **Clothing & Fabrics**

Dollfus Mieg et Compagnie (DMC) is a textile manufacturer that has activities spanning the apparel, household, and industrial sectors. Its main products include plain and printed fabrics for clothing and interior decoration, sportswear, threads, yarns, and household linens. It also owns spinning mills serving clients outside the company. DMC markets its Descamps bed linen and babywear through 200 retail outlets, located mainly in Europe. DMC has operations in 120 countries but its businesses focus on France and Germany. European sales generate 76% of revenues.

FFr mil	12/92	12/93	12/94	US$mil 12/94				
Sales	**8,635.0**	**7,982.0**	**7,970.0**	**1,445.1**	P/E Ratio	**NMF**	Price (9/30/95)	**248.90**
Net Income	**50.0**	**51.0**	**-150.0**	**-27.2**	P/B Ratio	**0.7**	52 Wk Hi-Low	**355.00-230.00**
Book Value	**2,601.0**	**2,606.0**	**2,415.0**	**452.2**	Yield %	**1.6**	Market Cap	**US$329.8mil**

Address **10 avenue Ledru-Rollin**
75012 Paris
Tel **1-49-28-10-00**
Fax **1-43-42-54-86**
ADR
SEDOL No. **4273808**
CEO **Jacques Boubal**
Chairman **Julien R. Charlier**

Ecco

Industry: **General Industrial & Commercial Services**

Ecco offers business-support services. The company specializes in employment services (providing temporary placement and human-resources management), which represent more than 80% of its revenues. It also offers security and surveillance services and contract cleaning. Ecco manages 1,100 agencies in more than 30 countries. Its majority-owned Ecco Travail Temporaire subsidiary operates employment services in Europe. In December 1994 the firm acquired German company Tautges GmbH and in early 1995 acquired Montreal-based Léonard & Parisien.

FFr mil	12/92	12/93	12/94	US$mil 12/94				
Sales	**13,076.0**	**12,474.0**	**16,584.7**	**3,007.2**	P/E Ratio	**53.5**	Price (9/30/95)	**856.00**
Net Income	**219.0**	**242.0**	**491.9**	**89.2**	P/B Ratio	**3.1**	52 Wk Hi-Low	**880.00-551.00**
Book Value	**1,894.0**	**2,063.0**	**2,810.7**	**526.3**	Yield %	**1.4**	Market Cap	**US$1,743.3mil**

Address **16 blvd. des Invalides**
75007 Paris
Tel **1-47-53-84-84**
Fax **1-45-51-74-37**
ADR
SEDOL No. **4303277**
CEO **Philippe Foriel-Destezet**
Chairman **Philippe Foriel-Destezet**

Elf Aquitaine

Industry: **Oil - Integrated Majors**

Elf Aquitaine, privatized in 1994, is a diversified oil and chemicals firm. It explores for, produces, distributes, and markets oil and natural gas. It explores in 28 countries, with production mainly in West Africa and the North Sea. Elf's natural-gas and crude-oil reserves total 3,343 million barrels. It distributes gas through a network of more than 6,300 gas stations. Elf also produces petrochemicals, bulk plastic, and chlorinated chemicals. It holds a majority interest in health-care company Elf Sanofi, which makes pharmaceuticals, perfumes, and cosmetics.

FFr mil	12/92	12/93	12/94	US$mil 12/94				
Sales	**200,563.0**	**209,675.0**	**207,674.0**	**37,656.2**	P/E Ratio	**NMF**	Price (9/30/95)	**332.30**
Net Income	**6,177.0**	**1,070.0**	**-5,439.0**	**-986.2**	P/B Ratio	**1.1**	52 Wk Hi-Low	**412.50-328.70**
Book Value	**87,012.0**	**84,088.0**	**76,472.0**	**14,320.6**	Yield %	**3.9**	Market Cap	**US$17,803mil**

Address **Tour Elf, place de la Coupole**
92400 Courbevoie
Tel **1-47-44-45-46**
Fax **1-47-44-69-46**
ADR **ELF**
SEDOL No. **4824080**
CEO **Philippe Jaffré**
Chairman **Philippe Jaffré**

Elf Sanofi

Industry: **Pharmaceuticals**

Elf Sanofi operates in two business sectors: health care and perfumes and beauty products. The company conducts beauty-product and pharmaceutical operations for the privatized petrochemical firm Elf Aquitaine. The acquisition of Sterling Winthrop, a prescription pharmaceutical company previously owned by Eastman Kodak, has enabled Sanofi to establish its presence in the U.S. pharmaceutical market. In early 1995 the company sold its Asian and American veterinary-product businesses to Rhone Poulenc. Exports account for two thirds of Elf Sanofi's sales.

FFr mil	12/92	12/93	12/94	US$mil 12/94				
Sales	**21,441.0**	**23,501.0**	**26,105.0**	**4,733.5**	P/E Ratio	**18.8**	Price (9/30/95)	**315.00**
Net Income	**1,046.0**	**823.0**	**1,505.0**	**272.9**	P/B Ratio	**1.7**	52 Wk Hi-Low	**323.20-233.00**
Book Value	**12,604.0**	**16,077.0**	**17,359.0**	**3,250.7**	Yield %	**1.9**	Market Cap	**US$5,846.5mil**

Address **32-34 rue Marbeuf**
75008 Paris
Tel **1-40-73-40-73**
Fax **1-40-73-26-38**
ADR
SEDOL No. **4887704**
CEO **Jean-François Dehecq**
Chairman **Jean-François Dehecq**

Eridania Béghin-Say

Industry: **Other Food**

Eridania Béghin-Say processes sugar, starch, oil, and animal feed. The company also owns several branded consumer products such as salad dressings and sauces, pastry ingredients, consumer oils, and herbs and spices. Eridania Béghin-Say is the result of a merger between two Gruppo Ferruzzi members: French agricultural company Béghin-Say and its Italian parent Eridania. In 1994 the group sold the condiments operations of its Lesieur and Ducros subsidiary. It also took a majority stake in the olive-oil producer Elousa, making Eridania the world's largest olive-oil producer.

FFr mil	12/92	12/93	12/94	US$mil 12/94				
Sales	**49,741.0**	**50,908.0**	**50,786.0**	**9,208.7**	P/E Ratio	**NMF**	Price (9/30/95)	**744.00**
Net Income	**1,278.0**	**1,344.0**	**1,208.0**	**219.0**	P/B Ratio	**1.1**	52 Wk Hi-Low	**794.00-676.00**
Book Value	**15,109.0**	**15,634.0**	**17,632.0**	**3,301.9**	Yield %	**4.0**	Market Cap	**US$3,877.1mil**

Address **54 ave. Hoche**
75360 Paris
Tel **1-40-53-56-56**
Fax **N/A**
ADR
SEDOL No. **4089403**
CEO **Stefano Meloni**
Chairman **Stefano Meloni**

Essilor

Industry: **Medical Supplies**

Essilor International manufactures and sells optical products, including contact lenses, eyeglass lenses and frames, protective glasses, and eye-examination equipment. Its eye-wear brand names include Fred, Kickers, Alain Delon, and Tann's. Sales of corrective lenses contribute 84% of Essilor's total revenues. In early 1995, Essilor acquired Gentex Optics, the world's largest maker of unbreakable plastic lenses. French holding company Saint-Gobain has a 20% interest in Essilor. Activities outside of France account for three fourths of total sales.

	FFr mil 12/92	12/93	12/94	US$mil 12/94				
Sales	5,630.0	5,910.0	6,304.6	1,143.2	P/E Ratio	19.8	Price (9/30/95)	840.00
Net Income	123.0	285.0	385.7	69.9	P/B Ratio	2.0	52 Wk Hi-Low	895.00-694.00
Book Value	2,561.0	2,870.0	3,115.1	583.4	Yield %	1.4	Market Cap	US$1,277.4mil

Address **147 rue de Paris** **94227 Charenton** Tel **1-49-77-42-24** Fax **N/A** ADR SEDOL No. **4303761** CEO **Gérard Cottet** Chairman **Gérard Cottet**

Eurafrance

Industry: **Financial Services - Diversified**

Eurafrance is a holding company for investment and insurance concerns. Its holdings include companies involved in real estate, asset trading, money brokering, corporate finance, and mergers-and-acquisition consulting. The firm holds large investments in the French firms SOVAC, La France, Société Financière et Industrielle Gaz et Eaux, and Société Française Générale Immobilière, as well as Assicurazioni Generali of Italy and U.S.-based Lazard Partners. Roughly two thirds of Eurafrance's revenues are derived from holdings in SOVAC, Gaz et Eaux, and Lazard Partners.

	FFr mil 06/92	06/93	06/94	US$mil 06/94				
Revenues	263.0	255.0	281.4	48.9	P/E Ratio	17.3	Price (9/30/95)	1,460.00
Net Income	242.0	285.0	279.2	48.5	P/B Ratio	0.9	52 Wk Hi-Low	1,815.5-1,375.0
Book Value	4,888.0	5,030.0	5,282.6	967.5	Yield %	3.3	Market Cap	US$1,031.8mil

Address **12 ave. Percier** **75008 Paris** Tel **1-44-13-01-11** Fax **N/A** ADR SEDOL No. **4321547** CEO **Antoine Bernheim** Chairman **Michel David-Weill**

Euro Disney

Industry: **Other Recreational Products & Services**

Euro Disney developed and operates the Euro Disney resort outside Paris, which contains a theme park, golf course, hotels, and an entertainment center. The company also operates tours through its Euro Disney Vacances subsidiary. EDL Holding Company, a subsidiary of The Walt Disney Company (United States), owns 39% of Euro Disney. Saudi Prince Alwaleed acquired roughly a 10% share of Euro Disney in 1994. Euro Disney has resumed its real-estate development activities through an agreement with Georges V Habitat to build 600 housing units on Euro Disney property.

	FFr mil 09/92	09/93	09/94	US$mil 09/94				
Sales	8,463.0	5,725.0	4,261.0	754.4	P/E Ratio	NMF	Price (9/30/95)	15.85
Net Income	-188.0	-5,337.0	-1,797.0	-318.2	P/B Ratio	2.2	52 Wk Hi-Low	19.40-6.50
Book Value	7,027.0	1,517.0	5,496.0	1,038.9	Yield %	0.0	Market Cap	US$2,464.6mil

Address **Route Nationale 34** **77700 Chessy** Tel **1-49-41-49-10** Fax **1-49-32-40-12** ADR SEDOL No. **4320878** CEO **Philippe Bourguigon** Chairman **Philippe Bourguignon**

EURO RSCG

Industry: **Advertising**

EURO RSCG offers a full range of advertising services. It runs 20 European subsidiaries and has 21 major clients in more than seven countries. Advertising firms Comart Associates and EWDB North America are among EURO RSCG's wholly-owned subsidiaries. Group agencies include Synergie-Equateur, Australie, and Perceval. EURO RSCG is 38%-owned by French media company Havas. In 1993, international business accounted for more than 57% of the gross margin generated by EURO RSCG.

	FFr mil 12/92	12/93	12/94	US$mil 12/94				
Sales	17,969.0	13,026.0	12,087.6	2,191.8	P/E Ratio	44.1	Price (9/30/95)	465.00
Net Income	20.0	34.0	55.9	10.1	P/B Ratio	1.4	52 Wk Hi-Low	640.00-437.20
Book Value	1,837.0	1,799.0	1,739.3	325.7	Yield %	2.5	Market Cap	US$500.5mil

Address **84 rue de Villiers** **92683 Levallois-Perret** Tel **41-34-34-34** Fax **47-47-90-96** ADR SEDOL No. **4301594** CEO **Alain de Pouzilhac** Chairman **Alain de Pouzilhac**

Foncière Lyonnaise

Industry: **Real-Estate Investment**

Société Foncière Lyonnaise is a real-estate company with the majority of its holdings located in the 16th district of Paris and the surrounding western suburbs (primarily Neuilly). The company manages and rents residential and commercial properties. Société Foncière Lyonnaise manages approximately 200,000 square meters of property, 52% of which is residential, 37% retail, and 11% commercial. The company also holds stock in other property and investment firms, including real-estate firm UNIBAIL and real-estate developer GFC.

	FFr mil 12/92	12/93	12/94	US$mil 12/94				
Sales	163.0	160.0	162.7	29.5	P/E Ratio	38.4	Price (9/30/95)	637.00
Net Income	82.0	72.0	61.6	11.2	P/B Ratio	4.0	52 Wk Hi-Low	849.00-532.00
Book Value	569.0	586.0	588.4	110.2	Yield %	2.5	Market Cap	US$480.9mil

Address **37 rue de Rome** **75008 Paris** Tel **1-44-70-21-10** Fax **1-43-87-37-34** ADR SEDOL No. **4344157** Managing Director **Yves Defline** Chairman **Henri Katz**

Gaz et Eaux

Industry: **Gas Utilities**

Société Financière et Industrielle Gaz et Eaux is a diversified holding company that derives its income from business investments in Luxembourg, France, the United States, and the United Kingdom. Its investments are spread across the financial, food, industrial, distribution, and communication sectors. French holdings include financial-services provider SOVAC, and building-materials firm Saint Gobain Groupe. It also invests in U.K. publisher Pearson and Luxembourg holding company Euralux. Its U.S. interests include Centre Capital Investors and Lazard Partners.

FFr mil	12/92	12/93	12/94	US$mil 12/94				
Sales	**253.0**	**362.0**	**242.8**	**44.0**	P/E Ratio	**17.5**	Price (9/30/95)	**1,838.00**
Net Income	**273.0**	**543.0**	**283.8**	**51.5**	P/B Ratio	**0.8**	52 Wk Hi-Low	**1,908.0-1,609.5**
Book Value	**5,175.0**	**5,588.0**	**5,757.5**	**1,078.2**	Yield %	**3.0**	Market Cap	**US$1,043.4mil**

Address **3 rue Jacques Bingen**
75017 Paris
Tel **1-47-66-02-64**
Fax **1-47-66-84-41**
ADR
SEDOL No. **4337317**
CEO **G.F. Brandford Griffith**
Chairman **Bruno Roger**

Généfim

Industry: **Real-Estate Investment**

Généfim leases hotel, corporate, and commercial properties. Office buildings compose more than two thirds of the company's property portfolio. Généfim's properties are mainly concentrated in Paris and the surrounding area. The company also owns real estate in the United Kingdom and Spain, including office buildings in London and Madrid. Généfim leases its hotel properties to the Accor and Pullman hoteliers. The company is controlled by the banking group Société Générale de France, which owns a 66% stake.

FFr mil	12/92	12/93	12/94	US$mil 12/94				
Sales	**650.0**	**799.0**	**782.9**	**142.0**	P/E Ratio	**7.2**	Price (9/30/95)	**130.00**
Net Income	**136.0**	**135.0**	**135.1**	**24.5**	P/B Ratio	**0.6**	52 Wk Hi-Low	**271.00-122.00**
Book Value	**1,078.0**	**1,095.0**	**932.2**	**174.6**	Yield %	**15.4**	Market Cap	**US$120.2mil**

Address **50 blvd. Haussmann**
75009 Paris
Tel **1-40-98-38-80**
Fax **1-40-98-57-10**
ADR
SEDOL No. **4806754**
CEO **G. Druhen-Charnaux**
Chairman **Alain Lamboley**

Générale des Eaux

Industry: **Water Utilities**

Compagnie Générale des Eaux is a diversified water distributor with additional activities in energy, construction, health care, public service, and communications. The firm distributes water in France, the United Kingdom, Spain, and the United States. It also generates and distributes electricity in France. The firm operates one of France's two mobile-phone networks and has formed an alliance with the German utility RWE to provide telecommunication services in Germany. Générale des Eaux owns a 99% stake in property developer Compagnie Immobilière Phénix.

FFr mil	12/91	12/92	12/93	US$mil 12/93				
Sales	**134,922.0**	**143,385.0**	**147,609.0**	**26,065.5**	P/E Ratio	**16.2**	Price (9/30/95)	**473.00**
Net Income	**2,613.0**	**2,907.0**	**3,205.0**	**566.0**	P/B Ratio	**1.6**	52 Wk Hi-Low	**591.00-425.00**
Book Value	**18,364.0**	**23,971.0**	**31,613.0**	**5,358.1**	Yield %	**0.6**	Market Cap	**US$10,827mil**

Address **52 rue d'Anjou**
75384 Paris
Tel **1-49-24-49-24**
Fax **1-49-24-69-99**
ADR
SEDOL No. **4175926**
CEO **Paul-Louis Girardot**
Chairman **Guy Dejouany**

Géophysique

Industry: **Oilfield Equipment & Services - Other**

Compagnie Générale de Géophysique uses reflection-seismic technology to explore hydrocarbon reservoirs. Its activities fall into five categories: land seismology, marine seismology, seismic data processing, reservoir description, and geophysical equipment. Its surface-geophysics operations contribute more than 80% of revenues, while geophysical equipment represents 14%. Europe accounts for more than one third of total revenues; the company's operations span five continents overall.

FFr mil	12/92	12/93	12/94	US$mil 12/94				
Sales	**3,012.0**	**2,679.0**	**2,506.3**	**454.5**	P/E Ratio	**NMF**	Price (9/30/95)	**208.00**
Net Income	**97.0**	**-137.0**	**-305.3**	**-55.4**	P/B Ratio	**1.1**	52 Wk Hi-Low	**398.50-208.00**
Book Value	**1,053.0**	**912.0**	**597.3**	**111.9**	Yield %	**0.0**	Market Cap	**US$130.0mil**

Address **1 rue Léon Migaux**
91341 Massy
Tel **64-47-30-00**
Fax **69-20-32-53**
ADR
SEDOL No. **4215394**
CEO **Yves Lesage**
Chairman **Yves Lesage**

GFC

Industry: **Financial Services - Diversified**

Groupement pour le Financement de la Construction (GFC) develops and manages real estate. Its activities also include property rental and leasing, land acquisition, and real-estate financing. Its property holdings are 81% residential and 19% commercial and professional. Approximately half of the company's properties are located in and around Paris. Groupement pour le Financement de la Construction is a partially-owned subsidiary of French-government-controlled insurer Assurances Générales de France (AGF).

FFr mil	12/92	12/93	12/94	US$mil 12/94				
Revenues	**510.0**	**497.0**	**507.1**	**91.9**	P/E Ratio	**16.9**	Price (9/30/95)	**350.00**
Net Income	**262.0**	**181.0**	**181.3**	**32.9**	P/B Ratio	**1.7**	52 Wk Hi-Low	**420.00-337.10**
Book Value	**2,062.0**	**2,000.0**	**1,855.8**	**347.5**	Yield %	**5.3**	Market Cap	**US$623.3mil**

Address **Tour Franklin**
92042 Paris-La Défense
Tel **1-49-01-02-88**
Fax **1-47-73-99-23**
ADR
SEDOL No. **4391807**
CEO **Eliane Sermondadaz**
Chairman **Eliane Sermondadaz**

Groupe de la Cité

Industry: **Publishing**

Groupe de la Cité publishes books in French, English, and Spanish. Its publications include Bordas and Dalloz Sirey textbooks, Nathan educational books and games for children, and Larousse and Le Robert dictionaries. Its novels are published under the Presses de la Cité and Robert Laffont names. The firm's France Loisirs mail-order and retail-book businesses have more than five million customers in France, Belgium, Switzerland, and Canada. Groupe de la Cité has signed an agreement to acquire Masson, the largest medical publisher in Mediterranean Europe.

	FFr mil 12/92	12/93	12/94	US$mil 12/94				
Sales	**6,781.0**	**7,085.0**	**7,285.7**	**1,321.1**	P/E Ratio	**14.4**	Price (9/30/95)	**780.00**
Net Income	**244.0**	**305.0**	**403.1**	**73.1**	P/B Ratio	**2.0**	52 Wk Hi-Low	**916.00-687.00**
Book Value	**2,561.0**	**2,734.0**	**2,976.8**	**557.4**	Yield %	**3.5**	Market Cap	**US$1,237.4mil**

Address	**20 ave. Hoche**	Tel	**1-42-25-05-98**	ADR		CEO	**Christian Brégou**
	75008 Paris	Fax	**1-42-25-16-01**	SEDOL No.	**4700919**	Chairman	**Christian Brégou**

GTM-Entrepose

Industry: **Heavy Construction**

GTM-Entrepose is an international construction and public-works firm. The majority of its services are in civil engineering and road and building construction. Secondary activities include industrial and electrical installations, offshore oil facilities, and real estate. In 1994, GTM-Entrepose and Dumez, in agreement with its main shareholder Lyonnaise des Eaux, combined their building and civil-engineering activities into a new, equally held Dumez-GTM subsidiary. The group is part of the consortium building the Oeresund Tunnel linking Sweden to Denmark.

	FFr mil 12/92	12/93	12/94	US$mil 12/94				
Sales	**26,608.0**	**30,182.0**	**30,880.0**	**5,599.3**	P/E Ratio	**14.4**	Price (9/30/95)	**329.00**
Net Income	**202.0**	**171.0**	**202.0**	**36.6**	P/B Ratio	**NMF**	52 Wk Hi-Low	**458.00-320.00**
Book Value	**2,132.0**	**2,311.0**	**N/A**	**N/A**	Yield %	**2.4**	Market Cap	**US$644.6mil**

Address	**61 ave. Jules-Quentin**	Tel	**1-46-95-76-93**	ADR		CEO	**André Jarrosson**
	92000 Nanterre	Fax	**1-46-95-77-95**	SEDOL No.	**4358794**	Chairman	**André Jarrosson**

Guichard-Perrachon

Industry: **Food Retailers & Wholesalers**

Casino Guichard-Perrachon et Compagnie is the holding company for Groupe Casino, which owns retail, restaurant, food-processing, and real- estate businesses in France and the United States. The company operates convenience stores, warehouse stores, supermarkets, and hypermarkets. It also operates 220 Casino Cafeteria restaurants. Casino Guichard-Perrachon manages its majority-owned Smart and Final retailer, with more than 100 Smart and Final stores in the United States and one in Mexico. The company is also developing hypermarkets in Poland.

	FFr mil 12/92	12/93	12/94	US$mil 12/94				
Sales	**61,587.0**	**63,010.0**	**62,501.0**	**11,332.9**	P/E Ratio	**22.6**	Price (9/30/95)	**146.40**
Net Income	**441.0**	**453.0**	**489.0**	**88.7**	P/B Ratio	**1.2**	52 Wk Hi-Low	**173.00-129.00**
Book Value	**7,101.0**	**7,364.0**	**7,141.0**	**1,337.3**	Yield %	**2.7**	Market Cap	**US$1,765.5mil**

Address	**24 rue de la Montat**	Tel	**77-45-31-31**	ADR		CEO	**Georges Plassat**
	42008 Saint-Etienne	Fax	**77-21-85-15**	SEDOL No.	**4178419**	Chairman	**Antoine Guichard**

Guilbert

Industry: **Other Specialty Retailers**

Guilbert is a business-to-business office-supplies retailer. Its products include papers, adhesives, writing instruments, furniture, and equipment. Its catalog lists 10,000 different items, about 15% of which carry the Guilbert brand name. Guilbert receives an average of 6,000 orders per day. It operates a network of 10 delivery agencies and a fleet of 370 delivery vans, and has retail offices in Spain, Belgium, and the United Kingdom. More than 85% of all sales are generated in France. Guilbert has five subsidiaries in France and five abroad.

	FFr mil 12/92	12/93	12/94	US$mil 12/94				
Revenues	**1,809.0**	**2,056.0**	**2,215.5**	**401.7**	P/E Ratio	**21.7**	Price (9/30/95)	**520.00**
Net Income	**198.0**	**181.0**	**199.0**	**36.1**	P/B Ratio	**3.6**	52 Wk Hi-Low	**554.00-388.00**
Book Value	**820.0**	**1,011.0**	**1,190.2**	**222.9**	Yield %	**2.3**	Market Cap	**US$877.8mil**

Address	**126 ave. du Poteau**	Tel	**1-44-54-54-54**	ADR		CEO	**Philippe Cuvelier**
	60451 Senlis	Fax	**1-44-54-54-70**	SEDOL No.	**4395779**	Chairman	**André M. Guilbert**

Havas

Industry: **Publishing**

Havas is a diversified media and communications firm. Its information and publicity division represents 20 TV channels, 180 radio stations, and magazines available in 18 nations. It owns 35% of Euro RSCG, an advertising firm; 24% of French TV broadcaster Canal Plus; and 42% of French publisher C.E.P. Communication. Havas owns 80% of Havas Voyages American Express, a business-travel venture with American Express. Havas, New Line Cinema, and Island Trading Company formed software-development firm Anonymous Entertainment.

	FFr mil 12/92	12/93	12/94	US$mil 12/94				
Sales	**28,183.0**	**34,957.0**	**37,751.0**	**6,845.1**	P/E Ratio	**19.3**	Price (9/30/95)	**368.40**
Net Income	**691.0**	**567.0**	**936.0**	**169.7**	P/B Ratio	**1.9**	52 Wk Hi-Low	**445.00-348.90**
Book Value	**8,561.0**	**9,001.0**	**9,840.0**	**1,842.7**	Yield %	**2.3**	Market Cap	**US$3,705.4mil**

Address	**136 ave. Charles-de-Gaulle**	Tel	**1-47-47-30-00**	ADR	**HAVSY**	CEO	**Pierre Dauzier**
	92522 Neuilly-sur-Seine	Fax	**1-47-47-32-23**	SEDOL No.	**4415473**	Chairman	**Pierre Dauzier**

Imétal

Industry: **Non-Ferrous Metals - Other (Exc. Aluminum)**

Imétal produces building materials and processes industrial minerals and metals. Its products include clay and ceramic tiles, bricks, clay for ceramic and sanitary industries, mechanical and structural tubing, and bimetallic wires. Its Huguenot Fenal, IRB, Gélis-Poudenx-Sans, and Financière D'Angers subsidiaries produce building materials. The diversified holding company Parfinance owns 50% of Imétal. In mid-1995 the company agreed to purchase Georgia Marble Holdings Corp., which owns several calcium carbonate quarries in the United States.

FFr mil	12/92	12/93	12/94	US$mil 12/94				
Sales	**5,839.0**	**6,291.0**	**7,510.0**	**1,361.7**	P/E Ratio	**13.8**	Price (9/30/95)	**585.00**
Net Income	**283.0**	**294.0**	**550.0**	**99.7**	P/B Ratio	**1.5**	52 Wk Hi-Low	**630.00-451.00**
Book Value	**4,039.0**	**4,672.0**	**5,060.0**	**947.6**	Yield %	**2.1**	Market Cap	**US$1,603.0mil**

Address **33 ave. du Maine**
75755 Paris
Tel **1-45-38-48-48**
Fax **1-45-38-74-78**
ADR
SEDOL No. **4457765**
CEO **René Mitieus**
Chairman **René Mitieus**

Immeubles de France

Industry: **Real-Estate Investment**

Société des Immeubles de France manages, rents, and leases more than 110,000 square meters of residential, commercial, and parking space in Paris. It also invests in other leasing and renting companies. The firm also has property interests in suburban Paris, Lyon, and London. By size, commercial properties constitute more than 62% of its holdings and generate 60% of its revenue. The company is a member of the property-management arm of the French real-estate and mortgage firm Crédit Foncier de France, which owns 55% of Société des Immeubles de France.

FFr mil	12/92	12/93	12/94	US$mil 12/94				
Sales	**76.0**	**176.0**	**192.6**	**34.9**	P/E Ratio	**15.8**	Price (9/30/95)	**238.00**
Net Income	**71.0**	**89.0**	**91.8**	**16.6**	P/B Ratio	**0.7**	52 Wk Hi-Low	**458.00-231.00**
Book Value	**801.0**	**2,087.0**	**2,154.6**	**403.5**	Yield %	**6.3**	Market Cap	**US$316.8mil**

Address **18-20 place de la Madeleine**
75008 Paris
Tel **1-44-71-34-00**
Fax **1-40-17-05-82**
ADR
SEDOL No. **4801533**
CEO **Georges Bonin**
Chairman **Georges Bonin**

Interbail

Industry: **Real-Estate Investment**

Société Financière Interbail principally leases and rents industrial and commercial property, and provides financial and consulting services. Interbail rents offices, warehouses, hotels, and retail outlets. The company has roughly FFr 12.6 billion in total assets. In 1993 Interbail as a whole moved away from its Specialized Credit Institution (Sicomi) status, by expanding its finance and long- and medium-term credit operations. It created Interbail Sicomi, allowing the parent company to continue financing real-estate leasing projects through the end of 1995.

FFr mil	12/92	12/93	12/94	US$mil 12/94				
Sales	**1,144.0**	**1,376.0**	**1,445.5**	**262.1**	P/E Ratio	**8.6**	Price (9/30/95)	**325.00**
Net Income	**255.0**	**235.0**	**201.8**	**36.6**	P/B Ratio	**0.9**	52 Wk Hi-Low	**389.00-325.00**
Book Value	**2,211.0**	**2,302.0**	**1,896.9**	**355.2**	Yield %	**9.8**	Market Cap	**US$343.5mil**

Address **14 rue Pergolèse**
75116 Paris
Tel **1-40-67-18-08**
Fax **1-40-67-17-16**
ADR
SEDOL No. **4463289**
Chairman Exec Bd **Jean Baptiste Pascal**
Chairman Supv Bd **Jean Martineau**

Labinal

Industry: **Electrical Components & Equipment**

Labinal manufactures small- and medium-size gas turbines, connectors, and other equipment for the aeronautics, space, defense, electronics, and automobile industries. The company's connectors are designed for the aerospace, automotive, defense, and telecommunications sectors. Labinal's aerospace division supplies filters, electrical wiring, and electrical motors. Its automotive products include filters, valves, cables, and switches for cars and all commercial vehicles. In 1994, the company generated roughly half its sales in France and 10% in the United States.

FFr mil	12/92	12/93	12/94	US$mil 12/94				
Sales	**9,150.0**	**8,541.0**	**9,477.5**	**1,718.5**	P/E Ratio	**26.5**	Price (9/30/95)	**758.00**
Net Income	**82.0**	**6.0**	**117.6**	**21.3**	P/B Ratio	**0.8**	52 Wk Hi-Low	**884.00-672.00**
Book Value	**2,799.0**	**2,846.0**	**3,668.2**	**686.9**	Yield %	**2.8**	Market Cap	**US$632.9mil**

Address **Pas du Lac, 5 ave. Newton**
78051 Yvelines
Tel **1-30-85-30-85**
Fax **1-30-43-41-71**
ADR
SEDOL No. **4699404**
CEO **Amaury Halna**
Chairman **Amaury Halna**

Lafarge

Industry: **Building Materials**

Lafarge (formerly Lafarge Coppee), a holding company, has 500 affiliates in 40 countries that produce concrete, aggregates, gypsum, and specialty building products. Cement and concrete aggregates account for nearly 70% of total revenues. Lafarge also develops vegetable and flower seeds, and produces chemical additives for food (such as MSG). The company sold its stake in U.S.-based plasterboard manufacturer National Gypsum in May 1995. Exports generate two thirds of Lafarge's sales; North America, its largest export market, accounts for a third of revenues.

FFr mil	12/92	12/93	12/94	US$mil 12/94				
Sales	**30,451.0**	**30,430.0**	**32,841.0**	**5,954.9**	P/E Ratio	**12.5**	Price (9/30/95)	**323.80**
Net Income	**1,228.0**	**1,553.0**	**2,225.0**	**403.4**	P/B Ratio	**1.3**	52 Wk Hi-Low	**394.00-299.45**
Book Value	**13,584.0**	**18,988.0**	**21,643.0**	**4,053.0**	Yield %	**2.8**	Market Cap	**US$5,917.3mil**

Address **28 rue Emile-Menier**
75116 Paris
Tel **1-44-34-11-11**
Fax **1-47-27-54-57**
ADR **LFCPF**
SEDOL No. **4502706**
CEO **Betrand Collomb**
Chairman **Betrand Collomb**

Lagardère

Industry: **Publishing**

Lagardère Groupe is a diversified company with interests in the publishing, distribution, communication, technology, and media industries. It has a 93% holding in Matra Hachette. The Matra division is active in the areas of space, defense, automobiles, telecommunications, and transit technologies. Hachette is active in print media, book publishing, distribution services, and broadcasting. The distribution-services division contributes 24% of sales and print media 16%. Lagardère holds a majority interest in Banque Arjil & Cie.

	FFr mil 12/92	12/93	12/94	US$mil 12/94				
Sales	**55,102.0**	**53,981.0**	**53,018.0**	**9,613.4**	P/E Ratio	**12.8**	Price (9/30/95)	**91.80**
Net Income	**96.0**	**155.0**	**615.0**	**111.5**	P/B Ratio	**1.5**	52 Wk Hi-Low	**132.90-85.30**
Book Value	**1,945.0**	**2,633.0**	**5,331.0**	**998.3**	Yield %	**N/A**	Market Cap	**US$1,600.2mil**

Address **4 rue de Presbourg**
75116 Paris
Tel **1-40-69-16-00**
Fax **1-40-69-18-54**
ADR
SEDOL No. **4547213**
Managing Director **Jean-Luc Lagardère**
Chairman **Raymond H. Levy**

Legrand

Industry: **Electrical Components & Equipment**

Legrand makes electrical fittings and accessories for household, commercial, and industrial uses. Its home electrical products include switches, sockets, circuit breakers, information signs, and remote and programmable controls. It also supplies programmable thermostats, broadcast-music systems, and theft-protection equipment for industrial use. Legrand has subsidiaries and offices in 40 countries. In early 1995 it bought two electric-cable-accessory companies: RTGamma (Italy) and Power Centre (United Kingdom). Sales outside France represent 57% of total revenues.

	FFr mil 12/92	12/93	12/94	US$mil 12/94				
Sales	**10,249.0**	**9,983.0**	**10,370.0**	**1,880.3**	P/E Ratio	**26.7**	Price (9/30/95)	**778.00**
Net Income	**657.0**	**578.0**	**785.0**	**142.3**	P/B Ratio	**3.6**	52 Wk Hi-Low	**821.00-622.00**
Book Value	**4,249.0**	**4,462.0**	**4,577.0**	**857.1**	Yield %	**0.9**	Market Cap	**US$3,385.6mil**

Address **128 ave. de Lattre de Tassigny**
87045 Limoges
Tel **55-06-87-87**
Fax **55-06-13-41**
ADR
SEDOL No. **4558583**
CEO **François Grappotte**
Chairman **François Grappotte**

Legris

Industry: **Building Materials**

Groupe Legris Industries provides equipment for industrial use and construction. It generates about 63% of its sales from the production of tower cranes and hydraulic mobile cranes. The remaining sales are in regulators and controls for industrial and domestic liquid-distribution systems. The firm generates one third of its sales in France, 21% in Germany, and 10% each in the United States and Asia. In 1995 Legris sold PPM Cranes, its U.S.-based mobile cranes subsidiary. Legris has subsidiaries throughout the world, including China, Taiwan, Mexico, and the U.S.

	FFr mil 12/92	12/93	12/94	US$mil 12/94				
Sales	**4,854.0**	**4,249.0**	**4,453.5**	**807.5**	P/E Ratio	**31.6**	Price (9/30/95)	**170.40**
Net Income	**27.0**	**-172.0**	**44.8**	**8.1**	P/B Ratio	**1.1**	52 Wk Hi-Low	**411.10-160.00**
Book Value	**1,409.0**	**1,235.0**	**1,255.2**	**235.1**	Yield %	**0.0**	Market Cap	**US$288.1mil**

Address **74 rue de Paris**
35014 Rennes
Tel **99-25-55-00**
Fax **99-25-56-50**
ADR
SEDOL No. **4510408**
CEO **Yvon Jacob**
Chairman **Pierre-Yves Legris**

LVMH

Industry: **Distillers & Brewers**

LVMH Moet Hennessy Louis Vuitton manufactures alcoholic beverages, beauty products, perfumes, luggage, leather goods, and apparel. Its products include Moet & Chandon, Veuve Clicquot, and Dom Perignon champagnes; Hennessy and Hine cognacs; Givenchy, Christian Dior, and Kenzo perfumes and cosmetics; Givenchy, Christian Lacroix, and Kenzo couture; and Louis Vuitton luggage and leather goods. Each of LVMH's four luxury divisions contributes roughly one fourth of sales. Exports account for 80% of revenues; the Far East generates nearly 40% of sales.

	FFr mil 12/92	12/93	12/94	US$mil 12/94				
Sales	**24,658.0**	**23,819.0**	**27,967.0**	**5,071.1**	P/E Ratio	**12.4**	Price (9/30/95)	**929.00**
Net Income	**3,007.0**	**3,574.0**	**6,421.0**	**1,164.3**	P/B Ratio	**2.6**	52 Wk Hi-Low	**967.00-787.00**
Book Value	**20,558.0**	**23,397.0**	**29,624.0**	**5,547.6**	Yield %	**1.9**	Market Cap	**US$16,419mil**

Address **30 Ave. Hoche**
75008 Paris
Tel **1-44-13-22-22**
Fax **1-44-13-22-23**
ADR **LVMHY**
SEDOL No. **4535649**
Chief Executive **Bernard Arnault**
Chairman **Bernard Arnault**

Lyonnaise des Eaux

Industry: **Water Utilities**

Lyonnaise des Eaux-Dumez is an urban-development and environmental-services group. Involved in all aspects of water collection, purification, and distribution, the group has 28 million customers, half of whom are in France. Lyonnaise provides waste-management and recycling services, and manages construction for large civil projects such as hydroelectric dams, the Channel Tunnel, and the Saint Denis sports stadium in Paris. The company also has holdings in mortuary-service and media/communication companies. More than 43% of Lyonnaise's sales are generated outside France.

	FFr mil 12/92	12/93	12/94	US$mil 12/94				
Sales	**71,991.0**	**93,556.0**	**99,965.0**	**18,126.0**	P/E Ratio	**32.4**	Price (9/30/95)	**451.00**
Net Income	**1,425.0**	**804.0**	**1,061.0**	**192.4**	P/B Ratio	**1.6**	52 Wk Hi-Low	**534.00-411.10**
Book Value	**12,533.0**	**15,026.0**	**16,186.0**	**3,031.1**	Yield %	**2.5**	Market Cap	**US$5,205.6mil**

Address **72 ave. de la Liberté**
92022 Nanterre
Tel **1-46-95-50-00**
Fax **1-46-95-51-86**
ADR
SEDOL No. **4540438**
CEO **Jérôme Monod**
Chairman **Jérôme Monod**

Michelin

Industry: **Tires & Rubber**

Compagnie Générale des Etablissements Michelin manufactures tires and wheels for passenger and commercial vehicles worldwide. It is the world's largest tire manufacturer by sales. The company generates 57% of sales in Western Europe, and 36% in North and South America. Its secondary products include bicycle tires, aircraft tires, tubes, steel cables, and maps. In April 1995 the company signed a co-operation agreement with German tire manufacturer Continental. Both companies, however, will remain independent and in competition.

	FFr mil 12/92	12/93	12/94	US$mil 12/94				
Sales	**66,847.0**	**63,298.0**	**67,221.4**	**12,188.8**	P/E Ratio	**93.9**	Price (9/30/95)	**215.90**
Net Income	**79.0**	**-3,670.0**	**1,290.8**	**234.0**	P/B Ratio	**2.7**	52 Wk Hi-Low	**233.10-188.50**
Book Value	**11,088.0**	**7,275.0**	**8,703.8**	**1,629.9**	Yield %	**1.0**	Market Cap	**US$4,713.9mil**

Address **12 Cours Sablon**
63000 Clermont-Ferrand
Tel **73-92-41-95**
Fax **73-90-28-94**
ADR
SEDOL No. **4588364**
CEO **François Michelin**
Chairman **Daniel Michelin**

Moulinex

Industry: **Other Home Furnishings**

Moulinex, through its wholly-owned German subsidiary Krups, is a manufacturer and distributor of household electric and nonelectric appliances. About 80% of its products are sold on the European market under the Moulinex and Krups brand names. It has over 20 factories worldwide, making food processors, microwave ovens, toasters, coffee makers, irons, and pressure cookers. The firm is 40% owned by French holding company FINAP. In 1995 Moulinex sold its share in U.K.-based Regal Swan and announced its intention to buy back remaining shares in Moulinex Spain.

	FFr mil 03/93 *	03/94	03/95	US$mil 03/95				
Sales	**9,939.0**	**8,098.0**	**7,681.7**	**1,441.2**	P/E Ratio	**NMF**	Price (9/30/95)	**100.90**
Net Income	**-138.0**	**-564.0**	**-212.7**	**-39.9**	P/B Ratio	**2.1**	52 Wk Hi-Low	**128.90-98.10**
Book Value	**1,242.0**	**643.0**	**1,335.3**	**278.2**	Yield %	**0.0**	Market Cap	**US$594.9mil**

Address **11 rue Jules Ferry**
93171 Bagnolet
Tel **1-49-20-71-00**
Fax **1-48-57-12-72**
ADR
SEDOL No. **4608121**
CEO **Jules Coulon**
Chairman **Gilbert Torelli**

*Irregular period due to fiscal year change.

Navigation Mixte

Industry: **Conglomerates**

Compagnie de Navigation Mixte is a holding company with activities in five areas: food, banking and finance, insurance, transportation and tourism, and technology. Its wholly-owned subsidiaries Compagnie Française de Sucrerie, Champagne de Venoge, and CICCO, and partially-owned Saupiquet, make sugar, champagne, orange juice, and tuna, respectively. Its Hurel-Dubois and SFIM affiliates make engine components for aerospace companies such as Rolls-Royce. The firm's Via Général de Transport et d'Industrie subsidiary operates tour buses.

	FFr mil 12/92	12/93	12/94	US$mil 12/94				
Sales	**15,666.0**	**15,922.0**	**15,645.5**	**2,836.9**	P/E Ratio	**17.4**	Price (9/30/95)	**728.00**
Net Income	**423.0**	**700.0**	**786.7**	**142.7**	P/B Ratio	**0.6**	52 Wk Hi-Low	**1,057.0-727.0**
Book Value	**16,714.0**	**17,475.0**	**17,815.3**	**3,336.2**	Yield %	**5.5**	Market Cap	**US$2,275.3mil**

Address **1 La Canebière**
13001 Marseille
Tel **1-49-26-26-00**
Fax **N/A**
ADR
SEDOL No. **4627665**
Managing Director **Jean-Pierre d'Araquy**
Chairman **Marc Fournier**

L'Oréal

Industry: **Cosmetics & Personal Care**

L'Oreal is the world's largest producer of cosmetic products, perfumes, and hair-care products, most of which it markets under the L'Oreal name. It also makes and markets a range of Lancome, Vichy, and Helena Rubinstein beauty products, as well as Ralph Lauren, Paloma Picasso, Cacharel, Armani, and Guy Laroche perfumes. Its subsidiaries include wholly-owned U.S. distributor Cosmair and 56%-owned pharmaceutical manufacturer and distributor Synthelabo. France accounts for 24% of the firm's cosmetics sales, the rest of Europe 39%, and North America 21%.

	FFr mil 12/92	12/93	12/94	US$mil 12/94				
Sales	**37,568.0**	**40,163.0**	**47,623.7**	**8,635.3**	P/E Ratio	**24.7**	Price (9/30/95)	**1,256.00**
Net Income	**2,194.0**	**2,430.0**	**2,883.4**	**522.8**	P/B Ratio	**3.5**	52 Wk Hi-Low	**1,337.0-1,031.0**
Book Value	**14,413.0**	**16,146.0**	**22,006.2**	**4,121.0**	Yield %	**1.0**	Market Cap	**US$15,685mil**

Address **41 rue Martre**
92117 Clichy
Tel **1-47-56-70-00**
Fax **1-47-76-80-02**
ADR **LORLY**
SEDOL No. **4534787**
CEO **Lindsay Owen-Jones**
Chairman **Lindsay Owen-Jones**

Oxygène et Acétylène

Industry: **Specialty Chemicals**

Société d'Oxygène et d'Acétylène d'Extrême-Orient (SOAEO) provides gases and welding equipment to the industrial sector, and medical equipment to the health-care industry. SOAEO operates in Southeast Asia, the Middle East, India, and the Pacific Rim. Its joint ventures include Guangzhou Iron & Steel and Shenzen Industrial Gases, both in southern China. Its affiliates include Hong Kong Oxygen, Singapore Oxygen Air Liquide, and Société d'Oxygène et d'Acétylène de La Reunion.

	FFr mil 12/92	12/93	12/94	US$mil 12/94				
Sales	**120.0**	**123.0**	**113.4**	**20.6**	P/E Ratio	**39.2**	Price (9/30/95)	**4,580.00**
Net Income	**122.0**	**170.0**	**179.3**	**32.5**	P/B Ratio	**7.0**	52 Wk Hi-Low	**4,746.0-2,751.7**
Book Value	**802.0**	**942.0**	**1,010.0**	**189.1**	Yield %	**2.6**	Market Cap	**US$1,426.1mil**

Address **75 Quai d'Orsay**
75007 Paris
Tel **1-40-62-55-55**
Fax **N/A**
ADR
SEDOL No. **4664929**
CEO **Jean Delorme**
Chairman **Jean Delorme**

Parfinance

Industry: **Industrial - Diversified**

Parfinance is a diversified holding company. The company, 27% owned by Groupe Bruxelles Lambert, maintains a 53% stake in Imétal, a producer of construction materials, industrial minerals, and metals. The company also invests in packaging company CarnaudMetalbox and banking group Compagnie Financière de Parabis. In May 1994 Parfinance, through one of its wholly-owned subsidiaries, acquired an interest in the newly privatized insurance company UAP.

FFr mil	12/92	12/93	12/94	US$mil 12/94				
Sales	**280.0**	**244.0**	**135.3**	**24.5**	P/E Ratio	**13.8**	Price (9/30/95)	**170.00**
Net Income	**258.0**	**296.0**	**386.9**	**70.2**	P/B Ratio	**0.7**	52 Wk Hi-Low	**203.00-170.00**
Book Value	**7,424.0**	**7,497.0**	**8,094.2**	**1,515.8**	Yield %	**4.4**	Market Cap	**US$1,084.4mil**

Address **1 Rond-Point Champs-Elysées**
75008 Paris
Tel **1-42-25-34-40**
Fax **N/A**
ADR
SEDOL No. **4671640**
CEO **A. Langlois- Meurinne**
Chairman **Paul Desmarais**

Paribas

Industry: **Banks - Money Center**

Compagnie Financière de Paribas is the holding company of Groupe Paribas, which is made up primarily of banks and financial-services and investment firms. Through its partially owned subsidiaries Banque Paribas, Compagnie Bancaire, Crédit du Nord, and Paribas Affaires Industrielles, Paribas offers banking and other financial services including financing, stock-exchange services, asset management, and equity investment. The group had assets of 1,295 billion FF in 1994 and is represented in more than 60 countries.

FFr mil	12/92	12/93	12/94	US$mil 12/94				
Revenues	**116,020.0**	**119,081.0**	**105,202.0**	**19,075.6**	P/E Ratio	**16.0**	Price (9/30/95)	**249.00**
Net Income	**886.0**	**1,449.0**	**1,715.0**	**311.0**	P/B Ratio	**0.6**	52 Wk Hi-Low	**391.50-248.30**
Book Value	**38,996.0**	**41,364.0**	**45,261.0**	**8,475.8**	Yield %	**4.8**	Market Cap	**US$5,866.0mil**

Address **5 rue d'Antin**
75002 Paris
Tel **1-42-98-12-34**
Fax **1-42-98-11-42**
ADR
SEDOL No. **4214410**
Managing Director **André Levy-Lang**
Chairman **Michel Francois-Poncet**

Pechiney

Industry: **Aluminum**

Pechiney is a government-controlled manufacturer of packaging materials for the food, beverage, and cosmetics industries; a producer of primary aluminum; and a manufacturer of components for aircraft and industrial gas-turbine engines. Its 67%-owned Pechiney International subsidiary generates most of its revenues and profits from its wholly-owned subsidiary American National Can (ANC). ANC produces glass beverage bottles and aluminum and steel beverage cans. Pechiney's packaging division generates approximately 42% of total revenues.

FFr mil	12/92	12/93	12/94	US$mil 12/94				
Sales	**65,374.0**	**63,025.0**	**70,741.0**	**12,827.0**	P/E Ratio	**N/A**	Price (9/30/95)	**315.00**
Net Income	**203.0**	**-980.0**	**-3,753.0**	**-680.5**	P/B Ratio	**N/A**	52 Wk Hi-Low	**399.00-276.50**
Book Value	**17,441.0**	**16,827.0**	**11,131.0**	**2,084.5**	Yield %	**0.0**	Market Cap	**US$796.7mil**

Address **10 place des Vosges**
92048 Paris-La Défense
Tel **1-46-91-46-91**
Fax **1-46-91-51-42**
ADR
SEDOL No. **4676849**
CEO **Jean-Pierre Rodier**
Chairman **Jean-Pierre Rodier**

Pechiney International

Industry: **Containers & Packaging**

Pechiney International is the largest European manufacturer of containers and packaging by market capitalization and sales. It is also a leading producer of beverage cans. It produces metal, glass, plastic, and paper containers for the food, beverage, and cosmetics industries. Its packaging sector generates 85% of total revenues. At the beginning of 1995 the group announced its desire to dispose of all or part of certain assets in the turbine-components, beverage-glass, and food-metal divisions. Pechiney International is 67% owned by the government-controlled Pechiney.

FFr mil	12/92	12/93	12/94	US$mil 12/94				
Sales	**35,328.0**	**34,451.0**	**35,130.0**	**6,369.9**	P/E Ratio	**NMF**	Price (9/30/95)	**117.80**
Net Income	**1,966.0**	**294.0**	**-4,543.0**	**-823.8**	P/B Ratio	**1.1**	52 Wk Hi-Low	**170.50-108.50**
Book Value	**15,649.0**	**15,985.0**	**8,914.0**	**1,669.3**	Yield %	**2.5**	Market Cap	**US$2,056.5mil**

Address **10 place des Vosges**
92400 Courbevoie
Tel **1-46-91-46-91**
Fax **1-46-91-46-46**
ADR
SEDOL No. **4676872**
Managing Director **Franck Considine**
Chairman **Jean-Pierre Rodier**

Pernod Ricard

Industry: **Distillers & Brewers**

Pernod Ricard manufactures and distributes alcoholic and nonalcoholic beverages. The company's products include Pernod, Ricard, Dubonnet, Aberlour Single Malt and Clan Campbell Scotch whiskies, and Wild Turkey bourbon. Pernod also produces Crus et Domaines de France table wines, and Carlton and Blancs de Fruits flavored wines. Citrus soft drink Orangina leads the firm's sales of nonalcoholic drinks, which account for more than half of its revenues. Exports, mostly to other European countries, generated 48% of the company's 1994 sales.

FFr mil	12/92	12/93	12/94	US$mil 12/94				
Sales	**14,497.0**	**15,053.0**	**15,832.0**	**2,870.7**	P/E Ratio	**25.0**	Price (9/30/95)	**278.20**
Net Income	**1,100.0**	**1,064.0**	**1,147.0**	**208.0**	P/B Ratio	**1.7**	52 Wk Hi-Low	**354.20-276.10**
Book Value	**7,663.0**	**8,418.0**	**8,994.0**	**1,684.3**	Yield %	**2.9**	Market Cap	**US$3,188.4mil**

Address **142 blvd. Haussmann**
75008 Paris
Tel **1-40-76-77-78**
Fax **1-42-25-95-66**
ADR **PDRDY**
SEDOL No. **4682329**
President **Thierry Jacquillat**
Chairman **Patrick Ricard**

Peugeot

Industry: **Automobile Manufacturers**

PSA Peugeot Citroen manufactures automobiles and auto components, including diesel engines, exhaust systems, and seats. The company also manufactures aerospace and defense technology and wheeled light armored vehicles. It controls about 31% of the French passenger-car market, and 13% of the European market. The company produced more than 1.8 million passenger vehicles and nearly 200,000 commercial vehicles in 1994. Nearly 55% of its sales are generated outside of France. It also provides financing for individual buyers and dealerships.

FFr mil	12/92	12/93	12/94	US$mil 12/94				
Sales	**155,431.0**	**145,431.0**	**166,195.0**	**30,135.1**	P/E Ratio	**10.9**	Price (9/30/95)	**673.00**
Net Income	**3,372.0**	**-1,413.0**	**3,102.0**	**562.5**	P/B Ratio	**0.6**	52 Wk Hi-Low	**828.00-629.00**
Book Value	**53,144.0**	**50,539.0**	**53,524.0**	**10,023.2**	Yield %	**N/A**	Market Cap	**US$6,844.8mil**

Address **75 ave. de la Grande-Armée**
75116 Paris
Tel **1-40-66-55-11**
Fax **1-40-66-41-85**
ADR **PEUGY**
SEDOL No. **4683827**
CEO **Pierre Peugeot**
Chairman **Jacques Calvet**

Pinault-Printemps-Redoute

Industry: **Retailers - Broadline**

Groupe Pinault-Printemps-Redoute is the result of a merger between consumer-goods retailer Pinault-Printemps and catalog retailer La Redoute. The company provides specialized and consumer-goods distribution, international-trade operations, and credit and financial services. The company operates Printemps department stores, Prisunic convenience shops, Conforama furniture stores, and La Redoute and Cyrillus electronics and appliance stores. Its CDME wholesale subsidiary distributes electrical equipment.

FFr mil	12/92	12/93	12/94	US$mil 12/94				
Revenues	**70,234.0**	**63,300.0**	**70,796.0**	**12,837.0**	P/E Ratio	**17.9**	Price (9/30/95)	**1,044.00**
Net Income	**586.0**	**511.0**	**1,212.0**	**219.8**	P/B Ratio	**1.9**	52 Wk Hi-Low	**1,155.0-895.0**
Book Value	**5,608.0**	**7,772.0**	**12,222.0**	**2,288.8**	Yield %	**2.2**	Market Cap	**US$4,647.9mil**

Address **102 rue de Provence**
75009 Paris
Tel **1-44-11-20-20**
Fax **1-44-11-20-18**
ADR
SEDOL No. **4703844**
Chairman Exec Bd **Pierre Blayau**
Chairman Supv Bd **Ambroise Roux**

Plaine Monceau

Industry: **Real-Estate Investment**

Compagnie des Immeubles de la Plaine Monceau, a majority-owned subsidiary of diversified French insurer Axa Groupe, owns and manages real estate. Its property portfolio, consisting of more than 565,000 square meters of professional and residential space, is located primarily in Paris and the surrounding area. Plaine Monceau's majority-owned holdings include real-estate subsidiaries Fincosa, Parigest, SCI Paris St. Michel, and SCI Ternes Opéra. Residential properties represent more than 55% of all rental income generated by the group.

FFr mil	12/92	12/93	12/94	US$mil 12/94				
Sales	**424.0**	**420.0**	**498.7**	**90.4**	P/E Ratio	**36.6**	Price (9/30/95)	**204.00**
Net Income	**454.0**	**171.0**	**397.0**	**72.0**	P/B Ratio	**1.1**	52 Wk Hi-Low	**302.00-179.00**
Book Value	**2,391.0**	**2,549.0**	**4,939.4**	**925.0**	Yield %	**2.4**	Market Cap	**US$1,142.2mil**

Address **21-23 ave. Matignon**
75008 Paris
Tel **1-40-75-57-00**
Fax **1-44-57-98-10**
ADR
SEDOL No. **4457981**
CEO **Hubert Marchal**
Chairman **Betrand de Feydeau**

Primagaz

Industry: **Gas Utilities**

Compagnie des Gaz de Pétrole Primagaz distributes fuel for heating, automotive, industrial, agricultural, and domestic uses. The company is a major distributor of liquefied petroleum gas, controlling 16% of the European market. Primagaz distributes its products to 54,500 sales points, which serve 14 million customers in 12 countries. These products include Viff motor fuel, Freon refrigerator gas, and Suva coolants. Primagaz's subsidiaries include Belgian holding company European Trading Gas.

FFr mil	12/92	12/93	12/94	US$mil 12/94				
Sales	**5,440.0**	**5,323.0**	**5,606.8**	**1,016.6**	P/E Ratio	**27.9**	Price (9/30/95)	**339.00**
Net Income	**222.0**	**252.0**	**284.0**	**51.5**	P/B Ratio	**2.2**	52 Wk Hi-Low	**364.80-265.00**
Book Value	**2,422.0**	**2,579.0**	**2,702.1**	**506.0**	Yield %	**2.0**	Market Cap	**US$1,235.3mil**

Address **64 ave. Hoche**
75008 Paris
Tel **1-42-67-30-00**
Fax **1-46-22-75-94**
ADR
SEDOL No. **4678771**
CEO **Jean-Charles Inglessi**
Chairman **Jean-Charles Inglessi**

Promodès

Industry: **Food Retailers & Wholesalers**

Promodès is a food retailer that operates hypermarkets, supermarkets, and convenience stores. Its 168 Continente hypermarkets generate 49% of the company's sales. Its supermarkets, which produce 25% of sales, include 870 Shopis and 518 Champion franchises. The 8 à Huit convenience-store chain has more than 1,000 outlets. The company operates in Spain, Germany, Portugal, Italy, and Greece. Promodès sold its U.S. Red Food supermarket chain in 1994 to Dutch-based Royal Ahold. France accounted for 66% of all sales in 1993.

FFr mil	12/92	12/93	12/94	US$mil 12/94				
Sales	**84,200.0**	**90,200.0**	**94,681.0**	**17,167.9**	P/E Ratio	**NMF**	Price (9/30/95)	**1,193.00**
Net Income	**555.0**	**701.0**	**900.0**	**163.2**	P/B Ratio	**4.0**	52 Wk Hi-Low	**1,253.0-890.0**
Book Value	**3,681.0**	**4,684.0**	**5,283.0**	**989.3**	Yield %	**0.9**	Market Cap	**US$4,242.2mil**

Address **Z.I. - Route de Paris**
14120 Mondeville
Tel **31-70-60-00**
Fax **31-83-56-19**
ADR
SEDOL No. **4706672**
CEO **Paul L. Halley**
Chairman **Paul L. Halley**

Rhône-Poulenc

Industry: **Commodity Chemicals**

Rhone-Poulenc is an international pharmaceutical and chemical company. It develops, produces, and markets specialty chemicals, polymers, organic- and inorganic-chemical intermediates, and pharmaceuticals. The health-care division, accounting for more than 41% of sales, manufactures products for the treatment of cardiovascular illnesses, cancer, and allergies. Rhone-Poulenc also produces animal-nutrition products and veterinary pharmaceuticals. Overseas exports generated nearly half of revenues; the U.S., its largest market, generates 22% of sales.

	FFr mil 12/92	12/93	12/94	US$mil 12/94				
Sales	**81,709.0**	**80,564.0**	**86,304.0**	**15,649.0**	P/E Ratio	**15.5**	Price (9/30/95)	**99.50**
Net Income	**2,184.0**	**1,844.0**	**3,038.0**	**550.9**	P/B Ratio	**0.8**	52 Wk Hi-Low	**138.00-96.50**
Book Value	**26,221.0**	**34,723.0**	**41,595.0**	**7,789.3**	Yield %	**2.8**	Market Cap	**US$6,351.7mil**

Address **25 Quai Paul-Doumer** **92408 Courbevoie** Tel **1-47-68-12-34** Fax **1-47-68-16-00** ADR **RP** SEDOL No. **4736817** CEO **Jean-René Fourtou** Chairman **Jean-René Fourtou**

Roussel Uclaf

Industry: **Pharmaceuticals**

Roussel Uclaf develops, produces, manufactures, and markets pharmaceuticals, fine chemicals, agrichemical, and animal-health products. Rulid and Claforan antibiotics are its best-selling products. It also manufactures anti-inflammatory and anti-arrhythmia drugs, analgesics, and immunostimulants. Its animal-health division produces vaccines, growth factors, and antibiotics. Its health-care division generated 74% of sales in 1994. Overseas exports accounted for 38% of revenues in 1994. German pharmaceutical firm Hoechst controls 56% of Roussel Uclaf.

	FFr mil 12/92	12/93	12/94	US$mil 12/94				
Sales	**14,812.0**	**15,893.0**	**16,266.0**	**2,949.4**	P/E Ratio	**14.5**	Price (9/30/95)	**764.00**
Net Income	**1,026.0**	**987.0**	**1,818.5**	**329.7**	P/B Ratio	**2.5**	52 Wk Hi-Low	**845.00-545.00**
Book Value	**6,693.0**	**7,307.0**	**8,388.9**	**1,571.0**	Yield %	**1.9**	Market Cap	**US$4,213.0mil**

Address **102 route de Noisy** **93235 Romainville** Tel **1-49-91-49-91** Fax **1-49-91-34-49** ADR SEDOL No. **4754206** CEO **Jean-Pierre Godard** Chairman **Edouard Sakiz**

SAGEM

Industry: **Diversified Technology**

Société d'Applications Générales d'Electricité et de Mécanique (SAGEM) manufactures navigation, defense, telecommunication, and electronic equipment. The company's products include military-guidance systems, aircraft-recognition equipment, facsimile machines, and mobile telephones. SAGEM owns 100% of Morpho Systémes, a world leader in the field of automatic fingerprint-identification systems. It also owns a 70% interest in automobile electronics firm SAGEM-Lucas.

	FFr mil 12/92	12/93	12/94	US$mil 12/94				
Sales	**12,253.9**	**13,038.1**	**13,691.2**	**2,482.5**	P/E Ratio	**20.0**	Price (9/30/95)	**2,729.00**
Net Income	**366.4**	**423.4**	**487.1**	**88.3**	P/B Ratio	**2.2**	52 Wk Hi-Low	**2,880.0-2,481.0**
Book Value	**1,959.6**	**2,303.4**	**3,325.8**	**622.8**	Yield %	**0.8**	Market Cap	**US$1,508.2mil**

Address **6 avenue d'Iéna** **75783 Paris** Tel **40-70-63-63** Fax **47-20-39-46** ADR SEDOL No. **4771410** CEO **Pierre Faure** Chairman **Pierre Faure**

Saint-Gobain

Industry: **Building Materials**

Saint-Gobain operates glass and building-materials businesses in 37 countries. The company produces flat glass, glass containers for the food and pharmeceuticals industry, glass and rock-wool insulation products, fiber reinforcements, industrial ceramics, abrasives, pipes, and roofing and cladding products. Its building-materials businesses are concentrated in the United States and Brazil. Most of its sales are made outside France. In 1994, Saint-Gobain acquired Clark United, an American manufacturer of ventilation products, and sold its own paper operations.

	FFr mil 12/92	12/93	12/94	US$mil 12/94				
Sales	**74,007.0**	**71,539.0**	**74,494.0**	**13,507.5**	P/E Ratio	**12.8**	Price (9/30/95)	**600.00**
Net Income	**2,377.0**	**1,314.0**	**3,625.0**	**657.3**	P/B Ratio	**1.3**	52 Wk Hi-Low	**682.00-568.00**
Book Value	**32,278.0**	**32,459.0**	**38,725.0**	**7,251.9**	Yield %	**2.6**	Market Cap	**US$9,901.6mil**

Address **Les Miroirs, 18 ave. d'Alsace** **92096 Courbevoie** Tel **1-47-62-30-00** Fax **1-47-62-30-30** ADR SEDOL No. **4768371** CEO **Jean-Louis Beffa** Chairman **Jean-Louis Beffa**

Saint Louis

Industry: **Other Food**

Groupe Saint Louis is an industrial holding company with interests in the paper, food, and agricultural sectors. Paper-producing affiliate Arjomari-Prioux accounts for roughly two thirds of the firm's profits. Sugar-producers Générale Sucrière and Euralin, makers of prepared foods, account for the remainder. Saint Louis is a minority partner in Panzalim, a joint venture to produce ready-frozen meals, with food and beverage company Danone. The company holds a 39% interest in the U.K. paper-products manufacturer Arjo Wiggins Appleton.

	FFr mil 12/92	12/93	12/94	US$mil 12/94				
Sales	**35,271.0**	**34,165.0**	**33,571.0**	**6,087.2**	P/E Ratio	**7.1**	Price (9/30/95)	**1,302.00**
Net Income	**774.0**	**717.0**	**1,466.0**	**265.8**	P/B Ratio	**1.0**	52 Wk Hi-Low	**1,594.0-1,290.0**
Book Value	**6,194.0**	**7,664.0**	**10,213.0**	**1,912.5**	Yield %	**2.9**	Market Cap	**US$2,117.9mil**

Address **23 ave. Franklin D. Roosevelt** **75008 Paris** Tel **1-40-76-74-72** Fax **1-45-63-46-33** ADR SEDOL No. **4768519** CEO **Bernard Dumon** Chairman **Bernard Dumon**

Salomon

Industry: **Other Recreational Products & Services**

Groupe Salomon manufactures and distributes sports equipment. The firm's primary market is alpine ski equipment (including skis, ski boots, and bindings), which represents 68% of all revenue. Its Taylor Made golf-equipment subsidiary contributes another 19%. The company is also involved in cross-country bindings and boots, hiking boots, and skiing accessories. Its largest market is Japan, which represents 39% of sales. In June 1994 Salomon acquired bicycle-component manufacturer Mavic. The Salomon family owns 38% of the company's share capital.

FFr mil	03/93	03/94	03/95	US$mil 03/95				
Sales	**3,154.0**	**3,603.0**	**3,810.0**	**714.8**	P/E Ratio	**24.0**	Price (9/30/95)	**2,599.00**
Net Income	**95.0**	**132.0**	**161.0**	**30.2**	P/B Ratio	**2.5**	52 Wk Hi-Low	**2,609.0-1,690.0**
Book Value	**1,137.0**	**1,367.0**	**1,532.9**	**319.4**	Yield %	**0.0**	Market Cap	**US$815.6mil**

Address **La Ravoire**
74370 Metz-Tessy
Tel **50-65-41-41**
Fax **50-65-42-56**
ADR
SEDOL No. **4771904**
CEO **Jean-François Gautier**
Chairman **Georges Salomon**

SEB

Industry: **Other Home Furnishings**

SEB manufactures electrical appliances and household goods. Its products include small kitchen appliances such as Rowenta coffee makers and toasters, Tefal cooking equipment, and bathroom appliances such as Tefal scales and electric toothbrushes. SEB also sells Calor vacuum cleaners and irons. While SEB's business is concentrated in France and Germany, it has expanded into Eastern Europe, North America, and Asia. Electrical cooking appliances and household goods represent 66% of SEB's sales. Overseas exports accounted for 22% of revenues in 1994.

FFr mil	12/92	12/93	12/94	US$mil 12/94				
Sales	**8,279.0**	**8,388.0**	**8,707.1**	**1,578.8**	P/E Ratio	**22.3**	Price (9/30/95)	**600.00**
Net Income	**314.0**	**331.0**	**400.1**	**72.6**	P/B Ratio	**3.3**	52 Wk Hi-Low	**601.00-448.00**
Book Value	**2,074.0**	**2,384.0**	**2,727.9**	**510.8**	Yield %	**1.5**	Market Cap	**US$1,825.1mil**

Address **Les 4 M-Chemin du Petit-Bois**
69132 Ecully
Tel **72-20-16-16**
Fax **72-20-16-55**
ADR
SEDOL No. **4792132**
CEO **Jacques Gairard**
Chairma **Jacques Gairard**

SEFIMEG

Industry: **Real-Estate Investment**

SEFIMEG (Société Française d'Investissements Immobiliers et de Gestion), a real-estate investment company, constructs and manages commercial and residential rental space. The company owns warehouses, offices, retail space, and parking lots throughout France. The company's portfolio consists of more than 829,000 square meters, nearly 70% of which are in Paris and surrounding areas. Apartments compose 67% of holdings, and commercial properties 33%. SEFIMEG's vacancy rate for business and commercial sites is 12%; for residential sites it is 2%.

FFr mil	12/92	12/93	12/94	US$mil 12/94				
Sales	**552.0**	**535.0**	**542.8**	**98.4**	P/E Ratio	**15.0**	Price (9/30/95)	**299.00**
Net Income	**511.0**	**340.0**	**316.0**	**57.3**	P/B Ratio	**1.1**	52 Wk Hi-Low	**418.80-276.00**
Book Value	**4,220.0**	**4,125.0**	**4,142.5**	**775.8**	Yield %	**4.7**	Market Cap	**US$963.5mil**

Address **4 place de Rio de Janeiro**
75008 Paris
Tel **1-40-75-30-30**
Fax **1-42-56-01-25**
ADR
SEDOL No. **4764302**
President --
Chairman **Marc L. de Lacharrière**

SGE

Industry: **Heavy Construction**

Société Générale d'Entreprises (SGE) is a construction and public-works company. Operating through 83 consolidated subsidiaries, most of which are in France, the firm constructs roads, tunnels, bridges, underground installations, railroads, airports, waterworks, and waste systems. In the energy sector, the company builds nuclear-, thermal-, and hydroelectric-power stations. Générale des Eaux holds more than 80% of the company's shares. SGE's General Enterprises division generates nearly half of the group's total sales.

FFr mil	12/92	12/93	12/94	US$mil 12/94				
Sales	**44,430.0**	**43,271.0**	**45,807.0**	**8,305.9**	P/E Ratio	**11.1**	Price (9/30/95)	**119.90**
Net Income	**405.4**	**305.7**	**290.0**	**52.6**	P/B Ratio	**0.8**	52 Wk Hi-Low	**225.60-118.00**
Book Value	**2,690.3**	**2,981.6**	**4,256.1**	**797.0**	Yield %	**6.3**	Market Cap	**US$711.6mil**

Address **1 Cours Ferdinand de Lesseps**
92500 Rueil-Malmaison
Tel **1-47-16-35-00**
Fax **1-47-16-91-02**
ADR
SEDOL No. **4818083**
Chief Executive **Antoine Zacharias**
Chairman **Guy Dejouany**

Simco

Industry: **Real-Estate Investment**

Simco-Union pour l'Habitation develops and manages residential, office, and commercial property. The company also undertakes construction and refurbishment work. Over 90% of its holdings are located in the Paris area. Simco's assets were estimated at FFr 10 billion in 1994, and its property portfolio consisted of almost 901,500 square meters. Residential properties made up about 76% of Simco's property portfolio in square footage in 1994. French insurer Union des Assurances de Paris (UAP) is Simco's major shareholder, owning about a third of its stock.

FFr mil	12/92	12/93	12/94	US$mil 12/94				
Sales	**600.0**	**627.0**	**609.3**	**110.5**	P/E Ratio	**15.7**	Price (9/30/95)	**378.00**
Net Income	**505.0**	**346.0**	**361.0**	**65.5**	P/B Ratio	**1.5**	52 Wk Hi-Low	**473.00-378.00**
Book Value	**3,761.0**	**4,046.0**	**3,817.1**	**714.8**	Yield %	**8.2**	Market Cap	**US$1,150.2mil**

Address **34 rue de la Fédération**
75737 Paris
Tel **1-40-61-66-20**
Fax **1-40-61-65-06**
ADR
SEDOL No. **4809689**
CEO **Jean-Paul Sorand**
Chairman **Georges Mazaud**

Société Générale

Industry: **Banks - Regional**

Société Générale, the largest private bank in France by total assets, provides its retail and corporate clients with a wide range of services. It offers loans, financing, insurance, asset-management services, lease-financing, and capital-market operations at its network of 2,000 branch offices. The bank operates in roughly 70 countries, oversees more than 250 consolidated subsidiaries, and had assets totaling FFr1.48 trillion at year-end 1994. Société Générale also holds significant real-estate interests through its wholly-owned Genefimmo subsidiary.

	FFr mil 12/92	12/93	12/94	US$mil 12/94				
Revenues	**155,195.0**	**126,194.0**	**101,279.0**	**18,364.3**	P/E Ratio	**10.2**	Price (9/30/95)	**504.00**
Net Income	**3,268.0**	**3,610.0**	**3,847.0**	**697.6**	P/B Ratio	**0.9**	52 Wk Hi-Low	**621.00-469.00**
Book Value	**40,114.0**	**46,438.0**	**49,258.0**	**9,224.3**	Yield %	**3.2**	Market Cap	**US$8,532.5mil**

Address **29 blvd. Haussmann**
75009 Paris
Tel **1-40-98-52-16**
Fax **1-40-98-38-28**
ADR **SEGLY**
SEDOL No. **4817756**
CEO **Marc Viénot**
Chairman **Marc Viénot**

SODEXHO

Industry: **General Industrial & Commercial Services**

Sodexho provides remote-site management services; issues service vouchers for food, gasoline, and gifts; offers contract food and management services; and operates boat cruises, restaurants, and spas. Nearly 85% of sales are generated by its contract food services. In 1994, 39% of its sales were generated in France, 29% in the rest of Europe, 19% in the U.S., and 13% in the rest of the world. Sodexho acquired U.K. contract caterer Gardner Merchant in January 1995, making it the world's largest contract-catering group. Financière Sodexho owns 48% of the company.

	FFr mil 08/92	08/93	08/94	US$mil 08/94				
Sales	**9,105.0**	**10,611.0**	**11,239.0**	**1,978.7**	P/E Ratio	**13.0**	Price (9/30/95)	**1,200.00**
Net Income	**218.0**	**230.0**	**635.7**	**111.9**	P/B Ratio	**3.5**	52 Wk Hi-Low	**1,242.0-735.0**
Book Value	**1,556.0**	**1,762.0**	**2,316.7**	**429.0**	Yield %	**1.4**	Market Cap	**US$1,680.7mil**

Address **3 ave. Newton**
78180 Montigny-le-Breton
Tel **1-30-85-75-00**
Fax **1-30-43-09-58**
ADR
SEDOL No. **4818306**
CEO **Pierre Bellon**
Chairman **Pierre Bellon**

Sommer Allibert

Industry: **Building Materials**

Sommer Allibert supplies coverings and plastic products for household, industrial, and medical uses. Its products include tiles and bathroom fixtures, containers and packaging materials for the cosmetics industry, and trolleys and tables for the medical industry. It also produces automobile fittings for companies such as BMW and General Motors. Sommer Allibert export to markets in Europe, North America and Asia. In 1994 it acquired a controlling interest in Domco, one of the leading North American manufacturers of vinyl floor coverings.

	FFr mil 12/92	12/93	12/94	US$mil 12/94				
Sales	**9,870.0**	**9,791.0**	**10,545.4**	**1,912.1**	P/E Ratio	**11.6**	Price (9/30/95)	**1,710.00**
Net Income	**164.0**	**220.0**	**316.7**	**57.4**	P/B Ratio	**1.3**	52 Wk Hi-Low	**2,190.0-1,628.0**
Book Value	**2,381.0**	**2,535.0**	**2,785.7**	**521.7**	Yield %	**2.2**	Market Cap	**US$746.6mil**

Address **2 rue de l'Égalité**
92748 Nanterre
Tel **1-41-20-40-40**
Fax **1-47-21-49-09**
ADR
SEDOL No. **4822147**
Chairman Exec Bd **Marc Assa**
Chairman Supv Bd **Bernard Deconinck**

SOVAC

Industry: **Financial Services - Diversified**

SOVAC, a holding company for a range of banking and finance organizations, offers financing and financial services to corporate and business clients. The company offers automobile financing, personal credit, business investment and property investment services, and insurance. The company has majority holdings in a number of companies, including CAVIA, an automobile-finance company, Banque SOVAC Immoblier, a commercial-finance company, and SOVAC finance, a services company. SOVAC operates primarily in France but also in Italy and Spain.

	FFr mil 12/92	12/93	12/94	US$mil 12/94				
Revenues	**11,117.0**	**9,709.0**	**8,181.0**	**1,483.4**	P/E Ratio	**8.8**	Price (9/30/95)	**345.60**
Net Income	**461.0**	**479.0**	**496.0**	**89.9**	P/B Ratio	**0.8**	52 Wk Hi-Low	**456.90-327.10**
Book Value	**5,299.0**	**5,722.0**	**5,778.0**	**1,082.0**	Yield %	**4.1**	Market Cap	**US$885.1mil**

Address **19/21 rue de la Bienfaisance**
75008 Paris
Tel **1-40-08-28-28**
Fax **1-42-94-91-05**
ADR
SEDOL No. **4232412**
Managing Director **André Wormser**
Chairman **Michel David-Weill**

Suez

Industry: **Financial Services - Diversified**

Compagnie de Suez is a diversified holding company with interests in banking and financial services, insurance, real estate, and building materials. Its main holdings include Banque Indosuez, Credisuez, Compagnie de Saint-Gobain, and the minerals, metal, and cement operations of Societe Generale de Belgique. Suez recently decided to close its loss-making real-estate development business. Suez's major shareholders include Union des Assurances de Paris, Societe Nationale Elf Aquitaine, Banque Nationale de Paris, and Saint-Gobain.

	FFr mil 12/92	12/93	12/94	US$mil 12/94				
Revenues	**182,689.0**	**194,463.0**	**108,639.0**	**19,698.8**	P/E Ratio	**NMF**	Price (9/30/95)	**189.80**
Net Income	**-1,869.0**	**1,575.0**	**-4,784.0**	**-867.5**	P/B Ratio	**0.6**	52 Wk Hi-Low	**275.40-189.60**
Book Value	**45,899.0**	**50,665.0**	**46,089.0**	**8,630.9**	Yield %	**4.3**	Market Cap	**US$5,988.0mil**

Address **1 rue d'Astorg**
75008 Paris
Tel **1-40-06-64-00**
Fax **1-40-06-66-88**
ADR **CSUZY**
SEDOL No. **4858205**
CEO **Gérard Worms**
Chairman **Gérard Worms**

Thomson-CSF

Industry: **Aerospace & Defense**

Thomson-CSF is the defense-electronics subsidiary of government-controlled Thomson S.A. Thomson-CSF manufactures electronic equipment for defense, aeronautical, navigation, communication, and industrial uses. The group's other products include short- and medium-range missiles, information systems, radio systems, and electronic components such as semiconductors and electron tubes. The company recently acquired a 25% stake in the Spanish data-processing and defense electronics venture Indra. Overseas exports account for nearly half of the company's revenues.

	FFr mil 12/92	12/93	12/94	US$mil 12/94				
Sales	**34,199.0**	**34,291.0**	**36,388.0**	**6,598.0**	P/E Ratio	**NMF**	Price (9/30/95)	**107.10**
Net Income	**1,518.0**	**-2,305.0**	**-962.0**	**-174.4**	P/B Ratio	**0.9**	52 Wk Hi-Low	**169.30-102.00**
Book Value	**19,129.0**	**15,046.0**	**13,256.0**	**2,482.4**	Yield %	**1.9**	Market Cap	**US$2,504.3mil**

Address **173 blvd. Haussmann**
75415 Paris
Tel **1-53-77-80-00**
Fax **1-53-77-89-44**
ADR **TCSFY**
SEDOL No. **4162791**
CEO **Alain Gomez**
Chairman **Alain Gomez**

Total

Industry: **Oil - Integrated Majors**

Total is a petroleum company that explores for, produces, refines, ships, distributes, and markets oil and natural gas. The company also produces petrochemicals and coal. Petroleum products account for nearly 90% of sales. Total produces roughly 633,000 barrels of oil per day and has proven crude-oil reserves of more than 4 billion barrels. The firm plans to merge its Euridep paint subsidiary with U.K. paint manufacturer Kalon, making Total the second-largest decorative-paints producer in Europe by sales. Overseas sales generate roughly half of Total's revenues.

	FFr mil 12/92	12/93	12/94	US$mil 12/94				
Sales	**136,608.0**	**135,478.0**	**136,743.0**	**24,794.7**	P/E Ratio	**20.4**	Price (9/30/95)	**298.00**
Net Income	**2,847.0**	**2,965.0**	**3,385.0**	**613.8**	P/B Ratio	**1.2**	52 Wk Hi-Low	**339.40-257.00**
Book Value	**44,667.0**	**51,394.0**	**55,106.0**	**10,319.5**	Yield %	**2.7**	Market Cap	**US$13,707mil**

Address **24 Cours Michelet**
92800 Puteaux
Tel **1-41-35-52-29**
Fax **N/A**
ADR **TOT**
SEDOL No. **4905413**
CEO **T. Desmarest**
Chairman **T. Desmarest**

UAP

Industry: **Insurance - Full Line**

Union des Assurances de Paris (UAP), France's largest insurance company, was recently privatized. It provides services in all lines of insurance and reinsurance, fund management, property management, banking, and real estate. UAP's partially-owned Banque Worms subsidiary offers commercial, merchant, and investment banking. Insurance operations account for nearly 90% of UAP's revenues. UAP owns a majority interest in Groupe Victoire, the insurance arm of Compagnie de Suez.

	FFr mil 12/92	12/93	12/94	US$mil 12/94				
Revenues	**189,795.0**	**228,138.0**	**192,865.0**	**34,971.0**	P/E Ratio	**21.4**	Price (9/30/95)	**113.30**
Net Income	**1,080.0**	**1,423.0**	**1,568.0**	**284.3**	P/B Ratio	**0.8**	52 Wk Hi-Low	**152.00-110.30**
Book Value	**33,170.0**	**32,870.0**	**39,499.0**	**7,396.8**	Yield %	**2.6**	Market Cap	**US$6,810.5mil**

Address **9 place Vendôme**
75052 Paris
Tel **1-42-86-71-71**
Fax **N/A**
ADR
SEDOL No. **4921077**
Managing Director **Didier Pfeiffer**
Chairman **Jacques Friedman**

UIF

Industry: **Real-Estate Investment**

Union Immobilèire de France (UIF), one of France's largest real-estate investment companies in terms of rental income, builds and manages commercial and residential rental space. The firm currently manages 369,000 square meters of space. Of this 76% are residential properties, 23% commercial properties, and 1% parking. Half of its property holdings are in Paris and the surrounding area. In 1994, the firm undertook two new developments, one in Paris and the other in Boulogne. Both will be completed by the summer of 1996.

	FFr mil 12/92	12/93	12/94	US$mil 12/94				
Sales	**377.0**	**377.0**	**299.9**	**54.4**	P/E Ratio	**18.0**	Price (9/30/95)	**418.90**
Net Income	**275.0**	**188.0**	**191.0**	**34.6**	P/B Ratio	**1.8**	52 Wk Hi-Low	**503.00-388.00**
Book Value	**1,794.0**	**1,808.0**	**1,950.4**	**365.2**	Yield %	**5.3**	Market Cap	**US$685.2mil**

Address **16 rue Duphot**
75001 Paris
Tel **1-49-27-92-14**
Fax **N/A**
ADR
SEDOL No. **4913546**
Managing Director **Henri Pochon**
Chairman **Claude Rivé**

UIS

Industry: **Real-Estate Investment**

Union pour le Financement d'Immeubles de Sociétés (UIS) manages real-estate leasing businesses. UIS, a member of Groupe Percier, leases and rents residential, commercial and retail properties. Over 80% of its property portfolio is concentrated in Paris and the surrounding area. Within Paris the company primarily leases office space. In 1991 the French-government-controlled insurer Groupes des Assurances Nationales (GAN) gained a controlling interest in UIS.

	FFr mil 12/92	12/93	12/94	US$mil 12/94				
Sales	**1,104.0**	**1,262.0**	**N/A**	**N/A**	P/E Ratio	**8.4**	Price (9/30/95)	**136.00**
Net Income	**259.0**	**270.0**	**194.6**	**35.3**	P/B Ratio	**0.9**	52 Wk Hi-Low	**240.00-135.20**
Book Value	**1,847.0**	**1,895.0**	**1,895.4**	**354.9**	Yield %	**10.6**	Market Cap	**US$333.4mil**

Address **5 ave. Percier**
75008 Paris
Tel **1-44-13-15-00**
Fax **1-42-25-02-29**
ADR
SEDOL No. **4917849**
CEO **Yves Bonnet**
Chairman **Alan Juliard**

Unibail

Industry: **Real-Estate Investment**

Union du Crédit-Bail Immobilier (Unibail) is active in property rental and leasing, finance, and construction. Office and retail space accounts for 85% of its property portfolio, with light industrial parks and residential property representing the remainder. The company's properties are concentrated in Paris and the surrounding area. Other Unibail holdings are located in 10 additional French cities and in London. In 1994, the company earned FFr 573 million net rental income on a portfolio valued at FFr 10 billion.

	FFr mil 12/92	12/93	12/94	US$mil 12/94				
Sales	**1,455.0**	**1,659.0**	**1,014.9**	**184.0**	P/E Ratio	**15.4**	Price (9/30/95)	**452.00**
Net Income	**171.0**	**207.0**	**241.9**	**43.9**	P/B Ratio	**1.1**	52 Wk Hi-Low	**540.00-430.00**
Book Value	**3,268.0**	**3,574.0**	**3,602.3**	**674.6**	Yield %	**6.0**	Market Cap	**US$759.3mil**

Address **108 rue de Richelieu**	Tel **1-40-15-21-21**	ADR		CEO	**Léon Bressler**
75002 Paris	Fax **1-40-15-23-04**	SEDOL No.	**4911346**	Chairman	**Léon Bressler**

Valeo

Industry: **Other Auto Parts**

Valeo manufactures automotive systems and components for passenger cars and trucks. Its main products include engine-cooling systems, lighting components, climate-control systems, and clutches and clutch facings. Additional products include electrical, security, and wiper systems. Valeo supplies several automakers, including Chrysler, Renault, Mercedes, Peugeot Citroen, Volkswagen, and Honda. Valeo Climatisation, a joint-venture heating and air-conditioning operation with Siemens, is 80%-controlled by Valeo. Roughly 20% of Valeo's sales are generated overseas.

	FFr mil 12/92	12/93	12/94	US$mil 12/94				
Sales	**20,645.0**	**20,235.0**	**23,050.0**	**4,179.5**	P/E Ratio	**15.9**	Price (9/30/95)	**231.80**
Net Income	**700.0**	**705.0**	**990.0**	**179.5**	P/B Ratio	**1.7**	52 Wk Hi-Low	**301.00-210.10**
Book Value	**7,213.0**	**8,240.0**	**9,308.0**	**1,743.1**	Yield %	**0.9**	Market Cap	**US$3,237.3mil**

Address **43 rue Bayen**	Tel **1-40-55-20-20**	ADR	**VLEEY**	CEO	**Noël Goutard**
75017 Paris	Fax **1-40-55-21-71**	SEDOL No.	**4937579**	Chairman	**Noël Goutard**

Vallourec

Industry: **Steel**

Groupe Vallourec is a steel company that primarily manufactures steel tubing. Its Valtubes division makes steel tubes and other related products, and its Valinox division produces stainless-steel tubes and specialty alloys. Its Valmont division makes containers for transporting and storing high-pressure gases. In 1994, Vallourec, Italian steel company Dalmine, and German steel company Mannesmann combined their stainless-steel-tubing businesses to form the equal partnership DMV Stainless Company.

	FFr mil 12/92	12/93	12/94	US$mil 12/94				
Sales	**6,605.0**	**5,793.0**	**6,893.5**	**1,250.0**	P/E Ratio	**42.8**	Price (9/30/95)	**213.00**
Net Income	**45.0**	**23.0**	**34.8**	**6.3**	P/B Ratio	**0.6**	52 Wk Hi-Low	**309.00-205.00**
Book Value	**2,803.0**	**2,830.0**	**2,840.6**	**531.9**	Yield %	**0.0**	Market Cap	**US$354.3mil**

Address **130 rue de Silly**	Tel **1-49-09-38-24**	ADR		Managing Director	**Jean-Claude Verdière**
92103 Boulogne, Billancourt	Fax **N/A**	SEDOL No.	**4926447**	Chairman	**Jean-Claude Cabre**

Worms & Cie.

Industry: **Banks - Regional**

Worms & Cie. is a holding company that invests mainly in the insurance, banking, real-estate, food, and paper sectors. The company has a 27% holding in Groupe Saint Louis, a French industrial holding company with paper, food, and agriculture interests. Its holdings in the financial sector include Athena Assurances, the investment-banking company Demachy Worms & Cie., and real-estate company Unibail. Worms also has an interest in Compagnie Nationale de Navigation, a services and transport company operating primarily in the petroleum industry.

	FFr mil 12/91	12/92	12/93	US$mil 12/93				
Revenues	**N/A**	**N/A**	**N/A**	**N/A**	P/E Ratio	**9.8**	Price (9/30/95)	**212.00**
Net Income	**1,002.0**	**571.0**	**714.0**	**129.5**	P/B Ratio	**0.6**	52 Wk Hi-Low	**264.10-200.00**
Book Value	**10,390.0**	**11,002.0**	**11,753.0**	**2,200.9**	Yield %	**3.5**	Market Cap	**US$1,417.7mil**

Address **55 rue la Boétie**	Tel **1-42-66-90-80**	ADR		President	--
75009 Paris	Fax **N/A**	SEDOL No.	**4981424**	Chairman	**F. Essig**

Zodiac

Industry: **Industrial - Diversified**

Groupe Zodiac manufactures equipment for air-transport and recreational marine uses. The company has three business segments: Aeronautical Equipment, which manufactures and markets emergency evacuation systems, deceleration systems, de-icing systems, and fuel tanks for civil and military aircraft; Airline Equipment, which manufactures seats for civil aircraft; and Marine Leisure, which produces inflatable and semi-rigid craft, a variety of swimming pools, and beach gear. North America, its largest market, accounts for 48% of sales.

	FFr mil 08/92	08/93	08/94	US$mil 08/94				
Sales	**2,273.0**	**2,678.0**	**2,966.6**	**522.3**	P/E Ratio	**5.4**	Price (9/30/95)	**662.00**
Net Income	**122.0**	**122.0**	**137.0**	**24.1**	P/B Ratio	**3.0**	52 Wk Hi-Low	**702.00-503.00**
Book Value	**623.0**	**924.0**	**1,021.2**	**189.1**	Yield %	**4.8**	Market Cap	**US$620.4mil**

Address **58 blvd. Galliéni**	Tel **1-41-23-23-23**	ADR		CEO	**Jean-Louis Gerondeau**
92137 Issy-les-Moulineaux	Fax **1-41-23-23-62**	SEDOL No.	**4994693**	Chairman	**Didier Domange**

Germany

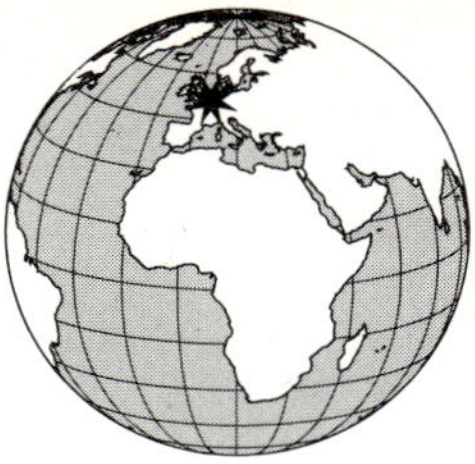

Germany

Dagmar Aalund, Frankfurt

Local Trading Hours	Time Difference from New York	Population (Est. 94)
10:30-1:30 (Frankfurt Stock Exchange) 8:30-5:00 (IBIS)	6 hours ahead of EST	81,418,000

Germany in 1995 introduced sweeping reforms in its stock market in a bid to compete with other international trading centers for worldwide investment capital.

Both the government and German corporations are taking actions to promote Finanzplatz Frankfurt — the Frankfurt financial center — and ease foreign investors' fears that the nation's exchanges are dominated by a few big German banks and institutions.

Also in 1995, the government's Second Financial Markets Promotion Law made insider trading illegal — finally bringing Germany closer to the international standard — and toughened reporting requirements for companies. An investigation by Germany's new trading watchdog agency, modeled on the U.S. Securities and Exchange Commission, led to a first-ever insider trading conviction in August 1995.

The changes won't stop here. Germany's Finance Ministry is drafting a new law that will cover a range of market liberalization measures not addressed in earlier legislation. The Third Financial Markets Promotion Law will institute European Union (E.U.) standards on investment services and capital adequacy in Germany.

On the corporate front, more and more German companies have joined a trend of reducing their shares' nominal value in order to cut their market price, increase their liquidity in the stock market and make them more attractive to the small investor. Shares in German companies tend to be held by large institutions.

But reforms have so far failed to spark enthusiasm among the traditionally risk-averse German public. They remain lukewarm to stock investments, with just over 5% of households investing compared with about 20% in the U.S.

Dow Jones Germany Equity Market Index Performance

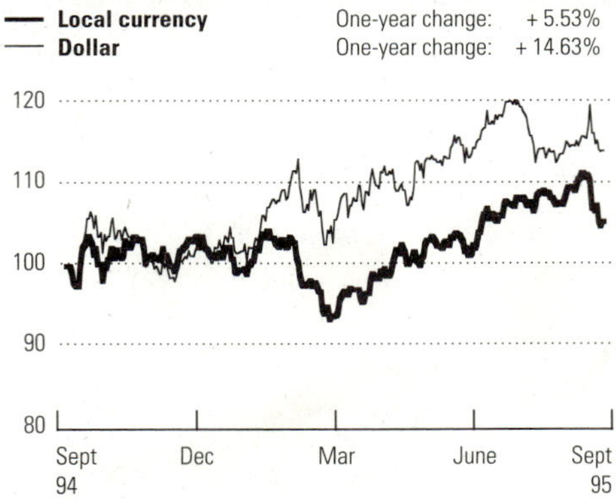

No official figures exist on foreign participation in Germany's share trading, but exchange officials and traders estimate a third to a half of turnover comes from London or other centers. Among foreign participants, U.K. investment houses are the most active. Investors based in other financial capitals, such as Tokyo and New York, often channel their orders through London.

Gross Domestic Product (94, inflation adjusted)	Three-Year Average GDP Growth (92-94)	Main Industries	Consumer Price Index (93-94)	Monetary Unit	Exchange Rate (9/95)
All-Germany 2.97 trillion DEM Western Germany: 2.71 trillion DEM Eastern Germany: 258.3 billion DEM	All-Germany: up 1.3% Western Germany: up 0.7% Eastern Germany: up 7.8%	Motor-vehicle production, electrical equipment, mechanical engineering, machinery, chemicals	Western Germany: up 3.0% Eastern Germany: up 3.4%	Deutsche mark	DM1.43 to US$1.00

Indeed, Germany's stock market in 1994 retained its rank as Europe's second-largest behind London's. Total equities turnover on all eight of the country's regional exchanges in 1994 came to a record 2.12 trillion marks in 1994, up from 1.98 trillion marks in 1993.

In 1994, the Frankfurt Stock Exchange increased its domination over Germany's other seven regional exchanges: By August 1994, Frankfurt boasted 74.24% of total share trading volume in Germany, up from 72% in mid-1993.

Frankfurt's exchange lists 417 of the total 666 German companies whose shares are traded on exchanges here. Those include all Germany's major corporations. The smaller companies often are listed only on regional exchanges.

Plans are afoot for major changes in the structure of Germany's exchanges. The stock exchanges in Frankfurt, Duesseldorf and Munich are planning to merge their operations in the coming months. Under that merger plan, shares represented in Germany's broad "DAX-100" weighted index will be traded and quoted simultaneously on all three exchanges and the IBIS electronic trading system. Other German shares will be listed on only one of the three exchanges, in a move the exchanges say is aimed at concentrating trading and buoying liquidity in second-tier stocks.

The three exchanges also want to institute a system requiring floor brokers to enter price spreads into the electronic trading system alongside the IBIS quotes, further increasing market transparency.

Ten Largest Capitalized Companies
as of 9/30/95

Stock	Market Cap. US$Mil
Allianz	40,145,969.2
Siemens	27,777,616.1
Daimler-Benz	25,254,892.3
Deutsche Bank	22,561,697.6
VEBA	19,273,468.5
Bayer	17,962,509.1
Munich Reinsurance	15,254,097.9
BASF	13,312,500.0
Dresdner Bank	12,041,772.4
Mannesmann	12,010,991.6

The Frankfurt stock and options exchanges, as well as securities clearing houses, are held by an umbrella company called Deutsche Bourse AG, which is spearheading the stock exchange reforms.

Another of the Deutsche Bourse's proposals this year unleashed a storm of protest from the floor brokers on the stock exchange. The German bourse is considering switching to a fully electronic nationwide trading system that would make the floor brokers' current role as market makers obsolete. Already, Germany's electronic IBIS trading system, which is a market place parallel to the daily three-hour floor trading session in Frankfurt, has won a growing share of German stock transactions since starting up in April 1991.

On average, 34.1% of the 1994 turnover on all bourses in shares on Germany's weighted

DAX index of 30 blue-chips stemmed from IBIS trades, compared with 11.7% four years ago. IBIS lists 40 major German stocks, 18 stock warrants, 30 fixed-income securities and 19 foreign bonds. Minimum lot size is usually 500 shares. There are plans to expand the number of IBIS-listed stocks to 100 as soon as possible, although IBIS would disappear in three to five years, when the new nationwide electronic trading network starts.

For large transactions, IBIS can be significantly cheaper for an investor than floor trading. IBIS transactions cost 3.50 marks each, regardless of size, while a broker's floor commission on a DAX share would be 0.04% of turnover. There are drawbacks, however, for some foreign investors. Under German regulations, IBIS can be set up in foreign cities, but only at subsidiaries of German-based institutions.

Settlement periods for both floor and IBIS trading are generally two days.

In addition to the stock exchanges and IBIS, the third pillar of German securities trading is the DTB, which entered its sixth year of operation in 1995. In 1994, it retained its position as Europe's second-largest options and futures exchange, behind London.

Trading is conducted on its own nationwide electronic network that allows traders to carry out transactions in DAX options, DAX futures, options on DAX futures and stock options, among other derivatives. DTB turnover rose 18% in 1994, to 59.2 million contracts. Average daily volume was 234,955 contracts in 1994, compared with 199,115 contracts the previous year. Simultaneous automatic clearing of transactions is integrated into the DTB system.

Industry Group Performance
1 Year Change Through 9/30/95

Industry	Change % (US$)
Best Performing	
Non-Ferrous Metals - Other (Excludes Aluminum)	31.55
Pharmaceuticals	26.69
Insurance - Full Line	26.64
Aluminum	25.52
Diversified Technology	22.38
Worst Performing	
Heavy Machinery	-37.35
Office Equipment	-28.91
Shipbuilding	-28.55
Transportation Equipment - All	-28.55
Heavy Construction	-22.77

In September 1994, the DAX hit an all-time high of 2,317.01 points on optimism that the dollar's recovery will take the pressure off earnings at Germany's heavily export-oriented companies. Improvements on the inflation front also bolstered speculation the Deutsche Bundesbank could follow its August cut in key rates with yet another ease. The market has rebounded dramatically from its March low of 1910.96 points, reached as the dollar drifted below 1.40 marks.

On the German exchanges, trading in domestic companies overshadows that in the

801 foreign corporate listings. The 30 DAX shares alone accounted for 84.3% of German equities trading in 1994. Foreign investors are known to concentrate almost solely on the DAX stocks.

Turnover for Deutsche Bank AG, Siemens AG and Daimler-Benz AG constituted 32.6% of all domestic share trading in 1994.

The most actively traded German shares in 1994 were Deutsche Bank with 224.59 billion marks worth of transactions, or 12.01% of all domestic share trading, diversified auto maker Daimler-Benz with 11.28%, electronics group Siemens with 9.27%, insurer Allianz Holding with 6.59%, auto maker Volkswagen with 5.96% and chemicals and pharmaceuticals company Bayer at 4.04%.

German stocks fall into three categories, based on listing requirements. The first segment makes up about 90% of trading volume. The criteria for this listing are: a company must have total nominal, or par, value of its capital stock of at least 2.5 million marks, be at least three years old, have at least 25% of its shares broadly distributed, and must publish an interim report that provides enough information for an investor to formulate an informed opinion.

To be traded in the second segment, a company must have a share capitalization of at least a nominal 500,000 marks. Most German companies have nominal per-share values of either 5 marks or 50 marks. The firm must also publish a sales prospectus and an interim report before listing on the stock exchange. There isn't any age requirement.

The third segment requires only that a sales brochure be available to potential investors. Corporations traded in that segment haven't formally applied to be listed but have agreed to brokers' requests to be allowed to trade their shares.

Allianz

Industry: **Insurance - Full Line**

Allianz Holding, Europe's largest insurer, sells property, casualty, and life insurance to customers around the world. Its property and casualty insurance includes auto, fire, storm, homeowner's, marine, and aviation coverage. The company offers property and casualty insurance in Germany through its subsidiary Allianz Versicherung, which forms the core of its operations. It has expanded internationally by acquiring the U.S. insurance company Fireman's Fund Insurance. Foreign operations contribute about half of Allianz's premium income.

DM mil	12/92	12/93	12/94	US$mil 12/94				
Revenues	46,635.0	57,484.0	66,100.0	40,979.5	P/E Ratio	44.4	Price (9/30/95)	2,576.00
Net Income	507.0	963.0	1,340.0	830.8	P/B Ratio	3.3	52 Wk Hi-Low	2,751.5-2,035.9
Book Value	11,094.0	11,963.0	17,742.6	11,446.8	Yield %	0.6	Market Cap	US$40,146mil

Address **Königinstr. 28, 80802 Munich** Tel **089-3800-0** Fax **089-349941** ADR SEDOL No. **4016326** Chairman Exec Bd **H. Schulte-Noelle** Chairman Supv Bd **Dr. Wolfgang Schieren**

AMB

Industry: **Insurance - Full Line**

AMB Aachener und Münchener Beteiligungs is a financial-services company that offers insurance, and banking services. The company's insurance activities include reinsurance and life, health, property, motor, and casualty insurance. AMB provides banking services including mortgage lending through its Badenia Bausparkasse building- society subsidiary. Its life-insurance activities accounted for 39% of premium income, property and casualty insurance 29%, and health insurance and reinsurance 19% in 1994. Its building-society activities contributed 13% of revenues.

DM mil	12/92	12/93	12/94	US$mil 12/94				
Revenues	506.0	267.0	233.9	145.0	P/E Ratio	7.4	Price (9/30/95)	945.00
Net Income	73.0	85.0	127.9	79.3	P/B Ratio	1.5	52 Wk Hi-Low	1,175.0-870.0
Book Value	2,879.0	2,906.0	3,120.2	2,013.0	Yield %	1.5	Market Cap	US$2,507.9mil

Address **Aachener & Münchener Allee 9, 52074 Aachen** Tel **0241-461-01** Fax **0241-461-1805** ADR SEDOL No. **4001924** CEO **Wolfgang Kaske** Chairman **Hans Krämer**

AVA

Industry: **Retailers - Broadline**

Allgemeine Handelsgesellschaft der Verbraucher (AVA) runs specialty-retail stores and shopping centers. It operates self-service hypermarkets and home-improvement stores under the Marktkauf name; Krane Optics eyecare stores; Dixi home, garden, and hobby stores; and Helco fresh-food markets. AVA's Marktkauf stores contribute 58% of all sales revenues. The company sold its 50% stake in the Backstube Siebrecht bakery chain in December 1994. AVA owns 40% of German supermaket operator Nanz. AVA is 49% controlled by German holding company Edeka Zentrale.

DM mil	12/92	12/93	12/94	US$mil 12/94				
Revenues	6,159.0	6,777.0	7,495.1	4,646.7	P/E Ratio	36.6	Price (9/30/95)	544.00
Net Income	81.0	90.0	45.7	28.3	P/B Ratio	2.2	52 Wk Hi-Low	615.00-451.00
Book Value	683.0	795.0	775.9	500.6	Yield %	2.6	Market Cap	US$1,180.4mil

Address **Fuggerstr. 11, 33689 Bielefeld** Tel **05205-9401** Fax **05205-941029** ADR SEDOL No. **4016490** Chairman Exec Bd **Klaus Daudel** Chairman Supv Bd **Dr. Gerhard Laule**

Babcock

Industry: **Industrial - Diversified**

Deutsche Babcock is a holding company that provides plant- and mechanical-engineering services, distributes power, and makes a variety of rolled-steel and nonferrous-metal products. It provides services to the recycling, oil and natural-gas, steel, textile, power-transmission, and other industries. The company's power-and-environment and process-and-system engineering divisions account for roughly 60% of its turnover. Overseas exports, mainly to North America, accounted for one-fourth of revenues in 1994.

DM mil	09/92	09/93	09/94	US$mil 09/94				
Sales	7,644.0	8,203.0	8,165.6	4,933.9	P/E Ratio	NMF	Price (9/30/95)	145.30
Net Income	67.0	-6.0	35.0	21.1	P/B Ratio	2.0	52 Wk Hi-Low	238.50-138.00
Book Value	650.0	375.0	416.7	268.8	Yield %	0.0	Market Cap	US$584.2mil

Address **Duisburger Str. 375, 46049 Oberhausen** Tel **0208-833-0** Fax **0208-260-91** ADR SEDOL No. **4267005** President & CEO **Heyo Schmiedeknecht** Chairman Supv Bd **Friedel Neuber**

BASF

Industry: **Commodity Chemicals**

BASF, the world's second-largest chemicals company by sales, manufactures products for the consumer, industrial, and agricultural sectors. It also explores for and sells crude oil and natural gas. Additional products include pharmaceuticals, plastics, fibers, dyestuffs, coatings, and fertilizers. It produces industrial chemicals, chemical intermediates, fiber intermediates, and fine chemicals. BASF also manufactures computers and printing systems. BASF recently acquired the pharmaceuticals division of U.K.-based Boots. Overseas exports generate nearly 40% of sales.

DM mil	12/92	12/93	12/94	US$mil 12/94				
Sales	44,522.0	43,123.0	46,564.6	28,868.3	P/E Ratio	14.8	Price (9/30/95)	312.50
Net Income	615.0	858.0	1,284.0	796.0	P/B Ratio	1.2	52 Wk Hi-Low	337.50-277.00
Book Value	14,497.0	14,784.0	15,740.4	10,155.1	Yield %	3.2	Market Cap	US$13,313mil

Address **Carl-Bosch-Str. 38, 67056 Ludwigshafen** Tel **0621-60-0** Fax **0621-6042525** ADR **BASFY** SEDOL No. **4083483** Chairman Exec Bd **Dr. Jürgen Strube** Chairman Supv Bd **Dr. Hans Albers**

Bayer

Industry: **Commodity Chemicals**

Bayer manufactures pharmaceuticals, chemicals, industrial and organic products, polymers, photographic film, and imaging systems for medical diagnosis, materials testing, and micrographics. Its U.S. interests include Miles, now operating under the Bayer name, and Sterling Winthrop's North American over-the-counter pharmaceutical business. Its products include Bayer Aspirin and Alka-Seltzer. Bayer's industrial-products and polymers divisions produce pigments, ceramics, polyurethanes, and synthetic products. Overseas exports account for nearly 50% of sales.

DM mil	12/92	12/93	12/94	US$mil 12/94				
Sales	**41,195.0**	**41,007.0**	**43,420.0**	**26,918.8**	P/E Ratio	**12.1**	Price (9/30/95)	**364.00**
Net Income	**1,516.0**	**1,327.0**	**1,970.0**	**1,221.3**	P/B Ratio	**1.5**	52 Wk Hi-Low	**387.80-330.20**
Book Value	**17,078.0**	**17,681.0**	**16,602.0**	**10,711.0**	Yield %	**3.6**	Market Cap	**US$17,963mil**

Address **Bayerwerk**
51368 Leverkusen
Tel **0214-3081753**
Fax **0214-3071985**
ADR **BAYZY**
SEDOL No. **4085304**
Chairman Exec Bd **Manfred Schneider**
Chairman Supv Bd **Hermann J. Strenger**

Bayer Hypo und Wechsel

Industry: **Banks - Regional**

Bayerische Hypotheken- und Wechsel-Bank (Hypo-Bank) is a Munich-based bank that primarily provides international mortgage-banking services. The bank also offers demand- and savings-deposits, commercial-lending, and custodial services. The company's principal lending activities include real estate lending for commercial and residential development. It operates almost 650 domestic branches and 22 overseas branches. Hypo-Bank is among Germany's five-largest banks in terms of assets.

DM mil	12/92	12/93	12/94	US$mil 12/94				
Revenues	**19,011.0**	**19,859.0**	**20,065.0**	**12,439.6**	P/E Ratio	**18.2**	Price (9/30/95)	**35.70**
Net Income	**366.0**	**515.0**	**503.0**	**311.8**	P/B Ratio	**10.7**	52 Wk Hi-Low	**414.00-35.70**
Book Value	**6,092.0**	**7,576.0**	**8,793.0**	**5,672.9**	Yield %	**4.1**	Market Cap	**US$5,834.1mil**

Address **Theatinerstr. 11**
80333 Munich
Tel **08992-442325**
Fax **N/A**
ADR
SEDOL No. **4085348**
Chairman Exec Bd **Eberhard Martini**
Chairman **--**

Bayerische Vereinsbank

Industry: **Banks - Regional**

Bayerische Vereinsbank offers commercial and mortgage banking, investment banking, and securities trading for private and institutional investors. Mortgage-banking activities account for 53% of the company's assets, which totaled DM318 billion at year-end 1994, and commercial-banking activities account for 47%. Bayerische operates through 788 German and 50 foreign branches and offices. Its subsidiaries include 75%-owned investment bank Vereinsbank Capital Corporation (U.S.) and 90%-owned Vereinsbank International (Luxembourg).

DM mil	12/92	12/93	12/94	US$mil 12/94				
Revenues	**21,462.0**	**22,891.0**	**22,550.9**	**13,980.7**	P/E Ratio	**19.1**	Price (9/30/95)	**40.70**
Net Income	**398.0**	**532.0**	**524.2**	**325.0**	P/B Ratio	**1.3**	52 Wk Hi-Low	**46.28-38.34**
Book Value	**6,743.0**	**6,872.0**	**7,797.8**	**5,030.9**	Yield %	**3.2**	Market Cap	**US$6,616.7mil**

Address **Kardinal-Faulhaber-Str. 1-14**
80311 Munich
Tel **089-2132-1**
Fax **089-21-326-415**
ADR **BAVNY**
SEDOL No. **4325419**
Chairman Exec Bd **Albrecht Schmidt**
Chairman Supv Bd **Maximilian Hackl**

Beiersdorf

Industry: **Pharmaceuticals**

Beiersdorf manufactures cosmetics, personal- and health-care products, pharmaceuticals, and adhesives. Its personal-care line includes Nivea, Nivea Visage, and pH5-Eucerin products for skin and hair care, and a variety of soaps, toothpastes, and deodorants. The company also produces Tesa adhesive tapes, glue, packaging and electrical tapes, Hansaplast bandages, and hospital supplies and medicines. Nearly two thirds of Beiersdorf's sales are generated outside Germany; overseas exports account for one fourth of all revenues.

DM mil	12/92	12/93	12/94	US$mil 12/94				
Sales	**4,552.0**	**4,763.0**	**5,152.6**	**3,194.4**	P/E Ratio	**22.6**	Price (9/30/95)	**1,090.00**
Net Income	**156.0**	**176.0**	**202.1**	**125.3**	P/B Ratio	**3.2**	52 Wk Hi-Low	**1,225.0-955.0**
Book Value	**1,161.0**	**1,277.0**	**1,409.7**	**909.5**	Yield %	**1.5**	Market Cap	**US$3,201.4mil**

Address **Unnastr. 48**
20245 Hamburg
Tel **040-569-0**
Fax **040-569-3434**
ADR
SEDOL No. **4089306**
Chairman Exec Bd **Dr. Rolf Kunisch**
Chairman Supv Bd **Dr. Wolfgang Schieren**

BHF-Bank

Industry: **Banks - Regional**

Berliner Handels und Frankfurter Bank (BHF-Bank) is a commercial bank with activities in securities operations, corporate finance, foreign exchange, and portfolio management. Its customers are private investors, medium- and large-size companies, financial institutions, and government organizations. The bank operates through 12 branches in Germany and one branch each in Tokyo, London, New York, Singapore, and the Cayman Islands. BHF-Bank has a 45% interest in British merchant bank Charterhouse.

DM mil	12/92	12/93	12/94	US$mil 12/94				
Revenues	**4,064.0**	**4,330.0**	**4,205.3**	**2,607.2**	P/E Ratio	**17.6**	Price (9/30/95)	**37.00**
Net Income	**117.0**	**154.0**	**173.1**	**107.3**	P/B Ratio	**0.9**	52 Wk Hi-Low	**40.30-35.60**
Book Value	**2,239.0**	**2,837.0**	**3,411.3**	**2,200.8**	Yield %	**3.9**	Market Cap	**US$2,086.2mil**

Address **Bockenheimer Landstr. 10**
60323 Frankfurt
Tel **069-718-0**
Fax **069-718-2296**
ADR
SEDOL No. **4737564**
Chairman Exec Bd **Klaus Subjetzki**
Chairman Supv Bd **Klaus Subjetzki**

Bilfinger & Berger

Industry: **Heavy Construction**

Bilfinger & Berger is a construction company. It also operates project-development, machinery, environmental-technology, construction-materials, and businesses. The company's engineering activities include bridge construction, tunneling, and plant development. 42% of its work is outside Germany, mainly in Africa, North America, Southeast Asia, and Australia. Its subsidiaries include the construction groups Fru-Con in the United States and A.W. Baulderstone and Australia. The company has made recent acquisitions in France, Poland, and the Czech Republic.

	DM mil 12/92	12/93	12/94	US$mil 12/94				
Sales	**4,693.0**	**5,220.0**	**5,895.7**	**3,655.1**	P/E Ratio	**17.4**	Price (9/30/95)	**630.00**
Net Income	**79.0**	**103.0**	**130.0**	**80.6**	P/B Ratio	**1.7**	52 Wk Hi-Low	**882.00-590.00**
Book Value	**1,023.0**	**1,039.0**	**1,355.8**	**874.7**	Yield %	**2.1**	Market Cap	**US$1,586.0mil**

Address	**Carl-Reiá-Platz 1-5**	Tel	**0621-459-0**	ADR		Chairman Exec Bd	**Dr. Christian Roth**
	68165 Mannheim	Fax	**0621-4592366**	SEDOL No.	**4098302**	Chairman Supv Bd	**Jürgen Sarrazin**

BMW

Industry: **Automobile Manufacturers**

Bayerische Motoren Werke (BMW) manufactures automobiles and motorcycles. It also manufactures aircraft engines through a joint venture with Rolls-Royce. The Rover Group, a U.K. car manufacturer, became a wholly-owned subsidiary in 1994 following BMW's purchase from British aerospace for £800 million. BMW has plants in 20 countries, sales subsidiaries and importers in 120 countries, and about 4,870 dealerships worldwide. More than 20% of its customers arrange financing with BMW's wholly-owned financing subsidiaries.

	DM mil 12/92	12/93	12/94	US$mil 12/94				
Sales	**31,241.0**	**29,016.0**	**42,125.0**	**26,115.9**	P/E Ratio	**20.7**	Price (9/30/95)	**783.00**
Net Income	**726.0**	**516.0**	**697.0**	**432.1**	P/B Ratio	**1.8**	52 Wk Hi-Low	**837.00-675.00**
Book Value	**6,627.0**	**6,915.0**	**7,800.0**	**5,032.3**	Yield %	**1.8**	Market Cap	**US$10,080mil**

Address	**Petuelring 130**	Tel	**089-3895-0**	ADR		Chairman Exec Bd	**Bernd Pischetsrieder**
	80809 Munich	Fax	**089-38955858**	SEDOL No.	**4085229**	Chairman Supv Bd	**Dr. E. von Kuenheim**

Bremer Vulkan

Industry: **Shipbuilding**

Bremer Vulkan Verbund builds ships for the civilian and defense markets. The company also manufactures machine tools, engines, and marine-electronics products such as systems for nautical communication and navigation. Bremer Vulkan has six civilian shipyards concentrating on new orders, repairs, and large-scale conversions. It also operates two naval shipyards. Bremer's shipbuilding division accounted for 43% of turnover, the electronics division 29%, and engineering and machine tools 16% in 1994. Overseas exports account for 30% of revenues.

	DM mil 12/92	12/93	12/94	US$mil 12/94				
Sales	**4,108.0**	**6,141.0**	**6,018.1**	**3,731.0**	P/E Ratio	**15.3**	Price (9/30/95)	**59.20**
Net Income	**82.0**	**-198.0**	**56.5**	**35.0**	P/B Ratio	**0.7**	52 Wk Hi-Low	**103.80-59.20**
Book Value	**1,125.0**	**842.0**	**1,316.2**	**849.2**	Yield %	**0.0**	Market Cap	**US$606.1mil**

Address	**Domshof 18-20**	Tel	**0421-33-370**	ADR		Chairman Exec Bd	**Dr. Friedrich Hennemann**
	28195 Bremen	Fax	**0421-33-37131**	SEDOL No.	**4121565**	Chairman Supv Bd	**Walter Behrmann**

Commerzbank

Industry: **Banks - Money Center**

Commerzbank, Germany's third-largest bank with assets totaling DM342 billion in December 1994, provides commercial and investment banking and related financial services. It offers home loans, real-estate leasing, life insurance, and asset- management services. The bank owns 51% of the municipal- and mortgage-loan lender Hypothekenbank. It owns four fund-management firms: Commerzbank Investment Management, Commerzbank International Capital Management, New York-based Commerzbank Capital Markets, and 75% of U.K.-based Jupiter Tyndall.

	DM mil 12/92	12/93	12/94	US$mil 12/94				
Revenues	**20,959.0**	**22,405.0**	**20,961.9**	**12,995.6**	P/E Ratio	**20.4**	Price (9/30/95)	**325.00**
Net Income	**683.0**	**627.0**	**1,052.2**	**652.3**	P/B Ratio	**0.8**	52 Wk Hi-Low	**350.50-303.50**
Book Value	**7,291.0**	**8,237.0**	**14,123.6**	**9,112.0**	Yield %	**3.7**	Market Cap	**US$8,431.8mil**

Address	**Neue Mainzer Str. 32-36**	Tel	**069-1-36-20**	ADR	**CRZBY**	Chairman Exec Bd	**Martin Kohlhaussen**
	60261 Frankfurt	Fax	**069-28-53-89**	SEDOL No.	**4213428**	Chairman Supv Bd	**Walter Seipp**

Concordia

Industry: **Real-Estate Investment**

Concordia Construction and Land (Concordia Bau und Boden) owns real-estate-investment and project-development businesses. The majority of its nearly 500,000 square meters of property is located in western Germany. Residential properties represent more than half of the firm's holdings and generate more than one third of revenues, while office buildings, retail property, and commercial real estate make up the remaining 48% and generate nearly two thirds of revenues. Concordia is building the Oceania residential complex in Miami.

	DM mil 12/91	12/92	12/93	US$mil 12/93				
Sales	**172.0**	**177.0**	**224.0**	**134.9**	P/E Ratio	**5.4**	Price (9/30/95)	**93.00**
Net Income	**9.0**	**12.0**	**17.0**	**10.2**	P/B Ratio	**0.7**	52 Wk Hi-Low	**100.00-91.00**
Book Value	**81.0**	**84.0**	**91.0**	**52.3**	Yield %	**25.8**	Market Cap	**US$650.3mil**

Address	**Lothringer Str. 21-23**	Tel	**0208-260-21**	ADR		Chairman Exec Bd	**Dr. Günter Minninger**
	46045 Oberhausen	Fax	**0208-855-932**	SEDOL No.	**4178129**	Chairman	**Dr. Sven Kratz**

Continental

Industry: **Tires & Rubber**

Continental produces and markets tires and automotive components for commercial and passenger vehicles. Its ContiTech division manufactures airsprings, antivibration and sealing systems, hose assemblies, and vehicle interiors. The firm makes tires under the Continental, General Tire, and Uniroyal brand names. Continental sells its passenger-car tires to independent dealers, and markets them through its own European network of nearly 1,000 tire dealers. The firm commands 8% of the world tire market; overseas exports, primarily to the U.S., account for 28% of sales.

DM mil	12/92	12/93	12/94	US$mil 12/94				
Sales	**9,690.0**	**9,369.0**	**9,876.9**	**6,123.3**	P/E Ratio	**27.0**	Price (9/30/95)	**20.23**
Net Income	**135.0**	**78.0**	**37.9**	**23.5**	P/B Ratio	**1.3**	52 Wk Hi-Low	**23.90-18.75**
Book Value	**1,466.0**	**1,502.0**	**1,479.8**	**954.7**	Yield %	**2.0**	Market Cap	**US$1,315.5mil**

Address **Vahrenwalder Str. 9**
30165 Hannover
Tel **0511-938-01**
Fax **0511-938-2766**
ADR **CTTAY**
SEDOL No. **4598589**
Chairman Exec Bd **Hubertus von Grünberg**
Chairman Supv Bd **Ulrich Weiss**

Daimler-Benz

Industry: **Automobile Manufacturers**

Daimler-Benz is Germany's largest automobile manufacturer by sales. Its Mercedes-Benz subsidiary produced 291,854 commercial vehicles and 590,060 passenger cars in 1994. Mercedes also owns U.S.-based Freightliner trucks. The firm owns 81% of AEG, an electrical-engineering firm that makes automation systems, rail systems, power tools, and electronics; and owns Daimler-Benz Aerospace, a manufacturer of aircraft and space systems and Debis, which offers financial, insurance, and mobile-communication services. Overseas exports account for 37% of revenues.

DM mil	12/92	12/93	12/94	US$mil 12/94				
Sales	**98,549.0**	**97,737.0**	**104,075.0**	**64,522.6**	P/E Ratio	**32.7**	Price (9/30/95)	**704.00**
Net Income	**1,418.0**	**602.0**	**895.0**	**554.9**	P/B Ratio	**1.8**	52 Wk Hi-Low	**789.00-607.00**
Book Value	**18,491.0**	**17,584.0**	**20,251.0**	**13,065.2**	Yield %	**1.6**	Market Cap	**US$25,255mil**

Address **PO Box 80 02 30**
70546 Stuttgart
Tel **0711-17-92287**
Fax **0711-17-94109**
ADR **DAI**
SEDOL No. **4252409**
Chairman Exec Bd **Edzard Reuter**
Chairman **Hilmar Kopper**

Degussa

Industry: **Precious Metals**

Degussa manufactures chemicals, pharmaceuticals, and precious metals. It refines, purchases, and sells precious metals for the jewelry and electronics market. Pharmaceutical products include dental equipment and alloys, prosthetic attachments, and generic and over-the-counter medicines through its ASTA Medica subsidiary. Its chemicals division manufactures hydrogen peroxide, adhesives and resins, rubber chemicals and pigments, and automotive-exhaust-gas catalysts. Overseas exports, primarily to North America, accounted for 46% of turnover in 1994.

DM mil	09/92	09/93	09/94	US$mil 09/94				
Sales	**12,815.0**	**14,901.0**	**13,815.8**	**8,347.9**	P/E Ratio	**20.3**	Price (9/30/95)	**446.50**
Net Income	**111.0**	**104.0**	**156.6**	**94.6**	P/B Ratio	**3.7**	52 Wk Hi-Low	**483.00-389.00**
Book Value	**1,663.0**	**1,640.0**	**1,033.3**	**666.6**	Yield %	**2.2**	Market Cap	**US$2,678.7mil**

Address **Weissfrauenstr. 9**
60311 Frankfurt
Tel **069-218-3618**
Fax **069-218-3743**
ADR
SEDOL No. **4260372**
President & CEO **Gert Becker**
Chairman **Helmut Sihler**

Deutsche Bank

Industry: **Banks - Money Center**

Deutsche Bank is Germany's largest bank, with assets totaling DM573 billion. It provides retail, private, and institutional banking. The bank also offers mortgage and investment banking, fund management, capital-market exchange, corporate financing, and mergers-and-acquisitions consulting. Commercial banking accounts for 70% of Deutsche Bank's assets and mortgage banking accounts for 13%. The bank operates more than 1,700 offices in Germany and 697 abroad. Subsidiaries include investment firms ITT Commercial Finance and Morgan Grenfell.

DM mil	12/92	12/93	12/94	US$mil 12/94				
Revenues	**47,709.0**	**55,029.0**	**41,656.0**	**25,825.2**	P/E Ratio	**14.8**	Price (9/30/95)	**68.03**
Net Income	**1,830.0**	**2,243.0**	**1,336.0**	**828.3**	P/B Ratio	**1.4**	52 Wk Hi-Low	**76.20-64.68**
Book Value	**18,775.0**	**20,472.0**	**23,401.0**	**15,097.4**	Yield %	**2.4**	Market Cap	**US$22,562mil**

Address **Taunusanlage 12**
60262 Frankfurt
Tel **069-7150-0**
Fax **069-71504225**
ADR **DBKAY**
SEDOL No. **4326672**
Chairman Exec Bd **Hilmar Kopper**
Chairman Supv Bd **F. Wilhelm Christians**

Dresdner Bank

Industry: **Banks - Money Center**

Dresdner Bank is a full-service bank that provides mortgage, commercial, and investment banking; portfolio management; and securities, foreign-exchange, and precious-metals trading. Dresdner is Germany's second-largest bank, with 1,600 branch offices worldwide and total assets of DM400 billion at year-end 1994. The bank serves more than 6 million German private customers and 190,000 German corporate customers. Its subsidiaries include U.K. merchant bank Kleinwort Benson and Deutsche Hypothekenbank. Allianz Holding has a 22% stake in Dresdner Bank.

DM mil	12/92	12/93	12/94	US$mil 12/94				
Revenues	**27,825.0**	**30,088.0**	**26,882.6**	**16,666.2**	P/E Ratio	**16.7**	Price (9/30/95)	**38.65**
Net Income	**949.0**	**1,026.0**	**598.8**	**371.2**	P/B Ratio	**1.2**	52 Wk Hi-Low	**41.75-37.40**
Book Value	**10,317.0**	**12,342.0**	**13,940.0**	**8,993.5**	Yield %	**3.5**	Market Cap	**US$12,042mil**

Address **Jürgen-Ponto-Platz 1**
60329 Frankfurt
Tel **069-26-30**
Fax **069-263-4831**
ADR **DRSDY**
SEDOL No. **4280604**
Chairman Exec Bd **Jürgen Sarrazin**
Chairman Supv Bd **Dr. Wolfgang Röller**

FAG

Industry: **Industrial - Diversified**

FAG Kugelfischer Georg Schäfer is an engineering and manufacturing company that specializes in the production of bearings. It supplies rolling bearings to the automotive, steel, and mechanical-engineering industries, and precision bearings to the aerospace, machine-tools, and textile-machinery industries. FAG's components unit makes products primarily for the company's bearings businesses, and its subsidiary DÜrkopp Adler makes sewing machines. FAG Kugelfischer also operates a specialized distribution business. About 45% of FAG's sales occur outside Europe.

DM mil	12/92	12/93	12/94	US$mil 12/94				
Sales	**3,563.0**	**3,115.0**	**2,697.6**	**1,672.4**	P/E Ratio	**NMF**	Price (9/30/95)	**197.00**
Net Income	**-440.0**	**-30.0**	**1.2**	**0.7**	P/B Ratio	**1.9**	52 Wk Hi-Low	**255.00-156.50**
Book Value	**406.0**	**341.0**	**343.4**	**221.6**	Yield %	**0.0**	Market Cap	**US$454.6mil**

Address **Georg-Schäfer-Str. 30**, **97421 Schweinfurt**
Tel **09721-91-0**
Fax **09721-913435**
ADR
SEDOL No. **4498474**
Chairman Exec Bd **Peter J. Kreher**
Chairman Supv Bd **Dr. Karl J. Neukirchen**

Gehe

Industry: **Pharmaceuticals**

GEHE is a pharmeceuticals company that produces hormonal medication, oral contraceptives, and generic products, including treatments for high blood pressure and heart disease. The company's health-care division, established in 1995, provides special beds, wheelchairs, and other equipment required for domestic patient care. GEHE's wholesale business operates through 84 branches in France, Germany, eastern Europe, Italy, Spain, Portugal, Belgium, and Luxemburg. GEHE's mail-order division supplies office and warehouse fittings in Europe and North America.

DM mil	12/92	12/93	12/94	US$mil 12/94				
Sales	**5,434.8**	**10,175.8**	**15,200.6**	**9,423.8**	P/E Ratio	**28.4**	Price (9/30/95)	**671.50**
Net Income	**89.4**	**93.2**	**137.9**	**85.5**	P/B Ratio	**3.1**	52 Wk Hi-Low	**695.00-474.03**
Book Value	**817.9**	**1,158.4**	**1,273.5**	**821.6**	Yield %	**1.5**	Market Cap	**US$3,423.2mil**

Address **Neckartalstrasse 155**, **70376 Stuttgart**
Tel **07-1150-0100**
Fax **07-1150-01500**
ADR
SEDOL No. **4357230**
Chairman Exec Bd **Dieter Kämmerer**
Chairman Supv Bd **Dr. Dieter Schadt**

Heidelberger Zement

Industry: **Building Materials**

Heidelberger Zement produces cement and concrete and manufactures building materials. The company provides specialty cements, limestone and lime products, and aggregates such as sand and gravel. It makes concrete bricks and paving stones, plasters, sealing agents, insulation systems, and interior fittings and provides specialty products and services for waste-management. The company also operates a shipping and air-freight business. Heidelberger has subsidiaries in North America and in Europe. North America accounted for about 28% of the company's 1994 revenues.

DM mil	12/92	12/93	12/94	US$mil 12/94				
Sales	**3,003.0**	**3,149.0**	**6,260.8**	**3,881.5**	P/E Ratio	**16.0**	Price (9/30/95)	**939.00**
Net Income	**130.0**	**146.0**	**214.0**	**132.6**	P/B Ratio	**1.6**	52 Wk Hi-Low	**1,172.6-909.0**
Book Value	**1,001.0**	**1,490.0**	**2,111.9**	**1,362.5**	Yield %	**1.5**	Market Cap	**US$2,528.1mil**

Address **Berliner Str. 6**, **69120 Heidelberg**
Tel **06221-481-0**
Fax **06221-481554**
ADR
SEDOL No. **4418706**
Chairman Exec Bd **Peter Schuhmacher**
Chairman Supv Bd **Dr. Wolfgang Röller**

Henkel

Industry: **Specialty Chemicals**

Henkel is a specialty-chemical manufacturer. The company manufactures general chemicals, metal chemicals, industrial adhesives, technical consumer products, cosmetics, toiletries, and detergents and household cleaners. Through its subsidiary Henkel-Ecolab, it has a joint venture with U.S. Henkel Ecolab to produce industrial- and institutional hygiene products. Henkel holds a 28% interest in U.S. household-products manufacturer Clorox, and a 30% interest in U.S. adhesives manufacturer Loctite.

DM mil	12/92	12/93	12/94	US$mil 12/94				
Sales	**14,101.0**	**13,867.0**	**14,069.0**	**8,722.3**	P/E Ratio	**11.0**	Price (9/30/95)	**540.00**
Net Income	**344.0**	**311.0**	**394.0**	**244.3**	P/B Ratio	**1.3**	52 Wk Hi-Low	**599.00-510.00**
Book Value	**2,918.0**	**3,022.0**	**3,429.0**	**2,212.3**	Yield %	**1.7**	Market Cap	**US$2,492.3mil**

Address **Henkelstr. 67**, **40191 Dusseldorf**
Tel **0211-7-97-0**
Fax **0211-7-98-40-4**
ADR
SEDOL No. **4420314**
CEO **Hans-Dietrich Winkhaus**
Chairman **Albrecht Woeste**

Philipp Holzmann

Industry: **Heavy Construction**

Philipp Holzmann, a general construction company, constructs housing and industrial buildings, provides structural engineering for the public sector, and offers specialized civil-engineering services. Commercial-building projects contribute over half of its domestic construction output, bolstered by a backlog of construction orders in the former East Germany. The company constructs road, rail, and waterway-traffic systems, and designs and manufactures fuel-feed systems for power plants. About two thirds of the company's construction activity is in Germany.

DM mil	12/92	12/93	12/94	US$mil 12/94				
Sales	**10,325.0**	**11,604.0**	**10,583.6**	**6,561.4**	P/E Ratio	**14.5**	Price (9/30/95)	**590.00**
Net Income	**81.0**	**86.0**	**107.3**	**66.5**	P/B Ratio	**1.3**	52 Wk Hi-Low	**865.00-581.00**
Book Value	**964.0**	**1,281.0**	**2,060.0**	**1,329.0**	Yield %	**2.3**	Market Cap	**US$1,809.2mil**

Address **Taunusanlage 1**, **60299 Frankfurt**
Tel **069-262-1**
Fax **069-262-433**
ADR
SEDOL No. **4434100**
Chairman Exec Bd **Dr. Lothar Mayer**
Chairman Supv Bd **Hermann Becker**

IVG

Industry: **General Industrial & Commercial Services**

Industrieverwaltungsgesellschaft (IVG) operates real-estate, transport, storage, and site- and facility-management businesses. IVG's real-estate activities generated DM 148 million in 1994, and account for about 75% of earnings. The company also rents out freight vans, railway wagons, and oil tank wagons. It operates caverns for crude oil and gas storage and supplies tanks and transport facilities to the petroleum industry. IVG sold its shipbuilding and propulsion-systems business in 1994. The German government completed the privitization of IVG in December 1993.

DM mil	12/92	12/93	12/94	US$mil 12/94				
Sales	**388.0**	**389.0**	**441.3**	**273.6**	P/E Ratio	**22.0**	Price (9/30/95)	**498.00**
Net Income	**32.0**	**35.0**	**7.2**	**4.5**	P/B Ratio	**3.0**	52 Wk Hi-Low	**553.00-483.00**
Book Value	**276.0**	**362.0**	**432.8**	**279.2**	Yield %	**2.6**	Market Cap	**US$905.5mil**

Address **Zanderstr. 5**
53137 Bonn
Tel **0228-844-0**
Fax **0228-844-107**
ADR
SEDOL No. **4459426**
Chairman Exec Bd **Dr. Eckart J. von Freyend**
Chairman Supv Bd **Dr. Manfred Lennings**

IWKA

Industry: **Factory Equipment**

Industrie-Werke Karlsruhe Augsburg (IWKA) is a mechanical-engineering firm that manufactures welding and assembly systems, machine tools, packaging machinery, and defense equipment. Its wholly-owned subsidiary, Bopp and Reuther, manufactures expansion joints and measuring equipment. Its KUKA-Vaz joint venture with Avto-Vaz provides engineering services to Russian automotive companies. IWKA owns engineering firm Formenbau Schwarzenberg, which specializes in welding systems.

DM mil	12/92	12/93	12/94	US$mil 12/94				
Sales	**1,748.0**	**1,689.0**	**1,767.2**	**1,095.6**	P/E Ratio	**23.3**	Price (9/30/95)	**306.00**
Net Income	**41.0**	**36.0**	**29.5**	**18.3**	P/B Ratio	**1.5**	52 Wk Hi-Low	**358.00-284.70**
Book Value	**424.0**	**436.0**	**443.0**	**285.8**	Yield %	**2.6**	Market Cap	**US$479.3mil**

Address **Gartenstr. 71**
76135 Karlsruhe
Tel **0721-143-0**
Fax **0721-143-243**
ADR
SEDOL No. **4462844**
Chairman Exec Bd **Dr. Wolf H. Prellwitz**
Chairman Supv Bd **Dr. Helmut Wolf**

Karstadt

Industry: **Retailers - Broadline**

Karstadt is a retail group with over-the-counter, mail-order, and wholesale businesses. It also owns travel agencies and other consumer-service businesses. The company operates 245 Karstadt and Hertie department stores and six chains, including sports-goods retailer Runners Point and consumer-electronics specialist Schürmann. Its mail-order business, Neckermann Versand, has a significant market share in countries such as Belgium and the Netherlands as well as in Germany. NUR Touristic, the company's travel-agency business, has subsidiaries in Austria and Belgium.

DM mil	12/92	12/93	12/94	US$mil 12/94				
Revenues	**18,498.0**	**18,714.0**	**24,181.7**	**14,991.7**	P/E Ratio	**131.6**	Price (9/30/95)	**633.00**
Net Income	**224.0**	**227.0**	**110.4**	**68.5**	P/B Ratio	**2.3**	52 Wk Hi-Low	**678.00-525.00**
Book Value	**2,533.0**	**2,659.0**	**2,333.4**	**1,505.4**	Yield %	**2.1**	Market Cap	**US$3,718.3mil**

Address **Theodor-Althoff-Str. 2**
45133 Essen
Tel **0201-7271**
Fax **0201-7275696**
ADR
SEDOL No. **4484105**
Chairman Exec Bd **Dr. Walter Deuss**
Chairman Supv Bd **Dr. Guido Sandler**

Kaufhof

Industry: **Retailers - Broadline**

Kaufhof, Germany's second-largest department-store chain by sales, operates the Kaufhof Mode und Sport, Kaufhalle, Kaufhof Warenhaus, and Horten department stores. It also owns specialty stores Media Markt (electronics), Vobis (microcomputers), Mac Fash (midprice clothing), and Reno (shoes). Its Media Markt and Vobis stores generate nearly half of its revenues and department store trading accounts for more than 40% of sales. Kaufhof has retail outlets throughout Europe. The company recently divested its loss-making Kuoni and ITS travel businesses.

DM mil	12/92	12/93	12/94	US$mil 12/94				
Revenues	**17,344.0**	**19,114.0**	**22,087.5**	**13,693.4**	P/E Ratio	**33.4**	Price (9/30/95)	**506.00**
Net Income	**179.0**	**188.0**	**70.4**	**43.6**	P/B Ratio	**2.3**	52 Wk Hi-Low	**540.00-432.00**
Book Value	**1,432.0**	**1,367.0**	**1,664.6**	**1,073.9**	Yield %	**2.4**	Market Cap	**US$2,650.7mil**

Address **Leonhard-Tietz-Str. 1**
50676 Cologne
Tel **0221-223-0**
Fax **0221-223-2548**
ADR **KAAGY**
SEDOL No. **4484707**
Chairman Exec Bd **Dr. Jens Odewald**
Chairman Supv Bd **Erwin Conradi**

KHD

Industry: **Heavy Machinery**

Klöckner-Humboldt-Deutz (KHD) manufactures engines and energy systems. It also engineers and installs plant, machine systems and components for ore, mineral and coal dressing, cement manufacture, and food processing. The company provides pollution-control processes and technologies for industrial and municipal wastewater and plans, supplies, and installs pipeline systems. The company's Tractors & Agricultural Machinery division (Deutz Fahr) was sold off in an agreement retroactive to January 1, 1995.

DM mil	12/92	12/93	12/94	US$mil 12/94				
Sales	**3,665.0**	**3,247.0**	**2,694.9**	**1,670.7**	P/E Ratio	**NMF**	Price (9/30/95)	**10.40**
Net Income	**0.0**	**0.0**	**-308.0**	**-190.9**	P/B Ratio	**2.4**	52 Wk Hi-Low	**25.90-6.68**
Book Value	**323.0**	**579.0**	**253.8**	**163.7**	Yield %	**0.0**	Market Cap	**US$433.6mil**

Address **Nikolaus-August-Otto-Allee 2**
51057 Cologne
Tel **0221-822-0**
Fax **0221-822-5405**
ADR
SEDOL No. **4557847**
Chairman Exec Bd **Werner Kirchgässer**
Chairman Supv Bd **Dr. Michael Endres**

Klöckner-Werke

Industry: **Steel**

Kloeckner-Werke manufactures packaging and bottling machines, plastic products, and steel. Kloeckner-Werke produces injection-molding, packaging, and labeling machines for the food and beverage industries. Its subsidiaries supply the European automobile industry with large plastic systems such as bumpers, dashboards, and door panels, and the North American auto industry with plastic fuel tank systems. The company's plastics processing activities account for 60% of its sales. Foreign sales account for two thirds of Kloeckner-Werke's revenues.

DM mil	09/92	09/93	09/94	US$mil 09/94				
Sales	**7,102.0**	**6,102.0**	**4,136.1**	**2,499.1**	P/E Ratio	**96.0**	Price (9/30/95)	**48.00**
Net Income	**-560.0**	**-196.0**	**4.6**	**2.8**	P/B Ratio	**1.1**	52 Wk Hi-Low	**147.30-48.00**
Book Value	**591.0**	**381.0**	**387.1**	**249.7**	Yield %	**0.0**	Market Cap	**US$307.6mil**

Address **Klöcknerhaus, Klöcknerstr. 29**, **47057 Duisburg**
Tel **0203-396-1**
Fax **0203-3963535**
ADR **KKWAY**
SEDOL No. **4496003**
Chairman Exec Bd **Hans C. von Rohr**
Chairman Supv Bd **Karl J. Neukirchen**

Linde

Industry: **Industrial - Diversified**

Linde is an engineering and industrial-gases company. The company's gas activities include the development of air-separation processes (mainly into liquid oxygen, nitrogen, and argon), and gas distribution. Its engineering division constructs gas plants and provides wastewater treatment. Linde manufactures forklifts, industrial trucks, earthmoving machinery, and hydraulic components. Linde also makes display cabinets and refrigerated display cases for the retail sector. Linde's industrial-gases and material-handling divisions accounts for two thirds of sales.

DM mil	12/92	12/93	12/94	US$mil 12/94				
Sales	**7,534.0**	**7,172.0**	**7,967.7**	**4,939.6**	P/E Ratio	**29.5**	Price (9/30/95)	**863.00**
Net Income	**236.0**	**156.0**	**245.8**	**152.4**	P/B Ratio	**2.6**	52 Wk Hi-Low	**912.00-725.00**
Book Value	**2,731.0**	**2,742.0**	**2,840.9**	**1,832.8**	Yield %	**1.4**	Market Cap	**US$4,960.1mil**

Address **Abraham-Lincoln-Str. 21**, **65189 Wiesbaden**
Tel **0611-770-0**
Fax **0611-770-269**
ADR
SEDOL No. **4517001**
Chairman Exec Bd **Dr. Hans Meinhardt**
Chairman Supv Bd **Dr. Wolfgang Schieren**

Linotype-Hell

Industry: **Office Equipment**

Linotype-Hell manufactures prepress equipment, software, and fonts. It ranks as the world's largest manufacturer of image-setting and reproduction equipment in terms of sales. Its product lines include the Series 1000 image- and data-processing equipment, the LinoPress system for newspaper publishing, and ChromaCom 1000 Orion image-processing software for personal computers. The company has subsidiaries in the United Kingdom, Switzerland, the United States, Canada, and Japan. In 1994, systems and equipment generated 72% of sales.

DM mil	12/92	12/93	12/94	US$mil 12/94				
Sales	**1,024.0**	**946.0**	**991.3**	**614.6**	P/E Ratio	**103.5**	Price (9/30/95)	**222.50**
Net Income	**32.0**	**-153.0**	**5.2**	**3.2**	P/B Ratio	**2.3**	52 Wk Hi-Low	**369.00-222.50**
Book Value	**402.0**	**231.0**	**232.2**	**149.8**	Yield %	**0.0**	Market Cap	**US$373.4mil**

Address **Mergenthaler Allee 55-75**, **65760 Eschborn**
Tel **06196-98-0**
Fax **06196-922597**
ADR
SEDOL No. **4518253**
Chairman Exec Bd **Dr. Erwin Königs**
Chairman Supv Bd **Dietrich K. Frowein**

Löwenbräu

Industry: **Distillers & Brewers**

Löwenbräu produces, markets, and distributes both alcoholic and nonalcoholic beers worldwide. Beers produced by the company include Pilsners, Bavarian weiss beers, Oktoberfest lagers, and alcohol-free brands. Löwenbräu's wholly-owned brewing and distribution subsidiaries operate in Spain, Greece, Switzerland, Italy, Malta, the United Kingdom, and the United States. Löwenbräu is controlled by the August von Frick family, who hold 89% of its shares. Löwenbräu's beer sales generate 79% of revenues and alcohol-free brands generate 7% of revenues.

DM mil	09/92	09/93	09/94	US$mil 09/94				
Sales	**343.0**	**375.0**	**330.0**	**199.4**	P/E Ratio	**NMF**	Price (9/30/95)	**2,640.00**
Net Income	**-8.0**	**51.0**	**-22.4**	**-13.5**	P/B Ratio	**5.8**	52 Wk Hi-Low	**3,165.4-2,474.0**
Book Value	**28.0**	**80.0**	**90.9**	**58.6**	Yield %	**0.2**	Market Cap	**US$444.9mil**

Address **Nymphenburger Str. 4**, **80335 Munich**
Tel **089-5200-0**
Fax **089-5200-412**
ADR
SEDOL No. **4536460**
Chairman Exec Bd **Dr. Franz J. Leibenfrost**
Chairman Supv Bd **Dr. Hubert Mennacher**

Lufthansa

Industry: **Airlines**

Deutsche Lufthansa provides passenger and cargo airline services. Its fleet consists of more than 300 aircraft. The firm's secondary interests are tourism, hotels, catering, and aviation-related insurance. It owns 25% of the DHL International express-delivery service. Lufthansa's wholly-owned Condor and Lufthansa CityLine subsidiaries provide passenger service in Europe. Lufthansa's code-sharing agreements with Thai Airways and United Airlines forms the world's largest air traffic network. It recently announced an alliance with SAS airlines to combine flight networks.

DM mil	12/92	12/93	12/94	US$mil 12/94				
Sales	**17,239.0**	**17,731.0**	**18,835.7**	**11,677.4**	P/E Ratio	**24.1**	Price (9/30/95)	**198.00**
Net Income	**-394.0**	**-101.0**	**292.3**	**181.2**	P/B Ratio	**1.9**	52 Wk Hi-Low	**227.50-165.00**
Book Value	**2,275.0**	**2,121.0**	**3,640.7**	**2,348.9**	Yield %	**2.0**	Market Cap	**US$4,915.4mil**

Address **Von-Gablenz-Str. 2-6**, **50679 Cologne**
Tel **0221-8260**
Fax **0221-8263356**
ADR **DLAGY**
SEDOL No. **4537708**
CEO **Jürgen Weber**
Chairman **Dr. Wolfgang Röller**

MAN

Industry: **Diversified Technology**

MAN's core businesses involve the production of commercial vehicles, diesel engines, printing presses, and other machinery for industrial plants. Its products include trucks; buses; sheet-fed offset presses; rotary web presses; and automotive, industrial, and marine engines. MAN also provides logistics and construction- engineering services to the construction industry. Commercial-vehicle sales generated 37% of revenues, and industrial machines and facilities combined to generate 25% in 1994. Overseas exports generate more than one third of revenues.

	DM mil 06/92	06/93	06/94	US$mil 06/94				
Sales	**19,171.0**	**18,972.0**	**18,144.4**	**10,781.0**	P/E Ratio	**NMF**	Price (9/30/95)	**400.20**
Net Income	**408.0**	**222.0**	**150.1**	**89.2**	P/B Ratio	**1.3**	52 Wk Hi-Low	**436.00-326.00**
Book Value	**3,434.0**	**3,402.0**	**3,434.1**	**2,159.8**	Yield %	**1.7**	Market Cap	**US$3,086.3mil**

Address **Ungererstr. 69**
80805 Munich
Tel **089-36098-0**
Fax **089-36098250**
ADR
SEDOL No. **4398303**
Chairman Exec Bd **Klaus Götte**
Chairman Supv Bd **Karlheinz Kaske**

Mannesmann

Industry: **Industrial - Diversified**

Mannesmann builds plants and machinery, makes systems and components for the automotive industry, provides telecommunication services, and produces steel tube and pipe. Its mobile-phone operations have nearly 1 million customers. Mannesmann builds plants for steel companies, manufactures materials-handling equipment for the construction industry, injection-molding machines for the plastics industry, and compressed air systems for petrochemical and transportation companies. Non-European exports account for 28% of revenues.

	DM mil 12/92	12/93	12/94	US$mil 12/94				
Sales	**28,018.0**	**27,963.0**	**30,397.4**	**18,845.3**	P/E Ratio	**31.3**	Price (9/30/95)	**469.00**
Net Income	**204.0**	**-344.0**	**211.5**	**131.1**	P/B Ratio	**2.7**	52 Wk Hi-Low	**494.50-354.50**
Book Value	**5,729.0**	**6,209.0**	**6,250.4**	**4,032.5**	Yield %	**1.3**	Market Cap	**US$12,011mil**

Address **Mannesmannufer 2**
40213 Dusseldorf
Tel **0211-820-0**
Fax **0211-8202163**
ADR **MNSMY**
SEDOL No. **4562896**
Chairman Exec Bd **Dr. Joachim Funk**
Chairman Supv Bd **Dr. F.Wilhelm Christians**

Metallgesellschaft

Industry: **Non-Ferrous Metals - Other (Exc. Aluminum)**

Metallgesellschaft is a diversified industrial company that provides trading, financial, and plant-engineering and -contracting services. The firm's chemicals division manufactures explosives, plastics, ceramics, and specialty and pigment chemicals. It provides private-, wholesale-, and investment-banking services to its customers. The company's trading business, accounting for 40% of sales, trades steel, steel scrap, metal, and chemicals. It constructs recycling and power-generation facilities. Overseas exports accounted for 46% of revenues in 1994.

	DM mil 09/92	09/93	09/94	US$mil 09/94				
Sales	**25,558.0**	**26,094.0**	**20,492.6**	**12,382.2**	P/E Ratio	**NMF**	Price (9/30/95)	**29.70**
Net Income	**41.0**	**-2,025.0**	**-2,697.7**	**-1,630.1**	P/B Ratio	**NMF**	52 Wk Hi-Low	**33.49-19.01**
Book Value	**1,706.0**	**-367.0**	**-116.5**	**-75.2**	Yield %	**0.0**	Market Cap	**US$1,499.1mil**

Address **Reuterweg 14**
60271 Frankfurt
Tel **069-159-0**
Fax **069-159-2125**
ADR
SEDOL No. **4557104**
Chairman Exec Bd **Karl-Josef Neukirchen**
Chairman Supv Bd **Ronaldo H. Schmitz**

Munich Reinsurance

Industry: **Insurance - Property & Casualty**

Munich Reinsurance (Münchener Rückversicherungs- Gesellschaft) is a reinsurance company that specializes in industrial and commercial coverage. Its reinsurance-underwriting services include life, fire, and motor-vehicle insurance (which together represent nearly 60% of the firm's total premium income), and personal-liability, natural-disaster, marine, and aviation coverage. It has reinsurance subsidiaries in Italy, the United States, United Kingdom, Australia, Canada, South Africa, and Switzerland. The firm has a 25% stake in German insurance company Allianz.

	DM mil 06/92	06/93	06/94	US$mil 06/94				
Revenues	**20,194.0**	**22,589.0**	**24,981.0**	**14,843.1**	P/E Ratio	**112.8**	Price (9/30/95)	**2,910.00**
Net Income	**197.0**	**170.0**	**191.7**	**113.9**	P/B Ratio	**6.3**	52 Wk Hi-Low	**3,148.0-2,450.0**
Book Value	**2,593.0**	**2,688.0**	**3,453.6**	**2,172.0**	Yield %	**0.4**	Market Cap	**US$15,254mil**

Address **Königinstr. 107**
80802 Munich
Tel **089-3891-0**
Fax **089-3990-56**
ADR
SEDOL No. **4610751**
Chairman Exec Bd **Dr. Hans J. Schinzler**
Chairman Supv Bd **Dr. Dieter Spethmann**

Preussag

Industry: **Steel**

Preussag is a large diversified manufacturing company. It produces steel, lead, zinc, crude oil, and natural gas, and manufactures tank cars, trucks, container ships, rail vehicles, building materials, automotive-soundproofing equipment, mobile buildings, and fire-extinguishing systems for buildings. Preussag also engages in drilling contracting, construction, and engineering, and is one of Germany's leading copper traders. Its steel-producing subsidiaries include Preussag Stahl and 51%-owned Metaleurop. Its transport and trade division generates more than 47% of sales.

	DM mil 09/92	09/93	09/94	US$mil 09/94				
Sales	**24,474.0**	**23,290.0**	**23,210.5**	**14,024.5**	P/E Ratio	**23.4**	Price (9/30/95)	**421.50**
Net Income	**440.0**	**193.0**	**245.3**	**148.2**	P/B Ratio	**2.0**	52 Wk Hi-Low	**471.50-387.50**
Book Value	**3,118.0**	**3,180.0**	**3,207.1**	**2,069.1**	Yield %	**2.4**	Market Cap	**US$4,489.7mil**

Address **Karl-Wiechert-Allee 4**
30625 Hannover
Tel **0511-566-00**
Fax **0511-566-1997**
ADR
SEDOL No. **4701707**
Chairman Exec Bd **Michael Frenzel**
Chairman Supv Bd **Friedel Neuber**

PWA

Industry: **Paper Products**

Papierwerke Waldhof-Aschaffenburg (PWA) manufactures, processes, and markets paper. Its main business areas are graphics and hygiene paper, which account for 72% of sales. The firm also manufactures and sells packaging, specialty papers, and corrugated board. Its brand-name products include Zewa Softis tissues, Danke toilet paper, and Artex paper towels. The company has wholly-owned subsidiaries in the U.S., the U.K., Spain, Ireland, and France. Overseas exports accounted for roughly 18% of sales in 1994.

DM mil	12/92	12/93	12/94	US$mil 12/94				
Sales	**4,241.0**	**3,857.0**	**4,445.3**	**2,755.9**	P/E Ratio	**38.4**	Price (9/30/95)	**230.50**
Net Income	**18.0**	**-241.0**	**30.5**	**18.9**	P/B Ratio	**2.4**	52 Wk Hi-Low	**290.00-221.50**
Book Value	**795.0**	**569.0**	**671.7**	**433.4**	Yield %	**0.0**	Market Cap	**US$1,038.4mil**

Address **PWA Haus**
83064 Raubling
Tel **08035-80-0**
Fax **08035-80-598**
ADR
SEDOL No. **4671167**
Chairman Exec Bd **Alfred H. Heinzel**
Chairman Supv Bd **Klaus Götte**

RWE

Industry: **Oil - Secondary**

RWE produces and distributes electric power, natural gas, and water. The company also provides telecommunication services, processes petroleum products, operates waste-disposal and construction businesses, and manufactures printing machines and medical appliances. Hochtief is RWE's international construction and civil-engineering arm. The firm owns 50% of DuPont's Consul Energy, the United States' second-largest coal producer and has a 27% stake in a consortium that acquired 75% of VEAG, the former East German electricity company.

DM mil	06/92	06/93	06/94	US$mil 06/94				
Sales	**51,737.0**	**53,094.0**	**55,750.0**	**33,125.4**	P/E Ratio	**21.5**	Price (9/30/95)	**488.50**
Net Income	**877.0**	**881.0**	**922.0**	**547.8**	P/B Ratio	**2.1**	52 Wk Hi-Low	**520.00-415.00**
Book Value	**5,557.0**	**7,690.0**	**7,807.0**	**4,910.1**	Yield %	**2.7**	Market Cap	**US$11,285mil**

Address **Kruppstr. 5**
45128 Essen
Tel **0201-185-0**
Fax **0201-185-5199**
ADR **RWEOY**
SEDOL No. **4735502**
Chairman Exec Bd **Friedhelm Gieske**
Chairman Supv Bd **Wolfgang Roller**

Salamander

Industry: **Footwear**

Salamander manufactures and sells footwear, textile products, leather goods, porcelain, and chemicals. It also provides technical services to the automobile-upholstery industry. Footwear accounts for more than two thirds of the company's total sales. The sales network for the company's footwear, shoe-care goods, leather goods, and porcelain includes more than 100 retail outlets located in major German cities. Salamander has 23 wholly-owned subsidiaries, five West European affiliates, and five joint ventures located primarily in former Eastern Bloc countries.

DM mil	12/92	12/93	12/94	US$mil 12/94				
Sales	**1,352.0**	**1,335.0**	**1,350.6**	**837.3**	P/E Ratio	**21.4**	Price (9/30/95)	**254.00**
Net Income	**19.0**	**23.0**	**22.2**	**13.8**	P/B Ratio	**1.2**	52 Wk Hi-Low	**344.00-253.00**
Book Value	**345.0**	**397.0**	**401.5**	**259.0**	Yield %	**3.9**	Market Cap	**US$330.0mil**

Address **Stammheimer Str. 10**
70806 Kornwestheim
Tel **07154-15-0**
Fax **07154-152763**
ADR
SEDOL No. **4771108**
Chairman Exec Bd **Dr. Gerhard Wacker**
Chairman Supv Bd **Dr. Franz J. Dazert**

SAP

Industry: **Software**

SAP Systems develops and markets standard-application business-software systems. The company also offers consulting and training services. SAP's R/2 system is designed for the mainframe environment, and its R/3 software for client/server technology. These products, which generated 71% of SAP's 1994 sales, cover application areas such as accounting, logistics, and human-resources management. SAP has subsidiaries in Europe, the Americas, Australasia, Africa, and the Middle East. In 1994, 42% of the company's sales were made outside Europe.

DM mil	12/92	12/93	12/94	US$mil 12/94				
Sales	**831.2**	**1,101.7**	**1,831.1**	**1,135.2**	P/E Ratio	**84.8**	Price (9/30/95)	**235.70**
Net Income	**126.3**	**145.8**	**280.3**	**173.7**	P/B Ratio	**11.6**	52 Wk Hi-Low	**266.50-85.50**
Book Value	**896.8**	**1,007.8**	**1,233.8**	**796.0**	Yield %	**0.4**	Market Cap	**US$10,054mil**

Address **Neurottstrasse 16**
69190 Walldorf
Tel **06227-34-0**
Fax **06227-34-1282**
ADR
SEDOL No. **4846288**
Chairman Exec Bd **Dietmar Hopp**
Chairman Supv Bd **Dr. Bernd Thiemann**

Schering

Industry: **Pharmaceuticals**

Schering develops, manufactures, and distributes pharmaceuticals. The company operates primarily through its 40% share in agrichemical company Hoechst Schering AgriEvo, a joint venture with chemicals manufacturer Hoechst. Schering produces oral contraceptives, diagnostic agents, cancer-treatment drugs, insecticides, and cereal fungicides. It holds the patent on Magnevist, the only contrast component used in magnetic resonance imaging, and Betaseron, the only preparatory treatment for multiple sclerosis.

DM mil	12/92	12/93	12/94	US$mil 12/94				
Sales	**6,267.0**	**5,363.0**	**4,692.1**	**2,908.9**	P/E Ratio	**22.9**	Price (9/30/95)	**105.40**
Net Income	**262.0**	**254.0**	**284.7**	**176.5**	P/B Ratio	**2.3**	52 Wk Hi-Low	**113.80-88.70**
Book Value	**2,747.0**	**2,912.0**	**3,080.3**	**1,987.3**	Yield %	**1.5**	Market Cap	**US$5,046.7mil**

Address **Müllerstr. 170-178**
13353 Berlin
Tel **030-468-0**
Fax **030-468-5305**
ADR
SEDOL No. **4845757**
Chairman Exec Bd **Giuseppe Vita**
Chairman Supv Bd **Klaus Subjetzki**

Schmalbach-Lubeca

Industry: **Containers & Packaging**

Schmalbach-Lubeca is a packaging company that is among the world's largest manufacturers of metal vacuum-holding closures for bottles and jars. The firm's PET Packaging and White Cap subsidiaries manufacture and distribute refillable bottles, food and pharmaceuticals packaging, and metal and plastic closures for vacuum-packed foods and beverages. Its beverage-packaging and metal-packaging divisions account for nearly 60% of sales. It operates a joint venture in China which produces beverage cans. The firm is 51%-owed by energy company VIAG.

	DM mil 12/92	12/93	12/94	US$mil 12/94				
Sales	**3,457.0**	**3,567.0**	**3,884.9**	**2,408.5**	P/E Ratio	**16.6**	Price (9/30/95)	**287.00**
Net Income	**90.0**	**8.0**	**65.0**	**40.3**	P/B Ratio	**1.7**	52 Wk Hi-Low	**408.00-240.50**
Book Value	**634.0**	**631.0**	**633.0**	**408.4**	Yield %	**1.7**	Market Cap	**US$752.6mil**

Address **Schmalbachstr. 1**
38112 Braunschweig
Tel **0531-394-0**
Fax **0531-394-515**
ADR
SEDOL No. **4779577**
Chairman Exec Bd **Erich Kanofsky**
Chairman Supv Bd **Rainer Grohe**

Siemens

Industry: **Diversified Technology**

Siemens is Europe's largest electronics- engineering company by market capitalization. Its products include electronic components and telecommunication systems, power-plant engineering products (including turbines), automotive electronics, transportation systems, and medical-engineering products. Siemens' industry and communications divisions account for roughly half of the company's turnover. Siemens owns Sylvania through its U.S.-based Osram lighting subsidiary. Non-European exports account for roughly one third of revenues.

	DM mil 09/92	09/93	09/94	US$mil 09/94				
Sales	**78,509.0**	**81,648.0**	**84,598.0**	**51,116.6**	P/E Ratio	**22.5**	Price (9/30/95)	**721.30**
Net Income	**1,795.0**	**1,803.0**	**1,769.0**	**1,068.9**	P/B Ratio	**2.0**	52 Wk Hi-Low	**769.00-598.50**
Book Value	**18,034.0**	**19,119.0**	**20,352.0**	**13,130.3**	Yield %	**1.8**	Market Cap	**US$27,778mil**

Address **Wittelsbacherplatz 2**
80333 Munich
Tel **089-234-2812**
Fax **089-234-2830**
ADR **SMAWY**
SEDOL No. **4807100**
President & CEO **Heinrich von Pierer**
Chairman **Hermann Franz**

Thüga

Industry: **Electrical Utilities - All**

Thüga, a 53%-owned subsidiary of PreussenElektra, heads a group of energy companies that supply electricity, gas, and water to Germany's private and public sectors. Half of the company's revenues originate from the distribution of natural gas, 42% from the generation and distribution of electricity, and 6% from consulting. Thüga has 42 subsidiaries and affiliates, and has ties to an additional 25 companies through its 40% interest in the energy firm Rhenag Rheinische Energie. Thüga is majority held by the German holding company VEBA.

	DM mil 12/92 P	12/93 P	12/94 P	US$mil 12/94				
Sales	**247.0**	**250.0**	**362.0**	**224.4**	P/E Ratio	**46.5**	Price (9/30/95)	**490.00**
Net Income	**55.0**	**85.0**	**61.1**	**37.9**	P/B Ratio	**2.5**	52 Wk Hi-Low	**575.00-470.00**
Book Value	**906.0**	**952.0**	**1,153.6**	**744.2**	Yield %	**2.2**	Market Cap	**US$1,781.8mil**

Address **Mandlstr. 3**
80802 Munich
Tel **089-38197-0**
Fax **089-38197568**
ADR
SEDOL No. **4889603**
Chairman Exec Bd **Dr. Dieter Nagel**
Chairman Supv Bd **Dr. Hans Dieter Harig**

P=Parent company data.

Thyssen

Industry: **Steel**

Thyssen is a diversified steel producer that oversees 310 consolidated companies. Its Thyssen Stahl subsidiary operates the group's steel-manufacturing businesses. Thyssen's products, which include spare parts, brake components, cement, and machine tools, supply the automotive, construction, and industrial sectors. Its U.S.-based Budd automotive-parts subsidiary supplies U.S. automobile makers. The firm has a 28% stake in E-Plus, a German mobile-phone company. The company generates 47% of its sales from abroad, and 23% from outside Europe.

	DM mil 09/92	09/93	09/94	US$mil 09/94				
Sales	**35,755.0**	**33,502.0**	**34,948.7**	**21,117.0**	P/E Ratio	**NMF**	Price (9/30/95)	**276.50**
Net Income	**319.0**	**-1,040.0**	**-1,039.8**	**-628.3**	P/B Ratio	**2.4**	52 Wk Hi-Low	**305.00-245.00**
Book Value	**4,832.0**	**3,544.0**	**3,544.0**	**2,286.5**	Yield %	**0.0**	Market Cap	**US$6,052.1mil**

Address **Kaiser-Wilhelm-Str. 100**
47166 Duisburg
Tel **0203-52-1**
Fax **0203-52-25102**
ADR
SEDOL No. **4891084**
Chairman Exec Bd **Heinz Kriwet**
Chairman Supv Bd **Günter Vogelsang**

VEBA

Industry: **Conglomerates**

VEBA is a diversified holding company with its business activities including the production and distribution of electricity, oil, chemicals, and natural gas. The company also provides paging, mobile-phone, satellite-communication, and cable-television telecommunication services through its Vebacom subsidiary. Its wholly-owned PreussenElektra subsidiary supplies electricity, gas, and water to its customers in western Germany. VEBA's majority-owned Hüls subsidiary manufactures chemical products such as lotions, adhesives, and silicons (for semiconductors).

	DM mil 12/92	12/93	12/94	US$mil 12/94				
Sales	**65,419.0**	**66,349.0**	**64,992.6**	**40,293.0**	P/E Ratio	**18.1**	Price (9/30/95)	**56.71**
Net Income	**952.0**	**775.0**	**1,383.9**	**858.0**	P/B Ratio	**1.8**	52 Wk Hi-Low	**60.45-48.50**
Book Value	**14,253.0**	**15,087.0**	**15,576.6**	**10,049.4**	Yield %	**2.6**	Market Cap	**US$19,273mil**

Address **Bennigsenplatz 1**
40474 Dusseldorf
Tel **0211-4579-1**
Fax **0211-4579532**
ADR
SEDOL No. **4942904**
Chairman Exec Bd **Ulrich Hartmann**
Chairman Supv Bd **Hermann J. Strenger**

VIAG

Industry: **Aluminum**

VIAG is a diversified industrial company whose major interests are in the energy, chemicals, packaging, and logistics businesses. Bayernwerk, acquired in 1994, manages the company's energy operations, providing electricity, natural gas, and waste-management services. VIAG subsidiary SKW Trostberg supplies chemicals to the food additives, construction, agricultural, and pharmaceuticals industries. VIAG makes a range of glass, plastic, and metal packaging products and offers steel-trading, transport, and chemicals- and energy-distribution services.

	DM mil 12/92	12/93	12/94	US$mil 12/94				
Sales	**24,311.0**	**23,734.0**	**28,956.7**	**17,952.1**	P/E Ratio	**10.1**	Price (9/30/95)	**550.00**
Net Income	**288.0**	**296.0**	**1,119.9**	**694.3**	P/B Ratio	**2.1**	52 Wk Hi-Low	**598.50-450.00**
Book Value	**3,556.0**	**4,427.0**	**5,307.1**	**3,424.0**	Yield %	**1.8**	Market Cap	**US$8,478.5mil**

Address **Georg-von-Böselager-Str. 25**
53117 Bonn
Tel **0228-522-01**
Fax **0228-5522977**
ADR
SEDOL No. **4929242**
Chairman Exec Bd **Dr. Alfred Pfeiffer**
Chairman Supv Bd **Dr. Jochen Holzer**

Volkswagen

Industry: **Automobile Manufacturers**

Volkswagen manufactures more than 3 million passenger cars and 177,000 commercial vehicles a year. The company's automaking divisions include Audi, Spain's SEAT, and the Czech Republic's Skoda. It also offers credit-banking, consumer-financing, and leasing services. Volkswagen has 24 plants in operation, 11 of which are outside Europe. Subsidiary V.A.G. imports and distributes Audi, VW, Skoda, and SEAT parts and automobiles to franchises throughout the U.K. Two thirds of sales originate in Germany; Non-European exports account for 17% of revenues.

	DM mil 12/92	12/93	12/94	US$mil 12/94				
Sales	**85,403.0**	**76,586.0**	**80,041.0**	**49,622.4**	P/E Ratio	**77.3**	Price (9/30/95)	**463.50**
Net Income	**147.0**	**-1,940.0**	**150.0**	**93.0**	P/B Ratio	**1.1**	52 Wk Hi-Low	**485.00-336.50**
Book Value	**13,535.0**	**11,263.0**	**10,987.0**	**7,088.4**	Yield %	**0.6**	Market Cap	**US$8,751.4mil**

Address **Volkswagenwerk**
38436 Wolfsburg
Tel **05361-90**
Fax **05361-928282**
ADR **VLKAY**
SEDOL No. **4930307**
Chairman Exec Bd **Ferdinand Piëch**
Chairman Supv Bd **Klaus Liesen**

Hong Kong

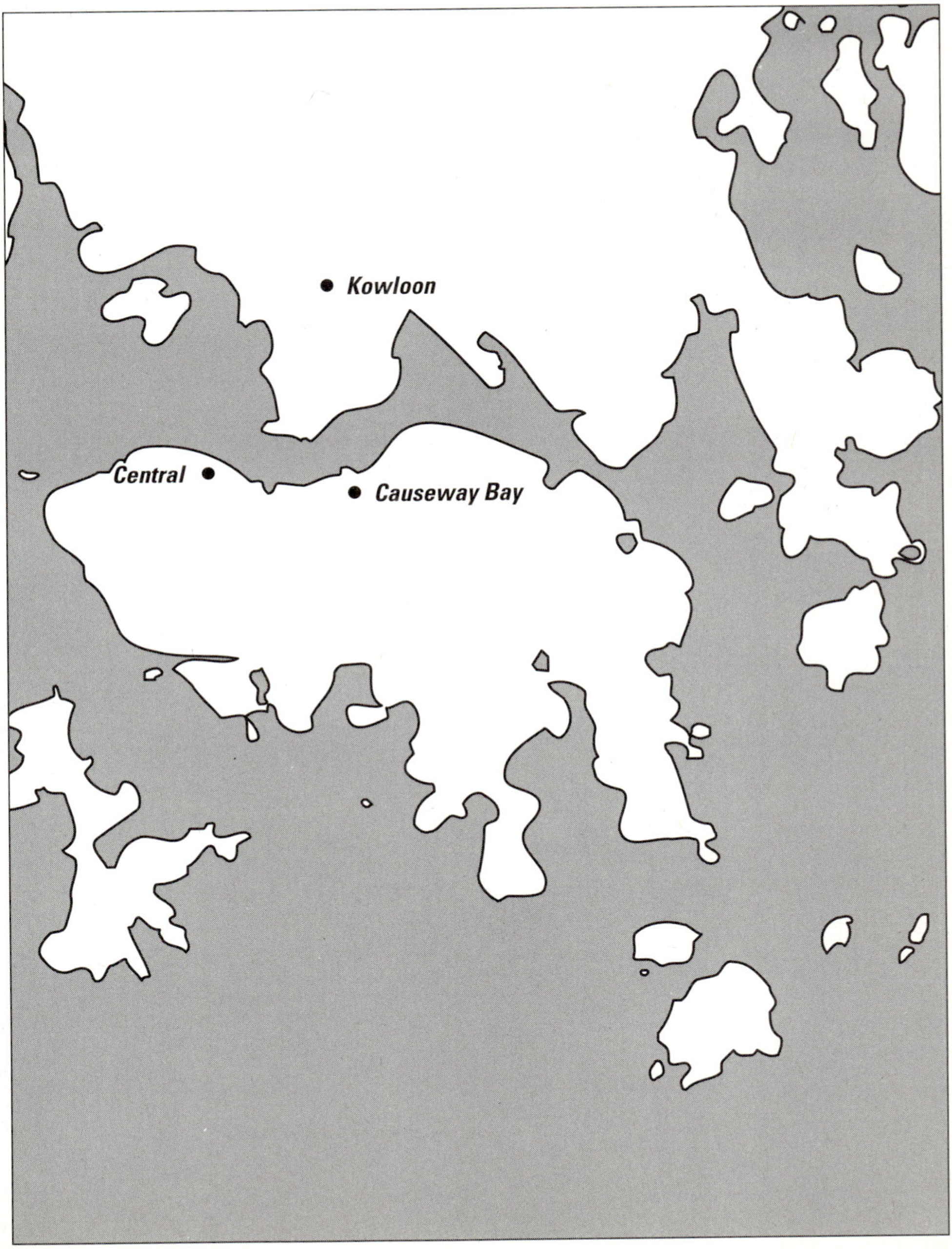

Hong Kong

James T. Areddy,
Hong Kong

Local Trading Hours	**Time Difference with New York**	**Population (Est. 94)**
0200-0430 GMT and 0630-0755 GMT	8 hours ahead of GMT	5,800,000

When the Stock Exchange of Hong Kong listed its first state-owned Chinese companies in mid-1993, it took a big step toward solidifying its position as the fund raising center for the mainland.

As the British colony prepares itself for rule from Beijing and as China makes its economy market oriented, the exchange says the key to its growth lies in listing more mainland enterprises.

Accommodating Chinese companies has coincided with an effort to improve corporate governance in the territory, for example in requiring groups to provide shareholders with more information about their property development interests across the border.

The exchange has listed 17 so-called class "H" shares of Chinese companies, with another dozen shortlisted for initial public offerings.

The special yuan-denominated class of stock only represents 1.0% of Hong Kong's total capitalization and the company numbers are still small compared with the 531 stock listings boasted by the exchange.

Selected by Beijing as much for their political connections as their business acumen, the "H" share listings nevertheless impart enormous prestige on the stock exchange and on China's central government, which controls each of them.

The groups emanate from China's most important industries, including manufacturers of power generation and telecommunications equipment, steel, petrochemicals, autos, shipbuilding, machinery, and even beer.

After nearly half a century of central planning, Chinese banks can't keep financing the expansion of these core industries and they will go to where they can get the best terms, be it Hong Kong, New York or even the foreign banks and brokerages moving to Shanghai.

Adding share-purchase warrants, debt securities and other types of securities, almost 1000 securities trade in Hong Kong, with significant growth recorded for bonds in recent years.

Dow Jones Hong Kong Equity Market Index Performance

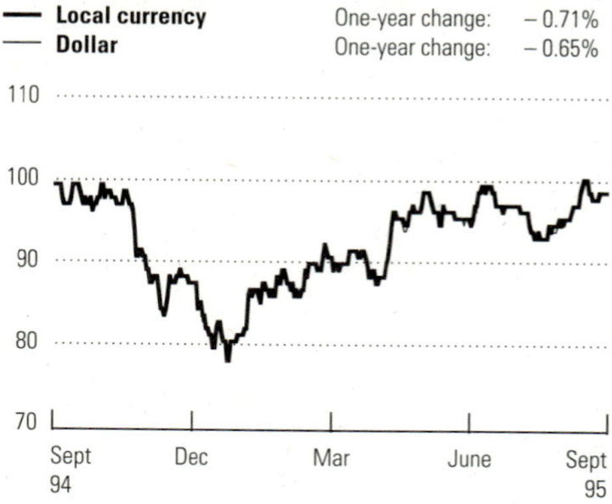

The value of average daily volume this year is running around HK$3.21 billion, far shy of the HK$4.36 billion traded on the average day in 1994, the year foreign buying pushed the

Gross Domestic Product (94)	Three-Year Average GDP Growth (92-94)	Main Industries	Consumer Price Index (94)	Monetary Unit	Exchange Rate (9/95)
$131.03 billion	5.9%	Wholesale, retail, hotel and restaurant services, real estate and financial services, and manufacturing	8.1%	Hong Kong Dollar	HK$7.73 to US$1.00

market to its record high following a "maximum bullish" assessment by U.S. brokerage Morgan Stanley & Co.

The firm's top strategists subsequently tempered their initial enthusiasm for China's economic growth prospects, and the benefits of it for Hong Kong stocks, knocking the territory's market back to earth just as interest rate worries set in.

After doubling in 1993 and pulling back some during 1994, market capitalization stands around HK$2.23 billion, with the property, conglomerate and banking sectors each accounting for about 25%. After Tokyo, the Stock Exchange of Hong Kong is the biggest in Asia, and claims to have the world's eighth largest capitalization, after Switzerland and before Amsterdam.

The Hang Seng Index, published by the territory's second-biggest bank, Hang Seng Bank Ltd., is the main market indicator. Two China-backed companies, Citic Pacific Ltd. and Guangdong Investment Ltd., are among the 33 stocks graded blue chip.

The index topped out at 12201.39 in early 1994 after more than doubling in 1993. The index then plunged more than 30% in 1994. Since Hong Kong's dollar is pegged to the U.S. currency and its interest rates to Federal Reserve Board policy, the market has gyrated on interest rate perceptions during 1995 in a range of 6967.93 and 9742.44.

Banking group HSBC Holdings PLC and Hongkong Telecommunications Ltd. lead in market capitalization, respectively with about 12% and 7.0% of the total. The two often set the direction for the market.

Ten Largest Capitalized Companies
as of 9/30/95

Stock	Market Cap. US$Mil
HSBC Holdings	24,395,073.7
Hong Kong Telecom	20,271,241.8
Hutchison Whampoa	19,620,068.0
Sun Hung Kai Properties	18,869,972.2
First Pacific	16,179,743.3
Cheung Kong	13,384,619.4
China Light & Power	10,300,936.6
Henderson Land Development	9,642,009.4
Swire Pacific	7,693,134.7
Hong Kong Electric	6,756,230.2

Both, however, are U.K. controlled and listed. Since their turnover levels on the London Stock Exchange rival the local activity, the Hang Seng Index's direction is often dictated by overnight moves in London.

Moving the closing bell closer to the London open, Hong Kong exchange authorities over the past two years have tacked an additional 25 minutes to the trading day.

Hong Kong's two-hour lunch break between 0430 GMT and 0630 GMT, remains sacrosanct, however, as apparently does the late-morning start, at 0200 GMT. Trading ends at 0755 GMT. The market is open five days a week.

Regulator efforts to win back trading of big stocks from London by pushing for negotiated commissions that would appeal to institutional investors have failed in the face of opposition from small, local brokerages. Some trading fees have been reduced in recent years, but the minimum commission remains at the greater of 0.25% or HK$50, per side, per trade. Hong Kong has no tax on capital gains.

Among the fees done away with in recent years was the "lifeboat levy," a tax that for seven years funded bailout of the Hong Kong Futures Exchange, which failed during the global stock market crash of 1987.

The Stock Exchange of Hong Kong was created in April 1986 through the merger of four trading centers, in an effort to do away with the chaos that prevailed at the decentralized arenas and to make Hong Kong a leading financial center.

Eighteen months later, however, such hopes were dashed by the way Hong Kong dealt with the October 1987 global stock market crash: by closing for four days, in an ill-fated attempt by exchange management to sidestep the meltdown and protect their interests.

Exchange Chairman Ronald Li got defrocked in the aftermath — spending four years in prison on market-related corruption charges — and the exchange management was restructured. Regulators were given more powers.

These days, stepping toward a floorless exchange, electronic order matching has been introduced and all members are being equipped to trade off the exchange, in their offices.

With their red jackets, gold numbers emblazoned across the back, floor traders who input trades on behalf of brokerages won't vacate the hushed, rectangular shaped exchange anytime soon. But as much as any business in the territory, the exchange worries about spiraling property prices, maybe particularly so because it is housed in Exchange Square — the most expensive office building in Hong Kong, if not the world.

Electronic trading will also help the exchange in linking with the fledgling Shenzhen and Shanghai markets, should Beijing mandate a national stock market or otherwise forge links between the bourses.

Talk of creating a secondary-level listing board to attract small companies, particularly those from China, has split exchange management, but doesn't appear likely to result in a new listing venue for Hong Kong.

Exchange turnover is tilted roughly 90% in favor of stocks and about 9.0% for warrants, or call options listed by companies themselves or sold by brokerages. Bonds, mutual funds and rights issues hardly trade.

Analysts variously say Hong Kong investors lack sophistication or are purists, preferring easy-to-understand trading possibilities.

As a result, the stock and futures exchanges in recent years have chalked up mixed records in introducing new products. Investor appetite for short selling of stock, permitted for more than a year on just 18 blue chips, has been poor. And other than its mainstay Hang Seng Index futures and options contracts, the futures exchange hasn't had much luck whetting investor appetite with anything new.

In contrast, a cautious introduction by the stock exchange of put and call options trading on a single stock, HSBC Holdings, got off to a better-than-expected start in September 1995. Options on a handful more blue chips are pending.

The upcoming change in Hong Kong's sovereignty may bode well for the exchange's ability to list more China-based enterprises, but the "1997 factor" may frighten some others. Jardine Matheson Holdings Ltd. and four other members of Hong Kong's original British trading house delisted from the exchange in the past year.

Most of the investment community speculated the upcoming power shift worries the venerable group which suffered on the mainland when the communists took control of China in 1949. Throughout, the Jardines group has insisted intransigent Hong Kong market regulators were to blame.

No other companies have followed Jardines in cancelling their Hong Kong share listings, but plenty have changed their domicile to Bermuda and other offshore havens, while a few have opted to spin off subsidiaries on the Stock Exchange of Singapore.

Amoy Properties

Industry: **Real-Estate Investment**

Amoy Properties is one of Hong Kong's largest property-investment companies, with a portfolio totaling 493,000 square meters. About two thirds of its rental income comes from commercial properties in central Hong Kong, central Kowloon, and Causeway Bay. Amoy also holds office buildings and residential, commercial, and industrial properties. The company has a 42% equity stake in a joint venture to develop a shopping center in Shanghai. Amoy is a subsidiary of Hang Lung Development (held through Prosperland Housing).

HK$ mil	06/92	06/93	06/94	US$mil 06/94				
Sales	1,422.2	1,763.5	2,477.1	320.3	P/E Ratio	11.0	Price (9/30/95)	7.30
Net Income	916.3	1,212.7	1,583.6	204.8	P/B Ratio	0.6	52 Wk Hi-Low	10.05-6.35
Book Value	17,353.5	21,273.2	29,541.4	3,821.7	Yield %	5.6	Market Cap	US$2,152.1mil

Address **4 Des Voeux Rd. Central**
Tel **879-0111**
Fax **576-3105**
ADR **AWOZY**
SEDOL No. **6030506**
Managing Director **Nelson W.L. Yuen**
Chairman **Ronnie C. Chan**

Bank of East Asia

Industry: **Banks - Money Center**

Bank of East Asia is one of Hong Kong's largest banking institutions; it provides a wide range of financial services, including the sale of insurance products. The bank operates 60 domestic branches as well as branches in mainland China, Singapore, the United States, and Canada. Its subsidiaries include Oakreed Financial Services, a joint venture that founded a debt-instrument trading company with the Long Term Credit Bank of Japan. The bank has a 35% equity stake in AEA Development, an investment bank and depository operating in the Philippines.

HK$ mil	12/92	12/93	12/94	US$mil 12/94				
Revenues	0.0	0.0	0.0	0.0	P/E Ratio	14.3	Price (9/30/95)	25.05
Net Income	685.3	1,006.0	1,965.4	254.3	P/B Ratio	2.7	52 Wk Hi-Low	28.54-18.90
Book Value	4,902.1	5,590.3	8,297.4	1,072.0	Yield %	3.0	Market Cap	US$2,861.9mil

Address **10 Des Voeux Rd. Central**
Tel **842-3200**
Fax **845-9333**
ADR **BKEAY**
SEDOL No. **6075648**
CEO **David K.P. Li**
Chairman **Li Fook-Wo**

Cathay Pacific Airways

Industry: **Airlines**

Cathay Pacific Airways serves some 40 destinations from its base of operations in Hong Kong's Kai Tak Airport. It operates a fleet of 55 aircraft, composed of Lockheed 1011 Tristars, Boeing 747s, and Airbuses. The company owns a 30% interest in Hong Kong Dragon Airlines, a regional carrier. Its other subsidiaries provide computerized reservation systems, airline catering, airport ground support, and airport security. It also has a joint venture developing and managing China's fourth-busiest airport in Xiamen. Hong Kong-based Swire Pacific has a 52% stake in Cathay Pacific.

HK$ mil	12/92	12/93	12/94	US$mil 12/94				
Sales	23,306.0	24,008.0	27,215.0	3,521.2	P/E Ratio	14.1	Price (9/30/95)	11.75
Net Income	3,008.0	2,293.0	2,388.0	309.0	P/B Ratio	2.2	52 Wk Hi-Low	12.70-10.20
Book Value	13,320.0	14,410.0	15,454.0	1,996.6	Yield %	3.6	Market Cap	US$4,354.2mil

Address **Swire Hse., 9 Connaught Rd. Central**
Tel **840-8873**
Fax **845-5445**
ADR **CPCAY**
SEDOL No. **6179755**
Managing Director **Rod Eddington**
Chairman **Peter Sutch**

CDL Hotels

Industry: **Lodging**

CDL Hotels manages and develops hotels and leisure centers. In Singapore, it operates the King's Hotel, Novotel Orchid Singapore, and the Orchard Hotel. CDL also manages 20 hotels throughout New Zealand, most a part of the Quality Hotel chain, three in London, two each in Malaysia and New York, and one each in Hong Kong, the Philippines, Australia, and China. The company has a 50% interest in Kingsgate International, which manages a shopping center and marina complex in Sydney, and a joint-venture with Lippo Group (Indonesia) which operates Seaworld Lippo Life.

HK$ mil	12/92	12/93	12/94	US$mil 12/94				
Sales	1,087.2	1,578.7	2,713.8	351.1	P/E Ratio	14.0	Price (9/30/95)	3.50
Net Income	149.2	224.8	387.9	50.2	P/B Ratio	1.0	52 Wk Hi-Low	4.30-3.03
Book Value	4,050.6	4,616.7	5,243.7	677.5	Yield %	1.4	Market Cap	US$693.9mil

Address **Great Eagle Ctr., 23 Harbour Rd. Wanchai**
Tel **N/A**
Fax **N/A**
ADR
SEDOL No. **6160180**
Managing Director **Kwek Leng Beng**
Chairman **Kwek Leng Beng**

Cheung Kong

Industry: **Conglomerates**

Cheung Kong Holdings is an investment firm with primary interests in the development and sale of properties. The company is currently developing a total of roughly 339,000 square meters of commercial, residential, and industrial floor space in Hong Kong and approximately 426,000 more in China. Cheung Kong also holds 95,000 square meters of space in Hong Kong for investment or its own use. Through its wholly-owned subsidiaries, it also has cement and quarry operations. Cheung Kong owns 44% of fellow Hong Kong firm Hutchison Whampoa.

HK$ mil	12/92	12/93	12/94	US$mil 12/94				
Sales	10,278.0	10,693.0	14,841.0	1,920.2	P/E Ratio	9.2	Price (9/30/95)	42.10
Net Income	6,218.0	9,781.0	10,113.0	1,308.4	P/B Ratio	2.1	52 Wk Hi-Low	42.50-24.85
Book Value	27,335.0	35,417.0	43,253.0	5,588.2	Yield %	2.6	Market Cap	US$13,385mil

Address **China Bldg., 29 Queen's Rd. Central**
Tel **526-6911**
Fax **845-2940**
ADR **CHEUY**
SEDOL No. **6190273**
President **--**
Chairman **Li Ka-Shing**

China Light & Power

Industry: **Electrical Utilities - All**

China Light and Power is one of two Hong Kong electric utilities. It services 1.7 million customers in Kowloon and the New Territories of Hong Kong, and supplies surplus electricity to Guangdong Province in China. The firm's profits from electricity generation are regulated under a scheme-of-control agreement with Hong Kong's government. The company owns stakes in the five power stations that supply it with electricity, two of which are in China: Guangdong Nuclear Power Station and Guangzhou Pumped Storage Power Station.

HK$ mil	09/92	09/93	09/94	US$mil 09/94				
Sales	13,402.0	14,767.0	15,445.0	1,998.6	P/E Ratio	19.0	Price (9/30/95)	40.00
Net Income	3,173.0	3,552.0	4,206.0	544.3	P/B Ratio	4.9	52 Wk Hi-Low	42.50-30.40
Book Value	12,864.0	14,425.0	16,342.0	2,114.1	Yield %	2.9	Market Cap	US$10,301mil

Address **147 Argyle St.** **Kowloon**
Tel **760-6111** Fax **760-4448**
ADR **CHLWY** SEDOL No. **6190916**
President -- Chairman **Sidney Gordon**

China Motor Bus

Industry: **Household Services**

China Motor Bus (CMB) operates a franchised bus system on Hong Kong island. CMB's bus-route system is composed of 64 routes over 45 million kilometres, and the company has a monopoly over these routes in part of the colony. Its fleet of 1,002 buses, 103 of which are air-conditioned, carries approximately 208 million passagers each year. The company competes directly with Singapore Bus Service and Citybus, the two other bus operators in the territory. CMB's two-year operating franchise will be up for renewal by the government in September 1995.

HK$ mil	06/92	06/93	06/94	US$mil 06/94				
Sales	792.4	814.5	761.1	98.4	P/E Ratio	11.9	Price (9/30/95)	66.50
Net Income	654.3	82.2	258.1	33.4	P/B Ratio	2.9	52 Wk Hi-Low	73.00-50.50
Book Value	801.4	795.3	1,060.1	137.1	Yield %	2.2	Market Cap	US$398.0mil

Address **391 Chai Wan Rd.** **Chai Wan**
Tel **561-6171** Fax **N/A**
ADR SEDOL No. **6190897**
Managing Director **Shing-kwan Ngan** Chairman **Shing-kwan Ngan**

Chinese Estates

Industry: **Real-Estate Investment**

Chinese Estates is a holding company that specializes in property and securities investments. The company derives the majority of its income from real-estate activities, including the holding, development, leasing, and sale of residential, commercial, and industrial properties. Among its investment properties in Hong Kong are the Entertainment Building, a 34-level commercial building with 211,000 square feet of space, and the Silvercord shopping mall. Its 40%-owned Asian Win Realty joint venture is developing approximately 11 million square feet of property in China.

HK$ mil	12/92	12/93	12/94	US$mil 12/94				
Sales	2,920.4	2,433.2	2,299.4	297.5	P/E Ratio	7.6	Price (9/30/95)	5.55
Net Income	639.5	593.2	1,183.0	153.1	P/B Ratio	0.4	52 Wk Hi-Low	8.20-4.48
Book Value	9,453.2	23,461.6	20,600.0	2,661.5	Yield %	4.5	Market Cap	US$1,138.9mil

Address **Harcourt Hse., 39 Gloucester Rd.** **Wanchai**
Tel **866-6999** Fax **866-2822**
ADR SEDOL No. **6191180**
President -- Chairman **Joseph Lau**

CITIC Pacific

Industry: **Real-Estate Investment**

CITIC Pacific is a diversified holding company with interests in infrastructure, trading, consumer-credit, property, and manufacturing businesses. The firm distributes and sells automobiles, food products, building materials, and consumer electronics through its wholly-owned Dah Chong Hong subsidiary. Its aviation and telecommunication interests include Dragonair (46%), Cathay Pacific (12.5%), and Hongkong Telecom (12%). It also has interests in two power stations and four steel-manufacturing operations in China, and waste-management and tunnel facilities in Hong Kong.

HK$ mil	12/92	12/93	12/94	US$mil 12/94				
Sales	8,394.1	11,538.6	12,123.0	1,568.5	P/E Ratio	17.6	Price (9/30/95)	23.35
Net Income	1,040.0	1,886.6	2,570.0	332.5	P/B Ratio	1.9	52 Wk Hi-Low	24.30-14.80
Book Value	10,124.9	21,339.4	25,096.0	3,242.4	Yield %	2.1	Market Cap	US$6,025.2mil

Address **Two Pacific Pl., 88 Queensway** **Central**
Tel **820-2111** Fax **877-2771**
ADR SEDOL No. **6196152**
Managing Director **Henry Fan Hung Ling** Chairman **Larry Yung Chi Kin**

Cross Harbour Tunnel

Industry: **General Industrial & Commercial Services**

Cross Harbour Tunnel is an infrastructure-construction company. It operates Hong Kong's two harbor tunnels. The company, together with Citic, the foreign-investment arm of the People's Republic of China, has a partnership to build Hong Kong's third tunnel. Cross Harbour Tunnel's 37%-owned Western Harbour Tunnel subsidiary is presently working on the third tunnel, which will link Hong Kong's western district with western Kowloon peninsula. Completion is set for 1997. The Hong Kong conglomerate Wharf Holdings owns a 26.7% interest in Cross Harbour Tunnel.

HK$ mil	12/92	12/93	12/94	US$mil 12/94				
Sales	492.5	672.8	728.3	94.2	P/E Ratio	12.7	Price (9/30/95)	15.00
Net Income	220.5	221.6	227.0	29.4	P/B Ratio	2.5	52 Wk Hi-Low	16.90-13.90
Book Value	282.1	1,131.5	1,132.4	146.3	Yield %	7.9	Market Cap	US$371.9mil

Address **19 Dex Voeux Rd.** **Central**
Tel **333-4141** Fax **845-9029**
ADR SEDOL No. **6235367**
President -- Chairman **G.A. Higginson**

Dah Sing Financial

Industry: **Financial Services - Diversified**

Dah Sing Financial provides banking, financial, and insurance services. The firm's banking services are offered through its main financing subsidiary, Dah Sing Bank. Its total banking network has 50 branches in Hong Kong and one each in Los Angeles, San Francisco, and Shenzhen, China. The company has a 40% interest in Jian Sing Bank, a joint-venture with state-owned People's Construction Bank of China to develop retail and wholesale banking in China. A 51%-owned joint-venture with M & G (U.K.), will offer investment- and fund-management services in Hong Kong and China.

HK$ mil	12/92	12/93	12/94	US$mil 12/94				
Revenues	**N/A**	**1,523.5**	**1,938.0**	**250.7**	P/E Ratio	**10.0**	Price (9/30/95)	**17.40**
Net Income	**213.9**	**303.1**	**396.6**	**51.3**	P/B Ratio	**1.6**	52 Wk Hi-Low	**23.00-12.30**
Book Value	**1,124.1**	**1,344.1**	**2,553.7**	**329.9**	Yield %	**4.1**	Market Cap	**US$514.3mil**

Address **Dah Sing Financial Ctr.**
Central
Tel **507-8866**
Fax **598-5052**
ADR
SEDOL No. **6249799**
Managing Director **Ronald Carstairs**
Chairman **David S.Y. Wong**

Dao Heng Bank

Industry: **Banks - Regional**

Dao Heng Bank Group is an investment-holding company for banking and financial-services businesses. Its two main subsidiaries, the Dao Heng Bank and the Overseas Trust Bank, combine to make the group the third-largest banking operation in Hong Kong. The Overseas Trust Bank operates 90 domestic and nine overseas branches. The banking group has HK$67 billion in total assets, holds approximately HK$58.7 billion in deposits, and has HK$36.3 billion loans outstanding. Other services Dao Heng offers include commercial banking and trustee and nominee services.

HK$ mil	06/92	06/93	06/94	US$mil 06/94				
Revenues	**N/A**	**1,918.2**	**4,071.8**	**526.5**	P/E Ratio	**13.9**	Price (9/30/95)	**25.65**
Net Income	**320.2**	**401.3**	**1,000.5**	**129.4**	P/B Ratio	**2.8**	52 Wk Hi-Low	**28.20-19.30**
Book Value	**1,257.1**	**1,597.9**	**6,016.7**	**778.4**	Yield %	**2.4**	Market Cap	**US$2,177.2mil**

Address **213 Queen's Rd. E.**
Central
Tel **831-7700**
Fax **891-6822**
ADR
SEDOL No. **6287131**
Managing Director **Kwek Leng Hai**
Chairman **Quek Leng Chan**

Dickson Concepts

Industry: **Apparel Retailers**

Dickson Concepts (International) is a wholesaler and retailer of designer-label merchandise in more than 30 countries. It sells watches, jewelry, clothing, leather products, lighters, and writing instruments. The company's chains include Bvlgari watch boutiques and Polo/Ralph Lauren and Adolfo Dominquez fashion boutiques. It owns the upscale Harvey Nichols department store in London and is opening another store in Leeds in third-quarter 1996. Under exclusive license from Warner Brothers, Dickson is planning to open Warner Brothers Studio Stores in Hong Kong and Singapore.

HK$ mil	03/93	03/94	03/95	US$mil 03/95				
Revenues	**2,568.7**	**2,914.9**	**3,266.8**	**422.6**	P/E Ratio	**11.5**	Price (9/30/95)	**5.60**
Net Income	**300.5**	**366.3**	**332.2**	**43.0**	P/B Ratio	**1.7**	52 Wk Hi-Low	**5.75-4.00**
Book Value	**1,876.1**	**2,053.6**	**2,239.6**	**289.7**	Yield %	**5.0**	Market Cap	**US$492.2mil**

Address **East Ocean Ctr., 98 Granville Rd.**
Tsimshatsui East, Kowloon
Tel **311-3888**
Fax **311-3323**
ADR
SEDOL No. **6271781**
President --
Chairman **Dickson Poon**

Esprit Asia

Industry: **Apparel Retailers**

Esprit Asia Holdings is a wholesaler and retailer of clothing, shoes, accessories, and bed and bath goods. All its garments are sold under the Esprit brand name. It operates 30 retail stores in Hong Kong, 42 in Taiwan, 39 in South Korea, 18 in Singapore, nine in China. Esprit operates six stores in Tokyo, Osaka, and Kobe, and also offers its goods at a Tokyo department store of Japanese retailer Mitsukoshi. Sales in Hong Kong account for approximately 58% of the company's revenue. Esprit holds the exclusive license to distribute Red Earth body-care products in Asia.

HK$ mil	06/92	06/93	06/94	US$mil 06/94				
Revenues	**485.5**	**769.7**	**1,144.9**	**148.1**	P/E Ratio	**11.6**	Price (9/30/95)	**2.78**
Net Income	**45.8**	**78.9**	**167.4**	**21.6**	P/B Ratio	**4.5**	52 Wk Hi-Low	**3.38-2.60**
Book Value	**N/A**	**134.2**	**467.1**	**60.4**	Yield %	**2.9**	Market Cap	**US$269.5mil**

Address **11 Yuk Yat St.**
Kowloon
Tel **765-4321**
Fax **N/A**
ADR
SEDOL No. **6321642**
President --
Chairman **M. Ying Lee Yuen**

First Pacific

Industry: **Overseas Trading**

First Pacific manages diverse operations in 25 countries, from airport security to the sale of pharmaceuticals. Marketing and distribution of consumer goods account for almost half of the company's profits, particularly through its 50% stake in Hagemeyer, a Dutch subsidiary. The firm also has retail-banking and real-estate subsidiaries in Hong Kong, Thailand, and the United States. It also operates telecommunication ventures in Hong Kong (where subsidiaries control one fourth of the cellular-telephone market), the Philippines, and Indonesia.

$ mil	12/92	12/93	12/94	US$mil 12/94				
Sales	**2,786.9**	**3,084.4**	**3,681.9**	**3,681.9**	P/E Ratio	**18.0**	Price (9/30/95)	**8.25**
Net Income	**78.6**	**101.2**	**130.3**	**130.3**	P/B Ratio	**4.7**	52 Wk Hi-Low	**8.65-4.30**
Book Value	**326.1**	**405.9**	**439.8**	**439.8**	Yield %	**0.0**	Market Cap	**US$2,093.1mil**

Address **2 Exchange Sq., 8 Connaught Pl.**
Central
Tel **842-4388**
Fax **845-9243**
ADR **FPAFY**
SEDOL No. **6339872**
Managing Director **Manuel V. Pangilinan**
Chairman **Soedono Salim**

Giordano

Industry: **Clothing & Fabrics**

Giordano manufactures and retails a range of casual apparel, including knitwear and woven garments, under its own Giordano label. It operates in 12 countries in the Pacific Rim, including Japan, South Korea, and New Zealand. Taiwan is Giordano's largest retailing market. Its products are sold from more than 700 outlets, 283 of which the company directly manages. Its 51%-owned Tiger Enterprises subsidiary operates six stores in China, and franchises another 34. Giordano also has a 20%-owned joint venture in Dubai with one of its franchisees in the Middle East.

HK$ mil	12/92	12/93	12/94	US$mil 12/94				
Sales	**1,661.4**	**2,334.1**	**2,863.7**	**370.5**	P/E Ratio	**22.9**	Price (9/30/95)	**7.10**
Net Income	**115.1**	**137.6**	**195.3**	**25.3**	P/B Ratio	**8.3**	52 Wk Hi-Low	**7.20-4.00**
Book Value	**361.7**	**454.7**	**544.5**	**70.3**	Yield %	**1.5**	Market Cap	**US$581.9mil**

Address **777-779 Cheung Sha Wan Rd. Kowloon**
Tel **746-5168**
Fax **785-0343**
ADR
SEDOL No. **6369619**
Chief Executive **P. Lau Kwok Kuen**
Chairman **P. Lau Kwok Kuen**

Great Eagle

Industry: **Real-Estate Investment**

Great Eagle principally invests in and develops property in Hong Kong. It manages more than two million square feet of property, roughly 71% of which is commercial. Among its major property interests in Hong Kong are a 69.5% stake in the Citibank Plaza office complex, 100% of the London Plaza shopping center, and 100% of the Eaton Hotel. The firm has subsidiaries engaged in advertising, building-materials trading, parking garages, insurance, and shipping. Great Eagle also has joint ventures to develop and renovate property in Sichuan and Guangzhou, China.

HK$ mil	09/92	09/93	09/94	US$mil 09/94				
Sales	**1,545.0**	**879.4**	**1,793.9**	**232.1**	P/E Ratio	**10.1**	Price (9/30/95)	**19.10**
Net Income	**378.3**	**450.0**	**780.0**	**100.9**	P/B Ratio	**0.5**	52 Wk Hi-Low	**22.85-13.40**
Book Value	**9,125.8**	**11,888.7**	**18,243.2**	**2,360.1**	Yield %	**3.7**	Market Cap	**US$1,055.1mil**

Address **Great Eagle Ctr., 23 Harbour Rd. Wanchai**
Tel **831-0668**
Fax **834-5799**
ADR
SEDOL No. **6387406**
Managing Director **Ka Shui Lo**
Chairman **Ying Shek Lo**

Guangdong Investment

Industry: **Lodging**

Guangdong Investment is an investment-holding company with interests in leisure, manufacturing, and property in Hong Kong and China. Through its subsidiaries, it owns seven hotels, and operates tours in Southeast Asia. The firm's holdings in China include 52% of malt manufacturer Guangzhou Malting, 80% of aluminum producer Full Arts Metal, and 64.5% of Shenzhen Brewery. It also owns HK Environmental Pollution Control Services and Union Globe Development, a finance and property firm. Its infrastructure investments include two power plants, one bridge, and a landfill.

HK$ mil	12/92	12/93	12/94	US$mil 12/94				
Sales	**1,039.1**	**2,751.7**	**3,760.7**	**486.6**	P/E Ratio	**17.2**	Price (9/30/95)	**4.63**
Net Income	**160.2**	**330.5**	**437.2**	**56.6**	P/B Ratio	**1.8**	52 Wk Hi-Low	**5.20-3.08**
Book Value	**2,394.5**	**2,452.1**	**5,062.2**	**654.0**	Yield %	**1.9**	Market Cap	**US$1,189.4mil**

Address **Admiralty Ctr., 18 Harcourt Rd. Central**
Tel **860-4368**
Fax **528-4386**
ADR
SEDOL No. **6913168**
President **--**
Chairman **He Keqin**

Guoco

Industry: **Securities Brokers**

Guoco Group is active in financial services, manufacturing, and property investment and development. Its 71%-owned Dao Heng Bank Group provides such services as general banking, insurance and insurance brokerage, securities and commodities brokerage, and fund management. It also owns a 60% interest in Malaysia's Hong Leong Credit. Guoco's manufacturing subsidiaries, mostly located in China, produce ceramic tiles, conventional and fiberoptic cables, air conditioners, and micromotors. The company also has property-development and investment interests in Southeast Asia.

HK$ mil	06/92	06/93	06/94	US$mil 06/94				
Sales	**1,680.5**	**2,018.6**	**3,300.3**	**426.8**	P/E Ratio	**11.3**	Price (9/30/95)	**38.70**
Net Income	**372.2**	**573.8**	**1,355.9**	**175.3**	P/B Ratio	**2.1**	52 Wk Hi-Low	**40.80-24.00**
Book Value	**3,190.4**	**4,544.8**	**7,207.3**	**932.4**	Yield %	**1.7**	Market Cap	**US$2,135.9mil**

Address **No. 213 Queen's Rd. E. Kowloon**
Tel **831-7700**
Fax **891-6822**
ADR
SEDOL No. **6390363**
Managing Director **Kwek Leng Hai**
Chairman **Quek Leng Chan**

Hang Lung Development

Industry: **Real-Estate Investment**

Hang Lung Development is an investment holding company with operations primarily in property development and investment. More than half of the floor space that the company is developing is located in Shanghai, China. Its property investment interests are mainly held by 55%-owned Amoy Properties. Hang Lung also has a 61% interest in Grand Hotel Holdings, which owns and operates Hong Kong's Grand Tower Hotel, Grand Plaza Hotel and Apartments, and the Wesley. Among the firm's other holdings are carparks, restaurants, laundries, and department stores.

HK$ mil	06/92	06/93	06/94	US$mil 06/94				
Sales	**3,619.1**	**4,179.8**	**5,464.1**	**706.6**	P/E Ratio	**7.6**	Price (9/30/95)	**12.45**
Net Income	**1,318.2**	**1,602.5**	**2,020.9**	**261.3**	P/B Ratio	**0.8**	52 Wk Hi-Low	**14.50-9.50**
Book Value	**11,775.1**	**15,377.1**	**19,625.7**	**2,538.9**	Yield %	**5.2**	Market Cap	**US$2,171.2mil**

Address **4 Des Voeux Rd. Central**
Tel **890-4111**
Fax **576-3105**
ADR **HANLY**
SEDOL No. **6408352**
President **Nelson W.L. Yuen**
Chairman **Ronnie C. Chan**

Harbour Centre

Industry: **Lodging**

Harbour Centre Development is a hotel-investment company. Its main real-estate holding is the Omni Hongkong Hotel in Hong Kong, a hotel complex with office space and retail shops, which represents more than 70% of total assets. The company owns seven hotels in the United States, including the Omni Houston Hotel and the Omni Mandalay Hotel, both in Texas, and the Omni Hotel in Chicago. All of Harbour Centre's hotels are managed by Omni Hotels (Asia Pacific), a wholly-owned Wharf subsidiary. The company is 57%-owned by Wharf Holdings, a major Hong Kong holding company.

HK$ mil	12/92	12/93	12/94	US$mil 12/94				
Sales	**847.6**	**997.8**	**1,256.2**	**162.5**	P/E Ratio	**16.4**	Price (9/30/95)	**8.60**
Net Income	**137.7**	**127.0**	**165.3**	**21.4**	P/B Ratio	**0.6**	52 Wk Hi-Low	**10.60-7.60**
Book Value	**3,230.8**	**1,250.6**	**4,764.1**	**615.5**	Yield %	**4.9**	Market Cap	**US$350.5mil**

Address **19 Des Voeux Rd.**
Central
Tel **738-8222**
Fax **736-6133**
ADR
SEDOL No. **6408954**
President --
Chairman **Gonzaga W.J. Li**

Henderson Investment

Industry: **Real-Estate Investment**

Henderson Investment has interests in residential and commercial real estate, retail companies, and utilities. It holds 32% of Hong Kong and China Gas and 25% of a power plant in China. It also owns 33% of Hong Kong Ferry and 35% of hotel and real-estate concern Miramar Hotel & Investment. Henderson's property-investment portfolio includes such commercial complexes as the wholly-owned Trend Plaza (195,000 square feet) and 25%-owned City One Plaza (413,000 square feet). Henderson Investment is a 72%-owned subsidiary of Henderson Land Development.

HK$ mil	06/92	06/93	06/94	US$mil 06/94				
Sales	**773.6**	**1,131.9**	**1,275.1**	**164.9**	P/E Ratio	**13.8**	Price (9/30/95)	**6.45**
Net Income	**736.2**	**977.0**	**1,130.5**	**146.2**	P/B Ratio	**0.9**	52 Wk Hi-Low	**7.10-3.98**
Book Value	**7,141.5**	**9,670.6**	**18,969.7**	**2,454.0**	Yield %	**4.5**	Market Cap	**US$2,140.1mil**

Address **19 Des Voeux Rd.**
Central
Tel **826-5222**
Fax **810-6292**
ADR
SEDOL No. **6972341**
Managing Director **Lee Shau Kee**
Chairman **Lee Shau Kee**

Henderson Land Development

Industry: **Home Construction**

Henderson Land Development's main activities include property development and investment, project and property management, construction, finance, and investment holding. Approximately three fourths of Henderson's 17-million-square-foot property portfolio is composed of residential space in Hong Kong's New Territories. The company also has property-development joint ventures in China. Henderson holds 30% stakes in Hong Kong and China Gas and Hong Kong Ferry. It is also the parent company of Henderson Investment, which owns property, retail, and utilities operations.

HK$ mil	06/92	06/93	06/94	US$mil 06/94				
Sales	**4,157.6**	**6,113.9**	**9,967.8**	**1,289.0**	P/E Ratio	**12.4**	Price (9/30/95)	**46.70**
Net Income	**2,437.0**	**4,006.8**	**6,038.0**	**780.8**	P/B Ratio	**2.6**	52 Wk Hi-Low	**51.50-31.60**
Book Value	**13,898.0**	**17,753.9**	**28,598.9**	**3,699.7**	Yield %	**3.4**	Market Cap	**US$9,642.0mil**

Address **19 Des Voeux Rd.**
Central
Tel **525-1033**
Fax **810-6292**
ADR **HLDCY**
SEDOL No. **6420538**
President --
Chairman **Lee Shau Kee**

HKR International

Industry: **Real-Estate Investment**

HKR International is a real-estate firm with a property portfolio of roughly 3 million square feet. Its principal property is its Discovery Bay project on Lantau Island, the site of Hong Kong's new airport. The property has roughly 4,500 completed residential units and more than 165,000 square feet of commercial space. HKR owns companies active in restaurants, recreational facilities, ferries, bus services, and sanitaryware. The company also has interests in hotels in Australia, Thailand, and Singapore. Hong Kong investment company Mingly owns 58% of HKR's share capital.

HK$ mil	03/93	03/94	03/95	US$mil 03/95				
Sales	**928.6**	**1,626.0**	**1,919.7**	**248.3**	P/E Ratio	**13.5**	Price (9/30/95)	**6.55**
Net Income	**329.7**	**2,994.2**	**444.3**	**57.5**	P/B Ratio	**0.7**	52 Wk Hi-Low	**7.70-4.45**
Book Value	**5,675.4**	**10,142.0**	**8,721.8**	**1,128.3**	Yield %	**3.1**	Market Cap	**US$772.4mil**

Address **Jardine Hse., 1 Connaught Pl.**
Central
Tel **524-9181**
Fax **N/A**
ADR
SEDOL No. **6159672**
Managing Director **Payson Mou Sing Cha**
Chairman **Cha Chi Ming**

Hong Kong Aircraft

Industry: **Aerospace & Defense**

Hong Kong Aircraft Engineering Company (Haeco) provides maintenance and repair services for commercial aircraft and related equipment at Hong Kong's Kai Tak Airport. Services for Cathay Pacific Airways account for roughly two thirds of Haeco's revenues. Other customers include Dragonair, American Trans Air, Air India, Xiamen Airlines, and Lowa. Other activities include aircraft-refueling services, aircraft-brake services, hangar operations in Australia and China, and aircraft-tire retreading. Haeco's major shareholders are Swire Pacific (53%) and Cathay Pacific (25%).

HK$ mil	12/92	12/93	12/94	US$mil 12/94				
Sales	**2,097.1**	**2,307.1**	**2,418.4**	**312.9**	P/E Ratio	**9.4**	Price (9/30/95)	**20.95**
Net Income	**387.9**	**447.0**	**413.7**	**53.5**	P/B Ratio	**2.3**	52 Wk Hi-Low	**36.00-18.20**
Book Value	**1,223.1**	**1,483.1**	**1,722.7**	**222.6**	Yield %	**4.5**	Market Cap	**US$501.9mil**

Address **Swire Hse., 9 Connaught Rd.**
Central
Tel **840-8867**
Fax **845-5445**
ADR
SEDOL No. **6435264**
Managing Director **A.J. Herdman**
Chairman **P.D.A. Sutch**

Hong Kong Electric

Industry: **Electrical Utilities - All**

Hong Kong Electric Holdings owns energy-generation and energy-supply operations. Its principal subsidiary, Hong Kong Electric Company, generates and supplies electricity to approximately 500,000 customers in Hong Kong. Of these, 70% are commercial customers, 23% are residential, and the remainder are industrial. The firm's profits from electricity generation are regulated under a scheme-of-control agreement with Hong Kong's government. The company is also active in engineering consulting through its Associated Technical Services subsidiary.

HK$ mil	12/92	12/93	12/94	US$mil 12/94				
Sales	**5,332.0**	**5,946.0**	**6,670.0**	**863.0**	P/E Ratio	**13.6**	Price (9/30/95)	**25.85**
Net Income	**3,050.0**	**3,380.0**	**3,848.0**	**497.9**	P/B Ratio	**3.8**	52 Wk Hi-Low	**28.05-18.95**
Book Value	**10,242.0**	**11,804.0**	**13,632.0**	**1,761.2**	Yield %	**3.9**	Market Cap	**US$6,756.2mil**

Address **Electric Hse., 44 Kennedy Rd. Central** Tel **843-3111** Fax **N/A**
ADR **HONGY** SEDOL No. **6435327**
Managing Director **Ewan Yee Lup-Yuen**
Chairman **George C. Magnus**

Hong Kong Telecom

Industry: **Telephone Systems - All**

Hongkong Telecommunications runs communication and information-technology businesses. The firm has approximately 3 million telephone, fax, and data circuits and more than 61,000 kilometers of fiber-optic cable servicing residences and businesses. Its 1010 GSM digital mobile network and UNITACS analog system provide mobile-communication services in Hong Kong and China. The firm is part of the APC Cable system, involving 40 telecom companies, which links Hong Kong, Japan, Singapore, Malaysia, and Taiwan using Asia's longest fiber-optic submarine cable.

HK$ mil	03/93	03/94	03/95	US$mil 03/95				
Sales	**21,645.3**	**24,279.8**	**26,909.6**	**3,480.7**	P/E Ratio	**18.0**	Price (9/30/95)	**14.05**
Net Income	**6,429.9**	**7,557.7**	**8,698.7**	**1,125.2**	P/B Ratio	**8.8**	52 Wk Hi-Low	**16.55-13.25**
Book Value	**13,763.1**	**15,632.9**	**17,718.0**	**2,292.1**	Yield %	**4.2**	Market Cap	**US$20,271mil**

Address **HK Telecom Twr., 979 King's Rd. Quarry Bay** Tel **888-6373** Fax **296-5003**
ADR **HKT** SEDOL No. **6436461**
CEO **Linus Cheung Wing-Lum**
Chairman **Lord Young of Graffham**

Hong Kong & China Gas

Industry: **Gas Utilities**

Hong Kong and China Gas is the sole provider of natural gas in Hong Kong, supplying natural gas for domestic and commercial use, as well as heating fuel for the industrial sector. The total length of its distribution networks is approximately 1,700 kilometers, including twin cross-harbor pipelines. Hong Kong and China Gas' plant in Tai Po produces about 85% of the company's gas supply. The company provides natural gas to about 90% of newly constructed homes, and markets gas appliances, water heaters, fireplaces, and rice cookers under the Towngas Select brand name.

HK$ mil	12/92	12/93	12/94	US$mil 12/94				
Sales	**2,960.5**	**3,259.6**	**3,718.4**	**481.1**	P/E Ratio	**22.3**	Price (9/30/95)	**12.45**
Net Income	**936.1**	**1,135.6**	**1,367.9**	**177.0**	P/B Ratio	**3.0**	52 Wk Hi-Low	**12.75-9.17**
Book Value	**3,203.3**	**8,635.6**	**10,235.4**	**1,322.4**	Yield %	**2.3**	Market Cap	**US$3,999.8mil**

Address **Leighton Ctr., 77 Leighton Rd. Causeway Bay** Tel **890-1433** Fax **577-5969**
ADR **HOKCY** SEDOL No. **6436557**
Managing Director **M.J. Matthews**
Chairman **Lee Shau Kee**

H.K. & Shanghai Hotels

Industry: **Lodging**

Hongkong and Shanghai Hotels develops and manages hotel, recreation, and consumer-service properties. It operates The Peninsula and The Kowloon in Hong Kong, The Peninsula Manila, The Peninsula New York, The Peninsula Beverly Hills, The Landmark in Ho Chi Minh City, and The Palace Hotel in Beijing. The company is currently constructing The Peninsula Bangkok and The Peak (Hong Kong) hotels. It also develops residential and commercial complexes in Hong Kong, Thailand, Taiwan, and the United States. The company also operates clubs, restaurants, and laundries in Hong Kong.

HK$ mil	12/92	12/93	12/94	US$mil 12/94				
Sales	**1,834.0**	**1,690.0**	**1,785.0**	**230.9**	P/E Ratio	**20.5**	Price (9/30/95)	**9.65**
Net Income	**479.0**	**535.0**	**691.0**	**89.4**	P/B Ratio	**0.6**	52 Wk Hi-Low	**11.65-7.00**
Book Value	**10,095.0**	**12,123.0**	**16,053.0**	**2,074.0**	Yield %	**2.5**	Market Cap	**US$1,346.9mil**

Address **St. George's Bldg., 2 Ice House St. Central** Tel **840-7788** Fax **N/A**
ADR SEDOL No. **6436386**
President --
Chairman **Michael D. Kadoorie**

Hopewell Holdings

Industry: **Heavy Construction**

Hopewell Holdings is an international holding company with interests in property, construction, transportation infrastructure, hotels, power stations, and civil engineering. In 1994, it opened a 123-kilometer superhighway between Hong Kong and Guangzhou, China. It is also building an elevated-rail and road project in Bangkok. Through 62%-owned Consolidated Electric Power Asia, Hopewell has plans to build power plants throughout Asia. The firm also owns the Kowloon Panda Hotel, Hopewell Center office building, and Allway Garden Shopping Arcade, all in Hong Kong.

HK$ mil	06/92	06/93	06/94	US$mil 06/94				
Sales	**1,622.9**	**2,889.8**	**2,305.3**	**298.1**	P/E Ratio	**9.3**	Price (9/30/95)	**5.25**
Net Income	**1,623.0**	**2,028.3**	**2,438.3**	**315.3**	P/B Ratio	**1.0**	52 Wk Hi-Low	**8.15-5.05**
Book Value	**17,413.3**	**17,188.0**	**21,629.4**	**2,798.1**	Yield %	**6.5**	Market Cap	**US$3,017.1mil**

Address **183 Queen's Rd. E. Central** Tel **528-4975** Fax **529-8602**
ADR **HOWWY** SEDOL No. **6436999**
President **Gordon Wu**
Chairman **James Wu**

HSBC Holdings

Industry: **Banks - Money Center**

HSBC is the largest banking company in Hong Kong, operating primarily in commercial banking, but also in investment banking, private banking, and insurance. It conducts the majority of its business in Hong Kong and the U.K. Its major banking subsidiaries are Hang Seng (Hong Kong), Midland (U.K.), Marine Midland (U.S.), the British Bank of the Middle East, and their parent company, Hongkong and Shanghai. Continental Europe, North America, and the Asia Pacific generate 29% of the bank's pretax profit, with the remainder coming from Hong Kong (39%) and the U.K. (32%).

HK$ mil	12/91	12/92	12/93	US$mil 12/93				
Revenues	**N/A**	**175,486.0**	**166,446.0**	**21,515.8**	P/E Ratio M	**8.9**	Price (9/30/95) M	**107.50**
Net Income	**5,664.0**	**14,321.0**	**20,624.0**	**2,666.0**	P/B Ratio M	**1.7**	52 Wk Hi-Low M	**110.00-71.25**
Book Value	**56,286.0**	**93,952.0**	**106,594.0**	**13,789.7**	Yield % M	**2.5**	Market Cap M	**US$24,395mil**

Address	**1 Queen's Rd.**	Tel	**822-1111**	ADR	**HSBHY**	President	**J.R.H. Bond**
	Central	Fax	**868-1646**	SEDOL No.	**6436502**	Chairman	**Sir William Purves**

M=Multiple issues in index; reflects most active.

Hutchison Whampoa

Industry: **Conglomerates**

Hutchison Whampoa is an international conglomerate with property-investment, energy, retail, media, container-terminal, telecommunication, and finance businesses. It holds a 70% stake in Hutchison Telephone, a Hong Kong cellular-phone service, and owns 35% of Hongkong Electric Holdings. It also owns 77% of Hongkong International Terminals, the world's largest private terminal operator, and 75% of the U.K.'s Felixstowe Port. In 1994, Hutchison launched Orange, a U.K. digital mobile-phone system. The firm's retail network includes about 380 stores in Hong Kong and Taiwan.

HK$ mil	12/92	12/93	12/94	US$mil 12/94				
Sales	**21,030.0**	**24,748.0**	**30,168.0**	**3,903.2**	P/E Ratio	**18.9**	Price (9/30/95)	**41.90**
Net Income	**3,052.0**	**6,304.0**	**8,021.0**	**1,037.8**	P/B Ratio	**2.7**	52 Wk Hi-Low	**42.10-25.05**
Book Value	**35,843.0**	**49,061.0**	**57,157.0**	**7,384.6**	Yield %	**2.2**	Market Cap	**US$19,620mil**

Address	**Hutchison Hse., 10 Harcourt Rd.**	Tel	**523-0161**	ADR	**HUWHY**	President	--
	Central	Fax	**810-0705**	SEDOL No.	**6448068**	Chairman	**Li Ka-Shing**

Hysan Development

Industry: **Real-Estate Investment**

Hysan Development is active in property investment and development, as well as in capital-market investment. It depends on rentals for the bulk of its income. Although the majority of its holdings are in Hong Kong, the company has a joint venture with First Capital, a subsidiary of Hong Kong banker and property investor Guoco Group, for a 1.63-million-square-foot residential development in Singapore. Hysan also has a 50-50 joint venture with Jebson & Co. to develop a residential property in Hong Kong, and is investing in commercial properties in Shanghai.

HK$ mil	12/92	12/93	12/94	US$mil 12/94				
Sales	**1,220.9**	**1,558.0**	**1,636.3**	**211.7**	P/E Ratio	**17.5**	Price (9/30/95)	**18.55**
Net Income	**980.2**	**1,501.7**	**1,063.8**	**137.6**	P/B Ratio	**0.6**	52 Wk Hi-Low	**22.65-13.55**
Book Value	**15,703.1**	**29,916.9**	**32,931.9**	**4,254.8**	Yield %	**5.1**	Market Cap	**US$2,405.9mil**

Address	**Caroline Ctr., 28 Yun Ping Rd.**	Tel	**895-5777**	ADR	**HYSNY**	President	--
	Kowloon	Fax	**577-5153**	SEDOL No.	**6449629**	Chairman	**Hon Chiu Lee**

IMC

Industry: **Marine Transportation**

IMC Holdings is a global shipping company. The company owns and operates five Panamax, six Handymax, and eight Handysize cargo vessels. IMC also has 50% interests in two other Panamax ships. The fleet has a total dead weight tonnage of approximately 844,000 tonnes. One more Handymax ship is scheduled for delivery in January 1996. IMC's ships primarily carry dry-bulk freight, mainly grain, coal, iron ore, steel products, and cement. The company also holds a 25% stake in Unithai Shipyard & Engineering, a shipyard operator located in Thailand.

HK$ mil	12/92 *	12/93	12/94	US$mil 12/94				
Sales	**210.9**	**315.7**	**354.7**	**45.9**	P/E Ratio	**12.2**	Price (9/30/95)	**5.00**
Net Income	**66.9**	**121.1**	**154.1**	**19.9**	P/B Ratio	**1.0**	52 Wk Hi-Low	**7.00-4.75**
Book Value	**1,746.1**	**1,792.4**	**1,893.6**	**244.7**	Yield %	**4.0**	Market Cap	**US$242.0mil**

Address	**One Pacific Pl., 88 Queensway**	Tel	**820-1100**	ADR		President	--
	Hong Kong	Fax	**596-0050**	SEDOL No.	**6464202**	Chairman	**Chavalit Tsao**

*Irregular period due to fiscal year change.

Jardine Intl Motors

Industry: **Other Specialty Retailers**

Jardine International Motors sells and services new and used automobiles, with an emphasis on Mercedes-Benz vehicles. It sells approximately 50,000 passenger cars and 1,400 commercial vehicles per year. Its wholly-owned Zung Fu and 49%-owned Southern Star Motor subsidiaries are the sole Mercedes-Benz distributors in Hong Kong and southern China, respectively. Jardine International Motors also has dealerships and distribution networks in Australia, the United States, the United Kingdom, Macao, Malaysia, France, and Japan. Jardine Matheson has a 75% stake in the firm.

$ mil	12/92	12/93	12/94	US$mil 12/94				
Revenues	**910.9**	**927.4**	**1,574.6**	**1,574.6**	P/E Ratio	**6.3**	Price (9/30/95)	**8.40**
Net Income	**59.5**	**73.2**	**81.5**	**81.5**	P/B Ratio	**1.9**	52 Wk Hi-Low	**10.70-7.20**
Book Value	**141.8**	**219.4**	**270.6**	**270.6**	Yield %	**0.1**	Market Cap	**US$518.7mil**

Address	**Bonaventure Hse., Leighton Rd.**	Tel	**895-7288**	ADR		Managing Director	**A. Nightingale / R. Lee**
	Quarry Bay	Fax	**890-7017**	SEDOL No.	**6990008**	Chairman	**Simon Keswick**

Johnson Electric

Industry: **Electrical Components & Equipment**

Johnson Electric Holdings designs, manufactures, and markets micromotors. Its main clients are makers of automobile components and home and personal-care appliances. Automotive applications for micromotors include climate-control and engine-management systems. The firm's motors are also used in kitchen appliances, hand-held tools, toys, and business machines such as word processors. Johnson Electric has wholly-owned manufacturing subsidiaries in Germany, Hong Kong, Thailand, Switzerland, and China. Exports to North America and Europe represent 51% of sales.

HK$ mil	03/93	03/94	03/95	US$mil 03/95				
Sales	**1,478.4**	**1,506.9**	**1,942.7**	**251.3**	P/E Ratio	**17.3**	Price (9/30/95)	**15.40**
Net Income	**331.6**	**338.3**	**338.7**	**43.8**	P/B Ratio	**2.2**	52 Wk Hi-Low	**21.90-14.60**
Book Value	**2,137.7**	**2,349.3**	**2,717.2**	**351.5**	Yield %	**1.6**	Market Cap	**US$759.4mil**

Address **14-16 Lee Chung St.**
Chai Wan
Tel **556-8211**
Fax **897-2054**
ADR **JELCY**
SEDOL No. **6475873**
Managing Director **P. Wang Shui Chung**
Chairman **Wang Seng Liang**

Kowloon Motor Bus

Industry: **Household Services**

Kowloon Motor Bus operates public buses in Kowloon and the New Territories of Hong Kong. Kowloon Motor Bus operates more than 3,349 licensed public buses servicing 355 bus routes. Most of the buses are double-deckers, and roughly 22% of the buses are air-conditioned. The company carries approximately 977 million passengers a year. The leading Hong Kong property developer Sun Hung Kai Properties holds a 32% stake in the firm. The company's franchise with the government expires in August 1997, and applications have been submitted to extend the agreement 10 years.

HK$ mil	12/92	12/93	12/94	US$mil 12/94				
Sales	**2,774.6**	**2,998.2**	**3,500.1**	**452.9**	P/E Ratio	**2.6**	Price (9/30/95)	**13.85**
Net Income	**330.5**	**321.9**	**2,116.8**	**273.9**	P/B Ratio	**4.0**	52 Wk Hi-Low	**15.70-12.50**
Book Value	**1,059.7**	**1,136.9**	**1,392.9**	**180.0**	Yield %	**5.8**	Market Cap	**US$723.2mil**

Address **No. 1, Po Lun St.,**
Lai Chi Kok, Kowloon
Tel **786-8888**
Fax **745-0300**
ADR
SEDOL No. **6497026**
Managing Director **John Cho Chak Chan**
Chairman **Pak Chuen Woo**

Lai Sun Garment

Industry: **Clothing & Fabrics**

Lai Sun Garment (International) manufactures clothing and invests in real estate. The firm's Lai Sun Development subsidiary invests in and develops properties in Hong Kong and China, accounting for the majority of profits. Its Glynhill International subsidiary holds its hotel interests and its North American property. Lai Sun Garment exports approximately 95% of its garments to the United States. It also operates 50 retail clothing shops in Hong Kong and 10 franchises in China. The firm has a controlling stake in Crocodile Garments, which operates 37 shops in Hong Kong.

HK$ mil	07/92	07/93	07/94	US$mil 07/94				
Sales	**4,612.6**	**3,410.9**	**4,695.9**	**607.5**	P/E Ratio	**3.5**	Price (9/30/95)	**7.90**
Net Income	**598.8**	**738.3**	**580.4**	**75.1**	P/B Ratio	**0.1**	52 Wk Hi-Low	**15.45-7.25**
Book Value	**5,648.5**	**13,327.8**	**16,838.7**	**2,178.4**	Yield %	**10.8**	Market Cap	**US$261.7mil**

Address **680 Cheung Sha Wan Rd.**
Kowloon
Tel **785-6011**
Fax **N/A**
ADR
SEDOL No. **6509802**
Managing Director **Lim Por Yen**
Chairman **Lim Por Yen**

Lei Shing Hong

Industry: **Financial Services - Diversified**

Lei Shing Hong is an investment-holding company for automobile trading, property investment, and general-trading businesses. The company generates 51% of its revenue in China, 24% in Southeast Asia, and 22% in Japan. It generates 85% of its revenue from automobile sales and general trading. The company partially owns five property developers in China, and wholly owns a vehicle-parts distributor in Singapore. Lei Shing Hong also has an agreement with Caterpillar China to distribute Caterpillar products in eastern China. The company is 30%-owned by Victon Investments.

HK$ mil	03/93	03/94	12/94 *	US$mil 12/94				
Revenues	**61.4**	**943.1**	**922.7**	**119.4**	P/E Ratio	**33.6**	Price (9/30/95)	**9.20**
Net Income	**50.6**	**176.6**	**140.8**	**18.2**	P/B Ratio	**5.2**	52 Wk Hi-Low	**10.10-8.70**
Book Value	**263.5**	**791.4**	**918.2**	**118.6**	Yield %	**0.7**	Market Cap	**US$612.4mil**

Address **New World Twr., 18 Queen's Rd.**
Central
Tel **526-1051**
Fax **524-1538**
ADR
SEDOL No. **6774008**
Chief Executive **Chee Kee Leong**
Chairman **Chee Kee Leong**

*Irregular period due to fiscal year change.

Miramar Hotel & Investment

Industry: **Lodging**

Miramar Hotel & Investment manages real estate, restaurants, catering services, and travel agencies. Its main holding is the 542-room Miramar Hotel and Shopping Arcade in Hong Kong. The company's other operations in Hong Kong include travel agencies, a chain of nine restaurants, food catering, and the management of the City Club recreation facility. Miramar's investment and development properties are located in Hong Kong, China, Canada, and the United States. Its interests in China include three hotels, a restaurant chain, laundries, a health spa, and eight villas.

HK$ mil	03/93	03/94	03/95	US$mil 03/95				
Sales	**860.8**	**1,094.3**	**1,103.6**	**142.7**	P/E Ratio	**NMF**	Price (9/30/95)	**16.65**
Net Income	**61.5**	**70.5**	**56.8**	**7.3**	P/B Ratio	**4.1**	52 Wk Hi-Low	**20.00-12.70**
Book Value	**4,402.2**	**14,170.1**	**2,340.4**	**302.8**	Yield %	**0.5**	Market Cap	**US$1,243.3mil**

Address **118-130 Nathan Rd.**
Kowloon
Tel **368-1111**
Fax **736-4975**
ADR
SEDOL No. **6596451**
Managing Director **Albert B.C. Young**
Chairman **Tim Ho**

New Asia Realty & Trust

Industry: **Real-Estate Investment**

New Asia Realty & Trust (formerly Hongkong Realty & Trust) invests in and develops residential, commercial, and industrial properties. The company's portfolio includes interests in approximately 5 million square feet of development property. The firm has a joint venture in Hong Kong with two companies, Sino Land and China Overseas Building Development. New Asia is 42%-controlled by Hong Kong conglomerate Wheelock & Co. In May 1995, Wheelock arranged for Wharf Holdings to trade its Marco Polo Holdings in Singapore for New Asia's land holdings on Hong Kong's Victoria Peak.

HK$ mil	03/93	03/94	03/95	US$mil 03/95				
Sales	**2,947.4**	**1,860.4**	**1,605.1**	**207.6**	P/E Ratio	**6.8**	Price (9/30/95)	**14.55**
Net Income	**1,110.3**	**1,124.9**	**889.3**	**115.0**	P/B Ratio	**0.6**	52 Wk Hi-Low	**19.75-10.20**
Book Value	**8,464.1**	**9,368.4**	**9,548.5**	**1,235.3**	Yield %	**4.9**	Market Cap	**US$684.1mil**

Address **Wheelock Hse., 20 Pedder St. Kowloon** Tel **524-9191** Fax **524-8574** ADR SEDOL No. **6435781** President -- Chairman **William J. Lees**

New World Development

Industry: **Real-Estate Investment**

New World Development is a diversified property group managing more than 869,000 square meters of floor area. Its Asia Terminal joint venture with U.S.-based Sea Land Orient Terminal holds the world's largest multilevel industrial warehouse. The group also holds 47.5% of Asia Television, one of Hong Kong's two licensed stations. The group has two hotel subsidiaries, New World Hotels International and Ramada Hotels & Resorts International; together they own 150 hotels around the world. New World dedicates between 20% and 25% of its assets to development in China.

HK$ mil	06/92	06/93	06/94	US$mil 06/94				
Sales	**12,459.2**	**13,320.1**	**19,557.2**	**2,529.1**	P/E Ratio	**11.2**	Price (9/30/95)	**30.50**
Net Income	**2,363.0**	**3,461.7**	**4,296.3**	**555.6**	P/B Ratio	**1.0**	52 Wk Hi-Low	**31.90-15.25**
Book Value	**30,356.1**	**36,315.9**	**47,733.0**	**6,175.0**	Yield %	**3.5**	Market Cap	**US$6,410.4mil**

Address **New World Twr., 18 Queen's Rd. Central** Tel **523-1056** Fax **810-4673** ADR **NDVLY** SEDOL No. **6633767** Managing Director **Cheng Kar-Shun** Chairman **Cheng Yu-Tung**

Oriental Press

Industry: **Publishing**

Oriental Press Group is Hong Kong's largest Chinese-language newspaper and magazine publisher. It publishes The Oriental Daily News, Hong Kong's best-selling newspaper with daily circulation of 450,000. Other publications include Oriental Sunday, the Sunday version of the Oriental Daily, Eastweek, a consumer magazine, and The Sun Racing Journal, a horse-racing sheet. Oriental Press also publishes an English-language newspaper, Eastern Express. Its property investments include the Capital Center hotel complex in Sydney, and Trevelyan House, an office building in London.

HK$ mil	03/93	03/94	03/95	US$mil 03/95				
Sales	**1,192.1**	**1,500.2**	**1,623.1**	**209.9**	P/E Ratio	**12.0**	Price (9/30/95)	**3.35**
Net Income	**420.2**	**471.9**	**405.0**	**52.4**	P/B Ratio	**2.8**	52 Wk Hi-Low	**5.08-2.95**
Book Value	**1,205.9**	**1,548.3**	**1,767.6**	**228.7**	Yield %	**7.2**	Market Cap	**US$629.8mil**

Address **Oriental Press Ctr., 7 Wang Tai Rd. Kowloon Bay, Kowloon** Tel **795-1111** Fax **795-2299** ADR SEDOL No. **6661490** President -- Chairman **Ma Ching Kwan**

Pacific Concord

Industry: **Other Specialty Retailers**

Pacific Concord Holding manufactures consumer products and is active in wholesaling, property development, and telecommunication. Its products include toys, children's clothing, Tempo and Harpo watches, and La Prairie cosmetics. The firm operates seven department stores in China; it plans 23 more department stores, 30 International Children City stores, and several supermarkets by 1998. Pacific Concord has an interest in a Hong Kong residential development joint venture (with Cheung Kong) and holdings in China and Thailand. Exports to China represent 35% of sales.

HK$ mil	12/92	12/93	12/94	US$mil 12/94				
Revenues	**848.8**	**1,291.2**	**863.2**	**111.7**	P/E Ratio	**6.3**	Price (9/30/95)	**1.19**
Net Income	**210.4**	**346.6**	**354.0**	**45.8**	P/B Ratio	**0.5**	52 Wk Hi-Low	**2.63-1.00**
Book Value	**2,551.8**	**5,749.4**	**4,499.6**	**581.3**	Yield %	**3.9**	Market Cap	**US$288.5mil**

Address **Wing On Plz., 62 Mody Rd. Kowloon** Tel **311-6788** Fax **N/A** ADR **PFCHY** SEDOL No. **6666086** Managing Director **Wong Sai Wa** Chairman **Wong Sai Chung**

Peregrine Investments

Industry: **Securities Brokers**

Peregrine Investments Holdings is an investment-banking group. The group's principal activities include investment banking, securities dealing, and investment management. The company is authorized by the Chinese government to act as a dealer in B shares on the Shanghai and Shenzhen exchanges. Its newly formed Peregrine Capital subsidiary in the United States advises American companies on Asian acquisitions and joint ventures. The company owns 51% of Peregrine Sewu Securities, a licensed Indonesian securities firm.

HK$ mil	12/92	12/93	12/94	US$mil 12/94				
Sales	**4,238.0**	**11,438.0**	**28,901.0**	**3,739.3**	P/E Ratio	**9.6**	Price (9/30/95)	**11.60**
Net Income	**676.1**	**855.6**	**650.7**	**84.2**	P/B Ratio	**1.4**	52 Wk Hi-Low	**15.00-7.45**
Book Value	**3,459.6**	**4,100.5**	**4,699.3**	**607.1**	Yield %	**4.3**	Market Cap	**US$833.4mil**

Address **New World Twr., 18 Queen's Rd. Central** Tel **825-1888** Fax **845-9411** ADR **PGIQY** SEDOL No. **6682930** Managing Director **Francis Pak To Leung** Chairman **Philip Tose**

C.P. Pokphand Co.

Industry: **Other Food**

C.P. Pokphand leads a group of agricultural and industrial businesses. In China, its activities include the operation of feed mills, poultry farms, meat-processing plants, and Shanghai's Kentucky Fried Chicken outlets, as well as forging steel and producing automotive air-conditioner compressors. Its Ek Chor Motorcycle joint venture produces approximately 15% of the motorcycles made in China. Pokphand also supplies the feed and poultry markets in Thailand, Indonesia, and Turkey.

$ mil	12/92	12/93	12/94	US$mil 12/94				
Sales	**199.9**	**237.8**	**449.7**	**449.7**	P/E Ratio	**14.5**	Price (9/30/95)	**3.15**
Net Income	**44.3**	**44.3**	**58.5**	**58.5**	P/B Ratio	**3.0**	52 Wk Hi-Low	**3.40-1.67**
Book Value	**178.5**	**261.0**	**286.7**	**286.7**	Yield %	**0.1**	Market Cap	**US$861.0mil**

Address **16 Harcourt Rd.** **Central** Tel **520-1601** Fax **861-2514** ADR **CPPKY** SEDOL No. **6693512** President **Sumet Jiaravanon** Chairman **Dhanin Chearavanont**

Regal Hotels

Industry: **Lodging**

Regal Hotels International Holdings owns and manages hotels in Hong Kong, China and North America. Its properties include the Regal Hongkong Hotel, the Shanghai Hotel, St. Louis' Regal Riverfront Hotel, and Toronto's Regal Constellation Hotel. Regal and an affiliate hold stakes in 22 hotels in the U.S. It operates a joint venture with China's Ministry of Internal Trade to provide management services, training, and consultancy to hotels in China, and is also expanding into restaurants, food, and beverages. Property developer Paliburg International Holdings owns 55% of Regal.

HK$ mil	12/92	12/93	12/94	US$mil 12/94				
Sales	**1,204.3**	**1,428.1**	**1,830.2**	**236.8**	P/E Ratio	**14.0**	Price (9/30/95)	**1.40**
Net Income	**192.8**	**720.5**	**328.3**	**42.5**	P/B Ratio	**0.3**	52 Wk Hi-Low	**2.03-1.30**
Book Value	**6,056.6**	**11,606.0**	**11,746.2**	**1,517.6**	Yield %	**4.3**	Market Cap	**US$526.5mil**

Address **Paliburg Plz., 68 Yee Wo St.** **Causeway Bay** Tel **894-7888** Fax **890-1697** ADR SEDOL No. **6730204** Managing Director **Lo Yuk Sui** Chairman **Lo Yuk Sui**

Semi-Tech (Global)

Industry: **Consumer Electronics**

Semi-Tech (Global) produces consumer electronics through subsidiaries in Japan and Germany and distributes them globally. Its holdings include a 72% stake in Germany's G.M. Pfaff, Europe's largest producer and distributor of industrial and commercial sewing machines, and controlling interests in Japan's Akai Electric and Sansui Electric, home-electronics producers and retailers. Semi-Tech's distribution network includes a 51% stake in Singer, the sewing-machine concern, and extends to 130 countries. Semi-Tech is 42%-owned by Canada's Semi-Tech Corporation.

HK$ mil	01/93	01/94	01/95	US$mil 01/95				
Sales	**9,832.0**	**6,520.0**	**4,187.0**	**541.6**	P/E Ratio	**3.2**	Price (9/30/95)	**11.65**
Net Income	**952.0**	**2,226.0**	**1,194.0**	**154.4**	P/B Ratio	**0.5**	52 Wk Hi-Low	**14.95-11.50**
Book Value	**5,347.0**	**6,670.0**	**7,974.0**	**1,030.2**	Yield %	**7.1**	Market Cap	**US$520.8mil**

Address **2 Exchange Sq., 8 Connaught Pl.** **Central** Tel **524-1043** Fax **845-3558** ADR SEDOL No. **6794891** Chief Executive **James H. Ting** Chairman **James H. Ting**

Shangri-La Asia

Industry: **Lodging**

Shangri-La Asia owns and manages hotels in Hong Kong, China, and southeast Asia. The company operates two hotels in Hong Kong, the Kowloon Shangri-La Hotel and the Island Shangri-La Hotel. It also owns eight in China, three in the Philippines, two in Fiji and one in Indonesia. It is currently involved in development projects for the construction of 12 hotels scheduled to be completed by 1999. The company also has interests in real-estate holdings in China, including a 50% interest in Beijing's China World Trade Center and a 30% interest in the Shanghai Center.

HK$ mil	12/92	12/93	12/94	US$mil 12/94				
Sales	**957.2**	**1,187.2**	**1,504.4**	**194.6**	P/E Ratio	**13.8**	Price (9/30/95)	**8.50**
Net Income	**222.4**	**472.9**	**632.0**	**81.8**	P/B Ratio	**0.8**	52 Wk Hi-Low	**9.80-7.90**
Book Value	**5,984.1**	**9,015.3**	**11,043.9**	**1,426.9**	Yield %	**3.5**	Market Cap	**US$1,164.6mil**

Address **Bank of China Twr., 1 Garden Rd.** **Central** Tel **525-9146** Fax **523-8842** ADR SEDOL No. **6771032** Managing Director **Paul J.C. Bush** Chairman **Tai Fung Liu**

Shun Tak Holdings

Industry: **Marine Transportation**

Shun Tak Holdings (previously Shun Tak Enterprises) runs transportation, property, and hospitality businesses. Its property holdings are located in Hong Kong, China, Australia, and Macao. The firm's Far East Hydrofoil Company holds a 75% share of the Hong Kong-Macao ferry market. Shun Tak owns 50% of the 433-room Mandarin Hotel and 34.9% of the 208-room Westin Resort, both located in Macao. The firm also has a 5% interest in Sociedade de Turismo e Diversoes de Macao (STDM), a diversified tourism and leisure conglomerate that holds Macao's only casino license.

HK$ mil	12/92	12/93	12/94	US$mil 12/94				
Sales	**1,662.4**	**1,859.3**	**1,872.8**	**242.3**	P/E Ratio	**12.2**	Price (9/30/95)	**6.10**
Net Income	**324.2**	**719.8**	**721.4**	**93.3**	P/B Ratio	**1.9**	52 Wk Hi-Low	**7.00-3.63**
Book Value	**2,558.4**	**4,136.7**	**4,677.3**	**604.3**	Yield %	**5.3**	Market Cap	**US$1,135.5mil**

Address **Shun Tak Ctr., 200 Connaught Rd.** **Central** Tel **859-3111** Fax **858-2964** ADR **SHTGY** SEDOL No. **6806633** Managing Director **Ambrose So** Chairman **Stanley Ho**

Sime Darby Hong Kong

Industry: **Other Specialty Retailers**

Sime Darby Hong Kong (SDHK) distributes motor vehicles and construction equipment. The passenger cars it distributes come from such manufacturers as Mitsubishi, BMW, Ford, Suzuki, and Alfa Romeo. SDHK's network of showrooms and service centers has 23 locations throughout Hong Kong, and one in China. Its construction-equipment division distributes Caterpillar products in Hong Kong and China. The company's other operations include manufacturing packaging products, rice trading, printing, and providing travel services. Malaysia's Sime Darby holds a 75% stake in SDHK.

HK$ mil	06/92	06/93	06/94	US$mil 06/94				
Revenues	**4,551.2**	**5,562.4**	**7,312.9**	**945.7**	P/E Ratio	**7.7**	Price (9/30/95)	**9.35**
Net Income	**377.5**	**694.2**	**562.9**	**72.8**	P/B Ratio	**4.8**	52 Wk Hi-Low	**12.00-8.10**
Book Value	**781.9**	**797.1**	**898.6**	**116.2**	Yield %	**11.3**	Market Cap	**US$563.9mil**

Address **Hennessy Ctr., 500 Hennessy Rd.** Tel **895-0777** ADR Managing Director **John Hickman Bell**
Causeway Bay Fax **890-5896** SEDOL No. **6808844** Chairman **Tun Ismail**

Sino Land

Industry: **Real-Estate Investment**

Sino Land is an investment-holding company with interests in property development and investment. Its property portfolio, including developments held for sale and sites kept for rental, consists of nearly 13 million square feet of gross floor area. Residential properties account for roughly 34% of this land, commerial space for 30%, and industrial sites for 25%. The majority of the firm's property is in Hong Kong, but 22% of it is in China and Singapore. In March 1995, the firm spun off its hotel operations into a separately listed company in which it holds no interest.

HK$ mil	06/92	06/93	06/94	US$mil 06/94				
Sales	**3,672.0**	**1,800.0**	**3,655.1**	**472.7**	P/E Ratio	**7.3**	Price (9/30/95)	**5.30**
Net Income	**1,164.1**	**900.6**	**1,476.7**	**191.0**	P/B Ratio	**1.1**	52 Wk Hi-Low	**8.27-4.58**
Book Value	**8,374.6**	**11,770.5**	**10,642.3**	**1,376.8**	Yield %	**4.5**	Market Cap	**US$1,681.3mil**

Address **Tsim Sha Tsui Ctr., Salisbury Rd.** Tel **721-8388** ADR **SNLAY** President **--**
Tsim Sha Tsui, Kowloon Fax **723-5901** SEDOL No. **6810429** Chairman **Robert Ng Chee Siong**

South China Morning Post

Industry: **Publishing**

South China Morning Post Holdings (SCMP) prints, publishes, and distributes newspapers. Its Morning Post, Hong Kong's dominant English-language newspaper, has a daily circulation of 102,000. Newspaper and magazine printing and publishing contribute 90% of turnover. SCMP markets its International Weekly Edition in Canada and the western U.S. It holds a 15% stake in Post Publishing, producer of the Bangkok Post. SCMP also owns 27% of Asia Magazines. Wah Kiu Yat Po, a Chinese-language newspaper in which the firm had a 19.8% stake, shut down in January 1995.

HK$ mil	06/92	06/93	06/94	US$mil 06/94				
Sales	**921.6**	**1,041.2**	**1,221.0**	**157.9**	P/E Ratio	**12.2**	Price (9/30/95)	**4.58**
Net Income	**531.7**	**586.4**	**564.1**	**72.9**	P/B Ratio	**2.3**	52 Wk Hi-Low	**5.05-4.03**
Book Value	**2,714.1**	**2,806.0**	**3,010.1**	**389.4**	Yield %	**6.6**	Market Cap	**US$887.8mil**

Address **Tong Chong St.** Tel **565-2222** ADR **SCHPY** CEO **Lindley John Holloway**
Quarry Bay Fax **565-9833** SEDOL No. **6824657** Chairman **Kuok Hock Nien**

Stelux

Industry: **Apparel Retailers**

Stelux has operations in real estate, optical retailing and wholesaling, and watch manufacturing and retailing. The firm derives 79% of profits from real-estate operations. It has an 11% stake in Thai real-estate developer Bangkok Land; it also owns Kowloon's Ambassador Hotel. Stelux operates roughly 120 City Chain watch stores and 60 Optical 88 eyewear stores in Hong Kong, Macau, Thailand, Singapore, Taiwan, and China. It exports watches to Europe and North America, and produces watch components in Hong Kong, Japan, Switzerland, and China.

HK$ mil	03/93	03/94	03/95	US$mil 03/95				
Revenues	**1,538.1**	**1,733.4**	**1,670.0**	**216.0**	P/E Ratio	**34.2**	Price (9/30/95)	**2.05**
Net Income	**315.6**	**327.2**	**56.6**	**7.3**	P/B Ratio	**N/A**	52 Wk Hi-Low	**3.30-1.84**
Book Value	**3,751.6**	**4,196.3**	**-9,999.3**	**-1,293.6**	Yield %	**1.5**	Market Cap	**US$248.3mil**

Address **15 Queen's Rd.** Tel **327-8261** ADR Managing Director **Wong Chong Po**
Central Fax **352-0188** SEDOL No. **6864448** Chairman **Wong Chue Meng**

Sun Hung Kai & Co.

Industry: **Securities Brokers**

Sun Hung Kai & Co. is an investment-holding and trading company. Its activities include insurance, stockbroking, and fund management. The insurance arm is among the five largest independent brokers in Hong Kong. The group's Jakarta operation is licensed for securities trading and underwriting in China. It has an interest in investment holding company SHK Hong Kong Industries and property developer Tian An China. The group has branches in Shanghai and Shenzhen, offices in London and New York, and operations in the Philippines, Thailand, Singapore, and Malaysia.

HK$ mil	12/92	12/93	12/94	US$mil 12/94				
Sales	**739.9**	**919.9**	**640.6**	**82.9**	P/E Ratio	**5.0**	Price (9/30/95)	**2.30**
Net Income	**324.9**	**410.2**	**315.1**	**40.8**	P/B Ratio	**0.7**	52 Wk Hi-Low	**4.25-2.28**
Book Value	**1,581.0**	**2,099.2**	**2,172.4**	**280.7**	Yield %	**10.9**	Market Cap	**US$205.8mil**

Address **Admiralty Ctr., 18 Harcourt Rd.** Tel **822-5678** ADR **SHGKY** Managing Director **Yip Lai Shing**
Central Fax **822-5664** SEDOL No. **6859789** Chairman **Tony Fung Wing Cheung**

Sun Hung Kai Properties

Industry: **Home Construction**

Sun Hung Kai Properties is a leading Hong Kong property developer. The company's portfolio is primarily composed of shopping centers, luxury residences, and parking garages. Its holdings also include small residential units, offices, and industrial buildings. Most of the company's retail portfolio is located in the outlying new territories. The group has expanded its activities into China, but has pledged to limit its interests there to less than 10% of its total investments. Sun Hung Kai's Hong Kong land holdings total approximately 40 million square feet.

HK$ mil	06/92	06/93	06/94	US$mil 06/94				
Sales	**10,657.0**	**13,475.0**	**17,780.0**	**2,299.2**	P/E Ratio	**16.5**	Price (9/30/95)	**62.75**
Net Income	**4,681.0**	**6,692.0**	**8,819.0**	**1,140.4**	P/B Ratio	**1.5**	52 Wk Hi-Low	**62.75-38.10**
Book Value	**39,972.0**	**57,930.0**	**95,702.0**	**12,380.6**	Yield %	**3.1**	Market Cap	**US$18,870mil**

Address	**30 Harbor Rd.**	Tel	**891-2111**	ADR	**SUHKY**	President	**Lee Shau-kee**
	Wanchai	Fax	**834-5862**	SEDOL No.	**6859927**	Chairman	**Walter Kwok**

Swire Pacific

Industry: **Conglomerates**

Swire Pacific is active in aviation, real estate, oil, shipping, and insurance. Major holdings include Cathay Pacific (52%) and Hong Kong United Dockyards (50%). Its wholly-owned Swire Properties owns or is developing more than 11 million square feet of office, retail, industrial, and residential properties in Hong Kong. Other Asian-Pacific subsidiaries bottle Coca-Cola and Schweppes products, sell Reebok shoes and Volvo automobiles, and operate support vessels for the offshore oil industry. Exports to North America and Southeast Asia each represent 6% of sales.

HK$ mil	12/92	12/93	12/94	US$mil 12/94				
Sales	**38,924.4**	**40,763.0**	**47,627.0**	**6,162.1**	P/E Ratio M	**17.5**	Price (9/30/95) M	**61.25**
Net Income	**4,418.6**	**4,658.0**	**5,561.0**	**719.5**	P/B Ratio M	**1.4**	52 Wk Hi-Low M	**63.00-38.30**
Book Value	**45,813.9**	**61,094.0**	**71,013.0**	**9,174.8**	Yield % M	**2.3**	Market Cap M	**US$7,693.1mil**

Address	**Swire Hse., 9 Connaught Rd.**	Tel	**840-8869**	ADR	**SWRAY**	Managing Director	**H.J. Conybeare**
	Central	Fax	**845-5445**	SEDOL No.	**6867748**	Chairman	**P.D.A. Sutch**

M=Multiple issues in index; reflects most active.

Tai Cheung

Industry: **Lodging**

Tai Cheung Holdings is one of Hong Kong's smaller property developers to trade through ADRs. The company specializes in developing office and retail space in the colony, though it also has several ongoing projects in Santa Monica, California. The firm has a 35% stake in the Sheraton-Hong Kong Hotel. As of March 1994, the company reported 13 properties held for development or sale: 11 in Hong Kong and two in California. The company planned to have 943,000 square feet of space coming to market in calendar 1995, 747,000 in 1996, and 430,000 in 1997.

HK$ mil	03/93	03/94	03/95	US$mil 03/95				
Sales	**912.1**	**1,520.2**	**694.6**	**89.8**	P/E Ratio	**4.8**	Price (9/30/95)	**6.80**
Net Income	**464.5**	**1,050.6**	**878.8**	**113.7**	P/B Ratio	**0.9**	52 Wk Hi-Low	**10.85-5.95**
Book Value	**2,557.9**	**5,143.9**	**4,438.9**	**574.2**	Yield %	**6.2**	Market Cap	**US$543.2mil**

Address	**3A Chater Rd.**	Tel	**532-2688**	ADR	**CAICY**	Managing Director	**Ivy Sau Ching Chan**
	Central	Fax	**810-4108**	SEDOL No.	**6869852**	Chairman	**David Pun Chan**

Television Broadcasts

Industry: **Broadcasting**

Television Broadcasts operates television-broadcast, -production, and -licensing businesses. Its Cantonese-language Jade channel commands an average audience share of about 75% in Hong Kong, while its Pearl channel maintains a 97% English-language audience share. The company's TVB Superchannel broadcasts Mandarin-language programs via cable to Taiwan. Its licensing business distributes programs in North America, Australia, and Europe. The company is launching a new Mandarin-language sports, special-events, and current-affairs channel for the Taiwanese market.

HK$ mil	12/92	12/93	12/94	US$mil 12/94				
Sales	**1,824.8**	**2,071.1**	**2,650.3**	**342.9**	P/E Ratio	**20.5**	Price (9/30/95)	**31.10**
Net Income	**365.6**	**519.7**	**639.1**	**82.7**	P/B Ratio	**11.9**	52 Wk Hi-Low	**36.30-25.60**
Book Value	**718.5**	**902.3**	**1,099.9**	**142.1**	Yield %	**3.4**	Market Cap	**US$1,689.8mil**

Address	**TV City, Clear Water Bay Rd.**	Tel	**719-7212**	ADR	**TVBSY**	Managing Director	**Kuok Khoon Ho**
	Kowloon	Fax	**581-1300**	SEDOL No.	**6881674**	Chairman	**Run Run Shaw**

Tsim Sha Tsui

Industry: **Real-Estate Investment**

Tsim Sha Tsui Properties is engaged in property development and investment, share investment and dealing, and hotel and restaurant operation. Its principal holding is a 62% equity stake in Hong Kong-based Sino Land, which holds a total of approximately 4.4 million square feet of investment property. Sino Land's major properties include Hong Kong's City Garden Hotel, the Omega Plaza commercial complex, and the 1 May Road luxury apartment complex. Tsim Sha Tsui holds interests in residential, commercial, and industrial properties in Hong Kong, Singapore, and China.

HK$ mil	06/92	06/93	06/94	US$mil 06/94				
Sales	**3,723.0**	**1,851.6**	**3,741.5**	**483.8**	P/E Ratio	**7.6**	Price (9/30/95)	**5.45**
Net Income	**654.4**	**516.4**	**847.3**	**109.6**	P/B Ratio	**0.4**	52 Wk Hi-Low	**7.55-4.78**
Book Value	**6,613.9**	**8,824.8**	**14,837.9**	**1,919.5**	Yield %	**4.4**	Market Cap	**US$866.5mil**

Address	**Tsim Sha Tsui Ctr., Salisbury Rd.**	Tel	**721-8388**	ADR		President	**--**
	Tsim Sha Tsui, Kowloon	Fax	**723-5901**	SEDOL No.	**6813008**	Chairman	**Robert Ng Chee Siong**

Wharf

Industry: **Real-Estate Investment**

Wharf Holdings' four core business areas are property, infrastructure, communication, and hotels. Its property portfolio totals more than 23 million square feet, with projects in Hong Kong, Singapore, China, and the U.S. Its infrastructure interests in Hong Kong include the operation of shipping-container, cruise-liner, and air-cargo terminals, as well as ferry services and the Cross-Harbour Tunnel. Wharf also owns U.S.-based Omni Hotels, with 50 hotels worldwide, and Wharf Cable, licensed to be the sole distributor of cable television in Hong Kong until October 1996.

	HK$ mil 12/92	12/93	12/94	US$mil 12/94				
Sales	**4,391.6**	**6,266.2**	**8,143.6**	**1,053.6**	P/E Ratio	**16.9**	Price (9/30/95)	**24.10**
Net Income	**2,051.4**	**2,725.7**	**3,100.6**	**401.2**	P/B Ratio	**0.6**	52 Wk Hi-Low	**31.70-21.25**
Book Value	**44,749.9**	**78,712.9**	**82,929.3**	**10,714.4**	Yield %	**3.9**	Market Cap	**US$6,746.8mil**

Address **19 Des Voeux Rd.** **Central** Tel **738-8222** Fax **736-3003** ADR **WARFY** SEDOL No. **6435576** President -- Chairman **Gonzaga W.J. Li**

Wheelock & Co.

Industry: **Overseas Trading**

Wheelock & Co is principally engaged in retail and distribution, financial services, and property development. In 1994, Hong Kong operations provided more than 90% of turnover and operating profit, but the company has sizable assets in Singapore and China. The group holds a 45% equity stake in Wharf Holdings and a 25% stake in Lane Crawford International. Other subsidiaries include New Asia Realty and Trust, Climax International, and Wheelock NatWest.

	HK$ mil 03/93	03/94	03/95	US$mil 03/95				
Sales	**2,205.2**	**2,226.1**	**2,432.9**	**314.7**	P/E Ratio	**10.1**	Price (9/30/95)	**11.55**
Net Income	**1,468.3**	**2,204.6**	**2,306.0**	**298.3**	P/B Ratio	**0.5**	52 Wk Hi-Low	**17.30-10.40**
Book Value	**24,100.8**	**40,638.4**	**42,332.9**	**5,476.4**	Yield %	**3.2**	Market Cap	**US$3,015.7mil**

Address **Wheelock Hse., 20 Pedder St.** **Central** Tel **N/A** Fax **N/A** ADR **WHELY** SEDOL No. **6981488** Managing Director **Raymong C.O. Tse** Chairman **Peter K.C. Woo**

Wing Lung Bank

Industry: **Banks - Regional**

Wing Lung Bank is one of the oldest local Chinese banks in Hong Kong. It operates banking and financial services in Hong Kong for commercial and industrial clients. The bank controls assets of approximately HK$33 billion. Wing Lung's services include securities brokerage, insurance underwriting and brokerage, trustee and nominee services, and investment holding. The bank operates 28 banking offices in Hong Kong. Its also operated one overseas office in Los Angeles and one representative office in Guangzhou, China.

	HK$ mil 12/92	12/93	12/94	US$mil 12/94				
Revenues	**N/A**	**N/A**	**N/A**	**N/A**	P/E Ratio	**11.4**	Price (9/30/95)	**43.10**
Net Income	**391.1**	**472.8**	**611.4**	**79.1**	P/B Ratio	**3.5**	52 Wk Hi-Low	**48.20-33.75**
Book Value	**1,436.2**	**1,716.4**	**2,006.7**	**259.3**	Yield %	**3.3**	Market Cap	**US$899.0mil**

Address **45 Des Voeux Rd.** **Central** Tel **826-8333** Fax **810-0592** ADR SEDOL No. **6972211** Managing Director **Che-shum Chung** Chairman **Michael Po-ko Wu**

Wing On International

Industry: **Retailers - Broadline**

Wing On Company International has operations in retail stores, restaurants, and property investment. It owns 12 Wing On department stores, five Muji specialty stores, and four restaurants in Hong Kong. It has joint ventures to develop and operate department stores in Singapore and China, as well as property-development and investment operations in the United States and New Zealand. It owns 40% of Seiyu department store in Singapore, a joint venture with Japanese retailer Seiyu. Among its property interests are 88% stakes in two commercial developments in Houston.

	HK$ mil 12/92	12/93	12/94	US$mil 12/94				
Revenues	**2,570.3**	**2,845.2**	**2,683.8**	**347.2**	P/E Ratio	**1.9**	Price (9/30/95)	**7.65**
Net Income	**309.0**	**269.4**	**1,198.2**	**155.0**	P/B Ratio	**0.3**	52 Wk Hi-Low	**11.55-7.00**
Book Value	**3,674.7**	**5,676.0**	**6,719.5**	**868.2**	Yield %	**7.2**	Market Cap	**US$293.0mil**

Address **Wing On Ctr., 211 Des Vouex Rd.** **Central** Tel **523-4091** Fax **868-0118** ADR SEDOL No. **6972244** Managing Director **Lester Kwok** Chairman **Angela Chan**

Winsor Industrial

Industry: **Clothing & Fabrics**

Winsor Industrial is a textile and clothing manufacturer with factories in Hong Kong and Malaysia. The company's operations include cotton and wool spinning, bleaching, and dyeing; cotton weaving; wool knitting; and the production of finished garments. Plants are located in Hong Kong, Macao, China, Malaysia, and Myanmar (Burma). Winsor's principal markets are Hong Kong (roughly 40% of sales) and North America (30% of sales and 50% of exports); it also exports to Europe and Asia. Winsor also has minor real-estate interests in Hong Kong, Singapore, and China.

	HK$ mil 03/93	03/94	03/95	US$mil 03/95				
Sales	**2,423.1**	**2,143.7**	**2,137.2**	**276.4**	P/E Ratio	**13.3**	Price (9/30/95)	**7.60**
Net Income	**262.1**	**171.4**	**148.2**	**19.2**	P/B Ratio	**0.7**	52 Wk Hi-Low	**10.90-7.45**
Book Value	**2,710.7**	**2,918.0**	**2,682.4**	**347.0**	Yield %	**7.2**	Market Cap	**US$255.3mil**

Address **Yu To Sang Bldg., 37 Queen's Rd.** **Central** Tel **810-0668** Fax **810-1199** ADR **WIINY** SEDOL No. **6972909** Managing Director **W.H. Chou** Chairman **T.K. Ann**

Indonesia

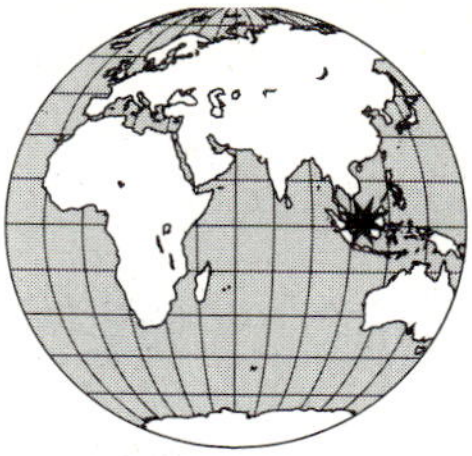

Indonesia

Peter Halesworth, Jakarta

Local Trading Hours	Time Difference from New York	Population (Est. 12/94)
9:30-12:00, 1:30-4:00 Mon.-Thurs. 9:30-11:30, 2:00-4:00 Friday	12 hours ahead of EST	192,000,000

There are two views of Indonesia's young stock market. An unkind view is that the shares of only around 20 of 230 listed companies are worth buying. Most others are too illiquid to unload in bearish times, and few Indonesians invest in domestic companies listed on the Jakarta Stock Exchange (JSX).

A second view is more benevolent. Indonesia, by sheer force of its population and rich resources, is a mega-economy in the making. The 50-year-old nation hungers for investment and needs a total of around 815 trillion rupiah through 1999. President Suharto has made it clear that capital markets must play a big role in mobilizing investment funds to continue the economic development of the world's fourth most-populous nation into a newly industrialized country.

Gross domestic product (GDP) is seen growing by an annual average of 7.1% through 1999, privatizations of large state-owned companies are in the pipeline, and the economy continues to open up to record amounts of direct foreign investment.

As of July 1995, the JSX's total market capitalization hit $60.10 billion, up 13% from $53 billion as of December 1994, just a fraction or around 35% of the nation's GDP, which shows plenty of room for growth compared with neighbors in the region.

For example, as of 1994 Malaysia's market capitalization was 283% of its GDP, Singapore's 217%, and Thailand's 94%. In terms of market capitalization, at the end of 1994 Indonesia had the seventh-largest of the eight emerging Asian markets, just edging out China, according to a World Bank study.

In preparation for future growth, in May 1995 the JSX moved into a new building and instituted a computerized order-matching system to replace the white boards where floor traders once met and made their deals.

Dow Jones Indonesia Equity Market Index Performance

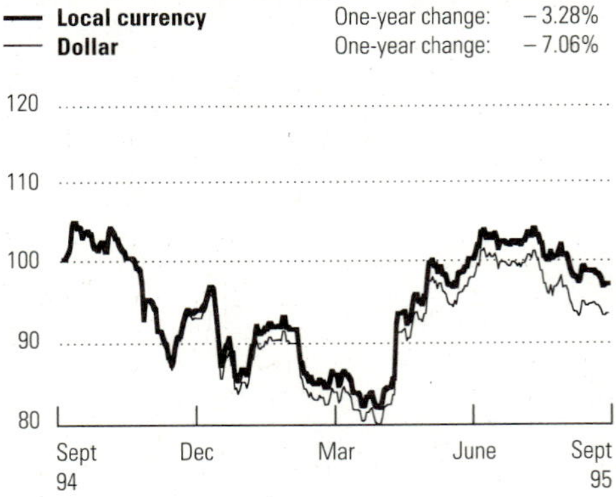

The scene at the JSX is tamer now, and also more efficient. The hurly-burly of big elbowed, marker-wielding traders rushing from board to board is gone, supplanted by traders seated studiously in front of computers. The new system has expanded the capacity of the JSX's transactions to around 12,000 an hour from a peak of around 5,000 daily under the old manual system.

Trading hours in the morning and afternoon sessions were extended to overlap with

Gross Domestic Product (94)	Three-Year Average GDP Growth (92-94)	Main Industries	Consumer Price Index (93-94)	Monetary Unit	Exchange Rate (9/95)
$173.2 billion	6.7%	Agriculture, manufacturing, oil and natural gas extraction, wood products, tourism	+ 9.3%	Rupiah	Rp2262.44 to US$1.00

investors in Hong Kong during the morning session, and also with investors in London during the afternoon session.

This internationalization of the JSX shows the exchange has come a long way since late 1987, when the Indonesian government injected some life into the sleepy stock exchange by allowing foreigners to buy shares of its 24 listed companies, removed the 4% limit on daily share price fluctuations, and relaxed listing requirements.

Prior to 1987, Indonesia's capital markets were at the mercy of political upheavals, which inevitably brought monetary instability and the downfall of fledgling exchanges. Dutch colonists as early as the 17th century informally traded shares in the opium regie of the Dutch East Indies Company. The first formal stock exchange, where stocks and bonds were traded, was organized in Jakarta in 1912 but was shut down in 1942 when the Japanese army forced out the Dutch and occupied Indonesia through 1945.

Trading in sovereign and bank bonds resumed after Indonesian independence in 1949, but the government's nationalization of Dutch companies in 1958 and triple-digit inflation in the 1960s again felled Indonesia's capital markets. Political turmoil in 1965 led to the emergence of President Suharto's New Order government, which reopened the Jakarta stock market in 1977.

By 1988, the Jakarta exchange had a mere 24 listed companies and trading was moribund. By 1990, the liberalization and opening of the stock market to foreign trade attracted 123 companies to list with a total market capitalization of 13.140 trillion rupiah.

Ten Largest Capitalized Companies
as of 9/30/95

Stock	Market Cap. US$Mil
Indocement Tunggal	4,402,159.9
HM Sampoerna	4,196,796.4
Astra International	1,387,389.3
Bank Internasional Indonesia	1,090,487.9
Barito Pacific Timber	1,036,491.6
Kalbe Farma	864,022.9
Indah Kiat Paper & Pulp	810,828.5
Modern Photo Film	766,431.4
Gudang Garam	765,400.2
Lippobank	678,657.8

Companies on the JSX are organized into nine broad sectors, with subsectors of industry, consumer goods and finance accounting for a majority of the trading volume and offering investors the best opportunities for liquidity.

Indonesia has 22 of its 234 private banks listed, several of which are key holdings of foreign institutional investors, who dominate trade on the JSX with around 70% of the market's daily transactions. Also regarded as constituent stocks for investors in Indonesia's stock market are several large consumer shares which are considered plays on the nation's robust economic growth and expanding middle class, as well as infrastructure and cement companies which should benefit from massive investment.

To buy shares in Indonesia, brokers charge a maximum fee of 1% of the total value of the transaction, which also includes a value-added tax (VAT). The government also charges a 0.07% fee for the transaction. On the sale of shares, the government charges a 0.1% sales tax.

The Indonesian currency, the rupiah, is fully convertible with major international currencies. The central bank, Bank Indonesia, through a crawling peg, manages a steady annual depreciation of the rupiah of 3%-5% versus the U.S. dollar to help keep the price of its growing non-oil and gas exports competitive on international markets.

However, the rupiah has been devalued three times in the past 20 years, with the most recent in 1986. Devaluations of the rupiah were mostly in response to sharp declines in oil prices. In 1983, around 75% of Indonesia's total exports were in oil and gas. By 1995, it had fallen to 25%, with 75% taken up by manufacturing. Although rumors of devaluation of the rupiah still worry some investors, most analysts believe it is highly unlikely and would be counterproductive considering Indonesia's huge investment needs.

Foreign investors are barred, under Indonesian law, from owning more than 49% of a listed company. Those who want to invest in a company which already is 49% foreign owned must buy shares from other foreigners on the foreign board. These shares usually trade at a premium to those on the regular board.

The capital markets regulator, Bapepam, is in the midst of an overhaul. A new capital markets law, the first to be legislated since 1952, is expected to be approved by Indonesia's parliament at the end of 1995. The new law is expected to give Bapepam for the first time the authority to investigate possible violations. Currently this is done exclusively by police.

Market players hope the long-awaited capital markets law will provide minority shareholders better protection, require full disclosure by listed companies and lead to what will be regarded as a more even playing field for minority shareholders.

Such reform is the product of success and has the JSX playing catch-up with the rest of the world after a spectacular bull run in 1993. That sent the Jakarta composite index soaring by 115% and landed the fledgling market in the international investor limelight.

Reform is not just for foreign consumption, however. Stronger surveillance and enforcement also will give more comfort to local investors. There are only around 200,000 domestic shareholders of listed companies in Indonesia, and many of these local shareholders are inactive players.

As foreign institutional investors dominate the stock market, the lack of a base of local players came sharply into focus after the Mexican peso and Barings crises caused international investors to withdraw from emerging markets such as Indonesia — leaving an important mobilizer of investment funds dangerously beholden to the whims of fickle international fund managers.

Expected to help boost domestic investor participation is a new pension fund law enacted in 1993, which expanded the amount of investment capital from domestic funds to the market. Another recent step forward is the government's raising of the limit of investment domestic pension funds can make in equities, to 10% from 5%. Studies estimate only around 5% of all Indonesian pension fund assets, around $7 billion, are invested in the stock market. Most pension fund holdings are invested in bonds, real estate and time deposits.

Argha Karya Prima Industry

Industry: **Containers & Packaging**

Argha Karya Prima Industry manufactures films for flexible packaging. The company makes 52 types of film for packaging of products ranging from candies, snacks, and cigarettes, to graphic-arts materials, audiovisual tapes, plywood overlays, and cable wraps. Argha Karya is also involved in packaging laminating, printing, and delivery. It has subsidiaries in Hong Kong and the United States, as well as an affiliate in Malaysia. Argha Karya exports packaging products to Asia; North, Central and South America; Africa; Australia; New Zealand; and the United Kingdom.

	Rp bil 12/92	12/93	12/94	US$mil 12/94				
Sales	**124.9**	**163.0**	**189.9**	**88.0**	P/E Ratio	**10.6**	Price (9/30/95)	**1,925.00**
Net Income	**12.9**	**22.7**	**23.7**	**11.0**	P/B Ratio	**1.7**	52 Wk Hi-Low	**3,175.0-1,550.0**
Book Value	**132.8**	**152.3**	**152.3**	**70.3**	Yield %	**2.9**	Market Cap	**US$112.3mil**

Address	**Jl. Jendral Sudirman**	Tel	**021-570-3778**	ADR		President	**Ibrahim Risjad**
	Jakarta 12910	Fax	**021-251-2068**	SEDOL No.	**6048952**	Chairman	**Henry Pribadi**

Astra International

Industry: **Other Specialty Retailers**

Astra International is a holding company with interests in 70 subsidiaries and affiliates. It has investments in the automotive, financial-services, heavy-machinery, forestry-products, and agriculture industries. Astra derives 75% of revenues from the automotive industry and supplies 56% of all automobiles sold in Indonesia, primarily Toyota, Daihatsu, BMW, Peugeot, and Isuzu cars; Nissan diesel trucks; and Honda motorcycles. Its Bank Universal subsidiary has 32 branches in 13 cities in Indonesia and offers consumer credit, leasing, and insurance services.

	Rp bil 12/92	12/93	12/94	US$mil 12/94				
Revenues	**5,017.4**	**6,415.3**	**9,506.9**	**4,404.3**	P/E Ratio	**10.9**	Price (9/30/95)	**2,700.00**
Net Income	**81.5**	**132.4**	**279.0**	**129.3**	P/B Ratio	**1.3**	52 Wk Hi-Low	**3,550.0-2,025.0**
Book Value	**1,282.0**	**1,390.2**	**2,336.0**	**1,078.7**	Yield %	**3.0**	Market Cap	**US$1,387.4mil**

Address	**Jl. Ir. H. Juanda No.22**	Tel	**021-231-2555**	ADR		Managing Director	**T.P. Rachmat**
	Jakarta 10120	Fax	**021-345-3358**	SEDOL No.	**6060666**	Chairman	**A.R. Ramly**

Bank Bali

Industry: **Banks - Regional**

Bank Bali is an individual, commercial, and investment bank with a network of 106 retail branches and 180 ATMs in Indonesia. Bank Bali's subsidiaries include a consumer-financing and -leasing firm, Bali Tunas Finance, an investment-advisory firm, Bali Securities, and Bali International Finance, a deposit-taking company in Hong Kong. Bank Bali also has two general-insurance affiliates and one insurance-brokerage affiliate. The bank has an international network of 255 correspondent banks in 92 countries, as well as branch offices in Los Angeles and on the Cayman Islands.

	Rp bil 12/92	12/93	12/94	US$mil 12/94				
Revenues	**579.3**	**527.3**	**653.1**	**302.6**	P/E Ratio	**12.7**	Price (9/30/95)	**3,650.00**
Net Income	**57.5**	**61.6**	**72.4**	**33.6**	P/B Ratio	**2.5**	52 Wk Hi-Low	**5,307.0-3,000.0**
Book Value	**300.5**	**325.4**	**361.2**	**166.8**	Yield %	**4.1**	Market Cap	**US$405.3mil**

Address	**Jl. Jend. Sudirman Kav.27**	Tel	**021-523-7899**	ADR		President	**Rudy Ramli**
	Jakarta 12920	Fax	**N/A**	SEDOL No.	**6075983**	Chairman	**Djaja Ramli**

Bank Internasional Indonesia

Industry: **Banks - Regional**

Bank Internasional Indonesia (BII) is the country's largest private bank by profits and shareholders' equity, and its third-largest bank by assets. It is the 51%-owned flagship bank of the Sinar Mas group, Indonesia's second-largest business conglomerate. The bank offers commercial banking, treasury operations, and credit-card services. BII has 143 branches throughout Indonesia, where it makes about 90% of revenues. It has branch offices in Singapore, the Cayman Islands, and Australia, a depository bank in Hong Kong, and a subsidiary in China.

	Rp bil 12/92	12/93	12/94	US$mil 12/94				
Revenues	**788.1**	**852.6**	**1,094.0**	**506.8**	P/E Ratio	**16.7**	Price (9/30/95)	**7,800.00**
Net Income	**83.2**	**112.4**	**141.9**	**65.7**	P/B Ratio	**2.9**	52 Wk Hi-Low	**8,350.0-4,425.0**
Book Value	**430.5**	**517.7**	**841.9**	**388.8**	Yield %	**1.3**	Market Cap	**US$1,090.5mil**

Address	**Wisma BII, Jl. M.H. Thamrin**	Tel	**021-310-4646**	ADR		President	**Indra Widjaja**
	Jakarta 10350	Fax	**021-390-2228**	SEDOL No.	**6076931**	Chairman	**Kamardy Arief**

Barito Pacific Timber

Industry: **Forest Products**

Barito Pacific Timber (BPT) is the largest plywood producer and exporter in Indonesia. It is the flagship company of the Barito Pacific Group, one of Indonesia's most-powerful business conglomerates. BPT currently accounts for almost 10% of worldwide trade in hardwood plywood. Its other products include block board, particle board, sawn timber, adhesives, and woodworking products. It controls forest concessions for 2.2 million hectares of forest area in Indonesia. BPT owns 36% of Sumalindo Lestari Jaya, the only other listed plywood company in Indonesia.

	Rp bil 12/92	12/93 R	12/94	US$mil 12/94				
Sales	**769.4**	**978.6**	**862.0**	**399.3**	P/E Ratio	**16.0**	Price (9/30/95)	**1,675.00**
Net Income	**79.8**	**310.2**	**147.2**	**68.2**	P/B Ratio	**1.2**	52 Wk Hi-Low	**3,900.0-1,625.0**
Book Value	**546.7**	**1,809.3**	**1,924.0**	**888.4**	Yield %	**4.0**	Market Cap	**US$1,036.5mil**

Address	**Jl. Let. Jend. S. Parman Kav. 62-63**	Tel	**021-530-6711**	ADR		Managing Director	**Joso Abdullah Gotama**
	Jakarta 11410	Fax	**021-530-6680**	SEDOL No.	**6070706**	Chairman	**Prajogo Pangestu**

R=Restated.

BDNI

Industry: **Banks - Regional**

Bank Danang Nasional Indonesia (BDNI) is Indonesia's fourth-largest private bank by assets--which total about 5 billion rupiah--and one of its most profitable. It is the wholly-owned banking arm of diversified tire-making conglomerate Gajah Tunggal. The bank offers both domestic and international lending services at 165 branches. BDNI has a 20% stake in Parma Ventura Indonesia, a venture-capital company run by Prudential Asia. The bank also runs a joint-venture bank with Commercial Bank of Vietnam, and has branch offices in Hong Kong, Los Angeles, and the Philippines.

Rp bil	12/91	12/92	12/93	US$mil 12/93				
Revenues	**565.4**	**672.6**	**756.3**	**358.6**	P/E Ratio	**11.9**	Price (9/30/95)	**2,075.00**
Net Income	**34.0**	**48.2**	**61.5**	**29.2**	P/B Ratio	**1.0**	52 Wk Hi-Low	**2,875.0-1,485.7**
Book Value	**271.2**	**292.2**	**750.3**	**349.6**	Yield %	**6.0**	Market Cap	**US$392.9mil**

Address **Jl., Hayam Wuruk 8**
Jakarta 10120
Tel **021-345-5208**
Fax **021-372-846**
ADR
SEDOL No. **6069964**
President **Sjamsul Nursalim**
Chairman **Makmun Murod**

Branta Mulia

Industry: **Tires & Rubber**

Branta Mulia manufactures tire yarn and cord, and is the largest tire-reinforcement company in the Asia Pacific region. The company operates tire-cord fabric plants in Indonesia, Thailand, and Malaysia, and distributes its tire products to 11 countries on two continents. In a joint venture with Japan's Teijin, it is currently building a polyester-tire-yarn plant in Indonesia that will be operational in October 1996. Branta Mulia has a license from DuPont (U.S.) to manufacture its Nylon-66 tire yarn, and manufacturing agreements with Goodyear (U.S.) and Bridgestone (Japan).

Rp bil	12/92	12/93	12/94	US$mil 12/94				
Sales	**221.4**	**281.9**	**309.0**	**143.1**	P/E Ratio	**13.4**	Price (9/30/95)	**2,900.00**
Net Income	**46.5**	**35.2**	**37.1**	**17.2**	P/B Ratio	**1.9**	52 Wk Hi-Low	**3,800.0-2,575.0**
Book Value	**300.6**	**323.3**	**342.4**	**158.1**	Yield %	**2.8**	Market Cap	**US$288.4mil**

Address **Jl. Jend., Sudirman Kav. 70-71**
Jakarta 12910
Tel **021-570-3778**
Fax **021-251-0210**
ADR
SEDOL No. **6120645**
President **Ibrahim Risjad**
Chairman **Ir. Soekrisman**

Dharmala Intiland

Industry: **Real-Estate Investment**

Dharmala Intiland is a property-development company with commercial, residential, retail, industrial, and hotel properties on the island of Java. Its primary asset is the Wisma Dharmala Sakti, a 24-story office building in Jakarta. Dharmala Intiland also owns two other office buildings and four housing developments in Jakarta. In Surabaya, it owns two housing developments, one apartment building, a convention center, and a three-star hotel. The company also has a joint venture with Singapore Technologies Industrial Corp. to develop a four-star hotel in Surabaya.

Rp bil	12/92	12/93	12/94	US$mil 12/94				
Sales	**44.9**	**146.1**	**252.6**	**117.0**	P/E Ratio	**4.8**	Price (9/30/95)	**1,300.00**
Net Income	**12.2**	**22.6**	**55.4**	**25.7**	P/B Ratio	**0.6**	52 Wk Hi-Low	**3,125.0-1,200.0**
Book Value	**289.8**	**304.6**	**560.7**	**258.9**	Yield %	**16.5**	Market Cap	**US$140.0mil**

Address **Jl. Jend. Sudirman 32**
Jakarta 10220
Tel **021-570-1912**
Fax **021-570-0015**
ADR
SEDOL No. **6268794**
President **Hendro Gondokusumo**
Chairman **Suhargo Gondokusumo**

Duta Anggada Realty

Industry: **Real-Estate Investment**

Duta Anggada Realty is the property-development and -investment arm of the Gunung Sewu Group. Its property portfolio includes office, residential, retail, and hotel properties in Bali and Jakarta, and other Indonesian cities. The firm derives 47% of its rental revenues from eight leasable office properties, including the Bank One Market Center in Dallas. It owns seven housing complexes, which contribute 26% of rental revenues, and six shopping malls (27% of rental revenues). It has a joint venture with Marriott to build a hotel and shopping complex in Jakarta.

Rp bil	12/92	12/93	12/94	US$mil 12/94				
Sales	**39.8**	**52.5**	**78.0**	**36.1**	P/E Ratio	**9.4**	Price (9/30/95)	**1,475.00**
Net Income	**36.4**	**19.6**	**30.5**	**14.1**	P/B Ratio	**1.1**	52 Wk Hi-Low	**2,700.0-1,150.0**
Book Value	**185.9**	**352.3**	**375.3**	**173.3**	Yield %	**3.4**	Market Cap	**US$179.3mil**

Address **Jl. Jend. Sudirman**
Jakarta 12910
Tel **021-520-8000**
Fax **021-520-8100**
ADR
SEDOL No. **6289386**
President **Hartadi Angkosubroto**
Chairman **Dasuki Angkosubroto**

Gadjah Tunggal

Industry: **Tires & Rubber**

Gadjah Tunggal is a tire maker that produces bias and radial tires and tire cord for cars and motorcycles. In Indonesia, it has the top market share for motorcycle tires (80%) and four-wheel-vehicle tires (31%). The company produces 4.2 million four-wheel-vehicle tires and 6.7 million motorcycle tires annually; its marketing and distribution network includes 65 local and 60 worldwide distributors. Gadjah Tunggal has manufacturing joint ventures with Inoue Rubber Company of Japan for motorcycle tires, and with Yokohama Rubber Company (Japan) for four-wheel-vehicle tires.

Rp bil	12/92	12/93	12/94	US$mil 12/94				
Sales	**269.7**	**364.6**	**487.3**	**225.7**	P/E Ratio	**12.0**	Price (9/30/95)	**1,500.00**
Net Income	**36.0**	**46.6**	**90.3**	**41.8**	P/B Ratio	**1.2**	52 Wk Hi-Low	**2,000.0-975.0**
Book Value	**264.4**	**310.0**	**1,004.2**	**463.7**	Yield %	**3.3**	Market Cap	**US$525.1mil**

Address **Jalan Hayam Wuruk 8**
Jakarta 10120
Tel **021-345-9302**
Fax **021-380-4908**
ADR
SEDOL No. **6358480**
President **Makmun Murod**
Chairman **Sjamsul Nursalim**

Gudang Garam

Industry: **Tobacco**

Gudang Garam is the largest clove-cigarette producer in Indonesia, by both output and market share. The company controls 49% of the clove-cigarette market, and has the capacity to produce 90 billion machine-made and 15 billion hand-rolled clove cigarettes annually. Gudang Garam owns three main domestic distributors, and has a marketing network of more than 450,000 retailers throughout Indonesia. It also exports more than 3 billion clove cigarettes. Gudang Garam's wholly-owned Surya Pamenang subsidiary manufactures industrial- and packaging-papers.

Rp bil	12/92 R	12/93	12/94	US$mil 12/94				
Sales	**3,294.8**	**3,874.5**	**4,783.7**	**2,216.2**	P/E Ratio	**34.8**	Price (9/30/95)	**18,000**
Net Income	**149.0**	**159.0**	**248.7**	**115.2**	P/B Ratio	**4.9**	52 Wk Hi-Low	**19,700.0-11,300.0**
Book Value	**1,509.2**	**1,596.0**	**1,770.1**	**817.4**	Yield %	**0.9**	Market Cap	**US$765.4mil**

Address **Jl. Jend. A Yani 79**, **Jakarta 10510**
Tel **021-420-2460**
Fax **021-421-2024**
ADR
SEDOL No. **6665652**
President **Rachman Halim**
Chairman **Imam Soebagio**

R=Restated.

HM Sampoerna

Industry: **Tobacco**

Hanjaya Mandala Sampoerna (HM Sampoerna) is the third-largest producer of hand- and machine-rolled clove cigarettes in Indonesia, where clove cigarettes make up 90% of annual cigarette consumption. It is the fourth-largest producer by market share, with a domestic share of nearly 6%. The company manufactures Indonesia's only low-tar clove cigarette. HM Sampoerna also makes Salem cigarettes for United States tobacco company RJ Reynolds. Its Alfa Retailindo subsidiary runs a network of nine Warehouse Store discount tobacco outlets in major cities throughout Indonesia.

Rp bil	12/92	12/93	12/94	US$mil 12/94				
Sales	**682.2**	**886.4**	**1,353.1**	**641.5**	P/E Ratio	**39.1**	Price (9/30/95)	**21,100**
Net Income	**54.3**	**105.5**	**242.7**	**115.1**	P/B Ratio	**11.1**	52 Wk Hi-Low	**21,650.0-9,000.0**
Book Value	**595.7**	**655.9**	**855.3**	**398.5**	Yield %	**1.7**	Market Cap	**US$4,196.8mil**

Address **Jl. Rungkut Industri Raya 14-18**, **Surabaya 60293**
Tel **031-818-190**
Fax **N/A**
ADR
SEDOL No. **6407887**
President **--**
Chairman **Puerta Sampoerna**

Hadtex Indosyntec

Industry: **Clothing & Fabrics**

Hadtex Indosyntec is Indonesia's fourth-largest textile manufacturer by production. The company produces polyester fiber and fabric for women's garments. It has a textile spinning, weaving, printing, dyeing, and finishing plant in West Java, with an average monthly polyester-fabric output of 5 million yards. Its primary market is Indonesia, but Hadtex also exports to Asia Pacific countries, the Middle East, Europe, North America, and Brazil. Hadtex has textile-weaving operations in China, and runs a worsted-spinning plant in Indonesia with Spinner Stohr of Germany.

Rp bil	12/92	12/93	12/94	US$mil 12/94				
Sales	**N/A**	**N/A**	**N/A**	**N/A**	P/E Ratio	**N/A**	Price (9/30/95)	**1,225.00**
Net Income	**N/A**	**N/A**	**N/A**	**N/A**	P/B Ratio	**N/A**	52 Wk Hi-Low	**1,625.0-1,050.0**
Book Value	**N/A**	**N/A**	**N/A**	**N/A**	Yield %	**N/A**	Market Cap	**US$102.9mil**

Address **Jl. Garuda 153/74**, **Bandung, Jawa Barat**
Tel **022-61-1281**
Fax **N/A**
ADR
SEDOL No. **6009885**
President **John Walker**
Chairman **Awong Hidjaja**

Indah Kiat Paper & Pulp

Industry: **Paper Products**

Indah Kiat Paper & Pulp is Southeast Asia's largest pulp producer, with annual production of 300,000 tonnes. It is 67%-owned by the Sinar Mas Group, a diversified Indonesia conglomerate with more than 200 companies. Pulp accounts for about 20% of Indah Kiat's total sales. The company also makes industrial paper and boxes, printing paper, and writing paper. Indah Kiat and another Sinar Mas subsidiary, Tjiwi Kimiah, together control 70% of the nation's market for writing and printing papers. Indah Kiat has a financial-services subsidiary, Indah Kiat International Finance.

Rp bil	12/91	12/92	12/93	US$mil 12/93				
Sales	**419.0**	**424.8**	**650.5**	**308.4**	P/E Ratio	**43.7**	Price (9/30/95)	**2,725.00**
Net Income	**159.9**	**121.8**	**90.0**	**42.7**	P/B Ratio	**1.9**	52 Wk Hi-Low	**3,625.0-2,150.0**
Book Value	**1,337.7**	**1,407.9**	**1,498.0**	**697.9**	Yield %	**N/A**	Market Cap	**US$810.8mil**

Address **Gedung Eka Life, Jl.M.T. Haryono**, **Jakarta 12780**
Tel **021-797-6345**
Fax **021-797-6312**
ADR
SEDOL No. **6462422**
President **Teguh Ganda Wijaya**
Chairman **Eka Tjipta Widjaja**

Indocement Tunggal

Industry: **Building Materials**

Indocement Tunggal Prakarsa is a multibusiness group with three major divisions: cement, food, and property. Its cement division is the leader in Indonesia's cement industry, with an annual capacity of almost 10 million tons and a market share of nearly 45%. Its food division manages Bogarsi, Indonesia's largest flour miller, and Indofood Group, the country's largest processed-food company. The Indofood Group produces instant noodles, food seasonings, snacks, baby foods, and beverages. The company's property division owns Wisma Indocement, an office tower in Jakarta.

Rp bil	12/92 R	12/93	12/94	US$mil 12/94				
Sales	**2,206.1**	**2,890.4**	**3,388.0**	**1,569.6**	P/E Ratio	**31.6**	Price (9/30/95)	**8,250.00**
Net Income	**327.4**	**312.4**	**367.8**	**170.4**	P/B Ratio	**4.4**	52 Wk Hi-Low	**9,100.0-6,100.0**
Book Value	**1,739.8**	**1,902.4**	**2,278.9**	**1,052.3**	Yield %	**2.5**	Market Cap	**US$4,402.2mil**

Address **Jl. Jend. Sudirman, Kav.70-71**, **Jakarta 12910**
Tel **021-251-2121**
Fax **021-251-0066**
ADR
SEDOL No. **6462262**
President **Sudwikatmono**
Chairman **Soedono Salim**

R=Restated.

Indorama Synthetics

Industry: **Clothing & Fabrics**

Indorama Synthetics is a polyester-yarn and fabric manufacturer which also produces bottle-, textile-, and film-grade resins. Its factory has a daily polyester-production capacity of 185 tonnes. Indorama is in the process of a $150 million expansion that will triple its polyester-yarn capacity by the end of 1995. Indo-rama Synthetics, the company's wholly-owned polyester-staple-fiber production subsidiary in India, is one of that country's largest exporters of synthetic-spun yarn. Indorama has marketing and technology agreements with the United States' Chemtex and Du Pont.

Rp bil	12/92	12/93	12/94	US$mil 12/94				
Sales	**242.1**	**301.5**	**381.5**	**176.7**	P/E Ratio	**11.8**	Price (9/30/95)	**7,575.00**
Net Income	**44.9**	**50.3**	**62.2**	**28.8**	P/B Ratio	**2.4**	52 Wk Hi-Low	**7,875.0-4,666.6**
Book Value	**183.1**	**252.7**	**311.8**	**144.0**	Yield %	**2.5**	Market Cap	**US$324.9mil**

Address	**Jl. H.R. Rasuna Said Kav 1-2**	Tel	**021-526-1555**	ADR		President	**Mohanlal Lohia**
	Jakarta 12950	Fax	**021-526-1501**	SEDOL No.	**6462336**	Chairman	**Gani Djemat**

Inti Indorayon Utama

Industry: **Paper Products**

Inti Indorayon Utama is Indonesia's second-largest pulp producer and one of the lowest-cost producers in the world. The company produces pulp and rayon fibers for the paper and textiles industries. Exports account for more than 60% of its annual sales. Indorayon operates a reforestation program to replenish its supply of raw material, and also has an estate where it grows eucalyptus timber. It intends to be self-sufficient in timber by the year 2000. The firm has expanded its production base from one factory to three through a contract with Ocean Sky Company (Hong Kong).

Rp bil	12/92	12/93	12/94	US$mil 12/94				
Sales	**163.0**	**157.2**	**387.5**	**179.5**	P/E Ratio	**NMF**	Price (9/30/95)	**3,400.00**
Net Income	**92.5**	**65.2**	**64.6**	**29.9**	P/B Ratio	**1.7**	52 Wk Hi-Low	**6,050.0-3,350.0**
Book Value	**703.6**	**736.4**	**850.0**	**392.5**	Yield %	**2.4**	Market Cap	**US$608.8mil**

Address	**Jl. Letjend. Haryono MT**	Tel	**061-532-532**	ADR	**PTIDY**	President	**Polar Yanto Tanoto**
	Medan 20231	Fax	**061-630-967**	SEDOL No.	**6465614**	Chairman	**Sukanto Tanoto**

Jakarta International Hotels

Industry: **Lodging**

Jakarta International Hotels & Development is a hotel and land development company. It owns and operates the Borobudur Inter-Continental, the Dai-ichi and Hilton Lagoon Tower, and the Shangri La Hotel, which are all in Jakarta. Its wholly-owned Danayasa Arthatama subsidiary is developing Jakarta's 440,000-square-meter Sudirman Central Business District (SCBD). Danayasa Arthatama's telecommunication subsidiary Artha Telekomindo has a joint venture with Indonesia's Telkom to provide Integrated Services Digital Network (ISDN) telecommunication services to SCBD.

Rp bil	12/92	12/93	12/94	US$mil 12/94				
Sales	**306.9**	**248.0**	**105.5**	**48.9**	P/E Ratio	**37.7**	Price (9/30/95)	**2,525.00**
Net Income	**57.1**	**42.2**	**26.1**	**12.1**	P/B Ratio	**0.6**	52 Wk Hi-Low	**3,050.0-1,850.0**
Book Value	**1,468.9**	**1,498.3**	**1,514.7**	**699.4**	Yield %	**1.0**	Market Cap	**US$430.8mil**

Address	**Jl. Lapangan Banteng Selatan**	Tel	**021-384-2229**	ADR		President	--
	Jakarta 10710	Fax	**021-384-2289**	SEDOL No.	**6272353**	Chairman	**H. Jusuf Indradewa**

Japfa Comfeed

Industry: **Other Food**

Japfa Comfeed is a diversified agribusiness company. Its operations include animal-feed manufacturing, chicken breeding, poultry processing, and shrimp farming and processing. The company breeds 50 million chicks annually, and its feed-mill capacity exceeds 1 million tonnes per year. It is the largest exporter of shrimp to Japan. It is also involved in trading raw materials, shipping, and manufacturing plastic-woven bags for use in feed mills. Japfa Comfeed exports woven bags to Singapore, Europe, the Middle East, and the United States.

Rp bil	12/92	12/93	12/94	US$mil 12/94				
Sales	**634.1**	**591.3**	**730.4**	**338.4**	P/E Ratio	**5.9**	Price (9/30/95)	**1,250.00**
Net Income	**23.8**	**31.1**	**31.5**	**14.6**	P/B Ratio	**0.6**	52 Wk Hi-Low	**3,300.0-1,225.0**
Book Value	**209.9**	**259.2**	**302.2**	**139.5**	Yield %	**5.2**	Market Cap	**US$72.7mil**

Address	**Jl. Letjen. MT Haryono Kav. 16**	Tel	**021-831-0310**	ADR		Managing Director	**Ferry Teguh Santosa**
	Jakarta 12810	Fax	**021-831-0309**	SEDOL No.	**6472391**	Chairman	**Somala Wiria**

Kalbe Farma

Industry: **Pharmaceuticals**

Kalbe Farma is the largest pharmaceuticals company in Indonesia by revenues. Through its primary Dankos (71%-owned) and Pfrimmer (49%-owned) subsidiaries, the company manufactures and markets human- and animal-health-care products. Its partially-owned Igar Jaya, Avesta, and Helios Foods subsidiaries manufacture glass vials, ampules, disposable syringes, packaging materials, confectioneries and snack foods. Nonpharmaceuticals products account for about 40% of total revenues. Kalbe Farma exports its pharmaceuticals products to Nigeria, Sri Lanka, Singapore, and Hong Kong.

Rp bil	12/92	12/93	12/94	US$mil 12/94				
Sales	**235.6**	**310.1**	**428.6**	**198.6**	P/E Ratio	**26.9**	Price (9/30/95)	**9,050.00**
Net Income	**34.1**	**50.1**	**59.0**	**27.4**	P/B Ratio	**6.2**	52 Wk Hi-Low	**10,850.0-7,575.0**
Book Value	**166.8**	**277.6**	**317.8**	**146.7**	Yield %	**1.0**	Market Cap	**US$864.0mil**

Address	**Jl. Jend. A. Yani**	Tel	**021-489-2808**	ADR		President	**B.D. Wreksoatmodjo**
	Pulo Mas, Jakarta 13210	Fax	**021-489-3549**	SEDOL No.	**6482204**	Chairman	**Boenjamin Setiawan**

Lippobank

Industry: **Banks - Regional**

Lippo Bank is a financial-services company offering retail, corporate, and consumer-banking services. Retail commercial banking composes 57% of the bank's loan portfolio. Lippo Bank has a wholly-owned merchant-banking subsidiary in Australia, and offices in Sydney, Bangkok, Kuala Lumpur, Hanoi, and Ho Chi Minh City. It is a member of the Lippo Group, and has financial-services affiliates in Hong Kong, Singapore, Thailand, China, Australia, and the United States. Lippo Bank has domestic joint ventures with Banque National de Paris, Tokai Bank, Daiwa Bank, and Bankers Trust.

	Rp bil 12/91	12/92	12/93	US$mil 12/93				
Revenues	**609.1**	**648.6**	**737.7**	**349.8**	P/E Ratio	**36.2**	Price (9/30/95)	**5,375.00**
Net Income	**22.2**	**32.1**	**42.4**	**20.1**	P/B Ratio	**4.0**	52 Wk Hi-Low	**5,700.0-2,525.0**
Book Value	**181.7**	**204.2**	**383.3**	**178.6**	Yield %	**0.6**	Market Cap	**US$678.7mil**

Address	**Jl. Gatot Subroto, Kav.35-36**	Tel	**021-520-1099**	ADR		President	**Markus Parmadi**
	Jakarta 12950	Fax	**021-520-5375**	SEDOL No.	**6519362**	Chairman	**H.M.N.M. Hasjim Ning**

Lippoland

Industry: **Real-Estate Investment**

Lippo Land Development is a property-development and -management company. It develops residential, commercial, and retail properties in the Jakarta area comprising the cities of Jakarta, Bogor, Tangerang, and Bekasi. Lippo Land's primary business is creating planned residential and commercial communities in suburban areas. Its largest developments are Lippo City (5,000 acres) and Lippo Village (1,250 acres). Lippo Land also manages five office buildings in Jakarta and develops condominiums, office complexes, and medical facilities through several joint ventures.

	Rp bil 06/91 R	06/92	06/93	US$mil 06/93				
Sales	**N/A**	**11.6**	**64.2**	**31.1**	P/E Ratio	**6.0**	Price (9/30/95)	**1,550.00**
Net Income	**N/A**	**23.0**	**28.2**	**13.6**	P/B Ratio	**0.5**	52 Wk Hi-Low	**5,200.0-1,350.0**
Book Value	**N/A**	**121.8**	**149.7**	**72.1**	Yield %	**6.5**	Market Cap	**US$170.5mil**

Address	**Jl. Jenderal Gatot Subroto**	Tel	**021-520-7500**	ADR		President	**Roy E. Tirtadji**
	Jakarta 12950	Fax	**021-520-0900**	SEDOL No.	**6519243**	Chairman	**Dr. H.M. Ning**

R=Restated.

Mayora Indah

Industry: **Other Food**

Mayora Indah is Indonesia's largest confectionery company by sales. A member of the Nabisco group, the company makes candy, chocolates, biscuits, wafers, and cookies. Mayora Indah has more than 20 brands, including Choki-choki chocolate, Kopiko candy, Danisa Danish cookies, and Beng Beng wafers. It has two plants and will complete a third in 1995, boosting capacity by 40%. Mayora Indah's Indonesian subsidiaries include wafer-maker Timur; Barat, a biscuit and wafer maker; and Torabika, which makes coffee. Its primary markets are Indonesia and Denmark.

	Rp bil 12/92	12/93	12/94	US$mil 12/94				
Sales	**120.1**	**162.3**	**250.0**	**115.8**	P/E Ratio	**29.7**	Price (9/30/95)	**3,550.00**
Net Income	**13.5**	**26.4**	**43.6**	**20.2**	P/B Ratio	**2.7**	52 Wk Hi-Low	**4,008.3-2,658.3**
Book Value	**N/A**	**154.8**	**509.2**	**235.1**	Yield %	**0.6**	Market Cap	**US$601.4mil**

Address	**Jl. Tomang Raya 21-23**	Tel	**021-565-5311**	ADR		President	**Halim Atmadja**
	Jakarta, Barat 11840	Fax	**021-565-5323**	SEDOL No.	**6572967**	Chairman	**Jogi Hendra Atmadja**

Modern Photo Film

Industry: **Other Recreational Products & Services**

Modern Photo Film is the sole maker and marketer of Fuji brand cameras and film in Indonesia, where Fuji cameras hold an 85% market share and Fuji film an 80% share. Its Honoris Industry subsidiary manufactures and exports nine types of Fuji cameras, accounting for 60% of Fuji cameras sold throughout the world. Modern Photo's retail arm, Modern PutraIndonesia, owns and operates 202 Fuji Image Plaza photo-processing outlets in Indonesia. The company also sells photographic paper, chemicals, medical x-ray film, phototypesetting film, and black-and-white scanners.

	Rp bil 12/92	12/93	12/94	US$mil 12/94				
Sales	**369.4**	**468.3**	**563.8**	**261.2**	P/E Ratio	**34.4**	Price (9/30/95)	**13,000**
Net Income	**31.6**	**40.0**	**50.4**	**23.3**	P/B Ratio	**7.4**	52 Wk Hi-Low	**13,200.0-8,800.0**
Book Value	**183.7**	**207.7**	**235.4**	**108.7**	Yield %	**1.3**	Market Cap	**US$766.4mil**

Address	**Jl. Matraman Raya 12**	Tel	**021-850-9882**	ADR		Managing Director	**Sungkono Honoris**
	Jakarta 13150	Fax	**021-858-1620**	SEDOL No.	**6598833**	Chairman	**Samadikun Hartono**

Modernland Realty

Industry: **Real-Estate Investment**

Modernland Realty develops housing units and land plots. It specializes in acquiring land and adding infrastructure such as roads, telephone lines, sewage systems, and water and electricity supplies. It also builds houses and sells plots for private homebuilding. The company has two major residential projects: Modernland Cipondoh, a residential and golf complex in west Jakarta, and Taman Modern, a residential and shopping complex in east Jakarta. The company's founder, the Modern Group, owns 68.8% of Modernland Realty via the holding company Inti Putramodern.

	Rp bil 12/92 R	12/93	12/94	US$mil 12/94				
Sales	**73.1**	**73.8**	**153.0**	**70.9**	P/E Ratio	**5.9**	Price (9/30/95)	**3,175.00**
Net Income	**33.6**	**20.1**	**40.1**	**18.6**	P/B Ratio	**1.0**	52 Wk Hi-Low	**7,900.0-2,600.0**
Book Value	**74.1**	**200.2**	**235.0**	**108.5**	Yield %	**2.2**	Market Cap	**US$105.0mil**

Address	**Jalan Matraman Raya 12**	Tel	**021-280-1000**	ADR		President	**Samadikun Hartono**
	Jakarta 13150	Fax	**021-858-1620**	SEDOL No.	**6579979**	Chairman	**Sungkono Honoris**

R=Restated.

Panin Bank

Industry: **Banks - Regional**

Panin Bank is a commercial bank with total assets of $1.5 billion. It operates 100 branch offices throughout Indonesia and two offshore branches on the Cook Islands and the Cayman Islands. Its primary business is providing financing to medium-sized retail businesses. As part of its international-banking services, Panin Bank offers international foreign-exchange transactions conducted through correspondent banks in 63 countries, and offshore commercial foreign borrowing. Its joint-venture partners include ANZ Bank Group of Australia, Bank Indonesia, and Nippon Credit Bank.

Rp bil	12/92	12/93	12/94	US$mil 12/94				
Revenues	**369.7**	**397.6**	**418.9**	**194.1**	P/E Ratio	**9.2**	Price (9/30/95)	**1,450.00**
Net Income	**29.1**	**38.7**	**47.3**	**21.9**	P/B Ratio	**1.2**	52 Wk Hi-Low	**3,100.0-1,450.0**
Book Value	**306.8**	**316.6**	**356.7**	**164.7**	Yield %	**6.6**	Market Cap	**US$192.8mil**

Address **Jalan Jenderal Sudirman Senayan, Jakarta 10270** Tel **021-270-0545** Fax **021-270-0340** ADR SEDOL No. **6668606** President **H. Rostian Sjamsudin** Chairman **A. Kemal Idris**

Plaza Indonesia Realty

Industry: **Lodging**

Plaza Indonesia Realty is a property-development company that builds and manages hotels and retail centers. It owns the Grand Hyatt Jakarta hotel and retail complex, a five-star hotel with more than 400 rooms. The company also owns the Plaza Indonesia Shopping Center in downtown Jakarta, with more than 40,000 square feet in leasable space and more than 300 retail shops and 17 restaurants, and sponsors merchandise and services promotions and exhibitions. The company has plans to construct a shopping mall and two 45-story towers in Jakarta's central business district.

Rp bil	12/92	12/93	12/94	US$mil 12/94				
Sales	**117.2**	**124.4**	**140.4**	**65.0**	P/E Ratio	**18.9**	Price (9/30/95)	**2,100.00**
Net Income	**10.5**	**24.0**	**31.8**	**14.7**	P/B Ratio	**1.4**	52 Wk Hi-Low	**2,550.0-1,025.0**
Book Value	**279.3**	**297.5**	**522.8**	**241.4**	Yield %	**1.0**	Market Cap	**US$320.2mil**

Address **Jl. M.H. Thamrin Kav. 28-30 Jakarta 10350** Tel **021-390-3728** Fax **021-310-7644** ADR SEDOL No. **6704094** President **Bambang Trihatmodjo** Chairman **Eka T. Widjaja**

Polysindo Eka Perkasa

Industry: **Clothing & Fabrics**

Polysindo Eka Perkasa is Indonesia's largest integrated textile producer. It manufactures polyester chips, fiber, and filament yarn. Through its 80%-owned Texmaco Jaya and Texmaco Perkasa Engineering subsidiaries, it also weaves, processes, and finishes textiles and manufactures light-engineering equipment; Texmaco Perkasa is Indonesia's only producer of textile machinery. Polysindo Eka Perkasa also has a joint venture with Eastman Kodak (U.S.) to produce specialty chips and fiber. Its distribution and marketing network spans Asia, Africa, Europe, and North America.

Rp bil	12/92	12/93	12/94	US$mil 12/94				
Sales	**597.7**	**671.4**	**821.6**	**380.6**	P/E Ratio	**13.3**	Price (9/30/95)	**1,300.00**
Net Income	**100.2**	**105.1**	**108.0**	**50.0**	P/B Ratio	**2.1**	52 Wk Hi-Low	**1,350.0-912.5**
Book Value	**354.1**	**620.1**	**678.1**	**313.1**	Yield %	**3.5**	Market Cap	**US$634.4mil**

Address **BDN Tower, Jl. Kebon Sirih 83 Jakarta 10340** Tel **021-380-0124** Fax **021-380-0352** ADR SEDOL No. **6693426** President **Marimutu Sinivasan** Chairman **H. Somala Wiria**

Semen Cibinong

Industry: **Building Materials**

Semen Cibinong is the second-largest cement manufacturer in Indonesia, accounting for one fourth of the production capacity in western Java. It has an annual-production capacity of more than 3.6 million tonnes, and markets its cement under the Kujang name. Semen Cibinong's wholly-owned Semen Nusantara subsidiary has a 21% cement market share in western Java and a 40% market share in central Java. Its Trumix Beton subsidiary runs a ready-mix cement business in the Jakarta area. Semen Cibinong is building a 2.6 million tonne cement plant that is scheduled to open in 1996.

Rp bil	12/92	12/93	12/94	US$mil 12/94				
Sales	**192.6**	**394.1**	**536.6**	**248.6**	P/E Ratio	**10.7**	Price (9/30/95)	**4,700.00**
Net Income	**25.2**	**27.9**	**53.3**	**24.7**	P/B Ratio	**0.8**	52 Wk Hi-Low	**6,400.0-4,150.0**
Book Value	**278.8**	**481.7**	**970.2**	**448.0**	Yield %	**2.1**	Market Cap	**US$341.1mil**

Address **Jl. Jenderal Sudirman Kav. 44-46 Jakarta 10210** Tel **021-251-2377** Fax **021-251-2394** ADR SEDOL No. **6795270** President **H. Djojohadikusumo** Chairman **Suyono Sosrodarsono**

SMART

Industry: **Other Food**

Sinar Mas Agro Resources & Technology (SMART) is the agribusiness arm of Indonesia's second-largest conglomerate, Sinar Mas Group. It produces bananas, edible oils, margarines, canned tuna, and fats. Smart's Filma oil has a 50% share of Indonesia's branded cooking-oil market; the firm also holds 35% of its market for industrial margarines and fats. Smart owns more than 7,000 hectares of oil palm, and produces 108,000 tonnes of bananas annually. It has a joint venture with Australian food maker Goodman Fielder Wattie to produce margarine products, tea bags, and snacks.

Rp bil	12/92 R	12/93	12/94	US$mil 12/94				
Sales	**518.0**	**455.2**	**524.0**	**242.8**	P/E Ratio	**7.7**	Price (9/30/95)	**1,475.00**
Net Income	**30.3**	**39.1**	**40.1**	**18.6**	P/B Ratio	**1.0**	52 Wk Hi-Low	**3,700.0-1,400.0**
Book Value	**241.1**	**271.2**	**302.2**	**139.6**	Yield %	**3.4**	Market Cap	**US$136.9mil**

Address **JITC Bldg., Jalan Mangga Dua Raya, Jakarta 14430** Tel **021-260-1088** Fax **021-260-1059** ADR SEDOL No. **6814056** President **Tan Siauw Liang** Chairman **Franky Oesman Widjaja**

R=Restated.

Unggul Indah

Industry: **Specialty Chemicals**

Unggul Indah (UIC) is one of the world's largest producers of alkybenzene, a principal ingredient in manufacturing detergents. It also manufactures heavy and light alkylates. UIC has the capacity to produce 150,000 tonnes of alkylbenzene each year. Its Petrocentral subsidiary is Indonesia's only producer of sodium tripolyphosphate, another raw material used in detergents. It yielded more than 50,000 tonnes in 1994. UIC operates an alkybenzene plant and a sulphonation plant in Vietnam. It also operates under licensing agreements with firms in Japan and the United States.

Rp bil	12/92 R	12/93	12/94	US$mil 12/94				
Sales	**168.2**	**238.8**	**282.4**	**130.8**	P/E Ratio	**8.1**	Price (9/30/95)	**1,875.00**
Net Income	**38.5**	**34.4**	**30.5**	**14.1**	P/B Ratio	**1.1**	52 Wk Hi-Low	**3,300.0-1,725.0**
Book Value	**188.2**	**207.1**	**227.9**	**105.2**	Yield %	**4.0**	Market Cap	**US$109.4mil**

Address	**Jl. Gatot Subroto Kav 6-7**	Tel	**021-525-6510**	ADR		President	**Johannes Kotjo**
	Jakarta 12930	Fax	**021-520-0829**	SEDOL No.	**6911270**	Chairman	**Anthony Salim**

R=Restated.

Ireland

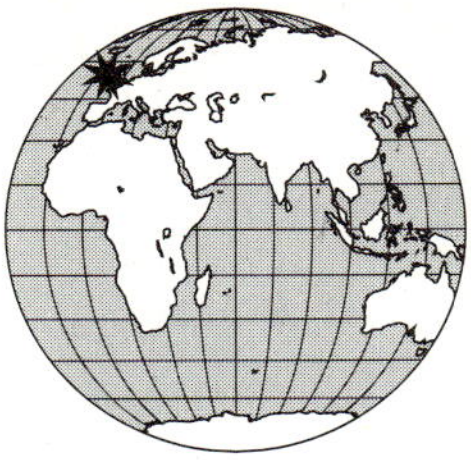

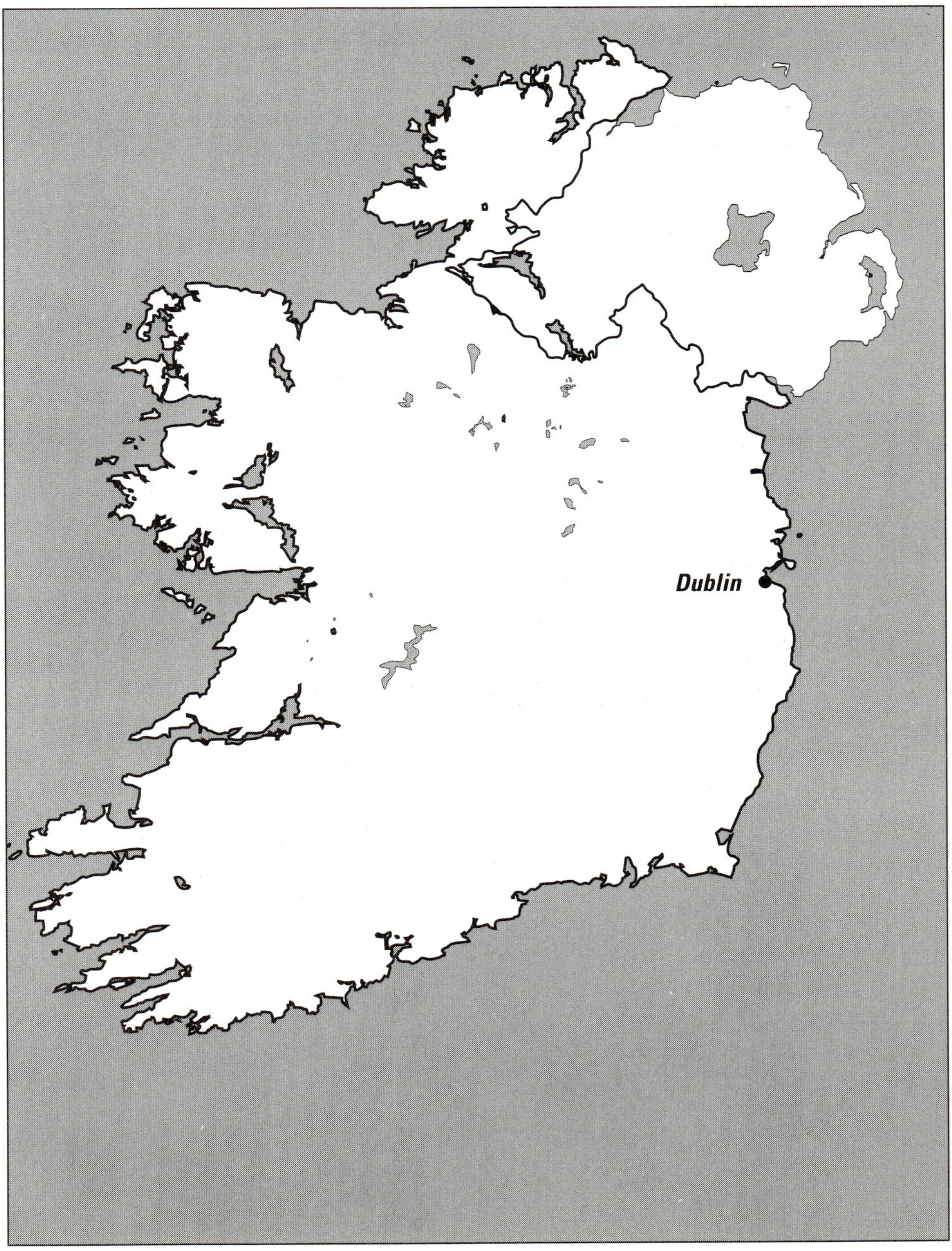

Ireland

Debra L. Marks, Dublin

Local Trading Hours	**Time Difference with New York**	**Population (Est. 94)**
10:30-3:30	5 hours ahead	3,539,000

The origins of the Dublin stock exchange stretch back over 200 years. These roots can be seen today at the stock exchange on Anglesea Street, where prices are still marked manually on a large chalk board twice a day during two floor trading sessions at 9:30 am and 2:15 pm, lasting about one hour each.

This isn't to say, however, that Dublin is stuck in the past. In 1995, the Irish stock exchange will see the most far-reaching structural changes in its history.

The pending demerger of the Dublin stock exchange from its big brother in London shouldn't be noticed at all — if officials at the Dublin exchange are correct.

Much advance planning has been put into the separation of the two exchanges — mandated by the European Union's investment services directive (ISD) — so that there should be little, if any disruption, stock exchange officials on both sides of the Irish Sea contend.

But the planned separation has been delayed to an unknown date, with computer and settlement wrangles said to be holding up the process. By law, the split has to take place by the end of this year, according to E.U. law.

Legislation in Ireland's Dail — or parliament — approving the move came only in late June although it had been on lawmakers' desks for over a year.

The E.U.'s ISD requires each member to have a national authority overseeing stock exchange transactions and regulating brokers' activities.

As such, Ireland crafted a stock exchange bill that appoints the Central Bank of Ireland as its authority. At the same time, the bill allows the central bank to delegate certain functions back to the exchange, including regulation of brokers' relations with their clients as well as relations with between brokers through the central bank.

Dow Jones Ireland Equity Market Index Performance

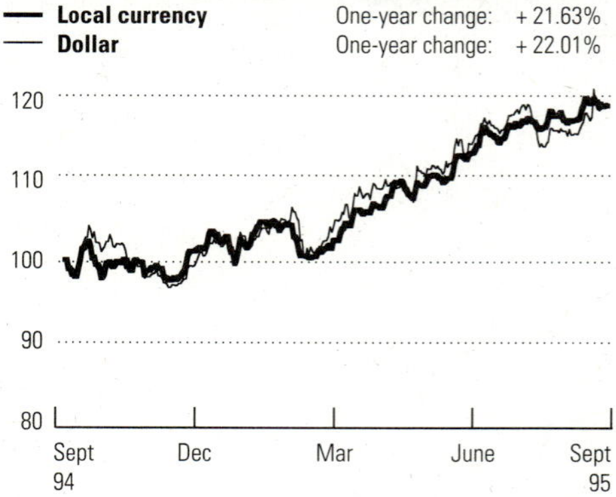

"The separation is more of a regulatory issue than a trading one," said Tom Healy, the general manager of the Dublin stock exchange. "Our objective is to make the changeover as seamless as possible so that the market knows no change."

Gross Domestic Product (94)	Three-Year Average GDP Growth (92-94)	Main Industries	Consumer Price Index (94)	Monetary Unit	Exchange Rate (9/95)
$51 billion	5.6%	Services, tourism and agriculture	2.4%	Punt	IR149.90 to US$1.00

Stock exchange and central bank officials continue to stress that there will be no practical effect on funds or companies listed in Dublin. Under the present system, most large Irish companies have their primary listing in Dublin and a secondary quotation in London. Dublin has been using the same listing criteria as London since 1985.

At the moment, Ireland lists about 80 companies with a total market capitalization of about 15 billion Irish punts, making it the third smallest stock market in the E.U. behind Lisbon and Luxembourg.

After the split, Irish stock prices will still be displayed on the Stock Exchanged Automated Quotation (SEAQ) system.

At the moment, about 1,000 transactions take place each day worth about 25-30 million punts. Trading in Irish stocks is on an "order driven" system. Irish government securities — or gilts — are also traded on the Irish stock exchange with about 400 trades a day and typical daily turnover of about 300-400 million punts.

The summer rally in Irish equity prices put Dublin stocks among some of Europe's best performing markets.

Only stock markets in Britain, Finland and Sweden have performed better so far this year. Stripping out currency factors, Dublin's gains have been the most pronounced across Europe.

So far this year, Ireland's ISEQ Overall index, the main barometer of Ireland's 65 most highly capitalized issues, has advanced 15.2%. The key barometer — calculated on a base where 1000 equals January 1983 — hit an all-time peak of 2134.58 in August, outstripping its earlier maximum trading level of 2088.87 reached in January 20, 1994.

Ten Largest Capitalized Companies
as of 9/30/95

Stock	Market Cap. US$Mil
Allied Irish Banks	14,024.3
Jefferson Smurfit	13,478.0
Bank of Ireland	12,655.8
CRH	10,201.5
Kerry Group	5,225.0
Irish Life	4,582.2
Independent Newspapers	3,069.2
Waterford Wedgewood	2,979.2
Greencore	2,822.5
Woodchester Investments	2,420.1

Analysts say that while expectations for economic growth across Europe and the U.S. have been pared back, forecasts for Ireland continue to rise. Ireland is the fastest growing economy in the European Union (EU), with EU growth rate estimates at 6.9% this year and 5.5% in 1996. Both figures have been revised upwards.

In its summer economic review and outlook, Ireland's Department of Finance forecasts 1995 gross national product (GNP) growth at a more conservative 5.25%. It also expects private consumption to grow by 5.25% while underlying lending growth should rise to

9.0%, all above current EU averages. Major brokerages in Dublin predict even higher levels.

On the corporate front, too, Ireland offers some success stories that even its closest neighbors can't match.

Fund managers at Irish Life PLC are forecasting corporate profitability for Irish companies in 1995 at a whopping 33%, largely as a result of smart gains in Dublin's top four stocks that account for over 50% of the entire market capitalization.

These are (with market weighting as of end July 1995 in brackets: Jefferson Smurfit Group PLC (15%); Allied Irish Banks PLC (14%); Bank of Ireland PLC (13%); and CRH PLC (11%). These are also the most actively traded issues.

There are no restrictions on foreign investment on the Irish stock exchange. Dividends accrued by a foreign investor aren't subject to income, corporation or withholding tax in Ireland.

However, companies have to pay advanced corporation tax on any dividends paid. Additionally, these dividend payments come with a tax credit to offset the effect of double taxation on the dividend in the hands of the investor.

A foreign investor in Ireland may be able to get relief from double taxation but this will depend on any taxation treaties between Ireland and the investor's country of residence.

Only member firms — of which there are 10 — are allowed to trade quoted securities directly on the exchange. All trades are published on the SEAQ electronic system. Official settlement for equities takes place within 5 working days of the deal while gilt settlement is the next day.

Allied Irish Banks

Industry: **Financial Services - Diversified**

Allied Irish Banks (AIB) is active in retail and investment banking and related financial services. The bank provides corporate-finance, leasing, custodial, unit-trust-management, and stock-brokerage services. The company also offers life insurance and pensions through its Ark Life Assurance subsidiary. AIB's assets totaled more than $31 billion at year-end 1994. The bank owns state-chartered York Bank and Trust and First Maryland Bancorp, both located in the United States. AIB and U.K.-based TSB bank operate Northern Ireland's First Trust Bank.

	IR£ mi 12/92 *	12/93	12/94	US$mil 12/94				
Revenues	**2,425.0**	**2,746.0**	**N/A**	**N/A**	P/E Ratio	**10.4**	Price (9/30/95)	**3.15**
Net Income	**118.0**	**145.0**	**212.5**	**318.6**	P/B Ratio	**1.6**	52 Wk Hi-Low	**3.18-2.35**
Book Value	**991.0**	**1,145.0**	**1,321.2**	**2,032.6**	Yield %	**3.5**	Market Cap	**US$14.0mil**

Address **Bankcentre, Ballsbridge**
Dublin 4
Tel **01-875-0222**
Fax **01-679-7127**
ADR **AIB**
SEDOL No. **19783**
Chairman Exec Bd **Thomas P. Mulcahy**
Chairman **James P. Culliton**

*Irregular period due to fiscal year change.

Bank of Ireland

Industry: **Banks - Regional**

Bank of Ireland and its subsidiaries offer retail and corporate banking and other financial services. It also operates a private bank and provides treasury and international banking services. The company owns the Irish building society ICS and the life-insurance and pensions firm Lifetime Assurance Co. Its wholly-owned First New Hampshire subsidiaries provide banking services in the United States. In fiscal 1993, Bank of Ireland generated 59% of its gross income in Ireland, 20% in Great Britain, and 14% in the United States.

	IR£ mi 03/93	03/94	03/95	US$mil 03/95				
Revenues	**1,848.0**	**1,678.0**	**1,582.7**	**2,442.4**	P/E Ratio	**9.0**	Price (9/30/95)	**3.99**
Net Income	**73.0**	**182.0**	**224.2**	**346.0**	P/B Ratio	**1.8**	52 Wk Hi-Low	**3.99-2.63**
Book Value	**1,311.0**	**1,496.0**	**1,031.4**	**1,690.8**	Yield %	**3.1**	Market Cap	**US$12.7mil**

Address **Lower Baggot St.**
Dublin 2
Tel **01-661-5933**
Fax **01-661-5671**
ADR
SEDOL No. **75600**
CEO **Patrick J.A. Molloy**
Chairman **Howard E. Kilroy**

CRH

Industry: **Building Materials**

CRH manufactures and supplies building materials. Its main products include cement, ready-mix concrete, aggregates, stone, sand, gravel, and clay. It also makes insulation products, security gates, fencing, and glass products, and is active in civil engineering, road surfacing, and construction. CRH has operations throughout Europe, the United States, and Argentina. Its wholly-owned U.S. subsidiaries include glass manufacturers Tempglass and HGP Industries and concrete masonry firm Superlite. Exports to the U.S. account for 26% of CRH's turnover.

	IR£ mi 12/92	12/93	12/94	US$mil 12/94				
Sales	**1,114.0**	**1,427.0**	**1,612.5**	**2,417.6**	P/E Ratio	**16.4**	Price (9/30/95)	**4.34**
Net Income	**47.0**	**62.0**	**92.9**	**139.3**	P/B Ratio	**2.6**	52 Wk Hi-Low	**4.52-3.33**
Book Value	**370.0**	**579.0**	**596.7**	**918.0**	Yield %	**1.9**	Market Cap	**US$10.2mil**

Address **Belgard Castle, Clondalkin**
Dublin 2
Tel **01-4591111**
Fax **01-4591702**
ADR **CRHCY**
SEDOL No. **182704**
CEO **Don Godson**
Chairman **Anthony D. Barry**

Fyffes

Industry: **Food Retailers & Wholesalers**

Fyffes obtains fresh produce from all over the world and distributes it in the United Kingdom, Ireland, Continental Europe and the United States. The company's wholly-owned Vangen Logistics Division provides warehousing and distribution services to retail and catering companies. Among numerous acquisitions in 1994 the company acquired 50% of Velleman & Tas, a Netherlands-based fruit company that also has substantial storage facilities. The company also owns 50% interests in Brdr. Lambeke, a Danish importer of produce, and EurobananCanarias, a Canary Islands banana producer.

	IR£ mi 10/92	10/93	10/94	US$mil 10/94				
Sales	**524.0**	**611.0**	**874.6**	**1,291.8**	P/E Ratio	**15.3**	Price (9/30/95)	**1.07**
Net Income	**21.0**	**22.0**	**24.5**	**36.1**	P/B Ratio	**1.7**	52 Wk Hi-Low	**1.13-0.97**
Book Value	**178.0**	**187.0**	**178.6**	**288.1**	Yield %	**1.4**	Market Cap	**US$2.0mil**

Address **1 Beresford St.**
Dublin 7
Tel **01-8730200**
Fax **01-8730068**
ADR
SEDOL No. **329523**
Managing Director **David V. McCann**
Chairman **Neil V. McCann**

Greencore

Industry: **Other Food**

Greencore Group supplies primary foods and related products, food ingredients, and prepared foods to industrial and commercial markets. The company is the Irish Republic's only sugar processor and is a supplier of flour, malt, and consumer foods. Wholly-owned subsidiary Interchem is the largest distributor of crop-protection products in Ireland. The company's other subsidiaries are involved in the production of agricultural products, chemicals, machinery, and fertilizers. Greencore Group also has a number of wholly-owned distributors and wholesalers.

	IR£ mi 09/92	09/93	09/94	US$mil 09/94				
Sales	**387.8**	**392.3**	**404.3**	**591.1**	P/E Ratio	**12.9**	Price (9/30/95)	**4.96**
Net Income	**24.1**	**28.4**	**32.2**	**47.1**	P/B Ratio	**2.6**	52 Wk Hi-Low	**5.00-3.77**
Book Value	**115.5**	**137.2**	**161.3**	**252.0**	Yield %	**2.0**	Market Cap	**US$2.8mil**

Address **Earlsfort Terrace**
Dublin 2
Tel **01-605-1000**
Fax **01-605-1100**
ADR
SEDOL No. **387628**
CEO **Gerry M. Murphy**
Chairman **Bernie M. Cahill**

Independent Newspapers

Industry: **Publishing**

Independent Newspapers is an international media and communications group that publishes newspapers and magazines in Ireland, the United Kingdom, Continental Europe, and Australia. The firm manages outdoor advertising for its publications and distributes television signals in Ireland. It publishes the Irish Independent, an Irish newspaper. In 1994, The firm acquired a 29% stake in Newspaper Publishing, U.K. publishers of The Independent and The Independent On Sunday. It also has a majority interest in Argus Newspapers, the largest newspaper group in South Africa.

IR£ mi	12/91	12/92	12/93	US$mil 12/93				
Sales	**156.0**	**170.0**	**174.0**	**254.0**	P/E Ratio	**NMF**	Price (9/30/95)	**3.83**
Net Income	**7.0**	**12.0**	**22.0**	**32.1**	P/B Ratio	**2.4**	52 Wk Hi-Low	**3.98-2.48**
Book Value	**138.0**	**144.0**	**186.0**	**262.0**	Yield %	**1.9**	Market Cap	**US$3.1mil**

Address **1/2 Upper Hatch St.**
Dublin 2
Tel **01-475-8432**
Fax **N/A**
ADR
SEDOL No. **461481**
CEO **Liam P. Healy**
Chairman **Dr. A.J.F. O'Reilly**

Irish Life

Industry: **Insurance - Life & Health**

Irish Life is an insurance and financial-services firm. It provides investment-management and asset-financing services to businesses as well as offering life insurance, mortgages, and personal pension and savings plans. Its wholly-owned U.S. subsidiary Interstate Assurance Company offers fixed annuities and has acquired the variable-annuity specialist First Variable Life. In France, the company is sole owner of Xaar, a financial-services company that operates 34 branches. In May 1994, the company exited the Norwegian market, selling its subsidiary DAVID.

IR£ mi	12/92	12/93	12/94	US$mil 12/94				
Revenues	**666.0**	**1,826.0**	**1,011.8**	**1,516.9**	P/E Ratio	**20.2**	Price (9/30/95)	**2.26**
Net Income	**32.0**	**33.0**	**34.0**	**50.9**	P/B Ratio	**9.9**	52 Wk Hi-Low	**2.31-1.78**
Book Value	**55.0**	**61.0**	**69.4**	**106.7**	Yield %	**4.4**	Market Cap	**US$4.6mil**

Address **Irish Life Ctr., Lower Abbey St.**
Dublin 1
Tel **01-704-2000**
Fax **01-704-1900**
ADR
SEDOL No. **459389**
Managing Director **David Kingston**
Chairman **Conor McCarthy**

Kerry Group

Industry: **Other Food**

Kerry Group provides food ingredients and consumer foods. In Europe and North America, the company produces and markets specialty food ingredients, food coatings, bakery mixes, fruit preparations and flavorings, and proteins. In Europe, the company also manufactures added-value products for the dairy, beef, pork, specialist poultry, gourmet, and convenience markets. In 1994, the company acquired the food-ingredients business of Allied Domecq, consisting of DCA Food Industries and Margett Foods. It also acquired Mattesson Wall's chilled-meats business in the U.K.

IR£ mi	12/92	12/93	12/94	US$mil 12/94				
Sales	**826.7**	**879.9**	**882.7**	**1,323.4**	P/E Ratio	**23.3**	Price (9/30/95)	**4.78**
Net Income	**24.7**	**28.9**	**32.3**	**48.4**	P/B Ratio	**2.5**	52 Wk Hi-Low	**4.80-3.22**
Book Value	**217.2**	**255.3**	**307.8**	**473.6**	Yield %	**0.6**	Market Cap	**US$5.2mil**

Address **Prince's Street, Tralee**
Co. Kerry
Tel **066-22433**
Fax **066-22353**
ADR
SEDOL No. **490656**
Managing Director **Denis Brosnan**
Chairman **Michael Hanrahan**

Jefferson Smurfit

Industry: **Paper Products**

Jefferson Smurfit is a paper and board manufacturer. It makes corrugated cardboard, folding cartons, cigarette packets, paper bags, paper tubes, and containerboard. The company also provides printing and waste-reclamation services. Jefferson Smurfit has overseas operations in the United Kingdom, the Netherlands, Germany, France, Italy, Spain, the United States, Colombia, Mexico, and Venezuela. In 1994, the company purchased the paper and packaging operations of French company Saint-Gobain and a 27.5% shareholding in Austrian paper manufacturer Nettingsdorfer.

IR£ mi	01/93	01/94	12/94 *	US$mil 12/94				
Sales	**1,260.0**	**1,468.0**	**1,710.1**	**2,563.9**	P/E Ratio	**6.4**	Price (9/30/95)	**1.88**
Net Income	**35.0**	**35.0**	**290.9**	**436.2**	P/B Ratio	**1.7**	52 Wk Hi-Low	**2.09-1.71**
Book Value	**831.0**	**823.0**	**1,226.0**	**1,886.1**	Yield %	**14.2**	Market Cap	**US$13.5mil**

Address **Beech Hill, Clonskeagh**
Dublin 4
Tel **01-269-6622**
Fax **01-269-4481**
ADR
SEDOL No. **819143**
CEO **Michael W.J. Smurfit**
Chairman **Michael W.J. Smurfit**

*Irregular period due to fiscal year change.

Waterford Wedgewood

Industry: **Other Home Furnishings**

Waterford Wedgwood is a fine-glass and ceramics manufacturer that distributes and retails its products throughout Europe, North and South America, the Middle East, Japan, Australia, and South Africa. The company's main products are Waterford Crystal handcrafted stemware and giftware, and Wedgwood bone-china tableware and decorative ware. Additional products include Coalport hand-painted figurines and giftware, Marquis contemporary crystal, and Johnson Brothers earthen tableware. Foreign sales, primarily to North America, account for 62% of revenues.

IR£ mi	12/92	12/93	12/94	US$mil 12/94				
Sales	**274.0**	**319.0**	**325.0**	**487.3**	P/E Ratio	**21.7**	Price (9/30/95)	**0.63**
Net Income	**-19.0**	**9.0**	**20.6**	**30.9**	P/B Ratio	**3.4**	52 Wk Hi-Low	**0.65-0.51**
Book Value	**101.0**	**122.0**	**132.6**	**204.0**	Yield %	**1.3**	Market Cap	**US$3.0mil**

Address **Kilbarry**
Waterford
Tel **051-73311**
Fax **051-78539**
ADR **WATFZ**
SEDOL No. **942038**
President **--**
Chairman **Anthony J.F O'Reilly**

Woodchester Investments

Industry: **Financial Services - Diversified**

Woodchester Group offers credit financing and international asset financing. It also provides banking, brokerage, insurance, leasing, commercial-mortgage and foreign-currency services. Woodchester Credit Lyonnais, its wholly-owned U.K. subsidiary, specializes in business-equipment and automobile financing. Woodchester's international division offers asset financing, fund management, and corporate treasury services. In 1994, Woodchester acquired Portuguese vehicle and equipment-leasing company Slibail Portuguesa. Woodchester is 53% owned by Crédit Lyonnais.

IR£ mi	12/92	12/93	12/94	US$mil 12/94				
Revenues	**208.0**	**211.0**	**188.6**	**282.8**	P/E Ratio	**15.7**	Price (9/30/95)	**1.73**
Net Income	**31.0**	**18.0**	**23.7**	**35.5**	P/B Ratio	**1.6**	52 Wk Hi-Low	**1.73-1.18**
Book Value	**233.0**	**249.0**	**228.7**	**351.8**	Yield %	**3.5**	Market Cap	**US$2.4mil**

Address	**Woodchester Hse., Golden Ln.**	Tel	**01-478-4299**	ADR		CEO	**Craig McKinney**
	Dublin 8	Fax	**01-475-6681**	SEDOL No.	**979092**	Chairman	**Craig McKinney**

Italy

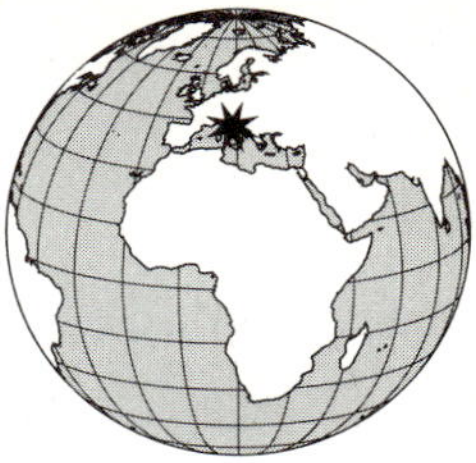

Italy

Heather O'Brian,
Milan

Local Trading Hours	Time Difference with New York	Population (Est. 94)
8:00-3:00	6 hours ahead	58,138,000

Rome wasn't built in a day, and an ongoing drive to modernize Italy's bourse is also proceeding at a less-than-frenzied pace. Nevertheless, there are clear signs that change is in the air at Piazza Affari, the site of Milan's stock market.

Since April 1994, all share trading has been conducted on a screen-based system. Only stock options are still traded through an open outcry system, and those are expected to be transferred to screen-based trading in early 1996.

And with the introduction in November 1994 of the FIB 30 stock futures contract, linked to the MIB 30 index of Milan's blue chip stocks, Italy's stock market completed another important step in its push to compete with other bourses in increasingly globalized equity markets.

One of the more resounding steps in Italy's own drawn-out Big Bang is expected to come in February 1996 with the extension of a five-day rolling settlement system to all shares quoted on Milan's stock market.

Currently, 191 of 326 stocks are already traded on the rolling settlement system, but they represent only a small percentage of trading activity in terms of volume. The aim of the change is to reduce price risk, boost liquidity and foreign interest, and encourage more efficient pricing. But thus far, those shares which have been moved to the new system have been characterized mainly by a sharp drop in trading volumes as market participants adapt to the new system.

Among other foreseen developments is the introduction of new derivatives products. The FIB 30 is the only equity derivative product which is now available on the Italian Derivatives Market (IDEM). An index option on the MIB 30 is set to begin in the autumn of 1995 while derivative products tied to interest rates and the lira are also under study.

In addition, Italy's Stock Exchange Council (ISEC) is examining the idea of using specialists in the stock market to enhance liquidity for a certain number of small and thinly-traded stocks.

Dow Jones Italy Equity Market Index Performance

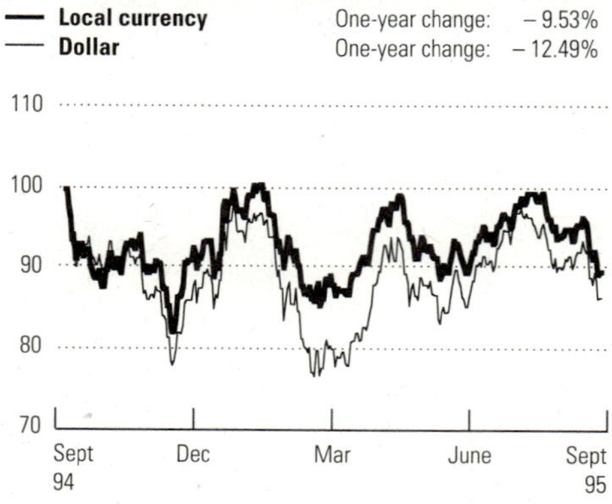

At 1995's midpoint, 223 companies, including four foreign companies, had their shares listed on Milan's stock market. This is only one

Gross Domestic Product (94)	Three-Year Average GDP Growth (92-94)	Main Industries	Consumer Price Index (93-94)	Monetary Unit	Exchange Rate (9/95)
$1.031 trillion	0.7%	Engineering, telecommunications, textiles and clothing, transportation equipment, chemicals, agriculture and food, insurance and banking, construction, tourism	3.9%	Lire	Lire1612.90 to US$1.00

more company than the 222 which were listed at 1994's end. While nine new companies were listed, eight exited from the stock market due to mergers or financial difficulties.

The categories of stock traded in Italy include ordinary shares, preferred shares, and so called savings shares, which are cumulative non-voting preferred shares.

As of June 30, 1995, total stock market capitalization stood at 289.306 trillion lire, down from 330.661 trillion lire at the end of 1994.

As a percentage of the country's 1,655 trillion lire economy, these figures underscore the traditional reluctance with which Italian companies, many of which are small or medium-sized family-controlled groups, have approached a potential stock market listing.

At the same time, tax and other financial incentives launched in the spring of 1994 to encourage companies with net equity of less than 500 billion lire to seek listings have started to bear some fruit.

Luxury jewelry and watch maker Bulgari SpA, machine tools company Stayer SpA, disk brake producer Brembo SpA and IMA SpA, a producer of machinery for the packaging industry, were among the new small and mid-sized additions to the stock market over the summer of 1995. Other new arrivals included regional banks Banca Carige, Banco di Desio, Credito Agrario Bresciano and Banca Briantea.

Meanwhile, plans to create a separate market for small and medium-sized companies, the so-called Nasdaq all'italiano, are at a preliminary state.

Ten Largest Capitalized Companies
as of 9/30/95

Stock	Market Cap. US$Mil
Generali	18,473,805.7
Fiat	12,185,299.8
STET	11,596,363.0
Telecom Italia	10,780,487.0
Alleanza	4,993,866.2
Montedison	3,695,736.8
Mediobanca	3,501,015.6
Banca Commerciale	3,476,238.8
RAS	2,908,224.1
Credito Italiano	2,616,947.5

One development welcomed by investors on Milan's bourse in 1995 was the split-off of cellular phone company Telecom Italia Mobile (TIM) from its Telecom Italia parent. TIM shares, which were quoted on the Milan stock market, have drawn both domestic and foreign interest, boosted by strong growth prospects and the dearth of pure cellular phone plays in Europe.

But aside from interest in selected stocks such as TIM, foreigners were said to have been largely absent from Milan's market. Politics, higher interest rates, a crippled lire and inflation concerns proved daunting for the first half of the year. Trading volumes averaged 604.3 billion lire in the first half of 1995 compared with 754 billion lire in 1994, amid general foreign disinterest in the market.

While investors applauded the arrival of the new prime minister, Lamberto Dini, (the Minister of the Treasury in the previous government) and his technocratic ministerial team in January 1995, political factors helped to restrain the stock market, with the Banca Commerciale Italiana (BCI) index losing about 5% in the first three months of the year.

Discussions about when the round of national elections would be held began almost immediately after Dini's arrival, with former prime minister and media magnate Silvio Berlusconi lifting his voice the loudest in the electoral battle cry. The Deutsche mark set an all-time high against the lira, surging to a level of 1,280 lire in March. The mark has since dropped back to below the 1,100 lire level.

In a move designed to combat the risk of higher inflation, the Bank of Italy stepped in to raise key interest rates in late May, and promised it wouldn't hesitate to act again if inflation didn't show signs of subsiding after the summer.

Nine months into 1995, however, Milan's market had scraped back earlier losses and even registered a gentle rise. Signs that inflation really might recede after August, a strengthening lira, and surprising calm on Italy's frequently stormy political front were behind the gains. Observers began to agree that Dini would likely see the parliament pass his government's 1996 budget and an increasing number of once confrontational politicians started to discuss the possibility that elections could take place as late as June 1996.

As the last leg of 1995 began, the government also showed timid signs that its privatization plans were going forward, although delays are still a key characteristic of the program.

A second tranche of shares in merchant bank and financial services group Istituto Mobiliare Italiano (IMI) was placed with a stable shareholding group of private investors in July. By the end of 1995, the Treasury is expected to sell off most of its remaining stake, through a private placement and privatization bond issue, in the insurer Istituto Nazionale delle Assicurazioni (INA).

Industry Group Performance
1 Year Change Through 9/30/95

Industry	Change % (US$)
Best Performing	
Paper Products	7.83
Retailers - Broadline	-0.94
Telephone Systems - All	-1.10
Oilfield Equipment & Services - Other	-3.12
Banks - Regional	-6.74
Worst Performing	
Computers	-35.52
Congolomerates	-30.57
Financial Services - Diversified	-28.00
Commodity Chemicals	-24.62
Chemicals - All	-24.62

As far as state sales go, however, those of electric utility Ente Nazionale per l'Energia Elettrica (ENEL), energy producer Ente Nazionale Idrocarburi (ENI) and telecommunications holding company Societa Finanziaria Telefonica per Azioni (Stet), are the most widely anticipated. They are expected to add significant bulk to the market and should help shake up the hierarchy in Milan's MIB 30. The ordering of Italy's privatization lineup is uncertain due to the necessity of Parliamentary approval of regulatory authorities, but the government's latest aim is to sell a first tranche of ENI within 1995.

In September, financial services and holding company Gemina SpA and Ferruzzi Finanziaria SpA announced plans for a mega-merger, which will result in Italy's second largest private industrial group. The operation, which also involves companies in industrial giant Fiat's circle, has been roundly criticized for a lack of stock market transparency. It has also highlighted the fact that the same handful of companies, starting with powerful merchant bank Mediobanca, continue to dictate the most important Italian financial deals.

Milan's stock market is also dominated by a few names. As of June 30, 1995, the stock market's largest 30 companies made up about 76% of the market's capitalization.

The Fiat group, insurer Assicurazioni Generali SpA, subsidiaries of the giant state holding company Istituto per la Ricostruzione Industriale SpA (IRI) and companies in the ENI group are the most liquid, with the Ras, Ferruzzi, Ligresti, De Benedetti and Pirelli groups following closely behind. The rest tend to be rather illiquid, small to medium-sized groups.

Alleanza

Industry: **Insurance - Life & Health**

Alleanza Assicurazioni offers insurance and financial services. It provides life insurance and all classes of non-life insurance, including accident and health, throughout Europe. The company's financial services include investment management and annuities. Its wholly-owned subsidiaries include Edicom and Crespim. It also acquired a 12% stake in Banco Ambrosiano Veneto with which it collaborates in the selling of a range of insurance policies. In 1995, Alleanza completed the purchased of Fincral-Finanziamenti al Lavoro and La Venezia Assicurazioni.

lire bil	12/92	12/93	12/94	US$mil 12/94				
Revenues	**978.7**	**1,970.8**	**2,543.0**	**1,583.6**	P/E Ratio	**67.4**	Price (9/30/95)	**14,624**
Net Income	**161.2**	**190.2**	**140.6**	**87.6**	P/B Ratio	**6.1**	52 Wk Hi-Low	**17,886.0-14,199.0**
Book Value	**1,134.7**	**1,123.9**	**1,564.2**	**964.2**	Yield %	**0.9**	Market Cap	**US$4,993.9mil**

Address **Viale Luigi Sturzo 35**
20154 Milan
Tel **02-6296345**
Fax **02-653778**
ADR
SEDOL No. **4015970**
Co-Chairman **Valerio Florio**
Co-Chairman **Roberto Pennisi**

Ambrosiano Veneto

Industry: **Banks - Regional**

Banco Ambrosiano Veneto offers banking and financial services from 538 branches. Its main subsidiaries specialize in leasing, factoring, mutual funds, and portfolio management. Its Caboto Group subsidiary is its securities-trading and -brokerage arm. In 1994, the bank acquired Società di Banche Siciliane, which has a network of 29 retail banks in Sicily. It also established Ambroveneto International Bank to support group funding activities. The bank has representative offices in London, New York, Hong Kong, and Beijing.

lire bil	12/92	12/93	12/94	US$mil 12/94				
Revenues	**4,438.7**	**5,195.7**	**4,989.2**	**3,106.9**	P/E Ratio M	**N/A**	Price (9/30/95) M	**4,083.00**
Net Income	**153.4**	**188.7**	**148.8**	**92.6**	P/B Ratio M	**N/A**	52 Wk Hi-Low M	**6,169.0-3,878.0**
Book Value	**2,169.8**	**2,219.4**	**2,370.8**	**1,461.4**	Yield % M	**N/A**	Market Cap M	**US$1,258.9mil**

Address **Piazza Paolo Ferrari 10**
20121 Milan
Tel **02-859-41**
Fax **02-859-47326**
ADR
SEDOL No. **4076836**
Managing Director **Carlo Salvatori**
Chairman **Giovanni Bazoli**

M=Multiple issues in index; reflects most active.

Autostrade

Industry: **Heavy Construction**

Freeway Concession and Construction (Concessioni e Construzione Autostrade) operates a group of transport-infrastructure businesses that construct, manage, and maintain roadways. Concessioni e Construzione Autostrade is also responsible for the collection of tolls on over half of Italy's highways. Autostrade works on approximately 50% of the Italian national roadway network, with more than 3,000 kilometers of roadway consigned to the company.

lire bil	12/92	12/93	12/94	US$mil 12/94				
Sales	**2,530.0**	**2,547.0**	**2,814.4**	**1,752.6**	P/E Ratio	**15.4**	Price (9/30/95)	**1,830.00**
Net Income	**29.3**	**82.3**	**140.2**	**87.3**	P/B Ratio	**0.4**	52 Wk Hi-Low	**2,290.0-1,574.0**
Book Value	**2,961.2**	**3,022.9**	**3,086.9**	**1,902.9**	Yield %	**6.0**	Market Cap	**US$671.1mil**

Address **Via A Bergamini 50**
00159 Rome
Tel **06-43631**
Fax **06-43634157**
ADR
SEDOL No. **4065317**
Managing Director **Dr. Domenico Cempella**
Chairman **Dr. Mario Schiavone**

Banca Commerciale

Industry: **Banks - Regional**

Banca Commerciale Italiana (BCI), one of Italy's largest banks by assets, offers extensive corporate- and retail-banking services in the domestic and international markets. In addition, the bank offers asset-management, life-insurance, investment-banking, mutual-fund marketing, and other financial services. The company is known as COMIT in Italy and as BCI overseas. The bank operates 928 branches in Italy and 303 branches and 29 representative offices abroad. BCI has operations in more than 46 countries.

lire bil	12/92	12/93	12/94	US$mil 12/94				
Revenues	**14,654.8**	**11,964.6**	**15,871.9**	**9,883.8**	P/E Ratio	**17.1**	Price (9/30/95)	**3,572.00**
Net Income	**218.5**	**301.2**	**329.4**	**205.1**	P/B Ratio	**0.7**	52 Wk Hi-Low	**4,112.0-3,189.0**
Book Value	**5,968.5**	**6,099.9**	**8,017.0**	**4,941.9**	Yield %	**3.5**	Market Cap	**US$3,476.2mil**

Address **Piazza della Scala 6**
20121 Milan
Tel **02-88501**
Fax **N/A**
ADR
SEDOL No. **4072942**
Managing Director **Luigi Fausti**
Chairman **Lionello Adler**

Banca Toscana

Industry: **Banks - Regional**

Banca Toscana operates in the banking and financial-services industries. Its businesses include lending, depository, and related services. The company also provides securities-trading, foreign-transaction, and cash-management services. Banca Toscana's operations are centered in Tuscany, but it has branches throughout Italy. The company's majority shareholder is Monte dei Paschi di Siena, and it is part of the Monte dei Oaschi Banking Group, one of the largest banking groups in Italy.

lire bil	12/91	12/92	12/93	US$mil 12/93				
Revenues	**2,293.4**	**1,993.9**	**2,453.3**	**1,527.7**	P/E Ratio	**27.5**	Price (9/30/95)	**3,353.00**
Net Income	**113.2**	**45.6**	**35.9**	**22.3**	P/B Ratio	**0.6**	52 Wk Hi-Low	**4,297.0-2,404.0**
Book Value	**1,502.1**	**1,487.9**	**1,521.0**	**937.6**	Yield %	**1.5**	Market Cap	**US$612.0mil**

Address **Via Leone Pancaldo 4**
50121 Florence
Tel **055-43911**
Fax **055-2398299**
ADR
SEDOL No. **4072210**
CEO **B. Bronzetti**
Chairman **Giuseppe Bartolomei**

Bonifiche Siele

Industry: **Banks - Regional**

Bonifiche Siele Finanziaria heads a group of banking and financial-services businesses. Its banking activities operate through its partially-owned Banca Nazionale dell'Agricoltura and Interbanca subsidiaries. Banca Nazionale consists of 283 branches and three international representative offices. Other holdings include the banking business Sielefin, the insurance-consulting agency Assiaudit, and the financial-services company Gestifondi. Bonifiche Siele has branches in New York and Hong Kong, and representative offices in Frankfurt and Paris.

lire bil	12/92	12/93	12/94	US$mil 12/94				
Revenues	**N/A**	**4,884.8**	**3,998.2**	**2,489.8**	P/E Ratio	**NMF**	Price (9/30/95)	**35,080**
Net Income	**6.7**	**-34.3**	**-221.6**	**-138.0**	P/B Ratio	**1.6**	52 Wk Hi-Low	**35,900.0-19,100.0**
Book Value	**550.9**	**983.6**	**579.7**	**357.4**	Yield %	**0.0**	Market Cap	**US$564.2mil**

Address **Via Guido d'Arezzo 32**	Tel **06-854-1441**	ADR	Managing Director **Massimo Lombardi**
00198 Rome	Fax **06-6749-070**	SEDOL No. **4865681**	Chairman **Giuliano Monterastelli**

Cartiere Burgo

Industry: **Paper Products**

Cartiere Burgo manufactures paper, paper pulp, and packaging. About 70% of the company's output consists of coated papers. Cartiere di Chieti, the parent company, and its wholly-owned subsidiary Burgo Ardennes focus on the production of coated graphic papers. Comecart, another subsidiary, designs and builds paper mills. Burgo Ardennes also owns S.E.F.E., a French forest-management company established in 1994. The company's products are sold mainly to the magazine and newspaper industries. In 1994, 75% of its paper sales were to other European Community countries.

lire bil	12/92	12/93	12/94	US$mil 12/94				
Sales	**1,570.4**	**1,705.0**	**2,402.1**	**1,495.9**	P/E Ratio	**95.6**	Price (9/30/95)	**10,900**
Net Income	**-136.3**	**0.2**	**19.5**	**12.1**	P/B Ratio	**1.0**	52 Wk Hi-Low	**11,732.0-8,807.0**
Book Value	**996.7**	**993.4**	**1,364.1**	**840.9**	Yield %	**0.0**	Market Cap	**US$851.9mil**

Address **Via del Freidano 8**	Tel **011-26071**	ADR	CEO **Giuseppe Lignana**
10099 San Mauro Torinese	Fax **011-266930**	SEDOL No. **4152822**	Chairman **Lionello Adler**

CIR

Industry: **Conglomerates**

Compagnie Industriali Riunite (CIR), partially owned by Cofide (a member of the De Benedetti group), is a financial-services and manufacturing company. Its holdings include the computer manufacturer Olivetti (24.5%), the electronics firm Sasib (53%), and the publisher Editoriale L'Espresso (58.5%). The company is also active in tourism through its 46% holding in Spanish hotelier Cofir. In addition, CIR owns a majority stake in the Italian automobile-parts group Sogefi.

lire bil	12/92	12/93	12/94	US$mil 12/94				
Sales	**964.0**	**1,113.3**	**9,812.3**	**6,110.3**	P/E Ratio	**NMF**	Price (9/30/95)	**1,043.00**
Net Income	**-539.9**	**16.0**	**-377.3**	**-235.0**	P/B Ratio	**0.5**	52 Wk Hi-Low	**2,141.0-1,038.0**
Book Value	**1,743.8**	**1,719.4**	**1,290.7**	**795.6**	Yield %	**0.0**	Market Cap	**US$364.1mil**

Address **Via Ciovassino 1**	Tel **02-722-701**	ADR	Managing Director **Rodolfo de Benedetti**
20121 Milan	Fax **N/A**	SEDOL No. **4162371**	Chairman **Carlo de Benedetti**

Cofide

Industry: **Conglomerates**

Cofide (Compagnia Finanziaria De Benedetti), a member of the De Benedetti group, is a financial-services, communications, and public-relations holding company. Its principal holdings include the financial-services and manufacturing firm Compagnie Industriali Riunite (CIR) and the real-estate firm Lasa. Finanza & Futuro Holding S.p.A., a subsidiary of Cofide set up in 1986, was listed on the Stock Exchange in 1994. In 1995, Deutsche Bank bought a controlling interest in Finanza & Futuro from Cofide.

lire bil	12/91	12/92	12/93	US$mil 12/93				
Sales	**206.3**	**497.5**	**297.6**	**185.3**	P/E Ratio	**95.7**	Price (9/30/95)	**481.50**
Net Income	**39.7**	**-281.3**	**3.2**	**2.0**	P/B Ratio	**0.3**	52 Wk Hi-Low	**1,198.0-467.5**
Book Value	**1,187.0**	**878.4**	**983.7**	**606.4**	Yield %	**0.0**	Market Cap	**US$169.1mil**

Address **Via Ciovassino 1**	Tel **02-722-701**	ADR	CEO **Carlo De Benedetti**
20121 Milan	Fax **02-722-70270**	SEDOL No. **4207636**	Chairman **Carlo De Benedetti**

Credito Italiano

Industry: **Banks - Regional**

Credito Italiano, privatized in the last quarter of 1993, is a savings and loan institution, primarily for retail customers. Credito Italiano also provides brokerage services and manages mutual funds through its partially-owned Gesticredit subsidiary. In a joint venture with Banca Commerciale Italiana and Credito Fondiario, Credito Italiano created Serfinim, a financial company with a majority interest in real-estate firm Immobiliare Italia. In January 1995, Credito Italiano took over the regional bank Credito Romagnolo.

lire bil	12/91	12/92	12/93	US$mil 12/93				
Revenues	**9,689.9**	**11,887.3**	**11,182.7**	**6,963.8**	P/E Ratio	**16.5**	Price (9/30/95)	**1,902.00**
Net Income	**297.0**	**202.2**	**274.9**	**171.2**	P/B Ratio	**0.9**	52 Wk Hi-Low	**2,157.0-1,547.0**
Book Value	**4,331.9**	**4,598.3**	**4,797.9**	**2,957.6**	Yield %	**3.0**	Market Cap	**US$2,616.9mil**

Address **Piazza Cordusio 2**	Tel **02-88-62-1**	ADR	Managing Director **Egidio G. Bruno**
20123 Milan	Fax **N/A**	SEDOL No. **4232445**	Chairman **Lucio Rondelli**

Ferruzzi Finanziaria

Industry: **Conglomerates**

Ferruzzi Finanziaria (Ferfin), part of the Ferruzzi Group, is an investment holding company that focuses primarily on the agriculture industry. It also has interests in the chemical, energy, and engineering industries as well as concrete and cement. In mid-1993, due to continuing financial problems, Ferruzzi Finanziaria handed control of its affairs to a group of its creditor banks and undertook a substantial program of reorganization and consolidation.

lire bil	12/91	12/92	12/93	US$mil 12/93				
Sales	**17,790.0**	**19,900.0**	**22,804.0**	**14,398.0**	P/E Ratio M	**12.8**	Price (9/30/95) M	**936.80**
Net Income	**115.0**	**-1,667.0**	**-2,419.0**	**-1,527.3**	P/B Ratio M	**NMF**	52 Wk Hi-Low M	**1,651.0-863.9**
Book Value	**3,096.0**	**847.0**	**-1,690.0**	**-987.1**	Yield % M	**0.0**	Market Cap M	**US$857.3mil**

Address **Via XIII Giugno 8**, **48100 Ravenna** — Tel **0544-514-111** — Fax **N/A** — ADR — SEDOL No. **4385907** — Managing Director **Enrico Bondi** — Chairman **Guido Rossi**

M=Multiple issues in index; reflects most active.

Fiat

Industry: **Automobile Manufacturers**

Fiat (Fabbrica Italiana di Automobili Torino), a diversified automobile and industrial manufacturer, is Europe's third-largest automotive company in terms of revenue. It manufactures and distributes autos and automotive components, commercial vehicles, and agricultural and construction equipment. It produces Alfa Romeo, Ferrari, Innocenti, and Lancia cars and Iveco commercial vehicles. Fiat's holdings include construction firm Cogefar-Impresit, insurer Toro, and financial firm Fidis. Sales outside of Italy account for roughly 60% of Fiat's revenues.

lire bil	12/92	12/93	12/94	US$mil 12/94				
Sales	**59,106.0**	**54,556.0**	**65,240.0**	**40,626.5**	P/E Ratio M	**28.9**	Price (9/30/95) M	**5,984.00**
Net Income	**551.0**	**-1,783.0**	**1,011.0**	**629.6**	P/B Ratio M	**1.2**	52 Wk Hi-Low M	**6,882.0-5,416.0**
Book Value	**16,170.0**	**17,427.0**	**20,021.0**	**12,341.5**	Yield % M	**0.8**	Market Cap M	**US$12,185mil**

Address **Corso G. Marconi 10**, **10125 Turin** — Tel **011-666-111** — Fax **011-666-3400** — ADR **FIA** — SEDOL No. **4335601** — CEO **Cesare Romiti** — Chairman **Giovanni Agnelli**

M=Multiple issues in index; reflects most active.

Fidis

Industry: **Financial Services - Diversified**

Fidis Finanziaria di Sviluppo, which is majority-owned by Fiat, is the holding company responsible for Fiat's interests in financial services, investment, and real-estate management. The company's subsidiaries include wholly-owned financial-services firms operating under the Fiat and Sava names and the majority-owned investment-management firms Fidisgestioni and Prime. The company has financial-services operations in Italy, the major European countries, and the United States (New York).

lire bil	12/92	12/93	12/94	US$mil 12/94				
Revenues	**2,970.2**	**2,894.4**	**2,872.6**	**1,788.8**	P/E Ratio	**9.7**	Price (9/30/95)	**3,213.00**
Net Income	**140.6**	**50.7**	**124.2**	**77.3**	P/B Ratio	**0.8**	52 Wk Hi-Low	**4,383.8-3,196.0**
Book Value	**2,447.2**	**1,113.3**	**1,520.9**	**937.5**	Yield %	**5.6**	Market Cap	**US$747.0mil**

Address **Via Giacosa 16 Bis**, **10125 Turin** — Tel **011-835102** — Fax **N/A** — ADR — SEDOL No. **4329671** — Managing Director **Gian Luigi Garrino** — Chairman **Francesco P. Mattioli**

La Fondiaria

Industry: **Insurance - Full Line**

La Fondiaria is a private-sector insurance company. It provides insurance and reinsurance services, including life insurance and all classifications of nonlife insurance, in Italy and abroad. The company's partially-owned insurance subsidiaries include La Previdente, Milano, and Dominion Insurance Holdings in London. In 1994, La Fondiaria bought the French insurer Groupama's 20% stake in La Fondiaria Assicurazioni. La Fondiaria is controlled by Ferruzzi Finanziaria, which holds shares both directly and through its majority-owned subsidiary GAIC.

lire bil	12/92	12/93	12/94	US$mil 12/94				
Revenues	**5,458.3**	**6,015.6**	**5,666.0**	**3,528.4**	P/E Ratio	**N/A**	Price (9/30/95)	**7,969.00**
Net Income	**-575.6**	**-464.8**	**-431.0**	**-268.4**	P/B Ratio	**N/A**	52 Wk Hi-Low	**12,366.0-7,713.0**
Book Value	**520.0**	**1,344.0**	**N/A**	**N/A**	Yield %	**N/A**	Market Cap	**US$1,206.2mil**

Address **Via L. il Magnifico 1**, **50129 Florence** — Tel **055-479-41** — Fax **055-47-6026** — ADR — SEDOL No. **4344771** — CEO **Arrigo Bianchi** — Chairman **Alberto Pecci**

GAIC

Industry: **Financial Services - Diversified**

GAIC is a holding company for insurance and financial-services companies. The firm's majority-owned subsidiaries include the holding companies GAIC International and Maslora, and the securities-management and interagency firm GAIC Commissionaria. In 1994, GAIC sold 49% of its 61% share of the merchant banker Monforte and sold off its 25% stake in Trade Factoring. The company also holds a 30% stake in the insurer La Fondiaria and has interests in Cartiere Burgo, Cofide, Assirein, and Situr. GAIC is 78%-owned by the financial holding company Ferruzzi Finanziaria.

lire bil	12/91 P	12/92 P	12/93 P	US$mil 12/93				
Revenues	**31.7**	**659.4**	**557.3**	**351.9**	P/E Ratio	**67.8**	Price (9/30/95)	**411.00**
Net Income	**5.7**	**-1,723.3**	**-550.3**	**-347.4**	P/B Ratio	**0.4**	52 Wk Hi-Low	**833.90-352.90**
Book Value	**3,100.2**	**1,579.4**	**1,029.2**	**601.1**	Yield %	**0.0**	Market Cap	**US$251.7mil**

Address **Via Cerva 28**, **20122 Milan** — Tel **02-76-009272** — Fax **N/A** — ADR — SEDOL No. **4357553** — President **--** — Chairman **Lamberto J. Celesia**

P=Parent company data.

Generali

Industry: **Insurance - Full Line**

Assicurazioni Generali, the largest insurance firm in Italy in terms of market capitalization, heads a group of 86 insurance companies and 145 other companies that operate in the financial, real-estate, and agricultural sectors. Approximately two thirds of Generali's consolidated premiums are derived from non-life insurance policies. With operations worldwide, Generali generates more than 60% of its insurance sales outside Italy. The company owns a 75% stake in Central Hispano-Generali, a Spanish insurance company.

	lire bil 12/91	12/92	12/93	US$mil 12/93				
Revenues	**9.5**	**13.5**	**12.9**	**8.1**	P/E Ratio	**52.8**	Price (9/30/95)	**37,170**
Net Income	**0.4**	**0.4**	**0.4**	**0.2**	P/B Ratio	**NMF**	52 Wk Hi-Low	**41,051.0-34,616.0**
Book Value	**5.7**	**6.0**	**5.3**	**3.1**	Yield %	**0.0**	Market Cap	**US$18,474mil**

Address **piazza Duca degli Abruzzi 2**, **34132 Trieste**
Tel **04-6710**
Fax **04-671600**
ADR
SEDOL No. **4056719**
Managing Director **Fabio Fegitz**
Chairman **Eugenio Coppola**

IFIL

Industry: **Other Food**

IFIL is the industrial holding company of Fiat. It invests in food, industrial, service, and tourism companies. Its food holdings include the French food manufacturer Danone, Italian cheese and processed-meat company Galbani, and Saint Louis, a holding company investing in the food and agriculture sectors. IFIL also has exposure to French food, insurance, and financial-services company Worms & Cie., French hotel operator Accor, and a minority interest in Fiat S.p.A. It has a controlling interest in retail and distribution company La Rinascente.

	lire bil 12/92	12/93	12/94	US$mil 12/94				
Sales	**388.1**	**374.0**	**5,189.3**	**3,231.5**	P/E Ratio M	**13.1**	Price (9/30/95) M	**5,540.00**
Net Income	**192.8**	**231.2**	**280.1**	**174.4**	P/B Ratio M	**0.7**	52 Wk Hi-Low M	**6,876.0-5,088.0**
Book Value	**2,026.3**	**2,314.5**	**3,236.4**	**1,995.0**	Yield % M	**2.0**	Market Cap M	**US$1,316.0mil**

Address **Piazza Solferino 11**, **10121 Turin**
Tel **011-55411**
Fax **N/A**
ADR
SEDOL No. **4455736**
Managing Director **Gabriele G. di Genola**
Chairman **Umberto Agnelli**

M=Multiple issues in index; reflects most active.

Italcementi

Industry: **Building Materials**

Italcementi is one of Europe's largest producers of cement. It also produces other building and hydraulic materials, and provides engineering design and construction services. Ciments Francais, its wholly-owned French cement and ready-mix concrete producer, generates nearly 40% of the company's revenues. Italcementi's other holdings include wholly-owned Cemensud, 72% of Cementerie Siciliane, and 77% of Cementerie di Sardegna. Non-European exports, mainly to North America, account for 23% of Italcementi's sales.

	lire bil 12/91	12/92	12/93	US$mil 12/93				
Sales	**1,648.7**	**1,712.8**	**5,161.4**	**3,214.1**	P/E Ratio M	**NMF**	Price (9/30/95) M	**10,441**
Net Income	**184.5**	**24.7**	**-126.1**	**-78.5**	P/B Ratio M	**0.9**	52 Wk Hi-Low M	**12,747.0-8,423.0**
Book Value	**2,388.4**	**2,912.7**	**2,623.3**	**1,617.1**	Yield % M	**0.8**	Market Cap M	**US$1,053.0mil**

Address **Via G. Camozzi 124**, **24100 Bergamo**
Tel **035-39-6111**
Fax **035-24-4905**
ADR **ILMNY**
SEDOL No. **4450076**
Managing Director **Giampiero Pesenti**
Chairman **Giovanni Giavazzi**

M=Multiple issues in index; reflects most active.

Italgas

Industry: **Gas Utilities**

Italgas (Società Italiana per il Gas) holds full and partial interests in water-distribution, natural-gas, and waste-management businesses. The company, with operations in 1,436 Italian municipalities, has 1,170 natural-gas-distribution concessions. These represent 33% of the Italian market for natural gas. An additional 391 concessions manage water-distribution services, while 57 treat wastewater and 29 manage sewage systems. Italgas holds interests in gas suppliers in Argentina and Portugal. In 1994, it supplied gas to over four million customers.

	lire bil 12/91	12/92	12/93	US$mil 12/93				
Sales	**3,352.6**	**3,381.0**	**3,580.6**	**2,229.7**	P/E Ratio	**31.9**	Price (9/30/95)	**4,775.00**
Net Income	**86.8**	**77.2**	**84.8**	**52.8**	P/B Ratio	**1.6**	52 Wk Hi-Low	**5,503.0-3,590.0**
Book Value	**1,235.9**	**1,256.3**	**1,678.0**	**1,034.4**	Yield %	**2.1**	Market Cap	**US$1,959.3mil**

Address **Via XX Settembre 41**, **10121 Turin**
Tel **011-23951**
Fax **011-239-4795**
ADR
SEDOL No. **4468206**
CEO **Giacomo Vitali**
Chairman **Carlo Damolo**

Italmobiliare

Industry: **Financial Services - Diversified**

Italmobiliare is a holding company for organizations involved in cement manufacturing, iron metallurgy, paper and cardboard production, financial services, publishing, and real estate. Its principal holdings include partial interests in the cement and building-materials manufacturer Italcementi; the iron-metallurgy, mechanical, and engineering firm Franco Tosi; the paper producer Cartiere Burgo; and the accounting firm Compagnia Fiduciaria Nazionale. Italmobiliare's associated companies include Mittel, Fincomind, and Acciaierie e Ferriere Lombarde.

	lire bil 03/92	03/93	12/94 *	US$mil 12/94				
Revenues	**124.0**	**168.2**	**5,539.0**	**3,449.3**	P/E Ratio	**71.2**	Price (9/30/95)	**28,300**
Net Income	**44.8**	**37.2**	**12.0**	**7.5**	P/B Ratio	**NMF**	52 Wk Hi-Low	**40,158.0-26,254.0**
Book Value	**744.0**	**792.0**	**N/A**	**N/A**	Yield %	**1.9**	Market Cap	**US$357.8mil**

Address **Via Borgonuovo 20**, **20121 Milan**
Tel **02-29-02-41**
Fax **02-6554-318**
ADR
SEDOL No. **4492216**
CEO **Giampiero Pesenti**
Chairman **Giampiero Pesenti**

*Irregular period due to fiscal year change.

Lloyd Adriatico

Industry: **Insurance - Full Line**

Lloyd Adriatico owns life and non-life-insurance and reinsurance businesses, and also holds interests in finance, agribusiness, and property-management companies. Its insurance products include health, liability, and motor-vehicle insurance. Motor-vehicle premiums contribute more than half of the company's total premiums. It also offers a full line of insurance through its majority-owned Spanish subsidiary. Lloyd Adriatico operates a sales network of approximately 600 agencies and 850 subagencies.

lire bil	12/90	12/91	12/92	US$mil 12/92				
Revenues	**940.2**	**1,173.0**	**1,466.2**	**1,180.4**	P/E Ratio	**19.3**	Price (9/30/95)	**19,010**
Net Income	**47.3**	**53.5**	**49.3**	**39.7**	P/B Ratio	**1.5**	52 Wk Hi-Low	**20,434.0-14,721.0**
Book Value	**515.9**	**608.4**	**624.8**	**423.6**	Yield %	**1.9**	Market Cap	**US$589.3mil**

Address **Largo Ugo Irneri 1**
34143 Trieste
Tel **040-77-81-1**
Fax **040-77-81-311**
ADR
SEDOL No. **4520270**
Managing Director **Antonio Sodaro**
Chairman **Antonio Sodaro**

Magneti Marelli

Industry: **Other Auto Parts**

Magneti Marelli is an automotive-components manufacturer that is partially owned by Fiat. The company manufactures electronic and electromechanical products for automobiles, including carburetors, instrumentation, engine-control, lighting, and climate-control products. Its customers include Fiat, Ford, BMW, and Toyota. The company is involved in a joint venture with U.S. automotive firm Walbro to produce fuel systems in Brazil. Magneti Marelli makes about one third of its sales to Italian companies and one fourth to French companies.

lire bil	12/92	12/93	12/94	US$mil 12/94				
Sales	**2,881.2**	**2,935.4**	**5,243.4**	**3,265.2**	P/E Ratio	**31.8**	Price (9/30/95)	**3,341.00**
Net Income	**-17.1**	**-157.4**	**27.2**	**16.9**	P/B Ratio	**1.0**	52 Wk Hi-Low	**4,454.0-3,056.0**
Book Value	**594.4**	**456.9**	**1,374.7**	**847.4**	Yield %	**2.1**	Market Cap	**US$816.8mil**

Address **Viale Aldo Borletti 61-63**
Corbetta, Milan
Tel **02-972001**
Fax **02-97200523**
ADR
SEDOL No. **4369161**
CEO **Domenico Bordone**
Chairman **Luigi Francione**

Mediobanca

Industry: **Financial Services - Diversified**

Mediobanca, a Milan-based merchant bank, provides medium- and long-term credit. Clients include companies in the insurance, finance, engineering, transport, telecommunication, electricity, and textiles and clothing industries. The bank also underwrites and places securities, and provides advisory services for mergers and acquisitions. As of June 1994, the bank had assets totaling L27,661 billion. Banca Commerciale Italiana, Banca di Roma, and Credito Italiano have a controlling interest in Mediobanca. Its holdings include a 3.5% stake in Ferruzzi and a 3.6% in Montedison.

lire bil	06/92	06/93	06/94	US$mil 06/94				
Revenues	**2,403.7**	**2,782.5**	**2,544.6**	**1,558.4**	P/E Ratio	**18.8**	Price (9/30/95)	**11,863**
Net Income	**262.1**	**200.1**	**301.1**	**184.4**	P/B Ratio	**1.4**	52 Wk Hi-Low	**14,438.0-11,279.0**
Book Value	**1,909.3**	**2,486.1**	**3,943.2**	**2,490.9**	Yield %	**1.7**	Market Cap	**US$3,501.0mil**

Address **Via Filodrammatici 10**
20121 Milan
Tel **02-8829-1**
Fax **02-8829-367**
ADR
SEDOL No. **4574813**
Managing Director **Vincenzo Maranghi**
Chairman **Francesco Cingano**

Milano Assicurazioni

Industry: **Insurance - Full Line**

Milano Assicurazioni, 42%-owned by the insurance company La Fondiaria, provides all categories of insurance and reinsurance, including life, accident, health, automobile, theft, fire, and transport. Through its majority-owned subsidiaries, Acquaviva, Ector, Elmar, Immobiliare Lauro, San Giulianese Sud, and Systema Terra, it also has interests in real estate. Milano Assicurazioni has a network of agencies across Italy, including Rome, Milan, Naples, and Genoa. The company also has operations in Germany.

lire bil	12/91	12/92	12/93	US$mil 12/93				
Revenues	**840.4**	**1,163.0**	**1,401.0**	**872.4**	P/E Ratio	**NMF**	Price (9/30/95)	**5,925.00**
Net Income	**27.3**	**-335.7**	**-88.7**	**-55.2**	P/B Ratio	**1.0**	52 Wk Hi-Low	**8,038.0-4,652.0**
Book Value	**672.9**	**7,505.8**	**1,045.6**	**644.5**	Yield %	**0.0**	Market Cap	**US$531.2mil**

Address **Via del Lauro 7**
20100 Milan
Tel **02-88401**
Fax **02-884-02389**
ADR
SEDOL No. **4215101**
CEO **G. Introvigne**
Chairman **Alberto M. Ferrari**

Montedison

Industry: **Conglomerates**

Montedison, an affiliate of Ferruzzi Finanziaria, is an industrial holding company active in chemical production, agroindustry, and energy production. Its chemical operations make polymers and fluoride chemicals, while its agroindustrial operations mainly produce sugar, oils, and starch. The firm owns 50% of the French agroindustrial firm Eridania Beghin-Say. In 1995, Montedison and Royal Dutch/Shell formed Montell, the largest polypropylene maker in the world. Non-European sales account for about one third of Montedison's total revenues.

lire bil	12/91	12/92	12/93	US$mil 12/93				
Sales	**15,732.0**	**16,968.0**	**20,415.0**	**12,889.6**	P/E Ratio	**NMF**	Price (9/30/95)	**1,120.00**
Net Income	**168.0**	**-1,679.0**	**-1,366.0**	**-862.5**	P/B Ratio	**3.3**	52 Wk Hi-Low	**1,393.0-1,060.0**
Book Value	**5,096.0**	**3,322.0**	**1,964.0**	**1,147.2**	Yield %	**0.0**	Market Cap	**US$3,695.7mil**

Address **Foro Buonaparte 31**
20121 Milan
Tel **02-63331**
Fax **02-63-335967**
ADR **MNT**
SEDOL No. **4009939**
Managing Director **Enrico Bondi**
Chairman **Guido Rossi**

Olivetti

Industry: **Computers**

Olivetti manufactures information-technology products such as local-area networks, workstations, and PCs, and has telecommunication interests. It also makes printers, typewriters, copiers, calculators, facsimile machines, and cash registers. Under an agreement with Microsoft, Olivetti provides service and support for Microsoft's international customers. It is a major shareholder in Omnitel Pronto Italia, Italy's second digital mobile-phone network. In a joint venture, Olivetti and Bell Atlantic operate Infostrada, data- and voice-transmission service.

	lire bil 12/91	12/92	12/93	US$mil 12/93				
Sales	8,607.1	8,025.5	8,612.6	5,437.8	P/E Ratio	NMF	Price (9/30/95)	1,392.00
Net Income	-459.8	-649.9	-464.6	-293.3	P/B Ratio	0.6	52 Wk Hi-Low	2,295.0-1,230.0
Book Value	3,083.5	2,361.2	2,550.4	1,489.7	Yield %	0.0	Market Cap	US$1,087.5mil

Address **Via Jervis 77**
10015 Ivrea
Tel **0125-525**
Fax **0125-52-2008**
ADR **OLIVY**
SEDOL No. **4659408**
Managing Director **Corrado Passera**
Chairman **Carlo De Benedetti**

Pirelli

Industry: **Tires & Rubber**

Pirelli manufactures tires for automobiles and cables for the telecommunication, power, and construction industries. The tire division generates more than half of Pirelli's sales, while the cable division generates 49%. The company produces tires in 31 factories and cables in 71 factories in 10 countries. In 1994, the company sold its entire interest in German tire manufacturer Continental, ending its takeover bid. Pirelli makes about 56% of its sales in Europe, 16% in North America, 18% in Central and South America, and 10% in Australia, Asia, and Africa.

	lire bil 12/92	12/93	12/94	US$mil 12/94				
Sales	8,251.6	9,247.0	9,790.2	6,096.6	P/E Ratio	31.0	Price (9/30/95)	2,229.00
Net Income	-104.9	-62.2	109.7	68.3	P/B Ratio	1.2	52 Wk Hi-Low	2,592.0-1,941.0
Book Value	2,531.8	2,604.1	2,876.9	1,773.4	Yield %	0.0	Market Cap	US$1,982.6mil

Address **Piazzale Cadorna 5**
20123 Milan
Tel **02-64421**
Fax **02-89010-406**
ADR **PIREY**
SEDOL No. **4689900**
Managing Director **Marco Provera**
Chairman **Leopoldo Pirelli**

Pirelli & Co.

Industry: **Financial Services - Diversified**

Pirelli & Company is a financial holding and investment company, involved mainly in the cable and tire-manufacturing sectors. The company (along with its Luxembourg affiliate) holds 38% of Société Internationale Pirelli, which, in turn, holds 49% of the tire maker Pirelli S.p.A. Pirelli & Co., in turn, is majority-controlled by a shareholding group led by Pirelli S.p.A. Chairman Leopoldo Pirelli. The Pirelli family directly owns 5% of Pirelli & Company. Assicurazioni Generali acquired a 7% stake in the company in 1995.

	lire bil 12/91	12/92	12/93	US$mil 12/93				
Revenues	205.7	174.8	131.7	83.1	P/E Ratio	30.6	Price (9/30/95)	2,376.00
Net Income	20.2	-95.7	41.3	26.1	P/B Ratio	1.2	52 Wk Hi-Low	3,815.9-2,282.0
Book Value	545.8	568.1	728.2	425.3	Yield %	0.0	Market Cap	US$572.2mil

Address **Via Gaetano Negri 10**
20123 Milan
Tel **02-85351**
Fax **02-89010406**
ADR
SEDOL No. **4689803**
Managing Director **Bruno Reboa**
Chairman **Leopoldo Pirelli**

Premafin Finanziaria

Industry: **Financial Services - Diversified**

Premafin Finanziaria is a holding company for businesses active in real-estate management, construction, insurance, and motorway operations. The company's real-estate portfolio consists of residential, commercial, and retail properties concentrated in the Milan area. Its majority-owned Grassetto subsidiary constructs residential developments and vacation facilities, and its partially-owned Società Assicuratrice Industriale (SAI) subsidiary provides insurance and reinsurance products in Italy and other European countries.

	lire bil 12/92	12/93	12/94	US$mil 12/94				
Revenues	772.0	389.3	459.2	285.9	P/E Ratio	NMF	Price (9/30/95)	796.20
Net Income	-56.2	-235.1	-152.4	-94.9	P/B Ratio	0.6	52 Wk Hi-Low	2,090.0-733.5
Book Value	663.7	712.6	715.1	440.8	Yield %	0.0	Market Cap	US$258.2mil

Address **Via Locatelli 1**
20124 Milan
Tel **02-667041**
Fax **02-66710045**
ADR
SEDOL No. **4699556**
President --
Chairman **Salvatore Ligresti**

Previdente

Industry: **Insurance - Property & Casualty**

La Previdente is an insurance company that provides a full line of life and non-life coverage. Its non-life-insurance products include automobile, aeronautical, injury, health, fire, and theft coverage. Its life-insurance businesses operate through its majority-owned Latina Vita and La Previdente Vita subsidiaries. Through its wholly-owned subsidiaries, Previdente has major interests in real-estate and financial businesses. La Previdente is controlled by Italy's Fondiaria insurance and reinsurance company.

	lire bil 12/92	12/93	12/94	US$mil 12/94				
Revenues	850.7	1,142.1	1,240.4	772.4	P/E Ratio	NMF	Price (9/30/95)	11,715
Net Income	-57.3	30.1	-29.6	-18.4	P/B Ratio	1.0	52 Wk Hi-Low	15,748.0-10,256.0
Book Value	530.4	671.7	670.3	413.2	Yield %	1.7	Market Cap	US$574.6mil

Address **Via Copernico 38**
20125 Milan
Tel **02-66-70-61**
Fax **N/A**
ADR
SEDOL No. **4499563**
Managing Director **Giorgio Lanz**
Chairman **A. Luigi Molinari**

RAS

Industry: **Insurance - Full Line**

Riunione Adriatica di Sicurtà (RAS) is a diversified insurance company that provides a full range of insurance and reinsurance coverage. A large part of its business is automobile insurance, but it also offers life, health, accident, fire, and general-liability coverage. Through its subsidiaries RAS also provides investment and banking services, and manages its own property portfolio, which has extensive holdings in the agriculture and service sectors. German insurance company Allianz has an interest of over 50% in RAS.

lire bil	12/92	12/93	12/94	US$mil 12/94				
Revenues	**6,792.6**	**7,727.8**	**84.4**	**52.5**	P/E Ratio M	**20.4**	Price (9/30/95) M	**17,392**
Net Income	**116.7**	**354.5**	**326.0**	**203.0**	P/B Ratio M	**0.9**	52 Wk Hi-Low M	**21,590.5-14,560.6**
Book Value	**3,331.9**	**3,724.6**	**5,209.1**	**3,211.1**	Yield % M	**1.4**	Market Cap M	**US$2,908.2mil**

Address **Corso Italia 23**, **20122 Milan**
Tel **02-72161**
Fax **02-890-0740**
ADR
SEDOL No. **4718246**
Managing Director **Giulio Baseggio**
Chairman **Angelo Marchiò**

M=Multiple issues in index; reflects most active.

La Rinascente

Industry: **Retailers - Broadline**

La Rinascente is a retail and distribution company that operates department and discount stores and supermarkets. Its wholly-owned sales centers include the Grandi Magazzini Rinascente department stores, UPIM discount stores, and specialized stores such as Trony electrical-appliances stores, Croff home-furnishings stores, and Bricocenter hardware stores. La Rinascente operates food-retailing SMA-Citta Mercato hypermarkets and SMA-Supermercati supermarkets. It announced the formation of a joint venture with Dutch Habitat Holdings to develop a chain of retail stores.

lire bil	12/92	12/93	12/94	US$mil 12/94				
Revenues	**4,498.7**	**4,969.2**	**5,189.3**	**3,231.5**	P/E Ratio M	**22.3**	Price (9/30/95) M	**9,542.00**
Net Income	**99.1**	**96.8**	**95.9**	**59.7**	P/B Ratio M	**2.1**	52 Wk Hi-Low M	**9,780.0-7,931.0**
Book Value	**791.0**	**830.9**	**932.3**	**574.7**	Yield % M	**2.1**	Market Cap M	**US$935.4mil**

Address **Palazzo Z - Strada 5**, **20089 Rozzano, Milan**
Tel **02-57581**
Fax **02-236-4220**
ADR **LARCY**
SEDOL No. **4740034**
CEO **Giovanni C. Gigli**
Chairman **Franzo G. Stevens**

M=Multiple issues in index; reflects most active.

SAI

Industry: **Insurance - Full Line**

Società Assicuratrice Industriale (SAI) provides insurance and reinsurance products in Italy and other European countries. The company manages mutual funds through its Saifinanziaria subsidiary. Automobile insurance accounts for roughly half of the company's premiums. The company also offers life, commercial, private, accident, health, fire, and theft insurance. SAI runs more than 950 offices, and operates a wholly-owned subsidiary in the United Kingdom. The company also provides real-estate services. SAI acquired auto insurer MAA Assicurazioni in 1995.

lire bil	12/92	12/93	12/94	US$mil 12/94				
Revenues	**N/A**	**N/A**	**91.0**	**56.7**	P/E Ratio M	**36.3**	Price (9/30/95) M	**17,987**
Net Income	**75.2**	**84.2**	**89.5**	**55.7**	P/B Ratio M	**NMF**	52 Wk Hi-Low M	**21,946.0-15,717.0**
Book Value	**1,355.5**	**1,402.0**	**N/A**	**N/A**	Yield % M	**1.1**	Market Cap M	**US$1,368.3mil**

Address **Corso Galileo Galilei 12**, **10125 Turin**
Tel **011-665-7111**
Fax **011-665-7685**
ADR
SEDOL No. **4767884**
CEO **P. Bovone**
Chairman **Salvatore Ligresti**

M=Multiple issues in index; reflects most active.

Saipem

Industry: **Oilfield Equipment & Services - Other**

Saipem provides specialized services for the oil industry. Its main activities include exploration and drilling for oil, gas, and minerals, land and marine construction, and infrastructure development. The company constructs plants, pipelines, and refineries for the chemical and petrochemical companies. It also provides research services for the oil, gas, and mineral industries. Saipem also offers civil and industrial construction. The company is indirectly held by the Italian government through its ENI (Ente Nazionale Idrocarburi) subsidiary.

lire bil	12/92	12/93	12/94	US$mil 12/94				
Sales	**1,922.0**	**2,114.2**	**2,008.9**	**1,251.0**	P/E Ratio	**18.1**	Price (9/30/95)	**3,654.00**
Net Income	**57.6**	**58.2**	**80.2**	**50.0**	P/B Ratio	**1.8**	52 Wk Hi-Low	**3,809.0-2,563.0**
Book Value	**636.6**	**711.1**	**787.3**	**485.3**	Yield %	**N/A**	Market Cap	**US$902.2mil**

Address **Via Di Cefalonia 67**, **20097 Milan**
Tel **02-53531**
Fax **02-520-23130**
ADR
SEDOL No. **4768768**
Managing Director **Francesco Nanotti**
Chairman **Luciano Sgubini**

Sasib

Industry: **Factory Equipment**

Sasib manufactures industrial equipment, including signalling, telecommunication, and safety equipment for the railway industry. In addition, Sasib manufactures and installs industrial-process equipment in tobacco, bakery, beverage, and food-packaging plants. It manufactures automated ovens, measuring, packaging, and pasteurizing machinery. Sasib's railway operations generated 32% of sales in 1994. Over 23% of its revenues were generated in North America. In 1994, the company acquired the Wrapper business unit of American based FMC group.

lire bil	12/92	12/93	12/94	US$mil 12/94				
Sales	**865.1**	**980.3**	**1,037.7**	**646.2**	P/E Ratio M	**21.1**	Price (9/30/95) M	**7,776.00**
Net Income	**41.6**	**51.1**	**51.5**	**32.1**	P/B Ratio M	**1.0**	52 Wk Hi-Low M	**8,678.0-6,566.0**
Book Value	**413.4**	**458.0**	**632.1**	**389.7**	Yield % M	**2.7**	Market Cap M	**US$404.4mil**

Address **Via di Corticella 87/89**, **40128 Bologna**
Tel **051-529-111**
Fax **051-529-419**
ADR
SEDOL No. **4776493**
CEO **Gian Carlo Vaccari**
Chairman **Vittorio Ripa di Meana**

M=Multiple issues in index; reflects most active.

Sirti

Industry: **Communications Technology**

Sirti offers services for the design, construction, control, and maintenance of telecommunication networks. Sirti provides telecommunication and signaling systems for the Italian railway, collection systems for motorway tolls, and equipment cables for trunk lines, radio links, portable radio systems, and satellite communications. Sirti has subsidiaries in the United Kingdom, Spain, France, Portugal and Germany. In 1994, the company acquired German company WS Montague and Italian company AET Telecommunications S.p.A.

lire bil	12/92	12/93	12/94	US$mil 12/94				
Sales	**1,524.3**	**1,561.1**	**1,690.0**	**1,052.4**	P/E Ratio	**10.5**	Price (9/30/95)	**10,158**
Net Income	**273.5**	**285.2**	**242.2**	**150.8**	P/B Ratio	**1.3**	52 Wk Hi-Low	**12,990.0-8,602.0**
Book Value	**1,425.1**	**1,594.9**	**1,740.9**	**1,073.1**	Yield %	**5.1**	Market Cap	**US$1,385.6mil**

Address **Via G.B. Pirelli 20**
20124 Milan
Tel **02-67741**
Fax **02-677-4326**
ADR
SEDOL No. **4811899**
Managing Director **Luigi Montella**
Chairman **Francesco Gelfi**

SNIA BPD

Industry: **Commodity Chemicals**

SNIA BPD is a holding company whose main subsidiaries manufacture fiber, primarily for the apparel industry; chemicals for water-treatment and detergent products; polymers, used primarily for packaging; and bioengineering products. Its majority-owned SNIA Fiber subsidiary manufactures polyamide filament used in hosiery, woven fabrics, and umbrellas. SNIA BPD has interests in two joint ventures with French chemicals company Rhône-Poulenc in the areas of textile filaments and technical polymers.

lire bil	12/92	12/93	12/94	US$mil 12/94				
Sales	**2,038.2**	**2,282.9**	**2,576.2**	**1,604.2**	P/E Ratio	**52.3**	Price (9/30/95)	**1,725.00**
Net Income	**-59.8**	**11.0**	**25.2**	**15.7**	P/B Ratio	**1.1**	52 Wk Hi-Low	**2,316.0-1,659.0**
Book Value	**1,224.6**	**1,221.4**	**1,220.7**	**752.5**	Yield %	**0.0**	Market Cap	**US$728.6mil**

Address **Via Borgonuovo 14**
20121 Milan
Tel **02-63321**
Fax **N/A**
ADR
SEDOL No. **4819406**
Managing Director **Umberto Rosa**
Chairman **Antonio Coppi**

STET

Industry: **Telephone Systems - All**

STET (Societa Finanziaria Telefonica) is a telecommunication holding company that is 61% owned by the Italian government agency Instituto per la Ricostruzione Industriale. STET owns 62% of Telecom Italia, which includes the state-controlled domestic and long-distance telephone concerns. Telecom Italia spun off its cellular-phone business to form Telecom Italia Mobile. STET has 24 million telephone subscribers and 1.8 million cellular-phone subscribers. Its publishing division sells advertising space in the yellow pages.

lire bil	12/92	12/93	12/94	US$mil 12/94				
Sales	**27,167.0**	**29,782.0**	**33,752.0**	**21,018.2**	P/E Ratio M	**16.1**	Price (9/30/95) M	**4,878.00**
Net Income	**965.0**	**1,014.0**	**1,165.0**	**725.5**	P/B Ratio M	**1.1**	52 Wk Hi-Low M	**5,342.0-4,244.0**
Book Value	**12,275.0**	**12,810.0**	**16,601.0**	**10,233.3**	Yield % M	**2.3**	Market Cap M	**US$11,596mil**

Address **Corso d'Italia 41**
00198 Rome
Tel **06-8589-277**
Fax **06-8543-965**
ADR **STE**
SEDOL No. **4846501**
CEO **Ernesto Pascale**
Chairman **Biagio Agnes**

M=Multiple issues in index; reflects most active.

Telecom Italia

Industry: **Telephone Systems - All**

Telecom Italia, Italy's state-controlled telephone company, provides national and international telecommunication services in Italy. Telecom Italia was formed in 1994 from the merger of Italy's main telecom operators - SIP, Iritel, Italcable, Telespazio, and SIRM. The company is controlled by STET, which was privitized in early 1995. Telecom Italia is spending more than $31 billion in the development of Italy's phone network and multimedia technology. It manages all telecommunications services at Pirelli, one of its main suppliers of cable.

lire bil	12/92	12/93	12/94	US$mil 12/94				
Sales	**21,555.0**	**23,404.0**	**29,162.5**	**18,160.2**	P/E Ratio M	**14.2**	Price (9/30/95) M	**2,619.00**
Net Income	**460.6**	**657.4**	**1,517.3**	**944.8**	P/B Ratio M	**1.8**	52 Wk Hi-Low M	**2,888.0-1,978.2**
Book Value	**13,758.0**	**14,815.0**	**21,621.3**	**13,328.0**	Yield % M	**4.0**	Market Cap M	**US$10,780mil**

Address **Via Flaminia 189**
00144 Rome
Tel **06-36881**
Fax **06-368-83361**
ADR
SEDOL No. **4811565**
Chief Executive **Vito Gamberale**
Chairman **Ernesto Pascale**

M=Multiple issues in index; reflects most active.

Toro

Industry: **Insurance - Full Line**

Toro Assicurazioni is an insurance company controlled by Fiat. The company offers a variety of insurance products in the personal-accident, life, transportation, and reinsurance areas. Its sales network in Italy includes 429 Toro agents and 43 agents in its majority-owned Augusta Assicurazioni subsidiary. The company provides insurance products in France through its Continent group subsidiary. Toro Assicurazioni also holds a number of real-estate interests through its subsidiaries, including Italian Istituto Piemontese Immobiliare and D. Féau, in France.

lire bil	12/92	12/93	12/94	US$mil 12/94				
Revenues	**2,198.9**	**2,481.2**	**2,144.6**	**1,335.5**	P/E Ratio M	**27.9**	Price (9/30/95) M	**21,682**
Net Income	**139.1**	**153.2**	**154.7**	**96.3**	P/B Ratio M	**0.8**	52 Wk Hi-Low M	**27,810.0-21,375.0**
Book Value	**1,533.2**	**1,664.7**	**1,779.0**	**1,096.6**	Yield % M	**1.5**	Market Cap M	**US$854.0mil**

Address **Via Arcivescovada 16**
10121 Turin
Tel **011-57331**
Fax **011-543587**
ADR
SEDOL No. **4898085**
Managing Director **Francesco Torri**
Chairman **Benedetto Salaroli**

M=Multiple issues in index; reflects most active.

Unicem

Industry: **Building Materials**

Unicem serves as the parent company for businesses that produce cement, ready-mix concrete, premixed plaster, and other building materials. The company also has interests in plant-engineering operations, clay mining, real estate, and finance. Unicem, Italy's second-largest cement producer, recently acquired the remaining 33% stake in U.S. company RC Cement in July 1995 and now wholly owns the firm. RC Cement operates four cement plants in the United States. Unicem only markets its products in Italy and the United States.

lire bil	12/92	12/93	12/94	US$mil 12/94				
Sales	**860.6**	**781.5**	**806.0**	**501.9**	P/E Ratio M	**NMF**	Price (9/30/95) M	**10,330**
Net Income	**47.9**	**25.1**	**-98.3**	**-61.2**	P/B Ratio M	**1.2**	52 Wk Hi-Low M	**12,110.0-8,566.0**
Book Value	**675.6**	**676.9**	**561.9**	**346.4**	Yield % M	**0.0**	Market Cap M	**US$406.5mil**

Address **Via Carlo Marenco 25**
10126 Turin
Tel **011-65641**
Fax **011-6564445**
ADR
SEDOL No. **4910398**
CEO **Luca Paveri Fontana**
Chairman **Giovanni Nasi**

M=Multiple issues in index; reflects most active.

Japan

Japan

James Paradise,
Tokyo

Local Trading Hours	Time Difference with New York	Population (Est. 94)
9:00-11:00; 12:30-3:00	14 hours ahead	125,107,000

It was an annus horribilis for Japan, with a major earthquake at the beginning of 1995 in the country's second major industrial center of Kansai, a poison gas attack on Tokyo subway commuters by a doomsday religious cult and the first failure of a bank since the end of World War II. But on the Tokyo stock market there have been signs of recovery.

The stock market has been struggling to recover from the aftermath of the collapse of the "bubble economy" of the 1980s when asset values skyrocketed to astronomical levels. Share prices, as measured by the two most widely watched stock indexes, the Nikkei 225 and the Tokyo Stock Price Index (TOPIX), have moved higher in the second half of 1995, encouraged by lower interest rates, a weaker yen and additional spending measures by the Japanese government — all of which were seen as pushing corporate profits up.

Trading volumes were also rising. On an average day in July 1995, 411 million shares were changing hands, up from 342 million shares in 1994, 353 million shares in 1993 and 269 million shares in 1992.

The Tokyo Stock Exchange (TSE) was also working to restore its credibility. Hit by a rash of delistings by foreign firms who claimed there was little "bang for the buck" by trading their shares on the exchange's "foreign section," and a general feeling that Japan's financial industry was suffering a "hollowing out" effect akin to what the manufacturing sector was going through, the exchange partially deregulated brokerage commissions in 1994. It is now considering setting up a special second section with less stringent listing requirements to allow more Japanese companies to raise money through equity finance. The exchange also relaxed listing requirements for foreign companies on Jan. 1, 1995, in a bid to attract more Asian companies to list their shares on the TSE. As of late September, no Asian companies had yet been listed.

Dow Jones Japan
Equity Market Index Performance

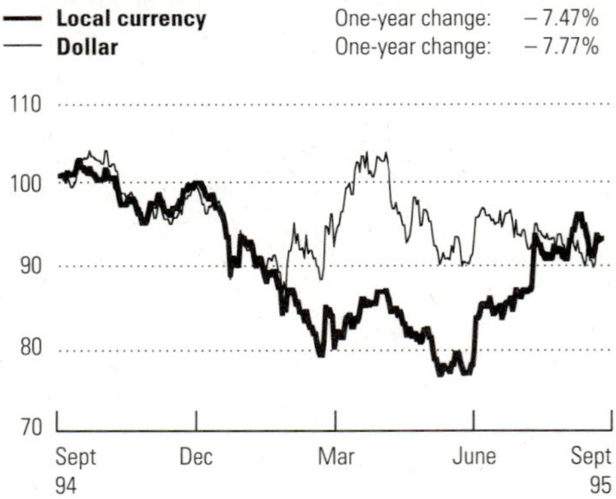

Founded in its present form in 1949, the Tokyo Stock Exchange is now divided into two sections — a first section of around 1,235 listed companies and a second section of around 465. There is also an over-the-counter market in Japan operated by the Japan Securities Dealers Association (JSDA) that is comprised of around 627 companies. The

Gross Domestic Product (94)	Three-Year Average GDP Growth (92-94)	Main Industries	Consumer Price Index (94)	Monetary Unit	Exchange Rate (9/95)
$4,097 trillion	0.2%	Automobiles, electronics, textiles, steel and financial services	0.4%	Yen	Y99.42 to US$1.00

OTC market has seen a wave of new registrations, helped partly by a regulatory change in April 1995 that allowed as many companies as wanted to register their shares on the OTC each month. (Previously, there were restrictions.) The JSDA also set up a new section on July 19, 1995, with easier registration requirements, and in the autumn was awaiting its first registration.

Despite its problems, the Tokyo Stock Exchange is still the second largest stock market in the world — though down from its No. 1 ranking when share prices zoomed to historical highs in 1989. The market is capitalized at around 311 trillion yen, and 445.1 million shares are outstanding. Of those shares, 43.5% are owned by financial institutions, 23.8% by industrial corporations, 23.5% by individuals and others, 7.4% by foreigners, 1.1% by securities companies and 0.7% by governmental bodies.

The Tokyo exchange is comprised of 124 member companies, 100 of which are Japanese and 24 of which are foreigners. The 150 most active stocks are traded on the floor of the exchange, and the rest on an automated system. Settlement for nearly all stocks is three business days after the day of transaction.

There is also trading of futures and options contracts based on the TOPIX on the TSE, as well as Japanese government bond futures, options on Japanese government bond futures and U.S. T-Bond futures. Trading of futures contracts based on the Nikkei 225 stock index takes place on the Osaka Securities Exchange. The TSE is now studying the possibility of introducing options on individual stocks, but has not yet made any decision.

Ten Largest Capitalized Companies

as of 9/30/95

Stock	Market Cap. US$Mil
Nippon Telegraph and Telephone	136,521,182.9
Toyota Motor	71,062,859.4
Industrial Bank of Japan	68,353,703.3
Fuji Bank	61,489,818.6
Sumitomo Bank	60,660,219.7
Mitsubishi Bank	57,369,992.2
Dai-Ichi Kangyo Bank	56,500,356.1
Sanwa Bank	54,271,552.2
Nomura Securities	38,296,657.6
Tokyo Electric Power	36,511,484.9

Foreigners, who had previously been blamed for pushing the stock market lower with their arbitrage-related transactions, were in 1995 being cited for their strong buying of Japanese stocks. The biggest net buyer in 1994 to the tune of 3.699 trillion yen on the TSE, foreign investors had in the first seven months of 1995 bought 1.196 trillion yen of shares more than they had sold. Overseas investors were anticipating the start of a new business cycle in Japan, and weren't scared away by a price-earnings ratio of over 70 times on first section listed issues.

Many market watchers feel that the key to the long-term recovery of the Tokyo stock market is the return of the individual investor.

Burned by the collapse of stock prices in the early 1990s, some brokers say that regaining the confidence of cash-laden households will be an uphill battle, though one made easier by interest rates on banking deposits in Japan of under 1%. Others say that marketing efforts should be focused on first-time investors, ones who have not experienced the bear market of the early 1990s. Still others say that much will depend on what life insurance companies and other institutional investors do. Banks will be constrained by huge amounts of problem loans, a prolonged situation that is having a negative impact on the economy as a whole.

The economy, all seem to agree, is the key to the stock market.

Industry Group Performance
1 Year Change Through 9/30/95

Industry	Change % (US$)
Best Performing	
Semiconductors	21.32
Computers	17.72
Industrial Technology	12.20
Broadcasting	10.95
Toy Manufacturers	8.05
Worst Performing	
Publishing	-26.58
Biotechnology	-25.70
Medical & Biological Technology - All	-25.70
Restaurants	-25.07
Footwear	-24.15

Achilles

Industry: **Footwear**

Achilles manufactures footwear, plastics, urethane, and industrial materials. Specific products include film, synthetic leathers, sheets, flooring and wall materials, health-care products, insulation, electrostatic removers, and interior materials. Achilles-brand footwear holds about a 20% share of the Japanese market. The company has technical-cooperation agreements with I.C.I. (United Kingdom), Bata Industries (Canada), Tarkett (Sweden), Technisynthese (France), Eccolet (Denmark), and AS Creation (Germany). Achilles is expanding into the construction-materials market.

	¥bil 03/93	03/94	03/95	US$mil 03/95				
Sales	**128.1**	**123.7**	**121.4**	**1,230.1**	P/E Ratio	**54.3**	Price (9/30/95)	**375.00**
Net Income	**2.2**	**1.7**	**1.5**	**15.0**	P/B Ratio	**1.5**	52 Wk Hi-Low	**488.00-311.00**
Book Value	**53.1**	**53.2**	**52.9**	**612.2**	Yield %	**1.6**	Market Cap	**US$814.0mil**

Address	**22-5, Daikyo-cho**	Tel	**03-3341-5111**	ADR		President	**Sadao Nakajima**
	Shinjuku-ku, Toyko 160	Fax	**03-3353-5322**	SEDOL No.	**6496045**	Chairman	**Masao Tonooka**

Advantest

Industry: **Industrial Technology**

Advantest, an affiliate of Fujitsu, produces precision testing and measuring instruments, and designs test systems for the semiconductor industry. Its testing equipment is used primarily for cellular telephones and mobile radios. More than one tenth of parent-company sales are to Midoriya Electric. Advantest develops software for its testing equipment through its affiliate, Advansoft Research in the United States, along with four other subsidiaries in Japan. A French subsidiary, Giga Instrumentation, produces electronic-measuring equipment for the European market.

	¥bil 03/93	03/94	03/95	US$mil 03/95				
Sales	**62.0**	**62.0**	**80.5**	**815.8**	P/E Ratio	**140.5**	Price (9/30/95)	**5,860.00**
Net Income	**0.0**	**0.3**	**3.1**	**31.5**	P/B Ratio	**4.2**	52 Wk Hi-Low	**6,300.0-2,270.0**
Book Value	**102.7**	**102.0**	**103.7**	**1,200.3**	Yield %	**0.2**	Market Cap	**US$4,390.6mil**

Address	**2-4-1, Nishi-Shinjuku**	Tel	**03-3342-7500**	ADR		President	**Hiroshi Ohura**
	Shinjuku-ku, Tokyo 163-08	Fax	**03-3342-7509**	SEDOL No.	**6870490**	Chairman	--

Aisin Seiki

Industry: **Other Auto Parts**

Aisin Seiki produces automotive and die-cast parts and electromechanical products. The company supplies engine, electronic, and auto-body parts; steering and driving devices; electronically controlled suspensions and transmissions; brakes; clutches; mechatronic products; and ornaments to Toyota Motor. More than 60% of the parent company's products are sold to Toyota, which owns 22% of Aisin's stock. It also supplies Suzuki Motor, Mitsubishi Motors, and Isuzu Motors. Aisin Seiki also manufactures home appliances, gas heat-pump air conditioners, and apparel machinery.

	¥bil 03/93	03/94	03/95	US$mil 03/95				
Sales	**838.5**	**787.1**	**789.2**	**7,999.3**	P/E Ratio	**29.6**	Price (9/30/95)	**1,300.00**
Net Income	**11.7**	**9.0**	**12.2**	**123.2**	P/B Ratio	**1.5**	52 Wk Hi-Low	**1,470.0-913.0**
Book Value	**226.2**	**233.3**	**248.0**	**2,870.3**	Yield %	**0.9**	Market Cap	**US$3,623.0mil**

Address	**2-1, Asahi-machi**	Tel	**0566-24-8266**	ADR		President	**Kanshiro Toyoda**
	Kariya City, Aichi 448	Fax	**0566-24-8848**	SEDOL No.	**6010702**	Chairman	**Shigeo Aiki**

Ajinomoto

Industry: **Other Food**

Ajinomoto is one of Japan's largest and most diversified food makers. The company manufactures processed and frozen foods, beverages, seasonings (such as monosodium glutamate), cooking oils, amino acids, and pharmaceuticals and sells them under the Ajinomoto, Knorr, and AGF brand names. Ajinomoto has 54 consolidated subsidiaries. The company has operations throughout Southeast Asia and Europe, Peru, the U.S., and China. Ajinomoto owns a 20% stake in beverage producer Calpis Food Industry. In fiscal 1993, sales within Japan accounted for 88% of the company's revenues.

	¥bil 03/93	03/94	03/95	US$mil 03/95				
Sales	**687.3**	**674.9**	**725.7**	**7,356.1**	P/E Ratio	**58.3**	Price (9/30/95)	**1,050.00**
Net Income	**11.5**	**10.5**	**11.7**	**118.6**	P/B Ratio	**1.9**	52 Wk Hi-Low	**1,340.0-864.0**
Book Value	**361.1**	**364.8**	**367.9**	**4,258.5**	Yield %	**1.0**	Market Cap	**US$6,852.5mil**

Address	**1-15-1, Kyobashi**	Tel	**03-5250-8111**	ADR	**AJINY**	President	**Shunsuke Inamori**
	Chuo-ku, Tokyo 104	Fax	**03-5250-8378**	SEDOL No.	**6010906**	Chairman	**Yasuhiko Ikeda**

All Nippon Airways

Industry: **Airlines**

All Nippon Airways (ANA) is Japan's leading domestic airline and the eighth-largest airline in the world by passenger volume. With subsidiary Air Nippon, the company controls about half of Japan's market, and also operates international flights. Altogether, the company flies nearly 20 international routes and 73 domestic routes. ANA has branched out into travel and transport services through subsidiaries. It also operates 31 luxury hotels in Japan and abroad. In 1995, ANA joined a frequent-flyer program with Delta (U.S.) and three Asian airlines.

	¥bil 03/93	03/94	03/95	US$mil 03/95				
Sales	**888.8**	**857.2**	**914.2**	**9,267.1**	P/E Ratio	**NMF**	Price (9/30/95)	**950.00**
Net Income	**-1.2**	**-9.4**	**-7.5**	**-75.7**	P/B Ratio	**8.9**	52 Wk Hi-Low	**1,150.0-902.0**
Book Value	**184.7**	**170.2**	**154.2**	**1,784.8**	Yield %	**0.3**	Market Cap	**US$13,786mil**

Address	**3-2-5, Kasumigaseki**	Tel	**03-3592-3065**	ADR		President	**Seiji Fukatsu**
	Chiyoda-ku, Tokyo 100	Fax	**03-3592-3039**	SEDOL No.	**6014908**	Chairman	**Takaya Sugiura**

Alps Electric

Industry: **Electrical Components & Equipment**

Alps Electric (Alps Denki) is one of Japan's leading comprehensive electronic-component makers. Products include keyboard switches, magnetic heads, television tuners, cassette mechanisms, VCR-field-reversing modulators, variable condensers, resistors, printers, and floppy-disk drives. Its new products include microtrackballs for notebook-size computers. Alps Electric has plants in the United States, Brazil, Germany, the United Kingdom, South Korea, Taiwan, and Malaysia, and five plants in Japan. Overseas production makes up roughly 20% of the company's total.

	¥bil 03/93	03/94	03/95	US$mil 03/95				
Sales	**419.1**	**393.9**	**399.7**	**4,051.5**	P/E Ratio	**41.3**	Price (9/30/95)	**1,040.00**
Net Income	**-1.9**	**-9.2**	**4.5**	**45.7**	P/B Ratio	**1.4**	52 Wk Hi-Low	**1,380.0-826.0**
Book Value	**137.7**	**127.3**	**131.2**	**1,519.0**	Yield %	**0.3**	Market Cap	**US$1,873.9mil**

Address	**1-7, Yukigaya-Otsukacho**	Tel	**03-3726-1211**	ADR	**ALPSY**	President	**Masataka Kataoka**
	Ota-ku, Tokyo 145	Fax	**03-3727-3878**	SEDOL No.	**6021500**	Chairman	**Katsutaro Kataoka**

Amada

Industry: **Factory Equipment**

Amada is a comprehensive manufacturer of metalworking machinery. Products include pressing machines, sheet-metal-working machines, and bandsaws. The firm supplies the auto, electronics, and construction industries. The parent company has one plant in Japan, in Hyogo Prefecture. The Amada group consists of 27 subsidiaries (including four in the United States and one each in Germany, France, the United Kingdom, and Taiwan) and 16 affiliated companies. Overseas sales account for approximately 38% of consolidated revenues.

	¥bil 03/93	03/94	03/95	US$mil 03/95				
Sales	**132.1**	**104.9**	**113.5**	**1,150.7**	P/E Ratio	**NMF**	Price (9/30/95)	**982.00**
Net Income	**4.1**	**-4.6**	**-4.0**	**-40.8**	P/B Ratio	**1.2**	52 Wk Hi-Low	**1,290.0-725.0**
Book Value	**244.3**	**237.1**	**232.2**	**2,687.0**	Yield %	**0.3**	Market Cap	**US$2,863.4mil**

Address	**200, Ishida**	Tel	**0463-96-1111**	ADR	**AMDLY**	President	**Nobuyuki Ueda**
	Isehara City, Kanagawa 259-11	Fax	**0463-93-1323**	SEDOL No.	**6022105**	Chairman	**Ryuharu Emori**

Amada Metrecs

Industry: **Industrial Technology**

Amada Metrecs, an affiliate of Amada, produces electronic equipment and metal molds, and maintains metal-processing machines. Its other products include automated-manufacturing systems. The parent company, Amada, accounts for the majority of Amada Metrecs' electrical-assembly, repair, and maintenance business. Amada and Amadasonoike own 25.6% and 7.6% of the company's stock, respectively. The firm has two consolidated subsidiaries in the U.S., Amada Engineering & Service and Elba Electronics, and unconsolidated subsidiaries in the U.K., Germany, and France.

	¥bil 03/93	03/94	03/95	US$mil 03/95				
Sales	**68.9**	**58.0**	**63.6**	**644.7**	P/E Ratio	**NMF**	Price (9/30/95)	**1,410.00**
Net Income	**1.3**	**-1.2**	**-0.3**	**-2.9**	P/B Ratio	**1.4**	52 Wk Hi-Low	**1,850.0-1,010.0**
Book Value	**79.0**	**77.3**	**76.0**	**879.8**	Yield %	**0.4**	Market Cap	**US$1,044.8mil**

Address	**806, Takamori**	Tel	**0463-91-8000**	ADR		President	**Yutaka Omura**
	Isehara City, Kanagawa 259-11	Fax	**0463-91-8113**	SEDOL No.	**6022116**	Chairman	**Mitsusaburo Shindo**

Amano

Industry: **Office Equipment**

Amano produces dust collectors, other environmental machinery, and information-control devices. It holds the largest market share in time-card recorders in Japan. The firm's other products include parking-lot traffic-control equipment, data-system equipment, production-control systems, patrol systems, time stamps, and industrial vacuum cleaners. Its major customers include ITO, Hitachi Credit, Kokuyo, and Sharp Finance. Amano operates four plants in Japan. It has five consolidated subsidiaries in North America and unconsolidated subsidiaries in Europe and Southeast Asia.

	¥bil 03/93	03/94	03/95	US$mil 03/95				
Sales	**48.4**	**45.7**	**48.5**	**491.4**	P/E Ratio	**46.4**	Price (9/30/95)	**1,240.00**
Net Income	**2.2**	**2.2**	**2.5**	**25.8**	P/B Ratio	**1.6**	52 Wk Hi-Low	**1,660.0-1,000.0**
Book Value	**72.1**	**73.3**	**74.2**	**859.3**	Yield %	**1.0**	Market Cap	**US$1,187.0mil**

Address	**275, Omamedo-cho**	Tel	**045-401-1441**	ADR		President	**Yasuyoshi Komoto**
	Kohoku-ku, Yokohama 222	Fax	**045-439-1151**	SEDOL No.	**6027304**	Chairman	**Ikuya Iwai**

Aoki

Industry: **Heavy Construction**

Aoki (Aoki Kensetsu) is a general contractor involved in civil engineering, building construction, and real estate. It builds airports, industrial plants, office buildings, and hotels. Aoki develops real estate, and does civil-engineering projects, such as waterworks and power plants. Real-estate and resort developers and public-works agencies are its primary clients. Overseas sales account for 37% of consolidated sales. Aoki has 65 subsidiaries, 25 of which are consolidated. Its subsidiaries and affiliates are particularly active in hotel-management operations overseas.

	¥bil 03/93	03/94	03/95	US$mil 03/95				
Sales	**412.0**	**362.5**	**379.1**	**3,842.7**	P/E Ratio	**NMF**	Price (9/30/95)	**461.00**
Net Income	**1.9**	**0.2**	**-7.4**	**-75.2**	P/B Ratio	**1.1**	52 Wk Hi-Low	**695.00-305.00**
Book Value	**216.1**	**207.4**	**186.5**	**2,158.2**	Yield %	**0.0**	Market Cap	**US$1,969.6mil**

Address	**1-4-15, Oyodo-Minami**	Tel	**06-458-5851**	ADR		President	**Soichi Miyawaki**
	Kita-ku, Osaka 531	Fax	**03-3486-3584**	SEDOL No.	**6045760**	Chairman	**Hiroyoshi Aoki**

Aoyama Trading

Industry: **Apparel Retailers**

Aoyama Trading (Aoyama Shoji) is a clothing retailer that specializes in menswear and is known for its retailing of inexpensive business suits. Its other product lines include blazers, formal wear, casual clothes, shirts, Western-style accessories, slacks, and coats. The firm has expanded its chain of stores to more than 530 branches throughout Japan. Aoyama is strengthening its presence in urban centers such as the Ginza area of Tokyo, New York, Paris, and Hong Kong, and plans to open three more in Taiwan. Its main suppliers include Nissho Iwai, Tomita, and Wako Sangyo.

¥bil	03/93 P	03/94 P	03/95 P	US$mil 03/95				
Revenues	**150.9**	**182.3**	**167.7**	**1,700.2**	P/E Ratio	**18.5**	Price (9/30/95)	**2,720.00**
Net Income	**15.3**	**15.9**	**10.7**	**108.4**	P/B Ratio	**1.0**	52 Wk Hi-Low	**3,380.0-1,260.0**
Book Value	**152.7**	**190.5**	**198.1**	**2,292.7**	Yield %	**1.3**	Market Cap	**US$1,990.4mil**

Address	**1-3-5, Ohji-cho**	Tel	**0849-20-0050**	ADR		President	**Goro Aoyama**
	Fukuyama City, Hiroshima 721	Fax	**0849-21-8129**	SEDOL No.	**6045878**	Chairman	--

P=Parent company data.

Arabian Oil

Industry: **Oil - Secondary**

Arabian Oil (Arabia Sekiyu) is a crude-oil producer that engages in the exploration, processing, and trading of oil. Petroleum accounts for more than 90% of consolidated sales; its other areas of activity are natural gas, uranium ore, and other minerals. Primary customers include Cosmo Oil and Tonen. The company operates the Khafji oil field on the Saudi-Kuwaiti border. Saudi Arabia and Kuwait each hold about 11% of equity. It has operations in China, Niger, and Malaysia, as well as a joint venture with Teikoku Oil and Mobil in an offshore exploration project in Vietnam.

¥bil	12/92	12/93	12/94	US$mil 12/94				
Sales	**226.0**	**156.5**	**158.3**	**1,550.6**	P/E Ratio	**133.0**	Price (9/30/95)	**4,150.00**
Net Income	**2.2**	**0.2**	**1.7**	**16.2**	P/B Ratio	**3.9**	52 Wk Hi-Low	**4,930.0-3,530.0**
Book Value	**58.1**	**56.7**	**56.3**	**564.5**	Yield %	**1.0**	Market Cap	**US$2,218.1mil**

Address	**3-2-3, Marunouchi**	Tel	**03-3214-4319**	ADR		President	**Keiichi Konaga**
	Chiyoda-ku, Tokyo 100	Fax	**03-3214-7019**	SEDOL No.	**6047108**	Chairman	--

Asahi Bank

Industry: **Banks - Regional**

Asahi Bank (Asahi Ginko) is Japan's ninth-largest bank by assets. The bank's strength lies in retail banking and meeting the needs of small and midsize companies. It offers a variety of services, including guidance in bond placements. Asahi bank became the first city bank to establish a securities firm when it opened Asahi Securities in June 1994. The bank's main business region is Tokyo and the adjacent prefectures of Kanagawa, Saitama, and Chiba. The bank has 373 domestic branches and 53 representative offices.

¥bil	03/93	03/94	03/95	US$mil 03/95				
Revenues	**1,500.9**	**1,390.5**	**1,295.2**	**13,128.7**	P/E Ratio	**138.5**	Price (9/30/95)	**1,080.00**
Net Income	**36.1**	**20.5**	**18.2**	**184.1**	P/B Ratio	**2.3**	52 Wk Hi-Low	**1,130.0-890.0**
Book Value	**1,067.1**	**1,072.0**	**1,075.1**	**12,443.0**	Yield %	**0.6**	Market Cap	**US$25,222mil**

Address	**1-1-2, Otemachi**	Tel	**03-3287-2111**	ADR	**ASBKY**	President	**Shigehiko Yoshino**
	Chiyoda-ku, Tokyo 100	Fax	**03-3212-3663**	SEDOL No.	**6499367**	Chairman	**Kosuke Yokote**

Asahi Breweries

Industry: **Distillers & Brewers**

Asahi Breweries (Asahi Biru) is Japan's second-largest brewer, with about 25% of the Japanese beer market. Other products include soft drinks, coffee, tea, fruit juice, liquors, foods, and pharmaceuticals. Asahi's biggest seller is Super Dry which accounts for 20% of its sales. In Japan, the firm also markets beers for Miller, Molson, and Fosters (of which it is the second-largest shareholder), in addition to operating golf courses and restaurants. Its domestic network consists of 74 sales offices and seven breweries. It has 95 subsidiaries, 15 of which are consolidated.

¥bil	12/92	12/93	12/94	US$mil 12/94				
Sales	**949.1**	**951.2**	**1,075.5**	**10,538.7**	P/E Ratio	**71.6**	Price (9/30/95)	**1,110.00**
Net Income	**3.9**	**3.4**	**6.5**	**63.6**	P/B Ratio	**1.6**	52 Wk Hi-Low	**1,170.0-942.0**
Book Value	**290.0**	**288.1**	**294.5**	**2,952.1**	Yield %	**0.9**	Market Cap	**US$4,701.8mil**

Address	**1-23-1, Azumabashi**	Tel	**03-5608-5116**	ADR		President	**Yuzo Seto**
	Sumida-ku, Tokyo 130	Fax	**03-5608-7121**	SEDOL No.	**6054409**	Chairman	**Hirotaro Higuchi**

Asahi Chemical Industry

Industry: **Commodity Chemicals**

Asahi Chemical Industry (Asahi Kasei Kogyo) is a leading producer of chemicals, construction materials, and plastics. It is Japan's second-largest chemicals maker by sales. The firm also makes drugs (such as the osteoporosis treatment Elcitonin), medical equipment, synthetic fibers, and rubber products. Asahi Chemical participates in joint ventures with Clark Schwebel Fiber Glass (U.S.), Ciba-Geigy (Switzerland), and Siemens (Germany). It also plans to form a joint venture with a wholly-owned subsidiary of Du Pont to market flash-spun nonwoven materials in Japan.

¥bil	03/93	03/94	03/95	US$mil 03/95				
Sales	**1,232.0**	**1,151.5**	**1,154.9**	**11,706.5**	P/E Ratio	**126.9**	Price (9/30/95)	**685.00**
Net Income	**18.2**	**8.7**	**7.8**	**78.7**	P/B Ratio	**2.3**	52 Wk Hi-Low	**787.00-551.00**
Book Value	**434.9**	**430.5**	**428.9**	**4,963.6**	Yield %	**0.9**	Market Cap	**US$9,937.7mil**

Address	**1-1-2, Yuraku-cho**	Tel	**03-3507-2204**	ADR	**ASHCY**	President	**Reiichi Yumikura**
	Chiyoda-ku, Tokyo 100	Fax	**03-3507-2495**	SEDOL No.	**6054603**	Chairman	**Nobuo Yamaguchi**

Asahi Glass

Industry: **Building Materials**

Asahi Glass is Japan's largest glass manufacturer, with nearly 50% of the domestic sheet-glass market. The firm is also a major world supplier of television cathode-ray tubes. Chemicals, ceramics, and electronic equipment are among the company's other major product areas. It has overseas manufacturing subsidiaries and affiliates in Singapore, Indonesia, the United States, the Netherlands, and Belgium, among others. Asahi Glass has an equity stake in AFG Industries, a U.S. float-glass manufacturer. In 1994, overseas sales accounted for 28.3% of total consolidated revenues.

¥bil	12/92	12/93	12/94	US$mil 12/94				
Sales	**1,316.8**	**1,227.3**	**1,240.9**	**12,159.0**	P/E Ratio	**71.8**	Price (9/30/95)	**1,070.00**
Net Income	**24.3**	**11.0**	**17.4**	**170.6**	P/B Ratio	**2.1**	52 Wk Hi-Low	**1,260.0-928.0**
Book Value	**596.7**	**591.1**	**596.3**	**5,977.2**	Yield %	**0.8**	Market Cap	**US$12,628mil**

Address **2-1-2, Marunouchi** **Chiyoda-ku, Tokyo 100**
Tel **03-3218-5555** Fax **03-3201-5390**
ADR **ASGLY** SEDOL No. **6055208**
President **Hiromichi Seya** Chairman **Jiro Furumoto**

Ashikaga Bank

Industry: **Banks - Regional**

Ashikaga Bank (Ashikaga Ginko) is the fifth-largest regional bank by total assets. The bank serves Tochigi Prefecture, an area inhabited by more than two million people. It handles securities trading and investment in government and municipal bonds, and is also active in mergers and acquisitions through its retail-banking and information networks. The services and distribution industries account for the largest portion of the bank's lending activities. Ashikaga has branches in New York and London, and two overseas representative offices.

¥bil	03/93 P	03/94 P	03/95 P	US$mil 03/95				
Revenues	**357.0**	**321.6**	**326.2**	**3,306.7**	P/E Ratio	**101.6**	Price (9/30/95)	**620.00**
Net Income	**8.1**	**3.5**	**3.8**	**38.2**	P/B Ratio	**1.4**	52 Wk Hi-Low	**750.00-571.00**
Book Value	**266.9**	**267.0**	**267.7**	**3,098.1**	Yield %	**0.8**	Market Cap	**US$3,879.0mil**

Address **4-1-25, Sakura** **Utsunomiya City, Tochigi 320**
Tel **0286-22-0111** Fax **0286-25-5546**
ADR SEDOL No. **6056977**
President **Hideo Tsunemi** Chairman **Hisao Mukae**

P=Parent company data.

Asics

Industry: **Footwear**

Asics is one of Japan's foremost makers of sportswear and athletic equipment. It specializes in sports shoes, which dominate the domestic market and sell in the United States (through its subsidiary Asics Tiger), Europe, and Asia. Its other products include ski, baseball, tennis, and golf equipment, and a wide variety of general-leisure and sporting goods. Asics also markets nutritional foods under the Savas brand name. The firm has 22 consolidated subsidiaries, as well as 12 unconsolidated subsidiaries. In 1994, 26.7% of Asic's consoldiated sales were made overseas.

¥bil	01/93	01/94	01/95	US$mil 01/95				
Sales	**177.7**	**158.3**	**145.1**	**1,436.5**	P/E Ratio	**NMF**	Price (9/30/95)	**280.00**
Net Income	**-0.3**	**-4.8**	**-6.8**	**-67.3**	P/B Ratio	**0.9**	52 Wk Hi-Low	**420.00-229.00**
Book Value	**76.1**	**70.6**	**63.2**	**638.3**	Yield %	**0.0**	Market Cap	**US$602.6mil**

Address **7-1-1, Minatojima-Nakamachi** **Chuo-ku, Kobe 650**
Tel **078-303-3333** Fax **078-303-2241**
ADR SEDOL No. **6057378**
President **Seiji Mihara** Chairman **Kihachiro Onitsuka**

Atsugi Nylon Industrial

Industry: **Clothing & Fabrics**

Atsugi Nylon Industrial (Atsugi Nylon Kogyo) manufactures hosiery, underwear, sleepwear, and lingerie. Men and women's hosiery accounts for about 78% of sales and includes socks, pantyhose, and tights. Support pantyhose are its core product, and is sold in Japan under the Full Supporty brand name. Headquartered in Kanagawa Prefecture, Atsugi Nylon operates 59 factories nationwide and 13 distribution centers. The firm supplements its apparel operations with the manufacture of textile machinery and real-estate operations, mainly housing construction and sales.

¥bil	03/93 *P	03/94 P	03/95 P	US$mil 03/95				
Sales	**51.4**	**46.2**	**42.0**	**425.3**	P/E Ratio	**47.1**	Price (9/30/95)	**433.00**
Net Income	**5.6**	**3.9**	**2.5**	**25.4**	P/B Ratio	**0.9**	52 Wk Hi-Low	**612.00-396.00**
Book Value	**133.6**	**134.5**	**134.0**	**1,550.9**	Yield %	**2.5**	Market Cap	**US$1,191.7mil**

Address **3905, Oya** **Ebina City, Kanagawa 243-04**
Tel **0462-35-8102** Fax **0462-31-4460**
ADR SEDOL No. **6063687**
President **Yoshiro Hori** Chairman --

*Irregular period due to fiscal year change; P=Parent company data.

Autobacs Seven

Industry: **Other Specialty Retailers**

Autobacs Seven, an Osaka-based auto-parts dealer, ranks first in sales of car parts and accessories in Japan. The company operates a nationwide chain of franchised outlets that carry more than 1,800 items under the Autobacs Seven name, such as tires, wheels, car-audio equipment, motor oil, and batteries. It imports, produces, and installs the parts it sells. The company also makes car interiors for Burns Corporation (U.S.) in Japan. As of March 1994, Autobacs Seven's network consisted of 307 franchised stores and 54 direct-management stores in Japan, and a store in Taiwan.

¥bil	03/93	03/94	03/95	US$mil 03/95				
Revenues	**146.9**	**163.4**	**181.1**	**1,835.4**	P/E Ratio	**41.6**	Price (9/30/95)	**9,800.00**
Net Income	**6.1**	**7.3**	**8.4**	**84.8**	P/B Ratio	**3.8**	52 Wk Hi-Low	**12,700.0-8,150.0**
Book Value	**54.9**	**81.6**	**98.0**	**1,134.0**	Yield %	**0.2**	Market Cap	**US$3,720.5mil**

Address **1-5-3, Shinsenri-Higashimachi** **Toyonaka City, Osaka 565**
Tel **06-873-2767** Fax **06-873-2774**
ADR SEDOL No. **6068422**
President **Koichi Sumino** Chairman **Toshio Sumino**

Bandai

Industry: **Toy Manufacturers**

Bandai is one of Japan's largest toymakers. The firm develops TV and animation characters (Ultraman, Godzilla, and Power Rangers) into character toys, plastic-model kits, video games and software, and radio- controlled toys. Bandai also sells character-based merchandise such as children's clothing, candy toys, and skin-care products. Over the long term, the firm sees its growth in multimedia, and has expanded into the production of motion pictures. In 1994, 23.1% of Bandai's consolidated sales were made overseas, up from 9.0% in 1993. It has 22 consolidated subsidiaries.

¥bil	03/93	03/94	03/95	US$mil 03/95				
Sales	**242.5**	**180.3**	**235.0**	**2,382.0**	P/E Ratio	**16.2**	Price (9/30/95)	**3,980.00**
Net Income	**3.0**	**-1.9**	**11.2**	**113.4**	P/B Ratio	**1.9**	52 Wk Hi-Low	**4,360.0-2,260.0**
Book Value	**84.9**	**82.9**	**94.7**	**1,096.0**	Yield %	**0.5**	Market Cap	**US$1,834.3mil**

Address **2-5-4, Komagata**
Taito-ku, Tokyo 111-81
Tel **03-3847-5011**
Fax **03-3847-5067**
ADR
SEDOL No. **6075057**
President **Makoto Yamashina**
Chairman --

Bank of Fukuoka

Industry: **Banks - Regional**

Bank of Fukuoka (Fukuoka Ginko) is Kyushu's largest regional bank. It is Japan's seventh-largest regional bank by deposits. The Bank of Fukuoka also serves corporate clients that are expanding international activities in Asia. The bank is currently entering the Chinese market through tie-ups with Shanghai Bank and Trust and Bank of China Trust and Consultants. The bank is active in Southeast Asia, with offices in Seoul, Hong Kong, and Bangkok, and also has branch offices in London and New York. About 60% of the bank's loans are made to small- or medium-size companies.

¥bil	03/93 P	03/94 P	03/95 P	US$mil 03/95				
Revenues	**340.2**	**282.5**	**251.7**	**2,550.8**	P/E Ratio	**105.8**	Price (9/30/95)	**730.00**
Net Income	**10.3**	**5.8**	**4.0**	**40.9**	P/B Ratio	**1.7**	52 Wk Hi-Low	**930.00-697.00**
Book Value	**245.8**	**248.7**	**249.8**	**2,891.0**	Yield %	**0.8**	Market Cap	**US$4,304.0mil**

Address **2-13-1, Tenjin**
Chuo-ku, Fukuoka 810
Tel **092-723-2622**
Fax **092-721-5863**
ADR
SEDOL No. **6075693**
President **Ryoji Tsukuda**
Chairman **Toyohiko Goto**

P=Parent company data.

Bank of Tokyo

Industry: **Banks - Money Center**

Bank of Tokyo (Tokyo Ginko) is Japan's foremost international financial institution. It specializes in corporate finance, investment-advisory services, and project services, and leads in foreign-exchange transactions. It also offers currency-risk hedging services, is a market maker for forward contracts in currencies, and plays a key role in the government's distribution of foreign-aid funds. Bank of Tokyo participates in the secondary market for third-world debt and consults with clients interested in third-world investment.

¥bil	03/93	03/94	03/95	US$mil 03/95				
Revenues	**2,125.7**	**1,837.2**	**1,687.6**	**17,105.7**	P/E Ratio	**75.3**	Price (9/30/95)	**1,490.00**
Net Income	**37.8**	**50.6**	**40.1**	**406.3**	P/B Ratio	**2.8**	52 Wk Hi-Low	**1,610.0-1,210.0**
Book Value	**1,007.9**	**1,048.4**	**1,078.7**	**12,484.5**	Yield %	**0.6**	Market Cap	**US$30,487mil**

Address **1-3-2, Nihonbashi-Hongokucho**
Chuo-ku, Tokyo 103
Tel **03-3245-1111**
Fax **03-3270-7761**
ADR **BTKYY**
SEDOL No. **6894081**
President **Tasuku Takagaki**
Chairman **Toyoo Gyoten**

Bank of Yokohama

Industry: **Banks - Regional**

Bank of Yokohama (Yokohama Ginko) is Japan's largest regional bank by assets. Its activities include commodity-securities dealing, trustee services, registration of bonds and debentures, and securities loans. Most of its lending is to the manufacturing and distribution industries. Loans to small- and medium-size firms account for almost three fourths of all loans. The bank has a total of 200 domestic offices and 15 overseas bases in 10 countries. It has an extensive network of 66 financial subsidiaries in the United Kingdom, including investment firm Guiness Mahon Holdings.

¥bil	03/93	03/94	03/95	US$mil 03/95				
Revenues	**702.3**	**589.6**	**535.6**	**5,429.5**	P/E Ratio	**132.1**	Price (9/30/95)	**740.00**
Net Income	**7.1**	**4.9**	**6.3**	**64.1**	P/B Ratio	**1.7**	52 Wk Hi-Low	**905.00-670.00**
Book Value	**501.8**	**501.9**	**503.2**	**5,823.6**	Yield %	**0.7**	Market Cap	**US$8,467.4mil**

Address **3-1-1, Minato-Mirai**
Nishi-ku, Yokohama, 220
Tel **045-225-1111**
Fax **045-225-1160**
ADR
SEDOL No. **6986449**
President **Sadaaki Hirasawa**
Chairman **Takashi Tanaka**

Banyu Pharmaceutical

Industry: **Pharmaceuticals**

Banyu Pharmaceutical (Banyu Seiyaku), a subsidiary of Merck & Co. (U.S.), is a leading Japanese pharmaceuticals manufacturer. The company purchases and markets drugs developed by Merck. Roughly 85% of Banyu's sales are in prescription drugs. Among the company's major drugs are Lipovas (an anti-lipemia agent), Renivace (an antihypertensive agent), Tienam (a carbapenem antibiotic), and Timoptol (an antiglaucoma and anti-ocular-hypertension agent). The company makes about 16% of its parent sales to Suzuken, one of the largest of Japan's pharmaceutical wholesalers.

¥bil	03/93 P	03/94 P	03/95 P	US$mil 03/95				
Sales	**114.7**	**122.5**	**129.0**	**1,307.8**	P/E Ratio	**32.9**	Price (9/30/95)	**1,160.00**
Net Income	**6.3**	**7.5**	**9.3**	**94.5**	P/B Ratio	**1.8**	52 Wk Hi-Low	**1,170.0-850.0**
Book Value	**160.6**	**166.1**	**173.2**	**2,005.0**	Yield %	**0.9**	Market Cap	**US$3,080.2mil**

Address **2-2-3, Nihonbashi-Honcho**
Chuo-ku, Tokyo 103
Tel **03-5203-8111**
Fax **03-3241-5585**
ADR **BNYUY**
SEDOL No. **6077309**
President **Kenjiro Nagasaka**
Chairman **Noriyuki Toyama**

P=Parent company data.

Best Denki

Industry: **Other Specialty Retailers**

Best Denki is one of Japan's largest consumer-electronics retailers by volume. The Kyushu-based company sells household electrical appliances, audio equipment, office equipment, pharmaceuticals, and cosmetics through 180 wholly-owned stores and 288 (including 23 overseas) franchises. Best Denki is expanding its operations in southern Japan and Southeast Asia. The retailer has a joint agreement with Yaohan to sell consumer electronics at Yaohan outlets in the U.S. Its major customers include Yaohan Best, Nippon Shinpan, Kakoi Electro, and Minami Nippon Shinpan.

¥bil	02/93	02/94	02/95	US$mil 02/95				
Revenues	**201.9**	**207.9**	**233.0**	**2,325.0**	P/E Ratio	**40.3**	Price (9/30/95)	**1,500.00**
Net Income	**3.6**	**4.5**	**4.7**	**46.8**	P/B Ratio	**1.9**	52 Wk Hi-Low	**1,640.0-1,210.0**
Book Value	**96.9**	**98.8**	**101.7**	**1,051.3**	Yield %	**1.7**	Market Cap	**US$1,908.1mil**

Address **2-1-12, Nanotsu**
Chuo-ku, Fukuoka 810
Tel **092-781-7161**
Fax **092-712-9540**
ADR
SEDOL No. **6098184**
President **Yasumitsu Kitada**
Chairman **Mitsuo Kitada**

Bridgestone

Industry: **Tires & Rubber**

Bridgestone is one of the world's largest tire manufacturers. It also makes a variety of nonrubber products. It is Japan's largest tire maker by sales and has a 48% share of Japan's tire market. Among its better-known brand names are Firestone, Dayton, and Road King. Other products include industrial-rubber goods such as conveyor belts, chemical products including building materials, marine products, and sporting goods, mainly tennis and golf equipment. Bridgestone acquired Ohio-based Firestone in 1988. In 1994, sales abroad accounted for 54% of total revenues.

¥bil	12/92	12/93	12/94	US$mil 12/94				
Sales	**1,745.2**	**1,599.2**	**1,595.1**	**15,629.5**	P/E Ratio	**35.8**	Price (9/30/95)	**1,470.00**
Net Income	**28.4**	**28.4**	**31.9**	**312.2**	P/B Ratio	**2.2**	52 Wk Hi-Low	**1,600.0-1,230.0**
Book Value	**455.4**	**489.3**	**526.8**	**5,279.7**	Yield %	**0.8**	Market Cap	**US$11,561mil**

Address **1-10-1, Kyobashi**
Chuo-ku, Tokyo 104
Tel **03-3563-6822**
Fax **03-3567-4615**
ADR **BRDCY**
SEDOL No. **6132101**
President **Yoichiro Kaizaki**
Chairman **--**

CSK

Industry: **Software**

CSK is Japan's largest independent information-processing-services firm. Its operations include computer programming, software development, facilities management, and data-entry services. It is also involved in computer-system maintenance, computer leasing, software sales, and computer-network servicing. CSK has franchise systems in Hokkaido, Nagano, and Hokuriku, and has 25 bases in 15 countries. In Japan, the firm has joint ventures with IBM Japan, Computer Systems Integration, and Japan Information Engineering. CSK has a 20% stake in Sega Enterprises.

¥bil	09/92	03/94 *	03/95	US$mil 03/95				
Sales	**125.9**	**46.0**	**85.1**	**862.7**	P/E Ratio	**NMF**	Price (9/30/95)	**2,970.00**
Net Income	**2.0**	**-0.6**	**-8.1**	**-82.4**	P/B Ratio	**1.4**	52 Wk Hi-Low	**3,530.0-1,920.0**
Book Value	**136.3**	**141.9**	**134.3**	**1,554.5**	Yield %	**0.4**	Market Cap	**US$1,915.9mil**

Address **2-6-1, Nishi-Shinjuku**
Shinjuku-ku, Tokyo 163-02
Tel **03-3344-1811**
Fax **03-3344-1874**
ADR **CSKKY**
SEDOL No. **6215552**
President **Isao Ohkawa**
Chairman **Isao Ohkawa**

*Irregular period due to fiscal year change.

Calpis Food Industry

Industry: **Soft Drinks**

Calpis Food Industry, a member of the Ajinomoto group, is a leading Japanese soft-drink maker. Calpis Water, a milk-based drink, accounts for roughly half of consolidated sales. In addition, the company produces cream, butter, liquor jelly, rice gruel, and biochemical agents. Calpis operates a vending-machine network throughout Japan that accounts for most of its soft-drink sales. Major customers include wholesalers Kokubun, Niseki Shoji, and Nihon Shurui Hanbai. The firm completed a new research facility in early 1994. Calpis is 20% owned by Ajinomoto.

¥bil	12/92	12/93	12/94	US$mil 12/94				
Sales	**122.2**	**104.7**	**106.4**	**1,042.7**	P/E Ratio	**NMF**	Price (9/30/95)	**660.00**
Net Income	**0.4**	**-0.2**	**0.2**	**2.3**	P/B Ratio	**1.1**	52 Wk Hi-Low	**935.00-560.00**
Book Value	**46.6**	**46.0**	**45.2**	**453.1**	Yield %	**0.6**	Market Cap	**US$522.8mil**

Address **2-20-3, Ebisu-Nishi**
Shibuya-ku, Tokyo 150
Tel **03-3780-2104**
Fax **03-3770-5374**
ADR **CPISY**
SEDOL No. **6161309**
President **Kimio Kobayashi**
Chairman **Shunsuke Inamori**

Canon

Industry: **Office Equipment**

Canon is one of the world's leading manufacturers of office equipment and optical products. Its product lines include photocopiers, computer equipment, photographic equipment, and telecommunication devices for office, home, and industrial use. Products include laser and bubble-jet printers, facsimile machines, telephones, workstations, desktop-publishing systems, cameras, camcorders, and semiconductor-manufacturing steppers. Canon holds 25% of the U.S. photocopier market. Exports contribute 79% of sales. About 68% of revenues come from Europe and the U.S.

¥bil	12/92	12/93	12/94	US$mil 12/94				
Sales	**1,914.4**	**1,836.1**	**1,933.3**	**18,943.6**	P/E Ratio	**46.5**	Price (9/30/95)	**1,770.00**
Net Income	**35.9**	**21.1**	**31.0**	**304.0**	P/B Ratio	**1.9**	52 Wk Hi-Low	**1,860.0-1,230.0**
Book Value	**707.8**	**721.4**	**781.2**	**7,829.6**	Yield %	**0.7**	Market Cap	**US$14,833mil**

Address **3-30-2, Shimomaruko**
Ohta-ku, Tokyo 146
Tel **03-3758-2111**
Fax **03-5482-5135**
ADR **CANNY**
SEDOL No. **6172323**
President **Hajime Mitarai**
Chairman **Ryuzaburo Kaku**

Canon Sales

Industry: **Overseas Trading**

Canon Sales (Canon Hanbai) holds exclusive rights to Japanese sales of Canon products. The firm's main sales lines include cameras, video systems, lenses, copiers, facsimile machines, word processors, semiconductor-manufacturing equipment, and laser printers. It directly manages 77 Zero-One Shops, where it sells Macintosh and IBM products. The firm is the primary Japanese distributor for Apple Computer. It also has an agreement with IMT (U.S.) to distribute interactive-multimedia equipment. Canon Sales is developing computer-systems integration with Yokogawa-Hewlett Packard.

	¥bil 12/92	12/93	12/94	US$mil 12/94				
Sales	**529.7**	**543.1**	**609.9**	**5,976.0**	P/E Ratio	**47.2**	Price (9/30/95)	**2,560.00**
Net Income	**6.4**	**5.6**	**6.3**	**61.3**	P/B Ratio	**1.5**	52 Wk Hi-Low	**3,270.0-1,980.0**
Book Value	**155.9**	**181.4**	**196.1**	**1,965.0**	Yield %	**0.6**	Market Cap	**US$3,054.7mil**

Address	**3-11-28, Mita**	Tel	**03-3455-9021**	ADR		President	**Hideharu Takemoto**
	Minato-ku, Tokyo 108	Fax	**043-211-9057**	SEDOL No.	**6172453**	Chairman	**Seiichi Takikawa**

Casio Computer

Industry: **Office Equipment**

Casio Computer (Casio Keisanki) is one of the world's leading manufacturers of digital watches and desktop-electronic calculators. Its other products include electronic keyboards and pianos, personal computers, computer printers, integrated-circuit cards, electronic cash registers, and liquid-crystal-display televisions. Major customers include Casio (a New Jersey sales affiliate), Casio Joho Kiki, and Casio Denshi Device. Casio Computer has 55 consolidated subsidiaries. In fiscal 1994, 49% of Casio's total consolidated sales were made overseas.

	¥bil 03/93	03/94	03/95	US$mil 03/95				
Sales	**431.7**	**383.8**	**401.7**	**4,071.5**	P/E Ratio	**50.8**	Price (9/30/95)	**929.00**
Net Income	**7.0**	**5.3**	**5.0**	**50.9**	P/B Ratio	**1.5**	52 Wk Hi-Low	**1,300.0-716.0**
Book Value	**164.0**	**170.7**	**175.1**	**2,026.4**	Yield %	**1.4**	Market Cap	**US$2,579.5mil**

Address	**2-6-1, Nishi-Shinjuku**	Tel	**03-3347-4852**	ADR	**CSIOF**	President	**Kazuo Kashio**
	Shinjuku-ku, Tokyo 163-02	Fax	**03-3347-4533**	SEDOL No.	**6178967**	Chairman	**Toshio Kashio**

Chiba Bank

Industry: **Banks - Regional**

Chiba Bank (Chiba Ginko) is one of the three largest regional banks in Japan by assets. This prefecture's leading bank, it has 162 branches and offices in Chiba and 10 offices in Tokyo. Its client base is primarily made up of individuals and small- and medium-size companies. The bank's emphasis has been on loans to the service sector, with 60% of its loans going to customers in Chiba Prefecture. Chiba Bank maintains overseas branches in New York, Los Angeles, London, and Hong Kong, and operates a subsidiary in London that is involved in securities transactions.

	¥bil 03/93 P	03/94 P	03/95 P	US$mil 03/95				
Revenues	**429.1**	**359.9**	**337.9**	**3,425.1**	P/E Ratio	**82.7**	Price (9/30/95)	**835.00**
Net Income	**14.8**	**9.9**	**7.9**	**79.7**	P/B Ratio	**1.7**	52 Wk Hi-Low	**934.00-717.00**
Book Value	**378.7**	**383.8**	**387.7**	**4,487.4**	Yield %	**0.6**	Market Cap	**US$6,533.2mil**

Address	**1-2, Chiba-Minato, Chuo-ku**	Tel	**043-245-1111**	ADR		President	**Takashi Tamaki**
	Chiba City, Chiba 260	Fax	**043-244-6654**	SEDOL No.	**6190563**	Chairman	--

P=Parent company data.

Chichibu Onoda Cement

Industry: **Building Materials**

Cichibuonoda Cement is one of Japan's largest cement makers by sales. Primary products include portland, white, and mixed cement. Other products include plaster, limestone, quicklime, silicon nitride, and engineering ceramics. It also produces building materials, and manufactures and sells chemical products and electronic components. On October 1, 1994, Onoda Cement merged with Japan's sixth-largest cement manufacturer, Chichibu Cement. The firm has over 100 subsidiaries. Overseas production and marketing are targeted to the U.S., China, Southeast Asia, and Australia.

	¥bil 03/93	03/94	03/95	US$mil 03/95				
Sales	**528.2**	**491.3**	**528.2**	**5,353.8**	P/E Ratio	**NMF**	Price (9/30/95)	**523.00**
Net Income	**9.0**	**0.8**	**-6.0**	**-61.3**	P/B Ratio	**1.6**	52 Wk Hi-Low	**651.00-366.00**
Book Value	**126.2**	**125.9**	**187.0**	**2,164.9**	Yield %	**1.1**	Market Cap	**US$3,035.4mil**

Address	**2-14-1, Nishi-Shinbashi**	Tel	**03-5512-5222**	ADR		President	**Kazusuke Imamura**
	Minato-ku, Tokyo 105	Fax	**03-5512-5239**	SEDOL No.	**6660204**	Chairman	**Ken Moroi**

Chiyoda Company

Industry: **Apparel Retailers**

Chiyoda Company is the largest Japanese retailer of shoes by sales, net income, and number of stores. The firm sells men's, women's, and children's sandals and sports shoes through 1,639 specialty stores throughout Japan. Chiyoda also specializes in toys, and has a chain of toy stores, Hello Mac in the Tokyo metropolitan area. The Hello Mac chain receives half of its sales from electronic-game software. As of the fiscal year ending February 1994, shoes and toys accounted for 64.2% and 31.4% of sales, respectively. Chiyoda also sells clothing, food, and sundries, and leases real estate.

	¥bil 02/93	02/94	02/95	US$mil 02/95				
Revenues	**203.8**	**218.7**	**220.7**	**2,202.7**	P/E Ratio	**24.1**	Price (9/30/95)	**2,150.00**
Net Income	**6.1**	**4.4**	**4.1**	**41.4**	P/B Ratio	**1.9**	52 Wk Hi-Low	**2,200.0-1,160.0**
Book Value	**45.5**	**49.2**	**52.7**	**545.4**	Yield %	**0.6**	Market Cap	**US$1,004.7mil**

Address	**4-39-8, Narita-Higashi**	Tel	**03-3316-4131**	ADR		President	**Masao Funabashi**
	Suginami-ku, Tokyo 166	Fax	**03-3317-2852**	SEDOL No.	**6191801**	Chairman	--

Chiyoda Corporation

Industry: **Oil - Secondary**

Chiyoda Corporation (Chiyoda Kako Kensetsu), a leading plant-engineering firm in Japan, specializes in oil-refining, utility, and petrochemical projects. It builds plants for processing petroleum and natural and liquefied petroleum gas, chemicals, fertilizers, pharmaceuticals, and textiles. Chiyoda also makes oil-storage facilities and handles projects related to automobile factories, environmental conservation, and regional development. Overseas sales make up 51% of consolidated sales; the firm is particularly active in Southeast Asia. It has 10 consolidated subsidiaries.

¥bil	03/93	03/94	03/95	US$mil 03/95				
Sales	**441.2**	**393.6**	**342.4**	**3,470.6**	P/E Ratio	**47.2**	Price (9/30/95)	**921.00**
Net Income	**11.6**	**4.2**	**3.8**	**38.6**	P/B Ratio	**1.6**	52 Wk Hi-Low	**1,360.0-691.0**
Book Value	**105.1**	**107.5**	**112.8**	**1,305.2**	Yield %	**0.9**	Market Cap	**US$1,808.5mil**

Address **2-13-19, Shiba**
Minato-ku, Tokyo 105
Tel **03-3456-1211**
Fax **03-5476-8478**
ADR
SEDOL No. **6191704**
President **Masaaki Kashiwara**
Chairman **Masakazu Tamaki**

Chiyoda Fire & Marine Insurance

Industry: **Insurance - Property & Casualty**

Chiyoda Fire & Marine Insurance (Chiyoda Kasai Kaijo Hoken) is a medium-size non-life-insurance company that specializes in automobile insurance. The firm's products include marine, casualty, transport, aviation, workers' compensation, natural-disaster, and medical insurance. Golf-course weather insurance, nursing-care-expense insurance, and comprehensive insurance with a maturity refund for homeowners are among the firm's newer offerings. It has overseas subsidiaries in the U.S., the U.K., and Luxembourg. Chiyoda Fire & Marine has close ties with the Toyota Motor Group.

¥bil	03/93	03/94	03/95	US$mil 03/95				
Revenues	**361.9**	**382.9**	**518.9**	**5,260.1**	P/E Ratio	**48.6**	Price (9/30/95)	**583.00**
Net Income	**5.8**	**5.3**	**4.2**	**42.6**	P/B Ratio	**1.5**	52 Wk Hi-Low	**674.00-451.00**
Book Value	**129.9**	**132.3**	**134.1**	**1,551.6**	Yield %	**1.2**	Market Cap	**US$2,054.2mil**

Address **2-1-9, Kyobashi**
Chuo-ku, Tokyo 104
Tel **03-3281-3311**
Fax **03-3281-3524**
ADR
SEDOL No. **6191760**
President **Takashi Toyabe**
Chairman **Hideo Kamio**

Chubu Electric Power

Industry: **Electrical Utilities - All**

Chubu Electric Power (Chubu Denryoku) ranks third among electric-power companies in Japan in terms of generating capacity, kilowatt-hour sales, and revenues. It serves eight million consumers in the Aichi, Gifu, Mie, Nagano, and Shizuoka regions, accounting for about 20% of Japan's total power output. The firm's principal facilities consist of 16 hydroelectric-, six fossil-fired, and one nuclear-power plant. Almost 75% of its energy is generated from fossil fuels, primarily, oils and liquefied natural gas. The firm and its three main subsidiaries are all based in Nagano.

¥bil	03/93	03/94	03/95	US$mil 03/95				
Sales	**1,962.6**	**1,955.7**	**2,067.5**	**20,956.7**	P/E Ratio	**39.3**	Price (9/30/95)	**2,400.00**
Net Income	**55.0**	**26.2**	**45.6**	**462.0**	P/B Ratio	**1.9**	52 Wk Hi-Low	**2,500.0-2,188.1**
Book Value	**904.2**	**893.4**	**929.2**	**10,754.2**	Yield %	**2.1**	Market Cap	**US$18,174mil**

Address **1, Higashi-Shincho**
Higashi-ku, Nagoya 461-91
Tel **052-951-8211**
Fax **N/A**
ADR
SEDOL No. **6195609**
President **Hiroji Ota**
Chairman **Kohei Abe**

Chudenko

Industry: **Electrical Components & Equipment**

Chudenko is a comprehensive electrical-engineering company affiliated with Chugoku Electric Power. It installs duct work for air-conditioning systems, telecommunication lines, and cables for transforming, transmitting, and distributing power. In addition to general-wiring work, Chudenko is expanding into fiberoptic-network construction and automatic-control devices and services for air conditioners. It has six subsidiaries, including two domestic subsidiaries: Gyoden sells electrical-construction materials, and Sanshin Electric Materials sells electric-manufacturing materials.

¥bil	03/93	03/94	03/95	US$mil 03/95				
Sales	**195.9**	**201.9**	**212.0**	**2,148.9**	P/E Ratio	**15.1**	Price (9/30/95)	**3,900.00**
Net Income	**17.0**	**16.9**	**15.8**	**160.6**	P/B Ratio	**1.5**	52 Wk Hi-Low	**4,050.0-2,980.0**
Book Value	**116.1**	**132.4**	**149.0**	**1,724.1**	Yield %	**0.3**	Market Cap	**US$2,411.0mil**

Address **1-15, Kami-Tenmacho, Nishi-ku**
Hiroshima, 733
Tel **082-291-7415**
Fax **082-293-6903**
ADR
SEDOL No. **6195869**
President **Koichi Ikeuchi**
Chairman **Toshio Miyazaki**

Chugai Pharmaceutical

Industry: **Pharmaceuticals**

Chugai Pharmaceutical (Chugai Seiyaku) is a pharmaceutical manufacturer that specializes in circulatory- and immune-system drugs. Prescription drugs account for about 70% of the company's consolidated sales and over-the-counter medications for about 20%. Chugai's best-selling drugs include Epogin (bioengineered erythropoietin), Neutrogin (a granulocyte-colony-stimulating factor), and Picibanil (an anticancer agent). Of the company's five consolidated subsidiaries, two are located in the United States. It has a technology-sharing agreement with Rhône-Poulenc (France).

¥bil	12/92	12/93	12/94	US$mil 12/94				
Sales	**151.5**	**159.5**	**171.4**	**1,679.4**	P/E Ratio	**30.6**	Price (9/30/95)	**1,020.00**
Net Income	**4.9**	**6.9**	**8.2**	**80.4**	P/B Ratio	**2.1**	52 Wk Hi-Low	**1,100.0-820.0**
Book Value	**108.3**	**114.2**	**120.8**	**1,211.2**	Yield %	**1.1**	Market Cap	**US$2,528.5mil**

Address **2-1-9, Kyobashi**
Chuo-ku, Tokyo 104
Tel **03-3281-6611**
Fax **03-3281-2828**
ADR
SEDOL No. **6196408**
President **Osamu Nagayama**
Chairman **Kimio Ueno**

Chugoku Bank

Industry: **Banks - Regional**

Chugoku Bank (Chugoku Ginko), based in Okayama, is a medium-size regional bank. Its area of operations is the Seto Inland Sea region, including Hiroshima and Kagawa prefectures. The officially designated bank of Okayama Prefecture, it has one of the highest equity ratios among regional banks. More than half the bank's loans are to the manufacturing and distribution sectors. Chugoku Bank has a network of 185 branches in Japan, a branch in New York, and representative offices in Hong Kong and London. The bank belongs to a network of 144 corresponding banks in 59 countries.

¥bil	03/93 P	03/94 P	03/95 P	US$mil 03/95				
Revenues	228.5	197.9	190.9	1,935.2	P/E Ratio	24.9	Price (9/30/95)	1,710.00
Net Income	9.2	12.2	14.0	141.9	P/B Ratio	1.5	52 Wk Hi-Low	1,770.0-1,510.0
Book Value	208.0	219.0	231.7	2,682.0	Yield %	0.4	Market Cap	US$3,501.2mil

Address	**1-15-20, Marunouchi**	Tel **086-223-3111**	ADR	President	**Kanji Inaba**
	Okayama City, Okayama 700	Fax **086-234-6582**	SEDOL No. **6195803**	Chairman	--

P=Parent company data.

Chukyo Coca-Cola Bottling

Industry: **Soft Drinks**

Chukyo Coca-Cola Bottling, a member of the Mitsubishi group, supplies soft drinks to the Nagoya area, which includes Aichi, Gifu, and Mie prefectures. Its single best-selling product is Georgia brand coffee. Other products include Coca-Cola, Fanta, Sprite, Hi-C, and Aquarius. It also markets vending machines. Beverage sales account for more than 90% of total sales. Though Chukyo is affiliated with Coca-Cola Japan, that company owns no stock in Chukyo. Chukyo has three bottling facilities, 29 sales-outlet offices, and a vending-machine management office in Japan.

¥bil	12/92 P	12/93 P	12/94 P	US$mil 12/94				
Sales	78.7	75.6	82.6	809.3	P/E Ratio	17.7	Price (9/30/95)	985.00
Net Income	3.0	2.2	2.7	26.4	P/B Ratio	1.4	52 Wk Hi-Low	1,200.0-850.0
Book Value	31.1	32.4	34.5	345.5	Yield %	1.5	Market Cap	US$478.6mil

Address	**4-1-47, Sunadabashi**	Tel **052-723-3130**	ADR	President	**Yoshiaki Shoji**
	Higashi-ku Nagoya, Aichi 461	Fax **052-723-3191**	SEDOL No. **6196420**	Chairman	--

P=Parent company data.

Citizen Watch

Industry: **Clothing & Fabrics**

Citizen Watch (Citizen Tokei) manufactures precision instruments including wristwatches, industrial machinery, clocks, eyeglass frames, jewelry, and information equipment (such as liquid-crystal displays and personal-computer hardware). The company is one of the world's largest producers of wristwatches, including designer-licensed watches, sports watches, and low-end watches. Its major customers include Marubeni, Yamasaki Seiki, Fuji Photo Film, Yuasa, CBM, KGK, Tokki, and Toshiba. Citizen Watch has 33 consolidated subsidiaries throughout Japan, and 10 located overseas.

¥bil	03/93	03/94	03/95	US$mil 03/95				
Sales	408.3	377.8	362.7	3,676.6	P/E Ratio	64.4	Price (9/30/95)	715.00
Net Income	12.1	7.4	3.5	35.2	P/B Ratio	1.3	52 Wk Hi-Low	840.00-496.00
Book Value	168.9	177.6	178.5	2,065.9	Yield %	1.3	Market Cap	US$2,254.7mil

Address	**2-1-1, Nishi-Shinjuku**	Tel **03-3342-1231**	ADR	President	**Michio Nakajima**
	Shinjuku-ku, Tokyo 163-04	Fax **03-3342-1280**	SEDOL No. **6197304**	Chairman	--

Clarion

Industry: **Other Auto Parts**

Clarion, a member of the Nissan group, is a leading manufacturer of car-audio equipment. The company is the major supplier of car-audio equipment to Nissan Motor. Its products include car compact-disc and digital-audiotape players, car air conditioners, modular kitchen units, car phones, karaoke machines, home stereos, and car electronics. Clarion has also entered the housing-equipment market. Sales of car-audio equipment account for 78% of consolidated sales. The firm has 56 consolidated subsidiaries. In 1994, 40% of Clarion's consolidated sales were made overseas.

¥bil	03/93	03/94	03/95	US$mil 03/95				
Sales	182.8	174.6	164.1	1,663.4	P/E Ratio	NMF	Price (9/30/95)	444.00
Net Income	-13.5	-3.8	-0.4	-4.4	P/B Ratio	1.9	52 Wk Hi-Low	532.00-315.00
Book Value	40.2	37.3	36.3	419.6	Yield %	0.0	Market Cap	US$695.0mil

Address	**2-22-3, Shibuya**	Tel **03-3400-1121**	ADR	President	**Ichizo Ishitsubo**
	Shibuya-ku, Tokyo 150	Fax **03-3400-8505**	SEDOL No. **6201164**	Chairman	--

Cleanup

Industry: **Household Products (Durable)**

Cleanup, a major vendor of household fixtures, is the leading manufacturer of systemized kitchens in Japan. Kitchen equipment, including luxury systemized kitchens, represent its main source of sales. The company is diversifying into color stainless-steel home furnishings, commercial-kitchen units, and is developing lines of bath and washstand products. With headquarters in Tokyo, Cleanup has a domestic network of five factories, 13 branches, and 10 wholly-owned consolidated subsidiaries. It also has a wholly-owned subsidiary in Hong Kong and a branch office in Beijing.

¥bil	03/93	03/94	03/95	US$mil 03/95				
Sales	89.5	91.1	94.9	961.5	P/E Ratio	24.7	Price (9/30/95)	1,320.00
Net Income	2.4	2.1	2.6	26.5	P/B Ratio	1.3	52 Wk Hi-Low	1,760.0-1,300.0
Book Value	42.0	48.0	50.2	581.2	Yield %	1.2	Market Cap	US$649.8mil

Address	**6-22-22, Nishi-Nippori**	Tel **03-3894-4771**	ADR	President	**Kyoichi Inoue**
	Arakawa-ku, Tokyo 116	Fax **03-3893-9577**	SEDOL No. **6203513**	Chairman	**Noboru Inoue**

Cosmo Oil

Industry: **Oil - Secondary**

Cosmo Oil (Cosmo Sekiyu) is Japan's third-largest oil refiner by sales. The company produces heavy fuel oil, diesel-gas oil, kerosene, gasoline, naphtha, lubricants, and other petroleum products. It distributes and sells gasoline through its chain of about 561 dealers and 7,104 service stations throughout Japan. The company is also involved in operating a real-estate business and in manufacturing pharmaceuticals. Its major clients include Kyushu Shoji, Hino Motors, and Isuzu Motors. Cosmo Oil has two joint exploration and procurement activities in the United Arab Emirates.

¥bil	03/93	03/94	03/95	US$mil 03/95				
Sales	**1,736.1**	**1,609.1**	**1,588.0**	**16,096.5**	P/E Ratio	**23.1**	Price (9/30/95)	**492.00**
Net Income	**17.5**	**8.7**	**13.1**	**132.4**	P/B Ratio	**1.7**	52 Wk Hi-Low	**776.00-461.00**
Book Value	**134.6**	**158.3**	**183.5**	**2,123.5**	Yield %	**1.6**	Market Cap	**US$3,126.1mil**

Address **1-1-1, Shibaura** Tel **03-3798-3211** ADR President **Keiichiro Okabe**
Minato-ku, Tokyo 105 Fax **03-3798-3411** SEDOL No. **6226338** Chairman **Hiroto Sumiyoshi**

Credit Saison

Industry: **Financial Services - Diversified**

Credit Saison, Japan's second-largest credit company, provides monthly-installment-payment plans, consumer-credit sales, financing, loan guarantees, and consignment operations. It issues credit cards for the Seibu Saison department stores, as well as under the names Saison-VISA and Saison-MasterCard, for the latter two of which it has more than 9.3 million cardholders. Credit Saison's credit cards are also used on Japan Telecom's telephone network. In its non-credit-related business, the firm retails clothing, household goods, and sundries, and publishes Skier magazine.

¥bil	03/93 P	03/94 P	03/95 P	US$mil 03/95				
Revenues	**131.9**	**126.4**	**128.8**	**1,305.9**	P/E Ratio	**34.3**	Price (9/30/95)	**2,060.00**
Net Income	**6.6**	**7.0**	**7.7**	**77.7**	P/B Ratio	**2.3**	52 Wk Hi-Low	**2,350.0-1,470.0**
Book Value	**104.5**	**110.2**	**116.5**	**1,348.9**	Yield %	**0.5**	Market Cap	**US$2,642.5mil**

Address **3-1-1, Higashi-Ikebukuro** Tel **03-3988-2112** ADR President **Kazuo Toriumi**
Toshima-ku, Tokyo 170 Fax **03-5391-4392** SEDOL No. **6591809** Chairman **Toshio Takeuchi**

P=Parent company data.

Dai Nippon Printing

Industry: **General Industrial & Commercial Services**

Dai Nippon Printing (DNP) is Japan's largest printing company by sales, with a market share of about 12%. Its main lines of business are commercial and specialty printing. DNP prints books, magazines, catalogs, and advertising materials, and has expanded into packaging and electronics. It markets photomasks (used in semiconductor manufacturing) in the U.S. through Du Pont Photomask. The company has 17 plants in Japan. DNP has a joint venture with France's Bull CP8 to produce integrated-circuit cards. Its U.S. subsidiary will begin production in 1995.

¥bil	03/93	03/94	03/95	US$mil 03/95				
Sales	**1,192.1**	**1,145.5**	**1,192.8**	**12,090.9**	P/E Ratio	**23.9**	Price (9/30/95)	**1,570.00**
Net Income	**44.6**	**40.8**	**49.2**	**498.7**	P/B Ratio	**1.6**	52 Wk Hi-Low	**1,870.0-1,270.0**
Book Value	**676.3**	**699.9**	**738.2**	**8,544.5**	Yield %	**1.0**	Market Cap	**US$11,840mil**

Address **1-1-1, Ichigaya-Kagacho** Tel **03-3266-2201** ADR **DNPCY** President **Yoshitoshi Kitajima**
Shinjuku-ku, Tokyo 162-01 Fax **03-3266-2129** SEDOL No. **6250906** Chairman --

Daicel Chemical

Industry: **Specialty Chemicals**

Daicel Chemical Industries (Daicel Kagaku Kogyo), an affiliate of Mitsui & Co., produces organic chemicals, cellulose, and other chemical-related products. It is a leading maker of acetic acids, acetic-acid cellulose, and cellulosics for use in cigarette-filter production. The company also produces air-bag inflators for automobiles and ABS plastics for makers of consumer electronics and general machinery. Daicel Chemical has seven plants and three research centers in Japan. Overseas subsidiaries are located in the United States, Europe, Taiwan, Hong Kong, and Singapore.

¥bil	03/93	03/94	03/95	US$mil 03/95				
Sales	**232.3**	**216.3**	**235.6**	**2,387.9**	P/E Ratio	**63.3**	Price (9/30/95)	**570.00**
Net Income	**2.9**	**-3.1**	**3.4**	**34.0**	P/B Ratio	**1.5**	52 Wk Hi-Low	**600.00-415.00**
Book Value	**143.4**	**138.1**	**140.2**	**1,622.5**	Yield %	**0.9**	Market Cap	**US$2,144.0mil**

Address **1, Teppo-cho** Tel **0722-27-3111** ADR President **Akiro Kojima**
Sakai City, Osaka 590 Fax **0722-27-3000** SEDOL No. **6250542** Chairman --

Dai-Dan

Industry: **Electrical Components & Equipment**

Dai-Dan designs and builds electrical, air-conditioning, plumbing, fire-prevention, and water-treatment systems. It ranks among Japan's top four air-conditioning-engineering companies by total sales, providing more than 50% of Dai-Dan's annual revenues. Private-sector orders generally account for about 75% of total revenues. The firm opened a research institute in Kyoto to promote joint research in building-maintenance software with Osaka-based manufacturers and universities. Dai-Dan has two subsididaries and 10 affiliates, including one affiliate in Thailand.

¥bil	03/93 P	03/94 P	03/95 P	US$mil 03/95				
Sales	**207.3**	**227.0**	**208.5**	**2,113.2**	P/E Ratio	**12.1**	Price (9/30/95)	**1,260.00**
Net Income	**6.4**	**6.6**	**4.8**	**48.2**	P/B Ratio	**1.2**	52 Wk Hi-Low	**1,980.0-1,050.0**
Book Value	**37.3**	**43.1**	**47.0**	**544.5**	Yield %	**1.3**	Market Cap	**US$577.3mil**

Address **1-9-25, Edobori** Tel **06-441-8231** ADR President **Setsu Sugaya**
Nishi-ku, Osaka 550 Fax **06-448-5628** SEDOL No. **6661735** Chairman --

P=Parent company data.

Daido Steel

Industry: **Steel**

Daido Steel (Daido Tokushuko) is a top Japanese specialty-steels maker. The firm's products include cast- and forged-steel products, cold-finished steel hoops, industrial furnaces, and environmentally oriented devices. Its newer products are stainless-steel castings with thin walls and stainless-steel cold- and warm-forging parts. The auto industry, Nissan Motor in particular, accounts for the majority of the firm's sales. Daido Steel holds a 33% share of CSC Industries, a U.S. steel-materials maker, and founded Ohio Star Forge in the U.S. as a joint venture with CSC.

¥bil	03/93	03/94	03/95	US$mil 03/95				
Sales	**407.7**	**369.4**	**400.3**	**4,057.1**	P/E Ratio	**51.1**	Price (9/30/95)	**485.00**
Net Income	**3.7**	**-2.3**	**4.1**	**41.4**	P/B Ratio	**1.6**	52 Wk Hi-Low	**587.00-365.00**
Book Value	**134.7**	**129.7**	**131.5**	**1,522.0**	Yield %	**1.2**	Market Cap	**US$2,095.5mil**

Address **1-11-18, Nishiki**
Naka-ku, Nagoya 460
Tel **052-201-5111**
Fax **052-221-9268**
ADR
SEDOL No. **6250627**
President **Kanji Tomita**
Chairman **Motoi Yasue**

Daiei

Industry: **Retailers - Broadline**

Daiei is Japan's largest retailer by sales. It is known for its supermarket chain, but it also runs department, discount, and convenience stores. The firm also has businesses in the restaurant, hotel, credit-card, real-estate, and tourism industries. Daiei sells its own lines of apparel, dry goods, and stationery. The parent company makes about 40% of sales in the Osaka area. Daiei Convenience Systems, a consolidated subsidiary of Daiei, operates Daiei's 5,000 Lawson convenience stores. In 1994, Daiei merged with three affiliates: Chujitsuya, Uneed Daiei, and Dainaha.

¥bil	02/93	02/94	02/95	US$mil 02/95				
Revenues	**2,515.1**	**2,653.7**	**3,223.9**	**32,168.9**	P/E Ratio	**NMF**	Price (9/30/95)	**1,130.00**
Net Income	**7.2**	**5.4**	**-50.7**	**-505.5**	P/B Ratio	**5.5**	52 Wk Hi-Low	**1,610.0-993.0**
Book Value	**146.2**	**115.7**	**147.0**	**1,520.0**	Yield %	**1.5**	Market Cap	**US$8,111.8mil**

Address **4-1-1, Minatojima-Nakamachi**
Chuo-ku, Kobe 650
Tel **078-302-5001**
Fax **03-3433-9226**
ADR **DAIEY**
SEDOL No. **6249982**
President **Isao Nakauchi**
Chairman **Isao Nakauchi**

Daifuku

Industry: **Factory Equipment**

Daifuku, a maker of factory-automation equipment, specializes in conveyor and storage systems. Its automated warehouses, which have a 40% share of the Japanese market, are supplied mainly to the auto industry. Its other clients include semiconductor, pharmaceutical, and light-electrical-machinery firms. Daifuku has a production joint venture with a Kanematsu subsidiary in Thailand, as well as a U.S. sales office and service plant. The firm also has technical and marketing agreements with Comau (Italy) and AEG (Germany). It is a member of the Dai-Ichi Kangyo Bank group.

¥bil	03/93	03/94	03/95	US$mil 03/95				
Sales	**147.9**	**128.2**	**108.0**	**1,094.7**	P/E Ratio	**NMF**	Price (9/30/95)	**1,210.00**
Net Income	**6.2**	**1.8**	**-1.0**	**-10.2**	P/B Ratio	**2.4**	52 Wk Hi-Low	**1,680.0-880.0**
Book Value	**59.6**	**59.8**	**57.5**	**665.4**	Yield %	**0.8**	Market Cap	**US$1,383.2mil**

Address **3-2-11, Mitejima**
Nishi-Yodogawa-ku, Osaka 555
Tel **06-472-1261**
Fax **06-476-2567**
ADR
SEDOL No. **6250025**
President **Susumu Ito**
Chairman **Shoichiro Masuda**

Daihatsu Motor

Industry: **Automobile Manufacturers**

Daihatsu Motor (Daihatsu Kogyo), a member of the Toyota group, manufactures compact passenger cars and minivehicles. It trails only Suzuki in the domestic production of minicars, and it also produces small trucks, sport-utility vehicles, vans, and auto parts. The assembly of vans, light trucks, and subcompacts on consignment for Toyota and Hino Motors accounts for about one fourth of parent-company sales. It has a joint venture with Piaggio (Italy), a joint venture in Indonesia, a technical tie-up with Asia Motors in South Korea, and a joint venture with the Malaysian government.

¥bil	03/93	03/94	03/95	US$mil 03/95				
Sales	**875.0**	**816.7**	**812.0**	**8,230.6**	P/E Ratio	**NMF**	Price (9/30/95)	**521.00**
Net Income	**-4.4**	**-1.0**	**1.2**	**12.3**	P/B Ratio	**2.2**	52 Wk Hi-Low	**659.00-346.00**
Book Value	**107.2**	**102.6**	**101.9**	**1,179.0**	Yield %	**0.6**	Market Cap	**US$2,233.7mil**

Address **1-1, Daihatsu-cho**
Ikeda City, Osaka 563
Tel **0727-54-3062**
Fax **0727-53-6880**
ADR
SEDOL No. **6250304**
President **Iichi Shingu**
Chairman **Takashi Toyozumi**

Daihen

Industry: **Electrical Components & Equipment**

Daihen, a member of the Sumitomo group, manufactures electrical equipment and welding machines. The firm is the world's leading producer of arc-welding robots. Its specific products include transformers, power switches, on-load tap-changers, plasma-cutting machines, laser welders, diffusion furnaces, and industrial robots. Daihen is currently developing advanced production-control systems and fine ceramics. Kansai Electric Power is the company's main customer. Daihen has tie-ups with TWI and Electrox, both of the United Kingdom, in carbon-dioxide laser-processing systems.

¥bil	03/93	03/94	03/95	US$mil 03/95				
Sales	**88.5**	**79.8**	**79.8**	**808.5**	P/E Ratio	**50.8**	Price (9/30/95)	**488.00**
Net Income	**1.7**	**1.2**	**1.3**	**13.5**	P/B Ratio	**1.9**	52 Wk Hi-Low	**601.00-386.00**
Book Value	**35.4**	**35.6**	**36.1**	**417.3**	Yield %	**1.4**	Market Cap	**US$679.9mil**

Address **2-1-11, Tagawa**
Yodogawa-ku, Osaka 532
Tel **06-390-5505**
Fax **06-308-6342**
ADR
SEDOL No. **6661843**
President **Daizo Nishimatsu**
Chairman **Keijiro Kobayashi**

Daiichi Chuo Kisen Kaisha

Industry: **Marine Transportation**

Daiichi Chuo Kisen, a member of Mitsui O.S.K. Lines group, is a tramp operator. Iron ore, oil, timber, steel, coal, and grains are its primary cargoes. The firm transports more than half of Sumitomo Metal Industries' raw materials used in their crude-steel production. Its mainstays, tramp and container shipping, account for about 85% of revenues. Ship charters are its next-largest source of revenue. Mitsui O.S.K. Lines and Sumitomo Metal own 24.4% and 20.1% of the firm's stock, respectively. In 1994, overseas sales consisted 86.7% of its total consolidated revenues.

	¥bil 03/93	03/94	03/95	US$mil 03/95				
Sales	64.6	59.3	66.3	671.7	P/E Ratio	NMF	Price (9/30/95)	240.00
Net Income	1.3	-0.6	0.0	0.5	P/B Ratio	2.7	52 Wk Hi-Low	388.00-190.00
Book Value	26.0	23.8	23.4	271.0	Yield %	0.0	Market Cap	US$636.2mil

Address **3-5-15, Nihonbashi Chuo-ku, Tokyo 103** Tel **03-3278-6761** Fax **03-3278-6746** ADR SEDOL No. **6250100** President **Mahiko Sotome** Chairman --

Dai-Ichi Kangyo Bank

Industry: **Banks - Money Center**

Dai-ichi Kangyo Bank (DKB) is the world's largest bank in terms of assets and deposits. Unlike most large Japanese banks, DKB does not have close ties with any particular industrial group. Loans to large corporations represent about 20% of DKB's corporate lending, and loans to small and midsize firms account for 70%. It also provides financial services to small companies, including swaps and hedging schemes, consultation on stock placements, and services related to mergers and acquisitions. The bank is also involved in project finance and arranging syndicated loans.

	¥bil 03/93	03/94	03/95	US$mil 03/95				
Revenues	2,952.3	2,751.9	2,416.5	24,494.7	P/E Ratio	NMF	Price (9/30/95)	1,800.00
Net Income	53.1	11.6	28.0	284.1	P/B Ratio	2.8	52 Wk Hi-Low	1,910.0-1,500.0
Book Value	1,894.0	1,986.5	1,986.1	22,987.4	Yield %	0.5	Market Cap	US$56,500mil

Address **1-1-5, Uchi-Saiwaicho Chiyoda-ku, Tokyo 100** Tel **03-3596-1111** Fax **03-3596-2179** ADR **DAIKY** SEDOL No. **6250241** President **Tadashi Okuda** Chairman **Kuniji Miyazaki**

Daiichi Pharmaceutical

Industry: **Pharmaceuticals**

Daiichi Pharmaceutical (Daiichi Seiyaku) is a pharmaceutical manufacturer specializing in circulatory, gastrointestinal, and infectious-disease treatments. Prescription drugs account for about 75% of the firm's consolidated sales. Its major drugs include Tarivid and its more potent successor, Cravit (both quinolone-antibacterial agents), and Panaldine (an anti-platelet-aggregation agent). Daiichi develops approximately 45% of its drugs in-house. Major customers include Toho Pharmaceutical and Nakagawayasu. The firm has eight consolidated subsidiaries overseas.

	¥bil 03/93	03/94	03/95	US$mil 03/95				
Sales	239.7	245.7	254.7	2,581.6	P/E Ratio	18.5	Price (9/30/95)	1,370.00
Net Income	17.6	18.6	20.1	203.9	P/B Ratio	1.5	52 Wk Hi-Low	1,600.0-1,220.0
Book Value	208.9	223.9	242.7	2,809.3	Yield %	1.0	Market Cap	US$3,747.4mil

Address **3-14-10, Nihonbashi Chuo-ku, Tokyo 103** Tel **03-3272-0611** Fax **03-3281-8427** ADR SEDOL No. **6250218** President **Tadashi Suzuki** Chairman --

Daikin Industries

Industry: **Electrical Components & Equipment**

Daikin Industries (Daikin Kogyo) produces air conditioners for home and commercial use, refrigeration equipment, hydraulic and lubrication equipment, chemicals, and defense products. The firm holds about one third of the Japanese commercial market for air conditioners. It produces fluoropolymers and is developing chlorofluorocarbon substitutes. Daikin also supplies ammunition and missile warheads to Japan's Defense Agency. It has sales and production subsidiaries in Belgium, the United States, Australia, Singapore, and Thailand, along with a sales subsidiary in Hong Kong.

	¥bil 03/93	03/94	03/95	US$mil 03/95				
Sales	429.3	370.8	384.3	3,895.9	P/E Ratio	82.7	Price (9/30/95)	844.00
Net Income	4.4	0.9	2.7	27.2	P/B Ratio	1.7	52 Wk Hi-Low	970.00-650.00
Book Value	135.3	133.5	134.2	1,553.2	Yield %	1.2	Market Cap	US$2,239.6mil

Address **2-4-12, Nakazaki-Nishi Kita-ku, Osaka 530** Tel **06-373-1201** Fax **06-373-4380** ADR SEDOL No. **6250724** President **Noriyuki Inoue** Chairman **Noriyuki Inoue**

Dainippon Ink & Chemicals

Industry: **Specialty Chemicals**

Dainippon Ink & Chemicals (Dainippon Inki Kagaku Kogyo) produces printing inks, thermosetting resins, and organic pigments. The company also makes chemical products, building materials, plastics, printing devices, and petrochemical products. It is moving into the production of biochemicals. Dainippon Ink & Chemicals heads the DIC group, a major producer of inks, pigments, and resins that encompasses 53 Japanese and 146 foreign companies. The company absorbed its consolidated DIC Hozai subsidiary in October 1994 to strengthen its plastic-film and plastic-sheet division.

	¥bil 03/93	03/94	03/95	US$mil 03/95				
Sales	889.1	848.2	849.7	8,612.4	P/E Ratio	57.7	Price (9/30/95)	467.00
Net Income	-4.2	5.3	6.4	65.1	P/B Ratio	1.9	52 Wk Hi-Low	540.00-356.00
Book Value	185.1	189.2	193.8	2,243.5	Yield %	1.3	Market Cap	US$3,724.3mil

Address **3-7-20, Nihonbashi Chuo-ku, Tokyo 103** Tel **03-3272-4511** Fax **03-3273-7586** ADR SEDOL No. **6250821** President **Takemitsu Takahashi** Chairman --

Dainippon Pharmaceutical

Industry: **Pharmaceuticals**

Dainippon Pharmaceutical (Dainippon Seiyaku) specializes in cardiovascular, antibacterial, and central-nervous-system drugs. Its major brands include Flumark (an antibacterial chemotherapeutic agent), Excegran (an antiepileptic drug), and Cetapril (an antihypertensive drug). Drugs account for about 75% of consolidated sales. Other businesses include animal-health products and industrial chemicals. Major customers include Gokyo, Sanseido, and Nakakita Seisakusho. Dainippon has business ties with Warner-Lambert (U.S.), Rhône-Poulenc Rorer (France) and H. Ludbeck (Denmark).

¥bil	03/93	03/94	03/95	US$mil 03/95				
Sales	**131.9**	**134.8**	**142.3**	**1,442.8**	P/E Ratio	**39.5**	Price (9/30/95)	**940.00**
Net Income	**4.3**	**4.4**	**4.0**	**40.6**	P/B Ratio	**1.9**	52 Wk Hi-Low	**1,110.0-786.0**
Book Value	**75.5**	**78.6**	**81.6**	**944.6**	Yield %	**0.8**	Market Cap	**US$1,590.1mil**

Address	**2-6-8, Dosho-machi Chuo-ku, Osaka 541**	Tel **06-203-5309**	ADR		President	**Takeshi Tomotake**
		Fax **06-203-6581**	SEDOL No.	**6250865**	Chairman	**Tomio Fujiwara**

Dainippon Screen Mfg

Industry: **Industrial Technology**

Dainippon Screen Manufacturing (Dainippon Screen Seizo) is a leading comprehensive manufacturer of precision equipment. The firm's product line includes equipment and software compatible with desktop-publishing systems, including scanner systems. Its products are electronic color scanners, television shadow masks, ultrafine metal meshes for electron tubes, semiconductor-manufacturing equipment, and liquid-crystal displays. The firm has 18 consoliated overseas subsidiaries, including 10 in the United States and two in the United Kingdom.

¥bil	03/93	03/94	03/95	US$mil 03/95				
Sales	**136.5**	**134.3**	**161.8**	**1,639.6**	P/E Ratio	**NMF**	Price (9/30/95)	**810.00**
Net Income	**-15.8**	**-18.1**	**-8.2**	**-83.1**	P/B Ratio	**2.5**	52 Wk Hi-Low	**848.00-489.00**
Book Value	**77.3**	**59.6**	**52.4**	**606.3**	Yield %	**0.0**	Market Cap	**US$1,337.4mil**

Address	**4-1-1, Tenjin Kitamachi, Horika-wadori , Kamigyo-ku, Kyoto 602**	Tel **075-414-7151**	ADR		President	**Akira Ishida**
		Fax **075-441-9208**	SEDOL No.	**6251028**	Chairman	--

Daishowa Paper Manufacturing

Industry: **Paper Products**

Daishowa Paper Manufacturing (Daishowa Seishi) produces newsprint, printing paper, wrapping paper, and paperboard. It is among the top paper makers not formerly affiliated with the now-defunct Oji Paper. Main customers are Okura Paper Pulp, Okamoto, and Komine. Its domestic production facilities include five pulp and paper mills and one particle-board plant. Daishowa has eight consolidated subsidiaries in North America, including joint ventures with Cariboo Pulp & Paper and Quesnel River Pulp. Its offices in North America and in Pacific Rim countries procure raw materials.

¥bil	03/93	03/94	03/95	US$mil 03/95				
Sales	**342.6**	**299.2**	**314.5**	**3,188.0**	P/E Ratio	**NMF**	Price (9/30/95)	**679.00**
Net Income	**-12.3**	**-34.5**	**-15.4**	**-156.3**	P/B Ratio	**3.4**	52 Wk Hi-Low	**850.00-371.00**
Book Value	**84.2**	**54.0**	**44.3**	**513.3**	Yield %	**0.0**	Market Cap	**US$1,501.1mil**

Address	**4-1-1, Imai Fuji City, Shizuoka 417**	Tel **0545-30-3000**	ADR		President	**Shogo Nakano**
		Fax **0545-32-0005**	SEDOL No.	**6250984**	Chairman	**Kiminori Saito**

Daito Trust Construction

Industry: **Heavy Construction**

Daito Trust Construction (Daito Kentaku) is active in construction and real estate. The company's specialty is the development of condominiums and other rental housing and its construction division also builds warehouses and factories. Daito Trust's construction undertakings together account for 90% of annual sales. It constructs buildings for leasing on consignment and supports leasing operations in such areas as tenant recruitment, building maintenance, and rent collection. They also perform the afore-listed functions for rental properties owned by Daito Trust itself.

¥bil	03/93	03/94	03/95	US$mil 03/95				
Sales	**278.0**	**274.1**	**216.8**	**2,198.0**	P/E Ratio	**17.2**	Price (9/30/95)	**1,150.00**
Net Income	**20.1**	**23.5**	**9.5**	**96.4**	P/B Ratio	**1.1**	52 Wk Hi-Low	**1,460.0-740.0**
Book Value	**124.0**	**142.8**	**149.0**	**1,724.7**	Yield %	**2.2**	Market Cap	**US$1,643.7mil**

Address	**4-7-35, Kita-Shinagawa Shinagawa-ku, Tokyo 140**	Tel **03-3473-9111**	ADR		President	**Katsumi Tada**
		Fax **03-5488-3348**	SEDOL No.	**6250508**	Chairman	--

Dai-Tokyo Fire & Marine Insurance

Industry: **Insurance - Property & Casualty**

Dai-Tokyo Fire & Marine Insurance (Dai-Tokyo Kasai Kaijo Hoken) is a non-life-insurance company that holds one of the top domestic market shares in auto-insurance premiums. It offers premiums for fire, marine, personal-accident, transport, movable-property, workers' compensation, and theft insurance. Dai-Tokyo also offers product-liability-information services for firms operating in Japan and the United States. Its overseas network includes four underwriting agencies, three liaison offices, and more than 1,200 claims agents. It has close ties with Nomura Securities.

¥bil	03/93 P	03/94 P	03/95 P	US$mil 03/95				
Revenues	**393.4**	**592.1**	**479.9**	**4,864.8**	P/E Ratio	**40.4**	Price (9/30/95)	**670.00**
Net Income	**8.4**	**7.5**	**6.7**	**68.4**	P/B Ratio	**1.4**	52 Wk Hi-Low	**750.00-580.00**
Book Value	**179.7**	**184.3**	**188.1**	**2,177.6**	Yield %	**1.0**	Market Cap	**US$2,743.7mil**

Address	**3-1-6, Nihonbashi Chuo-ku, Tokyo 103**	Tel **03-3272-8811**	ADR		President	**Hajime Ozawa**
		Fax **03-3272-9523**	SEDOL No.	**6251169**	Chairman	**Isao Kosaka**

P=Parent company data.

Daiwa Bank

Industry: **Banks - Regional**

Daiwa Bank is the 12th-largest city bank in Japan based on assets. In 1993, Daiwa became the first Japanese bank to establish a securities subsidiary with its acquisition of a majority stake in Cosmo securities. Daiwa Bank is the main banker to the Osaka city government, and is involved in financing for the Kansai International Airport. It offers services in trust banking, securities, real estate, and electronic banking. The bank has 15 main consolidated subsidiaries including Daiwa International Finance (U.S.), Daiwa Bank (Germany), and Daiwa Merchant Bank (Singapore).

¥bil	03/93	03/94	03/95	US$mil 03/95				
Revenues	**1,021.8**	**936.7**	**1,142.9**	**11,584.9**	P/E Ratio	**NMF**	Price (9/30/95)	**796.00**
Net Income	**18.1**	**12.7**	**1.6**	**16.7**	P/B Ratio	**1.9**	52 Wk Hi-Low	**875.00-750.00**
Book Value	**621.5**	**636.8**	**633.7**	**7,334.0**	Yield %	**0.9**	Market Cap	**US$12,096mil**

Address **2-2-1, Bingo-machi**
Chuo-ku, Osaka 541
Tel **06-271-1221**
Fax **06-268-1337**
ADR
SEDOL No. **6251341**
President **Akira Fujita**
Chairman **Sumio Abekawa**

Daiwa House Industry

Industry: **Home Construction**

Daiwa House Industry is a major builder of prefabricated housing. The company is Japan's second-largest homebuilder and a leading general-building contractor. It also builds warehouses, factories, hospitals, office and commercial buildings, corporate housing and dormitories, condominiums, and rental apartments. Daiwa House participates in urban-development projects and operates 20 domestic Daiwa Royal Hotel resorts, which include golf courses, ski slopes, and tennis courts. Overseas sales account for less than 10% of consolidated revenues.

¥bil	03/93	03/94	03/95	US$mil 03/95				
Sales	**932.1**	**943.2**	**980.6**	**9,939.9**	P/E Ratio	**19.5**	Price (9/30/95)	**1,560.00**
Net Income	**43.0**	**40.1**	**38.3**	**387.8**	P/B Ratio	**1.6**	52 Wk Hi-Low	**1,620.0-1,280.0**
Book Value	**394.0**	**426.0**	**456.0**	**5,277.3**	Yield %	**1.1**	Market Cap	**US$7,509.8mil**

Address **1-5-16, Awaza**
Nishi-ku, Osaka 550
Tel **06-532-5111**
Fax **06-538-5117**
ADR **DWAHY**
SEDOL No. **6251363**
President **Keiichi Uemura**
Chairman **Shunichi Ishibashi**

Daiwa Kosho Lease

Industry: **General Industrial & Commercial Services**

Daiwa Kosho Lease, an affiliate of Daiwa House Industry, specializes in short-term building leasing and real-estate sales. The firm's activities include the leasing of office buildings, temporary classrooms, cars, temporary structures for construction sites, motor vehicles, and office-automation equipment. It also sells real estate and the sales of office buildings account for about 30% of parent-company revenues. The firm is 20.4% owned by Daiwa House Industry, one of Japan's major builders of prefabricated housing. It has three affiliates, two of which are based in Osaka.

¥bil	03/93 P	03/94 P	03/95 P	US$mil 03/95				
Sales	**107.5**	**102.1**	**106.0**	**1,074.9**	P/E Ratio	**28.0**	Price (9/30/95)	**980.00**
Net Income	**5.2**	**5.0**	**5.2**	**53.1**	P/B Ratio	**1.8**	52 Wk Hi-Low	**1,070.0-740.0**
Book Value	**74.0**	**77.5**	**81.1**	**938.5**	Yield %	**1.1**	Market Cap	**US$1,476.9mil**

Address **5-20, Honmachibashi**
Chuo-ku, Osaka 540
Tel **06-942-8012**
Fax **06-942-8051**
ADR
SEDOL No. **6251415**
President **Osamu Hirayama**
Chairman **Nobuo Ishibashi**

P=Parent company data.

Daiwa Securities

Industry: **Securities Brokers**

Daiwa Securities (Daiwa Shoken) is the second-largest of Japan's Big Four securities firms by sales and assets. The company is traditionally strong in bond transactions. It offers a full array of brokerage services, including equity and bond trading, underwriting, market making, and investment advice. Daiwa Securities has 130 offices located throughout Japan, as well as overseas branches in Seoul, Beijing, Shanghai, Bangkok, Kuala Lumpur, Vancouver, and Berlin. In 1994, overseas activities accounted for 49.5% of Daiwa's consolidated revenues.

¥bil	03/93	03/94	03/95	US$mil 03/95				
Sales	**462.6**	**464.8**	**422.7**	**4,284.6**	P/E Ratio	**NMF**	Price (9/30/95)	**1,250.00**
Net Income	**-13.3**	**29.1**	**-44.5**	**-450.9**	P/B Ratio	**1.8**	52 Wk Hi-Low	**1,480.0-878.0**
Book Value	**970.5**	**984.5**	**927.2**	**10,731.6**	Yield %	**0.6**	Market Cap	**US$16,903mil**

Address **2-6-4, Otemachi**
Chiyoda-ku, Tokyo 100
Tel **03-3276-3181**
Fax **03-3242-9370**
ADR **DSECY**
SEDOL No. **6251448**
President **Motoo Esaka**
Chairman **Sadakane Doi**

Denki Kagaku Kogyo

Industry: **Specialty Chemicals**

Denki Kagaku Kogyo is a producer of lime chemicals and petrochemicals. The company produces more than 200 kinds of chemicals, including organic chemicals, inorganic chemicals, cement, plastics, fine chemicals, specialty rubber products, electronic materials, semiconductor-processing materials, and fertilizers. More than half of the calcium carbide sold in Japan is produced by Denki Kagaku. Denki Kagaku has four domestic production facilities and a research center. The company also has 33 consolidated subsidiaries and one each in the United States and Singapore.

¥bil	03/93	03/94	03/95	US$mil 03/95				
Sales	**247.3**	**210.2**	**229.9**	**2,330.6**	P/E Ratio	**NMF**	Price (9/30/95)	**340.00**
Net Income	**-8.9**	**-11.7**	**0.1**	**0.8**	P/B Ratio	**2.2**	52 Wk Hi-Low	**440.00-270.00**
Book Value	**83.3**	**72.1**	**72.1**	**834.1**	Yield %	**0.0**	Market Cap	**US$1,625.6mil**

Address **1-4-1, Yuraku-cho**
Chiyoda-ku, Tokyo 100
Tel **03-3507-5130**
Fax **03-3508-9479**
ADR
SEDOL No. **6309820**
President **Tsuneo Yano**
Chairman **Bunichiro Shimura**

Denny's Japan

Industry: **Restaurants**

Denny's Japan, a consolidated subsidiary of supermarket giant Ito-Yokado, operates a chain of 471 Denny's restaurants (including 27 franchises) under a licensing agreement with Denny's Inc. (U.S.); it plans to open 32 more by February 1996. Nearly 75% of the company's restaurants are located within Tokyo and its environs. The restaurants offer Western-style breakfast, lunch, dinner, and late-night menus. Denny's Japan acquired 23 Famil restaurants, which are subsidiaries of Ito-Yokado and will continue serving Japanese-style food. Families are the firm's target market.

¥bil	02/93 P	02/94 P	02/95 P	US$mil 02/95				
Sales	**85.8**	**93.0**	**95.1**	**948.5**	P/E Ratio	**31.6**	Price (9/30/95)	**2,920.00**
Net Income	**3.3**	**3.0**	**2.7**	**27.2**	P/B Ratio	**2.0**	52 Wk Hi-Low	**3,710.0-2,050.0**
Book Value	**39.6**	**41.8**	**43.6**	**451.0**	Yield %	**1.0**	Market Cap	**US$863.9mil**

Address **4-1-4, Shiba-Koen**
Minato-ku, Tokyo 105
Tel **03-3459-3548**
Fax **03-3459-3558**
ADR
SEDOL No. **6262990**
President **Yoshiharu Ohara**
Chairman --

P=Parent company data.

Dowa Fire & Marine Insurance

Industry: **Insurance - Property & Casualty**

Dowa Fire & Marine Insurance (Dowa Kasai Kaijo Hoken) is a medium-scale non-life-insurance firm noted for its flight insurance. Its line includes compulsory-auto-liability, machine, construction-works, flight, transport, and medical-payments insurance, among others. New products are comprehensive insurance for homeowners and married couples, weather insurance for businesses, and nursing-care-expense insurance. Dowa was the first Japanese firm to offer space insurance for satellite programs. It recently signed a mutual-operation agreement with Vietnam Insurance.

¥bil	03/93	03/94	03/95	US$mil 03/95				
Revenues	**210.1**	**220.4**	**357.7**	**3,625.9**	P/E Ratio	**43.5**	Price (9/30/95)	**487.00**
Net Income	**5.0**	**3.8**	**3.7**	**37.9**	P/B Ratio	**1.4**	52 Wk Hi-Low	**675.00-420.00**
Book Value	**112.7**	**114.3**	**115.7**	**1,339.4**	Yield %	**1.3**	Market Cap	**US$1,637.5mil**

Address **2-3-16, Imabashi**
Chuo-ku, Osaka 541
Tel **06-363-1121**
Fax **06-208-6809**
ADR
SEDOL No. **6278209**
President **Masao Okazaki**
Chairman --

Dowa Mining

Industry: **Non-Ferrous Metals - Other (Exc. Aluminum)**

Dowa Mining (Dowa Kogyo) is a smelter of copper and other nonferrous metals, such as zinc. Its main activities are refining and metal processing. The company holds leading market shares in iron oxides and metal particles used in magnetic-recording media. Electrolytic copper, zinc, and rolled-copper products are the parent company's largest segments. It is diversifying into powder metallurgy and electronic parts. Major customers include Marubeni, Tokyo Shoji, Komatsu, and Koyo Metals. Dowa Mining operates four mines, nine plants, and 29 consolidated subsidiaries in Japan.

¥bil	03/93	03/94	03/95	US$mil 03/95				
Sales	**236.4**	**220.9**	**256.5**	**2,599.5**	P/E Ratio	**NMF**	Price (9/30/95)	**447.00**
Net Income	**-3.5**	**-3.7**	**-1.7**	**-17.5**	P/B Ratio	**3.9**	52 Wk Hi-Low	**580.00-332.00**
Book Value	**32.6**	**30.4**	**29.2**	**337.5**	Yield %	**1.2**	Market Cap	**US$1,157.9mil**

Address **1-8-2, Marunouchi**
Chiyoda-ku, Tokyo 100
Tel **03-3201-1072**
Fax **03-3215-5170**
ADR
SEDOL No. **6278306**
President **Kenzo Harada**
Chairman **Sadaharu Niratani**

Ebara

Industry: **Factory Equipment**

Ebara (Ebara Seisakusho) is one of the world's largest producers of pneumatic machinery. The company holds about 5% of the world market in industrial pumps. It also specializes in fans, air blowers, and compressors. The company's other products include vacuum pumps, refrigeration equipment, air conditioners, boilers, heat pumps for trash incinerators, fluidized-bed incineration systems, and nuclear-power equipment. The firm supplies local governments, electric-power plants, steel and semiconductor makers, petrochemical firms, and the paper and pulp industry.

¥bil	03/93	03/94	03/95	US$mil 03/95				
Sales	**413.9**	**440.8**	**467.7**	**4,740.3**	P/E Ratio	**74.3**	Price (9/30/95)	**1,420.00**
Net Income	**3.9**	**10.0**	**5.5**	**55.5**	P/B Ratio	**3.3**	52 Wk Hi-Low	**1,770.0-997.0**
Book Value	**115.9**	**122.8**	**125.0**	**1,446.5**	Yield %	**0.7**	Market Cap	**US$4,103.8mil**

Address **11-1, Haneda-Asahicho**
Ota-ku, Tokyo 144
Tel **03-3743-6111**
Fax **03-3745-3010**
ADR **EBCOY**
SEDOL No. **6302700**
President **Hiroyuki Fujimura**
Chairman --

Eisai

Industry: **Pharmaceuticals**

Eisai is a midsize pharmaceutical company that specializes in circulatory, neurological, and digestive drugs. Eisai develops about 85% of its products in-house. Its leading products include Selbex (used to treat gastric ulcers) and Methycobal (used to treat peripheral nerve damage). The firm also makes veterinary drugs, chemical reagents, and machinery for drugmakers. Most of Eisai's over-the-counter drugs are based on vitamins such as B2 and E. The firm's OTC line includes products for skin care and the treatment of ailments associated with aging.

¥bil	03/93	03/94	03/95	US$mil 03/95				
Sales	**230.8**	**236.3**	**258.3**	**2,618.7**	P/E Ratio	**25.6**	Price (9/30/95)	**1,730.00**
Net Income	**15.1**	**15.1**	**17.4**	**176.2**	P/B Ratio	**2.1**	52 Wk Hi-Low	**1,770.0-1,390.0**
Book Value	**183.2**	**195.2**	**211.9**	**2,453.1**	Yield %	**0.8**	Market Cap	**US$4,475.8mil**

Address **4-6-10, Koishikawa**
Bunkyo-ku, Tokyo 112-88
Tel **03-3817-3700**
Fax **03-3811-3077**
ADR **EISAY**
SEDOL No. **6307200**
President **Haruo Naito**
Chairman **Yuji Naito**

Ezaki Glico

Industry: **Other Food**

Ezaki Glico produces and sells confectionery, ice cream, and other foodstuffs. Confectionery products include the Pocky brand of chocolate snacks and Glico caramels, and account for about 55% of sales. The company has a 14.6% of the Japanese ice-cream market. Its other products include baked goods, dairy products, soft drinks, and processed foods such as instant curry. Ezaki Glico operates more than 10,000 vending machines. Major customers include Kokuhun, Meikan, and Shinsei. It has production subsidiaries in the United States and Thailand, and a joint venture in France.

¥bil	03/93	03/94	03/95	US$mil 03/95				
Sales	**292.7**	**279.4**	**278.5**	**2,822.8**	P/E Ratio	**23.4**	Price (9/30/95)	**848.00**
Net Income	**4.6**	**4.5**	**4.8**	**48.2**	P/B Ratio	**1.2**	52 Wk Hi-Low	**1,090.0-720.0**
Book Value	**87.6**	**90.9**	**96.2**	**1,113.5**	Yield %	**1.2**	Market Cap	**US$1,122.9mil**

Address	**4-6-5, Utajima**	Tel	**06-477-8404**	ADR		President	**Katsuhisa Ezaki**
	Nishi-Yodogawa-ku, Osaka 555	Fax	**06-477-5670**	SEDOL No.	**6327703**	Chairman	--

FamilyMart

Industry: **Food Retailers & Wholesalers**

FamilyMart, a subsidiary of Seiyu, is Japan's third-largest operator of convenience stores by number of stores. The company's outlets are concentrated in the Tokyo area, with additional stores located throughout Japan and in Taiwan. Its more than 2,700 stores are equipped with point-of-sales systems and offer FamilyMart's line of merchandise. By establishing franchised outlets, the chain has been able to expand quickly without large capital outlays; the firm collects a share of each franchised outlet's operating income. FamilyMart directly controls 83 stores.

¥bil	02/93	02/94	02/95	US$mil 02/95				
Sales	**74.6**	**77.8**	**85.2**	**850.5**	P/E Ratio	**46.4**	Price (9/30/95)	**4,300.00**
Net Income	**8.6**	**8.6**	**8.7**	**86.4**	P/B Ratio	**4.3**	52 Wk Hi-Low	**5,341.7-3,710.0**
Book Value	**58.2**	**65.4**	**79.0**	**817.1**	Yield %	**0.4**	Market Cap	**US$3,397.8mil**

Address	**4-26-10, Higashi-Ikebukuro**	Tel	**03-3989-6653**	ADR		President	**Shigeru Goto**
	Toshima-ku, Tokyo 170	Fax	**03-3590-0497**	SEDOL No.	**6331276**	Chairman	**Sueaki Takaoka**

Fanuc

Industry: **Electrical Components & Equipment**

Fanuc is the top manufacturer of numerically controlled devices, with about 50% of the world market. The firm produces computer-numerical controllers for machine tools, cell controllers, servomotors, industrial robots, wire-electronic-discharge machines, laser equipment, and plastic-injection molding machines. Its products are primarily used in the automobile and other metalworking-intensive industries. Fanuc has joint ventures in the U.S. with General Electric and General Motors in China, and in India, as well as an affiliate in South Korea. Fanuc is 39% owned by Fujitsu.

¥bil	03/93	03/94	03/95	US$mil 03/95				
Sales	**139.4**	**125.3**	**141.3**	**1,432.0**	P/E Ratio	**60.5**	Price (9/30/95)	**4,420.00**
Net Income	**17.0**	**10.7**	**17.5**	**177.0**	P/B Ratio	**2.3**	52 Wk Hi-Low	**4,830.0-3,420.0**
Book Value	**439.4**	**446.5**	**459.9**	**5,322.9**	Yield %	**0.5**	Market Cap	**US$10,640mil**

Address	**3580, Shibokusa, Oshinomura**	Tel	**0555-84-5555**	ADR		President	**Ryoichiro Nozawa**
	Minamitsuru, Yamanashi 401	Fax	**0555-84-5515**	SEDOL No.	**6356934**	Chairman	**Seiuemon Inaba**

Fudo Construction

Industry: **Heavy Construction**

Fudo Construction (Fudo Kensetsu) is a general-construction company. Its operations include building construction, civil engineering, soil engineering, city planning, urban redevelopment, regional development, marine development, environmental engineering, waste-water treatment, and pollution control. The firm has engineered and constructed industrial plants such as refineries, thermal-power plants, steel works, waste-water treatment facilities, and civil projects. It is also engaged in resort development. Fudo Construction has three wholly-owned consolidated subsidiaries.

¥bil	03/93	03/94	03/95	US$mil 03/95				
Sales	**243.4**	**246.6**	**237.5**	**2,407.8**	P/E Ratio	**98.5**	Price (9/30/95)	**955.00**
Net Income	**1.4**	**1.3**	**1.2**	**12.3**	P/B Ratio	**4.4**	52 Wk Hi-Low	**1,390.0-658.0**
Book Value	**20.1**	**20.8**	**28.7**	**332.4**	Yield %	**0.5**	Market Cap	**US$1,263.2mil**

Address	**4-2-16, Hirano-machi**	Tel	**06-201-9203**	ADR		President	**Masanobu Ichiyoshi**
	Chuo-ku, Osaka 541	Fax	**03-3831-9255**	SEDOL No.	**6355005**	Chairman	**Takeshi Shikimura**

Fuji Bank

Industry: **Banks - Money Center**

Fuji Bank (Fuji Ginko) is Japan's third-largest bank by deposits and fifth-largest by loans. The bank is the financial center of the Fuyo group. It has 290 domestic branches and 56 domestic representative offices, as well as 18 branches overseas. The bank operates an east European desk that provides consulting services for eastern Europe and the former republics of the Soviet Union. It also provides aircraft financing for such companies as Air China, Air France, and British Aerospace. The bank is expanding its operations into Australia and Thailand through joint ventures.

¥bil	03/93	03/94	03/95	US$mil 03/95				
Revenues	**3,067.4**	**2,714.6**	**2,990.3**	**30,310.8**	P/E Ratio	**NMF**	Price (9/30/95)	**2,110.00**
Net Income	**58.3**	**32.9**	**4.6**	**47.1**	P/B Ratio	**3.1**	52 Wk Hi-Low	**2,240.0-1,650.0**
Book Value	**1,987.0**	**2,001.5**	**1,984.9**	**22,973.4**	Yield %	**0.4**	Market Cap	**US$61,490mil**

Address	**1-5-5, Ohtemachi**	Tel	**03-3216-2211**	ADR	**FUJPY**	President	**Tooru Hashimoto**
	Chiyoda-ku, Tokyo 100	Fax	**03-3201-0527**	SEDOL No.	**6356280**	Chairman	--

Fuji Electric

Industry: **Electrical Components & Equipment**

Fuji Electric (Fuji Denki) manufactures heavy electrical machinery and holds a more than 50% Japanese market share in the production of beverage-vending machines. Its heavy electrical machinery products include motors and power-conversion equipment, induction furnaces, clean rooms for semiconductor makers, and substation equipment. The company also produces electronic parts, including solar batteries and power transistors. Electric and hydropower plants, sewage- and water-treatment plants, the iron and steel industries, and railways use Fuji Electric's products.

¥bil	03/93	03/94	03/95	US$mil 03/95				
Sales	**900.0**	**834.0**	**856.3**	**8,679.8**	P/E Ratio	**91.9**	Price (9/30/95)	**496.00**
Net Income	**7.7**	**3.6**	**3.8**	**38.7**	P/B Ratio	**2.0**	52 Wk Hi-Low	**566.00-407.00**
Book Value	**179.7**	**175.0**	**177.0**	**2,048.6**	Yield %	**1.6**	Market Cap	**US$3,555.5mil**

Address	**1-12-1, Yuraku-cho**	Tel	**03-3211-7111**	ADR		President	**Yoshihiko Nakazato**
	Chiyoda-ku, Tokyo 100	Fax	**03-3215-8321**	SEDOL No.	**6356365**	Chairman	--

Fuji Heavy Industries

Industry: **Automobile Manufacturers**

Fuji Heavy Industries (Fuji Jukogyo), a member of the Nissan group, makes subcompact and passenger cars, including the Subaru Impreza and Legacy lines. The company is traditionally strong in front-wheel- and four-wheel-drive vehicles. It also makes rolling stock, tanker trucks, containers, conveyors, buses, and industrial machinery. The company makes aircraft parts for the Japan Defense Agency (its prime contractor), Boeing, McDonnell Douglas, and Fokker. Overseas sales account for about 43% of the firm's total revenues.

¥bil	03/93	03/94	03/95	US$mil 03/95				
Sales	**1,047.8**	**1,015.8**	**1,103.3**	**11,183.3**	P/E Ratio	**NMF**	Price (9/30/95)	**381.00**
Net Income	**-27.3**	**-25.5**	**1.2**	**12.5**	P/B Ratio	**2.5**	52 Wk Hi-Low	**465.00-300.00**
Book Value	**142.1**	**122.4**	**88.0**	**1,019.0**	Yield %	**0.0**	Market Cap	**US$2,243.2mil**

Address	**1-7-2, Nishi-Shinjuku**	Tel	**03-3347-2005**	ADR	**FUJHY**	President	**Isamu Kawai**
	Shinjuku-ku, Tokyo 160	Fax	**03-3347-2126**	SEDOL No.	**6356406**	Chairman	--

Fuji Machine Manufacturing

Industry: **Factory Equipment**

Fuji Machine Manufacturing (Fuji Kikai Seizo) is a leading producer of specialized machinery. The firm is among the major Japanese manufacturers of automated assembly lines for electronic parts and other industries. Fuji Machine also produces labor-saving equipment. Its chip-type electronic-parts installing machines are popular in overseas markets. The firm has a sales subsidiary in the U.S., Fuji America Corporation, an office in Singapore, and a subsidiary in Germany, Fuji Machine Manufacturing (Europe), which is jointly financed by Nichimen, a general-trading company.

¥bil	03/93	03/94	03/95	US$mil 03/95				
Sales	**56.3**	**57.8**	**67.9**	**688.8**	P/E Ratio	**57.0**	Price (9/30/95)	**3,930.00**
Net Income	**3.5**	**3.1**	**3.4**	**34.1**	P/B Ratio	**4.2**	52 Wk Hi-Low	**4,250.0-1,910.0**
Book Value	**40.6**	**43.1**	**45.9**	**530.9**	Yield %	**0.4**	Market Cap	**US$1,931.0mil**

Address	**19, Chausuyama, Yama-machi**	Tel	**0566-81-2111**	ADR		President	--
	Chiryu City, Aichi 472	Fax	**0566-83-0861**	SEDOL No.	**6356592**	Chairman	--

Fuji Photo Film

Industry: **Other Recreational Products & Services**

Fuji Photo Film is Japan's largest maker of photosensitive materials. It has a domestic market share of nearly 75% in film, while competitors Konica and Kodak have shares of roughly 17% and 8%, respectively. Fuji's share of the world film market is about 20%. Fuji also produces magnetic tape, cameras, medical equipment, film for liquid- crystal-display production, and 8mm video cameras. The company markets many of its products through its affiliate, Process Shisai (14.1% of 1994 parent sales). Overseas sales accounted for 39% of revenues in 1994.

¥bil	10/92	10/93	10/94	US$mil 10/94				
Sales	**1,142.3**	**1,086.8**	**1,066.7**	**10,294.7**	P/E Ratio	**19.9**	Price (9/30/95)	**2,470.00**
Net Income	**75.7**	**60.9**	**63.8**	**615.4**	P/B Ratio	**1.1**	52 Wk Hi-Low	**2,580.0-1,900.0**
Book Value	**1,067.1**	**1,103.9**	**1,155.6**	**11,919.3**	Yield %	**0.8**	Market Cap	**US$12,785mil**

Address	**2-26-30, Nishi-Azabu**	Tel	**03-3406-2111**	ADR	**FUJIY**	President	**Minoru Ohnishi**
	Minato-ku, Tokyo 106	Fax	**03-3406-2193**	SEDOL No.	**6356525**	Chairman	--

Fujikura

Industry: **Electrical Components & Equipment**

Fujikura (formerly Fujikura Densen) is one of the leading manufacturers of electric wire and cable by revenues. It also produces fiberoptic cable. Its clients include Nippon Telegraph and Telephone (which accounts for 14% of parent-company sales), electric-power companies, electronics companies, and automobile manufacturers. The firm is expanding into optoelectronics and superconductive ceramics. Fujikura has 37 consolidated subsidiaries, some located in Singapore, Thailand, and Malaysia. Overseas business consists 18% of consolidated sales.

¥bil	03/93	03/94	03/95	US$mil 03/95				
Sales	**317.5**	**315.1**	**311.6**	**3,158.4**	P/E Ratio	**17.4**	Price (9/30/95)	**691.00**
Net Income	**3.5**	**-1.6**	**13.5**	**136.6**	P/B Ratio	**2.0**	52 Wk Hi-Low	**811.00-466.00**
Book Value	**110.1**	**107.8**	**118.9**	**1,376.3**	Yield %	**0.9**	Market Cap	**US$2,351.3mil**

Address	**1-5-1, Kiba**	Tel	**03-5606-1111**	ADR		President	**Shigenobu Tanaka**
	Koto-ku, Tokyo 135	Fax	**03-5606-1502**	SEDOL No.	**6356707**	Chairman	--

Fujisawa Pharmaceutical

Industry: **Pharmaceuticals**

Fujisawa Pharmaceutical (Fujisawa Yakuhin Kogyo) is a drug manufacturer specializing in antibiotics. Its major products (in order of sales) include Cefspan, an oral cephalosporin; Tagamet, an antiulcer drug licensed from SmithKline & French (U.S.); and Intal, an antiallergy drug. Products developed in-house account for about 50% of sales. One major customer is Suzuken, a Kanto-based pharmaceutical wholesaler that sells mainly to medical practitioners. Fujisawa has five plants and two research facilities in Japan. Of its 31 consolidated subsidiaries, 12 are based overseas.

¥bil	03/93	03/94	03/95	US$mil 03/95				
Sales	**282.8**	**271.9**	**284.1**	**2,879.8**	P/E Ratio	**67.6**	Price (9/30/95)	**980.00**
Net Income	**-1.4**	**12.2**	**4.6**	**47.1**	P/B Ratio	**1.3**	52 Wk Hi-Low	**1,150.0-873.0**
Book Value	**224.2**	**229.3**	**235.4**	**2,724.0**	Yield %	**0.8**	Market Cap	**US$3,164.7mil**

Address	**3-4-7, Dosho-machi**	Tel	**06-206-7867**	ADR		President	**Akira Fujiyama**
	Chuo-ku, Osaka 541	Fax	**06-206-7926**	SEDOL No.	**6356804**	Chairman	**Tomokichiro Fujisawa**

Fujita

Industry: **Heavy Construction**

Fujita ranks among Japan's second-tier construction companies based on revenues but is an industry leader in urban redevelopment, especially in the Tokyo area. The company also provides civil-engineering services, develops and markets real estate, and manages industrial and residential buildings and resorts. Fujita has 12 consolidated subsidiaries, one of which is based in South Korea and engages in construction, real-estate leasing, and resort management. Fujita is a financial partner in the construction of a geothermal power plant in Kyushu.

¥bil	03/93	03/94	03/95	US$mil 03/95				
Sales	**877.4**	**757.9**	**704.9**	**7,144.9**	P/E Ratio	**53.7**	Price (9/30/95)	**483.00**
Net Income	**13.3**	**9.2**	**4.5**	**45.1**	P/B Ratio	**1.1**	52 Wk Hi-Low	**659.00-399.00**
Book Value	**208.4**	**211.9**	**212.0**	**2,453.2**	Yield %	**1.6**	Market Cap	**US$2,401.9mil**

Address	**4-6-15, Sendagaya**	Tel	**03-3402-1911**	ADR	**FTACY**	President	**Kazunori Fujita**
	Shibuya-ku, Tokyo 151	Fax	**03-3478-0729**	SEDOL No.	**6356882**	Chairman	**Keijiro Kaitsuka**

Fujita Kanko

Industry: **Lodging**

Fujita Kanko is a major operator of tourism-related businesses. The firm, an affiliate of Dowa Mining, owns and operates resort facilities, restaurants, and hotel chains. Its hotels are located in popular Japanese tourist spots such as Kyoto, Nara, and Hakone. Its popular Washington Hotel chain has more than 50 hotels serving middle-market customers. Fujita also has hotels in New York, Guam, and South Korea. It has 12 consolidated subsidiaries; nine are involved in the hotel business, and the rest are involved in food sales, golf-course management, and real-estate sales.

¥bil	12/92	12/93	12/94	US$mil 12/94				
Sales	**100.7**	**99.3**	**98.6**	**966.2**	P/E Ratio	**136.9**	Price (9/30/95)	**2,190.00**
Net Income	**1.7**	**1.1**	**2.0**	**19.1**	P/B Ratio	**7.2**	52 Wk Hi-Low	**2,190.0-1,780.0**
Book Value	**36.9**	**36.4**	**37.4**	**374.6**	Yield %	**0.3**	Market Cap	**US$2,689.0mil**

Address	**1-9-15, Kaigan**	Tel	**03-3433-5151**	ADR		President	**Masayoshi Matsuzawa**
	Minato-ku, Tokyo 105	Fax	**03-3435-0640**	SEDOL No.	**6356923**	Chairman	--

Fujitsu

Industry: **Computers**

Fujitsu is Japan's largest computer manufacturer, controlling roughly 25% of the domestic market. The company maintains a strong position in semiconductors, communication equipment, mainframes, and office computers. Fujitsu holds an 80% stake in ICL, a British computer maker that is one of the world's largest producers of in-store retail systems. Fujitsu's major customers include Nintendo, Uchida Yako, and Memorex Telex. Fujitsu has 423 consolidated subsidiaries in Japan and around the world. In 1994, overseas sales made up 30% of Fujitsu's total consolidated revenues.

¥bil	03/93	03/94	03/95	US$mil 03/95				
Sales	**3,461.9**	**3,139.3**	**3,257.7**	**33,021.2**	P/E Ratio	**50.4**	Price (9/30/95)	**1,250.00**
Net Income	**-32.6**	**-37.7**	**45.0**	**456.3**	P/B Ratio	**2.1**	52 Wk Hi-Low	**1,250.0-748.0**
Book Value	**1,101.2**	**1,057.9**	**1,100.3**	**12,735.1**	Yield %	**0.8**	Market Cap	**US$22,843mil**

Address	**1-6-1, Marunouchi**	Tel	**03-3216-7953**	ADR	**FJTSY**	President	**Tadashi Sekizawa**
	Chiyoda-ku, Tokyo 100	Fax	**03-3216-9365**	SEDOL No.	**6356945**	Chairman	**Takuma Yamamoto**

Fukuyama Transporting

Industry: **Trucking**

Fukuyama Transporting (Fukuyama Tsuun) is a Hiroshima-based trucking firm that serves mainly corporate customers. It is noted for its small-cargo transport in western Japan. The firm transports items such as construction materials, food, and textiles. It has cooperative agreements with several companies, including TNT Skypak International (U.K.), Airborne Freight (U.S.), and Kintetsu World Express (Japan) to deliver goods abroad. It is a member of the Kinki Nippon Railway group, which holds 28% of its outstanding stock. Fukuyama has 14 subsidiaries and four affiliates.

¥bil	03/93 P	03/94 P	03/95 P	US$mil 03/95				
Sales	**256.1**	**255.6**	**259.5**	**2,630.4**	P/E Ratio	**47.6**	Price (9/30/95)	**890.00**
Net Income	**9.9**	**8.2**	**5.3**	**53.7**	P/B Ratio	**1.7**	52 Wk Hi-Low	**1,170.0-767.0**
Book Value	**143.8**	**148.8**	**151.0**	**1,747.1**	Yield %	**1.2**	Market Cap	**US$2,541.0mil**

Address	**4-20-1, Higashi-Fukatsucho**	Tel	**0849-24-2000**	ADR		President	**Tokihiro Kato**
	Fukuyama City, Hiroshima 721	Fax	**0849-31-4865**	SEDOL No.	**6357120**	Chairman	**Noriyuki Komaru**

P=Parent company data.

Furukawa

Industry: **Heavy Machinery**

Furukawa (Furukawa Kikai Kinzoku) produces construction machinery, smelts nonferrous metals, and manufactures finished metal products and chemicals. The company's products include rock drills, bulldozers, parking systems, castings, and sewage pumps. Its metals division produces copper cathode, gold, silver, sulfuric acid, wire, and rolled copper. Furukawa also markets petroleum and runs four electric-power plants in Japan (mainly for its own use). The company has 15 consolidated subsidiaries, including Furukawa Equipement in France and 16 unconsolidated subsidiaries.

¥bil	03/93	03/94	03/95	US$mil 03/95				
Sales	**167.1**	**144.8**	**154.8**	**1,568.7**	P/E Ratio	**136.1**	Price (9/30/95)	**490.00**
Net Income	**1.6**	**0.2**	**0.9**	**9.0**	P/B Ratio	**2.0**	52 Wk Hi-Low	**670.00-379.00**
Book Value	**61.9**	**62.3**	**62.4**	**722.4**	Yield %	**1.2**	Market Cap	**US$1,235.9mil**

Address	**2-6-1, Marunouchi**	Tel	**03-3212-6561**	ADR		President	**Arashi Sasaki**
	Chiyoda-ku, Tokyo 100	Fax	**03-3287-0696**	SEDOL No.	**6357603**	Chairman	**Yutaka Okumura**

Furukawa Electric

Industry: **Electrical Components & Equipment**

Furukawa Electric (Furukawa Denki Kogyo) is a leading wire and cable company. It manufactures fiber optic cable, insulated wire, uncoated wire, magnet wire, copper sheets, tubes, superconducting material, and memory alloys. It also makes passive components such as mechanical switches, couplers, and connectors. Its products supply public utilities, telecommunication firms, automakers, electrical-appliance manufacturers, and electric railways. One of its U.S. subsidiaries is 100% owned International Components Technology, which makes magnetic disks and auto parts.

¥bil	03/93	03/94	03/95	US$mil 03/95				
Sales	**722.3**	**659.9**	**671.0**	**6,801.2**	P/E Ratio	**106.1**	Price (9/30/95)	**520.00**
Net Income	**5.4**	**0.9**	**3.2**	**32.6**	P/B Ratio	**1.8**	52 Wk Hi-Low	**683.00-395.00**
Book Value	**191.8**	**194.5**	**194.4**	**2,249.7**	Yield %	**1.2**	Market Cap	**US$3,432.3mil**

Address	**2-6-1 Marunouchi**	Tel	**03-3286-3038**	ADR	**FUWAY**	President	**Kengo Tomomatsu**
	Chiyoda-ku, Tokyo 100	Fax	**03-3286-3694**	SEDOL No.	**6357562**	Chairman	--

Futaba

Industry: **Electrical Components & Equipment**

Futaba (Futaba Denshi Kogyo) is the world's largest producer of vacuum-fluorescent displays (VFDs). It also makes radio-control equipment, metal-mold parts, and digital-readout systems. Futaba supplies the automotive, consumer-electronics, office-automation, metal-forming, and machine-tool industries. VFDs and keyboards together make up about 60% of the firm's exported goods. It has 18 subsidiaries, including sales subsidiaries in the U.S. and Hong Kong, and manufacturing subsidiaries in Taiwan and South Korea. 48% of Futaba's consolidated sales were made overseas in 1994.

¥bil	03/93	03/94	03/95	US$mil 03/95				
Sales	**81.3**	**79.5**	**91.3**	**925.4**	P/E Ratio	**27.5**	Price (9/30/95)	**4,460.00**
Net Income	**7.6**	**7.2**	**8.2**	**83.5**	P/B Ratio	**1.7**	52 Wk Hi-Low	**5,400.0-3,500.0**
Book Value	**124.8**	**130.2**	**136.8**	**1,583.7**	Yield %	**0.6**	Market Cap	**US$2,279.6mil**

Address	**629, Oshiba**	Tel	**0475-24-1111**	ADR		President	**Reiji Hosoya**
	Mobara City, Chiba 297	Fax	**0475-23-1346**	SEDOL No.	**6357733**	Chairman	--

Gakken

Industry: **Publishing**

Gakken (Gakushu Kenkyusha) is a major educational-publishing company. Textbooks and the firm's approximately 80 magazines are its main sources of revenues, with one fourth of all Japanese schoolchildren reading Gakken's monthly study magazines. It publishes dictionaries, reference books, encyclopedias, and art books. Other products and services include educational software and exam-preparation materials. Gakken exports gift items, and also imports office equipment, Montessori educational supplies, and other items from the United States, Europe, and Asia.

¥bil	03/93	03/94	03/95	US$mil 03/95				
Sales	**163.5**	**149.0**	**151.9**	**1,539.5**	P/E Ratio	**78.7**	Price (9/30/95)	**590.00**
Net Income	**-2.9**	**-4.3**	**0.8**	**7.7**	P/B Ratio	**0.6**	52 Wk Hi-Low	**802.00-510.00**
Book Value	**98.5**	**93.7**	**93.2**	**1,078.4**	Yield %	**0.0**	Market Cap	**US$604.1mil**

Address	**4-40-5, Kami-Ikedai**	Tel	**03-3726-8111**	ADR		President	**Kazuhiko Sawada**
	Ohta-ku, Tokyo 145	Fax	**03-3727-3424**	SEDOL No.	**6359739**	Chairman	--

General Sekiyu

Industry: **Oil - Secondary**

General Sekiyu is a Japanese refiner and distributor of oil and oil-related products. Petroleum products make up nearly 98% of the parent company's total sales. The company is affiliated with Exxon (U.S.) and has business ties with Esso Sekiyu. It controls about 5% of the gasoline market in Japan through a chain of 2,300 affiliated gas stations. General Sekiyu has two refineries, in Okinawa and Sakai. Its network in Japan consists of five automatic order-receiving centers and 28 distribution centers. It is diversifying into engineering, real estate, and electronic products.

¥bil	03/93	03/94	03/95	US$mil 03/95				
Sales	**522.6**	**488.5**	**513.7**	**5,207.2**	P/E Ratio	**31.7**	Price (9/30/95)	**929.00**
Net Income	**10.1**	**15.0**	**11.1**	**113.0**	P/B Ratio	**2.8**	52 Wk Hi-Low	**1,050.0-860.0**
Book Value	**112.5**	**120.6**	**125.4**	**1,451.2**	Yield %	**2.7**	Market Cap	**US$3,556.7mil**

Address	**2-8-6, Nishi-Shinbashi**	Tel	**03-3595-8278**	ADR		President	**Masayoshi Okai**
	Minato-ku, Tokyo 105	Fax	**03-3595-8316**	SEDOL No.	**6366007**	Chairman	--

Godo Steel

Industry: **Steel**

Godo Steel (Godo Seitetsu) is a major electric-furnace steel manufacturer. Its mainstay products include wire rods, steel bars, and H-beams, I-beams, and other steel shapes for use in building construction. The firm is Japan's third-largest steel-wire maker by volume. Its steelmaking works at Osaka and Himeji are each equipped with one blast furnace and two electric-arc furnaces. In 1991, the company merged with Funabashi Steel and now runs that company's plant near Tokyo. In 1994, more than 20% of its products were sold to Mitsui & Co. Godo is affiliated with Nippon Steel.

¥bil	03/93 P	03/94 P	03/95 P	US$mil 03/95				
Sales	**113.6**	**94.7**	**88.6**	**897.7**	P/E Ratio	**NMF**	Price (9/30/95)	**580.00**
Net Income	**4.8**	**-14.7**	**-12.4**	**-125.8**	P/B Ratio	**1.0**	52 Wk Hi-Low	**879.00-440.00**
Book Value	**124.0**	**107.6**	**93.9**	**1,087.3**	Yield %	**1.0**	Market Cap	**US$936.1mil**

Address **2-3-24, Umeda, Kita-ku, Osaka 530**
Tel **06-346-1031**
Fax **06-341-1994**
ADR
SEDOL No. **6374345**
President **Tokio Mitamura**
Chairman **Yoshiro Sasaki**

P=Parent company data.

Green Cross

Industry: **Pharmaceuticals**

Green Cross (Midori Juji) is Japan's leading manufacturer of blood-derived products, by market share. Albumin and venoglobulin are the firm's major blood-derived products. It also licenses Liple, a peripheral vasodilator, to pharmaceutical companies in the U.S. and Europe. It has two wholly-owned U.S. subsidiaries, Alpha Therapeutic and Green Cross Corporation of America, and seven other consolidated subsidiaries. Green Cross has research agreements with U.S. organizations, such as Stanford University and Biogen. It has three plants and two research facilities in Japan.

¥bil	12/92	12/93	12/94	US$mil 12/94				
Sales	**106.6**	**110.2**	**114.3**	**1,119.6**	P/E Ratio	**93.0**	Price (9/30/95)	**735.00**
Net Income	**1.2**	**1.8**	**1.6**	**16.1**	P/B Ratio	**1.9**	52 Wk Hi-Low	**1,000.00-615.00**
Book Value	**77.9**	**78.4**	**78.7**	**789.0**	Yield %	**0.7**	Market Cap	**US$1,529.1mil**

Address **1-3-3, Imabashi, Chuo-ku, Osaka 541**
Tel **06-227-4635**
Fax **06-229-3639**
ADR
SEDOL No. **6386306**
President **Takehiko Kawano**
Chairman --

Gunma Bank

Industry: **Banks - Regional**

Gunma Bank (Gunma Ginko), the ninth-largest regional bank in Japan by assets, is the designated financial institution for the Gunma Prefectural government and for several municipalities. The bank's domestic network consists of 173 branches. It has a branch in New York and a representative office in Hong Kong, along with overseas affiliated companies in Hong Kong and Amsterdam. Offering foreign-exchange services, the bank provides financial services focusing on corporate investment overseas. It belongs to a correspondent-banking network of 217 foreign banks in 62 countries.

¥bil	03/93 P	03/94 P	03/95 P	US$mil 03/95				
Revenues	**281.2**	**239.2**	**222.9**	**2,259.6**	P/E Ratio	**67.1**	Price (9/30/95)	**1,060.00**
Net Income	**10.6**	**7.4**	**8.1**	**81.7**	P/B Ratio	**2.4**	52 Wk Hi-Low	**1,140.0-953.0**
Book Value	**220.2**	**224.9**	**230.5**	**2,668.4**	Yield %	**0.5**	Market Cap	**US$5,455.7mil**

Address **194, Motosoja-machi, Maebashi City, Gunma 371**
Tel **0272-52-1111**
Fax **0272-51-4399**
ADR
SEDOL No. **6398088**
President **Takuji Tsuchikane**
Chairman --

P=Parent company data.

Gunze

Industry: **Clothing & Fabrics**

Gunze produces apparel, fabrics, industrial materials, machinery, and health foods. It is best known in Japan as a manufacturer of knit underwear. The firm's textile products, which account for about 80% of sales, include pantyhose, socks, lingerie, pajamas, and sportswear. It also makes synthetic sewing thread and textiles. Its licensed brand names include Calvin Klein, Montana, Fiorucci Sport, and Levi's. Gunze's domestic network includes 12 factories and 43 subsidiaries; it also has overseas offices in North America, Europe, Southeast Asia, China, and South Korea.

¥bil	03/93	03/94	03/95	US$mil 03/95				
Sales	**208.5**	**203.4**	**190.4**	**1,929.6**	P/E Ratio	**43.7**	Price (9/30/95)	**551.00**
Net Income	**3.6**	**3.4**	**2.7**	**27.5**	P/B Ratio	**1.0**	52 Wk Hi-Low	**707.00-503.00**
Book Value	**115.4**	**116.8**	**116.2**	**1,345.5**	Yield %	**1.4**	Market Cap	**US$1,196.0mil**

Address **1-8-17, Umeda, Kita-ku, Osaka 530**
Tel **06-348-1312**
Fax **06-348-4814**
ADR
SEDOL No. **6398709**
President **Yoshiaki Hamuro**
Chairman --

Hachijuni Bank

Industry: **Banks - Regional**

Hachijuni Bank is based in Nagano Prefecture, is ranked eighth among regional banks in assets. The manufacturing, distribution, and service sectors make up the largest portions of the bank's lending. The bank is authorized financial institution for prefectual-and municipal-tax receipts in the area. Hachijuni is also a clearing member of the Tokyo Financial Futures Market. Loans to small- and medium-size companies account for more than 65% of the bank's outstanding loans. The bank controls six subsidiaries and six affiliates, including Nagano Diamond Lease.

¥bil	03/93 P	03/94 P	03/95 P	US$mil 03/95				
Revenues	**288.6**	**239.8**	**221.7**	**2,247.6**	P/E Ratio	**59.4**	Price (9/30/95)	**1,110.00**
Net Income	**13.2**	**10.5**	**10.7**	**108.5**	P/B Ratio	**2.5**	52 Wk Hi-Low	**1,220.0-1,000.0**
Book Value	**235.0**	**242.8**	**250.6**	**2,900.7**	Yield %	**0.5**	Market Cap	**US$6,392.6mil**

Address **178-8, Okada, Nakagosho, Nagano City, Nagano 380**
Tel **0262-27-1182**
Fax **N/A**
ADR
SEDOL No. **6400626**
President **Minoru Chino**
Chairman **Tomitaro Nakayama**

P=Parent company data.

Hankyu

Industry: **Railroads**

Hankyu (Hankyu Dentetsu) is a railway operator in the Kansai region that has diversified into real estate and leisure-related fields. The company is the transportation wing and core member of the Hankyu and Toho groups. Based in Osaka, its passenger trains connect Osaka with Kobe, Takarazuka, and Kyoto. Its leisure division manages Nishinomiya Stadium, Takarazuka Ice Arena, Takarazuka theaters and several amusement parks. The company's real-estate division sells homes and leases commercial property. Hankyu also manages department stores and operates hotels.

¥bil	03/93	03/94	03/95	US$mil 03/95				
Sales	**355.7**	**375.2**	**364.1**	**3,690.8**	P/E Ratio	**NMF**	Price (9/30/95)	**555.00**
Net Income	**7.1**	**3.2**	**-13.0**	**-132.3**	P/B Ratio	**3.1**	52 Wk Hi-Low	**605.00-498.00**
Book Value	**180.3**	**179.4**	**154.3**	**1,786.1**	Yield %	**0.5**	Market Cap	**US$4,791.6mil**

Address	**1-16-1, Shibata**	Tel	**06-373-5162**	ADR		President	**Motohiro Sugai**
	Kita-ku, Osaka 530	Fax	**06-373-5669**	SEDOL No.	**6408664**	Chairman	**Kohei Kobayashi**

Hanshin Electric Railway

Industry: **Railroads**

Hanshin Electric Railway (Hanshin Denki Tetsudo) is a leading private railway company that is involved in real-estate and amusement-park activities. Based in the Kinki area, its rail network runs through the heart of Osaka and Kobe. It operates bus lines, taxi services, trucking firms, and air-freight services. Hanshin also manages a baseball team (Hanshin Tigers), a sports stadium, amusement parks, bowling alleys, department stores, and hotels. It sells and leases real estate along its track lines. Hanshin has 49 subsidiaries, including the Hanshin Department Store.

¥bil	03/93	03/94	03/95	US$mil 03/95				
Sales	**279.0**	**269.4**	**274.6**	**2,783.6**	P/E Ratio	**NMF**	Price (9/30/95)	**340.00**
Net Income	**4.4**	**5.2**	**-2.6**	**-26.8**	P/B Ratio	**1.4**	52 Wk Hi-Low	**494.00-307.00**
Book Value	**82.0**	**85.4**	**82.5**	**954.6**	Yield %	**0.7**	Market Cap	**US$1,174.7mil**

Address	**1-1-24, Ebie**	Tel	**06-457-2160**	ADR		President	**Masatoshi Tezuka**
	Fukushima-ku, Osaka 553	Fax	**06-457-2141**	SEDOL No.	**6408802**	Chairman	**Shunjiro Kuma**

Hanwa

Industry: **Overseas Trading**

Hanwa (Hanwa Kogyo) is a trading company specializing in steel products. The firm also markets machinery, information equipment, petrochemical products, frozen seafood, and timber. It is Japan's top importer of marine products. Major customers include the construction, steel, fabric, electrical-appliance, machinery, and ship-building industries. Hanwa deals in nonferrous ingots and imported steel scrap, and purchases steel from most major Japanese mills to sell in Japan and abroad. Hanwa has five consolidated subsidiaries, including Hanwa American, in the United States.

¥bil	03/93	03/94	03/95	US$mil 03/95				
Sales	**639.4**	**543.6**	**546.0**	**5,534.2**	P/E Ratio	**NMF**	Price (9/30/95)	**312.00**
Net Income	**6.0**	**-125.3**	**-201.2**	**-2,039.7**	P/B Ratio	**1.7**	52 Wk Hi-Low	**445.00-152.00**
Book Value	**402.9**	**272.4**	**71.3**	**825.0**	Yield %	**0.0**	Market Cap	**US$1,229.1mil**

Address	**1-13-10, Tsukiji**	Tel	**03-3544-2196**	ADR		President	**Shuji Kita**
	Chuo-ku, Tokyo 104	Fax	**03-3544-2230**	SEDOL No.	**6408824**	Chairman	--

Haseko

Industry: **Home Construction**

Haseko is a general contractor involved primarily in building construction and real estate. The company is a leading builder of high-rise condominiums, hotels, and office buildings in the Tokyo and Kinki areas. Haseko has constructed more than 200,000 condominium units. Haseko also provides comprehensive real-estate consulting services, including site selection, planning, and design. Also among its real-estate activities are hotel and resort management, land acquisition, and building development. Haseko has 42 consolidated subsidiaries, including Haseko in the U.S.

¥bil	03/93	03/94	03/95	US$mil 03/95				
Sales	**534.0**	**433.3**	**425.7**	**4,314.8**	P/E Ratio	**NMF**	Price (9/30/95)	**443.00**
Net Income	**0.6**	**1.0**	**-4.6**	**-46.4**	P/B Ratio	**0.7**	52 Wk Hi-Low	**674.00-392.00**
Book Value	**290.2**	**287.4**	**281.7**	**3,260.3**	Yield %	**1.1**	Market Cap	**US$1,912.9mil**

Address	**2-32-1, Shiba**	Tel	**03-3456-3901**	ADR		President	**Kohei Goda**
	Minato-ku, Tokyo 105	Fax	**03-3769-5947**	SEDOL No.	**6414401**	Chairman	**Yoshimi Mizukami**

Hazama

Industry: **Heavy Construction**

Hazama (Hazama Gumi) is a contractor involved in building construction and civil engineering, particularly dam construction. The company constructs office and residential buildings, some of which employ intelligent-building technology. Other projects include railways, bridges, and large-scale land reclamation. Hazama has lost its status as a government-designated contractor and has consequently expanded its overseas operations, which represent less than 10% of consolidated revenues. The company has 38 subsidiaries and 25 affiliates, including seven overseas subsidiaries.

¥bil	03/93	03/94	03/95	US$mil 03/95				
Sales	**696.3**	**593.7**	**568.2**	**5,759.8**	P/E Ratio	**40.1**	Price (9/30/95)	**429.00**
Net Income	**0.5**	**2.0**	**3.5**	**35.0**	P/B Ratio	**1.4**	52 Wk Hi-Low	**606.00-349.00**
Book Value	**98.3**	**96.8**	**99.2**	**1,148.1**	Yield %	**1.2**	Market Cap	**US$1,385.5mil**

Address	**2-5-8, Kita-Aoyama**	Tel	**03-3405-1111**	ADR		President	**Mikio Matsumoto**
	Minato-ku, Tokyo 107	Fax	**03-3405-1814**	SEDOL No.	**6416708**	Chairman	--

Heiwa Real Estate

Industry: **Real-Estate Investment**

Heiwa Real Estate (Heiwa Fudosan), leases office space and other property. The company derives the bulk of its revenues from leasing buildings to Japanese stock exchanges. Heiwa owns the buildings that house the Tokyo, Osaka, Nagoya, and Fukuoka exchanges. Rental fees from the Tokyo Stock Exchange are the firm's main revenue source. Heiwa also develops and leases office buildings, department stores, single-family houses, and residential lots in the Tokyo region. It has four unconsolidated subsidiaries: Heiwa Housing, Heiwa Birumen, Heiwa Jitsugyo, and Heiwa Resort.

¥bil	03/93 P	03/94 P	03/95 P	US$mil 03/95				
Sales	**14.7**	**16.9**	**15.9**	**161.6**	P/E Ratio	**39.0**	Price (9/30/95)	**725.00**
Net Income	**2.2**	**2.1**	**2.1**	**21.2**	P/B Ratio	**2.7**	52 Wk Hi-Low	**864.00-551.00**
Book Value	**27.7**	**29.0**	**30.4**	**351.3**	Yield %	**0.8**	Market Cap	**US$821.0mil**

Address **1-10, Nihonbashi-Kabutocho**, **Chuo-ku, Tokyo 103** | Tel **03-3666-0181** | Fax **03-3666-4930** | ADR | SEDOL No. **6419600** | President **Masaru Aratani** | Chairman --

P=Parent company data.

Hino Motors

Industry: **Land Transportation**

Hino Motors (Hino Jidosha Kogyo), a key member of the Toyota group, is one of Japan's major makers of trucks and buses. The company holds top domestic market shares in medium and large trucks; overall, it commands roughly 29% of Japan's truck market. Hino Motors also assembles trucks for Toyota, including the Hilux (a small truck) model. Hino Automobile Sales, a partially-owned subsidiary, is its other main customer. In 1994, overseas sales accounted for 16.5% of the company's total consolidated revenues. Its main lender is the Japan Development Bank.

¥bil	03/93	03/94	03/95	US$mil 03/95				
Sales	**632.3**	**535.5**	**650.8**	**6,597.1**	P/E Ratio	**52.0**	Price (9/30/95)	**780.00**
Net Income	**3.4**	**2.6**	**5.4**	**55.2**	P/B Ratio	**2.2**	52 Wk Hi-Low	**1,010.0-620.0**
Book Value	**118.9**	**122.1**	**130.7**	**1,513.0**	Yield %	**0.8**	Market Cap	**US$2,843.1mil**

Address **3-1-1, Hinodai**, **Hino City, Tokyo 191** | Tel **0425-86-5011** | Fax **03-3272-4822** | ADR **HINOY** | SEDOL No. **6428305** | President **Tomio Futami** | Chairman **Kaneyoshi Kusunoki**

Hirose Electric

Industry: **Electrical Components & Equipment**

Hirose Electric (Hirose Denki) is a specialized manufacturer of connectors for information and electronic equipment. Its main products are multipin and nylon connectors used in cellular phones, videocassette recorders, cameras, and other electronic equipment. The firm also produces coaxial and optical connectors for use in communication equipment and measuring instruments. Members of the Hirose family are among the firm's top shareholders. Hirose Electric operates four plants in Japan; it has ten subsidiaries. In 1994, 11.7% of its consolidated sales were made overseas.

¥bil	03/93	03/94	03/95	US$mil 03/95				
Sales	**42.0**	**44.6**	**51.6**	**522.9**	P/E Ratio	**35.6**	Price (9/30/95)	**6,220.00**
Net Income	**4.9**	**5.7**	**6.5**	**66.0**	P/B Ratio	**3.0**	52 Wk Hi-Low	**6,542.9-4,447.6**
Book Value	**67.1**	**72.0**	**77.9**	**902.1**	Yield %	**0.3**	Market Cap	**US$2,335.1mil**

Address **5-5-23, Osaki**, **Shinagawa-ku, Tokyo 141** | Tel **03-3491-5300** | Fax **03-3495-5230** | ADR | SEDOL No. **6428725** | President **Hideki Sakai** | Chairman --

Hiroshima Bank

Industry: **Banks - Regional**

Hiroshima Bank (Hiroshima Ginko) is one of the top 10 regional banks by assets. The bank is broadening its financial services and commissions business through tie-ups with Nikko Securities and Toyo Securities. It is the first regional bank to deal in commodity-fund transactions. Its loans are largely to the manufacturing, distribution, and service sectors. With over 220 offices in the Chugoku and Shikoku regions, it has one branch each in London and New York, and has subsidiaries in Hong Kong and Amsterdam. The bank is part of a worldwide correspondence-banking network.

¥bil	03/93 P	03/94 P	03/95 P	US$mil 03/95				
Revenues	**323.6**	**270.3**	**248.8**	**2,522.0**	P/E Ratio	**79.2**	Price (9/30/95)	**507.00**
Net Income	**6.4**	**5.1**	**3.9**	**39.5**	P/B Ratio	**1.4**	52 Wk Hi-Low	**623.00-491.00**
Book Value	**219.9**	**221.9**	**222.7**	**2,577.1**	Yield %	**1.0**	Market Cap	**US$3,123.8mil**

Address **1-3-8, Kamiya-cho, Naka-ku**, **Hiroshima City, Hiroshima 730** | Tel **082-247-5151** | Fax **082-248-1550** | ADR | SEDOL No. **6075723** | President **Makoto Uda** | Chairman **Shunsuke Kishida**

P=Parent company data.

Hitachi

Industry: **Diversified Technology**

Hitachi (Hitachi Seisakusho) is the largest Japanese manufacturer of electrical machinery by sales and one of the world's largest semiconductor makers. The firm's industrial products are sold to the power, manufacturing, construction, transportation, and automobile industries. Major customers include Hitachi Kaden (10.0% of parent-company sales), Hitachi Higashi Building Systems, and Nissei Sangyo. Hitachi has 844 consolidated subsidiaries. In April 1995 Hitachi acquired Hitachi Sales, a consolidated subsidiary that sells home appliances.

¥bil	03/93	03/94	03/95	US$mil 03/95				
Sales	**7,536.2**	**7,400.2**	**7,592.3**	**76,957.7**	P/E Ratio	**31.1**	Price (9/30/95)	**1,080.00**
Net Income	**77.3**	**65.3**	**113.9**	**1,154.7**	P/B Ratio	**1.2**	52 Wk Hi-Low	**1,130.0-785.0**
Book Value	**2,940.2**	**2,959.2**	**3,033.4**	**35,108.5**	Yield %	**1.0**	Market Cap	**US$35,708mil**

Address **4-6, Kanda-Surugadai**, **Chiyoda-ku, Tokyo 101** | Tel **03-3258-1111** | Fax **03-3258-5480** | ADR **HIT** | SEDOL No. **6429104** | President **Tsutomu Kanai** | Chairman **Katsushige Mita**

Hitachi Cable

Industry: **Electrical Components & Equipment**

Hitachi Cable (Hitachi Densen), a subsidiary of Hitachi, is Japan's third-largest electrical-wire and cable manufacturer. Its products include power cables, fiberoptic and communication cables, covered wires, chemical-compound integrated circuits (IC), and IC lead-frame material. The firm supplies the communication, electric-power, automobile, electronics, and construction industries. In 1994, 17% of its consolidated sales were made overseas where it is promoting the sales of high-voltage power cables and submarine cables. The company has 29 consolidated subsidiaries.

¥bil	03/93	03/94	03/95	US$mil 03/95				
Sales	**358.6**	**336.8**	**352.8**	**3,576.1**	P/E Ratio	**32.4**	Price (9/30/95)	**712.00**
Net Income	**7.1**	**6.0**	**8.3**	**83.8**	P/B Ratio	**1.6**	52 Wk Hi-Low	**872.00-541.00**
Book Value	**166.5**	**168.1**	**172.7**	**1,999.2**	Yield %	**1.3**	Market Cap	**US$2,695.8mil**

Address **2-1-2, Marunouchi**	Tel **03-5252-3261**	ADR	President	**Seiji Hara**
Chiyoda-ku, Tokyo 100	Fax **03-3214-5779**	SEDOL No. **6429148**	Chairman	**Hiroji Hashimoto**

Hitachi Chemical

Industry: **Commodity Chemicals**

Hitachi Chemical (Hitachi Kasei Kogyo), a subsidiary of Hitachi, makes a variety of chemical products, many for the semiconductor industry. Electronic parts and materials make up about 45% of its consolidated sales. Other products include organic and inorganic chemical products, synthetic-resin-processed goods, pharmaceuticals, and housing fixtures. Hitachi Chemical also supplies molded parts and nonasbestos disc-brake pads to the auto industry. Hitachi owns 56% of Hitachi Chemical's equity. In 1994, 12% of its consolidated sales consisted of overseas sales.

¥bil	03/93	03/94	03/95	US$mil 03/95				
Sales	**492.6**	**466.2**	**487.4**	**4,940.0**	P/E Ratio	**47.3**	Price (9/30/95)	**931.00**
Net Income	**2.2**	**2.4**	**4.0**	**40.3**	P/B Ratio	**2.3**	52 Wk Hi-Low	**1,220.0-760.0**
Book Value	**80.1**	**80.3**	**82.8**	**958.4**	Yield %	**0.8**	Market Cap	**US$1,893.0mil**

Address **2-1-1, Nishi-Shinjuku**	Tel **03-5381-2349**	ADR	President	**Takeshi Tanno**
Shinjuku-ku, Tokyo 163-04	Fax **03-3343-3498**	SEDOL No. **6429126**	Chairman	--

Hitachi Construction Machinery

Industry: **Heavy Machinery**

Hitachi Construction Machinery, a member of the Hitachi group, manufactures hydraulic excavators, minishovels, crawler cranes, tunnel excavators, wheel loaders, machines for foundation work, road-construction machines, and shield machines. It holds a majority stake in Toyosha, a Japanese maker of agricultural machinery and hydraulic excavators. The company also produces hydraulic excavators in the United States in a joint venture with Deere & Co., and in Italy in a joint venture with Fiat Geotech. Other plants are located in the Netherlands, Malaysia, and Indonesia.

¥bil	03/93	03/94	03/95	US$mil 03/95				
Sales	**237.8**	**238.6**	**271.0**	**2,747.4**	P/E Ratio	**40.5**	Price (9/30/95)	**1,110.00**
Net Income	**-0.9**	**-2.2**	**3.9**	**39.9**	P/B Ratio	**2.0**	52 Wk Hi-Low	**1,370.0-724.0**
Book Value	**79.8**	**77.1**	**80.8**	**935.2**	Yield %	**0.5**	Market Cap	**US$1,604.9mil**

Address **2-6-2, Otemachi**	Tel **03-3245-6305**	ADR	President	**Hajime Okada**
Chiyoda-ku, Tokyo 100	Fax **03-3246-2607**	SEDOL No. **6429405**	Chairman	--

Hitachi Credit

Industry: **Financial Services - Diversified**

Hitachi Credit, a consolidated subsidiary of Hitachi, is a credit company that specializes in providing financing for manufacturing companies. Its services include loan guarantees, the leasing of office-automation equipment, installment-credit sales, credit-card operations, and purchased installment receivables. Its installment-sales services enable individuals to purchase automobiles, home appliances, home furnishings, and insurance policies. Hitachi Credit has subsidiaries in the United Kingdom, the United States, Canada, and Hong Kong, and a branch office in Singapore.

¥bil	03/93	03/94	03/95	US$mil 03/95				
Revenues	**403.4**	**407.6**	**418.1**	**4,238.2**	P/E Ratio	**27.7**	Price (9/30/95)	**1,680.00**
Net Income	**6.2**	**6.6**	**7.2**	**73.0**	P/B Ratio	**1.5**	52 Wk Hi-Low	**1,960.0-1,370.0**
Book Value	**119.6**	**125.0**	**130.1**	**1,505.3**	Yield %	**1.0**	Market Cap	**US$2,006.9mil**

Address **2-15-12, Nishi-Shinbashi**	Tel **03-3503-2118**	ADR	President	**Masayoshi Hanabusa**
Minato-ku, Tokyo 105	Fax **03-3580-7267**	SEDOL No. **6429159**	Chairman	--

Hitachi Metals

Industry: **Steel**

Hitachi Metals (Hitachi Kinzoku), a member of the Hitachi group, makes special steels for the auto, aircraft, nuclear, and space industries. Other products include office-automation equipment, optical-telecommunication parts, auto parts such as ductile-iron castings and aluminum wheels, piping components, and feed-production plants. The firm is the top domestic maker of malleable cast-iron fittings. It has 44 consolidated subsidiaries, 12 of which are overseas. Nissan Motor is one of its main customers. Overseas sales account for over 20% of the firm's consolidated sales.

¥bil	03/93	03/94	03/95	US$mil 03/95				
Sales	**422.3**	**396.5**	**430.3**	**4,361.9**	P/E Ratio	**41.6**	Price (9/30/95)	**1,170.00**
Net Income	**3.1**	**4.0**	**9.9**	**100.1**	P/B Ratio	**2.3**	52 Wk Hi-Low	**1,310.0-888.0**
Book Value	**160.3**	**161.0**	**180.6**	**2,090.0**	Yield %	**0.9**	Market Cap	**US$4,203.3mil**

Address **2-1-2, Marunouchi**	Tel **03-3284-4571**	ADR	President	**Tetsuya Eda**
Chiyoda-ku, Tokyo 100	Fax **03-3214-1029**	SEDOL No. **6429201**	Chairman	**Koji Matsuno**

Hitachi Software Engineering

Industry: **Software**

Hitachi Software Engineering, a subsidiary of Hitachi,is the largest software firm in Japan. As a full-service supplier to the information industry, its products include software for everything from supercomputers to personal computers, as well as information-management equipment and consulting services. Sales to Hitachi account for more than 70% of its revenues. The firm also develops software for defense and other government projects. Hitachi Software is currently expanding into applications for Microsoft Windows. It has six subsidiaries and eight affiliates.

¥bil	03/93 P	03/94 P	03/95 P	US$mil 03/95				
Sales	90.5	82.0	87.2	883.4	P/E Ratio	77.7	Price (9/30/95)	2,330.00
Net Income	2.7	2.8	1.7	17.0	P/B Ratio	1.9	52 Wk Hi-Low	3,318.2-1,454.5
Book Value	60.2	62.1	67.9	786.0	Yield %	0.5	Market Cap	US$1,331.5mil

Address **6-81, Onoe-cho, Naka-ku, Yokohama, 231** Tel **045-681-2111** Fax **045-681-2209** ADR SEDOL No. **6429502** President **Tsutomu Sato** Chairman --

P=Parent company data.

Hitachi Zosen

Industry: **Shipbuilding**

Hitachi Zosen, a member of the Sanwa group, is a midsize shipbuilder and is also involved in machinery production and plant engineering. The firm's major lines include ships, offshore structures, construction machinery, prime movers, bridges and other steel structures, and incineration plants. Most of its ship orders are for large-scale tankers. Major customers include Asahi Chemical, Obayashi, Hitachi Zosen Development, and Shinagawa. Hitachi Zosen has a consolidated subsidiary in Singapore and a technical tie-up with Switzerland's Von Roll in the field of plant construction.

¥bil	03/93	03/94	03/95	US$mil 03/95				
Sales	447.8	524.5	547.5	5,549.5	P/E Ratio	72.2	Price (9/30/95)	484.00
Net Income	12.0	6.0	6.7	68.3	P/B Ratio	4.9	52 Wk Hi-Low	567.00-329.00
Book Value	98.4	98.9	99.7	1,154.1	Yield %	1.2	Market Cap	US$4,878.6mil

Address **5-3-28, Nishi-kujo, Konohana-ku, Osaka 554** Tel **06-466-7515** Fax **06-466-7576** ADR SEDOL No. **6429308** President **Iso Minami** Chairman **Yoshihiro Fujii**

Hokuetsu Paper Mills

Industry: **Paper Products**

Hokuetsu Paper Mills (Hokuetsu Seishi) is a midsize paper firm and a leading manufacturer of whiteboard. Its product lines include paperboard, printing paper, and specialty paper for facsimile machines, computers, and other information-processing equipment. Hokuetsu also sells lumber. It imports raw materials from Australia, North and South America, and New Zealand. Main customers include Marudai Paper, Okura Paper Pulp Shoji, Nittsu, and Okamoto. Hokuetsu also markets its products through Mitsubishi. It operates four plants and has 13 consolidated subsidiaries in Japan.

¥bil	03/93	03/94	03/95	US$mil 03/95				
Sales	114.5	107.2	110.8	1,123.2	P/E Ratio	54.6	Price (9/30/95)	824.00
Net Income	1.7	1.8	1.9	19.4	P/B Ratio	2.0	52 Wk Hi-Low	910.00-666.00
Book Value	47.8	49.5	51.3	594.0	Yield %	0.9	Market Cap	US$1,052.7mil

Address **3-2-2, Nihonbashi-Hongokucho, Chuo-ku, Tokyo 103** Tel **03-3245-4581** Fax **03-3245-4588** ADR SEDOL No. **6433105** President **Ukichi Inomata** Chairman **Toshio Tanaka**

Hokuriku Bank

Industry: **Banks - Regional**

Hokuriku Bank (Hokuriku Ginko) is one of the largest regional banks in Japan, based on assets. The bank is active in regional development projects, including the construction of public facilities. It also underwrites local-government bonds and lends to municipalities. Loans to small- and medium-size companies account for nearly 80% of total loans outstanding. The bank has four domestic subsidiaries and one overseas subsidiary, Hokuriku Finance (Hong Kong). In 1994, revenues from overseas operations accounted for 20.6% of total consolidated revenues.

¥bil	03/93	03/94	03/95	US$mil 03/95				
Revenues	466.5	372.5	341.9	3,465.8	P/E Ratio	95.5	Price (9/30/95)	630.00
Net Income	8.0	6.8	4.5	45.7	P/B Ratio	1.3	52 Wk Hi-Low	745.00-585.00
Book Value	329.0	332.4	333.5	3,860.5	Yield %	0.8	Market Cap	US$4,347.6mil

Address **1-2-26, Tsutsumicho-dori, Toyama City, Toyama 930** Tel **0764-23-7111** Fax **0764-91-6198** ADR SEDOL No. **6433161** President **Kenso Yashima** Chairman **Teruo Kubota**

Honda Motor

Industry: **Automobile Manufacturers**

Honda Motor (Honda Giken Kogyo) is Japan's third-largest automaker by sales, and the world's largest maker of motorcycles. The firm holds the fifth-largest share of the Japanese car market, while its U.S. market share in cars and trucks is the second-largest for a Japanese automaker. Popular models include the Accord series, the Civic series, and the Acura Integra. Honda also makes small engines, generators, and lawn mowers. In May 1994, Honda dissolved its agreements with the Rover Group (U.K.), but it still has manufacturing facilities in the United Kingdom.

¥bil	03/93	03/94	03/95	US$mil 03/95				
Sales	4,132.4	3,862.7	3,966.2	40,202.4	P/E Ratio	28.2	Price (9/30/95)	1,780.00
Net Income	38.3	23.7	61.5	623.6	P/B Ratio	1.7	52 Wk Hi-Low	1,800.0-1,150.0
Book Value	1,036.6	967.3	1,017.5	11,776.2	Yield %	0.8	Market Cap	US$17,442mil

Address **2-1-1, Minami-Aoyama, Minato-ku, Tokyo 107** Tel **03-3423-1111** Fax **03-5412-1515** ADR **HMC** SEDOL No. **6435145** President **Nobuhiko Kawamoto** Chairman --

Honshu Paper

Industry: **Paper Products**

Honshu Paper (Honshu Seishi), a leading paper manufacturer, holds the largest share of the Japanese paperboard market. The firm's other products include additional paper goods, pulp, lumber, building materials, plastics, chemicals, and pharmaceuticals. It also offers afforestation, forestation, gardening, and paper-consulting services. Main customers include Japan Pulp and Paper, a large paper distributor and exporter. It also imports woodchips from the United States for papermaking. Honshu Paper has nine paper mills and 23 plants for making corrugated-paper containers.

	¥bil 03/93	03/94	03/95	US$mil 03/95				
Sales	**468.4**	**447.5**	**470.2**	**4,765.9**	P/E Ratio	**77.1**	Price (9/30/95)	**601.00**
Net Income	**3.2**	**3.3**	**2.7**	**27.4**	P/B Ratio	**2.2**	52 Wk Hi-Low	**722.00-490.00**
Book Value	**94.2**	**94.7**	**95.0**	**1,099.7**	Yield %	**1.0**	Market Cap	**US$2,089.1mil**

Address	**1-26-20, Higashi**	Tel	**03-5467-1012**	ADR		President	**Takao Otsubo**
	Shibuya-ku, Tokyo 150	Fax	**03-5467-6653**	SEDOL No.	**6435703**	Chairman	**Yoshinobu Yonezawa**

Hosokawa Micron

Industry: **Factory Equipment**

Hosokawa Micron is the world's leading producer of particle-processing equipment, used in air-purification systems and other environmental-protection-related systems, with about 40% of the world market share. Its product lines include dust collectors, mixing and drying equipment, and crushing and classifying equipment. Major customers include Mitsubishi Kasei Engineering, Kanebo, and Canon. The firm has consolidated subsidiaries in the U.S., the Netherlands, Australia, Canada, Germany, Switzerland, the U.K., France, Italy, and Spain.

	¥bil 09/92	09/93	09/94	US$mil 09/94				
Sales	**55.5**	**48.9**	**42.9**	**411.2**	P/E Ratio	**NMF**	Price (9/30/95)	**1,630.00**
Net Income	**-2.3**	**-4.5**	**-0.1**	**-1.3**	P/B Ratio	**2.2**	52 Wk Hi-Low	**2,140.0-1,200.0**
Book Value	**25.3**	**20.4**	**20.4**	**206.4**	Yield %	**0.3**	Market Cap	**US$444.3mil**

Address	**2-5-14, Kawara-machi**	Tel	**06-233-3967**	ADR		President	**Masuo Hosokawa**
	Chuo-ku, Osaka 541	Fax	**06-229-9256**	SEDOL No.	**6439879**	Chairman	--

House Foods

Industry: **Other Food**

House Foods (House Shokuhin), previously House Foods Industrial, produces food flavorings, microwave foods, and other foodstuffs. The firm is Japan's largest maker of spices, holding 60% of market share. Its other products include drinks, snacks, desserts, and instant noodles. It holds 50% of the Japanese market in mineral water for home use. Overseas, House Foods has tie-ups with Keebler and General Mills in the U.S, and Marie Brizard et Roger International in France. House Foods & Yamaichi, a joint venture, is the largest producer and distributor of tofu products in the U.S.

	¥bil 03/93	03/94	03/95	US$mil 03/95				
Sales	**194.3**	**196.4**	**189.8**	**1,923.9**	P/E Ratio	**20.9**	Price (9/30/95)	**1,830.00**
Net Income	**8.9**	**9.9**	**10.0**	**101.3**	P/B Ratio	**1.5**	52 Wk Hi-Low	**2,060.0-1,650.0**
Book Value	**123.6**	**131.5**	**139.2**	**1,611.4**	Yield %	**1.0**	Market Cap	**US$2,097.1mil**

Address	**1-5-7, Mikuriya-Sakaemachi**	Tel	**06-788-1231**	ADR		President	**Kunihiko Ohtsuka**
	Higashi-Osaka City, Osaka 577	Fax	**06-788-1271**	SEDOL No.	**6440503**	Chairman	--

Hoya

Industry: **Medical Supplies**

Hoya is a major manufacturer of optical glass. The company has a worldwide network for the production and sale of eyeglasses that generates about 40% of net sales. Hoya is also known for optics (such as optical-lens blanks for cameras) and optical electronics (such as photomasks and large-scale masks for high-resolution liquid-crystal-display screens). The company's other lines of business include crystal products and contact lenses. Its major customers are Hoya Electronics, Hoya Optics, Toshiba, and Eye City. Hoya has five domestic plants and 29 consolidated subsidiaries.

	¥bil 03/93	03/94	03/95	US$mil 03/95				
Sales	**139.8**	**134.5**	**151.5**	**1,535.4**	P/E Ratio	**38.5**	Price (9/30/95)	**2,920.00**
Net Income	**5.3**	**6.1**	**8.8**	**89.3**	P/B Ratio	**2.8**	52 Wk Hi-Low	**2,940.0-1,980.0**
Book Value	**110.9**	**114.1**	**122.2**	**1,414.6**	Yield %	**0.6**	Market Cap	**US$3,410.6mil**

Address	**2-7-5, Naka-Ochiai**	Tel	**03-3952-1151**	ADR		President	**Mamoru Yamanaka**
	Shinjuku-ku, Tokyo 161	Fax	**03-3952-1314**	SEDOL No.	**6441506**	Chairman	**Tetsuo Suzuki**

Iino Kaiun Kaisha

Industry: **Marine Transportation**

Iino Kaiun is a tanker, LPG carrier, and specialized carrier operator. The firm's fleet consists of 93 ships and its typical cargoes are crude oil, lubricating oils, animal and vegetable oils, chemical products, liquefied natural gas, lumber, coal, grain, and fertilizer. Iino Kaiun has a tie-up with Reuters in England for information on shipping by introducing Reuters Monitor to its customers. It also operates Iino Sports clubs and convenience-store services. Its consolidated subsidiary, Iino Fudosan Kaisha, deals in real estate. It has close ties with Kawasaki Kisen.

	¥bil 03/93	03/94	03/95	US$mil 03/95				
Sales	**57.0**	**51.1**	**49.1**	**497.7**	P/E Ratio	**NMF**	Price (9/30/95)	**500.00**
Net Income	**-0.1**	**-0.7**	**-5.1**	**-52.0**	P/B Ratio	**2.6**	52 Wk Hi-Low	**722.00-442.00**
Book Value	**28.0**	**26.9**	**21.8**	**252.5**	Yield %	**0.0**	Market Cap	**US$559.8mil**

Address	**2-1-1, Uchi-Saiwaicho**	Tel	**03-3506-3033**	ADR		President	**Akira Karino**
	Chiyoda-ku, Tokyo 100	Fax	**03-3593-7884**	SEDOL No.	**6457008**	Chairman	--

Inax

Industry: **Building Materials**

Inax, a member of the Morimura group, is the top Japanese manufacturer of interior and exterior tiles, controlling about half of the market share. The firm also produces sanitary earthenware. It is attempting to become an integrated housing-equipment and -materials maker. Main customers include Aberuko, Hirata Tile, Marunishi Shoji, and Komatsu Bussan. Inax runs 15 plants throughout Japan and has 12 subsidiaries. It also has a joint venture, Sime Inax, with Sime Darby (Malaysia) and a cooperative agreement in technology and distribution with Interpace (U.S.).

¥bil	10/92 P	10/93 P	10/94 P	US$mil 10/94				
Sales	**270.8**	**267.7**	**271.0**	**2,615.3**	P/E Ratio	**60.7**	Price (9/30/95)	**989.00**
Net Income	**4.3**	**3.8**	**3.9**	**37.7**	P/B Ratio	**1.4**	52 Wk Hi-Low	**1,130.0-805.0**
Book Value	**164.7**	**166.5**	**168.5**	**1,738.0**	Yield %	**0.8**	Market Cap	**US$2,387.5mil**

Address **5-1, Koie-Honmachi**
Tokoname City, Aichi 479
Tel **0569-36-0226**
Fax **0569-34-2045**
ADR
SEDOL No. **6461504**
President **Teruzo Ina**
Chairman --

P=Parent company data.

Industrial Bank of Japan

Industry: **Banks - Money Center**

The Industrial Bank of Japan (Nippon Kogyo Ginko) is the largest of Japan's three long-term credit banks, and the leader of the IBJ group. It supplies long-term funds to many leading companies in conjunction with city banks. The financial and manufacturing sectors represent the largest portions of the bank's lending. IBJ also has a robust business in securities and international loans. It maintains transaction relationships with 90% of the top 200 Japanese companies. In 1994, overseas operations accounted for 40% of consolidated ordinary income.

¥bil	03/93	03/94	03/95	US$mil 03/95				
Revenues	**2,906.6**	**3,063.1**	**3,086.6**	**31,286.5**	P/E Ratio	**NMF**	Price (9/30/95)	**2,890.00**
Net Income	**40.9**	**21.9**	**29.7**	**300.9**	P/B Ratio	**4.8**	52 Wk Hi-Low	**3,130.0-1,940.0**
Book Value	**1,397.1**	**1,398.7**	**1,408.9**	**16,306.3**	Yield %	**0.3**	Market Cap	**US$68,354mil**

Address **1-3-3, Marunouchi**
Chiyoda-ku, Tokyo 100
Tel **03-3214-1111**
Fax **03-3213-6066**
ADR **ILBKY**
SEDOL No. **6462842**
President **Yo Kurosawa**
Chairman --

Isetan

Industry: **Retailers - Broadline**

Isetan is a major Japanese department-store chain of upper-tier merchandise whose flagship store in Shinjuku records one of the largest earnings in Japan's retail industry, generally consisting over 60% of parent sales. The firm sells luxury goods, fine art, jewelry, household goods, furniture, accessories, foodstuffs, and apparel. Isetan operates six major department stores in Japan. The firm has 14 consolidated subsidiaries including the Netherlands-based Isetan International Finance, the New York-based Isetan of America, and department stores in Hong Kong and Singapore.

¥bil	03/93	03/94	03/95	US$mil 03/95				
Revenues	**567.5**	**549.0**	**552.6**	**5,601.8**	P/E Ratio	**NMF**	Price (9/30/95)	**1,390.00**
Net Income	**3.3**	**3.2**	**1.9**	**19.1**	P/B Ratio	**2.0**	52 Wk Hi-Low	**1,850.0-1,070.0**
Book Value	**149.3**	**150.2**	**149.9**	**1,735.0**	Yield %	**0.7**	Market Cap	**US$3,080.6mil**

Address **3-14-1, Shinjuku**
Shinjuku-ku, Tokyo 160
Tel **03-3352-1111**
Fax **N/A**
ADR
SEDOL No. **6466844**
President **Kazumasa Koshiba**
Chairman **Shigekiyo Mukai**

Ishihara Sangyo Kaisha

Industry: **Commodity Chemicals**

Ishihara Sangyo Kaisha is a chemical company that specializes in titanium oxide, of which it is the largest producer in Japan. Agrichemicals and magnetic materials are the other two main areas of production. Its research and development efforts emphasize biotechnology, including the development of biopharmaceuticals. Ishihara Sangyo is involved in joint ventures with ICI (U.K.) to develop and market agrichemicals in Europe, and with Dupont (U.S.) to produce and market a new corn herbicide. The firm has 20 subsidiaries, eight of which are consolidated, and eight affiliates.

¥bil	03/93	03/94	03/95	US$mil 03/95				
Sales	**101.4**	**93.1**	**93.9**	**951.5**	P/E Ratio	**NMF**	Price (9/30/95)	**325.00**
Net Income	**-5.7**	**-5.3**	**-10.2**	**-103.9**	P/B Ratio	**1.8**	52 Wk Hi-Low	**444.00-235.00**
Book Value	**74.1**	**68.6**	**58.4**	**676.2**	Yield %	**0.0**	Market Cap	**US$1,036.7mil**

Address **1-3-15, Edobori**
Nishi-ku, Osaka 550
Tel **06-444-1853**
Fax **N/A**
ADR
SEDOL No. **6466866**
President **Takashi Akizawa**
Chairman **Kenzo Ishihara**

Ishikawajima-Harima Heavy Ind

Industry: **Heavy Machinery**

Ishikawajima-Harima Heavy Industries (Ishikawajima-Harima Jukogyo) manufactures an array of heavy machinery. The firm has top Japanese market shares in airplane engines and sky-parking systems. Its other products include iron- and steel-making equipment, industrial robots, gas turbines, and construction equipment. The firm is also active in the construction of thermal- and nuclear-power plants, oil- and gas-storage facilities, and ships. Ishikawajima-Harima has close ties with its main shareholder, Toshiba, in the construction of power plants, especially nuclear-power plants.

¥bil	03/93	03/94	03/95	US$mil 03/95				
Sales	**1,037.9**	**1,081.0**	**1,023.2**	**10,371.5**	P/E Ratio	**37.3**	Price (9/30/95)	**410.00**
Net Income	**17.8**	**11.6**	**14.3**	**145.4**	P/B Ratio	**2.8**	52 Wk Hi-Low	**488.00-301.00**
Book Value	**183.4**	**190.5**	**188.4**	**2,180.3**	Yield %	**1.5**	Market Cap	**US$5,354.9mil**

Address **2-2-1, Otemachi**
Chiyoda-ku, Tokyo 100
Tel **03-3244-5247**
Fax **03-3244-5139**
ADR
SEDOL No. **6466985**
President **Toshifumi Takei**
Chairman **Kosaku Inaba**

Isuzu Motors

Industry: **Automobile Manufacturers**

Isuzu Motors (Isuzu Jidosha), one of Japan's oldest automakers, specializes in the manufacture of small-, medium-, and large-size trucks. The firm ranks third in Japan in truck-production volume, with more than 350,000 units per year. In the five months through March 1995, overseas businesses generated 23% of total revenues, but operated at a loss. Isuzu made an agreement with GM to produce NPR trucks (marketed under the Elf name in Japan) in early 1994 in the U.S. Its cooperation with GM goes back to 1971, and GM holds a large equity stake in the company.

	¥bil 10/92	10/93	10/94	US$mil 10/94				
Sales	**1,580.1**	**1,561.8**	**1,597.4**	**15,415.7**	P/E Ratio	**NMF**	Price (9/30/95)	**454.00**
Net Income	**-29.0**	**-4.3**	**3.0**	**29.1**	P/B Ratio	**7.0**	52 Wk Hi-Low	**536.00-298.00**
Book Value	**70.6**	**63.5**	**66.8**	**689.4**	Yield %	**0.0**	Market Cap	**US$4,706.9mil**

Address	**6-26-1, Minami-Oi**	Tel	**03-5471-1111**	ADR	**ISUZY**	President	**Kazuhira Seki**
	Shinagawa-ku, Tokyo 140	Fax	**03-5471-1036**	SEDOL No.	**6467104**	Chairman	**Junji Takahashi**

Ito-Yokado

Industry: **Retailers - Broadline**

Ito-Yokado is Japan's second-largest supermarket operator; it also runs restaurants. The firm is known for its point-of-sales inventory-control system. Its restaurants include Denny's Japan and Famil. As of February 1995, the firm's network included 257 supermarkets and 265 other various specialty stores. Its affiliate Seven-Eleven Japan has a chain of 5,952 convenience stores. Ito-Yokado and Seven-Eleven Japan jointly own 64% of the Southland Corporation (U.S.). In fiscal 1994, North American operations accounted for 24% of revenues and 7% of operating income.

	¥bil 02/93	02/94	02/95	US$mil 02/95				
Revenues	**3,035.0**	**2,884.5**	**2,878.9**	**28,726.7**	P/E Ratio	**31.8**	Price (9/30/95)	**5,480.00**
Net Income	**64.8**	**58.7**	**71.3**	**711.4**	P/B Ratio	**3.0**	52 Wk Hi-Low	**5,600.0-4,140.0**
Book Value	**633.6**	**679.2**	**755.3**	**7,810.6**	Yield %	**0.6**	Market Cap	**US$22,856mil**

Address	**4-1-4, Shiba-Koen**	Tel	**03-3459-2111**	ADR	**IYCOY**	President	**Toshifumi Suzuki**
	Minato-ku, Tokyo 105	Fax	**03-3459-6873**	SEDOL No.	**6467944**	Chairman	--

Itochu

Industry: **Overseas Trading**

Itochu is ranked number one in sales among Japan's general-trading companies. The company's activities include the sale of textiles, machinery, and metals; the construction of housing and hotels; and civil-engineering work. It is expanding into the telecommunication field through its affiliates, Japan Communications Satellite and International Digital Communications. Worldwide, Itochu has more than 650 subsidiaries. China is one of the firm's fastest-growing overseas markets. In 1994, 42.8 % of Itochu's consolidated sales were made overseas.

	¥bil 03/93	03/94	03/95	US$mil 03/95				
Sales	**19,277.7**	**16,742.5**	**16,670.9**	**168,981.4**	P/E Ratio	**107.2**	Price (9/30/95)	**611.00**
Net Income	**4.0**	**-14.1**	**8.1**	**82.2**	P/B Ratio	**2.0**	52 Wk Hi-Low	**763.00-469.00**
Book Value	**503.5**	**465.3**	**446.3**	**5,165.3**	Yield %	**1.0**	Market Cap	**US$8,759.7mil**

Address	**4-1-3, Kyutaro-machi**	Tel	**06-241-2121**	ADR	**ITOCY**	President	**Minoru Murofushi**
	Chuo-ku, Osaka 541-77	Fax	**03-3497-7915**	SEDOL No.	**6467803**	Chairman	**Isao Yonekura**

Itoham Foods

Industry: **Other Food**

Itoham Foods (Ito Ham) is one of Japan's largest processors of ham. It sells sliced ham under the Hojun and Jun brand names. The company also makes processed and fresh-meat products, pizza, dairy foods such as butter and cheese, dressings, soft drinks, and snacks. Its sales network consists of 123 offices and 252 direct-sales outlets, with its products distributed through almost 80,000 wholesalers and retailers. Itoham imports processed beef from wholly-owned subsidiaries in the United States, and in Australia and New Zealand, where it operates livestock farms.

	¥bil 03/93	03/94	03/95	US$mil 03/95				
Sales	**486.0**	**463.0**	**452.1**	**4,582.6**	P/E Ratio	**49.2**	Price (9/30/95)	**757.00**
Net Income	**5.3**	**3.0**	**3.5**	**35.7**	P/B Ratio	**1.4**	52 Wk Hi-Low	**805.00-633.00**
Book Value	**123.2**	**123.8**	**125.1**	**1,447.8**	Yield %	**1.4**	Market Cap	**US$1,739.6mil**

Address	**4-27, Takahata-cho**	Tel	**0798-66-1231**	ADR		President	**Kenichi Ito**
	Nishinomiya City, Hyogo 663	Fax	**N/A**	SEDOL No.	**6467900**	Chairman	--

Iwatani International

Industry: **Overseas Trading**

Iwatani International (Iwatani Sangyo), a trading arm of the Sanwa group, is a specialty-gas trader. The company commands a large domestic market share in liquefied petroluem gas (LPG). It also trades in machinery, chemical products, agricultural and marine foods, consumer goods, building materials, and welding products. It has a joint venture with Union Carbide (U.S.), two joint ventures in Dalian (China), and an LPG-import contract with SAMAREC (Saudi Arabia). Iwatani is planning to consolidate and eliminate distribution bases through a business tie-up with Daido Hoxan.

	¥bil 03/93	03/94	03/95	US$mil 03/95				
Sales	**558.5**	**551.5**	**557.2**	**5,648.4**	P/E Ratio	**NMF**	Price (9/30/95)	**485.00**
Net Income	**1.6**	**0.8**	**0.4**	**3.6**	P/B Ratio	**2.4**	52 Wk Hi-Low	**629.15-390.00**
Book Value	**54.1**	**53.4**	**49.1**	**567.8**	Yield %	**1.2**	Market Cap	**US$1,226.2mil**

Address	**3-4-8, Honmachi**	Tel	**06-267-3322**	ADR		President	**Koji Saito**
	Chuo-ku, Osaka 541	Fax	**03-3555-5876**	SEDOL No.	**6468204**	Chairman	**Naoji Iwatani**

JACCS

Industry: **Financial Services - Diversified**

JACCS, the Japan Consumer Credit Service, is one of Japan's major credit companies. Its main services include loan guarantees, credit-card issuances, and personal loans. It has 126 branches, more than seven million cardholders, and 196,786 member retailers. JACCS issues MasterCard, VISA, and Japan Credit Bureau credit cards. It is also involved in car leasing and prepaid credit-card businesses. The firm has a cash-dispenser-sharing agreement with Dai-ichi Mutual Life Ins. and is a member of the Mitsubishi group. Its subsidiary, JACCS International, is in Delaware.

	¥bil 03/93 P	03/94 P	03/95 P	US$mil 03/95				
Revenues	**131.3**	**137.8**	**137.4**	**1,392.8**	P/E Ratio	**32.4**	Price (9/30/95)	**969.00**
Net Income	**3.2**	**4.1**	**4.6**	**46.3**	P/B Ratio	**2.4**	52 Wk Hi-Low	**1,140.0-730.0**
Book Value	**54.5**	**57.4**	**60.4**	**699.1**	Yield %	**0.9**	Market Cap	**US$1,487.2mil**

Address	**1-31-1, Nishi-Gotanda**	Tel	**03-3490-0971**	ADR		President	**Kenzo Kojima**
	Shinagawa-ku, Tokyo 141	Fax	**03-3490-4340**	SEDOL No.	**6468624**	Chairman	**Akira Watanabe**

P=Parent company data.

Japan Aircraft Manufacturing

Industry: **Aerospace & Defense**

Japan Aircraft Manufacturing (Nippon Hikoki), a Kawasaki Heavy Industries affiliate, produces aircraft bodies and parts, industrial machinery, and watercraft. The company's parts are used in Boeing 747s, 757s, and 767s, as well as virtually every plane assembled in Japan. Aircraft repair is another significant source of revenues. Its major customers are the Japanese Defense Agency and Kawasaki Heavy Machinery. It also does work for McDonnell Douglas. Many of its products are used in rockets and combat aircraft. Dai-ichi Mutual Life Insurance is the company's main lender.

	¥bil 03/93	03/94	03/95	US$mil 03/95				
Sales	**35.6**	**29.4**	**31.8**	**321.9**	P/E Ratio	**NMF**	Price (9/30/95)	**651.00**
Net Income	**0.2**	**0.1**	**0.2**	**1.9**	P/B Ratio	**2.0**	52 Wk Hi-Low	**790.00-400.00**
Book Value	**16.7**	**16.6**	**16.6**	**191.9**	Yield %	**0.6**	Market Cap	**US$331.9mil**

Address	**3175, Showa-machi**	Tel	**045-773-5110**	ADR		President	**Kanji Sonoda**
	Kanazawa-ku, Yokohama 236	Fax	**045-773-5102**	SEDOL No.	**6470340**	Chairman	**Teruaki Yamada**

Japan Airlines

Industry: **Airlines**

Japan Airlines (JAL), one of the world's major airlines, provides international and domestic air transport for passengers, cargo, and mail. The firm and its subsidiaries control about 30% of the Japanese international passenger market, serving more than 70 international and domestic destinations. The company also operates the Hotel Nikko chain through a subsidiary. Its computerized reservation system, Axess, dominates the Japanese market for the issue of international airline tickets. Japan Airlines is second to rival All Nippon Airways in passenger volume within Japan.

	¥bil 03/93	03/94	03/95	US$mil 03/95				
Sales	**1,283.8**	**1,256.6**	**1,348.4**	**13,668.0**	P/E Ratio	**NMF**	Price (9/30/95)	**639.00**
Net Income	**-47.9**	**-37.5**	**-14.6**	**-148.2**	P/B Ratio	**4.1**	52 Wk Hi-Low	**750.00-556.00**
Book Value	**339.6**	**302.8**	**279.8**	**3,239.0**	Yield %	**0.0**	Market Cap	**US$11,434mil**

Address	**2-7-3, Marunouchi**	Tel	**03-3284-2310**	ADR	**JAPNY**	President	**Akira Kondo**
	Chiyoda-ku, Tokyo 100	Fax	**03-3284-2528**	SEDOL No.	**6471871**	Chairman	**Susumu Yamaji**

Japan Airport Terminal

Industry: **Other Specialty Retailers**

Japan Airport Terminal (Nihonkuko Building) owns and leases property at Japan's major airports. It owns and operates the terminal building at Tokyo's Haneda airport, and leases retail space and runs gift shops at Narita and Haneda airports. Merchandise sales at these two airports account for over 50% of its consolidated sales. The company also provides other airport-related services such as information, parking, airline-ticket sales, travel insurance, hotel reservations, and baggage storage. Japan Airport Terminal has eight consolidated subsidiaries and two affiliates.

	¥bil 03/93	03/94	03/95	US$mil 03/95				
Revenues	**91.3**	**84.8**	**91.1**	**923.5**	P/E Ratio	**91.7**	Price (9/30/95)	**1,210.00**
Net Income	**3.2**	**1.1**	**1.3**	**13.5**	P/B Ratio	**1.6**	52 Wk Hi-Low	**1,360.0-1,000.0**
Book Value	**77.1**	**77.4**	**78.0**	**902.7**	Yield %	**0.6**	Market Cap	**US$1,223.6mil**

Address	**1-5-1, Marunouchi**	Tel	**03-3201-7116**	ADR		President	**Hiroshi Nagai**
	Chiyoda-ku, Tokyo 100	Fax	**03-3201-7110**	SEDOL No.	**6472175**	Chairman	**Hisao Takahashi**

Japan Energy

Industry: **Oil - Secondary**

Japan Energy, formerly called Nikko Kyodo, smelts nonferrous metals, and produces, refines, and distributes oil. The firm's metal-refining division produces zinc, aluminum, titanium, brass, and bronze in sheet and coil form. Its petroleum division produces naphtha, gasoline, jet fuel, kerosene, and heavy fuel oil. The firm is the fifth-largest Japanese producer of gasoline, with a market share of about 11%. It obtains oil from fields in China, Southeast Asia, and the Middle East. Japan Energy's main customers include Kyodo Oil, Nippon Mechatron, Mitsui Oil, and Nikko Sekiyu.

	¥bil 03/93	03/94	03/95	US$mil 03/95				
Sales	**1,317.5**	**1,803.3**	**1,868.2**	**18,936.5**	P/E Ratio	**NMF**	Price (9/30/95)	**290.00**
Net Income	**-28.9**	**6.8**	**-16.6**	**-167.8**	P/B Ratio	**2.5**	52 Wk Hi-Low	**436.00-265.00**
Book Value	**156.4**	**154.3**	**127.5**	**1,476.3**	Yield %	**1.7**	Market Cap	**US$3,190.9mil**

Address	**2-10-1, Toranomon**	Tel	**03-5573-6188**	ADR		President	**Kazushige Nagashima**
	Minato-ku, Tokyo 105	Fax	**03-5573-6773**	SEDOL No.	**6641209**	Chairman	**Yukio Kasahara**

Japan Securities Finance

Industry: **Financial Services - Diversified**

Japan Securities Finance (Nihon Shoken Kinyu) supplies short-term funds to securities houses and provides bond loans and other lending services. The call-loan market is the company's main source of funds, but it also borrows from the Bank of Japan and other financial services. It is one of the only independent companies, aside from brokerages, permitted to extend loans to securities companies for margin transactions. Japan Securities Finance is closely connected with and with regard to margin trading, acts as an unofficial regulatory body for the Tokyo Stock Exchange.

¥bil	03/93	03/94	03/95	US$mil 03/95				
Revenues	**57.4**	**50.4**	**43.3**	**438.9**	P/E Ratio	**62.2**	Price (9/30/95)	**1,430.00**
Net Income	**4.3**	**5.2**	**2.9**	**28.9**	P/B Ratio	**1.6**	52 Wk Hi-Low	**1,670.0-950.0**
Book Value	**94.5**	**102.9**	**109.7**	**1,270.2**	Yield %	**0.5**	Market Cap	**US$1,779.9mil**

Address **1-2-10, Nihonbashi-Kayabacho**
Chuo-ku, Tokyo 103
Tel **03-3666-0571**
Fax **03-3666-1403**
ADR
SEDOL No. **6470760**
President **Akira Aoki**
Chairman **Tatsuo Tajima**

Japan Steel Works

Industry: **Steel**

Japan Steel Works (Nihon Seikosho) is a malleable-cast-steel manufacturer. The company's products include cast and forged steel, steel sheets, resin machinery, plastics, and construction machinery. The company is also active in plant engineering. It produces military-related products, including tank guns, for the Japan Defense Agency (roughly 16% of parent-company revenues). In fiscal year 1994, 30.4% of Japan Steel Work's consolidated sales were made overseas, compared with 23.9% in 1993.

¥bil	03/93	03/94	03/95	US$mil 03/95				
Sales	**223.7**	**159.2**	**121.5**	**1,231.3**	P/E Ratio	**NMF**	Price (9/30/95)	**267.00**
Net Income	**2.7**	**-1.0**	**-4.2**	**-42.8**	P/B Ratio	**1.6**	52 Wk Hi-Low	**365.00-184.00**
Book Value	**69.1**	**66.6**	**62.2**	**720.1**	Yield %	**0.0**	Market Cap	**US$997.6mil**

Address **1-1-2, Yuraku-cho**
Chiyoda-ku, Tokyo 100
Tel **03-3501-6111**
Fax **03-3595-4629**
ADR **JPSWY**
SEDOL No. **6470685**
President **Keizo Ohnishi**
Chairman --

Japan Storage Battery

Industry: **Other Auto Parts**

Japan Storage Battery (Nippon Denchi), a member of the Mitsubishi group, specializes in manufacturing electronic equipment, which is marketed under the GS trademark. The company holds the top domestic market share (more than 30%) in automotive batteries. It also manufactures traction and industrial batteries, power-supply systems, lighting equipment, and cordless power tools. Japan Storage Battery supplies Nippon Yusoki and Toyoda Automatic Loom Works with traction batteries for forklifts, and also supplies products for portable electronic equipment to Sony and Aiwa.

¥bil	03/93	03/94	03/95	US$mil 03/95				
Sales	**107.6**	**103.0**	**108.7**	**1,101.6**	P/E Ratio	**90.9**	Price (9/30/95)	**609.00**
Net Income	**1.3**	**1.3**	**1.2**	**12.2**	P/B Ratio	**2.5**	52 Wk Hi-Low	**835.00-436.00**
Book Value	**41.6**	**42.0**	**43.3**	**501.4**	Yield %	**0.8**	Market Cap	**US$1,092.5mil**

Address **1, Inobanba-cho, Nishinosho**
Kisshoin Minami-ku, Kyoto 601
Tel **075-312-1211**
Fax **075-311-6704**
ADR
SEDOL No. **6470726**
President **Shigeru Negishi**
Chairman **Kensho Suematsu**

Japan Synthetic Rubber

Industry: **Tires & Rubber**

Japan Synthetic Rubber (Nihon Gosei Gomu), an affiliate of Bridgestone, is the third-largest synthetic rubber manufacturer in the world. The company is also Japan's leading maker of ABS plastics and paper-coating lattices. Synthetic rubbers and plastics are its best-selling products, providing about 55% and 35% of sales, respectively. The company is also diversifying into fine chemicals and electronic materials. Its major customers include Nichigo and Bridgestone. Japan Synthetic Rubber has three plants, two research facilities, and 10 consolidated subsidiaries in Japan.

¥bil	03/93	03/94	03/95	US$mil 03/95				
Sales	**204.6**	**180.2**	**191.7**	**1,943.5**	P/E Ratio	**80.8**	Price (9/30/95)	**590.00**
Net Income	**4.4**	**-2.2**	**1.9**	**19.3**	P/B Ratio	**1.5**	52 Wk Hi-Low	**688.00-390.00**
Book Value	**102.2**	**98.5**	**99.1**	**1,146.9**	Yield %	**0.8**	Market Cap	**US$1,539.8mil**

Address **2-11-24, Tsukiji**
Chuo-ku, Tokyo 104
Tel **03-5565-6500**
Fax **N/A**
ADR
SEDOL No. **6470986**
President **Eiichi Matsumoto**
Chairman **Tatsuo Asakura**

Japan Tobacco

Industry: **Tobacco**

Japan Tobacco (Nihon Tabako Sangyo) is the sole producer of tobacco products in Japan. The former government-owned monopoly, privatized in 1985, first sold stock to the public in October of 1994. The company trades on the first section of the Tokyo Stock Exchange. Japan Tobacco is currently four-fifths owned by the Japanese government and has a domestic market share of about 80%. The company is currently diversifying into pharmaceuticals, biochemicals, and foods. Japan Tobacco also has marketing associations with Philip Morris (U.S.).

¥bil	03/93	03/94	03/95	US$mil 03/95				
Sales	**3,333.5**	**3,393.6**	**3,502.5**	**35,502.3**	P/E Ratio	**NMF**	Price (9/30/95)	**853,000**
Net Income	**50.4**	**63.7**	**69.5**	**704.0**	P/B Ratio	**1.4**	52 Wk Hi-Low	**914,000-720,000**
Book Value	**1,070.9**	**1,124.3**	**1,196.9**	**13,853.0**	Yield %	**0.0**	Market Cap	**US$5,722.7mil**

Address **2-2-1, Toranomon**
Minato-ku, Tokyo 105
Tel **03-3582-3111**
Fax **03-5572-1441**
ADR
SEDOL No. **6474535**
President **Masaru Mizuno**
Chairman **Takeshi Hijikata**

Japan Wool Textile

Industry: **Clothing & Fabrics**

Japan Wool Textile (Nippon Keori) is a leading manufacturer of woolen textiles, which account for more than 50% of sales. Its products include yarns, fabrics, blankets, carpets, and uniforms. The company also leases land and operates shopping malls, fairways, and golf driving ranges. Its major customers include Chikuma, Nakahiro, and Akatsuki Shoji. Government agencies are the largest customers for the company's uniforms. Japan Wool Textile has 13 consolidated subsidiaries, 22 unconsolidated subsidiaries, and eight affiliates throughout Japan.

¥bil	11/92	11/93	11/94	US$mil 11/94				
Sales	**82.8**	**72.0**	**74.6**	**725.3**	P/E Ratio	**33.5**	Price (9/30/95)	**711.00**
Net Income	**4.0**	**2.2**	**2.0**	**19.4**	P/B Ratio	**1.3**	52 Wk Hi-Low	**1,210.0-711.0**
Book Value	**47.4**	**48.9**	**50.2**	**507.1**	Yield %	**1.0**	Market Cap	**US$674.9mil**

Address **3-3-10, Kawara-machi, Chuo-ku, Osaka 541**
Tel **06-205-6640** Fax **06-205-6644**
ADR SEDOL No. **6470704**
President **Yuichi Tomita** Chairman **Mitsuo Shiraha**

JDC

Industry: **Heavy Construction**

JDC (Nihon Kokudo Kaihatsu) is a general contractor that specializes in civil engineering. Among its projects are dams, hydroelectric-power plants, railways, agricultural facilities, waterworks, sewers, erosion control for waterways, and airports. Private contracts make up 60% of its current contracts. Building-construction projects include office buildings, amusement facilities, department stores, and hospitals. All four of its subsidiaries are located overseas: two in Singapore, and one each in Brazil and Brunei. JDC is involved in several construction projects overseas.

¥bil	03/93 P	03/94 P	03/95 P	US$mil 03/95				
Sales	**353.1**	**318.5**	**315.8**	**3,200.6**	P/E Ratio	**43.5**	Price (9/30/95)	**435.00**
Net Income	**3.6**	**3.0**	**1.8**	**18.0**	P/B Ratio	**1.8**	52 Wk Hi-Low	**669.00-340.00**
Book Value	**41.7**	**43.1**	**43.3**	**501.2**	Yield %	**1.7**	Market Cap	**US$772.8mil**

Address **4-9-9, Akasaka, Minato-ku, Tokyo 107**
Tel **03-3403-3311** Fax **03-5410-5621**
ADR SEDOL No. **6470607**
President **Akihiro Tsujioka** Chairman **--**

P=Parent company data.

Joyo Bank

Industry: **Banks - Regional**

Joyo Bank is the fourth-largest regional bank in Japan by assets. As the designated financial institution for the government of Ibaraki Prefecture, the bank is involved in a number of local-development projects. Joyo Bank offers comprehensive services to its customers through tie-up agreements with a securities firm, a trust bank, and life- and non-life-insurance companies. The distribution and service industries account for the largest portion of its loans. It has 149 branches and 27 representative offices in Japan, and representative offices in New York and Brussels.

¥bil	03/93 P	03/94 P	03/95 P	US$mil 03/95				
Revenues	**392.9**	**323.1**	**302.5**	**3,066.3**	P/E Ratio	**69.4**	Price (9/30/95)	**750.00**
Net Income	**13.4**	**10.2**	**8.7**	**87.8**	P/B Ratio	**1.9**	52 Wk Hi-Low	**865.00-681.00**
Book Value	**314.1**	**320.4**	**325.0**	**3,761.2**	Yield %	**0.7**	Market Cap	**US$6,065.9mil**

Address **2-5-5, Minami-machi, Mito City, Ibaraki 310**
Tel **0292-31-2151** Fax **0292-24-7525**
ADR SEDOL No. **6479767**
President **Toranosuke Nishino** Chairman **Itaru Ishikawa**

P=Parent company data.

Jusco

Industry: **Retailers - Broadline**

Jusco is Japan's third-largest supermarket-chain operator by revenues. In addition to supermarkets, the retailer and its subsidiaries operate discount stores, specialty shops, bookstores, department stores, restaurants, and consumer-credit services. The firm has 54 consolidated subsidiaries, including Wellmart, a supermarket chain in Hyogo Prefecture, and 66 subsidiaries. The firm acquired U.S. based Talbots in 1988, and has joint ventures with Laura Ashley and The Body Shop. In Asia, the firm operates more than a dozen Jusco superstores through subsidiaries.

¥bil	02/93	02/94	02/95	US$mil 02/95				
Revenues	**1,609.3**	**1,713.2**	**1,881.9**	**18,778.6**	P/E Ratio	**31.6**	Price (9/30/95)	**2,370.00**
Net Income	**8.3**	**25.9**	**23.2**	**231.0**	P/B Ratio	**2.9**	52 Wk Hi-Low	**2,370.0-1,560.0**
Book Value	**221.0**	**240.0**	**256.5**	**2,652.1**	Yield %	**0.8**	Market Cap	**US$7,355.9mil**

Address **1-5-1, Nakase, Minami-ku, Chiba 261**
Tel **043-212-6085** Fax **043-212-6809**
ADR **JUSCY** SEDOL No. **6480048**
President **Hidenori Futagi** Chairman **Takuya Okada**

Kajima

Industry: **Heavy Construction**

Kajima is a top general contractor involved in urban redevelopment, building construction, and civil engineering. The firm's civil-engineering works include railways, roads, sewerage, water- supply, and airport-related facilities. Construction projects, which include factories and office buildings, generate about 90% of consolidated sales. Kajima has 78 consolidated subsidiaries, with 28 in the U.S., 11 in France, seven in the Netherlands, four in the U.K., three in Germany, and one in Canada. Overseas revenues represent less than 10% of consolidated sales.

¥bil	03/93	03/94	03/95	US$mil 03/95				
Sales	**2,158.3**	**1,974.6**	**2,090.5**	**21,190.3**	P/E Ratio	**41.4**	Price (9/30/95)	**976.00**
Net Income	**17.1**	**1.2**	**22.7**	**230.1**	P/B Ratio	**2.4**	52 Wk Hi-Low	**1,040.0-790.0**
Book Value	**387.5**	**378.3**	**389.9**	**4,512.4**	Yield %	**0.9**	Market Cap	**US$9,437.1mil**

Address **1-2-7, Mota-Akasaka, Minato-ku, Tokyo 107**
Tel **03-3404-3311** Fax **03-3470-1444**
ADR **KAJMY** SEDOL No. **6481320**
President **Akira Miyazaki** Chairman **--**

Kamigumi

Industry: **Marine Transportation**

Kamigumi is a port-harbor transporter at the major ports of Tokyo, Yokohama, Nagoya, Osaka, Kobe, and Kanmon. Main activities include factory- and warehouse-cargo handling, road transport, warehouse and silo storage, freight forwarding, and customs clearance. The firm's network consists of 200 warehouses with 561,000 square meters of storage space and 467,000 square meters of silo space. Kamigumi is particularly strong in steel and heavy-cargo transport. It has three consolidated and 12 unconsolidated subsidiaries, and a network of affiliates throughout Southeast Asia.

¥bil	03/93	03/94	03/95	US$mil 03/95				
Sales	**140.6**	**147.9**	**148.3**	**1,503.2**	P/E Ratio	**35.5**	Price (9/30/95)	**929.00**
Net Income	**8.5**	**8.4**	**6.9**	**69.8**	P/B Ratio	**1.9**	52 Wk Hi-Low	**1,130.0-735.0**
Book Value	**106.1**	**121.2**	**125.8**	**1,455.9**	Yield %	**0.9**	Market Cap	**US$2,453.7mil**

Address	**4-1-11, Hamabedori**	Tel	**078-271-5110**	ADR		President	**Mutsumi Ozaki**
	Chuo-ku, Kobe 651	Fax	**N/A**	SEDOL No.	**6482668**	Chairman	**Tadashi Nagamine**

Kandenko

Industry: **Electrical Components & Equipment**

Kandenko is an electrical-engineering and construction contractor. It builds power stations, substations, and line equipment, and constructs cable tunnels and pits, manholes, and conduit lines. The firm also lays multicore fiberoptic cable and optical ground wire for digital-network telecommunication systems. It designs, installs, and maintains building equipment for private customers. Tokyo Electric Power, the firm's largest shareholder, is also its biggest customer, accounting for 50% of total sales. Kandenko has four subsidiaries, seven affiliates, and two offices in Asia.

¥bil	03/93 P	03/94 P	03/95 P	US$mil 03/95				
Sales	**546.0**	**580.1**	**531.9**	**5,391.7**	P/E Ratio	**23.4**	Price (9/30/95)	**1,340.00**
Net Income	**12.6**	**13.0**	**11.8**	**119.1**	P/B Ratio	**1.7**	52 Wk Hi-Low	**1,763.5-1,060.0**
Book Value	**129.0**	**140.5**	**150.3**	**1,739.8**	Yield %	**0.6**	Market Cap	**US$2,515.4mil**

Address	**4-8-33, Shibaura**	Tel	**03-5476-2111**	ADR		President	**Satoshi Hoshino**
	Minato-ku, Tokyo 108	Fax	**03-5476-3946**	SEDOL No.	**6483586**	Chairman	**Shojiro Komaki**

P=Parent company data.

Kanebo

Industry: **Clothing & Fabrics**

Kanebo is the second-largest textile firm in Japan by revenues, and has the second-largest domestic market share in cosmetics after Shiseido. In 1994, sales of Cosmetics and Textiles consisted of 34.3% and 34.1% of Kanebo's conosolidated sales, respectively. The firm makes silk, wool, cotton, nylon, polyester, and acrylic, as well as men's and women's apparel. Its licensed brand names include FILA, Christian Dior, and Hathaway. The company's nontextile goods include toiletries, drugs, foods, chemicals, and software. Kanebo has 72 subsudiaries and 26 affiliates.

¥bil	03/93	03/94	03/95	US$mil 03/95				
Sales	**659.7**	**583.6**	**590.0**	**5,980.3**	P/E Ratio	**NMF**	Price (9/30/95)	**222.00**
Net Income	**-10.3**	**-4.6**	**-0.7**	**-6.7**	P/B Ratio	**NMF**	52 Wk Hi-Low	**370.00-179.00**
Book Value	**4.9**	**1.7**	**2.3**	**27.2**	Yield %	**0.0**	Market Cap	**US$1,145.1mil**

Address	**1-5-90, Tomobuchi-cho**	Tel	**06-922-8055**	ADR		President	**Soichi Ishihara**
	Miyakojima-ku, Osaka 534	Fax	**06-922-8093**	SEDOL No.	**6483241**	Chairman	**Masao Nagata**

Kaneka

Industry: **Specialty Chemicals**

Kaneka (Kanegafuchi Kagaku Kogyo) is a chemical maker specializing in polyvinyl chloride. The firm's production line includes special-purpose resins, resin products, foodstuffs, medicine, electronic materials, and synthetic fibers. Currently, the firm is diversifying into biochemicals. Kaneka's largest customers are the medical, home-electronics, construction, electronic-cable, and office-automation industries. Kaneka has 26 consolidated subsidiaries, 20 of which are wholly-owned. Four subsidiaries are overseas plants in Singapore, the United States (two), and Belgium.

¥bil	03/93	03/94	03/95	US$mil 03/95				
Sales	**258.4**	**261.1**	**273.2**	**2,769.1**	P/E Ratio	**66.3**	Price (9/30/95)	**630.00**
Net Income	**4.2**	**3.0**	**3.3**	**33.6**	P/B Ratio	**1.6**	52 Wk Hi-Low	**821.00-510.00**
Book Value	**135.8**	**135.4**	**139.2**	**1,611.3**	Yield %	**1.1**	Market Cap	**US$2,217.6mil**

Address	**3-2-4, Nakanoshima**	Tel	**06-226-5169**	ADR		President	**Takeshi Furuta**
	Kita-ku, Osaka 530	Fax	**06-226-5177**	SEDOL No.	**6483360**	Chairman	**Tadasu Tachi**

Kanematsu

Industry: **Overseas Trading**

Kanematsu is one of the nine largest general-trading companies in Japan by sales. Its trading operations center around the import of raw materials, including fuels, chemicals, and metals. The firm also trades machinery, general merchandise, textiles, and foodstuffs and provisions; develops real estate; and exports Honda automobiles. Compared with Japan's other trading firms, Kanematsu depends heavily on domestic demand. It has operations in 54 countries, including Russia and eastern Europe. The company's joint ventures include ties with Telnet and a die-cast maker (U.S.).

¥bil	03/93	03/94	03/95	US$mil 03/95				
Sales	**5,916.8**	**5,691.5**	**5,548.5**	**56,241.1**	P/E Ratio	**NMF**	Price (9/30/95)	**360.00**
Net Income	**3.0**	**-6.5**	**-15.2**	**-154.0**	P/B Ratio	**1.3**	52 Wk Hi-Low	**551.00-300.00**
Book Value	**107.2**	**96.1**	**81.9**	**948.0**	Yield %	**1.4**	Market Cap	**US$1,052.6mil**

Address	**1-2-1, Shibaura**	Tel	**03-5440-8869**	ADR		President	**Masao Yosomiya**
	Minato-ku, Tokyo 105-05	Fax	**03-5440-6503**	SEDOL No.	**6483467**	Chairman	--

Kansai Electric Power

Industry: **Electrical Utilities - All**

Kansai Electric Power (Kansai Denryoku) is Japan's second-largest electric-power company in terms of generating capacity, kilowatt-hours sales, and revenues. It serves 11 million customers in Osaka, Kyoto, and Kobe, who consume about 20% of the nation's total electricity output. Kansai Electric is a pioneer in nuclear-power generation and is actively expanding its nuclear-energy capabilities. The utility's principal facilities consist of 20 hydroelectric-, 17 fossil-fuel, and three nuclear-power plants. The company has seven consolidated subsidiaries.

¥bil	03/93	03/94	03/95	US$mil 03/95				
Sales	2,367.3	2,371.8	2,541.5	25,761.7	P/E Ratio	54.1	Price (9/30/95)	2,460.00
Net Income	78.0	50.3	44.1	446.9	P/B Ratio	2.0	52 Wk Hi-Low	2,475.2-2,049.5
Book Value	1,072.6	1,074.3	1,203.4	13,928.8	Yield %	2.0	Market Cap	US$23,975mil

Address	**3-3-22, Nakanoshima**	Tel	**06-441-8821**	ADR		President	**Yoshihisa Akiyama**
	Kita-ku, Osaka 530-70	Fax	**06-441-8598**	SEDOL No.	**6483489**	Chairman	**Shoichiro Kobayashi**

Kansai Paint

Industry: **Specialty Chemicals**

Kansai Paint, part of the Sanwa group, is the largest paint manufacturer in Japan by sales. Its main product is synthetic-resin paint, which is used by automakers and accounts for more than 80% of parent-company sales. Other products include oil paints, lacquer, and paint thinner. The housing industry is also a major market for the firm's products. Its network includes six factories and 29 sales offices in Japan, and 12 offices and factories overseas. In addition, the firm has 23 consolidated subsidiaries in Japan and one each in Hong Kong, Taiwan, and Singapore.

¥bil	03/93	03/94	03/95	US$mil 03/95				
Sales	190.0	176.8	179.7	1,822.0	P/E Ratio	55.1	Price (9/30/95)	474.00
Net Income	4.4	2.5	2.4	24.3	P/B Ratio	1.7	52 Wk Hi-Low	614.00-400.00
Book Value	77.2	77.8	78.6	909.6	Yield %	1.3	Market Cap	US$1,330.8mil

Address	**4-3-6, Fushimi-machi**	Tel	**06-203-5531**	ADR		President	**Yoshio Sasaki**
	Chuo-ku, Osaka 541	Fax	**06-203-5018**	SEDOL No.	**6483746**	Chairman	**Masuo Tanaka**

Kao

Industry: **Cosmetics & Personal Care**

Kao is a leading maker of household goods, including personal-care, cosmetic, laundry, cleansing, and hygienic products. It has also diversified into floppy diskettes and fatty- and specialty chemicals. Kao has eight plants and 60 subsidiaries, which are located throughout the world. It owns the Andrew Jergens Company (U.S.) and Jergens Canada. Kao also has a joint venture with Guhl Kosmetik in Germany. It markets more than half of its goods through its own sales subsidiaries. In 1994, overseas sales accounted for 20% of total consolidated revenues.

¥bil	03/93	03/94	03/95	US$mil 03/95				
Sales	771.3	773.9	796.7	8,075.9	P/E Ratio	31.1	Price (9/30/95)	1,230.00
Net Income	20.4	22.2	23.7	240.1	P/B Ratio	2.2	52 Wk Hi-Low	1,230.0-960.0
Book Value	307.3	324.4	342.0	3,958.4	Yield %	0.9	Market Cap	US$7,426.6mil

Address	**1-14-10, Nihonbashi-Kayabacho**	Tel	**03-3660-7080**	ADR	**KAOCY**	President	**Fumikatsu Tokiwa**
	Chuo-ku, Tokyo 103	Fax	**03-3660-7092**	SEDOL No.	**6483809**	Chairman	**Hiromi Nakagawa**

Katokichi

Industry: **Other Food**

Katokichi produces frozen foods, including fish products. The company ranks second among Japanese producers of frozen food, holding about 11% of the domestic market. Nonfish products, such as noodles and mixes, account for 70% of the firm's sales. Katokichi is also known for operating the Eitaro restaurant chain. All of the company's production facilities are concentrated in Kagawa Prefecture. It is starting up new facilities for frozen-food production at plants in Ryugasaki and Koyo Seika. It has 24 subsidiaries, eight of which are consolidated.

¥bil	11/92	11/93	11/94	US$mil 11/94				
Sales	127.3	135.5	144.9	1,408.8	P/E Ratio	27.2	Price (9/30/95)	1,890.00
Net Income	2.2	2.9	3.9	37.4	P/B Ratio	1.2	52 Wk Hi-Low	2,490.0-1,700.0
Book Value	77.2	87.7	90.4	913.8	Yield %	1.3	Market Cap	US$1,054.5mil

Address	**Ko-1490-1, Kanonji-machi**	Tel	**0875-56-1131**	ADR		President	**Yoshio Matsuda**
	Kanonji City, Kagawa 768	Fax	**0875-56-1139**	SEDOL No.	**6484244**	Chairman	**Yoshikazu Kato**

Kawasaki Heavy Industries

Industry: **Industrial - Diversified**

Kawasaki Heavy Industries (Kawasaki Jukogyo) manufactures heavy machinery and provides plant-engineering services. The company's products include rolling stock, ships, aircraft, steel structures, motorcycles, and engines. It holds 20% of the world market for large motorcycles, and the largest share (about 35%) of the domestic rolling-stock market. The firm supplies the Japan Defense Agency with patrol planes, helicopters, and missiles. It also collaborates with Boeing to produce the B777 airplane. The company has plants in the United States, the Philippines, and Brazil.

¥bil	03/93	03/94	03/95	US$mil 03/95				
Sales	1,090.5	1,070.3	1,070.4	10,850.4	P/E Ratio	53.7	Price (9/30/95)	408.00
Net Income	14.4	17.1	10.2	103.6	P/B Ratio	3.6	52 Wk Hi-Low	484.00-288.00
Book Value	131.6	148.3	153.0	1,770.7	Yield %	1.2	Market Cap	US$5,522.3mil

Address	**1-1-3, Higashi-Kawasakicho**	Tel	**078-371-9551**	ADR		President	**Hiroshi Ohba**
	Chuo-ku Kobe, Hyogo 650	Fax	**03-3432-4759**	SEDOL No.	**6484620**	Chairman	--

Kawasaki Kisen Kaisha

Industry: **Marine Transportation**

Kawasaki Kisen, or "K" Line, is Japan's third-largest shipping firm in terms of sales. The company operates liners, bulk carriers, and oil tankers along scheduled and unscheduled shipping routes but it is especially well-established as a car carrier. The trans-Pacific and inter-Asian routes are its key markets. Container terminals and double-stack trains integrate its marine-transport services with its land-bound network in America. Kawasaki Kisen also has diversified into transport agencies and luxury resorts.

	¥bil 03/93	03/94	03/95	US$mil 03/95				
Sales	**498.8**	**444.1**	**449.0**	**4,550.9**	P/E Ratio	**47.6**	Price (9/30/95)	**300.00**
Net Income	**-2.7**	**2.8**	**3.7**	**37.6**	P/B Ratio	**3.1**	52 Wk Hi-Low	**328.00-219.00**
Book Value	**51.6**	**53.9**	**57.2**	**661.6**	Yield %	**0.0**	Market Cap	**US$1,766.8mil**

Address **1-2-9, Nishi-Shinbashi**
Minato-ku, Tokyo 0105
Tel **03-3595-5634**
Fax **03-3595-6155**
ADR
SEDOL No. **6484686**
President **Isao Shintani**
Chairman **Shiro Nagumo**

Kawasaki Steel

Industry: **Steel**

Kawasaki Steel (Kawasaki Seitetsu), a major blast-furnace steelmaker, specializes in manufacturing thin plates for the automotive and industrial- and electrical-machinery industries. The company also makes other steel products, chemical products, and has a sizable engineering and construction division. The firm produces about 10% of Japan's crude steel annually. Kawasaki Steel's largest customer (more than falf of parent-company sales) is steel-specialist-trader Kawasho. The firm is diversifying into nonsteel businesses such as electronics, robotics, and advanced materials.

	¥bil 03/93	03/94	03/95	US$mil 03/95				
Sales	**1,310.2**	**1,185.1**	**1,148.8**	**11,644.3**	P/E Ratio	**NMF**	Price (9/30/95)	**356.00**
Net Income	**-30.0**	**-22.0**	**-31.7**	**-321.5**	P/B Ratio	**2.5**	52 Wk Hi-Low	**457.00-275.00**
Book Value	**549.3**	**501.4**	**466.5**	**5,399.5**	Yield %	**0.0**	Market Cap	**US$11,643mil**

Address **2-2-3, Uchi-Saiwaicho**
Chiyoda-ku, Tokyo 100
Tel **03-3597-3270**
Fax **03-3597-4911**
ADR **KSKSY**
SEDOL No. **6484664**
President **Kanji Emoto**
Chairman **Shinobu Tosaki**

Kayaba Industry

Industry: **Other Auto Parts**

Kayaba Industry (Kayaba Kogyo) produces hydraulic components and shock absorbers. The company holds the largest share of the Japanese market in shock absorbers for cars, and the second-largest for motorcycles. It also makes hydraulic systems for trains and construction machinery, and is the only Japanese supplier of aircraft brakes. Boeing is a major customer. Kayaba's products are sold in more than 90 countries under the KYB brand. The auto industry accounts for about 87% of Kayaba's consolidated revenues. It has seven wholly-owned overseas production and sales units.

	¥bil 03/93	03/94	03/95	US$mil 03/95				
Sales	**192.8**	**185.4**	**209.5**	**2,123.3**	P/E Ratio	**21.7**	Price (9/30/95)	**465.00**
Net Income	**1.6**	**1.3**	**4.8**	**48.5**	P/B Ratio	**1.8**	52 Wk Hi-Low	**673.00-398.00**
Book Value	**49.1**	**49.1**	**60.7**	**703.1**	Yield %	**1.5**	Market Cap	**US$1,080.3mil**

Address **2-4-1, Hamamatsu-cho**
Minato-ku, Tokyo 105
Tel **03-3435-3541**
Fax **03-3436-6759**
ADR
SEDOL No. **6485009**
President **Takashi Chano**
Chairman **Yaichi Iso**

Keihan Electric Railway

Industry: **Railroads**

Keihan Electric Railway (Keihan Denki Tetsudo) is a major Kanto-area rail company that is involved in real-estate and leisure-related activities. Its railway lines connect Tokyo, Yokohama, and the Miura peninsula, and an express line links Narita International Airport and Haneda Airport. The firm realizes substantial revenues from its real-estate activities. It designs, constructs, and manages residential and commercial complexes, and operates department stores, restaurants, hotels, and amusement facilities. Keihan has 24 consolidated and 33 unconsolidated subsidiaries.

	¥bil 03/93	03/94	03/95	US$mil 03/95				
Sales	**229.2**	**227.7**	**240.4**	**2,436.7**	P/E Ratio	**102.9**	Price (9/30/95)	**432.00**
Net Income	**3.8**	**2.8**	**2.3**	**23.6**	P/B Ratio	**2.2**	52 Wk Hi-Low	**449.00-385.56**
Book Value	**102.9**	**103.6**	**104.4**	**1,207.8**	Yield %	**1.1**	Market Cap	**US$2,397.0mil**

Address **1-2-27, Shiromi**
Chuo-ku, Osaka 540
Tel **06-944-2527**
Fax **06-944-2501**
ADR
SEDOL No. **6487232**
President **Minoru Miyashita**
Chairman **Hiroshi Sumita**

Keihin Electric Express Railway

Industry: **Railroads**

Keihin Electric Express Railway (Keihin Kyuko Dentetsu) is a midsize private railroad company that is also active in railways, real-estate development, and leisure-related services. Its train lines provide service between Kyoto and Osaka. The company operates an express service connecting New Tokyo International Airport and Haneda Airport and provides regular and chartered bus service. Keihin Electric also owns hotels, restaurants, sports facilities, bus lines, taxi companies, a travel agency, and department stores. It has 31 consolidated subsidiaries.

	¥bil 03/93	03/94	03/95	US$mil 03/95				
Sales	**238.8**	**243.7**	**256.2**	**2,596.8**	P/E Ratio	**NMF**	Price (9/30/95)	**597.00**
Net Income	**4.0**	**2.4**	**1.0**	**10.5**	P/B Ratio	**3.0**	52 Wk Hi-Low	**644.00-536.00**
Book Value	**97.5**	**97.3**	**98.6**	**1,141.4**	Yield %	**0.8**	Market Cap	**US$2,986.4mil**

Address **2-20-20, Takanawa**
Minato-ku, Tokyo 108
Tel **03-3280-9135**
Fax **03-3280-9195**
ADR
SEDOL No. **6487306**
President **Ichiro Hiramatsu**
Chairman --

Keio Teito Electric Railway

Industry: **Railroads**

Keio Teito Electric Railway (Keio Teito Dentetsu) is a leading railroad company operating in the Kanto area. The company is also active in real estate and leisure-related fields. It operates two main lines, the Keio and the Inokashira. Its Sagamihara Line is linked to Japan Railway's Yokohama and Sagami Line, and connects Tokyo to Kanagawa Prefecture. Keio runs local bus routes and offers taxi services and sightseeing, as well as nationwide express-bus service. The firm also owns hotels, department stores, and shops in train stations. It has 25 consolidated subsidiaries.

¥bil	03/93	03/94	03/95	US$mil 03/95				
Sales	**441.1**	**428.1**	**450.3**	**4,564.2**	P/E Ratio	**75.1**	Price (9/30/95)	**571.00**
Net Income	**5.8**	**5.2**	**4.9**	**49.7**	P/B Ratio	**2.8**	52 Wk Hi-Low	**594.00-496.00**
Book Value	**117.5**	**129.0**	**133.3**	**1,543.1**	Yield %	**0.9**	Market Cap	**US$3,709.1mil**

Address **1-9-1, Sekido**
Tama City, Tokyo 206
Tel **0423-37-3132**
Fax **0423-74-9810**
ADR
SEDOL No. **6487362**
President **Hiroichi Nishiyama**
Chairman **Kenichi Kuwayama**

Keisei Electric Railway

Industry: **Railroads**

Keisei Electric Railway (Keisei Dentetsu) is a Kanto-based railway firm that has diversified into real estate and leisure-related activities. The company operates in Tokyo and Chiba Prefecture. It runs the Tokyo-Chiba railway line, two express lines to Narita Airport, an express service connecting Narita Airport to Haneda Airport, and a bus fleet. Keisei also operates movie theaters, hotels, and restaurants. The firm is a major shareholder of Oriental Land, which manages Tokyo Disneyland. Altogether it has 19 consolidated and 26 unconsolidated subsidiaries.

¥bil	03/93	03/94	03/95	US$mil 03/95				
Sales	**197.1**	**197.4**	**204.5**	**2,072.5**	P/E Ratio	**51.9**	Price (9/30/95)	**815.00**
Net Income	**1.9**	**3.2**	**4.3**	**43.2**	P/B Ratio	**8.0**	52 Wk Hi-Low	**854.00-559.00**
Book Value	**21.1**	**23.1**	**27.5**	**318.7**	Yield %	**0.5**	Market Cap	**US$2,227.0mil**

Address **1-10-3, Oshiage**
Sumida-ku, Tokyo 131
Tel **03-3621-2242**
Fax **03-3621-2292**
ADR
SEDOL No. **6487425**
President **Hiroto Senoo**
Chairman **Kurao Murata**

Keiyo

Industry: **Household Products (Durable)**

Keiyo operates home-center chain stores in Japan. The stores sell home-improvement products, household utensils, and sporting goods. Principal items sold include hardware, paints, building materials, and gardening supplies. In 1994, Keiyo had 82 home centers in its store network. Secondary activities are real-estate leasing and the sale of petroleum products. Keiyo has a joint venture with Jusco to operate discount stores. It has one consolidated and eight unconsolidated subsidiaries, and five affiliates. Keiyo's expansion plans are concentrated in the Kanto region.

¥bil	02/93	02/94	02/95	US$mil 02/95				
Sales	**115.8**	**123.4**	**132.5**	**1,322.1**	P/E Ratio	**43.6**	Price (9/30/95)	**1,050.00**
Net Income	**2.3**	**1.5**	**1.4**	**13.9**	P/B Ratio	**1.4**	52 Wk Hi-Low	**1,940.0-795.0**
Book Value	**39.1**	**44.1**	**45.2**	**466.9**	Yield %	**1.2**	Market Cap	**US$628.1mil**

Address **1-28-1, Mitsuwadai, Wakaba-ku**
Chiba City, Chiba 264
Tel **043-255-1111**
Fax **043-253-5951**
ADR
SEDOL No. **6487458**
President **Ken Nagai**
Chairman **Koki Nagai**

Keyence

Industry: **Industrial Technology**

Keyence manufactures sensors and measuring equipment. It produces magnetic and optical sensors for factory automation, with its products serving automobile, semiconductor, and communication-equipment manufacturers. Main customers include its own subsidiaries, Keyence Corporation of America and Keyence Deutschland, as well as Toshiba, Canon, and Scigate. Most of the firm's production is conducted through subcontractors; distribution is handled by a direct-sales network that operates in 35 countries. In 1994, overseas sales accounted for 13% of its consolidated sales.

¥bil	03/93 *	03/94	03/95 *	US$mil 03/95				
Sales	**29.9**	**31.3**	**38.7**	**392.6**	P/E Ratio	**54.1**	Price (9/30/95)	**12,300**
Net Income	**6.2**	**6.6**	**7.8**	**79.0**	P/B Ratio	**4.1**	52 Wk Hi-Low	**13,100.0-8,550.0**
Book Value	**90.4**	**96.5**	**103.7**	**1,200.1**	Yield %	**0.1**	Market Cap	**US$4,246.1mil**

Address **2-13, Aketa-cho**
Takatsuki City, Osaka 569
Tel **0726-84-1111**
Fax **0726-84-0111**
ADR
SEDOL No. **6490995**
President **Takemitsu Takizaki**
Chairman --

*Irregular period due to fiscal year change.

Kikkoman

Industry: **Other Food**

Kikkoman is a major soy-sauce brewer, controlling 30% of Japan's market. Other products include wine, tofu, health foods, mirin (cooking wine), sauces, miso, and soups. The firm holds about 10% of the domestic wine market, and it also imports and markets wines from Europe and the U.S. It has marketing rights to Del Monte juices and tomato products, Ragu sauces, Ocean Spray cranberry drinks, and Lea & Perrins Worcestershire sauce in Japan. One of its main customers is Kokubu & Co., a food wholesaler. Kikkoman has plants in the U.S., Singapore, Taiwan, and Brazil.

¥bil	12/92	12/93	12/94	US$mil 12/94				
Sales	**211.7**	**203.5**	**201.0**	**1,969.3**	P/E Ratio	**20.2**	Price (9/30/95)	**711.00**
Net Income	**4.9**	**4.7**	**6.6**	**64.8**	P/B Ratio	**1.6**	52 Wk Hi-Low	**845.00-583.00**
Book Value	**78.4**	**81.7**	**86.0**	**861.7**	Yield %	**1.0**	Market Cap	**US$1,343.1mil**

Address **339, Noda**
Noda City, Chiba 278
Tel **0471-23-5111**
Fax **0471-23-5200**
ADR
SEDOL No. **6490809**
President **Yuzaburo Mogi**
Chairman --

Kinden

Industry: **Electrical Components & Equipment**

Kinden, an affiliate of Kansai Electric Power, is the second-largest electrical-engineering company in Japan by sales. The company's areas of business include electrical and telecommunication engineering, air-conditioning-piping work, instrumentation, interior-wiring work, security-system installation, and civil engineering. General-wiring projects make up more than 65% of total sales, and work on power-distribution lines accounts for 20%. Kinden is currently increasing its optical-communication and office-automation-wiring work. It has 25 subsidiaries and affiliates.

¥bil	03/93 P	03/94 P	03/95 P	US$mil 03/95				
Sales	**501.3**	**540.8**	**560.6**	**5,682.6**	P/E Ratio	**23.5**	Price (9/30/95)	**1,710.00**
Net Income	**17.1**	**18.1**	**19.4**	**196.5**	P/B Ratio	**1.7**	52 Wk Hi-Low	**1,863.5-1,390.8**
Book Value	**207.0**	**225.0**	**241.9**	**2,799.5**	Yield %	**0.5**	Market Cap	**US$4,157.2mil**

Address **2-3-41, Honjo-Higashi, Kita-ku, Osaka 531**
Tel **06-375-6000** Fax **06-375-6370**
ADR SEDOL No. **6492924**
President **Taizo Oka** Chairman **Yasushi Aramaki**

P=Parent company data.

Kinki Nippon Railway

Industry: **Railroads**

Kinki Nippon Railway (Kinki Nippon Tetsudo) is a leading railway operator in the Osaka and Nagoya regions that has diversified into retail and real-estate operations. Its rail network is located in the Kinki and Tokai districts. The firm runs a nationwide bus service, a taxi service, and owns a fleet of trucks. Most of the firm's revenues come from retail sales, leisure-related activities, and real-estate operations. Kinki Nippon also manages hotels, department stores, aerial trams, ferries, and sightseeing cruises. It forms the Kintetsu group with over 85 subsidiaries.

¥bil	03/93	03/94	03/95	US$mil 03/95				
Sales	**877.2**	**870.8**	**922.4**	**9,349.8**	P/E Ratio	**NMF**	Price (9/30/95)	**810.00**
Net Income	**9.1**	**4.2**	**2.1**	**21.2**	P/B Ratio	**6.0**	52 Wk Hi-Low	**840.00-713.00**
Book Value	**225.7**	**222.1**	**213.0**	**2,465.6**	Yield %	**0.6**	Market Cap	**US$12,814mil**

Address **6-1-55, Ue-Honmachi, Tennoji-ku, Osaka 543**
Tel **06-775-3511** Fax **06-775-3467**
ADR SEDOL No. **6492968**
President **Wa Tashiro** Chairman **Shigeichiro Kanamori**

Kirin Brewery

Industry: **Distillers & Brewers**

Kirin Brewery is Japan's largest brewer, controlling almost 50% of the domestic beer market. It ranks fifth worldwide in beer-sales volume. Its main brands are Kirin Lager (the top-selling beer in Japan), Ichiban Shibori, and Kirin Draft. Kirin has joint ventures with Seagram and Molson (Canada), Tropicana Products (U.S.), and San Miguel Brewery (Hong Kong). The company has a joint venture with Anheuser-Busch (U.S.) to market Budweiser beer in Japan. It also has technical tie-ups with Netherlands-based Heineken and the Czech Republic's Pilsner Urquell Brewery.

¥bil	12/92	12/93	12/94	US$mil 12/94				
Sales	**1,601.9**	**1,574.8**	**1,698.6**	**16,643.8**	P/E Ratio	**21.0**	Price (9/30/95)	**1,040.00**
Net Income	**47.8**	**42.9**	**52.2**	**511.7**	P/B Ratio	**1.6**	52 Wk Hi-Low	**1,170.0-900.0**
Book Value	**620.9**	**652.4**	**693.0**	**6,945.5**	Yield %	**1.1**	Market Cap	**US$11,010mil**

Address **6-26-1, Jingumae, Shibuya-ku, Tokyo 150**
Tel **03-3499-6111** Fax **03-3499-6190**
ADR **KNBWY** SEDOL No. **6493745**
President **Keisaku Manabe** Chairman --

Kitano Construction

Industry: **Heavy Construction**

Kitano Construction (Kitano Kensetsu) is a general contractor involved in general construction, civil-engineering works, and real estate. The company is active in redevelopment projects in Tokyo and Nagano City, where it is based. Local construction projects account for 50% of its work. Private-sector orders account for 76% of its current contracts; many of these are for hotel and condominium construction. Kitano Construction has 12 subsidiaries and affiliates. Three of Kitano's subsidiaries operate hotels and golf courses in the Solomon Islands, Samoa, and Australia.

¥bil	03/93	03/94	03/95	US$mil 03/95				
Sales	**90.3**	**82.8**	**85.3**	**864.3**	P/E Ratio	**33.6**	Price (9/30/95)	**698.00**
Net Income	**2.3**	**1.8**	**1.6**	**16.6**	P/B Ratio	**1.7**	52 Wk Hi-Low	**924.00-502.00**
Book Value	**30.7**	**31.6**	**32.6**	**377.6**	Yield %	**1.3**	Market Cap	**US$552.4mil**

Address **524, Agata-machi, Nagano City, Nagano 380**
Tel **0262-33-5111** Fax **0262-35-3113**
ADR SEDOL No. **6494168**
President **Tsuguto Kitano** Chairman --

Kobe Steel

Industry: **Steel**

Kobe Steel (Kobe Seikosho) is one of Japan's five largest steelmakers, accounting for about 6% of Japan's total annual crude-steel production. The company manufactures aluminum and aluminum-alloy products, welding equipment, cutting tools, and construction machinery. It has also expanded into semiconductor manufacturing, factory-automation machinery and robotics, and information systems. Kobe Steel has the largest domestic market share for rolled aluminum and aluminum sheets. The company's main steelworks in Kakogawa and Kobe have a total of six blast furnaces.

¥bil	03/93	03/94	03/95	US$mil 03/95				
Sales	**1,334.1**	**1,249.0**	**1,335.6**	**13,537.9**	P/E Ratio	**NMF**	Price (9/30/95)	**279.00**
Net Income	**-14.3**	**-8.3**	**-92.4**	**-936.8**	P/B Ratio	**3.0**	52 Wk Hi-Low	**335.00-196.00**
Book Value	**389.9**	**371.5**	**264.8**	**3,064.3**	Yield %	**0.0**	Market Cap	**US$7,957.0mil**

Address **1-3-18, Wakinohama-cho, Chuo-ku, Kobe 651**
Tel **078-261-5206** Fax **03-5252-7961**
ADR **KBSTY** SEDOL No. **6496023**
President **Sokichi Kametaka** Chairman **Yugoro Komatsu**

Koito Manufacturing

Industry: **Other Auto Parts**

Koito Manufacturing (Koito Seisakusho), a member of the Toyota group, produces headlights and taillights, sealed-beam lamps, and halogen light bulbs for automobiles. It also makes aircraft parts, such as electronic equipment, displays, lighting, and hydraulic equipment. Other products include printed circuit boards, power-window regulators, electronic components, and resin products. About 45% of the parent company's sales are to Toyota, which owns about 20% of its shares. Koito Manufacturing has six manufacturing plants and five consolidated subsidiaries in Japan.

	¥bil 03/93	03/94	03/95	US$mil 03/95				
Sales	**242.3**	**232.1**	**225.1**	**2,281.9**	P/E Ratio	**25.1**	Price (9/30/95)	**690.00**
Net Income	**2.9**	**2.9**	**4.4**	**44.7**	P/B Ratio	**1.5**	52 Wk Hi-Low	**850.00-525.00**
Book Value	**67.8**	**69.3**	**72.9**	**843.7**	Yield %	**1.3**	Market Cap	**US$1,113.6mil**

Address **4-8-3, Takanawa, Minato-ku, Tokyo 108**
Tel **03-3443-7111**
Fax **03-3447-1520**
ADR
SEDOL No. **6496324**
President **Yoshiro Nagamura**
Chairman --

Kokusai Electric

Industry: **Electrical Components & Equipment**

Kokusai Electric (Kokusai Denki) manufactures pagers, wireless-communication equipment, data-communication systems, semiconductor integrated circuits, and semiconductor manufacturing equipment. Hitachi, its top shareholder (20.9%), is also the firm's major customer. Other customers include Sony, the Japanese government, Intel Semiconductor, and Nippon Telegraph and Telephone. Kokusai Electric also supplies stock-price-information systems to the Tokyo Stock Exchange. The firm has eight consolidated subsidiaries, including Bruce Technologies International (U.S.).

	¥bil 03/93	03/94	03/95	US$mil 03/95				
Sales	**120.7**	**129.1**	**143.8**	**1,457.2**	P/E Ratio	**50.2**	Price (9/30/95)	**2,260.00**
Net Income	**0.5**	**0.8**	**3.3**	**33.0**	P/B Ratio	**2.8**	52 Wk Hi-Low	**2,450.0-1,410.0**
Book Value	**55.0**	**54.8**	**57.9**	**670.5**	Yield %	**0.6**	Market Cap	**US$1,645.6mil**

Address **3-14-20, Higashi-Nakano, Nakano-ku, Tokyo 164**
Tel **03-3368-6111**
Fax **03-3365-9119**
ADR
SEDOL No. **6496368**
President **Shotaro Shibata**
Chairman --

Kokuyo

Industry: **Other Home Furnishings**

Kokuyo manufactures a wide range of office-related materials. Its product line of about 120,000 items includes stationery, school supplies, office equipment, and home and office furniture. The firm is Japan's leading office-stationery maker. The Kuroda family holds top management positions and is among the top shareholders. Kokuyo has a national distribution network of 25 delivery centers, 66 sales companies (at least one in every prefecture), and about 350 sales agents. It has eight consolidated and 9 unconsolidated subsidiaries, all of which are located in Japan.

	¥bil 03/93	03/94	03/95	US$mil 03/95				
Sales	**309.1**	**290.5**	**299.1**	**3,032.0**	P/E Ratio	**30.5**	Price (9/30/95)	**2,100.00**
Net Income	**11.1**	**8.6**	**9.0**	**91.1**	P/B Ratio	**1.7**	52 Wk Hi-Low	**2,650.0-1,890.0**
Book Value	**146.1**	**152.6**	**160.9**	**1,861.8**	Yield %	**0.8**	Market Cap	**US$2,760.8mil**

Address **6-1-1, Oimazato-Minami, Higashinari-ku, Osaka 537**
Tel **06-976-1221**
Fax **06-972-9589**
ADR
SEDOL No. **6496506**
President **Akihiro Kuroda**
Chairman **Shonosuke Kuroda**

Komatsu

Industry: **Heavy Machinery**

Komatsu (Komatsu Seisakusho) is Japan's largest construction-machinery maker, second only to Caterpillar (U.S.) worldwide. The company holds the largest Japanese market shares in bulldozers (60%), hydraulic shovels (32%), and mini-backhoes (30%). It also makes cranes, tunnel machinery, presses, cutting machines, and turret-punch presses. Komatsu has a controlling interest in Hanomag, a German maker of construction equipment, and has a joint venture with Dresser Industries in the U.S. The company has five plants in Japan, and others in the U.K., Indonesia, and Brazil.

	¥bil 03/93	03/94	03/95	US$mil 03/95				
Sales	**869.9**	**845.9**	**918.9**	**9,314.4**	P/E Ratio	**78.0**	Price (9/30/95)	**796.00**
Net Income	**3.0**	**1.3**	**10.2**	**103.6**	P/B Ratio	**1.4**	52 Wk Hi-Low	**924.00-574.00**
Book Value	**516.4**	**505.9**	**575.5**	**6,661.3**	Yield %	**1.0**	Market Cap	**US$8,037.8mil**

Address **2-3-6, Akasaka, Minato-ku, Tokyo 107**
Tel **03-5561-2604**
Fax **03-3505-9662**
ADR **KMATY**
SEDOL No. **6496584**
President **Satoru Anzaki**
Chairman **Tetsuya Katada**

Komori

Industry: **Factory Equipment**

Komori, a manufacturer of commercial-printing equipment, specializes in offset presses. It supplies most of the major Japanese printing companies and is the sole supplier of currency-printing presses to the Ministry of Finance. The company also makes share-certificate presses and deals in used equipment. Its other products include automated-press changers, automatic sheet-fed offset presses, and double-face printing presses. Komori has 13 consolidated subsidiaries in the United States, the United Kingdom, the Netherlands, Denmark, Italy, Sweden, Germany, France, and Canada.

	¥bil 03/93	03/94	03/95	US$mil 03/95				
Sales	**88.4**	**71.5**	**69.9**	**709.0**	P/E Ratio	**NMF**	Price (9/30/95)	**2,350.00**
Net Income	**1.3**	**-1.4**	**0.5**	**4.9**	P/B Ratio	**1.5**	52 Wk Hi-Low	**2,810.0-1,680.0**
Book Value	**123.3**	**122.2**	**122.7**	**1,420.4**	Yield %	**0.8**	Market Cap	**US$1,845.7mil**

Address **3-11-1, Azumabashi, Sumida-ku, Tokyo 130**
Tel **03-5608-7811**
Fax **03-3624-7160**
ADR
SEDOL No. **6496658**
President **Yoshiharu Komori**
Chairman --

Konami

Industry: **Software**

Konami is a leading software-development company that specializes in computer-game software. The company's main products are software for Nintendo's arcade and home-video games, and it also supplies game software to Sega. Overseas sales account for about 25% of its total consolidated sales. Thus far, exports have largely been to the United States, but sales to the European market have steadily been increasing. Konami has 10 subsidiaries, including ones in the United States, United Kingdom, Germany, Hong Kong, and Taiwan that sell and distribute its electronic products.

¥bil	03/93 *	03/94	03/95	US$mil 03/95				
Sales	**31.9**	**41.1**	**39.9**	**404.7**	P/E Ratio	**NMF**	Price (9/30/95)	**2,200.00**
Net Income	**2.0**	**-2.9**	**-13.2**	**-133.5**	P/B Ratio	**2.8**	52 Wk Hi-Low	**2,770.0-1,360.0**
Book Value	**43.0**	**39.4**	**25.8**	**298.9**	Yield %	**0.8**	Market Cap	**US$732.6mil**

Address **4-3-1, Toranomon**
Minato-ku, Tokyo 105
Tel **03-3432-5678**
Fax **03-3432-5862**
ADR
SEDOL No. **6496681**
President **Kagemasa Kozuki**
Chairman **Kagemasa Kozuki**

*Irregular period due to fiscal year change.

Konica

Industry: **Other Recreational Products & Services**

Konica is the second-largest film manufacturer in Japan, with roughly 16% of Japan's market for photographic film. It also produces photographic materials, photo-related industrial equipment, business machines such as facsimile and copy machines, cameras, and optical equipment. Konica has production facilities in Japan, in the U.S. (one each for film and copiers), and in Germany for copiers. Konica's overseas manufacturing, service, and marketing operations encompass the U.S., Europe, and the Asia Pacific region. Overseas sales represent about 48% of revenues.

¥bil	03/93 *	03/94	03/95	US$mil 03/95				
Sales	**502.6**	**492.9**	**517.6**	**5,246.6**	P/E Ratio	**59.0**	Price (9/30/95)	**631.00**
Net Income	**3.7**	**4.2**	**3.8**	**38.9**	P/B Ratio	**1.3**	52 Wk Hi-Low	**840.00-512.00**
Book Value	**170.7**	**172.5**	**169.0**	**1,955.5**	Yield %	**1.6**	Market Cap	**US$2,269.7mil**

Address **1-26-2, Nishi-Shinjuku**
Shinjuku-ku, Tokyo 163
Tel **03-3349-5251**
Fax **03-3349-5290**
ADR **KNCAY**
SEDOL No. **6496700**
President **Takanori Yoneyama**
Chairman **Megumi Ide**

*Irregular period due to fiscal year change.

Koyo Seiko

Industry: **Other Auto Parts**

Koyo Seiko, an affiliate of Toyota Motor, is one of Japan's four largest makers of bearings and steering systems. It also makes industrial furnaces, machine tools, semiconductor-production systems, control units, and oil seals. Koyo Seiko has eight plants and 17 offices in Japan. About 29% of its consolidated revenues is generated abroad. It has overseas factories in the U.S., Brazil, South Korea, and Europe. Koyo Seiko also maintains several joint ventures abroad, including those with Siam Motors (Thailand), Yung Ho Shun (Taiwan), Borg Warner (U.S.), and Torrington (U.S.).

¥bil	03/93	03/94	03/95	US$mil 03/95				
Sales	**314.2**	**285.8**	**309.3**	**3,135.1**	P/E Ratio	**112.4**	Price (9/30/95)	**832.00**
Net Income	**-0.3**	**-1.6**	**1.5**	**14.8**	P/B Ratio	**1.5**	52 Wk Hi-Low	**1,000.00-630.00**
Book Value	**112.6**	**110.1**	**110.1**	**1,274.5**	Yield %	**0.7**	Market Cap	**US$1,641.6mil**

Address **3-5-8, Minami-Senba**
Chuo-ku, Osaka 542
Tel **06-271-8261**
Fax **06-245-7892**
ADR
SEDOL No. **6497082**
President **Hiroshi Inoue**
Chairman **Uzuhiko Tsuboi**

Kubota

Industry: **Heavy Machinery**

Kubota is Japan's largest maker of farm equipment, with more than a 40% domestic market share in tractors. It also makes piping for water-supply and sewer systems. Its other products include combines, engines, pumps, valves, industrial castings, construction machinery, housing materials, and septic tanks. It also makes waste-treatment plants and trash incinerators. The firm has equity stakes in several Silicon Valley computer and technology companies. Kubota has 18 Japanese production facilities and plants in the United States, Spain, Germany, Indonesia, and Thailand.

¥bil	03/93	03/94	03/95	US$mil 03/95				
Sales	**940.4**	**979.5**	**1,014.0**	**10,278.0**	P/E Ratio	**46.7**	Price (9/30/95)	**668.00**
Net Income	**5.6**	**8.2**	**20.1**	**203.8**	P/B Ratio	**2.9**	52 Wk Hi-Low	**744.00-518.00**
Book Value	**312.5**	**310.6**	**321.4**	**3,719.4**	Yield %	**1.0**	Market Cap	**US$9,471.4mil**

Address **1-2-47, Shikitsu-Higashi**
Naniwa-ku, Osaka 556
Tel **06-648-2622**
Fax **06-648-2398**
ADR **KUB**
SEDOL No. **6497509**
President **Kohei Mitsui**
Chairman **Shigekazu Mino**

Kumagai Gumi

Industry: **Heavy Construction**

Kumagai Gumi is a general contractor primarily engaged in building construction and civil engineering. The firm builds roads, railways, dams, tunnels, and hydroelectric-power plants. It constructs commercial buildings, hotels, houses, and condominiums. The company is also active in land development, electrical wiring, and piping construction. Overseas operations represent about 6% of Kumagai Gumi's sales. It has subsidiaries in Hong Kong, China, Taiwan, Indonesia, the Philippines, Australia, the United Kingdom, and the United States.

¥bil	03/93	03/94	03/95	US$mil 03/95				
Sales	**1,187.1**	**929.3**	**926.9**	**9,395.1**	P/E Ratio	**NMF**	Price (9/30/95)	**442.00**
Net Income	**1.0**	**-6.5**	**-9.3**	**-94.4**	P/B Ratio	**1.1**	52 Wk Hi-Low	**595.00-355.00**
Book Value	**330.6**	**323.4**	**286.4**	**3,315.4**	Yield %	**0.7**	Market Cap	**US$3,026.3mil**

Address **2-1, Tsukudo-cho**
Shinjuku-ku, Tokyo 162
Tel **03-3260-2111**
Fax **03-3235-5389**
ADR
SEDOL No. **6497565**
President **Taichiro Kumagai**
Chairman --

Kurabo Industries

Industry: **Clothing & Fabrics**

Kurabo Industries (Kurashiki Boseki) is a textiles firm that produces cotton and wool yarn and fabric, as well as specialized-synthetic fabrics such as those used in sportswear and fireproof clothing. Textiles account for about 70% of the company's consolidated revenues. It also produces chemical products such as polyurethane foam for use in furniture, carpeting, bedding materials, and insulation. Kurabo is diversifying into electronics, optoelectronics, functional high polymers, and biotechnology. The firm has 12 factories, 24 subsidiaries, and 13 affiliates.

	¥bil 03/93	03/94	03/95	US$mil 03/95				
Sales	**150.8**	**139.8**	**150.9**	**1,529.2**	P/E Ratio	**29.4**	Price (9/30/95)	**362.00**
Net Income	**0.7**	**0.5**	**3.3**	**33.7**	P/B Ratio	**1.2**	52 Wk Hi-Low	**473.00-299.00**
Book Value	**77.4**	**76.8**	**80.1**	**927.3**	Yield %	**1.1**	Market Cap	**US$982.8mil**

Address	**2-4-31, Kyutaromachi**	Tel	**06-266-5130**	ADR		President	**Kozo Shindo**
	Chuo-ku, Osaka 541	Fax	**06-266-5612**	SEDOL No.	**6497651**	Chairman	**Atsushi Fujita**

Kuraray

Industry: **Clothing & Fabrics**

Kuraray is a midsize manufacturer of synthetic-fiber products. Its major products include artificial leathers, chemicals, synthetic resins, and medical products such as artificial organs and dental equipment. The firm also makes optical-memory disks, food, cosmetics, and household furniture. Kuraray has real-estate-development and plant-engineering affiliates. Its main clients include Marubeni, Takashima, Toyoshima, and Morita. Kuraray has 11 consolidated and 41 unconsolidated subsidiaries in Japan. Its overseas offices are located in New York, Dusseldorf, and Hong Kong.

	¥bil 03/93	03/94	03/95	US$mil 03/95				
Sales	**353.2**	**326.8**	**327.3**	**3,317.3**	P/E Ratio	**32.1**	Price (9/30/95)	**991.00**
Net Income	**9.4**	**8.2**	**9.6**	**97.5**	P/B Ratio	**1.9**	52 Wk Hi-Low	**1,230.0-914.0**
Book Value	**150.0**	**157.3**	**164.9**	**1,908.9**	Yield %	**0.9**	Market Cap	**US$3,102.1mil**

Address	**1-12-39, Umeda**	Tel	**06-348-2097**	ADR		President	**Hiroto Matsuo**
	Kita-ku, Osaka 530	Fax	**06-348-2165**	SEDOL No.	**6497662**	Chairman	**Hisao Nakamura**

Kurita Water Industries

Industry: **Pollution Control, Waste Management**

Kurita Water Industries (Kurita Kogyo) specializes in the production of water-treatment equipment, holding roughly 30% of the Japanese market. The firm's major products are water-treatment chemicals, and facilities and equipment to treat sewage and wastewater. Its customers include the chemical, auto, iron, steel, and food industries. Kurita also supplies ultra-pure-water systems to the semiconductor industry. Itochu, a Japanese trading company, is its largest shareholder with a 16.4% share. Kurita has production subsidiaries in Germany, Brazil, Singapore, and Thailand.

	¥bil 03/93	03/94	03/95	US$mil 03/95				
Sales	**126.6**	**130.5**	**137.2**	**1,390.4**	P/E Ratio	**30.3**	Price (9/30/95)	**2,700.00**
Net Income	**9.2**	**9.2**	**10.4**	**105.9**	P/B Ratio	**4.6**	52 Wk Hi-Low	**2,780.0-1,900.0**
Book Value	**52.8**	**60.4**	**68.9**	**797.9**	Yield %	**0.5**	Market Cap	**US$3,186.1mil**

Address	**3-4-7, Nishi-Shinjuku**	Tel	**03-3347-3202**	ADR		President	**Kazuo Taketoshi**
	Shinjuku-ku, Tokyo 160	Fax	**N/A**	SEDOL No.	**6497963**	Chairman	**Kiyoshi Takaoka**

Kyocera

Industry: **Semiconductors & related**

Kyocera is the world's leading maker of ceramic integrated-circuit packaging, holding roughly 70% of the world market. It also makes semiconductor parts, electronic components, ceramic-applied tools, optical equipment, compact-disc players, hard-disk drives, printers, cameras, and computers. It recently began mass production of cellular phones and other cordless communication devices, such as personal handy phones. It owns 23% of DDI, a long-distance telecom firm in Japan. In 1994, the firm made half of its sales in overseas markets.

	¥bil 03/93	03/94	03/95	US$mil 03/95				
Sales	**431.6**	**427.7**	**498.6**	**5,053.6**	P/E Ratio	**35.1**	Price (9/30/95)	**8,140.00**
Net Income	**23.9**	**36.8**	**43.3**	**438.7**	P/B Ratio	**2.6**	52 Wk Hi-Low	**8,860.0-6,000.0**
Book Value	**511.2**	**539.7**	**578.3**	**6,693.5**	Yield %	**0.6**	Market Cap	**US$15,296mil**

Address	**5-22, Kita-Inouecho, Higashino**	Tel	**075-592-3851**	ADR	**KYO**	President	**Kensuke Ito**
	Yamashina-ku, Kyoto 607	Fax	**075-501-6536**	SEDOL No.	**6499260**	Chairman	**Kazuo Inamori**

Kyokuyo

Industry: **Fishing**

Kyokuyo, one of Japan'e five largest fishing companies, produces and exports processed, canned, and frozen foods. Marine products account for roughly 65% of it's consolidated sales. The company also manages restaurants and provides refrigerated-transport ships for seafood transportation. Its major customers are Kaisho, Toyo Suisan, and Hirayama. The company's U.S. activities include buying marine products and marketing fish paste on the East Coast and managing a seafood-processing firm. Kyokuyo's joint venture in Argentina with Mitsui exports fish products to Japan.

	¥bil 03/93	03/94	03/95	US$mil 03/95				
Sales	**185.0**	**164.3**	**173.8**	**1,761.7**	P/E Ratio	**81.7**	Price (9/30/95)	**572.00**
Net Income	**-1.3**	**0.4**	**0.8**	**8.1**	P/B Ratio	**6.7**	52 Wk Hi-Low	**609.00-302.00**
Book Value	**8.3**	**8.7**	**9.6**	**111.3**	Yield %	**0.0**	Market Cap	**US$651.8mil**

Address	**2-1-2, Marunouchi**	Tel	**03-3211-0134**	ADR		President	**Kazumasa Ishise**
	Chiyoda-ku, Tokyo 100	Fax	**03-3211-6921**	SEDOL No.	**6498706**	Chairman	**Hironori Shimizu**

Kyowa Hakko Kogyo

Industry: **Pharmaceuticals**

Kyowa Hakko Kogyo is known for its pioneering work in amino-acid production and fermentation technology used in the production of drugs, food seasonings (such as MSG), alcoholic drinks, biochemicals, and veterinary medicines. Pharmaceuticals are its main business, accounting for more than 50% of consolidated sales. Kyowa controls about 1,500 patents overseas and 270 in Japan. It has 13 consolidated subsidiaries, including two in the U.S., one in the U.K., and one in Germany. The firm has a joint venture with Cephalon (U.S.) to codevelop drugs for neurodegenerative diseases.

¥bil	12/92	12/93	12/94	US$mil 12/94				
Sales	**323.8**	**323.2**	**341.5**	**3,346.6**	P/E Ratio	**40.0**	Price (9/30/95)	**955.00**
Net Income	**4.8**	**6.3**	**10.6**	**104.3**	P/B Ratio	**2.7**	52 Wk Hi-Low	**990.00-800.00**
Book Value	**148.2**	**151.4**	**158.8**	**1,592.1**	Yield %	**0.7**	Market Cap	**US$4,287.5mil**

Address **1-6-1, Otemachi**
Chiyoda-ku, Tokyo 100
Tel **03-3201-7211**
Fax **03-3284-1968**
ADR
SEDOL No. **6499550**
President **Kannosuke Nakamura**
Chairman --

Kyudenko

Industry: **Electrical Components & Equipment**

Kyudenko is an electrical contractor that has close ties with Kyushu Electric Power. The firm's specific business activities include indoor wiring, telecommunication-network installation, air-conditioning ductwork, plumbing, cargo transport, and electrical-equipment sales. Its electrical-contracting division deals mainly with power-generation facilities and distribution networks. One half of Kyudenko's sales are derived from its interior-wiring activities. It also installs sewage- and water-treatment facilities. Kyushu Electric Power owns 21% of the company's stock.

¥bil	03/93	03/94	03/95	US$mil 03/95				
Sales	**223.0**	**229.4**	**245.8**	**2,491.3**	P/E Ratio	**15.1**	Price (9/30/95)	**1,340.00**
Net Income	**7.5**	**6.6**	**6.9**	**69.6**	P/B Ratio	**1.2**	52 Wk Hi-Low	**1,470.0-1,060.0**
Book Value	**75.2**	**81.1**	**91.4**	**1,058.1**	Yield %	**0.8**	Market Cap	**US$1,092.5mil**

Address **1-23-35, Nanokawa**
Minami-ku, Fukuoka 815
Tel **092-523-1231**
Fax **092-524-3269**
ADR
SEDOL No. **6499969**
President **Tsukasa Shiraishi**
Chairman **Keiji Koga**

Kyushu Electric Power

Industry: **Electrical Utilities - All**

Kyushu Electric Power (Kyushu Denryoku) serves more than seven million customers on the southern island of Kyushu. The company ranks fifth in revenues among the nation's nine power companies. Its ratio of nuclear-power generation is higher than the national average. Kyushu Electric's primary facilities include 16 hydroelectric-, 12 thermal-, and two nuclear-power plants. Two more nuclear-power plants are currently under construction at the company's Genkai facility, as part of the company's efforts to reduce its dependency on foreign oil.

¥bil	03/93	03/94	03/95	US$mil 03/95				
Sales	**1,261.9**	**1,277.0**	**1,387.3**	**14,062.6**	P/E Ratio	**25.3**	Price (9/30/95)	**2,510.00**
Net Income	**38.5**	**39.4**	**46.6**	**472.3**	P/B Ratio	**1.9**	52 Wk Hi-Low	**2,564.4-2,000.0**
Book Value	**543.4**	**559.2**	**613.1**	**7,096.1**	Yield %	**2.0**	Market Cap	**US$11,971mil**

Address **2-1-82, Watanabe, Chuo-ku**
Fukuoka City, Fukuoka 810
Tel **092-761-3031**
Fax **092-733-1435**
ADR
SEDOL No. **6499806**
President **Shigeru Ohno**
Chairman **Tatsuo Kawai**

Kyushu Matsushita Electric

Industry: **Electrical Components & Equipment**

Kyushu Matsushita Electric (Kyushu Matsushita Denki) is an electronics manufacturer that holds the world's largest market share for magnetic heads. The company is active in office automation, telecommunication, magnetic-recording components, and factory automation. Its products include cordless phones, facsimile machines, color-TV components, computer hard disks and floppy diskettes, integrated-circuit lead frames, typewriters, and water-treatment equipment. The firm has nine domestic plants, and four subsidiaries and one affiliate located in Malaysia, the U.K., and Japan.

¥bil	03/93	03/94	03/95	US$mil 03/95				
Sales	**356.3**	**323.7**	**316.3**	**3,206.4**	P/E Ratio	**86.1**	Price (9/30/95)	**1,920.00**
Net Income	**12.4**	**6.8**	**3.9**	**39.8**	P/B Ratio	**2.1**	52 Wk Hi-Low	**2,840.0-1,430.0**
Book Value	**154.8**	**158.8**	**160.7**	**1,860.0**	Yield %	**0.7**	Market Cap	**US$3,405.8mil**

Address **4-1-62, Minoshima**
Hakata-ku, Fukuoka 812
Tel **092-431-2111**
Fax **092-477-1225**
ADR
SEDOL No. **6499903**
President **Sumio Mori**
Chairman --

Lintec

Industry: **Household Products (Durable)**

Lintec, a Japan Paper affiliate, manufactures adhesive tape, specialty paper, converted paper and film, packaging tapes, automatic-packaging systems, label-printing systems, and semiconductor-producing equipment. The semiconductor industry is an important market for its adhesive products. Lintec is investing ¥1.3 billion to construct a research base in Saitama, to be completed within the next fiscal year. Its major overseas subsidiaries are Madico (U.S.) and Texim Europe (France). Lintec has joined with Sumitomo Chemical to increase its production of window coatings.

¥bil	03/93	03/94	03/95	US$mil 03/95				
Sales	**104.2**	**103.0**	**108.8**	**1,102.7**	P/E Ratio	**40.7**	Price (9/30/95)	**1,250.00**
Net Income	**2.1**	**2.2**	**1.9**	**19.6**	P/B Ratio	**1.2**	52 Wk Hi-Low	**1,710.0-1,160.0**
Book Value	**56.7**	**60.3**	**65.2**	**754.1**	Yield %	**1.0**	Market Cap	**US$804.1mil**

Address **23-23, Honcho**
Itabashi-ku, Tokyo 173
Tel **03-5248-7711**
Fax **03-5248-7760**
ADR
SEDOL No. **6330080**
President **Komei Shoji**
Chairman --

Lion

Industry: **Household Products (Non-Durable)**

Lion manufactures household products such as cosmetics, detergents, toiletries, pharmaceuticals, foodstuffs, and surfactants. The firm is Japan's leading maker of toothpaste, holding more than 50% of the domestic market. Lion sells its products through 270,000 retailers in Japan. Its major customers include Banyu Pharmaceutical, Tokyodo, and Meijiya. It has joint ventures in China, Thailand, Malaysia, and Germany for the production of toothpaste and other goods for local use and for export. It also has a household-products subsidiary, Lion Corporation, in the United States.

	¥bil 12/92	12/93	12/94	US$mil 12/94				
Sales	**308.8**	**321.6**	**332.0**	**3,252.9**	P/E Ratio	**23.7**	Price (9/30/95)	**552.00**
Net Income	**-1.5**	**0.4**	**6.6**	**64.2**	P/B Ratio	**1.7**	52 Wk Hi-Low	**656.19-477.00**
Book Value	**82.5**	**80.9**	**85.4**	**855.7**	Yield %	**1.4**	Market Cap	**US$1,562.5mil**

Address **1-3-7, Honjo** Tel **03-3621-6211** ADR President **Michinao Takahashi**
Sumida-ku, Tokyo 130 Fax **03-3621-6149** SEDOL No. **6518808** Chairman **Atsushi Kobayashi**

Long-Term Credit Bank

Industry: **Banks - Money Center**

The Long-Term Credit Bank of Japan (Nippon Choki Shinyo Ginko), or LTCB, is the country's second-largest long-term credit bank. The bank is one of seven financial companies allowed to issue debentures in Japan. It has 26 branches throughout Japan, and recently established a domestic securities subsidiary. Its international network consists of 12 branches, representative offices, and agencies, and 15 subsidiaries. Three subsidiaries are located in the United States. The bank's diversified interests in Asia include several joint ventures with the Liem Group in Southeast Asia.

	¥bil 03/93	03/94	03/95	US$mil 03/95				
Revenues	**2,299.1**	**2,364.1**	**2,444.2**	**24,774.7**	P/E Ratio	**NMF**	Price (9/30/95)	**869.00**
Net Income	**23.2**	**34.0**	**7.1**	**71.8**	P/B Ratio	**1.9**	52 Wk Hi-Low	**1,180.0-724.0**
Book Value	**1,102.5**	**1,121.2**	**1,109.7**	**12,843.6**	Yield %	**0.9**	Market Cap	**US$20,916mil**

Address **2-1-8, Uchi-Saiwaicho** Tel **03-5511-5111** ADR President **Katsunobu Onogi**
Chiyoda-ku, Tokyo 100 Fax **03-5511-5505** SEDOL No. **6524731** Chairman **Takao Masuzawa**

Mabuchi Motor

Industry: **Electrical Components & Equipment**

Mabuchi Motor is the world's largest manufacturer of small electric motors, holding a 50% share of the international market. It also makes motor parts and manufacturing equipment. The firm holds 617 patents in the field of small-motor technology. The company's direct-current motors, of which it has 282 models, are used in audiovisual, office-automation, and precision equipment. Its annual production capacity exceeds 700 million motors. The firm has overseas production bases in Taiwan, China, Hong Kong and Malaysia. The Mabuchi family holds 30% of the concern's shares.

	¥bil 12/92	12/93	12/94	US$mil 12/94				
Sales	**75.7**	**76.4**	**87.8**	**860.5**	P/E Ratio	**21.1**	Price (9/30/95)	**5,850.00**
Net Income	**9.6**	**7.1**	**12.8**	**125.7**	P/B Ratio	**2.0**	52 Wk Hi-Low	**7,570.0-5,370.0**
Book Value	**123.4**	**127.8**	**138.9**	**1,392.0**	Yield %	**0.4**	Market Cap	**US$2,752.2mil**

Address **430, Matsuhidai** Tel **0473-84-1111** ADR President **Takaichi Mabuchi**
Matsudo City, Chiba 270 Fax **0473-85-2662** SEDOL No. **6551030** Chairman **Kenichi Mabuchi**

Maeda

Industry: **Heavy Construction**

Maeda (Maeda Kensetsu Kogyo), a member of the Fuyo group, is a building and civil-engineering contractor. The firm constructs public and private buildings. Its civil-engineering works include power stations, railways, tunnels, bridges, and dams; harbors and levees; dredging, sewage, and irrigation systems; and land reclamation and development. Construction orders account for 55% of current contracts, and civil-engineering projects make up the rest. Maeda has 19 subsidiaries and affiliates, including four overseas. Overseas operations are largely centered in Southeast Asia.

	¥bil 03/93 P	03/94 P	03/95 P	US$mil 03/95				
Sales	**501.0**	**532.8**	**529.9**	**5,371.3**	P/E Ratio	**49.3**	Price (9/30/95)	**1,050.00**
Net Income	**3.8**	**4.0**	**3.8**	**38.5**	P/B Ratio	**1.2**	52 Wk Hi-Low	**1,160.0-929.0**
Book Value	**148.5**	**152.7**	**155.9**	**1,804.8**	Yield %	**0.9**	Market Cap	**US$1,883.9mil**

Address **2-10-26, Fujimi** Tel **03-3265-5551** ADR President **Yasuji Maeda**
Chiyoda-ku, Tokyo 102 Fax **N/A** SEDOL No. **6554705** Chairman **Kenji Maeda**

P=Parent company data.

Maeda Road Construction

Industry: **Heavy Construction**

Maeda Road Construction (Maeda Doro), an affiliate of Maeda Construction, ranks second in Japan for asphalt-mixture production and is one of the top three road-paving companies by total sales. The firm's operations include asphalt and concrete paving and civil-engineering construction. Its civil-engineering division participates in beautification and development projects for malls and municipal parks. Maeda provides its products and services mainly to other road pavers and construction companies. Maeda has one subsidiary, Maeda Pacific Corporation, and 13 affiliates.

	¥bil 03/93 P	03/94 P	03/95 P	US$mil 03/95				
Sales	**196.6**	**204.7**	**202.0**	**2,047.5**	P/E Ratio	**35.6**	Price (9/30/95)	**1,850.00**
Net Income	**7.8**	**6.7**	**5.3**	**53.3**	P/B Ratio	**2.0**	52 Wk Hi-Low	**2,000.0-1,550.0**
Book Value	**86.4**	**91.7**	**95.4**	**1,104.7**	Yield %	**0.8**	Market Cap	**US$1,882.0mil**

Address **3-14-12, Kami-Ohsaki** Tel **03-3447-0781** ADR President **Masatsugu Okabe**
Shinagawa-ku, Tokyo 141 Fax **03-3473-3529** SEDOL No. **6554727** Chairman **Hidetoshi Osakabe**

P=Parent company data.

Makita

Industry: **Other Home Furnishings**

Makita is the largest Japanese manufacturer of portable electric-power tools for woodworking. Its products include jig and circular saws, planers, drills, hammers, grinders, sanders, and stationary woodworking machines. Makita is diversifying into household equipment, pneumatic tools, and gasoline-powered garden tools. The firm's international operations are carried out through 26 subsidiaries in 15 countries. Its overseas operations are located in Brazil, the U.S., Canada, Australia, the U.K., Germany, Austria, Italy, Spain, Singapore, Taiwan, and Hong Kong.

	¥bil 03/93	03/94	03/95	US$mil 03/95				
Sales	**178.9**	**160.8**	**164.4**	**1,666.2**	P/E Ratio	**37.5**	Price (9/30/95)	**1,570.00**
Net Income	**9.8**	**8.2**	**6.7**	**68.3**	P/B Ratio	**1.4**	52 Wk Hi-Low	**1,950.0-1,120.0**
Book Value	**179.8**	**180.6**	**185.3**	**2,145.2**	Yield %	**1.2**	Market Cap	**US$2,542.5mil**

Address	**3-11-8, Sumiyoshi-cho**	Tel	**0566-98-1711**	ADR	**MKTAY**	President	**Masahiko Goto**
	Anjo City, Aichi 446	Fax	**0566-98-5580**	SEDOL No.	**6555805**	Chairman	--

Marubeni

Industry: **Overseas Trading**

Marubeni is a leading general-trading company at the center of the Fuyo group. The company trades in machinery, chemicals, metals, minerals, fuels, foodstuffs, textiles, sporting goods, and raw materials. Its activities also include home construction, plant construction, shipbuilding, and civil engineering. Marubeni has been active in eastern Europe and the former Soviet Republics, recently establishing subsidiaries to sell office equipment and Nissan automobiles in Poland and Russia. The company has 410 consolidated subsidiaries, 240 of which are located overseas.

	¥bil 03/93	03/94	03/95	US$mil 03/95				
Sales	**17,325.5**	**15,592.3**	**14,918.9**	**151,222.6**	P/E Ratio	**71.7**	Price (9/30/95)	**495.00**
Net Income	**1.1**	**5.5**	**10.4**	**105.1**	P/B Ratio	**1.5**	52 Wk Hi-Low	**564.00-415.00**
Book Value	**452.9**	**438.8**	**480.5**	**5,560.8**	Yield %	**1.2**	Market Cap	**US$7,435.1mil**

Address	**2-5-7, Honmachi**	Tel	**06-266-2304**	ADR	**MARUY**	President	**Iwao Toriumi**
	Chuo-ku, Osaka 541	Fax	**03-3282-2331**	SEDOL No.	**6569464**	Chairman	**Kazuo Haruna**

Marudai Food

Industry: **Other Food**

Marudai Food (Marudai Shokuhin) makes processed and fresh meat. The company is the third-largest fish-meat ham and sausage maker and holds about 10% of the Japanese market share in processed meat. It specializes in ham and sausage and also produces pork, chicken, and beef products; fish-meat ham and sausage; and a variety of Western-style and Japanese convenience foods. The company markets its products through department stores, supermarkets, and grocery stores. It also owns the second-largest meat packer in Taiwan and a meat and food processor in the U.S.

	¥bil 03/93	03/94	03/95	US$mil 03/95				
Sales	**221.1**	**221.0**	**228.0**	**2,310.8**	P/E Ratio	**NMF**	Price (9/30/95)	**691.00**
Net Income	**1.8**	**1.3**	**0.0**	**0.3**	P/B Ratio	**0.9**	52 Wk Hi-Low	**818.00-556.00**
Book Value	**103.0**	**102.3**	**100.1**	**1,158.7**	Yield %	**0.7**	Market Cap	**US$920.1mil**

Address	**21-3, Midori-cho**	Tel	**0726-75-1111**	ADR		President	**Yoshiyuki Komori**
	Takatsuki City, Osaka 569	Fax	**0726-61-5006**	SEDOL No.	**6569442**	Chairman	**Takashi Haga**

Maruetsu

Industry: **Food Retailers & Wholesalers**

Maruetsu operates a chain of over 170 supermarkets, all located in the Tokyo area. Its main sales lines include fruits and vegetables, fish, meats, processed perishable foods, miscellaneous foods, sundries, and clothing. Sales of foodstuffs account for roughly 80% of its revenue. Maruetsu is working to market new products toward health-conscious customers. The firm opened five stores and remodeled eight stores in 1994. Daiei, a retailer and supermarket operator, directly owns 21% of Maruetsu's stock and controls an even larger share through other Daiei group companies.

	¥bil 03/93	03/94	03/95	US$mil 03/95				
Sales	**325.5**	**330.0**	**330.4**	**3,348.8**	P/E Ratio	**53.9**	Price (9/30/95)	**819.00**
Net Income	**2.2**	**2.7**	**2.3**	**23.2**	P/B Ratio	**1.1**	52 Wk Hi-Low	**1,090.0-700.0**
Book Value	**113.5**	**113.8**	**111.8**	**1,294.4**	Yield %	**1.8**	Market Cap	**US$1,243.0mil**

Address	**5-51-12, Higashi-Ikebukuro**	Tel	**03-3590-1110**	ADR		President	**Jiro Fujii**
	Toshima-ku, Tokyo 170	Fax	**03-3590-4642**	SEDOL No.	**6569594**	Chairman	**Yataro Takahashi**

Maruha

Industry: **Fishing**

Maruha, previously Taiyo Fishery, is a major producer and trader of marine products. The company's products include canned and frozen foods, fish-meat hams and sausages, refined sugars, meat and livestock, feed and bait, and gelatin. As Japan's largest importer of seafood products, the firm operates cold-storage facilities and a large fleet of refrigerated ships. It also has 20 aquaculture farms in Japan. A new undertaking is restaurant management. Maruha's overseas subsidiaries include Western Alaska Fisheries, Trans-Ocean Products, New Eastern, and Taiyo Finance Europe.

	¥bil 03/93	03/94	03/95	US$mil 03/95				
Sales	**1,007.0**	**953.2**	**955.1**	**9,681.3**	P/E Ratio	**70.5**	Price (9/30/95)	**303.00**
Net Income	**-4.6**	**-3.9**	**1.3**	**13.2**	P/B Ratio	**4.6**	52 Wk Hi-Low	**442.00-277.00**
Book Value	**22.6**	**18.6**	**19.6**	**227.2**	Yield %	**0.0**	Market Cap	**US$914.3mil**

Address	**1-1-2, Otemachi**	Tel	**03-3216-1710**	ADR		President	**Keijiro Nakabe**
	Chiyoda-ku, Tokyo 100	Fax	**03-3216-0342**	SEDOL No.	**6870207**	Chairman	--

Marui

Industry: **Retailers - Broadline**

Marui is a midsize Japanese retailer that leads the industry in consumer-credit services. Marui department stores sell foodstuffs, furniture, household furnishings, jewelry, sporting goods, accessories, and clothing. The company's consumer-services division grants small loans and offers cash-dispensing services through Marui credit cards, of which it has issued more than 12 million. Marui operates some 34 department stores in Tokyo and throughout Japan. Marui has a joint venture with Virgin (U.K.) to develop the Virgin Megastore chain of audiovisual stores in Japan.

	¥bil 01/93	01/94	01/95	US$mil 01/95				
Revenues	**576.0**	**545.1**	**530.8**	**5,254.6**	P/E Ratio	**40.8**	Price (9/30/95)	**1,850.00**
Net Income	**20.7**	**18.6**	**16.7**	**165.2**	P/B Ratio	**1.9**	52 Wk Hi-Low	**1,850.0-1,210.0**
Book Value	**343.8**	**354.2**	**363.0**	**3,668.2**	Yield %	**1.2**	Market Cap	**US$6,853.9mil**

Address	**3-7-18, Nakano**	Tel	**03-3384-0101**	ADR	**MAURY**	President	**Tadao Aoi**
	Nakano-ku, Tokyo 164-01	Fax	**03-3380-0107**	SEDOL No.	**6569527**	Chairman	--

Matsushita Communication Industrial

Industry: **Communications Technology**

Matsushita Communication Industrial (Matsushita Tsushin Kogyo) manufactures electronic goods. The firm's main products are telephones, professional audiovisual systems, car stereos, floppy-disk drives, and electronic-measuring equipment. Its better-known brand names include Panasonic and National. The firm has production bases in the U.S., the U.K., Germany, and the Philippines. It also supplies the Japanese government with radios and information equipment. Matsushita is developing integrated circuits with National Semiconductor for Toyota's car stereos.

	¥bil 03/93	03/94	03/95	US$mil 03/95				
Sales	**523.7**	**505.7**	**524.1**	**5,312.2**	P/E Ratio	**65.8**	Price (9/30/95)	**2,390.00**
Net Income	**7.2**	**5.8**	**6.8**	**69.1**	P/B Ratio	**2.2**	52 Wk Hi-Low	**2,820.0-1,650.0**
Book Value	**199.1**	**201.8**	**206.9**	**2,394.4**	Yield %	**0.5**	Market Cap	**US$4,522.3mil**

Address	**4-3-1, Tsunashima-Higashi**	Tel	**045-531-1231**	ADR		President	**Takashi Kawada**
	Kohoku-ku, Yokohama 223	Fax	**045-544-3285**	SEDOL No.	**6572666**	Chairman	--

Matsushita Electric Industrial

Industry: **Consumer Electronics**

Matsushita Electric Industrial is the center of the Matsushita group and the world's largest consumer-electronics manufacturer. Its products include electronic components, audio and video equipment, appliances, and office- and factory- automation equipment. It sells products under the Panasonic, National, Quasar, and Technics brand names. Overseas sales account for about one half of total revenues. In April 1995, the firm sold 80% of its MCA subsidiary for $5.7 billion. It retains a 20% stake in the entertainment group, which includes Universal Pictures.

	¥bil 03/93	03/94	03/95	US$mil 03/95				
Sales	**7,055.9**	**6,623.6**	**6,948.2**	**70,428.9**	P/E Ratio	**35.2**	Price (9/30/95)	**1,520.00**
Net Income	**38.4**	**24.5**	**90.5**	**917.3**	P/B Ratio	**1.0**	52 Wk Hi-Low	**1,700.0-1,200.0**
Book Value	**3,429.6**	**3,288.9**	**3,255.2**	**37,676.2**	Yield %	**0.8**	Market Cap	**US$32,064mil**

Address	**1006, Kadoma**	Tel	**06-908-1121**	ADR	**MC**	President	**Yoichi Morishita**
	Kadoma City, Osaka 571	Fax	**06-908-2351**	SEDOL No.	**6572707**	Chairman	**Masaharu Matsushita**

Matsushita Electric Works

Industry: **Building Materials**

Matsushita Electric Works manufactures and installs construction materials and lighting equipment for home and factory use. The company makes lighting and wiring equipment, security systems, building-automation systems, personal-care appliances, electric-power tools, and bathroom and kitchen units. It has diversified into electronic and plastic materials, such as printed-circuit boards, industrial resins and ceramics, and factory-automation equipment. The firm's sales network includes about 238,000 stores and 48 catalog showrooms across Japan.

	¥bil 11/92	11/93	11/94	US$mil 11/94				
Sales	**1,062.5**	**1,032.1**	**1,054.4**	**10,248.5**	P/E Ratio	**44.2**	Price (9/30/95)	**1,030.00**
Net Income	**18.3**	**14.5**	**17.1**	**166.2**	P/B Ratio	**1.6**	52 Wk Hi-Low	**1,100.0-908.0**
Book Value	**445.0**	**459.1**	**472.2**	**4,772.4**	Yield %	**1.2**	Market Cap	**US$7,689.5mil**

Address	**1048, Kadoma**	Tel	**06-908-1131**	ADR	**MSEWY**	President	**Kiyosuke Imai**
	Kadoma City, Osaka 571	Fax	**06-906-1860**	SEDOL No.	**6572729**	Chairman	**Toshio Miyoshi**

Matsushita Refrigeration

Industry: **Other Home Furnishings**

Matsushita Refrigeration (Matsushita Reiki), a member of the Matsushita group, produces household and commercial refrigerators, industrial air conditioners, vending machines, and control components (heat exchangers, compressors, and thermostats). The company controls 20% of the refrigerator market in Japan. More than 98% of the firm's parent sales are from its parent company, Matsushita Electric Industrial. Matsushita Refrigeration has four domestic factories. The firm has two consolidated subsidiaries based in the U.S. and Singapore.

	¥bil 03/93	03/94	03/95	US$mil 03/95				
Sales	**205.3**	**171.4**	**190.4**	**1,930.0**	P/E Ratio	**31.1**	Price (9/30/95)	**682.00**
Net Income	**-29.0**	**2.1**	**3.9**	**39.2**	P/B Ratio	**1.5**	52 Wk Hi-Low	**899.00-571.00**
Book Value	**78.5**	**78.5**	**79.8**	**923.6**	Yield %	**1.5**	Market Cap	**US$1,211.3mil**

Address	**3-22, Takaida-Hondori**	Tel	**06-784-7011**	ADR		President	**Tadashi Kubota**
	Higashi-Osaka City, Osaka 577	Fax	**N/A**	SEDOL No.	**6572826**	Chairman	--

Matsushita Seiko

Industry: **Other Home Furnishings**

Matsushita Seiko, a member of the Matsushita group, manufactures air-conditioning equipment for residential and industrial use. Its air conditioners are sold under the KDK and National brand names. The firm also makes household appliances, water-treatment systems, and air purifiers. It depends on individual consumers for approximately 75% of its sales. Exports to the Middle East and Southeast Asia contribute about 4.2% of revenues. The firm is 59.1%-owned by Matsushita Electric. Matsushita Seiko has two consolidated subsidiares, including one each in Japan and Hong Kong.

	¥bil 03/93	03/94	03/95	US$mil 03/95				
Sales	**112.6**	**106.3**	**107.4**	**1,088.8**	P/E Ratio	**43.1**	Price (9/30/95)	**677.00**
Net Income	**3.1**	**2.8**	**2.8**	**28.3**	P/B Ratio	**1.4**	52 Wk Hi-Low	**805.00-550.00**
Book Value	**81.9**	**82.8**	**83.7**	**968.6**	Yield %	**1.5**	Market Cap	**US$1,209.9mil**

Address	**6-2-61, Imafuku-Nishi**	Tel	**06-939-1161**	ADR		President	**Sukeji Ito**
	Joto-ku, Osaka 536	Fax	**06-931-9457**	SEDOL No.	**6572763**	Chairman	--

Matsushita-Kotobuki Electronics Ind

Industry: **Consumer Electronics**

Matsushita-Kotobuki Electronics Industries (Matsushita Kotobuki Denshi Kogyo) is the Matsushita group's audiovisual-equipment maker for the North American market. The firm makes videocassette recorders on an original-equipment-manufacturer (OEM) basis, mostly under the Panasonic label, and supplies camcorders to Kodak on an OEM basis. Other products include hard-disk drives for Quantum, a U.S. computer maker, and laser printers. It has four subsidiaries in the U.S., Singapore, Indonesia, and Ireland. In 1994, Matsushita made 86.4% of its consolidated revenues overseas.

	¥bil 03/93	03/94	03/95	US$mil 03/95				
Sales	**321.1**	**362.4**	**448.5**	**4,546.5**	P/E Ratio	**42.4**	Price (9/30/95)	**2,280.00**
Net Income	**8.8**	**8.7**	**8.5**	**86.2**	P/B Ratio	**2.0**	52 Wk Hi-Low	**2,860.0-1,520.0**
Book Value	**166.5**	**172.9**	**179.7**	**2,079.7**	Yield %	**0.7**	Market Cap	**US$3,626.8mil**

Address	**8-1 Furujin-machi**	Tel	**0878-51-7228**	ADR		President	**Takashi Honjo**
	Takamatsu City, Kagawa 760	Fax	**N/A**	SEDOL No.	**6572848**	Chairman	--

Matsuzakaya

Industry: **Retailers - Broadline**

Matsuzakaya, is one of Japan's oldest department-store chains with operations including restaurants, tea shops, and catalog sales of European goods. The company sells art objects, glassware, Japanese porcelain, furniture, household utensils, foodstuffs, and clothing. Its brand names include Henry Poole and Nina Ricci. Matsuzakaya's sales network includes more than 11 stores in major Japanese cities. The company operates its flagship Nagoya store in cooperation with Galeries Lafayette Paris (France). Matsuzakaya has overseas offices in the United States, France, and Hong Kong.

	¥bil 02/93	02/94	02/95	US$mil 02/95				
Revenues	**575.0**	**539.9**	**509.0**	**5,078.8**	P/E Ratio	**NMF**	Price (9/30/95)	**992.00**
Net Income	**3.9**	**0.3**	**0.2**	**1.7**	P/B Ratio	**2.0**	52 Wk Hi-Low	**1,390.0-841.0**
Book Value	**86.7**	**85.8**	**84.6**	**875.3**	Yield %	**0.8**	Market Cap	**US$1,704.8mil**

Address	**3-16-1, Sakae**	Tel	**052-251-1111**	ADR		President	**Akira Ito**
	Naka-ku, Nagoya 460	Fax	**N/A**	SEDOL No.	**6572785**	Chairman	**Kiko Saito**

Mazda Motor

Industry: **Automobile Manufacturers**

Mazda Motor (Matsuda) is Japan's fifth-largest automaker by sales. Passenger vehicles and auto parts account for about 65% and 17% of sales, respectively. The firm has 18 consolidated subsidiaries; research and development centers in the U.S., Europe, and Japan; and factories in 19 foreign countries. Ford Motor holds a 25% equity stake, and the two firms cooperate in production in the U.S. and Europe. It also has a production tie-up for minicars with Suzuki Motor. The firm markets its vehicles in more than 120 countries, and imports Ford, Citroën, and Fiat cars into Japan.

	¥bil 03/93	03/94	03/95	US$mil 03/95				
Sales	**2,593.4**	**2,188.2**	**2,204.1**	**22,341.8**	P/E Ratio	**NMF**	Price (9/30/95)	**360.00**
Net Income	**1.3**	**-49.0**	**-41.2**	**-417.2**	P/B Ratio	**1.2**	52 Wk Hi-Low	**584.00-298.00**
Book Value	**412.2**	**361.1**	**321.8**	**3,724.8**	Yield %	**0.0**	Market Cap	**US$3,904.0mil**

Address	**3-1, Shinchi, Fuchu-cho**	Tel	**082-282-1111**	ADR		President	**Yoshihiro Wada**
	Aki-gun, Hiroshima 730-91	Fax	**082-287-5237**	SEDOL No.	**6900308**	Chairman	**Norimasa Furuta**

Meidensha

Industry: **Factory Equipment**

Meidensha, a member of the Sumitomo group, manufactures heavy electric machinery and is expanding into electronics and control equipment. Its products include rotary machines such as motors and AC/DC generators; nonrotary machines such as transformers, switches, and circuit breakers; water-treatment-control systems; and factory-automation systems and equipment such as exhaust-testing systems, programmable controllers, and automatic-transmission-testing systems. Its products are used in automobile factories, water- and sewage-treatment plants, and by power utilities.

	¥bil 03/93	03/94	03/95	US$mil 03/95				
Sales	**208.0**	**210.0**	**216.1**	**2,190.0**	P/E Ratio	**77.6**	Price (9/30/95)	**613.00**
Net Income	**4.2**	**1.8**	**1.6**	**16.3**	P/B Ratio	**2.0**	52 Wk Hi-Low	**795.00-486.00**
Book Value	**60.5**	**60.5**	**61.1**	**706.7**	Yield %	**1.3**	Market Cap	**US$1,245.6mil**

Address	**2-2-1, Otemachi**	Tel	**03-3246-7072**	ADR		President	**Keiji Kojima**
	Chiyoda-ku, Tokyo 100	Fax	**03-3246-7144**	SEDOL No.	**6575900**	Chairman	**Tokihisa Inokuma**

Meiji Milk Products

Industry: **Other Food**

Meiji Milk Products (Meiji Nyugyo), a member of Dai-Ichi Kangyo Bank group, is Japan's second-largest dairy-food producer. It dominates the domestic markets for milk, ice cream, and infant formula. Other products include yogurt, cheese, butter, jelly, margarine, beverages, pudding, frozen foods, and animal feed. It is also diversifying into biotechnology and pharmaceuticals, including AIDS-fighting drugs. The firm has a joint venture with Suntory, a production agreement with Thailand's largest dairy-products maker, and development projects with a Bulgarian yogurt maker.

¥bil	03/93	03/94	03/95	US$mil 03/95				
Sales	**473.7**	**482.4**	**524.6**	**5,318.0**	P/E Ratio	**43.8**	Price (9/30/95)	**561.00**
Net Income	**0.9**	**2.7**	**3.8**	**38.4**	P/B Ratio	**2.3**	52 Wk Hi-Low	**736.00-472.00**
Book Value	**68.9**	**69.8**	**72.1**	**834.1**	Yield %	**1.1**	Market Cap	**US$1,673.9mil**

Address **2-3-6, Kyobashi**
Chuo-ku, Tokyo 104
Tel **03-3281-6114**
Fax **03-3281-4717**
ADR
SEDOL No. **6576088**
President **Hisashi Nakayama**
Chairman --

Meiji Seika Kaisha

Industry: **Other Food**

Meiji Seika produces a wide variety of foodstuffs and pharmaceuticals. Food products include chocolate, cookies, canned foods, and beverages. The pharmaceuticals division makes anticancer drugs, antibiotics, digestives, and agricultural chemicals. The company's production through joint ventures includes confectionery in the United States, Taiwan, and Colombia; anticancer agents in China; and antibiotics in South Korea, Indonesia, and Thailand. Meiji Seika has tie-ups with United Biscuits (U.K.) and Merck (U.S.). It exports its products to more than 60 countries.

¥bil	03/93	03/94	03/95	US$mil 03/95				
Sales	**341.2**	**327.1**	**342.9**	**3,475.8**	P/E Ratio	**66.9**	Price (9/30/95)	**582.00**
Net Income	**29.3**	**2.4**	**3.4**	**34.3**	P/B Ratio	**1.6**	52 Wk Hi-Low	**664.00-487.00**
Book Value	**140.9**	**141.1**	**145.4**	**1,682.8**	Yield %	**1.0**	Market Cap	**US$2,279.7mil**

Address **2-4-16, Kyobashi**
Chuo-ku,, Tokyo 104
Tel **03-3272-6511**
Fax **03-3281-7046**
ADR
SEDOL No. **6576185**
President **Ichiro Kitasato**
Chairman **Akira Sasai**

Mikuni Coca-Cola Bottling

Industry: **Soft Drinks**

Mikuni Coca-Cola Bottling, a Mitsui subsidiary and member of the Coca-Cola Bottling group, supplies soft drinks to the area north of Tokyo, including Saitama, Gunma, and Niigata prefectures. Its primary activity is the production and marketing of Coca-Cola products, canned coffee, and syrup. Mikuni bottles carbonated beverages and imports and sells Western liquor and wine. The firm also has an extensive vending-machine network that markets, leases, and repairs the machines. Mitsui, its major owner, holds 32.5% of equity.

¥bil	12/92	12/93	12/94	US$mil 12/94				
Sales	**113.2**	**110.7**	**121.1**	**1,187.0**	P/E Ratio	**13.3**	Price (9/30/95)	**1,130.00**
Net Income	**4.6**	**4.1**	**5.2**	**50.9**	P/B Ratio	**1.5**	52 Wk Hi-Low	**1,440.0-1,050.0**
Book Value	**38.1**	**41.3**	**45.6**	**457.1**	Yield %	**1.3**	Market Cap	**US$695.6mil**

Address **180, Kano**
Okegawa City, Saitama 363
Tel **048-774-1114**
Fax **048-776-3471**
ADR
SEDOL No. **6592147**
President **Masayuki Ikeba**
Chairman --

Minebea

Industry: **Electrical Components & Equipment**

Minebea is the world's leading producer of miniature ball bearings. Minebea also makes a variety of electronic goods, such as small precision motors, electromagnetic brakes and clutches, calculators, computer keyboards, disk drives, and speakers. The company has transferred most of its bearings production to Singapore and Thailand, where the firm is the top foreign investor. In 1994, Minebea made 50% of its consolidated sales overseas. The company has 57 subsidiaries in Japan and worldwide. Minebea's main lender is Sumitomo Trust Bank.

¥bil	09/92	03/94 *	03/95	US$mil 03/95				
Sales	**278.7**	**121.6**	**239.1**	**2,423.9**	P/E Ratio	**113.6**	Price (9/30/95)	**750.00**
Net Income	**-13.6**	**0.6**	**2.6**	**26.1**	P/B Ratio	**2.6**	52 Wk Hi-Low	**878.00-500.00**
Book Value	**168.5**	**111.6**	**113.3**	**1,311.1**	Yield %	**0.8**	Market Cap	**US$2,933.2mil**

Address **1-8-1, Shimo-Meguro**
Meguro-ku, Tokyo 153
Tel **03-5434-8611**
Fax **03-5434-8601**
ADR **MBEAY**
SEDOL No. **6642406**
President **Goro Ogino**
Chairman **Iwao Ishizuka**

*Irregular period due to fiscal year change.

Minolta

Industry: **Office Equipment**

Minolta (previously Minolta Camera) is a major manufacturer of cameras and business machines. Among its products are camera lenses, telescopes, photocopiers, survey equipment, silicon-wafer inspection systems, optical glass, semiconductor-related equipment, and planetariums. Minolta is active overseas, with 74% of its consolidated company sales coming from exports. The company has 53 consolidated subsidiaries, including ones in the United States, Europe, and Malaysia. Minolta is increasing its camera production overseas, primarily in Malaysia and China.

¥bil	03/93	03/94	03/95	US$mil 03/95				
Sales	**348.4**	**321.1**	**333.7**	**3,382.0**	P/E Ratio	**NMF**	Price (9/30/95)	**483.00**
Net Income	**-10.3**	**-4.8**	**-0.9**	**-9.0**	P/B Ratio	**2.5**	52 Wk Hi-Low	**558.00-300.00**
Book Value	**59.2**	**54.7**	**54.8**	**634.1**	Yield %	**0.0**	Market Cap	**US$1,356.2mil**

Address **2-3-13, Azuchi-machi**
Chuo-ku, Osaka 541
Tel **06-271-2251**
Fax **06-271-8320**
ADR
SEDOL No. **6595867**
President **Osamu Kanaya**
Chairman **Hideo Tashima**

Misawa Homes

Industry: **Home Construction**

Misawa Homes, a member of the Tokai group, is a builder specializing in wooden and prefabricated homes. Most of its income comes from sales of housing materials, such as wood-frame and ceramic components. The company markets housing materials through a network of more than 200 franchised dealers in Japan. Misawa Homes also sells real estate, participates in urban-development projects, and sells memberships in golf courses it owns. The firm has 83 subsidiaries and 24 affiliates, including three U.S. consolidated subsidiaries that engage in resort construction.

	¥bil 03/93	03/94	03/95	US$mil 03/95				
Sales	**483.0**	**513.3**	**488.9**	**4,956.0**	P/E Ratio	**45.0**	Price (9/30/95)	**891.00**
Net Income	**2.3**	**2.3**	**2.5**	**25.6**	P/B Ratio	**2.1**	52 Wk Hi-Low	**1,340.0-696.0**
Book Value	**53.6**	**53.4**	**55.4**	**641.4**	Yield %	**1.3**	Market Cap	**US$1,145.7mil**

Address	**2-4-5, Takaido-Higashi**	Tel	**03-3331-1111**	ADR		President	**Chiyoji Misawa**
	Suginami-ku, Tokyo 168	Fax	**03-3349-8074**	SEDOL No.	**6596581**	Chairman	--

Mitsubishi

Industry: **Overseas Trading**

Mitsubishi (Mitsubishi Shoji) is Japan's second-largest general-trading company. Metals account for about 40% of the firm's consolidated trading activities. It also trades petroleum products, machinery, and foodstuffs, and is expanding into telecommunications, biotechnology, and new materials. Mitsubishi recently acquired Aristech Chemical (U.S.), a petrochemicals maker. The firm has a long-standing joint venture with Kentucky Fried Chicken, which has more than 900 outlets in Japan. Of Mitsubishi's 566 subsidiaries, 380 are consolidated.

	¥bil 03/93	03/94	03/95	US$mil 03/95				
Sales	**17,793.3**	**17,276.3**	**17,466.6**	**177,047.5**	P/E Ratio	**79.9**	Price (9/30/95)	**1,110.00**
Net Income	**28.7**	**18.4**	**21.7**	**220.2**	P/B Ratio	**1.7**	52 Wk Hi-Low	**1,320.0-896.0**
Book Value	**724.6**	**698.8**	**1,021.8**	**11,826.1**	Yield %	**0.7**	Market Cap	**US$17,495mil**

Address	**2-6-3, Marunouchi**	Tel	**03-3210-2121**	ADR	**MSBHY**	President	**Minoru Makihara**
	Chiyoda-ku, Tokyo 100-86	Fax	**03-3210-8051**	SEDOL No.	**6596785**	Chairman	**Shinroku Morohashi**

Mitsubishi Bank

Industry: **Banks - Money Center**

Mitsubishi Bank (Mitsubishi Ginko) is Japan's sixth-largest bank by assets. It is the financial center of the Mitsubishi group, and loans to group companies represent 3% of the bank's total domestic lending. Its other activities include commodities and transactions, domestic and foreign exchange, and the issuance and deposit of industrial bonds. Mitsubishi Bank has 50 consolidated subsidiaries including the Bank of California, BanCal Tri-State, and Inland Property (all in the United States). In April 1996, Mitsubishi Bank will merge with the Bank of Tokyo.

	¥bil 03/93	03/94	03/95	US$mil 03/95				
Revenues	**2,921.0**	**2,940.6**	**2,979.1**	**30,197.6**	P/E Ratio	**NMF**	Price (9/30/95)	**1,980.00**
Net Income	**62.8**	**47.5**	**25.2**	**255.8**	P/B Ratio	**3.1**	52 Wk Hi-Low	**2,620.0-1,810.0**
Book Value	**1,801.6**	**1,831.7**	**1,827.9**	**21,156.0**	Yield %	**0.4**	Market Cap	**US$57,370mil**

Address	**2-7-1, Marunouchi**	Tel	**03-3240-1111**	ADR	**MBK**	President	**Tsuneo Wakai**
	Chiyoda-ku, Tokyo 100	Fax	**03-3240-2820**	SEDOL No.	**6596688**	Chairman	**Kazuo Ibuki**

Mitsubishi Cable Industries

Industry: **Electrical Components & Equipment**

Mitsubishi Cable Industries (Mitsubishi Densen Kogyo), a core of Mitsubishi Materials group's optical communications project, is Japan's sixth-largest maker of electric wire and cable by sales. Its products include plastic-covered wires, electric cables, communication cables, fiber-optic cables, bare wires, electronic parts, and O-rings. The firm's main markets are the auto and aerospace industries. A leader in industrial fibers, Mitsubishi Cable has developed its own manufacturing method for optical fibers synthesized from quartz.

	¥bil 03/93	03/94	03/95	US$mil 03/95				
Sales	**165.6**	**152.6**	**145.2**	**1,472.2**	P/E Ratio	**78.8**	Price (9/30/95)	**567.00**
Net Income	**6.4**	**4.1**	**1.4**	**14.2**	P/B Ratio	**1.7**	52 Wk Hi-Low	**760.00-466.00**
Book Value	**57.1**	**63.1**	**63.7**	**737.2**	Yield %	**1.2**	Market Cap	**US$1,108.0mil**

Address	**3-4-1, Marunouchi**	Tel	**03-3216-1551**	ADR		President	**Harunosuke Fuji**
	Chiyoda-ku, Tokyo 100	Fax	**03-3201-3948**	SEDOL No.	**6250780**	Chairman	**Hayao Shigenari**

Mitsubishi Chemical

Industry: **Commodity Chemicals**

Mitsubishi Chemical, formed through the October 1994 merger of Mitsubishi Kasei and Mitsubishi Petrochemical, is Japan's largest integrated chemicals firm, with strengths in petrochemicals and carbon products. The company's petrochemical products include olefins, polyethylene, polypropylene, and vinyl-chloride monomers. It also produces medical equipment, agricultural chemicals, and plywoods. The company has 22 wholly-owned subsidiaries in North and South America, Europe, Southeast Asia, and Australia. About 17% of its revenues come from overseas.

	¥bil 03/93	03/94	03/95	US$mil 03/95				
Sales	**1,180.9**	**1,077.1**	**1,340.2**	**13,584.4**	P/E Ratio	**NMF**	Price (9/30/95)	**480.00**
Net Income	**6.0**	**-2.9**	**3.0**	**30.8**	P/B Ratio	**2.2**	52 Wk Hi-Low	**583.00-360.00**
Book Value	**290.3**	**283.0**	**486.7**	**5,632.9**	Yield %	**0.6**	Market Cap	**US$10,578mil**

Address	**2-5-2, Marunouchi**	Tel	**03-3283-6264**	ADR	**MKASY**	President	**Akira Miura**
	Chiyoda-ku, Tokyo 100	Fax	**03-3283-6287**	SEDOL No.	**6597001**	Chairman	**Masahiko Furukawa**

Mitsubishi Electric

Industry: **Diversified Technology**

Mitsubishi Electric produces information and telecommunication equipment, heavy machinery, consumer goods, and industrial equipment. The firm is a leading electric-machinery manufacturer and defense contractor by revenues. It also produces four-megabyte dynamic random-access-memory chips, and participates in a technical agreement with Motorola to develop semiconductors. Mitsubishi Electric has 109 consolidated subsidiaries, including operations in North America, Europe, and Asia. Overseas revenues represented nearly 23% of total consolidated sales in fiscal 1994.

¥bil	03/93	03/94	03/95	US$mil 03/95				
Sales	**3,260.3**	**3,105.4**	**3,250.9**	**32,952.0**	P/E Ratio	**39.5**	Price (9/30/95)	**775.00**
Net Income	**28.5**	**20.7**	**42.1**	**426.7**	P/B Ratio	**2.0**	52 Wk Hi-Low	**775.00-540.00**
Book Value	**815.4**	**809.9**	**833.0**	**9,641.3**	Yield %	**1.3**	Market Cap	**US$16,733mil**

Address	**2-2-3, Marunouchi**	Tel	**03-3218-2272**	ADR	**MIELY**	President	**Takashi Kitaoka**
	Chiyoda-ku, Tokyo 100	Fax	**03-3218-2431**	SEDOL No.	**6597045**	Chairman	--

Mitsubishi Estate

Industry: **Real-Estate Investment**

Mitsubishi Estate is Japan's second-largest comprehensive real-estate company by sales. The company owns, manages, and leases office buildings in urban areas throughout Japan. Tokyo's Marunouchi district generates 70% of Mitsubishi Estate's rental revenues. The company is active in commercial and residential development (including condominiums, houses, and resort sites), project supervision, and architectural design. It also operates resorts and hotels overseas. In fiscal 1994, less than 13% of Mitsubishi Estate's consolidated sales came from overseas.

¥bil	03/93	03/94	03/95	US$mil 03/95				
Sales	**468.8**	**558.9**	**563.4**	**5,711.1**	P/E Ratio	**95.7**	Price (9/30/95)	**1,110.00**
Net Income	**26.2**	**22.6**	**15.1**	**152.6**	P/B Ratio	**2.8**	52 Wk Hi-Low	**1,210.0-902.0**
Book Value	**499.6**	**504.3**	**513.1**	**5,939.2**	Yield %	**0.7**	Market Cap	**US$14,505mil**

Address	**2-4-1, Marunouchi**	Tel	**03-3287-5100**	ADR	**MITEY**	President	**Takeshi Fukuzawa**
	Chiyoda-ku, Tokyo 100	Fax	**03-3212-3757**	SEDOL No.	**6596729**	Chairman	**Jotaro Takagi**

Mitsubishi Gas Chemical

Industry: **Commodity Chemicals**

Mitsubishi Gas Chemical (Mitsubishi Gas Kagaku or MGC), a member of the Mitsubishi group, is a leading Japanese producer and supplier of methanol and methanol derivatives, including formalin, plastics, and gasoline additives. It controls more than 30% of the Asian methanol market. The company also produces hydrogen peroxide and electronics materials, such as multilayer printed circuit boards. It makes more than 18% of its sales to its parent company, Mitsubishi. Major customers also include Dai Nippon Ink & Chemical, Tokyo Shokai, Nippon Hydrogen, and Itochu Fine Chemical. In fiscal 1992, sales of chemicals accounted for 52% o

¥bil	03/93	03/94	03/95	US$mil 03/95				
Sales	**297.8**	**276.1**	**311.3**	**3,155.4**	P/E Ratio	**44.2**	Price (9/30/95)	**438.00**
Net Income	**1.0**	**-1.9**	**4.9**	**50.1**	P/B Ratio	**1.5**	52 Wk Hi-Low	**439.00-335.00**
Book Value	**146.0**	**142.4**	**147.9**	**1,711.6**	Yield %	**0.6**	Market Cap	**US$2,196.2mil**

Address	**2-5-2, Marunouchi**	Tel	**03-3283-5000**	ADR		President	**Akira Ohira**
	Chiyoda-ku, Tokyo 100	Fax	**03-3287-0833**	SEDOL No.	**6596923**	Chairman	**Reiji Nishikawa**

Mitsubishi Heavy Industries

Industry: **Industrial - Diversified**

Mitsubishi Heavy Industries (Mitsubishi Jukogyo) manufactures heavy machinery and engages in shipbuilding and plant engineering. The company's products include steel structures, aircraft, heavy machinery, and air conditioners. It is the Japan Defense Agency's largest supplier, providing helicopters, tanks, and aircraft. The company also participates in aeronautics and space projects with Japan's National Space Development Agency. It does subcontracting work for Boeing and McDonnell Douglas and participates in the development of new aircraft with Boeing and Pratt & Whitney.

¥bil	03/93	03/94	03/95	US$mil 03/95				
Sales	**2,824.8**	**2,784.3**	**2,848.5**	**28,873.6**	P/E Ratio	**32.9**	Price (9/30/95)	**760.00**
Net Income	**81.1**	**79.9**	**77.9**	**789.7**	P/B Ratio	**2.2**	52 Wk Hi-Low	**794.00-541.00**
Book Value	**1,066.2**	**1,119.1**	**1,178.2**	**13,636.1**	Yield %	**1.1**	Market Cap	**US$25,751mil**

Address	**2-5-1, Marunouchi**	Tel	**03-3212-3111**	ADR		President	**Nobuyuki Masuda**
	Chiyoda-ku, Tokyo 100	Fax	**03-3212-9860**	SEDOL No.	**6597067**	Chairman	**Kentaro Aikawa**

Mitsubishi Materials

Industry: **Non-Ferrous Metals - Other (Exc. Aluminum)**

Mitsubishi Materials, a member of the Mitsubishi group, smelts copper, refines gold, manufactures cement, fabricates metal products, and develops advanced materials. The firm's main products include copper tubing and aluminum-welded products, fine ceramics, electronic parts, special materials and alloys, and aluminum cans. Its major markets are the building-materials and construction-machinery industries. The firm has 90 consolidated subsidiaries, including 10 companies in the U.S. It participates in a Venezuelan aluminum-refining project with Reynolds Metals (U.S.).

¥bil	03/93	03/94	03/95	US$mil 03/95				
Sales	**1,145.4**	**1,064.3**	**1,151.3**	**11,669.6**	P/E Ratio	**NMF**	Price (9/30/95)	**487.00**
Net Income	**0.3**	**-2.8**	**-3.7**	**-38.0**	P/B Ratio	**1.9**	52 Wk Hi-Low	**555.00-364.00**
Book Value	**316.7**	**308.6**	**290.5**	**3,362.5**	Yield %	**1.0**	Market Cap	**US$5,555.2mil**

Address	**1-5-1, Otemachi**	Tel	**03-5252-5200**	ADR		President	**Yumi Akimoto**
	Chiyoda-ku, Tokyo 100	Fax	**03-5252-5280**	SEDOL No.	**6597089**	Chairman	**Masaya Fujimura**

Mitsubishi Motors

Industry: **Automobile Manufacturers**

Mitsubishi Motors (Mitsubishi Jidosha Kogyo) is Japan's fourth-largest automaker by sales. The firm was formed in 1970 as a joint venture between Mitsubishi Heavy Industries and Chrysler, but Chrysler has since sold off most of its stake. It makes a wide range of vehicles, including passenger cars, minicars, commercial vehicles, sport-utility vehicles, trucks, and buses. Mitsubishi Motors has 16 consolidated subsidiaries overseas. The company also has joint ventures with Hyundai and Daimler-Benz, and plans to produce automobiles in the Netherlands with Volvo in 1995.

¥bil	03/93	03/94	03/95	US$mil 03/95				
Sales	**3,180.4**	**2,946.9**	**3,414.1**	**34,606.8**	P/E Ratio	**58.7**	Price (9/30/95)	**833.00**
Net Income	**25.8**	**5.6**	**12.6**	**127.9**	P/B Ratio	**1.6**	52 Wk Hi-Low	**977.00-688.00**
Book Value	**401.5**	**408.5**	**479.2**	**5,546.0**	Yield %	**0.8**	Market Cap	**US$7,712.7mil**

Address **5-33-8, Shiba, Minato-ku, Tokyo 108**
Tel **03-3456-1111**
Fax **03-5232-7747**
ADR
SEDOL No. **6598446**
President **Nobuhisa Tsukahara**
Chairman **Hirokazu Nakamura**

Mitsubishi Oil

Industry: **Oil - Secondary**

Mitsubishi Oil (Mitsubishi Sekiyu) is an oil refiner and distributor. Its activities include importing oil, and manufacturing and distributing petrochemicals. The company's three refineries account for about 8% of the total crude-oil-refining capacity in Japan. Major customers include electric utilities and manufacturers of chemicals, pulp, and paper. Mitsubishi has ties with Nippon Oil and a joint venture with Fuji Kosan. It has consolidated subsidiaries in the United States, the United Kingdom, and the Netherlands. The firm also has a joint venture with Thai Oil Company.

¥bil	03/93	03/94	03/95	US$mil 03/95				
Sales	**1,134.2**	**1,098.0**	**1,117.1**	**11,323.6**	P/E Ratio	**26.4**	Price (9/30/95)	**848.00**
Net Income	**12.6**	**14.6**	**12.9**	**131.2**	P/B Ratio	**1.7**	52 Wk Hi-Low	**1,100.0-772.0**
Book Value	**108.6**	**136.5**	**227.5**	**2,632.6**	Yield %	**1.2**	Market Cap	**US$3,827.9mil**

Address **1-2-4, Toranomon, Minato-ku, Tokyo 105**
Tel **03-3595-7156**
Fax **03-3508-2521**
ADR
SEDOL No. **6597186**
President **Yoshihiko Izumitani**
Chairman **Kikuo Yamada**

Mitsubishi Paper Mills

Industry: **Paper Products**

Mitsubishi Paper Mills (Mitsubishi Seishi), a member of the Mitsubishi group, is a major producer of art and coated papers. Its main products are high-quality and specialty paper, business-communication paper, and graphic-arts materials, including photosensitive paper and the Silver Master brand of platemakers. The firm has six mills in Japan and two wholly-owned subsidiaries in the U.S. and Germany. It has a licensing agreement with Feldmuhle (Germany). Mitsubishi Paper also has manufacturing and marketing tie-ups with DuPont Japan for heat-resistant pressboards.

¥bil	03/93	03/94	03/95	US$mil 03/95				
Sales	**224.9**	**209.0**	**208.7**	**2,115.4**	P/E Ratio	**NMF**	Price (9/30/95)	**577.00**
Net Income	**1.3**	**1.0**	**0.4**	**4.0**	P/B Ratio	**1.7**	52 Wk Hi-Low	**758.00-446.00**
Book Value	**108.6**	**108.0**	**108.5**	**1,255.4**	Yield %	**0.9**	Market Cap	**US$1,892.3mil**

Address **3-4-2, Marunouchi, Chiyoda-ku, Tokyo 100**
Tel **03-3213-3762**
Fax **03-3214-4534**
ADR
SEDOL No. **6597142**
President **Yoshihiro Onda**
Chairman **Shigeru Uchimura**

Mitsubishi Rayon

Industry: **Commodity Chemicals**

Mitsubishi Rayon, a member of the Mitsubishi group, is a leading producer of acrylic and plastic optical fibers. It also makes suede-type fabrics, polyester, acetate, polypropylene filaments, monomers, and resins. Other products include high-density printed circuit boards, membranes, water purifiers, and carbon fibers. About 10% of the parent company's sales are made through the trading firm Mitsubishi. It has technology-licensing agreements with U.S. firms DuPont and Advanced Display Technologies covering optical-fiber and video-display-screen manufacturing techniques.

¥bil	03/93	03/94	03/95	US$mil 03/95				
Sales	**337.4**	**307.4**	**323.1**	**3,275.3**	P/E Ratio	**135.7**	Price (9/30/95)	**380.00**
Net Income	**2.2**	**0.2**	**1.8**	**18.1**	P/B Ratio	**1.9**	52 Wk Hi-Low	**458.00-312.00**
Book Value	**130.1**	**129.3**	**126.3**	**1,462.0**	Yield %	**0.7**	Market Cap	**US$2,398.1mil**

Address **2-3-19, Kyobashi, Chuo-ku, Tokyo 104**
Tel **03-3245-8667**
Fax **N/A**
ADR
SEDOL No. **6597164**
President **Eiichi Taguchi**
Chairman **Yataro Nagai**

Mitsubishi Warehouse & Transp.

Industry: **General Industrial & Commercial Services**

Mitsubishi Warehouse & Transportation (Mitsubishi Soko) is Japan's largest warehousing firm, with 650,000 square meters of storage space. A member of the Mitsubishi group, its major customers are Mitsubishi Corp. and Mitsubishi Heavy Industries. The firm has an agreement with Unitrans (Japan) to provide port-harbor and international-transport services. While transport and warehousing services accounted for 75% of consolidated sales in 1994, its real-estate activities made most of its profit, with a 33% operating margin. The firm has 39 subsidiaries.

¥bil	03/93	03/94	03/95	US$mil 03/95				
Sales	**145.4**	**150.0**	**158.1**	**1,602.1**	P/E Ratio	**50.2**	Price (9/30/95)	**1,460.00**
Net Income	**8.5**	**6.6**	**4.9**	**49.5**	P/B Ratio	**2.6**	52 Wk Hi-Low	**1,680.0-1,160.0**
Book Value	**87.7**	**92.3**	**96.1**	**1,112.0**	Yield %	**0.5**	Market Cap	**US$2,467.1mil**

Address **1-19-1, Nihonbashi, Chuo-ku, Tokyo 103**
Tel **03-3278-6611**
Fax **03-3278-6694**
ADR
SEDOL No. **6596848**
President **Tsuyoshi Miyazaki**
Chairman --

Mitsui Construction

Industry: **Heavy Construction**

Mitsui Construction (Mitsui Kensetsu), a Mitsui affiliate, is a medium-size contractor specializing in energy-related facilities and high rises. Mitsui group projects account for 30% of its orders. Its civil-engineering works include water-tunnel construction, sewage, cabling, and subways. The firm constructs medium-, high-, and super-high-rise buildings, and handles large-scale urban-development work. Energy-related construction projects include storage tanks for liquid-propane gas, oil, and coal. Mitsui Construction has a network of 12 subsidiaries and 33 affiliates.

¥bil	03/93 P	03/94 P	03/95 P	US$mil 03/95				
Sales	582.5	532.7	515.5	5,224.8	P/E Ratio	NMF	Price (9/30/95)	385.00
Net Income	1.8	1.2	0.2	2.3	P/B Ratio	1.6	52 Wk Hi-Low	644.00-301.00
Book Value	50.6	50.2	49.8	576.9	Yield %	0.8	Market Cap	US$805.8mil

Address **3-10-1, Iwamoto-cho, Chiyoda-ku, Tokyo 101**
Tel **03-5821-7052**
Fax **03-5821-7607**
ADR
SEDOL No. **6597249**
President **Kazuhiro Inamura**
Chairman **Naoshi Onizawa**

P=Parent company data.

Mitsui Engineering & Shipbuilding

Industry: **Shipbuilding**

Mitsui Engineering & Shipbuilding (Mitsui Zosen) is the heavy-machinery arm of the Mitsui group. The firm's products include marine-diesel engines, defense systems, very large crude-oil carriers, bridges, hybrid floating structures, and high-speed ocean craft such as hovercraft. The company also provides naval vessels to Japan's Maritime Self-Defense Agency and technical assistance to companies in Indonesia and China. It has subsidiaries in the United States and Denmark and representative offices in Singapore, Jakarta, Beijing, London, New York, Houston, and Hong Kong.

¥bil	03/93	03/94	03/95	US$mil 03/95				
Sales	336.2	347.4	366.3	3,712.8	P/E Ratio	NMF	Price (9/30/95)	238.00
Net Income	5.3	2.8	-2.9	-29.3	P/B Ratio	2.0	52 Wk Hi-Low	347.00-176.00
Book Value	99.1	98.6	97.0	1,122.4	Yield %	0.0	Market Cap	US$1,989.3mil

Address **5-6-4, Tsukiji, Chuo-ku, Tokyo 104**
Tel **03-3544-3213**
Fax **03-3544-3050**
ADR
SEDOL No. **6597380**
President **Jiro Hoshino**
Chairman **Yasunosuke Ishii**

Mitsui Fudosan

Industry: **Real-Estate Investment**

Mitsui Fudosan, a member of the Mitsui group, is a leading property developer and Japan's largest real-estate company by sales. The firm sells condominiums, houses, and office buildings, and owns nine hotels in Japan. It has more than 200 subsidiaries and affiliates, including several large construction firms such as majority-owned Mitsui Home, one of Japan's leading homebuilders. The firm owns Oriental Land, the operator of Tokyo Disneyland, jointly with Keisei Railways. About 90% of Mitsui Fudosan's overseas subsidiary assets are located in the United States.

¥bil	03/93	03/94	03/95	US$mil 03/95				
Sales	1,348.4	1,301.9	1,242.2	12,590.9	P/E Ratio	106.3	Price (9/30/95)	1,190.00
Net Income	19.1	10.2	9.1	92.1	P/B Ratio	1.6	52 Wk Hi-Low	1,280.0-910.0
Book Value	597.1	604.1	606.3	7,017.6	Yield %	0.8	Market Cap	US$9,701.0mil

Address **2-1-1, Nihonbashi-Muromachi, Chuo-ku, Tokyo 103**
Tel **03-3246-3055**
Fax **03-3275-2329**
ADR
SEDOL No. **6597603**
President **Junichiro Tanaka**
Chairman **Hajime Tsuboi**

Mitsui Marine & Fire Insurance

Industry: **Insurance - Property & Casualty**

Mitsui Marine & Fire Insurance (Mitsui Kaijo Kasai Hoken) is the third-largest non-life-insurance company in Japan by total premiums sold, controlling nearly a 9% share of the domestic non-life market. The firm is also known for its commercial-insurance coverage, and is strengthening its personal-insurance line. Its premium line includes fire, marine, personal-accident, medical, auto, and compulsory auto-liability insurance. Mitsui Marine & Fire recently established a joint venture with Goldman Sachs to gain direc access to the over-the-counter market for swaps and options.

¥bil	03/93	03/94	03/95	US$mil 03/95				
Revenues	548.6	583.1	924.1	9,366.6	P/E Ratio	50.1	Price (9/30/95)	621.00
Net Income	11.2	10.2	9.0	91.6	P/B Ratio	1.9	52 Wk Hi-Low	780.00-551.00
Book Value	214.9	220.0	233.6	2,703.8	Yield %	1.1	Market Cap	US$4,536.7mil

Address **3-9, Kanda-Surugadai, Chiyoda-ku, Tokyo 101-11**
Tel **03-3259-3111**
Fax **03-3292-5890**
ADR
SEDOL No. **6870122**
President **Ko Matsukata**
Chairman **Takeru Ishikawa**

Mitsui Mining

Industry: **Coal**

Mitsui Mining (Mitsui Kozan), a member of Mitsui group, is Japan's largest coal-mining company based on revenues. It also produces cokes and cement and markets coal, petroleum, tiles, building materials, and machinery. Fuels account for about 55% of sales. The company has begun to develop and market aluminum fiber, carbon fiber, and pollution-control equipment. Primary markets are power plants and manufacturers. Its overseas operations include participation in a Chinese joint venture to import a coal-water mixture, and development of coal mines in Australia and Canada.

¥bil	03/93	03/94	03/95	US$mil 03/95				
Sales	304.7	284.3	286.0	2,899.3	P/E Ratio	NMF	Price (9/30/95)	415.00
Net Income	0.9	-2.5	-0.2	-1.7	P/B Ratio	2.2	52 Wk Hi-Low	523.00-310.00
Book Value	30.7	28.8	28.6	331.0	Yield %	0.0	Market Cap	US$635.2mil

Address **2-1-1, Nihonbashi-Muromachi, Chuo-ku, Tokyo 103**
Tel **03-3241-1335**
Fax **03-3241-8684**
ADR
SEDOL No. **6597324**
President **Tadashi Harada**
Chairman **--**

Mitsui Mining & Smelting

Industry: **Non-Ferrous Metals - Other (Exc. Aluminum)**

Mitsui Mining & Smelting (Mitsui Kinzoku Kogyo) smelts, refines, processes, and fabricates nonferrous metals, including zinc, gold, copper, silver, cadmium, and tin. Other products include rolled copper, chemical products, electronic materials, auto parts, die-cast products, and construction materials. The firm also handles engineering projects and trading of non-ferrous-metal products. It owns the Kamioka zinc mine, known for the size and quality of its deposit. Overseas consolidated subsidiaries are located in Ireland, the Netherlands, Malaysia, the U.S., and France.

¥bil	03/93	03/94	03/95	US$mil 03/95				
Sales	**336.5**	**317.1**	**342.3**	**3,469.8**	P/E Ratio	**NMF**	Price (9/30/95)	**358.00**
Net Income	**-4.3**	**-5.2**	**-9.1**	**-92.5**	P/B Ratio	**9.1**	52 Wk Hi-Low	**448.00-250.00**
Book Value	**33.8**	**29.8**	**19.3**	**223.5**	Yield %	**0.0**	Market Cap	**US$1,764.5mil**

Address **2-1-1, Nihonbashi-Muromachi** **Chuo-ku, Tokyo 103**
Tel **03-3246-8051** Fax **03-3246-8050**
ADR SEDOL No. **6597346**
President **Shinpei Miyamura** Chairman --

Mitsui O.S.K. Lines

Industry: **Marine Transportation**

Mitsui O.S.K. Lines (Osaka Shosen Mitsui Senpaku) is one of Japan's largest shipping companies and a member of the Mitsui group. Among the company's main cargoes are containers (mainly carrying finished goods), autos, perishable foodstuffs, minerals, and fossil fuels. The company operates routes to and from the U.S., Europe, and the Pacific Rim. Its fleet consists of 346 ships, 46 of which are owned, while the rest are chartered. Mitsui O.S.K. Lines has 394 subsidiaries and affiliates. In 1994, overseas activities acounted for 75% of Mitsui's total consolidated revenues.

¥bil	03/93	03/94	03/95	US$mil 03/95				
Sales	**673.1**	**608.6**	**635.3**	**6,439.5**	P/E Ratio	**NMF**	Price (9/30/95)	**286.00**
Net Income	**7.0**	**-6.0**	**-4.4**	**-44.8**	P/B Ratio	**2.6**	52 Wk Hi-Low	**425.00-225.00**
Book Value	**142.0**	**134.0**	**118.6**	**1,372.2**	Yield %	**0.0**	Market Cap	**US$3,155.5mil**

Address **2-1-1, Toranomon** **Minato-ku, Tokyo 105-91**
Tel **03-3587-7017** Fax **03-3587-7702**
ADR SEDOL No. **6597584**
President **Masaharu Ikuta** Chairman **Susumu Tenporin**

Mitsui Petrochemical Industries

Industry: **Commodity Chemicals**

Mitsui Petrochemical Industries (Mitsui Sekiyu Kagaku Kogyo) is the leading producer of high-density polyethylene, terephthalic acid, and polypropylene in Japan. The company also makes synthetic resins, basic chemicals, and special-purpose chemicals. It supplies makers of auto parts, packaging materials, and medical appliances. Mitsui Petrochemical has 33 subsidiaries. Among its joint ventures are a project to develop gas-phase polyethylene with Exxon Chemical (U.S.) and an agreement to exchange raw materials with BHP Petroleum (Australia).

¥bil	03/93	03/94	03/95	US$mil 03/95				
Sales	**341.7**	**332.2**	**361.3**	**3,662.1**	P/E Ratio	**51.0**	Price (9/30/95)	**790.00**
Net Income	**5.8**	**1.8**	**4.8**	**49.0**	P/B Ratio	**1.6**	52 Wk Hi-Low	**938.00-625.00**
Book Value	**153.4**	**155.2**	**158.3**	**1,831.7**	Yield %	**0.8**	Market Cap	**US$2,476.6mil**

Address **3-2-5, Kasumigaseki** **Chiyoda-ku, Tokyo 100**
Tel **03-3580-2012** Fax **03-3593-0027**
ADR SEDOL No. **6597368**
President **Shigenori Koda** Chairman **Shogo Takebayashi**

Mitsui-Soko

Industry: **General Industrial & Commercial Services**

Mitsui-Soko, a member of the Mitsui group, offers warehousing and transport services. It is Japan's second-largest warehousing firm by capacity, operating 532,000 square meters of warehouse space. The firm's main business line is port-harbor transport, but it is also active in real-estate leasing, equipment leasing, and land transport. It has 10 consolidated and 12 unconsolidated subsidiaries. Mitsui-Soko has facilities in Europe, a cargo-container business in North America, and through a joint venture has established distribution centers in Beijing, Dalian, and Shanghai.

¥bil	03/93	03/94	03/95	US$mil 03/95				
Sales	**89.9**	**84.9**	**91.2**	**924.6**	P/E Ratio	**18.4**	Price (9/30/95)	**690.00**
Net Income	**4.3**	**3.8**	**5.2**	**52.9**	P/B Ratio	**2.6**	52 Wk Hi-Low	**875.00-591.00**
Book Value	**29.8**	**32.7**	**36.7**	**425.3**	Yield %	**0.9**	Market Cap	**US$967.6mil**

Address **1-13-12, Nihonbashi-Kayabacho** **Chuo-ku, Tokyo 103**
Tel **03-3667-5335** Fax **03-3639-5055**
ADR SEDOL No. **6597647**
President **Kimio Shiino** Chairman **Goro Hara**

Mitsui Toatsu Chemicals

Industry: **Specialty Chemicals**

Mitsui Toatsu Chemicals (Mitsui Toatsu Kagaku) is a major integrated-chemicals firm. It produces agrichemicals, biotech chemicals, pharmaceuticals, and electronic materials, and is a leading supplier of polyvinyl chloride film. The plastics division supplies plastic resin to automakers, the consumer-electronics industry, and the housing industry. The firm develops environmentally friendly products such as biodegradable plastics. Mitsui Toatsu has 28 consolidated subsidiaries. It has joint ventures in several Asian countries, including Thailand, Taiwan, and China.

¥bil	03/93	03/94	03/95	US$mil 03/95				
Sales	**496.3**	**455.0**	**495.5**	**5,022.2**	P/E Ratio	**NMF**	Price (9/30/95)	**373.00**
Net Income	**3.1**	**-3.1**	**0.0**	**0.5**	P/B Ratio	**2.0**	52 Wk Hi-Low	**430.00-301.00**
Book Value	**158.4**	**151.8**	**149.5**	**1,729.9**	Yield %	**0.8**	Market Cap	**US$2,931.8mil**

Address **3-2-5, Kasumigaseki** **Chiyoda-ku, Tokyo 100**
Tel **03-3592-4106** Fax **03-3592-4267**
ADR SEDOL No. **6597625**
President **Akio Sato** Chairman **Haruo Sawamura**

Mitsui & Co.

Industry: **Overseas Trading**

Mitsui & Co. (Mitsui Bussan) is Japan's top general-trading company by revenues and a leader of Japan's Mitsui group. The company trades in steel, machinery, chemicals, foodstuffs, nonferrous metals, and textiles. Mitsui is also active in real-estate development, construction, investment, finance, transportation, satellite communications, and international economic development. The firm has several large petroleum-related projects. In 1994, Mitsui made 46% of its consolidated sales overseas.

	¥bil 03/93	03/94	03/95	US$mil 03/95				
Sales	**17,156.3**	**17,637.1**	**17,035.0**	**172,672.5**	P/E Ratio	**45.5**	Price (9/30/95)	**769.00**
Net Income	**17.5**	**15.3**	**26.2**	**265.6**	P/B Ratio	**2.1**	52 Wk Hi-Low	**875.00-618.00**
Book Value	**598.2**	**577.9**	**572.5**	**6,626.7**	Yield %	**1.0**	Market Cap	**US$12,013mil**

Address	**1-2-1, Otemachi**	Tel	**03-3285-1111**	ADR	**MITSY**	President	**Naohiko Kumagai**
	Chiyoda-ku, Tokyo 100	Fax	**03-3285-9819**	SEDOL No.	**6597302**	Chairman	**Koichiro Ejiri**

Mitsukoshi

Industry: **Retailers - Broadline**

Mitsukoshi is a leading department-store chain based in Tokyo. Its domestic sales network includes its flagship Nihonbashi outlet, other stores in the Tokyo metropolitan area, and stores throughout the rest of Japan. Its Tokyo headquarters and other outlets there, including fashion boutiques and restaurants, make up by far the largest portion of its retail space. Mitsukoshi has about 100 satellite gift shops, and through its domestic subsidiaries is also involved in direct mail, travel agencies, sports-club management, wedding services, and interior decorating.

	¥bil 02/93	02/94	02/95	US$mil 02/95				
Revenues	**1,082.6**	**1,034.9**	**1,017.1**	**10,148.9**	P/E Ratio	**NMF**	Price (9/30/95)	**825.00**
Net Income	**-8.2**	**-8.9**	**-4.3**	**-42.6**	P/B Ratio	**4.7**	52 Wk Hi-Low	**1,060.0-606.0**
Book Value	**102.7**	**91.3**	**85.1**	**879.5**	Yield %	**0.7**	Market Cap	**US$3,991.5mil**

Address	**1-4-1, Nihonbashi-Muromachi**	Tel	**03-3241-3311**	ADR		President	**Shoji Tsuda**
	Chuo-ku, Tokyo 103-01	Fax	**03-3242-4559**	SEDOL No.	**6597487**	Chairman	**Yoshiaki Sakakura**

Mizuno

Industry: **Other Recreational Products & Services**

Mizuno is a major manufacturer and distributor of sporting goods and sportswear. The firm's products include golf clubs and shoes; ski and camping equipment; baseball gloves, bats, and uniforms; athletic shoes; and swimsuits. Mizuno also manages and develops track stadiums, tennis courts, gymnasiums, golf domes, and resort facilities. The firm has three plants, 13 sales offices, three distribution centers, and 23 direct-sales outlets in Japan. Mizuno has sales subsidiaries in the Netherlands, Germany, France, U.K., U.S., Mexico, Canada, Taiwan, and Hong Kong.

	¥bil 03/93	03/94	03/95	US$mil 03/95				
Sales	**215.1**	**204.4**	**190.0**	**1,925.9**	P/E Ratio	**NMF**	Price (9/30/95)	**925.00**
Net Income	**-0.6**	**-1.2**	**0.0**	**0.1**	P/B Ratio	**1.3**	52 Wk Hi-Low	**1,110.0-725.0**
Book Value	**103.9**	**101.4**	**100.3**	**1,160.7**	Yield %	**1.3**	Market Cap	**US$1,273.5mil**

Address	**1-12-35, Nanko-Kita**	Tel	**06-614-8014**	ADR		President	**Masato Mizuno**
	Suminoe-ku, Osaka 559	Fax	**06-614-8493**	SEDOL No.	**6597960**	Chairman	**Kenjiro Mizuno**

Morinaga Milk Industry

Industry: **Other Food**

Morinaga Milk Industry (Morinaga Nyugyo) is the third-largest Japanese dairy producer by sales. The company produces dairy foods and nutritional foods, such as tofu, that are marketed worldwide under the Mori-Nu name. It also makes anticancer drugs, pharmaceuticals, and eutrophic medicines. In addition, the company markets Creap powdered cream, Eskimo ice cream, Lipton tea, Sunkist fruit juices and desserts, and Lady Borden ice cream in Japan. Morinaga Milk Industry has a joint venture with Kraft General Foods to import and produce Kraft products in Japan.

	¥bil 03/93	03/94	03/95	US$mil 03/95				
Sales	**400.7**	**407.1**	**453.8**	**4,599.4**	P/E Ratio	**35.2**	Price (9/30/95)	**430.00**
Net Income	**2.4**	**2.2**	**3.1**	**31.1**	P/B Ratio	**1.7**	52 Wk Hi-Low	**580.00-383.00**
Book Value	**62.2**	**63.2**	**64.0**	**740.7**	Yield %	**1.3**	Market Cap	**US$1,085.6mil**

Address	**5-33-1, Shiba**	Tel	**03-3798-0116**	ADR		President	**Akira Ohno**
	Minato-ku, Tokyo 108	Fax	**03-3798-0101**	SEDOL No.	**6602648**	Chairman	--

Morinaga & Company

Industry: **Other Food**

Morinaga & Company (Morinaga Seika) manufactures confectionery, foodstuffs, and ice cream. The firm's principal products in the confectionery category include chocolates, cookies, candies, caramels, and snacks. Foodstuffs produced by the company include pancake mix, cocoa, and beverages (including Sunkist-brand juices produced under license). Morinaga is the largest domestic manufactuer of caramels, pancake mix, and cocoa, and holds the second-largest share of the Japanese ice-cream market. It is also active in real estate and the operation of sports clubs.

	¥bil 03/93	03/94	03/95	US$mil 03/95				
Sales	**203.0**	**204.6**	**211.4**	**2,142.4**	P/E Ratio	**NMF**	Price (9/30/95)	**390.00**
Net Income	**-1.4**	**1.0**	**-3.1**	**-31.2**	P/B Ratio	**2.0**	52 Wk Hi-Low	**498.00-321.00**
Book Value	**55.6**	**55.3**	**50.8**	**588.0**	Yield %	**1.3**	Market Cap	**US$1,042.3mil**

Address	**5-33-1, Shiba**	Tel	**03-3456-0115**	ADR		President	**Akio Matsuzaki**
	Minato-ku, Tokyo 108	Fax	**03-3769-6129**	SEDOL No.	**6602604**	Chairman	**Sadao Takagi**

Murata Manufacturing

Industry: **Electrical Components & Equipment**

Murata Manufacturing (Murata Seisakusho) is a leading maker of ceramic electronic components, piezolectric products, and coil and circuit components. The company also sells noise-suppression and high-frequency equipment. Its products are used in mobile-communication equipment, consumer and industrial electronics, and air conditioners. Overseas sales make up 54% of total consolidated sales. Murata has 44 consolidated subsidiaries, including wholly-owned manufacturing and sales subsidiaries in Southeast Asia, Brazil, Mexico, and the United States.

¥bil	03/93	03/94	03/95	US$mil 03/95				
Sales	**272.1**	**279.2**	**317.5**	**3,217.8**	P/E Ratio	**23.4**	Price (9/30/95)	**3,770.00**
Net Income	**23.7**	**24.7**	**37.9**	**384.3**	P/B Ratio	**2.2**	52 Wk Hi-Low	**4,260.0-2,860.0**
Book Value	**339.5**	**368.4**	**412.5**	**4,774.5**	Yield %	**0.4**	Market Cap	**US$9,046.6mil**

Address	**2-26-10, Tenjin**	Tel	**075-951-9111**	ADR		President	**Yasutaka Murata**
	Nagaokakyo City, Kyoto 617	Fax	**075-954-7720**	SEDOL No.	**6610403**	Chairman	**Osamu Murata**

Nagase & Company

Industry: **Overseas Trading**

Nagase & Company (Nagase Sangyo) is Japan's largest specialty-chemical trader. Its major business lines include dyestuffs, chemical products, plastics, and synthetic resins. Other products include medical products, raw materials, and special resins for the electronics industry. Dainippon Ink and Chemicals, Nippon Paint, Sumitomo Chemical, and Mitsubishi Paper Mills are among Nagase's major customers. Its major foreign-business partners include Union Carbide, Eastman Chemical International, Ciba-Geigy, and General Electric. Nagase has 13 consolidated subsidiaries.

¥bil	03/93	03/94	03/95	US$mil 03/95				
Sales	**574.3**	**535.6**	**546.7**	**5,541.2**	P/E Ratio	**21.7**	Price (9/30/95)	**867.00**
Net Income	**3.2**	**6.1**	**6.1**	**61.4**	P/B Ratio	**1.2**	52 Wk Hi-Low	**975.00-642.00**
Book Value	**97.9**	**102.7**	**109.4**	**1,266.5**	Yield %	**0.9**	Market Cap	**US$1,320.5mil**

Address	**1-1-17, Shinmachi**	Tel	**06-535-2066**	ADR		President	**Hideo Nagase**
	Nishi-ku, Osaka 550	Fax	**06-535-2160**	SEDOL No.	**6619820**	Chairman	**Shozo Nagase**

Nagoya Railroad

Industry: **Railroads**

Nagoya Railroad is Japan's second-largest railroad in terms of operation mileage and is the largest private-railway operator in the Chubu district. In addition to railway services, the company provides tramway, taxi, marine, and charter-bus services. It is also participating in a consortium that is developing a magnetic levitation (maglev) train. The firm is active in real estate, and also manages sports facilities, amusement parks, hotels, restaurants, and a chain of swimming schools. It also has a 21% stake in a 47-company high-speed train joint venture, HSST Development.

¥bil	03/93	03/94	03/95	US$mil 03/95				
Sales	**356.6**	**348.5**	**376.7**	**3,818.1**	P/E Ratio	**NMF**	Price (9/30/95)	**500.00**
Net Income	**11.6**	**3.6**	**0.3**	**3.4**	P/B Ratio	**2.6**	52 Wk Hi-Low	**525.00-430.00**
Book Value	**156.1**	**162.4**	**151.7**	**1,755.6**	Yield %	**0.9**	Market Cap	**US$4,004.6mil**

Address	**1-2-4, Meieki**	Tel	**052-571-2111**	ADR		President	**Sokichi Minoura**
	Nakamura-ku, Nagoya 450	Fax	**N/A**	SEDOL No.	**6619864**	Chairman	**Seitaro Taniguchi**

Nankai Electric Railway

Industry: **Railroads**

Nankai Electric Railway (Nankai Denki Tetsudo) is a railway operator based in Osaka. It operates local rail and bus lines in southern Osaka and northern Wakayama prefectures. The firm also is involved in various real-estate activities: it develops land, sells residential lots, and runs amusement facilities, hotels, restaurants, and shops. The Osaka Stadium is among its better-known amusement facilities. Nankai plans to build a rail line to the new Kansai International Airport from downtown Osaka. The firm has 21 consolidated subsidiaries and 15 unconsolidated subsidiaries.

¥bil	03/93	03/94	03/95	US$mil 03/95				
Sales	**161.9**	**162.7**	**170.8**	**1,731.1**	P/E Ratio	**NMF**	Price (9/30/95)	**688.00**
Net Income	**2.2**	**1.9**	**1.7**	**17.3**	P/B Ratio	**2.9**	52 Wk Hi-Low	**824.00-610.00**
Book Value	**90.0**	**106.8**	**108.9**	**1,260.9**	Yield %	**0.7**	Market Cap	**US$3,187.8mil**

Address	**5-1-60, Nanba**	Tel	**06-644-7121**	ADR		President	**Taiji Kawakatsu**
	Chuo-ku, Osaka 542	Fax	**06-644-7123**	SEDOL No.	**6621472**	Chairman	**Shigeo Yoshimura**

National House Industrial

Industry: **Building Materials**

National House Industrial (National Jyutaku Sangyo), a member of the Matsushita group, holds the fourth-largeset share of Japan's prefabricated-housing market. The company designs houses and interior fixtures; produces building materials; manufactures and markets building machines; sells and leases real estate; and brokers casualty insurance. It specializes in the development and leasing of expensive subdivisions that combine Japan's traditional-architectural style and modern technology. National House has 13 consolidated subsidiaries and two unconsolidated subsidiaries.

¥bil	03/93	03/94	03/95	US$mil 03/95				
Sales	**212.2**	**223.2**	**243.9**	**2,472.4**	P/E Ratio	**24.3**	Price (9/30/95)	**1,850.00**
Net Income	**9.7**	**11.8**	**13.0**	**131.9**	P/B Ratio	**2.5**	52 Wk Hi-Low	**1,940.0-1,400.0**
Book Value	**107.7**	**116.5**	**125.8**	**1,455.7**	Yield %	**0.8**	Market Cap	**US$3,178.5mil**

Address	**1-1-4, Shinsenri-Nishimachi**	Tel	**06-834-5111**	ADR		President	**Shohei Tsuji**
	Toyonaka City, Osaka 565	Fax	**06-834-1586**	SEDOL No.	**6625720**	Chairman	--

Navix Line

Industry: **Marine Transportation**

Navix Line is one of the world's largest oil-tanker operators and a major transporter of bulk cargoes. Oil and petrochemical transport to Japan is one of the company's mainstays. It has 32 tankers that carry liquefied petroleum and natural gases, plastics, fibers, and synthetic rubber; 113 tramp (bulk cargo) vessels that transport commodities, finished goods, and raw materials; and four containers. Navix has 46 consolidated, 73 unconsolidated subsidiaries, and 36 affiliates. The firm was established in 1989 with the merger of Yamashita-Shinnihon Steamship and Japan Line.

¥bil	03/93	03/94	03/95	US$mil 03/95				
Sales	**170.6**	**157.8**	**152.6**	**1,546.9**	P/E Ratio	**NMF**	Price (9/30/95)	**263.00**
Net Income	**-6.7**	**-5.8**	**-0.9**	**-9.4**	P/B Ratio	**7.4**	52 Wk Hi-Low	**388.00-174.00**
Book Value	**19.4**	**16.3**	**13.9**	**160.3**	Yield %	**0.0**	Market Cap	**US$1,036.9mil**

Address	**1-1-1, Hitotsubashi**	Tel	**03-3282-7500**	ADR		President	**Noriaki Hori**
	Chiyoda-ku, Tokyo 100	Fax	**03-3282-7741**	SEDOL No.	**6985424**	Chairman	**Kazuo Ishii**

NEC

Industry: **Computers**

NEC is the world's second-largest manufacturer of semiconductors, and Japan's primary maker of personal computers. NEC purchased a 20% stake in U.S.-based PC maker Packard Bell for $170 million in July 1995. The firm is also tapping China's computer market through Beijing-based joint venture Shougang NEC Electronics. NEC has 89 consolidated subsidiaries in Japan. The company also has overseas subsidiaries and affiliates in 30 countries, which accounted for 27% of its revenues in fiscal 1994.

¥bil	03/93	03/94	03/95	US$mil 03/95				
Sales	**3,515.0**	**3,579.8**	**3,769.4**	**38,207.5**	P/E Ratio	**60.3**	Price (9/30/95)	**1,380.00**
Net Income	**-45.2**	**6.6**	**35.3**	**358.0**	P/B Ratio	**2.7**	52 Wk Hi-Low	**1,500.0-859.0**
Book Value	**805.8**	**782.1**	**790.7**	**9,152.2**	Yield %	**0.7**	Market Cap	**US$21,394mil**

Address	**5-7-1, Shiba**	Tel	**03-3454-1111**	ADR	**NIPNY**	President	**Hisashi Kaneko**
	Minato-ku, Tokyo 108-01	Fax	**03-3457-7249**	SEDOL No.	**6640400**	Chairman	**Tadahiro Sekimoto**

New Oji Paper

Industry: **Paper Products**

New Oji Paper, formed by the October 1993 merger of Oji Paper and Kanzaki Paper, is Japan's top paper producer by sales. The company's products include newsprint, printing paper, packaging paper, high-grade bleached board, tissue, pulp, lumber, and packing materials. It also manufactures converted products, such as diapers, thermal paper, and information-processing paper. New Oji also brokers real estate and operates forestry ventures in Vietnam and New Zealand. It established a paper-container manufacturing joint venture in China in 1994. It has 80 subsidiaries in Japan.

¥bil	03/93	03/94	03/95	US$mil 03/95				
Sales	**627.5**	**673.2**	**779.7**	**7,903.6**	P/E Ratio	**128.8**	Price (9/30/95)	**940.00**
Net Income	**4.3**	**4.7**	**5.4**	**55.1**	P/B Ratio	**2.0**	52 Wk Hi-Low	**1,080.0-811.0**
Book Value	**255.0**	**341.4**	**343.2**	**3,972.7**	Yield %	**0.9**	Market Cap	**US$7,024.5mil**

Address	**4-7-5, Ginza**	Tel	**03-3563-1111**	ADR		President	**Masahiko Ohkuni**
	Chuo-ku, Tokyo 104	Fax	**03-3563-1132**	SEDOL No.	**6657701**	Chairman	**Kazuo Chiba**

NGK Insulators

Industry: **Other Auto Parts**

NGK Insulators (Nippon Gaishi) produces insulators, combustion equipment, ceramics, sewage systems, and metal and porcelain products. NGK is the world's largest maker of insulators. Other main products include combustion equipment, ceramics, sewage systems, metal products, and porcelain products. It holds a 30% world market share for metal products and purification systems. Major customers include the electric-power, electronics, and auto industries. The firm has 28 consolidated subsidiaries, including in the U.S., Belgium, Germany, France, the U.K., and Switzerland.

¥bil	03/93	03/94	03/95	US$mil 03/95				
Sales	**240.6**	**233.0**	**226.2**	**2,292.8**	P/E Ratio	**44.7**	Price (9/30/95)	**952.00**
Net Income	**5.2**	**4.4**	**7.6**	**76.6**	P/B Ratio	**2.0**	52 Wk Hi-Low	**1,060.0-751.0**
Book Value	**160.7**	**162.5**	**165.8**	**1,918.7**	Yield %	**0.8**	Market Cap	**US$3,403.8mil**

Address	**2-56, Suda-cho, Mizuho-ku**	Tel	**052-872-7171**	ADR		President	**Masaharu Shibata**
	Nagoya City, Aichi 467	Fax	**052-872-7160**	SEDOL No.	**6619507**	Chairman	**Toshihito Kohara**

NGK Spark Plug

Industry: **Other Auto Parts**

NGK Spark Plug (Nippon Tokushu Togyo) is the largest Japanese spark-plug maker in terms of market share (60%) and the second largest in the world (10%). Spark plugs and ceramic products account for the majority of its sales. It produces integrated-circuit packages and develops oxygen sensors through Ceramic Sensor, a joint venture with NGK Insulators. Major domestic customers include Nissan Motor, Mazda Motor, and NEC. Beikoku Tokushu Togyo, its wholly-owned U.S. subsidiary, supplies spark plugs to the U.S. operations of Honda Motor, Nissan Motor, and Toyota Motor.

¥bil	03/93	03/94	03/95	US$mil 03/95				
Sales	**116.7**	**122.4**	**158.2**	**1,603.6**	P/E Ratio	**42.0**	Price (9/30/95)	**1,340.00**
Net Income	**4.4**	**3.3**	**6.6**	**66.7**	P/B Ratio	**2.3**	52 Wk Hi-Low	**1,370.0-866.0**
Book Value	**96.7**	**105.0**	**124.5**	**1,441.5**	Yield %	**0.7**	Market Cap	**US$2,887.8mil**

Address	**14-18, Takatsuji-cho**	Tel	**052-872-5920**	ADR		President	**Kaneo Okamura**
	Mizuho-ku, Nagoya 467	Fax	**052-872-5999**	SEDOL No.	**6619604**	Chairman	**Teiichi Suzuki**

NHK Spring

Industry: **Other Auto Parts**

NHK Spring (Nippatsu) specializes in the production of springs used in the automobile industry. Suspension springs, precision valve springs for engines, and torsion springs for transmimssions are its main products. The firm is also Japan's largest supplier of car seats and seat parts. It also makes multilevel auto-parking systems, piping for nuclear-power stations, and electric components. Major customers include Toyota Motor, Fuji Heavy Industries, Isuzu, Nissan Motor, Suzuki, and Mazda. NHK has production subsidiaries in the U.S. and Canada and a spring plant in Spain.

¥bil	03/93	03/94	03/95	US$mil 03/95				
Sales	**239.4**	**216.9**	**220.1**	**2,230.6**	P/E Ratio	**34.6**	Price (9/30/95)	**460.00**
Net Income	**3.2**	**1.6**	**3.3**	**33.0**	P/B Ratio	**1.4**	52 Wk Hi-Low	**580.00-350.00**
Book Value	**76.8**	**76.8**	**77.5**	**896.9**	Yield %	**1.3**	Market Cap	**US$1,129.3mil**

Address **3-10, Fukuura, Kanazawa-ku**
Yokohama, Kanagawa 236
Tel **045-786-7519**
Fax **045-786-7598**
ADR
SEDOL No. **6619648**
President **Tsuguhiro Maeda**
Chairman **Shohei Hamada**

Nichido Fire & Marine Insurance

Industry: **Insurance - Property & Casualty**

Nichido Fire & Marine Insurance (Nichido Kasai Kaijo Hoken) is Japan's third-largest provider of fire insurance. Its products include marine, casualty, auto, auto-liability, transport, movable-property, theft, and workers' compensation insurance. Among its new products are nursing-care expense and third-party-liability insurance. It has developed a comprehensive asset-management system with Nomura Research Institute. Nichido has nine international offices, including three recently opened in Honolulu, Dusseldorf, and Sydney. It also has a wholly-owned subsidiary in England.

¥bil	03/93 P	03/94 P	03/95 P	US$mil 03/95				
Revenues	**N/A**	**567.3**	**565.5**	**5,732.2**	P/E Ratio	**47.6**	Price (9/30/95)	**814.00**
Net Income	**8.9**	**8.1**	**7.3**	**74.4**	P/B Ratio	**2.1**	52 Wk Hi-Low	**864.00-644.00**
Book Value	**159.6**	**164.8**	**169.0**	**1,956.5**	Yield %	**0.9**	Market Cap	**US$3,503.5mil**

Address **5-3-16, Ginza**
Chuo-ku, Tokyo 104
Tel **03-3571-5141**
Fax **03-3574-0823**
ADR
SEDOL No. **6638524**
President **Takashi Aihara**
Chairman **Ikuo Egashira**

P=Parent company data.

Nichii

Industry: **Retailers - Broadline**

Nichii is a major retailer specializing in supermarkets. Its operations include more than 200 Nichii superstores, 30 Saty department stores, 17 Vivre clothing boutiques, and various restaurants, health clubs, and other ventures, collectively known as the MYCAL Group. Arby's Japan is another MYCAL company. Nichii also has leasing, insurance, real-estate and finance subsidiaries. It is participating in joint development of multiscreen cinemas in Japan with Warner Brothers (United States). Nichii owns a majority interest in Nissan Construction, which builds many of its stores.

¥bil	02/93	02/94	02/95	US$mil 02/95				
Revenues	**1,307.7**	**1,419.3**	**1,486.3**	**14,830.4**	P/E Ratio	**NMF**	Price (9/30/95)	**1,250.00**
Net Income	**9.2**	**-1.5**	**-5.2**	**-51.4**	P/B Ratio	**1.6**	52 Wk Hi-Low	**1,430.0-880.0**
Book Value	**224.8**	**226.3**	**215.0**	**2,223.7**	Yield %	**1.6**	Market Cap	**US$3,463.7mil**

Address **2-2-9, Awaji-machi**
Chuo-ku, Osaka 541
Tel **06-203-5072**
Fax **06-203-6387**
ADR
SEDOL No. **6638449**
President **Toshimine Kobayashi**
Chairman **--**

Nichimen

Industry: **Overseas Trading**

Nichimen is one of Japan's nine largest general-trading firms by sales. It mainly trades metals, chemicals, and machinery. Its metals division, which accounts for about 40% of the firm's sales, trades a wide range of iron and steel products. It also deals in machinery, industrial plants, textiles, and foodstuffs. Nichimen is Japan's largest trader of timber. Worldwide, it has branches and offices in 98 cities, and several joint ventures in Southeast Asia for making machinery, electronics, and steel products. In 1994, 44% of its consolidated sales were made overseas.

¥bil	03/93	03/94	03/95	US$mil 03/95				
Sales	**6,377.0**	**5,771.0**	**5,582.9**	**56,590.0**	P/E Ratio	**41.4**	Price (9/30/95)	**385.00**
Net Income	**4.4**	**3.8**	**3.9**	**40.0**	P/B Ratio	**1.1**	52 Wk Hi-Low	**480.00-336.00**
Book Value	**144.2**	**146.4**	**147.2**	**1,703.9**	Yield %	**1.6**	Market Cap	**US$1,640.5mil**

Address **1-13-1, Kyobashi**
Chuo-ku, Tokyo 104
Tel **03-3277-8040**
Fax **03-3277-8740**
ADR
SEDOL No. **6638568**
President **Akira Watari**
Chairman **Yoshimi Tanaka**

Nichirei

Industry: **Other Food**

Nichirei imports marine and livestock products, holding the top Japanese market share in frozen foods. The firm is Japan's largest cold-storage operator and the third largest worldwide. It runs about 70 warehouses directly and through affiliates. Its other products include curry, soups, sauces, and beverages. Nichirei sells about 80% of its products to the food-service industry, and the remainder directly to consumers. Main customers are Toa Shoji, Toho, Marudai Foods, and Morinaga. It has 99 subsidiaries, including ones in the Netherlands, U.S., Germany, and Australia.

¥bil	03/93	03/94	03/95	US$mil 03/95				
Sales	**523.6**	**523.4**	**559.8**	**5,674.6**	P/E Ratio	**43.9**	Price (9/30/95)	**579.00**
Net Income	**3.8**	**5.0**	**4.1**	**41.6**	P/B Ratio	**1.9**	52 Wk Hi-Low	**720.00-506.00**
Book Value	**84.0**	**87.7**	**96.5**	**1,116.7**	Yield %	**1.0**	Market Cap	**US$1,810.3mil**

Address **6-19-20, Tsukiji**
Chuo-ku, Tokyo 104
Tel **03-3248-2165**
Fax **03-3248-2119**
ADR
SEDOL No. **6640864**
President **Tadashi Teshina**
Chairman **Kozo Kaneda**

Nichiro

Industry: **Fishing**

Nichiro is a marine-products company that specializes in fresh and frozen fish. Its other goods and services include chilled, frozen, and canned foods; processed foods; feed; marine transportation; and cold storage. Many of its products are sold under the Akebono brand name. The firm offers tramp services and operates more than 30 refrigerated-transport ships. Nichiro's overseas operations include processed-food manufacturers in Seattle and Guam, and joint ventures in Canada, the U.S., Thailand, and Europe. It also operates aquaculture facilities in Japan and Chile.

	¥bil 03/93	03/94	03/95	US$mil 03/95				
Sales	**254.7**	**236.1**	**235.0**	**2,382.4**	P/E Ratio	**68.0**	Price (9/30/95)	**347.00**
Net Income	**-2.0**	**-2.1**	**0.8**	**8.5**	P/B Ratio	**4.1**	52 Wk Hi-Low	**407.00-280.00**
Book Value	**14.6**	**12.4**	**13.9**	**161.0**	Yield %	**0.9**	Market Cap	**US$574.1mil**

Address **1-12-1, Yuraku-cho**	Tel **03-3240-6222**	ADR	President	**Keinosuke Hisai**
Chiyoda-ku, Tokyo 100	Fax **03-5252-7963**	SEDOL No. **6638609**	Chairman	--

Nihon Cement

Industry: **Building Materials**

Nihon Cement, a member of the Fujo group, is Japan's second-largest producer of cement by sales. Its primary products are building materials, mining products, and sludge solidifiers. It developed its Asano Clean Set, a cement-based material, for the purposes of improving weak ground and treating sewer mire, oil mire, and other industrial wastes by solidification. Nihon Cement has eight plants, 24 consolidated subsidiaries, a research laboratory, and more than 90 bulk-distribution points in Japan. It has a joint venture, ACC Japan Castings, with Associated Cement (India).

	¥bil 03/93	03/94	03/95	US$mil 03/95				
Sales	**315.4**	**299.9**	**314.6**	**3,189.4**	P/E Ratio	**NMF**	Price (9/30/95)	**607.00**
Net Income	**6.3**	**3.5**	**-5.1**	**-52.1**	P/B Ratio	**1.3**	52 Wk Hi-Low	**780.00-505.00**
Book Value	**156.7**	**157.8**	**149.7**	**1,732.3**	Yield %	**1.2**	Market Cap	**US$1,999.6mil**

Address **1-6-1, Otemachi**	Tel **03-3201-1731**	ADR	President	**Michio Kimura**
Chiyoda-ku, Tokyo 100	Fax **03-3215-4890**	SEDOL No. **6640046**	Chairman	**Tooru Kitaoka**

Nihon Unisys

Industry: **General Industrial & Commercial Services**

Nihon Unisys, a joint venture between Unisys Corporation of the United States (32%) and Mitsui & Company of Japan (32%), is a major computer-sales company. Computer sales and leasing, systems maintenance, and software production are the company's main activities. Many of the goods the company sells are UNIX-related products. Nihon Unisys purchases computers from Mitsui, Unisys, Mitsubishi Electric, Oki Electric, and Oki Unisys. Nihon Unisys has an applications-software joint venture, Kayu Soft Engineering, in China and a subsidiary, Nihon Unisys Supply, in Japan.

	¥bil 03/93	03/94	03/95	US$mil 03/95				
Sales	**341.5**	**313.6**	**293.0**	**2,970.2**	P/E Ratio	**80.5**	Price (9/30/95)	**990.00**
Net Income	**3.2**	**1.1**	**1.3**	**13.7**	P/B Ratio	**1.5**	52 Wk Hi-Low	**1,330.0-850.0**
Book Value	**69.7**	**69.9**	**71.6**	**829.2**	Yield %	**0.8**	Market Cap	**US$1,092.0mil**

Address **1-1-1, Toyosu**	Tel **03-5546-4111**	ADR	President	**Kazutami Ishiguri**
Koto-ku, Tokyo 135	Fax **03-5546-7800**	SEDOL No. **6642688**	Chairman	--

Niigata Engineering

Industry: **Heavy Machinery**

Niigata Engineering (Niigata Tekkosho) manufactures industrial equipment and offers plant-engineering services. It makes diesel engines, machine tools (such as machining centers), industrial and construction machinery, rolling stock, cogeneration systems, and ships. The company's plant-engineering projects center around chemical facilities, refineries, and pollution-control systems. Niigata Engineering's overseas units are located in the Netherlands, U.S., Germany, Saudi Arabia, Thailand, Indonesia, and Singapore. It has offices in Hong Kong, South Korea, and China.

	¥bil 03/93	03/94	03/95	US$mil 03/95				
Sales	**267.0**	**259.0**	**242.6**	**2,459.0**	P/E Ratio	**NMF**	Price (9/30/95)	**323.00**
Net Income	**1.8**	**1.4**	**-4.9**	**-49.5**	P/B Ratio	**2.8**	52 Wk Hi-Low	**462.00-243.00**
Book Value	**46.6**	**46.5**	**39.2**	**453.9**	Yield %	**0.0**	Market Cap	**US$1,085.1mil**

Address **1-4-1, Kasumigaseki**	Tel **03-3504-2115**	ADR	President	**Yoshihiro Muramatsu**
Chiyoda-ku, Tokyo 100	Fax **03-3508-8985**	SEDOL No. **6640187**	Chairman	--

Nikko Securities

Industry: **Securities Brokers**

Nikko Securities (Nikko Shoken) is one of Japan's Big Four securities companies. The company is involved in equity and bond trading, futures and options, underwriting, investment trusts, and mergers and acquisitions. Nikko Securities has three computer hubs, in Tokyo, Nagoya, and Yokohama. Its network includes 138 domestic branches and seven overseas offices. The company has 29 consolidated subsidiaries, all but two of which are based overseas. In 1994, overseas activities accounted for 25.1% of Nikko Securities' total consolidated revenues, compared to 33.4% in 1993.

	¥bil 03/93	03/94	03/95	US$mil 03/95				
Sales	**320.6**	**350.8**	**265.5**	**2,691.2**	P/E Ratio	**NMF**	Price (9/30/95)	**981.00**
Net Income	**-8.1**	**15.2**	**-30.0**	**-303.8**	P/B Ratio	**1.8**	52 Wk Hi-Low	**1,170.0-680.0**
Book Value	**831.7**	**834.2**	**792.1**	**9,167.5**	Yield %	**0.7**	Market Cap	**US$14,490mil**

Address **3-3-1, Marunouchi**	Tel **03-3283-2211**	ADR **NIKOY**	President	**Kichiro Takao**
Chiyoda-ku, Tokyo 100	Fax **03-3283-2859**	SEDOL No. **6640284**	Chairman	**Shoji Umemura**

Nikon

Industry: **Other Recreational Products & Services**

Nikon is a comprehensive manufacturer of optical equipment. Its products include cameras, camera lenses, telescopes, survey equipment, optical glass, silicon-wafer inspection systems, and semiconductor-related equipment. Nikon controls roughly half of the world market for steppers used in semiconductor manufacturing. It plans to increase its share of the compact-autofocus camera market by introducing new low-priced models. Nikon has 51 subsidiaries (23 consolidated). In fiscal 1994, 56% of its consolidated sales came from overseas, up from 55% in 1993.

¥bil	03/93	03/94	03/95	US$mil 03/95				
Sales	231.9	246.2	288.5	2,924.2	P/E Ratio	NMF	Price (9/30/95)	1,280.00
Net Income	-8.8	-4.4	1.5	15.6	P/B Ratio	3.6	52 Wk Hi-Low	1,390.0-680.0
Book Value	142.5	135.8	132.5	1,533.6	Yield %	0.4	Market Cap	US$4,762.7mil

Address **3-2-3, Marunouchi**
Chiyoda-ku, Tokyo 100
Tel **03-3214-5311**
Fax **03-3214-5320**
ADR **NINOY**
SEDOL No. **6642321**
President **Shigeo Ono**
Chairman **Koji Sho**

Nintendo

Industry: **Toy Manufacturers**

Nintendo is the world's leading maker of home-video games. More than one fourth of all U.S. households have purchased the Nintendo Entertainment System. Its Super Famicom has captured roughly 55% of the Japanese market, and the Super NES has captured more than half of the U.S. market. Nintendo also sells the hand-held Game Boy system. Its Nintendo Power magazine has a monthly circulation in the U.S. of nearly one million. In 1994, 46.9% of its consolidated sales were made overseas, down from 52.7% in 1993.

¥bil	03/93	03/94	03/95	US$mil 03/95				
Sales	634.7	485.6	415.7	4,213.5	P/E Ratio	24.5	Price (9/30/95)	7,200.00
Net Income	88.6	52.7	41.7	422.3	P/B Ratio	2.2	52 Wk Hi-Low	7,250.0-4,590.0
Book Value	404.3	444.2	464.8	5,379.4	Yield %	1.0	Market Cap	US$10,260mil

Address **60, Kami-Takamatsucho**
Higashiyama-ku, Kyoto 605
Tel **075-541-6111**
Fax **N/A**
ADR **NTDOY**
SEDOL No. **6639550**
President **Hiroshi Yamauchi**
Chairman --

Nippon Beet Sugar Manufacturing

Industry: **Other Food**

Nippon Beet Sugar Manufacturing (Nippon Tensai Seito), an affiliate of Meiji Seika Kaisha, is Japan's largest manufacturer of beet sugar. The company's other products include compound livestock feeds, beet pulp, seedling paper pots for beet cultures, yeast, and Japanese noodles using beet fiber. It recently began using raffinose and betaine (acquired from beet juice) to produce livestock feed and shampoo. It also conducts research to find medical applications for raffinose. Nippon Beet Sugar's sales to Meisho consists of more than 80% of the parent-company's revenues.

¥bil	03/93	03/94	03/95	US$mil 03/95				
Sales	63.6	57.6	54.8	555.6	P/E Ratio	40.1	Price (9/30/95)	413.00
Net Income	1.8	1.7	1.6	16.0	P/B Ratio	1.4	52 Wk Hi-Low	498.00-325.00
Book Value	42.3	43.3	45.6	527.3	Yield %	1.2	Market Cap	US$636.6mil

Address **2-3-13, Kyobashi**
Chuo-ku, Tokyo 104
Tel **03-3273-4388**
Fax **03-3281-3847**
ADR
SEDOL No. **6640660**
President **Kotaro Baba**
Chairman --

Nippon Credit Bank

Industry: **Banks - Regional**

Nippon Credit Bank is the smallest of Japan's three long-term credit banks. In addition to long-term lending, its other services include advisory investment management, treasury and securities management, and project promotion. Recent overseas activities include a partnership with a New York corporate M&A specialist, Morgan Lewis Githens & Ahn. Nippon Credit International Ltd., a subsidiary, has established a London investment-management joint venture with Gartmore Investment Management. The bank has 17 consolidated subsidiaries (one of which is in Japan).

¥bil	03/93	03/94	03/95	US$mil 03/95				
Revenues	1,190.5	1,201.7	1,312.8	13,307.3	P/E Ratio	87.0	Price (9/30/95)	409.00
Net Income	18.4	17.1	8.2	83.1	P/B Ratio	1.3	52 Wk Hi-Low	500.00-380.00
Book Value	560.9	566.2	561.3	6,496.7	Yield %	1.5	Market Cap	US$7,139.6mil

Address **1-13-10, Kudan-Kita**
Chiyoda-ku, Tokyo 102
Tel **03-3263-1111**
Fax **03-3239-8065**
ADR
SEDOL No. **6618913**
President **Hiroshi Kubota**
Chairman **Seishi Matsuoka**

Nippon Densetsu Kogyo

Industry: **Electrical Components & Equipment**

Nippon Densetsu Kogyo serves its affiliate, Japan Railways (JR), as a general electrical contractor. Its main activities are light and power engineering, constructing power-generation and transformer substations, and installing power-transmission lines, air-conditioning and plumbing systems, communication equipment, signals, and railway tracks. Projects for JR account for over 40% of total revenues. It also leases real estate. Nippon Dentetsu has five domestic subsidiaries. The firm is active overseas, providing technology transfers and various advisory capabilities.

¥bil	03/93	03/94	03/95	US$mil 03/95				
Sales	148.5	143.1	147.9	1,499.1	P/E Ratio	23.7	Price (9/30/95)	964.00
Net Income	4.1	3.5	2.7	27.8	P/B Ratio	1.3	52 Wk Hi-Low	1,430.0-865.0
Book Value	45.3	48.5	51.5	596.6	Yield %	1.0	Market Cap	US$652.9mil

Address **1-2-23, Ikenohata**
Taito-ku, Tokyo 110
Tel **03-3822-8811**
Fax **03-3822-8960**
ADR
SEDOL No. **6640325**
President **Tatsuyuki Enomoto**
Chairman **Ryuji Yukawa**

Nippon Electric Glass

Industry: **Electrical Components & Equipment**

Nippon Electric Glass (Nippon Denki Garasu) makes glass and related products for industrial and home use. It is the world's second-largest manufacturer of glass for television cathode-ray tubes. The firm exports about 47% of its cathode-ray-tube glass. Nippon Electric Glass also exports glass-blowing machinery to Germany in cooperation with Coltoh. Its major customers include Matsushita Electric Industrial and Toshiba. Its overseas operations include a wholly-owned unconsolidated subsidiary in Illinois, an Ohio-based sales affiliate, and a production subsidiary in Malaysia.

¥bil	03/93	03/94	03/95	US$mil 03/95				
Sales	**205.2**	**246.3**	**268.7**	**2,723.5**	P/E Ratio	**33.2**	Price (9/30/95)	**1,880.00**
Net Income	**2.6**	**3.2**	**10.0**	**100.9**	P/B Ratio	**2.6**	52 Wk Hi-Low	**1,963.4-1,100.0**
Book Value	**105.3**	**105.6**	**115.3**	**1,334.7**	Yield %	**0.4**	Market Cap	**US$3,021.2mil**

Address **2-7-1, Seiran, Otsu City, Shiga 520** Tel **0775-37-1700** Fax **0775-34-4967** ADR SEDOL No. **6642666** President **Kiyosaku Kishida** Chairman **Akira Yanai**

Nippon Express

Industry: **Trucking**

Nippon Express (Nippon Tsuun) is Japan's largest transport-services company, conveying goods for both corporate customers and individuals. In addition to trucking, its operations include warehousing and marine and air transport. Nippon Express has two million square meters of warehouse space in Japan. It offers courier, packing, customs-clearance, and parcel-delivery services. Nippon Express has 300 subsidiaries. Its overseas operations include 11 subsidiaries in North and South America, 16 European subsidiaries, and seven offices in Asia.

¥bil	03/93	03/94	03/95	US$mil 03/95				
Sales	**1,705.1**	**1,656.5**	**1,687.2**	**17,102.5**	P/E Ratio	**36.2**	Price (9/30/95)	**888.00**
Net Income	**28.9**	**28.1**	**26.4**	**267.2**	P/B Ratio	**3.6**	52 Wk Hi-Low	**1,070.0-716.0**
Book Value	**218.3**	**239.8**	**262.1**	**3,034.0**	Yield %	**0.7**	Market Cap	**US$9,593.1mil**

Address **3-12-9, Soto-Kanda, Chiyoda-ku, Tokyo 101** Tel **03-3253-1111** Fax **03-5294-5129** ADR SEDOL No. **6642127** President **Shoichiro Hamanaka** Chairman **Takeshi Nagaoka**

Nippon Fire & Marine Insurance

Industry: **Insurance - Property & Casualty**

Nippon Fire & Marine Insurance (Nippon Kasai Kaijo Hoken) specializes in fire insurance. The firm's products include household, marine, accident, auto, and transport policies. It offers risk-prevention services for individual and corporate clients. Nippon Fire & Marine has an overseas network that includes 30 offices in 23 countries, including regional headquarters in Singapore, London, and New York. Its subsidiaries include an asset-management firm in the United Kingdom, and investment firms in Luxembourg, the Bahamas, the Channel Islands, and the United States.

¥bil	03/93 P	03/94 P	03/95 P	US$mil 03/95				
Revenues	**394.9**	**409.3**	**654.6**	**6,635.2**	P/E Ratio	**43.3**	Price (9/30/95)	**567.00**
Net Income	**9.5**	**8.5**	**7.6**	**77.1**	P/B Ratio	**1.6**	52 Wk Hi-Low	**720.00-508.00**
Book Value	**198.0**	**202.3**	**205.8**	**2,381.6**	Yield %	**1.2**	Market Cap	**US$3,311.7mil**

Address **2-2-10, Nihonbashi, Chuo-ku, Tokyo 103** Tel **03-3272-8111** Fax **03-3231-3614** ADR SEDOL No. **6643380** President **Kiyoshi Hirose** Chairman **--**

P=Parent company data.

Nippon Flour Mills

Industry: **Other Food**

Nippon Flour Mills (Nippon Seifun), is Japan's second-largest flour miller by market share, holding nearly 22% of the domestic market. It produces and markets wheat flours, bran, corn grits, vegetable proteins, rice flour, frozen foods, powdered soups, tempura batter, health food, and pet foods under the Ohmy brand name. The firm also imports and markets Italian products such as Barilla pasta, Valfrutta tomatoes, and Carapelli olive oil. Nippon Flour Mills operates warehouses and restaurants in Japan, as well as a joint venture in Los Angeles that supplies donut shops.

¥bil	03/93	03/94	03/95	US$mil 03/95				
Sales	**155.8**	**158.3**	**156.4**	**1,585.7**	P/E Ratio	**87.0**	Price (9/30/95)	**470.00**
Net Income	**1.5**	**1.0**	**1.0**	**10.0**	P/B Ratio	**1.5**	52 Wk Hi-Low	**531.00-364.00**
Book Value	**55.8**	**55.8**	**56.1**	**648.7**	Yield %	**1.3**	Market Cap	**US$865.8mil**

Address **5-27-5, Sendagaya, Shibuya-ku, Tokyo 151** Tel **03-3350-2306** Fax **03-5269-9320** ADR SEDOL No. **6640745** President **Hiroshi Sawada** Chairman **Fujio Hasegawa**

Nippon Hodo

Industry: **Heavy Construction**

Nippon Hodo, an affiliate of Nippon Oil, is the largest road-pavement firm in Japan by sales. The company's business activities include asphalt and concrete paving, road repair, civil engineering, building construction, and the production and sale of asphalt mixtures and oil products. The company is a leading vendor of plywood, and is diversifying into resort development and real estate. In 1994, road paving and building accounted for 76.5% of consolidated sales, production sales made up 21%, and development 2.5%. Nippon Hodo has 107 subsidiaries and 20 affiliates.

¥bil	03/93	03/94	03/95	US$mil 03/95				
Sales	**358.7**	**344.6**	**344.9**	**3,496.5**	P/E Ratio	**63.0**	Price (9/30/95)	**1,700.00**
Net Income	**7.3**	**5.6**	**3.2**	**32.1**	P/B Ratio	**1.6**	52 Wk Hi-Low	**1,790.0-1,460.0**
Book Value	**125.9**	**129.9**	**127.4**	**1,475.0**	Yield %	**0.7**	Market Cap	**US$2,001.9mil**

Address **1-19-11, Kyobashi, Chuo-ku, Tokyo 104** Tel **03-3563-6752** Fax **03-3567-4086** ADR SEDOL No. **6640789** President **Yoshio Nibe** Chairman **Yukiyasu Monobe**

Nippon Light Metal

Industry: **Aluminum**

Nippon Light Metal (Nippon Keikinzoku), an affiliate of Alcan Aluminum (Canada), produces metals, chemical products, building materials, and a variety of finished products. Its metals activities include converting bauxite into alumina, and smelting and producing aluminum and aluminum alloys. The company has diversified into processed products for the construction, automobile, and electronics industries. It has a technical and contracting agreement with Harmon Contract WSA (U.S.) and technical and marketing tie-ups with Korean Aluminum Company and Nippon Steel Corporation.

¥bil	03/93	03/94	03/95	US$mil 03/95				
Sales	**637.9**	**584.2**	**607.2**	**6,155.2**	P/E Ratio	**NMF**	Price (9/30/95)	**590.00**
Net Income	**4.2**	**-6.2**	**-5.1**	**-51.3**	P/B Ratio	**2.2**	52 Wk Hi-Low	**744.00-378.00**
Book Value	**161.9**	**154.2**	**147.0**	**1,701.4**	Yield %	**0.3**	Market Cap	**US$3,185.7mil**

Address **3-13-12, Mita**
Minato-ku, Tokyo 108
Tel **03-3456-9211**
Fax **03-3769-2451**
ADR
SEDOL No. **6641124**
President **Yuko Masuda**
Chairman **--**

Nippon Oil

Industry: **Oil - Secondary**

Nippon Oil, also known as Nisseki, operates Japan's largest oil importing, refining, and distributing network, with about a 17% domestic market share. The firm sells gasoline, its largest source of revenue, through its chain of more than 10,000 service stations. Caltex (U.S.) supplies about 40% of its oil, but Nippon Oil recently set up a joint venture with Saudi Arabian Oil. It is engaged in development operations in the Gulf of Mexico, the North Sea, Malaysia, Indonesia, Australia, and Myanmar, as well as offshore exploration projects in Papua New Guinea and Vietnam.

¥bil	03/93	03/94	03/95	US$mil 03/95				
Sales	**2,844.9**	**2,579.5**	**2,654.2**	**26,903.9**	P/E Ratio	**31.4**	Price (9/30/95)	**534.00**
Net Income	**31.0**	**23.2**	**20.8**	**211.3**	P/B Ratio	**1.0**	52 Wk Hi-Low	**700.00-524.00**
Book Value	**601.8**	**618.7**	**634.8**	**7,347.4**	Yield %	**1.3**	Market Cap	**US$6,605.8mil**

Address **1-3-12, Nishi-Shinbashi**
Minato-ku, Tokyo 105
Tel **03-3502-1111**
Fax **03-3502-9352**
ADR
SEDOL No. **6641403**
President **Hidejiro Ohsawa**
Chairman **Yasuoki Takeuchi**

Nippon Paint

Industry: **Specialty Chemicals**

Nippon Paint is the second-largest and the oldest paint-manufacturing company in Japan. The auto industry is its largest customer base. The company also makes oil- and water-based paints, and is expanding into the pharmaceutical and electronic-materials fields. With nine domestic plants, the company has a long-term plan for additional powder-paint plants in Southeast Asia, the U.S., and Europe. Nippon Paint currently produces powder paints in the U.S., and has factories in Thailand and Hong Kong. The firm has 22 domestic consolidated subsidiaries and five U.S. subsidiaries.

¥bil	03/93	03/94	03/95	US$mil 03/95				
Sales	**222.9**	**206.5**	**202.5**	**2,052.7**	P/E Ratio	**62.3**	Price (9/30/95)	**492.00**
Net Income	**4.2**	**2.6**	**2.1**	**21.3**	P/B Ratio	**1.4**	52 Wk Hi-Low	**755.00-435.00**
Book Value	**93.2**	**93.0**	**92.4**	**1,069.8**	Yield %	**1.2**	Market Cap	**US$1,313.4mil**

Address **2-1-2, Ohyodo-Kita**
Kita-ku, Osaka 531
Tel **06-458-1111**
Fax **06-455-9261**
ADR
SEDOL No. **6640507**
President **Hiroshi Fujii**
Chairman **Kazuo Sasaki**

Nippon Paper Industries

Industry: **Paper Products**

Nippon Paper Industries (Nippon Seishi) is Japan's largest paper manufacturer by sales. It has large market shares in newsprint, printing paper, paper cartons, and paper for automated-office equipment. Its mainstays are high-quality paper and coated-construction paper. Other products include noncarbon paper, processed paper and goods, film wrapper, chemicals, and building materials. Joint biotechnology projects with Weyerhaeuser (U.S.) and Tokyo University have led to development of pollution-resistant poplars and low-lignin conifers. It operates 12 factories in Japan.

¥bil	03/93	03/94	03/95	US$mil 03/95				
Sales	**547.8**	**961.6**	**989.2**	**10,026.9**	P/E Ratio	**127.5**	Price (9/30/95)	**650.00**
Net Income	**-3.3**	**0.1**	**4.8**	**49.1**	P/B Ratio	**2.1**	52 Wk Hi-Low	**783.00-545.00**
Book Value	**160.0**	**294.4**	**292.5**	**3,385.8**	Yield %	**1.1**	Market Cap	**US$6,201.1mil**

Address **1-12-1, Yuraku-cho**
Chiyoda-ku, Tokyo 100
Tel **03-3218-8000**
Fax **N/A**
ADR
SEDOL No. **6479820**
President **Takeshiro Miyashita**
Chairman **Choji Kuramochi**

Nippon Road

Industry: **Heavy Construction**

Nippon Road (Nippon Doro), a Shimizu affiliate, is a construction firm that specializes in asphalt paving. It also sells asphalt emulsions and other road-paving materials. The firm maintains roads, sidewalks, bridge decks, and airport runways, and builds sports facilities such as courts and tracks. Its civil-engineering projects are airports, harbors, and breakwaters. Nippon Road develops land for factories and housing, and is active in construction consultation. It has 37 subsidiaries, including one domestic subsidiary, N.D. Leasing and Service, which leases automobiles.

¥bil	03/93	03/94	03/95	US$mil 03/95				
Sales	**177.5**	**189.6**	**195.1**	**1,977.9**	P/E Ratio	**43.6**	Price (9/30/95)	**928.00**
Net Income	**3.6**	**3.3**	**2.1**	**21.1**	P/B Ratio	**1.5**	52 Wk Hi-Low	**1,130.0-780.0**
Book Value	**57.3**	**59.4**	**60.1**	**695.2**	Yield %	**1.2**	Market Cap	**US$911.2mil**

Address **1-6-5, Shinbashi**
Minato-ku, Tokyo 105
Tel **03-3571-4051**
Fax **03-3289-4489**
ADR
SEDOL No. **6642462**
President **Tadao Okagami**
Chairman **Hiroshi Shimizu**

Nippon Sanso

Industry: **Specialty Chemicals**

Nippon Sanso is Japan's largest seller of industrial gas. It supplies oxygen to the steel, chemical, paper, and pulp industries, and nitrogen to the semiconductor and petrochemical industries. The firm also sells argon, acetylene, petroleum-related gases, specialized gases, and gas-related equipment. Nippon Sanso has 34 consolidated subsidiaries, 13 of which are based in North America and Europe. Its U.S. subsidiary, Tri-Gas, Inc., has recently acquired Welco, Inc. and Doussan, Inc., two U.S. industrial-gas distributors. Nippon Sanso also owns the The Thermos Co. (U.S.).

¥bil	03/93	03/94	03/95	US$mil 03/95				
Sales	**267.6**	**257.9**	**255.3**	**2,587.9**	P/E Ratio	**43.0**	Price (9/30/95)	**482.00**
Net Income	**2.1**	**2.1**	**3.4**	**34.6**	P/B Ratio	**1.6**	52 Wk Hi-Low	**598.00-370.00**
Book Value	**87.9**	**87.5**	**90.0**	**1,041.9**	Yield %	**1.2**	Market Cap	**US$1,470.7mil**

Address **1-16-7, Nishi-Shinbashi**
Minato-ku, Tokyo 105
Tel **03-3581-8313**
Fax **03-3581-8755**
ADR
SEDOL No. **6640541**
President **Hiroo Tsuchiya**
Chairman **Hideo Mabuchi**

Nippon Sharyo

Industry: **Land Transportation**

Nippon Sharyo (Nippon Sharyo Seizo) manufactures railway rolling stock, including passenger coaches and electric cars. The company also builds electrical and industrial machinery, including generators, hydraulic hammers, cranes, bulldozers, and pile and casing drivers. It also constructs bridges, silos, autoclaves, storage tanks, and agricultural elevators, as well as special vehicles. Nippon Sharyo supplies railroad cars to the Japan Railways group, including cars for Shinkansen bullet trains. Among its other customers are Nagoya Railroad and the Construction Ministry.

¥bil	03/93 P	03/94 P	03/95 P	US$mil 03/95				
Sales	**105.1**	**100.4**	**97.1**	**983.9**	P/E Ratio	**42.7**	Price (9/30/95)	**811.00**
Net Income	**3.7**	**3.4**	**2.8**	**28.3**	P/B Ratio	**2.4**	52 Wk Hi-Low	**1,110.0-668.0**
Book Value	**45.5**	**48.1**	**49.9**	**577.7**	Yield %	**0.7**	Market Cap	**US$1,197.1mil**

Address **1-1, Sanbonmatsu-cho**
Atsuta-ku, Nagoya 456-91
Tel **052-882-3316**
Fax **052-882-3781**
ADR
SEDOL No. **6642503**
President **Yasuo Shimizu**
Chairman **Osamu Shinohara**

P=Parent company data.

Nippon Sheet Glass

Industry: **Building Materials**

Nippon Sheet Glass (Nippon Itagarasu) is one of Japan's second largest sheet-glass manufacturers. Among the firm's other glass-related products are figured glass, heat-reflecting and -absorbing glass, wired glass, double-glazed glass, glass fiber, fine glass, and fiberoptic products. The auto and construction industries are its biggest customers. The firm has joint ventures with Taiwan Glass and the Vietnamese government for glass-productiion factories. Of its 58 consolidated subsidiaries, all but three, which are based in the U.S., are domestic.

¥bil	03/93	03/94	03/95	US$mil 03/95				
Sales	**286.6**	**258.8**	**258.6**	**2,621.1**	P/E Ratio	**NMF**	Price (9/30/95)	**425.00**
Net Income	**1.1**	**-0.9**	**-0.6**	**-5.6**	P/B Ratio	**1.3**	52 Wk Hi-Low	**583.00-351.00**
Book Value	**150.6**	**146.5**	**145.8**	**1,687.8**	Yield %	**0.7**	Market Cap	**US$1,878.6mil**

Address **2-1-7, Kaigan**
Minato-ku, Tokyo 105
Tel **03-5443-9527**
Fax **03-5443-9554**
ADR
SEDOL No. **6641447**
President **Minoru Matsumura**
Chairman --

Nippon Shinpan

Industry: **Financial Services - Diversified**

Nippon Shinpan, a member of the Sanwa group, is one of Japan's largest consumer-credit companies. The firm provides leasing and loans to individual and corporate customers. It also is involved in credit-card operations, installment sales, loan guarantees, personal lending and leasing, and other activities. Nippon Shinpan has issued more than 25 million credit cards, making it the largest single issuer of credit cards in Japan. The firm recently teamed up with Daiei Finance and Kokunai Shinpan, the two other Japanese issuers of MasterCard, to expand cardholder privileges.

¥bil	03/93	03/94	03/95	US$mil 03/95				
Revenues	**385.6**	**391.0**	**376.3**	**3,814.1**	P/E Ratio	**NMF**	Price (9/30/95)	**620.00**
Net Income	**1.5**	**0.7**	**0.5**	**5.3**	P/B Ratio	**1.0**	52 Wk Hi-Low	**845.00-532.00**
Book Value	**202.4**	**199.9**	**198.9**	**2,301.8**	Yield %	**1.3**	Market Cap	**US$1,937.9mil**

Address **3-33-5, Hongo**
Bunkyo-ku, Tokyo 113-91
Tel **03-3811-3111**
Fax **03-3815-6650**
ADR
SEDOL No. **6643528**
President **Yoji Yamada**
Chairman **Yoji Yamada**

Nippon Shokubai

Industry: **Commodity Chemicals**

Nippon Shokubai is a leader in oxidation and catalyst technology used in the manufacture of paint and plastic. Its products include absorbent polymers and moldable plastics. The firm supplies the auto industry with materials for catalytic converters. It also makes catalysts for pollution control in power and other industrial plants. The company controls five consolidated manufacturing subsidiaries, including one in the United States. Nippon Shokubai also has wholly-owned subsidiaries in Germany and the U.S. to provide technical services and research on global trends.

¥bil	11/92	11/93	11/94	US$mil 11/94				
Sales	**152.6**	**140.6**	**136.5**	**1,326.6**	P/E Ratio	**48.9**	Price (9/30/95)	**910.00**
Net Income	**3.9**	**2.7**	**3.7**	**35.7**	P/B Ratio	**1.8**	52 Wk Hi-Low	**1,070.0-720.0**
Book Value	**94.8**	**95.7**	**98.0**	**990.6**	Yield %	**0.8**	Market Cap	**US$1,802.1mil**

Address **4-1-1, Koraibashi**
Chuo-ku, Osaka 541
Tel **06-223-9140**
Fax **06-227-1475**
ADR
SEDOL No. **6470588**
President **Shozo Tanaka**
Chairman --

Nippon Steel

Industry: **Steel**

Nippon Steel (Shin Nippon Seitetsu), leader of the Nippon Steel group, is one of the world's largest steel producers by sales. It manufactures steel plates, pipes, ingots, and H-beams. The firm controls approximately one fourth of the crude-steel market and one fifth of the stainless-steelmarket in Japan. Nippon Steel depends on exports for about 18% of its total consolidated sales. Its joint venture with Inland Steel (U.S.) in the United States, I/N Tek, produces cold-rolled-steel sheets. The company recently began to produce silicon wafers and semiconductors.

	¥bil 03/93	03/94	03/95	US$mil 03/95				
Sales	**2,951.4**	**2,749.4**	**2,881.1**	**29,203.8**	P/E Ratio	**NMF**	Price (9/30/95)	**346.00**
Net Income	**1.8**	**-54.1**	**-4.0**	**-40.3**	P/B Ratio	**2.7**	52 Wk Hi-Low	**403.00-276.00**
Book Value	**1,045.4**	**971.9**	**868.2**	**10,048.4**	Yield %	**0.7**	Market Cap	**US$23,978mil**

Address	**2-6-3, Otemachi**	Tel	**03-3242-4111**	ADR		President	**Takashi Imai**
	Chiyoda-ku, Tokyo 100-71	Fax	**03-3275-5611**	SEDOL No.	**6642569**	Chairman	**Hiroshi Saito**

Nippon Steel Chemical

Industry: **Specialty Chemicals**

Nippon Steel Chemical (Shin Nittetsu Kagaku), principal chemical company of the Nippon Steel group, produces coal-based chemicals, petrochemicals, carbon materials (such as carbon fibers and carbon black), bottled gases such as oxygen and nitrogen, and construction materials. Its parent company, Nippon Steel, the world's largest steelmaker, owns 56.7% of Nippon Steel Chemical's stock. The company has an equally-owned joint venture with PPG Industries (U.S.) and a technical tie-up with Tenma Corporation (Japan). Nippon Steel Chemical has 30 consolidated subsidiaries.

	¥bil 03/93	03/94	03/95	US$mil 03/95				
Sales	**291.1**	**265.7**	**282.4**	**2,862.7**	P/E Ratio	**NMF**	Price (9/30/95)	**380.00**
Net Income	**-7.6**	**-19.4**	**-7.1**	**-71.8**	P/B Ratio	**3.3**	52 Wk Hi-Low	**467.00-287.00**
Book Value	**52.8**	**33.1**	**22.3**	**257.5**	Yield %	**0.0**	Market Cap	**US$731.8mil**

Address	**5-13-16, Ginza**	Tel	**03-3248-5053**	ADR		President	**Takeshi Miyazaki**
	Chuo-ku, Tokyo 104	Fax	**03-3248-5112**	SEDOL No.	**6641395**	Chairman	--

Nippon Suisan Kaisha

Industry: **Fishing**

Nippon Suisan is one of Japan's largest traders of marine foods, and one of two major domestic fisheries still operating deep-sea fishing trawlers. The firm makes ground fish meat and frozen and canned foods. It is one of the largest Japanese producers of fish-meat, ham, and sausage. The firm also makes fine chemicals, pharmaceuticals, and beef products. It has an Alaskan fish-mincing factory and other U.S. affiliates that make fish paste. It also has joint ventures with Nichii to operate passenger cruise ships, and with U.S.' ConAgra and Pillsbury to import frozen foods.

	¥bil 03/93	03/94	03/95	US$mil 03/95				
Sales	**488.5**	**457.6**	**470.4**	**4,767.8**	P/E Ratio	**NMF**	Price (9/30/95)	**424.00**
Net Income	**4.7**	**-6.7**	**-1.1**	**-11.5**	P/B Ratio	**1.8**	52 Wk Hi-Low	**495.00-377.00**
Book Value	**77.7**	**71.1**	**69.4**	**803.0**	Yield %	**0.0**	Market Cap	**US$1,266.7mil**

Address	**2-6-2, Otemachi**	Tel	**03-3244-7196**	ADR		President	**Yasuo Kunii**
	Chiyoda-ku, Tokyo 100	Fax	**03-3244-7085**	SEDOL No.	**6640927**	Chairman	--

Nippon Telegraph and Telephone

Industry: **Communications Technology**

Nippon Telegraph and Telephone (NTT) is Japan's largest telecommunication firm and the country's largest company by market cap. The firm was originally a government monopoly, but 34% of its shares are now privately held. NTT has a monopoly on local phone service in Japan, and also offers long-distance and cellular-phone services within the country. (It is not allowed to compete in the international long-distance market.) It also offers computer-outsourcing, leased-circuit, and videotex services, and has a monopoly on public phones in Japan.

	¥bil 03/93	03/94	03/95	US$mil 03/95				
Sales	**6,504.0**	**6,652.4**	**7,037.2**	**71,331.9**	P/E Ratio	**NMF**	Price (9/30/95)	**853,000**
Net Income	**167.5**	**49.9**	**76.3**	**773.2**	P/B Ratio	**3.1**	52 Wk Hi-Low	**930,392-674,510**
Book Value	**4,345.9**	**4,320.9**	**4,321.6**	**50,019.1**	Yield %	**0.6**	Market Cap	**US$136,521mil**

Address	**1-1-6, Uchi-Saiwaicho**	Tel	**03-3509-3322**	ADR	**NTT**	President	**Masashi Kojima**
	Chiyoda-ku, Tokyo 100	Fax	**03-3509-4598**	SEDOL No.	**6641373**	Chairman	**Haruo Yamaguchi**

Nippon Television Network

Industry: **Broadcasting**

Nippon Television Network (Nippon Terebi Hosomo) is a private television network affiliated with the Yomiuri Shimbun group, which publishes Japan's most widely circulated newspaper. The company is the base for NNN, a nationwide news network that produces, markets, and broadcasts television programs. Nippon Television also sponsors music concerts, art exhibits, and other cultural events. The company has 11 consolidated subsidiaries, the most of which are based in Tokyo and involved in the management of leisure-related facilities and the marketing of audio-video merchandise.

	¥bil 03/93	03/94	03/95	US$mil 03/95				
Sales	**218.4**	**217.0**	**241.3**	**2,446.3**	P/E Ratio	**43.0**	Price (9/30/95)	**24,600**
Net Income	**3.5**	**3.0**	**7.2**	**73.3**	P/B Ratio	**2.4**	52 Wk Hi-Low	**25,000.0-17,800.0**
Book Value	**122.2**	**124.2**	**132.4**	**1,532.2**	Yield %	**0.4**	Market Cap	**US$3,133.8mil**

Address	**14, Niban-cho**	Tel	**03-5275-1111**	ADR		President	**Seiichiro Ujiie**
	Chiyoda-ku, Tokyo 102-40	Fax	**N/A**	SEDOL No.	**6644060**	Chairman	**Yosoji Kobayashi**

Nippon Yusen

Industry: **Marine Transportation**

Nippon Yusen, or NYK, is Japan's largest shipping firm in terms of sales. The company specializes in container ships running on scheduled routes (or regularly scheduled routes devoted to manufactured goods, such as electronics). The company also operates trampers (which carry bulk cargoes) and tankers. The parent company's fleet consists of roughly 400 ships. The Mitsubishi group is a major client. It also operates transport agencies and provides intra-harbor-transport services. The company has established land-based distribution systems in the United States and Europe.

¥bil	03/93	03/94	03/95	US$mil 03/95				
Sales	896.7	857.8	867.7	8,795.4	P/E Ratio	NMF	Price (9/30/95)	587.00
Net Income	7.4	6.1	3.1	31.9	P/B Ratio	3.0	52 Wk Hi-Low	660.00-468.00
Book Value	231.6	229.7	228.2	2,641.6	Yield %	0.7	Market Cap	US$6,932.1mil

Address **2-3-2, Marunouchi, Chiyoda-ku, Tokyo 100**
Tel **03-3284-6020**
Fax **03-3284-6081**
ADR
SEDOL No. **6643960**
President **Kentaro Kawamura**
Chairman **Jiro Nemoto**

Nippondenso

Industry: **Other Auto Parts**

Nippondenso, a member of the Toyota group, is Japan's largest maker of electronic and electrical auto parts. The company's products include car air conditioners, fuel-injection systems, and radiators. In fiscal 1993, sales to Toyota (which owns 24% of the company's stock) generated 52% of Nippondenso's parent-company sales. Nippondenso also supplies Mitsubishi Motors, Suzuki Motor, Mazda Motor, Honda Motor, Fuji Heavy Industries, and Hino Motors. The company has 10 plants in Japan (one located in Mie, one in Hiroshima, and the rest in Toyota's home prefecture of Aichi).

¥bil	12/92	12/93	12/94	US$mil 12/94				
Sales	1,523.8	1,427.7	1,412.2	13,837.5	P/E Ratio	41.9	Price (9/30/95)	1,830.00
Net Income	42.0	27.3	37.2	364.7	P/B Ratio	1.9	52 Wk Hi-Low	2,100.0-1,470.0
Book Value	759.4	772.2	839.5	8,414.7	Yield %	0.8	Market Cap	US$16,001mil

Address **1-1, Showa-cho, Kariya City, Aichi 448**
Tel **0566-25-5846**
Fax **0566-25-4509**
ADR **NIPDY**
SEDOL No. **6640381**
President **Tsuneo Ishimaru**
Chairman **Teikichiro Toyoda**

Nishi-Nippon Railroad

Industry: **Railroads**

Nishi-Nippon Railroad (Nishi-Nippon Tetsudo), head of the Nishitetsu group, is a major transportation-services provider, including bus, railway, and air transport. It operates Japan's largest bus system, with a fleet of more than 3,000 vehicles that carry more than 900,000 passengers daily. Based in Kyushu, the bus lines link cities in Kyushu and the main island of Honshu. Among its other activities are real estate (housing development and commercial buildings), amusement parks, and air-freight transport. The firm has 82 consolidated and three unconsolidated subsidiaries.

¥bil	03/93	03/94	03/95	US$mil 03/95				
Sales	278.6	276.8	294.2	2,981.7	P/E Ratio	48.7	Price (9/30/95)	385.00
Net Income	3.0	2.8	3.0	30.6	P/B Ratio	2.2	52 Wk Hi-Low	455.00-378.00
Book Value	64.6	65.5	68.0	787.5	Yield %	1.2	Market Cap	US$1,491.5mil

Address **1-11-17, Tenjin, Chuo-ku, Fukuoka 810**
Tel **092-734-1552**
Fax **092-781-2583**
ADR
SEDOL No. **6642967**
President **Hisayuki Hashimoto**
Chairman **Reinosuke Ohya**

Nishimatsu Construction

Industry: **Heavy Construction**

Nishimatsu Construction (Nishimatsu Kensetsu) is a general contractor active in civil engineering and building construction. Its civil-engineering works include railways, highways, tunnels, dams, power plants, and harbors. The public sector makes up about 60% of its civil-engineering orders and 40% of its building-construction orders. It also constructs residential and commercial buildings. Nishimatsu has five subsidiaries, two domestic and one each in Hong Kong, the United States, and Malaysia. It has several overseas offices and is particularly active in Southeast Asia.

¥bil	03/93 P	03/94 P	03/95 P	US$mil 03/95				
Sales	602.6	561.6	623.2	6,316.7	P/E Ratio	24.9	Price (9/30/95)	1,210.00
Net Income	12.2	12.7	13.4	136.1	P/B Ratio	2.4	52 Wk Hi-Low	1,260.0-930.0
Book Value	117.2	127.4	136.9	1,584.4	Yield %	1.0	Market Cap	US$3,362.2mil

Address **1-20-10, Toranomon, Minato-ku, Tokyo 105**
Tel **03-3502-0211**
Fax **03-3580-2695**
ADR
SEDOL No. **6640983**
President **Yoshiharu Kanayama**
Chairman **Taira Shibata**

P=Parent company data.

Nissan Chemical Industries

Industry: **Specialty Chemicals**

Nissan Chemical Industries (Nissan Kagaku Kogyo) is a general chemical firm affiliated with the Industrial Bank of Japan group. Its main products are fertilizers and agrichemicals. The first Japanese chemical company involved in phosphate-fertilizer production, it has expanded into electronic materials and pharmaceuticals. Nissan Chemical markets a hypertension agent in the United States. Its other products include swimming-pool disinfectants, polishing agents for electronic materials, and acid-cleaning agents. Overseas sales accounts for 12.5% of its consolidated sales.

¥bil	03/93	03/94	03/95	US$mil 03/95				
Sales	131.3	124.4	133.5	1,352.9	P/E Ratio	60.4	Price (9/30/95)	586.00
Net Income	2.3	2.1	1.7	17.7	P/B Ratio	2.6	52 Wk Hi-Low	771.00-460.00
Book Value	38.3	39.5	39.8	461.0	Yield %	0.9	Market Cap	US$1,055.5mil

Address **3-7-1, Kanda-Nishikicho, Chiyoda-ku, Tokyo 101**
Tel **03-3296-8361**
Fax **03-3296-8210**
ADR
SEDOL No. **6641588**
President **Hideichi Tokushima**
Chairman **Takeo Nakai**

Nissan Motor

Industry: **Automobile Manufacturers**

Nissan Motor (Nissan Jidosha) is Japan's second-largest automaker and the fifth largest in the world. Its domestic market shares in cars and light trucks are about 18%. Main models include the Altima, Infiniti, March, Sentra, Maxima, and Quest minivan (a joint effort with Ford in the United States). The firm also makes buses, textile and industrial machinery, and aerospace and marine equipment. Its major overseas plants are in the U.S., Mexico, the U.K., Spain, Thailand, Taiwan, the Philippines, and Malaysia. In 1995, 50% of its revenues were made overseas.

	¥bil 03/93	03/94	03/95	US$mil 03/95				
Sales	**6,197.6**	**5,800.9**	**5,834.1**	**59,136.6**	P/E Ratio	**NMF**	Price (9/30/95)	**714.00**
Net Income	**-56.0**	**-86.9**	**-166.1**	**-1,683.2**	P/B Ratio	**1.3**	52 Wk Hi-Low	**852.00-485.00**
Book Value	**1,721.3**	**1,579.8**	**1,429.1**	**16,540.1**	Yield %	**1.0**	Market Cap	**US$18,045mil**

Address **6-17-1, Ginza**
Chuo-ku, Tokyo 104-23
Tel **03-3543-5523**
Fax **03-3544-0109**
ADR **NSANY**
SEDOL No. **6642860**
President **Yoshifumi Tsuji**
Chairman **Yutaka Kume**

Nissan Shatai

Industry: **Other Auto Parts**

Nissan Shatai assembles vans, light trucks, small buses, passenger cars, and vans on consignment for Nissan Motor. Its 12 models include the Sunny, Avenil, Datsun Truck, and Fairlady Z. Practically all of the company's sales are to Nissan Motor, which owns more than 40% of Nissan Shatai; the company's R&D and production technology are also closely tied to Nissan Motor. It has two joint ventures with Nissan Motor Sales: a painting factory and an auto-maintenance equipment-manufacturing plant. Nissan Shatai also has a joint venture with Kanto Seiki to make plastic parts.

	¥bil 03/93	03/94	03/95	US$mil 03/95				
Sales	**501.9**	**396.7**	**397.7**	**4,031.6**	P/E Ratio	**58.9**	Price (9/30/95)	**518.00**
Net Income	**1.9**	**1.5**	**1.4**	**14.0**	P/B Ratio	**1.3**	52 Wk Hi-Low	**699.00-445.00**
Book Value	**64.7**	**64.7**	**64.7**	**748.9**	Yield %	**1.7**	Market Cap	**US$819.3mil**

Address **10-1, Amanuma**
Hiratsuka City, Kanagawa 254
Tel **0463-21-8012**
Fax **0463-21-8155**
ADR
SEDOL No. **6642901**
President **Shigenori Asano**
Chairman **Satoshi Uemura**

Nisshin Flour Milling

Industry: **Other Food**

Nisshin Flour Milling (Nisshin Seifun) is Japan's largest flour miller by sales. Its main product is wheat flour, which generates 52% of parent-company revenues. Other products include food supplements, bran, processed wheat-flour products, prepared foods, and compound feeds. Nisshin is the second-largest producer of fish feed and the third-largest maker of livestock feed in Japan. Its joint ventures abroad include production of feed additives with BASF (Germany), a milling factory with Mitsubishi and the STC Group (Thailand), and marketing with DCA Food Industries (U.S.).

	¥bil 03/93	03/94	03/95	US$mil 03/95				
Sales	**363.7**	**364.6**	**357.6**	**3,624.6**	P/E Ratio	**45.8**	Price (9/30/95)	**1,040.00**
Net Income	**7.8**	**8.0**	**5.4**	**55.0**	P/B Ratio	**1.7**	52 Wk Hi-Low	**1,240.0-871.0**
Book Value	**132.5**	**139.1**	**145.4**	**1,683.0**	Yield %	**0.6**	Market Cap	**US$2,504.8mil**

Address **19-12, Nihonbashi-Koamicho**
Chuo-ku, Tokyo 103
Tel **03-3660-3166**
Fax **03-3660-3844**
ADR
SEDOL No. **6640961**
President **Osamu Shoda**
Chairman --

Nisshin Oil Mills

Industry: **Other Food**

Nisshin Oil Mills (Nisshin Seiyu) produces salad dressings, cooking oils, cereals, and a variety of foodstuffs. It is Japan's largest maker of edible oils, with about 20% of the domestic market share. The firm's other products include health and soft drinks, soybean proteins, fine chemicals for cosmetics and pharmaceuticals, marine seedlings, fertilizers, and soybean meal. It also manages restaurants, golf ranges, and fitness clubs. Its major customers include Nisshin, Meijiya, Kokubu, Yamamuro, and Shinsei. The company has production joint ventures in China and Taiwan.

	¥bil 03/93	03/94	03/95	US$mil 03/95				
Sales	**141.2**	**136.7**	**137.6**	**1,394.8**	P/E Ratio	**57.1**	Price (9/30/95)	**702.00**
Net Income	**5.1**	**2.5**	**1.8**	**18.3**	P/B Ratio	**1.2**	52 Wk Hi-Low	**841.00-583.00**
Book Value	**83.7**	**84.4**	**85.0**	**984.1**	Yield %	**1.1**	Market Cap	**US$1,037.8mil**

Address **1-23-1, Shinkawa**
Chuo-ku, Tokyo 104
Tel **03-3206-5037**
Fax **03-3206-6452**
ADR
SEDOL No. **6641049**
President **Mitsuo Fukawa**
Chairman --

Nisshin Steel

Industry: **Steel**

Nisshin Steel (Nisshin Seiko) is a blast-furnace steelmaker that specializes in thin plate for the automotive, construction, and industrial- and electrical-machinery industries. Its products include steel and stainless steel, hot- and cold-rolled plates, and special steel. The company is the domestic leader in stainless-steel rolling plate. Major customers include Nippon Teppan and the general-trading companies Nissho Iwai and Mitsubishi. Nisshin Steel recently established a semiconductor-research center. In 1994, 19.8% of the firm's consolidated sales were made overseas.

	¥bil 03/93	03/94	03/95	US$mil 03/95				
Sales	**441.6**	**413.3**	**429.1**	**4,349.1**	P/E Ratio	**52.3**	Price (9/30/95)	**413.00**
Net Income	**-16.9**	**7.7**	**8.0**	**81.4**	P/B Ratio	**1.7**	52 Wk Hi-Low	**516.00-300.00**
Book Value	**243.8**	**247.9**	**252.5**	**2,922.4**	Yield %	**0.7**	Market Cap	**US$4,222.8mil**

Address **3-4-1, Marunouchi**
Chiyoda-ku, Tokyo 100
Tel **03-3216-5511**
Fax **03-3214-1895**
ADR **NHISY**
SEDOL No. **6641641**
President **Kensuke Koga**
Chairman **Kensuke Koga**

Nisshinbo Industries

Industry: **Clothing & Fabrics**

Nisshinbo Industries (Nisshin Boseki) is a major textile company that produces denim and materials for shirts and bedding. Its other products include synthetic fibers, brake linings, machine tools, polyurethane foam, and fine paper. Nisshinbo also develops and manufactures modular units for hardware and software systems in the automotive, air-craft, and electronics industries. Its main customers include Nisshinbo Brake Sales and Itochu. The company has 17 plants in Japan and 16 main consolidated subsidiaries, including one each in the United States and the Netherlands.

	¥bil 03/93	03/94	03/95	US$mil 03/95				
Sales	**241.9**	**219.9**	**224.3**	**2,273.3**	P/E Ratio	**119.4**	Price (9/30/95)	**860.00**
Net Income	**10.1**	**3.9**	**1.7**	**17.3**	P/B Ratio	**1.0**	52 Wk Hi-Low	**1,170.0-663.0**
Book Value	**192.9**	**194.4**	**197.5**	**2,286.0**	Yield %	**0.8**	Market Cap	**US$2,045.2mil**

Address **2-31-11, Nihonbashi-Ningyo**
Chuo-ku, Tokyo 103
Tel **03-5695-8833**
Fax **03-5695-8970**
ADR
SEDOL No. **6642923**
President **Akihiro Mochizuki**
Chairman **Tatsuo Tanabe**

Nissho Iwai

Industry: **Steel**

Nissho Iwai, the trading arm of the Sanwa group, is the sixth-largest general-trading company in Japan. The firm is particularly active in trading aircraft, metals, and machinery. Its largest division is metals, including steel, ferrous metals and coal, ferro-alloys, nonferrous metals, and precious metals. Nissho Iwai also handles various fuels and food commodities, as well as hand textiles, apparel, wood products, paper and pulp, consumer goods, chemicals, plastics, ceramics, and minerals. Nissho Iwai has a worldwide network of 471 consolidated subsidiaries and affiliates.

	¥bil 03/93	03/94	03/95	US$mil 03/95				
Sales	**10,636.1**	**10,300.8**	**10,020.5**	**101,570.8**	P/E Ratio	**59.7**	Price (9/30/95)	**400.00**
Net Income	**3.2**	**10.7**	**5.2**	**53.1**	P/B Ratio	**1.3**	52 Wk Hi-Low	**449.00-332.00**
Book Value	**234.0**	**241.3**	**243.5**	**2,818.8**	Yield %	**1.3**	Market Cap	**US$3,153.8mil**

Address **2-5-8, Imabashi**
Chuo-ku, Osaka 541
Tel **06-209-2111**
Fax **03-3588-4919**
ADR
SEDOL No. **6643001**
President **Akira Nishio**
Chairman --

Nissin Electric

Industry: **Electrical Components & Equipment**

Nissin Electric (Nisshin Denki) manufactures, installs, and services heavy electric machinery. It supplies electric-power companies with electrical machinery, including power capacitors, for which it holds about 70% of the Japanese market. The firm's major customer is Kansai Electric. It also produces semiconductor-manufacturing equipment. Other applications for its products include water-drainage systems, highways, factories, and building projects. Nissin Electric markets high-tension equipment manufactured by Emily Haefely (Switzerland) in Japan.

	¥bil 03/93	03/94	03/95	US$mil 03/95				
Sales	**109.3**	**108.3**	**100.4**	**1,017.6**	P/E Ratio	**39.0**	Price (9/30/95)	**678.00**
Net Income	**3.6**	**2.4**	**1.9**	**19.0**	P/B Ratio	**1.6**	52 Wk Hi-Low	**822.00-481.00**
Book Value	**41.7**	**43.5**	**45.2**	**523.1**	Yield %	**1.2**	Market Cap	**US$735.4mil**

Address **47, Umezu-Takasecho**
Ukyo-ku, Kyoto 615
Tel **075-861-3151**
Fax **075-864-8312**
ADR
SEDOL No. **6641663**
President **Teizo Yasui**
Chairman **Shin Komatsu**

Nissin Food Products

Industry: **Other Food**

Nissin Food Products (Nissin Shokuhin) produces instant noodles, rice, Chinese-style buns, snacks, boil-in-bag foods, and microwave foods. It is Japan's largest instant-noodle maker, holding 38% of the market. The company controls U.S. market shares of 59% for cupped noodles and 35% for bagged noodles, which are sold under the Cup O' Noodles, Oodles of Noodles, and Top Ramen brand names. The firm also manages 22 restaurants. Its major customers include Itochu, Mitsubishi, and Toshuku. Nissin Food has 16 consolidated subsidiaries in Hong Kong and two in the U.S.

	¥bil 03/93	03/94	03/95	US$mil 03/95				
Sales	**243.7**	**258.1**	**265.6**	**2,692.6**	P/E Ratio	**42.7**	Price (9/30/95)	**2,220.00**
Net Income	**3.9**	**8.2**	**6.9**	**70.1**	P/B Ratio	**1.6**	52 Wk Hi-Low	**2,540.0-1,930.0**
Book Value	**178.7**	**183.0**	**186.4**	**2,157.8**	Yield %	**1.1**	Market Cap	**US$2,968.0mil**

Address **4-1-1, Nishi-Nakajima**
Yodogawa-ku, Osaka 532
Tel **06-305-7711**
Fax **06-304-1288**
ADR
SEDOL No. **6641760**
President **Koki Ando**
Chairman **Momofuku Ando**

Nittetsu Mining

Industry: **Non-Ferrous Metals - Other (Exc. Aluminum)**

Nittetsu Mining (Nittetsu Kogyo), a member of the Nippon Steel group, produces ores, metals, and fuels. The company also manufactures machinery primarily for use in mining. It supplies limestone, limestone powder, crushed stone for the domestic construction industry, electrolytic-copper refining, petroleum products, steel milling, and stone-crushing machinery. The company's major customers include Shin Nihon Seikan, Tomen, Tetsuhara, Shinwa, Nippon Steel, and Nippon Cement. Nittetsu has 12 consolidated subsidiaries and operates 12 production facilities throughout Japan.

	¥bil 03/93	03/94	03/95	US$mil 03/95				
Sales	**100.2**	**97.8**	**100.8**	**1,021.3**	P/E Ratio	**56.1**	Price (9/30/95)	**870.00**
Net Income	**4.5**	**2.0**	**1.3**	**13.2**	P/B Ratio	**1.2**	52 Wk Hi-Low	**1,010.0-686.0**
Book Value	**60.5**	**62.1**	**62.8**	**727.0**	Yield %	**0.7**	Market Cap	**US$730.9mil**

Address **2-3-2, Marunouchi**
Chiyoda-ku, Tokyo 100
Tel **03-3284-0511**
Fax **03-3215-8480**
ADR
SEDOL No. **6641027**
President **Jun Yoshida**
Chairman --

Nitto Boseki

Industry: **Building Materials**

Nitto Boseki is a leading manufacturer of rock-wool insulation materials, panels, ceiling tiles, glass fibers, fiberglass-reinforced plastic, and thermoplastic products. The firm also produces cotton, synthetic fiber, medical goods, and chemical products. Yaesu Shoji is its main customer. It is also involved in engineering and real-estate operations. Although Nitto Boseki is categorized as a textile firm, its construction-materials segment made up the largest portion of consolidated revenues in 1994 (45.8%). It has 19 consolidated and 37 unconsolidated subsidiaries.

¥bil	03/93	03/94	03/95	US$mil 03/95				
Sales	**183.9**	**163.2**	**156.3**	**1,584.4**	P/E Ratio	**NMF**	Price (9/30/95)	**237.00**
Net Income	**-1.9**	**-4.8**	**-4.5**	**-45.8**	P/B Ratio	**1.3**	52 Wk Hi-Low	**317.00-192.00**
Book Value	**53.1**	**46.8**	**44.7**	**517.8**	Yield %	**0.0**	Market Cap	**US$590.4mil**

Address **1-2-1, Nihonbashi-Hamacho**
Chuo-ku, Tokyo 103
Tel **03-3865-6677**
Fax **03-3865-6721**
ADR
SEDOL No. **6641083**
President **Atsuhiko Sagara**
Chairman --

Nitto Denko

Industry: **Electrical Components & Equipment**

Nitto Denko manufactures industrial and electronic materials. The company's primary products include tapes used for packaging, insulation, and rust protection. It also makes integrated-circuit packaging, flexible printed circuits, and liquid-crystal-display polarizing films. Its products are used in the electronic, engineering, medical, semiconductor, and construction industries. In addition to its domestic production facilities, the company has United States plants in New Jersey, Kansas, and California that produce adhesive tapes, bar-code labels, and osmosis membranes, respectively.

¥bil	03/93	03/94	03/95	US$mil 03/95				
Sales	**253.8**	**249.8**	**257.5**	**2,610.2**	P/E Ratio	**34.2**	Price (9/30/95)	**1,510.00**
Net Income	**4.0**	**4.4**	**6.7**	**67.9**	P/B Ratio	**1.5**	52 Wk Hi-Low	**1,620.0-1,250.0**
Book Value	**143.1**	**145.3**	**150.4**	**1,740.9**	Yield %	**0.8**	Market Cap	**US$2,301.5mil**

Address **1-1-2, Shimohozumi**
Ibaraki City, Osaka 567
Tel **0726-22-2981**
Fax **0726-26-0301**
ADR
SEDOL No. **6641801**
President **Goro Kamai**
Chairman --

NKK

Industry: **Steel**

NKK is Japan's second-largest steel manufacturer, and one of the world's top five, based on crude-steel-production volume. The company has a heavy-industry division that engages in civil and plant engineering, shipbuilding, and machinery production. NKK operates seven manufacturing facilities in Japan, including ones in Hiroshima, Toyama, Niigata, and Shizuoka prefectures. NKK's two largest customers are trading giants Marubeni (16% of parent-company sales) and Mitsubishi (13%). In 1994, 28.5% of NKK's consolidated sales were made overseas.

¥bil	03/93	03/94	03/95	US$mil 03/95				
Sales	**1,858.6**	**1,777.9**	**1,802.0**	**18,265.6**	P/E Ratio	**NMF**	Price (9/30/95)	**265.00**
Net Income	**-4.5**	**-40.3**	**-38.3**	**-388.2**	P/B Ratio	**2.4**	52 Wk Hi-Low	**301.00-192.00**
Book Value	**468.3**	**419.9**	**394.8**	**4,569.3**	Yield %	**0.0**	Market Cap	**US$9,392.0mil**

Address **1-1-2, Marunouchi**
Chiyoda-ku, Tokyo 100
Tel **03-3217-2027**
Fax **03-3214-8428**
ADR **NKKCY**
SEDOL No. **6640466**
President **Shunkichi Miyoshi**
Chairman **Yoshinari Yamashiro**

NOK

Industry: **Other Auto Parts**

NOK produces oil seals, auto sensors, and electronic parts. It is one of the few auto-parts suppliers in Japan that is not affiliated with a domestic automaker. The firm controls 80% of the Japanese market for oil seals used in auto and industrial machinery. NOK also makes mechanical seals and O-rings. Although Toyota is a large shareholder, it also supplies Nissan Motor, Mitsubishi Motors, Mazda Motor, and Honda Motor, and several other auto-parts makers. NOK has marketing ties with Freudenberg (Germany) and makes oil seals and industrial-use cameras with EG&G (U.S.).

¥bil	03/93	03/94	03/95	US$mil 03/95				
Sales	**198.4**	**186.9**	**201.5**	**2,042.6**	P/E Ratio	**23.7**	Price (9/30/95)	**693.00**
Net Income	**3.8**	**2.7**	**4.9**	**50.1**	P/B Ratio	**1.5**	52 Wk Hi-Low	**950.00-568.00**
Book Value	**72.4**	**73.7**	**77.8**	**900.0**	Yield %	**0.9**	Market Cap	**US$1,174.8mil**

Address **1-12-15, Shiba-Daimon**
Minato-ku, Tokyo 105
Tel **03-3434-1792**
Fax **03-3436-5904**
ADR
SEDOL No. **6642428**
President **Masato Tsuru**
Chairman **Masato Tsuru**

Nomura Securities

Industry: **Securities Brokers**

Nomura Securities is the largest of Japan's Big Four brokerage houses by assets and sales. The company earns revenue primarily from stock-brokerage commissions and convertible-bond transactions. In most years it is Japan's leading Eurobond underwriter by volume. Nomura's other activities include banking, asset management, leveraged leasing, real estate, and mergers and acquisitions. Nomura has 145 branches in Japan and 10 overseas branches in Prague, Vienna, Berlin, Rome, Bangkok, Kuala Lumpur, New Delhi, Beijing, Shanghai, and Seoul.

¥bil	03/93	03/94	03/95	US$mil 03/95				
Sales	**561.6**	**658.4**	**554.6**	**5,621.6**	P/E Ratio	**NMF**	Price (9/30/95)	**1,940.00**
Net Income	**3.6**	**42.6**	**-18.3**	**-185.1**	P/B Ratio	**2.2**	52 Wk Hi-Low	**2,100.0-1,460.0**
Book Value	**1,741.5**	**1,754.2**	**1,713.3**	**19,829.7**	Yield %	**0.5**	Market Cap	**US$38,297mil**

Address **1-9-1, Nihonbashi**
Chuo-ku, Tokyo 103
Tel **03-3211-1811**
Fax **03-3273-6376**
ADR **NRSCY**
SEDOL No. **6643108**
President **Hideo Sakamaki**
Chairman **Masashi Suzuki**

Noritake

Industry: **Household Products (Durable)**

Noritake, a member of the Morimura group, manufactures high-quality ceramics, tableware, and industrial products. Its industrial goods include grinding wheels, diamond tools, coated abrasives, and grinding machines. It also produces electronic components, industrial ceramics, thick-film printed-circuit substrates, and whetstones. Noritake has marketing subsidiaries in the United States, Canada, Australia, and Germany, a sales subsidiary in Singapore, and factories in Iceland, Sri Lanka, and the Philippines. It operates Noritake Corners in major Japanese department stores.

¥bil	03/93	03/94	03/95	US$mil 03/95				
Sales	**117.5**	**111.9**	**113.0**	**1,145.8**	P/E Ratio	**75.1**	Price (9/30/95)	**774.00**
Net Income	**2.8**	**1.7**	**1.7**	**16.8**	P/B Ratio	**2.0**	52 Wk Hi-Low	**823.00-547.00**
Book Value	**61.3**	**61.9**	**63.1**	**730.3**	Yield %	**1.2**	Market Cap	**US$1,252.9mil**

Address **3-1-36, Noritake-Shinmachi**
Nishi-ku Nagoya, Aichi 451
Tel **052-561-7111**
Fax **052-565-6056**
ADR
SEDOL No. **6641522**
President **Tetsuya Hino**
Chairman **Susumu Saeki**

NSK

Industry: **Industrial - Diversified**

NSK (Nippon Seiko) is Japan's leading bearings maker by revenues. The firm specializes in ball bearings, but also makes auto parts (such as steering components, seat belts, and clutches), machine-tool parts (ball screws, grinding spindles, and direct-acting parts), and assorted electronic equipment. In addition to 47 subsidiaries, 22 affiliates, and nine domestic plants, it has factories in the United States, the United Kingdom, Brazil, South Korea, Germany, and Switzerland. In 1994, 29% of NSK's consolidated sales were made outside Japan.

¥bil	03/93	03/94	03/95	US$mil 03/95				
Sales	**415.2**	**380.1**	**415.7**	**4,213.8**	P/E Ratio	**79.0**	Price (9/30/95)	**608.00**
Net Income	**0.7**	**-1.4**	**4.3**	**43.4**	P/B Ratio	**1.5**	52 Wk Hi-Low	**793.00-455.00**
Book Value	**233.7**	**227.0**	**227.6**	**2,634.4**	Yield %	**1.0**	Market Cap	**US$3,424.4mil**

Address **1-6-3, Osaki**
Shinagawa-ku, Tokyo 141
Tel **03-3779-7111**
Fax **03-3779-7445**
ADR **NPSKY**
SEDOL No. **6641544**
President **Tetsuo Sekiya**
Chairman **Toshio Arata**

NTN

Industry: **Industrial - Diversified**

NTN, a member of the Sanwa group, is one of Japan's top four bearings makers. It is the largest domestic producer of uniform-velocity joints, with a 50% market share. Other products include precision ball screws, optical-disc cutters, magnetic-bearing spindles, and various other machine parts. NTN sells primarily to automakers and heavy-industry and aircraft manufacturers. In 1994, 34% of NTN's consolidated sales were made overseas. It operates plants in Japan (five), North America, Germany, Taiwan, and Australia. NTN has 24 consolidated and 13 unconsolidated subsidiaries.

¥bil	03/93	03/94	03/95	US$mil 03/95				
Sales	**310.3**	**285.6**	**301.8**	**3,059.2**	P/E Ratio	**86.8**	Price (9/30/95)	**616.00**
Net Income	**4.7**	**3.3**	**3.3**	**33.2**	P/B Ratio	**1.8**	52 Wk Hi-Low	**787.00-476.00**
Book Value	**165.4**	**163.4**	**162.8**	**1,884.2**	Yield %	**1.5**	Market Cap	**US$2,869.1mil**

Address **1-3-17, Kyomachibori**
Nishi-ku, Osaka 550
Tel **06-443-5001**
Fax **06-443-3226**
ADR
SEDOL No. **6651189**
President **Toyoaki Ito**
Chairman **Yoshitsugi Suma**

Obayashi

Industry: **Heavy Construction**

Obayashi (Obayashi Gumi) is one of Japan's top five general contractors by revenues. Its operations include building construction (more than 95% of parent-company sales), civil engineering, and real estate. The company renovates buildings and constructs leisure facilities. Obayashi also works on urban-renewal construction projects, such as residential high-rise residential buildings and intelligent-building business centers. The company has 47 subsidiaries. Obayashi has subsidiaries, affiliates, and offices in 15 countries, including the United States, China, and Vietnam.

¥bil	03/93	03/94	03/95	US$mil 03/95				
Sales	**1,538.5**	**1,652.8**	**1,422.0**	**14,413.6**	P/E Ratio	**79.6**	Price (9/30/95)	**780.00**
Net Income	**21.0**	**10.0**	**7.3**	**74.1**	P/B Ratio	**2.0**	52 Wk Hi-Low	**865.00-608.00**
Book Value	**280.5**	**284.2**	**288.4**	**3,337.9**	Yield %	**1.0**	Market Cap	**US$5,846.0mil**

Address **4-33, Kitahama-Higashi**
Chuo-ku, Osaka 540
Tel **06-946-4568**
Fax **03-3219-2328**
ADR
SEDOL No. **6656407**
President **Takao Tsumuro**
Chairman **Yoshiro Obayashi**

Odakyu Electric Railway

Industry: **Railroads**

Odakyu Electric Railway (Odakyu Dentetsu) is a leading railroad company operating in the Kanto region. It provides railway service, and is involved in real estate, retailing, and resort development. The company's rail network consists of four lines in Tokyo and Kanagawa prefectures, plus three tracks served jointly by three operators. Odakyu's operations include real-estate development (including hotels, condos, and commercial buildings), construction, department stores, golf courses, and amusement parks. Odakyu has 22 consolidated and 38 unconsolidated subsidiaries.

¥bil	03/93	03/94	03/95	US$mil 03/95				
Sales	**546.0**	**538.7**	**563.4**	**5,711.3**	P/E Ratio	**NMF**	Price (9/30/95)	**687.00**
Net Income	**4.5**	**3.1**	**3.0**	**30.8**	P/B Ratio	**3.5**	52 Wk Hi-Low	**750.00-602.00**
Book Value	**136.5**	**136.5**	**138.4**	**1,602.2**	Yield %	**0.7**	Market Cap	**US$4,913.9mil**

Address **1-8-3, Nishi-Shinjuku**
Shinjuku-ku, Tokyo 160
Tel **03-3349-2160**
Fax **03-3346-1899**
ADR
SEDOL No. **6656106**
President **Takashi Takigami**
Chairman --

Okamoto Industries

Industry: **Footwear**

Okamoto Industries specializes in rubber and plastic products. Its product divisions include vinyls and films, medical and sundry goods, building and industrial materials, Riken-brand automobile tires, footwear, and clothes, including sportswear. It has a joint venture with Reebok International and a technical-assistance agreement with Uniroyal Plastic (U.S.). Okamoto is Japan's leading producer of condoms, sold under the Skinless Skin brand name, with a market share approaching 60%. It has two joint-venture tire companies with Compagnie Financière Michelin (France).

	¥bil 03/93	03/94	03/95	US$mil 03/95				
Sales	**101.9**	**87.8**	**84.3**	**854.4**	P/E Ratio	**56.4**	Price (9/30/95)	**620.00**
Net Income	**3.4**	**1.6**	**1.7**	**17.1**	P/B Ratio	**2.1**	52 Wk Hi-Low	**773.00-451.00**
Book Value	**40.8**	**45.4**	**45.6**	**527.6**	Yield %	**1.2**	Market Cap	**US$957.1mil**

Address	**3-27-12, Hongo**	Tel	**03-3817-4146**	ADR		President	**Takehiko Okamoto**
	Bunkyo-ku, Tokyo 113-91	Fax	**03-3814-2355**	SEDOL No.	**6657767**	Chairman	--

Okamura

Industry: **Other Home Furnishings**

Okamura (Okamura Seisakusho) manufactures a wide range of furniture for commercial use. The company dominates the Japanese market for office furniture and shop-display equipment. Okamura also makes home furnishings, refrigerated display cases and freezers, hydraulic transmissions for rolling stock, and warehouse-automation machinery. The company has an agreement with Hamilton Industries (U.S.) to market laboratory furniture and equipment. Okamura has six domestic plants and a plant in Thailand. It has eight subsidiaries and five affiliates.

	¥bil 03/93	03/94	03/95	US$mil 03/95				
Sales	**169.5**	**159.6**	**165.3**	**1,675.4**	P/E Ratio	**28.4**	Price (9/30/95)	**730.00**
Net Income	**-1.1**	**-0.9**	**3.2**	**32.3**	P/B Ratio	**1.5**	52 Wk Hi-Low	**910.00-574.00**
Book Value	**58.5**	**55.8**	**59.0**	**682.7**	Yield %	**0.7**	Market Cap	**US$910.6mil**

Address	**2-7-18, Kitasaiwai, Nishi-ku**	Tel	**045-319-3401**	ADR		President	**Kikuo Nakamura**
	Yokohama-shi, Kanagawa 220	Fax	**045-319-3450**	SEDOL No.	**6657842**	Chairman	--

Okuma

Industry: **Heavy Machinery**

Okuma manufactures machine tools. The company is among the top Japanese makers of machining centers by production value. Its other products include lathes, drilling machines, boring machines, and industrial machinery. It also makes computerized machine tools and flexible-manufacturing systems. Okuma has two plants, 24 sales offices, and five wholly-owned subsidiaries in the U.S. and Europe. The company has a licensing agreement with Schutte (Germany) to make lathes, and its joint venture with Krauss-Maffei (Germany) makes injection-molding machines.

	¥bil 03/93	03/94	03/95	US$mil 03/95				
Sales	**67.6**	**55.1**	**61.4**	**622.6**	P/E Ratio	**NMF**	Price (9/30/95)	**810.00**
Net Income	**-4.4**	**-13.4**	**-3.2**	**-32.6**	P/B Ratio	**2.3**	52 Wk Hi-Low	**980.00-521.00**
Book Value	**62.9**	**49.9**	**46.8**	**541.8**	Yield %	**0.0**	Market Cap	**US$1,096.3mil**

Address	**5-25-1, Oguchi-cho**	Tel	**0587-95-7822**	ADR		President	**Junro Kashiwa**
	Niwa-gun, Aichi 480-01	Fax	**0587-95-4807**	SEDOL No.	**6657789**	Chairman	**Etsuro Tsuchihashi**

Okumura

Industry: **Heavy Construction**

Okumura (Okumura Gumi) is a construction firm that specializes in building construction and civil-engineering works. The bulk of Okumura's construction projects are in commercial buildings, railroads, and highways. Building construction and civil engineering each account for 49% of Okumura's total revenues. The company has diversified into real-estate operations, which account for almost 2% of parent-company sales. Okumura has five subsidiaries, four in Tokyo and one in the United States, and two affiliates. In addition, it has eight plants in Japan.

	¥bil 03/93 P	03/94 P	03/95 P	US$mil 03/95				
Sales	**344.1**	**343.2**	**289.6**	**2,935.6**	P/E Ratio	**39.0**	Price (9/30/95)	**920.00**
Net Income	**7.8**	**5.7**	**5.9**	**59.4**	P/B Ratio	**1.6**	52 Wk Hi-Low	**1,010.0-713.0**
Book Value	**132.7**	**136.0**	**139.6**	**1,615.6**	Yield %	**1.0**	Market Cap	**US$2,294.4mil**

Address	**2-2-2, Matsuzaki-cho**	Tel	**06-621-1101**	ADR		President	**Shotaro Okumura**
	Abeno-ku, Osaka 545	Fax	**06-623-7459**	SEDOL No.	**6657808**	Chairman	**Takemasa Okumura**

P=Parent company data.

Olympus Optical

Industry: **Medical Supplies**

Olympus Optical is a major manufacturer of optoelectronic equipment. The firm's major product lines include cameras, camcorders, microscopes, endoscopes, and clinical analyzers. Olympus controls close to 80% of the world endoscope market and 60% of the market for pretransfusion blood testing. The firm also makes microcassette-tape recorders, disk drives, and laser-optical pickup systems. Olympus has 15 consolidated subsidiaries in the United States, Europe, and Asia. In fiscal 1994, 66% of Olympus' consolidated sales came from overseas.

	¥bil 03/93	03/94	03/95	US$mil 03/95				
Sales	**267.7**	**239.6**	**252.1**	**2,555.3**	P/E Ratio	**78.5**	Price (9/30/95)	**919.00**
Net Income	**3.8**	**0.6**	**3.1**	**31.4**	P/B Ratio	**1.3**	52 Wk Hi-Low	**1,130.0-670.0**
Book Value	**145.8**	**183.0**	**182.4**	**2,111.3**	Yield %	**1.5**	Market Cap	**US$2,442.3mil**

Address	**2-3-1, Nishi-Shinjuku**	Tel	**03-3340-2151**	ADR	**OLYOY**	President	**Masatoshi Kishimoto**
	Shinjuku-ku, Tokyo 163-09	Fax	**03-3340-2098**	SEDOL No.	**6658801**	Chairman	**Toshiro Shimoyama**

Omron

Industry: **Electrical Components & Equipment**

Omron is a top maker of control components such as switches, relays, and timers. It produces electronic fund-transfer systems, health equipment, car electronics, and factory- and office-automation equipment. Omron is a pioneer in fuzzy-logic technology (a technology that brings intuitive skills to machines) and recently began selling fuzzy-logic software for document retrieval. Catering to both the private and public sectors, it operates 68 sales subsidiaries and seven production subsidiaries abroad. It is establishing offices in eastern Europe and the former Soviet Union.

	¥bil 03/93	03/94	03/95	US$mil 03/95				
Sales	**462.7**	**460.9**	**489.7**	**4,963.8**	P/E Ratio	**46.0**	Price (9/30/95)	**2,270.00**
Net Income	**4.6**	**4.7**	**12.2**	**123.2**	P/B Ratio	**2.1**	52 Wk Hi-Low	**2,310.0-1,450.0**
Book Value	**234.0**	**230.7**	**288.1**	**3,334.3**	Yield %	**0.6**	Market Cap	**US$5,984.4mil**

Address **Nanajo-Sagaru, Karasuma-dori**
Shimogyo-ku, Kyoto 600
Tel **075-344-7070**
Fax **075-344-7131**
ADR **OMTEY**
SEDOL No. **6659428**
President **Yoshio Tateishi**
Chairman **Takao Tateishi**

Ono Pharmaceutical

Industry: **Pharmaceuticals**

Ono Pharmaceutical (Ono Yakuhin Kogyo) is an Osaka-based company that specializes in prostaglandin products and digestive medicines. Ono is a world leader in prostaglandin-related research. Its major drugs include Foipan (used in pancreatitis treatment), Opalmon (used to treat obstructive thrombus), and Cataclot (used to treat thrombosis). Main customers include Suzuken, Kuraya Pharmaceutical, Showa Pharmaceutical, and Sanseido. Ono jointly researches prostaglandin products with Upjohn (U.S.) and has joint research programs at the William Harvey Research Institute (U.K.).

	¥bil 03/93 P	03/94 P	03/95 P	US$mil 03/95				
Sales	**95.2**	**109.7**	**121.1**	**1,227.3**	P/E Ratio	**22.8**	Price (9/30/95)	**4,090.00**
Net Income	**15.6**	**18.4**	**22.0**	**223.1**	P/B Ratio	**3.1**	52 Wk Hi-Low	**4,980.0-3,580.0**
Book Value	**126.3**	**142.0**	**160.8**	**1,860.9**	Yield %	**0.7**	Market Cap	**US$5,056.7mil**

Address **2-1-5, Dosho-machi**
Chuo-ku, Osaka 541
Tel **06-222-5551**
Fax **06-222-7274**
ADR
SEDOL No. **6660107**
President **Toshio Ueno**
Chairman **Kazuo Sano**

P=Parent company data.

Onward Kashiyama

Industry: **Clothing & Fabrics**

Onward Kashiyama is Japan's third-largest apparel manufacturer by sales. The firm produces men's, women's, and children's clothing, sportswear, kimonos, and accessories. Brands include Kumikyoku women's clothes and Gotairiku men's suits. The firm also plans a Kumikyoku children's line for 1995. Onward owns J. Press retail outlets in the U.S., and is affiliated with Jean-Paul Gaultier. It also has a suit-production joint venture and a factory in China. Onward markets its products mainly through department stores such as Isetan, Marui, Hankyu, Tokyu, and Takashimaya in Japan.

	¥bil 02/93	02/94	02/95	US$mil 02/95				
Sales	**219.1**	**191.3**	**188.9**	**1,885.1**	P/E Ratio	**53.4**	Price (9/30/95)	**1,330.00**
Net Income	**5.1**	**3.0**	**3.7**	**37.2**	P/B Ratio	**1.5**	52 Wk Hi-Low	**1,410.0-1,150.0**
Book Value	**130.3**	**130.0**	**132.9**	**1,374.0**	Yield %	**1.2**	Market Cap	**US$2,017.1mil**

Address **3-10-5, Nihonbashi**
Chuo-ku, Tokyo 103
Tel **03-3272-2317**
Fax **03-3272-2333**
ADR **OKASY**
SEDOL No. **6483821**
President **Akira Baba**
Chairman --

Organo

Industry: **Pollution Control, Waste Management**

Organo, an affiliate of Tosoh, produces water-treatment equipment and provides plant-engineering services. Organo's major customers are utilities and semiconductor makers. Its products include ultra-pure-water-producing and sewage-treatment equipment, and chemical-spray systems for golf courses. Organo also designs facilities for water and sewage-treatment plants and provides refining processes for food and drug production. It has three plants and nine consolidated subsidiaries in Japan. Organo also has subsidiaries in the United States, the United Kingdom, and Malaysia.

	¥bil 03/93	03/94	03/95	US$mil 03/95				
Sales	**79.8**	**68.7**	**71.1**	**720.8**	P/E Ratio	**35.8**	Price (9/30/95)	**976.00**
Net Income	**1.0**	**0.5**	**1.6**	**16.1**	P/B Ratio	**2.4**	52 Wk Hi-Low	**1,150.0-770.0**
Book Value	**22.4**	**22.7**	**23.8**	**275.7**	Yield %	**0.7**	Market Cap	**US$568.9mil**

Address **5-5-16, Hongo**
Bunkyo-ku, Toyko 113
Tel **03-5689-5104**
Fax **03-3816-5520**
ADR
SEDOL No. **6470522**
President **Hirokatsu Maeda**
Chairman --

Orient

Industry: **Financial Services - Diversified**

Orient, a core member of the Orico group, is one of Japan's three largest consumer-credit companies by volume of new contracts, revenues, and net income. The firm provides consumer credit, credit cards, guarantee and loan-agent services, commercial financing, and direct-cash loans through a domestic network of 234 branch offices. It issues VISA, Diner's Club, MasterCard, and Japan Credit Bureau credit cards. Orient has about 6.3 million cardholders and about 200,000 member outlets. Orient's international operations include two finance subsidiaries in London and Amsterdam.

	¥bil 03/93 P	03/94 P	03/95 P	US$mil 03/95				
Revenues	**429.6**	**378.8**	**372.5**	**3,775.9**	P/E Ratio	**46.3**	Price (9/30/95)	**472.00**
Net Income	**4.7**	**3.5**	**3.5**	**35.6**	P/B Ratio	**0.6**	52 Wk Hi-Low	**658.00-385.00**
Book Value	**259.7**	**260.4**	**261.1**	**3,022.1**	Yield %	**1.7**	Market Cap	**US$1,628.5mil**

Address **3-1-1, Higashi-Ikebukuro**
Toshima-ku, Tokyo 170
Tel **03-3989-6111**
Fax **03-3985-3586**
ADR
SEDOL No. **6661122**
President **Hiroshi Arai**
Chairman --

P=Parent company data.

Orix

Industry: **Financial Services - Diversified**

Orix offers a wide range of financial services, including loans, leases, rentals, and insurance. The company began as a lessor of industrial equipment, but has since diversified into the leasing of computers, office-automation equipment, and aircraft. It has also diversified into consumer finance, housing loans, mortgage-backed securities, venture capital, stock and bond brokerage, real-estate rentals, and life insurance. Orix is involved in a joint venture with Commodities Corporation (United States). In 1994, the company made 11.1% of its consolidated sales overseas.

¥bil	03/93	03/94	03/95	US$mil 03/95				
Revenues	**1,012.7**	**979.3**	**974.4**	**9,877.1**	P/E Ratio	**34.0**	Price (9/30/95)	**3,650.00**
Net Income	**6.2**	**6.9**	**7.0**	**70.5**	P/B Ratio	**2.0**	52 Wk Hi-Low	**3,780.0-2,410.0**
Book Value	**112.2**	**116.0**	**120.6**	**1,395.9**	Yield %	**0.4**	Market Cap	**US$2,381.5mil**

Address **2-4-1, Hamamatsu-cho**
Minato-ku, Tokyo 105
Tel **03-3435-6641**
Fax **03-3434-1250**
ADR
SEDOL No. **6661144**
President **Yoshihiko Miyauchi**
Chairman --

Osaka Gas

Industry: **Gas Utilities**

Osaka Gas ranks second among Japan's four major gas utilities. It provides natural gas to 5.6 million customers in the Kansai region, which includes Osaka, Kyoto, Nara, and Kobe. More than 90% of the gas it produces comes from liquefied natural gas (LNG). Osaka Gas has 48,000 kilometers of pipeline connecting its service area to two LNG terminals; a third terminal is currently under construction. It has long-term supply contracts with producers in the United States, Brunei, Abu Dhabi, Indonesia, Malaysia, and Australia. Its 15 consolidated subsidiaries are based in Osaka.

¥bil	03/93	03/94	03/95	US$mil 03/95				
Sales	**686.2**	**704.1**	**711.6**	**7,212.6**	P/E Ratio	**NMF**	Price (9/30/95)	**338.00**
Net Income	**15.8**	**14.8**	**-9.1**	**-92.5**	P/B Ratio	**2.4**	52 Wk Hi-Low	**431.00-310.00**
Book Value	**378.5**	**380.8**	**360.4**	**4,171.5**	Yield %	**1.5**	Market Cap	**US$8,595.0mil**

Address **4-1-2, Hirano-machi**
Chuo-ku, Osaka 541
Tel **06-202-2221**
Fax **06-226-1681**
ADR
SEDOL No. **6661768**
President **Shinichiro Ryoki**
Chairman **Masafumi Ohnishi**

Penta-Ocean Construction

Industry: **Heavy Construction**

Penta-Ocean Construction (Goyo Kensetsu), a leader in marine-engineering technology, is the largest marine civil-engineering firm in Japan. Its projects include dredging and reclamation, underground and waterfront development, and port and harbor construction and installation. Civil-engineering orders are about 60% of current contracts. As a comprehensive construction company, it also offers services in landscaping, building construction, and urban and regional development (particularly resort development). Penta-Ocean Construction has five subsidiaries and 15 affiliates.

¥bil	03/93 P	03/94 P	03/95 P	US$mil 03/95				
Sales	**521.9**	**525.1**	**530.4**	**5,376.7**	P/E Ratio	**72.7**	Price (9/30/95)	**800.00**
Net Income	**4.1**	**3.9**	**3.7**	**37.0**	P/B Ratio	**3.5**	52 Wk Hi-Low	**946.00-524.00**
Book Value	**46.0**	**54.5**	**80.0**	**925.7**	Yield %	**0.9**	Market Cap	**US$2,838.1mil**

Address **2-2-8, Koraku**
Bunkyo-ku, Tokyo 112
Tel **03-3816-7111**
Fax **03-3816-7158**
ADR
SEDOL No. **6680804**
President **Rempei Mizuno**
Chairman **Rempei Mizuno**

P=Parent company data.

Pioneer Electronic

Industry: **Consumer Electronics**

Pioneer Electronic is one of Japan's largest makers of audiovisual equipment. Its principal products include compact-disc players, laser-disc players, projection televisions, and laser-karaoke (sing-along) machines. The company leads the market in car-navigation electronics. Pioneer supplies car stereos and multiplay compact-disc players to BMW of Germany. Its major licensers are RCA, Dolby Lab, Philips Export, and Thompson SA. The firm's product development is directed toward laser-disc software and hardware, including a disk drive with read and write capability.

¥bil	03/93	03/94	03/95	US$mil 03/95				
Sales	**589.7**	**509.9**	**509.8**	**5,167.4**	P/E Ratio	**NMF**	Price (9/30/95)	**1,790.00**
Net Income	**10.8**	**6.6**	**-1.2**	**-12.1**	P/B Ratio	**1.1**	52 Wk Hi-Low	**2,580.0-1,440.0**
Book Value	**319.7**	**309.2**	**295.2**	**3,417.1**	Yield %	**1.4**	Market Cap	**US$3,233.1mil**

Address **1-4-1, Meguro**
Meguro-ku, Tokyo 153
Tel **03-3494-1111**
Fax **03-3495-5081**
ADR **PIO**
SEDOL No. **6688745**
President **Seiya Matsumoto**
Chairman --

Q.P.

Industry: **Other Food**

Q.P. produces condiments, canned foods (marketed under Aohata and Verde brands), and bottled foods. It is Japan's largest maker of mayonnaise, with its Kewpie brand holding 70% of the Japanese market. The company also makes salad dressings, mustard, tartar sauce, pasta sauce, egg products, baby foods, and mineral water. Q.P. holds the top domestic market share in canned sweet corn. The firm markets Green Giant canned vegetables and Pillsbury foods in Japan. It has eight plants, 35 sales offices, 10 branch offices nationwide, and three subsidiaries in the U.S.

¥bil	11/92	11/93	11/94	US$mil 11/94				
Sales	**282.5**	**285.9**	**303.2**	**2,947.2**	P/E Ratio	**24.7**	Price (9/30/95)	**838.00**
Net Income	**4.7**	**5.3**	**5.5**	**53.1**	P/B Ratio	**1.4**	52 Wk Hi-Low	**1,110.0-772.0**
Book Value	**91.0**	**95.1**	**99.0**	**1,000.9**	Yield %	**1.1**	Market Cap	**US$1,359.8mil**

Address **1-4-13, Shibuya**
Shibuya-ku, Tokyo 150
Tel **03-3486-3331**
Fax **03-3498-1806**
ADR
SEDOL No. **6714509**
President **Shiro Tarui**
Chairman **Yuichi Nakashima**

Rengo

Industry: **Containers & Packaging**

Rengo is one of Japan's top manufacturers of paperboard and jute liners by sales. The firm produces corrugated cardboard, paperboard, corrugated cartons, folding cartons, and flexible packages. Its corrugated-product line includes water-resistant, colored, and patterned materials. Rengo also supplies beverage makers with cardboard containers. Main customers include Toppan Printing, Dainippon Printing, Hitachi, Toyobo, and Noritsu. It has 10 consolidated and 25 unconsolidated subsidiaries in Japan. Its joint ventures in Dalian and Beijing manufacture corrugated cardboard.

¥bil	03/93	03/94	03/95	US$mil 03/95				
Sales	**284.8**	**272.1**	**281.7**	**2,855.0**	P/E Ratio	**55.9**	Price (9/30/95)	**665.00**
Net Income	**3.3**	**3.0**	**2.3**	**23.2**	P/B Ratio	**1.4**	52 Wk Hi-Low	**860.00-567.00**
Book Value	**86.4**	**88.0**	**90.0**	**1,041.7**	Yield %	**1.1**	Market Cap	**US$1,288.8mil**

Address	**3-5-12, Hirano-machi**	Tel	**06-202-2371**	ADR		President	**Kaoru Hasegawa**
	Chuo-ku, Osaka 541	Fax	**06-226-0298**	SEDOL No.	**6732200**	Chairman	--

Renown

Industry: **Clothing & Fabrics**

Renown designs, manufactures, and distributes more than 300 brands of apparel. Among the company's brand names are J. Crew, Perry Ellis, and Aquascutum. Its products are based on original and licensed designs from the U.S. and Europe and include dresses, suits, coats, and sportswear. Renown's apparel is manufactured by subcontracted firms, affiliated companies, and the company itself, which operates eight factories. Almost 50% of its inventory goes directly to department stores; the rest goes to retail shops and mass-merchandising stores. It has 31 subsidiaries overseas.

¥bil	01/93 *	01/94	01/95	US$mil 01/95				
Sales	**236.5**	**216.2**	**208.3**	**2,062.1**	P/E Ratio	**NMF**	Price (9/30/95)	**328.00**
Net Income	**-32.9**	**-18.3**	**-36.4**	**-360.4**	P/B Ratio	**0.9**	52 Wk Hi-Low	**493.00-235.00**
Book Value	**152.3**	**133.5**	**97.3**	**983.4**	Yield %	**0.0**	Market Cap	**US$915.4mil**

Address	**2-34-18, Jingumae**	Tel	**03-3403-2211**	ADR		President	**Keiji Toyoda**
	Shibuya-ku, Tokyo 150-07	Fax	**03-3403-5366**	SEDOL No.	**6732545**	Chairman	**Yasuo Kaneda**

*Irregular period due to fiscal year change.

Ricoh

Industry: **Office Equipment**

Ricoh is one of the world's largest manufacturers of photocopiers. The firm also produces cameras, information equipment, and data-processing systems. Ricoh leads Japan's facsimile market, with a 16% market share. It has 150 subsidiaries, 25 affiliates, and six production facilities in Japan. Ricoh generates 73% of sales in Japan, with 27% coming from North America and Europe. The firm acquired two U.S.-based companies, Savin and Selective Business Systems, in 1994. It also has tie-ups with Microsoft, International Chip, and Yokogawa-Hewlett Packard.

¥bil	03/93	03/94	03/95	US$mil 03/95				
Sales	**1,021.9**	**968.3**	**1,020.3**	**10,342.1**	P/E Ratio	**34.7**	Price (9/30/95)	**992.00**
Net Income	**5.0**	**9.5**	**18.6**	**188.5**	P/B Ratio	**1.7**	52 Wk Hi-Low	**1,050.0-650.0**
Book Value	**351.6**	**349.9**	**377.8**	**4,373.1**	Yield %	**1.0**	Market Cap	**US$6,501.6mil**

Address	**1-15-5, Minami-Aoyama**	Tel	**03-3479-3111**	ADR	**RICOY**	President	**Hiroshi Hamada**
	Minato-ku, Tokyo 107	Fax	**03-3403-1578**	SEDOL No.	**6738220**	Chairman	--

Rohm

Industry: **Semiconductors & related**

Rohm is a leading supplier of custom linear-integrated circuits and thermal printheads for facsimile machines. The firm's integrated circuits, semiconductor devices, and electronic components are mainly used in the private sector, including the computer and mobile-communication industries. In 1994, overseas sales accounted for 46% of consolidated revenues. Rohm has 38 subsidiaries, about 20 of which are overseas. The latter include manufacturing and sales offices for electronic components in the U.S., Brazil, Malaysia, Singapore, Hong Kong, South Korea, and Thailand.

¥bil	03/93	03/94	03/95	US$mil 03/95				
Sales	**186.9**	**200.0**	**241.5**	**2,447.8**	P/E Ratio	**28.7**	Price (9/30/95)	**6,210.00**
Net Income	**8.1**	**12.5**	**22.7**	**229.9**	P/B Ratio	**2.8**	52 Wk Hi-Low	**6,690.0-3,060.0**
Book Value	**183.4**	**201.6**	**236.6**	**2,738.5**	Yield %	**0.3**	Market Cap	**US$6,691.5mil**

Address	**21, Mizozaki-cho, Saiin**	Tel	**075-311-2121**	ADR		President	**Kenichiro Sato**
	Ukyo-ku, Kyoto 615	Fax	**075-315-0172**	SEDOL No.	**6747204**	Chairman	--

Ryobi

Industry: **Other Auto Parts**

Ryobi manufactures die-cast products for automobiles, electric appliances, and office machinery. It supplies automotive die-cast products to Ford Motor and General Motors. The company also manufactures printing presses, power tools, phototypesetters, housing materials, and golfing equipment. Mitsubishi Motors is Ryobi's largest customer; other major customers include Suzuki Motor, Fuji Heavy Industries, and Kawasaki Heavy Industries. Ryobi has 26 consolidated subsidiaries, including eight in the U.S. and one each in Canada, Australia, the U.K., France, and the Netherlands.

¥bil	03/93	03/94	03/95	US$mil 03/95				
Sales	**205.9**	**192.5**	**197.6**	**2,003.2**	P/E Ratio	**NMF**	Price (9/30/95)	**508.00**
Net Income	**3.6**	**0.3**	**-0.5**	**-4.6**	P/B Ratio	**1.8**	52 Wk Hi-Low	**628.00-410.00**
Book Value	**47.3**	**48.2**	**48.2**	**557.7**	Yield %	**1.7**	Market Cap	**US$874.5mil**

Address	**3-15-1, Soto-Kanda**	Tel	**03-3257-1971**	ADR		President	**Hiroshi Urakami**
	Chiyoda-ku, Tokyo 101	Fax	**03-3257-1716**	SEDOL No.	**6762906**	Chairman	--

Sagami Railway

Industry: **Real-Estate Investment**

Sagami Railway (Sagami Tetsudo), known to consumers in Japan as Sotetsu, is a Yokohama-based railway with extensive real-estate holdings. It operates bus lines, is active in construction, and makes construction materials such as concrete and gravel. Sotetsu also has divisions that deal in office-automation equipment, recycled paper, the import and distribution of petroleum products, and automobile marketing. Real-estate activities account for the largest share of its revenues. The firm has five consolidated subsidiaries (all wholly-owned) and 16 unconsolidated subsidiaries.

¥bil	03/93	03/94	03/95	US$mil 03/95				
Sales	**169.3**	**174.5**	**172.6**	**1,749.2**	P/E Ratio	**NMF**	Price (9/30/95)	**432.00**
Net Income	**1.4**	**0.8**	**-0.2**	**-2.1**	P/B Ratio	**2.7**	52 Wk Hi-Low	**495.00-386.00**
Book Value	**65.4**	**68.8**	**66.7**	**771.4**	Yield %	**1.2**	Market Cap	**US$1,790.3mil**

Address **2-9-14, Kitasaiwai, Nishi-ku, Yokohama, Kanagawa 220-91**
Tel **045-319-2111** Fax **045-319-8989**
ADR SEDOL No. **6767202**
President **Masahiro Hoshino** Chairman **Kojiro Tsushima**

Sakata Seed

Industry: **Biotechnology**

Sakata Seed (Sakata No Tane) develops and sells a variety of seeds, seedlings, and bulbs. The company controls 70% of the world market in pansy seeds, and holds high U.S. market shares in broccoli and pansy seeds. Other major seeds include the Prince and Andes melons; Atlas spinach; Honey Bantam sweet corn and cabbage; petunias; and lisianthus. Its overseas operations include research stations in California, Arizona, Washington, and Florida; an affiliate in Europe; and a research farm in Denmark. Sakata has a mail-order division and publishes a garden journal.

¥bil	05/93	05/94	05/95	US$mil 05/95				
Sales	**38.2**	**38.6**	**40.2**	**407.3**	P/E Ratio	**35.7**	Price (9/30/95)	**2,460.00**
Net Income	**3.7**	**3.8**	**3.5**	**35.6**	P/B Ratio	**1.8**	52 Wk Hi-Low	**3,380.0-2,330.0**
Book Value	**65.0**	**68.0**	**70.7**	**817.8**	Yield %	**0.6**	Market Cap	**US$1,259.7mil**

Address **3-1-7, Nagata-Higashi Minami-ku, Yokohama 232**
Tel **045-715-2111** Fax **045-715-1755**
ADR SEDOL No. **6769811**
President **Zenichiro Kaneko** Chairman --

Sakura Bank

Industry: **Banks - Money Center**

Sakura Bank is the fifth-largest bank both in Japan and in the world (ranked by assets). It is the financial center of Japan's Mitsui group. In addition to its traditional lending operations, the bank's services include bond underwriting and dealing (particularly domestic and Samurai bond issues), investment consulting, and lease financing. The bank has more than 350 branches and offices in the Tokyo region, and more than 190 around Osaka. The bank has an agreement with Arthur Andersen to supply services to Sakura's customers doing business outside of Japan.

¥bil	03/93	03/94	03/95	US$mil 03/95				
Revenues	**2,995.3**	**2,626.8**	**2,618.0**	**26,536.7**	P/E Ratio	**NMF**	Price (9/30/95)	**1,080.00**
Net Income	**57.7**	**22.9**	**22.4**	**227.2**	P/B Ratio	**2.0**	52 Wk Hi-Low	**1,360.0-885.0**
Book Value	**1,729.4**	**1,827.1**	**1,826.5**	**21,139.7**	Yield %	**0.8**	Market Cap	**US$36,017mil**

Address **1-3-1, Kudan-Minami Chiyoda-ku, Tokyo 100-91**
Tel **03-3230-3111** Fax **03-3239-1022**
ADR **SAKUY** SEDOL No. **6598714**
President **Shunsaku Hashimoto** Chairman **Kenichi Suematsu**

Sanden

Industry: **Other Auto Parts**

Sanden is one of the world's three largest makers of automotive air conditioners, holding about 20% of the world market. The company also manufactures vending machines, household appliances, and food-display cases. It supplies automakers in Japan and the United States, and holds 50 % of the European market. Sanden's operations in the U.S. include plants in Texas and Tennessee, and Vendo, a vending-machine maker. The company is also expanding into electronics through joint ventures with Casio Computer. Altogether, Sanden has 35 subsidiaries.

¥bil	03/93	03/94	03/95	US$mil 03/95				
Sales	**178.0**	**163.2**	**182.0**	**1,844.8**	P/E Ratio	**58.2**	Price (9/30/95)	**524.00**
Net Income	**-2.1**	**-0.8**	**1.3**	**13.2**	P/B Ratio	**1.5**	52 Wk Hi-Low	**690.00-410.00**
Book Value	**53.2**	**50.4**	**51.6**	**596.7**	Yield %	**0.6**	Market Cap	**US$760.7mil**

Address **20, Kotobuki-cho Isesaki City, Gunma 372**
Tel **0270-24-1281** Fax **03-3835-2631**
ADR SEDOL No. **6775186**
President **Masayoshi Ushikubo** Chairman **Tomoaki Ushikubo**

Sanki Engineering

Industry: **Electrical Components & Equipment**

Sanki Engineering (Sanki Kogyo), a Mitsui affiliate, designs and installs infrastructure systems that include plumbing, air-conditioning, central-heating, and electrical systems. Construction and installation of infrastructures accounts for nearly 85% of the company's total revenues. Climate-control systems alone make up about 50% of its revenues. Sanki's non-design activities include selling AT&T computers in Japan: the firm also trains South Korean software engineers in a stated effort to standardize South Korean and Japanese computer programming.

¥bil	03/93	03/94	03/95	US$mil 03/95				
Sales	**281.9**	**278.3**	**272.1**	**2,757.8**	P/E Ratio	**22.9**	Price (9/30/95)	**1,070.00**
Net Income	**8.7**	**7.1**	**3.9**	**40.0**	P/B Ratio	**1.4**	52 Wk Hi-Low	**1,360.0-756.0**
Book Value	**57.7**	**63.0**	**67.0**	**775.2**	Yield %	**1.7**	Market Cap	**US$909.6mil**

Address **1-4-1, Yuraku-cho Chiyoda-ku, Tokyo 100**
Tel **03-3502-6111** Fax **03-3508-9658**
ADR SEDOL No. **6774826**
President **Takeshi Ohshima** Chairman **Seiji Shiratani**

Sankyo

Industry: **Pharmaceuticals**

Sankyo is Japan's second-largest pharmaceutical manufacturer by sales. The company produces prescription and over-the-counter drugs, medical supplies, and other chemicals. Its major drugs include Mevalotin (hyperlipemia treatment), Krestin (anticancer), and Zaditen (antiallergy). The Federation of Agricultural Co-op, Nakagawayasu, Seinasu, and Seiwa are among its major customers. Sankyo has licensing agreements with Bristol-Myers Squibb and Upjohn (U.S.). It has overseas consolidated subsidiaries in Germany and affiliates in the U.S., India, Taiwan, and Thailand.

	¥bil 03/93	03/94	03/95	US$mil 03/95				
Sales	**518.9**	**516.8**	**553.1**	**5,606.1**	P/E Ratio	**28.3**	Price (9/30/95)	**2,260.00**
Net Income	**29.1**	**37.9**	**39.2**	**396.9**	P/B Ratio	**2.9**	52 Wk Hi-Low	**2,320.0-1,872.5**
Book Value	**275.8**	**310.2**	**344.9**	**3,992.1**	Yield %	**0.6**	Market Cap	**US$10,133mil**

Address	**3-5-1, Nihonbashi-Honcho**	Tel	**03-5255-7111**	ADR		President	**Yoshibumi Kawamura**
	Chuo-ku, Tokyo 103	Fax	**03-5255-7069**	SEDOL No.	**6775283**	Chairman	--

Sanrio

Industry: **Other Recreational Products & Services**

Sanrio is a major vendor of gift merchandise. The retailer markets more than 12,000 gift items, many of which are based on company-created trademark characters such as Hello Kitty. Sanrio receives royalties from movie-and video-licensing agreements for its characters. The company also sells greeting cards, books, and magazines. Sanrio also directly manages some 149 stores and has more than 3,000 sales corners in department stores in Japan. Its subsidiary Sanrio Communication World facilitates theme-park development. Sanrio sells products in over 40 countries.

	¥bil 03/93	03/94	03/95	US$mil 03/95				
Sales	**114.2**	**102.5**	**92.3**	**936.1**	P/E Ratio	**NMF**	Price (9/30/95)	**1,090.00**
Net Income	**-5.6**	**-4.4**	**-24.0**	**-243.3**	P/B Ratio	**2.6**	52 Wk Hi-Low	**1,520.0-854.0**
Book Value	**61.7**	**57.3**	**33.0**	**381.6**	Yield %	**0.0**	Market Cap	**US$861.1mil**

Address	**1-6-1, Ohsaki**	Tel	**03-3779-8111**	ADR		President	**Shintaro Tsuji**
	Shinagawa-ku, Tokyo 141	Fax	**03-3779-8054**	SEDOL No.	**6776349**	Chairman	--

Sanwa Bank

Industry: **Banks - Regional**

Sanwa Bank is the fourth-largest bank in Japan (ranked by assets) and in the world. It is the financial center of Japan's Sanwa group, which includes Nissho Iwai, Kobe Steel, and NTN. Sanwa was the first Japanese bank to set up an investment-advisory firm in Japan. Among Japan's banks, Sanwa is a leader in the gold market. Its domestic network includes 280 branches, 62 offices, and 580 automated-service counters. In 1994, overseas activities accounted for 44% of consolidated revenues. Sanwa established a bond-underwriting subsidiary in 1994.

	¥bil 03/93	03/94	03/95	US$mil 03/95				
Revenues	**3,244.0**	**2,733.7**	**2,748.6**	**27,860.7**	P/E Ratio	**NMF**	Price (9/30/95)	**1,860.00**
Net Income	**95.2**	**45.7**	**22.3**	**226.4**	P/B Ratio	**2.7**	52 Wk Hi-Low	**2,060.0-1,570.0**
Book Value	**2,006.9**	**2,028.9**	**2,032.8**	**23,528.1**	Yield %	**0.5**	Market Cap	**US$54,272mil**

Address	**3-5-6, Fushimi-machi**	Tel	**06-206-8111**	ADR	**SANWY**	President	**Naotaka Saeki**
	Chuo-ku, Osaka 541	Fax	**03-3215-1776**	SEDOL No.	**6776747**	Chairman	**Hiroshi Watanabe**

Sanwa Shutter

Industry: **Building Materials**

Sanwa Shutter (Sanwa Shutter Kogyo) is Japan's largest shutter manufacturer by market share. The firm makes, installs, and repairs shutters, doors, and exterior sliding doors. It also manufactures balconies, handrails, and other window-related products. Shutters and Shutter related products accounted for about 47% of company sales in 1994; products for doors and windows were 35.9% of company sales, respectively. Sanwa Shutter has three consolidated and 11 unconsolidated subsidiaries, and 61 affiliates, including some in Hong Kong, Taiwan, Singapore, and Malaysia.

	¥bil 03/93	03/94	03/95	US$mil 03/95				
Sales	**232.2**	**210.3**	**195.9**	**1,985.7**	P/E Ratio	**29.2**	Price (9/30/95)	**759.00**
Net Income	**9.3**	**6.8**	**6.2**	**62.4**	P/B Ratio	**1.7**	52 Wk Hi-Low	**952.00-601.00**
Book Value	**96.1**	**101.2**	**104.5**	**1,209.0**	Yield %	**1.1**	Market Cap	**US$1,807.4mil**

Address	**2-1-1, Nishi-Shinjuku**	Tel	**03-3346-3378**	ADR		President	**Toshitaka Takayama**
	Shinjuku-ku, Tokyo 163-04	Fax	**03-3346-3177**	SEDOL No.	**6776781**	Chairman	--

Sanyo Chemical Industries

Industry: **Specialty Chemicals**

Sanyo Chemical Industries (Sanyo Kasei Kogyo) is a leading producer of high-performance specialty chemicals. Surfactants, urethane-related products, and high-molecular and special-purpose chemicals account for more than 97% of its sales. The firm is the world's top supplier of superabsorbent polymers, a principal ingredient in disposable diapers and feminine-hygiene products. Other products include medical reagents that are used to detect disease. Trading company Tomen is one of its major customers. Sanyo has seven subsidiaries and six affiliates throghout Japan.

	¥bil 03/93	03/94	03/95	US$mil 03/95				
Sales	**69.4**	**65.4**	**67.4**	**683.0**	P/E Ratio	**25.1**	Price (9/30/95)	**845.00**
Net Income	**4.1**	**4.0**	**4.0**	**41.0**	P/B Ratio	**1.7**	52 Wk Hi-Low	**1,090.0-740.0**
Book Value	**53.3**	**55.9**	**59.8**	**691.7**	Yield %	**1.4**	Market Cap	**US$1,017.5mil**

Address	**11-1, Ikkyo-Nomotocho**	Tel	**075-541-4311**	ADR		President	**Tetsuo Tsutsumi**
	Higashiyama-ku, Kyoto 605	Fax	**075-551-2557**	SEDOL No.	**6776800**	Chairman	**Takehiko Fujimoto**

Sanyo Electric

Industry: **Consumer Electronics**

Sanyo Electric (Sanyo Denki) is one of Japan's largest manufacturers of electrical equipment by revenues. It markets a wide range of products, including audiovisual equipment, home appliances, vending machines, refrigerated showcases, air conditioners, office-automation equipment, computers, semiconductors, and batteries. Sanyo is a world leader in the production of solar cells. It also leads in domestic production of nickel-cadmium and nickel-hydrogen batteries. In 1994, overseas sales made up 42.7% of consolidated sales.

	¥bil 11/92	11/93	11/94	US$mil 11/94				
Sales	**1,565.8**	**1,556.8**	**1,693.6**	**16,461.4**	P/E Ratio	**97.6**	Price (9/30/95)	**566.00**
Net Income	**-1.3**	**-1.6**	**11.3**	**110.1**	P/B Ratio	**1.5**	52 Wk Hi-Low	**590.00-400.00**
Book Value	**727.1**	**713.2**	**718.3**	**7,258.9**	Yield %	**0.9**	Market Cap	**US$11,103mil**

Address	**2-5-5, Keihan-Hondori**	Tel	**06-991-1181**	ADR	**SANYY**	President	**Yasuaki Takano**
	Moriguchi City, Osaka 570	Fax	**06-992-0009**	SEDOL No.	**6776769**	Chairman	**Satoshi Iue**

Sanyo Shokai

Industry: **Clothing & Fabrics**

Sanyo Shokai designs, manufactures, and markets more than 60 brands of coats, suits, dresses, and sportswear for men, women, and children. Best known as a coat manufacturer, the company commands more than half of the Japanese market for coats. The company distributes its products directly to department and specialty stores throughout Japan, and exports to Australia, Canada, the U.S., and Italy. Sanyo Shokai's products are sold under the names of several Japanese designers, under the Sanyo name, and in collections from Burberry, Yves Saint Laurent, and Bill Blass.

	¥bil 12/92	12/93	12/94	US$mil 12/94				
Sales	**158.6**	**144.5**	**141.0**	**1,381.4**	P/E Ratio	**125.6**	Price (9/30/95)	**565.00**
Net Income	**1.1**	**0.1**	**0.6**	**6.0**	P/B Ratio	**1.5**	52 Wk Hi-Low	**650.00-450.00**
Book Value	**52.6**	**51.1**	**50.2**	**503.6**	Yield %	**2.1**	Market Cap	**US$774.2mil**

Address	**14, Honshio-cho**	Tel	**03-3357-4111**	ADR		President	**Masamichi Nakase**
	Shinjuku-ku, Tokyo 160	Fax	**03-3226-8530**	SEDOL No.	**6776888**	Chairman	**Nobuyuki Yoshihara**

Sapporo Breweries

Industry: **Distillers & Brewers**

Sapporo Breweries (Sapporo Biru) is Japan's third-largest brewer, controlling about 20% of the market. Its popular Black Label brand accounts for more than 50% of its beer sales. The firm also produces whiskey, wine, soft drinks, juices, pharmaceuticals, and cattle feed, and imports a wide variety of beers, wines, and mineral waters. It has three vineyards in the U.S., and is a distributor for 11 German estate wineries. Sapporo's other operations include a chain of beer halls, restaurants, sports clubs, and hotels. It has eight consolidated and 29 unconsolidated subsidiaries.

	¥bil 12/92	12/93	12/94	US$mil 12/94				
Sales	**577.1**	**601.7**	**663.9**	**6,505.7**	P/E Ratio	**91.2**	Price (9/30/95)	**885.00**
Net Income	**3.2**	**3.4**	**3.3**	**32.2**	P/B Ratio	**2.1**	52 Wk Hi-Low	**970.00-781.00**
Book Value	**133.1**	**139.0**	**139.7**	**1,400.7**	Yield %	**1.0**	Market Cap	**US$3,013.5mil**

Address	**7-10-1, Ginza**	Tel	**03-3572-6111**	ADR		President	**Kenzo Yamamne**
	Chuo-ku, Tokyo 104	Fax	**03-3572-0221**	SEDOL No.	**6776907**	Chairman	**Kazuo Arakawa**

Sasebo Heavy Industries

Industry: **Shipbuilding**

Sasebo Heavy Industries (Sasebo Jukogyo) is a shipbuilder and heavy-machinery manufacturer. The company's activities include ship repair and remodeling, production and engineering of steel structures, and production of boilers, winches, and other machinery for marine use. Its major customers include Sumitomo, Perennial Motors Transport, and Triumph Sea. The firm also builds ships for the Japan Defense Agency and repairs U.S. naval ships. It has participated in civil-engineering projects in Japan and overseas. Financing is managed by the Industrial Bank of Japan.

	¥bil 03/93 P	03/94 P	03/95 P	US$mil 03/95				
Sales	**56.4**	**63.9**	**57.1**	**578.3**	P/E Ratio	**53.5**	Price (9/30/95)	**257.00**
Net Income	**3.5**	**2.1**	**0.8**	**8.2**	P/B Ratio	**1.9**	52 Wk Hi-Low	**415.00-155.00**
Book Value	**22.2**	**23.4**	**23.3**	**269.5**	Yield %	**1.9**	Market Cap	**US$435.0mil**

Address	**2-2-1, Otemachi**	Tel	**03-3211-2989**	ADR		President	**Ryutaro Hasegawa**
	Chiyoda-ku, Tokyo 100	Fax	**03-3279-0380**	SEDOL No.	**6777405**	Chairman	--

P=Parent company data.

Sato Kogyo

Industry: **Heavy Construction**

Sato Kogyo is a general contractor working primarily with building construction and engineering projects. Two thirds of its parent-company sales stem from building construction, including residences and office, industrial, medical, and leisure facilities. Civil-engineering projects include the design and construction of tunnels, dams, highways, railroads, oil refineries, and power-generation facilities. It has 24 subsidiaries, of which four are domestic consolidated subsidiaries. It has affiliates in Malaysia, Singapore, Thailand, the United States, and the United Kingdom.

	¥bil 03/93	03/94	03/95	US$mil 03/95				
Sales	**657.0**	**668.3**	**614.8**	**6,231.9**	P/E Ratio	**NMF**	Price (9/30/95)	**605.00**
Net Income	**2.1**	**1.2**	**-3.9**	**-39.5**	P/B Ratio	**3.2**	52 Wk Hi-Low	**840.00-525.00**
Book Value	**64.1**	**62.5**	**49.6**	**574.2**	Yield %	**1.0**	Market Cap	**US$1,591.3mil**

Address	**1-11, Sakuragi-cho**	Tel	**0764-31-6531**	ADR		President	**Yoshitake Sato**
	Toyama City, Toyama 930	Fax	**03-3661-5473**	SEDOL No.	**6777609**	Chairman	**Sukekuro Sato**

Secom

Industry: **General Industrial & Commercial Services**

Secom is Japan's largest security-service company. It operates the largest security-communication network in Japan, and offers systems and services for home and business security. It also provides home-medical-care and on-line information services, produces software systems, and operates a cable-TV station. In September 1994 Secom sold its medical-services subsidiary, HMSS (U.S.). Remaining subsidiaries in Australia, China, Taiwan, Korea, Singapore, Thailand, Malaysia, Indonesia, the U.S., and the U.K. generate 10% of consolidated revenues.

	¥bil 03/93	03/94	03/95	US$mil 03/95				
Sales	**244.0**	**257.5**	**250.7**	**2,541.3**	P/E Ratio	**61.5**	Price (9/30/95)	**6,600.00**
Net Income	**11.0**	**11.6**	**12.2**	**123.6**	P/B Ratio	**3.2**	52 Wk Hi-Low	**6,750.0-5,010.0**
Book Value	**181.3**	**225.5**	**235.6**	**2,726.4**	Yield %	**0.7**	Market Cap	**US$7,552.4mil**

Address	**1-26-2, Nishi-Shinjuku** **Shinjuku-ku, Tokyo 163-05**	Tel **03-3348-7511** Fax **03-3345-0219**	ADR **SOMLY** SEDOL No. **6791591**	President Chairman	**Toshitaka Sugimachi** **Makoto Iida**

Sega Enterprises

Industry: **Toy Manufacturers**

Sega Enterprises, an affiliate of CSK, develops and manufactures video games for both commercial and consumer use. The firm's main products are hardware and software for video-game systems, portable video games, toys, and amusement machines. It also manages amusement arcades. The company's Genesis home-video-game system competes with Nintendo's Super NES. Sega's new products include simulation games and an IBM-compatible PC. Sega earns additional income from royalty and copyright fees. In 1994, 54.7% of Sega's consolidated sales were made overseas.

	¥bil 03/93	03/94	03/95	US$mil 03/95				
Sales	**416.2**	**416.5**	**383.6**	**3,888.1**	P/E Ratio	**111.4**	Price (9/30/95)	**5,670.00**
Net Income	**30.8**	**11.2**	**5.1**	**51.8**	P/B Ratio	**3.7**	52 Wk Hi-Low	**6,180.0-2,840.0**
Book Value	**119.2**	**155.6**	**155.3**	**1,797.0**	Yield %	**0.7**	Market Cap	**US$5,731.0mil**

Address	**1-2-12, Haneda** **Ota-ku, Tokyo 144**	Tel **03-5736-7034** Fax **03-5736-7058**	ADR **SEGNY** SEDOL No. **6791955**	President Chairman	**Hayao Nakayama** **Isao Ohkawa**

Seibu Railway

Industry: **Railroads**

Seibu Railway (Seibu Tetsudo), in conjunction with Kokudo, is a core member of the Seibu Railway group, and a major provider of transportation and leisure related-activities by sales. Railway service and tourism are the company's main areas of activity. Real-estate sales and leasing form its third-largest sector. Seibu Railway's diverse tourism-related operations include resort development and hotel management. The Seibu group operates a department store, restaurants, sports facilities, a baseball team, and an amusement park. It has 63 consolidated subsidiaries in Japan.

	¥bil 03/93	03/94	03/95	US$mil 03/95				
Sales	**543.1**	**525.9**	**551.1**	**5,586.5**	P/E Ratio	**NMF**	Price (9/30/95)	**4,350.00**
Net Income	**0.3**	**-0.9**	**-2.3**	**-23.5**	P/B Ratio	**NMF**	52 Wk Hi-Low	**4,750.0-2,750.0**
Book Value	**44.1**	**41.9**	**38.1**	**440.6**	Yield %	**0.1**	Market Cap	**US$18,959mil**

Address	**1-11-1, Kusunokidai** **Tokorozawa City, Saitama 359**	Tel **0429-26-2040** Fax **0429-26-2237**	ADR SEDOL No. **6792709**	President Chairman	**Iwao Nisugi** **Yoshiaki Tsutsumi**

Seiko

Industry: **Clothing & Fabrics**

Seiko (Hattori Seiko), the nucleus of the Seiko group, is the world's largest supplier of watches and clocks. It holds a substantial share of the market for medium- and high-quality watches with its Lassale, Pulsar, Lorus, and Alba brands. Its subsidiaries produce quartz oscillators, integrated-circuit chips, batteries, and computer goods. Seiko also sells jewelry. Retailers are among the firm's major customers. It has consolidated subsidiaries in Europe, Hong Kong, North America, and Australia. Seiko also has technical agreements and joint ventures in about 100 countries.

	¥bil 03/93	03/94	03/95	US$mil 03/95				
Sales	**378.0**	**334.7**	**330.9**	**3,353.7**	P/E Ratio	**NMF**	Price (9/30/95)	**798.00**
Net Income	**-5.2**	**-6.3**	**-9.4**	**-95.1**	P/B Ratio	**7.3**	52 Wk Hi-Low	**982.00-625.00**
Book Value	**29.5**	**25.5**	**11.5**	**133.2**	Yield %	**0.9**	Market Cap	**US$847.6mil**

Address	**2-6-21, Kyobashi** **Chuo-ku, Tokyo 104**	Tel **03-3563-2111** Fax **03-3563-8493**	ADR SEDOL No. **6414809**	President Chairman	**Masahiro Sekimoto** **Reijiro Hattori**

Seino Transportation

Industry: **Trucking**

Seino Transportation (Seino Unyu) is a leading Japanese trucking company that offers commercial transport and overnight parcel delivery in major metropolitan areas. The firm operates a domestic and international air-transport service, provides marine-cargo service, and operates ferryboats between Japan's major ports. Seino Transportation's general-delivery division is its mainstay, bringing in approximately 95% of consolidated sales. It has 23 subsidiaries and 33 affiliates that are involved in transportation, information and sales, and real-estate leasing and management.

	¥bil 03/93 *	03/94	03/95	US$mil 03/95				
Sales	**289.1**	**289.3**	**304.4**	**3,085.7**	P/E Ratio	**38.1**	Price (9/30/95)	**1,680.00**
Net Income	**6.2**	**5.1**	**6.7**	**68.1**	P/B Ratio	**1.3**	52 Wk Hi-Low	**1,910.0-1,410.0**
Book Value	**192.1**	**195.6**	**202.8**	**2,346.9**	Yield %	**0.7**	Market Cap	**US$2,578.7mil**

Address	**1, Taguchi-cho** **Ohgaki City, Gifu 503**	Tel **0584-81-1111** Fax **0584-82-5045**	ADR SEDOL No. **6793423**	President Chairman	**Yoshikazu Taguchi** **Toshio Taguchi**

*Irregular period due to fiscal year change.

Seiyo Food Systems

Industry: **Restaurants**

Seiyo Food Systems is a major restaurant-chain operator. The company operates a total of 465 stores and its four most important chains include its mainstay, Casa, a Western-style restaurant; Shochibo, which serves Chinese cuisine; Han, which serves Japanese food; and Talk, a chain of golf-clubhouse restaurants. The firm's food-catering division manages more than 168 company cafeterias, employee-training facilities, resorts, and wedding halls. The firm also has a joint venture, Ace Cafeteria, with Ajinomoto. Seiyo Food's two consolidated subsidiaries both manage restaurants.

¥bil	03/93	03/94	03/95	US$mil 03/95				
Sales	**97.6**	**96.3**	**96.1**	**974.1**	P/E Ratio	**42.6**	Price (9/30/95)	**874.00**
Net Income	**2.0**	**2.1**	**1.6**	**16.4**	P/B Ratio	**1.2**	52 Wk Hi-Low	**1,310.0-750.0**
Book Value	**56.4**	**57.4**	**57.9**	**670.3**	Yield %	**1.5**	Market Cap	**US$694.0mil**

Address **3-1-1, Higashi-Ikebukuro Toshima-ku, Tokyo 170**
Tel **03-3980-2346**
Fax **03-3983-3475**
ADR
SEDOL No. **6733441**
President **Jun Sugimoto**
Chairman **Shigeaki Wada**

Seiyu

Industry: **Retailers - Broadline**

Seiyu markets food, clothing, and household products through its nine department stores, 228 superstores and supermarkets, and specialty stores. The firm has 12 consolidated subsidiaries, including the convenience-store operator FamilyMart (52% owned) and a finance subsidiary, Tokyo City Finance (50% owned). Seiyu has more than 50 stores in Taiwan and a department store in Hong Kong. The company is 40% owner of Inter-Continental Hotels. Seiyu also has a partnership with L.L. Bean to sell the U.S. firm's products through a chain of specialty stores in Japan.

¥bil	02/93	02/94	02/95	US$mil 02/95				
Revenues	**1,377.1**	**1,305.7**	**1,329.2**	**13,263.7**	P/E Ratio	**120.2**	Price (9/30/95)	**1,190.00**
Net Income	**10.3**	**7.3**	**2.2**	**22.1**	P/B Ratio	**2.5**	52 Wk Hi-Low	**1,400.0-990.0**
Book Value	**117.8**	**120.7**	**107.8**	**1,114.5**	Yield %	**1.3**	Market Cap	**US$2,678.8mil**

Address **3-1-1, Higashi-Ikebukuro Toshima-ku, Tokyo 170**
Tel **03-3989-5162**
Fax **03-3989-4947**
ADR
SEDOL No. **6793780**
President **Katsuhiro Fujiseki**
Chairman **Sueaki Takaoka**

Sekisui Chemical

Industry: **Home Construction**

Sekisui Chemical (Sekisui Kagaku Kogyo) is a building-materials manufacturer that specializes in injection-molded plastics for home and industrial use and prefabricated housing. The firm holds high market share in Japan for polyvinyl-chloride pipe and pipe fittings. Its other products include adhesives, packaging, industrial foams and tapes, and medical equipment. The firm supplies polyvinyl film to the auto industry for the manufacture of shatterproof glass. Sekisui Chemical has nine plants in Japan and 188 subsidiaries, including ones in the U.S., Europe, and Asia.

¥bil	03/93	03/94	03/95	US$mil 03/95				
Sales	**912.0**	**953.9**	**1,023.0**	**10,369.1**	P/E Ratio	**NMF**	Price (9/30/95)	**1,260.00**
Net Income	**17.8**	**21.1**	**2.3**	**23.1**	P/B Ratio	**1.8**	52 Wk Hi-Low	**1,380.0-935.0**
Book Value	**374.1**	**389.0**	**384.1**	**4,446.0**	Yield %	**0.9**	Market Cap	**US$6,994.9mil**

Address **2-4-4, Nishi-Tenma Kita-ku, Osaka 530**
Tel **06-365-4085**
Fax **06-365-4370**
ADR
SEDOL No. **6793821**
President **Susumu Nishizawa**
Chairman **Kaoru Hirota**

Sekisui House

Industry: **Home Construction**

Sekisui House is Japan's largest builder of houses. The firm designs, constructs, and sells commercial buildings and residential properties, such as hotels, shopping centers, model homes, and high-rise apartments and condominiums. Sekisui participates mainly in large-scale developments. The firm also owns and manages residential properties. Its 13 consolidated subsidiaries finance development projects, manufacture housing materials, and sell real estate. Sekisui will purchase the remainder of its 42%-owned wooden-house-building subsidiary in August 1995.

¥bil	01/93	01/94	01/95	US$mil 01/95				
Sales	**1,193.6**	**1,294.4**	**1,254.1**	**12,415.8**	P/E Ratio	**20.2**	Price (9/30/95)	**1,230.00**
Net Income	**39.1**	**40.3**	**40.7**	**402.9**	P/B Ratio	**1.2**	52 Wk Hi-Low	**1,250.0-1,010.0**
Book Value	**581.4**	**641.5**	**697.3**	**7,047.0**	Yield %	**1.5**	Market Cap	**US$8,385.6mil**

Address **1-1-88, Oyodonaka Kita-ku, Osaka 531**
Tel **06-440-3111**
Fax **06-440-3331**
ADR
SEDOL No. **6793906**
President **Isao Okui**
Chairman **Hiromu Ohhashi**

Settsu

Industry: **Paper Products**

Settsu is Japan's leading manufacturer of corrugated cardboard and ranks second in paperboard production. The firm also produces pulp and corrugated containers. Its recycled-paperboard products include tubeboard, chipboard, and gypsum linerboard. Settsu markets a large portion of its products through the trading company Ryodai Shoji. Its domestic operations include three paperboard mills and five corrugated-container plants. Settsu also has six wholly-owned consolidated subsidiaries in the U.S., Canada (including Crain-Drummond in Ontario), the Netherlands, and Brunei.

¥bil	03/93	03/94	03/95	US$mil 03/95				
Sales	**149.8**	**131.4**	**122.2**	**1,238.2**	P/E Ratio	**NMF**	Price (9/30/95)	**295.00**
Net Income	**-8.8**	**-8.6**	**-7.4**	**-75.1**	P/B Ratio	**0.9**	52 Wk Hi-Low	**427.00-238.00**
Book Value	**83.1**	**76.2**	**71.2**	**823.9**	Yield %	**0.0**	Market Cap	**US$649.8mil**

Address **1-4-1, Kuise-Minamishinmachi Amagasaki City, Hyogo 660**
Tel **06-488-2530**
Fax **06-489-1122**
ADR
SEDOL No. **6796983**
President **Toshio Kamada**
Chairman --

Seven-Eleven Japan

Industry: **Food Retailers & Wholesalers**

Seven-Eleven Japan, a subsidiary of Ito-Yokado, is Japan's largest convenience-store chain. It has 5,952 stores, nearly all of which are franchised. The outlets are organized in regional clusters of 50 or 60 to facilitate distribution. About 18% of the firm's sales are made in Tokyo, where it has 844 stores. Together with its parent company, the firm controls 64% of the shares of Southland (U.S.), owner of the U.S. chain of 7-Eleven stores. In fiscal 1994, total sales from franchised and corporate stores was $13.9 billion.

¥bil	02/93 P	02/94 P	02/95 P	US$mil 02/95				
Sales	182.0	195.7	214.6	2,141.0	P/E Ratio	56.0	Price (9/30/95)	6,660.00
Net Income	45.0	46.6	49.5	494.2	P/B Ratio	8.0	52 Wk Hi-Low	7,309.1-5,800.0
Book Value	242.8	278.9	316.6	3,274.5	Yield %	0.4	Market Cap	US$25,361mil

Address	**4-1-4, Shiba-Koen**	Tel	**03-3459-3711**	ADR	**SVELY**	President	**Hiroo Kurita**
	Minato-ku, Tokyo 105	Fax	**N/A**	SEDOL No.	**6797179**	Chairman	**Toshifumi Suzuki**

P=Parent company data.

77 Bank

Industry: **Banks - Regional**

77 Bank (Shichijushichi Ginko), based in Miyagi Prefecture, is the largest regional bank in the Tohoku region by assets. It offers comprehensive financial services including foreign exchange, financial futures and options brokerage, and credit guarantees. The bank's regional domestic network consists of 147 branches, 128 of which are located in Miyagi. Foreign-exchange services are offered at about 60 branches. The 77 Bank has a branch in New York, a representative office in London, and correspondent-banking relationships with 104 banks in 42 countries.

¥bil	03/93 P	03/94 P	03/95 P	US$mil 03/95				
Revenues	208.6	180.8	173.4	1,757.8	P/E Ratio	33.5	Price (9/30/95)	946.00
Net Income	9.1	9.2	10.8	109.6	P/B Ratio	2.1	52 Wk Hi-Low	1,060.0-860.0
Book Value	154.7	161.9	170.8	1,976.6	Yield %	0.5	Market Cap	US$3,640.9mil

Address	**3-3-20, Chuo, Aoba-ku**	Tel	**022-267-1111**	ADR		President	**Iwao Muramatsu**
	Sendai City, Miyagi 980	Fax	**022-264-3120**	SEDOL No.	**6804165**	Chairman	**Chigio Sato**

P=Parent company data.

Sharp

Industry: **Consumer Electronics**

Sharp is one of the world's leading manufacturers of office-automation and home-electronic equipment. The company, a world leader in liquid-crystal-display technology, produced the world's first LCD calculator. Its products include TVs, VCRs, stereos, cordless telephones, facsimile machines, copiers, semiconductors, and laptop computers. Internationally, the company has sales and manufacturing subsidiaries, joint ventures, and representative offices in more than 30 foreign countries. In 1994, overseas sales made up 48.8% of consolidated sales, compared with 49.2% in 1993.

¥bil	03/93	03/94	03/95	US$mil 03/95				
Sales	1,508.3	1,518.1	1,617.6	16,396.7	P/E Ratio	34.7	Price (9/30/95)	1,390.00
Net Income	29.6	31.8	44.5	451.1	P/B Ratio	1.8	52 Wk Hi-Low	1,830.0-1,050.0
Book Value	766.9	818.4	851.5	9,855.3	Yield %	0.9	Market Cap	US$15,563mil

Address	**22-22, Nagaike-cho**	Tel	**06-621-1221**	ADR	**SHCAY**	President	**Haruo Tsuji**
	Abeno-ku, Osaka 545	Fax	**06-628-1653**	SEDOL No.	**6800602**	Chairman	--

Shima Seiki Mfg

Industry: **Factory Equipment**

Shima Seiki Manufacturing (Shima Seiki Seisakusho) is a manufacturer of independent electronic weft-knitting machinery. The company controls about an 80% share of the Japanese market for industrial machines for wool and acrylic fibers. Its other products include computer-controlled glove-knitting machines and computer-aided-design systems for clothing and knitted goods. Computer-controlled weft-knitting machines generally account for about 70% of the company's annual sales. Shima Seiki depends on exports to the United States and Europe for about half of its revenues.

¥bil	03/93	03/94	03/95	US$mil 03/95				
Sales	46.4	43.2	46.6	472.6	P/E Ratio	42.5	Price (9/30/95)	5,350.00
Net Income	5.0	4.4	5.0	50.5	P/B Ratio	2.6	52 Wk Hi-Low	8,530.0-3,510.0
Book Value	72.9	76.3	80.2	928.4	Yield %	0.5	Market Cap	US$2,131.0mil

Address	**85, Sakata**	Tel	**0734-71-0511**	ADR		President	**Masahiro Shima**
	Wakayama City, Wakayama 641	Fax	**0734-74-8267**	SEDOL No.	**6806008**	Chairman	--

Shimachu

Industry: **Other Specialty Retailers**

Shimachu is a large-scale retailer that specializes in furniture. Tables and chairs, household utensils, and wardrobes are the company's three largest-selling product areas. Shimachu also sells do-it-yourself goods such as tools, paint, and gardening supplies. Its other sales lines include carpeting and sports equipment. The firm oprerates 58 hardware and furniture stores, are located in Saitama Prefecture and the company is now expanding its sales network into the Tokyo area. Shimachu's major suppliers are Katanuma, Nikko Shokai, and France Bed.

¥bil	08/92 P	08/93 P	08/94 P	US$mil 08/94				
Revenues	78.9	79.8	77.6	738.8	P/E Ratio	20.6	Price (9/30/95)	2,730.00
Net Income	2.8	5.7	6.7	63.4	P/B Ratio	1.7	52 Wk Hi-Low	3,590.0-2,000.0
Book Value	60.3	65.3	82.0	818.9	Yield %	0.5	Market Cap	US$1,409.9mil

Address	**5-1555, Mihashi**	Tel	**048-623-7711**	ADR		President	**Shojiro Shimamura**
	Ohmiya City, Saitama 331	Fax	**048-623-1700**	SEDOL No.	**6804455**	Chairman	**Masao Shimamura**

P=Parent company data.

Shimano

Industry: **Other Recreational Products & Services**

Shimano specializes in the production and sale of bicycle parts, including hubs, speed variators, freewheeling gears, and brakes. It also makes fishing tackle (mainly rods and reels) and cold-forged products that are marketed primarily to the auto industry. In 1994, sales of cycling equipment accounted for about 84% of Shimano's consolidated sales, while fishing gear made up 14%. In that same year, Shimano generated 78% of its consolidated sales overseas. The company has six domestic subsidiaries and 13 overseas subsidiaries based mainly in Singapore, Malaysia, and Europe.

¥bil	11/92	11/93	11/94	US$mil 11/94				
Sales	**142.4**	**168.0**	**130.2**	**1,265.2**	P/E Ratio	**31.3**	Price (9/30/95)	**1,960.00**
Net Income	**9.7**	**14.0**	**8.6**	**83.2**	P/B Ratio	**2.0**	52 Wk Hi-Low	**2,120.0-1,390.0**
Book Value	**105.2**	**125.4**	**133.6**	**1,350.7**	Yield %	**0.6**	Market Cap	**US$2,701.9mil**

Address **3-77, Oimatsu-cho**
Sakai City, Osaka 590
Tel **0722-23-3252**
Fax **0722-23-3259**
ADR
SEDOL No. **6804820**
President **Yoshizo Shimano**
Chairman **Shozo Shimano**

Shimizu

Industry: **Heavy Construction**

Shimizu (Shimizu Kensetsu) is Japan's largest general contractor by revenues. It is noted for its technological expertise on projects involving underground tanks. The firm also constructs high-rises and intelligent buildings (buildings with computerized facility management). It uses such techniques as stress-sensitive concrete; mass-damping systems for buildings to minimize swaying; and inflatable underwater wave barriers. In addition, the firm works on renovation and urban development. Shimizu has 103 subsidiaries, 30 of which are consolidated, and 26 affiliates.

¥bil	03/93	03/94	03/95	US$mil 03/95				
Sales	**2,369.9**	**2,304.7**	**2,082.2**	**21,106.2**	P/E Ratio	**NMF**	Price (9/30/95)	**994.00**
Net Income	**21.7**	**43.7**	**-3.9**	**-39.8**	P/B Ratio	**2.2**	52 Wk Hi-Low	**1,100.0-794.0**
Book Value	**338.7**	**370.8**	**355.4**	**4,113.2**	Yield %	**0.9**	Market Cap	**US$7,883.1mil**

Address **1-2-3, Shibaura**
Minato-ku, Tokyo 105-07
Tel **03-5441-1111**
Fax **03-5441-0070**
ADR
SEDOL No. **6804400**
President **Harusuke Imamura**
Chairman --

Shin-Etsu Chemical

Industry: **Commodity Chemicals**

Shin-Etsu Chemical (Shin Etsu Kagaku Kogyo) produces plastics, electronic materials, organic chemicals, and fertilizers. It is one of the world's leading producers of polyvinyl chloride, accounting for about 16% of world production. The company is also a leading producer of silicon for semiconductors, with roughly 25% of the world market. Shin-Etsu Chemical operates six manufacturing facilities in Japan. It has consolidated subsidiaries in the United States, Malaysia, and the United kingdom. Shin-Etsu Chemical also has 58 unconsolidated subsidiaries and affiliates.

¥bil	03/93	03/94	03/95	US$mil 03/95				
Sales	**460.9**	**464.4**	**522.9**	**5,300.5**	P/E Ratio	**23.2**	Price (9/30/95)	**1,920.00**
Net Income	**16.0**	**17.5**	**26.9**	**272.3**	P/B Ratio	**2.2**	52 Wk Hi-Low	**2,090.0-1,450.0**
Book Value	**257.1**	**265.0**	**285.4**	**3,302.8**	Yield %	**0.4**	Market Cap	**US$6,269.1mil**

Address **2-6-1, Otemachi**
Chiyoda-ku, Tokyo 100
Tel **03-3246-5011**
Fax **03-3246-5358**
ADR
SEDOL No. **6804585**
President **Chihiro Kanagawa**
Chairman --

ShinMaywa Industry

Industry: **Land Transportation**

ShinMaywa Industries (Shin Meiwa Kogyo) produces special-duty vehicles for construction companies, including dump trucks, mixing trucks, tanker trucks, garbage trucks, and cranes. The company holds the second-largest domestic market share in multilevel parking facilities. Its other products include airplane components, waste-treatment equipment, pumps, automatic wire processors, aerial platforms, welding and laser-cutting robots, and vacuum, refrigeration, and heating equipment. ShinMaywa assembles seaplanes and exports parts to Boeing and other aircraft manufacturers.

¥bil	03/93	03/94	03/95	US$mil 03/95				
Sales	**166.9**	**152.4**	**149.7**	**1,517.5**	P/E Ratio	**90.9**	Price (9/30/95)	**845.00**
Net Income	**2.7**	**2.1**	**1.1**	**10.9**	P/B Ratio	**1.2**	52 Wk Hi-Low	**1,200.0-670.0**
Book Value	**83.3**	**84.2**	**84.1**	**973.1**	Yield %	**1.1**	Market Cap	**US$980.7mil**

Address **1-5-25, Kosone-cho**
Nishinomiya City, Hyogo 663
Tel **0798-47-0331**
Fax **0798-41-0755**
ADR
SEDOL No. **6804488**
President **Shiko Saikawa**
Chairman **Shinji Tamagawa**

Shinwa Kaiun Kaisha

Industry: **Marine Transportation**

Shinwa Kaiun, an affiliate of Nippon Yusen, operates tramp ships. The transport of iron ore, coal, and crude oil accounts for nearly 80% of revenues. Its fleet consists of 69 tramp ships, 29 specialized carrier ships, and six tankers. Nippon Yusen and Nippon Steel, its main customers, hold 26.7% and 13.1% of its stock, respectively. Shinwa Kaiun has a regular shipping route to China, with which it has strong historical ties. It has offices in London, Houston, Jakarta, Singapore, Sydney, Beijing, and Hong Kong. A new coal carrier has been in operation since June 1995.

¥bil	03/93	03/94	03/95	US$mil 03/95				
Sales	**70.6**	**72.8**	**76.8**	**778.2**	P/E Ratio	**NMF**	Price (9/30/95)	**246.00**
Net Income	**-1.7**	**-2.8**	**-1.1**	**-11.3**	P/B Ratio	**9.8**	52 Wk Hi-Low	**398.00-181.00**
Book Value	**8.2**	**5.2**	**4.1**	**47.1**	Yield %	**0.0**	Market Cap	**US$400.8mil**

Address **2-2-2, Uchi-Saiwaicho**
Chiyoda-ku, Tokyo 100
Tel **03-3597-6108**
Fax **03-3597-6031**
ADR
SEDOL No. **6805005**
President **Akira Tanikawa**
Chairman --

Shionogi & Co.

Industry: **Pharmaceuticals**

Shionogi & Co. (Shionogi Seiyaku) specializes in manufacturing antibiotics. It holds more than a 35% market share for oral cephalosporin antibiotics and a more than 20% share for the injectable form. Its main drugs include antibiotics Flumarin and Kefral. Major customers are Suzuken, Omori Pharmaceutical, Toho Pharmaceutical, and Osaka Pharmaceutical. Shionogi also markets products developed by Rhone-Poulenc (France) and Merck & Company (U.S.). It has eight consolidated subsidiaries and 13 unconsolidated subsidiaries, including Shionogi Europe in Amsterdam.

	¥bil 03/93	03/94	03/95	US$mil 03/95				
Sales	**348.2**	**344.5**	**365.3**	**3,702.9**	P/E Ratio	**26.1**	Price (9/30/95)	**871.00**
Net Income	**8.8**	**11.1**	**11.7**	**118.9**	P/B Ratio	**1.5**	52 Wk Hi-Low	**940.00-712.00**
Book Value	**188.3**	**196.6**	**206.5**	**2,390.1**	Yield %	**0.9**	Market Cap	**US$3,076.2mil**

Address **3-1-8, Dosho-machi, Chuo-ku, Osaka 541**
Tel **06-202-2161**
Fax **06-229-9596**
ADR
SEDOL No. **6804682**
President **Yoshihiko Shiono**
Chairman --

Shiseido

Industry: **Cosmetics & Personal Care**

Shiseido is a top Japanese cosmetics firm, controlling roughly 27% of the domestic market. The firm also operates restaurants and fitness centers. Shiseido is expanding into toiletries and foodstuffs, and is rapidly moving into pharmaceuticals, opening branches in Sendai and Hiroshima in 1994. Shiseido's Japanese retail network encompasses about 25,000 shops. The firm has foreign subsidiaries and affiliates in the United States and throughout Europe and the Pacific Rim. In 1994, overseas sales accounted for about 7.5% of total revenues.

	¥bil 03/93	03/94	03/95	US$mil 03/95				
Sales	**561.5**	**549.2**	**540.4**	**5,477.3**	P/E Ratio	**36.3**	Price (9/30/95)	**1,030.00**
Net Income	**13.3**	**14.7**	**11.4**	**115.4**	P/B Ratio	**1.2**	52 Wk Hi-Low	**1,200.0-950.0**
Book Value	**327.3**	**338.7**	**346.1**	**4,006.0**	Yield %	**1.2**	Market Cap	**US$4,146.3mil**

Address **7-5-5, Ginza, Chuo-ku, Tokyo 104-10**
Tel **03-3572-5111**
Fax **03-3572-6973**
ADR **SSDOY**
SEDOL No. **6805265**
President **Shozo Kozawa**
Chairman **Seiji Ishino**

Shizuoka Bank

Industry: **Banks - Regional**

Shizuoka Bank ranks third among Japanese regional banks by assets. The bank benefits from its location in Shizuoka Prefecture with its proximity to industrial centers. Shizuoka Bank ranks first among Japanese banks on the basis of its equity/capital ratio. Its activities include securities investment, trustee business, registration of public and corporate bonds, and brokerage of futures and option trading. The bank is known in the Japanese banking community for its conservative asset management. It has 201 branches in Japan and branch offices in Los Angeles and Hong Kong.

	¥bil 03/93 P	03/94 P	03/95 P	US$mil 03/95				
Revenues	**427.5**	**374.4**	**359.1**	**3,640.2**	P/E Ratio	**49.3**	Price (9/30/95)	**1,360.00**
Net Income	**21.9**	**22.1**	**22.2**	**224.8**	P/B Ratio	**2.5**	52 Wk Hi-Low	**1,400.0-942.0**
Book Value	**403.0**	**419.8**	**437.2**	**5,059.6**	Yield %	**0.4**	Market Cap	**US$11,006mil**

Address **1-10, Gofuku-cho, Shizuoka City, Shizuoka 420**
Tel **054-261-3131**
Fax **054-345-6136**
ADR
SEDOL No. **6805328**
President **Soichiro Kamiya**
Chairman **Jikichiro Sakai**

P=Parent company data.

Showa Aircraft Industry

Industry: **Aerospace & Defense**

Showa Aircraft Industry (Showa Hikoki Kogyo), originally an aircraft manufacturer, now derives about 70% of its business from a specialization in vehicle assembly. It assembles trucks and produces plastic parts for Hino Motors as well as assembling specialty vehicles, such as tank transports. It also produces alamide-fiber honeycomb and light-alloy structures for use in aircraft, and engages in real-estate leasing. The Mitsui group firms, including Mitsui Engineering & Shipbuilding (25%), are the three major shareholders of Showa Aircraft, with 38.4% combined market share.

	¥bil 03/93	03/94	03/95	US$mil 03/95				
Sales	**45.3**	**40.1**	**44.2**	**448.1**	P/E Ratio	**NMF**	Price (9/30/95)	**985.00**
Net Income	**0.7**	**0.5**	**0.0**	**-0.2**	P/B Ratio	**1.3**	52 Wk Hi-Low	**1,520.0-850.0**
Book Value	**25.7**	**25.8**	**25.4**	**294.4**	Yield %	**1.0**	Market Cap	**US$332.9mil**

Address **1-13-12, Nishi-Shinjuku, Shinjuku-ku, Tokyo 160**
Tel **03-3347-0600**
Fax **03-3347-0615**
ADR
SEDOL No. **6805403**
President **Hisao Jinbo**
Chairman --

Showa Aluminum

Industry: **Aluminum**

Showa Aluminum, an affiliate of the chemical manufacturer Showa Denko, manufactures aluminum automotive heat exchangers, aluminum cans, building materials, commercial refrigerators, and packaging foils. The company supplies the automobile, transportation, electronics, pharmaceutical, and food industries. It collaborated with Honda Motor to develop lightweight aluminum radiators. Ford Motor owns the technology for Showa Aluminum's supercompact condensers, used in air-conditioning systems. It has subsidiaries in the United States and Germany.

	¥bil 11/92	03/94 *	03/95	US$mil 03/95				
Sales	**172.9**	**158.7**	**170.0**	**1,723.2**	P/E Ratio	**70.9**	Price (9/30/95)	**411.00**
Net Income	**1.7**	**0.5**	**1.2**	**11.8**	P/B Ratio	**2.0**	52 Wk Hi-Low	**524.00-330.00**
Book Value	**38.3**	**37.2**	**40.1**	**464.5**	Yield %	**0.7**	Market Cap	**US$826.2mil**

Address **3-6-5, Iidabashi, Chiyoda-ku, Tokyo 102**
Tel **03-3239-5334**
Fax **03-3239-5306**
ADR
SEDOL No. **6805384**
President **Ichiro Anzai**
Chairman **Makoto Murata**

*Irregular period due to fiscal year change.

Showa Denko

Industry: **Commodity Chemicals**

Showa Denko is one of Japan's largest diversified chemical manufacturers. It produces olefins, biochemicals, gases, organic and inorganic chemicals, electronic materials, ceramics, alumina, aluminum, and other metallic materials. The firm has the largest ethylene-production capacity among petrochemical makers in Japan. Showa Denko is currently emphasizing higher value-added specialty products, which make up over 25% of sales. It has seven plants in Japan; nine consolidated subsidiaries; and commercial subsidiaries in the United States, Germany, and Singapore.

	¥bil 12/92	12/93	12/94	US$mil 12/94				
Sales	**564.9**	**508.5**	**495.8**	**4,857.6**	P/E Ratio	**NMF**	Price (9/30/95)	**286.00**
Net Income	**-20.5**	**-26.9**	**-28.5**	**-279.0**	P/B Ratio	**3.2**	52 Wk Hi-Low	**370.00-235.00**
Book Value	**148.0**	**120.8**	**92.2**	**924.0**	Yield %	**0.0**	Market Cap	**US$2,986.1mil**

Address **1-13-9, Shiba-Daimon**
Minato-ku, Tokyo 105
Tel **03-5470-3385**
Fax **03-3431-6442**
ADR
SEDOL No. **6805469**
President **Makoto Murata**
Chairman --

Showa Electric Wire & Cable

Industry: **Electrical Components & Equipment**

Showa Electric Wire & Cable (Showa Densen Denran) manufactures electric wire and cable, and electromechanical parts. Its main wire and cable products include telecommunication and electric-power cables, insulated wires, and fiberoptic systems. Showa Electric also makes information-management systems and related electronic parts. Cable and wire products remain its biggest earners, with more than 56% of consolidated sales. The firm has 28 subsidiaries and 24 affiliates. It has a strong presence in the Asian market, and is a partner in several technological joint ventures.

	¥bil 03/93	03/94	03/95	US$mil 03/95				
Sales	**166.4**	**152.6**	**159.0**	**1,612.0**	P/E Ratio	**NMF**	Price (9/30/95)	**460.00**
Net Income	**2.4**	**1.8**	**-0.4**	**-3.7**	P/B Ratio	**1.6**	52 Wk Hi-Low	**611.00-357.00**
Book Value	**66.1**	**66.4**	**64.1**	**742.2**	Yield %	**1.5**	Market Cap	**US$1,008.0mil**

Address **1-1-18, Toranomon**
Minato-ku, Tokyo 105
Tel **03-3597-7011**
Fax **03-3503-4506**
ADR
SEDOL No. **6805481**
President **Kaoru Murata**
Chairman **Zennosuke Matsui**

Showa Line

Industry: **Marine Transportation**

Showa Line (Showa Kaiun) is among Japan's five largest shipping companies by total sales. Its fleet consists of 111 ships (eight owned, the rest leased), including bulk-cargo ships and oil tankers. The company concentrates on tramp (bulk cargo) services such as the transport of iron ore, coal, nonferrous ores, woodchips, grain, cement, fertilizer, and cars. It is one of Japan's two largest shipping firms devoted to tramp and oil shipping-the other is Navix Line. Showa Line has 34 consolidated subsidiaries. Overseas activities generate 95% of Showa's consolidated sales.

	¥bil 03/93	03/94	03/95	US$mil 03/95				
Sales	**82.0**	**82.0**	**82.2**	**833.5**	P/E Ratio	**NMF**	Price (9/30/95)	**173.00**
Net Income	**-0.1**	**-5.4**	**-2.3**	**-23.1**	P/B Ratio	**13.8**	52 Wk Hi-Low	**241.00-81.00**
Book Value	**4.7**	**1.6**	**3.9**	**45.0**	Yield %	**0.0**	Market Cap	**US$541.1mil**

Address **2-2-3, Uchi-Saiwaicho**
Chiyoda-ku, Tokyo 100
Tel **03-3581-8551**
Fax **03-3581-8538**
ADR
SEDOL No. **6805641**
President **Seiki Fushimi**
Chairman **Kozo Yoshida**

Showa Sangyo

Industry: **Other Food**

Showa Sangyo is a major flour miller and cooking-oil producer. The company's products include wheat flour, vegetable oils, feed for livestock and fish, and processed foodstuffs such as pasta, frozen foods, and bread. The firm is primarily involved in commercial-use products. Showa Sangyo also trades cattle, hogs, and eggs; operates warehouses; and leases company-owned real estate. Showa Sangyo has 26 subsidiaries, 10 of which are consolidated, and four affiliates in Japan. The firm has a joint venture with Cargill (United States) to market processed meat in Japan.

	¥bil 03/93	03/94	03/95	US$mil 03/95				
Sales	**189.4**	**188.6**	**185.5**	**1,880.1**	P/E Ratio	**NMF**	Price (9/30/95)	**410.00**
Net Income	**1.4**	**1.4**	**-2.3**	**-23.7**	P/B Ratio	**1.3**	52 Wk Hi-Low	**520.00-351.00**
Book Value	**64.8**	**65.4**	**61.4**	**711.2**	Yield %	**1.5**	Market Cap	**US$797.4mil**

Address **2-2-1, Uchi-Kanda**
Chiyoda-ku, Tokyo 101
Tel **03-3257-2036**
Fax **03-3257-2097**
ADR
SEDOL No. **6805607**
President **Tadashi Shirayama**
Chairman --

Showa Shell Sekiyu

Industry: **Oil - Secondary**

Showa Shell Sekiyu, an affiliate of the Royal Dutch/Shell group, is a petroleum distributor that ranks third in gasoline sales and fifth in total sales in Japan. The company's lesser lines of business include real-estate and rental-car ventures. Its major customers include Isuzu Motors and NTN, a leading bearings manufacturer. Its domestic distribution network is made up of 1,300 dealers and 7,100 service stations. Showa Shell Sekiyu has five refineries with a total capacity of about 500,000 barrels per standard day. Shell Petroleum (U.K.) owns 34.4% of the company's stock.

	¥bil 12/92	12/93	12/94	US$mil 12/94				
Sales	**1,636.3**	**1,516.2**	**1,515.3**	**14,847.9**	P/E Ratio	**24.6**	Price (9/30/95)	**778.00**
Net Income	**18.8**	**7.8**	**13.7**	**133.9**	P/B Ratio	**1.6**	52 Wk Hi-Low	**1,208.7-775.0**
Book Value	**165.8**	**170.9**	**181.6**	**1,820.3**	Yield %	**1.0**	Market Cap	**US$2,949.0mil**

Address **3-2-5, Kasumigaseki**
Chiyoda-ku, Tokyo 100
Tel **03-3580-0132**
Fax **03-3581-9347**
ADR
SEDOL No. **6805544**
President **Tamotsu Yamazaki**
Chairman **Haruyuki Niimi**

Skylark

Industry: **Restaurants**

Skylark is Japan's largest suburban restaurant chain and one of McDonald's main rivals in the Japanese hamburger market. The Skylark chain of Western-style family restaurants is its mainstay. Through its subsidiaries, the firm handles its own advertising, cleaning, linen, supply, transportation, and building needs. Skylark also operates the Red Robin chain of hamburger restaurants, headquartered in California. The company has additional overseas operations in Taiwan and Thailand. Flo Japon, Skylark's joint venture with Flo of France, operates French restaurants in Japan.

	¥bil 12/92	12/93	12/94	US$mil 12/94				
Sales	**204.9**	**208.2**	**224.9**	**2,204.1**	P/E Ratio	**30.4**	Price (9/30/95)	**1,610.00**
Net Income	**3.9**	**0.2**	**5.3**	**51.7**	P/B Ratio	**1.9**	52 Wk Hi-Low	**2,160.0-1,310.0**
Book Value	**82.8**	**82.6**	**86.0**	**862.3**	Yield %	**1.0**	Market Cap	**US$1,615.2mil**

Address **1-25-8 Nishikubo**
Musashino-shi, Tokyo
Tel **0422-51-8111**
Fax **N/A**
ADR
SEDOL No. **6813161**
President **Tasuku Chino**
Chairman **Tadashi Yokokawa**

SMC

Industry: **Factory Equipment**

SMC is Japan's top producer of air-pressure equipment. Its domestic market share exceeds 40%, and its share of the world market approaches 15%. SMC's products include directional-control valves, drive mechanisms, pneumatic auxiliary equipment, filters, compressors, and hydraulic devices. Its major customers include Shoketsu Finance, SMC Pneumatics, Nippon Kisai, and Nichiden. SMC has consolidated subsidiaries in the U.S., Australia, New Zealand, Europe, Singapore, Hong Kong, the Philippines, and Taiwan. Overseas sales account for about 28% of consolidated revenues.

	¥bil 03/93	03/94	03/95	US$mil 03/95				
Sales	**96.7**	**97.0**	**115.4**	**1,169.4**	P/E Ratio	**40.7**	Price (9/30/95)	**6,700.00**
Net Income	**4.8**	**5.7**	**10.0**	**101.1**	P/B Ratio	**3.7**	52 Wk Hi-Low	**6,900.0-4,050.0**
Book Value	**95.5**	**99.8**	**110.2**	**1,275.8**	Yield %	**0.2**	Market Cap	**US$4,080.4mil**

Address **1-16-4, Shinbashi**
Minato-ku, Tokyo 105
Tel **03-3502-8271**
Fax **03-3508-0035**
ADR
SEDOL No. **6763965**
President **Yoshiyuki Takada**
Chairman --

Snow Brand Milk Products

Industry: **Other Food**

Snow Brand Milk Products (Yukijirushi Nyugyo) is the largest Japanese maker of dairy products, with leading domestic market shares in butter, cheese, and milk. The firm also makes ice cream, yogurt, infant formula, ham, sausage, frozen foods, wine, and pharmaceuticals. It has subsidiaries abroad in the U.S., Europe, Australia, Singapore, Hong Kong, Thailand, and Taiwan. Snow Brand has licensing agreements to market Twinnings, Hershey, Quaker Oats, and Claudel products as well as a joint venture with Dole Packaged Foods to import fruit juices in Japan.

	¥bil 03/93	03/94	03/95	US$mil 03/95				
Sales	**1,102.7**	**1,109.6**	**1,160.6**	**11,764.1**	P/E Ratio	**21.3**	Price (9/30/95)	**665.00**
Net Income	**8.2**	**7.9**	**10.1**	**102.5**	P/B Ratio	**1.6**	52 Wk Hi-Low	**794.00-614.00**
Book Value	**116.3**	**122.6**	**133.7**	**1,547.3**	Yield %	**1.1**	Market Cap	**US$2,167.8mil**

Address **13, Honshio-cho**
Shinjuku-ku, Tokyo 160
Tel **03-3226-2114**
Fax **03-3226-2150**
ADR
SEDOL No. **6818401**
President **Sumio Katayama**
Chairman **Katsuya Shono**

Sony

Industry: **Consumer Electronics**

Sony, a preeminent manufacturer of consumer electronics and entertainment media, is one of Japan's top television makers. Its products include TVs, video monitors, VCRs, tape recorders, compact-disc players, and semiconductors. Sony owns Columbia Records, Epic Records, and Columbia Pictures Entertainment, which includes Columbia Pictures, TriStar Pictures, Merv Griffin Enterprises, and Loews Theatre Management. In 1994, Sony made 72.4% of its sales outside Japan. U.S. sales accounted for 30% of total revenues; sales in Europe made up 22.7%.

	¥bil 03/93	03/94	03/95	US$mil 03/95				
Sales	**3,992.9**	**3,733.7**	**3,983.4**	**40,377.5**	P/E Ratio	**NMF**	Price (9/30/95)	**5,140.00**
Net Income	**36.3**	**15.3**	**-293.4**	**-2,973.6**	P/B Ratio	**1.9**	52 Wk Hi-Low	**6,000.0-3,800.0**
Book Value	**1,428.2**	**1,329.6**	**1,007.8**	**11,664.4**	Yield %	**1.0**	Market Cap	**US$19,331mil**

Address **6-7-35, Kita-Shinagawa**
Shinagawa-ku, Tokyo 141
Tel **03-5448-2111**
Fax **03-5448-2183**
ADR **SNE**
SEDOL No. **6821506**
President **Nobuyuki Idei**
Chairman **Norio Ohga**

Stanley Electric

Industry: **Other Auto Parts**

Stanley Electric (Stanley Denki), a manufacturer of electrical parts for automobiles and motorcycles, specializes in lighting and display equipment. The company holds 90% of the domestic market share in motorcycle lamps, and also makes semiconductors, liquid-crystal displays, light-emitting diodes, office-automation equipment, and light bulbs. Honda Motor is its major customer as well as its major shareholder. It also supplies parts to Mazda Motor, Toyota Motor, and Suzuki Motor. Stanley Electric has consolidated subsidiaries in the U.S., France, Thailand, and Hong Kong.

	¥bil 03/93	03/94	03/95	US$mil 03/95				
Sales	**181.5**	**167.3**	**163.3**	**1,655.3**	P/E Ratio	**39.1**	Price (9/30/95)	**630.00**
Net Income	**1.8**	**2.8**	**3.0**	**30.6**	P/B Ratio	**1.2**	52 Wk Hi-Low	**790.00-522.00**
Book Value	**83.1**	**96.0**	**99.4**	**1,149.9**	Yield %	**1.3**	Market Cap	**US$1,199.5mil**

Address **2-9-13, Naka-Meguro**
Meguro-ku, Tokyo 153
Tel **03-3710-2222**
Fax **03-3792-0007**
ADR
SEDOL No. **6841106**
President **Masahiro Shinoda**
Chairman --

Sumitomo

Industry: **Overseas Trading**

Sumitomo (Sumitomo Shoji) numbers among Japan's primary general-trading companies by sales and concentrates its trading activity in the metals and materials industries, but it also trades in machinery and chemicals. Besides trading, the firm is also an investor in a wide range of businesses, including Satellite Japan Corporation in the satellite-communications field, holding a 33.5% share in the company. Sumitomo, at the center of the Sumitomo group, has 349 consolidated subsidiaries and 180 affiliates, and a worldwide network that spans 88 countries.

¥bil	03/93	03/94	03/95	US$mil 03/95				
Sales	**18,027.0**	**17,000.3**	**16,139.5**	**163,595.8**	P/E Ratio	**139.3**	Price (9/30/95)	**947.00**
Net Income	**20.5**	**7.3**	**7.3**	**73.7**	P/B Ratio	**1.4**	52 Wk Hi-Low	**1,030.0-742.0**
Book Value	**711.0**	**705.1**	**701.3**	**8,116.8**	Yield %	**0.8**	Market Cap	**US$10,139mil**

Address	**4-5-33, Kitahama**	Tel	**06-220-6000**	ADR		President	**Tomiichi Akiyama**
	Chuo-ku, Osaka 541	Fax	**03-3217-6842**	SEDOL No.	**6858946**	Chairman	--

Sumitomo Bakelite

Industry: **Commodity Chemicals**

Sumitomo Bakelite is a leading supplier of electronic materials that serves the electronics, electrical, and auto industries. The company makes circuit boards and semiconductor sealants for computers, manufactures molded products from melamine and phenol resins, and has a facility that produces liquid resins for semiconductor applications. The firm also manufactures medical products. Sumitomo Bakelite has four domestic factories, and 14 consolidated and 13 unconsolidated subsidiaries. It has a consolidated subsidiary in Singapore that produces semiconductor sealants.

¥bil	03/93	03/94	03/95	US$mil 03/95				
Sales	**181.4**	**172.7**	**176.8**	**1,791.7**	P/E Ratio	**34.1**	Price (9/30/95)	**741.00**
Net Income	**1.3**	**3.6**	**4.9**	**50.0**	P/B Ratio	**2.2**	52 Wk Hi-Low	**778.00-502.00**
Book Value	**73.3**	**75.5**	**77.9**	**902.0**	Yield %	**1.1**	Market Cap	**US$1,697.5mil**

Address	**1-2-2, Uchi-Saiwaicho**	Tel	**03-3506-7039**	ADR		President	**Naoto Enda**
	Chiyoda-ku, Tokyo 100	Fax	**03-3506-7331**	SEDOL No.	**6858504**	Chairman	**Masao Nomura**

Sumitomo Bank

Industry: **Banks - Money Center**

Sumitomo Bank, the core of the Sumitomo group, is the third-largest Japanese bank by assets. Most of the bank's lending is to service, distribution, and manufacturing firms. In the wake of domestic banking deregulation, the bank is moving into investment banking, including mergers, swaps, and securities underwriting. The bank has a 50/50 joint venture with American Express International, Amex Sumigin Service, to issue the Sumigin American Express Gold Card. In 1994, overseas activities made up 42% of Sumitomo Bank's consolidated revenues.

¥bil	03/93	03/94	03/95	US$mil 03/95				
Revenues	**3,341.6**	**2,793.8**	**2,942.4**	**29,824.7**	P/E Ratio	**NMF**	Price (9/30/95)	**1,920.00**
Net Income	**21.1**	**35.6**	**-283.8**	**-2,877.0**	P/B Ratio	**3.1**	52 Wk Hi-Low	**1,930.0-1,470.0**
Book Value	**2,241.1**	**2,245.8**	**1,929.6**	**22,333.4**	Yield %	**0.4**	Market Cap	**US$60,660mil**

Address	**4-6-5, Kitahama**	Tel	**06-227-2111**	ADR	**SUBJY**	President	**Toshio Morikawa**
	Chuo-ku, Osaka 541	Fax	**03-3282-8480**	SEDOL No.	**6858526**	Chairman	**Sotoo Tatsumi**

Sumitomo Chemical

Industry: **Commodity Chemicals**

Sumitomo Chemical (Sumitomo Kagaku Kogyo), a member of the Sumitomo group, is Japan's second-largest diversified maker of chemicals by sales. Its products include basic chemicals, fine chemicals, pharmaceuticals, agricultural chemicals, electronic materials, composite materials, and aluminum. The firm makes Japan's top-selling dye, Sumafix Supra, and supplies photoresists to DRAM-chip manufacturers. The electronics industry, the agricultural sector, and trading companies are its major customers. Sumitomo Chemical has a worldwide network of 176 subsidiaries and affiliates.

¥bil	12/92	12/93	12/94	US$mil 12/94				
Sales	**1,018.2**	**936.5**	**978.4**	**9,586.9**	P/E Ratio	**78.7**	Price (9/30/95)	**433.00**
Net Income	**16.4**	**12.8**	**8.9**	**86.9**	P/B Ratio	**2.8**	52 Wk Hi-Low	**580.00-332.00**
Book Value	**242.0**	**247.8**	**251.3**	**2,519.3**	Yield %	**0.7**	Market Cap	**US$7,062.8mil**

Address	**4-5-33, Kitahama**	Tel	**06-220-3287**	ADR		President	**Akio Kosai**
	Chuo-ku, Osaka 541	Fax	**06-220-3347**	SEDOL No.	**6858560**	Chairman	**Hideo Mori**

Sumitomo Coal Mining

Industry: **Coal**

Sumitomo Coal Mining (Sumitomo Sekitan Kogyo) produces coal and industrial and building materials. The company has diversified into real estate by leasing office buildings, supplying housing, and developing resorts, as well as managing supermarkets and leisure facilities. Its major customers include Sumitomo Construction, Daiwa House, Shinei Kajima, Fujiki Komuten, and Koike. The company owns five plants, one coal mine, and operates limestone and rock quarries throughout Japan. Altogether it has 21 consolidated subsidiaries, including two in Australia.

¥bil	03/93	03/94	03/95	US$mil 03/95				
Sales	**139.1**	**144.5**	**146.1**	**1,481.0**	P/E Ratio	**106.8**	Price (9/30/95)	**470.00**
Net Income	**-3.3**	**-4.4**	**0.3**	**3.4**	P/B Ratio	**N/A**	52 Wk Hi-Low	**765.00-354.00**
Book Value	**1.2**	**-2.9**	**-3.4**	**-39.5**	Yield %	**1.1**	Market Cap	**US$362.3mil**

Address	**3-20-4, Nishi-Nihonbashi**	Tel	**03-3216-0911**	ADR		President	**Yuji Momose**
	Minato-ku, Tokyo 105	Fax	**03-3216-2717**	SEDOL No.	**6858601**	Chairman	--

Sumitomo Construction

Industry: **Heavy Construction**

Sumitomo Construction (Sumitomo Kensetsu), a member of the Sumitomo group, is a medium-size general contractor that specializes in civil-engineering work, such as bridge design and construction. The firm also builds railways, expressways, tunnels, dams, and water and sewage facilities. It constructs a variety of private and public facilities, including high-rise, wide-span, and intelligent buildings. The firm has 19 subsidiaries and seven affiliates. Seven of its eight consolidated subsidiaries are overseas, six are in the United States, and one is in Singapore.

¥bil	03/93	03/94	03/95	US$mil 03/95				
Sales	303.0	294.7	308.8	3,129.9	P/E Ratio	NMF	Price (9/30/95)	622.00
Net Income	1.7	0.6	0.6	6.1	P/B Ratio	3.4	52 Wk Hi-Low	867.00-380.00
Book Value	38.8	38.1	37.9	438.7	Yield %	0.6	Market Cap	US$1,286.4mil

Address	**13-4, Araki-cho**	Tel	**03-3353-5111**	ADR		President	**Shinsaku Sanmoto**
	Shinjuku-ku, Tokyo 160	Fax	**03-3356-8402**	SEDOL No.	**6858645**	Chairman	**Sadamu Mino**

Sumitomo Electric Industries

Industry: **Electrical Components & Equipment**

Sumitomo Electric (Sumitomo Denki Kogyo) is a manufacturer of electric wire and cable. It also produces special steel wires, sintered-alloy products, antilock brake systems, and does cable-engineering work. The firm is expanding its capacity to make local-area networks and automobile-navigation systems. Its overseas operations include production of automobile parts in the United States. Sumitomo Electric cooperates with AT&T on projects, including Litspec, a joint venture to produce fiveroptic cables. In 1994, 11% of the firm's parent sales were made overseas.

¥bil	03/93	03/94	03/95	US$mil 03/95				
Sales	1,136.7	1,101.5	1,120.0	11,353.1	P/E Ratio	42.3	Price (9/30/95)	1,210.00
Net Income	29.1	29.5	20.3	205.6	P/B Ratio	2.0	52 Wk Hi-Low	1,490.0-944.0
Book Value	383.1	402.1	423.2	4,898.1	Yield %	0.8	Market Cap	US$8,642.1mil

Address	**4-5-33, Kitahama**	Tel	**06-220-4141**	ADR	**SMTOY**	President	**Noritaka Kurauchi**
	Chuo-ku, Osaka 541	Fax	**06-222-6478**	SEDOL No.	**6858708**	Chairman	**Tetsuro Kawakami**

Sumitomo Forestry

Industry: **Home Construction**

Sumitomo Forestry (Sumitomo Ringyo) is a supplier of forestry products and the largest maker of custom-built wooden housing in Japan. It markets timber, building materials, chips, wood pulp, and value-added products such as aluminum sashes, plywood, and household products. The company's extensive landholdings make up 0.1% of Japan's total land area. Forestry operations account for 46% of net sales and construction 50%. Sumitomo Forestry has 15 consolidated subsidiaries, and is currently involved in five joint ventures in New Zealand, Indonesia, and the United States.

¥bil	03/93	03/94	03/95	US$mil 03/95				
Sales	583.0	647.9	686.3	6,956.7	P/E Ratio	27.4	Price (9/30/95)	1,560.00
Net Income	8.8	11.2	10.1	101.9	P/B Ratio	2.3	52 Wk Hi-Low	1,860.0-1,310.0
Book Value	98.9	108.5	117.5	1,360.4	Yield %	0.6	Market Cap	US$2,767.6mil

Address	**6-14-1, Nishi-Shinjuku**	Tel	**03-5322-6662**	ADR		President	**Hiroto Yamaguchi**
	Shinjuku-ku, Tokyo 160	Fax	**03-5322-6762**	SEDOL No.	**6858861**	Chairman	**Kazuo Ohnishi**

Sumitomo Heavy Industries

Industry: **Factory Equipment**

Sumitomo Heavy Industries (Sumitomo Jukikai Kogyo), a member of the Sumitomo group, manufactures heavy machinery. The firm is Japan's leading producer of speed-reduction gears. Its other products include heavy ships, power-transmission equipment, plastic-injection-molding machines, logistics and handling systems, construction equipment, pulp- and paper-production equipment, iron- and steel-making equipment, forges, machine tools, industrial vehicles, and hydraulic devices. Sumitomo Heavy Industries' largest export markets are Liberia, Panama, Norway, and the United States.

¥bil	03/93	03/94	03/95	US$mil 03/95				
Sales	483.9	482.0	490.8	4,974.7	P/E Ratio	NMF	Price (9/30/95)	297.00
Net Income	-1.1	-1.2	-2.9	-29.0	P/B Ratio	2.7	52 Wk Hi-Low	427.00-238.00
Book Value	71.2	69.7	65.4	757.0	Yield %	0.0	Market Cap	US$1,758.6mil

Address	**2-2-1, Otemachi**	Tel	**03-3245-4135**	ADR		President	**Mitoshi Ozawa**
	Chiyoda-ku, Tokyo 100	Fax	**03-3245-4337**	SEDOL No.	**6858731**	Chairman	--

Sumitomo Light Metal Industries

Industry: **Aluminum**

Sumitomo Light Metal Industries (Sumitomo Keikinzoku Kogyo) manufactures rolled aluminum and copper. The firm's main products include aluminum coil for beverage cans, copper tubes for air conditioners, copper and titanium tubes for nuclear-power plants, and aluminum substrates for magnetic disks and computer components. Its products are also used in the production of autos, furniture, and building materials. Sumitomo's largest customers are the manufacturing and trading sectors. It has joint technical agreements with Reynolds Metal (U.S.) and Hydro Aluminum (Switzerland).

¥bil	03/93	03/94	03/95	US$mil 03/95				
Sales	230.2	205.7	240.0	2,432.3	P/E Ratio	NMF	Price (9/30/95)	350.00
Net Income	-1.7	-3.2	-1.5	-14.8	P/B Ratio	12.6	52 Wk Hi-Low	437.00-261.00
Book Value	16.7	13.4	7.9	91.6	Yield %	0.0	Market Cap	US$1,004.6mil

Address	**5-11-3, Shinbashi**	Tel	**03-3436-9700**	ADR		President	**Shiro Sato**
	Minato-ku, Tokyo 105	Fax	**N/A**	SEDOL No.	**6858764**	Chairman	**Katsumi Uchida**

Sumitomo Marine & Fire Insurance

Industry: **Insurance - Property & Casualty**

Sumitomo Marine & Fire Insurance (Sumitomo Kaijo Kasai Hoken) is a non-life-insurance company that specializes in corporate insurance. The firm's main line includes auto, compulsory auto-liability, marine, fire, personal-accident, movable-property, workers' compensation, construction, aviation, theft, and machine insurance. Some of its new products include insurance with maturity refunds and individual annuity and accident insurance. Overall, the company has nearly 50,000 insurance agents in Japan and overseas. Sumitomo Marine & Fire is a licensed insurer in 20 countries.

¥bil	03/93	03/94	03/95	US$mil 03/95				
Revenues	**N/A**	**841.0**	**845.0**	**8,565.5**	P/E Ratio	**50.1**	Price (9/30/95)	**751.00**
Net Income	**12.8**	**11.5**	**10.0**	**101.8**	P/B Ratio	**2.1**	52 Wk Hi-Low	**909.00-645.00**
Book Value	**228.9**	**235.3**	**240.9**	**2,788.6**	Yield %	**0.9**	Market Cap	**US$5,041.9mil**

Address	**2-27-2, Shinkawa**	Tel	**03-3297-1111**	ADR		President	**Takashi Onoda**
	Chuo-ku, Tokyo 104	Fax	**03-3297-6880**	SEDOL No.	**6858786**	Chairman	**Sumao Tokumasu**

Sumitomo Metal Industries

Industry: **Steel**

Sumitomo Metal Industries (Sumitomo Kinzoku Kogyo) is one of Japan's largest integrated-steel manufacturers. The company makes steel plates, pipes, and bars; rolling-stock components; and electronics. It also engages in steel-structure engineering and is developing an array of titanium products. Sumitomo Metal produces about 10 million tons of crude steel per year, tying it with Kawasaki Steel as the third-largest producer in Japan. The company has 85 consolidated subsidiaries. In 1994, 18.5% of the company's consolidated-company sales were made overseas.

¥bil	03/93	03/94	03/95	US$mil 03/95				
Sales	**1,687.6**	**1,222.8**	**1,329.6**	**13,477.4**	P/E Ratio	**NMF**	Price (9/30/95)	**288.00**
Net Income	**0.7**	**-38.8**	**-28.9**	**-293.2**	P/B Ratio	**1.8**	52 Wk Hi-Low	**367.00-218.00**
Book Value	**575.5**	**527.5**	**499.4**	**5,779.7**	Yield %	**0.0**	Market Cap	**US$9,111.5mil**

Address	**4-5-33, Kitahama**	Tel	**06-220-5111**	ADR	**SMMLY**	President	**Tameaki Nakamura**
	Chuo-ku, Osaka 541	Fax	**06-223-0563**	SEDOL No.	**6858827**	Chairman	**Yasuo Shingu**

Sumitomo Metal Mining

Industry: **Precious Metals**

Sumitomo Metal Mining (Sumitomo Kinzoku Kozan) produces gold, copper, and nickel. The firm also manufactures electronic and building materials. It operates four plants throughout Japan and owns the Hishikari gold mine, Japan's largest gold deposit. Major customers include Marubeni, Sumitomo, Nissho Iwai, Uchida and Tatsuta Electric Wire & Cable. The firm has 33 consolidated subsidiaries, including overseas subsidiaries in Singapore, United States, Malaysia and the Netherlands. Sumitomo Metal Mining has a joint venture with Phelps Dodge (U.S.) at the Morenci copper mine.

¥bil	03/93	03/94	03/95	US$mil 03/95				
Sales	**508.0**	**446.7**	**464.8**	**4,711.8**	P/E Ratio	**NMF**	Price (9/30/95)	**806.00**
Net Income	**6.2**	**1.9**	**1.3**	**13.1**	P/B Ratio	**2.2**	52 Wk Hi-Low	**995.00-608.00**
Book Value	**179.9**	**210.9**	**205.9**	**2,383.6**	Yield %	**0.6**	Market Cap	**US$4,510.3mil**

Address	**5-11-3, Shinbashi**	Tel	**03-3436-7926**	ADR		President	**Moriki Aoyagi**
	Minato-ku, Tokyo 105	Fax	**03-3436-7735**	SEDOL No.	**6858849**	Chairman	**Akihiko Shinozaki**

Sumitomo Osaka Cement

Industry: **Building Materials**

Sumitomo Cement, a member of Sumitomo group, is Japan's fourth largest cement producer, with 13% domestic market share. The firm is diversifying into electronics, optoelectronics, and ceramics businesses. Sales to Andes Cement, a domestic affiliate of Sumitomo Cement, consisted 82.6 % of consolidated-company sales in 1994. Sumitomo Cement merged with Osaka Cement in October, 1994. The firm has joint-development agreements with Ortel Corporation (U.S.) and a joint venture with Sumitomo Metal Industries. It has 29 consolidated subsidiaries in Japan.

¥bil	03/93	03/94	03/95	US$mil 03/95				
Sales	**167.4**	**162.0**	**191.2**	**1,938.1**	P/E Ratio	**NMF**	Price (9/30/95)	**375.00**
Net Income	**3.4**	**2.8**	**-1.8**	**-18.1**	P/B Ratio	**1.5**	52 Wk Hi-Low	**411.00-300.00**
Book Value	**93.4**	**94.5**	**117.7**	**1,362.1**	Yield %	**1.3**	Market Cap	**US$1,724.5mil**

Address	**1, Kanda-Mitoshirocho**	Tel	**03-3296-9683**	ADR		President	**Shoichi Tatemoto**
	Chiyoda-ku, Tokyo 101	Fax	**03-3295-5156**	SEDOL No.	**6858548**	Chairman	**Einosuke Hamada**

Sumitomo Precision Products

Industry: **Aerospace & Defense**

Sumitomo Precision Products (Sumitomo Seimitsu Kogyo) is one of Japan's top manufacturers of aerospace equipment. The company's main product areas are hydraulic aircraft equipment, heat-exchanger machines, and environmental equipment. Its main customers include Japan's Defense Agency, Mitsubishi Heavy Industries, and Kawasaki Heavy Industries. Its affiliate, Sumitomo Metal Industries, owns 42% of the company's stock. It has three main plants and three wholly-owned subsidiaries: Sumisho Industries, Sumisho Engineering, and Surface Techno System.

¥bil	03/93	03/94	03/95	US$mil 03/95				
Sales	**34.6**	**33.3**	**31.0**	**314.6**	P/E Ratio	**NMF**	Price (9/30/95)	**955.00**
Net Income	**0.9**	**0.4**	**0.1**	**1.0**	P/B Ratio	**1.7**	52 Wk Hi-Low	**970.00-470.00**
Book Value	**30.4**	**30.4**	**30.0**	**346.7**	Yield %	**0.7**	Market Cap	**US$510.4mil**

Address	**1-10, Fuso-cho**	Tel	**06-489-5816**	ADR		President	**Iwao Takai**
	Amagasaki City, Hyogo 660	Fax	**06-489-5801**	SEDOL No.	**6858883**	Chairman	--

Sumitomo Realty & Development

Industry: **Real-Estate Investment**

Sumitomo Realty & Development (Sumitomo Fudosan), a member of Sumitomo Group, is one of Japan's largest real-estate firms. The company leases buildings and sells housing, condominiums, and residential lots. Sumitomo Realty manages more than 100 office buildings, including 97 in Tokyo, and has more than 50 subsidiaries and affiliates. The company's foreign activities, which include leasing, development, management, and brokerage, are centered in the United States, but the company also has subsidiaries and affiliates in Hong Kong, Australia, Thailand, and the Netherlands.

¥bil	03/93	03/94	03/95	US$mil 03/95				
Sales	446.5	388.1	295.3	2,993.4	P/E Ratio	NMF	Price (9/30/95)	695.00
Net Income	3.0	-2.4	0.5	5.4	P/B Ratio	1.1	52 Wk Hi-Low	740.00-482.00
Book Value	260.4	255.1	254.1	2,941.1	Yield %	0.9	Market Cap	US$2,843.8mil

Address **2-4-1, Nishi-Shinjuku**
Shinjuku-ku, Tokyo 163-08
Tel **03-3346-1011**
Fax **03-3344-6090**
ADR
SEDOL No. **6858902**
President **Junji Takashima**
Chairman **Shinichiro Takagi**

Sumitomo Rubber Industries

Industry: **Tires & Rubber**

Sumitomo Rubber Industries (Sumitomo Gomu Kogyo), the third-largest Japanese automobile-tire maker, sells tires under the Dunlop trademark. The firm also produces tennis and golf equipment and clothing under the Dunlop and Maxfli brand names. It makes flooring for sports facilities and various marine products. Sumitomo Rubber has an agreement with Izod (France) to market Lacoste sportswear and has an agreement with Inbadelca (Spain) to produce marine fenders in Japan. The firm has four domestic plants and overseas plants in the United States, Europe, and Southeast Asia.

¥bil	12/92	12/93	12/94	US$mil 12/94				
Sales	578.4	503.4	487.8	4,779.3	P/E Ratio	NMF	Price (9/30/95)	827.00
Net Income	6.1	4.6	1.0	10.2	P/B Ratio	2.2	52 Wk Hi-Low	980.58-610.00
Book Value	60.0	68.5	75.0	751.9	Yield %	1.1	Market Cap	US$1,673.4mil

Address **1-1-1, Tsutsui-cho**
Chuo-ku, Kobe 651
Tel **078-231-4141**
Fax **078-232-0264**
ADR
SEDOL No. **6858991**
President **Naoto Saito**
Chairman **Tasuku Yokoi**

Sumitomo Trust & Banking

Industry: **Banks - Regional**

Sumitomo Trust & Banking (Sumitomo Shintaku Ginko), is Japan's second-largest trust bank by total available funds. It is the industry leader in land trusts and also deals in corporate finance, investment management, and fiduciary services. The bank acts as a trustee for 361 land-trust contracts, and as a stock-transfer agent for 437 companies. It has 59 branches in Japan and a joint venture with TMBS General (Thailand). The company has overseas operations in 66 locations worldwide including branches in New York, the Cayman Islands, Nassau, London, Hong Kong, and Singapore.

¥bil	03/93	03/94	03/95	US$mil 03/95				
Revenues	1,186.8	1,096.5	1,168.0	11,839.7	P/E Ratio	NMF	Price (9/30/95)	1,360.00
Net Income	24.8	20.1	4.0	40.5	P/B Ratio	2.0	52 Wk Hi-Low	1,480.0-1,010.0
Book Value	856.1	866.0	859.2	9,944.0	Yield %	0.6	Market Cap	US$17,019mil

Address **4-5-33, Kitahama**
Chuo-ku, Osaka 541
Tel **06-220-2121**
Fax **03-3286-8741**
ADR
SEDOL No. **6859002**
President **Atsushi Niira**
Chairman **Hiroshi Hayasaki**

Suzuki Motor

Industry: **Automobile Manufacturers**

Suzuki Motor is the largest producer of minicars and the third-largest maker of motorcycles (most of which are mopeds) in Japan. Automobiles account for more than 80% of the company's sales. The company has more than 50 plants in 28 foreign countries, and joint ventures in Canada, India, and Hungary. Suzuki supplies cars such as the Geo Metro and Tracker to General Motors, with which it has capital and technical ties, and vehicles and parts to Mazda Motor. It also produces vehicles in South Korea and China. Overseas sales accounted for about 43% of revenues in March 1995.

¥bil	03/93	03/94	03/95	US$mil 03/95				
Sales	1,259.1	1,227.0	1,258.3	12,754.4	P/E Ratio	23.9	Price (9/30/95)	1,070.00
Net Income	19.0	15.2	20.1	203.3	P/B Ratio	1.6	52 Wk Hi-Low	1,290.0-830.0
Book Value	243.1	280.0	296.3	3,428.9	Yield %	0.7	Market Cap	US$4,828.6mil

Address **300, Takatsuka-cho**
Hamamatsu City, Shizuoka 432-91
Tel **053-440-2097**
Fax **053-440-2776**
ADR
SEDOL No. **6865504**
President **Osamu Suzuki**
Chairman **Hisao Uchiyama**

Tadano

Industry: **Heavy Machinery**

Tadano manufactures and repairs construction cranes and related equipment, including heavy-duty truck cranes, truck-loader cranes, self-loaders, crane augers, and aerial platforms. The firm has factories in Takamatsu, Shido, and Sakura, and 17 domestic sales offices. Its subsidiary FAUN integrates the distribution and sales networks of its other European units: Tadano FAUN of Germany, Tadano International and Tadano FAUN Holland of the Netherlands. It also has an equity stake in Blackwood Hodge, an Australian construction-equipment sales company.

¥bil	03/93	03/94	03/95	US$mil 03/95				
Sales	147.8	118.1	118.4	1,200.1	P/E Ratio	66.7	Price (9/30/95)	800.00
Net Income	3.5	0.8	1.7	17.3	P/B Ratio	1.5	52 Wk Hi-Low	989.00-591.00
Book Value	72.8	72.5	74.0	855.9	Yield %	1.3	Market Cap	US$1,138.1mil

Address **Ko-34, Shinden-cho**
Takamatsu City, Kagawa 761-01
Tel **0878-39-5555**
Fax **0878-39-5522**
ADR
SEDOL No. **6869722**
President **Hisashi Tadano**
Chairman **Yasuo Tadano**

Taisei

Industry: **Heavy Construction**

Taisei is one of Japan's largest general construction-companies. Its operations include building and housing construction, civil engineering, and real estate. Taisei's construction division builds power-generating plants, subways, highways, and railways, as well as concrete and wooden single-family housing units. The development segment rents and sells land, and develops and manages condominiums, office buildings, and ready-built houses. The firm derives roughly 20% of its business from the public sector. Taisei has overseas operations all over the world.

¥bil	03/93	03/94	03/95	US$mil 03/95				
Sales	**2,351.5**	**2,279.6**	**1,998.3**	**20,255.0**	P/E Ratio	**40.9**	Price (9/30/95)	**658.00**
Net Income	**36.4**	**25.3**	**16.4**	**166.0**	P/B Ratio	**1.7**	52 Wk Hi-Low	**724.00-501.00**
Book Value	**381.1**	**393.7**	**402.8**	**4,661.8**	Yield %	**1.2**	Market Cap	**US$6,748.6mil**

Address **1-25-1, Nishi-Shinjuku**, **Shinjuku-ku, Tokyo 163-06**
Tel **03-3348-1111** Fax **03-3345-1386**
ADR **TISCY** SEDOL No. **6870100**
President **Hyozo Yamamoto** Chairman --

Taisei Prefab Construction

Industry: **Heavy Construction**

Taisei Prefab Construction (Taisei Prefab) builds prefabricated high-rise housing. The firm also engages in civil-engineering projects, makes concrete products, and leases, brokers, and manages real estate. Private construction provides the company with more than 60% of its revenues. Headquartered in Tokyo, the company has a branch office in Osaka and five domestic factories. Taisei Prefab Construction is a partially-owned subsidiary of Taisei Corporation. Overseas activity is centered in Southeast Asia, where the firm has construction ventures in Malaysia and Thailand.

¥bil	03/93 P	03/94 P	03/95 P	US$mil 03/95				
Sales	**127.4**	**122.1**	**99.2**	**1,005.5**	P/E Ratio	**19.8**	Price (9/30/95)	**690.00**
Net Income	**5.1**	**4.6**	**2.4**	**24.8**	P/B Ratio	**1.2**	52 Wk Hi-Low	**1,330.0-590.0**
Book Value	**34.6**	**38.4**	**39.9**	**462.2**	Yield %	**1.7**	Market Cap	**US$488.3mil**

Address **7-23-1, Nishi-Gotanda**, **Shinagawa-ku, Tokyo 141**
Tel **03-3493-4941** Fax **03-3490-5428**
ADR SEDOL No. **6870683**
President **Hirokuni Hatakawa** Chairman --

P=Parent company data.

Taisho Pharmaceutical

Industry: **Pharmaceuticals**

Taisho Pharmaceutical (Taisho Seiyaku) manufactures prescription and over-the-counter (OTC) drugs. The firm's OTC products, which make up about 75% of its sales, include the popular Lipovitan series of nutrient drinks, Pabron cold medicines, Taisho Kanpo Ichoyaku (a gastrointestinal drug), and Dermalin (an athlete's foot treatment). Taisho develops more than 50% of its products in-house. Primary customers are Kuraya Pharmaceutical and Sanseido. It has technological agreements with Knoll AG (Germany), Upjohn (U.S.), and Hafslund Nycomed Pharma AG (Austria).

¥bil	03/93 P	03/94 P	03/95 P	US$mil 03/95				
Sales	**204.0**	**200.3**	**210.9**	**2,138.1**	P/E Ratio	**22.9**	Price (9/30/95)	**1,860.00**
Net Income	**28.4**	**25.1**	**27.6**	**279.4**	P/B Ratio	**2.2**	52 Wk Hi-Low	**1,920.0-1,510.0**
Book Value	**244.4**	**261.7**	**282.5**	**3,269.5**	Yield %	**1.1**	Market Cap	**US$6,350.6mil**

Address **3-24-1, Takada**, **Toshima-ku, Tokyo 171**
Tel **03-3985-1111** Fax **03-3985-6485**
ADR SEDOL No. **6870144**
President **Akira Uehara** Chairman **Shoji Uehara**

P=Parent company data.

Takara Shuzo

Industry: **Distillers & Brewers**

Takara Shuzo is one of Japan's top producers of alcoholic beverages and the largest seller of shochu (distilled spirits) and mirin (cooking wine). The company also produces sake, industrial alcohol, health and soft drinks, seasonings, and biochemicals. With more than 200 products, it has 11 domestic factories and 36 subsidiaries and affiliates. Takara Shuzo imports wine, beer, U.S. bourbons, German fruit drinks, French cognacs, and Chinese liquors. Of its 36 subsidiaries, 15 are consolidated and two produce and market sake for consumption in the United States.

¥bil	03/93	03/94	03/95	US$mil 03/95				
Sales	**148.2**	**158.3**	**189.0**	**1,915.5**	P/E Ratio	**28.6**	Price (9/30/95)	**760.00**
Net Income	**1.9**	**4.4**	**5.3**	**53.4**	P/B Ratio	**3.1**	52 Wk Hi-Low	**815.00-610.00**
Book Value	**44.2**	**47.1**	**51.3**	**594.2**	Yield %	**1.0**	Market Cap	**US$1,614.2mil**

Address **60, Higashinotoin, Shijodori**, **Shimogyo-ku, Kyoto 600**
Tel **075-241-5100** Fax **075-241-5127**
ADR SEDOL No. **6870382**
President **Hisashi Ohmiya** Chairman **Akira Tanabe**

Takara Standard

Industry: **Other Home Furnishings**

Takara Standard, a subsidiary of Takara Belmont, is a leading manufacturer of barber chairs and Japan's leading producer of enamelled sinks. Its key product lines include bath units, cabinets, systematized kitchens, and automated electric and gas-burning heating equipments. Kitchen equipments account for 58% of the firm's consolidated sales and bath-related products make up 42%. The firm recently acquired land for constructing a new plant near the Fukuoka plant to step up production. The firm is involved in real-estate leasing and sales through one of its subsidiaries.

¥bil	03/93	03/94	03/95	US$mil 03/95				
Sales	**112.0**	**122.2**	**131.6**	**1,333.8**	P/E Ratio	**30.4**	Price (9/30/95)	**1,040.00**
Net Income	**4.2**	**4.5**	**4.8**	**48.9**	P/B Ratio	**1.6**	52 Wk Hi-Low	**1,210.0-890.0**
Book Value	**79.0**	**86.7**	**90.7**	**1,049.5**	Yield %	**1.0**	Market Cap	**US$1,480.3mil**

Address **1-2-1, Shigino-Higashi**, **Joto-ku, Osaka 536**
Tel **06-962-1531** Fax **06-969-4122**
ADR SEDOL No. **6870906**
President **Rokuro Watanabe** Chairman --

Takasago Thermal Engineering

Industry: **Electrical Components & Equipment**

Takasago Thermal Engineering (Takasago Netsugaku Kogyo) is the leading air-conditioning-engineering firm in Japan. It mainly supplies air-conditioning systems for offices, factories, retail stores, and other commercial facilities. The firm offers high-tech industrial clean rooms, and smaller systems such as thermal chambers, clean-dry rooms, and clean booths. Takasago also makes computerized systems for control, instrumentation, and industrial plants. The firm has four subsidiaries, including Takasago's sole consolidated subidiary, wholly-owned Nippon Primac in Tokyo.

	¥bil 03/93	03/94	03/95	US$mil 03/95				
Sales	269.8	241.1	238.8	2,420.7	P/E Ratio	21.6	Price (9/30/95)	1,490.00
Net Income	8.1	7.5	5.9	59.9	P/B Ratio	1.8	52 Wk Hi-Low	1,690.0-1,220.0
Book Value	61.3	67.0	70.6	817.3	Yield %	1.1	Market Cap	US$1,285.4mil

Address	**4-2-8, Kanda Surugadai**	Tel **03-3255-8212**	ADR	President	**Masaru Ishii**
	Chiyoda-ku, Tokyo 101	Fax **03-3251-0914**	SEDOL No. **6870520**	Chairman	--

Takashimaya

Industry: **Retailers - Broadline**

Takashimaya, is Japan's largest department store retailer by sales. The company's leading products are apparel and art objects. Its other merchandise includes household utensils, foodstuffs, jewelry, and sundries. Takashimaya's licensed apparel brand names are Fauchon, Thierry Mugler, Romeo Gigli, and Geoffrey Beene. The retailer manages 35 consolidated subsidiaries, 37 unconsolidated subsidiaries and 30 affiliates with its flagship stores located in Osaka and Tokyo. The company is also active in overseas operations. Takashimaya also provides real-estate leasing services.

	¥bil 02/93	02/94	02/95	US$mil 02/95				
Revenues	1,295.9	1,224.5	1,187.1	11,845.2	P/E Ratio	NMF	Price (9/30/95)	1,450.00
Net Income	-7.0	-2.6	-1.2	-12.4	P/B Ratio	2.8	52 Wk Hi-Low	1,510.0-1,070.0
Book Value	124.3	119.9	118.3	1,223.4	Yield %	0.5	Market Cap	US$3,222.1mil

Address	**5-1-5, Nanba**	Tel **06-631-1101**	ADR	President	**Hiroshi Hidaka**
	Chuo-ku, Osaka 542	Fax **06-631-9850**	SEDOL No. **6870401**	Chairman	--

Takeda Chemical Industries

Industry: **Pharmaceuticals**

Takeda Chemical Industries (Takeda Yakuhin Kogyo) is the largest maker of pharmaceuticals in Japan by sales. Its products include prescription and over-the-counter drugs, vitamins, and industrial chemicals. One of its mainstay drugs is Avan, used to treat cerebral-metabolism disorders. Main customers are Nakakita Pharmaceuticals, Unic, and Kuraya Pharmaceuticals. The firm has a joint venture in the U.S. with Abbott Laboratories, and other joint ventures in Europe. It runs a research center in Tsukuba Science City, as well as joint research projects with U.S. universities.

	¥bil 03/93	03/94	03/95	US$mil 03/95				
Sales	720.1	727.8	771.7	7,821.9	P/E Ratio	23.5	Price (9/30/95)	1,380.00
Net Income	48.0	47.6	51.4	521.3	P/B Ratio	1.9	52 Wk Hi-Low	1,410.0-1,020.0
Book Value	577.6	613.8	653.0	7,558.3	Yield %	1.0	Market Cap	US$12,155mil

Address	**4-1-1, Dosho-machi**	Tel **06-204-2169**	ADR	President	**Kunio Takeda**
	Chuo-ku, Osaka 541	Fax **06-204-2035**	SEDOL No. **6870445**	Chairman	**Katsura Morita**

Takuma

Industry: **Pollution Control, Waste Management**

Takuma is a leading maker of garbage incinerators and industrial boilers in Japan. The company manufactures waste-processing equipment and enters into contracts to build water-processing plants. The industrial machinery it makes includes laminated-board-manufacturing equipment. Takuma's main customers are government agencies. The company has six consolidated subsidiaries: Five domestic subsidiaries provide maintenance services and paper- and plastic-waste disposal, and one in Taiwan produces boilers and is active in environmental planning.

	¥bil 03/93	03/94	03/95	US$mil 03/95				
Sales	97.8	117.1	97.9	992.6	P/E Ratio	45.9	Price (9/30/95)	1,350.00
Net Income	1.4	2.6	2.5	25.5	P/B Ratio	3.5	52 Wk Hi-Low	1,940.0-788.0
Book Value	21.1	27.3	33.5	387.5	Yield %	0.6	Market Cap	US$1,184.6mil

Address	**1-3-23, Dojimahama**	Tel **06-346-5161**	ADR	President	**Akira Ushimaru**
	Kita-ku, Osaka 530	Fax **06-347-9146**	SEDOL No. **6870768**	Chairman	**Junkichi Fukuda**

Tanabe Seiyaku

Industry: **Pharmaceuticals**

Tanabe Seiyaku is a pharmaceutical company that specializes in circulatory drugs. The firm's drug Diltiazem is exported to more than 90 countries and is one of the best-selling cardiovascular drugs in the world. Its major customers include Marion Merrell Dow, Sanki, Kuraya Pharmaceutical, and Toho Pharmaceutical. Tanabe has manufacturing facilities in France, Indonesia, and Taiwan. Its joint ventures include agreements with Glaxo (U.K.), Rhone-Poulenc (France), and Marion Merrell Dow (U.S.). It also operates a research facility, Tanabe Research Laboratories, in San Diego.

	¥bil 03/93	03/94	03/95	US$mil 03/95				
Sales	243.5	217.7	211.2	2,140.9	P/E Ratio	42.8	Price (9/30/95)	710.00
Net Income	5.7	3.4	4.0	40.7	P/B Ratio	1.3	52 Wk Hi-Low	873.00-602.00
Book Value	128.0	129.2	132.0	1,528.0	Yield %	1.1	Market Cap	US$1,727.7mil

Address	**3-2-10, Dosho-machi**	Tel **06-205-5555**	ADR	President	**Ichiro Chibata**
	Chuo-ku, Osaka 541	Fax **06-205-5014**	SEDOL No. **6870984**	Chairman	--

TDK

Industry: **Electrical Components & Equipment**

TDK is the world's largest maker of magnetic materials (including audiotapes, videotapes, and floppy disks) and ferrite, a magnetic ceramic. It also produces various electronic components, including capacitors, inductors, and high-density circuits. Since acquiring Silicon Systems, a California-based maker of application-specific integrated circuits, TDK has invested heavily in semiconductor manufacturing. TDK has 65 subsidiaries, 57 of which are overseas, and 10 affiliates. In 1994, 56.8% of TDK's consolidated sales were made overseas.

¥bil	03/93	03/94	03/95	US$mil 03/95				
Sales	**526.4**	**457.4**	**485.1**	**4,917.3**	P/E Ratio	**51.5**	Price (9/30/95)	**5,100.00**
Net Income	**18.4**	**5.5**	**13.0**	**131.9**	P/B Ratio	**1.8**	52 Wk Hi-Low	**5,100.0-3,470.0**
Book Value	**386.4**	**374.8**	**371.3**	**4,297.4**	Yield %	**1.0**	Market Cap	**US$6,745.5mil**

Address	**1-13-1, Nihonbashi**	Tel	**03-5201-7106**	ADR	**TDK**	President	**Hiroshi Sato**
	Chuo-ku, Tokyo 103	Fax	**03-5201-7110**	SEDOL No.	**6869302**	Chairman	--

Teijin

Industry: **Clothing & Fabrics**

Teijin is Japan's leading maker of polyester. The company also produces nylon, acetate, aramid, and polyvinyl-chloride fibers, polyester-film products, electronic components, resins, pharmaceuticals, and medical products. Teijin markets a portion of its products through its Teijin Shoji subsidiary; major customers include Takisada, Seiren, Ichida, and Nishiyama Shoten. The company has 107 subsidiaries and 47 affiliates. In addition to its six domestic plants, Teijin has manufacturing facilities in Thailand and Indonesia that produce polyester fibers and synthetic textiles.

¥bil	03/93	03/94	03/95	US$mil 03/95				
Sales	**618.4**	**562.7**	**566.7**	**5,744.6**	P/E Ratio	**NMF**	Price (9/30/95)	**475.00**
Net Income	**12.0**	**3.8**	**2.0**	**19.9**	P/B Ratio	**1.5**	52 Wk Hi-Low	**574.00-400.00**
Book Value	**319.0**	**318.8**	**314.9**	**3,644.3**	Yield %	**1.3**	Market Cap	**US$4,655.7mil**

Address	**1-6-7, Minami-Honmachi**	Tel	**06-268-3201**	ADR		President	**Hiroshi Itagaki**
	Chuo-ku, Osaka 541	Fax	**06-268-3205**	SEDOL No.	**6880507**	Chairman	--

Tekken

Industry: **Heavy Construction**

Tekken (Tekken Kensetsu), one of Japan's leading civil-engineering firms by revenues, specializes in constructing subways, bullet-train lines, and magnetic-levitation test tracks. It works on a variety of large-scale civil-engineering works including land reclamation, road networks, sewer and water-supply systems, hydroelectric dams, and power stations. The world's longest undersea tunnel, connecting Honshu and Hokkaido, was built by Tekken. The firm also constructs residential and industrial complexes using intelligent-building technology. Tekken has 10 subsidiaries.

¥bil	03/93	03/94	03/95	US$mil 03/95				
Sales	**246.7**	**242.6**	**268.6**	**2,722.5**	P/E Ratio	**71.3**	Price (9/30/95)	**720.00**
Net Income	**1.7**	**1.6**	**1.6**	**16.2**	P/B Ratio	**2.1**	52 Wk Hi-Low	**999.00-661.00**
Book Value	**54.5**	**54.8**	**53.3**	**616.7**	Yield %	**1.0**	Market Cap	**US$1,145.8mil**

Address	**2-5-3, Misaki-cho**	Tel	**03-3262-3411**	ADR		President	**Koji Takahashi**
	Chiyoda-ku, Tokyo 101	Fax	**03-3264-2913**	SEDOL No.	**6881168**	Chairman	--

Terumo

Industry: **Medical Supplies**

Terumo produces pharmaceuticals, blood-transfusion equipment, injectors, and artificial internal-organ systems. It has the largest Japanese market share in disposable medical instruments and it produces more than 1,500 varieties of injection systems. Terumo recently entered the over-the-counter pharmaceuticals market. It has a high export ratio (31%) and strong overseas manufacturing networks, including six consolidated subsidiaries in Belgium, Germany, France, Australia, Mexico, and the United States. Suzuken, a pharmaceuticals wholesaler, is one of Terumo's main clients.

¥bil	03/93	03/94	03/95	US$mil 03/95				
Sales	**114.5**	**111.3**	**114.9**	**1,164.2**	P/E Ratio	**36.9**	Price (9/30/95)	**756.00**
Net Income	**0.5**	**0.7**	**3.9**	**39.6**	P/B Ratio	**1.7**	52 Wk Hi-Low	**998.00-630.00**
Book Value	**81.0**	**83.7**	**85.9**	**993.9**	Yield %	**1.0**	Market Cap	**US$1,445.9mil**

Address	**2-44-1, Hatagaya**	Tel	**03-3374-8111**	ADR		President	**Takashi Wachi**
	Shibuya-ku, Tokyo 151	Fax	**03-3374-8399**	SEDOL No.	**6885074**	Chairman	**Tetsuzo Akutsu**

Toa

Industry: **Heavy Construction**

Toa (Toa Kensetsu Kogyo), a member of the Fuyo group, is a midsize general contractor specializing in offshore civil engineering. The company designs and constructs ports and harbors, dredges, waterways, and reclaims submerged land. Its inland civil-engineering projects include railway design and development, waterworks construction, road building, and land development. Toa also builds plants, warehouses, shops, schools, office buildings, and houses. The company currently received an order to construct a trash disposal plant in Singapore.

¥bil	03/93	03/94	03/95	US$mil 03/95				
Sales	**260.5**	**264.6**	**280.4**	**2,842.6**	P/E Ratio	**51.4**	Price (9/30/95)	**740.00**
Net Income	**2.2**	**2.3**	**2.7**	**26.9**	P/B Ratio	**3.5**	52 Wk Hi-Low	**905.00-553.00**
Book Value	**26.9**	**28.1**	**40.6**	**470.1**	Yield %	**0.8**	Market Cap	**US$1,427.3mil**

Address	**5, Yonban-cho**	Tel	**03-3262-5102**	ADR		President	**Hiroshi Kitamura**
	Chiyoda-ku, Tokyo 102	Fax	**03-3262-9536**	SEDOL No.	**6894508**	Chairman	**Teruju Matsumoto**

Toagosei

Industry: **Specialty Chemicals**

Toagosei (formerly Toagosei Chemical Industries), a Mitsui & Co. affiliate, produces fine chemicals and related products that are marketed to the construction and semiconductor industries. The firm's chemicals include soda and chlorine products, fertilizers, and resins. Its instant glue is sold in Japan as Aron Alpha and marketed in the United States as Krazy Glue. It also produces polyvinyl-chloride pipes for sewer construction, and water-resistant coatings for brick, concrete, and tile. The company operates several production facilities and a research center in Japan.

¥bil	12/92	12/93	12/94	US$mil 12/94				
Sales	**153.9**	**152.7**	**149.9**	**1,468.9**	P/E Ratio	**55.1**	Price (9/30/95)	**496.00**
Net Income	**4.2**	**3.3**	**2.3**	**22.8**	P/B Ratio	**1.8**	52 Wk Hi-Low	**625.71-385.00**
Book Value	**63.9**	**66.8**	**67.5**	**676.9**	Yield %	**1.4**	Market Cap	**US$1,287.9mil**

Address **1-14-1, Nishi-Shinbashi, Minato-ku, Tokyo 105**
Tel **03-3597-7215** Fax **03-3597-7382**
ADR SEDOL No. **6894467**
President **Akira Senda** Chairman **Toshiaki Kametani**

Tobishima

Industry: **Heavy Construction**

Tobishima (Tobishima Kensetsu), a member of the Fuyo group, is a general contractor that specializes in civil-engineering projects such as subway and railway development and power-plant construction. It is also active in dam and tunnel construction (working with gas lines, water lines, and telephone cables), as well as real-estate sales and development. There are nine subsidiaries and affiliates, including ones in Brunei and the Philippines. It has participated in development projects overseas, many of which are financed by development grants from the Japanese government.

¥bil	03/93	03/94	03/95	US$mil 03/95				
Sales	**478.3**	**433.5**	**435.6**	**4,415.5**	P/E Ratio	**NMF**	Price (9/30/95)	**421.00**
Net Income	**0.6**	**0.5**	**0.3**	**3.3**	P/B Ratio	**3.6**	52 Wk Hi-Low	**615.00-325.00**
Book Value	**31.2**	**31.7**	**27.4**	**317.6**	Yield %	**0.0**	Market Cap	**US$996.6mil**

Address **2, Sanban-cho, Chiyoda-ku, Tokyo 102**
Tel **03-3263-3151** Fax **03-3262-7683**
ADR SEDOL No. **6893000**
President **Shoichiro Ishihara** Chairman **Takashi Baba**

Tobu Railway

Industry: **Railroads**

Tobu Railway (Tobu Tetsudo) is a large railway company that has branched into real estate and leisure-related services. It has the second-longest operating mileage of any railway in the Kanto region. The firm has a bus-route network that includes regular routes and tours in Tokyo and seven prefectures. Its real-estate operations primarily develop land along its railway lines, and lease both land and commercial buildings. The Tobu group also operates department stores and sports clubs. It has 28 consolidated and 42 nonconsolidated subsidiaries, and 53 affiliated companies.

¥bil	03/93	03/94	03/95	US$mil 03/95				
Sales	**313.8**	**334.1**	**346.1**	**3,508.3**	P/E Ratio	**NMF**	Price (9/30/95)	**611.00**
Net Income	**2.4**	**1.7**	**1.2**	**11.9**	P/B Ratio	**3.6**	52 Wk Hi-Low	**640.00-505.00**
Book Value	**150.5**	**148.6**	**145.7**	**1,686.4**	Yield %	**0.8**	Market Cap	**US$5,277.1mil**

Address **1-1-2, Oshiage, Sumida-ku, Tokyo 131**
Tel **03-3621-5055** Fax **03-3621-5161**
ADR SEDOL No. **6895169**
President **Takashige Uchida** Chairman **Kaichiro Nezu**

Toda

Industry: **Heavy Construction**

Toda (Toda Kensetsu), a member of the Mitsubishi group, is a general contractor that constructs office buildings, industrial plants, warehouses, hospitals, and houses. Its civil-engineering projects include urban and land development, roads, and railways. Orders from the private sector account for almost 70% of its current contracts, with government contracts making up the rest. The firm's real estate activity is about 7.0 % of parent-company sales. Toda has 12 subsidiaries and nine affiliates; these include overseas operations in China, Thailand, Malaysia, and Brazil.

¥bil	03/93 P	03/94 P	03/95 P	US$mil 03/95				
Sales	**753.5**	**733.8**	**641.3**	**6,500.6**	P/E Ratio	**35.1**	Price (9/30/95)	**857.00**
Net Income	**14.1**	**10.2**	**7.9**	**79.7**	P/B Ratio	**1.7**	52 Wk Hi-Low	**985.00-725.00**
Book Value	**148.9**	**156.0**	**160.8**	**1,860.8**	Yield %	**1.1**	Market Cap	**US$2,771.4mil**

Address **1-7-1, Kyobashi, Chuo-ku, Tokyo 104**
Tel **03-3562-6111** Fax **03-3564-6713**
ADR SEDOL No. **6893884**
President **Moriji Toda** Chairman **Junnosuke Toda**

P=Parent company data.

Toho

Industry: **Other Recreational Products & Services**

Toho is a motion-picture producer and distributor affiliated with the Sanwa and Hankyu groups. It has several directly-owned theaters in the Tokyo area. About 50% of consolidated sales are from its movie division, real-estate and leasing activities account for about 30%, and its theater operations contribute 12%. It also manages concession stands, sports facilities, hotels, and traditional inns. Toho holds the highest market share for film distribution (including many U.S. films) in Japan. Toho's 33 consolidated and 48 unconsolidated subsidiaries are largely based in Tokyo.

¥bil	02/93	02/94	02/95	US$mil 02/95				
Sales	**166.0**	**165.2**	**159.2**	**1,588.8**	P/E Ratio	**39.7**	Price (9/30/95)	**15,500**
Net Income	**7.8**	**7.8**	**6.7**	**66.7**	P/B Ratio	**2.4**	52 Wk Hi-Low	**17,543.7-12,453.3**
Book Value	**100.3**	**106.6**	**111.5**	**1,152.8**	Yield %	**0.6**	Market Cap	**US$2,671.3mil**

Address **1-2-1, Yuraku-cho, Chiyoda-ku, Tokyo 100**
Tel **03-3591-1221** Fax **03-3591-2414**
ADR SEDOL No. **6895200**
President **Toshihiko Ishida** Chairman **Isao Matsuoka**

Toho Zinc

Industry: **Non-Ferrous Metals - Other (Exc. Aluminum)**

Toho Zinc (Toho Aen) is a smelter of zinc and lead. The company is Japan's largest lead manufacturer by sales. Its other products include processed-metal products, electronic materials and parts, sulfuric acid, cadmium, sound-proof construction materials, iron, gold, silver, and electrolytic zinc and lead. Toho Zinc holds a leading domestic market share in high-purity electrolytic iron for nuclear reactors. The firm also does civil-engineering work. Its products are mainly supplied to the steel and automobile industries. Toho Zinc has three production facilities in Japan.

¥bil	03/93	03/94	03/95	US$mil 03/95				
Sales	**59.8**	**47.2**	**51.5**	**521.6**	P/E Ratio	**NMF**	Price (9/30/95)	**510.00**
Net Income	**0.4**	**-0.1**	**0.0**	**0.3**	P/B Ratio	**4.9**	52 Wk Hi-Low	**575.00-264.00**
Book Value	**8.8**	**10.8**	**11.3**	**130.8**	Yield %	**0.6**	Market Cap	**US$552.0mil**

Address **3-12-2, Nihonbashi** **Chuo-ku, Tokyo 103** | Tel **03-3272-5611** | Fax **N/A** | ADR | SEDOL No. **6895567** | President **Hironobu Tsuchiya** | Chairman **Ukitsu Ito**

Tohoku Electric Power

Industry: **Electrical Utilities - All**

Tohoku Electric Power (Tohoku Denryoku) supplies electricity to the Tohoku area in northeastern Japan and Niigata Prefecture. The firm serves nearly five million residences and more than one million industrial and commercial customers. Its principal operations consist of 14 hydroelectric-, seven thermal-, and one nuclear-power station. Most of its power is generated by thermal plants, but like many of Japan's electric utilities, the firm is pursuing the use of nuclear power. It has 21 main subsidiaries (three wholly owned), one of which imports natural gas from Indonesia.

¥bil	03/93	03/94	03/95	US$mil 03/95				
Sales	**1,276.5**	**1,343.5**	**1,440.3**	**14,599.6**	P/E Ratio	**22.6**	Price (9/30/95)	**2,420.00**
Net Income	**46.1**	**35.8**	**53.3**	**540.3**	P/B Ratio	**2.0**	52 Wk Hi-Low	**2,574.3-2,168.3**
Book Value	**545.2**	**555.9**	**608.8**	**7,046.8**	Yield %	**2.1**	Market Cap	**US$12,120mil**

Address **3-7-1, Ichiban-cho, Aoba-ku** **Sendai City, Sendai 980** | Tel **022-225-2111** | Fax **N/A** | ADR | SEDOL No. **6895266** | President **Toshiaki Yashima** | Chairman **Teruyuki Akema**

Tokai Bank

Industry: **Banks - Money Center**

Tokai Bank is ranked eighth among Japanese banks by total assets. The bank is the financial center of the Tokai group and the primary bank for Toyota Motor. In addition to lending, the bank offers advisory services for mergers and acquisitions, computerized-banking systems, and electronic-information services. It has 285 branches in Japan and 17 overseas branches. It has operations in 25 countries, including joint ventures with large local financial institutions in Thailand, Malaysia, and Hong Kong. In 1994, overseas sales contributed 38% to Tokai's consolidated revenues.

¥bil	03/93	03/94	03/95	US$mil 03/95				
Revenues	**1,894.6**	**1,944.6**	**1,520.6**	**15,413.6**	P/E Ratio	**NMF**	Price (9/30/95)	**1,210.00**
Net Income	**25.3**	**33.9**	**4.6**	**46.9**	P/B Ratio	**2.2**	52 Wk Hi-Low	**1,260.0-913.0**
Book Value	**1,097.5**	**1,124.6**	**1,113.2**	**12,884.7**	Yield %	**0.7**	Market Cap	**US$24,694mil**

Address **3-21-24, Nishiki** **Naka-ku Nagoya City, Aichi 460** | Tel **052-211-1111** | Fax **052-219-1007** | ADR | SEDOL No. **6895341** | President **Satoru Nishigaki** | Chairman **Kiichiro Ito**

Tokimec

Industry: **Aerospace & Defense**

Tokimec is a precision-machinery maker that specializes in marine and aircraft instruments. The firm also produces measuring equipment for scientific and medical applications, and hydraulic- and pneumatic-control devices for use in construction machinery, automation systems, and various types of vehicles. Major customers include the Ministry of Defense and companies in the shipbuilding, aerospace, and machine-tool industries. Tokimec has 10 consolidated subsidiaries and five plants. It has technology transfer agreements with Honeywell and Allied Signal of the United States.

¥bil	03/93	03/94	03/95	US$mil 03/95				
Sales	**60.9**	**54.3**	**55.0**	**557.5**	P/E Ratio	**NMF**	Price (9/30/95)	**455.00**
Net Income	**-0.9**	**-1.9**	**0.1**	**1.2**	P/B Ratio	**1.3**	52 Wk Hi-Low	**590.00-340.00**
Book Value	**32.6**	**30.8**	**30.9**	**357.6**	Yield %	**0.0**	Market Cap	**US$390.8mil**

Address **2-16-46, Minami-Kamata** **Ohta-ku, Tokyo 144** | Tel **03-3732-2111** | Fax **03-3490-8453** | ADR | SEDOL No. **6895943** | President **Keijiro Morita** | Chairman **Nobue Hirono**

Tokuyama

Industry: **Commodity Chemicals**

Tokuyama (formerly Tokuyama Soda), a member of the Sanwa group, is an integrated-chemical company that produces organic and inorganic chemicals, medical products, and plastics. The firm also produces fine chemicals and electronics, and is a leading producer of caustic soda and chlorine. Building materials account for its largest sales segment. The company's primary clients are the construction, auto, and electronic-components industries. Tokuyama has 17 wholly-owned consolidated and 18 unconsolidated subsidiaries, and 54 affiliates in Japan and abroad.

¥bil	03/93	03/94	03/95	US$mil 03/95				
Sales	**183.6**	**179.2**	**191.1**	**1,936.7**	P/E Ratio	**39.5**	Price (9/30/95)	**604.00**
Net Income	**0.3**	**1.0**	**3.9**	**39.5**	P/B Ratio	**1.7**	52 Wk Hi-Low	**619.00-394.00**
Book Value	**89.8**	**89.3**	**91.2**	**1,055.1**	Yield %	**1.0**	Market Cap	**US$1,549.0mil**

Address **3-3-1, Shibuya** **Shibuya-ku, Tokyo 150** | Tel **03-3499-8710** | Fax **N/A** | ADR | SEDOL No. **6895761** | President **Kaoru Tsuji** | Chairman **--**

Tokyo Dome

Industry: **Other Recreational Products & Services**

Tokyo Dome operates amusement parks and sports stadiums, and engages in facilities leasing, retailing, restaurant operations, fitness and health businesses, and financing. Its Korakuen Leisure Land attracts 30 million visitors annually. The company's domed arena is visited by almost 10 million people annually, and is home to two baseball teams. Toyko Dome's other enterprises include the Osaka Korakuen Hotel, the TPC Batoh Korakuen Golf Course, and the Maiko Kogen Ski Resort. The company has a joint venture with Brockum of Canada to promote rock concerts in Japan.

	¥bil 01/93	01/94	01/95	US$mil 01/95				
Sales	**120.6**	**119.7**	**115.2**	**1,140.2**	P/E Ratio	**NMF**	Price (9/30/95)	**1,620.00**
Net Income	**-0.5**	**-0.1**	**-0.4**	**-4.4**	P/B Ratio	**3.5**	52 Wk Hi-Low	**1,850.0-1,250.0**
Book Value	**77.9**	**76.1**	**75.5**	**763.5**	Yield %	**0.7**	Market Cap	**US$2,645.2mil**

Address **1-3-61, Koraku**
Bunkyo-ku, Tokyo 112
Tel **03-3811-2111**
Fax **N/A**
ADR
SEDOL No. **6496744**
President **Makoto Hosaka**
Chairman --

Tokyo Electric Power

Industry: **Electrical Utilities - All**

Tokyo Electric Power (Tokyo Denryoku) is the largest private electric-power company in Japan by revenues. Its 22 million customers account for one third of Japan's electricity consumption. The company is the world's largest consumer of liquefied natural gas, accounting for 25% of the global trade. Tokyo Electric's principal facilities consist of 17 hydroelectric-, 14 thermal-, and three nuclear-power plants. The company is currently replacing traditional supplies of energy with nuclear power. Tokyo Electric has 30 subsidiaries (eight consolidated), all based in Tokyo.

	¥bil 03/93	03/94	03/95	US$mil 03/95				
Sales	**4,700.0**	**4,721.1**	**5,002.5**	**50,706.5**	P/E Ratio	**42.0**	Price (9/30/95)	**2,710.00**
Net Income	**73.8**	**62.0**	**86.5**	**876.8**	P/B Ratio	**2.4**	52 Wk Hi-Low	**2,901.0-2,485.1**
Book Value	**1,404.2**	**1,399.1**	**1,496.6**	**17,322.1**	Yield %	**1.8**	Market Cap	**US$36,511mil**

Address **1-1-3, Uchi-Saiwaicho**
Chiyoda-ku, Tokyo 100
Tel **03-3501-8111**
Fax **03-3592-1795**
ADR
SEDOL No. **6895404**
President **Hiroshi Araki**
Chairman **Sho Nasu**

Tokyo Electron

Industry: **Semiconductors & related**

Tokyo Electron, a Tokyo Broadcasting affiliate, sells semiconductor-production equipment, computer systems, and electronic components. It is the world's leading supplier of oxidation/diffusion furnaces and is the leading domestic supplier of ion implanters. Other sales lines are wafer probes, and coaters and developers for the photoresist treatment process. Main clients are the high-tech manufacturers such as Seiko Epson and Sanken Electric. It has a wholly-owned U.S. subsidiary, TEL America, a joint venture with Varian (U.S.), and a license from Asyst Technologies (U.S.).

	¥bil 03/93	03/94	03/95	US$mil 03/95				
Sales	**153.9**	**189.7**	**251.7**	**2,551.1**	P/E Ratio	**66.3**	Price (9/30/95)	**4,310.00**
Net Income	**1.8**	**5.1**	**9.7**	**98.6**	P/B Ratio	**4.2**	52 Wk Hi-Low	**4,640.0-2,330.0**
Book Value	**144.3**	**146.1**	**153.3**	**1,773.9**	Yield %	**0.4**	Market Cap	**US$6,488.6mil**

Address **2-3-1, Nishi-Shinjuku**
Shinjuku-ku, Tokyo 163-09
Tel **03-3340-8111**
Fax **03-3340-8400**
ADR
SEDOL No. **6895675**
President **Akira Inoue**
Chairman **Toshio Kodaka**

Tokyo Gas

Industry: **Gas Utilities**

Tokyo Gas is Japan's largest gas utility, serving 7.7 million households mainly in the Kanto region. Its activities include the production and supply of natural gas, cokes, tars, tar products, and aluminum sulfates. It also makes and sells gas appliances. Tokyo Gas derives about 85% of its gas from liquefied natural gas imported from the U.S., Brunei, Australia, and Malaysia. It transports gas through a 43,000-kilometer pipeline that links Tokyo to two terminals in Tokyo Bay. It has 12 consolidated subsidiaries (10 wholly-owned) and five representative offices overseas.

	¥bil 03/93	03/94	03/95	US$mil 03/95				
Sales	**844.4**	**909.7**	**915.9**	**9,283.5**	P/E Ratio	**93.1**	Price (9/30/95)	**363.00**
Net Income	**16.4**	**16.2**	**11.1**	**112.2**	P/B Ratio	**2.5**	52 Wk Hi-Low	**457.00-334.00**
Book Value	**404.8**	**409.7**	**411.2**	**4,758.8**	Yield %	**1.4**	Market Cap	**US$10,260mil**

Address **1-5-20, Kaigan**
Minato-ku, Tokyo 105
Tel **03-3433-2111**
Fax **03-437-9190**
ADR
SEDOL No. **6895448**
President **Kunio Anzai**
Chairman **Hiroshi Watanabe**

Tokyo Ohka Kogyo

Industry: **Semiconductors & related**

Tokyo Ohka Kogyo, a chemical company, is the leading producer of photoresists for semiconductors in Japan. Other products include printing materials, processing devices, and chemical compounds used in such items as printing equipment, semiconductor-manufacturing machinery, and cathode-ray tubes. About 85% of parent-company revenues are from the manufacture of photosensitive resins and related chemical products. Tokyo Ohka has seven subsidiaries, including six wholly-owned consolidated subsidiaries in the United States and the United Kingdom.

	¥bil 03/93	03/94	03/95	US$mil 03/95				
Sales	**56.9**	**59.2**	**68.6**	**695.4**	P/E Ratio	**31.1**	Price (9/30/95)	**3,000.00**
Net Income	**4.7**	**4.6**	**4.9**	**49.4**	P/B Ratio	**1.8**	52 Wk Hi-Low	**3,750.0-2,090.0**
Book Value	**79.1**	**82.8**	**86.7**	**1,003.2**	Yield %	**0.6**	Market Cap	**US$1,526.9mil**

Address **1-403, Kosugi-cho, Nakahara-ku**
Kawasaki City, Kanagawa 211
Tel **044-722-7181**
Fax **044-722-7179**
ADR
SEDOL No. **6894898**
President **Hisashi Nakane**
Chairman **Takeo Ito**

Tokyo Steel Manufacturing

Industry: **Steel**

Tokyo Steel Manufacturing (Tokyo Seitetsu), a major electric-furnace steelmaker, leads Japan in producing H-beams, with a 30% market share. The firm's products include steel bars, plates, and specialty steel, with an emphasis on thin-plate sheet. Its Okayama facility now sports a hot-coil continuous-production line. The firm is building two new plants, one in Mie Prefecture and one in Utsunomiya. The new facilities are scheduled to be completed by the end of 1996. It has a U.S. joint venture, TAMCO, to produce steel products with Mitsui & Co. and Amelon (U.S.).

¥bil	03/93 P	03/94 P	03/95 P	US$mil 03/95				
Sales	**203.3**	**152.7**	**140.3**	**1,421.9**	P/E Ratio	**NMF**	Price (9/30/95)	**1,910.00**
Net Income	**14.6**	**-12.3**	**-8.7**	**-88.4**	P/B Ratio	**1.6**	52 Wk Hi-Low	**2,640.0-1,380.0**
Book Value	**209.9**	**193.7**	**182.7**	**2,114.0**	Yield %	**0.5**	Market Cap	**US$2,998.2mil**

Address **2-2-2, Uchi-Saiwaicho**
Chiyoda-ku, Tokyo 100
Tel **03-3580-8521**
Fax **03-3501-3675**
ADR
SEDOL No. **6895879**
President **Masanari Iketani**
Chairman --

P=Parent company data.

Tokyo Style

Industry: **Clothing & Fabrics**

Tokyo Style is a leading manufacturer and retailer of women's apparel in Japan. The sale of casual wear provides more than 60% of sales. Its other products include coats, dresses, and suits. Tokyo Style sells various British and French brands such as Nicole Farhi, Wolsey, and Jean Claude. The company manufactures clothing in six domestic factories. It is expanding its international operations through its Mosaique stores in Paris; Turin, Italy; and New York; and a production base in Hong Kong. The firm announced a venture to manufacture women's clothes in China.

¥bil	02/93	02/94	02/95	US$mil 02/95				
Sales	**79.4**	**77.7**	**71.9**	**717.2**	P/E Ratio	**34.9**	Price (9/30/95)	**1,540.00**
Net Income	**6.8**	**7.1**	**4.5**	**44.9**	P/B Ratio	**1.1**	52 Wk Hi-Low	**1,920.0-1,160.0**
Book Value	**132.3**	**138.2**	**141.5**	**1,463.2**	Yield %	**0.8**	Market Cap	**US$1,584.2mil**

Address **5-7-1, Kojimachi**
Chiyoda-ku, Tokyo 102
Tel **03-3262-8111**
Fax **03-3262-5510**
ADR
SEDOL No. **6896645**
President **Yoshio Takano**
Chairman --

Tokyotokeiba

Industry: **Other Recreational Products & Services**

Tokyotokeiba is a horse- and motorcycle-racetrack lessor and operator. Its primary sources of income include leasing a horse racetrack in Tokyo and leasing a motorcycle racetrack in Gunma Prefecture. The firm also operates various warehouses, sports facilities, and amusement parks. It has four consolidated subsidiaries: Oi Kogyo, a concession-stand operator; Tokyo Summer Land, an amusement-park operator; Kanto Kosan, a motorcycle-racetrack operator; and Tokyo Soko, a warehouse-management firm. The Tokyo metropolitan government is its top shareholder.

¥bil	12/92	12/93	12/94	US$mil 12/94				
Sales	**24.0**	**21.4**	**19.3**	**189.2**	P/E Ratio	**61.3**	Price (9/30/95)	**380.00**
Net Income	**3.4**	**2.3**	**1.8**	**17.4**	P/B Ratio	**2.3**	52 Wk Hi-Low	**560.00-320.00**
Book Value	**44.9**	**46.4**	**47.2**	**473.2**	Yield %	**0.8**	Market Cap	**US$1,098.1mil**

Address **3-3-9, Nihonbashi**
Chuo-ku, Tokyo 103
Tel **03-3271-9105**
Fax **N/A**
ADR
SEDOL No. **6896065**
President **Tsutomu Manita**
Chairman **Fumio Takahashi**

Tokyu

Industry: **Railroads**

Tokyu (Tokyo Kyuko Dentetsu), a key member of the Tokyu group, is a diversified railway and real-estate company. It provides railway and bus services, and is involved in tourism-related businesses and real-estate sales and leasing activities. Its railway operations link Tokyo to the southwestern region of Japan. Tokyu operates department stores, hotels, sports facilities, and a cable-television company. A quadruple-tracking project of the firm's railway network is scheduled for completion in 1997. The firm has 113 consolidated subsidiaries and 59 affiliates.

¥bil	03/93	03/94	03/95	US$mil 03/95				
Sales	**476.6**	**458.7**	**469.7**	**4,760.5**	P/E Ratio	**NMF**	Price (9/30/95)	**668.00**
Net Income	**2.1**	**1.0**	**1.9**	**19.1**	P/B Ratio	**3.1**	52 Wk Hi-Low	**705.00-521.00**
Book Value	**239.8**	**235.6**	**238.2**	**2,757.5**	Yield %	**0.7**	Market Cap	**US$7,379.7mil**

Address **5-6, Nanpeidai-cho**
Shibuya-ku, Tokyo 150
Tel **03-3477-6074**
Fax **03-3462-1690**
ADR
SEDOL No. **6896548**
President **Shinobu Shimizu**
Chairman --

Tokyu Construction

Industry: **Heavy Construction**

Tokyu Construction (Tokyu Kensetsu) is a medium-size general contractor that builds residential, factory, civic, and commercial buildings, and develops resort towns, parks, hotels, and condominiums. The firm's public and private civil-engineering works include dams, railways, roads, and tunnels. It also offers real-estate brokerage and services such as sports-facility maintenance and hotel management through its affiliates. Overseas sales account for less than 10% of its net revenues. Tokyu Construction has 18 consolidated subsidiaries and eight affiliates.

¥bil	03/93	03/94	03/95	US$mil 03/95				
Sales	**672.8**	**684.5**	**635.2**	**6,438.2**	P/E Ratio	**NMF**	Price (9/30/95)	**465.00**
Net Income	**1.3**	**-1.8**	**-0.5**	**-5.1**	P/B Ratio	**1.2**	52 Wk Hi-Low	**574.00-433.00**
Book Value	**79.9**	**89.0**	**85.7**	**992.1**	Yield %	**2.5**	Market Cap	**US$1,076.7mil**

Address **1-16-14, Shibuya**
Shibuya-ku, Tokyo 150
Tel **03-5466-5111**
Fax **03-3400-4580**
ADR
SEDOL No. **6895802**
President **Tetsu Goto**
Chairman --

Tokyu Hotel Chain

Industry: **Lodging**

Tokyu Hotel Chain is an urban luxury-hotel group that owns and operates 21 hotels throughout Japan. Its hotel operations account for 88% of the company's total consolidated sales, and its linen and cleaning services make up the remaining 12%. The hotels' clientele consists mostly of business travelers. Tokyu Hotel has eight domestic consolidated subsidiaries, six are involved in the hotel business, and one each in linen- supplying services and building-maintenance operations, respectively. Tokyu Hotel also has nine unconsolidated subsidiaries and four affiliates.

¥bil	12/92	12/93	12/94	US$mil 12/94				
Sales	82.4	78.8	75.9	743.9	P/E Ratio	NMF	Price (9/30/95)	650.00
Net Income	1.3	0.8	0.3	3.4	P/B Ratio	1.7	52 Wk Hi-Low	915.00-560.00
Book Value	42.0	41.7	41.3	414.2	Yield %	0.9	Market Cap	US$705.0mil

Address	**6-6, Koji-machi**	Tel	**03-3264-2262**	ADR		President	**Mitsugi Nakajima**
	Chiyoda-ku, Tokyo 102	Fax	**03-3239-2959**	SEDOL No.	**6893969**	Chairman	**Tadatake Ebina**

Tomen

Industry: **Overseas Trading**

Tomen is a leading trading company that specializes in metals, chemicals, petroleum, textiles, machinery, and foodstuffs. Its largest sales segment, metals, involves offshore trading of precious metals and steel. Amont the firm's activities in the textile division are exporting Southeast Asian fabrics to North America and Europe and importing garments and bedding materials. Tomen also trades construction materials and lumber and timber products. Its overseas network consists of six branches, 64 representative offices, 16 trading subsidiaries, and 17 subsidiary offices.

¥bil	03/93	03/94	03/95	US$mil 03/95				
Sales	7,675.7	6,973.9	6,943.7	70,383.3	P/E Ratio	NMF	Price (9/30/95)	335.00
Net Income	3.6	1.6	1.0	10.3	P/B Ratio	2.0	52 Wk Hi-Low	403.00-283.00
Book Value	119.0	115.9	114.4	1,323.9	Yield %	1.6	Market Cap	US$2,256.6mil

Address	**1-6-7, Kawara-machi**	Tel	**06-208-2401**	ADR		President	**Yasuo Matsukawa**
	Chuo-ku, Osaka 541	Fax	**03-3588-9980**	SEDOL No.	**6900386**	Chairman	--

Tonen

Industry: **Oil - Secondary**

Tonen is a specialized refiner of oil, importing most of its crude oil through its affiliates Exxon and Mobil. The firm specializes in white oils such as gasoline, and produces naphtha, kerosene, diesel oil, heavy oil, and lubricants. Tonen's total crude-oil-refining capacity is greater than 360,000 barrels per standard day. Primary customers are Esso Eastern and Mobil Petroleum. Its main refineries are located in Wakayama and Kawasaki. Tonen is entering the pharmaceuticals market through joint-development projects with International Reagent and Yamanouchi Pharmaceutical.

¥bil	12/92	12/93	12/94	US$mil 12/94				
Sales	681.9	619.0	574.1	5,624.9	P/E Ratio	41.9	Price (9/30/95)	1,430.00
Net Income	17.4	16.8	22.0	215.8	P/B Ratio	2.8	52 Wk Hi-Low	1,630.0-1,270.0
Book Value	359.7	339.0	328.6	3,293.5	Yield %	3.5	Market Cap	US$9,299.5mil

Address	**1-1-1, Hitotsubashi**	Tel	**03-3286-5053**	ADR		President	**Tamehiko Tamahori**
	Chiyoda-ku, Tokyo 100	Fax	**03-3286-5120**	SEDOL No.	**6894520**	Chairman	**Osamu Ikeda**

Toppan Printing

Industry: **General Industrial & Commercial Services**

Toppan Printing is Japan's second-largest printing firm by revenues, with a 10.4% share of the Japanese market. The company prints books, posters, catalogs, stock certificates, and checks. It also produces advertisements, credit cards, ID cards, magnetic cards, electronic publications, and periodicals on CD-ROM. Toppan has 18 plants in Japan, and operations in China, Australia, Southeast Asia, Europe, and the United States. It owns a 30% stake in Tosho Printing, a medium-size printing firm. Its 90%-owned Toppan Moore holds 1.7% of Japan's printing market.

¥bil	03/93	03/94	03/95	US$mil 03/95				
Sales	1,098.5	1,090.0	1,130.6	11,459.8	P/E Ratio	54.5	Price (9/30/95)	1,260.00
Net Income	29.5	31.8	15.9	161.0	P/B Ratio	1.5	52 Wk Hi-Low	1,450.0-1,050.0
Book Value	507.9	533.3	570.3	6,600.4	Yield %	1.0	Market Cap	US$8,861.9mil

Address	**1, Kanda-Izumicho**	Tel	**03-3835-5671**	ADR	**TONPY**	President	**Hiromichi Fujita**
	Chiyoda-ku, Tokyo 101	Fax	**03-3837-7675**	SEDOL No.	**6897024**	Chairman	--

Topy Industries

Industry: **Factory Equipment**

Topy Industries (Topy Kogyo), a member of the Nippon Steel group, processes metal for machinery, construction materials, and steel structures. It commands a leading share of the domestic market for automobile wheels, which account for about 45% of parent-company sales. Other products include steel beams for construction use, flat bars for shipbuilding, structural shapes and sections, mill plates, and bridge superstructures. It supplies all major Japanese automakers, as well as Caterpillar, GM Saturn, and the United States subsidiaries of Mazda Motor and Mitsubishi Motors.

¥bil	03/93	03/94	03/95	US$mil 03/95				
Sales	243.5	219.8	227.1	2,302.3	P/E Ratio	NMF	Price (9/30/95)	420.00
Net Income	2.0	-2.2	-1.3	-13.1	P/B Ratio	2.0	52 Wk Hi-Low	538.00-362.00
Book Value	51.0	48.4	46.2	535.0	Yield %	0.7	Market Cap	US$952.5mil

Address	**5-9, Yonban-cho**	Tel	**03-3265-0111**	ADR		President	**Tomokatsu Kotani**
	Chiyoda-ku, Tokyo 102	Fax	**03-3262-0400**	SEDOL No.	**6897121**	Chairman	--

Toray Industries

Industry: **Clothing & Fabrics**

Toray Industries is Japan's leading maker of synthetic fibers. The company's main products include polyester, acrylic, synthetic suede, resins, and carbon fibers. Toray also produces chemicals, printing equipment, pharmaceuticals, measuring instruments, and electronic parts; builds condominiums and homes; and is active in engineering and real estate. Major customers include Mitsui (14% of parent-company sales) and Nissei. Its 33 overseas consolidated subsidiaries produce 30% of its output of fiber and plastics. In 1994, Toray made 27% of its consolidated sales overseas.

¥bil	03/93	03/94	03/95	US$mil 03/95				
Sales	970.5	884.1	900.5	9,127.8	P/E Ratio	83.6	Price (9/30/95)	602.00
Net Income	26.9	14.3	10.0	101.8	P/B Ratio	1.8	52 Wk Hi-Low	782.00-495.00
Book Value	452.1	456.1	456.2	5,279.9	Yield %	1.2	Market Cap	US$8,486.1mil

Address **2-2-1, Nihonbashi-Muromachi**, **Chuo-ku, Tokyo 103**
Tel **03-3245-5201** Fax **03-3245-5459**
ADR **TRAYY** SEDOL No. **6897143**
President **Katsunosuke Maeda** Chairman --

Toshiba

Industry: **Diversified Technology**

Toshiba is Japan's second-largest manufacturer of general-electrical machinery by sales, and one of the world's largest producers of semiconductors. The company's products include power generators, factory-automation equipment, facsimile machines, computers, integrated circuits, camcorders, cameras, metals, and ceramics. These are marketed primarily to industrial manufacturers, power-plant builders, and trading companies. The company operates 27 plants and research centers in Japan. It has more than 850 subsidiaries and affiliates throughout Asia, North America, and Europe.

¥bil	03/93	03/94	03/95	US$mil 03/95				
Sales	4,627.5	4,630.9	4,790.8	48,560.8	P/E Ratio	52.2	Price (9/30/95)	725.00
Net Income	20.6	12.1	44.7	453.0	P/B Ratio	2.1	52 Wk Hi-Low	774.00-495.00
Book Value	1,148.8	1,117.7	1,118.8	12,949.2	Yield %	1.4	Market Cap	US$23,464mil

Address **1-1-1, Shibaura**, **Minato-ku, Tokyo 105-01**
Tel **03-3457-2148** Fax **03-3456-4776**
ADR SEDOL No. **6897217**
President **Fumio Sato** Chairman **Joichi Aoi**

Toshiba Machine

Industry: **Factory Equipment**

Toshiba Machine (Toshiba Kikai), an affiliate of Toshiba, ranks second in total sales among Japanese machine-tool makers. Its major machine-tool products include plastic-processing machinery, die-casting machines, hydraulic machinery, machining centers, injection-molding machines, and precision molds. The company also manufactures beverage dispensers, printing presses, and semiconductor-manufacturing equipment. Its major customers include the automobile, iron, steel, and non-ferrous-metals industries. Exports account for roughly 40% of the company's sales.

¥bil	03/93	03/94	03/95	US$mil 03/95				
Sales	129.1	105.9	116.7	1,182.6	P/E Ratio	NMF	Price (9/30/95)	491.00
Net Income	0.4	-9.1	-8.3	-84.0	P/B Ratio	1.8	52 Wk Hi-Low	779.00-389.00
Book Value	63.2	53.5	44.5	514.7	Yield %	0.0	Market Cap	US$813.8mil

Address **4-2-11, Ginza**, **Chuo-ku, Tokyo 104**
Tel **03-3567-8739** Fax **03-3562-5220**
ADR SEDOL No. **6897262**
President **Sadao Okano** Chairman --

Toshoku

Industry: **Overseas Trading**

Toshoku imports and sells a variety of products-primarily food products-in Japan. The company's principal customers include alcoholic-beverage manufacturers (hops, malt, and grapes) and restaurants (frozen vegetables). Foodstuffs account for 90% of total sales and the firm handles about 30% of Japan's total volume of cocoa-product imports. Toshoku also trades in chemical products, machinery, and commodities, and is involved in construction and real estate. Its overseas consolidated subsidiaries are located in the United States, the United Kingdom, Germany, and Australia.

¥bil	10/92	10/93	10/94	US$mil 10/94				
Sales	917.3	890.9	862.7	8,325.5	P/E Ratio	43.4	Price (9/30/95)	477.00
Net Income	2.2	2.7	2.3	22.6	P/B Ratio	1.3	52 Wk Hi-Low	777.20-395.00
Book Value	58.0	75.0	80.5	830.8	Yield %	1.2	Market Cap	US$1,039.0mil

Address **2-4-3, Nihonbashi-Muromachi**, **Chuo-ku, Tokyo 103**
Tel **03-3245-2084** Fax **03-3245-2870**
ADR SEDOL No. **6897347**
President **Tetsuya Sato** Chairman **Mitsuo Iizuka**

Tosoh

Industry: **Specialty Chemicals**

Tosoh, an affiliate of the Industrial Bank of Japan, is an integrated chemical maker that produces caustic soda and polyvinyl-chloride products, synthetic rubber, fine chemicals, ceramics, and analysis equipment. It has 35 consolidated subsidiaries, including ones in the U.S. and Europe. The firm wholly owns Weiss Scientific Glass, a U.S. maker of miconductor-production equipment. Among Tosoh's current joint ventures are a project in Indonesia with Mitsui (Japan) and local firms, and an agreement with DSM, N.V. (the Netherlands) to market an artificial sweetener in the U.S.

¥bil	03/93	03/94	03/95	US$mil 03/95				
Sales	358.8	326.8	351.5	3,563.3	P/E Ratio	149.7	Price (9/30/95)	434.00
Net Income	-10.5	-22.2	1.8	17.7	P/B Ratio	4.4	52 Wk Hi-Low	471.00-318.00
Book Value	81.2	61.4	59.6	689.9	Yield %	0.0	Market Cap	US$2,622.1mil

Address **1-7-7, Akasaka**, **Minato-ku, Tokyo 107**
Tel **03-3585-6916** Fax **03-3582-0972**
ADR SEDOL No. **6900289**
President **Madoka Tashiro** Chairman **Tatsuro Goda**

Tostem

Industry: **Building Materials**

Tostem is the largest seller of aluminum sashes in Japan. It manufactures other aluminum housing products such as closets, steel shutters, steel sliding doors, balconies, and household appliances. Tostem sells more than 65,000 catalog items and has a network of 20,000 retail dealers. The firm also supplies the commercial-building market. Tostem has 197 subsidiaries and affiliates and six domestic distribution centers. Most of its 21 production facilities are located in northern Japan. An overseas subsidiary manufactures and markets aluminum products for the Thai market.

¥bil	03/93	03/94	03/95	US$mil 03/95				
Sales	**507.4**	**524.3**	**555.8**	**5,633.5**	P/E Ratio	**27.3**	Price (9/30/95)	**3,190.00**
Net Income	**15.3**	**17.9**	**25.5**	**258.5**	P/B Ratio	**2.1**	52 Wk Hi-Low	**3,350.0-2,460.0**
Book Value	**294.0**	**307.0**	**325.9**	**3,772.1**	Yield %	**0.6**	Market Cap	**US$7,017.1mil**

Address	**2-1-1, Ohjima**	Tel	**03-3638-8112**	ADR		President	**Kenjiro Ushioda**
	Koto-ku, Tokyo 136	Fax	**03-3638-8343**	SEDOL No.	**6900212**	Chairman	--

Toto

Industry: **Building Materials**

Toto manufactures sanitary-ware, faucets and metal fittings, bathtubs, prefabricated bathrooms, computer-controlled toilet seats, modular kitchens, water heaters, swimming pools, and tiles. Toto has 10 plants in Japan for production and has 37 showrooms and 66 sales offices in Japan for retailing. It has 35 subsidiaries, 20 of which are consolidated. Among its products are automatic-flush urinals and its Washlet line of computer-controlled toilets, featuring ozonic deodorizing, washing, drying, and bidet functions. Less than 10% of its consolidated sales are made overseas.

¥bil	03/93	03/94	03/95	US$mil 03/95				
Sales	**423.2**	**427.2**	**454.6**	**4,608.3**	P/E Ratio	**44.9**	Price (9/30/95)	**1,360.00**
Net Income	**14.9**	**12.1**	**10.2**	**103.6**	P/B Ratio	**1.9**	52 Wk Hi-Low	**1,740.0-1,210.0**
Book Value	**226.4**	**235.0**	**241.9**	**2,799.3**	Yield %	**0.8**	Market Cap	**US$4,620.9mil**

Address	**2-1-1, Nakanoshima, Kokurakitku,**	Tel	**093-951-2109**	ADR		President	**Shigeru Ezoe**
	Kitakyushu-City, Fukuoka 802	Fax	**093-951-2718**	SEDOL No.	**6897466**	Chairman	**Yoshine Koga**

Toyo Engineering

Industry: **Heavy Construction**

Toyo Engineering is a leading international plant-engineering contractor, offering services in gas, petrochemicals, chemical fertilizers, computer-integrated manufacturing, factory automation, and nuclear power. More than 79% of its parent sales come from overseas (mainly Indonesia, China, and Malaysia), and more than 65% of its order backlog is for overseas projects. Toyo Engineering plans to concentrate on projects in China, Southeast Asia, and the Indian subcontinent. The firm has 16 subsidiaries and 16 affiliates in Japan and abroad, and 15 offices abroad.

¥bil	03/93	03/94	03/95	US$mil 03/95				
Sales	**165.0**	**132.7**	**190.5**	**1,931.3**	P/E Ratio	**57.9**	Price (9/30/95)	**567.00**
Net Income	**3.5**	**1.8**	**1.7**	**17.5**	P/B Ratio	**1.1**	52 Wk Hi-Low	**750.00-469.00**
Book Value	**86.4**	**87.2**	**88.4**	**1,022.7**	Yield %	**1.1**	Market Cap	**US$1,002.0mil**

Address	**3-2-5, Kasumigaseki**	Tel	**03-3592-7411**	ADR		President	**Morio Sonoda**
	Chiyoda-ku, Tokyo 100	Fax	**03-3593-0749**	SEDOL No.	**6899718**	Chairman	**Uzuhiko Uwatoko**

Toyo Exterior

Industry: **Building Materials**

Toyo Exterior, a subsidiary of Tostem, makes a wide variety of metal exterior home products. The firm controls large shares of the Japanese aluminum sash, gate, door, and fence markets. It also manufactures and sells carports, terraces, balconies, pipes, road signs, and garden products. The company's new carports (introduced in May 1994) are expected to do well, in part because they are one third less expensive than competing products. Toyo Exterior operates five factories and four distribution centers and has more than 60 sales agents throughout Japan.

¥bil	03/93	03/94	03/95	US$mil 03/95				
Sales	**57.6**	**55.1**	**59.4**	**602.4**	P/E Ratio	**37.9**	Price (9/30/95)	**2,260.00**
Net Income	**3.6**	**2.6**	**3.1**	**31.1**	P/B Ratio	**1.9**	52 Wk Hi-Low	**3,090.0-1,800.0**
Book Value	**55.4**	**57.5**	**59.9**	**693.5**	Yield %	**0.6**	Market Cap	**US$1,172.5mil**

Address	**1-4-12, Shinjuku**	Tel	**03-3354-3101**	ADR		President	**Hidenori Sugimoto**
	Shinjuku-ku, Tokyo 160	Fax	**03-3354-3069**	SEDOL No.	**6899730**	Chairman	**Kenjiro Ushioda**

Toyo Ink Mfg

Industry: **Specialty Chemicals**

Toyo Ink Manufacturing (Toyo Ink Seizo) is one of Japan's largest producers of printing ink, which accounts for about 47% of consolidated sales. The firm's products include inks for offset printing, color-newsprint ink, printing machines, synthetic resins, and adhesive tapes. Its R&D projects include the development and production of environmentally safe coatings and the development of recordable optical discs and other computer applications. Toyo Ink has nine domestic plants. The company has 42 consolidated subsidiaries in the United States, Europe, and Hong Kong.

¥bil	03/93	03/94	03/95	US$mil 03/95				
Sales	**225.2**	**216.6**	**234.7**	**2,379.2**	P/E Ratio	**36.2**	Price (9/30/95)	**547.00**
Net Income	**3.7**	**3.8**	**4.4**	**44.4**	P/B Ratio	**1.4**	52 Wk Hi-Low	**698.00-455.00**
Book Value	**110.4**	**111.4**	**114.8**	**1,328.6**	Yield %	**1.3**	Market Cap	**US$1,605.0mil**

Address	**2-3-13, Kyobashi**	Tel	**03-3272-5731**	ADR		President	**Mutsuo Nagashima**
	Chuo-ku, Tokyo 104	Fax	**03-3278-8688**	SEDOL No.	**6900104**	Chairman	--

Toyo Seikan Kaisha

Industry: **Containers & Packaging**

Toyo Seikan Kaisha manufactures containers, mainly for food and beverage use, and related machinery. The company produces food cans, decorative cans, plastic containers, 18-liter cans, and canning and bottling machines. It holds the leading share of the domestic market for food and beverage cans. Through its subsidiaries, the company manufactures paper containers, glass bottles, bottle caps, and other paper, machine, and oil products. Toyo Seikan has 13 consolidated and 27 unconsolidated subsidiaries, and 14 affiliates, including 17 production facilities throughout Japan.

¥bil	03/93	03/94	03/95	US$mil 03/95				
Sales	**770.0**	**755.0**	**779.2**	**7,897.9**	P/E Ratio	**19.9**	Price (9/30/95)	**3,090.00**
Net Income	**27.7**	**23.8**	**31.3**	**317.7**	P/B Ratio	**1.6**	52 Wk Hi-Low	**3,420.0-2,350.0**
Book Value	**337.8**	**359.8**	**393.9**	**4,559.4**	Yield %	**0.2**	Market Cap	**US$6,269.5mil**

Address **1-3-1, Uchi-Saiwaicho**
Chiyoda-ku, Tokyo 100
Tel **03-3508-2111**
Fax **N/A**
ADR
SEDOL No. **6900267**
President **Hirofumi Miki**
Chairman **Yoshiro Takasaki**

Toyo Suisan Kaisha

Industry: **Other Food**

Toyo Suisan is Japan's second-largest instant-noodle maker. The company produces both bagged and cupped noodles (including the Maru-chan brand). It is also a major producer, importer, and wholesaler of frozen and processed foods, including fish-paste products. It operates refrigerated warehouses throughout Japan. The firm has 17 consolidated subsidiaries, two of which (in Virginia and California) hold roughly one quarter of the U.S. instant-noodle market. Toyo Suisan'snoodles made in the United States are also exported to Western Europe, Russia, and Hungary.

¥bil	03/93	03/94	03/95	US$mil 03/95				
Sales	**208.3**	**219.9**	**244.0**	**2,473.5**	P/E Ratio	**25.8**	Price (9/30/95)	**1,040.00**
Net Income	**10.6**	**5.7**	**4.6**	**46.5**	P/B Ratio	**1.3**	52 Wk Hi-Low	**1,220.0-833.0**
Book Value	**79.0**	**85.3**	**88.8**	**1,027.9**	Yield %	**1.2**	Market Cap	**US$1,191.2mil**

Address **2-13-40, Konan**
Minato-ku, Tokyo 108
Tel **03-3458-5111**
Fax **N/A**
ADR
SEDOL No. **6899967**
President **Teruaki Hashimoto**
Chairman **Kazuo Mori**

Toyo Tire & Rubber

Industry: **Tires & Rubber**

Toyo Tire & Rubber (Toyo Gomu Kogyo) is a rubber-products manufacturer that specializes in tires for trucks and buses. Its other products include conveyor belts, rubber linings, reinforced plastic, chemical products, apparel, airbags, and waterproof sheets. The firm developed antivibration rubber for use in earthquake-resistant building foundations. Main customers include Toyota Motor and Mitsubishi. It also markets bedclothes under license from Minardi (Italy). Toyo Tire has technical tie-ups with Continental (Germany), General Tire (U.S.), and Yokohama Tire & Rubber.

¥bil	03/93	03/94	03/95	US$mil 03/95				
Sales	**275.4**	**255.4**	**249.9**	**2,533.3**	P/E Ratio	**77.6**	Price (9/30/95)	**396.00**
Net Income	**-0.5**	**-2.5**	**1.1**	**10.8**	P/B Ratio	**1.6**	52 Wk Hi-Low	**567.00-309.00**
Book Value	**56.4**	**52.6**	**53.0**	**613.7**	Yield %	**0.0**	Market Cap	**US$833.6mil**

Address **1-17-18, Edobori**
Nishi-ku, Osaka 550
Tel **06-441-8801**
Fax **06-441-1974**
ADR
SEDOL No. **6900182**
President **Shozo Katayama**
Chairman --

Toyo Trust & Banking

Industry: **Banks - Regional**

Toyo Trust & Banking (Toyo Shintaku Ginko), Japan's fifth-largest trust bank by assets, specializes in the security-transfer-agency business. The bank offers stock-transfer and registration services. It controls about 14% of all corporate-pension funds held by trust banks in Japan. Toyo is also involved in lending, investment-management services, corporate-agency services, real estate, and systems engineering. The firm has more than 60 branches in Japan. Its operations abroad include six wholly-owned subsidiaries in Hong Kong, London, Sydney, Zurich, New York, and Brussels.

¥bil	03/93	03/94	03/95	US$mil 03/95				
Revenues	**632.2**	**529.5**	**494.8**	**5,015.1**	P/E Ratio	**99.2**	Price (9/30/95)	**754.00**
Net Income	**11.9**	**5.4**	**6.0**	**60.5**	P/B Ratio	**1.2**	52 Wk Hi-Low	**1,150.0-700.0**
Book Value	**479.0**	**478.6**	**478.8**	**5,541.1**	Yield %	**0.9**	Market Cap	**US$5,960.6mil**

Address **1-4-3, Marunouchi**
Chiyoda-ku, Tokyo 100
Tel **03-3287-2211**
Fax **03-3201-3785**
ADR
SEDOL No. **6900472**
President **Nobuyoshi Takeuchi**
Chairman **Mitsuo Imose**

Toyobo

Industry: **Clothing & Fabrics**

Toyobo (Toyo Boseki) is a comprehensive textile manufacturer. It produces cotton, polyester, nylon, acrylic, and other synthetic fibers. The company also manufactures uniforms, household goods, and sportswear. Its nontextile products include films, resins, printing plates, electronic materials, biochemicals, medical instruments, and pharmaceuticals. Nontextile businesses account for about 40% of consolidated sales. Its main customers include Dainippon Printing, Mantsune, Toppan Printing, and Seiren. Toyobo has 21 factories, seven of which contain weaving facilities.

¥bil	03/93	03/94	03/95	US$mil 03/95				
Sales	**548.9**	**497.1**	**505.5**	**5,123.9**	P/E Ratio	**53.7**	Price (9/30/95)	**322.00**
Net Income	**4.3**	**0.4**	**4.1**	**41.9**	P/B Ratio	**2.0**	52 Wk Hi-Low	**438.00-270.00**
Book Value	**102.6**	**106.9**	**109.7**	**1,269.2**	Yield %	**1.6**	Market Cap	**US$2,238.0mil**

Address **2-2-8, Dojimahama**
Kita-ku, Osaka 530
Tel **06-348-3091**
Fax **06-348-3192**
ADR
SEDOL No. **6900502**
President **Minoru Shibata**
Chairman **Saburo Takizawa**

Toyoda Automatic Loom Works

Industry: **Factory Equipment**

Toyoda Automatic Loom Works (Toyoda Jidoshokki Seisakusho), a founding member of the Toyota group, holds equity stakes in several Toyota-group firms. Originally a maker of spinning and weaving machines, the the company's main activity is now automobile production. It assembles the Sprinter, Starlet, and Corolla models for Toyota, which owns nearly one-fourth of the company, and supplies Toyota-group firms with compressors for air conditioners. About 75% and 25% of its sales go to Toyota and Nippondenso, respectively. It holds the largest domestic market share in forklifts.

¥bil	03/93	03/94	03/95	US$mil 03/95				
Sales	**571.5**	**494.1**	**479.1**	**4,855.9**	P/E Ratio	**43.2**	Price (9/30/95)	**1,630.00**
Net Income	**15.4**	**10.7**	**10.6**	**107.8**	P/B Ratio	**1.8**	52 Wk Hi-Low	**2,050.0-1,410.0**
Book Value	**241.7**	**248.6**	**255.5**	**2,957.6**	Yield %	**0.8**	Market Cap	**US$4,624.8mil**

Address **2-1, Toyoda-cho, Kariya City, Aichi 448**
Tel **0566-22-2511** Fax **0566-23-3255**
ADR SEDOL No. **6900546**
President **Chisei Isogai**
Chairman **Yoshitoshi Toyoda**

Toyoda Machine Works

Industry: **Other Auto Parts**

Toyoda Machine Works (Toyoda Koki) manufactures auto parts and machine tools. The company sells most of its products to its affiliate, Toyota Motor; other customers include Nagoya Tech and Kawasaki Heavy Industries. It supplies automakers with specialized machine tools and power-steering systems; the latter constitutes the largest segment (72%) of parent-company sales. Toyoda has the largest Japanese market share in grinding machines. It also makes computer-integrated-manufacturing equipment. Toyoda has a wholly-owned machine tool manufacturer in France.

¥bil	03/93	03/94	03/95	US$mil 03/95				
Sales	**184.8**	**149.6**	**155.2**	**1,573.1**	P/E Ratio	**4.3**	Price (9/30/95)	**685.00**
Net Income	**-4.3**	**-2.1**	**20.3**	**205.8**	P/B Ratio	**0.9**	52 Wk Hi-Low	**895.00-547.00**
Book Value	**75.1**	**73.0**	**94.3**	**1,091.3**	Yield %	**0.9**	Market Cap	**US$875.6mil**

Address **1-1, Asahi-machi, Kariya City, Aichi 448**
Tel **0566-25-5198** Fax **0566-25-5470**
ADR SEDOL No. **6900568**
President **Toyo Kato**
Chairman **Tamotsu Arashima**

Toyota Motor

Industry: **Automobile Manufacturers**

Toyota Motor, Japan's largest automaker, ranks third worldwide in sales among car makers. The company makes a wide range of cars and trucks, including the Corolla, Corona, and Camry models. Its Lexus division produces luxury cars. In Japan, Toyota sells its cars through more than 5,000 outlets; the compay commands roughly 40% of the domestic passenger-car market. Toyota has 29 production companies in 26 countries, including two plants in the United Kingdom, which make passenger cars and engines, and a plant in Kentucky.

¥bil	06/93	06/94	03/95 *	US$mil 03/95				
Sales	**10,210.7**	**9,362.7**	**8,121.0**	**82,316.9**	P/E Ratio	**53.4**	Price (9/30/95)	**1,890.00**
Net Income	**176.5**	**125.8**	**132.0**	**1,337.5**	P/B Ratio	**1.4**	52 Wk Hi-Low	**2,140.0-1,600.0**
Book Value	**4,762.5**	**4,829.8**	**5,020.8**	**58,111.6**	Yield %	**0.8**	Market Cap	**US$71,063mil**

Address **1, Toyota-cho, Toyota City, Aichi 471**
Tel **0565-28-2121** Fax **0565-23-5708**
ADR **TOYOY** SEDOL No. **6900643**
President **Tatsuro Toyoda**
Chairman **Shoichiro Toyoda**

*Irregular period due to fiscal year change.

Toyota Tsusho

Industry: **Overseas Trading**

Toyota Tsusho is the principal trading company of the Toyota group. It markets automobiles for Toyota Motors; trades in steel, nonferrous metals, vehicles, machinery, fuel, and fibers; and offers distribution, telecommunication, insurance, and real-estate services. The vast majority of the firm's business involves the Toyota group. Toyota group companies hold a 32.7% stake in Toyota Tsusho. Among its other major customers are Nippondenso, Koyo Seiko, Kanto Auto Works, and Aisin Seiki. It has 23 consolidated subsidiaries in Japan, the U.S., and Europe.

¥bil	03/93	03/94	03/95	US$mil 03/95				
Sales	**2,046.1**	**1,705.6**	**1,642.5**	**16,648.4**	P/E Ratio	**103.3**	Price (9/30/95)	**630.00**
Net Income	**6.1**	**2.2**	**1.6**	**15.7**	P/B Ratio	**1.2**	52 Wk Hi-Low	**793.00-495.00**
Book Value	**131.8**	**131.8**	**134.7**	**1,559.0**	Yield %	**1.2**	Market Cap	**US$1,604.5mil**

Address **4-7-23, Meieki, Nakamura-ku, Nagoya 450**
Tel **052-584-5432** Fax **052-584-5663**
ADR SEDOL No. **6900580**
President **Eizo Takeyama**
Chairman **Keiji Nogami**

Tsubakimoto Chain

Industry: **Factory Equipment**

Tsubakimoto Chain is Japan's largest producer of industrial chains, based on market share. Chains and transmission equipment account for about 77% of sales. The company also makes materials-handling systems, including conveyors and sorting and packaging equipment. It supplies the automobile, machine-tool, electronics, apparel, newspaper, paper and pulp, and multilevel auto-parking industries. Tsubakimoto Chain has four plants and 17 sales offices in Japan. It has consolidated subsidiaries in the U.S., Canada, China, Singapore, the Netherlands, and the U.K.

¥bil	03/93	03/94	03/95	US$mil 03/95				
Sales	**120.9**	**109.0**	**101.7**	**1,030.6**	P/E Ratio	**NMF**	Price (9/30/95)	**501.00**
Net Income	**2.5**	**1.1**	**-0.6**	**-6.4**	P/B Ratio	**1.6**	52 Wk Hi-Low	**595.00-368.00**
Book Value	**63.1**	**62.4**	**60.8**	**703.3**	Yield %	**1.2**	Market Cap	**US$969.4mil**

Address **4-17-96, Tsurumi, Tsurumi-ku, Osaka 538**
Tel **06-911-1221** Fax **06-913-0505**
ADR SEDOL No. **6906704**
President **Michio Noguchi**
Chairman **--**

Ube Industries

Industry: **Commodity Chemicals**

Ube Industries (Ube Kosan) is Japan's third-largest integrated chemical manufacturer by sales. The company manufactures chemical products, machinery, cement, and coal, and provides plant-engineering services. It supplies the auto industry with polypropylene composites and die-casting machines used in the manufacture of panels and bumpers. Ube also supplies materials to semiconductor makers, and intermediate materials to pharmaceutical manufacturers. The company's domestic network consists of 11 factories and plants. It has 79 consolidated subsidiaries.

	¥bil 03/93	03/94	03/95	US$mil 03/95				
Sales	**646.7**	**585.5**	**613.6**	**6,219.9**	P/E Ratio	**NMF**	Price (9/30/95)	**335.00**
Net Income	**-2.8**	**-3.9**	**-3.2**	**-32.0**	P/B Ratio	**3.8**	52 Wk Hi-Low	**430.00-275.00**
Book Value	**85.5**	**81.6**	**74.7**	**864.2**	Yield %	**0.0**	Market Cap	**US$2,823.2mil**

Address	**1-12-32, Nishi-Honmachi**	Tel	**03-5460-3207**	ADR		President	**Maomi Nagahiro**
	Ube City, Yamaguchi 755	Fax	**03-5460-3390**	SEDOL No.	**6910705**	Chairman	**Motoo Nagahigashi**

Unitika

Industry: **Clothing & Fabrics**

Unitika, a member of the Sanwa group, is a leading textile manufacturer that is also involved in the chemical, engineering, and real-estate businesses. Its major products include cotton, wool, nylon, rayon, polyester, and polyvinyl alcohol. The firm makes apparel, carpets, fiberglass, and resins, and nylon, polyester, and vinylon film. It also produces environmental equipment such as waste-disposal systems and water-drainage facilities. Its major customers include Takisada, Fuji Jigyo, and Itochu. Unitika has nine main factories and 53 consolidated subsidiaries in Japan.

	¥bil 03/93	03/94	03/95	US$mil 03/95				
Sales	**343.8**	**328.2**	**352.0**	**3,568.2**	P/E Ratio	**NMF**	Price (9/30/95)	**264.00**
Net Income	**0.6**	**-6.9**	**-8.0**	**-81.4**	P/B Ratio	**5.3**	52 Wk Hi-Low	**395.00-215.00**
Book Value	**40.5**	**31.9**	**23.6**	**272.9**	Yield %	**0.0**	Market Cap	**US$1,263.9mil**

Address	**4-1-3, Kyutaromachi**	Tel	**06-281-5232**	ADR		President	**Keita Taguchi**
	Chuo-ku, Osaka 541	Fax	**06-281-5697**	SEDOL No.	**6918301**	Chairman	--

Uny

Industry: **Retailers - Broadline**

Uny is a leading operator of supermarkets and superstores, with most of its stores in the Osaka and Nagoya areas. The company's stores include 82 Uny superstores, 15 Sun Terrace shopping centers, 18 Apita superstores, and other more-specialized outlets. Uny's superstores carry a full line of merchandise including food, clothing, and household goods. The company has 15 consolidated subsidiaries, including Sagami (a kimono retailer with more than 250 outlets), Circle K (with nearly 1,300 convenience stores), U Store (a supermarket chain), and a superstore in Hong Kong.

	¥bil 02/93	02/94	02/95	US$mil 02/95				
Revenues	**804.4**	**824.5**	**871.0**	**8,691.4**	P/E Ratio	**26.0**	Price (9/30/95)	**1,610.00**
Net Income	**8.3**	**-0.2**	**11.7**	**117.0**	P/B Ratio	**1.7**	52 Wk Hi-Low	**1,660.0-1,310.0**
Book Value	**175.3**	**172.0**	**182.0**	**1,882.3**	Yield %	**0.7**	Market Cap	**US$3,065.4mil**

Address	**1, Amaike-Gotandacho**	Tel	**0587-24-8009**	ADR		President	**Michio Ieda**
	Inazawa City, Aichi 492	Fax	**0587-24-8024**	SEDOL No.	**6918624**	Chairman	**Toshio Nishikawa**

Ushio

Industry: **Industrial Technology**

Ushio (Ushio Denki), a maker of industrial- and commercial-lighting equipment, specializes in the production of halogen and xenon lamps. Bulb manufacturing accounts for almost 64% of revenues. It supplies lighting equipment to the automotive, audiovisual, semiconductor, office-automation, health, and fishery industries. It also makes optical equipment for semiconductor production. Ushio has overseas plants in Hong Kong, Taiwan, Germany, the Netherlands, and the United States. Ushio is among the firms that are financing Motorola's Iridium satellite-communications project.

	¥bil 03/93	03/94	03/95	US$mil 03/95				
Sales	**49.4**	**49.0**	**55.2**	**559.2**	P/E Ratio	**42.1**	Price (9/30/95)	**1,100.00**
Net Income	**1.2**	**1.5**	**3.6**	**36.9**	P/B Ratio	**2.5**	52 Wk Hi-Low	**1,160.0-781.0**
Book Value	**59.0**	**59.4**	**61.1**	**707.3**	Yield %	**0.8**	Market Cap	**US$1,544.9mil**

Address	**2-6-1, Otemachi**	Tel	**03-3242-1811**	ADR		President	**Akihiro Tanaka**
	Chiyoda-ku, Tokyo 100	Fax	**03-3245-0589**	SEDOL No.	**6918981**	Chairman	**Jiro Ushio**

Victor Company of Japan

Industry: **Consumer Electronics**

Victor Company of Japan (JVC), a member of the Matsushita group, manufactures VCRs and other audiovisual equipment. JVC's consumer products include camcorders, hi-fidelity stereos, compact-disc players, cassette decks, wide-screen televisions, and car-audio equipment. Its nonconsumer product line includes professional audiovisual equipment, computer monitors, electronic news-gathering services, closed-circuit television, and compression technology. About 53% of JVC's revenues come from overseas. JVC has subsidiaries and affiliates throughout Europe, Asia, and the U.S.

	¥bil 03/93	03/94	03/95	US$mil 03/95				
Sales	**768.9**	**726.5**	**767.2**	**7,776.8**	P/E Ratio	**NMF**	Price (9/30/95)	**1,010.00**
Net Income	**-43.1**	**-19.6**	**0.6**	**6.0**	P/B Ratio	**1.1**	52 Wk Hi-Low	**1,470.0-838.0**
Book Value	**264.5**	**241.7**	**242.7**	**2,809.5**	Yield %	**0.0**	Market Cap	**US$2,582.3mil**

Address	**3-12, Moriya-cho**	Tel	**045-450-1561**	ADR	**VJAPY**	President	**Takeo Shuzui**
	Kanagawa-ku, Yokohama 221	Fax	**N/A**	SEDOL No.	**6929109**	Chairman	--

Wacoal

Industry: **Clothing & Fabrics**

Wacoal is the world's largest manufacturer of women's underwear and lingerie. It also makes cosmetics and interior-decoration goods. In 1994, 89% of parent-company sales came from lingerie and sleepwear. Wacoal sells 40% of its merchandise through department stores. It has the largest market share of lingerie in Asia. Wacoal has manufacturing subsidiaries in North America, Asia, and Europe. In the U.S., Wacoal markets its lingerie under the Wacoal, Parfage, and Donna Karan Intimates brands. Less than 10% of the company's revenues come from overseas.

	¥bil 03/93	03/94	03/95	US$mil 03/95				
Sales	**153.6**	**150.8**	**153.2**	**1,552.6**	P/E Ratio	**27.6**	Price (9/30/95)	**1,200.00**
Net Income	**6.7**	**7.2**	**6.7**	**67.8**	P/B Ratio	**1.4**	52 Wk Hi-Low	**1,220.0-948.0**
Book Value	**127.3**	**131.7**	**135.6**	**1,569.1**	Yield %	**1.1**	Market Cap	**US$1,860.2mil**

Address	**29, Nakajima, Kisshoin**	Tel	**075-682-1017**	ADR	**WACLY**	President	**Yoshikata Tsukamoto**
	Minami-ku, Kyoto 601	Fax	**075-682-1199**	SEDOL No.	**6932204**	Chairman	**Koichi Tsukamoto**

Yakult Honsha

Industry: **Other Food**

Yakult Honsha is a beverage manufacturer specializing in fermented milk products. It also makes pharmaceuticals and cosmetics, such as skin-care and hair-care products and perfumes. Yakult distributes products through 162 sales companies, vending machines, and a sales network of 58,000 Yakult Ladies who deliver fermented milk beverages and 33,000 Yakult Beauties who sell cosmetics door-to-door. The company has 52 subsidiaries in Japan and abroad, including Taiwan, Thailand, South Korea, the Philippines, Singapore, Hong Kong, and Mexico.

	¥bil 03/93	03/94	03/95	US$mil 03/95				
Sales	**178.2**	**190.4**	**198.5**	**2,012.4**	P/E Ratio	**22.3**	Price (9/30/95)	**1,230.00**
Net Income	**9.8**	**9.0**	**9.7**	**98.1**	P/B Ratio	**1.2**	52 Wk Hi-Low	**1,670.0-1,150.0**
Book Value	**172.3**	**179.3**	**187.3**	**2,167.7**	Yield %	**1.2**	Market Cap	**US$2,176.3mil**

Address	**1-1-19, Higashi-Shinbashi**	Tel	**03-3574-8960**	ADR		President	**Jun Kuwahara**
	Minato-ku, Tokyo 105	Fax	**03-3574-7253**	SEDOL No.	**6985112**	Chairman	--

Yamaguchi Bank

Industry: **Banks - Regional**

Yamaguchi Bank (Yamaguchi Ginko) is a medium-size regional bank and the only regional bank in Yamaguchi Prefecture. Small- and medium-size companies account for more than 50% of its loans. The bank has been underwriting public bonds since 1983 and has expanded its securities operations to include trading in bond options and futures. In addition to 159 domestic branches, it has branches in South Korea, Hong Kong, and China, as well as offices in Bangkok, Jakarta, and China. It is a member of a correspondent-banking network of 162 banks in 65 countries.

	¥bil 03/93 P	03/94 P	03/95 P	US$mil 03/95				
Revenues	**209.8**	**184.7**	**179.5**	**1,819.6**	P/E Ratio	**33.9**	Price (9/30/95)	**1,700.00**
Net Income	**11.7**	**11.5**	**10.0**	**101.5**	P/B Ratio	**1.7**	52 Wk Hi-Low	**1,840.0-1,500.0**
Book Value	**184.6**	**194.8**	**203.4**	**2,354.0**	Yield %	**0.4**	Market Cap	**US$3,419.8mil**

Address	**4-2-36, Takezaki-cho**	Tel	**0832-23-3411**	ADR		President	**Kozo Tanaka**
	Shimonoseki, Yamaguchi 750	Fax	**0832-33-5850**	SEDOL No.	**6985219**	Chairman	**Hikaru Imura**

P=Parent company data.

Yamaha

Industry: **Other Recreational Products & Services**

Yamaha is the world's largest maker of musical instruments and controls nearly 50% of the piano market in Japan. Its other products include electronic instruments, audio and audiovisual equipment, sporting goods, household furnishings, and electronic parts and equipment, such as magnetic heads for use in computer disk drives. Yamaha has a network of nine domestic factories and 16 factories overseas. The firm has 58 consolidated subsidiaries and 31 unconsolidated subsidiaries based throughout the world. In 1994, 30.5% of its sales were made overseas.

	¥bil 03/93	03/94	03/95	US$mil 03/95				
Sales	**483.5**	**445.6**	**482.6**	**4,891.3**	P/E Ratio	**53.8**	Price (9/30/95)	**1,480.00**
Net Income	**1.8**	**-4.0**	**5.3**	**54.1**	P/B Ratio	**1.8**	52 Wk Hi-Low	**1,500.0-925.0**
Book Value	**162.1**	**154.7**	**157.2**	**1,819.9**	Yield %	**0.4**	Market Cap	**US$2,889.1mil**

Address	**10-1, Nakazawa-machi**	Tel	**053-460-2141**	ADR		President	**Seisuke Ueshima**
	Hamamatsu City, Shizuoka 430	Fax	**053-464-8554**	SEDOL No.	**6642387**	Chairman	--

Yamaha Motor

Industry: **Other Recreational Products & Services**

Yamaha Motor (Yamaha Hatsudoki) manufactures motorcycles, boats, and outboard motors. It is second only to Honda in worldwide motorcycle sales. Yamaha also makes marine engines and produces car engines for Toyota and Ford; it also produces small engines for golf carts, snowplows, and lawn mowers. More than 65% of Yamaha's total sales are exports; about 70% of its motorcycles are sold abroad. Its overseas operations include manufacturing bases in Southeast Asia, the U.S., Brazil, France, Italy, Spain, Sweden, and India, and a joint venture to supply motorcycles in China.

	¥bil 03/93	03/94	03/95	US$mil 03/95				
Sales	**676.8**	**652.8**	**666.3**	**6,753.5**	P/E Ratio	**45.4**	Price (9/30/95)	**795.00**
Net Income	**6.1**	**2.6**	**4.0**	**40.9**	P/B Ratio	**1.8**	52 Wk Hi-Low	**949.00-582.00**
Book Value	**101.6**	**100.2**	**99.6**	**1,152.8**	Yield %	**0.8**	Market Cap	**US$1,842.3mil**

Address	**2500, Shingai**	Tel	**0538-32-1115**	ADR		President	**Takehiko Hasegawa**
	Iwata City, Shizuoka 438	Fax	**0538-37-4252**	SEDOL No.	**6985264**	Chairman	**Hideto Eguchi**

Yamaichi Securities

Industry: **Securities Brokers**

Yamaichi Securities (Yamaichi Shoken) is the third-largest of Japan's Big Four securities houses by asset size. It provides services in capital markets, mergers and acquisitions, asset management, financial technology, information services, and other banking activities. The company is traditionally strong in bond and equity underwriting, both domestic and international. The company is also a primary dealer in U.S. Treasury securities. Yamaichi has 118 domestic branches and 31 overseas offices. Most of its subsidiaries are involved in securities trading.

¥bil	03/93	03/94	03/95	US$mil 03/95				
Sales	**267.8**	**280.2**	**198.2**	**2,009.0**	P/E Ratio	**NMF**	Price (9/30/95)	**561.00**
Net Income	**-42.3**	**14.1**	**-70.7**	**-717.1**	P/B Ratio	**1.1**	52 Wk Hi-Low	**796.00-446.00**
Book Value	**686.3**	**691.4**	**613.8**	**7,104.0**	Yield %	**0.5**	Market Cap	**US$6,820.1mil**

Address **2-4-1, Yaesu, Chuo-ku, Tokyo 104** Tel **03-3276-3181** Fax **03-3276-3930** ADR **YAMAY** SEDOL No. **6985305** President **Atsuo Miki** Chairman **Tsugio Yukihira**

Yamamura Glass

Industry: **Containers & Packaging**

Yamamura Glass is a leading manufacturer of glass containers in Japan. The company's mainstays are glass bottles for beverages such as beer and milk, seasonings, and pharmaceuticals. These products accounted for 77% of its sales in fiscal year 1994. Additionally, the firm is expanding its involvement in the production of plastic bottles such as PET bottles and metal cans such as soft-drink cans. Yamamura Glass recently started new operations in the pharmaceutical and real-estate industries. The company has seven subsidiaries and eight affiliates in Japan.

¥bil	03/93	03/94	03/95	US$mil 03/95				
Sales	**77.3**	**76.3**	**82.6**	**837.6**	P/E Ratio	**28.1**	Price (9/30/95)	**612.00**
Net Income	**2.8**	**3.4**	**2.6**	**26.8**	P/B Ratio	**1.3**	52 Wk Hi-Low	**655.00-524.00**
Book Value	**53.9**	**56.5**	**58.9**	**682.2**	Yield %	**1.1**	Market Cap	**US$746.1mil**

Address **2-21, Hamamatsubara-cho, Nishinomiya City, Hyogo 662** Tel **0798-32-2300** Fax **0798-36-0725** ADR SEDOL No. **6985349** President **Takeshi Yamamura** Chairman --

Yamanouchi Pharm

Industry: **Pharmaceuticals**

Yamanouchi Pharmaceutical (Yamanouchi Seiyaku) manufactures circulatory and digestive drugs. Major drugs developed in-house include Gaster, an antiulcer drug, and the hypertension agent Perdipine. Pharmaceuticals account for more than 80% of the firm's sales. Another major line is nutritional products. Yamanouchi owns nutritional-product makers Shaklee (U.S.) and Shaklee Japan, as well as the pharmaceutical division of Royal Gistbrocades (the Netherlands). It holds 28% equity stake in Roberts Pharmaceutical (U.S.). One of its main customers is Kuraya Pharmaceutical.

¥bil	03/93	03/94	03/95	US$mil 03/95				
Sales	**357.5**	**368.7**	**384.3**	**3,895.6**	P/E Ratio	**17.4**	Price (9/30/95)	**2,140.00**
Net Income	**30.1**	**34.8**	**39.7**	**402.6**	P/B Ratio	**1.7**	52 Wk Hi-Low	**2,150.0-1,840.0**
Book Value	**347.4**	**376.2**	**411.0**	**4,756.6**	Yield %	**1.0**	Market Cap	**US$6,959.8mil**

Address **2-3-11, Nihonbashi-Honcho, Chuo-ku, Tokyo 103** Tel **03-3244-3087** Fax **03-3244-3054** ADR SEDOL No. **6985383** President **Masayoshi Onoda** Chairman **Shigeo Morioka**

Yamatake-Honeywell

Industry: **Industrial Technology**

Yamatake-Honeywell manufactures industrial-process-automation equipment. The company is the largest Japanese manufacturer of building-automation systems, including air-conditioning controls, security systems, and fire-alarm systems. It also makes sensors and control products such as programmable and combustion controllers. The firm's products are used in building maintenance, semiconductor manufacturing, food processing, environmental protection, supermarket operations, and industrial automation. Yamatake-Honeywell is 24.2% owned by Honeywell (U.S.).

¥bil	09/92	09/93	09/94	US$mil 09/94				
Sales	**196.7**	**196.8**	**178.7**	**1,710.7**	P/E Ratio	**20.5**	Price (9/30/95)	**1,380.00**
Net Income	**6.3**	**7.2**	**5.7**	**54.2**	P/B Ratio	**1.4**	52 Wk Hi-Low	**1,600.0-1,080.0**
Book Value	**74.0**	**80.4**	**85.0**	**859.3**	Yield %	**0.8**	Market Cap	**US$1,166.0mil**

Address **2-12-19, Shibuya, Shibuya-ku, Tokyo 150** Tel **03-3486-2031** Fax **03-3409-7388** ADR SEDOL No. **6985543** President **Ichiro Ido** Chairman --

Yamato Transport

Industry: **Trucking**

Yamato Transport (Yamato Unyu) is one of Japan's largest trucking firms. It specializes in door-to-door delivery, which accounts for more than 80% of total sales. Its operations include night, express, and moving services, and luggage transport to and from the New Tokyo International Airport. The firm is active in air-cargo and marine transport, and provides international service in cooperation with United Parcel Service (U.S.). It has 11 consolidated subsidiaries, three of which are based in the U.S., to handle transport and customs-brokerage services.

¥bil	03/93	03/94	03/95	US$mil 03/95				
Sales	**541.0**	**564.8**	**604.0**	**6,121.9**	P/E Ratio	**41.3**	Price (9/30/95)	**1,120.00**
Net Income	**7.9**	**9.3**	**10.8**	**109.2**	P/B Ratio	**2.1**	52 Wk Hi-Low	**1,145.3-899.9**
Book Value	**151.3**	**179.6**	**192.2**	**2,224.7**	Yield %	**0.9**	Market Cap	**US$4,103.7mil**

Address **2-16-10, Ginza, Chuo-ku, Tokyo 104** Tel **03-3541-3411** Fax **03-3542-3887** ADR SEDOL No. **6985565** President **Koji Miyauchi** Chairman **Takuo? Kanetani**

Yamazaki Baking

Industry: **Other Food**

Yamazaki Baking is Japan's leading baker, with a 30% share of the market for bread. The firm distributes breads, pastries, and confections through retail outlets throughout Japan. It has three consolidated subsidiaries: wholly-owned Delica, a baker and marketer; wholly-owned convenience-store chain Sunshop Yamazaki; and partially-owned Yamazaki Nabisco, which markets Nabisco cookies and snacks. The firm has 22 plants in Japan and bakeries in France, Australia, Taiwan, Hong Kong, Thailand, and the U.S. Yamazaki bought U.S.-based Vie de France's restaurant chain in 1994.

¥bil	12/92	12/93	12/94	US$mil 12/94				
Sales	**582.9**	**607.7**	**623.3**	**6,107.9**	P/E Ratio	**27.9**	Price (9/30/95)	**1,810.00**
Net Income	**13.5**	**14.9**	**14.3**	**140.0**	P/B Ratio	**2.1**	52 Wk Hi-Low	**2,040.0-1,510.0**
Book Value	**170.2**	**182.3**	**193.8**	**1,942.7**	Yield %	**0.7**	Market Cap	**US$4,010.4mil**

Address **3-2-4, Iwamoto-cho**
Chiyoda-ku, Tokyo 101
Tel **03-3864-3171**
Fax **N/A**
ADR
SEDOL No. **6985509**
President **Nobuhiro Iijima**
Chairman --

Yaskawa Electric

Industry: **Factory Equipment**

Yaskawa Electric (Yasukawa Denki) manufactures electrical motors and their controllers for industrial use, and also offers systems-engineering services. The company produces industrial-automation products, including servomotors, programmable controllers, industrial robots, and other components for factory-automation systems. Its major customers include Yaskawa Shoji, Nissho Iwai, Nittetsu Shoji, Chuo Koki Sangyo, and Koyo Denki Industries. Yaskawa Electric operates four plants and has 13 consolidated subsidiaries in Japan and one in the U.S.

¥bil	03/93	03/94	03/95 *	US$mil 03/95				
Sales	**194.3**	**185.4**	**185.7**	**1,882.4**	P/E Ratio	**NMF**	Price (9/30/95)	**449.00**
Net Income	**-7.5**	**-3.8**	**-1.8**	**-18.4**	P/B Ratio	**2.7**	52 Wk Hi-Low	**573.00-319.00**
Book Value	**43.9**	**40.1**	**38.2**	**441.7**	Yield %	**0.0**	Market Cap	**US$1,038.0mil**

Address **2-1, Kurosaki-shiroishi**
Yahata-Nishiku, Kitakyushu 806
Tel **093-645-8800**
Fax **093-631-8837**
ADR
SEDOL No. **6986041**
President **Ko Kikuchi**
Chairman --

*Irregular period due to fiscal year change.

Yasuda Fire & Marine Insurance

Industry: **Insurance - Property & Casualty**

Yasuda Fire & Marine Insurance (Yasuda Kasai Kaijo Hoken), a member of the Fuyo group, is Japan's second-largest property and casualty insurer, handling about 30 million policies annually. Its products include fire, marine, personal-accident, voluntary auto, workers' compensation, property, transport, fidelity, theft, and construction-works policies, plus a new long-term comprehensive insurance with maturity refund. It has more than 500 branch and subbranch offices in Japan. The firm's worldwide network has its head offices in London, New York, Sao Paulo, and Singapore.

¥bil	03/93	03/94	03/95	US$mil 03/95				
Revenues	**768.9**	**852.1**	**1,273.4**	**12,907.1**	P/E Ratio	**52.9**	Price (9/30/95)	**640.00**
Net Income	**14.1**	**12.2**	**10.7**	**108.9**	P/B Ratio	**2.3**	52 Wk Hi-Low	**756.00-526.00**
Book Value	**232.9**	**238.8**	**243.7**	**2,821.1**	Yield %	**1.1**	Market Cap	**US$5,717.2mil**

Address **1-26-1, Nishi-Shinjuku**
Shinjuku-ku, Tokyo 160
Tel **03-3349-3111**
Fax **03-3349-4697**
ADR
SEDOL No. **6986063**
President **Koichi Ariyoshi**
Chairman **Yasuo Goto**

Yasuda Trust & Banking

Industry: **Banks - Regional**

Yasuda Trust & Banking is Japan's fourth-largest trust bank by assets. It is the trustee for more than 17% of all assets in securities-investment trusts in Japan. The financial and services sectors account for the largest portions of Yasuda's loan portfolio. The bank has 58 branches in Japan and eight overseas. It is currently establishing an aircraft-financing company with six European government-affiliated financial institutions. Yasuda controls 13 consolidated subsidiaries, the largest of which is Yasuda Trust and Banking (Switzerland).

¥bil	03/93	03/94	03/95	US$mil 03/95				
Revenues	**815.1**	**739.7**	**728.2**	**7,381.5**	P/E Ratio	**141.2**	Price (9/30/95)	**579.00**
Net Income	**8.6**	**3.9**	**4.6**	**46.2**	P/B Ratio	**1.2**	52 Wk Hi-Low	**885.00-534.00**
Book Value	**556.6**	**552.8**	**549.9**	**6,364.4**	Yield %	**1.2**	Market Cap	**US$6,424.8mil**

Address **1-2-1, Yaesu**
Chuo-ku, Tokyo 103
Tel **03-3278-8111**
Fax **03-3274-4670**
ADR
SEDOL No. **6986085**
President **Masami Tachikawa**
Chairman **Fujio Takayama**

Yodogawa Steel Works

Industry: **Steel**

Yodogawa Steel Works (Yodogawa Seikosho) is a major Japanese manufacturer of surface-treated steel plates. Its products include steel sheets and plates, construction materials, rolled-cast steel, steel ingots, and cast products, with an emphasis on finished products such as sheds and zinc-coated steel plates. Parcel-delivery lockers and stainless-steel billets are among its newest products. Yodogawa operates five factories, including a new facility in Fukui Prefecture, which produces home products. It also has equity participation in a rolled-steel manufacturer in Taiwan.

¥bil	03/93	03/94	03/95	US$mil 03/95				
Sales	**168.1**	**148.7**	**168.3**	**1,706.2**	P/E Ratio	**29.3**	Price (9/30/95)	**796.00**
Net Income	**5.6**	**4.4**	**5.7**	**57.8**	P/B Ratio	**1.4**	52 Wk Hi-Low	**860.00-640.00**
Book Value	**109.0**	**112.0**	**118.4**	**1,370.6**	Yield %	**0.9**	Market Cap	**US$1,694.1mil**

Address **4-1-1, Minami-Honmachi**
Chuo-ku, Osaka 541
Tel **06-245-1113**
Fax **06-282-0541**
ADR
SEDOL No. **6986364**
President **Tosuke Shibata**
Chairman **Masao Ohmori**

Yokogawa Electric

Industry: **Industrial Technology**

Yokogawa Electric (Yokogawa Denki) manufactures factory-control systems such as test and measuring equipment, analytical instruments, system controllers, and information-processing equipment. Its products are used in the steel, chemical, oil, automobile, and pharmaceutical industries. Major customers of the parent company include Yokogawa Shoji, Shingawa Denki, Nishigawa Keisoku, and Tokyo Denki Sangyo. The company is involved in joint ventures with General Electric, Hewlett-Packard, and Johnson Controls. In 1994, 22.5% of its consolidated sales were made overseas.

¥bil	03/93	03/94	03/95	US$mil 03/95				
Sales	**247.0**	**242.2**	**242.9**	**2,462.2**	P/E Ratio	**95.2**	Price (9/30/95)	**885.00**
Net Income	**1.7**	**0.9**	**2.4**	**24.6**	P/B Ratio	**1.3**	52 Wk Hi-Low	**1,120.0-582.0**
Book Value	**176.6**	**175.0**	**176.8**	**2,046.2**	Yield %	**0.8**	Market Cap	**US$2,308.2mil**

Address **2-9-32, Nakamachi**
Musashino City, Tokyo 180
Tel **0422-52-5555**
Fax **0422-52-9803**
ADR
SEDOL No. **6986427**
President **Eiji Mikawa**
Chairman **Takashi Yamanaka**

Yokohama Rubber

Industry: **Tires & Rubber**

Yokohama Rubber (Yokohama Gomu), a member of Furukawa group, is Japan's second-largest automobile-tire maker by sales volume. The firm also makes industrial products, sporting equipment, and airplane parts. Its main customers include Mitsubishi Motors and Fuji Heavy Industries. Yokohama's high-performance tires are standard on Acura's NSX sports car and on Porsche's production line. The firm has technical-cooperation agreements with Aeroquip (Switzerland), Courtaulds Aerospace (U.S.), Continental (Germany), and Toyo Tire & Rubber (Japan).

¥bil	12/92	12/93	12/94	US$mil 12/94				
Sales	**432.3**	**400.2**	**379.4**	**3,717.2**	P/E Ratio	**85.7**	Price (9/30/95)	**583.00**
Net Income	**4.8**	**-0.2**	**2.1**	**20.5**	P/B Ratio	**1.8**	52 Wk Hi-Low	**687.00-440.00**
Book Value	**88.3**	**87.7**	**96.7**	**968.9**	Yield %	**1.3**	Market Cap	**US$1,856.9mil**

Address **5-36-11, Shinbashi**
Minato-ku, Tokyo 105
Tel **03-5400-4518**
Fax **03-3432-5616**
ADR
SEDOL No. **6986461**
President **Seiji Hagiwara**
Chairman **Kazuo Motoyama**

York-Benimaru

Industry: **Food Retailers & Wholesalers**

York-Benimaru, an Ito-Yokado affiliate, is the Tohoku region's largest supermarket chain. Its network includes 62 stores and 14 Denny's restaurant franchises. The firm owns exclusive franchise rights to Denny's in Fukushima Prefecture. It opened four supermarkets and one Denny's during 1994. Foodstuffs account for more than half of the company's sales. Other lines include clothing and household utensils. The firm also derives revenues by renting its real-estate holdings. To bolster name recognition and reduce transportation costs, the firm concentrates stores in limited areas.

¥bil	02/93	02/94	02/95	US$mil 02/95				
Sales	**210.3**	**240.4**	**263.1**	**2,625.3**	P/E Ratio	**24.2**	Price (9/30/95)	**3,340.00**
Net Income	**5.7**	**6.1**	**6.9**	**69.3**	P/B Ratio	**2.7**	52 Wk Hi-Low	**4,390.0-2,980.0**
Book Value	**51.6**	**56.3**	**61.8**	**639.2**	Yield %	**0.8**	Market Cap	**US$1,687.5mil**

Address **2-18-2, Asahi**
Koriyama City, Fukushima 963
Tel **0249-24-3211**
Fax **0249-25-3439**
ADR
SEDOL No. **6986955**
President **Zenjiro Ohtaka**
Chairman **Hiroei Masukawa**

Yuasa

Industry: **Other Auto Parts**

Yuasa is a battery manufacturer that specializes in automobile and industrial-use batteries. It holds the largest domestic share of the market for motorcycle batteries and ranks among the top three Japanese companies in the production of automobile batteries. Yuasa also supplies industrial-use batteries and power sources for electric cars, office-automation equipment, and computers. Its major customers include Kansai Yuasa Battery, Toshiba Battery, and Kyusyu Yuasa Battery Sales. Yuasa has 32 subsidiaries, including two manufacturing company in Europe and a plant in U.S.

¥bil	03/93	03/94	03/95	US$mil 03/95				
Sales	**124.9**	**134.5**	**137.5**	**1,393.6**	P/E Ratio	**NMF**	Price (9/30/95)	**531.00**
Net Income	**1.7**	**1.3**	**0.5**	**5.1**	P/B Ratio	**2.6**	52 Wk Hi-Low	**667.00-376.00**
Book Value	**37.4**	**37.6**	**36.5**	**422.9**	Yield %	**0.8**	Market Cap	**US$946.3mil**

Address **6-6, Josai-cho**
Takatsuki City, Osaka 569
Tel **0726-61-9811**
Fax **0726-61-9814**
ADR
SEDOL No. **6988508**
President **Teruhisa Yuasa**
Chairman **Kiyoshi Sekiguchi**

Yurtec

Industry: **Electrical Components & Equipment**

Yurtec is an electrical contractor that installs indoor wiring, air conditioners, and plumbing. The firm also constructs power-distribution lines and power-transmission and -transformation lines. Orders to Tohoku Electric Power, of which it is a subsidiary, account for about 50% of total parent sales. It has branch offices in Osaka and Tokyo and has been active in Africa, Southeast Asia, and the Middle East. It has 11 subsidiaries, including two domestic subsidiaries: New Lease leases machines and vehicles and Tokusu installs outdoor wiring and sells electrical materials.

¥bil	03/93	03/94	03/95	US$mil 03/95				
Sales	**190.8**	**208.6**	**229.9**	**2,330.8**	P/E Ratio	**14.0**	Price (9/30/95)	**2,050.00**
Net Income	**7.5**	**7.7**	**8.6**	**86.8**	P/B Ratio	**1.9**	52 Wk Hi-Low	**2,238.1-1,600.0**
Book Value	**48.6**	**55.7**	**63.8**	**738.3**	Yield %	**0.5**	Market Cap	**US$1,261.2mil**

Address **4-1-1, Tsutsujigaoka**
Miyagino-ku, Sendai, Miyagi 980
Tel **022-296-2111**
Fax **022-296-2121**
ADR
SEDOL No. **6894672**
President **Hiroshi Nakazawa**
Chairman **Tojiro Kinoshita**

Zexel

Industry: **Other Auto Parts**

Zexel is Japan's leading maker of fuel-injection pumps for diesel engines and of air conditioners for automobiles. The company's other products include emission-control systems, diesel starters, turbocharge-control systems, hydraulic equipment, remote valve-control systems, and differential torque systems. Zexel is an affiliate of Isuzu Motors and has close ties with Nissan Motor. It has consolidated subsidiaries overseas in U.S., South Korea, and Belgium. Zexel was formed after acquiring patent rights for fuel injection production from Robert Bosch (Germany).

	¥bil 03/93	03/94	03/95	US$mil 03/95				
Sales	**276.1**	**259.3**	**283.4**	**2,873.0**	P/E Ratio	**59.0**	Price (9/30/95)	**625.00**
Net Income	**0.7**	**0.3**	**2.6**	**26.4**	P/B Ratio	**1.8**	52 Wk Hi-Low	**700.00-547.00**
Book Value	**83.3**	**82.2**	**84.3**	**975.7**	Yield %	**0.8**	Market Cap	**US$1,546.1mil**

Address **3-6-7, Shibuya**
Shibuya-ku, Tokyo 150

Tel **03-3400-1551**
Fax **03-5992-2615**

ADR
SEDOL No. **6269504**

President **Yutaka Ota**
Chairman --

Malaysia

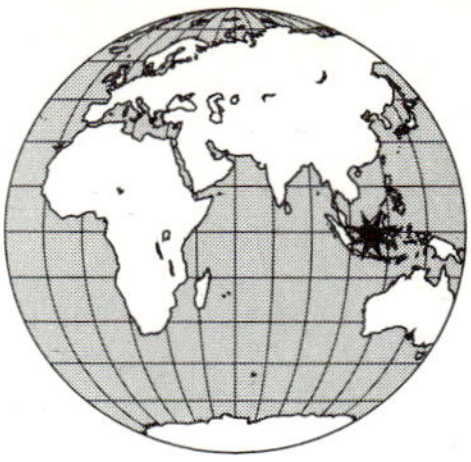

Malaysia

Lim Mui Khi,
Kuala Lumpur

Local Trading Hours	Time Difference with New York	Population (Est. 94)
9:30-5:00	13 hours ahead of EST (12 hours ahead during Daylight Savings Time)	19,283,000

The Kuala Lumpur Stock Exchange (KLSE), which split from the Singapore exchange in 1990, has already overtaken its more dominant neighbor in terms of market capitalization. At 553.08 billion ringgit (at September 15), it is one of the largest markets in Southeast Asia.

In terms of trading, however, dealings often continue to be dictated by the more established exchange in Singapore, which still trades a substantial number of Malaysian shares on its over-the-counter market.

Lower costs of transactions and a restructured fee-sharing schedule between local and foreign brokerages, and a string of other incentives designed to put the Kuala Lumpur market on the fast track were introduced in the middle of 1995.

More local brokerage firms will be given access to capital funds through public listings. Foreign firms will thus find it easier to take a stake, normally at a 30% maximum, although Ministry of Finance approval is still needed. Incentives are also being provided for more fund managers, both local and foreign, to be based in Malaysia. To increase local retail participation, smaller trading lots are also allowed which will make trading of larger blue chips more affordable.

While these measures were seen as generally positive, the market's response has so far been flat.

Turmoil in financial markets elsewhere as well as domestic factors—including uninspiring corporate earnings and apparent contradictions in government policies towards privatized concerns—have pulled the market's valuations down.

Overheating issues in the economy and a persistent belief the central bank, Bank Negara Malaysia, would tighten credit facilities to cool consumption spending, have also damped the market's performance.

Dow Jones Malaysia Equity Market Index Performance

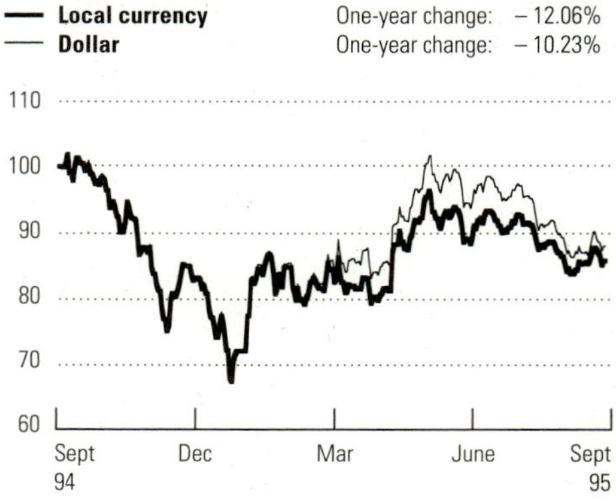

Compared with the last two years, when the market's rise culminated in a sharp rally following a lifting of liquidity-tightening measures by the central bank, 1995 has seen generally listless dealings, marked by occasional bursts of short-lived volatility.

Gross Domestic Product (94)	Three-Year Average GDP Growth (92-94)	Main Industries	Consumer Price Index (94)	Monetary Unit	Exchange Rate (9/95)
$46.69 billion	8.3%	Services, manufacturing, semiconductors, agriculture, forestry, fishing, mining and quarrying, and construction	3.7%	Ringgit	MR2.51 to US$1.00

The market languished further in the third quarter of this year when investors reacted to uncertainties created by the restructured fee sharing system between local and foreign brokerages, and the eventual conversion to a paperless trading system by trimming their positions and then staying out of the market. This threatened the trading of Malaysian shares at the Singapore exchange, and sparked bitter exchanges between dealers on both sides.

As an indication of how dependent the market still is on Singapore investors, a plan announced by the rival exchange to allow the trading of Malaysian shares even after they have been converted to a paperless system sparked a sharp rally.

The KLSE trading system has been fully automated since 1992, but it wants delivery and settlement to be on a paperless, book-entry system by end of 1996. When finished, all trading will be performed between electronically maintained accounts, and share certificates will be stored in a KLSE central vault. Of the 511 stocks traded, 152 listed on the second board are trading on the paperless system, but just 22 of the 362 main board shares have so far been converted.

Companies on the main board need track records of between three and five years, while second board listings need a track record of two to three years.

Foreign investors can freely trade in all listed securities and repatriate income, capital gains and capital. Some companies, however, impose limits on foreign shareholdings, which, when reached, frequently entails the creation of a separate foreign issue —identical in rights to its domestic counterpart—that is traded only amongst foreigners.

Ten Largest Capitalized Companies
as of 9/30/95

Stock	Market Cap. US$Mil
Telekom Malaysia	14,979,778.6
Tenaga Nasional	11,626,567.6
Malayan Banking	9,263,949.5
Genting	6,067,121.2
Sime Darby	5,641,845.8
Resorts World	5,437,465.1
United Engineers (Malaysia)	3,476,143.9
Malaysian International Shipping	3,007,968.1
Renong	2,863,232.8
AMMB Holdings	2,402,425.9

Malaysian law requires that shareholders declare their holdings in a company when they amount to more than 5% of issued share capital. But investors can otherwise remain anonymous through the use of nominee services, provided by brokerages and other financial institutions.

In 1995, through Sept. 30, some 44 new companies were listed on the exchange, of which 13 are on the main board. The largest was the privatized gas processor and distributor, Petronas Gas Bhd., which was listed in early September. Petronas Gas is a 75% owned subsidiary of the state-owned oil company, Petroliam Nasional Bhd. or Petronas, and is the second in the group after Petronas Dagangan Bhd., the retailing arm, to be listed.

The market also witnessed the trading of call warrants from June when the first warrant on Malayan Banking Bhd. stock was listed. Since then, warrants on the stock of Renong Bhd. and Sime Darby Bhd. have also been listed. A futures contract on the key market index, the KLSE Composite Index, was also being planned for the end of 1995.

The market lists a variety of securities, ordinary stocks, preference shares, a class of stock warrants, bonds and loan stocks.

The companies listed range from national utilities and regional conglomerates to family-controlled companies with narrowly focused businesses. The range represents fairly well the diversity of Malaysia's economy, with the notable exception of the giant state oil company and the foreign semiconductor manufacturers, which produce the nation's single largest export. No semiconductor maker is listed on the exchange.

Though the KLSE divides the market into outdated sectors that hark back to Malaysia's days as a tin and rubber economy, Japanese-controlled electrical goods concerns and national car manufacturers are listed alongside plantation companies. Such major economic sectors as construction, services, manufacturing, property development, finance, agriculture and other natural resources are all represented.

The KLSE's ten sectors are: consumer products, industrial products, construction, trading and services, finance, hotels, properties, mining, plantations, and loans, notes and bonds.

About 100 of the listed concerns attract a relatively consistent degree of foreign-investor interest, and many of those are core, blue-chip holdings in fund managers' regional portfolios. Increasingly, the smaller companies, which traditionally help to drive robust speculative activity amongst retail investors, are also drawing institutional interest, not just for shorter term trading.

Commissions, previously on a set scale, are now fixed on a sliding scale, with the rate falling from 1% on the first 0.5 million ringgit of shares traded, to 0.75% on the next 0.5 million to 2 million ringgit of trades, to 0.5% on the trades exceeding 2 million ringgit.

Sharing of fees between local and foreign brokerages was also changed from the equal split before to an increasing scale in favor of the local firm. Local firms get half of fees when 1% is imposed, two-thirds for trades charged at 0.75%, and seven-tenths for charges at 0.5%.

Dealing is performed by about 50 licensed brokerages, some joint ventures with international securities houses. Orders are matched by computer and share certificates processed through a central clearing house that is part of the KLSE.

In 1993, the Securities Commission was set up to provide for the regulation of and to advise the Minister of Finance on matters relating to the securities and futures contracts industries.

AMMB Holdings

Industry: **Banks - Regional**

AMMB Holdings is Malaysia's largest merchant bank. With two billion ringgits under management, it has a market share of 30%. It provides services in merchant banking, leasing, investment brokerage, consulting, and insurance. Its Security Pacific Asia Bank and Arab-Malaysian Finance subsidiaries provide commercial-banking services. Merchant-banking services are provided by its Arab-Malaysian Merchant Bank subsidiary. Arab-Malaysian Credit and majority-owned Arab-Malaysian Eagle Assurance offer credit-leasing and insurance services, respectively.

	MR mil 03/91 R	03/92	03/93	US$mil 03/93				
Revenues	**716.2**	**929.8**	**1,109.4**	**435.7**	P/E Ratio	**51.8**	Price (9/30/95)	**31.00**
Net Income	**70.5**	**136.7**	**115.3**	**45.3**	P/B Ratio	**9.7**	52 Wk Hi-Low	**35.50-20.30**
Book Value	**383.6**	**522.2**	**612.1**	**236.3**	Yield %	**0.6**	Market Cap	**US$2,402.4mil**

Address	**55 Jalan Raja Chulan**	Tel	**03-238-2633**	ADR		President	**Cheah Tek Kuang**
	50708 Kuala Lumpur	Fax	**03-238-2842**	SEDOL No.	**6047023**	Chairman	**Azman Hashim**

R=Restated.

Amsteel

Industry: **Steel**

Amsteel, formerly Amalgamated Steel Mills, is a holding company and member of Malaysia's Lion Group. In 1994, it divested its steel business to Lion Land in exchange for a majority stake in that property company; through its stake in Lion Land, it retains an indirect interest in the steel industry. Amsteel also distributes Suzuki cars and scooters, manufactures and sells Silverstone tires, and operates a chain of 30 Parkson stores and 18 convenience stores. Amsteel is also active in the property, financial services, and food indusries.

	MR mil 06/92	06/93	06/94	US$mil 06/94				
Sales	**2,067.1**	**2,324.1**	**2,775.8**	**1,057.8**	P/E Ratio	**21.6**	Price (9/30/95)	**2.22**
Net Income	**63.9**	**77.3**	**127.6**	**48.6**	P/B Ratio	**2.5**	52 Wk Hi-Low	**2.82-1.69**
Book Value	**563.3**	**949.9**	**1,073.6**	**412.9**	Yield %	**0.9**	Market Cap	**US$1,068.5mil**

Address	**Menara Lion, 165 Jl. Ampang**	Tel	**03-262-2155**	ADR		Managing Director	**William H.J. Cheng**
	50450 Kuala Lumpur	Fax	**03-264-1036**	SEDOL No.	**6025706**	Chairman	**Zain Hashim**

Antah Holdings

Industry: **Conglomerates**

Antah Holdings, through its subsidiaries, provides financial services, manufactures consumer products, operates hotels and resorts, and provides industrial services. Its financial services include underwriting insurance policies and providing lease-purchasing services. The company's consumer products include snack foods, fruit, canned food, sports drinks, bottled water, furniture, and Hoover vacuum cleaners. Antah provides industrial clients with advertising, security, and engineering services. The company also operates 7-Eleven stores in Malaysia.

	MR mil 06/92	06/93	06/94	US$mil 06/94				
Sales	**722.7**	**706.7**	**701.9**	**267.5**	P/E Ratio	**39.9**	Price (9/30/95)	**2.71**
Net Income	**95.0**	**-16.9**	**4.6**	**1.8**	P/B Ratio	**1.5**	52 Wk Hi-Low	**2.97-1.58**
Book Value	**277.8**	**244.5**	**260.8**	**100.3**	Yield %	**1.1**	Market Cap	**US$248.5mil**

Address	**Bangunan BNH**	Tel	**03-254-5144**	ADR		Chief Executive	**Imran ibni T. Ja'afar**
	50490 Kuala Lumpur	Fax	**03-255-8464**	SEDOL No.	**6044734**	Chairman	**Naquiah btr T. Ja'afar**

Aokam Perdana

Industry: **Forest Products**

Aokam Perdana produces timber and related products. Its forestry products include veneer-wrapped moldings and plywood and lumber products. The company's production facilities comprise about 1 million square feet and can produce more than 24,000 cubic meters per month of plywood and veneer-wrapped products. Aokam Perdana markets these products in Malaysia and abroad, with the majority of its exports going to Europe, North America, Japan, and Taiwan. The company also owns a slicing plant, Pacific Wood Products, as well as a waste recovery plant.

	MR mil 06/92	06/93	06/94	US$mil 06/94				
Sales	**72.4**	**135.7**	**223.1**	**85.0**	P/E Ratio	**8.3**	Price (9/30/95)	**5.05**
Net Income	**26.0**	**64.8**	**113.5**	**43.3**	P/B Ratio	**2.5**	52 Wk Hi-Low	**22.50-5.05**
Book Value	**163.4**	**239.9**	**373.1**	**143.5**	Yield %	**1.4**	Market Cap	**US$395.8mil**

Address	**Jalan Sultan Ismail**	Tel	**03-244-1266**	ADR		Managing Director	**Teh Soon Seng**
	50250 Kuala Lumpur	Fax	**03-244-1173**	SEDOL No.	**6045704**	Chairman	**Abdul Rahman**

Asia Pacific Land

Industry: **Real-Estate Investment**

Asia Pacific Land (AP Land) invests in and develops real estate in the hotel, retail, agricultural, and corporate sectors. AP Land's hotel subsidiaries include APL Hotel and Ferringhi Beach Hotel. Its properties include the Crown Princess Kuala Lumpur hotel, City Square Shopping Complex, Marina Terrace Sports and Recreational Complex, and the Empire Tower building. AP Land's current development projects include a 1,068 hectare township in Selangor, a luxury apartment complex in Australia, and villas and apartments at Mount Pleasure Resort, Penang.

	MR mil 01/93	01/94	01/95	US$mil 01/95				
Sales	**63.7**	**92.3**	**194.2**	**74.7**	P/E Ratio	**47.1**	Price (9/30/95)	**1.46**
Net Income	**18.5**	**18.5**	**22.3**	**8.6**	P/B Ratio	**1.2**	52 Wk Hi-Low	**2.44-1.39**
Book Value	**459.2**	**602.9**	**890.9**	**348.0**	Yield %	**1.4**	Market Cap	**US$352.1mil**

Address	**City Sq. Ctr., Jalan Tun Razak**	Tel	**03-262-1566**	ADR		President	--
	50400 Kuala Lumpur	Fax	**03-262-1494**	SEDOL No.	**6050935**	Chairman	**Low Yow Chuan**

Asiatic Development

Industry: **Plantations**

Asiatic Development, a majority-owned subsidiary of the Malaysian company Genting, manages plantation and property businesses. The plantation division produces rubber, fruit, cocoa, and oil palms. It currently owns more than 68,000 acres of oil palms, 12,000 acres of rubber trees, and 1,600 acres of cocoa beans. The company develops real estate, primarily for housing and industrial developments. Asiatic Development and Australia's Airboss formed a joint venture that manufactures nonpneumatic tires.

	MR mil 12/92 R	12/93	12/94	US$mil 12/94				
Sales	**124.9**	**153.1**	**152.1**	**58.1**	P/E Ratio	**54.2**	Price (9/30/95)	**2.71**
Net Income	**39.5**	**27.8**	**36.3**	**13.9**	P/B Ratio	**3.6**	52 Wk Hi-Low	**3.46-2.36**
Book Value	**511.4**	**535.7**	**562.9**	**220.7**	Yield %	**1.5**	Market Cap	**US$800.5mil**

Address **Jalan Sultan Ismail** / **50250 Kuala Lumpur** — Tel **03-261-3733** — Fax **03-261-6149** — ADR — SEDOL No. **6057680** — Chief Executive **L.G. Tong / B. Musa** — Chairman **Mohamed Amin**

R=Restated.

Bandar Raya Developments

Industry: **Home Construction**

Bandar Raya Developments develops and manages residential and commercial real estate, and manufactures particle board and melamine-impregnated paper. It builds houses, shopping centers, condominiums, recreation complexes, hotels, office buildings, and vacation resorts. Its Mieco Chipboard subsidiary is Malaysia's largest producer of particle board. It supplies 50,000 cubic meters of rubberwood and moisture-resistant particle board and more than 12 million square meters of melamine-impregnated paper to domestic and international markets.

	MR mil 12/92	12/93	12/94	US$mil 12/94				
Sales	**165.5**	**202.9**	**571.3**	**218.2**	P/E Ratio	**17.8**	Price (9/30/95)	**4.74**
Net Income	**15.4**	**47.8**	**109.8**	**41.9**	P/B Ratio	**2.9**	52 Wk Hi-Low	**5.70-3.10**
Book Value	**339.7**	**378.2**	**478.6**	**187.7**	Yield %	**1.1**	Market Cap	**US$550.3mil**

Address **285 Jl. Ma'arof** / **59000 Kuala Lumpur** — Tel **03-294-6622** — Fax **03-294-1922** — ADR **BROBY** — SEDOL No. **6074902** — CEO **Lim Kim Wah** — Chairman **Lim Bok Yeng**

Batu Kawan

Industry: **Plantations**

Batu Kawan operates plantations, produces industrial chemicals, and provides stock-brokerage services. It owns 42% of Kuala Lumpur Kepong, a plantation business that cultivates oil palms, rubber trees, and cocoa. Batu Kawan produces sulfuric acid through its 35% stake in Malay-Sino Chemical Industries, and chlor-alkaline products through a 61% stake in See Sen Chemical. It also has a 25% stake in both Laporte (Malaysia) and KL-Kepong Cocoa Products. Through other interests, Batu Kawan develops real estate and makes rubber examination gloves and three-ply parquet.

	MR mil 09/92	09/93	09/94	US$mil 09/94				
Sales	**66.2**	**25.4**	**32.1**	**12.2**	P/E Ratio	**21.1**	Price (9/30/95)	**6.10**
Net Income	**69.8**	**93.6**	**47.7**	**18.2**	P/B Ratio	**1.8**	52 Wk Hi-Low	**6.95-4.98**
Book Value	**573.2**	**647.2**	**674.6**	**263.5**	Yield %	**1.6**	Market Cap	**US$472.1mil**

Address **1 Jalan S.P. Seenivasagam** / **30000 Ipoh, Perak** — Tel **05-241-7844** — Fax **05-241-5312** — ADR — SEDOL No. **6084622** — Managing Director **Lee Hau Hian** — Chairman **Lee Oi Hian**

Berjaya Group

Industry: **Conglomerates**

Berjaya Group is a diversified industrial company engaged in property development, construction, the manufacture and trade of consumer durables, and the provision of general insurance services. It holds a 61% stake in Berjaya Industrial, a company that manufactures textiles and steel-wire products, provides marketing services, and operates gaming facilities. The company's Berjaya Hotels & Resorts operates two resort hotels. Berjaya also owns 51% of the consumer-goods company Berjaya Singer and 40% of Hutchinson Bangladesh Telecom.

	MR mil 04/93	04/94	04/95	US$mil 04/95				
Sales	**1,842.6**	**2,438.1**	**3,284.9**	**1,281.2**	P/E Ratio	**11.2**	Price (9/30/95)	**1.98**
Net Income	**201.4**	**244.3**	**136.7**	**53.3**	P/B Ratio	**1.4**	52 Wk Hi-Low	**4.12-1.80**
Book Value	**658.5**	**984.2**	**1,077.9**	**436.4**	Yield %	**2.4**	Market Cap	**US$668.3mil**

Address **30 Jalan Sultan Ismail** / **50250 Kuala Lumpur** — Tel **03-242-2622** — Fax **03-243-2246** — ADR — SEDOL No. **6721468** — Managing Director **Tan Chee Sing** — Chairman **Tan Chee Yioun**

Cement Industries of Malaysia

Industry: **Building Materials**

Cement Industries of Malaysia (CIMA) manufactures and markets cement and ready-mix concrete under the brand name Blue Lion. The company is Malaysia's second-largest cement company, accounting for 17% of the country's cement output. CIMA currently holds quarries with an aggregate area of more than 108 hectares. Its wholly-owned Perlis Paper Products subsidiary manufactures and sells bags for cement, and 60%-owned Cimaco Quarry operates limestone quarries. CIMA is a 54%-owned subsidiary of United Engineers.

	MR mil 12/92 R	12/93	12/94	US$mil 12/94				
Sales	**158.5**	**206.6**	**293.0**	**111.9**	P/E Ratio	**16.9**	Price (9/30/95)	**8.05**
Net Income	**57.6**	**72.4**	**62.7**	**23.9**	P/B Ratio	**2.2**	52 Wk Hi-Low	**9.05-6.40**
Book Value	**431.4**	**457.7**	**480.9**	**188.6**	Yield %	**3.7**	Market Cap	**US$423.1mil**

Address **Bukit Ketri, Mukim of Chuping** / **02450 Perlis, Kangar** — Tel **04-938-2006** — Fax **04-938-2722** — ADR — SEDOL No. **6182827** — Managing Director **Badarudin Khalid** — Chairman **Yahya bin Ismail**

R=Restated.

Commerce Asset Holding

Industry: **Banks - Regional**

Commerce Asset offers services in commercial and merchant banking, stock brokerage, lease financing, and property-trust management. It owns 98% of Bank of Commerce, a Kuala Lumpur-based bank; and has a 64% stake in Commerce International Merchant Bankers, a merchant-banking and securities firm. The firm also offers investment-advisory services through its minority interest in Malaysian Issuing House. Commercial-banking activities provide Commerce Asset with more than 60% of total revenues, and its brokerage businesses generate nearly 35%.

MR mil	12/92	12/93	12/94	US$mil 12/94				
Revenues	**829.4**	**971.8**	**1,145.3**	**437.5**	P/E Ratio	**20.0**	Price (9/30/95)	**13.20**
Net Income	**90.0**	**126.8**	**147.4**	**56.3**	P/B Ratio	**3.9**	52 Wk Hi-Low	**14.70-8.05**
Book Value	**495.0**	**613.2**	**764.6**	**299.8**	Yield %	**0.8**	Market Cap	**US$1,184.8mil**

Address **Commerce Sq., Jalan Semantan** **50490 Kuala Lumpur** Tel **03-253-5333** Fax **03-253-3335** ADR SEDOL No. **6075745** President -- Chairman **Mohamed Desa Pachi**

DCB Holdings

Industry: **Banks - Regional**

DCB Holdings is the holding company for the Development & Commercial Bank and its six subsidiaries. DCB provides banking and other financial services including lease financing, credit-card purchasing, merchant banking, unit-trust management, and insurance underwriting. It operates more than 50 commercial-banking branches. DCB also invests in and develops real estate. Banking provides the firm with more than 89% of its total revenues, and leasing operations generate the remainder.

MR mil	12/92	12/93	12/94	US$mil 12/94				
Revenues	**957.9**	**1,220.8**	**N/A**	**N/A**	P/E Ratio	**27.3**	Price (9/30/95)	**7.00**
Net Income	**88.2**	**143.7**	**200.3**	**76.5**	P/B Ratio	**4.7**	52 Wk Hi-Low	**8.00-4.72**
Book Value	**827.1**	**966.2**	**1,145.6**	**449.3**	Yield %	**1.0**	Market Cap	**US$2,176.5mil**

Address **161B Jalan Ampang** **50450 Kuala Lumpur** Tel **03-261-7177** Fax **03-261-9541** ADR SEDOL No. **6244675** Managing Director **Ismail Bin Zakaria** Chairman **Geh Ik Cheong**

Dunlop Estates

Industry: **Plantations**

Dunlop Estates operates gaming and real-estate-development businesses. The company operates its gaming businesses through majority ownership of the Magnum Corporation, which conducts a licensed lottery game and owns pari-mutuel betting facilities. Its Dunlop Agro-Management subsidiary provides agriculture consulting services. The firm also operates resorts and hotels, provides landscaping services, and refines palm oil. Dunlop Estates is a subsidiary of Multi-Purpose Holdings, which holds more than 58% of the company's shares.

MR mil	12/92	12/93	12/94	US$mil 12/94				
Sales	**1,572.7**	**2,252.4**	**2,234.8**	**853.6**	P/E Ratio	**20.8**	Price (9/30/95)	**6.15**
Net Income	**54.6**	**315.7**	**138.6**	**52.9**	P/B Ratio	**2.2**	52 Wk Hi-Low	**10.00-4.98**
Book Value	**581.1**	**893.7**	**1,070.2**	**419.7**	Yield %	**0.8**	Market Cap	**US$952.9mil**

Address **Jl. Munshi Abdullah** **50100 Kuala Lumpur** Tel **03-294-8333** Fax **03-294-1380** ADR SEDOL No. **6286439** Chief Executive **Lim Thian Kiat** Chairman **Lim Ah Tam**

Edaran Otomobil Nasional

Industry: **Other Specialty Retailers**

Edaran Otomobil Nasional sells automobiles, offers financial services, and has interests in the manufacturing and telecommunication industries. It distributes Proton automobiles and related parts through its 54 service centers. Proton has 71% of the country's passenger-car market. Eon Bank, a 61%-owned subsidiary, provides commercial-banking services through 48 branches. Edaran holds 30% of Mobikom, a joint venture with Telekom Malaysia, Permodalan Nasional, and Sapura Holdings that provides cellular-telephone services to more than 70,000 subscribers.

MR mil	12/92	12/93	12/94	US$mil 12/94				
Revenues	**2,683.7**	**3,642.6**	**4,440.4**	**1,696.1**	P/E Ratio	**19.7**	Price (9/30/95)	**20.10**
Net Income	**108.4**	**177.6**	**225.6**	**86.2**	P/B Ratio	**4.6**	52 Wk Hi-Low	**25.25-16.00**
Book Value	**631.6**	**772.9**	**968.6**	**379.8**	Yield %	**1.7**	Market Cap	**US$1,780.7mil**

Address **Jl. Kerjaya, Seksyen Utara Satu** **40000 Shah Alam** Tel **03-703-1111** Fax **03-703-0009** ADR SEDOL No. **6303617** Managing Director **Adzmi Bin Abdul Wahab** Chairman **Jamil Bin Mohamed Jan**

Ekran

Industry: **Heavy Construction**

Ekran is among the largest turnkey contractors in Malaysia. It engages in construction, manufactures cables, and provides telecommunications services. Its Woodhouse subsidiary specializes in the construction of hotels and resorts. Federal Cables, Wires, and Metal Manufacturing produces telecommunications and power cables, distributes telecommunications equipment, and provides paging services. Ekran is currently constructing a hydroelectric facility in Borneo; the project requires clearing nearly 80,000 hectares of forest--timber that Ekran plans to extract and process.

MR mil	06/92 R	06/93	06/94	US$mil 06/94				
Sales	**163.3**	**220.0**	**257.6**	**98.2**	P/E Ratio	**37.4**	Price (9/30/95)	**7.00**
Net Income	**28.1**	**31.6**	**50.2**	**19.1**	P/B Ratio	**6.6**	52 Wk Hi-Low	**12.10-6.40**
Book Value	**179.6**	**216.3**	**273.4**	**105.2**	Yield %	**1.7**	Market Cap	**US$717.1mil**

Address **Amoda Bldg., 22 Jalan Imbi** **55100 Kuala Lumpur** Tel **03-241-0111** Fax **03-244-8944** ADR SEDOL No. **6306984** President -- Chairman **Ting Pek Khiing**

R=Restated.

Faber Group

Industry: **Lodging**

Faber Group is a holding company with activities in the property-development, hospitality, hospital-services, infrastructure-construction, and transportation industries. The company's hotel business consists of eight hotels in Malaysia, and a joint venture to build a hotel in Hanoi, Vietnam. It has entered into a licensing agreement with ITT Sheraton to brand six of its hotels. The company has seven subsidiaries that construct single- and multi-family housing in Malaysian townships. Faber also builds infrastructure projects and operates a fleet of cargo-transport trucks.

MR mil	06/92	06/93	06/94	US$mil 06/94				
Sales	**105.8**	**75.7**	**127.0**	**48.4**	P/E Ratio	**19.9**	Price (9/30/95)	**2.35**
Net Income	**32.5**	**54.3**	**100.0**	**38.1**	P/B Ratio	**1.9**	52 Wk Hi-Low	**3.30-1.60**
Book Value	**903.1**	**958.6**	**1,067.2**	**410.5**	Yield %	**0.0**	Market Cap	**US$789.7mil**

Address **Faber Twrs., Jalan Desa Bahagia** Tel **03-783-8855** ADR Managing Director **Aminuddin Y. Lana**
58100 Kuala Lumpur Fax **03-781-3578** SEDOL No. **6330778** Chairman **Abdullah M. Yusof**

Federal Flour Mills

Industry: **Other Food**

Federal Flour Mills produces flour, animal feed, and cooking oils. The company operates six flour mills throughout Malaysia. It also manages five animal-feed factories, two soybean-processing plants, and an animal-breeder farm. The company supplies flour to noodle, bread, and cookie manufacturers, and directly to consumers. Through its Federal Computer Services subsidiary, the company develops and markets software, multimedia applications, and telecommunication products. Federal Flour Mills is a 50%-owned subsidiary of Perlis Plantations.

MR mil	12/92	12/93	12/94	US$mil 12/94				
Sales	**2,254.5**	**2,284.7**	**3,298.8**	**1,260.0**	P/E Ratio	**10.4**	Price (9/30/95)	**7.80**
Net Income	**82.2**	**83.7**	**133.3**	**50.9**	P/B Ratio	**2.0**	52 Wk Hi-Low	**9.50-6.00**
Book Value	**513.4**	**586.4**	**697.0**	**273.3**	Yield %	**1.3**	Market Cap	**US$554.7mil**

Address **38 Jalan Sultan Ismail** Tel **03-242-4077** ADR Managing Director **Oh Siew Nam**
50250 Kuala Lumpur Fax **03-241-8242** SEDOL No. **6333120** Chairman **Haji M. Shamsudin**

Genting

Industry: **Casinos**

Genting is a holding company active in hotels and resorts, plantations, transportation, and property development. Resorts and leisure contribute 86% of the company's revenues. Its 55%-owned Resorts World subsidiary operates theme parks and resorts, including the Awana Hotel and Golf and Country Resort. Genting's majority-owned Asiatic Development plantation subsidiary cultivates nearly 34,000 hectares, with oil palm composing 84% of the crop and rubber composing 14% of the crop. Asiatic also has a joint venture to develop a palm-oil-production facility in China.

MR mil	12/92	12/93	12/94	US$mil 12/94				
Sales	**1,638.5**	**2,004.2**	**2,378.0**	**908.3**	P/E Ratio	**27.9**	Price (9/30/95)	**21.70**
Net Income	**370.8**	**597.8**	**607.5**	**232.0**	P/B Ratio	**5.1**	52 Wk Hi-Low	**27.50-18.90**
Book Value	**1,968.3**	**2,488.6**	**3,002.4**	**1,177.4**	Yield %	**0.9**	Market Cap	**US$6,067.1mil**

Address **Wisma Genting, Jl. Sultan Ismail** Tel **03-261-2288** ADR **GEBEY** Managing Director **Colin Au Fook Yew**
50250 Kuala Lumpur Fax **03-261-5304** SEDOL No. **6366676** Chairman **Lim Goh Tong**

Golden Hope Plantations

Industry: **Plantations**

Golden Hope Plantations manages plantations and develops residential property. Covering more than 100,000 hectares, the company's plantations cultivate oil palms, cocoa, fruit, and rubber trees. The company also processes palm oil, palm kernels, cocoa, and rubber. It has processing plants worldwide, including ones in Vietnam and China. Golden Hope also produces fruit juices marketed under the Morjus brand name. Its Golden Hope Agrotech Consultancy and Perkhidmatan Komputer Perladangan subsidiaries provide agricultural and computer consulting services.

MR mil	03/92	03/93	03/94	US$mil 03/94				
Sales	**502.1**	**593.4**	**850.8**	**326.0**	P/E Ratio	**17.2**	Price (9/30/95)	**4.50**
Net Income	**73.8**	**100.2**	**261.5**	**100.2**	P/B Ratio	**1.9**	52 Wk Hi-Low	**4.96-3.76**
Book Value	**1,831.9**	**2,073.7**	**2,383.6**	**889.4**	Yield %	**2.7**	Market Cap	**US$1,794.1mil**

Address **201-A Jalan Tun Razak** Tel **03-261-9022** ADR Managing Director **Abdul Rahman bin Ramli**
50400 Kuala Lumpur Fax **03-261-8221** SEDOL No. **6411929** Chairman **Ismail bin Mohamed Ali**

Highlands & Lowlands

Industry: **Plantations**

Highlands & Lowlands manages plantation and property-development businesses. Its principal business is the cultivation of rubber trees, cocoa, coconuts, and oil palms on plantations in Malaysia. The company's crops cover more than 55,000 hectares, with 42,800 dedicated to oil palms, 9,000 to rubber trees, 2,500 to cocoa, and the balance to coconuts. Sales of oil palm products generate more than half of the company's revenues. Highlands & Lowlands is a 51%-owned subsidiary of Kumpulan Guthrie, Malaysia's largest plantation company by market capitalization.

MR mil	12/92	12/93	12/94	US$mil 12/94				
Sales	**331.3**	**382.7**	**351.0**	**134.1**	P/E Ratio	**37.2**	Price (9/30/95)	**4.28**
Net Income	**444.7**	**63.2**	**94.9**	**36.2**	P/B Ratio	**2.2**	52 Wk Hi-Low	**5.05-3.70**
Book Value	**1,124.6**	**1,141.7**	**1,188.5**	**466.1**	Yield %	**2.8**	Market Cap	**US$1,030.5mil**

Address **21 Jalan Gelenggang** Tel **03-254-1644** ADR Managing Director **Abdul Khalid**
50490 Kuala Lumpur Fax **03-255-7934** SEDOL No. **6425856** Chairman **Abdul Khalid**

Hong Leong Credit

Industry: **Financial Services - Diversified**

Hong Leong Credit provides financial services, invests in and develops real estate, and provides other companies with management-consulting services. The firm's financial services include fund management, financing, insurance, and investment brokerage. Hong Leong Credit owns 100% of the commercial bank MUI Bank and 49% of the real-estate concern Hong Leong Properties. Its Hong Leong Computer Services subsidiary markets information-technology services. Hong Leong Credit is a majority-owned subsidiary of diversified conglomerate Hong Leong Industries.

MR mil	06/92	06/93 R	06/94	US$mil 06/94				
Revenues	**438.5**	**N/A**	**1,021.7**	**389.4**	P/E Ratio	**19.7**	Price (9/30/95)	**12.00**
Net Income	**53.4**	**97.4**	**186.2**	**71.0**	P/B Ratio	**3.9**	52 Wk Hi-Low	**17.00-8.95**
Book Value	**428.7**	**511.0**	**1,046.4**	**402.5**	Yield %	**0.8**	Market Cap	**US$1,644.2mil**

Address **117 Jalan Tun H.S. Lee**, **50000 Kuala Lumpur**
Tel **03-232-1511**
Fax **03-238-8105**
ADR
SEDOL No. **6436450**
Managing Director **J. Lim Cheng Poh**
Chairman **Quek Leng Chan**

R=Restated.

Hong Leong Industries

Industry: **Building Materials**

Hong Leong Industries is a diversified holding company. Its subsidiaries manufacture and distribute motor vehicles, automotive components, ceramic tiles, steel, semiconductors and packaging materials. It also invests in and develops real estate. Hong Leong is engaged in a joint venture with NTUC Fairprice Co-operative, a supermarket chain in Singapore, to operate retail chains in Malaysia. The company is also involved in two joint ventures in China: it owns 51% of a motorcycle manufacturer and 42% of a ceramic-manufacturing plant.

MR mil	06/92	06/93	06/94	US$mil 06/94				
Sales	**774.8**	**1,024.2**	**1,164.9**	**443.9**	P/E Ratio	**19.1**	Price (9/30/95)	**13.20**
Net Income	**70.7**	**82.4**	**96.8**	**36.9**	P/B Ratio	**3.1**	52 Wk Hi-Low	**16.20-11.20**
Book Value	**432.9**	**508.0**	**595.1**	**228.9**	Yield %	**0.5**	Market Cap	**US$738.0mil**

Address **18 Jalan Perak**, **50450 Kuala Lumpur**
Tel **03-264-2631**
Fax **03-238-8105**
ADR
SEDOL No. **6436308**
President & CEO **Kwek Leng San**
Chairman **Quek Leng Chan**

Hong Leong Properties

Industry: **Real-Estate Investment**

Hong Leong Properties is a holding company whose subsidiaries invest in and develop real estate. The company also operates travel and tourism businesses and holds interests in the restaurant, entertainment, and fashion industries. Its Guoman Hotels subsidiary develops and operates resorts and hotels. Hong Leong Properties also owns 30% of Guoco Properties, a joint venture with Hong Kong's Guoco Group and Singapore's First Capital that constructs residential properties. The company is 33% owned by Hong Leong Credit, a subsidiary of Hong Leong Industries.

MR mil	06/92 *	06/93	06/94	US$mil 06/94				
Sales	**253.3**	**235.3**	**356.0**	**135.7**	P/E Ratio	**42.7**	Price (9/30/95)	**3.12**
Net Income	**20.9**	**23.7**	**56.4**	**21.5**	P/B Ratio	**5.5**	52 Wk Hi-Low	**4.82-2.43**
Book Value	**321.1**	**332.1**	**398.6**	**153.3**	Yield %	**0.3**	Market Cap	**US$928.7mil**

Address **18 Jalan Perak**, **50450 Kuala Lumpur**
Tel **03-264-1818**
Fax **N/A**
ADR
SEDOL No. **6089360**
Managing Director **Isham bin Nyak Arif**
Chairman **Quek Leng Chan**

*Irregular period due to fiscal year change.

Hume Industries

Industry: **Building Materials**

Hume Industries manufactures building materials, air conditioners, refrigerators, and rubber- and wood-based products. It also publishes Chinese-language newspapers and magazines. Hume produces a range of concrete products, including ready-mix concrete, roof tiles, and prefabricated building components. It also makes wood furniture, rubber gaskets, and pipes for oil, gas, and water distribution. It has entered into a joint venture with Guoco Group (Hong Kong) and the provincial government of Fujian, China to construct an international airport.

MR mil	06/92	06/93	06/94	US$mil 06/94				
Sales	**840.9**	**970.2**	**1,027.5**	**391.6**	P/E Ratio	**58.3**	Price (9/30/95)	**14.10**
Net Income	**49.6**	**92.5**	**59.9**	**22.8**	P/B Ratio	**6.0**	52 Wk Hi-Low	**14.30-9.50**
Book Value	**483.1**	**552.3**	**584.5**	**224.8**	Yield %	**0.8**	Market Cap	**US$1,391.9mil**

Address **18 Jalan Perak**, **50450 Kuala Lumpur**
Tel **03-264-2300**
Fax **03-776-8818**
ADR
SEDOL No. **6444754**
President & CEO **Roger Tan Kim Hock**
Chairman **Quek Leng Chan**

IGB

Industry: **Real-Estate Investment**

IGB Corporation is a real-estate and investment holding company. The firm's real-estate portfolio includes retail, residential, and commercial properties in Malaysia, Australia, Singapore, Vietnam, the United Kingdom, and the United States. These properties include condominiums, hotels, shopping centers, restaurants, and parking garages. IGB, in partnership agreements with the New World Group, is currently erecting the New World Kuala Lumpur and the Kuala Lumpur Renaissance in Malaysia, as well as the New World Saigon Inn in Ho Chi Minh City, Vietnam.

MR mil	12/92	12/93	12/94	US$mil 12/94				
Sales	**763.0**	**807.6**	**609.9**	**233.0**	P/E Ratio	**18.3**	Price (9/30/95)	**2.19**
Net Income	**68.8**	**91.0**	**55.4**	**21.2**	P/B Ratio	**1.4**	52 Wk Hi-Low	**2.64-1.78**
Book Value	**578.7**	**681.2**	**729.9**	**286.2**	Yield %	**1.4**	Market Cap	**US$402.5mil**

Address **IGB Plz., 6 Jalan Kampar**, **50400 Kuala Lumpur**
Tel **03-442-6111**
Fax **03-441-1468**
ADR
SEDOL No. **6455273**
Managing Director **Tan Boon Seng**
Chairman **Tan Kim Yeow**

Industrial Oxygen

Industry: **Plantations**

Industrial Oxygen grows and processes a variety of crops, holds interests in property-development concerns, and produces industrial and medical gases. It owns more than 100,000 hectares of land, 85% dedicated to oil-palm cultivation, 11% to rubber-tree production, and the balance to cocoa-bean cultivation. The company's 70%-owned Nissan-Industrial Oxygen subsidiary operates its medical and industrial gas business. Nearly 62% of revenues are derived from the company's agricultural concerns, and 33% from its property-development businesses.

	MR mil 06/92	06/93	06/94	US$mil 06/94				
Sales	**190.2**	**227.8**	**330.1**	**125.8**	P/E Ratio	**14.0**	Price (9/30/95)	**2.90**
Net Income	**26.7**	**30.9**	**136.0**	**51.8**	P/B Ratio	**2.6**	52 Wk Hi-Low	**3.50-2.35**
Book Value	**513.2**	**615.7**	**739.0**	**284.2**	Yield %	**0.7**	Market Cap	**US$761.7mil**

Address **Bangunan IOI, 8 Jalan Kenari 5**
47100 Puchong
Tel **03-575-2288**
Fax **03-575-3997**
ADR
SEDOL No. **6464514**
Managing Director **Lee Shin Cheng**
Chairman **Abdul Rahman**

Island & Peninsular

Industry: **Real-Estate Investment**

Island & Peninsular is a holding company whose subsidiaries own and develop property, construct residential and commercial buildings, provide financial services, and operate rubber tree and oil palm plantations. The company also provides landscaping services and operates a plant nursery. Its Austral Enterprises subsidiary produces 330,000 tonnes of oil-palm products annually. Island & Peninsular's financial services include mortgage financing, leasing, and investment brokerage. Pemegang Amanah Raya Malaysia holds a controlling interest in Island & Peninsular.

	MR mil 01/93	01/94	01/95	US$mil 01/95				
Sales	**N/A**	**343.6**	**347.8**	**133.7**	P/E Ratio	**14.9**	Price (9/30/95)	**7.00**
Net Income	**25.3**	**51.6**	**57.4**	**22.1**	P/B Ratio	**1.2**	52 Wk Hi-Low	**7.40-5.90**
Book Value	**N/A**	**597.0**	**661.4**	**258.4**	Yield %	**2.9**	Market Cap	**US$319.6mil**

Address **24-31 Jalan 8/55A**
54200 Kuala Lumpur
Tel **03-456-7100**
Fax **03-457-2786**
ADR
SEDOL No. **6467148**
Managing Director **Yusof Hussin**
Chairman **Mohamed Farid**

Kamunting

Industry: **Real-Estate Investment**

Kamunting Corporation is a holding company for a broad range of companies. One of Kamunting's core businesses is the operation of toll plazas at the Kepong Toll Interchange. It also underwrites insurance policies through KSM Insuran, a majority-owned subsidiary. The company's real-estate-development business is conducted through Kamunting Construction, a subsidiary that heads the construction division and Petani Housing Development, a property-development company. Kamunting also operates hotels, golf courses, and horse-racing facilities.

	MR mil 03/92	03/93	03/94	US$mil 03/94				
Sales	**78.4**	**135.7**	**126.9**	**48.6**	P/E Ratio	**5.6**	Price (9/30/95)	**1.91**
Net Income	**32.8**	**49.7**	**267.8**	**102.6**	P/B Ratio	**1.4**	52 Wk Hi-Low	**2.82-1.56**
Book Value	**773.9**	**821.0**	**1,086.2**	**405.3**	Yield %	**0.5**	Market Cap	**US$598.1mil**

Address **285 Jalan Ma'arof**
59000 Kuala Lumpur
Tel **03-254-7333**
Fax **03-254-1380**
ADR
SEDOL No. **6483230**
Managing Director **Lin Thian Kiat**
Chairman **Lim Ah Tam**

Kedah Cement

Industry: **Building Materials**

Kedah Cement manufactures bagged and bulk cement. The company has a cement-grinding capacity of 2 million tonnes a year. It hopes to increase its capacity to 3.8 million tonnes a year through an expansion project currently underway. It leases limestone and shale quarries covering an area of 1,000 acres and operates five processing plants across Malaysia. In addition to the sale and transportation of cement, Kedah also invests in rental properties through its 49.9% interest in Lam Huat Properties. The government-owned industrial investor Hicom holds a 32% stake in Kedah.

	MR mil 03/92	03/93	03/94	US$mil 03/94				
Sales	**308.6**	**239.0**	**268.1**	**102.7**	P/E Ratio	**25.4**	Price (9/30/95)	**4.22**
Net Income	**40.6**	**53.3**	**48.0**	**18.4**	P/B Ratio	**4.5**	52 Wk Hi-Low	**4.82-2.88**
Book Value	**257.2**	**263.2**	**271.0**	**101.1**	Yield %	**3.6**	Market Cap	**US$490.1mil**

Address **98 Jalan Dang Wangi**
50100 Kuala Lumpur
Tel **03-298-1366**
Fax **03-292-7707**
ADR
SEDOL No. **6602938**
Managing Director **Heng Keah Yong**
Chairman **Jamil Mohamed Jan**

Kelanamas Industries

Industry: **Other Food**

Kelanamas Industries is a diversified industrial and consumer-products group with interests in timber, tin plates, sugar and beverages, and stockbroking. Kelanamas Industries has operations in the construction, engineering, and quarrying industries. It manufactures, trades, and distributes consumer food products such as fruit juice. It also owns a 90% stake in stockbroker Alor Star Securities and a 100% stake in plywood and veneer firm Veracity, which has a factory that produces a monthly average of 7,000 cubic meters of timber.

	MR mil 10/92 *	10/93	09/94 *	US$mil 09/94				
Sales	**248.0**	**386.4**	**267.7**	**101.9**	P/E Ratio	**NMF**	Price (9/30/95)	**4.50**
Net Income	**10.6**	**9.1**	**-1.4**	**-0.5**	P/B Ratio	**1.8**	52 Wk Hi-Low	**7.60-3.68**
Book Value	**96.7**	**104.2**	**289.7**	**113.2**	Yield %	**0.7**	Market Cap	**US$205.7mil**

Address **Wisma Perdana, Jalan Dungun**
50490 Kuala Lumpur
Tel **03-253-8282**
Fax **N/A**
ADR
SEDOL No. **6860714**
President --
Chairman **Esa Mohamed**

*Irregular period due to fiscal year change.

Kuala Lumpur Kepong

Industry: **Plantations**

Kuala Lumpur Kepong (KLK) owns plantations and industrial businesses. The company cultivates 250,000 acres in Malaysia. It devotes 61% of its land to oil palm. The remainder is planted with rubber and cocoa. KLK owns a 29% interest in Yule Catto, a U.K.-based specialty-chemicals and building-products manufacturer, and holds a 40% stake in rubber-gloves producer Masif Healthcare Products. Exports generated 70% of the company's sales in fiscal 1994. Sales to the Asian-Pacific region generated 42% of total revenues and 18% came from Europe.

MR mil	09/92	09/93	09/94	US$mil 09/94				
Sales	**441.6**	**501.1**	**672.6**	**255.9**	P/E Ratio	**33.5**	Price (9/30/95)	**7.75**
Net Income	**76.8**	**157.3**	**118.9**	**45.2**	P/B Ratio	**2.5**	52 Wk Hi-Low	**8.00-6.00**
Book Value	**1,306.9**	**1,399.2**	**1,460.5**	**570.5**	Yield %	**1.9**	Market Cap	**US$1,467.3mil**

Address **Wisma Taiko, 1 Jl. Seenivasagam** Tel **05-241-7844** ADR **KLKBY** Managing Director **Ong Beng Kee**
30000 Ipoh Fax **05-255-5312** SEDOL No. **6497446** Chairman **Lee Oi Hian**

Kumpulan Guthrie

Industry: **Plantations**

Kumpulan Guthrie is Malaysia's largest plantation company by market capitalization. The company cultivates palm oil, cocoa, rubber trees, and coconuts, and operates commodities-trading, livestock, manufacturing, and property-development businesses. Its plantations encompass approximately 150,000 hectares in Malaysia and Indonesia, oil palms are planted on 67% of this land, rubber trees are on 26%, and the remainder is dedicated to cocoa and coconuts. The company also owns a controlling interest in Malaysian plantation operator Highlands & Lowlands.

MR mil	12/92	12/93	12/94	US$mil 12/94				
Sales	**945.3**	**1,056.6**	**1,268.5**	**484.5**	P/E Ratio	**62.0**	Price (9/30/95)	**3.72**
Net Income	**28.4**	**79.5**	**79.9**	**30.5**	P/B Ratio	**2.7**	52 Wk Hi-Low	**4.80-3.56**
Book Value	**1,332.1**	**1,345.9**	**1,368.0**	**536.5**	Yield %	**2.4**	Market Cap	**US$1,482.1mil**

Address **21 Jalan Gelenggang** Tel **03-254-1644** ADR Managing Director **Abdul Khalid Ibrahim**
50490 Damansara Heights Fax **03-255-7934** SEDOL No. **6498933** Chairman **J. Ghazali Haki Che Mat**

Land & General

Industry: **Forest Products**

Land & General heads a diversified group of property, industrial, marine-services, timber, education, and financial-services businesses. Its range of activities include developing real estate, building homes, oil exploration, and manufacturing industrial resins, furniture, and precision tools. It also operates kindergartens, language centers, and technical-education courses. The company's real-estate businesses generate 56% of earnings. Land & General owns 22% of Rashid Hussain, which provides commercial and merchant banking and financial services.

MR mil	12/92	12/93	12/94	US$mil 12/94				
Sales	**460.3**	**552.8**	**749.9**	**286.4**	P/E Ratio	**19.6**	Price (9/30/95)	**6.60**
Net Income	**59.8**	**112.9**	**159.5**	**60.9**	P/B Ratio	**4.1**	52 Wk Hi-Low	**8.90-5.57**
Book Value	**386.9**	**500.0**	**703.5**	**275.9**	Yield %	**2.0**	Market Cap	**US$1,133.5mil**

Address **61 Jalan Raja Abdullah** Tel **03-291-1726** ADR Managing Director **Abdul Karim**
50300 Kuala Lumpur Fax **03-292-7711** SEDOL No. **6365491** Chairman **Azmi Wan Hamzah**

Landmarks

Industry: **Lodging**

Landmarks is a holding company that is principally engaged in real-estate development, hotel operation, and infrastructure construction. The company develops real estate for residential and commercial use. The company plans to develop a 700-hectare site near Johannesburg, South Africa for residential use. With Time Engineering and Yayasam Islam Perlis, a government agency, Landmarks participates in a consortium that overseas the operation of a natural-gas-fired power plant. The company also owns a 27% stake in South Africa's Boland Bank.

MR mil	12/92	12/93	12/94	US$mil 12/94				
Sales	**145.6**	**153.0**	**187.5**	**71.6**	P/E Ratio	**38.5**	Price (9/30/95)	**3.16**
Net Income	**42.3**	**36.5**	**34.4**	**13.1**	P/B Ratio	**1.7**	52 Wk Hi-Low	**5.55-2.90**
Book Value	**709.6**	**751.6**	**775.7**	**304.2**	Yield %	**1.6**	Market Cap	**US$527.0mil**

Address **Jalan Sultan Ismail** Tel **03-242-0311** ADR President **--**
50250 Kuala Lumpur Fax **N/A** SEDOL No. **6504960** Chairman **Samsudin Abu Hassan**

Leader Universal

Industry: **Steel**

Leader Universal Holdings manufactures aluminum and copper rods and low-voltage, high-voltage, and telecommunications cables. The firm has exclusive contracts for the purchase of its telecommunications and power cables with Telekom Malaysia and Tenaga Nasional. Leader has agreed to produce magnetic and electric wires for the South Korean firm GoldStar Cable. The firm also develops real estate and operates a cocoa and oil palm plantation. Through a joint venture with Kim Long Enterprises, Leader is constructing a digital wireless-communication system in China.

MR mil	12/92	12/93	12/94	US$mil 12/94				
Sales	**464.3**	**662.6**	**732.0**	**279.6**	P/E Ratio	**15.4**	Price (9/30/95)	**7.70**
Net Income	**79.4**	**109.1**	**127.6**	**48.7**	P/B Ratio	**2.8**	52 Wk Hi-Low	**9.45-7.60**
Book Value	**307.1**	**562.1**	**723.5**	**283.7**	Yield %	**0.9**	Market Cap	**US$1,323.3mil**

Address **Wisma Leader, 8 Jalan Larut** Tel **04-229-2888** ADR Managing Director **H. H'ng Bak Seah**
10050 Penang Fax **04-229-2333** SEDOL No. **6918516** Chairman **H'ng Bok San**

Leong Hup Holdings

Industry: **Other Food**

Leong Hup Holdings operates a poultry-farming firm and a construction company. The company's poultry-farming operation specializes in chicken breeding. With a 30% share of the Malaysian poultry market, it is the country's largest fully integrated poultry farmer. The company operates its own chicken farms and hatcheries. Its activities include chick breeding, parent stock farming, contract farming, processing, and retailing. Leong Hup owns 30% of KFC Holdings (Malaysia), a Kentucky Fried Chicken franchise holder. The company also constructs hotels, housing, and resorts.

MR mil	03/91	03/92	03/93	US$mil 03/93				
Sales	**64.0**	**93.6**	**140.9**	**55.3**	P/E Ratio	**48.8**	Price (9/30/95)	**3.90**
Net Income	**7.1**	**7.7**	**4.1**	**1.6**	P/B Ratio	**2.2**	52 Wk Hi-Low	**6.40-3.46**
Book Value	**44.6**	**48.7**	**117.3**	**45.3**	Yield %	**N/A**	Market Cap	**US$157.6mil**

Address **Jalan Ah Fook**, **80000 Johor Baru** | Tel **N/A** | Fax **N/A** | ADR | SEDOL No. **6512598** | Managing Director **Lau Chong Wang** | Chairman **Lau Chong Wang**

Lingui Developments

Industry: **Plantations**

Lingui Developments is a holding company whose subsidiaries invest in and manage real estate, operate plantations, and manufacture rubber products. Its plantation businesses cultivate oil palm and cocoa on more than 11,200 hectares of land in Malaysia. Lingui's Hock Lee Rubber Products subsidiary manufactures rubber products and provides tire-retreading services. Real-estate investment and management services are provided through its Hock Lee Enterprises and Medan Ria subsidiaries. Lingui Developments also operates six quarry sites in Sarawak.

MR mil	06/92	06/93	06/94	US$mil 06/94				
Sales	**19.9**	**28.3**	**85.9**	**32.7**	P/E Ratio	**57.6**	Price (9/30/95)	**5.30**
Net Income	**6.7**	**8.0**	**21.9**	**8.3**	P/B Ratio	**4.8**	52 Wk Hi-Low	**9.30-4.38**
Book Value	**96.2**	**106.2**	**210.8**	**81.1**	Yield %	**0.4**	Market Cap	**US$1,029.6mil**

Address **Wisma Inai, 241 Jalan Tun Razak**, **50400 Kuala Lumpur** | Tel **03-241-6333** | Fax **03-244-2188** | ADR | SEDOL No. **6518648** | Managing Director **Chee Kee Leong** | Chairman **Chan Hua Eng**

Magnum

Industry: **Casinos**

Magnum is one of Malaysia's largest gaming companies. It also owns significant financial, hospitality, and real-estate interests. The firm operates the licensed 4-D lottery game, and manages horse-racing and betting facilities. In addition, Magnum owns a condominium and hotel-resort complex in Ampang and operates a printing firm. It also holds approximately 88% of Magnum Finance, a 26-branch financial-services company, and 23% of TA Enterprise, a brokerage firm. The Malaysian conglomerate Multi-Purpose Holdings owns more than 53% of Magnum's stock.

MR mil	12/92	12/93	12/94	US$mil 12/94				
Sales	**1,556.0**	**2,248.5**	**2,229.8**	**851.7**	P/E Ratio	**16.6**	Price (9/30/95)	**4.66**
Net Income	**186.2**	**369.3**	**279.6**	**106.8**	P/B Ratio	**4.5**	52 Wk Hi-Low	**6.30-3.80**
Book Value	**518.2**	**791.4**	**1,025.7**	**402.2**	Yield %	**1.1**	Market Cap	**US$1,848.2mil**

Address **Magnum Hse., 111 Jalan Pudu**, **55100 Kuala Lumpur** | Tel **03-238-8033** | Fax **03-232-6685** | ADR | SEDOL No. **6554006** | Chief Executive **Lim Sze Guan** | Chairman **Lim Ah Tam**

Malayan Banking

Industry: **Banks - Regional**

Malayan Banking is the parent company to the Maybank Group, the largest commercial bank in Malaysia. The group comprises nearly 20 subsidiaries that provide services in merchant banking, offshore banking, lease purchasing, venture capital, securities brokerage, unit-trust management, and insurance. Maybank operates 226 branch offices and 18 service centers in Malaysia and abroad. Operations in Malaysia account for 86% of revenues; business in Singapore contributes 9%. It also has operations in Brunei, Hong Kong, London, and New York.

MR mil	06/92	06/93	06/94	US$mil 06/94				
Revenues	**4,320.2**	**5,010.9**	**5,752.4**	**2,192.2**	P/E Ratio	**36.3**	Price (9/30/95)	**20.30**
Net Income	**276.3**	**391.2**	**643.8**	**245.4**	P/B Ratio	**6.0**	52 Wk Hi-Low	**21.30-14.10**
Book Value	**3,104.8**	**3,373.6**	**3,886.1**	**1,494.7**	Yield %	**0.9**	Market Cap	**US$9,263.9mil**

Address **100 Jalan Tun Perak**, **50050 Kuala Lumpur** | Tel **03-230-8833** | Fax **03-238-1464** | ADR | SEDOL No. **6556325** | Managing Director **Amirsham A. Aziz** | Chairman **Mohamed Basir**

Malayan Cement

Industry: **Building Materials**

Malayan Cement primarily manufactures cement, concrete, other aggregate materials, and precast-concrete products. Other businesses include investment holdings, property rental, and agricultural interests. It derives 70% of its profits from Malaysian cement producer APMC, a joint venture with Pan Malaysia Cement Works. The company also conducts business in Singapore through its Cement Marketing subsidiary. Associated International Cement, a subsidiary of the United Kingdom's Blue Circle Industries, holds more than 57% of Malayan Cement's stock.

MR mil	11/92	11/93	11/94	US$mil 11/94				
Sales	**439.5**	**403.4**	**451.0**	**171.5**	P/E Ratio	**21.7**	Price (9/30/95)	**4.60**
Net Income	**63.2**	**64.1**	**69.9**	**26.6**	P/B Ratio	**3.5**	52 Wk Hi-Low	**4.84-3.60**
Book Value	**367.9**	**402.5**	**437.8**	**171.0**	Yield %	**2.6**	Market Cap	**US$606.1mil**

Address **Jalan Semantan**, **50490 Kuala Lumpur** | Tel **03-254-0177** | Fax **03-255-8632** | ADR | SEDOL No. **6556518** | Managing Director **Jeffery C. Pope** | Chairman **Tunku Abdullah**

Malayan United Industries

Industry: **Financial Services - Diversified**

Malayan United Industries (MUI) is a diversified Malaysian firm with operations in the property, construction, manufacturing, hotel, and media industries. In 1993, MUI sold two subsidiaries, MUI Bank and MUI Finance, that previously generated most of MUI's profits. MUI's holdings include the South China Morning Post (25%-owned) and a controlling stake in Hong Kong hotelier Morning Star. Its affiliate, Pan Malaysia Cement (57%) is Malaysia's largest cement maker. MUI also owns 40% of Asia Pacific Media, a joint venture with the U.S. Christian Broadcasting Network.

MR mil	12/92	12/93	12/94	US$mil 12/94				
Revenues	**645.7**	**656.6**	**659.1**	**251.7**	P/E Ratio	**35.6**	Price (9/30/95)	**2.24**
Net Income	**43.2**	**680.4**	**136.6**	**52.2**	P/B Ratio	**1.7**	52 Wk Hi-Low	**2.32-1.42**
Book Value	**956.9**	**1,592.7**	**1,684.1**	**660.4**	Yield %	**1.1**	Market Cap	**US$1,157.4mil**

Address	**MUI Plz., Jl. P. Ramlee**	Tel	**03-248-2566**	ADR	**MYLUY**	CEO	**Khoo Kay Peng**
	50250 Kuala Lumpur	Fax	**03-245-9216**	SEDOL No.	**6556756**	Chairman	**Khoo Kay Peng**

Malayawata Steel

Industry: **Steel**

Malayawata Steel operates a steel mill that is the largest producer of steel bars in Malaysia. Its main products are milled-steel round bars, high-tensile deformed bars, wire rods, and flat and angle bars; the company produces more than 1.4 million tonnes of these products per year. Its Malayawata Charcoal subsidiary manufactures charcoal for its parent company's operations. The subsidiary also operates a sawmill and markets lumber products. Malayawata Steel holds a 60% stake in Empresa, which owns oil-palm plantations in Malaysia that cover 6,000 hectares.

MR mil	03/92	03/93	03/94	US$mil 03/94				
Sales	**384.9**	**392.5**	**414.7**	**158.9**	P/E Ratio	**15.6**	Price (9/30/95)	**5.10**
Net Income	**30.6**	**52.4**	**44.0**	**16.8**	P/B Ratio	**1.9**	52 Wk Hi-Low	**5.70-3.70**
Book Value	**302.6**	**331.8**	**359.6**	**134.2**	Yield %	**3.1**	Market Cap	**US$273.1mil**

Address	**Lot 236, Prai, Wellesley**	Tel	**04-307-144**	ADR		President	--
	12700 Pulau Pinang	Fax	**04-308-863**	SEDOL No.	**6556864**	Chairman	**Shahriman T. Sulaiman**

Malaysia Mining

Industry: **Non-Ferrous Metals - Other (Exc. Aluminum)**

Malaysia Mining operates mining and engineering businesses. The company produces tin and its by-products in concentrate form, and explores for minerals such as base- and precious-metal ore. Malaysia Mining also holds a 30% stake in Plutonic Resources, an Australian gold miner, and a 47% interest in Ashton Mining, an Australian diamond miner; revenues from these two miners contribute greatly to the company's profits. Malaysia Mining owns domestic tin-smelting operations, and also owns mining interests in Papua New Guinea, Thailand, and Japan.

MR mil	01/93	01/94	01/95	US$mil 01/95				
Sales	**504.1**	**489.4**	**479.1**	**184.2**	P/E Ratio	**31.3**	Price (9/30/95)	**3.76**
Net Income	**53.0**	**180.0**	**50.2**	**19.3**	P/B Ratio	**1.2**	52 Wk Hi-Low	**5.85-3.38**
Book Value	**1,113.2**	**1,238.2**	**1,315.4**	**513.8**	Yield %	**1.1**	Market Cap	**US$626.3mil**

Address	**201A Jalan Tun Razak**	Tel	**03-261-6000**	ADR		Managing Director	**Ibrahim Menudin**
	50400 Kuala Lumpur	Fax	**03-261-2951**	SEDOL No.	**6556648**	Chairman	**Nasruddin bin Mohamed**

Malaysian Airline System

Industry: **Airlines**

Malaysian Airline System, the largest Malaysian airline by market capitalization, operates a fleet of 70 passenger and cargo aircraft. The company has destinations throughout Asia and Australia, and in parts of Europe and North America. It also provides trucking services and bus transportation, and develops computerized reservation systems and computer software for travel services. Passenger flights contribute about two thirds of company revenues. Malaysian Helicopter Services has a 32% interest in Malaysian Airline System.

MR mil	03/93 R	03/94	03/95	US$mil 03/95				
Sales	**3,791.8**	**4,081.1**	**4,780.1**	**1,857.8**	P/E Ratio	**36.2**	Price (9/30/95)	**7.20**
Net Income	**143.6**	**8.4**	**263.1**	**102.3**	P/B Ratio	**1.4**	52 Wk Hi-Low	**8.95-6.40**
Book Value	**3,277.0**	**3,279.3**	**3,494.1**	**1,381.1**	Yield %	**1.0**	Market Cap	**US$2,008.0mil**

Address	**Jalan Sultan Ismail**	Tel	**03-261-0555**	ADR		Managing Director	**Wan Malek Ibrahim**
	50250 Kuala Lumpur	Fax	**03-261-3472**	SEDOL No.	**6556682**	Chairman	**Tajudin Ramli**

R=Restated.

Malaysian International Shipping

Industry: **Marine Transportation**

Malaysian International Shipping (MISC) provides marine-transportation services. Its principal business is the ownership and operation of a fleet of 53 ships. This fleet, which has a capacity of more than 1.8 million deadweight tonnes, is used to transport goods from port to port. Among the materials that Malaysian International Shipping transports are liquefied natural gas, chemicals, oil, and woodchips. The company also holds minority interest in Malaysia's Port Klang. Its land-based subsidiaries provide haulage, warehousing, trucking, and container repair services.

MR mil	12/92	12/93	12/94	US$mil 12/94				
Sales	**1,979.2**	**2,017.1**	**2,410.6**	**920.8**	P/E Ratio	**13.2**	Price (9/30/95)	**7.55**
Net Income	**503.3**	**520.2**	**570.9**	**218.1**	P/B Ratio	**1.8**	52 Wk Hi-Low	**8.60-5.60**
Book Value	**3,359.3**	**3,729.4**	**4,102.0**	**1,608.6**	Yield %	**2.6**	Market Cap	**US$3,008.0mil**

Address	**Wisma MISC, 2 Jalan Conlay**	Tel	**03-242-8088**	ADR		Managing Director	**Ariffin Alias**
	50450 Kuala Lumpur	Fax	**03-248-6602**	SEDOL No.	**6558031**	Chairman	**R.M. Alias**

Malaysian Oxygen

Industry: **Specialty Chemicals**

Malaysian Oxygen produces industrial gases, welding rods, medical gases and equipment, and related products for use in the electronics, industrial, and medical sectors. Sales of industrial and medical gases generate most of the company's revenues, accounting for 75% of the total. Its welding subsidiary, Malaysian Oxygen Welding Products, is the country's largest producer of electrodes in terms of volume and range. Alboc, a joint venture between industrial-gas producers The BOC Group (U.K.) and L'Air Liquide (France), owns 45% of Malaysian Oxygen.

MR mil	09/92	09/93	09/94	US$mil 09/94				
Sales	**185.1**	**209.3**	**244.2**	**92.9**	P/E Ratio	**30.0**	Price (9/30/95)	**9.60**
Net Income	**39.8**	**41.6**	**44.7**	**17.0**	P/B Ratio	**6.5**	52 Wk Hi-Low	**9.65-6.75**
Book Value	**152.6**	**176.9**	**203.3**	**79.4**	Yield %	**1.8**	Market Cap	**US$529.4mil**

Address **13 Jalan 222**
46100 Petaling Jaya
Tel **03-755-4233**
Fax **03-756-6389**
ADR
SEDOL No. **6556927**
Managing Director **Roderick H. Duke**
Chairman **H. Omar Yoke Lin Ong**

MBF Capital

Industry: **Financial Services - Diversified**

MBF Capital is the holding company for financial-service companies. It operates financing, stockbroking, unit-trust management, leasing, credit-card, and insurance businesses. MBF Finance, a subsidiary offering deposit and loan services, is Malaysia's largest finance company in terms of total assets. MBF Finance operates 127 branches in Malaysia. The company is also developing three major real-estate projects, one of which is a hotel and commercial complex, and two of which are residential projects. MBF Holdings has a controlling 32% interest in the company.

MR mil	12/92	12/93	12/94	US$mil 12/94				
Revenues	**1,065.5**	**1,213.3**	**1,249.9**	**477.4**	P/E Ratio	**10.0**	Price (9/30/95)	**2.70**
Net Income	**27.1**	**157.5**	**206.9**	**79.0**	P/B Ratio	**1.9**	52 Wk Hi-Low	**3.42-1.99**
Book Value	**754.0**	**889.2**	**1,106.8**	**434.0**	Yield %	**1.9**	Market Cap	**US$835.4mil**

Address **Plaza MBF, Jalan Ampang**
50450 Kuala Lumpur
Tel **03-261-8066**
Fax **03-261-3280**
ADR
SEDOL No. **6551278**
President & CEO **Loy Hean Heong**
Chairman **Tunku Abdullah**

Metroplex

Industry: **Home Construction**

Metroplex is a holding company engaged in procuring and developing real estate. Its subsidiaries are a diversified group of property developers and construction firms that build commercial complexes, apartments, townhouses, and retail projects. Metroplex rents and leases these properties to individuals and commercial users. It also markets building materials, offers financial services, and owns a cruise line. Metroplex's construction businesses operate in Malaysia and Singapore through subsidiaries Metroplex Construction and Metrobilt Construction.

MR mil	01/93	01/94	01/95	US$mil 01/95				
Sales	**139.2**	**152.0**	**244.6**	**94.0**	P/E Ratio	**38.2**	Price (9/30/95)	**2.18**
Net Income	**34.5**	**34.4**	**43.6**	**16.8**	P/B Ratio	**2.7**	52 Wk Hi-Low	**2.80-1.69**
Book Value	**491.4**	**535.2**	**628.0**	**245.3**	Yield %	**1.4**	Market Cap	**US$686.5mil**

Address **150 Jalan Ampang**
50450 Kuala Lumpur
Tel **03-244-8911**
Fax **03-241-9638**
ADR
SEDOL No. **6584683**
Managing Director **Chan Teik Huat**
Chairman **Lim Siew Kim**

Mulpha International Trading

Industry: **Overseas Trading**

Mulpha International is a securities- and general-trading company that engages in property development, concrete manufacturing, and hotel operations. The company sells engineering equipment, provides rental construction equipment, and develops and manages residential and commercial properties. It also sells apparel, shoes, and cosmetics under the Pierre Cardin name, and sports equipment under the Rossignol name. In Malaysia, Australia, and Vietnam, Mulpha International operates hotels, resorts, and parking garages.

MR mil	12/92	12/93	12/94	US$mil 12/94				
Sales	**122.5**	**279.5**	**457.4**	**174.7**	P/E Ratio	**35.2**	Price (9/30/95)	**2.71**
Net Income	**7.9**	**24.7**	**44.1**	**16.8**	P/B Ratio	**3.8**	52 Wk Hi-Low	**4.48-2.12**
Book Value	**142.8**	**166.5**	**453.4**	**177.8**	Yield %	**0.4**	Market Cap	**US$1,040.4mil**

Address **17 Jalan Semangat**
46200 Petaling Jaya
Tel **06-755-1344**
Fax **06-757-2234**
ADR
SEDOL No. **6609597**
President --
Chairman **M. Chen Wing Sum**

Multi-Purpose

Industry: **Casinos**

Multi-Purpose Holdings is the investment arm of the Multi-Purpose Group. The firm is active in the finance, real-estate, technology, and shipping industries. It also operates a numbers-forecasting game and horse races. Its financial activities include commercial banking, general insurance, and property investment. The firm owns 52% of Dunlop Estates, a holding company for real-estate and gaming operations that has a 51% stake in Magnum. Multi-Purpose also owns a 38% stake in property-developer Bandar Raya Developments.

MR mil	12/92	12/93	12/94	US$mil 12/94				
Sales	**1,841.5**	**2,548.4**	**2,612.1**	**997.7**	P/E Ratio	**23.4**	Price (9/30/95)	**3.90**
Net Income	**83.1**	**326.2**	**264.7**	**101.1**	P/B Ratio	**2.3**	52 Wk Hi-Low	**4.92-2.59**
Book Value	**796.1**	**1,061.6**	**1,265.9**	**496.4**	Yield %	**0.3**	Market Cap	**US$1,167.0mil**

Address **8 Jalan Munshi Abdullah**
50100 Kuala Lumpur
Tel **03-294-8333**
Fax **03-294-1380**
ADR
SEDOL No. **6609627**
Chief Executive **T.K. Lim**
Chairman **T.K. Lim**

Mycom

Industry: **Real-Estate Investment**

Mycom is a diversified holding company. Its subsidiaries are involved in gaming, property development, plantations, construction, timber, industrial materials, automobiles, and investment brokerage. The company is involved in gaming through its 51%-owned Olympia Industries subsidiary. This subsidiary manages gaming and property activities for Lotteries (Sabah). Mycom's UNP Plywood unit owns timberland and processes lumber used in construction. Mycom also owns a 30% interest in Italy's Automobili Lamborghini and intends to develop commercial vehicles in Indonesia.

MR mil	06/92	06/93	06/94	US$mil 06/94				
Sales	**314.3**	**333.0**	**614.5**	**234.2**	P/E Ratio	**11.3**	Price (9/30/95)	**3.06**
Net Income	**48.9**	**356.7**	**66.9**	**25.5**	P/B Ratio	**2.1**	52 Wk Hi-Low	**5.48-2.98**
Book Value	**139.4**	**306.9**	**355.6**	**136.8**	Yield %	**2.3**	Market Cap	**US$400.3mil**

Address	**Wisma Hamzah-Kwong Hing 1**	Tel	**03-230-0033**	ADR		Managing Director	**Yap Yong Seong**
	50100 Kuala Lumpur	Fax	**03-230-2285**	SEDOL No.	**6612487**	Chairman	**Jaffar bin Abdul**

Nestlé (Malaysia)

Industry: **Other Food**

Nestlé (Malaysia) produces milk and food products. Nestlé (Malaysia) produces condensed milk, powdered milk, juices, instant coffee, instant noodles, cereals, condiments, chocolate, snack foods, and other food products. The company markets these products in Malaysia under the Nestlé, Carnation, Crunch, Teapot, and other brand names. It also exports these products to other countries in the region. Nestlé (Malaysia) operates five production plants in Malaysia. The Swiss food and beverage producer Nestlé owns 51% of the company's outstanding shares.

MR mil	12/92	12/93	12/94	US$mil 12/94				
Sales	**1,202.6**	**1,319.1**	**1,460.8**	**558.0**	P/E Ratio	**28.5**	Price (9/30/95)	**17.80**
Net Income	**116.5**	**134.4**	**149.3**	**57.0**	P/B Ratio	**10.2**	52 Wk Hi-Low	**19.40-15.50**
Book Value	**358.9**	**385.5**	**410.0**	**160.8**	Yield %	**3.0**	Market Cap	**US$1,663.0mil**

Address	**4 Lorong Pesiaran Barat**	Tel	**03-755-4466**	ADR		Managing Director	**Ajit Saran**
	46918 Petaling Jaya	Fax	**03-755-0992**	SEDOL No.	**6629335**	Chairman	**Mohamed Ghazali Seth**

New Straits Times Press

Industry: **Publishing**

The New Straits Times Press publishes newspapers, periodicals, journals, and books in Malaysia. It also manages chains of retail outlets through its Berita Book Centre and its majority-owned Marican subsidiaries. The company's newspapers include a daily, The New Straits Times; a weekly, The New Sunday Times; and a business daily, Malaysia's Business Times. The New Straits Times Press' other subsidiaries invest in and develop real estate, underwrite life-insurance policies, and market computers, peripherals, and software to customers throughout Malaysia.

MR mil	08/92	08/93	08/94	US$mil 08/94				
Sales	**380.8**	**422.6**	**532.4**	**202.6**	P/E Ratio	**16.9**	Price (9/30/95)	**7.10**
Net Income	**66.1**	**71.4**	**69.9**	**26.6**	P/B Ratio	**3.6**	52 Wk Hi-Low	**10.30-6.50**
Book Value	**385.7**	**416.3**	**351.0**	**137.1**	Yield %	**1.3**	Market Cap	**US$510.1mil**

Address	**Balai Berita, 31 Jalan Riong**	Tel	**03-282-3131**	ADR		Managing Director	**Mohamed Noor**
	59100 Kuala Lumpur	Fax	**03-282-1434**	SEDOL No.	**6633002**	Chairman	**Mohamed Ghazali**

Nylex

Industry: **Specialty Chemicals**

Nylex manufactures industrial films and coated fabrics such as vinyl fabrics, injection-molded products, and suede products. The company's suede products are used in footwear, furniture, automotive, luggage, and packaging applications. Nylex also produces PVC products, power-generation equipment, glass containers, roofing tiles, and insulation products. Its Tamco Cutler-Hammer subsidiary operates switchgear-manufacturing ventures in the United Arab Emirates and China. Australian industrial manufacturer BTR Nylex owns a 50% equity interest in Nylex.

MR mil	12/92 R	12/93	12/94	US$mil 12/94				
Sales	**335.1**	**369.8**	**441.4**	**168.6**	P/E Ratio	**25.0**	Price (9/30/95)	**7.35**
Net Income	**42.1**	**37.5**	**44.0**	**16.8**	P/B Ratio	**3.3**	52 Wk Hi-Low	**8.50-4.38**
Book Value	**292.1**	**308.1**	**332.5**	**130.4**	Yield %	**2.7**	Market Cap	**US$438.2mil**

Address	**Shah Alam Industrial Estate**	Tel	**03-559-1706**	ADR		Managing Director	**Heah Kok Soon**
	40910 Shah Alam	Fax	**03-550-0088**	SEDOL No.	**6652375**	Chairman	**Alan R. Jackson**

R=Restated.

Oriental Holdings

Industry: **Automobile Manufacturers**

Oriental Holdings is a diversified Malaysian holding company with subsidiaries that primarily manufacture motor vehicles and related components. Through its Oriental Assemblers and Kah Motor subsidiaries, Oriental makes and markets Honda cars, motorcycles, and components. The company also invests in and develops real estate, manages hotels and golf courses, provides lending services, and cultivates and processes rubber and palm oil. In addition, Oriental Holdings manufactures wire, building materials, and injection-molded plastic parts for use in automotive applications.

MR mil	12/92	12/93	12/94	US$mil 12/94				
Sales	**1,278.2**	**1,527.9**	**2,060.3**	**787.0**	P/E Ratio	**9.3**	Price (9/30/95)	**12.60**
Net Income	**122.1**	**131.0**	**196.5**	**75.1**	P/B Ratio	**1.5**	52 Wk Hi-Low	**15.20-11.00**
Book Value	**774.4**	**893.0**	**1,182.6**	**463.8**	Yield %	**2.1**	Market Cap	**US$724.3mil**

Address	**42 Jalan Sultan, Ahmad Shah**	Tel	**04-376-915**	ADR		Managing Director	**Loh Boon Siew**
	10050 Penang	Fax	**04-360-713**	SEDOL No.	**6661434**	Chairman	**Loh Boon Siew**

Pacific Chemical

Industry: **Forest Products**

Pacific Chemical is an holding company that engages in log trading and timber production. It operates its timber business through its wholly-owned Usama Industries subsidiary, which sells a large portion of its timber to Woodhouse, a subsidiary of Ekran. Pacific Chemical is also part of a consortium of companies involved in a $6-billion hydroelectric-power project in Bakun--Asia's largest power project to date. The company will use the timber it harvests from the project site to produce paper products. Pacific Chemical is an affiliate of Malaysia's Ting industrial group.

MR mil	12/91	12/92	12/93	US$mil 12/93				
Sales	**N/A**	**N/A**	**149.7**	**58.0**	P/E Ratio	**33.2**	Price (9/30/95)	**6.10**
Net Income	**N/A**	**N/A**	**11.1**	**4.3**	P/B Ratio	**3.7**	52 Wk Hi-Low	**10.44-5.10**
Book Value	**N/A**	**N/A**	**182.5**	**67.8**	Yield %	**0.9**	Market Cap	**US$394.7mil**

Address **8-3 Jalan Segambut**
51200 Kuala Lumpur
Tel **03-443-9266**
Fax **03-559-9791**
ADR
SEDOL No. **6666592**
President **Mun Chiew Foong**
Chairman **Ting Pek Khiing**

Pelangi

Industry: **Home Construction**

Pelangi develops commercial and residential property, manufactures building products, and cultivates rubber and oil palm. The rental of space in its Menara Pelangi office building and the sale of retail sites and luxury single- and multifamily housing units account for most of the company's profits. Pelangi's residential properties, sold primarily through its Taman Gunong Hijau subsidiary, are concentrated in the Malaysian state of Johore. Pelangi also manufactures and markets ready-mix concrete, concrete roof tiles, medical-examination gloves, and lime products.

MR mil	03/93	03/94	03/95	US$mil 03/95				
Sales	**143.6**	**161.1**	**183.9**	**71.5**	P/E Ratio	**20.8**	Price (9/30/95)	**2.96**
Net Income	**23.0**	**36.4**	**45.9**	**17.8**	P/B Ratio	**N/A**	52 Wk Hi-Low	**3.60-2.60**
Book Value	**245.4**	**268.4**	**N/A**	**N/A**	Yield %	**1.0**	Market Cap	**US$380.7mil**

Address **Menara Pelangi, Jalan Kuning**
80400 Johor Bahru
Tel **07-332-4366**
Fax **07-332-4968**
ADR
SEDOL No. **6679352**
Managing Director **Goon Swee Kheong**
Chairman **Tunku Osman Ahmad**

Perlis Plantations

Industry: **Plantations**

Perlis Plantations is a diversified holding company that cultivates and refines sugarcane and oil palm. The firm is also active in commodity trading, food processing, hotel management, and cinema operations. Perlis owns and operates a 4,560-hectare sugarcane plantation along the Malaysian-Thai border. The company has a 50% stake in Federal Flour Mills, which operates Malaysia's leading soybean-crushing plants and palm-oil refinery. Perlis also operates 70 cinemas. Its 24%-owned Shangri-La Hotels subsidiary operates hotels with a total of 2,200 rooms.

MR mil	12/92	12/93	12/94	US$mil 12/94				
Sales	**3,329.1**	**3,445.1**	**4,805.8**	**1,835.7**	P/E Ratio	**14.8**	Price (9/30/95)	**8.00**
Net Income	**172.3**	**272.1**	**178.6**	**68.2**	P/B Ratio	**1.6**	52 Wk Hi-Low	**9.05-7.70**
Book Value	**1,123.6**	**1,369.6**	**1,510.3**	**592.3**	Yield %	**2.0**	Market Cap	**US$938.2mil**

Address **38 Jl. Sultan Ismail**
50250 Kuala Lumpur
Tel **03-241-2077**
Fax **03-241-8242**
ADR **PPBHY**
SEDOL No. **6681669**
President **--**
Chairman **Kuok Khoon Ean**

Perusahaan Otomobil Nasional

Industry: **Automobile Manufacturers**

Perusahaan Otomobil Nasional (Proton) is Malaysia's largest automobile manufacturer by market capitalization. The company has a production capacity of 120,000 units per year, and markets its cars under the Proton Saga and Wira model names. Proton also produces replacement parts and a line of accessories for its automobiles through a minority interest in PHN Industry and Aluminium Alloy Castings. The company markets its cars in Malaysia and 17 other countries, including Australia and the United Kingdom. Edaran Otomobil Nasional is Proton's sole distributor in Malaysia.

MR mil	03/93 R	03/94 R	03/95	US$mil 03/95				
Sales	**2,286.5**	**3,087.0**	**3,708.4**	**1,441.3**	P/E Ratio	**19.7**	Price (9/30/95)	**9.00**
Net Income	**265.3**	**246.9**	**232.1**	**90.2**	P/B Ratio	**3.3**	52 Wk Hi-Low	**9.80-7.65**
Book Value	**1,072.0**	**1,308.0**	**1,403.7**	**554.8**	Yield %	**1.8**	Market Cap	**US$1,826.5mil**

Address **Kawasan Perindustrian HICOM**
40000 Shah Alam
Tel **03-511-1055**
Fax **03-511-1252**
ADR
SEDOL No. **6697558**
Managing Director **Nadzmi bin Mohd Salleh**
Chairman **Jamil bin Mohd Jan**

R=Restated.

Petaling Garden

Industry: **Real-Estate Investment**

Petaling Garden invests in and develops real estate and housing, and is also active in the hotels and resorts and oil-palm-plantation industries. The majority of the company's income comes from its plantations; it grows oil palms on 1,050 hectares of land. Petaling also sells and leases commercial, industrial, and residential property. Its 56%-owned Lanjut Golf Resort subsidiary operates a resort that includes a 66-room hotel and two golf courses. Petaling's Komtar Hotel venture with Rasa Sayang Beach Hotels operates the Shangri-La hotel in Penang.

MR mil	12/92 R	12/93	12/94	US$mil 12/94				
Sales	**74.4**	**85.3**	**97.6**	**37.3**	P/E Ratio	**97.4**	Price (9/30/95)	**3.02**
Net Income	**11.7**	**59.6**	**59.6**	**22.8**	P/B Ratio	**2.6**	52 Wk Hi-Low	**4.92-2.47**
Book Value	**216.9**	**224.1**	**223.9**	**87.8**	Yield %	**1.0**	Market Cap	**US$229.4mil**

Address **49-B Jalan 6/31**
46000 Petaling Jaya
Tel **03-792-0518**
Fax **03-791-2726**
ADR
SEDOL No. **6683364**
Managing Director **Ang Guan Seng**
Chairman **Ang Guan Seng**

R=Restated.

Promet

Industry: **Marine Transportation**

Promet is a diversified marine contractor. It operates marine-contracting and -consulting services, and engages in civil engineering, construction, and property-investment and development activities. The company also owns interests in granite-quarry businesses and provides specialized services for the petroleum industry. Its marine-construction services include shipbuilding and ship repair; civil engineering projects include a housing project in the Philippines and the construction and management of an oil terminal in Pakistan.

MR mil	12/92	12/93	12/94	US$mil 12/94				
Sales	73.2	222.5	286.2	109.3	P/E Ratio	93.9	Price (9/30/95)	3.10
Net Income	-29.3	27.3	17.7	6.8	P/B Ratio	3.7	52 Wk Hi-Low	3.46-1.83
Book Value	385.0	422.5	448.3	175.8	Yield %	0.0	Market Cap	US$658.5mil

Address **Jalan Sultan Ismail**, **50250 Kuala Lumpur**
Tel **03-248-4899**
Fax **03-248-2902**
ADR
SEDOL No. **6114488**
Managing Director **Benety Chang**
Chairman **Brian Chang**

Public Bank

Industry: **Banks - Regional**

Public Bank provides banking and financial services, including corporate-banking, retail-banking, commodity-trading, and stock-brokerage services. In addition, Public Bank manages unit investment trusts through its 55%-owned Kuala Lumpur Mutual Fund subsidiary. Commercial banking services account for 34% of profits. The company has branches in Malaysia, Hong Kong, Sri Lanka, and Cambodia. Its Asian operations include Hong Kong-based JCG Finance and a bank in Vietnam established in a joint venture with the Bank for Investment and Development of Vietnam.

MR mil	12/92	12/93	12/94	US$mil 12/94				
Revenues	1,580.5	2,242.6	2,250.7	859.7	P/E Ratio	20.9	Price (9/30/95)	4.66
Net Income	139.7	287.0	256.0	97.8	P/B Ratio	3.1	52 Wk Hi-Low	6.45-4.08
Book Value	947.3	1,219.6	1,859.5	729.2	Yield %	1.7	Market Cap	US$630.6mil

Address **6 Jalan Sultan Sulaiman**, **50000 Kuala Lumpur**
Tel **03-273-3333**
Fax **03-274-2179**
ADR
SEDOL No. **6707093**
President & CEO **Teh Hong Piow**
Chairman **Thong Yaw Hong**

Rashid Hussain

Industry: **Securities Brokers**

Rashid Hussain engages in banking and investment activities. Its Rashid Hussain Securities, RHB Futures, RHB Equities, and 51%-owned Straits Securities subsidiaries provide investment advice and brokerage services. The company owns a 20% interest in Development & Commercial Bank. This bank and its affiliates provide commercial, merchant, and offshore banking, and underwrite insurance. Its Rashid Hussain Asset Management subsidiary manages more than 1.1 billion ringgits in assets for investors. The company also develops and manages real-estate holdings.

MR mil	05/92	05/93	05/94	US$mil 05/94				
Sales	109.9	203.0	402.3	153.4	P/E Ratio	9.2	Price (9/30/95)	7.20
Net Income	41.1	70.8	201.5	76.8	P/B Ratio	2.8	52 Wk Hi-Low	8.90-5.45
Book Value	403.2	464.2	670.1	259.7	Yield %	1.0	Market Cap	US$825.0mil

Address **RHB 1, 424 Jalan Tun Razak**, **50400 Kuala Lumpur**
Tel **03-985-2233**
Fax **03-985-5522**
ADR
SEDOL No. **6724735**
President --
Chairman **Abdul Rashid Hussain**

Renong

Industry: **Conglomerates**

Renong is a holding company that focuses on infrastructure development. It is active in construction, engineering, telecommunications, finance, oil and gas, and property development. Renong owns 33% of United Engineers (Malaysia), a contractor specializing in infrastructure projects. Its Prolink Development subsidiary is currently building a 10,900 hectare township in southwest Johor. It provides telecommunications services through its Time Telecommunications subsidiary, which has a fiberoptic network spanning more than 3,000 kilometers.

MR mil	06/92	06/93	06/94	US$mil 06/94				
Sales	149.3	334.1	400.3	152.6	P/E Ratio	42.3	Price (9/30/95)	4.36
Net Income	114.9	449.2	282.8	107.8	P/B Ratio	2.6	52 Wk Hi-Low	5.05-2.38
Book Value	2,214.0	2,651.3	2,661.5	1,023.7	Yield %	0.2	Market Cap	US$2,863.2mil

Address **42 Jalan Syed Putra**, **50460 Kuala Lumpur**
Tel **03-274-2166**
Fax **03-274-3979**
ADR
SEDOL No. **6732374**
Managing Director **Yusli Mohamed Yusoff**
Chairman **Halim Bin Saad**

Resorts World

Industry: **Casinos**

Resorts World develops and manages hotels, restaurants, recreation and amusement facilities, and gaming operations. It operates the Genting Highlands Resort, which is located outside of Kuala Lumpur. This resort features the 821-room Resort Hotel, the 300-room Awana Hotel, the Genting Convention Center, a golf course, and an indoor theme park. The firm is also building an outdoor theme park. Resorts World has a total of 1,700 available rooms and an average occupancy rate of more than 80%. Resorts World is also the only holder of a casino license in Malaysia.

MR mil	12/92	12/93	12/94	US$mil 12/94				
Sales	1,347.6	1,704.5	1,925.2	735.4	P/E Ratio	24.5	Price (9/30/95)	12.50
Net Income	386.3	451.1	555.7	212.3	P/B Ratio	6.9	52 Wk Hi-Low	17.40-12.00
Book Value	1,239.5	1,567.8	1,984.3	778.2	Yield %	1.0	Market Cap	US$5,437.5mil

Address **Wisma Genting, Jl. Sultan Ismail**, **50250 Kuala Lumpur**
Tel **03-261-3833**
Fax **03-261-5304**
ADR **RSWSY**
SEDOL No. **6731962**
President --
Chairman **Lim Goh Tong**

Rothmans of Pall Mall

Industry: **Tobacco**

Rothmans of Pall Mall (Malaysia) manufactures tobacco products and provides packaging services. It makes, imports, and sells cigarettes and other tobacco products through its subsidiaries, Cigarette Importers and Distributors, Rothmans Brands, The Leaf Tobacco Development, and Tobacco Importers and Manufacturers. Its subsidiaries have a combined market share of more than 50% of cigarette sales in Malaysia. It also holds 35% of the printing and packaging firm Tien Wah Press. Rothmans International (U.K.) owns 50% of Rothmans of Pall Mall.

MR mil	03/93	03/94	03/95	US$mil 03/95				
Sales	**1,123.7**	**1,329.2**	**1,444.5**	**561.4**	P/E Ratio	**18.4**	Price (9/30/95)	**19.50**
Net Income	**229.8**	**273.7**	**303.9**	**118.1**	P/B Ratio	**NMF**	52 Wk Hi-Low	**20.20-15.00**
Book Value	**728.3**	**353.5**	**217.7**	**86.0**	Yield %	**7.9**	Market Cap	**US$2,218.3mil**

Address **Jalan Universiti, Petaling Jaya**
46200 Selangor
Tel **03-756-6899**
Fax **03-755-8416**
ADR
SEDOL No. **6752349**
Managing Director **Anthony Jones**
Chairman **Talib bin Othman**

Selangor Properties

Industry: **Real-Estate Investment**

Selangor Properties is a property-investment and development company operating solely in Malaysia. It owns or has significant interests in 12 major residential, retail, and office properties, mostly in the Damansara Heights area of Kuala Lumpur. The company's primary revenue source is rental income. Selangor's T.K. Weng, Chong Chook Yew, and Bungsar Hill Holdings subsidiaries engage in property-investment and investment-holding activities. It also has an interest in Singapore-based Pointworth Management, an investment- and fund-management concern.

MR mil	10/92	10/93	10/94	US$mil 10/94				
Sales	**63.1**	**60.7**	**65.3**	**24.8**	P/E Ratio	**37.1**	Price (9/30/95)	**2.52**
Net Income	**15.9**	**22.4**	**89.8**	**34.2**	P/B Ratio	**1.2**	52 Wk Hi-Low	**3.60-2.10**
Book Value	**606.3**	**621.6**	**693.3**	**270.8**	Yield %	**2.0**	Market Cap	**US$345.0mil**

Address **Jalan Semantan**
50490 Kuala Lumpur
Tel **03-255-7188**
Fax **03-255-0441**
ADR **SEL**
SEDOL No. **6794040**
Managing Director **Chong Chook Yew**
Chairman **Wen Tien Kuang**

Sime Darby

Industry: **Conglomerates**

Sime Darby, Malaysia's largest conglomerate by market capitalization, has interests in more than 200 companies. It operates plantations, develops property, and distributes cars and heavy machinery. The firm cultivates oil-palm, rubber, and cocoa crops, and manufactures tires for sale in Malaysia, Europe, and the Middle East. It distributes Ford, BMW, and Land Rover vehicles and Caterpillar construction equipment. Almost half of Sime Darby's revenue comes from Hong Kong, Singapore, and Australia. It owns 75% of the publicly traded Sime Darby Hong Kong.

MR mil	06/92	06/93	06/94	US$mil 06/94				
Sales	**6,197.5**	**7,041.4**	**8,212.5**	**3,129.8**	P/E Ratio	**23.3**	Price (9/30/95)	**6.70**
Net Income	**353.5**	**403.2**	**449.7**	**171.4**	P/B Ratio	**3.1**	52 Wk Hi-Low	**7.20-5.00**
Book Value	**2,930.6**	**3,142.4**	**3,423.2**	**1,316.6**	Yield %	**2.4**	Market Cap	**US$5,641.8mil**

Address **Jalan Raja Laut**
50350 Kuala Lumpur
Tel **03-291-4122**
Fax **03-298-7398**
ADR **SIDBY**
SEDOL No. **6808769**
President **Tunku Tan**
Chairman **Tun Ismail**

Sime UEP Properties

Industry: **Real-Estate Investment**

Sime UEP Properties is the division of Malaysia's Sime Darby that handles real-estate investment and development. The company primarily constructs single-family houses for middle-income buyers. It sells approximately 2,000 of these houses per year. It also develops commercial properties and sells industrial plots and shop offices. Sime UEP operates a movie theater, a plant nursery, and an amusement park. Its Subang Jaya subsidiary constructed the Tai-Pan Triangle retail and office development in the Subang Jaya Town Center commercial complex.

MR mil	06/92	06/93	06/94	US$mil 06/94				
Sales	**507.5**	**442.9**	**376.6**	**143.5**	P/E Ratio	**29.6**	Price (9/30/95)	**4.44**
Net Income	**79.3**	**79.0**	**60.9**	**23.2**	P/B Ratio	**2.9**	52 Wk Hi-Low	**6.10-4.02**
Book Value	**608.5**	**626.2**	**626.6**	**241.0**	Yield %	**3.4**	Market Cap	**US$715.4mil**

Address **Wisma Tractors, 7 Jalan SS 16/1**
47500 Petaling Jaya
Tel **03-733-0088**
Fax **03-733-2122**
ADR
SEDOL No. **6915250**
Managing Director **Mohamed Haji Said**
Chairman **Syed N. Shahabuddin**

TA Enterprise

Industry: **Securities Brokers**

TA Enterprise is an investment holding company with interests in retail investment brokerage, fund management, property development, and construction. The company underwrites securities in Malaysia through its TA Securities and Botly Securities subsidiaries. It offers regional brokerage services through its subsidiaries in Hong Kong, the Philippines, and Australia. The company holds a 40% stake in Serendib Trust Services (a brokerage firm in Sri Lanka) and 6% interest in Global Trust Bank of India. The company also has offices in London and New York.

MR mil	10/92	10/93	01/95 *	US$mil 01/95				
Sales	**136.8**	**683.4**	**1,156.1**	**444.5**	P/E Ratio	**5.8**	Price (9/30/95)	**3.54**
Net Income	**34.8**	**307.5**	**365.5**	**140.5**	P/B Ratio	**2.8**	52 Wk Hi-Low	**4.75-2.68**
Book Value	**157.6**	**449.1**	**775.0**	**302.7**	Yield %	**1.4**	Market Cap	**US$851.0mil**

Address **UBN Twr., Jl. P. Ramlee**
50250 Kuala Lumpur
Tel **03-232-1277**
Fax **03-201-4929**
ADR
SEDOL No. **6872032**
Managing Director **Tiah Thee Kian**
Chairman **Tiah Thee Kian**

*Irregular period due to fiscal year change.

Tan Chong Motor Holdings

Industry: **Automobile Manufacturers**

Tan Chong Motor Holdings distributes automobiles for Japan's Nissan Motor and makes automotive parts, such as shock absorbers and radiators. The company also sells trucks and heavy equipment, markets Shiseido cosmetics and Wacoal apparel, manages real estate, operates travel and tour businesses, and provides insurance and financial services. Its Comit Communication Technologies subsidiary distributes Motorola cellular phones and Apple Newton personal digital assistants. Tan Chong operates in Papua New Guinea, Brunei, Singapore, Hong Kong, and Australia.

MR mil	12/92	12/93	12/94	US$mil 12/94				
Sales	**1,623.1**	**1,726.4**	**1,827.0**	**697.9**	P/E Ratio	**19.7**	Price (9/30/95)	**2.76**
Net Income	**77.2**	**79.3**	**96.1**	**36.7**	P/B Ratio	**1.6**	52 Wk Hi-Low	**3.66-2.46**
Book Value	**927.4**	**1,013.3**	**1,124.5**	**441.0**	Yield %	**1.4**	Market Cap	**US$738.9mil**

Address **21 Jalan Ipoh Kecil, 50350 Kuala Lumpur**
Tel **03-442-7644**
Fax **03-441-8373**
ADR
SEDOL No. **6871125**
Managing Director **Tan Eng Soon**
Chairman **Tan Kim Hor**

Tasek Cement

Industry: **Building Materials**

Tasek Cement manufactures and sells cement and related products used in residential, commercial, and industrial construction, as well as in public infrastructure projects. The company markets its construction products throughout Malaysia under the Crocodile brand name. The company also operates five cement outlets. The company's production activities are centered around the Tasek Cement Factory and Tasek Industrial Estate in Ipoh. Tasek Cement also owns a bulk cement and packing plant in Selangor, as well as 850 acres of plantation land in Ulu Kinta.

MR mil	06/92	06/93	06/94	US$mil 06/94				
Sales	**205.6**	**205.0**	**213.9**	**81.5**	P/E Ratio	**20.6**	Price (9/30/95)	**6.00**
Net Income	**40.1**	**34.3**	**43.6**	**16.6**	P/B Ratio	**3.3**	52 Wk Hi-Low	**6.90-4.90**
Book Value	**221.3**	**240.8**	**275.9**	**106.1**	Yield %	**1.7**	Market Cap	**US$356.8mil**

Address **Jalan Sultan Idris Shah, 30000 Ipoh**
Tel **05-515-726**
Fax **N/A**
ADR
SEDOL No. **6874704**
Chief Executive **David Tan Sek Yin**
Chairman **Hamzah Sendut**

Technology Resources Industries

Industry: **Electrical Components & Equipment**

Technology Resources Industries (TRI) is an investment holding company active in telecommunications, transportation, property investment, securities dealing, and manufacturing. Its wholly-owned Celcom subsidiary has 450,000 subscribers making it Malaysia's largest cellular-network operator. TRI owns a 15% stake in the U.S. Orbcomm project, the world's first satellite-based two-way data-communication system. It operates the project in conjunction with Canada's Teleglobe. TCI also owns 32% of Malaysia Airlines and 62% of Malaysia Helicopter Services.

MR mil	12/92	12/93	12/94	US$mil 12/94				
Sales	**177.7**	**672.6**	**780.9**	**298.3**	P/E Ratio	**69.7**	Price (9/30/95)	**6.55**
Net Income	**9.3**	**18.7**	**63.2**	**24.1**	P/B Ratio	**N/A**	52 Wk Hi-Low	**10.90-6.10**
Book Value	**743.1**	**1,069.1**	**N/A**	**N/A**	Yield %	**0.0**	Market Cap	**US$1,764.8mil**

Address **Menara Twr. 161B, Jl. Ampang, 50450 Kuala Lumpur**
Tel **03-261-9555**
Fax **N/A**
ADR
SEDOL No. **6754453**
President --
Chairman **Tajuding Ramli**

Telekom Malaysia

Industry: **Telephone Systems - All**

Telekom Malaysia provides telecommunications services to commercial and residential customers. It is the primary provider of telephone services in Malaysia, serving a client base of 2.9 million customers. The company's cellular-telephone business provides services to 96,700 subscribers. Telekom Malaysia also provides teleconferencing and fax services. Its 60%-owned Fiberail subsidiary operates fiberoptic telecommunications system. Telekom Malaysia also provides international-paging and voice-mail services through its 40% interest in Skytel System.

MR mil	12/92	12/93	12/94	US$mil 12/94				
Sales	**3,413.8**	**3,930.9**	**4,491.7**	**1,715.7**	P/E Ratio	**26.9**	Price (9/30/95)	**18.90**
Net Income	**922.9**	**1,219.0**	**1,397.5**	**533.8**	P/B Ratio	**3.9**	52 Wk Hi-Low	**20.90-15.70**
Book Value	**7,279.5**	**8,352.7**	**9,567.9**	**3,752.1**	Yield %	**0.7**	Market Cap	**US$14,980mil**

Address **Jalan Pantai Baharu, 59200 Kuala Lumpur**
Tel **03-232-9494**
Fax **03-757-4747**
ADR
SEDOL No. **6868398**
President --
Chairman **Mohamed Rashdan**

Tenaga Nasional

Industry: **Electrical Utilities - All**

Tenaga Nasional is an electric utility providing service throughout Malaysia. The company is licensed as the country's sole transmitter and distributor of electrical energy. It holds minority stakes in Genting Sayen Malaysia and YTL, two independent power producers. Tenaga Nasional manufactures switchgears and electrical transformers used in its power-transmission grid. It is involved in a joint venture with Cellular Communication Network (Malaysia) to install a fiber-optic communication network. Malaysia's government owns 70% of the company.

MR mil	08/92	08/93	08/94	US$mil 08/94				
Sales	**N/A**	**5,030.4**	**5,629.4**	**2,142.1**	P/E Ratio	**16.8**	Price (9/30/95)	**9.60**
Net Income	**N/A**	**1,525.4**	**1,723.5**	**655.8**	P/B Ratio	**2.2**	52 Wk Hi-Low	**13.70-8.65**
Book Value	**N/A**	**11,566.0**	**13,310.4**	**5,199.4**	Yield %	**1.3**	Market Cap	**US$11,627mil**

Address **129 Jl. Bangsar, 59200 Kuala Lumpur**
Tel **03-282-5566**
Fax **N/A**
ADR **TNABY**
SEDOL No. **6904612**
President --
Chairman **Ani bin Arope**

UMW

Industry: **Automobile Manufacturers**

UMW Holdings manufactures industrial and commercial vehicles, passenger cars, and automotive components. Its products include automobiles, agricultural tractors, and trucks. It operates a Toyota-dealership franchise, sells Komatsu heavy equipment, and manufactures Kancil passenger cars. The company manufactures and distributes automotive filtration products and shock absorbers. The company also distributes Pennzoil motor-oil products. UMW-BFI Waste Services, a joint venture with Browning-Ferris Industries Asia-Pacific, provides non-hazardous-waste management.

	MR mil 12/92	12/93	12/94	US$mil 12/94				
Sales	**1,788.4**	**1,813.4**	**2,208.8**	**843.7**	P/E Ratio	**22.8**	Price (9/30/95)	**6.80**
Net Income	**75.5**	**54.7**	**70.5**	**26.9**	P/B Ratio	**3.1**	52 Wk Hi-Low	**8.40-5.44**
Book Value	**475.5**	**532.1**	**578.6**	**226.9**	Yield %	**1.9**	Market Cap	**US$707.7mil**

Address **The Corporate, Jalan Utas 15/7**
40200 Shah Alam
Tel **03-559-1911**
Fax **03-550-2282**
ADR
SEDOL No. **6910824**
Chief Executive **Haji Rahmay**
Chairman **Haji Rahmat**

Uniphoenix

Industry: **Specialty Chemicals**

Uniphoenix develops real estate, markets office equipment, provides engineering services, develops software, brokers investments, sterilizes medical products, and manufactures packaging materials, air compressors, and chemicals. Its Persoft subsidiary sells office supplies, computers, and peripherals, offering Microsoft, Fujitsu, Ricoh, and Pyramid products. Uniphoenix has an interest in Formglas (SEA), a joint venture with Canada's Formglas Interiors and Singapore's Framework Building Products that produces fiberglass-reinforced gypsum and cement.

	MR mil 12/92	12/93	12/94	US$mil 12/94				
Sales	**114.0**	**260.1**	**309.5**	**118.2**	P/E Ratio	**NMF**	Price (9/30/95)	**2.05**
Net Income	**9.2**	**14.3**	**-6.7**	**-2.6**	P/B Ratio	**1.7**	52 Wk Hi-Low	**4.02-2.04**
Book Value	**188.1**	**205.4**	**224.3**	**88.0**	Yield %	**1.0**	Market Cap	**US$154.0mil**

Address **86 Jalan Ampang**
50250 Kuala Lumpur
Tel **03-202-0888**
Fax **N/A**
ADR
SEDOL No. **6914558**
President **Ibrahim Mohamed**
Chairman **Jamil bin Mohamed Jan**

United Engineers (Malaysia)

Industry: **Heavy Construction**

United Engineers (Malaysia), Malaysia's largest construction company by market capitalization, builds bridges and institutional facilities, and develops civil-engineering projects. Major construction projects include the Malaysia Singapore Second Crossing, the National Sports Complex, and the North-South Expressway. It provides project-management and engineering services. United Engineers also manufactures cement, provides transportation services, and operates limestone quarries. The company is 33% owned by Renong, a Malaysian conglomerate.

	MR mil 12/92	12/93	12/94	US$mil 12/94				
Sales	**641.3**	**671.1**	**926.9**	**354.0**	P/E Ratio	**40.3**	Price (9/30/95)	**16.10**
Net Income	**117.0**	**222.2**	**237.4**	**90.7**	P/B Ratio	**6.9**	52 Wk Hi-Low	**18.70-10.60**
Book Value	**873.6**	**1,063.5**	**1,263.2**	**495.4**	Yield %	**0.4**	Market Cap	**US$3,476.1mil**

Address **UE Complex, 5 Jalan 217**
46700 Petaling Jaya
Tel **03-792-2600**
Fax **03-791-0381**
ADR
SEDOL No. **6917717**
Managing Director **Abdul Hamid**
Chairman **Radin Soenarno**

United Plantations

Industry: **Plantations**

United Plantations manages nine plantations that produce a variety of commodities. It cultivates oil palm, coconuts, bananas, and cocoa in western-peninsular Malaysia. Oil-palm production occupy more than 2,600 hectares; and cocoa fills nearly 250 hectares. The company also makes cooking oils, fats, and soap products. In addition, the company constructs turnkey oil-palm factories, and transports oil and molasses. Aarhus Oliefabrik of Denmark holds 31% of the company's share capital.

	MR mil 12/92	12/93	12/94	US$mil 12/94				
Sales	**213.6**	**200.6**	**187.9**	**71.8**	P/E Ratio	**31.9**	Price (9/30/95)	**5.45**
Net Income	**26.1**	**25.7**	**26.7**	**10.2**	P/B Ratio	**2.6**	52 Wk Hi-Low	**7.40-4.80**
Book Value	**301.0**	**308.4**	**314.6**	**123.4**	Yield %	**3.7**	Market Cap	**US$329.6mil**

Address **Jendarata Estate**
36009 Teluk Intan, Perak
Tel **05-646-1411**
Fax **05-641-1876**
ADR
SEDOL No. **6917148**
Chief Executive **Seri B. Bek-Nielsen**
Chairman **Haji Basir**

Mexico

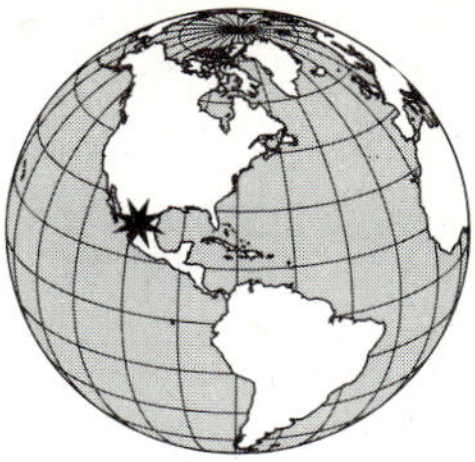

Mexico

Mike Esterl,
Mexico City

Local Trading Hours	Time Difference fom New York	Population (Est. 94)
8:30-14:00; 7:30-14:00 during Daylight Savings Time	1 hour behind EST	90,000,000

Awakened from the slumber of a decades-long state-controlled economy in the early 1990s, Mexico's Bolsa Mexicana de Valores has quickly roared to life as one of the world's largest and most active emerging stock markets.

And one of the most volatile.

Market capitalization ballooned from $22.48 billion in 1989 to $200.61 billion four years later, while foreign investment in the Bolsa swelled from $808.0 million to $54.63 billion during the same period as then-President Carlos Salinas de Gortari initiated spirited liberalization reforms.

Almost overnight the Mexican stock exchange became one of the world's most profitable, with the market's key IPC index posting a real increase of 37% in 1993. The gains appeared to rest on some solid foundations, with gross domestic product (GDP) having grown 3.5% during the year while inflation dropped into the single-digit range and the peso was transformed into a paradigm of stability.

The outlook was even more bullish for 1994, after the rocky path toward Mexican inclusion in the North American Free Trade Agreement (NAFTA) passed a big, last-minute U.S. Congress hurdle and plans to join the exclusive Organization of Economic Cooperation and Development (OECD) moved steadily forward.

Among other positive omens, a new Foreign Investment Law adopted in December 1993 eliminated reams of red tape, and a concerted automation drive led the United Kingdom's Securities and Investments Board to award the Bolsa the status of Designated Investment Exchange – the first Latin American exchange to win such a classification.

But for those investors who were beginning to see the Bolsa as the Big Easy, 1994 proved to be a rude wake-up call. A few minutes after the NAFTA New Year was rung in, several thousand armed Maya rebels sprang from the jungles of southern Chiapas and claimed sovereignty over large swaths of land bordering Guatemala while demanding wholescale changes to Mexico's political economy.

Dow Jones Mexico Equity Market Index Performance

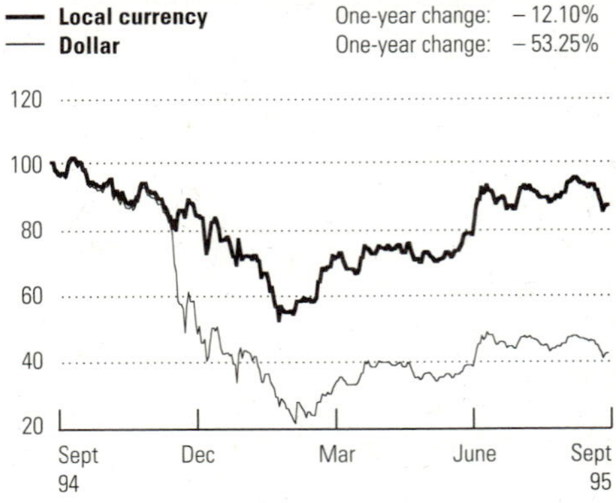

The financial markets appeared to right themselves soon after the self-styled and outgunned Zapatista National Liberation

Gross Domestic Product (94)	Three-Year Average GDP Growth (93-94)	Main Industries	Consumer Price Index (94)	Monitary Unit	Exchange Rate (9/95)
U.S.$377.1 billion (1.273 trillion pesos)	+2.33%	Petroleum, tourism, manufacturing, financial services, transportation and communications, construction, agriculture	+7.1%	Peso	Peso6.38 to US$1.00

Army (EZLN) agreed to an uneasy ceasefire in the wake of 12 days of skirmishes that had left at least 145 people dead. The IPC climbed to 2,881.17 points on February 8, after having closed 1993 at a record-high 2,602.60.

A social and political maelstrom quickly took hold on other fronts, though. The presidential candidate of the 65-year ruling Institutional Revolutionary Party (PRI) was assassinated in March during a campaign stop in Tijuana. The stock index sank to a year-low 1,957.33 by April 20 as international reserves began to decline and the government issued more dollar-linked debt in the form of Tesobonos.

Again the markets managed to right themselves somewhat, spurred on in part by the country's cleanest elections in decades that saw a young Yale-trained economist of the ruling party, Ernesto Zedillo, take the presidential helm.

Still, the Bolsa never regained its full splendor, with the IPC ending the year at 2,375.66 as the EZLN continued to produce a backdrop of threats amid a steady hum of ruling party fratricide allegations following the September slaying of PRI Secretary General Francisco Ruiz Massieu. Reports of huge carriers filled with cocaine shipments landing on Mexican soil under official sanction gathered steam, and editorials in mainstream newspapers about the country's rapid "Colombianization" became daily routine.

There was one final shock before the year was out. On December 20, with international reserves dwindling to precarious levels, the government did what it had promised foreign investors for years it would not do: it devalued the peso.

Ten Largest Capitalized Companies
as of 9/30/95

Stock	Market Cap. US$Mil
Industrias Penoles	9,918,360.0
Grupo Carso	5,421,159.9
Cemex	2,603,610.8
Grupo Televisa	2,260,470.6
Grupo Industrial Alfa	2,257,756.1
Cifra	1,557,818.2
CIFRA	1,557,818.2
Kimberly Clark de México	1,540,843.9
Grupo Industrial Bimbo	1,493,848.0
FEMSA	1,372,966.8

A lot of people jumped ship. Foreign investment in the stock market, which had dropped from $60.92 billion in January of 1994 to $50.39 billion in November, fell further to $34.40 billion by year's end. For the year, the IPC posted a nominal loss of 8.7% and a real decline of 15%.

As the inexperienced three-week-old Zedillo administration stumbled to outline a coherent emergency plan, just how dicey a bet the Bolsa and the Mexican economy had become was painfully clear even to the most casual observer.

The shockwaves continued to be felt in 1995. While foreign participation still made up about a quarter of market capitalization at the end of August, its stake had declined to some $27.18 billion. A 45% plunge in the value of the peso against the dollar since December had meanwhile wiped out any nominal gains derived from the IPC edging up to an August close of 2,516.99.

Widespread projections that accumulated 12-month inflation of around 50% would prompt the peso to lose another 5% or so against the U.S. currency in the final four months of 1995 were making short-term foreign earnings projections bleak. And despite Mexico's recording of its first quarterly current account surplus in seven years and a reduction in monthly inflation to around 2% by mid-year, a sharp 10.5% second-quarter GDP contraction and interest rates that remained stubbornly above 30% were prompting most analysts to discount positive economic growth until the second quarter of 1996.

Mexico's Bolsa, according to most observers, has now become a place for the long-haul investor. It's probably also a good idea if the faint-hearted keep their distance, amid a sea of socio-political variables that can make any investment an adventure.

Among the more surreal events of 1995 was the older brother of former President Carlos Salinas being charged with masterminding the murder of Francisco Ruiz Massieu, a high-ranking official of the ruling party. It didn't stop there; the murder victim's younger brother, who headed the original investigation into the killing, was held in the U.S. on suspected drug-trafficking links. In a separate imbroglio, a bunch of high-ranking officials involved in a widening public transportation scandal kept showing up dead. One of them had committed suicide by shooting himself twice, according to the official version.

Among other recent developments, the long-ruling PRI lost three of five gubernatorial elections and its two winning candidates were burdened with persistent vote fraud allegations. The national party leader had resigned before the end of August, as had several cabinet members.

Unemployment meanwhile doubled in the first six months of 1995 to 6.6%, according to official surveys. Most observers said the actual number was much higher. Those who had work were angrily watching their purchasing power plummet, and a rapidly growing debtors' rights group, El Barzon, continued to threaten banks with a national moratorium on loan payments.

Analysts admit it is impossible to calculate all those variables into investment earnings charts. But despite the recent hits and the future dangers, many insist that some solid winners are emerging from the 200 or so companies that trade on the Bolsa and the 35 issues that currently make up the IPC.

In fact, a weaker peso already has helped a crop of internationally diversified companies push Mexico's trade balance into the black for the first time since the late 1980s. Steel and petrochemical conglomerates such as Alfa have seen export levels soar, while construction companies such as Grupo ICA and Bufete Industrial have replaced domestic slack with foreign infrastructure projects. Companies such as steel giant Cemex, meanwhile, have maintained healthy cash flow levels through foreign holdings in countries stretching from Spain to Venezuela.

And national telephone monopoly Telefonos de Mexico (Telmex) – responsible for about a third of the Bolsa's 1994 average daily trading volume of 1.07 billion pesos – remains a favorite among many market observers despite the advent of long-distance competition in 1997.

Without discounting the turbulent recent past, most analysts agree the growing international presence of Mexican companies is indisputable. Of the 34 primary public offerings totaling 6.60 billion pesos that were made in 1994, 11 of them were placed abroad at a value of $1.37 billion. That pushed the number of Mexican issues abroad at year's end to 58. Successful international debt placements by several major Mexican firms in the summer of 1995 indicated that global castigation was beginning to wear off much more quickly than in the wake of the country's 1982 currency devaluation.

In what also should help, President Zedillo reiterated in September that his administration is not planning to introduce any Chilean-style foreign investment controls. Mexico's recent liberalization has translated into a foreign-friendly climate, with foreign individual equity investors being exempt from taxation on capital gains and after-tax profit dividends. Earnings derived from government Treasury bills are also tax free. Foreigners, however, are prevented from purchasing "A" voting shares and there is a 49% limit on foreign stakes.

Although the local stock market has become highly automated in recent years – including the introduction of the International Quotations System (SIC) in 1994 – transactions are still ultimately conducted via the trading floor on a cash settlement basis.

While trading volume on the Bolsa rose 45% in 1994 compared with the earlier year, the amount traded on a second-tier market soared to 585 million pesos last year, 100 times higher than in its inaugural 1993 year. Trading of derivative products also appeared to be on the rise, with 1994 volume in warrants doubling to 2.61 billion pesos from the year before.

Bolsa officials say they are planning new derivatives options to be traded on the local market next spring, including the introduction of currency futures. The Chicago Mercantile Exchange meanwhile introduced peso futures trading in the spring of 1995, and in August it announced plans for a slate of other options trading that would include a newly weighted index of 30 Mexican stocks.

Apasco

Industry: **Building Materials**

Apasco is Mexico's second-largest cement maker by sales. It produces and distributes cement, ready-mix concrete, and related products. In 1994, it produced and sold 6.7 million tons of cement, or a 23% share of the Mexican market. The company also sold 2.7 million cubic meters of ready-mix concrete, or a 28% share of the Mexican market. Apasco markets 67% of its cement through distributors, and sells the remainder directly to users. The firm operates six plants throughout Mexico. It expects to expand its annual cement production capacity to 9 million tons by 1996.

	N$ mil 12/92	12/93	12/94	US$mil 12/94				
Sales	**1,548,198**	**1,975.0**	**2,362.8**	**681.1**	P/E Ratio	**29.0**	Price (9/30/95)	**25.20**
Net Income	**295,177.0**	**313.2**	**242.1**	**69.8**	P/B Ratio	**1.9**	52 Wk Hi-Low	**34.90-13.80**
Book Value	**2,428,337**	**2,763.1**	**3,759.5**	**762.6**	Yield %	**1.2**	Market Cap	**US$1,087.8mil**

Address	**Campos Eliseos 345**	Tel	**05-724-0000**	ADR	**AASAY**	President & CEO	**P.A. Froidevaux**
	11560 Mexico DF	Fax	**05-724-0280**	SEDOL No.	**2045645**	Chairman	**Augustin Santamarina**

Cemex

Industry: **Building Materials**

Cemex is Mexico's largest and the world's fourth- largest cement maker. It produces and distributes mixed concrete and aggregates and operates subsidiaries in the United States, Spain, Venezuela, Panama, and the Caribbean. Altogether, the company has operations in 22 countries. Through its trading and distribution network, it does business in 54 countries. In 1994, Cemex's production capacity totaled 44 million metric tons. Cemex also operates Marriott CasaMagna Hotels in Mexico.

	N$ mil 12/92	12/93	12/94	US$mil 12/94				
Sales	**6,901,148**	**9,240.8**	**10,644.6**	**3,068.5**	P/E Ratio M	**13.8**	Price (9/30/95) M	**24.45**
Net Income	**1,713,729**	**1,666.0**	**1,903.7**	**548.8**	P/B Ratio M	**2.1**	52 Wk Hi-Low M	**32.50-10.50**
Book Value	**9,156,117**	**10,288.0**	**14,349.3**	**2,910.6**	Yield % M	**1.2**	Market Cap M	**US$2,603.6mil**

Address	**Ave Constitucion 444 Pte**	Tel	**08-328-3000**	ADR	**CMXBY**	CEO	**Lorenzo H. Zambrano**
	64000 Monterrey NL	Fax	**08-345-2025**	SEDOL No.	**2182939**	Chairman	**M. Zambrano Hellion**

M=Multiple issues in index; reflects most active.

CIFRA

Industry: **Retailers - Broadline**

Cifra is Mexico's largest retailer. It markets consumer goods such as food, furniture, and appliances through a total of 264 stores and restaurants. The company operates discount stores offering clothing, groceries, and general merchandise through its subsidiaries. It also runs a retail supermarket chain, clothing stores, and a chain of 34 restaurants specializing in typical Mexican cuisine. Cifra formed a joint venture with Wal-Mart Stores in 1991. Jointly, the two firms operate about 70 stores in Mexico, including two Wal-Mart Supercenters.

	N$ mil 12/92	12/93	12/94	US$mil 12/94				
Revenues	**11,496,711**	**14,231.2**	**15,637.3**	**4,507.7**	P/E Ratio M	**N/A**	Price (9/30/95) M	**8.12**
Net Income	**938,205.0**	**1,034.9**	**1,165.2**	**335.9**	P/B Ratio M	**3.2**	52 Wk Hi-Low M	**10.00-5.44**
Book Value	**4,245,786**	**6,213.2**	**8,200.3**	**1,663.4**	Yield % M	**1.0**	Market Cap M	**US$1,557.8mil**

Address	**Jose Ma. Castorena 470**	Tel	**05-327-9211**	ADR		President	--
	05200 Mexico, DF	Fax	**05-327-9259**	SEDOL No.	**2196985**	Chairman	**Jeronimo A. Arango**

M=Multiple issues in index; reflects most active.

Controladora Comercial Mexicana

Industry: **Retailers - Broadline**

Controladora Comercial Mexicana (Comerci) operates 131 retail outlets through five chains in Mexico. Comercial Mexicana, the company's flagship chain, operates 83 clothing and general-merchandise stores. In addition, the company runs 15 Bodega Comercial Mexicana wholesale stores, 19 Sumesa supermarkets, and 29 family-oriented California Restaurants. Through a joint venture with the United States-based Price/Costco, it operates 13 Price Club Mexico discount-membership shopping stores. It is also in a joint venture with French retailer Auchan to build hypermarkets in Mexico.

	N$ mil 12/92	12/93	12/94	US$mil 12/94				
Revenues	**5,636.9**	**7,160.5**	**9,058.7**	**2,611.3**	P/E Ratio	**NMF**	Price (9/30/95)	**4.97**
Net Income	**254.2**	**240.3**	**-220.6**	**-63.6**	P/B Ratio	**1.6**	52 Wk Hi-Low	**7.24-2.28**
Book Value	**2,144.4**	**2,689.1**	**3,134.9**	**635.9**	Yield %	**0.0**	Market Cap	**US$381.7mil**

Address	**Fernando de Alva 27, Col. Obrera**	Tel	**05-732-7282**	ADR	**CRRXY**	President	**Carlos G. Zabalegui**
	06800 Mexico, DF	Fax	**05-588-5024**	SEDOL No.	**2221661**	Chairman	**Carlos G. Nova**

Desc

Industry: **Conglomerates**

Desc Sociedad de Fomento Industrial is a holding company with interests in auto parts, chemicals, consumer products, food, agribusiness, and real estate. Its Unik subsidiary is Mexico's largest producer of auto parts. Grupo Irsa, Desc's chemicals and consumer-products subsidiary, makes synthetic rubber, industrial phosphates, polystyrene, and acrylics. Its glue and waterproofing materials hold top shares of Mexico's market. Desc also has a 10% stake in Grupo Financiero InverMexico, a financial-services company.

	N$ mil 12/92	12/93	12/94	US$mil 12/94				
Sales	**5,158.1**	**4,803.7**	**5,539.0**	**1,596.7**	P/E Ratio	**NMF**	Price (9/30/95)	**24.00**
Net Income	**354.1**	**352.7**	**-737.9**	**-212.7**	P/B Ratio	**1.8**	52 Wk Hi-Low	**28.95-9.64**
Book Value	**6,211.3**	**6,938.6**	**3,443.5**	**698.5**	Yield %	**0.0**	Market Cap	**US$426.0mil**

Address	**Bosque de Ciruelos #304**	Tel	**05-251-6918**	ADR	**DES**	President	--
	11700 Mexico, DF	Fax	**05-251-3431**	SEDOL No.	**2265120**	Chairman	**Fernando Mestre**

El Puerto de Liverpool

Industry: **Retailers - Broadline**

El Puerto de Liverpool operates retail stores and is involved in real-estate activities. Its hypermarkets and department stores, located in major cities throughout Mexico, sell furniture, clothing, and fabric. Through Kmart México, a joint venture with Kmart (U.S.), the firm operates two Kmart Super Center stores in Mexico City's northern suburbs. Kmart México plans to open at least five more stores near Mexico City in 1995. The company's real-estate division has interests in two shopping centers, and two development sites for stores and shopping centers.

N$ mil	12/92	12/93	12/94	US$mil 12/94				
Revenues	**2,833.8**	**3,023.7**	**3,545.3**	**1,022.0**	P/E Ratio	**37.2**	Price (9/30/95)	**4.80**
Net Income	**309.7**	**282.1**	**172.6**	**49.8**	P/B Ratio	**1.8**	52 Wk Hi-Low	**5.16-3.30**
Book Value	**2,700.9**	**3,041.7**	**3,572.6**	**724.7**	Yield %	**0.5**	Market Cap	**US$904.1mil**

Address **Mariano Excobedo No. 425**, **11560 Mexico DF**
Tel **05-254-6188**
Fax **05-254-6307**
ADR
SEDOL No. **2307185**
President --
Chairman **Enrique Bremond**

FEMSA

Industry: **Other Food**

Fomento Economico Mexicano (FEMSA) is Mexico's largest producer of soft drinks and beer. It distributes its beverages to drugstores, supermarkets, and retail stores in Mexico, and exports them to 63 countries, primarily in Asia and South America. The firm's beer division, Femsa Cerveza, holds a 47% share of Mexico's beer market. Its brands include Tecate, Carta Blanca, and Dos Equis. Its soft-drink division, Coca-Cola Femsa, produces brands such as Coke, Sprite, and Fanta. Femsa operates 677 Oxxo convenience stores, and makes packaging materials for bottled beverages.

N$ mil	12/92	12/93	12/94	US$mil 12/94				
Sales	**6,382.0**	**7,534.0**	**9,220.0**	**2,657.8**	P/E Ratio	**NMF**	Price (9/30/95)	**16.18**
Net Income	**508.0**	**684.0**	**-480.0**	**-138.4**	P/B Ratio	**1.4**	52 Wk Hi-Low	**19.04-7.40**
Book Value	**4,485.0**	**5,518.0**	**6,093.0**	**1,235.9**	Yield %	**0.6**	Market Cap	**US$1,373.0mil**

Address **Gral. Anaya 601 Pte.**, **64410 Monterrey NL**
Tel **08-328-6149**
Fax **08-328-6080**
ADR
SEDOL No. **2344397**
Chief Executive **José A.F. Carbajal**
Chairman **Eugino G. Lagüera**

Grupo Carso

Industry: **Conglomerates**

Grupo Carso is a holding company that has a 6% interest in Telefonos de Mexico, a telephone utility, and invests in a variety of industries. The firm's 75%-owned subsidiary, Condumex, makes products for the electromanufacturing, telecommunications, auto-parts, and plastics industries. Grupo Carso owns a 66% stake in Sanborn Hermanos, which operates specialty stores and restaurants. Its wholly-owned tile maker, Porcelanite, holds a 25% market share. Grupo Carso also has interests in mining, tobacco, paper and printing, food and beverages, and chemicals manufacturing.

N$ mil	12/92	12/93	12/94	US$mil 12/94				
Sales	**7,976.0**	**9,843.3**	**11,326.4**	**3,265.0**	P/E Ratio	**20.2**	Price (9/30/95)	**37.80**
Net Income	**1,121.2**	**1,484.2**	**1,705.6**	**491.7**	P/B Ratio	**2.6**	52 Wk Hi-Low	**42.30-19.76**
Book Value	**8,560.3**	**10,569.4**	**14,392.8**	**2,919.4**	Yield %	**0.0**	Market Cap	**US$5,421.2mil**

Address **Ave. Paseo de Las Palmas 265**, **11000 Lomas de Chapultepec**
Tel **05-202-8838**
Fax **N/A**
ADR
SEDOL No. **2393452**
President --
Chairman **Carlos Slim Helu**

Grupo Embotellador

Industry: **Other Food**

Grupo Embotellador de Mexico (GEMEX) is the largest bottler, outside the United States, of the soft-drink products of PepsiCo, Inc. The company has the exclusive rights to produce and sell Pepsi-Cola, Pepsi Light, Seven-Up, and Mirinda in the Mexico City area. Grupo Embotellador bottles and sells a wide range of other carbonated beverages and mineral waters under the trademarks Manzanita Sol, Squirt, Titan, Seagram, Clearly Canadian, Garci-Crespo, San Lorenzo, and TBC. The company also produces plastic bottles, bottle caps, and packaging materials and containers.

N$ mil	12/92	12/93	12/94	US$mil 12/94				
Sales	**1,269.4**	**1,477.5**	**2,049.3**	**590.8**	P/E Ratio	**N/A**	Price (9/30/95)	**37.00**
Net Income	**172.9**	**216.7**	**-107.4**	**-31.0**	P/B Ratio	**8.9**	52 Wk Hi-Low	**50.80-17.40**
Book Value	**913.4**	**993.1**	**1,472.2**	**298.6**	Yield %	**0.7**	Market Cap	**US$448.5mil**

Address **Calzada de la Viga 891, Iztacalco**, **08800 Mexico DF**
Tel **05-228-7119**
Fax **05-228-7197**
ADR **GEM**
SEDOL No. **2394262**
Managing Director **Rubén P. de Jong**
Chairman **E. C. Molina Sobrino**

Grupo Financiero Banamex-Accival

Industry: **Financial Services - Diversified**

Grupo Financiero Banamex Accival (Banacci) is Mexico's largest financial-services company. Banacci operates as a holding company with two primary subsidiaries, commercial bank Banco Nacional de Mexico (Banamex), and brokerage house Accival. Banamex is Mexico's largest bank by assets. It is active in retail banking, offering services such as money-market accounts and fixed-income funds. It operates 710 branches throughout Mexico. Accival is the leading trader on the Mexican Stock Exchange with a 12% market share in terms of volume traded.

N$ mil	12/92	12/93	12/94	US$mil 12/94				
Revenues	**N/A**	**25,977.0**	**26,360.0**	**7,598.7**	P/E Ratio M	**12.5**	Price (9/30/95) M	**11.90**
Net Income	**N/A**	**3,590.0**	**1,469.0**	**423.5**	P/B Ratio M	**1.7**	52 Wk Hi-Low M	**14.86-8.60**
Book Value	**N/A**	**12,370.0**	**13,063.0**	**2,649.7**	Yield % M	**4.2**	Market Cap M	**US$282.8mil**

Address **Paseo de la Reforma 420**, **06600 Mexico DF**
Tel **05-225-6301**
Fax **05-225-6755**
ADR
SEDOL No. **2387132**
Chief Executive **R. Hernández Ramírez**
Chairman **Alfredo Harp Hel£**

M=Multiple issues in index; reflects most active.

Grupo Financiero Bancomer

Industry: **Financial Services - Diversified**

Grupo Financiero Bancomer, Mexico's second-largest financial firm by assets, provides financial services and manages investments. The firm owns a bank, a brokerage house, two leasing companies, a foreign-exchange house, and a warehouse company. It has 934 branches and approximately 1,800 automatic-teller machines in Mexico. Bancomer is most active in lending, with a 27% share of Mexico's mortgage market. It also has a telecommunication joint venture with GTE. Mexico's government is expected to sell its $1 billion stake in the firm through a public offering in 1995.

N$ mil	12/92 R	12/93	12/94	US$mil 12/94				
Revenues	**274.9**	**10.4**	**20.3**	**5.9**	P/E Ratio	**8.8**	Price (9/30/95)	**1.89**
Net Income	**1,472.7**	**2,062.7**	**901.2**	**259.8**	P/B Ratio	**0.9**	52 Wk Hi-Low	**4.48-0.91**
Book Value	**14,056.3**	**9,413.1**	**9,427.3**	**1,912.2**	Yield %	**4.2**	Market Cap	**US$501.6mil**

Address **Av. Universidad 1200**, **03339 Mexico DF** | Tel **05-604-2745** | Fax **05-621-4756** | ADR | SEDOL No. **2074229** | Chief Executive **R. Guajardo Touché** | Chairman **E. Garza Lagüera**

R=Restated.

Grupo Gigante

Industry: **Retailers - Broadline**

Grupo Gigante operates stores and restaurants and manages real estate through its subsidiaries. Grupo Gigante operates a total of 189 supermarkets through five chains: Gigante, Bodega, Super G, Hiper G, and SuperMart. Each of these chains targets a clientele of a different income level. It also runs 29 Toks family-style and five specialty restaurants. The firm has a joint venture with Tandy International (U.S.) that operates 48 Radio Shack stores in Mexico. Grupo Gigante formed a joint venture with France's Carrefour in 1994 to develop hypermarket-style supermarkets.

N$ mil	12/92 R	12/93	12/94	US$mil 12/94				
Revenues	**6,288.8**	**7,861.0**	**8,966.7**	**2,584.8**	P/E Ratio	**NMF**	Price (9/30/95)	**1.53**
Net Income	**104.4**	**79.1**	**-51.3**	**-14.8**	P/B Ratio	**1.2**	52 Wk Hi-Low	**2.04-0.96**
Book Value	**2,222.3**	**2,745.2**	**2,739.6**	**555.7**	Yield %	**0.0**	Market Cap	**US$258.7mil**

Address **Av. Ejército Nacional No. 769-A**, **11520 Mexico DF** | Tel **05-724-8369** | Fax **05-724-8308** | ADR | SEDOL No. **2392749** | Vice-Chairman **Angel Losada Moreno** | Chairman **Angel Losada Gómez**

R=Restated.

Grupo Industrial Alfa

Industry: **Conglomerates**

Grupo Industrial Alfa is a holding company with interests in steel, petrochemicals, and food. Its Hylsamex steel unit operates a joint venture with U.S.-based Worthington Industries to make molded steel. Its Alpek petrochemical unit produces primary materials used in the manufacture of synthetic fibers, films, and packaging. Alfa's Sigma food unit distributes processed meats, yogurt, cheese, and prepared foods. Its brand names include Oscar Meyer and Yoplait. Alfa also manufactures carpets, operates Total HOME hardware stores, and produces Selther and Simmons mattresses.

N$ mil	12/92	12/93	12/94	US$mil 12/94				
Sales	**7,770.0**	**7,990.0**	**9,353.0**	**2,696.2**	P/E Ratio	**NMF**	Price (9/30/95)	**83.00**
Net Income	**220.0**	**210.0**	**-1,070.0**	**-308.4**	P/B Ratio	**1.7**	52 Wk Hi-Low	**89.20-42.00**
Book Value	**5,240.0**	**5,630.0**	**8,590.0**	**1,742.4**	Yield %	**1.0**	Market Cap	**US$2,257.8mil**

Address **Apartado Postal 111**, **66200 Garza Garcia NL** | Tel **08-335-3535** | Fax **08-335-8135** | ADR | SEDOL No. **2043423** | Chief Executive **D. Garza Medina** | Chairman **D. Garza Medina**

Grupo Industrial Bimbo

Industry: **Other Food**

Grupo Industrial Bimbo is Mexico's largest baking firm, with a 90% share of the packaged-breads market and a 60% share of the sweet snack-foods market. Its products include breads, biscuits, pies, pastries, appetizers, chocolates, jams, and confectionaries. Its products are marketed in Mexico and southern regions of the United States. The company operates a baking plant in Argentina and is further expanding its operations into the U.S. and Central and South America. Grupo Industrial Bimbo has a 40% interest in Grupo Quan, a Mexican ice cream and restaurant group.

N$ mil	12/92	12/93	12/94	US$mil 12/94				
Sales	**4,484.4**	**5,448.5**	**6,186.2**	**1,783.3**	P/E Ratio	**59.3**	Price (9/30/95)	**28.45**
Net Income	**255.3**	**355.1**	**161.1**	**46.4**	P/B Ratio	**2.3**	52 Wk Hi-Low	**30.00-19.00**
Book Value	**2,611.3**	**3,148.8**	**4,068.0**	**825.2**	Yield %	**0.7**	Market Cap	**US$1,493.8mil**

Address **Ejercito Nacional 533, 4 Piso**, **11520 Mexico DF** | Tel **05-250-8200** | Fax **05-250-8314** | ADR | SEDOL No. **2392471** | President **--** | Chairman **Roberto Servitje**

Grupo Industrial Maseca

Industry: **Other Food**

Grupo Industrial Maseca (Gimsa) is the leading Mexican producer of corn flour, with more than three fourths of the Mexican market. Its 16 plants manufacture more than 1.2 million tonnes of corn flour per year. It is also building new plants in Chiapas and Veracruz. The firm derives nearly 70% of its revenue from corn-flour sales to tortilla producers, and 30% from sales to consumers. It also holds 20% of the U.S. retail tortilla market. Gimsa plans to expand its operations to include the manufacture of bread as well as flour tortillas for the domestic market in 1995.

N$ mil	12/92	12/93	12/94	US$mil 12/94				
Sales	**928.5**	**1,158.4**	**1,131.9**	**326.3**	P/E Ratio	**21.7**	Price (9/30/95)	**5.00**
Net Income	**132.3**	**171.2**	**211.0**	**60.8**	P/B Ratio	**3.3**	52 Wk Hi-Low	**6.26-3.58**
Book Value	**639.5**	**1,043.3**	**1,398.0**	**283.6**	Yield %	**N/A**	Market Cap	**US$324.7mil**

Address **Av. La Clinica 2520**, **64000 Monterrey NL** | Tel **08-335-9900** | Fax **08-335-9935** | ADR **MSK** | SEDOL No. **2390572** | CEO **Eduardo Livas Cantu** | Chairman **Roberto G. Barrera**

Grupo Modelo

Industry: **Distillers & Brewers**

Grupo Modelo is Mexico's largest brewer, maintaining a 55% market share. It produces Corona Extra, Mexico's top-selling brand, Corona Light, Modelo Especial, Negra Modelo, Light Modelo, and Pacifico. Corona Extra is the second-best-selling imported beer in the United States. Overall, the company's brands make up 71% of the beer exported from Mexico. Modelo operates seven breweries, a malt factory, and canning and lid factories. It also owns 32 real-estate companies and promotional sports companies. Anheuser Busch of the U.S. owns 18% of Grupo Modelo.

N$ mil	12/92	12/93	12/94	US$mil 12/94				
Sales	**5,285.8**	**5,662.1**	**6,353.8**	**1,831.6**	P/E Ratio	**35.4**	Price (9/30/95)	**26.00**
Net Income	**347.7**	**374.6**	**597.3**	**172.2**	P/B Ratio	**2.9**	52 Wk Hi-Low	**28.75-17.45**
Book Value	**5,228.0**	**5,796.4**	**7,311.2**	**1,483.0**	Yield %	**0.3**	Market Cap	**US$662.6mil**

Address **Campos Eliseos 400 piso 18**
11000 Mexico DF
Tel **05-281-0114**
Fax **05-280-6718**
ADR
SEDOL No. **2380539**
Chief Executive **A. Fernández Rodríguez**
Chairman **A. Fernández Rodríguez**

Grupo Sidek

Industry: **Real-Estate Investment**

Grupo Sidek operates in the tourism, construction, steel, shipyard-services, and financial-services industries. The firm has two subsidiaries: Grupo Simec, which produces metal construction materials, and Grupo Situr, which develops and manages resorts, hotels, and housing complexes. Grupo Situr owns 47 hotels and 15 resorts, primarily along Mexico's coasts. Grupo Sidek also has two joint ventures, one with Grupo Sitra and Procomex and another with the United Kingdom's Trafalgar House. These joint ventures construct urban and commercial infrastructure.

N$ mil	12/92	12/93	12/94	US$mil 12/94				
Sales	**1,436.7**	**2,326.8**	**2,903.5**	**837.0**	P/E Ratio	**NMF**	Price (9/30/95)	**4.40**
Net Income	**248.2**	**504.1**	**-557.6**	**-160.7**	P/B Ratio	**0.3**	52 Wk Hi-Low	**16.30-2.44**
Book Value	**1,374.0**	**1,957.8**	**5,266.5**	**1,068.3**	Yield %	**0.0**	Market Cap	**US$117.8mil**

Address **Calzada L Cárdenas 601**
44440 Guadalajara
Tel **03-612-2092**
Fax **03-612-5480**
ADR **SDK**
SEDOL No. **2393076**
President **José Martínez Güitrón**
Chairman **Jorge Martínez Güitrón**

Grupo Situr

Industry: **General Industrial & Commercial Services**

Grupo Situr is a real-estate developer that owns and operates 15 hotels in Mexico City and on Mexico's coasts. It is also developing tourism-oriented real-estate projects in eight cities. Grupo Situr is participating in a joint venture with the Hong Kong-based Mandarin Oriental Hotel Group to open a hotel in Mexico City. It is also involved in a joint venture with Holiday Inn to construct and operate 10 hotels in Mexico. Grupo Situr is a subsidiary of Grupo Sidek, and Banco Nacional de Mexico holds a minority stake in the company.

N$ mil	12/92	12/93	12/94	US$mil 12/94				
Sales	**824.1**	**1,605.9**	**2,003.9**	**577.7**	P/E Ratio	**NMF**	Price (9/30/95)	**2.75**
Net Income	**276.4**	**434.7**	**-590.0**	**-170.1**	P/B Ratio	**0.5**	52 Wk Hi-Low	**11.64-1.66**
Book Value	**1,304.6**	**2,643.4**	**4,108.1**	**833.3**	Yield %	**0.0**	Market Cap	**US$155.6mil**

Address **Agustin Yanez 24343**
44100 Piso, Guadalajara
Tel **03-669-5551**
Fax **03-615-0734**
ADR **GPSRY**
SEDOL No. **2391876**
President --
Chairman **José Martínez Güitrón**

Grupo Televisa

Industry: **Broadcasting**

Grupo Televisa is the world's largest producer and broadcaster of Spanish-language television, holding 90% of Mexico's TV audience. Televisa operates three television networks in Mexico; its TV programs are licensed for broadcast in 63 countries. The firm derives 65% of its revenues from TV and radio advertising. It is also active in magazine publishing, cable TV, feature films, and music. Televisa holds a 50% interest in TV-broadcasting satellite PanAmSat through a joint venture with a TV-program producer. It also owns and operates magazine publisher Grupo America.

N$ mil	12/92	12/93	12/94	US$mil 12/94				
Sales	**4,230.6**	**5,981.5**	**6,442.0**	**1,857.0**	P/E Ratio	**107.6**	Price (9/30/95)	**63.50**
Net Income	**695.3**	**796.7**	**541.3**	**156.0**	P/B Ratio	**11.1**	52 Wk Hi-Low	**98.80-43.80**
Book Value	**2,937.5**	**3,680.9**	**5,324.9**	**1,080.1**	Yield %	**0.4**	Market Cap	**US$2,260.5mil**

Address **Av. Chapultepec 28**
06724 Mexico DF
Tel **05-709-3333**
Fax **05-709-8891**
ADR **TV**
SEDOL No. **2380108**
President --
Chairman **Emilio A. Milmo**

Empresas ICA

Industry: **Mining**

Empresas ICA-Sociedad Controladora does heavy, urban, and industrial construction. ICA has contracts to build sections of highway throughout Mexico, including Mazatlan, Guadalajara, and the Sierra Madre mountains. Its urban construction projects include hotels, government buildings, office buildings, museums, and theaters. ICA also builds and expands thermoelectric- and nuclear-power plants. Other ventures include hotel management, engineering, transportation, and auto parts. At December 31, 1994, its order backlog stood at $725 million.

N$ mil	12/92	12/93	12/94	US$mil 12/94				
Sales	**5,593.0**	**6,052.2**	**6,929.1**	**1,997.4**	P/E Ratio	**126.1**	Price (9/30/95)	**74.40**
Net Income	**502.2**	**597.9**	**61.8**	**17.8**	P/B Ratio	**1.4**	52 Wk Hi-Low	**111.00-29.40**
Book Value	**4,220.6**	**4,964.4**	**5,639.3**	**1,143.9**	Yield %	**0.8**	Market Cap	**US$1,209.9mil**

Address **Mineria 145, Col. Escandon**
11800 Mexico DF
Tel **05-272-9991**
Fax **05-227-5042**
ADR **ICA**
SEDOL No. **2314334**
President & CEO **Bernardo Quintana Isaac**
Chairman **Gilberto Borja Navarete**

Industrias Penoles

Industry: **Mining**

Industrias Penoles is a natural-resources industrial group involved in construction, metals, chemicals, and mining. The construction group explores for natural resources and provides construction and engineering services, primarily to the firm's other divisions. The firm's metals and mining subsidiaries produce gold, silver, lead, zinc, copper, tungsten, and nonferrous materials. The metals and mining group sold more than 161,500 tonnes of lead and 114,500 tonnes of zinc in 1994. The chemicals group produces magnesium oxide, sodium sulfate, fine chemicals, and fertilizers.

	$ mil 12/92 R	12/93	12/94	US$mil 12/94				
Sales	**792.8**	**687.8**	**704.6**	**704.6**	P/E Ratio	**NMF**	Price (9/30/95)	**24.00**
Net Income	**54.1**	**16.1**	**4.8**	**4.8**	P/B Ratio	**2.4**	52 Wk Hi-Low	**26.00-8.80**
Book Value	**956.6**	**875.9**	**638.8**	**638.8**	Yield %	**0.0**	Market Cap	**US$1,554.6mil**

Address	**Rio de la Plata No.48**	Tel	**05-286-8133**	ADR		President	**Jaime Lomelín**
	06500 Mexico DF	Fax	**05-286-7147**	SEDOL No.	**2448200**	Chairman	**Alberto Baillères**

R=Restated.

Kimberly Clark de México

Industry: **Paper Products**

Kimberly-Clark de Mexico is the 43%-owned Mexican arm of the $7 billion diversified U.S. household-products company, Kimberly Clark. Kimberly Mexico emphasizes consumer products, and has top market share in Mexico in disposable diapers and tissue products. It also sells Kotex-brand feminine products. The firm manufactures and sells industrial paper products, including Scribe notebooks and notepads, and bond and fax paper. Kimberly Mexico has plants in Orizaba, Veracruz; San Juan del Rio, Queretaro; Cuautilan, State of Mexico; and Ramos Arizpe, Coahuila.

	N$ mil 12/92	12/93	12/94	US$mil 12/94				
Sales	**2,792.4**	**3,221.2**	**3,878.8**	**1,118.1**	P/E Ratio	**N/A**	Price (9/30/95)	**89.00**
Net Income	**431.1**	**532.0**	**438.9**	**126.5**	P/B Ratio	**4.7**	52 Wk Hi-Low	**92.90-43.60**
Book Value	**2,524.0**	**2,824.4**	**3,763.1**	**763.3**	Yield %	**2.0**	Market Cap	**US$1,540.8mil**

Address	**Jose Luis Lagrange 103-3**	Tel	**05-282-7205**	ADR	**KCDMY**	Vice Chairman	--
	11510 Mexico DF	Fax	**05-282-7272**	SEDOL No.	**2491914**	Chairman	**C.X. Gonzales Laporte**

Telefonos de Mexico

Industry: **Telephone Systems - All**

Telefonos de Mexico (Telmex) provides telecommunication services to residential and commercial locations throughout Mexico. It operates both local and long-distance networks. Telmex has more than 8 million lines and 217,000 public telephones in service. By December 1994, Telmex's cellular subsidiary, Telcel, was providing service for more than 334,000 customers. Telmex is the primary investor in the Columbus II fiberoptic system, which involves 57 telephone companies in 41 countries.

	N$ mil 12/92	12/93	12/94	US$mil 12/94				
Sales	**20,704.7**	**24,601.6**	**29,213.1**	**8,421.2**	P/E Ratio M	**13.7**	Price (9/30/95) M	**10.22**
Net Income	**7,975.2**	**9,003.1**	**7,861.1**	**2,266.1**	P/B Ratio M	**1.9**	52 Wk Hi-Low M	**10.90-8.20**
Book Value	**30,955.6**	**37,049.1**	**55,242.7**	**11,205.4**	Yield % M	**2.5**	Market Cap M	**US$752.8mil**

Address	**Parque Via 198, #508**	Tel	**05-703-3990**	ADR	**TMX**	CEO	**Jaime Chico Pardo**
	06599 Mexico DF	Fax	**05-254-5955**	SEDOL No.	**2881731**	Chairman	**Carlos Slim Helu**

M=Multiple issues in index; reflects most active.

Tolmex

Industry: **Building Materials**

Tolmex manufactures and markets cement and ready- mix concrete. In 1994, Tolmex produced 10.2 million tons of cement and 3.8 million cubic meters of ready-mix concrete. The company exported 823,000 tons of cement in 1994, primarily to Far Eastern countries and the United States. As of December 1993, Tolmex had nine cement plants and 23 distribution terminals throughout Mexico. A new plant in central Mexico came online in the first quarter of 1995. Tolmex is a subsidiary of the Cemex Group, which is Mexico's leading and the world's fourth-largest producer of cement.

	N$ mil 12/91	12/92	12/93	US$mil 12/93				
Sales	**2,524.2**	**3,207.1**	**3,421.2**	**1,102.6**	P/E Ratio	**12.7**	Price (9/30/95)	**32.20**
Net Income	**620.9**	**795.9**	**1,011.1**	**325.8**	P/B Ratio	**1.8**	52 Wk Hi-Low	**54.00-13.98**
Book Value	**4,118.4**	**5,193.1**	**6,367.2**	**2,053.9**	Yield %	**1.1**	Market Cap	**US$741.9mil**

Address	**Ave. Constitucion 444**	Tel	**83-283-000**	ADR	**TLMXY**	President	**Lorenzo H. Zambrano**
	64000 Monterrey NL	Fax	**83-425-025**	SEDOL No.	**2896122**	Chairman	**Lorenzo H. Zambrano**

Vitro

Industry: **Industrial - Diversified**

Vitro manufactures and markets glass containers, automotive and architectural flat glass, kitchen glassware and enamelware, household appliances, chemical and fiberglass products, and mineral resources. Container sales account for approximately 60% of Vitro's revenue. The firm generates more than one half of consolidated sales abroad; one third of its assets are located outside of Mexico. Vitro's U.S. subsidiary, Anchor Glass Container, focuses on the American market and accounts for one third of consolidated sales. Vitro also has an interest in Grupo Financiero Serfin.

	N$ mil 12/92	12/93	12/94	US$mil 12/94				
Sales	**10,316.0**	**10,927.0**	**14,190.0**	**4,090.5**	P/E Ratio	**NMF**	Price (9/30/95)	**16.94**
Net Income	**602.0**	**585.0**	**-1,088.0**	**-313.6**	P/B Ratio	**0.7**	52 Wk Hi-Low	**29.20-15.90**
Book Value	**6,386.0**	**6,510.0**	**7,255.0**	**1,471.6**	Yield %	**3.5**	Market Cap	**US$796.6mil**

Address	**Av. Ricardo Margain 400**	Tel	**08-329-1280**	ADR	**VTO**	President & CEO	**Federico Sada G.**
	66250 Garza Garacia NL	Fax	**08-329-1290**	SEDOL No.	**2931324**	Chairman	--

The Netherlands

The Netherlands

Anya Shiffrin,
Amsterdam

Local Trading Hours	Time Difference from New York	Population (Est. 1/95)
9:30-4:30	6 hours ahead of EST (7 ahead March-May, 5 ahead Sept.-Oct)	15,422,842

The Amsterdam Stock Exchange has its roots in the open air trading of the early 17th century, when brokers started to take positions based on the fortunes of Dutch ships that travelled the world, returning home loaded with cargo.

Just as it does today, news and rumor played an important part in the transactions, with an informal network passing on gossip from overseas which in turn affected the price of the deals being made.

The Calvinistic city elders decried the mercenary impulses of the market speculators but the bourse expanded and today ranks as the fourth market in Europe in terms of capitalization and fifth in terms of turnover.

With its stable economy, and the strong guilder which is pegged to the Deutsche mark, the bourse is an attractive market for foreign investors.

In 1994 the bourse had a record volume of 312 billion guilders with 1.7 million registered share transactions. Foreign investors were responsible for 56% of the transactions, private investors for 25% of the transactions and institutional investors accounted for 14%.

The Dutch civil servant's pension fund, the ABP, one of the largest pension funds in the world, has said it will start investing more in stocks and this is expected to expand market liquidity.

The Dutch have historically been a mercantile and international people and their companies have retained these traits. Some of the most important bourse-listed companies are internationally owned such as the Anglo-Dutch Royal/Dutch Shell Group, consumer products company Unilever, publisher Reed Elsevier and Dutch-Swedish chemicals company Akzo Nobel.

These firms are part of the AEX index of top 25 companies which also includes KLM Royal Dutch Airlines, postal and telecom monopoly KPN, food retailer Ahold and the country's two largest banks, ABN Amro and the Internationale Nederlanden Groep.

Dow Jones Netherlands Equity Market Index Performance

Closed-end mutual funds are also traded in the bourse with five funds from the Rotterdam-based Robeco Groep family of mutual funds trading on the main market.

Gross Domestic Product (94)	Three Year Average GDP Growth (91-94)	Main Industries	Consumer Price Index (94)	Monetary Unit	Exchange Rate (9/95)
608.4 billion guilders	+1.6%	Commercial services, transportation, metals, banking and insurance	+2.7%	Guilder	NLG1.60 to US$1.00

Dutch multinationals tend to list their shares on overseas exchanges with companies like Philips also trading in New York. Other companies trade in the U.K. as well, making these stocks attractive for cross-border arbitrage.

Because Dutch companies, and especially the index heavyweights, derive so much of their income overseas, the market is highly dollar sensitive and investors keep a close eye on U.S. economic indicators and interest rate movements as well as interest rate trends in Germany.

As well as index companies there are four companies in the so-called "parallel" market which was merged with the main market on October 1, 1994.

Fearful of losing market share to London, where about 30-40% of trade in Dutch stocks takes place, the bourse authorities introduced a market maker system in the autumn of 1994 in order to improve liquidity and transparency as well as to narrow price spreads. The market split into wholesale and retail segments and the jobbers (or hoekman) were replaced by market makers in the wholesale market. Hoekman remain on the retail side of trade and the bourse says that the changes have improved the Dutch market's share in trade in Dutch stocks. The exchange wants to at least maintain the current level of domestic trading in Dutch equities – estimated at about 50% of total volumes in Dutch shares.

Trade is done by ASSET and AIDA dealing systems as well with a limit order book. Bourse hours are 9:30 am to 4:30 pm.

Ten Largest Capitalized Companies
as of 9/30/95

Stock	Market Cap. US$Mil
Royal Dutch Petroleum	65,870,092.7
Philips Electronics	16,499,535.0
PTT Nederland	16,260,488.1
ING Group	16,228,236.5
ABN Amro	12,557,064.3
Aegon	9,371,838.8
Akzo Nobel	8,532,841.9
Elsevier	8,425,333.4
Heineken	8,090,396.3
Robeco	8,032,543.8

In 1994 there were 60 billion guilders and 21 new institutions in new issues.

There have been fewer major share issues on the Dutch stock market in 1995 but the second tranche of shares in KPN is due to float in the autumn of this year. In general, investors prefer new issues from larger and more well-known companies than from smaller ones.

The first Dutch insider trading laws were implemented in 1989 but to date there has been only one conviction (now being re-tried) for insider trading, although there have been a number of ongoing investigations. Finance minister Gerrit Zalm has said repeatedly that if the bourse doesn't tighten its stance he will seek tougher legislation. Maximum penalties for insider trading are two years in prison and a 100,000 guilder fine for private investors and a 1 million guilder fine for institutions.

Another debate has been over the very strict defenses that Dutch companies' employ to ward off hostile takeovers. These include the sale of share certificates rather than shares themselves, poison pills and the ability of targeted companies to issue emergency preference shares. In 1995, the bourse proposed setting up a takeover panel to decide on possible takeovers but Zalm has said the possible reforms don't go far enough.

ABN Amro

Industry: **Banks - Money Center**

ABN Amro Holding offers a full range of banking services. Its main activities include domestic, international, credit, and investment banking. The bank has a network of 1,600 branches in 64 countries, 1,050 of which are in the Netherlands. It serves about 10,000 corporate clients in the Netherlands, and maintains an 18% share of the Dutch consumer-banking market. ABN Amro owns U.S. banks, including Chicago-based LaSalle Talman Bank, Cragin Federal, and European American Bank. The bank recently purchased Nordic investment bank Alfred Berg from Volvo.

	NLG mil 12/92	12/93	12/94	US$mil 12/94				
Revenues	**42,492.0**	**40,879.0**	**37,776.0**	**20,870.7**	P/E Ratio	**9.7**	Price (9/30/95)	**66.20**
Net Income	**1,684.0**	**2,024.0**	**2,286.0**	**1,263.0**	P/B Ratio	**1.0**	52 Wk Hi-Low	**66.50-53.90**
Book Value	**16,074.0**	**19,139.0**	**19,325.0**	**11,106.3**	Yield %	**4.8**	Market Cap	**US$12,557mil**

Address	**Foppingadreef 22**	Tel	**020-628-9898**	ADR	**ARBLY**	Chairman Exec Bd	**P.J. Kalff**
	1102 BS Amsterdam	Fax	**020-628-7837**	SEDOL No.	**4004224**	Chairman Supv Bd	**J.D. Hooglandt**

Aegon

Industry: **Insurance - Full Line**

Aegon is one of the world's 20 largest insurance firms by assets. Life insurance and associated financial services generate more than two thirds of revenues, but the company also offers accident, health, and general insurance, including auto and fire insurance. The company operates in the U.S. through its subsidiary Aegon USA, which offers life and health insurance. It has insurance subsidiaries in the United Kingdom, the Caribbean, Spain, Hungary, and Taiwan. Sales in the United States account for more than one third of Aegon's revenues.

	NLG mil 12/92	12/93	12/94	US$mil 12/94				
Revenues	**15,321.0**	**22,102.0**	**20,605.0**	**11,384.0**	P/E Ratio	**12.9**	Price (9/30/95)	**57.90**
Net Income	**909.0**	**1,004.0**	**1,151.0**	**635.9**	P/B Ratio	**1.9**	52 Wk Hi-Low	**59.40-39.20**
Book Value	**6,313.0**	**8,669.0**	**7,959.0**	**4,574.1**	Yield %	**3.4**	Market Cap	**US$9,371.8mil**

Address	**Mariahoeveplein 50**	Tel	**070-344-3210**	ADR	**AEG**	Chairman Exec Bd	**Kees J. Storm**
	2501 CE The Hague	Fax	**070-347-5238**	SEDOL No.	**4002057**	Chairman Supv Bd	**G. van Schaik**

Ahold

Industry: **Food Retailers & Wholesalers**

Royal Ahold (Koninklijke Ahold) is a food producer, retailer, and institutional supplier with operations in Europe and the United States. It operates more than 530 stores in the U.S. through five chains, including Bi-Lo, Giant Food Stores, and First National Supermarkets. In the Netherlands, Ahold owns six retail companies, and more than 1,450 stores. The company also owns 27 Mana supermarkets in the Czech Republic, Pingo Doce stores in Portugal, 24 health- and beauty-supply stores in Belgium, and 50% of the Spanish sherry producer Luis Paez.

	NLG mil 01/93	01/94	01/95	US$mil 01/95				
Sales	**21,594.0**	**27,093.0**	**28,977.9**	**16,197.8**	P/E Ratio	**17.4**	Price (9/30/95)	**60.10**
Net Income	**305.0**	**343.0**	**409.5**	**228.9**	P/B Ratio	**3.3**	52 Wk Hi-Low	**60.90-47.30**
Book Value	**1,483.0**	**2,137.0**	**2,220.4**	**1,306.1**	Yield %	**2.1**	Market Cap	**US$4,515.5mil**

Address	**Albert Heijnweg 1**	Tel	**075-599-111**	ADR		Chairman Exec Bd	**C.H. van der Hoeven**
	1507 EH Zaandam	Fax	**075-598-350**	SEDOL No.	**4025173**	Chairman Supv Bd	**J.H. Choufoer**

Akzo Nobel

Industry: **Commodity Chemicals**

Akzo Nobel produces chemicals, fibers, coatings, and pharmaceuticals. Its chemicals are used in oil, plastic, rubber, paper, and detergent. Akzo also provides coatings for aerospace, automotive, industrial, and consumer products. Its fibers are used in clothing, footwear, textiles for home furnishings, carpet, industrial fabrics, and tires. Its pharmaceutical division produces and markets generic drugs, veterinary products, and contraceptive and fertility drugs. Non-European exports, primarily to the U.S., account for nearly 40% of the company's revenues.

	NLG mil 12/92	12/93	12/94	US$mil 12/94				
Sales	**16,713.0**	**16,509.0**	**22,208.0**	**12,269.6**	P/E Ratio	**11.6**	Price (9/30/95)	**192.10**
Net Income	**646.0**	**549.0**	**1,178.0**	**650.8**	P/B Ratio	**2.2**	52 Wk Hi-Low	**212.90-166.00**
Book Value	**5,078.0**	**6,152.0**	**6,257.0**	**3,596.0**	Yield %	**3.6**	Market Cap	**US$8,532.8mil**

Address	**Velperweg 76**	Tel	**085-66-44-33**	ADR	**AKZOY**	Chairman Exec Bd	**Cees J.A. van Lede**
	6800 SB Arnhem	Fax	**085-66-32-50**	SEDOL No.	**4011901**	Chairman Supv Bd	**F.H. Fentener**

BolsWessanen

Industry: **Other Food**

Royal BolsWessanen (Koninklijke BolsWessanen) markets a wide range of food and beverages in Europe and North America. The company produces and sells dairy and breakfast products, frozen foods, prepared foods, and alcoholic and nonalcoholic beverages. The company's products include Kemps frozen desserts, Harrisons and Crosfield's cereals, Jonge Bols gin, and Adelbodner mineral water. It has a 35% stake in Italian spirits company Davide Campari-Milano. Exports to the United States account for half of the company's revenues; Europe generates the remaining revenues.

	NLG mil 12/92	12/93	12/94	US$mil 12/94				
Sales	**5,008.0**	**5,153.0**	**5,287.1**	**2,921.0**	P/E Ratio	**10.1**	Price (9/30/95)	**31.10**
Net Income	**284.0**	**201.0**	**254.1**	**140.4**	P/B Ratio	**2.3**	52 Wk Hi-Low	**35.40-27.30**
Book Value	**1,262.0**	**1,199.0**	**1,123.6**	**645.7**	Yield %	**4.1**	Market Cap	**US$1,603.1mil**

Address	**Prof. E.M. Meijerslaan 2**	Tel	**020-547-95-47**	ADR	**KNWSY**	Chairman Exec Bd	**R. Schipper**
	1183 AV Amstelveen	Fax	**020-645-91-60**	SEDOL No.	**4949477**	Chairman Supv Bd	**A. van der Stee**

Cap Volmac

Industry: **Software**

Cap Volmac Group (formerly Volmac Software Groep) provides computer software and information-technology services. The company's services include data processing, facilities management, and consultation services. Its custom solutions and consulting operations contribute nearly 90% of company revenues. Cap Volmac Group generates 80% of its revenues within the Netherlands, with most of the rest coming from operations in Belgium. The French consulting and computer-services company Cap Gemini Sogeti has a 58% interest in Cap Volmac Group.

NLG mil	12/92	12/93	12/94	US$mil 12/94				
Sales	**855.8**	**808.9**	**811.9**	**448.6**	P/E Ratio	**12.3**	Price (9/30/95)	**19.60**
Net Income	**74.6**	**55.1**	**66.0**	**36.5**	P/B Ratio	**3.8**	52 Wk Hi-Low	**27.20-19.50**
Book Value	**191.1**	**199.7**	**213.1**	**122.5**	Yield %	**6.4**	Market Cap	**US$508.8mil**

Address **Daltonlaan 300**, **3500 GN Utrecht**
Tel **030-526-526**
Fax **030-543-143**
ADR
SEDOL No. **4930802**
Chairman Exec Bd **C.J.A. van Breugel**
Chairman Supv Bd **R. van Ommeren**

CSM

Industry: **Other Food**

The Central Sugar Company (Centrale Suiker Maatschappij) (CSM) develops, manufactures, and distributes food products and ingredients. CSM's food division, its largest by sales, makes pasta, wheat flour, rice, soups, sauces, baking products, and processed-vegetable and -fruit products. Its sugar division produces sugar and agricultural fertilizer. Its ingredients division produces lactic acid, fruit fillings, icing, and bakery ingredients. Exports within Europe generate 23% of CSM's revenues, and overseas exports, primarily to North America, generate 36% of revenues.

NLG mil	09/92	09/93	09/94	US$mil 09/94				
Sales	**2,105.0**	**2,522.0**	**2,637.7**	**1,421.2**	P/E Ratio	**14.9**	Price (9/30/95)	**65.00**
Net Income	**129.0**	**147.0**	**164.1**	**88.4**	P/B Ratio	**3.1**	52 Wk Hi-Low	**72.10-63.60**
Book Value	**693.0**	**652.0**	**782.9**	**449.9**	Yield %	**2.3**	Market Cap	**US$1,526.4mil**

Address **Nienoord 13**, **1112 XE Diemen**
Tel **020-59-06-911**
Fax **020-69-51-942**
ADR
SEDOL No. **4158596**
Chairman Exec Bd **G.M.L. van Loon**
Chairman Supv Bd **F.H. Fentener**

DSM

Industry: **Commodity Chemicals**

DSM makes base and fine chemicals, polymers, resins, fertilizers, hydrocarbons, synthetic rubbers, and plastic goods. The firm also explores for oil and natural gas. DSM sells to automotive, computer, electronics, synthetic-fiber, paint, and drug firms. It produces Dyneema fibers for use in cycling helmets, windsurfing sails, and protective apparel, and makes ingredients for drugs such as Ampicillin, Amoxicillin, Diltiazem, Captopril, and Terbutaline. Hydrocarbons and polymers generate nearly 45% of sales. Non-European exports account for more than 26% of DSM's revenues.

NLG mil	12/92	12/93	12/94	US$mil 12/94				
Sales	**8,907.0**	**8,040.0**	**8,977.0**	**4,959.7**	P/E Ratio	**8.7**	Price (9/30/95)	**128.40**
Net Income	**224.0**	**-118.0**	**532.0**	**293.9**	P/B Ratio	**1.1**	52 Wk Hi-Low	**152.30-118.50**
Book Value	**4,252.0**	**4,089.0**	**4,379.0**	**2,516.7**	Yield %	**4.7**	Market Cap	**US$2,890.4mil**

Address **Het Overloon 1**, **6401 JH Heerlen**
Tel **045-788-111**
Fax **045-719-753**
ADR **DSMKY**
SEDOL No. **4249100**
Chairman Exec Bd **Simon D. de Bree**
Chairman Supv Bd **H.H.F. Wijffels**

Elsevier

Industry: **Publishing**

Elsevier co-owns with Reed International the publishing and information firm Reed Elsevier. Reed Elsevier publishes scientific, medical, professional, business, and consumer books, journals, newspapers, and magazines. Its titles include the American Journal of Medicine, Marie Claire, and Halsbury's Laws of England. Its online services include Excerpta Medica Database, an electronic database of medical literature, and U.S.-based Lexis-Nexis, which supplies legal and medical information. Non-European sales, mainly to the U.S., account for nearly half of its revenues.

NLG mil	12/92 P	12/93 P	12/94 P	US$mil 12/94				
Sales	**424.0**	**528.0**	**628.3**	**347.1**	P/E Ratio	**22.0**	Price (9/30/95)	**20.50**
Net Income	**434.0**	**552.0**	**650.2**	**359.2**	P/B Ratio	**7.4**	52 Wk Hi-Low	**21.60-14.80**
Book Value	**963.0**	**2,460.0**	**1,922.4**	**1,104.8**	Yield %	**2.7**	Market Cap	**US$8,425.3mil**

Address **PO Box 470**, **1000 AL Amsterdam**
Tel **020-515-2333**
Fax **020-683-2617**
ADR **ENL**
SEDOL No. **4148810**
Chairman Exec Bd **P.J. Vinken**
Chairman Supv Bd **A. Schuitemaker**

P=Parent company data.

Fokker Vliegtuigenfabriek

Industry: **Aerospace & Defense**

Fokker designs and manufactures passenger jets, turboprop planes, and military components and aircraft. It also performs maintenance on and repairs existing aircraft, and produces parts for the Airbus A310/300- and A300/600-series passenger planes. In 1994, it took orders for 335 jets and 205 turboprops, and delivered its first Fokker 70 model. Fokker's military division makes transport planes and fuselages for American-made F-16s. Its space division manufactures the parachute system and engine frames for the Ariane 5 rocket. Fokker is 51%-owned by Daimler-Benz Aerospace.

NLG mil	12/92	12/93	12/94	US$mil 12/94				
Sales	**4,082.5**	**3,697.6**	**2,348.1**	**1,297.3**	P/E Ratio	**NMF**	Price (9/30/95)	**8.40**
Net Income	**19.8**	**-459.6**	**-449.4**	**-248.3**	P/B Ratio	**0.6**	52 Wk Hi-Low	**15.90-6.90**
Book Value	**539.4**	**506.0**	**711.9**	**409.1**	Yield %	**0.0**	Market Cap	**US$249.4mil**

Address **Hoogoorddreef 15**, **1101 BA Amsterdam**
Tel **020-605-6666**
Fax **020-605-7022**
ADR **FOKKY**
SEDOL No. **4343938**
Chairman Exec Bd **B.J.A. van Schaik**
Chairman Supv Bd **J.E. Schrempp**

Fortis AMEV

Industry: **Insurance - Full Line**

Fortis AMEV is a holding company that primarily manages its 50% stake in the Fortis insurance and banking company. Through Fortis, AMEV offers life, accident, health, and general insurance. It offers retail banking and asset management through its Metropolitan, VSB, and ASLK-CGER banking subsidiaries. Its main markets are the Netherlands, Belgium, and the United States. Fortis AMEV generates 62% of its revenues from insurance activities and 38% from banking activities. Non-European insurance premiums account for nearly 30% of its revenues.

NLG mil	12/92	12/93	12/94	US$mil 12/94				
Revenues	**546.0**	**580.0**	**632.1**	**349.2**	P/E Ratio	**10.7**	Price (9/30/95)	**93.30**
Net Income	**532.0**	**574.0**	**626.4**	**346.1**	P/B Ratio	**1.2**	52 Wk Hi-Low	**96.50-66.50**
Book Value	**4,717.0**	**5,324.0**	**5,402.0**	**3,104.6**	Yield %	**4.1**	Market Cap	**US$4,179.7mil**

Address **Archimedeslaan 10**, **3584 BA Utrecht** | Tel **030-579-111** | Fax **030-522-394** | ADR **AMVNY** | SEDOL No. **4001690** | CEO **J.L.M. Bartelds** | Chairman **F. Roos**

Getronics

Industry: **Communications Technology**

Getronics is a telecommunication and information- systems services company. Its information-systems services include desktop and industrial automation, network and software services, and information-systems management. It also provides telecommunication services such as telematics installation and consultancy. It has a 15% stake in MobiNed, which is competing for a license to establish and operate the Netherlands' second mobile phone network. Getronics is active throughout Europe and has operations in Spain, the U.K., Scandinavia, and the Benelux countries.

NLG mil	12/92	12/93	12/94	US$mil 12/94				
Sales	**1,026.0**	**1,302.4**	**1,410.0**	**779.0**	P/E Ratio	**20.8**	Price (9/30/95)	**78.80**
Net Income	**60.7**	**65.6**	**80.2**	**44.3**	P/B Ratio	**5.2**	52 Wk Hi-Low	**79.50-50.50**
Book Value	**203.8**	**238.0**	**318.9**	**183.3**	Yield %	**1.1**	Market Cap	**US$1,041.0mil**

Address **Donauweg 10**, **1043 AJ Amsterdam** | Tel **020-586-1412** | Fax **020-586-1568** | ADR | SEDOL No. **4370345** | President & CEO **A.H.J. Risseeuw** | Chairman Supv Bd **J.C. Bakker**

Gist-Brocades

Industry: **Other Food**

Royal Gist-Brocades (Koninklijke Gist-Brocades) develops and manufactures biotechnology products. Its four divisions are food ingredients, biosynthetics, bulk pharmaceuticals, and agribusiness. The company produces baker's yeast, penicillin, and their intermediate derivatives and enzymes. It also provides raw materials to the pharmaceutical and cosmetics industries, and industrial enzymes to the detergent, starch, and textile industries. Sales to Europe account for 56% of Gist-Brocades' revenues; exports to non-European countries generate 36% of revenues.

NLG mil	12/92	12/93	12/94	US$mil 12/94				
Sales	**1,565.0**	**1,703.0**	**1,769.6**	**977.7**	P/E Ratio	**11.3**	Price (9/30/95)	**42.50**
Net Income	**104.0**	**135.0**	**141.2**	**78.0**	P/B Ratio	**1.4**	52 Wk Hi-Low	**47.40-35.50**
Book Value	**982.0**	**1,072.0**	**1,102.1**	**633.4**	Yield %	**3.5**	Market Cap	**US$1,001.5mil**

Address **Wateringseweg 1**, **2611 XT Delft** | Tel **015-799-111** | Fax **015-793-809** | ADR | SEDOL No. **4370282** | Chairman Exec Bd **H.C. Scheffer** | Chairman Supv Bd **G. van Schaik**

Heineken

Industry: **Distillers & Brewers**

Heineken produces and distributes beer, wine, spirits, and soft drinks in more than 170 countries. The company's beers include Heineken, Amstel, Amstel Light, and Murphy's Irish Stout. It also brews the nonalcoholic beers Buckler and Amstel Malt. It has 100 breweries in more than 55 countries. Europe and the U.S. are its main markets, but it also brews and distributes beer in Canada, Africa, and Asia. Heineken's subsidiaries include 65%-owned Spanish brewery El Aguila and 43%-owned Asia Pacific Breweries. Non-European exports account for nearly 30% of its revenues.

NLG mil	12/92	12/93	12/94	US$mil 12/94				
Sales	**8,944.0**	**9,049.0**	**9,974.2**	**5,510.6**	P/E Ratio	**21.5**	Price (9/30/95)	**258.00**
Net Income	**564.0**	**519.0**	**662.1**	**365.8**	P/B Ratio	**3.0**	52 Wk Hi-Low	**267.20-185.04**
Book Value	**3,650.0**	**3,973.0**	**4,354.0**	**2,502.3**	Yield %	**1.1**	Market Cap	**US$8,090.4mil**

Address **Tweede Weteringplantsoen 21**, **1017 ZD Amsterdam** | Tel **020-523-9239** | Fax **020-626-3503** | ADR **HINKY** | SEDOL No. **4419301** | Chairman Exec Bd **K. Vuursteen** | Chairman **A. Hazelhoff**

Hunter Douglas

Industry: **Other Home Furnishings**

Hunter Douglas manufactures window coverings, architectural products, and machine tools. The company's other activities include metal trading, particularly aluminum, and production and marketing of precision machinery. The company's products include blinds, shades, and other window coverings. Its window covering and architectural products generate the majority of its revenues. In 1994, sales in Europe, the Middle East, and Africa accounted for 42% of revenues, and exports to North America generated 38% of revenues.

NLG mil	12/92	12/93	12/94	US$mil 12/94				
Sales	**1,682.0**	**1,781.0**	**2,003.4**	**1,106.8**	P/E Ratio	**14.7**	Price (9/30/95)	**79.00**
Net Income	**33.0**	**63.0**	**90.4**	**50.0**	P/B Ratio	**2.4**	52 Wk Hi-Low	**84.50-64.00**
Book Value	**488.0**	**528.0**	**550.0**	**316.1**	Yield %	**2.5**	Market Cap	**US$821.6mil**

Address **Piekstraat 2**, **3071 EL Rotterdam** | Tel **010-486-9911** | Fax **010-485-0621** | ADR | SEDOL No. **4448628** | President & CEO **Ralph Sonnenberg** | Chairman **Ralph Sonnenberg**

ING Group

Industry: **Financial Services - Diversified**

Internationale Nederlanden Group (ING) provides banking, insurance, and related financial services. It offers life and general insurance, securities trading, loans, leasing, and debt conversion. ING operates more than 400 bank branches in the Netherlands and 75 offices in nearly 50 countries. It acquired the collapsed U.K. investment bank Barings, including its securities and asset-management businesses, in March 1995. ING's insurance activities account for 78% of revenues; 37% of its income is generated outside Europe.

	NLG mil 12/92	12/93	12/94	US$mil 12/94				
Revenues	**48,963.0**	**49,635.0**	**48,987.0**	**27,064.6**	P/E Ratio	**10.6**	Price (9/30/95)	**92.90**
Net Income	**1,829.0**	**2,029.0**	**2,302.0**	**1,271.8**	P/B Ratio	**1.2**	52 Wk Hi-Low	**94.50-72.70**
Book Value	**15,597.0**	**21,481.0**	**21,758.0**	**12,504.6**	Yield %	**4.0**	Market Cap	**US$16,228mil**

Address **Strawinskylaan 2631**
1000 AV Amsterdam
Tel **020-541-5462**
Fax **020-541-5451**
ADR **INLGY**
SEDOL No. **4488163**
Chairman Exec Bd **A.G. Jacobs**
Chairman Supv Bd **J.H. Choufoer**

KLM

Industry: **Airlines**

KLM Royal Dutch Airlines (Koninklijke Luchtvaart Maatschappij) is an international airline that offers scheduled and chartered services for passengers and cargo. The company also has interests in computer-reservation systems, helicopter ferrying, forwarding, and trucking. Along with its wholly-owned KLM Cityhopper subsidiary, the company flies to more than 150 destinations on six continents and operates a fleet of 152 planes. KLM owns 25% of NWA, the holding company for Northwest Airlines, 45% of Air UK, and 50% of charter airline Martinair.

	NLG mil 03/93	03/94	03/95	US$mil 03/95				
Sales	**8,222.0**	**8,672.0**	**9,188.0**	**5,289.6**	P/E Ratio	**11.0**	Price (9/30/95)	**56.10**
Net Income	**-562.0**	**103.0**	**470.0**	**270.6**	P/B Ratio	**1.3**	52 Wk Hi-Low	**60.40-41.60**
Book Value	**2,124.0**	**3,515.0**	**3,762.0**	**2,458.8**	Yield %	**2.7**	Market Cap	**US$2,984.7mil**

Address **Amsterdamseweg 55**
1117 ZL Amstelveen
Tel **020-649-9123**
Fax **020-641-2872**
ADR **KLM**
SEDOL No. **4480255**
Chairman Exec Bd **P. Bouw**
Chairman Supv Bd **C.J. Oort**

KNP BT

Industry: **Paper Products**

Royal KNP BT (Koninklijke KNP BT) produces paper, board, and packaging and distributes paper, graphic and information systems, and office products. The company's paper products include coated paper, pulp, flexible and protective packaging, and corrugated cardboard. One of Europe's largest paper companies, KNP manages 150 operating companies in more than 30 countries. European exports generate 60% of its revenues, and overseas exports, primarily to North America, account for 20% of revenues. The paper and office- products division generates roughly 55% of sales.

	NLG mil 01/93	12/93	12/94	US$mil 12/94				
Sales	**11,760.0**	**11,178.0**	**13,147.0**	**7,263.5**	P/E Ratio	**15.6**	Price (9/30/95)	**47.50**
Net Income	**116.0**	**-343.0**	**325.0**	**179.6**	P/B Ratio	**1.6**	52 Wk Hi-Low	**54.30-43.60**
Book Value	**2,362.0**	**2,324.0**	**2,929.0**	**1,683.3**	Yield %	**2.1**	Market Cap	**US$2,978.8mil**

Address **Paalbergweg 2**
1009 AA Amsterdam
Tel **020-567-2672**
Fax **020-567-2567**
ADR
SEDOL No. **4501242**
Chairman Exec Bd **Robert F.W. van Oordt**
Chairman Supv Bd **F.C. Rauwenhoff**

Nedlloyd Group

Industry: **Trucking**

Royal Nedlloyd Group (Koninklijke Nedlloyd Groep) engages primarily in ocean shipping and road cargo. Its ocean-shipping division consists of 18 vessels that specialize in container logistics; it has routes worldwide. Its road-cargo division operates a fleet of roughly 5,000 vehicles. It also offers storage, forwarding, and distribution services. Ocean shipping and European transport and distribution contribute 96% of revenues. The firm's Neddrill subsidiary provides drilling and related services to the offshore oil industry. Non-European sales account for 37% of revenues.

	NLG mil 12/92	12/93	12/94	US$mil 12/94				
Sales	**6,722.0**	**6,618.0**	**6,607.0**	**3,650.3**	P/E Ratio	**13.8**	Price (9/30/95)	**56.80**
Net Income	**-58.0**	**-112.0**	**92.0**	**50.8**	P/B Ratio	**0.8**	52 Wk Hi-Low	**60.80-43.30**
Book Value	**1,488.0**	**1,385.0**	**1,601.0**	**920.1**	Yield %	**2.2**	Market Cap	**US$796.2mil**

Address **Boompjes 40**
3011 XB Rotterdam
Tel **010-400-6818**
Fax **010-404-6190**
ADR **RNLGY**
SEDOL No. **4628839**
Chairman Exec Bd **L.J.M. Berndsen**
Chairman Supv Bd **O.H.A. van Royen**

Nutricia

Industry: **Other Food**

Verenigde Bedrijven Nutricia is a food company that specializes in nutritional products, reduced-calorie foods, infant formula, and personal-care products. Infant formula, produced in a joint venture with the Hungarian company EGIS Pharmaceuticals, generates more than one third of revenues. Nutricia also makes Galenco skin-care products, Chocomel chocolate milk, and Fristi yogurt drinks. U.K. food retailer Unigate has a 30% stake in the company. European exports account for 64% of revenues; exports to non-European countries account for 9% of revenues.

	NLG mil 12/92	12/93	12/94	US$mil 12/94				
Sales	**1,253.0**	**1,404.0**	**1,490.4**	**823.4**	P/E Ratio	**18.9**	Price (9/30/95)	**120.30**
Net Income	**87.0**	**101.0**	**136.2**	**75.2**	P/B Ratio	**4.4**	52 Wk Hi-Low	**120.30-84.60**
Book Value	**473.0**	**513.0**	**582.3**	**334.7**	Yield %	**1.6**	Market Cap	**US$1,611.8mil**

Address **Rokkeveenseweg 49**
2712 PJ Zoetermeer
Tel **079-539000**
Fax **079-539620**
ADR
SEDOL No. **4588126**
President **J.C.T. van der Wielen**
Chairman **E.J. van der Hagen**

Océ-van der Grinten

Industry: **Office Equipment**

Oce-van der Grinten markets a range of copiers, printers, and plotter systems as well as materials and imaging supplies for these systems. The company has operations in roughly 30 countries and markets its products in more than 80 countries. It leases and sells copiers, printers, and printing and reproduction systems through its Office and Engineering Systems divisions. It has roughly 20% of the worldwide market share of printing and copying systems. Exports to non-European countries account for nearly 30% of its revenues.

NLG mil	11/91	11/92	11/93	US$mil 11/93				
Sales	**2,576.0**	**2,664.0**	**2,626.0**	**1,419.5**	P/E Ratio	**16.6**	Price (9/30/95)	**91.00**
Net Income	**101.0**	**87.0**	**62.0**	**33.5**	P/B Ratio	**1.5**	52 Wk Hi-Low	**94.00-72.00**
Book Value	**949.0**	**968.0**	**998.0**	**519.8**	Yield %	**2.5**	Market Cap	**US$927.4mil**

Address **St. Urbanusweg 43**, **5900 MA Venlo** Tel **077-592-222** Fax **077-544-700** ADR **OCENY** SEDOL No. **4657952** Chairman Exec Bd **J.V.H. Pennings** Chairman Supv Bd **H.B. van Liemt**

Pakhoed

Industry: **Marine Transportation**

Royal Pakhoed (Koninklijke Pakhoed) provides worldwide distribution, tank storage, logistics, and support activities to shipping businesses and the chemical and oil industries. Its Pakhoed Shipping division provides shipping services. Its Pakhoed Corporation division offers storage and environmental-protection services and its Furness division provides land-transport services. In 1995, Pakhoed's U.S. subsidiary acquired storage firm Montank Transit of Canada. European exports account for 16% of revenues; exports to non- European countries account for 11% of revenues.

NLG mil	12/92	12/93	12/94	US$mil 12/94				
Sales	**1,415.0**	**1,449.0**	**1,365.3**	**754.3**	P/E Ratio	**14.7**	Price (9/30/95)	**46.90**
Net Income	**91.0**	**60.0**	**92.7**	**51.2**	P/B Ratio	**1.4**	52 Wk Hi-Low	**52.70-41.20**
Book Value	**845.0**	**843.0**	**1,015.3**	**583.5**	Yield %	**3.4**	Market Cap	**US$863.2mil**

Address **Blaak 333**, **3011 GB Rotterdam** Tel **010-400-2911** Fax **010-413-9829** ADR SEDOL No. **4492067** Chairman Exec Bd **N.J. Westdijk** Chairman Supv Bd **J.H. Choufoer**

Philips Electronics

Industry: **Diversified Technology**

Philips manufactures electronic products for industrial and consumer use. The company makes videocassette recorders, CD players, televisions, camcorders, kitchen and bathroom appliances, arena-lighting systems, and communication and industrial systems. Philips assembles discrete semiconductors in a joint venture with Motorola and operates a joint venture to make LCD panels with France's Thomson Consumer Electronics and Sagem. Philips' holdings include a 75% interest in PolyGram. Non-European sales account for more than 45% of its revenues.

NLG mil	12/92	12/93	12/94	US$mil 12/94				
Sales	**58,527.0**	**58,825.0**	**60,977.0**	**33,689.0**	P/E Ratio	**12.2**	Price (9/30/95)	**78.00**
Net Income	**-900.0**	**1,965.0**	**2,125.0**	**1,174.0**	P/B Ratio	**2.1**	52 Wk Hi-Low	**81.70-50.50**
Book Value	**9,071.0**	**11,449.0**	**12,683.0**	**7,289.1**	Yield %	**1.6**	Market Cap	**US$16,500mil**

Address **Groenewoudseweg 1**, **5621 BA Eindhoven** Tel **040-786-022** Fax **040-785-486** ADR **PHG** SEDOL No. **4685209** President **Jan D. Timmer** Chairman Supv Bd **F.A. Maljers**

PTT Nederland

Industry: **Telephone Systems - All**

Koninklijke PTT Nederland (KPN) is the Dutch postal and telecommunication company that is 65%-controlled by the Dutch government. The company's postal activities generate roughly 30% of its revenues, and the remaining sales are generated by its telecommunication activities. The Dutch government recently awarded KPN a license to provide cross-border paging services. KPN's joint venture with Swiss Telecom recently acquired a 27% stake in Czech telecom company SPT. KPN's other subsidiaries include Telecential, which provides cable services to nearly 300,000 U.K. customers.

NLG mil	12/92	12/93	12/94	US$mil 12/94				
Sales	**N/A**	**N/A**	**N/A**	**N/A**	P/E Ratio	**12.8**	Price (9/30/95)	**56.50**
Net Income	**N/A**	**N/A**	**N/A**	**N/A**	P/B Ratio	**1.8**	52 Wk Hi-Low	**59.20-51.90**
Book Value	**N/A**	**N/A**	**N/A**	**N/A**	Yield %	**4.1**	Market Cap	**US$16,260mil**

Address **Stationsplein 7**, **9726 AE Groningen** Tel **050-822-822** Fax **N/A** ADR SEDOL No. **4534561** President -- Chairman **J. Groenendijk**

Robeco

Industry: **Financial Services - Diversified**

Robeco is a holding company for a group of fund-management companies that offer financial products to clients and institutions. The company's fund family is led by its flagship equities fund, the Robeco fund. Robeco's other funds include a long-term bond fund, Rorento; an equities fund, Rolinco; and two medium-term bond funds, Florentine and Divirente. Robeco also runs property-investment businesses through group member Rodamco. In 1994, the group launched funds investing in Dutch equities, Dutch retail properties, and emerging-market equities.

NLG mil	12/92	12/93	12/94	US$mil 12/94				
Revenues	**320.0**	**303.0**	**307.0**	**169.6**	P/E Ratio	**36.3**	Price (9/30/95)	**110.00**
Net Income	**296.0**	**278.0**	**280.0**	**154.7**	P/B Ratio	**1.0**	52 Wk Hi-Low	**115.20-98.80**
Book Value	**8,945.0**	**10,931.0**	**9,937.0**	**5,710.9**	Yield %	**3.2**	Market Cap	**US$8,032.5mil**

Address **Coolsingel 120**, **3011 AG Rotterdam** Tel **010-224-1224** Fax **010-411-5288** ADR SEDOL No. **4744111** President **Pieter Korteweg** Chairman Supv Bd **Conrad J. Oort**

Rodamco

Industry: **Real-Estate Investment**

Rodamco, partially owned by the Robeco holding company, operates property-investment businesses. It has roughly 1.8 million square meters of retail, office, and industrial rental property. Retail property is Rodamco's primary management area, and the company holds Australian retail investments with that country's Westfield Trust. Australasian holdings are the focus of the Rodamco Pacific division. Overall, North America accounts for more than 40% of Rodamco's property portfolio; continental Europe accounts for 28%; and the United Kingdom, accounts for 23%.

NLG mil	02/93	02/94	02/95	US$mil 02/95				
Sales	**472.0**	**568.0**	**622.0**	**352.2**	P/E Ratio	**15.1**	Price (9/30/95)	**44.70**
Net Income	**429.0**	**452.0**	**453.0**	**256.5**	P/B Ratio	**0.9**	52 Wk Hi-Low	**53.50-44.00**
Book Value	**7,282.0**	**7,763.0**	**7,993.0**	**4,873.8**	Yield %	**6.6**	Market Cap	**US$4,280.3mil**

Address	**Coolsingel 120**	Tel	**010-224-1224**	ADR		President	--
	3011 AG Rotterdam	Fax	**010-224-2115**	SEDOL No.	**4746430**	Chairman	**Pieter Korteweg**

Rolinco

Industry: **Securities Brokers**

Rolinco is a global fund-management company that is partially owned by the holding company Robeco. The company invests in international equities and growth stocks. Rolinco has interests in the markets of European countries, the United States, Australia, Japan, Europe, and Hong Kong. By the end of 1994, Rolinco's investments in Southeast Asia and Australia amounted to 18%. Its major investments include real estate and utility companies. Rolinco manages 5.5 billion guilders in assets, which are concentrated in Japan (28%) and the United States (28%).

NLG mil	12/92	12/93	12/94	US$mil 12/94				
Sales	**140.0**	**123.0**	**112.0**	**61.9**	P/E Ratio	**64.6**	Price (9/30/95)	**116.40**
Net Income	**121.0**	**100.0**	**87.0**	**48.1**	P/B Ratio	**1.0**	52 Wk Hi-Low	**123.60-102.10**
Book Value	**4,843.0**	**5,846.0**	**5,400.0**	**3,103.4**	Yield %	**1.6**	Market Cap	**US$4,625.3mil**

Address	**Coolsingel 120**	Tel	**010-224-1224**	ADR		President	**Pieter Korteweg**
	3011 AG Rotterdam	Fax	**010-411-5288**	SEDOL No.	**4747079**	Chairman Supv Bd	**Conrad J. Oort**

Royal Dutch Petroleum

Industry: **Oil - Integrated Majors**

Royal Dutch Petroleum is a parent company for businesses that explore for, extract, process, and sell oil, natural gas, and chemicals. Nearly all of its income is derived from its 60% interest in Royal Dutch/Shell. Royal Dutch/Shell produces 2.2 million barrels of oil a day and its oil and gas reserves totaled nearly 9 billion barrels at year-end 1994. Its chemical division produces base and industrial chemicals, polymers, and crop-protection products. Exports to non-European countries account for roughly half of the company's revenues.

£ mil	12/92	12/93	12/94	US$mil 12/94				
Sales	**55,026.0**	**63,350.0**	**61,929.0**	**34,214.9**	P/E Ratio	**16.2**	Price (9/30/95)	**196.60**
Net Income	**3,064.0**	**3,000.0**	**4,070.0**	**2,248.6**	P/B Ratio	**1.2**	52 Wk Hi-Low	**205.00-180.00**
Book Value	**34,113.0**	**34,859.0**	**35,988.0**	**20,682.8**	Yield %	**1.6**	Market Cap	**US$65,870mil**

Address	**Carel van Bylandtlaan 30**	Tel	**070-377-4540**	ADR	**RD**	President	**C.A.J. Herkströter**
	2596 HR The Hague	Fax	**070-377-3115**	SEDOL No.	**4756097**	Chairman	**L.C. van Wachem**

Stork

Industry: **Industrial - Diversified**

Stork designs, manufactures, and maintains industrial-process installations. The company installs and maintains pipeline networks for factories, and refrigeration and transport systems for food-processing lines. It specializes in the overhaul of rotating equipment and electric motors. It produces machines for the printing and finishing of textiles, systems for meat and poultry processing, liquid-transport systems, and equipment for water-purification plants. European exports account for 36% of revenues; exports to non-European countries generate 29% of revenues.

NLG mil	12/92	12/93	12/94	US$mil 12/94				
Sales	**3,641.0**	**3,656.0**	**3,892.6**	**2,150.6**	P/E Ratio	**14.0**	Price (9/30/95)	**40.00**
Net Income	**50.0**	**56.0**	**81.3**	**44.9**	P/B Ratio	**1.5**	52 Wk Hi-Low	**46.50-38.60**
Book Value	**750.0**	**749.0**	**778.4**	**447.3**	Yield %	**2.8**	Market Cap	**US$713.4mil**

Address	**Amersfoortsestraatweg 7**	Tel	**021-595-7411**	ADR		CEO	**J.C.M. Hovers**
	1412 KA Naarden	Fax	**021-594-1184**	SEDOL No.	**4925701**	Chairman	**R.Hazelhoff**

Unilever

Industry: **Other Food**

UK-based Unilever PLC has a 50% interest in the Unilever group of companies; Netherlands-based Unilever NV controls the other 50% (both listings show the same consolidated data). Core businesses are the manufacture food products (roughly 50% of sales) and detergents (25% of sales). Food products include Country Crock spreads, Wishbone salad dressings, and Ragu sauces. Detergents include Wisk laundry detergent and Dove soap. Unilever also makes consumer goods through Elizabeth Arden and Calvin Klein Cosmetics subsidiaries. Nearly half of sales come from outside Europe.

£ mil	12/92	12/93	12/94	US$mil 12/94				
Sales	**24,700.0**	**27,863.0**	**29,666.0**	**45,640.0**	P/E Ratio	**98.0**	Price (9/30/95)	**208.00**
Net Income	**1,291.0**	**1,296.0**	**507.0**	**780.0**	P/B Ratio	**12.5**	52 Wk Hi-Low	**210.00-192.50**
Book Value	**4,583.0**	**4,703.0**	**5,333.0**	**8,332.8**	Yield %	**0.1**	Market Cap	**US$105,911mil**

Address	**Weena 455**	Tel	**010-464-5911**	ADR		President	--
	3000 DK Rotterdam	Fax	**010-464-4799**	SEDOL No.	**4912048**	Chairman	**Floris Maljers**

Wolters Kluwer

Industry: **Publishing**

Wolters Kluwer publishes mainly specialized publications such as legal, scientific, medical, business, educational, and professional-training journals and manuals. Tax, medical, and legal publishing account for more than half of sales. In addition to publishing books, journals, newsletters, and other printed material, Wolters Kluwer provides computer-based information on diskette and CD-ROM. Foreign sales account for nearly 70% of revenues. Its most important foreign markets are the United States, the United Kingdom, and Belgium.

	NLG mil 12/92	12/93	12/94	US$mil 12/94				
Sales	**2,355.0**	**2,616.0**	**2,735.8**	**1,511.5**	P/E Ratio	**25.4**	Price (9/30/95)	**146.90**
Net Income	**258.0**	**318.0**	**381.8**	**210.9**	P/B Ratio	**16.0**	52 Wk Hi-Low	**149.50-117.80**
Book Value	**644.0**	**557.0**	**606.1**	**348.3**	Yield %	**1.2**	Market Cap	**US$6,059.5mil**

Address	**Stadhouderskade 1**	Tel	**020-607-0400**	ADR	**WTKWY**	Chairman Exec Bd	**M. Ververs**
	1000 AV Amsterdam	Fax	**020-607-0490**	SEDOL No.	**4977111**	Chairman Supv Bd	**O. Hattink**

New Zealand

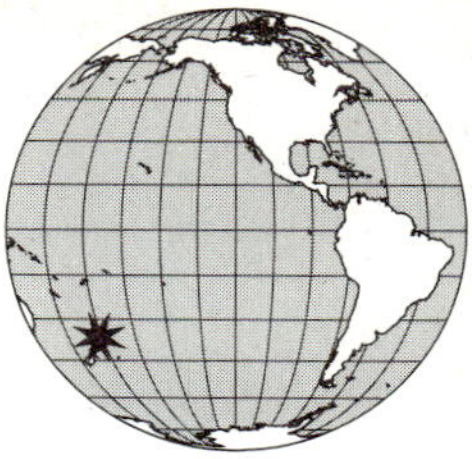

New Zealand

Ed Lane,
Wellington

Local Trading Hours	Time Difference from New York	Population (Est. 6/95)
9:30-3:30	17 hours ahead of EST	3,500,000

The New Zealand Stock Exchange (NZSE) is a screen-based system that operates with little regulation from the government and acts as an independent entity on behalf of members and listed companies.

The market is also in a unique position because New Zealand is the first country across the International Dateline with an exchange and hence the first to kick off the global trading day.

The first stock exchanges in New Zealand served the capital needs of the early gold fields that dotted the island nation. But as gold fever waned, the forerunner of today's exchange was formed by combining the regional exchanges into a loosely knit operating group known as the Stock Exchange Association of New Zealand. The current exchange evolved from that operation.

The NZSE is an independent body that operates under its own by-laws as outlined in the Sharebrokers Act of 1981, which came into effect in 1983. In June of 1991, the NZSE made a major leap forward with the development of a screen-based system that abolished the need for floor trading and created a national market.

Changes to the Companies Act of 1955 as amended by Parliament in 1993 now require listed companies to re-register by July 1997 under more open disclosure rules of ownership and structure than previously. In addition, the government also passed a Takeovers Act in 1993 that set up a panel to recommend a consistent code for company takeovers. The panel's recommendations were effectively tabled by the current government. But in the past year, most New Zealand companies have instituted some form of "pause and notify" provisions in company charters in response to new NZSE listing rules that basically require shareholders to be notified when someone increases a shareholding above a certain percentage.

Dow Jones New Zealand Equity Market Index Performance

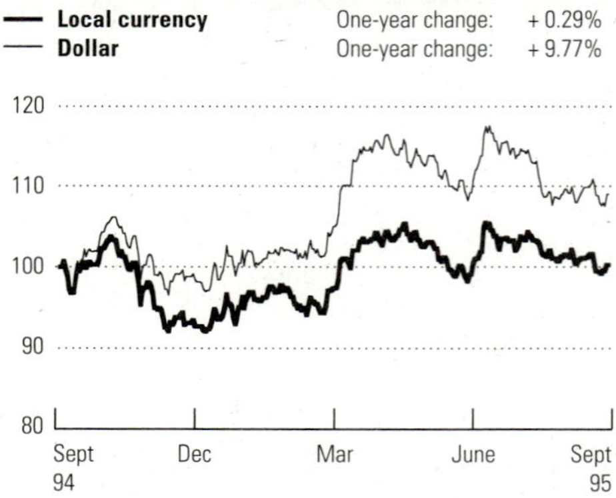

The New Zealand economy is unusual in the world: Government budget surpluses are projected for the foreseeable future, and they are being used to reduce debt and cut taxes. In addition, the Reserve Bank of New Zealand has an agreement with the government to keep underlying inflation below 2% annually.

Gross Domestic Product (6/95, 2nd Qtr.)	Three Year Average GDP Growth (91-94)	Main Industries	Consumer Price Index (94)	Monetary Unit	Exchange Rate (9/95)
NZ$88.64 billion	+4.5%	Forestry, fruit, dairy, fisheries, aluminum, livestock production	+1.8%	New Zealand dollar	NZ$1.52 to US$1.00

The 2% limit was breached in the second quarter of 1995 at 2.2%. The Reserve Bank's desire to get back under 2% has been expressed by keeping short-term money market rates generally above 9% for most of 1995. The attractive yields have tended to draw cash that might otherwise be invested on the NZSE and the market has seen a notable decrease in activity for the year as a result.

Market capitalization as of June 30, 1995, was NZ$45.4 billion, up from NZ$43.3 billion in 1994. But the number of trades for the year ended June 30, 1995, fell to 381.7 million from 520.1 million the previous year, and market turnover slipped to NZ$13.7 billion from NZ$14.4 billion.

There are currently 138 equity listings and 11 debt listings on the NZSE, compared with 131 equity listings and 11 debt listings reported in the previous year. There are 62 foreign-based companies as of the year ended June 30, 1995, compared with 57 the previous year.

Market leaders in New Zealand are mostly involved in resource-based sectors, particularly forestry. Current worldwide high pulp and paper prices have made these stocks particularly active in the past year, including the acquisition of a majority stake in Carter Holt Harvey Ltd. by U.S.-based International Paper Co. But the largest company by market capitalization is telephone utility Telecom Corp. at NZ$11.4 billion.

Types of shares traded on the exchange include fully, or partially-paid ordinary shares, preferred shares, rights, equity warrants, convertible notes and share options in selected companies.

The New Zealand Futures and Options Exchange, a separate entity, offers trading in a share-index futures contract and share options on selected companies.

Ten Largest Capitalized Companies
as of 9/30/95

Stock	Market Cap. US$Mil
Telecom of New Zealand	7,371,926.3
Fletcher Challenge	4,155,948.8
Carter Holt Harvey	4,018,903.8
Brierley Investment	2,027,998.2
Lion Nathan	1,145,795.8
Fletcher Challenge Forestry	728,118.3
Wilson & Horton	534,024.7
Fernz	386,339.5
Independent Newspapers	372,161.8
Fisher & Paykel	334,779.1

Settlement of orders is for cash on demand unless otherwise agreed, with the maximum delivery time being five working days. But the NZSE does not impose a penalty on late delivery up to eight days. Brokerage commission rates are negotiable, with a top rate of around 2.5%.

The NZSE is moving to a paperless settlement cash system envisaged for the current year. As a further enhancement to the requirements placed on members for the protection of clients, the NZSE will also include a requirement for the operation of client funds to be separate from other assets of the firm, in the same way that client securities are held in nominee accounts now.

A withholding tax is imposed on New Zealand dividends paid to non-resident shareholders at the rate of 33%, but if the non-resident is from a country with which New Zealand has a tax treaty, the withholding tax is around 15%. There is no capital gains tax in New Zealand. The tax structure can also be affected by a request for a supplementary dividend, or reduced to 24% if the shares are not bought by what is termed a regular trader.

Brierley Investment

Industry: **Conglomerates**

Brierley Investments is a holding company with investments principally in New Zealand, Australia, the United Kingdom, the United States, and Asia. It has a 70% stake in the U.K.'s second-largest hotel company, Mount Charlotte, which owns 101 hotels. Mount Charlotte is the largest hotelier in Scotland and in London, where it has 24 hotels and a 17% market share. Brierley also owns 96% of Australian Consolidated Investments, which has interests in brewing and petroleum. Brierley holds 43% of regional carrier Air New Zealand and 30% of Skellerup, an industrial concern.

NZ$ mil	06/93	06/94	06/95	US$mil 06/95				
Sales	**2,334.3**	**1,585.3**	**2,576.3**	**1,610.2**	P/E Ratio	**7.5**	Price (9/30/95)	**1.16**
Net Income	**193.7**	**342.1**	**340.7**	**212.9**	P/B Ratio	**0.9**	52 Wk Hi-Low	**1.28-1.04**
Book Value	**3,015.8**	**3,220.1**	**3,335.1**	**2,223.4**	Yield %	**7.8**	Market Cap	**US$2,028.0mil**

Address	**CML Bldg., 22-24 Victoria St.**	Tel	**04-473-8199**	ADR	**BYILY**	CEO	**Paul D. Collins**
	Wellington	Fax	**04-473-1631**	SEDOL No.	**6132189**	Chairman	**Robert H. Matthew**

Carter Holt Harvey

Industry: **Forest Products**

Carter Holt Harvey is a diversified forestry company that makes products for the building industry. The company manufactures forestry and wood products, pulp and paper, paperboard packaging, and steel and fiberglass products. It is New Zealand's largest forest-plantation owner, holding 325,000 hectares, or 25%, of New Zealand's plantation forests. The firm owns Baigent Forest Industries and Australia-based paper merchant Raleigh Paper. It also holds a 30% interest in the Chilean energy company Copec. Carter Holt Harvey is 50% owned by New York-based International Paper Co.

NZ$ mil	03/93	03/94	03/95	US$mil 03/95				
Sales	**2,461.0**	**2,476.0**	**2,718.0**	**1,671.6**	P/E Ratio	**13.5**	Price (9/30/95)	**3.54**
Net Income	**243.0**	**325.0**	**445.0**	**273.7**	P/B Ratio	**1.3**	52 Wk Hi-Low	**4.07-3.12**
Book Value	**3,647.0**	**4,367.0**	**4,827.0**	**3,154.9**	Yield %	**2.5**	Market Cap	**US$4,018.9mil**

Address	**640 Great South Rd.**	Tel	**09-262-6000**	ADR		Chief Executive	**David W. Oskin**
	Manukau City, Auckland 1	Fax	**09-262-0956**	SEDOL No.	**6178406**	Chairman	**Wilson J. Whineray**

DB Group

Industry: **Distillers & Brewers**

DB Group operates brewing, wine, retail, and wholesale businesses. DB Breweries produces brands such as DB Draught, DB Natural, Export Gold, and Mako Special Bitter. Its wine-producing subsidiary, Corban Wines, holds a 35% market share in New Zealand. DB Group also operates Robbie Burns and Liquorland stores, and Green Bottle Wholesale liquor outlets. In 1994, the company implemented a divestment program to sell its assets in hotels and taverns. Asia Pacific Breweries of Japan, controlled by Heineken (Netherlands) and Fraser & Neave (Singapore), owns 54% of DB Group.

NZ$ mil	06/92 R	06/93	09/94 *	US$mil 09/94				
Sales	**820.9**	**761.4**	**872.9**	**504.3**	P/E Ratio	**NMF**	Price (9/30/95)	**0.86**
Net Income	**-233.4**	**-23.4**	**-93.2**	**-53.8**	P/B Ratio	**0.9**	52 Wk Hi-Low	**1.00-0.72**
Book Value	**461.1**	**422.7**	**293.2**	**176.6**	Yield %	**0.0**	Market Cap	**US$172.0mil**

Address	**Citibank Ctr., 23 Customs St.**	Tel	**09-377-8990**	ADR		President	**Erik J. K. Altes**
	Auckland 1	Fax	**09-309-9422**	SEDOL No.	**6555582**	Chairman	**David Sadler**

*Irregular period due to fiscal year change; R=Restated.

Fernz

Industry: **Commodity Chemicals**

Fernz manufactures agricultural and industrial chemicals, fertilizers, pharmaceuticals, and animal-health products. Agricultural chemicals and animal-health products together account for 60% of sales. The firm's major products include Nufarm herbicides, Ichem water-purifying chemicals, Chemicca timber-preservative chemicals, and Captec animal-health-care products. Fernz has developed an anti-hepatitis tablet, Inferon, which it markets in China. It is applying for registration of the drug in other countries. Fernz holds 40% of New Zealand Technology Developments' shares.

NZ$ mil	05/93	05/94	05/95	US$mil 05/95				
Sales	**401.0**	**445.7**	**484.5**	**302.8**	P/E Ratio	**14.6**	Price (9/30/95)	**4.17**
Net Income	**30.5**	**38.3**	**40.5**	**25.3**	P/B Ratio	**2.3**	52 Wk Hi-Low	**5.88-4.05**
Book Value	**169.9**	**236.2**	**252.3**	**167.1**	Yield %	**3.6**	Market Cap	**US$386.3mil**

Address	**81 Carlton Gore Rd.**	Tel	**09-379-3001**	ADR		Managing Director	**Kerry M. Hoggard**
	Newmarket,, Auckland 1	Fax	**09-366-1394**	SEDOL No.	**6355328**	Chairman	**William Wilson**

Fisher & Paykel

Industry: **Other Home Furnishings**

Fisher & Paykel Industries manufactures, distributes, and sells household appliances and consumer electronics. The company's products include refrigerators, washers and dryers, stoves, and dishwashers. The company offers repair services for all of its household appliances. It also distributes and markets consumer electronics, including Panasonic products, and AT&T telecommunication products and personal computers. Fisher & Paykel provides telecommunication and office-automation services to businesses and produces humidifiers for the health-care industry.

NZ$ mil	03/93	03/94	03/95	US$mil 03/95				
Sales	**597.8**	**669.6**	**767.6**	**472.1**	P/E Ratio	**11.8**	Price (9/30/95)	**4.70**
Net Income	**28.0**	**26.9**	**49.7**	**30.6**	P/B Ratio	**1.7**	52 Wk Hi-Low	**4.79-3.90**
Book Value	**251.8**	**267.5**	**305.4**	**199.6**	Yield %	**3.8**	Market Cap	**US$334.8mil**

Address	**78 Springs Rd.**	Tel	**09-273-0600**	ADR		Chief Executive	**Gary A. Paykel**
	East Tamaki, Auckland	Fax	**09-273-0538**	SEDOL No.	**6340250**	Chairman	**Sir Colin Maiden**

Fletcher Challenge

Industry: **Forest Products**

Fletcher Challenge manages paper-production, construction, and energy-supply businesses. The firm has 25 paper-manufacturing facilities in seven countries, and produces pulp, newsprint, and specialty papers. Its building-industries division distributes products such as cement, steel, wood, and gypsum plasterboard. Its Fletcher Homes subsidiary is New Zealand's largest builder of houses. Fletcher Challenge also sells building materials and produces oil and natural gas. It generates approximately 60% of its revenues abroad, primarily in North America and Asia.

NZ$ mil	06/93	06/94	06/95	US$mil 06/95				
Sales	9,486.4	8,116.5	8,401.0	5,317.1	P/E Ratio	15.1	Price (9/30/95)	4.10
Net Income	374.0	675.0	464.0	293.7	P/B Ratio	1.3	52 Wk Hi-Low	4.61-3.56
Book Value	455.8	4,340.1	4,703.0	3,135.3	Yield %	3.0	Market Cap	US$4,155.9mil

Address	**810 Great South Rd.**	Tel	**09-525-9000**	ADR	**FLC**	CEO	**Hugh Fletcher**
	Penrose, Auckland	Fax	**09-525-0559**	SEDOL No.	**6342018**	Chairman	**Ronald Trotter**

Fletcher Challenge Forestry

Industry: **Forest Products**

Fletcher Challenge Forestry Division (FCFD), a 49.5%-owned subsidiary of Fletcher Challenge, breeds tree seedlings and maintains and harvests forests in New Zealand and Chile. The firm has an equity interest in 194,000 hectares of plantation forests, mostly of radiata pine. Its Hikurangi Forest Farms subsidiary, on New Zealand's North Island, comprises 31,250 hectares of land, 23,500 of which are planted. Excluding sales to Fletcher Challenge, FCFD generates roughly 25% of its sales by volume in New Zealand, 22% in Japan, and 16% in South Korea.

NZ$ mil	06/93	06/94	06/95	US$mil 06/95				
Sales	374.6	319.5	351.0	222.2	P/E Ratio	22.1	Price (9/30/95)	2.03
Net Income	188.3	61.7	68.0	43.0	P/B Ratio	1.4	52 Wk Hi-Low	2.34-1.73
Book Value	744.0	710.6	840.0	560.0	Yield %	3.0	Market Cap	US$728.1mil

Address	**810 Great South Rd.**	Tel	**09-525-9000**	ADR	**FFS**	CEO	**Hugh Fletcher**
	Penrose, Auckland	Fax	**09-525-0599**	SEDOL No.	**6342278**	Chairman	**Ronald Trotter**

Independent Newspapers

Industry: **Publishing**

Independent Newspapers owns a group of publishing businesses that specialize in community newspapers. Its wholly-owned Independent News Auckland subsidiary publishes 10 newspapers, with a total weekly circulation of more than one million. Its Gordon and Gotch subsidiary publishes more than 3,000 titles and distributes 60 million magazines yearly. Independent Newspapers also runs the daily Nelson Evening Mail, two community newspapers, and the New Zealand Gardener magazine. The firm owns other operations in New Zealand, Australia, and the United States.

NZ$ mil	06/92	06/93	06/94	US$mil 06/94				
Sales	924.5	965.6	939.6	531.1	P/E Ratio	11.7	Price (9/30/95)	4.40
Net Income	30.6	41.2	47.0	26.6	P/B Ratio	1.7	52 Wk Hi-Low	5.65-4.40
Book Value	191.5	194.6	341.1	203.0	Yield %	4.1	Market Cap	US$372.2mil

Address	**NZI Hse., 25-33 Victoria St.**	Tel	**04-496-9800**	ADR		Managing Director	**John M. Robson**
	Wellington	Fax	**04-496-9841**	SEDOL No.	**6462024**	Chairman	**Sir Colin Maiden**

Lion Nathan

Industry: **Distillers & Brewers**

Lion Nathan produces beer, wine, spirits, and soft drinks. Its beer brands include Tooheys, Castlemaine, Lion Ale, XXXX, Swan, and Emu. It holds nearly 62% of New Zealand's beer market and 44% of Australia's. The company operates a joint venture with Coors to brew and market XXXX in the U.S. Lion Nathan has the exclusive right to bottle and distribute PepsiCo's soft-drink products in Australia. In April 1995, the company acquired a 60% interest in a joint venture that owns the Taihushui Brewery in China. Lion Nathan is the sole owner of Australia's SA Brewing.

NZ$ mil	08/92	08/93	08/94	US$mil 08/94				
Sales	1,806.5	2,288.6	2,514.1	1,441.6	P/E Ratio	7.1	Price (9/30/95)	3.18
Net Income	20.9	32.1	221.1	126.8	P/B Ratio	0.8	52 Wk Hi-Low	3.24-2.60
Book Value	1,280.4	1,548.7	1,890.0	1,138.6	Yield %	4.7	Market Cap	US$1,145.8mil

Address	**55-65 Shortland St.**	Tel	**09-303-3388**	ADR		President	**Douglas Myers**
	Auckland 1	Fax	**09-303-3307**	SEDOL No.	**6518950**	Chairman	**Sir Gordon Tait**

Progressive Entreprises

Industry: **Food Retailers & Wholesalers**

Progressive Enterprises owns and operates Foodtown, Countdown, and Rattrays supermarket chains, Farmers Deka department and discount stores, and 22 Georgie Pie restaurants throughout New Zealand. The company's stores rank second among New Zealand's supermarkets, claiming a 34% market share in sales. It serves on average more than one million customers each week. It also claims a 50% share of the grocery market in Western Australia and a 5% share of Australia's grocery market overall. Australia's Foodland owns 57% of Progressive's shares.

NZ$ mil	07/92	07/93	07/94	US$mil 07/94				
Sales	1,080.8	964.6	2,179.3	1,240.4	P/E Ratio	30.3	Price (9/30/95)	1.21
Net Income	8.4	28.1	9.2	5.2	P/B Ratio	1.1	52 Wk Hi-Low	1.43-1.10
Book Value	129.9	142.4	262.1	157.9	Yield %	5.8	Market Cap	US$187.4mil

Address	**80 Favona Rd.**	Tel	**09-275-0499**	ADR		Chief Executive	**Trevor W. Herd**
	Mangere, Auckland	Fax	**09-275-0508**	SEDOL No.	**6707695**	Chairman	**David G. Sadler**

Sanford

Industry: **Fishing**

Sanford is a fishing company that harvests, processes, and stores seafood. Its products include fish, oysters, scallops, mussels, and lobster. The company operates three oyster farms in northern New Zealand, more than 50 fishing vessels, and more than 50 mussel farms on New Zealand's South Island. It manages eight seafood-processing plants in New Zealand. Sanford owns Big Glory Seafoods and a processing plant on Stewart Island. It also manages inshore and deep-water catching and fishmeal production in Chile. The firm exports the majority of its products, primarily to Japan.

NZ$ mil	08/92	08/93	08/94	US$mil 08/94				
Sales	**239.9**	**257.4**	**325.1**	**186.4**	P/E Ratio	**9.7**	Price (9/30/95)	**3.35**
Net Income	**25.3**	**26.7**	**28.6**	**16.4**	P/B Ratio	**1.5**	52 Wk Hi-Low	**5.16-3.10**
Book Value	**152.3**	**171.5**	**201.5**	**121.4**	Yield %	**3.0**	Market Cap	**US$189.8mil**

Address **22 Jellicoe St.**
Auckland 1
Tel **09-379-4720**
Fax **09-309-1190**
ADR
SEDOL No. **6774183**
Managing Director **David G. Anderson**
Chairman **W.D. Goodfellow**

Steel & Tube

Industry: **Steel**

Steel & Tube Holdings produces, sells, and installs steel products, and markets, installs, and services technical machinery. It distributes cars, auto parts, and accessories to car manufacturers, and holds Jaguar franchising rights in New Zealand. The firm's holdings include 100% of petrochemical-services business Robt. Stone and 50% of automotive supplier Motorcorp Holdings. It also owns steel producer Stewart Steel's merchandising operations, and manages a maintenance contract for Shell Todd Oil Services in Hawaii. Tubemakers of Australia owns 50% of Steel & Tube.

NZ$ mil	03/92	03/93	06/94 *	US$mil 06/94				
Sales	**250.6**	**275.2**	**367.3**	**207.6**	P/E Ratio	**11.6**	Price (9/30/95)	**7.05**
Net Income	**8.0**	**12.3**	**26.4**	**14.9**	P/B Ratio	**3.2**	52 Wk Hi-Low	**7.60-5.80**
Book Value	**107.9**	**86.5**	**95.5**	**56.8**	Yield %	**5.7**	Market Cap	**US$201.4mil**

Address **15-17 King's Crescent**
Lower Hutt, Wellington
Tel **04-725-623**
Fax **04-737-736**
ADR
SEDOL No. **6843823**
Chief Executive **Nick Calavrias**
Chairman **Keith T. Cocks**

*Irregular period due to fiscal year change.

Telecom of New Zealand

Industry: **Telephone Systems - All**

Telecom Corp. of New Zealand, the country's largest telephone-service firm, provides domestic and international telecommunication service. Telecom operates approximately 1.7 million telephone lines and serves more than 157,400 cellular and 38,000 pager customers. It also publishes telephone directories and distributes them to 4.6 million clients. Telecom serves 95% of its customers through digital exchanges. Telecom is 49.5% owned by U.S.-based Bell Atlantic and Ameritech. It holds a 51% stake in Australia's Pacific Star Communications.

NZ$ mil	03/93	03/94	03/95	US$mil 03/95				
Sales	**2,474.3**	**2,497.0**	**2,840.5**	**1,746.9**	P/E Ratio	**18.1**	Price (9/30/95)	**5.93**
Net Income	**107.7**	**528.1**	**620.2**	**381.4**	P/B Ratio	**5.4**	52 Wk Hi-Low	**6.25-5.06**
Book Value	**2,446.5**	**2,030.3**	**2,085.2**	**1,362.9**	Yield %	**5.1**	Market Cap	**US$7,371.9mil**

Address **68 Jervois Quay**
Wellington
Tel **04-801-9000**
Fax **04-473-5428**
ADR **NZT**
SEDOL No. **6881436**
CEO **Roderick Deane**
Chairman **Peter Shirtcliffe**

Wilson & Horton

Industry: **Publishing**

Wilson & Horton operates publishing and printing businesses. Its daily newspaper, The New Zealand Herald, has a circulation of more than 245,000. Its other publications include The Christchurch Star and N.Z. Woman's Weekly, New Zealand's largest-circulation women's magazine. Its subsidiaries, Shortland and United Publishing and Printing, publish books and educational materials. The Wilson & Horton Print Group is the largest commercial printing firm in New Zealand. The firm also produces credit and security cards, data forms, and graphic designs.

NZ$ mil	03/93	03/94	03/95	US$mil 03/95				
Sales	**320.5**	**367.4**	**400.4**	**246.2**	P/E Ratio	**24.3**	Price (9/30/95)	**8.25**
Net Income	**36.9**	**41.5**	**32.5**	**20.0**	P/B Ratio	**2.5**	52 Wk Hi-Low	**10.20-7.20**
Book Value	**276.8**	**302.3**	**317.8**	**207.7**	Yield %	**2.2**	Market Cap	**US$534.0mil**

Address **46 Albert St.**
Auckland 1
Tel **09-379-5050**
Fax **09-377-5266**
ADR
SEDOL No. **6970367**
Managing Director **H. Michael Horton**
Chairman **P.F. Clapshaw**

Norway

Norway

Marius Meland,
Oslo

Local Trading Hours	Time Difference with New York	Population (Est. 94)
10:00-4:00	6 hours ahead	4,315,000

It may well be small, but the Oslo Stock Exchange is an increasingly attractive market place for foreign investors. Norway's open economy, coupled with a recent tax reform and relaxed rules on foreign ownership, has attracted a greater share of foreign investors than any other European exchange except Luxembourg. Almost one third of the capitalized value of shares listed in Oslo are owned by foreign investors. And after Norway rejected European Union (E.U.) membership in 1994, many portfolio managers have come to regard the market as an interesting alternative investment arena within Europe.

Opened in 1819, the Oslo Stock Exchange is the only bourse in Norway, with regional offices in Bergen and Trondheim. For the past 166 years, it has been located in an easily recognizible, neo-classic building in downtown Oslo. Its importance is illustrated by the fact that the stock exchange was the first institutional building to be constructed in Oslo, even before the royal palace, the parliament and the university.

It's no coincidence that the stock exchange is situated close to what used to be the main harbor in Oslo. Throughout history, Norway has harvested its greatest wealth from the sea, be it from fishing, maritime commerce, shipping or, most recently, offshore oil and natural gas production. The sea is also the key to why Norway has one of Europe's most open economies, with exports accounting for as much as 40% of gross domestic product.

Foreign investors played an important role in financing Norway's hydro-powered industry around the turn of this century. In the mid-1970s, foreign investors were once again invited to take part in another industrial revolution in Norway, when the discovery of offshore petroleum turned Norway into one of Western Europe's wealthiest nations.

Dow Jones Norway Equity Market Index Performance

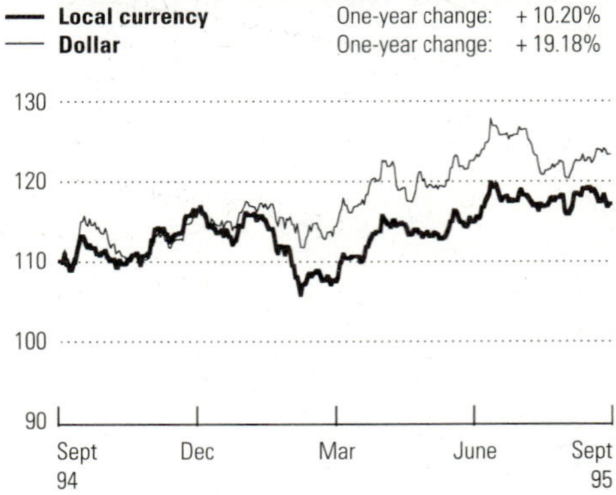

Because of Norway's commodity-oriented economy, the country is generally more advanced in the global economic cycle than the E.U. That means the Norwegian economy trails the U.S. economy much more closely than almost all European countries. Norway's economy grew by 5.1% in 1994 and was expected to rise almost as much in 1995. Growth is projected to subside some in 1996, but will still be higher than in most of Norway's European trading partners. The Norwegian central bank foresees that the

Gross Domestic Product (94)	Three-Year Average GDP Growth (92-94)	Main Industries	Consumer Price Index (9/95)	Monetary Unit	Exchange Rate (9/95)
$125 billion	3.7%	Petroleum, hydro power, metals and chemicals	2.3%	Norwegian Krone	NOK6.28 to US$1.00

economy will come to a "soft landing" slightly after the U.S.

Meanwhile, inflation is lower than the European average at a projected 2.5% in 1995 and 2.25% in 1996, although the Organization for Economic Cooperation and Development (OECD) has warned against the risk of economic overheating. In the long term, many economists worry over the consequences of Norway's rejection of E.U. membership, but in the short term the country is assured access to the common market through the European Economic Area agreement between the E.U. and the European Free Trade Association.

Surfing on the strong growth in the economy, Norwegian share prices rose to all-time-highs in record turnover in mid-1995. On the corporate level, strong growth translated into the highest earnings in history.

But that wasn't the only reason why stock prices soared in most of 1995. A string of corporate mergers and takeovers, especially in the financial sector, also helped lift the market as competing bids raised share prices. Competing bids for the insurance company Vital Forsikring AS from Den norske Bank AS, the country's largest commercial bank, and Dutch insurer Aegon NV, caused a frenzied rally to financial stocks. The market also focused much of its attention on new, technology-oriented companies, which saw their stocks rise at a mind-boggling pace over the summer.

Meanwhile, the traditional heavyweights such as state-controlled fertilizer, aluminum and oil conglomerate Norsk Hydro AS saw their share price grow steadily, albeit at a somewhat slower pace than the market.

Ten Largest Capitalized Companies
as of 9/30/95

Stock	Market Cap. US$Mil
Norsk Hydro	9,830,441.6
Orkla	1,902,089.2
Hafslund Nycomed	1,571,254.8
Kvaerner	1,411,028.3
Saga Petroleum	1,233,792.5
Bergesen	881,499.0
Schibsted	804,976.1
Aker	602,085.2
Dyno Industrier	570,758.1
Leif Höegh & Co.	458,598.7

In Norway, like in most of Scandinavia, the presence of the state is more easily felt than in most European countries. The Oslo Stock Exchange is no exception; in fact, the level of state ownership in the stock market is extraordinarily high even by Scandinavian standards. While the public sector holds about 19% of the capitalized value of shares at the Oslo Stock Exchange, the corresponding figures for Stockholm and Copenhagen are 8% and 1%. Norway's biggest company, Statoil AS, is fully owned by the state and isn't publicly traded even though it's organized as a corporation. The second largest company, the industrial giant Norsk Hydro AS, is owned 51% by the state and 49% by private investors.

Moreover, the state holds a majority of shares in the commercial banks following massive bail-outs during the banking crisis in the early 1990s, although parliament has decided to lower the state's stake to 50% by 1997. The state also has significant holdings in many other companies through the National Insurance Scheme Fund. Institutional investors account for a large share of stock ownership, whereas private households are all but absent from the market.

Industrial blue chips such as Norsk Hydro, pharmaceutical company Hafslund Nycomed and Europe's largest shipbuilder, Kvaerner AS, are by far the market's biggest companies by capitalized value. Often referred to as "the locomotive of the Oslo Stock Exchange," Norsk Hydro determines the market trend by its sheer size and its position as the market's most actively traded stock. Many Norwegian shipping companies have "flagged out"—registered their ships under foreign flags—but the Oslo Stock Exchange still likes to call itself "the world's biggest shipping exchange." Shipping companies listed in Oslo include Bergesen d.y. AS, Unitor AS, and Wilh. Wilhelmsen Ltd., as well as the cruise company Vard AS. All the blue chips appear on the main list, while smaller and mid-sized companies appear on the SMB list, with less stringent criteria for capitalization and distribution.

The Oslo Stock Exchange calculates two main indexes and four sector indices. They are calculated automatically every minute during the stock exchange session. The Oslo All-Share Index, composed of all the shares on the main list, gives a general overview of movements in the stock market. The OBX index, consisting of the 25 most listed share classes on the Oslo Stock Exchange, was drawn up to serve as an underlying instrument for trading in derivatives. The sector indices are the Bank Index, the Insurance Index, the Shipping Index and the Industry Index. All indices except the OBX Index had the same basis value of 100 on Jan. 1, 1983, while the OBX had a basis value of 200 on Jan. 1, 1987.

It was the end of an era when the Oslo Stock Exchange introduced its first electronic trading system in 1988. The current system will be replaced again at the end of 1996, although at present it's not certain the stock exchange will be able to stick to its time table. All dealers have their offices at the stock exchange, although the requirement for a physical presence is under debate and may be dropped soon. The trading session lasts from 10 a.m. to 4 p.m., but dealers are allowed to punch in their bids and offers from 9 in the morning. Since May 1991 all listed securities have been registered electronically in the Norwegian Registry of Securities, which acts as a central register of ownership.

On Jan. 1, 1995, all rules that discriminated against foreign ownership of shares were abolished as Norway entered the European Economic Area. Foreign investors pay no turnover or capital gains tax, but pay a witholding tax on dividends according to tax agreements between Norway and their country. Normally, the tax rate is about 15% for countries with a tax agreement; otherwise, the tax rate is 25%. Corporate tax rates are currently at 28%, while the maxiumum personal tax rate on earned income is at 49.5%.

Aker

Industry: **Oilfield Equipment & Services - Other**

Aker manufactures building materials, and supplies technology to the oil and gas industry. Building materials including cement, ready-mix concrete, light clinker, aggregates, and bricks account for 41% of sales, and its oil- and gas-technology interests account for 59%. Aker and Sweden's Euroc AB jointly own cement firm Sancem Group, which operates in Africa, the United Kingdom, and the United States. Aker's technology sector builds oil platforms and provides electrical and engineering services. Exports, primarily to the U.S., accounted for roughly 44% of revenues in 1994.

NOK mil	12/92	12/93	12/94	US$mil 12/94				
Sales	**17,332.0**	**18,143.0**	**16,568.0**	**2,361.1**	P/E Ratio M	**11.8**	Price (9/30/95) M	**95.00**
Net Income	**453.0**	**506.0**	**356.0**	**50.7**	P/B Ratio M	**1.0**	52 Wk Hi-Low M	**97.50-69.50**
Book Value	**4,024.0**	**4,367.0**	**4,403.0**	**651.3**	Yield % M	**3.7**	Market Cap M	**US$602.1mil**

Address **Fjordalléen 16**
0250 Oslo
Tel **022-94-50-00**
Fax **022-94-50-16**
ADR
SEDOL No. **4012283**
President & CEO **Tom Ruud**
Chairman **Gerhard Heiberg**

M=Multiple issues in index; reflects most active.

Bergesen

Industry: **Marine Transportation**

Bergesen D.Y. owns and operates large tankers, cargo carriers, and liquefied-petroleum-gas (LPG) vessels. The firm operates a fleet of 20 crude- oil tankers, 18 LPG vessels, and six dry-cargo carriers. Bergesen D.Y. owns 32 of the vessels it operates and has a majority stake in the other 12. It is building a multipurpose shuttle tanker in a joint venture with Statoil. Twenty-eight of its ships operate in the spot market. Bergesen D.Y. also has interests in real estate and finance. It owns more than 105,000 square meters of commercial and residential real estate in Norway.

NOK mil	12/92	12/93	12/94	US$mil 12/94				
Sales	**2,641.0**	**2,926.0**	**2,705.0**	**385.5**	P/E Ratio M	**92.7**	Price (9/30/95) M	**139.00**
Net Income	**25.0**	**133.0**	**84.0**	**12.0**	P/B Ratio M	**1.7**	52 Wk Hi-Low M	**165.00-126.50**
Book Value	**4,478.0**	**4,554.0**	**4,599.0**	**680.3**	Yield % M	**0.7**	Market Cap M	**US$881.5mil**

Address **Drammensveien 106**
0205 Oslo
Tel **022-12-05-05**
Fax **022-12-05-00**
ADR
SEDOL No. **4100898**
Managing Director **Morten Sig. Bergesen**
Chairman **Petter C.G. Sundt**

M=Multiple issues in index; reflects most active.

Dyno Industrier

Industry: **Commodity Chemicals**

Dyno Industrier (DI) is a diversified chemical company that produces explosives, chemicals, and plastic products. The coal, metal, and construction industries buy 92% of the company's explosives. The firm also produces resins and oil field chemicals and makes plastic packaging and fuel-tank systems. Its plastic division provides components for the automotive and electronics industries. Dyno Industrier and Dutch companies Akzo Nobel and DSM jointly own the methanol producer Methanor. Overseas exports accounted for nearly half of DI's sales in 1994.

NOK mil	12/92	12/93	12/94	US$mil 12/94				
Sales	**7,480.0**	**8,225.0**	**9,698.0**	**1,382.1**	P/E Ratio	**8.4**	Price (9/30/95)	**141.00**
Net Income	**51.0**	**151.0**	**418.0**	**59.6**	P/B Ratio	**1.5**	52 Wk Hi-Low	**198.00-132.50**
Book Value	**2,023.0**	**2,128.0**	**2,387.0**	**353.1**	Yield %	**2.8**	Market Cap	**US$570.8mil**

Address **Tollbugaten 22, Sentrum**
0106 Oslo
Tel **022-31-70-00**
Fax **022-31-78-56**
ADR
SEDOL No. **4294274**
President & CEO **Arild Ingierd**
Chairman **Ragnar Halvorsen**

Hafslund Nycomed

Industry: **Pharmaceuticals**

Hafslund Nycomed produces medical-imaging agents and pharmaceuticals. Its medical-imaging agents are used mainly in x-rays, magnetic-resonance imaging, and ultrasound procedures. Nycomed is the world leader in the sale and distribution of imaging contrast agents. Its pharmaceuticals division produces and markets both prescription and over-the-counter drugs in Europe and Japan. The company also generates approximately 2,500 GWh of electricity per year, primarily at five hydroelectric plants in Norway. Exports generate more than three fourths of revenues.

NOK mil	12/92	12/93	12/94	US$mil 12/94				
Sales	**5,184.0**	**5,776.0**	**7,153.0**	**1,019.4**	P/E Ratio M	**18.2**	Price (9/30/95) M	**168.00**
Net Income	**1,005.0**	**1,112.0**	**901.0**	**128.4**	P/B Ratio M	**2.7**	52 Wk Hi-Low M	**168.00-111.00**
Book Value	**5,075.0**	**5,694.0**	**6,186.0**	**915.1**	Yield % M	**2.6**	Market Cap M	**US$1,571.3mil**

Address **Slemdalsveien 37**
0301 Oslo
Tel **022-96-34-00**
Fax **022-96-36-00**
ADR **HN**
SEDOL No. **4401751**
President & CEO **Svein Aaser**
Chairman **Terje Mikalsen**

M=Multiple issues in index; reflects most active.

Leif Höegh & Co.

Industry: **Marine Transportation**

Leif Höegh and Company (LHC) is one of Norway's leading shipping companies. The company operates 74 ships, of which 27 are owned or partially owned, and 16 are chartered. It also operates eight container vessels and two dry-bulk carriers, most of which are leased to charterers. Leif Höegh transports oil, coal, liquefied natural gas, steel, and other container and bulk products. LHC and Ugland jointly own Hual, which transports cars by sea. LHC owns 42% of Bona Shipholding, which operates 10 Panamax OBO vessels, and 50% of Cool, which operates 48 reefer vessels.

NOK mil	12/92	12/93	12/94	US$mil 12/94				
Sales	**2,088.0**	**2,433.0**	**2,800.0**	**399.0**	P/E Ratio	**NMF**	Price (9/30/95)	**96.00**
Net Income	**173.0**	**244.0**	**276.0**	**39.3**	P/B Ratio	**1.6**	52 Wk Hi-Low	**104.00-78.00**
Book Value	**1,454.0**	**1,608.0**	**1,761.0**	**260.5**	Yield %	**3.1**	Market Cap	**US$458.6mil**

Address **Wergelandsveien 7**
0203 Oslo
Tel **022-86-97-00**
Fax **022-20-14-08**
ADR
SEDOL No. **4512017**
President **Thor J. Guttormsen**
Chairman **Westye Höegh**

Kvaerner

Industry: **Conglomerates**

Kvaerner is a shipbuilding and engineering company that manufactures passenger, naval, and container ships, including refrigerated and bulk carriers, gas carriers, and chemical tankers. Kvaerner's engineering projects include manufacturing hydropower equipment and propulsion engines and performing construction and engineering work on North Sea oil platforms. Kvaerner also provides chemical-pulp manufacturers with chemical- and energy-recovery systems. In 1995, the company sold its interest in gas tankers to Havtor Shipping in exchange for a 45% stake in the company.

	NOK mil 12/92	12/93	12/94	US$mil 12/94				
Sales	**19,993.0**	**24,530.0**	**26,152.0**	**3,726.9**	P/E Ratio M	**12.8**	Price (9/30/95) M	**266.00**
Net Income	**729.0**	**977.0**	**901.0**	**128.4**	P/B Ratio M	**1.5**	52 Wk Hi-Low M	**327.00-250.00**
Book Value	**6,379.0**	**6,954.0**	**7,751.0**	**1,146.6**	Yield % M	**2.3**	Market Cap M	**US$1,411.0mil**

Address **Hoffsveien 1, Skoyen**
0212 Oslo
Tel **022-96-70-00**
Fax **022-52-01-22**
ADR
SEDOL No. **4502029**
President & CEO **Erik Tonseth**
Chairman **Kaspar K. Kielland**

M=Multiple issues in index; reflects most active.

Norsk Hydro

Industry: **Conglomerates**

Norsk Hydro manufactures products for agriculture and the light-metals, energy, and petrochemical industries. The company produces mineral-based fertilizer and supplies aluminum and magnesium. It also extracts and sells oil and gas, generates electrical power, and produces raw materials for plastics. Norsk Hydro's oil and gas operations, concentrated in the North Sea, produced 11.5 million tons of oil equivalent in 1994. Europe, outside of Norway itself, accounts for the majority of the company's revenue.

	NOK mil 12/91	12/92	12/93	US$mil 12/93				
Sales	**60,608.0**	**58,062.0**	**62,350.0**	**8,741.1**	P/E Ratio	**NMF**	Price (9/30/95)	**269.50**
Net Income	**-675.0**	**167.0**	**3,406.0**	**477.5**	P/B Ratio	**2.9**	52 Wk Hi-Low	**288.50-218.50**
Book Value	**16,820.0**	**16,407.0**	**19,307.0**	**2,567.4**	Yield %	**1.3**	Market Cap	**US$9,830.4mil**

Address **Bygdoy Allé 2**
0240 Oslo
Tel **022-43-21-00**
Fax **022-43-27-25**
ADR **NHY**
SEDOL No. **4645805**
President & CEO **Egil Myklebust**
Chairman **Torvild Aakvaag**

Norske Skog

Industry: **Paper Products**

Norske Skogindustrier (Norske Skog) produces paper, pulp, and building materials. Norske Skog and A/S Union, of which Norske Skog owns 57%, together produced more than 1.3 million tons of paper products in 1994. Norske Skog also produced 429,000 tons of magazine paper and 423,000 tons of bleached pulp in 1994. The firm's building-products business, which generated 21% of turnover in 1994, produces sawn timber, chipboard, parquet flooring, tiles, and high-pressure laminates. The paper division accounted for 63% of the company's total revenues.

	NOK mil 12/92	12/93	12/94	US$mil 12/94				
Sales	**7,557.0**	**7,338.0**	**9,170.0**	**1,306.8**	P/E Ratio M	**28.9**	Price (9/30/95) M	**200.00**
Net Income	**-516.0**	**-47.0**	**206.0**	**29.4**	P/B Ratio M	**1.3**	52 Wk Hi-Low M	**219.50-166.00**
Book Value	**3,769.0**	**3,861.0**	**4,727.0**	**699.3**	Yield % M	**0.8**	Market Cap M	**US$177.1mil**

Address **Norske Skogindustrier**
7620 Skogn
Tel **074-08-70-00**
Fax **074-08-71-00**
ADR
SEDOL No. **4647447**
President & CEO **Jan Reinås**
Chairman **Lage Westerbo**

M=Multiple issues in index; reflects most active.

Orkla

Industry: **Conglomerates**

Orkla is a foods, consumer-goods, and chemicals company. Among its consumer products are cookies, confectionery, oils, detergents, clothing, footwear, and cosmetics. Orkla's chemical products include pharmaceutical intermediates and specialty pulp. Orkla also produces and markets fresh bread and bakery products. The company holds majority stakes in 15 Norwegian local newspapers. In 1995, Orkla purchased the Procordia and Abba Seafood food operations of Volvo, and created a beverages joint-venture with Volvo that produces soft drinks and alcoholic beverages.

	NOK mil 12/92	12/93	12/94	US$mil 12/94				
Sales	**16,807.0**	**17,858.0**	**20,780.0**	**2,961.4**	P/E Ratio M	**12.6**	Price (9/30/95) M	**302.50**
Net Income	**211.0**	**984.0**	**1,149.0**	**163.7**	P/B Ratio M	**2.0**	52 Wk Hi-Low M	**308.50-180.00**
Book Value	**5,837.0**	**6,573.0**	**7,229.0**	**1,069.4**	Yield % M	**1.7**	Market Cap M	**US$1,902.1mil**

Address **PO Box 308**
1324 Lysaker
Tel **022-50-10-80**
Fax **022-50-16-91**
ADR
SEDOL No. **4657673**
President & CEO **Jens P. Heyerdahl**
Chairman **Svein Ribe-Anderssen**

M=Multiple issues in index; reflects most active.

Saga Petroleum

Industry: **Oil - Secondary**

Saga Petroleum operates primarily in the Norwegian sector of the North Sea. Its main products are oil and liquefied petroleum gas. The firm has long-term contracts to supply gas via pipeline to buyers in France, Belgium, Germany, and the Netherlands. In 1994, the firm produced 6 million tons of oil equivalent, representing 3.9% of proved and probable reserves. It sold 34.4 million barrels of oil and 512 million cubic meters of gas. Average daily oil production is more than 108,000 barrels. Saga sells most of its products to other Western European countries.

	NOK mil 12/92	12/93	12/94	US$mil 12/94				
Sales	**4,924.0**	**5,667.0**	**5,839.0**	**832.1**	P/E Ratio M	**13.3**	Price (9/30/95) M	**81.00**
Net Income	**277.0**	**388.0**	**549.0**	**78.2**	P/B Ratio M	**2.1**	52 Wk Hi-Low M	**93.50-72.50**
Book Value	**4,436.0**	**4,553.0**	**4,874.0**	**721.0**	Yield % M	**2.5**	Market Cap M	**US$1,233.8mil**

Address **Kjorboveien 16**
1301 Sandvika
Tel **067-12-66-00**
Fax **067-12-66-66**
ADR **SPM.A**
SEDOL No. **4768025**
President & CEO **Asbjorn Larsen**
Chairman **Wilhelm Wilhelmsen**

M=Multiple issues in index; reflects most active.

Schibsted

Industry: **Publishing**

Schibsted is a newspaper-publishing company that also has interests in the film and television industries. The company obtains more than 60% of its revenues from subscription and retail sales of its newspapers; advertising revenues account for the remaining sales. It sells nearly 3 million newspapers weekly and a further 1.75 million on weekends. Schibsted's wholly-owned Schibsted Film subsidiary is the holding company for its interests in the Scandinavian film and television market. Its TV Pluss cable and satellite entertainment channel transmits throughout Norway.

NOK mil	12/92	12/93	12/94	US$mil 12/94				
Sales	**2,626.0**	**2,753.0**	**3,041.8**	**433.5**	P/E Ratio	**16.0**	Price (9/30/95)	**73.00**
Net Income	**167.0**	**315.0**	**316.1**	**45.0**	P/B Ratio	**3.8**	52 Wk Hi-Low	**85.00-69.00**
Book Value	**1,020.0**	**1,266.0**	**1,342.9**	**198.6**	Yield %	**1.6**	Market Cap	**US$805.0mil**

Address **Akersgt. 55, Sentrum**
0107 Oslo
Tel **022-86-41-00**
Fax **022-86-38-80**
ADR
SEDOL No. **4790534**
CEO **Kjell Aamot**
Chairman **Tinius Nagell-Erichsen**

Unitor

Industry: **Specialty Chemicals**

Unitor provides comprehensive ship maintenance at 920 ports. It handles gas-cylinder exchange and furnishes corrosion protection and welding products. It also supplies refrigerants, oil-spill-protection devices, and fire, safety, and rescue equipment. Its Ticon Isolering subsidiary provides insulation for refrigeration and freezer systems. Kjemi-Service and Unitor supply marine chemicals and agricultural, industrial, household, and auto-care products to clients such as Texaco, Shell, and Unilever.

NOK mil	12/92	12/93	12/94	US$mil 12/94				
Sales	**1,403.0**	**1,604.0**	**1,762.0**	**251.1**	P/E Ratio	**12.6**	Price (9/30/95)	**96.00**
Net Income	**88.0**	**113.0**	**146.0**	**20.8**	P/B Ratio	**2.2**	52 Wk Hi-Low	**123.50-86.00**
Book Value	**793.0**	**871.0**	**851.0**	**125.9**	Yield %	**3.1**	Market Cap	**US$317.9mil**

Address **Trollåsveien 4**
1410 Kolbotn
Tel **066-81-88-00**
Fax **066-80-79-75**
ADR **UTORY**
SEDOL No. **4918347**
Managing Director **Karsten Houm**
Chairman **Stein H. Annexstad**

Vard

Industry: **Marine Transportation**

Vard is a marine-transportation holding company for a cruise operator. Vard's Kloster Cruise subsidiary, which offers a variety of cruises worldwide, deploys 10 ships among its Royal Cruise lines and Norwegian Cruise lines, for a total capacity of more than 10,400 passengers. Royal Cruise lines operate three ships with 2,239 berths. Norwegian Cruise lines operate seven cruise ships containing 8,229 berths. Vard sold its ferry operations and its Royal Viking Sun Cruise line in 1993.

NOK mil	12/92	12/93	12/94	US$mil 12/94				
Sales	**5,471.0**	**7,301.0**	**6,404.5**	**912.7**	P/E Ratio	**1.2**	Price (9/30/95)	**9.40**
Net Income	**-214.0**	**-313.0**	**285.4**	**40.7**	P/B Ratio	**0.4**	52 Wk Hi-Low	**25.18-6.18**
Book Value	**1,029.0**	**804.0**	**932.8**	**138.0**	Yield %	**0.0**	Market Cap	**US$52.9mil**

Address **Munkedamsveien 45 C**
0123 Oslo
Tel **022-83-03-10**
Fax **022-83-04-18**
ADR
SEDOL No. **4926931**
President & CEO **Bernt S. Karlsen**
Chairman **Einar Kloster**

Philippines

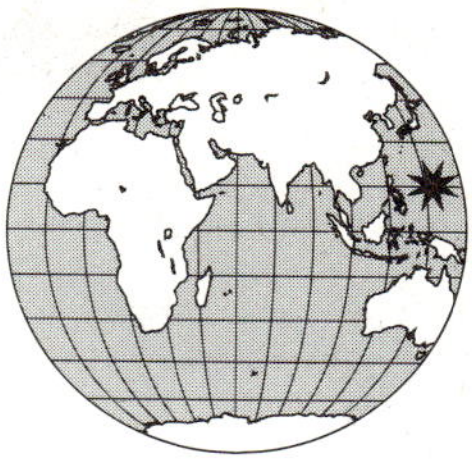

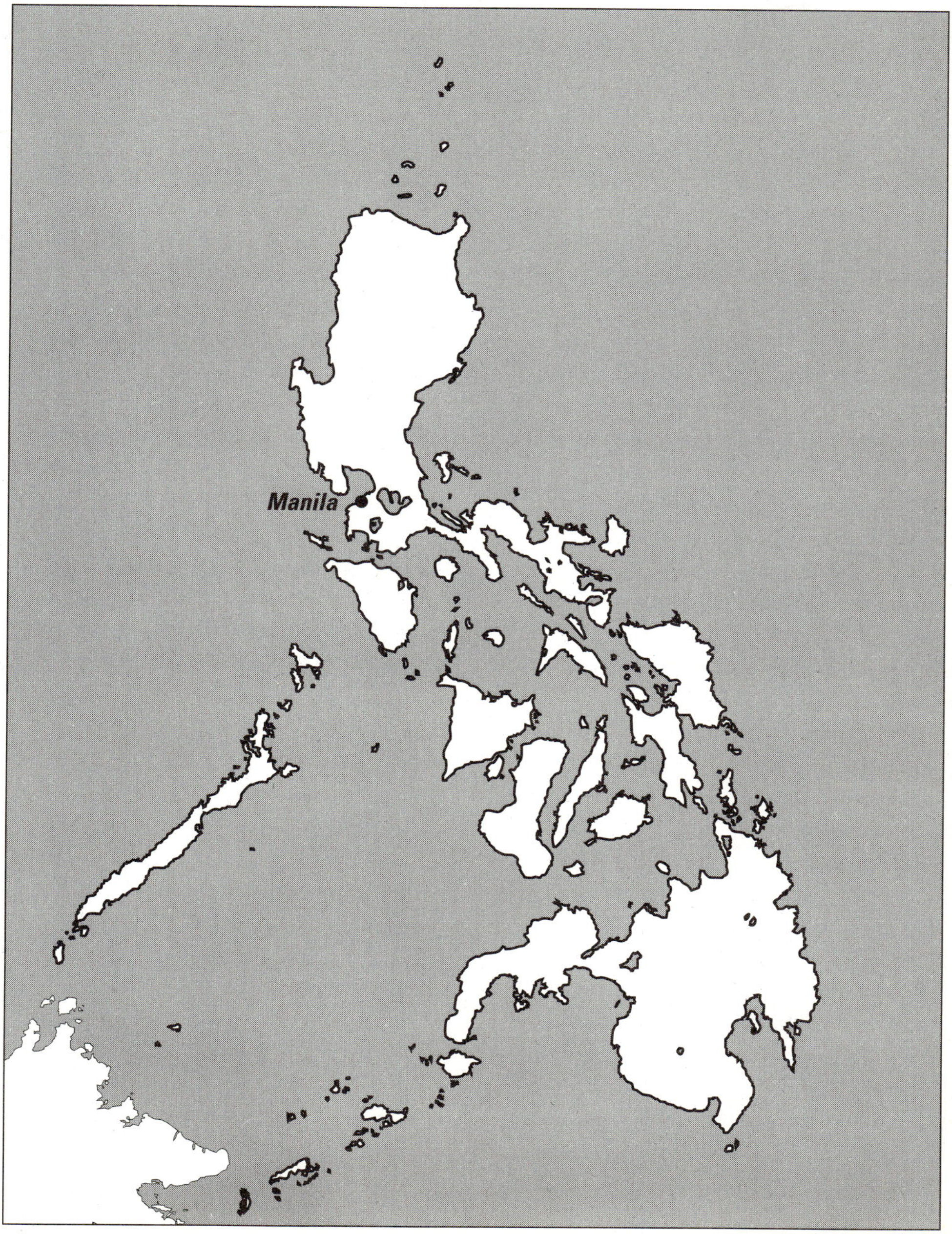

Philippines

Lilian Karunungan,
Manila

Local Trading Hours	**Time Difference from New York**	**Population (Est. 94)**
01:30-04:15 GMT	12 hours ahead of EST	69,809,000

Though the Philippines had a stock market since the late 1920s, it was only in recent years that it has captured foreign investors' interest.

The Philippines is located centrally in the booming Southeast Asian region, and investor concerns about the country's unstable political climate have been slowly calmed since the relatively peaceful Presidential elections in May 1992, won by the current Philippine President Fidel Ramos.

Investor confidence in the country was also reinforced as Mr. Ramos implemented liberal economic policies when he opened the telecommunications industry to more players in 1993, further lifted foreign exchange restrictions and allowed ten foreign banks in early 1995 to operate in the country in his bid to attract more foreign investments.

At the same time, the Ramos administration is being credited with the swift action it undertook to solve the country's electricity shortage problem in 1993 through a novel build-operate-and-transfer scheme which attracted many foreign companies to build power plants.

The results were impressive, and the Philippine stock market zoomed to record highs with share prices rising by as much as 154% in 1993. The market's composite index reached a record high of 3,385 points on Jan. 4, 1994.

Since then, however, the stock market spent most of 1994 consolidating. Like other Asian markets, the Philippine stock market was hit badly in early 1995 by Mexico's financial crisis and the collapse of the British bank Barings PLC.

The market started to recover in May 1995 after the Congressional elections were won by the government slate, which should help ensure the implementation of liberal economic policies laid down by President Ramos such as the tax reform package, and the deregulation of the oil industry. The reforms are intended to wean away the country from foreign assistance in 1997 when it graduates from the International Monetary Fund's extended fund facility.

Dow Jones Philippines Equity Market Index Performance

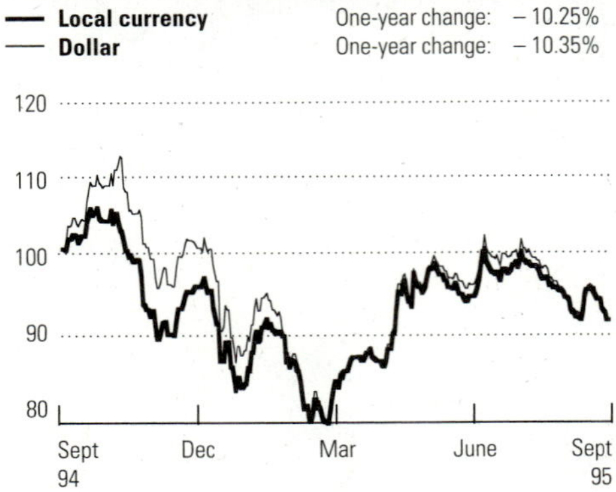

Concerns on inflation and the slow growth of the agricultural sector due to a recent

Gross Domestic Product (94)	Three-Year Average GDP Growth (92-94)	Main Industries	Consumer Price Index (93-94)	Monetary Unit	Exchange Rate (9/95)
$63.96 billion	+ 2.2%	Manufacturing, wholesale and retail trade, transportation, communications, real estate, construction, banking	+ 9%	Philippine Peso	PPeso26.03 to US$1.00

drought, however, kept the market from rising substantially since August 1995.

Most analysts still rate the Philippine market a buy because of the country's strong growth prospects as the government implements more reforms to sustain the country's growth in the coming years amidst lower inflation.

The government is targeting a Gross National Product (GNP) growth rate of 7% to 7.5% in 1996 from 6% to 6.5% in 1995. Inflation is envisioned to slow to 6.5% in 1996 from the range of 6.5% to 7.5% expected in 1995.

The Philippines' stock market used to have two exchanges — the Manila Stock Exchange, which was established as far back as in 1927 and is considered one of the oldest in the Far East; and the Makati Stock Exchange, which was set up in 1965. The existence of the two stock exchanges, however, discouraged foreign investment because of differing prices on the two bourses. To attract more foreign participation, a computerized linkup of the two floors was effected on March 25, 1994, resulting in a uniform opening and closing of stock prices for all traded stocks. In April 1995, the Philippine Stock Exchange widened its reach to other parts in the country with the start of computerized trading from regional trading centers in key cities to encourage more local participation.

To sustain investor interest in the country's stock exchange, the Asian Development Bank agreed in September 1995 to provide a $150 million loan to the Philippines in exchange for the implementation of key reforms. This would involve the change in the Philippine Securities and Exchange Commission into a "disclosure-oriented regulatory" body that would require full disclosure by all publicly-listed companies in an accurate, clear and timely way of all material events and corporate actions.

Ten Largest Capitalized Companies
as of 9/30/95

Stock	Market Cap. US$Mil
Philippine Long Distance	4,043,010.0
Petron	2,941,317.7
SM Prime	2,481,194.1
Metropolitan Bank & Trust	2,011,858.8
San Miguel	1,874,647.6
Philippine Commercial Intl Bank	1,410,481.5
Ayala	1,252,676.0
JG Summit	1,246,169.4
Philippine National Bank	1,046,729.4
Benpres	957,016.9

The ADB loan also aims to finance the establishment of a central depository system to help modernize back-office systems and result in the efficient transfer of securities. The private sector is hoping to have this in place by February 1996.

As of August 1995, the companies listed at the Philippine Stock Exchange numbered 201, up from 189 in 1994 and 178 in 1993 as more companies opted to go to the stock market to raise funds for their expansions. A total of 11 companies had listed at the Philippine Stock Exchange in 1995, as of August, raising a total of 21.2 billion pesos from their initial public offerings (IPOs). The year 1994 registered a record number of IPOs with 21 companies collecting a total of 37.3 billion pesos. In 1993, eleven companies went public, taking 8.7 billion pesos from IPOs.

The market's movement is tracked by the Philippine Stock Exchange composite index which now is comprised of 41 selected issues after several companies declassified their A and B shares to boost share liquidity by allowing more foreign ownership of shares. The A shares are exclusive to Filipinos, while only foreign investors can buy B shares.

In October 1994, shares comprising the index were expanded to 43 from 31, which included for the first time B shares to reflect the strong participation of foreign investors. Foreign buying had catapulted the Philippine stock market into third place in world performance in 1993. The computation of the index is based on the number of shares outstanding of the 41 issues and their closing prices.

The index covers four sectors: commercial and industrial, properties, mining and oil. The commercial and industrial issues have the heaviest weighing at 77.84%; the property stocks at 20.80%; the mining shares at 0.84%; and the oil issues at 0.52%.

The Philippine stock market had a market capitalization of 1.53 trillion pesos at the end of August 1995, up from the year-end 1994 level of 1.39 billion pesos.

As of the end of August 1995, the company with the largest share in terms of market capitalization was San Miguel Corp., a food, beverage and packaging conglomerate, with 134.6 billion pesos.

Next was Ayala Land, Inc., the country's leading real estate company, with 120.4 billion pesos; Ayala Corp., a conglomerate with interests in property development, banking, food manufacturing, and telecommunications, at 104 billion pesos; Petron Corp., an oil refiner, 90.63 billion pesos; and Manila Electric Co., the country's largest electric distribution concern, 87.61 billion pesos.

Aside from common shares of stocks listed at the Philippine Stock Exchange, preferred stocks, bonds and warrants are also traded, but they comprise a negligible portion of the daily trading turnover.

To encourage the active trading of these instruments, the Philippine Stock Exchange is pushing for the lowering of taxes on bond transactions from the current 20% to 0.375%, and possibly as low as 0.125%. Stock transactions are taxed at 0.5%.

Cash dividends are not taxable but stock dividends are taxed 0.375% when they are sold. Buyers of stocks also bear the cost of the documentary stamp tax, which is 2 pesos for every 200 pesos at par or nominal value of the stock certificate.

Brokers get a minimum commission fee of 45 pesos whether it is a buy or sell transaction. The maximum fee is 1.5% of the gross value of the transaction.

The Philippine Stock Exchange had 184 member-brokers as of September 15, 1995, of which 167 are active, including 36 foreign brokerage houses. Due to the keen interest in the country's stock market, the Philippine Stock Exchange said the cost of one brokerage seat has almost doubled to 85 million pesos as of September 15, 1995, up from 50 million pesos in December 1994.

Alaska Milk

Industry: **Other Food**

Alaska Milk Corporation produces liquid and powdered milk products and fruit juices. The company markets its products under the Alaska, Frisian Girl, and Granny Goose brand names. Its products include evaporated milk, sweetened condensed milk, and chocolate-flavored milk. Liquid milk sales account for approximately 65% of revenues, and powdered milk sales account for 34%. Ultrahigh temperature milk and fruit-juice products contribute the remaining portion of revenues. Alaska Milk is a subsidiary of the Philippines' General Milling, a diversified food manufacturer.

P$ mil	12/92 R	12/93 R	12/94	US$mil 12/94				
Sales	**1,767.0**	**1,833.9**	**1,805.8**	**68.5**	P/E Ratio	**18.3**	Price (9/30/95)	**5.30**
Net Income	**158.6**	**117.9**	**149.5**	**5.7**	P/B Ratio	**4.9**	52 Wk Hi-Low	**6.50-4.85**
Book Value	**350.3**	**468.2**	**617.9**	**25.3**	Yield %	**0.0**	Market Cap	**US$130.5mil**

Address **121 Paseo de Roxas, Makati, Metro Manila**
Tel **02-819-5451**
Fax **02-819-5477**
ADR
SEDOL No. **6014771**
President **George K. Young**
Chairman & CEO **Wilfred Uytengsu**

R=Restated.

Ayala

Industry: **Conglomerates**

Ayala Corporation is an investment-holding company with interests in the property-development, hotels, banking, insurance, food manufacturing, electronics, telecommunications, and agriculture industries. Ayala Land, the company's 89%-owned property arm, is the country's largest property developer. Approximately 60% of Ayala's revenues come from Ayala Land. Ayala also owns a 42% stake in the Bank of the Philippine Islands, and has a 36% interest in a joint venture with Singapore Telecom to provide cellular telephone service and an international digital gateway facility.

P$ mil	12/92	12/93	12/94	US$mil 12/94				
Sales	**12,297.6**	**13,988.4**	**22,555.4**	**855.1**	P/E Ratio	**10.6**	Price (9/30/95)	**25.50**
Net Income	**1,604.1**	**2,040.1**	**5,195.2**	**197.0**	P/B Ratio	**2.7**	52 Wk Hi-Low	**36.50-19.64**
Book Value	**11,905.6**	**13,853.6**	**20,332.1**	**833.3**	Yield %	**0.2**	Market Cap	**US$1,252.7mil**

Address **Makati S.E. Bldg., Ayala Ave., Makati, Metro Manila**
Tel **02-814-7701**
Fax **02-815-0764**
ADR
SEDOL No. **6069113**
President **J. Zobel de Ayala II**
Chairman **J. Zobel de Ayala**

Bacnotan Consolidated

Industry: **Building Materials**

Bacnotan Consolidated Industries is an investment holding company in the cement and galvanized iron-sheet manufacturing sectors. The company also invests in an pulp and paper mill that produces paper for cement bags and packaging materials. Its main subsidiaries include 68%-owned Davao Union Cement, 60%-owned Bacnotan Cement, and 53%-owned Atlas Cement. Bacnotan Cement is engaged in a 2.3 billion-peso plant expansion that will increase its annual production capacity to 30 million bags of cement. This will make it the Philippine's largest cement manufacturer by volume.

P$ mil	06/92	06/93	06/94	US$mil 06/94				
Sales	**4,738.2**	**4,904.8**	**5,592.7**	**201.1**	P/E Ratio	**25.0**	Price (9/30/95)	**178.00**
Net Income	**394.5**	**378.5**	**356.0**	**12.8**	P/B Ratio	**2.2**	52 Wk Hi-Low	**198.33-140.00**
Book Value	**2,558.7**	**3,600.2**	**4,018.2**	**148.8**	Yield %	**0.5**	Market Cap	**US$341.6mil**

Address **Phinma Bldg., 166 Salcedo St., Makati, Metro Manila**
Tel **02-810-9526**
Fax **02-817-9807**
ADR
SEDOL No. **6076823**
President **Oscar J. Hilado**
Chairman **Ernesto O. Escaler**

Benpres

Industry: **Conglomerates**

Benpres Holdings was formed in September 1993 to act as a holding company for the Lopez Group of companies. The company holds interests in broadcasting, telecommunications, financial services, and energy businesses. It owns a 71% stake in television broadcaster ABS-CBN and a 20% stake in SkyCable, a cable-television broadcaster. Its telecommunications subsidiaries maintain and develop communications networks and provide phone service to individuals. Benpres' other activities include property development, transportation, electricity generation, and commercial banking.

P$ mil	09/93	12/93 *	12/94	US$mil 12/94				
Sales	**N/A**	**2,121.9**	**3,231.9**	**122.5**	P/E Ratio	**16.9**	Price (9/30/95)	**7.60**
Net Income	**N/A**	**182.3**	**1,200.8**	**45.5**	P/B Ratio	**4.3**	52 Wk Hi-Low	**12.73-7.27**
Book Value	**N/A**	**3,233.8**	**4,756.8**	**195.0**	Yield %	**0.0**	Market Cap	**US$957.0mil**

Address **Benpres Bldg., Exchange Rd., Pasig, Metro Manila**
Tel **02-631-3111**
Fax **02-631-3104**
ADR
SEDOL No. **6092313**
President & CEO **Eugenio Lopez, Jr.**
Chairman **Oscar M. Lopez**

*Irregular period due to fiscal year change.

Filinvest Land

Industry: **Real-Estate Investment**

Filinvest Land owns real estate and specializes in the development of residential property. The company has a land inventory of more than 1,000 hectares. Filinvest is currently developing its 20%-owned Alabang Corporate City project, a 244-hectare residential area south of Manila. This project is a joint venture with Filinvest Development and the Philippine government to build 21,000 housing units. The company also provides mortgage-financing services to purchasers of its houses and lots, and participates in some commercial-development projects.

P$ mil	12/92	12/93	12/94	US$mil 12/94				
Sales	**N/A**	**224.9**	**898.9**	**34.1**	P/E Ratio	**10.5**	Price (9/30/95)	**8.40**
Net Income	**N/A**	**125.5**	**631.6**	**23.9**	P/B Ratio	**6.7**	52 Wk Hi-Low	**10.25-4.48**
Book Value	**N/A**	**2,535.0**	**3,166.6**	**129.8**	Yield %	**0.0**	Market Cap	**US$812.1mil**

Address **FDC Bldg., 173 P. Gomez St., San Juan, Metro Manila**
Tel **02-70-0611**
Fax **02-70-0674**
ADR
SEDOL No. **6341446**
President **Andrew L. Gotianun**
Chairman **Andrew L. Gotianun**

International Container

Industry: **General Industrial & Commercial Services**

International Container Terminal Services (ICTSI) manages the Manila International Container Terminal which handles approximately 85% of the container traffic passing through the port of Manila. The company provides cargo-handling, ship-maintenance, customs-coordination, and loose-cargo-tracking services. It also operates a terminal at Subic Bay and is currently developing an inland container depot in Cabuyao, Laguna. ICTSI owns 51% of a development project to build a terminal in Cebu, Philippines and manages a recently privatized terminal in Buenos Aires, Argentina.

P$ mil	12/92	12/93	12/94	US$mil 12/94				
Sales	1,000.9	1,142.7	1,283.5	48.7	P/E Ratio	32.4	Price (9/30/95)	16.50
Net Income	232.4	345.5	205.3	7.8	P/B Ratio	4.7	52 Wk Hi-Low	20.40-13.20
Book Value	1,077.8	1,398.7	1,570.6	64.4	Yield %	1.2	Market Cap	US$320.2mil

Address	**MICT S. Access Rd.**	Tel	**02-213-651**	ADR		President	**Carlos T. Soriano**
	North Harbour, Metro Manila	Fax	**02-286-0004**	SEDOL No.	**6455819**	Chairman	**Enrique K. Razon, Jr.**

JG Summit

Industry: **Conglomerates**

JG Summit is an investment-holding company with interests in the branded consumer-food, agriculture, textiles, real-estate, financial-services, electronics, petroleum, and power-generation industries. The company owns the largest textile mill in the country, and also operates clothing-manufacturing facilities. JG Summit's other interests include a 60% stake in property- and hotel-developer Robinson's Land, a 60% stake in phone-service provider Digital Communications, a 20% stake in oil-driller Oriental Petroleum, and a 19% stake in Far East Bank.

P$ mil	12/92	12/93	12/94	US$mil 12/94				
Sales	9,310.7	10,561.8	12,121.1	459.6	P/E Ratio	5.7	Price (9/30/95)	7.70
Net Income	1,577.0	1,876.2	6,024.1	228.4	P/B Ratio	1.7	52 Wk Hi-Low	11.00-6.00
Book Value	9,719.9	12,599.6	18,565.0	760.9	Yield %	0.3	Market Cap	US$1,246.2mil

Address	**Galleria Ctr., Ortigas Ave.**	Tel	**02-633-7631**	ADR		President	**James L. Go**
	Quenzon, Metro Manila	Fax	**02-633-9387**	SEDOL No.	**6466457**	Chairman & CEO	**John Gokongwei, Jr.**

Jollibee Food

Industry: **Restaurants**

Jollibee Foods Corporation develops, operates, and franchises fast-food restaurants under the name Jollibee. In the Philippines, it manages or franchises 160 stores. The company also has eight overseas outlets: five in Brunei, two in Indonesia, and one in the United Arab Emirates. Its restaurants serve fast food ranging from cheeseburgers and chicken to noodles and mango pie. Jollibee owns the franchise rights to manage Royal Copenhagen Danish ice cream food stores in selected Asian countries, and has a global franchise for the Donut King and Donut Magic fast-food stores.

P$ mil	12/92	12/93	12/94	US$mil 12/94				
Sales	2,296.0	2,702.2	3,606.2	136.7	P/E Ratio	32.3	Price (9/30/95)	16.75
Net Income	201.1	292.8	403.8	15.3	P/B Ratio	10.3	52 Wk Hi-Low	18.00-6.67
Book Value	520.5	1,029.2	1,411.8	57.9	Yield %	0.5	Market Cap	US$538.6mil

Address	**Araneta Center Cubao**	Tel	**02-634-1111**	ADR		President & CEO	**Tony Tan Caktiong**
	Quenzon, Metro Manila	Fax	**02-633-3697**	SEDOL No.	**6474494**	Chairman	**Tony Tan Caktiong**

Manila Electric

Industry: **Electrical Utilities - All**

Manila Electric (Meralco) purchases electricity from National Power and distributes it to customers in Metro Manila, Bulacan, Rizal, Cavite, and parts of the Laguna, Quezon, Batangas, and Pampanga provinces. In 1994, the firm served 2.5 million customers and had sales of 14,555 million kilowatt hours. Meralco is also active in power generation through its 40%-owned First Private Power consortium. FPP completed construction of its Bauang-based 215-megawatt diesel-fired baseload power plant in 1994. Meralco is the Philippines' fourth-largest firm by revenues.

P$ mil	12/92	12/93	12/94	US$mil 12/94				
Sales	31,482.1	33,841.6	43,834.9	1,661.9	P/E Ratio	19.0	Price (9/30/95)	199.00
Net Income	1,863.4	1,631.0	3,622.4	137.3	P/B Ratio	2.3	52 Wk Hi-Low	241.67-166.67
Book Value	19,293.9	22,533.0	27,382.1	1,122.2	Yield %	0.5	Market Cap	US$935.3mil

Address	**Lopez Bldg., Ortigas Ave.**	Tel	**02-631-2222**	ADR	**MERAY**	President	**Manuel M. Lopez**
	Pasig, Metro Manila	Fax	**02-632-8885**	SEDOL No.	**6574833**	Chairman	**Felipe B. Alfonso**

Manila Mining

Industry: **Precious Metals**

Manila Mining explores for and mines gold and silver. The company is the Philippines' largest mining company in terms of market capitalization. Its mining operation at Surigao del Norte, Philippines produces a monthly average of more than 9,000 ounces of gold and 5,000 ounces of silver. The company has reserves of 30 million tonnes with a grade of 1.8 grams per tonne. This reserve level will ensure a mine life of at least 10 years. Manila Mining carries out both drilling and depth-probing exploration programs.

P$ mil	12/92	12/93	12/94	US$mil 12/94				
Sales	400.9	731.8	1,106.2	41.9	P/E Ratio	6.1	Price (9/30/95)	0.09
Net Income	197.2	420.4	560.5	21.3	P/B Ratio	4.0	52 Wk Hi-Low	0.20-0.08
Book Value	386.8	788.4	1,310.3	53.7	Yield %	0.0	Market Cap	US$79.8mil

Address	**Paseo de Roxas**	Tel	**02-815-9447**	ADR		President	**Felipe U. Yap**
	Makati, Metro Manila	Fax	**02-815-4693**	SEDOL No.	**6561943**	Chairman	**Felipe U. Yap**

Megaworld Properties

Industry: **Real-Estate Investment**

Megaworld Properties & Holdings invests in and develops real estate in Manila and the surrounding areas. The company specializes in large-scale development projects such as high-rise residential and office buildings and townhouse-community developments. Its projects include a 45-story office tower in the Makati business district to serve as Petron's headquarters; the development of 2,300 hectares of land for Manila Bank; and the World Center, a 32-story office tower located in Makati. The company was listed on the Philippine Stock Exchange on June 15, 1994.

	P$ mil 12/92	12/93	12/94	US$mil 12/94				
Sales	**N/A**	**608.0**	**1,885.8**	**71.5**	P/E Ratio	**26.7**	Price (9/30/95)	**13.50**
Net Income	**N/A**	**118.3**	**415.9**	**15.8**	P/B Ratio	**11.9**	52 Wk Hi-Low	**14.25-7.35**
Book Value	**N/A**	**300.5**	**1,472.9**	**60.4**	Yield %	**0.0**	Market Cap	**US$841.4mil**

Address	**777 Paseo de Roxas**	Tel	**02-813-0036**	ADR		President	**Andrew L. Tan**
	Makati, Metro Manila	Fax	**02-817-4850**	SEDOL No.	**6563648**	Chairman	**Andrew L. Tan**

Metropolitan Bank & Trust

Industry: **Banks - Regional**

Metropolitan Bank & Trust Company (MBTC) offers a full range of banking services to both individual and corporate customers. It also provides financial services such as investment management, leasing, credit cards, and insurance. The company operates approximately 220 domestic branches and nine overseas branches. MBTC owns a 73% interest in Philippine Savings Bank, a bank which specializes in savings and mortgage services. The company also owns a stake in First Metro Investment, a property-investment concern.

	P$ mil 12/91	12/92	12/93	US$mil 12/93				
Revenues	**8,289.1**	**8,394.3**	**9,039.7**	**334.5**	P/E Ratio	**8.9**	Price (9/30/95)	**485.00**
Net Income	**1,026.9**	**1,231.2**	**1,657.8**	**61.3**	P/B Ratio	**2.1**	52 Wk Hi-Low	**546.09-397.83**
Book Value	**3,855.8**	**5,503.9**	**7,076.9**	**255.9**	Yield %	**1.9**	Market Cap	**US$2,011.9mil**

Address	**Sen. Gil J. Puyat Ave.**	Tel	**02-810-3311**	ADR		President	**Antonia S. Abacan, Jr.**
	Makati, Metro Manila	Fax	**N/A**	SEDOL No.	**6584359**	Chairman	**George S.K. Ty**

Petron

Industry: **Oil - Secondary**

Petron Corporation produces and distributes petroleum and liquified-petroleum-gas (LPG) products through consumer service-stations and directly to industrial customers. It holds 45% of the market for petroleum and LPG products in the Philippines. Petron operates a 250-hectare refinery in Limay that has an average daily production capacity of 155,000 barrels. Privatized in September 1994, Petron is still 40%-owned by the government oil concern Philippine National Oil Company. Saudi Aramco, the world's largest exporter of crude oil, also owns 40% of the company.

	P$ mil 12/92	12/93	12/94	US$mil 12/94				
Sales	**40,712.6**	**44,938.1**	**45,943.6**	**1,741.9**	P/E Ratio	**20.4**	Price (9/30/95)	**12.25**
Net Income	**1,472.4**	**2,777.3**	**3,736.7**	**141.7**	P/B Ratio	**6.2**	52 Wk Hi-Low	**21.60-12.25**
Book Value	**7,927.6**	**8,551.8**	**12,288.5**	**503.6**	Yield %	**0.0**	Market Cap	**US$2,941.3mil**

Address	**7901 Makati Ave.**	Tel	**02-892-9061**	ADR		President	**Abdulaziz F. Al-Khayyal**
	Makati, Metro Manila 1200	Fax	**02-815-3094**	SEDOL No.	**6684130**	Chairman & CEO	**Monico V. Jacob**

Philippine Commercial Intl Bank

Industry: **Banks - Regional**

Philippine Commercial International Bank (PCIBank) offers commercial banking services through a domestic network of 263 bank branches and 155 automated-teller machines. It is the country's fourth-largest commercial bank, with total assets of 72 billion pesos. The company's financial services include U.S. dollar checking accounts, credit cards, international capital trading, securities underwriting, insurance, and lease financing. PCIBank is majority-owned by the Lopez family, controllers of Benpres Holdings, and John Gokongwei, Jr., JG Summit's largest shareholder.

	P$ mil 12/92	12/93	12/94	US$mil 12/94				
Revenues	**5,408.3**	**5,375.3**	**6,950.2**	**263.5**	P/E Ratio	**23.6**	Price (9/30/95)	**235.00**
Net Income	**1,239.7**	**1,314.6**	**1,558.6**	**59.1**	P/B Ratio	**4.0**	52 Wk Hi-Low	**245.00-165.73**
Book Value	**5,499.4**	**6,637.2**	**9,160.0**	**375.4**	Yield %	**0.5**	Market Cap	**US$1,410.5mil**

Address	**PCIBank Twr. 1, Makati Ave.**	Tel	**02-817-1021**	ADR		President & CEO	**Rafael Buenaventura**
	Makati, Metro Manila	Fax	**02-817-4147**	SEDOL No.	**6685564**	Chairman	**Eugenio Lopez, Jr.**

Philippine Long Distance

Industry: **Telephone Systems - All**

Philippine Long Distance Telephone is the leading provider of long-distance and local telephone service in the Philippines. The company serves nearly 1.5 million telephones, which is about 90% of the country's total. The company handles more than 92 million domestic calls and nearly 32 million international calls each year. It owns 142 exchanges covering the Metro Manila area and 145 other cities and municipalities. The company also offers cellular-telephone service and operates dedicated digital facilities for facsimile service.

	P$ mil 12/92	12/93	12/94	US$mil 12/94				
Sales	**17,621.2**	**20,501.4**	**22,249.4**	**843.5**	P/E Ratio	**20.8**	Price (9/30/95)	**1,740.00**
Net Income	**4,977.9**	**5,546.8**	**5,217.4**	**197.8**	P/B Ratio	**2.1**	52 Wk Hi-Low	**1,970.0-1,205.0**
Book Value	**28,968.2**	**34,076.9**	**44,297.9**	**1,815.5**	Yield %	**0.4**	Market Cap	**US$4,043.0mil**

Address	**PLDT Bldg., Legaspi St.**	Tel	**02-816-8121**	ADR	**PHI**	President	**Antonio O. Cojuangco**
	Makati, Metro Manila	Fax	**02-818-7597**	SEDOL No.	**6685661**	Chairman	**Alfonso Yuchengco**

Philippine National Bank

Industry: **Banks - Regional**

Philippine National Bank (PNB) is the country's largest commercial bank, with assets of more than 100 billion pesos. It provides financial services to individual, corporate, and institutional customers, and serves as the official depository of the Republic of the Philippines. PNB's network comprises 305 domestic branches and 135 automated-teller machines. The company's services include foreign exchange, trust-fund management, securities underwriting, and mutual-fund management. The national government of the Philippines owns approximately 45% of PNB's share capital.

P$ mil	12/92	12/93	12/94	US$mil 12/94				
Revenues	**10,808.1**	**12,307.3**	**13,869.7**	**525.8**	P/E Ratio	**13.2**	Price (9/30/95)	**272.50**
Net Income	**2,304.1**	**2,443.9**	**2,007.1**	**76.1**	P/B Ratio	**1.4**	52 Wk Hi-Low	**420.00-202.00**
Book Value	**13,737.1**	**15,485.3**	**19,898.1**	**815.5**	Yield %	**1.8**	Market Cap	**US$1,046.7mil**

Address **PNB Ctr., Roxas Blvd.**
Manila
Tel **02-526-3310**
Fax **02-833-1241**
ADR
SEDOL No. **6685694**
President **Peter Favila**
Chairman **D.L. Lacson, Jr.**

Picop Resources

Industry: **Forest Products**

Picop Resources (formerly Paper Industries Corporation of the Philippines) manufactures wood and paper products. The company operates one of the largest fully integrated timber, pulp, and paper mills in Southeast Asia. Its products include plywood, veneer, lumber, newsprint, kraft paper, linerboard, mechanical-printing paper, and telephone-directory paper. Sales of timber products account for 42% of the company's revenue. Picop Resources is 39% owned by Picop Holdings, a joint venture controlled by Guoco Philippines and Malaysia's Hong Leong Industries.

P$ mil	12/92	12/93	12/94	US$mil 12/94				
Sales	**2,972.1**	**3,075.1**	**3,373.4**	**127.9**	P/E Ratio	**16.7**	Price (9/30/95)	**8.70**
Net Income	**-136.4**	**4.2**	**179.0**	**6.8**	P/B Ratio	**1.6**	52 Wk Hi-Low	**14.75-8.50**
Book Value	**1,244.7**	**1,254.4**	**2,770.0**	**113.5**	Yield %	**0.0**	Market Cap	**US$175.0mil**

Address **Julia Vargas Ave.**
Pasig, Metro Manila
Tel **02-633-5935**
Fax **02-633-9959**
ADR
SEDOL No. **6687720**
President & CEO **Evaristo M. Narvaez, Jr.**
Chairman **Jose P. Magno**

RFM

Industry: **Other Food**

RFM Corporation manufactures packaged-foods, bottles soft drinks, processes meat, and produces milk and juice drinks. Its brands include White King specialty mixes, Carol Ann's snacks, Sunkist juice drinks, Swift frozen poultry and processed meats, and Selecta dairy products. The company is the Philippine's largest supplier of tuna to the United States. RFM owns 73% of Selecta Dairy Products, 68% of Swift Foods, and 60% of Cosmos Bottling Corporation. It also is the majority owner of Pacific Semiconductors, the Philippine's largest exporter of electronic power devices.

P$ mil	12/92	12/93	12/94	US$mil 12/94				
Sales	**6,700.3**	**7,284.3**	**9,193.7**	**348.6**	P/E Ratio	**6.8**	Price (9/30/95)	**6.90**
Net Income	**302.5**	**186.0**	**1,431.2**	**54.3**	P/B Ratio	**2.2**	52 Wk Hi-Low	**8.40-5.90**
Book Value	**2,913.0**	**3,069.0**	**4,481.6**	**183.7**	Yield %	**0.2**	Market Cap	**US$371.0mil**

Address **Pioneer & Sheridan Sts.**
Mandaluyong, Metro Manila
Tel **05-631-8101**
Fax **05-631-5007**
ADR
SEDOL No. **6736213**
President & CEO **Jose A. Concepcion III**
Chairman **Rafael G. Hechanova**

Robinson's Land

Industry: **Real-Estate Investment**

Robinson's Land Corporation owns and develops real estate. It specializes in the development of residential properties and commercial real estate such as shopping centers, office towers, and hotels. Its flagship property is Robinson's Galleria, a retail, commercial, and residential complex in Manila. It is also building a planned community of 3,700 houses east of Manila, and is planning the construction of three shopping centers in the provinces. The company manages the property investments of conglomerate JG Summit, which owns 70% of Robinson's share capital.

P$ mil	09/92	09/93	09/94	US$mil 09/94				
Sales	**380.0**	**375.8**	**357.3**	**13.1**	P/E Ratio	**26.6**	Price (9/30/95)	**3.70**
Net Income	**209.5**	**237.0**	**194.0**	**7.1**	P/B Ratio	**1.5**	52 Wk Hi-Low	**4.40-2.32**
Book Value	**3,005.1**	**3,242.1**	**3,436.1**	**131.7**	Yield %	**0.0**	Market Cap	**US$255.9mil**

Address **EDSA & Ortigas Ave.**
Quenzon City, Metro Manila
Tel **02-633-7641**
Fax **02-632-0667**
ADR
SEDOL No. **6744722**
President **James L. Go**
Chairman **John Gokongwei, Jr.**

San Miguel

Industry: **Distillers & Brewers**

San Miguel produces beverages, food, and packaging materials. The company manufactures San Miguel beer at breweries in the Philippines, Hong Kong, Indonesia, Vietnam, and China. Its other products include juice drinks, mineral water, chicken, pork, prawns, dairy products and processed foods. San Miguel has a 70% equity stake in Coca-Cola Bottlers Philippines, which supplies Coca-Cola, Sprite, and Fanta soft drinks. It owns 50% of Magnolia Nestle, which markets ice cream, chocolate milk, and desserts under the Nestle name.

P$ mil	12/92	12/93	12/94	US$mil 12/94				
Sales	**58,230.8**	**60,853.0**	**68,429.7**	**2,594.4**	P/E Ratio	**34.7**	Price (9/30/95)	**92.00**
Net Income	**3,595.3**	**4,028.9**	**11,860.8**	**449.7**	P/B Ratio	**5.7**	52 Wk Hi-Low	**111.00-80.77**
Book Value	**17,950.7**	**21,416.6**	**30,432.5**	**1,247.2**	Yield %	**0.6**	Market Cap	**US$1,874.6mil**

Address **40 San Miguel Ave.**
Mandaluyong City, Metro Manila
Tel **02-632-3000**
Fax **02-632-3099**
ADR **SMGBY**
SEDOL No. **6775777**
President **Francisco C. Eizmendi**
Chairman & CEO **Andres Soriano III**

SM Prime

Industry: **Real-Estate Investment**

SM Prime Holdings was formed in January 1994 as a holding company for SM shopping, dining, and entertainment malls and related real-estate investments. The company operates a chain of five malls and is active in acquiring land for mall development. Its malls together house 1,700 tenants, including SM-affiliates SM Department Stores and SM Supermarkets, and offer almost 1.1 million square meters of floor area. It also owns 42 cinemas, 78 bowling lanes, 180 restaurants, and 90 food counters, and is the only operator of ice skating rinks in the Philippines.

P$ mil	12/92	12/93	12/94	US$mil 12/94				
Sales	**N/A**	**N/A**	**2,263.4**	**85.8**	P/E Ratio	**63.9**	Price (9/30/95)	**7.80**
Net Income	**N/A**	**N/A**	**1,014.1**	**38.4**	P/B Ratio	**4.6**	52 Wk Hi-Low	**8.40-5.23**
Book Value	**N/A**	**N/A**	**14,048.3**	**575.8**	Yield %	**0.0**	Market Cap	**US$2,481.2mil**

Address	**Makati S.E. Bldg., Ayala Ave.**	Tel	**02-813-0274**	ADR		President	**Henry Sy, Sr.**
	Makati, Metro Manila	Fax	**02-818-1208**	SEDOL No.	**6818843**	Chairman	**Henry Sy, Sr.**

Southeast Asia Cement

Industry: **Building Materials**

Southeast Asia Cement Holdings (SEACEM) manufactures and markets cement. The company was incorporated in May 1994, and subsequently listed on the stock exchange in December 1994. Its average cement production capacity is 1,900 metric tons per day. It owns 98% of FR Cement, a cement manufacturer that operates clinker-processing and cement-finishing facilities. FR Cement is currently building a power plant to satisfy the energy demands of its cement factories. SEACEM also has a strategic alliance with Tong Yang Cement, South Korea's second-largest cement group.

P$ mil	12/92	12/93	12/94	US$mil 12/94				
Sales	**N/A**	**N/A**	**902.7**	**34.2**	P/E Ratio	**132.0**	Price (9/30/95)	**3.30**
Net Income	**N/A**	**N/A**	**78.7**	**3.0**	P/B Ratio	**3.0**	52 Wk Hi-Low	**3.70-1.84**
Book Value	**N/A**	**N/A**	**4,456.1**	**182.6**	Yield %	**0.0**	Market Cap	**US$516.6mil**

Address	**Emmanuel Hse., 115 Aguirre St.**	Tel	**02-894-0612**	ADR		President	**J.M.J. Lopez-Vito III**
	Makati, Metro Manila	Fax	**02-893-6345**	SEDOL No.	**6826192**	Chairman	**Benito R. Araneta**

Swift Foods

Industry: **Other Food**

Swift Foods manufactures, markets, and distributes processed meats, poultry, and commercial animal feeds. Its products include broiler chickens, frankfurters, sausages, ham, bacon, and customized meat products for fast food restaurants. The company's products sell under brand names such as Swift Premium, Swift Sariwanok, and Blue Ribbon. Swift Food also operates chick-breeding farms. The company began operations in July 1994, when RFM Corporation spun off its poultry, meat, and feeds division. RFM retains a 68% holding in Swift Foods.

P$ mil	06/91	06/92	06/93	US$mil 06/93				
Sales	**4,414.6**	**4,085.9**	**3,670.6**	**147.0**	P/E Ratio	**10.4**	Price (9/30/95)	**7.50**
Net Income	**144.9**	**223.3**	**328.8**	**13.2**	P/B Ratio	**8.7**	52 Wk Hi-Low	**14.00-7.50**
Book Value	**N/A**	**N/A**	**391.2**	**14.5**	Yield %	**0.0**	Market Cap	**US$154.2mil**

Address	**Pioneer & Sheridan Sts.**	Tel	**02-645-5011**	ADR		President	**José A. Concepcion III**
	Mandaluyong, Metro Manila	Fax	**02-941-8282**	SEDOL No.	**6861698**	Chairman	**José A. Concepcion III**

Vitarich

Industry: **Other Food**

Vitarich Corporation breeds and sells poultry, processes meat, and manufactures animal health products. The company derives 69% of its revenues from sales of chickens, and 30% from animal feed sales. Its processed-meat products include chicken hot dogs, chicken steak, ham, corned beef, and tocino. Its animal health division produces animal medicines and veterinary products, as well as a variety of animal feeds. Vitarich also operates breeder farms and hatcheries, provides veterinary services, and runs the Vitarich Poultry school which trains poultry farmers.

P$ mil	12/92	12/93	12/94	US$mil 12/94				
Sales	**2,306.0**	**2,891.7**	**3,957.0**	**150.0**	P/E Ratio	**19.6**	Price (9/30/95)	**9.60**
Net Income	**36.0**	**85.6**	**148.2**	**5.6**	P/B Ratio	**4.2**	52 Wk Hi-Low	**11.25-7.00**
Book Value	**530.0**	**624.0**	**691.6**	**28.3**	Yield %	**1.0**	Market Cap	**US$151.2mil**

Address	**Sarmiento Bldg., Pasong Tamo**	Tel	**02-816-7229**	ADR		President	**Renato P. Sarmiento**
	Makati, Metro Manila	Fax	**02-816-7236**	SEDOL No.	**6930509**	Chairman	**Rogelio M. Sarmiento**

Singapore

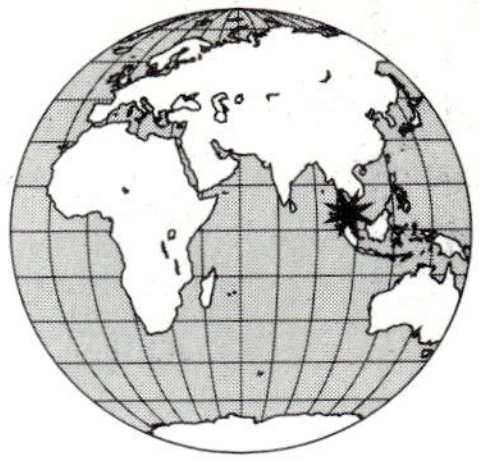

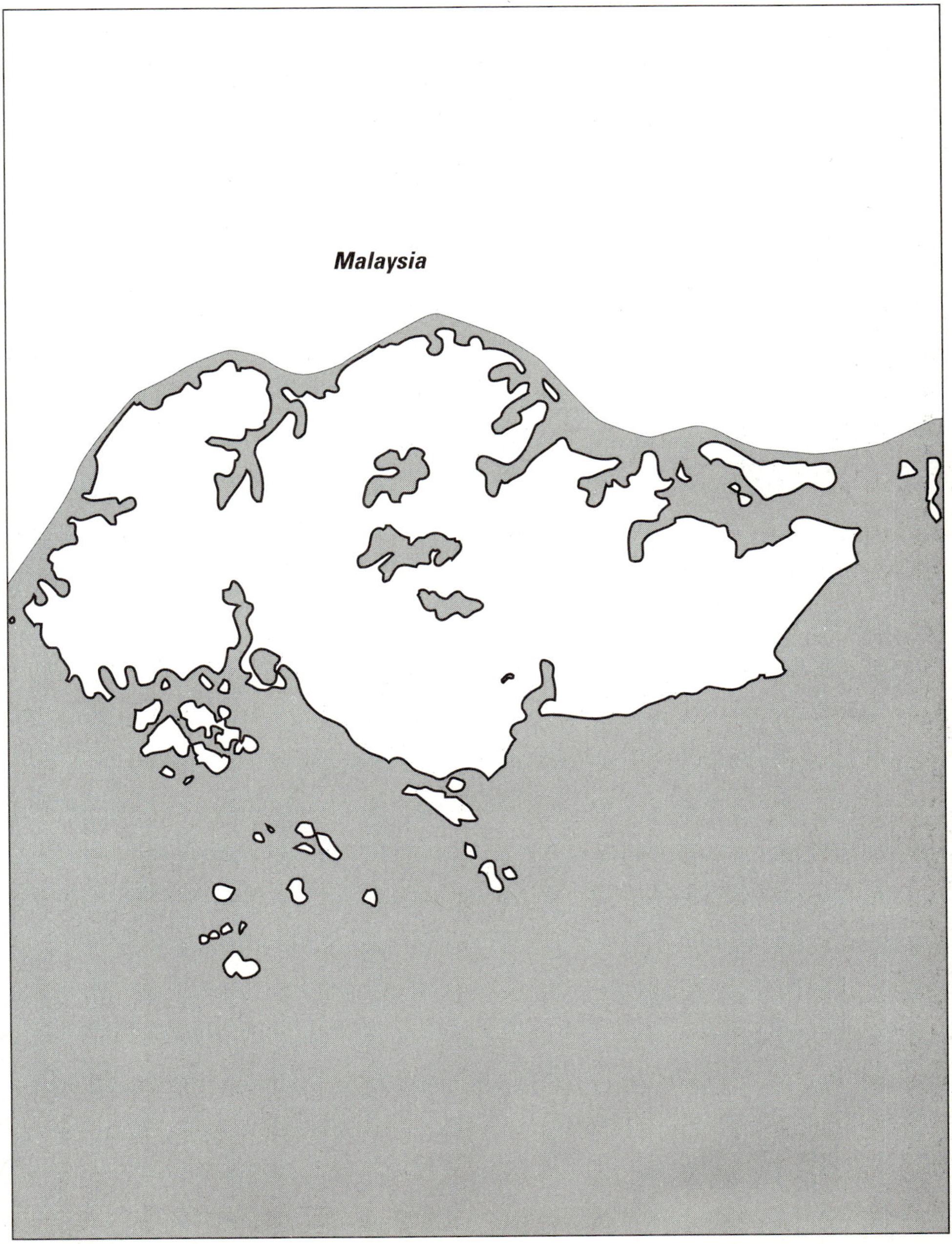

Singapore

Darren McDermott, Singapore

Local Trading Hours	Time Difference from New York	Population (Est. 12/94)
9:00-12:30, 2:00-5:00	13 hours ahead of EST	2,900,000

The main products have shifted from rubber and palm oil to electronics and refined petroleum products, but since Sir Stamford Raffles picked it as a convenient trading center, Singapore has remained faithful to – and prospered from – its entrepot status.

The Stock Exchange of Singapore, like the tiny but wealthy island nation that is its home, has built much of its strength on this status as a trade hub for the region.

With precious few natural resources and a well-paid work force that has priced it out of the market for simple manufacturing, Singapore is successfully carving out a niche for itself as a comfortable and well-oiled gateway to the rich infrastructure projects and burgeoning consumer markets of its larger neighbors. Even before the republic's technocratic government embarked on a regionalization campaign, many Singapore-listed companies were deriving large profits from the island's role in regional trade.

In fact, half of the exchange's volume on many days takes place in the regional stocks – mostly Malaysian – that are traded on a special over-the-counter system at the exchange. The other half comes from the main board of Singapore-listed companies and secondary listings of foreign companies, and a secondary board, Sesdaq, for small-capitalization companies with shorter earnings records.

The Stock Exchange of Singapore was born in May 1973 when the Singapore and Malaysian currencies split, although trading of shares in rubber companies dates back to the 19th century. From its modest beginnings, employing chalk boards and hundreds of young clerks in the 1950s, Singapore has grown into one of the biggest and most modern stock exchanges in Asia.

At the end of June 1995 there were 276 companies listed on the main board, accounting for about U.S.$179 billion in market capitalization. Sesdaq, with 43 companies listed, accounts for another U.S.$2.23 billion. Options are traded on four stocks, but volumes remain thin.

Dow Jones Singapore Equity Market Index Performance

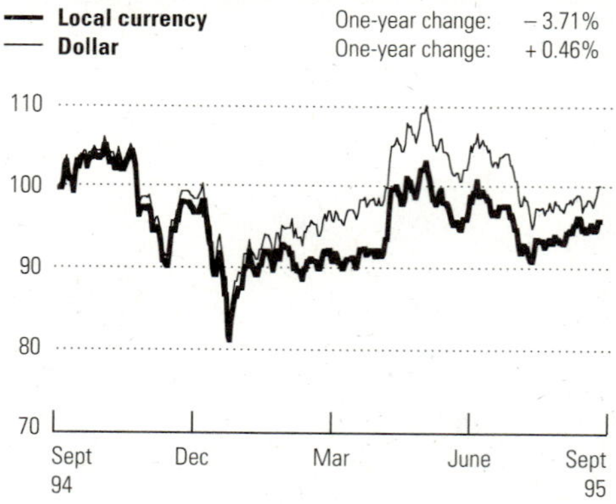

But many Malaysian companies remained listed in Singapore until another split in January 1990 that removed them from the Singapore market. Eager to maintain

Gross Domestic Product (94 nominal)	Three-Year Average GDP Growth (92-94)	Main Industries	Consumer Price Index (93-94)	Monetary Unit	Exchange Rate (9/95)
$105.31 billon	+ 8.7%	Manufacturing (particularly electronics), financial services, commerce, entrepot trade.	+ 3.1%	Singapore dollar	S$1.42 to US$1.00

brokerage commissions on trading Malaysian shares for the many institutions based in Singapore, dealers turned to the over-the-counter market, called CLOB International. Here, 113 Malaysian shares, 10 Hong Kong and 3 other regional stocks are traded in Singapore dollars, although they are not formally listed and do not conform to Singapore listing requirements.

True to Singapore's penchant for technological innovation and order, in March 1989 the exchange moved to a floorless, fully automated, screen-based trading system. Trading is conducted over the telephone or through the computer system, which automatically matches bids and offers on the screen and sends confirmation to the brokerages.

Settlement is now also fully computerized, with the last of the Singapore-listed companies completing the three-year-old conversion process to scripless settlement in June 1994. Now all actively traded stock certificates are held in a central depository, completely doing away with delivery.

Clearing and settlement takes place through brokers' book orders to the depository where clients must open accounts; statements are sent regularly to shareholders. Settlement takes place exactly a week after the trade.

Shareholdings above 5% must be declared, and all subsequent transactions must be reported to the SES. It is possible to establish anonymous ownership through the nominee services of a broker, but the exchange does require the nationality of the owner.

Ten Largest Capitalized Companies
as of 9/30/95

Stock	Market Cap. US$Mil
Singapore Airlines	43,443,030.7
OCBC	22,261,651.4
DBS Bank	21,823,168.3
United Overseas Bank	17,639,737.5
Singapore Press Holdings	10,551,851.7
Overseas Union Bank	10,373,503.3
City Developments	4,752,297.5
Keppel	3,926,738.0
Hong Leong Finance	3,466,477.0
Fraser & Neave	2,725,893.0

In addition to brokerage commissions, transactions are charged clearing fees, 0.05% stamp duties, and the national 3% goods-and-services tax. Singapore does not tax dividends per se, although the 27% corporate tax applies to gross dividends payable, representing tax on the listed company's profits.

There are no foreign-exchange controls, limitations on repatriation of income or capital gains taxes for non-residents. Share purchases are mostly unrestricted, although there is a 40% foreign-shareholding limit on the banking stocks and a range of limits on some other "strategic" companies. The government also maintains a so-called "golden share" through the Ministry of Finance in a number of companies it deems strategically sensitive, giving it veto power over major corporate decisions despite its lack of majority ownership.

Still, many of Singapore's "government-linked" companies, core industrial enterprises that were state-run and have been privatized over the years, still have a small free-floating segment of the government's remaining large stake.

The latest of these companies to hit the market was Singapore Telecommunications Ltd., the national telephone company that was listed with great fanfare in November 1993. A massive publicity campaign sold shares in the company to nearly every adult on the island, increasing the 300,000 Singaporean shareholders by nearly five fold and raising about U.S.$3 billion for the company.

To handle the volume, the exchange built a share-purchase system through the automated teller machine network of six local banks. And with the scripless share system now in place, this plan has been extended and trading shares can be as easy as going to the bank.

But Singapore Telecom's share price has slumped badly since its listing; few investors expect it to recover soon and many fund managers track "ex-Telecom" indices because the share weighs so heavily on the market.

This year will see the listing of the next state-run entity, the Public Utilities Board, although few details have been announced.

Like many Southeast Asian markets, Singapore suffered in 1995 compared with its surge in 1993 and early 1994. A slight firming in the second half of 1994 ended abruptly as regional markets went into a tailspin, largely victims of the panic that swept through emerging markets in the wake of the devaluation of the Mexican peso and the collapse of financial markets there.

A moderate return of international investment flows as interest rates in the United States have eased has helped push Singapore's key indices near their 1995 opening levels. But the market is suffering from a fairly deep malaise, which dealers blame mostly on high price-earnings levels and expectations of slower earnings growth as the economy picks its way down from two years of lofty 10% growth.

Amcol Holdings

Industry: **Electrical Components & Equipment**

Amcol Holdings is a Singapore-based property investor and developer, manufacturer, and trading company. It manufactures and sells electronic products including televisions and compact-disc players. Amcol has a 30% stake in Hock Der, a Malaysian property developer that is building a 24-story office complex in Johor Baru. It also holds a 36% interest in Zhongshan Square, a Shanghai office and residential development. Amcol began construction of a Tanjong Rhu-based condominium complex in late 1994. It also operates in investment-holding and portfolio investment businesses.

S$ mil	12/92	12/93	12/94	US$mil 12/94				
Sales	**774.6**	**844.0**	**1,151.0**	**757.7**	P/E Ratio	**25.2**	Price (9/30/95)	**3.76**
Net Income	**16.1**	**38.9**	**44.2**	**29.1**	P/B Ratio	**2.4**	52 Wk Hi-Low	**4.64-2.10**
Book Value	**321.9**	**428.1**	**452.9**	**310.2**	Yield %	**1.3**	Market Cap	**US$845.4mil**

Address **Chiat Hong Bldg., 110 Middle Rd. Tukang Lima 0718** Tel **337-1722** Fax **338-1480** ADR SEDOL No. **6028879** Managing Director **K.T. Leng / C.H. Tiu** Chairman **Cheng Yu Tung**

City Developments

Industry: **Real-Estate Investment**

City Developments (CityDev) invests in, develops, and manages residential, commercial, and hotel properties. It holds more than 800,000 sq. meters of land. CityDev also develops condominiums and entertainment complexes in Singapore. It receives rental income, primarily from office-building and shopping complexes in Singapore. The company's 51%-owned subsidiary, CDL Hotels (which trades in Hong Kong), manages 35 hotels with a total of more than 10,000 rooms. These include the Grand Hyatt Taipei (Taiwan), the Novotel Orchid Singapore, and the Manila Plaza Hotel (Philippines).

S$ mil	12/92	12/93	12/94	US$mil 12/94				
Sales	**506.3**	**751.8**	**1,139.3**	**750.0**	P/E Ratio	**N/A**	Price (9/30/95)	**8.80**
Net Income	**89.6**	**114.8**	**228.2**	**150.2**	P/B Ratio	**3.9**	52 Wk Hi-Low	**9.40-7.55**
Book Value	**984.7**	**1,110.6**	**1,765.8**	**1,209.5**	Yield %	**0.9**	Market Cap	**US$4,752.3mil**

Address **36 Robinson Rd., 20-01 City Hse. Singapore 0106** Tel **221-2266** Fax **227-9751** ADR **CDEVY** SEDOL No. **6197928** Managing Director **Kwek Leng Joo** Chairman **Kwek Leng Beng**

Cycle & Carriage

Industry: **Other Specialty Retailers**

Cycle & Carriage (C&C) is a diversified group that is involved in vehicle sales, property, and food and retail. It sells Mercedes-Benz and Mitsubishi cars in Singapore, Mazda and Mercedes vehicles in Malaysia, Hyundai cars in Australia, and Ford cars in Thailand and Vietnam. C&C commands about 25% of Singapore's passenger-car market. The property division is run largely through 60%-owned public subsidiary Malayan Credit. C&C's 43%-owned public subsidiary Cold Storage produces and sells Nestle dairy foods in Malaysia and also operates supermarkets and pharmacies there.

S$ mil	09/92	12/93 *	12/94	US$mil 12/94				
Revenues	**1,564.5**	**2,333.0**	**2,477.0**	**1,630.7**	P/E Ratio	**23.9**	Price (9/30/95)	**12.70**
Net Income	**59.3**	**112.0**	**123.7**	**81.4**	P/B Ratio	**2.9**	52 Wk Hi-Low	**14.20-9.55**
Book Value	**740.6**	**881.0**	**1,037.5**	**710.6**	Yield %	**1.8**	Market Cap	**US$2,084.9mil**

Address **78 Shenton Way #33-00 Singapore 0207** Tel **223-3886** Fax **223-8633** ADR **CYCRY** SEDOL No. **6242260** Managing Director **Boon Yoon Chiang** Chairman **Dato' Paduka**

*Irregular period due to fiscal year change.

DBS Bank

Industry: **Banks - Money Center**

Development Bank of Singapore (DBS) is Singapore's largest bank by assets. DBS provides retail-banking and investment-banking services. It is Singapore's most active underwriter, lead-managing nearly half of the country's initial public offerings. It has 47 local branches and 13 overseas offices. DBS holds a 50% stake in Hong Kong advisory-services firm PruAsia, and a 30% interest in Malaysian securities firm Hwang-DBS. It also has subsidiaries and affiliates in Singapore, Hong Kong, and London.

S$ mil	12/92	12/93	12/94	US$mil 12/94				
Revenues	**1,919.4**	**1,867.6**	**2,239.1**	**1,474.0**	P/E Ratio	**20.3**	Price (9/30/95)	**16.20**
Net Income	**328.4**	**467.9**	**532.9**	**350.8**	P/B Ratio	**2.0**	52 Wk Hi-Low	**17.20-12.20**
Book Value	**3,973.5**	**4,599.6**	**5,349.4**	**3,664.0**	Yield %	**1.0**	Market Cap	**US$21,823mil**

Address **6 Shenton Way, DBS Bldg. Singapore 0106** Tel **220-1111** Fax **221-1306** ADR **DEVBY** SEDOL No. **6265513** President **Patrick Yeoh Khwai Hoh** Chairman & CEO **Ngiam Tong Dow**

DBS Land

Industry: **Real-Estate Investment**

DBS Land develops and manages hotels as well as commercial, residential, and industrial property through its 56 domestic and overseas subsidiaries. The company is now developing 23 projects in Malaysia, Indonesia, Hong Kong, China, Thailand, Vietnam, Cambodia, and Sri Lanka. The company's Raffles International subsidiary designs and markets hotels. It is restoring the Royal Hotel in Phnom Penh, Cambodia. It also owns and operates a Raffles hotel in Singapore and the Galle Face Hotel in Sri Lanka. DBS Land owns Siam Holdings, which develops property in Thailand.

S$ mil	12/92	12/93	12/94	US$mil 12/94				
Sales	**289.8**	**301.6**	**520.7**	**342.8**	P/E Ratio	**20.5**	Price (9/30/95)	**4.22**
Net Income	**66.4**	**78.7**	**149.1**	**98.2**	P/B Ratio	**1.3**	52 Wk Hi-Low	**5.20-3.28**
Book Value	**1,463.6**	**1,533.2**	**2,657.0**	**1,819.9**	Yield %	**1.9**	Market Cap	**US$2,613.0mil**

Address **Plz. Singapura, 68 Orchard Rd. Singapore 0923** Tel **336-3300** Fax **336-1204** ADR SEDOL No. **6244772** Managing Director **Han Cheng Fong** Chairman **P. Yeoh Khwai Hoh**

Far East Levingston Shipbuilding

Industry: **Shipbuilding**

Far East Levingston Shipbuilding (FELS) manufactures and repairs offshore-drilling rigs and floating production systems. It makes bulk carriers, semisubmersible platforms, mobile rigs, workboats, barges, drilling ships, and other steel marine craft for the oil-production industry. The company operates or has investments in the Middle East, Indochina, North America, the Philippines, China, and the North Sea. FELS derived 76% of 1994 production revenues from its offshore and marine operations and 12% from its power-generation operations. Keppel Corporation owns 52% of FELS.

S$ mil	12/92	12/93	12/94	US$mil 12/94				
Sales	**318.8**	**337.4**	**500.8**	**329.7**	P/E Ratio	**24.0**	Price (9/30/95)	**6.25**
Net Income	**26.6**	**36.6**	**43.3**	**28.5**	P/B Ratio	**1.8**	52 Wk Hi-Low	**7.40-5.40**
Book Value	**404.8**	**437.8**	**737.4**	**505.1**	Yield %	**0.6**	Market Cap	**US$868.1mil**

Address **31 Shipyard Rd.**
Jurong Town 2262
Tel **265-2144**
Fax **261-7719**
ADR
SEDOL No. **6331469**
Managing Director **Choo Chiau Beng**
Chairman **Loh Wing Siew**

Fraser & Neave

Industry: **Soft Drinks**

Fraser & Neave produces, packages, and markets beverages and dairy products that it distributes throughout Australasia. It also develops residential and commercial properties and theme parks. The firm's dairy operations are Singapore's largest by production. Its soft-drink division holds Coca-Cola, Sprite, and Fanta franchises in Singapore, Malaysia, Indonesia, Cambodia, and Vietnam. Fraser & Neave produces Tiger Beer, Singapore's market leader, through its Asia Pacific Breweries. It also produces Reeb beer through China's Shanghai Mila Brew.

S$ mil	09/92	09/93	09/94	US$mil 09/94				
Sales	**1,420.4**	**1,465.7**	**2,087.0**	**1,343.9**	P/E Ratio	**27.5**	Price (9/30/95)	**16.50**
Net Income	**35.1**	**93.6**	**146.9**	**94.6**	P/B Ratio	**2.2**	52 Wk Hi-Low	**18.00-12.90**
Book Value	**1,090.0**	**1,439.2**	**1,787.8**	**1,208.0**	Yield %	**0.9**	Market Cap	**US$2,725.9mil**

Address **438 Alexandra Rd.**
Singapore 0511
Tel **272-9488**
Fax **271-0811**
ADR
SEDOL No. **6350602**
Managing Director **Tan Yam Pin**
Chairman **Michael Fam**

Great Eastern Life Assurance

Industry: **Insurance - Life & Health**

The Great Eastern Life Assurance Company is Singapore's largest insurance company, with almost $1.5 billion in policies. The company derives 83% of its total revenues from insurance premiums. It offers life, personal-accident, and health insurance; individual annuities; employee-benefit packages; home-loan financing; and investment management. It operates branch offices in Singapore, Malaysia, and Brunei, and has overseas agencies in Australia, Canada, Hong Kong, and the United Kingdom. The firm is 46%-owned by Singapore's Oversea-Chinese Banking Corporation.

S$ mil	12/92	12/93	12/94	US$mil 12/94				
Revenues	**1,335.3**	**1,665.6**	**2,024.8**	**1,333.0**	P/E Ratio	**4.9**	Price (9/30/95)	**30.30**
Net Income	**45.8**	**46.1**	**60.6**	**39.9**	P/B Ratio	**0.9**	52 Wk Hi-Low	**30.60-24.60**
Book Value	**230.7**	**277.1**	**334.3**	**229.0**	Yield %	**6.3**	Market Cap	**US$2,073.5mil**

Address **OCBC Ctr., 65 Chulia St.**
Singapore 0104
Tel **532-4331**
Fax **532-2214**
ADR
SEDOL No. **6384021**
President --
Chairman **Howe Yoon Chong**

Hai Sun Hup

Industry: **Marine Transportation**

Hai Sun Hup owns and operates cargo ships, and is active in warehousing, trading, and hotel management. Its fleet of 13 vessels includes car carriers, container ships, and oil tankers. The company has joint ventures with shipping and trading companies from Japan, Sweden, Germany, and Switzerland. It operates shipping-terminal facilities and warehouses throughout the Far East. Hai Sun Hup owns four hotels in Australia, and has diversified into the production of furniture and interior decorations, the distribution of foods, and the operation of a travel agency.

S$ mil	03/93	03/94	03/95	US$mil 03/95				
Sales	**162.0**	**175.1**	**244.4**	**164.8**	P/E Ratio	**20.5**	Price (9/30/95)	**0.97**
Net Income	**24.7**	**23.9**	**20.2**	**13.6**	P/B Ratio	**1.9**	52 Wk Hi-Low	**1.18-0.79**
Book Value	**190.4**	**213.2**	**220.4**	**156.3**	Yield %	**1.0**	Market Cap	**US$291.4mil**

Address **200 Cantonment Rd.**
Singapore 0208
Tel **220-4906**
Fax **225-5948**
ADR
SEDOL No. **6424206**
President --
Chairman **Ow Chio Kiat**

Haw Par Brothers

Industry: **Overseas Trading**

Haw Par Brothers International is a diversified firm that operates pharmaceuticals, sports and leisure, and industrial-manufacturing divisions. Its pharmaceuticals division produces and markets proprietary drugs and dietary supplements, including Tiger brand balms. Its 75%-owned Drug Houses of Australia is Singapore's largest generic drug producer. Wholly-owned Haw Par Leisure makes and retails sporting goods. The company's industrial division produces power generators, repairs aviation equipment, supplies building materials, and retails computer equipment.

S$ mil	12/92	12/93	12/94	US$mil 12/94				
Sales	**333.0**	**360.3**	**341.6**	**224.9**	P/E Ratio	**21.3**	Price (9/30/95)	**3.00**
Net Income	**19.1**	**26.8**	**48.3**	**31.8**	P/B Ratio	**1.3**	52 Wk Hi-Low	**3.52-2.62**
Book Value	**378.9**	**380.3**	**411.6**	**281.9**	Yield %	**2.7**	Market Cap	**US$384.8mil**

Address **180 Clemenceau Ave.**
Singapore 0923
Tel **337-9102**
Fax **336-9232**
ADR
SEDOL No. **6415523**
President & CEO **Hong Hai**
Chairman **Wee Cho Yaw**

Hong Fok

Industry: **Real-Estate Investment**

Hong Fok is an holding company that invests in, develops, and manages commercial and residential property in Singapore and throughout Asia. It owns two major commercial properties, its flagship mixed-use complex, The Concourse, and Henderson Industrial Park. The firm's Winfoong Investments subsidiary, which is based in Hong-Kong, is active in property projects in Guangdong, China, as well as in Hong Kong. Its carries out construction projects through its wholly-owned subsidiary, Sui Chong International. Other activities include property management and gardening services.

S$ mil	12/92	12/93	12/94	US$mil 12/94				
Sales	**248.9**	**95.0**	**204.9**	**134.9**	P/E Ratio	**NMF**	Price (9/30/95)	**2.22**
Net Income	**43.7**	**-12.6**	**-13.8**	**-9.1**	P/B Ratio	**0.4**	52 Wk Hi-Low	**2.76-1.78**
Book Value	**380.9**	**406.4**	**761.9**	**521.8**	Yield %	**0.5**	Market Cap	**US$213.1mil**

Address	**The Concourse, 300 Beach Rd.**	Tel	**292-8181**	ADR		Managing Director	**Cheong Pin Chuan**
	Singapore 0719	Fax	**733-4937**	SEDOL No.	**6435178**	Chairman	**Cheong Kim Pong**

Hong Leong Finance

Industry: **Financial Services - Diversified**

Hong Leong Finance is Singapore's largest financial-services company by market capitalization. It offers investment holding and trading, automobile and home financing, and factoring and nominee services through its network of 13 branches located throughout Singapore. The firm also has operations in Brunei and Hong Kong. It owns 74% of Singapore Finance which offers deposit and financing services. Development Bank of Singapore is the partial owner of Hong Leong Finance. Hong Leong Investment Holdings is the company's ultimate holding company.

S$ mil	12/92	12/93	12/94	US$mil 12/94				
Revenues	**211.7**	**227.7**	**244.6**	**161.0**	P/E Ratio	**15.6**	Price (9/30/95)	**4.38**
Net Income	**36.6**	**55.9**	**107.6**	**70.8**	P/B Ratio	**1.8**	52 Wk Hi-Low	**5.30-3.56**
Book Value	**451.8**	**510.8**	**563.2**	**385.8**	Yield %	**1.6**	Market Cap	**US$3,466.5mil**

Address	**Hong Leong Bldg., 16 Raffles Quay**	Tel	**220-9433**	ADR		Managing Director	**Kwek Leng Beng**
	Singapore 0104	Fax	**224-6773**	SEDOL No.	**6424336**	Chairman	**Kwek Leng Beng**

Hotel Properties

Industry: **Lodging**

Hotel Properties is a hotelier and property developer. It owns or holds stakes in hotels in Singapore, Australia, Sri Lanka, Malaysia, Cambodia, Indonesia, Maldives and Burma. Major properties include the Hilton International Singapore, Singapore's Four Seasons Hotel and the Four Seasons Resort Bali. Hotel Properties operates Hard Rock Cafe franchises throughout the Asian Pacific, Haagen-Dazs outlets in Singapore, Malaysia, and Hong Kong, and Planet Hollywood franchises in Australia and Hong Kong. The company is 28%-owned by the Oversea-Chinese Bank Nominees.

S$ mil	12/92	12/93	12/94	US$mil 12/94				
Sales	**167.3**	**282.0**	**588.8**	**387.6**	P/E Ratio	**10.1**	Price (9/30/95)	**2.11**
Net Income	**30.2**	**80.5**	**92.6**	**61.0**	P/B Ratio	**1.1**	52 Wk Hi-Low	**3.00-2.05**
Book Value	**518.1**	**628.2**	**741.6**	**507.9**	Yield %	**1.9**	Market Cap	**US$584.7mil**

Address	**HPL Hse., 50 Cuscaden Rd.**	Tel	**734-5250**	ADR		President	**Ong Beng Seng**
	Singapore 1024	Fax	**235-0729**	SEDOL No.	**6440183**	Chairman	**Peter Y.S. Fu**

Hwa Hong

Industry: **Heavy Construction**

Hwa Hong is a diversified holding company with operations in warehousing, trading, investing, insurance, civil engineering, commercial construction, and the manufacture of oils, soap, and packaging materials. The firm's subsidiaries manage warehouses and industrial space in Singapore, Malaysia, Hong Kong, the United Kingdom, and the British Virgin Islands. Hwa Hong provides insurance through 99.6%-owned People's Insurance and Global Trade Insurance Management. It has subsidiaries in Singapore and China and a property-development joint venture in Vietnam.

S$ mil	12/92	12/93	12/94	US$mil 12/94				
Sales	**280.6**	**223.9**	**221.0**	**145.5**	P/E Ratio	**36.3**	Price (9/30/95)	**2.25**
Net Income	**8.0**	**9.1**	**9.0**	**5.9**	P/B Ratio	**1.1**	52 Wk Hi-Low	**2.64-1.70**
Book Value	**255.2**	**248.1**	**298.8**	**204.7**	Yield %	**1.3**	Market Cap	**US$231.6mil**

Address	**60 Martin Rd. #07-38**	Tel	**235-5088**	ADR		President	**Ong Choo Eng**
	Singapore 0923	Fax	**733-3664**	SEDOL No.	**6449049**	Chairman	**Ong Choo Eng**

Inchcape

Industry: **Other Specialty Retailers**

Inchcape distributes and sells motor vehicles, consumer products, and health-care and industrial equipment. It holds Toyota, Lexus, and Iveco franchises in Singapore, sells Suzuki motorcycles in Myanmar, and supplies Land Rover and Volkswagen vehicles in Brunei. Inchcape sells Rolex watches and Ferragamo and Timberland shoes. It also sells irrigation systems, cellular phones, and kitchen appliances. In 1994, Inchcape generated 76% of its sales in Singapore; 16% came from Brunei, and 7% from Malaysia and other countries. The firm plans to sell its office-automation business.

S$ mil	12/92	12/93	12/94	US$mil 12/94				
Revenues	**1,080.7**	**1,196.2**	**1,259.4**	**829.1**	P/E Ratio	**10.7**	Price (9/30/95)	**4.54**
Net Income	**50.8**	**75.6**	**63.7**	**41.9**	P/B Ratio	**1.6**	52 Wk Hi-Low	**5.70-4.44**
Book Value	**385.9**	**434.8**	**465.5**	**318.9**	Yield %	**4.4**	Market Cap	**US$523.4mil**

Address	**11 Keppel Rd. #09-01**	Tel	**220-6933**	ADR		CEO	**P.R. McCready**
	Singapore 0208	Fax	**220-6433**	SEDOL No.	**6461805**	Chairman	**D.G. John**

IPC

Industry: **Computers**

IPC Corporation is a computer and electronic-products manufacturer. It also develops software and produces communications equipment, and computer peripherals. Its distribution network includes more than 100 IPC retail centers throughout the Asia-Pacific and a mobile sales team that sells to corporate and individual customers. IPC is involved in a joint venture with France's Groupe Bull to develop smartcard technology. It is also involved in a joint venture with the Netherland's Philips Electronics to manufacture computers that can read both audio and visual compact discs.

	S$ mil 12/92	12/93	12/94	US$mil 12/94				
Sales	**274.5**	**579.4**	**1,359.4**	**894.9**	P/E Ratio	**14.7**	Price (9/30/95)	**1.06**
Net Income	**41.1**	**53.6**	**72.3**	**47.6**	P/B Ratio	**3.0**	52 Wk Hi-Low	**1.10-0.74**
Book Value	**49.4**	**246.5**	**355.5**	**243.5**	Yield %	**0.9**	Market Cap	**US$746.5mil**

Address	**IPC Bldg., 23 Tai Seng Dr.**	Tel	**744-2688**	ADR		Managing Director	**Benjamin M.K. Ngiam**
	Singapore 1953	Fax	**N/A**	SEDOL No.	**6461344**	Chairman	**Patrick M.J. Ngiam**

Jurong Shipyard

Industry: **Marine Transportation**

Jurong Shipyard is Singapore's third-largest ship repair company in terms of volume. It also builds about three to four new vessels each year, and retains equity interests in a portion of them. Jurong is involved in a joint venture with Singapore's Neptune Orient Lines, which charters ships to oil operators working in the region. It also owns a 35% interest in Atlantis Shipyard, a company that specializes in the repair of smaller vessels. The company's affiliate Jurong 24 Hours operates three manufacturing facilities that produce printed circuit boards.

	S$ mil 12/92	12/93	12/94	US$mil 12/94				
Sales	**379.8**	**333.9**	**334.1**	**219.9**	P/E Ratio	**21.4**	Price (9/30/95)	**10.20**
Net Income	**68.4**	**64.6**	**52.9**	**34.8**	P/B Ratio	**2.2**	52 Wk Hi-Low	**12.40-9.35**
Book Value	**423.5**	**477.7**	**520.9**	**356.8**	Yield %	**1.3**	Market Cap	**US$795.9mil**

Address	**5 Jalan Samulun**	Tel	**265-1766**	ADR		Managing Director	**Kwi Kin Tan**
	Jurong Town 2262	Fax	**261-0738**	SEDOL No.	**6480037**	Chairman	**Cheng Eng Lua**

Keppel

Industry: **Shipbuilding**

Keppel repairs, builds, and converts ships; develops property; offers consumer- and investment-banking services; and is active in telecommunication. The firm runs shipyards and service installations through subsidiaries in Singapore, Southeast Asia, Australia, the Middle East, and the U.S. Two of its subsidiaries, Far East Levingston Shipbuilding and Straits Steamship Land, produce oil rigs and develop and rent properties. Keppel also holds a 35% stake in telecom concern MobileOne Asia. The firm's banking division owns 26% of India's Centurion Bank.

	S$ mil 12/92	12/93	12/94	US$mil 12/94				
Sales	**1,559.5**	**1,528.9**	**2,103.4**	**1,384.7**	P/E Ratio	**26.1**	Price (9/30/95)	**11.40**
Net Income	**173.8**	**262.8**	**211.4**	**139.2**	P/B Ratio	**2.2**	52 Wk Hi-Low	**13.50-10.30**
Book Value	**1,817.5**	**2,171.1**	**2,624.9**	**1,797.9**	Yield %	**1.1**	Market Cap	**US$3,926.7mil**

Address	**325 Telek Blangah Rd.**	Tel	**270-6666**	ADR	**KPELY**	Managing Director	**Loh Wing Siew**
	Singapore 0409	Fax	**274-2176**	SEDOL No.	**6490263**	Chairman	**Sim Kee Boon**

Malayan Credit

Industry: **Real-Estate Investment**

Malayan Credit is a holding company with stakes in firms engaged in commercial- and residential- property investment and development, securities investment, and real-estate management. Cycle & Carriage, a Singapore-based diversified automobile retailer, owns a 66% share of the company. Malayan Credit's two main properties are a 34-story commercial and office complex and a 303-apartment luxury residential complex, both in Singapore. Almost 100% of the company's revenue-generating property is in Singapore. Most of its Malaysian holdings are as yet undeveloped.

	S$ mil 09/92 *	12/93 *	12/94	US$mil 12/94				
Sales	**23.7**	**120.0**	**99.9**	**65.8**	P/E Ratio	**30.7**	Price (9/30/95)	**2.73**
Net Income	**-2.0**	**19.7**	**28.7**	**18.9**	P/B Ratio	**0.9**	52 Wk Hi-Low	**3.88-2.44**
Book Value	**786.8**	**799.0**	**961.4**	**658.5**	Yield %	**4.0**	Market Cap	**US$621.0mil**

Address	**78 Shenton Way**	Tel	**221-8111**	ADR	**MYANY**	Managing Director	**Ang Ah Lay**
	Singapore 0207	Fax	**225-3383**	SEDOL No.	**6556574**	Chairman	**Rin Kei Mei**

*Irregular period due to fiscal year change.

Metro

Industry: **Retailers - Broadline**

Metro Holdings distributes and sells consumer products, develops real estate, and manages construction interests. It operates two Metro department stores and 22 Factory Outlet retail stores in Singapore, Indonesia, and Malaysia. Metro also has real-estate developments throughout Southeast Asia. Its Orchard Square Development subsidiary manages a commercial complex, and its 25%-owned Etika Cekap associate is currently developing a residential area. Through a joint venture with U.S.-based Kmart, Metro operates Kmart discount stores in Singapore.

	S$ mil 03/93 R	03/94	03/95	US$mil 03/95				
Revenues	**397.9**	**430.3**	**303.4**	**204.6**	P/E Ratio	**88.1**	Price (9/30/95)	**5.90**
Net Income	**4.7**	**19.9**	**49.3**	**33.2**	P/B Ratio	**0.9**	52 Wk Hi-Low	**6.35-4.08**
Book Value	**585.9**	**658.4**	**715.1**	**507.2**	Yield %	**0.7**	Market Cap	**US$436.8mil**

Address	**391B Orchard Rd.**	Tel	**733-3000**	ADR		Managing Director	**Jopie Ong Hie Koan**
	Ngee Ann City 0923	Fax	**735-3515**	SEDOL No.	**6584285**	Chairman	**Ong Tjoe Kim**

R=Restated.

NatSteel

Industry: **Steel**

NatSteel manufactures steel, electronic, and chemical products, and operates engineering, construction, and resort-development businesses. It specializes in the manufacture of steel reinforcing bars and wire rods. NatSteel's chemical operations specialize in lime and refractory products. The company's wholly-owned NatSteel Engineering subsidiary has a joint venture with Intraco, a power company, to develop and operate electric-power projects in China, Vietnam, and Myanmar. NatSteel has subsidiaries and affiliates in Malaysia, Indonesia, and the United Kingdom.

S$ mil	12/92	12/93	12/94	US$mil 12/94				
Sales	**958.9**	**1,418.5**	**1,527.9**	**1,005.9**	P/E Ratio	**25.2**	Price (9/30/95)	**2.95**
Net Income	**13.2**	**48.6**	**33.4**	**22.0**	P/B Ratio	**1.4**	52 Wk Hi-Low	**3.46-2.76**
Book Value	**442.2**	**462.2**	**701.5**	**480.5**	Yield %	**2.0**	Market Cap	**US$672.4mil**

Address **22 Tanjong Kling Rd., Jurong**
Singapore 2262
Tel **265-1233**
Fax **265-8317**
ADR
SEDOL No. **6623616**
Managing Director **Kong Hua Ang**
Chairman **Michael Wee**

Neptune Orient Lines

Industry: **Marine Transportation**

Neptune Orient Lines (NOL) provides containerized liner and chartering services. It runs a fleet of 27 container ships with a total carrying capacity of 771,655 deadweight tonnes. NOL offers container services worldwide, focusing on links inside Asia and from the Far East to the U.S. East Coast. It also operates 32 cargo, oil, product, bulk, and combination carriers with a total capacity of roughly 2.16 million deadweight tons. NOL's average fleet age, 7.9 years, is low for the industry. The company generates 41% of sales outside the Asia-Pacific region.

S$ mil	12/92	12/93	12/94	US$mil 12/94				
Sales	**1,586.2**	**1,871.6**	**1,941.6**	**1,278.2**	P/E Ratio	**17.5**	Price (9/30/95)	**1.52**
Net Income	**36.3**	**73.2**	**63.0**	**41.5**	P/B Ratio	**1.0**	52 Wk Hi-Low	**2.31-1.52**
Book Value	**874.8**	**1,050.4**	**1,067.4**	**731.1**	Yield %	**3.3**	Market Cap	**US$731.5mil**

Address **NOL Bldg., 456 Alexandra Rd.**
Singapore 0511
Tel **278-9000**
Fax **278-4900**
ADR **NTOLY**
SEDOL No. **6628859**
CEO **Lua Cheng Eng**
Chairman **Herman R. Hochstadt**

OCBC

Industry: **Banks - Money Center**

Oversea-Chinese Banking Corporation (OCBC), Singapore's second-largest bank by capital, provides retail and investment banking, treasury operations, and stock brokerage at 114 branches in 11 countries, including the Philippines, Malaysia, the United States, and China. OCBC operates 218 automated-teller machines (ATMs). These machines constitute the largest ATM network in Singapore. It also offers services in life insurance, unit-trust fund management, and real estate. The bank's subsidiaries include the Singapore-based Bank of Singapore, Four Seas Bank, and Focal Finance.

S$ mil	12/92	12/93	12/94	US$mil 12/94				
Revenues	**2,291.0**	**2,136.8**	**2,335.7**	**1,537.7**	P/E Ratio	**26.4**	Price (9/30/95)	**16.10**
Net Income	**295.5**	**434.3**	**646.1**	**425.3**	P/B Ratio	**3.3**	52 Wk Hi-Low	**17.40-12.10**
Book Value	**3,249.2**	**3,643.7**	**4,335.1**	**2,969.2**	Yield %	**0.7**	Market Cap	**US$22,262mil**

Address **OCBC Ctr., 65 Chulia St.**
Singapore 0104
Tel **535-7222**
Fax **533-7955**
ADR
SEDOL No. **6663690**
Chief Executive **Tony Tan Keng Yam**
Chairman **Tony Tan Keng Yam**

Overseas Union Bank

Industry: **Banks - Money Center**

Overseas Union Bank (OUB) offers banking and financial services. It is the smallest of Singapore's Big Four banks. Its national division offers consumer-credit and banking services, and provides a variety of life-insurance products through a 50%-owned joint venture with Canada's Manulife Financial. The corporate division handles business-financing needs. OUB is also active in fund management, stockbroking, risk management, and underwriting. OUB operates 35 branches in Singapore and 13 in Malaysia. It has 12 other foreign offices, including two in China.

S$ mil	12/92	12/93	12/94	US$mil 12/94				
Revenues	**830.5**	**962.2**	**1,208.0**	**795.3**	P/E Ratio	**24.9**	Price (9/30/95)	**9.10**
Net Income	**106.5**	**163.4**	**218.6**	**143.9**	P/B Ratio	**2.4**	52 Wk Hi-Low	**9.30-7.35**
Book Value	**1,395.6**	**1,619.0**	**2,312.4**	**1,583.8**	Yield %	**1.0**	Market Cap	**US$10,374mil**

Address **OUB Centre, 1 Raffles Pl.**
Singapore 0104
Tel **533-8686**
Fax **533-2293**
ADR **OUBLY**
SEDOL No. **6664057**
President & CEO **Peter Seah Lim Huat**
Chairman **Dr. Lien Ying Chow**

Overseas Union Enterprise

Industry: **Lodging**

Overseas Union Enterprise manages hotels, rents commercial offices and shopping centers, and invests in a range of operating subsidiaries. Its main hotel operation is the Mandarin Singapore. Its three hotel-management subsidiaries opened four new hotels in 1994 and are scheduled to open three more in 1995. Its wholly-owned SMI Hospitality Services subsidiary manages service apartments, a health club, and two restaurants. Its subsidiary Hotel Investment (Hainan) is currently developing the Hainin Mandarin Hotel. Overseas Union Bank owns 26% of the company's share capital.

S$ mil	12/92	12/93	12/94	US$mil 12/94				
Sales	**152.0**	**152.3**	**166.0**	**109.3**	P/E Ratio	**32.1**	Price (9/30/95)	**7.20**
Net Income	**23.4**	**23.6**	**26.3**	**17.3**	P/B Ratio	**1.7**	52 Wk Hi-Low	**8.90-7.10**
Book Value	**465.6**	**522.9**	**538.8**	**369.0**	Yield %	**2.2**	Market Cap	**US$635.8mil**

Address **333 Orchard Rd.**
Singapore 0923
Tel **737-4411**
Fax **N/A**
ADR
SEDOL No. **6663827**
Managing Director **Lien Ying Chow**
Chairman **Lien Ying Chow**

Pacific Carriers

Industry: **Marine Transportation**

Pacific Carriers (PCL) is a marine-transport company that manages, charters, and trades ships, and owns and operates freight-trading businesses throughout the world. The company's fleet consists of 24 vessels, mainly dry-bulk carriers, with a capacity range of 4.2 to 138 billion dead-weight tonnes. It manages an additional 20 vessels for independent clients. Its joint venture, Pac Lines S.A., offers a parcel service for steel and steel products from Europe and South America to the Far East. The Kuok Group (Singapore) owns 36.6% of the company.

S$ mil	12/92	12/93	12/94	US$mil 12/94				
Sales	**111.8**	**141.1**	**133.8**	**88.1**	P/E Ratio	**30.2**	Price (9/30/95)	**1.36**
Net Income	**34.8**	**14.3**	**13.6**	**9.0**	P/B Ratio	**1.3**	52 Wk Hi-Low	**1.56-1.27**
Book Value	**331.9**	**325.1**	**316.5**	**216.8**	Yield %	**2.9**	Market Cap	**US$287.3mil**

Address **111 N. Bridge Rd., Peninsula Plz.** Tel **338-5000** ADR Managing Director **Tan Gim Hoe**
Singapore 0617 Fax **339-7609** SEDOL No. **6666688** Chairman **Teo Joo Kim**

Parkway

Industry: **Real-Estate Investment**

Parkway Holdings builds and manages private hospitals. It is also active in advertising and the management of commercial air and freight terminals. The firm owns Gleneagles Hospital, one of Singapore's largest hospitals. Parkway has entered into joint ventures to build hospitals in Malaysia and Indonesia. It also develops and invests in property in Hong Kong, and has interests in residential property in the United Kingdom and the United States. Parkway is currently constructing a fashion mart through a joint venture with the diversified holding company Hwa Hong.

S$ mil	12/92	12/93	12/94	US$mil 12/94				
Sales	**186.3**	**197.7**	**189.6**	**124.8**	P/E Ratio	**34.9**	Price (9/30/95)	**3.56**
Net Income	**22.6**	**50.3**	**32.0**	**21.1**	P/B Ratio	**1.2**	52 Wk Hi-Low	**3.80-3.06**
Book Value	**696.6**	**766.6**	**863.2**	**591.2**	Yield %	**1.4**	Market Cap	**US$707.7mil**

Address **80 Marine Parade Rd.** Tel **345-8822** ADR Managing Director **Tony Tan Choon Keat**
Singapore 1544 Fax **344-0366** SEDOL No. **6811143** Chairman **Tan Chin Nam**

QAF

Industry: **Other Food**

QAF manufactures and distributes food products, publishes newspapers, provides oil-field support services, and sells consumer products. QAF's food division, which accounts for 90% of sales, produces bread, frozen meat, spices, and canned food. The company retails these products through its Singapore-based Smart Supermarket chain. QAF is involved in joint ventures to distribute a variety of food products, including meat, fruits, and vegetables, in China and India. Its subsidiaries in Brunei publish newspapers, produce industrial gases, and distribute Saab cars.

S$ mil	03/92	03/93	03/94	US$mil 03/94				
Sales	**219.5**	**264.4**	**300.9**	**188.3**	P/E Ratio	**43.3**	Price (9/30/95)	**1.99**
Net Income	**6.3**	**12.3**	**14.1**	**8.8**	P/B Ratio	**5.1**	52 Wk Hi-Low	**1.99-1.40**
Book Value	**62.8**	**84.6**	**122.2**	**77.8**	Yield %	**1.0**	Market Cap	**US$438.1mil**

Address **510 Thomson Rd.** Tel **258-7888** ADR Managing Director **Wong Fong Fui**
Singapore 1129 Fax **258-4093** SEDOL No. **6091202** Chairman **Didi Dawis**

Republic Hotels & Resorts

Industry: **Lodging**

Republic Hotels & Resorts manages hotels and rental properties in Singapore and Malaysia. Two of the company's primary hotel holdings, King's Hotel Clarion and the Novotel Orchid, are located in Singapore. Another primary hotel holding, the Novotel Penang, is located in Malaysia. Another major property interest is the Tanglin Shopping Centre, in which Republic owns 111 stores and 10 commercial offices. It also owns 20% of a Chinese venture to develop the Suzhou International Commercial Center. Republic is 68% owned by Hong Kong's CDL Hotels International.

S$ mil	12/91	12/92	12/93	US$mil 12/93				
Sales	**55.4**	**58.1**	**57.1**	**35.4**	P/E Ratio	**29.0**	Price (9/30/95)	**1.68**
Net Income	**4.4**	**6.0**	**6.8**	**4.2**	P/B Ratio	**0.8**	52 Wk Hi-Low	**2.85-1.65**
Book Value	**161.1**	**166.9**	**168.3**	**104.5**	Yield %	**2.4**	Market Cap	**US$338.5mil**

Address **Anson Ctr., 51 Anson Rd.** Tel **220-7377** ADR President --
Singapore 0207 Fax **N/A** SEDOL No. **6490746** Chairman **Kwek Leng Beng**

Robinson and Co.

Industry: **Retailers - Broadline**

Robinson and Company manages chains of retail outlets and operates wholesale and advertising businesses. Its department stores include Robinsons, Marks & Spencer, and John Little. Marks & Spencer stores account for one third of the company's revenue and one half of its profit. It carries Marks & Spencer clothing in its Singapore and Malaysia outlets through an exclusive agreement with the U.K.-based company. Its John Little stores target the discount market; they sells sports apparel as well as casual and dress clothes for women, men, and children under the JL brand name.

S$ mil	06/93 R	06/94	06/95	US$mil 06/95				
Revenues	**197.7**	**208.7**	**215.5**	**145.3**	P/E Ratio	**12.6**	Price (9/30/95)	**6.00**
Net Income	**26.2**	**29.1**	**28.2**	**19.0**	P/B Ratio	**1.3**	52 Wk Hi-Low	**6.90-5.15**
Book Value	**228.9**	**249.5**	**268.8**	**192.0**	Yield %	**2.5**	Market Cap	**US$252.2mil**

Address **Centrepoint, 176 Orchard Rd.** Tel **733-0888** ADR Chief Executive **P.N. Husum**
Singapore 0923 Fax **732-7203** SEDOL No. **6744409** Chairman **Teo Cheng Guan**

R=Restated.

Rothmans Industries

Industry: **Tobacco**

Rothmans Industries produces and retails tobacco products for markets in Singapore, Thailand, Vietnam, Cambodia, and Myanmar (Burma). The firm's products include cigarettes, pipe tobacco, and cigars. Its brand names include Rothmans, Dunhill, Captain Black, Cartier, and Peter Stuyvesant. The company has manufacturing facilities in Myanmar, Vietnam, and Singapore. Its Rothmans of Pall Mall subsidiary is the first foreign company licensed to market tobacco products in Vietnam. U.K.-based Rothmans International holds a 50% stake in Rothmans Industries.

S$ mil	03/93	03/94	03/95	US$mil 03/95				
Sales	**218.8**	**261.6**	**249.7**	**168.4**	P/E Ratio	**17.5**	Price (9/30/95)	**5.70**
Net Income	**43.3**	**46.8**	**201.1**	**135.6**	P/B Ratio	**2.4**	52 Wk Hi-Low	**6.25-4.64**
Book Value	**239.6**	**101.1**	**270.8**	**192.1**	Yield %	**4.7**	Market Cap	**US$460.6mil**

Address **905 Bukit Timah Rd.** **Singapore 2158**
Tel **466-0077** Fax **469-3882**
ADR
SEDOL No. **6752275**
President --
Chairman **Alan Yeo Chee Yeow**

Sembawang Shipyard

Industry: **Shipbuilding**

Sembawang builds, repairs, and manages ships, and operates construction and engineering companies. The company's customers include Mobil Oil Singapore and Swedish marine-transport firm Wallenius. Sembawang provides engineering services to environmental, oil and gas, construction, and industrial markets. Its wholly-owned Sembawang Engineering subsidiary builds offshore platforms, mooring systems, and drilling modules. The company owns 50% of Sembawang Johnson Management, which manages 44 ships, including bulk carriers, tankers, and container vessels.

S$ mil	12/92	12/93	12/94	US$mil 12/94				
Sales	**707.9**	**666.1**	**1,105.2**	**727.6**	P/E Ratio	**20.3**	Price (9/30/95)	**7.45**
Net Income	**90.5**	**92.2**	**126.0**	**83.0**	P/B Ratio	**1.8**	52 Wk Hi-Low	**12.10-7.40**
Book Value	**757.9**	**851.3**	**916.6**	**627.8**	Yield %	**1.2**	Market Cap	**US$1,223.5mil**

Address **391A Orchard Rd. #18-00** **Ngee Ann City 0923**
Tel **735-2222** Fax **735-2006**
ADR **SBAWY**
SEDOL No. **6795128**
Managing Director **Er Kwong Wah**
Chairman **Philip Yeo**

Sime Singapore

Industry: **Overseas Trading**

Sime Singapore's operations include consumer services, engineering, and heavy-equipment retail. It also operates motor dealerships, and provides packaging-production, insurance, and real-estate services. Its consumer services include travel-agency operations, warehousing, and pharmaceuticals and food retailing. Its retail franchises include BMW, Ford, and Land Rover vehicles, Dunlop tires, Caterpillar machinery, Chubb security and fire-protection equipment, and Hertz car rentals. Sime Singapore is 69% owned by Malaysia's Sime Darby.

S$ mil	06/92	06/93	06/94	US$mil 06/94				
Sales	**522.7**	**498.2**	**554.8**	**351.4**	P/E Ratio	**18.2**	Price (9/30/95)	**1.04**
Net Income	**20.3**	**44.2**	**30.8**	**19.5**	P/B Ratio	**1.8**	52 Wk Hi-Low	**1.21-0.90**
Book Value	**263.8**	**293.8**	**310.4**	**204.2**	Yield %	**3.8**	Market Cap	**US$398.2mil**

Address **896 Dunearn Rd., #04-01** **Singapore 2158**
Tel **468-8880** Fax **469-0832**
ADR
SEDOL No. **6808888**
Managing Director **Yip Jon Khiam**
Chairman **M. Wong Pakshong**

Singapore Airlines

Industry: **Airlines**

Singapore Airlines (SIA) is a commercial airline that provides passenger and cargo services. It also operates aircraft-engineering and aircraft-maintenance services. The company's international network, centered in Southeast Asia, reaches 75 cities in 40 countries. Its fleet of 66 aircraft carries 10 million passengers and 550.5 million kilograms of cargo each year. SIA has an alliance with Swissair and Delta Air Lines, through which the companies make joint purchases and share airport facilities. SIA is Singapore's largest company by market capitalization.

S$ mil	03/93 R	03/94	03/95	US$mil 03/95				
Sales	**5,648.2**	**6,236.4**	**6,555.9**	**4,420.7**	P/E Ratio	**18.5**	Price (9/30/95)	**13.20**
Net Income	**850.6**	**801.7**	**917.5**	**618.7**	P/B Ratio	**1.9**	52 Wk Hi-Low	**15.00-11.80**
Book Value	**7,689.0**	**8,279.2**	**8,986.1**	**6,373.1**	Yield %	**1.2**	Market Cap	**US$43,443mil**

Address **Airline Hse., 25 Airline Rd.** **Singapore 1781**
Tel **542-3333** Fax **545-5034**
ADR
SEDOL No. **6811983**
Managing Director **Cheong Choong Kong**
Chairman **J.Y. Pillay**

R=Restated.

Singapore Bus Service

Industry: **Household Services**

Singapore Bus Service provides public-transportation and bus-chartering services. The company offers more than 200 bus routes and runs a fleet of 2,700 buses throughout Singapore. Ridership is approximately 906 million passenger trips per year. Its wholly-owned SBS Taxi and 96%-owned SABS Taxi subsidiaries maintain a combined fleet of 1,540 taxis. The company also operates commercial-vehicle service facilities. In July 1995, Singapore Bus Service merged its taxi operations with those of Singapore Technologies Automotive to form a joint-venture company, CityCab.

S$ mil	12/92	12/93	12/94	US$mil 12/94				
Sales	**450.7**	**473.7**	**502.4**	**330.7**	P/E Ratio	**9.6**	Price (9/30/95)	**9.40**
Net Income	**63.3**	**84.4**	**72.9**	**48.0**	P/B Ratio	**1.1**	52 Wk Hi-Low	**13.00-9.00**
Book Value	**518.8**	**597.8**	**665.2**	**455.6**	Yield %	**1.1**	Market Cap	**US$2,462.5mil**

Address **205 Braddell Rd.** **Singapore 2057**
Tel **284-8866** Fax **281-3267**
ADR
SEDOL No. **6810968**
Managing Director **Phua Tin How**
Chairman **Michael W.S. Lock**

Singapore Land

Industry: **Real-Estate Investment**

Singapore Land develops and manages commercial property. It owns four office towers in Singapore with a total of 1.9 million square feet of leaseable space. The company has a 44% stake in the Marina Square complex, which consists of three hotels, two department stores, a supermarket, and entertainment and mall complexes. Singapore Land also owns an office building in Glasgow; has a 20% interest in Aymet Singapore Land Turizm, a Turkish hotel and convention-center developer; and has a 20% stake in Orchid Lodge Company, a Thai hotel-development and -management company.

S$ mil	12/92	12/93	12/94	US$mil 12/94				
Sales	**164.3**	**146.6**	**132.1**	**87.0**	P/E Ratio	**32.5**	Price (9/30/95)	**8.25**
Net Income	**77.2**	**63.7**	**84.5**	**55.6**	P/B Ratio	**0.9**	52 Wk Hi-Low	**9.85-7.65**
Book Value	**2,003.0**	**2,064.6**	**3,272.9**	**2,241.7**	Yield %	**N/A**	Market Cap	**US$1,997.7mil**

Address **UIC Bldg., 5 Shenton Way** **Singapore 0106** Tel **222-9312** Fax **225-1004** ADR **SINPY** SEDOL No. **6811295** President & CEO **Lim Hock San** Chairman **S.P. Tao**

Singapore Petroleum

Industry: **Oil - Secondary**

Singapore Petroleum refines, distributes, and markets crude oil and petroleum products. It sells roughly 85 million barrels of oil per year. The company's facilities in Singapore include a residue catalytic cracker and a lubricant-blending plant. Fuel sales to Singapore's Public Utilities Board Seraya Power Station account for 15% of its sales. The company is also the largest supplier of fuel to Singapore's Changi Airport. Singapore Petroleum has supply and trading outlets in Tokyo, Hong Kong, and Oslo. It also has a joint venture to refine and market oil and gas in China.

S$ mil	12/92	12/93	12/94	US$mil 12/94				
Sales	**1,540.3**	**1,754.6**	**2,016.5**	**1,327.5**	P/E Ratio	**17.1**	Price (9/30/95)	**1.92**
Net Income	**41.0**	**55.8**	**47.5**	**31.3**	P/B Ratio	**1.6**	52 Wk Hi-Low	**3.10-1.82**
Book Value	**334.1**	**481.3**	**515.2**	**352.9**	Yield %	**1.6**	Market Cap	**US$1,078.3mil**

Address **DBS Bldg., 6 Shenton Way** **Singapore 0106** Tel **221-3166** Fax **221-3691** ADR SEDOL No. **6812403** President & CEO **Cheng Hong Kok** Chairman **Tan Boon Teik**

Singapore Press Holdings

Industry: **Publishing**

Singapore Press Holdings (SPH) prints and publishes newspapers and periodicals in English, Malay, and Chinese. The firm's newspaper-related operations account for nearly 95% of its sales. Its Singapore-based Malay-language publications include The Sunday Times, Business Times, and The Straits Times. Other publications include The New Paper, which is printed in English, and Lianhe Zaobao, which is printed in Chinese. The publications' daily circulation is more than 1 million copies. It also offers electronic information services through Audiotex and Newslink.

S$ mil	08/92	08/93	08/94	US$mil 08/94				
Sales	**607.4**	**661.0**	**767.5**	**491.4**	P/E Ratio	**20.2**	Price (9/30/95)	**21.80**
Net Income	**192.7**	**226.3**	**304.2**	**194.8**	P/B Ratio	**5.0**	52 Wk Hi-Low	**23.08-17.58**
Book Value	**753.4**	**927.1**	**1,179.7**	**786.5**	Yield %	**1.0**	Market Cap	**US$10,552mil**

Address **News Ctr., 82 Genting Ln.** **Singapore 1334** Tel **743-8800** Fax **744-9949** ADR SEDOL No. **6811745** Chief Executive **Denis Tay Koon Tek** Chairman **Lim Kim San**

Singapore Technologies Aerospace

Industry: **Aerospace & Defense**

Singapore Technologies Aerospace (formerly Singapore Aerospace) manufactures aircraft components, and provides aircraft-maintenance and engineering services to such customers as Boeing, McDonnell Douglas, the United States Navy, and Netherlands-based Fokker. Its Singapore Aviation Services subsidiary provides aircraft maintenance in Singapore. Its foreign subsidiaries include Mobile Aerospace Engineering, which provides maintenance for commercial airlines in the U.S. and Airline Rotables, which provides component-management services in the United Kingdom.

S$ mil	12/92	12/93	12/94	US$mil 12/94				
Sales	**421.3**	**454.1**	**492.6**	**324.3**	P/E Ratio	**19.9**	Price (9/30/95)	**1.65**
Net Income	**24.0**	**30.7**	**17.7**	**11.7**	P/B Ratio	**1.2**	52 Wk Hi-Low	**2.80-1.60**
Book Value	**390.1**	**415.0**	**417.7**	**286.1**	Yield %	**2.4**	Market Cap	**US$2,393.8mil**

Address **540 Airport Rd., Paya Lebar** **Singapore 1953** Tel **287-1111** Fax **289-3235** ADR SEDOL No. **6807540** President **Boon Swan Foo** Chairman **Quek Poh Huat**

Straits Steamship Land

Industry: **Real-Estate Investment**

Straits Steamship Land, a member of the Keppel group, develops property and provides shipping, warehousing, transportation, and telecommunications services. Its real-estate division constructs, manages, and sells offices, hotels, health facilities, and retail and residential sites throughout Southeast Asia. The company operates its shipping and telecom interests through Steamers Maritime Holdings, in which it holds a 36% stake. The firm derives 65% of profit from its property division. It has operations in China, Malaysia, Australia, Indonesia, and Vietnam.

S$ mil	12/92	12/93	12/94	US$mil 12/94				
Sales	**67.8**	**59.1**	**198.4**	**130.6**	P/E Ratio	**32.5**	Price (9/30/95)	**3.90**
Net Income	**35.5**	**39.1**	**59.3**	**39.0**	P/B Ratio	**1.0**	52 Wk Hi-Low	**5.55-3.64**
Book Value	**1,112.4**	**1,387.0**	**2,127.4**	**1,457.1**	Yield %	**0.8**	Market Cap	**US$1,432.7mil**

Address **Ocean Bldg., 10 Collyer Quay** **Singapore 0104** Tel **535-0066** Fax **535-0996** ADR SEDOL No. **6853468** Managing Director **Lim Chee Onn** Chairman **Sim Kee Boon**

Straits Trading

Industry: **Overseas Trading**

Straits Trading, a member of the OCBC group, processes, sells, and distributes tin, and manages property through its subsidiaries in Singapore and Malaysia. Its holdings include mines, plantations, office buildings, and residential developments. The firm also purchases, smelts, and warehouses tin concentrates in Malaysia through its 37.5%-owned Malaysia Smelting affiliate (MSC). Straits Trading's wholly-owned Sword Properties subsidiary owns a hotel and recreational facility in Perth, Australia. The Oversea-Chinese Banking Corporation has 32.5% interest in Straits Trading.

S$ mil	12/92	12/93	12/94	US$mil 12/94				
Sales	**162.7**	**209.6**	**240.1**	**158.1**	P/E Ratio	**33.6**	Price (9/30/95)	**3.26**
Net Income	**47.0**	**74.0**	**80.0**	**52.7**	P/B Ratio	**1.2**	52 Wk Hi-Low	**4.06-2.96**
Book Value	**716.9**	**763.0**	**787.7**	**539.5**	Yield %	**4.0**	Market Cap	**US$681.8mil**

Address **Straits Trading Bldg., 9 Battery Rd.** Tel **535-4722** ADR Chief Executive **Howe Yoon Chong**
Singapore 0104 Fax **532-7939** SEDOL No. **6853521** Chairman **Howe Yoon Chong**

Tat Lee Bank

Industry: **Banks - Regional**

Tat Lee Bank is Singapore's fifth-largest bank, with assets totalling more than S$7.5 billion. It provides a variety of financial services, including general banking, nominee services, investment trading, gold and futures dealing, stock and securities brokerage, insurance, and property development. Tat Lee Bank has 27 branches in Singapore, as well as offices in Jakarta, Tokyo, Hong Kong, Beijing, and Bangkok. Its ATM network includes 77 machines. The bank's China Walden Venture Investments joint venture with U.S.-based Walden invests in developing industries in China.

S$ mil	12/92	12/93	12/94	US$mil 12/94				
Revenues	**242.3**	**337.9**	**433.1**	**285.1**	P/E Ratio	**30.1**	Price (9/30/95)	**3.76**
Net Income	**29.9**	**46.5**	**53.7**	**35.4**	P/B Ratio	**1.8**	52 Wk Hi-Low	**4.01-3.25**
Book Value	**549.7**	**865.2**	**900.9**	**617.1**	Yield %	**1.7**	Market Cap	**US$1,210.7mil**

Address **63 Market St.** Tel **533-9292** ADR President & CEO **Goh Eng Chew**
Singapore 0104 Fax **533-1043** SEDOL No. **6875406** Chairman **Goh Eng Chew**

Times Publishing

Industry: **Publishing**

Times Publishing's core businesses are publishing, commercial printing, marketing, and distribution. The company has printing facilities in Singapore, Malaysia, Hong Kong, and the United Kingdom. Its books and magazines are also distributed and retailed in Germany, Thailand, Indonesia, Japan, Australia, and the United States. The company also operates 43 bookstores in Singapore, Malaysia, Brunei, and Indonesia. Times Publishing's Australian subsidiaries distribute and market home-entertainment products such as videocassettes and compact discs.

S$ mil	08/92	08/93	08/94	US$mil 08/94				
Sales	**494.7**	**430.8**	**475.4**	**304.4**	P/E Ratio	**13.5**	Price (9/30/95)	**3.30**
Net Income	**24.9**	**21.4**	**29.7**	**19.0**	P/B Ratio	**0.9**	52 Wk Hi-Low	**4.08-3.20**
Book Value	**458.1**	**453.8**	**469.2**	**312.8**	Yield %	**3.0**	Market Cap	**US$282.7mil**

Address **1 New Industrial Rd.** Tel **284-8844** ADR President & CEO **Kua Hong Pak**
Singapore 1953 Fax **284-4733** SEDOL No. **6891855** Chairman **Lim Kim San**

United Industrial

Industry: **Real-Estate Investment**

United Industrial (UIC) is a property, manufacturing, and electronics group. It invests in commercial property; manufactures electronic systems, detergents, toiletry products, and packaging materials; distributes computers; and operates travel and cargo-shipping services. UIC has stakes in rental office space in Singapore, Turkey, the United Kingdom, and Canada. It has interests in hotel operations in Thailand and China. It also owns 56% of property-developer Singapore Land and operates Beijing United Computer Systems in partnership with China's government.

S$ mil	12/92	12/93	12/94	US$mil 12/94				
Sales	**357.8**	**315.1**	**303.3**	**199.7**	P/E Ratio	**21.7**	Price (9/30/95)	**1.26**
Net Income	**39.5**	**81.4**	**1.2**	**0.8**	P/B Ratio	**0.8**	52 Wk Hi-Low	**1.52-1.10**
Book Value	**1,328.0**	**1,398.1**	**2,132.1**	**1,460.3**	Yield %	**0.8**	Market Cap	**US$1,399.2mil**

Address **UIC Bldg., 5 Shenton Way** Tel **220-1352** ADR President & CEO **Lim Hock San**
Singapore 0106 Fax **224-0278** SEDOL No. **6916532** Chairman **Wee Cho Yaw**

United Overseas Bank

Industry: **Banks - Regional**

United Overseas Bank (UOB) offers banking and financial services, including commercial and merchant banking, stock brokerage, fund management, derivatives and precious-metals trading, and insurance. The company's banking network includes UOB, Chung Khiaw Bank, Lee Wah Bank, Far Eastern Bank, and Industrial & Commercial Bank. UOB operates 78 branches in Singapore and 59 offices abroad--the largest network among Singapore-incorporated banks. UOB also owns 22% of United Overseas Land, a Singapore property- and hotel-development company.

S$ mil	12/92	12/93	12/94	US$mil 12/94				
Revenues	**1,827.9**	**2,039.7**	**2,391.9**	**1,574.7**	P/E Ratio	**15.6**	Price (9/30/95)	**12.30**
Net Income	**300.8**	**456.6**	**601.3**	**395.9**	P/B Ratio	**2.5**	52 Wk Hi-Low	**14.60-10.83**
Book Value	**2,653.3**	**3,040.5**	**3,681.3**	**2,521.5**	Yield %	**1.2**	Market Cap	**US$17,640mil**

Address **UOB Plz., 80 Raffles Place** Tel **533-9898** ADR **UOVEY** President **Wong Yuen Weng**
Singapore 0104 Fax **534-2334** SEDOL No. **6916770** Chairman & CEO **Wee Cho Yaw**

WBL Corporation

Industry: **Industrial - Diversified**

WBL Corporation (formerly Wearne Brothers) manufactures agricultural, industrial, and electronic products. It also distributes automotive and industrial products and develops offices, industrial parks, and residential properties. Its technology and manufacturing division produces agricultural and chemical equipment, building materials, and electronic components. The firm also sells luxury cars, trucks, and industrial equipment. It has a 87% stake in Wearnes International, which has operations in commercial and industrial materials.

S$ mil	09/92	09/93	09/94	US$mil 09/94				
Sales	**959.5**	**906.2**	**834.0**	**537.0**	P/E Ratio	**18.4**	Price (9/30/95)	**3.42**
Net Income	**-39.0**	**-17.3**	**8.3**	**5.3**	P/B Ratio	**1.3**	52 Wk Hi-Low	**3.80-2.90**
Book Value	**362.5**	**328.8**	**291.0**	**196.6**	Yield %	**1.5**	Market Cap	**US$273.6mil**

Address **OCBC Ctr., 65 Chulia St.**
Singapore 0104
Tel **533-3444**
Fax **534-1443**
ADR
SEDOL No. **6944908**
President --
Chairman **Tang I-Fang**

Wing Tai

Industry: **Home Construction**

Wing Tai manufactures and retails clothing, trades fabric, and invests in and develops property. Its garment-retailing division operates 36 Stock-Mart stores in Singapore, Malaysia, and Brunei, as well as the G2000 and U2 clothing chains. It retails such brand names as Domani, Bosmar, and City Jeans. Wing Tai also has property interests in Singapore and Malaysia, including the Inchcape House office building, the Cherryhill condominium project, and the Maplewood residential development. The firm currently has three commercial and residential development projects in China.

S$ mil	06/92 R	06/93	06/94	US$mil 06/94				
Sales	**202.1**	**167.8**	**211.7**	**134.1**	P/E Ratio	**25.7**	Price (9/30/95)	**2.42**
Net Income	**14.7**	**20.7**	**38.7**	**24.5**	P/B Ratio	**1.4**	52 Wk Hi-Low	**3.00-2.02**
Book Value	**425.1**	**435.9**	**936.9**	**616.4**	Yield %	**1.2**	Market Cap	**US$1,071.0mil**

Address **107 Tampines Rd.**
Singapore 1953
Tel **280-9111**
Fax **286-8338**
ADR
SEDOL No. **6972385**
Managing Director **Cheng Wai Keung**
Chairman **Edgar Cheng Wai Kin**

R=Restated.

Yeo Hiap Seng

Industry: **Other Food**

Yeo Hiap Seng (YHS) manufactures, distributes, and markets food and beverages worldwide. Its brand-name products include Yeo's beverages and Chun King oriental foods. YHS is the sole manifacturer and distributor of Pepsi, Schweppes, Mirinda, and Seven-Up products in Singapore and Malaysia. It is also the sole distributor of Budweiser in Singapore, Malaysia, and Hong Kong. Its other products include chrysanthemum tea, and beef and chicken curries. The company markets its products throughout the Far East, the Middle East, and North America.

S$ mil	12/92	12/93	12/94	US$mil 12/94				
Sales	**265.7**	**266.6**	**262.6**	**172.9**	P/E Ratio	**NMF**	Price (9/30/95)	**5.35**
Net Income	**6.6**	**3.1**	**-42.7**	**-28.1**	P/B Ratio	**1.8**	52 Wk Hi-Low	**5.40-3.12**
Book Value	**219.3**	**214.4**	**422.2**	**289.2**	Yield %	**0.7**	Market Cap	**US$535.4mil**

Address **950 Dunearn Rd.**
Singapore 2158
Tel **466-2266**
Fax **466-4641**
ADR
SEDOL No. **6986160**
Managing Director **Alex Meng Wah Chan**
Chairman **Yip Yan Wong**

South Africa

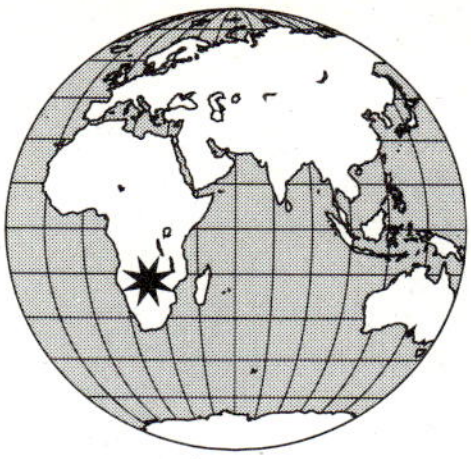

South Africa

Matthew Curtin,
Johannesburg

Local Trading Hours	Time Difference from New York	Population (Est. 10/94)
9:30-4:30	6 hours ahead of EST	40,650,000

The Johannesburg Stock Exchange (JSE) has gained significantly in stature in the past year as a mixture of political change, economic reform and regulatory upheaval in South Africa galvanized foreign and domestic interest in the bourse.

South Africa's successful transition to democracy and the lifting of sanctions — particularly those preventing U.S. investors buying South African equities, and the deregulation of the stock market — promise to entrench the JSE's position as the preeminent exchange on the African continent and a leading emerging market bourse.

The JSE itself dislikes the emerging market tag, and fancies itself as a "re-emerging" market. The bourse opened its doors for trading in 1887, boasts more than 640 companies, and in July this year was the world's 12th largest stock exchange with a market capitalization of $241 billion.

However, the JSE acknowledges that until this year its potential was hobbled by South Africa's exchange controls, a vestige of the country's political troubles in the mid-1980s which has led to the bourse's dubious distinction of being one of the world's most illiquid stock markets.

Controls, which required foreigners to buy and sell shares through the financial rand mechanism, deterred offshore investment and prevented the bourse from embracing fully fledged reform akin to the "Big Bang" on the London Stock Exchange in 1986.

Foreign investors are no longer restricted by exchange controls. But until government abolished them on March 10, 1995, the JSE was planning only slow reform, after commissioning a research report to investigate how the bourse might be restructured.

That go-slow approach frustrated local merchant banks, which at one stage considered setting up a rival bourse. Those plans fell away when the JSE committed itself to far-reaching changes once exchange controls were relaxed.

Dow Jones South Africa Equity Market Index Performance

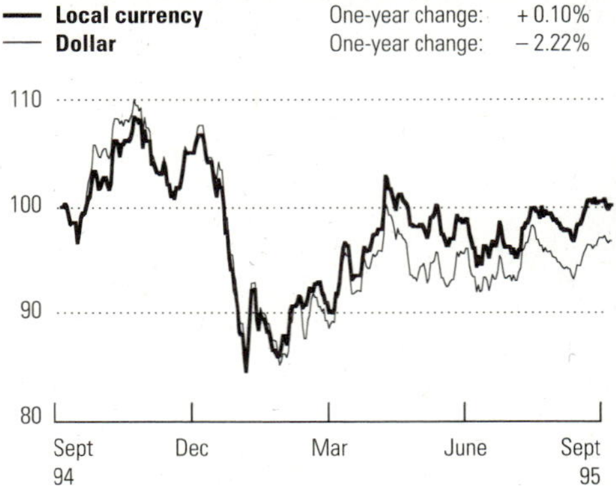

The JSE's big bang was to occur on Nov. 8, 1995, following approval by the bourse's board of changes to JSE regulations, coupled with a

Gross Domestic Product (94)	Three-Year GDP Growth (92-94)	Main Industries	Consumer Price Index (94)	Monetary Unit	Exchange Rate (9/95)
$110 billion	+1%	Mining, agriculture, manufacturing, energy, banking and insurance, retailing	+ 9.1%	Rand	Rand3.65 to US$1.00

number of legislative amendments. The thrust of the reforms is to bring the JSE into line with international standards.

A major development is the opening up of the JSE's membership to outsiders, allowing foreign, non-stockbroking, and corporate membership with limited liability.

It's a change that has been seized upon by a number of stock brokerages and international finance houses.

James Capel & Co., Deutsche Morgan Grenfell, SmithNewcourt PLC, Robert Fleming Holdings Ltd., and Natwest Securities Ltd. are among the international companies that have taken stakes in local stock brokerages. South African merchant banks have also entered the fray, either by buying stock brokerages, or setting up their own equity operations.

But change is also on its way for how the JSE operates. In 1996, the reforms will lead to the introduction of dual capacity trading, with members able to deal as a principal or agent, subject to the disclosure of the capacity in which they are acting.

The JSE will also install an order-driven automated trading system, which is likely to lead to the demise of the bourse's trading floor and open-outcry system of share dealings.

Brokerage rates will also become fully negotiable next year. Currently there is a fixed scale for transactions of less than 3 million rand, with negotiable fees allowed only for larger deals.

Ten Largest Capitalized Companies
as of 9/30/95

Stock	Market Cap. US$Mil
Anglo American	12,913,508.2
DeBeers Consolidated Mines	10,286,368.2
South African Breweries	8,630,072.6
Foschini	6,010,630.1
Liberty Life Association	5,909,837.7
Sasol	5,214,961.6
Gencor	5,127,483.2
Rembrandt	4,361,917.8
Standard Bank Investment	4,065,692.5
Liberty Holdings	3,090,356.2

The bourse plans to move to a rolling settlement from a fixed settlement system, with a central depository to be set up to hold share certificates in line with the planned electronic share registry and payments system.

In a separate development, the government has removed a 15% non-resident shareholders' tax on dividends declared on or after Oct. 1, 1995. The JSE continues to campaign for the lifting of a 1% marketable securities tax on share transactions.

There are just two clouds immediately on the JSE's horizon. One is that government is committed to only a slow relaxation of exchange controls on resident South Africans, which prevent domestic institutional and individual investors from investing abroad. Initial relaxation introduced in July allows institutions to swap South African assets for foreign securities with foreign counter parties, with central bank approval.

However, the JSE's liquidity is likely to be constrained until free movement of capital is allowed. Full liberalization of exchange controls is being held back by the low level of South Africa's foreign exchange reserves, currently equivalent to around six weeks of import cover, which might be put at risk by a sudden outflow of funds.

The initial relaxation also promotes contributing to the economic empowerment of the black majority. The JSE is encouraging companies raising funds specifically for the government's reconstruction and development program, aimed at improving living standards for South Africa's blacks, to list on the exchange.

The bourse has long been a symbol of the control South Africa's white-owned companies hold over the private sector, with the JSE buildings being a favorite destination for trade union marches. Just 11 companies on the JSE are in black hands, and several have been listed only recently.

The other cloud is debate about future antitrust policy. Government is in the process of drawing up draft competition legislation, which some business people fear will reflect recent criticism by Trade and Industry Minister Trevor Manuel and Cyril Ramaphosa, secretary-general of the African National Congress, the alleged stranglehold South Africa's conglomerates have over the economy.

Five family and institutional groups control four fifths of companies listed on the JSE, with companies controlled by Anglo American Corp. of South Africa, the country's biggest mining industrial group, accounting for around a third of the JSE's market capitalization.

These uncertainties aside, good trading volumes and steady performance of stocks amid strong foreign demand for shares this year are signs of the confidence international investors have in the South African economy and the bourse itself.

The value of shares traded in the JSE's financial year ended Feb. 28, 1995, rose nearly 60% to a record high of 61.9 billion rand from 39.5 billion rand in 1994.

JSE figures show that through most of 1995 there was strong offshore buying, with net purchases by foreigners up to Sept. 8 standing at 3.92 billion rand against 516.3 million rand in the same period in 1994.

Also significant is the JSE's inclusion in important emerging market indices, used as benchmarks by international portfolio investors to guide their investment decisions. The JSE was included in the Morgan Stanley

Capital International and International Finance Corp. emerging market indices in March this year, with a weighting of 16% and 25% respectively, and in the Dow Jones World Stock Index on Oct. 1.

Foreign interest has been concentrated in blue chip industrial shares, which have shown impressive earnings growth as the South African economy has recovered, showing average growth in gross domestic production of 3% in the past two years.

Mining and industrial shares have climbed steadily since February when the fallout on emerging market investment sentiment after Mexico's currency crisis in December 1994 faded, but a persistent weak spot on the JSE has been the gold mining sector. Dull bullion prices, a relatively strong rand, and persistent labor troubles have combined to put investors off the shares.

By September 1995, the JSE's All Gold Index had fallen by a quarter since the start of the year, but industrial shares had returned to record highs set in January and February.

AECI

Industry: **Specialty Chemicals**

AECI is one of South Africa's major industrial groups. Its holdings include 40%-owned Polifin, a joint venture with Sasol that manufactures plastics, chlor-alkali, and organic chemicals. AECI also owns 51% of AECI Explosives, a joint venture with Imperial Chemical Industries (U.K.) that makes explosives for the mining industry. In addition, the group produces fertilizers and high-quality industrial yarns. AECI has a joint venture to produce lysine, an amino acid used in animal feed. The domestic market accounts for 85% of sales.

	R mil 12/92	12/93	12/94	US$mil 12/94				
Sales	**5,359.0**	**5,968.0**	**5,547.0**	**1,563.4**	P/E Ratio	**12.9**	Price (9/30/95)	**24.00**
Net Income	**164.0**	**237.0**	**287.0**	**80.9**	P/B Ratio	**1.6**	52 Wk Hi-Low	**34.00-24.00**
Book Value	**2,004.0**	**2,199.0**	**2,308.0**	**652.0**	Yield %	**2.8**	Market Cap	**US$1,017.0mil**

Address **Office Twr., Carlton Ctr.** **Johannesburg 2000**
Tel **011-223-9111**
Fax **011-223-1456**
ADR **AECLY**
SEDOL No. **6009205**
Managing Director **N.C. Axelson**
Chairman **M.A. Sander**

African Oxygen

Industry: **Specialty Chemicals**

African Oxygen (Afrox) manufactures and markets gases, welding equipment, fluid-handling devices, and other specialized industrial products. The company sells and rents its products through 78 trading outlets under the Handigas brand name. Its healthcare division has interests in 14 private hospitals in the country, and the company distributes its products directly to these hospitals. Afrox's liquified petroleum gas (LPG) interests make it the southern Africa's leading distributor of LPG. BOC Holdings of the United Kingdom owns nearly 58% of Afrox's share capital.

	R mil 09/92	09/93	09/94	US$mil 09/94				
Sales	**1,113.2**	**1,209.9**	**1,439.2**	**410.1**	P/E Ratio	**31.6**	Price (9/30/95)	**124.00**
Net Income	**94.3**	**115.6**	**124.8**	**35.6**	P/B Ratio	**4.9**	52 Wk Hi-Low	**124.00-95.00**
Book Value	**686.0**	**748.3**	**760.0**	**212.9**	Yield %	**1.9**	Market Cap	**US$1,017.7mil**

Address **Afrox Hse., 23 Webber St.** **Selby, Johannesburg 2001**
Tel **011-490-0400**
Fax **011-493-8828**
ADR
SEDOL No. **6009506**
Managing Director **Royden T. Vice**
Chairman **Royden T. Vice**

Amalgamated Beverage Industries

Industry: **Soft Drinks**

Amalgamated Beverage Industries (ABI) produces and distributes carbonated soft drinks. It operates five bottling plants that produce beverages under franchise licenses with Coca-Cola, Schweppes, and Sparletta. Its brand names include Coca-Cola, Diet Coke, Tab, Fanta, Sprite, Iron Brew, Lemon Twist, and Granadilla. ABI provides beverages, coolers, and sign-writing services to more than 23,000 soft-drink shops and similar small outlets. ABI is 68%-owned by beverage and leisure company South African Breweries, South Africa's largest brewer.

	R mil 03/91	03/92	03/93	US$mil 03/93				
Sales	**884.3**	**1,045.4**	**1,157.4**	**396.4**	P/E Ratio	**23.7**	Price (9/30/95)	**18.25**
Net Income	**58.7**	**71.6**	**84.0**	**28.8**	P/B Ratio	**5.5**	52 Wk Hi-Low	**22.50-17.25**
Book Value	**266.7**	**309.5**	**349.2**	**110.2**	Yield %	**2.1**	Market Cap	**US$530.0mil**

Address **14 Pongola Crescent** **Sandton 2199**
Tel **011-333-8181**
Fax **011-337-5522**
ADR
SEDOL No. **6023573**
Managing Director **H.A. Reid**
Chairman **R.L. Lloyd**

Anglo-Alpha

Industry: **Building Materials**

Anglo-Alpha manufactures cement, construction materials, ready-mix concrete, lime, limestone products, industrial minerals, and paper bags. The company's other activities include the manufacture of fly ash, plastic bags, fertilizer, and explosives. It operates eight cement factories that have a combined average production capacity of 3.6 million tons each year. The company also has 32 ready-mix concrete facilities that have a production capacity of 1.2 million cubic meters annually. Anglo-Alpha is 30%-owned by Switzerland-based cement producer Holderbank Financière Glaris.

	R mil 12/92	12/93	12/94	US$mil 12/94				
Sales	**757.0**	**877.2**	**1,140.5**	**321.4**	P/E Ratio	**21.0**	Price (9/30/95)	**117.00**
Net Income	**45.5**	**80.6**	**115.9**	**32.7**	P/B Ratio	**3.7**	52 Wk Hi-Low	**120.00-93.00**
Book Value	**784.8**	**857.2**	**962.6**	**271.9**	Yield %	**1.8**	Market Cap	**US$964.1mil**

Address **94 Rivonia Rd.** **Sandton 2199**
Tel **011-780-1000**
Fax **011-783-8950**
ADR
SEDOL No. **6032201**
Managing Director **J.G. Pretorius**
Chairman **P. Byland**

Anglo American

Industry: **Precious Metals**

Anglo American Corporation of South Africa is the country's largest mining finance group, investing in gold, diamond, coal, platinum, and base-metal production. It owns 20% of De Beers Consolidated Mines and 18% of De Beers Centenary. Other associate companies include Johannesburg Consolidated Investment and Europe-based mining company Minorco. The company also has major interests in steel, paper, chemicals, motor manufacturing, food processing, real estate, banking, and insurance. Anglo American earns 35% of its investment income outside of South Africa.

	R mil 03/93	03/94	03/95	US$mil 03/95				
Sales	**1,466.0**	**2,477.0**	**2,949.0**	**824.4**	P/E Ratio	**23.0**	Price (9/30/95)	**202.50**
Net Income	**1,692.0**	**1,681.0**	**2,057.0**	**575.1**	P/B Ratio	**2.1**	52 Wk Hi-Low	**247.00-183.00**
Book Value	**18,304.0**	**20,349.0**	**22,475.0**	**6,277.9**	Yield %	**2.3**	Market Cap	**US$12,914mil**

Address **44 Main St.** **Johannesburg 2001**
Tel **011-638-9111**
Fax **011-638-2455**
ADR **ANGLY**
SEDOL No. **6032524**
President **--**
Chairman **J. Ogilvie Thompson**

Anglo American Coal

Industry: **Coal**

Anglo American Coal Corporation (Amcoal) is a private-sector coal-mining group. It operates eight plants, four of which supply steam coal for power generation to Eskom, which supplies 90% of the electricity generated in South Africa. In the year ended March 1995, Amcoal produced 45.7 million tons of coal. The firm's Verref division produces refractory and building materials, including ceramic tiles, clay pipes and fittings, and concrete roof tiles. Anglo American Corporation of South Africa owns 51.5% of Amcoal.

	R mil 03/93	03/94	03/95	US$mil 03/95				
Sales	**1,941.9**	**1,926.9**	**2,261.5**	**632.2**	P/E Ratio	**17.1**	Price (9/30/95)	**264.00**
Net Income	**461.9**	**255.7**	**389.7**	**108.9**	P/B Ratio	**3.1**	52 Wk Hi-Low	**290.00-200.00**
Book Value	**1,768.0**	**1,897.7**	**2,121.2**	**592.5**	Yield %	**2.5**	Market Cap	**US$1,822.1mil**

Address **44 Main St. Johannesburg 2001** Tel **011-638-5428** Fax **011-638-9111** ADR **ANAMY** SEDOL No. **6032342** Managing Director **K.J. Trueman** Chairman **D. Rankin**

Anglo American Gold

Industry: **Precious Metals**

Anglo American Gold Investment Company (Amgold) is an investment-holding company with interests in gold and uranium mines in South Africa, Namibia, and Mali. It main assets are a 3% interest in Minorco, a natural resources concern, and an 11% interest in Gold Fields of South Africa. Its other investments include a 19% interest in Free State Consolidated Gold Mines, a 19% interest in Vaal Reefs Exploration and Mining Company, and a 12% interest in Driefontein Consolidated. Anglo American Corporation of South Africa owns 50% of the company's share capital.

	R mil 03/93	03/94	03/95	US$mil 03/95				
Sales	**N/A**	**500.0**	**599.0**	**167.5**	P/E Ratio	**14.5**	Price (9/30/95)	**330.00**
Net Income	**248.0**	**466.0**	**548.0**	**153.2**	P/B Ratio	**6.0**	52 Wk Hi-Low	**483.00-296.00**
Book Value	**968.0**	**1,108.0**	**1,318.0**	**368.2**	Yield %	**4.2**	Market Cap	**US$2,183.2mil**

Address **44 Main St. Johannesburg 2001** Tel **011-638-9111** Fax **011-638-2455** ADR SEDOL No. **6032643** President -- Chairman **N.F. Oppenheimer**

Anglo American Industrial

Industry: **Steel**

Anglo American Industrial Corporation (AMIC) is a diversified industrial-holding company with interests in iron, steel, aluminum, chemicals, mining, paper, forest products, electronics, furniture, and construction businesses. It has a 40% equity interest in AECI, a South African industrial group, and a 35% interest in McCarthy Group, a diversified retailer. Through its 44% interest in the Tongaat-Hulett Group, AMIC produces sugar and consumer foods, textiles, building materials, and aluminum. Anglo American Corporation of South Africa owns 48% of AMIC.

	R mil 12/92	12/93	12/94	US$mil 12/94				
Sales	**6,782.0**	**8,789.0**	**16,938.0**	**4,774.0**	P/E Ratio	**15.9**	Price (9/30/95)	**176.00**
Net Income	**354.0**	**476.0**	**730.0**	**205.7**	P/B Ratio	**1.9**	52 Wk Hi-Low	**222.50-167.00**
Book Value	**4,238.0**	**4,866.0**	**6,014.0**	**1,698.9**	Yield %	**2.6**	Market Cap	**US$3,145.0mil**

Address **44 Main St. Johannesburg 2001** Tel **011-638-3221** Fax **011-638-9111** ADR SEDOL No. **6033301** President -- Chairman **Leslie Boyd**

Anglo American Investment Trust

Industry: **Precious Metals**

Anglo American Investment Trust (Anamint) is an investment-holding company with interests in diamond-trading concerns. Its major assets are a 26% interest in De Beers Consolidated Mines and a 23% interest in De Beers Centenary AG. Anamint's other investments are privately-owned South African diamond companies. They include 10% of Cymberline's common equity and 100% of its preference shares, 19% of The Diamond Purchasing and Trading Company, 19% of The Diamond Trading Company, and 13% of Industrial Distributors common equity and 30% of its preference shares.

	R mil 03/93	03/94	03/95	US$mil 03/95				
Sales	**N/A**	**384.0**	**409.0**	**114.3**	P/E Ratio	**25.9**	Price (9/30/95)	**103.00**
Net Income	**312.0**	**372.0**	**397.0**	**111.0**	P/B Ratio	**2.0**	52 Wk Hi-Low	**115.00-88.00**
Book Value	**4,267.0**	**4,740.0**	**5,194.0**	**1,450.8**	Yield %	**3.9**	Market Cap	**US$2,821.9mil**

Address **44 Main St. Johannesburg 2001** Tel **011-638-9111** Fax **011-638-2455** ADR SEDOL No. **6033527** President -- Chairman **J. Ogilvie Thompson**

Anglovaal

Industry: **Financial Services - Diversified**

Anglovaal Ltd. is an industrial and mining holding company. Its industrial interests include engineering, textile, packaging, cement, food, and consumer-goods companies. Anglovaal holds a 60% stake in Anglovaal Industries, which in turn owns 60% of Consol, a glass, paper, and plastics maker, and 65% of National Brands, maker of biscuits and other food products. The firm's mining division owns a 54% interest in Middle Witwatersrand, a precious-metals and coal-mining firm. Anglovaal also provides management-consulting services to its mining units.

	R mil 06/92	06/93	06/94	US$mil 06/94				
Revenues	**8,205.8**	**8,509.5**	**9,969.1**	**2,883.7**	P/E Ratio M	**23.8**	Price (9/30/95) M	**135.00**
Net Income	**262.3**	**286.5**	**351.7**	**101.7**	P/B Ratio M	**0.8**	52 Wk Hi-Low M	**143.00-103.00**
Book Value	**2,328.9**	**2,558.2**	**3,168.2**	**868.0**	Yield % M	**0.9**	Market Cap M	**US$665.8mil**

Address **Anglovaal Hse., 56 Main St. Johannesburg 2001** Tel **011-634-9111** Fax **011-634-0038** ADR **ANAVY** SEDOL No. **6041122** Managing Director **Basil E. Hersov** Chairman **Basil E. Hersov**

M=Multiple issues in index; reflects most active.

Barlows

Industry: **Conglomerates**

Barlow focuses on infrastructural businesses. In October 1993, Barlow Rand, formerly South Africa's largest industrial company, split into five independent companies: Barlow, C.G. Smith, Reunert, Rand Mines, and Rand Mine Properties. Barlow's subsidiaries produce steel tubes, paint, cement, earthmoving equipment, consumer durables, and construction supplies. Its wholly-owned subsidiary Barlow Motor Investments is South Africa's second-largest motor-vehicle retailing group. It also owns Plascon, which ranks among the world's 20 largest paint manufacturers.

	R mil 09/92	09/93	09/94	US$mil 09/94				
Sales	**35,165.0**	**37,978.0**	**12,873.6**	**3,668.7**	P/E Ratio	**24.2**	Price (9/30/95)	**41.25**
Net Income	**475.0**	**623.0**	**372.3**	**106.1**	P/B Ratio	**2.7**	52 Wk Hi-Low	**41.25-28.75**
Book Value	**4,487.0**	**4,759.0**	**3,087.0**	**864.7**	Yield %	**1.4**	Market Cap	**US$2,253.6mil**

Address **Barlow Pk., Katherine St.** **Sandton 2146**
Tel **011-801-9111** Fax **011-444-3643**
ADR **BRRAY** SEDOL No. **6079123**
Managing Director **R.K.J Chambers** Chairman **Warren Clewlow**

Bateman Industrial

Industry: **Industrial - Diversified**

Bateman Industrial Corporation manufactures heavy construction and engineering equipment primarily for companies in the mining, chemicals, and infrastructure-construction industries. Its products include drill rigs, utility vehicles, and earth-moving equipment. The company is one of the main operating subsidiaries of South Africa's Edward L. Bateman, a process- and project-engineering company. Shares of Bateman Industrial began trading on the Johannesburg Stock Exchange in late 1994.

	R mil 06/92	06/93	06/94	US$mil 06/94				
Sales	**N/A**	**N/A**	**522.5**	**151.1**	P/E Ratio	**14.2**	Price (9/30/95)	**4.40**
Net Income	**N/A**	**N/A**	**15.4**	**4.5**	P/B Ratio	**7.3**	52 Wk Hi-Low	**6.00-4.20**
Book Value	**N/A**	**N/A**	**57.6**	**15.8**	Yield %	**1.8**	Market Cap	**US$115.7mil**

Address **Bartlett Rd.** **Boksburg 1460**
Tel **011-899-9111** Fax **011-892-1198**
ADR SEDOL No. **6082819**
CEO **H. Brereton** Chairman **H. Brereton**

Bidvest

Industry: **General Industrial & Commercial Services**

Bidvest Group is an investment-holding company with interests in distribution, service, and trading businesses. Its service subsidiaries offer linen and uniform rental, property and washroom cleaning, and pest-control services. Its trading subsidiaries manufacture and distribute bakery supplies, spices and seasonings, butchery equipment, packaging, and stationery products. The company's distribution network supplies frozen foods, groceries, and food-service equipment to the hospitality industry. Bidvest also offers sea and airfreight transport and warehousing services.

	R mil 06/92	06/93	06/94	US$mil 06/94				
Sales	**596.0**	**775.2**	**2,560.7**	**740.7**	P/E Ratio	**2.6**	Price (9/30/95)	**21.00**
Net Income	**21.1**	**40.2**	**91.6**	**26.5**	P/B Ratio	**0.4**	52 Wk Hi-Low	**21.00-16.00**
Book Value	**156.3**	**497.9**	**605.5**	**165.9**	Yield %	**13.1**	Market Cap	**US$617.9mil**

Address **Milner Pl., 4 Carse O'Gowrie Rd.** **Parktown 2193**
Tel **011-643-3042** Fax **011-643-4517**
ADR SEDOL No. **6100089**
President -- Chairman **Brian Joffe**

Clicks

Industry: **Other Specialty Retailers**

Clicks Group owns and manages three chains of retail outlets specializing in the sale of health, home beauty, and confectionery products. In addition to healthcare products, its stores also sell electrical goods, radios, cameras, stationery and paper products, toys, cleaners, kitchenware, and music cassettes and compact discs. The company operates 154 Clicks stores, 110 Diskom Stores, and 87 Musica stores throughout South Africa. Clicks' ultimate holding company is South Africa's Premier Group, which directly and indirectly owns 48% of the company.

	R mil 04/93	04/94	04/95	US$mil 04/95				
Revenues	**949.8**	**1,061.4**	**1,247.8**	**348.4**	P/E Ratio	**22.5**	Price (9/30/95)	**3.20**
Net Income	**31.3**	**17.4**	**32.2**	**9.0**	P/B Ratio	**3.5**	52 Wk Hi-Low	**3.50-2.60**
Book Value	**149.2**	**166.2**	**212.9**	**58.8**	Yield %	**1.6**	Market Cap	**US$198.7mil**

Address **Searle & Pontac Sts.** **Cape Town 8001**
Tel **021-460-1911** Fax **021-461-8221**
ADR SEDOL No. **6198965**
Chief Executive **Trevor C. Honneysett** Chairman **Doug Band**

DeBeers Consolidated Mines

Industry: **Precious Metals**

De Beers Consolidated Mines, together with its partners in Namibia and Botswana, is the world's leading producer of gem diamonds. These ADRs represent De Beers/Centenary linked units, which combine a share in De Beers Consolidated Mines with a share in De Beers Centenary, a Swiss-based group that represents the company's international operations. De Beers owns 39% of Anglo American Corporation of South Africa, a mining finance group, as well as other investments. As of Dec. 31,1994, the net asset value of these holdings totaled $40.30 per ADR.

	R mil 12/92	12/93	12/94	US$mil 12/94				
Sales	**2,754.0**	**3,163.0**	**3,083.0**	**868.9**	P/E Ratio	**12.8**	Price (9/30/95)	**98.75**
Net Income	**2,178.0**	**2,867.0**	**2,924.0**	**824.1**	P/B Ratio	**1.3**	52 Wk Hi-Low	**105.00-81.00**
Book Value	**24,389.0**	**27,657.0**	**29,924.0**	**8,453.1**	Yield %	**3.0**	Market Cap	**US$10,286mil**

Address **36 Stockdale St.** **Kimberly 8301**
Tel **0531-807-111** Fax **0531-807-210**
ADR **DBRSY** SEDOL No. **6259118**
President -- Chairman **J. Ogilvie Thompson**

Del Monte Royal Foods

Industry: **Other Food**

Del Monte Royal Foods (Delfood) cans fruit and manufactures confectionery products and grocery goods. Its two main subsidiaries are Royal Beech Nut, which makes biscuits and snacks under the Royal brand name, and South African Preserving Company, which cans pineapple, seasonal fruit, fruit drinks, and tomato products under the Del Monte label for export to the United Kingdom and continental Europe. The company's products also include jam, fruit preserves, desserts, and teas. Delfood is a partially-owned subsidiary of Anglo-American Corporation, an industrial conglomerate.

R mil	05/90	08/91 *	11/92 *	US$mil 11/92				
Sales	**N/A**	**248.6**	**374.0**	**131.6**	P/E Ratio	**14.4**	Price (9/30/95)	**5.25**
Net Income	**N/A**	**23.9**	**35.7**	**12.6**	P/B Ratio	**2.5**	52 Wk Hi-Low	**7.50-4.00**
Book Value	**N/A**	**188.2**	**203.6**	**71.4**	Yield %	**2.3**	Market Cap	**US$140.1mil**

Address **161 Rivonia Rd.**
Morningside, Sandton 2128
Tel **011-883-6970**
Fax **011-884-7088**
ADR
SEDOL No. **6754635**
Chief Executive **V.S. Imerman**
Chairman **V.S. Imerman**

*Irregular period due to fiscal year change.

Dorbyl

Industry: **Land Transportation**

Dorbyl is a mechanical engineering company specializing in structural, civil, and mining engineering. The company also manufactures rolling stock, railway wheels and axles, automotive components, and general engineering equipment. Its other activities include shipbuilding and ship repair, foundry operations, and commercial vehicle bodywork. The company also markets steel and tubing. Its ship-repair subsidiary, Dorbyl Marine, operates shipyards in Durban, Cape Town, and East London. Dorbyl's ultimate holding company is Metkor, a South African steel and engineering company.

R mil	09/92	09/93	09/94	US$mil 09/94				
Sales	**2,977.1**	**2,590.4**	**2,884.6**	**822.1**	P/E Ratio	**86.8**	Price (9/30/95)	**44.25**
Net Income	**81.7**	**-4.8**	**-20.1**	**-5.7**	P/B Ratio	**1.9**	52 Wk Hi-Low	**44.25-15.00**
Book Value	**848.3**	**796.3**	**743.9**	**208.4**	Yield %	**0.5**	Market Cap	**US$391.1mil**

Address **Dorbyl Pk., Skeen Blvd.**
Bedfordview 2008
Tel **011-607-9111**
Fax **011-607-2037**
ADR
SEDOL No. **6277057**
Chief Executive **D.B. Mostert**
Chairman **J.H. de Loor**

Driefontein Consolidated

Industry: **Precious Metals**

Driefontein Consolidated is one of South Africa's leading gold-mining companies. It operates two independently managed mines, the East Driefontein mine and the older West Driefontein mine. Driefontein produced 57,619 kilograms of gold in fiscal 1993. The company has focused capital expenditures on a new subvertical shaft at West Driefontein and has begun full-scale sinking operations. The company's ore reserves total approximately 40,700 kilograms of gold. Gold Fields of South Africa, a mining finance group, owns approximately one third of Driefontein.

R mil	06/92	06/93	06/94	US$mil 06/94				
Sales	**1,861.1**	**1,893.9**	**2,587.3**	**748.4**	P/E Ratio	**12.9**	Price (9/30/95)	**49.75**
Net Income	**551.0**	**526.0**	**785.0**	**227.1**	P/B Ratio	**3.5**	52 Wk Hi-Low	**68.00-46.00**
Book Value	**2,409.5**	**2,629.4**	**2,924.9**	**801.3**	Yield %	**4.8**	Market Cap	**US$2,780.5mil**

Address **75 Fox St.**
Johannesburg 2001
Tel **011-639-9111**
Fax **011-639-2101**
ADR **DRFNY**
SEDOL No. **6280215**
Managing Director **M.R. Fuller-Good**
Chairman **A.H. Munro**

Duiker Exploration

Industry: **Mining**

Duiker Exploration operates collieries and produces both bituminous coal and anthracite. It runs four bituminous coal mines that produce 8.1 tons of coal annually, and two anthracite coal mines that produce 248,700 tons of coal annually. It also operates a gold mine in the Piet Retief area that has an average annual production of 323 kilograms. Duiker terminated operations at its two asbestos properties and these sites are currently being rehabilitated. 55% of Duiker's share capital is owned by WPH International. WPH's ultimate holding company is Lonrho (United Kingdom).

R mil	09/92	09/93	09/94	US$mil 09/94				
Sales	**176.9**	**190.9**	**351.0**	**100.0**	P/E Ratio	**19.4**	Price (9/30/95)	**76.00**
Net Income	**16.3**	**36.2**	**59.1**	**16.8**	P/B Ratio	**6.0**	52 Wk Hi-Low	**87.00-56.00**
Book Value	**154.5**	**180.3**	**182.7**	**51.2**	Yield %	**1.6**	Market Cap	**US$300.1mil**

Address **19 Girton Rd., Parktown**
Johannesburg 2000
Tel **011-642-7691**
Fax **011-484-2882**
ADR
SEDOL No. **6284206**
Managing Director **E.H.J. Stoyell**
Chairman **T.A. Wilkinson**

Edgars Stores

Industry: **Apparel Retailers**

Edgar Stores manufactures and retails clothing, footwear, accessories, and household textiles. It operates 164 Edgars clothing stores that target middle- to high-income customers, 278 Sales House clothing stores that target low- to middle-income customers, and 78 Jet high-volume stores that sell clothing and footwear. The company has five factories that are operated by Celrose and Lee. These factories make denim jeans, men's shirts, and womenswear. The company recently purchased Lauré, a jacket manufacturer. South African Breweries holds 65% of Edgar's share capital.

R mil	03/93	03/94	03/95	US$mil 03/95				
Revenues	**3,175.9**	**3,678.8**	**4,265.2**	**1,192.4**	P/E Ratio	**23.6**	Price (9/30/95)	**130.00**
Net Income	**185.8**	**231.8**	**284.3**	**79.5**	P/B Ratio	**5.9**	52 Wk Hi-Low	**142.00-113.00**
Book Value	**685.6**	**858.3**	**1,137.1**	**317.6**	Yield %	**1.6**	Market Cap	**US$1,837.7mil**

Address **Press Ave., Crown Mines**
Johannesburg 2025
Tel **011-495-6000**
Fax **N/A**
ADR
SEDOL No. **6304892**
Managing Director **D.W. Etheridge**
Chairman **J.M. Kahn**

Fedsure

Industry: **Insurance - Property & Casualty**

Fedsure Holdings is a holding company for financial-services companies. Its principal subsidiary, Fedlife Assurance, offers life insurance, group-benefits plans, pension programs, and funeral-benefit services. Its 85%-owned subsidiary, Fedgen Insurance, offers short-term insurance policies. Fedsure also owns 100% of Fedsure Asset Management, which manages portfolios for corporate and institutional clients, and 65% of Fedgrowth Management Company, which manages mutual funds. Its other subsidiaries are active in mortgage participation, banking, and property management.

R mil	12/92	12/93	12/94	US$mil 12/94				
Revenues	**N/A**	**N/A**	**N/A**	**N/A**	P/E Ratio	**25.0**	Price (9/30/95)	**19.25**
Net Income	**42.4**	**64.4**	**81.8**	**23.1**	P/B Ratio	**3.3**	52 Wk Hi-Low	**19.25-15.50**
Book Value	**348.3**	**371.1**	**522.6**	**147.6**	Yield %	**2.9**	Market Cap	**US$458.5mil**

Address **Fedlife Hse., 1 de Villiers St.**
Johannesburg 2001
Tel **011-332-6500**
Fax **011-492-1102**
ADR
SEDOL No. **6333971**
Chief Executive **Arnold I. Basserabie**
Chairman **J.A. Barrow**

Fintech

Industry: **Software**

Fintech is an investment holding company that has interests in the office-automation, data-processing, computer-hardware, and computer-software companies. Its principal subsidiary is XeraTech, which has an alliance with Rank Xerox to distribute office equipment. It also manufactures automated-teller machines and other electronic equipment for the banking industry. It shares ownership of business-communication specialist Alcatel STC Business Systems with France's Alcatel Alsthom. Fintech is 67% owned by Allied Electronics Corporation.

R mil	02/93	02/94	02/95	US$mil 02/95				
Sales	**602.2**	**629.0**	**743.9**	**208.5**	P/E Ratio	**18.7**	Price (9/30/95)	**65.00**
Net Income	**6.3**	**28.8**	**39.5**	**11.1**	P/B Ratio	**6.1**	52 Wk Hi-Low	**65.00-42.50**
Book Value	**78.1**	**99.8**	**127.5**	**35.4**	Yield %	**1.6**	Market Cap	**US$211.7mil**

Address **Old Pretoria Rd.**
Midrand 1685
Tel **011-315-0090**
Fax **011-805-3393**
ADR
SEDOL No. **6337702**
President --
Chairman **David Redshaw**

First National Bank

Industry: **Banks - Regional**

First National Bank Holdings provides retail and commercial banking services. Its banking network includes 474 branch offices, 62 service branches, 236 agencies, and 1,100 automated-teller machines in South Africa, Botswana, and Namibia. The company's corporate banking division offers electronic transmission services, financing, and risk-management services. Its two main subsidiaries are First National Trust, a fund-management and trust company, and First Bowring, an insurance broker. First National also has subsidiaries in 10 countries in Europe, the Caribbean, and Asia.

R mil	09/92	09/93	09/94	US$mil 09/94				
Revenues	**7,621.1**	**8,053.9**	**9,185.5**	**2,617.7**	P/E Ratio	**14.5**	Price (9/30/95)	**25.50**
Net Income	**451.9**	**593.7**	**736.4**	**209.9**	P/B Ratio	**3.0**	52 Wk Hi-Low	**26.50-19.50**
Book Value	**2,505.3**	**3,129.9**	**3,662.8**	**1,026.0**	Yield %	**2.2**	Market Cap	**US$3,041.3mil**

Address **1 First Pl., BankCity**
Johannesburg 2001
Tel **011-371-2111**
Fax **011-371-2257**
ADR
SEDOL No. **6342784**
Managing Director **Barend J. Swart**
Chairman **Basil E. Hersov**

Foodcorp

Industry: **Other Food**

Foodcorp is a holding company active in the manufacture of grain-based foods, edible oils, prepared foods and snacks, and high-protein foods. Its brand-name products include Nola's salad dressings, Bobtail dog food, Sunbake bread, Ruto's Supreme cake flour, Enterprise and Herti prepared meats, Simba snack foods, and Harvestime frozen vegetables. Foodcorp also manages livestock slaughtering and auctioneering as well as the manufacturing of bovine leather. PepsiCo has taken a 50% holding in Foodcorp's Simba subsidiary, South Africa's largest maker of snack foods.

R mil	08/92	08/93	08/94	US$mil 08/94				
Sales	**2,430.0**	**2,657.0**	**2,755.0**	**787.6**	P/E Ratio	**16.8**	Price (9/30/95)	**37.00**
Net Income	**59.0**	**92.0**	**87.0**	**24.9**	P/B Ratio	**2.5**	52 Wk Hi-Low	**37.00-26.50**
Book Value	**513.0**	**663.0**	**725.0**	**202.5**	Yield %	**1.6**	Market Cap	**US$487.4mil**

Address **P.O. Box 1816**
Bedfordview 2008
Tel **011-493-1501**
Fax **011-853-1747**
ADR
SEDOL No. **6333443**
Managing Director **Dave Kennealy**
Chairman **Grant Thomas**

Foschini

Industry: **Apparel Retailers**

Foschini operates chains of retail stores that specialize in the sale of clothing, jewelry, and accessories. The company manages more than 800 stores that operate under the Foschini, Markhams, American Swiss, Pages, and Sterns store names. Foschini controls Oceana Investments, the company's overseas-investment arm, which has a 37% stake in Etam, a U.K.-based clothing retailer. Etam has more than 220 stores throughout the United Kingdom. Foschini is ultimately controlled by the Lewis Family through a 50% holding by Lewis Foschini Investment Company.

R mil	03/93	03/94	03/95	US$mil 03/95				
Revenues	**1,161.4**	**1,442.4**	**1,787.5**	**499.7**	P/E Ratio	**25.5**	Price (9/30/95)	**25.00**
Net Income	**103.3**	**143.8**	**188.4**	**52.7**	P/B Ratio	**6.3**	52 Wk Hi-Low	**27.00-19.66**
Book Value	**445.7**	**575.6**	**763.7**	**213.3**	Yield %	**0.0**	Market Cap	**US$1,314.7mil**

Address **LEFIC Ctr., Voortrekker Rd.**
Parow East 7500
Tel **021-938-1911**
Fax **021-927-0630**
ADR
SEDOL No. **6349688**
Managing Director **Neville Goodwin**
Chairman **Stanley Lewis**

Freegold

Industry: **Precious Metals**

Freegold (Free State Consolidated Gold Mines) is an investment holding company that invests in gold-mining operations throughout South Africa. The company's operations include 27 mining shafts and nine metallurgical plants. The company has a mining area of more than 27,900 hectares. Fiscal year 1994 gold production was more than 101 tons, representing about 17% of South African production and making the company the largest gold producer in the world.

	R mil 03/93	03/94	03/95	US$mil 03/95				
Sales	**3,971.4**	**4,482.4**	**4,518.1**	**1,263.1**	P/E Ratio	**15.6**	Price (9/30/95)	**42.25**
Net Income	**293.0**	**470.4**	**309.7**	**86.6**	P/B Ratio	**0.8**	52 Wk Hi-Low	**74.00-35.75**
Book Value	**5,565.2**	**5,833.3**	**6,063.0**	**1,693.6**	Yield %	**6.4**	Market Cap	**US$1,377.3mil**

Address **44 Main St.**
Johannesburg 2001
Tel **011-638-9111**
Fax **011-638-5281**
ADR **FSCNY**
SEDOL No. **6351111**
Managing Director **N. Mayer**
Chairman **C.L. Sunter**

Gencor

Industry: **Precious Metals**

Gencor is an investment company with stategic holdings in mining and metals businesses. The company has interests in Gengold, Impala Platinum Holdings, Ingwe Coal, Samancor, Alusaf, and Richards Bay Minerals. These companies are engaged in the mining of gold, platinum, coal, aluminium, ferro alloys, titanium, and base minerals. In 1994, Gencor acquired mining-company Billiton from Royal Dutch Shell Group for $1.2 billion, and merged its Trans-Natal Coal subsidary with Randcoal to form Ingwe Coal. The group disposed of its nonmining assets in 1993.

	R mil 08/92	08/93	06/94 *	US$mil 06/94				
Sales	**N/A**	**474.0**	**630.0**	**182.2**	P/E Ratio	**30.0**	Price (9/30/95)	**13.60**
Net Income	**N/A**	**1,357.0**	**760.0**	**219.8**	P/B Ratio	**2.5**	52 Wk Hi-Low	**15.50-11.55**
Book Value	**N/A**	**11,499.0**	**7,438.0**	**2,037.8**	Yield %	**1.1**	Market Cap	**US$5,127.5mil**

Address **6 Hollard St.**
Johannesburg 2001
Tel **011-376-9111**
Fax **011-836-8708**
ADR **GNCLY**
SEDOL No. **6365811**
President --
Chairman **B.P. Gilbertson**

*Irregular period due to fiscal year change.

Gold Fields of South Africa

Industry: **Precious Metals**

Gold Fields of South Africa is a mining finance company investing in gold, platinum, copper, coal, zinc, base metal, and mineral producers. Gold Fields owns approximately one third of three gold producers: Doornfontein Gold Mining, Driefontein Consolidated, and Kloof Gold Mining. Gold Fields also has a 49% equity stake in Deelkraal Gold Mining, a 65% stake in Northam Platinum, and a 79% stake in Gold Fields Coal. The company's Gold Fields Mining and Development subsidiary finances exploration costs and receives fee income for technical and administrative assistance.

	R mil 06/93	06/94	06/95	US$mil 06/95				
Sales	**492.0**	**562.0**	**628.0**	**184.7**	P/E Ratio	**24.0**	Price (9/30/95)	**98.00**
Net Income	**300.0**	**-293.0**	**408.0**	**120.0**	P/B Ratio	**3.6**	52 Wk Hi-Low	**131.00-90.50**
Book Value	**2,901.0**	**2,413.0**	**2,617.0**	**719.0**	Yield %	**2.2**	Market Cap	**US$2,592.2mil**

Address **75 Fox St.**
Johannesburg 2001
Tel **011-639-9111**
Fax **011-639-2101**
ADR **GLDFY**
SEDOL No. **6376266**
Managing Director **J.A. Stegmann**
Chairman **A.J. Wright**

IBM South Africa

Industry: **Software**

IBM South Africa (formerly Information Services Group) markets and distributes IBM computer products in South Africa. The company sells mainframes, automated-teller machines, systems servers, personal computers and related equipment. It also provides maintenance, cabling, power-supply installation, and consulting services. IBM South Africa is also involved in two joint ventures. It works with Standard Bank to provide data-interchange and network-management services, and with Times Media to maintain a database connection between purchasers and suppliers.

	R mil 09/92	09/93	12/94 *	US$mil 12/94				
Sales	**1,048.5**	**1,238.0**	**1,709.0**	**481.7**	P/E Ratio	**20.4**	Price (9/30/95)	**8.75**
Net Income	**51.6**	**45.1**	**14.2**	**4.0**	P/B Ratio	**10.9**	52 Wk Hi-Low	**9.50-4.50**
Book Value	**145.6**	**141.2**	**120.1**	**33.9**	Yield %	**3.0**	Market Cap	**US$360.0mil**

Address **70 Rivonia Rd.**
Sandhurst 2196
Tel **011-320-8277**
Fax **011-320-9988**
ADR
SEDOL No. **6879806**
President --
Chairman **Derek Cooper**

*Irregular period due to fiscal year change.

Impala Platinum Holdings

Industry: **Precious Metals**

Impala Platinum Holdings (Implats) is the second- largest producer of platinum in the world. Among the minerals extracted from the company's three primary mines are platinum, palladium, rhodium, iridium, ruthenium, gold, silver, nickel, copper, and cobalt. The largest market for platinum is the automotive industry, where the metal is used in catalytic converters, which reduce engine emissions. Other markets include the jewelry, glass, chemical, and electronics industries.

	R mil 06/92	06/93	06/94	US$mil 06/94				
Sales	**2,263.8**	**2,213.9**	**2,183.7**	**631.7**	P/E Ratio	**33.2**	Price (9/30/95)	**90.50**
Net Income	**260.3**	**186.4**	**143.7**	**41.6**	P/B Ratio	**2.1**	52 Wk Hi-Low	**102.00-72.00**
Book Value	**2,409.0**	**2,556.6**	**2,666.3**	**730.5**	Yield %	**1.5**	Market Cap	**US$1,542.2mil**

Address **Unicorn Hse., 70 Marshall St.**
Johannesburg 2001
Tel **011-376-2800**
Fax **011-836-5954**
ADR **IMPAY**
SEDOL No. **6457804**
President --
Chairman **J. Michael McMahon**

Imperial Holdings

Industry: **General Industrial & Commercial Services**

Imperial Holdings is a holding company with interests in motor-vehicle rental and sales, transport, and financial services. Its Imperial Car Rental and Tempest Car Hire subsidiaries operate a fleet of 5,100 cars and a total of 84 branch offices. Imperial's motor-vehicle unit sells Toyota, Mercedes, and Honda passenger and commercial vehicles. Its transport unit maintains a fleet of 2,255 bulk-product and refrigerated vehicles. Imperial also offers insurance, investment-management, and property-rental services, and operates two coach-touring and charter businesses.

	R mil 06/92	06/93	06/94	US$mil 06/94				
Sales	**781.3**	**1,086.7**	**1,489.0**	**430.7**	P/E Ratio	**44.9**	Price (9/30/95)	**34.50**
Net Income	**27.7**	**47.3**	**70.8**	**20.5**	P/B Ratio	**6.0**	52 Wk Hi-Low	**34.50-22.50**
Book Value	**117.5**	**267.5**	**584.3**	**160.1**	Yield %	**0.8**	Market Cap	**US$960.7mil**

Address **140 Boeing Rd. E.**
Elma Park, Edenvale 1610
Tel **011-453-0945**
Fax **011-453-0960**
ADR
SEDOL No. **6458874**
President --
Chairman **William G. Lynch**

Ingwe Coal

Industry: **Coal**

Ingwe Coal Corporation (formerly Randcoal) is the world's third-largest privately-owned producer of hard coal, and the world's largest exporter of steam coal. It operates 14 mines that produce hard coal and steam coal that is sold to domestic customers and exported. Two of the company's collieries are dedicated to the production of coal for Eskom, South Africa's national supplier of electricity. Ingwe was created when the coal-mining interests of Rand Mines and Gencor merged in October 1994. Gencor owns a 50% interest in Ingwe, and Rand Mines holds a 46% stake.

	R mil 09/92	09/93	09/94	US$mil 09/94				
Sales	**1,620.9**	**1,649.5**	**1,656.2**	**472.0**	P/E Ratio	**30.7**	Price (9/30/95)	**29.50**
Net Income	**172.4**	**92.0**	**124.2**	**35.4**	P/B Ratio	**2.8**	52 Wk Hi-Low	**30.00-22.00**
Book Value	**1,138.9**	**1,311.1**	**1,370.8**	**384.0**	Yield %	**1.7**	Market Cap	**US$1,041.9mil**

Address **Randcoal Hse., 21 Chaplin Rd.**
Illovo 2196
Tel **011-441-1611**
Fax **011-880-3855**
ADR
SEDOL No. **6974488**
President --
Chairman **John C. Hall**

Investec Bank

Industry: **Banks - Regional**

Investec Bank is southern Africa's fifth-largest bank in terms of assets. In addition to retail banking, it offers a range of services, including merchant banking, investment management, and property trading. The company's South African subsidiaries include Metboard Management, Investec Merchant Bank, and Investec Property Group. It also has two subsidiaries in the United Kingdom, Allied Trust Bank and Clive Discount, the latter of which is a bond broker. The company is 48% owned by Investec Holdings, a holding company whose sole activity is investment in Investec Bank.

	R mil 03/93	03/94	03/95	US$mil 03/95				
Revenues	**N/A**	**881.4**	**1,664.4**	**465.3**	P/E Ratio	**22.1**	Price (9/30/95)	**73.50**
Net Income	**54.0**	**88.2**	**157.5**	**44.0**	P/B Ratio	**2.0**	52 Wk Hi-Low	**76.50-58.00**
Book Value	**636.9**	**941.0**	**1,841.4**	**514.4**	Yield %	**2.0**	Market Cap	**US$1,027.0mil**

Address **55 Fox St.**
Johannesburg 2001
Tel **011-498-2000**
Fax **011-498-2100**
ADR
SEDOL No. **6465959**
Chief Executive **Hugh Herman**
Chairman **Bas Kardol**

Iscor

Industry: **Steel**

Iscor markets and produces a wide range of iron and steel. The company has mining operations located in Pretoria, Vanderbijlpark, Newcastle, Vereeniging, and Kuils River. Iscor mines 8.5 million tons of iron ore a year in Sishen and Thabazimbi, and 3.4 million tons of coal a year in Grootegeluk, Durnacol, Hlobane, and Tshikondeni. Iscor also has investments in property-holding, manufacturing, recycling, and service companies. The company ranks twenty-second in the world on the basis of metric tons crude steel output, with 1994 liquid-steel production of 7.3 million tons.

	R mil 06/92	06/93	06/94	US$mil 06/94				
Sales	**8,616.0**	**9,041.1**	**9,827.1**	**2,842.7**	P/E Ratio	**17.6**	Price (9/30/95)	**3.95**
Net Income	**336.0**	**-176.9**	**512.3**	**148.2**	P/B Ratio	**1.3**	52 Wk Hi-Low	**4.77-3.95**
Book Value	**6,643.0**	**6,383.5**	**6,902.4**	**1,891.1**	Yield %	**0.0**	Market Cap	**US$2,541.6mil**

Address **Roger Dyason Rd.**
Pretoria West 0001
Tel **N/A**
Fax **N/A**
ADR **ISCRY**
SEDOL No. **6466695**
Managing Director **Hans Smith**
Chairman **Marius de Waal**

JD Group

Industry: **Other Specialty Retailers**

JD Group sells furniture through its network of seven major retail chains. It operates 67 Bradlows, 136 Russells, 100 Score, and 25 Montana Harmony furniture stores throughout South Africa. JD also manages 77 Price 'N Pride discount furniture outlets and 21 Giddys appliance and entertainment-products stores. Its Joshua Doore discount furniture chain includes 28 hyperstores, 17 mid-sized stores, and 48 catalogue showrooms. The company also operates twelve distribution centers and has interests in a retailer in Namibia.

	R mil 12/91	12/92	06/94 *	US$mil 06/94				
Revenues	**542.3**	**457.3**	**1,638.3**	**473.9**	P/E Ratio	**8.2**	Price (9/30/95)	**15.25**
Net Income	**32.4**	**36.8**	**127.3**	**36.8**	P/B Ratio	**1.6**	52 Wk Hi-Low	**16.00-11.25**
Book Value	**237.4**	**262.4**	**656.9**	**180.0**	Yield %	**1.8**	Market Cap	**US$296.3mil**

Address **29 De Beer St.**
Braamfontein 2001
Tel **011-408-0408**
Fax **011-403-1487**
ADR
SEDOL No. **6479648**
Managing Director **I. David Sussman**
Chairman **I. David Sussman**

*Irregular period due to fiscal year change.

Johannesburg Consolidated Investment

Industry: **Precious Metals**

Johannesburg Consolidated Investment (Johnnies) is a mining and finance group. The group has major investments in platinum, gold, chrome, coal, diamonds, base metals, property, media, and a variety of consumer-based industries. Johnnies has investments in a number of South African companies including Rustenburg Platinum, Randfontein Estates, Consolidated Metallurgical Industries, DeBeers, Free State Development & Investment, and Argus Newspapers. About 40% of the company's equity is controlled by Anglo American.

R mil	06/92	06/93	06/94	US$mil 06/94				
Sales	**N/A**	**N/A**	**2,919.1**	**844.4**	P/E Ratio	**8.8**	Price (9/30/95)	**44.25**
Net Income	**N/A**	**N/A**	**761.5**	**220.3**	P/B Ratio	**1.9**	52 Wk Hi-Low	**58.00-37.25**
Book Value	**N/A**	**N/A**	**3,521.3**	**964.7**	Yield %	**4.5**	Market Cap	**US$1,803.2mil**

Address **Fox & Harrison Sts.**
Johannesburg 2001
Tel **081-650-4866**
Fax **081-658-3430**
ADR **JICPY**
SEDOL No. **6475141**
President --
Chairman **P.F. Retief**

Kloof Gold Mining

Industry: **Precious Metals**

Kloof Gold Mining conducts gold-mining operations on 13,411 hectares leased from the South African government. The company milled more than 2.1 million tons of ore in fiscal 1993, producing 48,200 kilograms of fine gold. Production costs amounted to about $243 per ounce. The company is focusing capital expenditure on the No. 4 Vertical Shaft at the Kloof division, which accounts for one half of the company's total tonnage milled. Other divisions include the Leeudoorn and Libanon sites. Kloof is a member of Gold Fields of South Africa, a mining finance group.

R mil	06/92	06/93	06/94	US$mil 06/94				
Sales	**1,101.4**	**1,669.5**	**2,018.2**	**583.8**	P/E Ratio	**N/A**	Price (9/30/95)	**40.75**
Net Income	**318.2**	**480.6**	**747.9**	**216.3**	P/B Ratio	**1.6**	52 Wk Hi-Low	**71.75-38.00**
Book Value	**2,189.8**	**2,978.8**	**3,596.8**	**985.4**	Yield %	**4.4**	Market Cap	**US$1,547.4mil**

Address **75 Fox St.**
Johannesburg 2001
Tel **011-639-9111**
Fax **011-639-2101**
ADR **KLOFY**
SEDOL No. **6495785**
Managing Director **M.R. Fuller-Good**
Chairman **A.H. Munro**

Liberty Holdings

Industry: **Insurance - Life & Health**

Liberty Holdings serves as a parent company to Liberty Life Association of Africa. It owns 53% of Liberty Life's equity, and it provides Liberty Life with financial consultation and management services. The company is jointly controlled by Liberty Investors and Standard Bank Investment, parent to the Standard Bank of South Africa. Liberty Holdings' other activities include property construction and development and unit-trust management. Together with Guardian Royal Exchange (United Kingdom), it jointly owns Guardian National Insurance Company of South Africa.

R mil	12/92	12/93	12/94	US$mil 12/94				
Revenues	**4,869.2**	**14,219.6**	**15,904.4**	**4,482.6**	P/E Ratio	**33.7**	Price (9/30/95)	**245.00**
Net Income	**241.2**	**414.2**	**461.1**	**130.0**	P/B Ratio	**2.5**	52 Wk Hi-Low	**270.00-220.00**
Book Value	**2,958.5**	**4,179.1**	**4,611.9**	**1,302.8**	Yield %	**2.3**	Market Cap	**US$3,090.4mil**

Address **1 Ameshoff St.**
Braamfontein, Johannesburg 2001
Tel **011-408-3911**
Fax **N/A**
ADR
SEDOL No. **6515058**
President --
Chairman **D. Gordon**

Liberty Life Association

Industry: **Insurance - Life & Health**

Liberty Life Association is South Africa's largest life-insurance company in terms of assets. Its subsidiaries offer international insurance and investment-based financial services. Its strategic investments include a 39% interest in Standard Bank Investment, a 28% interest in Premier Group, a food and pharmaceutical concern, and a 58% interest in the United Kingdom's TransAtlantic Holdings, a life-insurance provider. Because Liberty Life is 53% owned by Liberty Holdings, its ultimate parent companies are Standard Bank Investment and Liberty Investors.

R mil	12/92	12/93	12/94	US$mil 12/94				
Revenues	**4,852.2**	**14,548.7**	**16,282.5**	**4,589.2**	P/E Ratio	**28.6**	Price (9/30/95)	**92.50**
Net Income	**352.8**	**441.8**	**565.4**	**159.4**	P/B Ratio	**2.8**	52 Wk Hi-Low	**106.00-83.75**
Book Value	**4,989.3**	**7,184.1**	**7,908.1**	**2,233.9**	Yield %	**2.2**	Market Cap	**US$5,909.8mil**

Address **Liberty Life Ctr., 1 Ameshoff St.**
Braamfontein 2001
Tel **N/A**
Fax **N/A**
ADR **LTYLY**
SEDOL No. **6515047**
Managing Director **Alan Romanis**
Chairman **Donald Gordon**

Liblife Strategic Investments

Industry: **Financial Services - Diversified**

Liblife Strategic Investments acts as the holding company for a portion of the strategic investments of Liberty Life Association of Africa. It holds a 24% interest in Standard Bank Investment, a 23% interest in The Premier Group, and a 28% interest in Beverage and Consumer Industry Holdings, a company that in turn owns 34% of South African Breweries. The company also owns a 4.6% interest in GFSA Holdings, which owns 42% of Gold Fields of South Africa. Liberty Life has an 80% stake in Liblife Strategic.

R mil	12/92	12/93	12/94	US$mil 12/94				
Revenues	**137.5**	**146.3**	**155.7**	**43.9**	P/E Ratio	**16.5**	Price (9/30/95)	**12.25**
Net Income	**202.0**	**324.6**	**373.3**	**105.2**	P/B Ratio	**0.9**	52 Wk Hi-Low	**13.75-10.00**
Book Value	**4,211.1**	**7,135.8**	**7,351.4**	**2,076.7**	Yield %	**2.2**	Market Cap	**US$1,872.7mil**

Address **Liberty Life Ctr., 1 Ameshoff St.**
Braamfontein 2001
Tel **N/A**
Fax **N/A**
ADR
SEDOL No. **6518897**
President --
Chairman **Donald Gordon**

Malbak

Industry: **Conglomerates**

Malbak manufactures food, packaging and paper products, healthcare products, and branded consumer products. Through its 75% interest in Foodcorp, the company produces grain-based foods, snacks, and prepared foods. Its consumer products division operates through three main companies: Ellerines, a retail furniture and appliance chain, Malbak Motor Holdings, a motor vehicle retailer, and Tedelex, a distributor of household and business appliances. Malbak has a 75% interest SA Druggist, a pharmaceutical producer, and a 68% interest in Holdains, a packaging concern.

	R mil 08/92	08/93	08/94	US$mil 08/94				
Sales	**10,031.0**	**11,002.0**	**12,611.0**	**3,605.2**	P/E Ratio	**18.4**	Price (9/30/95)	**24.75**
Net Income	**329.0**	**301.0**	**80.0**	**22.9**	P/B Ratio	**2.7**	52 Wk Hi-Low	**25.75-15.75**
Book Value	**2,350.0**	**2,741.0**	**2,829.0**	**790.2**	Yield %	**1.5**	Market Cap	**US$2,086.3mil**

Address	**Protea Pl., Off Fredman Dr.**	Tel **011-783-4480**	ADR	President	--
	Sandton 2146	Fax **011-783-0408**	SEDOL No. **6705871**	Chairman	**Grant S. Thomas**

McCarthy Group

Industry: **Other Specialty Retailers**

McCarthy Group is a holding company whose sole investment is in McCarthy Retail. It owns 85% of McCarthy Retail's shares and 55% of its convertible debentures. McCarthy Retail sells motor vehicles, furniture, household appliances, electronic equipment, and clothing. Its motor division is South Africa's sole importer of Yamaha motorcycles, engines, sports equipment, and musical instruments. The company also owns 80% of Midas (South Africa), which markets and distributes automotive products. McCarthy Group's only source of revenue is from distributions of McCarthy Retail.

	R mil 06/92	06/93	06/94	US$mil 06/94				
Revenues	**N/A**	**5,266.6**	**6,171.9**	**1,785.3**	P/E Ratio	**25.0**	Price (9/30/95)	**17.85**
Net Income	**N/A**	**70.3**	**112.6**	**32.6**	P/B Ratio	**3.8**	52 Wk Hi-Low	**19.25-10.50**
Book Value	**N/A**	**633.4**	**744.7**	**204.0**	Yield %	**0.2**	Market Cap	**US$782.7mil**

Address	**203 North Ridge Rd.**	Tel **031-290222**	ADR	President	--
	Durban 4001	Fax **031-290950**	SEDOL No. **6551245**	Chairman	**Brian C. McCarthy**

Metro Cash & Carry

Industry: **Food Retailers & Wholesalers**

Metro Cash and Carry operates more than 200 wholesale-distributor outlets throughout South Africa. Its wholesale stores trade under the Metro, Trador, Trade Centre, Stax, and Metbuild names. The company primarily wholesales groceries, consumer goods, and hardware. It also operates retail consumer-goods stores through its Stax Superstore chain, and manages The Lucky Seven franchise of grocery and consumer-goods stores. Metro sells its own products primarily under the Family Favourite brand name. South Africa's Premier Group owns a 68% interest in Metro.

	R mil 06/91	04/92 *	04/93	US$mil 04/93				
Sales	**4,064.4**	**4,074.8**	**5,202.9**	**1,766.1**	P/E Ratio	**35.3**	Price (9/30/95)	**12.00**
Net Income	**-244.0**	**34.1**	**49.3**	**16.7**	P/B Ratio	**6.7**	52 Wk Hi-Low	**12.85-9.75**
Book Value	**75.1**	**269.6**	**295.8**	**93.6**	Yield %	**1.2**	Market Cap	**US$541.0mil**

Address	**Crownwood and Amethyst Rds.**	Tel **011-490-2000**	ADR	Managing Director	**C.S. dos Santos**
	Johannesburg 2001	Fax **011-835-2301**	SEDOL No. **6584337**	Chairman	**P.G.A. Wrighton**

*Irregular period due to fiscal year change.

Murray & Roberts

Industry: **Building Materials**

Murray & Roberts Holdings (M&R) manufactures construction materials and provides engineering and transport services in Africa. Its products include stainless-steel containers, heat exchangers, forklift trucks, automotive components, test and measurement equipment, and cargo-transport equipment. M&R's construction division is a general contractor in southern Africa that builds infrastructure projects, residential developments, pipelines, and railways. M&R also develops and manages retail and industrial properties and operates Unitrans, a land-based freight transporter.

	R mil 06/92	06/93	06/94	US$mil 06/94				
Sales	**5,841.9**	**6,779.0**	**7,765.2**	**2,246.2**	P/E Ratio	**22.0**	Price (9/30/95)	**23.75**
Net Income	**265.0**	**333.2**	**339.5**	**98.2**	P/B Ratio	**3.0**	52 Wk Hi-Low	**24.00-18.20**
Book Value	**2,150.4**	**2,264.4**	**2,503.0**	**685.8**	Yield %	**1.8**	Market Cap	**US$2,076.0mil**

Address	**Douglas Roberts Ctr., Skeen Blvd.**	Tel **011-455-1410**	ADR	Chief Executive	**André van der Colff**
	Bedfordview 2008	Fax **011-455-2222**	SEDOL No. **6582546**	Chairman	**Dave Brink**

Nampak

Industry: **Paper Products**

Nampak manufactures and markets packaging products. The company's packaging division produces tin-plated beverage and food cans, glass bottles, polycoated cartons for liquids, plastic bottles, metal cans and drums, flexible packs for confectionery products, plastic shopping bags, and bread wrappers. Nampak's paper and printing division manufactures corrugated boxes and partitions, cartons, paper bags, and sanitary products. It also prints business forms and distributes paper and graphics materials. CG Smith owns 62% of the company's share capital.

	R mil 09/92	09/93	09/94	US$mil 09/94				
Sales	**4,364.2**	**4,543.7**	**4,790.8**	**1,365.3**	P/E Ratio	**23.6**	Price (9/30/95)	**17.00**
Net Income	**255.3**	**296.9**	**349.9**	**99.7**	P/B Ratio	**5.1**	52 Wk Hi-Low	**18.00-12.75**
Book Value	**1,199.5**	**1,390.4**	**1,613.6**	**452.0**	Yield %	**1.6**	Market Cap	**US$2,273.0mil**

Address	**Nampak Ctr., 114 Dennis Rd.**	Tel **011-444-7418**	ADR	Managing Director	**Trevor Evans**
	Atholl Gardens, Sandton 2196	Fax **011-444-4794**	SEDOL No. **6621397**	Chairman	**Brian Connellan**

Nasional Pers Beperk

Industry: **Publishing**

Nasional Pers Beperk (Naspers) publishes and distributes both English and Afrikaans newspapers, magazines, and books. The company's consumer magazine titles include Huisgenoot, which has a weekly circulation of more than 500,000 copies, and You, which has a weekly circulation of almost 300,000 copies. Naspers publishes three daily newspapers, Die Burger, Die Beeld, and Die Volksblad. The company has operations in electronic media, has entered the cellular telephone industry, and provides subscription television services. South Africa's Servgo holds a 20% stake in Naspers.

	R mil 03/93	03/94	03/95	US$mil 03/95				
Sales	**N/A**	**N/A**	**N/A**	**N/A**	P/E Ratio	**N/A**	Price (9/30/95)	**20.75**
Net Income	**N/A**	**N/A**	**N/A**	**N/A**	P/B Ratio	**N/A**	52 Wk Hi-Low	**20.75-14.75**
Book Value	**N/A**	**N/A**	**N/A**	**N/A**	Yield %	**N/A**	Market Cap	**US$633.4mil**

Address **P.O. Box 2271**	Tel **021-406-2121**	ADR		President	--
Cape Town 8000	Fax **021-406-2921**	SEDOL No.	**6622668**	Chairman	--

Nedcor

Industry: **Banks - Regional**

Nedcor is an investment-holding company with interests in the banking and financial-services industries. Its main banking subsidiaries are Nedcor Bank, UAL Merchant Bank, and Cape of Good Hope Bank. Its other subsidiaries are active in lending, investment management, mutual funds, and insurance. Nedcor has subsidiaries in 21 African countries. It also has operations in the United States, and its NedFinance Asia subsidiary has an office in Beijing, making it the first African bank set up operations in China. Nedcor is 53% owned by SA Mutual Life Assurance Society.

	R mil 09/92	09/93	09/94	US$mil 09/94				
Revenues	**7,582.0**	**7,547.0**	**8,351.0**	**2,379.9**	P/E Ratio	**14.6**	Price (9/30/95)	**45.00**
Net Income	**408.0**	**486.0**	**603.0**	**171.8**	P/B Ratio	**2.6**	52 Wk Hi-Low	**46.50-30.00**
Book Value	**2,464.0**	**2,872.0**	**3,410.0**	**955.2**	Yield %	**2.1**	Market Cap	**US$2,417.1mil**

Address **100 Main St.**	Tel **011-630-7111**	ADR		Chief Executive	**R.C.M. Laubscher**
Johannesburg 2000	Fax **011-630-7558**	SEDOL No.	**6628008**	Chairman	**J.B. Maree**

Omni Media

Industry: **General Industrial & Commercial Services**

Omni Media Corporation (formerly Argus Holdings) is an investment-holding company with subsidiaries that operate in the publishing and media industries. Its main interests are a 36% stake in Times Media, a publisher of newspapers and magazines, a 50% stake in CTP Holdings, a printing and packaging concern, and a 32% stake in CNA Gallo, a chain of entertainment and stationery shops. Omni's other holdings include minority interests in programming and broadcasting companies, a cellular phone company, and the sole distributor of telephone directories and yellow pages.

	R mil 03/93	03/94	03/95	US$mil 03/95				
Sales	**1,653.0**	**1,823.6**	**1,708.3**	**477.6**	P/E Ratio	**NMF**	Price (9/30/95)	**37.50**
Net Income	**99.6**	**170.1**	**-29.3**	**-8.2**	P/B Ratio	**3.7**	52 Wk Hi-Low	**37.50-32.75**
Book Value	**426.7**	**572.5**	**584.1**	**163.2**	Yield %	**1.2**	Market Cap	**US$598.4mil**

Address **28 Harrison St.**	Tel **011-373-7111**	ADR		Chief Executive	**D.D.B. Band**
Johannesburg 2001	Fax **011-373-5063**	SEDOL No.	**6049494**	Chairman	**V.G. Bray**

Palabora Mining

Industry: **Mining**

Palabora Mining is the leading producer of copper in South Africa. The company extracts copper from one open-pit mine, which supplies more than 125,000 tons of copper concentrate per year. Palabora also operates a copper smelter, which produces approximately 105,000 tons of anodes annually and more than 100,000 tons of sulfuric acid. The company also produces zirconia, uranium oxide, and vermiculite as by-products. Palabora supplies more than half of the world's supply of vermiculite. The company's open-pit mine is expected to remain productive to the year 2000.

	R mil 12/92	12/93	12/94	US$mil 12/94				
Sales	**1,115.6**	**1,098.8**	**1,386.3**	**390.7**	P/E Ratio	**8.1**	Price (9/30/95)	**57.00**
Net Income	**198.7**	**169.9**	**214.7**	**60.5**	P/B Ratio	**4.6**	52 Wk Hi-Low	**82.00-47.00**
Book Value	**342.8**	**344.8**	**348.5**	**98.4**	Yield %	**13.3**	Market Cap	**US$442.2mil**

Address **Rio Tinto Hse., 122 Pybus Rd.**	Tel **011-883-3860**	ADR	**PBOMY**	Managing Director	**F. Fenwick**
Sandton 2199	Fax **011-883-2703**	SEDOL No.	**6667904**	Chairman	**A.J. Leroy**

Pepkor

Industry: **Food Retailers & Wholesalers**

Pepkor operates more than 1,700 outlets, making it the largest retail group in Africa. It manages 1,097 Pep clothing and semidurables stores, 135 Smart Centre and 151 Ackerman's family-fashion stores, 91 Cashbuild basic building-materials outlets, 8 Stuttafords fashion-housewares stores, and 234 Shoprite and Checkers food retail centers. In 1994, Pepkor acquired Brown & Jackson, a U.K.-listed retailer which operates more than 200 Poundstretcher discount stores in the United Kingdom. South African investment company Pepgro owns 50% of Pepkor.

	R mil 02/93	02/94	02/95	US$mil 02/95				
Sales	**7,763.9**	**8,247.1**	**9,684.6**	**2,714.3**	P/E Ratio	**18.8**	Price (9/30/95)	**22.00**
Net Income	**143.4**	**162.9**	**207.4**	**58.1**	P/B Ratio	**3.9**	52 Wk Hi-Low	**24.75-18.00**
Book Value	**509.0**	**639.1**	**1,026.6**	**285.2**	Yield %	**1.6**	Market Cap	**US$967.2mil**

Address **36 Stellenberg Rd.**	Tel **021-933-5137**	ADR		President	--
Parow Industria 7500	Fax **021-931-0848**	SEDOL No.	**6681755**	Chairman	**Christo Wiese**

Pick 'n Pay Stores

Industry: **Food Retailers & Wholesalers**

Pick 'n Pay Stores is a retailer of food and general merchandise. The company operates Pick 'n Pay hypermarkets and supermarkets, Score supermarkets, RiteValu franchise-operated stores. Price Club wholesale stores, and Boardmans household-goods retail shops. It has also diversified into the operation of auto centers. Pick 'n Pay's property division comprises 14 property-owning subsidiaries, and manages more than 16 shopping centers that it owns or leases in South Africa. Pick 'n Pay Holdings owns 52% of the company's share capital.

R mil	02/93	02/94	02/95	US$mil 02/95				
Sales	**6,423.5**	**6,685.9**	**7,919.5**	**2,219.6**	P/E Ratio	**22.2**	Price (9/30/95)	**11.25**
Net Income	**93.0**	**96.4**	**67.0**	**18.8**	P/B Ratio	**4.3**	52 Wk Hi-Low	**11.75-8.00**
Book Value	**348.0**	**386.9**	**405.4**	**112.6**	Yield %	**2.8**	Market Cap	**US$482.4mil**

Address **Main & Campground Rds.**
Claremont 7700
Tel **021-658-1000**
Fax **021-683-2514-**
ADR
SEDOL No. **6688068**
Managing Director **G.M. Ackerman**
Chairman **R.D. Ackerman**

Plate Glass & Shatterprufe Industries

Industry: **Building Materials**

Plate Glass & Shatterprufe Industries (PGSI) manufactures glass and board products for the automotive, construction, and furniture industries. Its wholly-owned subsidiary Glass SA is South Africa's leading exporter of float and automotive glass. PGSI owns 81% of Belron International, which repairs and replaces automotive glass through more than 800 branches in 11 countries. The company also has a 75% interest in PG Bison, a manufacturer of wood-based board products, and a 45% interest in PG Industries, a maker of building materials in Zimbabwe and Botswana.

R mil	03/93	03/94	03/95	US$mil 03/95				
Sales	**2,774.6**	**3,237.0**	**3,772.4**	**1,054.6**	P/E Ratio	**15.2**	Price (9/30/95)	**129.00**
Net Income	**79.1**	**189.2**	**246.9**	**69.0**	P/B Ratio	**5.2**	52 Wk Hi-Low	**160.00-115.00**
Book Value	**301.3**	**439.6**	**617.9**	**172.6**	Yield %	**2.2**	Market Cap	**US$873.3mil**

Address **20 Baker St., Rosebank**
Johannesburg 2196
Tel **011-880-4801**
Fax **011-788-0665**
ADR
SEDOL No. **6692401**
Chief Executive **Ronnie Lubner**
Chairman **Ronnie Lubner**

Power Technologies

Industry: **Electrical Components & Equipment**

Power Technologies (Powertech) is a holding company with interests in energy-control equipment, power and telecommunications cables, domestic appliances, lighting products, batteries, and solar energy. ABB Powertech, a joint venture with Swiss-based ABB Asea Brown Boveri, manufactures power-generation, -transmisson, and -distribution equipment. Powertech's general technologies division manufactures Hoover appliances, and has alliances with Maytag and Whirlpool of the United States, as well as with Hitachi of Japan. Powertech is a member of South Africa's Altron Group.

R mil	02/93	02/94	02/95	US$mil 02/95				
Sales	**1,148.3**	**1,537.8**	**1,813.9**	**508.4**	P/E Ratio	**17.3**	Price (9/30/95)	**7.65**
Net Income	**45.7**	**62.7**	**72.3**	**20.3**	P/B Ratio	**3.0**	52 Wk Hi-Low	**8.70-6.50**
Book Value	**308.6**	**372.7**	**428.8**	**119.1**	Yield %	**1.7**	Market Cap	**US$346.5mil**

Address **Knightsbridge, 33 Sloane St.**
Bryanston 2152
Tel **011-706-7184**
Fax **011-706-7890**
ADR
SEDOL No. **6698023**
Chief Executive **Johan P. van den Bergh**
Chairman **Peter A. Watt**

Premier Group

Industry: **Other Food**

Premier Group manufactures and distributes food products, dairy products, cooking oils and fats, and animal feed. Through its subsidiaries, the company operates maize and wheat mills, manages cotton farms, processes cotton, manufactures pharmaceuticals, and operates wholesale businesses. Premier also retails tools, home-improvement products, videos, and other consumer products. Food manufacturing accounts for 44% of the company's earnings, and pharmaceutical sales account for 24%. Its partially-owned subsidiaries include Clicks Group and Metro Cash and Carry.

R mil	04/92 *	04/93	04/94	US$mil 04/94				
Sales	**10,638.2**	**10,151.1**	**14,430.8**	**4,253.1**	P/E Ratio	**16.6**	Price (9/30/95)	**5.15**
Net Income	**190.5**	**200.3**	**204.6**	**60.3**	P/B Ratio	**3.2**	52 Wk Hi-Low	**5.65-4.50**
Book Value	**1,104.8**	**1,268.5**	**1,327.4**	**377.1**	Yield %	**1.9**	Market Cap	**US$1,166.1mil**

Address **1 Newtown Ave.**
Killarney 2193
Tel **011-446-9111**
Fax **011-446-2239**
ADR
SEDOL No. **6699899**
Chief Executive **P.G.A. Wrighton**
Chairman **P.G.A. Wrighton**

*Irregular period due to fiscal year change.

Pretoria Portland Cement

Industry: **Building Materials**

Pretoria Portland Cement Company (PPC) manufactures and distributes cement, lime, and limestone products. Its six factories produce 5.5 million tons of cement each year, accounting for 45% of the market share in South Africa. The company operates a lime plant at Lime Acres in the Northern Cape that produces 2.2 million tons of lime annually. PPC also invests in a range of companies that manufacture cement-based products, paper bags, and containers. These investments include cement companies in Namibia and Natal. Barlow, an infrastructure builder, owns 59% of PPC.

R mil	09/92	09/93	09/94	US$mil 09/94				
Sales	**810.0**	**1,102.3**	**1,327.6**	**378.3**	P/E Ratio	**23.1**	Price (9/30/95)	**86.50**
Net Income	**107.0**	**160.6**	**141.1**	**40.2**	P/B Ratio	**5.1**	52 Wk Hi-Low	**111.00-84.00**
Book Value	**579.0**	**655.0**	**696.9**	**195.2**	Yield %	**2.9**	Market Cap	**US$973.0mil**

Address **11 Sherborne Rd., Parktown**
Johannesburg 2193
Tel **011-488-1700**
Fax **011-726-3537**
ADR
SEDOL No. **6701749**
Managing Director **John E. Gomersall**
Chairman **W.A.M. Clewlow**

Q Data

Industry: **Software**

Q Data manufacturers computer equipment and peripherals and offers computer-related services. The company's main activities are the development of software programs, the sale and rental of computer software packages, and the provision of support for software programs. The company operates through 15 main software and consulting subsidiaries, including Q Packaged Programs, Knowledge Systems International, Payroll Software Holdings, and Automated Reasoning. Q Data is 43%-owned by computer hardware and software manufacturer Siltek.

R mil	06/93	06/94	06/95	US$mil 06/95				
Sales	**203.7**	**271.2**	**510.3**	**150.1**	P/E Ratio	**22.0**	Price (9/30/95)	**31.00**
Net Income	**13.0**	**17.7**	**26.3**	**7.7**	P/B Ratio	**7.6**	52 Wk Hi-Low	**32.00-25.00**
Book Value	**25.5**	**33.1**	**75.9**	**20.9**	Yield %	**1.1**	Market Cap	**US$138.9mil**

Address	**230 16th Rd., Randjiespark**	Tel	**011-313-5111**	ADR		Managing Director	**P. den Boer**
	Halfway House 1685	Fax	**011-313-5120**	SEDOL No.	**6713584**	Chairman	**P. den Boer**

Rembrandt

Industry: **Distillers & Brewers**

Rembrandt Group is a diversified holding company with its main businesses in tobacco, liquor, and mining. The firm also has equity stakes in companies engaged in banking and financial services, forestry and timber processing, printing and packaging, engineering, medical services, and food. The Trade Mark Group, which accounts for half of the firm's total earnings, consists of four wholly-owned tobacco and liquor subsidiaries, including Intercontinental Tobacco and Matindus. Tegniese Mynbeleggings, a mining subsidiary, accounts for one fourth of total earnings.

R mil	03/93	03/94	03/95	US$mil 03/95				
Sales	**1,388.8**	**1,640.7**	**5,365.0**	**1,499.9**	P/E Ratio	**14.4**	Price (9/30/95)	**30.50**
Net Income	**987.5**	**1,032.9**	**949.0**	**265.3**	P/B Ratio	**2.1**	52 Wk Hi-Low	**30.75-23.50**
Book Value	**6,354.4**	**7,089.3**	**7,718.0**	**2,155.9**	Yield %	**1.6**	Market Cap	**US$4,361.9mil**

Address	**Coetzier St.**	Tel	**021-883-2333**	ADR	**RBDGY**	Managing Director	**M.H. Visser**
	Stellenbosch 7599	Fax	**021-887-1645**	SEDOL No.	**6731928**	Chairman	**Johan P. Rupert**

Reunert

Industry: **Diversified Technology**

Reunert is an investment-holding company active in the electrical engineering, defense, electronics, and telecommunications industries. Its electrical engineering holdings include wholly-owned Circuit Breaker Industries, a maker of circuit breakers and earth leakage-protection products, 41%-owned African Cables, a producer of electrical and communication cables, and a 50%-owned GEC Alsthom South Africa, a manufacturer of power-generation equipment. Its other interests include the manufacture of armored vehicles, radar equipment, and fiberoptic cable.

R mil	09/92	09/93	09/94	US$mil 09/94				
Sales	**2,277.6**	**2,367.6**	**3,512.2**	**1,000.9**	P/E Ratio	**25.9**	Price (9/30/95)	**20.50**
Net Income	**53.0**	**99.7**	**144.1**	**41.1**	P/B Ratio	**7.5**	52 Wk Hi-Low	**21.50-13.25**
Book Value	**257.4**	**322.3**	**522.8**	**146.4**	Yield %	**1.3**	Market Cap	**US$1,072.4mil**

Address	**Lincoln Wood, Woodlands Dr.**	Tel	**011-804-5888**	ADR		Chief Executive	**A.J. Ellingford**
	Woodmead, Sandton 2146	Fax	**011-804-5997**	SEDOL No.	**6728726**	Chairman	**C.C. Parker**

Rustenburg Platinum

Industry: **Precious Metals**

Rustenburg Platinum is the largest producer of platinum in the world. Among the products extracted from the company's three primary mines are platinum, palladium, rhodium, iridium, ruthenium, osmium, gold, silver, copper, and nickel. Processing and refining of the mines' output is carried out by Rustenburg Base Metals Refiners, a wholly-owned subsidiary. The largest market for platinum is the automotive industry, where the metal is used in catalytic converters to reduce engine emissions. Other markets include the jewelry, chemical, and electronics industries.

R mil	06/92	06/93	06/94	US$mil 06/94				
Sales	**2,732.8**	**2,814.9**	**2,956.4**	**855.2**	P/E Ratio	**34.7**	Price (9/30/95)	**79.50**
Net Income	**402.3**	**281.4**	**287.4**	**83.1**	P/B Ratio	**4.9**	52 Wk Hi-Low	**119.00-74.00**
Book Value	**1,745.4**	**1,857.4**	**2,051.4**	**562.0**	Yield %	**2.1**	Market Cap	**US$2,729.6mil**

Address	**Fox & Harrison Sts.**	Tel	**011-373-9111**	ADR	**RPATY**	Managing Director	**B.E. Davison**
	Johannesburg 2001	Fax	**011-834-4962**	SEDOL No.	**6761000**	Chairman	**P.F. Retief**

Safmarine & Rennies

Industry: **Marine Transportation**

Safmarine and Rennies Holdings (Safren) offers industrial services in the transport and leisure sectors. Through its three main subsidiaries, wholly-owned Safmarine, 75%-owned Rennies Group, and 73%-owned Kersaf Investments, the company engages in shipping and air transport, travel services, hotel and cinema management, and liquor and water distribution. Kersaf Investments accounts for 44% of the company's revenue, and Safmarine accounts for 36%. The Rennies Group represents travel agent Thomas Cook and transport company Federal Express in South Africa.

R mil	06/92	06/93	06/94	US$mil 06/94				
Sales	**4,294.7**	**4,502.6**	**5,075.9**	**1,468.3**	P/E Ratio	**1.7**	Price (9/30/95)	**10.75**
Net Income	**269.9**	**297.2**	**325.8**	**94.2**	P/B Ratio	**0.3**	52 Wk Hi-Low	**13.50-9.75**
Book Value	**1,276.4**	**1,701.5**	**2,040.2**	**559.0**	Yield %	**25.6**	Market Cap	**US$163.3mil**

Address	**Safmarine Hse., 22 Riebeek St.**	Tel	**021-408-6015**	ADR		Chief Executive	**D.A. Hawton**
	Cape Town 8001	Fax	**021-419-6844**	SEDOL No.	**6766685**	Chairman	**D.A. Hawton**

Sage

Industry: **Insurance - Full Line**

Sage Group provides life insurance and financial services and develops property throughout South Africa. The company's core business activity is life insurance, but it also offers a range of financial services, including investment management, mutual-fund management, personal financial planning, and banking. Its property division owns property, develops land, and builds houses. Sage's main subsidiaries are Amalgamated Insurance Holdings, Sage Life, Sage Capital Managers, Investor Mutual Funds, and Sage Property Holdings.

	R mil 03/93	03/94	03/95	US$mil 03/95				
Revenues	**727.4**	**830.4**	**1,111.2**	**310.7**	P/E Ratio	**17.3**	Price (9/30/95)	**15.00**
Net Income	**58.2**	**95.7**	**82.9**	**23.2**	P/B Ratio	**3.0**	52 Wk Hi-Low	**15.00-8.93**
Book Value	**346.4**	**402.7**	**511.2**	**142.8**	Yield %	**3.0**	Market Cap	**US$392.5mil**

Address **Sage Ctr., 10 Fraser St.** **Johannesburg 2001**
Tel **011-377-5555** Fax **011-834-2107**
ADR SEDOL No. **6767321**
President -- Chairman **H. Louis Shill**

Samancor

Industry: **Mining**

Samancor owns and operates two manganese mines,two chrome mines, and nine plants to process the mines' output. Most of its chrome ore is converted into ferrochrome for use in making stainless steel. Samancor is the largest ferrochrome producer in the world. It also supplies 40% of the world's consumption of manganese for use in the desulfurization and strengthening of steel and aluminum. The company also produces dolomite and silica from two mines and two processing plants. Its main competitors are in Russia and China.

	R mil 06/92	06/93	06/94	US$mil 06/94				
Sales	**2,063.9**	**1,790.9**	**2,189.6**	**633.4**	P/E Ratio	**33.8**	Price (9/30/95)	**50.00**
Net Income	**275.0**	**176.7**	**280.2**	**81.1**	P/B Ratio	**4.2**	52 Wk Hi-Low	**58.00-46.00**
Book Value	**2,057.0**	**2,141.7**	**2,252.4**	**617.1**	Yield %	**1.3**	Market Cap	**US$2,588.6mil**

Address **Samancor Hse., 88 Marshall St.** **Johannesburg 2001**
Tel **011-491-7368** Fax **011-491-7911**
ADR **SMNCY** SEDOL No. **6823052**
Managing Director **G.P. Gilbertson** Chairman **Mike Salamon**

Sappi

Industry: **Paper Products**

Sappi is South Africa's largest pulp and paper producer, holding about half of that country's paper market. The company manages about 340,000 hectares of plantations in Africa, which supply about 50% of its timber requirements. Sappi, which is the world's top maker of coated wood-free papers, has overseas operations in the United Kingdom, the United States, and Germany. In October 1994, Sappi acquired a leading manufacturer of coated free-sheet paper, S.D. Warren, from Scott Paper.

	R mil 02/93	02/94	02/95	US$mil 02/95				
Sales	**4,677.0**	**5,540.6**	**7,804.1**	**2,187.2**	P/E Ratio	**20.4**	Price (9/30/95)	**71.75**
Net Income	**351.2**	**95.1**	**117.3**	**32.9**	P/B Ratio	**1.8**	52 Wk Hi-Low	**76.50-55.25**
Book Value	**5,077.3**	**5,822.5**	**6,035.8**	**1,676.6**	Yield %	**1.4**	Market Cap	**US$2,977.0mil**

Address **48 Ameshoff St.** **Braamfontein 2001**
Tel **011-407-8111** Fax **011-339-1846**
ADR **SAPIY** SEDOL No. **6777007**
President -- Chairman **Eugene van As**

Sasol

Industry: **Oil - Secondary**

Sasol produces and markets liquid fuels, pipeline gas, petrochemicals, fertilizers, and coal. Its synthetic-fuels business accounts for roughly 40% of the company's profits. Other activities include the manufacture of waxes, alpha olefins, solvents, phenolics, tar products, solvents, and mining explosives. Its subsidiaries include National Petroleum Refiners of South Africa and Tosas, a manufacturer of road-binding materials. Sasol conducts most of its business in South Africa, but the firm also has petrochemical operations in Europe and the Far East.

	R mil 06/92	06/93	06/94	US$mil 06/94				
Sales	**7,853.9**	**8,247.4**	**9,841.8**	**2,846.9**	P/E Ratio	**11.5**	Price (9/30/95)	**30.00**
Net Income	**1,153.0**	**1,303.6**	**1,497.5**	**433.2**	P/B Ratio	**2.3**	52 Wk Hi-Low	**37.50-29.00**
Book Value	**5,541.1**	**6,363.3**	**7,366.8**	**2,018.3**	Yield %	**3.0**	Market Cap	**US$5,215.0mil**

Address **1 Sturdee Ave.** **Rosebank 2196**
Tel **011-441-3111** Fax **011-788-5092**
ADR **SASOY** SEDOL No. **6777450**
Managing Director **Paul Kruger** Chairman **J.A. Stegmann**

Sentrachem

Industry: **Specialty Chemicals**

Sentrachem is an investment holding company that has interests primarily in the chemicals industry. The company's subsidiaries manufacture agricultural chemicals, veterinary products, animal feeds, industrial chemicals, foodstuffs, plastics, and rubber. In July 1995, the company acquired U.S.-based chemical manufacturer Hampshire Chemicals. It also has a joint-venture agreement with Germany's Hoechst to build a polypropylene plant in South Africa. South African holding company Sankorp owns a 37% interest in the company.

	R mil 08/92	08/93	08/94	US$mil 08/94				
Sales	**2,433.2**	**2,623.3**	**2,795.3**	**799.1**	P/E Ratio	**17.2**	Price (9/30/95)	**15.50**
Net Income	**56.5**	**76.2**	**119.2**	**34.1**	P/B Ratio	**3.1**	52 Wk Hi-Low	**17.75-12.50**
Book Value	**597.8**	**636.8**	**758.1**	**211.8**	Yield %	**1.8**	Market Cap	**US$637.5mil**

Address **5 Protea Pl.** **Sandton 2196**
Tel **011-783-2121** Fax **011-783-2180**
ADR SEDOL No. **6795708**
Managing Director **J.L. Job** Chairman **D. Hunt-Davis**

Servgro

Industry: **Other Recreational Products & Services**

Servgro International invests primarily in the hotel and leisure industries. The company's main interests include an 85% stake in Zeda Holdings, a provider of Avis car-rental services in southern Africa; a 55% stake in Price Forbes Group, an insurance broker and financial consultant; a 48% stake in Fedics Group, a contract caterer and food-retailer; a 41% stake in Interleisure, a film and video distributor; and a 43% stake in Interpark, a parking developer. Servgro also has interests in the television-rental and -repair, cellular-communications, and publishing sectors.

	R mil 03/93	03/94	03/95	US$mil 03/95				
Sales	**921.4**	**966.3**	**1,139.2**	**318.5**	P/E Ratio	**24.4**	Price (9/30/95)	**16.25**
Net Income	**50.8**	**54.7**	**74.0**	**20.7**	P/B Ratio	**3.9**	52 Wk Hi-Low	**16.25-10.00**
Book Value	**347.6**	**378.3**	**483.1**	**134.9**	Yield %	**1.5**	Market Cap	**US$491.6mil**

Address	**President Pl., 148 Jan Smuts Ave.**	Tel	**011-442-6320**	ADR		President	--
	Rosebank 2196	Fax	**011-442-6335**	SEDOL No.	**6796916**	Chairman	**P.J.J. van der Walt**

Siltek

Industry: **Computers**

Siltek designs, manufactures, and distributes computer hardware and software for information communication technology. The company also provides support and consulting services. Its main systems and networking subsidiaries are HiPerformance Systems and Centera, South Africa's largest networking company. Its main distribution subsidiaries are M&PD and Electronic Back-up Systems. Through subsidiaries, it also manufactures automated-teller machines and credit-card and check verification terminals. Siltek is 64% owned by Grintek, an electronics company.

	R mil 06/93	06/94	06/95	US$mil 06/95				
Sales	**1,120.4**	**1,412.3**	**1,747.6**	**514.0**	P/E Ratio	**14.5**	Price (9/30/95)	**21.00**
Net Income	**39.4**	**45.8**	**69.9**	**20.6**	P/B Ratio	**4.4**	52 Wk Hi-Low	**23.00-14.50**
Book Value	**174.1**	**205.5**	**255.6**	**70.2**	Yield %	**2.0**	Market Cap	**US$292.4mil**

Address	**275 Kent Ave.**	Tel	**011-886-2410**	ADR		Managing Director	**Patrick A. Landey**
	Ferndale, Randburg 2194	Fax	**011-886-1976**	SEDOL No.	**6900803**	Chairman	**A.N. Saulez**

C.G. Smith

Industry: **Other Food**

C.G. Smith is the parent company of a diversified group of businesses focused primarily in the nondurable consumer-goods sector. The group operates in a broad range of industries covering food, fishing, pharmaceuticals, packaging, paper, textiles, and bulk liquid storage. The firm is one of the largest industrial companies quoted on the Johannesburg Stock Exchange. C.G. Smith holds about 65% of the shares of Nampak, the largest packing company in South Africa.

	R mil 09/92	09/93	09/94	US$mil 09/94				
Sales	**17,836.3**	**19,191.7**	**20,876.5**	**5,949.4**	P/E Ratio	**21.6**	Price (9/30/95)	**22.90**
Net Income	**471.4**	**391.7**	**364.5**	**103.9**	P/B Ratio	**3.9**	52 Wk Hi-Low	**23.75-15.00**
Book Value	**2,327.4**	**2,599.3**	**2,802.5**	**785.0**	Yield %	**1.6**	Market Cap	**US$2,956.7mil**

Address	**36 Wierda Rd. W.**	Tel	**011-883-0575**	ADR	**CGSMY**	President	--
	Sandton 2146	Fax	**011-883-3100**	SEDOL No.	**6816137**	Chairman	**Derek Cooper**

South African Breweries

Industry: **Distillers & Brewers**

South African Breweries' main interests are beer, hotels, and retailing. Its beer operations hold a virtual monopoly in South Africa. Subsidiaries making plate glass, furniture, textiles, safety matches, and footwear account for 22% of sales. The firm sells clothing, textiles, and footwear through its Edgars, Sales House, and Jet retail chains. It owns and operates 56 hotels and resorts in South Africa. It also produces carbonated beverages and fruit juices, and makes Coca-Cola and Schweppes products for the South African market.

	R mil 03/93	03/94	03/95	US$mil 03/95				
Sales	**19,410.1**	**21,966.7**	**27,882.0**	**7,794.8**	P/E Ratio	**24.7**	Price (9/30/95)	**115.00**
Net Income	**893.8**	**990.5**	**1,372.0**	**383.6**	P/B Ratio	**6.3**	52 Wk Hi-Low	**116.00-83.50**
Book Value	**4,498.5**	**4,783.5**	**5,063.0**	**1,414.2**	Yield %	**1.7**	Market Cap	**US$8,630.1mil**

Address	**2 Jan Smuts Ave.**	Tel	**011-407-1700**	ADR	**SBWRY**	President	--
	Johannesburg 2001	Fax	**011-339-1830**	SEDOL No.	**6822101**	Chairman	**J. Meyer Kahn**

Southern Life

Industry: **Insurance - Life & Health**

Southern Life Association offers services that include life and health-care insurance, employee-benefits administration, and asset-management. The company manages more than 5 billion rand in employee-benefits accounts. It also manages four mutual funds. Southern Life has a joint venture with First Bowring Insurance Brokers and First National Bank to market insurance services to First National Bank customers. Its other affiliates include 13%-owned Medi-Clinic Group, a private hospital group, and 25%-owned Hansard Financial Trust, a financial-services company.

	R mil 03/93	03/94	03/95	US$mil 03/95				
Revenues	**3,704.0**	**4,834.2**	**4,783.5**	**1,337.3**	P/E Ratio	**19.0**	Price (9/30/95)	**33.00**
Net Income	**196.2**	**240.3**	**305.5**	**85.4**	P/B Ratio	**5.1**	52 Wk Hi-Low	**40.00-31.00**
Book Value	**683.2**	**872.2**	**1,143.0**	**319.3**	Yield %	**3.5**	Market Cap	**US$1,565.6mil**

Address	**Great Westerford, Main Rd.**	Tel	**021-658-0911**	ADR		Managing Director	**Johannes R. Calitz**
	Rondbosch 7700	Fax	**021-686-4921**	SEDOL No.	**6829997**	Chairman	**Thomas N. Chapman**

Standard Bank Investment

Industry: **Banks - Regional**

Standard Bank Investment Corporation (SBIC) is South Africa's largest banking group in terms of market capitalization and revenue. The company's assets total more than 84 billion rand. Its main subsidiary, The Standard Bank of South Africa, provides individual and corporate banking at 490 branches. SBIC has operations throughout southern Africa, as well as in London, New York, Hong Kong, and Taipei. The company owns 50% of Liblife Controlling, the ultimate holding company of Liberty Life Association. Liberty Life group owns 37% of SBIC.

R mil	12/92	12/93	12/94	US$mil 12/94				
Revenues	**9,661.1**	**10,169.7**	**11,506.0**	**3,243.0**	P/E Ratio	**14.5**	Price (9/30/95)	**124.50**
Net Income	**625.5**	**828.5**	**1,027.0**	**289.5**	P/B Ratio	**2.5**	52 Wk Hi-Low	**145.00-95.00**
Book Value	**3,855.5**	**5,389.9**	**5,852.0**	**1,653.1**	Yield %	**2.1**	Market Cap	**US$4,065.7mil**

Address **5 Simmonds St.** **Johannesburg 2001**
Tel **011-636-6086**
Fax **011-636-6084**
ADR
SEDOL No. **6838829**
Managing Director **E.P. Theron**
Chairman **C.B. Strauss**

Stocks & Stocks

Industry: **Industrial - Diversified**

Stocks & Stocks engages in property development and construction. Its construction division designs and constructs commercial buildings and homes and operates civil engineering projects. Construction accounts for 51% of the company's income and property development accounts for 39%. Current projects include Sandton Square, Portswood Ridge in Cape Town, Woolworths' head office in Cape Town, and a new Makro outlet in Sandton. The company also manages timeshare homes, owns and manages hotels, reinforces and trades steel, and develops information technology.

R mil	04/92	04/93	04/94	US$mil 04/94				
Sales	**1,439.0**	**1,104.0**	**1,334.2**	**393.2**	P/E Ratio	**13.1**	Price (9/30/95)	**4.60**
Net Income	**20.0**	**11.9**	**27.8**	**8.2**	P/B Ratio	**1.8**	52 Wk Hi-Low	**5.35-3.00**
Book Value	**164.0**	**173.8**	**200.5**	**57.0**	Yield %	**2.0**	Market Cap	**US$101.4mil**

Address **23A 10th Ave.** **Rivonia 2128**
Tel **011-806-4000**
Fax **011-806-4009**
ADR
SEDOL No. **6853112**
President --
Chairman **Reginald A. Edwards**

Suncrush

Industry: **Soft Drinks**

Suncrush is a Natal-based bottler of soft drinks and fruit juices. It has bottling licenses for Coca-Cola, Fanta, Krest, Schweppes, and Sparletta. The company also markets fruit juices under the Appletiser label. Its beverage and bottling subsidiaries include Queenstown Bottlers, Mmabatho Mineral Waters, Havrey. It also has interests in distributor Intertruck Holdings, and holding companies Tempora Investments and Ettington Investments. The company is 50% owned by Dalys, a South African holding company whose main source of income is dividend payments by Suncrush.

R mil	06/93	06/94	06/95	US$mil 06/95				
Sales	**572.0**	**616.2**	**708.1**	**208.3**	P/E Ratio	**19.3**	Price (9/30/95)	**12.75**
Net Income	**60.4**	**81.3**	**98.8**	**29.1**	P/B Ratio	**3.9**	52 Wk Hi-Low	**14.50-10.75**
Book Value	**361.5**	**419.0**	**491.9**	**135.1**	Yield %	**1.5**	Market Cap	**US$547.6mil**

Address **491 Ridge Rd.** **Durban 4000**
Tel **031-29-4371**
Fax **011-29-9125**
ADR
SEDOL No. **6806536**
Managing Director **R.D. Hamilton**
Chairman **R.D. Hamilton**

Tiger Oats

Industry: **Other Food**

Tiger Oats is an investment holding company operating in the food-processing and distribution industry. Operations include milling, baking, confectionery, agribusiness and food processing, edible oils and derivatives, trading, shipping, and distribution. The company holds controlling interests in the pharmaceutical company Adcock Ingram and food company Oceana Fishing. Tiger Oats is a subsidiary of C.G. Smith, a South African consumer-goods manufacturer.

R mil	09/92	09/93	09/94	US$mil 09/94				
Sales	**9,211.8**	**10,039.4**	**10,975.5**	**3,127.8**	P/E Ratio	**21.7**	Price (9/30/95)	**53.00**
Net Income	**298.1**	**325.3**	**222.8**	**63.5**	P/B Ratio	**3.7**	52 Wk Hi-Low	**56.00-40.00**
Book Value	**1,821.4**	**2,046.7**	**2,154.4**	**603.5**	Yield %	**1.6**	Market Cap	**US$2,183.6mil**

Address **85 Bute Ln.** **Sandton 2146**
Tel **011-320-0111**
Fax **011-884-2029**
ADR **TIOAY**
SEDOL No. **6891297**
President --
Chairman **R.A. Williams**

Tongaat-Hulett

Industry: **Other Food**

Tongaat-Hulett Group is an holding company with interests in the manufacture of sugar, building materials, consumer foods, aluminum, textiles, starch, and glucose. The company operates five sugar mills and one sugar refinery. It also operates plants that produce food products such as edible oils, mushrooms, cordials, and dehydrated food. The company's building-materials division produces bricks, clay roofing materials, and ceramic tiles and also owns 20 wholesale outlets and 21 Brick 'n Tile retail stores. Anglo American Industrial owns 43% of Tongaat-Hulett's shares.

R mil	03/93	03/94	03/95	US$mil 03/95				
Sales	**3,872.8**	**3,972.3**	**4,417.5**	**1,235.0**	P/E Ratio	**16.4**	Price (9/30/95)	**45.00**
Net Income	**196.6**	**153.7**	**286.2**	**80.0**	P/B Ratio	**1.9**	52 Wk Hi-Low	**51.50-39.00**
Book Value	**1,872.5**	**1,963.1**	**2,229.4**	**622.7**	Yield %	**2.2**	Market Cap	**US$1,123.6mil**

Address **Amanzimnyama Hill** **Tongaat, Natal 4400**
Tel **0322-21000**
Fax **0322-21094**
ADR
SEDOL No. **6443502**
Managing Director **C.M.L. Savage**
Chairman **C.J. Saunders**

Trans-Natal Coal

Industry: **Coal**

Trans-Natal Coal Corporation serves as the investment-holding arm for Gencor's mining interests. Its principal holding is a 50% interest in Ingwe Coal Corporation, the world's largest exporter of steam coal. Ingwe was created when Rand Mines and Gencor merged their coal-mining subsidiaries, Randcoal and Trans-Natal Coal, in October 1994. Gencor manages Ingwe through its 50% controlling interest in Trans-Natal. The company also markets coal and finances coal-mining projects. Trans-Natal Coal owns a 41% interest in the Richards Bay Coal Terminal.

	R mil 06/92	06/93	06/94	US$mil 06/94				
Sales	**1,564.1**	**1,638.7**	**1,728.5**	**500.0**	P/E Ratio	**21.4**	Price (9/30/95)	**28.00**
Net Income	**143.6**	**98.5**	**104.4**	**30.2**	P/B Ratio	**N/A**	52 Wk Hi-Low	**33.00-24.50**
Book Value	**679.0**	**713.8**	**N/A**	**N/A**	Yield %	**2.9**	Market Cap	**US$611.2mil**

Address **80 Marshall St.** **Johannesburg 2001**
Tel **011-376-9111**
Fax **011-376-2419**
ADR
SEDOL No. **6901107**
Managing Director **D.J.K. Murray**
Chairman **B.P. Gilbertson**

Trencor

Industry: **Trucking**

Trencor manufactures, exports, owns, leases, and finances the purchase of transport containers in South Africa and abroad. It also manufactures truck trailers, road tankers, and trailer components. Its transport division offers cargo-shipment, express-parcel, and air-courier services. The company also exports automotive products and general commodities. Trencor owns a 28% interest in W & A Investment Corporation, a South African holding company for industrial and consumer businesses. Mobile Industries, a South African holding company, owns 47% of the company.

	R mil 06/92	06/93	06/94	US$mil 06/94				
Sales	**644.0**	**740.6**	**853.9**	**247.0**	P/E Ratio	**17.0**	Price (9/30/95)	**16.00**
Net Income	**130.0**	**252.3**	**34.1**	**9.9**	P/B Ratio	**3.8**	52 Wk Hi-Low	**20.00-14.00**
Book Value	**443.0**	**587.1**	**613.4**	**168.1**	Yield %	**1.5**	Market Cap	**US$636.9mil**

Address **1313 Main Twr., Heerengracht** **Cape Town 8001**
Tel **021-21-7310**
Fax **021-419-3692**
ADR
SEDOL No. **6905336**
President --
Chairman **N.I. Jowell**

Vaal Reefs Exploration & Mining

Industry: **Precious Metals**

Vaal Reefs Exploration & Mining is involved in the exploration and mining of gold, uranium oxide, and sulphuric acid. The company has over 10 operating shafts in the Klerksdorp district, North West Province, Transvaal, and the Viljoenskroon district in Orange Free State, South Africa. Vaal Reefs has five gold plant complexes, two uranium plants, and two acid plants. In 1994, the company produced 70.7 tons of gold and 1.2 tons of uranium. The company's main subsidiary is wholly-owned Western Reefs Exploration & Development.

	R mil 12/92	12/93	12/94	US$mil 12/94				
Sales	**N/A**	**2,926.1**	**3,108.6**	**876.2**	P/E Ratio	**NMF**	Price (9/30/95)	**240.00**
Net Income	**N/A**	**637.2**	**676.7**	**190.7**	P/B Ratio	**1.0**	52 Wk Hi-Low	**478.00-194.50**
Book Value	**N/A**	**4,147.5**	**4,643.8**	**1,311.8**	Yield %	**N/A**	Market Cap	**US$1,256.9mil**

Address **44 Main St.** **Johannesburg 2001**
Tel **011-638-9111**
Fax **011-638-5281**
ADR **VAALY**
SEDOL No. **6926100**
Managing Director **L. Hewitt**
Chairman **C.L. Sunter**

Wooltru

Industry: **Food Retailers & Wholesalers**

Wooltru operates a range of clothing, food, and housewares stores. It manages 82 Woolworths department stores that offer food and general merchandise under the Woolworths label. The company operates 202 Truworths and 150 Topics clothing stores, 18 Dion general-merchandise stores, and 12 Makro warehouse clubs. Its home-shopping business, Leading Concepts, offers catalogue shopping and manages two retail showrooms. Wooltru is also active in property development, and has a joint venture with Investec Property to develop a new retail area in Stellenbosch.

	R mil 06/92	06/93	06/94	US$mil 06/94				
Sales	**3,804.0**	**5,560.5**	**6,676.5**	**1,931.3**	P/E Ratio	**31.5**	Price (9/30/95)	**21.25**
Net Income	**92.0**	**151.9**	**255.7**	**74.0**	P/B Ratio	**7.5**	52 Wk Hi-Low	**25.00-18.00**
Book Value	**776.5**	**825.8**	**1,001.7**	**274.4**	Yield %	**1.3**	Market Cap	**US$868.6mil**

Address **Wooltru Hse., 93 Longmarket St.** **Cape Town 8001**
Tel **021-407-9114**
Fax **021-461-9246**
ADR
SEDOL No. **6980913**
Chief Executive **Colin Hall**
Chairman **Henri Kuiper**

South Korea

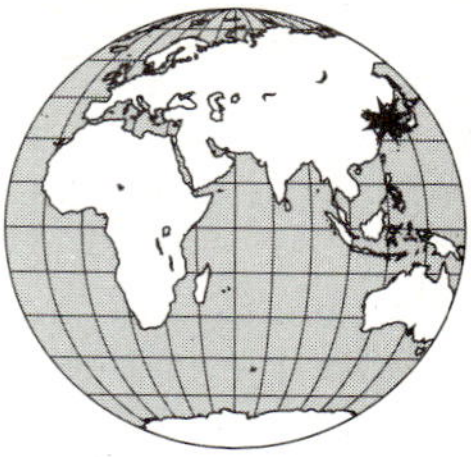

South Korea

Kim Soo-Mi,
Seoul

Local Trading Hours	Time Difference from New York	Population (Est. 94)
9:30-11:30 and 1:00-3:00 Mon.-Fri. 9:30-11:30 Sat.	13 hours ahead of EST	44,450,000

Since its establishment in November 1956 with only 12 listed companies, the Korea Stock Exchange (KSE) has undergone a great expansion in line with the nation's overall economy — which has grown into one of Asia's major economic powerhouses from a poor agricultural nation over the past three decades.

The KSE, the nation's only stock exchange, has now grown to become the fourth biggest in Asia and 16th in the world. At the end of 1994 there were 699 companies listed and a combined market capitalization of 151.17 trillion won.

Despite recent rapid growth, Korea's total market capitalization is still only 49.6% of GDP, low compared with other Asian emerging markets. In terms of market capitalization, the largest of the 27 sectors on the exchange at end 1994 was the electric and electronics sector at 17.17 trillion won, followed by electric power and gas at 17.01 trillion won, banks at 16.40 trillion won, chemicals 11.33 trillion won and securities 10.45 trillion won.

Korea Electric Power Corp. (Kepco) topped the list with a market capitalization of 16.78 trillion won, followed by Samsung Electronics, 6.72 trillion won, and Pohang Iron & Steel Co. (Posco), 6.01 trillion won. At the end of 1994, the 10 largest companies on the exchange accounted for 31% of the total value of the Korean market.

The KSE is composed of the first section, which trades big listed companies with 80% or more of the total shares, and the second section. The second section trades the newly listed companies with less than 20% of the total outstanding shares publicly offered.

Companies listed on the second section can move to the first section later if they satisfy certain requirements, which, among other things, call upon them to have 40% or more of their equity publicly traded, distribute a certain level of dividends and have a debt ratio below the average in their sector during the latest three fiscal years. Any stock in the first section that fails to meet these requirements will be downgraded to the second section.

Dow Jones South Korea Equity Market Index Performance

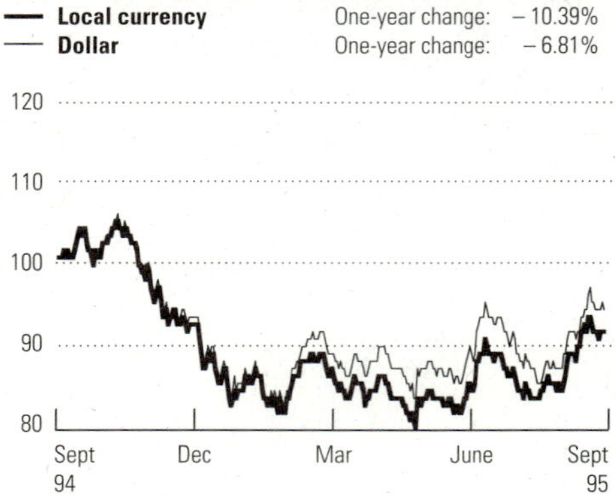

To protect investors from excessive fluctuations in stock prices, the exchange has adopted daily price fluctuation limits under

Gross Domestic Product (94)	Three-Year Average GDP Growth (92-94)	Main Industries	Consumer Price Index (93-94)	Monetary Unit	Exchange Rate (9/95)
US$379.5 billion	+ 7.1%	Electric and electronics, automobiles, chemicals, shipbuilding and steel	+6.2%	Korean Won	Won768.05 to US$1.00

which stock prices may not move by more than 6% of the previous day's closing price.

The average stock price on the KSE was 21,977 won in 1994, up 12.4% from a year before, while the average market price/earnings ratio was 18 times. Domestic individual investors held 40.2% of the total number of shares on the KSE, down from the previous year's 41.3%. The number of shares held by domestic institutional investors also declined to 33.4% from 36.8% in the previous year. Foreign investors accounted for 7.3% of total outstanding shares, up from 7.0% a year earlier.

After a series of measures to ease foreign stock ownership limits, foreign investors can currently purchase up to 15% of the issued shares of any listed company, with a 3% ceiling for each foreign investor. Kepco and Posco are subject to a stricter 10% cap in combined foreign stock ownership and a 1% ceiling for each foreign investor. Stocks that have reached their investment limit can be traded among foreign investors on the over-the-counter market.

From the opening of the stock market to foreigners in January 1992 until the end of 1994, foreign investors purchased 14.91 trillion won of shares and sold 8.14 trillion won, resulting in a net purchase of 6.77 trillion won of stock. In the first eight months of 1995, foreign investors bought 5.37 trillion won and sold 4.32 trillion won, resulting in a net purchase of 1.05 trillion won.

Foreign securities firms wanting to trade in South Korea have to deposit 10 billion won with the Korean government to do each of three securities business activities — brokering, dealing or underwriting — with a total of 30 billion won needed to do all three. Since the first two branch offices were opened in Seoul by Baring Securities and Jardine Fleming of the U.K. in October 1991, the total of foreign branch offices had risen to 14 by August 1995.

Ten Largest Capitalized Companies
as of 9/30/95

Stock	Market Cap. US$Mil
Dong-Ah Construction	871,104,000.0
Korea Electric Power	19,308,997.9
Samsung Electronics	13,888,028.1
Pohang Iron & Steel	6,693,607.2
Daewoo Heavy Industries	4,743,753.7
Korea Mobil Telecom	3,498,340.0
LG Electronics	2,753,424.0
Shinhan Bank	2,719,494.8
Hyundai Engineering & Construction	2,469,719.4
Yukong	2,421,986.4

Taxation for non-residents and foreign corporations varies according to whether they have a permanent establishment in Korea and whether they are the residents of a country having a tax treaty with Korea. If there is a tax treaty, taxation is carried out in accordance with the conditions of the treaty. Otherwise, Korean laws are applied, and non-residents and foreign corporations without a permanent establishment in Korea are subject to a 25% withholding tax for dividends and interest.

Investors from the U.S. and most European nations don't pay this capital gains tax, thanks to tax agreements between their countries and South Korea. But Korea has no such agreements with most Asian countries including Japan, Hong Kong, Singapore, Thailand and Taiwan. For this reason, Japanese investment in South Korean shares is minuscule compared with the inflow from other countries. As of May 1995, the cumulative, net Japanese capital inflow for investment in Korean stocks was $29.7 million, compared with $2.92 billion for the U.S. and $1.97 billion for the U.K.

At present, Korea has no equity derivatives market, but officials have been testing a stock index futures market since April, 3, 1995, with a plan to open it in January 1996. Kospi 200 index futures will trade with four delivery months, March, June, September and December.

The Korean stock market has experienced several changes since its opening to foreign investments. Before the opening, trading was dominated by construction, commercial and financial stocks, which were favored by domestic investors due to their good liquidity. But foreign investors paid more attention to stocks with low price/earnings ratios, favoring shares such as Korea Mobile Telecom and Tae Kwang Ind., and resulting in a more than doubling of their prices.

The KSE put a computerized order-routing system into full operation in 1983, enabling member firms to transmit orders directly to the trading floor. To cope with the expanding trading volume, the Stock Market Automated Trading System, called Smats, the first computerized trading system of the exchange, was introduced in March 1988. Smats has grown since that time and has handled more than 95% of the total stock trading volume since 1991.

Securities companies can impose their trading commission within the KSE specified ceilings: 0.6% for shares and 0.3% for bonds and beneficiary certificates. But, in fact, all domestic brokers now charge the same commission: 0.5% of the contract amount in stock trading of less than 200 million won, with a discount rate for contract amounts above 200 million won.

In 1994, the Korean stock market rose strongly, thanks to a sustained recovery in the economy. The Kospi reached a record high of 1,138.75 points in November 1994, and ended the year at 1,027.37 points, up 18.6% from the end of 1993.

Coming into 1995, the Korean stock market slipped into a correction, dragged down by a combination of poor liquidity and rising interest rates, before it bottomed out in early July. Stock analysts expected the market to continue advancing for the rest of 1995, largely driven by inflow of more funds thanks to the new global composite tax system planned to take effect Jan. 1, 1996.

The new tax system imposes taxes on combined financial gains, except income from stock investment, as opposed to taxing separate financial income under the current tax system.

Anam Industrial

Industry: **Semiconductors & related**

Anam Industrial assembles semiconductors and manufactures watches and optical products. Semiconductors account for almost 96% of the company's sales. The company produces Nikon cameras and products under license from the Japanese optical-equipment manufacturer. It is the flagship company for South Korea's Anam Group and owns 48% of Anam Semiconductor Technology and 29% of Anam Construction. Anam exports 94% of its products, and it is currently developing additional manufacturing facilities in China and making investments in the Philippines.

Won bil	12/92 P	12/93 P	12/94 P	US$mil 12/94				
Sales	**482.4**	**623.2**	**768.4**	**959.1**	P/E Ratio	**21.6**	Price (9/30/95)	**21,400**
Net Income	**7.4**	**11.5**	**14.4**	**17.9**	P/B Ratio	**1.9**	52 Wk Hi-Low	**25,202.9-16,021.2**
Book Value	**124.7**	**147.8**	**158.2**	**202.3**	Yield %	**0.9**	Market Cap	**US$376.1mil**

Address **151-122 Hwayang-dong, Seoul** Tel **02-460-5114** Fax **02-465-2607** ADR SEDOL No. **6001397** President **Hwang In-Gil** Chairman **Hwang In-Gil**

P=Parent company data.

Asia Cement Manufacturing

Industry: **Building Materials**

Asia Cement Manufacturing operates limestone mines and produces cement and ready-mixed concrete mainly for the construction industry in South Korea. Cement accounts for 77% of the company's sales. It is currently constructing a concrete plant in Dalian, China, which will have an average production capacity of 200,000 cubic meters per year. Asia Cement also has interests in paper, finance, telecommunications, construction materials, and retailing. Its subsidiaries include wholly-owned Daesung Industrial Development, 96%-owned Digicom, and 71%-owned Ahjin Constructs.

Won bil	12/92	12/93	12/94	US$mil 12/94				
Sales	**193.6**	**203.2**	**207.2**	**258.6**	P/E Ratio	**8.6**	Price (9/30/95)	**33,000**
Net Income	**11.4**	**10.1**	**15.2**	**18.9**	P/B Ratio	**0.7**	52 Wk Hi-Low	**45,100.0-30,000.0**
Book Value	**102.3**	**152.9**	**176.1**	**225.2**	Yield %	**2.0**	Market Cap	**US$171.9mil**

Address **726, Yoksam-dong, Kangnam-gu, Seoul** Tel **02-527-6400** Fax **02-563-5839** ADR SEDOL No. **6057152** President **Lee Yun-Mu** Chairman **Lee Yun-Mu**

Asia Motors

Industry: **Land Transportation**

Asia Motors manufactures motor vehicles, specializing in trucks, buses, and other heavy-duty vehicles. Its major customers include domestic and overseas military organizations. The company also produces the Pride passenger car. Truck sales account for 34% of the company's revenue, bus sales account for 17% of revenue, and sales of Pride cars make up the remainder. Asia Motors is currently planning the construction of a large-bus manufacturing plant in Kwangju, South Korea. Kia Motors, South Korea's second-largest automaker, owns a 25% interest in Asia Motors.

Won bil	12/92 P	12/93 P	12/94 P	US$mil 12/94				
Sales	**970.5**	**1,023.9**	**1,353.4**	**1,689.3**	P/E Ratio	**48.4**	Price (9/30/95)	**10,800**
Net Income	**7.4**	**8.1**	**7.3**	**9.1**	P/B Ratio	**1.0**	52 Wk Hi-Low	**16,000.0-8,700.0**
Book Value	**290.1**	**365.7**	**429.4**	**549.0**	Yield %	**0.9**	Market Cap	**US$533.9mil**

Address **15 Youido-dong, Yongdungpo-gu, Seoul** Tel **02-788-8497** Fax **02-780-1037** ADR SEDOL No. **6056881** President **Cho Rae-Sung** Chairman **Cho Rae-Sung**

P=Parent company data.

Central Investment & Finance

Industry: **Financial Services - Diversified**

Central Investment & Finance provides short-term financing and related services to small business and corporate clients. The company's services include deposit taking, corporate lending, issuing of corporate notes, and fund management. It is also involved in the factoring business, trade-note discounting, and securities trading. The company owns 96% of Shinchoonggang Mutual Savings & Finance, a savings and loan concern, and has recently set up an offshore futures fund. Central Investment & Finance is 17%-owned by Dongkuk Steel Mill.

Won bil	06/92 P	06/93 P	06/94 P	US$mil 06/94				
Revenues	**390.2**	**327.9**	**324.7**	**400.3**	P/E Ratio	**5.5**	Price (9/30/95)	**16,900**
Net Income	**21.8**	**23.1**	**21.3**	**26.3**	P/B Ratio	**0.8**	52 Wk Hi-Low	**23,500.0-14,000.0**
Book Value	**N/A**	**159.3**	**194.3**	**241.1**	Yield %	**3.6**	Market Cap	**US$211.2mil**

Address **65-2 Myong-dong 1-ga, Chung-gu, Seoul** Tel **02-771-1700** Fax **02-773-6931** ADR SEDOL No. **6184339** President **Yun Jang-Su** Chairman **Yun Jang-Su**

P=Parent company data.

Cheil Foods & Chemicals

Industry: **Other Food**

Cheil Foods & Chemicals manufactures processed foods, seasonings, and animal feed. The company's product range includes sugar, wheat powder, cooking oil, and beverages. Sugar sales account for 26% of the company's revenues, processed meats account for 15% of revenues, and feedstuffs account for 12% of revenues. The company also produces detergents and pharmaceuticals. Its major subsidiaries include 94%-owned Cheil Frozen Foods, 28%-owned Samsung Engineering, and 22%-owned Joongang Daily News. It also has an interest in a motion-picture-distribution business.

Won bil	12/92 P	12/93 P	12/94 P	US$mil 12/94				
Sales	**1,264.8**	**1,306.3**	**1,431.9**	**1,787.3**	P/E Ratio	**49.6**	Price (9/30/95)	**50,000**
Net Income	**7.0**	**7.4**	**8.5**	**10.6**	P/B Ratio	**1.8**	52 Wk Hi-Low	**63,000.0-41,200.0**
Book Value	**188.8**	**219.4**	**221.9**	**283.7**	Yield %	**0.3**	Market Cap	**US$513.0mil**

Address **150 Taepyongno 2-ga, Chung-gu, Seoul** Tel **02-726-8114** Fax **02-751-8529** ADR SEDOL No. **6189516** President **Son Kyong-Shik** Chairman **Son Kyong-Shik**

P=Parent company data.

Cheil Industries

Industry: **Commodity Chemicals**

Cheil Industries is South Korea's largest wool-spinning company and the world's fourth-largest tailoring-fabric manufacturer. The company specializes in the production of combed wool yarn and wool textiles. It also produces synthetic resins, engineering plastics, and finished garments. The company generates 41% of its revenues from the sale of synthetic resins, while apparel sales accounts for 31% of revenues, and wool-fabric sales account for 22% of revenues. Cheil Industries main affiliates include 51%-owned Hi Creation and 16%-owned Samsung Petrochemical.

Won bil	12/92 P	12/93 P	12/94 P	US$mil 12/94				
Sales	**554.5**	**579.7**	**724.3**	**904.0**	P/E Ratio	**10.5**	Price (9/30/95)	**19,400**
Net Income	**6.4**	**8.7**	**28.7**	**35.8**	P/B Ratio	**0.9**	52 Wk Hi-Low	**26,129.4-16,000.0**
Book Value	**252.0**	**282.9**	**336.7**	**430.5**	Yield %	**2.1**	Market Cap	**US$409.2mil**

Address **105 Chimsan-dong, Buk-gu**
Daegu
Tel **053-358-7123**
Fax **053-356-7160**
ADR
SEDOL No. **6189538**
President **Yu Hyon-Shik**
Chairman **Yu Hyon-Shik**

P=Parent company data.

Cho Hung Bank

Industry: **Banks - Regional**

Cho Hung Bank offers retail- and corporate-banking services through a network of 356 domestic branches, 500 automatic cash lobbies, and 15 overseas offices. Its assets at year-end 1994 totalled 35.2 trillion won. Its services include deposit taking, foreign exchange, credit cards, stock trading, and trust accounts. In addition, it offers financing, advisory, and custodian services to corporate clients. Cho Hung Bank's six subsidiaries engage in leasing, securities investment, mutual-fund management, investment consulting, economic research, and computer-systems design.

Won bil	12/92	12/93	12/94	US$mil 12/94				
Revenues	**2,077.7**	**2,211.7**	**3,165.1**	**3,950.5**	P/E Ratio	**11.1**	Price (9/30/95)	**10,900**
Net Income	**92.5**	**103.2**	**147.7**	**184.3**	P/B Ratio	**1.1**	52 Wk Hi-Low	**14,700.0-8,050.0**
Book Value	**1,264.7**	**1,331.4**	**1,650.3**	**2,110.1**	Yield %	**2.8**	Market Cap	**US$2,327.5mil**

Address **14, 1-ka, Namdaemun-ro**
Seoul
Tel **02-733-2000**
Fax **02-723-6475**
ADR
SEDOL No. **6192741**
President **Chan Mok Woo**
Chairman **Chan Mok Woo**

Choong Nam Spinning

Industry: **Clothing & Fabrics**

Choong Nam Spinning is South Korea's largest manufacturer of cotton yarn. The company also produces dyed fabrics, wool fabrics, and other textile products. The company generates approximately 48% of its revenue from the sale of cotton yarns and fabrics. Choong Nam operates mainly from its textile factory in Taejon, South Korea. It also owns a plant in Vietnam and is involved in joint-venture plants in both Vietnam and India. Choong Nam also owns a significant amount of land in South Korea.

Won bil	12/92 P	12/93 P	12/94 P	US$mil 12/94				
Sales	**234.3**	**143.0**	**189.8**	**236.9**	P/E Ratio	**78.2**	Price (9/30/95)	**17,200**
Net Income	**1.4**	**-21.7**	**1.7**	**2.1**	P/B Ratio	**0.4**	52 Wk Hi-Low	**25,600.0-15,300.0**
Book Value	**383.7**	**361.9**	**369.3**	**472.2**	Yield %	**0.9**	Market Cap	**US$174.4mil**

Address **1 Wonnae-dong, Yusung-gu**
Taejon
Tel **042-541-0121**
Fax **042-541-6500**
ADR
SEDOL No. **6192956**
President **Lee Jun-Ho**
Chairman **Lee Jun-Ho**

P=Parent company data.

Choong Wae Pharmaceutical

Industry: **Pharmaceuticals**

Choong Wae Pharmaceuticals produces prescription and over-the-counter medications primarily for hospitals. Sales of prescription drugs account for approximately 70% of the company's revenues. Its main products include general and nutritional intravenous solutions and antibiotics. Its wholly-owned Choongwae Industrial subsidiary manufactures automobile parts, and its 72%-owned Choongwae Medical subsidiary makes medical equipment. The company also owns a 50% interest in C & C Laboratory, which is research facility.

Won bil	12/92	12/93	12/94	US$mil 12/94				
Sales	**83.4**	**98.4**	**110.0**	**137.3**	P/E Ratio	**34.4**	Price (9/30/95)	**38,000**
Net Income	**3.2**	**3.4**	**3.7**	**4.7**	P/B Ratio	**2.6**	52 Wk Hi-Low	**69,166.6-29,250.0**
Book Value	**27.4**	**30.1**	**54.3**	**69.4**	Yield %	**1.3**	Market Cap	**US$187.0mil**

Address **698 Shindaebang-dong**
Seoul
Tel **02-840-6777**
Fax **02-847-0010**
ADR
SEDOL No. **6192978**
President **Byong-On Lee**
Chairman **--**

Chosun Brewery

Industry: **Distillers & Brewers**

Chosun Brewery is South Korea's second-largest brewer in terms of sales. The company's products satisfy 35% of the country's market demand for beer. Its beers are marketed under the Crown and Hite brand names. In association with United Distillers of the United Kingdom, Chosun Brewery markets whiskey in South Korea. The company moved its Youngdeungpo manufacturing facilities and is currently planning to build a residential and commercial building on the site. Chosun also has interests in the glass-manufacturing and food-production industries.

Won bil	12/92 P	12/93 P	12/94 P	US$mil 12/94				
Sales	**195.3**	**204.9**	**273.7**	**341.6**	P/E Ratio	**31.6**	Price (9/30/95)	**27,500**
Net Income	**3.5**	**1.8**	**5.0**	**6.3**	P/B Ratio	**2.1**	52 Wk Hi-Low	**29,000.0-19,104.1**
Book Value	**54.4**	**74.3**	**78.8**	**100.8**	Yield %	**1.0**	Market Cap	**US$230.6mil**

Address **640 Yongdungpo-dong**
Yongdungpo-gu, Seoul
Tel **02-833-5111**
Fax **02-841-3640**
ADR
SEDOL No. **6193573**
President **Park Mun-Dok**
Chairman **Park Mun-Dok**

P=Parent company data.

Commercial Bank of Korea

Industry: **Banks - Regional**

The Commercial Bank of Korea is Korea's largest commercial bank in terms of capital. At year-end 1994, the bank's assets totalled 33.5 trillion won. It operates 322 domestic branches and 14 overseas offices located in New York, Los Angeles, Chicago, London, Frankfurt, Tokyo, Osaka, Singapore, Jakarta, and Shanghai. Its international banking division arranges and acts as lead manager of financing arrangements for clients such as Samsung Electronics and First Bangkok City Bank. The bank also offers foreign-exchange, trust-banking, and securities-investment services.

Won bil	12/92	12/93	12/94	US$mil 12/94				
Revenues	2,281.7	2,292.1	2,993.8	3,736.8	P/E Ratio	27.6	Price (9/30/95)	8,850.00
Net Income	37.5	18.2	32.4	40.4	P/B Ratio	1.0	52 Wk Hi-Low	9,600.0-6,950.0
Book Value	1,179.3	1,188.2	1,451.8	1,856.4	Yield %	1.1	Market Cap	US$1,958.9mil

Address **111-1, 2-ka, Namdaemun-ro**
Seoul
Tel **02-754-3920**
Fax **02-318-5225**
ADR
SEDOL No. **6213307**
President **Jee-Tae Chung**
Chairman **Jee-Tae Chung**

Coryo Securities

Industry: **Securities Brokers**

Coryo Securities provides brokerage, second-market dealing, underwriting, and other finance-related services. Commission income composes 56% of the company's revenues, while interest and dividends account for 22% of revenues. Coryo has the largest number of overseas branches and was the first South Korea brokerage firm to open a branch in Tokyo. The company also manages offshore funds in Ireland and Hong Kong, as well as managing an offshore futures fund. Coryo's operations in international finance provide assistance to overseas firms investing in South Korea.

Won bil	03/92 P	03/93 P	03/94 P	US$mil 03/94				
Sales	133.7	156.2	213.3	263.2	P/E Ratio	15.5	Price (9/30/95)	14,500
Net Income	-8.8	17.5	26.1	32.2	P/B Ratio	0.9	52 Wk Hi-Low	16,100.0-8,500.0
Book Value	N/A	396.9	415.8	509.4	Yield %	2.1	Market Cap	US$469.6mil

Address **25-5 Chungmuro 1-ga, Chung-gu**
Seoul
Tel **02-771-3600**
Fax **02-752-7221**
ADR
SEDOL No. **6226082**
President **Lee Jong-U**
Chairman **Lee Jong-U**

P=Parent company data.

Dae Ryung Industrial

Industry: **Communications Technology**

Dae Ryung Industrial manufactures satellite video receivers (SVR), cordless phones, radar detectors, and other electronic products. The company holds more than 30% of the world's SVR market. Sales of SVRs account for more than 60% of the company's revenues, sales of cordless phones account for almost 10%, and sales of radar detectors account for almost 6%. The company exports approximately 98% of its products. In addition to its South Korean-based manufacturing facilities, Dae Ryung operates a production plant in the Philippines and overseas sales offices worldwide.

Won bil	12/92	12/93	12/94	US$mil 12/94				
Sales	80.1	102.2	125.7	156.9	P/E Ratio	29.2	Price (9/30/95)	39,300
Net Income	1.6	2.0	3.2	4.0	P/B Ratio	2.3	52 Wk Hi-Low	66,600.0-30,800.0
Book Value	29.7	30.6	41.5	53.1	Yield %	0.3	Market Cap	US$122.1mil

Address **459-21 Karibong-dong, Kuro-gu**
Seoul
Tel **02-857-0001**
Fax **02-864-2111**
ADR
SEDOL No. **6249283**
President **Song-U Kwon**
Chairman **--**

Daegu Bank

Industry: **Banks - Regional**

Daegu Bank provides commercial-banking services in the Taegu city area and the Kyongsang province. The bank offers deposit-taking services and household and corporate loans, and is South Korea's largest provincial bank in terms of both of these activities. Daegu Bank generates more than 54% of its revenue from interest on loans while earning only 8% of its revenue from commission income. Its wholly-owned subsidiaries include Daegu Mutual Saving & Finance and Daegu Banking Institute. The company owns 57% of the financing company Daegu Leasing.

Won bil	12/92 P	12/93 P	12/94 P	US$mil 12/94				
Revenues	414.9	432.8	525.9	656.4	P/E Ratio	12.6	Price (9/30/95)	12,600
Net Income	41.4	41.9	42.1	52.5	P/B Ratio	1.1	52 Wk Hi-Low	13,100.0-8,429.8
Book Value	435.3	460.8	486.4	621.9	Yield %	3.1	Market Cap	US$689.0mil

Address **118 Susong-dong, Susong-gu**
Taegu
Tel **053-756-2001**
Fax **053-756-7028**
ADR
SEDOL No. **6249476**
President **Hong Hui-Hum**
Chairman **Hong Hui-Hum**

P=Parent company data.

Daelim Industrial

Industry: **Heavy Construction**

Daelim Industrial is a construction company that specializes in building manufacturing facilities and energy-generating plants. Through an affiliate, the company also markets petrochemicals. Civil and industrial construction accounts for 42% of the company's revenues, sales of petrochemicals account for 34% of revenues, and housing construction accounts for 24% of revenues. Daelim is currently in two consortiums that are building a gas-processing plant on the east coast of Malaysia and converting a electric-power plant for Malaysia's Tenaga Nasional.

Won bil	12/92	12/93	12/94	US$mil 12/94				
Sales	1,719.0	1,560.5	1,820.8	2,272.7	P/E Ratio	36.5	Price (9/30/95)	18,200
Net Income	7.2	6.9	15.2	19.0	P/B Ratio	1.1	52 Wk Hi-Low	25,007.2-14,316.4
Book Value	459.4	465.7	463.1	592.1	Yield %	0.5	Market Cap	US$664.0mil

Address **23-9 Youido-dong**
Seoul
Tel **02-368-7114**
Fax **02-368-7700**
ADR
SEDOL No. **6249584**
President **Lee Jong-Guk**
Chairman **Lee Jong-Guk**

Daewoo

Industry: **Overseas Trading**

Daewoo Corporation is a general trading company with interests in the import and export of heavy machinery, automobiles, ships, and textiles. The company also has domestic and overseas construction operations. Daewoo derives almost 70% of its revenues from its heavy machinery, chemicals and electronics businesses. It has operations in more than 120 countries including China, where it owns a cement plant in the Shandong province, Indonesia where it is working on an oil refinery project, and Vietnam, where it operates an antiseptic factory.

Won bil	12/92 P	12/93 P	12/94 P	US$mil 12/94				
Sales	**8,151.2**	**9,533.5**	**10,528.6**	**13,141.5**	P/E Ratio	**25.3**	Price (9/30/95)	**11,300**
Net Income	**40.3**	**48.6**	**48.1**	**60.1**	P/B Ratio	**0.9**	52 Wk Hi-Low	**15,238.1-9,400.0**
Book Value	**1,250.0**	**1,380.0**	**1,426.2**	**1,823.6**	Yield %	**2.2**	Market Cap	**US$1,664.7mil**

Address **541 Namdaemunno 5-ga**
Seoul
Tel **02-759-2114**
Fax **02-753-9489**
ADR
SEDOL No. **6249647**
President **Kang Byong-Hun**
Chairman **Kang Byong-Hun**

P=Parent company data.

Daewoo Electronics

Industry: **Consumer Electronics**

Daewoo Electronics manufactures consumer electrical appliances and industrial electronic products. The company's product range includes home automation equipment, facsimiles, color and closed-circuit televisions, refrigerators, videocassette recorders, car audio equipment, and nonmemory semiconductors. The company's overseas manufacturing facilities include a television plant in Mexico, a car-audio facility in China, and a VCR plant in Northern Ireland. It is currently building additional manufacturing facilities in China, Vietnam, Poland, and Mexico.

Won bil	12/92	12/93	12/94	US$mil 12/94				
Sales	**1,740.9**	**2,033.5**	**2,545.1**	**3,176.8**	P/E Ratio	**14.1**	Price (9/30/95)	**10,100**
Net Income	**13.5**	**31.9**	**55.9**	**69.8**	P/B Ratio	**1.0**	52 Wk Hi-Low	**12,952.4-8,800.0**
Book Value	**566.1**	**699.3**	**759.6**	**971.2**	Yield %	**2.5**	Market Cap	**US$1,023.1mil**

Address **541 Namdaemunro 5-ga**
Seoul
Tel **02-360-7114**
Fax **02-364-5588**
ADR
SEDOL No. **6249669**
President **Sun Hun Bae**
Chairman **Sun Hun Bae**

Daewoo Heavy Industries

Industry: **Transportation Equipment - All**

Daewoo Heavy Industries manufactures industrial equipment including diesel engines, industrial vehicles, railroad carriages, construction equipment, automatized machinery, and airplane components. It is also engaged in shipbuilding, industrial plant construction, and minivehicle passenger-cars manufacturing. The company is planning the construction of a forklift-truck plant in the United States that would be operational by early 1997. Daewoo Heavy Industries is 40%-owned by the South Korean industrial conglomerate Daewoo Corporation.

Won bil	12/92 P	12/93 P	12/94 P	US$mil 12/94				
Sales	**904.7**	**882.2**	**1,618.5**	**2,020.2**	P/E Ratio	**20.8**	Price (9/30/95)	**10,200**
Net Income	**10.6**	**16.7**	**74.4**	**92.8**	P/B Ratio	**1.3**	52 Wk Hi-Low	**17,600.0-9,000.0**
Book Value	**564.7**	**1,058.0**	**2,744.0**	**3,508.6**	Yield %	**4.9**	Market Cap	**US$4,743.8mil**

Address **6 Mansok-dong, Tong-gu**
Ichon
Tel **032-760-1114**
Fax **032-756-2679**
ADR
SEDOL No. **6249700**
President **Yong Sok Yun**
Chairman **Yong Sok Yun**

P=Parent company data.

Daewoo Securities

Industry: **Securities Brokers**

Daewoo Securities offers financial services to domestic and overseas investors. It is South Korea's largest brokerage firm in terms of assets and operating revenues. The company's range of services includes dealing, underwriting, securities distribution, mergers and aquisitions consulting, currency trading, and futures and options dealing. Daewoo Securities is active in global markets including the emerging markets of India, China, and eastern Europe. The company also has a subsidiary office in New York and is a member of the National Association of Securities Dealers.

Won bil	03/92 P	03/93 P	03/94 P	US$mil 03/94				
Sales	**284.2**	**285.6**	**435.6**	**537.6**	P/E Ratio	**20.1**	Price (9/30/95)	**25,400**
Net Income	**9.6**	**40.8**	**87.6**	**108.1**	P/B Ratio	**1.1**	52 Wk Hi-Low	**38,100.0-18,600.0**
Book Value	**N/A**	**957.7**	**1,031.5**	**1,263.7**	Yield %	**0.0**	Market Cap	**US$1,514.6mil**

Address **34-3 Youido-dong**
Seoul
Tel **02-768-3355**
Fax **02-782-3155**
ADR
SEDOL No. **6249658**
President **Chang Hui Kim**
Chairman **Chang Hui Kim**

P=Parent company data.

Daewoo Telecom

Industry: **Communications Technology**

Daewoo Telecom manufactures telephone and telecommunication equipment, fiberoptic cables, electronic switching systems, transmission equipment, personal computers, and computer peripherals. The company is developing a 900 megahertz cordless phone, and has released portable facsimiles and pentium-chip personal computers. Daewoo Telecom generates almost 40% of its sales in overseas markets. Its wholly-owned Leading Edge subsidiary serves as the company's U.S.-based computer sales company. It also has sales subsidiaries in Europe and Japan.

Won bil	12/92	12/93	12/94	US$mil 12/94				
Sales	**381.4**	**473.8**	**590.5**	**737.0**	P/E Ratio	**31.2**	Price (9/30/95)	**13,300**
Net Income	**6.6**	**7.4**	**9.4**	**11.7**	P/B Ratio	**1.1**	52 Wk Hi-Low	**14,800.0-8,250.0**
Book Value	**197.6**	**251.9**	**301.6**	**385.6**	Yield %	**1.1**	Market Cap	**US$431.1mil**

Address **531 Gajwa-dong, So-gu**
Ichon
Tel **02-589-2114**
Fax **02-756-1225**
ADR
SEDOL No. **6249357**
President **Song Gyu Park**
Chairman **Song Gyu Park**

Daihan Investment & Finance

Industry: **Financial Services - Diversified**

Daihan Investment & Finance offers short-term investment financing services. The company also engages in factoring, securities investment and trading, fund management, deposit taking, and corporate-note issuing. It derives approximately 70% of its revenue from interest income. The company's 83%-owned Daihan Venture Capital supplies its corporate clients with venture capital to fund their development projects. Daihan Investment & Finance is affiliated with the Miwon group of companies. Sun Won Construction owns 31% of the company's share capital.

Won bil	06/92 P	06/93 P	06/94 P	US$mil 06/94				
Revenues	**314.5**	**291.8**	**290.8**	**358.5**	P/E Ratio	**8.9**	Price (9/30/95)	**22,200**
Net Income	**21.8**	**22.4**	**20.5**	**25.3**	P/B Ratio	**0.7**	52 Wk Hi-Low	**31,800.0-14,100.0**
Book Value	**N/A**	**241.1**	**263.3**	**326.7**	Yield %	**2.7**	Market Cap	**US$231.2mil**

Address **54 Myong-dong 1-ga, Chung-gu** **Seoul**
Tel **02-771-9000** Fax **02-754-8184**
ADR SEDOL No. **6249744**
President **Jong Hwan Kim** Chairman **Jong Hwan Kim**

P=Parent company data.

Daishin Securities

Industry: **Securities Brokers**

Daishin Securities is the second-largest brokerage house in South Korea in terms of revenues and holds a 7.6% market share. It operates through a network of 55 domestic branches, one London-based subsidiary, and four representative offices in Tokyo, New York, Zurich, and Hong Kong. In addition to stock trading, the company is also active in underwriting stock and bond placements, arranging and underwriting mergers and acquisitions, and futures and options trading. Daishin Securities serves as the parent company for the Daishin Group of finance companies.

Won bil	03/92	03/93	03/94	US$mil 03/94				
Sales	**255.0**	**261.5**	**298.3**	**368.1**	P/E Ratio	**8.8**	Price (9/30/95)	**14,500**
Net Income	**-11.1**	**35.9**	**56.8**	**70.1**	P/B Ratio	**0.5**	52 Wk Hi-Low	**18,400.0-9,650.0**
Book Value	**770.2**	**807.1**	**851.8**	**1,043.6**	Yield %	**1.7**	Market Cap	**US$549.9mil**

Address **34-8 Yoido-dong** **Seoul**
Tel **02-769-2000** Fax **02-786-6913**
ADR SEDOL No. **6251200**
President & CEO **Choon Ho Lee** Chairman **Jae Bong Yang**

Dong Bang

Industry: **Other Food**

Dong Bang manufactures cooking oil, soybean grits, and formulated food products. The company is South Korea's largest processor of soybean. Sales of cooking oil account for more than 34% of the company's revenues, sales of feedstuffs account for almost 24%, and sales of soybean meal account for more than 23%. The company operates a joint venture with the British-Dutch food company Unilever to sell its cooking oils. Dong Bang also owns a 41% interest in brokering company Dongbang Peregrin Securities. The company's president, Myong-Su Shin, owns a 16% interest in Dong Bang.

Won bil	12/92	12/93	12/94	US$mil 12/94				
Sales	**276.6**	**251.9**	**290.7**	**362.8**	P/E Ratio	**22.5**	Price (9/30/95)	**31,700**
Net Income	**3.9**	**1.8**	**3.3**	**4.1**	P/B Ratio	**1.7**	52 Wk Hi-Low	**57,000.0-24,700.0**
Book Value	**43.4**	**45.0**	**49.7**	**63.5**	Yield %	**0.3**	Market Cap	**US$107.6mil**

Address **2 Yangpyong-dong 4-ga** **Seoul**
Tel **02-676-9123** Fax **02-675-4961**
ADR SEDOL No. **6276173**
President **Myong-Su Shin** Chairman --

Dong Hae Pulp

Industry: **Paper Products**

Dong Hae Pulp is South Korea's largest pulp manufacturer in terms of production. The company has an annual average production capacity of 380,000 tonnes of pulp, satisfying 20% of the country's market demand. Most of the company's production is sold in the domestic market with exports accouting for only 2.8% of sales. It derives 100% of its revenue from the sale of bleached kraft pulp for printing, art, and wood-free paper. Dong Hae Pulp's major shareholders include Hankook Paper Manufacturing (20%) and the Morim Group (16%).

Won bil	12/92 P	12/93 P	12/94 P	US$mil 12/94				
Sales	**68.6**	**88.2**	**151.5**	**189.1**	P/E Ratio	**NMF**	Price (9/30/95)	**21,300**
Net Income	**2.7**	**-45.8**	**-19.4**	**-24.3**	P/B Ratio	**10.9**	52 Wk Hi-Low	**31,100.0-18,100.0**
Book Value	**85.6**	**38.1**	**18.6**	**23.8**	Yield %	**0.0**	Market Cap	**US$264.6mil**

Address **1 Dangwol-ri, Onsan-myon** **Ulsan-shi, Kyongnam**
Tel **052-238-2181** Fax **052-238-2190**
ADR SEDOL No. **6275738**
President **Byong Myon Choe** Chairman **Byong Myon Choe**

P=Parent company data.

Dong Shin Pharmaceutical

Industry: **Pharmaceuticals**

Dong Shin Pharmaceutical manufactures prescription drugs, vaccines, and other pharmaceuticals for use primarily in hospitals. The company's products include albumin injections, blood-plasma separators, and medicinal drinks. It also produces an insulin patch that can be surgically inserted under the skin. Sales of albumin injections account for more than 30% of the company's revenues. Dong Shin Pharmaceutical exports only 3% of its products. These exports are made up mainly of albumin products sent to China.

Won bil	12/92	12/93	12/94	US$mil 12/94				
Sales	**38.5**	**40.6**	**44.4**	**55.4**	P/E Ratio	**103.4**	Price (9/30/95)	**36,000**
Net Income	**1.1**	**1.1**	**1.0**	**1.2**	P/B Ratio	**2.7**	52 Wk Hi-Low	**60,491.2-28,400.0**
Book Value	**20.5**	**29.0**	**39.6**	**50.6**	Yield %	**0.2**	Market Cap	**US$127.2mil**

Address **994 Taechi-dong, Kangnam-gu** **Seoul**
Tel **02-556-9966** Fax **02-557-8898**
ADR SEDOL No. **6276258**
President **Wan-Shik Park** Chairman --

Dong-A Pharmaceutical

Industry: **Pharmaceuticals**

Dong-A Pharmaceutical is South Korea's largest pharmaceuticals manufacturer. The company produces both prescription and over-the-counter medications including Bacchus health drinks. Bacchus drinks account for almost 37% of the company's revenue. Dong-A is also beginning clinical testing on its cancer-treatment drug and is hoping to begin commercial production of it in 1996. It has also agreed to purchase a Japanese company's patent for a nontoxic pain reliever. Dong-A is also engaged in the manufacture of ceramic products and the production of personal-care items.

Won bil	12/92 P	12/93 P	12/94 P	US$mil 12/94				
Sales	**188.3**	**204.5**	**236.9**	**295.7**	P/E Ratio	**32.5**	Price (9/30/95)	**19,600**
Net Income	**2.1**	**0.7**	**4.5**	**5.6**	P/B Ratio	**1.6**	52 Wk Hi-Low	**26,700.0-16,900.0**
Book Value	**86.6**	**91.5**	**95.1**	**121.6**	Yield %	**0.5**	Market Cap	**US$200.6mil**

Address **252 Yongdu 2-dong**
Seoul
Tel **02-920-8114**
Fax **02-924-2662**
ADR
SEDOL No. **6273163**
President **Chung Shik Yu**
Chairman **Chung Sam Son**

P=Parent company data.

Dong-Ah Construction

Industry: **Heavy Construction**

Dong Ah Contruction Industrial engages in engineering projects on 20 construction sites, and through a network of 60 domestic and 18 overseas branch offices. Its major projects include the Dangjin thermoelectric power station, subway construction for the Bundang Line, and a hydroelectric power station in Laos. The company recently completed phase one of Libya's man-made river project. It also constructs housing and commercial and retail locations. Dong Ah plans to build a future-oriented urban area for tourism and information processing in the Inchon-western Seoul region.

$ mil	12/92	12/93	12/94	US$mil 12/94				
Sales	**1,600.0**	**1,895.3**	**2,546.9**	**2,546.9**	P/E Ratio	**22.1**	Price (9/30/95)	**31,200**
Net Income	**24.6**	**24.8**	**39.4**	**39.4**	P/B Ratio	**1.2**	52 Wk Hi-Low	**40,000.0-18,600.0**
Book Value	**449.7**	**640.0**	**749.4**	**749.4**	Yield %	**N/A**	Market Cap	**US$1,134.2mil**

Address **120-23, Seosomun-Dong**
Seoul
Tel **02-3709-2114**
Fax **02-3709-3000**
ADR
SEDOL No. **6276140**
President **Ryu Sung-Yong**
Chairman **Choi Won-Suk**

Dongah Tire

Industry: **Tires & Rubber**

Dong Ah Tire Industrial manufactures automobile-tires, automobile tire tubes, mud flaps, and other rubber products. The company generates 65% of its revenue from the sale of tire tubes and the remainder from the sale of tires. Almost 71% of its revenue is generated by overseas sales. With technical assistance from France's Michelin, the company plans to start reprocessing used tires. The company also owns 22% of Dongnam Housing Industrial, a construction concern. Dong Ah Tire is 30%-owned by the company's chairman, Man Su Kim.

Won bil	12/92 P	12/93 P	12/94 P	US$mil 12/94				
Sales	**73.8**	**70.7**	**85.1**	**106.2**	P/E Ratio	**8.0**	Price (9/30/95)	**49,500**
Net Income	**10.1**	**11.1**	**13.2**	**16.5**	P/B Ratio	**1.3**	52 Wk Hi-Low	**69,800.0-41,400.0**
Book Value	**57.7**	**69.1**	**82.3**	**105.2**	Yield %	**0.2**	Market Cap	**US$137.9mil**

Address **90 Yusan-ri, Yangsan-up**
Kyongnam
Tel **052-389-0011**
Fax **052-382-7736**
ADR
SEDOL No. **6276087**
President **Man Su Kim**
Chairman **Man Su Kim**

P=Parent company data.

Dongkuk Steel Mill

Industry: **Steel**

Dongkuk Steel Mill produces concrete reinforcing bars, section steel, and steel wire rods for the construction industry. The company also produces steel sheets for the shipbuilding industry. It also plans to begin processing scrap iron and has purchased land in the Asan Bay area for the construction of a new steel plant. In a joint venture with Japan's Kobe Steel, Dongkuk Steel Mill is building a steel-slab factory in Venezeula that will produce 1 million tonnes of steel slabs annually mainly for export to South Korea.

Won bil	12/92 P	12/93 P	12/94 P	US$mil 12/94				
Sales	**669.3**	**800.0**	**905.9**	**1,130.7**	P/E Ratio	**14.7**	Price (9/30/95)	**20,600**
Net Income	**24.8**	**16.0**	**28.1**	**35.1**	P/B Ratio	**1.1**	52 Wk Hi-Low	**27,900.0-18,000.0**
Book Value	**331.3**	**342.0**	**448.4**	**573.3**	Yield %	**2.9**	Market Cap	**US$627.6mil**

Address **50 Suha-dong, Chung-gu**
Seoul
Tel **02-317-1114**
Fax **02-317-1391**
ADR
SEDOL No. **6276117**
President **Sang-Tae Chang**
Chairman **Sang-Tae Chang**

P=Parent company data.

Dongsuh Securities

Industry: **Securities Brokers**

Dongsuh Securities provides brokerage services through a network of more than 50 branches in South Korea. The company is also engaged in closed-end fund management, bond dealing, and futures and options trading. More than 53% of the company's revenue is derived from commission and fee income. The company owns 99% of both Dongsuh Research Institute and Dongsuh Investment Management, as well as holding a 20% stake in Kukdong Mutual Savings & Finance. Dongsuh Securities is an affiliate of the Kuk Dong Construction group of companies.

Won bil	03/92 P	03/93 P	03/94 P	US$mil 03/94				
Sales	**185.3**	**224.0**	**290.4**	**358.4**	P/E Ratio	**39.5**	Price (9/30/95)	**15,600**
Net Income	**-5.9**	**37.2**	**47.8**	**59.0**	P/B Ratio	**0.7**	52 Wk Hi-Low	**17,900.0-9,300.0**
Book Value	**N/A**	**792.6**	**827.8**	**1,014.2**	Yield %	**0.0**	Market Cap	**US$709.1mil**

Address **34-1 Youido-dong, Yongdunpo-gu**
Seoul
Tel **02-784-1211**
Fax **02-784-2946**
ADR
SEDOL No. **6276463**
President **Gwan-Jong Kim**
Chairman **Gwan-Jong Kim**

P=Parent company data.

Haitai Confectionery

Industry: **Other Food**

Haitai Confectionery is South Korea's second-largest producer of confectionery goods. It also produces a variety of ice-cream products and Dent-Q chewing gum. The firm also serves as the parent company for the Haitai Group, which includes a 70% stake in Haitai Industrial, a 63% stake in Haitai Beverage, and a 22% stake in Haitai Trading. The Haitai group is trying to diversify into the electronics industry. In December 1994, Haitai Confectionery, together with its Haitai Electronics and Haitai Mart affiliates, took over Inkel, a manufacturer of audio products.

Won bil	06/92	06/93	06/94	US$mil 06/94				
Sales	**436.1**	**486.1**	**529.4**	**652.7**	P/E Ratio	**15.4**	Price (9/30/95)	**12,300**
Net Income	**26.5**	**25.5**	**6.6**	**8.1**	P/B Ratio	**0.1**	52 Wk Hi-Low	**18,200.0-12,100.0**
Book Value	**N/A**	**138.7**	**157.4**	**195.3**	Yield %	**3.3**	Market Cap	**US$122.4mil**

Address	**131 Namyong-dong, Yongsan-gu**	Tel	**02-709-7766**	ADR		President	**Jong-Sok Yang**
	Seoul	Fax	**02-790-8123**	SEDOL No.	**6402279**	Chairman	--

Hanil Bank

Industry: **Banks - Regional**

Hanil Bank provides a range of financial services including deposits; loans; foreign exchange; retail, corporate, and trust banking; and securities investment. At year-end 1994, the bank had assets totalling 34.3 trillion won. The company's banking network includes 330 domestic branches, 419 ATMs, and 17 overseas offices. Its international banking division offers custodian services to overseas firms, arranges for securities and bonds issues, and manages lease financing. Hanil Bank is the parent for the Hanil finance and investment group of companies.

Won bil	12/92	12/93	12/94	US$mil 12/94				
Revenues	**2,285.5**	**2,562.9**	**3,357.3**	**4,190.4**	P/E Ratio	**9.7**	Price (9/30/95)	**10,100**
Net Income	**152.5**	**148.4**	**143.1**	**178.7**	P/B Ratio	**0.9**	52 Wk Hi-Low	**12,800.0-7,800.0**
Book Value	**1,421.7**	**1,526.5**	**1,879.6**	**2,403.3**	Yield %	**3.0**	Market Cap	**US$2,182.9mil**

Address	**130 Namdaemun-no 2-ga**	Tel	**02-259-6114**	ADR		President & CEO	**Kwan Woo Lee**
	Seoul	Fax	**02-754-0479**	SEDOL No.	**6408404**	Chairman	**Yong Ju Kim**

Hanil Cement

Industry: **Building Materials**

Hanil Cement Manufacturing manufactures cement and ready-mix concrete mainly for use in the South Korean construction industry. Its annual production capacity is approximately 6 million tonnes of cement and 3 million cubic meters of ready-mix concrete. The company owns an 80% stake in Handuck Development, a construction company, an 83% stake in Hanil Industrial, and a 43% stake in Joungwon Industrial. Hanil Cement also engages in auto-parts manufacturing and distribution through a joint venture with Okihara of Japan and has investments in leisure businesses.

Won bil	12/92	12/93	12/94	US$mil 12/94				
Sales	**242.6**	**285.8**	**321.2**	**400.9**	P/E Ratio	**14.3**	Price (9/30/95)	**46,500**
Net Income	**15.6**	**13.3**	**13.3**	**16.6**	P/B Ratio	**0.7**	52 Wk Hi-Low	**65,000.0-39,100.0**
Book Value	**125.0**	**244.8**	**254.3**	**325.2**	Yield %	**1.4**	Market Cap	**US$247.0mil**

Address	**832-2 Yoksam 1-dong**	Tel	**02-531-7114**	ADR		President	**Byong-Guk Lee**
	Seoul	Fax	**02-531-7115**	SEDOL No.	**6407713**	Chairman	**Byong-Guk Lee**

Hanil Synthetic Fiber

Industry: **Clothing & Fabrics**

Hanil Synthetic Fiber is South Korea's largest manufacturer of acrylic products. The company's products include acrylic yarns, acrylic fibers, sewing equipment, sweaters, and other apparel. Almost 63% of the company's sales come from exports of its products. Hanil Synthetic Fiber has moved some of its acrylic-yarn manufacturing facilities to China, and it is building apartments on the old factory sites. The company has investments in the construction business through an 84% stake in Hanil Leisure Development and an 80% stake in Namju Development.

Won bil	12/92	12/93	12/94	US$mil 12/94				
Sales	**430.0**	**419.6**	**471.5**	**588.5**	P/E Ratio	**17.5**	Price (9/30/95)	**8,500.00**
Net Income	**-62.9**	**-90.6**	**6.3**	**7.9**	P/B Ratio	**1.1**	52 Wk Hi-Low	**14,400.0-6,400.0**
Book Value	**167.0**	**79.8**	**108.8**	**139.1**	Yield %	**0.0**	Market Cap	**US$143.7mil**

Address	**222 Yangdok-dong, Hoiwon-gu**	Tel	**0551-90-3114**	ADR		President	**Jong-Jae Kim**
	Kyongnam	Fax	**0551-90-3115**	SEDOL No.	**6407702**	Chairman	--

Hankook Tire

Industry: **Tires & Rubber**

Hankook Tire Manufacturing produces automobile tires and rubber tubes. The company also engages in the manufacture of batteries and aluminum-alloy wheels. It generates almost 91% of its revenue from the sale of automobile tires, and exports account for more than 55% of the company's sales. Hankook is currently constructing a new tire-manufacturing plant in Kumsan, South Korea, and is looking for sites overseas to set up production facilities. Yokohama Rubber, Japan's second-largest automobile-tire maker, owns a 13% stake in the company.

Won bil	12/92 P	12/93 P	12/94 P	US$mil 12/94				
Sales	**623.2**	**701.6**	**843.9**	**1,053.3**	P/E Ratio	**12.3**	Price (9/30/95)	**57,000**
Net Income	**29.5**	**18.8**	**21.4**	**26.7**	P/B Ratio	**1.3**	52 Wk Hi-Low	**91,300.0-50,100.0**
Book Value	**171.2**	**186.8**	**204.8**	**261.9**	Yield %	**1.2**	Market Cap	**US$341.4mil**

Address	**647-15 Yoksam-dong**	Tel	**02-222-1000**	ADR		President	**Gon-Hui Hong**
	Seoul	Fax	**02-222-1100**	SEDOL No.	**6408589**	Chairman	**Gon-Hui Hong**

P=Parent company data.

Hankuk Glass Industries

Industry: **Industrial - Diversified**

Hankuk Glass Industries (Hanglas) manufactures flat glass for architectural and automotive uses, tube glass for lighting fixtures and medical applications, and glass wool for insulation and sound-absorption products. The company produces other glass-related products including MARBLITE crystallized glass, liquid sealants used as adhesives, and polycarbonate sheets. Hanglas has a joint venture with Daewoo and a local Chinese government authority to build a flat glass plant in Nanjing, China, and a subsidiary in Hong Kong that markets glass products in Southeast Asia.

Won bil	06/92	06/93	06/94	US$mil 06/94				
Sales	**N/A**	**459.3**	**532.5**	**656.6**	P/E Ratio	**8.0**	Price (9/30/95)	**25,700**
Net Income	**N/A**	**17.3**	**31.9**	**39.3**	P/B Ratio	**0.6**	52 Wk Hi-Low	**35,144.0-21,800.0**
Book Value	**N/A**	**177.6**	**429.4**	**532.9**	Yield %	**2.3**	Market Cap	**US$357.4mil**

Address **45-1 Yoido-dong, Yungdungpo-gu** **Seoul**
Tel **02-785-0311** Fax **02-786-2170**
ADR
SEDOL No. **6407746**
President & CEO **Yung-Zung Choi**
Chairman **Bong-Soo Lee**

Hankuk Paper

Industry: **Paper Products**

Hankuk Paper Manufacturing makes paper products mainly for printing, art, and writing. The company also manufactures paper for use in the production of packaging cartons. By the end of 1995, it will open a new manufacturing facility in Osan, South Korea, which will add 300,000 tonnes to its current production capacity. The company owns a packaging company, Hankuk Package, and has minority interests in Keyang Electric Machinery, an electrical-power-tool maker, and Donghae Pulp, South Korea's largest pulp manufacturer. Hankuk Paper is a major affiliate of the Haesung Group.

Won bil	12/92 P	12/93 P	12/94 P	US$mil 12/94				
Sales	**133.0**	**128.1**	**147.5**	**184.1**	P/E Ratio	**18.4**	Price (9/30/95)	**27,500**
Net Income	**2.3**	**-4.0**	**7.4**	**9.3**	P/B Ratio	**2.2**	52 Wk Hi-Low	**38,349.5-21,559.7**
Book Value	**58.3**	**54.0**	**61.1**	**78.1**	Yield %	**1.8**	Market Cap	**US$179.0mil**

Address **1358-6 Socho-dong, Socho-gu** **Seoul**
Tel **02-528-7200** Fax **02-554-2133**
ADR
SEDOL No. **6408578**
President **Yon-Gi Lee**
Chairman **Yon-Gi Lee**

P=Parent company data.

Hansol Paper

Industry: **Paper Products**

Hansol Paper Manufacturing produces newsprint and wood-printing paper. The company is South Korea's largest paper manufacturer in terms of market share. It also produces varieties of art paper, printing paper, and paperboards. Through its newly constructed Taejon plant and its Dong Chang Paper subsidiary, the company manufactures more than 24,000 tonnes of white duplex paperboard. Hansol has interests in merchant banks, a savings and loan bank, and other financial-services companies. It also has investments in leisure-related, construction, and chemical businesses.

Won bil	12/92 P	12/93 P	12/94 P	US$mil 12/94				
Sales	**444.0**	**484.0**	**628.0**	**783.9**	P/E Ratio	**21.7**	Price (9/30/95)	**33,000**
Net Income	**9.8**	**12.1**	**19.8**	**24.8**	P/B Ratio	**1.4**	52 Wk Hi-Low	**44,400.0-26,700.0**
Book Value	**103.6**	**172.2**	**335.5**	**429.0**	Yield %	**2.0**	Market Cap	**US$602.7mil**

Address **64-8 Taepyongno 1-ga, Chung-gu** **Seoul**
Tel **02-399-4161** Fax **02-399-4050**
ADR
SEDOL No. **6192945**
President **Hyong-U Ku**
Chairman **Hyong-U Ku**

P=Parent company data.

Hanwha

Industry: **Specialty Chemicals**

Hanwha is an integrated chemicals manufacturer and the sole producer of explosives in South Korea. The company generates almost 30% of its revenues from the sale of explosives, detonators, and fuses. It owns a 50% stake in Pacific Construction and a 38% stake in Taipyung Development, a real-estate development concern. Hanwha has obtained its own general-construction license and plans to participate in infrastructure-construction projects. The company is also involved in the telecommunication industry through its Golden Bell and Oriental Telecommunications subsidiaries.

Won bil	12/92 P	12/93 P	12/94 P	US$mil 12/94				
Sales	**270.8**	**281.6**	**383.3**	**478.4**	P/E Ratio	**91.3**	Price (9/30/95)	**13,700**
Net Income	**3.7**	**-18.2**	**2.9**	**3.6**	P/B Ratio	**1.1**	52 Wk Hi-Low	**18,621.5-10,800.0**
Book Value	**225.0**	**234.3**	**238.0**	**304.3**	Yield %	**0.4**	Market Cap	**US$402.5mil**

Address **1 Changgyo-dong, Chung-gu** **Seoul**
Tel **02-729-1881** Fax **02-752-3475**
ADR
SEDOL No. **6496755**
President **Yong-Gu Kim**
Chairman **Yong-Gu Kim**

P=Parent company data.

Hanwha Chemical

Industry: **Commodity Chemicals**

Hanwha Chemical (formerly Hanyang Chemical) is a diversified manufacturer of petrochemicals. Its products include polyethylene, octane, lubricating oil, plastics, caustic soda, chlorine, and hydrochloric acid. The company operates a 50%-owned joint venture with German chemical manufacturer BASF to produce urethane. It also owns 20% of Sammi Precision, an industrial-machinery producer. Hanwha's other interests include a 48% stake in Hanyang Stores and a 24% stake in Hanwha Energy. Hanwha Corporation owns 18% of the company's share capital.

Won bil	12/92	12/93	12/94	US$mil 12/94				
Sales	**886.7**	**1,026.2**	**1,216.9**	**1,518.9**	P/E Ratio	**31.5**	Price (9/30/95)	**14,200**
Net Income	**20.1**	**-33.9**	**20.2**	**25.2**	P/B Ratio	**1.1**	52 Wk Hi-Low	**23,200.0-12,900.0**
Book Value	**515.5**	**535.2**	**565.5**	**723.1**	Yield %	**0.1**	Market Cap	**US$804.9mil**

Address **1 Changgyo-dong, Chung-gu** **Seoul**
Tel **02-729-2700** Fax **02-729-3000**
ADR
SEDOL No. **6407768**
President **Won-Bae Park**
Chairman **Won-Bae Park**

Honam Petrochemical

Industry: **Commodity Chemicals**

Honam Petrochemical manufactures synthetic resins and other petrochemicals. The company's products include polypropylene, high-density polyethylene, and ethylene glycol. More than 52% of the company's revenues is derived from the sale of synthetic resins. Raw-material sales account for 26% of revenues and synthetic-raw-material sales make up the remainder. The company exports 45% of its products. Currently, Honam is building a ethylene glycol plant due to open in 1996. Japanese chemical firm First Chemical owns a 34% interest in the company.

Won bil	12/92 P	12/93 P	12/94 P	US$mil 12/94				
Sales	308.0	320.2	454.4	567.2	P/E Ratio	20.1	Price (9/30/95)	17,900
Net Income	-22.1	-68.8	28.3	35.3	P/B Ratio	2.7	52 Wk Hi-Low	30,200.0-16,100.0
Book Value	251.3	182.2	210.5	269.2	Yield %	1.7	Market Cap	US$742.5mil

Address **191 Hangangno 2-ga, Yongsan-gu** **Seoul**
Tel **02-791-0333** Fax **02-796-5800**
ADR SEDOL No. **6440020**
President **Bo-Yong Chong** Chairman **Bo-Yong Chong**

P=Parent company data.

Hotel Shilla

Industry: **Lodging**

Hotel Shilla operates two hotels in South Korea. One hotel is located in Seoul and has 620 rooms, and the other is located in Cheju and has 330 rooms. The company's other activities include the operation of a duty-free store and involvement in a take-out food business. It also has contracts to provide the food service in Samsung General Hospital and to supply food products to Samsung Group's employee cafeterias. More than 40% of the company's revenue comes from sales in the duty-free store and 27% comes from the provision of food and beverages.

Won bil	12/92 P	12/93 P	12/94 P	US$mil 12/94				
Sales	136.2	168.3	199.8	249.4	P/E Ratio	38.5	Price (9/30/95)	12,000
Net Income	4.2	5.5	4.7	5.9	P/B Ratio	1.0	52 Wk Hi-Low	18,100.0-9,250.0
Book Value	175.1	176.5	218.2	279.0	Yield %	2.1	Market Cap	US$285.0mil

Address **202 Changchung-dong, Chung-gu** **Seoul**
Tel **02-233-3131** Fax **02-233-5073**
ADR SEDOL No. **6440332**
President **Yong-Il Lee** Chairman **Yong-Il Lee**

P=Parent company data.

Hwa Sung Industrial

Industry: **Retailers - Broadline**

Hwa Sung Industrial manages department stores, shopping arcades, and other retail outlets. Its retail chains include Dong-A Department Store, Dong-A Shopping Center, and Pretemps Department Store all of which are in Seoul. The company recently opened a shopping center in Daegu's Jisan area, and plans to open another in the Chilkok area by the end of 1995. Hwa Sung Industrial is also involved in the construction sector, which generates 34% of the company's revenues, and the financial-services industry through its 54% stake in Dong-A Mutual Savings & Finance.

Won bil	12/92 P	12/93 P	12/94 P	US$mil 12/94				
Revenues	404.3	513.8	561.1	700.3	P/E Ratio	10.6	Price (9/30/95)	33,800
Net Income	10.1	13.7	19.3	24.1	P/B Ratio	2.0	52 Wk Hi-Low	47,200.9-27,462.3
Book Value	62.6	88.7	103.4	132.2	Yield %	1.5	Market Cap	US$265.5mil

Address **53-3 Toksan-dong, Chung-gu** **Taegu**
Tel **053-252-2111** Fax **053-252-9746**
ADR SEDOL No. **6959593**
President **In-Jung Lee** Chairman **In-Jung Lee**

P=Parent company data.

Hyundai Cement

Industry: **Building Materials**

Hyundai Cement is South Korea's third-largest cement manufacturer with an annual production capacity of 7 million tonnes. It operates two cement-manufacturing facilities, one located in Youngweol and the other in Tangyang. Hyundai Cement serves as the parent company to the Sung Woo group of companies. As a result, it has investment interests in the tourism, civil-engineering, and automotive-component industries. Hyundai cement owns a 72% stake in Sungwoo General Leisure, a 76% stake in Sungwoo Construction, and a 71% stake in Sungwoo Allied Signal.

Won bil	12/92 P	12/93 P	12/94 P	US$mil 12/94				
Sales	175.7	218.1	295.3	368.6	P/E Ratio	13.8	Price (9/30/95)	34,000
Net Income	6.2	5.3	8.9	11.0	P/B Ratio	1.1	52 Wk Hi-Low	45,200.0-29,200.0
Book Value	104.4	104.4	109.7	140.3	Yield %	1.9	Market Cap	US$159.4mil

Address **1424-2 Socho-dong, Socho-gu** **Seoul**
Tel **02-520-2114** Fax **02-520-2119**
ADR SEDOL No. **6450869**
President **Sun-Yong Chong** Chairman **Sun-Yong Chong**

P=Parent company data.

Hyundai Engineering & Construction

Industry: **Heavy Construction**

Hyundai Engineering & Construction (HDEC) participates in civil-, architectural-, industrial-, and electrical-engineering projects in South Korea and overseas. Its major current projects include the Sabiya Power Station and transmission line in Kuwait, Eastern General Hospital in Singapore, Jamuna Bridge in Bangladesh, and a fertilizer plant in Thailand. It is also involved in the construction of nuclear-power stations, refineries, pipelines, housing, hotels, and airports. HDEC is a member of The Hyundai Group of Companies, which controls the company's management.

Won bil	12/92	12/93	12/94	US$mil 12/94				
Sales	2,712.8	2,791.9	3,123.8	3,899.1	P/E Ratio	81.7	Price (9/30/95)	39,800
Net Income	19.0	20.7	23.5	29.4	P/B Ratio	2.6	52 Wk Hi-Low	46,376.6-30,071.5
Book Value	651.6	668.1	724.5	926.4	Yield %	0.2	Market Cap	US$2,469.7mil

Address **140-2 Kyedong, Chongro-ku** **Seoul**
Tel **02-746-1114** Fax **02-743-8963**
ADR SEDOL No. **6450988**
President & CEO **Kwang Myung Kim** Chairman **Jae Myun Park**

Hyundai Marine & Fire Insurance

Industry: **Insurance - Property & Casualty**

Hyundai Marine & Fire Insurance offers a full range of insurance services. More than 54% of the company's premium earnings are generated by its automobile-liability coverage. The company also offers long-term and general insurance policies, as well as savings-type insurance programs. Based on direct premiums, it has a 15% share of the domestic insurance market. The company has minority interests in investment-management and commercial-banking concerns. Chairman and president Mong Yun Chung owns almost 22% of the company's share capital.

Won bil	03/92 P	03/93 P	03/94 P	US$mil 03/94				
Revenues	571.8	742.4	875.1	1,080.0	P/E Ratio	NMF	Price (9/30/95)	45,300
Net Income	3.0	3.2	0.0	0.0	P/B Ratio	6.6	52 Wk Hi-Low	47,387.4-28,500.0
Book Value	N/A	62.5	61.4	75.2	Yield %	0.0	Market Cap	US$492.7mil

Address **178 Sejongno, Chongno-gu Seoul** Tel **02-732-1212** Fax **02-732-4897** ADR SEDOL No. **6451077** President **Mong-Yun Chong** Chairman **Mong-Yun Chong**

P=Parent company data.

Hyundai Motor

Industry: **Automobile Manufacturers**

Hyundai Motor Company is the largest automobile manufacturer in Korea, holding 46% of the domestic market. The company's passenger-vehicle models include the Accent economy car, and the Elantra, Sonata, and Grandeur sedans. It is also Korea's leading supplier of commercial vehicles, satisfying 47.9% of the domestic demand. Hyundai exports an average of 390,000 cars and commercial vehicles to more than 180 countries. It produces most of its units at its plant in Ulsan, and is building another passenger-vehicle plant in Yulchon and a commercial-vehicle plant in Chunjoo.

Won bil	12/92 P	12/93 P	12/94 P	US$mil 12/94				
Sales	6,079.0	7,181.2	9,052.3	11,298.8	P/E Ratio	13.3	Price (9/30/95)	41,400
Net Income	41.6	58.2	136.8	170.7	P/B Ratio	1.1	52 Wk Hi-Low	49,700.0-33,500.0
Book Value	1,000.3	1,407.3	1,513.6	1,935.4	Yield %	1.4	Market Cap	US$2,163.3mil

Address **140-2 Kye-dong, Chongro-ku Seoul** Tel **02-746-1114** Fax **02-741-0470** ADR SEDOL No. **6451055** President **Song Won Chon** Chairman **Se Yung Chung**

P=Parent company data.

Hyundai Motor Service

Industry: **Other Specialty Retailers**

Hyundai Motor Service provides maintenance and repair services to vehicles and equipment manufactured by Hyundai Motor and Hyundai Precision Industries. The company also sells automobiles, auto parts, heavy machinery, and oil and gasoline products. It established an auto-finance company, 35%-owned Hyundai Auto Finance, to manage billing for its products. Hyundai Motor Service also holds a 20% stake in Hyundai Research Institute. All its products and services are supplied to the domestic market. Hyundai Precision Industries owns 11% of the company's capital.

Won bil	12/92 P	12/93 P	12/94 P	US$mil 12/94				
Revenues	3,220.1	3,903.4	4,711.4	5,880.6	P/E Ratio	14.9	Price (9/30/95)	40,500
Net Income	25.5	17.3	30.2	37.7	P/B Ratio	1.2	52 Wk Hi-Low	45,818.2-36,000.0
Book Value	310.5	348.0	429.3	548.9	Yield %	1.4	Market Cap	US$493.6mil

Address **113-25 Wonhyoro 4-ga Seoul** Tel **02-717-6111** Fax **02-715-8265** ADR SEDOL No. **6450911** President **Yang-Rae Cho** Chairman **Yang-Rae Cho**

P=Parent company data.

Hyundai Securities

Industry: **Securities Brokers**

Hyundai Securities provides brokerage and other financial services to individual and corporate clients. The company offers securities trading, investment management, financial consulting, and underwriting services. More than 60% of the company's revenue is derived from commission and fee income. Hyundai Securities holds the financial interests of the Hyundai group of companies, including 20% of Hyundai Research Institute and 65% of Hyundai Investment Management. Hyundai Motor owns a 14% stake in the company.

Won bil	03/92 P	03/93 P	03/94 P	US$mil 03/94				
Sales	145.3	158.4	206.9	255.3	P/E Ratio	11.7	Price (9/30/95)	17,200
Net Income	-18.4	8.7	32.7	40.4	P/B Ratio	0.9	52 Wk Hi-Low	25,700.0-12,500.0
Book Value	N/A	388.1	417.5	511.5	Yield %	0.6	Market Cap	US$510.3mil

Address **34-4 Youido-dong Seoul** Tel **02-768-0011** Fax **02-782-0009** ADR SEDOL No. **6497888** President **Dong-Yun Kim** Chairman **Dong-Yun Kim**

P=Parent company data.

Inchon Iron & Steel

Industry: **Steel**

Inchon Iron & Steel is South Korea's largest electrical-furnace steel manufacturer. The company's main products include stainless cold-rolled steel sections, concrete-reinforcing steel bars, H beams, and stainless-steel sheets. It is currently waiting for government approval of a plan to construct an additional steel facility in Pusan, South Korea. Inchon Iron & Steel is part of the Hyundai group of companies, and Hyundai Heavy Industries owns 42% of its share capital. Inchon Iron & Steel owns minority interests in Hyundai Petrochemical and Hyundai Precision Industries.

Won bil	12/92 P	12/93 P	12/94 P	US$mil 12/94				
Sales	917.5	1,083.9	1,213.5	1,514.7	P/E Ratio	12.8	Price (9/30/95)	32,300
Net Income	14.4	11.5	27.8	34.7	P/B Ratio	1.0	52 Wk Hi-Low	42,200.0-27,000.0
Book Value	332.1	337.0	358.2	458.0	Yield %	1.9	Market Cap	US$462.6mil

Address **1 Songhyun-dong, Tong-gu Inchon** Tel **032-760-2114** Fax **032-763-5046** ADR SEDOL No. **6461850** President **Chang-Gi Paek** Chairman **Chang-Gi Paek**

P=Parent company data.

Isu Chemical

Industry: **Specialty Chemicals**

Isu Chemical manufactures industrial chemicals. The company's products include kerosene, alkyl benzene, paraffin, and lubricating oil. Isu Chemical is South Korea's sole manufacturer and supplier of alkyl benzene. Sales of kerosene account for 56% of the company's revenues, and sales of alkyl benzene make up 35% of revenues. The company is diversifying into the electronics industry by taking a stake in a Chinese venture to produce parts for color televisions. Isu Chemical's subsidiaries include wholly-owned Dong Inchon Motor Service and 46%-owned Isu Ceramics.

Won bil	12/92	12/93	12/94	US$mil 12/94				
Sales	**212.5**	**219.3**	**231.7**	**289.2**	P/E Ratio	**20.2**	Price (9/30/95)	**10,800**
Net Income	**3.5**	**2.7**	**4.4**	**5.5**	P/B Ratio	**1.1**	52 Wk Hi-Low	**18,800.0-10,100.0**
Book Value	**77.1**	**80.2**	**86.3**	**110.3**	Yield %	**1.7**	Market Cap	**US$115.8mil**

Address **112 Banpo-dong, Socho-gu**
Seoul
Tel **02-590-6600**
Fax **02-590-6666**
ADR
SEDOL No. **6467568**
President **Chan-Uk Kim**
Chairman --

Jaeil Investment & Finance

Industry: **Financial Services - Diversified**

Jaeil Investment & Finance offers short-term financing and other financial services. The company is South Korea's largest short-term financing company in terms of deposits taken and money lent. Deposits taken by the company amount to 4.5 trillion won. The company generates more than 78% of its revenue from interest income. Jaeil Investment & Finance works in close collaboration with South Korea's Shinhan Bank and owns a 10% stake in Shinhan Research Institute. The company also owns a 76% stake in Shineun Mutual Savings & Finance.

Won bil	06/92 P	06/93 P	06/94 P	US$mil 06/94				
Revenues	**354.7**	**273.1**	**167.9**	**207.0**	P/E Ratio	**11.9**	Price (9/30/95)	**16,400**
Net Income	**13.6**	**18.5**	**8.2**	**10.1**	P/B Ratio	**1.1**	52 Wk Hi-Low	**19,200.0-11,700.0**
Book Value	**N/A**	**144.0**	**151.6**	**188.1**	Yield %	**3.7**	Market Cap	**US$213.5mil**

Address **199-40 Ulchiro 2-ga, Chung-gu**
Seoul
Tel **02-771-7400**
Fax **02-777-0571**
ADR
SEDOL No. **6469092**
President **Gwi-Jae Lee**
Chairman **Gwi-Jae Lee**

P=Parent company data.

Jinro

Industry: **Distillers & Brewers**

Jinro produces distilled liquors, whiskey, wine, beer, and brandy. It is South Korea's largest distiller of soju (a rice-, grain-, or sweet-potato-based liquor similar to vodka), holding a 48% market share. Sales of soju account for approximately 94% of the company's revenue. Jinro also has interests in advertising, pharmaceuticals, financing, and construction businesses. The company has a joint venture with Adolph Coors of the United States, 67%-owned Jinro Coors Brewing, which produces Cass cold-filtered beer. Cass brand beers have a 10% market share in South Korea.

Won bil	09/92 P	09/93 P	09/94 P	US$mil 09/94				
Sales	**217.4**	**255.2**	**302.2**	**374.6**	P/E Ratio	**13.0**	Price (9/30/95)	**20,800**
Net Income	**2.5**	**6.4**	**13.1**	**16.3**	P/B Ratio	**1.0**	52 Wk Hi-Low	**27,500.0-18,300.0**
Book Value	**118.3**	**156.3**	**174.8**	**217.5**	Yield %	**2.9**	Market Cap	**US$217.7mil**

Address **1448-3 Socho-dong, Socho-gu**
Seoul
Tel **02-520-3114**
Fax **02-584-6868**
ADR
SEDOL No. **6474159**
President **Son-Jung Kim**
Chairman **Son-Jung Kim**

P=Parent company data.

Keum Kang Development

Industry: **Retailers - Broadline**

Keum Kang Development Industries operates department stores, hotels, and highway rest-area facilities. The company's three Hyundai Department Stores are located in upscale areas of Seoul and its surrounding suburbs. It is currently planning to open a fourth department store in Pusan, South Korea. Revenue generated by retail sales accounts for more than 90% of the company's revenue. Keum Kang Development is affiliated with the Hyundai group of companies and owns a 11% stake in shipper Hyundai Merchant Marine.

Won bil	12/92 P	12/93 P	12/94 P	US$mil 12/94				
Revenues	**430.0**	**481.9**	**622.5**	**777.0**	P/E Ratio	**31.9**	Price (9/30/95)	**17,400**
Net Income	**3.1**	**-5.0**	**7.4**	**9.2**	P/B Ratio	**2.4**	52 Wk Hi-Low	**23,150.3-13,311.4**
Book Value	**93.0**	**84.4**	**98.8**	**126.3**	Yield %	**0.0**	Market Cap	**US$305.4mil**

Address **456 Apkujong-dong, Kangnam-gu**
Seoul
Tel **02-549-2233**
Fax **02-540-5604**
ADR
SEDOL No. **6489302**
President **Yong-Il Kim**
Chairman **So Sueng Ahn**

P=Parent company data.

Keumkang

Industry: **Building Materials**

Keumkang is South Korea's largest manufacturer of construction materials in terms of quantities supplied. The company's products include automotive safety glass, sheet glass, slate, rock wool, and gypsum board. It is the first South Korean company to develop a water-resistant gypsum board. It has also invested in manufacturing facilities of polyvinyl-chloride construction materials such as PVC windows and doors. Keumkang has a 62% stake in Keumkang Construction, a 40% stake in Korea Silica, and a 8% stake in Keumkang Country Club.

Won bil	12/92 P	12/93 P	12/94 P	US$mil 12/94				
Sales	**356.9**	**374.2**	**441.1**	**550.6**	P/E Ratio	**10.6**	Price (9/30/95)	**61,200**
Net Income	**29.3**	**30.9**	**34.8**	**43.4**	P/B Ratio	**1.7**	52 Wk Hi-Low	**83,700.0-55,000.0**
Book Value	**155.9**	**180.8**	**210.5**	**269.2**	Yield %	**1.6**	Market Cap	**US$478.1mil**

Address **1301-4 Socho-dong, Socho-gu**
Seoul
Tel **02-345-5000**
Fax **02-552-2139**
ADR
SEDOL No. **6490917**
President **Kang-Bong Sok**
Chairman **Kang-Bong Sok**

P=Parent company data.

Kia Motors

Industry: **Automobile Manufacturers**

Kia Motors designs and manufactures passenger cars, trucks, vans, minibuses, specialty vehicles, and automobile components. It is South Korea's second-largest auto manufacturer in terms of market share. Its passenger cars are marketed under the Avella, Sephia, and Sportage names. The company has also set up a 60%-owned joint venture with Ford of the United States. Upon obtaining regulatory approval, Kia Ford Credit Finance will provide retail and wholesale financing, retail leasing, and fleet leasing. Ford is Kia Motors largest shareholder with a 9% interest.

Won bil	12/92 P	12/93 P	12/94 P	US$mil 12/94				
Sales	**3,282.3**	**4,112.9**	**4,730.8**	**5,904.8**	P/E Ratio	**NMF**	Price (9/30/95)	**17,800**
Net Income	**15.0**	**18.7**	**-69.6**	**-86.8**	P/B Ratio	**1.4**	52 Wk Hi-Low	**19,200.0-10,800.0**
Book Value	**822.3**	**941.8**	**963.9**	**1,232.5**	Yield %	**0.0**	Market Cap	**US$1,726.9mil**

Address **15-21 Youido-dong, Seoul** Tel **02-788-1114** Fax **02-784-0746** ADR SEDOL No. **6490928** President **Sung-Jun Han** Chairman **Sung-Jun Han**

P=Parent company data.

Kohap

Industry: **Clothing & Fabrics**

Kohap manufactures integrated synthetic fabrics and yarns. Approximately 70% of the company revenue is generated by the sale of textiles. Synthetic resins and other products make up the remainder. Its other products include home and car interior textiles and plastic packaging bottles. The company exports more than 58% of its goods. Kohap has a minority interest in Eastern Telecommunications, which develops and sells telecommunication products and systems. The company's other holdings include a 92% stake in Kohap Engineering Plastics and a 69% stake in Kohap Petrochemical.

Won bil	12/92 P	12/93 P	12/94 P	US$mil 12/94				
Sales	**660.0**	**705.0**	**885.7**	**1,105.5**	P/E Ratio	**44.7**	Price (9/30/95)	**12,700**
Net Income	**6.6**	**4.8**	**5.7**	**7.2**	P/B Ratio	**1.1**	52 Wk Hi-Low	**17,000.0-11,900.0**
Book Value	**187.7**	**190.0**	**220.1**	**281.4**	Yield %	**1.6**	Market Cap	**US$295.0mil**

Address **61 Kochon-dong, Uiwang-shi, Kyonggi** Tel **034-352-0101** Fax **034-352-4022** ADR SEDOL No. **6496197** President **Sang-Un Lee** Chairman **Sang-Un Lee**

P=Parent company data.

Kolon Industries

Industry: **Clothing & Fabrics**

Kolon Industries is South Korea's largest manufacturer of nylon and synthetic products in terms of production capacity. The company produces polyester yarn, polyester fabrics, water-resistant fabric, and tire cord as well as polyester film, videotapes, and engineering plastic resins. It has also developed a specialized fabric for use in automobile airbags. Kolon Industries has invested in a cable-television business and purchased Lawsons, a 24-hour convenience-store chain. Toray Industries, Japan's leading maker of synthetic fibers, has a 12% interest in the company.

Won bil	12/92 P	12/93 P	12/94 P	US$mil 12/94				
Sales	**775.6**	**727.1**	**761.5**	**950.5**	P/E Ratio	**17.6**	Price (9/30/95)	**23,500**
Net Income	**13.0**	**27.1**	**12.4**	**15.4**	P/B Ratio	**0.6**	52 Wk Hi-Low	**35,000.0-18,700.0**
Book Value	**241.3**	**290.0**	**321.3**	**410.8**	Yield %	**0.6**	Market Cap	**US$260.9mil**

Address **45 Mugyo-dong, Chung-gu, Seoul** Tel **02-311-7114** Fax **02-311-8912** ADR SEDOL No. **6496539** President **Ung-Yol Lee** Chairman **Ung-Yol Lee**

P=Parent company data.

Korea Chemical

Industry: **Specialty Chemicals**

Korea Chemical Company manufactures paint mainly for the automobile, marine, and shipping-container industries. Its major customer is the Hyundai group of companies. The company operates production facilities in Singapore and the Netherlands, and exports almost 30% of its paint products. Its products include multisided inorganic paint and a specially developed paint for use by semiconductor manufacturers. The company has a research laboratory to promote the development of fine chemicals. Its affiliates include 38%-owned Keum Kang Construction and 20%-owned Korea Silica.

Won bil	12/92	12/93	12/94	US$mil 12/94				
Sales	**304.5**	**321.2**	**393.1**	**490.7**	P/E Ratio	**8.6**	Price (9/30/95)	**72,700**
Net Income	**22.0**	**26.7**	**33.8**	**42.2**	P/B Ratio	**1.4**	52 Wk Hi-Low	**132,000-62,000**
Book Value	**103.6**	**176.0**	**205.9**	**263.3**	Yield %	**1.4**	Market Cap	**US$378.6mil**

Address **777 Yompo-dong, Chung-gu, Ulsan-shi, Kyongnam** Tel **02-345-5000** Fax **02-289-0502** ADR SEDOL No. **6498331** President **Chung-Se Kim** Chairman **Chung-Se Kim**

Korea Development Leasing

Industry: **Financial Services - Diversified**

Korea Development Leasing offers capital-equipment leasing services to small and midsize companies. The company has an overseas, wholly-owned subsidiary in Hong Kong, KDLC Lease & Finance (H.K.), a 24% interest in a Thai leasing concern, and offers leasing services in several other Southeast Asian countries including Indonesia. Korea Development Leasing was setup as a joint venture between Korea Long-Term Credit Bank and Orix Corporation of Japan, which now have shareholdings of 21% and 26%, respectively.

Won bil	03/92 P	03/93 P	03/94 P	US$mil 03/94				
Revenues	**409.9**	**515.4**	**566.7**	**699.4**	P/E Ratio	**8.4**	Price (9/30/95)	**25,500**
Net Income	**21.2**	**25.9**	**30.5**	**37.6**	P/B Ratio	**1.4**	52 Wk Hi-Low	**39,900.0-22,300.0**
Book Value	**N/A**	**155.1**	**179.1**	**219.4**	Yield %	**2.4**	Market Cap	**US$332.7mil**

Address **88 Sorin-dong, Chongno-gu, Seoul** Tel **02-370-0114** Fax **02-736-2387** ADR SEDOL No. **6498900** President **Il-Gyu Kang** Chairman **Il-Gyu Kang**

P=Parent company data.

Korea Electric Power

Industry: **Electrical Utilities - All**

Korea Electric Power (Kepco) generates and supplies electric power to industrial, commercial, and residential customers. Kepco has a monopoly on the transmission and distribution of electricity in South Korea, and owns 95.2% of the country's total electricity-generating capacity. In 1994, Kepco's installed capacity was 28,750 megawatts. The firm generated 165 billion kilowatt hours of electricity during that year. Kepco's nuclear facilities generate 35.5% of the company's electricity, and coal-fired facilities generate 25.4%.

Won bil	12/92	12/93	12/94	US$mil 12/94				
Sales	6,717.5	7,526.0	8,864.6	11,064.5	P/E Ratio	20.0	Price (9/30/95)	28,900
Net Income	763.6	419.4	881.8	1,100.7	P/B Ratio	1.6	52 Wk Hi-Low	37,000.0-23,500.0
Book Value	9,194.1	9,817.6	11,165.2	14,276.3	Yield %	1.7	Market Cap	US$19,309mil

Address	**167 Samsong-dong, Kangnam-gu**	Tel **02-550-3114**	ADR	**KEP**	President	**Chong-Hun Rieh**
	Seoul	Fax **02-550-5981**	SEDOL No.	**6495730**	Chairman	**Chong-Hun Rieh**

Korea Electronics

Industry: **Semiconductors & related**

Korea Electronics manufactures semiconductors and electronics equipment. The company's principal products include transistors, integrated circuits, liquid crystal displays, and color-television components. Sales of semiconductors account for 61% of the company's revenue, and sales of electronics equipment make up the remainder. The company generates more than 87% of its revenues from exporting its products. Korea Electronics owns a subsidiary in Hong Kong, as well as production facilities in Thailand.

Won bil	09/92	09/93	09/94	US$mil 09/94				
Sales	258.0	266.2	293.1	363.4	P/E Ratio	15.9	Price (9/30/95)	27,200
Net Income	2.4	3.7	6.8	8.5	P/B Ratio	1.1	52 Wk Hi-Low	43,000.0-25,000.0
Book Value	84.8	86.5	95.9	119.3	Yield %	1.8	Market Cap	US$141.7mil

Address	**45 Namdaemunno 4-ga, Chung-gu**	Tel **02-757-5700**	ADR		President	**Jong-So Kwak**
	Seoul	Fax **02-756-5800**	SEDOL No.	**6496733**	Chairman	--

Korea Exchange Bank

Industry: **Banks - Regional**

Korea Exchange Bank was set up to specialize in foreign exchange transactions. Now it also offers a range of financial services including household loans and stock investing. The company generates 45% of its revenue from interest income, 19% of its revenue from gains on securities, and 10% of its revenue from commission and fee income. Korea Exchange Bank has introduced a global dealing system for its foreign-exchange treasury operations, and is setting up a brokerage house and investment research institute. The Bank of Korea owns 65% of the company's share capital.

Won bil	12/92 P	12/93 P	12/94 P	US$mil 12/94				
Revenues	1,638.2	1,549.0	1,911.2	2,385.5	P/E Ratio	14.2	Price (9/30/95)	9,110.00
Net Income	61.7	83.5	100.4	125.3	P/B Ratio	0.9	52 Wk Hi-Low	10,741.6-6,690.0
Book Value	1,133.5	1,566.1	1,640.2	2,097.2	Yield %	2.6	Market Cap	US$1,852.7mil

Address	**181 Ulchiro 2-ga, Chung-gu**	Tel **02-729-0114**	ADR		President	**Myong-Son Chang**
	Seoul	Fax **02-757-7897**	SEDOL No.	**6495042**	Chairman	**Myong-Son Chang**

P=Parent company data.

Korea Express

Industry: **Marine Transportation**

Korea Express is South Korea's largest land cargo-transportation company in terms of revenues. It specializes in the transportation of industrial cargo, shipping containers, and packages. The company also provides transportation services for domestic and overseas construction projects and loading services to sea-freight shipping companies. Korea Express is currently building a wharf in Asan Bay and an intermodal cargo terminal in Taejon. The company owns a 75% stake in Korea Express Tourist, a 33% stake in Dong Ah General Development, and a 32% stake in Dong Ah Television.

Won bil	12/92 P	12/93 P	12/94 P	US$mil 12/94				
Sales	426.1	496.0	573.3	715.6	P/E Ratio	20.0	Price (9/30/95)	31,200
Net Income	13.8	10.3	14.2	17.7	P/B Ratio	1.9	52 Wk Hi-Low	40,869.2-25,300.0
Book Value	112.7	150.9	193.1	246.9	Yield %	1.9	Market Cap	US$380.0mil

Address	**58-12 Sosomun-dong, Chung-gu**	Tel **02-753-2141**	ADR		President	**Yo-Hwan Kim**
	Seoul	Fax **02-753-0361**	SEDOL No.	**6497112**	Chairman	**Yo-Hwan Kim**

P=Parent company data.

Korea First Bank

Industry: **Banks - Regional**

Korea First Bank provides retail- and commercial-banking services throughout South Korea. The company derives 50% of its revenue from interest on loans. It also provides international banking services and operates branches in London, Tokyo, and New York. It has entered into a joint venture with the Industrial and Commercial Bank of China and will begin operations in the city of Qingdao, China by the end of 1996. Korea First Bank has a 55% interest in KFB Mutual Saving & Finance, a 49% interest in First Citicorp Leasing, and a 49% interest in KFB Securities.

Won bil	12/92 P	12/93 P	12/94 P	US$mil 12/94				
Revenues	1,487.5	1,555.4	2,017.8	2,518.6	P/E Ratio	8.4	Price (9/30/95)	8,400.00
Net Income	146.8	154.1	131.3	163.8	P/B Ratio	0.7	52 Wk Hi-Low	14,000.0-6,650.0
Book Value	1,333.3	1,443.2	1,865.4	2,385.2	Yield %	3.6	Market Cap	US$1,421.8mil

Address	**100 Kongpyong-dong, Chongno-gu**	Tel **02-733-0070**	ADR		President	**Chol-Su Lee**
	Seoul	Fax **02-734-5976**	SEDOL No.	**6496788**	Chairman	**Chol-Su Lee**

P=Parent company data.

Korea Green Cross

Industry: **Other Food**

Korea Green Cross Corporation manufactures prescription and over-the-counter pharmaceuticals. Prescription medication accounts for approximately 80% of the company's total sales. Sales of blood-fraction materials account for approximately 26% of the company's revenues and microbiological products account for more than 25% of revenues. Its products include hepatitis vaccines, anticancer drugs, antiviral agents, chicken-pox vaccines, and AIDS testing kits. Most of the company's products are sold to hospitals throughout South Korea.

Won bil	12/92	12/93	12/94	US$mil 12/94				
Sales	127.9	146.3	155.5	194.0	P/E Ratio	36.0	Price (9/30/95)	85,700
Net Income	5.8	5.3	4.8	6.0	P/B Ratio	2.0	52 Wk Hi-Low	148,668-68,100
Book Value	72.6	76.5	87.0	111.3	Yield %	0.7	Market Cap	US$234.3mil

Address **227 Kugal-ri, Kihung-up**
Yongin-gun, Kyonggi
Tel **02-584-0131**
Fax **031-282-4522**
ADR
SEDOL No. **6497134**
President **Yong-Sop Ho**
Chairman **Yong-Sop Ho**

Korea Iron & Steel

Industry: **Steel**

Korea Iron & Steel manufactures steel bars and steel sheets. Its products are sold primarily to businesses in the construction industry. Sales of reinforcing bars account for 65% of the company's revenues, sales of steel sheets account for 10% of revenues, and sales of steel pipes account for 9% of revenues. The company also holds minority interests in Dongkuk Industries, Kyongnam Daily, and Kukje Transportation. Korea Iron & Steel is 48% owned by Dongkuk Steel Mill, South Korea's largest producer of concrete-reinforcement bars.

Won bil	12/92	12/93	12/94	US$mil 12/94				
Sales	315.2	447.6	527.4	658.3	P/E Ratio	23.0	Price (9/30/95)	14,800
Net Income	10.1	2.6	6.4	7.9	P/B Ratio	0.8	52 Wk Hi-Low	25,600.0-12,200.0
Book Value	152.8	153.3	209.1	267.4	Yield %	2.7	Market Cap	US$231.2mil

Address **621 Wolyong-dong, Happo-gu**
Kyongnam
Tel **0551-49-3000**
Fax **0551-44-9212**
ADR
SEDOL No. **6497178**
President **Sang-Don Chang**
Chairman --

Korea Kumho Petrochemical

Industry: **Commodity Chemicals**

Korea Kumho Petrochemical is South Korea's largest manufacturer of synthetic rubber in terms of domestic market share. Its main products are styrenen butadiene rubber and butadiene rubber used in synthetic-rubber tires, shoes, and industrial raw materials. The company also produces latex and elastomer. It exports approximately 77% of its synthetic-rubber products. Korea Kumho Petrochemical has two 50%-owned petrochemical joint ventures, Kumho Mitsui Toatsu and Kumho Shell Chemical. It also owns 14% of Asiana Airlines.

Won bil	12/92 P	12/93 P	12/94 P	US$mil 12/94				
Sales	187.3	210.7	243.1	303.4	P/E Ratio	12.3	Price (9/30/95)	9,600.00
Net Income	13.7	18.5	18.3	22.9	P/B Ratio	0.8	52 Wk Hi-Low	13,700.0-8,330.0
Book Value	247.3	255.1	260.7	333.3	Yield %	5.2	Market Cap	US$255.0mil

Address **70 Sorin-dong, Chongno-gu**
Seoul
Tel **02-399-7551**
Fax **02-720-9742**
ADR
SEDOL No. **6499323**
President **Hung-Gi Kim**
Chairman **Hung-Gi Kim**

P=Parent company data.

Korea Long-Term Credit

Industry: **Banks - Regional**

Korea Long-Term Credit Bank (KLB) provides commercial-banking services to corporate clients. The company specializes in extending medium- and long-term credit to South Korean businesses. It issues long-term bonds to fund industrial-development projects and raises capital funds overseas and loans them to South Korean companies for long-term investments. Through its wholly-owned KLB Credit Card subsidiary, the company issues Visa credit cards. KLB also owns a 38% stake in brokerage firm KLB Securities and a 21% stake in finance company Korea Development Leasing.

Won bil	12/92 P	12/93 P	12/94 P	US$mil 12/94				
Revenues	930.4	1,021.6	1,267.4	1,581.9	P/E Ratio	8.9	Price (9/30/95)	23,400
Net Income	77.8	72.3	105.8	132.1	P/B Ratio	0.1	52 Wk Hi-Low	28,249.7-20,300.0
Book Value	633.9	719.0	9,407.7	12,029.1	Yield %	10.2	Market Cap	US$1,569.4mil

Address **15-22 Youido-dong**
Seoul
Tel **02-782-0111**
Fax **02-784-7310**
ADR
SEDOL No. **6496670**
President **Jung-Hyon Bong**
Chairman **Jung-Hyon Bong**

P=Parent company data.

Korea Mobil Telecom

Industry: **Telephone Systems - All**

Korea Mobil Telecommunications (KMT) provides mobile-communication and radio-paging services throughout South Korea. The company is South Korea's sole provider of cellular-phone service, but it expects more companies to enter the market in 1996. It offer wireless-communication services to more than 1.4 million subscribers and paging services to more than 4.5 million subscribers. In August 1995, KMT signed a contract with AT&T as a supplier of its wireless-phone equipment. Korea Telecom and Yukong both have 20% interests in the company.

Won bil	12/92 P	12/93 P	12/94 P	US$mil 12/94				
Sales	258.3	428.1	782.9	977.2	P/E Ratio	20.9	Price (9/30/95)	485,000
Net Income	48.7	76.9	128.7	160.7	P/B Ratio	6.5	52 Wk Hi-Low	652,000-352,000
Book Value	210.8	284.9	411.0	525.5	Yield %	0.2	Market Cap	US$3,498.3mil

Address **16-49 Hangangno 3-ga**
Seoul
Tel **02-705-0114**
Fax **02-705-0499**
ADR
SEDOL No. **6495655**
President **Byong-Il Cho**
Chairman **Byong-Il Cho**

P=Parent company data.

Korea Zinc

Industry: **Non-Ferrous Metals - Other (Exc. Aluminum)**

Korea Zinc produces zinc ingots, electrolytic lead, and electrolytic gold. The company has an average annual smelting capacity of 180,000 tonnes of zinc and 90,000 tonnes of lead. It is currently constructing a new zinc smelter that will increase its capacity to 225,000 tonnes of zinc. It is also developing zinc materials for use in the manufacturing of semiconductors. Korea Zinc's wholly-owned subsidiaries are involved in heavy machinery, recycling, and chemical businesses. The company is an affiliate of Young Poong, which owns 26% of its share capital.

Won bil	12/92 P	12/93 P	12/94 P	US$mil 12/94				
Sales	**273.4**	**255.4**	**311.2**	**388.4**	P/E Ratio	**17.8**	Price (9/30/95)	**19,400**
Net Income	**12.7**	**15.5**	**18.8**	**23.4**	P/B Ratio	**1.5**	52 Wk Hi-Low	**26,000.0-17,100.0**
Book Value	**204.8**	**211.6**	**221.8**	**283.6**	Yield %	**2.6**	Market Cap	**US$434.5mil**

Address	**142 Nonhyon-dong, Kangnam-gu**	Tel	**02-519-3416**	ADR		President	**Jae-Gu Lee**
	Seoul	Fax	**02-549-8245**	SEDOL No.	**6495428**	Chairman	**Jae-Gu Lee**

P=Parent company data.

Korean Air Lines

Industry: **Airlines**

Korean Air is an international commercial airline. Its fleet of 95 aircraft services 55 overseas and 14 domestic destinations. The airline transports 19 million passengers and 763,000 tonnes of cargo annually. Its catering division produces meals for 31 customer airlines. Its aerospace division manufactures and maintains aircraft for South Korea's and the United States' military. Currently, Korean Air is taking a part in building the nation's first communication satellite. The company also manages duty-free shops, shuttle-bus service, a training institute, and four hotels.

Won bil	12/92	12/93	12/94	US$mil 12/94				
Sales	**2,337.7**	**2,701.0**	**3,058.4**	**3,817.4**	P/E Ratio	**31.4**	Price (9/30/95)	**25,900**
Net Income	**1.2**	**11.8**	**36.9**	**46.1**	P/B Ratio	**2.0**	52 Wk Hi-Low	**30,500.0-20,500.0**
Book Value	**472.6**	**484.7**	**621.1**	**794.2**	Yield %	**0.6**	Market Cap	**US$1,646.3mil**

Address	**41-3 Seosomoon-dong, Chung-gu**	Tel	**02-756-2000**	ADR		President & CEO	**Yang Ho Cho**
	Seoul	Fax	**02-755-5220**	SEDOL No.	**6496766**	Chairman	**Choong Hoon Cho**

Korean Reinsurance

Industry: **Insurance - Property & Casualty**

Korean Reinsurance is the sole provider of reinsurance in South Korea. It provides fire, marine, motor, casualty, and life insurance. It generates approximately 40% of its revenue from casualty- and property-insurance policies and 32% from fire-insurance policies. The company has wholly-owned subsidiaries in London and New York and a 25%-owned affiliate in Malaysia. It also has a reinsurance agreement with a firm based in Bermuda. It offers services to domestic clients as well as to clients in London, Tokyo, Singapore, Hong Kong, and Jakarta.

Won bil	03/92 P	03/93 P	03/94 P	US$mil 03/94				
Revenues	**298.2**	**323.2**	**392.3**	**484.1**	P/E Ratio	**NMF**	Price (9/30/95)	**38,000**
Net Income	**-6.1**	**-2.9**	**0.7**	**0.9**	P/B Ratio	**2.0**	52 Wk Hi-Low	**48,000.0-32,000.0**
Book Value	**N/A**	**89.4**	**130.7**	**160.1**	Yield %	**1.1**	Market Cap	**US$336.8mil**

Address	**80 Susong-dong, Chongro-gu**	Tel	**02-739-6141**	ADR		President	**Hyong-Sop Shim**
	Seoul	Fax	**02-739-3753**	SEDOL No.	**6497253**	Chairman	**Hyong-Sop Shim**

P=Parent company data.

Kuk Dong Engineering & Construction

Industry: **Home Construction**

Kuk Dong Engineering & Construction is a general contractor that specializes in domestic housing construction. It is currently constructing residential apartment buildings as part of city-redevelopment programs. The company is also involved in infrastructure and environmental projects including the construction of the Hanam-Chunchon highway. Kuk Dong is planning to build an elevated road in Jakarta and a housing development in Kobe, Japan. The company has a 8% stake in Dong Suh Securities and other interests in golf courses, resorts, and hotels.

Won bil	12/92 P	12/93 P	12/94 P	US$mil 12/94				
Sales	**429.2**	**398.3**	**342.0**	**426.9**	P/E Ratio	**29.7**	Price (9/30/95)	**14,800**
Net Income	**2.2**	**2.1**	**6.4**	**8.0**	P/B Ratio	**1.1**	52 Wk Hi-Low	**19,465.6-10,900.0**
Book Value	**131.1**	**146.6**	**163.4**	**208.9**	Yield %	**1.1**	Market Cap	**US$240.1mil**

Address	**60-1 Chungmuro 3-ga, Chung-gu**	Tel	**02-273-1141**	ADR		President	**Myong-Gun Kim**
	Seoul	Fax	**02-273-4719**	SEDOL No.	**6497338**	Chairman	**Myong-Gun Kim**

P=Parent company data.

Kumho

Industry: **Tires & Rubber**

Kum Ho manufactures tires and other rubber products. The company specializes in the production of tires for high-speed vehicles and tires for Boeing 737s. It is currently planning the construction of a second plant in South Korea. It also operates a joint-venture manufacturing facility in Nanjing, China that has an annual production capacity of 3 million tires. The company exports approximately 50% of its rubber products. Kumho holds a 17% interest in Asiana Air Lines, and a 12% interest in Korea Kumho Petrochemical.

Won bil	12/92 P	12/93 P	12/94 P	US$mil 12/94				
Sales	**826.5**	**885.4**	**850.6**	**1,061.7**	P/E Ratio	**NMF**	Price (9/30/95)	**9,500.00**
Net Income	**25.1**	**3.2**	**-46.9**	**-58.5**	P/B Ratio	**0.7**	52 Wk Hi-Low	**14,100.0-7,730.0**
Book Value	**253.3**	**246.4**	**202.8**	**259.3**	Yield %	**0.0**	Market Cap	**US$182.8mil**

Address	**10-1 Hoehyon-dong 2-ga**	Tel	**02-758-1114**	ADR		President	**Il Nam**
	Seoul	Fax	**02-758-1515**	SEDOL No.	**6497684**	Chairman	**Il Nam**

P=Parent company data.

Kun Young Construction

Industry: **Home Construction**

Kun Young Construction is a domestic residential constructor that specializes in building high-quality apartment buildings. Sales of the units it constructs account for almost 60% of the company's revenue. Construction contracts account for 38% of its revenue. Through its wholly-owned U.S. subsidiary, the company is currently working on a housing complex in Hawaii. It also plans to enter the housing-construction market in China. Kun Young Construction is an affiliate of the Kun Young group of companies.

Won bil	12/92 P	12/93 P	12/94 P	US$mil 12/94				
Sales	323.1	350.8	600.6	749.7	P/E Ratio	9.6	Price (9/30/95)	13,400
Net Income	7.2	8.9	13.7	17.1	P/B Ratio	1.1	52 Wk Hi-Low	22,000.0-9,800.0
Book Value	109.8	105.7	150.1	191.9	Yield %	4.1	Market Cap	US$212.9mil

Address **46-3 Jamwon-dong, Socho-gu Seoul**
Tel **02-369-7114**
Fax **02-369-7439**
ADR
SEDOL No. **6499312**
President **Jong-Il Om**
Chairman **Jong-Il Om**

P=Parent company data.

Kyungwon-Century

Industry: **Consumer Electronics**

Kyungwon-Century manufactures freezers, heaters, air conditioners, and related equipment. The company holds between 25% and 40% of the South Korean market for each of these products. Sales of air conditioners account for 32% of the company's revenues, sales of freezers account for 24% of revenues, and sales of air-conditioning equipment account for almost 18% of revenues. The firm has a 45% interest in cable-television company Mirae CATV, and a 51% interest in Kyungwon-Century U.S.A. subsidiary The company's president, Yun-Hui Won, owns 10% of its shares.

Won bil	03/92	03/93	03/94	US$mil 03/94				
Sales	172.1	167.1	101.7	125.5	P/E Ratio	46.3	Price (9/30/95)	29,000
Net Income	9.0	8.5	4.8	5.9	P/B Ratio	2.2	52 Wk Hi-Low	36,600.0-25,958.3
Book Value	N/A	79.9	80.0	98.0	Yield %	2.1	Market Cap	US$226.5mil

Address **222-22 Nae-dong, Ochung-gu Kyonggi**
Tel **02-316-7114**
Fax **02-316-7011**
ADR
SEDOL No. **6499345**
President **Yun-Hui Won**
Chairman --

LG Chemical

Industry: **Specialty Chemicals**

LG Chemical (formerly Lucky Ltd.) is South Korea's largest manufacturer of petrochemicals and household products in terms of volume. Approximately 30% of the company's revenue is derived from industrial-material sales. Petrochemical sales account for another 30% of revenue, and the sale of household goods accounts for 22%. Its range of 8,000 products includes cosmetics, food seasonings, plastic fuel tanks, polyvinyl chloride, octane, and fine chemicals. LG Chemical is licensed to produce 2-propylheptanol, a C10 alcohol used to make plasticizers.

Won bil	12/92 P	12/93 P	12/94 P	US$mil 12/94				
Sales	2,096.0	2,280.7	2,802.6	3,498.1	P/E Ratio	13.6	Price (9/30/95)	16,800
Net Income	31.0	44.5	91.6	114.4	P/B Ratio	1.1	52 Wk Hi-Low	28,800.0-15,100.0
Book Value	832.7	915.7	1,065.8	1,362.8	Yield %	3.0	Market Cap	US$1,594.1mil

Address **20 Youido-dong, Yongdungpo-gu Seoul**
Tel **02-787-1114**
Fax **02-787-7039**
ADR
SEDOL No. **6537030**
President **Jae-Gap Song**
Chairman **Jae-Gap Song**

P=Parent company data.

LG Electronics

Industry: **Consumer Electronics**

LG Electronics (formerly Goldstar) manufactures consumer electronics. The company is South Korea's largest maker of home appliances in terms of sales. Its products include televisions, microwave ovens, and computers. It has more than 20 overseas subsidiaries and export sales account for more than 55% of the company's revenue. The company owns almost 58% of the U.S. television maker Zenith Electronics, which gives it a 12% share of the U.S. television market. The company is also currently building television-manufacturing facilities in Hai Hung, Vietnam.

Won bil	12/92 P	12/93 P	12/94 P	US$mil 12/94				
Sales	3,787.5	4,323.6	5,149.2	6,427.1	P/E Ratio	20.6	Price (9/30/95)	25,700
Net Income	26.5	65.6	104.6	130.6	P/B Ratio	1.6	52 Wk Hi-Low	37,350.2-22,500.0
Book Value	823.1	1,252.8	1,250.2	1,598.6	Yield %	1.9	Market Cap	US$2,753.4mil

Address **20 Youido-dong, Yongdungpo-gu Seoul**
Tel **02-787-5114**
Fax **02-787-3400**
ADR
SEDOL No. **6375779**
President **Ja-Hong Ku**
Chairman **Ja-Hong Ku**

P=Parent company data.

LG Insurance

Industry: **Insurance - Property & Casualty**

LG Insurance Company is a non-life insurer. It provides fire, marine, transit, and cargo coverage to business clients, and accident, travel, automobile, and private-pension coverage to individual customers. LG Insurance has a branch office in New York, and liaison offices in London, Jakarta, Tokyo, and Los Angeles. It is the only Korean insurer that can directly underwrite business in the state of California. It also has a cooperation agreement with Grupo Nacional Provincial of Mexico to operate in North America.

Won bil	03/92	03/93	03/94	US$mil 03/94				
Revenues	463.2	594.3	706.3	871.7	P/E Ratio	NMF	Price (9/30/95)	62,200
Net Income	4.6	4.7	0.0	0.0	P/B Ratio	2.3	52 Wk Hi-Low	63,200.0-34,800.0
Book Value	146.3	150.4	118.8	145.6	Yield %	0.0	Market Cap	US$351.5mil

Address **85 Da-Dong, Chung-gu Seoul**
Tel **02-310-2114**
Fax **02-753-1002**
ADR
SEDOL No. **6668899**
Chief Executive **Whee-Young Lee**
President **Whee-Young Lee**

LG International

Industry: **Overseas Trading**

LG International (formerly Lucky-Goldstar International) is the trading arm of the LG group of companies. It distributes electronic products, machinery, chemicals, oil, fabric, and sewing products. The company also manufactures garments including ready-to-wear men's and women's apparel. LG International derives more than 85% of its sales from exports and operates from 38 offices worldwide. In addition to its trading operations, LG International is involved in overseas natural-resource development projects and invests in infrastructure projects.

Won bil	12/92 P	12/93 P	12/94 P	US$mil 12/94				
Sales	**3,867.5**	**4,106.3**	**5,361.1**	**6,691.6**	P/E Ratio	**62.8**	Price (9/30/95)	**12,400**
Net Income	**9.0**	**3.8**	**5.2**	**6.4**	P/B Ratio	**1.6**	52 Wk Hi-Low	**14,272.2-9,331.8**
Book Value	**161.4**	**199.0**	**201.9**	**258.2**	Yield %	**0.6**	Market Cap	**US$422.0mil**

Address **20 Youido-dong, Yongdungpo-gu** **Seoul**
Tel **02-787-1114** Fax **02-785-7762**
ADR SEDOL No. **6537115**
President **Su-Hwan Park** Chairman **Jin-Hwan Chun**

P=Parent company data.

LG Metals

Industry: **Non-Ferrous Metals - Other (Exc. Aluminum)**

LG Metals is South Korea's largest nonferrous-metal smelter in terms of volume produced. Its annual production capacity is 220,000 tons of electrolytic copper, 20,000 tons of gold ingots, and 20,000 tons of copper and stainless-steel pipes. It is the sole supplier of eletrolytic copper to domestic cable manufacturers and holds a 50% domestic market share. The company also produces silver ingots, lead, platinum, tin, and sulfuric acid, and sells gold coins through Korea First Bank. LG Cable & Machinery owns a 19% stake in LG Metals.

Won bil	12/92 P	12/93 P	12/94 P	US$mil 12/94				
Sales	**756.3**	**791.3**	**1,007.5**	**1,257.5**	P/E Ratio	**22.4**	Price (9/30/95)	**17,200**
Net Income	**3.5**	**0.5**	**9.2**	**11.5**	P/B Ratio	**1.7**	52 Wk Hi-Low	**21,600.0-12,000.0**
Book Value	**40.5**	**115.0**	**124.2**	**158.8**	Yield %	**0.9**	Market Cap	**US$268.7mil**

Address **20 Youido-dong, Yongdungpo-gu** **Seoul**
Tel **02-787-1114** Fax **02-761-3188**
ADR SEDOL No. **6497231**
President **Jong-Song Lee** Chairman **Jong-Song Lee**

P=Parent company data.

LG Securities

Industry: **Securities Brokers**

LG Securities (formerly Lucky Securities) offers brokerage, dealership, underwriting, international investment-banking, investment-management, and mergers and acquisitions services. It operates 59 domestic branches, owns three overseas subsidiaries in London, New York, and Hong Kong, and maintains two representative offices in Tokyo and Zurich. The company holds a 7% market share of the total brokerage volume, and a 9.1% market share of bond underwriting in South Korea. Its underwriting clients include Korea Electric Power, Ssangyong Motors, and Hansol Paper Manufacturing.

Won bil	03/93	03/94	03/95	US$mil 03/95				
Sales	**216.5**	**282.4**	**303.5**	**382.3**	P/E Ratio	**19.6**	Price (9/30/95)	**17,400**
Net Income	**38.8**	**48.7**	**38.9**	**49.0**	P/B Ratio	**0.8**	52 Wk Hi-Low	**24,500.0-11,700.0**
Book Value	**856.7**	**892.6**	**884.2**	**1,145.1**	Yield %	**0.6**	Market Cap	**US$880.8mil**

Address **34-36 Yeoido-dong** **Seoul**
Tel **02-768-7000** Fax **02-784-8621**
ADR SEDOL No. **6537085**
President & CEO **Youn-Il Jin** Chairman **Youn-Il Jin**

Lotte Chilsung Beverage

Industry: **Soft Drinks**

Lotte Chilsung Beverage is South Korea's largest bottler of soft drinks in terms of volume. It produces its own brand, Chilsung cider, as well as bottling Pepsi cola. The company's other products include fruit juices, sports drinks, and soybean-based drinks. Lotte Chilsung is also planning the construction of a bottled drinking-water plant in the Kangwon area to be operational in 1996. More than 50% of the company's revenue comes from juice sales, while cider and cola account for 28% of revenue. Lotte Confectionery holds a 10% stake in the company.

Won bil	12/92 P	12/93 P	12/94 P	US$mil 12/94				
Sales	**527.4**	**518.2**	**619.2**	**772.9**	P/E Ratio	**14.6**	Price (9/30/95)	**110,000**
Net Income	**2.2**	**5.6**	**9.4**	**11.7**	P/B Ratio	**3.5**	52 Wk Hi-Low	**151,900-69,000**
Book Value	**27.7**	**31.7**	**39.3**	**50.3**	Yield %	**0.5**	Market Cap	**US$177.6mil**

Address **1322-1 Socho-dong, Socho-gu** **Seoul**
Tel **02-536-0222** Fax **02-591-8531**
ADR SEDOL No. **6535443**
President **Jun-Ik Park** Chairman **Jun-Ik Park**

P=Parent company data.

Lotte Confectionery

Industry: **Other Food**

Lotte Confectionery produces chewing-gum, hard candy, ice-cream, dairy products, chocolates, cookies, cakes, and dairy products. It derives more than 47% of its total sales from ice cream products, 33% from cookies and chocolates, and almost 20% from gum and candy. Lotte Confectionery is the flagship of the Lotte group of companies. The company holds minority interests in several of the Korean-listed Lotte companies, including soft-drink firm Lotte Chilsung Beverage, food maker Lotte Sam Kang, and provincial bank Pusan Bank. Lotte Aluminum owns a 16% stake in the company.

Won bil	12/92 P	12/93 P	12/94 P	US$mil 12/94				
Sales	**528.2**	**577.2**	**650.8**	**812.3**	P/E Ratio	**15.1**	Price (9/30/95)	**95,000**
Net Income	**4.0**	**5.3**	**8.9**	**11.1**	P/B Ratio	**1.9**	52 Wk Hi-Low	**123,600-77,100**
Book Value	**62.5**	**66.3**	**69.5**	**88.9**	Yield %	**0.6**	Market Cap	**US$175.6mil**

Address **23 Yangpyong-dong 4-ga** **Seoul**
Tel **02-675-9311** Fax **02-675-6600**
ADR SEDOL No. **6535432**
President **Gyu-Shik Kim** Chairman **Gyu-Shik Kim**

P=Parent company data.

Mando Machinery

Industry: **Other Auto Parts**

Mando Machinery produces auto parts and components, particularly climate-control devices, and distributes them to South Korean automobile and farm-equipment manufacturers. The company's auto products include air conditioners, steering components, and brake parts. It also manufactures guns and sells household air conditioners. Mando Machinery is affiliated with the Halla group of companies. It owns a 63% interest in Halla Venture Capital and a 50% interest in Halla Climate Control. Halla Engineering & Construction holds a 19% stake in the company.

Won bil	12/92 P	12/93 P	12/94 P	US$mil 12/94				
Sales	619.5	750.6	1,007.3	1,257.3	P/E Ratio	8.6	Price (9/30/95)	46,000
Net Income	9.2	9.4	23.9	29.8	P/B Ratio	1.0	52 Wk Hi-Low	58,700.0-42,000.0
Book Value	174.1	178.6	193.3	247.2	Yield %	1.3	Market Cap	US$241.2mil

Address **730 Tang-dong, Kunpo-shi Kyonggi** Tel **034-350-6114** Fax **034-359-6380** ADR SEDOL No. **6560940** President **Mong-Won Chong** Chairman **Mong-Won Chong**

P=Parent company data.

Miwon

Industry: **Other Food**

Miwon is South Korea's largest producer of monosodium glutamate, with a more than 50% domestic market share. The company also manufactures animal feed, fertilizers, and chemical resins. Miwon is currently introducing a drink to reduce the influence of alcohol and planning the construction of a facility to produce its antibiotics and anticancer drugs. It is also planning to construct a drug-manufacturing plant in the Umsung industrial estate. Miwon's goal is that pharmaceuticals will be one of its main product lines by the year 2000.

Won bil	12/92 P	12/93 P	12/94 P	US$mil 12/94				
Sales	415.2	481.3	533.8	666.3	P/E Ratio	5.3	Price (9/30/95)	21,800
Net Income	4.9	7.4	33.5	41.8	P/B Ratio	1.3	52 Wk Hi-Low	33,300.0-20,200.0
Book Value	81.2	82.2	140.6	179.8	Yield %	0.8	Market Cap	US$229.3mil

Address **96-48 Shinsol-dong Seoul** Tel **02-220-9500** Fax **02-232-3719** ADR SEDOL No. **6796518** President **Yong-Hak Yu** Chairman **Yong-Hak Yu**

P=Parent company data.

Oriental Chemical Industries

Industry: **Commodity Chemicals**

Oriental Chemical Industries (OCI) manufactures industrial chemicals, specialty chemicals, agrochemicals, and petrochemicals. Its major basic chemical products include soda ash, calcium chloride, phosphoric acid, and white carbon. The company is South Korea's largest supplier of calcium phosphate, a basic ingredient of livestock feed. OCI maintains a joint-venture with Japan's Sumitomo Chemicals and Itochu to produce high-purity grade reagents. The company also designs automation systems and manufactures of semiconductor components.

Won bil	12/92	12/93	12/94	US$mil 12/94				
Sales	453.1	501.9	551.5	688.3	P/E Ratio	23.4	Price (9/30/95)	23,800
Net Income	8.2	16.4	8.6	10.7	P/B Ratio	1.1	52 Wk Hi-Low	33,500.0-18,800.0
Book Value	177.2	171.6	175.1	223.9	Yield %	1.5	Market Cap	US$240.3mil

Address **50 Sokong-dong, Chung-gu Seoul** Tel **02-727-9500** Fax **02-757-4111** ADR SEDOL No. **6661304** President **Kwon Suk-myung** Chairman & CEO **Lee Hoi-rim**

Orion Electric

Industry: **Electrical Components & Equipment**

Orion Electric manufactures cathode ray tubes, color picture tubes, computer monitors, and liquid-crystal displays. It supplies most of its products to Daewoo Electric Components and Daewoo Electronics. More than 89% of its sales revenue is generated by exports. The company has contracts to supply color picture tubes to Philips, Sanyo, and Mitsubishi. Orion Electric owns 70% of a joint venture with Vietnam's state-run Hanel Electric, which runs a Hanoi plant that is producing picture tubes and computer monitors. Daewoo Heavy Industries owns 10% of Orion Electric's shares.

Won bil	12/92 P	12/93 P	12/94 P	US$mil 12/94				
Sales	405.3	477.1	668.6	834.5	P/E Ratio	13.5	Price (9/30/95)	18,600
Net Income	13.2	8.3	20.0	25.0	P/B Ratio	0.9	52 Wk Hi-Low	25,100.0-16,500.0
Book Value	165.5	202.5	289.2	369.8	Yield %	1.1	Market Cap	US$355.2mil

Address **165 Kongdan-dong, Kumi-shi Kyonbuk** Tel **05-469-5000** Fax **05-461-8779** ADR SEDOL No. **6661371** President **Kil-Yong Om** Chairman **Kil-Yong Om**

P=Parent company data.

Pacific

Industry: **Cosmetics & Personal Care**

Pacific is South Korea's largest manufacturers of cosmetics. The company's other products include toiletries, household goods, food, and enzymes. Cosmetic sales account for 70% of the company's revenue; sales of household and health-care products and biochemicals make up the remainder. Pacific serves as the parent company for the Pacific group of companies. It owns more than 52% of Pacific Dolphins, 44% of Pacific System, and 30% of Pacific Pharmaceutical. The company also holds a 79% stake in Youmee Cosmetics.

Won bil	12/92 P	12/93 P	12/94 P	US$mil 12/94				
Sales	450.9	513.0	603.4	753.1	P/E Ratio	12.5	Price (9/30/95)	20,800
Net Income	18.7	18.0	15.2	18.9	P/B Ratio	1.1	52 Wk Hi-Low	39,000.0-17,300.0
Book Value	137.8	147.5	156.5	200.1	Yield %	2.6	Market Cap	US$230.2mil

Address **181 Hangangno 2-ga, Yongsan-gu Seoul** Tel **02-709-5114** Fax **02-798-4612** ADR SEDOL No. **6665931** President **Dong-Gun Han** Chairman **Dong-Gun Han**

P=Parent company data.

Pang Rim Spinning

Industry: **Clothing & Fabrics**

Pang Rim is a cotton-spinning company that manufactures processed textiles, cotton yarns, and cotton fibers. The company generates more than 55% of its revenue from export sales. It is South Korea's third-largest cotton-spinning company in terms of volume, but sales of cotton yarns only account for 6% of the company's revenue. More than 81% of the company's revenue is derived from the sale of processed textiles such as polyester fibers. Private investor Sang Gun So owns more than 47% of the Pang Rim's share capital.

Won bil	09/92 P	09/93 P	09/94 P	US$mil 09/94				
Sales	**190.3**	**181.0**	**213.6**	**264.8**	P/E Ratio	**51.8**	Price (9/30/95)	**49,600**
Net Income	**5.1**	**1.0**	**2.9**	**3.6**	P/B Ratio	**0.7**	52 Wk Hi-Low	**74,200.0-43,200.0**
Book Value	**201.2**	**200.5**	**203.0**	**252.6**	Yield %	**0.7**	Market Cap	**US$193.7mil**

Address	**54 Mullae-dong 3-ga**	Tel	**02-630-2114**	ADR		President	**Jae-Hui So**
	Seoul	Fax	**02-675-5854**	SEDOL No.	**6669427**	Chairman	**Jae-Hui So**

P=Parent company data.

Pohang Iron & Steel

Industry: **Steel**

Pohang Iron & Steel (Posco) manufactures hot- and cold-rolled steel, heavy plates, wire rods, silicon-steel sheets, and stainless steel. It also makes specialized products for the construction and shipbuilding industries. The company produces all of its steel in South Korea at Pohang Works and Kwangyang Works. Posco is the second-largest steel producer in the world based on annual crude-steel production. In 1994, the company produced more than 23 million tonnes of crude steel. Posco is the largest and the only fully integrated steel producer in South Korea.

Won bil	12/92	12/93	12/94	US$mil 12/94				
Sales	**6,182.1**	**6,920.9**	**7,314.0**	**9,129.1**	P/E Ratio	**15.7**	Price (9/30/95)	**65,700**
Net Income	**185.1**	**294.6**	**383.2**	**478.3**	P/B Ratio	**1.2**	52 Wk Hi-Low	**89,000.0-54,500.0**
Book Value	**4,815.9**	**5,051.6**	**5,269.8**	**6,738.2**	Yield %	**1.0**	Market Cap	**US$6,693.6mil**

Address	**1 Koedong-dong, Pohang-shi**	Tel	**0562-220-0114**	ADR	**PKX**	President	**Chong-Chin Kim**
	Kyongbuk	Fax	**0562-72-7590**	SEDOL No.	**6693233**	Chairman	**Mahn-Je Kim**

Poongsan

Industry: **Non-Ferrous Metals - Other (Exc. Aluminum)**

Poongsan manufactures copper and copper-alloy products such as sheets, pipes, and blank coins. The company has production facilities in South Korea, Thailand, and the United States, and is the world's leading copper-alloy producer in terms of capacity. Poongsan also makes stainless-steel strips, welded titanium tubes, and defense-related products. It sells more than 70% of its products to individual companies, while it sells almost 30% of its products to military organizations. Individual investor Chan U Ryu owns a 36% stake in Poongsan.

Won bil	12/92 P	12/93 P	12/94 P	US$mil 12/94				
Sales	**554.9**	**515.2**	**604.8**	**754.9**	P/E Ratio	**21.9**	Price (9/30/95)	**13,900**
Net Income	**8.9**	**8.3**	**12.2**	**15.2**	P/B Ratio	**1.2**	52 Wk Hi-Low	**20,000.0-12,200.0**
Book Value	**210.7**	**214.2**	**220.7**	**282.2**	Yield %	**2.9**	Market Cap	**US$347.4mil**

Address	**239-1 Hyosong-dong, Puk-gu**	Tel	**02-273-3021**	ADR		President	**Hun-Bo Chong**
	Inchon	Fax	**02-273-3835**	SEDOL No.	**6694474**	Chairman	**Hun-Bo Chong**

P=Parent company data.

STC

Industry: **Household Products (Non-Durable)**

STC Corporation's main products are packaging film, batteries, and packaging tape. It also manufactures hairpieces and other consumer goods. The company operates one manufacturing facility in Kumi, South Korea, and is planning the construction of a second in the same area. It also has plants in Indonesia and the Philippines, and it exports its products to North America, South America, Southeast Asia, and Africa. STC's main subsidiaries include 75%-owned Hallim Investment Finance, 51%-owned STC Plastics, and 45%-owned STC Brands.

Won bil	12/92 P	12/93 P	12/94 P	US$mil 12/94				
Sales	**161.9**	**169.1**	**190.4**	**237.7**	P/E Ratio	**107.1**	Price (9/30/95)	**18,200**
Net Income	**8.4**	**20.8**	**1.7**	**2.1**	P/B Ratio	**1.1**	52 Wk Hi-Low	**33,900.0-15,300.0**
Book Value	**82.3**	**122.4**	**121.6**	**155.5**	Yield %	**2.2**	Market Cap	**US$179.6mil**

Address	**32 Mullae-dong 3-ga**	Tel	**02-675-0621**	ADR		President	**Jwa-Jin Choe**
	Seoul	Fax	**02-675-1595**	SEDOL No.	**6764849**	Chairman	**Jwa-Jin Choe**

P=Parent company data.

Sam Yang

Industry: **Commodity Chemicals**

Sam Yang Company began as a refiner of sugar and has diversified to become South Korea's highest-volume manufacturer of polyester yarns and fabrics. Sales of polyester account for 45% of the company's revenue, while sugar sales account for only 19%. It also produces animal feed, engineering plastics, and livestock products. In addition to domestic manufacturing plants, the company has an interest in a Vietnamese plant that exports yarns and fabrics to markets in Southeast Asia. Sam Yang also has investments in merchant banking and pharmaceuticals.

Won bil	06/92 P	06/93 P	06/94 P	US$mil 06/94				
Sales	**698.7**	**725.0**	**769.7**	**949.0**	P/E Ratio	**32.3**	Price (9/30/95)	**28,200**
Net Income	**21.0**	**15.8**	**7.3**	**9.0**	P/B Ratio	**1.0**	52 Wk Hi-Low	**39,800.0-25,500.0**
Book Value	**N/A**	**213.4**	**225.1**	**279.3**	Yield %	**2.1**	Market Cap	**US$290.8mil**

Address	**263 Yonji-dong, Chongno-gu**	Tel	**02-740-7114**	ADR		President	**Sang-Ung Kim**
	Seoul	Fax	**02-743-7720**	SEDOL No.	**6771816**	Chairman	**Sang-Ung Kim**

P=Parent company data.

Sammi Steel

Industry: **Steel**

Sammi Steel manufactures stainless-steel sheets and steel bars and tubes. Its annual production capacity is 1.5 million tons of steel products. The company manufactures 1,800 steel products, and supplies specialty items to the automobile, shipbuilding, and machinery industries. It is diversifying its product range to include materials for semiconductors, electronic parts, and cable- and wireless-telecommunication products. Sammi Steel is a member of the Sammi group of companies. Sammi Corporation owns 9% of the company's share capital.

Won bil	12/92 P	12/93 P	12/94 P	US$mil 12/94				
Sales	**479.2**	**654.1**	**758.3**	**946.5**	P/E Ratio	**NMF**	Price (9/30/95)	**8,300.00**
Net Income	**-79.0**	**-89.6**	**-68.5**	**-85.5**	P/B Ratio	**2.3**	52 Wk Hi-Low	**12,400.0-7,390.0**
Book Value	**232.5**	**149.4**	**137.4**	**175.7**	Yield %	**0.0**	Market Cap	**US$313.4mil**

Address **1004 Taechi-dong, Kangnam-gu Seoul** Tel **02-222-4114** Fax **02-563-1291** ADR SEDOL No. **6771333** President **Hyon-Chol Kim** Chairman **Hyon-Chol Kim**

P=Parent company data.

Samsung

Industry: **Overseas Trading**

Samsung is South Korea's largest general trading company by revenue. Its products include electronics, chemicals, heavy industrial equipment, semiconductors, and textiles. It also engages in natural-resource development and offshore trading for other Samsung affiliates. The company has operations worldwide, including a television tube plant and semiconductor facility in India, and a consumer-electronics factory in the United Kingdom. The Samsung group consists of 28 affiliated businesses with activities that range from electronics to financial services.

Won bil	12/92 P	12/93 P	12/94 P	US$mil 12/94				
Sales	**12,055.7**	**13,320.5**	**15,576.5**	**19,442.1**	P/E Ratio	**32.1**	Price (9/30/95)	**26,500**
Net Income	**15.9**	**12.2**	**13.7**	**17.1**	P/B Ratio	**2.0**	52 Wk Hi-Low	**33,400.0-20,300.0**
Book Value	**273.1**	**273.1**	**329.1**	**420.8**	Yield %	**1.9**	Market Cap	**US$739.7mil**

Address **250 Taepyongno 2-ga, Chung-gu Seoul** Tel **02-751-2114** Fax **02-752-7926** ADR SEDOL No. **6771601** President **Se-Gil Shin** Chairman **Se-Gil Shin**

P=Parent company data.

Samsung Aerospace

Industry: **Aerospace & Defense**

Samsung Aerospace designs and manufactures defense-related equipment, lead frames, and cameras. The company is the designated systems integrator for the South Korean government's production of F-16 fighter aircraft in conjunction with the United States' Lockheed Martin. It also provides aircraft-engine maintenance to the U.S. military. The company is developing industrial-use cameras and high-speed printing machinery. Samsung Aerospace is a member of the Samsung group of companies. Samsung Electronics is the company's largest shareholder with a 9% interest.

Won bil	12/92	12/93	12/94	US$mil 12/94				
Sales	**484.9**	**680.9**	**810.5**	**1,011.6**	P/E Ratio	**65.4**	Price (9/30/95)	**23,900**
Net Income	**4.4**	**5.2**	**7.1**	**8.9**	P/B Ratio	**1.7**	52 Wk Hi-Low	**27,823.9-17,300.0**
Book Value	**210.7**	**253.5**	**303.7**	**388.3**	Yield %	**1.0**	Market Cap	**US$653.5mil**

Address **28 Songju-dong, Changwon-shi Kyongnam** Tel **0551-60-2251** Fax **0551-60-5220** ADR SEDOL No. **6772671** President **Dae-Won Lee** Chairman --

Samsung Electro-Mechanics

Industry: **Electrical Components & Equipment**

Samsung Electro-Mechanics designs and manufactures precision equipment and parts for electronic products. More than 50% of the company's revenue is derived from the production of parts for video recorders and television equipment. The company operates five overseas manufacturing facilities and nine sales offices worldwide. Samsung Electro-Mechanics has a 49% interest in the newly formed automobile manufacturer Samsung Motors, and plans to begin production of electronic automobile components for that company. Samsung Electronics has a 16% stake in the company.

Won bil	12/92 P	12/93 P	12/94 P	US$mil 12/94				
Sales	**604.1**	**731.6**	**948.7**	**1,184.1**	P/E Ratio	**42.5**	Price (9/30/95)	**38,000**
Net Income	**7.4**	**8.1**	**17.8**	**22.3**	P/B Ratio	**2.1**	52 Wk Hi-Low	**46,677.6-28,600.0**
Book Value	**241.4**	**277.9**	**350.6**	**448.3**	Yield %	**1.6**	Market Cap	**US$620.4mil**

Address **314 Maetan 3-dong, Paldal-gu Suwon-shi, Kyonggi** Tel **0331-210-5114** Fax **0331-210-5087** ADR SEDOL No. **6771689** Chairman **Hyong-Do Lee** Chairman **Hyong-Do Lee**

P=Parent company data.

Samsung Electronics

Industry: **Semiconductors & related**

Samsung Electronics manufactures consumer and industrial electronic equipment such as computers, memory chips, semiconductors, television sets, and telecommunication equipment. It is the world's largest supplier of memory chips in terms of market share. In September 1995, Samsung Electronics established a joint venture with Crosna, a Russian telecommunication equipment maker, to produce switching systems. Its other investments include a 22% stake in industrial equipment maker Samsung Heavy Industries and a 40% interest in computer manufacturer AST.

Won bil	12/92 P	12/93 P	12/94 P	US$mil 12/94				
Sales	**6,102.8**	**8,154.8**	**11,518.1**	**14,376.5**	P/E Ratio	**10.9**	Price (9/30/95)	**165,000**
Net Income	**72.4**	**154.6**	**945.1**	**1,179.6**	P/B Ratio	**3.8**	52 Wk Hi-Low	**169,500-77,897**
Book Value	**1,172.2**	**1,626.4**	**2,864.4**	**3,662.5**	Yield %	**0.1**	Market Cap	**US$13,888mil**

Address **250 Taepyengnp 2-ga, Chung-gu Seoul** Tel **02-727-7114** Fax **02-753-0967** ADR SEDOL No. **6771720** President **Gwang-Ho Kim** Chairman **Gwang-Ho Kim**

P=Parent company data.

Samsung Engineering & Construction

Industry: **Heavy Construction**

Samsung Engineering & Construction is a general contractor with both domestic and overseas building projects. Its work has included 12 infrastructure projects for the South Korean government and the construction of temporary housing units for the Kobe earthquake victims. The company is also active in the construction of petrochemical-manufacturing facilities. Samsung Engineering & Construction is expected to be merged with Samsung as a result of a restructuring program. Samsung and Samsung Life Insurance together own 12% of the company.

Won bil	12/92 P	12/93 P	12/94 P	US$mil 12/94				
Sales	**1,353.4**	**1,378.6**	**1,838.5**	**2,294.8**	P/E Ratio	**20.1**	Price (9/30/95)	**25,500**
Net Income	**28.3**	**14.5**	**32.9**	**41.0**	P/B Ratio	**1.7**	52 Wk Hi-Low	**30,353.6-19,100.0**
Book Value	**258.0**	**283.3**	**532.4**	**680.7**	Yield %	**0.4**	Market Cap	**US$1,143.9mil**

Address	**677-25 Yoksam-dong**	Tel **02-527-0114**	ADR		President	**Hun Choe**
	Seoul	Fax **02-527-0117**	SEDOL No.	**6771612**	Chairman	**Hun Choe**

P=Parent company data.

Samsung Fine Chemicals

Industry: **Specialty Chemicals**

Samsung Fine Chemicals is a manufacturer of fertilizers that has diversified its products to include general fine-chemicals. The company recently completed the construction of a fine chemicals plant in the Ulsan Industrial Complex. The company derives approximately 20% of its revenue from the sale of urea fertilizer. Samsung Fine Chemicals is a member of the Samsung group of companies, and Samsung Display Devices and Samsung Life Insurance together own a 23% stake in the company. Cheil Industries, a South Korean textile company, owns a 10% interest in the company.

Won bil	12/92 P	12/93 P	12/94 P	US$mil 12/94				
Sales	**191.1**	**211.7**	**235.1**	**293.4**	P/E Ratio	**NMF**	Price (9/30/95)	**62,100**
Net Income	**4.5**	**5.0**	**0.5**	**0.6**	P/B Ratio	**2.3**	52 Wk Hi-Low	**136,724-50,000**
Book Value	**76.3**	**80.1**	**79.4**	**101.5**	Yield %	**0.3**	Market Cap	**US$243.1mil**

Address	**190 Yochon-dong, Nam-gu**	Tel **052-270-6114**	ADR		President	**Sung-Ung Lee**
	Ulsan-shi, Kyongnam	Fax **052-272-7925**	SEDOL No.	**6496432**	Chairman	**Sung-Ung Lee**

P=Parent company data.

Samsung Fire & Marine Insurance

Industry: **Insurance - Property & Casualty**

Samsung Fire & Marine Insurance is South Korea's largest fire- and marine-insurance company with an 18% share in the domestic earned premium market. The company also offers automobile, casualty, property, and long-term insurance services, and is active in pension-related insurance programs, asset management, and property owning. Almost 46% of the company's revenue is generated from automobile-insurance policies. Long-term insurance accounts for 37% of revenues. Samsung Life Insurance owns 9% of the company's share capital.

Won bil	03/92 P	03/93 P	03/94 P	US$mil 03/94				
Revenues	**657.1**	**904.2**	**1,112.5**	**1,373.0**	P/E Ratio	**NMF**	Price (9/30/95)	**337,000**
Net Income	**3.9**	**5.5**	**5.1**	**6.3**	P/B Ratio	**15.5**	52 Wk Hi-Low	**337,000-180,000**
Book Value	**N/A**	**44.5**	**48.3**	**59.2**	Yield %	**0.1**	Market Cap	**US$977.0mil**

Address	**87 Ulchiro 1-ga, Chung-gu**	Tel **02-758-7114**	ADR		President	**Jong-Gi Lee**
	Seoul	Fax **02-752-4875**	SEDOL No.	**6042363**	Chairman	**Jong-Gi Lee**

P=Parent company data.

Samsung Heavy Industries

Industry: **Shipbuilding**

Samsung Heavy Industries manufactures heavy machinery and transportation equipment. It builds ships and offshore production facilities at its shipyard on Koje island, construction and industrial equipment at its facilities in Changwon, and commercial transportation vehicles at its plant in Taegu. The company's construction division is responsible for the construction of Samsung's new passenger-car plant in Pusan and the building of a gas-exploration platform in Vietnam for France's Bouygeus Offshore. Samsung Electronics owns a 22% stake in the company.

Won bil	12/92 P	12/93 P	12/94 P	US$mil 12/94				
Sales	**1,607.3**	**1,617.6**	**2,038.3**	**2,544.1**	P/E Ratio	**19.8**	Price (9/30/95)	**24,300**
Net Income	**94.5**	**73.0**	**71.9**	**89.8**	P/B Ratio	**1.9**	52 Wk Hi-Low	**44,092.1-19,600.0**
Book Value	**322.9**	**550.1**	**820.4**	**1,049.0**	Yield %	**1.8**	Market Cap	**US$2,083.1mil**

Address	**25 Pongrae-dong 1-ga, Chung-gu**	Tel **02-728-6200**	ADR		President	**Ju-Hyon Kyong**
	Seoul	Fax **02-728-6161**	SEDOL No.	**6772217**	Chairman	**Ju-Hyon Kyong**

P=Parent company data.

Seoul Bank

Industry: **Banks - Regional**

Seoul Bank (formerly Bank of Seoul) offers both retail- and corporate-banking services. Total assets at the end of 1994 amounted to 30,900 billion won. At the same time, the bank held deposits totalling 18,900 billion won and had loans outstanding of approximately 12,600 billion won. The bank operates 319 domestic branches and 11 overseas offices. It offers credit-card services to more than 1.2 million cardholders. Seoul Bank also offers international-banking, trust-fund, securities-investment, and custodian services to individual and corporate clients.

Won bil	12/92	12/93	12/94	US$mil 12/94				
Revenues	**1,942.4**	**2,132.2**	**2,756.1**	**3,440.1**	P/E Ratio	**23.3**	Price (9/30/95)	**8,110.00**
Net Income	**69.9**	**9.2**	**51.5**	**64.3**	P/B Ratio	**1.0**	52 Wk Hi-Low	**8,940.0-6,670.0**
Book Value	**1,185.5**	**1,141.3**	**1,391.1**	**1,778.7**	Yield %	**0.0**	Market Cap	**US$1,731.7mil**

Address	**10-11 Namdaemun-no 2-ka**	Tel **02-771-6000**	ADR		President & CEO	**Hong Kyun Sohn**
	Seoul	Fax **02-775-4983**	SEDOL No.	**6076470**	Chairman	**Sung Hwan Suh**

Seoul Securities

Industry: **Securities Brokers**

Seoul Securities offers brokerage services to individual and corporate clients. The company manages 12 trillion won in stock accounts and 4.7 trillion won in bond accounts. Almost 46% of the company's revenue is generated from commission and fee income. It also has a futures trading department and a investment-management team, and offers securities-trading services to international clients. The company is a member of the Daelim group of companies, and construction and petrochemical company Daelim Industries owns 22% of the company's share capital.

Won bil	03/92 P	03/93 P	03/94 P	US$mil 03/94				
Sales	**58.5**	**72.3**	**108.5**	**133.9**	P/E Ratio	**17.4**	Price (9/30/95)	**12,600**
Net Income	**3.5**	**11.2**	**13.2**	**16.3**	P/B Ratio	**0.7**	52 Wk Hi-Low	**16,300.0-8,300.0**
Book Value	**N/A**	**320.2**	**329.6**	**403.8**	Yield %	**0.8**	Market Cap	**US$303.1mil**

Address	**23-9 Youido-dong**	Tel	**02-368-6000**	ADR		President	**In-Jik Chong**
	Seoul	Fax	**02-368-6702**	SEDOL No.	**6819556**	Chairman	**In-Jik Chong**

P=Parent company data.

Shin Poong Paper Manufacturing

Industry: **Paper Products**

Shin Poong Paper Manufacturing produces bleached paperboard for use in the manufacture of packaging products for groceries, food products, and medical goods. It is South Korea's leading supplier of white duplex board with a domestic market share of about 20%. The company exports approximately 67% of its paperboard products. Shin Poong is currently constructing its sixth manufacturing facility, which is scheduled to commence operations by the end of 1995. The company's chairman, Il-Hong Chong, owns a 17% stake in Shin Poong.

Won bil	12/92 P	12/93 P	12/94 P	US$mil 12/94				
Sales	**71.0**	**67.6**	**73.5**	**91.7**	P/E Ratio	**2.9**	Price (9/30/95)	**39,000**
Net Income	**12.2**	**10.0**	**27.1**	**33.8**	P/B Ratio	**0.9**	52 Wk Hi-Low	**63,400.0-34,000.0**
Book Value	**60.3**	**69.1**	**90.0**	**115.1**	Yield %	**2.6**	Market Cap	**US$102.6mil**

Address	**15 Haechang-ri, Koduk-myon**	Tel	**0333-669-8100**	ADR		President	**Il-Hong Chong**
	Pyungteak-gun, Kyonggi	Fax	**0333-62-7760**	SEDOL No.	**6804671**	Chairman	**Il-Hong Chong**

P=Parent company data.

Shin Won

Industry: **Clothing & Fabrics**

Shin Won is South Korea's largest exporter of sweaters. The company also produces other apparel, accessories, and bags. It exports approximately 50% of its products. The company also distributes DKNY brand fashions in South Korea. Shin Won has an agreement with North Korea to set up a joint- venture sweater plant in that country. Its apparel-manufacturing subsidiaries include wholly-owned Shinwon-Hongkong, wholly-owned Qingdao Shinwon Garment, and 49%-owned Shinwon Oxford. The company's president Song-Chol Park is Shin Won's largest shareholder with an 18% stake.

Won bil	12/92	12/93	12/94	US$mil 12/94				
Sales	**167.8**	**222.7**	**359.8**	**449.1**	P/E Ratio	**9.2**	Price (9/30/95)	**30,600**
Net Income	**5.3**	**8.0**	**13.2**	**16.4**	P/B Ratio	**1.2**	52 Wk Hi-Low	**43,600.0-28,300.0**
Book Value	**50.3**	**66.6**	**96.7**	**123.6**	Yield %	**2.3**	Market Cap	**US$146.9mil**

Address	**532 Tohwa-dong, Mapo-gu**	Tel	**02-716-7611**	ADR		President	**Song-Chol Park**
	Seoul	Fax	**02-716-8374**	SEDOL No.	**6805823**	Chairman	--

Shinhan Bank

Industry: **Banks - Regional**

Shinhan Bank operates a commercial-banking network of 165 domestic branches, 152 ATMs, eight overseas offices, and one overseas subsidiary. The bank provides retail- and international-banking services to more than 2.2 million customers. Its loan activity is focused on loans to small- and midsize companies which account for 59% of the loans outstanding. The bank's assets totalled almost 25.1 trillion won at the end of 1994. Shinhan Bank also provides foreign-exchange services, custodian services for foreign investors, and pension-trust management.

Won bil	12/92	12/93	12/94	US$mil 12/94				
Revenues	**1,992.8**	**1,610.4**	**2,235.4**	**2,790.1**	P/E Ratio	**13.3**	Price (9/30/95)	**17,100**
Net Income	**168.8**	**136.4**	**157.3**	**196.3**	P/B Ratio	**1.4**	52 Wk Hi-Low	**23,782.0-14,000.0**
Book Value	**1,691.1**	**1,366.6**	**1,448.8**	**1,852.5**	Yield %	**2.5**	Market Cap	**US$2,719.5mil**

Address	**120, 2-ka, Taepyung-ro, Chung-ku**	Tel	**02-756-0505**	ADR		President	**Eung-Chan Ra**
	Seoul	Fax	**02-774-7013**	SEDOL No.	**6805986**	Chairman	**Heui-Keon Lee**

Shinsegae Department Store

Industry: **Retailers - Broadline**

Shinsegae Department Store sells clothing, household goods, food, and other consumer items through its seven branch department stores in Seoul. The company's total sales are composed of 36% apparel, 21% foodstuffs, and 18% household goods. It also operates provincial department stores and discount stores, and has an apparel factory that makes its own-label products. Through a joint venture with Price/Costco of the United States, Shinsegae manages wholesale membership discount stores. The company owns a 15% interest in Samsung Life Insurance.

Won bil	12/92 P	12/93 P	12/94 P	US$mil 12/94				
Revenues	**564.2**	**701.9**	**864.1**	**1,078.5**	P/E Ratio	**46.0**	Price (9/30/95)	**66,500**
Net Income	**7.8**	**12.8**	**14.0**	**17.5**	P/B Ratio	**4.3**	52 Wk Hi-Low	**85,774.1-50,000.0**
Book Value	**108.2**	**140.4**	**149.3**	**190.9**	Yield %	**0.7**	Market Cap	**US$836.4mil**

Address	**52-5 Chungmuro 1-ga, Chung-gu**	Tel	**02-727-1631**	ADR		President	**Han-Sop Yu**
	Seoul	Fax	**02-774-1309**	SEDOL No.	**6805049**	Chairman	**Han-Sop Yu**

P=Parent company data.

Ssangyong Cement

Industry: **Building Materials**

Ssangyong Cement is South Korea's largest cement manufacturer in terms of production capacity. Its manufacturing facilities have an annual production capacity of 15 million tonnes of cement. Almost 60% of the company's revenue is generated by sales of cement. Sales of ready-mixed concrete make up approximately 22% of its revenue. It is also engaged in the production of fine ceramics and telecommunication equipment. The company has operations in Japan and Singapore, and owns minority stakes in Ssangyong Construction and Ssangyong Oil Refining.

Won bil	12/92 P	12/93 P	12/94 P	US$mil 12/94				
Sales	911.6	952.6	1,078.0	1,345.5	P/E Ratio	29.1	Price (9/30/95)	24,800
Net Income	35.9	27.1	29.8	37.1	P/B Ratio	1.2	52 Wk Hi-Low	33,300.0-18,900.0
Book Value	584.8	657.0	657.7	841.0	Yield %	2.6	Market Cap	US$1,062.1mil

Address **24-1 Cho-dong 2-ga, Chung-gu Seoul** Tel **02-270-5114** Fax **02-275-7040** ADR SEDOL No. **6837280** President **Dok-Chang U** Chairman **Dok-Chang U**

P=Parent company data.

Ssangyong Investment & Securities

Industry: **Securities Brokers**

Ssangyong Investment & Securities provides brokerage services, investment management, securities underwriting, and financial consulting. It also has departments involved in futures trading, mergers and acquisitions consulting, corporate financial planning, and international investing. The company derives more than 45% of its revenue from commission and fee income and approximately 40% from gains on trading. Ssangyong Investment & Securities operates through a network of 43 domestic branches. Ssangyong Cement owns 25% of the company's share capital.

Won bil	03/92 P	03/93 P	03/94 P	US$mil 03/94				
Sales	164.5	190.0	247.1	305.0	P/E Ratio	11.2	Price (9/30/95)	17,000
Net Income	-19.6	26.2	41.3	51.0	P/B Ratio	1.0	52 Wk Hi-Low	24,400.0-10,800.0
Book Value	N/A	485.0	519.4	636.3	Yield %	0.9	Market Cap	US$587.4mil

Address **198 Ulchiro 2-ga, Chung-gu Seoul** Tel **02-771-1200** Fax **02-755-5521** ADR SEDOL No. **6837332** President **Ho-Gun Myong** Chairman **Ho-Gun Myong**

P=Parent company data.

Ssangyong Oil Refining

Industry: **Oil - Secondary**

Ssangyong Oil Refining produces refined petroleum products and lubricants. It derives more than 90% of its revenue from the sale of refined oil. The company is also investing in desulfurization and other plants to produce light distillates. Ssangyong Oil Refining owns a 15% interest in Ssangyong Motor, a manufacturer of commercial vehicles, and a 9% interest in Daehan Oil Pipeline. The company is 35%-owned by the Saudi Arabian petroleum company Aramco, and 28%-owned by South Korea's Ssangyong Cement.

Won bil	12/92 P	12/93 P	12/94 P	US$mil 12/94				
Sales	2,042.9	2,078.4	2,415.4	3,014.8	P/E Ratio	11.0	Price (9/30/95)	21,900
Net Income	77.2	79.4	112.7	140.7	P/B Ratio	1.2	52 Wk Hi-Low	29,000.0-19,300.0
Book Value	836.5	906.4	1,005.7	1,285.9	Yield %	4.1	Market Cap	US$1,605.1mil

Address **24-1 Cho-dong 2-ga, Chung-gu Seoul** Tel **02-270-6114** Fax **02-273-2170** ADR SEDOL No. **6837321** President **Son-Dong Kim** Chairman **Son-Dong Kim**

P=Parent company data.

Sung Chang

Industry: **Forest Products**

Sung Chang is an integrated wood-products manufacturer. Its main products include plywood and hardboard. The company also produces furniture-manufacturing equipment and Sunwood brand furniture products. The company derives more than 64% of its revenue from the sale of plywood. More than 24% of its revenue comes from furniture sales and the remainder comes from hardboard sales. Sung Chang is currently constructing additional manufacturing facilities for hardwood and furniture products. Private investor Hae-Su Chong controls 32% of the company's capital.

Won bil	09/92 P	09/93 P	09/94 P	US$mil 09/94				
Sales	140.8	173.8	192.4	238.5	P/E Ratio	NMF	Price (9/30/95)	50,500
Net Income	-2.7	1.7	0.5	0.6	P/B Ratio	2.1	52 Wk Hi-Low	91,000.0-41,400.0
Book Value	72.3	72.5	71.4	88.9	Yield %	1.0	Market Cap	US$197.3mil

Address **380 Tadae-dong, Saha-gu Pusan** Tel **051-260-3333** Fax **051-263-2120** ADR SEDOL No. **6860673** President **Hae-Rin Chong** Chairman **Hae-Rin Chong**

P=Parent company data.

Sunkyong

Industry: **Overseas Trading**

Sunkyong Industries manufactures synthetic textiles including polyester and acetate. It is South Korea's sole supplier of acetate filament yarn. Its other products include polyester yarns and polyester staple fibers. Its chemicals division produces high-tech polymers and processes crude oil. The company is currently developing fine chemicals and new materials such as pigments used in paint production, adhesives, and engineering plastics. The company has a polyester plant and is building a plant to produce plastic chips for packaging bottles in Indonesia.

Won bil	12/92 P	12/93 P	12/94 P	US$mil 12/94				
Sales	2,639.3	3,029.4	3,469.6	4,330.7	P/E Ratio	41.9	Price (9/30/95)	23,300
Net Income	7.5	10.0	9.0	11.3	P/B Ratio	1.4	52 Wk Hi-Low	23,300.0-12,016.6
Book Value	243.2	245.0	252.4	322.7	Yield %	0.5	Market Cap	US$612.8mil

Address **36-1 Ulchiro 2-ga, Chung-gu Seoul** Tel **02-758-2114** Fax **02-754-9414** ADR SEDOL No. **6860015** President **Sung-Jong Kim** Chairman **Sung-Jong Kim**

P=Parent company data.

Sunkyong Industries

Industry: **Clothing & Fabrics**

Sunkyong is the trading arm of the Sunkyong group of companies. Its distribution network exports more than 2,000 of the Sunkyong group's products to 130 countries. More than 69% of the company's revenue in 1994 was generated by export sales. The company's sales in 1994 were made up principally of heavy industrial equipment and chemical products (62%), commodities (22%), and fabrics (10%). The company also has interests in the mobile-telecommunication industry and infrastructure-development projects. It also owns a 17% interest in oil refiner Yukong.

Won bil	12/92 P	12/93 P	12/94 P	US$mil 12/94				
Sales	**513.8**	**561.7**	**666.1**	**831.4**	P/E Ratio	**25.6**	Price (9/30/95)	**25,900**
Net Income	**10.5**	**7.8**	**10.4**	**13.0**	P/B Ratio	**0.6**	52 Wk Hi-Low	**34,400.0-22,200.0**
Book Value	**355.9**	**356.5**	**359.6**	**459.8**	Yield %	**1.9**	Market Cap	**US$296.8mil**

Address	**600 Chongia-dong, Changan-gu**	Tel	**033-145-3131**	ADR		President	**Jun-Ung Kim**
	Suwon-shi, Kyonggi	Fax	**033-145-3158**	SEDOL No.	**6859916**	Chairman	**Jun-Ung Kim**

P=Parent company data.

Taihan Electric Wire

Industry: **Communications Technology**

Taihan Electric Wire manufactures principally electric cables and wires. Its other products include special and optical-fiber cables, watt meters, time switches, gas meters, and portable telephones. The company operates overseas manufacturing facilities in India, China, and Saudi Arabia, and is currently building a fiber-optic-cable plant near Beijing. Taihan Electric Wire has a 55% stake in Daijing Capital Telecommunication Cable and a 33% stake in Sam Yang Metal, a stainless-steel manufacturer.

Won bil	12/92 P	12/93 P	12/94 P	US$mil 12/94				
Sales	**454.2**	**443.6**	**706.6**	**882.0**	P/E Ratio	**21.8**	Price (9/30/95)	**24,500**
Net Income	**13.8**	**18.2**	**18.9**	**23.6**	P/B Ratio	**1.8**	52 Wk Hi-Low	**33,500.0-18,500.0**
Book Value	**188.6**	**223.5**	**233.1**	**298.1**	Yield %	**2.4**	Market Cap	**US$535.9mil**

Address	**194-15 Hoehyon-dong 1-ga**	Tel	**02-316-9114**	ADR		President	**Chae-Jun Yu**
	Seoul	Fax	**02-754-5240**	SEDOL No.	**6869799**	Chairman	**Chae-Jun Yu**

P=Parent company data.

Tong Yang Confectionery

Industry: **Other Food**

Tong Yang Confectionery manufactures a variety of confectionery products including candies, chocolates, cookies, snack foods, and chewing gum. The company has also diversified into the manufacturing of soft drinks and bottled water, and into the production of cartoons for cable television. Its principal subsidiaries include 99%-owned Orion Beverage and 95%-owned Tong Yang Mart. The company also owns 50% of Orion Frito-Lay, a joint venture to produce and distribute snack foods. Tong Yang Confectionery is part of the Tong Yang Cement group of companies.

Won bil	12/92	12/93	12/94	US$mil 12/94				
Sales	**272.5**	**297.7**	**316.2**	**394.7**	P/E Ratio	**28.6**	Price (9/30/95)	**22,700**
Net Income	**3.7**	**4.2**	**2.7**	**3.4**	P/B Ratio	**1.4**	52 Wk Hi-Low	**39,300.0-21,700.0**
Book Value	**36.9**	**50.1**	**69.5**	**88.9**	Yield %	**2.2**	Market Cap	**US$125.9mil**

Address	**30-10 Munbae-dong, Yongsan-gu**	Tel	**02-710-6000**	ADR		President	**Chol-Gon Tam**
	Seoul	Fax	**02-719-2582**	SEDOL No.	**6896849**	Chairman	--

Tongyang Cement

Industry: **Building Materials**

Tongyang Cement is South Korea's second-largest manufacturer of cement in terms of capacity. Its annual production capacity is 11 million tonnes of cement. The company also produces ready-mixed concrete and is involved in construction projects. Its other investments are in the food-processing, distribution, data-communication, and financial-services industries. Sales of cement account for approximately 70% of the company's revenue, while ready-mixed concrete sales account for 20%. A group of investors led by Hye Gyong Lee controls 32% of Tong Yang Cement.

Won bil	12/92 P	12/93 P	12/94 P	US$mil 12/94				
Sales	**510.1**	**560.6**	**580.4**	**724.4**	P/E Ratio	**15.1**	Price (9/30/95)	**26,700**
Net Income	**25.3**	**18.6**	**18.1**	**22.5**	P/B Ratio	**0.6**	52 Wk Hi-Low	**34,500.0-21,100.0**
Book Value	**363.0**	**376.6**	**391.9**	**501.1**	Yield %	**2.4**	Market Cap	**US$283.4mil**

Address	**Youido-dong, Yongdungpo-gu**	Tel	**02-370-3000**	ADR		President	**Jae-Bok Lee**
	Seoul	Fax	**02-739-2579**	SEDOL No.	**6896452**	Chairman	**Jae-Bok Lee**

P=Parent company data.

Tongyang Nylon

Industry: **Commodity Chemicals**

Tongyang Nylon manufactures nylon filament and tire cord. The company also produces engineering plastics, personal computers, and plastic packaging bottles. More than 55% of the company's products are exported. Its current business-development projects include producing tile carpet, constructing a port in Onsan, South Korea, and building a plastic packaging plant in China. Tong Yang Nylon holds minority interests in Tong Yan Polyester, Hyosun Heavy Industries, and Hankook Caprolactum.

Won bil	12/92 P	12/93 P	12/94 P	US$mil 12/94				
Sales	**752.9**	**682.2**	**805.1**	**1,004.9**	P/E Ratio	**22.6**	Price (9/30/95)	**28,800**
Net Income	**4.0**	**3.2**	**10.2**	**12.8**	P/B Ratio	**0.7**	52 Wk Hi-Low	**35,700.0-23,300.0**
Book Value	**304.4**	**303.4**	**311.4**	**398.2**	Yield %	**1.9**	Market Cap	**US$301.0mil**

Address	**450 Kongdok-dong, Mapo-gu**	Tel	**02-707-7000**	ADR		President	**Yong-Bae Paek**
	Seoul	Fax	**02-707-3155**	SEDOL No.	**6896838**	Chairman	**Yong-Bae Paek**

P=Parent company data.

Yuhan

Industry: **Pharmaceuticals**

Yuhan manufactures prescription drugs, cosmetics, and personal-hygiene products. Sales of prescription and over-the-counter medicines account for 30% of the company's revenue. Its main pharmaceuticals products include Almagel, Acopex, and Beecom-C. The company has patented its high-blood-pressure treatment in Japan, and is developing a new formula to increase its market share in that country. Yuhan distributes Clorox insecticides in South Korea and has a joint venture with the U.S. company to produce liquid bleach and home-cleaning products.

Won bil	12/92 P	12/93 P	12/94 P	US$mil 12/94				
Sales	**127.7**	**136.9**	**148.0**	**184.7**	P/E Ratio	**37.2**	Price (9/30/95)	**48,000**
Net Income	**3.7**	**3.0**	**3.7**	**4.7**	P/B Ratio	**2.4**	52 Wk Hi-Low	**76,190.5-40,381.0**
Book Value	**44.9**	**57.1**	**61.9**	**79.1**	Yield %	**1.0**	Market Cap	**US$188.7mil**

Address	**49-6 Taebang-dong, Tongjak-gu Seoul**	Tel **02-815-0181**	ADR		President	**Tae-Hun Kim**
		Fax **02-813-5607**	SEDOL No.	**6988337**	Chairman	**Tae-Hun Kim**

P=Parent company data.

Yukong

Industry: **Oil - Secondary**

Yukong refines oil and produces petroleum products, petrochemicals, and lubricants. It is South Korea's leading oil refiner with a 39% market share in petroleum and a 23% market share in lubricants. The company also operates a network of gas service stations throughout South Korea, and is involved in oil and natural-gas exploration projects in Ecuador. Yukong is constructing desulfurization plants to refine low-priced heavy crude into lighter distillates. Sunkyong and Sunkyong Industry have a combined 20% interest in the company.

Won bil	12/92 P	12/93 P	12/94 P	US$mil 12/94				
Sales	**4,720.9**	**5,327.0**	**5,865.7**	**7,321.4**	P/E Ratio	**33.6**	Price (9/30/95)	**31,000**
Net Income	**29.3**	**35.4**	**53.0**	**66.1**	P/B Ratio	**1.1**	52 Wk Hi-Low	**44,931.0-26,800.0**
Book Value	**1,424.0**	**1,509.8**	**1,720.4**	**2,199.8**	Yield %	**1.6**	Market Cap	**US$2,422.0mil**

Address	**Youido-dong, Yongdungpo-gu Seoul**	Tel **02-788-5114**	ADR		President	**Hang-Dok Kim**
		Fax **02-784-6075**	SEDOL No.	**6988371**	Chairman	**Hang-Dok Kim**

P=Parent company data.

Spain

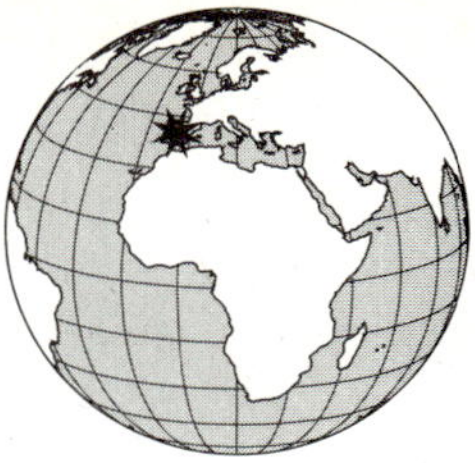

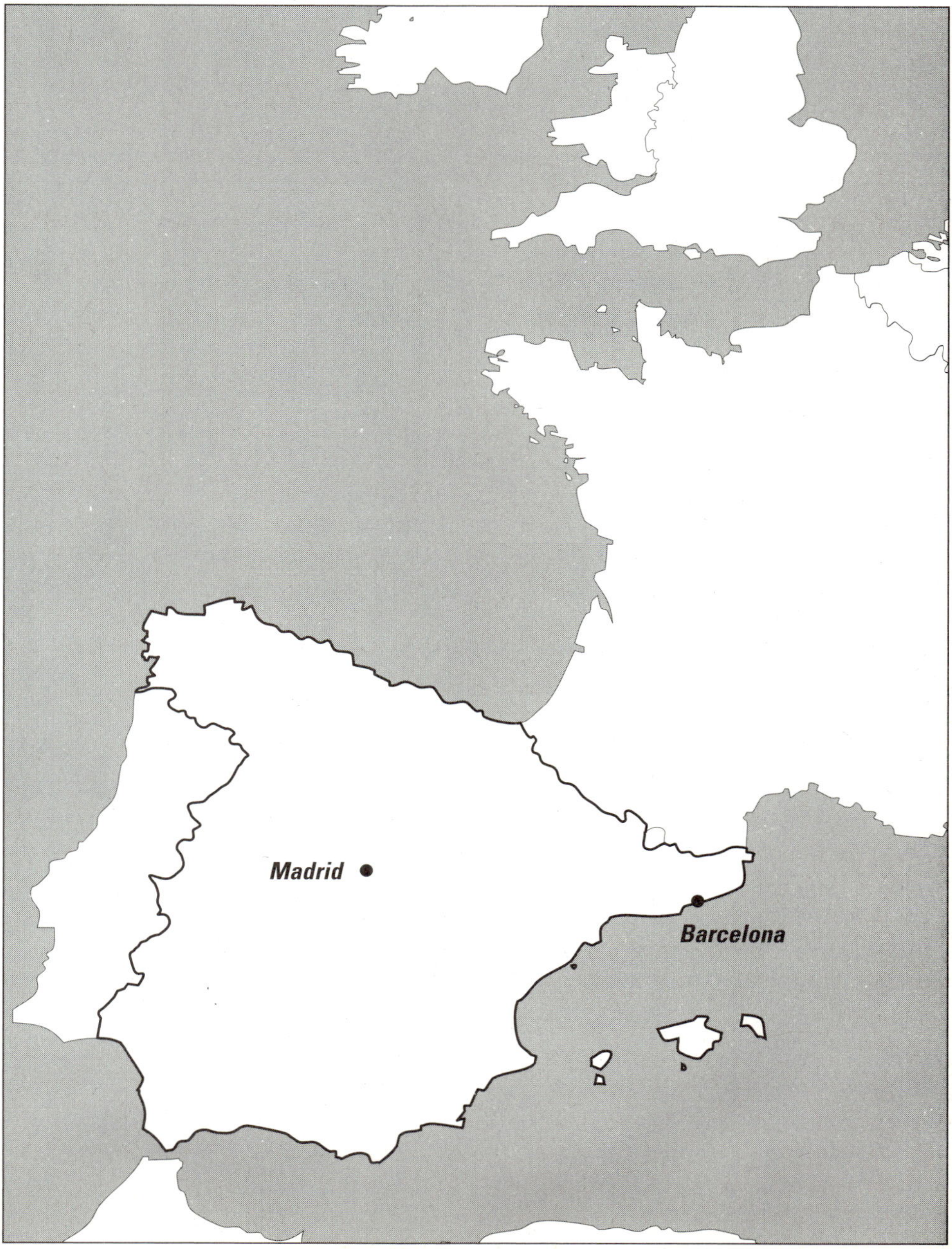

Spain

Mary Milliken,
Madrid

Local Trading Hours	Time Difference with New York	Population (Est. 94)
11:00-5:00	6 hours ahead	39,303,000

The turn-of-the-century palace housing the Bolsa de Madrid looks like an elegant gentlemen's club with its polished wood floors and intricate glass and iron ceiling. A handful of brokers casually mill around on the parquet, while the old school of investors contemplate the scene from the second floor railing.

The atmosphere is so calm because only a fraction of Spain's equity trading takes place here after an advanced computer trading system was introduced in the late 1980s, gradually replacing the old open-outcry system. Now the action is in the fast-paced dealing rooms, where young and eager traders hardly have time for lunch and much less for a siesta.

While not considered an emerging market nor a fully matured market, Spain has made great leaps in becoming a respectable European trading center in the past 10 years. It offers higher yields than the more developed markets, but it also provides a growing sense of security and transparency. Spain ranks eighth in terms of equity volume and market capitalization in Europe, behind the U.K., France, Germany, the Netherlands, Italy, Switzerland and Sweden.

Spain's stocks are traded on four exchanges — Madrid, Barcelona, Bilbao and Valencia — but Madrid is by far the largest, accounting for around 85% of the 8.50 trillion pesetas record volume in 1994.

Spain's markets had their own Big Bang in July 1989, when they installed the Toronto Stock Exchange's Computer-Assisted Trading System (CATS) to electronically link up the four bourses and the country's trading rooms. In September 1995, the market phased out the CATS after a series of breakdowns during heavy trading periods. In its place came Spain's own system, called the Spanish Bourse Connection System, known by its acronym SIBE. By end of that month, all companies quoted on CATS were operating on the SIBE. The umbrella market authority, Sociedad de Bolsas, claims equity trading will be much more agile with SIBE.

Dow Jones Spain
Equity Market Index Performance

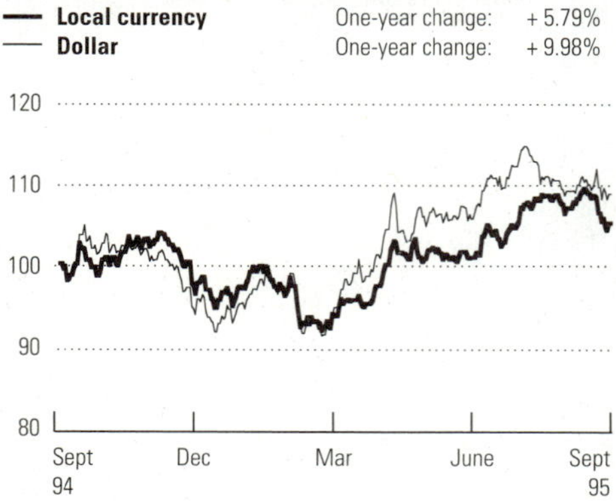

Other reforms since the Big Bang have been the installment of a computerized settlements system in 1993, an improvement in market transparency under the auspices of the National Stock Market Commission and the

Gross Domestic Product (94)	Three-Year Average GDP Growth (92-94)	Main Industries	Consumer Price Index (94)	Monetary Unit	Exchange Rate (9/95)
$64.8 billion	0.5%	Food processing, automobiles, energy and mining, tourism, banking and insurance, and retail	4.7%	Peseta	Pesetas123.46 to US$1.00

abolishment of the monopoly of government-appointed stockbrokers, who have been replaced with professional brokerage houses. The settlements system has reduced the time it takes to settle share transactions to seven days from the previous 10 to 15 days.

The continuous market operates between 11 a.m. and 5 p.m., although there is after-hours trading as well. Early trading in the other European stock exchanges is normally the main factor determining the market trend at the outset. Brokerages begin entering their bids in earnest after 10:30 a.m., based largely on what direction London, Paris and Frankfurt are taking. After a lull in activity around lunch time, the market players await the opening of Wall Street, which usually determines how the market will end the day.

While each bourse has its general index, the IBEX-35 index of the 35 most liquid stocks in the market has taken over as the major stock market indicator. These 35 stocks account for some 90% of trading on an average day.

With the introduction of electronic trading and important share offerings in the last few years, Spain is overcoming its traditional lack of liquidity. But trading is still heavily concentrated in the blue-chip stocks, including the semi-public telecommunications group Telefonica de Espana SA, the state-run energy group Repsol SA and the state-controlled electricity company Empresa Nacional de Electricidad SA (Endesa). On average, these three stocks account for 30% of trading volume. But when the market turns volatile, the safe-haven blue-chips can account for as much as 50% of total volume.

Ten Largest Capitalized Companies
as of 9/30/95

Stock	Market Cap. US$Mil
ENDESA	13,352,001.0
Telefónica de España	12,936,179.3
Repsol	9,440,304.6
Banco Bilbao Vizcaya	6,986,878.3
Iberdrola	6,928,568.8
Banco de Santander	6,701,147.7
Gas Natural	4,705,933.5
Banco Popular Español	4,499,092.8
Argentaria	4,472,703.7
Banco Central Hispano	3,422,439.2

Telefonica, Repsol, Endesa, the state-run bank Argentaria Corporacion Bancaria de Espana, Banco Bilbao Vizcaya and Banco Santander also trade American depositary receipts (ADRs) on Wall Street. ADR dealing accounts for around 30% of total trading in these companies and generates a substantial amount of arbitrage trading in Madrid.

Bourse activity has also been boosted by the introduction of futures and options trading on the IBEX-35 and individual blue-chip stocks. Derivatives trading has added volume to the cash market, but it has also increased the volatility of prices, especially on key contract expiration dates.

The Spanish stock market has been criticized for not fairly representing the country's economy. The banking sector accounts for 31% of the market's capitalization of 16 trillion pesetas, while the electric utilities' weight stands at 22%. There are many construction and building materials stocks on the market, but they only account for 5% of capitalization. The tourism sector, which generates almost 10% of Spain's gross domestic product, is hardly represented on the market. Media and entertainment are also largely absent from the exchange. On a more positive note, the retail sector, one of the fastest-growing of the Spanish economy, has stepped up its presence through recent listings.

In recent years, the majority of share offerings have come from the state-run companies as the government privatizes packages of strategic industries and banks on the Spanish market. Family-run companies have traditionally shied away from listing on the equity market owing to the high tax burden of capital gains, but there have been some exceptions. In 1994, the family-run retailer and textile manufacturer Cortefiel successfully floated a stake of the company on the market to broaden its shareholder base, making it an example for future listings by family-owned companies.

In 1994, the Spanish stock market showed a weak performance as the Madrid General Index posted a 12% drop at the end of the year from end-1993 levels. Higher fixed-income interest rates and political scandals shook investor confidence. While the political turmoil has worsened into 1995, lower interest rates, a heady economic recovery and good corporate earnings have helped bring the market out of the doldrums in 1995.

The Spanish market has shown a steady rise since hitting its low for 1995 in April. In the first nine months of the year, the Madrid General Index has jumped 9% from the end-1994 levels, while the IBEX-35 index has increased 11%. The best performances have been in the water, electricity and gas utilities, and in motorways and telecommunications. Two major privatization offerings in oil group Repsol SA in June and in telecommunications conglomerate Telefonica de Espana SA in September are signals of the Spanish equity market's current buoyancy.

Argentaria

Industry: **Banks - Money Center**

Argentaria Corp. Bancaria de Espana is one of the three largest banking groups in Spain by total assets. Its areas of business include corporate, retail, international, and investment banking, as well as mortgage-lending, money-market trading, fund management, and life insurance. It operates more than 3,300 branches in Spain, and is also active in the United States, Central and South America, and the rest of Europe. The bank manages mutual-fund assets of more than $4.6 billion. The bank has five main banking subsidiaries, including Banco Exterior and Caja Postal.

	ptas mil 12/91	12/92	12/93	US$mil 12/93				
Revenues	**401,948.0**	**1,049,974**	**1,154,860**	**8,682.6**	P/E Ratio	**8.5**	Price (9/30/95)	**4,400.00**
Net Income	**20,214.0**	**56,174.0**	**64,844.0**	**487.5**	P/B Ratio	**1.0**	52 Wk Hi-Low	**5,170.0-3,645.0**
Book Value	**569,736.0**	**613,929.0**	**660,991.0**	**5,021.6**	Yield %	**2.3**	Market Cap	**US$4,472.7mil**

Address	**Paseo de Recoletos 10**	Tel	**N/A**	ADR		President	--
	28001 Madrid	Fax	**N/A**	SEDOL No.	**4049720**	Chairman	**F. Luzon Lopez**

Aumar

Industry: **General Industrial & Commercial Services**

Autopistas del Mare Nostrum (Aumar) builds and operates roads, service roads and areas, and provides related services under license from the Spanish government. Aumar maintains the operation of toll highways. It also provides road-surfacing and drainage services, renovates service areas, and offers a breakdown service. The company's contract to maintain three tollways, from Tarragona to Valencia, Valencia to Alicante, and Seville to Cádiz, covering 468 kilometers, will expire in 2006. The construction firm Dragados y Construcciones owns 26% of the company.

	ptas mil 12/92	12/93	12/94	US$mil 12/94				
Sales	**25,790.0**	**25,352.0**	**26,998.2**	**203.0**	P/E Ratio	**14.8**	Price (9/30/95)	**1,480.00**
Net Income	**6,672.0**	**6,672.0**	**6,672.5**	**50.2**	P/B Ratio	**1.2**	52 Wk Hi-Low	**1,580.0-1,205.0**
Book Value	**80,773.0**	**81,441.0**	**82,107.8**	**623.8**	Yield %	**7.0**	Market Cap	**US$799.9mil**

Address	**Martínez Cubells 5**	Tel	**06-337-20-02**	ADR		Managing Director	**José Luis Cerón Ayuso**
	46002 Valencia	Fax	**06-337-20-03**	SEDOL No.	**4065629**	Chairman	**José Luis Cerón Ayuso**

Autopistas

Industry: **General Industrial & Commercial Services**

Autopistas Concesionaria Española (Acesa) constructs, manages, and maintains tollways. The company's activities are centered in the northeastern region of Catalonia, where Acesa has maintained and operated the motorway network since 1967. Its tollway concessions include several of Spain's primary tourist roads, such as La Jonquera-Barcelona-Tarragona, Zaragoza-Mediterranean, and Montgat-Malgrat, totalling more than 509 kilometers. These concessions will expire in 2016 when Acesa's fixed assets will revert to the Spanish government.

	ptas mil 12/92	12/93	12/94	US$mil 12/94				
Sales	**42,228.0**	**49,861.0**	**46,103.0**	**346.6**	P/E Ratio	**12.6**	Price (9/30/95)	**1,210.00**
Net Income	**16,153.0**	**16,220.0**	**19,554.0**	**147.0**	P/B Ratio	**1.8**	52 Wk Hi-Low	**1,295.0-921.6**
Book Value	**119,296.0**	**136,573.0**	**133,763.0**	**1,016.2**	Yield %	**N/A**	Market Cap	**US$2,136.5mil**

Address	**Plaza Gala Placídia 1**	Tel	**03-217-28-00**	ADR		Managing Director	**J.M. Basañez**
	08006 Barcelona	Fax	**N/A**	SEDOL No.	**4065663**	Chairman	**Josep Vilarasau Salat**

Banco Bilbao Vizcaya

Industry: **Banks - Money Center**

Banco Bilbao Vizcaya provides banking, insurance, and other financial services in Spain and Portugal. The bank operated more than 2,800 banking branches in Spain and nearly 200 more in locations worldwide at year-end 1994. The firm services more than 6 million customers, including roughly 3,000 large companies, as well as individuals and small- and medium-size businesses. More then 80% of its assets are in Spain. The bank acquired a majority stake in Mexican bank Probursa in June 1995.

	ptas mil 12/92	12/93	12/94	US$mil 12/94				
Revenues	**1,148,116**	**1,360,894**	**1,123,541**	**8,447.1**	P/E Ratio	**12.1**	Price (9/30/95)	**3,800.00**
Net Income	**69,478.0**	**71,085.0**	**72,330.0**	**543.8**	P/B Ratio	**1.4**	52 Wk Hi-Low	**3,900.0-3,090.0**
Book Value	**620,848.0**	**674,267.0**	**631,560.0**	**4,798.0**	Yield %	**4.6**	Market Cap	**US$6,986.9mil**

Address	**Plaza de San Nicolás 4**	Tel	**04-487-55-55**	ADR	**BBV**	CEO	**Emilio Ybarra Churruca**
	48005 Bilbao	Fax	**N/A**	SEDOL No.	**4099855**	Chairman	**Emilio Ybarra Churruca**

Banco Central Hispano

Industry: **Banks - Money Center**

Banco Central Hispanoamericano offers commercial-banking services to approximately 8 million clients. The firm has 15 subsidiary banks, five of which are in Spain. Its 3,454 branches and subsidiaries operate throughout Spain and 27 other countries. The bank offers a range of services, including leasing, factoring, asset management, insurance, pension plans, and investment funds. In 1993 it obtained a stake in the private television station Antena 3. The bank, one of Spain's largest, was formed through the merger of Banco Central and Banco Hispano Americano in 1991.

	ptas mil 12/92	12/93	12/94	US$mil 12/94				
Revenues	**1,137,780**	**1,316,999**	**1,011,595**	**7,605.5**	P/E Ratio	**12.7**	Price (9/30/95)	**2,580.00**
Net Income	**52,597.0**	**48,403.0**	**32,785.0**	**246.5**	P/B Ratio	**N/A**	52 Wk Hi-Low	**3,195.0-2,475.0**
Book Value	**649,492.0**	**648,881.0**	**N/A**	**N/A**	Yield %	**N/A**	Market Cap	**US$3,422.4mil**

Address	**Alcalá 49**	Tel	**01-532-88-10**	ADR		CEO	**José María Amusátegui**
	28014 Madrid	Fax	**01-532-76-59**	SEDOL No.	**4074346**	Chairman	**José María Amusátegui**

Banco Exterior de España

Industry: **Banks - Regional**

Banco Exterior de España (BEX) provides corporate, commercial, institutional, and investment banking, including international services. The bank also engages in leasing, factoring, insurance, and capital-market operations. BEX specializes in export and structural financing for small- and medium-size companies. The bank operates 641 branches in Spain, including its network of five regional banks. Overseas, BEX operates in 27 countries through its branches and representative offices. Argentaria, a government-controlled financial holding company, owns 73% of BEX.

ptas mil	12/92	12/93	12/94	US$mil 12/94				
Revenues	**492,265.0**	**540,932.0**	**438,345.0**	**3,295.6**	P/E Ratio	**15.1**	Price (9/30/95)	**2,990.00**
Net Income	**32,574.0**	**32,626.0**	**20,857.0**	**156.8**	P/B Ratio	**1.2**	52 Wk Hi-Low	**4,440.0-2,980.0**
Book Value	**283,788.0**	**298,391.0**	**257,872.0**	**1,959.1**	Yield %	**3.8**	Market Cap	**US$2,551.8mil**

Address **Goya 14**
28001 Madrid
Tel **01-537-85-59**
Fax **01-537-83-17**
ADR
SEDOL No. **4072641**
Managing Director **José I. Rivero Pradera**
Chairman **Francisco Luzón López**

Banco Popular Español

Industry: **Banks - Regional**

Banco Popular Español offers commercial-banking services to corporate and private investors, primarily in the Spanish retail market, as well as financial services. The bank consists of five regional banks, France's Banco Popular Comercial, and other financial-services subsidiaries. It has branches throughout Spain, Europe, and South America. Banco Popular Español recently formed Popular Rabobank, a joint-venture agribusiness bank with Dutch Rabobank, and maintains its joint-venture mortgage bank, Banco Popular Hypotecario, with Germany's Bayerische Hypotheken.

ptas mil	12/92	12/93	12/94	US$mil 12/94				
Revenues	**368,904.0**	**396,526.0**	**347,422.0**	**2,612.0**	P/E Ratio	**10.2**	Price (9/30/95)	**19,220**
Net Income	**50,263.0**	**53,917.0**	**54,631.0**	**410.7**	P/B Ratio	**1.9**	52 Wk Hi-Low	**19,990.0-15,040.0**
Book Value	**235,452.0**	**269,065.0**	**297,657.0**	**2,261.3**	Yield %	**4.4**	Market Cap	**US$4,499.1mil**

Address **Velázquez 34**
28001 Madrid
Tel **01-520-70-00**
Fax **01-577-92-08**
ADR
SEDOL No. **4073600**
CEO **Ildefonso Ayala**
Chairman **Luis Valls**

Banco de Santander

Industry: **Banks - Money Center**

Grupo Santander provides retail-banking, financial, and investment services. Santander has increased its assets by 44% since its purchase of 49% of Banesto in 1994. Holdings include 10% of The Royal Bank of Scotland, with whom it operates Banco de Comercio e Industria, a commercial-banking joint venture in Portugal. Santander also owns 30% of First Fidelity Bancorp, one of the 25 largest banks in the U.S. by assets. It holds a 13.5% stake in Airtel, a consortium led by U.S.-based AirTouch and British Telecom that won Spain's second mobile-communication license.

ptas mil	12/92	12/93	12/94	US$mil 12/94				
Revenues	**798,042.0**	**1,085,677**	**1,140,961**	**8,578.1**	P/E Ratio	**11.9**	Price (9/30/95)	**5,180.00**
Net Income	**59,189.0**	**66,381.0**	**69,636.0**	**523.5**	P/B Ratio	**1.4**	52 Wk Hi-Low	**5,390.0-4,160.0**
Book Value	**365,857.0**	**408,355.0**	**606,536.0**	**4,607.9**	Yield %	**5.0**	Market Cap	**US$6,701.1mil**

Address **Paseo de la Castellana 75**
28046 Madrid
Tel **01-342-48-87**
Fax **01-342-48-94**
ADR **STD**
SEDOL No. **4072287**
President --
Chairman **Emilio Botín-Sanz**

Bankinter

Industry: **Banks - Regional**

Bankinter provides traditional banking services to personal, commercial, and public-sector customers through a 253-branch Spanish network. The bank offers telephone and electronic banking, private banking, mortgage loans, mutual funds and other companies' insurance products. It arranges securities transactions through Mercavalor, a securities company in which it has a 17% interest. Bankinter's branch offices are concentrated in Madrid, Central Spain, and Catalonia. Bankinter, established by Banco Santander and Bank America, was known as Banco Intercontinental Espanol.

ptas mil	12/92	12/93	12/94	US$mil 12/94				
Revenues	**162,916.0**	**195,907.0**	**140,452.0**	**1,056.0**	P/E Ratio	**10.2**	Price (9/30/95)	**10,770**
Net Income	**18,433.0**	**18,620.0**	**16,210.0**	**121.9**	P/B Ratio	**1.4**	52 Wk Hi-Low	**11,820.0-9,610.0**
Book Value	**124,964.0**	**118,039.0**	**116,563.0**	**885.5**	Yield %	**4.3**	Market Cap	**US$1,345.9mil**

Address **Paseo de la Castellana 29**
28046 Madrid
Tel **01-319-95-00**
Fax **01-339-76-24**
ADR
SEDOL No. **4071411**
Managing Director **Juan Arena**
Chairman **Jaime Botín-Sanz**

CEPSA

Industry: **Oil - Secondary**

Compañía Española de Petróleos (CEPSA), the largest private oil refiner in Spain by market capitalization, explores for, extracts, and refines oil. It then manufactures and distributes petroleum products such as lubricants, plastics, polymers, and other refined chemicals. About one third of the company's revenues come from petrochemicals and plastics. Banco Central Hispanoamericano (BCH) has a direct stake of 11% in the company but controls it by retaining the voting rights on the CEPSA shares it sold in 1994. France's Elf Aquitaine owns one third of CEPSA.

ptas mil	12/92	12/93	12/94	US$mil 12/94				
Sales	**521,343.0**	**612,310.0**	**704,218.0**	**5,294.5**	P/E Ratio	**16.8**	Price (9/30/95)	**3,375.00**
Net Income	**11,410.0**	**13,271.0**	**17,909.0**	**134.6**	P/B Ratio	**1.7**	52 Wk Hi-Low	**3,540.0-2,890.0**
Book Value	**167,650.0**	**170,451.0**	**177,370.0**	**1,347.5**	Yield %	**3.3**	Market Cap	**US$2,438.2mil**

Address **Avda. de América 32**
28028 Madrid
Tel **01-337-60-00**
Fax **01-255-41-16**
ADR
SEDOL No. **4684121**
CEO **E. Marín García**
Chairman **L. Magana Martínez**

Cristalería Española

Industry: **Building Materials**

Cristalería Española manufactures glass, synthetic fibers, insulation, and foundation pipes. The company's main division makes glassware for the construction and auto industries under the Cristanola Plata, Stapid, and Parsol brand names. The company also sells rock-wool and fiberglass insulation under the Roclaine and Isover brand names. The company's glassware products include security, decorative, plate, and sheet glass. Its glassware division generated nearly three fourths of sales in 1994. International Saint-Gobain has a controlling share of Cristalería Española.

ptas mil	12/92	12/93	12/94	US$mil 12/94				
Sales	**126,222.0**	**116,285.0**	**124,807.4**	**938.3**	P/E Ratio	**39.0**	Price (9/30/95)	**7,700.00**
Net Income	**2,392.0**	**-9,152.0**	**2,592.1**	**19.5**	P/B Ratio	**2.4**	52 Wk Hi-Low	**8,700.0-5,090.0**
Book Value	**48,024.0**	**38,469.0**	**42,870.3**	**325.7**	Yield %	**0.0**	Market Cap	**US$818.2mil**

Address **Paseo de la Castellana 77**
28046 Madrid
Tel **01-397-20-00**
Fax **01-397-23-99**
ADR
SEDOL No. **4234548**
Managing Director **Philippe Crouzet**
Chairman **J.L. Leal Maldonado**

Cubiertas y Mzov

Industry: **Heavy Construction**

Cubiertas y Mzov is engaged in civil engineering, construction, and real-estate development, almost exclusively in Spain. Its operations are divided into three segments: urban construction and maintenance, rail and road infrastructure, and maritime works. The company specializes in large-scale public-works projects, generating over half of its revenues in this area. Cubiertas' nonconstruction businesses represent roughly 10% of its total revenue. The company offered its shareholders a 1-for-20 bonus rights issue in June 1994.

ptas mil	12/92	12/93	12/94	US$mil 12/94				
Sales	**207,547.0**	**187,908.0**	**194,941.0**	**1,465.6**	P/E Ratio	**9.6**	Price (9/30/95)	**7,850.00**
Net Income	**5,066.0**	**4,053.0**	**4,263.0**	**32.1**	P/B Ratio	**0.9**	52 Wk Hi-Low	**9,750.0-6,240.0**
Book Value	**41,922.0**	**45,070.0**	**45,510.0**	**345.7**	Yield %	**2.8**	Market Cap	**US$331.9mil**

Address **Via Augusta 81-85**
08006 Barcelona
Tel **03-217-22-16**
Fax **N/A**
ADR
SEDOL No. **4239327**
CEO **A. Mesa Buxareu**
Chairman **J.M. Urgoiti**

Dragados

Industry: **Heavy Construction**

Dragados y Construcciones is a construction company with activities that include civil engineering and industrial work, building maintenance, infrastructure conservation, and toll-road construction and maintenance. Dragados undertook North and South American projects worth 16 million pesetas in 1994. Its second-largest international market is North Africa. In 1994, Dragados acquired Spanish construction companies Comylsa and Tecsa to reinforce its presence in the residential-construction area. Banco Central Hispanoamericano owns 23% of the company.

ptas mil	12/92	12/93	12/94	US$mil 12/94				
Sales	**326,263.0**	**300,170.0**	**311,349.0**	**2,340.8**	P/E Ratio	**11.0**	Price (9/30/95)	**1,855.00**
Net Income	**11,115.0**	**9,680.0**	**10,051.0**	**75.6**	P/B Ratio	**0.9**	52 Wk Hi-Low	**2,130.0-1,475.0**
Book Value	**115,364.0**	**119,009.0**	**121,927.0**	**926.3**	Yield %	**3.6**	Market Cap	**US$892.9mil**

Address **Paseo Alameda de Osuna 50**
28042 Madrid
Tel **01-583-30-00**
Fax **01-742-77-53**
ADR
SEDOL No. **4280143**
CEO **Enrique D. López-Jamar**
Chairman **Santiago F. Casaus**

Ebro Agrícolas

Industry: **Other Food**

Ebro Agrícolas, Compañía de Alimentación is a food company that manufactures, markets, exports, and imports sugar and other agriculture products. Owning 13 sugar mills in Spain, it also produces rice, soya, cotton, wheat, spices, baking products, bananas, and ornamental plants, and has a 50% interest in Portugese tinned-fish group Vasco da Gama. Ebro Agrícolas also blends composite animal feed for the farming industry. Serunion, its institutional-catering business, feeds more than 90,000 people a day. Kokmeeuw Holdings owns 39% of the company.

ptas mil	09/92	09/93	09/94	US$mil 09/94				
Sales	**144,461.0**	**139,347.0**	**152,605.0**	**1,125.5**	P/E Ratio	**14.5**	Price (9/30/95)	**1,240.00**
Net Income	**5,306.0**	**3,204.0**	**4,104.8**	**30.3**	P/B Ratio	**0.9**	52 Wk Hi-Low	**1,565.0-1,225.0**
Book Value	**63,986.0**	**65,252.0**	**67,677.8**	**526.4**	Yield %	**N/A**	Market Cap	**US$483.3mil**

Address **Balmes 103**
08008 Barcelona
Tel **03-454-68-00**
Fax **03-323-75-41**
ADR
SEDOL No. **4300085**
Vice-Chairman **Alfonso Carner Suñol**
Chairman **Manuel Guasch Molins**

ENDESA

Industry: **Electrical Utilities - All**

Empresa Nacional de Electricidad (Endesa) is an electric utility that serves more than 3 million customers and accounts for roughly 27% of Spain's electricity output. It operates plants throughout Spain, including 10 fossil-fuel plants that generate approximately 28,000 GWh of electricity (representing 40% of Spain's fossil fuel output), three nuclear-power plants that produce 11,163 GWh of electricity, and five hydroelectric-power plants that produce 1,600 GWh of electricity per year. Endesa also has mining operations and owns two coal-production centers.

ptas mil	12/92	12/93	12/94	US$mil 12/94				
Sales	**700,515.0**	**736,572.0**	**811,533.0**	**6,101.3**	P/E Ratio	**12.4**	Price (9/30/95)	**6,340.00**
Net Income	**106,299.0**	**116,813.0**	**132,728.0**	**997.9**	P/B Ratio	**2.1**	52 Wk Hi-Low	**6,750.0-5,030.0**
Book Value	**600,748.0**	**682,202.0**	**776,511.0**	**5,899.2**	Yield %	**2.5**	Market Cap	**US$13,352mil**

Address **Príncipe de Vergara 187**
28002 Madrid
Tel **01-563-09-23**
Fax **01-563-81-81**
ADR **ELE**
SEDOL No. **4315368**
CEO **Feliciano Fuster Jaume**
Chairman **Feliciano Fuster Jaume**

Financiera Alba

Industry: **Financial Services - Diversified**

Corporación Financiera Alba is a holding company that operates banks and retail outlets; acquires, develops, and leases real estate; and produces food, beverages, building materials, and chemicals. Its main holdings include the French cable-television station Canal Plus (13%), Spanish construction firm Ginés Navarro (30%), and Banco Urquijo (77%). In 1994, Corporación Financiera Alba acquired a 2.6% stake in the AIRTEL consortium, which won a contract to provide Spain's second mobile-telephone network. The March family controls about 32% of the company's shares.

ptas mil	12/92	12/93	12/94	US$mil 12/94				
Revenues	**5,106.0**	**5,131.0**	**8,983.0**	**67.5**	P/E Ratio	**19.6**	Price (9/30/95)	**6,550.00**
Net Income	**6,188.0**	**3,350.0**	**6,011.0**	**45.2**	P/B Ratio	**1.1**	52 Wk Hi-Low	**6,940.0-5,200.0**
Book Value	**101,901.0**	**103,077.0**	**101,516.0**	**771.2**	Yield %	**1.8**	Market Cap	**US$882.1mil**

Address **Nuñez de Balboa 70**
28006 Madrid
Tel **01-3-62-61-00**
Fax **01-5-75-67-37**
ADR
SEDOL No. **4182432**
Vice-Chairman **Pablo V. Vadell**
Chairman **Juan M. Delgado**

Gas Natural

Industry: **Gas Utilities**

Gas Natural SDG is a natural-gas distributor. In 1994, it made about three fourths of its total revenues in Spain and the remainder in Argentina. The company accounts for more than 90% of the natural-gas distributed in Spain. The company's partially-owned subsidiary, Gas Natural BAN, provides gas services to a 15,000 square-kilometer area in Argentina. The company acquired 91% of Enagas, Spain's leading nationalized gas company, in 1993, incorporating it fully with the rest of the company in 1994. Repsol S.A., a Spanish oil refiner, has a 45% interest in Gas Natural.

ptas mil	12/92	12/93	12/94	US$mil 12/94				
Sales	**100,626.0**	**155,297.0**	**213,215.0**	**1,603.0**	P/E Ratio	**24.4**	Price (9/30/95)	**15,570**
Net Income	**12,334.0**	**14,699.0**	**23,852.0**	**179.3**	P/B Ratio	**3.7**	52 Wk Hi-Low	**16,700.0-10,200.0**
Book Value	**129,450.0**	**141,598.0**	**158,894.0**	**1,207.1**	Yield %	**1.0**	Market Cap	**US$4,705.9mil**

Address **Avda. Portal de l'Angel 22**
08002 Barcelona
Tel **03-402-51-00**
Fax **03-402-58-70**
ADR
SEDOL No. **4179865**
Managing Director **Juan Badosa Pagés**
Chairman **Pedro Duran Farell**

Iberdrola

Industry: **Electrical Utilities - All**

Iberdrola is a diversified electric company that produces hydroelectric, conventional thermal, and thermonuclear energy. Iberdrola's other businesses include insurance, real estate, and construction. Serving nearly eight million customers, the company provides electricity to just over 40% of the Spanish market. Iberdrola has interests in other Spanish electric companies, including a 54% share in Compania Electrica Conquense, a 96% stake in Hidroelectrica de Cataluna, and 100% ownership of Valores Mobiliarios y Energia. Banco Bilbao Vizcaya has a 10% interest in Iberdrola.

ptas mil	12/92	12/93	12/94	US$mil 12/94				
Sales	**781,162.0**	**795,161.0**	**754,311.0**	**5,671.1**	P/E Ratio	**15.3**	Price (9/30/95)	**934.00**
Net Income	**58,702.0**	**60,539.0**	**69,522.0**	**522.7**	P/B Ratio	**0.9**	52 Wk Hi-Low	**1,010.0-700.0**
Book Value	**893,193.0**	**921,603.0**	**949,096.0**	**7,210.3**	Yield %	**8.0**	Market Cap	**US$6,928.6mil**

Address **Gardoqui 8**
Vizcaya, Bilbao
Tel **N/A**
Fax **N/A**
ADR
SEDOL No. **4424640**
Vice-Chairman **José A. Garrido Martínez**
Chairman **Iñigo de Oriol Ybarra**

Mapfre

Industry: **Insurance - Full Line**

Mapfre operates in the insurance, banking, and real-estate sectors. The company offers reinsurance and life and general insurance, including family, fire, homeowners', auto, civil-liability, and personal-accident products. Through its wholly-owned Mapfre Internacional subsidiary, the company has interests in 45 insurance companies in 23 countries, with the emphasis on Latin America. The firm's partially owned Banco Mapfre subsidiary provides retail banking services for Spanish individuals and businesses at 60 branches.

ptas mil	12/92	12/93	12/94	US$mil 12/94				
Revenues	**174,400.0**	**244,105.0**	**248,527.0**	**1,868.5**	P/E Ratio	**24.6**	Price (9/30/95)	**6,380.00**
Net Income	**5,102.0**	**5,308.0**	**7,043.0**	**53.0**	P/B Ratio	**1.8**	52 Wk Hi-Low	**7,200.0-4,810.0**
Book Value	**75,701.0**	**88,811.0**	**95,176.0**	**723.1**	Yield %	**2.6**	Market Cap	**US$1,317.0mil**

Address **Paseo de Recoletos 25**
28004 Madrid
Tel **01-581-11-00**
Fax **01-419-91-95**
ADR **CRFEY**
SEDOL No. **4182540**
Mng Dir & CEO **José M. M. Martínez**
Chairman **Carlos Alvarez Jiménez**

Metrovacesa

Industry: **Real-Estate Investment**

Inmobiliaria Metropolitana Vasco Central S.A (Metrovacesa) develops and manages real estate in Spain and Portugal. In terms of rental revenues, it is the leading Spanish real-estate group. In 1994, 45% of its rental revenues came from office space, with the remainder generated by residential and commercial sites, hotels, shopping malls, parking lots, and industrial sites. Metrovacesa also develops some housing and industrial properties for sale. Banco Bilbao Vizcaya (BBV) owns 25% of the company.

ptas mil	12/92	12/93	12/94	US$mil 12/94				
Sales	**8,776.0**	**16,187.0**	**15,354.5**	**115.4**	P/E Ratio	**20.6**	Price (9/30/95)	**3,860.00**
Net Income	**4,374.0**	**3,802.0**	**4,219.1**	**31.7**	P/B Ratio	**1.3**	52 Wk Hi-Low	**4,615.0-3,135.0**
Book Value	**53,199.0**	**67,097.0**	**69,090.9**	**524.9**	Yield %	**2.7**	Market Cap	**US$702.7mil**

Address **Pza. Carlos Trías Betrán 7**
28020 Madrid
Tel **01-597-43-36**
Fax **01-597-45-29**
ADR
SEDOL No. **4585268**
CEO **Fernando Vara Herrero**
Chairman **José A. Sáenz**

Portland Valderrivas

Industry: **Building Materials**

Portland Valderrivas is a construction company that is active in both the private and public sectors. The company constructs, develops, and sells private housing, apartments, and commercial property in the Madrid area. It also builds roads, bridges, and other public works for the Spanish government. It produces and distributes cement, ready-mix concrete, clinker, ceramic tiles, prefabricated building materials, and pavement to the general public and its construction subsidiaries. Fomento de Construcciones y Contratos has a 30% interest in Portland Valderrivas.

ptas mil	12/92	12/93	12/94	US$mil 12/94				
Sales	N/A	33,488.0	37,476.0	281.8	P/E Ratio	14.0	Price (9/30/95)	8,550.00
Net Income	N/A	2,010.0	4,422.0	33.2	P/B Ratio	1.5	52 Wk Hi-Low	10,500.0-7,510.0
Book Value	N/A	38,664.0	41,628.0	316.3	Yield %	2.3	Market Cap	US$502.8mil

Address **José Abascal 59** **28003 Madrid**
Tel **01-396-01-00**
Fax **01-396-01-70**
ADR
SEDOL No. **4696847**
CEO **R. Martínez Ynzenga**
Chairman **A. Cortina de Alcocer**

Repsol

Industry: **Oil - Integrated Majors**

Repsol produces, transports, refines, and explores for oil and natural gas. On average, the company produced more than 205,000 barrels of gas and oil per day in 1993 and its reserves stood at 165 million barrels of oil. The retail arm of the firm consists of a network of 3,500 service stations in Spain, France, and the U.K. Repsol also produces bulk chemicals derived from petroleum such as ethylene, propylene, and benzene. Repsol's joint venture Total and OMV will explore three Libyan oilfields with reserves estimated between 800 million and 1 billion barrels of oil.

ptas mil	12/92	12/93	12/94	US$mil 12/94				
Sales	1,907,898	2,216,631	2,329,447	17,513.5	P/E Ratio	12.1	Price (9/30/95)	3,885.00
Net Income	71,917.0	80,114.0	96,803.0	727.8	P/B Ratio	2.0	52 Wk Hi-Low	4,130.0-3,475.0
Book Value	480,957.0	528,024.0	588,606.0	4,471.7	Yield %	3.6	Market Cap	US$9,440.3mil

Address **Paseo de la Castellana 278** **28046 Madrid**
Tel **01-348-81-00**
Fax **01-314-28-21**
ADR **REP**
SEDOL No. **4733227**
CEO **Oscar Fanjul**
Chairman **Oscar Fanjul**

Sevillana de Electricidad

Industry: **Electrical Utilities - All**

Sevillana de Electricidad produces, transmits, and distributes electrical power in southern Spain. It has nine provincial electricity departments in Andalusia's eight provinces and in the Badajoz province. It also operates electricity production plants in the Andalusia, Extremadura, and Castilla-La Mancha communities. In 1994, it generated net power of 10,946 GWh. Total power installed is approximately 5,000 MW. The firm provides service to 8 million people in a 100,000-square-kilometer area.

ptas mil	12/92	12/93	12/94	US$mil 12/94				
Sales	250,200.0	259,506.0	268,477.0	2,018.5	P/E Ratio	14.7	Price (9/30/95)	802.00
Net Income	13,530.0	12,809.0	16,211.0	121.9	P/B Ratio	0.8	52 Wk Hi-Low	857.00-517.00
Book Value	293,650.0	292,420.0	289,025.0	2,195.7	Yield %	4.7	Market Cap	US$1,929.8mil

Address **Avda. de la Borbolla 5** **41004 Sevilla**
Tel **05-441-73-11**
Fax **05-441-21-28**
ADR **COVDY**
SEDOL No. **4800466**
CEO **E. Zurutuza Reigosa**
Chairman **Fernando de Ybarra**

Tabacalera

Industry: **Tobacco**

Tabacalera, a state-controlled tobacco company, produces and markets tobacco products and manages food and postage-stamp-distribution businesses. Through its partially-owned CETARSA and Compañía de Filipinas subsidiaries, Tabacalera imports and sells tobacco from the United States, Cuba, the Philippines, and Indonesia. It also administers the state monopoly of wholesale postage-stamp distribution. More than 80% of the company's income is generated by its tobacco products. In 1994, Tabacalera acquired a 32% interest in Spanish leaf-tobacco company Intabex.

ptas mil	12/92	12/93	12/94	US$mil 12/94				
Sales	700,266.0	668,111.0	783,101.0	5,887.6	P/E Ratio	14.7	Price (9/30/95)	4,395.00
Net Income	12,593.0	4,810.0	11,031.0	82.9	P/B Ratio	1.7	52 Wk Hi-Low	4,985.0-3,100.0
Book Value	88,190.0	85,781.0	92,499.0	702.7	Yield %	3.3	Market Cap	US$1,310.8mil

Address **Calle del Barquillo 5** **28000 Madrid**
Tel **01-532-76-00**
Fax **01-522-75-86**
ADR
SEDOL No. **4869627**
President --
Chairman **Pedro Pérez Fernández**

Telefónica de España

Industry: **Telephone Systems - All**

Telefonica de Espana is Spain's partially privatized telecommunication firm. It operates more than 13 million local telephone lines, 481,600 integrated business-communication lines, and nearly 43,000 public phone booths. Telefonica is building a digital mobile-communication network to which it already has more than 250,000 subscribers. South American subsidiaries include Telefonica de Argentina and Telefonos de Chile. It also owns 80% of Puerto Rico's long-distance service. Telefonica leads a consortium that controls 95% of Peru's telecommunications.

ptas mil	12/92	12/93	12/94	US$mil 12/94				
Sales	1,208,938	1,297,437	1,578,850	11,870.2	P/E Ratio	14.2	Price (9/30/95)	1,700.00
Net Income	80,761.0	96,367.0	112,608.0	846.6	P/B Ratio	1.1	52 Wk Hi-Low	1,780.0-1,490.0
Book Value	1,392,005	1,437,055	1,512,031	11,487.0	Yield %	3.9	Market Cap	US$12,936mil

Address **General Perón 38** **28020 Madrid**
Tel **01-584-62-18**
Fax **01-597-40-75**
ADR **TEF**
SEDOL No. **4880822**
CEO **Germán Ancochea Soto**
Chairman **C. Velázquez-Gaztelu**

Uralita

Industry: **Building Materials**

Uralita has interests in the construction and chemicals sectors. It manufactures and distributes a range of building materials, including paint, concrete, tile, ceramics, and plastics. Building materials represented 70% of the company's sales in 1994. Uralita's chemicals business operates through the subsidiary Energía y Industrias Aragonesas, which produces agrochemicals and chlorates. In 1995, 51% of Aragonesas was listed on the Madrid Stock Exchange. In May 1994, Uralita acquired Cercalda, a Portuguese manufacturer of clay roof tiles.

ptas mil	12/92	12/93	12/94	US$mil 12/94				
Sales	**114,174.0**	**104,422.0**	**120,405.0**	**905.2**	P/E Ratio	**NMF**	Price (9/30/95)	**1,315.00**
Net Income	**2,814.0**	**-7,470.0**	**-751.0**	**-5.6**	P/B Ratio	**1.4**	52 Wk Hi-Low	**1,645.0-1,140.0**
Book Value	**51,276.0**	**50,683.0**	**49,668.0**	**377.3**	Yield %	**0.0**	Market Cap	**US$558.0mil**

Address **Mejía Lequerica 10**
28004 Madrid
Tel **01-448-10-00**
Fax **01-593-37-93**
ADR
SEDOL No. **4922155**
Managing Director **Eugenio Ruiz-Gálvez**
Chairman **Juan A. García Díez**

Vallehermoso

Industry: **Real-Estate Investment**

Vallehermoso is the largest property-investment and -development company in Spain. It specializes in commercial and residential urban real estate. Vallehermoso also engages in telecommunication, retail-property, and office-maintenance operations. The company owns office property in Paris, Lisbon, and London. Vallehermoso also has in excess of 646,000 square meters of rental space located primarily in Barcelona, Madrid, and Seville. The sale of residential and commercial properties generated more than 80% of total revenues in 1994.

ptas mil	12/92	12/93	12/94	US$mil 12/94				
Sales	**45,881.0**	**36,373.0**	**41,532.0**	**312.2**	P/E Ratio	**22.5**	Price (9/30/95)	**2,180.00**
Net Income	**7,748.0**	**3,757.0**	**4,159.0**	**31.3**	P/B Ratio	**1.1**	52 Wk Hi-Low	**2,475.0-1,675.0**
Book Value	**69,025.0**	**81,497.0**	**83,754.0**	**636.3**	Yield %	**2.3**	Market Cap	**US$759.6mil**

Address **Paseo de la Castellana 83-85**
28046 Madrid
Tel **01-556-10-64**
Fax **01-597-01-90**
ADR
SEDOL No. **4926704**
President --
Chairman **Martín Eyries**

Sweden

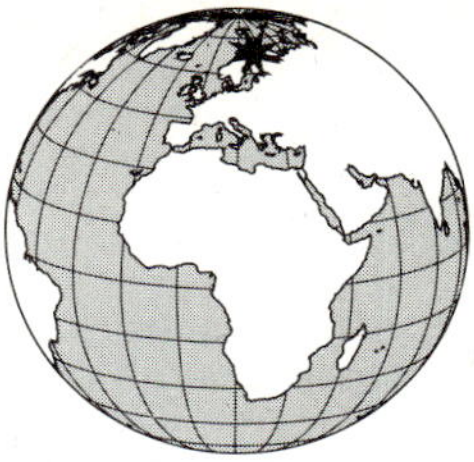

Sweden

Birgitta Forsberg, Stockholm

Local Trading Hours	Time Difference with New York	Population (Est. 94)
10:00-4:00	6 hours ahead	8,778,000

A general index surge of 25% from the beginning of 1995 through mid-September made the Stockholm Stock Exchange one of the best-performing bourses in the world during that period.

Lower interest rates and growing corporate earnings are the two major factors supporting prices. The stock market's strength also reflects growing investor confidence in the minority Social-Democratic government's ability to restore battered state finances through their fiscal policies.

The exchange's turnover has likewise continued to be strong, amounting to about 450 billion kronor after the first eight months of 1995, which is merely 0.8% less than during the corresponding period in the record year 1994. This makes the Stockholm exchange the largest in the Nordic region and the seventh largest in Europe.

Heavily influencing both turnover and market developments are pharmaceutical company Astra and telecommunications group L.M. Ericsson, by far the two largest and most traded shares. A dive or rally in one or both of the shares generally depresses or lifts the whole market, often offsetting other shares' movements.

Because of their size, Ericsson and Astra make the market sectors they belong to dominant in the Swedish market. Engineering accounts for 41% of total market capitalization, while chemicals and pharmaceuticals weighs in at 20%. In distant third place trails the forestry sector with 9%, followed by the banking and insurance sector and other industry with 7% each. Of remaining sectors, the investment company sector's slice amounts to 6%, while the service and construction & real estate sectors have 4% each and the retail sector 2%.

A total of 229 companies are listed on the exchange with 288 share issues. The total market capitalization was 1.10 trillion kronor after the first six months in 1995, up 13% from 977 billion kronor at the end of 1994. The 25 most active issues on the main A list accounted for 89% of market turnover during the first six months of 1995 and 80% of total market value.

Dow Jones Sweden Equity Market Index Performance

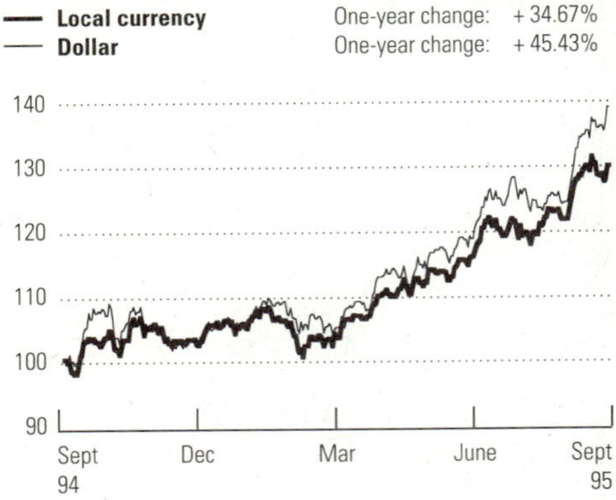

Apart from the A list, which is the main market list and consists of 123 major companies, the bourse has two parallel market

Gross Domestic Product (94)	Three-Year Average GDP Growth (92-94)	Main Industries	Consumer Price Index (94)	Monetary Unit	Exchange Rate (9/95)
$208.37 million	– 0.6%	Engineering, pharmaceutical, forestry, banking and insurance	2.6%	Krona	SEK6.93 to US$1.00

lists. The unofficial O list contains 57 companies and the over-the-counter (OTC) list 49. Turnover on the O list was 16.4 billion kronor in the first six months of 1995, corresponding to 5% of total turnover, while the OTC list's turnover in the period amounted to 4.4 billion kronor, or 1.4% of the total. Companies on the O and OTC lists are quoted but not registered with the exchange.

Different indices show the development for the different lists, or part of the lists. The OMX index, most quoted by traders, encompasses 30 large shares and is compiled, as a basis for estimating index futures, by the OM Group, which operates trading, clearing and settlement activities in Swedish equity derivatives. The exchange's SX-General index contains all the A list's shares and is based on the last price paid for those stocks, while its SX-16 index tracks the 16 most actively traded share issues by value.

Although the main market has a larger number of companies listed than the parallel markets together and also has about 94% of total turnover, foreign trading in shares on the OTC and O lists is increasing. In addition, more companies are entering the parallel markets. Since September 1994, five new companies have emerged on the OTC list and 11 on the O list.

Privatization of fully or partly state-owned companies have added four groups to the market in the past two years: steel group Svenskt Stal AB (SSAB), defense and information technology group Celsius Industrier AB, pharmaceutical company Pharmacia AB and forest group AssiDomaen AB. Other broad share introductions, mainly directed toward Swedish households, have also boosted the number of listed companies. Those introductions include banking groups Foereningsbanken AB and Swedbank, or Sparbankernas bank, as well as mortgage bank Stadshypotek AB.

Ten Largest Capitalized Companies
as of 9/30/95

Stock	Market Cap. US$Mil
Astra	17,984,622.7
ASEA	6,701,284.3
Pharmacia	4,956,011.9
Sandvik	4,196,596.5
Swedish Commercial	3,590,718.6
Skanska	3,572,704.8
Stora	3,569,931.8
Volvo	3,466,597.3
Electrolux	3,407,513.9
S-E Banken	3,247,481.6

Despite Sweden holding a world record through almost half of its population, or 4 million persons, owning shares, households keep decreasing their slice of the share market. On June 30, 1995, households owned 13% of the total amount of shares directly and another 10% through funds — primarily tax incentive funds — managed by large institutional investors, down from a total of 50% in the mid-1970s. The biggest owners on the Stockholm exchange are instead domestic institutional investors, which held about 50% of shares on June 30, 1995, while foreigners, who keep increasing their stake, had 27%, up from 26% at the end of 1994 and 21% at the beginning of 1994.

When trading in Stockholm, most foreigners choose to register their stock transactions through a nominee account, instead of using a direct share account, as it's generally more convenient and enables them to stay anonymous.

No deals are put down on paper and trading is fully automated with computers matching buyers with sellers since the call over market. Continuous floor trading completely ended in 1990, after having played a minor role following the introduction of electronic trading in the mid-1970s. As of 1993, the rolling settlement period is set at three banking days. The exchange is order-driven rather than quote-driven and Swedish security brokers don't usually function as market makers.

As of Jan. 1, 1996, foreign traders won't have to go through a Swedish broker to buy or sell shares as 16 European countries, including Sweden, ease regulations to increase competition, in accordance with the European Union's (E.U.) investment services directive (ISD). This could lead to a larger part of deals being settled without contact with the exchange. Currently, 95% of trading in Swedish shares in Sweden passes through the bourse, while 60% of worldwide trading in Swedish shares is done through the Stockholm Stock Exchange, as world trading includes Swedish shares listed abroad.

Competition has also increased within the country as the Stockholm Stock Exchange lost its monopoly position regarding securities trading in Sweden in 1993. Since then it has been possible, in theory, for others to set up stock trading places, but no new rivals have emerged.

In 1993, the exchange was transformed into a limited company, owned by the 34 bourse members and the companies with shares listed on the exchange. Six of the members are foreign-owned Stockholm-based firms, which are overseen by the Swedish financial supervisory authority, and five are remote members with no activity in Stockholm. The latter stay under the supervision of their respective countries of origin, under the ISD regime.

Irrespective of through whom they trade, foreigners are not affected by Swedish tax regulations. They don't pay capital gains tax in Sweden and although they are subjected to withholding tax on dividends, rules in most cases assure that they are not taxed more than they would be in their native countries.

For domestic investors, taxes again became stricter as of Jan. 1, 1995, when taxes on dividends were reinstated at 30% and the capital gains tax was raised to 30% after having been 12.5% for one year, in 1994.

AGA

Industry: **Specialty Chemicals**

AGA produces and distributes industrial and medical gases, generates energy, and provides support services to the food industry. The firm sells air gases via pipes and in cylinder form to hospitals and to steel, chemical, and engineering companies. It provides liquid gas mainly to the food, glass, and health-care industries. The firm holds a 34% stake in Gullspangs Kraft, which provides power to 192,000 customers in Sweden. Europe excluding Sweden generates more than 55% of sales, the U.S. 12%, and the rest of the world 19%.

	SEK mil 12/92	12/93	12/94	US$mil 12/94				
Sales	**11,870.0**	**16,063.0**	**12,544.0**	**1,636.1**	P/E Ratio M	**17.2**	Price (9/30/95) M	**91.00**
Net Income	**1,007.0**	**1,136.0**	**1,269.0**	**165.5**	P/B Ratio M	**2.8**	52 Wk Hi-Low M	**98.00-65.50**
Book Value	**7,578.0**	**8,310.0**	**7,771.0**	**1,045.9**	Yield % M	**2.5**	Market Cap M	**US$1,707.6mil**

Address **AGA**
181 81 Lidingo
Tel **08-731-10-00**
Fax **08-767-63-44**
ADR **AGAXY**
SEDOL No. **4034618**
President & CEO **Marcus Storch**
Chairman **Sven Ågrup**

M=Multiple issues in index; reflects most active.

ASEA

Industry: **Electrical Components & Equipment**

Asea is a holding company with a 50% stake in Zurich-based power and industrial firm ABB Asea Brown Boveri, which is its only principal asset. Swiss holding company BBC Brown Boveri owns the other 50% of ABB. ABB is the world's largest electrical engineering group, composed of more than 1,300 companies operating in 140 countries. ABB serves customers in electrical power generation, industrial and building systems, and rail transportation. In 1994, 56% of ABB's sales came from Europe, 17% from North America, and 14% from Asia.

	SEK mil 12/92	12/93	12/94	US$mil 12/94				
Sales	**3,079.0**	**4,493.0**	**5,381.6**	**701.9**	P/E Ratio M	**21.7**	Price (9/30/95) M	**695.00**
Net Income	**1,490.0**	**252.0**	**2,923.3**	**381.3**	P/B Ratio M	**4.2**	52 Wk Hi-Low M	**705.00-507.00**
Book Value	**14,424.0**	**14,710.0**	**15,028.5**	**2,022.7**	Yield % M	**1.7**	Market Cap M	**US$6,701.3mil**

Address **Hamngatan 2**
103 91 Stockholm
Tel **08-613-65-60**
Fax **08-613-65-65**
ADR **ASEAY**
SEDOL No. **4052966**
President **Kjell Högfelt**
Chairman **Peter Wallenberg**

M=Multiple issues in index; reflects most active.

Astra

Industry: **Pharmaceuticals**

Astra, the largest pharmaceuticals company in the Nordic region, manufactures and markets local anesthetics, anti-infective medicines, and medicines for the treatment of intestinal, respiratory, and cardiovascular diseases. Ulcer medication Prilosec and anti-inflammatory inhalation drug Pulmicort are two of the firm's brand-name products. Astra recently purchased half of a joint venture with U.S.-based pharmaceuticals group Merck. Europe accounts for more than half of Astra's sales, the U.S. 13%, and the Asia-Pacific region and the Nordic countries 17% each.

	SEK mil 12/92	12/93	12/94	US$mil 12/94				
Sales	**15,568.0**	**22,600.0**	**28,030.0**	**3,655.9**	P/E Ratio M	**22.5**	Price (9/30/95) M	**248.50**
Net Income	**3,527.0**	**6,092.0**	**6,795.0**	**886.3**	P/B Ratio M	**6.6**	52 Wk Hi-Low M	**259.00-174.00**
Book Value	**11,650.0**	**17,142.0**	**23,301.0**	**3,136.1**	Yield % M	**0.9**	Market Cap M	**US$17,985mil**

Address **Astra AB**
151 85 Sodertalje
Tel **08-553-260-00**
Fax **08-553-288-10**
ADR **ARRAY**
SEDOL No. **4051208**
President & CEO **Håkan Mogren**
Chairman **Bo Berggren**

M=Multiple issues in index; reflects most active.

Atlas Copco

Industry: **Industrial - Diversified**

Atlas Copco manufactures tools for construction, mining, and compressor- and industrial-technology applications. It makes about 20% of its products in Sweden; 95% of its sales come from outside the country. The company supplies compressors for the manufacture of industrial gases to customers such as French gas producer L'Air Liquide and Danish gas concern Hede Nielsen. Its subsidiaries include electric-power-tool manufacturer Kango (U.K.) and U.S.-based Robbins, a manufacturer of tunnel-boring machines. Atlas Copco acquired Milwaukee Electric Tool (U.S.) in July 1995.

	SEK mil 12/92	12/93	12/94	US$mil 12/94				
Sales	**16,007.0**	**18,906.0**	**20,914.0**	**2,727.8**	P/E Ratio M	**17.7**	Price (9/30/95) M	**115.50**
Net Income	**604.0**	**867.0**	**1,194.0**	**155.7**	P/B Ratio M	**2.3**	52 Wk Hi-Low M	**125.00-87.00**
Book Value	**7,295.0**	**8,394.0**	**9,183.0**	**1,235.9**	Yield % M	**2.0**	Market Cap M	**US$2,041.6mil**

Address **Sicka Industrivag 3**
105 23 Stockholm
Tel **08-743-8000**
Fax **08-644-9045**
ADR **ATLKY**
SEDOL No. **4050971**
President & CEO **Michael Treschow**
Chairman **Peter Wallenberg**

M=Multiple issues in index; reflects most active.

Electrolux

Industry: **Other Home Furnishings**

Electrolux is Europe's market leader in the production of household appliances. The company also manufactures food-service equipment, industrial laundry equipment, and forestry and garden equipment. Its brand-name products include Electrolux and Zanussi appliances and vacuum cleaners and Weed Eater garden tools. The company and Germany's AEG jointly develop and manufacture washers, dryers, and dishwashers. Electrolux wholly owns the U.S. household-appliance manufacturer Frigidaire. Europe generates 45% of sales and North America one third.

	SEK mil 12/92	12/93	12/94	US$mil 12/94				
Sales	**80,436.0**	**100,121.0**	**108,004.0**	**14,086.9**	P/E Ratio	**5.0**	Price (9/30/95)	**331.50**
Net Income	**183.0**	**584.0**	**4,830.0**	**630.0**	P/B Ratio	**1.2**	52 Wk Hi-Low	**395.00-313.00**
Book Value	**16,772.0**	**16,853.0**	**20,465.0**	**2,754.4**	Yield %	**3.8**	Market Cap	**US$3,407.5mil**

Address **Lilla Essingen**
105 45 Stockholm
Tel **08-738-6000**
Fax **08-656-4478**
ADR **ELUXY**
SEDOL No. **4308993**
President & CEO **Leif Johansson**
Chairman **Anders Scharp**

LM Ericsson

Industry: **Communications Technology**

Ericsson Telephone, the world's leading supplier of mobile-telephone systems, operates telecommunication services and produces wired- and mobile-communication systems; it also manufactures electronic defense systems. The firm supplies mobile-telephone systems to 22 million customers in 74 countries and operates a telecommunication base of 82 million AXE lines. It also manufactures land-based air-defense radar, naval surveillance radar, and airborne early-warning radar. Exports to Europe account for 40% of sales; 50% of revenues come from non-European exports.

	SEK mil 12/92	12/93	12/94	US$mil 12/94				
Sales	47,020.0	62,954.0	82,554.0	10,767.4	P/E Ratio M	43.3	Price (9/30/95) M	176.00
Net Income	478.0	2,835.0	3,949.0	515.1	P/B Ratio M	7.2	52 Wk Hi-Low M	182.04-96.17
Book Value	17,720.0	21,305.0	23,302.0	3,136.2	Yield % M	0.7	Market Cap M	US$2,083.3mil

Address **LM Ericsson AB**
126 25 Stockholm
Tel **08-719-00-00**
Fax **08-719-19-76**
ADR **ERICY**
SEDOL No. **4321558**
President & CEO **Lars Ramqvist**
Chairman **Björn Svedberg**

M=Multiple issues in index; reflects most active.

Esselte

Industry: **Office Equipment**

Esselte manufactures and markets office products, identification and marking systems, graphic-art supplies, and framing products. Its products include Bensons binding mechanisms, Dymo and Pendaflex office supplies, Letraset graphic-art materials, and Metro price-marking, bar-coding, electronic article-surveillance, and retail-display equipment. Its office-products division generates 64% of revenues. The United States, Esselte's largest market, generates 24% of revenues. Exports to Europe and the rest of the world account for 70% of revenues.

	SEK mil 12/92	12/93	12/94	US$mil 12/94				
Sales	9,909.0	11,843.0	12,123.0	1,581.2	P/E Ratio M	14.9	Price (9/30/95) M	99.50
Net Income	-251.0	147.0	230.0	30.0	P/B Ratio M	1.4	52 Wk Hi-Low M	104.00-86.00
Book Value	2,164.0	2,225.0	2,362.0	317.9	Yield % M	3.0	Market Cap M	US$274.7mil

Address **Sundbybergsvägen 1**
171 27 Solna
Tel **08-27-27-60**
Fax **08-83-32-98**
ADR **ESLTY**
SEDOL No. **4313771**
President **Bo Lundquist**
Chairman **Rune Andersson**

M=Multiple issues in index; reflects most active.

Gambro

Industry: **Advanced Medical Technology**

Gambro is a medical-technology firm that manufactures products for cardiovascular surgery, renal care, and blood-component technology. The firm makes products such as kidney-dialysis machines, plate dialyzers, heart and lung oxygenators, and blood-component equipment. Medical equipment accounts for nearly 90% of its sales. Gambro also provides health-care services through its U.S.-based dialysis clinic chain Ren. More than half of Gambro's revenues come from non-European countries, primarily the United States.

	SEK mil 12/92	12/93	12/94	US$mil 12/94				
Sales	6,312.0	9,046.0	9,807.0	1,279.1	P/E Ratio	19.7	Price (9/30/95)	115.50
Net Income	454.0	600.0	690.0	90.0	P/B Ratio	3.5	52 Wk Hi-Low	116.00-77.00
Book Value	2,293.0	3,347.0	3,861.0	519.7	Yield %	1.4	Market Cap	US$1,768.5mil

Address **Magistratsvägen 16**
220 10 Lund
Tel **046-16-90-00**
Fax **N/A**
ADR **GAMBY**
SEDOL No. **4392651**
CEO **Berthold Lindqvist**
Chairman **Lennart Nilsson**

Gullspångs Kraft

Industry: **Electrical Utilities - All**

Gullspångs Kraft produces and distributes electricity to companies and private individuals in central and northern Sweden. The company has nearly 200,000 retail customers. Most of its production is hydroelectric and nuclear power, though it also distributes energy from coal, oil, and biomass fuels. It also distributes heat through district heating networks. The company has the capacity to generate 10,726 GWh of electricity a year. It has 153 wholly- and partially-owned hydroelectric power plants. AGA, a gas-producing company, owns a 34% stake of Gullspångs Kraft.

	SEK mil 12/92	12/93	12/94	US$mil 12/94				
Sales	2,806.0	3,127.0	3,336.1	435.1	P/E Ratio	14.2	Price (9/30/95)	96.50
Net Income	360.0	524.0	483.3	63.0	P/B Ratio	1.7	52 Wk Hi-Low	98.50-78.00
Book Value	3,183.0	3,587.0	3,923.1	528.0	Yield %	3.1	Market Cap	US$907.7mil

Address **Box 1643**
701 16 Orebro
Tel **019-21-81-00**
Fax **019-26-24-23**
ADR
SEDOL No. **4396341**
CEO **Olof G. Wikström**
Chairman **Olof G. Wikström**

Incentive

Industry: **Industrial - Diversified**

Incentive is an industrial holding company with subsidiaries operating in the fields of medical technology, transportation, environment, materials handling, and power generation. Its Gambro medical-technology subsidiary provides products for renal care, cardiovascular surgery, blood-component technology, and health-care services. Its Hägglunds Vehicle subsidiary makes military and civilian tracked-vehicles. Incentive has stakes in energy company ASEA and electrical-goods manufacturer Electrolux. Exports to non-European countries accounted for 35% of revenues in 1994.

	SEK mil 12/92	12/93	12/94	US$mil 12/94				
Sales	11,771.0	12,271.0	18,389.0	2,398.5	P/E Ratio M	10.4	Price (9/30/95) M	331.00
Net Income	388.0	462.0	2,186.0	285.1	P/B Ratio M	2.1	52 Wk Hi-Low M	332.00-213.50
Book Value	9,500.0	9,922.0	10,976.0	1,477.3	Yield % M	2.4	Market Cap M	US$2,393.7mil

Address **Hamngatan 2**
103 91 Stockholm
Tel **08-613-65-00**
Fax **08-611-28-30**
ADR
SEDOL No. **4506117**
President & CEO **Mikael Lilius**
Chairman **Anders Scharp**

M=Multiple issues in index; reflects most active.

Investor

Industry: **Land Transportation**

Investor is a holding company for industrial corporations. It owns the Saab and Scania manufacturing companies, which make Scania heavy vehicles and Saab aircraft. The company also operates a Saab automobile joint venture with General Motors. Investor has interests in pharmaceuticals-firm Astra, forestry company Stora, banking firm S-E Banken, and telecommunication company L.M. Ericsson. Investor also holds 36% of the voting rights in Incentive, an industrial holding company that has 33% of the voting rights in the energy company ASEA.

	SEK mil 12/92	12/93	12/94	US$mil 12/94				
Sales	**29,809.0**	**29,454.0**	**32,322.0**	**4,215.7**	P/E Ratio M	**16.9**	Price (9/30/95) M	**238.50**
Net Income	**1,163.0**	**474.0**	**2,812.0**	**366.8**	P/B Ratio M	**2.6**	52 Wk Hi-Low M	**241.00-166.00**
Book Value	**13,136.0**	**13,060.0**	**18,466.0**	**2,485.3**	Yield % M	**3.4**	Market Cap M	**US$2,681.8mil**

Address **Arsenalsgatan 8 C**
103 32 Stockholm
Tel **08-614-20-00**
Fax **08-614-21-50**
ADR
SEDOL No. **4466288**
CEO **Claes Dahlbäck**
Chairman **Peter Wallenberg**

M=Multiple issues in index; reflects most active.

NCC

Industry: **Heavy Construction**

NCC is a construction company that builds, repairs, and maintains roads, railroads, and airports; maintains streets, parks, and sewage plants for municipalities; and builds and renovates houses, hospitals, schools, and industrial properties. NCC produces ballast, liquid asphalt, and concrete, and also provides the construction industry with equipment and supplies. Its construction activities account for 88% of revenues. NCC also has significant real-estate interests. It owns and manages more than 1.1 million square meters of property.

	SEK mil 12/92	12/93	12/94	US$mil 12/94				
Sales	**20,082.0**	**17,604.0**	**16,549.0**	**2,158.5**	P/E Ratio	**7.2**	Price (9/30/95)	**74.00**
Net Income	**-1,313.0**	**221.0**	**817.0**	**106.6**	P/B Ratio	**2.5**	52 Wk Hi-Low	**76.00-53.50**
Book Value	**4,231.0**	**4,572.0**	**2,370.0**	**319.0**	Yield %	**1.4**	Market Cap	**US$469.9mil**

Address **Vallgatan 3**
171 80 Solna
Tel **08-655-20-00**
Fax **08-83-15-70**
ADR
SEDOL No. **4645731**
CEO **Jan Sjöqvist**
Chairman **Jan Sjöqvist**

Perstorp

Industry: **Specialty Chemicals**

Perstorp is a chemical company that produces surface materials, acoustics, plastics, specialty chemicals, and biotechnology. The company's surface materials include laminate flooring, decorative laminate, and foils, all of which it supplies to the construction industry. It supplies noise-control and acoustic-related components to the automotive industry. It makes instruments used to analyze food and animal feed, and supplies systems that handle plastics for the materials- and waste-handling industries. Sales outside of Europe account for nearly one third of revenues.

	SEK mil 08/92	08/93	08/94	US$mil 08/94				
Sales	**7,286.0**	**8,502.0**	**10,241.0**	**1,289.0**	P/E Ratio	**19.4**	Price (9/30/95)	**320.00**
Net Income	**168.0**	**232.0**	**392.9**	**49.5**	P/B Ratio	**2.3**	52 Wk Hi-Low	**320.00-257.00**
Book Value	**2,632.0**	**3,039.0**	**3,267.3**	**422.7**	Yield %	**1.8**	Market Cap	**US$970.2mil**

Address **Perstorp AB**
284 80 Perstorp
Tel **0435-380-00**
Fax **0435-381-00**
ADR
SEDOL No. **4682459**
President & CEO **Gösta Wiking**
Chairman **Karl-Erik Sahlberg**

Pharmacia

Industry: **Pharmaceuticals**

Pharmacia is a pharmaceuticals and biotechnology company that sells its products in more than 100 countries. The company markets oncology, allergy, ophthalmic, nutrition, therapeutic, and hormone products. Pharmacia's name-brand products include growth hormone Genotropin; ophthalmic viscous liquid Healon; tumor-treatment drug Farmorubicin; and smoking-cessation drug Nicorette, which is available in skin patches, chewing gum, and nasal spray. European exports account for more than half of revenues; exports to non-European countries generate 40% of the company's revenues.

	SEK mil 12/92	12/93	12/94	US$mil 12/94				
Sales	**15,488.0**	**24,708.0**	**26,450.0**	**3,449.9**	P/E Ratio M	**16.1**	Price (9/30/95) M	**208.50**
Net Income	**3,433.0**	**2,667.0**	**3,279.0**	**427.7**	P/B Ratio M	**2.9**	52 Wk Hi-Low M	**210.00-113.50**
Book Value	**20,609.0**	**15,697.0**	**18,132.0**	**2,440.4**	Yield % M	**1.2**	Market Cap M	**US$4,956.0mil**

Address **Frösundaviks allé 15**
171 97 Stockholm
Tel **08-624-50-00**
Fax **08-655-80-10**
ADR **PHARY**
SEDOL No. **4704461**
President & CEO **Jan Ekberg**
Chairman **Sören Gyll**

M=Multiple issues in index; reflects most active.

Sandvik

Industry: **Industrial - Diversified**

Sandvik manufactures rock-drilling and metalworking tools, and engineering components. The firm's metalworking-tools division produces tools for drilling, turning, and milling, as well as systems, equipment, and software used to automate steelworking processes. The rock-drilling segment serves the mining and civil-engineering industries. Sandvik's engineering-components division makes production lines for specialized tasks, such as parcel sorting. European exports account for half of its sales; 43% of revenues come from outside Europe, and 7% from Sweden.

	SEK mil 12/92	12/93	12/94	US$mil 12/94				
Sales	**17,217.0**	**21,770.0**	**25,285.0**	**3,297.9**	P/E Ratio M	**15.1**	Price (9/30/95) M	**139.00**
Net Income	**1,112.0**	**1,069.0**	**2,436.0**	**317.7**	P/B Ratio M	**2.4**	52 Wk Hi-Low M	**147.00-108.00**
Book Value	**13,538.0**	**14,364.0**	**16,013.0**	**2,155.2**	Yield % M	**2.7**	Market Cap M	**US$4,196.6mil**

Address **Sandvik AB**
811 81 Sandviken
Tel **026-26-00-00**
Fax **026-26-13-50**
ADR **SAVKY**
SEDOL No. **4784883**
President & CEO **Clas Åke Hedström**
Chairman **Percy Barnevik**

M=Multiple issues in index; reflects most active.

SCA

Industry: **Paper Products**

Svenska Cellulosa (SCA) is Sweden's second-largest forestry and packaging group. The company operates through four main divisions: SCA Mölnlycke, which generated 45% of SCA's revenues in 1994, produces toiletries and tissue and clinical products; SCA Packaging produces corrugated board and container board; SCA Graphic Paper manufactures printing paper, fine paper, and pulp; and the SCA Timber division transports wood and provides sawn timber. Export sales to Europe account for 81% revenues, exports to the rest of the world 3%, and Sweden generates the remaining sales.

SEK mil	12/92	12/93	12/94	US$mil 12/94				
Sales	**32,137.0**	**33,420.0**	**33,676.0**	**4,392.3**	P/E Ratio M	**43.9**	Price (9/30/95) M	**125.50**
Net Income	**6,200.0**	**1,071.0**	**555.0**	**72.4**	P/B Ratio M	**1.2**	52 Wk Hi-Low M	**140.00-109.00**
Book Value	**18,284.0**	**19,963.0**	**19,590.0**	**2,636.6**	Yield % M	**3.0**	Market Cap M	**US$2,387.6mil**

Address **Stureplan 3**
103 97 Stockholm
Tel **08-788-51-00**
Fax **08-660-74-30**
ADR
SEDOL No. **4865379**
President & CEO **Sverker Martin-Löf**
Chairman **Bo Rydin**

M=Multiple issues in index; reflects most active.

S-E Banken

Industry: **Banks - Regional**

Skandinaviska Enskilda Banken (SE Banken) provides a full range of banking services to its private and institutional customers. The bank's SE Banken division offers its private customers (including small- and medium-size companies) deposit, loan, mortgage, life-insurance, mutual-fund, bond, and foreign-exchange trading services at more than 300 branches. Its Enskilda division provides services for large corporations, banks, and institutions. Its Diligentia division manages the bank's property portfolio. As of March 1995, SE Banken's total assets amounted to SEK411 billion.

SEK mil	12/92	12/93	12/94	US$mil 12/94				
Revenues	**57,188.0**	**46,148.0**	**36,349.0**	**4,741.0**	P/E Ratio	**86.3**	Price (9/30/95)	**44.90**
Net Income	**-4,762.0**	**1,172.0**	**211.0**	**27.5**	P/B Ratio	**1.0**	52 Wk Hi-Low	**48.90-33.40**
Book Value	**16,788.0**	**23,328.0**	**23,503.0**	**3,163.3**	Yield %	**3.3**	Market Cap	**US$3,247.5mil**

Address **Kungsträdgårdsgatan 8**
106 40 Stockholm
Tel **08-763-80-00**
Fax **08-763-83-93**
ADR
SEDOL No. **4813345**
Mng Dir & CEO **Björn Svedberg**
Chairman **Curt G. Olsson**

Skandia

Industry: **Insurance - Property & Casualty**

Skandia Group Forsikring is an insurance and financial-services company. Skandia offers pensions, reinsurance, and investment-management services. Its Skandia Norden subsidiary, which accounted for 54% of the company's premium income in 1994, offers life, health, marine, motor, and aviation insurance to individual and commercial customers. Its Skandia International division provides life and general insurance throughout Scandinavia, Europe, and the United States. Its SkandiaBanken subsidiary offers a full range of banking services to its Swedish customers.

SEK mil	12/92	12/93	12/94	US$mil 12/94				
Revenues	**28,915.0**	**27,269.0**	**22,095.0**	**2,881.8**	P/E Ratio	**NMF**	Price (9/30/95)	**163.50**
Net Income	**-2,369.0**	**1,384.0**	**-24.0**	**-3.1**	P/B Ratio	**2.0**	52 Wk Hi-Low	**168.50-110.00**
Book Value	**4,011.0**	**6,180.0**	**8,182.0**	**1,101.2**	Yield %	**1.2**	Market Cap	**US$2,414.8mil**

Address **Sveavägen 44**
103 50 Stockholm
Tel **08-788-10-00**
Fax **08-788-30-80**
ADR
SEDOL No. **4813141**
President & CEO **Björn Wolrath**
Chairman **Sven Söderberg**

Skanska

Industry: **Heavy Construction**

Skanska is a construction and real-estate company. It builds houses, commercial and industrial buildings, roads, railroads, and bridges. The company also supplies products such as prefabricated concrete, steel frames, roofs, and steel and glass doors and windows to the construction industry. The firm has operations in 44 countries, including real-estate interests in the U.K, the U.S., and Germany. Its construction division generates 76% of the company's total revenues. Non-European exports, primarily to the U.S., account for 23% of its revenues.

SEK mil	12/92	12/93	12/94	US$mil 12/94				
Sales	**32,178.0**	**31,635.0**	**37,527.0**	**4,894.6**	P/E Ratio	**9.9**	Price (9/30/95)	**212.00**
Net Income	**-3,101.0**	**517.0**	**2,691.0**	**351.0**	P/B Ratio	**2.7**	52 Wk Hi-Low	**216.50-138.00**
Book Value	**7,283.0**	**7,789.0**	**10,038.0**	**1,351.0**	Yield %	**1.8**	Market Cap	**US$3,572.7mil**

Address **Skanska AB**
182 25 Danderyd
Tel **08-753-88-00**
Fax **08-755-12-56**
ADR
SEDOL No. **4813431**
President & CEO **Melker Schörling**
Chairman **Percy Barnevik**

SKF

Industry: **Industrial - Diversified**

SKF is the world's largest manufacturer of roller bearings by market share. The company produces ball- and roller bearings for engines, machines, and wheels; lubricants; seals for machine components; measuring and control instruments; and specialty steels for the roller-bearing, auto, and engineering industries. Its customers include Caterpillar, Fiat, Volkswagen, Chrysler, and Ford. The ETR 500, an Italian high-speed train, also uses SKF bearings. Exports within Europe accounted for half of SKF's 1994 sales; non-European countries generated 45%, and Sweden 5%.

SEK mil	12/92	12/93	12/94	US$mil 12/94				
Sales	**26,649.0**	**29,200.0**	**33,273.0**	**4,339.8**	P/E Ratio M	**13.8**	Price (9/30/95) M	**153.00**
Net Income	**-1,704.0**	**-331.0**	**1,248.0**	**162.8**	P/B Ratio M	**1.8**	52 Wk Hi-Low M	**167.00-121.00**
Book Value	**8,930.0**	**9,009.0**	**9,872.0**	**1,328.7**	Yield % M	**2.8**	Market Cap M	**US$1,407.3mil**

Address **SKF AB**
415 50 Gothenburg
Tel **031-37-10-00**
Fax **031-37-28-32**
ADR **SKFRY**
SEDOL No. **4767066**
President & CEO **Mauritz Sahlin**
Chairman **Anders Scharp**

M=Multiple issues in index; reflects most active.

Stora

Industry: **Paper Products**

Stora Kopparbergs Bergslags is a forestry company that produces newsprint, fine paper, board and packaging paper, pulp, and sawn-timber products. The company's building-products division manufactures and markets doors, windows, and kitchen fittings. Its paper operations account for two-thirds of its sales revenue. Stora's total production capacity for pulp and paper products is 7.4 million tons. It supplies 5% of Sweden's electricity through its interest in thermal-, hydroelectric-, and nuclear-power stations. Stora markets its products in Europe and North America.

	SEK mil 12/92	12/93	12/94	US$mil 12/94				
Sales	**47,623.0**	**50,435.0**	**48,894.0**	**6,377.2**	P/E Ratio	**14.9**	Price (9/30/95)	**94.50**
Net Income	**-1,115.0**	**651.0**	**2,038.0**	**265.8**	P/B Ratio	**1.2**	52 Wk Hi-Low	**110.00-78.80**
Book Value	**21,803.0**	**21,789.0**	**24,131.0**	**3,247.8**	Yield %	**2.1**	Market Cap	**US$3,569.9mil**

Address	**Åsgatan 22**	Tel	**023-78-00-00**	ADR		President & CEO	**Lars-Åke Helgesson**
	791 80 Falun	Fax	**023-138-58**	SEDOL No.	**4810584**	Chairman	**Bo Berggren**

Svedala Industri

Industry: **Heavy Machinery**

Svedala Industri develops, manufactures, and markets equipment and systems for mineral processing and materials handling. It also manufactures screens, noise-supression systems, and conveyor belts for the construction industry. Svedala has subsidiaries in more than 40 countries. In 1995, the company acquired Skega, producers of abrasive-resistant rubber products and South African pump- and processing-systems manufacturer Unique Engineering. In 1994, Europe generated 42% of Svedala's revenues, North America 27%, and the rest of the world 31%.

	SEK mil 12/92	12/93	12/94	US$mil 12/94				
Sales	**8,149.0**	**10,318.0**	**10,344.0**	**1,349.2**	P/E Ratio	**11.6**	Price (9/30/95)	**209.00**
Net Income	**-129.0**	**-14.0**	**426.0**	**55.6**	P/B Ratio	**2.1**	52 Wk Hi-Low	**225.00-153.00**
Book Value	**1,615.0**	**2,016.0**	**2,388.0**	**321.4**	Yield %	**2.4**	Market Cap	**US$713.8mil**

Address	**PO Box 4004**	Tel	**040-24-58-00**	ADR		President & CEO	**Thomas Oldér**
	203 11 Malmo	Fax	**040-97-92-80**	SEDOL No.	**4863016**	Chairman	**Rune Andersson**

Swedish Commercial

Industry: **Banks - Regional**

Swedish Commercial Bank (Svenska Handelsbanken) is one of the largest commercial banks in Sweden. The bank lends to both individuals and companies. Svenska Handelsbanken also offers life insurance and pensions, and provides investment-banking services. Its wholly-owned Handelsbanken Hypotek subsidiary provides mortgages. The company has about 487 branches in Sweden, 22 elsewhere in Europe, several in the Far East, and one each in Australia and the United States. At year-end 1994, the bank had assets totaling roughly SEK400 billion.

	SEK mil 12/92	12/93	12/94	US$mil 12/94				
Revenues	**46,824.0**	**40,414.0**	**34,441.0**	**4,492.1**	P/E Ratio M	**11.8**	Price (9/30/95) M	**120.00**
Net Income	**-525.0**	**1,704.0**	**2,404.0**	**313.6**	P/B Ratio M	**1.2**	52 Wk Hi-Low M	**124.00-85.50**
Book Value	**17,089.0**	**21,577.0**	**22,771.0**	**3,064.7**	Yield % M	**2.5**	Market Cap M	**US$3,590.7mil**

Address	**Kungsträdgårdsgatan 2**	Tel	**08-701-10-00**	ADR		President & CEO	**Arne Mårtensson**
	106 70 Stockholm	Fax	**08-723-06-25**	SEDOL No.	**4868635**	Chairman	**Tom Hedelius**

M=Multiple issues in index; reflects most active.

Sydkraft

Industry: **Electrical Utilities - All**

Sydkraft is a utilities holding company. Its 70 wholly- or partially-owned subsidiaries operate in the electric, natural-gas, solid-fuel, consulting, and liquefied-petroleum-gas industries. Nuclear-power plants generate 38% of its 6,500 MW electricity capacity, hydropower plants 35%, fossil-fuel plants 18%, and gas-turbine plants 9%. Sydkraft distributes natural and liquefied petroleum gas and sells heating systems and products. The company provides consulting and contracting services to the electricity and telecommunication industries.

	SEK mil 12/92	12/93	12/94	US$mil 12/94				
Sales	**9,500.0**	**11,637.0**	**12,118.0**	**1,580.5**	P/E Ratio M	**18.5**	Price (9/30/95) M	**141.00**
Net Income	**1,185.0**	**2,122.0**	**1,358.0**	**177.1**	P/B Ratio M	**2.0**	52 Wk Hi-Low M	**141.00-91.00**
Book Value	**10,103.0**	**11,827.0**	**13,712.0**	**1,845.5**	Yield % M	**2.3**	Market Cap M	**US$2,260.6mil**

Address	**Carl Gustafs Väg 1**	Tel	**040-25-50-00**	ADR		President & CEO	**Göran Ahlström**
	205 09 Malmo	Fax	**040-97-60-69**	SEDOL No.	**4869337**	Chairman	**Joakim Ollén**

M=Multiple issues in index; reflects most active.

Trelleborg

Industry: **Non-Ferrous Metals - Other (Exc. Aluminum)**

Trelleborg mines and processes copper, lead, zinc, nickel, silver, and gold, and manufactures rubber products. Its Boliden Mineral subsidiary, which accounts for 25% of sales in 1994, operates 12 mines in Sweden and abroad, producing nonferrous metals and concentrates. Boliden Metals manufactures brass-rod, tubings, and lead alloys. Trelleborg Industri makes rubber products for a range of industries. The company's 70 Ahlsell stores make it Sweden's largest heating and plumbing wholesaler. Trelleborg also operates a steel and metals wholesale business.

	SEK mil 12/92	12/93	12/94	US$mil 12/94				
Sales	**23,125.0**	**21,617.0**	**19,135.0**	**2,495.8**	P/E Ratio	**14.6**	Price (9/30/95)	**82.00**
Net Income	**-1,239.0**	**-1,142.0**	**652.0**	**85.0**	P/B Ratio	**1.5**	52 Wk Hi-Low	**120.50-79.50**
Book Value	**6,171.0**	**5,964.0**	**6,470.0**	**870.8**	Yield %	**1.2**	Market Cap	**US$1,141.2mil**

Address	**Nygatan 102**	Tel	**0410-670-00**	ADR		President & CEO	**Kjell Nilsson**
	231 22 Trelleborg	Fax	**0410-427-63**	SEDOL No.	**4902384**	Chairman	**Rune Andersson**

Volvo

Industry: **Automobile Manufacturers**

Volvo is a diversified industrial firm that manufactures cars, trucks, and buses. It produced 351,700 cars, 69,200 trucks, and 5,770 buses in 1994. Volvo also makes generators and marine and industrial engines for commercial and leisure craft. It gained full ownership of construction- and earthmoving-equipment maker VME (now Volvo Construction Equipment) in 1995 after buying out U.S. partner Clark Equipment. It also acquired bus manufacturer Prevost Car of Canada. Europe accounted for 59% of Volvo's 1994 sales, North America 25%, and the rest of the world 16%.

	SEK mil 12/92	12/93	12/94	US$mil 12/94				
Sales	**83,002.0**	**111,155.0**	**155,866.0**	**20,329.5**	P/E Ratio M	**5.3**	Price (9/30/95) M	**169.00**
Net Income	**-3,320.0**	**-3,466.0**	**13,230.0**	**1,725.6**	P/B Ratio M	**1.7**	52 Wk Hi-Low M	**177.00-122.50**
Book Value	**29,721.0**	**27,088.0**	**43,332.0**	**5,832.0**	Yield % M	**2.0**	Market Cap M	**US$3,466.6mil**

Address **Volvo AB**
405 08 Gothenburg
Tel **031-59-00-00**
Fax **031-54-79-59**
ADR **VOLVY**
SEDOL No. **4937728**
Managing Director **Sören Gyll**
Chairman **Bert-Olof Svanholm**

M=Multiple issues in index; reflects most active.

Switzerland

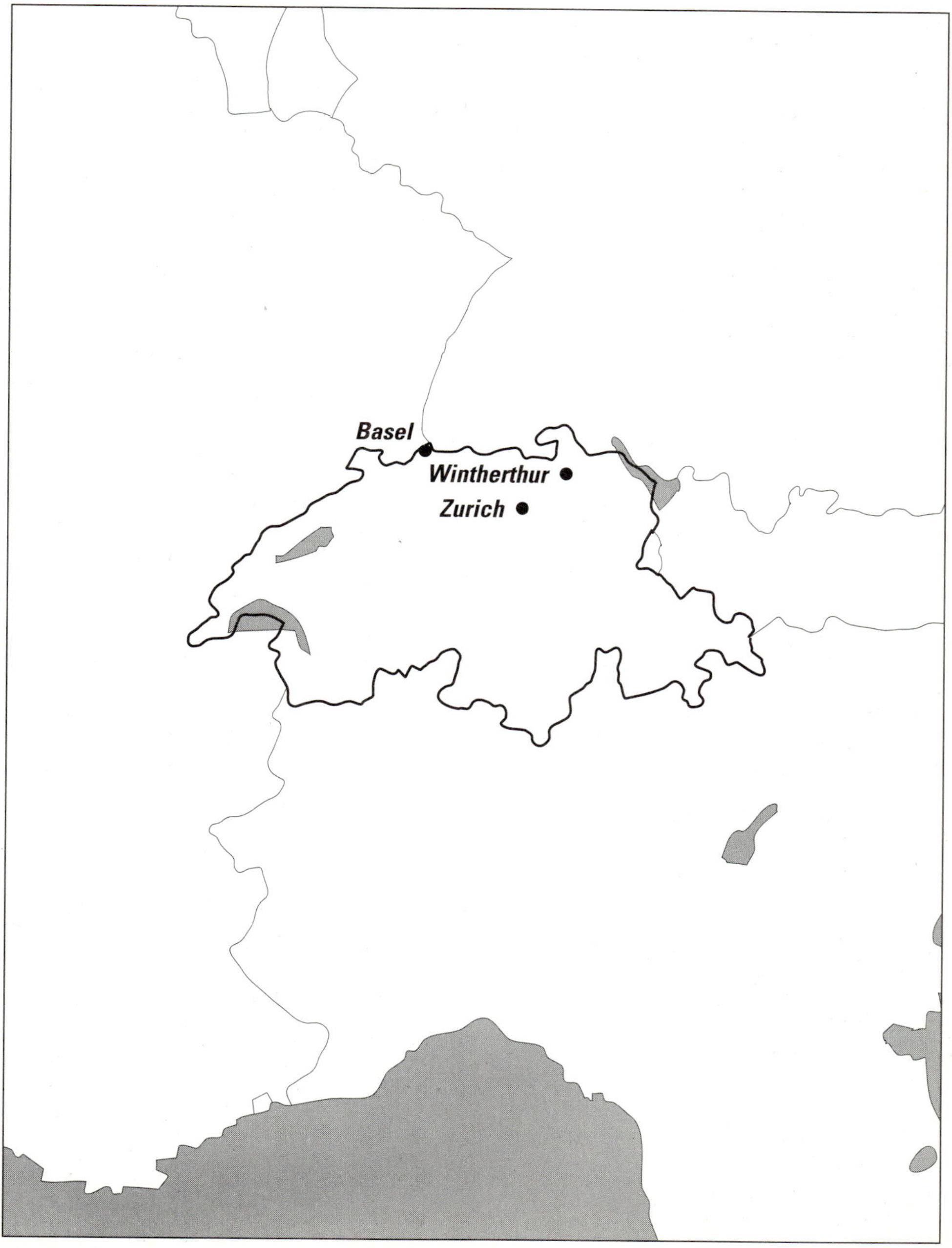

Switzerland

**Alastair McIndoe,
Zurich**

Local Trading Hours	Time Difference with New York	Population (Est. 94)
10:00-1:00 and 2:00-4:00	6 hours ahead	7,040,000

The foyer of a Zurich theatre provided an untypically flamboyant venue for the first meeting in 1855 of the "Friday Exchange," where Swiss stocks were first traded. Switzerland once had seven different bourses, but these have been whittled down to three — Zurich, Basel and Geneva, with Zurich being biggest by far.

The open-outcry system still being practiced on Swiss trading floors will shortly be replaced by electronic trading. As a result, the three bourses will be integrated into a single network operated by the Swiss Exchange.

Electronic trading, which has suffered numerous start-up setbacks, is likely to be launched in early 1996. Once running, it should increase liquidity and give investors a clearer picture of what is happening in the market. The Swiss Options and Financial Futures Exchange (SOFFEX) has been automated since its inception in 1988. Swiss Exchange has owned SOFFEX since 1994 and it will also operate the Swiss Electronic Exchange. A common trading system for underlying and standardized derivatives will be available by 1997.

The Zurich stock exchange is dominated by a clutch of heavyweights, most notably food group Nestle SA — the market's main defensive stock — and pharmaceutical major Roche Holding AG. Both stocks accounted for a combined 35% of the total market capitalization of 282 billion francs at end-July 1995 of the Swiss Market Index (SMI). The index comprises the 21 leading issues of 17 Swiss companies and is the most widely followed market indicator by foreign investors. Some 252 companies are listed on the all-share Swiss Performance Index (SPI). The SMI has a strong showing in financial stocks, including the banking majors Union Bank of Switzerland, Swiss Bank Corp. and CS Holding and the country's three main insurance groups. All these stocks are easily tradeable, as are the stocks of the Basel-based drug companies Roche, Ciba-Geigy AG and Sandoz AG. BBC Brown Boveri AG, co-owner of heavy engineering group ABB Asea Brown Boveri AG, is the SMI's main industrial issue.

Dow Jones Switzerland Equity Market Index Performance

Local currency One-year change: + 19.43%
Dollar One-year change: + 33.07%

Within the SMI's three main sectors — banks, insurers and pharmaceuticals — investors have a varied choice of highly-liquid blue chips. This, however, is not the case with other sectors, such as food, construction and services. Cementmaker Holderbank

Gross Domestic Product (94)	Three-Year Average GDP Growth (92-94)	Main Industries	Consumer Price Index (94)	Monetary Unit	Exchange Rate (9/95)
$259 billion	0.1%	Pharmaceuticals, chemicals, financial services, machinemaking, tourism and watchmaking	0.9%	Swiss franc	Sfr1.16 to US$1.00

Financiere Glarus AG, for instance, accounts for around two-thirds of the market capitalization of the construction sector and Nestle 95% of the foods.

The make-up of the broad SPI is heavily skewed towards the industrial sector, which includes a batch of important second-line issues, such as construction chemicals group Sika Finanz AG, and engineers, such as liftmaker Schindler AG.

Trading is dominated by British and U.S. institutional investors — the Anglo-Saxons as they are termed by Swiss "boersianer" — and the large Swiss pension funds. What differentiates the two is that foreign investors are more demanding of a company's transparency. Similarly, the foreign lobby has exerted the most pressure on corporate Switzerland to provide a higher standard of reporting and shareholder information. Most blue chips now adhere to International Accounting Standards or to European Union accounting norms. Past accounting practice was highly arbitrary.

Official trading on the Zurich bourse is between 10:00 a.m and 4:00 p.m, with an hour's recess from 1:00 p.m. All stocks can be handled prebourse, which is often marked by block trades. The market for second address-issues is usually thin. The daily trade volume of Swiss stocks varies from 700 million to just under 2 billion francs.

The bigger Swiss companies have striven in recent years to simplify their share structures by generally opting for one category of share. Hitherto, three types of issues — registered, bearer and participation certificates — were possible. In essence, granting or withholding voting rights differentiates the three classes. Streamlining this structure was aimed primarily at making Swiss shares more attractive to foreign investors and — a distant second — to coopt small investors. This process is largely complete. Meanwhile, medium and smaller-sized companies are also reforming their share structure, but at a more leisurely pace.

Ten Largest Capitalized Companies
as of 9/30/95

Stock	Market Cap. US$Mil
Nestlé	41,152,082.8
Union Bank of Switzerland	21,139,503.4
Roche	19,448,275.9
CS Holding	17,125,415.5
Zurich Insurance	13,878,931.0
Swiss Reinsurance	13,661,310.3
Swiss Bank	9,115,869.0
BBC Brown Boveri	8,933,207.8
Richemont	6,660,000.0
Winterthur	4,737,200.0

One drawback of the Swiss market is the absence of a large scale privatization programme by the Bern government that would lead to the flotation of state enterprises. Such a programme would undeniably enhance the attractiveness of the Swiss market for foreign investors. For one, it means that compared with Britain and Germany, investors have fewer choices of telecommunication, transport and utility issues. However, a long dearth of new listings appears to have been recently broken by a sprinkling of small flotations and, more importantly, Sandoz spinning off its speciality chemicals activities into a new medium-sized company.

Another long-standing bone of contention is Switzerland's loophole-ridden takeover code. However, a new stock exchange law that is to be implemented by mid-1996 to replace the code is expected to bring improvements, particularly for leveraged buyouts. People trading on the Zurich bourse say that Swiss companies have so far been reluctant to change their statutes limiting investor voting rights to 3-7% of total votes. This means that investors, and most notably the large institutions, have a limited voice in how a company is run and in influencing strategy. This situation is also aggravated by the lethargic attitude of domestic institutions in trying to change a company's policy even if a clear need for change is indeed perceived.

No major changes in the tax treatment of foreign investors have been made in the last few years. In essence, foreign investors pay a 35% witholding tax on dividends but this is retrievable — albeit in a lengthy process. A small stamp duty is also levied on share transactions, but this is not regarded as punitive. From 1996, Switzerland's labyrinthal tax laws relating to share ownership, which often vary from canton to canton, will also be harmonized under the federal stock exchange law.

After a very strong 1993 and a lackluster 1994, Swiss shares, driven by falling interest rates, are likely to advance markedly in 1995 despite an extremely detrimental currency situation. The strong Swiss franc has made Swiss stocks relatively expensive for some foreign investors, while the weak dollar has depressed many export-orientated issues. A strong performance is also being pencilled in for 1996 on a favorable interest rate environment and a robuster dollar. A further fillip for Swiss stocks in 1996 may also come from the increased participation of institutional investors from continental Europe, and especially Germany. Any rekindling of uncertainty within the European exchange rate mechanism will enhance the attractiveness of the Swiss market as a safe haven for foreign investor funds.

Aare-Tessin

Industry: **Electrical Utilities - All**

Aare-Tessin für Elektrizität produces, transports, and distributes energy. It serves customers in Switzerland's northwestern and southern regions, including the cantons of Solothurn, Basel-Land, Aargau, and Ticino. It has interests in 11 hydroelectric-, one thermal-, and three nuclear-power plants. Its wholly-owned subsidiary Colenco produces energy-distribution systems. Diversified energy firm Motor-Columbus has a 55% stake in parent company Aare-Tessin. European Community countries generate more than 55% of the company's total revenue.

	SFr mil 12/92 *	12/93	12/94	US$mil 12/94				
Sales	**1,405.0**	**1,516.0**	**1,532.0**	**1,125.6**	P/E Ratio	**16.0**	Price (9/30/95)	**750.00**
Net Income	**93.0**	**117.0**	**142.0**	**104.3**	P/B Ratio	**2.6**	52 Wk Hi-Low	**780.00-560.00**
Book Value	**723.0**	**780.0**	**878.0**	**670.2**	Yield %	**2.4**	Market Cap	**US$1,635.8mil**

Address	**Bahnhofquai 12**	Tel	**062-31-71-11**	ADR		CEO	**Walter Bürgi**
	4601 Olten	Fax	**062-31-73-73**	SEDOL No.	**4002790**	Chairman	**Angelo Pozzi**

*Irregular period due to fiscal year change.

Adia

Industry: **General Industrial & Commercial Services**

Adia is an international temporary-personnel agency that provides local, regional, and global services in auditing, consulting, placement, outplacement, and temporary help. It specializes in the areas of business administration, data processing, engineering and construction, and tourism. In 1995, Adia merged with its U.S.-based subsidiary Adia Services. The company has offices in 27 countries, but operates primarily in Europe, North America, and the Far East. Europe accounts for about 43% of revenues, North America 46%, and the rest of the world 11%.

	SFr mil 12/92	12/93	12/94	US$mil 12/94				
Sales	**3,212.0**	**3,114.0**	**3,541.9**	**2,602.4**	P/E Ratio	**42.2**	Price (9/30/95)	**210.00**
Net Income	**-219.0**	**-127.0**	**32.4**	**23.8**	P/B Ratio	**6.9**	52 Wk Hi-Low	**246.00-198.00**
Book Value	**31.0**	**324.0**	**221.9**	**169.4**	Yield %	**0.0**	Market Cap	**US$1,174.0mil**

Address	**Place Chauderon 4**	Tel	**021-341-02-00**	ADR	**ADIAY**	CEO	**John P. Bowmer**
	1003 Lausanne	Fax	**021-23-40-90**	SEDOL No.	**4007029**	Chairman	**Klaus J. Jacobs**

Alusuisse-Lonza

Industry: **Aluminum**

Alusuisse-Lonza Holding is a diversified holding company with subsidiaries that manufacture chemicals, aluminum and graphite materials, packaging, and automotive components. Its organic chemicals are used in the production of pharmaceuticals, food additives, and fertilizers. Alusuisse-Lonza's Canadian subsidiary Lawson Mardin provides packaging for clients in the food, pharmaceutical, and cosmetics industries. In 1994, the company's packaging interests generated 37% of its profits, aluminum activities 34%, and chemical subsidiaries 22%

	SFr mil 12/92	12/93	12/94	US$mil 12/94				
Sales	**6,547.0**	**6,188.0**	**7,499.0**	**5,509.9**	P/E Ratio M	**25.3**	Price (9/30/95) M	**861.00**
Net Income	**119.0**	**82.0**	**207.0**	**152.1**	P/B Ratio M	**3.0**	52 Wk Hi-Low M	**898.00-605.00**
Book Value	**1,608.0**	**1,853.0**	**1,775.0**	**1,355.0**	Yield % M	**1.7**	Market Cap M	**US$1,502.3mil**

Address	**Feldeggstr. 4**	Tel	**01-386-22-22**	ADR		CEO	**Theodor M. Tschopp**
	8034 Zurich	Fax	**01-386-25-85**	SEDOL No.	**4023984**	Chairman	**Hans K. Jucker**

M=Multiple issues in index; reflects most active.

BBC Brown Boveri

Industry: **Electrical Components & Equipment**

BBC Brown Boveri is a holding company with a 50% stake in the power and industrial firm ABB Asea Brown Boveri. ABB serves customers in the areas of electrical power generation, transmission and distribution, industrial and building systems, and rail-transportation. In 1995, ABB Brown Boveri and Daimler-Benz announced plans to merge their rail-transportation operations. Daimler agreed to make a cash payment of $900 million to ABB as part of the transaction. More than half of ABB's sales come from Europe, 20% from North America, and 24% from Africa and Australasia.

	SFr mil 12/92	12/93	12/94	US$mil 12/94				
Sales	**41,165.0**	**41,906.0**	**40,714.0**	**29,914.8**	P/E Ratio M	**116.8**	Price (9/30/95) M	**1,339.00**
Net Income	**347.0**	**88.0**	**1,041.2**	**765.0**	P/B Ratio M	**11.8**	52 Wk Hi-Low M	**1,399.0-1,023.0**
Book Value	**3,155.0**	**3,079.0**	**5,262.0**	**4,016.8**	Yield % M	**0.3**	Market Cap M	**US$8,933.2mil**

Address	**BBC Brown Boveri**	Tel	**056-757-700**	ADR	**BBCBY**	President	**B.H. Müller-Berghoff**
	5401 Baden	Fax	**056-221-026**	SEDOL No.	**4127187**	Chairman	**David de Pury**

M=Multiple issues in index; reflects most active.

Bobst

Industry: **Factory Equipment**

Bobst is an engineering firm that specializes in machinery for the printing and packaging industries. The company manufactures printing presses, offset presses, paperboard-processing machinery, and electronic equipment for rotary presses. Its machinery is used to produce packaging for Toblerone chocolate, Kodak film, and Rothmans cigarettes. Bobst has operations in 100 countries. More than half of its 1994 sales were generated in Europe, the United States accounted for 22% of sales, and the rest of the world generated 17%.

	SFr mil 12/92	12/93	12/94	US$mil 12/94				
Sales	**1,013.0**	**933.0**	**1,052.6**	**773.4**	P/E Ratio M	**16.5**	Price (9/30/95) M	**1,780.00**
Net Income	**65.0**	**45.0**	**60.5**	**44.5**	P/B Ratio M	**1.2**	52 Wk Hi-Low M	**1,950.0-1,480.0**
Book Value	**795.0**	**813.0**	**844.6**	**644.7**	Yield % M	**1.4**	Market Cap M	**US$537.1mil**

Address	**50 route des Flumeaux**	Tel	**021-621-2111**	ADR		CEO	**Pierre Baroffio**
	1008 Prilly-Lausanne	Fax	**021-24-11-70**	SEDOL No.	**4130613**	Chairman	**Bruno de Kalbermatten**

M=Multiple issues in index; reflects most active.

Ciba-Geigy

Industry: **Pharmaceuticals**

Ciba-Geigy is a diversified chemical firm that makes pharmaceutical, agricultural, consumer, and industrial products. The company produces agents that treat cardiovascular diseases, diseases of the central nervous systems, and allergies. Its brand-name products include NewVues contact lenses, Maalox antacid, and the Habitrol nicotine transdermal patch. Ciba-Geigy owns a 50% stake in U.S.-based biotechnology firm Chiron and owns the U.S. and Canadian over-the-counter business of Rhone-Polenc Rorer. Non-European exports generate 52% of Ciba-Geigy's revenues.

	SFr mil 12/92	12/93	12/94	US$mil 12/94				
Sales	**22,204.0**	**22,647.0**	**22,049.0**	**16,200.6**	P/E Ratio M	**13.6**	Price (9/30/95) M	**923.00**
Net Income	**1,520.0**	**1,779.0**	**1,913.0**	**1,405.6**	P/B Ratio M	**1.8**	52 Wk Hi-Low M	**932.00-705.00**
Book Value	**18,064.0**	**17,080.0**	**15,480.0**	**11,816.8**	Yield % M	**1.8**	Market Cap M	**US$2,979.9mil**

Address	**Klybeckstr. 141**	Tel	**061-696-1111**	ADR	**CBGXY**	CEO	**Alex Krauer**
	4057 Basel	Fax	**061-697-2539**	SEDOL No.	**4193445**	Chairman	**Alex Krauer**

M=Multiple issues in index; reflects most active.

CS Holding

Industry: **Financial Services - Diversified**

CS Holding is a major diversified banking and financial-services holding company. The company offers full-service banking, investment banking, life insurance, securities trading, asset management, and other nonfinancial services. Its holdings include full-service bank Credit Suisse, investment bank CS First Boston Group, insurer CS Life, and investment advisor Leu Holding. CS Holding also has a 48% stake in Electrowatt, a holding company for utility, service, and industrial operations.

	SFr mil 12/92	12/93	12/94	US$mil 12/94				
Revenues	**8,980.0**	**13,813.0**	**19,476.0**	**14,310.1**	P/E Ratio	**13.9**	Price (9/30/95)	**108.50**
Net Income	**1,028.0**	**1,709.0**	**1,331.0**	**978.0**	P/B Ratio	**1.2**	52 Wk Hi-Low	**114.00-90.75**
Book Value	**8,467.0**	**13,370.0**	**16,299.0**	**12,442.0**	Yield %	**3.3**	Market Cap	**US$17,125mil**

Address	**Nüschelerstr. 1**	Tel	**01-212-16-16**	ADR	**CSHKY**	CEO	**Rainer E. Gut**
	8021 Zurich	Fax	**01-212-06-69**	SEDOL No.	**4245614**	Chairman	**Rainer E. Gut**

Elektrowatt

Industry: **Electrical Utilities - All**

Elektrowatt is a holding company with interests in the energy, construction, engineering, and information-technology industries. It owns hydroelectric-, nuclear-, and solar-power plants in Switzerland and southern Germany. Electrowatt also makes electronic components, and installs fire-protection and power-distribution equipment and security systems. The industrial products division contributed 45% of the company's net income. The company is 44%-owned by diversified banking and financial-services firm CS Holding.

	SFr mil 09/92	09/93	09/94	US$mil 09/94				
Sales	**4,608.0**	**4,739.0**	**4,943.0**	**3,513.1**	P/E Ratio	**16.4**	Price (9/30/95)	**355.00**
Net Income	**153.0**	**176.0**	**172.0**	**122.2**	P/B Ratio	**2.0**	52 Wk Hi-Low	**370.00-280.00**
Book Value	**1,665.0**	**1,641.0**	**1,678.0**	**1,300.8**	Yield %	**3.2**	Market Cap	**US$2,434.2mil**

Address	**Bellerivestr. 36**	Tel	**01-385-22-11**	ADR		President	**Oskar K. Ronner**
	8022 Zurich	Fax	**01-385-25-55**	SEDOL No.	**4279215**	Chairman	**Adolf Gugler**

EMS-Chemie

Industry: **Commodity Chemicals**

EMS-Chemie Holding is a diversified chemicals company that produces engineering polymers, adhesives, and protective coatings for a range of industries. EMS-TOGO supplies coating, bonding and sealing products to the automotive industry and EMS-Dottikon produces intermediate substances for chemicals and pharmaceuticals companies. The company also makes electric-ignition systems, builds industrial plants specializing in polymer and fiber production, and operates its own power stations. In 1994, 30% of EMS' sales were to non-European countries.

	SFr mil 12/92	12/93	12/94	US$mil 12/94				
Sales	**845.0**	**830.0**	**856.5**	**629.3**	P/E Ratio	**23.0**	Price (9/30/95)	**5,270.00**
Net Income	**176.0**	**202.0**	**144.0**	**105.8**	P/B Ratio	**3.2**	52 Wk Hi-Low	**5,360.0-3,485.0**
Book Value	**815.0**	**944.0**	**846.7**	**646.3**	Yield %	**0.0**	Market Cap	**US$2,189.8mil**

Address	**Selnaustr. 16**	Tel	**01-284-18-80**	ADR		CEO	**Christoph Blocher**
	8039 Zurich	Fax	**01-284-18-99**	SEDOL No.	**4295523**	Chairman	**Christoph Blocher**

Holderbank

Industry: **Building Materials**

Holderbank Financière Glarus is a holding company with operations in the building-materials industry by sales. It provides ready-mix concrete, cement, aggregates, and concrete chemicals. Holderbank's cement and clinker operations account for 57% of sales, and readymix concrete and aggregates sales account for 24%. The company's subsidiaries include French cement producer Cedest, St. Lawrence Cement of Canada, and cement producer Holnam of the United States. Non-European exports account for more than half of the company's revenues.

	SFr mil 12/92	12/93	12/94	US$mil 12/94				
Sales	**7,836.0**	**8,428.0**	**8,428.0**	**6,192.5**	P/E Ratio M	**66.5**	Price (9/30/95) M	**908.00**
Net Income	**261.0**	**287.0**	**287.0**	**210.9**	P/B Ratio M	**4.0**	52 Wk Hi-Low M	**1,068.0-782.0**
Book Value	**3,005.0**	**3,319.0**	**3,319.0**	**2,533.6**	Yield % M	**0.4**	Market Cap M	**US$3,075.5mil**

Address	**Zürcherstr. 170**	Tel	**055-27-01-01**	ADR		Managing Director	**Thomas Schmidheiny**
	8645 Jona	Fax	**055-27-01-27**	SEDOL No.	**4420499**	Chairman	**Thomas Schmidheiny**

M=Multiple issues in index; reflects most active.

Landis & Gyr

Industry: **Diversified Technology**

Landis & Gyr manufactures energy-management, climate-control, and communication products. The company's main divisions produce metering and billing devices for utilities companies and control systems for heating, ventilation, and air-conditioning equipment. The company's communication division makes intercoms and coin- and card-operated payphones. In 1994, Europe accounted for two thirds of revenues. Landis & Gyr's commercial- and residential-building-control divisions accounted for nearly 60% of revenues in 1994. Unotec Holding owns 35% of Landis & Gyr.

	SFr mil 09/92	09/93	09/94	US$mil 09/94				
Sales	**2,982.0**	**2,897.0**	**2,900.0**	**2,061.1**	P/E Ratio	**11.8**	Price (9/30/95)	**705.00**
Net Income	**78.0**	**97.0**	**111.7**	**79.4**	P/B Ratio	**1.2**	52 Wk Hi-Low	**820.00-625.00**
Book Value	**1,070.0**	**1,120.0**	**1,154.2**	**894.7**	Yield %	**2.0**	Market Cap	**US$1,145.6mil**

Address **Grafenauweg 10**	Tel **042-24-11-24**	ADR	President & CEO	**Dr. Willy Kissling**
6301 Zug	Fax **042-24-35-22**	SEDOL No. **4510936**	Chairman	**Dr. Georg Krneta**

Merkur

Industry: **Restaurants**

Merkur is a diversified retailer that operates kiosk and mail-order retail businesses and vending machines. It also has wholesale trade operations in newspapers and books; produces and sells beds and mattresses; and invests in commercial real estate. Merkur's bedding interests are represented by market leaders Müller-Imhoof in Switzerland and Epéda and Mérinos in France. Retail trade and restaurants account for more than 40% of revenues. Merkur won a bid to supply more than 2,000 vending machines throughout the Paris Metro.

	SFr mil 12/92	12/93	12/94	US$mil 12/94				
Sales	**2,528.0**	**2,708.0**	**2,917.5**	**2,143.6**	P/E Ratio	**11.5**	Price (9/30/95)	**266.00**
Net Income	**71.0**	**83.0**	**93.6**	**68.7**	P/B Ratio	**1.6**	52 Wk Hi-Low	**350.00-266.00**
Book Value	**606.0**	**623.0**	**671.3**	**512.4**	Yield %	**3.0**	Market Cap	**US$963.1mil**

Address **Fellerstr. 15**	Tel **031-990-2020**	ADR	CEO	**Fritz Frohofer**
3027 Bern	Fax **031-990-2801**	SEDOL No. **4581619**	Chairman	**Georg Krneta**

Motor-Columbus

Industry: **Electrical Utilities - All**

Motor-Columbus is a holding company and through its subsidiaries generates, transmits, and distributes electricity, and operates environmental-consulting and engineering services. After restructuring the company, Motor-Columbus now focuses on its electricity and engineering operations. It is 74% owned by Union Bank of Switzerland (UBS). Motor-Columbus has a 54% stake in Swiss energy producer Aare-Tessin für Elektrizität (Atel). Atel supplies and distributes electricity to southern Switzerland and Italy.

	SFr mil 12/92	12/93	12/94	US$mil 12/94				
Sales	**1,861.0**	**1,540.0**	**1,532.0**	**1,125.6**	P/E Ratio	**7.6**	Price (9/30/95)	**1,900.00**
Net Income	**-225.0**	**181.0**	**126.0**	**92.6**	P/B Ratio	**4.3**	52 Wk Hi-Low	**2,160.0-1,660.0**
Book Value	**N/A**	**148.0**	**223.0**	**170.2**	Yield %	**0.0**	Market Cap	**US$982.8mil**

Address **Parkstr. 27**	Tel **056-30-11-11**	ADR	CEO	**Dr. Ernst Thomke**
5401 Baden	Fax **056-21-13-29**	SEDOL No. **4606523**	Chairman	**Dr. Heinrich Steinmann**

Nestlé

Industry: **Other Food**

Nestlé is one of the world's largest food producers, and is also a leading producer of beverages, dairy products, pharmaceuticals, and pet foods. The firm's drinks, which account for more than 28% of its sales, include Nescafé instant coffee, Hills Brothers coffee, and Perrier mineral water. Additional products include Nestlé, KitKat, and Baci chocolate; Stouffer and Lean Cuisine frozen foods; Carnation Good Start infant formula; and Friskies and Fancy Feast cat food. European sales generate 46% of revenues, North and South America 36%, and the rest of the world 18%.

	SFr mil 12/92	12/93	12/94	US$mil 12/94				
Sales	**54,500.0**	**57,486.0**	**56,894.0**	**41,803.1**	P/E Ratio	**14.1**	Price (9/30/95)	**1,183.00**
Net Income	**2,698.0**	**2,887.0**	**3,250.0**	**2,388.0**	P/B Ratio	**2.8**	52 Wk Hi-Low	**1,268.0-1,087.0**
Book Value	**13,930.0**	**15,660.0**	**16,944.0**	**12,934.4**	Yield %	**2.2**	Market Cap	**US$41,152mil**

Address **Ave. Nestlé 55**	Tel **021-924-2526**	ADR **NSRGY**	CEO	**Helmut O. Maucher**
1800 Vevey	Fax **021-921-1885**	SEDOL No. **4616696**	Chairman	**Helmut O. Maucher**

Oerlikon-Bührle

Industry: **Conglomerates**

Oerlikon-Bührle, a conglomerate that operates defense businesses, retailing activities, and hotels, also offers contracting services and manages real estate. Its Oerlikon-Contraves subsidiary produces antiaircraft guns and missile systems, ammunition, aircraft, and aircraft parts. Its Bally retail division operates 506 stores that sell shoes, accessories, and clothing. Its Kunz and Dietfurt division sells yarns, threads, and grey fabrics. The firm owns the Hotel Zürich, zum Storchen, and Ascot hotels. Overseas exports accounted for 21% of revenues in 1994.

	SFr mil 12/92	12/93	12/94	US$mil 12/94				
Sales	**3,568.0**	**2,993.0**	**3,573.0**	**2,625.3**	P/E Ratio	**15.2**	Price (9/30/95)	**91.00**
Net Income	**33.0**	**55.0**	**70.0**	**51.4**	P/B Ratio	**0.9**	52 Wk Hi-Low	**141.00-85.00**
Book Value	**1,165.0**	**1,203.0**	**1,192.0**	**909.9**	Yield %	**0.0**	Market Cap	**US$959.4mil**

Address **Hofwiesenstr. 135**	Tel **01-363-40-60**	ADR	President	**--**
8021 Zurich	Fax **01-363-72-60**	SEDOL No. **4612757**	Chairman	**Dr. Hans Widmer**

Richemont

Industry: **Tobacco**

Compagnie Financière Richemont is a holding company whose main businesses are in tobacco and luxury goods. The company also has interests in the retail and electronic-media industries. Richemont holds a 60% interest in tobacco company Rothmans International and a 70% interest in Vendôme Luxury Group, whose products include jewelry, watches, leather goods, fragrances, menswear, and womens' fashions, marketed under brand names such as Cartier, Alfred Dunhill, and Karl Lagerfeld. In 1994, Richemont acquired 25% of Telepiù, the Italian pay-television operator.

	SFr mil 03/93	03/94	03/95	US$mil 03/95				
Sales	**3,443.0**	**3,665.0**	**3,852.1**	**2,951.8**	P/E Ratio	**30.4**	Price (9/30/95)	**1,480.00**
Net Income	**208.0**	**115.0**	**279.6**	**214.3**	P/B Ratio	**NMF**	52 Wk Hi-Low	**1,520.0-1,135.0**
Book Value	**1,138.0**	**1,221.0**	**1,525.8**	**1,350.3**	Yield %	**0.5**	Market Cap	**US$6,660.0mil**

Address **Rigistr. 2**, **6300 Zug**
Tel **042-22-33-22**
Fax **042-21-71-38**
ADR
SEDOL No. **4738211**
Managing Director **Johann Rupert**
Chairman **Nikolaus Senn**

Rieter Holding

Industry: **Factory Equipment**

Rieter Holding manufactures spinning systems and chemical-fiber systems for the textile industry, and noise-control and thermal-insulation products for automobiles. It manufactures machines and integrated installations for staple-fiber spinning and for the manufacture and processing of synthetic fibers. Its wholly-owned Unikeller subsidiary, which generated 37% of sales in 1994, supplies automotive products to such customers as Volkswagen, BMW, and Ford. Its spinning-systems operations generated 40% of revenues. Overseas exports accounted for 45% of revenues in 1994.

	SFr mil 12/92	12/93	12/94	US$mil 12/94				
Sales	**1,693.0**	**1,655.0**	**1,615.5**	**1,187.0**	P/E Ratio	**3.4**	Price (9/30/95)	**340.00**
Net Income	**33.0**	**41.0**	**43.6**	**32.0**	P/B Ratio	**1.1**	52 Wk Hi-Low	**369.00-282.00**
Book Value	**713.0**	**726.0**	**713.8**	**544.9**	Yield %	**8.8**	Market Cap	**US$696.4mil**

Address **Klosterstr. 20**, **8406 Winterthur**
Tel **052-208-7171**
Fax **052-208-7060**
ADR
SEDOL No. **4716154**
CEO **Kurt Feller**
Chairman **Dr. Heinrich Steinmann**

Roche

Industry: **Pharmaceuticals**

Roche Holding produces pharmaceuticals, vitamins, fine chemicals, diagnostic products, fragrances, and flavors. Its pharmaceuticals, which account for more than 55% of total sales, treat infectious, cardiovascular, inflammatory, and autoimmune diseases, among others. Its Rocephin ranks as the best-selling injectable antibiotic worldwide. Roche has agreed to acquire the medicinal feed-additive business of American Cyanamid from American Home Products. European exports make up 32% of revenues, North America and Latin America 49%, and the rest of the world 17%.

	SFr mil 12/92	12/93	12/94	US$mil 12/94				
Sales	**12,953.0**	**14,315.0**	**14,748.0**	**10,836.1**	P/E Ratio M	**42.5**	Price (9/30/95) M	**14,100**
Net Income	**1,916.0**	**2,478.0**	**2,860.0**	**2,101.4**	P/B Ratio M	**7.4**	52 Wk Hi-Low M	**14,300.0-10,800.0**
Book Value	**16,046.0**	**17,914.0**	**16,422.0**	**12,535.9**	Yield % M	**0.4**	Market Cap M	**US$19,448mil**

Address **Roche Holding**, **4002 Basel**
Tel **061-688-8888**
Fax **061-691-0014**
ADR **ROHHY**
SEDOL No. **4745749**
CEO **Fritz Gerber**
Chairman **Fritz Gerber**

M=Multiple issues in index; reflects most active.

Sandoz

Industry: **Pharmaceuticals**

Sandoz manufactures pharmaceuticals, chemicals, and food products. The firm produces drugs such as the immunosuppressant Neoral, the antidepressant Pamelor, and the antischizophrenic Clozaril. It also produces and markets vegetable and flower seeds. Sandoz's brand-name food products include Gerber baby food, Roland crispbread, and Ovaltine drink mix. The firm recently announced that it is selling its Clariant specialty-chemicals division. Sandoz's pharmaceuticals division generated 45% of revenues in 1994. Sales in Europe account for 40% of revenues.

	SFr mil 12/92	12/93	12/94	US$mil 12/94				
Sales	**14,416.0**	**15,100.0**	**15,870.0**	**11,660.5**	P/E Ratio M	**19.4**	Price (9/30/95) M	**893.00**
Net Income	**1,495.0**	**1,706.0**	**1,734.0**	**1,274.1**	P/B Ratio M	**4.8**	52 Wk Hi-Low M	**916.00-639.00**
Book Value	**9,328.0**	**10,557.0**	**6,887.0**	**5,257.3**	Yield % M	**1.3**	Market Cap M	**US$3,138.6mil**

Address **Lichtstr. 35**, **4002 Basel**
Tel **061-324-11-11**
Fax **061-324-80-01**
ADR **SDOZY**
SEDOL No. **4809399**
CEO **Rolf W. Schweizer**
Chairman **Marc Moret**

M=Multiple issues in index; reflects most active.

Schindler

Industry: **Industrial - Diversified**

Schindler Holding manufactures elevators and escalators (which account for more than 90% of sales), people movers, and related equipment. It installs its equipment in airports, cruise ships, and large buildings. Its majority-owned ALSO Holding subsidiary distributes computer software and hardware for IBM, COMPAQ, and Hewlett-Packard. Schindler's other products include moving walkways, passenger-train cars, and remote monitoring systems. The company generates 63% of its revenues in Europe, 24% in North America and South America, and 13% in the rest of the world.

	SFr mil 12/92	12/93	12/94	US$mil 12/94				
Sales	**4,511.0**	**4,516.0**	**4,713.6**	**3,463.3**	P/E Ratio M	**9.4**	Price (9/30/95) M	**1,060.00**
Net Income	**111.0**	**169.0**	**146.5**	**107.6**	P/B Ratio M	**1.1**	52 Wk Hi-Low M	**1,620.0-990.0**
Book Value	**1,173.0**	**1,268.0**	**1,352.4**	**1,032.4**	Yield % M	**2.6**	Market Cap M	**US$686.3mil**

Address **Seestr. 55**, **6052 Hergiswil**
Tel **041-95-85-50**
Fax **041-39-31-34**
ADR
SEDOL No. **4778842**
President --
Chairman **Alfred N. Shindler**

M=Multiple issues in index; reflects most active.

SMH

Industry: **Clothing & Fabrics**

Swiss Corporation for Microelectronics and Watchmaking (SMH) produces wristwatches, watch components, integrated circuits for battery-operated appliances, and laser tools. It is the world's largest clock and watch manufacturer in terms of sales and finished-watch production. Its luxury brands include Omega, Rado, and Longines. Tissot and Swatch are among the company's less- expensive brands. SMH and Mercedes-Benz operate MC Micro Compact Car, a joint venture to manufacture the Swatch Car. Overseas exports made up 42% of sales in 1994.

SFr mil	12/92	12/93	12/94	US$mil 12/94				
Sales	**2,762.0**	**2,770.0**	**2,588.0**	**1,901.5**	P/E Ratio M	**78.9**	Price (9/30/95) M	**750.00**
Net Income	**413.0**	**441.0**	**315.0**	**231.4**	P/B Ratio M	**11.5**	52 Wk Hi-Low M	**830.00-550.00**
Book Value	**1,575.0**	**1,932.0**	**2,165.0**	**1,652.7**	Yield % M	**1.1**	Market Cap M	**US$2,340.5mil**

Address **Seevorstadt 6**, **2502 Biel** — Tel **032-22-97-22**, Fax **032-23-15-95** — ADR — SEDOL No. **4762403** — CEO **Nicolas G. Hayek** — Chairman **Nicolas G. Hayek**

M=Multiple issues in index; reflects most active.

Sulzer

Industry: **Building Materials**

Sulzer Brothers (Gebrüder Sulzer) produces heavy machinery and medical devices. The company's manufacturing products include weaving machinery, reciprocating compressors, air-separation machinery, and boiler plants. Its medical products include pacemakers, artificial joints, and heart valves. The Sulzer Infra Group (accounting for 25% of sales) designs, installs, and manages building equipment such as air-flow and ventilation systems. European exports make up 42% of revenues, North America and Latin America generate 23%, and the rest of the world makes up 17%.

SFr mil	12/92	12/93	12/94	US$mil 12/94				
Sales	**6,801.0**	**6,657.0**	**6,038.0**	**4,436.4**	P/E Ratio M	**12.0**	Price (9/30/95) M	**670.00**
Net Income	**168.0**	**186.0**	**195.0**	**143.3**	P/B Ratio M	**1.1**	52 Wk Hi-Low M	**916.00-649.00**
Book Value	**2,178.0**	**2,178.0**	**2,131.0**	**1,626.7**	Yield % M	**3.0**	Market Cap M	**US$1,316.3mil**

Address **Zurcherstr. 9**, **8401 Winterthur** — Tel **052-262-1122**, Fax **052-262-0101** — ADR — SEDOL No. **4854719** — President & CEO **Fritz Fahrni** — Chairman **Pierre Borgeaud**

M=Multiple issues in index; reflects most active.

Surveillance

Industry: **General Industrial & Commercial Services**

Société Générale de Surveillance Holding (SGS) operates inspection, verification, and testing services. It operates safety inspections for industrial installations, and provides import- and export-verification services for minerals, oil, and petrochemical firms. The company also samples and measures agricultural products, and tests the quality of consumer products. SGS provides environmental-damage assessments and loss- adjustment services to insurers. The company has operations in more than 140 countries. Overseas exports accounted for 56% of revenues in 1994.

SFr mil	12/92	12/93	12/94	US$mil 12/94				
Sales	**2,474.0**	**2,642.0**	**2,674.1**	**1,964.8**	P/E Ratio M	**91.9**	Price (9/30/95) M	**2,140.00**
Net Income	**194.0**	**196.0**	**207.4**	**152.4**	P/B Ratio M	**18.8**	52 Wk Hi-Low M	**2,180.0-1,620.0**
Book Value	**1,130.0**	**996.0**	**1,069.4**	**816.3**	Yield % M	**0.5**	Market Cap M	**US$2,132.6mil**

Address **8 rue des Alpes**, **1211 Geneva** — Tel **022-739-9498**, Fax **022-732-3522** — ADR — SEDOL No. **4824767** — President -- — Chairman **Elisabeth S. Amorini**

M=Multiple issues in index; reflects most active.

Swiss Bank

Industry: **Banks - Money Center**

Swiss Bank Corporation, one of Switzerland's three largest banks, provides a full range of banking services at its more than 310 Swiss branches and 2,700 branches and offices abroad. Its services include retail banking, asset management, and foreign exchange. Its Swiss banking subsidiaries include Langenthal and Seeland Banks. U.S. interests include derivatives firm O'Connor Partners, and investment-management firm Brinson Partners. In July 1995, the bank acquired the investment-banking business of S.G. Warburg.

SFr mil	12/92	12/93	12/94	US$mil 12/94				
Revenues	**17,881.0**	**17,753.0**	**13,679.0**	**10,050.7**	P/E Ratio M	**24.0**	Price (9/30/95) M	**442.00**
Net Income	**1,006.0**	**1,365.0**	**811.0**	**595.9**	P/B Ratio M	**2.2**	52 Wk Hi-Low M	**452.00-338.00**
Book Value	**12,369.0**	**13,129.0**	**15,014.0**	**11,461.1**	Yield % M	**1.8**	Market Cap M	**US$9,115.9mil**

Address **Aeschenplatz 6**, **4002 Basel** — Tel **061-288-2020**, Fax **061-288-9099** — ADR **SWBKY** — SEDOL No. **4780609** — CEO **George Blum** — Chairman **Walter G. Frehner**

M=Multiple issues in index; reflects most active.

Swiss Reinsurance

Industry: **Insurance - Full Line**

Swiss Reinsurance (Schweizerische Rückversicherungs-Gesellschaft) is a reinsurance company that provides life, fire, accident, motor, marine, aviation, nuclear-energy, and engineering reinsurance. It also offers risk-management services to other companies through its subsidiary International Risk Management. U.S. subsidiary Swiss Reinsurance accounts for about one third of the company's total reinsurance business. In 1994, the company sold its majority holdings in European direct insurance companies to the Allianz Group and Winterthur Insurance.

SFr mil	12/92	12/93	12/94	US$mil 12/94				
Revenues	**25,017.0**	**15,566.0**	**15,298.0**	**11,240.3**	P/E Ratio	**18.4**	Price (9/30/95)	**1,130.00**
Net Income	**281.0**	**545.0**	**923.0**	**678.2**	P/B Ratio	**NMF**	52 Wk Hi-Low	**1,157.0-577.0**
Book Value	**3,664.0**	**N/A**	**N/A**	**N/A**	Yield %	**1.3**	Market Cap	**US$13,661mil**

Address **Mythenquai 50/60**, **8022 Zurich** — Tel **01-285-21-21**, Fax **01-285-29-99** — ADR — SEDOL No. **4850029** — CEO **Lukas Mühlemann** — Chairman **Ulrich Bremi**

Swissair

Industry: **Airlines**

Swiss Air Transport Company (Schweizerische Luftverkehr) is an international passenger, mail, and cargo airline. The company also has hotel, food-service, and real-estate interests. Swissair and its subsidiaries operate a fleet of 115 airplanes, flying to more than 110 destinations worldwide. Its partially-owned subsidiaries include regional carrier Crossair and charter airline Balair/CTA. Swissair has cooperative agreements with Austrian Airlines, Delta Air Lines, and Singapore Airlines. Swissair has agreed to purchase 49.5% of Belgium's Sabena airlines.

	SFr mil 12/92	12/93	12/94	US$mil 12/94				
Sales	**6,214.0**	**6,403.0**	**4,363.0**	**3,205.7**	P/E Ratio	**80.0**	Price (9/30/95)	**800.00**
Net Income	**113.0**	**59.0**	**23.0**	**16.9**	P/B Ratio	**0.9**	52 Wk Hi-Low	**877.00-605.00**
Book Value	**2,883.0**	**2,907.0**	**2,928.0**	**2,235.1**	Yield %	**0.0**	Market Cap	**US$1,591.7mil**

Address **Hirschengraben 84**	Tel **01-812-12-12**	ADR	President & CEO	**Otto Loepfe**
8001 Zurich	Fax **01-810-80-46**	SEDOL No. **4866662**	Chairman	**Hanes Goetz**

Union Bank of Switzerland

Industry: **Banks - Money Center**

Union Bank of Switzerland (UBS) is an independent financial-services company. Its core areas of activity are corporate and institutional banking, corporate finance, and securities trading; foreign exchange, precious metals, commodities, and related derivatives; and investment advisory and asset-management services. UBS has 399 offices, 335 of which are located outside of Switzerland. The bank has 21 consolidated subsidiaries in Switzerland, through which it indirectly holds a number of other companies. Its main U.S. subsidiary holding company is UBS Inc.

	SFr mil 12/92	12/93	12/94	US$mil 12/94				
Revenues	**20,516.0**	**20,922.0**	**19,990.0**	**14,687.7**	P/E Ratio	**18.6**	Price (9/30/95)	**1,184.00**
Net Income	**1,343.0**	**2,268.0**	**1,613.0**	**1,185.2**	P/B Ratio	**1.1**	52 Wk Hi-Low	**1,290.0-1,001.0**
Book Value	**19,317.0**	**21,720.0**	**22,770.0**	**17,381.7**	Yield %	**2.7**	Market Cap	**US$21,140mil**

Address **Bahnholfstrasse 45**	Tel **01-234-11-11**	ADR	CEO	**Robert Studer**
8021 Zurich	Fax **01-236-51-11**	SEDOL No. **4783727**	Chairman	**Nikolaus Senn**

Winterthur

Industry: **Insurance - Full Line**

Winterthur Swiss Insurance (Winterthur Schweizerische Versicherungs-Gesellschaft) provides life, health, motor, property, accident, and general-liability insurance. It also has reinsurance operations. Its non-life-insurance operations account for more than 60% of total gross premiums. Its life-insurance premiums are roughly evenly divided between groups and individuals. Winterthur owns Germany's DBV Insurance firm, and U.S. non-life-insurance firm Unigard. The company has branches in Munich, Barcelona, Paris, Amsterdam, Luxembourg and Tokyo.

	SFr mil 12/92	12/93	12/94	US$mil 12/94				
Revenues	**14,419.0**	**15,020.0**	**20,462.0**	**15,034.5**	P/E Ratio	**17.5**	Price (9/30/95)	**754.00**
Net Income	**247.0**	**324.0**	**364.2**	**267.6**	P/B Ratio	**1.6**	52 Wk Hi-Low	**777.00-566.00**
Book Value	**4,306.0**	**5,416.0**	**4,106.6**	**3,134.8**	Yield %	**2.3**	Market Cap	**US$4,737.2mil**

Address **General Guisan-Str. 40**	Tel **052-261-1111**	ADR	CEO	**Peter Spälti**
8401 Winterthur	Fax **052-213-6620**	SEDOL No. **4972989**	Chairman	**Peter Spälti**

Zurich Insurance

Industry: **Insurance - Full Line**

Zurich Insurance (Zürich Versicherungsgesellschaft) is an insurance company that offers life and non-life insurance services worldwide. The company's general coverage includes motor, property, accident and sickness, worker's compensation, and general-liability insurance. Its life-insurance activities account for one fourth of its premium revenues and general insurance generates 64%. It purchased U.S. insurance company Home Insurance in June 1995 and has agreed to purchase two life insurance companies from the U.S.-based financial company Kemper.

	SFr mil 12/92	12/93	12/94	US$mil 12/94				
Revenues	**19,594.0**	**22,793.0**	**23,285.1**	**17,108.8**	P/E Ratio	**113.0**	Price (9/30/95)	**324.00**
Net Income	**491.0**	**613.0**	**695.4**	**510.9**	P/B Ratio	**0.3**	52 Wk Hi-Low	**338.00-225.60**
Book Value	**8,710.0**	**10,207.0**	**69,976.8**	**53,417.4**	Yield %	**0.3**	Market Cap	**US$13,879mil**

Address **Mythenquai 2**	Tel **01-205-21-21**	ADR	CEO	**Rolf Hüppi**
8002 Zurich	Fax **01-201-33-97**	SEDOL No. **4995599**	Chairman	**Fritz Gerber**

Taiwan

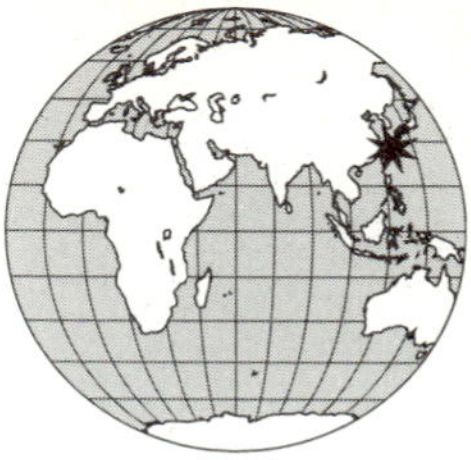

Taiwan

Shirley Lai,
Taipei

Local Trading Hours	Time Difference from New York	Population (Est. 12/94)
9:00-12:00 weekdays, 9:00-11:00 Saturdays	13 hours ahead of EST, (12 hours ahead during Daylight savings)	21,000,000

The inception of Taiwan's securities market was linked with the land reforms on this island in 1950s, when the government released bonds and shares of state-owned companies to acquire land for redistribution to peasants.

To expand the securities market, the government established the Securities and Exchange Commission (SEC) in 1960 to draw guidelines for the market. Taiwan Stock Exchange, the only centralized securities trading market, was set up in 1961 and began operations in 1962 with prices of 18 companies written on a blackboard.

The market has adopted a fully automated computerized system to conduct all transactions electronically. As of August 31, 1995, 369 stocks were listed on the exchange with a market capitalization of NT$4.19 trillion.

Share price fluctuations are subject to a 7% limit of the closing price on the previous day, a measure designed to curb volatile trading.

The exchange probably has the shortest trading hours in the world. Trading begins at 9:00 a.m. and ends at noon on weekdays and on Saturdays runs from 9:00 a.m. to 11:00 a.m. The government since 1994 has said it will extend the hours, but didn't announce any timetable for the plan.

Daily volume in Taiwan shares averaged NT$65.78 billion in 1994, or about U.S.$2.5 billion, up from NT$31.23 billion in 1993. The daily turnover has tumbled in 1995, averaging about NT$37.34 billion during the first eight months.

Retail investors remain the major force in the market, contributing over 90% of the market's transactions.

The market's key barometer, the Taiwan Stock Exchange Weighted Stock Index, was weighted for the number of outstanding shares, patterning after the NYSE Composite Index.

Dow Jones Taiwan Equity Market Index Performance

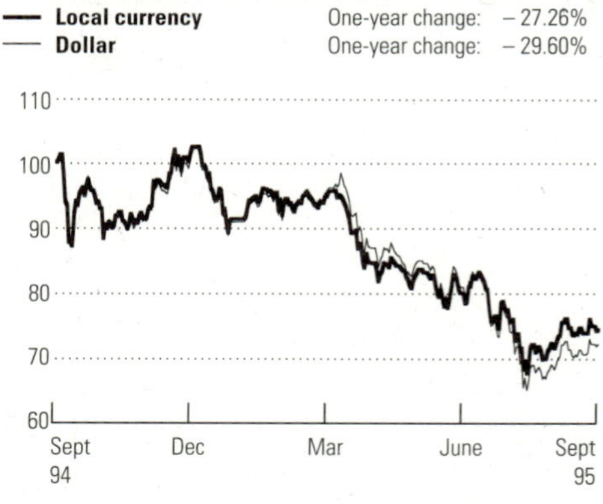

The stock exchange in August 1995 increased the sub-indexes to 22 from eight to better reflect changes in various industries, though banking and insurance take about a 30% weighting and continue to hold the largest chunk of the index.

Gross Domestic Product (94)	Three-Year Average GDP Growth (92-94)	Main Industries	Consumer Price Index (93-94)	Monetary Unit	Exchange Rate (9/95)
U.S.$241.0 billion	+ 6.54% (inflation adjusted)	Electronics, petrochemicals, plastics, electric machinery	+ 4.09%	New Taiwan dollar	NT$27.02 to US$1.00

Movement of banking, electronics and plastics stocks have controlled the performance of the market. Electronics shares, backed by strong earnings, have been the market leader, as Taiwan has emerged as a major manufacturing base of personal computer products.

Stock of China Steel Corp., this island's only integrated steel company, has often been ranked one of the most actively traded issues in terms of volume for its huge number of outstanding shares. Other stocks on the spotlight include Acer Inc., Taiwan's largest and the world's No. 7 personal computer maker, and leading semiconductor companies. Evergreen Marine Corp., one of the largest container shipping companies in the world, has attracted strong buying interest from foreigners.

The government has gradually eased restrictions to encourage foreign equity investment, which accounts for less than 2% of the overall trading.

Taiwan in 1991 opened the stock market to foreign institutions, including banks, insurance companies, fund management firms and securities brokers, for direct investment. But Taiwan remains a semi-closed market for foreigners, as it imposes various restrictions on capital flows and prohibits foreign individuals from buying shares on Taiwan's bourse.

The government in September 1995 raised the ceiling of combined foreign ownership in Taiwan shares to 15% of total market capitalization, after it lifted the cap to 12% from 10% in February.

Ten Largest Capitalized Companies
as of 9/30/95

Stock	Market Cap. US$Mil
ACER	55,685,500.0
Hua Nan Commercial Bank	7,186,154.1
First Bank	6,347,153.4
Chang Hwa Commercial Bank	5,717,527.4
Nan Ya Plastics	4,151,942.6
China Development	3,988,165.8
International Commercial Bank	3,887,352.0
United Micro Electronics	3,534,565.4
Formosa Plastic	3,349,520.9
Tatung	3,132,124.4

Five foreign securities brokerage houses have opened branches in Taiwan this year to execute orders from overseas clients after the SEC eased some requirements.

Meanwhile, the Ministry of Finance and Taiwan's central bank have announced plans to lift the ban, either later this year or in early 1996, to allow direct equity investment by foreign individuals.

Qualified foreign institutional investors have to remit money and convert it into New Taiwan dollar four months after it gets government approval.

Foreign institutions can repatriate income from capital gains and stock dividends from stock investment one year after realization. If a foreign institution decides to withdraw from the Taiwan market, it can expatriate the funds three months after the money is remitted into this island. Authorities have said they will loosen up regulations on remittances for foreign investors later in 1995.

Foreign investors are required to pay 20% tax on dividends and other income earned from equity investment, on top of a 0.3% transaction tax paid upon share sales.

The capital gains tax on securities transactions was suspended in 1990 after a string of street protests by investors. In 1995, legislators boycotted the Ministry of Finance's attempt to reimpose the capital gains tax, at a rate of 0.6% for individual investors and 0.3% for institutions.

After active foreign buying pushed the market's index to the high of 7124 points at the end of 1994, the market turned bearish to become one of the few laggards in Asia. The market's key index fell about one third in the first nine months of 1995. Early in the year, financial troubles at construction companies, which suffered from a sluggish property market, sent jitters into the stock market. Later, Taiwan's worst bank run and an embezzlement case in a major commercial paper underwriter kept the market unsettled.

But the most serious blows came from the deteriorating political tension between Taiwan and mainland China. Share prices tumbled to a 20-month low in early August when China announced the second round of missile tests in a month in seas north of Taiwan, a gesture to vent anger over Taiwan's efforts to break diplomatic isolation.

Taiwan is the seat of Kuomintang, or Nationalist Party, which fled to the island after losing a civil war to Communist forces on mainland China. Beijing regards the island as a renegade province and doesn't rule out the use of force against Taiwan for reunification. Taipei, which boasts the world's second largest foreign reserves of U.S.$98 billion, tries to gain international recognition as a political entity, seen by Beijing as moving toward independence.

Fears about possible Chinese retaliation have unnerved the market, as Taiwanese businesses with heavy investment in mainland China are vulnerable to changes in Beijing.

China's reaction toward Taiwan's first direct presidential election next March could have significant impact on the market.

Despite the market's downtrend, most analysts think share prices will eventually rebound on Taiwan's good economic fundamentals after political disputes across the Taiwan Strait fade away.

Taiwan projected its economy, measured by gross domestic product (GDP), would grow 6.62% in 1995, up from 6.54% in 1994 and 6.32% in 1993. Per capita gross national product was seen rising to U.S.$12,469 in 1995 from U.S.$11,597 a year before. Inflation is moderating, with the Consumer Price Index expected to grow at 3.9% in 1995, compared with 4.1% in the previous year.

Taiwan's exports have enjoyed brisk growth in the wake of global economic recovery, though rising imports may have reduced this island's trade surplus in 1995 to an estimated U.S.$6.8 billion from 1993's U.S.$7.7 billion, an 11-year low.

The central bank's moderate monetary policy, which has shown strong support for the local currency to prevent capital outflow, is seen as a stabilizing force for Taiwan's financial markets.

ACER

Industry: **Computers**

Acer manufactures computers and other related products. Its product line includes personal computers, client/server systems, computer peripherals, software products, and network systems. The company markets these devices under the AcerAltos and other trademarks primarily in Taiwan, North America, and Europe. Its Hong Kong-based Acer Market Services subsidiary manufactures and markets computers throughout mainland China. Acer also has controlling interest in TI-Acer, a joint venture with Texas Instruments and China Development that makes semiconductors and components.

$ mil	12/91	12/92	12/93	US$mil 12/93				
Sales	**985.2**	**1,192.2**	**1,883.3**	**1,883.3**	P/E Ratio	**0.4**	Price (9/30/95)	**65.00**
Net Income	**-22.7**	**2.2**	**40.6**	**40.6**	P/B Ratio	**1.1**	52 Wk Hi-Low	**72.50-49.30**
Book Value	**316.8**	**327.6**	**358.0**	**358.0**	Yield %	**N/A**	Market Cap	**US$2,060.9mil**

Address **156 Min Sheng E. Rd.**, **Taipei** | Tel **02-545-5288** | Fax **02-545-5308** | ADR | SEDOL No. **6000673** | President **--** | Chairman **Stan Shih**

ASE

Industry: **Semiconductors & related**

Advanced Semiconductor Engineering (ASE) manufactures integrated-circuit packages and chips for computer and industrial applications. It also produces notebook computers. ASE sells its products in Taiwan and exports them to Europe and the United States. It has two subsidiaries in Taiwan: 55.5%-owned ASE Technologies, which designs and manufactures notebook PCs, and ASE Test, which performs final tests on the firm's integrated-circuit products. It also operates ASE Electronics, which is based in Malaysia. Foreign financial firms own 3% of the company's stock.

NT$ mil	12/92	12/93	12/94	US$mil 12/94				
Sales	**1,891.5**	**5,823.3**	**9,491.0**	**358.3**	P/E Ratio	**15.8**	Price (9/30/95)	**63.00**
Net Income	**-34.0**	**524.9**	**932.0**	**35.2**	P/B Ratio	**3.9**	52 Wk Hi-Low	**82.50-49.60**
Book Value	**2,188.8**	**2,728.4**	**3,759.0**	**142.8**	Yield %	**0.0**	Market Cap	**US$831.9mil**

Address **333 Keelung Rd.**, **Taipei** | Tel **02-757-6355** | Fax **02-757-6121** | ADR | SEDOL No. **6056074** | President **Richard H.P. Chang** | Chairman **Jason C.S. Chang**

Asia Cement

Industry: **Building Materials**

Asia Cement is Taiwan's second-largest cement company by revenues. It manufactures and trades cement, premixed concrete, hardened bricks, and clinker. Its average annual cement-production is 6.25 million tonnes. Asia Cement exports its products to Japan, Hong Kong, Singapore, and other Asian countries. The Far Eastern Group, Taiwan's third-largest business group by income, owns a 26% share of Asia Cement through its textile-manufacturing subsidiary Far Eastern Textile. Asia Cement has environmental-engineering operations in Taiwan, and has investments in Singapore.

NT$ mil	12/92 P	12/93 P	12/94 P	US$mil 12/94				
Sales	**13,133.3**	**15,702.6**	**15,329.9**	**578.7**	P/E Ratio	**13.1**	Price (9/30/95)	**44.00**
Net Income	**3,654.8**	**3,389.0**	**4,010.1**	**151.4**	P/B Ratio	**2.2**	52 Wk Hi-Low	**55.91-43.90**
Book Value	**19,802.6**	**21,080.8**	**23,845.2**	**906.0**	Yield %	**5.7**	Market Cap	**US$2,138.3mil**

Address **333 Tunhwa S. Rd.**, **Taipei** | Tel **02-733-8000** | Fax **02-735-9797** | ADR | SEDOL No. **6056331** | President **T. H. Chang** | Chairman **Douglas Tong Hsu**

P=Parent company data.

Cathay Construction

Industry: **Heavy Construction**

Cathay Construction is the largest construction company in Taiwan, with annual revenues exceeding NT$9 billion. Its activities include commercial, hotel, and parking-garage construction, as well as urban planning, contracting, consulting, surveying, and property leasing and sales. Headquartered in Taipei, Cathay Construction has branch offices in Taiching, Tainan, and Kaohsiung. Its most recent projects include two office buildings and three hotel complexes. Cathay Construction and Cathay Life Insurance make up the Cathay Group, Taiwan's most profitable business group.

NT$ mil	12/91	12/92	12/93	US$mil 12/93				
Sales	**9,626.3**	**8,424.6**	**9,458.3**	**359.2**	P/E Ratio	**12.7**	Price (9/30/95)	**31.10**
Net Income	**2,537.7**	**1,936.6**	**1,918.4**	**72.9**	P/B Ratio	**2.1**	52 Wk Hi-Low	**39.25-26.58**
Book Value	**13,636.8**	**14,671.8**	**15,696.7**	**590.1**	Yield %	**6.7**	Market Cap	**US$1,799.8mil**

Address **218 Tun Hua S. Rd., Sec. 2**, **Taipei** | Tel **02-377-9968** | Fax **02-377-8399** | ADR | SEDOL No. **6179733** | President **Chao-Chi Lee** | Chairman **Chao-Chi Lee**

Chang Hwa Commercial Bank

Industry: **Banks - Regional**

Chang Hwa Commercial Bank is one of the top six banks in Taiwan by assets. The bank takes deposits and conducts commercial banking. It is also active in trade-finance and lending operations. Chang Hwa Bank is one of 11 financial institutions that are majority-owned by the Taiwan provincial government. The bank has branches in Taiwan, Hong Kong, New York, Los Angeles, London, and Amsterdam, and additional representative offices in Hong Kong and London. Chang Hwa Bank is one of five Taiwan banks with permission to do business with China through offshore branches.

NT$ mil	12/91	12/92	12/93	US$mil 12/93				
Revenues	**49,133.2**	**52,234.5**	**53,418.9**	**2,028.8**	P/E Ratio	**29.8**	Price (9/30/95)	**94.00**
Net Income	**3,915.1**	**2,906.0**	**3,989.5**	**151.5**	P/B Ratio	**N/A**	52 Wk Hi-Low	**162.31-84.50**
Book Value	**18,524.2**	**N/A**	**N/A**	**N/A**	Yield %	**0.0**	Market Cap	**US$5,717.5mil**

Address **57 Chungshan N. Rd., Sec. 2**, **Taipei** | Tel **02-536-2951** | Fax **02-561-0771** | ADR | SEDOL No. **6187855** | President **K.H. Yeh** | Chairman **Chi-Shuan Lo**

Cheng Loong

Industry: **Paper Products**

Cheng Loong is one of Taiwan's largest paper manufacturers, with annual sales of more than $360 million. The company manufactures paper products such as paperboard, linerboard, corrugated board, boxes, and art papers. It leads the paper-products industry in the price setting of paper in Taiwan. Cheng Loong sells its paper products in Taiwan, Japan, Southeast Asia, Hong Kong, and the United States. The company has significant landholdings in Taiwan. Foreign financial institutions own 7.7% of Cheng Loong's total shares.

NT$ mil	12/92	12/93	12/94	US$mil 12/94				
Sales	**9,698.6**	**9,905.5**	**12,539.4**	**473.3**	P/E Ratio	**9.1**	Price (9/30/95)	**22.30**
Net Income	**48.3**	**632.0**	**1,402.1**	**52.9**	P/B Ratio	**1.4**	52 Wk Hi-Low	**38.75-21.00**
Book Value	**6,200.4**	**6,974.0**	**8,873.6**	**337.1**	Yield %	**9.0**	Market Cap	**US$562.8mil**

Address	**1 Min Sheng Rd., Panchiao**	Tel	**02-222-5131**	ADR		President	**Tony-Ho Tsai**
	Taipei Hsien	Fax	**02-222-6110**	SEDOL No.	**6190239**	Chairman	**Cheng-Loong Cheng**

Cheng Shin Rubber

Industry: **Tires & Rubber**

Cheng Shin Rubber Industry manufactures bicycle, automobile, truck, and motorcycle tires and tire tubes. It is one of the world's largest makers of bicycle tires and tubes. Cheng Shin Rubber sells its tires and tubes in Taiwan, North America, Europe, Asia, and Central America. Cheng Shin Rubber invested $20 million to establish a plant and sales unit to manufacture and market motorcycle and bicycle tires and tubes in Xiamen, China. Cheng Shin is also planning to build a $200 million tire plant in the Philippines and has a joint venture with Japan's Toyo Rubber.

NT$ mil	12/92	12/93	12/94	US$mil 12/94				
Sales	**231.0**	**225.0**	**235.0**	**8.9**	P/E Ratio	**NMF**	Price (9/30/95)	**31.90**
Net Income	**28.0**	**34.0**	**30.0**	**1.1**	P/B Ratio	**NMF**	52 Wk Hi-Low	**36.22-23.95**
Book Value	**166.0**	**202.0**	**237.0**	**9.0**	Yield %	**0.0**	Market Cap	**US$592.1mil**

Address	**215 Meei-Kong Rd., Ta-Tsun**	Tel	**04-852-5151**	ADR		President	**Yun-Hwa Chen**
	Chang-Hwa	Fax	**04-852-6468**	SEDOL No.	**6190228**	Chairman	**Jye Luo**

Chia Hsin Cement

Industry: **Building Materials**

Chia Hsin Cement is Taiwan's third-largest cement company by revenues. It produces Portland cement, hardened bricks, and other building materials. It is also active in quarrying and distributing limestone, and contructing and leasing commercial buildings. Chia Hsin is a member of the diversified conglomerate Koos Group, through which it has securities and banking-industry investments. The company owns the U.S. terminal maker Wyse Technologies, and has a joint venture with Tong Yang Cement of South Korea to build storage silos and an import terminal in Taichung.

NT$ mil	12/92 R	12/93	12/94	US$mil 12/94				
Sales	**4,827.0**	**5,199.9**	**4,830.6**	**182.3**	P/E Ratio	**25.2**	Price (9/30/95)	**22.70**
Net Income	**713.9**	**1,285.6**	**425.8**	**16.1**	P/B Ratio	**1.5**	52 Wk Hi-Low	**41.73-19.10**
Book Value	**6,581.8**	**7,394.2**	**7,139.3**	**271.3**	Yield %	**2.2**	Market Cap	**US$445.5mil**

Address	**96 Chung Shan Rd. N.**	Tel	**02-551-5211**	ADR		President	**Nelson An-Ping Chang**
	Taipei	Fax	**02-581-8320**	SEDOL No.	**6190626**	Chairman	**Yung-Ping Chang**

R=Restated.

Chia Hsin Flour

Industry: **Other Food**

Chia Hsin Flour is one of Taiwan's leading food producers. The company manufactures and sells animal feed, salad oil, wheat powder, and soybean powder. Chia Hsin Flour also engages in the construction and housing industries, manufacturing various building materials, and has significant investments in the petrochemicals industry. It is planning to invest up to $10 million in China's petrochemical industry in the next few years. The company makes all of its sales domestically. Chia Hsin Flour is a member of the diversified conglomerate China Rebar Group.

NT$ mil	12/91	12/92	12/93	US$mil 12/93				
Sales	**3,762.8**	**3,938.8**	**4,392.6**	**166.8**	P/E Ratio	**27.9**	Price (9/30/95)	**14.85**
Net Income	**370.2**	**420.3**	**316.7**	**12.0**	P/B Ratio	**1.0**	52 Wk Hi-Low	**21.75-12.28**
Book Value	**7,014.2**	**7,419.1**	**8,563.4**	**321.9**	Yield %	**0.0**	Market Cap	**US$510.2mil**

Address	**219 Chung Hsiao E. Rd., Sec 4**	Tel	**02-752-5321**	ADR		President	**N/A**
	Taipei	Fax	**02-721-5825**	SEDOL No.	**6190637**	Chairman	**N/A**

Chia Hsin Livestock

Industry: **Clothing & Fabrics**

Chia Hsin Livestock manufactures textiles, primarily fabrics and cotton yarns. The company also raises hogs, produces animal feed, and sells eggs. Chia Hsin Livestock is in the process of ending its livestock operations to concentrate on textile production. Chia Hsin Livestock is a member of the diversified conglomerate Hualon Group, Taiwan's ninth-largest business group with assets of more than $4 billion. The company has invested $420 million to build a computer-wafer-manufacturing plant, to be completed by 1997.

NT$ mil	12/91	12/92	12/93	US$mil 12/93				
Sales	**2,523.9**	**2,126.2**	**1,735.8**	**65.9**	P/E Ratio	**NMF**	Price (9/30/95)	**15.50**
Net Income	**85.1**	**-599.6**	**-264.8**	**-10.1**	P/B Ratio	**2.5**	52 Wk Hi-Low	**28.10-13.50**
Book Value	**4,268.3**	**3,668.8**	**3,404.0**	**128.0**	Yield %	**0.0**	Market Cap	**US$324.1mil**

Address	**5 Fl., 42 Chung Shan N. Rd., Sec. 2**	Tel	**02-521-6252**	ADR		President	**Wencheng Li**
	Taipei	Fax	**02-537-4837**	SEDOL No.	**6190499**	Chairman	**Zhihui He**

Chien Tai Cement

Industry: **Building Materials**

Chien Tai Cement manufactures cement and markets it in Taiwan, Southeast Asia, and the Middle East. It is also owns silos where it stores imported Japanese cement, and is active in domestic real-estate development and construction. The company owns Kaohsiung's 85-story, multiuse T & C Tower in partnership with Tuntex, a holding company with an 11% interest in Chien Tai. The company also owns a cement-manufacturing company located in the Philippines. Chien Tai is 23%-owned by Central Investment Holding, the investment arm of the ruling Nationalist Party.

NT$ mil	12/91	12/92	12/93	US$mil 12/93				
Sales	**2,682.3**	**2,853.6**	**3,013.3**	**114.4**	P/E Ratio	**14.7**	Price (9/30/95)	**17.60**
Net Income	**679.0**	**698.1**	**798.4**	**30.3**	P/B Ratio	**1.3**	52 Wk Hi-Low	**27.83-15.10**
Book Value	**5,883.7**	**6,575.6**	**7,367.8**	**277.0**	Yield %	**0.0**	Market Cap	**US$435.0mil**

Address **14 F, 29 Anho Rd., Sec 4, Taipei** | Tel **02-700-1880** | Fax **02-706-1393** | ADR | SEDOL No. **6190660** | President -- | Chairman --

China Development

Industry: **Banks - Regional**

China Development (CDC) provides financial services, including investment-banking for corporations and industries throughout Taiwan and in other Asian markets. The company underwrites public offerings of stock and other securities and provides brokerage services. It has an interest in the China Securities Investment Trust Company, which manages seven Taiwan- and China-oriented investment funds listed on the American Stock Exchange. CDC partially owns TI-Acer, a joint venture with Texas Instruments and Acer that manufactures semiconductors and other electronic components.

NT$ mil	12/92	12/93	12/94	US$mil 12/94				
Revenues	**2,625.5**	**2,961.6**	**4,929.6**	**186.1**	P/E Ratio	**20.6**	Price (9/30/95)	**80.00**
Net Income	**931.3**	**1,306.2**	**3,002.6**	**113.3**	P/B Ratio	**3.1**	52 Wk Hi-Low	**99.74-68.45**
Book Value	**9,945.5**	**11,276.4**	**22,929.2**	**871.2**	Yield %	**2.0**	Market Cap	**US$3,988.2mil**

Address **CDC Tower, 125 Nanking E. Rd., Taipei** | Tel **02-763-8800** | Fax **02-768-6060** | ADR | SEDOL No. **6190994** | President **Benny T. Hu** | Chairman & CEO **Tai-Ying Liu**

China Petrochemical Development

Industry: **Commodity Chemicals**

China Petrochemical Development is a petrochemicals manufacturer. It produces on average 150,000 tonnes of caprolactam, 171,000 tonnes of acrylonitrile, and 66,000 tonnes of methanol per year. The company is in negotiations to establish a joint venture with U.S.-based BP Chemicals, a subsidiary of London-based British Petroleum. The venture would construct an acrylonitrile plant in China to be operational by the year 2000. China Petrochemical is 33%-owned by Chinese Petroleum Corporation, the state-run Taiwan oil company.

NT$ mil	06/91	06/92	06/93	US$mil 06/93				
Sales	**9,573.1**	**7,946.8**	**6,856.4**	**268.0**	P/E Ratio	**NMF**	Price (9/30/95)	**19.60**
Net Income	**620.4**	**-253.2**	**233.5**	**9.1**	P/B Ratio	**1.0**	52 Wk Hi-Low	**44.60-16.00**
Book Value	**13,360.3**	**13,107.1**	**18,178.0**	**688.8**	Yield %	**N/A**	Market Cap	**US$696.2mil**

Address **9/F #6, Roosevelt Rd., Sec 1, Taipei** | Tel **03-396-9600** | Fax **N/A** | ADR | SEDOL No. **6206084** | President **P.L. Wu** | Chairman **Y.S. Kuan**

China Rebar

Industry: **Building Materials**

China Rebar is a holding company active in the construction-materials, fabric-manufacturing, retail, and hospitality industries. It is one of Taiwan's 10 largest companies in terms of assets, and it has interests in more than 27 firms. The company produces cement, aluminum doors, windows, and curtain walls, which it sells mainly in Taiwan and East Asia. It also operates textile factories, hotels, and a department store. China Rebar is currently constructing a residential development in Taipei and negotiating a joint venture with Formosa Plastics to develop land in Taipei.

NT$ mil	12/91	12/92	12/93	US$mil 12/93				
Sales	**N/A**	**N/A**	**N/A**	**N/A**	P/E Ratio	**16.3**	Price (9/30/95)	**13.45**
Net Income	**989.2**	**832.5**	**824.1**	**31.3**	P/B Ratio	**N/A**	52 Wk Hi-Low	**22.27-10.95**
Book Value	**N/A**	**N/A**	**N/A**	**N/A**	Yield %	**0.0**	Market Cap	**US$587.7mil**

Address **219 Chung Hsiao E. Rd., Sec 4, Taipei** | Tel **02-711-2131** | Fax **02-781-8257** | ADR | SEDOL No. **6190983** | President **Wang Yutseng** | Chairman **Wang Yutseng**

China Steel

Industry: **Steel**

China Steel is an integrated steel producer. It manufactures more than six million tonnes of steel per year; construction is underway to increase output by 40% late in the decade. The company also produces aluminum, chemicals, and environmental-engineering products. China Steel has a 35% interest in a joint venture with MEMC Electronics, a U.S.-based firm, that will produce silicon wafers. The company also holds minority interests in coal-mining and iron-ore-mining concerns abroad. Taiwan's government controls more than 50% of China Steel.

NT$ mil	06/92 R	06/93	06/94	US$mil 06/94				
Sales	**57,508.4**	**60,191.1**	**66,547.4**	**2,501.0**	P/E Ratio	**17.6**	Price (9/30/95)	**21.50**
Net Income	**8,120.2**	**5,388.1**	**8,851.4**	**332.7**	P/B Ratio	**1.5**	52 Wk Hi-Low	**33.40-20.20**
Book Value	**102,897.4**	**103,444.1**	**104,361.1**	**3,892.6**	Yield %	**5.1**	Market Cap	**US$584.6mil**

Address **Lin Hai Industrial District, Kaohsiung** | Tel **07-802-1111** | Fax **07-801-9427** | ADR | SEDOL No. **6190950** | President **J.Y. Chen** | Chairman **C.Y. Wang**

R=Restated.

Chung Hsing Bills Finance

Industry: **Financial Services - Diversified**

Chung Hsing Bills Finance is a bill-financing firm that specializes in short-term money-market management. As the first bills-finance company established in Taiwan, Chung Hsing dominates the territory's short-term money market and is one of three companies allowed to trade in securities of one year or less. The company is involved in the trading of short-term commercial paper, Treasury bills, bankers' acceptances, and negotiable certificates of deposit. Chung Hsing has seven branches throughout Taiwan. It is affiliated with the far-flung Kuomintang (KMT) business group.

NT$ mil	12/91	12/92	12/93	US$mil 12/93				
Revenues	2,822.0	2,813.5	3,219.4	122.3	P/E Ratio	20.3	Price (9/30/95)	30.60
Net Income	1,433.8	1,436.1	1,525.7	57.9	P/B Ratio	2.2	52 Wk Hi-Low	39.25-23.42
Book Value	7,334.2	6,740.4	11,734.7	441.2	Yield %	0.0	Market Cap	US$1,378.3mil

Address **125 Nanking E. Rd., Sec. 2**, **Taipei**
Tel **02-508-1658**
Fax **02-507-7229**
ADR
SEDOL No. **6196282**
President **Guanglun Zeng**
Chairman **Leshan Wang**

Chung Hwa Pulp

Industry: **Paper Products**

Chung Hwa Pulp manufactures wood pulp and paper. The company annually produces roughly 232,000 tons of wood pulp and 115,000 tons of paper from its mills located in Taiwan. It also produces organic fertilizer as a byproduct of its manufacturing operations. Products include bleached hardwood sulphate pulp, bleached softwood sulfate pulp, wood-free paper, and coated paper. Approximately 42% of the company's sales go to Taiwan's Yuen Foong Yu Paper Manufacturing, a major shareholder of the company. Chung Hwa Pulp's primary timber suppliers are located in China and Vietnam.

NT$ mil	12/92	12/93	12/94	US$mil 12/94				
Sales	3,502.9	3,234.7	5,094.6	192.3	P/E Ratio	37.1	Price (9/30/95)	33.40
Net Income	-739.6	-575.1	361.1	13.6	P/B Ratio	2.6	52 Wk Hi-Low	66.50-32.80
Book Value	4,578.5	4,383.6	5,094.1	193.5	Yield %	0.0	Market Cap	US$497.3mil

Address **4th Fl., 20 Pa-Teh Rd., Sec. 3**, **Taipei**
Tel **02-579-4001**
Fax **02-579-0175**
ADR
SEDOL No. **6196538**
Managing Director **Lee How-Kau**
Chairman **Liu Yue-Yao**

Chung Shing Textile

Industry: **Clothing & Fabrics**

Chung Shing Textile produces and sells undergarments under its own There Gun and YIshur labels. It is also the only company licensed to produce and sell BVD-brand undergarments in Taiwan. Other products include printed and dyed fabrics, cotton thread, and synthetic fibers. Its main export markets are Hong Kong and the United States. Chung Shing's retail operations include its own There Gun Hypermarkets, as well as an 18% stake in Taiwan's Sunrise department store chain and a 94% stake in San Chiang Enterprise, a Taiwanese supermarket chain.

NT$ mil	12/92	12/93	12/94	US$mil 12/94				
Sales	10,564.3	9,582.7	10,362.5	391.2	P/E Ratio	54.2	Price (9/30/95)	13.00
Net Income	30.6	-1,460.2	200.4	7.6	P/B Ratio	1.1	52 Wk Hi-Low	24.40-11.20
Book Value	9,439.7	9,642.7	9,841.5	373.9	Yield %	0.0	Market Cap	US$408.5mil

Address **123 Chung Hsiao E. Rd., Sec. 2**, **Taipei**
Tel **02-397-1188**
Fax **02-396-3346**
ADR
SEDOL No. **6196613**
President --
Chairman **C.Y. Baw**

Chuntex Electronic

Industry: **Computers**

Chuntex Electronic Co. is one of the world's largest computer-monitor makers. The company makes 14-, 15-, and 16-inch monitors, as well as other electronic components. Chuntex has its CTX U.S.A. subsidiary, a manufacturing subsidiary in Thailand, and a marketing subsidiary in the Netherlands. CTX U.S.A. distributes Chuntex's products in North America and accounts for 73% of the company's total sales. Chuntex also owns a 51% stake in Prior Industrial, a Thailand monitor maker, and a 51% stake in Veridata Electronics, a local notebook-computer maker.

NT$ mil	12/92 R	12/93	12/94	US$mil 12/94				
Sales	6,245.9	8,124.2	9,872.9	372.7	P/E Ratio	33.3	Price (9/30/95)	30.80
Net Income	323.8	401.7	193.2	7.3	P/B Ratio	2.3	52 Wk Hi-Low	40.04-24.20
Book Value	1,687.4	2,670.5	2,854.1	108.4	Yield %	0.0	Market Cap	US$293.0mil

Address **2 Alley 6, Lane 235, Pao-Chiao Rd.**, **Hsien-Tien, Taipei**
Tel **02-917-5055**
Fax **02-917-2736**
ADR
SEDOL No. **6172196**
President --
Chairman --

R=Restated.

Compeq Manufacturing

Industry: **Semiconductors & related**

Compeq Manufacturing produces approximately 14% of the world's printed-circuit boards, and 26% of Taiwan's. The company manufactures approximately 3 million circuit boards per year, roughly 20% of which are made for notebook computers. It also manufactures tailored circuit boards for communication cards, process-control equipment, and engineering work stations. Its major customers include Intel, Siemens, IBM, Acer, Quanta, Apple, Dell, and Compaq. The firm's operations in the United States are managed through its wholly-owned Compeq International.

NT$ mil	12/92	12/93	12/94	US$mil 12/94				
Sales	2,854.6	3,575.3	4,234.3	159.8	P/E Ratio	17.7	Price (9/30/95)	79.00
Net Income	159.8	382.3	627.4	23.7	P/B Ratio	3.6	52 Wk Hi-Low	81.50-58.75
Book Value	2,317.8	2,598.8	3,088.5	117.3	Yield %	3.8	Market Cap	US$494.1mil

Address **Ta-Hsin Rd., Shin Chuang Village**, **Lu Chu Hsiang, Taoyuan Hsien**
Tel **03-323-1111**
Fax **03-323-5566**
ADR
SEDOL No. **6215273**
President **Charles Wu**
Chairman **H.W. Chen**

Delta Electronic Industrial

Industry: **Computers**

Delta Electronic Industrial manufactures power-supply equipment and monitors. Its products include intermediate-frequency transmitters, electronic components, color monitors, and electronic filters. It recently began producing power-supply units for notebook computers. The company sells its products in Taiwan and exports to the United States, Southeast Asia, Japan, and Europe. Delta supplies parts to U.S. computer makers IBM, Apple, and Hewlett-Packard. It also owns a transformer and coil factory in mainland China.

NT$ mil	12/92	12/93	12/94	US$mil 12/94				
Sales	**5,592.4**	**6,363.6**	**9,058.0**	**341.9**	P/E Ratio	**15.3**	Price (9/30/95)	**42.10**
Net Income	**366.6**	**736.5**	**676.7**	**25.5**	P/B Ratio	**2.4**	52 Wk Hi-Low	**68.33-34.60**
Book Value	**2,436.4**	**3,591.7**	**4,299.6**	**163.4**	Yield %	**0.0**	Market Cap	**US$464.0mil**

Address **144 Minchuan E. Rd., Sec. 3**
Taipei
Tel **02-716-4822**
Fax **02-716-9764**
ADR
SEDOL No. **6260734**
Managing Director **Mengxiong Chen**
Chairman **Conghua Zheng**

Eagle Food

Industry: **Soft Drinks**

Eagle Holding is a processed-food manufacturer that has overseas land-development operations as well. Its products include soybean powder and meal; beverages such as milk, juice and soft drinks; salad oil; and feedstuffs. Through its primary Eagle Food Industry subsidiary, the company also runs price-club operations in Taiwan. Eagle Holding owns two hotels in the United States, and is developing a shopping mall there. The company has investments in mainland China as well. Eagle Holding's principal shareholders are Fortune Investment Company of Taiwan and Taiwan Vespa.

NT$ mil	12/91	12/92	12/93	US$mil 12/93				
Sales	**3,040.0**	**3,243.0**	**3,505.0**	**133.1**	P/E Ratio	**9.1**	Price (9/30/95)	**15.60**
Net Income	**100.3**	**150.4**	**457.4**	**17.4**	P/B Ratio	**1.2**	52 Wk Hi-Low	**28.83-14.15**
Book Value	**2,855.0**	**3,003.0**	**3,470.0**	**130.5**	Yield %	**0.0**	Market Cap	**US$184.5mil**

Address **14 F, 57 Fuhsing N. Rd.**
Taipei
Tel **02-752-8931**
Fax **02-781-0485**
ADR
SEDOL No. **6296698**
President **Zhenfeng Wang**
Chairman **Zhenkui Wang**

Evergreen Marine

Industry: **Marine Transportation**

Evergreen Marine provides marine transportation of containerized cargo. The company operates a fleet of more than 85 ships, making it one of the largest container-shipping company in the world. It maintains offices in more than 100 countries and operates ports in Asia, Europe, North America, and South America. Evergreen Marine is engaged in a joint venture with General Electric that will construct container ports, terminals, and other facilities in China. Evergreen Marine is also affiliated with Uniglory Marine, which operates a fleet of more than 25 container ships.

NT$ mil	12/92	12/93	12/94	US$mil 12/94				
Sales	**30,159.4**	**31,399.8**	**29,195.1**	**1,102.0**	P/E Ratio	**15.1**	Price (9/30/95)	**39.50**
Net Income	**2,707.0**	**2,811.3**	**2,574.6**	**97.2**	P/B Ratio	**1.9**	52 Wk Hi-Low	**54.09-33.91**
Book Value	**20,889.1**	**23,301.7**	**25,810.7**	**980.6**	Yield %	**3.8**	Market Cap	**US$2,034.2mil**

Address **166 Minsheng E. Rd., Sec. 2**
Taipei
Tel **02-505-7766**
Fax **02-505-5256**
ADR
SEDOL No. **6324500**
President **George Msu**
Chairman **Sun-san Lin**

Far Eastern Department Stores

Industry: **Retailers - Broadline**

Far Eastern Department Stores is a retailer that operates Taiwan's largest chain of department stores. Its stores, located throughout Taiwan, sell clothing, household appliances, groceries, and other items. Far Eastern Department Stores has a joint venture with the French retailer Promodes to develop shopping malls in Taiwan. It has holdings in overseas supermarkets, shopping centers, and department stores as well. The company is a member of the Far Eastern Group, Taiwan's third-largest business group by profits. It is 21%-owned by group member Far Eastern Textile.

NT$ mil	12/91	12/92	12/93	US$mil 12/93				
Revenues	**12,256.6**	**15,165.0**	**16,811.2**	**638.5**	P/E Ratio	**15.6**	Price (9/30/95)	**28.00**
Net Income	**812.0**	**531.9**	**791.3**	**30.1**	P/B Ratio	**1.9**	52 Wk Hi-Low	**43.33-25.20**
Book Value	**6,179.0**	**6,241.5**	**6,270.3**	**235.7**	Yield %	**4.3**	Market Cap	**US$464.3mil**

Address **27 Paoking Rd.**
Taipei
Tel **02-381-6155**
Fax **02-375-3908**
ADR
SEDOL No. **6331373**
President **Heming Ying**
Chairman **Xudong Xu**

Far Eastern Textiles

Industry: **Commodity Chemicals**

Far Eastern Textile manufactures polyester, fabrics, and yarn. Its products include polyester staples, polyester filaments, staple yarns, textiles, polyester-textured yarns, fabrics, color cloths, polyester chips, and polyester bottles. The company is a member of the Far Eastern Group, and owns 26% of Asian Cement and 21% of Far Eastern Department Stores, both of which are Far Eastern Group members. Through a joint venture with the United States' E.I. Du Pont de Nemours, Far Eastern Textile is constructing a nylon plant scheduled to open in 1996.

NT$ mil	12/91	12/92	12/93	US$mil 12/93				
Sales	**20,700.0**	**21,183.1**	**20,186.5**	**766.7**	P/E Ratio	**42.5**	Price (9/30/95)	**30.30**
Net Income	**2,349.3**	**2,002.0**	**1,157.6**	**44.0**	P/B Ratio	**2.1**	52 Wk Hi-Low	**40.87-24.35**
Book Value	**21,897.7**	**22,203.3**	**21,876.2**	**822.4**	Yield %	**1.3**	Market Cap	**US$1,939.8mil**

Address **16 Fl., 333 Tunhua S. Rd., Sec 2**
Taipei
Tel **02-733-8000**
Fax **02-736-9934**
ADR
SEDOL No. **6331470**
President --
Chairman --

First Bank

Industry: **Banks - Regional**

First Commercial Bank is one of the Big Three commercial banks controlled by the Taiwanese provincial government, which holds 50% of the bank's total shares. First Commercial has the largest branch network in Taiwan, with 128 branches and 23 representative offices throughout the island. The bank also has branch offices in Frankfurt, Guam, London, Los Angeles, Singapore, Hong Kong, and Tokyo, and representative offices in Manila, Bangkok, and New York. The bank is in the process of expanding its U.S. business from primarily wholesale banking to include retail operations.

NT$ mil	12/91	12/92	12/93	US$mil 12/93				
Revenues	**59,060.1**	**57,393.3**	**55,806.1**	**2,119.5**	P/E Ratio	**28.3**	Price (9/30/95)	**94.00**
Net Income	**4,637.3**	**2,604.7**	**4,669.7**	**177.4**	P/B Ratio	**4.4**	52 Wk Hi-Low	**162.31-84.00**
Book Value	**21,753.7**	**22,329.3**	**30,030.9**	**1,129.0**	Yield %	**0.0**	Market Cap	**US$6,347.2mil**

Address **30 Chun King S. Rd., Sec. 1**
Taipei
Tel **02-311-1111**
Fax **02-331-0582**
ADR
SEDOL No. **6339526**
President **Kenneth Tsan**
Chairman **Hsiao-Yao Chen**

Formosa Chemical & Fibre

Industry: **Commodity Chemicals**

Formosa Chemical & Fibre manufactures artificial fibers for the textile industry. The company's products include rayon, rayon and blended cloths, spin-draw nylon filaments, and nylon cloths. Formosa Chemical sells its products in Taiwan, Europe, Hong Kong, Indonesia, the United States, the Philippines, and Japan. Formosa Chemical's affiliates include textile manufacturer Taroko Textile and Taih Yung Enterprises, which produces garments, diapers, and sanitary products. The company is a subsidiary of the Formosa Plastics Group, Taiwan's largest private industrial group.

NT$ mil	12/91 R	12/92	12/93	US$mil 12/93				
Sales	**29,550.9**	**26,134.9**	**25,524.0**	**969.4**	P/E Ratio	**15.8**	Price (9/30/95)	**26.00**
Net Income	**5,013.1**	**3,928.0**	**3,376.2**	**128.2**	P/B Ratio	**1.5**	52 Wk Hi-Low	**42.44-24.10**
Book Value	**30,067.6**	**32,082.9**	**34,187.6**	**1,285.2**	Yield %	**2.5**	Market Cap	**US$2,100.1mil**

Address **201 Tun Hwa N. Rd.**
Taipei
Tel **02-712-2211**
Fax **02-712-9211**
ADR
SEDOL No. **6348715**
President --
Chairman **Y.C. Wang**

R=Restated.

Formosa Plastic

Industry: **Commodity Chemicals**

Formosa Plastics is the largest privately-owned industrial group in Taiwan. It manufactures PVC resins and bags, acrylic staples, ethylene, polypropylene, polymers, and liquid caustic soda. Formosa sells its products in Taiwan and exports them internationally. Its affiliates include Nan Ya Plastics in Taiwan and the U.S.' Formosa Plastics America and Formosa Petrochemical. Formosa owns five chemical tankers for ethylene transport. It is building an $8.6 billion petrochemical plant in central Taiwan to be completed in 1997.

NT$ mil	12/92 R	12/93	12/94	US$mil 12/94				
Sales	**26,125.5**	**25,482.9**	**0.0**	**0.0**	P/E Ratio	**21.0**	Price (9/30/95)	**43.70**
Net Income	**3,860.1**	**3,877.3**	**0.0**	**0.0**	P/B Ratio	**NMF**	52 Wk Hi-Low	**54.50-42.52**
Book Value	**26,350.0**	**28,774.1**	**0.0**	**0.0**	Yield %	**2.3**	Market Cap	**US$3,349.5mil**

Address **201 Tun Hwa N. Rd.**
Taipei
Tel **02-712-2211**
Fax **02-712-9211**
ADR
SEDOL No. **6348544**
President --
Chairman **Y.C. Wang**

R=Restated.

Formosa Taffeta

Industry: **Commodity Chemicals**

Formosa Taffeta manufactures products from nylon and other materials. Its products include nylon taffeta, tire cords, cotton weaving, and umbrella ribs. It is a member of Formosa Plastics, Taiwan's leading industrial group. Formosa Taffeta is building its first cement plant in China, a $6 million ready-mixed cement factory that will have an annual production capacity of 1 million tonnes. It is also building a taffeta plant, an umbrella-parts plant, and a tire-cords plant in China, and setting up a plant for testing and packaging integrated circuits in Taiwan.

NT$ mil	12/91	12/92	12/93	US$mil 12/93				
Sales	**N/A**	**N/A**	**N/A**	**N/A**	P/E Ratio	**14.0**	Price (9/30/95)	**19.90**
Net Income	**1,954.9**	**1,264.9**	**1,486.6**	**56.5**	P/B Ratio	**N/A**	52 Wk Hi-Low	**34.09-18.20**
Book Value	**N/A**	**N/A**	**N/A**	**N/A**	Yield %	**3.5**	Market Cap	**US$777.0mil**

Address **11 F, 201 Tun Hwa N. Rd.**
Taipei
Tel **02-715-5354**
Fax **02-713-1329**
ADR
SEDOL No. **6348588**
President --
Chairman --

Goldsun Development & Const.

Industry: **Building Materials**

Goldsun Development and Construction is a concrete-products maker and distributor. The company produces ready-mixed concrete, asbestos cement, silica sheet, fly ash, and gravel. Its operations include reinforcing steel and pile-engineering work, and the quarrying, processing, and distributing of gravel and sand. The company also leases and sells public housing and commercial buildings. Goldsun has 13 subsidiaries and affiliates, including several construction and engineering firms, an investment company, a securities firm, and a concrete-products company in Saudi Arabia.

NT$ mil	12/91	12/92	12/93	US$mil 12/93				
Sales	**N/A**	**N/A**	**N/A**	**N/A**	P/E Ratio	**13.7**	Price (9/30/95)	**19.20**
Net Income	**397.9**	**559.8**	**943.4**	**35.8**	P/B Ratio	**N/A**	52 Wk Hi-Low	**28.22-15.71**
Book Value	**N/A**	**N/A**	**N/A**	**N/A**	Yield %	**2.6**	Market Cap	**US$561.3mil**

Address **10 Fl., 139 Chengchow Rd.**
Taipei
Tel **02-553-9000**
Fax **02-553-7890**
ADR
SEDOL No. **6375564**
President --
Chairman --

Grand Pacific Petrochemical

Industry: **Commodity Chemicals**

Grand Pacific Petrochemical (GPPC) produces materials used in manufacturing plastics, such as styrene monomer and acrylonitrile butadiene styrene (ABS). The firm's total annual Taiwan-based ABS-production capacity is currently 70,000 tonnes. GPPC also has a plant in Thailand, which has an ABS-production capacity of 8,000 tonnes per year. The company sells its products in Taiwan, Hong Kong, Malaysia, Thailand, and North America. The United World Chinese Commercial Bank owns 10% of GPPC's share capital and Overseas Trust, a Taiwanese investment company, holds 6.3%.

	NT$ mil 12/91	12/92	12/93	US$mil 12/93				
Sales	**N/A**	**N/A**	**N/A**	**N/A**	P/E Ratio	**67.5**	Price (9/30/95)	**28.50**
Net Income	**32.4**	**94.1**	**202.6**	**7.7**	P/B Ratio	**N/A**	52 Wk Hi-Low	**70.00-23.14**
Book Value	**N/A**	**N/A**	**N/A**	**N/A**	Yield %	**0.7**	Market Cap	**US$553.8mil**

Address **9 F, 42-1 Hsuchang St.**	Tel **02-311-4731**	ADR	President	**--**
Taipei	Fax **02-361-4240**	SEDOL No. **6381237**	Chairman	**Daniel Wu**

Great Wall Enterprise

Industry: **Other Food**

Great Wall Enterprises is a food company that produces livestock feeds, salad oil, flour, noodles, canned and frozen food, and soft drinks, and distributes them throughout Taiwan. Livestock feeds are the company's main line, accounting for more than 60% of its annual revenues. It is currently negotiating with Arkansas-based Tyson Foods the details of a joint investment in a Chinese poultry farm. The company has 13 subsidiaries, including a holding company and a securities firm, operates Burger King franchises in Taiwan, and runs a flour mill in mainland China.

	NT$ mil 12/91	12/92	12/93	US$mil 12/93				
Sales	**4,861.5**	**4,834.4**	**5,163.3**	**196.1**	P/E Ratio	**108.3**	Price (9/30/95)	**15.70**
Net Income	**317.6**	**135.0**	**37.0**	**1.4**	P/B Ratio	**1.3**	52 Wk Hi-Low	**26.60-13.55**
Book Value	**2,818.9**	**2,950.7**	**3,002.3**	**112.9**	Yield %	**0.0**	Market Cap	**US$157.2mil**

Address **3 Niao Sung 2 St.**	Tel **06-253-1111**	ADR	President	**Han Chiahuan**
Yung Kang Hsiang, Tainan	Fax **06-253-1686**	SEDOL No. **6384344**	Chairman	**Han Haojan**

G.T.M.

Industry: **Clothing & Fabrics**

G.T.M. is a textile producer that is also involved in trading activities. The company manufactures worsted and woolen yarn, fabric, and related products such as cloth, clothing, and bedding. The company also produces and trades raw materials for textiles. G.T.M. has four factories and seven branches, all located in Taiwan. The company distributes its products in Taiwan, Hong Kong, Japan, and Singapore. G.T.M. makes approximately 90% of its total sales in Taiwan, and 10% overseas.

	NT$ mil 12/92	12/93	12/94	US$mil 12/94				
Sales	**527.3**	**467.1**	**453.9**	**17.1**	P/E Ratio	**NMF**	Price (9/30/95)	**36.30**
Net Income	**52.5**	**65.7**	**9.3**	**0.4**	P/B Ratio	**2.2**	52 Wk Hi-Low	**67.00-28.60**
Book Value	**1,923.7**	**1,989.1**	**1,970.7**	**74.9**	Yield %	**0.2**	Market Cap	**US$157.3mil**

Address **300 Chung Hsiao Rd., Sec 2.**	Tel **02-741-5000**	ADR	President	**Ku Chaochi**
Taipei	Fax **02-776-5073**	SEDOL No. **6357993**	Chairman	**Ku Hsingchung**

Hsin Chu Bank

Industry: **Banks - Regional**

Medium Business Bank of Hsin Chu is a regional bank offering deposit, loan, financing, credit-card, securities, and investing services mainly in the Taoyun, Hsinchu, and Miaoli areas of Taiwan. The bank has 66 regional branches. In 1995, Hsin Chu Bank opened a branch office in Taipei, its first branch outside its regional territory. Its is the largest regional bank in Taiwan taking NT$180 billion in deposits and offering NT$138.2 billion in loans. The main service of the bank's loan operations is to provide business customers with mid- and long-term credit.

	NT$ mil 12/92	12/93	12/94	US$mil 12/94				
Revenues	**11,833.6**	**14,190.5**	**16,175.4**	**610.6**	P/E Ratio	**20.2**	Price (9/30/95)	**84.00**
Net Income	**1,341.9**	**1,824.4**	**2,116.8**	**79.9**	P/B Ratio	**3.3**	52 Wk Hi-Low	**145.19-75.50**
Book Value	**5,473.8**	**7,509.3**	**9,847.8**	**374.2**	Yield %	**0.0**	Market Cap	**US$1,600.8mil**

Address **106 Chung-Yang Rd.**	Tel **035-245-131**	ADR	President	**Shuan Yung Chan**
Hsinchu	Fax **035-251-531**	SEDOL No. **6575096**	Chairman	**Shad-Hwa Chan**

Hua Engineering Wire & Cable

Industry: **Electrical Components & Equipment**

Hua Engineering Wire & Cable manufactures communication cables and electrical wire. Its products include power cables, communication cables, and copper wires. Hua Engineering is an affiliate of the wire and steel company First Copper & Rubber. The company has $30 million in investments in wire factories in Ningbo, Shanghai, Fujian, Xinjiang, Wuxi, and Shenyang province, China. The company sells its products domestically, and exports them to Southeast Asia and the Middle East as well. Hua Engineering is controlled by the Wang family of Kaohsiung.

	NT$ mil 12/92	12/93	12/94	US$mil 12/94				
Sales	**4,725.6**	**5,225.5**	**5,764.7**	**217.6**	P/E Ratio	**15.8**	Price (9/30/95)	**20.10**
Net Income	**592.6**	**642.6**	**555.6**	**21.0**	P/B Ratio	**1.4**	52 Wk Hi-Low	**32.90-17.90**
Book Value	**5,989.2**	**6,077.2**	**6,125.6**	**232.7**	Yield %	**5.0**	Market Cap	**US$346.9mil**

Address **170 Chung Cheng 4th Rd.**	Tel **07-281-4161**	ADR	President	**Lien-Fang Tsai**
Kaoshiung	Fax **07-281-0110**	SEDOL No. **6441885**	Chairman	**Yu-Cheng Wang**

Hua Nan Commercial Bank

Industry: **Banks - Regional**

Hua Nan Commercial Bank is a deposit-taking and commercial bank that also offers general-banking and securities-brokerage services. It has assets of about NT$798 billion and operates 142 branches in Taiwan. Hua Nan maintains offices domestically in Taipei County, Taoyuan, and Hsinchu, and overseas in Los Angeles, New York, Tokyo, Frankfurt, Hong Kong, and London. Majority-owned by Taiwan's government, Hua Nan is one of the country's three leading commercial banks. It also conducts trade finance and remittances with mainland China through its offshore branches.

NT$ mil	06/92	06/93	06/94	US$mil 06/94				
Revenues	**55,012.6**	**53,235.9**	**54,253.6**	**2,039.0**	P/E Ratio	**24.3**	Price (9/30/95)	**91.00**
Net Income	**2,952.5**	**5,269.0**	**5,334.9**	**200.5**	P/B Ratio	**3.8**	52 Wk Hi-Low	**154.67-87.00**
Book Value	**23,425.5**	**28,864.5**	**34,200.2**	**1,275.7**	Yield %	**0.0**	Market Cap	**US$7,186.2mil**

Address **38 Chung-king S. Rd.**
Taipei
Tel **02-371-3111**
Fax **02-331-5737**
ADR
SEDOL No. **6449102**
President **Edward H.T. Chien**
Chairman **James C. T. Lo**

Hualon-Teijran

Industry: **Commodity Chemicals**

Hualon-Teijran, a textile manufacturer, is the flagship company for the Hualon Group, Taiwan's ninth-largest business group, with $4 billion in assets. It produces polyester filaments, taffeta, nylon-filament yarns and cloths, and blended yarns. Other affiliates include Taiwan Tea, textile maker Chia Hsin Livestock, Min Hsu Cotton, semiconductor firm Hualon Microelectronics, and E-Hsin International, a trading firm. Hualon has two textile plants in Malaysia, and is currently building a $247 million textile plant in Vietnam and a $250 million factory in Ireland.

NT$ mil	12/91	12/92	12/93	US$mil 12/93				
Sales	**20,155.1**	**19,505.8**	**21,985.5**	**835.0**	P/E Ratio	**NMF**	Price (9/30/95)	**19.70**
Net Income	**3,472.6**	**850.1**	**-384.0**	**-14.6**	P/B Ratio	**1.4**	52 Wk Hi-Low	**38.00-14.39**
Book Value	**19,653.9**	**21,489.5**	**21,324.7**	**801.7**	Yield %	**0.0**	Market Cap	**US$1,408.4mil**

Address **7-8 Fl., 42 Chungshan N. Rd.**
Sec. 2, Taipei
Tel **02-537-7811**
Fax **02-537-2380**
ADR
SEDOL No. **6441937**
President **Qingxiong Liang**
Chairman **Youming Weng**

International Bills Finance

Industry: **Financial Services - Diversified**

International Bills Finance is a financial-services company that is active in money-market investment and bill financing. It underwrites commercial paper primarily for manufacturers and construction firms, extends credit, and conducts trading operations. Commercial paper and negotiable certificates of deposit contribute approximately 97% of the firm's trading volume; roughly 90% of its transactions involve banks or private enterprises. International Bills Finance is controlled by Taiwanese government-owned concerns.

NT$ mil	12/91	12/92	12/93	US$mil 12/93				
Revenues	**1,484.9**	**1,610.3**	**1,645.8**	**62.5**	P/E Ratio	**7.1**	Price (9/30/95)	**15.50**
Net Income	**1,361.4**	**1,420.5**	**1,491.7**	**56.7**	P/B Ratio	**1.0**	52 Wk Hi-Low	**39.42-11.00**
Book Value	**6,596.9**	**9,691.0**	**11,088.7**	**416.9**	Yield %	**N/A**	Market Cap	**US$639.9mil**

Address **Taipei Fin. Ctr., 62 Tun Hwa Rd.**
Taipei
Tel **02-772-5335**
Fax **02-741-8411**
ADR
SEDOL No. **6464503**
President **Kenneth K.T. Chao**
Chairman **K.H. King**

International Commercial Bank

Industry: **Financial Services - Diversified**

International Commercial Bank of China (ICBC) is a commercial-banking business offering deposits, loans, foreign-exchange and offshore banking, securities investments, guarantees, agency services, and stockbroking. It has 45 branch offices in Taiwan, the United States, Japan, Panama, the Philippines, Vietnam, Bahrain, and Europe. Its overseas subsidiaries include International Commercial Bank of Cathay in Canada, the Chinese American Bank in New York, Cathay Finance International Holdings in Sydney, and ICBC Europe in Amsterdam. ICBC is 48%-owned by the cabinet of Taiwan.

NT$ mil	12/92	12/93	12/94	US$mil 12/94				
Revenues	**17,417.8**	**19,554.1**	**24,454.2**	**923.1**	P/E Ratio	**34.0**	Price (9/30/95)	**62.50**
Net Income	**2,359.9**	**2,490.7**	**3,081.7**	**116.3**	P/B Ratio	**4.1**	52 Wk Hi-Low	**100.00-45.60**
Book Value	**21,085.1**	**23,180.4**	**25,534.2**	**970.1**	Yield %	**0.5**	Market Cap	**US$3,887.4mil**

Address **100 Chi-lin Rd.**
Taipei
Tel **02-563-3156**
Fax **02-561-1216**
ADR
SEDOL No. **6455057**
President **Theodore S.S. Cheng**
Chairman **P. Y. Pai**

Kwong Fong Industries

Industry: **Clothing & Fabrics**

Kwong Fong Industries is a conglomerate that manufactures textiles. Its products include towels, bed linens, and yarn. Kwong Fong sells its products in Taiwan and exports them to Thailand, Canada, Europe, Australia, Asia, and the U.S. It has two Hong-Kong-based subsidiaries, Great China Metal Industry and Chinney Investment. Great China manufactures aluminum and tin cans, which it sells in Taiwan, Hong Kong, Japan, and South Korea. Chinney is active in trading, apparel manufacturing, and building construction. Kwong Fong also has textiles and dyeing operations in China.

NT$ mil	12/92	12/93	12/94	US$mil 12/94				
Sales	**N/A**	**N/A**	**0.0**	**0.0**	P/E Ratio	**NMF**	Price (9/30/95)	**15.90**
Net Income	**-134.0**	**-296.5**	**0.0**	**0.0**	P/B Ratio	**NMF**	52 Wk Hi-Low	**27.57-14.20**
Book Value	**N/A**	**N/A**	**0.0**	**0.0**	Yield %	**0.0**	Market Cap	**US$184.4mil**

Address **72 Nanking E. Rd., Sec. 2**
Taipei
Tel **02-561-5100**
Fax **02-521-6071**
ADR
SEDOL No. **6498193**
President **Yamin Wang**
Chairman **Yingcai He**

Lien Hwa Industrial

Industry: **Other Food**

Lien Hwa Industrial is a holding company with interests in food, shipbuilding, tools, computers, and industrial gases. It makes agricultural equipment, motor and sailing yachts, petrochemicals, personal computers, and processed foods such as wheat flour and flaked barley. Lien Hwa has branch offices in Japan, the United States, Hong Kong, and Singapore. Its major markets are Taiwan, Thailand, Hong Kong, Malaysia, Japan, and the U.S. Lien Hwa has three domestic subsidiaries: Lien Hwa Industrial Gases, Union Petrochemical, and personal-computer maker Mitac International.

NT$ mil	12/91	12/92	12/93	US$mil 12/93				
Sales	**730.5**	**889.6**	**902.5**	**34.3**	P/E Ratio	**NMF**	Price (9/30/95)	**25.80**
Net Income	**404.6**	**203.9**	**-54.1**	**-2.1**	P/B Ratio	**1.9**	52 Wk Hi-Low	**48.33-21.90**
Book Value	**5,639.5**	**5,719.5**	**5,581.0**	**209.8**	Yield %	**0.8**	Market Cap	**US$478.5mil**

Address **77 Changan W. Road**
Taipei
Tel **02-511-5981**
Fax **02-541-9152**
ADR
SEDOL No. **6515144**
President --
Chairman --

Liton Electronic

Industry: **Electrical Components & Equipment**

Taiwan Liton Electronic is an electronic-component manufacturer. Its products include light-emitting diodes, numeric displays, switch power supplies, and lamps. Taiwan Liton has factories in Taiwan, Thailand, Malaysia, and mainland China. The firm sells its products in Taiwan, Europe, Hong Kong, northeast and Southeast Asia, and the United States. A member of the Taiwanese conglomerate Liton Group, its affiliates include semiconductor-wafer producer Silitek Corp.; Lite-On, a U.S. semiconductor-component maker; and Diodes, a U.S. producer of light-emitting diodes.

NT$ mil	12/91	12/92	12/93	US$mil 12/93				
Sales	**3,246.3**	**3,669.6**	**4,707.8**	**178.8**	P/E Ratio	**33.8**	Price (9/30/95)	**40.50**
Net Income	**150.1**	**130.8**	**339.5**	**12.9**	P/B Ratio	**3.7**	52 Wk Hi-Low	**59.57-35.60**
Book Value	**2,034.0**	**2,155.2**	**2,566.8**	**96.5**	Yield %	**1.1**	Market Cap	**US$362.3mil**

Address **12 Fl., 25 Tunhwa S. Rd.**
Taipei
Tel **02-771-4321**
Fax **02-751-1962**
ADR
SEDOL No. **6519737**
President **Warren Chen**
Chairman **Raymong Soong**

Mercuries & Associates

Industry: **Retailers - Broadline**

Mercuries & Associates is a food-processing, retailing, and electronic-services company. The company produces processed foods and drinks, and is involved in the manufacturing, trading, and services industries as well. It operates department stores and fast-food restaurants. Mercuries & Associates operates more than 100 divisions located throughout Taiwan and Hong Kong. The company distributes its products locally and exports them to overseas markets. Mercuries & Associates is also involved in gift production and distribution and services electronic paging equipment.

NT$ mil	12/91	12/92	12/93	US$mil 12/93				
Revenues	**9,002.0**	**9,429.0**	**9,879.0**	**375.2**	P/E Ratio	**21.4**	Price (9/30/95)	**37.60**
Net Income	**234.9**	**396.9**	**539.7**	**20.5**	P/B Ratio	**2.3**	52 Wk Hi-Low	**57.08-33.40**
Book Value	**2,355.2**	**3,629.9**	**3,988.9**	**150.0**	Yield %	**2.7**	Market Cap	**US$408.0mil**

Address **145 Chien-Kuo N. Rd., Sec. 2**
Taipei
Tel **02-503-1111**
Fax **02-505-7050**
ADR
SEDOL No. **6580454**
President **Hotung Chen**
Chairman **Chaohshi Loeng**

Microtek International

Industry: **Computers**

Microtek designs and manufactures computer peripherals and telecommunication equipment. Its line of computer peripherals includes optical-image scanners, computer printers, and monitors. The company holds approximately a 20% share of the world image-scanner market. Microtek's 70%-owned Advanced Communications Technology subsidiary manufactures cordless telephones and other communication products. Microtek markets its products in Europe, the United States, and Asia. The company is currently constructing manufacturing facilities in several cities in mainland China.

NT$ mil	12/92	12/93	12/94	US$mil 12/94				
Sales	**2,083.7**	**2,342.7**	**2,995.2**	**113.1**	P/E Ratio	**56.6**	Price (9/30/95)	**38.50**
Net Income	**54.8**	**221.4**	**124.5**	**4.7**	P/B Ratio	**2.9**	52 Wk Hi-Low	**43.20-29.45**
Book Value	**2,188.2**	**2,426.4**	**2,460.2**	**93.5**	Yield %	**2.6**	Market Cap	**US$290.3mil**

Address **6 Industry E. Rd. 3**
Hsinchu
Tel **02-501-6699**
Fax **02-505-7026**
ADR
SEDOL No. **6592062**
President **Benny Hsu**
Chairman **Benny Hsu**

Nan Kang Rubber Tire

Industry: **Tires & Rubber**

Nan Kang Rubber Tire manufactures and distributes rubber tires and tubes for automobiles and trucks. The company sells its products in Taiwan, the United States, Europe, Asia, and the Middle East. Nan Kang's affiliates include Shihlin Electrical and Motor and the Ambassador Hotel. Nan Kang Rubber Tire is nearly 24%-owned by Kuo Feng Corporation, a Taiwanese manufacturer of computer monitors. Both Kuo Feng and Shihlin Electronics and Engineering are bidding for a controlling interest in the company.

NT$ mil	12/91	12/92	12/93	US$mil 12/93				
Sales	**N/A**	**N/A**	**N/A**	**N/A**	P/E Ratio	**NMF**	Price (9/30/95)	**39.40**
Net Income	**-124.2**	**-169.9**	**-94.3**	**-3.6**	P/B Ratio	**N/A**	52 Wk Hi-Low	**92.50-39.30**
Book Value	**N/A**	**N/A**	**N/A**	**N/A**	Yield %	**0.0**	Market Cap	**US$188.7mil**

Address **9 Chang An E. Rd., Sec. 1**
Taipei
Tel **02-511-7171**
Fax **02-541-3642**
ADR
SEDOL No. **6621427**
President **Tongmaolang Pian**
Chairman **Shuzhen Xu**

Nan Ya Plastics

Industry: **Commodity Chemicals**

Nan Ya Plastics manufactures petrochemical products and electronic components. Its petrochemical products include polyester fibers used in fabrics, polyvinyl chloride (PVC) for plumbing and other piping, and polyethylene terephthalate (PET) used in plastic containers. The company makes electronic components for computers and peripherals, including memory chips, liquid crystal displays, and printed-circuit boards. Nan Ya Plastics is planning to begin production of medical equipment and small cars. The company is a majority-owned subsidiary of Formosa Plastics.

NT$ mil	12/91 R	12/92	12/93	US$mil 12/93				
Sales	62,106.0	62,188.4	63,125.5	2,397.5	P/E Ratio	17.1	Price (9/30/95)	46.00
Net Income	5,038.8	4,999.6	5,892.5	223.8	P/B Ratio	2.7	52 Wk Hi-Low	57.40-43.90
Book Value	26,141.2	29,313.2	33,507.2	1,259.7	Yield %	2.2	Market Cap	US$4,151.9mil

Address **201 Tun Hwa N. Rd.**
Taipei
Tel **02-712-2211**
Fax **02-712-9211**
ADR
SEDOL No. **6621580**
President **--**
Chairman **Y.C. Wang**

R=Restated.

Pacific Construction

Industry: **Heavy Construction**

Pacific Construction is one of the largest real-estate developers in Taiwan. The company focuses on public-works construction projects throughout Taiwan. Pacific Construction owns 55% of a joint-venture consulting company in Taiwan with the Japanese contractor Fujita. The company, Pacific-Fujita, handles urban-planning, environmental-protection, and national infrastructure projects. Pacific Construction owns a holding company in the United States, which invests in luxury residential property, and a 26% interest in Artif Technology, a multimedia-products manufacturer.

NT$ mil	12/91	12/92	12/93	US$mil 12/93				
Sales	7,245.4	8,746.3	7,476.1	283.9	P/E Ratio	24.7	Price (9/30/95)	19.40
Net Income	781.3	1,039.2	696.5	26.5	P/B Ratio	1.4	52 Wk Hi-Low	27.95-16.10
Book Value	9,218.8	10,222.0	10,800.6	406.0	Yield %	0.0	Market Cap	US$636.2mil

Address **285 Chung Hsiao E. Rd., Sec. 4**
Taipei
Tel **02-751-0051**
Fax **02-776-4391**
ADR
SEDOL No. **6665964**
President **Chu Wen Jeng**
Chairman **Chaig Minchiang**

Pacific Electric Wire & Cable

Industry: **Electrical Components & Equipment**

Pacific Electric Wire & Cable (PEWC) has diversified operations that include the manufacture of wires and cables, banking, telecommunications, real estate, and hotels. The company's core business produces roughly 191,000 tonnes of wire and cable per year in Taiwan and Thailand. Its 93%-owned Pacific USA subsidiary manages the company's U.S. investments, including Pacific Southwest Bank in Texas. PEWC's joint ventures include the Hotel Conrad Hong Kong with Swire Properties and Hilton Hotels, and Pacific Iridium, a satellite-telecommunication venture with Motorola.

NT$ mil	12/92	12/93	12/94	US$mil 12/94				
Sales	15,442.2	13,053.2	14,434.5	544.9	P/E Ratio	29.4	Price (9/30/95)	20.90
Net Income	1,937.4	188.7	775.4	29.3	P/B Ratio	1.5	52 Wk Hi-Low	27.45-18.00
Book Value	13,033.6	13,436.5	16,305.7	619.5	Yield %	6.2	Market Cap	US$987.8mil

Address **285 Chung Hsiao E. Rd., Sec 4**
Taipei
Tel **02-741-0211**
Fax **02-752-0480**
ADR
SEDOL No. **6666138**
President **Jack T. Sun**
Chairman **Yu-jeh Tung**

President Enterprises

Industry: **Other Food**

President Enterprises is an integrated food-processing company. Its products include beverages, instant noodles, processed fruits, vegetable oils, snack foods, and animal feed. Its 63%-owned President Chain Store subsidiary operates convenience stores throughout Taiwan, including more than 900 7-Eleven stores. President Enterprises and PepsiCo market Pepsi and Frito-Lay products on the island through their President-PepsiCo Bottling joint venture. Through a joint venture with Japan's Duskin Serve, the company provides janitorial services and cleaning-equipment rental.

NT$ mil	12/92	12/93	12/94	US$mil 12/94				
Sales	45,706.0	51,319.5	56,388.0	2,128.5	P/E Ratio	5.5	Price (9/30/95)	32.30
Net Income	2,106.0	2,714.3	6,943.0	262.1	P/B Ratio	1.7	52 Wk Hi-Low	50.38-29.00
Book Value	13,281.0	15,994.1	22,716.9	863.1	Yield %	1.5	Market Cap	US$1,839.0mil

Address **310 Chungcheng Rd.**
Yungkang, Tainan
Tel **06-253-2121**
Fax **06-253-2661**
ADR
SEDOL No. **6700393**
President **Chang Sheng Lin**
Chairman **Shiu Chi Wu**

Ruentex Industries

Industry: **Clothing & Fabrics**

Ruentex Industries' diversified interests include textile manufacture and retail, construction, and property development. The firm's six textile mills in Taiwan annually produce 60 million yards of cloth for such customers as Levi-Strauss, Marks & Spencer, and Wal-Mart. It sells Nautica products, of which it is Taiwan's sole retailer, through three outlets in Taipei. Ruentex also holds a 50% stake in Ruentex Cement and a 24% stake in Ever Pioneer Steel. The company develops residential and commercial properties through its 18%-owned Ruentex Construction & Development.

NT$ mil	12/92 R	12/93	12/94	US$mil 12/94				
Sales	2,128.6	2,659.1	3,598.9	135.8	P/E Ratio	8.8	Price (9/30/95)	14.15
Net Income	84.4	-57.9	190.9	7.2	P/B Ratio	1.1	52 Wk Hi-Low	30.77-13.00
Book Value	3,642.7	3,584.8	4,095.9	155.6	Yield %	7.1	Market Cap	US$225.7mil

Address **76 Tun-Hua S. Rd., Sec 2**
Taipei
Tel **02-705-8181**
Fax **02-703-1170**
ADR
SEDOL No. **6758422**
President **Ming-Tuan Huang**
Chairman **Leda W. Yin**

R=Restated.

Sampo

Industry: **Electrical Components & Equipment**

Sampo manufactures consumer electronics, electric devices, and communication equipment, and also designs plastic products. The company's products include televisions, air-conditioners, computer peripherals, videocassette recorders, and various electric household appliances. Sampo markets these products under the Sampo, AlphaScan, OfficePro, and other trademarks. In addition, it distributes Chrysler automobiles on the island of Taiwan and is constructing a VCR-manufacturing facility in China. Sharp of Japan owns 8% of the company's shares.

NT$ mil	12/91	12/92	12/93	US$mil 12/93				
Sales	**10,259.0**	**11,630.5**	**12,677.5**	**481.5**	P/E Ratio	**21.5**	Price (9/30/95)	**23.00**
Net Income	**222.2**	**489.9**	**664.7**	**25.2**	P/B Ratio	**1.8**	52 Wk Hi-Low	**38.12-19.60**
Book Value	**5,727.6**	**6,229.6**	**7,082.8**	**266.3**	Yield %	**2.2**	Market Cap	**US$537.5mil**

Address **217 Nanking E. Rd., Sec. 3**, **Taipei**
Tel **02-715-2111** Fax **02-717-2900**
ADR
SEDOL No. **6771924**
President --
Chairman --

Shihlin Electric & Engineering

Industry: **Electrical Components & Equipment**

Shihlin Electric and Engineering makes electrical appliances and machinery. Its main line is machines for factory automation. Its products include power transformers, capacitors, switchgear and control panels, magnetic switches, nonfuse breakers, electric auto parts, and other electronic products. Shihlin Electric has five branch offices in Taiwan and two subsidiaries, Fulin Industrial and Fung Lin Engineering. The company sells its products in Taiwan, Southeast Asia, Japan, North America, and Latin America. Mitsubishi Electric of Japan is one of its major shareholders.

NT$ mil	12/92	12/93	12/94	US$mil 12/94				
Sales	**6,692.7**	**7,211.6**	**7,700.1**	**290.7**	P/E Ratio	**22.3**	Price (9/30/95)	**44.50**
Net Income	**416.6**	**436.7**	**541.5**	**20.4**	P/B Ratio	**2.3**	52 Wk Hi-Low	**62.13-39.20**
Book Value	**3,924.1**	**4,191.8**	**4,596.3**	**174.6**	Yield %	**1.1**	Market Cap	**US$465.3mil**

Address **75 Chung Shan N. Rd., Sec. 6**, **Taipei**
Tel **02-834-2662** Fax **02-836-6187**
ADR
SEDOL No. **6804198**
President **Tsang-Ming Chou**
Chairman **Chin-Te Hsu**

Shihlin Paper

Industry: **Paper Products**

Shihlin Paper is a paper-products and packaging manufacturer. The company produces roughly 195,000 tonnes of paper per year from its two mills located in Taiwan. Shihlin Paper's products include coated board and ivory board for high-quality paper products and packaging, color board for stationery, and wallpaper. The company's primary customers are located in Taiwan, China, and Hong Kong. Shihlin Paper has a wholly-owned subsidiary, Shihlin Environmental Purification, that processes wastewater from the company's manufacturing facilities.

NT$ mil	12/91 R	12/92	12/93	US$mil 12/93				
Sales	**2,523.1**	**2,396.3**	**2,221.7**	**84.4**	P/E Ratio	**138.1**	Price (9/30/95)	**48.20**
Net Income	**20.2**	**97.0**	**64.4**	**2.4**	P/B Ratio	**3.6**	52 Wk Hi-Low	**73.66-33.95**
Book Value	**2,289.9**	**2,436.4**	**2,492.5**	**93.7**	Yield %	**1.8**	Market Cap	**US$370.6mil**

Address **18 Futeh Rd., Shihlin District**, **Taipei**
Tel **02-881-1111** Fax **02-882-3800**
ADR
SEDOL No. **6804530**
President **C.S. Lin**
Chairman **Chen Chaw Chuan**

R=Restated.

Shinkong Synthetic Fiber

Industry: **Commodity Chemicals**

Shinkong Synthetic Fiber is a textile manufacturer that produces polyester fibers, chips, filament yarns, and films. It also makes video tapes, engineering plastics, bottle-grade chip, polyester bottles, and nylon filament. Shinkong Synthetic Fiber sells its products in Taiwan and internationally. It operates three factory sites that together produce 1,050 metric tonnes of polymers daily. A member of the diversified Taiwanese Shinkong Group conglomerate, the company's affiliates include Shinkong Spinning and Shinkong Co.

NT$ mil	12/92	12/93	12/94	US$mil 12/94				
Sales	**11,602.1**	**11,698.7**	**14,131.6**	**533.4**	P/E Ratio	**21.4**	Price (9/30/95)	**28.70**
Net Income	**358.5**	**387.9**	**1,055.4**	**39.8**	P/B Ratio	**2.2**	52 Wk Hi-Low	**51.00-20.10**
Book Value	**9,156.0**	**9,278.2**	**10,215.2**	**388.1**	Yield %	**0.0**	Market Cap	**US$821.6mil**

Address **123 Nan King E. Rd.**, **Taipei**
Tel **02-507-1251** Fax **02-507-2264**
ADR
SEDOL No. **6804886**
President **Thomas T.L. Wu**
Chairman **Eugene T.C. Wu**

Sinkong Spinning

Industry: **Clothing & Fabrics**

Sinkong Spinning is a textile manufacturer. The company's textile products include fabrics, blended yarns, and cotton. The company distributes its textile products in Taiwan, Hong Kong, the Philippines, Singapore, Thailand, South Africa, the Netherlands, and Germany. Sinkong Spinning has plans to invest $38.5 million in a joint-venture gauze factory on mainland China before the end of 1995. Sinkong Spinning has interests in the supermarket industry as well.

NT$ mil	12/91	12/92	12/93	US$mil 12/93				
Sales	**1,513.5**	**1,222.5**	**2,725.0**	**103.5**	P/E Ratio	**10.7**	Price (9/30/95)	**22.80**
Net Income	**-163.5**	**-577.2**	**563.0**	**21.4**	P/B Ratio	**1.7**	52 Wk Hi-Low	**31.91-16.80**
Book Value	**3,540.5**	**2,997.7**	**3,548.8**	**133.4**	Yield %	**0.0**	Market Cap	**US$245.0mil**

Address **123 Nanking E. Rd., Sec. 2**, **Taipei**
Tel **02-507-1251** Fax **02-564-2224**
ADR
SEDOL No. **6811693**
President **Qiaorong Hu**
Chairman **Dongjin Wu**

Tainan Spinning

Industry: **Commodity Chemicals**

Tainan Spinning is a polyester-textile-products manufacturer, and is one of Taiwan's largest textile makers by sales. Its products include polyester yarns, fibers, filaments, and staples. Tainan Spinning is a leading manufacturer of cotton yarns as well. The company sells its products in Taiwan, and exports them to Hong Kong, Australia, the Philippines, Singapore, and Thailand. Tainan Spinning has significant landholdings in the southern region of Taiwan. The company plans to invest $40 million to set up textile-production facilities in mainland China.

NT$ mil	12/91	12/92	12/93	US$mil 12/93				
Sales	**7,827.1**	**6,508.6**	**6,791.3**	**257.9**	P/E Ratio	**52.6**	Price (9/30/95)	**22.00**
Net Income	**1,150.5**	**877.2**	**455.3**	**17.3**	P/B Ratio	**1.7**	52 Wk Hi-Low	**38.81-19.00**
Book Value	**11,111.7**	**12,494.0**	**12,927.0**	**486.0**	Yield %	**0.0**	Market Cap	**US$1,122.6mil**

Address **511 Yu-Nung Rd. E. District**
Tainan
Tel **06-237-6161**
Fax **06-235-6629**
ADR
SEDOL No. **6871824**
President --
Chairman --

Taipei Business Bank

Industry: **Banks - Regional**

Taipei Business Bank is a regional bank that provides general banking and financial services. The bank caters to individuals and small- and medium-size businesses. The company operates 62 branches and two sub-branches located throughout northern Taiwan, including the Taipei area. Five of the branches are locations for international banking business and 29 branches offer foreign currencies and traveler's checks. The bank also operates a representitive office in Hong Kong. Lien Chan, the premier of Taiwan, has significant investment links with Taipei Business Bank.

NT$ mil	12/92 R	12/93	12/94	US$mil 12/94				
Revenues	**12,150.6**	**14,971.9**	**16,980.6**	**641.0**	P/E Ratio	**24.2**	Price (9/30/95)	**73.50**
Net Income	**1,490.9**	**1,863.0**	**2,603.9**	**98.3**	P/B Ratio	**4.7**	52 Wk Hi-Low	**94.07-58.50**
Book Value	**9,901.8**	**11,269.7**	**13,482.8**	**512.3**	Yield %	**0.0**	Market Cap	**US$2,754.8mil**

Address **36 Nanking E. Rd., Sec 3**
Taipei
Tel **02-506-3333**
Fax **02-506-2462**
ADR
SEDOL No. **6869993**
President **K.C. Yu**
Chairman **S.C. Ho**

R=Restated.

Taiwan Cement

Industry: **Building Materials**

Taiwan Cement is Taiwan's largest cement company by revenues. It produces cement, hardened bricks, and ready-mixed concrete, and has an annual cement-production capacity of 5.6 million tonnes. The company has a cement joint venture in Thailand with Bangkok Bank, and another in Vietnam to construct a sugar-processing plant. It also has an agreement with Singapore's Government Investment Corporation and France's Lafarge Coppee to build cement plants in Southeast Asia. Taiwan Cement is the industrial arm of the Koos Group, a family-run banking and industrial conglomerate.

NT$ mil	12/91	12/92	12/93	US$mil 12/93				
Sales	**15,283.7**	**17,481.1**	**20,180.8**	**766.5**	P/E Ratio	**10.8**	Price (9/30/95)	**35.10**
Net Income	**2,883.9**	**2,993.8**	**3,725.7**	**141.5**	P/B Ratio	**1.8**	52 Wk Hi-Low	**50.89-32.10**
Book Value	**16,362.3**	**17,743.8**	**19,232.6**	**723.0**	Yield %	**5.7**	Market Cap	**US$1,863.4mil**

Address **16-5 Tehwei St.**
Taipei
Tel **02-586-5101**
Fax **02-586-2337**
ADR
SEDOL No. **6869937**
President **Koo Cheng-yun**
Chairman **Koo Chen-fu**

Taiwan Glass

Industry: **Containers & Packaging**

Taiwan Glass owns and operates three factories in Taiwan, producing roughly 600,000 tonnes of glass per annum. The company produces float, tempered, laminated, mirrored, rolled, laminated, container, tableware, and heat-resistant glass. It also manufactures glass fabric for use in the production of circuit boards. Its joint-venture interests in China, undertaken with U.K.-based Pilkington and Japan's Nippon Sheet Glass, include a 54% stake in factories producing float glass and rolled glass.

NT$ mil	12/92 R	12/93	12/94	US$mil 12/94				
Sales	**6,836.2**	**7,509.7**	**9,052.7**	**341.7**	P/E Ratio	**16.8**	Price (9/30/95)	**48.90**
Net Income	**806.5**	**1,279.1**	**1,834.0**	**69.2**	P/B Ratio	**2.3**	52 Wk Hi-Low	**55.22-43.04**
Book Value	**10,622.4**	**11,838.5**	**13,365.4**	**507.8**	Yield %	**3.7**	Market Cap	**US$1,322.1mil**

Address **261 Nanking E. Rd.**
Taipei
Tel **02-713-0333**
Fax **02-715-0333**
ADR
SEDOL No. **6870865**
President **Por-Fong Lin**
Chairman **Yu-Chia Lin**

R=Restated.

Taiwan Kolin

Industry: **Other Home Furnishings**

Taiwan Kolin is a household- and electronic-appliance manufacturer. The company's products include air conditioners, color televisions, washing machines, videocassette recorders, and refrigerators. Taiwan Kolin has a joint venture with the Japanese audio-equipment and recordings producer Nippon Columbia. The K and D Music joint venture, of which Taiwan Kolin owns 60%, produces and sells recordings of Japanese music in Taiwan. Taiwan Kolin imports components for production from Japan. The company sells its products in Taiwan and Japan.

NT$ mil	12/91	12/92	12/93	US$mil 12/93				
Sales	**5,825.2**	**6,393.9**	**6,706.9**	**254.7**	P/E Ratio	**25.2**	Price (9/30/95)	**16.90**
Net Income	**206.2**	**226.8**	**235.5**	**8.9**	P/B Ratio	**1.2**	52 Wk Hi-Low	**28.58-15.00**
Book Value	**3,969.4**	**4,077.2**	**4,511.6**	**169.6**	Yield %	**3.0**	Market Cap	**US$211.8mil**

Address **83 Chungking S. Rd., Sec. 1**
Taipei
Tel **02-314-3151**
Fax **02-361-4037**
ADR
SEDOL No. **6496380**
President --
Chairman --

Taiwan Paper

Industry: **Paper Products**

Taiwan Pulp & Paper manufactures and distributes paper, pulp, and pharmaceuticals. The company's products include pulp, wood-free paper, poster paper, and high-quality paper such as home or office stationery. Taiwan Paper sells its products in Taiwan, Hong Kong, Southeast Asia, and South Korea. The company is expanding its overseas operations; in 1995 it invested $30 million in two plastics and construction-materials companies in Hong Kong. Also in 1995, Taiwan Paper invested $101 million in a pulp plant and sales operation in Vietnam.

NT$ mil	12/91	12/92	12/93	US$mil 12/93				
Sales	**2,931.5**	**1,185.0**	**1,133.5**	**43.0**	P/E Ratio	**NMF**	Price (9/30/95)	**21.60**
Net Income	**-95.8**	**-349.2**	**-927.9**	**-35.2**	P/B Ratio	**2.2**	52 Wk Hi-Low	**47.60-17.50**
Book Value	**5,078.3**	**4,729.2**	**4,307.6**	**161.9**	Yield %	**0.0**	Market Cap	**US$348.5mil**

Address **53 Nanking E. Rd., Sec. 2, Taipei**
Tel **02-511-5181**
Fax **02-531-5797**
ADR
SEDOL No. **6871084**
President **Bohong Zhang**
Chairman **Neng Cai**

Taiwan Pineapple

Industry: **Other Food**

Taiwan Pineapple is a canned-food manufacturer that also engages in land-development operations. It makes canned pineapple and other fruits, juices, and vegetables. Taiwan Pineapple is developing a golf course, a hotel, and an amusement park in Taiwan. The company has offices in Tokyo and Jakarta. Taiwan Pineapple has several subsidiaries, including Ta Tung Paper Container Corp., Phoenix Enterprise Corp., Typhone Silk Corp., Phoenix Recreational Corp., Typhone Investment Corp., and Typhone Allied ABC Co.

NT$ mil	12/91	12/92	12/93	US$mil 12/93				
Sales	**816.1**	**873.5**	**1,026.5**	**39.0**	P/E Ratio	**7.5**	Price (9/30/95)	**35.40**
Net Income	**88.0**	**-229.4**	**800.7**	**30.4**	P/B Ratio	**2.3**	52 Wk Hi-Low	**56.96-27.12**
Book Value	**2,044.0**	**1,814.5**	**2,622.2**	**98.6**	Yield %	**0.0**	Market Cap	**US$377.7mil**

Address **15 Chungking S. Rd., Sec. 1, Taipei**
Tel **02-381-1711**
Fax **02-381-1725**
ADR
SEDOL No. **6870650**
President **Zonghong Huang**
Chairman **Yedongmei Huang**

Taiwan Synthetic Rubber

Industry: **Tires & Rubber**

Taiwan Synthetic Rubber is Taiwan's sole synthetic-rubber manufacturer. It produces styrene-butadiene rubber (SBR) and butadiene rubber (BR), which are raw materials used in making car, motorcycle, and bicycle tires. Its annual production capacity is 83,000 tonnes of SBR and 48,000 tonnes of BR. The company also produces thermoplastics elastromer (TPE), which is used to produce shoe soles. Taiwan Synthetic Rubber has a joint venture with the provincial government of Jiangsu in China to build a $60 million SBR plant, with an annual production capacity of 100,000 tonnes.

NT$ mil	12/92	12/93	12/94	US$mil 12/94				
Sales	**3,160.9**	**3,420.5**	**4,583.8**	**173.0**	P/E Ratio	**14.5**	Price (9/30/95)	**36.00**
Net Income	**311.5**	**432.5**	**759.8**	**28.7**	P/B Ratio	**2.5**	52 Wk Hi-Low	**48.33-29.80**
Book Value	**3,956.0**	**4,085.4**	**4,470.5**	**169.9**	Yield %	**3.3**	Market Cap	**US$492.6mil**

Address **285 Chung Hsiao E. Rd., Sec 4, Taipei**
Tel **02-772-5656**
Fax **02-772-3404**
ADR
SEDOL No. **6870876**
President **Qi Yin**
Chairman **Nita Ing**

Taiwan Tea

Industry: **Other Specialty Retailers**

Taiwan Tea is a food producer and land developer. The company produces tea and other foods, raises livestock, operates fisheries, trades tea leaves, and leases land to amusement-park operators. Taiwan Tea is also active in the domestic retail-car market. The company trades and sells its products in Taiwan, and exports them to the United States and Japan. Taiwan Tea is a member of the diversified conglomerate Hualon Group, Taiwan's ninth-largest business group by assets. Its affiliates include textile manufacturer Chia Hsin Livestock and cotton producer Min Hsin Cotton.

NT$ mil	12/91	12/92	12/93	US$mil 12/93				
Revenues	**1,096.5**	**1,557.0**	**1,207.3**	**45.9**	P/E Ratio	**26.1**	Price (9/30/95)	**37.80**
Net Income	**-320.2**	**-227.2**	**337.7**	**12.8**	P/B Ratio	**2.0**	52 Wk Hi-Low	**74.40-28.40**
Book Value	**2,482.4**	**2,255.2**	**4,342.9**	**163.3**	Yield %	**0.0**	Market Cap	**US$408.4mil**

Address **61 Chungshan N. Rd., Sec. 2, Taipei**
Tel **02-563-9921**
Fax **02-581-2099**
ADR
SEDOL No. **6871073**
President --
Chairman --

Tatung

Industry: **Electrical Components & Equipment**

Tatung produces computers, peripherals, and home appliances. The company's computer products include personal computers, monitors, optical-image scanners, workstations, and servers. Tatung markets these products directly and through resellers under the Tatung, Omniscan, TPC-5510, Audio 15, SuperCOMP, and other trademarks in Taiwan, Europe, Asia, and the U.S. Its Tatung Science & Technology subsidiary produces the company's work-stations and servers. Tatung holds a minority interest in Chung Hwa Picture Tube, which accounts for a significant portion of revenues.

NT$ mil	12/91	12/92	12/93	US$mil 12/93				
Sales	**30,373.5**	**33,103.7**	**N/A**	**N/A**	P/E Ratio	**15.6**	Price (9/30/95)	**45.50**
Net Income	**294.7**	**1,215.9**	**3,508.6**	**133.3**	P/B Ratio	**N/A**	52 Wk Hi-Low	**54.44-39.52**
Book Value	**14,513.1**	**16,489.6**	**N/A**	**N/A**	Yield %	**0.0**	Market Cap	**US$3,132.1mil**

Address **22 Chungshan N. Rd., Sec. 3, Taipei**
Tel **02-592-5252**
Fax **02-591-5185**
ADR
SEDOL No. **6875677**
President **Weishan Lin**
Chairman **Tingsheng Lin**

Tay Feng

Industry: **Tires & Rubber**

Tay Feng Tire manufactures rubber industrial and vehicle products. The company is one of Taiwan's largest makers of automobile tires. Tay Feng's other products include conveyer-ply and -tube rubber, and bicycle and other tires. The company is also involved in trading and investing. Tay Feng Tire has one factory and one subsidiary in Taiwan. The company's customers are located domestically, as well as in European, Asian, Australian, and North American markets. Tay Feng is 5.4%-owned by Japan's Sumitomo Rubber Industries.

NT$ mil	12/92	12/93	12/94	US$mil 12/94				
Sales	**1,933.6**	**1,980.2**	**2,115.9**	**79.9**	P/E Ratio	**46.4**	Price (9/30/95)	**47.80**
Net Income	**134.6**	**130.0**	**132.9**	**5.0**	P/B Ratio	**2.9**	52 Wk Hi-Low	**78.18-32.82**
Book Value	**1,887.1**	**2,013.1**	**2,141.5**	**81.4**	Yield %	**0.0**	Market Cap	**US$252.3mil**

Address **1 Nanking E. Rd., Sec. 3**
Taipei
Tel **02-506-1211**
Fax **02-506-0027**
ADR
SEDOL No. **6877316**
President **Shaoxiang Ma**
Chairman **Shaoji Ma**

Teco Electric & Machinery

Industry: **Other Home Furnishings**

Teco Electric & Machinery manufactures industrial electric motors and home appliances. It also produces computer peripherals and other related accessories, such as color monitors for desktop computers, optical image scanners, and liquid crystal displays for notebook computers. Through a joint venture with Japan's Royal, Teco Electric & Machinery operates a chain of Royal Host restaurants throughout Taiwan. The company operates a cathode-ray-tube-manufacturing plant in China, and owns Westinghouse Motor, a Texas-based manufacturer of motors for industrial applications.

NT$ mil	12/91	12/92	12/93	US$mil 12/93				
Sales	**11,004.4**	**12,861.7**	**14,934.1**	**567.2**	P/E Ratio	**15.0**	Price (9/30/95)	**48.10**
Net Income	**1,376.4**	**1,347.5**	**1,567.5**	**59.5**	P/B Ratio	**2.3**	52 Wk Hi-Low	**71.84-46.20**
Book Value	**8,664.3**	**9,379.2**	**10,425.2**	**391.9**	Yield %	**5.0**	Market Cap	**US$1,143.9mil**

Address **156-2 Sung Chiang Rd.**
Taipei
Tel **02-562-1111**
Fax **02-521-8341**
ADR
SEDOL No. **6879851**
President **T.S. Shieh**
Chairman **Theodore M.H. Huang**

Tuntex Distinct

Industry: **Commodity Chemicals**

Tuntex Distinct is the only listed company of the diversified investment and industrial conglomerate Tuntex Group. The firm makes textiles and develops and sells real estate. Its products include polyester and chemical fibers; pure terephthalic acid, a raw material for polyester-fiber production; and polyester-staple fiber, a raw material for making clothes. Its affiliates include the Thai petrochemical firms Tuntex Thailand, Tuntex Petrochemical, and Tuntex Distinct BVI, a Taiwan investment and trading firm. Its primary markets are in Asia and the United States.

NT$ mil	12/91	12/92	12/93	US$mil 12/93				
Sales	**7,012.0**	**13,996.3**	**10,457.3**	**397.2**	P/E Ratio	**20.7**	Price (9/30/95)	**18.20**
Net Income	**1,362.8**	**2,427.9**	**1,351.6**	**51.3**	P/B Ratio	**1.6**	52 Wk Hi-Low	**33.02-16.70**
Book Value	**9,001.5**	**13,615.2**	**14,961.2**	**562.5**	Yield %	**0.0**	Market Cap	**US$1,067.1mil**

Address **376 Jen-Ai Rd., Sec. 4**
Taipei
Tel **02-755-9827**
Fax **02-391-3551**
ADR
SEDOL No. **6907398**
President **Youxian Chen**
Chairman **Youhao Chen**

Uniglory Marine

Industry: **Marine Transportation**

Uniglory Marine provides marine-transportation services. The company operates a fleet of more than 25 container ships. Uniglory Marine and its agents maintain offices in Asia, South America, and Africa and operate out of ports around the world, including Taiwan, Malaysia, Hong Kong, the Philippines, Brazil, Argentina, Uruguay, Mauritius, Panama, Vietnam, Indonesia, and the People's Republic of China. The company is investing in the construction of a new port in China. Uniglory Marine is 34%-owned by the Evergreen Group, the world's largest shipping company by fleet size.

NT$ mil	12/92	12/93	12/94	US$mil 12/94				
Sales	**6,214.2**	**6,777.9**	**10,415.1**	**393.1**	P/E Ratio	**29.2**	Price (9/30/95)	**39.40**
Net Income	**210.8**	**194.6**	**321.2**	**12.1**	P/B Ratio	**2.3**	52 Wk Hi-Low	**54.08-34.50**
Book Value	**3,617.9**	**3,801.2**	**4,107.4**	**156.1**	Yield %	**0.0**	Market Cap	**US$463.4mil**

Address **172 Minsheng E. Rd.**
Taipei
Tel **02-508-6025**
Fax **02-508-6108**
ADR
SEDOL No. **6911764**
President **Mun-Chi Lee**
Chairman **Yao-Fon Loh**

United Micro Electronics

Industry: **Semiconductors & related**

United Microelectronics (UMC) is Taiwan's second-largest semiconductor producer by revenues, with annual sales of approximately $380 million. It makes computer memory chips and peripherals, and photoelectric components such as liquid crystal displays. The firm will complete construction of a $940 million eight-inch-silicon-wafer plant in Taiwan in 1995, and is currently working on a joint venture with United States' Alliance Semiconductor and S3 to build a chip facility in Taiwan. UMC's markets are Taiwan, South Korea, Hong Kong, Japan, the U.S., and Europe.

NT$ mil	12/91	12/92	12/93	US$mil 12/93				
Sales	**5,661.0**	**6,427.6**	**9,897.8**	**375.9**	P/E Ratio	**57.4**	Price (9/30/95)	**74.00**
Net Income	**601.2**	**1,227.8**	**2,458.0**	**93.4**	P/B Ratio	**10.0**	52 Wk Hi-Low	**92.67-67.33**
Book Value	**6,553.5**	**8,762.6**	**10,668.5**	**401.1**	Yield %	**0.4**	Market Cap	**US$3,534.6mil**

Address **233-1 Pao-Chiao Rd.**
Hsin-Tien
Tel **02-918-1589**
Fax **02-918-0188**
ADR
SEDOL No. **6916628**
President **John Hsuan**
Chairman **Robert H.C. Tsao**

Universal Cement

Industry: **Building Materials**

Universal Cement is a cement manufacturer. The company's primary products include portland cement, cement products, and gypsum board. Universal Cement has four factories, five division offices, and five subsidiaries all of which are in Taiwan. The company's primary customers are construction and infrastructure-construction companies. Universal Cement distributes its cement and related products domestically, and exports a small amount of its production to Brunei.

NT$ mil	12/91	12/92	12/93	US$mil 12/93				
Sales	3,078.9	3,578.6	3,658.7	139.0	P/E Ratio	10.7	Price (9/30/95)	24.10
Net Income	699.4	1,117.4	900.6	34.2	P/B Ratio	1.7	52 Wk Hi-Low	41.12-20.20
Book Value	3,652.0	4,436.1	4,827.3	181.5	Yield %	4.1	Market Cap	US$330.8mil

Address **125 Nanking E. Rd., Sec. 2, Taipei** Tel **02-507-7801** Fax **02-507-5870** ADR SEDOL No. **6918549** President **Yen Hsiufeng** Chairman **Wu Tsiunhsien**

USI Far East

Industry: **Commodity Chemicals**

USI Far East's core business is the manufacture of polyethylene raw materials for the plastics industry in the Asia Pacific region. The company's products include ethylene vinyl acetate copolymer resins and high- and low-density polyethylene resins. USI produces approximately 185,000 tonnes of resin per year. The company sells roughly 80% of its production in Taiwan, while it exports 15% to Hong Kong. The company has agreed to invest in the newly formed Vanguard International Semiconductor Corporation, which will begin mass production of DRAM chips in 1995.

NT$ mil	12/92	12/93	12/94	US$mil 12/94				
Sales	3,345.6	3,591.6	4,071.0	153.7	P/E Ratio	19.2	Price (9/30/95)	23.20
Net Income	220.0	145.9	549.1	20.7	P/B Ratio	1.7	52 Wk Hi-Low	51.90-19.00
Book Value	5,953.1	5,889.6	6,265.0	238.0	Yield %	2.2	Market Cap	US$409.0mil

Address **212 Chung-Hsiao E. Rd., Sec. 4, Taipei** Tel **02-721-6511** Fax **02-751-6639** ADR SEDOL No. **6919003** President **Sidney H. Chow** Chairman **Antonio T. Chong**

Walsin Lihwa

Industry: **Electrical Components & Equipment**

Walsin Lihwa Wire & Cable manufactures electric wire and cable products, including bare-copper cables, power cables, and aluminum-alloy transmission-line conductors for industrial applications. Through Walsin-CarTech Specialty Steel, a joint venture with U.S.-based specialty steelmaker Carpenter Technology, the company produces more than 200,000 tonnes of specialty and carbon-steel products annually. Other products include integrated circuits, fine ceramics for electronic use, engineering plastics, and cable-television equipment and accessories.

NT$ mil	12/92	12/93	12/94	US$mil 12/94				
Sales	10,160.3	10,381.5	12,759.4	481.6	P/E Ratio	16.9	Price (9/30/95)	32.50
Net Income	602.4	926.1	2,298.4	86.8	P/B Ratio	1.9	52 Wk Hi-Low	42.86-25.71
Book Value	17,673.0	18,161.8	20,412.6	775.6	Yield %	2.5	Market Cap	US$1,618.1mil

Address **117 Min Sheng E. Rd., Sec. 3, Taipei** Tel **02-719-2211** Fax **02-718-5452** ADR SEDOL No. **6936574** President **Hiroaki Baba** Chairman **Ting-Piao Chiao**

Wei-Chuan Food

Industry: **Other Food**

Wei-Chuan Foods is a diversified food-processing company. It also distributes automobiles, sells electric home appliances, provides printing services, operates retail chains, transports goods, provides computer services, and engages in construction and engineering. The company's food products include dairy products, baked goods, seasonings, sauces, juices, and frozen foods. Wei-Chuan operates the Sung-Ching Supermarket store chain through a joint venture with Masei of Japan. Through a joint venture with Arco-USA, the company operates a convenience-store chain.

NT$ mil	12/91	12/92	12/93	US$mil 12/93				
Sales	11,388.5	8,658.9	8,905.5	338.2	P/E Ratio	76.7	Price (9/30/95)	22.00
Net Income	160.7	144.5	126.7	4.8	P/B Ratio	1.7	52 Wk Hi-Low	39.54-18.00
Book Value	4,737.6	4,846.5	4,989.5	187.6	Yield %	0.0	Market Cap	US$346.8mil

Address **125 Sungchiang Rd., Taipei** Tel **02-507-8221** Fax **02-507-0623** ADR SEDOL No. **6949312** President **Nantu Huang** Chairman **Keming Huang**

Yuen Foong Yu Paper

Industry: **Paper Products**

Yuen Foong Yu is a diversified manufacturer of paper products. Its principal products include paperboard and art, writing, and covering paper. The company also offers environment-friendly products, such as recycled paper, cardboard, and toilet tissue. Yuen Foong Yu's Prime View International subsidiary is constructing a color liquid crystal display (LCD) factory that will have production capabilities of more than 24,000 LCD panels per month upon completion in 1997. The company operates paper-manufacturing plants in Kaohsiung and Taoyuan, Taiwan.

NT$ mil	12/91	12/92	12/93	US$mil 12/93				
Sales	15,095.3	15,303.3	14,543.2	552.3	P/E Ratio	14.4	Price (9/30/95)	23.10
Net Income	260.0	528.7	1,336.2	50.7	P/B Ratio	1.4	52 Wk Hi-Low	35.48-21.50
Book Value	12,004.2	12,218.8	13,493.6	507.3	Yield %	4.3	Market Cap	US$821.8mil

Address **51 Chungking E. Rd., Sec. 2, Taipei** Tel **02-396-1166** Fax **02-396-6771** ADR SEDOL No. **6988616** President **Shouchuan He** Chairman **Shoushan He**

Yungtay Engineering

Industry: **Industrial - Diversified**

Yungtay Engineering is Taiwan's largest elevator manufacturer. The company manufactures and sells elevators, escalators, construction machinery, freezers, air conditioners, inverters, and parking equipment. Yungtay trades and sells its products in Taiwan and exports them to the United States and Japan. Yungtay also distributes elevators, escalators, and construction machinery manufactured by Hitachi in Taiwan and overseas. The company has production facilities in Taiwan and on mainland China. Yungtay is 8%-owned by the Japanese electronics manufacturer Hitachi.

NT$ mil	12/91	12/92	12/93	US$mil 12/93				
Sales	**3,233.2**	**4,316.8**	**4,963.3**	**188.5**	P/E Ratio	**12.3**	Price (9/30/95)	**62.00**
Net Income	**890.4**	**1,157.9**	**1,650.3**	**62.7**	P/B Ratio	**3.4**	52 Wk Hi-Low	**121.30-56.00**
Book Value	**2,744.0**	**3,622.3**	**4,826.0**	**181.4**	Yield %	**4.8**	Market Cap	**US$704.8mil**

Address **99 Fuhsing N. Rd.**
Taipei

Tel **02-717-2217**
Fax **02-716-5511**

ADR
SEDOL No. **6988694**

President **Shuqi Han**
Chairman **Yunxia Yu**

Thailand

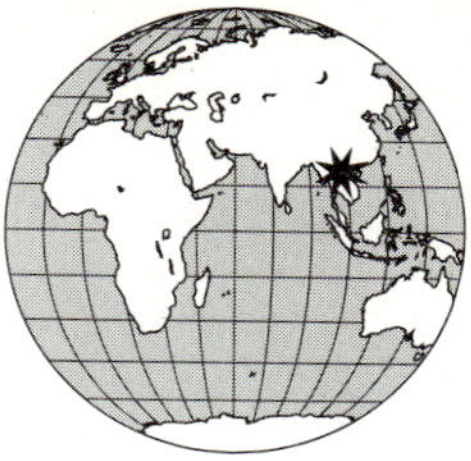

Thailand

Joseph Rebello,
Bangkok

Local Trading Hours	Time Difference from New York	Population (Est. 12/94)
10:00-12:30 and 2:30-4:30, Monday-Friday	12 hours ahead of EST; 11 hours during Daylight savings	59,100,000

Foreign brokers are apt to grumble about the roller-coaster swerves of the stock market, the frustrating curbs on foreign investment, and the haphazard use of accounting standards among Thai companies.

But even the stubbornest of critics will concede one thing: For sheer money-making capacity, it's hard to find a more rewarding market in Asia.

The 407 corporations and 67 mutual funds listed on the Stock Exchange of Thailand, for example, have been on a tear lately. Their average profit growth is expected to touch 23% in 1996, according to one estimate, more than the average of listed stocks on every other regional stock exchange.

Trading activity isn't bad, either. Although the market capitalization of listed Thai stocks - 3.4 trillion baht in September 1995 - is considerably smaller than those of listed Hong Kong stocks, for example, trading volume in Bangkok often exceeds Hong Kong's.

That brings a tidy income for the exchange's 44 member brokerage firms, whose fees are set at 0.5% of trade value. Consider the arithmetic: Trading volume reached 2 trillion baht in 1994, which generated total brokers fees of 10 billion baht. An average cut, in other words, of 227.3 million baht per firm.

No doubt, the price of membership is astronomically high. The Stock Exchange of Thailand charges brokerages 300 million baht a pop, about $12 million, for the privilege of joining - one of the steepest fees of its kind in the world.

But that's a bargain, says Suvicha Mingkwan, a vice president at the exchange. "You can break even within two years," he says. "It's quite an attractive proposition."

There are other attractions. Floor trading, for one thing, doesn't exist. A computerized-order matching system, installed in 1991, permits traders to buy and sell without disclosing the identities of interested parties until a deal is complete. Confirmation of trades comes instantly. Settlement is three days after trading.

Dow Jones Thailand Equity Market Index Performance

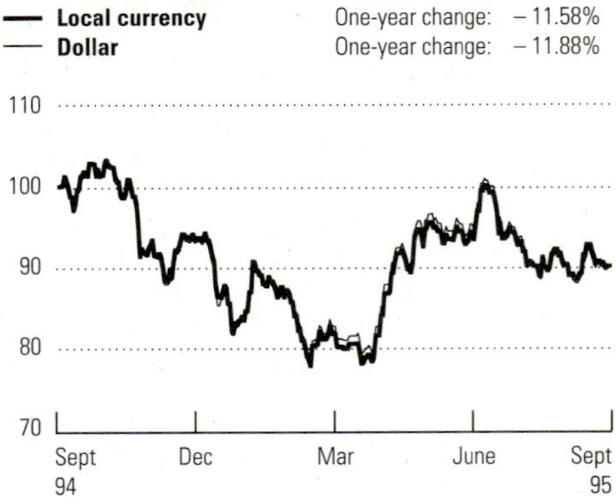

The high-tech gloss illustrates just how much the market has advanced in two decades. In April 1975, the exchange opened for the first time with just nine listed stocks and 16

Gross Domestic Product (94)	Three-Year Average GDP Growth (93-94)	Main Industries	Consumer Price Index (92-94)	Monetary Unit	Exchange Rate (9/95)
$164 billion	+8.5%	Manufacturing, textiles, machinery/computers, electrical appliances, wholesale and retail trade, services, agriculture	+5%	Baht	B25.05 to US$1.00

securities. The early years were hardly encouraging - by 1976, the SET index had dropped to 82.7 points from its starting level of 100 in 1975.

Back then, traders used a "board knocking" system: prices were scribbled on a marker board, which interested parties rapped with a wooden stick to indicate a desire to trade. Confirmation took at least a day.

Today, trading isn't merely more efficient. It's also considerably more varied. The exchange divides its stocks into 30 categories, including agribusiness, electronics, property development, transportation, chemicals, printing, pharmaceuticals and entertainment.

Three sectors, however, dominate trading activity: finance and securities, which accounts for 29% of turnover value; banking which accounts for 17.5%; and communications, which accounts for 10.6%. Two thirds of all trading occurs in 100 stocks with the biggest market capitalization.

Banking, which includes all 16 of Thailand's commercial banks, also happens to be the sector with the heftiest market capitalization: 781.8 billion baht, or 23.7% of the total, at the end of 1994. Communications follows a bit behind, with 15.5 of total market capitalization.

Despite the technical advances of the SET, the market tends to fluctuate wildly. The SET index, for example, roared to a historic high of 1,753.73 points on Jan. 4, 1994. But it's bounced downhill ever since, hurt by alarms about inflation or political instability that fade in and out of the market. In September 1995, the SET index hovered between 1275 and 1350.

Ten Largest Capitalized Companies
as of 9/30/95

Stock	Market Cap. US$Mil
Bangkok Bank	8,226,184.4
Siam Cement	6,716,167.7
Thai Farmers Bank	5,237,525.0
Shinawatra Computer & Comm.	3,430,419.2
Siam Commercial Bank	3,337,325.3
Finance One	2,223,172.5
Land & House	2,213,937.1
Siam City Cement	1,953,002.8
Bank of Ayudhya	1,916,167.7
Phatra Thanakit	1,859,093.8

One reason for the big swings in the index, experts say, is structural. Individual investors account for close to 70% of trading activity, and SET officials say such investors are easily stampeded into buying or dumping stock. The SET hopes to increase the role of institutional investors; the goal is to boost their share of activity to 50%.

To that end, the SET and the Securities and Exchange Commission have been deregulating rapidly. Rules regarding the operation of mutual funds and private investment funds have been relaxed.

The SEC is also considering launching an over-the-counter stock exchange, possibly early in 1996, to help small- and medium-sized companies finance their expansion plans. Futures and options markets, now nonexistent in Thailand, are also under consideration.

One aspect of the market, however, doesn't appear likely to see liberalization anytime soon. As the Thai economy booms, foreign investors have come to play an increasingly powerful role in the stock market - to the great consternation of regulators. In 1994, foreign investors accounted for 19.9% of the exchange's transactions, up from 12.9% in 1988.

Many regulators see foreigners as a source of instability in the market, since they've proved just as likely to pump up the market as to deflate it. As a result, the SET recently raised the specter of clamping down on foreign investment - by reducing limits on foreign ownership of listed companies. It hasn't, however, carried out the threat, and experts think it isn't likely to.

Restrictions, in any case, are already tight. Foreign investors can repatriate income freely: The baht is uncommonly stable against the dollar (it hasn't fluctuated more than 2% in the last three years), and there is no tax on capital gains. But Thai law forbids foreigners to own more than 49% of a company. The limit is even lower for banks and finance companies - 25%.

Foreigners who want to invest in a company that has already filled its foreign allotment must buy stock from other foreigners. Those transactions occur on the SET's foreign board - and the buyer usually pays a stiff premium. Unlike local stocks, which aren't allowed to rise or fall more than 10% in a day, stocks on the foreign board trade without a floor or ceiling.

Despite the curbs, however, foreign investors continue to flock to the market. So do local investors, in ever increasing numbers. The Thai economy is expected to grow by 8.6% this year and inflation is mostly in check at an estimated 5.2% for 1995. Analysts remain bullish on the market.

So is the exchange. In its clearest signal of self-confidence the SET is erecting ostentatious new digs in the heart of Bangkok: an 18-story building that will cost $40 million. The building will provide badly needed space as the exchange expands, a SET official says. But it will also bring "prestige," he says, underscoring Thailand's newfound status as a world-class stock market.

American Standard Sanitaryware

Industry: **Building Materials**

American Standard Sanitaryware manufactures a variety of products, including sanitary-ware fixtures and plastic seat covers, bathtubs, whirlpools, and shower enclosures and trays. Its plant is the largest in Southeast Asia and is Thailand's leading sanitary-ware producer. The company is the sole importer of American Standard and Ideal Standard bath and kitchen fittings from the United States, Germany, Italy, and South Korea. It is also an agent for Sloan Valve, an American manufacturer of flush valves. American Standard Sanitaryware is a subsidiary of American Standard.

	B mil 12/92 R	12/93	12/94	US$mil 12/94				
Sales	**1,387.3**	**1,453.8**	**1,686.9**	**67.3**	P/E Ratio	**8.9**	Price (9/30/95)	**452.00**
Net Income	**419.6**	**409.2**	**380.4**	**15.2**	P/B Ratio	**5.2**	52 Wk Hi-Low	**664.00-330.00**
Book Value	**682.1**	**749.3**	**657.3**	**26.5**	Yield %	**13.9**	Market Cap	**US$135.3mil**

Address **392 Sukhumvit Rd.**
Bangkok 10110
Tel **02-258-0175**
Fax **02-258-9675**
ADR
SEDOL No. **6029474**
Managing Director **David W. Van Hise**
Chairman **Chalermbhand Srivikorn**

R=Restated.

Asia Credit

Industry: **Financial Services - Diversified**

Asia Credit finances projects related to land and business development. It also conducts securities-brokerage operations, including buying and selling securities and underwriting securities issues; provides investment advice; and leases commercial vehicles. The company obtained permission from the government to open nine provincial credit offices scheduled to open in 1995. Asia Credit is the main brokerage and investment subsidiary of Bangkok Bank, Thailand's largest commercial bank. France's Société Generale is another major shareholder.

	B mil 12/92	12/93	12/94	US$mil 12/94				
Revenues	**4,772.1**	**5,256.1**	**5,964.0**	**237.9**	P/E Ratio	**10.3**	Price (9/30/95)	**168.00**
Net Income	**837.6**	**907.7**	**1,157.1**	**46.2**	P/B Ratio	**2.0**	52 Wk Hi-Low	**308.00-117.00**
Book Value	**3,519.1**	**4,181.8**	**6,304.0**	**253.8**	Yield %	**2.7**	Market Cap	**US$510.7mil**

Address **320 Rama 4 Rd.**
Bangkok 10500
Tel **02-235-1477**
Fax **02-238-4721**
ADR
SEDOL No. **6056405**
President **Banthorn Lewprasert**
Chairman **Chancai Leetavorn**

Asia Securities Trading

Industry: **Securities Brokers**

Asia Securities Trading provides brokerage, investment-advisory, and underwriting services in Thailand. It has a 4.2% market share of the country's trading, with a volume of more than 475,840 million baht. Trading in the provinces accounted for nearly 11% of this volume. The firm's investment-advisory division provides assistance to institutions and individual investors in Thailand and abroad. Its research-services division provides clients with published documents and on-line information. Asia Securities Trading underwrote or co-underwrote 35 public offerings in 1994.

	B mil 12/92	12/93	12/94	US$mil 12/94				
Sales	**911.6**	**1,190.1**	**1,316.4**	**52.5**	P/E Ratio	**14.6**	Price (9/30/95)	**73.50**
Net Income	**468.5**	**659.2**	**652.8**	**26.0**	P/B Ratio	**3.2**	52 Wk Hi-Low	**97.50-45.00**
Book Value	**2,152.7**	**2,584.4**	**2,977.3**	**119.9**	Yield %	**2.7**	Market Cap	**US$381.4mil**

Address **175 S. Sathorn Rd.**
Bangkok 10120
Tel **02-285-1666**
Fax **02-285-1900**
ADR
SEDOL No. **6057141**
President & CEO **Chali Sophonpanich**
Chairman **Deja Tulananda**

Ayudhya Insurance

Industry: **Insurance - Property & Casualty**

Ayudhya Insurance is Thailand's fifth-largest insurance company, controlling 1.5% of its non-life-insurance premiums. Its policies include fire, marine, accident, and automobile insurance and reinsurance. Fire insurance contributes nearly 50% of the firm's total underwriting revenues and 62% of its underwriting profits. Motor insurance accounts for nearly 33% of revenues and more than 15% of profits. Marine insurance and miscellaneous policies together account for the remainder. Ayudhya Insurance derives 79% of its profits from investment income and 21% from net premiums.

	B mil 12/92 R	12/93	12/94	US$mil 12/94				
Revenues	**112.6**	**170.4**	**172.2**	**6.9**	P/E Ratio	**8.5**	Price (9/30/95)	**171.00**
Net Income	**436.3**	**466.2**	**505.8**	**20.2**	P/B Ratio	**0.8**	52 Wk Hi-Low	**260.00-162.00**
Book Value	**4,616.7**	**4,831.8**	**5,036.1**	**202.7**	Yield %	**7.0**	Market Cap	**US$170.7mil**

Address **Ploenchit Twr., 898 Ploenchit Rd.**
Bangkok 10330
Tel **02-263-0335**
Fax **02-263-0589**
ADR
SEDOL No. **6069221**
President **--**
Chairman **Krit Ratanarak**

R=Restated.

Ban Pu Coal

Industry: **Coal**

Ban Pu Coal primarily exlores for and mines coal. The company produces approximately 2 million tonnes of coal per year, and commands almost 50% of the Thai coal market. It also generates electricity through its 72%-owned Thai Cogeneration subsidiary. Most coal sales are to the Electricity Generating Authority of Thailand. The company also has coal operations in Indonesia, Australia, Vietnam, and China. Other interests include a 60% stake in Silamani, a producer and retailer of decorative stones, and a 30% stake in Newmont Ban-Kham, a gold-exploration joint venture.

	B mil 06/91	06/92	06/93	US$mil 06/93				
Sales	**106.4**	**742.3**	**1,485.7**	**58.4**	P/E Ratio	**50.2**	Price (9/30/95)	**580.00**
Net Income	**69.4**	**191.7**	**545.5**	**21.4**	P/B Ratio	**10.1**	52 Wk Hi-Low	**648.00-410.00**
Book Value	**1,038.6**	**1,670.2**	**2,718.1**	**107.7**	Yield %	**0.7**	Market Cap	**US$1,137.6mil**

Address **Grand Amarin, New Petchburi Rd.**
Rachatevee, Bangkok 10310
Tel **02-207-0688**
Fax **02-207-0695**
ADR
SEDOL No. **6074849**
President **Chanin Vongkusolkit**
Chairman **Metha Auapinyakul**

Bangkok Bank

Industry: **Banks - Regional**

Bangkok Bank is Thailand's largest commercial bank by assets, controlling 899 billion baht. The bank's services include general banking, mutual-fund management, insurance, securities brokerage, financial advisory, and custodian services. The bank operates approximately 130 branches in Bangkok, 304 branches throughout the rest of Thailand, and 19 branches and three representitive offices overseas. Its overseas locations include China, Myanmar (Burma), Cambodia, Taiwan, Hong Kong, Singapore, Malaysia, Vietnam, Japan, Germany, the United Kingdom, and the United States.

	B mil 12/92	12/93	12/94	US$mil 12/94				
Revenues	**75,884.4**	**83,747.8**	**91,968.2**	**3,668.2**	P/E Ratio	**11.8**	Price (9/30/95)	**206.00**
Net Income	**10,540.1**	**13,903.8**	**17,448.1**	**695.9**	P/B Ratio	**2.6**	52 Wk Hi-Low	**228.00-169.00**
Book Value	**45,335.3**	**66,845.9**	**78,266.4**	**3,150.8**	Yield %	**2.2**	Market Cap	**US$8,226.2mil**

Address	**333 Silom Rd.**	Tel	**02-231-4333**	ADR		President	**Chatri Sophonpanich**
	Bangkok 10500	Fax	**02-236-4806**	SEDOL No.	**6077008**	Chairman	**Prasit Kanchanawat**

Bangkok Insurance

Industry: **Insurance - Property & Casualty**

Bangkok Insurance has operations in general insurance and reinsurance. It is Thailand's largest underwriter of commercial and industrial policies, with total premiums of more than 2,3 billion baht. The firm holds 8% of the market for direct-written premiums. Its main lines are fire, motor, and marine insurance, but it also offers general-accident, personal, engineering, and aviation policies. Fire insurance accounted for 26.9% of the firm's 1994 premiums and 64.2% of its underwriting profits; motor insurance accounted for 43.3% of premiums and 15.9% of underwriting profits.

	B mil 12/92 R	12/93	12/94	US$mil 12/94				
Revenues	**1,640.5**	**1,996.6**	**2,325.8**	**92.8**	P/E Ratio	**9.0**	Price (9/30/95)	**420.00**
Net Income	**549.3**	**606.0**	**736.2**	**29.4**	P/B Ratio	**2.4**	52 Wk Hi-Low	**604.00-388.00**
Book Value	**2,725.1**	**3,012.3**	**3,489.7**	**140.5**	Yield %	**4.3**	Market Cap	**US$335.3mil**

Address	**302 Silom Rd.**	Tel	**02-234-1155**	ADR		President	**Chai Sophonpanich**
	Bangkok 10500	Fax	**02-236-6541**	SEDOL No.	**6078971**	Chairman	**Chatri Sophonpanich**

R=Restated.

Bangkok Land

Industry: **Real-Estate Investment**

Bangkok Land invests in residential and commercial property-development projects, including infrastructure development and development for rental, sale, and investment purposes. It is currently developing a $10 billion satellite-town project in suburban Bangkok, Muang Thong Thani. Muang Thong Thani will be the location for some athletics facilities and the athletes' village for the 1998 Asian Games. Bangkok Land is controlled by the Kanjanpas family, who also control Tanayong, another property-development firm, and Stelux, a Hong Kong-based retailer.

	B mil 03/92	03/93	03/94	US$mil 03/94				
Sales	**11,699.4**	**16,811.0**	**12,774.5**	**502.8**	P/E Ratio	**4.4**	Price (9/30/95)	**37.25**
Net Income	**4,019.6**	**4,868.2**	**5,028.9**	**197.9**	P/B Ratio	**1.0**	52 Wk Hi-Low	**78.50-29.75**
Book Value	**15,989.5**	**18,877.7**	**21,506.6**	**844.4**	Yield %	**10.7**	Market Cap	**US$892.2mil**

Address	**Metro Ctr., New Petchburi Rd.**	Tel	**02-254-1031**	ADR		President	**Montri Kosiyakul**
	Bangkok 10400	Fax	**02-254-1025**	SEDOL No.	**6074560**	Chairman	**Mongkol Kanjanapas**

Bangkok Metropolitan Bank

Industry: **Banks - Regional**

Bangkok Metropolitan Bank is Thailand's 10th-largest commercial bank, with assets totalling 134 billion baht. It operates 65 branches in the Bangkok metropolitan area and 70 branches in provincial areas throughout Thailand. The bank has 53 ATMs in the metropolitan area and 34 located in the provinces. It also offers business-financing, foreign-exchange, and credit-card services. It has international operations in Hong Kong, New York, and San Francisco. Bangkok Metropolitan Bank is one of 47 banks to be issued a license to bank offshore by Thailand's Ministry of Finance.

	B mil 12/92	12/93	12/94	US$mil 12/94				
Revenues	**8,410.4**	**10,436.3**	**12,253.2**	**488.7**	P/E Ratio	**15.2**	Price (9/30/95)	**26.50**
Net Income	**324.8**	**723.1**	**1,424.2**	**56.8**	P/B Ratio	**2.0**	52 Wk Hi-Low	**31.66-20.95**
Book Value	**8,080.2**	**8,657.2**	**11,190.8**	**450.5**	Yield %	**1.4**	Market Cap	**US$879.9mil**

Address	**2 Chalermkhet 4 St., Pomprab**	Tel	**02-223-0561**	ADR		President	**Vichien Tegapaibul**
	Bangkok 10100	Fax	**02-224-3768**	SEDOL No.	**6076641**	Chairman	**Udane Tejapaibul**

Bank of Asia

Industry: **Banks - Regional**

Bank of Asia provides commercial-, corporate-, and consumer-banking services through 49 branches in Bangkok and 44 in Thailand's provinces. The bank's wholesale division also offers investment-banking, risk-management, and foreign-trading services. It also markets derivative-based products to its retail customers. Bank of Asia had nearly 83,300 million baht in assets and 53,600 million in deposits at year-end 1994. It owns a 25% interest in both the Thai Asia Mutual Fund Company and Vendome Insurance, a joint venture with Union des Assurances de Paris and Swedish Motors.

	B mil 12/92 R	12/93	12/94	US$mil 12/94				
Revenues	**7,573.4**	**7,174.4**	**8,006.1**	**319.3**	P/E Ratio	**18.1**	Price (9/30/95)	**63.00**
Net Income	**326.7**	**713.2**	**1,238.8**	**49.4**	P/B Ratio	**3.6**	52 Wk Hi-Low	**73.00-41.98**
Book Value	**3,950.4**	**5,126.6**	**6,406.2**	**257.9**	Yield %	**2.0**	Market Cap	**US$904.1mil**

Address	**191 S. Sathorn Rd., Khet Sathorn**	Tel	**02-287-2211**	ADR		President	**Chulakorn Singhakowin**
	Bangkok 10120	Fax	**02-287-2973**	SEDOL No.	**6079264**	Chairman	**Snoh Unakul**

R=Restated.

Bank of Ayudhya

Industry: **Banks - Regional**

Bank of Ayudhya is Thailand's fifth-largest commercial bank and its largest real-estate lender. It operates a network of 279 full-service branches and 45 smaller branches in Thailand. The bank has two branch offices in Hong Kong and Laos, and two representative offices in Vietnam and Myanmar. In collaboration with Ayudhya Life Assurance, the bank issues the Ayudhya Life Visa Card for insurance policyholders. Bank of Ayudhya has interests in a variety of commercial, manufacturing, financial, and real-estate companies throughout Thailand.

	B mil 12/92	12/93	12/94	US$mil 12/94				
Revenues	**20,434.2**	**21,953.6**	**26,105.5**	**1,041.2**	P/E Ratio	**14.1**	Price (9/30/95)	**120.00**
Net Income	**2,500.1**	**2,723.5**	**3,410.1**	**136.0**	P/B Ratio	**2.5**	52 Wk Hi-Low	**129.00-88.00**
Book Value	**14,911.4**	**17,154.5**	**19,411.1**	**781.4**	Yield %	**3.3**	Market Cap	**US$1,916.2mil**

Address **550 Ploenchit Rd. Bangkok 10330**
Tel **02-208-2080**
Fax **02-253-8589**
ADR
SEDOL No. **6075938**
President **Anant Tangtatswas**
Chairman & CEO **Krit Ratanarak**

Charoen Pokphand Feedmill

Industry: **Other Food**

Charoen Pokphand Feedmill (CPF), a member of the Charoen Pokphand Group, produces and distributes prawn and animal feed to customers throughout Thailand. The company also has its own prawn farms and cold-storage processing plants, and engages in animal husbandry, raising chickens, swine, and cattle. CPF has six subsidiaries, which are involved in farming and the preparation of seafood products for the consumer market. For the future, CPF plans to invest in Thailand's petrochemical, telecommunication, and retail markets.

	B mil 12/91	12/92	12/93	US$mil 12/93				
Sales	**11,476.8**	**18,681.5**	**18,768.5**	**735.4**	P/E Ratio	**10.9**	Price (9/30/95)	**111.00**
Net Income	**623.7**	**1,195.1**	**1,221.8**	**47.9**	P/B Ratio	**2.3**	52 Wk Hi-Low	**176.00-107.00**
Book Value	**3,026.1**	**5,008.0**	**5,679.7**	**220.2**	Yield %	**4.3**	Market Cap	**US$531.7mil**

Address **313 C.P. Twr., Silom Rd. Bangkok 10500**
Tel **02-231-0221**
Fax **02-231-0212**
ADR **CPOKY**
SEDOL No. **6160481**
President **Phong Visedpaitoon**
Chairman **Dhanin Chearavanont**

Christiani & Nielsen

Industry: **Heavy Construction**

Christiani & Nielson is one of Thailand's leading construction firms. It is involved in heavy engineering and construction, civil and marine works, and residential, light-industrial, commercial, and real-estate development. The firm has projects in Thailand, Denmark, Germany, China, and Vietnam. It currently holds a 72% stake in Nobleclear GmbH, a joint venture that is developing a satellite town near Berlin. The company owns 98% of the Danish construction company Christiani & Nielsen, its former parent company, and now serves as the parent company for the group.

	B mil 12/92	12/93	12/94	US$mil 12/94				
Sales	**1,221.6**	**6,213.9**	**9,178.7**	**366.1**	P/E Ratio	**17.9**	Price (9/30/95)	**45.25**
Net Income	**342.6**	**201.2**	**227.7**	**9.1**	P/B Ratio	**6.1**	52 Wk Hi-Low	**117.11-44.00**
Book Value	**1,061.7**	**1,001.8**	**672.9**	**27.1**	Yield %	**2.0**	Market Cap	**US$163.0mil**

Address **93/1 Wireless Rd. Bangkok 10330**
Tel **02-252-2246**
Fax **02-256-6278**
ADR
SEDOL No. **6194792**
Managing Director **John R. Millard**
Chairman **Isarangkun Na Ayuthaya**

CMIC Finance & Securities

Industry: **Financial Services - Diversified**

CMIC Finance & Securities is involved in commercial and housing development, retail trading, and investment banking. It also provides securities-brokerage services, offers investment advice, and underwrites securities. Loans receivable account for 70% of the company's total assets, and investments in securities make up 12%. CMIC has the second-largest share of Thailand's auto-leasing sector. In October 1994 CMIC signed a professional-services agreement with Smith New Court of Singapore to establish cooperation in securities trading, research, and investment banking.

	B mil 12/92	12/93	12/94	US$mil 12/94				
Revenues	**4,994.0**	**4,816.7**	**5,127.6**	**204.5**	P/E Ratio	**17.1**	Price (9/30/95)	**85.50**
Net Income	**942.3**	**961.2**	**913.9**	**36.5**	P/B Ratio	**3.1**	52 Wk Hi-Low	**118.00-57.00**
Book Value	**4,135.9**	**4,377.1**	**5,245.9**	**211.2**	Yield %	**4.7**	Market Cap	**US$645.8mil**

Address **54 B.B. Bldg., Asoke Rd. Bangkok 10110**
Tel **02-259-9000**
Fax **02-259-1849**
ADR
SEDOL No. **6190466**
President & CEO **Suthep Wongvorazathe**
Chairman **Gen. N. Mahanonda**

Dhana Siam Finance & Securities

Industry: **Financial Services - Diversified**

Dhana Siam Finance and Securities offers banking and brokerage services through nine offices in Thailand. The firm accepts deposits, sells financial instruments, and provides fund management, securities brokerage, and loans for businesses, housing, and automobiles. It has approximately 45 billion baht in total assets and 22 billion baht in deposits. The company also operates an investment-consulting business and acts as an intermediary in business alliances. Dhana Siam is a partially-owned subsidiary of Siam Commercial Bank.

	B mil 12/91	12/92	12/93	US$mil 12/93				
Revenues	**3,628.8**	**4,622.2**	**5,733.8**	**224.7**	P/E Ratio	**21.6**	Price (9/30/95)	**123.00**
Net Income	**471.9**	**956.5**	**1,365.8**	**53.5**	P/B Ratio	**5.6**	52 Wk Hi-Low	**203.64-75.50**
Book Value	**2,334.8**	**4,418.7**	**5,304.5**	**205.7**	Yield %	**1.6**	Market Cap	**US$1,238.5mil**

Address **132 Wireless Rd., Lumpini Bangkok 10330**
Tel **02-250-0250**
Fax **02-254-6820**
ADR
SEDOL No. **6268705**
President **Rutt Phanijphand**
Chairman **Prachitr Yossundara**

Dusit Thani

Industry: **Lodging**

Dusit Thani owns and operates hotels, mainly in Thailand. The company owns or manages 45 hotels under the Dusit Thani, Princess, Kempinski, and Thani names. It also owns The Melrose hotel in Dallas, and two restaurants in Thailand. The company owns 46% of Philippine Hoteliers, has formed a joint venture to open a hotel in Indonesia, and is exploring projects in Laos, Vietnam, Malaysia, China, and Nepal. Dusit Thani also partially-owns Kempenski Hotels, a German luxury-hotel chain. The company runs its own Dusit Thani College, a hotel-industry training facility.

B mil	12/91 R	12/92	12/93	US$mil 12/93				
Sales	**N/A**	**1,022.8**	**1,027.9**	**40.3**	P/E Ratio	**10.1**	Price (9/30/95)	**44.00**
Net Income	**N/A**	**228.0**	**214.1**	**8.4**	P/B Ratio	**1.1**	52 Wk Hi-Low	**74.00-38.50**
Book Value	**N/A**	**1,651.0**	**1,731.4**	**67.1**	Yield %	**7.4**	Market Cap	**US$78.3mil**

Address **946 Rama IV Rd.**
Bangkok 10500
Tel **02-238-0032**
Fax **02-238-3680**
ADR
SEDOL No. **6284381**
President **Khunying Chanut Piyaoui**
Chairman **Khunying Chanut Piyaoui**

R=Restated.

Finance One

Industry: **Financial Services - Diversified**

Finance One is Thailand's largest nonbank financial-services company. It provides real-estate, commercial, development, and consumer financing, as well as investment banking. The company's investment-banking division underwrites and trades debt and corporate issues, assesses and manages risk, and structures derivatives. Its capital-markets subdivision provides advice on equity and debt-related financing. Finance One trades securities through its wholly-owned Securities One subsidiary. It also owns nearly 93% of Thana One Finance and Securities and 10% of One Holding.

B mil	12/92	12/93	12/94	US$mil 12/94				
Revenues	**5,273.2**	**6,933.4**	**12,340.3**	**492.2**	P/E Ratio	**7.3**	Price (9/30/95)	**135.00**
Net Income	**861.5**	**1,298.3**	**2,390.4**	**95.3**	P/B Ratio	**2.2**	52 Wk Hi-Low	**173.00-100.00**
Book Value	**4,522.4**	**5,995.1**	**8,126.2**	**327.1**	Yield %	**2.6**	Market Cap	**US$2,223.2mil**

Address **119 S. Sathorn Rd.**
Bangkok 10120
Tel **02-287-0880**
Fax **02-285-6565**
ADR
SEDOL No. **6336914**
President **Pin Chakkaphak**
Chairman **Thanat Khoman**

First Bangkok City Bank

Industry: **Banks - Regional**

First Bangkok City Bank is the seventh-largest of Thailand's 15 commercial banks by assets with approximately $7 billion (180 billion baht) in total assets. The bank offers a variety of commercial-banking services at 78 branches in Thailand and one overseas branch in the Cayman Islands. The bank participates in a joint venture with the Bangkok branch of France's Banque Indosuez, manager of the $180 million Siam Fund, its subsidiary Indosuez Assets Management Asia (Hong Kong), and a Thai insurance company to provide fund management in Thailand.

B mil	12/92 R	12/93	12/94	US$mil 12/94				
Revenues	**13,418.5**	**15,996.1**	**17,527.7**	**699.1**	P/E Ratio	**12.0**	Price (9/30/95)	**21.25**
Net Income	**766.0**	**2,101.6**	**2,889.6**	**115.3**	P/B Ratio	**1.9**	52 Wk Hi-Low	**24.50-16.25**
Book Value	**9,061.5**	**12,854.7**	**19,213.8**	**773.5**	Yield %	**4.7**	Market Cap	**US$1,465.9mil**

Address **20 Yukhon 2 Rd., Suan Mali**
Bangkok 10100
Tel **02-223-0501**
Fax **02-225-3036**
ADR
SEDOL No. **6339496**
Chief Executive **Manoch Kanchanachaya**
Chairman **Gen. Sithi Chirarochana**

R=Restated.

First City Investment

Industry: **Financial Services - Diversified**

First City Investment (FCI) provides commercial, development, and housing financing. In December 1994, the company's total assets amounted to 13,165 million baht and its loans total 8,735 million baht. It offers credit approval totalling 4,400 million baht to 150 clients. FCI signed a contract with the Industrial Finance Corporation of Thailand and the Fund for Rehabilitation and Development of Financial Institutions in March 1993. According to this agreement, these institutions will manage the company and hold a total of 75.8% of the company's shares until 1998.

B mil	06/93 R	06/94	12/94 *	US$mil 12/94				
Revenues	**1,141.5**	**965.0**	**637.8**	**25.4**	P/E Ratio	**100.0**	Price (9/30/95)	**39.00**
Net Income	**51.2**	**164.2**	**103.8**	**4.1**	P/B Ratio	**3.3**	52 Wk Hi-Low	**45.50-25.75**
Book Value	**2,857.1**	**3,021.3**	**3,125.1**	**125.8**	Yield %	**0.0**	Market Cap	**US$412.6mil**

Address **2884 New Petchburi Rd.**
Bangkok 10310
Tel **02-319-0020**
Fax **02-318-3675**
ADR
SEDOL No. **6339571**
President **Kavee Tovijit**
Chairman **Anothai Techamontrikul**

*Irregular period due to fiscal year change; R=Restated.

General Finance & Securities

Industry: **Financial Services - Diversified**

General Finance & Securities is a brokerage firm and investment bank that provides securities brokerage and commercial, development, and consumer-finance services. It is among Thailand's 10 largest nonbank financial-services companies, with 34.7 billion baht in assets. The company derives 80% of its revenue from its lending operations. Its joint venture with New Zealand's Brierley Investments, General Finance Brierley, invests in agribusinesses and resource industries in Thailand and Indochina. The firm's affiliate, Abico Holding, produces palm oil in Bangkok.

B mil	12/92 R	12/93	12/94	US$mil 12/94				
Revenues	**2,295.9**	**3,081.8**	**4,190.1**	**167.1**	P/E Ratio	**6.8**	Price (9/30/95)	**112.00**
Net Income	**338.8**	**516.1**	**739.9**	**29.5**	P/B Ratio	**5.0**	52 Wk Hi-Low	**139.73-79.00**
Book Value	**2,029.1**	**2,320.3**	**3,018.4**	**121.5**	Yield %	**4.5**	Market Cap	**US$603.6mil**

Address **1 SG Twr., Rajadamri Rd.**
Lumpini, Bangkok 10330
Tel **02-651-8585**
Fax **02-651-8580**
ADR
SEDOL No. **6364528**
President **S. Pravitra**
Chairman **Narongchai Akrasanee**

R=Restated.

Hana Microelectronics

Industry: **Semiconductors & related**

Hana Microelectronics assembles integrated circuits, semiconductors, and printed-circuit boards for the electronics industry. The company also winds microcoils for use in cameras, disk drives, clocks, and watches. Hana produces cache memory boards and software-protection devices. Hana's assembly facilities are centered in Lamphun province, Thailand. Its wholly-owned Hana Trading subsidiary sells finished watches from Hong Kong in Thailand. It owns a 26% stake in Hong Kong's Astron Group, manufacturer of laminates used in the chip-on-board production process.

	B mil 12/92	12/93	12/94	US$mil 12/94				
Sales	**1,624.1**	**1,640.0**	**1,887.3**	**75.3**	P/E Ratio	**12.2**	Price (9/30/95)	**101.00**
Net Income	**158.0**	**243.6**	**278.7**	**11.1**	P/B Ratio	**1.7**	52 Wk Hi-Low	**190.00-88.50**
Book Value	**798.0**	**986.6**	**2,120.0**	**85.3**	Yield %	**2.1**	Market Cap	**US$148.0mil**

Address **10/4 Moo 7, Vibhavadi-Rangsit Rd.** **Khet Donmuang, Bangkok 10210**
Tel **02-551-1297** Fax **02-551-1299**
ADR SEDOL No. **6409463**
President & CEO **Richard D. Han**
Chairman **S.Y. Han**

Hemaraj Land & Development

Industry: **Real-Estate Investment**

Hemaraj Land and Development has operations in industrial-property development and infrastructure. The company's two principal developments are the Chonburi Industrial Estate and the Eastern Industrial Estate, located southeast of Bangkok. The developments' total area equals roughly 11 million square meters; they are part of the Thai government's Eastern Seaboard Development Program. In addition to commercial, residential, and industrial facilities, Hemeraj provides site grading, roads, drainage, and power infrastructure for the sites.

	B mil 12/92	12/93	12/94	US$mil 12/94				
Sales	**768.0**	**939.0**	**643.4**	**25.7**	P/E Ratio	**49.8**	Price (9/30/95)	**108.00**
Net Income	**262.2**	**329.3**	**153.1**	**6.1**	P/B Ratio	**2.9**	52 Wk Hi-Low	**135.00-50.50**
Book Value	**2,098.5**	**2,287.7**	**2,579.3**	**103.8**	Yield %	**1.9**	Market Cap	**US$305.1mil**

Address **Banchang Glas Haus, Sukhumvit** **Bangkok 10110**
Tel **02-260-6510** Fax **02-260-6297**
ADR SEDOL No. **6419718**
Managing Director **Prateep Trilohaka**
Chairman **Manoch Kanchanachaya**

Industrial Finance of Thailand

Industry: **Banks - Regional**

The Industrial Finance Corporation of Thailand (ICFT) provides services for industrial projects, including financing, equity investment, and loan syndication and guarantee. It also offers investment-advisory and investment-banking services. Loans have been approved for 954 projects amounting to almost 28 billion baht. The company had 90 billion baht in total assets at year-end 1994. ICFT holds nearly 100% of Asset Development, which leases machinery and equipment to commercial and industrial businesses. The government of Thailand holds 30% of the company's shares.

	B mil 12/92	12/93	12/94	US$mil 12/94				
Revenues	**5,825.2**	**6,205.4**	**7,572.3**	**302.0**	P/E Ratio	**18.6**	Price (9/30/95)	**77.00**
Net Income	**1,068.4**	**1,256.7**	**1,720.0**	**68.6**	P/B Ratio	**3.2**	52 Wk Hi-Low	**78.00-43.75**
Book Value	**7,324.8**	**8,693.3**	**13,154.4**	**529.6**	Yield %	**2.3**	Market Cap	**US$1,657.1mil**

Address **1770 New Petchburi Rd.** **Bangkok 10310**
Tel **02-253-7111** Fax **02-253-9677**
ADR SEDOL No. **6458829**
President **Aswin Kongsiri**
Chairman **Aran Thammano**

International Cosmetics

Industry: **Overseas Trading**

International Cosmetics distributes and sells a wide variety of brand-name consumer products in Thailand. The company's products include cosmetics, toiletries, perfumes, clothing, footwear, watches, electronics, consumer appliances, sporting goods, and foods. Brand names include Arrow and Guy Laroche menswear, Wacoal and Elle womenswear, Catalina and Speedo sportswear, Sapporo beer, Samsung and SiliconGraphics computers, and Konica film and cameras. The company also develops, owns, and leases retail outlets for its products thoughout Thailand.

	B mil 12/92	12/93	12/94	US$mil 12/94				
Sales	**7,254.8**	**8,481.2**	**10,165.2**	**405.4**	P/E Ratio	**6.5**	Price (9/30/95)	**386.00**
Net Income	**601.7**	**617.3**	**857.8**	**34.2**	P/B Ratio	**1.2**	52 Wk Hi-Low	**496.00-296.00**
Book Value	**2,830.0**	**3,765.9**	**4,636.4**	**186.7**	Yield %	**2.6**	Market Cap	**US$226.3mil**

Address **Soi Pradoo, 1 Sathupradit Rd.** **Yannawa, Bangkok 10210**
Tel **02-294-0281** Fax **02-294-3024**
ADR SEDOL No. **6464707**
President **Boonkiet Chokwatana**
Chairman **Boonsithi Chokwatana**

International Engineering

Industry: **Communications Technology**

International Engineering distributes telecommunication and electronic products in Thailand. The company is Thailand's sole distributor of Nokia and Fujitsu cellular phones, and Westinghouse generators, tranformers, and circuit breakers. It also distributes Foster Wheeler boilers and Hathaway digital-fault recorders for utilities and other industries. Its wholly-owned Micronetic subsidiary distributes and services DEC computers in Thailand, and designs electronic financial systems in a joint venture with U.S.-based Midwest Stock Exchange Integrated System.

	B mil 12/92 R	12/93	12/94	US$mil 12/94				
Sales	**2,026.5**	**1,911.4**	**2,729.6**	**108.9**	P/E Ratio	**9.1**	Price (9/30/95)	**130.00**
Net Income	**274.3**	**275.7**	**350.2**	**14.0**	P/B Ratio	**3.2**	52 Wk Hi-Low	**254.00-116.00**
Book Value	**949.3**	**1,033.0**	**1,611.5**	**64.9**	Yield %	**4.2**	Market Cap	**US$206.8mil**

Address **SM Twr., 388 Phaholyothin Rd.** **Bangkok 10400**
Tel **02-298-0070** Fax **02-298-0808**
ADR SEDOL No. **6465841**
President **Kanak Abhiradee**
Chairman **C.A. Samudavanija**

R=Restated.

Krisda Mahanakorn

Industry: **Real-Estate Investment**

Krisda Mahanakorn invests in real-estate and property development in Bangkok. It specializes in residential property, but is also involved in infrastructure development. In addition to land sales, Krisda Mahanakorn also provides construction services to its customers. The company has 51% stake in a joint venture with Hong Kong-based construction company New World Development, which invests in property in Thailand. The company also owns KMC Marina Business, developer and owner of club houses and other marina-recreation and sports complexes.

B mil	12/91	12/92	12/93	US$mil 12/93				
Sales	**728.0**	**3,192.3**	**1,461.1**	**57.3**	P/E Ratio	**18.7**	Price (9/30/95)	**50.00**
Net Income	**516.3**	**1,435.4**	**499.4**	**19.6**	P/B Ratio	**1.7**	52 Wk Hi-Low	**77.50-47.00**
Book Value	**2,866.4**	**3,956.6**	**4,003.6**	**155.2**	Yield %	**1.9**	Market Cap	**US$279.4mil**

Address **97/4 Sukhothai Rd.** **Bangkok 10400**
Tel **02-243-5454**
Fax **02-243-5292**
ADR
SEDOL No. **6499873**
President **Tanade Singkalawanji**
Chairman **Meechai Ruchupan**

Land & House

Industry: **Home Construction**

Land & House is Thailand's second-largest real-estate developer, specializing in high-end home construction. The firm also owns a 33% stake in Quality Houses, and a 40% stake in Bangkok Chain Hospital, which owns and operates hospitals in metropolitan Bangkok. Land & House has also expanded into the lower-income housing market, building houses that will sell for 600,000 baht or less. Land & House is a member of a consortium, including Hong Kong's First Pacific and Manila-based Metro Pacific, which won rights to develop a 530-acre site near Manila's financial district.

B mil	12/92	12/93	12/94	US$mil 12/94				
Sales	**3,664.3**	**6,274.9**	**8,313.0**	**331.6**	P/E Ratio	**24.8**	Price (9/30/95)	**362.00**
Net Income	**1,241.9**	**1,707.2**	**2,217.0**	**88.4**	P/B Ratio	**5.7**	52 Wk Hi-Low	**482.00-308.00**
Book Value	**5,519.7**	**7,174.8**	**9,765.0**	**393.1**	Yield %	**1.4**	Market Cap	**US$2,213.9mil**

Address **38 Convent Rd., Q Hse.** **Bangkok 10500**
Tel **02-237-8900**
Fax **02-237-8860**
ADR
SEDOL No. **6523921**
President **Anan Asavabhokhin**
Chairman **Anan Asavabhokhin**

Matichon

Industry: **Publishing**

Matichon is a media firm that mainly publishes Thai-language newspapers and magazines. Its publications include Matichon Daily, the twice-weekly Prachachart Business, Matichon Weekly Review, the biweekly Technology Chaobarn, and Art and Culture Monthly. The company also publishes books and other printed material, which it distributes through its Ngarndee subsidiary. Its research division, which provides research information to the editorial departments, has experimentally launched a newspaper-clipping service available to subscribers outside the company.

B mil	12/92	12/93	12/94	US$mil 12/94				
Sales	**949.4**	**1,096.0**	**1,433.8**	**57.2**	P/E Ratio	**10.2**	Price (9/30/95)	**107.00**
Net Income	**100.1**	**173.4**	**188.7**	**7.5**	P/B Ratio	**2.2**	52 Wk Hi-Low	**185.00-78.00**
Book Value	**409.5**	**825.2**	**885.6**	**35.7**	Yield %	**6.5**	Market Cap	**US$76.9mil**

Address **12 Tethsaban-naruemarn Rd.** **Bangkok 10900**
Tel **02-580-0021**
Fax **02-589-9112**
ADR
SEDOL No. **6572321**
Managing Director **N. Joonjuasuparerk**
Chairman **Khanchai Boonpan**

MDX

Industry: **Real-Estate Investment**

MDX is primarily involved in real-estate and infrastructure development that specializes in the construction of industrial facilities. The company is currently building Gateway City Industrial Estate, a major development project. Approximately 70% of the completed facilities have been sold; purchasers include Toyota Motor Thailand. MDX has five 99%-owned subsidiaries that develop commercial and residential real estate, including Orchid Plaza, Central Apartment, Gateway Development, Unity Realty, and Petchkasame Place, and two that provide basic utilities.

B mil	12/91	12/92	12/93	US$mil 12/93				
Sales	**731.4**	**2,329.6**	**1,729.3**	**67.8**	P/E Ratio	**5.3**	Price (9/30/95)	**42.00**
Net Income	**253.0**	**1,196.5**	**1,297.0**	**50.8**	P/B Ratio	**1.3**	52 Wk Hi-Low	**114.00-32.00**
Book Value	**1,769.0**	**3,954.6**	**5,293.2**	**205.2**	Yield %	**7.1**	Market Cap	**US$277.7mil**

Address **1 Wireless Rd., Pathumwan** **Bangkok 10330**
Tel **02-253-0428**
Fax **02-253-0427**
ADR
SEDOL No. **6550112**
President **Precha Sekhararidhi**
Chairman **Pracha Hetrakul**

Modernform

Industry: **Other Home Furnishings**

Modernform Group consists of nine companies that manufacture and distribute furniture for offices and households. The company's Moflex office furniture accounts for approximately 45% of its sales, and its Klasse household furniture accounts for 20%. Modernform manufactures Metro and Brayton household furniture, as well as office furniture under license from U.S.-based Steelcase Design, and exports its products to other countries throughout the Pacific. It derives 12% of its sales from exports. Modernform has a distribution network of 43 outlets, 38 of which are in Bangkok.

B mil	12/92 R	12/93	12/94	US$mil 12/94				
Sales	**1,337.9**	**1,451.9**	**1,808.3**	**72.1**	P/E Ratio	**6.7**	Price (9/30/95)	**36.75**
Net Income	**242.9**	**245.5**	**257.3**	**10.3**	P/B Ratio	**1.3**	52 Wk Hi-Low	**65.00-34.75**
Book Value	**1,219.7**	**1,315.2**	**1,703.5**	**68.6**	Yield %	**7.5**	Market Cap	**US$88.0mil**

Address **33/2 Moo 7, Banga-Trat Rd.** **Samut Prakan 10540**
Tel **02-379-3181**
Fax **02-379-3461**
ADR
SEDOL No. **6578772**
President & CEO **J. Dhammarungruang**
Chairman **Adul Usanachitt**

R=Restated.

Multi Credit of Thailand

Industry: **Financial Services - Diversified**

Multi-Credit Corporation of Thailand (MCC) offers financial services such as securities trading, investment banking, corporate and consumer lending, and mortgage financing. It has 29,000 million baht in total assets. The firm trades securities for institutions and individuals through its main office in Bangkok, and through five branches. It also underwrites new equity issues. MCC's mortgage-financing department focuses on house contractors, developers, and refinancing; refinancing accounts for about 50% of its business. MCC is the sole owner of Credit Foncier Premruethani.

B mil	12/92 R	12/93	12/94	US$mil 12/94				
Revenues	**2,028.6**	**2,859.6**	**3,507.8**	**139.9**	P/E Ratio	**7.5**	Price (9/30/95)	**164.00**
Net Income	**601.3**	**702.7**	**657.1**	**26.2**	P/B Ratio	**2.1**	52 Wk Hi-Low	**412.22-164.00**
Book Value	**1,695.2**	**2,100.0**	**2,376.1**	**95.7**	Yield %	**7.3**	Market Cap	**US$196.4mil**

Address **140/1 Wireless Rd.** **Pathumwan, Bangkok 10330**
Tel **02-256-0170** Fax **02-253-5594**
ADR
SEDOL No. **6609672**
President **Theodor V. Heyermann**
Chairman **Bangkok Chowkwanyun**

R=Restated.

Natural Park

Industry: **Real-Estate Investment**

Natural Park develops apartments and hotels for rental and sale. The company's current projects include The Natural Park luxury apartments, The Monarch-Lee Gardens business hotel, and The Natural Home Rangsit residential housing and sports complex. The company holds 51% of Nomanan, a property-development firm. Natural Park uses Nomanan's land resources to develop condominiums and office buildings. Natural Park also owns 100% of residential and commercial real-estate developer Santisin, which is currently developing a residential project on Ramindra Road.

B mil	12/92	12/93	12/94	US$mil 12/94				
Sales	**219.3**	**523.6**	**800.6**	**31.9**	P/E Ratio	**NMF**	Price (9/30/95)	**141.00**
Net Income	**38.3**	**54.4**	**32.2**	**1.3**	P/B Ratio	**5.9**	52 Wk Hi-Low	**162.00-129.00**
Book Value	**1,114.6**	**1,153.2**	**3,037.5**	**122.3**	Yield %	**0.0**	Market Cap	**US$709.6mil**

Address **88 Sukhumvit 49, Sukumvit Rd.** **Bangkok 10110**
Tel **02-259-4800** Fax **02-259-4819**
ADR
SEDOL No. **6617374**
Managing Director **Thosapong Jaruthavee**
Chairman **Viravudh Assakul**

Nava Finance & Securities

Industry: **Securities Brokers**

Nava Finance and Securities provides development, commercial, and consumer-finance services; brokers and trades securities; and offers investment advice and management. It is Thailand's fourth-largest securities trader, with 5.36% of the total trading volume. In 1994, the investment-banking division served as an underwriter and managed the sale of equity and debt for eight companies including Property Perfect and Bangkok Expressway. The company was the first to be granted permission to open a representative securities office in Vietnam.

B mil	12/92	12/93	12/94	US$mil 12/94				
Sales	**2,926.2**	**4,073.8**	**4,790.6**	**191.1**	P/E Ratio	**14.7**	Price (9/30/95)	**72.50**
Net Income	**555.7**	**917.8**	**1,110.4**	**44.3**	P/B Ratio	**4.0**	52 Wk Hi-Low	**94.95-44.25**
Book Value	**2,477.4**	**3,245.2**	**4,055.6**	**163.3**	Yield %	**1.8**	Market Cap	**US$651.2mil**

Address **422 Phayathai Rd.** **Bangkok 10330**
Tel **02-215-0969** Fax **02-215-2944**
ADR
SEDOL No. **6627641**
Chief Executive **Thanadee Sophonsiri**
Chairman **Thanadee Sophonsiri**

New Imperial Hotel

Industry: **Lodging**

New Imperial Hotel is Thailand's second-largest hotelier. It owns and operates eight hotels throughout Thailand. The company's flagship Imperial Hotel is located in Bangkok and has 400 rooms. Its 4.5 billion-baht Queen's Park Hotel, also in Bangkok, has 1,400 rooms. The company also owns 34 boat houses, three other hotels in Bangkok, and three hotels in Mae Hon Son province, near Myanmar (Burma). Privately held Maha Thanakit Finances owns 70% of New Imperial Hotel's shares.

B mil	12/92	12/93	12/94	US$mil 12/94				
Sales	**928.4**	**1,135.3**	**1,309.3**	**52.2**	P/E Ratio	**NMF**	Price (9/30/95)	**20.00**
Net Income	**93.2**	**-134.7**	**-538.1**	**-21.5**	P/B Ratio	**4.5**	52 Wk Hi-Low	**34.50-18.75**
Book Value	**1,573.0**	**1,438.2**	**884.7**	**35.6**	Yield %	**0.0**	Market Cap	**US$79.8mil**

Address **199 Sukhumvit Soi 22** **Bangkok 10110**
Tel **02-261-9000** Fax **02-261-9527**
ADR
SEDOL No. **6631288**
President **Sarisdiguna Kitiyakara**
Chairman **Gen. Prem Tinasolanon**

NTS Steel Group

Industry: **Steel**

NTS Steel Group operates blast furnaces and manufactures steel round bars, steel deformed bars, and steel wire rods for sale in Thailand and in overseas markets. The company uses other industries' scrap metal in producing steel. Its major customers are businesses from the construction industry. NTS operates two plants in Samutprakan, and opened a third plant in Chonburi in August 1994. The Chonburi plant is managed by BSE and BSW, a German producer of minimill steel bars and wire rods.

B mil	12/92 R	12/93	12/94	US$mil 12/94				
Sales	**998.9**	**2,673.9**	**3,259.3**	**130.0**	P/E Ratio	**37.4**	Price (9/30/95)	**43.00**
Net Income	**81.4**	**195.4**	**242.6**	**9.7**	P/B Ratio	**2.5**	52 Wk Hi-Low	**64.00-42.50**
Book Value	**3,294.3**	**3,489.8**	**3,629.0**	**146.1**	Yield %	**1.1**	Market Cap	**US$363.1mil**

Address **UM Twr., 9 Ramkhamhaeng Rd.** **Suanluang, Bangkok 10250**
Tel **02-719-9800** Fax **02-719-9820**
ADR
SEDOL No. **6635730**
Managing Director **Sawai Horrungruang**
Chairman **Sawasdi Horrungruang**

R=Restated.

One Holding

Industry: **Clothing & Fabrics**

One Holding has interests in latex-thread manufacturing, property development, and investment management. Its joint venture Regency One is constructing a high-rise apartment building in Bangkok. Other property activities include a 40% stake in Pladaeng, a Thai property developer, and a joint-venture with Ital-Thai to develop a former United States military base in the Philippines. The firm's latex-thread division, Filatex, has a production capacity of 8,000 tonnes. One Holding's investment division has holdings in finance, banks, property, and insurance securities.

B mil	12/92	12/93	12/94	US$mil 12/94				
Sales	**216.3**	**260.1**	**487.4**	**19.4**	P/E Ratio	**21.7**	Price (9/30/95)	**67.00**
Net Income	**87.5**	**210.2**	**473.2**	**18.9**	P/B Ratio	**2.9**	52 Wk Hi-Low	**102.00-50.50**
Book Value	**1,302.8**	**1,453.0**	**3,638.2**	**146.5**	Yield %	**2.4**	Market Cap	**US$427.9mil**

Address **Bldg. One, 99 Wireless Rd.** Tel **02-256-7300** ADR Managing Director **Santi Grachangnetara**
Bangkok 10330 Fax **02-256-7160** SEDOL No. **6336345** Chairman **Thanat Khoman**

Padaeng Industry

Industry: **Mining**

Padaeng Industry is Thailand's largest mineral-mining company by production. It holds a government-granted monopoly on zinc refining. The firm mines and refines zinc ore, and produces zinc ingots, zinc alloys, cadmium balls, and cadmium sticks. It holds a 51% stake in Puthep, a joint venture with U.S.-based Phelps Dodge Mining to develop a copper mine in northeast Thailand. The mine's estimated copper-ore content is 185 million tonnes. It also operates an joint venture with Thailand's Ban Pu Coal to explore for base metals in Laos and Myanmar.

B mil	12/92	12/93	12/94	US$mil 12/94				
Sales	**2,482.5**	**1,952.9**	**2,038.4**	**81.3**	P/E Ratio	**NMF**	Price (9/30/95)	**21.50**
Net Income	**725.6**	**207.9**	**13.3**	**0.5**	P/B Ratio	**0.5**	52 Wk Hi-Low	**62.00-20.75**
Book Value	**4,452.3**	**4,400.6**	**4,168.0**	**167.8**	Yield %	**5.1**	Market Cap	**US$89.3mil**

Address **CTI Twr., 191 Pachadaphisek Rd.** Tel **02-261-1111** ADR President **Pravit Kingwathanakith**
Bangkok 10110 Fax **02-261-1108** SEDOL No. **6666989** Chairman **Aran Thammano**

Pakpanang Cold Storage

Industry: **Fishing**

Pakpanang Coldstorage manufactures and distributes frozen seafood products. Its products include frozen shrimp, squid, fish, crab, and other seafood. Frozen goods account for 80% of the company's total production, and semicooked products account for the remainder. It exports its products to Japan, France, Italy, and the United States under such brand names as Blue Sky, Laidam, Top Maco, Okeanos, Rymer, and T & T. Pakpanang has four factories in Thailand with a total annual production capacity of 19,000 tonnes. It also manages a subsidiary in the U.S., Asia Pacific Seafood.

B mil	06/92	06/93	06/94	US$mil 06/94				
Sales	**2,753.7**	**3,914.7**	**3,328.4**	**131.2**	P/E Ratio	**14.1**	Price (9/30/95)	**35.75**
Net Income	**104.4**	**150.9**	**143.2**	**5.6**	P/B Ratio	**3.3**	52 Wk Hi-Low	**48.00-31.00**
Book Value	**410.7**	**631.8**	**654.7**	**26.1**	Yield %	**5.6**	Market Cap	**US$85.6mil**

Address **103 Soi Ruammitr, Nonsee Rd.** Tel **02-295-1991** ADR Chief Executive **W. Kanokwatanawan**
Bangkok, Yannawa 10120 Fax **02-295-2002** SEDOL No. **6668156** Chairman **Yong Areecharoenlert**

Phatra Thanakit

Industry: **Financial Services - Diversified**

Phatra Thankit is a finance company with securities trading and investment, underwriting, commercial-lending, investment-consulting, and fund-management businesses. The company's total assets amounted to 52,900 million baht in 1994, and its portfolio of investments in listed and unlisted firms totals 9,948 million baht. It is among Thailand's top-five most-active brokers, with a market share of 5.7% of the average trading volume. Phatra was the financial advisor and managing underwriter for issues of 10 companies in 1994, including the Thai Farmers Bank.

B mil	12/92	12/93	12/94	US$mil 12/94				
Revenues	**4,201.4**	**5,157.8**	**6,311.8**	**251.7**	P/E Ratio	**5.7**	Price (9/30/95)	**175.00**
Net Income	**911.8**	**1,263.3**	**2,399.5**	**95.7**	P/B Ratio	**4.7**	52 Wk Hi-Low	**262.00-135.00**
Book Value	**2,888.3**	**3,651.6**	**10,093.9**	**406.4**	Yield %	**8.3**	Market Cap	**US$1,859.1mil**

Address **Ratchadaphisek Rd.** Tel **02-265-1000** ADR President --
Huaykwang, Bangkok 10310 Fax **02-275-3666** SEDOL No. **6684970** Chairman **Photipong Lamsam**

Property Perfect

Industry: **Real-Estate Investment**

Property Perfect is a real-estate company that develops residential properties at five locations in the Bangkok metropolitan area. Its current projects include townhouses and single-family properties. The company owns more than 99% of the shares of Krungthep Land, 65% of Estate Perfect Company, and 22% of Thai Factory Development, all real-estate developers. It also holds 9% of Granito, a manufacturer of granite slabs. Property Perfect's land investment was more than 3,500 million baht at year-end 1994, and total assets amounted to 11,454 million baht.

B mil	12/92 R	12/93	12/94	US$mil 12/94				
Sales	**897.3**	**1,229.6**	**1,666.0**	**66.4**	P/E Ratio	**25.1**	Price (9/30/95)	**240.00**
Net Income	**187.7**	**246.6**	**345.6**	**13.8**	P/B Ratio	**2.5**	52 Wk Hi-Low	**330.00-184.00**
Book Value	**661.6**	**1,496.2**	**3,451.8**	**139.0**	Yield %	**1.0**	Market Cap	**US$345.1mil**

Address **Vongvanij Bldg., Rama IX Rd.** Tel **02-245-6640** ADR Managing Director **Chainid Ngow-Sirmanee**
Bangkok 10310 Fax **02-247-3328** SEDOL No. **6705752** Chairman **Tawatchai Nakhata**

R=Restated.

Quality House

Industry: **Home Construction**

Quality House is a real-estate developer that designs and builds apartments for businessmen, as well as condominiums, houses, offices, and shopping centers in Bangkok and its bordering provinces. It also develops existing residential property for investment purposes. The company's current projects include four housing complexes, one city condominium, one apartment building, and one office building. It also has a joint venture with G.S. Property Management to develop a shopping center, Gaysorn Plaza, in Bangkok. It has three offices in metropolitan Bangkok.

B mil	12/91	12/92	12/93	US$mil 12/93				
Sales	**389.7**	**581.8**	**828.7**	**32.5**	P/E Ratio	**82.0**	Price (9/30/95)	**117.00**
Net Income	**63.3**	**111.1**	**145.6**	**5.7**	P/B Ratio	**5.1**	52 Wk Hi-Low	**139.00-63.80**
Book Value	**854.7**	**1,392.2**	**2,319.9**	**90.0**	Yield %	**0.6**	Market Cap	**US$476.4mil**

Address **9 S. Sathorn Rd., Tungmahamek** Tel **02-679-1999** ADR President **Joompol Meesook**
Bangkok 10120 Fax **02-679-1998** SEDOL No. **6716594** Chairman **Pol. Gen. Pow Sarasin**

Renown Leatherwears

Industry: **Clothing & Fabrics**

Renown Leatherwears manufactures and exports tanned leather, finished leather, and leather gloves for industrial use. The company's major export markets include Singapore, Taiwan, and Europe. It derives approximately 80% of its revenue from finished leather, and the remainder from industrial gloves. It obtains roughly 95% of its raw materials overseas. Renown has an average annual tanned-leather production capacity of 20.8 million square feet. It 95%-owned LS Holding subsidiary was established to hold the company's leather-production interests in Myanmar.

B mil	12/92	12/93	12/94	US$mil 12/94				
Sales	**726.0**	**838.3**	**1,031.8**	**41.2**	P/E Ratio	**23.8**	Price (9/30/95)	**145.00**
Net Income	**106.4**	**130.1**	**194.8**	**7.8**	P/B Ratio	**3.7**	52 Wk Hi-Low	**170.00-133.00**
Book Value	**463.0**	**518.1**	**1,380.4**	**55.6**	Yield %	**2.8**	Market Cap	**US$202.6mil**

Address **Green Twr. Bldg., Rama 4 Rd.** Tel **02-367-3850** ADR Managing Director **Lertsak Nopburanand**
Bangkok 10110 Fax **02-367-3865** SEDOL No. **6732620** Chairman **Boonsom Tunchumrus**

Robinsons Department Store

Industry: **Retailers - Broadline**

Robinson Department Store owns and operates nine retail outlets in Bangkok and is opening 10 provincial stores in 1996. Robinson also owns nearly 75% of Sapan Mai Department Store. Its R.I.S. subsidiary operates information systems and technology for all of the Robinson stores, and its CR (Thailand) joint venture owns and develops department stores in the provinces. Robinson, the only department-store operator listed on the Stock Exchange of Thailand, plans to merge with Central, operator of 12 upscale department stores, one Zen store, and a supermarket.

B mil	12/91	12/92	12/93	US$mil 12/93				
Revenues	**7,363.1**	**7,400.1**	**8,184.4**	**320.7**	P/E Ratio	**36.5**	Price (9/30/95)	**48.75**
Net Income	**223.2**	**217.7**	**192.3**	**7.5**	P/B Ratio	**2.9**	52 Wk Hi-Low	**62.50-39.00**
Book Value	**1,505.2**	**1,679.2**	**2,443.7**	**94.8**	Yield %	**2.1**	Market Cap	**US$280.5mil**

Address **2 Silom Rd., Suriwong** Tel **02-245-4811** ADR President --
Bangkok 10110 Fax **02-246-0151** SEDOL No. **6745093** Chairman **Prayoon Kovirulskul**

Saha-Union

Industry: **Overseas Trading**

Saha-Union's core business is manufactuting textiles, garments, and footwear, but its diversified interests range from real estate and computer repair to plastics production and agriculture. In addition to its own Venus brand-name textiles and garments, the company is also licensed to manufacture Van Heusen, Grand Slam, and Nike garments and footwear. Its 25%-owned Thai Plastic makes plastic components for consumer products. Saha-Union's 50%-owned Union Rubber Products manufactures elastic braid and shoe soles. The firm also cultivates cotton and rubber.

B mil	12/91 R	12/92	12/93	US$mil 12/93				
Sales	**-999.0**	**12,586.2**	**12,260.0**	**480.4**	P/E Ratio	**18.3**	Price (9/30/95)	**29.00**
Net Income	**-999.0**	**769.2**	**569.9**	**22.3**	P/B Ratio	**1.4**	52 Wk Hi-Low	**37.75-26.75**
Book Value	**-999.0**	**5,903.5**	**6,065.0**	**235.2**	Yield %	**5.2**	Market Cap	**US$347.3mil**

Address **1828 Sukhumvit Rd.** Tel **02-311-5111** ADR President **Sumeth Darakananda**
Bangkok 10250 Fax **02-331-5668** SEDOL No. **6767428** Chairman **Anand Panyarachun**

R=Restated.

Securities One

Industry: **Securities Brokers**

Securities One, a subsidiary of Finance One, offers securities brokerage and trading and investment advice, primarily to institutions. It holds 7% of Thailand's securities-trading market, and has the highest trading volume of any Thai firm. Its corporate-finance and investment division provides fund-raising, derivative-structuring, and underwriting services. Commissions and fees contributed 52.1% to the firm's 1994 revenue; interest income and dividends accounted for 27.2%. Securities One owns 24% of Nithipat Capital, an investment bank and brokerage house.

B mil	12/92 R	12/93	12/94	US$mil 12/94				
Sales	**889.7**	**1,598.3**	**2,110.8**	**84.2**	P/E Ratio	**7.5**	Price (9/30/95)	**220.00**
Net Income	**382.5**	**766.9**	**1,015.3**	**40.5**	P/B Ratio	**4.5**	52 Wk Hi-Low	**284.00-114.00**
Book Value	**1,862.9**	**2,394.8**	**4,428.3**	**178.3**	Yield %	**2.8**	Market Cap	**US$790.4mil**

Address **153/3 Soi Mahardlekluang 1** Tel **02-652-1234** ADR President **P. Kovithvathanaphong**
Bangkok 10330 Fax **02-652-1250** SEDOL No. **6791795** Chairman **Thanat Khoman**

R=Restated.

Shangri-La Hotel

Industry: **Lodging**

Shangri-La Hotel is a Bangkok-based hotel owner and operator. It provides lodging, serves food and beverages, and arranges conferences and parties. The company's flagship Shangri-La Bangkok hotel has 871 rooms and 44,050 square feet of function space. Its Chao Phraya tower also houses 10 floors of executive offices and a shopping arcade. The hotel's major customers are from Europe and Japan. Shangri-La Hotel holds a 5% stake in Singapore's Shangri-La Hotel, and a 14.6% stake in Shangri-La International Hotels (Beihai) through its wholly-owned Apizaco (Hong Kong) subsidiary.

	B mil 12/92	12/93	12/94	US$mil 12/94				
Sales	**937.3**	**946.0**	**1,126.4**	**44.9**	P/E Ratio	**24.4**	Price (9/30/95)	**21.00**
Net Income	**575.1**	**196.8**	**224.7**	**9.0**	P/B Ratio	**1.3**	52 Wk Hi-Low	**26.75-19.00**
Book Value	**4,024.1**	**4,237.2**	**4,265.3**	**171.7**	Yield %	**2.4**	Market Cap	**US$218.0mil**

Address **89 Soi Wat Suan Plu, New Rd.** **Bangrak, Bangkok 10500**
Tel **02-236-7777** Fax **02-236-8579**
ADR
SEDOL No. **6799959**
Managing Director **Thomas L.M. Shing**
Chairman **Suree Asdathorn**

Shinawatra Computer & Comm.

Industry: **Computers**

Shinawatra Computer & Communications provides telecommunication services, markets computer systems and telecommunication equipment, and offers cable-TV and radio broadcasting. Shinawatra has a 20% stake in Smart Satcom, a Thai producer of satellite dishes. The firm also holds 58% of Advanced Info Service, which operates Thailand's largest mobile-phone network, and 36% of Shinawatra Paging, the Thai market leader in paging services. Shinawatra also has a stake in International Broadcasting, which has a 90% share of Thailand's cable-TV business and 76,000 subscribers.

	B mil 12/92	12/93	12/94	US$mil 12/94				
Sales	**2,532.4**	**5,595.1**	**8,700.6**	**347.0**	P/E Ratio	**28.8**	Price (9/30/95)	**620.00**
Net Income	**511.5**	**1,472.1**	**2,765.4**	**110.3**	P/B Ratio	**13.2**	52 Wk Hi-Low	**784.00-438.00**
Book Value	**2,601.4**	**3,692.5**	**6,508.3**	**262.0**	Yield %	**N/A**	Market Cap	**US$3,430.4mil**

Address **Phanon Yothin Rd.** **Bangkok 10400**
Tel **02-299-5000** Fax **02-299-5196**
ADR **SHWCY**
SEDOL No. **6805964**
Chairman Exec Bd **Paiboon Limpaphayom**
Chairman **Potjaman Shinawatra**

Siam Cement

Industry: **Building Materials**

Siam Cement manufactures cement, construction materials, machinery, petrochemicals, paper, and packaging. The company derives 57% of its revenue from cement sales; 25% from construction materials; 10% from steel, electricals, and vehicle accessories; and the remainder from petrochemicals and other businesses. Its 25 wholly-owned and 19 partly-owned subsidiaries are active in the acquisition of land and factories, as well as the manufacturing of refractories, steel, pipes, decorative products, glass, fiberglass, sanitaryware, and floor, wall, and ceiling tiles.

	B mil 12/92 R	12/93	12/94	US$mil 12/94				
Sales	**50,468.2**	**56,418.8**	**65,409.1**	**2,608.9**	P/E Ratio	**31.1**	Price (9/30/95)	**1,402.00**
Net Income	**3,987.9**	**3,164.3**	**5,398.0**	**215.3**	P/B Ratio	**7.1**	52 Wk Hi-Low	**1,540.0-1,228.0**
Book Value	**17,388.5**	**18,653.0**	**23,735.4**	**955.5**	Yield %	**1.3**	Market Cap	**US$6,716.2mil**

Address **1 Siam Cement Rd., Bangsue** **Bangkok 10800**
Tel **02-586-3333** Fax **02-586-4444**
ADR
SEDOL No. **6806785**
President **Chumpol NaLamlieng**
Chairman **Sanya Dharmasakti**

R=Restated.

Siam City Bank

Industry: **Banks - Regional**

Siam City Bank is a commercial bank with assets totaling roughly 162 billion baht. The company operates 40 branches in Bangkok, 123 in the Thai provinces, and an office in Phnom Penh, Cambodia. Siam City also has two overseas representative offices in Myanmar and China. A branch in the Cayman Islands manages the company's offshore banking operations. The bank also operates 91 ATMs throughout Thailand. Siam City offers insurance services in association with Thailand's Muangthai Life Insurance, and credit cards with Visa International.

	B mil 12/92	12/93	12/94	US$mil 12/94				
Revenues	**10,884.4**	**13,090.1**	**16,715.5**	**666.7**	P/E Ratio	**11.7**	Price (9/30/95)	**27.75**
Net Income	**1,176.2**	**1,980.7**	**2,862.3**	**114.2**	P/B Ratio	**2.8**	52 Wk Hi-Low	**34.00-21.25**
Book Value	**7,004.5**	**9,247.1**	**11,859.8**	**477.4**	Yield %	**1.8**	Market Cap	**US$1,331.6mil**

Address **1101 New Petchburi Rd.** **Bangkok 10400**
Tel **02-208-5000** Fax **02-253-1240**
ADR
SEDOL No. **6807056**
President **Som Jatusipitak**
Chairman **Chalerm Cheo-Sakul**

Siam City Cement

Industry: **Building Materials**

Siam City Cement is Thailand's second-largest cement producer and its largest clinker and cement exporter, exporting 2 million tonnes in 1994. The company manufactures and distributes cement products, asbestos-concrete tiles and pipes, sanitary ware, chinaware, porcelain, brass fittings, and corrugated paper boxes. In September 1994, Siam City Cement formed Gulf Electric, a joint venture with Lanna Lignite, to produce and sell electricity to the Electricity Generating Authority of Thailand. Siam City Cement has business in other construction-related industries as well.

	B mil 12/92	12/93	12/94	US$mil 12/94				
Sales	**9,309.0**	**11,074.2**	**11,966.1**	**477.3**	P/E Ratio	**20.6**	Price (9/30/95)	**418.00**
Net Income	**1,131.7**	**1,470.7**	**2,125.6**	**84.8**	P/B Ratio	**4.0**	52 Wk Hi-Low	**530.00-334.00**
Book Value	**6,273.3**	**7,058.3**	**12,111.5**	**487.6**	Yield %	**1.9**	Market Cap	**US$1,953.0mil**

Address **888/180-189 Ploenchit Rd.** **Bangkok 10330**
Tel **02-253-0104** Fax **02-253-2891**
ADR
SEDOL No. **6806376**
Chief Executive **Somkiart Limsong**
Chairman **Krit Ratanarak**

Siam Commercial Bank

Industry: **Banks - Regional**

Siam Commercial Bank offers commercial-banking services such as deposit accounts, loans, credit cards, travel insurance, and unit trusts. It offers an ATM gold card together with MasterCard International. Siam Commercial Bank has 353 branches and 44 foreign-exchange centers in Thailand, and branches abroad in New York, Chicago, Los Angeles, London, Hong Kong, Singapore, and Laos. It also has a joint venture with Cambodia's government, the Cambodian Commerce Bank. The bank holds 100% of Singburi Sugar and almost 100% of Hong Kong-based Siam Commercial Finance.

	B mil 12/92	12/93	12/94	US$mil 12/94				
Revenues	**27,659.6**	**32,209.0**	**37,662.6**	**1,502.2**	P/E Ratio	**13.5**	Price (9/30/95)	**220.00**
Net Income	**4,180.3**	**4,847.5**	**6,203.6**	**247.4**	P/B Ratio	**2.8**	52 Wk Hi-Low	**230.00-170.00**
Book Value	**19,391.2**	**26,165.3**	**30,219.3**	**1,216.6**	Yield %	**3.0**	Market Cap	**US$3,337.3mil**

Address **1060 Phetchaburi Rd.**
Bangkok 10400
Tel **02-256-1234**
Fax **02-253-6697**
ADR
SEDOL No. **6889924**
President & CEO **Olarn Chaipravat**
Chairman **Prachitr Yossundara**

Siam Food Products

Industry: **Plantations**

Siam Food Products manufactures and exports canned pineapple, pineapple-juice concentrate, and other canned fruit and vegetables. The company derives the majority of its revenue from its exports under its own Siam Food label, as well as those under its clients' brand names including Libby's, St. Michael, Empress, Geisha, and Dairy Queen. Major export markets include Germany, the Netherlands, France, the United States, and the United Kingdom. Siam Food's plantations contribute 20% of its pineapples. It purchases the remaining 80% from contracted pineapple growers.

	B mil 09/91 R	09/92	09/93	US$mil 09/93				
Sales	**1,287.4**	**1,354.1**	**866.1**	**33.9**	P/E Ratio	**NMF**	Price (9/30/95)	**51.00**
Net Income	**265.8**	**282.2**	**-73.3**	**-2.9**	P/B Ratio	**1.8**	52 Wk Hi-Low	**75.00-45.50**
Book Value	**711.9**	**826.7**	**580.9**	**22.8**	Yield %	**15.4**	Market Cap	**US$42.8mil**

Address **235/9 Asoke Rd., Sukhumvit 21**
Bangkok 10110
Tel **02-258-0120**
Fax **02-259-0512**
ADR
SEDOL No. **6806956**
President **Adul Pinsuvana**
Chairman **Nam Phoonwathu**

R=Restated.

Singer Thailand

Industry: **Other Home Furnishings**

Singer Thailand assembles and distributes Singer brand household and artisan sewing machines, and is one of the country's largest manufacturers of household appliances. The company assembles, trades in, and distributes refrigerators, televisions, gas stoves, stereos, videocassette recorders, and washing machines in Thailand. Refrigerators account for approximately 32% of sales, and televisions account for 28%. Singer Thailand has a total sales force of 11,000 people based in more than 290 Singer stores throughout Thailand. The company is 48% owned by Singer Sewing Machine.

	B mil 06/92	06/93	06/94	US$mil 06/94				
Sales	**5,319.2**	**6,218.2**	**6,711.4**	**264.6**	P/E Ratio	**10.6**	Price (9/30/95)	**212.00**
Net Income	**320.7**	**487.0**	**540.6**	**21.3**	P/B Ratio	**3.4**	52 Wk Hi-Low	**264.00-166.00**
Book Value	**1,095.7**	**1,582.7**	**1,662.7**	**66.3**	Yield %	**6.1**	Market Cap	**US$228.5mil**

Address **321 Siphaya Rd.**
Bangrak, Bangkok 10500
Tel **02-236-0138**
Fax **02-236-4242**
ADR
SEDOL No. **6811013**
Managing Director **George E. Chyc-Magdzin**
Chairman **Banyong Lamsam**

Sino-Thai Engineering & Construction

Industry: **Heavy Construction**

Sino-Thai Engineering & Construction (STECON) manufactures construction materials and does infrastructure construction. Its projects include construction of a cooling-tower substructure for the Electricity Generating Authority of Thailand; refinery construction for Shell, Caltex, and Esso; and development of flood-control systems for Thailand's Public Works Department. Another major project will develop treatment facilities for one third of central Bangkok's wastewater. Its 40%-owned Sino-Thai Pressure Vessels and Iron Works subsidiary manufactures steel building products.

	B mil 12/92 R	12/93	12/94	US$mil 12/94				
Sales	**2,525.4**	**2,326.2**	**4,318.4**	**172.2**	P/E Ratio	**23.8**	Price (9/30/95)	**262.00**
Net Income	**329.6**	**284.7**	**330.5**	**13.2**	P/B Ratio	**4.1**	52 Wk Hi-Low	**346.00-250.00**
Book Value	**1,024.9**	**1,249.7**	**1,487.6**	**59.9**	Yield %	**1.7**	Market Cap	**US$240.6mil**

Address **Asoke Rd., Sukhumvit 21**
Bangkok 10110
Tel **02-260-1321**
Fax **02-260-1339**
ADR
SEDOL No. **6835370**
Managing Director **Chavarat Charnvirakul**
Chairman **Chavarat Charnvirakul**

R=Restated.

Srithai Superware

Industry: **Household Products (Durable)**

Srithai Superware manufactures plastic and melamine consumer products, such as utensils, dishes, baskets, and various household items. It holds 65% of Thailand's melamine-product market. The company also has subsidiaries and operations in investment holding and trading, and the manufacture of molds, plastic, and melamine powder. It also operates a packaging-materials joint venture, Srithai Packaging. Srithai Superware exports its products to 30 countries, including Australia, Japan, the United States, Singapore, China, and Poland.

	B mil 12/92 R	12/93	12/94	US$mil 12/94				
Sales	**1,896.3**	**2,289.6**	**2,730.5**	**108.9**	P/E Ratio	**19.9**	Price (9/30/95)	**178.00**
Net Income	**243.7**	**304.0**	**357.5**	**14.3**	P/B Ratio	**4.0**	52 Wk Hi-Low	**188.00-136.00**
Book Value	**1,104.0**	**1,668.7**	**1,800.1**	**72.5**	Yield %	**2.4**	Market Cap	**US$284.2mil**

Address **355 Suksawat Rd., Soi 36**
Bangkok 10140
Tel **02-427-0200**
Fax **02-427-7168**
ADR
SEDOL No. **6837268**
President **Sanan Angubolkul**
Chairman **Sumit Lertsumitkul**

R=Restated.

Sun Tech Group

Industry: **Plantations**

Sun Tech Group is Thailand's leading exporter of canned-tomato products, including peeled, diced, and crushed tomatoes, and tomato paste and juice. The company farms tomatoes on its own plantations, and processes and cans them at its factory. It exports approximately 85% of its output to Australia, Japan, Europe, and North America under its customers' trademarks. Sun Tech's other products include pineapple and pineapple-juice concentrate, mushrooms, baby corn, and asparagus. The company also owns a 10% stake in Nakorn Thai Strip Mill, a hot-rolled steel-coil producer.

B mil	12/90	12/91	12/92	US$mil 12/92				
Sales	**N/A**	**25.3**	**116.6**	**4.6**	P/E Ratio	**NMF**	Price (9/30/95)	**38.50**
Net Income	**N/A**	**-142.8**	**-127.3**	**-5.0**	P/B Ratio	**7.7**	52 Wk Hi-Low	**46.50-37.00**
Book Value	**N/A**	**191.3**	**413.9**	**16.0**	Yield %	**0.0**	Market Cap	**US$126.8mil**

Address **1 Sukhumvit 25 Rd.**
Bangkok 10110
Tel **02-260-6464**
Fax **02-260-6290**
ADR
SEDOL No. **6863047**
President **C. Horrungruang**
Chairman **Prayoon Chindapradit**

Tanayong

Industry: **Real-Estate Investment**

Tanayong is active in property development and investment, hotels, and infrastructure construction. Its two largest projects are its 6,000-unit Thana City residential complex, and the Bangkok Transit System, a mass-transit rail project. The firm holds roughly 160 million square feet of land, 35% of which is under development. Its Thai hotel interests include a 40% stake in the 378-room Empress Hotel, and a 21% stake in the 415-room Regent Bangkok. It also owns Bangkok's TST Tower office complex. Hong Kong-based Hwa Kay Thai Holdings has a 30% stake in Tanayong.

B mil	03/91 R	12/92 *	12/93	US$mil 12/93				
Sales	**N/A**	**2,325.3**	**1,126.7**	**44.1**	P/E Ratio	**22.5**	Price (9/30/95)	**38.00**
Net Income	**N/A**	**1,284.5**	**518.6**	**20.3**	P/B Ratio	**0.9**	52 Wk Hi-Low	**68.00-30.00**
Book Value	**N/A**	**12,470.3**	**12,702.5**	**492.5**	Yield %	**2.6**	Market Cap	**US$464.9mil**

Address **25 Soi Chidlom, Ploenchit Rd.**
Bangkok 10330
Tel **02-251-6788**
Fax **02-255-8651**
ADR
SEDOL No. **6872203**
President **Keeree Kanjanapas**
Chairman **Mongkol Kanjanapas**

*Irregular period due to fiscal year change; R=Restated.

Thai Central Chemical

Industry: **Specialty Chemicals**

Thai Central Chemical Corporation (TCCC) produces, imports, and distributes fertilizers for Thailand's agriculture market. It has a production capacity of 500,000 tonnes and sells 1.14 million tonnes of fertilizer per year. It is Thailand's largest producer of chemical fertilizers, maintaining a 40% market share. TCCC also operates four distribution centers for its products throughout Thailand. Its 51%-owned subsidiaries include chemical importer MC Industrial Chemical, dye importer MC Textile, and plastics importer MC Plastics. Thailand's Metro holds a 34% stake in TCCC.

B mil	12/92	12/93	12/94	US$mil 12/94				
Sales	**7,272.8**	**7,121.4**	**8,097.6**	**323.0**	P/E Ratio	**11.0**	Price (9/30/95)	**31.75**
Net Income	**595.5**	**346.4**	**283.3**	**11.3**	P/B Ratio	**1.0**	52 Wk Hi-Low	**49.25-31.25**
Book Value	**3,327.5**	**3,916.8**	**3,887.5**	**156.5**	Yield %	**6.3**	Market Cap	**US$152.1mil**

Address **180-184 Metro, Rajawongse Rd.**
Bangkok 10100
Tel **02-225-0135**
Fax **02-224-9839**
ADR
SEDOL No. **6886282**
President **Takashi Hirabayashi**
Chairman **Niran Sirinavin**

Thai Farmers Bank

Industry: **Banks - Regional**

Thai Farmers Bank (TFB) is a commercial bank that offers loans, credit cards, and deposit services. It had 508,800 million baht in assets and had issued 360,000 credit cards at year-end 1994. TFB has 45 currency-exchange offices, 454 branches (134 of which are in metropolitan Bangkok) and 295 ATMs throughout Thailand. It operates overseas offices in 10 countries including Laos, Myanmar (Burma), Cambodia, and China. TFB also owns 75% of Thanakorn Vegetable Oil Products, 50% of Progress Software, and smaller stakes in a variety of other companies.

B mil	12/92	12/93	12/94	US$mil 12/94				
Revenues	**39,565.4**	**44,833.2**	**50,215.0**	**2,002.8**	P/E Ratio	**12.6**	Price (9/30/95)	**164.00**
Net Income	**5,212.7**	**7,942.2**	**10,419.4**	**415.6**	P/B Ratio	**2.8**	52 Wk Hi-Low	**188.00-152.00**
Book Value	**26,978.0**	**35,635.3**	**46,641.5**	**1,877.7**	Yield %	**2.8**	Market Cap	**US$5,237.5mil**

Address **400 Phahon Yothin Ave.**
Bangkok 10400
Tel **02-270-1122**
Fax **02-271-4033**
ADR
SEDOL No. **6888783**
President **Banthoon Lamsam**
Chairman **Banyong Lamsam**

Thai-German Ceramic Industry

Industry: **Building Materials**

Thai-German Ceramic Industry is Thailand's largest tile producer; it also has interests in hotels and real-estate development. The company manufactures and distributes decoratively glazed floor tiles, as well as unglazed floor tiles. Its brand names include Campana, Casa, and T-GCI. Thai-German Ceramic plans to spend 4.8 billion baht over the next three years to expand both its production facilities and its real-estate and hotel operations. The company issued 2.5 billion baht in bonds and warrants to finance this expansion.

B mil	12/92	12/93	12/94	US$mil 12/94				
Sales	**N/A**	**N/A**	**N/A**	**N/A**	P/E Ratio	**N/A**	Price (9/30/95)	**82.00**
Net Income	**N/A**	**N/A**	**N/A**	**N/A**	P/B Ratio	**N/A**	52 Wk Hi-Low	**128.00-56.00**
Book Value	**N/A**	**N/A**	**N/A**	**N/A**	Yield %	**N/A**	Market Cap	**US$245.6mil**

Address **139 Robinson Rachada Bldg.**
Bangkok 10310
Tel **02-246-0084**
Fax **N/A**
ADR
SEDOL No. **6886237**
President --
Chairman --

Thai Investment & Securities

Industry: **Financial Services - Diversified**

Thai Investment and Securities (Tisco) provides retail-investment services to consumers and investment and financial-advisory services to institutional clients. It offers underwriting, corporate lending, securities investing, and mortgage and automobile loans. The company has more than 41 billion baht in assets. Tisco owns 100% of Thai Securities, a brokerage firm. It also owns and manages Thai Capital Management (TCM), a mutual-fund company, in conjunction with Krung Thai Thanakit, Krung Thai Bank, and Bankers Trust. Each of these firms holds 25% of TCM's shares.

B mil	12/92	12/93	12/94	US$mil 12/94				
Revenues	**3,263.1**	**3,517.1**	**4,341.5**	**173.2**	P/E Ratio	**8.7**	Price (9/30/95)	**724.00**
Net Income	**974.1**	**1,215.2**	**1,392.7**	**55.5**	P/B Ratio	**2.0**	52 Wk Hi-Low	**980.00-586.00**
Book Value	**3,914.8**	**4,823.3**	**6,036.6**	**243.0**	Yield %	**4.1**	Market Cap	**US$482.7mil**

Address	**138 Silom Rd.**	Tel	**02-237-7788**	ADR		President	**Pliu Mangkornkanck**
	Bangkok 10500	Fax	**02-236-2768**	SEDOL No.	**6886776**	Chairman	**Timothy S. Rattray**

Thai Military Bank

Industry: **Banks - Regional**

Thai Military Bank is a commercial bank that offers consumer-oriented services through its network of 272 branches. It also has branches abroad in Vietnam, Hong Kong, Laos, and the Cayman Islands, and a representative office in Myanmar (Burma). The bank has a 6% market share in consumer loans. It had nearly 228 billion baht in assets and 178.5 billion baht in deposits at year-end 1994. The bank has two 99%-owned property-development subsidiaries and holds stakes in a variety of financial, industrial, and service companies throughout Thailand.

B mil	12/92	12/93	12/94	US$mil 12/94				
Revenues	**17,103.5**	**19,897.3**	**23,630.0**	**942.5**	P/E Ratio	**12.7**	Price (9/30/95)	**86.50**
Net Income	**1,800.2**	**2,812.5**	**3,505.5**	**139.8**	P/B Ratio	**2.8**	52 Wk Hi-Low	**98.50-60.24**
Book Value	**9,337.5**	**14,571.6**	**15,944.0**	**641.9**	Yield %	**2.9**	Market Cap	**US$1,772.2mil**

Address	**3000 Phahon Yothin Rd.**	Tel	**02-299-1111**	ADR		President	**Gen. W. Wongwanich**
	Bangkok 10900	Fax	**02-273-7121**	SEDOL No.	**6887876**	Chairman	**Gen. P. Charumani**

Thai Pineapple

Industry: **Plantations**

Thai Pineapple is Thailand's largest manufacturer and exporter of processed pineapple products by revenues. The company produces more than 5 million standard cases of canned pineapple and 2.5 million gallons of pineapple-juice concentrate annually. Taiwan Pineapple sells its products under its own Tipco brand name, in addition to brand names such as Sysco, Libby's, and Geisha. The company's primary markets are the United States, Europe, Korea, and Japan. The company owns 100% of Delaware-registered Tipco Marketing, which acts as a sales agent for the company in the U.S.

B mil	12/92 R	12/93	12/94	US$mil 12/94				
Sales	**1,505.0**	**993.6**	**1,078.6**	**43.0**	P/E Ratio	**7.4**	Price (9/30/95)	**34.50**
Net Income	**216.3**	**-75.7**	**163.8**	**6.5**	P/B Ratio	**1.6**	52 Wk Hi-Low	**41.25-27.00**
Book Value	**595.5**	**519.8**	**742.5**	**29.9**	Yield %	**2.9**	Market Cap	**US$48.2mil**

Address	**118/1 Rama 6 Rd.**	Tel	**02-271-0041**	ADR		President	**Phanporn Dabbaransi**
	Bangkok 10400	Fax	**02-271-4304**	SEDOL No.	**6887489**	Chairman	**Prasit Supsakorn**

R=Restated.

Thai Plastic & Chemical

Industry: **Commodity Chemicals**

Thai Plastic and Chemical is Thailand's largest producer of polyvinyl chloride (PVC). It manufactures PVC in resin and compounded-pallet form, and distributes it to industrial manufacturers of plastic products such as pipes, wires, and cables. It has formed a joint venture with a unit of U.S.-based Occidental Petroleum to build a PVC plant in Rayong. The company is 51% owned by a conglomerate of Japanese companies, including Asahi Chemical Industry and trading firm Mitsui & Co., each of which has a 20% stake. Siam Cement also owns 10% of Thai Plastic and Chemical.

B mil	12/92	12/93	12/94	US$mil 12/94				
Sales	**N/A**	**N/A**	**N/A**	**N/A**	P/E Ratio	**N/A**	Price (9/30/95)	**138.00**
Net Income	**N/A**	**N/A**	**N/A**	**N/A**	P/B Ratio	**N/A**	52 Wk Hi-Low	**240.96-116.00**
Book Value	**N/A**	**N/A**	**N/A**	**N/A**	Yield %	**N/A**	Market Cap	**US$413.2mil**

Address	**191 S. Sathorn Rd.**	Tel	**02-287-2985**	ADR		President	--
	Yannawa, Bangkok 10120	Fax	**02-287-2983**	SEDOL No.	**6887111**	Chairman	--

TPI Polene

Industry: **Commodity Chemicals**

T.P.I. Polene is a Bangkok-based manufacturer of cement and petrochemical products. It is Thailand's third-largest producer of cement with a market share of 12%. It also produces and distributes low-density polyethylene-plastic pellets to other manufacturers, who use them in the manufacture of plastic bags, bottles, water pipes, and coating materials. The company sells its products domestically and also exports them to countries throughout the Pacific Rim under the Polene name. T.P.I. Polene is majority-owned by Thai Petrochemical Industry.

B mil	12/92	12/93	12/94	US$mil 12/94				
Sales	**N/A**	**N/A**	**N/A**	**N/A**	P/E Ratio	**N/A**	Price (9/30/95)	**190.00**
Net Income	**N/A**	**N/A**	**N/A**	**N/A**	P/B Ratio	**N/A**	52 Wk Hi-Low	**270.00-124.00**
Book Value	**N/A**	**N/A**	**N/A**	**N/A**	Yield %	**N/A**	Market Cap	**US$1,782.4mil**

Address	**175-177 Surawongse Rd.**	Tel	**02-235-0310**	ADR		President	**P. Leophairatana**
	Bangkok 10500	Fax	**N/A**	SEDOL No.	**6869056**	Chairman	**S. Hongladarom**

Tropical Canning

Industry: **Fishing**

Tropical Canning produces canned seafood, primarily for export markets in the United States. The company's products, including tuna, baby clams, shrimp, and crabmeat, are marketed under the TCB and TC Boy Tuna labels. Tropical Canning operates through its wholly-owned Tropical Seafood Products and 49%-owned Tropical Packaging subsidiaries. In addition to seafood canning, its subsidiaries are active in frozen-seafood processing, can making, and label printing. The company is also involved in property development and operates a joint-venture to produce fiberglass boats.

B mil	12/92 R	12/93	12/94	US$mil 12/94				
Sales	**1,303.3**	**1,539.4**	**1,451.7**	**57.9**	P/E Ratio	**32.5**	Price (9/30/95)	**7.80**
Net Income	**58.2**	**42.3**	**16.1**	**0.6**	P/B Ratio	**0.5**	52 Wk Hi-Low	**17.75-7.70**
Book Value	**981.9**	**1,004.4**	**989.1**	**39.8**	Yield %	**3.2**	Market Cap	**US$20.6mil**

Address **1/1 Kanjanavanich Rd.**
Hatyai 90110
Tel **074-212-330**
Fax **074-212-338**
ADR
SEDOL No. **6904719**
Managing Director **Kampol Watcharanimit**
Chairman **Tan Boon Pin**

R=Restated.

Unicord

Industry: **Fishing**

Unicord is the world's largest producer and exporter of canned tuna by revenues. The company also produces and exports canned salmon and sardines, cat food, and frozen shrimp, prawns, and tuna loins. Unicord sells more than 350 seafood brand names worldwide. The company owns Bumble Bee Seafoods of the United States, and its Bumble Bee brand tuna is the second-biggest seller in the $1 billion U.S. tuna market, with a 26% market share. Unicord has a second subsidiary in the U.S. and one in Thailand as well. It recently began a distribution business in the U.S.

B mil	12/91	12/92	12/93	US$mil 12/93				
Sales	**6,755.2**	**6,171.1**	**13,859.9**	**543.1**	P/E Ratio	**30.8**	Price (9/30/95)	**3.70**
Net Income	**336.9**	**-753.6**	**33.5**	**1.3**	P/B Ratio	**0.5**	52 Wk Hi-Low	**7.70-3.70**
Book Value	**3,506.6**	**4,247.7**	**2,206.0**	**85.5**	Yield %	**0.0**	Market Cap	**US$41.4mil**

Address **404 Phayathai Rd.**
Bangkok 10330
Tel **02-216-0020**
Fax **02-216-1468**
ADR
SEDOL No. **6911344**
President --
Chairman **Kamchom Sathirakul**

Union Asia Finance

Industry: **Financial Services - Diversified**

Union Asia Finance is Thailand's sixth-largest nonbank financial company by assets. It has more than 37 billion baht in assets. The company provides financing for commercial development, as well as mortgages for consumers. It also underwrites and brokers securities, and provides investment advice. Union Asia Finance is 20%-owned by Bangkok Bank, Thailand's largest commercial bank by assets. Union Asia Finance holds 12.5% of BBL Asset Management, in addition to 10% stakes in Bangkok Grand Pacific Lease and Bangkok Sakura Leasing.

B mil	12/92 R	12/93	12/94	US$mil 12/94				
Revenues	**3,757.0**	**4,149.3**	**4,305.3**	**171.7**	P/E Ratio	**10.4**	Price (9/30/95)	**118.00**
Net Income	**805.2**	**901.5**	**913.5**	**36.4**	P/B Ratio	**2.0**	52 Wk Hi-Low	**195.00-80.00**
Book Value	**2,310.5**	**3,835.7**	**4,690.6**	**188.8**	Yield %	**3.4**	Market Cap	**US$381.1mil**

Address **Sathorn City Twr., S. Sathorn Rd.**
Sathorn, Bangkok 10120
Tel **02-236-7511**
Fax **02-236-7518**
ADR
SEDOL No. **6912273**
President **Chaiyut Pilun-Owad**
Chairman **Phuchong Bhengsri**

R=Restated.

Univest Land

Industry: **Real-Estate Investment**

Univest Land develops and manages real-estate projects. Its largest development is Muang Ake, a 1,600-acre residential community consisting of 10,000 houses. The company's properties in Bangkok include Fortune Town, a shopping and hotel complex, and Ratchada Square. It also jointly owns Chaophya Marble Granite, a construction-materials firm, with Finance One. The company has a 40%-owned joint venture with Singapore's Alliance Technology to build a 9,000 square meter Bangkok Underwater World theme park inside a mega-shopping mall that Univest is constructing.

B mil	12/92	12/93	12/94	US$mil 12/94				
Sales	**1,437.9**	**1,750.9**	**2,202.9**	**87.9**	P/E Ratio	**24.1**	Price (9/30/95)	**51.00**
Net Income	**337.0**	**150.7**	**309.1**	**12.3**	P/B Ratio	**2.9**	52 Wk Hi-Low	**103.00-43.25**
Book Value	**1,094.6**	**1,054.8**	**3,144.3**	**126.6**	Yield %	**2.5**	Market Cap	**US$366.5mil**

Address **1 Ratchadaphisek Rd.**
Bangkok 10310
Tel **02-247-3737**
Fax **02-246-8973**
ADR
SEDOL No. **6807131**
President & CEO **Thatree Boondicharern**
Chairman **Chanchai Leetavorn**

Wattachak

Industry: **Publishing**

Wattachak is a multimedia company involved in publishing, television, and radio. It publishes six weekly and two daily Thai-language newspapers. The company also owns the English-language daily Thailand Times, which has a circulation of approximately 1,000. Wattachak jointly owns TV-broadcasting satellite Thai Sky with satellite company Samart, and operates 76 radio stations. Thai Sky provides pay-for-view services to approximately 70,000 households. The company also sells second-hand electrical appliances, as well as audio and photo equipment.

B mil	12/92	12/93	12/94	US$mil 12/94				
Sales	**431.1**	**1,184.6**	**2,359.1**	**94.1**	P/E Ratio	**11.4**	Price (9/30/95)	**47.25**
Net Income	**73.5**	**341.8**	**343.0**	**13.7**	P/B Ratio	**2.2**	52 Wk Hi-Low	**61.50-35.50**
Book Value	**421.4**	**1,390.2**	**3,813.6**	**153.5**	Yield %	**1.6**	Market Cap	**US$347.1mil**

Address **88 Bomrajchonnee Rd.**
Taling-Chan, Bangkok 10170
Tel **02-434-0330**
Fax **02-435-0900**
ADR
SEDOL No. **6971069**
Managing Director **Praphan Boonyakiat**
Chairman **Nikorn Pornsatit**

United Kingdom

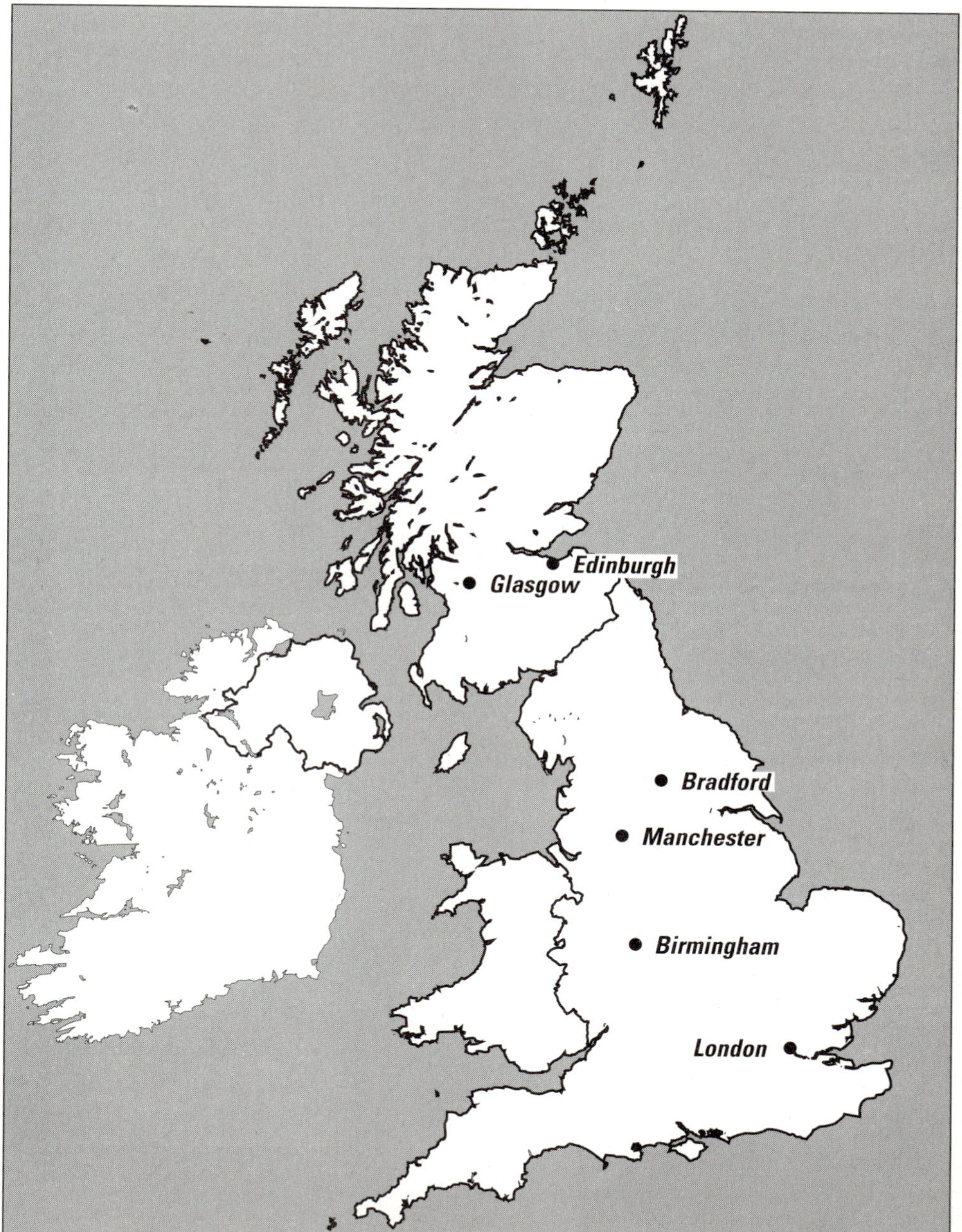

United Kingdom

Local Trading Hours	Time Difference with New York	Population (Est. 94)
8:30-4:30	5 hours ahead	58,135,000

Paul Beckett,
London

From its roots in Seventeenth Century coffee parlors, the London Stock Exchange has grown over the centuries into the world's leading center for trading foreign shares and the world's third-largest market by capitalization.

There were once as many as 20 stock exchanges around Great Britain, but the regional exchanges banded together to become a united Stock Exchange in the early 1970s. Since the "Big Bang" in 1986, trading on the London exchange has been done entirely on an electronic basis through the Stock Exchange Automated Quotation system, for U.K. and Irish equities, and through SEAQ International for foreign equities. The landmark Stock Exchange Tower on Threadneedle Street — the site of the exchange since 1773 — is occupied by exchange administrators.

The exchange operates on a market-making system, where 30 so-called market-makers are obliged to trade at the prices they quote. Market-makers are obliged to quote prices from 8:30 a.m. to 2:30 p.m. local time Monday to Friday.

At the end of 1994, there were more than 2,000 Irish and U.K. companies listed on the exchange with an equity capital value of 775 billion pounds. There were also 464 listed foreign companies with a total equity market value of 1.98 trillion pounds.

On Sept. 13, 1995, the London exchange's benchmark FT-SE 100 index set a new all-time record closing high of 3,570.8 points, up from 3065.5 at the end of 1994. Investors were encouraged that Britain's economic growth will be slow but steady and inflation subdued. The upturn in market fortunes was particularly welcome after a dismal 1994, when the FT-SE 100, colloquially termed "the Footsie," fell 10% over the course of the year.

The index comprises the largest 100 companies by market capitalization. By rule of thumb they are worth more than 1.5 billion pounds, with the constituents reviewed quarterly.

Dow Jones United Kingdom Equity Market Index Performance

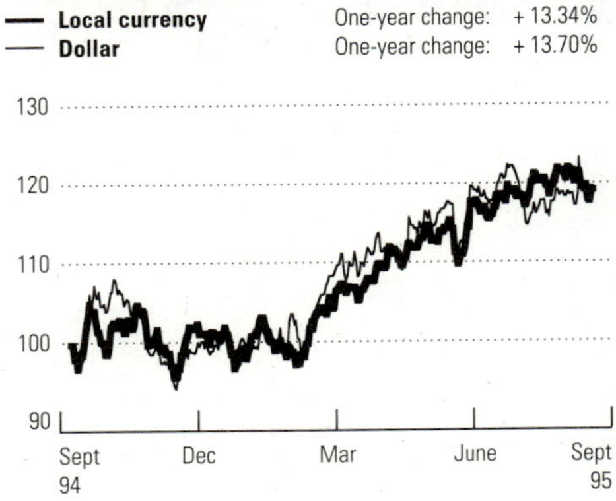

As of August 1995, the largest company was British Petroleum PLC, the oil major, with a market value of 26.8 billion pounds. It was closely followed by pharmaceuticals giant Glaxo Wellcome PLC, formed by the 1995 merger of Glaxo PLC and Wellcome PLC, at 26.7 billion pounds. Third was British

Gross Domestic Product (94)	Three-Year Average GDP Growth (92-94)	Main Industries	Consumer Price Index (94)	Monetary Unit	Exchange Rate (9/95)
$1.1 trillion	1.9%	Engineering, energy, pharmaceuticals and banking	2.4%	Sterling	UKS0.63 to US$1.00

Telecommunications PLC, the formerly state-owned telecoms group, at 25.4 billion.

The largest sector by market turnover in August was retail banks, followed by diversified industrial companies, pharmaceuticals and integrated oil companies — namely BP and the Shell Transport & Trading Co. PLC, the London-listed arm of the Royal Dutch/Shell Group of Companies.

Shell, whose counterpart, Royal Dutch Petroleum, is listed on the Amsterdam Stock Exchange, is just one of a number of dual-nationality concerns that have halfheadquarters in London. Others include Anglo-Dutch publishing group Reed Elsevier and Anglo-Dutch consumer goods giant Unilever.

Turnover in foreign equities totaled a record 719 billion pounds in 1994, the stock exchange says, up 24% from 1993 and above the 606 billion pounds of turnover in U.K. and Irish equities. (The London exchange was supposed to decouple from the Irish Stock Exchange in the summer of 1995, but computer problems in Dublin delayed the move to independence until at least the end of that year.)

European issues made up most of the foreign share turnover, in spite of efforts from other European bourses to attract companies back to their home markets. Turnover totalled 103 billion pounds in French equities, 81 billion pounds in German equities and 55 billion pounds in Dutch equities. The most actively traded European shares by turnover were Germany's Deutsche Bank, France's Elf Aquitaine, Royal Dutch Petroleum, and Switzerland's Roche Holdings and Nestle.

Ten Largest Capitalized Companies
as of 9/30/95

Stock	Market Cap. US$Mil
Glaxo Wellcome	42,276,796.5
British Petroleum	41,598,087.3
BT	39,190,913.1
Shell Transport & Trading	39,142,702.1
BAT Industries	25,900,318.6
Barclays	19,461,635.6
Marks & Spencer	19,238,496.0
BTR	18,870,207.4
British Gas	18,416,378.0
NatWest	17,436,569.0

Japanese shares attracted the most interest for an individual country, with 165 billion pounds in turnover in 1994, up 44% from 1993.

Turnover in emerging market equities has also been growing steadily in London. It reached record levels in 1994, with 3.7 billion pounds in Indian shares, 2.7 billion in Argentinian shares, 2.6 billion in South Korean shares, 2.3 billion in Thai shares, 1.8 billion in Brazilian shares, and 1.2 billion in Taiwanese shares.

Trading in foreign shares on SEAQ International is dominated by institutional business. The shares are divided into 20 separate country sectors with 52 market makers from major international securities houses. Trading in the international equity market can be done around the clock, but quotations can be put into SEAQ International only between 7 a.m. and 8:30 p.m. London time.

In June 1995, the exchange launched an equity market designed to cater to the special funding needs of small, young or developing companies that want to raise finance and have their shares more widely traded. AIM, as the market is called, has simpler application and listing rules than the Official List and replaces the Unlisted Securities Market.

On the whole, the market's listing rules are regarded as strict. For instance, the exchange requires companies to publish price-sensitive information such as corporate results and takeover announcements through its own information service first.

But its stringency does not appear to have deterred new listers, in part because there is no other viable alternative in the U.K. In 1994, a record 256 U.K. and Irish companies and 12 foreign companies joined the Official List, and 17 joined the Unlisted Securities Market.

In recent years, the exchange has also increased its market share of world eurobond listings, holding more than 25% of the market compared with around 12% in 1988. A eurobond is a long-term loan issued in a currency other than that of the country or market in which the loan is issued. The exchange also provides markets in U.K. gilts (government securities) as well as fixed interest stocks.

Industry Group Performance
1 Year Change Through 9/30/95

Industry	Change % (US$)
Best Performing	
Retailers - Specialty Apparel	73.26
Entertainment	50.12
Industrial Technology	46.78
Pharmaceuticals	45.31
Advertising	37.13
Worst Performing	
Railroads	-65.14
Air Freight & Couriers	-33.41
Heavy Construction	-29.84
Overseas Trading	-18.69
Trucking	-17.70

Non-resident individuals and companies are potentially liable to income tax of 25% on dividends in the U.K. though tax credits are available, depending on the terms of any anti-double taxation agreements.

Abbey National

Industry: **Banks - Regional**

Abbey National provides retail-banking and financial services and invests in treasury assets. The company has interests in commercial real estate and investment companies. It serves more than 10 million customers in the United Kingdom and provides residential mortgages, loans, and real-estate services in France, Spain, Italy, and the Channel Islands. The firm's wholly-owned subsidiaries, Abbey National Life and Scottish Mutual, offer life-insurance services. In 1995, the company acquired Pegasus Assurance Group, which offers healthcare and disability insurance.

£ mil	12/92	12/93	12/94	US$mil 12/94				
Revenues	6,308.0	5,363.0	5,726.0	8,809.2	P/E Ratio	0.1	Price (9/30/95)	5.42
Net Income	317.0	390.0	610.0	938.5	P/B Ratio	1.9	52 Wk Hi-Low	5.46-3.81
Book Value	3,184.0	3,386.0	3,704.0	5,787.5	Yield %	3.3	Market Cap	US$11,296mil

Address	**Abbey Hse., Baker St.**	Tel	**0171-612-4000**	ADR		CEO	**Peter Birch**
	London NW1 6XL	Fax	**0171-612-4230**	SEDOL No.	**4455**	Chairman	**Lord Tugendhat**

ABP

Industry: **Marine Transportation**

Associated British Ports Holdings (ABP) operates ports and transportation businesses. It also invests in retail and industrial property through its principal subsidiary, Grosvenor Square Properties Group. In 1994, ABP's 22 ports and two container businesses handled 110 million tonnes of cargo, and Red Funnel, its vehicle and passenger ferry subsidiary, carried over 1.8 million passengers. The group also provides research and consultancy and offshore insurance services. Its major property holdings are located in Cardiff, Hull, Southampton and Fleetwood.

£ mil	12/92	12/93	12/94	US$mil 12/94				
Sales	220.0	227.0	197.7	304.2	P/E Ratio	19.2	Price (9/30/95)	3.15
Net Income	-27.0	48.0	61.7	94.9	P/B Ratio	1.6	52 Wk Hi-Low	3.19-2.60
Book Value	580.0	657.0	736.2	1,150.3	Yield %	174.9	Market Cap	US$1,893.4mil

Address	**150 Holborn**	Tel	**0171-430-1177**	ADR		Managing Director	**Sir Keith Stuart**
	London EC1N 2LR	Fax	**0171-430-1384**	SEDOL No.	**56434**	Chairman	**Sir Keith Stuart**

Allied Colloids

Industry: **Specialty Chemicals**

Allied Colloids Group manufactures and markets specialty industrial chemicals for the paper, mining, oil and pollution-control industries. The company also produces chemicals for the textiles, coatings, and agricultural markets. Its wholly-owned U.S. subsidiary Hydrolabs manufactures and sells industrial chemicals to the textile industry. Allied Colloids has operations throughout Europe, Canada, the United States, Australia, Singapore, Hong Kong, and Mexico. More than 50% of the company's sales are generated outside the United Kingdom.

£ mil	04/93	04/94	04/95	US$mil 04/95				
Sales	295.0	327.0	356.0	559.7	P/E Ratio	17.7	Price (9/30/95)	1.26
Net Income	30.0	33.0	37.5	58.9	P/B Ratio	3.1	52 Wk Hi-Low	1.43-1.11
Book Value	169.0	190.0	213.1	343.7	Yield %	2.1	Market Cap	US$1,056.8mil

Address	**Cleckheaton Rd., Low Moor**	Tel	**01274-671267**	ADR		CEO	**Peter Flesher**
	Bradford, West Yorks BD12 0JZ	Fax	**01274-606499**	SEDOL No.	**19084**	Chairman	**Sir Trevor Holdsworth**

Allied Domecq

Industry: **Distillers & Brewers**

Allied Domecq is a food and beverage company. Its beverage brands include Canadian Club, Ballantine's, Courvoisier, Beefeater, Kahlua, and Tetley Tea. Notable retail interests include Baskin Robbins (4,026 stores), Dunkin' Donuts (3,948 stores), Victoria Wine liquor stores (1,500 stores), and more than 4,300 pubs. Its alcoholic-beverage subsidiaries include Domecq and Carlsberg-Tetley, and food subsidiaries Panrico and Continental Bakeries. Its spirits and wine activities account for 43% of revenues, retailing 29%, and Carlsberg-Tetley alone generates 17%.

£ mil	03/93	03/94	03/95	US$mil 03/95				
Sales	5,266.0	5,526.0	6,126.0	9,601.9	P/E Ratio	14.0	Price (9/30/95)	5.39
Net Income	260.0	325.0	387.0	606.6	P/B Ratio	2.3	52 Wk Hi-Low	6.12-4.93
Book Value	2,382.0	2,331.0	2,342.0	3,839.3	Yield %	3.7	Market Cap	US$8,825.8mil

Address	**24 Portland Pl.**	Tel	**0171-323-9000**	ADR	**ALDCY**	CEO	**Anthony J. Hales**
	London W1N 4BB	Fax	**0171-323-1742**	SEDOL No.	**18508**	Chairman	**Michael C.J. Jackaman**

Allied Textile

Industry: **Clothing & Fabrics**

Allied Textile Companies is a holding company for textile manufacturers, processors, and distributors. Its subsidiaries operate in Belgium, France, Germany, North America, and the United Kingdom. Its products include fibers, yarns, worsted cloths, knitwear, and dyers. Over 57% of revenues originate in the U.K., with 24% of revenues coming from North America. In the fiscal year ending October 1994, the company acquired Coating Applications (Textiles) Ltd., a maker of PVC coatings, Cleyn & Tinker Inc., a manufacturer of worsted fabrics, and Carleton Woolen Mills Inc.

£ mil	09/92	09/93	09/94	US$mil 09/94				
Sales	129.1	127.4	168.3	255.0	P/E Ratio	12.3	Price (9/30/95)	2.23
Net Income	8.7	9.4	11.7	17.7	P/B Ratio	2.0	52 Wk Hi-Low	2.65-2.23
Book Value	59.2	66.5	78.8	125.0	Yield %	3.0	Market Cap	US$247.3mil

Address	**Highburton**	Tel	**01484-604301**	ADR		CEO	**J.R. Corrin**
	Huddersfield HD8 0QJ	Fax	**01484-605740**	SEDOL No.	**20644**	Chairman	**J.P. Honeysett**

AMEC

Industry: **Heavy Construction**

AMEC is an international group operating in the areas of building and civil engineering, mechanical and electrical engineering, and housing and development. Its mechanical and electrical engineering businesses represent approximately 52% of group revenues. The firm also fabricates and maintains oil platforms and refineries, builds houses and offices in England, and supplies air-conditioning systems. Exports to non-European countries account for about 11% of group revenues. The group recently acquired U.S. construction company Morse Diesel International.

£ mil	12/92	12/93	12/94	US$mil 12/94				
Sales	2,122.0	2,184.0	1,962.4	3,019.1	P/E Ratio	14.3	Price (9/30/95)	0.60
Net Income	-78.0	19.0	17.7	27.2	P/B Ratio	0.5	52 Wk Hi-Low	1.10-0.56
Book Value	242.0	240.0	233.4	364.7	Yield %	5.0	Market Cap	US$192.7mil

Address **Sandiway Hse., Hartford**
Northwich, Cheshire CW8 2YA
Tel **01606-883885**
Fax **01606-883996**
ADR
SEDOL No. **28262**
President --
Chairman **Sir Alan Cockshaw**

Anglian Water

Industry: **Water Utilities**

Anglian Water supplies and distributes water and provides sewage treatment, disposal, process engineering. In terms of area covered, the company is the largest of the ten regional water companies in England and Wales. It provides services to more than two million properties. The company's international business has operations in the United States, South America, Europe, Asia, and Australasia. In March 1995, Anglian Water International secured a £50m contract to design and build sewage treatment facilities for Wellington, New Zealand.

£ mil	03/93	03/94	03/95	US$mil 03/95				
Sales	583.0	687.9	720.1	1,128.7	P/E Ratio	8.6	Price (9/30/95)	5.69
Net Income	166.0	115.3	196.8	308.5	P/B Ratio	1.1	52 Wk Hi-Low	5.78-4.56
Book Value	1,369.0	1,412.8	1,530.6	2,509.2	Yield %	4.6	Market Cap	US$2,686.1mil

Address **Anglian Hse., Ambury Rd.**
Huntingdon, Cambs PE18 6NZ
Tel **01480-443000**
Fax **01480-443115**
ADR
SEDOL No. **32412**
Managing Director **Alan Smith**
Chairman **Robin Gourlay**

APV

Industry: **Factory Equipment**

APV designs and manufactures products for fluid-handling, heat-exchange and homogenization processes. Its Sales and Engineering division provides general engineering services to customers mainly in the dairy, brewing, soft drink, processed food, and personal products industries. The company's specialist operations provide plants and installations for customers in the industrial dry foods, ice cream, and cheese businesses. In 1994, about 44% of APV's revenues were generated outside the United Kingdom and continental Europe.

£ mil	12/92	12/93	12/94	US$mil 12/94				
Sales	809.0	834.0	874.6	1,345.5	P/E Ratio	NMF	Price (9/30/95)	0.95
Net Income	9.0	3.0	-24.5	-37.7	P/B Ratio	2.7	52 Wk Hi-Low	0.95-0.50
Book Value	126.0	127.0	102.8	160.6	Yield %	2.8	Market Cap	US$445.7mil

Address **1 Lygon Pl.**
London SW1W 0JR
Tel **0171-730-7244**
Fax **0171-730-2660**
ADR
SEDOL No. **4950**
CEO **Neil French**
Chairman **Sir Peter Cazalet**

Argyll

Industry: **Food Retailers & Wholesalers**

Argyll Group is a food retailer operating in the United Kingdom. The company is best known for its Safeway grocery-stores and supermarkets, which number more than 350 in the U.K. It also runs 106 Presto grocery stores, which concentrate on serving the needs of smaller communities in the Northern United Kingdom. Safeway accounts for more than 90% of company sales. Last year, Safeway generated average sales per square foot of £12.86. Argyll sold its Lo-Cost discount food retailing business, its two wholesaling businesses, and Presto's older and smaller branches in 1994.

£ mil	04/93	04/94	04/95	US$mil 04/95				
Sales	5,196.0	5,608.0	6,217.7	9,776.3	P/E Ratio	40.5	Price (9/30/95)	3.36
Net Income	303.0	253.0	93.4	146.9	P/B Ratio	2.2	52 Wk Hi-Low	3.64-2.37
Book Value	1,644.0	1,776.0	1,754.7	2,830.2	Yield %	3.6	Market Cap	US$6,033.0mil

Address **8 Chesterfield Hill**
London W1X 7RG
Tel **0171-493-0808**
Fax **0171-493-3794**
ADR
SEDOL No. **49241**
CEO **Colin Smith**
Chairman **Sir Alistair Grant**

Arjo Wiggins Appleton

Industry: **Paper Products**

Arjo Wiggins Appleton manufactures and distributes paper products. The company produces carbonless paper for business forms and credit-card receipts, thermal paper for fax machines, stationery, and fine coated and specialty paper. Its Appleton paper subsidiaries produce carbonless and thermal paper in North America. Its wholly-owned subsidiary CEASA and partially-owned subsidiary SOPORCEL produce pulp in Spain and Portugal, respectively. Arjo Wiggins Appleton has operations throughout Europe and in North America.

£ mil	12/92	12/93	12/94	US$mil 12/94				
Sales	2,623.0	2,727.0	2,915.1	4,484.8	P/E Ratio	13.7	Price (9/30/95)	2.46
Net Income	94.0	75.0	146.4	225.2	P/B Ratio	1.6	52 Wk Hi-Low	2.88-2.21
Book Value	1,207.0	1,181.0	1,285.0	2,007.8	Yield %	3.0	Market Cap	US$3,194.5mil

Address **Gateway House, Basing View**
Basingstoke, Hamps RG21 4EE
Tel **01256-723000**
Fax **01256-723723**
ADR
SEDOL No. **965411**
CEO **Alain Soulas**
Chairman **Cob Stenham**

BAA

Industry: **General Industrial & Commercial Services**

BAA operates seven U.K. airports that account for more than 70% of the United Kingdom's passenger traffic and more than 80% of its cargo transport. Although the company has interests in property development, its main revenue sources are from airport operations such as airport landing and takeoff charges, retail and duty-free stores, and car-parking fees. BAA also manages operates at Pittsburgh International Airport (U.S.). BAA McArthur/Glen, a retailing joint venture, opened its first brand-name and designer-goods outlet center in April 1995.

	£ mil 03/93	03/94	03/95	US$mil 03/95				
Sales	**952.0**	**1,098.0**	**1,159.0**	**1,816.6**	P/E Ratio	**18.3**	Price (9/30/95)	**5.00**
Net Income	**211.0**	**240.0**	**279.0**	**437.3**	P/B Ratio	**1.8**	52 Wk Hi-Low	**5.35-4.19**
Book Value	**2,047.0**	**2,543.0**	**2,845.0**	**4,663.9**	Yield %	**2.0**	Market Cap	**US$8,160.1mil**

Address **130 Wilton Rd.**
London SW1V 1LQ
Tel **0171-834-9449**
Fax **0171-932-6699**
ADR **BAAPY**
SEDOL No. **67340**
CEO **Sir John Egan**
Chairman **Dr. N. Brian Smith**

William Baird

Industry: **Clothing & Fabrics**

William Baird is primarily produces contract clothing and designs, manufactures, and retails branded clothing. It makes the Windsmoor, Planet, and Precis Petites name brands of women's apparel, and the Dannimac brand of men's and women's rainwear. In 1994, the company acquired lingerie producer Morris Cohen, and Melka Tenson, the European leisurewear and sportswear group. The company has also sold off most of its Darchem Group wholly-owned engineering and building-services subsidiary. Operations in the United Kingdom account for 90% of total revenues.

	£ mil 12/92	12/93	12/94	US$mil 12/94				
Sales	**542.0**	**493.0**	**526.9**	**810.6**	P/E Ratio	**15.7**	Price (9/30/95)	**2.32**
Net Income	**9.0**	**12.0**	**16.9**	**25.9**	P/B Ratio	**1.8**	52 Wk Hi-Low	**2.44-2.00**
Book Value	**168.0**	**157.0**	**151.0**	**236.0**	Yield %	**4.1**	Market Cap	**US$427.0mil**

Address **79 Mount St.**
London W1Y 5HJ
Tel **0171-409-1785**
Fax **0171-499-6788**
ADR
SEDOL No. **71114**
CEO **J. M. Green-Armytage**
Chairman **T. Donald Parr**

Barclays

Industry: **Banks - Money Center**

Barclays offers personal and investment banking, life insurance, pensions, and mortgage processing. The bank operates more than 2,000 personal-banking networks in the United Kingdom, as well as offices in Spain, France, and Portugal. Barclays issues the Barclaycard credit card to more than 8 million people. Barclays de Zoete Wedd (BZW), its investment-banking division, specializes in trading and asset-management services. Barclays owns the German bank Merck Fink and recently acquired the Wells Fargo Nikko Investment Advisors and the MasterWorks division of Wells Fargo Bank.

	£ mil 12/92	12/93	12/94	US$mil 12/94				
Revenues	**15,192.0**	**14,788.0**	**13,459.0**	**20,706.2**	P/E Ratio	**10.3**	Price (9/30/95)	**7.49**
Net Income	**-343.0**	**313.0**	**1,179.0**	**1,813.8**	P/B Ratio	**2.0**	52 Wk Hi-Low	**7.66-5.42**
Book Value	**5,279.0**	**5,312.0**	**6,161.0**	**9,626.6**	Yield %	**2.8**	Market Cap	**US$19,462mil**

Address **54 Lombard St.**
London EC3P 3AH
Tel **0171-699-5000**
Fax **0171-699-2437**
ADR **BCS**
SEDOL No. **78201**
CEO **J. Martin Taylor**
Chairman **Andrew R.F. Buxton**

Bardon

Industry: **Building Materials**

Evered Bardon is an aggregates company that produces and supplies stone and concrete products, sand and gravel, sea-dredged aggregates, ready-mix concrete, and road-surfacing materials. The company also has contracting and waste-disposal businesses. Its wholly-owned civil and marine subsidiary operates in the United Kingdom and continental Europe. Bardon also produces aggregates in the United States through its wholly-owned Mid-Atlantic and Trimount subsidiaries. About 45% of the company's revenue's is generated in the U.S.

	£ mil 12/92	12/93	12/94	US$mil 12/94				
Sales	**336.0**	**326.0**	**331.7**	**510.3**	P/E Ratio	**16.8**	Price (9/30/95)	**0.29**
Net Income	**-43.0**	**-51.0**	**13.3**	**20.5**	P/B Ratio	**0.5**	52 Wk Hi-Low	**0.40-0.27**
Book Value	**346.0**	**354.0**	**346.4**	**541.3**	Yield %	**7.0**	Market Cap	**US$250.9mil**

Address **Blenheim Ct., Lode Ln.**
Solihull B91 2AA
Tel **0121-711-1717**
Fax **0121-711-1505**
ADR
SEDOL No. **323826**
CEO **Peter W.G. Tom**
Chairman **Frank Davies**

Barratt Developments

Industry: **Home Construction**

Barratt Developments is a building and property-development company. Its core activity is homebuilding, and it completed 5,800 sales of houses in 1994. It is also involved in partnership developments with the U.K. central government, local authorities, and housing associations. Barratt is active in the Southern California housing market. It also operates nine leisure resorts in Spain and the U.K. that are used by 28,000 time-share owners. Barratt also sells and leases commercial property. In 1994, about 12% of its revenues were generated in the United States.

	£ mil 06/92	06/93	06/94	US$mil 06/94				
Sales	**438.0**	**405.0**	**498.9**	**748.0**	P/E Ratio	**15.0**	Price (9/30/95)	**1.94**
Net Income	**14.0**	**17.0**	**23.3**	**34.9**	P/B Ratio	**1.7**	52 Wk Hi-Low	**2.06-1.41**
Book Value	**180.0**	**193.0**	**205.4**	**316.0**	Yield %	**3.1**	Market Cap	**US$562.9mil**

Address **Wingrove Hse., Ponteland Rd.**
Newcastle-upon-Tyne NE5 3DP
Tel **0191-286-6811**
Fax **0191-271-2242**
ADR
SEDOL No. **81180**
CEO **Frank Eaton**
Chairman **Sir Lawrence Barratt**

Bass

Industry: **Distillers & Brewers**

Bass produces and distributes beer and soft drinks, and operates hotels, pubs, betting shops, and liquor stores. Bass is the United Kingdom's largest brewer. Its brands of beer include Bass Ale, Worthington's Best Bitter, Tennent's Lager, and Carling Black Label. The firm ranks as the U.K.'s second-largest producer of soft drinks (sold under the Britvic brand name). Its hotel operations include the international Holiday Inn chain. Bass also operates the Bass Ginsber Beer joint venture in China. In 1994, Bass generated 13.7% of its revenues overseas.

	£ mil 09/92	09/93	09/94	US$mil 09/94				
Sales	4,307.0	4,451.0	4,452.0	6,745.5	P/E Ratio	16.0	Price (9/30/95)	6.40
Net Income	433.0	314.0	349.0	528.8	P/B Ratio	1.6	52 Wk Hi-Low	6.88-4.90
Book Value	3,343.0	3,413.0	3,582.0	5,685.7	Yield %	3.3	Market Cap	US$8,895.1mil

Address **20 N. Audley St.**, **London W1Y 1WE** Tel **0171-409-1919** Fax **0171-409-8503** ADR **BAS** SEDOL No. **83205** CEO **Ian M.G. Prosser** Chairman **Ian M.G. Prosser**

BAT Industries

Industry: **Tobacco**

B.A.T Industries is a diversified conglomerate that manufactures cigarettes and provides financial services. It offers general-insurance products in the United Kingdom through its Eagle Star and Allied Dunbar subsidiaries, and in the United States through Farmers Insurance Group. B.A.T. controls about 11% of the world cigarette market and 18% of the U.S. market, with cigarette brands including Lucky Strike, Kool, and Pall Mall. Its U.S. subsidiaries include American Tobacco and Brown & Williamson. Non-European exports account for more than 55% of revenues.

	£ mil 12/92	12/93	12/94	US$mil 12/94				
Sales	18,647.0	20,767.0	21,136.0	32,516.9	P/E Ratio	13.5	Price (9/30/95)	5.29
Net Income	869.0	1,169.0	1,205.0	1,853.8	P/B Ratio	3.6	52 Wk Hi-Low	5.35-4.11
Book Value	3,975.0	5,000.0	4,588.0	7,168.8	Yield %	5.2	Market Cap	US$25,900mil

Address **Windsor Hse., 50 Victoria St.**, **London SW1H 0NL** Tel **0171-222-7979** Fax **0171-222-0122** ADR **BTI** SEDOL No. **68116** CEO **Martin F. Broughton** Chairman **Sir Patrick Sheehy**

BBA Group

Industry: **Other Auto Parts**

BBA Group is an international association of transportation and industrial companies that supply engineering products and services to the automotive, aviation, industrial textile, and electrical-contracting businesses. In 1994, about 40% of the group's revenues were generated in North America, and about 35% came from continental Europe. BBA Group sold Angus, a fire protection group, in 1994, and it sold Scandura, a conveyor belting company, in 1995. It acquired Terram, a U.S.-based geopolymer company, in 1995.

	£ mil 12/92	12/93	12/94	US$mil 12/94				
Sales	1,323.0	1,393.0	1,228.0	1,889.2	P/E Ratio	45.3	Price (9/30/95)	2.90
Net Income	18.0	-29.0	32.0	49.2	P/B Ratio	3.0	52 Wk Hi-Low	2.90-1.78
Book Value	322.0	349.0	388.2	606.6	Yield %	1.7	Market Cap	US$1,879.4mil

Address **Whitechapel Rd.**, **Cleckheaton, W. Yorks BD19 6HP** Tel **01274-874444** Fax **01274-869916** ADR SEDOL No. **67748** CEO **Roberto Quarta** Chairman **Vanni E. Treves**

Berkeley

Industry: **Home Construction**

The Berkeley Group builds and sells upscale private homes primarily in southern, northwestern, and central England. St. George, its wholly-owned subsidiary, builds private homes in the London area. The company is also involved in commercial-property development. In 1994, Berkeley owned or controlled 5500 plots of land, of which 1000 were joint-venture sites. Its houses were sold for an average of more than £150,000. Berkeley Eastoak Investments, a Berkeley Group associate, sold part of its commercial-property investment portfolio in 1994.

	£ mil 04/93	04/94	04/95	US$mil 04/95				
Sales	182.0	228.1	283.4	445.6	P/E Ratio	12.8	Price (9/30/95)	4.10
Net Income	10.0	25.8	25.0	39.3	P/B Ratio	1.4	52 Wk Hi-Low	4.19-3.16
Book Value	180.0	203.4	224.0	361.3	Yield %	2.0	Market Cap	US$504.2mil

Address **The Old House, 4 Heath Rd.**, **Weybridge, Surrey KT13 8TB** Tel **01932-847222** Fax **01932-858596** ADR SEDOL No. **94177** CEO **Anthony W. Pidgley** Chairman **Graham J. Roper**

BET

Industry: **General Industrial & Commercial Services**

BET provides specialized support services to industrial, commercial, and public-sector customers primarily in Europe and North America. Services include scaffolding, crane, and other equipment rental, as well as road tanker, container, and distribution. Business services, the firm's largest sector, generate 45% of its sales. BET's general-business division performs a variety of services including textile rental, security, cleaning, and catering. North America accounts for more than 30% of revenues and continental Europe accounts for 18%.

	£ mil 03/93	04/94	04/95	US$mil 04/95				
Sales	2,003.0	1,785.0	1,761.3	2,769.3	P/E Ratio	12.8	Price (9/30/95)	1.33
Net Income	-27.0	64.0	97.4	153.1	P/B Ratio	4.0	52 Wk Hi-Low	1.44-0.99
Book Value	333.0	260.0	313.6	505.8	Yield %	3.0	Market Cap	US$1,973.8mil

Address **Stratton Hse., Piccadilly**, **London W1X 6AS** Tel **0171-629-8886** Fax **0171-499-5118** ADR **BEP** SEDOL No. **133025** CEO **L. John Clark** Chairman **Sir Christopher Harding**

BICC

Industry: **Heavy Construction**

BICC Group manufactures cables and provides engineering and construction services. It is also involved in property-development. BICC's cables division manufactures and distributes cables and cable-systems in the United Kingdom, North America, continental Europe, Australasia, and the Asia Pacific region. Balfour Beatty, its wholly-owned engineering and construction subsidiary, operates in more than 45 countries and produces about 44% of BICC's revenues. In 1994, about 43% of the group's revenues were generated outside the U.K. and Europe.

	£ mil 12/92	12/93	12/94	US$mil 12/94				
Sales	**3,388.0**	**3,614.0**	**3,674.0**	**5,652.3**	P/E Ratio	**15.4**	Price (9/30/95)	**3.02**
Net Income	**13.0**	**53.0**	**69.0**	**106.2**	P/B Ratio	**2.0**	52 Wk Hi-Low	**3.62-2.94**
Book Value	**420.0**	**341.0**	**542.0**	**846.9**	Yield %	**4.8**	Market Cap	**US$1,694.3mil**

Address **Devonshire Hse., Mayfair Pl.**
London W1X 5FH
Tel **0171-629-6622**
Fax **0171-409-0070**
ADR
SEDOL No. **96162**
Managing Director **Sir Robin Biggam**
Chairman **Sir Robin Biggam**

Bilton

Industry: **Real-Estate Investment**

Bilton is primarily involved in property investment. Its other divisions operate in the housing, civil-engineering, and plant-hire businesses. Bilton's property investments, which are concentrated in Southeast England, generated net rental income of more than £25 million in 1994. Industrial properties comprise 85% of the company's portfolio. Glenhazel Investment Trust owns more than 29% of Bilton. Schroder Nominees and Schroder Unit Trusts own about 13% of the company. The National Coal Board and The Percy Bilton Charity are also major shareholders.

	£ mil 12/92	12/93	12/94	US$mil 12/94				
Sales	**24.0**	**22.0**	**22.6**	**34.7**	P/E Ratio	**15.5**	Price (9/30/95)	**2.30**
Net Income	**12.0**	**12.0**	**13.0**	**19.9**	P/B Ratio	**0.7**	52 Wk Hi-Low	**2.57-2.11**
Book Value	**320.0**	**282.0**	**286.4**	**447.5**	Yield %	**4.3**	Market Cap	**US$320.8mil**

Address **Bilton Hse., 54 Uxbridge Rd.**
London W5 2TL
Tel **0181-567-7777**
Fax **0181-840-0249**
ADR
SEDOL No. **97143**
Managing Director **R.W.A. Groom**
Chairman **H.D. Free**

Peter Black

Industry: **Clothing & Fabrics**

Peter Black Holdings manufactures and supplies retailers with personal-care products, footwear, and accessories. Its wholly-owned subsidiary English Grains (Holdings) produces health foods and vitamins. The company is currently building a new £10m plant for English Grains. Peter Black distributes goods for third-party retailers with almost two thirds of the company's sales being to Marks and Spencer. Approximately 10% of the company's total revenue comes from exports.In 1994, as part of a refocusing policy, the company sold its retail and leisure businesses.

	£ mil 05/92	06/93	06/94	US$mil 06/94				
Sales	**106.0**	**105.0**	**117.0**	**175.4**	P/E Ratio	**NMF**	Price (9/30/95)	**2.85**
Net Income	**4.0**	**6.0**	**9.0**	**13.5**	P/B Ratio	**3.3**	52 Wk Hi-Low	**2.88-2.27**
Book Value	**36.0**	**41.0**	**48.0**	**73.8**	Yield %	**1.4**	Market Cap	**US$250.9mil**

Address **Keighley**
West Yorkshire BD21 3JQ
Tel **01535-661177**
Fax **01535-609973**
ADR
SEDOL No. **101743**
CEO **Gordon L. Black**
Chairman **Thomas S. Black**

Blue Circle Industries

Industry: **Building Materials**

Blue Circle Industries invests in property and makes cement, concrete, and heating and bathroom products. It owns 50% of Aalborg Portland, Denmark's only cement maker, and has cement operations in Chile, Africa, and Southeast Asia. Blue Circle makes boilers, radiators, gas fires, and ceramic and brass bathroom fixtures. It owns the French heating-products firms CICH and the German company Brotje, which makes floor-standing boilers and hot-water radiators. More than 55% of Blue Circle's sales are exports and 27% of total sales are generated outside of Europe.

	£ mil 12/92	12/93	12/94	US$mil 12/94				
Sales	**1,331.0**	**1,679.0**	**1,750.6**	**2,693.2**	P/E Ratio	**24.3**	Price (9/30/95)	**3.08**
Net Income	**34.0**	**108.0**	**99.2**	**152.6**	P/B Ratio	**2.0**	52 Wk Hi-Low	**3.39-2.56**
Book Value	**963.0**	**981.0**	**1,112.6**	**1,738.4**	Yield %	**3.8**	Market Cap	**US$3,563.6mil**

Address **84 Eccleston Sq.**
London SW1V 1PX
Tel **0171-828-3456**
Fax **0171-245-8169**
ADR **BCLEY**
SEDOL No. **105853**
CEO **Keith Orrell-Jones**
Chairman **Sir Peter Walters**

The BOC Group

Industry: **Specialty Chemicals**

BOC Group produces and markets gases and related products, health-care products, and vacuum technology. The company supplies compressed gas to the brewing, electronic, food-preservation, and leisure industries, and it provides high-purity gases and delivery systems to Japan's and Taiwan's semiconductor industries. BOC Group's health-care products also include a variety of anesthetic gases and equipment. Exports outside Europe represent nearly 70% of BOC's sales, with Asia and the Americas each generating 30% of turnover. Only 15% of revenues come from the U.K.

	£ mil 09/92	09/93	09/94	US$mil 09/94				
Sales	**2,656.0**	**3,235.5**	**3,462.3**	**5,245.9**	P/E Ratio	**33.6**	Price (9/30/95)	**7.99**
Net Income	**91.0**	**203.9**	**113.6**	**172.1**	P/B Ratio	**2.5**	52 Wk Hi-Low	**8.59-6.70**
Book Value	**1,388.0**	**1,488.8**	**1,509.8**	**2,396.5**	Yield %	**2.9**	Market Cap	**US$6,079.5mil**

Address **Chertsey Rd.**
Windlesham, Surrey GU20 6HJ
Tel **01276-477222**
Fax **01276-471333**
ADR **BOCNY**
SEDOL No. **108120**
CEO **Alexander P. Dyer**
Chairman **Richard V. Giordano**

The Body Shop

Industry: **Other Specialty Retailers**

Body Shop International makes natural skin- and hair-care products. The firm operates more than 1,200 outlets worldwide, about 900 of which are located outside the United Kingdom. Its wholly-owned subsidiaries include Soapworks, which produces about 28 million bars of soap a year; Colourings, a manufacturer of cosmetics; and Cos-Tec, a producer of cosmetics, skin-care products, and toiletries. Exports made up more than 70% of sales in 1994; continental Europe accounted for 26% of revenues, with 28% from North America and 16% from the rest of the world.

	£ mil 02/93	02/94	02/95	US$mil 02/95				
Revenues	**168.0**	**195.0**	**219.7**	**341.7**	P/E Ratio	**12.4**	Price (9/30/95)	**1.43**
Net Income	**14.0**	**19.0**	**21.8**	**33.9**	P/B Ratio	**2.5**	52 Wk Hi-Low	**2.31-1.09**
Book Value	**82.0**	**97.0**	**110.6**	**175.6**	Yield %	**1.7**	Market Cap	**US$430.9mil**

Address **Watersmead**	Tel **01903-731500**	ADR	**BDSPY**	CEO	**Anita Roddick**
Littlehampton BN17 6LS	Fax **01903-726250**	SEDOL No.	**108313**	Chairman	**T. Gordon Roddick**

Booker

Industry: **Other Food**

Booker processes, packs, and distributes wholesale food products. It specializes in fish products and prepared foods. Booker is also involved in agribusiness activities such as animal husbandry, forest and farm management, and horticulture. In 1994, Booker purchased U.S.-based fish-farming group Marine Harvest International, making it the world's largest farmer of Atlantic salmon. Booker also acts as a marketing agent for the sugar industries of Guyana and St. Kitts. It owns Booker Entertainment, which produces television programs based on Agatha Christie books.

	£ mil 12/92	01/94	12/94	US$mil 12/94				
Sales	**3,395.0**	**3,531.0**	**3,699.2**	**5,691.1**	P/E Ratio	**18.9**	Price (9/30/95)	**4.00**
Net Income	**41.0**	**60.0**	**45.8**	**70.5**	P/B Ratio	**5.2**	52 Wk Hi-Low	**4.44-3.74**
Book Value	**158.0**	**170.0**	**171.0**	**267.2**	Yield %	**5.6**	Market Cap	**US$1,427.6mil**

Address **Portland Hse., Stag Pl.**	Tel **0171-828-9850**	ADR	**BKERY**	CEO	**Charles J. Bowen**
London SW1E 5AY	Fax **0171-630-8029**	SEDOL No.	**110523**	Chairman	**Jonathan F. Taylor**

Boots

Industry: **Drug-based Retailers**

Boots develops, produces, and markets health- and personal-care products. Although best known for its U.K. retail drugstore chain, Boots The Chemists (1,134 stores), it also runs Boots Opticians (272 stores), A.G. Stanley (397 home-decorating stores), and Halfords (403 car- parts stores). Boots also owns 39 Children's World toy and clothing stores and operates 219 Do It All stores in a joint venture with WH Smith. Boots recently sold its pharmaceutical business to Germany's BASF. Exports to Europe and the U.S. account for roughly 12% of Boots' sales.

	£ mil 03/93	03/94	03/95	US$mil 03/95				
Revenues	**3,962.0**	**4,167.0**	**3,894.1**	**6,103.6**	P/E Ratio	**8.6**	Price (9/30/95)	**5.67**
Net Income	**279.0**	**288.0**	**659.2**	**1,033.2**	P/B Ratio	**2.7**	52 Wk Hi-Low	**5.94-4.59**
Book Value	**1,479.0**	**1,609.0**	**2,006.9**	**3,290.0**	Yield %	**3.0**	Market Cap	**US$8,541.1mil**

Address **1 Thane Rd. W.**	Tel **01602-506111**	ADR	**BOOOY**	CEO	**Sir James Blyth**
Nottingham NG2 3AA	Fax **01602-592727**	SEDOL No.	**111441**	Chairman	**Sir Michael Angus**

Bowthorpe

Industry: **Diversified Technology**

Bowthorpe provides products and services for electric utilities and the electronic-products industry. The company provides data-acquisition and thermal-management services, as well as aerospace and position sensors, electro-ceramic products, electronic instrumentation, and electronic subsystems. The group also produces cable accessories and provides cable-fixing and protection services. In 1995, Bowthorpe acquired Metrosonics, a U.S.-based instrumentation company. The United States produced 38% of the group's revenues in 1994.

	£ mil 12/92	12/93	12/94	US$mil 12/94				
Sales	**265.0**	**334.0**	**417.6**	**642.5**	P/E Ratio	**21.1**	Price (9/30/95)	**4.20**
Net Income	**24.0**	**30.0**	**36.9**	**56.7**	P/B Ratio	**4.9**	52 Wk Hi-Low	**4.32-2.81**
Book Value	**91.0**	**77.0**	**160.2**	**250.4**	Yield %	**2.0**	Market Cap	**US$1,242.7mil**

Address **Gatwick Rd.**	Tel **01293-528888**	ADR		CEO	**John M. Westhead**
Crawley, West Sussex RH10 2RZ	Fax **01293-541905**	SEDOL No.	**116402**	Chairman	**H. Anthony Vice**

BPB Industries

Industry: **Building Materials**

BPB Industries manufactures building materials. One of the world's largest gypsum companies, BPB operates 80 manufacturing plants worldwide and serving markets in more than 35 countries. It also makes plasterboard liner, plaster, plasterboard, paper, and packaging products. The company's principal customers are in the building industry. During the past twelve months, the company has expanded into Eastern Europe. It has acquired a gypsum quarry in Poland and has started construction on a major plasterboard plant in Berlin.

	£ mil 03/93	03/94	03/95	US$mil 03/95				
Sales	**1,125.0**	**1,151.0**	**1,328.3**	**2,082.0**	P/E Ratio	**14.5**	Price (9/30/95)	**3.18**
Net Income	**40.0**	**75.0**	**109.9**	**172.3**	P/B Ratio	**2.2**	52 Wk Hi-Low	**3.40-2.68**
Book Value	**633.0**	**654.0**	**725.3**	**1,189.0**	Yield %	**2.8**	Market Cap	**US$2,528.5mil**

Address **Langley Pk. Hse., Uxbridge Rd.**	Tel **01753-573273**	ADR		CEO	**Jean-Pierre Cuny**
Slough, Berkshire SL3 6DU	Fax **01753-823397**	SEDOL No.	**68707**	Chairman	**Alan Turner**

Bradford Property Trust

Industry: **Real-Estate Investment**

Bradford Property Trust develops, renovates, and manages residential property. It operates 10 wholly-owned subsidiaries and two associate companies in England and Scotland. In the year ending April 1995, the company purchased a number of properties. Its most significant purchase was a portfolio of nine commercial properties and 370 residential sites in Harborne, Birmingham. Rental income accounts for 54% of revenues, with property sales generating the remainder. Warner Estate Holdings is the company's largest shareholder, with a 13% share.

	£ mil 04/93	04/94	04/95	US$mil 04/95				
Sales	34.0	49.0	39.7	62.5	P/E Ratio	16.8	Price (9/30/95)	1.92
Net Income	14.0	21.0	16.6	26.1	P/B Ratio	1.9	52 Wk Hi-Low	2.02-1.71
Book Value	116.0	129.0	145.6	234.8	Yield %	3.8	Market Cap	US$452.6mil

Address **69 Market St.**
Bradford, West Yorks BD1 1NE
Tel **01274-723181**
Fax **01274-395304**
ADR
SEDOL No. **117568**
Managing Director **David G. Baker**
Chairman **Philip C.T. Warner**

British Aerospace

Industry: **Aerospace & Defense**

British Aerospace (BAE) is a defense and commercial aerospace company. It is also involved in the management of business-park property through its wholly-owned subsidiary, Arlington Securities. BAE's defense division finished 1994 orders total £9.7 billion. Air systems accounted for more than 50% of sales. The company's commercial aircraft business includes a 20% stake in Airbus Industrie and a regional-aircraft joint venture with German, French, Italian, and Spanish aerospace companies. BAE sold Rover Group, its civilian-automobile production division, in 1994.

	£ mil 12/92	12/93	12/94	US$mil 12/94				
Sales	9,411.0	10,146.0	6,346.0	9,763.1	P/E Ratio	23.7	Price (9/30/95)	7.32
Net Income	-888.0	-214.0	140.0	215.4	P/B Ratio	3.5	52 Wk Hi-Low	7.61-4.20
Book Value	1,780.0	1,510.0	876.0	1,368.8	Yield %	1.4	Market Cap	US$4,943.7mil

Address **Farnborough Aerospace Ctr.**
Farnborough, Hamps GU14 6YU
Tel **01252-373232**
Fax **N/A**
ADR
SEDOL No. **127158**
CEO **Richard H. Evans**
Chairman **Robert Bauman**

British Airways

Industry: **Airlines**

British Airways (BA) provides scheduled and chartered passenger flights, and air-cargo services. It flies to 155 destinations in 72 countries. In fiscal 1994, the airline carried 35 million passengers and 660,000 tons of cargo. International flights accounted for about 54% of BA's revenues in 1994. It holds a 25% interest in Australian airline Qantas Airways, a 50% stake in TAT European Airlines (France), and a 22% interest in USAir. Roughly 40% of BA's revenue is generated in Europe, and one third is generated in North America.

	£ mil 03/93	03/94	03/95	US$mil 03/95				
Sales	5,566.0	6,303.0	7,177.0	11,249.2	P/E Ratio	17.2	Price (9/30/95)	4.51
Net Income	178.0	286.0	250.0	391.8	P/B Ratio	2.1	52 Wk Hi-Low	4.61-3.44
Book Value	1,214.0	1,827.0	2,090.0	3,426.2	Yield %	2.8	Market Cap	US$6,834.5mil

Address **Speedbird Hse., Heathrow**
Hounslow TW6 2JA
Tel **0181-759-5511**
Fax **0181-562-5557**
ADR **BAB**
SEDOL No. **129057**
Managing Director **Robert Ayling**
Chairman **Sir Colin Marshall**

British Gas

Industry: **Gas Utilities**

British Gas purchases, distributes, and sells natural gas to residential, industrial, and commercial customers. It supplies gas to more than 18 million domestic customers (75% of households) in the United Kingdom, and it owns 39% of Natural Gas Clearinghouse, the United States' largest independent marketer of natural gas. It also produces oil and natural gas; BG and the Italian oil company Agip are developing a gas and oil field in Kazakhstan. In 1994, British Gas sold its interests in Canadian natural-gas companies Bow Valley Energy and Consumers' Gas.

	£ mil 12/92	12/93	12/94	US$mil 12/94				
Sales	10,254.0	10,386.0	9,029.0	13,890.8	P/E Ratio	15.6	Price (9/30/95)	2.66
Net Income	681.0	-285.0	737.0	1,133.8	P/B Ratio	1.5	52 Wk Hi-Low	3.17-2.62
Book Value	8,123.0	7,211.0	7,601.0	11,876.6	Yield %	5.5	Market Cap	US$18,416mil

Address **Rivermill Hse., 152 Grosvenor Rd.**
London SW1V 3JL
Tel **0171-821-1444**
Fax **0171-821-8522**
ADR **BRG**
SEDOL No. **134330**
CEO **Cedric Brown**
Chairman **Richard V. Giordano**

British Land

Industry: **Real-Estate Investment**

British Land is a property-investment company that specializes in long-term income-producing commercial properties, mainly offices and retail outlets, in the United Kingdom. Approximately 84% of the company's real-estate holdings are properties to which it owns permanent title. British Land has entered into a £198m joint venture with Scottish & Newcastle to buy 306 rental units. The company has additional holdings in Ireland, the Netherlands, and the United States. The company also owns interests in supermarkets, including 46 Sainsbury and 39 Somerfield stores.

	£ mil 03/93	03/94	03/95	US$mil 03/95				
Sales	168.0	201.0	228.5	358.2	P/E Ratio	48.6	Price (9/30/95)	4.13
Net Income	28.8	33.7	34.5	54.1	P/B Ratio	1.0	52 Wk Hi-Low	4.34-3.43
Book Value	775.5	1,307.3	1,579.5	2,589.3	Yield %	2.0	Market Cap	US$2,412.7mil

Address **10 Cornwall Terr.**
London NW1 4QP
Tel **0171-486-4466**
Fax **0171-935-5552**
ADR
SEDOL No. **136701**
CEO **John Ritblat**
Chairman **John Ritblat**

British Petroleum

Industry: **Oil - Integrated Majors**

The British Petroleum Company (BP) is a petroleum and chemicals company that also has agricultural interests. It explores for, refines, produces, and markets oil and natural gas. It operates 15,700 service stations throughout the world. BP supplies acrylonitrile and acetic acid to manufacturers worldwide. Its chemicals are used in synthetic fibers, paints, and pharmaceuticals. BP has decided to float its BP Antwerp and U.S.-based Carborundum chemicals plant subsidiaries. Two thirds of sales are exports and nearly 40% of all sales are made outside of Europe.

£ mil	12/92	12/93	12/94	US$mil 12/94				
Sales	33,250.0	34,950.0	33,116.0	50,947.7	P/E Ratio	16.5	Price (9/30/95)	4.75
Net Income	-458.0	615.0	1,577.0	2,426.2	P/B Ratio	2.4	52 Wk Hi-Low	4.98-3.93
Book Value	9,979.0	9,748.0	11,057.0	17,276.6	Yield %	2.2	Market Cap	US$41,598mil

Address	**Britannic Hse., 1 Finsbury Circus**	Tel	**0171-496-4000**	ADR	**BP**	CEO	**John Browne**
	London EC2M 7BA	Fax	**0171-496-5656**	SEDOL No.	**138495**	Chairman	**David A.G. Simon**

British Steel

Industry: **Steel**

British Steel, Europe's second-largest steelmaker, manufactures and distributes steel products, including seamless pipes for oil exploration and production, railway tracks, steel sheets for automobiles and domestic appliances, and tin plate for canning. Its Tuscaloosa Steel (U.S.) subsidiary produces coil and cut plate steel for the construction, transportation, and energy industries. British Steel's automotive customers include Ford, Honda, and Jaguar. Nearly half of its sales are exports, with Europe representing its single largest market.

£ mil	04/93	04/94	04/95	US$mil 04/95				
Sales	4,303.0	4,191.0	6,228.0	9,792.5	P/E Ratio	7.8	Price (9/30/95)	1.82
Net Income	-130.0	69.0	468.0	735.8	P/B Ratio	0.9	52 Wk Hi-Low	1.89-1.45
Book Value	3,720.0	3,754.0	4,087.0	6,591.9	Yield %	4.1	Market Cap	US$5,814.6mil

Address	**9 Albert Embankment**	Tel	**0171-735-7654**	ADR	**BST**	CEO	**Brian S. Moffat**
	London SE1 7SN	Fax	**0171-587-1142**	SEDOL No.	**141147**	Chairman	**Brian S. Moffat**

Brixton Estate

Industry: **Real-Estate Investment**

Brixton Estate is a property investment and development company. More than 83% of its investments are U.K.-based, but it also has properties in Belgium, Germany, Australia, the United States, and France. The firm's portfolio was valued at more than £900 million at the end of 1994 and generated £70 million in net rental income. Industrial and warehouse investments make up 54% of the company's portfolio, and office properties account for 44%. Brixton Estate acquired £62 million of new property investments in Southeast England and London in 1994.

£ mil	12/92	12/93	12/94	US$mil 12/94				
Sales	56.0	61.0	70.0	107.7	P/E Ratio	16.7	Price (9/30/95)	1.80
Net Income	23.0	24.0	25.3	38.8	P/B Ratio	0.9	52 Wk Hi-Low	2.02-1.65
Book Value	302.0	447.0	471.6	736.8	Yield %	4.7	Market Cap	US$665.7mil

Address	**22-24 Ely Pl.**	Tel	**0171-242-6898**	ADR		Managing Director	**Terence J. Nagle**
	London EC1N 6TQ	Fax	**0171-405-1630**	SEDOL No.	**143002**	Chairman	**Douglas F. Gardner**

N. Brown

Industry: **Other Specialty Retailers**

N. Brown Group sells retail goods in the United Kingdom through direct-mail catalogs. It also operates warehouse-storage facilities and several consulting services. Its catalogs, which are predominantly targeted at women in the over-45 age group, offer clothing, footwear, and household products. The company recently purchased Sander & Kay Plc, a mail-order company specializing in menswear. Its wholly-owned consulting firms include Dunlop Heywood, which provides property-survey services, and Morfitt & Turnbull, a financial advisor.

£ mil	02/93	02/94	02/95	US$mil 02/95				
Revenues	171.0	187.0	208.2	323.7	P/E Ratio	20.8	Price (9/30/95)	2.56
Net Income	13.0	15.0	18.0	28.0	P/B Ratio	4.1	52 Wk Hi-Low	2.63-2.05
Book Value	72.0	82.0	91.5	145.2	Yield %	1.9	Market Cap	US$593.4mil

Address	**53 Dale St.**	Tel	**0161-236-8256**	ADR		CEO	**James Martin**
	Manchester M60 6ES	Fax	**0161-238-2308**	SEDOL No.	**147297**	Chairman	**Sir David Alliance**

Bryant

Industry: **Home Construction**

Bryant Group builds homes and business complexes, and manages properties. It derives 78% of its revenues and 90% of its operating profit from the construction and sale of homes in the United Kingdom. In 1994, the company's residential division completed 3,255 homes, with an average price of £95,000 per home. The property-management group is also developing more than 9,800 parcels of real estate. Bryant Group holds a 50% stake in Slateplace, a property developer, which it jointly owns with Boots Development Properties.

£ mil	05/92	05/93	05/94	US$mil 05/94				
Sales	323.0	310.0	391.7	586.4	P/E Ratio	12.5	Price (9/30/95)	1.11
Net Income	14.0	13.0	24.7	37.0	P/B Ratio	1.4	52 Wk Hi-Low	1.44-1.06
Book Value	196.0	215.0	228.0	345.5	Yield %	4.5	Market Cap	US$491.8mil

Address	**Cranmore Blvd.**	Tel	**0121-711-1212**	ADR		CEO	**Andrew MacKenzie**
	Solihull, W. Midlands B90 4SD	Fax	**0121-711-2610**	SEDOL No.	**149408**	Chairman	**Colin F.N. Hope**

BSS Group

Industry: **Real-Estate Investment**

The BSS Group markets and distributes products and services for industrial, commercial, and domestic heating and plumbing installations. It produces industrial and commercial-heating and mechanical-services equipment, domestic-heating, sanitary ware and plumbing products, and industrial process valves and control equipment. The company's industrial divisions, BSS and Manor, operate 49 branches in the U.K. Domestic division Zenith Plumbpoint has a network of 55 branches. In January 1995, BSS Group acquired copper-tube and -fittings distributor Rokker and Stanton.

£ mil	03/93	03/94	03/95	US$mil 03/95				
Sales	**244.0**	**258.0**	**293,923.0**	**460,694.4**	P/E Ratio	**17.4**	Price (9/30/95)	**6.04**
Net Income	**4.0**	**6.0**	**9,070.0**	**14,216.3**	P/B Ratio	**0.0**	52 Wk Hi-Low	**6.23-5.14**
Book Value	**60.0**	**62.0**	**66,544.0**	**109,088.5**	Yield %	**3.2**	Market Cap	**US$251.0mil**

Address **Fleet Hse., Lee Circle, Leicester LE1 3QQ**
Tel **01533-623232** Fax **01533-531343**
ADR SEDOL No. **140100**
CEO **Peter Cooper**
Chairman **Ian H. Phillips**

BT

Industry: **Telephone Systems - All**

British Telecommunications (BT) is the United Kingdom's main provider of telecommunication services. The company operates more than 120,000 pay phones in the U.K. and has issued more than 3 million BT charge cards. BT owns a 60% stake in Telecom Securicor Cellular Radio, which operates a cellular network serving more than 1.5 million mobile-phone users. BT has a 20% interest in U.S. long-distance telecommunication company MCI, and has formed a joint venture with Germany's Viag to provide voice and data services to local and international customers.

£ mil	03/93	03/94	03/95	US$mil 03/95				
Sales	**13,242.0**	**13,675.0**	**13,893.0**	**21,775.9**	P/E Ratio	**14.2**	Price (9/30/95)	**3.96**
Net Income	**1,220.0**	**1,767.0**	**1,736.0**	**2,721.0**	P/B Ratio	**2.1**	52 Wk Hi-Low	**4.14-3.60**
Book Value	**12,218.0**	**13,026.0**	**11,997.0**	**19,667.2**	Yield %	**4.5**	Market Cap	**US$39,191mil**

Address **81 Newgate St., London EC1A 7AJ**
Tel **0171-356-5000** Fax **0171-356-5520**
ADR **BTY** SEDOL No. **140843**
Managing Director **Michael L. Hepher**
Chairman **Sir Iain D.T. Vallance**

BTP

Industry: **Specialty Chemicals**

BTP produces specialized chemicals and materials, primarily in Europe, Australasia and the United States. The group operates four business divisions: biocides and chemicals, performance chemicals, adhesive and textile coatings, and industrial. The adhesive and textile coatings division consists of 12 companies with manufacturing locations in the United Kingdom, Germany, Italy, France, and Singapore. It generates 30% of BTP's revenues. The industrial unit contains a polymers division as well as a safety division that produces arrest systems.

£ mil	03/93	03/94	03/95	US$mil 03/95				
Sales	**208.0**	**290.0**	**346.9**	**543.8**	P/E Ratio	**15.2**	Price (9/30/95)	**2.76**
Net Income	**14.0**	**21.0**	**25.9**	**40.6**	P/B Ratio	**2.7**	52 Wk Hi-Low	**3.03-2.37**
Book Value	**83.0**	**109.0**	**162.2**	**265.9**	Yield %	**3.9**	Market Cap	**US$698.4mil**

Address **Hayes Rd., Cadishead, Manchester M44 5BX**
Tel **0161-775-3945** Fax **0161-775-3970**
ADR SEDOL No. **140724**
CEO **Stephen J. Hannam**
Chairman **John Ketteley**

BTR

Industry: **Conglomerates**

BTR manufactures industrial equipment, building materials, car and airplane components, control and electrical systems, and consumer goods. BTR recently created the world's largest automated baggage-handling system for Denver International Airport. The company manufactures sealing systems for construction, automotive, and industrial applications. BTR owns the U.K. sports-products firm Dunlop Slazenger, which makes Maxfli golf equipment. BTR recently announced that it has acquired U.S.-based Formica. Nearly two thirds of sales are from exports outside of Europe.

£ mil	12/92	12/93	12/94	US$mil 12/94				
Sales	**8,690.0**	**8,422.0**	**9,111.0**	**14,016.9**	P/E Ratio	**13.3**	Price (9/30/95)	**3.27**
Net Income	**677.0**	**807.0**	**871.0**	**1,340.0**	P/B Ratio	**4.4**	52 Wk Hi-Low	**3.47-2.76**
Book Value	**1,840.0**	**2,102.0**	**2,690.0**	**4,203.1**	Yield %	**4.1**	Market Cap	**US$18,870mil**

Address **Silvertown Hse., Vincent Sq., London SW1P 2PL**
Tel **0171-834-3848** Fax **0171-834-3879**
ADR **BTRUY** SEDOL No. **67889**
Managing Director **Alan R. Jackson**
Chairman **Norman C. Ireland**

Bunzl

Industry: **Paper Products**

Bunzl is involved in the distribution, conversion, and manufacture of paper and plastic-based products in Europe and the United States. The company produces disposable paper and plastic products for supermarkets, fast-food chains, airlines, and hotels. It is a major distributor of fine paper in Europe and manufactures cigarette filters for worldwide sale. Bunzl supplies plastic products to the engineering and oil industries and makes packaging, automotive components, housewares, and gardening products. The United States accounts for 60% of the company's revenues.

£ mil	12/92	12/93	12/94	US$mil 12/94				
Sales	**1,289.0**	**1,505.0**	**1,513.6**	**2,328.6**	P/E Ratio	**NMF**	Price (9/30/95)	**2.07**
Net Income	**28.0**	**34.0**	**-33.8**	**-52.0**	P/B Ratio	**3.6**	52 Wk Hi-Low	**2.17-1.60**
Book Value	**215.0**	**233.0**	**243.9**	**381.1**	Yield %	**2.4**	Market Cap	**US$1,399.3mil**

Address **110 Park St., London W1Y 3RB**
Tel **0171-495-4950** Fax **0171-495-4953**
ADR SEDOL No. **154004**
CEO **Anthony Habgood**
Chairman **Alexander P. Dyer**

Burmah Castrol

Industry: **Oil - Secondary**

Burmah Castrol produces lubricants, chemicals, and fuels, and transports liquefied natural gas. The company manufactures Castrol GTX motor oil and Simoniz International car-care products, and operates service-station networks in seven countries. Its wholly-owned U.S. subsidiary Dryden Oil makes commercial lubricants. Burmah Castrol and the Japanese companies Mitsui OSK Lines and Nissho Iwai own LNG Transportation, which transports liquefied natural gas from Indonesia to Japan. Exports represent more than 80% of Burmah's revenue.

	£ mil 12/92	12/93	12/94	US$mil 12/94				
Sales	**2,355.0**	**2,758.0**	**2,934.4**	**4,514.5**	P/E Ratio	**14.1**	Price (9/30/95)	**9.77**
Net Income	**86.0**	**103.0**	**138.0**	**212.3**	P/B Ratio	**3.2**	52 Wk Hi-Low	**9.95-7.84**
Book Value	**548.0**	**592.0**	**617.8**	**965.3**	Yield %	**3.3**	Market Cap	**US$3,100.1mil**

Address **Burmah Castrol Hse., Pipers Way** Tel **01793-511521** ADR **BURMY** CEO **Jonathan M. Fry**
Swindon, Wiltshire SN3 1RE Fax **01793-513723** SEDOL No. **155405** Chairman **Lawrence M. Urquhart**

Burton

Industry: **Apparel Retailers**

Burton Group is a clothing and home-furnishings retailer. It operates approximately 408 Burtons menswear outlets and 87 Debenham department stores. The company also runs 532 Dorothy Perkins women's clothing outlets, Top Man and Top Shop for young men and women, Evans larger-size womenswear stores, and Principles shops for men and women. Some of the company's outlets are located within its Debenham stores or in other department stores. Nearly half of the company's sales come from its Debenham department stores.

	£ mil 08/92	08/93	09/94	US$mil 09/94				
Revenues	**1,765.0**	**1,893.0**	**1,909.6**	**2,893.3**	P/E Ratio	**52.1**	Price (9/30/95)	**1.10**
Net Income	**9.0**	**14.0**	**30.2**	**45.8**	P/B Ratio	**1.8**	52 Wk Hi-Low	**1.10-0.58**
Book Value	**701.0**	**853.0**	**838.4**	**1,330.8**	Yield %	**1.8**	Market Cap	**US$2,454.1mil**

Address **214 Oxford St.** Tel **0171-636-8040** ADR **BURUY** CEO **John L. Hoerner**
London W1N 9DF Fax **0171-927-0580** SEDOL No. **156301** Chairman **Sir John Hoskyns**

Cable & Wireless

Industry: **Telephone Systems - All**

Cable & Wireless is a global telecommunication firm. Its international and domestic telephone services generated 48% and 29% of sales, respectively, in fiscal 1994. The firm has a 58% stake in Hongkong Telecom, and owns 80% of the U.K. firm Mercury Communications, which handles more than 15 million telephone calls each day. The company's global network includes operations in Russia and the other ex-Communist states, Australia, South Africa, Latin America, and the Caribbean. More than two thirds of the firm's sales are generated outside of Europe.

	£ mil 03/93	03/94	03/95	US$mil 03/95				
Sales	**3,826.0**	**4,699.0**	**5,132.8**	**8,045.1**	P/E Ratio	**36.3**	Price (9/30/95)	**4.17**
Net Income	**514.0**	**514.0**	**252.1**	**395.1**	P/B Ratio	**2.7**	52 Wk Hi-Low	**4.48-3.54**
Book Value	**3,018.0**	**3,275.0**	**3,338.6**	**5,473.1**	Yield %	**2.2**	Market Cap	**US$14,535mil**

Address **124 Theobalds Rd.** Tel **0171-315-4000** ADR **CWP** CEO **James H. Ross**
London WC1X 8RX Fax **0171-315-5000** SEDOL No. **162557** Chairman **Lord Young**

Cadbury Schweppes

Industry: **Other Food**

Cadbury Schweppes is a confectionery and beverage company. Its products include Schweppes, Canada Dry, and Crush soft drinks; Motts and Capri-Sun fruit drinks; and Dairy Milk and Flake chocolate. Cadbury Schweppes and Coca-Cola distribute their drinks in the U.K. through a Cadbury Schweppes & Coca-Cola Beverages joint venture. In March 1995, Cadbury acquired U.S. soft drinks company Dr. Pepper/Seven Up, making it the largest non-cola soft-drink supplier in the world. Exports represent roughly half of sales and nearly one third of all sales are made outside Europe.

	£ mil 01/93	01/94	12/94	US$mil 12/94				
Sales	**3,372.0**	**3,725.0**	**4,029.6**	**6,199.4**	P/E Ratio	**15.2**	Price (9/30/95)	**4.79**
Net Income	**203.0**	**243.0**	**269.3**	**414.3**	P/B Ratio	**2.7**	52 Wk Hi-Low	**5.01-3.89**
Book Value	**1,084.0**	**1,365.0**	**1,499.0**	**2,342.2**	Yield %	**3.3**	Market Cap	**US$7,497.2mil**

Address **25 Berkeley Sq.** Tel **0171-262-1212** ADR **CADBY** CEO **David Wellings**
London W1X 6HT Fax **0171-706-0530** SEDOL No. **161242** Chairman **Dominic Cadbury**

CAMAS

Industry: **Building Materials**

Camas is a diversified building-materials company. The company produces crushed rock, sand, and gravel for private-sector house construction, coated stone and road surfacing for the construction and maintenance of roads, and precast concrete for the construction industry. Its Camas Associated Asphalt subsidiary provides road surfacing services. The company's U.S. building-materials subsidiaries include Kost and C&M Ready Mix Concrete. Europe accounts for three fourths of Camas' revenues, the remaining revenues are generated in the United States.

	£ mil 12/92	12/93	12/94	US$mil 12/94				
Sales	**337.5**	**365.2**	**449.9**	**692.2**	P/E Ratio	**16.1**	Price (9/30/95)	**0.71**
Net Income	**5.0**	**12.2**	**13.3**	**20.4**	P/B Ratio	**1.0**	52 Wk Hi-Low	**0.83-0.67**
Book Value	**214.7**	**129.9**	**223.3**	**348.9**	Yield %	**5.4**	Market Cap	**US$344.0mil**

Address **Regent Hse., Rodney Rd.** Tel **01242-227722** ADR CEO **Alan Shearer**
Cheltenham, Gloucs GL50 1HX Fax **01242-229050** SEDOL No. **165619** Chairman **Maurice Warren**

Caradon

Industry: **Containers & Packaging**

Caradon manufactures building products and automobile components in Europe and North America, and prints financial and business forms in the United States. The company makes Stelrad radiators, Mira commercial shower systems, and Everest doors and windows. The company's building-products subsidiary Pillar has bolstered profits in the European building-products division. Its wholly-owned U.S. subsidiaries Clarke American and Checks in the Mail print checks and financial forms. Caradon generates about 38% of its revenues in North America and 10% in Europe.

£ mil	12/92	12/93	12/94	US$mil 12/94				
Sales	551.0	952.0	1,987.8	3,058.2	P/E Ratio	10.9	Price (9/30/95)	2.17
Net Income	84.0	170.0	130.4	200.6	P/B Ratio	2.4	52 Wk Hi-Low	2.93-1.94
Book Value	525.0	482.0	539.8	843.4	Yield %	4.4	Market Cap	US$2,056.5mil

Address	**Caradon House, 24 Queens Rd.**	Tel	**01932-850850**	ADR	**CRDOY**	CEO	**Peter J. Jansen**
	Weybridge, Surrey KT13 9UX	Fax	**01932-823328**	SEDOL No.	**583299**	Chairman	**Antony P. Hichens**

Carlton Communications

Industry: **Broadcasting**

Carlton Communications is involved in digital- signal processing, sound mixing, television broadcasting, the manufacture of video cassettes, and the processing and postproduction of films and TV programs. It owns Carlton Television, which broadcasts to 11 million viewers in the London area, and Central Independent Television, which broadcasts to 9 million people in central England. Carlton's wholly-owned Technicolor subsidiaries produce prerecorded video cassettes and compact disks. The U.K. generates 47% of sales, and the U.S. generates more than 40% of sales.

£ mil	09/92	09/93	09/94	US$mil 09/94				
Sales	635.0	1,005.0	1,404.7	2,128.3	P/E Ratio	19.2	Price (9/30/95)	10.35
Net Income	75.0	94.0	129.8	196.7	P/B Ratio	6.9	52 Wk Hi-Low	10.82-8.14
Book Value	383.0	425.0	340.5	540.5	Yield %	2.0	Market Cap	US$3,783.0mil

Address	**15 St. George St., Hanover Sq.**	Tel	**0171-499-8050**	ADR	**CCTVY**	Managing Director	**June F. de Moller**
	London W1R 9DE	Fax	**0171-895-9575**	SEDOL No.	**341925**	Chairman	**Michael P. Green**

Clyde Petroleum

Industry: **Oil - Secondary**

Clyde Petroleum explores for and extracts oil and gas reserves. The company has onshore and offshore production and exploration interests in and around the United Kingdom and the Netherlands. It has minority exploration interests in Malaysia, Syria and Yemen. In 1994, company reserves amounted to about 177 million barrels of oil, of which 110 million are currently in production. Its U.K. operations accounted for more than 70% of revenues and the Netherlands accounted for about 29%. Clyde and the Austrian oil company OMV jointly own St. James's Oil and Gas.

£ mil	12/92	12/93	12/94	US$mil 12/94				
Sales	83.0	82.0	116.6	179.4	P/E Ratio	17.3	Price (9/30/95)	0.52
Net Income	-40.0	-23.0	12.1	18.6	P/B Ratio	1.1	52 Wk Hi-Low	0.56-0.36
Book Value	167.0	172.0	191.0	298.4	Yield %	1.9	Market Cap	US$336.9mil

Address	**Coddington Ct., Coddington**	Tel	**01531-640811**	ADR		Managing Director	**Roy A. Franklin**
	Ledbury HR8 1JL	Fax	**01531-640519**	SEDOL No.	**204857**	Chairman	**J. Malcolm Gourlay**

Coats Viyella

Industry: **Clothing & Fabrics**

Coats Viyella manufactures textile products and precision-engineered components. It makes thread, zippers, and fabric. Coats Viyella sells clothes under such brand names as Van Heuser and Berghaus and makes uniforms for British Rail and British Telecom. Coats Viyella operates more than 60 Jaeger menswear shops and approximately 120 Viyella womenswear shops. It makes aluminum, magnesium, and zinc die-cast components. Continental Europe generates 24% of sales, and nearly 40% of all sales are recorded outside Europe.

£ mil	12/92	12/93	12/94	US$mil 12/94				
Sales	2,095.0	2,444.0	2,183.9	3,359.8	P/E Ratio	25.7	Price (9/30/95)	2.01
Net Income	59.0	91.0	55.0	84.6	P/B Ratio	1.8	52 Wk Hi-Low	2.20-1.67
Book Value	707.0	791.0	787.2	1,230.0	Yield %	2.5	Market Cap	US$2,218.3mil

Address	**28 Savile Row**	Tel	**0171-734-4030**	ADR	**COATY**	CEO	**Neville C. Bain**
	London W1X 2DD	Fax	**0171-437-2016**	SEDOL No.	**927057**	Chairman	**Sir David Alliance**

Commercial Union

Industry: **Insurance - Full Line**

Commercial Union (CU) offers life insurance, general insurance, pensions, and fund management services. Life insurance accounts for more than 63% of the group's premium income. CU derives about 41% of its premium income from the United Kingdom, 20% from continental Europe, and 27% from North America. The company owns the Dutch life- and general-insurer Delta Lloyd and has a 98% stake in the French life-insurance company L'Epargne de France. CU acquired French insurance company Groupe Victoire in 1994. Six percent of CU is owned by French bank Sociètè Gènèrale.

£ mil	12/92	12/93	12/94	US$mil 12/94				
Revenues	5,572.0	5,970.0	6,762.0	10,403.1	P/E Ratio	10.4	Price (9/30/95)	5.85
Net Income	236.0	321.0	349.0	536.9	P/B Ratio	1.2	52 Wk Hi-Low	6.43-4.74
Book Value	1,501.0	2,529.0	3,173.0	4,957.8	Yield %	4.5	Market Cap	US$6,158.5mil

Address	**St. Helen's, 1 Undershaft**	Tel	**0171-283-7500**	ADR		CEO	**John G.T. Carter**
	London EC3P 3DQ	Fax	**0171-662-8070**	SEDOL No.	**216238**	Chairman	**Nicholas H. Baring**

Cookson

Industry: **Industrial - Diversified**

Cookson Group manufactures specialized industrial materials for the circuit-board, steel, plastics, and jewelry-fabrication industries. In the United States, Cookson also makes dental products and stampings for electric and electronic applications. Its ceramic supplies business includes Cookson Matthey Ceramics (CMC), a joint venture formed in 1994 with Johnson Matthey to supply materials to the tile, tableware and sanitaryware industries. The company eliminated its lead, aluminium and magnets business in 1994, and is planning to sell its plastic-additives operations.

£ mil	12/92	12/93	12/94	US$mil 12/94				
Sales	1,238.0	1,431.0	1,525.4	2,346.8	P/E Ratio	3.4	Price (9/30/95)	2.83
Net Income	42.0	65.0	14.5	22.3	P/B Ratio	3.4	52 Wk Hi-Low	2.96-1.88
Book Value	462.0	627.0	566.7	885.5	Yield %	2.0	Market Cap	US$3,044.3mil

Address **130 Wood St.**
London EC2V 6EQ
Tel **0171-606-4400**
Fax **0171-606-2851**
ADR
SEDOL No. **508407**
CEO **Richard Oster**
Chairman **Robert Malpas**

Courtaulds

Industry: **Specialty Chemicals**

Courtaulds manufactures chemical-based materials. Its products include coatings for ships, buildings, and oil-production equipment. The company supplies sealants and coatings to aircraft manufacturers and to airlines such as British Airways. Courtaulds makes packaging tubes from plastic, metal, and laminated materials for the pharmaceutical, food, and beverage industries. It produces colored acrylic fibers and acetate-filament yarns for clothing. Nearly two thirds of sales are exports and more than 40% of all sales are exports outside Europe.

£ mil	03/93	03/94	03/95	US$mil 03/95				
Sales	2,050.0	1,952.0	2,130.8	3,339.8	P/E Ratio	15.7	Price (9/30/95)	3.98
Net Income	151.0	82.0	102.4	160.5	P/B Ratio	2.6	52 Wk Hi-Low	4.83-3.95
Book Value	542.0	577.0	606.3	993.9	Yield %	3.9	Market Cap	US$2,543.5mil

Address **50 George St.**
London W1A 2BB
Tel **0171-612-1000**
Fax **0171-612-1500**
ADR **COU**
SEDOL No. **228482**
CEO **Sipko Huismans**
Chairman **Sir Christopher Hogg**

Courtaulds Textiles

Industry: **Clothing & Fabrics**

Courtaulds Textiles is a textile and clothing company that produces lace, stretch fabric, car upholstery, yarns, and home furnishings. Berlei and Gossard bras, Aristoc tights, and Jockey underwear are among its branded clothing operations. It also supplies retailers such as Marks & Spencer with private-label clothing. The company is the United Kingdom's largest producer of lingerie and underwear. Continental Europe accounts for 23% of its sales, and North America accounts for 12%. Courtaulds Textiles spun off from Courtaulds PLC in 1990.

£ mil	12/92	12/93	12/94	US$mil 12/94				
Sales	890.0	923.0	1,053.2	1,620.3	P/E Ratio	13.4	Price (9/30/95)	4.53
Net Income	30.0	30.0	34.3	52.8	P/B Ratio	1.7	52 Wk Hi-Low	5.12-4.16
Book Value	264.0	262.0	263.8	412.2	Yield %	3.3	Market Cap	US$731.8mil

Address **13/14 Margaret St.**
London W1A 3DA
Tel **0171-331-4500**
Fax **0171-331-4600**
ADR
SEDOL No. **228794**
CEO **Noel Jervis**
Chairman **John Eccles**

Dalgety

Industry: **Other Food**

Dalgety is a food company that produces and distributes snack foods, grocery and agricultural products, food ingredients, and pet foods. Its products include Golden Wonder snack products, Homepride baking mixes and flour, and Spillers pet foods. It owns Lucas Ingredients, a supplier of spices and foods for the convenience-food industry. McDonald's is the largest client of its wholly-owned U.S.-based fast-food distribution subsidiary, Martin-Brower. The company acquired United Kingdom pet food producer Paragon Petcare in 1994.

£ mil	06/92	06/93	06/94	US$mil 06/94				
Sales	3,982.0	4,470.0	4,955.3	7,429.2	P/E Ratio	12.1	Price (9/30/95)	4.43
Net Income	88.0	81.0	84.4	126.5	P/B Ratio	2.7	52 Wk Hi-Low	4.84-3.96
Book Value	370.0	413.0	382.0	587.7	Yield %	4.8	Market Cap	US$2,021.1mil

Address **100 George St.**
London W1H 5RH
Tel **0171-486-0200**
Fax **0171-493-0892**
ADR
SEDOL No. **251325**
CEO **Richard Clothier**
Chairman **Maurice E. Warren**

Dawson

Industry: **Clothing & Fabrics**

Dawson International is a textiles company. It produces cashmere and woolen goods, hosiery carpet yarns, and various fabrics. Its UK Apparel division, which accounted for about a third of the company's 1994 sales, includes brands such as Pringle of Scotland and Ballantyne Cashmere. In the United States, Dawson makes thermal and performance wear under the J.E. Morgan and Duofold labels. It also has interests in two Far East cashmere businesses. Dawson closed its fleece and jersey operations in 1994, and sold its U.S.-based bathroom-accessories business in 1995.

£ mil	03/93	03/94	04/95	US$mil 04/95				
Sales	432.0	385.0	328.4	516.4	P/E Ratio	NMF	Price (9/30/95)	1.23
Net Income	21.0	-101.0	-2.9	-4.6	P/B Ratio	1.6	52 Wk Hi-Low	1.42-0.97
Book Value	163.0	115.0	150.5	242.7	Yield %	2.4	Market Cap	US$379.9mil

Address **9 Charlotte Sq.**
Edinburgh EH2 4DR
Tel **0131-220-1919**
Fax **0131-459-1786**
ADR
SEDOL No. **258564**
Managing Director **Peter Forrest**
Chairman **R. Derek Finlay**

De La Rue

Industry: **General Industrial & Commercial Services**

De La Rue prints bank-notes and securities and manufactures payment-systems equipment. It supplies bank notes to more than 100 issuing authorities. It also produces coins, bonds, checks, and financial-payment cards. De La Rue manufactures passports, identification cards, security holograms, and lottery tickets. It has a 23% stake in Camelot, the operator of the United Kingdom's national lottery. De La Rue recently acquired the specialist paper manufacturer Portals. Nearly 90% of its sales are exports and 45% of all sales are generated outside of Europe.

£ mil	03/93	03/94	03/95	US$mil 03/95				
Sales	**560.0**	**587.0**	**747.1**	**1,171.0**	P/E Ratio	**16.5**	Price (9/30/95)	**9.09**
Net Income	**74.0**	**96.0**	**108.8**	**170.5**	P/B Ratio	**10.7**	52 Wk Hi-Low	**10.52-8.61**
Book Value	**272.0**	**322.0**	**188.6**	**309.2**	Yield %	**2.5**	Market Cap	**US$3,217.4mil**

Address	**6 Agar St.**	Tel	**0171-836-8383**	ADR	**DERUY**	CEO	**Jeremy J.S. Marshall**
	London WC2N 4DE	Fax	**0171-240-4224**	SEDOL No.	**259471**	Chairman	**Lord Limerick**

Delta

Industry: **Electrical Components & Equipment**

Delta is an engineering and industrial-services company than manufactures and distributes cables, circuit-protection equipment, and plumbing and engineering products. In Australia, Delta is a distributor of electric and electronic products and protective coatings. In Africa, its three associated companies repair motors and transformers, engage in manganese-related production, and manufacture plumbing products. In 1994, about 35% of Delta's sales were to countries outside the United Kingdom and continental Europe.

£ mil	01/93	01/94	12/94	US$mil 12/94				
Sales	**786.0**	**833.0**	**898.6**	**1,382.5**	P/E Ratio	**15.3**	Price (9/30/95)	**4.24**
Net Income	**34.0**	**34.0**	**41.2**	**63.4**	P/B Ratio	**1.8**	52 Wk Hi-Low	**5.33-4.17**
Book Value	**318.0**	**329.0**	**342.9**	**535.8**	Yield %	**3.7**	Market Cap	**US$1,001.2mil**

Address	**1 Kingsway**	Tel	**0171-836-3535**	ADR		CEO	**Robert A. Easton**
	London WC2B 6XF	Fax	**0171-836-4511**	SEDOL No.	**261506**	Chairman	**Sir Martin Jacomb**

Diploma

Industry: **Overseas Trading**

Diploma distributes semiconductors and other electronic equipment in the United Kingdom and the United States. The company also manufactures building products such as doors and handmade bricks; supplies carbon and alloy products to the oil and engineering industries; distributes water, electric, and gas fittings, and supplies and services laboratory instrumentation. About 90% of the company's revenues are generated in the U.K. Diploma acquired a 70% share in Rayfast Ltd, a U.K. distributor of high-technology wiring and associated products, in 1994.

£ mil	09/92	09/93	09/94	US$mil 09/94				
Sales	**132.0**	**158.0**	**191.5**	**290.2**	P/E Ratio	**14.9**	Price (9/30/95)	**4.30**
Net Income	**7.0**	**14.0**	**16.1**	**24.4**	P/B Ratio	**3.0**	52 Wk Hi-Low	**5.00-4.08**
Book Value	**67.0**	**74.0**	**81.0**	**128.6**	Yield %	**3.1**	Market Cap	**US$381.3mil**

Address	**20 Bunhill Row**	Tel	**0171-638-0934**	ADR		CEO	**Christopher Thomas**
	London EC1Y 8LP	Fax	**0171-638-7651**	SEDOL No.	**270472**	Chairman	**Christopher Thomas**

Dixons

Industry: **Other Specialty Retailers**

Dixons Group sells electronic consumer goods through a network of retail outlets and invests in real estate. Its electronics goods include cameras, personal computers, stereo systems, televisions, home-office equipment, and kitchen and laundry appliances. Dixons operates consumer-electronics stores in the United Kingdom, as well as the chains Currys Superstores and PC World. The firm sold its U.S.-based Silo consumer-electronics stores to Fretter (U.S.) in 1993. Dixons generates more than 10% of its sales from commercial-property developments in Europe.

£ mil	05/93	04/94	04/95	US$mil 04/95				
Revenues	**1,944.0**	**1,578.0**	**1,646.9**	**2,589.5**	P/E Ratio	**20.8**	Price (9/30/95)	**3.46**
Net Income	**-16.0**	**-165.0**	**75.1**	**118.1**	P/B Ratio	**7.4**	52 Wk Hi-Low	**3.57-1.76**
Book Value	**290.0**	**285.0**	**186.0**	**300.0**	Yield %	**2.1**	Market Cap	**US$2,186.6mil**

Address	**29 Farm St.**	Tel	**0171-499-3494**	ADR	**DXN**	CEO	**John Clare**
	London W1X 7RD	Fax	**0171-629-1404**	SEDOL No.	**272304**	Chairman	**Stanley Kalms**

Electrocomponents

Industry: **Overseas Trading**

Electrocomponents is a holding company for electronics distributors. Its wholly-owned subsidiaries RS Components U.K. and RS Components International distribute tools, instruments, and electronic, electrical, and mechanical components in Europe, Australia, New Zealand, India, and Hong Kong. Sales from these subsidiaries account for 92% of revenues. Pact International (70% owned) provides electrical and audio accessories to retailers. Operations in the United Kingdom and Ireland account for roughly 84% of total revenues.

£ mil	03/93	03/94	03/95	US$mil 03/95				
Sales	**347.0**	**397.0**	**472.6**	**740.8**	P/E Ratio	**23.7**	Price (9/30/95)	**3.25**
Net Income	**31.0**	**48.0**	**57.7**	**90.4**	P/B Ratio	**6.7**	52 Wk Hi-Low	**3.29-2.22**
Book Value	**141.0**	**168.0**	**204.0**	**334.4**	Yield %	**1.8**	Market Cap	**US$2,170.0mil**

Address	**21 Knightsbridge**	Tel	**0171-245-1277**	ADR		CEO	**Robert A. Lawson**
	London SW1X 7LY	Fax	**0171-235-4458**	SEDOL No.	**309644**	Chairman	**Roy Cotterill**

English China Clays

Industry: **Specialty Chemicals**

English China Clays (ECC) produces clays, minerals, specialty chemicals, pigments, and paint. The company mines and processes kaolin and produces aggregates in the United Kingdom and the United States. ECC supplies specialty chemicals to the paper and surface-treatment industries through its U.S subsidiary EZE Products. Calgon, another U.S. subsidiary, produces water-management chemicals, paper chemicals, and industrial biocides. Exports represent 87% of sales, and nearly half of all sales are made outside of Europe, primarily in North America.

£ mil	12/92	12/93	12/94	US$mil 12/94				
Sales	**966.0**	**1,131.0**	**877.6**	**1,350.2**	P/E Ratio	**18.1**	Price (9/30/95)	**3.63**
Net Income	**75.0**	**61.0**	**61.0**	**93.8**	P/B Ratio	**2.2**	52 Wk Hi-Low	**4.13-3.23**
Book Value	**819.0**	**743.0**	**513.4**	**802.2**	Yield %	**4.5**	Market Cap	**US$1,759.9mil**

Address **1015 Arlington Business Pk.**
Reading, Berkshire RG7 4SA
Tel **01734-304010**
Fax **01734-309500**
ADR **ENC**
SEDOL No. **316707**
CEO **Andrew H. Teare**
Chairman **Lord Chilver**

Enterprise Oil

Industry: **Oil - Secondary**

Enterprise Oil explores for and produces oil and natural gas in 17 countries in Europe, Australia, and Southeast Asia. Most of its wells are in the North Sea. The firm has major exploration interests in the Black Sea, the Gulf of Thailand, and the South China Sea. It owns one third of Elf Enterprise Petroleum, an oil- and gas-exploration and production joint venture with the French oil firm Societe Nationale Elf Aquitaine. Enterprise Oil has proven and probable reserves of 882 million barrels of oil and oil equivalent. Exports represent nearly two thirds of revenues.

£ mil	12/92	12/93	12/94	US$mil 12/94				
Sales	**538.0**	**546.0**	**651.3**	**1,002.0**	P/E Ratio	**30.6**	Price (9/30/95)	**3.58**
Net Income	**87.0**	**95.0**	**71.0**	**109.2**	P/B Ratio	**1.9**	52 Wk Hi-Low	**4.22-3.53**
Book Value	**902.0**	**951.0**	**936.3**	**1,463.0**	Yield %	**4.5**	Market Cap	**US$2,799.1mil**

Address **Grand Bldgs, Trafalgar Sq.**
London WC2N 5EJ
Tel **0171-925-4000**
Fax **0171-925-4321**
ADR **ETP**
SEDOL No. **318866**
CEO **Graham J. Hearne**
Chairman **Graham J. Hearne**

Eurotherm

Industry: **Industrial Technology**

Eurotherm manufactures industrial process-control equipment, including products for controlling temperature and atmosphere, measuring and controlling the thickness of material, and controlling integrated industrial processes. Eurotherm also makes DC and AC drives, which control electric motors, and recorders, which collect and record process parameters. The company has subsidiaries in Europe, the United States, Japan, Australia, Korea, and Hong Kong. About 38% of the company's revenues was generated outside Europe in 1994.

£ mil	10/92	10/93	10/94	US$mil 10/94				
Sales	**155.0**	**158.0**	**168.0**	**256.5**	P/E Ratio	**27.7**	Price (9/30/95)	**5.37**
Net Income	**10.0**	**13.0**	**17.2**	**26.3**	P/B Ratio	**6.4**	52 Wk Hi-Low	**5.40-3.62**
Book Value	**57.0**	**65.0**	**74.9**	**122.8**	Yield %	**1.0**	Market Cap	**US$761.8mil**

Address **Leonardslee, Lower Beeding**
Horsham, West Sussex RH13 6PP
Tel **01403-891665**
Fax **01403-891689**
ADR
SEDOL No. **323116**
CEO **Claes A. Hultman**
Chairman **Dr. Jack L. Leonard**

Eurotunnel

Industry: **Railroads**

Eurotunnel is the parent company for the Channel Tunnel project connecting the United Kingdom and France. It designs, finances, and constructs the tunnel. The firm has a concession from the British and French governments to construct and operate the tunnel until 2051. It operates three types of railcars: passenger wagons, double-deck tourist wagons for motorcycles and small cars, and single-deck wagons for large freight-carrying vehicles. The tunnel was officially opened in May 1994, but full freight and passenger services did not begin until November 1994.

£ mil	12/92	12/93	12/94	US$mil 12/94				
Sales	**0.0**	**0.0**	**13.8**	**21.2**	P/E Ratio	**NMF**	Price (9/30/95)	**0.90**
Net Income	**-2.0**	**-2.0**	**-191.4**	**-294.5**	P/B Ratio	**0.8**	52 Wk Hi-Low	**3.21-0.84**
Book Value	**1,241.0**	**1,367.0**	**958.4**	**1,497.5**	Yield %	**0.0**	Market Cap	**US$1,269.7mil**

Address **The Adelphi, John Adam St.**
London WC2N 6JT
Tel **0171-747-6747**
Fax **0171-747-6666**
ADR
SEDOL No. **316893**
Co-Chairman **Patrick Ponsolle**
Co-Chairman **Sir Alastair Morton**

Farnell

Industry: **Electrical Components & Equipment**

Farnell Electronics distributes electronic components to the professional and industrial sectors. The company has operations in 18 countries, and about 48% of its revenues were generated outside the United Kingdom in 1994.It recently established an international purchasing office in Singapore to buy components directly from Far East manufacturers. It acquired Spelec, a French components distributor, in 1994. In 1995, Farnell's manufacturing division was sold intact to a company controlled by CINVen Funds.

£ mil	01/93	01/94	01/95	US$mil 01/95				
Sales	**254.0**	**320.0**	**514.2**	**794.7**	P/E Ratio	**23.4**	Price (9/30/95)	**6.73**
Net Income	**31.0**	**33.0**	**38.6**	**59.7**	P/B Ratio	**6.2**	52 Wk Hi-Low	**6.95-4.92**
Book Value	**108.0**	**116.0**	**146.7**	**232.8**	Yield %	**1.3**	Market Cap	**US$1,445.5mil**

Address **Farnell Hse., Sandbeck Way**
Wetherby, West Yorks LS22 4DH
Tel **01937-587241**
Fax **01937-580070**
ADR
SEDOL No. **331841**
CEO **Howard Poulson**
Chairman **Richard E. Hanwell**

Fine Art Developments

Industry: **Other Specialty Retailers**

Fine Art Developments makes greeting cards, stationery, and educational toys. It sells these products and other merchandise mainly through mail-order catalogs. The company also operates the stationery retail-chain Papertree, a Christmas hampers business, and charity trading services. It generates 87% of its revenues in the United Kingdom. Mail-order operations account for 57% of revenues. In 1995, Fine Art Developments acquired The Dee Group, which principally sells womens' and children's clothing.

£ mil	03/93	03/94	03/95	US$mil 03/95				
Revenues	**312.0**	**317.0**	**340.1**	**533.1**	P/E Ratio	**13.8**	Price (9/30/95)	**4.51**
Net Income	**23.0**	**26.0**	**26.0**	**40.7**	P/B Ratio	**3.1**	52 Wk Hi-Low	**4.98-3.21**
Book Value	**101.0**	**106.0**	**117.1**	**192.0**	Yield %	**3.4**	Market Cap	**US$573.0mil**

Address **Dawson Ln., Dudley Hill**
Bradford, West Yorks BD4 6HW
Tel **01274-651188**
Fax **01274-687386**
ADR
SEDOL No. **337407**
Managing Director **D.A. Johnson**
Chairman **Keith Chapman**

First Leisure

Industry: **Other Recreational Products & Services**

First Leisure Corporation is a diversified leisure company that operates resort facilities, discotheques, bowling alleys, snooker clubs, and bingo clubs. It operates two major London theaters through a joint venture with Cameron Mackintosh. It has interests in the marina business through another joint venture. The company, which has plans to develop health and fitness operations, acquired 75% of the Royal County of Berkshire Racquets and Health Club in 1994. First Leisure's discotheques generated about 35% of its revenues in 1994, and resort facilities generated 32%.

£ mil	10/92	10/93	10/94	US$mil 10/94				
Sales	**108.0**	**122.0**	**141.8**	**216.5**	P/E Ratio	**19.5**	Price (9/30/95)	**3.23**
Net Income	**25.0**	**24.0**	**27.1**	**41.4**	P/B Ratio	**2.2**	52 Wk Hi-Low	**3.45-2.47**
Book Value	**274.0**	**232.0**	**242.8**	**398.0**	Yield %	**2.2**	Market Cap	**US$837.8mil**

Address **7 Soho St.**
London W1V 5FA
Tel **0171-437-9727**
Fax **0171-439-0088**
ADR
SEDOL No. **340494**
CEO **John O. Conlan**
Chairman **Lord Rayne**

Albert Fisher

Industry: **Other Food**

Albert Fisher processes, sources, and distributes food, operating in Europe and North America in the fruit, vegetable, and seafood sectors. The company's divisions include fresh produce, frozen foods, and food processing and distribution. Its Albert Fisher Larios joint venture prepares and cans fruits and vegetables. Albert Fisher's U.S. subsidiaries include seafood company Aqua Star and produce company Fresh Western. North American exports account for one third of sales and exports to continental Europe generate roughly 30% of sales.

£ mil	08/92	08/93	08/94	US$mil 08/94				
Sales	**1,176.0**	**1,256.0**	**1,372.9**	**2,070.7**	P/E Ratio	**16.1**	Price (9/30/95)	**0.53**
Net Income	**11.0**	**15.0**	**21.5**	**32.4**	P/B Ratio	**1.9**	52 Wk Hi-Low	**0.56-0.38**
Book Value	**230.0**	**179.0**	**194.5**	**299.2**	Yield %	**7.0**	Market Cap	**US$597.4mil**

Address **'C' Sefton Pk., Bells Hill**
Stoke Poges, Bucks SL2 4HS
Tel **01753-677877**
Fax **01753-664481**
ADR **AFHGY**
SEDOL No. **339607**
President --
Chairman **Stephen R. Walls**

FKI

Industry: **Electrical Components & Equipment**

FKI is a group of manufacturing businesses serving the materials-handling, hardware, automotive, engineering, and process-control markets. Its hardware operations supply furniture fittings, door and window fasteners, and security products. FKI also makes control cables, vehicle lighting systems, and trim components. Its engineering businesses make equipment used primarily by the electricity industry. Its process-control products monitor traffic flows, gas flows, and engine performance. Operations in the United States generated 58% of profits in 1994.

£ mil	03/93	03/94	03/95	US$mil 03/95				
Sales	**721.0**	**794.0**	**768.6**	**1,204.7**	P/E Ratio	**23.2**	Price (9/30/95)	**1.76**
Net Income	**27.0**	**36.0**	**34.1**	**53.5**	P/B Ratio	**3.5**	52 Wk Hi-Low	**1.84-1.36**
Book Value	**232.0**	**201.0**	**227.6**	**373.0**	Yield %	**2.6**	Market Cap	**US$1,252.2mil**

Address **West Hse., King Cross Rd.**
Halifax HX1 1EB
Tel **01422-330267**
Fax **01422-330084**
ADR
SEDOL No. **329459**
CEO **Robert G. Beeston**
Chairman **Jeff Whalley**

Forte

Industry: **Lodging**

Forte operates approximately 940 hotels and 600 restaurants in 60 countries. The company has interests in The Savoy Hotel PLC, AFI Hotels, and ALPHA Airports, the airline caterer and retail operator. Forte operates Travelodge budget motels in the United Kingdom and the United States. Its Posthouse hotels stress value for money and an informal style while the company's Forte Grand chain and the Mèridien group, acquired in 1994, offer luxury hotels. Forte operates the U.K. roadside-restaurant chain Little Chef and owns the U.K. sporting-goods retailer Lillywhites.

£ mil	01/93	01/94	01/95	US$mil 01/95				
Sales	**1,936.0**	**1,638.0**	**1,789.0**	**2,765.1**	P/E Ratio	**24.7**	Price (9/30/95)	**2.49**
Net Income	**115.0**	**86.0**	**89.0**	**137.6**	P/B Ratio	**1.0**	52 Wk Hi-Low	**2.75-2.22**
Book Value	**2,637.0**	**2,316.0**	**2,375.0**	**3,769.8**	Yield %	**3.0**	Market Cap	**US$3,733.5mil**

Address **166 High Holborn**
London WC1V 6TT
Tel **0171-836-7744**
Fax **0171-240-9993**
ADR
SEDOL No. **905804**
President **Lord Forte**
Chairman **Sir Rocco Forte**

Frogmore Estates

Industry: **Real-Estate Investment**

Frogmore Estates is a property-investment company with interests in London and Southeast England. In 1994, its property assets, which were valued at £346 million, generated more than £20 million in net rental and service income. Retail property accounts for 38% of Frogmore's £230 million investment portfolio. Industrial property and Central London offices each account for 20% of the portfolio. The company's trading portfolio, 34% of its total property assets, includes housebuilding, joint developments, and residential and commerical trading properties.

	£ mil 06/92	06/93	06/94	US$mil 06/94				
Sales	**42.0**	**46.0**	**66.9**	**100.3**	P/E Ratio	**15.8**	Price (9/30/95)	**4.70**
Net Income	**7.0**	**8.0**	**14.7**	**22.1**	P/B Ratio	**0.9**	52 Wk Hi-Low	**4.97-4.05**
Book Value	**164.0**	**154.0**	**252.6**	**388.6**	Yield %	**3.6**	Market Cap	**US$382.9mil**

Address	**8 Manchester Sq.**	Tel **0171-224-4343**	ADR		Managing Director **Phillip G. Davies**
	London W1A 2JZ	Fax **0171-935-6476**	SEDOL No.	**331078**	Chairman **Dennis J. Cope**

General Accident

Industry: **Insurance - Full Line**

General Accident financial services offers all types of insurance except for industrial life policies. The company provides property services through General Accident Property Services, its wholly-owned residential real-estate business. General Accident operates in continental Europe, the United States, Canada, and the Asia-Pacific. The company recently opened a representative office in China. About 57% of its premium income is generated outside the United Kingdom and continental Europe; 29% is generated in the U.S. alone.

	£ mil 12/92	12/93	12/94	US$mil 12/94				
Revenues	**4,690.0**	**5,108.0**	**4,787.5**	**7,365.4**	P/E Ratio	**9.1**	Price (9/30/95)	**6.18**
Net Income	**-27.0**	**245.0**	**329.4**	**506.8**	P/B Ratio	**1.3**	52 Wk Hi-Low	**6.50-4.91**
Book Value	**1,629.0**	**2,710.0**	**2,182.3**	**3,409.8**	Yield %	**4.7**	Market Cap	**US$4,466.5mil**

Address	**Pitheavlis**	Tel **01738-21202**	ADR		CEO **W. Nelson Robertson**
	Perth, Perthshire PH2 0NH	Fax **01738-21843**	SEDOL No.	**368537**	Chairman **Earl of Airlie**

General Electric

Industry: **Diversified Technology**

General Electric Company (GEC) is an electronics manufacturer. Its products include electronic and power systems, integrated circuits, consumer goods, medical equipment, and electronic metrology products. GEC also produces telecommunication switching equipment, pay phones, and industrial marking and coding products. It also manufactures home appliances and produces radiology equipment and magnetic-resonance systems. GEC owns the military and civilian avionics company GEC- Marconi. Exports represent 70% of sales, and 41% of all sales are made outside of Europe.

	£ mil 03/93	03/94	03/95	US$mil 03/95				
Sales	**5,612.0**	**5,791.0**	**5,843.0**	**9,158.3**	P/E Ratio	**15.4**	Price (9/30/95)	**3.18**
Net Income	**536.0**	**540.0**	**564.0**	**884.0**	P/B Ratio	**2.6**	52 Wk Hi-Low	**3.36-2.60**
Book Value	**3,101.0**	**3,328.0**	**3,348.0**	**5,488.5**	Yield %	**3.6**	Market Cap	**US$13,831mil**

Address	**1 Stanhope Gate**	Tel **0171-493-8484**	ADR	**GNELY**	Managing Director **Lord Weinstock**
	London W1A 1EH	Fax **0171-493-1974**	SEDOL No.	**365334**	Chairman **Lord Prior**

GKN

Industry: **Other Auto Parts**

GKN manufactures automotive, agritechnical, aerospace, and military products and vehicles, and provides industrial and distribution services. The firm's products include universal joints, automotive driveline systems, and axles. Its 50%-owned Chep subsidiary supplies pallets throughout Europe and North America. GKN Defence manufactures Piranha and Warrior armored vehicles, and its wholly-owned Westland aerospace subsidiary manufactures Sea King, Apache, and EH101 helicopters. Nearly 60% of GKN's sales are generated outside the U.K.

	£ mil 12/92	12/93	12/94	US$mil 12/94				
Sales	**1,984.0**	**1,994.0**	**3,059.4**	**4,706.8**	P/E Ratio	**29.2**	Price (9/30/95)	**8.27**
Net Income	**48.0**	**39.0**	**92.3**	**142.0**	P/B Ratio	**3.6**	52 Wk Hi-Low	**8.27-5.44**
Book Value	**655.0**	**656.0**	**799.8**	**1,249.7**	Yield %	**2.6**	Market Cap	**US$4,554.2mil**

Address	**Ipsley Hse., Church Ln.**	Tel **01527-517715**	ADR	**GKNPY**	Managing Director **Sir David B. Lees**
	Redditch B98 0TL	Fax **01527-517715**	SEDOL No.	**395182**	Chairman **Sir David B. Lees**

Glaxo Wellcome

Industry: **Pharmaceuticals**

Glaxo Wellcome develops and manufactures pharmaceuticals. Anti-ulcer drug Zantac is the company's most lucrative product, generating about a third of revenues. The company also produces respiratory drugs, systemic antibiotics, migraine treatments, antiemisis drugs, and antiviral compounds including best-selling Zovirax (anti-herpes) and Retrovir (anti-HIV). Glaxo acquired the U.K.-based drug company Wellcome for $15 billion in March 1995. Exports represent about two thirds of revenue and 43% of all sales are generated in the United States.

	£ mil 06/92	06/93	06/94	US$mil 06/94				
Sales	**4,096.0**	**4,930.0**	**5,656.0**	**8,479.8**	P/E Ratio	**17.9**	Price (9/30/95)	**7.67**
Net Income	**1,033.0**	**1,207.0**	**1,303.0**	**1,953.5**	P/B Ratio	**4.6**	52 Wk Hi-Low	**7.99-5.68**
Book Value	**3,572.0**	**4,546.0**	**5,043.0**	**7,758.5**	Yield %	**3.5**	Market Cap	**US$42,277mil**

Address	**Lansdowne Hse., Berkeley Sq.**	Tel **0171-493-4060**	ADR	**GLX**	CEO **Sir Richard Sykes**
	London W1X 6BP	Fax **0171-408-0228**	SEDOL No.	**371784**	Chairman **Sir Colin Corness**

Glynwed

Industry: **Building Materials**

Glynwed processes specialty metals and plastics, makes finished products for residential and industrial uses, and develops and leases property. Its consumer products include Falcon catering equipment, Aga domestic cookers, a range of gas cookers and fires, and synthetic sinks. Glynwed makes iron and steel covers and gratings, cable TV adapters and cables, and a range of pipes and drainage systems. It also supplies hot- and cold-rolled metal products. In 1994, more than 84% of the company's revenues were generated in the United Kingdom and continental Europe.

£ mil	12/92	12/93	12/94	US$mil 12/94				
Sales	**906.0**	**900.0**	**1,024.9**	**1,576.8**	P/E Ratio	**16.8**	Price (9/30/95)	**3.59**
Net Income	**19.0**	**30.0**	**44.4**	**68.3**	P/B Ratio	**3.4**	52 Wk Hi-Low	**3.77-2.93**
Book Value	**206.0**	**203.0**	**221.9**	**346.7**	Yield %	**3.4**	Market Cap	**US$1,187.2mil**

Address **Headland Hse., New Coventry Rd.** **Sheldon, Birmingham B26 3AZ**
Tel **0121-742-2366** Fax **0121-742-0403**
ADR SEDOL No. **374288**
CEO **Bruce Ralph**
Chairman **Gareth Davies**

Granada

Industry: **Broadcasting**

Granada Group has interests in electrics and electronics rental, computer services, television, and leisure-related services. Its Granada shops lease and sell televisions, VCRs, satellite-reception equipment, and mobile phones. Granada Television holds the Channel 3 license for northwest England and London (weekend) and produces national TV programs. The company's leisure division provides services such as contract catering, expressway assistance, and textile rental. The division also offers air-travel services and operates hotels.

£ mil	09/92	10/93	10/94	US$mil 10/94				
Sales	**1,340.0**	**1,615.0**	**2,097.7**	**3,202.6**	P/E Ratio	**18.9**	Price (9/30/95)	**6.35**
Net Income	**79.0**	**126.0**	**192.0**	**293.1**	P/B Ratio	**7.3**	52 Wk Hi-Low	**6.57-4.81**
Book Value	**562.0**	**464.0**	**502.3**	**823.4**	Yield %	**1.6**	Market Cap	**US$5,873.6mil**

Address **36 Golden Sq.** **London W1R 4AH**
Tel **0171-734-8080** Fax **0171-494-2893**
ADR SEDOL No. **381125**
CEO **Gerry Robinson**
Chairman **Alex Bernstein**

Grand Metropolitan

Industry: **Distillers & Brewers**

Grand Metropolitan is an international food, beverages, and retail group. Among its food and beverage brand names are Haagen-Dazs ice-cream products, Pillsbury baked goods, Green Giant vegetables, J&B scotch whiskey, Bailey's Original Irish Cream, Malibu rum, and Smirnoff vodka. It also operates roughly 7,150 Burger King fast-food restaurants in 44 countries. The company recently acquired the U.S. food group Pet, which produces El Paso Mexican food and Progresso soups. Exports make up 90% of the company's sales, with nearly 60% of sales coming from the United States.

£ mil	09/92	09/93	09/94	US$mil 09/94				
Sales	**7,045.0**	**7,637.0**	**7,742.0**	**11,730.3**	P/E Ratio	**20.6**	Price (9/30/95)	**4.45**
Net Income	**624.0**	**413.0**	**450.0**	**681.8**	P/B Ratio	**2.6**	52 Wk Hi-Low	**4.45-3.55**
Book Value	**3,759.0**	**3,715.0**	**3,540.0**	**5,619.0**	Yield %	**3.1**	Market Cap	**US$14,747mil**

Address **20 St. James's Sq.** **London SW1Y 4RR**
Tel **0171-321-6000** Fax **0171-321-6001**
ADR **GRM** SEDOL No. **381932**
CEO **George J. Bull**
Chairman **Sir Allen Sheppard**

Great Portland Estates

Industry: **Real-Estate Investment**

Great Portland Estates invests in and develops freehold and leasehold properties throughout the United Kingdom. The company's holdings are concentrated in London. It owns 8.7 million square feet of commercial space and has approximately 1,200 tenants. Its portfolio was valued at over £1.1 billion in 1994. Freehold properties and leashold properties with tenants greater than 900 years made up 86% of its holdings. Offices and commercial space accounts for 59% of the company's property; retail space accounts for 30%; and industrial space accounts for 11%.

£ mil	03/93	03/94	03/95	US$mil 03/95				
Sales	**84.0**	**84.0**	**93.6**	**146.6**	P/E Ratio	**13.5**	Price (9/30/95)	**1.72**
Net Income	**27.0**	**16.0**	**40.3**	**63.2**	P/B Ratio	**0.8**	52 Wk Hi-Low	**1.97-1.65**
Book Value	**412.0**	**637.0**	**657.4**	**1,077.7**	Yield %	**5.1**	Market Cap	**US$883.4mil**

Address **Knighton Hse., 56 Mortimer St.** **London W1N 8BD**
Tel **0171-580-3040** Fax **0171-631-5169**
ADR SEDOL No. **384607**
Managing Director **Richard Peskin**
Chairman **Richard Peskin**

Great Universal Stores

Industry: **Other Specialty Retailers**

Great Universal Stores sells clothing and accessories through its home-shopping catalog business and retail outlets. It also invests in property. Its principal catalogs include Great Universal and Kays (both in the United Kingdom), and Wehkamp (in the Netherlands). Its Burberry clothing stores have locations throughout Europe and the United States. The company's property portfolio includes nearly 1,200 sites, of which 80% are occupied by retailers. More than three fourths of the company's revenues are generated in the U.K.

£ mil	03/93	03/94	03/95	US$mil 03/95				
Revenues	**2,810.4**	**3,094.3**	**2,660.0**	**4,169.3**	P/E Ratio	**16.2**	Price (9/30/95)	**5.96**
Net Income	**316.7**	**345.1**	**371.1**	**581.7**	P/B Ratio	**1.7**	52 Wk Hi-Low	**6.37-4.96**
Book Value	**3,297.7**	**3,617.0**	**3,540.6**	**5,804.3**	Yield %	**2.5**	Market Cap	**US$9,514.9mil**

Address **Universal Hse., Devonshire St.** **Manchester M60 1XA**
Tel **0161-273-8282** Fax **0161-273-5290**
ADR **GRUSY** SEDOL No. **384704**
President **--**
Chairman **Lord Wolfson**

Greenalls

Industry: **Restaurants**

The Greenalls Group operates pubs, liquor stores, hotels, and restaurants. The firm manages nearly 2,000 pubs, which generated almost 40% of revnues in 1994. Its liquor stores operation accounted for about 21% of revenues last year. Greenall's wholly-owned De Vere Hotels subsidiary, which operates the Grand Hotel in Brighton, concentrates on the luxury standard sector. The company operates six hotels in the United States. It also operates gaming machines, and manufactures soft drinks, and branded gin and vodka for the United Kingdom and overseas markets.

	£ mil 09/92	09/93	09/94	US$mil 09/94				
Sales	**529.0**	**596.0**	**716.2**	**1,085.2**	P/E Ratio	**18.7**	Price (9/30/95)	**4.98**
Net Income	**35.0**	**53.0**	**55.9**	**84.7**	P/B Ratio	**1.4**	52 Wk Hi-Low	**5.27-4.02**
Book Value	**767.0**	**807.0**	**718.6**	**1,140.7**	Yield %	**2.6**	Market Cap	**US$1,654.2mil**

Address **Wilderspool Hse., Greenalls Ave.** Tel **01925-51234** ADR Managing Director **Peter Greenall**
Warrington, Cheshire WA4 6RH Fax **01925-413137** SEDOL No. **387004** Chairman **Andrew G. Thomas**

Guardian Royal Exchange

Industry: **Insurance - Full Line**

Guardian provides life insurance and financial products such as corporate pensions. Its main personal-insurance products are household- and motor-insurance policies. The company provides its services in more than 50 countries, and about 24% of the company's premium income was derived from countries outside the United Kingdom and continental Europe in 1994. The company owns U.S.-based motor-insurer American Ambassador Casualty Company. It completed the acquisition of motor-insurer National Corporation of Indianapolis in 1994.

	£ mil 12/92	12/93	12/94	US$mil 12/94				
Revenues	**3,062.0**	**3,368.0**	**4,222.0**	**6,495.4**	P/E Ratio	**NMF**	Price (9/30/95)	**2.18**
Net Income	**114.0**	**647.0**	**-123.0**	**-189.2**	P/B Ratio	**1.3**	52 Wk Hi-Low	**2.34-1.61**
Book Value	**1,132.0**	**1,681.0**	**1,494.0**	**2,334.4**	Yield %	**3.8**	Market Cap	**US$3,026.4mil**

Address **Royal Exchange** Tel **0171-283-7101** ADR CEO **John Robbins**
London EC3V 3LS Fax **0171-621-2596** SEDOL No. **394231** Chairman **Lord Charles Hambro**

Guinness

Industry: **Distillers & Brewers**

Guinness is an international beverage company that distills spirits and brews beer; its brands include Guinness and Harp beers, Dewar's scotch whiskey, and Tanqueray gins. Its 100%-owned United Distillers subsidiary makes Bell's Scotch whiskey, Johnnie Walker scotch, and Gordon's gin. French beverage and luxury-product firm LVMH Moet-Hennessy Louis Vuitton holds 20% of Guinness, which, in turn, owns 34% of Moet-Hennessy's champagne and cognac divisions. Exports represent 80% of revenues; the company generates 45% of total sales outside of Europe.

	£ mil 12/92	12/93	12/94	US$mil 12/94				
Sales	**4,363.0**	**4,663.0**	**4,690.0**	**7,215.4**	P/E Ratio	**16.3**	Price (9/30/95)	**5.18**
Net Income	**524.0**	**433.0**	**641.0**	**986.2**	P/B Ratio	**2.6**	52 Wk Hi-Low	**5.32-4.05**
Book Value	**3,571.0**	**3,729.0**	**3,947.0**	**6,167.2**	Yield %	**2.7**	Market Cap	**US$16,604mil**

Address **39 Portman Sq.** Tel **0171-486-0288** ADR **GURSY** Managing Director **Brian F. Baldock**
London W1H 0EE Fax **0171-486-0002** SEDOL No. **396000** Chairman **Anthony A. Greener**

Halma

Industry: **Industrial - Diversified**

Halma is a holding company with interests in safety-interlocking, environmental-control, gas-detection, fire-detection, and security firms in Europe, North America, Australia, and Singapore. Its Castell Safety International subsidiary manufactures captive key and valve interlocks used to control industrial equipment. Halma's other holdings include water-analysis firm Palintest, electronic-sensor-maker Memco, and fire-detector-manufacturer Apollo. Acquisitions in 1995 include Zircoa, a sensor maker, and Bio-Chem Valve Corporation, and Monitor Controls Inc.

	£ mil 03/93	04/94	04/95	US$mil 04/95				
Sales	**116.0**	**135.0**	**153.7**	**241.7**	P/E Ratio	**23.1**	Price (9/30/95)	**1.71**
Net Income	**14.0**	**17.0**	**19.8**	**31.1**	P/B Ratio	**7.1**	52 Wk Hi-Low	**1.74-1.37**
Book Value	**46.0**	**56.0**	**63.8**	**103.0**	Yield %	**1.3**	Market Cap	**US$705.3mil**

Address **Misbourne Ct., Rectory Way** Tel **01494-721111** ADR CEO **David S. Barber**
Amersham, Bucks HP7 0DE Fax **01494-728032** SEDOL No. **405207** Chairman **David S. Barber**

Hambro Countrywide

Industry: **Real-Estate Investment**

Hambro Countrywide operates real estate agencies and provides property-related and financial services. The company's network of 762 residential-estate agencies makes it the largest estate agency group in England. Its Commercial and Professional Division comprises its property-management and valuation services and commercial agency Wright Oliphant. Its Hambro Guardian subsidiaries provide life insurance, pensions, investment products, and mortgages. Hambro owns 48% of Hambro Countrywide Security, which installs and maintains security systems.

	£ mil 12/92	12/93	12/94	US$mil 12/94				
Sales	**80.9**	**94.5**	**0.0**	**0.0**	P/E Ratio	**NMF**	Price (9/30/95)	**0.31**
Net Income	**-2.2**	**14.6**	**-6.1**	**-9.4**	P/B Ratio	**1.4**	52 Wk Hi-Low	**0.46-0.24**
Book Value	**56.1**	**68.7**	**77.4**	**120.9**	Yield %	**0.0**	Market Cap	**US$173.8mil**

Address **Queensgate, 1 Myrtle Rd.** Tel **01277-264466** ADR CEO **Harry D. Hill**
Brentwood, Essex CM14 5EG Fax **01277-217916** SEDOL No. **405412** Chairman **Christopher H. Sporborg**

Hambros

Industry: **Financial Services - Diversified**

Hambros is a holding company for an international group of companies operating in the banking, direct-investments, insurance-services and retail financial services sectors. It specializes in rights issues, mergers, and acquisitions. Hambros spun off Hambro Insurance Services Group in 1993, but has retained a majority interest in the group. Its subsidiaries include retail financial-services firm Hambro Countrywide and real-estate investor Berkeley Hambro Property Company. In August 1994, the company bought Nationwide's real-estate business.

£ mil	03/93	03/94	03/95	US$mil 03/95				
Revenues	**N/A**	**755.0**	**780.0**	**1,222.6**	P/E Ratio	**48.8**	Price (9/30/95)	**1.95**
Net Income	**47.0**	**60.0**	**7.0**	**11.0**	P/B Ratio	**0.7**	52 Wk Hi-Low	**2.65-1.82**
Book Value	**494.0**	**510.0**	**474.8**	**778.4**	Yield %	**3.8**	Market Cap	**US$546.6mil**

Address **41 Tower Hill**
London EC3N 4HA
Tel **0171-480-5000**
Fax **0171-702-4424**
ADR
SEDOL No. **405672**
President --
Chairman **Charles E.A. Hambro**

Hammerson

Industry: **Real-Estate Investment**

Hammerson is a property-investment and development company that owns property throughout the United Kingdom, Europe, and North America. More than 50% of the company's portfolio consists of U.K. properties, and properties in North America account for 27%. This portfolio, more than half of which is now invested in retail properties, was valued at £1634 million and produced net rental income of more than £120 million in 1994. Hammerson sold its Australian interests in 1994 and acquired 11 major properties in the U.K., France and Canada for a total of £351 million.

£ mil	12/92	12/93	12/94	US$mil 12/94				
Sales	**132.0**	**119.0**	**107.8**	**165.8**	P/E Ratio	**10.3**	Price (9/30/95)	**3.55**
Net Income	**78.0**	**29.0**	**94.0**	**144.6**	P/B Ratio	**0.9**	52 Wk Hi-Low	**3.93-3.04**
Book Value	**742.0**	**860.0**	**1,061.1**	**1,658.0**	Yield %	**2.8**	Market Cap	**US$1,595.5mil**

Address **100 Park Ln.**
London W1Y 4AR
Tel **0171-887-1000**
Fax **0171-887-1010**
ADR
SEDOL No. **406501**
CEO **Roland R. Spinney**
Chairman **Geoffrey M. Smith**

Hanson

Industry: **Conglomerates**

Hanson is an industrial-management company that produces coal, chemicals, tobacco products, and aggregates. Its U.K. holdings include cigarette manufacturer Imperial Tobacco and London Brick. Its U.S. interests include Peabody Coal, the world's largest private coal company; lumber producer Cavenham Forest Industries; and chemicals manufacturer Quantum. Hanson recently spun off many of its U.S. companies, including Farberware cookware and Jacuzzi whirlpools, to form U.S. Industries. Nearly 60% of sales come from outside Europe, mainly from the U.S.

£ mil	09/92	09/93	09/94	US$mil 09/94				
Sales	**8,711.0**	**9,668.0**	**10,837.0**	**16,419.7**	P/E Ratio	**9.6**	Price (9/30/95)	**2.03**
Net Income	**1,089.0**	**734.0**	**1,065.0**	**1,613.6**	P/B Ratio	**2.3**	52 Wk Hi-Low	**2.42-1.99**
Book Value	**4,224.0**	**3,953.0**	**4,598.0**	**7,298.4**	Yield %	**5.8**	Market Cap	**US$16,645mil**

Address **1 Grosvenor Pl.**
London SW1X 7JH
Tel **0171-245-1245**
Fax **0171-235-9795**
ADR **HAN**
SEDOL No. **408808**
CEO **Derek C. Bonham**
Chairman **Lord Hanson**

Hays

Industry: **General Industrial & Commercial Services**

Hays provides business-to-business mail, storage, distribution, and personnel-recruitment services. Its distribution division, which transports chemicals, furniture, foods, and other goods, generates nearly two thirds of revenues. Its wholly-owned Britdoc and Data Express subsidiaries deliver mail and parcels for businesses in the United Kingdom. Hays operates accountant-recruitment agencies in the U.K. and Australia, and also recruits technical staff in the U.K. Its Hays Fril subsidiary provides transport services in France.

£ mil	06/92	06/93	06/94	US$mil 06/94				
Sales	**680.0**	**784.0**	**631.9**	**947.4**	P/E Ratio	**23.5**	Price (9/30/95)	**3.45**
Net Income	**38.0**	**46.0**	**59.3**	**88.8**	P/B Ratio	**11.1**	52 Wk Hi-Low	**3.63-2.67**
Book Value	**143.0**	**130.0**	**126.4**	**194.4**	Yield %	**1.8**	Market Cap	**US$2,225.9mil**

Address **Hays Hse., Millmead**
Guildford, Surrey GU2 5HJ
Tel **01483-302203**
Fax **01483-300388**
ADR
SEDOL No. **416102**
Managing Director **John A. Napier**
Chairman **Ronnie E. Frost**

Hepworth

Industry: **Building Materials**

Hepworth is a building materials and industrial group. It manufactures pipes for the building, civil-engineering, and agricultural markets. It also makes refractory products, as well as processing sands that are used in various industries. Hepworth Saunier Duval, a continental European subsidiary that makes gas boilers and water heaters, accounts for more than 30% of the company's revenues. Hepworth's home products include boilers, heaters, sliding doors, and domestic hardware products. Less than 10% of Hepworth's customers are outside Europe.

£ mil	12/92	12/93	12/94	US$mil 12/94				
Sales	**628.0**	**655.0**	**695.9**	**1,070.6**	P/E Ratio	**12.9**	Price (9/30/95)	**2.79**
Net Income	**31.0**	**40.0**	**52.3**	**80.5**	P/B Ratio	**3.1**	52 Wk Hi-Low	**3.29-2.54**
Book Value	**96.0**	**201.0**	**218.9**	**342.0**	Yield %	**5.3**	Market Cap	**US$1,076.1mil**

Address **Tapton Park Rd.**
Sheffield S10 3FS
Tel **01142-306599**
Fax **01142-608642**
ADR
SEDOL No. **421902**
CEO **John D. Carter**
Chairman **Sir Roland Smith**

Hillsdown

Industry: **Other Food**

Hillsdown Holdings is one of Europe's largest food processors. Its products cover a wide range of items, such as beverages and processed turkey meat. Sales of food products generate nearly 90% of revenues. The company's food division includes HL Foods, a British canned-goods supplier, and Materne Fruibourg, a preserve manufacturer. Its Fairview subsidiary builds homes and flats in the London area and makes housing fixtures such as ceiling systems and lighting products. Exports represent more than half of all revenues, and 38% of all sales are made in North America.

	£ mil 12/92	12/93	12/94	US$mil 12/94				
Sales	**4,373.0**	**4,182.0**	**4,261.6**	**6,556.3**	P/E Ratio	**12.2**	Price (9/30/95)	**1.77**
Net Income	**2.0**	**94.0**	**101.4**	**156.0**	P/B Ratio	**1.9**	52 Wk Hi-Low	**2.00-1.62**
Book Value	**631.0**	**632.0**	**654.3**	**1,022.3**	Yield %	**5.2**	Market Cap	**US$1,952.3mil**

Address **32 Hampstead High St.** Tel **0171-794-0677** ADR **HDNHY** CEO **David A. Newton**
London NW3 1QD Fax **0171-435-1355** SEDOL No. **427870** Chairman **Sir John Nott**

Hogg Robinson

Industry: **General Industrial & Commercial Services**

Hogg Robinson provides business-travel management, and financial, and international-transport services. It is a major shareholder in British Travel International (BTI), one of Britain's largest business-travel agents. The company also offers international-freight services. Hogg Robinson's financial services include employee-benefits consulting, pension administration, and auto and property insurance. In 1994, the company acquired Benelux contract distribution and warehouse operation Snel BV.

	£ mil 03/93	03/94	03/95	US$mil 03/95				
Sales	**142.0**	**144.0**	**198.2**	**310.7**	P/E Ratio	**18.1**	Price (9/30/95)	**2.14**
Net Income	**10.0**	**16.0**	**8.2**	**12.9**	P/B Ratio	**3.4**	52 Wk Hi-Low	**2.20-1.45**
Book Value	**51.0**	**55.0**	**44.1**	**72.3**	Yield %	**3.6**	Market Cap	**US$236.2mil**

Address **Church Gate, Church St. W.** Tel **01483-730311** ADR Managing Director **David Radcliffe**
Woking, Surrey GU21 1DJ Fax **01483-728926** SEDOL No. **430492** Chairman **Brian R. Perry**

Ibstock Johnsen

Industry: **Building Materials**

Ibstock manufactures building materials in the United Kingdom, United States, and Portugal. The company makes facing bricks, architectural stoneware, and clay roof tiles in the U.K. It also makes these products through its U.S.-based subsidiary Glen-Gery. In Portugal, Ibstock owns eucalyptus plantations and a woodpulp mill, and manufactures timber products and ceramic sanitaryware. More than 40% of revenues were generated outside Europe in 1994. Ibstock acquired Scottish Brick in 1994. M & G Group owns about 13% of the company's issued share capital.

	£ mil 12/92	12/93	12/94	US$mil 12/94				
Sales	**277.0**	**187.0**	**210.1**	**323.3**	P/E Ratio	**20.5**	Price (9/30/95)	**0.68**
Net Income	**-25.0**	**-14.0**	**9.2**	**14.2**	P/B Ratio	**1.1**	52 Wk Hi-Low	**0.85-0.68**
Book Value	**229.0**	**199.0**	**196.3**	**306.8**	Yield %	**2.1**	Market Cap	**US$331.2mil**

Address **Lutterworth Hse.** Tel **01455-553071** ADR Managing Director **Ian D. Maclellan**
Lutterworth LE17 4PS Fax **01455-553182** SEDOL No. **455406** Chairman **Colin F.N. Hope**

ICI

Industry: **Commodity Chemicals**

Imperial Chemical Industries (ICI) makes industrial chemicals and materials, paints, and explosives. Its chemical products include titanium-dioxide pigments, used in paint, ink, paper, and plastics; and acrylics used for coatings, baths, and car components. ICI also produces CFC replacements, PVC tubing, catalysts, and manufactures Glidden and Dulux paints. Its explosives serve customers in the mining and quarrying sectors, and are used in safety airbags for cars. Exports represent 78% of revenues and nearly 60% of sales come from outside Europe.

	£ mil 12/92	12/93	12/94	US$mil 12/94				
Sales	**12,061.0**	**8,430.0**	**9,189.0**	**14,136.9**	P/E Ratio	**30.9**	Price (9/30/95)	**8.03**
Net Income	**-570.0**	**138.0**	**188.0**	**289.2**	P/B Ratio	**1.6**	52 Wk Hi-Low	**8.44-6.70**
Book Value	**4,286.0**	**3,983.0**	**3,736.0**	**5,837.5**	Yield %	**3.4**	Market Cap	**US$9,228.5mil**

Address **9 Millbank** Tel **0171-834-4444** ADR **ICI** CEO **Charles Miller Smith**
London SW1P 3JF Fax **0171-834-2042** SEDOL No. **459497** Chairman **Sir Ronald Hampel**

IMI

Industry: **Industrial - Diversified**

IMI manufactures building products, beverage dispensers, food-service equipment, point-of-purchase displays, and pneumatic products. Its specialized-engineering division makes special-purpose valves, alloys, casino tokens, and sporting ammunition. IMI's building products include copper tubing, heating and air conditioning systems and burner controls. More than 42% of the company's revenues are generated outside the United Kingdom and the European Union. IMI sold Brook Street Computers and more than 80% of Redwood, another computer operation, in 1994.

	£ mil 12/92	12/93	12/94	US$mil 12/94				
Sales	**1,006.0**	**1,065.0**	**1,155.4**	**1,777.5**	P/E Ratio	**54.7**	Price (9/30/95)	**3.28**
Net Income	**44.0**	**45.0**	**19.5**	**30.0**	P/B Ratio	**2.7**	52 Wk Hi-Low	**3.32-2.86**
Book Value	**378.0**	**386.0**	**394.7**	**616.7**	Yield %	**3.2**	Market Cap	**US$1,700.7mil**

Address **P.O. Box 216, Witton** Tel **0121-356-4848** ADR CEO **Gary J. Allen**
Birmingham, W. Midlands B6 7BA Fax **0121-356-3526** SEDOL No. **457963** Chairman **Sir Eric Pountain**

Inchcape

Industry: **Overseas Trading**

Inchcape distributes and sells motor vehicles, consumer products, and health-care and industrial equipment. It holds Toyota, Lexus, and Iveco franchises in Singapore, sells Suzuki motorcycles in Myanmar, and supplies Land Rover and Volkswagen vehicles in Brunei. Inchcape sells Rolex watches and Ferragamo and Timberland shoes. It also sells irrigation systems, cellular phones, and kitchen appliances. In 1994, Inchcape generated 76% of its sales in Singapore; 16% came from Brunei, and 7% from Malaysia and other countries. The firm plans to sell its office-automation business.

	£ mil 12/92	12/93	12/94	US$mil 12/94				
Sales	**4,959.0**	**5,834.0**	**6,008.0**	**3,955.2**	P/E Ratio	**16.9**	Price (9/30/95)	**4.54**
Net Income	**155.0**	**176.0**	**141.0**	**92.8**	P/B Ratio	**3.8**	52 Wk Hi-Low	**5.70-4.44**
Book Value	**642.0**	**769.0**	**632.4**	**433.2**	Yield %	**3.3**	Market Cap	**US$1,179.8mil**

Address **St. James's Hse., 23 King St.**	Tel **0171-321-0110**	ADR **INCHY**	CEO	**Charles Mackay**
London SW1Y 6QY	Fax **0171-321-0604**	SEDOL No. **6461805**	Chairman	**Sir David Plastow**

Invesco

Industry: **Financial Services - Diversified**

Invesco is an international investment-management firm. The company manages portfolios of equity, balanced, fixed-income, money-market, and real-estate investments for institutional and retail investors. Institutional assets make up the bulk of Invesco's holdings. As of June 1995, the company held $51.3 billion in institutional assets. Invesco is the parent company of Invesco Funds Group, a mutual-fund company based in Denver. Invesco Funds has $10.4 billion in total assets.

	£ mil 12/92	12/93	12/94	US$mil 12/94				
Revenues	**3,442.0**	**4,538.0**	**178.6**	**274.8**	P/E Ratio	**18.3**	Price (9/30/95)	**2.21**
Net Income	**6.0**	**24.0**	**30.8**	**47.3**	P/B Ratio	**8.7**	52 Wk Hi-Low	**2.60-1.51**
Book Value	**18.0**	**40.0**	**66.9**	**104.5**	Yield %	**2.2**	Market Cap	**US$921.9mil**

Address **11 Devonshire Sq.**	Tel **0171-626-3434**	ADR	President	--
London EC2M 4YR	Fax **0171-623-3339**	SEDOL No. **128269**	Chairman	**Charles W. Brady**

Johnson Matthey

Industry: **Precious Metals**

Johnson Matthey is an advanced materials technology company. It manufactures catalysts and pollution-control systems; produces electronic materials, specialty chemicals, and pharmaceutical compounds; refines, fabricates, and markets precious metals; and manufactures decorative and specialized materials for the ceramics, plastics, paint, ink, and construction industries. The company controls more than one third of the world market for autocatalysts. Its joint venture with Cookson Group is the world's largest manufacturer of decorative ceramic transfers.

	£ mil 03/93	03/94	03/95	US$mil 03/95				
Sales	**1,851.0**	**1,844.0**	**2,261.2**	**3,544.2**	P/E Ratio	**19.7**	Price (9/30/95)	**5.86**
Net Income	**50.0**	**45.0**	**63.9**	**100.2**	P/B Ratio	**3.3**	52 Wk Hi-Low	**5.94-5.00**
Book Value	**333.0**	**372.0**	**380.2**	**623.3**	Yield %	**2.0**	Market Cap	**US$2,006.8mil**

Address **2-4 Cockspur St., Trafalgar Sq.**	Tel **0171-269-8400**	ADR	CEO	**David J. Davies**
London SW1Y 5BQ	Fax **0171-269-8433**	SEDOL No. **476407**	Chairman	**David J. Davies**

Kingfisher

Industry: **Retailers - Broadline**

Kingfisher is one of the largest retailers in Europe. Its U.K. subsidiaries include Superdrug; B&Q, a do-it-yourself home-improvement center; Woolworths, an established chain of variety stores; and Comet, a home-appliance and consumer electronics retailer. It operates in Europe through its wholly-owned French electronics subsidiary Darty. The company owns office-supply store Staples, music and video wholesaler Entertainment U.K., and video-rental chain Titles, which operates 96 locations in the U.K. It manages nearly 23 million square feet of store space.

	£ mil 01/93	01/94	01/95	US$mil 01/95				
Revenues	**3,548.0**	**4,479.0**	**4,887.7**	**7,554.4**	P/E Ratio	**19.5**	Price (9/30/95)	**5.04**
Net Income	**148.0**	**230.0**	**172.5**	**266.6**	P/B Ratio	**2.8**	52 Wk Hi-Low	**5.04-3.89**
Book Value	**1,158.0**	**1,091.0**	**1,219.2**	**1,935.2**	Yield %	**3.0**	Market Cap	**US$5,340.0mil**

Address **119 Marylebone Rd.**	Tel **0171-724-7749**	ADR **KNGFY**	CEO	**Geoffrey Mulcahy**
London NW1 5PX	Fax **0171-724-1160**	SEDOL No. **981116**	Chairman	**Nigel Mobbs**

Ladbroke

Industry: **Casinos**

Ladbroke Group operates retail gambling casinos, and hotels. Its gaming business accounts for 70% of revenue, operating through nearly 2,000 racing shops and several casinos in the United Kingdom, Ireland, Belgium, and the United States. Ladbroke's Hilton International subsidiary manages 162 hotels worldwide and generates 24% of the company's revenues. The company recently announced the sale of its Texas Homecare Superstores subsidiary. Exports represent more than 40% of revenues and 23% of all sales come from outside Europe.

	£ mil 12/92	12/93	12/94	US$mil 12/94				
Sales	**4,167.0**	**4,269.0**	**3,703.0**	**5,696.9**	P/E Ratio	**NMF**	Price (9/30/95)	**1.69**
Net Income	**1.0**	**26.0**	**-304.0**	**-467.7**	P/B Ratio	**1.0**	52 Wk Hi-Low	**1.87-1.47**
Book Value	**2,513.0**	**2,164.0**	**1,904.3**	**2,975.5**	Yield %	**3.6**	Market Cap	**US$3,121.3mil**

Address **10 Cavendish Pl.**	Tel **0171-323-5000**	ADR **LADGY**	CEO	**Peter M. George**
London W1M 0DJ	Fax **0171-436-1300**	SEDOL No. **500254**	Chairman	**John B.H. Jackson**

Land Securities

Industry: **Real-Estate Investment**

Land Securities is a property-investment and -development group. Its holdings and development projects include offices, shopping centers, supermarkets, and industrial-warehouse buildings. The company's portfolio is valued in excess of £5billion. Most of the company's portfolio holdings are based in central London. Property, offices, and retail shops make up 83% of the portfolio and approximately 75% of it is freehold. Land Securities owns more than 3,500 stores, including more than 100 supermarkets, each of which has an area in excess of 10,000 square feet.

	£ mil 03/93	03/94	03/95	US$mil 03/95				
Sales	**381.0**	**389.0**	**400.0**	**627.0**	P/E Ratio	**17.5**	Price (9/30/95)	**6.15**
Net Income	**170.0**	**181.0**	**179.7**	**281.7**	P/B Ratio	**0.9**	52 Wk Hi-Low	**6.45-5.45**
Book Value	**2,544.0**	**3,453.0**	**3,533.8**	**5,793.1**	Yield %	**4.1**	Market Cap	**US$4,978.5mil**

Address **5 Strand**
London WC2N 5AF
Tel **0171-413-9000**
Fax **0171-925-0202**
ADR
SEDOL No. **504502**
Managing Director **Peter J. Hunt**
Chairman **Peter J. Hunt**

Laporte

Industry: **Specialty Chemicals**

Laporte produces specialty chemicals. It supplies chemicals and related services to the electronics industry. Its plastic-compounds products include specialized PVC materials, flexible cords, and beverage-can liners. It supplies organic chemicals to the pharmaceutical, agrochemical, polymer, and semiconductor industries; adhesives, coatings, and concrete products to the construction industry; and hygiene products to the swimming-pool maintenance, dairy, and food-production industries. About 54% of the company's revenues are generated outside Europe.

	£ mil 01/93	01/94	01/95	US$mil 01/95				
Sales	**522.0**	**877.0**	**964.5**	**1,490.7**	P/E Ratio	**17.5**	Price (9/30/95)	**8.09**
Net Income	**64.0**	**78.0**	**88.3**	**136.5**	P/B Ratio	**3.9**	52 Wk Hi-Low	**8.39-6.26**
Book Value	**233.0**	**306.0**	**403.0**	**639.7**	Yield %	**2.8**	Market Cap	**US$2,465.5mil**

Address **Laporte Hse., Kingsway**
Luton, Bedfordshire LU4 8EW
Tel **01582-21212**
Fax **01582-31818**
ADR
SEDOL No. **506133**
Mng Dir & CEO **Ken J. Minton**
Chairman **Roger Bexon**

Lasmo

Industry: **Oil - Secondary**

Lasmo is an international oil and gas exploration and production company. The company's oil and gas fields are concentrated in the United Kingdom and Indonesia; it also has fields are in Algeria, Libya, Colombia, and Vietnam. Lasmo's substantial liquefied-natural-gas (LNG) holdings are located primarily in Indonesia. The company announced major oil and gas discoveries in Algeria and Colombia in August 1994. The company has proven and probable reserves of 745 million barrels. Nearly two thirds of sales are made outside of the U.K.

	£ mil 12/92	12/93	12/94	US$mil 12/94				
Sales	**621.0**	**678.0**	**648.0**	**996.9**	P/E Ratio	**NMF**	Price (9/30/95)	**1.66**
Net Income	**-386.0**	**-118.0**	**-3.0**	**-4.6**	P/B Ratio	**1.2**	52 Wk Hi-Low	**1.84-1.37**
Book Value	**1,090.0**	**1,118.0**	**1,295.0**	**2,023.4**	Yield %	**0.8**	Market Cap	**US$2,543.8mil**

Address **100 Liverpool St.**
London EC2M 2BB
Tel **0171-945-4545**
Fax **0171-606-2893**
ADR
SEDOL No. **531696**
CEO **Joseph Darby**
Chairman **Rudolph Agnew**

Legal & General

Industry: **Insurance - Life & Health**

Legal & General Group offers life insurance, pensions, general insurance, and investment-management services. It has operations in the United Kingdom, the United States, Australia, France, and the Netherlands. The company generates more than 80% of its income from its life-insurance and pensions business. Legal & General has £33 billion in funds under management, and offers investments in managed funds. Legal & General also provides mortgage lending and operates real-estate agencies in the United Kingdom.

	£ mil 12/92	12/93	12/94	US$mil 12/94				
Revenues	**2,829.0**	**4,548.0**	**4,070.5**	**6,262.3**	P/E Ratio	**26.3**	Price (9/30/95)	**5.97**
Net Income	**90.0**	**149.0**	**111.0**	**170.8**	P/B Ratio	**8.8**	52 Wk Hi-Low	**6.00-4.15**
Book Value	**262.0**	**324.0**	**332.0**	**518.8**	Yield %	**3.6**	Market Cap	**US$4,651.7mil**

Address **Temple Ct., 11 Queen Victoria St.**
London EC4N 4TP
Tel **0171-528-6200**
Fax **0171-528-6222**
ADR
SEDOL No. **511524**
CEO **David J. Prosser**
Chairman **Sir Christopher Harding**

Lloyds Abbey Life

Industry: **Insurance - Life & Health**

Lloyds Abbey Life, a majority-owned subsidiary of Lloyds Bank, is a holding company for insurance and financial-services firms. The company's subsidiaries offer real-estate, mortgage, and general insurance services. The company's Black Horse Financial Services and Abbey Life subsidiaries offer pensions, unit trusts, and investment and savings plans. Trans Leben offers pensions and life insurance to personal and small-business customers in Germany, and its Lloyds Bowmaker subsidiary offers leasing and hire-purchase services.

	£ mil 12/92	12/93	12/94	US$mil 12/94				
Revenues	**2,276.0**	**3,048.0**	**2,145.1**	**3,300.2**	P/E Ratio	**15.1**	Price (9/30/95)	**4.51**
Net Income	**125.0**	**138.0**	**207.0**	**318.5**	P/B Ratio	**2.4**	52 Wk Hi-Low	**4.58-3.13**
Book Value	**1,169.0**	**1,243.0**	**1,302.3**	**2,034.8**	Yield %	**4.3**	Market Cap	**US$4,983.6mil**

Address **205 Brooklands Rd.**
Weybridge, Surrey KT13 0PE
Tel **01932-850888**
Fax **01932-846597**
ADR
SEDOL No. **4154**
CEO **Stephen Maran**
Chairman **Sir Simon Hornby**

Lloyds Bank

Industry: **Banks - Money Center**

Lloyds Bank offers a wide range of financial services, including asset management, insurance, and corporate electronic payments. The bank provides mortgage services, life and health insurance, and pension plans. It operates approximately 1,900 retail branches in the United Kingdom. It also offers worldwide banking services to both private and corporate clients. It owns 62% of Lloyds Abbey Life, and recently purchased the Cheltenham & Gloucester Building Society (C&G).

£ mil	12/92	12/93	12/94	US$mil 12/94				
Revenues	**8,400.0**	**6,644.0**	**6,504.0**	**10,006.2**	P/E Ratio	**11.2**	Price (9/30/95)	**6.90**
Net Income	**441.0**	**605.0**	**797.0**	**1,226.2**	P/B Ratio	**2.4**	52 Wk Hi-Low	**7.09-5.38**
Book Value	**2,730.0**	**3,063.0**	**3,661.0**	**5,720.3**	Yield %	**3.7**	Market Cap	**US$14,251mil**

Address **71 Lombard St.** **London EC3P 3BS** | Tel **0171-626-1500** | Fax **0171-357-4926** | ADR | SEDOL No. **521103** | CEO **Brian I. Pitman** | Chairman **Sir Robin Ibbs**

Lloyds Chemists

Industry: **Drug-based Retailers**

Lloyds Chemists is a health-care company engaged in retailing, distributing, and manufacturing pharmaceutical, medical, and related products. It sells toiletries, cosmetics, prescriptions, and over-the-counter medicines through approximately 906 Lloyds Chemist stores and 319 Lloyds Supersave Drugstores. It also operates around 313 Holland and Barrett health-food stores. The company also distributes and retails veterinary supplies. By merging several of its subsidiaries, it has created Daniels Pharmaceutical, a national pharmaceutical wholesaling business.

£ mil	06/92	06/93	06/94	US$mil 06/94				
Revenues	**509.0**	**802.0**	**939.7**	**1,408.9**	P/E Ratio	**7.2**	Price (9/30/95)	**2.44**
Net Income	**26.0**	**35.0**	**41.0**	**61.5**	P/B Ratio	**2.4**	52 Wk Hi-Low	**3.23-1.87**
Book Value	**94.0**	**115.0**	**120.3**	**185.1**	Yield %	**3.9**	Market Cap	**US$470.4mil**

Address **Britannia Hse., Centurion Pk.** **Tamworth, Staffords B77 5TZ** | Tel **01827-260011** | Fax **01827-261593** | ADR | SEDOL No. **520412** | CEO **Peter E. Lloyd** | Chairman **Allen J. Lloyd**

Lonrho

Industry: **Conglomerates**

Lonrho is an international conglomerate with interests in natural-resources mining and refining, hotels, general trade, and agriculture. The firm mines gold and platinum in four African countries, Colombia, and Uzbekistan. It also explores for coal, oil, and natural-gas in Ghana, South Africa, and the United States. Lonrho produces fruits, coffee, cotton, sugar, tea, timber, and wheat in Africa. It owns and operates the U.K.'s Metropole, North America's Princess Hotels, and several hotels and lodges in Africa. About 66% of sales come from outside the U.K.

£ mil	09/92	09/93	09/94	US$mil 09/94				
Sales	**2,923.0**	**1,732.0**	**1,964.0**	**2,975.8**	P/E Ratio	**25.2**	Price (9/30/95)	**1.67**
Net Income	**86.0**	**112.0**	**51.0**	**77.3**	P/B Ratio	**1.2**	52 Wk Hi-Low	**1.69-1.31**
Book Value	**1,057.0**	**1,060.0**	**1,043.0**	**1,655.6**	Yield %	**2.9**	Market Cap	**US$2,046.3mil**

Address **Cheapside Hse., 138 Cheapside** **London EC2V 6BL** | Tel **0171-606-9898** | Fax **0171-606-2285** | ADR **LNROY** | SEDOL No. **534101** | Mng Dir & CEO **D. Block** | Chairman **Sir John Leahy**

Low & Bonar

Industry: **Containers & Packaging**

Low & Bonar manufactures consumer and industrial packaging, plastic products, and specialist materials such as polypropylene yarns and floor coverings. It has operations in the United Kingdom, continental Europe, the United States, and Canada. The company's films and industrial packaging division accounts for 36% of sales, and its consumer cartons and flexible packaging accounts for 27%. About 28% of Low & Bonar's revenues are generated in North America. The company acquired industrial packaging interests from Twinpak of Canada in 1994.

£ mil	11/92	11/93	11/94	US$mil 11/94				
Sales	**307.0**	**369.0**	**420.9**	**644.6**	P/E Ratio	**16.6**	Price (9/30/95)	**4.99**
Net Income	**3.0**	**20.0**	**29.5**	**45.2**	P/B Ratio	**3.7**	52 Wk Hi-Low	**5.46-3.81**
Book Value	**104.0**	**120.0**	**132.1**	**206.4**	Yield %	**2.3**	Market Cap	**US$779.5mil**

Address **Bonar Hse., Faraday St.** **Dundee DD1 9JA** | Tel **01382-818171** | Fax **01382-816262** | ADR | SEDOL No. **536301** | CEO **James W. Leng** | Chairman **Hugh W. Laughland**

Lucas

Industry: **Diversified Technology**

Lucas Industries is an engineering firm that manufactures products for the automotive and aerospace industries. The company manufactures Colette disc- and anti-lock brakes and powertrain, and electrical systems for cars. It also controls 24% of Europe's truck-brake market. It provides Boeing and Airbus with flight-control, engine-control, and communication systems. Lucas also makes robot-control equipment and CAD software for the automobile industry. The company is increasing its exposure to both the Eastern European and Asia Pacific markets.

£ mil	07/92	07/93	07/94	US$mil 07/94				
Sales	**2,253.0**	**2,434.0**	**2,487.9**	**3,746.8**	P/E Ratio	**NMF**	Price (9/30/95)	**1.96**
Net Income	**-9.0**	**25.0**	**-167.0**	**-251.5**	P/B Ratio	**2.4**	52 Wk Hi-Low	**2.11-1.73**
Book Value	**725.0**	**731.0**	**621.8**	**956.6**	Yield %	**3.6**	Market Cap	**US$2,495.2mil**

Address **Brueton Hse., New Rd.** **Solihull, W. Midlands B91 3TX** | Tel **0121-627-6000** | Fax **0121-627-6171** | ADR | SEDOL No. **537575** | CEO **George Simpson** | Chairman **Sir Brian Pearse**

M & G Group

Industry: **Financial Services - Diversified**

M & G Group is an investment-management company that offers products such as unit trusts, personal equity plans, investment trusts, and unit-linked life-insurance and pension plans. It also offers investment-management services to company pension funds, charities, and other institutional clients. The company has £11.8 billion under management of which £5.8 billion is in unit trusts. Its wholly-owned subsidiaries include M & G Pensions and Annuity Company, M & G Securities, and M & G Financial Services.

£ mil	09/92	09/93	09/94	US$mil 09/94				
Revenues	**59.0**	**64.0**	**77.0**	**116.7**	P/E Ratio	**19.6**	Price (9/30/95)	**11.28**
Net Income	**28.0**	**36.0**	**43.0**	**65.2**	P/B Ratio	**5.2**	52 Wk Hi-Low	**11.80-9.08**
Book Value	**104.0**	**148.0**	**160.9**	**255.4**	Yield %	**2.7**	Market Cap	**US$1,331.7mil**

Address **Three Quays, Tower Hill**
London EC3R 6BQ
Tel **0171-626-4588**
Fax **0171-623-8615**
ADR
SEDOL No. **549763**
Managing Director **David L. Morgan**
Chairman **Sir David Money-Coutts**

MAI

Industry: **Financial Services - Diversified**

MAI broadcasts television programs in the United Kingdom and provides financial services and products in the U.K. and abroad. Its wholly-owned U.K. subsidiary Wagon Finance provides automobile loans. Its money- and securities-brokerage services accounted for more than half its revenues in 1994. About 37% of MAI's revenues are generated outside the U.K. In 1994, the firm acquired Anglia Television, which broadcasts to the eastern regions of England. In acquiring Anglia, MAI also gained control of airtime sales company TSMS.

£ mil	06/92	06/93	06/94	US$mil 06/94				
Revenues	**389.0**	**528.0**	**695.3**	**1,042.4**	P/E Ratio	**19.5**	Price (9/30/95)	**3.24**
Net Income	**44.0**	**51.0**	**55.9**	**83.8**	P/B Ratio	**6.0**	52 Wk Hi-Low	**3.24-2.18**
Book Value	**161.0**	**194.0**	**174.5**	**268.5**	Yield %	**2.4**	Market Cap	**US$1,682.4mil**

Address **8 Montague Close**
London SE1 9RD
Tel **0171-407-7627**
Fax **0171-407-0002**
ADR
SEDOL No. **594019**
Managing Director **Lord Clive Hollick**
Chairman **James McKinnon**

Marks & Spencer

Industry: **Retailers - Broadline**

Marks & Spencer (M&S) is an international retailer of clothing, household goods, and food items, most of which appear under the St. Michael and Marks & Spencer trademarks. The firm operates 283 stores in the U.K., and 25 throughout Europe. M&S also owns Brooks Brothers clothing stores (U.S. and Japan), and Kings Super Markets (U.S.). It also markets its St. Michael merchandise in Canada through the company's Marks & Spencer and D'Aillard's chains, and in Hong Kong. M&S' Brooks Brothers lines are its best sellers overseas, with a 41% share of its foreign operations' sales.

£ mil	03/93	03/94	03/95	US$mil 03/95				
Revenues	**5,925.0**	**6,541.0**	**6,806.5**	**10,668.5**	P/E Ratio	**19.4**	Price (9/30/95)	**4.34**
Net Income	**496.0**	**578.0**	**623.8**	**977.7**	P/B Ratio	**3.3**	52 Wk Hi-Low	**4.51-3.69**
Book Value	**2,950.0**	**3,324.0**	**3,714.9**	**6,090.0**	Yield %	**2.4**	Market Cap	**US$19,238mil**

Address **Michael Hse., 37-67 Baker St.**
London W1A 1DN
Tel **0171-935-4422**
Fax **0171-487-2679**
ADR
SEDOL No. **565402**
President --
Chairman **Sir Richard Greenbury**

Marley

Industry: **Building Materials**

Marley manufactures plastic, concrete, and clay building products, and supplies automotive components. Its products include plumbing and drainage pipes; siding, frames, and flooring for homes; and paving and roofing materials. Marley makes instrument panels and exterior car components for companies such as Ford, Nissan, Saab, and Jaguar. In 1994, Marley generated more than half of its sales in the United Kingdom. The company has subsidiaries operating in the United States, Germany, Australia, South Africa, and Brazil.

£ mil	12/92	12/93	12/94	US$mil 12/94				
Sales	**569.0**	**617.0**	**661.5**	**1,017.7**	P/E Ratio	**11.1**	Price (9/30/95)	**1.09**
Net Income	**-2.0**	**-12.0**	**43.4**	**66.8**	P/B Ratio	**1.5**	52 Wk Hi-Low	**1.50-1.08**
Book Value	**211.0**	**223.0**	**246.2**	**384.7**	Yield %	**3.7**	Market Cap	**US$579.1mil**

Address **London Rd., Riverhead**
Sevenoaks, Kent TN13 2DS
Tel **01732-455255**
Fax **01732-740694**
ADR
SEDOL No. **565703**
CEO **David Trapnell**
Chairman **Sir George Russell**

Alfred McAlpine

Industry: **Heavy Construction**

Alfred McAlpine is an engineering, construction, and mining group. The services it provides in the United Kingdom and abroad include specialist civil engineering, slate production, and private- and public-sector construction. In the United States, the group operates mainly through its two wholly-owned subsidiaries. Blythe Construction and Becker Minerals. About 13% of McAlpine's revenues were generated outside the U.K. in 1994. Its subsidiary Alfred McAlpine Quarry Products, a supplier of sand, gravel, and other construction materials was sold in 1994.

£ mil	10/92	10/93	12/94 *	US$mil 12/94				
Sales	**561.0**	**619.0**	**894.2**	**1,375.7**	P/E Ratio	**12.2**	Price (9/30/95)	**1.24**
Net Income	**3.0**	**1.0**	**6.9**	**10.6**	P/B Ratio	**0.5**	52 Wk Hi-Low	**2.24-1.09**
Book Value	**170.0**	**156.0**	**183.3**	**286.4**	Yield %	**5.6**	Market Cap	**US$136.0mil**

Address **8 Suffolk St.**
London SW1Y 4HG
Tel **0171-930-6255**
Fax **0171-839-6902**
ADR
SEDOL No. **564539**
CEO **Oliver Whitehead**
Chairman **Sir John Milne**

*Irregular period due to fiscal year change.

McKechnie

Industry: **Industrial - Diversified**

McKechnie manufactures plastic and metal components for the electronics, automotive, aerospace, and telecommunication industries. Its consumer-products division, offering window furnishings, doors, screens, trimmings, and prepacked hardware, serves the home-improvement and do-it-yourself market. The company made 24% of its sales in the Pacific region and 17% in the United States in 1994. McKechnie acquired Linread, the United Kingdom-based producer of engineering bolts and fasteners, and sold its South African interests and U.K. packaging operations in 1994.

	£ mil 07/92	07/93	07/94	US$mil 07/94				
Sales	**286.0**	**314.0**	**402.6**	**606.3**	P/E Ratio	**17.0**	Price (9/30/95)	**4.62**
Net Income	**16.0**	**18.0**	**24.9**	**37.5**	P/B Ratio	**3.4**	52 Wk Hi-Low	**4.70-3.80**
Book Value	**118.0**	**128.0**	**133.0**	**204.7**	Yield %	**3.2**	Market Cap	**US$716.5mil**

Address **Leighswood Rd., Aldridge**
Walsall, W Midlands WS9 8DS
Tel **01922-743887**
Fax **01922-51045**
ADR
SEDOL No. **552404**
CEO **Michael S. Ost**
Chairman **Vanni E. Treves**

MEPC

Industry: **Real-Estate Investment**

MEPC owns, develops and manages commercial property. The company has operations in the United Kingdom, continental Europe, the United States, and Australia. MEPC generated £347 million gross rental income on a portfolio of £3365 million in 1994. Office space accounted for 55% of this portfolio and retail property for 34%. About 27% of the company's holdings consist of properties located outside the United Kingdom, and MEPC's strategy is to increase this overseas exposure during the next few years. Recent acquisitions are concentrated in the U.S. and Australia.

	£ mil 09/92	09/93	09/94	US$mil 09/94				
Sales	**229.0**	**226.0**	**234.3**	**355.0**	P/E Ratio	**19.6**	Price (9/30/95)	**3.94**
Net Income	**63.0**	**53.0**	**81.2**	**123.0**	P/B Ratio	**0.8**	52 Wk Hi-Low	**4.45-3.54**
Book Value	**1,505.0**	**1,616.0**	**1,925.9**	**3,057.0**	Yield %	**5.1**	Market Cap	**US$2,545.3mil**

Address **12 St. James's Sq.**
London SW1Y 4LB
Tel **0171-911-5300**
Fax **0171-839-2340**
ADR
SEDOL No. **549804**
CEO **James L. Tuckey**
Chairman **Michael Blakenham**

Mercury Asset

Industry: **Financial Services - Diversified**

Mercury Asset Management (MAM) manages money for institutions and individuals. It has £63.5 billion of funds under management, including £9.6 billion of funds for private investors. Mercury Fund Managers is the fourth-largest unit-trust manager in the United Kingdom. The management of U.K. institutional funds makes up 67% of its business, while 17% of the funds it manages are for clients based outside the U.K. As a result of the sale of S.G. Warburg (which owned 75% of its shares) to Swiss Bank, MAM is demerging from Warburg to become a fully independent company.

	£ mil 03/93	03/94	03/95	US$mil 03/95				
Revenues	**169.0**	**221.0**	**255.0**	**399.7**	P/E Ratio	**20.9**	Price (9/30/95)	**8.99**
Net Income	**59.0**	**78.0**	**78.3**	**122.8**	P/B Ratio	**7.1**	52 Wk Hi-Low	**9.07-5.83**
Book Value	**176.0**	**212.0**	**231.8**	**380.0**	Yield %	**2.9**	Market Cap	**US$2,596.0mil**

Address **33 King William St.**
London EC4R 9AS
Tel **0171-280-2800**
Fax **0171-280-2820**
ADR
SEDOL No. **580858**
CEO **David W.J. Price**
Chairman **Hugh A. Stevenson**

Meyer

Industry: **Building Materials**

Meyer International distributes and sells timber, timber products, and building materials in the United Kingdom, the United States, the Netherlands, and Germany. Its building products include timber, wood panels and laminates, doors, flooring, and fences. The company supplies these products to the small-building company and home-improvement markets through approximately 190 Jewson stores in the U.K. and 65 Pontmeyer home-improvement stores in the Netherlands. Many of the Jewson branches also contain outlets for the company's Hire Point tool-rental business.

	£ mil 03/93	03/94	03/95	US$mil 03/95				
Sales	**1,070.0**	**1,193.0**	**1,302.5**	**2,041.5**	P/E Ratio	**11.3**	Price (9/30/95)	**3.20**
Net Income	**10.0**	**29.0**	**35.7**	**56.0**	P/B Ratio	**1.1**	52 Wk Hi-Low	**4.15-2.90**
Book Value	**255.0**	**324.0**	**351.2**	**575.7**	Yield %	**3.6**	Market Cap	**US$640.7mil**

Address **Villiers Hse., 41-47 Strand**
London WC2N 5JG
Tel **0171-839-7766**
Fax **0171-839-5520**
ADR
SEDOL No. **587213**
CEO **John M. Dobby**
Chairman **Harry Langman**

Morgan Crucible

Industry: **Industrial - Diversified**

The Morgan Crucible Company manufactures technical- and thermal-ceramics products, carbon products, electronic components, and chemical products. The company makes carbon brushes and commutators for electric motors. Morgan's range of ceramic products includes domestic-heating components, textile-machine threadguides, crucibles, and insulating fiber. Its chemical products include specialty lubricants. Morgan generates more than 80% of its profits outside the United Kingdom. In August 1994, the company sold its Holt Lloyd car-care subsidiary.

	£ mil 01/93	01/94	01/95	US$mil 01/95				
Sales	**680.0**	**793.0**	**738.1**	**1,140.8**	P/E Ratio	**18.1**	Price (9/30/95)	**3.99**
Net Income	**43.0**	**46.0**	**50.5**	**78.1**	P/B Ratio	**3.1**	52 Wk Hi-Low	**4.04-3.00**
Book Value	**233.0**	**236.0**	**281.1**	**446.2**	Yield %	**3.3**	Market Cap	**US$1,387.7mil**

Address **Morgan Hse., Madeira Walk**
Windsor, Berkshire SL4 1EP
Tel **01753-837000**
Fax **01753-850872**
ADR
SEDOL No. **602729**
Managing Director **Dr. Edwin B. Farmer**
Chairman **Sir James Spooner**

John Mowlem & Co.

Industry: **Heavy Construction**

John Mowlem & Company is an engineering, construction, and property-management firm. It is involved in large scale construction projects, including the London Underground Jubilee Line extension. Its wholly-owned SGB subsidiaries lease scaffolding and other construction equipment. John Mowlem owns 90% of London City Airport. The company also has operations in the United States, Australia, Germany, and the Middle East. In 1994, as part of a major restructuring, the company sold its housing business, John Mowlem Homes, and two small SGB businesses.

£ mil	12/92	12/93	12/94	US$mil 12/94				
Sales	**1,245.0**	**1,317.0**	**1,330.0**	**2,046.2**	P/E Ratio	**20.0**	Price (9/30/95)	**0.62**
Net Income	**-32.0**	**-124.0**	**4.8**	**7.4**	P/B Ratio	**0.7**	52 Wk Hi-Low	**1.14-0.62**
Book Value	**179.0**	**91.0**	**153.4**	**239.7**	Yield %	**3.2**	Market Cap	**US$171.8mil**

Address **White Lion Ct., Swan St.** **Isleworth, Middlesex TW7 6RN**
Tel **0181-568-9111** Fax **0181-847-4802**
ADR SEDOL No. **608307**
CEO **John R. Marshall** Chairman **Sir Philip Beck**

A & J Mucklow

Industry: **Real-Estate Investment**

A & J Mucklow Group invests in and develops industrial and commercial. It owns 5.4 million square feet of industrial property and 311,000 square feet of commercial property. These properties generate £15 million and £4 million in gross annual rental income, respectively. The group owns 47 industrial estates, 13 office properties, and two retail warehouses. The group is planning to build an additional 260,000 sqaure feet of property. Properties in the West Midlands area of central England account for 70% of the value of the firm's portfolio.

£ mil	06/92	06/93	06/94	US$mil 06/94				
Sales	**19.0**	**20.0**	**20.5**	**30.8**	P/E Ratio	**19.6**	Price (9/30/95)	**1.47**
Net Income	**8.0**	**6.0**	**7.4**	**11.1**	P/B Ratio	**0.9**	52 Wk Hi-Low	**1.51-1.24**
Book Value	**152.0**	**142.0**	**154.1**	**237.0**	Yield %	**4.3**	Market Cap	**US$227.8mil**

Address **Haden Cross, Halesowen Rd.** **Warley, West Midlands B64 7JB**
Tel **0121-550-1841** Fax **0121-550-7532**
ADR SEDOL No. **609140**
Managing Director **G. Clive Evans** Chairman **Albert J. Mucklow**

National Power

Industry: **Electrical Utilities - All**

National Power is one of the largest generators of electricity in the United Kingdom. The company has coal, oil, and combined-cycle gas-turbine plants. It has a capacity of 21,000 megawatts. Most of its sales are to regional United Kingdom electricity companies. It also wholly owns power-generator American National Power, which operates power plants in Virginia, Georgia, New Jersey, and Texas. The firm also owns stakes in Portuguese power-generator Tejo and the Pego power station in Portugal. The British government recently sold its interest in National Power.

£ mil	03/93	03/94	03/95	US$mil 03/95				
Sales	**4,348.0**	**3,641.0**	**3,953.0**	**6,195.9**	P/E Ratio	**12.5**	Price (9/30/95)	**5.16**
Net Income	**420.0**	**522.0**	**525.0**	**822.9**	P/B Ratio	**2.4**	52 Wk Hi-Low	**5.58-4.24**
Book Value	**2,314.0**	**2,643.0**	**2,548.0**	**4,177.0**	Yield %	**3.0**	Market Cap	**US$9,716.4mil**

Address **85 Queen Victoria St.** **London EC4V 4DP**
Tel **0171-454-9494** Fax **0171-615-3331**
ADR **NP** SEDOL No. **632016**
CEO **Keith Henry** Chairman **John Baker**

NatWest

Industry: **Banks - Money Center**

NatWest Group, one of the largest of London's clearing banks, operates in the United Kingdom and 27 other countries. The bank's NatWest Markets subsidiary provides corporate and investment banking throughout Europe. Other operations include a wide range of mortgage- and investment-banking activities. The bank has several subsidiaries, including Ulster Bank in Northern Ireland. NatWest recently announced the sale of Bancorp, its U.S. retail-banking arm. More than half of group income is generated domestically.

£ mil	12/92	12/93	12/94	US$mil 12/94				
Revenues	**15,203.0**	**13,437.0**	**12,121.0**	**18,647.7**	P/E Ratio	**10.0**	Price (9/30/95)	**6.32**
Net Income	**210.0**	**617.0**	**1,093.0**	**1,681.5**	P/B Ratio	**1.7**	52 Wk Hi-Low	**6.51-4.58**
Book Value	**5,540.0**	**5,726.0**	**6,421.0**	**10,032.8**	Yield %	**3.4**	Market Cap	**US$17,437mil**

Address **41 Lothbury** **London EC2P 2BP**
Tel **0171-726-1000** Fax **0171-726-1035**
ADR **NW** SEDOL No. **625395**
CEO **Derek Wanless** Chairman **Lord Alexander**

Next

Industry: **Other Specialty Retailers**

Next retails its own branded goods through approximately 300 stores in the United Kingdom and through mail-order catalogs. Next Retailing offers family apparel, home-interior goods, accessories, and fashion jewelry. Next Directory offers similar products through a home-shopping catalog. Next operates four stores in both the United States and the Middle East and plans to open two stores in France in 1995. Its Club 24 subsidiary provides financial and management services. In 1994, Next acquired consumer-credit business Clydesdale, which it integrated into Club 24.

£ mil	01/93	01/94	01/95	US$mil 01/95				
Revenues	**485.0**	**544.0**	**652.9**	**1,009.1**	P/E Ratio	**18.6**	Price (9/30/95)	**4.06**
Net Income	**37.0**	**64.0**	**81.3**	**125.7**	P/B Ratio	**5.2**	52 Wk Hi-Low	**4.15-2.32**
Book Value	**199.0**	**243.0**	**291.5**	**462.7**	Yield %	**2.2**	Market Cap	**US$2,411.3mil**

Address **Desford Rd., Enderby** **Leicester LE9 5AT**
Tel **01533-866411** Fax **01533-848998**
ADR SEDOL No. **421861**
CEO **David Jones** Chairman **Lord Wolfson**

NFC

Industry: **Trucking**

NFC offers moving, transport, logistics, and storage services in Europe, North America, and the Far East. Its subsidiaries include National Carriers, a European delivery and logistics service; North American Allied Van Lines removal and storage services; and Exel Logistics, a warehousing and transport service for the food, media, and apparel industries. NFC's customers in Europe include Burger King, Pizza Hut, Kraft, Marks & Spencer, and J Sainsbury. Exports represent roughly half of NFC's revenues, and 40% of all sales are made outside Europe.

	£ mil 10/92	10/93	10/94	US$mil 10/94				
Sales	**1,724.0**	**1,892.0**	**2,034.9**	**3,106.7**	P/E Ratio	**13.3**	Price (9/30/95)	**1.49**
Net Income	**78.0**	**88.0**	**73.4**	**112.1**	P/B Ratio	**1.8**	52 Wk Hi-Low	**1.85-1.43**
Book Value	**332.0**	**313.0**	**582.7**	**955.2**	Yield %	**4.8**	Market Cap	**US$1,636.0mil**

Address **66 Chiltern St.**	Tel **0171-317-0123**	ADR **NFC**	President	--
London W1M 1PR	Fax **0171-224-2385**	SEDOL No. **618715**	Chairman	**Sir Christopher Bland**

North West Water

Industry: **Water Utilities**

North West Water Group operates water- and wastewater-treatment facilities worldwide. Its services include solids extraction, disinfection, and water- and wastewater-process engineering. The company provides drinking water to 7 million people in northwest England. The company's wholly-owned subsidiary, Wallace & Tiernan, designs and manufactures water- and wastewater-treatment equipment. As part of its international expansion policy, the company has embarked upon a partnership with Bechtel, one of the world's largest construction companies.

	£ mil 03/93	03/94	03/95	US$mil 03/95				
Sales	**878.0**	**924.0**	**1,011.8**	**1,585.9**	P/E Ratio	**8.5**	Price (9/30/95)	**5.90**
Net Income	**222.0**	**260.0**	**259.2**	**406.3**	P/B Ratio	**1.0**	52 Wk Hi-Low	**6.58-4.85**
Book Value	**1,834.0**	**2,051.0**	**2,246.4**	**3,682.6**	Yield %	**4.3**	Market Cap	**US$3,512.4mil**

Address **Dawson Hse., Great Sankey**	Tel **01925-234000**	ADR	CEO	**Brian Staples**
Warrington, Cheshire WA5 3LW	Fax **01925-233361**	SEDOL No. **646233**	Chairman	**Sir Desmond Pitcher**

Northern Foods

Industry: **Other Food**

Northern Foods is a fresh-food manufacturer specializing in dairy products and prepared foods. The company is Britain's largest supplier of liquid milk to households and shops. It also produces Eden Vale cottage cheese and Ski yogurt. Other products include Pork Farms, Bowyers, and Holland's meat products; Fox's and Elkes cookies; and Falconis and Kara Foods breads. It also makes foods for the Marks and Spencer (St. Michael), J. Sainsbury, and Tesco brands. In June 1995, the company acquired control of Irish frozen food manufacturer Green Isle Food Group Limited.

	£ mil 03/93	03/94	03/95	US$mil 03/95				
Sales	**2,026.0**	**2,049.0**	**1,971.3**	**3,089.8**	P/E Ratio	**NMF**	Price (9/30/95)	**1.83**
Net Income	**114.0**	**117.0**	**0.6**	**0.9**	P/B Ratio	**3.3**	52 Wk Hi-Low	**2.20-1.79**
Book Value	**321.0**	**370.0**	**321.3**	**526.7**	Yield %	**4.8**	Market Cap	**US$1,672.4mil**

Address **Beverley Hse., St. Stephen's Sq.**	Tel **01482-25432**	ADR	President	--
Hull, E. Yorkshire HU1 3XG	Fax **01482-226136**	SEDOL No. **646608**	Chairman	**Christopher R. Haskins**

Ocean

Industry: **Marine Transportation**

Ocean Group provides international freight management, distribution, environmental services, and support to the offshore oil industry. Its wholly-owned subsidiaries include MSAS Cargo, an international air-freight forwarder; McGregor Cory, a supplier of contract-distribution services in the United Kingdom and Europe; Cory Environmental, which provides refuse collection, transport and disposal services; OIL, a supplier of support vessels to the offshore oil industry; and National Environmental Testing, a leading United States environmental testing service.

	£ mil 12/92	12/93	12/94	US$mil 12/94				
Sales	**1,394.0**	**953.0**	**1,026.1**	**1,578.6**	P/E Ratio	**69.6**	Price (9/30/95)	**3.55**
Net Income	**3.0**	**31.0**	**7.8**	**12.0**	P/B Ratio	**2.6**	52 Wk Hi-Low	**3.72-2.45**
Book Value	**238.0**	**245.0**	**209.5**	**327.3**	Yield %	**4.0**	Market Cap	**US$869.4mil**

Address **Ocean Hse., The Ring**	Tel **01344-302000**	ADR	CEO	**John Allan**
Bracknell, Berkshire RG12 1AN	Fax **01344-710031**	SEDOL No. **655422**	Chairman	**Peter I. Marshall**

P & O

Industry: **Marine Transportation**

The Peninsular and Oriental Steam Navigation Company (P&O) operates passenger-cruise, ferry, and marine-cargo lines and also has construction and property interests. Cruise and ferry services, including the wholly-owned U.S. subsidiary Princess Cruises, generate almost 50% of the company's income. The company's U.K. subsidiaries, P&O Containers and P&O Bulk Shipping, control most of the U.K. cargo market. P&O operates in the United Kingdom, the United States, China, and Australia. Exports account for 66% of revenues. Half of all sales are made outside Europe.

	£ mil 12/92	12/93	12/94	US$mil 12/94				
Sales	**5,044.4**	**5,586.8**	**5,989.6**	**9,214.8**	P/E Ratio	**12.4**	Price (9/30/95)	**4.78**
Net Income	**191.9**	**403.3**	**238.7**	**367.2**	P/B Ratio	**1.1**	52 Wk Hi-Low	**6.43-4.78**
Book Value	**2,254.8**	**2,677.1**	**2,653.9**	**4,146.7**	Yield %	**6.4**	Market Cap	**US$4,581.8mil**

Address **79 Pall Mall**	Tel **0171-930-4343**	ADR **POSNY**	Managing Director	**Sir Bruce MacPhail**
London SW1Y 5EJ	Fax **0171-930-8572**	SEDOL No. **680048**	Chairman	**Lord Sterling**

Pearson

Industry: **Publishing**

Pearson publishes books and periodicals, manages tourist attractions, and produces television programs. Its book-publishing interests include Penguin Books and Longmans. The company also publishes the Financial Times and has a 50% stake in The Economist. Its television interests include Thames Television, producers and distributors of programs, and a 14% stake in BSkyB. It owns Alton Towers theme park, and Madame Tussaud's wax museum. In 1994 the company purchased Mindscape, a U.S. software publisher, and Future Publishing, a publisher of consumer magazines.

	£ mil 12/92	12/93	12/94	US$mil 12/94				
Sales	**1,636.0**	**1,320.0**	**1,550.1**	**2,384.8**	P/E Ratio	**14.6**	Price (9/30/95)	**5.89**
Net Income	**105.0**	**148.0**	**222.9**	**342.9**	P/B Ratio	**3.1**	52 Wk Hi-Low	**6.57-5.43**
Book Value	**1,068.0**	**997.0**	**1,036.1**	**1,618.9**	Yield %	**2.5**	Market Cap	**US$5,176.2mil**

Address **3 Burlington Gardens**	Tel **0171-411-2000**	ADR	Managing Director	**Frank Barlow**
London W1X 1LE	Fax **0171-411-2390**	SEDOL No. **677608**	Chairman	**Michael Blakenham**

Pentland

Industry: **Footwear**

Pentland Group is a holding company with interests in footwear, athletic clothing, stationery, and home-appliances. Its Speedo, Ellesse, and Pony subsidiaries specialize in swimwear, ski and tennis clothing, and sports clothing, respectively. Holmes, a U.S. subsidiary, manufactures small electrical appliances such as air purifiers. The company's Hanson White subsidiary produces stationery and greeting cards. Its EMS Publications subsidiary produces Christmas cards. In 1994, Pentland acquired Reusch, a German manufacturer of skiing and goalkeeping gloves.

	£ mil 12/92	12/93	12/94	US$mil 12/94				
Sales	**327.0**	**470.0**	**632.5**	**973.1**	P/E Ratio	**18.5**	Price (9/30/95)	**1.22**
Net Income	**57.0**	**10.0**	**23.7**	**36.5**	P/B Ratio	**1.5**	52 Wk Hi-Low	**1.46-0.94**
Book Value	**403.0**	**310.0**	**294.0**	**459.4**	Yield %	**2.5**	Market Cap	**US$699.5mil**

Address **Lakeside, Squires Ln.**	Tel **0181-346-2600**	ADR	President	**--**
Finchley, London N3 2QL	Fax **0181-346-2700**	SEDOL No. **94553**	Chairman	**R. Stephen Rubin**

Persimmon

Industry: **Home Construction**

Persimmon is a residential developer and homebuilder in England and Scotland. The company builds a broad range of residences, including small townhouses, apartments, and larger detached houses. It is also involved in the housing sector, completing 421 homes for Housing Associations last year. The average selling price of its homes is £65,159. Persimmon currently owns about 17,000 building plots with planning permission. A further 1,900 acres without planning permission are either owned or under option. The company sold more than 3,000 residences in 1994.

	£ mil 12/92	12/93	12/94	US$mil 12/94				
Sales	**144.0**	**169.0**	**206.2**	**317.3**	P/E Ratio	**10.6**	Price (9/30/95)	**1.67**
Net Income	**7.0**	**13.0**	**17.6**	**27.1**	P/B Ratio	**1.0**	52 Wk Hi-Low	**2.36-1.64**
Book Value	**129.0**	**145.0**	**197.6**	**308.7**	Yield %	**5.7**	Market Cap	**US$309.7mil**

Address **Persimmon Hse.**	Tel **01904-642199**	ADR	CEO	**John White**
Fulford, York YO1 4RE	Fax **01904-610014**	SEDOL No. **682538**	Chairman	**Duncan H. Davidson**

Photo-Me

Industry: **Other Recreational Products & Services**

Photo-Me International is the world's largest manufacturer and operator of coin-operated photographic booths. The company's Automatic Photo Studios are found in more than 100 countries. Its PMI Express Systems division operates a service that enables clients to obtain business cards in several minutes. The company also produces a wide range of photo-identity cards through its PMI Identification Systems division. In 1994, Photo-Me acquired KIS, a French company specializing in technology that freezes video images into high-quality still photographs.

	£ mil 04/92	04/93	04/94	US$mil 04/94				
Sales	**115.0**	**134.0**	**172.4**	**258.8**	P/E Ratio	**16.9**	Price (9/30/95)	**1.74**
Net Income	**11.0**	**10.0**	**7.4**	**11.0**	P/B Ratio	**1.4**	52 Wk Hi-Low	**2.63-1.74**
Book Value	**49.0**	**58.0**	**74.0**	**112.1**	Yield %	**2.8**	Market Cap	**US$167.6mil**

Address **Church Rd.**	Tel **01372-453399**	ADR	Managing Director	**David W. Miller**
Bookham, Surrey KT23 3EU	Fax **01372-459064**	SEDOL No. **687179**	Chairman	**Daniel David**

Pilkington

Industry: **Building Materials**

Pilkington manufactures glass and plastic products used in the building, transport, ophthalmic, and electronics industries. More than 50% of its revenue comes from building products such as energy- efficient glass for residential, commercial, and industrial buildings. It also produces windshields for General Motors, Nissan, and Volvo cars and cockpit windows for McDonnell Douglas. Pilkington manufactures contact lenses, glass for liquid-crystal displays, optic fibers, and insulation materials. Approximately 85% of the company's business is outside the United Kingdom.

	£ mil 03/93	03/94	03/95	US$mil 03/95				
Sales	**2,301.0**	**2,515.0**	**2,663.0**	**4,174.0**	P/E Ratio	**NMF**	Price (9/30/95)	**1.99**
Net Income	**-20.0**	**40.0**	**-323.0**	**-506.3**	P/B Ratio	**1.9**	52 Wk Hi-Low	**2.16-1.43**
Book Value	**908.0**	**880.0**	**826.0**	**1,354.1**	Yield %	**2.1**	Market Cap	**US$2,523.2mil**

Address **Prescot Rd.**	Tel **01744-692448**	ADR	CEO	**Roger F. Leverton**
St. Helens WA10 3TT	Fax **01744-613329**	SEDOL No. **688462**	Chairman	**Sir Antony Pilkington**

PowerGen

Industry: **Electrical Utilities - All**

PowerGen generates electricity in the United Kingdom. The company accounts for 28% of the total electricity-generation market in England and Wales. The U.K.'s regional electricity companies are the firm's principal customers. The company is involved in joint ventures in eastern Germany, Portugal, and East Java. Kinetica, a joint venture between PowerGen and Conoco, supplies gas to more than 15,000 customers. The British government sold its shares in PowerGen in March 1995.

£ mil	04/93	04/94	04/95	US$mil 04/95				
Sales	3,188.0	2,932.0	2,885.0	4,536.2	P/E Ratio	11.3	Price (9/30/95)	5.59
Net Income	285.0	345.0	388.0	610.1	P/B Ratio	2.2	52 Wk Hi-Low	6.07-4.63
Book Value	1,670.0	1,919.0	1,880.0	3,032.3	Yield %	2.7	Market Cap	US$6,435.3mil

Address **53 New Broad St.** **London EC2M 1JJ** Tel **0171-826-2826** Fax **0171-826-2890** ADR **PWG** SEDOL No. **697822** CEO **Edmund A. Wallis** Chairman **Sir Colin Southgate**

Provident Financial

Industry: **Financial Services - Diversified**

Provident Financial is a personal financial-services company that specializes in credit and insurance. Its wholly-owned subsidiaries, Provident Personal Credit and H.T. Greenwood, lend money to approximately 1.1 million people, many of them in low-income groups. The company owns the car insurer Provident Insurance, which has more than 800,000 policyholders. It also owns the insurance retailer Colonnade Insurance Brokers, which operates in both the high street and through a 24 hour telephone brokerage service.

£ mil	12/92	12/93	12/94	US$mil 12/94				
Revenues	371.0	400.0	445.3	685.0	P/E Ratio	18.8	Price (9/30/95)	7.64
Net Income	29.0	42.0	54.4	83.6	P/B Ratio	5.1	52 Wk Hi-Low	7.70-4.95
Book Value	154.0	176.0	200.2	312.9	Yield %	2.7	Market Cap	US$1,633.5mil

Address **Colonnade, Sunbridge Rd.** **Bradford BD1 2LQ** Tel **01274-731111** Fax **01274-727300** ADR SEDOL No. **701433** CEO **John van Kuffeler** Chairman **Antony Warde-Norbury**

Prudential

Industry: **Insurance - Life & Health**

Prudential is the United Kingdom's largest life-insurance provider by market capitalization, serving more than 8 million customers worldwide. Prudential provides life and reinsurance services through its Mercantile & General subsidiary. Prudential also has interests in the investment-management and retail-investment industries. Jackson National Life, the firm's largest U.S. subsidiary, mainly sells fixed-rate annuities and life products. Prudential generates more than 47% of the company's premium income overseas, mainly in the United States.

£ mil	12/92	12/93	12/94	US$mil 12/94				
Revenues	13,151.0	14,427.0	12,048.0	18,535.4	P/E Ratio	17.7	Price (9/30/95)	3.78
Net Income	282.0	396.0	406.0	624.6	P/B Ratio	9.8	52 Wk Hi-Low	3.82-2.90
Book Value	504.0	788.0	733.0	1,145.3	Yield %	3.8	Market Cap	US$11,408mil

Address **142 Holborn Bars** **London EC1N 2NH** Tel **0171-405-9222** Fax **0171-548-3725** ADR **PPLCY** SEDOL No. **709954** CEO **Peter Davis** Chairman **Sir Brian Corby**

PSIT

Industry: **Real-Estate Investment**

PSIT (formerly Property Security Investment Trust) invests in and deals property and other securities. Rental income from its more than four million feet of retail, corporate, and industrial investment properties contributes approximately 99% of its revenues. Its properties in the United Kingdom generate 79% of its profits, Australian properties generate 11%, and the remaining properties in Belgium, Germany, the Netherlands, and the U.S. generate 10%. Management focuses on buying properties that generate current income but also provide scope for further development.

£ mil	03/92	03/93	03/94	US$mil 03/94				
Sales	18.0	20.0	21.0	31.6	P/E Ratio	27.6	Price (9/30/95)	1.38
Net Income	6.0	7.0	9.0	13.6	P/B Ratio	0.9	52 Wk Hi-Low	1.51-1.26
Book Value	161.0	163.0	197.0	294.0	Yield %	3.6	Market Cap	US$266.7mil

Address **Fetcham Park Hse., Lower Rd.** **Fetcham, Surrey KT22 9HD** Tel **01372-376155** Fax **01372-362338** ADR SEDOL No. **705349** CEO **Geoffrey H. Caines** Chairman **Albert R. Perry**

Raine

Industry: **Home Construction**

Raine Industries is a construction company that engages in residential and commercial building and contracting activities. In 1994, the company's wholly-owned Hassall Homes subsidiary sold approximately 2,000 homes in the United Kingdom. The average selling price of these homes was £70,220. Raine's Hall & Tawse Group subsidiary builds homes for housing authorities and also serves as the company's main contractor. Its Plumb Group subsidiary, with operations in the U.K. and Germany, finishes interiors for retailers, leisure and commercial centers, and hotels.

£ mil	06/92	06/93	06/94	US$mil 06/94				
Sales	364.0	446.0	456.5	684.3	P/E Ratio	4.9	Price (9/30/95)	0.23
Net Income	5.0	8.0	8.8	13.1	P/B Ratio	0.4	52 Wk Hi-Low	0.65-0.20
Book Value	118.0	118.0	120.3	185.1	Yield %	13.0	Market Cap	US$68.7mil

Address **Raine Hse., Ashbourne Rd.** **Derby DE22 4NB** Tel **01332-824000** Fax **01332-824824** ADR SEDOL No. **720728** Managing Director **David S. Vincent** Chairman **Peter W. Parkin**

Rank Organisation

Industry: **Other Recreational Products & Services**

Rank Organisation supplies products and services to the film and television industries, and owns holiday-package businesses, resorts, casinos, and nightclubs. It owns a 50% stake in the Universal Studios theme park in Florida and a 29% interest in Rank Xerox, a joint venture that makes document-processing systems. The company processes film and duplicates video for major film studios, operates 300 Odeon theaters in the United Kingdom, and owns and franchises a number of Hard Rock Cafe restaurants in the United States. Overseas sales generates about 33% of all revenues.

£ mil	10/92	10/93	10/94	US$mil 10/94				
Sales	**2,096.0**	**2,106.8**	**2,169.1**	**3,311.6**	P/E Ratio	**23.7**	Price (9/30/95)	**4.25**
Net Income	**135.5**	**168.2**	**168.1**	**256.6**	P/B Ratio	**2.3**	52 Wk Hi-Low	**4.61-3.63**
Book Value	**1,382.7**	**1,485.7**	**1,558.8**	**2,555.4**	Yield %	**3.1**	Market Cap	**US$5,601.8mil**

Address **6 Connaught Pl.** **London W2 2EZ**
Tel **0171-706-1111** Fax **0171-262-9886**
ADR **RANKY** SEDOL No. **724593**
Mng Dir & CEO **Michael B. Gifford**
Chairman **Sir Denys Henderson**

Reckitt & Colman

Industry: **Household Products (Non-Durable)**

Reckitt & Colman manufactures household consumer products, personal-care products, and food and beverages. Its brands include Harpic, Dettol and Lemsip. Household and toiletry products constitute its major market, representing almost 70% of sales. In 1994, the company purchased L&F Household, which sells the Lysol brand and other products. In the same year the company sold off Colman's of Norwich food business to Unilever. The company is selling off non-core business lines to focus on household products.

£ mil	01/93	01/94	12/94	US$mil 12/94				
Sales	**1,854.0**	**2,096.0**	**2,070.8**	**3,185.8**	P/E Ratio	**30.8**	Price (9/30/95)	**6.57**
Net Income	**94.0**	**169.0**	**82.1**	**126.2**	P/B Ratio	**3.6**	52 Wk Hi-Low	**7.12-5.29**
Book Value	**618.0**	**704.0**	**686.2**	**1,072.2**	Yield %	**2.8**	Market Cap	**US$4,413.3mil**

Address **One Burlington Ln.** **London W4 2RW**
Tel **0181-994-6464** Fax **0181-994-8920**
ADR SEDOL No. **727699**
CEO **Vernon L. Sankey**
Chairman **Michael J. Colman**

Redland

Industry: **Building Materials**

Redland is a producer of construction materials, and has manufacturing operations in 35 countries. The company's main products are roof tiles, clay bricks, and construction aggregates. Roofing products account for 70% of Redland's operating profits. Its U.S. subsidiaries Western Mobile, which surfaces roads and makes ready-mix concrete, and roof-tile manufacturer Monier. Redland also has operations in the United Kingdom, continental Europe, and the Far East. Exports account for 80% of sales. Continental Europe and North America are the company's primary markets for exports.

£ mil	12/92	12/93	12/94	US$mil 12/94				
Sales	**2,090.0**	**2,216.0**	**2,468.8**	**3,798.2**	P/E Ratio	**11.5**	Price (9/30/95)	**3.79**
Net Income	**83.0**	**129.0**	**170.4**	**262.2**	P/B Ratio	**1.3**	52 Wk Hi-Low	**4.94-3.64**
Book Value	**1,408.0**	**1,457.0**	**1,519.5**	**2,374.2**	Yield %	**5.1**	Market Cap	**US$3,117.4mil**

Address **Redland Hse.** **Reigate, Surrey RH2 0SJ**
Tel **01737-242488** Fax **01737-221938**
ADR **REDPY** SEDOL No. **728700**
CEO **Robert S. Napier**
Chairman **Sir Colin Corness**

Reed International

Industry: **Publishing**

Reed International is a holding company that derives the majority of its income from its 50% stake in publishing and information firm Reed Elsevier. Reed Elsevier provides electronic information services and publishes newspapers, magazines, and scientific, medical, professional, business, and consumer books. Reed International also has a significant stake in financial-services company Elsevier Reed Finance. Reed Elsevier owns U.S.-based Lexis-Nexis (formerly Mead Data Central), the largest provider of legal, business, and news online information services.

£ mil	12/92 *P	12/93 P	12/94 P	US$mil 12/94				
Sales	**1,196.6**	**282.0**	**328.0**	**504.6**	P/E Ratio	**21.7**	Price (9/30/95)	**9.55**
Net Income	**73.7**	**197.0**	**233.5**	**359.2**	P/B Ratio	**7.2**	52 Wk Hi-Low	**10.15-7.14**
Book Value	**1,430.3**	**907.0**	**750.7**	**1,173.0**	Yield %	**2.3**	Market Cap	**US$8,543.1mil**

Address **6 Chesterfield Gardens** **London W1A 1EJ**
Tel **0171-499-4020** Fax **0171-491-8212**
ADR **RUK** SEDOL No. **730879**
President **--**
Chairman **Ian Irvine**

*Irregular period due to fiscal year change; P=Parent company data.

Rentokil

Industry: **Pollution Control, Waste Management**

Rentokil is an environmental and property-services group that provides environmental, security, personnel, express-delivery, medical, and health-care services. It also provides indoor decorative plants and trees to businesses, hotels, and shopping centers; pest-control services; water and ventilation services; and manufactures timber-preservation products. Its wholly-owned Securiguard subsidiary provides security and janitorial services in the United Kingdom. Overseas sales represent 55% of revenues, and one third of all sales come from outside Europe.

£ mil	12/92	12/93	12/94	US$mil 12/94				
Sales	**466.0**	**588.0**	**734.6**	**1,130.2**	P/E Ratio	**27.4**	Price (9/30/95)	**3.20**
Net Income	**70.0**	**94.0**	**114.6**	**176.3**	P/B Ratio	**18.0**	52 Wk Hi-Low	**3.21-2.13**
Book Value	**144.0**	**108.0**	**174.5**	**272.7**	Yield %	**1.1**	Market Cap	**US$4,972.4mil**

Address **Felcourt** **East Grinstead RH19 2JY**
Tel **01342-833022** Fax **01342-326229**
ADR **RTOKY** SEDOL No. **733038**
CEO **Clive M. Thompson**
Chairman **H. E. St L King**

Reuters

Industry: **Publishing**

Reuters provides real-time financial data, news, historical databases, and information-management systems to businesses and the news media. Financial news and information sales account for 70% of its revenues. It offers electronic brokerage services such as Instinet for equities, Globex for futures and options, and Dealing 2000-1 for foreign exchange. It provides U.S.-based Fox Broadcasting and U.K.-based Sky News with news programming. Reuters' U.S. subsidiaries include Teknekron Software Systems and Quotron Systems. Exports account for nearly 84% of revenues.

	£ mil 12/92	12/93	12/94	US$mil 12/94				
Sales	**1,568.0**	**1,874.0**	**2,309.0**	**3,552.3**	P/E Ratio	**25.8**	Price (9/30/95)	**5.59**
Net Income	**236.0**	**299.0**	**347.0**	**533.8**	P/B Ratio	**13.0**	52 Wk Hi-Low	**5.94-4.08**
Book Value	**951.0**	**739.0**	**715.0**	**1,117.2**	Yield %	**1.4**	Market Cap	**US$14,815mil**

Address **85 Fleet St.**
London EC4P 4AJ
Tel **0171-250-1122**
Fax **0171-324-5874**
ADR **RTRSY**
SEDOL No. **733812**
Mng Dir & CEO **Peter Job**
Chairman **Sir Christopher Hogg**

Rexam

Industry: **Paper Products**

Rexam (formerly Bowater) is a print and packaging firm that operates in Europe, Australasia, North America, and South America. It makes corrugated packaging, plastic and paper bags, beverage cartons, and plastic containers. Rexam makes packaging for Johnnie Walker Scotch, Elida Gibbs Vaseline petroleum jelly, and Guerlain cosmetics. The firm's BroadPrint and Causton Envelopes subsidiaries print direct-mail products. North America and Australasia generate more than 45% of Rexam's sales and the remaining sales are made in Europe and the United Kingdom.

	£ mil 12/92	12/93	12/94	US$mil 12/94				
Sales	**1,568.0**	**2,113.0**	**2,210.0**	**3,400.0**	P/E Ratio	**13.2**	Price (9/30/95)	**4.04**
Net Income	**106.0**	**142.0**	**161.0**	**247.7**	P/B Ratio	**3.1**	52 Wk Hi-Low	**5.17-3.88**
Book Value	**470.0**	**642.0**	**655.0**	**1,023.4**	Yield %	**3.4**	Market Cap	**US$3,234.2mil**

Address **Bowater Hse., Knightsbridge**
London SW1X 7NN
Tel **0171-584-7070**
Fax **0171-581-1149**
ADR **REXMY**
SEDOL No. **115971**
Mng Dir & CEO **David Lyon**
Chairman **Michael Woodhouse**

RMC Group

Industry: **Building Materials**

RMC Group manufactures construction materials and operates home-improvement stores and builders' merchants. It produces ready-mix concrete, aggregates, cement, lime, and concrete products. The company also operates more than 90 Great Mills home-improvement stores in the United Kingdom. RMC's wholly-owned subsidiary Hales Waste Control disposes of construction, industrial, and trade waste. RMC has operations throughout western Europe, the United States, Hungary, the Czech Republic, and Israel. In 1994, over 50% of its operating revenue was generated in Germany.

	£ mil 12/92	12/93	12/94	US$mil 12/94				
Sales	**3,140.0**	**3,123.0**	**3,678.0**	**5,658.5**	P/E Ratio	**19.8**	Price (9/30/95)	**10.86**
Net Income	**61.0**	**77.0**	**135.1**	**207.8**	P/B Ratio	**3.0**	52 Wk Hi-Low	**11.79-8.75**
Book Value	**761.0**	**781.0**	**896.5**	**1,400.8**	Yield %	**1.7**	Market Cap	**US$4,261.8mil**

Address **RMC Hse., Coldharbour Ln.**
Egham, Surrey TW20 8TD
Tel **01932-568833**
Fax **01932-568933**
ADR
SEDOL No. **726641**
Managing Director **Peter L. Young**
Chairman **James Owen**

Rolls-Royce

Industry: **Aerospace & Defense**

Rolls-Royce is an engineering company that provides products and services to the aerospace, defense, and industrial-power-systems industries. Its Aerospace Group specializes in gas turbines for aircraft. Its industrial power group produces transmission, power-generation, and distribution systems and equipment for the marine-propulsion, oil, natural gas, offshore, and defense markets. It owns U.S.-based Allison Engine, a supplier of military transport and small helicopter engines. Exports generate about 75% of sales and more than 63% of sales are made outside Europe.

	£ mil 12/92	12/93	12/94	US$mil 12/94				
Sales	**3,562.0**	**3,518.0**	**3,163.0**	**4,866.2**	P/E Ratio	**31.1**	Price (9/30/95)	**1.74**
Net Income	**-202.0**	**63.0**	**81.0**	**124.6**	P/B Ratio	**2.0**	52 Wk Hi-Low	**1.94-1.48**
Book Value	**899.0**	**1,225.0**	**1,242.0**	**1,940.6**	Yield %	**2.4**	Market Cap	**US$4,018.6mil**

Address **65 Buckingham Gate**
London SW1E 6AT
Tel **0171-222-9020**
Fax **0171-233-1733**
ADR **RYCEY**
SEDOL No. **747761**
CEO **Dr. Terence Harrison**
Chairman **Sir Ralph Robins**

Royal Bank of Scotland

Industry: **Banks - Regional**

The Royal Bank of Scotland Group offers retail and corporate banking and insurance. In addition, the bank provides financial services such as treasury, capital markets, and securities investments. It also provides services to U.K. banking businesses such as real-estate, personnel and training, and money-transmission services, as well as business consultancy. The bank's Direct Line Insurance subsidiary controls more than 10% of its market. Royal Bank's Citizen Financial Services subsidiary operates bank branches in the United States.

	£ mil 09/92	09/93	09/94	US$mil 09/94				
Revenues	**N/A**	**N/A**	**3,045.0**	**4,613.6**	P/E Ratio	**10.9**	Price (9/30/95)	**4.50**
Net Income	**31.0**	**182.0**	**383.0**	**580.3**	P/B Ratio	**0.1**	52 Wk Hi-Low	**4.71-3.78**
Book Value	**1,780.0**	**1,897.0**	**45,320.0**	**71,936.5**	Yield %	**3.1**	Market Cap	**US$5,730.2mil**

Address **42 St. Andrew Sq.**
Edinburgh EH2 2YE
Tel **0131-556-8555**
Fax **0131-557-6140**
ADR
SEDOL No. **754783**
CEO **George R. Mathewson**
Chairman **Lord Younger**

Royal Insurance

Industry: **Insurance - Full Line**

Royal Insurance is one of the two principal subsidiaries of Royal Insurance Holdings. The company provides general and life insurance and reinsurance. It offers a range of insurance types, including motor, household, property, marine, fire, and liability insurance. Royal Insurance Global issues policies and manages claims in approximately 90 countries. The company operates real-estate agencies through Royal Insurance Property Services and investment services through Royal Insurance Asset Management.

	£ mil 12/92	12/93	12/94	US$mil 12/94				
Revenues	6,131.0	6,884.0	5,009.0	7,706.2	P/E Ratio	6.7	Price (9/30/95)	3.53
Net Income	9.0	137.0	342.0	526.2	P/B Ratio	1.2	52 Wk Hi-Low	3.72-2.53
Book Value	1,462.0	2,177.0	1,877.0	2,932.8	Yield %	3.4	Market Cap	US$3,660.2mil

Address **1 Cornhill**	Tel **0171-283-4300**	ADR		CEO	**Richard A. Gamble**
London EC3V 3QR	Fax **0171-623-5282**	SEDOL No.	**755214**	Chairman	**Allan G. Gormly**

RTZ

Industry: **Mining**

RTZ, the world's largest mining group, explores for and processes natural resources and precious metals. The firm's coal operations include CRA, the 49%-owned holding company for RTZ's mining operations in Asia and Australia; and U.S. coal-mining companies Nerco, Cordero Mining, and Powder River Basin. RTZ's precious-metals mining operations include U.S.-based subsidiaries Kennecott and Flambeau Gold. RTZ plans to buy an stake in U.S.-based Freeport McMoRan. Overseas sales make up 92% of total revenues; three fourths of sales come from outside Europe.

	£ mil 12/92	12/93	12/94	US$mil 12/94				
Sales	3,012.0	2,022.0	2,288.0	3,520.0	P/E Ratio	16.1	Price (9/30/95)	9.27
Net Income	249.0	287.0	612.0	941.5	P/B Ratio	2.9	52 Wk Hi-Low	9.29-7.21
Book Value	2,899.0	3,190.0	3,448.0	5,387.5	Yield %	3.0	Market Cap	US$15,706mil

Address **6 St. James's Sq.**	Tel **0171-930-2399**	ADR	**RTZ**	CEO	**Robert P. Wilson**
London SW1Y 4LD	Fax **0171-930-3249**	SEDOL No.	**718875**	Chairman	**Sir Derek Birkin**

Rugby

Industry: **Building Materials**

Rugby Group manufactures building materials throughout Europe, Australia, and the United States. The company is divided into three divisions. Its joinery division produces doors, windows, and related products. The company's cement-and-lime division manufactures cement-based products. The company's Australia-based Cockburn Cement subsidiary also produces quicklime for use in the aluminum, gold, and other resource-based industries. Rugby Group's metal-products division manufactures steel products for use in construction.

	£ mil 12/92	12/93	12/94	US$mil 12/94				
Sales	650.0	735.0	1,010.6	1,554.8	P/E Ratio	13.0	Price (9/30/95)	1.05
Net Income	38.0	43.0	49.6	76.3	P/B Ratio	1.7	52 Wk Hi-Low	1.27-1.02
Book Value	302.0	322.0	398.7	623.0	Yield %	3.4	Market Cap	US$1,061.2mil

Address **Crown Hse.**	Tel **01788-542666**	ADR		Managing Director	**Peter J. Carr**
Rugby, Warwickshire CV21 2DT	Fax **01788-540256**	SEDOL No.	**758707**	Chairman	**Geoffrey A. Higham**

J. Sainsbury

Industry: **Food Retailers & Wholesalers**

J. Sainsbury, the United Kingdom's largest supermarket retailer by market capitalization, operates about 460 Sainsbury's grocery stores in the U.K., holding close to 11% of that market. Its subsidiary stores include Savacentre Department Store and Homebase, both in the U.K., and Shaw's Supermarkets in the United States. Sainsbury also has a partial interest in Giant, a U.S. food retailer that has 159 stores. Its U.S. operations generate nearly 10% of group revenues. Sainsbury recently announced the acquisition of more than 200 Texas Homecare stores from Ladbroke Group.

	£ mil 03/93	03/94	03/95	US$mil 03/95				
Sales	9,686.0	10,583.0	11,357.0	17,800.9	P/E Ratio	14.6	Price (9/30/95)	4.37
Net Income	503.0	142.0	535.5	839.3	P/B Ratio	2.4	52 Wk Hi-Low	4.77-3.84
Book Value	3,029.0	3,040.0	3,289.0	5,391.8	Yield %	2.7	Market Cap	US$12,528mil

Address **Stamford Hse., Stamford St.**	Tel **0171-921-6000**	ADR	**JSNSY**	Managing Director	**D.A. Quarmby**
London SE1 9LL	Fax **0171-921-6132**	SEDOL No.	**767640**	Chairman	**David J. Sainsbury**

St. James's Place

Industry: **Financial Services - Diversified**

Saint James's Place Capital runs investment- holding, life-insurance, and fund-management businesses. Its wholly-owned J. Rothschild Investment Management subsidiary manages the company's £180 million investment portfolio and third-party funds totaling £330 million. It also provides mergers and acquisitions consulting with the American investment bank James D. Wolfensohn. St. James's Place has formed a joint venture with New York Life (United States) that will purchase small and medium-size life- insurance companies and manage their existing funds.

	£ mil 03/93	03/94	03/95	US$mil 03/95				
Revenues	26.0	49.0	32.9	51.6	P/E Ratio	19.6	Price (9/30/95)	1.12
Net Income	14.0	75.0	15.5	24.3	P/B Ratio	1.3	52 Wk Hi-Low	1.32-1.06
Book Value	291.0	219.0	228.4	374.4	Yield %	2.7	Market Cap	US$487.1mil

Address **27 St. James's Pl.**	Tel **0171-493-8111**	ADR		Co-Chairman	**Sir Mark Weinberg**
London SW1A 1NR	Fax **0171-493-5765**	SEDOL No.	**766959**	Co-Chairman	**Lord Rothschild**

Scapa

Industry: **Industrial - Diversified**

Scapa Group designs, engineers, and manufactures consumable materials for the paper, printing, pharmaceuticals, chemicals, food, oil, and mining industries. The paper industry is its principal market. It manufactures paper-machine clothing, and roll covers and provides roll servicing for the paper industry. It also produces a range of tapes and compounds, filters, industrial textiles, stainless-steel wire, adhesive tape, and computer-printer tapes. The United States is Scapa's largest market, generating more than 44% of its operating profit.

£ mil	03/93	03/94	03/95	US$mil 03/95				
Sales	347.0	392.0	437.3	685.4	P/E Ratio	19.2	Price (9/30/95)	2.34
Net Income	31.0	31.0	28.9	45.3	P/B Ratio	2.3	52 Wk Hi-Low	2.49-1.90
Book Value	228.0	237.0	245.8	403.0	Yield %	2.6	Market Cap	US$882.4mil

Address **Oakfield Hse., 93 Preston New Rd.** Tel **01254-580123** ADR CEO **David M. Dunn**
Blackburn, Lancashire BB2 6AY Fax **01254-51764** SEDOL No. **779098** Chairman **Harry Tuley**

Schroders

Industry: **Securities Brokers**

Schroders is an international merchant-banking, investment-banking, and fund-management company. The company specializes in corporate finance and is involved in about 100 mergers and acquisitions per year. It provides capital markets, project-financing, securities, banking and leasing, treasury and trading, and investment-management services to clients. Schroders manages funds totaling more than £57 billion and is the second-largest UK unit-trust group. The company owns the U.S. investment management and securities firm Wertheim Schroder.

£ mil	12/92	12/93	12/94	US$mil 12/94				
Sales	697.0	753.0	988.8	1,521.2	P/E Ratio	19.8	Price (9/30/95)	13.55
Net Income	64.0	140.0	132.3	203.5	P/B Ratio	3.6	52 Wk Hi-Low	14.78-8.57
Book Value	462.0	675.0	731.3	1,142.7	Yield %	1.0	Market Cap	US$3,240.8mil

Address **120 Cheapside** Tel **0171-382-6000** ADR CEO **Win F.W. Bischoff**
London EC2V 6DS Fax **0171-382-3950** SEDOL No. **779407** Chairman **George W. Mallinckrodt**

Scottish Power

Industry: **Electrical Utilities - All**

Scottish Power supplies electricity to southern and central Scotland. In addition to the company's core electricity-generation, -transmission, and -distribution businesses, Scottish Power provides electrical-contracting services and sells electric appliances. Electricity exports to England, Wales, and Ireland account for more than 10% of its total electricity output. The firm also supplies gas through its CaledonianGas subsidiary. In November 1994, it launched Scottish Telecom, a telecommunications subsidiary.

£ mil	03/93	03/94	03/95	US$mil 03/95				
Sales	1,485.9	1,568.6	1,715.8	2,689.3	P/E Ratio	10.5	Price (9/30/95)	3.52
Net Income	219.5	257.7	274.0	429.5	P/B Ratio	2.6	52 Wk Hi-Low	3.78-3.10
Book Value	799.6	941.8	1,105.9	1,813.0	Yield %	3.9	Market Cap	US$4,564.0mil

Address **1 Atlantic Quay** Tel **0141-248-8200** ADR **SPYAY** CEO **Ian Robinson**
Glasgow G2 8SP Fax **0141-248-8300** SEDOL No. **790828** Chairman **Murray Stuart**

Sears

Industry: **Retailers - Broadline**

Sears operates 3,642 retail stores that sell shoes and clothing. It operates a mail-order business, and owns Selfridges, the United Kingdom's second-largest department store. The company's British Shoe subsidiary is the largest footwear retailer in the U.K., controlling about 34% of the market. Sears' retail-clothing chains include Adams (children's wear), Olympus (sportswear), Miss Selfridge (womenswear), and Wallis (womenswear). Freemans, its home-shopping subsidiary, holds 16% of the U.K. mail-order market. Sears' property division rents space to other retailers.

£ mil	01/93	01/94	01/95	US$mil 01/95				
Revenues	1,935.0	2,008.0	2,143.7	3,313.3	P/E Ratio	14.7	Price (9/30/95)	1.10
Net Income	-70.0	103.0	114.5	177.0	P/B Ratio	1.4	52 Wk Hi-Low	1.19-0.97
Book Value	1,088.0	1,132.0	1,194.4	1,895.9	Yield %	3.6	Market Cap	US$2,647.7mil

Address **40 Duke St.** Tel **0171-408-1180** ADR **SPLCY** CEO **Liam G. Strong**
London W1A 2HP Fax **0171-408-1027** SEDOL No. **787002** Chairman **Geoffrey M. Smith**

Security Services

Industry: **General Industrial & Commercial Services**

Security Services operates security-services, delivery and communications businesses worldwide. Its security-services division, which generates 30% of sales, provides guarding, cash-delivery, alarm-installation, janitorial, prison-management, and airport-security services. The company's parcels division provides mail, overnight and same-day delivery, and executive chauffeur services. Cellnet Group, of which Security Services owns 27%, operates one of the world's largest cellular-communications networks. Securicor owns 51% of Security Services.

£ mil	09/92	09/93	09/94	US$mil 09/94				
Sales	563.0	615.0	772.5	1,170.5	P/E Ratio	28.7	Price (9/30/95)	10.10
Net Income	16.0	29.0	38.6	58.4	P/B Ratio	5.9	52 Wk Hi-Low	10.58-7.15
Book Value	153.0	170.0	188.7	299.6	Yield %	0.6	Market Cap	US$1,757.3mil

Address **15 Carshalton Rd.** Tel **0181-770-7000** ADR CEO **Roger Wiggs**
Sutton, Surrey SM1 4LD Fax **0181-643-1059** SEDOL No. **792727** Chairman **Peter A.C. Smith**

Severn Trent

Industry: **Water Utilities**

Severn Trent provides waste-management services and is the United Kingdom's second-largest water company in terms of its service area. The company designs and implements advanced disinfection systems for water and sewage treatment. It provides water-distribution and waste-management services to about 20 million customers in the U.K., continental Europe, and North America. Severn Trent's wholly-owned Biffa Waste Services subsidiary operates waste-management services in the U.K. and Belgium.

	£ mil 03/93	03/94	03/95	US$mil 03/95				
Sales	**905.0**	**998.0**	**1,076.4**	**1,687.1**	P/E Ratio	**9.5**	Price (9/30/95)	**6.27**
Net Income	**248.0**	**260.0**	**238.0**	**373.0**	P/B Ratio	**1.0**	52 Wk Hi-Low	**6.56-4.81**
Book Value	**1,980.0**	**2,139.0**	**2,290.0**	**3,754.1**	Yield %	**4.6**	Market Cap	**US$3,627.7mil**

Address **2308 Coventry Rd.** Tel **0121-722-6000** ADR CEO **Vic Cocker**
Birmingham B26 3JZ Fax **0121-722-6150** SEDOL No. **798510** Chairman **Richard Ireland**

Shanks & McEwan

Industry: **Pollution Control, Waste Management**

Shanks & McEwan Group is a waste-management and -disposal company that also offers construction services. It operates approximately 40 waste-management sites in the United Kingdom. Its waste-services division manages landfill sites and accounts for 60% of revenues. The company's environmental-services division, led by the firm's wholly-owned Rechem subsidiary, specializes in the high-temperature destruction of hazardous waste. Its technical-services division develops the firm's waste treatment facilities.

	£ mil 03/93	03/94	04/95	US$mil 04/95				
Sales	**131.0**	**120.0**	**139.1**	**218.7**	P/E Ratio	**23.1**	Price (9/30/95)	**0.97**
Net Income	**7.0**	**-9.0**	**7.7**	**12.1**	P/B Ratio	**2.6**	52 Wk Hi-Low	**1.04-0.74**
Book Value	**83.0**	**67.0**	**69.1**	**111.4**	Yield %	**3.4**	Market Cap	**US$283.6mil**

Address **Astor Hse., Station Rd.** Tel **01628-524523** ADR CEO **M.C.E. Averill**
Bourne End, Bucks SL8 5YP Fax **01628-524114** SEDOL No. **799524** Chairman **G.H. Waddell**

Shell Transport & Trading

Industry: **Oil - Integrated Majors**

Shell Transport & Trading holds a 40% interest in the Royal Dutch/Shell Group. The other 60% is held by Royal Dutch Petroleum of the Netherlands. The Royal Dutch/Shell Group comprises companies that explore for, extract, process, and sell oil, natural gas, chemicals, coal, and metals. Royal Dutch/Shell Group produces approximately 2.2 million barrels of crude oil per day, and sells approximately 7.3 billion cubic feet of natural gas per day. It has proven crude-oil reserves of 9 billion barrels. More than half of its sales are made outside Europe.

	£ mil 12/92	12/93	12/94	US$mil 12/94				
Sales	**55,026.0**	**63,350.0**	**61,929.0**	**95,275.4**	P/E Ratio	**16.5**	Price (9/30/95)	**7.44**
Net Income	**3,064.0**	**3,000.0**	**4,070.0**	**6,261.5**	P/B Ratio	**0.7**	52 Wk Hi-Low	**7.83-6.82**
Book Value	**34,113.0**	**34,859.0**	**35,988.0**	**56,231.3**	Yield %	**3.6**	Market Cap	**US$39,143mil**

Address **Shell Ctr.** Tel **0171-934-3856** ADR **SC** Managing Director **Mark Moody-Stuart**
London SE1 7NA Fax **0171-934-8060** SEDOL No. **803414** Chairman **John S. Jennings**

Siebe

Industry: **Industrial - Diversified**

Siebe is one of the United Kingdom's largest diversified engineering groups. The company specializes in the manufacture of electromechanical and electronic controls for the appliance, automotive, and industrial markets. Its other products include compressed-air and pneumatic equipment; transfer and filtration equipment for gases and liquids; valves; electronics; and safety and life-support products. The firm generates more than 90% of its sales outside the U.K. Half of its sales are made from the United States.

	£ mil 04/93	04/94	04/95	US$mil 04/95				
Sales	**1,619.0**	**1,864.0**	**2,146.2**	**3,374.5**	P/E Ratio	**19.3**	Price (9/30/95)	**7.24**
Net Income	**106.0**	**127.0**	**160.3**	**252.0**	P/B Ratio	**3.2**	52 Wk Hi-Low	**7.40-4.99**
Book Value	**811.0**	**950.0**	**966.2**	**1,558.4**	Yield %	**1.7**	Market Cap	**US$4,924.5mil**

Address **Saxon Hse., 2-4 Victoria St.** Tel **01753-855411** ADR **SIBEY** CEO **Allen M. Yurko**
Windsor, Berkshire SL4 1EN Fax **01753-840638** SEDOL No. **807041** Chairman **Barrie Stephens**

Simon Engineering

Industry: **Heavy Machinery**

Simon Engineering manufactures specialized materials-handling and industrial equipment. It operates three core companies. Simon Access manufactures airport emergency vehicles, firefighting aerial ladders and platforms, and digger derricks and other access platforms. Simon Storage specializes in the storage of bulk liquids, gases, solids, and Simon-Carves specializes in chemical and process-plant engineering. As part of a major restructuring process, the company sold 10 businesses for a total of £26.5 million in 1994.

	£ mil 12/92	12/93	12/94	US$mil 12/94				
Sales	**401.0**	**340.0**	**294.5**	**453.1**	P/E Ratio	**NMF**	Price (9/30/95)	**0.90**
Net Income	**-3.0**	**-164.0**	**-15.1**	**-23.2**	P/B Ratio	**1.9**	52 Wk Hi-Low	**1.03-0.68**
Book Value	**106.0**	**37.0**	**74.2**	**115.9**	Yield %	**0.0**	Market Cap	**US$223.4mil**

Address **Simon Hse., 6 Eaton Gate** Tel **0171-730-0777** ADR CEO **Maurice C. Dixson**
London SW1W 9BJ Fax **0171-881-2200** SEDOL No. **809702** Chairman **Michael Davies**

Slough Estates

Industry: **Real-Estate Investment**

Slough Estates is a real-estate investor and developer specializing in the development of industrial property. The company acquires, develops, manages, and owns properties in major business centers throughout the world. It currently operates in the United Kingdom, Canada, the United States, Australia, Belgium, France, and Germany. The company manages approximately 31 million square feet of industrial, office, and retail space occupied by about 2,400 tenants. In 1994, the company became the majority shareholder of Bredero Properties.

	£ mil 12/92	12/93	12/94	US$mil 12/94				
Sales	**181.0**	**190.0**	**179.4**	**276.0**	P/E Ratio	**23.6**	Price (9/30/95)	**2.15**
Net Income	**27.0**	**25.0**	**46.7**	**71.8**	P/B Ratio	**0.7**	52 Wk Hi-Low	**2.41-2.08**
Book Value	**924.0**	**1,180.0**	**1,223.0**	**1,910.9**	Yield %	**3.8**	Market Cap	**US$1,331.9mil**

Address **234 Bath Rd.**	Tel **01753-537171**	ADR	CEO	**Roger W. Carey**
Slough, Berkshire SL1 4EE	Fax **01753-820585**	SEDOL No. **814104**	Chairman	**Nigel Mobbs**

Smith & Nephew

Industry: **Medical Supplies**

Smith & Nephew is a worldwide manufacturer of health-care products. Its products include wound dressings, artificial hips and joints, casting products, eye and ear implants, and arthroscopy equipment. It manufactures consumer healthcare goods such as Elastoplast first-aid dressings, Lil-lets tampons, and Simple skin-care products. In 1994, 44% of the company's annual sales were generated in America, 38% in the United Kingdom and Continental Europe and 18% in Africa, Asia, and Australasia. The company acquired Wrights Coal Tar Soap in 1994.

	£ mil 12/92	12/93	12/94	US$mil 12/94				
Sales	**832.0**	**931.0**	**949.9**	**1,461.4**	P/E Ratio	**NMF**	Price (9/30/95)	**1.89**
Net Income	**103.0**	**109.0**	**-53.9**	**-82.9**	P/B Ratio	**4.6**	52 Wk Hi-Low	**2.03-1.39**
Book Value	**282.0**	**348.0**	**445.9**	**696.7**	Yield %	**2.8**	Market Cap	**US$3,275.3mil**

Address **2 Temple Pl., Victoria Embkmt.**	Tel **0171-836-7922**	ADR	CEO	**John H. Robinson**
London WC2R 3BP	Fax **0171-240-7088**	SEDOL No. **816605**	Chairman	**Eric Kinder**

W.H. Smith

Industry: **Other Specialty Retailers**

W.H. Smith Group operates retail stores selling products such as books, stationery, recorded music, and videos. It owns and operates approximately 300 Our Price Music outlets, 35 Our Price Video stores, and 24 Virgin Megastores. Its Do It All hardware-supplies chain is operated as a joint venture with Boots throughout the United Kingdom. W.H. Smith owns 82% of United Kingdom bookselling chain Waterstone's, which has Chicago and Boston branches. It also operates 167 W.H. Smith retail and W.H. Smith music stores in the United States.

	£ mil 05/92	05/93	05/94	US$mil 05/94				
Revenues	**2,128.0**	**2,312.0**	**2,441.6**	**3,655.1**	P/E Ratio	**18.3**	Price (9/30/95)	**3.69**
Net Income	**81.0**	**84.0**	**55.2**	**82.6**	P/B Ratio	**2.1**	52 Wk Hi-Low	**4.81-3.24**
Book Value	**435.0**	**482.0**	**476.2**	**721.5**	Yield %	**4.2**	Market Cap	**US$1,633.2mil**

Address **Strand Hse., 7 Holbein Pl.**	Tel **0171-730-1200**	ADR	CEO	**Sir Malcolm Field**
London SW1W 8NR	Fax **0171-259-9075**	SEDOL No. **817653**	Chairman	**Jeremy Hardie**

SmithKline Beecham

Industry: **Pharmaceuticals**

SmithKline Beecham (SB) is a major manufacturer of health-care products. Its pharmaceutical products include Augmentin and Amoxil antibiotics, the antidepressant Paxil/Seroxat, and the anti-inflammatory Relafen. Its consumer products include Tums antacids, Contac cold capsules, and Oxy skin-care treatments. In 1994, SB bought U.S.-based Sterling Winthrop's international over-the-counter business; SB also sold its animal health division to U.S. drug-producer Pfizer. Exports outside Europe account for 70% of revenues; half of all sales are made in the U.S.

	£ mil 12/92	12/93	12/94	US$mil 12/94				
Sales	**4,924.0**	**6,040.0**	**6,071.0**	**9,340.0**	P/E Ratio	**NMF**	Price (9/30/95)	**6.40**
Net Income	**728.0**	**813.0**	**90.0**	**138.5**	P/B Ratio	**NMF**	52 Wk Hi-Low	**6.40-4.02**
Book Value	**1,080.0**	**1,254.0**	**570.0**	**890.6**	Yield %	**2.0**	Market Cap	**US$14,081mil**

Address **New Horizons Ct.**	Tel **0181-975-2000**	ADR **SBH**	CEO	**Jan Leschly**
Brentford, Middlesex TW8 9EP	Fax **0181-847-0830**	SEDOL No. **819392**	Chairman	**Sir Peter Walters**

Smiths Industries

Industry: **Aerospace & Defense**

Smiths Industries is an international aerospace-electronics, medical-systems, and specialized industrial company. It supplies cockpit displays, data recorders, and navigation systems to the U.S. military and civil-aviation industries. Through Smiths Industries Medical Systems, the company produces single-use products for anaesthesia, respiratory therapy, and intensive-care appplications. It is currently expanding its involvement in community healthcare and recently purchased Deltec, a producer of intravenous drug delivery systems for non-hospitalized patients.

	£ mil 08/92	07/93	07/94	US$mil 07/94				
Sales	**635.0**	**726.0**	**742.4**	**1,118.1**	P/E Ratio	**21.9**	Price (9/30/95)	**5.82**
Net Income	**69.0**	**71.0**	**79.5**	**119.7**	P/B Ratio	**8.2**	52 Wk Hi-Low	**5.83-4.11**
Book Value	**330.0**	**267.0**	**212.0**	**326.2**	Yield %	**2.2**	Market Cap	**US$2,774.7mil**

Address **765 Finchley Rd., Childs Hill**	Tel **0181-458-3232**	ADR	CEO	**Roger Hurn**
London NW11 8DS	Fax **0181-458-4380**	SEDOL No. **818270**	Chairman	**Roger Hurn**

Industry: **Industrial - Diversified**

Spirax-Sarco

Spirax-Sarco Engineering develops fluid-control equipment that controls the flow of steam, hot water, oil, and compressed air for industrial and commercial applications. Spirax-Sarco owns 34 companies with 100 sales offices in 35 countries and has authorized distributors in approximately 50 countries. More than 70% of its operating profits are generated outside the United Kingdom. It owns Watson-Marlow, which manufactures and repairs a variety of industrial pumps in the United Kingdom and North America.

£ mil	12/92	12/93	12/94	US$mil 12/94				
Sales	154.0	193.0	217.9	335.2	P/E Ratio	21.5	Price (9/30/95)	5.99
Net Income	13.0	16.0	21.7	33.3	P/B Ratio	4.7	52 Wk Hi-Low	6.11-4.27
Book Value	87.0	85.0	98.2	153.4	Yield %	1.9	Market Cap	US$741.5mil

Address **Charlton Hse., Cirencester Rd. Cheltenham, Gloucs GL53 8ER**
Tel **01242-521361**
Fax **01242-573342**
ADR
SEDOL No. **834704**
CEO **Timothy B. Fortune**
Chairman **Chris J. Tappin**

Industry: **Building Materials**

Spring Ram

The Spring Ram Corporation primarily builds and supplies kitchen and bathroom furniture as well as fully fitted kitchens and complete bathrooms. Its special products division includes Regency Doors and Meredrew Cabinets. Its wholly-owned Stag Furniture subsidiary manufactures hand-carved dining-room and bedroom furniture. GT Rackstraw produces handcrafted cabinet furniture primarily for the export market. During 1994, the company purchased bedding, upholstery, and furniture-maker Rest Assured and closed its Artisan Tile subsidiary.

£ mil	01/93	01/94	12/94	US$mil 12/94				
Sales	193.0	240.0	256.6	394.8	P/E Ratio	48.6	Price (9/30/95)	0.34
Net Income	18.0	-41.0	2.9	4.5	P/B Ratio	1.2	52 Wk Hi-Low	0.46-0.34
Book Value	139.0	89.0	128.7	201.1	Yield %	1.5	Market Cap	US$244.7mil

Address **Euroway Hse., Roydsdale Way Bradford BD4 6SJ**
Tel **01274-686888**
Fax **01274-682099**
ADR
SEDOL No. **836131**
President --
Chairman **B. Roger Regan**

Industry: **Insurance - Full Line**

Sun Alliance

Sun Alliance is a holding company for the Sun Alliance group of companies. These companies provide all major types of insurance, including mortgage-indemnity, automobile, household, and commercial insurance, as well as life insurance and pensions. Although the company operates mainly in the United Kingdom, it has operations in Europe, the Middle East, South America, Africa, and the Far East. In addition to the Sun Alliance Group, the company has other subsidiaries, which include the wholly-owned Swinton (Holdings) Ltd in the UK and the 72%-owned Codan Bank in Denmark.

£ mil	12/92	12/93	12/94	US$mil 12/94				
Revenues	5,760.0	7,174.0	4,650.8	7,155.1	P/E Ratio	12.3	Price (9/30/95)	3.65
Net Income	-129.0	181.0	249.4	383.7	P/B Ratio	1.7	52 Wk Hi-Low	3.75-2.84
Book Value	1,548.0	2,012.0	1,755.6	2,743.1	Yield %	4.3	Market Cap	US$4,690.8mil

Address **1 Bartholomew Ln. London EC2N 2AB**
Tel **0171-588-2345**
Fax **0171-588-1078**
ADR
SEDOL No. **859633**
CEO **Roger Taylor**
Chairman **Sir Christopher Benson**

Industry: **Other Auto Parts**

T & N

T&N mainly produces auto parts. The company also makes engineering and industrial materials for the aerospace, petrochemical, electrical, and power-generation industries. It produces Glacier, Clevite, and Vandervell bearings, and also produces clutch facings and drum-brake linings. Its Goetze subsidiary produces pistons in Germany. T&N holds a stake in Kolbenschmidt, a German automobile-parts manufacturer. T&N's customers include Ford Motor, Chrysler, Peugeot, Citroen, and BMW. Exports represent 82% of revenues; 44% of all sales are made outside Europe.

£ mil	12/92	12/93	12/94	US$mil 12/94				
Sales	1,390.0	1,662.0	1,936.1	2,978.6	P/E Ratio	NMF	Price (9/30/95)	1.79
Net Income	26.0	41.0	-16.5	-25.4	P/B Ratio	1.8	52 Wk Hi-Low	2.29-1.44
Book Value	516.0	559.0	513.4	802.2	Yield %	6.1	Market Cap	US$1,504.8mil

Address **Ashburton Rd. W., Trafford Pk. Manchester M17 1RA**
Tel **0161-872-0155**
Fax **0161-872-8884**
ADR **TNNSY**
SEDOL No. **907606**
CEO **Colin F.N. Hope**
Chairman **Colin F.N. Hope**

Industry: **Banks - Regional**

TSB Group

TSB Group provides retail-banking and insurance services to individuals. Its retail-banking division provides traditional banking services such as loans, mortgages, banking by phone, and unit-trust sales. Its insurance division provides pensions and life, homeowner's, liability, fire, and theft insurance. Its wholly-owned Hill Samuel Bank specializes in the provision of merchant banking and fund management. UDT provides retail and commercial-vehicle financing. Mortgage Express subsidiary has a loan portfolio of £2 billion.

£ mil	10/92	10/93	10/94	US$mil 10/94				
Revenues	3,105.0	2,658.0	2,718.0	4,149.6	P/E Ratio	12.8	Price (9/30/95)	2.76
Net Income	-25.0	184.0	312.0	476.3	P/B Ratio	2.3	52 Wk Hi-Low	2.76-2.14
Book Value	1,638.0	1,740.0	1,932.0	3,167.2	Yield %	3.3	Market Cap	US$6,708.6mil

Address **25 Milk St. London EC2V 8LU**
Tel **0171-606-7070**
Fax **0171-606-0510**
ADR
SEDOL No. **870612**
CEO **Peter B. Ellwood**
Chairman **Sir Nicholas Goodison**

Tarmac

Industry: **Heavy Construction**

Tarmac operates construction services and manufactures quarry products and other building materials. It is one of the United Kingdom's largest private-enterprise homebuilding organizations. It also contracts to provide building, civil-engineering, and mechanical services. Tarmac provides road materials, aggregates, ready-mix concrete, and clay bricks to the construction industry. The company operates primarily in the U.K. but also provides services in Europe and Asia. Tarmac America produces construction materials in the United States.

£ mil	12/92	12/93	12/94	US$mil 12/94				
Sales	**2,935.0**	**2,453.0**	**2,510.3**	**3,862.0**	P/E Ratio	**12.1**	Price (9/30/95)	**0.94**
Net Income	**-264.0**	**-62.0**	**71.8**	**110.5**	P/B Ratio	**0.9**	52 Wk Hi-Low	**1.32-0.87**
Book Value	**1,021.0**	**1,086.0**	**954.5**	**1,491.4**	Yield %	**5.9**	Market Cap	**US$1,375.2mil**

Address **Hilton Hall, Essington**
Wolverhampton WV11 2BQ
Tel **01902-307407**
Fax **01902-307408**
ADR
SEDOL No. **874120**
CEO **Neville I. Simms**
Chairman **Sir John Banham**

Tate & Lyle

Industry: **Other Food**

Tate & Lyle manufactures sugar and cereal sweeteners and processes starch products. Its wholly-owned U.S. subsidiaries include cane-sugar producer Domino, and beet-sugar producer Western Sugar. The company's cereal-sweetener and starch division includes Belgium-based Amylum; Prignitz-Starke, a German potato-starch producer; and A.E. Staley Manufacturing, a U.S.-based company that makes the Stellar fat substitute and Krystar reduced-calorie sweetener. Exports generate 80% of revenues; 60% of sales are made outside of Europe.

£ mil	09/92	09/93	09/94	US$mil 09/94				
Sales	**3,294.0**	**3,698.0**	**4,074.0**	**6,172.7**	P/E Ratio	**10.2**	Price (9/30/95)	**4.49**
Net Income	**116.0**	**149.0**	**171.1**	**259.2**	P/B Ratio	**2.1**	52 Wk Hi-Low	**4.77-3.99**
Book Value	**630.0**	**710.0**	**786.3**	**1,248.1**	Yield %	**3.2**	Market Cap	**US$2,796.9mil**

Address **Sugar Quay, Lower Thames St.**
London EC3R 6DQ
Tel **0171-626-6525**
Fax **0171-623-5213**
ADR **TATYY**
SEDOL No. **875413**
President --
Chairman **Neil M. Shaw**

Taylor Woodrow

Industry: **Heavy Construction**

Taylor Woodrow is a construction, housing, property-development, and trading conglomerate. It provides construction consulting to major British service firms such as the London Underground, but recently has focused more heavily on its property portfolio. The company's wholly-owned Greenham subsidiaries distribute janatorial supplies, video equipment, construction materials, and personal-protection equipment. By March 1995, it had sold nearly all of its shares in the loss-making Eurotunnel channel-tunnel rail company.

£ mil	12/92	12/93	12/94	US$mil 12/94				
Sales	**1,226.0**	**1,150.0**	**1,146.3**	**1,763.5**	P/E Ratio	**13.6**	Price (9/30/95)	**1.06**
Net Income	**-90.0**	**17.0**	**32.4**	**49.8**	P/B Ratio	**0.8**	52 Wk Hi-Low	**1.34-1.04**
Book Value	**525.0**	**531.0**	**517.5**	**808.6**	Yield %	**2.2**	Market Cap	**US$647.9mil**

Address **Taywood Hse., 345 Ruislip Rd.**
Southall, Middlesex UB1 2QX
Tel **0181-578-2366**
Fax **0181-575-4701**
ADR
SEDOL No. **878230**
CEO **H. A. Palmer**
Chairman **C J. Parsons**

Tesco

Industry: **Food Retailers & Wholesalers**

Tesco is a food-retailing company that produces Tesco-brand food and operates a chain of 464 stores in England, Scotland, and Wales. It subsidiaries include the William Low grocery chain, which operates 45 stores in Scotland and 12 in England; the French food retailer Catteau, which operates 103 outlets in northern France; and Hungarian food retailer Global TH. The total retail-sales area of Tesco's stores exceeds 11.2 million square feet. Roughly 95% of its revenue is generated in the United Kingdom.

£ mil	02/93	02/94	02/95	US$mil 02/95				
Sales	**7,581.5**	**8,600.0**	**10,101.0**	**15,709.2**	P/E Ratio	**16.6**	Price (9/30/95)	**3.13**
Net Income	**417.6**	**298.0**	**380.0**	**591.0**	P/B Ratio	**2.1**	52 Wk Hi-Low	**3.38-2.34**
Book Value	**2,752.9**	**2,749.0**	**3,104.0**	**4,927.0**	Yield %	**2.7**	Market Cap	**US$10,230mil**

Address **Delamare Rd., Cheshunt**
Hertfordshire EN8 9SL
Tel **01992-632222**
Fax **01992-644481**
ADR **TSCPY**
SEDOL No. **884709**
Managing Director **David Malpas**
Chairman **Sir Ian MacLaurin**

Thames Water

Industry: **Water Utilities**

Thames Water, the largest of the United Kingdom's privatized water companies, supplies water and treats waste for customers in and around London. The company also provides water services to customers in Africa, Asia, continental Europe, and South America. Its other services include sewer surveying, drainage consultancy, and landscaping. Its wholly-owned Thames Water Utilities subsidiary operates the company's water-supply and sewerage activities. The company also provides insurance and property-development services.

£ mil	03/93	03/94	03/95	US$mil 03/95				
Sales	**1,044.0**	**1,105.0**	**1,173.6**	**1,839.5**	P/E Ratio	**7.5**	Price (9/30/95)	**5.34**
Net Income	**230.0**	**222.0**	**282.2**	**442.3**	P/B Ratio	**1.0**	52 Wk Hi-Low	**5.67-4.38**
Book Value	**1,691.0**	**1,833.0**	**2,035.2**	**3,336.4**	Yield %	**4.7**	Market Cap	**US$3,388.5mil**

Address **14 Cavendish Pl.**
London W1M 9DJ
Tel **0171-636-8686**
Fax **0171-436-6755**
ADR
SEDOL No. **886006**
CEO **Michael R. Hoffman**
Chairman **Sir Robert Clarke**

Industry: **Entertainment**

Thorn EMI

Thorn EMI develops and retails music products and operates a consumer-electronics rental business. Its music-division subsidiaries include Virgin Music, Capital Records, and Chrysalis Records. The company's rental businesses, including Radio Rentals (U.K. and Australia) and Remco (U.S.), rent consumer-electronics products. Its HMV subsidiary operates 200 music stores worldwide. Thorn EMI recently sold its Rumbelows consumer-electronics stores and acquired book-retailer Dillons. Exports generate 66% of revenues; almost 40% of sales are made from outside Europe.

	£ mil 03/93	03/94	03/95	US$mil 03/95				
Sales	**4,381.0**	**4,084.0**	**4,329.0**	**6,785.3**	P/E Ratio	**59.0**	Price (9/30/95)	**14.74**
Net Income	**179.0**	**202.0**	**266.5**	**417.7**	P/B Ratio	**10.8**	52 Wk Hi-Low	**15.35-9.63**
Book Value	**477.0**	**735.0**	**583.8**	**957.0**	Yield %	**2.5**	Market Cap	**US$10,014mil**

Address **4 Tenterden St., Hanover Sq.**
London W1A 2AY
Tel **0171-355-4848**
Fax **0171-355-1308**
ADR **THOMY**
SEDOL No. **889403**
President --
Chairman **Colin Southgate**

Industry: **Industrial - Diversified**

TI Group

TI Group is an engineering company that operates three core businesses across five continents. Its John Crane division produces sealing systems and operates in 42 countries. TI's Bundy division manufactures and markets small-diameter fluid systems for the automotive and refrigeration industries. Its Dowty division makes aircraft components such as landing gear, propellers, and hydraulic systems for civilian and military aircraft worldwide. Exports represent about 85% of revenues; the United States is its largest export market, generating 43% of all sales.

	£ mil 12/92	12/93	12/94	US$mil 12/94				
Sales	**1,039.0**	**1,323.0**	**1,420.2**	**2,184.9**	P/E Ratio	**20.0**	Price (9/30/95)	**4.51**
Net Income	**57.0**	**84.0**	**104.9**	**161.4**	P/B Ratio	**6.2**	52 Wk Hi-Low	**4.51-3.32**
Book Value	**269.0**	**289.0**	**342.9**	**535.8**	Yield %	**2.7**	Market Cap	**US$3,349.6mil**

Address **Lambourn Ct.**
Abingdon, Oxon OX14 1UH
Tel **0123-555-5570**
Fax **0123-555-5818**
ADR **TIGUY**
SEDOL No. **868673**
President --
Chairman **Sir Christopher Lewinton**

Industry: **Air Freight & Couriers**

Tibbett & Britten

Tibbett & Britten Group is a distributor for manufacturers and retailers. Tibbett & Britten Ltd deals with clothing and textiles, groceries, and other consumer products in the UK. Axial Holdings (formerly Silcock Express) provides the car industry with distribution and predelivery inspection services. Tibbett & Britten International manages the group's nonautomotive activities outside the UK. The company has acquired holdings in Eskimo-Iglo Tiefkühlogistik GmbH in Austria and Clef in France. In 1994, 33% of the company's revenue was generated overseas.

	£ mil 12/92	12/93	12/94	US$mil 12/94				
Sales	**232.0**	**360.0**	**464.0**	**713.8**	P/E Ratio	**10.9**	Price (9/30/95)	**4.68**
Net Income	**10.0**	**16.0**	**18.9**	**29.1**	P/B Ratio	**2.8**	52 Wk Hi-Low	**7.40-4.50**
Book Value	**69.0**	**75.0**	**74.6**	**116.6**	Yield %	**3.5**	Market Cap	**US$328.4mil**

Address **1 Shirley Rd., Windmill Hill**
Enfield, Middlesex EN2 6SB
Tel **0181-367-9955**
Fax **0181-366-7042**
ADR
SEDOL No. **891107**
CEO **John A. Harvey**
Chairman **John A. Harvey**

Industry: **Conglomerates**

Tomkins

Tomkins is an investment-management company with holdings in companies that make food products, guns, building materials, professional and leisure products, fluid controls (valves, faucets), and auto equipment. Brand-name products include Smith & Wesson handguns, Pegler faucets, Murray bicycles and lawnmowers. Its Ranks Hovis McDougall subsidiary manufactures brand-name food products such as Bisto, McDougall, and Just Juice. Its Canadian-based Noma Industries subsidiary produces lawnmowers, snowblowers, and garden tractors. Nearly half of sales are made overseas.

	£ mil 05/92	05/93	04/94	US$mil 04/94				
Sales	**1,274.0**	**2,060.0**	**3,245.1**	**4,872.5**	P/E Ratio	**16.2**	Price (9/30/95)	**2.52**
Net Income	**93.0**	**120.0**	**179.4**	**269.4**	P/B Ratio	**3.1**	52 Wk Hi-Low	**2.60-2.03**
Book Value	**450.0**	**802.0**	**897.8**	**1,360.3**	Yield %	**2.9**	Market Cap	**US$4,730.8mil**

Address **84 Upper Richmond Rd.**
London SW15 2ST
Tel **0181-871-4544**
Fax **0181-877-9700**
ADR **TKS**
SEDOL No. **896265**
CEO **Gregory Hutchings**
Chairman **Michael Moore**

Industry: **Heavy Construction**

Trafalgar House

Trafalgar House is a construction and engineering company that serves the power, oil, gas, and metal industries. It also develops commercial and residential property in the U.K. and the U.S. The company provides offshore-contracting services for oil, factory-automation, and bridge-building companies; it also provides engineering services for Shell and British Steel. Its Cunard Steam-Ship subsidiary operates luxury cruise ships such as the QE2, and hotels in London, including the Ritz. Exports make up 71% of revenues; more than 60% of all sales come from outside Europe.

	£ mil 09/92	09/93	09/94	US$mil 09/94				
Sales	**3,890.0**	**3,877.0**	**3,763.5**	**5,702.3**	P/E Ratio	**25.5**	Price (9/30/95)	**0.28**
Net Income	**-85.0**	**-367.0**	**30.0**	**45.5**	P/B Ratio	**0.4**	52 Wk Hi-Low	**0.89-0.28**
Book Value	**542.0**	**281.0**	**699.2**	**1,109.8**	Yield %	**3.6**	Market Cap	**US$478.9mil**

Address **1 Berkeley St.**
London W1A 1BY
Tel **0171-499-9020**
Fax **0171-493-5484**
ADR **TFLHY**
SEDOL No. **901040**
CEO **Nigel Rich**
Chairman **Simon Keswick**

UniChem

Industry: **Drug-based Retailers**

UniChem is a distributor of pharmaceutical, medical and health-care products operating in the United Kingdom and Europe. It is a pharmaceutical wholesaler in Portugal and, through IPSO, is linked with wholesalers in major European markets. The company distributes pharmaceuticals to approximately 5,500 retail and hospital pharmacies in the U.K. Its Moss Chemists subsidiary operates 353 pharmacies. Since its acquisition of Hospital Management & Supplies in 1994, the company has been involved in wholesaling medical and surgical supplies to hospitals.

£ mil	12/92	12/93	12/94	US$mil 12/94				
Revenues	1,048.0	1,178.0	1,324.7	2,037.9	P/E Ratio	14.0	Price (9/30/95)	2.71
Net Income	19.0	25.0	29.6	45.6	P/B Ratio	3.4	52 Wk Hi-Low	2.85-2.34
Book Value	93.0	98.0	139.0	217.2	Yield %	6.9	Market Cap	US$739.6mil

Address	**UniChem Hse., Cox Ln.**	Tel	**0181-391-2323**	ADR		CEO	**Jeffrey F. Harris**
	Chessington, Surrey KT9 1SN	Fax	**0181-974-1707**	SEDOL No.	**916572**	Chairman	**Lord Rippon**

Unigate

Industry: **Other Food**

Unigate produces and distributes food and beverages, owns U.S.-based Black-eyed Pea and Taco Bueno restaurants, operates car dealerships, and provides transportation services. The company's Unigate Dairies subsidiary processes milk and distributes it to retailers in southern England. Its U.K. subsidiaries include the St. Ivel dairy operation, animal-feed producer W.J. Oldacre, and transport company Wincanton. Unigate has an agreement with Cadbury Schweppes to make desserts containing Cadbury's chocolate. Exports, which are mainly to the U.S., generate 14% of revenues.

£ mil	03/93	03/94	03/95	US$mil 03/95				
Sales	1,825.0	1,823.0	1,886.0	2,956.1	P/E Ratio	21.4	Price (9/30/95)	4.24
Net Income	73.0	73.0	46.6	73.0	P/B Ratio	3.7	52 Wk Hi-Low	4.39-3.19
Book Value	335.0	327.0	267.6	438.7	Yield %	4.3	Market Cap	US$1,578.8mil

Address	**Unigate Hse., Wood Ln.**	Tel	**0181-749-8888**	ADR	**UNGAY**	CEO	**Ross Buckland**
	London W12 7RP	Fax	**0181-576-6071**	SEDOL No.	**911704**	Chairman	**Ian A. Martin**

Unilever

Industry: **Other Food**

UK-based Unilever PLC has a 50% interest in the Unilever group of companies; Netherlands-based Unilever NV controls the other 50% (both listings show the same consolidated data). Core businesses are the manufacture food products (roughly 50% of sales) and detergents (25% of sales). Food products include Country Crock spreads, Wishbone salad dressings, and Ragu sauces. Detergents include Wisk laundry detergent and Dove soap. Unilever also makes consumer goods through Elizabeth Arden and Calvin Klein Cosmetics subsidiaries. Nearly half of sales come from outside Europe.

£ mil	12/92	12/93	12/94	US$mil 12/94				
Sales	24,700.0	27,863.0	29,666.0	45,640.0	P/E Ratio	15.1	Price (9/30/95)	12.64
Net Income	1,291.0	1,296.0	507.0	780.0	P/B Ratio	1.9	52 Wk Hi-Low	13.01-10.76
Book Value	4,583.0	4,703.0	5,333.0	8,332.8	Yield %	2.1	Market Cap	US$16,346mil

Address	**Unilever Hse., Blackfriars**	Tel	**0171-822-5252**	ADR	**UL**	President	--
	London EC4P 4BQ	Fax	**0171-822-5951**	SEDOL No.	**913216**	Chairman	**Michael S. Perry**

United Biscuits

Industry: **Other Food**

United Biscuits is a food manufacturer specializing in cookies, snacks, confections, and frozen foods. Its McVitie's subsidiary is the second-largest manufacturer of cookies in the United Kingdom. Keebler, its wholly-owned U.S. subsidiary, is the second-largest manufacturer of cookies and crackers in the United States. United Biscuits' brand-name products include KP nuts, Chips Ahoy cookies, and Young's frozen seafood. It owns Smith's Snackfood, which has a 55% share of the Australian snack market, and Dutch-based Dalgety Snacks. Exports represent 56% of revenues.

£ mil	01/93	01/94	12/94	US$mil 12/94				
Sales	2,942.0	3,374.0	3,397.0	5,226.2	P/E Ratio	16.6	Price (9/30/95)	2.77
Net Income	111.0	67.0	87.8	135.1	P/B Ratio	2.0	52 Wk Hi-Low	3.65-2.61
Book Value	866.0	745.0	723.3	1,130.2	Yield %	5.5	Market Cap	US$2,319.0mil

Address	**Church Rd.**	Tel	**01895-432100**	ADR	**UTBTY**	CEO	**Eric L. Nicoli**
	W. Drayton, Middlesex UB7 7PR	Fax	**01895-448848**	SEDOL No.	**914123**	Chairman	**Sir Robert C. Clarke**

United News & Media

Industry: **Publishing**

United News & Media, formerly United Newspapers, publishes newspapers and business and consumer magazines; operates information services; and manages exhibitions in Europe, the United States, and the Far East. It publishes three national newspapers in the United Kingdom, as well as a variety of regional newspapers. Magazine titles include OS/2 Magazine and The Bike Mag. Overseas subsidiaries include U.S.-based magazine publisher Harmon Homes and Hong Kong International Trade Fair Group. Exports account for more than a third of revenues.

£ mil	12/92	12/93	12/94	US$mil 12/94				
Sales	828.0	875.0	1,013.4	1,559.1	P/E Ratio	13.2	Price (9/30/95)	5.21
Net Income	80.0	100.0	96.4	148.2	P/B Ratio	4.1	52 Wk Hi-Low	5.62-4.71
Book Value	167.0	417.0	307.3	480.1	Yield %	4.4	Market Cap	US$2,020.8mil

Address	**Ludgate Hse., 245 Blackfriars Rd.**	Tel	**0171-921-5000**	ADR	**UNEWY**	Managing Director	**Graham J.S. Wilson**
	London SE1 9UY	Fax	**0171-928-2728**	SEDOL No.	**916721**	Chairman	**Lord Stevens**

Industry: **Telephone Systems - All**

Vodafone

Vodafone Group is a telecommunication company that provides cellular-radio-network, voice-mail, radio-paging, and data-communication services. It also manufactures digital cellular telephones. Nearly all of its sales are generated in the United Kingdom, where its cellular network has more than 1.8 million subscribers. Vodafone has a 35% stake in the MT-2 consortium, which has won a license to develop a second mobile-communication network in the Netherlands. Vodafone also has communication interests in Greece, South Africa, Australia, Fiji, and continental Europe.

£ mil	03/93	03/94	03/95	US$mil 03/95				
Sales	**664.0**	**851.0**	**1,152.6**	**1,806.6**	P/E Ratio	**34.0**	Price (9/30/95)	**2.66**
Net Income	**222.0**	**245.0**	**237.4**	**372.1**	P/B Ratio	**9.9**	52 Wk Hi-Low	**2.80-1.82**
Book Value	**596.0**	**698.0**	**817.3**	**1,339.8**	Yield %	**1.2**	Market Cap	**US$12,842mil**

Address **The Courtyard, 2-4 London Rd.**
Newbury, Berkshire RG13 1JL
Tel **01635-33251**
Fax **01635-45713**
ADR **VOD**
SEDOL No. **719210**
CEO **George A. Whent**
Chairman **Sir Ernest Harrison**

Industry: **Real-Estate Investment**

Wates City of London

Wates City of London Properties invests in and develops property in London. It has interests in eight office sites. The Wates portfolio currently contains 599,000 square feet of floorspace either leased, vacant, or under development. At the end of February 1995, Wates' rental income, including their share of rent from associated companies totaled £10.2 million. The company is redeveloping 60 Gracechurch Street for Societe Generale. It will also construct a new building with 115,360 square feet of retail space. The company plans to complete this building in 1997.

£ mil	12/92	12/93	12/94	US$mil 12/94				
Sales	**17.0**	**12.0**	**7.8**	**12.0**	P/E Ratio	**NMF**	Price (9/30/95)	**0.70**
Net Income	**-73.0**	**-1.0**	**-1.0**	**-1.6**	P/B Ratio	**0.9**	52 Wk Hi-Low	**0.78-0.62**
Book Value	**89.0**	**112.0**	**150.9**	**235.8**	Yield %	**0.0**	Market Cap	**US$220.4mil**

Address **City Tower, 40 Basinghall St.**
London EC2V 5DE
Tel **0171-588-2888**
Fax **0171-588-3799**
ADR
SEDOL No. **942298**
Managing Director **J.D. Nettleton**
Chairman **Paul C.R. Wates**

Industry: **Factory Equipment**

Weir

Weir Group produces engineering products and provides specialized engineering services. Its engineering products are mainly consist of pumps that it produces for the power, oil, water, and shipping industries. Its engineering services include the rental of specialized equipment to the oil industry and the provision of computer services to a variety of industries. In September 1994, the company acquired EnviroTech Pumpsystems. It also owns two valve manufacturers which operate in the United Kingdom and the United States.

£ mil	01/93	12/93	12/94	US$mil 12/94				
Sales	**425.0**	**449.0**	**475.5**	**731.6**	P/E Ratio	**20.5**	Price (9/30/95)	**2.67**
Net Income	**27.0**	**27.0**	**22.0**	**33.9**	P/B Ratio	**3.1**	52 Wk Hi-Low	**2.93-2.22**
Book Value	**138.0**	**149.0**	**172.3**	**269.2**	Yield %	**260.7**	Market Cap	**US$835.7mil**

Address **149 Newlands Rd., Cathcart**
Glasgow G44 4EX
Tel **0141-637-7111**
Fax **0141-637-2221**
ADR
SEDOL No. **946580**
Mng Dir & CEO **Sir Ronald Garrick**
Chairman **Lord Weir**

Industry: **Building Materials**

Williams

Williams Holdings manufactures building and security products and fire-protection equipment. Its Kidde and Fenwal Safety Systems subsidiaries specialize in fire-detection, fire-extinguishing, and burner-management products. The company's building products include paint, electronic appliances, and ventilation equipment. The firm also builds garages, conservatories, and kitchens. Its Yale and Corbin Russwin subsidiaries produce door locks, safes, and alarm systems. Overseas sales account for 70% of revenues; half of all sales are made in the United States.

£ mil	12/92	12/93	12/94	US$mil 12/94				
Sales	**1,034.0**	**1,164.0**	**1,393.1**	**2,143.2**	P/E Ratio	**16.1**	Price (9/30/95)	**3.30**
Net Income	**115.0**	**100.0**	**136.3**	**209.7**	P/B Ratio	**3.9**	52 Wk Hi-Low	**3.58-3.04**
Book Value	**395.0**	**319.0**	**484.5**	**757.0**	Yield %	**4.1**	Market Cap	**US$3,035.9mil**

Address **Sir Frank Whittle Rd.**
Derby DE2 4XA
Tel **01332-202020**
Fax **01332-349139**
ADR **WIHLY**
SEDOL No. **967666**
CEO **Roger M. Carr**
Chairman **Nigel R. Rudd**

Industry: **Home Construction**

Wilson Bowden

Wilson Bowden builds homes and invests in and develops property. It operates in seven regions within the United Kingdom. In 1994, the company sold more than 2,000 homes, an increase of almost 11% from the previous year. It also completed industrial, retail and office developments totaling approximately 500,000 square feet. The company generates almost 80% of its operating profit from housebuilding. It is currently undertaking its largest project to date, a £25 million shopping center in Northampton.

£ mil	12/92	12/93	12/94	US$mil 12/94				
Sales	**128.0**	**185.0**	**241.7**	**371.8**	P/E Ratio	**12.4**	Price (9/30/95)	**3.35**
Net Income	**11.0**	**21.0**	**25.3**	**38.9**	P/B Ratio	**1.3**	52 Wk Hi-Low	**3.71-3.08**
Book Value	**162.0**	**232.0**	**248.4**	**388.1**	Yield %	**3.0**	Market Cap	**US$496.8mil**

Address **207 Leicester Rd.**
Ibstock, Leicester LE67 6HP
Tel **01530-60777**
Fax **01530-62805**
ADR
SEDOL No. **970073**
CEO **David W. Wilson**
Chairman **David W. Wilson**

Wilson Connolly

Industry: **Home Construction**

Wilson Connolly Holdings is a holding company that co-ordinates the activities of its subsidiaries. These subsidiaries are engaged in private housing, building contracting and property development. Its wholly-owned subsidiary Wilcon Holmes sold 4,200 private houses in 1994 and is the fifth-largest housebuilder in the United Kingdom. Wilson Connolly Properties also developed two retail warehouse complexes in Taunton and Bristol. These complexes include multiscreen cinemas, bowling alleys, and fast-food outlets. Both complexes were rented before construction began.

£ mil	12/92	12/93	12/94	US$mil 12/94				
Sales	**201.0**	**274.0**	**316.0**	**486.1**	P/E Ratio	**11.0**	Price (9/30/95)	**1.48**
Net Income	**12.0**	**19.0**	**25.8**	**39.7**	P/B Ratio	**1.2**	52 Wk Hi-Low	**1.95-1.24**
Book Value	**214.0**	**227.0**	**244.7**	**382.3**	Yield %	**3.0**	Market Cap	**US$448.1mil**

Address **Thomas Wilson Hse., Tenter Rd. Northampton NN3 1QJ**
Tel **01604-790909** Fax **01604-492387**
ADR SEDOL No. **970404**
Managing Director **I.C. Black**
Chairman **L.A. Wilson**

George Wimpey

Industry: **Heavy Construction**

George Wimpey is a construction, property, and minerals company. Almost 40% of Wimpey's 1994 revenues were generated by construction projects, and about 35% by private home-building. About 28% of Wimpey's home completions took place outside the United Kingdom. In 1995, the company plans to pull out of its property interests in France, Canada, Spain and the Canaries. Wimpey's minerals business concentrates on the production of dry and coated stone. Wimpey sold its marine positioning operations in 1994, and acquired the minerals business of Alfred McAlpine in 1995.

£ mil	12/92	12/93	12/94	US$mil 12/94				
Sales	**1,639.0**	**1,587.0**	**1,684.2**	**2,591.1**	P/E Ratio	**12.4**	Price (9/30/95)	**1.08**
Net Income	**-119.0**	**22.0**	**31.5**	**48.5**	P/B Ratio	**0.7**	52 Wk Hi-Low	**1.50-1.02**
Book Value	**446.0**	**536.0**	**521.5**	**814.8**	Yield %	**5.1**	Market Cap	**US$618.8mil**

Address **27 Hammersmith Grove London W6 7EN**
Tel **0181-748-2000** Fax **0181-748-0076**
ADR SEDOL No. **971344**
CEO **Joseph A. Dwyer**
Chairman **Sir John Quinton**

Wolseley

Industry: **Building Materials**

Wolseley, the world's largest distributor of heating and plumbing supplies by market share, also distributes and retails bathroom accessories. Of its 444 U.K. retail outlets, 219 operate as Plumb Centers. Its European outlets include Brossette BTI in France and ÖAG, Austria's largest distributor of heating and sanitary products. Wolseley manufactures pumps, lighting products, electrical accessories, boilers, and burners. Through its Calumet Holdings subsidiary, it also distributes professional photographic equipment in Europe and the United States.

£ mil	07/92	07/93	07/94	US$mil 07/94				
Sales	**1,954.0**	**2,491.0**	**3,254.1**	**4,900.7**	P/E Ratio	**14.5**	Price (9/30/95)	**3.69**
Net Income	**59.0**	**81.0**	**135.2**	**203.6**	P/B Ratio	**3.6**	52 Wk Hi-Low	**4.10-3.29**
Book Value	**343.0**	**423.0**	**558.0**	**858.5**	Yield %	**2.3**	Market Cap	**US$3,222.4mil**

Address **Vines Ln. Droitwich, Worcesters WR9 8ND**
Tel **01905-794444** Fax **01905-776704**
ADR SEDOL No. **976402**
Managing Director **Jeremy Lancaster**
Chairman **Jeremy Lancaster**

WPP Group

Industry: **Advertising**

WPP Group provides advertising and marketing services in 78 countries. Media advertising, accounting for 54% of revenues, is conducted primarily through its wholly-owned Ogilvy & Mather Worldwide and J. Walter Thompson subsidiaries. WPP is also active in market and public-opinion research, public relations, nonmedia advertising, direct marketing, and business-to-business marketing. WPP Group counts more than 300 companies in the Fortune 500 among its clients. Exports generate roughly 80% of revenues; 43% of sales come from North America.

£ mil	12/92	12/93	12/94	US$mil 12/94				
Sales	**5,367.0**	**6,030.0**	**1,426.9**	**2,195.2**	P/E Ratio	**18.9**	Price (9/30/95)	**1.49**
Net Income	**-12.0**	**23.0**	**47.4**	**72.9**	P/B Ratio	**NMF**	52 Wk Hi-Low	**1.64-1.01**
Book Value	**-253.0**	**-162.0**	**-109.9**	**-171.7**	Yield %	**0.7**	Market Cap	**US$1,730.9mil**

Address **27 Farm St. London W1X 6RD**
Tel **0171-408-2204** Fax **0171-493-6819**
ADR **WPPGY** SEDOL No. **974042**
CEO **Martin S. Sorrell**
Chairman **Gordon K.G. Stevens**

Yorkshire Water

Industry: **Water Utilities**

Yorkshire Water supplies drinking water to 4.5 million residential and industrial customers in Yorkshire. It operates environmental-protection and -engineering activities. The company also manages the disposal of medical waste, and builds and operates incineration plants. Its Babcock Water Engineering joint venture with Babcock International Group designs water- and sewage-treatment plants. Its joint venture with U.S. company Ogden Projects designs and constructs waste-to-energy facilities serving 16 million customers nationwide.

£ mil	03/93	03/94	03/95	US$mil 03/95				
Sales	**482.0**	**531.0**	**549.3**	**861.0**	P/E Ratio	**9.5**	Price (9/30/95)	**6.25**
Net Income	**129.0**	**136.0**	**131.5**	**206.1**	P/B Ratio	**0.9**	52 Wk Hi-Low	**6.39-4.73**
Book Value	**1,179.0**	**1,266.0**	**1,348.6**	**2,210.8**	Yield %	**4.4**	Market Cap	**US$2,010.1mil**

Address **2 Embankment, Sovereign St. Leeds LS1 4BG**
Tel **01532-343234** Fax **01532-342322**
ADR SEDOL No. **987880**
Managing Director **Trevor Newton**
Chairman **Sir Gordon Jones**

Industry: **Pharmaceuticals**

Zeneca

Zeneca develops, produces, and markets pharmaceuticals, chemicals, and seeds. Its prescription pharmaceuticals include Tenormin and Zestril cardiovascular treatments and Zoladex and Metastron cancer treatments. Its agrichemicals division produces herbicides, insecticides, fungicides, and many other compounds. The company also produces dyes, inks, biocides, resins, and solvents. It agreed to buy 50% of the U.S. company Salick Health Care in December 1994. Exports account for more than 90% of revenues; nearly two thirds of sales are made outside Europe.

	£ mil 12/92	12/93	12/94	US$mil 12/94				
Sales	**3,979.0**	**4,440.0**	**4,480.0**	**6,892.3**	P/E Ratio	**24.5**	Price (9/30/95)	**11.45**
Net Income	**80.0**	**440.0**	**443.0**	**681.5**	P/B Ratio	**6.4**	52 Wk Hi-Low	**11.70-7.97**
Book Value	**55.0**	**1,602.0**	**1,685.0**	**2,632.8**	Yield %	**2.5**	Market Cap	**US$17,195mil**

Address **15 Stanhope Gate**
London W1Y 6LN

Tel **0171-304-5000**
Fax **0171-304-5151**

ADR **ZEN**
SEDOL No. **989529**

CEO **David Barnes**
Chairman **Sir Denys Henderson**

United States

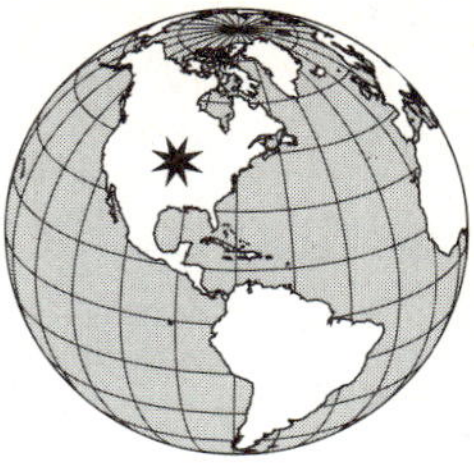

United States

Dave Kansas,
New York

Local Trading Hours	Time Difference with New York	Population (Est. 6/93)
9:30-4:00 EST (Pacific Exchange is open until 4:30 p.m. EST)	No difference from EST	258,300,000

The U.S. equity markets are the largest in the world. And, to the surprise of many market seers, it was also one of the top-performing equity markets in the world for the first nine months of 1995.

Falling interest rates and a slowing economy combined for what many economists said was impossible in 1994: an economic "soft landing" following the boost in interest rates to forestall inflation. This utopian environment of slow growth with no inflation helped spur a powerful rally in U.S. stocks.

By mid-year, major market barometers had smashed old records and risen more than 25%. The most popular measure, the Dow Jones Industrial Average, rose past 4000 in February and crossed 4800 in September. Technology and financial stocks performed the strongest. But as any seasoned Wall Streeter knows, what comes up must come down. Or at least a little bit down. When was the question as 1995's fourth quarter began. U.S. stock prices haven't suffered a standard 20% bear market decline since October 1990.

The bull market's success has sparked all kinds of new business-related activities. Media companies, including Dow Jones, plan to start new business cable television networks. Business books about folks like investor Warren Buffett top bestseller lists. And, it seems, most everybody owns at least one mutual fund.

With stocks performing so strongly, there was little surprise that mutual fund inflows remain strong. Defined-contribution plans, which allow individuals to choose their style of retirement investing, helped keep mutual fund inflows steady throughout the first nine months of the year. Strategists expect such inflows will continue, especially as more and more retirement-minded baby boomers near the end of their working days.

Mergers dominated the stock markets on several occasions as arbitrageurs and other investors sought to capitalize on the takeover binge of 1995. Among the bigger deals: Walt Disney buying Capital Cities/ABC for $19 billion, Chemical Banking announcing a $10 billion merger with Chase Manhattan and International Business Machines' $3.3 billion purchase of Lotus Development.

Dow Jones United States Equity Market Index Performance

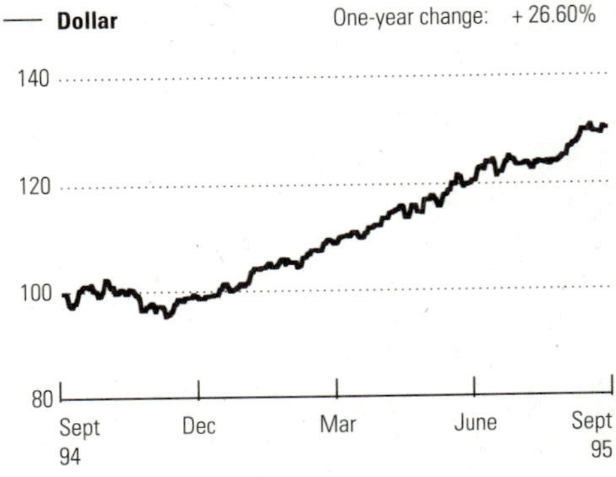

The merger activity, along with record corporate stock buyback efforts, helped stock supply shrink, many analysts say. With supply

Gross Domestic Product (94) (based on constant dollars)	Three-Year Average GDP Growth (92-94) (based on constant dollars)	Main Industries	Consumer Price Index (12/93-12/94)	Monetary Unit	Exchange Rate (9/95)
$5,344 billion	3.2%	Services, finance, insurance, real estate, durable and non-durable manufacturing, retail and wholesale trade, and construction	3.6%	United States dollar	US$1.00 to US$1.00

shrinking, investor dollars chase fewer issues, helping to push prices higher.

But rising prices stir the juices in the initial public offering market. Though lazy in the beginning of 1995, the IPO market accelerated rapidly into the summer. The most spectacular moment came when Netscape, an internet software firm, went public at $28 a share, soared to $74, and settled in the low $50 range a few days following the offering. Also having successful offerings: Red Hook Ale, a microbrewery and Premisys Communications, an equipment maker.

Netscape's success stemmed from its internet and technology labels, a hot ticket in the U.S. markets. While the broad market rose to record levels, technology issues—especially semiconductor and personal computer concerns—had stupendous years. By some measures, the semiconductor sector rose 75% in the first nine months of 1995.

The U.S. equity markets consist primarily of two competing operations: the New York Stock Exchange and the Nasdaq Stock Market. The older NYSE has an actual trading floor and utilizes a so-called auction market, in which a single specialist matches buyers and sellers in each of the NYSE's listings. The Nasdaq Stock Market is a dealer-based market, with several market-makers matching buyers and sellers in a screen-based environment.

Both operations have battled hard for listings, dominance and moral supremacy in the lucrative U.S. financial markets. By mid-1995, both markets traded more than 300 million shares on a typical day.

Ten Largest Capitalized Companies
as of 9/30/95

Stock	Market Cap. US$Mil
General Electric	107,254,721.3
AT&T	104,302,315.3
Exxon	89,717,521.3
Coca-Cola	87,021,558.0
Philip Morris	70,140,584.5
Merck & Co.	69,254,808.0
Wal-Mart Stores	57,146,456.9
IBM	53,673,233.1
Microsoft	53,000,420.0
Procter & Gamble	52,927,721.0

The rivalry between the two markets took an interesting turn in the past year when the U.S. Justice Department accused Nasdaq market makers of illegally fixing spreads between the bid and ask price on certain stocks. The NYSE has long maintained that their own auction-based system provided better spreads. Nasdaq has cooperated with the investigation and a resolution of some sort was anticipated in the fall.

Nasdaq trades many of the premier technology companies in the country, including Microsoft, Oracle, Cisco Systems and Intel. Beyond the big names, Nasdaq also trades many smaller-capitalization issues, a group that many analysts think is due for a strong showing in the next several years.

The New York Stock Exchange, meanwhile, has concentrated more on non-U.S. listings to build its list of stocks. The NYSE now lists close to 300 non-U.S. companies among its more than 2,700 issues, creating a virtual world market in New York. Currently, those shares trade as American depositary receipts or other types of programs that convert non-U.S. shares into dollar denominated units. The NYSE, however, says it is testing ways to trade non-U.S. issues in their native currencies, perhaps by late 1996.

The push to increase non-U.S. listings, however, has stumbled in some areas. Only Daimler-Benz is listed from Germany, and the other German companies complain about the requirement to adhere to different accounting and regulatory standards in the U.S. Controversy about U.S. regulations and accounting standards has also hampered efforts to list companies from Switzerland and France. Most of the Big Board's new listings in recent years have come from Latin America, but that market suffered when the Mexican economy stumbled on the heels of the peso's devaluation in late 1994. NYSE officials are lobbying the Securities and Exchange Commission to ease their rules on accounting standards.

Away from the skirmishes between the Big Board and the Nasdaq, smaller markets have also started increasing their presence in the U.S. Through "preferencing," regional exchanges have grabbed larger—though still relatively small—shares of the trading action. Preferencing permits a brokerage firm to internalize order flow to themselves, thereby reaping a larger profit on each transaction.

Industry Group Performance
1 Year Change Through 9/30/95

Industry	Change % (US$)
Best Performing	
Semiconductors	109.03
Advanced Technology Medical Devices	61.42
Medical & Biological Technology - All	58.61
Securities Brokers	56.80
Aerospace & Defense	56.26
Worst Performing	
Steel	-28.13
Trucking	-14.33
Precious Metals	-13.47
Coal	-8.88
Retailers - Other Specialty	-4.81

The practice of preferencing has come under scrutiny because it permits a firm to execute a trade at the edge of the spread, rather than somewhere in between. Some critics say this hurts some investors, usually small retail clients, who sometimes pay 12.5 to 25 cents more per share on a "preferenced" trade. The Cincinnati Stock Exchange has the largest preferencing operation in the country, but it remains a test case. The Securities and Exchange Commission had yet to rule on the Cincinnati model as of Sept. 30, 1995.

But not just preferencing operations threaten to siphon of trade volume from the NYSE, and, to a lesser degree, Nasdaq. The Boston Stock Exchange and the Pacific Stock Exchange have also built their trading business in NYSE and Nasdaq stocks. The Chicago Stock Exchange has proposed an all-electronic U.S. Stock Exchange that will specialize in stocks already traded on other exchanges. And third-market operators, such as Bernard Madoff, trade large stocks in large blocks for large clients, further trimming the Big Board and Nasdaq's share of the action.

The venerable American Stock Exchange continues to battle against obscurity. While the NYSE and the Nasdaq traded consistently more than 300 million shares per day, the AMEX trailed badly with less than 30 million shares traded a day. Still, with names like Hasbro, Viacom and Turner Broadcasting, and a strong derivatives business, the AMEX continues to struggle ahead.

Abbott Laboratories

Industry: **Medical Supplies**

Abbott Laboratories manufactures health-care products for consumers, hospitals, and laboratories. The company's pharmaceutical- and nutritional-products division makes prescription drugs that include antibiotics and oral estrogen; infant formulas sold under the names Similac and Isomil; personal-care products such as Selsun Blue dandruff shampoo; and agricultural chemicals such as insecticides and plant-growth regulators. Its hospital- and laboratory-products division produces intravenous solutions and equipment, injectable drugs, and diagnostic instruments.

$ mil	12/92	12/93	12/94	% Change				
Sales	7,851.9	8,407.8	9,156.0	8.9	P/E Ratio	22.8	Price (9/30/95)	42.63
Net Income	1,239.1	1,399.1	1,516.7	8.4	P/B Ratio	8.5	52 Wk Hi-Low	43.38-30.13
Book Value	3,347.6	3,674.9	4,049.4	10.2	Yield %	1.8	Market Cap	US$33,825mil

Address **100 Abbott Park Rd.**
Abbott Park, IL 60064-3500
Tel **708-937-6100**
Fax **708-937-1511**
Exchange **NYSE**
Ticker **ABT**
President & COO **Thomas R. Hodgson**
Chairman & CEO **Duane L. Burnham**

Acclaim Entertainment

Industry: **Toy Manufacturers**

Acclaim Entertainment publishes interactive software. Its principal software products are games programmed under license from Nintendo and Sega for use with the Super Nintendo Entertainment System, Nintendo Game Boy, Nintendo Entertainment System, Sega Genesis, Sega Game Gear, and Sega Master System. Current titles include Mortal Kombat, Mortal Kombat II, Alien 3, X-Men, and NBA All-Star Challenge. Acclaim markets its products in the United States and abroad. Business outside the U.S. accounts for 36% of sales. The company also publishes comic books.

$ mil	08/92	08/93	08/94	% Change				
Sales	214.6	327.1	480.8	47.0	P/E Ratio	25.8	Price (9/30/95)	25.75
Net Income	13.8	28.2	45.1	59.8	P/B Ratio	5.8	52 Wk Hi-Low	28.19-13.44
Book Value	64.7	96.9	175.2	80.8	Yield %	0.0	Market Cap	US$1,156.2mil

Address **71 Audrey Ave.**
Oyster Bay, NY 11771
Tel **516-624-8888**
Fax **516-624-2885**
Exchange **NASDA**
Ticker **AKLM**
Chief Executive **Gregory Fischbach**
Chairman **James Scoroposki**

Actava

Industry: **Household Services**

Actava Group primarily manufactures lawn-and-garden equipment. The company's lawn-and-garden division makes lawnmowers, tractors, and snowblowers and distributes similar products made by others, under the Snapper and Blackhawk names. The company also owns approximately 39% of Roadmaster, a sporting-goods manufacturer. Actava Group has entered into a collaborative agreement with Orion Pictures, MCEG Sterling, and Metromedia International Telecommunications to form a new global media, entertainment, and communications company.

$ mil	12/92	12/93	12/94	% Change				
Sales	1,148.7	1,241.1	551.8	-55.5	P/E Ratio	NMF	Price (9/30/95)	18.38
Net Income	11.6	-47.6	-65.8	38.1	P/B Ratio	2.5	52 Wk Hi-Low	19.13-8.63
Book Value	239.8	195.9	124.7	-36.4	Yield %	0.0	Market Cap	US$318.7mil

Address **4900 Georgia-Pacific Ctr.**
Atlanta, GA 30303
Tel **404-658-9000**
Fax **404-524-4713**
Exchange **NYSE**
Ticker **ACT**
President & CEO **John D. Phillips**
Chairman **--**

Acuson

Industry: **Advanced Medical Technology**

Acuson manufactures medical diagnostic ultrasound-imaging systems. Its products include ultrasound equipment and related software used in radiology, obstetrics/gynecology, cardiology, and other medical specialties. The company markets its products primarily to community and teaching hospitals and clinics in the U.S., Australia, Canada, Finland, France, Germany, Italy, Japan, Norway, Sweden, Russia, and the U.K. Business activity outside the U.S. accounts for approximately 20% of sales. Acuson operates manufacturing facilities in California and Pennsylvania.

$ mil	12/92	12/93	12/94	% Change				
Sales	342.8	295.3	350.5	18.7	P/E Ratio	21.6	Price (9/30/95)	13.38
Net Income	36.8	3.7	18.3	393.8	P/B Ratio	1.9	52 Wk Hi-Low	18.38-10.88
Book Value	201.1	183.3	207.8	13.4	Yield %	0.0	Market Cap	US$373.4mil

Address **1220 Charleston Rd.**
Mountain View, CA 94039
Tel **415-969-9112**
Fax **415-961-4726**
Exchange **NYSE**
Ticker **ACN**
President & CEO **Samuel H. Maslak**
Chairman **--**

Addington Resources

Industry: **Coal**

Addington Resources operates landfills and natural-resource mines and manufactures mining equipment. The company operates nonhazardous solid-waste landfills and recyclable-material sorting centers under government contracts in Georgia, Kentucky, and North Carolina. It manages coal, sulfur and limestone mines primarily in Kentucky. Its Mining Technologies subsidiary makes mining machinery and their related components. Addington Resources also owns and manages citrus-farm property in Belize. Its primary customer is the electric-utility industry.

$ mil	12/92	12/93	12/94	% Change				
Sales	301.5	384.1	151.2	-60.6	P/E Ratio	NMF	Price (9/30/95)	15.38
Net Income	11.0	-16.2	-7.1	-56.0	P/B Ratio	2.0	52 Wk Hi-Low	15.38-8.25
Book Value	136.8	124.9	120.2	-3.7	Yield %	0.0	Market Cap	US$244.8mil

Address **1500 North Big Run Rd.**
Ashland, KY 41102
Tel **606-928-3433**
Fax **606-928-9527**
Exchange **NASDA**
Ticker **ADDR**
President & COO **Kirby J. Taylor**
Chairman & CEO **Larry Addington**

Adobe Systems

Industry: **Software**

Adobe Systems develops software applications for its PostScript page-description language. PostScript is a computer language that communicates descriptions of computer-generated graphics and text to any output device with a PostScript interpreter. More than 5,000 applications support PostScript language output. These applications are available for every major computer-operating system and hardware configuration. Products are marketed through various channels, including distribution through retail channels and direct original equipment manufacturer licenses.

$ mil	11/92	11/93	11/94	% Change				
Sales	**265.9**	**313.5**	**597.8**	**90.7**	P/E Ratio	**NMF**	Price (9/30/95)	**51.75**
Net Income	**43.6**	**57.0**	**6.3**	**-88.9**	P/B Ratio	**6.9**	52 Wk Hi-Low	**65.50-28.75**
Book Value	**224.6**	**272.3**	**456.8**	**67.7**	Yield %	**0.4**	Market Cap	**US$3,278.1mil**

Address **1585 Charleston Rd.**
Mountain View, CA 94039-7900
Tel **415-961-4400**
Fax **415-961-5707**
Exchange **NASDA**
Ticker **ADBE**
President **Charles M. Geschke**
Chairman & CEO **John E. Warnock**

ADP

Industry: **Software**

Automatic Data Processing (ADP) offers computer services that enable clients to process and distribute data, using the company's computer programs for interactive manipulation of ADP and third-party databases and information. The company's employer-services group offers payroll and payroll-related services including payroll processing, payroll-tax filing, human-resource record keeping and reporting from regional offices throughout the U.S. The brokerage services group provides front-office database and quotation services for the investment and brokerage industries.

$ mil	06/93	06/94	06/95	% Change				
Sales	**2,223.3**	**2,469.0**	**2,893.7**	**17.2**	P/E Ratio	**24.6**	Price (9/30/95)	**68.13**
Net Income	**294.2**	**329.3**	**394.8**	**19.9**	P/B Ratio	**4.7**	52 Wk Hi-Low	**70.50-52.75**
Book Value	**1,494.5**	**1,691.3**	**2,096.6**	**24.0**	Yield %	**0.9**	Market Cap	**US$9,798.1mil**

Address **One ADP Blvd.**
Roseland, NJ 07068
Tel **201-994-5000**
Fax **201-994-5387**
Exchange **NYSE**
Ticker **AUD**
President **Arthur F. Weinbach**
Chairman **Josh S. Weston**

Advanced Micro Devices

Industry: **Semiconductors & related**

Advanced Micro Devices manufactures integrated circuits, microprocessors, and related peripheral memory devices and circuits. These products are used in telecommunication, office-automation, and computer-networking applications. Its microprocessor products include the AM486 central-processing units used in personal computers. Advanced Micro Devices markets these products to original-equipment manufacturers of computers, peripherals, and communication equipment in the United States and in international markets. Foreign sales account for 55% of the total.

$ mil	12/92	12/93	12/94	% Change				
Sales	**1,514.5**	**1,648.3**	**2,134.7**	**29.5**	P/E Ratio	**9.6**	Price (9/30/95)	**29.13**
Net Income	**245.0**	**228.8**	**305.3**	**33.4**	P/B Ratio	**1.6**	52 Wk Hi-Low	**38.63-22.50**
Book Value	**1,046.7**	**1,352.3**	**1,735.3**	**28.3**	Yield %	**0.0**	Market Cap	**US$3,022.4mil**

Address **One AMD Pl.**
Sunnyvale, CA 94088-3453
Tel **408-732-2400**
Fax **408-894-0547**
Exchange **NYSE**
Ticker **AMD**
President & COO **Richard Previte**
Chairman & CEO **W.J. Sanders III**

Aetna Life & Casualty

Industry: **Insurance - Full Line**

Aetna Life & Casualty provides insurance and financial services. Its insurance products include life, health, automobile, homeowner's, fire, liability, and workers' compensation policies. Its Aetna Financial Services and Aetna Capital Management subsidiaries offer pension and annuity products, and investment-advisory and asset-management services. Although the company operates in the United States and abroad, 90% of its total revenues are derived from U.S. sources. Based on assets, Aetna is one of the nation's largest insurance and financial-services organizations.

$ mil	12/92	12/93	12/94	% Change				
Revenues	**17,497.2**	**17,117.7**	**17,524.7**	**2.4**	P/E Ratio	**17.7**	Price (9/30/95)	**73.38**
Net Income	**56.0**	**-365.9**	**467.5**	**-227.8**	P/B Ratio	**1.5**	52 Wk Hi-Low	**74.38-43.25**
Book Value	**7,238.3**	**7,043.1**	**5,503.0**	**-21.9**	Yield %	**3.8**	Market Cap	**US$8,307.5mil**

Address **151 Farmington Ave.**
Hartford, CT 06156
Tel **203-273-0123**
Fax **203-273-0079**
Exchange **NYSE**
Ticker **AET**
President **Ronald E. Compton**
Chairman **Ronald E. Compton**

AFLAC

Industry: **Insurance - Life & Health**

AFLAC sells supplemental health insurance in six countries, primarily in the United States and Japan. The company's primary subsidiary, American Family Life Assurance Company of Columbus, writes medical-insurance policies, including policies for hospital intensive care, accident and disability, long-term care, home health care, and Medicare supplements. In addition, AFLAC offers several life-insurance plans in the U.S. Insurance operations outside the U.S. account for about 84% of the company's total revenues. AFLAC also owns seven network-affiliated television stations.

$ mil	12/92	12/93	12/94	% Change				
Revenues	**3,986.5**	**5,000.6**	**6,110.8**	**22.2**	P/E Ratio	**14.6**	Price (9/30/95)	**41.50**
Net Income	**183.4**	**255.3**	**292.8**	**14.7**	P/B Ratio	**2.4**	52 Wk Hi-Low	**44.50-31.75**
Book Value	**1,081.9**	**1,365.6**	**1,751.8**	**28.3**	Yield %	**1.1**	Market Cap	**US$3,996.3mil**

Address **1932 Wynnton Rd.**
Columbus, GA 31999
Tel **706-323-3431**
Fax **706-324-6330**
Exchange **NYSE**
Ticker **AFL**
President & CEO **Daniel P. Amos**
Chairman **Paul S. Amos**

H.F. Ahmanson & Co.

Industry: **Savings & Loans (U.S. Only)**

H.F. Ahmanson & Company is the holding company of Home Savings of America, the largest federally chartered savings bank by assets in the U.S. Home Savings operates 357 branches in six states (mainly in California), and 82 lending offices in 12 states. All of these offer consumer-savings and mortgage-banking services. Adjustable-rate mortgages (secured by residential real estate) which the company also develops, make up most of its mortgage portfolio. Home Savings conducts certain savings and lending operations through the company's Savings of America subsidiary.

$ mil	12/92	12/93	12/94	% Change				
Revenues	**3,637.5**	**3,100.0**	**3,381.4**	**9.1**	P/E Ratio	**16.0**	Price (9/30/95)	**25.38**
Net Income	**204.1**	**-159.6**	**237.4**	**-248.7**	P/B Ratio	**1.0**	52 Wk Hi-Low	**25.63-15.88**
Book Value	**2,745.6**	**2,949.0**	**2,964.6**	**0.5**	Yield %	**3.5**	Market Cap	**US$2,981.1mil**

Address	**4900 Rivergrade Rd.**	Tel	**818-960-6311**	Exchange	**NYSE**	President	**Charles R. Rinehart**
	Irwindale, CA 91706	Fax	**818-962-9679**	Ticker	**AHM**	Chairman	**Charles R. Rinehart**

Air Express International

Industry: **Air Freight & Couriers**

Air Express International provides freight services. It offers delivery of all shipment sizes, concentrating on industrial equipment. The company also provides express delivery among 18 European cities and forwards cargo for shipment by air, land, and sea. Air Express operates terminal facilities, or is represented by other companies acting as agents, in 230 U.S. and 320 foreign cities. Business activities outside the United States account for approximately 63% of revenues. The company operates facilities in 188 locations in the U.S. and 50 locations abroad.

$ mil	12/92	12/93	12/94	% Change				
Sales	**672.3**	**725.7**	**997.4**	**37.4**	P/E Ratio	**19.7**	Price (9/30/95)	**25.25**
Net Income	**18.6**	**17.3**	**22.6**	**30.8**	P/B Ratio	**4.4**	52 Wk Hi-Low	**26.50-15.92**
Book Value	**65.4**	**78.1**	**99.4**	**27.2**	Yield %	**0.6**	Market Cap	**US$467.1mil**

Address	**120 Tokeneke Rd.**	Tel	**203-655-7900**	Exchange	**NASDA**	President & CEO	**Guenter Rohrmann**
	Darien, CT 06820	Fax	**203-655-5779**	Ticker	**AEIC**	Chairman	**Hendrik J. Hartong, Jr.**

Air Products & Chemicals

Industry: **Specialty Chemicals**

Air Products & Chemicals recovers industrial gases and specialty chemicals and provides related services. It also operates waste-to-energy and electricity-generating facilities and designs cryogenic systems. Markets for its industrial gases include the oil and chemical industries. The company's specialty chemicals are used in the manufacture of adhesives, textiles, paper, and construction materials. Air Products & Chemicals markets its products worldwide, with foreign sales accounting for 25% of revenues.

$ mil	09/92	09/93	09/94	% Change				
Sales	**3,217.3**	**3,327.7**	**3,485.3**	**4.7**	P/E Ratio	**23.9**	Price (9/30/95)	**52.13**
Net Income	**271.0**	**200.9**	**247.8**	**23.3**	P/B Ratio	**2.7**	52 Wk Hi-Low	**59.25-43.13**
Book Value	**2,097.7**	**2,101.9**	**2,206.4**	**5.0**	Yield %	**1.8**	Market Cap	**US$5,825.3mil**

Address	**7201 Hamilton Blvd.**	Tel	**610-481-4911**	Exchange	**NYSE**	President & CEO	**Harold A. Wagner**
	Allentown, PA 18195-1501	Fax	**610-481-5900**	Ticker	**APD**	Chairman	**Harold A. Wagner**

Airborne Freight

Industry: **Air Freight & Couriers**

Airborne Freight is an international express-parcel company. Its primary service is overnight-express delivery, which accounts for 63% of the company's domestic shipments. The company mainly serves corporate customers. Airborne also provides general air-freight and door-to-door service, and acts as a freight forwarder in the United States and abroad. It accomplishes these services through a company-owned fleet of trucks, vans, and airplanes, and through independent contractors. Business conducted outside the U.S. accounts for 14% of total revenues.

$ mil	12/92	12/93	12/94	% Change				
Sales	**1,484.3**	**1,720.0**	**1,970.8**	**14.6**	P/E Ratio	**13.5**	Price (9/30/95)	**24.50**
Net Income	**5.2**	**39.1**	**38.8**	**-0.7**	P/B Ratio	**1.3**	52 Wk Hi-Low	**26.00-18.25**
Book Value	**285.6**	**318.8**	**392.4**	**23.1**	Yield %	**1.2**	Market Cap	**US$515.7mil**

Address	**3101 Western Ave.**	Tel	**206-285-4600**	Exchange	**NYSE**	President & COO	**Robert G. Brazier**
	Seattle, WA 98111	Fax	**206-281-3890**	Ticker	**ABF**	Chairman & CEO	**Robert S. Cline**

AirTouch Communications

Industry: **Mobile Communication Systems**

AirTouch Communications provides cellular-telephone communication services and related products. The company has cellular interests in the U.S., Germany, Portugal, Sweden, Belgium, and Japan, and offers paging services in Thailand and France. It provides cellular-telephone service, wireless data transmission, and paging services to more than 1.9 million subscribers worldwide. AirTouch Communications' domestic revenues are primarily derived from customers in California, Kansas, Missouri, Michigan, Ohio, and Georgia.

$ mil	12/92 R	12/93	12/94	% Change				
Sales	**880.2**	**988.0**	**1,235.4**	**25.0**	P/E Ratio	**NMF**	Price (9/30/95)	**30.63**
Net Income	**10.2**	**34.5**	**98.1**	**184.3**	P/B Ratio	**4.4**	52 Wk Hi-Low	**34.63-25.00**
Book Value	**-9,999.1**	**3,337.3**	**3,459.6**	**3.7**	Yield %	**0.0**	Market Cap	**US$15,158mil**

Address	**One California St.**	Tel	**415-658-2000**	Exchange	**NYSE**	Chief Executive	**Sam Ginn**
	San Francisco, CA 94111	Fax	**415-658-2034**	Ticker	**ATI**	Chairman	**Sam Ginn**

R=Restated.

Alaska Air

Industry: **Airlines**

Alaska Air is the parent company of Alaska Airlines and Horizon Air Industries. Alaska Airlines operates routes between the continental U.S. and Alaska. Horizon Air Industries is a commuter airline operating in the Pacific Northwest. Alaska Airlines serves 36 airports in six states, three cities in Mexico, and three cities in Russia from its hubs in Seattle; Anchorage, Alaska; and Portland, Oregon. Horizon services 33 airports in six states and British Columbia. Services provided through the Alaska Airlines subsidiary account for approximately 80% of total revenues.

$ mil	12/92	12/93	12/94	% Change				
Sales	**1,115.4**	**1,128.3**	**1,315.6**	**16.6**	P/E Ratio	**9.3**	Price (9/30/95)	**15.63**
Net Income	**-84.8**	**-30.9**	**22.5**	**-172.9**	P/B Ratio	**1.1**	52 Wk Hi-Low	**20.88-13.50**
Book Value	**196.7**	**166.8**	**191.3**	**14.7**	Yield %	**0.0**	Market Cap	**US$210.0mil**

Address **19300 Pacific Hwy. S.**
Seattle, WA 98188
Tel **206-431-7040**
Fax **206-433-3379**
Exchange **NYSE**
Ticker **ALK**
President & CEO **John F. Kelly**
Chairman **John F. Kelly**

Albemarle

Industry: **Specialty Chemicals**

Albemarle is a chemical-manufacturing company. The company's products include chemicals for polymers, detergents, personal-care products, pharmaceuticals, agriculture, and petroleum applications. These chemicals are used in plastics, insulation, soaps, bleaches, lubricants, pesticides, analgesics, herbicides, and fungicides. Albemarle markets its products in the United States and abroad. International operations account for approximately 40% of the company's sales. Albemarle operates research and manufacturing facilities in the U.S., Belgium, Japan, and Singapore.

$ mil	12/92 R	12/93 R	12/94	% Change				
Sales	**818.2**	**903.4**	**1,080.9**	**19.7**	P/E Ratio	**23.7**	Price (9/30/95)	**18.75**
Net Income	**39.8**	**21.8**	**51.3**	**135.2**	P/B Ratio	**2.3**	52 Wk Hi-Low	**19.13-12.38**
Book Value	**589.8**	**700.2**	**545.0**	**-22.2**	Yield %	**1.1**	Market Cap	**US$1,238.8mil**

Address **330 S. Fourth St.**
Richmond, VA 23210
Tel **804-788-6000**
Fax **804-788-5688**
Exchange **NYSE**
Ticker **ALB**
President & COO **E. Gary Cook**
Chairman & CEO **Floyd D. Gottwald, Jr.**

R=Restated.

Albertson's

Industry: **Food Retailers & Wholesalers**

Albertson's operates a chain of retail food and drug stores. The company is the fourth-largest retail food and drug chain in the U.S., with operations in 19 western, midwestern, and southern states. It currently operates 720 stores: 588 combination food and drug stores, 88 conventional supermarkets, and 44 warehouse stores. Retail operations are supported by 11 company-owned distribution centers. The combination food and drug stores range in size from 35,000 to 75,000 square feet. The company's conventional supermarkets range from 15,000 to 35,000 square feet.

$ mil	01/93	01/94	01/95	% Change				
Sales	**10,173.7**	**11,283.7**	**11,894.6**	**5.4**	P/E Ratio	**21.6**	Price (9/30/95)	**34.13**
Net Income	**269.2**	**340.0**	**400.4**	**17.8**	P/B Ratio	**5.1**	52 Wk Hi-Low	**34.13-27.63**
Book Value	**1,388.4**	**1,389.4**	**1,687.9**	**21.5**	Yield %	**1.3**	Market Cap	**US$8,669.1mil**

Address **250 Parkcenter Blvd.**
Boise, ID 83726
Tel **208-385-6200**
Fax **208-385-6110**
Exchange **NYSE**
Ticker **ABS**
President **John B. Carley**
Chairman & CEO **Gary G. Michael**

Alco Standard

Industry: **General Industrial & Commercial Services**

Alco Standard distributes paper, packaging products, and office equipment. Unisource Worldwide, a subsidiary, distributes office and printing papers to printers and other businesses, paper and plastic packaging and related equipment to food processors, and janitorial supplies to commercial facilities. Alco Office Products, another subsidiary, sells and leases copiers, fax machines, and other office equipment, and offers related maintenance services, facilities management, and specialized document-copying services. The company markets its products and services worldwide.

$ mil	09/92	09/93	09/94	% Change				
Sales	**4,882.9**	**6,387.1**	**7,925.8**	**24.1**	P/E Ratio	**77.0**	Price (9/30/95)	**84.75**
Net Income	**95.8**	**0.1**	**70.6**	**NMF**	P/B Ratio	**3.4**	52 Wk Hi-Low	**86.88-64.25**
Book Value	**860.4**	**1,020.6**	**1,367.1**	**34.0**	Yield %	**1.2**	Market Cap	**US$4,715.7mil**

Address **825 Duportail Rd.**
Wayne, PA 19087-5589
Tel **610-296-8000**
Fax **610-296-8419**
Exchange **NYSE**
Ticker **ASN**
President & CEO **John E. Stuart**
Chairman **Ray B. Mundt**

Alcoa

Industry: **Aluminum**

Aluminum Company of America (Alcoa) manufactures and sells primary aluminum and semi fabricated and finished aluminum products. It also produces and sells alumina and alumina-based chemicals, a variety of other finished products, and components and systems for various applications. Customers for these products include the international packaging, transportation, building, and industrial industries. The company's non-aluminum products include electrical, ceramic, plastic, vinyl, composite materials, manufacturing equipment, gold, magnesium, steel, and titanium forgings.

$ mil	12/92	12/93	12/94	% Change				
Sales	**9,491.5**	**9,055.9**	**9,904.3**	**9.4**	P/E Ratio	**25.2**	Price (9/30/95)	**52.88**
Net Income	**-1,139.2**	**4.8**	**375.2**	**NMF**	P/B Ratio	**2.4**	52 Wk Hi-Low	**59.75-37.25**
Book Value	**3,604.3**	**3,583.8**	**3,999.2**	**11.6**	Yield %	**1.5**	Market Cap	**US$9,437.9mil**

Address **Alcoa Bldg., 425 Sixth Ave.**
Pittsburgh, PA 15219-1850
Tel **412-553-4545**
Fax **412-553-4498**
Exchange **NYSE**
Ticker **AA**
Chief Executive **Paul H. O'Neill**
Chairman **Paul H. O'Neill**

Alexander & Baldwin

Industry: **Marine Transportation**

Alexander & Baldwin provides ocean-transportation services, makes food products, leases cargo containers, and develops real estate. Its ocean-transportation services, which generate the majority of revenues, include transporting freight between Hawaii and the Pacific Coast of the U.S., providing tugboat services, and loading and unloading cargoes. As for food products, the company grows and processes sugarcane and coffee. It sells these commodities in raw and processed forms. Alexander & Baldwin also sells and manages residential and commercial properties.

$ mil	12/92	12/93	12/94	% Change				
Sales	730.9	962.0	1,185.2	23.2	P/E Ratio	14.8	Price (9/30/95)	24.00
Net Income	19.0	67.0	74.6	11.4	P/B Ratio	1.7	52 Wk Hi-Low	26.00-21.00
Book Value	559.1	587.0	632.6	7.8	Yield %	3.7	Market Cap	US$1,092.3mil

Address **822 Bishop St.**
Honolulu, HI 96801-3440
Tel **808-525-6611**
Fax **808-525-6652**
Exchange **NASDA**
Ticker **ALEX**
President & CEO **John C. Couch**
Chairman **R.J. Pfeiffer**

Allegheny Ludlum

Industry: **Steel**

Allegheny Ludlum manufactures specialty materials including stainless-steel. The company manufactures stainless steel sheet, strip, plate, foil, welded tubing, and stampings; grain-oriented silicon electrical steel sheet and strip; and other specialty steel and metal alloys. Stainless steel represents approximately 78% of total sales. ALstrip, a subsidiary, is the company's distributor outlet for stainless-steel strip (less than 24" wide). Common uses of the company's products are in automobiles, appliances, communications, chemical processing, and medical equipment.

$ mil	12/92	12/93	12/94	% Change				
Sales	1,036.0	1,100.2	1,076.9	-2.1	P/E Ratio	78.4	Price (9/30/95)	20.38
Net Income	-78.4	70.8	18.2	-74.3	P/B Ratio	4.0	52 Wk Hi-Low	22.88-18.13
Book Value	256.9	403.4	361.7	-10.3	Yield %	2.4	Market Cap	US$1,408.2mil

Address **1000 Six PPG Pl.**
Pittsburgh, PA 15222
Tel **412-394-2800**
Fax **412-394-3034**
Exchange **NYSE**
Ticker **ALS**
President & CEO **Arthur H. Aronson**
Chairman **Richard P. Simmons**

Allegheny Power System

Industry: **Electrical Utilities - Eastern U.S.**

Allegheny Power System provides electricity through four subsidiaries (Monongahela Power, Potomac Edison, West Penn Power, and Allegheny Generating) that serve 1.3 million customers. Its service area includes five states: Pennsylvania (about 45% of sales), West Virginia (28%), Maryland (20%), Virginia (5%), and Ohio (2%). Residential customers account for roughly 35% of revenues. The company operates 54 generation units. Approximately 88% of its electricity is supplied by coal-fired plants; the remainder is supplied via storage reserves and hydroelectric generators.

$ mil	12/92	12/93	12/94	% Change				
Sales	2,306.7	2,331.5	2,451.7	5.2	P/E Ratio	11.4	Price (9/30/95)	25.50
Net Income	185.3	198.7	243.1	22.4	P/B Ratio	1.3	52 Wk Hi-Low	25.50-19.75
Book Value	2,105.9	2,232.3	2,384.6	6.8	Yield %	6.4	Market Cap	US$3,061.2mil

Address **12 E. 49th St.**
New York, NY 10017-1028
Tel **212-752-2121**
Fax **212-836-4340**
Exchange **NYSE**
Ticker **AYP**
President **Alan J. Noia**
Chairman & CEO **Klaus Bergman**

AlliedSignal

Industry: **Industrial - Diversified**

AlliedSignal manufactures aerospace and automotive products and engineered materials that are marketed in the U.S. and worldwide. Its aerospace division produces parts including turbofan, turboshaft, turbojet and turboprop engines, climate-control equipment, and aircraft-landing systems, as well as weather and collision-avoidance radar systems. The company's automotive division manufactures brakes, engine parts, and safety restraints for automobile producers. AlliedSignal's engineered-materials division makes plastics, chemicals, circuit-board laminates, and nylon yarns.

$ mil	12/92	12/93	12/94	% Change				
Sales	12,042.0	11,827.0	12,817.0	8.4	P/E Ratio	16.5	Price (9/30/95)	44.13
Net Income	-712.0	411.0	759.0	84.7	P/B Ratio	4.2	52 Wk Hi-Low	46.75-30.88
Book Value	2,251.0	2,390.0	2,982.0	24.8	Yield %	1.5	Market Cap	US$12,494mil

Address **101 Columbia Rd.**
Morristown, NJ 07962
Tel **201-455-2000**
Fax **201-455-6069**
Exchange **NYSE**
Ticker **ALD**
Chief Executive **Lawrence A. Bossidy**
Chairman **Lawrence A. Bossidy**

Allstate

Industry: **Insurance - Property & Casualty**

Allstate underwrites property and casualty and life insurance. The company is the second-largest property-liability insurer in the United States based on premiums earned. Personal automobile and homeowner's insurance lines constitute the bulk of Allstate's property and casualty business, which accounts for roughly 90% of the company's property and liability premiums. Allstate also sells life insurance, group pension plans, and annuity products. The company markets its insurance policies through about 14,500 Allstate-affiliated agents in the U.S. and Canada.

$ mil	12/92	12/93	12/94	% Change				
Revenues	20,228.1	20,946.3	21,464.3	2.5	P/E Ratio	32.8	Price (9/30/95)	35.38
Net Income	-825.2	1,301.5	483.8	-62.8	P/B Ratio	1.9	52 Wk Hi-Low	36.00-29.88
Book Value	7,182.7	10,299.7	8,426.0	-18.2	Yield %	2.0	Market Cap	US$15,861mil

Address **2775 Sanders Rd.**
Northbrook, IL 60062-6127
Tel **708-402-5000**
Fax **N/A**
Exchange **NYSE**
Ticker **ALL**
President **Edward M. Liddy**
Chairman & CEO **Jerry D. Choate**

Alumax

Industry: **Aluminum**

Alumax is an integrated aluminum company. The company produces and markets primary aluminum ingot and billet, and fabricates value-added aluminum products used in the building and construction, transportation, and container and packaging industries. It is currently the third-largest U.S. aluminum company and the fourth-largest aluminum company in North America, and operates more than 100 plants and facilities in the U.S., Canada, and western Europe. The company also makes fabricated-aluminum products and aluminum extrusions through its Kawneer subsidiary.

$ mil	12/92	12/93	12/94	% Change				
Sales	**2,431.0**	**2,347.3**	**2,754.5**	**17.3**	P/E Ratio	**40.2**	Price (9/30/95)	**33.75**
Net Income	**-38.9**	**-138.3**	**46.7**	**-133.8**	P/B Ratio	**1.3**	52 Wk Hi-Low	**37.13-24.00**
Book Value	**1,191.4**	**1,099.6**	**1,162.1**	**5.7**	Yield %	**0.0**	Market Cap	**US$1,508.0mil**

Address **5655 Peachtree Pkwy. Norcross, GA 30092-2812**
Tel **404-246-6600** Fax **404-246-6756**
Exchange **NYSE** Ticker **AMX**
President **--**
Chairman & CEO **Allen Born**

Alza

Industry: **Advanced Medical Technology**

Alza manufactures pharmaceutical products, including controlled-dosage and electrotransport-system agents. Its OROS technology allows patients to take remedies in a once-daily, time-release form that would otherwise have to be taken several times per day. The company's main OROS-technology agents include Procardia XL and Minipress XL, which treat hypertension, and Volmax, which fights asthma. Alza makes transdermal-delivery systems, including Nicoderm, which delivers nicotine to the bloodstream through the skin, and Transderm-Nitro, which transports nitroglycerin.

$ mil	12/92	12/93	12/94	% Change				
Sales	**250.5**	**234.2**	**278.8**	**19.0**	P/E Ratio	**32.4**	Price (9/30/95)	**23.00**
Net Income	**72.2**	**45.6**	**58.1**	**27.5**	P/B Ratio	**5.2**	52 Wk Hi-Low	**26.50-17.38**
Book Value	**407.5**	**306.7**	**364.5**	**18.8**	Yield %	**0.0**	Market Cap	**US$1,894.1mil**

Address **950 Page Mill Rd., P.O. Box 10950 Palo Alto, CA 94303-0802**
Tel **415-494-5000** Fax **415-494-8811**
Exchange **NYSE** Ticker **AZA**
President **Ernest Mario**
Chairman **Alejandro Zaffaroni**

AmSouth

Industry: **Banks - Southern U.S.**

AmSouth Bancorporation is a holding company with approximately 369 banking offices in Alabama, Florida, Georgia, and Tennessee. The company offers retail and commercial banking, and trust, mortgage, and brokerage services. The company's AmSouth Bank of Alabama, Alabama's second-largest bank, operates 149 branches in the state. Its other subsidiaries include AmSouth Bank of Florida (137 offices), AmSouth Bank of Georgia (8 offices), and AmSouth Bank of Tennessee (22 offices). AmSouth also offers first mortgage loans through its AmSouth Mortgage subsidiary.

$ mil	12/92	12/93	12/94	% Change				
Revenues	**829.7**	**971.3**	**1,226.8**	**26.3**	P/E Ratio	**16.9**	Price (9/30/95)	**38.00**
Net Income	**102.0**	**146.2**	**127.3**	**-12.9**	P/B Ratio	**1.7**	52 Wk Hi-Low	**39.13-25.50**
Book Value	**782.8**	**1,090.0**	**1,310.5**	**20.2**	Yield %	**3.8**	Market Cap	**US$2,219.4mil**

Address **1900 Fifth Ave. N. Birmingham, AL 35203**
Tel **205-320-7151** Fax **205-326-4072**
Exchange **NYSE** Ticker **ASO**
President **C. Dowd Ritter**
Chairman & CEO **John W. Woods**

Amax Gold

Industry: **Precious Metals**

Amax Gold, a majority-held subsidiary of Cyprus AMAX Minerals, operates gold mines, mainly in North America. The company's principal property in terms of production is the Sleeper mine in Nevada; it produces about 100,000 ounces of gold per year. Amax holds 7.1 million ounces of reserves at sites in the U.S., Chile, and New Zealand, more than half of which is at the Fort Knox mine in Alaska. Its Amax Precious Metals subsidiary coordinates Amax Gold's refining contracts with other companies and sells the company's refined gold to bullion dealers, primarily in Europe.

$ mil	12/92	12/93	12/94	% Change				
Sales	**99.7**	**81.9**	**94.6**	**15.5**	P/E Ratio	**NMF**	Price (9/30/95)	**6.13**
Net Income	**11.5**	**-104.2**	**-35.5**	**-65.9**	P/B Ratio	**2.0**	52 Wk Hi-Low	**7.63-4.50**
Book Value	**257.2**	**173.3**	**245.5**	**41.7**	Yield %	**0.0**	Market Cap	**US$498.1mil**

Address **9100 E. Mineral Circle Englewood, CO 80112**
Tel **303-643-5500** Fax **303-643-5507**
Exchange **NYSE** Ticker **AU**
President **Roger A. Kauffman**
Chairman & CEO **Milton H. Ward**

Amerada Hess

Industry: **Oil - Secondary**

Amerada Hess operates oil and natural-gas wells and related businesses in North America, the United Kingdom, and the North Sea. The company owns an average 16% interest in about 20,000 wells and holds net reserves of approximately 2.6 trillion cubic feet of natural gas and 644 million barrels of oil. It operates refineries at St. Croix, U.S. Virgin Islands, and Port Reading, New Jersey at which it principally produces gasoline and fuel oil for sale in the eastern United States. The company operates 540 Hess gasoline stations primarily in New York, New Jersey, and Florida.

$ mil	12/92	12/93	12/94	% Change				
Sales	**5,875.0**	**5,851.6**	**6,602.0**	**12.8**	P/E Ratio	**61.6**	Price (9/30/95)	**48.63**
Net Income	**7.5**	**-268.2**	**73.7**	**-127.5**	P/B Ratio	**1.5**	52 Wk Hi-Low	**53.00-43.75**
Book Value	**3,387.6**	**3,028.9**	**3,099.6**	**2.3**	Yield %	**1.2**	Market Cap	**US$4,522.3mil**

Address **1185 Ave. of the Americas New York, NY 10036**
Tel **212-997-8500** Fax **212-536-8930**
Exchange **NYSE** Ticker **AHC**
President **Robert F. Wright**
Chairman & CEO **Leon Hess**

American Brands

Industry: **Tobacco**

American Brands manufactures tobacco products and other consumer goods. The company markets cigarettes, cigars, and loose tobacco primarily in the United Kingdom under the Benson & Hedges, Condor, Old Holborn, and Hamlet brands. Its other products include Jim Beam whiskey, Lord Calvert Canadian whiskey, Gilbey's gin and vodka, Moen plumbing supplies, Masterlock locks, ACCO office products, Titleist golf balls and clubs, and Foot-Joy leisure and athletic products. American Brands' tobacco business accounts for approximately 50% of the company's total sales.

$ mil	12/92	12/93	12/94	% Change				
Sales	**14,623.6**	**13,701.4**	**13,146.5**	**-4.0**	P/E Ratio	**11.6**	Price (9/30/95)	**42.25**
Net Income	**883.8**	**469.8**	**734.1**	**56.3**	P/B Ratio	**1.8**	52 Wk Hi-Low	**43.50-33.00**
Book Value	**4,301.6**	**4,271.4**	**4,637.5**	**8.6**	Yield %	**4.7**	Market Cap	**US$7,978.3mil**

Address **1700 E. Putnam Ave.**
Old Greenwich, CT 06870-0811
Tel **203-698-5000**
Fax **203-637-2580**
Exchange **NYSE**
Ticker **AMB**
President **John T. Ludes**
Chairman & CEO **Thomas C. Hays**

American Electric Power

Industry: **Electrical Utilities - Central U.S.**

American Electric Power generates electricity. The company provides electricity to approximately seven million customers in Indiana, Kentucky, Michigan, Ohio, Tennessee, Virginia, and West Virginia. Its largest subsidiary, Appalachian Power, contributes 26% of revenues. Most of the company's electricity sales are to commercial and industrial users. Approximately 83% of its electricity is supplied by coal-fired plants, the remainder by nuclear and hydroelectric sources. The company also supplies electrical power to municipal electric systems and rural energy cooperatives.

$ mil	12/92	12/93	12/94	% Change				
Sales	**5,044.8**	**5,268.8**	**5,504.7**	**4.5**	P/E Ratio	**13.4**	Price (9/30/95)	**36.38**
Net Income	**527.7**	**412.6**	**500.0**	**21.2**	P/B Ratio	**1.6**	52 Wk Hi-Low	**36.38-30.63**
Book Value	**5,011.5**	**4,921.0**	**4,229.6**	**-14.0**	Yield %	**6.6**	Market Cap	**US$6,763.4mil**

Address **1 Riverside Plz.**
Columbus, OH 43215-2373
Tel **614-223-1000**
Fax **614-223-1823**
Exchange **NYSE**
Ticker **AEP**
President & CEO **E. Linn Draper, Jr.**
Chairman **E. Linn Draper, Jr.**

American Express

Industry: **Financial Services - Diversified**

American Express Company is a major provider of travel and financial services. The company's Travel Related Services division issues the American Express and Optima cards and American Express Travelers Cheques, and provides corporate and consumer travel products and services through 2,277 offices in more than 160 countries. Its subsidiaries, Centurion Bank and IDS Financial, provide investment products and lending, insurance, and information-processing services. The company also publishes various magazines, including Travel & Leisure.

$ mil	12/92	12/93	12/94	% Change				
Revenues	**26,961.0**	**14,173.0**	**14,282.0**	**0.8**	P/E Ratio	**16.1**	Price (9/30/95)	**44.38**
Net Income	**461.0**	**1,478.0**	**1,413.0**	**-4.4**	P/B Ratio	**3.4**	52 Wk Hi-Low	**44.63-28.25**
Book Value	**7,499.0**	**8,734.0**	**6,433.0**	**-26.3**	Yield %	**2.1**	Market Cap	**US$21,642mil**

Address **World Financial Ctr., 200 Vesey St.**
New York, NY 10285
Tel **212-640-2000**
Fax **212-619-9802**
Exchange **NYSE**
Ticker **AXP**
President **Jeffrey E. Stiefler**
Chairman & CEO **Harvey Golub**

American Financial

Industry: **Insurance - Property & Casualty**

American Financial Group provides specialty property and casualty insurance. Its principal operations are conducted by the NSA Group, a group of private-passenger automobile-insurance companies that insure non-standard-risk individuals who are unable to obtain insurance through major-market carriers because of age, occupation, driving-record, or vehicle-type constraints. American Financial Group also owns Republic Indemnity of America, which provides workers' compensation and employer's liability insurance policies to California and Arizona employers.

$ mil	12/92	12/93	12/94	% Change				
Revenues	**998.7**	**1,273.6**	**1,557.9**	**22.3**	P/E Ratio	**NMF**	Price (9/30/95)	**30.00**
Net Income	**305.4**	**232.0**	**0.3**	**-99.9**	P/B Ratio	**0.9**	52 Wk Hi-Low	**31.88-22.25**
Book Value	**1,502.8**	**1,722.3**	**1,548.7**	**-10.1**	Yield %	**3.0**	Market Cap	**US$1,582.4mil**

Address **One E. Fourth St.**
Cincinnati, OH 45202
Tel **513-579-6600**
Fax **513-579-0108**
Exchange **NYSE**
Ticker **APZ**
President **Carl H. Lindner III**
Chairman & CEO **Carl H. Lindner**

American General

Industry: **Insurance - Life & Health**

American General provides consumer financial services throughout the United States, Puerto Rico, the Virgin Islands, and Canada. The company's primary subsidiaries are AGC Life Insurance, American General Finance, and American General Investment, providing annuities, consumer loans, credit-card services, and life, accident, health, and property and casualty insurance. The company's Variable Annuity Life Insurance subsidiary offers tax-deferred retirement plans for teachers and employees of nonprofit organizations. Life insurance represents 40% of the company's revenues.

$ mil	12/92	12/93	12/94	% Change				
Revenues	**4,602.0**	**4,829.0**	**4,841.0**	**0.2**	P/E Ratio	**15.3**	Price (9/30/95)	**37.38**
Net Income	**533.0**	**204.0**	**513.0**	**151.5**	P/B Ratio	**2.2**	52 Wk Hi-Low	**38.38-25.88**
Book Value	**4,616.0**	**5,137.0**	**3,457.0**	**-32.7**	Yield %	**3.1**	Market Cap	**US$7,656.6mil**

Address **2929 Allen Pkwy.**
Houston, TX 77019-2155
Tel **713-522-1111**
Fax **713-523-8531**
Exchange **NYSE**
Ticker **AGC**
President **James R. Tuerff**
Chairman & CEO **Harold S. Hook**

American Greetings

Industry: **Publishing**

American Greetings manufactures greeting cards and other paper products. The company's primary products are cards, gift wrappings, party goods, and stationery. CreataCard, a subsidiary, operates in-store machines that allow customers to create individual personalized greeting cards. Other subsidiaries include Wilhold, which makes hair accessories; Acme Frame Products, which manufactures picture frames; and Magnivision, which makes nonprescription eyeglasses. The company operates about 30 manufacturing plants and distribution facilities in North America and Europe.

$ mil	02/93	02/94	02/95	% Change				
Sales	**1,671.7**	**1,770.0**	**1,868.9**	**5.6**	P/E Ratio	**15.3**	Price (9/30/95)	**30.50**
Net Income	**112.3**	**133.7**	**148.8**	**11.3**	P/B Ratio	**2.0**	52 Wk Hi-Low	**32.13-25.94**
Book Value	**952.5**	**1,053.4**	**1,159.5**	**10.1**	Yield %	**1.8**	Market Cap	**US$2,269.5mil**

Address **1 American Rd.**
Cleveland, OH 44144-2398
Tel **216-252-7300**
Fax **216-252-6777**
Exchange **NASDA**
Ticker **AGREA**
President **Edward Fruchtenbaum**
Chairman & CEO **Morry Weiss**

American Home Products

Industry: **Pharmaceuticals**

American Home Products is a diversified manufacturer. Its brand-name lines include Norplant contraceptives; Advil and Anacin analgesics; Dristan, Robitussin, and Dimetapp cough, cold, and allergy medicine; Denorex shampoo; and Chap Stick lip balm. The company also makes organ-transplant-rejection agents, such as Rapamune, and prescription pain relievers, such as Lodine. It produces veterinary drugs, including animal antibiotics; generic pharmaceuticals; agricultural products such as herbicides; and specialty-food products under the Chef Boyardee and Jiffy Pop names.

$ mil	12/92	12/93	12/94	% Change				
Sales	**7,873.7**	**8,304.9**	**8,966.2**	**8.0**	P/E Ratio	**17.1**	Price (9/30/95)	**84.88**
Net Income	**1,460.8**	**1,469.3**	**1,528.3**	**4.0**	P/B Ratio	**6.1**	52 Wk Hi-Low	**86.13-58.00**
Book Value	**3,562.6**	**3,876.5**	**4,254.1**	**9.7**	Yield %	**3.5**	Market Cap	**US$26,302mil**

Address **5 Giralda Farms**
Madison, NJ 07940
Tel **201-660-5000**
Fax **201-660-6671**
Exchange **NYSE**
Ticker **AHP**
President & CEO **John R. Stafford**
Chairman **John R. Stafford**

American International

Industry: **Insurance - Property & Casualty**

American International Group specializes in commercial- and industrial-insurance coverage. It offers property, casualty, marine, life, and financial-services insurance in approximately 130 countries, with a special emphasis on markets of the Far East. The company's U.S. operations account for slightly less than 50% of total revenues. Its noninsurance activities include commodities trading, premium and equipment financing, private banking, and interest-rate and currency swaps. The company operates 250 offices in the U.S. and numerous offices throughout the world.

$ mil	12/92	12/93	12/94	% Change				
Revenues	**18,389.0**	**20,135.7**	**22,441.7**	**11.5**	P/E Ratio	**18.6**	Price (9/30/95)	**85.00**
Net Income	**1,657.0**	**1,938.8**	**2,175.5**	**12.2**	P/B Ratio	**2.5**	52 Wk Hi-Low	**86.50-58.42**
Book Value	**12,782.2**	**15,224.2**	**16,421.7**	**7.9**	Yield %	**0.3**	Market Cap	**US$40,306mil**

Address **70 Pine St.**
New York, NY 10270
Tel **212-770-7000**
Fax **212-727-5662**
Exchange **NYSE**
Ticker **AIG**
President **Thomas R. Tizzio**
Chairman & CEO **Maurice R. Greenberg**

American National

Industry: **Insurance - Life & Health**

American National Insurance (ANI) provides insurance and investment-management services. It offers individual and group insurance products, including life, accident, health, and property and casualty coverage. Accident- and health-insurance premiums generate more revenues than any other line, accounting for nearly 28% of the total. The company's Securities Management and Research subsidiary offers variable-annuity accounts and provides management-consulting services to mutual funds. ANI is licensed to do business in the U.S., Guam, American Samoa, and western Europe.

$ mil	12/92	12/93	12/94	% Change				
Revenues	**1,318.1**	**1,329.0**	**1,395.4**	**5.0**	P/E Ratio	**7.2**	Price (9/30/95)	**58.25**
Net Income	**168.6**	**185.5**	**215.1**	**16.0**	P/B Ratio	**0.7**	52 Wk Hi-Low	**66.75-45.00**
Book Value	**1,856.7**	**1,961.7**	**2,072.3**	**5.6**	Yield %	**3.8**	Market Cap	**US$1,542.4mil**

Address **One Moody Plz.**
Galveston, TX 77550
Tel **409-763-4661**
Fax **409-766-6663**
Exchange **NASDA**
Ticker **ANAT**
President **Orson C. Clay**
Chairman & CEO **Robert L. Moody**

American President

Industry: **Marine Transportation**

American President provides container-transportation services in and among Asia, North America, and the Middle East by ship, truck, and rail. American President has an 11% share of the transpacific container-shipping market. U.S. import cargoes consist largely of clothing, electronics, and automotive components. Export cargoes include refrigerated goods, military shipments, and lower-value materials such as wastepaper and lumber. The company's largest export customer is the U.S. government. Transportation within North America accounts for about 25% of revenues.

$ mil	12/92	12/93	12/94	% Change				
Sales	**2,504.7**	**2,594.2**	**2,793.5**	**7.7**	P/E Ratio	**12.3**	Price (9/30/95)	**29.25**
Net Income	**56.5**	**80.1**	**74.2**	**-7.4**	P/B Ratio	**1.3**	52 Wk Hi-Low	**31.50-21.13**
Book Value	**472.2**	**550.5**	**616.4**	**12.0**	Yield %	**1.4**	Market Cap	**US$919.8mil**

Address **1111 Broadway**
Oakland, CA 94607
Tel **510-272-8000**
Fax **510-272-7941**
Exchange **NYSE**
Ticker **APS**
President & CEO **John M. Lillie**
Chairman **John M. Lillie**

American Stores

Industry: **Food Retailers & Wholesalers**

American Stores sells food and drug merchandise. Its principal food operations are Lucky Stores' Northern California Division and Southern California Division, Jewel-Osco-New Mexico, Acme Markets, Jewel Food Stores, and Star Market. The company operates about 1,600 stores in 26 states, including Jewel-Osco combination stores, which are jointly operated by Osco Drug and Jewel Food Stores. The combination stores include specialty departments such as delicatessens, bakeries, and pharmacies. Private-label and name-brand products are sold in the company's stores.

$ mil	01/93	01/94	01/95	% Change				
Sales	**19,051.2**	**18,763.4**	**18,355.1**	**-2.2**	P/E Ratio	**11.7**	Price (9/30/95)	**28.38**
Net Income	**206.4**	**247.1**	**345.2**	**39.7**	P/B Ratio	**2.0**	52 Wk Hi-Low	**30.63-23.50**
Book Value	**1,692.0**	**1,742.3**	**2,050.9**	**17.7**	Yield %	**1.7**	Market Cap	**US$4,212.7mil**

Address **709 E. South Temple**
Salt Lake City, UT 84102
Tel **801-539-0112**
Fax **801-531-0768**
Exchange **NYSE**
Ticker **ASC**
President & CEO **Victor L. Lund**
Chairman **L.S. Skaggs**

American Water Works

Industry: **Water Utilities**

American Water Works is a holding company for its water-service subsidiaries. These 23 subsidiaries provide water-supply service to approximately six million people in 734 communities in 21 states. Its American Commonwealth Management Services subsidiary provides management services to nonaffiliated water and wastewater systems. Its other subsidiaries own land, buildings, and equipment leased to companies affiliated with American Water Works. Residential customers account for approximately 56% of water-service revenues; commercial and industrial users provide about 29%.

$ mil	12/92	12/93	12/94	% Change				
Sales	**657.4**	**717.5**	**770.2**	**7.4**	P/E Ratio	**13.1**	Price (9/30/95)	**30.63**
Net Income	**68.2**	**75.4**	**78.7**	**4.3**	P/B Ratio	**1.2**	52 Wk Hi-Low	**32.75-25.25**
Book Value	**719.1**	**759.8**	**835.1**	**9.9**	Yield %	**3.5**	Market Cap	**US$1,023.0mil**

Address **1025 Laurel Oak Rd.**
Voorhees, NJ 08043
Tel **609-346-8200**
Fax **609-346-8360**
Exchange **NYSE**
Ticker **AWK**
President & CEO **George W. Johnstone**
Chairman **Marilyn W. Lewis**

Ameritech

Industry: **Regional Telephone Systems**

Ameritech provides communication services in the U.S. and internationally. Through its subsidiaries in Illinois, Indiana, Michigan, Ohio, and Wisconsin, the company provides telephone service to 13 million customers. Other services include paging, mobile-telephone service, directory publishing, and business consulting. It is the largest paging-service provider in the Midwest. The company also owns interests in foreign companies, including Telecom and Sky Network Television in New Zealand, MATAV in Hungary, NetCom in Norway, and Polska Telefonia Komorkowa in Poland.

$ mil	12/92	12/93	12/94	% Change				
Sales	**11,153.0**	**11,710.4**	**12,569.5**	**7.3**	P/E Ratio	**NMF**	Price (9/30/95)	**52.13**
Net Income	**-400.4**	**1,512.8**	**-1,063.6**	**-170.3**	P/B Ratio	**4.7**	52 Wk Hi-Low	**52.50-38.25**
Book Value	**6,992.2**	**7,844.6**	**6,055.1**	**-22.8**	Yield %	**3.7**	Market Cap	**US$28,888mil**

Address **30 S. Wacker Dr.**
Chicago, IL 60606
Tel **312-750-5000**
Fax **312-207-1601**
Exchange **NYSE**
Ticker **AIT**
Chief Executive **Richard C. Notebaert**
Chairman **Richard C. Notebaert**

Ametek

Industry: **Industrial Technology**

Ametek manufactures electrical, electronic, and plastic products. Its electromechanical division makes motors and blowers for use in vacuum cleaners, furnaces, lawn tools, business machines, computers, and medical equipment. Its precision-instruments group makes instruments and sensors, primarily for the aerospace, petroleum, and truck-manufacturing industries. Its industrial-materials group produces filters, housings, and materials for automotive, appliance, and telecommunication applications. Ametek markets its products in the United States and abroad.

$ mil	12/92	12/93	12/94	% Change				
Sales	**769.5**	**732.2**	**808.0**	**10.3**	P/E Ratio	**20.4**	Price (9/30/95)	**17.13**
Net Income	**44.4**	**-7.3**	**31.0**	**-524.7**	P/B Ratio	**8.1**	52 Wk Hi-Low	**19.00-15.88**
Book Value	**210.3**	**165.3**	**73.2**	**-55.7**	Yield %	**1.4**	Market Cap	**US$564.1mil**

Address **Station Sq.**
Paoli, PA 19301
Tel **610-647-2121**
Fax **610-296-3412**
Exchange **NYSE**
Ticker **AME**
Chief Executive **Walter E. Blankley**
Chairman **Walter E. Blankley**

Amgen

Industry: **Biotechnology**

Amgen is a manufacturer of biotechnology products. It makes human-therapeutic agents that aid the growth, multiplication, and maturation of red and white blood cells. The company's Epogen product, which spurs the production of red blood cells, is used to treat chronic renal failure associated with anemia in AIDS-related AZT therapy. Its Neupogen agent, which stimulates the production of white blood cells, is used by patients undergoing chemotherapy or receiving bone-marrow transplants. Amgen markets its products in the U.S., Australia, Canada, China, and Europe.

$ mil	12/92	12/93	12/94	% Change				
Sales	**1,050.7**	**1,306.3**	**1,647.9**	**26.2**	P/E Ratio	**43.6**	Price (9/30/95)	**49.88**
Net Income	**357.6**	**383.3**	**319.7**	**-16.6**	P/B Ratio	**10.4**	52 Wk Hi-Low	**52.00-25.44**
Book Value	**933.7**	**1,172.0**	**1,274.3**	**8.7**	Yield %	**0.0**	Market Cap	**US$13,141mil**

Address **1840 DeHavilland Dr.**
Thousand Oaks, CA 91320-1789
Tel **805-447-1000**
Fax **805-499-9315**
Exchange **NASDA**
Ticker **AMGN**
President **Kevin W. Sharer**
Chairman & CEO **Gordon M. Binder**

Amoco

Industry: **Oil - Integrated Majors**

Amoco is an integrated petroleum company with operations worldwide. The company owns, on average, a 45% interest in 49,000 wells, primarily in North America, and holds net reserves of 2.2 billion barrels of oil and 18.5 trillion cubic feet of natural gas, making it the largest private holder of gas reserves in North America. It operates five refineries, and supplies gasoline to 9,700 retail outlets, including about 3,500 company-operated Amoco stations. Amoco's chemical products include lubricating oil, plastics, paint, and additives used in the production of polyester.

$ mil	12/92	12/93	12/94	% Change				
Sales	**25,280.0**	**25,336.0**	**26,048.0**	**2.8**	P/E Ratio	**17.8**	Price (9/30/95)	**64.13**
Net Income	**-74.0**	**1,820.0**	**1,789.0**	**-1.7**	P/B Ratio	**2.2**	52 Wk Hi-Low	**69.75-57.00**
Book Value	**12,960.0**	**13,665.0**	**14,382.0**	**5.2**	Yield %	**3.4**	Market Cap	**US$31,481mil**

Address	**200 E. Randolph Dr.**	Tel	**312-856-6111**	Exchange	**NYSE**	President & CEO	**H. Laurance Fuller**
	Chicago, IL 60601-7125	Fax	**312-856-2460**	Ticker	**AN**	Chairman	**H. Laurance Fuller**

AMP

Industry: **Electrical Components & Equipment**

AMP manufactures electrical- and electronic-connection devices. The company produces more than 100,000 types of electrical splices, connectors, cable assemblies, switches, and related application tools and machines. AMP's products are used in electronics manufacturing and in the installation and maintenance of electrical equipment. The company markets its products in the United States and internationally. Sales within the U.S. account for approximately 42% of revenues. AMP operates manufacturing and warehousing facilities in the U.S. and 32 other countries.

$ mil	12/92	12/93	12/94	% Change				
Sales	**3,337.1**	**3,450.6**	**4,027.5**	**16.7**	P/E Ratio	**21.9**	Price (9/30/95)	**38.50**
Net Income	**290.3**	**296.7**	**369.4**	**24.5**	P/B Ratio	**3.5**	52 Wk Hi-Low	**45.00-34.75**
Book Value	**1,943.3**	**2,056.4**	**2,334.4**	**13.5**	Yield %	**2.2**	Market Cap	**US$8,377.1mil**

Address	**Eisenhower Blvd.**	Tel	**717-564-0100**	Exchange	**NYSE**	President & CEO	**William J. Hudson**
	Harrisburg, PA 17105	Fax	**717-780-6130**	Ticker	**AMP**	Chairman	**James E. Marley**

AMR

Industry: **Airlines**

AMR is the parent company of American Airlines and other aviation companies. American Airlines accounts for more than 82% of the company's revenues; it provides passenger and cargo service to about 170 destinations in the United States and abroad, and sells reservation- and data-processing services to travel vendors. American Eagle, a subsidiary, also owns four regional airlines and provides services including consulting and leasing to the aviation industry. Revenues resulting from operations outside the U.S. account for approximately 25% of the company's total.

$ mil	12/92	12/93	12/94	% Change				
Sales	**14,396.0**	**15,816.0**	**16,137.0**	**2.0**	P/E Ratio	**16.0**	Price (9/30/95)	**72.13**
Net Income	**-935.0**	**-110.0**	**228.0**	**-307.3**	P/B Ratio	**1.6**	52 Wk Hi-Low	**79.75-48.25**
Book Value	**3,349.0**	**4,276.0**	**3,380.0**	**-21.0**	Yield %	**0.0**	Market Cap	**US$5,504.1mil**

Address	**4333 Amon Carter Blvd.**	Tel	**817-963-1234**	Exchange	**NYSE**	President & CEO	**Robert L. Crandall**
	Fort Worth, TX 76155	Fax	**817-976-9641**	Ticker	**AMR**	Chairman	**Robert L. Crandall**

Anadarko Petroleum

Industry: **Oil - Secondary**

Anadarko Petroleum operates oil and natural-gas wells, primarily in the western United States. The company owns an average 50% interest in approximately 8,700 wells and holds net reserves of 1.9 trillion cubic feet of natural gas and 157 million barrels of oil. It owns five gas-gathering systems, two gas-processing plants, and interests in pipelines and other facilities related to the natural-gas industry. Anadarko operates wells and explores for additional reserves in Algeria, China, Indonesia, and Yemen, and is developing potential geothermal-energy sources.

$ mil	12/92	12/93	12/94	% Change				
Sales	**375.2**	**476.3**	**482.5**	**1.3**	P/E Ratio	**67.7**	Price (9/30/95)	**47.38**
Net Income	**27.3**	**117.4**	**41.1**	**-65.0**	P/B Ratio	**3.1**	52 Wk Hi-Low	**50.25-35.88**
Book Value	**656.9**	**864.2**	**899.6**	**4.1**	Yield %	**0.6**	Market Cap	**US$2,791.5mil**

Address	**17001 Northchase Dr.**	Tel	**713-875-1101**	Exchange	**NYSE**	President & CEO	**Robert J. Allison, Jr.**
	Houston, TX 77060	Fax	**713-874-3385**	Ticker	**APC**	Chairman	**Robert J. Allison, Jr.**

Analog Devices

Industry: **Semiconductors & related**

Analog Devices manufactures data converters and operational amplifiers. The company's products include linear, digital, and mixed-signal integrated circuits for signal-processing applications. Analog Devices markets its products through distributors and a direct-sales force to original-equipment manufacturers in the defense, aerospace, computer, telecommunication, and consumer-electronics industries worldwide. Business operations outside the United States accounts for approximately 56% of revenues. Analog Devices operates manufacturing facilities in the U.S. and abroad.

$ mil	10/92	10/93	10/94	% Change				
Sales	**567.3**	**666.3**	**773.5**	**16.1**	P/E Ratio	**36.1**	Price (9/30/95)	**34.63**
Net Income	**14.9**	**44.5**	**74.5**	**67.4**	P/B Ratio	**5.0**	52 Wk Hi-Low	**38.75-20.25**
Book Value	**375.0**	**432.0**	**521.9**	**20.8**	Yield %	**0.0**	Market Cap	**US$2,620.4mil**

Address	**One Technology Way**	Tel	**617-329-4700**	Exchange	**NYSE**	President	**Jerald G. Fishman**
	Norwood, MA 02062-9106	Fax	**617-329-8703**	Ticker	**ADI**	Chairman & CEO	**Ray Stata**

Anheuser-Busch

Industry: **Distillers & Brewers**

Anheuser-Busch, the world's largest brewer in terms of sales, also produces food products and operates entertainment businesses. The company's beer brands include Budweiser, Michelob, and Busch, produced at 13 breweries in the United States, and Carlsberg, imported from Denmark. Its food products include Colonial, Rainbo, and Earth Grains breads; Merico brand refrigerated dough, salad dressings, and dairy products; and Eagle brand snacks. Anheuser-Busch's other holdings include the Busch Gardens and Sea World theme parks, the St. Louis Cardinals, and Busch Stadium.

$ mil	12/92	12/93	12/94	% Change				
Sales	**11,393.7**	**11,505.3**	**12,053.8**	**4.8**	P/E Ratio	**16.0**	Price (9/30/95)	**62.38**
Net Income	**917.5**	**594.5**	**1,032.1**	**73.6**	P/B Ratio	**3.6**	52 Wk Hi-Low	**63.75-49.00**
Book Value	**4,620.4**	**4,255.5**	**4,415.5**	**3.8**	Yield %	**2.4**	Market Cap	**US$15,934mil**

Address **1 Busch Pl.** **St. Louis, MO 63118** Tel **314-577-2000** Fax **314-577-2900** Exchange **NYSE** Ticker **BUD** President & CEO **August A. Busch III** Chairman **August A. Busch III**

Aon

Industry: **Insurance - Full Line**

Aon is an international insurance holding company. It offers insurance brokerage and consulting services, including reinsurance, underwriting management, actuarial services, proprietary risk-management information systems, and loss-control consulting. The company's insurance subsidiaries provide traditional- and specialty-life, accident and health, and specialty-property and -casualty insurance products and coverage. Aon also manages an investment portfolio that includes mortgage and real-estate loans, fixed-income securities, annuities, and guaranteed investment contracts.

$ mil	12/92	12/93	12/94	% Change				
Revenues	**3,336.5**	**3,844.8**	**4,156.9**	**8.1**	P/E Ratio	**13.0**	Price (9/30/95)	**40.88**
Net Income	**126.6**	**323.8**	**360.0**	**11.2**	P/B Ratio	**1.9**	52 Wk Hi-Low	**41.38-29.75**
Book Value	**2,103.9**	**2,287.8**	**2,307.4**	**0.9**	Yield %	**3.1**	Market Cap	**US$4,376.9mil**

Address **123 N. Wacker Dr.** **Chicago, IL 60606** Tel **312-701-3000** Fax **312-701-3100** Exchange **NYSE** Ticker **AOC** President & CEO **Patrick G. Ryan** Chairman **Patrick G. Ryan**

Apple Computer

Industry: **Computers**

Apple Computer designs and produces personal-computer hardware, software, and peripherals. It is best known for its Macintosh personal computers, which use Apple's proprietary operating system. It also sells operating systems and applications software. In addition, Apple markets the Newton hand-held computer. The company markets its products to business, education, government, and individual users in the United States and internationally. Business activities outside the U.S. account for approximately 45% of sales. Apple operates manufacturing facilities worldwide.

$ mil	09/92	09/93	09/94	% Change				
Sales	**7,086.5**	**7,977.0**	**9,188.8**	**15.2**	P/E Ratio	**14.3**	Price (9/30/95)	**37.25**
Net Income	**530.4**	**86.6**	**310.2**	**258.2**	P/B Ratio	**1.9**	52 Wk Hi-Low	**49.38-33.13**
Book Value	**2,187.4**	**2,026.4**	**2,383.3**	**17.6**	Yield %	**1.3**	Market Cap	**US$4,570.2mil**

Address **1 Infinite Loop** **Cupertino, CA 95014** Tel **408-996-1010** Fax **408-996-0275** Exchange **NASDA** Ticker **AAPL** President & CEO **Michael H. Spindler** Chairman **A.C. Markkula, Jr.**

Applied Materials

Industry: **Semiconductors & related**

Applied Materials manufactures systems that produce silicon wafer circuits using several different technologies, including chemical vapor-deposition, physical vapor-deposition, and epitaxial and polysilicon deposition. It is currently developing systems used in the production of flat-panel displays. Applied Materials markets these products to users in the semiconductor-manufacturing industry in the U.S. and abroad. Operations in the U.S. account for 38% of sales. The company operates manufacturing and engineering facilities in California, Texas, England, Japan, and Israel.

$ mil	10/92	10/93	10/94	% Change				
Sales	**751.4**	**1,080.0**	**1,659.8**	**53.7**	P/E Ratio	**39.3**	Price (9/30/95)	**102.25**
Net Income	**39.5**	**99.7**	**220.7**	**121.4**	P/B Ratio	**8.9**	52 Wk Hi-Low	**118.25-38.50**
Book Value	**474.1**	**598.8**	**966.3**	**61.4**	Yield %	**0.0**	Market Cap	**US$9,022.9mil**

Address **3050 Bowers Ave.** **Santa Clara, CA 95054-3299** Tel **408-727-5555** Fax **408-748-9943** Exchange **NASDA** Ticker **AMAT** President **Dan Maydan** Chairman & CEO **James C. Morgan**

Aquarion

Industry: **Water Utilities**

Aquarion is a water-service utility holding company. Its Bridgeport Hydraulic and Stamford Water subsidiaries supply water to about 496,000 Connecticut customers. Reservoirs provide 89% of its water supply; most of the remainder comes from wells. Residential customers consumed roughly 50% of water supplied by Aquarion; commercial and industrial clients used an additional 34%. The firm also provides environmental-testing and engineering services to other utilities, and owns Timco, a forest-products and electricity- and steam-cogeneration company in New Hampshire.

$ mil	12/92	12/93	12/94	% Change				
Sales	**103.7**	**107.4**	**122.0**	**13.6**	P/E Ratio	**13.0**	Price (9/30/95)	**24.25**
Net Income	**9.4**	**11.0**	**12.2**	**11.1**	P/B Ratio	**1.4**	52 Wk Hi-Low	**26.13-21.63**
Book Value	**97.2**	**110.5**	**115.1**	**4.2**	Yield %	**6.7**	Market Cap	**US$161.8mil**

Address **835 Main St.** **Bridgeport, CT 06601-2353** Tel **203-335-2333** Fax **203-337-5938** Exchange **NYSE** Ticker **WTR** President & CEO **Jack E. McGregor** Chairman **William S. Warner**

Archer-Daniels-Midland

Industry: **Other Food**

Archer-Daniels-Midland (ADM) markets agricultural commodities and related products. It processes corn, wheat, rice, barley, and oilseeds. The company's operations include milling wheat and rice into flour; processing corn to produce corn sugar, syrup, starch, and alcohol; and refining cane sugar. Processing oilseeds generates about 60% of the company's revenues. ADM also operates a fleet of trucks and railcars to transport its products. It owns and operates approximately 168 processing plants worldwide. ADM markets these commodities in the U.S. and around the world.

$ mil	06/93	06/94	06/95	% Change				
Sales	**9,811.4**	**11,374.4**	**12,671.9**	**11.4**	P/E Ratio	**10.5**	Price (9/30/95)	**15.38**
Net Income	**567.5**	**484.1**	**795.9**	**64.4**	P/B Ratio	**1.4**	52 Wk Hi-Low	**19.88-15.00**
Book Value	**4,883.3**	**5,045.4**	**5,854.2**	**16.0**	Yield %	**0.6**	Market Cap	**US$8,331.3mil**

Address **4666 Faries Pkwy. Decatur, IL 62525** | Tel **217-424-5200** | Fax **217-424-5839** | Exchange **NYSE** | Ticker **ADM** | President **James R. Randall** | Chairman & CEO **Dwayne O. Andreas**

Armco

Industry: **Steel**

Armco produces carbon, stainless, flat-rolled and electrical steels; steel products; snowplows; and tubular steel goods. Through a 50% joint venture with Acerinox, Armco finishes chrome, nickel, flat-rolled, and stainless steels. The company also owns a 50%-partnership interest in National-Oil well, a distributor of oil country tubular goods and a manufacturer of drilling and other oil and gas equipment. Armco manufactures snowplows through its Dogulas Dynamics subsidiary. Douglas Dynamics produces the snowplows for four-wheel drive pick-up trucks and utility vehicles.

$ mil	12/92	12/93	12/94	% Change				
Sales	**2,073.6**	**1,664.0**	**1,437.6**	**-13.6**	P/E Ratio	**11.4**	Price (9/30/95)	**6.50**
Net Income	**-429.9**	**-641.8**	**77.7**	**-112.1**	P/B Ratio	**NMF**	52 Wk Hi-Low	**7.63-5.88**
Book Value	**342.3**	**-313.1**	**-218.5**	**-30.2**	Yield %	**0.0**	Market Cap	**US$689.9mil**

Address **One Oxford Ctr., 301 Grant St. Pittsburgh, PA 15219-1415** | Tel **412-255-9800** | Fax **412-225-9849** | Exchange **NYSE** | Ticker **AS** | President & CEO **James F. Will** | Chairman **John C. Haley**

Armstrong

Industry: **Building Materials**

Armstrong World Industries manufactures interior furnishings, including floor coverings, building products, and furniture. Products are sold primarily for the furnishing, refurbishing, repair, modernization, and construction of residential, commercial, and institutional buildings. It also manufactures industrial products. Ceramic products are sold through sales-service centers operated by American Olean Tile, a subsidiary. Thomasville Furniture Industries, another subsidiary, manufactures traditional-style, as well as contemporary wooden and upholstered furniture.

$ mil	12/92	12/93	12/94	% Change				
Sales	**2,549.8**	**2,525.4**	**2,752.7**	**9.0**	P/E Ratio	**10.6**	Price (9/30/95)	**55.50**
Net Income	**-234.2**	**63.5**	**210.4**	**231.3**	P/B Ratio	**2.8**	52 Wk Hi-Low	**60.13-36.38**
Book Value	**562.8**	**569.5**	**735.1**	**29.1**	Yield %	**2.3**	Market Cap	**US$2,061.8mil**

Address **313 W. Liberty St. Lancaster, PA 17604-3001** | Tel **717-397-0611** | Fax **717-396-2126** | Exchange **NYSE** | Ticker **ACK** | Chief Executive **George A. Lorch** | Chairman **George A. Lorch**

Arnold Industries

Industry: **Trucking**

Arnold Industries is a holding company engaged in trucking and warehousing businesses. Its New Penn Motor Express subsidiary is a less-than-truckload transportation company operating primarily in New England and mid-Atlantic states. The business of New Penn Motor Express contributes approximately 53% of company operating revenues. Commodities transported include paper products, food products, textiles, building products, metal products, and pharmaceuticals. Other subsidiaries provide truckload services and warehousing and warehouse-related trucking services.

$ mil	12/92	12/93	12/94	% Change				
Sales	**233.6**	**272.9**	**302.4**	**10.8**	P/E Ratio	**15.6**	Price (9/30/95)	**17.75**
Net Income	**25.8**	**29.9**	**30.4**	**1.5**	P/B Ratio	**2.7**	52 Wk Hi-Low	**19.00-16.75**
Book Value	**136.0**	**156.9**	**176.5**	**12.5**	Yield %	**2.3**	Market Cap	**US$472.8mil**

Address **625 South Fifth Avenue Lebanon, PA 17042** | Tel **717-274-2521** | Fax **N/A** | Exchange **NASDA** | Ticker **AIND** | President **E.H. Arnold** | Chairman **E.H. Arnold**

ASARCO

Industry: **Non-Ferrous Metals - Other (Exc. Aluminum)**

ASARCO manages nonferrous metal mines, including copper, silver, lead, and zinc mines, as well as smelters and refineries to process their production. The company owns 1.3 billion tons of copper reserves, which it supplies to the construction, electrical-products, and industrial-machinery industries. It produces silver for photographic and electronic goods, lead for automotive and industrial batteries, and zinc for galvanized-metal products and zinc-based alloys. ASARCO's American Limestone division makes ready-mix concrete for construction and agricultural use.

$ mil	12/92	12/93	12/94	% Change				
Sales	**1,908.5**	**1,736.4**	**2,031.9**	**17.0**	P/E Ratio	**20.6**	Price (9/30/95)	**31.50**
Net Income	**-83.1**	**15.6**	**64.0**	**310.4**	P/B Ratio	**0.9**	52 Wk Hi-Low	**36.50-24.38**
Book Value	**1,357.5**	**1,471.6**	**1,517.4**	**3.1**	Yield %	**1.3**	Market Cap	**US$1,336.4mil**

Address **180 Maiden Ln. New York, NY 10038** | Tel **212-510-2000** | Fax **212-510-1855** | Exchange **NYSE** | Ticker **AR** | President & CEO **Richard de J. Osborne** | Chairman **Richard de J. Osborne**

Ashland

Industry: **Oil - Secondary**

Ashland operates energy and construction businesses. The company holds, on average, a 90% interest in 3,000 oil and natural-gas wells in the U.S. and Nigeria, and holds net reserves of nine million barrels of oil and 352 billion cubic feet of gas. It owns three refineries, 700 SuperAmerica and Rich Oil gas stations, and 315 Valvoline quick-oil-change centers, and produces lubricants and automotive fluids under the Valvoline and Pyroil names. APAC, the company's construction division, builds highways and other large-scale projects. Ashland also has coal-mining interests.

$ mil	09/92	09/93	09/94	% Change				
Sales	**10,210.8**	**10,198.8**	**10,334.0**	**1.3**	P/E Ratio	**11.4**	Price (9/30/95)	**33.38**
Net Income	**-335.7**	**142.2**	**197.0**	**38.5**	P/B Ratio	**1.3**	52 Wk Hi-Low	**39.50-32.13**
Book Value	**1,086.0**	**1,161.6**	**1,595.0**	**37.3**	Yield %	**3.0**	Market Cap	**US$2,121.7mil**

Address	**1000 Ashland Dr.**	Tel	**606-329-3333**	Exchange	**NYSE**	President	**Paul W. Chellgren**
	Ashland, KY 41169	Fax	**606-329-5274**	Ticker	**ASH**	Chairman & CEO	**John R. Hall**

AT&T

Industry: **Communications Technology**

AT&T provides domestic and international communication services and products to business and residential customers. AT&T offers networking software and equipment for telephone and cable-television companies, data-communication systems, and equipment leasing. AT&T also provide on-line services to Internet users. Its McCaw Cellular subsidiary provides cellular-communication services. AT&T plans to split into three separate companies by the end of 1996. The separate companies will include AT&T's current communication services, network systems, and computer divisions.

$ mil	12/92	12/93	12/94	% Change				
Sales	**64,904.0**	**67,156.0**	**75,094.0**	**11.8**	P/E Ratio	**21.8**	Price (9/30/95)	**65.75**
Net Income	**3,807.0**	**-3,794.0**	**4,710.0**	**-224.1**	P/B Ratio	**5.8**	52 Wk Hi-Low	**66.25-47.25**
Book Value	**18,921.0**	**13,850.0**	**17,921.0**	**29.4**	Yield %	**2.0**	Market Cap	**US$104,302mil**

Address	**32 Ave. of the Americas**	Tel	**212-387-5400**	Exchange	**NYSE**	Chief Executive	**Robert E. Allen**
	New York, NY 10013	Fax	**212-387-6646**	Ticker	**T**	Chairman	**Robert E. Allen**

Atlantic Richfield

Industry: **Oil - Integrated Majors**

Atlantic Richfield produces oil, natural gas, and coal. The company owns an average 43% interest in approximately 16,000 oil and natural-gas wells worldwide, holds net reserves of approximately 2.4 billion barrels of oil and eight trillion cubic feet of natural gas, and operates two refineries on the west coast of the United States. Its primary coal operations include two mines in Wyoming, and it has net reserves of 1.5 billion tons. It sells coal and natural gas primarily to utilities, and distributes petroleum products through more than 1,600 Arco service stations.

$ mil	12/92	12/93	12/94	% Change				
Sales	**18,668.0**	**18,487.0**	**16,552.0**	**-10.5**	P/E Ratio	**19.1**	Price (9/30/95)	**107.38**
Net Income	**801.0**	**269.0**	**919.0**	**241.6**	P/B Ratio	**2.7**	52 Wk Hi-Low	**117.50-97.63**
Book Value	**6,721.0**	**6,127.0**	**6,278.0**	**2.5**	Yield %	**5.1**	Market Cap	**US$17,268mil**

Address	**515 S. Flower St.**	Tel	**213-486-3511**	Exchange	**NYSE**	President & CEO	**Mike R. Bowlin**
	Los Angeles, CA 90071	Fax	**213-486-2063**	Ticker	**ARC**	Chairman	**Lodwrick M. Cook**

Autodesk

Industry: **Software**

Autodesk develops and supports design-automation and multimedia software products for personal computers and work stations. Principal software products include AutoCAD, AutoCAD LT, AutoSketch, and Generic CADD. These products are design, sketching, and drafting tools and are used by architects, engineers, and in the construction industry. In fiscal 1994, sales of AutoCAD and its updates comprised 85% of company revenues. AutoCAD is a general-purpose design and drafting software tool for personal computers and work stations and is available in 85 countries.

$ mil	01/93	01/94	01/95	% Change				
Sales	**367.7**	**418.7**	**465.3**	**11.1**	P/E Ratio	**38.4**	Price (9/30/95)	**43.75**
Net Income	**43.9**	**62.2**	**56.6**	**-9.0**	P/B Ratio	**6.4**	52 Wk Hi-Low	**52.00-31.25**
Book Value	**267.8**	**296.9**	**323.5**	**9.0**	Yield %	**0.5**	Market Cap	**US$2,057.1mil**

Address	**111 McInnis Parkway**	Tel	**415-507-5000**	Exchange	**NASDA**	President & CEO	**Carol Bartz**
	San Rafael, CA 94903	Fax	**N/A**	Ticker	**ACAD**	Chairman	**Carol Bartz**

Avnet

Industry: **Semiconductors & related**

Avnet manufactures electronic and electromechanical components. The company also distributes computer products for industrial and military customers. Its products include television-signal-processing and audio equipment, magnet wire, electrical motors, measuring instruments, control equipment, and industrial-maintenance products. In addition, the company produces trophy component parts and markets giftware. Avnet's principal suppliers of semiconductors include Advanced Micro Devices, Hewlett-Packard, Integrated Device Technology, and others.

$ mil	06/92	06/93	06/94	% Change				
Sales	**1,759.0**	**2,238.0**	**3,547.7**	**58.5**	P/E Ratio	**24.6**	Price (9/30/95)	**51.63**
Net Income	**50.5**	**69.1**	**85.3**	**23.4**	P/B Ratio	**1.9**	52 Wk Hi-Low	**55.13-33.88**
Book Value	**837.2**	**868.2**	**1,108.5**	**27.7**	Yield %	**1.2**	Market Cap	**US$2,104.4mil**

Address	**80 Cutter Mill Rd.**	Tel	**516-466-7000**	Exchange	**NYSE**	President	**Roy Vallee**
	Great Neck, NY 11021	Fax	**516-466-1203**	Ticker	**AVT**	Chairman & CEO	**Leon Machiz**

Avon

Industry: **Cosmetics & Personal Care**

Avon Products manufactures cosmetics, perfumes, jewelry, and gift items. Cosmetics, fragrances, and toiletries account for approximately 61% of the company's total net sales. Avon's principal distribution channel is a network of about 1.9 million independent representatives in 30 countries; these representatives primarily make sales in customers' homes or places of business. The company operates manufacturing facilities and distribution centers in North America, Latin America, Europe, and the Pacific Rim, and it produces almost all of the products it sells.

$ mil	12/92	12/93	12/94	% Change				
Sales	3,809.9	4,007.6	4,266.5	6.5	P/E Ratio	25.9	Price (9/30/95)	71.75
Net Income	175.0	132.1	195.8	48.2	P/B Ratio	NMF	52 Wk Hi-Low	75.00-54.63
Book Value	310.5	314.0	185.6	-40.9	Yield %	2.6	Market Cap	US$4,885.7mil

Address	**9 W. 57th St.**	Tel	**212-546-6015**	Exchange	**NYSE**	President	**Edward J. Robinson**
	New York, NY 10019-2683	Fax	**212-546-6136**	Ticker	**AVP**	Chairman & CEO	**James E. Preston**

Aztar

Industry: **Casinos**

Aztar operates casino hotels in Atlantic City, New Jersey, and in Las Vegas and Laughlin, Nevada. The company's TropWorld complex covers 10 acres in Atlantic City. TropWorld's 92,191-square-foot casino contains 2,780 slot machines, 95 table games, and 1,020 hotel rooms. Tropicana, in Las Vegas, occupies 45,000 square feet and contains 1,510 slot machines, 52 table games, and 1,907 hotel rooms. Tropicana is 50%-owned by the company's Adamar subsidiary. Ramada Express in Laughlin contains 1,545 slot machines, 33 gaming tables, and 1,500 rooms on 50,000 square feet.

$ mil	12/92	12/93	12/94	% Change				
Sales	512.0	518.8	541.4	4.4	P/E Ratio	23.9	Price (9/30/95)	8.38
Net Income	19.8	11.4	14.1	23.7	P/B Ratio	0.9	52 Wk Hi-Low	10.13-5.50
Book Value	333.7	347.0	366.1	5.5	Yield %	0.0	Market Cap	US$319.1mil

Address	**Ste. 400, 2390 E. Camelback Rd.**	Tel	**602-381-4100**	Exchange	**NYSE**	President & CEO	**Paul E. Rubeli**
	Phoenix, AZ 85016-3452	Fax	**602-381-4107**	Ticker	**AZR**	Chairman	**Paul E. Rubeli**

Baker Hughes

Industry: **Oilfield Equipment & Services - Other**

Baker Hughes manufactures products for the petroleum, mineral-production, water-treatment, chemical, and food-processing markets. It makes rock-drilling bits and drilling-fluid additives for the specialty-chemical and oil- and gas-drilling industries, and offers chemical-formulation and -application services at its on-site laboratories. Baker Hughes also supplies liquid/solid separation equipment, drilling and control systems, pumps, flow-regulation devices, and other related equipment to its customers. International sales account for about 66% of its revenues.

$ mil	09/92	09/93	09/94	% Change				
Sales	2,538.6	2,701.7	2,504.8	-7.3	P/E Ratio	92.6	Price (9/30/95)	20.38
Net Income	5.0	58.9	42.7	-27.6	P/B Ratio	1.8	52 Wk Hi-Low	23.38-17.00
Book Value	1,645.6	1,610.6	1,638.5	1.7	Yield %	2.3	Market Cap	US$2,877.1mil

Address	**3900 Essex Ln.**	Tel	**713-439-8600**	Exchange	**NYSE**	President & CEO	**James D. Woods**
	Houston, TX 77027	Fax	**713-439-8699**	Ticker	**BHI**	Chairman	**James D. Woods**

Ball

Industry: **Containers & Packaging**

Ball manufactures packaging products for food and beverages. The company also provides aerospace and communication systems and professional services to governmental and commercial customers. These products and services include satellite design and radio-frequency antennae. Most of the company's packaging sales are made to major companies in the packaged-food and beverage business, including Anheuser-Busch. It also has contracts for services to the U.S. Department of Defense. Ball-InCon Glass Packaging, a subsidiary, manufactures glass containers.

$ mil	12/92	12/93	12/94	% Change				
Sales	2,177.8	2,440.9	2,594.7	6.3	P/E Ratio	12.6	Price (9/30/95)	29.63
Net Income	69.1	-65.1	73.0	-212.1	P/B Ratio	1.4	52 Wk Hi-Low	38.50-27.25
Book Value	596.0	548.6	616.7	12.4	Yield %	2.0	Market Cap	US$890.8mil

Address	**345 S. High St.**	Tel	**317-747-6100**	Exchange	**NYSE**	President & CEO	**George A. Sissel**
	Muncie, IN 47307-0407	Fax	**317-747-6203**	Ticker	**BLL**	Chairman	**Alvin Owsley**

Bally Entertainment

Industry: **Casinos**

Bally Entertainment operates fitness centers and hotels. Bally's Health & Tennis, a subsidiary, operates about 330 centers in metropolitan areas under Holiday Health, Jack LaLanne, Vic Tanny, and Chicago Health Clubs names. The company is planning to spin-off this subsidiary during 1995. Bally Manufacturing's casino-hotel division operates the 2,800-room Bally's Casino Resort in Las Vegas, the 1,200-room Bally's Park Place in Atlantic City, and the 500-room Bally's Grand in Atlantic City. It also owns a 50% interest in Bally's New Orleans, a 130,000 square foot riverboat.

$ mil	12/92	12/93	12/94	% Change				
Sales	1,230.5	1,313.9	942.3	-28.3	P/E Ratio	NMF	Price (9/30/95)	10.88
Net Income	11.8	-46.5	-68.4	47.1	P/B Ratio	1.7	52 Wk Hi-Low	12.88-7.38
Book Value	410.2	364.1	293.6	-19.4	Yield %	0.0	Market Cap	US$513.4mil

Address	**8700 W. Bryn Mawr Ave.**	Tel	**312-399-1300**	Exchange	**NYSE**	President & CEO	**Arthur M. Goldberg**
	Chicago, IL 60631	Fax	**N/A**	Ticker	**BLY**	Chairman	**Arthur M. Goldberg**

Baltimore Gas & Electric

Industry: **Electrical Utilities - Eastern U.S.**

Baltimore Gas and Electric is an electric and natural-gas utility that generates and distributes electricity and natural gas in Maryland. Residential customers account for approximately 44% of electric and 61% of natural-gas revenues. The company produces about 39% of its electricity using nuclear energy and 56% using coal. It owns a nuclear-power plant, 13 fossil-fuel-power plants, interest in two coal-fired plants, a hydroelectric-generation company, and a geothermal-energy station. The company has agreed to merge with Potomac Electric Power.

$ mil	12/92	12/93	12/94	% Change				
Sales	**2,491.3**	**2,668.7**	**2,783.0**	**4.3**	P/E Ratio	**13.4**	Price (9/30/95)	**25.88**
Net Income	**264.3**	**309.9**	**323.6**	**4.4**	P/B Ratio	**1.2**	52 Wk Hi-Low	**26.38-21.38**
Book Value	**3,099.3**	**3,172.2**	**3,206.6**	**1.1**	Yield %	**5.8**	Market Cap	**US$3,817.3mil**

Address	**Gas and Electric Bldg.**	Tel	**410-783-5920**	Exchange	**NYSE**	President	**Edward A. Crooke**
	Baltimore, MD 21201	Fax	**410-234-5367**	Ticker	**BGE**	Chairman & CEO	**Christian H. Poindexter**

Banc One

Industry: **Banks - Central U.S.**

Banc One, a bank holding company, manages 79 banks in 16 states, which are located primarily in the Midwest and West. The company offers retail and middle-market banking services, including corporate and mortgage banking, bank-card services, and trust management. Banc One also operates a number of mutual funds. The company has affiliates that provide data-processing, merchant and investment-banking, venture-capital, and insurance services. Consumer and real-estate loans each account for approximately 31% of the company's total loan portfolio.

$ mil	12/92	12/93	12/94	% Change				
Revenues	**5,999.0**	**7,226.8**	**7,857.1**	**8.7**	P/E Ratio	**15.1**	Price (9/30/95)	**36.50**
Net Income	**781.3**	**1,140.0**	**1,005.1**	**-11.8**	P/B Ratio	**1.9**	52 Wk Hi-Low	**36.50-24.63**
Book Value	**5,213.5**	**7,033.6**	**7,564.9**	**7.6**	Yield %	**3.4**	Market Cap	**US$14,324mil**

Address	**100 E. Broad St.**	Tel	**614-248-5944**	Exchange	**NYSE**	President	**Richard J. Lehmann**
	Columbus, OH 43271	Fax	**614-248-5624**	Ticker	**ONE**	Chairman & CEO	**John B. McCoy**

Bancorp Hawaii

Industry: **Banks - Western U.S.**

Bancorp Hawaii is a bank holding company with banking, insurance, investment-advisory, and real-estate subsidiaries that provide a variety of financial services to customers in Hawaii and other areas of the Pacific Basin, and in selected markets outside that region. Its Bank of Hawaii subsidiary provides commercial- and retail-banking services throughout the Far East. The company's other businesses include FirstFed America, First National Bank of Arizona, and Bancorp Life Insurance of Hawaii. Bancorp Hawaii also provides full-service brokerage and investment products.

$ mil	12/92	12/93	12/94	% Change				
Revenues	**940.0**	**938.1**	**941.4**	**0.4**	P/E Ratio	**12.3**	Price (9/30/95)	**33.75**
Net Income	**127.5**	**132.6**	**117.7**	**-11.2**	P/B Ratio	**1.5**	52 Wk Hi-Low	**36.25-24.13**
Book Value	**828.3**	**938.1**	**966.8**	**3.1**	Yield %	**3.1**	Market Cap	**US$1,401.3mil**

Address	**130 Merchant St.**	Tel	**808-537-8111**	Exchange	**NYSE**	President	**Richard J. Dahl**
	Honolulu, HI 96813	Fax	**808-537-8440**	Ticker	**BOH**	Chairman & CEO	**Lawrence M. Johnson**

Bank of Boston

Industry: **Banks - Eastern U.S.**

Bank of Boston provides retail- and corporate-banking services. The company offers corporate- and personal-trust services, home and commercial mortgages, overseas banking (in approximately 26 countries), domestic corporate and investment banking, and merchant-banking services, mainly in the New England area. The company's subsidiaries include Bank of Boston Connecticut and Rhode Island Hospital Trust. Bank of Boston operates more than 300 branches in approximately 20 states. Operations in the United States account for about 77% of the company's revenues.

$ mil	12/92	12/93	12/94	% Change				
Revenues	**5,291.7**	**7,395.6**	**4,546.0**	**-38.5**	P/E Ratio	**12.8**	Price (9/30/95)	**47.63**
Net Income	**263.1**	**299.0**	**435.0**	**45.5**	P/B Ratio	**1.6**	52 Wk Hi-Low	**47.63-24.63**
Book Value	**2,230.6**	**2,911.7**	**3,142.0**	**7.9**	Yield %	**2.0**	Market Cap	**US$5,318.9mil**

Address	**100 Federal St.**	Tel	**617-434-2200**	Exchange	**NYSE**	President	**Charles K. Gifford**
	Boston, MA 02110	Fax	**617-434-7706**	Ticker	**BKB**	Chairman & CEO	**Ira Stepanian**

Bank of New York

Industry: **Banks - Eastern U.S.**

Bank of New York is a bank holding company with worldwide operations. Its principal subsidiary, The Bank of New York, is the leading retail bank in the New York City area and the largest provider of securities-processing services in the U.S. The company issues bank credit cards, with 5.1 million credit-card accounts outstanding. It also offers commercial and residential real-estate mortgages. In addition, Bank of New York, through its BNY Associates subsidiary, provides investment-banking and financial-advisory services to middle-market companies throughout the U.S.

$ mil	12/92	12/93	12/94	% Change				
Revenues	**3,583.0**	**3,822.0**	**4,251.0**	**11.2**	P/E Ratio	**11.9**	Price (9/30/95)	**46.50**
Net Income	**369.0**	**559.0**	**749.0**	**34.0**	P/B Ratio	**2.0**	52 Wk Hi-Low	**46.50-26.75**
Book Value	**3,515.0**	**4,072.0**	**4,296.0**	**5.5**	Yield %	**2.4**	Market Cap	**US$8,931.7mil**

Address	**48 Wall St.**	Tel	**212-495-1784**	Exchange	**NYSE**	President	**Thomas A. Renyi**
	New York, NY 10286	Fax	**212-495-2546**	Ticker	**BK**	Chairman & CEO	**J. Carter Bacot**

BankAmerica

Industry: **Banks - Money Center**

BankAmerica is the second-largest bank holding company in the U.S., by assets. The company's banks operate about 2,000 branches in 10 western states, Illinois, and Hawaii, and have finance offices in 36 countries. It provides consumer-, commercial-, and international-banking services and products. BankAmerica has a dominant market share in California, Washington, and Nevada. The company operates 133 supermarket and other in-store branches in nine states. Its BA Investment Services division distributes investment products, including the Pacific Horizon mutual-fund family.

$ mil	12/92	12/93	12/94	% Change				
Revenues	**15,262.0**	**15,900.0**	**16,531.0**	**4.0**	P/E Ratio	**11.2**	Price (9/30/95)	**59.88**
Net Income	**1,492.0**	**1,954.0**	**2,176.0**	**11.4**	P/B Ratio	**1.2**	52 Wk Hi-Low	**61.13-38.88**
Book Value	**15,488.0**	**17,144.0**	**18,891.0**	**10.2**	Yield %	**2.7**	Market Cap	**US$22,410mil**

Address	**Bank of America Ctr.**	Tel	**415-622-3530**	Exchange	**NYSE**	President & CEO	**David A. Coulter**
	San Francisco, CA 94104	Fax	**415-624-0690**	Ticker	**BAC**	Chairman	**Richard M. Rosenberg**

Bankers Trust

Industry: **Banks - Money Center**

Bankers Trust New York provides banking, investment-management, and insurance services. Its Bankers Trust subsidiary provides commercial-banking, advisory, and securities-trading services. The company's other businesses include PROFITCo, an asset-management company; Financial Services, a global-banking- and -trading-service provider; and Consorico, a Chilean insurance underwriter. In addition, Bankers Trust New York, through its BT Securities subsidiary, is a primary dealer in U.S. government securities, and underwrites securities for commercial and municipal clients.

$ mil	12/92	12/93	12/94	% Change				
Revenues	**6,550.0**	**7,800.0**	**7,503.0**	**-3.8**	P/E Ratio	**9.8**	Price (9/30/95)	**70.25**
Net Income	**761.0**	**995.0**	**615.0**	**-38.2**	P/B Ratio	**1.2**	52 Wk Hi-Low	**71.38-50.63**
Book Value	**3,809.0**	**4,534.0**	**4,704.0**	**3.7**	Yield %	**5.3**	Market Cap	**US$5,506.5mil**

Address	**280 Park Ave.**	Tel	**212-250-2500**	Exchange	**NYSE**	President	**Eugene B. Shanks, Jr.**
	New York, NY 10017	Fax	**212-454-1704**	Ticker	**BT**	Chairman & CEO	**Charles S. Sanford, Jr.**

C.R. Bard

Industry: **Medical Supplies**

C.R. Bard manufactures single-patient-use health-care products for cardiovascular, urological, and surgical applications. Products include Foley catheters, procedural kits, and surgical-drainage and wound-management devices. Cardiovascular products account for about 50% of sales, surgical tools and implements generate 28%, and urological products provide the balance. The company markets its products to hospitals, clinics, and other health-care providers in the U.S. and internationally. Business activities outside the U.S. account for approximately 19% of revenues.

$ mil	12/92	12/93	12/94	% Change				
Sales	**990.2**	**970.9**	**1,018.2**	**4.9**	P/E Ratio	**21.2**	Price (9/30/95)	**30.50**
Net Income	**75.0**	**56.0**	**74.9**	**33.8**	P/B Ratio	**3.6**	52 Wk Hi-Low	**31.63-24.00**
Book Value	**392.4**	**383.1**	**439.8**	**14.8**	Yield %	**1.9**	Market Cap	**US$1,594.3mil**

Address	**730 Central Ave.**	Tel	**908-277-8000**	Exchange	**NYSE**	President & CEO	**William H. Longfield**
	Murray Hill, NJ 07974	Fax	**908-277-8078**	Ticker	**BCR**	Chairman	**William H. Longfield**

Barnett Banks

Industry: **Banks - Southern U.S.**

Barnett Banks is Florida's largest bank holding company, with 31 commercial banks and more than 600 branches in Florida and Georgia. The company commands Florida's and many of its counties' largest market share. Barnett Banks' loan portfolio is weighted toward residential mortgages, and installment and commercial loans. The company's nonbanking subsidiaries provide such services as trust, insurance, loan-collection, mortgage-banking, full-service brokerage, and credit-card services. Barnett Banks also manages the Emerald family of mutual funds.

$ mil	12/92	12/93	12/94	% Change				
Revenues	**3,456.5**	**3,129.9**	**3,110.6**	**-0.6**	P/E Ratio	**11.8**	Price (9/30/95)	**56.63**
Net Income	**207.7**	**421.0**	**488.0**	**15.9**	P/B Ratio	**1.7**	52 Wk Hi-Low	**58.88-37.63**
Book Value	**2,556.1**	**2,874.1**	**3,134.2**	**9.0**	Yield %	**2.8**	Market Cap	**US$5,462.3mil**

Address	**50 N. Laura St.**	Tel	**904-791-7720**	Exchange	**NYSE**	President	**Allen L. Lastinger, Jr.**
	Jacksonville, FL 32202-3638	Fax	**904-791-5356**	Ticker	**BBI**	Chairman & CEO	**Charles E. Rice**

Battle Mountain Gold

Industry: **Precious Metals**

Battle Mountain Gold operates gold, silver, and copper mines in the United States, Latin America, Australia, and New Guinea. Its principal property is the Battle Mountain complex in Nevada, which generates about one quarter of the company's revenues. The company's other mining operations include the San Luis mine in Colorado, the Pajingo and Red Dome mines in Australia, the San Cristobal mine in Chile, and the Kori Kollo mine in Bolivia. It holds net reserves of about 8.1 million ounces of gold (more than half of which are at Kori Kollo) and 29.8 million ounces of silver.

$ mil	12/92	12/93	12/94	% Change				
Sales	**181.8**	**193.4**	**229.7**	**18.8**	P/E Ratio	**NMF**	Price (9/30/95)	**9.88**
Net Income	**-36.4**	**-4.4**	**9.6**	**-317.5**	P/B Ratio	**2.1**	52 Wk Hi-Low	**13.00-8.88**
Book Value	**269.8**	**369.6**	**375.6**	**1.6**	Yield %	**0.5**	Market Cap	**US$799.9mil**

Address	**42nd Fl., 333 Clay St.**	Tel	**713-650-6400**	Exchange	**NYSE**	President	**Kenneth R. Werneburg**
	Houston, TX 77002	Fax	**713-650-3636**	Ticker	**BMG**	Chairman & CEO	**Karl E. Elers**

Bausch & Lomb

Industry: **Medical Supplies**

Bausch & Lomb manufactures personal-health and medical products. Its principal products include contact lenses, lens-care and eye-care solutions, Ray-Ban sunglasses, and eyeglass frames. The company also makes OptiPranolol, a beta-blocker used to fight glaucoma; Interplak toothpaste and dental-care accessories; Bushnell binoculars; and Miracle Ear hearing aids. Bausch & Lomb also sells the Curel and Soft Sense lines of skin-care products. The company markets its products worldwide. Sales outside the United States account for approximately 45% of the company's total.

$ mil	12/92	12/93	12/94	% Change				
Sales	**1,709.1**	**1,872.2**	**1,850.6**	**-1.2**	P/E Ratio	**NMF**	Price (9/30/95)	**41.38**
Net Income	**171.4**	**156.5**	**13.5**	**-91.4**	P/B Ratio	**2.7**	52 Wk Hi-Low	**44.13-31.00**
Book Value	**898.2**	**926.8**	**914.4**	**-1.3**	Yield %	**2.3**	Market Cap	**US$2,369.3mil**

Address **1 Chase Sq.**
Rochester, NY 14601-0054
Tel **716-338-6000**
Fax **716-338-8859**
Exchange **NYSE**
Ticker **BOL**
Chief Executive **Daniel E. Gill**
Chairman **Daniel E. Gill**

Baxter International

Industry: **Medical Supplies**

Baxter International produces health-care products and services used in hospitals and other health-care settings. The company distributes more than 200,000 different items, including bandages, fluid-collection devices, intravenous solutions, precision surgical instruments, and specialized products used to treat blood, cardiac, and kidney disorders. It sells these products through a direct-sales force and distributors to health-care professionals and institutions in the United States and approximately 100 countries. Sales in the U.S. account for 75% of the company's total.

$ mil	12/92	12/93	12/94	% Change				
Sales	**8,471.0**	**8,879.0**	**9,324.0**	**5.0**	P/E Ratio	**19.3**	Price (9/30/95)	**41.13**
Net Income	**441.0**	**-198.0**	**596.0**	**-401.0**	P/B Ratio	**3.1**	52 Wk Hi-Low	**41.13-24.88**
Book Value	**3,795.0**	**3,185.0**	**3,720.0**	**16.8**	Yield %	**2.5**	Market Cap	**US$11,381mil**

Address **One Baxter Pkwy.**
Deerfield, IL 60015
Tel **708-948-2000**
Fax **708-948-3948**
Exchange **NYSE**
Ticker **BAX**
Chief Executive **Vernon R. Loucks, Jr.**
Chairman **Vernon R. Loucks, Jr.**

BayBanks

Industry: **Banks - Eastern U.S.**

BayBanks provides banking, brokerage, and investment-management services to individuals, businesses, governmental units, and other New England banks. The company manages a network of 205 full-service banking offices and 366 automated-banking facilities serving 151 cities and towns in Massachusetts and two in Connecticut. Its subsidiaries include BayBank Systems, which operates the company's automated-teller network and issues loans and credit cards, and BayBanks Mortgage. BayBanks also serves as investment advisor and servicing agent for the BayFunds mutual fund family.

$ mil	12/92	12/93	12/94	% Change				
Revenues	**911.3**	**789.0**	**865.1**	**9.6**	P/E Ratio	**13.5**	Price (9/30/95)	**75.88**
Net Income	**59.2**	**67.7**	**107.4**	**58.7**	P/B Ratio	**1.8**	52 Wk Hi-Low	**83.75-51.00**
Book Value	**644.2**	**703.3**	**788.6**	**12.1**	Yield %	**2.1**	Market Cap	**US$1,484.9mil**

Address **175 Federal St.**
Boston, MA 02110
Tel **617-482-1040**
Fax **617-876-4734**
Exchange **NASDA**
Ticker **BBNK**
President **William M. Crozier**
Chairman **William M. Crozier**

Bear Stearns

Industry: **Securities Brokers**

Bear Stearns is the holding company for Bear Stearns & Company, which provides financial services including investment banking, securities trading, and brokerage, through 17 offices in the U.S. and overseas. The company underwrites share issues and provides assistance in mergers, acquisitions, restructurings, and securities clearance. Bear Stearns trades mainly U.S. government obligations, institutional equities, corporate fixed-income securities, and mortgage-related instruments on the major U.S. commodites and stock exchanges, including the New York Stock Exchange.

$ mil	06/92	06/93	06/94	% Change				
Sales	**2,677.0**	**2,856.9**	**3,441.1**	**20.4**	P/E Ratio	**6.3**	Price (9/30/95)	**21.50**
Net Income	**294.6**	**362.4**	**387.0**	**6.8**	P/B Ratio	**1.1**	52 Wk Hi-Low	**23.13-14.05**
Book Value	**1,277.0**	**1,766.5**	**2,167.0**	**22.7**	Yield %	**2.8**	Market Cap	**US$2,409.5mil**

Address **245 Park Ave.**
New York, NY 10167
Tel **212-272-2000**
Fax **212-272-8239**
Exchange **NYSE**
Ticker **BSC**
President & CEO **James E. Cayne**
Chairman **Alan C. Greenberg**

Beckman

Industry: **Advanced Medical Technology**

Beckman Instruments manufactures instruments, reagents, and other products used in biological research and in medical laboratories and clinics. Its main products include the Biomek automated laboratory work station (which manipulates and analyzes liquid compounds), the Optima line of centrifuges, and various chromatography, spectrophotometry, and other analytical equipment. Beckman Instruments also produces computer software to support its own clinical and laboratory equipment as well as that manufactured by others. The company markets its products worldwide.

$ mil	12/92	12/93	12/94	% Change				
Sales	**908.8**	**875.7**	**888.6**	**1.5**	P/E Ratio	**20.2**	Price (9/30/95)	**30.25**
Net Income	**43.8**	**-37.6**	**42.2**	**-212.2**	P/B Ratio	**2.7**	52 Wk Hi-Low	**31.38-26.63**
Book Value	**357.4**	**275.5**	**317.0**	**15.1**	Yield %	**1.3**	Market Cap	**US$877.6mil**

Address **2500 Harbor Blvd.**
Fullerton, CA 92634-3100
Tel **714-871-4848**
Fax **714-773-8111**
Exchange **NYSE**
Ticker **BEC**
President **John P. Wareham**
Chairman & CEO **Louis T. Rosso**

Becton Dickinson

Industry: **Medical Supplies**

Becton, Dickinson & Company produces medical supplies, including hypodermic products, gloves, catheters, surgical blades, thermometers, and elastic support products. Becton, Dickinson also manufactures diagnostic equipment, including blood-collection devices, hematology instruments, microbiology systems, and other medical apparatus. The company markets its products to health-care professionals, medical institutions, and the public in the United States, Canada, Latin America, Japan, and Europe. International sales account for about 44% of the company's revenues.

$ mil	09/92	09/93	09/94	% Change				
Sales	**2,365.3**	**2,465.4**	**2,559.5**	**3.8**	P/E Ratio	**20.6**	Price (9/30/95)	**62.88**
Net Income	**200.8**	**71.8**	**227.2**	**216.4**	P/B Ratio	**3.0**	52 Wk Hi-Low	**63.25-45.25**
Book Value	**1,594.9**	**1,457.0**	**1,481.7**	**1.7**	Yield %	**1.2**	Market Cap	**US$4,146.0mil**

Address **1 Becton Dr.**
Franklin Lakes, NJ 07417-1880
Tel **201-847-6800**
Fax **201-847-6475**
Exchange **NYSE**
Ticker **BDX**
President & CEO **Clateo Castellini**
Chairman **Clateo Castellini**

Bell Atlantic

Industry: **Regional Telephone Systems**

Bell Atlantic, a regional Bell company, provides communication and information services. The company has seven telephone subsidiaries that service six Atlantic states and Washington, D.C. Other subsidiaries provide cellular telecommunications, software, paging services, computer maintenance, network support, and business services. Bell Atlantic also has interests in communications concerns doing business in New Zealand and Czechoslovakia. Bell Atlantic, NYNEX, AirTouch, and U.S. West have formed partnerships to provide nationwide wireless communications services.

$ mil	12/92	12/93	12/94	% Change				
Sales	**12,093.2**	**12,534.8**	**13,791.4**	**10.0**	P/E Ratio	**NMF**	Price (9/30/95)	**61.38**
Net Income	**1,340.6**	**1,403.4**	**-754.8**	**-153.8**	P/B Ratio	**4.4**	52 Wk Hi-Low	**61.75-48.88**
Book Value	**7,816.3**	**8,224.4**	**6,081.3**	**-26.1**	Yield %	**4.5**	Market Cap	**US$26,796mil**

Address **1717 Arch St.**
Philadelphia, PA 19103
Tel **215-963-6000**
Fax **215-963-6470**
Exchange **NYSE**
Ticker **BEL**
Chief Executive **Raymond W. Smith**
Chairman **Raymond W. Smith**

BellSouth

Industry: **Regional Telephone Systems**

BellSouth, a regional Bell holding company, provides communication and information services. It delivers local and long-distance phone service to about 67% of the population in nine southeastern states. It also provides cellular-phone, electronic-mail, credit-card-validation, and paging services in the United States and abroad. In addition, the company publishes approximately 500 telephone directories. The company has ownership interests in foreign telecommunication companies in Argentina, Australia, Denmark, Germany, Uruguay, Venezuela, Chile, New Zealand, and China.

$ mil	12/92	12/93	12/94	% Change				
Sales	**15,201.6**	**15,880.3**	**16,844.5**	**6.1**	P/E Ratio	**16.8**	Price (9/30/95)	**73.13**
Net Income	**1,617.7**	**880.1**	**2,159.8**	**145.4**	P/B Ratio	**2.5**	52 Wk Hi-Low	**73.25-50.75**
Book Value	**13,798.6**	**13,494.2**	**14,367.3**	**6.5**	Yield %	**3.8**	Market Cap	**US$36,309mil**

Address **1155 Peachtree St. N.E.**
Atlanta, GA 30309-3610
Tel **404-249-2000**
Fax **404-249-5597**
Exchange **NYSE**
Ticker **BLS**
President & CEO **John L. Clendenin**
Chairman **John L. Clendenin**

A.H. Belo

Industry: **Publishing**

A.H. Belo operates newspapers and television stations. The company's main newspaper is The Dallas Morning News, which has a daily circulation of about 525,000 and a Sunday circulation of 800,000. Its DFW Suburban Newspapers subsidiary publishes six paid-circulation and two free community newspapers that serve Dallas-Fort Worth suburbs. A.H. Belo's television operations include an unaffiliated station in Seattle, ABC-affiliated stations in Dallas-Fort Worth and in Norfolk-Hampton, Virginia, and CBS-affiliated stations in Texas, California, Louisiana, and Oklahoma.

$ mil	12/92	12/93	12/94	% Change				
Sales	**515.9**	**544.8**	**628.1**	**15.3**	P/E Ratio	**20.2**	Price (9/30/95)	**34.38**
Net Income	**37.2**	**51.1**	**68.9**	**34.8**	P/B Ratio	**3.6**	52 Wk Hi-Low	**36.75-23.88**
Book Value	**281.2**	**346.1**	**382.5**	**10.5**	Yield %	**0.9**	Market Cap	**US$1,359.5mil**

Address **400 S. Record St.**
Dallas, TX 75265-5237
Tel **214-977-6606**
Fax **214-977-6603**
Exchange **NYSE**
Ticker **BLC**
President & CEO **Robert W. Decherd**
Chairman **Robert W. Decherd**

Bemis

Industry: **Containers & Packaging**

Bemis manufactures flexible packaging, specialty coating, and graphics products. The company's flexible-packaging products include coated and laminated films, packaging machinery, multiwall and small paper bags, and plastic containers. Pressure-sensitive adhesive-labeling systems and materials, electronic-engraving systems, and nonwoven fabrics round out its principal specialty-coating and graphics lines. The company markets its products primarily to customers in the retail-food, agribusiness, chemicals, printing, and graphic-arts industries in the United States and abroad.

$ mil	12/92	12/93	12/94	% Change				
Sales	**1,181.3**	**1,203.5**	**1,390.5**	**15.5**	P/E Ratio	**19.7**	Price (9/30/95)	**27.63**
Net Income	**57.0**	**44.3**	**72.8**	**64.3**	P/B Ratio	**3.4**	52 Wk Hi-Low	**29.75-21.88**
Book Value	**361.0**	**370.5**	**418.0**	**12.8**	Yield %	**2.0**	Market Cap	**US$1,422.4mil**

Address **Ste. 2300, 222 S. Ninth St.**
Minneapolis, MN 55402
Tel **612-376-3000**
Fax **612-376-3180**
Exchange **NYSE**
Ticker **BMS**
President & CEO **John H. Roe**
Chairman **--**

Beneficial

Industry: **Financial Services - Diversified**

Beneficial is a financial-services and insurance holding company with more than 1,000 offices in the U.S., Canada, the U.K., and Germany. The company operates the Beneficial full-service commercial-bank network and consumer-finance insurance businesses. Its subsidiaries offer credit-insurance underwriting (through Central National Life Insurance of Omaha) and commercial banking, and make tax-refund-anticipation loans. Through its subsidiary, Harbour Island, Beneficial is involved in a 177-acre real-estate development near the southern waterfront of Tampa, Florida.

$ mil	12/92	12/93	12/94	% Change				
Revenues	**1,819.3**	**1,957.5**	**2,137.4**	**9.2**	P/E Ratio	**15.9**	Price (9/30/95)	**52.25**
Net Income	**45.3**	**183.2**	**177.7**	**-3.0**	P/B Ratio	**2.0**	52 Wk Hi-Low	**53.75-35.50**
Book Value	**1,207.6**	**1,312.2**	**1,400.3**	**6.7**	Yield %	**3.1**	Market Cap	**US$2,767.9mil**

Address **301 N. Walnut St.**
Wilmington, DE 19801
Tel **302-425-2500**
Fax **302-425-2518**
Exchange **NYSE**
Ticker **BNL**
President **David J. Farris**
Chairman & CEO **Finn M.W. Caspersen**

Bethlehem Steel

Industry: **Steel**

Bethlehem Steel is the second-largest steel producer in the United States in terms of sales. It also produces other raw materials, repairs ships and offshore drill rigs, and manufactures forgings and castings. Steel operations include hot-rolled, cold-rolled, and coated sheets and strip, plates, structural shapes, piling, tin-mill products, specialty blooms, carbon and alloy bars, rail, and pipe. Other operations include the BethForge subsidiary, which manufactures forgings and castings, and CENTEC, which produces centrifugally cast rolls for the metalworking industry.

$ mil	12/92	12/93	12/94	% Change				
Sales	**4,007.9**	**4,323.4**	**4,819.4**	**11.5**	P/E Ratio	**40.4**	Price (9/30/95)	**14.13**
Net Income	**-449.3**	**-266.3**	**80.5**	**-130.2**	P/B Ratio	**1.3**	52 Wk Hi-Low	**21.00-13.63**
Book Value	**379.1**	**696.6**	**1,155.8**	**65.9**	Yield %	**0.0**	Market Cap	**US$1,559.8mil**

Address **1170 8th Ave.**
Bethlehem, PA 18016-7699
Tel **610-694-2424**
Fax **610-694-5743**
Exchange **NYSE**
Ticker **BS**
President **Roger P. Penny**
Chairman & CEO **Curtis H. Barnette**

Betz Laboratories

Industry: **Specialty Chemicals**

Betz Laboratories engages in the chemical treatment of water. It diagnoses water-related problems and supplies specialty chemicals to treat water, wastewater, and industrial materials. The company's chemicals, services, and treatment programs minimize corrosion, scaling, deposits, and microbiological fouling. As an adjunct to its principal business, Betz also markets water-analysis test kits. It serves customers in the chemical, paper, automotive, electric-utility, and food-processing industries worldwide. International sales account for 24% of the total.

$ mil	12/92	12/93	12/94	% Change				
Sales	**707.0**	**684.9**	**708.3**	**3.4**	P/E Ratio	**16.8**	Price (9/30/95)	**40.88**
Net Income	**82.0**	**65.5**	**73.2**	**11.7**	P/B Ratio	**3.5**	52 Wk Hi-Low	**49.88-40.88**
Book Value	**297.7**	**299.3**	**324.0**	**8.2**	Yield %	**3.5**	Market Cap	**US$1,132.3mil**

Address **4636 Somerton Rd.**
Trevose, PA 19053-6783
Tel **215-355-3300**
Fax **215-953-2484**
Exchange **NYSE**
Ticker **BTL**
President & CEO **William R. Cook**
Chairman **John F. McCaughan**

Biogen

Industry: **Biotechnology**

Biogen develops and produces drugs through genetic engineering. Its main source of revenues is royalties received from licenses for products based on the company's technology. The company derives most of its royalties from sales of alpha-interferon and hepatitis-B products. It also receives a significant amount of interest income from its marketable-securities and cash portfolio. Biogen is seeking FDA approval for its Avonex product, which is used to treat multiple sclerosis. The company and Genovo have entered into a joint venture to develop human gene-therapy treatments.

$ mil	12/92	12/93	12/94	% Change				
Sales	**135.1**	**149.3**	**156.3**	**4.7**	P/E Ratio	**NMF**	Price (9/30/95)	**60.00**
Net Income	**38.3**	**32.4**	**-4.9**	**-115.1**	P/B Ratio	**6.0**	52 Wk Hi-Low	**61.00-32.25**
Book Value	**285.0**	**325.2**	**329.9**	**1.5**	Yield %	**0.0**	Market Cap	**US$2,002.1mil**

Address **14 Cambridge Ctr.**
Cambridge, MA 02142
Tel **617-679-2000**
Fax **617-679-2617**
Exchange **NASDA**
Ticker **BGEN**
President **James R. Tobin**
Chairman & CEO **James L. Vincent**

Biomet

Industry: **Advanced Medical Technology**

Biomet manufactures products used in orthopedic surgery and therapy. The company's products include reconstructive equipment, trauma-treatment devices, orthopedic supports, surgical instruments, arthroscopic devices, and general operating-room supplies. Electro-Biology, a subsidiary, manufactures electrical bone-growth and spinal-fusion stimulators, which generate pulsed electromagnetic signals to aid in healing fractures. Biomet markets its products under the Biomet, Arthrotek, and Effner trademarks, primarily in the United States, Germany, and the United Kingdom.

$ mil	05/93	05/94	05/95	% Change				
Sales	**335.4**	**373.3**	**452.3**	**21.2**	P/E Ratio	**25.0**	Price (9/30/95)	**17.25**
Net Income	**64.0**	**69.8**	**79.2**	**13.5**	P/B Ratio	**4.5**	52 Wk Hi-Low	**18.38-10.75**
Book Value	**301.3**	**357.3**	**444.6**	**24.4**	Yield %	**0.0**	Market Cap	**US$1,987.0mil**

Address **Airport Industrial Pk.**
Warsaw, IN 46581
Tel **219-267-6639**
Fax **219-267-8137**
Exchange **NASDA**
Ticker **BMET**
President & CEO **Dane A. Miller**
Chairman **Niles L. Noblitt**

Black & Decker

Industry: **Other Home Furnishings**

Black & Decker manufactures power tools, hardware, consumer household products, and commercial equipment. In addition, the company develops and markets information systems and software for business applications. Black & Decker major products include power tools, security hardware, small appliances, plumbing products, gardening equipment, and outdoor-recreational products, glass-container-making equipment, and industrial-fastening systems. Its main customers are the automotive, transportation, construction, electronics, aerospace, and machine-tool industries.

$ mil	12/92	12/93	12/94	% Change				
Sales	4,779.6	4,882.2	5,248.3	7.5	P/E Ratio	24.9	Price (9/30/95)	34.13
Net Income	-333.6	66.0	127.4	93.0	P/B Ratio	2.5	52 Wk Hi-Low	34.50-21.25
Book Value	1,074.0	1,048.9	1,169.4	11.5	Yield %	1.2	Market Cap	US$2,924.3mil

Address **701 E. Joppa Rd.**
Towson, MD 21286
Tel **410-716-3900**
Fax **410-716-7021**
Exchange **NYSE**
Ticker **BDK**
President & CEO **Nolan D. Archibald**
Chairman **Nolan D. Archibald**

H & R Block

Industry: **Household Services**

H & R Block is a diversified personal-services company. H & R Block Tax Services, a subsidiary, provides tax-return preparation and electronic-filing services in the United States and Australia; tax-return preparation and refund-discounting in Canada; and tax-preparation services at military installations outside the U.S. The CompuServe subsidiary provides communication and information services to computer users through the CompuServe Information Service. Interim Services provides temporary office personnel and other employment services throughout North America.

$ mil	04/93	04/94	04/95	% Change				
Sales	1,525.3	1,238.7	1,360.3	9.8	P/E Ratio	37.6	Price (9/30/95)	38.00
Net Income	180.7	200.5	107.3	-46.5	P/B Ratio	5.8	52 Wk Hi-Low	46.63-33.38
Book Value	650.5	707.9	685.9	-3.1	Yield %	3.2	Market Cap	US$3,984.8mil

Address **4410 Main St.**
Kansas City, MO 64111
Tel **816-753-6900**
Fax **816-753-5346**
Exchange **NYSE**
Ticker **HRB**
President & CEO **Thomas M. Bloch**
Chairman **Henry W. Bloch**

Boatmen's Bancshares

Industry: **Banks - Central U.S.**

Boatmen's Bancshares is Missouri's largest bank holding company. It owns 45 subsidiary banks in nine states. With core markets in Missouri, New Mexico, Oklahoma, and Texas, Boatmen's Bancshares operates more than 500 banking offices and 877 off-site automated-teller machines (some of which are located in Wal-Mart and Sam's Club stores). It also operates a trust company, a mortgage-banking company, a credit life-insurance company, and an insurance agency. Boatmen's Bancshares issues credit cards through another subsidiary. It agreed to acquire Fourth Financial in 1995.

$ mil	12/92	12/93	12/94	% Change				
Revenues	2,000.7	2,106.8	2,294.2	8.9	P/E Ratio	10.9	Price (9/30/95)	37.00
Net Income	215.4	317.3	355.3	11.9	P/B Ratio	1.8	52 Wk Hi-Low	38.44-26.25
Book Value	1,794.5	2,134.4	2,202.0	3.2	Yield %	3.5	Market Cap	US$4,783.0mil

Address **800 Market St.**
St. Louis, MO 63101
Tel **314-466-6000**
Fax **314-466-7333**
Exchange **NASDA**
Ticker **BOAT**
President **Samuel B. Hayes III**
Chairman & CEO **Andrew B. Craig III**

Boeing

Industry: **Aerospace & Defense**

Boeing is the largest aerospace firm in the United States, as measured by total sales. Its principal commercial-aircraft models include the 737, 747, 757, and 767. A new model, the 777, is in development. It makes versions of its civilian products for military use. Boeing is a major contractor for the U.S. Space Station and produces the V-22 Osprey helicopter, F-22 fighter plane, B-2 bomber, AWACS plane, electronic systems, and missiles for military use. The company sells its products to commercial airlines and governmental agencies in the U.S. and in foreign markets.

$ mil	12/92	12/93	12/94	% Change				
Sales	30,184.0	25,438.0	21,924.0	-13.8	P/E Ratio	27.2	Price (9/30/95)	68.25
Net Income	552.0	1,244.0	856.0	-31.2	P/B Ratio	2.4	52 Wk Hi-Low	71.75-43.13
Book Value	8,056.0	8,983.0	9,700.0	8.0	Yield %	1.5	Market Cap	US$23,372mil

Address **7755 E. Marginal Way S.**
Seattle, WA 98108
Tel **206-655-2121**
Fax **206-655-7004**
Exchange **NYSE**
Ticker **BA**
President **Philip M. Condit**
Chairman & CEO **Frank Shrontz**

Boise Cascade

Industry: **Paper Products**

Boise Cascade produces paper and forest products. The company manufactures uncoated free-sheet papers, newsprint, containerboard, coated papers, and pulp. Boise is also a major producer of plywood, lumber, and particle board. In addition, the company distributes office supplies and office furniture. To support these activities, the company has three million acres of timberland, primarily in the Pacific Northwest. Boise Cascade markets its paper and lumber to users in the U.S. and in foreign countries. Customers in the U.S. account for almost all of the company's revenues.

$ mil	12/92	12/93	12/94	% Change				
Sales	3,715.6	3,958.3	4,140.4	4.6	P/E Ratio	NMF	Price (9/30/95)	40.38
Net Income	-227.5	-77.1	-62.6	-18.8	P/B Ratio	1.1	52 Wk Hi-Low	45.88-23.00
Book Value	1,357.6	1,504.5	1,364.9	-9.3	Yield %	1.5	Market Cap	US$1,928.4mil

Address **1111 W. Jefferson St.**
Boise, ID 83702
Tel **208-384-6161**
Fax **208-384-7298**
Exchange **NYSE**
Ticker **BCC**
President & CEO **George J. Harad**
Chairman **John B. Fery**

Borland

Industry: **Software**

Borland International designs business software and object-oriented programming-language software. The company creates products for the MS-Window operating system, as well as for Unix-based systems, including DEC VAX VMS and SCO Xenix operating systems. Borland International's database-management products include dBASE IV, Paradox, and Interbase. Its products include computer-language-compilers such as Borland C++, Turbo C++, Borland Pascal, and Turbo Pascal, and client server tools such as ReportSmith. Export sales accounted for 45% of revenues in fiscal 1995.

$ mil	03/93	03/94	03/95	% Change				
Sales	**464.0**	**393.5**	**254.1**	**-35.4**	P/E Ratio	**NMF**	Price (9/30/95)	**14.63**
Net Income	**-49.2**	**-69.9**	**-12.2**	**-82.6**	P/B Ratio	**3.3**	52 Wk Hi-Low	**16.75-6.13**
Book Value	**188.3**	**120.4**	**123.0**	**2.2**	Yield %	**0.0**	Market Cap	**US$417.4mil**

Address **100 Borland Way, Scotts Valley, CA 95066-3249**
Tel **408-431-1000** Fax **408-431-4122**
Exchange **NASDA** Ticker **BORL**
President **Gary Wetsel**
Chairman **Philippe Kahn**

Bowater

Industry: **Paper Products**

Bowater manufactures forestry products including newsprint, directory paper, coated publication paper, market pulp, computer forms, and lumber. Newsprint generates roughly 44% of Bowater's sales. The company markets its products under the Bowater name in the United States and internationally. Export sales account for approximately 13% of the company's net sales. An integrated manufacturer, Bowater owns nearly four million acres of timberland, and operates manufacturing and processing plants throughout the United States and in Nova Scotia, Canada.

$ mil	12/92	12/93	12/94	% Change				
Sales	**1,493.9**	**1,353.7**	**1,359.0**	**0.4**	P/E Ratio	**NMF**	Price (9/30/95)	**46.63**
Net Income	**-82.0**	**-64.5**	**-4.8**	**-92.5**	P/B Ratio	**1.8**	52 Wk Hi-Low	**53.50-23.38**
Book Value	**892.2**	**806.9**	**961.9**	**19.2**	Yield %	**1.3**	Market Cap	**US$1,810.2mil**

Address **55 E. Camperdown Way, Greenville, SC 29602**
Tel **803-271-7733** Fax **803-282-9482**
Exchange **NYSE** Ticker **BOW**
President & CEO **Arnold M. Nemirow**
Chairman **Anthony P. Gammie**

Boyd Gaming

Industry: **Casinos**

Boyd Gaming owns and operates six properties in Las Vegas. These properties include the Stardust Resort and Casino, Sam's Town Hotel and Gambling Hall, the Eldorado Casino, Jokers Wild Casino, California Hotel and Casino, and Fremont Hotel and Casino. During fiscal 1994 the company also opened another Sam's Town Hotel and Gambling Hall in Mississippi, Silver Star Hotel and Casino in Mississippi, and Treasure Chest Casino. Treasure Chest is a riverboat gambling operation near New Orleans. The company currently owns or operates 388,300 square feet of casino space.

$ mil	06/92	06/93	06/94	% Change				
Sales	**406.8**	**431.2**	**468.2**	**8.6**	P/E Ratio	**64.7**	Price (9/30/95)	**14.88**
Net Income	**6.1**	**12.7**	**12.7**	**-0.4**	P/B Ratio	**5.1**	52 Wk Hi-Low	**18.63-10.63**
Book Value	**62.7**	**72.7**	**164.4**	**126.2**	Yield %	**0.0**	Market Cap	**US$846.7mil**

Address **2950 S. Industrial Rd., Las Vegas, NV 89109**
Tel **702-792-7200** Fax **N/A**
Exchange **NYSE** Ticker **BYD**
President **Charles L. Ruthe**
Chairman & CEO **William S. Boyd**

Brinker International

Industry: **Restaurants**

Brinker International operates 458 restaurants across the U.S., Canada, and Mexico. The company is principally engaged in the operation and development of the Southwestern-themed Chili's Grill & Bar, as well as the more-upscale Grady's American Grill, Romano's Macaroni Grill, and Spageddies Italian restaurants. Of the restaurants, 277 are company-operated, full-service Chili's establishments. Approximately 85% of revenues are derived from the sale of food and nonalcoholic beverages. In 1994 the company agreed to acquire the 21-unit chain of On the Border Cafes.

$ mil	06/92	06/93	06/94	% Change				
Sales	**519.3**	**652.9**	**878.5**	**34.6**	P/E Ratio	**17.2**	Price (9/30/95)	**14.88**
Net Income	**35.7**	**48.9**	**61.6**	**26.0**	P/B Ratio	**2.5**	52 Wk Hi-Low	**24.50-14.75**
Book Value	**254.1**	**334.7**	**417.3**	**24.7**	Yield %	**0.0**	Market Cap	**US$1,129.6mil**

Address **6820 LBJ Fwy., Dallas, TX 75240**
Tel **214-980-9917** Fax **214-770-9593**
Exchange **NYSE** Ticker **EAT**
President **Ronald A. McDougall**
Chairman & CEO **Norman E. Brinker**

Bristol-Myers Squibb

Industry: **Pharmaceuticals**

Bristol-Myers Squibb is a producer of pharmaceuticals, medical devices, and other health-care products, and household chemicals and beauty aids. It manufactures prescription drugs, antibiotics, orthopedic implants, bandages, and surgical instruments. The company's brand-name products include Enfamil infant formula, Bufferin and Excedrin pain relievers, Clairol hair-care products, Sea Breeze skin-care applications, Vitalis hair preparations, Windex household cleaner, and Drano drain opener. International sales account for approximately 35% of the company's revenues.

$ mil	12/92	12/93	12/94	% Change				
Sales	**11,156.0**	**11,413.0**	**11,984.0**	**5.0**	P/E Ratio	**20.1**	Price (9/30/95)	**72.88**
Net Income	**1,962.0**	**1,959.0**	**1,842.0**	**-6.0**	P/B Ratio	**6.5**	52 Wk Hi-Low	**74.25-56.13**
Book Value	**6,020.0**	**5,940.0**	**5,704.0**	**-4.0**	Yield %	**4.0**	Market Cap	**US$36,961mil**

Address **345 Park Ave., New York, NY 10154**
Tel **212-546-4000** Fax **212-546-4020**
Exchange **NYSE** Ticker **BMY**
President & CEO **Charles A. Heimbold**
Chairman **Richard L. Gelb**

Brown-Forman

Industry: **Distillers & Brewers**

Brown-Forman distributes wines, spirits, and consumer durables. The company produces, bottles, and exports the Jack Daniels, Early Times, Southern Comfort, and Korbel brands of alcoholic beverages, and imports Canadian Mist whiskey. It also manufactures fine-china dinnerware and crystal stemware, which it markets under the Lenox name. Its other consumer-durable products include luggage and leather accessories. Brown-Forman markets all of these products in the United States and internationally. Sales to customers outside the U.S. account for less than 10% of the total.

$ mil	04/93	04/94	04/95	% Change				
Sales	**1,691.7**	**1,665.1**	**1,679.6**	**0.9**	P/E Ratio	**18.1**	Price (9/30/95)	**38.88**
Net Income	**156.2**	**128.5**	**148.6**	**15.6**	P/B Ratio	**4.9**	52 Wk Hi-Low	**39.25-26.38**
Book Value	**818.1**	**463.7**	**545.8**	**17.7**	Yield %	**2.5**	Market Cap	**US$2,682.2mil**

Address **850 Dixie Hwy.**
Louisville, KY 40210
Tel **502-585-1100**
Fax **502-774-7876**
Exchange **NYSE**
Ticker **BFB**
President & CEO **Owsley Brown II**
Chairman **Owsley Brown II**

Brown Group

Industry: **Footwear**

Brown Group is a footwear company with operations in the supplying and retailing of footwear for men, women, and children. The company's major brand names include Air Step, Brittania, Dr. Scholl's, Naturalizer, DeLiso, Naturalizer, Regal, Penaljo, Jean Pier Clemente, Buster Brown, and Wildcats, among others. Company-owned retail footwear stores include 418 Naturalizer, 722 Famous Footwear, 14 F.X. LaSalle, and four Other Family Footwear stores. Fabri-Centers of America also operates 343 Cloth World retail-fabric stores.

$ mil	01/93	01/94	01/95	% Change				
Sales	**1,791.2**	**1,597.8**	**1,461.6**	**-8.5**	P/E Ratio	**8.2**	Price (9/30/95)	**18.38**
Net Income	**4.7**	**-31.6**	**39.4**	**-224.7**	P/B Ratio	**1.3**	52 Wk Hi-Low	**34.63-17.13**
Book Value	**289.0**	**233.9**	**249.7**	**6.8**	Yield %	**8.7**	Market Cap	**US$329.8mil**

Address **8300 Maryland Ave.**
St. Louis, MO 63166-0029
Tel **314-854-4000**
Fax **314-854-4274**
Exchange **NYSE**
Ticker **BG**
President & CEO **B.A. Bridgewater**
Chairman **B.A. Bridgewater**

Browning-Ferris

Industry: **Pollution Control, Waste Management**

Browning-Ferris Industries provides disposal services for nonhazardous and medical waste. The company, which operates in 400 North American and 250 overseas locations, provides waste recycling, transportation, and disposal, and operates 97 landfills in the U.S. It collects medical waste from approximately 114,000 customers. The company's subsidiaries offer portable-restroom services and manage municipal and commercial sweeping businesses. Browning-Ferris generates roughly 61% of consolidated revenues from the collection of solid wastes.

$ mil	09/92	09/93	09/94	% Change				
Sales	**3,287.5**	**3,494.9**	**4,314.5**	**23.5**	P/E Ratio	**20.4**	Price (9/30/95)	**30.38**
Net Income	**175.6**	**197.4**	**278.7**	**41.2**	P/B Ratio	**2.5**	52 Wk Hi-Low	**40.38-25.75**
Book Value	**1,460.4**	**1,532.6**	**2,391.7**	**56.1**	Yield %	**2.2**	Market Cap	**US$6,467.5mil**

Address **757 N. Eldridge**
Houston, TX 77079
Tel **713-870-8100**
Fax **713-870-7844**
Exchange **NYSE**
Ticker **BFI**
President **Bruce E. Ranck**
Chairman & CEO **William D. Ruckelshaus**

Brunswick

Industry: **Other Recreational Products & Services**

Brunswick manufactures marine and recreation products. The company's marine products include Bayliner marine-propulsion systems and Mercury and Mariner boat motors, which are marketed to the marina and boat-building industries. Its recreational product line includes Zebco fishing reels and accessories and Brunswick bowling equipment, golf clubs and bags, and billiard tables. In addition, Brunswick operates 126 recreation centers, primarily bowling centers, worldwide. The company also manages seven Circus World Pizza restaurants, which include children's recreation areas.

$ mil	12/92	12/93	12/94	% Change				
Sales	**2,059.4**	**2,206.8**	**2,700.1**	**22.4**	P/E Ratio	**15.0**	Price (9/30/95)	**20.25**
Net Income	**-26.3**	**23.1**	**129.0**	**458.4**	P/B Ratio	**2.1**	52 Wk Hi-Low	**23.50-16.38**
Book Value	**822.5**	**804.4**	**910.7**	**13.2**	Yield %	**2.2**	Market Cap	**US$1,939.9mil**

Address **1 N. Field Ct.**
Lake Forest, IL 60045-4811
Tel **708-735-4700**
Fax **708-735-4765**
Exchange **NYSE**
Ticker **BC**
President & CEO **Jack F. Reichert**
Chairman **Jack F. Reichert**

Burlington Northern

Industry: **Railroads**

Burlington Northern Santa Fe is a rail-transportation holding company. Its Burlington Northern Railroad subsidiary operates the longest railroad system in the United States, consisting of more than 24,000 miles of track in the West and Midwest. Transportation of coal accounts for about 33% of revenues, making it Burlington's largest source of income. The remaining revenues are generated by transporting other freight, including agricultural commodities and consumer products. In 1995, Burlington Northern merged with Santa Fe Pacific, a railroad and petroleum-pipeline operator.

$ mil	12/92	12/93	12/94	% Change				
Sales	**4,630.0**	**4,699.0**	**4,995.0**	**6.3**	P/E Ratio	**16.6**	Price (9/30/95)	**72.50**
Net Income	**278.0**	**296.0**	**416.0**	**40.5**	P/B Ratio	**2.9**	52 Wk Hi-Low	**76.25-46.63**
Book Value	**1,728.0**	**1,919.0**	**2,237.0**	**16.6**	Yield %	**1.7**	Market Cap	**US$11,031mil**

Address **3800 Continental Plz., 777 Main St.**
Fort Worth, TX 76102-5384
Tel **817-333-2000**
Fax **817-333-2130**
Exchange **NYSE**
Ticker **BNI**
Chief Executive **Gerald Grinstein**
Chairman **Gerald Grinstein**

Burlington Resources

Industry: **Oil - Secondary**

Burlington Resources operates oil and natural-gas wells in the south-central U.S. Meridian Oil, a subsidiary, owns, on average, a 45% interest in 32,000 wells and holds net reserves of 5.5 trillion cubic feet of gas and 184 million barrels of oil. Most of the company's petroleum production comes from the San Juan Basin of northwestern New Mexico and southwestern Colorado. It operates two natural-gas pipeline systems and seven natural-gas-gathering systems, from which it supplies gas to industrial customers, electric and gas utilities, and pipeline companies.

$ mil	12/92	12/93	12/94	% Change				
Sales	**1,141.4**	**1,249.0**	**1,054.9**	**-15.5**	P/E Ratio	**32.3**	Price (9/30/95)	**38.75**
Net Income	**257.8**	**256.3**	**154.3**	**-39.8**	P/B Ratio	**1.9**	52 Wk Hi-Low	**42.63-33.88**
Book Value	**2,405.8**	**2,608.1**	**2,568.0**	**-1.5**	Yield %	**1.4**	Market Cap	**US$4,904.4mil**

Address	**5051 Westheimer**	Tel	**713-624-9500**	Exchange	**NYSE**	President & CEO	**Thomas H. O'Leary**
	Houston, TX 77056	Fax	**713-624-9555**	Ticker	**BR**	Chairman	**Thomas H. O'Leary**

Cabletron Systems

Industry: **Communications Technology**

Cabletron Systems manufactures local-area-network (LAN) and wide-area-network (WAN) connectivity products. Network-interconnection products include smart hubs, which allow internetworking of various operating systems; multiport repeaters which regenerate network signals as they weaken along stretches of cable; transceivers which connect PCs to LANs and WANs; and network-management software which assists network administrators in correcting problems. The company also makes cables and test equipment used in the installation of its interconnection products.

$ mil	02/93	02/94	02/95	% Change				
Sales	**418.2**	**598.1**	**810.7**	**35.5**	P/E Ratio	**29.0**	Price (9/30/95)	**65.88**
Net Income	**83.5**	**119.2**	**162.0**	**35.9**	P/B Ratio	**8.0**	52 Wk Hi-Low	**68.75-37.50**
Book Value	**288.8**	**423.8**	**587.5**	**38.6**	Yield %	**0.0**	Market Cap	**US$4,719.2mil**

Address	**35 Industrial Way**	Tel	**603-332-9400**	Exchange	**NYSE**	President & CEO	**S. Robert Levine**
	Rochester, NH 03867	Fax	**603-337-2211**	Ticker	**CS**	Chairman	**Craig R. Benson**

Cablevision Systems

Industry: **Broadcasting**

Cablevision Systems provides cable-television services. It controls cable-television systems in six states, and has approximately 1.7 million subscribers. In addition, Cablevision manages or has ownership interests in other cable-television systems serving roughly 861,000 subscribers. The company also owns interests in companies that produce and distribute national and regional programming through the Sports Channel, Prime Sports Channel, Bravo, and American Movie Classics channels, and pay-per-view services. The company also owns a radio station in Cleveland, Ohio.

$ mil	12/92	12/93	12/94	% Change				
Sales	**572.5**	**666.7**	**837.2**	**25.6**	P/E Ratio	**NMF**	Price (9/30/95)	**59.63**
Net Income	**-250.5**	**-246.6**	**-315.2**	**27.8**	P/B Ratio	**NMF**	52 Wk Hi-Low	**68.88-46.25**
Book Value	**-1,250.2**	**-1,503.2**	**-1,818.5**	**21.0**	Yield %	**0.0**	Market Cap	**US$1,418.7mil**

Address	**1 Media Crossways**	Tel	**516-364-8450**	Exchange	**AMEX**	Chief Executive	**Charles F. Dolan**
	Woodbury, NY 11797	Fax	**516-496-1780**	Ticker	**CVC**	Chairman	**Charles F. Dolan**

Cabot

Industry: **Specialty Chemicals**

Cabot manufactures specialty chemicals and personal-safety equipment, and distributes natural gas and coal. The company makes carbon black, a powder made from oil and used in tires, printing inks, and industrial rubber products. It also produces thermoplastic concentrates, tantalum-based electrical-capacitor materials, fumed silica, and disposable safety products such as goggles and face shields. Cabot's energy subsidiaries include minority-held American Oil and Gas, which buys, processes, and resells natural gas, and Tuco, which handles and distributes coal.

$ mil	09/92	09/93	09/94	% Change				
Sales	**1,557.0**	**1,614.3**	**1,679.8**	**4.1**	P/E Ratio	**27.1**	Price (9/30/95)	**53.13**
Net Income	**62.2**	**11.3**	**78.7**	**596.4**	P/B Ratio	**3.6**	52 Wk Hi-Low	**57.88-25.63**
Book Value	**493.0**	**442.3**	**562.5**	**27.2**	Yield %	**1.0**	Market Cap	**US$2,015.9mil**

Address	**75 State St.**	Tel	**617-345-0100**	Exchange	**NYSE**	President & CEO	**Samuel W. Bodman**
	Boston, MA 02109-1806	Fax	**617-342-6103**	Ticker	**CBT**	Chairman	**Samuel W. Bodman**

California Water Service

Industry: **Water Utilities**

California Water Service is a public water utility that provides water service to 38 cities in the San Francisco, Los Angeles, Sacramento, and San Joaquin and Salinas valley areas. The company produces, purifies, and stores water for distribution to roughly 365,500 customers. Residential water consumption accounts for about 74% of revenues; commercial and industrial users make up another 20% of the total. The company is also developing drought-management and water-testing technologies. The utility obtains half its water from wells and the balance from third parties.

$ mil	12/92	12/93	12/94	% Change				
Sales	**139.8**	**151.7**	**157.3**	**3.7**	P/E Ratio	**13.5**	Price (9/30/95)	**32.88**
Net Income	**12.5**	**15.5**	**14.4**	**-7.0**	P/B Ratio	**1.4**	52 Wk Hi-Low	**33.13-29.50**
Book Value	**123.0**	**127.5**	**147.9**	**16.0**	Yield %	**6.0**	Market Cap	**US$205.4mil**

Address	**1720 N. First St.**	Tel	**408-451-8200**	Exchange	**NASDA**	President & CEO	**Donald L. Houck**
	San Jose, CA 95112	Fax	**408-437-9185**	Ticker	**CWT**	Chairman	**C.H. Stump**

CalMat

Industry: **Building Materials**

CalMat manufactures construction materials in the western U.S. The company's concrete and aggregates division mines aggregates from 1.8 billion tons of reserves; it processes these aggregates at 34 plants. The company also operates 28 ready-mix concrete plants and 375 mixer trucks. Its asphalt division operates 36 plants that manufacture hot-mix asphalt, in part from aggregates and oil that have been salvaged from roads and other surfaces. CalMat's primary customers are contractors who use its products to build homes, commercial buildings, roads, and transit systems.

$ mil	12/92	12/93	12/94	% Change				
Sales	341.5	348.4	365.2	4.8	P/E Ratio	22.2	Price (9/30/95)	18.00
Net Income	-16.5	9.2	18.7	103.6	P/B Ratio	1.2	52 Wk Hi-Low	21.25-17.00
Book Value	350.7	351.0	361.1	2.9	Yield %	2.2	Market Cap	US$416.8mil

Address **3200 San Fernando Rd.**
Los Angeles, CA 90065
Tel **213-258-2777**
Fax **213-258-1583**
Exchange **NYSE**
Ticker **CZM**
President & CEO **A. Frederick Gerstell**
Chairman **A. Frederick Gerstell**

Campbell Soup

Industry: **Other Food**

Campbell Soup manufactures prepared foods. The company's main products include Campbell's canned soups and pasta sauces, V-8 vegetable juice, Franco-American pasta products, Prego and Open Pit sauces, and Pepperidge Farm baked goods. It sells its products to grocery chains and other retailers, wholesale food-service distributors, institutional customers, and government agencies worldwide. Campbell also makes Godiva chocolates and operates approximately 120 Godiva retail shops. The company manufactures most of the packaging it uses for its canned and frozen products.

$ mil	07/92	07/93	07/94	% Change				
Sales	6,263.2	6,586.2	6,690.0	1.6	P/E Ratio	20.0	Price (9/30/95)	50.25
Net Income	490.5	8.2	630.0	NMF	P/B Ratio	6.3	52 Wk Hi-Low	51.25-38.13
Book Value	2,027.6	1,704.0	1,989.0	16.7	Yield %	2.2	Market Cap	US$12,543mil

Address **Campbell Pl.**
Camden, NJ 08103-1799
Tel **609-342-4800**
Fax **609-342-3878**
Exchange **NYSE**
Ticker **CPB**
President & CEO **David W. Johnson**
Chairman **David W. Johnson**

Capital Cities/ABC

Industry: **Broadcasting**

Capital Cities/ABC operates the ABC television and radio networks, affiliated stations, publications, and cable-television services. The company's television interests include eight TV stations, an 80% share of the cable sports network ESPN, and ownership interests in the Arts & Entertainment and Lifetime cable-television channels of 37.5% and 50%, respectively. In addition, Capital Cities/ABC owns 21 radio stations and publishes nine daily newspapers and several national magazines. In 1995, Walt Disney agreed to acquire the company.

$ mil	12/92	12/93	12/94	% Change				
Sales	5,344.1	5,673.7	6,379.2	12.4	P/E Ratio	26.6	Price (9/30/95)	117.63
Net Income	246.1	455.3	679.8	49.3	P/B Ratio	4.2	52 Wk Hi-Low	119.50-77.00
Book Value	3,805.7	3,572.1	4,288.6	20.1	Yield %	0.1	Market Cap	US$18,097mil

Address **77 W. 66th St.**
New York, NY 10023-6298
Tel **212-456-7777**
Fax **212-456-1285**
Exchange **NYSE**
Ticker **CCB**
President **Robert A. Iger**
Chairman & CEO **Thomas S. Murphy**

Cardinal Health

Industry: **Drug-based Retailers**

Cardinal Health distributes health- and beauty-care products. The company distributes pharmaceuticals, surgical and hospital supplies, and various other items sold by retail drugstores, hospitals, alternative-care centers, and the pharmacy departments of supermarkets and mass merchandisers. It also offers support services such as in-pharmacy computer systems. In addition, the company operates specialty wholesaling businesses including a pharmaceutical-repackaging program for independent and chain customers and a distribution network for therapeutic-plasma products.

$ mil	03/93	06/94 *	06/95	% Change				
Revenues	1,966.5	5,790.4	7,806.1	34.8	P/E Ratio	27.5	Price (9/30/95)	55.38
Net Income	33.6	35.1	85.0	142.1	P/B Ratio	4.2	52 Wk Hi-Low	56.50-41.13
Book Value	255.6	368.5	548.2	48.8	Yield %	0.2	Market Cap	US$2,321.8mil

Address **655 Metro Pl. S.**
Dublin, OH 43017
Tel **614-761-8700**
Fax **614-761-8919**
Exchange **NASDA**
Ticker **CAH**
President & COO **John C. Kane**
Chairman & CEO **Robert D. Walter**

*Irregular period due to fiscal year change.

Caremark

Industry: **Health Care Providers**

Caremark International provides alternative-site patient care and managed-care services. Alternative-site services are provided outside of traditional settings, such as a hospital. Services include infusion therapy, hemophilia and immune-deficiency therapy, among others. The company's managed-care segment provides services for prescription-drug benefit programs and multispecialty physician group practices, provides nephrology services, and operates a preferred-provider organization in Puerto Rico. Services are provided in the United States, Canada, Europe, and Japan.

$ mil	12/92	12/93	12/94	% Change				
Sales	1,461.2	1,783.2	2,426.0	36.0	P/E Ratio	19.9	Price (9/30/95)	21.50
Net Income	27.3	77.7	80.4	3.5	P/B Ratio	3.2	52 Wk Hi-Low	24.88-16.25
Book Value	332.2	409.6	486.7	18.8	Yield %	0.2	Market Cap	US$1,736.6mil

Address **2215 Sanders Rd.**
Northbrook, IL 60062
Tel **708-559-4700**
Fax **708-559-4648**
Exchange **NYSE**
Ticker **CK**
President **James G. Connelly III**
Chairman & CEO **C.A. Lance Piccolo**

Carolina Power & Light

Industry: **Electrical Utilities - Southern U.S.**

Carolina Power & Light generates electrical power and provides related services. The company sells electricity to approximately 3.5 million residential, commercial, and industrial customers in eastern and western North Carolina and central South Carolina. Approximately 55% of the company's electricity is generated from coal; 32% is nuclear; 2% is hydroelectric; and 11% is from other fuels. Residential customers account for 33% of the revenues, while industrial and commercial customers contribute about 46% of this figure; the remainder is from resale and other sales.

	$ mil 12/92	12/93	12/94	% Change				
Sales	**2,766.8**	**2,895.4**	**2,876.6**	**-0.6**	P/E Ratio	**16.6**	Price (9/30/95)	**33.63**
Net Income	**379.6**	**346.5**	**313.2**	**-9.6**	P/B Ratio	**1.9**	52 Wk Hi-Low	**34.00-25.25**
Book Value	**2,677.8**	**2,775.9**	**2,730.0**	**-1.7**	Yield %	**5.1**	Market Cap	**US$5,226.4mil**

Address **411 Fayetteville St.**
Raleigh, NC 27601
Tel **919-546-6111**
Fax **919-546-3805**
Exchange **NYSE**
Ticker **CPL**
President **William Cavanaugh III**
Chairman & CEO **Sherwood H. Smith, Jr.**

Catellus Development

Industry: **Real-Estate Investment**

Catellus Development is a real-estate-development firm with property holdings of 1 million acres in developed and undeveloped land and 14.7 million square feet of income-producing buildings in California and 11 states in the West, Southwest, and Midwest. The company's primary activity is developing industrial parks in major metropolitan areas. Approximately 84% of its holdings are industrial buildings such as warehouses and light manufacturing and research facilities.The company's activities also include asset management, other development activities, and property sales.

	$ mil 12/92	12/93	12/94	% Change				
Sales	**186.2**	**190.5**	**175.4**	**-7.9**	P/E Ratio	**NMF**	Price (9/30/95)	**6.38**
Net Income	**1.2**	**-52.8**	**-2.5**	**-95.4**	P/B Ratio	**0.9**	52 Wk Hi-Low	**7.25-5.38**
Book Value	**145.9**	**526.0**	**499.7**	**-5.0**	Yield %	**0.0**	Market Cap	**US$465.2mil**

Address **201 Mission St.**
San Francisco, CA 94105
Tel **415-974-4500**
Fax **415-974-4651**
Exchange **NYSE**
Ticker **CDX**
President & CEO **Nelson C. Rising**
Chairman **Joseph R. Seiger**

Caterpillar

Industry: **Heavy Machinery**

Caterpillar manufactures earthmoving, construction, and materials-handling machinery and engines. Its products include track and wheel tractors, lift trucks, track and wheel excavators, off-highway trucks, dump trucks, paving equipment, log loaders, and truck components. The company also makes engines used in earthmoving and construction machines; locomotives; and marine, petroleum, agricultural, and industrial applications. Caterpillar also offers financing and insurance services. Approximately 49% of the company's total sales are derived overseas.

	$ mil 12/92	12/93	12/94	% Change				
Sales	**9,840.0**	**11,235.0**	**13,863.0**	**23.4**	P/E Ratio	**12.1**	Price (9/30/95)	**56.88**
Net Income	**-2,435.0**	**652.0**	**955.0**	**46.5**	P/B Ratio	**3.9**	52 Wk Hi-Low	**73.88-48.38**
Book Value	**1,575.0**	**2,199.0**	**2,911.0**	**32.4**	Yield %	**1.1**	Market Cap	**US$11,316mil**

Address **100 N.E. Adams St.**
Peoria, IL 61629-7310
Tel **309-675-1000**
Fax **309-675-4225**
Exchange **NYSE**
Ticker **CAT**
Chief Executive **Donald V. Fites**
Chairman **Donald V. Fites**

CBI Industries

Industry: **Industrial - Diversified**

CBI Industries is a holding company for its subsidiaries in contracting services, industrial gases, and investments. Chicago Bridge & Iron handles contracting services. Chicago Bridge provides design, engineering, fabrication, project-management, general-contracting, and specialty-construction services. The industrial gases subsidiary is comprised of Liquid Carbonic Industries and its subsidiaries. The investments subsidiary includes CBI Investments, which has interests in oil and refined-product storage, blending, and transport; real estate; and financial investments.

	$ mil 12/92	12/93	12/94	% Change				
Sales	**1,672.8**	**1,671.7**	**1,890.9**	**13.1**	P/E Ratio	**19.8**	Price (9/30/95)	**23.75**
Net Income	**64.0**	**-34.0**	**51.5**	**-251.4**	P/B Ratio	**1.3**	52 Wk Hi-Low	**27.25-20.13**
Book Value	**715.5**	**676.6**	**715.8**	**5.8**	Yield %	**2.0**	Market Cap	**US$907.4mil**

Address **800 Jorie Blvd.**
Oak Brook, IL 60521-2268
Tel **708-572-7000**
Fax **708-572-7405**
Exchange **NYSE**
Ticker **CBH**
President & CEO **John E. Jones**
Chairman **John E. Jones**

CBS

Industry: **Broadcasting**

CBS is a television-broadcast network. It purchases and distributes news, sports, and entertainment programming to its 206 independently owned affiliates. The company also owns and operates seven television stations and 21 radio stations. Through partnerships with Twentieth Century-Fox Film and MTM Studios, CBS distributes feature-film videocassettes and manages television- and film-production facilities. The company also markets its programming internationally. In 1995, Westinghouse Electric agreed to acquire the company.

	$ mil 12/92	12/93	12/94	% Change				
Sales	**3,503.0**	**3,510.1**	**3,711.9**	**5.7**	P/E Ratio	**21.4**	Price (9/30/95)	**79.88**
Net Income	**81.0**	**326.2**	**281.6**	**-13.7**	P/B Ratio	**13.3**	52 Wk Hi-Low	**81.38-51.00**
Book Value	**571.3**	**1,262.7**	**367.0**	**-70.9**	Yield %	**0.5**	Market Cap	**US$5,176.2mil**

Address **51 W. 52nd St.**
New York, NY 10019
Tel **212-975-4321**
Fax **212-975-4299**
Exchange **NYSE**
Ticker **CBS**
President & CEO **Laurence A. Tisch**
Chairman **Laurence A. Tisch**

Centerior Energy

Industry: **Electrical Utilities - Central U.S.**

Centerior Energy generates electrical power. The company provides electricity to 2.4 million customers in an area of 4,200 square miles in Ohio through its Cleveland Electric Illuminating and Toledo Edison subsidiaries. Residential users account for about 31% of operating revenues; commercial and industrial users make up almost 60%. Centerior generates roughly 45% of its electricity using its three nuclear-power generating stations; the balance of the company's needs is produced with fossil fuels at its 12 fossil-fuel-fired plants or is purchased from third parties.

$ mil	12/92	12/93	12/94	% Change				
Sales	**2,438.0**	**2,474.0**	**2,421.0**	**-2.1**	P/E Ratio	**7.9**	Price (9/30/95)	**10.88**
Net Income	**212.0**	**-943.0**	**204.0**	**-121.6**	P/B Ratio	**0.9**	52 Wk Hi-Low	**10.88-8.25**
Book Value	**2,889.0**	**1,785.0**	**1,882.0**	**5.4**	Yield %	**7.4**	Market Cap	**US$1,609.8mil**

Address **6200 Oak Tree Blvd.**
Independence, OH 44131
Tel **216-447-3100**
Fax **216-447-3240**
Exchange **NYSE**
Ticker **CX**
President & CEO **Robert J. Farling**
Chairman **Robert J. Farling**

Centex

Industry: **Home Construction**

Centex builds residential and commercial buildings, manufactures building materials, and provides financial services. The company builds and provides mortgage financing for 12,000 single-family homes per year throughout the U.S. These houses have an average sales price of about $160,000. It also builds nonresidential projects such as hotels, medical facilities, office buildings, shopping centers, and government buildings. It manufactures construction products, including cement, ready-mix concrete, and gypsum wallboard. Centex also owns the Texas Trust Savings Bank.

$ mil	03/93	03/94	03/95	% Change				
Sales	**2,502.7**	**3,214.5**	**3,277.5**	**2.0**	P/E Ratio	**9.5**	Price (9/30/95)	**29.00**
Net Income	**61.0**	**85.2**	**92.3**	**8.3**	P/B Ratio	**1.2**	52 Wk Hi-Low	**31.00-20.13**
Book Value	**578.4**	**668.7**	**668.2**	**-0.1**	Yield %	**0.7**	Market Cap	**US$817.6mil**

Address **3333 Lee Pkwy.**
Dallas, TX 75219
Tel **214-559-6500**
Fax **214-522-7568**
Exchange **NYSE**
Ticker **CTX**
President **William J. Gillilan III**
Chairman & CEO **Laurence E. Hirsch**

Centocor

Industry: **Biotechnology**

Centocor is a manufacturer of in vitro diagnostic and antibody-based biotechnology products that are used to treat cancer and arthritis, and infectious, cardiovascular, and autoimmune diseases. It produces CentoRx, which prevents the formulation of blood clots in the cardiovascular system. The company has developed a therapeutic agent for the treatment of sepsis syndrome, and is testing several cardiovascular-therapy and cancer-fighting products. Centocor's diagnostic-imaging products, which use radioactive isotopes to record images of antibodies, are similar to x-rays.

$ mil	12/92	12/93	12/94	% Change				
Sales	**126.2**	**75.9**	**67.2**	**-11.4**	P/E Ratio	**NMF**	Price (9/30/95)	**10.88**
Net Income	**-194.1**	**-74.4**	**-126.7**	**70.2**	P/B Ratio	**NMF**	52 Wk Hi-Low	**20.75-10.88**
Book Value	**30.7**	**-19.2**	**5.3**	**-127.5**	Yield %	**0.0**	Market Cap	**US$634.2mil**

Address **200 Great Valley Pkwy.**
Malvern, PA 19355
Tel **610-651-6000**
Fax **610-651-6100**
Exchange **NASDA**
Ticker **CNTO**
President & CEO **David P. Holveck**
Chairman **Hubert J.P. Schoemaker**

Ceridian

Industry: **Software**

Ceridian provides technology-based and employer-management services. It also makes defense systems. The company's information-services division collects and analyzes data, and delivers the resulting information to customers. Its employer-services division offers payroll and payroll-related services, human-resource-information, and benefit-management services. The company's Computing Devices International subsidiary develops electronic systems for defense agencies. Its Arbitron subsidiary estimates audience size and demographics for radio stations and advertising agencies.

$ mil	12/92	12/93	12/94	% Change				
Sales	**830.3**	**886.1**	**916.3**	**3.4**	P/E Ratio	**31.0**	Price (9/30/95)	**44.38**
Net Income	**-392.5**	**-30.4**	**78.6**	**-358.6**	P/B Ratio	**10.8**	52 Wk Hi-Low	**45.88-23.63**
Book Value	**-100.9**	**111.3**	**186.5**	**67.6**	Yield %	**0.0**	Market Cap	**US$2,027.8mil**

Address **8100 34th Ave. S.**
Minneapolis, MN 55425
Tel **612-853-8100**
Fax **612-853-7896**
Exchange **NYSE**
Ticker **CEN**
President & CEO **Lawrence Perlman**
Chairman **Lawrence Perlman**

Champion International

Industry: **Paper Products**

Champion International manufactures forest products in the U.S., Canada, and Brazil. The company operates about 12 paper mills where it makes printing and writing papers, primarily for office use; coated papers, which are primarily used for magazines, advertising materials, and textbooks; newsprint, which is used for newspapers and directories; and kraft paper, which is used primarily for grocery bags. It also produces paper milk and juice cartons, oven-safe packaging, plywood, and dimensional lumber. The company owns or leases more than five million acres of timberland.

$ mil	12/92	12/93	12/94	% Change				
Sales	**4,926.5**	**5,068.9**	**5,318.2**	**4.9**	P/E Ratio	**141.8**	Price (9/30/95)	**53.88**
Net Income	**-440.4**	**-156.2**	**63.3**	**-140.5**	P/B Ratio	**1.5**	52 Wk Hi-Low	**60.13-33.50**
Book Value	**3,458.8**	**2,950.1**	**3,260.8**	**10.5**	Yield %	**0.4**	Market Cap	**US$5,204.3mil**

Address **1 Champion Plz.**
Stamford, CT 06921
Tel **203-358-7000**
Fax **203-358-7495**
Exchange **NYSE**
Ticker **CHA**
President **L.C. Heist**
Chairman & CEO **Andrew C. Sigler**

Charming Shoppes

Industry: **Apparel Retailers**

Charming Shoppes operates 1,428 women's specialty-apparel stores in 46 states. The company's Fashion Bug stores sell sportswear, dresses, coats, suits, and lingerie to women in the 15- to 45-year-old age group. Fashion Bug Plus stores sell similar merchandise in larger sizes. The company sells men's sportswear and accessories through its Fashion Bug stores. Stores sell brand-name merchandise and specially manufactured garments under one of the company's private labels. Approximately 77% of the merchandise sold is under the Stefano and Maggie Lawrence private-label names.

$ mil	01/93	01/94	01/95	% Change				
Revenues	**1,178.7**	**1,254.1**	**1,272.7**	**1.5**	P/E Ratio	**10.7**	Price (9/30/95)	**4.50**
Net Income	**81.1**	**79.8**	**44.7**	**-44.0**	P/B Ratio	**0.8**	52 Wk Hi-Low	**8.13-3.88**
Book Value	**445.3**	**522.1**	**558.8**	**7.0**	Yield %	**2.0**	Market Cap	**US$463.3mil**

Address	**450 Winks Lane**	Tel	**215-245-9100**	Exchange	**NASDA**	President	**Philip Wachs**
	Bensalem, PA 19020	Fax	**215-638-6914**	Ticker	**CHRS**	Chairman & CEO	**David V. Wachs**

Chase Manhattan

Industry: **Banks - Money Center**

Chase Manhattan is a major financial-services company. Its Chase Manhattan Bank subsidiary provides retail-, wholesale-, and investment-banking, as well as securities-trading, and investment-advisory services. The bank is also the second-largest bank credit-card issuer in the United States, as well as a mortgage servicer of a $66 billion portfolio. Chase Manhattan's global financial-services division offers trust, loan-origination, private-banking, and security-custodian services to customers throughout the world. In 1995, the company agreed to merge with Chemical Banking.

$ mil	12/92	12/93	12/94	% Change				
Revenues	**11,125.0**	**11,417.0**	**11,187.0**	**-2.0**	P/E Ratio	**10.4**	Price (9/30/95)	**61.13**
Net Income	**639.0**	**966.0**	**1,205.0**	**24.7**	P/B Ratio	**1.3**	52 Wk Hi-Low	**61.13-33.00**
Book Value	**6,511.0**	**8,122.0**	**8,359.0**	**2.9**	Yield %	**2.4**	Market Cap	**US$10,664mil**

Address	**1 Chase Manhattan Plz.**	Tel	**212-552-2222**	Exchange	**NYSE**	Chief Executive	**Thomas G. Labrecque**
	New York, NY 10081	Fax	**212-552-3529**	Ticker	**CMB**	Chairman	**Thomas G. Labrecque**

Chemical Banking

Industry: **Banks - Money Center**

Chemical Banking is a holding company that provides financial services through various subsidiaries, mainly Chemical Bank and Texas Commerce Bank National Association. The banks operate offices primarily in New York, New Jersey, and Texas. The banks provide consumer and real-estate financing, investment banking, discount brokerage, and credit-card issuance. The company also owns a 40% stake in CIT Group, which offers leasing services. Its Margaretten Financial subsidiary originates and services mortgages. In 1995, the company agreed to merge with Chase Manhattan.

$ mil	12/92	12/93	12/94	% Change				
Revenues	**12,174.0**	**12,427.0**	**12,685.0**	**2.1**	P/E Ratio	**13.1**	Price (9/30/95)	**60.88**
Net Income	**1,086.0**	**1,604.0**	**1,294.0**	**-19.3**	P/B Ratio	**1.4**	52 Wk Hi-Low	**61.00-34.00**
Book Value	**9,851.0**	**11,164.0**	**10,712.0**	**-4.0**	Yield %	**2.7**	Market Cap	**US$15,347mil**

Address	**270 Park Ave.**	Tel	**212-270-6000**	Exchange	**NYSE**	President	**Edward D. Miller**
	New York, NY 10017-2036	Fax	**212-270-1648**	Ticker	**CHL**	Chairman & CEO	**Walter V. Shipley**

Chevron

Industry: **Oil - Integrated Majors**

Chevron is a petroleum company with operations worldwide. The company owns an average 49% interest in 40,000 wells and holds reserves of 4.2 billion barrels of oil and ten trillion cubic feet of natural gas, mainly in the U.S., Canada, and Africa. Its refineries supply products to 10,000 retail outlets, including 2,000 company-operated Chevron, Gulf, and Caltex gas stations. Chevron's chemical plants produce olefin, fuel additives, and lubricants. The company's Pittsburgh & Midway Coal Mining subsidiary operates mines in the western U.S. with reserves of 560 million tons.

$ mil	12/92	12/93	12/94	% Change				
Sales	**41,428.0**	**36,191.0**	**35,130.0**	**-2.9**	P/E Ratio	**18.7**	Price (9/30/95)	**48.63**
Net Income	**1,569.0**	**1,265.0**	**1.693.0**	**33.8**	P/B Ratio	**2.2**	52 Wk Hi-Low	**50.25-41.25**
Book Value	**13,728.0**	**13,997.0**	**14,596.0**	**4.3**	Yield %	**3.8**	Market Cap	**US$31,702mil**

Address	**225 Bush St.**	Tel	**415-894-7700**	Exchange	**NYSE**	Chief Executive	**Kenneth T. Derr**
	San Francisco, CA 94104	Fax	**415-895-6017**	Ticker	**CHV**	Chairman	**Kenneth T. Derr**

Chrysler

Industry: **Automobile Manufacturers**

Chrysler is one of the three major U.S. manufacturers of cars, trucks, and related parts and accessories. It manufactures vehicles under the Chrysler, Dodge, Plymouth, Jeep, and Eagle names, and imports and distributes vehicles from Mitsubishi for sale under its brand names. The company also generates revenues from automotive retail, wholesale, and fleet financing, as well as from property and casualty insurance through its Chrysler Financial subsidiary. Chrysler provides car and truck rentals through its Thrifty Rent-A-Car System and Dollar Systems rental-car subsidiaries.

$ mil	12/92	12/93	12/94	% Change				
Sales	**33,548.0**	**40,831.0**	**49,363.0**	**20.9**	P/E Ratio	**5.2**	Price (9/30/95)	**53.00**
Net Income	**723.0**	**-2,551.0**	**3,713.0**	**-245.6**	P/B Ratio	**1.8**	52 Wk Hi-Low	**57.63-38.50**
Book Value	**7,538.0**	**6,836.0**	**10,694.0**	**56.4**	Yield %	**2.1**	Market Cap	**US$20,269mil**

Address	**12000 Chrysler Dr.**	Tel	**313-956-5741**	Exchange	**NYSE**	President	**Robert A. Lutz**
	Highland Park, MI 48288-0001	Fax	**313-956-1462**	Ticker	**C**	Chairman & CEO	**Robert J. Eaton**

Chubb

Industry: **Insurance - Property & Casualty**

Chubb is an insurance holding company that also has real-estate operations and annuity investment products. The company underwrites property and casualty insurance and sells individual, group-life, and health insurance in the United States and its territories, Canada, Europe, Australia, and the Far East. Business in the U.S. accounts for 80% of Chubb's revenues. Its Bellemead Development subsidiary develops residential and commercial real estate, primarily acquiring suburban parcels and developing land either to be held by the company or sold to third parties.

$ mil	12/92	12/93	12/94	% Change				
Revenues	**4,940.8**	**5,499.7**	**5,709.5**	**3.8**	P/E Ratio	**16.1**	Price (9/30/95)	**96.00**
Net Income	**617.1**	**324.2**	**528.5**	**63.0**	P/B Ratio	**2.0**	52 Wk Hi-Low	**96.88-68.88**
Book Value	**3,954.4**	**4,196.1**	**4,247.0**	**1.2**	Yield %	**1.9**	Market Cap	**US$8,354.9mil**

Address **15 Mountain View Rd.**
Warren, NJ 07061-1615
Tel **908-903-2000**
Fax **908-580-3430**
Exchange **NYSE**
Ticker **CB**
President **Dean R. O'Hare**
Chairman **Dean R. O'Hare**

CIGNA

Industry: **Insurance - Full Line**

CIGNA provides insurance and related financial services worldwide. Its insurance subsidiaries offer group and individual life, accident, and disability insurance; property-casualty coverage for businesses and individuals; and pension and retirement products and services. Its revenues are primarily derived from premiums, fees, and investments, which include equity securities, mortgage loans, real estate, and fixed-maturity instruments. CIGNA's health-maintenance organization serves approximately 5.3 million members throughout the United States.

$ mil	12/92	12/93	12/94	% Change				
Revenues	**18,582.0**	**18,402.0**	**18,392.0**	**-0.1**	P/E Ratio	**13.6**	Price (9/30/95)	**104.13**
Net Income	**311.0**	**234.0**	**554.0**	**136.8**	P/B Ratio	**1.3**	52 Wk Hi-Low	**105.88-59.63**
Book Value	**5,744.0**	**6,575.0**	**5,811.0**	**-11.6**	Yield %	**2.9**	Market Cap	**US$7,552.9mil**

Address **1 Liberty Pl., 1650 Market St.**
Philadelphia, PA 19192-1550
Tel **215-761-1000**
Fax **215-761-5618**
Exchange **NYSE**
Ticker **CI**
Chief Executive **Wilson H. Taylor**
Chairman **Wilson H. Taylor**

Cincinnati Financial

Industry: **Insurance - Property & Casualty**

Cincinnati Financial is an insurance holding company. Its Cincinnati Insurance, Cincinnati Casualty, and Cincinnati Indemnity subsidiaries underwrite property, casualty, life, accident, health, and fire insurance. It sells insurance in 46 states, primarily in the Midwest and Southeast. The company also owns real-estate properties in the Cincinnati area, and finances cars, trucks, computers, machine tools, and construction equipment through its subsidiary, CFC Investment. Investment income generates substantially all of the company's revenues.

$ mil	12/92	12/93	12/94	% Change				
Revenues	**1,304.2**	**1,422.2**	**1,512.5**	**6.4**	P/E Ratio	**13.9**	Price (9/30/95)	**54.38**
Net Income	**171.3**	**216.0**	**201.2**	**-6.8**	P/B Ratio	**1.4**	52 Wk Hi-Low	**58.00-44.05**
Book Value	**1,713.8**	**1,947.3**	**1,940.1**	**-0.4**	Yield %	**2.4**	Market Cap	**US$2,883.6mil**

Address **6200 S. Gilmore Rd.**
Fairfield, OH 45014-5141
Tel **513-870-2000**
Fax **513-870-2088**
Exchange **NASDA**
Ticker **CINF**
President & CEO **Robert B. Morgan**
Chairman **John J. Schiff**

Cincinnati Milacron

Industry: **Factory Equipment**

Cincinnati Milacron manufactures machine tools and other equipment for the metalworking, automotive, agricultural, and aerospace industries. The company makes metal-cutting equipment, and centerless-grinding and turning-center machinery. Plastics machinery, precision-grinding wheels, and metalworking fluids are some of its main products. The company produces computer controls and software for factory and machine-shop automation. Its brand names include Vista injection-molding machines, Sabre vertical-machining centers, and Maxin and Avenger turning centers.

$ mil	12/92	12/93	12/94	% Change				
Sales	**789.2**	**1,029.4**	**1,197.1**	**16.3**	P/E Ratio	**28.6**	Price (9/30/95)	**31.50**
Net Income	**21.5**	**-101.9**	**37.7**	**-137.0**	P/B Ratio	**6.7**	52 Wk Hi-Low	**33.50-20.13**
Book Value	**134.4**	**124.1**	**157.8**	**27.2**	Yield %	**1.1**	Market Cap	**US$1,078.3mil**

Address **4701 Marburg Ave.**
Cincinnati, OH 45209
Tel **513-841-8100**
Fax **513-841-8991**
Exchange **NYSE**
Ticker **CMZ**
President **Raymond E. Ross**
Chairman & CEO **Daniel J. Meyer**

CINergy

Industry: **Electrical Utilities - Central U.S.**

CINergy provides natural gas and electricity in southwestern Ohio and nearby areas in Kentucky and Indiana. Cincinnati Gas and Electric, a primary subsidiary, has a service area with an estimated population of 1.8 million and covers approximately 3,000 square miles in Ohio, Kentucky, and Indiana. Electricity sales constitute approximately 73% of revenues, natural-gas sales account for the remainder. The company's PSI Engergy subsidiary produces, transmits, and distributes electric energy to 1.9 million people throughout Indiana. It also invests in foreign utility companies.

$ mil	12/92 R	12/93 R	12/94	% Change				
Sales	**2,634.5**	**2,840.1**	**2,924.2**	**3.0**	P/E Ratio	**21.4**	Price (9/30/95)	**27.88**
Net Income	**270.8**	**62.6**	**191.1**	**205.6**	P/B Ratio	**1.8**	52 Wk Hi-Low	**27.88-21.00**
Book Value	**2,316.9**	**2,221.7**	**2,414.3**	**8.7**	Yield %	**5.4**	Market Cap	**US$4,366.3mil**

Address **139 E. Fourth St.**
Cincinnati, OH 45202
Tel **513-381-2000**
Fax **N/A**
Exchange **NYSE**
Ticker **CIN**
President **James E. Rogers**
Chairman & CEO **Jackson H. Randolph**

R=Restated.

Cintas

Industry: **General Industrial & Commercial Services**

Cintas manufactures corporate uniforms and provides related services. The company designs and produces uniforms at three manufacturing facilities, and rents, leases, and sells those uniforms through 33 company-owned locations, primarily in the eastern half of the United States. It serves approximately 100,000 medium- to large-size businesses, including PepsiCo and Southwest Airlines. In conjunction with its rental operations, Cintas provides cleaning and delivery services. The company is expanding its market into Canada through a joint venture with Cadet Uniform Services.

$ mil	05/93	05/94	05/95	% Change				
Sales	**452.7**	**523.2**	**615.1**	**17.6**	P/E Ratio	**32.8**	Price (9/30/95)	**44.00**
Net Income	**44.9**	**52.2**	**62.7**	**20.1**	P/B Ratio	**5.7**	52 Wk Hi-Low	**44.00-33.25**
Book Value	**264.9**	**309.7**	**364.3**	**17.6**	Yield %	**0.5**	Market Cap	**US$2,069.7mil**

Address **6800 Cintas Blvd.**
Cincinnati, OH 45262
Tel **513-459-1200**
Fax **513-573-4130**
Exchange **NASDA**
Ticker **CTAS**
President & CEO **Robert J. Kohlhepp**
Chairman **Richard T. Farmer**

CIPSCO

Industry: **Electrical Utilities - Central U.S.**

CIPSCO is a utility holding company. Its principal subsidiary, Central Illinois Public Service, provides electric service to about 317,000 customers and natural-gas service to about 166,000 customers in a 20,000-square-mile region of Illinois. Other energy services include supplying power to cooperative and municipal electric systems and transporting gas from suppliers to large-volume customers. Residential customers account for about 42% of the company's electric and 63% of natural-gas revenues. In 1995, the company agreed to merge with Union Electric.

$ mil	12/92	12/93	12/94	% Change				
Sales	**729.4**	**834.5**	**835.9**	**0.2**	P/E Ratio	**14.0**	Price (9/30/95)	**34.38**
Net Income	**72.5**	**85.5**	**84.0**	**-1.8**	P/B Ratio	**1.8**	52 Wk Hi-Low	**34.38-26.50**
Book Value	**616.6**	**634.3**	**647.6**	**2.1**	Yield %	**5.8**	Market Cap	**US$874.9mil**

Address **607 E. Adams St.**
Springfield, IL 62739
Tel **217-523-3600**
Fax **217-525-6783**
Exchange **NYSE**
Ticker **CIP**
President & CEO **Clifford L. Greenwalt**
Chairman **Clifford L. Greenwalt**

Circuit City

Industry: **Other Specialty Retailers**

Circuit City Stores is the largest specialty retailer of brand-name consumer electronics and major appliances in the United States. The company has more than 350 locations, including about 380 Circuit City Superstores (15,000 to 44,000 square feet in size), five Circuit City stores (4,000 to 15,000 square feet), and 33 mall stores (2,000 to 4,000 square feet) operating under the names of Impulse and Circuit City Express. The stores sell video equipment, audio equipment, and other consumer electronic products such as telephones and home computers. Most sell major appliances.

$ mil	02/93	02/94	02/95	% Change				
Revenues	**3,269.8**	**4,130.4**	**5,583.0**	**35.2**	P/E Ratio	**18.4**	Price (9/30/95)	**31.63**
Net Income	**110.2**	**132.4**	**167.9**	**26.8**	P/B Ratio	**3.5**	52 Wk Hi-Low	**37.13-21.25**
Book Value	**575.6**	**710.4**	**877.5**	**23.5**	Yield %	**0.3**	Market Cap	**US$3,069.0mil**

Address **9950 Mayland Dr.**
Richmond, VA 23233-1464
Tel **804-527-4000**
Fax **804-527-4187**
Exchange **NYSE**
Ticker **CC**
President & CEO **Richard L. Sharp**
Chairman **Richard L. Sharp**

Circus Circus

Industry: **Casinos**

Circus Circus Enterprises owns and operates casinos and hotels in Nevada and a riverboat casino. These properties include Las Vegas' Excalibur, Circus Circus, and Luxor; Reno's Circus Circus Hotel and Casino; and Laughlin's Colorado Belle and Edgewater. The Circus Circus riverboat casino, which is docked in Tunica County, Mississippi, contains 59,000 square feet of casino space. In the fiscal year that ended January 31, 1995, 58% of the company's revenues were derived from casino operations. Hotels, restaurants, bars, and other attractions contributed the remainder.

$ mil	01/93	01/94	01/95	% Change				
Sales	**843.0**	**954.9**	**1,170.2**	**22.5**	P/E Ratio	**17.6**	Price (9/30/95)	**28.00**
Net Income	**117.3**	**116.2**	**136.3**	**17.3**	P/B Ratio	**3.5**	52 Wk Hi-Low	**35.75-20.13**
Book Value	**490.0**	**560.0**	**686.1**	**22.5**	Yield %	**0.0**	Market Cap	**US$2,876.1mil**

Address **2880 Las Vegas Blvd. S.**
Las Vegas, NV 89109-1120
Tel **702-734-0410**
Fax **702-734-2268**
Exchange **NYSE**
Ticker **CIR**
President & CEO **Clyde T. Turner**
Chairman **Clyde T. Turner**

Cisco Systems

Industry: **Communications Technology**

Cisco Systems manufactures computer-networking equipment and software. The company's main products are multiprotocol routers which allow data communication between geographically dispersed computer networks that would otherwise be incompatible. It produces software that supports its routers and provides network-management, -diagnostic, and -security capabilities. Cisco markets its products in the U.S. and other countries to computer-equipment manufacturers who resell them under private labels directly to network users. The company also markets protocol translators.

$ mil	07/92	07/93	07/94	% Change				
Sales	**339.6**	**649.0**	**1,243.0**	**91.5**	P/E Ratio	**58.0**	Price (9/30/95)	**69.00**
Net Income	**84.4**	**172.0**	**314.9**	**83.1**	P/B Ratio	**NMF**	52 Wk Hi-Low	**72.13-25.63**
Book Value	**245.6**	**475.2**	**848.2**	**78.5**	Yield %	**0.0**	Market Cap	**US$18,722mil**

Address **170 W. Tasman Dr.**
San Jose, CA 95134
Tel **408-526-4000**
Fax **408-526-4100**
Exchange **NASDA**
Ticker **CSCO**
President & CEO **John P. Morgridge**
Chairman **Donald T. Valentine**

Citicorp

Industry: **Banks - Money Center**

Citicorp is the largest bank holding company in the United States, serving individuals, businesses, and governments through 3,400 locations in 94 countries. The company's core businesses are global-consumer services and global-financial services, with operations in 41 countries, comprising private and branch banking, and credit and charge cards. Citicorp offers commercial- and investment-banking, asset-management, brokerage, real-estate, and mortgage services. It also issues fixed-income securities and is a member of the Cirrus network of automated-teller machines.

$ mil	12/92	12/93	12/94	% Change				
Revenues	**31,948.0**	**32,196.0**	**31,650.0**	**-1.7**	P/E Ratio	**10.1**	Price (9/30/95)	**70.75**
Net Income	**722.0**	**2,219.0**	**3,366.0**	**51.7**	P/B Ratio	**1.6**	52 Wk Hi-Low	**71.88-38.88**
Book Value	**11,181.0**	**13,953.0**	**17,769.0**	**27.3**	Yield %	**0.6**	Market Cap	**US$29,319mil**

Address **399 Park Ave.**
New York, NY 10043
Tel **212-559-1000**
Fax **212-559-5138**
Exchange **NYSE**
Ticker **CCI**
President & CEO **John S. Reed**
Chairman **John S. Reed**

Clayton Homes

Industry: **Home Construction**

Clayton Homes produces and finances manufactured homes. The company operates 13 manufacturing plants, where it makes 13,000 homes per year that are priced between $13,000 and $75,000 and range in size from 400 to 1,900 square feet. It sells about half of these homes to 400 independent dealers and the remainder through 165 company-owned dealers. Vanderbilt Mortgage and Finance, a subsidiary, provides mortgage financing and acts as an agent for physical-damage and credit life insurance. Clayton also operates 33 manufactured-housing communities.

$ mil	06/92	06/93	06/94	% Change				
Sales	**296.8**	**384.5**	**510.2**	**32.7**	P/E Ratio	**19.8**	Price (9/30/95)	**23.75**
Net Income	**39.3**	**53.8**	**72.3**	**34.4**	P/B Ratio	**3.1**	52 Wk Hi-Low	**24.38-12.80**
Book Value	**292.9**	**348.6**	**462.2**	**32.6**	Yield %	**0.0**	Market Cap	**US$1,792.7mil**

Address **623 Market St.**
Knoxville, TN 37902
Tel **615-970-7200**
Fax **615-970-1238**
Exchange **NYSE**
Ticker **CMH**
President **Joseph H. Stegmayer**
Chairman & CEO **James L. Clayton**

Cleveland-Cliffs

Industry: **Mining**

Cleveland-Cliffs operates iron-ore-processing facilities and related businesses. The company produces iron-ore pellets from purchased ore at four plants and manages five mining operations in Michigan, Minnesota, and Quebec. It sells iron-ore pellets to primary steel manufacturers in North America and Europe, transporting its goods by company-owned or -managed railways. Cleveland-Cliffs also owns mining interests in Newfoundland and Tasmania that it leases to others, and owns undeveloped oil-shale reserves in Utah. The company has total iron-ore reserves of 1.7 billion tons.

$ mil	12/92	12/93	12/94	% Change				
Sales	**266.9**	**268.1**	**334.8**	**24.9**	P/E Ratio	**11.6**	Price (9/30/95)	**41.13**
Net Income	**-7.9**	**54.6**	**42.8**	**-21.6**	P/B Ratio	**1.6**	52 Wk Hi-Low	**46.75-34.13**
Book Value	**269.6**	**280.7**	**311.4**	**10.9**	Yield %	**3.0**	Market Cap	**US$489.1mil**

Address **1100 Superior Ave.**
Cleveland, OH 44114-2589
Tel **216-694-5700**
Fax **216-694-4880**
Exchange **NYSE**
Ticker **CLF**
Chief Executive **M. Thomas Moore**
Chairman **M. Thomas Moore**

Clorox

Industry: **Household Products (Non-Durable)**

Clorox principally manufactures chlorine and nonchlorine bleaches. The company also makes other well-known consumer products, including Pine Sol and Formula 409 household cleansers, S.O.S. soap pads, Kingsford and Match Light charcoal products, Hidden Valley Ranch salad dressings, K.C. Masterpiece barbecue sauce, Liquid-Plumr drain openers, and Combat insecticides. The company markets these products worldwide. Business in the U.S. accounts for more than 90% of sales. Clorox operates manufacturing facilities in the U.S., Canada, Mexico, Argentina, and South Korea.

$ mil	06/92	06/93	06/94	% Change				
Sales	**1,717.0**	**1,634.2**	**1,836.9**	**12.4**	P/E Ratio	**18.0**	Price (9/30/95)	**71.38**
Net Income	**98.7**	**167.1**	**212.1**	**26.9**	P/B Ratio	**4.2**	52 Wk Hi-Low	**72.25-51.50**
Book Value	**813.7**	**879.3**	**909.4**	**3.4**	Yield %	**2.5**	Market Cap	**US$3,791.9mil**

Address **1221 Broadway**
Oakland, CA 94612
Tel **510-271-7000**
Fax **510-832-1463**
Exchange **NYSE**
Ticker **CLX**
President & CEO **G. Craig Sullivan**
Chairman **G. Craig Sullivan**

CMS Energy

Industry: **Electrical Utilities - Central U.S.**

CMS Energy is an energy company with utility and petroleum operations. Its Consumers Power subsidiary provides electricity to 1.5 million customers and natural-gas service to 1.4 million customers in Michigan. CMS' other activities include international exploration for and production of oil and natural gas, operation of independent power plants, and management of natural-gas pipelines. Electric-utility revenues account for roughly 60% of the consolidated total; gas-utility revenues make up about 33%; the remainder is derived from oil and gas exploration and production.

$ mil	12/92	12/93	12/94	% Change				
Sales	**3,073.0**	**3,482.0**	**3,619.0**	**3.9**	P/E Ratio	**12.6**	Price (9/30/95)	**26.25**
Net Income	**-297.0**	**155.0**	**179.0**	**15.5**	P/B Ratio	**2.1**	52 Wk Hi-Low	**26.38-21.00**
Book Value	**727.0**	**966.0**	**1,107.0**	**14.6**	Yield %	**3.0**	Market Cap	**US$2,314.7mil**

Address **Ste. 1100, 330 Town Center Dr.**
Dearborn, MI 48126
Tel **313-436-9261**
Fax **313-436-9225**
Exchange **NYSE**
Ticker **CMS**
President **Victor J. Fryling**
Chairman & CEO **W.T. McCormick, Jr.**

Coastal

Industry: **Pipelines**

Coastal is a diversified energy company. The company owns, on average, a 39% interest in 6,200 petroleum wells and holds net reserves of 926 billion cubic feet of natural gas and 34 million barrels of oil in North America. It markets gas to industrial customers through 19,000 miles of pipelines, produces automotive and industrial fuels and lubricants at its four refineries, manufactures chemicals used in the agriculture and mining industries, and owns interests in four power plants. Its ANR Freight subsidiary provides cargo-transportation services using a fleet of trucks.

$ mil	12/92	12/93	12/94	% Change				
Sales	**10,062.9**	**10,136.1**	**10,215.3**	**0.8**	P/E Ratio	**16.4**	Price (9/30/95)	**33.63**
Net Income	**-126.8**	**115.8**	**232.6**	**100.9**	P/B Ratio	**1.4**	52 Wk Hi-Low	**34.00-24.88**
Book Value	**2,009.9**	**2,278.1**	**2,457.2**	**7.9**	Yield %	**1.2**	Market Cap	**US$3,526.1mil**

Address	**9 Greenway Plz.**	Tel	**713-877-1400**	Exchange	**NYSE**	President	**David A. Arledge**
	Houston, TX 77046-0995	Fax	**713-877-6752**	Ticker	**CGP**	Chairman & CEO	**Oscar S. Wyatt, Jr.**

Coca-Cola

Industry: **Soft Drinks**

Coca-Cola Company is the world's largest manufacturer of soft-drink concentrates and syrups, with a global market share of about 45%. The company's soft-drink brand names include Coke, Diet Coke, Sprite, Tab, Nestea, Fanta, and Barq's. It sells about two thirds of its concentrates and syrups to company-owned and independent bottlers in 200 countries, who prepare them for distribution to food stores, vending machines, wholesalers, and end users for fountain use. The company's foods division makes fruit juices under the Minute Maid, Hi-C, and Fruitopia names.

$ mil	12/92	12/93	12/94	% Change				
Sales	**13,073.9**	**13,957.0**	**16,172.0**	**15.9**	P/E Ratio	**34.8**	Price (9/30/95)	**69.00**
Net Income	**1,664.4**	**2,176.0**	**2,554.0**	**17.4**	P/B Ratio	**16.8**	52 Wk Hi-Low	**70.50-48.38**
Book Value	**3,888.4**	**4,584.0**	**5,235.0**	**14.2**	Yield %	**1.1**	Market Cap	**US$87,022mil**

Address	**1 Coca-Cola Plz.**	Tel	**404-676-2121**	Exchange	**NYSE**	President	**M. Douglas Ivester**
	Atlanta, GA 30313	Fax	**404-676-6792**	Ticker	**KO**	Chairman & CEO	**Roberto C. Goizueta**

Coca-Cola Enterprises

Industry: **Soft Drinks**

Coca-Cola Enterprises, which is 44% owned by the Coca-Cola Company, is the world's largest bottler of Coca-Cola soft-drink products. The company manufactures approximately 55% of the bottled and canned Coca-Cola products sold in the United States from soft-drink concentrates and syrups that it purchases from Coca-Cola. It sells reconstituted products through about 860,000 company-owned coolers, dispensers, and vending machines, accounting for approximately 85% of sales, and syrups to fountain users in the U.S. and internationally, which accounts for the remainder.

$ mil	12/92	12/93	12/94	% Change				
Sales	**5,127.0**	**5,465.0**	**6,011.0**	**10.0**	P/E Ratio	**47.4**	Price (9/30/95)	**24.63**
Net Income	**-186.0**	**-15.0**	**69.0**	**-560.0**	P/B Ratio	**2.4**	52 Wk Hi-Low	**25.13-16.63**
Book Value	**1,254.0**	**1,260.0**	**1,339.0**	**6.3**	Yield %	**0.2**	Market Cap	**US$3,194.4mil**

Address	**1 Coca-Cola Plz., N.W.**	Tel	**404-676-2100**	Exchange	**NYSE**	Chief Executive	**S.K. Johnston, Jr.**
	Atlanta, GA 30313-2100	Fax	**404-676-6792**	Ticker	**CCE**	Chairman	**M. Douglas Ivester**

Colgate-Palmolive

Industry: **Household Products (Non-Durable)**

Colgate-Palmolive produces household consumer goods. Its brand-name products include Colgate oral-hygiene products, Mennen Speed Stick deodorant, Irish Spring bar soap, Softsoap liquid soap, Palmolive dishwashing liquid, and Ajax household cleansers, and Fab laundry detergent. The company also produces Hill's Science Diet pet food, which it sells through veterinarians and pet stores. The company markets its products in the United States and more than 100 other countries. Sales in North America account for approximately 21% of the company's total sales.

$ mil	12/92	12/93	12/94	% Change				
Sales	**7,007.2**	**7,141.3**	**7,587.9**	**6.3**	P/E Ratio	**17.4**	Price (9/30/95)	**66.63**
Net Income	**477.0**	**189.9**	**580.2**	**205.5**	P/B Ratio	**5.3**	52 Wk Hi-Low	**77.00-57.25**
Book Value	**2,619.8**	**1,875.0**	**1,822.9**	**-2.8**	Yield %	**2.3**	Market Cap	**US$9,688.9mil**

Address	**300 Park Ave.**	Tel	**212-310-2000**	Exchange	**NYSE**	President	**William S. Shanahan**
	New York, NY 10022-7499	Fax	**212-310-3284**	Ticker	**CL**	Chairman & CEO	**Reuben Mark**

Columbia Gas System

Industry: **Gas Utilities**

Columbia Gas System is a public-utility holding company. Its subsidiaries explore for, produce, and distribute natural gas. The company operates a pipeline network and provides natural-gas service to more than 1.9 million residential, commercial, and industrial customers in Ohio, Pennsylvania, Virginia, Kentucky, and Maryland. Residential customers account for approximately two thirds of sales; commercial and industrial users comprise most of the balance. The company is going through reorganization proceedings since filing for Chapter 11 bankruptcy status in July 1991.

$ mil	12/92	12/93	12/94	% Change				
Sales	**2,922.0**	**3,391.2**	**2,833.4**	**-16.4**	P/E Ratio	**8.1**	Price (9/30/95)	**38.63**
Net Income	**51.2**	**152.2**	**240.6**	**58.1**	P/B Ratio	**1.3**	52 Wk Hi-Low	**39.25-22.63**
Book Value	**1,075.1**	**1,227.3**	**1,468.0**	**19.6**	Yield %	**0.0**	Market Cap	**US$1,953.4mil**

Address	**20 Montchanin Rd.**	Tel	**302-429-5000**	Exchange	**NYSE**	President & CEO	**John H. Croom**
	Wilmington, DE 19807-0020	Fax	**302-429-5730**	Ticker	**CG**	Chairman	**John H. Croom**

Columbia/HCA Healthcare

Industry: **Health Care Providers**

Columbia/HCA Healthcare is a health-care-services company that buys, sells and owns general, acute-care and specialty hospitals and related health-care facilities. The company operates approximately 170 hospitals located in 26 states and in England and Switzerland. Most of the company's general and acute-care hospitals provide medical and surgical services, including inpatient care, intensive and cardiac care, diagnostic services and emergency services. Its psychiatric hospitals provide therapeutic programs for psychiatric and chemically dependent patients of all ages.

$ mil	12/92	12/93	12/94	% Change				
Sales	**819.3**	**10,252.0**	**11,132.0**	**8.6**	P/E Ratio	**22.8**	Price (9/30/95)	**48.63**
Net Income	**25.4**	**507.0**	**630.0**	**24.3**	P/B Ratio	**3.4**	52 Wk Hi-Low	**49.88-34.38**
Book Value	**264.6**	**3,471.0**	**5,022.0**	**44.7**	Yield %	**0.2**	Market Cap	**US$21,573mil**

Address **1 Park Plz.**
Nashville, TN 37203
Tel **615-327-9551**
Fax **N/A**
Exchange **NYSE**
Ticker **COL**
President & CEO **Richard L. Scott**
Chairman **Thomas F. Frist, Jr.**

Comdisco

Industry: **General Industrial & Commercial Services**

Comdisco buys, sells, and leases new and used computer and other high-technology equipment. The company also provides technology-planning and asset-management services, integrating leasing and business-continuity services with asset acquisition; asset-management software tools; and data-center moves, consolidations, disposition, and migration strategies. These services are designed to provide integrated long-term asset and technological planning to high-technology equipment users. Customers include Fortune 1000 corporations and companies of similar or smaller sizes.

$ mil	09/92	09/93	09/94	% Change				
Sales	**2,205.0**	**2,153.0**	**2,098.0**	**-2.6**	P/E Ratio	**25.6**	Price (9/30/95)	**29.75**
Net Income	**-9.0**	**87.0**	**53.0**	**-39.1**	P/B Ratio	**1.5**	52 Wk Hi-Low	**32.38-19.75**
Book Value	**699.0**	**739.0**	**741.0**	**0.3**	Yield %	**1.2**	Market Cap	**US$1,041.0mil**

Address **6111 N. River Rd.**
Rosemont, IL 60018
Tel **708-698-3000**
Fax **708-518-5440**
Exchange **NYSE**
Ticker **CDO**
President & CEO **Jack Slevin**
Chairman --

Comerica

Industry: **Banks - Central U.S.**

Comerica is a bank holding company that owns and operates about 400 branches in Michigan, Illinois, Texas, California, and Florida. In addition to its full-service banking operations, the company also has subsidiaries that offer insurance, full-service brokerage, mortgages, commercial and consumer loans, lease financing, institutional trust, investment management, and international-finance and -trading services. Comerica also specializes in middle-market and private financial services, and is the second-largest bank based in Michigan by total assets and deposits.

$ mil	12/92	12/93	12/94	% Change				
Revenues	**2,269.8**	**2,245.4**	**2,558.6**	**13.9**	P/E Ratio	**11.1**	Price (9/30/95)	**36.38**
Net Income	**226.0**	**340.6**	**387.2**	**13.7**	P/B Ratio	**1.8**	52 Wk Hi-Low	**36.75-24.13**
Book Value	**2,029.4**	**2,181.7**	**2,391.8**	**9.6**	Yield %	**3.4**	Market Cap	**US$4,167.8mil**

Address **500 Woodward Ave.**
Detroit, MI 48226
Tel **313-222-4000**
Fax **313-222-4013**
Exchange **NYSE**
Ticker **CMA**
President **Michael T. Monahan**
Chairman & CEO **Eugene A. Miller**

Community Psychiatric

Industry: **Health Care Providers**

Community Psychiatric Centers provides psychiatric services for adults, adolescents, and children. Services are provided for patients with acute psychiatric, emotional, and other disorders. The company offers inpatient, partial-hospitalization, outpatient, and residential-treatment programs through 35 hospitals in 17 states in the U.S. and 13 hospitals in the U.K. Through its Transitional Hospitals subsidiary, it also offers long-term critical-care services in five states through four freestanding hospitals and three units within its psychiatric hospitals.

$ mil	11/92	11/93	11/94	% Change				
Sales	**344.3**	**335.6**	**424.0**	**26.3**	P/E Ratio	**49.0**	Price (9/30/95)	**11.75**
Net Income	**23.1**	**-24.9**	**10.2**	**-141.0**	P/B Ratio	**1.2**	52 Wk Hi-Low	**13.88-9.50**
Book Value	**450.9**	**422.5**	**440.0**	**4.2**	Yield %	**0.1**	Market Cap	**US$513.0mil**

Address **Ste. 118, 6600 W. Charleston Blvd.**
Las Vegas, NV 89102
Tel **702-259-3600**
Fax **702-259-3650**
Exchange **NYSE**
Ticker **CMY**
Chief Executive **Richard L. Conte**
Chairman **Richard L. Conte**

Compaq Computer

Industry: **Computers**

Compaq Computer manufactures personal computers, PC systems, printers, and related products. The company's product line includes desktop and notebook personal computers and laser printers designed for network environments, as well as operating-system software. Compaq also publishes versions of the BASIC computer-programming language that are compatible with its computers. The company operates manufacturing facilities in Texas, Singapore, Brazil, China, and Scotland. Compaq sells its products worldwide. Business outside North America accounts for 50% of revenues.

$ mil	12/92	12/93	12/94	% Change				
Sales	**4,099.8**	**7,191.0**	**10,866.0**	**51.1**	P/E Ratio	**15.0**	Price (9/30/95)	**48.38**
Net Income	**213.2**	**462.0**	**867.0**	**87.7**	P/B Ratio	**3.4**	52 Wk Hi-Low	**54.25-31.63**
Book Value	**2,006.7**	**2,654.0**	**3,674.0**	**38.4**	Yield %	**0.0**	Market Cap	**US$12,781mil**

Address **20555 State Hwy. 249**
Houston, TX 77070
Tel **713-370-0670**
Fax **713-374-1797**
Exchange **NYSE**
Ticker **CPQ**
President & CEO **Eckhard Pfeiffer**
Chairman **Benjamin M. Rosen**

Computer Associates

Industry: **Software**

Computer Associates International designs, develops, and supports standardized software products for use with a broad range of mainframe, midrange, and desktop computers. The software is designed to enable clients to use their data-processing resources more effectively by providing tools to measure and improve hardware and software performance. Products are sold internationally. The company also develops and supports database-management, business applications and graphics software for computers from various vendors including IBM, Compaq, Apple, and others.

$ mil	03/93	03/94	03/95	% Change				
Sales	**1,841.0**	**2,148.5**	**2,623.0**	**22.1**	P/E Ratio	**24.7**	Price (9/30/95)	**42.25**
Net Income	**245.5**	**401.3**	**431.9**	**7.6**	P/B Ratio	**6.4**	52 Wk Hi-Low	**50.83-29.08**
Book Value	**1,054.5**	**1,243.1**	**1,578.1**	**27.0**	Yield %	**0.3**	Market Cap	**US$10,198mil**

Address **1 Computer Associates Plz.**
Islandia, NY 11788-7000
Tel **516-342-5224**
Fax **516-342-5329**
Exchange **NYSE**
Ticker **CA**
Chief Executive **Charles B. Wang**
Chairman **Charles B. Wang**

Computer Sciences

Industry: **Software**

Computer Sciences provides information-technology consulting, systems integration, and outsourcing. Services include management-consulting and education and research programs, and the design, engineering, development, integration, installation, and operation of computer-based systems and communication systems. These services are provided in the U.S., and abroad, to financial, industrial, and service industries, and to many federal, state, and local governments. Contract services to the federal government comprised about 44% of the company's revenues in fiscal 1995.

$ mil	04/93	04/94	03/95	% Change				
Sales	**2,479.8**	**2,582.7**	**3,372.5**	**30.6**	P/E Ratio	**30.8**	Price (9/30/95)	**64.38**
Net Income	**78.1**	**95.8**	**110.7**	**15.6**	P/B Ratio	**3.1**	52 Wk Hi-Low	**65.38-41.25**
Book Value	**695.4**	**805.7**	**1,148.6**	**42.6**	Yield %	**0.0**	Market Cap	**US$3,570.8mil**

Address **2100 E. Grand Ave.**
El Segundo, CA 90245
Tel **310-615-0311**
Fax **310-322-9805**
Exchange **NYSE**
Ticker **CSC**
President & CEO **Van B. Honeycutt**
Chairman **William R. Hoover**

Comsat

Industry: **Communications Technology**

Comsat provides information and telecommunication services worldwide. The company offers satellite linkups for international transmission of voice, video, and data. It provides mobile-communication services through its ownership interest in the global Intelsat and Inmarsat communication-satellite networks. The company also distributes on-demand video-entertainment products to the hospitality industry, and owns the Denver Nuggets professional basketball team. Its international-communications division commands more income than any other division, generating 31% of revenues.

$ mil	12/92	12/93	12/94	% Change				
Sales	**563.6**	**640.4**	**826.9**	**29.1**	P/E Ratio	**13.7**	Price (9/30/95)	**22.50**
Net Income	**42.9**	**75.3**	**77.6**	**3.1**	P/B Ratio	**1.3**	52 Wk Hi-Low	**25.63-17.63**
Book Value	**621.1**	**679.4**	**826.9**	**21.7**	Yield %	**3.4**	Market Cap	**US$1,063.9mil**

Address **6560 Rock Spring Dr.**
Bethesda, MD 20817
Tel **301-214-3000**
Fax **301-428-7747**
Exchange **NYSE**
Ticker **CQ**
President & CEO **Bruce L. Crockett**
Chairman **Melvin R. Laird**

ConAgra

Industry: **Other Food**

ConAgra produces prepared-food products, trades and processes commodities, and distributes agricultural products. The company's prepared foods include Hunt's tomato products, Wesson oil, Orville Redenbacher's popcorn, Healthy Choice prepared foods, Butterball turkey, and Armour meat products. It trades grains, wool, legumes, chemicals, forest products, and machinery, and operates 70 grain mills and other processing facilities in the United States and internationally. Its agricultural-products division distributes crop-protection chemicals, fertilizers, and animal feed.

$ mil	05/93	05/94	05/95	% Change				
Sales	**21,519.1**	**23,512.2**	**24,108.9**	**2.5**	P/E Ratio	**19.2**	Price (9/30/95)	**39.63**
Net Income	**270.3**	**437.1**	**495.6**	**13.4**	P/B Ratio	**3.4**	52 Wk Hi-Low	**40.00-30.00**
Book Value	**2,410.4**	**2,582.5**	**2,850.3**	**10.4**	Yield %	**2.1**	Market Cap	**US$9,731.8mil**

Address **One ConAgra Dr.**
Omaha, NE 68102
Tel **402-595-4000**
Fax **402-595-4714**
Exchange **NYSE**
Ticker **CAG**
Chief Executive **Philip B. Fletcher**
Chairman **Philip B. Fletcher**

Conrail

Industry: **Railroads**

Conrail is a freight-railroad operator with a 13,000-mile system in the northeastern and midwestern United States. Through its contracts with the U.S. Postal Service and United Parcel Service, the company engages in the intermodal transport of mail and parcels. The company also transports goods for the chemical, coal, food and grain, forest products, automotive, and other industries. The transportation of chemicals accounts for approximately 18% of its revenues; automotive parts and finished vehicles make up about 15%; and coal contributes another 15% to the total.

$ mil	12/92	12/93	12/94	% Change				
Sales	**3,345.0**	**3,453.0**	**3,733.0**	**8.1**	P/E Ratio	**17.6**	Price (9/30/95)	**68.75**
Net Income	**282.0**	**160.0**	**324.0**	**102.5**	P/B Ratio	**1.8**	52 Wk Hi-Low	**70.00-48.25**
Book Value	**2,748.0**	**2,784.0**	**2,925.0**	**5.1**	Yield %	**2.0**	Market Cap	**US$5,692.8mil**

Address **2001 Market St., 2 Commerce Sq.**
Philadelphia, PA 19101-1417
Tel **215-209-4000**
Fax **215-209-4582**
Exchange **NYSE**
Ticker **CRR**
President & CEO **David M. Le Van**
Chairman **James A. Hagen**

Consolidated Edison

Industry: **Electrical Utilities - Eastern U.S.**

Consolidated Edison of New York is a public electric utility. It provides electricity to nearly three million customers and natural gas to more than one million customers in New York City and Westchester County. It also distributes steam. The company generates 65% of its electricity at fossil-fuel firing stations and 11% at stations using nuclear energy. It purchases the balance of its needs from third parties. Residential customers account for roughly 35% of electric and 62% of natural-gas revenues; commercial and industrial users make up 65% and 32% of these figures.

$ mil	12/92	12/93	12/94	% Change				
Sales	5,932.9	6,265.4	6,373.1	1.7	P/E Ratio	10.2	Price (9/30/95)	30.38
Net Income	604.1	658.5	734.3	11.5	P/B Ratio	1.2	52 Wk Hi-Low	30.75-24.38
Book Value	5,528.1	5,709.3	5,953.3	4.3	Yield %	6.6	Market Cap	US$7,136.2mil

Address **4 Irving Pl.**
New York, NY 10003
Tel **212-460-4600**
Fax **212-529-4542**
Exchange **NYSE**
Ticker **ED**
President & CEO **Eugene R. McGrath**
Chairman **Eugene R. McGrath**

Consolidated Freightways

Industry: **Trucking**

Consolidated Freightways is the holding company for freight-transportation companies. CF Motor Freight provides long-haul freight service in all 50 states and 89 foreign countries. Con-Way Transportation Services offers regional service to most of the U.S. and intermodal services to railroads. Emery Worldwide performs international air-cargo services and has a contract with the U.S. Postal Service to deliver express mail. CF Motor Freight generates more than 50% of the company's revenues. Activities outside the U.S. account for about 13% of company revenues.

$ mil	12/92	12/93	12/94	% Change				
Sales	4,055.6	4,191.8	4,680.5	11.7	P/E Ratio	25.8	Price (9/30/95)	24.75
Net Income	-81.1	50.6	54.8	8.2	P/B Ratio	1.3	52 Wk Hi-Low	26.63-18.13
Book Value	579.2	623.4	673.6	8.1	Yield %	0.4	Market Cap	US$1,071.7mil

Address **3240 Hillview Ave.**
Palo Alto, CA 94304
Tel **415-494-2900**
Fax **415-813-0160**
Exchange **NYSE**
Ticker **CNF**
President & CEO **Donald E. Moffitt**
Chairman **Raymond F. O'Brien**

Consolidated Natural Gas

Industry: **Gas Utilities**

Consolidated Natural Gas is a public-utility holding company. It operates six local natural-gas distribution subsidiaries, primarily in Ohio, Pennsylvania, Virginia, and West Virginia. Residential customers account for 38% of natural-gas sales; commercial and industrial users make up another 14%. The balance comes primarily from wholesale and nonregulated sales. The company is currently increasing its stake in the electrical-generation market and is developing technology for natural-gas-powered vehicles and the recycling of methane from landfills.

$ mil	12/92	12/93	12/94	% Change				
Sales	1,951.5	2,615.0	2,402.9	-8.1	P/E Ratio	20.5	Price (9/30/95)	40.38
Net Income	195.0	205.9	183.2	-11.0	P/B Ratio	1.7	52 Wk Hi-Low	40.63-33.88
Book Value	2,132.8	2,176.4	2,184.3	0.4	Yield %	4.8	Market Cap	US$3,765.9mil

Address **CNG Twr., 625 Liberty Ave.**
Pittsburgh, PA 15222-3199
Tel **412-227-1000**
Fax **412-227-1304**
Exchange **NYSE**
Ticker **CNG**
Chief Executive **George A. Davidson, Jr.**
Chairman **George A. Davidson, Jr.**

Consolidated Papers

Industry: **Paper Products**

Consolidated Papers produces paper products. Its products include coated papers used in magazines, books, brochures, advertisements, and other applications, as well as paperboard and corrugated products used in milk cartons and other food containers. The company markets its enamel printing paper to magazine publishers and commercial printers, and its coated specialty papers to users who package and label food and other consumer products in the U.S. It operates manufacturing plants in the Wisconsin towns of Wisconsin Rapids, Biron, Whiting, Stevens Point, and Adams.

$ mil	12/92	12/93	12/94	% Change				
Sales	904.2	947.3	1,027.6	8.5	P/E Ratio	28.4	Price (9/30/95)	55.88
Net Income	12.4	64.2	86.7	35.1	P/B Ratio	2.5	52 Wk Hi-Low	64.50-42.25
Book Value	921.6	939.0	975.9	3.9	Yield %	2.3	Market Cap	US$2,484.3mil

Address **P.O. Box 8050**
Wisconsin Rapids, WI 54495-8050
Tel **715-422-3111**
Fax **715-422-3052**
Exchange **NYSE**
Ticker **CDP**
President & CEO **Patrick F. Brennan**
Chairman **George W. Mead**

Consumers Water

Industry: **Water Utilities**

Consumers Water is a holding company that provides water-utility and related services. It owns at least 90% of the voting stock of 9 water companies providing service to 221,000 customers in six states in the northeastern United States. The company also owns C/P Utility Services, which provides meter, engineering, and water-conservation services, primarily to utilities, and Burlington Homes, which produces manufactured housing. Residential customers account for approximately 65% of total water-utility revenues; commercial and industrial users provide another 22%.

$ mil	12/92	12/93	12/94	% Change				
Sales	74.6	78.2	80.4	2.8	P/E Ratio	14.0	Price (9/30/95)	17.13
Net Income	8.0	5.9	10.0	69.5	P/B Ratio	1.4	52 Wk Hi-Low	18.50-14.75
Book Value	85.3	98.0	102.0	4.1	Yield %	6.8	Market Cap	US$143.8mil

Address **3 Canal Plz.**
Portland, ME 04101
Tel **207-773-6438**
Fax **207-761-7903**
Exchange **NASDA**
Ticker **CONW**
President & CEO **Peter L. Haynes**
Chairman **David R. Hastings II**

Cooper Industries

Industry: **Industrial - Diversified**

Cooper Industries manufactures electrical products, automotive parts, hand tools, and hardware. Its electrical products and equipment are used in power-distribution and lighting applications. It produces power tools, pliers, saws, files, torches, automotive brakes, spark plugs, air-conditioning components, and steering-control products. The company markets its products to original-equipment manufacturers, retailers, and end users in the United States and in foreign markets. Business outside the U.S. accounts for approximately 23% of the company's operating revenues.

$ mil	12/92	12/93	12/94	% Change				
Sales	**6,158.5**	**6,273.8**	**4,588.0**	**-26.9**	P/E Ratio	**NMF**	Price (9/30/95)	**35.25**
Net Income	**-228.7**	**367.1**	**-19.9**	**-105.4**	P/B Ratio	**1.5**	52 Wk Hi-Low	**40.38-31.75**
Book Value	**2,866.9**	**2,984.6**	**2,741.1**	**-8.2**	Yield %	**3.7**	Market Cap	**US$3,793.1mil**

Address	**Ste. 4000, 1001 Fannin**	Tel	**713-739-5400**	Exchange	**NYSE**	President	**H. John Riley, Jr.**
	Houston, TX 77210-4446	Fax	**713-739-5555**	Ticker	**CBE**	Chairman & CEO	**Robert Cizik**

Cooper Tire & Rubber

Industry: **Tires & Rubber**

Cooper Tire & Rubber produces tires and other automotive products. It makes automobile and truck tires, inner tubes, vibration-control products, automotive body sealers, and specialty-seating components. The company sells its products in the replacement-tire market and to original-equipment manufacturers, including automobile companies and mobile-home and travel-trailer makers in the U.S. and internationally. Sales from international operations account for approximately 6% of the consolidated total. Cooper operates 10 manufacturing facilities in the U.S. and Mexico.

$ mil	12/92	12/93	12/94	% Change				
Sales	**1,174.7**	**1,193.6**	**1,403.2**	**17.6**	P/E Ratio	**15.7**	Price (9/30/95)	**24.25**
Net Income	**43.2**	**102.2**	**128.5**	**25.8**	P/B Ratio	**3.1**	52 Wk Hi-Low	**29.25-22.00**
Book Value	**471.5**	**550.2**	**662.1**	**20.3**	Yield %	**0.9**	Market Cap	**US$2,028.5mil**

Address	**701 Lima Ave.**	Tel	**419-423-1321**	Exchange	**NYSE**	President & CEO	**Patrick W. Rooney**
	Findlay, OH 45840	Fax	**419-424-4212**	Ticker	**CTB**	Chairman	**Patrick W. Rooney**

Adolph Coors

Industry: **Distillers & Brewers**

Adolph Coors produces beer and nonalcoholic malt beverages through its subsidiary, Coors Brewing Company. Its main brands include Coors, Coors Light, Keystone, Steinlager, and George Killian's Irish Red beers, Zima clear malt beverage, and nonalcoholic Coors Cutter. Brewers licensed by the company to produce Coors outside the U.S. include Molson Breweries of Canada, Asahi Breweries in Japan, and Newcastle Breweries of Scotland. Coors markets its beverages worldwide, but currently its international operations and export sales do not contribute significantly to revenues.

$ mil	12/92	12/93	12/94	% Change				
Sales	**1,550.8**	**1,581.8**	**1,662.7**	**5.1**	P/E Ratio	**11.9**	Price (9/30/95)	**18.13**
Net Income	**-2.0**	**-41.9**	**58.1**	**-238.7**	P/B Ratio	**1.0**	52 Wk Hi-Low	**18.75-15.13**
Book Value	**685.4**	**631.9**	**674.2**	**6.7**	Yield %	**2.8**	Market Cap	**US$696.4mil**

Address	**Adolph Coors**	Tel	**303-279-6565**	Exchange	**NASDA**	CEO	**Peter H. Coors**
	Golden, CO 80401	Fax	**303-277-5308**	Ticker	**ACCO**	Chairman	**William K. Coors**

CoreStates Financial

Industry: **Banks - Eastern U.S.**

CoreStates Financial is a bank holding company that provides wholesale- and retail-banking through 400 branches in Pennsylvania, New Jersey, and Delaware. The company also offers credit-card services to more than 1.9 million customers in the United States. CoreStates Financial offers financial services for the consumer, small-business, and middle-market sectors. CoreStates Financial's other services include trust and investment management, electronic-payment services, and discount brokerage. Its Congress Financial division provides commercial financing.

$ mil	12/92	12/93	12/94	% Change				
Revenues	**2,133.9**	**2,013.6**	**2,497.1**	**24.0**	P/E Ratio	**21.2**	Price (9/30/95)	**36.63**
Net Income	**181.4**	**314.9**	**245.4**	**-22.1**	P/B Ratio	**2.3**	52 Wk Hi-Low	**38.63-24.25**
Book Value	**1,703.5**	**1,959.5**	**2,350.1**	**19.9**	Yield %	**3.4**	Market Cap	**US$5,107.4mil**

Address	**Broad & Chestnut Sts.**	Tel	**215-973-3827**	Exchange	**NYSE**	President	**Charles L. Coltman III**
	Philadelphia, PA 19101	Fax	**215-786-8294**	Ticker	**CFL**	Chairman & CEO	**Terrence A. Larsen**

Corning

Industry: **Diversified Technology**

Corning manufactures and sells products made from specialty glass and related inorganic materials. These materials have properties of chemical stability, electrical resistance, heat resistance, light transmission, and mechanical strength. The company annually produces approximately 60,000 different products at 41 plants in eight countries. In addition, Corning engages in laboratory services businesses at 50 facilities in 10 countries. Most of the company's products are marketed under the Corning, Corning Ware, Celcor, Corelle, Corguide, Pyrex, Visions, and Vycor trademarks.

$ mil	12/92	12/93	12/94	% Change				
Sales	**3,708.7**	**4,004.8**	**4,770.5**	**19.1**	P/E Ratio	**21.7**	Price (9/30/95)	**28.63**
Net Income	**-12.6**	**-15.2**	**281.3**	**NMF**	P/B Ratio	**2.9**	52 Wk Hi-Low	**37.25-28.25**
Book Value	**1,830.7**	**1,685.8**	**2,287.9**	**35.7**	Yield %	**2.4**	Market Cap	**US$6,578.1mil**

Address	**1 Riverfront Plz.**	Tel	**607-974-9000**	Exchange	**NYSE**	President	**Roger G. Ackerman**
	Corning, NY 14831	Fax	**607-974-6447**	Ticker	**GLW**	Chairman & CEO	**James R. Houghton**

CPC International

Industry: **Other Food**

CPC International is a food-processing company. Its products include Hellman's mayonnaise, Mazola corn oil, Skippy peanut butter, Knorr sauces and soups, Entenmann's bakery goods, and Mueller pasta. It also refines corn to produce cornstarch, which it markets under the Argo brand name, and sweeteners, including glucose, dextrose, and Karo brand corn syrup. The company markets these foodstuffs in the United States and internationally. CPC International operates 143 food-processing plants in the U.S., Canada, Europe, Africa, the Middle East, Latin America, and Asia.

$ mil	12/92	12/93	12/94	% Change				
Sales	**6,599.0**	**6,738.0**	**7,425.0**	**10.2**	P/E Ratio	**29.3**	Price (9/30/95)	**66.00**
Net Income	**223.8**	**454.5**	**345.0**	**-24.1**	P/B Ratio	**5.5**	52 Wk Hi-Low	**67.63-49.63**
Book Value	**1,661.8**	**1,769.1**	**1,749.0**	**-1.1**	Yield %	**2.1**	Market Cap	**US$9,637.5mil**

Address	**International Plz.**	Tel	**201-894-4000**	Exchange	**NYSE**	President & CEO	**Charles R. Shoemate**
	Englewood Cliffs, NJ 07632-9976	Fax	**201-894-2186**	Ticker	**CPC**	Chairman	**Charles R. Shoemate**

CPI

Industry: **Household Services**

CPI operates portrait studios, photographic-finishing laboratories, electronic-publishing stores, and Prints Plus wall-decor locations. Almost half of net sales and more than three fourths of its operating earnings are from the Sears Portrait Studio business. The company operates 660 photofinishing locations under the names of CPI Photo Finish, Fox Photo, and Proex. The company also owns 103 stores in the Prints Plus poster, print, and custom framing chain. CPI has 900 studios in all major North American Sears stores, and 92 studios in non-Sears shopping centers.

$ mil	02/93	02/94	02/95	% Change				
Sales	**449.4**	**475.5**	**533.2**	**12.1**	P/E Ratio	**21.1**	Price (9/30/95)	**22.13**
Net Income	**22.6**	**13.2**	**14.8**	**12.3**	P/B Ratio	**1.8**	52 Wk Hi-Low	**22.13-13.88**
Book Value	**171.9**	**175.5**	**166.0**	**-5.4**	Yield %	**2.5**	Market Cap	**US$306.7mil**

Address	**1706 Washington Ave.**	Tel	**314-231-1575**	Exchange	**NYSE**	President	**Russell Isaak**
	St. Louis, MO 63103-1717	Fax	**314-621-9286**	Ticker	**CPY**	Chairman & CEO	**Alyn V. Essman**

Cracker Barrel Old Country Store

Industry: **Restaurants**

Cracker Barrel Old Country Store owns and operates nearly 191 full-service country-style restaurants located primarily in the southwest, midwest, mid-Atlantic, and southwest U.S. The company's restaurants specialize in rural Southern cooking and offer breakfast, lunch, and dinner from a moderately priced menu with meals from $1.29 to $10.95. The restaurants also feature gift shops that sell handblown glassware, old-fashioned crockery, and children's toys, as well as various foodstuffs sold under the company's own Cracker Barrel Old Country Store brand name.

$ mil	07/92	07/93	07/94	% Change				
Sales	**400.6**	**517.6**	**640.9**	**23.8**	P/E Ratio	**21.0**	Price (9/30/95)	**20.13**
Net Income	**33.9**	**45.7**	**58.0**	**26.9**	P/B Ratio	**2.8**	52 Wk Hi-Low	**24.38-19.00**
Book Value	**222.1**	**366.8**	**429.9**	**17.2**	Yield %	**0.1**	Market Cap	**US$1,207.0mil**

Address	**Hartmann Drive**	Tel	**615-444-5533**	Exchange	**NASDA**	President & CEO	**Dan W. Evins**
	Lebanon, TN 37088-0787	Fax	**N/A**	Ticker	**CBRL**	Chairman	**Dan W. Evins**

Crane

Industry: **Industrial - Diversified**

Crane manufactures engineered-industrial products used in the aerospace, fluid-handling, automatic-merchandising, transportation, commercial-construction, and defense markets. Products include gate, globe, ball, and butterfly valves that are designed for use under various pressures and temperatures, along with pipefitting, actuators, pumps, and flow-measurement equipment. Subsidiaries include Resistoflex, Cor Tec, and others. Its Polyflon division manufactures radio-frequency components. Crane's Eldec subsidiary is a defense and aerospace subcontractor.

$ mil	12/92	12/93	12/94	% Change				
Sales	**1,307.0**	**1,310.2**	**1,653.5**	**26.2**	P/E Ratio	**18.5**	Price (9/30/95)	**34.50**
Net Income	**24.3**	**48.9**	**55.9**	**14.4**	P/B Ratio	**3.2**	52 Wk Hi-Low	**39.00-25.13**
Book Value	**271.4**	**290.8**	**328.0**	**12.8**	Yield %	**2.2**	Market Cap	**US$1,052.8mil**

Address	**100 First Stamford Pl.**	Tel	**203-363-7300**	Exchange	**NYSE**	President & CEO	**Robert S. Evans**
	Stamford, CT 06902	Fax	**203-363-7295**	Ticker	**CR**	Chairman	**Robert S. Evans**

Crestar Financial

Industry: **Banks - Southern U.S.**

Crestar Financial provides banking, insurance, and related services. Its primary subsidiary is Crestar Bank, which operates 336 branches in Virginia, Maryland, and Washington, D.C. Its other subsidiaries include Crestar Insurance Agency (insurance products and annuities), Crestar Securities (brokerage services), and Capitoline Investment Services (investment-advisory services). Crestar Financial manages the CrestFunds family of mutual funds. The company provides financial services and products to the consumer market, and to businesses, institutions, and governments.

$ mil	12/92	12/93	12/94	% Change				
Revenues	**1,082.1**	**1,080.9**	**1,180.3**	**9.2**	P/E Ratio	**12.5**	Price (9/30/95)	**55.88**
Net Income	**79.8**	**140.5**	**169.1**	**20.3**	P/B Ratio	**1.9**	52 Wk Hi-Low	**57.75-36.75**
Book Value	**958.9**	**1,062.5**	**1,126.1**	**6.0**	Yield %	**2.7**	Market Cap	**US$2,106.0mil**

Address	**919 E. Main St.**	Tel	**804-782-5000**	Exchange	**NYSE**	President	**James M. Wells III**
	Richmond, VA 23261-6665	Fax	**804-782-7744**	Ticker	**CF**	Chairman & CEO	**Richard G. Tilghman**

Crown Cork & Seal

Industry: **Containers & Packaging**

Crown Cork & Seal is a manufacturer of metal and plastic packaging products. These products include cans, crowns, and closures and machinery for filling. The company's products are manufactured in 84 plants in the United States. The products are sold to 82 domestic plants, and in 70 plants outside the U.S.; and are sold to the general food, brewing, soft-drink, paint, toiletry, drug, antifreeze, chemical, and pet-food industries. The company also provides technical and engineering services worldwide through its engineering group as well as parts and overhaul services.

$ mil	12/92	12/93	12/94	% Change				
Sales	3,780.7	4,162.6	4,452.2	7.0	P/E Ratio	26.4	Price (9/30/95)	38.75
Net Income	155.4	99.1	131.0	32.2	P/B Ratio	2.5	52 Wk Hi-Low	50.50-36.38
Book Value	1,143.6	1,251.8	1,365.2	9.1	Yield %	0.0	Market Cap	US$3,502.5mil

Address **9300 Ashton Rd.**
Philadelphia, PA 19136
Tel **215-698-5100**
Fax **215-698-5201**
Exchange **NYSE**
Ticker **CCK**
President & CEO **William J. Avery**
Chairman **William J. Avery**

CSX

Industry: **Railroads**

CSX provides transportation and related services to 100 ports in 70 countries. Its rail-transportation and -distribution services span 20 states in the eastern, midwestern, and southern regions of the United States, as well as Ontario, Canada. CSX provides inland-marine services and international freight transportation, including intermodal, barge, rail, and trucking services. The company has a 40% market share in the rail transportation of coal and a 70% share in phosphates and fertilizer transportation. Operations outside North America account for 69% of revenues.

$ mil	12/92	12/93	12/94	% Change				
Sales	8,734.0	8,940.0	9,608.0	7.5	P/E Ratio	13.5	Price (9/30/95)	84.13
Net Income	20.0	359.0	652.0	81.6	P/B Ratio	2.4	52 Wk Hi-Low	87.75-64.75
Book Value	2,975.0	3,180.0	3,731.0	17.3	Yield %	2.1	Market Cap	US$8,851.2mil

Address **1 James Ctr., 901 E. Cary St.**
Richmond, VA 23219-4031
Tel **804-782-1400**
Fax **804-783-1345**
Exchange **NYSE**
Ticker **CSX**
President & CEO **John W. Snow**
Chairman **John W. Snow**

Cummins Engine

Industry: **Land Transportation**

Cummins Engine manufactures diesel engines and engine-related components and power systems for trucks, buses, light-commercial vehicles including delivery trucks and vans, and other heavy equipment. The company's principal North American markets are the heavy-duty and midrange truck industries, while its other major customers include manufacturers of equipment for construction, mining, agriculture, and various industrial uses. Cummins Engine's Fleetguard subsidiary makes heavy-duty and specialty filters. Approximately 43% of the company's net sales originate overseas.

$ mil	12/92	12/93	12/94	% Change				
Sales	3,749.2	4,247.9	4,737.2	11.5	P/E Ratio	6.3	Price (9/30/95)	38.50
Net Income	-189.5	177.1	252.9	42.8	P/B Ratio	1.5	52 Wk Hi-Low	48.63-37.25
Book Value	501.1	821.1	1,072.6	30.6	Yield %	1.6	Market Cap	US$1,559.3mil

Address **500 Jackson St.**
Columbus, IN 47202-3005
Tel **812-377-5000**
Fax **812-377-3334**
Exchange **NYSE**
Ticker **CUM**
President **Theodore M. Solso**
Chairman & CEO **James A. Henderson**

Cyprus Amax Minerals

Industry: **Coal**

Cyprus Amax mines copper, coal, gold, and other minerals. The company's copper operations include copper-mining complexes in Arizona and South America. Its coal operations include surface and underground mines in the east-central U.S. and underground mines in the Rocky Mountain region. Cyprus AMAX also produces molybdenum, lithium carbonate, gold, iron ore, and zinc at mines in Nevada, North Carolina, Tennessee, and Virginia, and Chile. The company's customers include the construction, automotive, electrical, steel, electric-utility, specialty-glass, and drug industries.

$ mil	12/92	12/93	12/94	% Change				
Sales	1,641.4	1,763.5	2,788.0	58.1	P/E Ratio	16.6	Price (9/30/95)	28.13
Net Income	-333.6	100.2	175.0	74.7	P/B Ratio	1.1	52 Wk Hi-Low	32.63-23.88
Book Value	923.0	2,216.6	2,329.0	5.1	Yield %	3.2	Market Cap	US$2,613.1mil

Address **9100 E. Mineral Circle**
Englewood, CO 80112
Tel **303-643-5000**
Fax **303-643-5224**
Exchange **NYSE**
Ticker **CYM**
President & CEO **Milton H. Ward**
Chairman **Milton H. Ward**

Dames & Moore

Industry: **Pollution Control, Waste Management**

Dames & Moore provides environmental and other specialized consulting and engineering services. The company offers environmental services involving the assessment of site conditions and the design and implementation of solutions for issues related to hazardous waste, air pollution, water pollution, and regulatory compliance. The company also provides specialized consulting services related to civil and geotechnical engineering, water supply, and urban and transportation planning and design. Clients are principally large corporations.

$ mil	03/93	03/94	03/95	% Change				
Sales	251.9	253.8	269.0	6.0	P/E Ratio	20.3	Price (9/30/95)	16.00
Net Income	23.1	21.9	17.9	-18.3	P/B Ratio	2.2	52 Wk Hi-Low	16.00-11.38
Book Value	125.4	144.7	161.6	11.7	Yield %	0.8	Market Cap	US$363.1mil

Address **911 Wilshire Blvd., Ste. 700**
Los Angeles, CA 90017
Tel **213-683-1560**
Fax **N/A**
Exchange **NYSE**
Ticker **DM**
President & CEO **Arthur C. Darrow**
Chairman **--**

Dana

Industry: **Other Auto Parts**

Dana manufactures truck and industrial components. Its product line includes axles, driveshafts, clutches, transmissions, piston rings, pistons, filters, vehicular frames, side rails, pumps, control valves, and hydraulic cylinders. The company's products are marketed worldwide to vehicular, industrial, and mobile off-highway original-equipment markets. Vehicular components for use on automobiles, pickup trucks, vans, sport-utility vehicles, minivans, and medium and heavy trucks account for 80% of sales. Dana operates manufacturing and distribution facilities worldwide.

$ mil	12/92	12/93	12/94	% Change				
Sales	**4,872.3**	**5,460.1**	**6,613.8**	**21.1**	P/E Ratio	**12.5**	Price (9/30/95)	**28.88**
Net Income	**-382.0**	**79.6**	**228.2**	**186.7**	P/B Ratio	**3.0**	52 Wk Hi-Low	**32.13-20.13**
Book Value	**707.0**	**801.4**	**939.8**	**17.3**	Yield %	**2.9**	Market Cap	**US$2,924.3mil**

Address **4500 Dorr St.**
Toledo, OH 43697
Tel **419-535-4500**
Fax **419-535-4643**
Exchange **NYSE**
Ticker **DCN**
President & CEO **Southwood J. Morcott**
Chairman **Southwood J. Morcott**

Darden Restaurants

Industry: **Restaurants**

Darden Restaurants, formerly a subsidiary of General Mills, operates chains of restaurants across the United States. As of May 31, 1995, the company operated 1,177 restaurants, including 660 Red Lobster, 459 Olive Garden, and 51 China Coast restaurants. In addition, the company operated 55 Red Lobster units and 18 Olive Garden units in Canada. The Red Lobster restaurants feature seafood, Olive Garden features Italian entrees, and China Coast offers Chinese cuisine. All of these units are casual-dining restaurants and have an average capacity of 8,200 square feet.

$ mil	05/93 R	05/94	05/95	% Change				
Sales	**2,737.0**	**2,963.0**	**3,163.3**	**6.8**	P/E Ratio	**34.8**	Price (9/30/95)	**11.50**
Net Income	**91.6**	**126.8**	**52.4**	**-58.7**	P/B Ratio	**1.5**	52 Wk Hi-Low	**11.63-9.88**
Book Value	**1,211.4**	**1,407.3**	**1,174.0**	**-16.6**	Yield %	**0.0**	Market Cap	**US$1,817.0mil**

Address **5900 Lake Ellenor Dr.**
Orlando, FL 32809
Tel **407-245-4000**
Fax **N/A**
Exchange **NYSE**
Ticker **DRI**
President & CEO **Joe R. Lee**
Chairman **Joe R. Lee**

R=Restated.

Dayton Hudson

Industry: **Retailers - Broadline**

Dayton Hudson operates general-merchandise retailers across the United States through its subsidiaries. Target stores gave the company 64% of its fiscal 1994 revenues. Target is a discount merchandise chain with 611 stores in 32 states. These stores feature name-brand and private-label family apparel. The company's Mervyn chain is a moderate-price department store emphasizing name-brand and private-label casual apparel and home softgoods through 286 stores in 15 states. The department-store division operates 63 Dayton's, Hudson's, and Marshall Field's stores.

$ mil	01/93	01/94	01/95	% Change				
Revenues	**17,927.0**	**19,233.0**	**21,311.0**	**10.8**	P/E Ratio	**13.1**	Price (9/30/95)	**75.88**
Net Income	**383.0**	**375.0**	**434.0**	**15.7**	P/B Ratio	**1.7**	52 Wk Hi-Low	**84.00-64.50**
Book Value	**2,593.0**	**2,888.0**	**3,237.0**	**12.1**	Yield %	**2.2**	Market Cap	**US$5,446.1mil**

Address **777 Nicollet Mall**
Minneapolis, MN 55402
Tel **612-370-6948**
Fax **612-370-5502**
Exchange **NYSE**
Ticker **DH**
President **Stephen E. Watson**
Chairman & CEO **Robert J. Ulrich**

Dean Foods

Industry: **Other Food**

Dean Foods processes dairy products and makes specialty-food products. The company's dairy division produces milk, ice cream, yogurt, ultrapasteurized products, and aerosol toppings sold under the Dean, Fieldcrest, and private label trademarks. Its specialty-foods division makes Veg-All and Freshlike canned and frozen vegetables, Peter Piper and Aunt Jane's pickles and relishes, Dean sauces and dips, and private-label powdered coffee creamers. DFC Transportation, a subsidiary, provides refrigerated and frozen truck-freight services to the parent company and others.

$ mil	05/93	05/94	05/95	% Change				
Sales	**2,274.3**	**2,431.2**	**2,630.2**	**8.2**	P/E Ratio	**14.2**	Price (9/30/95)	**28.50**
Net Income	**68.4**	**71.9**	**80.1**	**11.4**	P/B Ratio	**2.0**	52 Wk Hi-Low	**31.63-26.38**
Book Value	**476.3**	**524.8**	**584.5**	**11.4**	Yield %	**2.4**	Market Cap	**US$1,138.0mil**

Address **3600 N. River Rd.**
Franklin Park, IL 60131
Tel **708-678-1680**
Fax **708-678-2779**
Exchange **NYSE**
Ticker **DF**
President **Thomas L. Rose**
Chairman **Howard M. Dean**

Dean Witter, Discover

Industry: **Financial Services - Diversified**

Dean Witter Discover is a financial-services company that provides a range of nationally marketed credit and investment products, with a focus on individuals. The company's two principal businesses are credit services and asset management. Its credit-services division issues and markets the Discover Card, a proprietary credit and financial-services card. Dean Witter's full-service securities business is operated primarily through its Dean Witter Reynolds subsidiary, and the company's Dean Witter InterCapital division provides asset-management services.

$ mil	12/92	12/93	12/94	% Change				
Revenues	**5,183.5**	**5,821.6**	**6,602.6**	**13.4**	P/E Ratio	**12.9**	Price (9/30/95)	**56.25**
Net Income	**410.5**	**603.6**	**740.9**	**22.7**	P/B Ratio	**2.3**	52 Wk Hi-Low	**57.88-32.25**
Book Value	**2,673.3**	**3,477.1**	**4,108.0**	**18.1**	Yield %	**0.9**	Market Cap	**US$9,500.6mil**

Address **2 World Trade Ctr.**
New York, NY 10048
Tel **212-392-2222**
Fax **212-392-8405**
Exchange **NYSE**
Ticker **DWD**
Chief Executive **Philip J. Purcell**
Chairman **Philip J. Purcell**

Deere & Co.

Industry: **Heavy Machinery**

Deere & Company manufactures agricultural, industrial, and lawn-care equipment. The company's product lines include tractors, riding, and walk-behind mowers, snowblowers, leaf blowers, excavators, loaders, diesel engines, utility-transport vehicles, and machinery components. Its primary industrial-machine products include construction, earthmoving, and forestry equipment, and cranes and trucks. The company provides credit, managed-health-care, and life-insurance services for businesses and consumers through its John Deere Credit and John Deere Insurance Group subsidiaries.

$ mil	10/92	10/93	10/94	% Change				
Sales	**5,723.4**	**6,479.3**	**7,663.1**	**18.3**	P/E Ratio	**11.6**	Price (9/30/95)	**81.38**
Net Income	**37.4**	**-920.9**	**603.6**	**-165.5**	P/B Ratio	**2.7**	52 Wk Hi-Low	**93.88-61.63**
Book Value	**2,650.3**	**2,085.4**	**2,557.9**	**22.7**	Yield %	**2.5**	Market Cap	**US$7,051.9mil**

Address **John Deere Rd.**
Moline, IL 61265
Tel **309-765-8000**
Fax **309-765-5671**
Exchange **NYSE**
Ticker **DE**
President **David H. Stowe, Jr.**
Chairman & CEO **Hans W. Becherer**

Dell Computer

Industry: **Computers**

Dell Computer is a manufacturer and vendor of computer equipment. The company markets its wares directly to the its customers, which include corporate, government, and education accounts, as well as small businesses and individuals. It also sells personal-computer systems through mass merchants, in order to supplement its direct-marketing strategy. In addition to computer systems, Dell Computer offers software, peripherals, and service and support programs. The company and its subsidiaries conduct business in the United States and abroad.

$ mil	01/93	01/94	01/95	% Change				
Sales	**2,013.9**	**2,873.2**	**3,475.3**	**21.0**	P/E Ratio	**25.1**	Price (9/30/95)	**85.00**
Net Income	**101.6**	**-35.8**	**149.2**	**-516.4**	P/B Ratio	**5.2**	52 Wk Hi-Low	**91.75-40.00**
Book Value	**369.2**	**471.1**	**651.7**	**38.3**	Yield %	**0.0**	Market Cap	**US$3,849.3mil**

Address **2112 Kramer Ln., Bldg. 1**
Austin, TX 78758-4012
Tel **512-338-4400**
Fax **512-728-3653**
Exchange **NASDA**
Ticker **DELL**
Chief Executive **Michael S. Dell**
Chairman **Michael S. Dell**

Delta Air Lines

Industry: **Airlines**

Delta Air Lines offers passenger and freight air-transportation services. It provides flights to 153 U.S. cities in 43 states, the District of Columbia, Puerto Rico, and the U.S. Virgin Islands; the airline also has service to 57 cities in 32 countries. Passenger transportation generates about 92% of the airline's total revenues. International passenger transportation makes up 19% of total revenues. The airline has hubs in Atlanta, Dallas/Ft. Worth, Los Angeles, New York, Cincinnati, Salt Lake City, Orlando, Portland, Oregon, and a European hub in Frankfurt, Germany.

$ mil	06/92	06/93	06/94	% Change				
Sales	**10,836.8**	**11,996.7**	**12,359.0**	**3.0**	P/E Ratio	**NMF**	Price (9/30/95)	**69.25**
Net Income	**-506.3**	**-1,001.9**	**-409.0**	**-59.2**	P/B Ratio	**2.4**	52 Wk Hi-Low	**80.50-43.13**
Book Value	**1,894.1**	**1,913.1**	**1,467.0**	**-23.3**	Yield %	**0.3**	Market Cap	**US$3,515.3mil**

Address **Hartsfield Atlanta Int'l Airport**
Atlanta, GA 30320
Tel **404-715-2600**
Fax **404-715-2233**
Exchange **NYSE**
Ticker **DAL**
President & CEO **Ronald W. Allen**
Chairman **Ronald W. Allen**

Deluxe

Industry: **General Industrial & Commercial Services**

Deluxe designs checks and other printed products, and provides business services. Through its five subsidiaries, the company provides goods and services that include business forms, software and processing services for automated-teller machines, account-verification services for financial institutions, and consumer products such as stationery, gift wrap, and greeting cards. It markets its products and services to financial institutions and through direct mail to individuals in the U.S. and internationally. Deluxe operates production facilities in North America and the U.K.

$ mil	12/92	12/93	12/94	% Change				
Sales	**1,534.4**	**1,581.8**	**1,747.9**	**10.5**	P/E Ratio	**19.4**	Price (9/30/95)	**33.13**
Net Income	**202.8**	**141.9**	**140.9**	**-0.7**	P/B Ratio	**3.4**	52 Wk Hi-Low	**34.00-26.13**
Book Value	**829.8**	**801.2**	**814.4**	**1.6**	Yield %	**4.4**	Market Cap	**US$2,737.5mil**

Address **1080 W. County Rd. F**
St. Paul, MN 55126-8201
Tel **612-483-7111**
Fax **612-483-7821**
Exchange **NYSE**
Ticker **DLX**
President & CEO **Harold V. Haverty**
Chairman **Harold V. Haverty**

Dentsply International

Industry: **Advanced Medical Technology**

Dentsply International manufactures dental and medical products, including artificial teeth, impression materials, root-canal products, crown and bridge materials, dental sealants, dental implants, handpieces, cutting instruments, ultrasonic scalers, ultrasonic polishers, video-imaging devices, and dental and medical x-ray machines. The company markets these products to dentists, dental clinics, and other health-care institutions in the United States and more than 100 foreign countries. Business outside the U.S. accounts for approximately 45% of sales.

$ mil	12/92 R	12/93 R	12/94	% Change				
Sales	**476.3**	**503.8**	**524.8**	**4.2**	P/E Ratio	**15.5**	Price (9/30/95)	**34.50**
Net Income	**34.3**	**14.1**	**62.0**	**341.3**	P/B Ratio	**3.2**	52 Wk Hi-Low	**39.88-32.75**
Book Value	**100.3**	**236.4**	**299.3**	**26.6**	Yield %	**0.4**	Market Cap	**US$933.7mil**

Address **570 W. College Ave.**
York, PA 17405-0872
Tel **717-845-7511**
Fax **N/A**
Exchange **NASDA**
Ticker **XRAY**
President **John C. Miles II**
Chairman & CEO **Burton C. Borgelt**

R=Restated.

Detroit Edison

Industry: **Electrical Utilities - Central U.S.**

Detroit Edison is a public electric utility. It serves roughly 1.9 million customers in an approximately 7,600-square-mile area in southeastern Michigan that includes the city of Detroit. Residential customers account for approximately 32% of operating revenues; commercial and industrial users provide about another 60%. Sales to customers in the automotive and related industries constitute roughly 11% of revenues. The company generates approximately 79% of its electricity with fossil fuels and about 17% with nuclear energy, and purchases the balance from third parties.

$ mil	12/92	12/93	12/94	% Change				
Sales	**3,558.1**	**3,555.2**	**3,519.3**	**-1.0**	P/E Ratio	**12.1**	Price (9/30/95)	**32.25**
Net Income	**588.0**	**521.9**	**419.9**	**-19.5**	P/B Ratio	**1.3**	52 Wk Hi-Low	**32.50-24.88**
Book Value	**3,447.9**	**3,676.6**	**3,706.4**	**0.8**	Yield %	**6.4**	Market Cap	**US$4,736.6mil**

Address **2000 Second Ave.**
Detroit, MI 48226-1279
Tel **313-237-8000**
Fax **313-237-8828**
Exchange **NYSE**
Ticker **DTE**
President **Anthony J. Earley, Jr.**
Chairman & CEO **John E. Lobbia**

Dexter

Industry: **Industrial - Diversified**

Dexter produces and sells specialty materials. Its products include adhesives, structural materials, and coatings for aircraft; acoustic materials and thermoplastic compounds used in auto manufacturing; printed wiring-board and specialty magnetic materials used in the electronics industry; coatings for beverage and food cans; and nonwoven fabrics used for surgical instruments, gowns, and operating-theater drapes. The company markets its products to research institutions, clinical laboratories, pharmaceutical companies, and other users worldwide.

$ mil	12/92	12/93	12/94	% Change				
Sales	**951.4**	**887.1**	**974.7**	**9.9**	P/E Ratio	**16.3**	Price (9/30/95)	**25.50**
Net Income	**38.2**	**24.2**	**37.9**	**56.6**	P/B Ratio	**1.8**	52 Wk Hi-Low	**25.88-20.00**
Book Value	**315.6**	**313.3**	**343.6**	**9.7**	Yield %	**3.5**	Market Cap	**US$625.1mil**

Address **1 Elm St.**
Windsor Locks, CT 06096-2334
Tel **203-627-9051**
Fax **203-627-9713**
Exchange **NYSE**
Ticker **DEX**
Chief Executive **K. Grahame Walker**
Chairman **K. Grahame Walker**

Dial

Industry: **Household Products (Non-Durable)**

Dial manufactures personal-care items, packaged foods, and household products, including soap, detergent, cleansers, and air fresheners. It also provides specialty services, such as airline catering, money-order processing (under the Travelers Express service mark), and convention services. Sales of consumer products account for 43% of the company's total revenues. Dial markets its products to consumers under the Dial, Pure & Natural, Borateem, Breck, Purex, Renuzit, Brillo, Parsons', Armour Star, and Lunch Bucket trademarks in the U.S. and internationally.

$ mil	12/92	12/93	12/94	% Change				
Sales	**3,388.6**	**3,000.3**	**3,546.9**	**18.2**	P/E Ratio	**15.4**	Price (9/30/95)	**24.75**
Net Income	**-81.5**	**120.5**	**140.3**	**16.4**	P/B Ratio	**4.1**	52 Wk Hi-Low	**26.13-19.63**
Book Value	**390.4**	**469.7**	**561.7**	**19.6**	Yield %	**2.4**	Market Cap	**US$2,306.9mil**

Address **Dial Tower**
Phoenix, AZ 85077
Tel **602-207-4000**
Fax **602-207-5455**
Exchange **NYSE**
Ticker **DL**
President & CEO **John W. Teets**
Chairman **John W. Teets**

Digital Equipment

Industry: **Computers**

Digital Equipment supplies networked computer systems, software, and services. The company manufactures personal computers, work stations and servers, peripheral hardware, and software products. Its systems are marketed for use in data-management, telecommunication, finance, publishing, and software-development applications. Digital Equipment also offers consulting, systems-integration, and support services to complement its product line. The company markets its products and services in the U.S. and internationally; foreign operations account for 65% of revenues.

$ mil	06/93	06/94	06/95	% Change				
Sales	**14,371.4**	**13,450.8**	**13,813.1**	**2.7**	P/E Ratio	**77.3**	Price (9/30/95)	**45.63**
Net Income	**-251.3**	**-2,156.1**	**121.8**	**-105.7**	P/B Ratio	**1.9**	52 Wk Hi-Low	**49.13-25.63**
Book Value	**4,885.4**	**3,279.8**	**3,528.3**	**7.6**	Yield %	**0.0**	Market Cap	**US$6,699.5mil**

Address **111 Powdermill Road**
Maynard, MA 01754
Tel **508-493-5111**
Fax **508-493-8780**
Exchange **NYSE**
Ticker **DEC**
President & CEO **Robert B. Palmer**
Chairman **Robert B. Palmer**

Dillard

Industry: **Retailers - Broadline**

Dillard Department Stores operates retail department stores located primarily in 20 southwestern, southeastern, and midwestern states. In fiscal 1994, 229 stores were in operation. All of the company's stores are owned or leased from a wholly-owned subsidiary or from third parties. These stores offer branded apparel and home furnishings. In addition, the company has a private label for shoes, Roundtree & Yorke. More than 86% of total sales came from apparel, cosmetics, accessories, and shoes. Other items sold include furniture, housewares, televisions, and appliances.

$ mil	01/93	01/94	01/95	% Change				
Revenues	**4,714.0**	**5,130.6**	**5,545.8**	**8.1**	P/E Ratio	**14.3**	Price (9/30/95)	**31.88**
Net Income	**236.4**	**241.1**	**251.8**	**4.4**	P/B Ratio	**1.6**	52 Wk Hi-Low	**33.75-24.38**
Book Value	**1,832.0**	**2,081.6**	**2,323.6**	**11.6**	Yield %	**0.3**	Market Cap	**US$3,603.3mil**

Address **1600 Cantrell Rd.**
Little Rock, AR 72201
Tel **501-376-5200**
Fax **501-376-5917**
Exchange **NYSE**
Ticker **DDS**
President **William Dillard II**
Chairman & CEO **William Dillard**

Dole Food

Industry: **Other Food**

Dole Food processes and distributes food products and operates real-estate interests. The company distributes bananas and other tropical fruits, vegetables, and nuts, which it procures from third-party sources and its own farms in the United States, Latin America, and Asia. Its processed products include canned pineapples and concentrates, fruit juices, frozen novelties, and raisins. The company's Castle & Cooke Homes subsidiary develops residential and commercial real estate, primarily in Arizona and California, and operates two resorts on the Hawaiian island of Lanai.

$ mil	12/92	12/93	12/94	% Change				
Sales	3,375.5	3,430.5	3,841.6	12.0	P/E Ratio	30.4	Price (9/30/95)	34.63
Net Income	15.7	77.9	67.9	-12.9	P/B Ratio	1.9	52 Wk Hi-Low	35.00-22.88
Book Value	1,001.0	1,052.1	1,080.6	2.7	Yield %	1.2	Market Cap	US$2,059.5mil

Address	**31355 Oak Crest Dr.**	Tel **818-879-6600**	Exchange **NYSE**	Chief Executive	**David H. Murdock**
	Westlake Village, CA 91361	Fax **818-879-6650**	Ticker **DOL**	Chairman	**David H. Murdock**

Dominion Resources

Industry: **Electrical Utilities - Southern U.S.**

Dominion Resources is an electric utility. Doing business as Virginia Power and North Carolina Power in a 30,000-square-mile area in Virginia and North Carolina, the company serves more than 1.8 million users. Dominion generates about 36% of its electricity with coal, 34% with nuclear energy, and 3% with oil; it purchases most of the balance from third parties. Residential customers account for about 43% of revenues; commercial and industrial users comprise 39%. The company develops natural-gas reserves and holds net reserves of 325 billion cubic feet of natural gas.

$ mil	12/92	12/93	12/94	% Change				
Sales	3,791.1	4,433.9	4,491.1	1.3	P/E Ratio	13.4	Price (9/30/95)	37.63
Net Income	444.5	516.6	478.2	-7.4	P/B Ratio	1.4	52 Wk Hi-Low	39.00-35.25
Book Value	4,131.3	4,435.9	4,586.1	3.4	Yield %	6.8	Market Cap	US$6,528.4mil

Address	**901 E. Byrd St.**	Tel **804-775-5700**	Exchange **NYSE**	President	**Tyndall L. Baucom**
	Richmond, VA 23261-6532	Fax **804-775-5819**	Ticker **D**	Chairman & CEO	**Thomas E. Capps**

Donaldson

Industry: **Pollution Control, Waste Management**

Donaldson produces filtration equipment used in industrial and electronic machinery. The company's engine-products division makes hydraulic-fluid, oil, and fuel filters; air cleaners; and mufflers for heavy equipment used in the construction, mining, and transportation industries. Donaldson's industrial-products division makes air-intake and exhaust-filtration systems for industrial turbines, and filters used in computer hard-disk drives, artificial respirators, and aircraft-ventilation systems. Domestic sales account for about 65% of the company's revenues.

$ mil	07/92	07/93	07/94	% Change				
Sales	482.1	533.3	593.5	11.3	P/E Ratio	19.7	Price (9/30/95)	24.63
Net Income	25.8	28.2	34.2	21.1	P/B Ratio	3.4	52 Wk Hi-Low	28.00-22.50
Book Value	160.3	174.0	189.7	9.0	Yield %	1.0	Market Cap	US$646.5mil

Address	**1400 W. 94th St.**	Tel **612-887-3131**	Exchange **NYSE**	President	**William G. Van Dyke**
	Minneapolis, MN 55431	Fax **N/A**	Ticker **DCI**	Chairman & CEO	**William A. Hodder**

R.R. Donnelly & Sons

Industry: **General Industrial & Commercial Services**

R.R. Donnelley & Sons is a commercial printer and supplier of print and digital-information services. The company operates under contracts with about 5,000 customers, including publishers of commercial and trade magazines, books, telephone and other directories, merchandise catalogs, and computer-equipment owner's manuals. Its provides printing, binding, prepress, and electronic-medium-duplication services worldwide. Metromail, a subsidiary, compiles mailing lists for sale to direct-mail companies and others, and carries out mass mailings for commercial customers.

$ mil	12/92	12/93	12/94	% Change				
Sales	4,193.1	4,387.8	4,888.8	11.4	P/E Ratio	22.3	Price (9/30/95)	39.00
Net Income	234.7	109.4	268.6	145.5	P/B Ratio	3.0	52 Wk Hi-Low	40.13-27.88
Book Value	1,849.0	1,844.0	1,978.4	7.3	Yield %	1.5	Market Cap	US$5,991.1mil

Address	**77 W. Wacker Dr.**	Tel **312-326-8000**	Exchange **NYSE**	Chief Executive	**John R. Walter**
	Chicago, IL 60601	Fax **312-326-8543**	Ticker **DNY**	Chairman	**John R. Walter**

Dover

Industry: **Industrial - Diversified**

Dover manufactures equipment for industrial, commercial, and municipal customers. Its Dover Elevator International subsidiary operates eight companies that manufacture, install, and service elevators in the United States, Puerto Rico, Canada, and Europe. Dover's other subsidiaries make hydraulic, laboratory, heat-transfer, and food-service equipment; fluid-delivery systems; power generators; electronic components; and parking meters. The company markets its products to the automotive, fuel-handling, petroleum-product, waste-management, and service industries.

$ mil	12/92	12/93	12/94	% Change				
Sales	2,271.6	2,483.9	3,085.3	24.2	P/E Ratio	21.6	Price (9/30/95)	38.25
Net Income	129.7	158.3	202.4	27.8	P/B Ratio	4.4	52 Wk Hi-Low	41.25-25.06
Book Value	804.9	870.0	995.9	14.5	Yield %	1.3	Market Cap	US$4,337.8mil

Address	**280 Park Ave.**	Tel **212-922-1640**	Exchange **NYSE**	President & CEO	**Thomas L. Reece**
	New York, NY 10017-1292	Fax **212-922-1656**	Ticker **DOV**	Chairman	**Gary L. Roubos**

Dow Chemical

Industry: **Commodity Chemicals**

Dow Chemical manufactures chemicals, plastic materials, pharmaceuticals, and consumer products. Plastics such as as thermoplastics, thermosets, and fabricated products generate roughly 37% of the company's sales. Consumer, pharmaceutical, and agricultural products such as Ziploc bags, Handi-Wrap, Dow bathroom cleaner, Nicoderm and Nicorette smoking-cessation aids, and Treflan herbicides contribute 29% of sales. The company markets these and its other products in the United States and internationally. Business operations in the U.S. account for approximately 51% of sales.

$ mil	12/92	12/93	12/94	% Change				
Sales	**18,971.0**	**18,060.0**	**20,015.0**	**10.8**	P/E Ratio	**22.1**	Price (9/30/95)	**74.50**
Net Income	**-489.0**	**644.0**	**938.0**	**45.7**	P/B Ratio	**2.5**	52 Wk Hi-Low	**78.50-61.63**
Book Value	**8,074.0**	**8,169.0**	**8,234.0**	**0.8**	Yield %	**3.5**	Market Cap	**US$20,038mil**

Address	**2030 Dow Ctr.**	Tel	**517-636-1000**	Exchange	**NYSE**	President	**William Stavropoulos**
	Midland, MI 48674	Fax	**517-636-0922**	Ticker	**DOW**	Chairman & CEO	**Frank P. Popoff**

Dow Jones

Industry: **Publishing**

Dow Jones & Company publishes business news in print and electronic format and and community newspapers. The company's main publication is The Wall Street Journal; along with The Wall Street Journal Europe and The Asian Wall Street Journal, circulation is more than 1.9 million. Dow Jones also publishes Barron's, Far Eastern Economic Review, SmartMoney and American Demographics. The Telerate division supplies real-time market data. The company also provides radio- and television-news programming.

$ mil	12/92	12/93	12/94	% Change				
Sales	**1,817.9**	**1,931.8**	**2,091.0**	**8.2**	P/E Ratio	**20.5**	Price (9/30/95)	**36.88**
Net Income	**107.6**	**147.5**	**178.2**	**20.8**	P/B Ratio	**2.4**	52 Wk Hi-Low	**38.00-28.25**
Book Value	**1,449.4**	**1,492.8**	**1,481.6**	**-0.7**	Yield %	**2.3**	Market Cap	**US$3,574.1mil**

Address	**200 Liberty St.**	Tel	**212-416-2000**	Exchange	**NYSE**	President	**Kenneth L. Burenga**
	New York, NY 10281	Fax	**212-416-2658**	Ticker	**DJ**	Chairman & CEO	**Peter R. Kann**

DPL

Industry: **Electrical Utilities - Central U.S.**

DPL is a holding company with Dayton Power & Light (DP&L) as its principal subsidiary. DP&L provides electricity and natural-gas service in Ohio. The company provides electricity to 470,000 retail customers and 12 municipalities on a wholesale basis. DP&L has 290,000 natural-gas customers and provides steam service. Residential customers account for approximately 42% of electric and 66% of natural-gas revenues; commercial and industrial consumers make up 45% and 24% of these figures, respectively. The company generates more than 92% of its electricity from coal.

$ mil	12/92	12/93	12/94	% Change				
Sales	**1,017.3**	**1,151.3**	**1,187.9**	**3.2**	P/E Ratio	**15.0**	Price (9/30/95)	**23.13**
Net Income	**138.8**	**139.0**	**154.9**	**11.4**	P/B Ratio	**2.2**	52 Wk Hi-Low	**23.13-19.00**
Book Value	**1,000.0**	**1,027.3**	**1,128.3**	**9.8**	Yield %	**5.1**	Market Cap	**US$2,473.3mil**

Address	**Courthouse Plz. S.W.**	Tel	**513-224-6000**	Exchange	**NYSE**	President & CEO	**Peter H. Forster**
	Dayton, OH 45402	Fax	**513-259-7385**	Ticker	**DPL**	Chairman	**Peter H. Forster**

Dresser Industries

Industry: **Oilfield Equipment & Services - Other**

Dresser Industries provides products and services to the petroleum industry. The company's oil-field-services division manufactures well-drilling bits and related oil-field equipment and provides pipe-coating and seismic resource-exploration services. Its hydrocarbon-processing segment makes compressors, pumps, turbines, generators, and related products and systems that are sold for use in power generation and petroleum processing. The company's M.W. Kellogg subsidiary provides engineering, construction, and related services, mainly to the hydrocarbon-processing industry.

$ mil	10/92	10/93	10/94	% Change				
Sales	**3,797.0**	**4,216.0**	**5,307.3**	**25.9**	P/E Ratio	**12.1**	Price (9/30/95)	**23.88**
Net Income	**-365.5**	**126.7**	**361.8**	**185.6**	P/B Ratio	**2.7**	52 Wk Hi-Low	**25.00-18.63**
Book Value	**949.4**	**943.6**	**1,632.3**	**73.0**	Yield %	**2.8**	Market Cap	**US$4,355.2mil**

Address	**2001 Ross Ave.**	Tel	**214-740-6000**	Exchange	**NYSE**	President	**William E. Bradford**
	Dallas, TX 75201	Fax	**214-740-6584**	Ticker	**DI**	Chairman & CEO	**John J. Murphy**

DSC Communications

Industry: **Communications Technology**

DSC Communications supplies telecommunication systems in the U.S. and internationally. The company's principal products are microprocessor-controlled switching, transmission, individual home- or business-access, and private-network systems that meet U.S. and international standards as well as the requirements of regional Bell operating companies, long-distance carriers, independent telephone companies, and private networks. DSC Communications operates manufacturing facilities in the U.S., Puerto Rico, England, Denmark, Poland, and India.

$ mil	12/92	12/93	12/94	% Change				
Sales	**536.3**	**730.8**	**1,003.1**	**37.3**	P/E Ratio	**42.6**	Price (9/30/95)	**59.25**
Net Income	**11.6**	**81.7**	**162.6**	**99.1**	P/B Ratio	**7.9**	52 Wk Hi-Low	**63.00-27.13**
Book Value	**202.6**	**617.8**	**851.1**	**37.8**	Yield %	**0.0**	Market Cap	**US$6,797.3mil**

Address	**1000 Coit Rd.**	Tel	**214-519-3000**	Exchange	**NASDA**	President & CEO	**James L. Donald**
	Plano, TX 75075-5813	Fax	**214-519-2321**	Ticker	**DIGI**	Chairman	**James L. Donald**

Duke Power

Industry: **Electrical Utilities - Southern U.S.**

Duke Power is a utility that supplies electricity to more than 1.7 million residential, commercial, and industrial customers in a 20,000-square-mile area in North Carolina and South Carolina. Its Nantahala Power & Light subsidiary provides electricity to 51,000 customers in North Carolina. Residential customers account for about 32% of revenues; commercial and industrial users make up 52%. Duke generates about 39% of its electricity using nuclear energy; another 43% comes from coal. The balance is produced at hydroelectric stations or bought from third parties.

$ mil	12/92	12/93	12/94	% Change				
Sales	**3,961.5**	**4,281.9**	**4,488.9**	**4.8**	P/E Ratio	**15.1**	Price (9/30/95)	**43.38**
Net Income	**508.1**	**626.4**	**638.9**	**2.0**	P/B Ratio	**1.7**	52 Wk Hi-Low	**43.75-37.75**
Book Value	**4,930.1**	**5,118.7**	**5,312.3**	**3.8**	Yield %	**4.4**	Market Cap	**US$8,885.8mil**

Address	**422 S. Church St.**	Tel	**704-594-0887**	Exchange	**NYSE**	President	**William A. Coley**
	Charlotte, NC 28242-0001	Fax	**704-373-3814**	Ticker	**DUK**	Chairman & CEO	**William H. Grigg**

Dun & Bradstreet

Industry: **General Industrial & Commercial Services**

Dun & Bradstreet markets information and software through five operations: marketing-information services, risk-management and business-marketing-information services, software services, directory-information services, and other business services. The company's IMS International division provides information and decision-support services to pharmaceutical and health-care industries. The Nielsen subsidiary is a marketing-information supplier, primarily measuring television audiences. Dun & Bradstreet Information Services supplies risk-management information.

$ mil	12/92	12/93	12/94	% Change				
Sales	**4,750.7**	**4,710.4**	**4,895.7**	**3.9**	P/E Ratio	**15.6**	Price (9/30/95)	**57.88**
Net Income	**553.5**	**38.1**	**629.5**	**NMF**	P/B Ratio	**7.5**	52 Wk Hi-Low	**59.88-49.00**
Book Value	**2,156.0**	**1,111.3**	**1,318.6**	**18.7**	Yield %	**4.4**	Market Cap	**US$9,807.7mil**

Address	**187 Danbury Rd.**	Tel	**203-834-4200**	Exchange	**NYSE**	President & CEO	**Robert E. Weissman**
	Wilton, CT 06897	Fax	**N/A**	Ticker	**DNB**	Chairman	**Charles W. Moritz**

Du Pont

Industry: **Commodity Chemicals**

E.I. du Pont de Nemours & Company (Du Pont) makes chemicals and related products. Its principal products include refrigerants, engineered materials, white-pigment chemicals, textiles, carpets, and industrial polymers and acrylics. The company also produces herbicides, printing and publishing supplies, and x-ray products and equipment, and its Conoco subsidiary produces petroleum products. Du Pont markets its products under the Teflon, Lycra, Dacron, Kevlar, Silverstone, and other trademarks in the United States and abroad. Foreign sales account for 47% of the total.

$ mil	12/92	12/93	12/94	% Change				
Sales	**37,799.0**	**37,098.0**	**39,333.0**	**6.0**	P/E Ratio	**17.2**	Price (9/30/95)	**68.75**
Net Income	**-3,927.0**	**555.0**	**2,727.0**	**391.4**	P/B Ratio	**3.7**	52 Wk Hi-Low	**72.38-52.38**
Book Value	**11,765.0**	**11,230.0**	**12,822.0**	**14.2**	Yield %	**2.6**	Market Cap	**US$38,154mil**

Address	**1007 Market St.**	Tel	**302-774-1000**	Exchange	**NYSE**	Chief Executive	**Edgar S. Woolard, Jr.**
	Wilmington, DE 19898	Fax	**302-774-7321**	Ticker	**DD**	Chairman	**Edgar S. Woolard, Jr.**

Eastman Chemical

Industry: **Specialty Chemicals**

Eastman Chemical manufactures plastic, chemical, and fiber products. Its performance products are plastics used in soft-drink containers and plastic packaging, raw materials for coatings and paints, photographic chemicals, engineered and compound plastics, and chemicals used in vitamins and food ingredients. Its industrial products include fibers used in cigarette filters, intermediate chemicals, plastics used for packaging, and acetate yarns used in the fabric industry. Eastman Chemical markets these products worldwide. Foreign sales account for 34% of the company's total.

$ mil	12/92 R	12/93	12/94	% Change				
Sales	**3,811.0**	**3,903.0**	**4,329.0**	**10.9**	P/E Ratio	**15.8**	Price (9/30/95)	**64.00**
Net Income	**371.0**	**-209.0**	**336.0**	**-260.8**	P/B Ratio	**4.1**	52 Wk Hi-Low	**68.75-45.75**
Book Value	**2,933.0**	**1,061.0**	**1,295.0**	**22.1**	Yield %	**2.5**	Market Cap	**US$5,205.3mil**

Address	**100 N. Eastman Rd.**	Tel	**423-229-2000**	Exchange	**NYSE**	Chief Executive	**Earnest W. Deavenport**
	Kingsport, TN 37662-5075	Fax	**423-229-2145**	Ticker	**EMN**	Chairman	**Earnest W. Deavenport**

R=Restated.

Eastman Kodak

Industry: **Other Recreational Products & Services**

Eastman Kodak develops and manufactures imaging and information systems. The company manufactures film, photographic papers, photographic chemicals, cameras and projectors, photographic plates and processing equipment, as well as other imaging products under the Kodak name. Its commercial products include graphic-arts films, microfilm products, applications software, copiers, printers, and other business equipment. Eastman Kodak markets its products to commercial users and individuals in the United States and abroad. It operates manufacturing facilities worldwide.

$ mil	12/92	12/93	12/94	% Change				
Sales	**20,183.0**	**16,364.0**	**13,557.0**	**-17.2**	P/E Ratio	**35.7**	Price (9/30/95)	**59.25**
Net Income	**1,146.0**	**-1,515.0**	**557.0**	**-136.8**	P/B Ratio	**5.0**	52 Wk Hi-Low	**63.88-44.63**
Book Value	**6,557.0**	**3,356.0**	**4,017.0**	**19.7**	Yield %	**2.7**	Market Cap	**US$20,253mil**

Address	**343 State St.**	Tel	**716-724-4000**	Exchange	**NYSE**	President & CEO	**George M.C. Fisher**
	Rochester, NY 14650	Fax	**716-412-3516**	Ticker	**EK**	Chairman	**George M.C. Fisher**

Eaton

Industry: **Land Transportation**

Eaton supplies components for automotive, appliance, aircraft, and industrial-machinery manufacturers. It produces automotive-engine components, heavy-duty truck axles and transmissions, timers, water valves, and pressure switches for appliances, controls for military and commercial aircraft, and controls and power-distribution systems for light-commercial and industrial-construction equipment. The company sells these products to users under a number of trademarks, including Eaton, Char-Lynn, Dill, Fuller, Roadranger, and Top Spec, in the U.S. and in foreign markets.

$ mil	12/92	12/93	12/94	% Change				
Sales	**3,869.0**	**4,401.0**	**6,052.0**	**37.5**	P/E Ratio	**12.0**	Price (9/30/95)	**53.00**
Net Income	**-128.0**	**173.0**	**333.0**	**92.5**	P/B Ratio	**2.5**	52 Wk Hi-Low	**62.25-44.25**
Book Value	**948.0**	**1,105.0**	**1,680.0**	**52.0**	Yield %	**2.3**	Market Cap	**US$4,128.7mil**

Address **Eaton Ctr.**
Cleveland, OH 44114-2584
Tel **216-523-5000**
Fax **216-523-4787**
Exchange **NYSE**
Ticker **ETN**
President **John S. Rodewig**
Chairman & CEO **William E. Butler**

Echlin

Industry: **Other Auto Parts**

Echlin is a worldwide supplier of automotive products, primarily for the replacement-part market. Its principal products include brake systems, engine systems, heavy-duty clutches, drive shafts, and suspension systems. The company manufactures components for 95% of the cars, trucks, and buses on the road as well as for off-road, industrial, agricultural, and recreational vehicles. It also manufactures home-security controls and industrial wire and cable products. Echlin operates manufacturing facilities throughout North America, South America, Europe, and Africa.

$ mil	08/92	08/93	08/94	% Change				
Sales	**1,783.4**	**1,944.5**	**2,229.5**	**14.7**	P/E Ratio	**17.0**	Price (9/30/95)	**35.75**
Net Income	**64.3**	**93.6**	**123.7**	**32.1**	P/B Ratio	**2.6**	52 Wk Hi-Low	**39.25-26.88**
Book Value	**693.9**	**713.8**	**799.0**	**11.9**	Yield %	**2.0**	Market Cap	**US$2,130.1mil**

Address **100 Double Beach Rd.**
Branford, CT 06405
Tel **203-481-5751**
Fax **203-488-0370**
Exchange **NYSE**
Ticker **ECH**
President **C. Scott Greer**
Chairman & CEO **Frederick J. Mancheski**

Ecolab

Industry: **General Industrial & Commercial Services**

Ecolab provides cleaning, sanitizing, and maintenance products and services. Its major customers are the food-service, lodging, health-care, dairy, and textile industries. Through Henkel-Ecolab, a joint venture with Henkel, a German services company, the company sells cleaning and sanitizing products to the European institutional and industrial markets. Ecolab sells its products and services under the Power Plus, Maxi-Clean, Quick Fill, Oasis, and other trademarks in 100 countries worldwide. Ecolab's operations outside the United States account for about 22% of sales.

$ mil	12/92	12/93	12/94	% Change				
Sales	**1,004.8**	**1,041.5**	**1,207.6**	**15.9**	P/E Ratio	**22.1**	Price (9/30/95)	**27.63**
Net Income	**64.3**	**76.6**	**84.6**	**10.4**	P/B Ratio	**4.0**	52 Wk Hi-Low	**27.75-19.25**
Book Value	**343.6**	**374.3**	**461.8**	**23.4**	Yield %	**1.7**	Market Cap	**US$1,779.5mil**

Address **Ecolab Ctr.**
St. Paul, MN 55102-1390
Tel **612-293-2233**
Fax **612-225-3123**
Exchange **NYSE**
Ticker **ECL**
President & CEO **Allan L. Schuman**
Chairman **Pierson M. Grieve**

A.G. Edwards

Industry: **Securities Brokers**

A.G. Edwards is a holding company whose subsidiaries provide securities and commodities brokerage, investment banking, trust, asset management, and insurance services. Its principal subsidiary, A.G. Edwards & Sons, operates more than 500 branch offices and provides financial products and services to individual and institutional investors, and investment-banking services, to corporate, governmental and municipal clients. The firm has roughly 1.58 million individual, corporate, and institutional customers. Retail-investment services account for about 95% of revenues.

$ mil	02/93	02/94	02/95	% Change				
Sales	**1,074.4**	**1,278.6**	**1,178.3**	**-7.8**	P/E Ratio	**13.3**	Price (9/30/95)	**26.63**
Net Income	**119.4**	**154.9**	**124.1**	**-19.9**	P/B Ratio	**1.8**	52 Wk Hi-Low	**26.63-16.75**
Book Value	**615.2**	**790.4**	**919.3**	**16.3**	Yield %	**2.1**	Market Cap	**US$1,660.7mil**

Address **One N. Jefferson Ave.**
St. Louis, MO 63103
Tel **314-289-3000**
Fax **314-289-2333**
Exchange **NYSE**
Ticker **AGE**
President & CEO **Benjamin F. Edwards III**
Chairman **Benjamin F. Edwards III**

EG&G

Industry: **Diversified Technology**

EG&G designs components and instruments for radiation detection, security systems, optoelectronics, and industrial measurement. It also provides nuclear-waste management, nuclear-weapons testing, fossil-fuel research, and equipment-fabrication services to the U.S. Department of Energy. In addition, EG&G offers technical services to the auto industry and manufactures aircraft components. The company markets its products and services internationally. Business activity in the United States generates most of EG&G's income, accounting for approximately 90% of revenues.

$ mil	12/92	12/93	12/94	% Change				
Sales	**2,788.8**	**2,697.9**	**1,332.6**	**-50.6**	P/E Ratio	**NMF**	Price (9/30/95)	**19.50**
Net Income	**87.8**	**59.1**	**-5.7**	**-109.6**	P/B Ratio	**2.4**	52 Wk Hi-Low	**20.00-13.25**
Book Value	**473.6**	**477.9**	**445.4**	**-6.8**	Yield %	**2.9**	Market Cap	**US$1,023.6mil**

Address **45 William St.**
Wellesley, MA 02181
Tel **617-237-5100**
Fax **617-431-4255**
Exchange **NYSE**
Ticker **EGG**
President & CEO **John M. Kucharski**
Chairman **John M. Kucharski**

El Paso Natural Gas

Industry: **Pipelines**

El Paso Natural Gas operates natural-gas pipelines in California and the southwestern United States. The company operates approximately 17,000 miles of pipeline, including processing facilities and compressor stations; this pipeline draws natural gas from 270 wells in Colorado, New Mexico, Oklahoma, and Texas. It mainly delivers gas to California utilities and industrial end users south of Sacramento, accounting for almost half of all the gas consumed in California. The company's El Paso Gas Marketing subsidiary buys and sells natural gas on behalf of the company.

$ mil	12/92	12/93	12/94	% Change				
Sales	**802.8**	**908.9**	**869.9**	**-4.3**	P/E Ratio	**11.2**	Price (9/30/95)	**27.50**
Net Income	**76.3**	**91.7**	**89.6**	**-2.3**	P/B Ratio	**1.4**	52 Wk Hi-Low	**34.63-24.88**
Book Value	**669.0**	**707.5**	**709.6**	**0.3**	Yield %	**4.4**	Market Cap	**US$938.2mil**

Address **100 N. Stanton St.** **El Paso, TX 79901** Tel **915-541-2600** Fax **915-541-3155** Exchange **NYSE** Ticker **EPG** President & CEO **William A. Wise** Chairman **William A. Wise**

Electronic Arts

Industry: **Toy Manufacturers**

Electronic Arts creates and distributes interactive-entertainment software for a variety of hardware platforms. As of March 31, 1995, the company marketed approximately 119 of its own titles and distributed more than 130 titles developed by other software publishers. The company has developed products for 32 different computer-hardware platforms, including the IBM personal computer, Commodore 64, Amiga, Apple II, Apple Macintosh, Sega Genesis video game system, and the Nintendo Entertainment System. The company is currently developing compact-disc (CD-ROM) products.

$ mil	03/93	03/94	03/95	% Change				
Sales	**298.4**	**418.3**	**493.4**	**17.9**	P/E Ratio	**34.3**	Price (9/30/95)	**36.75**
Net Income	**30.9**	**44.7**	**55.7**	**24.7**	P/B Ratio	**7.9**	52 Wk Hi-Low	**41.88-16.88**
Book Value	**181.3**	**172.2**	**237.1**	**37.7**	Yield %	**0.0**	Market Cap	**US$1,886.3mil**

Address **1450 Fashion Island Blvd.** **San Mateo, CA 94404** Tel **415-571-7171** Fax **415-570-5137** Exchange **NASDA** Ticker **ERTS** President & CEO **Lawrence F. Probst III** Chairman **Lawrence F. Probst III**

Eli Lilly & Co.

Industry: **Pharmaceuticals**

Eli Lilly & Company manufactures pharmaceuticals, medical devices, and diagnostic and animal-health supplies. Its products include antibiotics, anti-infectives, and diabetic-care products, and central-nervous-system and oncolytic agents used for the cancer treatment. It also makes diagnostic tests for pregnancy, cancer, and other medical conditions. The company's main drugs include Prozac (an antidepressant), Humulin (insulin), and Ceclor (an antibiotic). Eli Lilly's PCS Health Systems subsidiary provides prescription-management services to more than 55 million subscribers.

$ mil	12/92	12/93	12/94	% Change				
Sales	**6,167.3**	**6,452.4**	**5,711.6**	**-11.5**	P/E Ratio	**20.2**	Price (9/30/95)	**89.88**
Net Income	**708.7**	**480.2**	**1,286.1**	**167.8**	P/B Ratio	**4.9**	52 Wk Hi-Low	**91.88-57.63**
Book Value	**4,892.1**	**4,568.8**	**5,355.6**	**17.2**	Yield %	**2.8**	Market Cap	**US$26,244mil**

Address **Lilly Corporate Ctr.** **Indianapolis, IN 46285** Tel **317-276-2000** Fax **317-276-2095** Exchange **NYSE** Ticker **LLY** Chief Executive **Randall L. Tobias** Chairman **Randall L. Tobias**

EMC

Industry: **Computers**

EMC develops and services computer storage and retrieval products. These products improve the capacity and price performance of IBM Mainframe, IBM Midrange, Unisys, and Bull computer systems. The company sells its products to end-user customers and selected distributors, and through original equipment-manufacturer agreements. Integrated Cached Disk Array-based products represents more than 93% of company revenues. Some of the company's customers include American Express, Sony, and United Airlines. The company services its products in North America, Europe, and Asia.

$ mil	12/92	12/93	12/94	% Change				
Sales	**334.6**	**757.8**	**1,343.1**	**77.2**	P/E Ratio	**15.4**	Price (9/30/95)	**18.13**
Net Income	**28.7**	**127.1**	**250.7**	**97.2**	P/B Ratio	**5.0**	52 Wk Hi-Low	**27.13-15.25**
Book Value	**158.1**	**419.1**	**727.6**	**73.6**	Yield %	**0.0**	Market Cap	**US$3,865.5mil**

Address **171 South St.** **Hopkinton, MA 01748** Tel **508-435-1000** Fax **508-497-6915** Exchange **NYSE** Ticker **EMC** President & CEO **Michael C. Ruettgers** Chairman **Richard J. Egan**

Emerson Electric

Industry: **Electrical Components & Equipment**

Emerson Electric manufactures electrical and electronic products and components. The company produces computer power supplies, meters, instruments, valves, switches, and heating, ventilating, and air-conditioning equipment. Emerson also produces a line of electric motors. In addition, Emerson makes saws, grinders, battery-powered screwdrivers, drills, and sanders, which are sold under such brand names as Bosch, Sears, Craftsman, and Skil. The company markets these products in the U.S. and abroad. Business outside of the U.S. accounts for virtually all of net sales.

$ mil	09/92	09/93	09/94	% Change				
Sales	**7,706.0**	**8,173.8**	**8,607.2**	**5.3**	P/E Ratio	**20.3**	Price (9/30/95)	**71.50**
Net Income	**662.9**	**708.1**	**788.6**	**11.4**	P/B Ratio	**3.7**	52 Wk Hi-Low	**75.25-57.25**
Book Value	**3,729.8**	**3,915.1**	**4,341.8**	**10.9**	Yield %	**2.2**	Market Cap	**US$16,052mil**

Address **8000 W. Florissant Ave.** **St. Louis, MO 63136** Tel **314-553-2000** Fax **314-553-1605** Exchange **NYSE** Ticker **EMR** President **J.J. Adorjan** Chairman & CEO **Charles F. Knight**

Engelhard

Industry: **Specialty Chemicals**

Engelhard manufactures specialty chemicals and engineered products. The company's catalysts and chemicals division makes chemical additives used in petroleum products, paints, printing inks, and plastics, and in the power-generation industry to control fumes and exhaust. Its pigments and additives division makes chemicals used in the manufacture of paper, plastics, paints, and coatings. The engineered-materials and precious-metals division produces industrial temperature-sensing devices, crucibles, electroplating materials, and brazing alloys, and procures precious metals.

$ mil	12/92	12/93	12/94	% Change				
Sales	**2,399.7**	**2,150.9**	**2,385.8**	**10.9**	P/E Ratio	**30.9**	Price (9/30/95)	**25.38**
Net Income	**10.6**	**0.7**	**118.0**	**NMF**	P/B Ratio	**5.9**	52 Wk Hi-Low	**32.38-14.08**
Book Value	**647.2**	**531.3**	**614.7**	**15.7**	Yield %	**1.2**	Market Cap	**US$3,657.3mil**

Address **101 Wood Ave.**
Iselin, NJ 08830
Tel **908-205-5000**
Fax **908-321-1161**
Exchange **NYSE**
Ticker **EC**
President **L. Donald LaTorre**
Chairman & CEO **Orin R. Smith**

Enron

Industry: **Pipelines**

Enron is an oil and natural-gas company. The company operates through its subsidiaries and affiliates, which are engaged in gathering and transporting natural gas to markets throughout the United States and internationally. Four pipeline companies--Northern Natural Gas, Transwestern Pipeline, Florida Gas Transmission, and Houston Pipe Line--are included in Enron's operations. Enron Gas Services purchases natural gas through production payment transactions, and contractual arrangements. Enron's subsidiaries also construct and operate natural-gas-fired power plants.

$ mil	12/92	12/93	12/94	% Change				
Sales	**6,324.7**	**7,972.5**	**8,983.7**	**12.7**	P/E Ratio	**18.6**	Price (9/30/95)	**33.50**
Net Income	**306.2**	**332.5**	**453.4**	**36.4**	P/B Ratio	**2.9**	52 Wk Hi-Low	**36.75-27.00**
Book Value	**2,546.6**	**2,623.4**	**2,880.3**	**9.8**	Yield %	**2.3**	Market Cap	**US$8,442.2mil**

Address **1400 Smith St.**
Houston, TX 77002-7369
Tel **713-853-6161**
Fax **713-853-3129**
Exchange **NYSE**
Ticker **ENE**
President **Richard D. Kinder**
Chairman & CEO **Kenneth L. Lay**

ENSCO International

Industry: **Oil Drilling**

ENSCO International provides petroleum-exploration and -production products and services. It drills for oil and natural gas using a fleet of offshore rigs. The company operates 33 offshore-drilling rigs located along the Gulf Coast of the United States, in the North Sea, and Venezuela. ENSCO International also maintains a fleet of 35 oil-field support vessels and equipment-maintenance facilities for the oil and natural-gas industry. The company also provides contract-drilling services through its Penrod subsidiary, an international drilling contractor.

$ mil	12/92	12/93	12/94	% Change				
Sales	**162.0**	**246.2**	**262.0**	**6.4**	P/E Ratio	**27.9**	Price (9/30/95)	**17.00**
Net Income	**-29.6**	**16.5**	**37.2**	**125.5**	P/B Ratio	**2.1**	52 Wk Hi-Low	**19.13-11.00**
Book Value	**214.0**	**454.9**	**487.9**	**7.3**	Yield %	**0.0**	Market Cap	**US$1,027.4mil**

Address **2700 Fountain Pl., 1445 Ross Ave.**
Dallas, TX 75202
Tel **214-922-1500**
Fax **214-855-0080**
Exchange **AMEX**
Ticker **ESV**
Chief Executive **Carl F. Thorne**
Chairman **Carl F. Thorne**

Enserch

Industry: **Pipelines**

Enserch operates petroleum wells and related businesses. Enserch Exploration, a subsidiary, owns, on average, a 52% interest in about 2,400 petroleum wells and holds net reserves of 1.1 trillion cubic feet of natural gas and 46.1 million barrels of oil. Lone Star, a utility subsidiary, owns and operates 32,000 miles of gas pipelines, and distributes gas to more than one million customers. Other subsidiaries include Enserch Processing Partners, which produces butane, propane, and ethane, and Enserch Development, which builds power-generation plants for industrial clients.

$ mil	12/92	12/93	12/94	% Change				
Sales	**2,825.5**	**1,902.1**	**1,857.4**	**-2.3**	P/E Ratio	**12.1**	Price (9/30/95)	**16.50**
Net Income	**-28.0**	**59.2**	**102.3**	**72.8**	P/B Ratio	**1.2**	52 Wk Hi-Low	**18.25-12.13**
Book Value	**779.6**	**821.7**	**900.5**	**9.6**	Yield %	**1.2**	Market Cap	**US$1,128.6mil**

Address **300 S. St. Paul St.**
Dallas, TX 75201-5598
Tel **214-651-8700**
Fax **214-670-2520**
Exchange **NYSE**
Ticker **ENS**
Chief Executive **David W. Biegler**
Chairman **David W. Biegler**

Entergy

Industry: **Electrical Utilities - Southern U.S.**

Entergy is a utility holding company with four utilities that provide electrical service to more than 2.4 million customers in Arkansas, Mississippi, Louisiana, and Texas. The company's system consists of 54 power plants and more than 80,000 miles of distribution lines. Nuclear generators supply approximately 41% of its electrical energy, natural gas 22%; and coal-fired plants provide another 14% of the total. Most of the balance is purchased from third parties. In addition, the company is establishing ventures to provide electricity in Latin America and the Pacific Rim.

$ mil	12/92	12/93	12/94	% Change				
Sales	**4,116.5**	**4,485.3**	**5,963.3**	**33.0**	P/E Ratio	**17.5**	Price (9/30/95)	**26.13**
Net Income	**437.6**	**551.9**	**341.8**	**-38.1**	P/B Ratio	**0.9**	52 Wk Hi-Low	**26.13-20.13**
Book Value	**4,278.9**	**6,536.1**	**6,350.8**	**-2.8**	Yield %	**6.9**	Market Cap	**US$5,949.9mil**

Address **639 Loyola Ave.**
New Orleans, LA 70113
Tel **504-529-5262**
Fax **504-569-4269**
Exchange **NYSE**
Ticker **ETR**
President **Jerry L. Maulden**
Chairman & CEO **Edwin Lupberger**

Equifax

Industry: **General Industrial & Commercial Services**

Equifax provides information-based administrative services to businesses and governments throughout the U.S. and in nine foreign countries. The company's Equifax Credit Information Services and its Credit Northwest subsidiary provide information and administrative services for consumer and commercial credit-report services. Equifax Services provides information for insurance-underwriting purposes. Equifax Marketing Decision Systems, Elrick & Lavidge, Quick Test, Health Economics, Cooperative Healthcare Networks, and High Integrity Systems provide marketing-research.

$ mil	12/92	12/93	12/94	% Change				
Sales	**1,134.3**	**1,217.2**	**1,422.0**	**16.8**	P/E Ratio	**25.8**	Price (9/30/95)	**41.88**
Net Income	**85.3**	**63.5**	**120.4**	**89.5**	P/B Ratio	**8.8**	52 Wk Hi-Low	**41.88-24.00**
Book Value	**258.0**	**254.0**	**361.9**	**42.5**	Yield %	**1.5**	Market Cap	**US$3,337.4mil**

Address	**1600 Peachtree St. N.W.**	Tel	**404-885-8000**	Exchange	**NYSE**	President	**D.W. McGlaughlin**
	Atlanta, GA 30302	Fax	**404-888-5452**	Ticker	**EFX**	Chairman & CEO	**C.B. Rogers, Jr.**

Equitable

Industry: **Insurance - Life & Health**

Equitable is a diversified financial-services organization. The company provides insurance, investment-management, and investment-banking services. Insurance products, mutual funds, and annuities are provided by its subsidiary, Equitable Life Assurance Society of the United States, and that company's subsidiaries. Equitable renders investment services through its Equitable Real Estate Investment Management and Donaldson, Lufkin & Jenrette subsidiaries. Equitable markets its insurance products, including life insurance, health insurance, and annuities, throughout the U.S.

$ mil	12/92	12/93	12/94	% Change				
Revenues	**6,282.0**	**6,479.7**	**6,447.3**	**-0.5**	P/E Ratio	**16.2**	Price (9/30/95)	**24.50**
Net Income	**-128.6**	**234.5**	**296.8**	**26.6**	P/B Ratio	**1.5**	52 Wk Hi-Low	**26.38-16.88**
Book Value	**2,284.7**	**3,247.2**	**3,013.8**	**-7.2**	Yield %	**0.8**	Market Cap	**US$4,516.5mil**

Address	**787 Seventh Ave.**	Tel	**212-554-1234**	Exchange	**NYSE**	President	**Joseph J. Melone**
	New York, NY 10019	Fax	**N/A**	Ticker	**EQ**	Chairman & CEO	**Richard H. Jenrette**

Equitable Resources

Industry: **Gas Utilities**

Equitable Resources is an international petroleum-exploration, -development, and -production company. It currently holds about three million acres of natural-gas and oil properties. The company operates through its subsidiaries, Balcron Oil in the U.S. and Andex Energy in Colombia. Equitable maintains a pipeline system that spans nine states. The company also owns a natural-gas utility serving 265,000 users in Pennsylvania, West Virginia, and Kentucky. Utility services account for approximately 35% of total revenues. Residential utility customers make up about 23%.

$ mil	12/92	12/93	12/94	% Change				
Sales	**812.4**	**1,094.8**	**1,397.3**	**27.6**	P/E Ratio	**16.8**	Price (9/30/95)	**29.50**
Net Income	**60.0**	**73.5**	**60.7**	**-17.4**	P/B Ratio	**1.4**	52 Wk Hi-Low	**30.88-26.00**
Book Value	**589.4**	**728.0**	**750.0**	**3.0**	Yield %	**3.9**	Market Cap	**US$1,024.2mil**

Address	**420 Blvd. of the Allies**	Tel	**412-261-3000**	Exchange	**NYSE**	President & CEO	**Frederick H. Abrew**
	Pittsburgh, PA 15219	Fax	**412-553-6014**	Ticker	**EQT**	Chairman	--

Ethyl

Industry: **Specialty Chemicals**

Ethyl manufactures chemicals used in petroleum and industrial products, including additives for gasoline and diesel fuels, hydraulic fluids, lubricants, and automatic-transmission fluids. Ethyl also makes gasoline additives that contain intake-valve-deposit detergent, which must be added to all unleaded gasoline sold in the United States. The company markets its products in the U.S. and internationally. Business overseas accounts for nearly half of the company's sales. Ethyl operates production facilities in the United States, Canada, the United Kingdom, and Belgium.

$ mil	12/92	12/93	12/94	% Change				
Sales	**1,692.6**	**1,938.4**	**1,174.1**	**-39.4**	P/E Ratio	**13.4**	Price (9/30/95)	**11.13**
Net Income	**255.0**	**175.5**	**97.8**	**-44.3**	P/B Ratio	**3.4**	52 Wk Hi-Low	**11.88-9.63**
Book Value	**1,401.5**	**752.6**	**390.9**	**-48.1**	Yield %	**4.5**	Market Cap	**US$1,317.6mil**

Address	**330 S. Fourth St.**	Tel	**804-788-5000**	Exchange	**NYSE**	President	**Thomas E. Gottwald**
	Richmond, VA 23217	Fax	**804-788-5612**	Ticker	**EY**	Chairman & CEO	**Bruce C. Gottwald**

Expeditors

Industry: **Air Freight & Couriers**

Expeditors International of Washington (EIW) is a freight-shipping company. Its main source of revenue is air freight; it also provides ocean-freight and import services. EIW's air-freight business generates about 48% of revenues. The company's air-freight-forwarding business primarily involves shipments to and from Asia, the United States, and Europe through its offices and international service centers in 28 countries. Operations in the U.S. account for about 33% of revenues. The company has developed its own electronic-data interface, Contact, to track cargo.

$ mil	12/92	12/93	12/94	% Change				
Sales	**333.2**	**361.5**	**450.6**	**24.7**	P/E Ratio	**25.0**	Price (9/30/95)	**27.00**
Net Income	**11.3**	**10.2**	**13.2**	**29.6**	P/B Ratio	**3.2**	52 Wk Hi-Low	**28.00-18.38**
Book Value	**79.0**	**87.6**	**101.1**	**15.4**	Yield %	**0.4**	Market Cap	**US$324.6mil**

Address	**19119 16th Avenue S.**	Tel	**206-246-3711**	Exchange	**NASDA**	President	**Kevin M. Walsh**
	Seattle, WA 98188	Fax	**206-246-3197**	Ticker	**EXPD**	Chairman & CEO	**Peter J. Rose**

Exxon

Industry: **Oil - Integrated Majors**

Exxon is one of the world's largest oil companies. It owns, on average, a 42% interest in 42,000 wells in 80 countries and net proved reserves of 6.1 billion barrels of oil and 42.2 trillion cubic feet of gas. It sells motor fuels through 12,000 company-operated and 22,000 other retail service stations worldwide, and supplies aviation fuel and other distillates to wholesale markets. Exxon's chemical division produces plastics, rubber, solvents, and fertilizers. The company also mines coal and other minerals worldwide, and owns interests in power plants in Hong Kong.

$ mil	12/92	12/93	12/94	% Change				
Sales	**115,672.0**	**109,532.0**	**112,128.0**	**2.4**	P/E Ratio	**17.8**	Price (9/30/95)	**72.25**
Net Income	**4,770.0**	**5,280.0**	**5,100.0**	**-3.4**	P/B Ratio	**2.4**	52 Wk Hi-Low	**73.88-56.75**
Book Value	**33,776.0**	**34,792.0**	**37,415.0**	**7.5**	Yield %	**4.0**	Market Cap	**US$89,718mil**

Address **225 E. John W. Carpenter Fwy.**
Irving, TX 75062
Tel **214-444-1000**
Fax **214-444-1348**
Exchange **NYSE**
Ticker **XON**
President **Charles R. Sitter**
Chairman & CEO **Lee R. Raymond**

Federal Express

Industry: **Air Freight & Couriers**

Federal Express provides domestic and international expedited air-delivery services. It offers overnight and second-day delivery for heavy freight, packages, and documents throughout North America, Europe, Latin America, Asia, and Africa. Federal Express markets these services under the FedEx, International Priority, and FedEx Priority Overnight service marks. The company's service network includes more than 500 aircraft and 35,000 vehicles, sorting facilities, and service centers. Operations outside the United States account for about 28% of revenues.

$ mil	05/93	05/94	05/95	% Change				
Sales	**7,808.0**	**8,479.5**	**9,392.1**	**10.8**	P/E Ratio	**15.7**	Price (9/30/95)	**83.00**
Net Income	**53.9**	**204.4**	**297.6**	**45.6**	P/B Ratio	**2.1**	52 Wk Hi-Low	**83.50-53.88**
Book Value	**1,671.4**	**1,924.7**	**2,245.6**	**16.7**	Yield %	**0.0**	Market Cap	**US$4,662.4mil**

Address **2005 Corporate Ave.**
Memphis, TN 38132
Tel **901-369-3600**
Fax **901-922-2042**
Exchange **NYSE**
Ticker **FDX**
President & CEO **Frederick W. Smith**
Chairman **Frederick W. Smith**

Federal Paper Board

Industry: **Paper Products**

Federal Paper Board manufactures forest products, primarily in the midwestern and eastern United States. The company operates four paper mills, where it produces paperboard, bleached softwood pulps, and uncoated free-sheet paper; five lumber mills, where it makes dimensional lumber and woodchips; and 10 converting plants, where it manufactures paper and plastic cups and lids, paper plates, and milk and juice cartons. It distributes its products in the U.S. and the United Kingdom. Federal owns or leases 690,000 acres of timberland in Georgia and North Carolina.

$ mil	12/92	12/93	12/94	% Change				
Sales	**1,460.8**	**1,386.4**	**1,569.6**	**13.2**	P/E Ratio	**24.8**	Price (9/30/95)	**38.38**
Net Income	**91.6**	**20.8**	**72.0**	**246.2**	P/B Ratio	**1.8**	52 Wk Hi-Low	**44.63-25.88**
Book Value	**940.4**	**906.7**	**918.2**	**1.3**	Yield %	**2.7**	Market Cap	**US$1,757.8mil**

Address **75 Chestnut Ridge Rd.**
Montvale, NJ 07645
Tel **201-391-1776**
Fax **201-573-4426**
Exchange **NYSE**
Ticker **FBO**
President & CEO **John R. Kennedy**
Chairman --

Federal Realty

Industry: **Real-Estate Investment**

Federal Realty Investment Trust is a real-estate investment trust that invests mainly in shopping centers in the eastern United States, especially in the Washington, DC area. The shopping centers usually feature supermarket, drug, or discount-store chains. The trust generally acquires, renovates, and re-leases older shopping centers. The trust owns or has interests in 53 shopping centers with approximately 11.2 million leasable square feet. These account for approximately 90% of the trust's total revenue. The company also owns a 282-unit apartment building in Maryland.

$ mil	12/92	12/93	12/94	% Change				
Sales	**100.2**	**115.3**	**137.8**	**19.5**	P/E Ratio	**34.9**	Price (9/30/95)	**23.38**
Net Income	**9.4**	**18.1**	**20.5**	**13.1**	P/B Ratio	**2.1**	52 Wk Hi-Low	**23.38-19.75**
Book Value	**222.9**	**284.2**	**345.2**	**21.4**	Yield %	**6.7**	Market Cap	**US$741.1mil**

Address **Ste. 500, 4800 Hampden Ln.**
Bethesda, MD 20814
Tel **301-652-3360**
Fax **301-961-9328**
Exchange **NYSE**
Ticker **FRT**
President & CEO **Steven J. Guttman**
Chairman --

FHLMC

Industry: **Financial Services - Diversified**

Federal Home Loan Mortgage Corporation (FHLMC) is a shareholder-owned, U.S. government-sponsored enterprise that provides stability in the secondary market for residential mortgages. FHLMC purchases and securitizes conventional, residential mortgages from mortgage-lending institutions. FHLMC is one of two major sources of secondary-market funding for conventional mortgages, and has financed one out of every six homes in the U.S. Approximately 25% of FHLMC's purchased mortgages have financed homes for low- and moderate-income families.

$ mil	12/92	12/93	12/94	% Change				
Revenues	**4,461.0**	**5,456.0**	**6,923.0**	**26.9**	P/E Ratio	**13.6**	Price (9/30/95)	**69.13**
Net Income	**622.0**	**786.0**	**983.0**	**25.1**	P/B Ratio	**2.4**	52 Wk Hi-Low	**72.75-47.75**
Book Value	**3,570.0**	**4,437.0**	**5,162.0**	**16.3**	Yield %	**1.5**	Market Cap	**US$12,495mil**

Address **8200 Jones Branch Dr.**
McLean, VA 22102
Tel **703-903-2000**
Fax **703-903-2759**
Exchange **NYSE**
Ticker **FRE**
President **David W. Glenn**
Chairman & CEO **Leland C. Brendsel**

Fifth Third Bancorp

Industry: **Banks - Central U.S.**

Fifth Third Bancorp is a multibank and savings and loan holding company. Its Fifth Third Bank subsidiaries operate 353 branches in Ohio, Kentucky, and Indiana. The company, through its affiliates and the bank, provides a full line of banking services including retail, commercial, trust and investment, and data processing. Fifth Third Bancorp's Fountain Square Insurance subsidiary engages in underwriting credit life, accident, and health insurance and in reinsurance activities. Computer services are provided to the bank through its Midwest Payment Systems subsidiary.

$ mil	12/92	12/93	12/94	% Change				
Revenues	894.5	953.9	1,178.2	23.5	P/E Ratio	15.1	Price (9/30/95)	57.38
Net Income	164.1	196.4	244.5	24.5	P/B Ratio	2.7	52 Wk Hi-Low	58.25-46.50
Book Value	1,005.2	1,197.6	1,398.8	16.8	Yield %	2.1	Market Cap	US$3,743.0mil

Address	**Fifth Third Ctr., 38 Fountain Sq. Plz.**	Tel	**513-579-5300**	Exchange	**NASDA**	President & CEO	**George A. Schaefer, Jr.**
	Cincinnati, OH 45263	Fax	**513-579-6020**	Ticker	**FITB**	Chairman	--

First Bank System

Industry: **Banks - Central U.S.**

First Bank System is a holding company for bank and nonbank subsidiaries. The banks operates more than 300 offices, mainly in Colorado, Minnesota, North and South Dakota, and Wisconsin. First Bank System has four core businesses: retail and community banking, commercial banking, payment systems, and trust and investment. Its nonbanking divisions offer services such as insurance-brokerage and mortgage banking. First Bank System also owns Metropolitan Financial, a thrift holding company. In 1995, it agreed to acquire FirsTier Financial.

$ mil	12/92	12/93	12/94	% Change				
Revenues	1,864.2	2,231.4	2,847.0	27.6	P/E Ratio	22.4	Price (9/30/95)	48.13
Net Income	276.0	298.0	305.0	2.3	P/B Ratio	2.5	52 Wk Hi-Low	48.13-32.38
Book Value	2,076.0	2,245.0	2,612.0	16.3	Yield %	2.4	Market Cap	US$6,391.7mil

Address	**601 Second Ave. S.**	Tel	**612-973-1111**	Exchange	**NYSE**	President & CEO	**John F. Grundhofer**
	Minneapolis, MN 55402-4302	Fax	**612-973-3257**	Ticker	**FBS**	Chairman	**John F. Grundhofer**

First Chicago

Industry: **Banks - Money Center**

First Chicago is a bank holding company with subsidiaries that include First National Bank of Chicago, American National Bank and Trust, and several community banks in northern Illinois and southern Wisconsin. At more than 100 locations, its banks offer consumer, corporate, and institutional banking services such as credit cards, mortgage loans, and trust management. The company is also engaged in venture-capital operations and is a major underwriter and distributor of tax-exempt bonds. In 1995, First Chicago agreed to merge with NBD Bancorp.

$ mil	12/92	12/93	12/94	% Change				
Revenues	4,357.8	4,826.5	5,094.6	5.6	P/E Ratio	9.7	Price (9/30/95)	68.63
Net Income	93.5	804.5	689.7	-14.3	P/B Ratio	1.4	52 Wk Hi-Low	68.63-43.13
Book Value	3,401.0	4,264.0	4,533.0	6.3	Yield %	2.8	Market Cap	US$6,157.0mil

Address	**One First National Plz.**	Tel	**312-732-4000**	Exchange	**NYSE**	President	**Leo F. Mullin**
	Chicago, IL 60670	Fax	**312-732-3366**	Ticker	**FNB**	Chairman & CEO	**Richard L. Thomas**

First Colony

Industry: **Insurance - Life & Health**

First Colony is an insurance holding company. Its First Colony Life Insurance and American Mayflower Life Insurance subsidiaries sell individual life-insurance and annuity products. First Colony's insurance policies include annual-premium life, single-premium life, and impaired-risk business insurance. Annuity products include single-premium immediate annuities and single-premium deferred annuities. The company brokers its products through a network of independent agents throughout the United States. Annuity products account for 68% of First Colony's premiums.

$ mil	12/92	12/93	12/94	% Change				
Revenues	1,282.5	1,559.7	1,375.8	-11.8	P/E Ratio	12.9	Price (9/30/95)	27.00
Net Income	163.7	203.9	106.9	-47.6	P/B Ratio	1.3	52 Wk Hi-Low	27.63-21.00
Book Value	819.8	1,094.6	1,014.6	-7.3	Yield %	1.1	Market Cap	US$1,331.2mil

Address	**901 East Byrd St., Riverfront**	Tel	**804-775-0300**	Exchange	**NYSE**	President	**Ronald V. Dolan**
	Richmond, VA 23219	Fax	**N/A**	Ticker	**FCL**	Chairman & CEO	**Bruce C. Gottwald, Jr.**

First Fidelity

Industry: **Banks - Eastern U.S.**

First Fidelity Bancorporation is the bank holding company for First Fidelity, which operates branches in six states in the eastern United States. The bank's wholesale division serves more than 3,500 large businesses, while its community-business subsidiary serves about 3,500 small businesses. The company's consumer-banking division serves 1.6 million households through 550 branches. First Fidelity's money-center subsidiary trades U.S. government securities and short-term fixed-income instruments. The company has agreed to be acquired by First Union.

$ mil	12/92	12/93	12/94	% Change				
Revenues	2,461.7	2,428.7	2,553.1	5.1	P/E Ratio	13.0	Price (9/30/95)	67.50
Net Income	313.7	398.8	451.1	13.1	P/B Ratio	1.9	52 Wk Hi-Low	67.50-41.00
Book Value	2,257.6	2,738.4	2,877.0	5.1	Yield %	2.6	Market Cap	US$5,408.8mil

Address	**550 Broad St.**	Tel	**201-565-3200**	Exchange	**NYSE**	President & CEO	**Anthony P. Terracciano**
	Newark, NJ 07102	Fax	**N/A**	Ticker	**FFB**	Chairman	**Anthony P. Terracciano**

First Financial Management

Industry: **General Industrial & Commercial Services**

First Financial Management provides financial-information services. Services include credit card authorization, check verification, electronic database management, and health-care claims processing. The company operates primarily through its National Bancard, TeleCheck Services, Nationwide Credit, and MicroBilt units. National Bancard is the largest full-service provider of merchant credit-card authorization, processing, and settlement services in the United States. The company's Western Union subsidiary is an international automated money transfer network.

$ mil	12/92	12/93	12/94	% Change				
Sales	**1,388.1**	**1,659.8**	**2,204.1**	**32.8**	P/E Ratio	**38.1**	Price (9/30/95)	**97.63**
Net Income	**45.8**	**127.7**	**160.2**	**25.5**	P/B Ratio	**4.2**	52 Wk Hi-Low	**97.63-70.75**
Book Value	**1,118.3**	**1,248.0**	**1,429.8**	**14.6**	Yield %	**0.1**	Market Cap	**US$6,235.1mil**

Address **Ste. 700, 3 Corporate Sq.**
Atlanta, GA 30329
Tel **404-321-0120**
Fax **N/A**
Exchange **NYSE**
Ticker **FFM**
President & CEO **Patrick H. Thomas**
Chairman **Patrick H. Thomas**

First Hawaiian

Industry: **Banks - Western U.S.**

First Hawaiian is a bank holding company. Its First Hawaiian Bank subsidiary operates 61 branches throughout Hawaii, two in Guam, one in the Cayman Islands, and an office in Tokyo. The company's other subsidiaries include First Hawaiian Creditcorp, a financial-services provider, and First Hawaiian Leasing, which leases commercial equipment and vehicles. First Hawaiian owns Pioneer Federal Savings Bank, a federally chartered bank with 19 branch offices located on Hawaii's four major islands. First Hawaiian also offers trust and investment-management services.

$ mil	12/92	12/93	12/94	% Change				
Revenues	**547.0**	**511.7**	**562.4**	**9.9**	P/E Ratio	**13.1**	Price (9/30/95)	**29.50**
Net Income	**86.9**	**81.9**	**72.5**	**-11.5**	P/B Ratio	**1.5**	52 Wk Hi-Low	**30.50-23.00**
Book Value	**562.2**	**608.4**	**627.9**	**3.2**	Yield %	**4.0**	Market Cap	**US$940.4mil**

Address **1132 Bishop St.**
Honolulu, HI 96813
Tel **808-525-7000**
Fax **808-525-6204**
Exchange **NASDA**
Ticker **FHWN**
President **John A. Hoag**
Chairman & CEO **Walter A. Dods, Jr.**

First Interstate

Industry: **Banks - Western U.S.**

First Interstate Bancorp is a holding company of 16 banks that operate approximately 1,200 branches in 13 states. The company's banks offer consumer, corporate, and international banking services and products to customers in the western United States, primarily in California. The company also has several nonbanking divisions that provide financial services to third parties and affiliated banks. First Interstate Bancorp, through its subsidiaries, offers commercial loans, asset management and investment counseling, bank-card services, mortgage banking, and venture capital.

$ mil	12/92	12/93	12/94	% Change				
Revenues	**4,101.8**	**3,898.3**	**4,246.3**	**8.9**	P/E Ratio	**11.6**	Price (9/30/95)	**100.75**
Net Income	**282.3**	**736.7**	**733.5**	**-0.4**	P/B Ratio	**2.2**	52 Wk Hi-Low	**103.00-66.88**
Book Value	**3,251.1**	**3,548.3**	**3,436.0**	**-3.2**	Yield %	**2.7**	Market Cap	**US$7,655.5mil**

Address **633 W. Fifth St.**
Los Angeles, CA 90071
Tel **213-614-3001**
Fax **213-614-3741**
Exchange **NYSE**
Ticker **I**
President & CEO **William E.B. Siart**
Chairman **Edward M. Carson**

First Security

Industry: **Banks - Western U.S.**

First Security provides financial services to individuals and corporations through its bank and nonbank subsidiaries. Its subsidiary banks operate 261 banking branches in Idaho, Nevada, New Mexico, Oregon, Utah, and Wyoming. The company's First Security Investor Services division is a broker/dealer that offers both discount and full-service-brokerage products to retail customers. First Security's other subsidiaries provide insurance, leasing, mortgage banking, information technology, and investment management services.

$ mil	12/92	12/93	12/94	% Change				
Revenues	**679.7**	**811.9**	**980.1**	**20.7**	P/E Ratio	**11.2**	Price (9/30/95)	**31.38**
Net Income	**86.6**	**114.1**	**140.1**	**22.8**	P/B Ratio	**1.7**	52 Wk Hi-Low	**33.38-22.00**
Book Value	**642.7**	**835.7**	**889.5**	**6.4**	Yield %	**3.3**	Market Cap	**US$1,568.2mil**

Address **79 S. Main St.**
Salt Lake City, UT 84111
Tel **801-246-5706**
Fax **801-359-6928**
Exchange **NASDA**
Ticker **FSCO**
President **Morgan J. Evans**
Chairman & CEO **Spencer F. Eccles**

First Tennessee National

Industry: **Banks - Southern U.S.**

First Tennessee National is a bank holding company. Through its principal subsidiary, First Tennessee Bank National Association, and its other subsidiaries, the company provides a range of financial services. These services include general banking, bond division, underwriting of bank-eligible securities, check clearing, mutual-fund sales, and check-processing software. The company's subsidiary banks operate 223 branches in 20 Tennessee counties, including all of the major metropolitan areas of the state, and eight branches in Mississippi.

$ mil	12/92	12/93	12/94	% Change				
Revenues	**824.3**	**857.0**	**1,057.8**	**23.4**	P/E Ratio	**12.2**	Price (9/30/95)	**55.50**
Net Income	**89.2**	**120.7**	**146.4**	**21.3**	P/B Ratio	**2.4**	52 Wk Hi-Low	**55.63-41.25**
Book Value	**597.5**	**679.0**	**748.8**	**10.3**	Yield %	**3.1**	Market Cap	**US$1,919.3mil**

Address **165 Madison Ave.**
Memphis, TN 38103
Tel **901-523-4444**
Fax **N/A**
Exchange **NASDA**
Ticker **FTEN**
President & CEO **Ralph Horn**
Chairman **Ronald Terry**

First Union

Industry: **Banks - Southern U.S.**

First Union is the ninth-largest bank holding company, by assets, in the United States. The company operates more than 1,300 branches in the South Atlantic region of the United States, providing retail banking and trust services, as well as investment and commercial banking, to more than seven million customers. First Union also maintains 222 branches worldwide that offer mortgage-banking, home-equity lending, asset-based financing, insurance, and securities-brokerage services. In 1995, First Union agreed to acquire First Fidelity Bancorporation.

$ mil	12/92	12/93	12/94	% Change				
Revenues	**4,354.5**	**5,754.6**	**6,253.6**	**8.7**	P/E Ratio	**10.2**	Price (9/30/95)	**51.00**
Net Income	**515.2**	**817.5**	**925.4**	**13.2**	P/B Ratio	**1.7**	52 Wk Hi-Low	**51.38-39.38**
Book Value	**3,831.7**	**5,207.6**	**5,397.5**	**3.6**	Yield %	**3.4**	Market Cap	**US$8,764.5mil**

Address **2 First Union Ctr.**
Charlotte, NC 28288
Tel **704-374-6565**
Fax **704-374-3425**
Exchange **NYSE**
Ticker **FTU**
President **John R. Georgius**
Chairman & CEO **Edward E. Crutchfield**

First USA

Industry: **Financial Services - Diversified**

First USA is a financial-services company focusing exclusively on the credit card business. Through its subsidiary, First USA Bank, the company offers both MasterCard and Visa to more than 10.5 million members throughout the United States. The First USA Merchant Services subsidiary processes merchant credit-card transactions. First USA also provides investment services to other financial institutions through its First USA Capital Markets subsidiary, which also obtains funding for First USA Bank's credit-card loan portfolio and manages its investment portfolio.

$ mil	06/93	06/94	06/95	% Change				
Revenues	**479.7**	**726.6**	**1,082.4**	**49.0**	P/E Ratio	**19.8**	Price (9/30/95)	**54.25**
Net Income	**39.2**	**90.6**	**175.2**	**93.4**	P/B Ratio	**4.3**	52 Wk Hi-Low	**54.25-41.50**
Book Value	**209.8**	**522.0**	**709.0**	**35.8**	Yield %	**0.2**	Market Cap	**US$3,066.9mil**

Address **1601 Elm Street**
Dallas, TX 75201
Tel **214-849-2000**
Fax **N/A**
Exchange **NYSE**
Ticker **FUS**
President **Richard W. Vague**
Chairman & CEO **John C. Tolleson**

First of America Bank

Industry: **Banks - Central U.S.**

First of America Bank is a multi-bank holding company for two bank subsidiaries, which operate more than 600 branches in Florida, Michigan, Indiana, and Illinois. First of America's main subsidiaries offer a range of lending, depository, and related financial services to individual, commercial, and governmental customers. The company also owns nonbanking divisions that provide mortgage banking, trust services, data processing, pension consulting, revolving credit, discount-securities brokerage, and investment-advisory services.

$ mil	12/92	12/93	12/94	% Change				
Revenues	**1,857.4**	**1,803.2**	**1,885.3**	**4.6**	P/E Ratio	**11.7**	Price (9/30/95)	**43.00**
Net Income	**147.5**	**247.4**	**220.5**	**-10.9**	P/B Ratio	**1.7**	52 Wk Hi-Low	**44.63-29.75**
Book Value	**1,335.5**	**1,523.4**	**1,578.9**	**3.6**	Yield %	**3.8**	Market Cap	**US$2,718.1mil**

Address **211 S. Rose St.**
Kalamazoo, MI 49007
Tel **616-376-9000**
Fax **616-376-7273**
Exchange **NYSE**
Ticker **FOA**
President **Richard F. Chormann**
Chairman & CEO **Daniel R. Smith**

Firstar

Industry: **Banks - Central U.S.**

Firstar is a bank holding company principally engaged in consumer and commercial banking through 248 branches in Arizona, Illinois, Iowa, Minnesota, and Wisconsin. The company's main subsidiary is Firstar Bank Milwaukee, which is the largest commercial bank in Wisconsin. Other subsidiaries make business and personal loans, issue and service credit cards, and engage in other consumer- and commercial-banking activities. Firstar also offers international banking services, including foreign trade financing, and owns and manages the Portico family of mutual funds.

$ mil	12/92	12/93	12/94	% Change				
Revenues	**1,199.3**	**1,209.2**	**1,273.2**	**5.3**	P/E Ratio	**11.5**	Price (9/30/95)	**37.13**
Net Income	**166.0**	**204.3**	**207.7**	**1.7**	P/B Ratio	**1.9**	52 Wk Hi-Low	**38.25-25.63**
Book Value	**1,048.4**	**1,155.9**	**1,306.5**	**13.0**	Yield %	**3.1**	Market Cap	**US$2,843.1mil**

Address **777 E. Wisconsin Ave.**
Milwaukee, WI 53202
Tel **414-765-4321**
Fax **414-765-4349**
Exchange **NYSE**
Ticker **FSR**
President **John A. Becker**
Chairman & CEO **Roger L. Fitzsimonds**

Fleet Financial

Industry: **Banks - Eastern U.S.**

Fleet Financial Group is a diversified financial-services organization with 1,200 offices in 38 states. Its subsidiaries include seven banks in New England and New York and 10 financial-services companies located throughout the United States. The company is engaged in commercial- and consumer-banking and trust businesses through its bank subsidiaries. Fleet Financial Group also provides mortgage-banking, asset-based lending, securities-brokerage, municipal-securities-underwriting, and student-loan-processing services. A merger with Shawmut National is pending.

$ mil	12/92	12/93	12/94	% Change				
Revenues	**4,852.1**	**4,677.0**	**4,445.0**	**-5.0**	P/E Ratio	**10.1**	Price (9/30/95)	**37.75**
Net Income	**279.8**	**488.0**	**613.0**	**25.6**	P/B Ratio	**1.5**	52 Wk Hi-Low	**39.13-30.25**
Book Value	**3,010.4**	**3,639.0**	**3,380.0**	**-7.1**	Yield %	**3.7**	Market Cap	**US$5,357.6mil**

Address **50 Kennedy Plz.**
Providence, RI 02903
Tel **401-278-5800**
Fax **401-278-3685**
Exchange **NYSE**
Ticker **FLT**
President & CEO **Terrence Murray**
Chairman **Terrence Murray**

Fleming

Industry: **Food Retailers & Wholesalers**

Fleming distributes food and serves as the principal supply source for 3,700 supermarkets, in 43 states across the United States and in several foreign countries; the largest concentration is on the East Coast. In addition, the company owns and operates 350 supermarkets. The company distributes national and private-label brand groceries, meats, dairy and delicatessen products, frozen foods, fresh produce, and a variety of general merchandise and related items. Fleming's brands include Bonnie Hubbard, Captain's Cove, Fleming's, IGA, Marquee Premium, and Montco, among others.

$ mil	12/92	12/93	12/94	% Change				
Sales	**12,937.9**	**13,092.1**	**15,753.5**	**20.3**	P/E Ratio	**15.9**	Price (9/30/95)	**24.00**
Net Income	**113.0**	**35.2**	**56.2**	**59.6**	P/B Ratio	**0.8**	52 Wk Hi-Low	**29.75-19.38**
Book Value	**1,060.4**	**1,060.4**	**1,078.6**	**1.7**	Yield %	**5.0**	Market Cap	**US$902.3mil**

Address **6301 Waterford Blvd.**
Oklahoma City, OK 73126-0647
Tel **405-840-7200**
Fax **405-841-8749**
Exchange **NYSE**
Ticker **FLM**
President & CEO **Robert E. Stauth**
Chairman **Robert E. Stauth**

FlightSafety

Industry: **General Industrial & Commercial Services**

FlightSafety International provides technology training to operators of aircraft, ships, and power plants. The company owns and operates a fleet of more than 165 simulators and training devices. It also designs, manufactures, and sells full-motion flight simulators and other training equipment through its Simulation Systems Division, and visual displays and systems for flight simulators through its Visual Simulation Systems Division. The company's Instructional Systems Division develops classroom-presentation systems, interactive software, courseware, and manuals.

$ mil	12/92	12/93	12/94	% Change				
Sales	**278.4**	**297.1**	**301.3**	**1.4**	P/E Ratio	**19.5**	Price (9/30/95)	**45.88**
Net Income	**82.3**	**66.4**	**74.5**	**12.2**	P/B Ratio	**2.6**	52 Wk Hi-Low	**49.25-36.88**
Book Value	**564.4**	**526.4**	**560.4**	**6.5**	Yield %	**1.0**	Market Cap	**US$1,435.6mil**

Address **Marine Air, LaGuardia Airport**
Flushing, NY 11371
Tel **718-565-4100**
Fax **718-565-4134**
Exchange **NYSE**
Ticker **FSI**
President **Albert L. Ueltschi**
Chairman **Albert L. Ueltschi**

Fluor

Industry: **Heavy Construction**

Fluor provides engineering, procurement, construction, maintenance, and related services. The company operates worldwide through its subsidiaries, including Fluor Daniel, serving industrial, commercial, utility, natural resources, energy, and governmental clients. Projects include feasibility studies and conceptual design. The company also invests in coal-related businesses through its Massey Coal Company, which produces, processes, and sells bituminous, low-sulfur coal of steam and metallurgical grade from 16 mining complexes. The steam coal is sold to domestic utilities.

$ mil	10/92	10/93	10/94	% Change				
Sales	**6,600.7**	**7,850.2**	**8,485.3**	**8.1**	P/E Ratio	**24.1**	Price (9/30/95)	**56.00**
Net Income	**5.8**	**166.8**	**192.4**	**15.3**	P/B Ratio	**3.8**	52 Wk Hi-Low	**59.25-41.50**
Book Value	**880.8**	**1,044.1**	**1,220.5**	**16.9**	Yield %	**0.9**	Market Cap	**US$4,634.9mil**

Address **3333 Michelson Dr.**
Irvine, CA 92730
Tel **714-975-2000**
Fax **714-975-5981**
Exchange **NYSE**
Ticker **FLR**
Chief Executive **Leslie G. McCraw**
Chairman **Leslie G. McCraw**

FMC

Industry: **Industrial - Diversified**

FMC produces chemicals, defense systems, and machinery. Its chemicals include phosphorous compounds, lithium-based products, and crop-protection chemicals used by industrial and agricultural customers. FMC designs defense systems for the governments of the U.S. and its allies. These products include tanks, armaments, launching systems, and naval guns. The company also manufacturers a variety of machinery and equipment used in the petroleum, airline, automotive, and food-processing industries. In addition, FMC mines for gold and silver in the U.S. and in Latin America.

$ mil	12/92	12/93	12/94	% Change				
Sales	**3,973.7**	**3,753.9**	**4,010.8**	**6.8**	P/E Ratio	**16.3**	Price (9/30/95)	**76.00**
Net Income	**-75.7**	**36.3**	**173.4**	**377.7**	P/B Ratio	**6.7**	52 Wk Hi-Low	**79.50-56.25**
Book Value	**219.0**	**216.9**	**416.5**	**92.0**	Yield %	**0.0**	Market Cap	**US$2,781.5mil**

Address **200 E. Randolph Dr.**
Chicago, IL 60601
Tel **312-861-6000**
Fax **800-621-4500**
Exchange **NYSE**
Ticker **FMC**
President **Larry D. Brady**
Chairman & CEO **Robert N. Burt**

FNMA

Industry: **Financial Services - Diversified**

Federal National Mortgage Association (FNMA) is a federally chartered, stockholder-owned company and is the largest secondary buyer of real-estate mortgages in the U.S. It was chartered by the U.S. government to help provide low- and moderate-income-family housing by purchasing mortgage loans from lenders, thereby replenishing their funds for additional lending. The company also issues mortgage-backed securities in exchange for pools of mortgage loans from lenders. FNMA's income is mainly derived from the difference between interest rates on mortgages and borrowed money.

$ mil	12/92	12/93	12/94	% Change				
Revenues	**14,559.0**	**16,053.0**	**18,573.0**	**15.7**	P/E Ratio	**13.3**	Price (9/30/95)	**103.50**
Net Income	**1,623.0**	**1,873.0**	**2,132.0**	**13.8**	P/B Ratio	**3.0**	52 Wk Hi-Low	**105.38-68.13**
Book Value	**6,774.0**	**8,052.0**	**9,541.0**	**18.5**	Yield %	**2.3**	Market Cap	**US$28,235mil**

Address **3900 Wisconsin Ave. N.W.**
Washington, DC 20016-2899
Tel **202-752-7000**
Fax **202-752-6158**
Exchange **NYSE**
Ticker **FNM**
President **Lawrence M. Small**
Chairman & CEO **James A. Johnson**

Food Lion

Industry: **Food Retailers & Wholesalers**

Food Lion operates retail food supermarkets principally in the southeastern United States. The company has more than 1,000 supermarkets in operation averaging 26,500 square feet in size. These stores, which operate under the Food Lion name, sell groceries, fresh produce, meats and poultry, dairy products, seafood, frozen foods, deli and bakery, and nonfood items such as tobacco, health and beauty aids, and other household and personal products. It offers nationally and regionally advertised brand-name merchandise, as well as products under the private Food Lion label.

$ mil	12/92	12/93	12/94	% Change				
Sales	**7,195.9**	**7,609.8**	**7,932.6**	**4.2**	P/E Ratio	**18.9**	Price (9/30/95)	**6.06**
Net Income	**178.0**	**3.9**	**152.9**	**NMF**	P/B Ratio	**2.9**	52 Wk Hi-Low	**6.63-4.94**
Book Value	**955.7**	**917.6**	**1,027.4**	**12.0**	Yield %	**1.5**	Market Cap	**US$2,920.5mil**

Address **2110 Executive Dr.**
Salisbury, NC 28145-1330
Tel **704-633-8250**
Fax **704-636-5024**
Exchange **NASDA**
Ticker **FDLN**
President & CEO **Tom E. Smith**
Chairman **Tom E. Smith**

Ford Motor

Industry: **Automobile Manufacturers**

Ford Motor manufactures automobiles and provides financial services. It produces cars and trucks ranging from the subcompact class to the luxury class. It markets these vehicles under the Ford and Jaguar brands and the Taurus, Mustang, Thunderbird, Explorer, Escort, and other models in the United States and internationally. Ford also provides financial services through its Ford Motor Credit subsidiary; these services include automobile loans and leases, as well as personal loans and savings accounts. Business operations outside the U.S. account for 30% of revenues.

$ mil	12/92	12/93	12/94	% Change				
Sales	**100,132.3**	**108,521.0**	**128,439.0**	**18.4**	P/E Ratio	**6.3**	Price (9/30/95)	**31.13**
Net Income	**-7,385.0**	**2,529.0**	**5,308.0**	**109.9**	P/B Ratio	**1.5**	52 Wk Hi-Low	**32.88-24.75**
Book Value	**14,752.9**	**15,574.0**	**21,659.0**	**39.1**	Yield %	**2.9**	Market Cap	**US$33,431mil**

Address **The American Rd.**
Dearborn, MI 48121-1899
Tel **313-322-3000**
Fax **313-322-7896**
Exchange **NYSE**
Ticker **F**
President & CEO **Alexander J. Trotman**
Chairman **Alexander J. Trotman**

Foster Wheeler

Industry: **Heavy Construction**

Foster Wheeler builds industrial facilities worldwide and manufactures related equipment. The company's engineering and construction division builds chemical plants, refineries, and petroleum-field equipment, and provides related engineering, management, and environmental services. Its energy-equipment division manufactures steam generators, nuclear-power-plant equipment, and chemical-processing equipment. Its power-systems division offers venture-capital financing and builds, manages, and operates waste-to-energy, recycling, cogeneration, and water-treatment plants.

$ mil	12/92	12/93	12/94	% Change				
Sales	**2,494.8**	**2,583.0**	**2,234.4**	**-13.5**	P/E Ratio	**19.3**	Price (9/30/95)	**35.38**
Net Income	**-45.8**	**57.7**	**65.4**	**13.4**	P/B Ratio	**2.8**	52 Wk Hi-Low	**38.75-27.00**
Book Value	**387.3**	**400.2**	**456.5**	**14.1**	Yield %	**2.0**	Market Cap	**US$1,268.4mil**

Address **Perryville Corporate Pk.**
Clinton, NJ 08809-4000
Tel **908-730-4000**
Fax **908-730-5315**
Exchange **NYSE**
Ticker **FWC**
President & CEO **Richard J. Swift**
Chairman **Richard J. Swift**

FPL

Industry: **Electrical Utilities - Southern U.S.**

FPL Group is a holding company with utility, agricultural, and service operations in Florida. Its Florida Power & Light subsidiary supplies electric service to 3.4 million customers in a service area that covers much of Florida. Residential customers account for approximately 55% of revenues; commercial and industrial users contribute another 39% of the total. The company generates about 32% of its electricity with oil, 25% with nuclear energy, 17% with natural gas, and 5% with coal. FPL also provides cable-television services and manages 29,000 acres of citrus groves.

$ mil	12/92	12/93	12/94	% Change				
Sales	**5,193.3**	**5,316.3**	**5,422.7**	**2.0**	P/E Ratio	**14.0**	Price (9/30/95)	**40.88**
Net Income	**466.9**	**428.7**	**518.7**	**21.0**	P/B Ratio	**1.6**	52 Wk Hi-Low	**40.88-31.50**
Book Value	**4,387.4**	**4,648.8**	**4,742.5**	**2.0**	Yield %	**4.6**	Market Cap	**US$7,566.0mil**

Address **700 Universe Blvd.**
Juno Beach, FL 33408
Tel **407-694-4000**
Fax **407-694-4999**
Exchange **NYSE**
Ticker **FPL**
President & CEO **James L. Broadhead**
Chairman **James L. Broadhead**

Fruit of the Loom

Industry: **Clothing & Fabrics**

Fruit of the Loom is an integrated clothing manufacturer that specializes in underwear and activewear. The company is the largest underwear maker in the United States by market share, selling briefs, boxer shorts, and T-shirts under brands that include Fruit of the Loom, BVD, and Munsingwear, and supplying T-shirts to screen printers under the Screen Stars and Best labels. It produces imprinted sportswear through licensing agreements with colleges, professional athletic teams, the Walt Disney Company, and Warner Brothers. The company also makes socks and women's briefs.

$ mil	12/92	12/93	12/94	% Change				
Sales	**1,855.1**	**1,884.4**	**2,297.8**	**21.9**	P/E Ratio	**26.1**	Price (9/30/95)	**20.63**
Net Income	**178.6**	**207.5**	**60.3**	**-70.9**	P/B Ratio	**1.4**	52 Wk Hi-Low	**29.63-20.25**
Book Value	**855.0**	**1,047.0**	**1,125.8**	**7.5**	Yield %	**0.0**	Market Cap	**US$1,565.1mil**

Address **Sears Tower, 233 S. Wacker Dr.**
Chicago, IL 60606
Tel **312-876-1724**
Fax **312-993-1749**
Exchange **NYSE**
Ticker **FTL**
President **John B. Holland**
Chairman & CEO **William Farley**

Gannett

Industry: **Publishing**

Gannett provides news and information services throughout North America. The company publishes 83 daily newspapers, including USA Today and more than 50 nondaily publications. It also operates 10 television stations, 11 AM and FM radio stations, and the largest outdoor-advertising company in North America, with operations in 11 states and Canada. It also offers research, marketing, commercial-printing, newswire, and news-programming services. Newspaper publishing sales accounts for about 83% of the company's total revenues. In 1995, the company agreed to acquire Multimedia.

$ mil	12/92	12/93	12/94	% Change				
Sales	**3,469.0**	**3,641.6**	**3,824.5**	**5.0**	P/E Ratio	**16.9**	Price (9/30/95)	**54.63**
Net Income	**199.7**	**397.8**	**465.4**	**17.0**	P/B Ratio	**4.2**	52 Wk Hi-Low	**55.75-46.75**
Book Value	**1,580.1**	**1,907.9**	**1,822.2**	**-4.5**	Yield %	**2.5**	Market Cap	**US$7,656.1mil**

Address **1100 Wilson Blvd.**
Arlington, VA 22234
Tel **703-284-6000**
Fax **703-558-4634**
Exchange **NYSE**
Ticker **GCI**
President & CEO **John J. Curley**
Chairman **John J. Curley**

The Gap

Industry: **Apparel Retailers**

Gap is a specialty retailer that operates stores selling casual apparel for men, women, and children under private-label brand names. These brands are marketed under Gap, GapKids, babyGap, GapShoes, and Banana Republic names. The company operates 1,525 stores including 810 Gap, 330 GapKids, 192 Banana Republic, and 65 Old Navy Clothing Co. stores throughout the United States, United Kingdom, Canada, and France. Virtually all stores are leased; no stores are franchised or operated by others. About 70% of the dollar value of its merchandise is imported from overseas vendors.

$ mil	01/93	01/94	01/95	% Change				
Revenues	**2,960.4**	**3,295.7**	**3,722.9**	**13.0**	P/E Ratio	**16.4**	Price (9/30/95)	**36.00**
Net Income	**210.7**	**258.4**	**320.2**	**23.9**	P/B Ratio	**3.8**	52 Wk Hi-Low	**38.00-29.13**
Book Value	**887.8**	**1,126.5**	**1,375.2**	**22.1**	Yield %	**1.3**	Market Cap	**US$5,186.1mil**

Address **One Harrison**
San Francisco, CA 94105
Tel **415-952-4400**
Fax **415-952-4069**
Exchange **NYSE**
Ticker **GPS**
President **Millard S. Drexler**
Chairman & CEO **Donald G. Fisher**

GEICO

Industry: **Insurance - Property & Casualty**

GEICO is the parent company of the Government Employees Insurance Company, which offers motor-vehicle, homeowners', and other types of insurance to active and retired military personnel and federal-government employees. GEICO General Insurance, a subsidiary, provides auto insurance to standard- and preferred-risk individuals not employed by the government. GEICO, through another subsidiary, also engages in secured consumer and business lending. The company's offices are concentrated primarily in the eastern United States.

$ mil	12/92	12/93	12/94	% Change				
Revenues	**2,420.0**	**2,638.3**	**2,716.0**	**2.9**	P/E Ratio	**23.0**	Price (9/30/95)	**68.25**
Net Income	**172.8**	**273.7**	**207.8**	**-24.1**	P/B Ratio	**3.2**	52 Wk Hi-Low	**68.63-47.75**
Book Value	**1,292.5**	**1,534.6**	**1,445.9**	**-5.8**	Yield %	**1.5**	Market Cap	**US$4,621.9mil**

Address **1 Geico Plz.**
Washington, D.C. 20076-0001
Tel **301-986-2500**
Fax **301-986-2113**
Exchange **NYSE**
Ticker **GEC**
President **Louis A. Simpson**
Chairman **Olza M. Nicely**

Gencorp

Industry: **Aerospace & Defense**

GenCorp manufactures technology-based products for military and industrial customers. It has three primary divisions: Aerojet, which develops solid and liquid rocket-propulsion systems, defense electronics, and ordnance products; GenCorp Automotive, which produces rubber and plastic automotive parts; and GenCorp Polymer, which manufactures polymers and plastic products. Aerojet is a contractor for the U.S. Government's Titan, Peacekeeper, Minuteman, Small ICBM, Advanced Solid Rocket Motor, and Delta propulsion programs. GenCorp's customers include General Motors.

$ mil	11/92	11/93	11/94	% Change				
Sales	**1,937.0**	**1,905.0**	**1,740.0**	**-8.7**	P/E Ratio	**NMF**	Price (9/30/95)	**10.63**
Net Income	**22.0**	**43.0**	**-226.0**	**-625.6**	P/B Ratio	**NMF**	52 Wk Hi-Low	**14.13-10.00**
Book Value	**213.0**	**235.0**	**-7.0**	**-103.0**	Yield %	**5.6**	Market Cap	**US$348.4mil**

Address **175 Ghent Rd.**
Fairlawn, OH 44333-3300
Tel **216-869-4200**
Fax **216-869-4288**
Exchange **NYSE**
Ticker **GY**
President & CEO **John B. Yasinsky**
Chairman **A. William Reynolds**

General Dynamics

Industry: **Aerospace & Defense**

General Dynamics manufactures military vehicles and related products. The company's Electric Boat Division produces Trident and Seawolf nuclear submarines, and its Land Systems Division designs battle tanks, including the M1 Series Abrams tank. The company markets these vehicles to the U.S. Department of Defense and foreign defense agencies. Sales to foreign governments (including foreign military sales made through the U.S. government) account for roughly 24% of net sales. In addition, General Dynamics' Freeman subsidiary operates coal mines in Illinois and Kentucky.

$ mil	12/92	12/93	12/94	% Change				
Sales	**3,472.0**	**3,187.0**	**3,058.0**	**-4.0**	P/E Ratio	**14.6**	Price (9/30/95)	**54.88**
Net Income	**815.0**	**885.0**	**238.0**	**-73.1**	P/B Ratio	**2.6**	52 Wk Hi-Low	**55.75-38.63**
Book Value	**1,874.0**	**1,177.0**	**1,316.0**	**11.8**	Yield %	**2.6**	Market Cap	**US$3,455.4mil**

Address **3190 Fairview Pk. Dr.**
Falls Church, VA 22042-4523
Tel **703-876-3000**
Fax **703-876-3125**
Exchange **NYSE**
Ticker **GD**
Chief Executive **James R. Mellor**
Chairman **James R. Mellor**

Industry: **Conglomerates**

General Electric

General Electric (GE) provides financial services and produces industrial products, power-generation systems, aerospace systems, home appliances, and engineered materials. It provides consumer- and commercial-financial, as well as equipment-management services through its GE Capital subsidiary. In addition, it owns the National Broadcasting Company (NBC), which includes the broadcast network, its owned-and-operated stations, and cable-TV interests. The company markets its products and services worldwide. Operations abroad account for about 22% of revenues.

	$ mil 12/92	12/93	12/94	% Change				
Sales	57,073.0	60,562.0	60,109.0	-0.7	P/E Ratio	23.0	Price (9/30/95)	63.75
Net Income	4,725.0	4,315.0	4,726.0	9.5	P/B Ratio	4.1	52 Wk Hi-Low	64.63-45.50
Book Value	23,459.0	25,824.0	26,387.0	2.2	Yield %	2.3	Market Cap	US$107,255mil

Address **3135 Easton Turnpike, Fairfield, CT 06431**
Tel **203-373-2211** Fax **203-373-2884**
Exchange **NYSE** Ticker **GE**
Chief Executive **John F. Welch, Jr.** Chairman **John F. Welch, Jr.**

Industry: **Communications Technology**

General Instrument

General Instrument (GI) supplies systems and equipment to the cable- and satellite-television industries. Its communications division provides subscriber systems worldwide, with products including interactive digital cable converters, wireless systems, video on demand, satellite-television encryption systems, and fiber optic cables. In addition, GI has developed DigiCipher, a technology allowing greater amounts of information to be transmitted by existing satellite systems. GI's power semiconductor division produces power-control and voltage-suppression components.

	$ mil 12/92	12/93	12/94	% Change				
Sales	1,074.7	1,392.5	2,036.3	46.2	P/E Ratio	15.0	Price (9/30/95)	30.00
Net Income	-53.0	90.6	246.5	172.1	P/B Ratio	5.4	52 Wk Hi-Low	41.63-27.00
Book Value	291.3	389.1	677.2	74.0	Yield %	0.0	Market Cap	US$3,698.3mil

Address **181 W. Madison St., Chicago, IL 60602**
Tel **312-541-5000** Fax **312-541-8038**
Exchange **NYSE** Ticker **GIC**
President **Richard S. Friedland** Chairman & CEO **David F. Akerson**

Industry: **Other Food**

General Mills

General Mills produces packaged foods, including breakfast cereals, baking goods, snack and convenience foods, flour, frozen yogurt, and beverages that it markets under the Lucky Charms, Cheerios, Total, Wheaties, Betty Crocker, Hamburger Helper, Pop Secret, Bisquick, Bac*O's, Columbo, and Yoplait trademarks. Cereal Partners Worldwide, its joint venture with Nestle, markets breakfast cereal abroad. The company's Snack Ventures Europe joint venture with PepsiCo sells snack foods in Holland, France, Belgium, Spain, Portugal, and Greece.

	$ mil 05/93	05/94	05/95	% Change				
Sales	8,134.6	8,516.9	5,026.7	-41.0	P/E Ratio	23.9	Price (9/30/95)	55.75
Net Income	506.1	469.9	367.4	-21.8	P/B Ratio	NMF	52 Wk Hi-Low	56.75-44.11
Book Value	1,218.5	1,151.2	141.0	-87.8	Yield %	3.4	Market Cap	US$8,836.4mil

Address **One General Mills Blvd., Minneapolis, MN 55426**
Tel **612-540-2311** Fax **612-540-4925**
Exchange **NYSE** Ticker **GIS**
President **Charles W. Gaillard** Chairman & CEO **Stephen W. Sanger**

Industry: **Automobile Manufacturers**

General Motors

General Motors is one of the three largest U.S. manufacturers of automobiles, trucks, and related parts. Its vehicles are sold under the GMC Truck, Chevrolet, Oldsmobile, Pontiac, Buick, and Cadillac names. It also operates General Motors Acceptance Corporation, a car finance and insurance concern and GM Hughes Electronics, an automotive-electronics company. The company also produces military vehicles, weapon-control systems, guided-missiles, and defense and commercial satellites. General Motors plans to spin off its Electronic Data Systems subsidiary.

	$ mil 12/92	12/93	12/94	% Change				
Sales	132,429.4	138,219.5	154,951.2	12.1	P/E Ratio	9.1	Price (9/30/95)	46.88
Net Income	-23,498.3	2,465.8	4,900.6	98.7	P/B Ratio	2.8	52 Wk Hi-Low	51.88-36.63
Book Value	6,225.6	5,597.5	12,823.8	129.1	Yield %	1.7	Market Cap	US$35,035mil

Address **3044 W. Grand Blvd., Detroit, MI 48202-3091**
Tel **313-556-5000** Fax **313-556-5108**
Exchange **NYSE** Ticker **GM**
President & CEO **John F. Smith, Jr.** Chairman **John G. Smale**

Industry: **Electrical Utilities - Eastern U.S.**

General Public Utilities

General Public Utilities (GPU) generates electrical power and provides related services. The company provides electricity to approximately 1.9 million customers in New Jersey and Pennsylvania. Service is delivered through GPU's subsidiaries: Jersey Central Power & Light, Metropolitan Edison, and Pennsylvania Electric. Residential customers account for about 32% of electrical-energy sales, and industrial and commercial customers roughly 68%. GPU generates about 75% of its electricity from coal and other fossil fuels; the remainder comes primarily from nuclear-power plants.

	$ mil 12/92	12/93	12/94	% Change				
Sales	3,434.2	3,596.1	3,649.5	1.5	P/E Ratio	21.9	Price (9/30/95)	31.13
Net Income	251.6	295.7	163.7	-44.6	P/B Ratio	1.4	52 Wk Hi-Low	31.13-24.25
Book Value	2,379.3	2,610.4	2,572.6	-1.4	Yield %	5.7	Market Cap	US$3,620.5mil

Address **100 Interpace Pkwy., Parsippany, NJ 07054-1149**
Tel **201-263-6500** Fax **201-263-6822**
Exchange **NYSE** Ticker **GPU**
President & CEO **James R. Leva** Chairman **James R. Leva**

General Re

Industry: **Insurance - Property & Casualty**

General Re is the holding company for General Reinsurance and its affiliates, which together constitute the General Re Group. It provides reinsurance, insurance, and related services throughout the U.S. and in more than 30 other countries. The company's main business is domestic property and casualty reinsurance; it is the largest property and casualty reinsurer in the U.S. and the third largest in the world. In addition to insurance and reinsurance operations, the company operates in the securities derivatives market through its General Re Financial Products subsidiary.

$ mil	12/92	12/93	12/94	% Change				
Revenues	3,386.8	3,560.0	3,837.0	7.8	P/E Ratio	18.9	Price (9/30/95)	151.00
Net Income	657.4	711.0	665.0	-6.5	P/B Ratio	2.5	52 Wk Hi-Low	152.13-105.00
Book Value	4,227.4	4,762.0	4,860.0	2.1	Yield %	1.3	Market Cap	US$12,386mil

Address **Financial Ctr., 695 E. Main St.**
Stamford, CT 06904-2351
Tel **203-328-5000**
Fax **203-328-6423**
Exchange **NYSE**
Ticker **GRN**
President & CEO **Ronald E. Ferguson**
Chairman **Ronald E. Ferguson**

General Signal

Industry: **Industrial Technology**

General Signal makes instrumentation and systems used in a variety of industries. These products include automotive components, telecommunication components, industrial-fluid mixers, fire-detection systems, uninterruptible-power supplies, power-conditioning equipment, and industrial pumps and valves. These products are used in telecommunication transmission, electronic testing and measurement, management of electrical energy, and transportation. It markets its products to end users in the United States and internationally. Sales abroad account for 10% of revenues.

$ mil	12/92	12/93	12/94	% Change				
Sales	1,618.3	1,530.0	1,527.7	-0.2	P/E Ratio	17.1	Price (9/30/95)	29.25
Net Income	-83.2	34.7	80.7	132.6	P/B Ratio	2.5	52 Wk Hi-Low	42.25-28.50
Book Value	365.0	525.2	547.9	4.3	Yield %	3.1	Market Cap	US$1,389.3mil

Address **One High Ridge Pk.**
Stamford, CT 06904
Tel **203-329-4100**
Fax **203-329-4159**
Exchange **NYSE**
Ticker **GSX**
President **Michael D. Lockhart**
Chairman & CEO **Edmund M. Carpenter**

Genuine Parts

Industry: **Other Auto Parts**

Genuine Parts distributes replacement parts for automobiles, trucks, and industrial equipment. Its National Automotive Parts Association (NAPA) distribution centers sell to more than 5,800 auto-parts stores. The industrial-parts division distributes bearings, fluid-transmission equipment, and materials-handling components. The company also sells office products including furniture, desk supplies, and electronic business equipment such as calculators and copiers. Its Berry Bearing Company subsidiary distributes industrial replacement parts and related supplies.

$ mil	12/92	12/93	12/94	% Change				
Sales	3,668.8	4,384.3	4,858.4	10.8	P/E Ratio	17.2	Price (9/30/95)	40.13
Net Income	219.8	257.8	288.6	11.9	P/B Ratio	3.2	52 Wk Hi-Low	40.63-34.13
Book Value	1,235.4	1,445.3	1,526.2	5.6	Yield %	2.9	Market Cap	US$4,926.1mil

Address **2999 Circle 75 Pkwy.**
Atlanta, GA 30339
Tel **404-953-1700**
Fax **404-956-2212**
Exchange **NYSE**
Ticker **GPC**
President **Thomas C. Gallagher**
Chairman & CEO **Larry L. Prince**

Georgia-Pacific

Industry: **Forest Products**

Georgia-Pacific manufactures forest products and gypsum wallboard. It manages approximately six million acres of timberland, primarily in the southern United States. The company makes plywood, strand board, dimensional lumber, and gypsum wallboard, which it sells, along with similar goods purchased from outside companies, to the construction industry and the retail market. Georgia-Pacific also makes pulp, adhesives, and resins for use in papermaking, and paper products such as packaging materials, printing papers, Coronet paper towels, and Angel Soft bathroom tissue.

$ mil	12/92	12/93	12/94	% Change				
Sales	11,847.0	12,330.0	12,738.0	3.3	P/E Ratio	25.1	Price (9/30/95)	87.50
Net Income	-124.0	-34.0	310.0	NMF	P/B Ratio	3.0	52 Wk Hi-Low	95.00-67.50
Book Value	2,508.0	2,402.0	2,620.0	9.1	Yield %	1.8	Market Cap	US$7,963.0mil

Address **133 Peachtree St. N.E.**
Atlanta, GA 30303
Tel **404-652-4000**
Fax **404-827-7010**
Exchange **NYSE**
Ticker **GP**
Chief Executive **A.D. Correll**
Chairman **A.D. Correll**

Giant Food

Industry: **Food Retailers & Wholesalers**

Giant Food operates a chain of supermarkets. These 157 supermarkets are located in the Washington, DC area and other locations in Maryland and Virginia. The company's non-supermarket-support subsidiaries include stores operating under their own names as well as Cole Engineering, Warex-Jessup, Landover Wholesale Tobacco, LECO, Bursil, GFS Realty, GF McLean Shopping Center, Super G, Inc., Montrose Crossing, Friendship Macomb SC, Bayside Traffic Services, and the 85%-owned Shaw Community Supermarket. The company also operates three freestanding drugstores.

$ mil	02/93	02/94	02/95	% Change				
Sales	3,472.6	3,567.5	3,695.6	3.6	P/E Ratio	19.7	Price (9/30/95)	31.38
Net Income	81.5	95.2	94.2	-1.1	P/B Ratio	2.5	52 Wk Hi-Low	32.50-21.38
Book Value	663.0	713.4	755.5	5.9	Yield %	2.3	Market Cap	US$1,859.8mil

Address **6400 Sheriff Rd.**
Landover, MD 20785
Tel **301-341-4100**
Fax **301-341-4804**
Exchange **AMEX**
Ticker **GFS**
President **Pete L. Manos**
Chairman & CEO **Israel Cohen**

Giddings & Lewis

Industry: **Factory Equipment**

Giddings & Lewis manufactures industrial automation equipment and machine tools. The company's markets, which include the automotive, construction, aerospace, appliance, energy, and electronics industries, span approximately 250 industries in nearly 70 countries. Its automated-assembly systems are used to assemble automotive airbags, engines, and transmissions and household appliances. Giddings & Lewis' machine-tool products include lathes; boring, drilling, and milling machines; and machining centers. The company also provides consulting services to its customers.

$ mil	12/92	12/93	12/94	% Change				
Sales	**622.9**	**517.5**	**619.5**	**19.7**	P/E Ratio	**12.5**	Price (9/30/95)	**17.44**
Net Income	**35.5**	**43.7**	**47.9**	**9.6**	P/B Ratio	**1.2**	52 Wk Hi-Low	**18.88-13.88**
Book Value	**325.9**	**436.0**	**485.3**	**11.3**	Yield %	**0.7**	Market Cap	**US$599.9mil**

Address **142 Doty St.**
Fond du Lac, WI 54936-0590
Tel **414-921-9400**
Fax **414-929-4455**
Exchange **NASDA**
Ticker **GIDL**
Chief Executive **Joseph R. Coppola**
Chairman **Joseph R. Coppola**

Gillette

Industry: **Cosmetics & Personal Care**

Gillette produces toiletries, including razors, and writing instruments. Its Braun division is the largest seller of electric shavers in Germany, and is a major seller in Europe, North America, and Japan. The company's Oral-B toothbrushes are sold internationally. Other products include Right Guard deodorant, Gillette Sensor razors and blades, Braun coffeemakers, and Paper Mate, Parker and Liquid Paper stationery products. Products are manufactured at 62 facilities in 28 countries and distributed through wholesalers, retailers, and agents in more than 200 countries.

$ mil	12/92	12/93	12/94	% Change				
Sales	**5,162.8**	**5,410.8**	**6,070.2**	**12.2**	P/E Ratio	**30.3**	Price (9/30/95)	**47.63**
Net Income	**513.4**	**288.3**	**698.3**	**142.2**	P/B Ratio	**10.5**	52 Wk Hi-Low	**48.00-34.88**
Book Value	**1,496.4**	**1,479.0**	**2,017.3**	**36.4**	Yield %	**1.0**	Market Cap	**US$21,118mil**

Address **Prudential Tower Bldg.**
Boston, MA 02199
Tel **617-421-7000**
Fax **617-421-7123**
Exchange **NYSE**
Ticker **G**
Chief Executive **Alfred M. Zeien**
Chairman **Alfred M. Zeien**

Global Marine

Industry: **Oil Drilling**

Global Marine operates oil and natural-gas wells in the U.S. and provides worldwide oil-field services. The company owns, on average, a 15% interest in 46 wells in the Gulf of Mexico and on the Gulf Coast and holds net reserves of 12 billion cubic feet of gas and 655,000 barrels of oil. Its oil field-services subsidiaries include Global Marine Drilling, which operates a fleet of 56 offshore contract-drilling rigs, primarily in the North Sea, the Gulf of Mexico, and off the coast of West Africa; and Applied Drilling Technology, which offers oil-field-consulting services.

$ mil	12/92	12/93	12/94	% Change				
Sales	**260.3**	**269.0**	**359.0**	**33.5**	P/E Ratio	**NMF**	Price (9/30/95)	**7.13**
Net Income	**57.2**	**-26.5**	**1.3**	**-104.9**	P/B Ratio	**5.5**	52 Wk Hi-Low	**7.38-3.50**
Book Value	**154.5**	**205.4**	**212.3**	**3.4**	Yield %	**0.0**	Market Cap	**US$1,176.5mil**

Address **777 N. Eldridge Rd.**
Houston, TX 77079
Tel **713-596-5100**
Fax **713-531-1260**
Exchange **NYSE**
Ticker **GLM**
President & CEO **C. Russell Luigs**
Chairman **C. Russell Luigs**

Golden West Financial

Industry: **Savings & Loans (U.S. Only)**

Golden West Financial is a savings and loan holding company. Through its main subsidiary, World Savings and Loan, the company operates 263 savings branch offices and 198 loan-origination offices, primarily in California and Colorado. The company's other subsidiaries include Atlas Advisers and Atlas Securities. These companies provide services to Atlas Assets, an open-end registered investment company. Through its subsidiaries, Golden West Financial owns and manages the Atlas family of mutual funds, as well as being the sole distributor of Atlas fund shares.

$ mil	12/92	12/93	12/94	% Change				
Revenues	**2,025.6**	**1,932.2**	**1,914.0**	**-0.9**	P/E Ratio	**13.6**	Price (9/30/95)	**50.50**
Net Income	**283.5**	**273.9**	**230.5**	**-15.9**	P/B Ratio	**1.5**	52 Wk Hi-Low	**52.00-34.25**
Book Value	**1,727.4**	**2,065.6**	**2,000.3**	**-3.2**	Yield %	**0.6**	Market Cap	**US$2,964.0mil**

Address **1901 Harrison St.**
Oakland, CA 94612
Tel **510-446-3420**
Fax **510-446-4259**
Exchange **NYSE**
Ticker **GDW**
President **Russell W. Kettell**
Chairman & CEO **H. Sandler / M. Sandler**

BFGoodrich

Industry: **Commodity Chemicals**

B.F. Goodrich manufactures aerospace components and specialty chemicals, and provides related services. The company's aerospace division designs aircraft landing gear, cockpit instruments, and emergency-evacuation systems, and provides maintenance services for commercial and military aircraft. Its specialty-chemicals division produces polyurethane and other plastics with specialized thermal characteristics; chemical additives used by manufacturers of pharmaceuticals, soaps, and plastics; adhesives and sealants; and industrial water-purification systems.

$ mil	12/92	12/93	12/94	% Change				
Sales	**2,525.8**	**1,818.3**	**2,199.2**	**20.9**	P/E Ratio	**25.0**	Price (9/30/95)	**65.88**
Net Income	**-295.9**	**128.3**	**75.7**	**-41.0**	P/B Ratio	**1.8**	52 Wk Hi-Low	**65.88-41.50**
Book Value	**835.1**	**899.1**	**922.6**	**2.6**	Yield %	**3.3**	Market Cap	**US$1,709.1mil**

Address **3925 Embassy Pkwy.**
Akron, OH 44333-1799
Tel **216-374-2000**
Fax **216-374-2333**
Exchange **NYSE**
Ticker **GR**
President & CEO **John D. Ong**
Chairman **John D. Ong**

Goodyear Tire & Rubber

Industry: **Tires & Rubber**

Goodyear Tire & Rubber manufactures tires and rubber products and operates a petroleum pipeline. The company's tire division makes tires and inner tubes under brand names that include Aquatread, Eagle, Regatta, and Tiempo, and provides retreading services. Its general-products segment makes natural- and synthetic-rubber automotive components, industrial belts and hoses, brake-shoe components, and chemicals used in the rubber and plastic industries. Celeron, a subsidiary, operates a 1,225-mile heated crude-oil pipeline that extends from California to Texas.

$ mil	12/92	12/93	12/94	% Change				
Sales	11,784.9	11,643.4	12,288.2	5.5	P/E Ratio	10.5	Price (9/30/95)	39.38
Net Income	-658.6	387.8	567.0	46.2	P/B Ratio	2.1	52 Wk Hi-Low	45.00-31.88
Book Value	1,930.3	2,300.8	2,803.2	21.8	Yield %	1.9	Market Cap	US$5,998.3mil

Address **1144 E. Market St.**
Akron, OH 44316-0001
Tel **216-796-2121**
Fax **216-796-2222**
Exchange **NYSE**
Ticker **GT**
President **Hoyt M. Wells**
Chairman & CEO **Stanley C. Gault**

W.R. Grace & Co.

Industry: **Specialty Chemicals**

W.R. Grace & Company manufactures chemicals and food-service-packaging products, and provides specialized health-care services. Its core chemical lines include products used in the petroleum, construction, and water-treatment industries. The company manufactures plastic-packaging products that preserve food flavor and aroma and lengthen grocery-store shelf life. Its health-care division offers kidney-dialysis services, manufactures medical products, and provides home health-care services. W.R. Grace also produces emission-control equipment for industrial clients.

$ mil	12/92	12/93	12/94	% Change				
Sales	5,518.2	4,408.4	5,093.3	15.5	P/E Ratio	75.9	Price (9/30/95)	66.75
Net Income	-294.5	26.0	83.3	220.4	P/B Ratio	4.2	52 Wk Hi-Low	71.25-36.00
Book Value	1,545.0	1,517.6	1,504.5	-0.9	Yield %	2.1	Market Cap	US$6,444.2mil

Address **1 Town Center Rd.**
Boca Raton, FL 33486-1010
Tel **407-362-2000**
Fax **407-362-2193**
Exchange **NYSE**
Ticker **GRA**
President & CEO **Thomas A. Holmes**
Chairman **J. Peter Grace**

W.W. Grainger

Industry: **Electrical Components & Equipment**

W.W. Grainger distributes equipment and supplies to industrial, commercial, institutional, and contractor markets. The company's Grainger Division is a nationwide distributor of air compressors, air conditioners, refrigeration equipment and components, air tools and paint-spraying equipment, liquid pumps, and power and hand tools, as well as other items shown in its General Catalog. The Grainger Division sells 73,000 items principally to contractors, service shops, industrial and commercial departments, manufacturers, hotels, and health-care and education facilities.

$ mil	12/92	12/93	12/94	% Change				
Sales	2,364.4	2,628.4	3,023.1	15.0	P/E Ratio	24.2	Price (9/30/95)	60.38
Net Income	137.2	148.4	127.9	-13.8	P/B Ratio	3.0	52 Wk Hi-Low	64.25-51.75
Book Value	931.2	941.9	1,032.8	9.7	Yield %	1.3	Market Cap	US$3,068.9mil

Address **5500 W. Howard St.**
Skokie, IL 60077-2699
Tel **708-982-9000**
Fax **708-913-7101**
Exchange **NYSE**
Ticker **GWW**
President & CEO **Richard L. Keyser**
Chairman **David W. Grainger**

Grand Casinos

Industry: **Casinos**

Grand Casinos specializes in operating land-based casinos. The company owns and operates Grand Casino Gulfport, the largest dockside casino on the Mississippi Gulf Coast, as well as Grand Casino Biloxi on the Gulf Coast. It also manages two Las Vegas-style casinos on Native American land in Minnesota, the Grand Casino Mille Lacs and the Grand Casino Hinckley, which are owned by the Mille Lacs Band of the Ojibwe Tribe. The company has also approved management contracts with the Coushatta and Tunica-Biloxi Tribes in Louisiana, and owns 50% of Mississippi Development Corp.

$ mil	12/92 R	12/93	12/94	% Change				
Sales	9.2	117.0	285.8	144.2	P/E Ratio	31.3	Price (9/30/95)	40.63
Net Income	2.7	18.8	29.0	54.6	P/B Ratio	3.3	52 Wk Hi-Low	41.38-14.75
Book Value	55.2	247.9	276.9	11.7	Yield %	0.0	Market Cap	US$910.7mil

Address **13705 First Ave. N.**
Minneapolis, MN 55441-5444
Tel **612-449-9092**
Fax **N/A**
Exchange **NYSE**
Ticker **GND**
President **Patrick R Cruzen**
Chairman & CEO **Lyle Berman**

R=Restated.

Great Lakes Chemical

Industry: **Specialty Chemicals**

Great Lakes Chemical manufactures specialty chemicals and provides related services. The company produces flame retardants, antioxidants, plasticizers, and alcohols that are used in the electronic-equipment, textiles, construction, and pharmaceutical industries. Its water-treatment division makes sanitizing chemicals used in swimming pools, wastewater-treatment plants, papermaking, and food processing. The company also produces fuel additives, agricultural chemicals, industrial coatings, and oil-field chemicals, and provides contract research and testing services.

$ mil	12/92	12/93	12/94	% Change				
Sales	1,496.5	1,792.0	2,065.0	15.2	P/E Ratio	16.9	Price (9/30/95)	67.63
Net Income	232.7	272.8	278.7	2.2	P/B Ratio	3.5	52 Wk Hi-Low	69.00-52.13
Book Value	1,052.9	1,256.6	1,311.0	4.3	Yield %	0.6	Market Cap	US$4,377.2mil

Address **One Great Lakes Blvd.**
West Lafayette, IN 47906-0200
Tel **317-497-6100**
Fax **317-497-6234**
Exchange **NYSE**
Ticker **GLK**
President & CEO **Robert B. McDonald**
Chairman **Martin Hale**

Great Northern Iron Ore

Industry: **Mining**

Great Northern Iron Ore Properties is a trust that owns rights to mineral and nonmineral lands on the Mesabi Range in northeastern Minnesota. Its main source of income is royalties on the production of iron ore, primarily taconite, by mining companies that lease the approximately 12,000 acres of land under the trust's management. Principal lessees currently include National Steel, USX-U.S. Steel, M.A. Hanna, LTV Steel Mining, and Hibbing Taconite. The trust is scheduled to terminate 20 years after the death of the sole surviving person named in the trust agreement of 1906.

$ mil	12/92	12/93	12/94	% Change				
Sales	9.8	6.9	7.6	9.7	P/E Ratio	11.4	Price (9/30/95)	47.00
Net Income	8.4	5.5	6.2	12.7	P/B Ratio	5.3	52 Wk Hi-Low	49.00-40.50
Book Value	13.2	13.2	13.4	1.4	Yield %	8.5	Market Cap	US$70.5mil

Address **332 Minnesota St.**
St. Paul, MN 55101-1361
Tel **612-224-2385**
Fax **612-224-2387**
Exchange **NYSE**
Ticker **GNI**
President & CEO **Harry L. Holtz**
Chairman **Harry L. Holtz**

Great Western Financial

Industry: **Savings & Loans (U.S. Only)**

Great Western Financial is a bank holding company that specializes in retail services and operates about 1,400 offices in the U.S. Its Great Western Bank subsidiary operates more than 400 savings institutions in California and Florida. Great Western's real-estate-services division offers mortgages through 258 offices, primarily in California. Its Aristar subsidiary provides consumer installment loans and credit insurance under the Blazer Financial Services and City Finance names through more than 500 branches concentrated in the southern United States.

$ mil	12/92	12/93	12/94	% Change				
Revenues	3,210.4	2,760.8	2,997.6	8.6	P/E Ratio	14.1	Price (9/30/95)	23.75
Net Income	85.0	62.0	251.2	305.2	P/B Ratio	1.3	52 Wk Hi-Low	23.75-15.75
Book Value	2,449.7	2,423.4	2,483.8	2.5	Yield %	3.9	Market Cap	US$3,228.1mil

Address **9200 Oakdale Ave.**
Chatsworth, CA 91311-6519
Tel **818-775-3411**
Fax **818-775-3434**
Exchange **NYSE**
Ticker **GWF**
President **John F. Maher**
Chairman & CEO **James F. Montgomery**

Green Tree Financial

Industry: **Financial Services - Diversified**

Green Tree Financial finances manufactured homes. The company purchases, originates, pools, sells, or services conditional sales contracts for new and previously owned manufactured homes, FHA-insured home improvements, and Harley-Davidson motorcycles. In addition, the company services manufactured-home loans originated by other lenders and continues to service recreational-vehicle installment contracts. Green Tree Financial operates its business through 42 regional service centers throughout the United States.

$ mil	12/92	12/93	12/94	% Change				
Revenues	246.6	366.7	497.4	35.7	P/E Ratio	23.4	Price (9/30/95)	61.00
Net Income	55.0	116.4	181.3	55.7	P/B Ratio	5.7	52 Wk Hi-Low	61.75-38.38
Book Value	298.8	549.4	725.9	32.1	Yield %	0.4	Market Cap	US$4,176.2mil

Address **1100 Landmark Towers**
St. Paul, MN 55102-1639
Tel **612-293-3400**
Fax **N/A**
Exchange **NYSE**
Ticker **GNT**
President **Robert D. Potts**
Chairman & CEO **Lawrence M. Coss**

Grey Advertising

Industry: **Advertising**

Grey Advertising produces and places advertisements in various media including television, radio, newspaper, and magazines. It also offers services, such as marketing consultation, direct-response advertising, product publicity, public relations, and sales promotion. Clients include Celestial Seasonings, Sara Lee, Anheuser-Busch, Brown & Williamson, and others. The company serves its international clients through a network of 202 agencies in 51 countries outside the United States. Grey's media-company network, MediaCom, includes 22 media companies in 16 countries.

$ mil	12/92	12/93	12/94	% Change				
Sales	564.5	567.2	593.3	4.6	P/E Ratio	NMF	Price (9/30/95)	197.00
Net Income	16.5	17.7	-21.4	-220.8	P/B Ratio	2.1	52 Wk Hi-Low	209.00-145.00
Book Value	126.3	135.7	116.2	-14.4	Yield %	1.7	Market Cap	US$235.2mil

Address **777 Third Ave.**
New York, NY 10017
Tel **212-546-2000**
Fax **212-546-1495**
Exchange **NASDA**
Ticker **GREY**
President **Edward H. Meyer**
Chairman **Edward H. Meyer**

GTE

Industry: **Regional Telephone Systems**

GTE provides telephone services and telecommunication products and services. The company serves more than 17 million lines in the Americas. It also provides cellular service to approximately one million users, making it the second-largest provider of mobile-cellular telephone services in the U.S. in terms of population in areas served. In addition, GTE supplies communication, intelligence-support, and electronic-defense systems to the U.S. and other governments; it also offers satellite-communication services to businesses, and operates phones on-board commercial aircraft.

$ mil	12/92	12/93	12/94	% Change				
Sales	19,984.0	19,747.5	19,944.0	1.0	P/E Ratio	15.4	Price (9/30/95)	39.25
Net Income	-754.0	900.0	2,451.0	172.3	P/B Ratio	3.6	52 Wk Hi-Low	39.25-29.88
Book Value	10,171.0	9,677.0	10,592.0	9.5	Yield %	4.8	Market Cap	US$38,146mil

Address **1 Stamford Forum**
Stamford, CT 06904
Tel **203-965-2000**
Fax **203-965-2520**
Exchange **NYSE**
Ticker **GTE**
Chief Executive **Charles R. Lee**
Chairman **Charles R. Lee**

Halliburton

Industry: **Oilfield Equipment & Services - Other**

Halliburton provides technical and construction services, primarily to energy-related industries, and manufactures related products. Halliburton Energy Services, a subsidiary, makes drilling equipment and provides maintenance, testing, and data-processing services for the petroleum industry. The company's Brown & Root subsidiary provides engineering, design, and construction services for projects such as power-generation facilities, chemical plants, and underwater pipelines. Its Highlands Insurance subsidiary offers personal and corporate property and casualty insurance.

$ mil	12/92	12/93	12/94	% Change				
Sales	**6,565.9**	**6,350.8**	**5,740.5**	**-9.6**	P/E Ratio	**26.8**	Price (9/30/95)	**41.75**
Net Income	**-137.3**	**-161.0**	**177.8**	**-210.4**	P/B Ratio	**2.5**	52 Wk Hi-Low	**45.25-30.75**
Book Value	**1,907.3**	**1,887.7**	**1,942.2**	**2.9**	Yield %	**2.4**	Market Cap	**US$4,768.2mil**

Address **3600 Lincoln Plz., 500 N. Akard St.** **Dallas, TX 75201-3391**
Tel **214-978-2600** Fax **214-969-1046**
Exchange **NYSE** Ticker **HAL**
President **Dale P. Jones**
Chairman & CEO **Thomas H. Cruikshank**

Handy & Harman

Industry: **Precious Metals**

Handy & Harman refines precious metals, produces precious-metal alloys, and makes parts, components, and assemblies primarily for North American automobile original-equipment manufacturers. It also markets specialty wire and tubing, and plastic and steel fittings for natural-gas, electrical, and water utilities. These products are marketed to users in the United States and internationally. Business conducted in the U.S. accounts for virtually all of Handy & Harman's revenues. The company operates 32 manufacturing plants in North America, South America, Europe, and Asia.

$ mil	12/92	12/93	12/94	% Change				
Sales	**572.2**	**658.3**	**781.5**	**18.7**	P/E Ratio	**12.7**	Price (9/30/95)	**15.00**
Net Income	**11.7**	**9.5**	**16.5**	**73.8**	P/B Ratio	**2.0**	52 Wk Hi-Low	**17.13-13.75**
Book Value	**84.9**	**91.6**	**106.1**	**15.9**	Yield %	**1.3**	Market Cap	**US$211.5mil**

Address **250 Park Ave.** **New York, NY 10177**
Tel **212-661-2400** Fax **212-309-0682**
Exchange **NYSE** Ticker **HNH**
President **Frank E. Grzelecki**
Chairman & CEO **Richard N. Daniel**

Harcourt General

Industry: **Apparel Retailers**

Harcourt General's principal businesses are publishing and specialty retailing. The company also provides insurance services. Its Harcourt Brace subsidiary publishes books and scholarly journals for the educational, scientific, and medical markets. It also conducts a bar-examination review program. The company also owns 65% of The Nieman Marcus Group; that firm's Nieman Marcus and Bergdorf Goodman subsidiaries sell apparel, jewelry, and other assorted merchandise. Harcourt General's Drake Beam Morin subsidiary provides human resource consulting services.

$ mil	10/92	10/93	10/94	% Change				
Revenues	**3,716.9**	**3,655.7**	**3,154.2**	**-13.7**	P/E Ratio	**18.9**	Price (9/30/95)	**41.88**
Net Income	**494.5**	**171.3**	**177.5**	**3.6**	P/B Ratio	**3.1**	52 Wk Hi-Low	**45.25-32.50**
Book Value	**924.4**	**1,051.6**	**1,047.4**	**-0.4**	Yield %	**1.5**	Market Cap	**US$3,045.6mil**

Address **27 Boylston St.** **Chestnut Hill, MA 02167**
Tel **617-232-8200** Fax **617-738-4007**
Exchange **NYSE** Ticker **H**
President & CEO **Robert J. Tarr, Jr.**
Chairman **Richard A. Smith**

John H. Harland

Industry: **General Industrial & Commercial Services**

John H. Harland prints checks and other documents, and manufactures related equipment. The company's main products are personal and business checks, business forms, banking forms, and related documents, which it prints at facilities in the United States and Puerto Rico. Scantron, its affiliate, manufactures mark-reading equipment and forms, for scoring standardized tests; it also makes machine-read survey products. Harlan also collects and analyzes demographic consumer information for commercial use. Sales of checks and other forms generate 83% of the company's net sales.

$ mil	12/92	12/93	12/94	% Change				
Sales	**445.0**	**519.5**	**521.3**	**0.3**	P/E Ratio	**13.2**	Price (9/30/95)	**22.13**
Net Income	**56.6**	**52.5**	**51.2**	**-2.4**	P/B Ratio	**3.3**	52 Wk Hi-Low	**23.63-19.38**
Book Value	**256.2**	**183.7**	**203.4**	**10.7**	Yield %	**4.4**	Market Cap	**US$675.9mil**

Address **2939 Miller Rd.** **Decatur, GA 30035**
Tel **404-981-9460** Fax **404-593-5619**
Exchange **NYSE** Ticker **JH**
President & CEO **Robert R. Woodson**
Chairman **Robert R. Woodson**

Harnischfeger

Industry: **Heavy Machinery**

Harnischfeger Industries produces papermaking machinery and mining and materials-handling equipment. It owns an 80% stake in Beloit, which makes papermaking equipment, surface-mining shovels, and overhead cranes. The company also owns a 10% stake in Measurex, which offers computer-integrated manufacturing services to the paper and chemical industries. Its Syscon subsidiary supplies computer hardware and software to the private sector and the U.S. Department of Defense. The company's Joy Technologies subsidiary manufactures mining equipment.

$ mil	10/92	10/93	10/94	% Change				
Sales	**1,375.8**	**1,234.7**	**1,116.7**	**-9.6**	P/E Ratio	**NMF**	Price (9/30/95)	**33.38**
Net Income	**56.7**	**-17.7**	**-48.0**	**171.4**	P/B Ratio	**1.9**	52 Wk Hi-Low	**38.75-24.63**
Book Value	**591.4**	**503.3**	**486.2**	**-3.4**	Yield %	**1.2**	Market Cap	**US$1,601.3mil**

Address **13400 Bishops Ln.** **Brookfield, WI 53005**
Tel **414-671-4400** Fax **414-671-7604**
Exchange **NYSE** Ticker **HPH**
President **John A. McKay**
Chairman & CEO **Jeffrey T. Grade**

Harper

Industry: **Air Freight & Couriers**

Harper Group ships freight by land, sea, and air and provides customs brokerage, freight tracking, storage, and insurance. It has more than 300 offices in 45 countries on five continents. Harper's principal operating companies are Circle International (air/ocean imports and exports) and Sekin Transport International (air and ocean freight forwarding). Its principal cargoes are electronic equipment and consumer goods. The company markets its services through its senior executives, managers, and a sales force of more than 225 persons in the U.S. and internationally.

$ mil	12/92	12/93	12/94	% Change				
Sales	431.7	429.9	469.6	9.2	P/E Ratio	18.6	Price (9/30/95)	19.00
Net Income	5.0	19.1	16.7	-12.5	P/B Ratio	2.0	52 Wk Hi-Low	20.00-13.13
Book Value	130.7	145.2	151.4	4.2	Yield %	1.1	Market Cap	US$306.9mil

Address **260 Townsend St.**
San Francisco, CA 94107-0933
Tel **415-978-0600**
Fax **415-978-0699**
Exchange **NASDA**
Ticker **HARG**
President & CEO **Peter Gibert**
Chairman **Peter Gibert**

Harrahs Entertainment

Industry: **Casinos**

Harrahs Entertainment is a casino, entertainment, and hotel company. Its Harrah's casino-entertainment division operates 12 casino properties in five states, and has additional casino locations under development. The company's hotel division operates the Embassy Suites, Hampton Inn, and Homewood Suites hotels. Harrah's operates casino hotels in Reno, Lake Tahoe, Las Vegas, and Laughlin, Nevada; Atlantic City, New Jersey; as well as riverboat and dockside casinos. The company also own Harrah's Joliet, a riverboat casino in Illinois, as well as a 17% interest in Eagle Gaming.

$ mil	12/92	12/93	12/94	% Change				
Sales	1,113.1	1,251.9	1,339.4	7.0	P/E Ratio	38.5	Price (9/30/95)	29.25
Net Income	52.5	86.3	78.4	-9.2	P/B Ratio	4.8	52 Wk Hi-Low	32.85-18.85
Book Value	427.9	536.0	623.4	16.3	Yield %	0.0	Market Cap	US$2,999.1mil

Address **1023 Cherry Rd.**
Memphis, TN 38117
Tel **901-762-8600**
Fax **901-762-8637**
Exchange **NYSE**
Ticker **PRI**
President & CEO **Philip G. Satre**
Chairman **Michael D. Rose**

Harris

Industry: **Communications Technology**

Harris develops electronic equipment, systems, and components. The company produces electronic equipment, such as communication systems for military and space programs, semiconductors for various civilian and military customers, and communication equipment for the broadcast and telecommunication industries. Its Lanier Worldwide subsidiary manufactures office equipment, including copiers, dictation systems, and fax machines, as well as speech-recognition systems. Harris markets these products internationally. Business in the U.S. accounts for 30% of sales.

$ mil	06/93	06/94	06/95	% Change				
Sales	3,099.1	3,336.1	3,444.1	3.2	P/E Ratio	13.9	Price (9/30/95)	54.88
Net Income	111.1	111.8	154.5	38.2	P/B Ratio	1.7	52 Wk Hi-Low	61.25-38.00
Book Value	1,141.3	1,188.0	1,248.8	5.1	Yield %	2.3	Market Cap	US$2,146.8mil

Address **1025 W. NASA Blvd.**
Melbourne, FL 32919
Tel **407-727-9100**
Fax **407-727-9344**
Exchange **NYSE**
Ticker **HRS**
President **Phillip W. Farmer**
Chairman & CEO **Phillip W. Farmer**

Harsco

Industry: **Industrial - Diversified**

Harsco provides industrial services, construction products, and defense systems and vehicles. The company makes its products and services available through facilities in 30 countries. The company recycles scrap material from steelmaking companies to produce reclaimed steel and slag. It manufactures items including scaffolding, pipe fittings, and railway-maintenance equipment. Harsco also manufactures concrete-forming products, industrial-process equipment, roofing materials, and metal-fabrication products. Business outside the U.S. accounts for 36% of the company's sales.

$ mil	12/92	12/93	12/94	% Change				
Sales	1,624.9	1,422.3	1,357.7	-4.5	P/E Ratio	16.1	Price (9/30/95)	55.63
Net Income	84.3	87.6	86.6	-1.2	P/B Ratio	2.4	52 Wk Hi-Low	59.00-39.25
Book Value	495.1	523.1	581.2	11.1	Yield %	2.6	Market Cap	US$1,404.0mil

Address **P.O. Box 8888**
Camp Hill, PA 17001-8888
Tel **717-763-7064**
Fax **717-763-6424**
Exchange **NYSE**
Ticker **HSC**
President & CEO **Derek C. Hathaway**
Chairman **Derek C. Hathaway**

Hartford Steam Boiler

Industry: **Insurance - Property & Casualty**

Hartford Steam Boiler Inspection and Insurance is the largest underwriter of boiler and industrial-machinery insurance in North America. It also provides engineering and technical-consulting services. Approximately 38% of the company's total revenues comes from equipment inspection, safety certification, and loss-prevention engineering. The company markets its insurance products through contracts with independent agents in all 50 states, the District of Columbia, Puerto Rico, and Canada. The company maintains 17 branch offices throughout the United States.

$ mil	12/92	12/93	12/94	% Change				
Revenues	682.1	636.1	603.6	-5.1	P/E Ratio	19.0	Price (9/30/95)	48.38
Net Income	41.2	9.5	51.9	446.3	P/B Ratio	3.3	52 Wk Hi-Low	49.00-36.13
Book Value	374.3	324.7	299.5	-7.8	Yield %	4.4	Market Cap	US$985.4mil

Address **One State St.**
Hartford, CT 06102-5024
Tel **203-722-1866**
Fax **203-722-5770**
Exchange **NYSE**
Ticker **HSB**
President & CEO **Gordon W. Kreh**
Chairman **--**

Hasbro

Industry: **Toy Manufacturers**

Hasbro manufactures toy products and related items. The company markets its wares in the United States and internationally under brand names that include Hasbro, Kenner, Playskool, Tonka, Milton Bradley, and Parker Brothers. Its better-known products include Nerf toys, Tinkertoys, G.I. Joe action figures, Tonka toy trucks, Mr. Potato Head, and the Monopoly, Parcheesi, Candy Land, Yahtzee, The Game of Life, Trivial Pursuit, and Scrabble board games. Hasbro also makes the Playskool Baby line of products such as silicone pacifiers, bibs, and infant apparel.

$ mil	12/92	12/93	12/94	% Change				
Sales	2,541.1	2,747.2	2,670.3	-2.8	P/E Ratio	15.9	Price (9/30/95)	31.13
Net Income	179.2	200.0	175.0	-12.5	P/B Ratio	2.0	52 Wk Hi-Low	35.25-28.00
Book Value	1,105.6	1,276.7	1,395.4	9.3	Yield %	0.9	Market Cap	US$2,732.2mil

Address **1027 Newport Ave.**
Pawtucket, RI 02862
Tel **401-431-8697**
Fax **401-431-8535**
Exchange **AMEX**
Ticker **HAS**
Chief Executive **Alan G. Hassenfeld**
Chairman **Alan G. Hassenfeld**

Health & Retirement Properties Trust

Industry: **Real-Estate Investment**

Health and Retirement Properties Trust is a real-estate investment trust that invests in nursing homes and other health-care related real estate, primarily long-term care facilities. The company has real estate investments in 141 properties located in 27 states, of which the company owns 80 and has mortgage investments in the remaining 61. The properties consist of 77% nursing homes and long-term care facilities, 21% nursing homes with subacute services, and 2% are other facilities. These properties are concentrated in California, Nebraska, Colorado, and Iowa.

$ mil	12/92	12/93	12/94	% Change				
Sales	48.7	56.5	86.7	53.4	P/E Ratio	16.4	Price (9/30/95)	15.63
Net Income	27.2	33.4	49.9	49.4	P/B Ratio	1.5	52 Wk Hi-Low	16.00-14.75
Book Value	228.3	441.1	602.0	36.5	Yield %	8.4	Market Cap	US$924.8mil

Address **400 Centre St.**
Newton, MA 02158
Tel **617-332-3990**
Fax **N/A**
Exchange **NYSE**
Ticker **HRP**
President **David J. Hegarty**
Chairman --

Health Care Property

Industry: **Real-Estate Investment**

Health Care Property Investors invests in health-care-related real estate throughout the U.S. The real estate includes long-term care facilities, acute-care and rehabilitation hospitals, psychiatric hospitals, substance-abuse recovery centers, congregate-care and assisted-living facilities and medical office buildings. The company owns an interest in 170 properties located in 32 states, which are leased pursuant to long-term leases to 33 health-care providers, including Beverly Enterprises, Columbia/HCA Healthcare, Continental Medical Systems, and others.

$ mil	12/92	12/93	12/94	% Change				
Sales	83.7	92.6	99.0	7.0	P/E Ratio	18.1	Price (9/30/95)	33.88
Net Income	35.7	44.1	50.0	13.4	P/B Ratio	3.4	52 Wk Hi-Low	34.50-29.63
Book Value	271.4	269.9	269.4	-0.2	Yield %	5.9	Market Cap	US$966.9mil

Address **10990 Wilshire Blvd., Ste. 1200**
Los Angeles, CA 90024
Tel **310-473-1990**
Fax **N/A**
Exchange **NYSE**
Ticker **HCP**
President & CEO **Kenneth B. Roath**
Chairman **Kenneth B. Roath**

Hecla Mining

Industry: **Precious Metals**

Hecla Mining operates metal and industrial-mineral mines. The company's metals division manages mines in Alaska, California, Idaho, Nevada, and Mexico that contain total reserves of about 2.1 million ounces of gold, 76 million ounces of silver, 186,000 tons of lead, and 351,000 tons of zinc. Its industrial-minerals division mines clay, kaolin, and feldspar in the southern U.S.; these minerals are used mainly in ceramic and porcelain products. Hecla Mining also operates a plant in Utah that produces cobalt sulfate for use by the copper-processing industry.

$ mil	12/92	12/93	12/94	% Change				
Sales	100.7	81.8	128.8	57.4	P/E Ratio	NMF	Price (9/30/95)	12.13
Net Income	-49.3	-11.7	-24.6	110.3	P/B Ratio	2.1	52 Wk Hi-Low	13.25-8.75
Book Value	113.7	240.1	277.5	15.6	Yield %	0.0	Market Cap	US$584.9mil

Address **6500 Mineral Dr.**
Coeur d'Alene, ID 83814
Tel **208-769-4100**
Fax **208-769-4159**
Exchange **NYSE**
Ticker **HL**
President & CEO **Arthur Brown**
Chairman **Arthur Brown**

H.J. Heinz

Industry: **Other Food**

H.J. Heinz produces more than 3,000 consumer-food products, including ketchup and other condiments, canned soups, and baby food sold under the Heinz brand name. The company's other primary products include StarKist canned tuna, Ore-Ida frozen potato products, and Weight Watchers reduced-calorie foods. It sells these products to retail-food stores, restaurants, and institutional customers on five continents. Heinz also produces pet foods under brand names that include 9-Lives, Amore, and Vets. The company operates 95 production facilities in the United States and abroad.

$ mil	04/93	04/94	04/95	% Change				
Sales	7,103.4	7,046.7	8,086.8	14.8	P/E Ratio	19.2	Price (9/30/95)	45.75
Net Income	396.3	602.9	591.0	-2.0	P/B Ratio	4.5	52 Wk Hi-Low	46.88-35.88
Book Value	2,320.9	2,338.6	2,472.9	5.7	Yield %	3.1	Market Cap	US$11,723mil

Address **600 Grant St.**
Pittsburgh, PA 15219
Tel **412-456-5700**
Fax **412-456-6128**
Exchange **NYSE**
Ticker **HNZ**
President & CEO **Anthony J.F. O'Reilly**
Chairman **Anthony J.F. O'Reilly**

Industry: **Oil Drilling**

Helmerich & Payne

Helmerich & Payne operates oil and natural-gas wells, provides oil-field services, manufactures chemicals, and develops real estate. The company owns, on average, a 14% interest in 4,250 wells and net reserves of 284 billion cubic feet of gas and six million barrels of oil in Oklahoma, Kansas, Texas, and Louisiana. It operates 70 onshore and offshore contract-drilling rigs worldwide. Helmerich & Payne Properties, a subsidiary, develops commercial real estate in the Tulsa area. Natural Gas Odorizing, another subsidiary, makes odorants that are mixed with natural gas.

$ mil	09/92	09/93	09/94	% Change				
Sales	230.5	306.0	322.7	5.5	P/E Ratio	27.6	Price (9/30/95)	28.13
Net Income	10.8	24.6	25.0	1.5	P/B Ratio	1.3	52 Wk Hi-Low	31.25-24.50
Book Value	493.3	508.9	524.3	3.0	Yield %	1.7	Market Cap	US$696.3mil

Address **Utica at 21st St.**
Tulsa, OK 74114
Tel **918-742-5531**
Fax **918-743-2671**
Exchange **NYSE**
Ticker **HP**
President & CEO **Hans Helmerich**
Chairman **W.H. Helmerich III**

Industry: **Commodity Chemicals**

Hercules

Hercules manufactures chemicals and related products. The company's products include resins for inks and adhesives, wet-strength resins and sizing for the paper industry, natural gums for the food industry, water-soluble polymers for use as thickeners and stabilizers in paints and coatings, and resins for use in printed-circuit boards. Hercules markets these compounds and products in the United States and internationally. Foreign sales account for approximately 32% of the company's total sales. The company operates plants in the United States, and worldwide.

$ mil	12/92	12/93	12/94	% Change				
Sales	2,864.9	2,773.4	2,821.0	1.7	P/E Ratio	25.3	Price (9/30/95)	58.00
Net Income	167.9	-33.4	274.2	-920.8	P/B Ratio	5.2	52 Wk Hi-Low	60.75-33.33
Book Value	1,746.4	1,368.2	1,294.7	-5.4	Yield %	1.3	Market Cap	US$6,468.0mil

Address **1313 N. Market St.**
Wilmington, DE 19894-0001
Tel **302-594-5000**
Fax **302-594-7252**
Exchange **NYSE**
Ticker **HPC**
President & CEO **Thomas L. Gossage**
Chairman **Thomas L. Gossage**

Industry: **Other Food**

Hershey Foods

Hershey Foods manufactures food products, primarily chocolate and pasta. The company's major candy brands include Hershey's, Reese's, KitKat, Life Savers, and Twizzlers. Its grocery-products division produces cocoa, chocolate syrup, baking chocolate, and ice-cream toppings under the Hershey name, and peanut butter under the Reese's name. Hershey's pasta division manufactures pasta under brand names that include San Giorgio, American Beauty, Delmonico, and Skinner. The company operates manufacturing facilities in North America, and markets its products in 60 countries.

$ mil	12/92	12/93	12/94	% Change				
Sales	3,219.8	3,488.2	3,606.3	3.4	P/E Ratio	30.4	Price (9/30/95)	64.38
Net Income	242.6	193.3	184.2	-4.7	P/B Ratio	3.9	52 Wk Hi-Low	64.75-44.75
Book Value	1,465.3	1,412.3	1,441.1	2.0	Yield %	1.9	Market Cap	US$4,999.4mil

Address **100 Crystal A Dr.**
Hershey, PA 17033-0810
Tel **717-534-6799**
Fax **717-534-4078**
Exchange **NYSE**
Ticker **HSY**
President **Joseph P. Viviano**
Chairman & CEO **Kenneth L. Wolfe**

Industry: **Computers**

Hewlett-Packard

Hewlett-Packard manufactures computers and electronic equipment. The company offers more than 12,000 products, including computer systems, which are compatible with IBM equipment; computer peripherals, including HP LaserJet and HP DeskJet printers; and electronic instruments, including measurement systems for use in electronics, medicine, and analytical chemistry. Hewlett-Packard also produces semiconductors for sale to other electronics manufacturers. The company markets its products in the United States and more than 100 other countries.

$ mil	10/92	10/93	10/94	% Change				
Sales	16,410.0	20,317.0	24,991.0	23.0	P/E Ratio	27.2	Price (9/30/95)	83.38
Net Income	549.0	1,177.0	1,599.0	35.9	P/B Ratio	4.3	52 Wk Hi-Low	85.63-42.31
Book Value	7,499.0	8,511.0	9,926.0	16.6	Yield %	0.7	Market Cap	US$42,647mil

Address **3000 Hanover St.**
Palo Alto, CA 94304
Tel **415-857-1501**
Fax **415-857-7299**
Exchange **NYSE**
Ticker **HWP**
President & CEO **Lewis E. Platt**
Chairman **Lewis E. Platt**

Industry: **Lodging**

Hilton Hotels

Hilton Hotels operates an international chain of hotels, resorts, and gaming operations. As of December 31, 1994, the company owned or leased and operated 23 hotels, and managed 40 hotels partially- or wholly-owned by others. In addition, 160 hotels were operated under the Hilton, Hilton Garden Inn, and Hilton Suites names by others pursuant to franchises granted by a Hilton subsidiary. These properties are located in the United States, with the exception of four international hotels and two hotel casinos operated by the company's Conrad International Hotels subsidiary.

$ mil	12/92	12/93	12/94	% Change				
Sales	1,229.6	1,393.5	1,506.2	8.1	P/E Ratio	25.3	Price (9/30/95)	63.88
Net Income	103.9	106.1	121.7	14.7	P/B Ratio	2.7	52 Wk Hi-Low	79.25-57.00
Book Value	1,002.5	1,056.7	1,127.8	6.7	Yield %	1.9	Market Cap	US$3,085.3mil

Address **9336 Civic Center Dr.**
Beverly Hills, CA 90210
Tel **310-278-4321**
Fax **310-205-4613**
Exchange **NYSE**
Ticker **HLT**
President **R.C. Avansino, Jr.**
Chairman & CEO **Barron Hilton**

Home Depot

Industry: **Other Specialty Retailers**

Home Depot is a home-improvement retailer. The company operates stores that sell an assortment of building materials and home-improvement products. At the end of fiscal 1994, the company had 340 stores in 28 states. The 40,000 to 50,000 items stocked in a typical company store are name-brand merchandise. The largest segment of sales, 34.2%, is from building materials, lumber, and floor and wall coverings. In addition to these stores, the company's Depot Diners provide food services. The company is also planning to expand the number of its garden-supply stores.

$ mil	01/93	01/94	01/95	% Change				
Revenues	**7,148.4**	**9,238.8**	**12,476.7**	**35.0**	P/E Ratio	**30.2**	Price (9/30/95)	**39.88**
Net Income	**362.9**	**457.4**	**604.5**	**32.2**	P/B Ratio	**5.3**	52 Wk Hi-Low	**49.75-38.50**
Book Value	**2,304.1**	**2,814.1**	**3,442.2**	**22.3**	Yield %	**0.4**	Market Cap	**US$18,991mil**

Address **2727 Paces Ferry Rd.**
Atlanta, GA 30339-4089
Tel **404-433-8211**
Fax **404-431-2707**
Exchange **NYSE**
Ticker **HD**
President **Arthur M. Blank**
Chairman & CEO **Bernard Marcus**

Homestake Mining

Industry: **Precious Metals**

Homestake Mining operates gold, sulfur, silver, and other mineral mines and oil fields in the United States, Australia, Canada, Chile, and Mexico. The company, including its Canadian subsidiary International Corona, operates about 17 gold mines that contain total reserves of about 18 million ounces. Its mining operations include ore-processing facilities, wastewater-treatment plants, and tailings-disposal facilities. The company's Homestake Sulphur subsidiary owns an interest in Main Pass Block 299, a sulfur and oil deposit in the Gulf of Mexico offshore of Louisiana.

$ mil	12/92	12/93	12/94	% Change				
Sales	**659.6**	**703.5**	**656.1**	**-6.7**	P/E Ratio	**29.8**	Price (9/30/95)	**17.00**
Net Income	**-175.8**	**52.5**	**78.0**	**48.6**	P/B Ratio	**4.0**	52 Wk Hi-Low	**21.63-15.00**
Book Value	**465.4**	**515.2**	**588.8**	**14.3**	Yield %	**1.1**	Market Cap	**US$2,345.2mil**

Address **650 California St.**
San Francisco, CA 94108-2788
Tel **415-981-8150**
Fax **415-397-5038**
Exchange **NYSE**
Ticker **HM**
President **Jack E. Thompson**
Chairman & CEO **Harry M. Conger**

Honeywell

Industry: **Electrical Components & Equipment**

Honeywell specializes in control components, systems, and services for home, building, aerospace, and industrial uses. Its products for residential and commercial buildings include heating, air-conditioning, and security systems. The company also makes control and measurement systems for commercial and military aircraft and spacecraft. Honeywell's industrial-automation equipment is used in process plants and petroleum refineries. The company markets its products to retailers, industrial users, and government agencies worldwide. Sales abroad account for 37% of the total.

$ mil	12/92	12/93	12/94	% Change				
Sales	**6,222.6**	**5,963.0**	**6,057.0**	**1.6**	P/E Ratio	**19.9**	Price (9/30/95)	**42.88**
Net Income	**246.8**	**322.2**	**278.9**	**-13.4**	P/B Ratio	**2.9**	52 Wk Hi-Low	**45.75-28.88**
Book Value	**1,790.4**	**1,773.0**	**1,854.7**	**4.6**	Yield %	**2.3**	Market Cap	**US$5,453.8mil**

Address **Honeywell Plz.**
Minneapolis, MN 55408
Tel **612-951-1000**
Fax **612-870-5780**
Exchange **NYSE**
Ticker **HON**
President **D. Larry Moore**
Chairman & CEO **Michael R. Bonsignore**

Hormel Foods

Industry: **Other Food**

Geo. A. Hormel & Company produces food products for the consumer and industrial markets. Its fresh and frozen meat products include beef, pork, poultry, fish, hot dogs, and bacon. The company sells Spam canned luncheon meats, Dinty Moore stews, Hormel chili and hash, Jennie-O turkeys, and Top Shelf shelf-stable entrees. Hormel also sells ethnic foods such as its Chi-Chi's line of Mexican food and its House of Tsang Asian foods. It also produces gelatin, meat broths, and an egg substitute for food manufacturers, as well as proteins used in the cosmetics industry.

$ mil	10/92	10/93	10/94	% Change				
Sales	**2,813.7**	**2,854.0**	**3,064.8**	**7.4**	P/E Ratio	**17.1**	Price (9/30/95)	**26.38**
Net Income	**95.2**	**-26.8**	**118.0**	**-540.2**	P/B Ratio	**3.1**	52 Wk Hi-Low	**27.88-22.13**
Book Value	**644.3**	**570.9**	**661.1**	**15.8**	Yield %	**1.9**	Market Cap	**US$2,022.9mil**

Address **1 Hormel Pl.**
Austin, MN 55912-3680
Tel **507-437-5611**
Fax **507-437-5489**
Exchange **NYSE**
Ticker **HRL**
President & CEO **Joel W. Johnson**
Chairman **R.L. Knowlton**

Host Marriott

Industry: **Real-Estate Investment**

Host Marriott operates hotels and provides contract services for food and merchandise management. Its lodging segment consists of 123 operated or franchised hotels. The company operates more than 250 full-service hotels and resorts in the U.S. and 21 other countries and operates food and gift concession areas at 70 U.S. airports; 95 Marriot Travel Plazas on 14 highway systems; and 40 merchandise stores at arenas and major tourist attractions. In 1995, the company announced plans to form Host Marriott Services, which would operate its concessions businesses.

$ mil	12/92	12/93	12/94	% Change				
Sales	**8,722.0**	**1,791.0**	**1,501.0**	**-16.2**	P/E Ratio	**NMF**	Price (9/30/95)	**12.38**
Net Income	**85.0**	**50.0**	**-25.0**	**-150.0**	P/B Ratio	**2.7**	52 Wk Hi-Low	**13.75-8.50**
Book Value	**785.0**	**505.0**	**710.0**	**40.6**	Yield %	**0.0**	Market Cap	**US$1,966.9mil**

Address **10400 Fernwood Rd.**
Bethesda, MD 20817
Tel **301-380-9000**
Fax **301-380-8260**
Exchange **NYSE**
Ticker **HMT**
President & CEO **Stephen F. Bollenbach**
Chairman **Richard E. Marriott**

Household International

Industry: **Financial Services - Diversified**

Household International is a financial-services and insurance company. Its operations are divided into two business segments: finance and banking, and individual life insurance. The company's financial-service products include home-equity credit, mortgages, credit cards, loans, and checking, savings, and money-market accounts. Its Alexander Hamilton Life subsidiary offers life, disability, and specialty insurance and annuities. The company serves 19 million customers in the U.S., Canada, and the U.K. Finance and banking accounts for 86% of the company's total net income.

$ mil	12/92	12/93	12/94	% Change				
Revenues	**4,180.6**	**4,454.5**	**4,603.3**	**3.3**	P/E Ratio	**17.6**	Price (9/30/95)	**62.00**
Net Income	**190.9**	**298.7**	**367.6**	**23.1**	P/B Ratio	**2.4**	52 Wk Hi-Low	**62.00-33.75**
Book Value	**1,944.4**	**2,078.3**	**2,523.0**	**21.4**	Yield %	**2.0**	Market Cap	**US$6,068.4mil**

Address **2700 Sanders Rd.**
Prospect Heights, IL 60070-2799
Tel **708-564-5000**
Fax **708-564-7590**
Exchange **NYSE**
Ticker **HI**
President & CEO **William F. Aldinger**
Chairman **Donald C. Clark**

Houston Industries

Industry: **Electrical Utilities - Southern U.S.**

Houston Industries is an energy, communication, and related services holding company. It provides electricity to more than 1,000,000 customers in Texas; manages cable-television systems in four states through its KBLCOM subsidiary; and has a 50% interest in Paragon Communications, which serves 967,000 cable-television customers. Other subsidiaries provide power-plant testing and training to utility and industrial customers. About 34% of the company's electricity is generated with natural gas, 43% with coal, and the remainder is nulcear or purchased from third parties.

$ mil	12/92	12/93	12/94	% Change				
Sales	**4,596.4**	**4,323.9**	**4,001.9**	**-7.4**	P/E Ratio	**13.6**	Price (9/30/95)	**44.13**
Net Income	**434.7**	**416.3**	**399.3**	**-4.1**	P/B Ratio	**1.6**	52 Wk Hi-Low	**44.88-32.63**
Book Value	**3,284.7**	**3,274.0**	**3,369.3**	**2.9**	Yield %	**6.8**	Market Cap	**US$5,795.2mil**

Address **4400 Post Oak Pkwy.**
Houston, TX 77027
Tel **713-629-3000**
Fax **713-629-3129**
Exchange **NYSE**
Ticker **HOU**
President **Don D. Sykora**
Chairman & CEO **Don D. Jordan**

Hubbell

Industry: **Electrical Components & Equipment**

Hubbell manufactures electrical and electronic products. The company's low-voltage products include wiring devices, lighting fixtures, and industrial controls. Its high-voltage products include test and measurement equipment, wire and cable, insulators, and surge suppressors. Hubbell also manufactures electrical enclosures and fittings, and data-transmission and telecommunication equipment. The company markets these products in the United States and internationally. Business in the U.S. accounts for substantially all of the company's net sales.

$ mil	12/92	12/93	12/94	% Change				
Sales	**786.1**	**832.4**	**1,013.7**	**21.8**	P/E Ratio	**18.3**	Price (9/30/95)	**58.63**
Net Income	**77.6**	**66.3**	**106.5**	**60.7**	P/B Ratio	**3.2**	52 Wk Hi-Low	**60.13-50.24**
Book Value	**541.3**	**557.6**	**609.0**	**9.2**	Yield %	**2.8**	Market Cap	**US$1,929.9mil**

Address **584 Derby Milford Rd.**
Orange, CT 06477
Tel **203-799-4100**
Fax **203-799-4333**
Exchange **NYSE**
Ticker **HUB**
President & CEO **G. Jackson Ratcliffe**
Chairman **G. Jackson Ratcliffe**

Humana

Industry: **Health Care Providers**

Humana provides health-benefit plans for approximately two million subscribers. It is one of the largest for-profit managed-care providers in the United States. The company owns and manages health-maintenance organizations and preferred-provider organizations that provide services to subscribers through contract agreements with more than 28,000 physicians and 460 hospitals. Humana's products are primarily sold to employers and other groups, and Medicare-eligible individuals. The company also manages a dental-services subsidiary. Humana operates in 14 states.

$ mil	08/92	12/93 *	12/94	% Change				
Sales	**4,043.0**	**3,137.0**	**3,576.0**	**14.0**	P/E Ratio	**18.3**	Price (9/30/95)	**20.13**
Net Income	**122.0**	**89.0**	**176.0**	**97.8**	P/B Ratio	**3.1**	52 Wk Hi-Low	**27.13-17.25**
Book Value	**2,016.0**	**889.0**	**1,058.0**	**19.0**	Yield %	**0.0**	Market Cap	**US$3,256.7mil**

Address **500 W. Main St.**
Louisville, KY 40201-1438
Tel **502-580-1000**
Fax **502-580-4516**
Exchange **NYSE**
Ticker **HUM**
President **Wayne T. Smith**
Chairman & CEO **David A. Jones**

*Irregular period due to fiscal year change.

J.B. Hunt

Industry: **Trucking**

J.B. Hunt Transport Services is a freight-transportation company. It transports commodities in the United States, Canada, and Mexico by truck and combination truck and railroad service. The company's principal freight is foodstuffs, automotive parts, and chemicals. It is also licensed to transport hazardous waste. Business operations in Canada and Mexico account for approximately 5% of total revenues. Hunt operates 7,400 tractors and 8,600 trailers, as well as maintenance facilities in Atlanta, Chicago, Detroit, Houston, Oklahoma City, and other cities in the U.S.

$ mil	12/92	12/93	12/94	% Change				
Sales	**912.0**	**1,020.9**	**1,207.6**	**18.3**	P/E Ratio	**14.4**	Price (9/30/95)	**15.13**
Net Income	**38.8**	**38.2**	**40.4**	**5.7**	P/B Ratio	**1.5**	52 Wk Hi-Low	**20.13-15.00**
Book Value	**308.6**	**344.0**	**377.9**	**9.9**	Yield %	**1.3**	Market Cap	**US$583.4mil**

Address **615 J.B. Hunt Corporate Dr.**
Lowell, AR 72745
Tel **501-820-0000**
Fax **501-820-8395**
Exchange **NASDA**
Ticker **JBHT**
President & CEO **Kirk Thompson**
Chairman **J.B. Hunt**

Huntington Bancshares

Industry: **Banks - Central U.S.**

Huntington Bancshares is a bank holding company with banks that provide commercial and consumer banking, mortgage banking, and savings and loan services through 344 offices in Ohio, Florida, Illinois, Indiana, Kentucky, Michigan, Pennsylvania, and West Virginia. Its other financial-services companies provide automobile-financing, mortgage-trust, investment-banking, and loan-origination services through 75 offices in the Midwest and eastern United States. The company also owns and manages the Monitor family of mutual funds, with total assets of approximately $600 million.

$ mil	12/92	12/93	12/94	% Change				
Revenues	1,259.0	1,542.1	1,455.1	-5.6	P/E Ratio	12.0	Price (9/30/95)	22.50
Net Income	139.0	236.9	242.6	2.4	P/B Ratio	2.1	52 Wk Hi-Low	23.38-16.07
Book Value	941.4	1,324.6	1,411.8	6.6	Yield %	3.2	Market Cap	US$3,090.9mil

Address **Huntington Ctr., 41 S. High St.**
Columbus, OH 43287
Tel **614-480-8300**
Fax **614-463-5485**
Exchange **NASDA**
Ticker **HBAN**
President **Zuheir Sofia**
Chairman & CEO **Frank Wobst**

IBM

Industry: **Computers**

International Business Machines (IBM) designs computer systems, peripherals, software and provides related services. The company produces personal and mainframe computers, as well as networking and programming systems. It also designs microprocessor chips, hard drives, fax boards, and keyboards for its (and compatible) computers. IBM also offers customer and dealer financing for its products and services. It markets its products under the ThinkPad, PS/Note, Options, and PowerPC trademarks in the United States and abroad. IBM acquired Lotus Development in 1995.

$ mil	12/92	12/93	12/94	% Change				
Sales	64,523.0	62,716.0	64,052.0	2.1	P/E Ratio	18.8	Price (9/30/95)	94.38
Net Income	-4,965.0	-8,101.0	3,021.0	-137.3	P/B Ratio	2.4	52 Wk Hi-Low	113.75-68.38
Book Value	27,624.0	19,738.0	23,413.0	18.6	Yield %	1.1	Market Cap	US$53,673mil

Address **1 Old Orchard Rd.**
Armonk, NY 10504
Tel **914-765-1900**
Fax **914-765-6007**
Exchange **NYSE**
Ticker **IBM**
Chief Executive **Louis V. Gerstner, Jr.**
Chairman **Louis V. Gerstner, Jr.**

Illinois Central

Industry: **Railroads**

Illinois Central, through its subsidiary, Illinois Central Railroad Company operates a freight railroad between Chicago and the Gulf of Mexico. Including secondary main-, passing-, yard-, and switching-lines, the railroad's system totals about 5,000 miles of track. With customers engaged in various businesses, the company primarily transports chemicals, coal, grain, paper, grain-mill, and food products, and intermodal freight. The transportation of chemicals accounts for roughly 25% of total freight revenues; coal makes up about 15% of the total; and grain contributes 19%.

$ mil	12/92	12/93	12/94	% Change				
Sales	547.4	564.7	593.9	5.2	P/E Ratio	14.7	Price (9/30/95)	39.13
Net Income	95.9	68.2	113.9	67.0	P/B Ratio	3.7	52 Wk Hi-Low	40.75-39.13
Book Value	338.8	377.4	454.1	20.3	Yield %	2.2	Market Cap	US$1,634.3mil

Address **455 N. Cityfront Plaza Dr.**
Chicago, IL 60611-5504
Tel **312-755-7500**
Fax **N/A**
Exchange **NYSE**
Ticker **IC**
President & CEO **E. Hunter Harrison**
Chairman **Gilbert H. Lamphere**

Illinois Tool Works

Industry: **Industrial - Diversified**

Illinois Tool Works manufactures engineered components, industrial systems, and consumables. The company's engineered components segment includes short lead-time plastic and metal components and assemblies; plastic and metal fasteners, and fastening tools and equipment. Industrial systems and consumables' products include longer-lead-time systems and related consumables for consumer and industrial packaging, finishing, furniture, inspection, and quality-assurance applications. Illinois Tool Works markets its products to industrial customers worldwide.

$ mil	12/92	12/93	12/94	% Change				
Sales	2,811.6	3,159.2	3,461.3	9.6	P/E Ratio	24.0	Price (9/30/95)	58.88
Net Income	192.1	206.6	277.8	34.5	P/B Ratio	4.4	52 Wk Hi-Low	63.00-39.88
Book Value	1,339.7	1,258.7	1,541.5	22.5	Yield %	0.9	Market Cap	US$6,907.9mil

Address **3600 W. Lake Ave.**
Glenview, IL 60025-5811
Tel **708-724-7500**
Fax **708-657-4261**
Exchange **NYSE**
Ticker **ITW**
President **W. James Farrell**
Chairman & CEO **John D. Nichols**

Illinova

Industry: **Electrical Utilities - Central U.S.**

Illinova is a public utility providing electric-power and natural-gas service in Illinois. It delivers its services to approximately 555,000 residential and industrial customers in a service area that covers 15,000 square miles, or one fourth of the state. Residential customers account for approximately 41% of and 63% of electric and natural-gas revenues. Commercial and Industrial users make up the majority of the remainder. The company generates approximately 72% of its electricity at company-owned coal-fired plants; the remaining 28% comes from nuclear-energy stations.

$ mil	12/92	12/93	12/94	% Change				
Sales	1,479.5	1,581.2	1,589.5	0.5	P/E Ratio	13.0	Price (9/30/95)	27.13
Net Income	122.1	-55.8	158.2	-383.5	P/B Ratio	1.4	52 Wk Hi-Low	27.13-19.00
Book Value	1,825.8	1,672.7	1,450.2	-13.3	Yield %	2.9	Market Cap	US$2,051.8mil

Address **500 S. 27th St.**
Decatur, IL 62525-1805
Tel **217-424-6600**
Fax **217-424-7378**
Exchange **NYSE**
Ticker **ILN**
President & CEO **Larry D. Haab**
Chairman **Larry D. Haab**

Imo Industries

Industry: **Factory Equipment**

Imo Industries manufactures controls and engineered-power products and provides other related services. The company's products include actuators, window controls, latches, door panels, rotary and centrifugal pumps, electronic adjustable-speed motor drives, gears, speed reducers, motor controllers, transducers, and pump switches. Imo Industries markets its products to the defense, aviation, marine, oil- and gas-processing, and cogeneration industries in the United States and overseas. The company operates 45 facilities in North America, Europe, Asia, and Australia.

$ mil	12/92	12/93	12/94	% Change				
Sales	928.3	641.7	463.9	-27.7	P/E Ratio	40.2	Price (9/30/95)	9.25
Net Income	-82.6	-270.6	3.9	-101.5	P/B Ratio	NMF	52 Wk Hi-Low	9.88-6.25
Book Value	241.4	-34.0	-28.0	-17.6	Yield %	0.0	Market Cap	US$157.8mil

Address **1009 Lenox Dr.** **Lawrenceville, NJ 08648** Tel **609-896-7600** Fax **609-896-7688** Exchange **NYSE** Ticker **IMD** Chief Executive **Donald K. Farrar** Chairman **Donald K. Farrar**

Indresco

Industry: **Heavy Machinery**

Indresco operates in three segments: minerals and refractory products, mining equipment, and air equipment. The company's Harbison-Walker division mines, processes minerals, and manufactures more than 200 refractory products. Refractories are used to contain liquids, solids, or gasses at high temperatures. The Marion division produces walking and crawler draglines, rotary blast-hole drills and other equipment used in surface mining. The Jeffrey division produces underground-mining machines. The Cleco brand pneumatic tools include assembly tools used in electronic markets.

$ mil	10/92	10/93	10/94	% Change				
Sales	558.7	538.1	437.1	-18.8	P/E Ratio	17.5	Price (9/30/95)	17.88
Net Income	-65.7	-40.4	24.6	-160.9	P/B Ratio	1.5	52 Wk Hi-Low	18.13-11.25
Book Value	352.0	287.8	273.6	-4.9	Yield %	0.0	Market Cap	US$405.7mil

Address **Ste. 2500, 2121 San Jacinto St.** **Dallas, TX 75201** Tel **214-953-4500** Fax **214-953-4596** Exchange **NYSE** Ticker **ID** President & CEO **J.L. Jackson** Chairman **J.L. Jackson**

Informix

Industry: **Software**

Informix develops and supports distributed database-management systems and tools for the development of object-oriented graphics and character-based applications. These tools are used for delivering information to desktop platforms. In addition to software products, the company offers training, consulting, and system maintenance to its customers. Presently, Informix has operating subsidiaries in 30 foreign countries. The company's database-management software runs on the UNIX, Windows, NetWare, and Windows/NT operating software.

$ mil	12/92	12/93	12/94	% Change				
Sales	283.6	352.9	468.7	32.8	P/E Ratio	33.2	Price (9/30/95)	32.50
Net Income	47.8	56.1	66.2	18.0	P/B Ratio	7.7	52 Wk Hi-Low	34.00-26.50
Book Value	132.7	207.4	275.6	32.9	Yield %	0.0	Market Cap	US$4,350.4mil

Address **4100 Bohannon Dr.** **Menlo Park, CA 94025** Tel **415-926-6300** Fax **N/A** Exchange **NASDA** Ticker **IFMX** President & CEO **Phillip E. White** Chairman **Phillip E. White**

Ingersoll-Rand

Industry: **Industrial - Diversified**

Ingersoll-Rand manufactures industrial machinery, engineered equipment, and produces air-compression machinery used in refineries, chemical plants, and service stations. The company and Dresser Industries jointly own Dresser-Rand, which makes steam and gas turbines and gas compressors and engines. The company produces road-building equipment, drills, and pumps for use in construction and mining applications. It also supplies automated systems, including bearings and centrifugal air compressors, to the automotive market. In 1995, the company acquired Clark Equipment.

$ mil	12/92	12/93	12/94	% Change				
Sales	3,783.8	4,021.1	4,507.5	12.1	P/E Ratio	18.8	Price (9/30/95)	37.50
Net Income	-234.4	142.5	211.1	48.2	P/B Ratio	2.6	52 Wk Hi-Low	42.00-28.88
Book Value	1,293.4	1,349.8	1,531.3	13.4	Yield %	1.9	Market Cap	US$3,972.4mil

Address **200 Chestnut Ridge Rd.** **Woodcliff Lake, NJ 07675** Tel **201-573-0123** Fax **201-573-3448** Exchange **NYSE** Ticker **IR** President & CEO **James E. Perrella** Chairman **James E. Perrella**

Inland Steel

Industry: **Steel**

Inland Steel Industries produces various steels; approximately 99% of company products consist of carbon and high-strength low-alloy steel grades. Iron Steel Company, a subsidiary, produces and sells steel and related products, and transports iron ore and other commodities on the Great Lakes. The company's steel service center operations are conducted by its Inland Materials Distribution Group through its operating subsidiaries--Joseph T. Ryerson & Son and J. M. Tull Metals Company. Steel service centers sell carbon, alloy, and stainless steels and industrial plastics.

$ mil	12/92	12/93	12/94	% Change				
Sales	3,494.3	3,888.2	4,497.0	15.7	P/E Ratio	12.6	Price (9/30/95)	22.75
Net Income	-815.6	-37.6	107.4	-385.6	P/B Ratio	1.4	52 Wk Hi-Low	40.25-22.75
Book Value	506.3	623.4	732.1	17.4	Yield %	0.0	Market Cap	US$1,106.8mil

Address **30 W. Monroe St.** **Chicago, IL 60603** Tel **312-346-0300** Fax **312-899-3323** Exchange **NYSE** Ticker **IAD** President & CEO **Robert J. Darnall** Chairman **Robert J. Darnall**

Integra Financial

Industry: **Banks - Eastern U.S.**

Integra Financial is a bank holding company headquartered in Pittsburgh. Its Integra Bank subsidiary provides retail- and commercial-banking services through more than 260 branches in western Pennsylvania. The bank offers savings, interest- and non-interest-bearing checking, and money-market accounts, as well as certificates of deposit. Integra Financial's nonbanking subsidiaries offer trust, mortgage-banking, securities-brokerage, consumer-financing and credit life and disability reinsurance services. In 1995, the company agreed to be acquired by National City.

$ mil	12/92	12/93	12/94	% Change				
Revenues	890.3	1,083.7	1,079.1	-0.4	P/E Ratio	11.6	Price (9/30/95)	58.13
Net Income	113.4	212.8	169.0	-20.6	P/B Ratio	2.2	52 Wk Hi-Low	58.13-42.63
Book Value	663.0	1,032.3	858.6	-16.8	Yield %	2.9	Market Cap	US$1,908.0mil

Address **4 PPG Place**
Pittsburgh, PA 15222-5408
Tel **412-644-7669**
Fax **412-261-7279**
Exchange **NYSE**
Ticker **ITG**
President **Leonard M. Carroll**
Chairman & CEO **William F. Roemer**

Intel

Industry: **Semiconductors & related**

Intel designs microcomputer components and related products. The company's principal products are its microprocessors (the central processing units of a personal computer); it markets these to original-equipment manufacturers under the Pentium, Intel486, and Intel386 trademarks. Currently, approximately 87% of all personal computers have Intel-based architecture. The company also manufactures memory chips, computer modules and boards, network and communication products, personal-conferencing products, and parallel supercomputers.

$ mil	12/92	12/93	12/94	% Change				
Sales	5,844.0	8,782.0	11,521.0	31.2	P/E Ratio	11.5	Price (9/30/95)	60.13
Net Income	1,066.5	2,295.0	2,288.0	-0.3	P/B Ratio	2.7	52 Wk Hi-Low	76.44-28.91
Book Value	5,444.6	7,500.0	9,267.0	23.6	Yield %	0.4	Market Cap	US$49,513mil

Address **2200 Mission College Blvd.**
Santa Clara, CA 95052-8119
Tel **408-765-8080**
Fax **408-765-1402**
Exchange **NASDA**
Ticker **INTC**
President **Andrew S. Grove**
Chairman **Gordon E. Moore**

Intergraph

Industry: **Industrial Technology**

Intergraph sells systems for computer-aided design, computer-aided manufacturing, and computer-aided engineering in the United States and abroad. It develops computer-graphics systems used in technical applications by companies in the utilities, building, automotive, electronics, manufacturing, and publishing industries. The company provides industry-specific application software, work stations, servers, and support services. Intergraph markets its products and services in about 50 countries, and sales outside of the U.S. account for more than half of its revenues.

$ mil	12/92	12/93	12/94	% Change				
Sales	1,176.7	1,050.8	1,041.4	-0.9	P/E Ratio	NMF	Price (9/30/95)	12.13
Net Income	8.4	-116.0	-70.2	-39.5	P/B Ratio	1.0	52 Wk Hi-Low	13.75-7.50
Book Value	736.9	588.7	522.3	-11.3	Yield %	0.0	Market Cap	US$558.8mil

Address **Intergraph**
Huntsville, AL 35894-0001
Tel **205-730-2000**
Fax **205-730-2164**
Exchange **NASDA**
Ticker **INGR**
Chief Executive **James W. Meadlock**
Chairman **James W. Meadlock**

International Flavors & Fragrances

Industry: **Cosmetics & Personal Care**

International Flavors & Fragrances manufactures flavoring and fragrance agents for use in consumer goods. The company's fragrance products are used in cosmetics and other personal-care products; soaps, detergents, and other cleaning products; and room fresheners. Its flavors are used in processed foods, beverages, pharmaceutical products, tobacco products, and animal food. The company makes synthetic and organic products, primarily from organic chemicals, fruits, vegetables, flowers, and woods, and operates manufacturing plants and distribution facilities worldwide.

$ mil	12/92	12/93	12/94	% Change				
Sales	1,126.4	1,188.7	1,315.2	10.6	P/E Ratio	23.8	Price (9/30/95)	48.25
Net Income	170.6	202.5	226.0	11.6	P/B Ratio	5.3	52 Wk Hi-Low	53.00-40.75
Book Value	977.1	891.9	1,008.1	13.0	Yield %	2.2	Market Cap	US$5,369.4mil

Address **521 W. 57th St.**
New York, NY 10019-2960
Tel **212-765-5500**
Fax **212-708-7132**
Exchange **NYSE**
Ticker **IFF**
President **Eugene P. Grisanti**
Chairman **Eugene P. Grisanti**

Intl Game Technology

Industry: **Other Recreational Products & Services**

International Game Technology (IGT) manufactures computerized casino gaming products and proprietary systems. The company also develops and manufactures systems that monitor slot-machine play. In addition to gaming-product sales and leases, the company's computerized, linked proprietary systems monitor video-gaming terminals. The company has also developed specialized terminals for lotteries. In addition, the company offers spinning-reel slot machines, sold under the S-Plus trademark. IGT directly or indirectly owns subsidiaries in Europe, Australia, Japan, and Europe.

$ mil	09/92	09/93	09/94	% Change				
Sales	399.4	478.0	674.5	41.1	P/E Ratio	12.5	Price (9/30/95)	13.38
Net Income	64.8	119.0	140.5	18.0	P/B Ratio	3.4	52 Wk Hi-Low	20.75-12.63
Book Value	214.1	378.5	520.9	37.6	Yield %	0.9	Market Cap	US$1,726.5mil

Address **5270 Neil Rd.**
Reno, NV 89510-0120
Tel **702-686-1200**
Fax **702-688-0777**
Exchange **NYSE**
Ticker **IGT**
Chief Executive **John J. Russell**
Chairman **Charles N. Mathewson**

International Paper

Industry: **Paper Products**

International Paper is an integrated paper and forest-products manufacturer. It operates more than six million acres of forestland and has manufacturing plants in more than 26 countries. The company produces bleached board for milk and food packaging, and white and colored business papers, including those marketed under the Hammermill, Strathmore, Beckett, and Springhill brand names. Its other products include photographic films and papers, logs, and other wood items. International Paper operates production facilities in North America, Europe, Asia, and Latin America.

$ mil	12/92	12/93	12/94	% Change				
Sales	**13,598.0**	**13,685.0**	**14,966.0**	**9.4**	P/E Ratio	**29.4**	Price (9/30/95)	**42.00**
Net Income	**86.0**	**289.0**	**357.0**	**23.5**	P/B Ratio	**1.6**	52 Wk Hi-Low	**45.38-34.06**
Book Value	**6,189.0**	**6,225.0**	**6,514.0**	**4.6**	Yield %	**2.0**	Market Cap	**US$10,692mil**

Address	**2 Manhattanville Rd.**	Tel	**914-397-1500**	Exchange	**NYSE**	Chief Executive	**John A. Georges**
	Purchase, NY 10577	Fax	**914-397-1596**	Ticker	**IP**	Chairman	**John A. Georges**

Interpublic Group

Industry: **Advertising**

Interpublic Group operates three advertising agencies: McCann-Erickson Worldwide, Lintas Worldwide, and The Lowe Group. It offers advertising-agency services through association arrangements with local agencies in various parts of the world. The company conducts market research, sales promotion, product development, direct marketing, telemarketing, and other related services. The company also owns the Scali, McCabe, Sloves advertising agency, as well as a 19.9% equity interest in Atlantis Communications, a Canadian television-program distributor.

$ mil	12/92	12/93	12/94	% Change				
Sales	**1,855.0**	**1,793.9**	**1,984.3**	**10.6**	P/E Ratio	**32.1**	Price (9/30/95)	**39.75**
Net Income	**87.3**	**124.8**	**93.5**	**-25.1**	P/B Ratio	**4.8**	52 Wk Hi-Low	**40.00-29.88**
Book Value	**511.2**	**564.0**	**649.4**	**15.1**	Yield %	**1.4**	Market Cap	**US$3,103.1mil**

Address	**1271 Ave. of the Americas**	Tel	**212-399-8000**	Exchange	**NYSE**	President & CEO	**Philip H. Geier, Jr.**
	New York, NY 10020	Fax	**212-399-8130**	Ticker	**IPG**	Chairman	**Philip H. Geier, Jr.**

Ipalco

Industry: **Electrical Utilities - Central U.S.**

Ipalco Enterprises is the holding company for Indianapolis Power & Light Company and Mid-America Capital Resources. Indianapolis Power & Light is an electric and steam utility serving more than 400,000 customers, primarily in Indianapolis and Marion County, Indiana. Commercial and industrial users account for approximately 58% of its revenues. Mid-America operates a district-cooling system in Indianapolis and district-cooling and steam-heating systems in Cleveland. Mid-America's systems provide alternative climate control for businesses and governmental agencies.

$ mil	12/92	12/93	12/94	% Change				
Sales	**633.2**	**644.3**	**686.1**	**6.5**	P/E Ratio	**12.5**	Price (9/30/95)	**30.75**
Net Income	**88.3**	**75.4**	**93.0**	**23.3**	P/B Ratio	**1.4**	52 Wk Hi-Low	**36.13-28.63**
Book Value	**787.7**	**787.2**	**802.0**	**1.9**	Yield %	**6.9**	Market Cap	**US$1,163.0mil**

Address	**25 Monument Circle**	Tel	**317-261-8261**	Exchange	**NYSE**	President	**John R. Hodowal**
	Indianapolis, IN 46204	Fax	**317-261-8313**	Ticker	**IPL**	Chairman	**John R. Hodowal**

ITT

Industry: **Conglomerates**

ITT is a multi-industry conglomerate. Its largest business is insurance, conducted primarily through ITT Hartford, and focuses on property and casualty, life, and health coverage. The company's service division includes commercial and consumer finance, as well as telephone-directory publishing. In addition, the company operates technical schools and the ITT Sheraton chain of hotels and casinos. ITT also produces electronic and mechanical products for use in automotive, defense, and other applications. The company markets its products and operates hotels worldwide.

$ mil	12/92	12/93	12/94	% Change				
Sales	**21,651.0**	**22,762.0**	**23,620.0**	**3.8**	P/E Ratio	**14.5**	Price (9/30/95)	**124.00**
Net Income	**-885.0**	**913.0**	**1,022.0**	**11.9**	P/B Ratio	**2.4**	52 Wk Hi-Low	**128.50-77.00**
Book Value	**7,247.0**	**7,650.0**	**5,459.0**	**-28.6**	Yield %	**1.6**	Market Cap	**US$14,359mil**

Address	**1330 Ave. of the Americas**	Tel	**212-258-1000**	Exchange	**NYSE**	President & CEO	**Rand V. Araskog**
	New York, NY 10019-5490	Fax	**212-489-5196**	Ticker	**ITT**	Chairman	**Rand V. Araskog**

Jacobs Engineering

Industry: **Heavy Construction**

Jacobs Engineering Group provides engineering, construction, construction management, process-plant maintenance, and consulting services. The company markets these services to government agencies and users in the refining, chemical, food-processing, pharmaceutical, and biotechnology industries in the United States and internationally. Business outside North America accounts for approximately 6% of the company's total revenues. Jacobs Engineering has offices throughout the U.S. and in Ireland, England, and Scotland.

$ mil	09/92	09/93	09/94	% Change				
Sales	**1,106.4**	**1,142.9**	**1,165.8**	**2.0**	P/E Ratio	**33.2**	Price (9/30/95)	**24.88**
Net Income	**26.6**	**28.7**	**18.8**	**-34.5**	P/B Ratio	**3.1**	52 Wk Hi-Low	**25.63-18.75**
Book Value	**139.8**	**173.8**	**200.4**	**15.3**	Yield %	**0.0**	Market Cap	**US$629.9mil**

Address	**251 S. Lake Ave.**	Tel	**818-449-2171**	Exchange	**NYSE**	President & CEO	**Noel G. Watson**
	Pasadena, CA 91101	Fax	**N/A**	Ticker	**JEC**	Chairman	**Joseph J. Jacobs**

James River

Industry: **Household Products (Non-Durable)**

James River manufactures forest products in the United States and Europe from purchased timber stock. The company's consumer products include Northern and Nice 'N Soft bathroom tissue, Brawny paper towels, and Dixie and Vanity Fair plates, cups, and cutlery. Its food- and consumer-packaging division makes paperboard cartons, plastic packaging such as potato chip and bread bags, and barrier papers such as cereal-box liners. It also makes office and publishing papers. James River operates 116 manufacturing facilities in the United States and abroad.

$ mil	12/92	12/93	12/94*	% Change				
Sales	4,728.2	4,650.2	5,417.3	16.5	P/E Ratio	NMF	Price (9/30/95)	32.00
Net Income	-427.3	-0.4	-13.0	NMF	P/B Ratio	1.2	52 Wk Hi-Low	36.50-20.00
Book Value	2,113.7	1,968.2	2,161.6	9.8	Yield %	1.9	Market Cap	US$2,635.8mil

Address	**120 Tredegar St.**	Tel	**804-644-5411**	Exchange	**NYSE**	President & CEO	**Robert C. Williams**
	Richmond, VA 23219	Fax	**804-649-4428**	Ticker	**JR**	Chairman	**Robert C. Williams**

Jefferson-Pilot

Industry: **Insurance - Life & Health**

Jefferson-Pilot is a holding company primarily engaged in writing life, annuity, accident and health, property and casualty, and title insurance. Its primary business is individual life insurance, but it also offers group policies, including life, major-medical, and dental plans, and manages annuity and mutual-fund products. The company's communication division owns and operates three network-affiliated television stations and 12 radio stations. The division also provides information to advertising agencies and broadcasters, and produces college-athletics programming.

$ mil	12/92	12/93	12/94	% Change				
Revenues	1,202.3	1,246.6	1,268.8	1.8	P/E Ratio	13.1	Price (9/30/95)	64.25
Net Income	203.2	195.2	239.2	22.6	P/B Ratio	1.8	52 Wk Hi-Low	65.63-50.63
Book Value	1,686.8	1,733.1	1,732.5	0.0	Yield %	2.7	Market Cap	US$3,049.6mil

Address	**100 N. Greene St.**	Tel	**910-691-3000**	Exchange	**NYSE**	President & CEO	**David A. Stonecipher**
	Greensboro, NC 27420	Fax	**910-691-3938**	Ticker	**JP**	Chairman	**Robert H. Spilman**

Johnson & Johnson

Industry: **Pharmaceuticals**

Johnson & Johnson manufactures personal-care and health-care products worldwide. Its retail products include Band-Aid adhesive bandages, Johnson's baby products, Reach toothbrushes, Monistat-7 yeast-infection treatments, and Tylenol over-the-counter medications. The company manufactures prescription drugs, including Retin-A acne cream and Ortho-Novum oral contraceptives. It also provides medical supplies to physicians, hospitals, and clinics in 150 countries. Johnson & Johnson also owns Neutrogena, a manufacturer of skin- and hair-care products.

$ mil	12/92	12/93	12/94	% Change				
Sales	13,753.0	14,138.0	15,734.0	11.3	P/E Ratio	23.8	Price (9/30/95)	74.13
Net Income	1,030.0	1,787.0	2,006.0	12.3	P/B Ratio	6.7	52 Wk Hi-Low	74.63-50.13
Book Value	5,171.0	5,568.0	7,122.0	27.9	Yield %	1.5	Market Cap	US$48,014mil

Address	**1 Johnson & Johnson Plz.**	Tel	**908-524-0400**	Exchange	**NYSE**	Chief Executive	**Ralph S. Larsen**
	New Brunswick, NJ 08933	Fax	**908-828-3063**	Ticker	**JNJ**	Chairman	**Ralph S. Larsen**

Johnson Controls

Industry: **Other Auto Parts**

Johnson Controls manufactures control systems, automotive products, and plastics. The company makes control systems for temperature, lighting, energy management, security, and fire safety in residential and nonresidential buildings. Johnson Controls manufactures automotive-seating components, and also supplies automotive batteries in the United States. The company's plastic products include containers and personal-care items. Johnson Controls operates manufacturing facilities in 13 North American and European countries.

$ mil	09/92	09/93	09/94	% Change				
Sales	5,156.5	6,181.7	6,870.5	11.1	P/E Ratio	16.6	Price (9/30/95)	63.25
Net Income	123.0	15.9	165.2	939.0	P/B Ratio	2.1	52 Wk Hi-Low	65.00-46.13
Book Value	1,194.2	1,079.0	1,202.8	11.5	Yield %	2.3	Market Cap	US$2,589.3mil

Address	**5757 N. Green Bay Ave.**	Tel	**414-228-1200**	Exchange	**NYSE**	Chief Executive	**James H. Keyes**
	Milwaukee, WI 53201	Fax	**414-228-2443**	Ticker	**JCI**	Chairman	**James H. Keyes**

Jostens

Industry: **Other Specialty Retailers**

Jostens manufactures class rings, graduation announcements, diplomas, and student yearbooks marketed to more than 30,000 elementary schools, high schools, and colleges worldwide. It also produces student pictures for elementary and high school students in the United States and in 50 countries. Sales of school products account for about 85% of Jostens' sales. The company also designs similar products marketed to businesses; these products are used in promotion campaigns, as well as to recognize individual achievement. Jostens operates plants in the U.S., Canada, and the U.K.

$ mil	06/93	06/94	06/95	% Change				
Revenues	914.8	827.3	665.1	-19.6	P/E Ratio	21.2	Price (9/30/95)	23.50
Net Income	-12.1	-16.2	50.4	-410.9	P/B Ratio	3.9	52 Wk Hi-Low	24.00-16.88
Book Value	313.3	256.6	270.6	5.5	Yield %	3.7	Market Cap	US$1,069.4mil

Address	**5501 Norman Center Dr.**	Tel	**612-830-3300**	Exchange	**NYSE**	President & CEO	**Robert C. Buhrmaster**
	Minneapolis, MN 55437	Fax	**612-897-4136**	Ticker	**JOS**	Chairman	**Robert P. Jensen**

Kansas City Power

Industry: **Electrical Utilities - Central U.S.**

Kansas City Power & Light is an electric utility. It generates and distributes electricity to more than 424,000 residential, commercial, industrial, and municipal customers, as well as other electric utilities in a 4,700-square-mile area of Missouri and Kansas. Residential customers account for roughly 71% of revenues; commercial and industrial users provide the remainder. Approximately 74% of the company's operating capacity comes from coal-fired stations; nearly 25% comes from nuclear-power generators; and the remainder comes from natural-gas and oil-fired plants.

$ mil	12/92	12/93	12/94	% Change				
Sales	**802.7**	**857.5**	**868.3**	**1.3**	P/E Ratio	**14.4**	Price (9/30/95)	**23.63**
Net Income	**86.3**	**105.8**	**104.8**	**-1.0**	P/B Ratio	**1.5**	52 Wk Hi-Low	**24.38-21.13**
Book Value	**944.8**	**956.9**	**965.3**	**0.9**	Yield %	**6.3**	Market Cap	**US$1,462.4mil**

Address	**1201 Walnut St.**	Tel	**816-556-2200**	Exchange	**NYSE**	President	**Drue Jennings**
	Kansas City, MO 64106-2124	Fax	**816-556-2418**	Ticker	**KLT**	Chairman	**Drue Jennings**

Kasler

Industry: **Heavy Construction**

Kasler Holding provides construction, mining, and environmental-remediation services. Its subsidiaries construct dams, roadways, and bridges for federal and state agencies; mine for phosphate, silica, and limestone; and perform real-estate and industrial-construction work. Its public-works and infrastructure-construction projects account for approximately 82% of revenues. Contracts with local, state, and federal agencies generate roughly 67% of Kasler's income. The company currently holds licenses to work in 23 states in the U.S., as well as mining leases in California.

$ mil	10/92	11/93 *	11/94	% Change				
Sales	**161.9**	**210.2**	**258.7**	**23.1**	P/E Ratio	**NMF**	Price (9/30/95)	**6.13**
Net Income	**6.5**	**6.9**	**0.7**	**-90.4**	P/B Ratio	**1.5**	52 Wk Hi-Low	**6.63-3.88**
Book Value	**43.3**	**120.4**	**120.0**	**-0.4**	Yield %	**0.8**	Market Cap	**US$180.6mil**

Address	**27400 E. Fifth St.**	Tel	**909-884-4811**	Exchange	**NYSE**	President & CEO	**John H. Wimberly**
	Highland, CA 92346	Fax	**909-862-8433**	Ticker	**KAS**	Chairman	**Dorn Parkinson**

*Irregular period due to fiscal year change.

Kaufman & Broad

Industry: **Home Construction**

Kaufman & Broad Home builds single- and multifamily housing. The company generally builds single-family houses in medium-size developments close to major metropolitan areas. These houses are intended primarily for first-time buyers. It also constructs housing and commercial developments in France, and owns and operates a housing-construction division in Toronto, Canada. Houses in California represent roughly 88% of those sold by the company in the United States. Its Kaufman & Broad Mortgage subsidiary provides mortgage-financing services to purchasers of its houses.

$ mil	11/92	11/93	11/94	% Change				
Sales	**1,094.2**	**1,237.0**	**1,336.3**	**8.0**	P/E Ratio	**10.9**	Price (9/30/95)	**12.63**
Net Income	**28.2**	**39.9**	**46.6**	**16.7**	P/B Ratio	**1.0**	52 Wk Hi-Low	**15.88-11.25**
Book Value	**318.4**	**444.3**	**404.8**	**-8.9**	Yield %	**2.4**	Market Cap	**US$408.9mil**

Address	**10990 Wilshire Blvd.**	Tel	**310-231-4000**	Exchange	**NYSE**	Chief Executive	**Bruce Karatz**
	Los Angeles, CA 90024	Fax	**310-231-4222**	Ticker	**KBH**	Chairman	**Bruce Karatz**

Kellogg

Industry: **Other Food**

Kellogg is a major manufacturer of ready-to-eat cereal products and other breakfast and convenience foods. The company's principal products are breakfast cereals, which it sells under the Kellogg's name, and include products such as Corn Flakes, Rice Krispies, Special K, Nutri-Grain, Fruit Loops, and Frosted Flakes. Its other main products include Nutri-Grain granola and fruit bars, Pop Tarts toaster pastries, and Nutri-Grain and Eggo frozen waffles. The company distributes its products in the United States and abroad, primarily through retail-food stores.

$ mil	12/92	12/93	12/94	% Change				
Sales	**6,190.6**	**6,295.4**	**6,562.0**	**4.2**	P/E Ratio	**23.0**	Price (9/30/95)	**72.38**
Net Income	**431.2**	**680.7**	**705.4**	**3.6**	P/B Ratio	**8.9**	52 Wk Hi-Low	**73.25-53.38**
Book Value	**1,945.2**	**1,713.4**	**1,807.5**	**5.5**	Yield %	**1.9**	Market Cap	**US$15,865mil**

Address	**1 Kellogg Sq.**	Tel	**616-961-2000**	Exchange	**NYSE**	Chief Executive	**Arnold G. Langbo**
	Battle Creek, MI 49016-3599	Fax	**616-961-2871**	Ticker	**K**	Chairman	**Arnold G. Langbo**

Kelly Services

Industry: **General Industrial & Commercial Services**

Kelly Services provides temporary clerical, marketing, technical, light-industrial, and home-care services. The company hires and assigns temporary employees to work on the premises of its customers. Services are provided to a clientele located in cities of all 50 states, as well as in Canada, Europe, New Zealand, and Australia through approximately 1,000 offices. Staff-leasing services are provided in California through the company's Your Staff subsidiary. According to Kelly's records, more than 200,000 customers have used the company's services in recent years.

$ mil	12/92	12/93	12/94	% Change				
Sales	**1,722.5**	**1,954.5**	**2,362.6**	**20.9**	P/E Ratio	**16.6**	Price (9/30/95)	**26.75**
Net Income	**39.2**	**44.6**	**61.1**	**36.9**	P/B Ratio	**2.4**	52 Wk Hi-Low	**36.75-25.63**
Book Value	**367.3**	**386.2**	**431.5**	**11.7**	Yield %	**2.6**	Market Cap	**US$1,016.4mil**

Address	**999 W. Big Beaver Rd.**	Tel	**810-362-4444**	Exchange	**NASDA**	President & CEO	**Terence E. Adderley**
	Troy, MI 48084	Fax	**810-244-4154**	Ticker	**KELYA**	Chairman	**William R. Kelly**

Kemper

Industry: **Insurance - Full Line**

Kemper is a financial-services company that provides asset-, real-estate, and risk-management services, securities brokerage, reinsurance, and life, property, and casualty insurance. Among its offerings are life insurance, fixed and variable annuities, money-market funds, more than 30 fixed-income and equity mutual funds, risk-control and -analysis services, and full-service securities management for its retail clients and other customers. Kemper also owns and manages properties as investments, primarily in California and the Midwest.

$ mil	12/92	12/93	12/94	% Change				
Revenues	**2,200.6**	**1,549.2**	**1,601.8**	**3.4**	P/E Ratio	**24.5**	Price (9/30/95)	**48.25**
Net Income	**-203.4**	**235.5**	**91.4**	**-61.2**	P/B Ratio	**1.3**	52 Wk Hi-Low	**60.88-36.63**
Book Value	**1,766.1**	**1,619.0**	**1,257.4**	**-22.3**	Yield %	**1.9**	Market Cap	**US$1,676.3mil**

Address **1 Kemper Dr.**
Long Grove, IL 60049
Tel **708-320-4700**
Fax **708-320-4694**
Exchange **NYSE**
Ticker **KEM**
President **Stephen B. Timbers**
Chairman & CEO **David B. Mathis**

Kerr-McGee

Industry: **Oil - Secondary**

Kerr-McGee is a diversified energy and chemical company. The company owns, on average, a 10% interest in 13,500 petroleum wells worldwide and holds net reserves of 850 billion cubic feet of natural gas and 191 million barrels of oil. It operates refineries that provide motor fuels to 1,200 Kerr-McGee gas stations, of which it manages 51. The company operates four coal mines in Illinois, West Virginia, and Wyoming with recoverable reserves of 900 million tons. Its chemical division produces titanium-dioxide pigment, boron, ilmenite, zircon, and wood-treatment chemicals.

$ mil	12/92	12/93	12/94	% Change				
Sales	**3,382.0**	**3,281.0**	**3,353.0**	**2.2**	P/E Ratio	**31.9**	Price (9/30/95)	**55.50**
Net Income	**-101.0**	**77.0**	**90.0**	**16.9**	P/B Ratio	**1.9**	52 Wk Hi-Low	**59.88-44.00**
Book Value	**1,350.0**	**1,512.0**	**1,543.0**	**2.1**	Yield %	**2.7**	Market Cap	**US$2,877.0mil**

Address **123 Robert S. Kerr Ave.**
Oklahoma City, OK 73102
Tel **405-270-1313**
Fax **405-270-3940**
Exchange **NYSE**
Ticker **KMG**
Chief Executive **Frank A. McPherson**
Chairman **Frank A. McPherson**

KeyCorp

Industry: **Banks - Central U.S.**

KeyCorp is a bank holding company with full-service commercial banks that focus on individuals, small- to medium-size businesses, and municipalities. The company's banks offer services in mortgage banking, trust and esatate planning, private banking, credit reinsurance, discount brokerage, and asset management. The banks also offer automated-teller services and safe deposit box rentals, as well as savings, money-market, individual-retirement, and checking accounts. KeyCorp operates approximately 1,300 branch and affiliate offices in 25 states.

$ mil	12/92	12/93	12/94	% Change				
Revenues	**2,405.0**	**5,215.6**	**5,387.4**	**3.3**	P/E Ratio	**9.9**	Price (9/30/95)	**34.25**
Net Income	**301.2**	**709.9**	**853.5**	**20.2**	P/B Ratio	**1.8**	52 Wk Hi-Low	**35.00-24.00**
Book Value	**1,868.1**	**4,393.6**	**4,698.5**	**6.9**	Yield %	**3.7**	Market Cap	**US$7,793.1mil**

Address **127 Public Sq.**
Cleveland, OH 44114-1306
Tel **216-689-6300**
Fax **216-689-0519**
Exchange **NYSE**
Ticker **KEY**
President **Robert W. Gillespie**
Chairman & CEO **Victor J. Riley, Jr.**

Keystone International

Industry: **Factory Equipment**

Keystone International designs and manufactures valves and other products that control the flow of liquids, gases, and fibrous and slurry materials. Industrial valves, its largest product segment, comprises 40% of company sales. Products include butterfly valves, safety relief valves, and critical-service valves. These specialized industrial products are used in various industries including chemical, power, food and beverage, marine and government, petroleum production and refining, water, commercial construction, oil and gas pipeline, mining and metals, and pulp and paper.

$ mil	12/92	12/93	12/94	% Change				
Sales	**528.4**	**516.1**	**535.1**	**3.7**	P/E Ratio	**22.9**	Price (9/30/95)	**21.50**
Net Income	**42.5**	**41.0**	**33.0**	**-19.6**	P/B Ratio	**2.7**	52 Wk Hi-Low	**22.75-17.00**
Book Value	**252.6**	**270.6**	**286.4**	**5.8**	Yield %	**3.4**	Market Cap	**US$761.1mil**

Address **9600 W. Gulf Bank Dr.**
Houston, TX 77040
Tel **713-466-1176**
Fax **713-466-6328**
Exchange **NYSE**
Ticker **KII**
Chief Executive **Raymond A. LeBlanc**
Chairman **Raymond A. LeBlanc**

Kimberly-Clark

Industry: **Household Products (Non-Durable)**

Kimberly-Clark produces products from natural and synthetic fibers, and provides air-transportation services. The company operates 85 production plants worldwide. Its consumer products include Kleenex facial and bathroom tissues, Huggies diapers, Kotex and New Freedom feminine-hygiene products, and Depend adult undergarments. It also makes newsprint and technical and tobacco papers. The company owns Midwest Express Airlines, which provides regional airline service, and offers services to the aviation industry. In 1995, the company agreed to acquire Scott Paper.

$ mil	12/92	12/93	12/94	% Change				
Sales	**7,091.1**	**6,972.9**	**7,364.2**	**5.6**	P/E Ratio	**20.2**	Price (9/30/95)	**67.13**
Net Income	**135.0**	**510.9**	**535.1**	**4.7**	P/B Ratio	**4.1**	52 Wk Hi-Low	**67.75-47.25**
Book Value	**2,191.1**	**2,457.2**	**2,595.8**	**5.6**	Yield %	**2.6**	Market Cap	**US$10,765mil**

Address **P.O. Box 619100**
Dallas, TX 75261-9100
Tel **214-830-1200**
Fax **214-830-1490**
Exchange **NYSE**
Ticker **KMB**
Chief Executive **Wayne R. Sanders**
Chairman **Wayne R. Sanders**

Kimco Realty

Industry: **Real-Estate Investment**

Kimco Realty owns and operates a number of neighborhood and community shopping centers. The company specializes in the acquisition, development, and management of centers with strong growth potential. These neighborhood and community shopping centers are designed to attract local area customers and are typically anchored by a supermarket, discount department store or drugstore, offering day-to-day necessities rather than high-priced luxury items. Kimco has 166 properties comprising approximately 22.3 million square feet of leasable space in 24 states.

$ mil	12/92	12/93	12/94	% Change				
Sales	**78.8**	**98.9**	**125.3**	**26.7**	P/E Ratio	**23.2**	Price (9/30/95)	**39.88**
Net Income	**19.0**	**34.6**	**40.3**	**16.4**	P/B Ratio	**2.5**	52 Wk Hi-Low	**41.00-37.25**
Book Value	**154.8**	**336.2**	**320.7**	**-4.6**	Yield %	**5.0**	Market Cap	**US$894.4mil**

Address	**Ste. 100, 3333 New Hyde Park Rd.**	Tel	**516-869-9000**	Exchange	**NYSE**	President	**David M. Samber**
	New Hyde Park, NY 11042	Fax	**516-869-9001**	Ticker	**KIM**	Chairman	**Milton Cooper**

King World

Industry: **Entertainment**

King World Productions distributes and syndicates television programming. The company currently distributes programming to approximately 400 television stations in more than 200 designated television markets in the United States, Canada, and foreign countries. It distributes directly and through sales agents and subdistributors. The company derives its revenues from the first-run syndication of the television series "The Oprah Winfrey Show," "Inside Edition," and "Wheel of Fortune." The company distributes programming primarily to network-affiliated stations.

$ mil	08/92	08/93	08/94	% Change				
Sales	**503.2**	**474.3**	**480.7**	**1.3**	P/E Ratio	**15.7**	Price (9/30/95)	**36.63**
Net Income	**94.9**	**101.9**	**88.3**	**-13.3**	P/B Ratio	**2.9**	52 Wk Hi-Low	**43.38-32.75**
Book Value	**342.9**	**394.2**	**459.1**	**16.5**	Yield %	**0.0**	Market Cap	**US$1,345.4mil**

Address	**1700 Broadway**	Tel	**212-315-4000**	Exchange	**NYSE**	President & CEO	**Michael King**
	New York, NY 10019	Fax	**212-247-7674**	Ticker	**KWP**	Chairman	**Roger King**

Kirby

Industry: **Marine Transportation**

Kirby provides marine-transportation, diesel-engine repair, and insurance services. The company's principal business, conducted by 14 subsidiaries, is the inland and offshore marine transportation of industrial and agricultural chemicals, petroleum products, dry bulk cargoes, containerized cargoes, and palletized cargoes using more than 600 ships. It also overhauls and repairs diesel engines and sells related parts for customers in the marine- and rail-transportation industries. Kirby's Universal Insurance subsidiary underwrites property- and casualty-insurance policies.

$ mil	12/92	12/93	12/94	% Change				
Sales	**269.5**	**378.4**	**433.1**	**14.5**	P/E Ratio	**26.7**	Price (9/30/95)	**15.50**
Net Income	**0.7**	**22.8**	**16.7**	**-27.0**	P/B Ratio	**2.0**	52 Wk Hi-Low	**17.88-13.25**
Book Value	**122.8**	**211.8**	**223.0**	**5.3**	Yield %	**0.0**	Market Cap	**US$426.3mil**

Address	**Ste. 300, 1775 St. James Pl.**	Tel	**713-629-9370**	Exchange	**AMEX**	President	**George A. Peterkin, Jr.**
	Houston, TX 77251-1745	Fax	**713-964-2200**	Ticker	**KEX**	Chairman	**Robert G. Stone, Jr.**

Kmart

Industry: **Retailers - Broadline**

Kmart is a mass-merchandise retailer. Its primary operation is a chain of about 2,300 Kmart discount stores in the United States. The company also has retail operations in Canada, the Czech Republic, Slovakia, and joint ventures in Mexico and Singapore. It has an interest in Coles Myer, an Australian retailer, and the footwear retailer Meldisco. Kmart's specialty-retail groups consist of the Borders-Walden group (bookstores), the Builders Square group (home-improvement stores), the Office Max group (office-supply stores), and Planet Music (compact discs).

$ mil	01/93	01/94	01/95	% Change				
Revenues	**37,724.0**	**34,156.0**	**34,025.0**	**-0.4**	P/E Ratio	**23.0**	Price (9/30/95)	**14.50**
Net Income	**941.0**	**-974.0**	**296.0**	**-130.4**	P/B Ratio	**1.1**	52 Wk Hi-Low	**17.88-11.88**
Book Value	**7,536.0**	**6,093.0**	**6,032.0**	**-1.0**	Yield %	**6.6**	Market Cap	**US$6,653.9mil**

Address	**3100 W. Big Beaver Rd.**	Tel	**810-643-1000**	Exchange	**NYSE**	Interim President	**Anthony N. Palizzi**
	Troy, MI 48084-3163	Fax	**810-643-2514**	Ticker	**KM**	Chairman	**Donald S. Perkins**

Knight-Ridder

Industry: **Publishing**

Knight-Ridder publishes newspapers and provides electronic news-retrieval and information services. The company publishes The Philadelphia Inquirer, The Miami Herald, The Detroit Free Press, and 25 other daily newspapers in communities nationwide. Knight-Ridder's newspaper businesses generate 82% of the company's total revenues. Knight-Ridder's information services, including its Dialog databases and its MoneyCenter financial-information service, target users in the United States and abroad.

$ mil	12/92	12/93	12/94	% Change				
Sales	**2,329.5**	**2,451.3**	**2,649.0**	**8.1**	P/E Ratio	**18.6**	Price (9/30/95)	**58.63**
Net Income	**40.9**	**148.1**	**170.9**	**15.4**	P/B Ratio	**2.5**	52 Wk Hi-Low	**58.75-46.88**
Book Value	**1,181.8**	**1,243.2**	**1,224.7**	**-1.5**	Yield %	**2.5**	Market Cap	**US$2,879.6mil**

Address	**1 Herald Plz.**	Tel	**305-376-3800**	Exchange	**NYSE**	President	**P. Anthony Ridder**
	Miami, FL 33132	Fax	**305-376-3876**	Ticker	**KRI**	Chairman & CEO	**James K. Batten**

Kohl's

Industry: **Apparel Retailers**

Kohl's operates 109 family-oriented, specialty department stores located throughout the Midwest in Illinois, Indiana, Iowa, Michigan, Minnesota, Ohio, and Wisconsin. Targeting middle-income customers, the stores feature moderately-priced, nationally known brands of apparel, shoes, accessories, housewares, and soft home products such as towels, sheets, and pillows. In addition to Levi's, Lee, Nike, Reebok, Cannon, and other national brand merchandise, Kohl's stores also offer private-label merchandise in many departments, sold under several names.

$ mil	01/93	01/94	01/95	% Change				
Revenues	1,096.9	1,305.8	1,554.1	19.0	P/E Ratio	27.7	Price (9/30/95)	51.88
Net Income	26.6	53.9	68.5	27.1	P/B Ratio	5.7	52 Wk Hi-Low	54.50-39.88
Book Value	207.4	262.5	334.3	27.3	Yield %	0.0	Market Cap	US$1,907.1mil

Address **N54 W13600 Woodale Dr.**
Menomonee Falls, WI 53051
Tel **414-783-5800**
Fax **N/A**
Exchange **NYSE**
Ticker **KSS**
President **Jay H. Baker**
Chairman & CEO **William S. Kellogg**

Kroger

Industry: **Food Retailers & Wholesalers**

Kroger is a food retailer. The company currently operates more than 1,300 supermarkets in 24 states. About 1,000 supermarkets are operated principally under the Kroger name in the Midwest, South, Southeast, and Southwest, in 16 states. Dillon Companies, a subsidiary of the company, operates approximately 240 supermarkets in nine states. In addition, the company operates about 930 convenience stores in 16 states. These stores are named Kwik Shop, Quik Stop, Time Savers, Turkey Hill, Loaf 'N Jug, Mini Mart, and Tom Thumb. Products are private-label groceries.

$ mil	12/92	12/93	12/94	% Change				
Sales	22,144.6	22,384.3	22,959.1	2.6	P/E Ratio	16.0	Price (9/30/95)	34.13
Net Income	-5.9	-12.2	242.2	NMF	P/B Ratio	NMF	52 Wk Hi-Low	34.50-22.00
Book Value	-2,700.0	-2,459.6	-2,153.7	-12.4	Yield %	0.0	Market Cap	US$4,181.5mil

Address **1014 Vine St.**
Cincinnati, OH 45202
Tel **513-762-4000**
Fax **513-762-4554**
Exchange **NYSE**
Ticker **KR**
President **Richard L. Bere**
Chairman & CEO **Joseph A. Pichler**

La Quinta Inns

Industry: **Lodging**

La Quinta Inns operates a chain of 228 inns in 29 states, with concentrations in Texas, Florida, and California. The company wholly owns 176 inns, and owns 40% or more of an additional 50. The inns contain an average of 130 rooms, averaging 300 square feet each, and are generally located near interstate highways, major traffic arteries, or areas such as airports and convention centers. The inns are also generally located adjacent to free-standing restaurants. The company is in a licensing agreement with Desarrollos Turisticos Vanguardia for lodging operations in Mexico.

$ mil	12/92	12/93	12/94	% Change				
Sales	255.8	271.9	362.2	33.2	P/E Ratio	35.9	Price (9/30/95)	28.00
Net Income	-8.8	20.3	37.8	86.3	P/B Ratio	6.9	52 Wk Hi-Low	30.50-19.25
Book Value	124.3	149.1	189.2	26.9	Yield %	0.4	Market Cap	US$1,464.2mil

Address **Weston Ctr., 112 E. Pecan**
San Antonio, TX 78299-2636
Tel **210-302-6000**
Fax **210-366-6151**
Exchange **NYSE**
Ticker **LQI**
President & CEO **Gary L. Mead**
Chairman **Thomas M. Taylor**

LAM Research

Industry: **Industrial Technology**

Lam Research makes semiconductor-processing equipment used in the fabrication of integrated circuits. The company's products are used to deposit specific films on a semiconductor silicon wafer and selectively etch away portions of various films to create a circuit design. Lam Research's products include multichamber systems that integrate up to four circuit chambers on a single platform, and chemical-vapor systems that expose a silicon wafer to various gases containing material to be deposited. The company also manufactures four types of single-wafer plasma-etch systems.

$ mil	06/93	06/94	06/95	% Change				
Sales	260.5	484.9	798.2	64.6	P/E Ratio	18.3	Price (9/30/95)	59.75
Net Income	18.9	37.8	89.2	136.2	P/B Ratio	4.1	52 Wk Hi-Low	71.75-37.50
Book Value	130.3	176.8	395.3	123.5	Yield %	0.0	Market Cap	US$1,614.3mil

Address **4650 Cushing Parkway**
Fremont, CA 94538
Tel **510-659-0200**
Fax **510-490-5026**
Exchange **NASDA**
Ticker **LRCX**
Chief Executive **Roger D. Emerick**
Chairman **Roger D. Emerick**

Landstar System

Industry: **Trucking**

Landstar System provides over-the-road transportation services throughout North America. The company transports iron, steel, paper, lumber, building products, aluminum, chemicals, containers, foodstuffs, ammunitions, military hardware, and other cargoes using a fleet of more than 9,100 trucks and 12,800 trailers driven by a staff of company-employed drivers. Landstar employs electronic-document and data-interchange (EDI) technology, allowing the company's management and customers to track the location and assess the status of specific parcels or cargo shipments.

$ mil	12/92 R	12/93	12/94	% Change				
Sales	672.5	780.5	984.4	26.1	P/E Ratio	12.7	Price (9/30/95)	24.13
Net Income	6.4	11.7	24.4	108.1	P/B Ratio	2.9	52 Wk Hi-Low	37.50-21.44
Book Value	29.9	80.8	105.2	30.2	Yield %	0.0	Market Cap	US$308.3mil

Address **1000 Bridgeport Ave.**
Shelton, CT 06484-0898
Tel **203-925-2900**
Fax **203-925-2916**
Exchange **NASDA**
Ticker **LSTR**
President & CEO **Jeffrey C. Crowe**
Chairman **Jeffrey C. Crowe**

R=Restated.

Lee Enterprises

Industry: **Publishing**

Lee Enterprises operates newspapers and television stations. The company publishes 19 daily and 36 weekly newspapers with combined circulations of about 63.3 million. Its television operations include five CBS-affiliated stations in Hawaii, Nebraska, New Mexico, and Oregon; an NBC affiliate in Huntington, West Virginia; an ABC affiliate in Tucson, Arizona; and an independent station in Las Cruces, New Mexico. NAPP Systems, a subsidiary, manufactures photosensitive polymer printing plates and related equipment for use by newspaper and telephone-directory printers.

$ mil	09/92	09/93	09/94	% Change				
Sales	**363.9**	**372.9**	**402.6**	**8.0**	P/E Ratio	**20.0**	Price (9/30/95)	**43.38**
Net Income	**38.5**	**41.2**	**50.9**	**23.4**	P/B Ratio	**4.1**	52 Wk Hi-Low	**43.38-31.75**
Book Value	**203.8**	**223.5**	**241.9**	**8.2**	Yield %	**1.9**	Market Cap	**US$1,031.2mil**

Address	**215 N. Main St.**	Tel	**319-383-2100**	Exchange	**NYSE**	President & CEO	**Richard D. Gottlieb**
	Davenport, IA 52801	Fax	**319-323-9608**	Ticker	**LEE**	Chairman	**Lloyd G. Schermer**

Leggett & Platt

Industry: **Other Home Furnishings**

Leggett & Platt produces components used in the manufacture of bedding and other furniture. The company's main products include springs, lumber for box-spring frames, incliner mechanisms for reclining furniture, finished bed frames, and carpet-cushioning materials. It also makes nonfurniture items that include die-cast-aluminum ingots and finished products, industrial wire, metal shelving, and computerized cutting equipment. Hanes Holding Company, a subsidiary, produces industrial fabrics used in furniture manufacturing. Leggett & Platt markets its products worldwide.

$ mil	12/92	12/93	12/94	% Change				
Sales	**1,170.5**	**1,526.7**	**1,858.1**	**21.7**	P/E Ratio	**17.7**	Price (9/30/95)	**24.63**
Net Income	**62.5**	**85.9**	**115.4**	**34.3**	P/B Ratio	**3.3**	52 Wk Hi-Low	**26.38-16.81**
Book Value	**425.2**	**515.6**	**625.2**	**21.3**	Yield %	**1.3**	Market Cap	**US$2,068.2mil**

Address	**1 Leggett Rd.**	Tel	**417-358-8131**	Exchange	**NYSE**	President	**Felix E. Wright**
	Carthage, MO 64836	Fax	**417-358-8449**	Ticker	**LEG**	Chairman & CEO	**Harry M. Cornell, Jr.**

Lehman Brothers

Industry: **Securities Brokers**

Lehman Brothers Holdings is a holding company for Lehman Brothers investment bank. The company's businesses include raising capital through securities underwriting and direct placements, corporate-finance advisory services, merchant banking, securities sales and trading, institutional asset management, research services, and the trading of foreign securities, commodities, and derivative products. Its offices are located across the United States, Europe, the Middle East, Latin America, and South America.

$ mil	12/92	12/93	11/94 *	% Change				
Sales	**N/A**	**10,586.0**	**9,190.0**	**-13.2**	P/E Ratio	**33.5**	Price (9/30/95)	**23.13**
Net Income	**N/A**	**-102.0**	**113.0**	**-210.8**	P/B Ratio	**0.7**	52 Wk Hi-Low	**24.13-13.88**
Book Value	**N/A**	**2,052.0**	**3,395.0**	**65.4**	Yield %	**0.8**	Market Cap	**US$2,417.7mil**

Address	**3 World Financial Ctr.**	Tel	**212-526-7000**	Exchange	**NYSE**	President	**T. Christopher Pettit**
	New York, NY 10285	Fax	**212-619-7165**	Ticker	**LEH**	Chairman & CEO	**Richard S. Fuld, Jr.**

*Irregular period due to fiscal year change.

The Limited

Industry: **Apparel Retailers**

The Limited purchases, distributes, and sells women's apparel and, to a lesser degree, men's and children's apparel. The company sells its products through retail stores and mail-order catalogue operations. The company currently operates more than 4,800 stores and four catalog divisions. The stores include Express, The Limited, Lerner New York, Lane Bryant, Victoria's Secret, Structure, The Limited Too, Abercrombie & Fitch, Henri Bendel, Bath & Body Works, Cacique, and Penhaligon's. Catalogs include Victoria's Secret, Lane Bryant Direct, Roaman's, and Lerner Direct.

$ mil	01/93	01/94	01/95	% Change				
Revenues	**6,944.3**	**7,245.1**	**7,320.8**	**1.0**	P/E Ratio	**15.2**	Price (9/30/95)	**19.00**
Net Income	**455.5**	**391.0**	**448.3**	**14.7**	P/B Ratio	**2.5**	52 Wk Hi-Low	**23.13-16.75**
Book Value	**2,267.6**	**2,441.3**	**2,761.0**	**13.1**	Yield %	**1.9**	Market Cap	**US$6,789.1mil**

Address	**3 Limited Pkwy.**	Tel	**614-479-7000**	Exchange	**NYSE**	President & CEO	**Leslie H. Wexner**
	Columbus, OH 43216	Fax	**614-479-7225**	Ticker	**LTD**	Chairman	**Leslie H. Wexner**

Lincoln National

Industry: **Insurance - Full Line**

Lincoln National, an insurance holding company, sells insurance and investment products. The company has four major business segments: property and casualty insurance, life insurance and annuities, and life and health reinsurance. Its American States Insurance subsidiary writes property and casualty insurance. The company's Lincoln National Life Insurance subsidiary offers individual life insurance, annuities, and pension plans. Lincoln National's other subsidiaries reinsure life and health policies. The company markets its insurance and annuities in the U.S. and the U.K.

$ mil	12/92	12/93	12/94	% Change				
Revenues	**8,034.1**	**8,289.8**	**6,984.4**	**-15.7**	P/E Ratio	**14.0**	Price (9/30/95)	**47.13**
Net Income	**362.9**	**318.9**	**349.9**	**9.7**	P/B Ratio	**1.5**	52 Wk Hi-Low	**47.13-34.63**
Book Value	**2,951.2**	**4,072.3**	**3,042.1**	**-25.3**	Yield %	**3.5**	Market Cap	**US$4,457.2mil**

Address	**200 E. Berry St.**	Tel	**219-455-2000**	Exchange	**NYSE**	President	**Robert A. Anker**
	Fort Wayne, IN 46802	Fax	**219-455-7556**	Ticker	**LNC**	Chairman & CEO	**Ian M. Rolland**

Litton Industries

Industry: **Aerospace & Defense**

Litton Industries is a multi-industry, technology-based corporation. It produces command, control, communication, and intelligence systems and marine-combat vessels for the defense industry. The company makes oil-exploration and oil-field-services equipment. Litton also designs and installs systems for integrated manufacturing, automated data collection, and material handling. The company markets its products and services to users in the defense, commercial-aircraft, and other industries worldwide. Contracts with the U.S. government account for about 73% of revenues.

$ mil	07/92	07/93	07/94	% Change				
Sales	**5,692.6**	**3,474.2**	**3,446.1**	**-0.8**	P/E Ratio	**NMF**	Price (9/30/95)	**43.50**
Net Income	**174.4**	**65.2**	**-152.5**	**-333.9**	P/B Ratio	**3.3**	52 Wk Hi-Low	**43.50-33.00**
Book Value	**1,364.1**	**1,663.7**	**610.4**	**-63.3**	Yield %	**0.0**	Market Cap	**US$2,007.4mil**

Address **21240 Burbank Blvd.**
Woodland Hills, CA 91367
Tel **818-598-5000**
Fax **818-598-5940**
Exchange **NYSE**
Ticker **LIT**
President & CEO **John M. Leonis**
Chairman **Alton J. Brann**

Liz Claiborne

Industry: **Clothing & Fabrics**

Liz Claiborne designs clothing and related items. Its main products are women's apparel, accessories, cosmetics, and fragrances sold under the Liz Claiborne, Lizsport, Lizwear, Elisabeth, and Dana Buchman brand names. The company also makes women's shoes and jewelry and men's clothing, cologne, and furnishings. Liz Claiborne operates retail stores under the names Liz Claiborne, Elisabeth, and First Issue. The company markets its apparel and accessories in the United States and internationally. Sales to customers in the U.S. account for more than 94% of the total.

$ mil	12/92	12/93	12/94	% Change				
Sales	**2,194.3**	**2,204.3**	**2,162.9**	**-1.9**	P/E Ratio	**23.8**	Price (9/30/95)	**25.25**
Net Income	**218.8**	**126.9**	**82.9**	**-34.7**	P/B Ratio	**2.0**	52 Wk Hi-Low	**25.75-14.50**
Book Value	**997.8**	**978.3**	**983.0**	**0.5**	Yield %	**1.8**	Market Cap	**US$1,893.8mil**

Address **1441 Broadway**
New York, NY 10018
Tel **212-354-4900**
Fax **212-703-1827**
Exchange **NYSE**
Ticker **LIZ**
President **--**
Chairman **Jerome A. Chazen**

Lockheed Martin

Industry: **Aerospace & Defense**

Lockheed Martin provides aerospace and technology products and services for governments worldwide. Its Lockheed subsidiary manufactures spacecraft, missiles, and launch vehicles. Lockheed also makes cargo and special-mission aircraft and tactical fighters. The company's Martin Marietta subsidiary produces technology products for use in aerospace, defense, information-technology, and construction applications. Martin Marietta also provides products for NASA and the U.S. Postal Service. U.S. government contracts account for more than 75% of the company's total revenues.

$ mil	12/92 R	12/93 R	12/94	% Change				
Sales	**16,030.0**	**22,397.0**	**22,906.0**	**2.3**	P/E Ratio	**13.1**	Price (9/30/95)	**67.13**
Net Income	**-361.0**	**829.0**	**1,018.0**	**22.8**	P/B Ratio	**2.2**	52 Wk Hi-Low	**67.13-40.67**
Book Value	**3,482.0**	**5,201.0**	**6,086.0**	**17.0**	Yield %	**1.7**	Market Cap	**US$13,444mil**

Address **6801 Rockledge Dr.**
Bethesda, MD 20817-1877
Tel **301-897-6000**
Fax **N/A**
Exchange **NYSE**
Ticker **LMT**
President **Norman R. Augustine**
Chairman & CEO **Daniel M. Tellep**

R=Restated.

Loews

Industry: **Insurance - Property & Casualty**

Loews has a broad range of corporate interests. CNA Financial, its largest subsidiary, offers property, casualty, and life insurance. Loews' other operations include cigarette-maker Lorillard, with brands that include Newport and Kent; Loews Hotels, which manages 12 hotels in the U.S., one in Canada, and one in Monte Carlo; watchmaker Bulova; and Diamond Offshore Drilling, which owns and operates offshore oil rigs in the Gulf of Mexico. Loews also owns an 18% stake in CBS's common stock. More than 75% of Loews' revenues is derived from its various insurance businesses.

$ mil	12/92	12/93	12/94	% Change				
Revenues	**13,691.5**	**13,686.8**	**13,515.2**	**-1.3**	P/E Ratio	**32.7**	Price (9/30/95)	**145.50**
Net Income	**122.6**	**594.1**	**267.8**	**-54.9**	P/B Ratio	**1.6**	52 Wk Hi-Low	**145.50-86.00**
Book Value	**5,527.0**	**6,127.2**	**5,405.3**	**-11.8**	Yield %	**0.7**	Market Cap	**US$8,572.3mil**

Address **667 Madison Ave.**
New York, NY 10021-8087
Tel **212-545-2000**
Fax **212-545-2714**
Exchange **NYSE**
Ticker **LTR**
President **James S. Tisch**
Chairman & CEO **L. Tisch / P. Tisch**

Long Island Lighting

Industry: **Electrical Utilities - Eastern U.S.**

Long Island Lighting supplies electric and natural-gas service to about 2.7 million customers in Long Island, New York. Approximately 81% of the company's revenues come from the sale of electrical power, much of which it purchases from other generating companies (43%), or produces at its oil-fired plants (25%); it generates the remainder from natural-gas and nuclear sources. The company's electricity sales are split evenly between residential users and commercial and industrial users. Residential users account for approximately 66% of the company's natural-gas revenues.

$ mil	12/92	12/93	12/94	% Change				
Sales	**2,621.8**	**2,881.0**	**3,067.3**	**6.5**	P/E Ratio	**8.0**	Price (9/30/95)	**17.25**
Net Income	**302.0**	**296.6**	**301.9**	**1.8**	P/B Ratio	**0.7**	52 Wk Hi-Low	**18.00-13.63**
Book Value	**2,897.0**	**2,946.1**	**3,101.9**	**5.3**	Yield %	**10.3**	Market Cap	**US$2,053.5mil**

Address **175 E. Old Country Rd.**
Hicksville, NY 11801
Tel **516-755-6650**
Fax **516-935-1729**
Exchange **NYSE**
Ticker **LIL**
President & CEO **William J. Catacosinos**
Chairman **William J. Catacosinos**

Longs Drug Stores

Industry: **Drug-based Retailers**

Longs Drug Stores operates a drugstore chain with 324 stores in the western United States. The company has 278 stores in California, 32 in Hawaii, six each in Colorado and Nevada, and two in Alaska. The stores range in size from 15,000 to 25,000 square feet, with an average size of 22,000 square feet. More than one fourth of the company's sales volume is from its pharmacies; other business categories include photofinishing and supplies, cosmetics, and greeting cards. The stores sell nationally advertised name-brand merchandise and items marketed under a private label.

	$ mil 01/93	01/94	01/95	% Change				
Revenues	**2,475.5**	**2,499.2**	**2,558.3**	**2.4**	P/E Ratio	**17.7**	Price (9/30/95)	**41.50**
Net Income	**53.0**	**52.8**	**48.7**	**-7.7**	P/B Ratio	**1.6**	52 Wk Hi-Low	**42.00-30.38**
Book Value	**458.2**	**499.6**	**524.1**	**4.9**	Yield %	**2.7**	Market Cap	**US$847.9mil**

Address **141 N. Civic Dr.**
Walnut Creek, CA 94596
Tel **510-937-1170**
Fax **510-210-6330**
Exchange **NYSE**
Ticker **LDG**
President **Stephen D. Roath**
Chairman & CEO **Robert M. Long**

Loral

Industry: **Aerospace & Defense**

Loral manufactures defense electronics and communication systems. It designs electronic systems for military training, intelligence, reconnaissance, and tactical-weapons applications. Its products include radar-warning systems, radar-jamming systems, flight simulators, weapons simulators, rocket-launch systems, and flight-control software. The company also develops and manufactures private-sector products such as communication and weather satellites, flight simulators, and medical-diagnostic equipment. It markets these products primarily to the U.S. government.

	$ mil 03/93	03/94	03/95	% Change				
Sales	**3,335.4**	**4,008.7**	**5,484.4**	**36.8**	P/E Ratio	**16.9**	Price (9/30/95)	**57.00**
Net Income	**-92.1**	**228.3**	**288.4**	**26.3**	P/B Ratio	**2.9**	52 Wk Hi-Low	**57.88-37.00**
Book Value	**1,187.9**	**1,381.3**	**1,687.5**	**22.2**	Yield %	**1.0**	Market Cap	**US$4,883.0mil**

Address **600 Third Ave.**
New York, NY 10016
Tel **212-697-1105**
Fax **212-661-8988**
Exchange **NYSE**
Ticker **LOR**
President **Frank C. Lanza**
Chairman & CEO **Bernard L. Schwartz**

Louisiana Land & Exploration

Industry: **Oil - Secondary**

Louisiana Land & Exploration operates oil and natural-gas wells. The company owns, on average, an 16% interest in 1,800 wells and holds net reserves of 97 million barrels of oil and 984 billion cubic feet of natural gas. Its operating subsidiaries include LL&E Petroleum Marketing, which operates a refinery that uses feedstocks from the company and outside sources to produce gasoline, naphtha, and fuel oil for sale to wholesale distributors. Its LL&E Gas Marketing subsidiary sells three fourths of the parent company's natural-gas production, primarily to local distributors.

	$ mil 12/92	12/93	12/94	% Change				
Sales	**787.4**	**815.4**	**801.5**	**-1.7**	P/E Ratio	**NMF**	Price (9/30/95)	**35.63**
Net Income	**-6.8**	**9.6**	**-226.9**	**NMF**	P/B Ratio	**3.4**	52 Wk Hi-Low	**46.25-32.63**
Book Value	**416.6**	**599.8**	**352.4**	**-41.2**	Yield %	**2.8**	Market Cap	**US$1,192.4mil**

Address **909 Poydras St.**
New Orleans, LA 70112
Tel **504-566-6500**
Fax **504-566-6874**
Exchange **NYSE**
Ticker **LLX**
President & CEO **H. Leighton Steward**
Chairman **H. Leighton Steward**

Louisiana-Pacific

Industry: **Forest Products**

Louisiana-Pacific manufactures forest products in the United States, Canada, and Mexico. The company operates about 130 production facilities where it primarily makes dimensional lumber, plywood and other panel products, and wood pulp. It also makes gypsum wallboard, windows, doors, hardwood veneers, joists, and recycled-newspaper residential insulation. The company's main customers are builders, lumber retailers, papermakers, and the ready-to-assemble furniture and textile industries. Louisiana-Pacific owns or leases more than 1.5 million acres of U.S. timberland.

	$ mil 12/92	12/93	12/94	% Change				
Sales	**2,184.7**	**2,511.3**	**3,039.5**	**21.0**	P/E Ratio	**7.7**	Price (9/30/95)	**24.13**
Net Income	**176.9**	**244.0**	**346.9**	**42.2**	P/B Ratio	**1.5**	52 Wk Hi-Low	**33.50-21.63**
Book Value	**1,361.0**	**1,571.4**	**1,849.4**	**17.7**	Yield %	**2.0**	Market Cap	**US$2,601.4mil**

Address **111 S.W. Fifth Ave.**
Portland, OR 97204
Tel **503-221-0800**
Fax **503-796-0204**
Exchange **NYSE**
Ticker **LPX**
President **Harry A. Merlo**
Chairman **Harry A. Merlo**

Lowe's

Industry: **Other Specialty Retailers**

Lowe's is a specialty retailer serving the home-decor, home-electronics, and building-contractor markets. The company has more than 300 stores, predominantly across the South Atlantic and South Central regions of the United States. Each store combines the merchandise, sales, and service of a home-improvement center, a building-contractor-supply business, and a consumer-durables retailer. The stores are divided into big, medium, and small size categories. Big stores, which have more than 100,00 square feet of selling space, account for 69% of company sales.

	$ mil 01/93	01/94	01/95	% Change				
Revenues	**3,846.4**	**4,538.0**	**6,110.5**	**34.7**	P/E Ratio	**20.8**	Price (9/30/95)	**30.00**
Net Income	**84.7**	**131.8**	**223.6**	**69.6**	P/B Ratio	**3.4**	52 Wk Hi-Low	**40.63-26.50**
Book Value	**733.2**	**873.7**	**1,419.9**	**62.5**	Yield %	**0.6**	Market Cap	**US$4,803.6mil**

Address **State Highway 268 E.**
North Wilkesboro, NC 28659
Tel **910-651-4000**
Fax **910-651-4766**
Exchange **NYSE**
Ticker **LOW**
President & CEO **Leonard G. Herring**
Chairman **Robert L. Strickland**

LSI Logic

Industry: **Semiconductors & related**

LSI Logic designs application-specific integrated circuits. Its products include customized chips and chip-sets used in the electronics, computer, telecommunication, and entertainment industries worldwide. The company's circuits are used in direct-broadcast satellite equipment, cable-television decoders, and computer-network applications. Business activities outside the U.S. account for approximately 14% of the company's total revenues. LSI Logic operates research-and-development facilities in California, and manufacturing facilities in California, Hong Kong, and Japan.

$ mil	12/92	12/93	12/94	% Change				
Sales	617.5	718.8	901.8	25.5	P/E Ratio	58.3	Price (9/30/95)	57.75
Net Income	-110.2	53.8	108.7	102.3	P/B Ratio	12.1	52 Wk Hi-Low	60.63-41.88
Book Value	197.7	292.4	544.9	86.3	Yield %	0.0	Market Cap	US$7,394.0mil

Address **1551 McCarthy Blvd.**
Milpitas, CA 95035
Tel **408-433-8000**
Fax **408-433-7715**
Exchange **NYSE**
Ticker **LSI**
President & CEO **Wilfred J. Corrigan**
Chairman **Wilfred J. Corrigan**

LTV

Industry: **Steel**

LTV manufactures coated sheet and cold-rolled and hot-rolled sheet and strip steel, and tubular and tin mill products. It operates two integrated steel mills as well as tubular- and tin-mills. Sales of steel-mill products account for roughly 93% of sales. The automotive industry and steel service centers are the largest markets for the company's products. Most of its steel products are sold under annual contracts. Its Continental Emsco subsidiary provides oil-field equipment and supplies. LTV is also forming an international joint-venture with Sumitomo Metal Industries.

$ mil	12/92	12/93	12/94	% Change				
Sales	3,825.9	4,163.2	4,529.2	8.8	P/E Ratio	10.9	Price (9/30/95)	14.00
Net Income	598.7	4,314.9	127.1	-97.1	P/B Ratio	1.2	52 Wk Hi-Low	21.00-13.38
Book Value	-4,129.3	539.8	1,282.8	137.6	Yield %	0.0	Market Cap	US$1,469.2mil

Address **25 W. Prospect Ave.**
Cleveland, OH 44115
Tel **216-622-5000**
Fax **216-622-1066**
Exchange **NYSE**
Ticker **LTV**
President & CEO **David H. Hoag**
Chairman **David H. Hoag**

Lubrizol

Industry: **Specialty Chemicals**

Lubrizol manufactures specialty chemicals and vegetable oils. The company's main products are engine-oil additives for use in gasoline and diesel-powered engines. Its other specialty chemicals include additives for automatic-transmission fluids, gear oils, industrial fluids, metalworking compounds, and motor fuels. Lubrizol sells the majority of these products to the refining divisions of petroleum companies. In addition, the company produces specialty vegetable oils, including high-oleic sunflower and safflower oils, primarily for sale to food-processing companies.

$ mil	12/92	12/93	12/94	% Change				
Sales	1,544.7	1,517.6	1,592.8	5.0	P/E Ratio	12.2	Price (9/30/95)	32.63
Net Income	124.6	45.6	175.6	285.0	P/B Ratio	2.5	52 Wk Hi-Low	37.00-29.13
Book Value	819.4	732.2	832.0	13.6	Yield %	2.7	Market Cap	US$2,073.1mil

Address **29400 Lakeland Blvd.**
Wickliffe, OH 44092
Tel **216-943-4200**
Fax **216-943-5337**
Exchange **NYSE**
Ticker **LZ**
President **W.G. Bares**
Chairman & CEO **L.E. Coleman**

Magma Copper

Industry: **Non-Ferrous Metals - Other (Exc. Aluminum)**

Magma Copper operates copper and gold mines and related businesses. The company owns land in Arizona, where it manages underground and open-pit copper mines, as well as smelting and refining plants. It also owns about 12,500 acres near Ely, Nevada, where it operates gold mines and searches for additional copper reserves, and in Peru, where it operates copper mines. Total company reserves include about nine billion pounds of recoverable copper. Magma Copper's main products include copper cathode and copper rod, the basic stock of the copper-wire and -cable industries.

$ mil	12/92	12/93	12/94	% Change				
Sales	819.5	792.4	889.6	12.3	P/E Ratio	12.2	Price (9/30/95)	18.75
Net Income	55.3	21.9	87.4	299.1	P/B Ratio	1.1	52 Wk Hi-Low	20.63-14.13
Book Value	465.4	680.2	760.1	11.7	Yield %	0.0	Market Cap	US$865.2mil

Address **7400 N. Oracle Rd., Ste. 200**
Tucson, AZ 85704
Tel **520-575-5600**
Fax **520-575-5674**
Exchange **NYSE**
Ticker **MCU**
President & CEO **J. Burgess Winter**
Chairman **Donald J. Donahue**

Mallinckrodt

Industry: **Medical Supplies**

Mallinckrodt Group makes medical and veterinary health-care products and specialty chemicals. Its human health-care products include diagnostic and therapeutic products and vital-signs monitors. Its veterinary business sells more than 1,000 types of vaccines, antibacterial agents, and therapeutic preparations. The company also produces specialty chemicals used in analgesics, catalysts, and, through a joint venture with Hercules called Tastemaker, flavors. Mallinckrodt Group markets these products in the United States and abroad.

$ mil	06/93	06/94	06/95	% Change				
Sales	1,796.3	1,940.1	2,212.1	14.0	P/E Ratio	17.1	Price (9/30/95)	39.63
Net Income	-200.4	103.8	180.3	73.7	P/B Ratio	2.6	52 Wk Hi-Low	41.00-29.25
Book Value	910.5	1,015.9	1,171.5	15.3	Yield %	1.4	Market Cap	US$3,036.6mil

Address **7733 Forsyth Blvd.**
St. Louis, MO 63105
Tel **314-854-5200**
Fax **314-854-5380**
Exchange **NYSE**
Ticker **MKG**
President & CEO **C. Ray Holman**
Chairman **C. Ray Holman**

Manitowoc

Industry: **Heavy Machinery**

Manitowoc is a diversified manufacturer of capital goods. The company produces cranes, which are sold under the Manitowoc, Manitex, and Orley Meyer brand names. It also manufactures ice-making machines and refrigeration and freezing equipment for the food-service, lodging, convenience-store, and health-care industries. Manitowoc operates three ship-repair yards in Wisconsin and Ohio, which provide tank and cargo-hold replacement, hazardous-waste removal, tank-cleaning and -lining services, and hull, engine, and electrical-system repair for its customers.

$ mil	06/93	06/94	12/94 *	% Change				
Sales	**278.6**	**275.4**	**123.9**	**-55.0**	P/E Ratio	**NMF**	Price (9/30/95)	**29.63**
Net Income	**-3.9**	**14.0**	**-5.1**	**-136.2**	P/B Ratio	**3.0**	52 Wk Hi-Low	**30.00-21.00**
Book Value	**119.4**	**93.9**	**75.1**	**-20.1**	Yield %	**1.7**	Market Cap	**US$227.3mil**

Address	**700 E. Magnolia Ave., Ste. B**	Tel	**414-684-4410**	Exchange	**NYSE**	President & CEO	**Fred M. Butler**
	Manitowoc, WI 54220	Fax	**414-683-6277**	Ticker	**MTW**	Chairman	--

*Irregular period due to fiscal year change.

Manor Care

Industry: **Health Care Providers**

Manor Care is a holding company for the Manor Care Hotel Division and three subsidiaries: Manor Healthcare, Vitalink Pharmacy Services, and Choice Hotels International. The hotel division owns and operates the Quality, Clarion, and other lodging chains. Manor Healthcare develops and manages nursing centers principally for senior citizens. Healthcare also owns and operates an acute-care general hospital, nursing-assistant training schools, and has a 50% interest in a clinical laboratory. Vitalink, which is 82% company-owned, operates institutional pharmacies.

$ mil	05/93	05/94	05/95	% Change				
Sales	**1,009.7**	**1,163.1**	**1,322.0**	**13.7**	P/E Ratio	**22.5**	Price (9/30/95)	**34.00**
Net Income	**59.4**	**78.4**	**94.5**	**20.5**	P/B Ratio	**3.4**	52 Wk Hi-Low	**35.38-26.13**
Book Value	**362.0**	**533.8**	**624.9**	**17.1**	Yield %	**0.3**	Market Cap	**US$2,121.0mil**

Address	**10750 Columbia Pike**	Tel	**301-681-9400**	Exchange	**NYSE**	President	**Stewart Bainum, Jr.**
	Silver Spring, MD 20901	Fax	**301-680-4020**	Ticker	**MNR**	Chairman & CEO	**Stewart Bainum, Jr.**

Manpower

Industry: **General Industrial & Commercial Services**

Manpower is a holding company for Manpower International, the largest nongovernmental employment-services organization in the world. With more than 2,200 company-owned and franchise offices, Manpower's services include temporary help, contract services, and training and testing of temporary and permanent personnel. The company concentrates its operations in the U.S., continental Europe, and the U.K., and has other offices in Canada, Japan, and Israel. Another subsidiary, Brook Street Bureau, operates 94 offices in the U.K., providing temporary-placement services.

$ mil	12/92	12/93	12/94	% Change				
Sales	**3,186.6**	**3,180.4**	**4,296.4**	**35.1**	P/E Ratio	**25.9**	Price (9/30/95)	**29.00**
Net Income	**-46.7**	**-48.9**	**83.9**	**-271.6**	P/B Ratio	**10.6**	52 Wk Hi-Low	**34.13-24.50**
Book Value	**159.6**	**102.7**	**203.5**	**98.1**	Yield %	**0.4**	Market Cap	**US$2,182.2mil**

Address	**5301 N. Ironwood Rd.**	Tel	**414-961-1000**	Exchange	**NYSE**	President & CEO	**Mitchell S. Fromstein**
	Milwaukee, WI 53201	Fax	**414-332-0796**	Ticker	**MAN**	Chairman	**Mitchell S. Fromstein**

Manville

Industry: **Building Materials**

Manville manufactures packaging, paper, and fiberglass-based products. It operates through two principal subsidiaries: Riverwood International and Schuller International. Riverwood, which is 81.5% Manville-owned, is a packaging and paper-products company. Manville's building products and engineered products are manufactured through Schuller and its affiliated companies. The company owns or operates 62 facilities in the United States and eight other countries, about 540,000 acres of timberland in the U.S., 174,000 acres in Brazil, and holds an interest in platinum mines.

$ mil	12/92	12/93	12/94	% Change				
Sales	**2,223.8**	**2,275.9**	**2,560.3**	**12.5**	P/E Ratio	**131.3**	Price (9/30/95)	**13.13**
Net Income	**35.9**	**47.8**	**37.0**	**-22.6**	P/B Ratio	**1.5**	52 Wk Hi-Low	**15.25-8.13**
Book Value	**825.3**	**846.1**	**1,063.5**	**25.7**	Yield %	**0.0**	Market Cap	**US$1,613.4mil**

Address	**717 17th St.**	Tel	**303-978-2000**	Exchange	**NYSE**	President & CEO	**W. Thomas Stephens**
	Denver, CO 80202	Fax	**303-978-2041**	Ticker	**MVL**	Chairman	**W. Thomas Stephens**

Mapco

Industry: **Oil - Secondary**

Mapco processes and transports petroleum and chemicals and operates coal mines. The company's natural-gas-liquids division processes natural-gas liquids; operates pipelines for anhydrous ammonia, crude oil, and refined petroleum products; and distributes fertilizer. Its petroleum division manages refineries in Alaska and Tennessee, and operates Mapco Express gas station/convenience stores in Alaska and the southern United States. Mapco's coal division operates eight mines in Illinois, Kentucky, Maryland, and Virginia that hold reserves of 343 million tons of coal.

$ mil	12/92	12/93	12/94	% Change				
Sales	**2,786.8**	**2,715.3**	**3,059.3**	**12.7**	P/E Ratio	**19.5**	Price (9/30/95)	**51.50**
Net Income	**100.7**	**127.0**	**79.1**	**-37.7**	P/B Ratio	**2.5**	52 Wk Hi-Low	**59.13-50.00**
Book Value	**477.5**	**574.3**	**622.6**	**8.4**	Yield %	**1.9**	Market Cap	**US$1,535.8mil**

Address	**1800 S. Baltimore Ave.**	Tel	**918-581-1800**	Exchange	**NYSE**	President	**Robert M. Howe**
	Tulsa, OK 74101-0645	Fax	**918-599-3509**	Ticker	**MDA**	Chairman & CEO	**James E. Barnes**

Marriott International

Industry: **Lodging**

Marriott provides food-service and facilities management, operating in two business segments, lodging and contract services. Its lodging segment consists of 851 company-operated or franchised hotels, with a total of approximately 180,000 rooms. Lodgings operate under the names Marriott Hotels, Resorts and Suites; Courtyard hotels; Residence Inn; Fairfield Inn; and Marriott Ownership Resorts. The contract-services segment provides food- and facilities-management services through Marriott Management Services, Marriott Distribution Services, and the Senior Living Services.

$ mil	12/92	12/93	12/94	% Change				
Sales	**6,971.0**	**7,430.0**	**8,415.0**	**13.3**	P/E Ratio	**24.8**	Price (9/30/95)	**37.38**
Net Income	**134.0**	**126.0**	**200.0**	**58.7**	P/B Ratio	**6.0**	52 Wk Hi-Low	**39.00-26.25**
Book Value	**763.0**	**696.0**	**767.0**	**10.2**	Yield %	**0.7**	Market Cap	**US$4,682.5mil**

Address **Marriott Drive**
Washington, D.C. 20058
Tel **301-380-3000**
Fax **301-380-5067**
Exchange **NYSE**
Ticker **MAR**
President **J.W. Marriott, Jr.**
Chairman **J.W. Marriott, Jr.**

Marsh & McLennan

Industry: **Financial Services - Diversified**

Marsh & McLennan provides insurance-brokerage, consulting, and investment-management services. It offers insurance under the Marsh & McLennan, Guy Carpenter & Company, and Seabury & Smith names. Mercer Consulting Group, another subsidiary, provides management consulting, especially in the areas of human resources, employee benefits, and compensation. Marsh & McLennan also offers investment-management services through its Putnam Investments subsidiary, which has more than 80 mutual funds and $95 billion under management.

$ mil	12/92	12/93	12/94	% Change				
Revenues	**2,937.0**	**3,163.4**	**3,435.0**	**8.6**	P/E Ratio	**17.4**	Price (9/30/95)	**87.88**
Net Income	**263.7**	**332.4**	**371.5**	**11.8**	P/B Ratio	**4.4**	52 Wk Hi-Low	**88.75-71.75**
Book Value	**1,102.9**	**1,365.3**	**1,460.6**	**7.0**	Yield %	**3.2**	Market Cap	**US$6,380.9mil**

Address **1166 Ave. of the Americas**
New York, NY 10036
Tel **212-345-5000**
Fax **212-345-4812**
Exchange **NYSE**
Ticker **MMC**
President --
Chairman **A.J.C. Smith**

Marshall & Ilsley

Industry: **Banks - Central U.S.**

Marshall & Ilsley is a bank holding company. The company owns 35 banks, with 225 branches in Wisconsin and 12 branches in Arizona, the largest of which is M&I Marshall & Ilsley Bank. Marshall & Ilsley also owns a number of companies engaged in banking-related businesses, including investment and trust management, insurance sales, equipment leasing, mortgage banking, venture capital, brokerage and financial-advisory services, and data processing. The company's income is derived primarily from investments in, advances to, and service fees from its subsidiaries.

$ mil	12/92	12/93	12/94	% Change				
Revenues	**798.0**	**787.4**	**1,184.5**	**50.4**	P/E Ratio	**23.5**	Price (9/30/95)	**25.13**
Net Income	**109.2**	**125.5**	**105.9**	**-15.6**	P/B Ratio	**2.2**	52 Wk Hi-Low	**26.25-19.88**
Book Value	**760.6**	**750.4**	**1,061.3**	**41.4**	Yield %	**2.3**	Market Cap	**US$2,346.3mil**

Address **770 N. Water St.**
Milwaukee, WI 53202
Tel **414-765-7801**
Fax **N/A**
Exchange **NASDA**
Ticker **MRIS**
President **Dennis J. Kuester**
Chairman & CEO **James B. Wigdale**

Masco

Industry: **Building Materials**

Masco manufactures building, home-improvement, and home-furnishings products, and manufactures faucets, plumbing supplies, shower items, and kitchen and bath cabinets. Products include Delta and Peerless single- and double-handle faucets and the Merillat, Kraftmaid, Starmark, and Fieldstone brands of custom kitchen and bath cabinets. Other specialty kitchen and bath consumer products include Thermador ovens and related cooking equipment. Home-furnishing products include Universal, Benchcraft, Henredon, Drexel, and Heritage wood and upholstered furniture.

$ mil	12/92	12/93	12/94	% Change				
Sales	**3,525.0**	**3,886.0**	**4,468.0**	**15.0**	P/E Ratio	**22.5**	Price (9/30/95)	**27.50**
Net Income	**183.1**	**221.1**	**193.7**	**-12.4**	P/B Ratio	**2.0**	52 Wk Hi-Low	**29.50-21.75**
Book Value	**1,886.9**	**1,998.4**	**2,112.7**	**5.7**	Yield %	**2.5**	Market Cap	**US$4,357.7mil**

Address **21001 Van Born Rd.**
Taylor, MI 48180
Tel **313-274-7400**
Fax **313-374-6666**
Exchange **NYSE**
Ticker **MAS**
President **Wayne B. Lyon**
Chairman & CEO **Richard A. Manoogian**

MascoTech

Industry: **Other Auto Parts**

MascoTech manufactures original equipment and aftermarket parts for the transportation industry. The company manufactures commercial, institutional, and residential building products for the construction industry, and products for the defense industry. Defense products include large-diameter cold-formed cartridge cases, projectiles, casings for rocket motors, and other items. Through its subsidiaries, the company has businesses in the United States, the United Kingdom, Canada, Germany, and Italy. Business outside the U.S. accounts for 6% of the company's total sales.

$ mil	12/92	12/93	12/94	% Change				
Sales	**1,656.8**	**1,582.9**	**1,702.3**	**7.5**	P/E Ratio	**NMF**	Price (9/30/95)	**11.25**
Net Income	**38.4**	**47.6**	**-220.1**	**-562.4**	P/B Ratio	**1.7**	52 Wk Hi-Low	**13.63-10.63**
Book Value	**353.4**	**667.6**	**381.1**	**-42.9**	Yield %	**1.0**	Market Cap	**US$632.5mil**

Address **21001 Van Born Rd.**
Taylor, MI 48180
Tel **313-274-7405**
Fax **313-274-8959**
Exchange **NYSE**
Ticker **MSX**
President **Lee M. Gardner**
Chairman & CEO **Richard A. Manoogian**

Mattel

Industry: **Toy Manufacturers**

Mattel manufactures and sells children's toys and games in the U.S. and internationally. Its main products include the Barbie doll and related clothing and accessories, Fisher-Price toys and juvenile products, Hot Wheels toy vehicles and accessories, See 'N Say talking toys, and Disney-licensed preschool and infant toys and large dolls. The company has additional licensing agreements with McDonald's, Nickelodeon, and others. It also produces family and educational games, including Uno and Skip-Bo. Sales abroad account for approximately 41% of the Mattel's total revenues.

$ mil	12/92	12/93	12/94	% Change				
Sales	**1,847.9**	**2,704.4**	**3,205.0**	**18.5**	P/E Ratio	**26.2**	Price (9/30/95)	**29.38**
Net Income	**143.9**	**117.2**	**255.8**	**118.3**	P/B Ratio	**6.0**	52 Wk Hi-Low	**30.50-20.00**
Book Value	**526.0**	**817.8**	**1,085.7**	**32.8**	Yield %	**0.6**	Market Cap	**US$6,510.1mil**

Address	**333 Continental Blvd.**	Tel	**310-252-2000**	Exchange	**NYSE**	President	**Jill E. Barad**
	El Segundo, CA 90245-5012	Fax	**310-978-5913**	Ticker	**MAT**	Chairman & CEO	**John W. Amerman**

Maxxam

Industry: **Aluminum**

Maxxam has operations in aluminum production, forest products, and real-estate management and development. It produces alumina, primary aluminum, and fabricated aluminum goods through its subsidiary, Kaiser Aluminum. Maxxam's forest-products operations are conducted through the Pacific Lumber Company, which is a major producer of redwood and Douglas fir lumber. Maxxam's real-estate assets consist of community developments, single- and multifamily residential properties, and resorts located primarily in the southwestern United States and Puerto Rico.

$ mil	12/92	12/93	12/94	% Change				
Sales	**2,202.6**	**2,031.1**	**2,115.7**	**4.2**	P/E Ratio	**NMF**	Price (9/30/95)	**49.13**
Net Income	**-7.3**	**-600.2**	**-122.1**	**-79.7**	P/B Ratio	**NMF**	52 Wk Hi-Low	**67.00-27.25**
Book Value	**443.9**	**-167.9**	**-275.3**	**64.0**	Yield %	**0.0**	Market Cap	**US$427.8mil**

Address	**5847 San Felipe, Ste. 2600**	Tel	**713-975-7600**	Exchange	**AMEX**	President & CEO	**Charles E. Hurwitz**
	Houston, TX 77257-2887	Fax	**713-267-3710**	Ticker	**MXM**	Chairman	**Charles E. Hurwitz**

May Department Stores

Industry: **Retailers - Broadline**

May Department Stores operates regional-department store companies across the U.S., and is the largest department-store retailer in the country. At the end of fiscal 1994, the company operated 314 companies under the names Lord & Taylor, Foley's, Robinsons-May, Hecht's, Kaufmann's, Filene's, Famous-Barr, and Meier & Frank. In addition, the company operates 4,435 Payless ShoeSource stores. Merchandising efforts are focused on three major categories: cosmetics, shoes and accessories; women's, children's, and men's apparel; and home furnishings.

$ mil	01/93	01/94	01/95	% Change				
Revenues	**11,150.0**	**11,529.0**	**12,223.0**	**6.0**	P/E Ratio	**14.3**	Price (9/30/95)	**43.75**
Net Income	**603.0**	**711.0**	**782.0**	**10.0**	P/B Ratio	**2.6**	52 Wk Hi-Low	**45.38-33.00**
Book Value	**3,195.0**	**3,652.0**	**4,152.0**	**13.7**	Yield %	**2.3**	Market Cap	**US$10,878mil**

Address	**611 Olive St.**	Tel	**314-342-6300**	Exchange	**NYSE**	President	**Jerome T. Loeb**
	St. Louis, MO 63101-1799	Fax	**314-342-3066**	Ticker	**MA**	Chairman & CEO	**David C. Farrell**

Maytag

Industry: **Other Home Furnishings**

Maytag manufactures home appliances under the Maytag, Admiral, Jenn-Air, Magic Chef, and Hoover brand names. The company's products include home and coin-operated laundry equipment, gas and electric ranges, microwave ovens, refrigerators, freezers, dishwashers, food-waste disposals, dehumidifiers, trash compactors, and floor-care appliances. The company markets these products to laundromats, builders of single- and multifamily housing, recreational-vehicle manufacturers and owners, and consumers needing replacement appliances in the United States and internationally.

$ mil	12/92	12/93	12/94	% Change				
Sales	**3,041.2**	**2,987.1**	**3,372.5**	**12.9**	P/E Ratio	**12.6**	Price (9/30/95)	**17.50**
Net Income	**-315.4**	**51.3**	**148.0**	**188.4**	P/B Ratio	**2.6**	52 Wk Hi-Low	**18.00-14.25**
Book Value	**599.2**	**586.8**	**731.7**	**24.7**	Yield %	**2.9**	Market Cap	**US$1,883.2mil**

Address	**403 W. Fourth St. N.**	Tel	**515-792-8000**	Exchange	**NYSE**	Chief Executive	**Leonard A. Hadley**
	Newton, IA 50208	Fax	**515-791-8578**	Ticker	**MYG**	Chairman	**Leonard A. Hadley**

MBNA

Industry: **Banks - Eastern U.S.**

MBNA is a bank holding company and the parent company of MBNA America Bank. The bank issues standard and gold VISA and MasterCard credit cards, specializing in affinity credit cards marketed primarily to members of associations and financial institutions. MBNA also offers individual and second-mortgage loans, money-market deposit accounts, and certificates of deposit. The company operates two administrative and credit-card facilities, two information-processing operations, and several telemarketing offices. MBNA is the world's second-largest issuer of bank credit cards.

$ mil	12/92	12/93	12/94	% Change				
Revenues	**1,171.9**	**1,392.8**	**1,853.2**	**33.1**	P/E Ratio	**23.5**	Price (9/30/95)	**41.63**
Net Income	**172.7**	**207.8**	**266.6**	**28.3**	P/B Ratio	**6.7**	52 Wk Hi-Low	**41.63-21.88**
Book Value	**661.3**	**769.1**	**919.6**	**19.6**	Yield %	**1.7**	Market Cap	**US$6,181.3mil**

Address	**400 Christiana Rd.**	Tel	**302-453-9930**	Exchange	**NYSE**	President	**Charles M. Cawley**
	Newark, DE 19713	Fax	**302-453-2033**	Ticker	**KRB**	Chairman & CEO	**Alfred Lerner**

McCormick & Co.

Industry: **Other Food**

McCormick & Company manufactures food products and plastic packaging. The company's principal business is the manufacture of spices, seasonings, and flavorings for sale to the retail, industrial food-service, and food-processing markets, primarily under the McCormick and Schilling brand names. Its Setco and Tubed Products subsidiaries produce plastic packaging for the food, cosmetic, and health-care industries. McCormick markets these products primarily through a direct-sales force in the U.S. and abroad, with sales outside the U.S. accounting for about 17% of the total.

$ mil	11/92	11/93	11/94	% Change				
Sales	**1,471.4**	**1,556.6**	**1,694.8**	**8.9**	P/E Ratio	**31.8**	Price (9/30/95)	**23.88**
Net Income	**95.2**	**73.1**	**61.2**	**-16.3**	P/B Ratio	**4.0**	52 Wk Hi-Low	**24.00-18.00**
Book Value	**437.9**	**466.8**	**490.0**	**5.0**	Yield %	**2.0**	Market Cap	**US$1,938.0mil**

Address **18 Loveton Circle**
Sparks, MD 21152
Tel **410-771-7301**
Fax **410-771-7462**
Exchange **NASDA**
Ticker **MCCRK**
President & CEO **H. Eugene Blattman**
Chairman **C.P. McCormick, Jr.**

McDermott International

Industry: **Oilfield Equipment & Services - Other**

McDermott International builds power-generation equipment and offshore-industrial facilities. The company's power-generation-systems division makes steam-production and pollution-control equipment for use primarily in electricity generation and industrial processes; it also makes nuclear-reactor components and other equipment for the U.S. Navy. Its marine-construction-services division builds offshore platforms, pipelines, and processing facilities; makes and charters ships; and provides related engineering services for petroleum, petrochemical, and mining companies.

$ mil	03/93	03/94	03/95	% Change				
Sales	**3,172.6**	**3,059.9**	**3,043.7**	**-0.5**	P/E Ratio	**NMF**	Price (9/30/95)	**19.75**
Net Income	**-188.7**	**-10.8**	**9.1**	**-184.4**	P/B Ratio	**1.5**	52 Wk Hi-Low	**28.88-19.75**
Book Value	**460.4**	**542.3**	**710.6**	**31.0**	Yield %	**5.1**	Market Cap	**US$1,071.8mil**

Address **1450 Poydras St.**
New Orleans, LA 70112-6050
Tel **504-587-5400**
Fax **504-587-6433**
Exchange **NYSE**
Ticker **MDR**
Chief Executive **Robert E. Howson**
Chairman **Robert E. Howson**

McDonald's

Industry: **Restaurants**

McDonald's operates, franchises, and services an international system of more than 15,000 fast-food restaurants. The company's restaurants prepare, assemble, package, and sell a limited menu of low- to moderate-price foods. These restaurants are operated by the company with franchise agreements, by independent third parties, or joint-venture agreements between the company and local business people. The substantially uniform menu consists of hamburgers and cheeseburgers, salads, milk shakes, breakfast items, chicken sandwiches, French-fried potatoes, and soft drinks.

$ mil	12/92	12/93	12/94	% Change				
Sales	**7,133.3**	**7,408.1**	**8,320.8**	**12.3**	P/E Ratio	**22.8**	Price (9/30/95)	**38.25**
Net Income	**958.6**	**1,082.5**	**1,224.4**	**13.1**	P/B Ratio	**3.9**	52 Wk Hi-Low	**41.38-26.25**
Book Value	**5,892.4**	**6,274.1**	**6,885.4**	**9.7**	Yield %	**0.6**	Market Cap	**US$26,576mil**

Address **McDonald's Plz.**
Oak Brook, IL 60521
Tel **708-575-3000**
Fax **708-575-6942**
Exchange **NYSE**
Ticker **MCD**
Chief Executive **Michael R. Quinlan**
Chairman **Michael R. Quinlan**

McDonnell Douglas

Industry: **Aerospace & Defense**

McDonnell Douglas is the world's largest manufacturer of military aircraft by sales. It also produces civilian aircraft and other products, including missiles, space hardware, and electronic systems. Its better-known aircraft include the F-15 Eagle, C-17 Globemaster, and AH-64 Apache helicopter. The company is also working on NASA's space-station project. The company markets its products to commercial airlines and government agencies worldwide. Contracts with the U.S. government account for approximately 70% of revenues; international sales contribute about 32%.

$ mil	12/92	12/93	12/94	% Change				
Sales	**17,384.0**	**14,487.0**	**13,176.0**	**-9.0**	P/E Ratio	**16.4**	Price (9/30/95)	**82.75**
Net Income	**-781.0**	**396.0**	**598.0**	**51.0**	P/B Ratio	**2.5**	52 Wk Hi-Low	**85.00-38.25**
Book Value	**3,022.0**	**3,413.0**	**3,872.0**	**13.4**	Yield %	**0.7**	Market Cap	**US$9,349.3mil**

Address **P.O. Box 516**
St. Louis, MO 63166-0516
Tel **314-232-0232**
Fax **314-234-3826**
Exchange **NYSE**
Ticker **MD**
President & CEO **Harry C. Stonecipher**
Chairman **John F. McDonnell**

McGraw-Hill

Industry: **Publishing**

McGraw-Hill Companies is a major information-services company. The company's information and media-services division operates television stations in four cities, publishes Business Week Magazine, and provides commercial directories to the construction and import/export industries. Its financial-services divsion includes Standard & Poor's, which provides consulting and analysis related to worldwide markets and securities. Its MacMillan/McGraw-Hill subsidiary publishes textbooks and print and electronic information sources for legal, health, and business professionals.

$ mil	12/92	12/93	12/94	% Change				
Sales	**2,050.5**	**2,195.5**	**2,760.9**	**25.8**	P/E Ratio	**19.9**	Price (9/30/95)	**81.75**
Net Income	**28.6**	**11.4**	**203.1**	**NMF**	P/B Ratio	**4.4**	52 Wk Hi-Low	**83.38-64.00**
Book Value	**908.8**	**823.0**	**913.1**	**10.9**	Yield %	**2.8**	Market Cap	**US$4,081.9mil**

Address **1221 Ave. of the Americas**
New York, NY 10020
Tel **212-512-2000**
Fax **212-512-4702**
Exchange **NYSE**
Ticker **MHP**
President **Harold McGraw III**
Chairman & CEO **Joseph L. Dionne**

MCI Communications

Industry: **Long Distance Telephone Systems**

MCI Communications provides long-distance telephone and other information services in the United States. MCI markets its services under the Friends & Family, Best Friends, and 1-800-Collect service marks. The company also offers electronic-mail and data-transmission services, and calling cards that allow cardholders to place calls from any telephone in the contiguous U.S. Long-distance service is provided mainly through the company's fiberoptic and digital-microwave system; international calls are carried through submarine cable systems and satellite transmissions.

$ mil	12/92	12/93	12/94	% Change				
Sales	10,562.0	11,921.0	13,338.0	11.9	P/E Ratio	19.7	Price (9/30/95)	26.06
Net Income	609.0	582.0	795.0	36.6	P/B Ratio	2.0	52 Wk Hi-Low	26.88-17.50
Book Value	3,150.0	4,713.0	9,004.0	91.0	Yield %	0.2	Market Cap	US$17,665mil

Address **1801 Pennsylvania Ave. N.W.**
Washington, DC 20006
Tel **202-872-1600**
Fax **202-887-2967**
Exchange **NASDA**
Ticker **MCIC**
President **Gerald H. Taylor**
Chairman & CEO **Bert C. Roberts, Jr.**

McKesson

Industry: **Drug-based Retailers**

McKesson distributes ethical and proprietary drugs and health and beauty products in the United States and Canada. Its products are distributed to chain and independent drug stores, hospitals, food stores, and mass merchandisers. The company also processes and sells bottled drinking water, and develops Armor All brand aftermarket products to protect and enhance the appearance of car finishes. The company's bottled-water products are sold as the company's Sparkletts, Alhambra, and Crystal brands. McKesson also owns 22.7% of Nadro, a Mexican pharmaceutical wholesaler.

$ mil	03/93	03/94	03/95	% Change				
Revenues	11,669.4	12,428.2	13,189.1	6.1	P/E Ratio	4.9	Price (9/30/95)	45.00
Net Income	114.7	136.2	404.5	197.0	P/B Ratio	2.0	52 Wk Hi-Low	47.38-30.50
Book Value	619.4	678.6	1,013.5	49.4	Yield %	3.0	Market Cap	US$1,997.5mil

Address **1 Post St.**
San Francisco, CA 94104
Tel **415-983-8300**
Fax **415-983-8955**
Exchange **NYSE**
Ticker **MCK**
President **David E. McDowell**
Chairman & CEO **Alan Seelenfreund**

Mead

Industry: **Paper Products**

Mead manufactures paper products for printing, packaging, and other industries. It also provides on-line information services. Its products include office and school supplies sold under the Mead, Gilbert, and Cambridge brand names; publishing and specialty papers; and packaging materials and machines. As an adjunct to its paper-products business, Mead owns more than 1.3 million acres of timberlands. The company markets its products in the United States and abroad, and operates manufacturing facilities in the U.S. and 12 other countries.

$ mil	12/92	12/93	12/94	% Change				
Sales	4,703.2	4,790.3	4,557.5	-4.9	P/E Ratio	5.2	Price (9/30/95)	58.63
Net Income	71.6	124.1	695.7	460.6	P/B Ratio	1.6	52 Wk Hi-Low	63.63-44.13
Book Value	1,495.4	1,578.0	2,182.6	38.3	Yield %	1.7	Market Cap	US$3,141.2mil

Address **Courthouse Plz. N.E.**
Dayton, OH 45463
Tel **513-495-6323**
Fax **N/A**
Exchange **NYSE**
Ticker **MEA**
President & CEO **Steven C. Mason**
Chairman **Steven C. Mason**

Meditrust

Industry: **Real-Estate Investment**

Meditrust is a dedicated real-estate investment trust. The company invests in the subacute sector of the health-care industry, primarily in facilities providing long-term-care services. Investments are made primarily for the production of income, and include long-term care and substance-abuse treatment facilities, rehabilitation and psychiatric hospitals, and other health-care-related facilities. Meditrust owns and manages 274 health-care facilities containing about 33,000 beds, located throughout the U.S., making it one of the largest health-care REITs in the country.

$ mil	12/92	12/93	12/94	% Change				
Sales	132.4	150.8	173.0	14.7	P/E Ratio	15.2	Price (9/30/95)	34.63
Net Income	51.4	63.6	80.5	26.5	P/B Ratio	1.8	52 Wk Hi-Low	35.38-29.00
Book Value	431.5	585.8	770.2	31.5	Yield %	7.6	Market Cap	US$1,715.4mil

Address **197 First Ave.**
Needham, MA 02194-9127
Tel **617-433-6000**
Fax **617-433-1290**
Exchange **NYSE**
Ticker **MT**
President **David F. Benson**
Chairman & CEO **Abraham D. Gosman**

Medtronic

Industry: **Advanced Medical Technology**

Medtronic develops therapeutic medical devices for cardiovascular and neurological applications. The company's products include pacemakers, mechanical heart valves, and products for cardiopulmonary, vascular, and neurological stimulation. The company markets its products to health-care institutions and physicians in more than 120 countries. Business activity outside the United States accounts for approximately 31% of sales. Medtronic operates research and manufacturing facilities in the U.S., Puerto Rico, Canada, France, Germany, Italy, Japan, and the Netherlands.

$ mil	04/92	04/93	04/94	% Change				
Sales	1,176.9	1,328.2	1,390.9	4.7	P/E Ratio	53.1	Price (9/30/95)	53.75
Net Income	161.5	197.2	232.4	17.8	P/B Ratio	11.9	52 Wk Hi-Low	105.00-49.00
Book Value	796.5	841.5	1,053.5	25.2	Yield %	0.3	Market Cap	US$12,417mil

Address **7000 Central Ave. N.E.**
Minneapolis, MN 55432
Tel **612-574-4000**
Fax **612-574-4879**
Exchange **NYSE**
Ticker **MDT**
President & CEO **William W. George**
Chairman **Winston R. Wallin**

Mellon Bank

Industry: **Banks - Eastern U.S.**

Mellon Bank is a bank holding company that operates banks and various securities-related businesses in Delaware, Maryland, New Jersey, and Pennsylvania. Its banks manage 449 banking offices and engage in retail, worldwide-commercial, and trust banking. Its nonbank subsidiaries provide services such as equipment leasing, residential- and commercial-mortgage financing, and securities trading. The company's Boston Company subsidiary offers trust and investment-management services. Mellon Bank's Dreyfus subsidiary provides mutual funds and portfolio management.

$ mil	12/92	12/93	12/94	% Change				
Revenues	2,972.0	3,237.0	3,962.0	22.4	P/E Ratio	18.4	Price (9/30/95)	44.63
Net Income	437.0	361.0	433.0	19.9	P/B Ratio	1.6	52 Wk Hi-Low	47.75-30.63
Book Value	2,557.0	3,313.0	4,122.0	24.4	Yield %	3.5	Market Cap	US$6,537.0mil

Address **1 Mellon Bank Ctr.**
Pittsburgh, PA 15258-0001
Tel **412-234-5000**
Fax **412-234-6283**
Exchange **NYSE**
Ticker **MEL**
President & CEO **Frank V. Cahouet**
Chairman **Frank V. Cahouet**

Melville

Industry: **Other Specialty Retailers**

Melville operates 7,378 specialty-retail stores and leased departments across the United States and Canada, and has stores in the United Kingdom, Czech Republic, Slovakia, Mexico, and Singapore. The company also manufactures footwear. It sells prescription drugs, and health and beauty aids in stores operating under the CVS, Peoples, and Rea & Derick trade names. It sells apparel and accessories in chains of stores under the Marshalls, Bob's, Chess King, Chess King Garage, Garage, Wilsons Suede and Leather, Wilsons The Leather Experts, Pelle Cuir, and other trade names.

$ mil	12/92	12/93	12/94	% Change				
Revenues	10,432.8	10,435.4	11,285.6	8.1	P/E Ratio	12.5	Price (9/30/95)	34.50
Net Income	133.4	331.8	307.5	-7.3	P/B Ratio	1.5	52 Wk Hi-Low	39.88-29.63
Book Value	2,077.9	2,248.2	2,382.9	6.0	Yield %	4.4	Market Cap	US$3,624.5mil

Address **1 Theall Rd.**
Rye, NY 10580
Tel **914-925-4000**
Fax **914-925-4026**
Exchange **NYSE**
Ticker **MES**
President **Harvey Rosenthal**
Chairman & CEO **Stanley P. Goldstein**

Mercantile Bancorporation

Industry: **Banks - Central U.S.**

Mercantile Bancorporation is the bank holding company for Mercantile Bank of St. Louis and 40 other banks located in Missouri, Illinois, Iowa, and Kansas. The banks primarily offer services to commercial customers, including business, real-estate, and credit-card loans; deposit services; bond trading; equipment leasing; international banking; and safe-deposit-box rentals. Mercantile Bank of St. Louis provides banking services to other banks, including check processing, investment advisement, and bank-operation and loan assistance.

$ mil	12/92	12/93	12/94	% Change				
Revenues	815.5	892.9	1,023.3	14.6	P/E Ratio	12.0	Price (9/30/95)	44.75
Net Income	85.0	117.0	161.0	37.7	P/B Ratio	1.8	52 Wk Hi-Low	46.75-36.25
Book Value	669.3	841.1	1,068.3	27.0	Yield %	2.5	Market Cap	US$2,495.5mil

Address **1 Mercantile Ctr.**
St. Louis, MO 63166
Tel **314-425-2525**
Fax **N/A**
Exchange **NYSE**
Ticker **MTL**
Chief Executive **Thomas H. Jacobsen**
Chairman **Thomas H. Jacobsen**

Mercantile Bankshares

Industry: **Banks - Eastern U.S.**

Mercantile Bankshares is a bank holding company that owns most of the outstanding shares of 20 Maryland commercial and retail banks. The affiliated banks include Annapolis Banking and Trust, Baltimore Trust, Bank of Southern Maryland, Calvert Bank and Trust Company, Chestertown Bank of Maryland, and Potomac Valley Bank. Mercantile Bankshares also owns Mercantile Mortgage, a mortgage-banking company, MBC Agency, an insurance agency, and MBC Realty, which owns and operates various properties used by Merc-Safe, the holding company for Mercantile Pennsylvania.

$ mil	12/92	12/93	12/94	% Change				
Revenues	501.6	454.9	495.6	8.9	P/E Ratio	14.5	Price (9/30/95)	27.25
Net Income	76.3	82.4	90.4	9.7	P/B Ratio	1.8	52 Wk Hi-Low	27.75-21.13
Book Value	598.1	654.9	723.9	10.5	Yield %	2.7	Market Cap	US$1,291.9mil

Address **2 Hopkins Plz.**
Baltimore, MD 21203
Tel **410-237-5900**
Fax **N/A**
Exchange **NASDA**
Ticker **MRBK**
President **Edward K. Dunn, Jr.**
Chairman & CEO **H. Furlong Baldwin**

Mercantile Stores

Industry: **Apparel Retailers**

Mercantile Stores owns and leases retail department stores. As of January 1995, the company owned 60 and leased 43 stores across the midwestern and southern U.S. The stores operate under 13 different names and vary in size, the average store being approximately 170,000 square feet. Store names include McAlpin's, Lion, and Maison Blanche. Catering to middle- through upper-middle-income customers, the stores focus on fashion apparel and home furnishings. In addition to its department-store operations, Mercantile Stores is a partner in five shopping-center ventures.

$ mil	01/93	01/94	01/95	% Change				
Revenues	2,732.0	2,729.9	2,819.8	3.3	P/E Ratio	16.0	Price (9/30/95)	45.00
Net Income	69.1	89.7	103.4	15.3	P/B Ratio	1.2	52 Wk Hi-Low	48.75-37.50
Book Value	1,282.6	1,334.7	1,400.6	4.9	Yield %	2.3	Market Cap	US$1,658.0mil

Address **9450 Seward Rd.**
Fairfield, OH 45014
Tel **513-881-8000**
Fax **513-881-8689**
Exchange **NYSE**
Ticker **MST**
Chief Executive **David L. Nichols**
Chairman **David L. Nichols**

Merck & Co.

Industry: **Pharmaceuticals**

Merck & Company produces pharmaceuticals for humans and animals, and makes specialty chemicals. The company's drug products for humans include cardiovascular therapeutics, antiulcerants, antibiotics, and hepatitis B and pediatric-disease vaccines. Merck also is developing a vaccine for chicken pox, and makes antiparasitic drugs for animals. Its specialty-chemicals products, including alginates and biogums, are used in food and drug products and in oil exploration. The company's Merck-Medco Managed Care division provides managed-health-care and prescription-drug services.

$ mil	12/92	12/93	12/94	% Change				
Sales	**9,662.5**	**10,498.2**	**14,969.8**	**42.6**	P/E Ratio	**23.5**	Price (9/30/95)	**56.00**
Net Income	**1,984.2**	**2,166.2**	**2,997.0**	**38.4**	P/B Ratio	**6.3**	52 Wk Hi-Low	**57.50-34.38**
Book Value	**5,002.9**	**10,021.7**	**11,139.0**	**11.1**	Yield %	**2.0**	Market Cap	**US$69,255mil**

Address **1 Merck Dr.,Whitehouse Station NJ 08889-0100** Tel **908-423-1000** Fax **908-594-4459** Exchange **NYSE** Ticker **MRK** President & CEO **Raymond V. Gilmartin** Chairman **Raymond V. Gilmartin**

Meridian Bancorp

Industry: **Banks - Eastern U.S.**

Meridian Bancorp is a bank and financial-services holding company. The company's banks, Meridian Bank, Delaware Trust, and Meridian Bank New Jersey operate 325 branches in Delaware, southern New Jersey, and eastern and central Pennsylvania. Its Meridian Life Insurance subsidiary reinsures life, accident, and health insurance. The company's Meridian Asset Management subsidiary offers personal- and corporate-trust services, as well as asset-management and investment-advisory services.

$ mil	12/92	12/93	12/94	% Change				
Revenues	**1,082.3**	**1,247.0**	**1,225.9**	**-1.7**	P/E Ratio	**13.9**	Price (9/30/95)	**38.25**
Net Income	**114.7**	**157.8**	**159.4**	**1.0**	P/B Ratio	**1.8**	52 Wk Hi-Low	**40.38-25.75**
Book Value	**904.4**	**1,185.6**	**1,215.1**	**2.5**	Yield %	**3.5**	Market Cap	**US$2,193.1mil**

Address **35 N. Sixth St. Reading, PA 19603** Tel **610-655-2000** Fax **610-655-1585** Exchange **NASDA** Ticker **MRDN** President **Ezekiel S. Ketchum** Chairman & CEO **Samuel A. McCullough**

Merrill Lynch & Co.

Industry: **Securities Brokers**

Merrill Lynch & Company is a financial-services holding firm. Its subsidiaries provide investment, financing, and insurance services. Its Merrill Lynch, Pierce, Fenner & Smith subsidiary is a securities, options-contracts, and futures-contracts broker. Merrill Lynch also manages mutual funds, underwrites life-insurance products, and is a primary dealer in U.S.-government-issued obligations. In addition, the company participates in every aspect of investment banking, including underwriting the sale of securities and providing a broad range of corporate-advisory services.

$ mil	12/92	12/93	12/94	% Change				
Sales	**13,428.3**	**16,588.2**	**18,233.1**	**9.9**	P/E Ratio	**13.2**	Price (9/30/95)	**62.50**
Net Income	**893.8**	**1,358.9**	**1,016.8**	**-25.2**	P/B Ratio	**1.9**	52 Wk Hi-Low	**63.75-33.25**
Book Value	**4,569.1**	**5,485.9**	**5,817.6**	**6.0**	Yield %	**1.4**	Market Cap	**US$11,000mil**

Address **250 Vessey St. New York, NY 10281** Tel **212-449-1000** Fax **212-236-4384** Exchange **NYSE** Ticker **MER** President **David H. Komansky** Chairman & CEO **Daniel P. Tully**

Michigan National

Industry: **Banks - Central U.S.**

Michigan National, a subsidiary of National Australia Bank, is a bank holding company. Its largest subsidiary, Michigan National Bank, operates 191 branches in Michigan. The company's savings and loan association, Independence One Bank of California, manages five offices in southern California. The company also offers investment-banking services. Other subsidiaries originate residential mortgages and provide distressed-asset-management and loan services. Michigan National also offers real-estate-relocation benefit programs to corporate clients.

$ mil	12/92	12/93	12/94	% Change				
Revenues	**1,003.9**	**935.1**	**897.0**	**-4.1**	P/E Ratio	**9.8**	Price (9/30/95)	**108.63**
Net Income	**66.1**	**23.8**	**171.7**	**621.4**	P/B Ratio	**1.8**	52 Wk Hi-Low	**108.75-73.50**
Book Value	**805.8**	**815.6**	**795.0**	**-2.5**	Yield %	**1.8**	Market Cap	**US$1,482.3mil**

Address **27777 Inkster Rd. Farmington Hills, MI 48334** Tel **810-473-3000** Fax **810-477-3338** Exchange **NASDA** Ticker **MNCO** President **Douglas E. Ebert** Chairman & CEO **Robert J. Mylod**

Micron Technology

Industry: **Semiconductors & related**

Micron Technology manufactures microprocessor components and computers. Micron Semiconductor, a subsidiary, manufactures memory semiconductors for use primarily by computer manufacturers. Another subsidiary, Micron Custom Manufacturing Services, produces memory-expansion and video-enhancement modules for use in personal computers and peripherals. Through its Micron Computer subsidiary, the company also assembles personal computerss. It also develops and designs radio-frequency identification products and field-emission flat-panel displays.

$ mil	08/92	08/93	08/94	% Change				
Sales	**506.3**	**828.3**	**1,628.6**	**96.6**	P/E Ratio	**41.5**	Price (9/30/95)	**79.50**
Net Income	**6.6**	**104.1**	**400.5**	**284.8**	P/B Ratio	**15.4**	52 Wk Hi-Low	**94.38-22.06**
Book Value	**511.2**	**639.5**	**1,049.3**	**64.1**	Yield %	**0.1**	Market Cap	**US$16,382mil**

Address **2805 E. Columbia Rd. Boise, ID 83706-9698** Tel **208-368-4000** Fax **N/A** Exchange **NYSE** Ticker **MU** President **James W. Garrett** Chairman & CEO **Joseph L. Parkinson**

Microsoft

Industry: **Software**

Microsoft develops and supports microcomputer software. This software includes operating systems for personal computers, office machines, and personal-information devices; languages; and application programs; and personal-computer books, hardware, and multimedia products. These products are available for all personal computers and computers running Intel microprocessors. The company's operating systems are marketed under the names MS-DOS, Windows, and others. Microsoft's products are distributed through resellers and original equipment manufacturers.

	$ mil 06/92	06/93	06/94	% Change				
Sales	**2,758.7**	**3,753.0**	**4,649.0**	**23.9**	P/E Ratio	**45.9**	Price (9/30/95)	**90.50**
Net Income	**708.1**	**953.0**	**1,146.0**	**20.3**	P/B Ratio	**11.8**	52 Wk Hi-Low	**109.00-54.38**
Book Value	**2,193.0**	**3,242.0**	**4,450.0**	**37.3**	Yield %	**0.0**	Market Cap	**US$53,000mil**

Address **1 Microsoft Way**
Redmond, WA 98052
Tel **206-882-8080**
Fax **206-936-7329**
Exchange **NASDA**
Ticker **MSFT**
President & CEO **William H. Gates**
Chairman **William H. Gates**

Midlantic

Industry: **Banks - Eastern U.S.**

Midlantic is the holding company for Midlantic Bank, which operates 324 offices in New Jersey and southeastern Pennsylvania. The bank provides deposit and lending services to individual, corporate, and institutional customers, as well as automated teller machines. The company also has several nonbanking subsidiaries, such as Midlantic Securities, a discount broker/dealer. In addition, the company owns Lenders Life Insurance, which acts as a reinsurer for credit-related insurance, and Lease and Go, which leases automobiles. The company has agreed to be acquired PNC Bank.

	$ mil 12/92	12/93	12/94	% Change				
Revenues	**1,352.6**	**1,012.0**	**1,052.1**	**4.0**	P/E Ratio	**10.8**	Price (9/30/95)	**54.25**
Net Income	**7.0**	**170.4**	**271.6**	**59.4**	P/B Ratio	**2.1**	52 Wk Hi-Low	**54.75-24.25**
Book Value	**843.5**	**1,122.6**	**1,374.2**	**22.4**	Yield %	**0.7**	Market Cap	**US$2,816.9mil**

Address **Metro Park Plz.**
Edison, NJ 08818
Tel **908-321-8000**
Fax **908-205-4525**
Exchange **NASDA**
Ticker **MIDL**
President & CEO **Garry J. Scheuring**
Chairman **Garry J. Scheuring**

Millipore

Industry: **Industrial Technology**

Millipore manufactures separation-technology products. Its principal products are membrane filters and certain chemistries, resins, and enzymes used primarily for the analysis and purification of fluids by pharmaceutical, electronics, chemical, and food and beverage companies, as well as research and testing laboratories. The company markets these products through a direct-sales force to end users in the U.S. and internationally. Sales abroad account for 64% of the total. Millipore has research and production facilities at seven locations in the U.S., Europe, and Asia.

	$ mil 12/92	12/93	12/94	% Change				
Sales	**777.0**	**445.4**	**497.3**	**11.6**	P/E Ratio	**36.6**	Price (9/30/95)	**37.50**
Net Income	**33.2**	**34.6**	**56.2**	**62.5**	P/B Ratio	**7.8**	52 Wk Hi-Low	**38.88-23.00**
Book Value	**452.8**	**461.2**	**221.3**	**-52.0**	Yield %	**0.8**	Market Cap	**US$1,680.9mil**

Address **80 Ashby Rd.**
Bedford, MA 01730-2271
Tel **617-275-9200**
Fax **617-533-3301**
Exchange **NYSE**
Ticker **MIL**
President & CEO **John A. Gilmartin**
Chairman **John A. Gilmartin**

Mirage Resorts

Industry: **Casinos**

Mirage Resorts develops and operates casinos and hotels. It owns the Mirage, a Las Vegas casino and 29-story hotel with an adjacent 16,100-seat outdoor arena. Other properties in Las Vegas include the Treasure Island resort and the Golden Nugget and Dunes casino hotels. It also operates the Golden Nugget-Laughlin in Nevada, and owns undeveloped property in Nevada and in Atlantic City, New Jersey. Through a subsidiary, the company owns an additional 164-acre site on the Las Vegas strip, and announced plans for construction of another casino hotel on the property.

	$ mil 12/92	12/93	12/94	% Change				
Sales	**833.0**	**953.3**	**1,254.2**	**31.6**	P/E Ratio	**27.2**	Price (9/30/95)	**32.88**
Net Income	**28.4**	**29.2**	**114.3**	**291.5**	P/B Ratio	**2.9**	52 Wk Hi-Low	**34.63-18.38**
Book Value	**553.6**	**910.9**	**1,030.9**	**13.2**	Yield %	**0.0**	Market Cap	**US$2,996.4mil**

Address **3400 Las Vegas Blvd. S.**
Las Vegas, NV 89109
Tel **702-791-7111**
Fax **702-792-7676**
Exchange **NYSE**
Ticker **MIR**
President & CEO **Stephen A. Wynn**
Chairman **Stephen A. Wynn**

Mobil

Industry: **Oil - Integrated Majors**

Mobil is a major integrated petroleum company. It owns, on average, a 42% interest in 30,000 wells worldwide, and holds net reserves of 3.4 billion barrels of oil and 18 trillion cubic feet of natural gas. The company owns interests in 21 refineries, 29 oceangoing tankers, and 34,000 miles of pipeline, and it markets motor fuels through 20,000 retail outlets worldwide. Mobil's chemical division operates 43 plants, where it makes basic petrochemicals and fuel and lubricant additives. The company sold its plastics division to Tenneco in 1995.

	$ mil 12/92	12/93	12/94	% Change				
Sales	**63,564.0**	**63,474.0**	**66,757.0**	**5.2**	P/E Ratio	**38.8**	Price (9/30/95)	**99.63**
Net Income	**862.0**	**2,084.0**	**1,079.0**	**-48.2**	P/B Ratio	**2.3**	52 Wk Hi-Low	**103.13-77.75**
Book Value	**16,540.0**	**17,237.0**	**17,146.0**	**-0.5**	Yield %	**3.4**	Market Cap	**US$39,411mil**

Address **3225 Gallows Rd.**
Fairfax, VA 22037-0001
Tel **703-846-3000**
Fax **703-846-2313**
Exchange **NYSE**
Ticker **MOB**
President & CEO **Lucio A. Noto**
Chairman **Lucio A. Noto**

Monsanto

Industry: **Commodity Chemicals**

Monsanto manufactures chemicals and pharmaceutical products. Its products include herbicides, pesticides, food additives, synthetic carpet fibers, and plastics such as the Saflex plastic interlayer. Its NutraSweet subsidiary produces NutraSweet brand sweetener and Simplesse brand fat substitute. G.D. Searle, its pharmaceutical subsidiary, produces anti-infectives, oral contraceptives, and the Equal brand sweetener. Monsanto sells these products in the United States and in international markets. Its business operations in the U.S. account for approximately 65% of sales.

$ mil	12/92	12/93	12/94	% Change				
Sales	**7,763.0**	**7,902.0**	**8,272.0**	**4.7**	P/E Ratio	**18.9**	Price (9/30/95)	**100.75**
Net Income	**-88.0**	**494.0**	**622.0**	**25.9**	P/B Ratio	**3.8**	52 Wk Hi-Low	**104.13-68.50**
Book Value	**3,005.0**	**2,855.0**	**2,948.0**	**3.3**	Yield %	**2.5**	Market Cap	**US$11,613mil**

Address **800 N. Lindbergh Blvd.**
St. Louis, MO 63167
Tel **314-694-1000**
Fax **314-694-8748**
Exchange **NYSE**
Ticker **MTC**
President **Robert B. Shapiro**
Chairman & CEO **Richard J. Mahoney**

Montana Power

Industry: **Electrical Utilities - Western U.S.**

Montana Power has utility, coal-mining, and energy-production operations. The company provides electric and natural-gas service to roughly 593,000 customers in Montana. Utility operations produce about 51% of consolidated revenues. Montana Power generates about 27% of its electricity at hydroelectric stations and 44% using coal. It purchases the balance of its electric power from other suppliers. Through its other subsidiaries, the company mines and sells coal, explores for and markets oil and natural gas, and manages nonutility electricity-generation facilities.

$ mil	12/92	12/93	12/94	% Change				
Sales	**997.4**	**1,075.6**	**1,006.0**	**-6.5**	P/E Ratio	**11.6**	Price (9/30/95)	**23.13**
Net Income	**107.1**	**107.2**	**113.6**	**6.0**	P/B Ratio	**1.2**	52 Wk Hi-Low	**24.13-21.25**
Book Value	**918.9**	**1,012.7**	**1,056.9**	**4.4**	Yield %	**6.9**	Market Cap	**US$1,255.6mil**

Address **40 E. Broadway**
Butte, MT 59701-9989
Tel **406-723-5421**
Fax **406-496-5099**
Exchange **NYSE**
Ticker **MTP**
Chief Executive **Daniel T. Berube**
Chairman **Daniel T. Berube**

J.P. Morgan & Co.

Industry: **Banks - Money Center**

J.P. Morgan & Company is a financial-services holding company with operations that include commercial, investment, and merchant banking. The company provides corporate-advisory services, which include advising clients on mergers and acquisitions, divestitures, and privatizations, as well as underwriting equity and debt securities. It also offers asset-management and private-banking services. The company operates the Euroclear System, a securities-clearing and -settlement system that links participants from approximately 60 countries to more than 20 world stock markets.

$ mil	12/92	12/93	12/94	% Change				
Revenues	**10,231.0**	**11,941.0**	**11,915.0**	**-0.2**	P/E Ratio	**12.9**	Price (9/30/95)	**77.38**
Net Income	**1,382.0**	**1,586.0**	**1,215.0**	**-23.4**	P/B Ratio	**1.5**	52 Wk Hi-Low	**78.88-55.25**
Book Value	**7,066.0**	**9,859.0**	**9,568.0**	**-3.0**	Yield %	**3.6**	Market Cap	**US$14,538mil**

Address **60 Wall St.**
New York, NY 10260-0060
Tel **212-483-2323**
Fax **212-648-5209**
Exchange **NYSE**
Ticker **JPM**
President & CEO **Douglas A. Warner III**
Chairman **Douglas A. Warner III**

Morgan Stanley

Industry: **Securities Brokers**

Morgan Stanley provides a wide range of financial and research services to multinational companies, governments, financial institutions, and individual investors. It operates 28 principal offices in the U.S., Europe, and Pacific Rim. International sales account for more than half of Morgan Stanley's total revenues. The company's financial services include securities underwriting, mergers and acquisition, and trading; corporate finance; stock brokerage; and merchant banking. In addition, it manages open-end and closed-end funds for institutions and individuals.

$ mil	01/93 *	01/94	01/95	% Change				
Sales	**7,382.0**	**9,176.0**	**9,376.0**	**2.2**	P/E Ratio	**23.0**	Price (9/30/95)	**96.13**
Net Income	**510.5**	**786.0**	**395.0**	**-49.7**	P/B Ratio	**1.6**	52 Wk Hi-Low	**99.63-55.25**
Book Value	**3,434.0**	**4,469.0**	**4,555.0**	**1.9**	Yield %	**1.2**	Market Cap	**US$7,380.3mil**

Address **1251 Ave. of the Americas**
New York, NY 10020
Tel **212-703-4000**
Fax **212-703-6503**
Exchange **NYSE**
Ticker **MS**
President **John J. Mack**
Chairman **Richard B. Fisher**

*Irregular period due to fiscal year change.

Morrison Knudsen

Industry: **Heavy Construction**

Morrison Knudsen provides engineering and construction services and operates coal and lignite mines. Its engineering and construction division primarily serves the transportation, water-services, and waste-management industries. The company provides planning, design, engineering, construction, procurement, program-management, construction-management, and project-finance services. In 1995, Morrison Knudsen sold its stakes in MK Rail, which manufactures and rebuilds locomotives and railcars, and in MK Gold, a gold-mining company.

$ mil	12/92	12/93	12/94	% Change				
Sales	**2,284.9**	**2,722.5**	**2,504.3**	**-8.0**	P/E Ratio	**NMF**	Price (9/30/95)	**7.75**
Net Income	**-7.1**	**35.8**	**-349.6**	**NMF**	P/B Ratio	**4.4**	52 Wk Hi-Low	**17.50-5.38**
Book Value	**375.8**	**407.0**	**57.8**	**-85.8**	Yield %	**10.3**	Market Cap	**US$256.1mil**

Address **Morrison Knudsen Plz.**
Boise, ID 83729
Tel **208-386-5000**
Fax **208-386-7186**
Exchange **NYSE**
Ticker **MRN**
President & CEO **R.A. Tinstman**
Chairman **Robert S. Miller**

Morton International

Industry: **Specialty Chemicals**

Morton International produces salt, specialty chemicals, and automotive-safety products. While perhaps best known for its Morton and Windsor table salts, the company manufactures other salt products, adhesives and specialty polymers, coatings, electronic materials, and specialty dyes. It also develops and manufactures gas generators and airbag inflators and modules for use in automobile passenger-safety systems. Morton markets these products to commercial, industrial, governmental, and individual users worldwide. Business in the U.S. accounts for about 80% of sales.

$ mil	06/93	06/94	06/95	% Change				
Sales	**2,309.8**	**2,849.6**	**3,325.9**	**16.7**	P/E Ratio	**15.8**	Price (9/30/95)	**31.00**
Net Income	**32.5**	**226.5**	**294.1**	**29.8**	P/B Ratio	**2.8**	52 Wk Hi-Low	**33.50-26.00**
Book Value	**1,200.2**	**1,399.6**	**1,663.5**	**18.9**	Yield %	**1.4**	Market Cap	**US$4,588.2mil**

Address **100 N. Riverside Plz. Chicago, IL 60606**
Tel **312-807-2000** Fax **312-807-2228**
Exchange **NYSE** Ticker **MII**
President & CEO **S. Jay Stewart**
Chairman **S. Jay Stewart**

Motorola

Industry: **Communications Technology**

Motorola produces wireless-communication and electronic equipment, systems, and components. Its products include two-way radios, pagers, personal-communication systems, cellular telephones, semiconductors, microprocessors, electronic defense- and aerospace-systems, automotive equipment, and data-communication and information-handling equipment. The company markets these products primarily under the Motorola brand name in the United States and internationally. Motorola operates manufacturing facilities in North America, Europe, and Asia.

$ mil	12/92	12/93	12/94	% Change				
Sales	**13,303.0**	**16,963.0**	**22,245.0**	**31.1**	P/E Ratio	**28.8**	Price (9/30/95)	**76.38**
Net Income	**453.0**	**1,022.0**	**1,560.0**	**52.6**	P/B Ratio	**4.9**	52 Wk Hi-Low	**81.75-49.00**
Book Value	**5,144.0**	**6,409.0**	**9,096.0**	**41.9**	Yield %	**0.4**	Market Cap	**US$45,045mil**

Address **1303 E. Algonquin Rd. Schaumburg, IL 60196**
Tel **708-576-5000** Fax **708-576-8003**
Exchange **NYSE** Ticker **MOT**
Chief Executive **Gary L. Tooker**
Chairman **William J. Weisz**

Multimedia

Industry: **Broadcasting**

Multimedia publishes 11 daily and 50 nondaily newspapers and operates two radio stations, five network-affiliated television stations, 140 cable-television franchises, and a video-production company. Its cable-television franchises serve about 432,000 subscribers in five states. The company produces and syndicates television programming, including the Phil Donahue and Rush Limbaugh shows. Multimedia also manages a security-alarm business that monitors about 65,000 security-alarm customers. In 1995, the company agreed to be acquired by Gannett.

$ mil	12/92	12/93	12/94	% Change				
Sales	**576.8**	**634.6**	**630.5**	**-0.6**	P/E Ratio	**18.5**	Price (9/30/95)	**43.50**
Net Income	**60.5**	**99.9**	**90.0**	**-9.9**	P/B Ratio	**NMF**	52 Wk Hi-Low	**43.75-26.00**
Book Value	**-290.7**	**-177.5**	**-76.9**	**-56.7**	Yield %	**0.0**	Market Cap	**US$1,645.3mil**

Address **305 S. Main St. Greenville, SC 29601**
Tel **803-298-4373** Fax **803-298-4271**
Exchange **NASDA** Ticker **MMEDC**
President **Douglas J. Greenlaw**
Chairman & CEO **Donald D. Sbarra**

Murphy Oil

Industry: **Oil - Secondary**

Murphy Oil is a petroleum-production, agribusiness, and real-estate-development company. It owns, on average, a 24% interest in 6,400 oil and natural-gas wells, primarily in the U.S., Canada, Ecuador, and the U.K. The company holds net reserves of 220 million barrels of oil and 644 billion cubic feet of natural gas. Deltic Farm & Timber, a subsidiary, owns and operates 341,000 acres of timberland; two lumbermills; 36,000 acres of cotton, soybean, and grain fields; and a 4,300-acre residential community built around a golf course, all in Arkansas and Louisiana.

$ mil	12/92	12/93	12/94	% Change				
Sales	**1,596.4**	**1,599.8**	**1,679.2**	**5.0**	P/E Ratio	**16.9**	Price (9/30/95)	**40.00**
Net Income	**105.6**	**102.1**	**106.6**	**4.4**	P/B Ratio	**1.4**	52 Wk Hi-Low	**48.63-38.38**
Book Value	**1,200.1**	**1,222.4**	**1,270.7**	**3.9**	Yield %	**3.3**	Market Cap	**US$1,793.3mil**

Address **200 Peach St. El Dorado, AR 71731-7000**
Tel **501-862-6411** Fax **501-862-9057**
Exchange **NYSE** Ticker **MUR**
President & CEO **Claiborne P. Deming**
Chairman **R. Madison Murphy**

Nabors Industries

Industry: **Oil Drilling**

Nabors Industries provides petroleum drilling and related services. The company operates about 250 land-drilling rigs under contracts with petroleum-production companies in the U.S., South America, Africa, and Asia; international operations (excluding those in the North Sea) generate 24% of revenues. It operates a fleet of offshore drilling rigs, operating primarily in the North Sea and the Gulf of Mexico. Nabors also provides oil-field management, engineering, and construction; petroleum transportation; environmental remediation; and other oil-field support services.

$ mil	09/92	09/93	09/94	% Change				
Sales	**286.3**	**352.0**	**422.6**	**20.0**	P/E Ratio	**NMF**	Price (9/30/95)	**9.44**
Net Income	**33.8**	**34.3**	**0.7**	**-98.1**	P/B Ratio	**2.4**	52 Wk Hi-Low	**9.94-6.13**
Book Value	**184.8**	**267.7**	**276.8**	**3.4**	Yield %	**0.0**	Market Cap	**US$793.8mil**

Address **515 W. Greens Rd., Ste. 1200 Houston, TX 77067**
Tel **713-874-0035** Fax **713-872-5205**
Exchange **AMEX** Ticker **NBR**
President **Anthony G. Petrello**
Chairman & CEO **Eugene M. Isenberg**

NACCO

Industry: **Heavy Machinery**

NACCO Industries manufactures industrial equipment, housewares, and appliances, and operates coal mines. NACCO Materials Handling Group, a 97%-owned subsidiary, makes forklifts under the Hyster and Yale names. The company's other primary operating subsidiaries are 80%-owned Hamilton Beach/Proctor-Silex, a manufacturer of small household appliances; North American Coal, which operates four surface mines in Louisiana, North Dakota, and Texas and holds reserves of 2.2 billion tons; and Kitchen Collection, which operates approximately 120 retail stores in 37 states.

$ mil	12/92	12/93	12/94	% Change				
Sales	**1,467.0**	**1,538.8**	**1,853.5**	**20.4**	P/E Ratio	**12.6**	Price (9/30/95)	**59.38**
Net Income	**-85.9**	**8.3**	**42.1**	**406.6**	P/B Ratio	**1.9**	52 Wk Hi-Low	**63.63-46.88**
Book Value	**239.6**	**235.6**	**279.4**	**18.6**	Yield %	**1.1**	Market Cap	**US$532.3mil**

Address **5875 Landerbrook Dr.** **Mayfield Heights, OH 44124-4017**
Tel **216-449-9600** Fax **216-449-9607**
Exchange **NYSE** Ticker **NC**
President & CEO **Alfred M. Rankin, Jr.** Chairman **Alfred M. Rankin, Jr.**

Nalco Chemical

Industry: **Specialty Chemicals**

Nalco Chemical manufactures industrial specialty chemicals and provides related services worldwide. The company's products are used in applications that include controlling scale, corrosion, and foam in cooling systems and boilers; lubrication in metalworking; improving quality and production in the papermaking industry; clarifying water in water-treatment facilities; and enhancing efficiency in petroleum- and mineral-refining operations. Its engineering and analytical services include programs for materials recycling, chemical and waste handling, and water treatment.

$ mil	12/92	12/93	12/94	% Change				
Sales	**1,374.5**	**1,389.4**	**1,345.6**	**-3.2**	P/E Ratio	**27.3**	Price (9/30/95)	**34.13**
Net Income	**145.0**	**85.6**	**97.1**	**13.4**	P/B Ratio	**4.3**	52 Wk Hi-Low	**38.63-31.38**
Book Value	**576.3**	**550.6**	**544.2**	**-1.2**	Yield %	**2.8**	Market Cap	**US$2,305.3mil**

Address **1 Nalco Ctr.** **Naperville, IL 60563-1198**
Tel **708-305-1000** Fax **708-305-2900**
Exchange **NYSE** Ticker **NLC**
Chief Executive **Edward J. Mooney** Chairman **Edward J. Mooney**

Nashua

Industry: **Office Equipment**

Nashua manufactures coated-paper products, computer products, and office supplies and provides photofinishing services. The company manufactures facsimile and thermal papers, pressure-sensitive labels, specialty papers, data-storage disks, and copier and laser-printer supplies. Davac dry-gummed label paper and Stallion carbonless paper are the company's graphics products. The company also remanufactures laser-printer toner cartridges and operates mail-order photofinishing services under the York Photo name. Exports account for approximately 13% of the company's sales.

$ mil	12/92	12/93	12/94	% Change				
Sales	**552.5**	**555.7**	**478.6**	**-13.9**	P/E Ratio	**45.2**	Price (9/30/95)	**15.38**
Net Income	**-4.8**	**-19.2**	**2.1**	**-110.9**	P/B Ratio	**1.1**	52 Wk Hi-Low	**23.25-15.25**
Book Value	**117.2**	**93.1**	**92.7**	**-0.4**	Yield %	**4.7**	Market Cap	**US$98.0mil**

Address **44 Franklin St.** **Nashua, NH 03061-2002**
Tel **603-880-2323** Fax **603-880-5671**
Exchange **NYSE** Ticker **NSH**
President & CEO **William E. Mitchell** Chairman **Charles E. Clough**

National City

Industry: **Banks - Central U.S.**

National City is the third-largest bank holding company in Ohio by total assets. Its main subsidiaries are located in Ohio, Indiana, and Kentucky and offer credit cards, mortgage banking, and credit life insurance. The company's commercial-banking services include brokerage, investment management, leasing, mortgage banking, venture-capital services, small-business and community investment, and other related businesses. National City operates 10 commercial banks, with a total of 614 branch offices. In 1995, the company agreed to acquire Integra Financial.

$ mil	12/92	12/93	12/94	% Change				
Revenues	**2,783.7**	**2,701.9**	**2,905.2**	**7.5**	P/E Ratio	**11.4**	Price (9/30/95)	**30.88**
Net Income	**346.9**	**404.0**	**429.4**	**6.3**	P/B Ratio	**1.8**	52 Wk Hi-Low	**31.63-24.00**
Book Value	**2,499.9**	**2,763.3**	**2,601.1**	**-5.9**	Yield %	**3.8**	Market Cap	**US$4,548.5mil**

Address **1900 E. Ninth St.** **Cleveland, OH 44114-3484**
Tel **216-575-2000** Fax **216-575-9263**
Exchange **NYSE** Ticker **NCC**
President **David A. Daberko** Chairman & CEO **Edward B. Brandon**

National Semiconductor

Industry: **Semiconductors & related**

National Semiconductor manufactures more than 5,000 semiconductor products. The company and its subsidiaries focus on application-specific integrated circuits for use in computers, computer peripherals, telecommunication devices, and various analog applications such as data acquisition, audio/video systems, and automotive systems. It also makes digital-semiconductor products. National Semiconductor markets these semiconductors through distributors and a direct-sales force to original-equipment manufacturers in the United States and internationally.

$ mil	05/93	05/94	05/95	% Change				
Sales	**2,013.7**	**2,295.4**	**2,379.4**	**3.7**	P/E Ratio	**13.7**	Price (9/30/95)	**27.63**
Net Income	**130.3**	**264.0**	**264.2**	**0.1**	P/B Ratio	**2.4**	52 Wk Hi-Low	**33.00-14.50**
Book Value	**837.4**	**1,105.7**	**1,406.7**	**27.2**	Yield %	**0.0**	Market Cap	**US$3,416.2mil**

Address **2900 Semiconductor Dr.** **Santa Clara, CA 95052**
Tel **408-721-5000** Fax **408-721-7254**
Exchange **NYSE** Ticker **NSM**
President & CEO **Gilbert F. Amelio** Chairman **Gilbert F. Amelio**

National Service

Industry: **Industrial - Diversified**

National Service Industries (NSI) is a diversified manufacturing and services company. Through its Lithonia Lighting subsidiary, NSI manufactures lighting equipment for commercial, industrial, and residential uses. The company also makes maintenance, sanitation, and water-treatment chemicals; custom and standard envelopes and related office products; insulation materials; and merchandising tools for the home-furnishings industry. In addition, its National Linen Service subsidiary rents linens and uniforms to commercial users. It markets its products and services worldwide.

$ mil	08/92	08/93	08/94	% Change				
Sales	**1,633.8**	**1,804.8**	**1,881.9**	**4.3**	P/E Ratio	**17.5**	Price (9/30/95)	**29.25**
Net Income	**74.1**	**75.1**	**82.7**	**10.1**	P/B Ratio	**2.0**	52 Wk Hi-Low	**30.75-25.13**
Book Value	**683.0**	**704.0**	**727.4**	**3.3**	Yield %	**3.7**	Market Cap	**US$1,412.9mil**

Address **NSI Ctr., 1420 Peachtree St. N.E. Atlanta, GA 30309**
Tel **404-853-1000** Fax **404-853-6031**
Exchange **NYSE** Ticker **NSI**
President **Don W. Hubble**
Chairman & CEO **D. Raymond Riddle**

NationsBank

Industry: **Banks - Southern U.S.**

NationsBank is a financial-services holding company, that offers commercial- and retail-banking services, originates and manages home-mortgage loans, and operates full-service and discount-securities businesses. It also issues credit cards and provides trust and investment services. The company offers financial advisory, securities underwriting, and other investment-banking services to corporations. NationsBank manages nearly 2,000 branches under the NationsBank name primarily in the southeastern region of the United States. The company agreed to acquire Bank South in 1995.

$ mil	12/92	12/93	12/94	% Change				
Revenues	**9,942.0**	**10,392.0**	**13,113.0**	**26.2**	P/E Ratio	**11.0**	Price (9/30/95)	**67.25**
Net Income	**1,145.0**	**1,501.0**	**1,690.0**	**12.6**	P/B Ratio	**1.7**	52 Wk Hi-Low	**68.63-43.75**
Book Value	**7,814.0**	**9,979.0**	**11,011.0**	**10.3**	Yield %	**2.8**	Market Cap	**US$18,252mil**

Address **NationsBank Ctr., 100 N. Tryon St. Charlotte, NC 28255**
Tel **704-386-5000** Fax **704-386-6699**
Exchange **NYSE** Ticker **NB**
President **Kenneth D. Lewis**
Chairman & CEO **Hugh L. McColl, Jr.**

Navistar International

Industry: **Land Transportation**

Navistar International manufactures diesel vehicles and replacement parts. The company produces diesel-powered medium and heavy trucks and buses, used by common carriers as well as by the passenger-transportation, leasing, construction, and energy/petroleum industries. Navistar also produces diesel engines for use in its medium trucks and for sale to original-equipment manufacturers. These products are marketed in about 70 countries. Business in the United States accounts for 88% of revenues. Navistar operates eight manufacturing plants in North America.

$ mil	10/92	10/93	10/94	% Change				
Sales	**3,875.0**	**4,694.0**	**5,337.0**	**13.7**	P/E Ratio	**16.7**	Price (9/30/95)	**12.00**
Net Income	**-212.0**	**-501.0**	**82.0**	**-116.4**	P/B Ratio	**1.1**	52 Wk Hi-Low	**17.50-12.00**
Book Value	**338.0**	**775.0**	**817.0**	**5.4**	Yield %	**0.0**	Market Cap	**US$902.3mil**

Address **455 N. Cityfront Plaza Dr. Chicago, IL 60611**
Tel **312-836-2000** Fax **312-836-2227**
Exchange **NYSE** Ticker **NAV**
President **John R. Horne**
Chairman & CEO **James C. Cotting**

NBD Bancorp

Industry: **Banks - Central U.S.**

NBD Bancorp is a bank holding company with subsidiaries that operate approximately 630 branches in five states: Michigan, Illinois, Indiana, Ohio, and Florida. The company's main subsidiary is NBD Bank, which is the largest banking institution in Michigan by total assets, and which accounts for approximately 71% of the company's income. NBD Bancorp's other divisions are engaged in mortgage banking, trust services, insurance, leasing, consumer-credit processing, and securities trading. In 1995, NBD Bancorp agreed to merge with First Chicago.

$ mil	12/92	12/93	12/94	% Change				
Revenues	**3,373.0**	**3,208.2**	**3,463.4**	**8.0**	P/E Ratio	**11.4**	Price (9/30/95)	**38.25**
Net Income	**300.1**	**485.8**	**531.7**	**9.4**	P/B Ratio	**1.8**	52 Wk Hi-Low	**38.75-27.13**
Book Value	**2,940.9**	**3,248.6**	**3,291.5**	**1.3**	Yield %	**3.2**	Market Cap	**US$6,143.0mil**

Address **611 Woodward Ave. Detroit, MI 48226**
Tel **313-225-1000** Fax **617-225-2012**
Exchange **NYSE** Ticker **NBD**
President **Thomas H. Jeffs II**
Chairman & CEO **Verne G. Istock**

New England Electric

Industry: **Electrical Utilities - Eastern U.S.**

New England Electric System is a utility holding company providing electrical power to about 1.3 million customers in Rhode Island, Massachusetts, and New Hampshire. Its subsidiaries include three retail electric companies--New England Power, Massachusetts Electric, and Narragansett Electric; two wholesale electric-generating companies; an oil and natural-gas exploration and development company; three electric-transmission companies; and an operations- and management-consulting company. Roughly 37% of the company's electricity is generated by coal-firing plants.

$ mil	12/92	12/93	12/94	% Change				
Sales	**2,181.7**	**2,234.0**	**2,243.0**	**0.4**	P/E Ratio	**12.1**	Price (9/30/95)	**37.00**
Net Income	**185.0**	**190.2**	**199.4**	**4.9**	P/B Ratio	**1.5**	52 Wk Hi-Low	**37.00-29.75**
Book Value	**1,486.4**	**1,529.9**	**1,580.8**	**3.3**	Yield %	**6.2**	Market Cap	**US$2,402.2mil**

Address **25 Research Dr. Westborough, MA 01582**
Tel **508-366-9011** Fax **508-836-0276**
Exchange **NYSE** Ticker **NES**
President & CEO **John W. Rowe**
Chairman **Joan T. Bok**

New Plan Realty

Industry: **Real-Estate Investment**

New Plan Realty Trust is a self-administered and self-managed real-estate investment trust. The trust primarily develops and operates shopping and factory-outlet centers and apartment complexes. It owns interests in 97 shopping centers with an aggregate of 12.4 million gross rentable square feet; five factory outlets with 1.5 million gross rentable square feet; and 20 rental-apartment complexes containing 3,940 units, located in 20 states. The average occupancy rate for the trust's shopping and factory-outlet centers and apartments were 89%, 94%, and 97% respectively.

$ mil	07/92	07/93	07/94	% Change				
Sales	**64.7**	**76.3**	**101.0**	**32.3**	P/E Ratio	**20.9**	Price (9/30/95)	**22.13**
Net Income	**49.4**	**43.2**	**52.3**	**21.1**	P/B Ratio	**2.1**	52 Wk Hi-Low	**22.63-19.00**
Book Value	**506.3**	**500.6**	**565.5**	**13.0**	Yield %	**6.0**	Market Cap	**US$1,175.0mil**

Address **1120 Ave. of the Americas**
New York, NY 10036
Tel **212-869-3000**
Fax **212-302-4776**
Exchange **NYSE**
Ticker **NPR**
President **Arnold Laubich**
Chairman & CEO **William Newman**

New York Times

Industry: **Publishing**

New York Times is a publishing, broadcasting, and information-services company operating throughout North America. It also owns forest-products interests. In addition to The New York Times, the company publishes The Boston Globe, 28 regional newspapers, and magazines, including Golf World, Golf Digest, and Snow Country. It also operates television and radio stations. The company's newspaper businesses accounts for 84% of total revenues. Magazine publishing contributes about 12% of revenues, and the balance comes from its broadcasting and information-services businesses.

$ mil	12/92	12/93	12/94	% Change				
Sales	**1,773.5**	**2,019.7**	**2,357.6**	**16.7**	P/E Ratio	**13.4**	Price (9/30/95)	**27.38**
Net Income	**-44.7**	**6.1**	**213.4**	**NMF**	P/B Ratio	**1.7**	52 Wk Hi-Low	**28.50-20.38**
Book Value	**1,001.4**	**1,600.7**	**1,545.3**	**-3.5**	Yield %	**2.0**	Market Cap	**US$2,655.6mil**

Address **229 W. 43rd St.**
New York, NY 10036
Tel **212-556-1234**
Fax **212-556-7389**
Exchange **AMEX**
Ticker **NYT.A**
President **Lance R. Primis**
Chairman & CEO **Arthur O. Sulzberger**

Newell

Industry: **Household Products (Durable)**

Newell manufactures consumer products. The company makes housewares under the Anchor Hocking, Airbake, Cushionaire, Mirro, and WearEver labels; other products include picture frames, bathroom scales, hardware, stationery, and school and office supplies. Newell markets its wares worldwide, principally to volume purchasers, including chain-discount and variety stores, warehouse clubs, home centers, and hardware stores. Sales in the U.S. account for more than 90% of the company's total. Newell operates manufacturing facilities in the U.S. and Canada.

$ mil	12/92	12/93	12/94	% Change				
Sales	**1,451.7**	**1,645.0**	**2,074.9**	**26.1**	P/E Ratio	**20.0**	Price (9/30/95)	**24.75**
Net Income	**119.1**	**165.3**	**195.6**	**18.3**	P/B Ratio	**3.5**	52 Wk Hi-Low	**26.25-20.50**
Book Value	**859.4**	**979.1**	**1,125.3**	**14.9**	Yield %	**1.6**	Market Cap	**US$3,915.3mil**

Address **29 E. Stephenson St.**
Freeport, IL 61032
Tel **815-235-4171**
Fax **815-969-6141**
Exchange **NYSE**
Ticker **NWL**
Chief Executive **William P. Sovey**
Chairman **Daniel C. Ferguson**

Newhall Land & Farming

Industry: **Real-Estate Investment**

Newhall Land & Farming is a land-resource firm. Its primary business is developing master-planned communities, including residential, industrial, and commercial real estate in Valencia, California and Scottsdale, Arizona. The company is currently planning another community in Valencia. Its agricultural operations include farming alfalfa, cotton, wheat, tomatoes, melons, and barley crops. It also has cattle operations. The company owns approximately 100,000 acres of real estate in southern California. Master-planned communities generate 79% of Newhall's revenues.

$ mil	12/92	12/93	12/94	% Change				
Sales	**128.2**	**105.5**	**134.3**	**27.3**	P/E Ratio	**31.8**	Price (9/30/95)	**13.38**
Net Income	**17.2**	**12.8**	**15.6**	**21.6**	P/B Ratio	**4.4**	52 Wk Hi-Low	**14.88-12.00**
Book Value	**113.0**	**111.3**	**112.4**	**1.0**	Yield %	**3.0**	Market Cap	**US$483.8mil**

Address **23823 Valencia Blvd.**
Valencia, CA 91355
Tel **805-255-4000**
Fax **805-255-3960**
Exchange **NYSE**
Ticker **NHL**
President **Gary M. Cusumano**
Chairman & CEO **Thomas L. Lee**

Newmont Mining

Industry: **Precious Metals**

Newmont Mining is the holding company for 90%-owned Newmont Gold, which operates gold and silver mines. Newmont Gold operates six open-pit gold mines near Carlin, Nevada, that hold 19,000 ounces of reserves. It holds rights to an additional 7,600 ounces of reserves through mining interests in Peru, Uzbekistan, and Indonesia. The company produces bullion containing 85% to 95% gold and silver, which it sells for refining into pure bullion, jeweler's gold, and industrial materials. Newmont Gold also mines mercury, selling it as a by-product.

$ mil	12/92	12/93	12/94	% Change				
Sales	**613.2**	**634.3**	**597.4**	**-5.8**	P/E Ratio	**60.7**	Price (9/30/95)	**42.50**
Net Income	**79.0**	**133.1**	**76.1**	**-42.8**	P/B Ratio	**5.4**	52 Wk Hi-Low	**45.75-33.25**
Book Value	**528.6**	**629.8**	**673.5**	**6.9**	Yield %	**1.1**	Market Cap	**US$3,663.4mil**

Address **1700 Lincoln St.**
Denver, CO 80203
Tel **303-863-7414**
Fax **303-837-5837**
Exchange **NYSE**
Ticker **NEM**
President & CEO **Ronald C. Cambre**
Chairman **Ronald C. Cambre**

Nextel Communications

Industry: **Mobile Communication Systems**

Nextel Communications provides wireless-communication services and sells related equipment. The company offers fleet-dispatch, cellular-phone, and paging services to approximately 310,000 subscribers, primarily in Los Angeles, San Francisco, Dallas/Fort Worth, Chicago, and New York. It also provides management and consulting services to other wireless-communication companies. Its OneComm subsidiary provides wireless-communication services in the western U.S. Nextel Communications sells wireless-communication equipment through about 60 sales representatives.

$ mil	03/93	03/94	12/94 *	% Change				
Sales	**53.0**	**67.9**	**83.7**	**23.2**	P/E Ratio	**NMF**	Price (9/30/95)	**16.88**
Net Income	**-9.6**	**-56.9**	**-125.9**	**121.2**	P/B Ratio	**1.4**	52 Wk Hi-Low	**22.50-9.63**
Book Value	**255.2**	**846.3**	**1,268.6**	**49.9**	Yield %	**0.0**	Market Cap	**US$3,243.1mil**

Address **201 Rte. 17 N.**
Rutherford, NJ 07070
Tel **201-438-1400**
Fax **201-438-5540**
Exchange **NASDA**
Ticker **CALL**
President & CEO **Brian D. McAuley**
Chairman **Morgan E. O'Brien**

*Irregular period due to fiscal year change.

Niagara Mohawk Power

Industry: **Electrical Utilities - Eastern U.S.**

Niagara Mohawk Power operates utilities in New York and owns other energy-based businesses. The company provides electric service to 1.5 million residential, commercial, and industrial customers, and distributes natural gas to about 500,000 residential and business customers. Sales of electricity account for about 85% of total revenues. Residential customers account for 35% of electric revenues and 62% of natural-gas revenues. Other subsidiaries operate an oil- and natural-gas exploration company; an electric utility in Ontario, Canada; and cogeneration power plants.

$ mil	12/92	12/93	12/94	% Change				
Sales	**3,701.5**	**3,933.4**	**4,152.2**	**5.6**	P/E Ratio	**13.1**	Price (9/30/95)	**13.13**
Net Income	**256.4**	**271.8**	**177.0**	**-34.9**	P/B Ratio	**0.6**	52 Wk Hi-Low	**15.63-11.75**
Book Value	**2,700.8**	**2,869.7**	**3,008.4**	**4.8**	Yield %	**8.3**	Market Cap	**US$1,894.3mil**

Address **300 Erie Blvd. W.**
Syracuse, NY 13202
Tel **315-474-1511**
Fax **315-428-6126**
Exchange **NYSE**
Ticker **NMK**
President **John M. Endries**
Chairman & CEO **William E. Davis**

NICOR

Industry: **Gas Utilities**

NICOR is engaged in energy and shipping operations. Its Northern Illinois Gas subsidiary delivers natural gas to more than 1.7 million customers and provides gas transportation and backup gas to more than 12,000 commercial and industrial users. Natural-gas distribution contributes approximately 91% of the company's operating income. Residential customers account for 90% of natural-gas sales; commercial and industrial users make up the balance. Its other operations include an oil and natural-gas exploration and production company and a containerized-freight shipper.

$ mil	12/92	12/93	12/94	% Change				
Sales	**1,611.6**	**1,673.9**	**1,609.4**	**-3.9**	P/E Ratio	**13.2**	Price (9/30/95)	**27.25**
Net Income	**108.3**	**111.7**	**109.5**	**-2.0**	P/B Ratio	**2.0**	52 Wk Hi-Low	**27.88-22.00**
Book Value	**728.9**	**720.6**	**692.8**	**-3.9**	Yield %	**4.6**	Market Cap	**US$1,375.2mil**

Address **1844 Ferry Rd.**
Naperville, IL 60563
Tel **708-305-9500**
Fax **708-983-9328**
Exchange **NYSE**
Ticker **GAS**
President **Thomas L. Fisher**
Chairman & CEO **Richard G. Cline**

Nike

Industry: **Footwear**

Nike produces athletic and casual footwear, apparel, and accessories. The company sells its products to approximately 14,000 retail accounts in the United States and, through a combination of independent distributors, licensees, and subsidiaries, in 110 countries; it also operates about 60 retail outlets. In fiscal 1995, 63% of revenues were derived from domestic retail sales. Company products are sold under the Nike, and other brand names including Side 1 and i.e. footwear for women. Nike's Cole Haan Holdings division markets dress and casual footwear and accessories.

$ mil	05/93	05/94	05/95	% Change				
Sales	**3,931.0**	**3,789.7**	**4,760.8**	**25.6**	P/E Ratio	**20.4**	Price (9/30/95)	**111.13**
Net Income	**365.0**	**298.8**	**399.7**	**33.8**	P/B Ratio	**4.0**	52 Wk Hi-Low	**111.13-58.38**
Book Value	**1,646.0**	**1,740.9**	**1,964.7**	**12.9**	Yield %	**0.9**	Market Cap	**US$7,939.3mil**

Address **1 Bowerman Dr.**
Beaverton, OR 97005
Tel **503-671-6453**
Fax **503-671-6300**
Exchange **NYSE**
Ticker **NKE**
President **Thomas E. Clarke**
Chairman & CEO **Philip H. Knight**

NIPSCO

Industry: **Electrical Utilities - Central U.S.**

NIPSCO Industries is a utility holding company. Its principal subsidiary, Northern Indiana Public Service, supplies natural gas and electricity in northern Indiana. Sales of electricity account for roughly 58% of revenues. Northern Indiana Public Service serves a 12,000-square-mile area that has a population of about 2.2 million. Another subsidiary, Kokomo Gas and Fuel, serves the city of Kokomo and its surrounding rural territory. Approximately 97% of NIPSCO's electricity is generated at coal-fired stations; the balance is produced at natural-gas-fired plants.

$ mil	12/92	12/93	12/94	% Change				
Sales	**1,582.4**	**1,677.9**	**1,676.4**	**-0.1**	P/E Ratio	**14.1**	Price (9/30/95)	**34.88**
Net Income	**136.6**	**156.1**	**164.0**	**5.1**	P/B Ratio	**2.0**	52 Wk Hi-Low	**35.25-26.38**
Book Value	**1,069.5**	**1,129.7**	**1,142.9**	**1.2**	Yield %	**4.2**	Market Cap	**US$2,218.6mil**

Address **5265 Hohman Ave.**
Hammond, IN 46320
Tel **219-853-5200**
Fax **219-853-5352**
Exchange **NYSE**
Ticker **NI**
President & CEO **Gary L. Neale**
Chairman **Gary L. Neale**

Noble Affiliates

Industry: **Oil - Secondary**

Noble Affiliates operates oil and natural-gas wells worldwide. Samedan Oil, the company's primary operating subsidiary, owns, on average, a 34% interest in 5,600 wells and holds net reserves of 76 million barrels of oil and 778 billion cubic feet of natural gas, with the greatest concentration in the Gulf of Mexico. Noble Gas Marketing, another subsidiary, sells Samedan Oil's gas products directly to industrial end users under short-term contracts. Noble Affiliates is currently exploring for additional petroleum reserves in Tunisia, Equatorial Guinea, and Indonesia.

$ mil	12/92	12/93	12/94	% Change				
Sales	**259.8**	**278.0**	**306.2**	**10.1**	P/E Ratio	**NMF**	Price (9/30/95)	**26.38**
Net Income	**41.2**	**12.6**	**3.2**	**-74.8**	P/B Ratio	**3.2**	52 Wk Hi-Low	**30.13-21.63**
Book Value	**304.8**	**415.4**	**412.1**	**-0.8**	Yield %	**0.6**	Market Cap	**US$1,319.9mil**

Address **110 W. Broadway, P.O. Box 1967 Ardmore, OK 73402** Tel **405-223-4110** Fax **405-221-1210** Exchange **NYSE** Ticker **NBL** President & CEO **Robert Kelley** Chairman **Robert Kelley**

NorAm Energy

Industry: **Gas Utilities**

NorAm Energy is a public natural-gas utility that provides natural gas to 2.7 million customers in communities throughout Arkansas, Louisiana, Minnesota, Mississippi, Oklahoma, and Texas. The company's main divisions, Arkansas Louisiana Gas Company, Entex, and Minnegasco, operate approximately 51,000 miles of gas-distribution pipelines. Residential customers account for approximately 37% of NorAm Energy's natural-gas sales; commercial and industrial users provide another 46%. The company has the third-largest gas-distribution system in the U.S. in terms of customers.

$ mil	12/92	12/93	12/94	% Change				
Sales	**2,743.8**	**2,949.6**	**2,801.5**	**-5.0**	P/E Ratio	**23.9**	Price (9/30/95)	**7.88**
Net Income	**-228.5**	**36.1**	**48.1**	**33.2**	P/B Ratio	**1.3**	52 Wk Hi-Low	**8.00-5.25**
Book Value	**712.9**	**708.0**	**717.4**	**1.3**	Yield %	**3.6**	Market Cap	**US$976.0mil**

Address **1600 Smith St., 11th Fl. Houston, TX 77002** Tel **713-654-5100** Fax **713-654-7511** Exchange **NYSE** Ticker **NAE** President & CEO **T. Milton Honea** Chairman **T. Milton Honea**

Nord Resources

Industry: **Mining**

Nord Resources operates mines and related businesses in the United States, Africa, and Australia. Sierra Rutile, a 50%-owned subsidiary, mines titanium dioxide in Sierra Leone from 4 million metric tons of reserves for use as a pigment by paint, paper, and plastic-product manufacturers. Nord Kaolin, an 80%-owned subsidiary, mines kaolin clay in Georgia, which it processes into pigments, fillers, and coatings for the papermaking industry. Nord Pacific, a 35%-owned subsidiary, owns a 40% stake in the Girilambone copper mine in Australia and explores for other minerals.

$ mil	12/92	12/93	12/94	% Change				
Sales	**100.1**	**88.4**	**71.5**	**-19.1**	P/E Ratio	**NMF**	Price (9/30/95)	**2.38**
Net Income	**13.4**	**-9.1**	**-15.6**	**71.5**	P/B Ratio	**0.4**	52 Wk Hi-Low	**7.00-2.38**
Book Value	**115.2**	**108.8**	**97.5**	**-10.4**	Yield %	**0.0**	Market Cap	**US$37.6mil**

Address **8150 Washington Village Dr. Dayton, OH 45458** Tel **513-433-6307** Fax **513-435-7285** Exchange **NYSE** Ticker **NRD** President & CEO **Edgar F. Cruft** Chairman **Edgar F. Cruft**

Nordson

Industry: **Factory Equipment**

Nordson makes automated equipment used to apply adhesives, sealants, and coatings during manufacturing processes. Its products include automated adhesive- and sealing-dispensing systems, electrostatic-spray equipment for applying liquid and powder paints and coatings, and advanced gasketing machinery. The company also provides related software and application technologies. Markets for Nordson's application equipment include the automotive, appliance, bookbinding, defense, furniture, food-and-beverage, and telecommunication industries.

$ mil	10/92	10/93	10/94	% Change				
Sales	**425.6**	**461.6**	**506.7**	**9.8**	P/E Ratio	**24.0**	Price (9/30/95)	**58.75**
Net Income	**39.5**	**36.0**	**46.7**	**29.6**	P/B Ratio	**5.1**	52 Wk Hi-Low	**61.00-53.25**
Book Value	**177.7**	**196.4**	**212.4**	**8.2**	Yield %	**1.0**	Market Cap	**US$1,069.5mil**

Address **28601 Clemens Rd. Westlake, OH 44145** Tel **216-892-1580** Fax **216-892-9507** Exchange **NASDA** Ticker **NDSN** President & CEO **William P. Madar** Chairman **Eric T. Nord**

Nordstrom

Industry: **Apparel Retailers**

Nordstrom operates a chain of department stores. The company sells apparel, shoes, and accessories for women, men, and children through 55 large specialty stores and four smaller stores in the western, eastern, and midwestern regions of the U.S. The company operates clearance stores under the name Nordstrom Rack, which serve as outlets for clearance merchandise from the company's large specialty stores and also purchased merchandise directly from manufacturers. The company operates a men's specialty store in New York and leases shoe departments in 11 stores in Hawaii.

$ mil	01/93	01/94	01/95	% Change				
Revenues	**3,422.0**	**3,589.9**	**3,894.5**	**8.5**	P/E Ratio	**16.9**	Price (9/30/95)	**41.75**
Net Income	**136.6**	**140.4**	**203.0**	**44.6**	P/B Ratio	**2.6**	52 Wk Hi-Low	**49.25-36.13**
Book Value	**1,052.0**	**1,166.5**	**1,343.8**	**15.2**	Yield %	**0.9**	Market Cap	**US$3,435.1mil**

Address **1501 Fifth Ave. Seattle, WA 98101** Tel **206-628-2111** Fax **206-628-1795** Exchange **NASDA** Ticker **NOBE** President **R. Johnson / J. Whitacre** Chairman **B. & J. Nordstrom**

Norfolk Southern

Industry: **Railroads**

Norfolk Southern provides rail-transportation and motor-carrier transportation. Through its Norfolk Southern Railway subsidiary, the company operates more than 14,500 miles of track in 20 states in the southern, southeastern, midwestern, and eastern parts of the United States and in the province of Ontario, Canada. The railroad's main cargoes include coal, paper, forest products, chemicals, automotive parts, and agricultural commodities. Its North American Van Lines subsidiary provides residential-moving services in the U.S. and, to a lesser extent, internationally.

$ mil	12/92	12/93	12/94	% Change				
Sales	**4,606.6**	**4,460.1**	**4,581.3**	**2.7**	P/E Ratio	**15.3**	Price (9/30/95)	**74.75**
Net Income	**557.7**	**772.0**	**667.8**	**-13.5**	P/B Ratio	**2.1**	52 Wk Hi-Low	**77.13-59.75**
Book Value	**4,232.6**	**4,620.7**	**4,684.8**	**1.4**	Yield %	**2.6**	Market Cap	**US$9,794.2mil**

Address **3 Commercial Pl.**
Norfolk, VA 23510
Tel **804-629-2600**
Fax **804-629-2345**
Exchange **NYSE**
Ticker **NSC**
President & CEO **David R. Goode**
Chairman **David R. Goode**

Northeast Utilities

Industry: **Electrical Utilities - Eastern U.S.**

Northeast Utilities is a utility holding company. Through subsidiaries, it furnishes electric service in Connecticut, New Hampshire, and Massachusetts, and sells electricity to eight municipalities. Residential customers account for approximately 39% of revenues; commercial and industrial users supply another 48%. Northeast Utilities generates roughly 62% of its electricity with nuclear energy, 10% with coal, and 11% from natural gas and oil. The company also provides support services for other utilities, including accounting, operational, planning, and purchasing.

$ mil	12/92	12/93	12/94	% Change				
Sales	**3,216.9**	**3,629.1**	**3,642.7**	**0.4**	P/E Ratio	**10.6**	Price (9/30/95)	**24.38**
Net Income	**256.1**	**250.0**	**286.9**	**14.7**	P/B Ratio	**1.3**	52 Wk Hi-Low	**24.38-21.13**
Book Value	**2,174.0**	**2,224.1**	**2,309.1**	**3.8**	Yield %	**7.2**	Market Cap	**US$3,079.8mil**

Address **174 Brush Hill Ave.**
West Springfield, MA 01090
Tel **203-665-5000**
Fax **203-665-3652**
Exchange **NYSE**
Ticker **NU**
President & CEO **Bernard M. Fox**
Chairman **William B. Ellis**

Northern States Power

Industry: **Electrical Utilities - Central U.S.**

Northern States Power (NSP) is an electricity and natural-gas utility. The company produces and distributes electricity, distributes natural gas, and operates other energy-related companies. It operates five coal-burning and two nuclear electricity-generation stations, and provides electricity and natural-gas service in five northern states. NSP's nonutility operations include a coal-conversion processing plant, waste-derived fuel plants, and steam-supply lines. Residential users provide approximately 33% of electric and about 52% of electric and natural-gas revenues.

$ mil	12/92	12/93	12/94	% Change				
Sales	**2,159.5**	**2,404.0**	**2,486.6**	**3.4**	P/E Ratio	**13.1**	Price (9/30/95)	**45.38**
Net Income	**206.4**	**211.7**	**243.5**	**15.0**	P/B Ratio	**1.4**	52 Wk Hi-Low	**47.38-41.88**
Book Value	**1,897.6**	**2,067.9**	**2,137.4**	**3.4**	Yield %	**5.8**	Market Cap	**US$3,071.6mil**

Address **414 Nicollet Mall**
Minneapolis, MN 55401
Tel **612-330-5500**
Fax **612-330-1902**
Exchange **NYSE**
Ticker **NSP**
President & CEO **James J. Howard**
Chairman **James J. Howard**

Northern Trust

Industry: **Banks - Central U.S.**

Northern Trust is a bank holding company with subsidiaries in Illinois, Arizona, California, Florida, New York, Texas, and Georgia. Its principal subsidiary, Northern Trust Company, is a Chicago bank that is the third-largest bank in Illinois by assets. The company's banks offer fiduciary, investment-management, financial-consulting, credit, and trust services for individuals, institutions, and organizations. The company also manages a securities-brokerage firm, underwrites tax-exempt debt, and provides management-consulting services to nonaffiliated financial institutions.

$ mil	12/92	12/93	12/94	% Change				
Revenues	**1,231.3**	**1,258.8**	**1,478.6**	**17.5**	P/E Ratio	**14.5**	Price (9/30/95)	**46.00**
Net Income	**149.5**	**167.9**	**182.2**	**8.5**	P/B Ratio	**1.9**	52 Wk Hi-Low	**47.63-32.25**
Book Value	**1,010.5**	**1,151.7**	**1,280.7**	**11.2**	Yield %	**2.0**	Market Cap	**US$2,570.1mil**

Address **50 S. LaSalle St.**
Chicago, IL 60675
Tel **312-630-6000**
Fax **312-444-5592**
Exchange **NASDA**
Ticker **NTRS**
President & COO **William A. Osborn**
Chairman & CEO **David W. Fox**

Northrop Grumman

Industry: **Aerospace & Defense**

Northrop Grumman produces aircraft, special-purpose vehicles, and electronics for the defense and civilian markets. Its major defense products include the B-2 Stealth bomber and components for F/A-18 fighter aircraft. The company also manufactures fuselage sections for the Boeing 747. Its electronic products include missile-guidance systems, unmanned vehicles, and electronic-targeting devices. Northrop Grumman markets its products primarily to government agencies and aircraft manufacturers. Government contracts account for 84% of the company's revenues.

$ mil	12/92	12/93	12/94	% Change				
Sales	**5,550.0**	**5,063.0**	**6,711.0**	**32.5**	P/E Ratio	**84.5**	Price (9/30/95)	**60.88**
Net Income	**121.0**	**96.0**	**35.0**	**-63.5**	P/B Ratio	**2.3**	52 Wk Hi-Low	**62.50-40.25**
Book Value	**1,254.0**	**1,322.0**	**1,290.0**	**-2.4**	Yield %	**2.6**	Market Cap	**US$3,005.6mil**

Address **1840 Century Park E.**
Los Angeles, CA 90067
Tel **310-553-6262**
Fax **310-201-3023**
Exchange **NYSE**
Ticker **NOC**
President & CEO **Kent Kresa**
Chairman **Kent Kresa**

Norwest

Industry: **Banks - Central U.S.**

Norwest, a bank holding company, operates banks and financial-services and insurance subsidiaries through 2,788 offices in all 50 states, Canada, Central and South America, and Hong Kong. The company manages 258 branches in the Midwest and western United States, and banking-related divisions involved in mortgage banking, consumer and agricultural finance, leasing, and venture-capital investing. Norwest also provides investment-banking and securities-brokerage services. Its insurance subsidiaries offer life, disability, property, and unemployment insurance.

$ mil	12/92	12/93	12/94	% Change				
Revenues	**4,628.1**	**5,276.6**	**6,111.2**	**15.8**	P/E Ratio	**13.4**	Price (9/30/95)	**32.75**
Net Income	**446.7**	**653.6**	**800.4**	**22.5**	P/B Ratio	**2.6**	52 Wk Hi-Low	**32.75-21.13**
Book Value	**3,072.7**	**3,568.4**	**3,846.4**	**7.8**	Yield %	**2.4**	Market Cap	**US$10,653mil**

Address	**Sixth & Marquette**	Tel	**612-667-1234**	Exchange	**NYSE**	President & CEO	**Richard M. Kovacevich**
	Minneapolis, MN 55479	Fax	**612-667-7680**	Ticker	**NOB**	Chairman	**Lloyd P. Johnson**

Novell

Industry: **Software**

Novell develops and services specialized and general-purpose operating-system products and application-programming tools. The company's information-system software products include Novell's NetWare and AppWare families. These products provide matched software components for distributing information resources within local, wide-area and internetworked information systems. Products are sold through U.S. and foreign sales offices. Business outside the U.S. accounts for 43% of the company's total net sales. The company's Fluent subsidiary develops multimedia software.

$ mil	10/92	10/93	10/94	% Change				
Sales	**933.4**	**1,122.9**	**1,998.1**	**77.9**	P/E Ratio	**32.6**	Price (9/30/95)	**18.25**
Net Income	**249.0**	**-35.2**	**206.7**	**-687.3**	P/B Ratio	**4.5**	52 Wk Hi-Low	**22.88-14.31**
Book Value	**937.8**	**996.5**	**1,487.0**	**49.2**	Yield %	**0.0**	Market Cap	**US$6,735.9mil**

Address	**1555 N. Technology Way**	Tel	**801-429-7000**	Exchange	**NASDA**	President & CEO	**Robert J. Frankenberg**
	Orem, UT 84057	Fax	**801-429-5291**	Ticker	**NOVL**	Chairman	**Robert J. Frankenberg**

Nucor

Industry: **Steel**

Nucor manufactures and sells steel products, principally hot-rolled, cold-rolled, and cold-finished steel; steel joists and joist girders; steel deck; and steel grinding balls. The company sells 85% of hot- and cold-rolled steel products to nonaffiliated customers. It sells hot-rolled, cold-rolled, and cold-finished steel to steel service centers, fabricators, and manufacturers. It sells its steel grinding balls primarily to the mining industry. The company sells steel joists and joist girders, and steel deck to general contractors and fabricators throughout the U.S.

$ mil	12/92	12/93	12/94	% Change				
Sales	**1,619.2**	**2,253.7**	**2,975.6**	**32.0**	P/E Ratio	**17.2**	Price (9/30/95)	**44.75**
Net Income	**79.2**	**123.5**	**226.6**	**83.5**	P/B Ratio	**3.5**	52 Wk Hi-Low	**70.63-44.25**
Book Value	**784.2**	**902.2**	**1,122.6**	**24.4**	Yield %	**0.4**	Market Cap	**US$3,912.8mil**

Address	**2100 Rexford Rd.**	Tel	**704-366-7000**	Exchange	**NYSE**	President & COO	**John D. Correnti**
	Charlotte, NC 28211	Fax	**704-362-4208**	Ticker	**NUE**	Chairman & CEO	**F. Kenneth Iverson**

NYNEX

Industry: **Regional Telephone Systems**

NYNEX is a regional Bell company serving New York state and New England. Its subsidiaries, New York Telephone, New England Telephone, and NYNEX Mobile Communications, provide wireline- and wireless-telecommunication services to about 16.5 million customers. While the telephone companies account for about 86% of NYNEX's revenues, the company also offers directory-publishing, database-management, software, and consulting services throughout the U.S. and in 70 other countries. NYNEX and Bell Atlantic have combined their cellular-telephone businesses.

$ mil	12/92	12/93	12/94	% Change				
Sales	**13,155.0**	**13,407.8**	**13,306.6**	**-0.8**	P/E Ratio	**25.3**	Price (9/30/95)	**47.75**
Net Income	**1,311.2**	**-394.1**	**792.6**	**-301.1**	P/B Ratio	**2.4**	52 Wk Hi-Low	**48.63-36.13**
Book Value	**9,723.7**	**8,415.5**	**8,581.4**	**2.0**	Yield %	**4.9**	Market Cap	**US$20,404mil**

Address	**1095 Ave. of the Americas**	Tel	**212-395-2121**	Exchange	**NYSE**	President & CEO	**Ivan G. Seidenberg**
	New York, NY 10036	Fax	**212-921-2684**	Ticker	**NYN**	Chairman	**William C. Ferguson**

Oakwood Homes

Industry: **Home Construction**

Oakwood Homes produces manufactured housing and provides related services. The company operates 10 manufacturing plants, where it produces two- to four-bedroom homes at an average price of approximately $41,000. It sells its homes under the names Oakwood Mobile Homes, Freedom Homes, Victory Homes, and Golden Homes, primarily in the southeastern U.S. Oakwood Acceptance, a subsidiary, provides mortgage financing for the majority of the homes the company sells. Oakwood Homes also develops real estate for use in developing manufactured-housing communities.

$ mil	09/92	09/93	09/94	% Change				
Sales	**184.6**	**260.9**	**506.2**	**94.0**	P/E Ratio	**22.9**	Price (9/30/95)	**35.25**
Net Income	**14.0**	**24.5**	**33.9**	**38.4**	P/B Ratio	**2.7**	52 Wk Hi-Low	**36.38-20.75**
Book Value	**104.4**	**228.9**	**270.9**	**18.4**	Yield %	**0.2**	Market Cap	**US$780.6mil**

Address	**2225 S. Holden Rd.**	Tel	**910-855-2400**	Exchange	**NYSE**	President & CEO	**Nicholas J. St. George**
	Greensboro, NC 27417	Fax	**910-855-2504**	Ticker	**OH**	Chairman	**Ralph L. Darling**

Occidental Petroleum

Industry: **Oil - Secondary**

Occidental Petroleum is a petroleum and chemical company. It owns an average 57% interest in about 14,000 wells and holds net reserves of approximately 918 million barrels of oil and 2.3 trillion cubic feet of natural gas in North America, Latin America, the Middle East, and Russia. MidCon, a subsidiary, markets natural gas to utility, industrial, and municipal customers, and also operates 15,000 miles of gas pipeline in 12 states. Occidental Chemical, another subsidiary, manufactures basic manufacturing feedstocks that include chemicals, petrochemicals, and plastics.

$ mil	12/92	12/93	12/94	% Change				
Sales	**8,494.0**	**8,116.0**	**9,236.0**	**13.8**	P/E Ratio	**NMF**	Price (9/30/95)	**22.00**
Net Income	**-591.0**	**283.0**	**-36.0**	**-112.7**	P/B Ratio	**1.6**	52 Wk Hi-Low	**24.13-18.25**
Book Value	**3,440.0**	**3,958.0**	**4,457.0**	**12.6**	Yield %	**4.5**	Market Cap	**US$7,000.1mil**

Address	**10889 Wilshire Blvd.**	Tel	**310-208-8800**	Exchange	**NYSE**	President & CEO	**Dr. Ray R. Irani**
	Los Angeles, CA 90024	Fax	**310-443-6690**	Ticker	**OXY**	Chairman	**Dr. Ray R. Irani**

Office Depot

Industry: **Other Specialty Retailers**

Office Depot operates a chain of office supply warehouse stores in North America, with more than 400 stores and five delivery centers in the United States and western Canada. The stores carry a variety of brand-name merchandise, including paper products, computer hardware and software, and office furniture sold at discounts ranging from 30-60% off list prices. Its stores also offer businesses a private label credit card with revolving credit and other services, such as printing, copying, and faxing. The company's L.E. Muran and Yorkship Press subsidiaries print stationery.

$ mil	12/92	12/93	12/94	% Change				
Revenues	**1,733.0**	**2,579.5**	**4,266.2**	**65.4**	P/E Ratio	**43.7**	Price (9/30/95)	**30.13**
Net Income	**39.2**	**63.4**	**105.0**	**65.5**	P/B Ratio	**6.3**	52 Wk Hi-Low	**32.00-21.75**
Book Value	**382.5**	**554.7**	**715.3**	**28.9**	Yield %	**0.0**	Market Cap	**US$4,528.0mil**

Address	**2200 Old Germantown Rd.**	Tel	**407-278-4800**	Exchange	**NYSE**	President	**Mark D. Begelman**
	Delray Beach, FL 33445	Fax	**N/A**	Ticker	**ODP**	Chairman & CEO	**David I. Fuente**

Ogden

Industry: **Pollution Control, Waste Management**

Ogden provides aviation, entertainment, environmental, technical, and facility-management services. Ogden Projects, a subsidiary, provides waste-disposal services throughout the United States. The company's aviation-services division provides ground services, catering, and fueling of aircraft at domestic and foreign airports. The entertainment-services division provides facility management, concert promotion, and food and other concessions at arenas and other venues. Environmental and energy services provide independent power generation.

$ mil	12/92	12/93	12/94	% Change				
Sales	**1,768.8**	**2,039.3**	**2,110.2**	**3.5**	P/E Ratio	**15.5**	Price (9/30/95)	**23.50**
Net Income	**55.6**	**56.8**	**66.3**	**16.7**	P/B Ratio	**1.9**	52 Wk Hi-Low	**23.88-18.13**
Book Value	**481.1**	**486.3**	**596.8**	**22.7**	Yield %	**5.3**	Market Cap	**US$1,148.2mil**

Address	**2 Pennsylvania Plz.**	Tel	**212-868-6100**	Exchange	**NYSE**	President & CEO	**R. Richard Ablon**
	New York, NY 10121	Fax	**212-868-4578**	Ticker	**OG**	Chairman	**Ralph E. Ablon**

Ohio Casualty

Industry: **Insurance - Property & Casualty**

Ohio Casualty, through its subsidiaries, provides property and casualty insurance, life insurance, and insurance-premium finance products and services. Its property and casualty insurance product line includes auto-liability, workers' compensation, homeowner's, and commercial multiple-peril insurance policies. Ohio Casualty offers annuities and universal-life products and manages an investment portfolio. Property and casualty insurance accounts for more than 96% of its revenues. Approximately 5,200 independent insurance agencies in 38 states sell the products.

$ mil	12/92	12/93	12/94	% Change				
Revenues	**1,812.1**	**1,669.8**	**1,558.7**	**-6.7**	P/E Ratio	**13.3**	Price (9/30/95)	**35.75**
Net Income	**98.5**	**87.0**	**96.9**	**11.4**	P/B Ratio	**1.5**	52 Wk Hi-Low	**35.75-27.63**
Book Value	**825.2**	**862.3**	**850.8**	**-1.3**	Yield %	**4.1**	Market Cap	**US$1,277.7mil**

Address	**136 N. Third St.**	Tel	**513-867-3000**	Exchange	**NASDA**	President & CEO	**Lauren N. Patch**
	Hamilton, OH 45025	Fax	**513-867-3964**	Ticker	**OCAS**	Chairman	**Joseph L. Marcum**

Ohio Edison

Industry: **Electrical Utilities - Central U.S.**

Ohio Edison provides electrical power to consumers. The electric utility operates in a 7,500-square-mile area of Ohio with a population of about 2.5 million. Pennsylvania Power, a subsidiary, provides electric service in a 1,500-square-mile area of Pennsylvania. Ohio Edison serves more than one million customers. Residential customers account for more than 37% of electric-power sales revenues and commercial clients generate 27%. Approximately 75% of Ohio Edison's electric capacity comes from coal-fired plants; the remainder comes primarily from nuclear facilities.

$ mil	12/92	12/93	12/94	% Change				
Sales	**2,332.4**	**2,369.9**	**2,368.2**	**-0.1**	P/E Ratio	**11.5**	Price (9/30/95)	**22.75**
Net Income	**277.0**	**82.7**	**303.5**	**267.0**	P/B Ratio	**1.3**	52 Wk Hi-Low	**22.75-18.13**
Book Value	**2,750.0**	**2,545.6**	**2,619.5**	**2.9**	Yield %	**6.6**	Market Cap	**US$3,470.9mil**

Address	**76 S. Main St.**	Tel	**216-384-5100**	Exchange	**NYSE**	President & CEO	**Willard R. Holland**
	Akron, OH 44308	Fax	**216-384-5791**	Ticker	**OEC**	Chairman	**Willard R. Holland**

Oklahoma Gas & Electric

Industry: **Electrical Utilities - Central U.S.**

Oklahoma Gas & Electric (OG&E) is a public utility that provides electricity and natural gas. The company furnishes electric service to 670,000 customers in Oklahoma and Arkansas. Residential users account for approximately 38% of electricity revenues; commercial and industrial customers about 45%. Approximately 70% of OG&E's electricity is generated by coal-fired plants; the balance is from natural gas. Enogex, a subsidiary, gathers and transports natural gas to public utilities, other suppliers, and end users through a 3,000-mile natural-gas pipeline in Oklahoma.

$ mil	12/92	12/93	12/94	% Change				
Sales	1,315.0	1,447.3	1,355.2	-6.4	P/E Ratio	12.5	Price (9/30/95)	37.63
Net Income	99.7	114.3	123.8	8.3	P/B Ratio	1.6	52 Wk Hi-Low	37.63-32.13
Book Value	951.5	956.8	971.2	1.5	Yield %	7.1	Market Cap	US$1,518.3mil

Address **101 N. Robinson**
Oklahoma City, OK 73101
Tel **405-553-3000**
Fax **405-553-3760**
Exchange **NYSE**
Ticker **OGE**
President & CEO **James G. Harlow, Jr.**
Chairman **James G. Harlow, Jr.**

Omnicom

Industry: **Advertising**

Omnicom operates advertising agencies through its wholly- and partially-owned subsidiaries. These agencies produce and place advertising in various media, including television, radio, newspapers, and magazines. The company operates three independent agency networks: The BBDO Worldwide Network, the DDB Needham Worldwide Network, and the TBWA International Network. The agency also operates independent agencies, Altschiller Reitzfeld; and Goodby, Berlin and Silverstein; and marketing-service and specialty-advertising companies through Diversified Agency Services.

$ mil	12/92	12/93	12/94	% Change				
Sales	1,385.2	1,516.5	1,756.2	15.8	P/E Ratio	27.8	Price (9/30/95)	65.13
Net Income	69.3	85.3	80.1	-6.1	P/B Ratio	4.4	52 Wk Hi-Low	66.00-49.25
Book Value	308.9	402.2	540.7	34.4	Yield %	1.9	Market Cap	US$2,364.4mil

Address **437 Madison Ave.**
New York, NY 10022
Tel **212-415-3600**
Fax **212-415-3530**
Exchange **NYSE**
Ticker **OMC**
President & CEO **Bruce Crawford**
Chairman **Bruce Crawford**

Oneok

Industry: **Gas Utilities**

Oneok engages in the exploration, purchase, and sale of petroleum energy. The company gathers, stores, transports, and sells oil and natural gas and leases pipeline capacity to other utility companies for natural-gas distribution. The company owns interests in approximately 372 natural-gas wells, 140 oil wells, and 16 gas-processing plants in Oklahoma and Texas. Oneok's Oklahoma Natural Gas subsidiary also provides natural gas to residential, governmental, and industrial customers in 17 communities throughout Oklahoma.

$ mil	08/92	08/93	08/94	% Change				
Sales	677.1	789.1	792.4	0.4	P/E Ratio	17.4	Price (9/30/95)	23.25
Net Income	32.6	38.4	36.2	-5.7	P/B Ratio	1.6	52 Wk Hi-Low	23.88-16.88
Book Value	362.6	372.1	379.5	2.0	Yield %	4.8	Market Cap	US$628.2mil

Address **100 W. Fifth St.**
Tulsa, OK 74102
Tel **918-588-7000**
Fax **918-588-7273**
Exchange **NYSE**
Ticker **OKE**
President & CEO **Larry W. Brummett**
Chairman **Larry W. Brummett**

Oracle

Industry: **Software**

Oracle designs, develops, and supports computer-software products. This software is used for database-management and network products, applications-development productivity tools, and end-user applications. The company's principal product, the ORACLE relational-database-management system, runs on supercomputers, mainframes, minicomputers, microcomputers, and personal computers. The company also offers consulting, support, and systems-integration services for its customers. International customers provide 60% of revenues.

$ mil	05/93	05/94	05/95	% Change				
Sales	1,502.8	2,001.1	2,966.9	48.3	P/E Ratio	38.4	Price (9/30/95)	38.38
Net Income	98.3	283.7	441.5	55.6	P/B Ratio	13.7	52 Wk Hi-Low	46.00-25.33
Book Value	528.0	740.6	1,211.4	63.6	Yield %	0.0	Market Cap	US$16,634mil

Address **500 Oracle Pkwy.**
Redwood City, CA 94065
Tel **415-506-7000**
Fax **415-506-7200**
Exchange **NASDA**
Ticker **ORCL**
President & CEO **Lawrence J. Ellison**
Chairman **Lawrence J. Ellison**

Oryx Energy

Industry: **Oil - Secondary**

Oryx Energy operates oil and natural-gas wells, primarily in the U.S. and the U.K. The company owns an average 50% interest in about 5,400 petroleum wells and holds net reserves of roughly 470 million barrels of oil and 1.5 trillion cubic feet of natural gas. The majority of its operations are in the U.S. and are carried out through 98%-owned Sun Energy Partners of which the company is the managing general partner. Oryx Energy explores for additional reserves on about 14 million acres of undeveloped property in the U.S., Indonesia, the North Sea, Gabon, and Ecuador.

$ mil	12/92	12/93	12/94	% Change				
Sales	1,275.0	1,080.0	1,082.0	0.2	P/E Ratio	NMF	Price (9/30/95)	13.00
Net Income	14.0	-100.0	-1,025.0	925.0	P/B Ratio	NMF	52 Wk Hi-Low	14.63-9.88
Book Value	817.0	676.0	-347.0	-151.3	Yield %	0.0	Market Cap	US$1,343.7mil

Address **13155 Noel Rd.**
Dallas, TX 75240
Tel **214-715-4000**
Fax **214-715-3798**
Exchange **NYSE**
Ticker **ORX**
President & CEO **Robert L. Keiser**
Chairman **Robert L. Keiser**

Outboard Marine

Industry: **Other Recreational Products & Services**

Outboard Marine manufactures boats, recreational marine engines, accessories, and related services. The company sells its Chris-Craft, Stratos, Four Winns, and other powerboats and Johnson and Evinrude outboard motors, parts, and accessories to dealers and wholesale distributors in the United State and internationally. It sells its OMC Cobra and OMC King Cobra stern-drive engines and OMC turbojet-drive systems to boat builders worldwide. The company operates manufacturing facilities in the U.S. and nine other countries.

$ mil	09/92	09/93	09/94	% Change				
Sales	**1,064.6**	**1,034.6**	**1,078.4**	**4.2**	P/E Ratio	**8.9**	Price (9/30/95)	**21.50**
Net Income	**1.9**	**-282.5**	**48.5**	**-117.2**	P/B Ratio	**2.1**	52 Wk Hi-Low	**24.50-17.63**
Book Value	**454.5**	**160.9**	**209.0**	**29.9**	Yield %	**1.9**	Market Cap	**US$430.3mil**

Address **100 Sea-Horse Dr.**
Waukegan, IL 60085
Tel **708-689-6200**
Fax **708-689-5555**
Exchange **NYSE**
Ticker **OM**
President & CEO **James C. Chapman**
Chairman **James C. Chapman**

Overseas Shipholding

Industry: **Marine Transportation**

Overseas Shipholding is an international bulk-shipping company. It provides shipping service through a fleet of 61 vessels. The company charters its ships to commercial shippers and U.S. and foreign governmental agencies for the transport of petroleum products, iron ore, coal, and grain. Transport of petroleum and its derivatives accounts for about 78% of voyage revenues, while dry cargo makes up the balance. The company also has a 49% ownership interest in Celebrity Cruise Lines. Shipping activities outside the U.S. account for approximately 60% of revenues.

$ mil	12/92	12/93	12/94	% Change				
Sales	**370.9**	**389.4**	**364.1**	**-6.5**	P/E Ratio	**NMF**	Price (9/30/95)	**19.88**
Net Income	**16.1**	**17.9**	**-6.2**	**-134.6**	P/B Ratio	**0.9**	52 Wk Hi-Low	**24.38-18.63**
Book Value	**762.4**	**768.4**	**809.8**	**5.4**	Yield %	**3.0**	Market Cap	**US$720.0mil**

Address **1114 Ave. of the Americas**
New York, NY 10036
Tel **212-869-1222**
Fax **212-536-3776**
Exchange **NYSE**
Ticker **OSG**
President **Morton P. Hyman**
Chairman **Morton P. Hyman**

Owens-Corning Fiberglas

Industry: **Building Materials**

Owens-Corning Fiberglas develops glass filaments. The company's products are used in the construction, transportation, marine, aerospace, energy, appliance, packaging, and electronics industries. Construction products are sold for insulation, roofing materials, windows, and patio doors. Its products are also used for underground petroleum storage. The industrial-materials division makes fiberglass reinforcements, polyester resins and other products. The company has roughly 80 trademarks registered in the U.S. and about 290 trademarks registered in other countries.

$ mil	12/92	12/93	12/94	% Change				
Sales	**2,878.0**	**2,944.0**	**3,351.0**	**13.8**	P/E Ratio	**12.4**	Price (9/30/95)	**44.63**
Net Income	**73.0**	**131.0**	**159.0**	**21.4**	P/B Ratio	**NMF**	52 Wk Hi-Low	**46.25-27.88**
Book Value	**-1,008.0**	**-869.0**	**-680.0**	**-21.7**	Yield %	**0.0**	Market Cap	**US$2,263.9mil**

Address **Fiberglas Tower**
Toledo, OH 43659
Tel **419-248-8000**
Fax **419-248-5337**
Exchange **NYSE**
Ticker **OCF**
Chief Executive **Glen H. Hiner**
Chairman **Glen H. Hiner**

Owens-Illinois

Industry: **Containers & Packaging**

Owens-Illinois manufactures packaging products, including glass containers, glass bottles, plastic containers, plastic closures, prescription containers, labels, and multipack plastic carriers for beverage containers (primarily six-pack carriers). Through Kimble, a 49%-owned subsidiary, it also produces scientific and laboratory ware. The company markets these products under the Plasti-Shield and Micro-Serve trademarks to brewers, soft-drink bottlers, and food producers in the United States and abroad. Sales outside the U.S. account for approximately 19% of the total.

$ mil	12/92	12/93	12/94	% Change				
Sales	**3,672.1**	**3,535.0**	**3,567.3**	**0.9**	P/E Ratio	**19.7**	Price (9/30/95)	**12.63**
Net Income	**-134.2**	**4.9**	**78.3**	**NMF**	P/B Ratio	**4.0**	52 Wk Hi-Low	**14.13-10.38**
Book Value	**298.6**	**294.8**	**375.9**	**27.5**	Yield %	**0.0**	Market Cap	**US$1,503.4mil**

Address **One Seagate**
Toledo, OH 43666
Tel **419-247-5000**
Fax **419-247-1132**
Exchange **NYSE**
Ticker **OI**
Chief Executive **Joseph H. Lemieux**
Chairman **Joseph H. Lemieux**

Paccar

Industry: **Land Transportation**

Paccar manufactures heavy-duty on- and off-road trucks, industrial machinery, and automotive parts. Its Peterbilt, Kenworth, and Foden trucks hold about 22% of the Class 8 diesel-truck market in the United States. The company also markets Volkswagen trucks in Brazil, produces oil-field extraction pumps, and sells automotive components through its chain of Al's Auto Supply and Grand Auto retail stores. Paccar also provides financing and leasing services to dealers and customers. The company operates manufacturing facilities in North America, Australia, and the U.K.

$ mil	12/92	12/93	12/94	% Change				
Sales	**2,576.8**	**3,378.9**	**4,285.1**	**26.8**	P/E Ratio	**8.9**	Price (9/30/95)	**46.75**
Net Income	**65.2**	**142.2**	**204.5**	**43.8**	P/B Ratio	**1.5**	52 Wk Hi-Low	**54.00-40.00**
Book Value	**1,038.4**	**1,107.5**	**1,174.5**	**6.0**	Yield %	**6.4**	Market Cap	**US$1,816.7mil**

Address **777 106th Ave. N.E.**
Bellevue, WA 98004
Tel **206-455-7400**
Fax **206-453-4900**
Exchange **NASDA**
Ticker **PCAR**
President **David J. Hovind**
Chairman & CEO **Charles M. Pigott**

Pacific Enterprises

Industry: **Gas Utilities**

Pacific Enterprises is a natural-gas utility holding company. Southern California Gas Company (SoCal Gas), the company's principal operating subsidiary, is the country's largest distributor of natural gas, based on service area, and serves 4.7 million customers. Residential customers account for approximately 60% of natural-gas revenues; commercial and industrial customers make up another 30%. The remainder comes from wholesale sales, exchanges, and utility electricity generation. Pacific Enterprises also owns Pacific Interstate, which operates natural-gas pipelines.

$ mil	12/92	12/93	12/94	% Change				
Sales	**2,900.0**	**2,899.0**	**2,664.0**	**-8.1**	P/E Ratio	**12.9**	Price (9/30/95)	**25.13**
Net Income	**-550.0**	**181.0**	**172.0**	**-5.0**	P/B Ratio	**1.4**	52 Wk Hi-Low	**26.00-20.00**
Book Value	**969.0**	**1,284.0**	**1,428.0**	**11.2**	Yield %	**5.0**	Market Cap	**US$2,124.8mil**

Address **555 W. Fifth St.**
Los Angeles, CA 90013
Tel **213-895-5000**
Fax **213-629-1225**
Exchange **NYSE**
Ticker **PET**
President & COO **Richard D. Farman**
Chairman & CEO **Willis B. Wood, Jr.**

Pacific Gas & Electric

Industry: **Electrical Utilities - Western U.S.**

Pacific Gas and Electric (PG&E) is an electric-power and natural-gas utility. It serves about 13 million customers in California. The distribution of natural gas contributes about 30% of revenues. Residential customers account for about 38% of electric revenues and 42% of natural-gas revenues; commercial and industrial users make up about 52% and 30% of these figures, respectively. It generates roughly 19% of its electricity with fossil fuels, 17% with nuclear energy, 6% with geothermal energy, and 14% from hydroelectric stations; the balance is from third parties.

$ mil	12/92	12/93	12/94	% Change				
Sales	**10,296.1**	**10,582.4**	**10,447.4**	**-1.3**	P/E Ratio	**13.5**	Price (9/30/95)	**29.88**
Net Income	**1,170.6**	**1,065.5**	**1,007.5**	**-5.4**	P/B Ratio	**1.4**	52 Wk Hi-Low	**29.88-21.75**
Book Value	**9,220.8**	**9,329.0**	**9,505.5**	**1.9**	Yield %	**6.6**	Market Cap	**US$12,679mil**

Address **77 Beale St.**
San Francisco, CA 94177
Tel **415-973-7000**
Fax **415-973-9269**
Exchange **NYSE**
Ticker **PCG**
President & CEO **Stanley T. Skinner**
Chairman **Richard A. Clarke**

Pacific Telesis

Industry: **Regional Telephone Systems**

Pacific Telesis Group, a regional Bell holding company, provides telcommunication and information services. Its Pacific Bell and Nevada Bell subsidiaries deliver telephone service to more than 20 million customers in California and Nevada, which account for more than 90% of revenues. The company also publishes business and residential telephone directories. Other products offered by the company include voice mail, electronic messaging, and other services. It markets these products and services to residential, governmental, and commercial users in its service regions.

$ mil	12/92	12/93	12/94	% Change				
Sales	**9,935.0**	**9,244.0**	**9,235.0**	**-0.1**	P/E Ratio	**11.3**	Price (9/30/95)	**30.75**
Net Income	**1,142.0**	**-1,504.0**	**1,159.0**	**-177.1**	P/B Ratio	**2.5**	52 Wk Hi-Low	**31.75-26.00**
Book Value	**8,251.0**	**7,786.0**	**5,233.0**	**-32.8**	Yield %	**7.1**	Market Cap	**US$13,173mil**

Address **130 Kearny St.**
San Francisco, CA 94108
Tel **415-394-3000**
Fax **415-362-2913**
Exchange **NYSE**
Ticker **PAC**
President & CEO **Philip J. Quigley**
Chairman **Philip J. Quigley**

Pacificorp

Industry: **Electrical Utilities - Western U.S.**

Pacificorp is an electric-utility holding company. The utilities, Pacific Power and Utah Power, provide electric service to approximately 1.3 million retail and wholesale customers in seven western states. Residential customers account for about 28% of energy revenues; commercial and industrial users about 50%. Pacificorp also holds an 87% interest in Pacific Telecom, a telephone company that provides local telephone service in Washington, Montana, Iowa, Wisconsin, Idaho, Colorado, Wyoming, Oregon, and Alaska. Its telecommunication business provides 20% of revenues.

$ mil	12/92	12/93	12/94	% Change				
Sales	**3,242.0**	**3,412.4**	**3,506.5**	**2.8**	P/E Ratio	**12.6**	Price (9/30/95)	**19.00**
Net Income	**-340.4**	**479.1**	**468.0**	**-2.3**	P/B Ratio	**1.3**	52 Wk Hi-Low	**19.75-16.63**
Book Value	**3,544.6**	**3,849.0**	**4,046.2**	**5.1**	Yield %	**5.7**	Market Cap	**US$5,401.3mil**

Address **700 N.E. Multnomah St.**
Portland, OR 97232
Tel **503-731-2000**
Fax **503-731-2136**
Exchange **NYSE**
Ticker **PPW**
President & CEO **Frederick W. Buckman**
Chairman **Keith McKennon**

PaineWebber

Industry: **Securities Brokers**

PaineWebber is a full-service independent securities firm that operates 338 offices worldwide. The company brokers the purchase and sale of securities, including stocks, bonds, mutual funds, annuities, and other insurance-related products, and commodities. It also offers investment-banking, advisory, and asset-management services to individuals, corporations, institutions, and municipalities. Its Mitchell Hutchins Asset Management subsidiary oversees the company's investment products and services, including mutual funds and stock-portfolio management.

$ mil	12/92	12/93	12/94	% Change				
Sales	**3,363.7**	**4,004.7**	**3,964.1**	**-1.0**	P/E Ratio	**48.2**	Price (9/30/95)	**19.75**
Net Income	**213.2**	**246.2**	**31.6**	**-87.2**	P/B Ratio	**1.1**	52 Wk Hi-Low	**20.75-13.00**
Book Value	**1,080.7**	**1,195.0**	**1,816.5**	**52.0**	Yield %	**2.4**	Market Cap	**US$1,955.1mil**

Address **1285 Ave. of the Americas**
New York, NY 10019
Tel **212-713-2000**
Fax **212-713-4924**
Exchange **NYSE**
Ticker **PWJ**
President **Paul B. Guenther**
Chairman & CEO **Donald B. Marron**

Pall

Industry: **Industrial Technology**

Pall manufactures filters and microfiltration systems. The company's proprietary filter media and other fluid-clarification equipment are used to remove solid, liquid, and gaseous contaminants from liquids and gases in health-care, aerospace, and fluid-processing applications. It markets its products to commercial and industrial customers worldwide. Pall's health-care products account for 50% of total sales; its aerospace products contribute 26%, and sales to fluid-processing markets contribute 24%. Sales outside the Western Hemisphere account for 57% of total sales.

$ mil	07/92	07/93	07/94	% Change				
Sales	**685.1**	**687.2**	**700.8**	**2.0**	P/E Ratio	**27.1**	Price (9/30/95)	**23.25**
Net Income	**92.7**	**78.3**	**98.9**	**26.3**	P/B Ratio	**4.6**	52 Wk Hi-Low	**24.00-16.88**
Book Value	**545.6**	**542.9**	**587.2**	**8.2**	Yield %	**1.5**	Market Cap	**US$2,659.6mil**

Address **2200 Northern Blvd.**
East Hills, NY 11548
Tel **516-484-5400**
Fax **516-484-3529**
Exchange **NYSE**
Ticker **PLL**
President **Jeremy Hayward-Surry**
Chairman & CEO **Eric Krasnoff**

Panhandle Eastern

Industry: **Pipelines**

Panhandle Eastern transports natural gas and provides related services. The company's principal subsidiary pipeline companies--Texas Eastern Transmission, Algonquin Gas Transmission, Panhandle Eastern Pipe Line, and Trunkline Gas--operate pipeline connecting most major natural-gas-producing regions in North America to markets in the midwestern and eastern U.S. The company merged with Associated Natural Gas in 1994. The transportation of natural gas accounts for about 50% of revenues; sales make up 40%. The company also imports liquefied natural gas.

$ mil	12/92	12/93	12/94	% Change				
Sales	**2,430.5**	**2,120.9**	**4,585.1**	**116.2**	P/E Ratio	**18.0**	Price (9/30/95)	**27.25**
Net Income	**188.6**	**148.1**	**225.2**	**52.1**	P/B Ratio	**2.0**	52 Wk Hi-Low	**27.25-19.00**
Book Value	**1,438.6**	**1,665.6**	**2,035.2**	**22.2**	Yield %	**3.1**	Market Cap	**US$4,080.4mil**

Address **5400 Westheimer Ct.**
Houston, TX 77251
Tel **713-627-5400**
Fax **713-627-4145**
Exchange **NYSE**
Ticker **PEL**
President **Paul M. Anderson**
Chairman & CEO **Dennis Hendrix**

Parametric Technology

Industry: **Software**

Parametric Technology develops and supports a family of fully integrated software products that automate the mechanical-design-through-manufacturing process. Mechanical design uses a number of engineering procedures to develop virtually all manufactured products, ranging from basic consumer products to jet-propelled aircraft. The company's Pro/ENGINEER mechanical-design-automation system enables end users to reduce time-to-market and manufacturing costs for their products. Sales and support offices are located across the United States, Europe, and Pacific Rim.

$ mil	09/92	09/93	09/94	% Change				
Sales	**86.7**	**163.1**	**244.3**	**49.8**	P/E Ratio	**53.9**	Price (9/30/95)	**61.50**
Net Income	**21.1**	**43.0**	**66.9**	**55.6**	P/B Ratio	**14.5**	52 Wk Hi-Low	**63.25-31.50**
Book Value	**78.7**	**146.8**	**242.1**	**64.9**	Yield %	**0.0**	Market Cap	**US$3,788.0mil**

Address **128 Technology Dr.**
Waltham, MA 02154
Tel **617-398-5000**
Fax **617-398-6000**
Exchange **NASDA**
Ticker **PMTC**
President & COO **C. Richard Harrison**
Chairman & CEO **Steven C. Walske**

Parker Drilling

Industry: **Oil Drilling**

Parker Drilling provides land-drilling contractor services, specializing in difficult drilling conditions. It provides drilling-engineering and project-management services to oil companies, industrial and government users, and independent natural-gas producers who develop their own oil and natural-gas sources in the United States and abroad. Its Parker Technology and Parker Kinetic Designs subsidiaries design and manufacture drilling rigs and components and market new technologies for industrial and military purposes. Sales outside the U.S. account for 80% of revenues.

$ mil	08/92	08/93	08/94	% Change				
Sales	**123.3**	**100.8**	**152.4**	**51.2**	P/E Ratio	**NMF**	Price (9/30/95)	**6.00**
Net Income	**-11.2**	**-10.7**	**-28.8**	**169.3**	P/B Ratio	**1.8**	52 Wk Hi-Low	**6.38-4.50**
Book Value	**210.2**	**207.7**	**180.6**	**-13.1**	Yield %	**0.0**	Market Cap	**US$334.2mil**

Address **Parker Bldg., 8 E. Third St.**
Tulsa, OK 74103
Tel **918-585-8221**
Fax **918-585-1058**
Exchange **NYSE**
Ticker **PKD**
President & CEO **Robert L. Parker, Jr.**
Chairman **Robert L. Parker**

Parker Hannifin

Industry: **Industrial - Diversified**

Parker Hannifin manufactures fluid-power-system components and replacement parts for the industrial and aerospace markets. The company sells its motion-control products, including fluid-power systems and electromechanical controls, to the agricultural-, construction-, and food-processing-equipment industries. Its aerospace product line includes hydraulic, pneumatic, and fuel systems. The company manages plants throughout the United States and Puerto Rico, and in foreign countries such as Argentina, the Czech Republic, Hong Kong, Mexico, New Zealand, and South Korea.

$ mil	06/93	06/94	06/95	% Change				
Sales	**2,489.3**	**2,576.3**	**3,214.4**	**24.8**	P/E Ratio	**12.8**	Price (9/30/95)	**38.00**
Net Income	**65.1**	**47.7**	**218.2**	**357.5**	P/B Ratio	**2.4**	52 Wk Hi-Low	**41.25-25.67**
Book Value	**932.9**	**966.4**	**1,191.5**	**23.3**	Yield %	**1.8**	Market Cap	**US$2,804.2mil**

Address **17325 Euclid Ave.**
Cleveland, OH 44112
Tel **216-531-3000**
Fax **216-383-9414**
Exchange **NYSE**
Ticker **PH**
President & CEO **Duane E. Collins**
Chairman **Patrick S. Parker**

PECO Energy

Industry: **Electrical Utilities - Eastern U.S.**

PECO Energy is an electric and natural-gas utility that provides electricity to more than 3.7 million customers and natural gas to nearly 370,000 customers in Pennsylvania and Maryland. The company generates approximately 60% of its electricity using nuclear energy, 24% using fossil fuels, and 3% at hydroelectric stations. It purchases the balance of its electricity from third parties. Residential customers account for approximately 38% of electric and 58% of natural-gas revenues, respectively; commercial and industrial users make up 51% and 32% of these figures.

$ mil	12/92	12/93	12/94	% Change				
Sales	**3,962.5**	**3,988.1**	**4,040.6**	**1.3**	P/E Ratio	**16.3**	Price (9/30/95)	**28.63**
Net Income	**478.9**	**590.6**	**426.7**	**-27.8**	P/B Ratio	**1.4**	52 Wk Hi-Low	**29.75-23.75**
Book Value	**4,675.8**	**4,872.4**	**4,672.7**	**-4.1**	Yield %	**5.4**	Market Cap	**US$6,352.0mil**

Address **2301 Market St.**
Philadelphia, PA 19101
Tel **215-841-4000**
Fax **215-841-4241**
Exchange **NYSE**
Ticker **PE**
President & COO **Corbin A. McNeill, Jr.**
Chairman & CEO **Joseph F. Paquette, Jr.**

Penn Virginia

Industry: **Coal**

Penn Virginia engages in energy exploration and production, timber operations, and investment management. The company mines for coal primarily in Virginia, West Virginia, and Kentucky, and produces oil and natural gas in five states. Its coal reserves are estimated at approximately 258 million tons, and it has proven petroleum reserves of about 224 billion cubic feet of natural gas and oil (measured in terms of natural-gas energy). It also produces timber and pulpwood and, through its Penn Virginia Equities subsidiary, manages a portfolio of equity investments.

$ mil	12/92	12/93	12/94	% Change				
Sales	**20.3**	**33.3**	**35.5**	**6.5**	P/E Ratio	**10.3**	Price (9/30/95)	**32.50**
Net Income	**-17.1**	**10.3**	**13.5**	**31.1**	P/B Ratio	**1.0**	52 Wk Hi-Low	**35.00-27.75**
Book Value	**87.4**	**137.8**	**137.5**	**-0.3**	Yield %	**6.2**	Market Cap	**US$138.5mil**

Address **The Bellevue, 200 S. Broad St.**
Philadelphia, PA 19102
Tel **215-545-6600**
Fax **215-545-6608**
Exchange **NASDA**
Ticker **PVIR**
Chief Executive **Lennox K. Black**
Chairman **Lennox K. Black**

J.C. Penney

Industry: **Retailers - Broadline**

JCPenney operates a chain of retail stores predominantly selling family apparel, shoes, jewelry, accessories, and home furnishings. The company operates more than 1,750 retail stores; approximately 1,250 JCPenney department stores and 500 drugstores across the United States. In addition, the company operates six catalog distribution centers; four of which are owned, and operates and owns one store distribution center and an insurance-company corporate-office building. Subsidiaries include companies conducting business under the JCPenney name, as well as Thrift Drug.

$ mil	01/93	01/94	01/95	% Change				
Revenues	**18,009.0**	**18,983.0**	**20,380.0**	**7.4**	P/E Ratio	**11.6**	Price (9/30/95)	**49.63**
Net Income	**777.0**	**940.0**	**1,057.0**	**12.4**	P/B Ratio	**2.0**	52 Wk Hi-Low	**52.38-40.63**
Book Value	**4,705.0**	**5,365.0**	**5,615.0**	**4.7**	Yield %	**3.4**	Market Cap	**US$11,204mil**

Address **6501 Legacy Dr.**
Plano, TX 75024
Tel **214-431-1000**
Fax **214-431-1962**
Exchange **NYSE**
Ticker **JCP**
Chief Executive **James E. Oesterreicher**
Chairman **William R. Howell**

Pennzoil

Industry: **Oil - Secondary**

Pennzoil is an integrated petroleum company. The company owns an average 56% interest in about 11,000 wells and holds net reserves of approximately 220 million barrels of oil and 1.5 trillion cubic feet of natural gas, mostly in Texas and Louisiana. Pennzoil also owns three refineries, which produce motor oil, fuels, lubricants, and waxes. The company's Jiffy Lube subsidiary franchises oil-change centers in the United States and internationally. Refined products account for approximately 60% of the company's total revenues.

$ mil	12/92	12/93	12/94	% Change				
Sales	**2,222.7**	**2,477.5**	**2,474.8**	**-0.1**	P/E Ratio	**NMF**	Price (9/30/95)	**43.88**
Net Income	**128.2**	**141.9**	**-288.7**	**-303.4**	P/B Ratio	**1.7**	52 Wk Hi-Low	**52.38-42.88**
Book Value	**1,180.2**	**1,505.8**	**1,204.3**	**-20.0**	Yield %	**6.8**	Market Cap	**US$2,029.7mil**

Address **Pennzoil Pl.**
Houston, TX 77252
Tel **713-546-4000**
Fax **713-546-6169**
Exchange **NYSE**
Ticker **PZL**
President & CEO **James L. Pate**
Chairman **James L. Pate**

Peoples Energy

Industry: **Gas Utilities**

Peoples Energy is a utility holding company. Its subsidiaries produce and distribute natural gas to residential, commercial, and industrial customers. The company provides service to approximately 842,000 customers in Chicago through its operating public utility, Peoples Gas Light and Coke, and more than 129,000 customers in suburban communities north of the city through the North Shore Gas Company. Residential customers account for approximately 74% of the company's operating revenues; commercial and industrial customers generate about 16% of that figure.

$ mil	09/92	09/93	09/94	% Change				
Sales	**1,096.8**	**1,258.9**	**1,279.5**	**1.6**	P/E Ratio	**12.9**	Price (9/30/95)	**27.50**
Net Income	**70.4**	**73.4**	**74.4**	**1.4**	P/B Ratio	**1.5**	52 Wk Hi-Low	**28.38-24.13**
Book Value	**629.1**	**628.5**	**641.4**	**2.0**	Yield %	**6.5**	Market Cap	**US$960.1mil**

Address **122 S. Michigan Ave.**
Chicago, IL 60603
Tel **312-431-4000**
Fax **312-431-4082**
Exchange **NYSE**
Ticker **PGL**
President & COO **J. Bruce Hasch**
Chairman & CEO **Richard E. Terry**

Pep Boys

Industry: **Other Specialty Retailers**

Pep Boys-Manny, Moe & Jack sells about 24,000 automotive parts and accessories The company also services automobiles. It operates 435 stores in 32 states. In addition to branded products, the company sells oil, transmission fluid, chemicals, paints, tires, hoses, and batteries under the Pep Boys name. It sells antifreeze under the name Pure As Gold, starters and alternators are under the True Blue and Pro-Start names, and water pumps under the True Blue and Procool names. Its brakes are sold under the Shur Grip and Prostop names and tires under the names Cornell and Futura.

$ mil	01/93	01/94	01/95	% Change				
Revenues	1,155.6	1,241.1	1,407.0	13.4	P/E Ratio	21.7	Price (9/30/95)	27.13
Net Income	54.6	65.5	75.7	15.6	P/B Ratio	2.8	52 Wk Hi-Low	36.13-24.88
Book Value	509.8	547.8	586.3	7.0	Yield %	0.6	Market Cap	US$1,669.8mil

Address	**3111 W. Allegheny Ave.**	Tel	**215-229-9000**	Exchange	**NYSE**	President & CEO	**Mitchell G. Leibovitz**
	Philadelphia, PA 19132	Fax	**215-227-4067**	Ticker	**PBY**	Chairman	**Mitchell G. Leibovitz**

PepsiCo

Industry: **Soft Drinks**

PepsiCo manufactures soft drinks and snack foods and operates restaurants. The company makes soft drinks, including Pepsi Cola, Diet Pepsi, Mountain Dew, and Slice, which it distributes to independent and company-owned bottlers. PepsiCo's snack-foods business primarily consists of Frito-Lay, which manufactures Fritos, Doritos, and Tostitos corn chips, Lay's and Ruffles potato chips, Cheetos cheese-flavored snacks, and Rold Gold Pretzels. PepsiCo markets its products worldwide. The company's restaurant division owns the Pizza Hut, Taco Bell, and KFC restaurant chains.

$ mil	12/92	12/93	12/94	% Change				
Sales	21,970.0	25,020.7	28,472.4	13.8	P/E Ratio	23.4	Price (9/30/95)	51.00
Net Income	374.3	1,587.9	1,752.0	10.3	P/B Ratio	5.9	52 Wk Hi-Low	51.88-32.25
Book Value	5,355.7	6,338.7	6,856.1	8.2	Yield %	1.4	Market Cap	US$40,163mil

Address	**700 Anderson Hill Rd.**	Tel	**914-253-2000**	Exchange	**NYSE**	Chief Executive	**Wayne Calloway**
	Purchase, NY 10577	Fax	**914-253-2070**	Ticker	**PEP**	Chairman	**Wayne Calloway**

Perkin-Elmer

Industry: **Diversified Technology**

Perkin-Elmer manufactures analytical-instrumentation systems and supplies thermal-spray coatings. Its instrumentation systems are used for chemical analysis and measurement and are used in environmental, pharmaceutical, chemical, and agricultural applications. The company's thermal-spray equipment and supplies are used in aerospace, automotive, and industrial applications. The company markets these products through its own sales force to industrial, education, research, institutional, quality-control, medical, and other users in the United States and internationally.

$ mil	06/93 *	06/94	06/95	% Change				
Sales	1,011.3	1,024.5	1,063.5	3.8	P/E Ratio	22.7	Price (9/30/95)	35.63
Net Income	-56.9	51.1	66.9	30.9	P/B Ratio	4.9	52 Wk Hi-Low	38.00-25.38
Book Value	306.6	290.4	304.7	4.9	Yield %	1.9	Market Cap	US$1,491.3mil

Address	**761 Main Ave.**	Tel	**203-762-1000**	Exchange	**NYSE**	President & CEO	**Gaynor N. Kelley**
	Norwalk, CT 06859	Fax	**203-762-6000**	Ticker	**PKN**	Chairman	**Gaynor N. Kelley**

*Irregular period due to fiscal year change.

Pfizer

Industry: **Pharmaceuticals**

Pfizer is a diversified manufacturer of health-care and food-science products. Its pharmaceutical brand-name lines include Zoloft, an antidepressant; Glucotrol, an antidiabetic agent; and Procardia XL and Cardura, which regulate hypertension. The company manufactures food additives, including caffeine and flavor enhancers; medical equipment such as prosthetic implants, catheters, ultrasonic cutting devices, and monitoring systems; consumer-health-care products, including Visine eye drops and Ben-Gay ointment; and therapeutics for the veterinary-medicine industry.

$ mil	12/92	12/93	12/94	% Change				
Sales	7,230.2	7,477.7	8,281.3	10.7	P/E Ratio	25.5	Price (9/30/95)	53.38
Net Income	810.9	657.5	1,298.4	97.5	P/B Ratio	7.8	52 Wk Hi-Low	53.63-34.00
Book Value	4,718.6	3,865.5	4,323.9	11.9	Yield %	1.8	Market Cap	US$33,851mil

Address	**235 E. 42nd St.**	Tel	**212-573-2323**	Exchange	**NYSE**	Chief Executive	**William C. Steere, Jr.**
	New York, NY 10017	Fax	**212-573-7851**	Ticker	**PFE**	Chairman	**William C. Steere, Jr.**

Phelps Dodge

Industry: **Non-Ferrous Metals - Other (Exc. Aluminum)**

Phelps Dodge mines copper and other metals and manufactures chemicals and metal products. Phelps Dodge Mining, the company's mining and metals division, operates copper mines in Arizona, New Mexico, and Chile that contain about 10.6 million tons of reserves. It supplies copper to the wire and cable industry and mines other minerals, including gold, silver, molybdenum, and lead. Phelps Dodge Industries, its manufacturing division, makes carbon black for the rubber industry, alloys for the consumer-electronics and aerospace industries, and wheels for heavy equipment.

$ mil	12/92	12/93	12/94	% Change				
Sales	2,579.3	2,595.9	3,289.2	26.7	P/E Ratio	16.4	Price (9/30/95)	62.63
Net Income	221.7	187.9	271.0	44.2	P/B Ratio	2.0	52 Wk Hi-Low	70.13-52.00
Book Value	1,972.5	2,022.1	2,187.6	8.2	Yield %	2.7	Market Cap	US$4,355.1mil

Address	**2600 N. Central Ave.**	Tel	**602-234-8100**	Exchange	**NYSE**	President & CEO	**Douglas C. Yearley**
	Phoenix, AZ 85004	Fax	**602-234-8337**	Ticker	**PD**	Chairman	**Douglas C. Yearley**

Philip Morris

Industry: **Tobacco**

Philip Morris manufactures tobacco products, food products, and beer. The company's tobacco division, which holds a 45% United States market share, produces cigarettes under the Marlboro, Merit, and Virginia Slims brand names. Kraft General Foods, a subsidiary, makes food products under the Kraft, General Foods, Jell-O, Nabisco, Oscar Mayer, and Louis Rich trademarks, and produces flavorings and other food ingredients used by food manufacturers. Its Miller Brewing Company subsidiary brews beer sold under the Miller, Lowenbrau, Meister Brau, and Milwaukee's Best brands.

$ mil	12/92	12/93	12/94	% Change				
Sales	59,131.0	60,901.0	65,125.0	6.9	P/E Ratio	15.3	Price (9/30/95)	83.50
Net Income	4,939.0	3,091.0	4,725.0	52.9	P/B Ratio	5.6	52 Wk Hi-Low	83.63-56.25
Book Value	12,563.0	11,627.0	12,786.0	10.0	Yield %	3.6	Market Cap	US$70,141mil

Address	**120 Park Ave.**	Tel	**212-880-5000**	Exchange	**NYSE**	Chief Executive	**Geoffrey C. Bible**
	New York, NY 10017	Fax	**212-878-2165**	Ticker	**MO**	Chairman	**Geoffrey C. Bible**

Phillips Petroleum

Industry: **Oil - Integrated Majors**

Phillips Petroleum is a major integrated petroleum company. It owns, on average, a 33% interest in 24,000 wells worldwide, and holds net reserves of 877 million barrels of oil and 6.4 trillion cubic feet of natural gas. It operates refineries that primarily provide motor fuels to 8,500 Phillips 66 service stations, about 350 of which are company-operated. The company's subsidiaries include GPM Gas, which processes natural gas; Houston Chemical Complex, which produces chemicals and plastics; and Phillips Fibers, which manufactures synthetic cloth and carpet fibers.

$ mil	12/92	12/93	12/94	% Change				
Sales	11,933.0	12,309.0	12,211.0	-0.8	P/E Ratio	17.6	Price (9/30/95)	32.50
Net Income	180.0	243.0	484.0	99.2	P/B Ratio	2.9	52 Wk Hi-Low	37.00-30.13
Book Value	2,698.0	2,688.0	2,953.0	9.9	Yield %	3.4	Market Cap	US$8,520.0mil

Address	**Phillips Bldg., Fourth & Keeler**	Tel	**918-661-6600**	Exchange	**NYSE**	President & COO	**J.J. Mulva**
	Bartlesville, OK 74004	Fax	**918-661-7636**	Ticker	**P**	Chairman & CEO	**W.W. Allen**

Pioneer Hi-Bred

Industry: **Biotechnology**

Pioneer Hi-Bred International is an agricultural genetic-engineering company. Sales of hybrid seed corn and varietal soybeans account for approximately 89% of the company's revenues. The company's other crop products include hybrid strains of sorghum and sunflower, and nonhybrid varieties of soybean, alfalfa, wheat, canola, and vegetables. Pioneer Hi-Bred International also produces engineered strains of microorganisms used in crop production, animal breeding, and soil remediation. The company markets its products in the United States and internationally.

$ mil	08/92	08/93	08/94	% Change				
Sales	1,261.8	1,343.4	1,478.7	10.1	P/E Ratio	19.2	Price (9/30/95)	46.00
Net Income	152.2	120.5	212.7	76.5	P/B Ratio	4.5	52 Wk Hi-Low	47.00-30.63
Book Value	799.5	825.4	881.1	6.7	Yield %	1.3	Market Cap	US$3,867.9mil

Address	**700 Capital Sq., 400 Locust St.**	Tel	**515-248-4800**	Exchange	**NASDA**	President	**Thomas N. Urban**
	Des Moines, IA 50309	Fax	**N/A**	Ticker	**PHYB**	Chairman	**Thomas N. Urban**

Pitney Bowes

Industry: **Office Equipment**

Pitney Bowes provides equipment, supplies, and financial services to business and government organizations. Business equipment consists of mailing systems, copying systems, and voice-processing systems. Supplies and services include items manufactured by the company's Monarch Marketing Systems subsidiary, which are used to encode and track price and other merchandise information. The company also provides lease financing for its products and other financial services through its subsidiaries under its own name, Colonial Pacific Leasing, and Atlantic Mortgage & Investment.

$ mil	12/92	12/93	12/94	% Change				
Sales	3,434.1	3,542.9	3,270.6	-7.7	P/E Ratio	24.1	Price (9/30/95)	42.00
Net Income	100.2	353.2	274.1	-22.4	P/B Ratio	3.6	52 Wk Hi-Low	42.63-30.63
Book Value	1,652.9	1,871.6	1,745.1	-6.8	Yield %	2.5	Market Cap	US$6,363.7mil

Address	**1 Elmcroft Rd.**	Tel	**203-356-5000**	Exchange	**NYSE**	President & CEO	**George B. Harvey**
	Stamford, CT 06926	Fax	**203-351-7644**	Ticker	**PBI**	Chairman	**George B. Harvey**

Pittston Minerals

Industry: **Coal**

Pittston Minerals consists of Pittston Coal Company and Pittston Mineral Ventures Company, both of which are engaged in natural resources. It sells coal for the electricity-generation market to customers throughout North America, and sells metallurgical coal in the United States and internationally. Pittston Mineral Ventures interests are principally in gold mining and exploration in Nevada and Australia. Its partner in gold exploration is Mining Projects Investors. Business operations outside the U.S. account for approximately 45% of the company's total revenues.

$ mil	12/92 R	12/93	12/94	% Change				
Sales	657.9	687.1	795.0	15.7	P/E Ratio	NMF	Price (9/30/95)	10.88
Net Income	21.8	-33.0	-52.9	60.3	P/B Ratio	NMF	52 Wk Hi-Low	26.25-9.75
Book Value	12.3	-24.9	-8.6	-65.5	Yield %	6.0	Market Cap	US$92.3mil

Address	**100 First Stamford Pl.**	Tel	**203-978-5200**	Exchange	**NYSE**	President & CEO	**Joseph C. Farrell**
	Stamford, CT 06912	Fax	**203-978-5315**	Ticker	**PZM**	Chairman	**Joseph C. Farrell**

R=Restated.

Pittston Services

Industry: **Air Freight & Couriers**

Pittston Services conducts business through Burlington Air Express, Brink's, and Brink's Home Security. Burlington provides air-freight and logistics-management services, and has operations in more than 100 countries. It markets its services to large companies in a variety of industries. Brink's is a security-transportation company, and Brink's Home Security is a home-security-services company. Brink's operates a fleet of approximately 1,800 armored trucks for carrying valuable cargo, and Brink's Home Security installs electronic home-security systems throughout the U.S.

$ mil	12/92 R	12/93	12/94	% Change				
Sales	**1,415.2**	**1,569.0**	**1,872.3**	**19.3**	P/E Ratio	**12.9**	Price (9/30/95)	**27.13**
Net Income	**27.3**	**47.1**	**79.9**	**69.5**	P/B Ratio	**2.5**	52 Wk Hi-Low	**29.25-22.63**
Book Value	**329.2**	**378.4**	**456.4**	**20.6**	Yield %	**0.7**	Market Cap	**US$1,127.8mil**

Address **100 First Stamford Pl.**
Stamford, CT 06912
Tel **203-978-5200**
Fax **203-978-5315**
Exchange **NYSE**
Ticker **PZS**
President & CEO **Joseph C. Farrell**
Chairman **Joseph C. Farrell**

R=Restated.

PNC Bank

Industry: **Banks - Eastern U.S.**

PNC Bank is a bank holding company with businesses in investment management and trust, and corporate, retail, and investment banking. The company operates about 604 offices in the eastern and midwestern United States, including banks and subsidiaries that specialize in brokerage, mortgage origination, securities underwriting, credit-card issuance, international banking, and investment management. In addition, PNC Bank manages the PNC family of 29 mutual funds, with assets of more than $5 billion. The company has agreed to acquire Midlantic.

$ mil	12/92	12/93	12/94	% Change				
Revenues	**4,105.7**	**4,146.4**	**4,819.4**	**16.2**	P/E Ratio	**10.8**	Price (9/30/95)	**27.88**
Net Income	**426.9**	**725.9**	**610.1**	**-16.0**	P/B Ratio	**1.5**	52 Wk Hi-Low	**28.63-20.13**
Book Value	**3,745.6**	**4,325.0**	**4,394.0**	**1.6**	Yield %	**4.7**	Market Cap	**US$6,413.0mil**

Address **Fifth Ave. & Wood St.**
Pittsburgh, PA 15265
Tel **412-762-3900**
Fax **412-762-4507**
Exchange **NYSE**
Ticker **PNC**
President **James E. Rohr**
Chairman & CEO **Thomas H. O'Brien**

Polaroid

Industry: **Other Recreational Products & Services**

Polaroid manufactures photographic and other optical products. Its principal products are instant cameras sold under the Captiva, JobPro, and Vision trademarks and instant-camera film. The company also produces other photographic film products, film holders, and medical laser-imaging systems. Polaroid sells these products under the Hybrid IV, Polacolor PRO, and Helios trademarks. It markets all of its products to individuals and industries in the United States and in international markets. Business operations outside the U.S. account for approximately 50% of sales.

$ mil	12/92	12/93	12/94	% Change				
Sales	**2,152.3**	**2,244.9**	**2,312.5**	**3.0**	P/E Ratio	**16.0**	Price (9/30/95)	**39.75**
Net Income	**99.0**	**-51.3**	**117.2**	**-328.5**	P/B Ratio	**2.1**	52 Wk Hi-Low	**44.88-29.00**
Book Value	**808.9**	**767.3**	**864.4**	**12.7**	Yield %	**1.5**	Market Cap	**US$1,796.3mil**

Address **549 Technology Sq.**
Cambridge, MA 02139
Tel **617-386-2000**
Fax **617-386-5618**
Exchange **NYSE**
Ticker **PRD**
President & CEO **I. MacAllister Booth**
Chairman **I. MacAllister Booth**

Policy Management

Industry: **Software**

Policy Management Systems provides software and related support and information services to the insurance industry. Through its nationwide network, the company provides the property- and casualty-insurance industry with information to assist insurers in making decisions on risk-selection, pricing, and claims adjusting. The company offers more than 135 business support systems, which include more than 90 IBM-compatible application-software systems, outsourcing, and information services. While operations are worldwide, 85% of revenues are generated in the United States.

$ mil	12/92	12/93	12/94	% Change				
Sales	**497.1**	**453.1**	**492.7**	**8.7**	P/E Ratio	**NMF**	Price (9/30/95)	**51.25**
Net Income	**59.4**	**-56.1**	**-9.7**	**-82.8**	P/B Ratio	**2.6**	52 Wk Hi-Low	**53.88-37.25**
Book Value	**574.0**	**477.0**	**376.9**	**-21.0**	Yield %	**0.0**	Market Cap	**US$993.1mil**

Address **One PMS Ctr.**
Blythewood, SC 29016
Tel **803-735-4000**
Fax **803-735-6499**
Exchange **NYSE**
Ticker **PMS**
President & CEO **G. Larry Wilson**
Chairman **G. Larry Wilson**

Potlatch

Industry: **Forest Products**

Potlatch manufactures forest products for sale in the U.S., Australia, and Japan. The company operates 23 manufacturing facilities and owns or leases approximately 1.5 million acres of timberland in the U.S. This timberland provides about 60% of the logs it uses in its manufacturing operations. Its primary wood products include dimensional lumber, plywood, oriented strand board, particleboard, and hardwood flooring. Potlatch also produces printing papers; market pulp; paperboard food cartons; and consumer products, including bathroom tissue, paper towels, and napkins.

$ mil	12/92	12/93	12/94	% Change				
Sales	**1,326.6**	**1,368.9**	**1,471.3**	**7.5**	P/E Ratio	**24.3**	Price (9/30/95)	**40.88**
Net Income	**78.9**	**6.6**	**49.0**	**642.4**	P/B Ratio	**1.3**	52 Wk Hi-Low	**44.00-36.00**
Book Value	**955.6**	**919.7**	**920.2**	**0.1**	Yield %	**3.8**	Market Cap	**US$1,194.4mil**

Address **One Maritime Plz.**
San Francisco, CA 94119
Tel **415-576-8800**
Fax **415-576-8840**
Exchange **NYSE**
Ticker **PCH**
President & COO **L. Pendleton Siegel**
Chairman & CEO **John M. Richards**

Potomac Electric

Industry: **Electrical Utilities - Eastern U.S.**

Potomac Electric Power produces electrical power in the eastern United States. The utility provides service to the Washington, DC area and part of Maryland, and sells electricity wholesale to the Southern Maryland Electric Cooperative. The company generates 76% of its power with coal, 16% with oil, 5% with natural gas; and purchases the remainder from other generating companies, including the Ohio Edison System and Panda Energy. Residential customers account for approximately 30% of electricity revenues. The company has agreed to merge with Baltimore Gas & Electric.

$ mil	12/92	12/93	12/94	% Change				
Sales	**1,562.2**	**1,702.4**	**1,790.6**	**5.2**	P/E Ratio	**13.5**	Price (9/30/95)	**24.25**
Net Income	**216.8**	**241.6**	**227.2**	**-6.0**	P/B Ratio	**1.3**	52 Wk Hi-Low	**24.38-18.25**
Book Value	**2,096.9**	**2,227.7**	**2,224.3**	**-0.2**	Yield %	**6.8**	Market Cap	**US$2,873.3mil**

Address	**1900 Pennsylvania Ave. N.W.**	Tel	**202-872-2000**	Exchange	**NYSE**	President & COO	**John M. Derrick, Jr.**
	Washington, DC 20068	Fax	**202-331-6874**	Ticker	**POM**	Chairman & CEO	**Edward F. Mitchell**

PP&L Resources

Industry: **Electrical Utilities - Eastern U.S.**

PP and Light Resources Holding Company is an electric utility serving industrial and residential customers within an area of Pennsylvania that includes Allentown, Harrisburg, Scranton, and Lancaster. It is also a member of the Pennsylvania-New Jersey-Maryland Interconnection Association. About 57% of the energy generated by the company comes from coal-fired stations, 36% from nuclear operations, and the remainder from oil-fired and hydroelectric stations. Sales to residential users account for about 35% of energy revenues; commercial and industrial make up 48%.

$ mil	12/92	12/93	12/94	% Change				
Sales	**2,744.1**	**2,727.0**	**2,725.1**	**-0.1**	P/E Ratio	**16.6**	Price (9/30/95)	**23.38**
Net Income	**346.7**	**348.1**	**244.3**	**-29.8**	P/B Ratio	**1.2**	52 Wk Hi-Low	**23.38-18.00**
Book Value	**2,916.2**	**2,932.2**	**2,920.8**	**-0.4**	Yield %	**7.1**	Market Cap	**US$3,655.7mil**

Address	**2 N. Ninth St.**	Tel	**215-774-5151**	Exchange	**NYSE**	President	**William F. Hecht**
	Allentown, PA 18101	Fax	**215-770-5408**	Ticker	**PPL**	Chairman	**William F. Hecht**

PPG Industries

Industry: **Industrial - Diversified**

PPG Industries produces coatings and resins, glass, and chemicals. The company supplies protective and decorative finishes for autos, appliances, industrial equipment, and containers; factory-finished aluminum extrusions; and coils for architectural uses. Its glass products are used in the automotive, construction, and other industries. Major chlor-alkali products of PPG's chemicals division are chlorine, caustic soda, and vinyl-chloride monomer. Most of the chemicals are sold directly to other manufacturing companies in chemical processing and plastics industries.

$ mil	12/92	12/93	12/94	% Change				
Sales	**5,813.9**	**5,753.9**	**6,331.2**	**10.0**	P/E Ratio	**19.1**	Price (9/30/95)	**46.50**
Net Income	**319.4**	**22.2**	**514.6**	**NMF**	P/B Ratio	**3.8**	52 Wk Hi-Low	**46.88-33.88**
Book Value	**2,698.9**	**2,473.1**	**2,557.0**	**3.4**	Yield %	**2.4**	Market Cap	**US$9,432.2mil**

Address	**One PPG Pl.**	Tel	**412-434-3131**	Exchange	**NYSE**	Chief Executive	**Jerry E. Dempsey**
	Pittsburgh, PA 15272	Fax	**412-434-2448**	Ticker	**PPG**	Chairman	**Jerry E. Dempsey**

Praxair

Industry: **Specialty Chemicals**

Praxair is the largest supplier of industrial gases in North and South America. The gases are used in the metal-fabrication, primary-metals, chemicals, electronics, oil-and-gas, food-processing, and pulp-and-paper industries. The company has also developed non-cryogenic air-separation technologies, including pressure swing adsorption and vacuum pressure swing adsorption. Praxair markets its products in the United States and internationally. Business outside the U.S. accounts for approximately 46% of the company's sales. Praxair operates gas-processing facilities worldwide.

$ mil	12/92	12/93	12/94	% Change				
Sales	**2,604.0**	**2,438.0**	**2,711.0**	**11.2**	P/E Ratio	**18.4**	Price (9/30/95)	**26.75**
Net Income	**-60.0**	**118.0**	**203.0**	**72.0**	P/B Ratio	**4.4**	52 Wk Hi-Low	**28.75-19.13**
Book Value	**544.0**	**635.0**	**839.0**	**32.1**	Yield %	**1.0**	Market Cap	**US$3,703.8mil**

Address	**39 Old Ridgebury Rd.**	Tel	**716-879-4077**	Exchange	**NYSE**	President	**Edgar G. Hotard**
	Danbury, CT 06810	Fax	**N/A**	Ticker	**PX**	Chairman & CEO	**H.W. Lichtenberger**

Precision Castparts

Industry: **Aerospace & Defense**

Precision Castparts supplies the aerospace industry with large and complex structural investment casting. The company also supplies other investment castings from stainless steel and alloys of nickel, cobalt, and titanium. In addition, the company manufactures precision-cast airfoils through its subsidiary, PCC Airfoils. The airfoils division manufactures and sells blades and vanes used as replacement parts and as original equipment in commercial and military aircraft jet engines. Advanced Forming Technology, another subsidiary, produces metal-injected molded parts.

$ mil	03/93	03/94	04/95	% Change				
Sales	**461.4**	**420.4**	**436.4**	**3.8**	P/E Ratio	**25.2**	Price (9/30/95)	**36.50**
Net Income	**1.8**	**22.2**	**29.0**	**30.6**	P/B Ratio	**2.9**	52 Wk Hi-Low	**36.50-18.13**
Book Value	**203.3**	**222.8**	**258.4**	**16.0**	Yield %	**0.6**	Market Cap	**US$743.2mil**

Address	**4600 S.E. Harney Dr.**	Tel	**503-777-3881**	Exchange	**NYSE**	President & CEO	**William C. McCormick**
	Portland, OR 97206	Fax	**503-653-4665**	Ticker	**PCP**	Chairman	**William C. McCormick**

Premark

Industry: **Household Products (Durable)**

Premark International manufactures consumer goods and commercial food-processing equipment. Dart Industries, a subsidiary, makes Tupperware plastic food-storage containers, tableware, microwave cookware, and educational toys, which are sold directly to consumers through demonstrations. Premark makes commercial dishwashers, mixers, slicers, and other appliances, sold under the Hobart, Vulcan, and Foster names. Its consumer- and decorative-products division makes glazed-tile products, prefinished oak flooring, and decorative laminates for countertops and cabinetry.

$ mil	12/92	12/93	12/94	% Change				
Sales	**2,946.0**	**3,097.3**	**3,450.8**	**11.4**	P/E Ratio	**15.0**	Price (9/30/95)	**50.88**
Net Income	**-79.3**	**172.5**	**225.5**	**30.7**	P/B Ratio	**3.3**	52 Wk Hi-Low	**54.38-39.00**
Book Value	**710.3**	**811.9**	**972.3**	**19.8**	Yield %	**1.5**	Market Cap	**US$3,110.2mil**

Address **1717 Deerfield Rd.**
Deerfield, IL 60015
Tel **708-405-6000**
Fax **708-408-6013**
Exchange **NYSE**
Ticker **PMI**
President & COO **James M. Ringler**
Chairman & CEO **Warren L. Batts**

Price/Costco

Industry: **Other Specialty Retailers**

Price/Costco operates a chain of cash-and-carry membership warehouses. The warehouses sell nationally branded and private-label merchandise to businesses for commercial use, personal use, or resale, and to individuals who are members of selected employee groups. Total inventories per warehouse are limited to approximately 3,500 to 4,000 active stock-keeping units. The company operates 221 warehouses in 21 states, Canada, and the U.K. Store chains include Price Club and others. The company also operates three stores in Mexico through a 50%-owned joint venture.

$ mil	08/92	08/93	08/94	% Change				
Revenues	**7,511.8**	**15,497.7**	**16,481.0**	**6.3**	P/E Ratio	**NMF**	Price (9/30/95)	**17.13**
Net Income	**129.1**	**223.2**	**-112.4**	**-150.3**	P/B Ratio	**2.2**	52 Wk Hi-Low	**18.50-12.25**
Book Value	**802.0**	**1,796.7**	**1,685.0**	**-6.2**	Yield %	**0.0**	Market Cap	**US$3,339.3mil**

Address **10809 120th Ave. N.E.**
Kirkland, WA 98033
Tel **206-803-8100**
Fax **N/A**
Exchange **NNM**
Ticker **PCCW**
President & CEO **Jim Sinegal**
Chairman **Jeffrey H. Brotman**

Procter & Gamble

Industry: **Household Products (Non-Durable)**

Procter & Gamble is a major manufacturer of consumer products. Its personal-care products include Ivory, Camay, and Zest soaps; Cover Girl and Max Factor cosmetics; Pampers diapers; and Crest toothpaste. The company's laundry- and cleaning-products division makes Bold, Cheer, Era, and Tide laundry detergents; Cascade and Dawn dishwashing detergents; and Mr. Clean household cleaners. Procter and Gamble's food-and-beverage division's products include Crisco shortening, Folger's coffee, and Pringle's potato chips. The company also makes paper pulp and industrial chemicals.

$ mil	06/93	06/94	06/95	% Change				
Sales	**30,433.0**	**30,296.0**	**33,434.0**	**10.4**	P/E Ratio	**20.8**	Price (9/30/95)	**77.00**
Net Income	**-656.0**	**2,211.0**	**2,645.0**	**19.6**	P/B Ratio	**5.0**	52 Wk Hi-Low	**78.13-58.88**
Book Value	**7,441.0**	**8,832.0**	**10,589.0**	**19.9**	Yield %	**1.8**	Market Cap	**US$52,928mil**

Address **One Procter & Gamble Plz.**
Cincinnati, OH 45202
Tel **513-983-1100**
Fax **513-983-9369**
Exchange **NYSE**
Ticker **PG**
President & COO **Durk I. Jager**
Chairman & CEO **John E. Pepper**

Progressive

Industry: **Insurance - Property & Casualty**

Progressive is an insurance holding company that owns 60 subsidiaries and has one mutual insurance company affiliate. It underwrites insurance for private-passenger automobiles and small commercial vehicles for people whose insurance has been canceled or who have been rejected by another insurer. It also underwrites property-casualty insurance. The company sells its policies in the U.S. and Canada through independent agents, vehicle dealers, and direct mailings. Its Progressive Partners division provides investment- and capital-management services for the company.

$ mil	12/92	12/93	12/94	% Change				
Revenues	**1,738.9**	**1,954.8**	**2,415.3**	**23.6**	P/E Ratio	**12.5**	Price (9/30/95)	**44.75**
Net Income	**153.8**	**267.3**	**274.3**	**2.6**	P/B Ratio	**2.8**	52 Wk Hi-Low	**47.88-32.25**
Book Value	**629.0**	**997.9**	**1,151.9**	**15.4**	Yield %	**0.5**	Market Cap	**US$3,217.4mil**

Address **6300 Wilson Mills Rd.**
Mayfield Village, OH 44143
Tel **216-461-5000**
Fax **216-446-7481**
Exchange **NYSE**
Ticker **PGR**
President & CEO **Peter B. Lewis**
Chairman **Peter B. Lewis**

Provident Life

Industry: **Insurance - Life & Health**

Provident Life & Accident Insurance is a holding company that offers life and health insurance and pension plans through its subsidiaries: Provident Life & Accident Insurance, Provident National Assurance, and Provident Life and Casualty. The company offers individual life insurance, employee benefits for large and small groups, group pension plans, and group or individual disability-income insurance. The company also offers health-maintenance organizations and certain managed-health-care services through its its indirect subsidiary Provident Health Care Plans.

$ mil	12/92	12/93	12/94	% Change				
Revenues	**2,866.7**	**2,938.0**	**2,762.2**	**-6.0**	P/E Ratio	**10.0**	Price (9/30/95)	**27.13**
Net Income	**112.6**	**-81.2**	**135.3**	**-266.6**	P/B Ratio	**1.1**	52 Wk Hi-Low	**27.50-20.75**
Book Value	**1,387.5**	**1,401.6**	**1,169.1**	**-16.6**	Yield %	**3.8**	Market Cap	**US$1,231.2mil**

Address **1 Fountain Sq.**
Chattanooga, TN 37402
Tel **615-755-1011**
Fax **615-755-1755**
Exchange **NYSE**
Ticker **PVB**
President & CEO **J. Harold Chandler**
Chairman **--**

Providian

Industry: **Insurance - Life & Health**

Providian is an insurance holding company. Through its subsidiaries, the company provides insurance, annuity products, and financial services in the U.S. Providian's insurance products include universal life, interest-sensitive life, term-life, accidental death and dismemberment, disability, individual-health, and accident policies. Its annuity products include variable annuities, single-premium deferred annuities, flexible-premium deferred annuities, and individual retirement annuities. The company offers secured and unsecured loans through a banking subsidiary.

$ mil	12/92	12/93	12/94	% Change				
Revenues	**2,853.3**	**2,884.2**	**2,959.1**	**2.6**	P/E Ratio	**13.7**	Price (9/30/95)	**41.50**
Net Income	**322.5**	**322.7**	**300.9**	**-6.8**	P/B Ratio	**1.9**	52 Wk Hi-Low	**41.50-30.13**
Book Value	**2,185.9**	**2,492.9**	**2,121.9**	**-14.9**	Yield %	**1.9**	Market Cap	**US$3,954.1mil**

Address **400 W. Market St.**
Louisville, KY 40202
Tel **502-560-2000**
Fax **502-560-2550**
Exchange **NYSE**
Ticker **PVN**
President & COO **Shailesh J. Mehta**
Chairman & CEO **Irving W. Bailey II**

Public Service Enterprise

Industry: **Electrical Utilities - Eastern U.S.**

Public Service Enterprise Group is a utility holding company. Operating through its Public Service Electric & Gas subsidiary it provides electric and natural-gas service to more than two million customers in New Jersey. The company's other subsidiaries explore for and produce oil and natural gas, and participate in the development of power-generation and -supply companies, and manage real-estate investments. Residential users account for about 45% of electricity and 49% of natural-gas revenues. Commercial and industrial customers account for most of the balance.

$ mil	12/92	12/93	12/94	% Change				
Sales	**5,356.8**	**5,705.6**	**5,915.8**	**3.7**	P/E Ratio	**10.7**	Price (9/30/95)	**29.75**
Net Income	**504.1**	**600.9**	**679.0**	**13.0**	P/B Ratio	**1.4**	52 Wk Hi-Low	**30.00-25.13**
Book Value	**4,782.1**	**5,133.7**	**5,311.2**	**3.5**	Yield %	**7.3**	Market Cap	**US$7,279.8mil**

Address **80 Park Plz.**
Newark, NJ 07101-1171
Tel **201-430-7000**
Fax **201-430-5328**
Exchange **NYSE**
Ticker **PEG**
President **Lawrence R. Codey**
Chairman & CEO **E. James Ferland**

Public Service of Colorado

Industry: **Electrical Utilities - Western U.S.**

Public Service Company of Colorado is an electric and natural-gas utility. It provides electric and gas service in Colorado and Wyoming, and explores for oil and gas in Texas, Montana, and Wyoming. The company generates approximately 95% of its electric power from fossil fuels and the remainder from hydroelectric sources. It purchases additional electricity during the summer. Residential customers account for about 26% of electricity revenues and 59% of natural-gas revenues. In 1995, Public Service Company of Colorado agreed to merge with Southwestern Public Service.

$ mil	12/92	12/93	12/94	% Change				
Sales	**1,862.3**	**1,998.7**	**2,057.4**	**2.9**	P/E Ratio	**13.3**	Price (9/30/95)	**34.25**
Net Income	**136.6**	**157.4**	**170.3**	**8.2**	P/B Ratio	**1.5**	52 Wk Hi-Low	**34.25-26.00**
Book Value	**1,284.1**	**1,367.1**	**1,450.2**	**6.1**	Yield %	**5.8**	Market Cap	**US$2,161.2mil**

Address **1225 17th St.**
Denver, CO 80201
Tel **303-571-7511**
Fax **303-294-2019**
Exchange **NYSE**
Ticker **PSR**
President & COO **Wayne H. Brunetti**
Chairman & CEO **D.D. Hock**

Puget Sound Power

Industry: **Electrical Utilities - Western U.S.**

Puget Sound Power & Light is a public electric-power utility. The utility provides service to nearly 823,000 residential, commercial, and industrial customers in the Puget Sound region of Washington. The company purchases about 69% of its power from outside sources and supplies the balance of its needs from hydroelectric, coal-fired, natural-gas-fired, and oil-fired stations owned jointly with other public electric utilities. Residential customers account for approximately 47% of the utility's electric-power revenues; commercial and industrial users roughly 47%.

$ mil	12/92	12/93	12/94	% Change				
Sales	**1,025.0**	**1,112.9**	**1,194.1**	**7.3**	P/E Ratio	**14.2**	Price (9/30/95)	**23.25**
Net Income	**135.7**	**138.3**	**120.1**	**-13.2**	P/B Ratio	**1.1**	52 Wk Hi-Low	**23.38-19.38**
Book Value	**1,299.0**	**1,394.7**	**1,389.0**	**-0.4**	Yield %	**7.9**	Market Cap	**US$1,479.7mil**

Address **411 - 108th Ave. N.E.**
Bellevue, WA 98004
Tel **206-454-6363**
Fax **206-454-3300**
Exchange **NYSE**
Ticker **PSD**
President & CEO **Richard R. Sonstelie**
Chairman **--**

Pulte Corp

Industry: **Home Construction**

Pulte builds single- and multifamily housing and provides financial services in the southern and eastern United States. Pulte Home, a subsidiary, builds 10,000 houses per year, primarily single-family detached homes, priced between $50,000 and $600,000 (with an average price of $147,000), in subdivisions developed by outside companies. The company's financial subsidiaries include ICM Mortgage, which provides mortgage financing, primarily to buyers of Pulte homes, and Pulte Financial, which engages in the acquisition and sale of mortgages and mortgage-backed securities.

$ mil	12/92	12/93	12/94	% Change				
Sales	**1,369.9**	**1,632.8**	**1,755.9**	**7.5**	P/E Ratio	**4.9**	Price (9/30/95)	**28.38**
Net Income	**70.1**	**79.4**	**162.8**	**105.0**	P/B Ratio	**1.1**	52 Wk Hi-Low	**30.13-18.75**
Book Value	**481.4**	**556.3**	**710.6**	**27.7**	Yield %	**0.8**	Market Cap	**US$763.9mil**

Address **33 Bloomfield Hills Pkwy.**
Bloomfield Hills, MI 48304
Tel **810-647-2750**
Fax **810-433-4598**
Exchange **NYSE**
Ticker **PHM**
President & CEO **Robert K. Burgess**
Chairman **William J. Pulte**

Quaker Oats

Industry: **Other Food**

Quaker Oats produces beverages and food products. Its beverages include Gatorade sports drinks and Snapple iced teas and juices. The company's brand-name food products include Quaker Oats oat products, Cap'n Crunch and Life cereals, and Rice-A-Roni and Near East rice and pasta products. It also manufactures cereals, juices, baked goods, and ice-cream toppings for the food-service industry. Quaker Oats markets its products to consumers and food-service customers worldwide. The company operates manufacturing facilities in the United States and abroad.

$ mil	06/93	06/94	06/95	% Change				
Sales	5,730.6	5,955.0	6,365.2	6.9	P/E Ratio	5.5	Price (9/30/95)	33.13
Net Income	171.3	231.5	802.0	246.4	P/B Ratio	3.9	52 Wk Hi-Low	38.44-30.06
Book Value	562.5	461.1	1,147.6	148.9	Yield %	3.4	Market Cap	US$4,441.3mil

Address **321 N. Clark St.**
Chicago, IL 60610

Tel **312-222-7111**
Fax **312-222-8200**

Exchange **NYSE**
Ticker **OAT**

President & COO **Philip A. Marineau**
Chairman & CEO **William D. Smithburg**

Questar

Industry: **Gas Utilities**

Questar is an integrated natural-gas company. It owns, on average, a 25% interest in 3,200 wells and holds net gas reserves of 620 billion cubic feet. Its Mountain Fuel subsidiary provides gas-utility services to more than 570,000 customers in Utah, southwestern Wyoming, and a portion of southeastern Idaho. Questar operates a 2,580-mile company-owned pipeline that spans Utah, Wyoming, and Colorado, with which it aggregates gas for resale, primarily to Mountain Fuel. Interstate Land, a subsidiary, owns and manages commercial real estate in the western United States.

$ mil	12/92	12/93	12/94	% Change				
Sales	604.8	660.4	670.3	1.5	P/E Ratio	14.9	Price (9/30/95)	32.13
Net Income	80.6	81.7	87.5	7.1	P/B Ratio	2.0	52 Wk Hi-Low	32.88-26.63
Book Value	562.5	609.5	659.9	8.3	Yield %	3.5	Market Cap	US$1,301.7mil

Address **180 E. First S.**
Salt Lake City, UT 84147

Tel **801-534-5000**
Fax **801-534-5483**

Exchange **NYSE**
Ticker **STR**

President & CEO **R.D. Cash**
Chairman **R.D. Cash**

Ralston Purina

Industry: **Other Food**

Ralston Purina produces pet foods, food additives, chemical products, and consumer products. Its products include dog food, cat food, other pet foods, batteries, dietary soy proteins, fiber food ingredients, and polymer products. It markets these products under the Purina, Dog Chow, Puppy Chow, Cat Chow, Meow Mix, Eveready, Energizer, Supro, Pro-Cote, and Fibrim trademarks in the United States and in international markets. Ralston Purina also produces baked goods through its Continental Baking subsidiary, whose shares trade separately from those of the company.

$ mil	09/92	09/93	09/94	% Change				
Sales	7,752.4	5,915.4	5,759.3	-2.6	P/E Ratio	28.4	Price (9/30/95)	57.88
Net Income	313.2	153.4	223.2	45.5	P/B Ratio	10.1	52 Wk Hi-Low	58.63-40.50
Book Value	809.9	668.2	572.2	-14.4	Yield %	2.1	Market Cap	US$6,029.6mil

Address **Checkerboard Sq.**
St. Louis, MO 63164

Tel **314-982-1000**
Fax **314-982-4031**

Exchange **NYSE**
Ticker **RAL**

President & CEO **William P. Stiritz**
Chairman **William P. Stiritz**

Raychem

Industry: **Industrial - Diversified**

Raychem develops products for the electronics, industrial, and telecommunication markets. Its electronic products include interconnection systems, wire and cable, and circuit-protection devices. The company makes electrical-insulation products and leak-detection systems for industrial applications. It also supplies telecommunication customers with telephone and cable-television cable connectors, closures, and accessories. Raychem and LM Ericsson have formed Ericsson Raynet, which produces fiberoptic systems. Foreign sales account for about 65% of the company's total sales.

$ mil	06/93	06/94	06/95	% Change				
Sales	1,385.7	1,461.5	1,530.6	4.7	P/E Ratio	NMF	Price (9/30/95)	45.00
Net Income	9.6	1.7	-29.2	NMF	P/B Ratio	2.6	52 Wk Hi-Low	46.75-33.25
Book Value	689.5	732.9	749.7	2.3	Yield %	0.7	Market Cap	US$1,975.4mil

Address **300 Constitution Dr.**
Menlo Park, CA 94025

Tel **415-361-4180**
Fax **415-361-7377**

Exchange **NYSE**
Ticker **RYC**

President & CEO **Robert J. Saldich**
Chairman **Paul M. Cook**

Rayonier Inc.

Industry: **Forest Products**

Rayonier manufactures specialty pulp and building products. The company's specialty pulp goods are used in the manufacture of circuit boards, shoe components, battery separators, and air and oil filters. The company's 1.5 million acres of forestland, which is located in the Southeast and Pacific Northwest regions of the U.S. and in New Zealand, provide lumber and plywood for the construction industry. Rayonier's international sales account for approximately 12% of the company's total sales. Rayonier operates manufacturing and research facilities worldwide.

$ mil	12/92 R	12/93	12/94	% Change				
Sales	974.0	936.3	1,069.5	14.2	P/E Ratio	16.6	Price (9/30/95)	39.13
Net Income	-103.0	52.5	70.0	33.4	P/B Ratio	1.8	52 Wk Hi-Low	39.88-27.13
Book Value	676.0	606.3	655.2	8.1	Yield %	1.8	Market Cap	US$1,159.3mil

Address **1177 Summer St.**
Stamford, CT 06905

Tel **203-348-7000**
Fax **203-964-4333**

Exchange **NYSE**
Ticker **RYN**

President & CEO **Ronald M. Gross**
Chairman **Ronald M. Gross**

R=Restated.

Raytheon

Industry: **Diversified Technology**

Raytheon designs electronics, power-generation facilities, aircraft, and major household appliances. The company primarily makes electronic devices for government and commercial use. These devices include radar, air-traffic-control, and autopilot systems, as well as integrated circuits. Its energy and environmental division constructs petroleum refineries, chemical-processing plants, and cogeneration facilities. Raytheon's Aircraft Division produces Hawker, Beechcraft, and other jet aircraft. Raytheon also manufactures appliances under the Amana and Speed Queen brands.

$ mil	12/92	12/93	12/94	% Change				
Sales	9,058.2	9,201.2	10,012.9	8.8	P/E Ratio	18.8	Price (9/30/95)	85.00
Net Income	635.1	693.0	596.9	-13.9	P/B Ratio	2.7	52 Wk Hi-Low	85.00-61.25
Book Value	3,843.2	4,297.9	3,928.2	-8.6	Yield %	1.7	Market Cap	US$10,366mil

Address	**141 Spring St.**	Tel	**617-862-6600**	Exchange	**NYSE**	President	**Max E. Bleck**
	Lexington, MA 02173	Fax	**617-860-2172**	Ticker	**RTN**	Chairman & CEO	**Dennis J. Picard**

Reader's Digest

Industry: **Publishing**

Reader's Digest Association publishes magazines, books, and home-entertainment products. The company's Reader's Digest magazine is published in 17 languages in the United States and internationally. It also publishes Moneywise and American Health magazines. Through direct-mail solicitations, it sells magazine subscriptions, condensed versions of books, series books, recorded music collections, and home videos. Business operations outside the U.S. account for approximately 60% of revenues. The company's books and home-entertainment products generate 68% of revenues.

$ mil	06/92	06/93	06/94	% Change				
Sales	2,614.0	2,868.6	2,806.4	-2.2	P/E Ratio	21.8	Price (9/30/95)	47.13
Net Income	234.4	207.3	246.3	18.8	P/B Ratio	6.8	52 Wk Hi-Low	49.25-38.75
Book Value	934.9	806.3	791.0	-1.9	Yield %	2.9	Market Cap	US$5,221.5mil

Address	**Reader's Digest Rd.**	Tel	**914-238-1000**	Exchange	**NYSE**	President & CEO	**James P. Schadt**
	Pleasantville, NY 10570	Fax	**914-238-4559**	Ticker	**RDA**	Chairman	**George V. Grune**

Reebok

Industry: **Footwear**

Reebok International manufactures footwear and leisure apparel and equipment. The company makes athletic shoes, apparel, and accessories under the Reebok and Avia names, and casual, dress, and walking shoes under the Rockport and Boks names. It sells these products worldwide through shoe stores, department stores, and company-owned specialty-retail stores. The company also makes golf footwear and clothing under the Greg Norman name, sold mostly at golf pro shops and golf-specialty stores. The majority of its products are produced by contractors in the Pacific Rim.

$ mil	12/92	12/93	12/94	% Change				
Sales	3,022.6	2,893.9	3,280.4	13.4	P/E Ratio	11.4	Price (9/30/95)	34.38
Net Income	114.8	223.4	254.5	13.9	P/B Ratio	2.8	52 Wk Hi-Low	40.00-31.25
Book Value	838.7	846.6	990.5	17.0	Yield %	0.9	Market Cap	US$2,695.3mil

Address	**100 Technology Center Dr.**	Tel	**617-341-5000**	Exchange	**NYSE**	President & CEO	**Paul B. Fireman**
	Stoughton, MA 02072	Fax	**617-341-5087**	Ticker	**RBK**	Chairman	**Paul B. Fireman**

Regal Beloit

Industry: **Factory Equipment**

Regal-Beloit manufactures power-transmission products and cutting tools. Its product line includes standard and custom gearboxes, specialized off-highway transmissions, forklift axles, high-performance transmissions, taps, drills, end mills, reamers, and gauges. The company markets its products to original-equipment manufacturers and independent distributors. The company operates 18 manufacturing, office, service, and distribution facilities in Illinois, Wisconsin, Indiana, South Carolina, South Dakota, California, New York, Pennsylvania, Texas, England, and Germany.

$ mil	12/92	12/93	12/94	% Change				
Sales	199.8	219.9	242.7	10.3	P/E Ratio	16.5	Price (9/30/95)	18.63
Net Income	9.4	14.2	23.1	62.9	P/B Ratio	3.4	52 Wk Hi-Low	20.75-12.25
Book Value	83.9	92.7	110.6	19.3	Yield %	1.7	Market Cap	US$382.1mil

Address	**200 State St.**	Tel	**608-364-8800**	Exchange	**AMEX**	President & CEO	**James L. Packard**
	Beloit, WI 53511	Fax	**N/A**	Ticker	**RBC**	Chairman	**James L. Packard**

Regions Financial

Industry: **Banks - Southern U.S.**

Regions Financial is a bank holding company that operates more than 200 banking offices in Alabama, Florida, Georgia, Louisiana, Mississippi, South Carolina, and Tennessee. In addition to providing commercial-banking services, the company's banks offer mortgage-banking, leasing, credit-related insurance, and securities-brokerage services, as well as automated-teller machines. Regions Financial also owns a number of bank-related subsidiaries, including Regions Life Insurance Company, a reinsurer of credit, life, accident, and health insurance, and First Alabama Investments.

$ mil	12/92	12/93	12/94	% Change				
Revenues	655.8	687.7	929.2	35.1	P/E Ratio	11.9	Price (9/30/95)	40.63
Net Income	95.0	112.0	145.9	30.3	P/B Ratio	1.8	52 Wk Hi-Low	41.25-30.00
Book Value	656.7	851.0	1,013.9	19.1	Yield %	3.0	Market Cap	US$1,844.7mil

Address	**417 N. 20th St.**	Tel	**205-326-7100**	Exchange	**NNM**	Chief Executive	**J. Stanley Mackin**
	Birmingham, AL 35202	Fax	**205-326-7099**	Ticker	**RGBK**	Chairman	**J. Stanley Mackin**

Republic New York

Industry: **Banks - Money Center**

Republic New York is a bank holding company. Its Republic National Bank of New York subsidiary operates 34 branches in the United States that provide banking and financial services to corporations, financial institutions, and individuals. The bank also manages eight overseas branches and 13 foreign-representative offices. Its international-banking services include accepting deposits, extending credit, buying and selling foreign currencies, and issuing letters of credit. The company's Safra Republic Holdings subsidiary offers private-banking services to wealthy individuals.

$ mil	12/92	12/93	12/94	% Change				
Revenues	**2,340.8**	**2,328.4**	**2,559.7**	**9.9**	P/E Ratio	**10.1**	Price (9/30/95)	**58.50**
Net Income	**258.9**	**301.2**	**340.0**	**12.9**	P/B Ratio	**1.2**	52 Wk Hi-Low	**60.00-42.13**
Book Value	**2,263.4**	**2,747.2**	**2,639.4**	**-3.9**	Yield %	**2.3**	Market Cap	**US$3,281.6mil**

Address **452 Fifth Ave.**
New York, NY 10018
Tel **212-525-6100**
Fax **212-525-5569**
Exchange **NYSE**
Ticker **RNB**
President **Jeffrey C. Keil**
Chairman & CEO **Walter H. Weiner**

Reynolds Metals

Industry: **Aluminum**

Reynolds Metals supplies and recycles aluminum and other products, the core business is integrated production of value-added aluminum. The company produces alumina, carbon products, and primary and reclaimed aluminum to supply its fabricating operations. The fabricating operations produce aluminum foil, sheet, plate, cans and extruded products, flexible packaging, and wheels, among other items. Products are marketed under the Reynolds brand name, including Reynolds Wrap aluminum foil. The company also produces gold through Australian operations.

$ mil	12/92	12/93	12/94	% Change				
Sales	**5,592.6**	**5,269.2**	**5,879.1**	**11.6**	P/E Ratio	**40.7**	Price (9/30/95)	**57.75**
Net Income	**-748.8**	**-322.1**	**121.7**	**-137.8**	P/B Ratio	**1.6**	52 Wk Hi-Low	**64.13-46.38**
Book Value	**2,060.0**	**1,622.9**	**2,271.7**	**40.0**	Yield %	**1.7**	Market Cap	**US$3,664.1mil**

Address **6601 W. Broad St.**
Richmond, VA 23261
Tel **804-281-2000**
Fax **804-281-4160**
Exchange **NYSE**
Ticker **RLM**
President & COO **Jeremiah J. Sheehan**
Chairman & CEO **Richard G. Holder**

Rite Aid

Industry: **Drug-based Retailers**

Rite Aid operates a chain of 2,829 drugstores in the U.S., which are located in 23 eastern states. Half of its pharmacy sales are in third-party prescriptions. The company's drugstores offer brand-name health and personal-care products, seasonal merchandise, and a private-label product line. Express-mail, photocopy, money-order, packaging services, and photo departments are in selected locations. Eagle Managed Care, a subsidiary, markets prescription plans and sells other managed health-care services to employers and government-sponsored employee-benefit programs.

$ mil	02/93	02/94	03/95	% Change				
Revenues	**4,085.1**	**4,058.7**	**4,533.9**	**11.7**	P/E Ratio	**16.8**	Price (9/30/95)	**28.00**
Net Income	**132.4**	**9.3**	**141.3**	**NMF**	P/B Ratio	**2.3**	52 Wk Hi-Low	**30.13-20.50**
Book Value	**1,035.6**	**954.7**	**1,011.8**	**6.0**	Yield %	**2.2**	Market Cap	**US$2,345.2mil**

Address **30 Hunter Ln.**
Camp Hill, PA 17011
Tel **717-761-2633**
Fax **717-975-5871**
Exchange **NYSE**
Ticker **RAD**
President & COO **Timothy J. Noonan**
Chairman & CEO **Martin L. Grass**

Roadway Services

Industry: **Trucking**

Roadway Services provides trucking and air transportation through its subsidiaries. Its Roadway Express subsidiary provides long-haul general freight service in the United States, Canada, Mexico, Europe, and the Pacific Rim. Its Roadway Package System subsidiary transports small packages. Roadway Regional Group, a subsidiary, is the parent company of Coles Express, Spartan Express, Central Freight Lines, and Viking Freight. The company's Roadway Global Air subsidiary provides heavyweight air-cargo transportation, including overnight, second-day, and third-day delivery.

$ mil	12/92	12/93	12/94	% Change				
Sales	**3,577.6**	**4,155.9**	**4,572.0**	**10.0**	P/E Ratio	**99.5**	Price (9/30/95)	**49.75**
Net Income	**147.4**	**101.2**	**19.6**	**-80.7**	P/B Ratio	**1.9**	52 Wk Hi-Low	**57.75-43.00**
Book Value	**1,021.4**	**1,047.2**	**1,015.4**	**-3.0**	Yield %	**2.8**	Market Cap	**US$1,944.1mil**

Address **1077 Gorge Blvd.**
Akron, OH 44309
Tel **216-384-8184**
Fax **216-258-6042**
Exchange **NASDA**
Ticker **ROAD**
President & COO **Daniel J. Sullivan**
Chairman & CEO **Joseph M. Clapp**

Rockwell International

Industry: **Diversified Technology**

Rockwell International manufactures components and systems for use in electronics, defense, aerospace, automotive, and graphics applications. It produces manufacturing-plant-automation systems, avionics, data and facsimile modems, and defense electronics for weapons, communication, and guidance systems. Rockwell also builds spacecraft-propulsion systems, and produces axles and brakes for passenger and heavy-duty vehicles. In addition, the company makes high-speed printing presses and other graphic-arts equipment. Rockwell markets its products worldwide.

$ mil	09/92	09/93	09/94	% Change				
Sales	**10,909.7**	**10,840.0**	**11,123.3**	**2.6**	P/E Ratio	**16.5**	Price (9/30/95)	**47.25**
Net Income	**-1,036.0**	**561.9**	**634.1**	**12.8**	P/B Ratio	**3.1**	52 Wk Hi-Low	**47.63-33.88**
Book Value	**2,778.0**	**2,956.0**	**3,355.6**	**13.5**	Yield %	**2.2**	Market Cap	**US$10,258mil**

Address **2201 Seal Beach Blvd.**
Seal Beach, CA 90740
Tel **310-797-3311**
Fax **310-797-5595**
Exchange **NYSE**
Ticker **ROK**
Chief Executive **Donald R. Beall**
Chairman **Donald R. Beall**

Rohm and Haas

Industry: **Commodity Chemicals**

Rohm and Haas manufactures plastics and chemicals. The company's principal products include polymers, resins, plastics, biocides, automotive fluids, and agricultural and water-treatment chemicals. Rohm and Haas produces these goods from basic petrochemical commodities such as propylene, acetone, and styrene. It sells its compounds as finished products or as raw materials to manufacturers of consumer goods such as paint, furniture fabrics, carpets, shampoo, leather goods, fruit juices, magazines, and newspapers. Rohm and Haas markets its products in the U.S. and abroad.

$ mil	12/92	12/93	12/94	% Change				
Sales	3,063.0	3,269.0	3,534.0	8.1	P/E Ratio	15.9	Price (9/30/95)	60.38
Net Income	-5.0	107.0	264.0	146.7	P/B Ratio	2.5	52 Wk Hi-Low	61.63-52.00
Book Value	1,428.0	1,441.0	1,620.0	12.4	Yield %	2.4	Market Cap	US$4,077.5mil

Address **100 Independence Mall W.**
Philadelphia, PA 19106
Tel **215-592-3000**
Fax **215-592-3377**
Exchange **NYSE**
Ticker **ROH**
President **John P. Mulroney**
Chairman & CEO **J. Lawrence Wilson**

Rollins

Industry: **Household Services**

Rollins provides termite and pest control, plantscaping, lawn care, and protective services to residential and commercial customers. Orkin Exterminating Company, a subsidiary, provides customized pest-control services to approximately 1.4 million customers through a network of 367 company-owned and -operated branches in the U.S. and Mexico. Orkin's plantscaping division designs, and maintains green and flowering plants from 9 branches and one supply outlet. Rollins' protective services provides customized wired- and wireless- electronic-security systems.

$ mil	12/92	12/93	12/94	% Change				
Sales	527.7	575.8	605.3	5.1	P/E Ratio	17.6	Price (9/30/95)	24.50
Net Income	38.0	44.5	49.6	11.4	P/B Ratio	4.5	52 Wk Hi-Low	28.50-22.13
Book Value	129.9	160.5	193.6	20.6	Yield %	2.0	Market Cap	US$878.3mil

Address **2170 Piedmont Rd. N.E.**
Atlanta, GA 30324
Tel **404-888-2000**
Fax **404-888-2730**
Exchange **NYSE**
Ticker **ROL**
President & COO **Gary W. Rollins**
Chairman & CEO **R. Randall Rollins**

Rollins Environmental

Industry: **Pollution Control, Waste Management**

Rollins Environmental Services provides waste-management services. The company transports, treats, stores, and disposes of industrial waste; operates recycling and repackaging facilities; and maintains environmental-testing laboratories. It operates chemical-waste-treatment and incineration plants in New Jersey, Louisiana, Colorado, and Texas. It also owns a landfill at the Colorado plant, where it disposes of waste including incinerator ash and construction debris. Rollins Environmental operates recycling facilities in Missouri and California.

$ mil	09/92	09/93	09/94	% Change				
Sales	240.5	214.8	181.5	-15.5	P/E Ratio	NMF	Price (9/30/95)	4.88
Net Income	32.0	11.9	-9.9	-183.4	P/B Ratio	1.5	52 Wk Hi-Low	6.13-4.13
Book Value	206.6	212.8	203.0	-4.6	Yield %	0.0	Market Cap	US$294.3mil

Address **One Rollins Plz.**
Wilmington, DE 19899
Tel **302-426-3314**
Fax **302-426-3339**
Exchange **NYSE**
Ticker **REN**
President & COO **Nicholas Pappas**
Chairman & CEO **John W. Rollins**

Rollins Truck Leasing

Industry: **Trucking**

Rollins Truck Leasing is engaged in full-service leasing and short-term rental of tractors, trailers, and trucks and related services. Under the leases, Rollins purchases vehicles and components that are custom-engineered to its customers' requirements. This equipment is then leased to the customer for periods ranging from three to eight years. In addition, the company arranges for licenses and insurance, pays highway and use taxes and supplies an emergency road service to its customers. Principal subsidiaries are Rollins Leasing and Rollins Dedicated Carriage Services.

$ mil	09/92	09/93	09/94	% Change				
Sales	380.4	408.8	450.9	10.3	P/E Ratio	12.4	Price (9/30/95)	10.63
Net Income	24.6	30.4	39.8	30.9	P/B Ratio	1.9	52 Wk Hi-Low	14.13-10.25
Book Value	191.0	216.8	251.2	15.9	Yield %	1.2	Market Cap	US$483.5mil

Address **1 Rollins Plz.**
Wilmington, DE 19803
Tel **302-426-2700**
Fax **N/A**
Exchange **NYSE**
Ticker **RLC**
President **John W. Rollins, Jr.**
Chairman & CEO **John W. Rollins**

Rouse

Industry: **Real-Estate Investment**

Rouse develops and manages real estate, which it leases to long-term tenants. The company develops and renovates retail centers and mixed-use projects, primarily for ownership. The company owns and/or manages more than 200 properties in the U.S. and one in Canada. These include retail centers such as Baltimore's Harborplace and Boston's Faneuil Hall Marketplace, office and industrial-use buildings, hotels, and mixed-use complexes. Rouse also develops and sells land to builders for various types of use through its Howard Research and Development subsidiary.

$ mil	12/92	12/93	12/94	% Change				
Sales	597.1	646.8	671.2	3.8	P/E Ratio	NMF	Price (9/30/95)	21.88
Net Income	-16.2	-9.3	2.2	-123.7	P/B Ratio	10.9	52 Wk Hi-Low	22.31-17.50
Book Value	-34.8	113.2	95.1	-16.0	Yield %	3.1	Market Cap	US$1,046.7mil

Address **10275 Little Patuxent Pkwy.**
Columbia, MD 21044
Tel **410-992-6000**
Fax **410-992-6363**
Exchange **NASDA**
Ticker **ROUS**
President & CEO **Anthony W. Deering**
Chairman **Mathias J. DeVito**

Rowan

Industry: **Oil Drilling**

Rowan provides contract oil- and natural-gas-well drilling and charter-aircraft services. The company operates 24 offshore-drilling rigs, primarily in the Gulf of Mexico and the North Sea, and 17 onshore rigs, primarily in the U.S. and Venezuela. It also owns 101 helicopters and 17 airplanes and provides charter-aircraft service, primarily in Alaska and the Gulf of Mexico. The company holds a 49% interest in KLM Helikopters (a subsidiary of KLM Royal Dutch Airlines). The company also operates a heavy-equipment-manufacturing operation and a marine-rig construction yard.

$ mil	12/92	12/93	12/94	% Change				
Sales	**250.0**	**353.2**	**438.2**	**24.1**	P/E Ratio	**NMF**	Price (9/30/95)	**7.50**
Net Income	**-73.8**	**-13.3**	**-23.0**	**72.9**	P/B Ratio	**1.4**	52 Wk Hi-Low	**8.50-5.63**
Book Value	**375.8**	**460.3**	**442.4**	**-3.9**	Yield %	**0.0**	Market Cap	**US$633.1mil**

Address **Transco Twr., 2800 Post Oak Blvd.** **Houston, TX 77056** Tel **713-621-7800** Fax **713-960-7660** Exchange **NYSE** Ticker **RDC** President & CEO **C.R. Palmer** Chairman **C.R. Palmer**

Rubbermaid

Industry: **Household Products (Durable)**

Rubbermaid manufactures household, office, and industrial products, made primarily of plastic. The company's main product lines include Rubbermaid plastic trash containers, food- and household-storage products, and cleaning accessories; Little Tikes toys; Iron Mountain Forge playground equipment; and Eldon and Davson office products. Sales of household products, largely through mass merchandisers, provide about 80% of company revenues. Rubbermaid markets its products worldwide, and operates manufacturing facilities in the United States and in five other countries.

$ mil	12/92	12/93	12/94	% Change				
Sales	**1,805.3**	**1,960.2**	**2,169.4**	**10.7**	P/E Ratio	**19.5**	Price (9/30/95)	**27.63**
Net Income	**164.1**	**211.4**	**228.1**	**7.9**	P/B Ratio	**3.5**	52 Wk Hi-Low	**34.13-25.75**
Book Value	**987.6**	**1,130.5**	**1,285.8**	**13.7**	Yield %	**1.7**	Market Cap	**US$4,367.4mil**

Address **1147 Akron Rd.** **Wooster, OH 44691** Tel **216-264-6464** Fax **216-287-2739** Exchange **NYSE** Ticker **RBD** President & COO **Charles A. Carroll** Chairman & CEO **Wolfgang R. Schmitt**

Russell

Industry: **Clothing & Fabrics**

Russell is an integrated clothing manufacturer that specializes in athletic uniforms and casualwear. The company's athletic division makes uniforms for amateur and professional sports, is the primary supplier of uniforms to the National Football League and Major League Baseball, and produces imprinted sportswear under license from athletic teams. Russell makes clothing such as sweatpants and T-shirts under the Russell and Jerzees trademarks, and produces woven fabrics for sale to other clothing manufacturers. Cross Creek Apparel, a subsidiary, makes knit clothing.

$ mil	01/93	01/94	12/94	% Change				
Sales	**899.1**	**930.8**	**1,098.3**	**18.0**	P/E Ratio	**13.0**	Price (9/30/95)	**25.50**
Net Income	**82.2**	**49.1**	**78.8**	**60.5**	P/B Ratio	**1.6**	52 Wk Hi-Low	**31.50-25.50**
Book Value	**570.0**	**587.7**	**628.7**	**7.0**	Yield %	**1.6**	Market Cap	**US$993.4mil**

Address **755 Lee St.** **Alexander City, AL 35010** Tel **205-329-4000** Fax **205-329-4474** Exchange **NYSE** Ticker **RML** President & CEO **John C. Adams** Chairman **John C. Adams**

Ryder System

Industry: **General Industrial & Commercial Services**

Ryder System provides highway-transportation services. Through its subsidiaries, the company engages in full-service leasing and short-term rental of trucks, tractors, and trailers; logistics services; public-transit management and student transportation; and transportation by truck of automobiles and light trucks. Its services are provided throughout the United States, Canada, the United Kingdom, Germany, and Poland. The company serves more than 11,100 customers. General Motors is the largest single customer of the company, accounting for approximately 10% of its revenue.

$ mil	12/92	12/93	12/94	% Change				
Sales	**4,029.8**	**4,217.0**	**4,685.6**	**11.1**	P/E Ratio	**13.0**	Price (9/30/95)	**25.38**
Net Income	**123.9**	**-61.4**	**153.5**	**-350.0**	P/B Ratio	**1.8**	52 Wk Hi-Low	**26.50-20.13**
Book Value	**1,475.1**	**990.2**	**1,129.0**	**14.0**	Yield %	**2.4**	Market Cap	**US$1,999.7mil**

Address **3600 N.W. 82nd Ave.** **Miami, FL 33166** Tel **305-593-3726** Fax **305-593-3336** Exchange **NYSE** Ticker **R** President & CEO **M. Anthony Burns** Chairman **M. Anthony Burns**

Ryland

Industry: **Home Construction**

Ryland Group builds single-family homes and condominiums and provides financial services. It builds about 8,000 homes per year, at an average price of about $160,000, under the names Larchmont Homes and Brock Homes in California, Scott Felder in Texas, and Ryland Homes in most of the rest of the continental United States. The company's Ryland Mortgage originates and services mortgages and issues mortgage-backed securities and issues builder and multi-builder bonds. Most of the homes built by Ryland Group are financed by Ryland Mortgage.

$ mil	12/92	12/93	12/94	% Change				
Sales	**1,442.3**	**1,474.4**	**1,642.7**	**11.4**	P/E Ratio	**10.9**	Price (9/30/95)	**15.50**
Net Income	**27.5**	**-2.7**	**24.5**	**NMF**	P/B Ratio	**0.8**	52 Wk Hi-Low	**17.25-13.00**
Book Value	**305.7**	**293.2**	**312.1**	**6.5**	Yield %	**3.9**	Market Cap	**US$241.8mil**

Address **11000 Broken Land Pkwy.** **Columbia, MD 21044** Tel **410-715-7000** Fax **410-715-7909** Exchange **NYSE** Ticker **RYL** President & CEO **R. Chad Dreier** Chairman **R. Chad Dreier**

SCEcorp

Industry: **Electrical Utilities - Western U.S.**

SCEcorp is a utility holding company. Its main subsidiary, Southern California Edison, is an electric utility that serves 4.1 million customers in California. The company generates about 63% of its electricity from natural gas, 18% from nuclear energy, 12% from coal, and 7% from hydroelectric stations. Residential customers make up approximately 34% of electrical-energy revenues, commercial and industrial users about 48%. SCEcorp's other subsidiary, the Mission Group, builds cogeneration plants, manages energy-related investments, and develops commercial real estate.

$ mil	12/92	12/93	12/94	% Change				
Sales	7,984.0	7,821.0	8,344.6	6.7	P/E Ratio	11.7	Price (9/30/95)	17.75
Net Income	739.0	639.0	680.7	6.5	P/B Ratio	1.3	52 Wk Hi-Low	17.88-12.88
Book Value	5,954.0	5,958.0	6,144.0	3.1	Yield %	6.3	Market Cap	US$7,917.3mil

Address **2244 Walnut Grove Ave.**
Rosemead, CA 91770
Tel **818-302-2222**
Fax **818-302-4815**
Exchange **NYSE**
Ticker **SCE**
Chief Executive **John E. Bryson**
Chairman **John E. Bryson**

SAFECO

Industry: **Insurance - Property & Casualty**

SAFECO provides insurance, real-estate, commercial-credit, and asset-management services and manages the SAFECO family of mutual funds. The company's largest business is property and casualty insurance; it also offers auto, homeowner's, fire, recreational-property, and commercial insurance. Its real-estate division specializes in shopping-center and nursing-home development and management. SAFECO provides loans and equipment financing to commercial businesses through its SAFECO Credit subsidiary. The company has 100 offices throughout the United States.

$ mil	12/92	12/93	12/94	% Change				
Revenues	3,294.7	3,516.7	3,537.1	0.6	P/E Ratio	13.2	Price (9/30/95)	65.63
Net Income	311.3	428.8	314.4	-26.7	P/B Ratio	1.5	52 Wk Hi-Low	67.13-47.38
Book Value	2,448.1	2,774.4	2,829.5	2.0	Yield %	2.9	Market Cap	US$4,133.9mil

Address **Safeco Plz.**
Seattle, WA 98185
Tel **206-545-5000**
Fax **206-545-5995**
Exchange **NASDA**
Ticker **SAFC**
President & CEO **Roger H. Eigsti**
Chairman **Roger H. Eigsti**

Safety-Kleen

Industry: **General Industrial & Commercial Services**

Safety-Kleen provides liquid-waste management, parts-cleaning services, and related products to approximately 400,000 industrial and commercial customers in the U.S. and in foreign countries through 236 branch facilities. The company supplies solvent-based equipment for cleaning tools and parts to automotive-repair facilities, paint shops, and fiberglass-product manufacturers. It also collects and recycles used industrial solvents, including used automotive lubricants and dry-cleaning fluids. Business operations outside the U.S. generate approximately 84% of revenues.

$ mil	12/92	12/93	12/94	% Change				
Sales	794.5	795.5	791.3	-0.5	P/E Ratio	16.8	Price (9/30/95)	14.63
Net Income	45.6	-101.3	50.1	-149.4	P/B Ratio	2.1	52 Wk Hi-Low	18.00-12.88
Book Value	492.1	362.7	396.3	9.3	Yield %	2.5	Market Cap	US$844.7mil

Address **1000 N. Randall Rd.**
Elgin, IL 60123
Tel **708-697-8460**
Fax **708-697-2783**
Exchange **NYSE**
Ticker **SK**
President & CEO **John G. Johnson, Jr.**
Chairman **Donald W. Brinckman**

Salomon

Industry: **Securities Brokers**

Salomon conducts global investment banking, global securities and commodities trading, and U.S. oil-refining activities. Its primary subsidiaries are Salomon Brothers Holding Company, which performs securities-trading and investment-banking activities; Phibro Division of Salomon, which trades energy securities; and Phibro Energy USA, which operates oil refineries in the U.S. Gulf Coast region. Salomon maintains 35 offices in the U.S and throughout the world. The company also provides money-management services through its Salomon Brothers Asset Management subsidiary.

$ mil	12/92	12/93	12/94	% Change				
Sales	8,196.0	8,799.0	6,278.0	-28.7	P/E Ratio	NMF	Price (9/30/95)	38.25
Net Income	550.0	827.0	-399.0	-148.2	P/B Ratio	0.9	52 Wk Hi-Low	42.88-32.50
Book Value	4,308.0	5,331.0	4,492.0	-15.7	Yield %	1.7	Market Cap	US$4,069.3mil

Address **7 World Trade Ctr.**
New York, NY 10048
Tel **212-783-7000**
Fax **212-783-2107**
Exchange **NYSE**
Ticker **SB**
Chief Executive **Robert E. Denham**
Chairman **Robert E. Denham**

San Diego Gas & Electric

Industry: **Electrical Utilities - Western U.S.**

San Diego Gas & Electric is a public utility that provides natural-gas and electric service in San Diego County and Orange County, California. Approximately 24% of the company's electricity is generated by natural-gas-fired plants, 17% comes from nuclear energy, and 55% is purchased from third parties. The utility also produces power from oil-fired stations. It provides electricity to about 1.1 million customers and natural gas to more than 690,000 customers. Residential customers account for approximately 41% of electricity revenues and 56% of natural-gas revenues.

$ mil	12/92	12/93	12/94	% Change				
Sales	1,870.9	1,980.1	1,982.0	0.1	P/E Ratio	19.8	Price (9/30/95)	23.13
Net Income	210.7	218.7	143.5	-34.4	P/B Ratio	1.7	52 Wk Hi-Low	23.13-18.63
Book Value	1,579.8	1,634.7	1,592.9	-2.6	Yield %	6.6	Market Cap	US$2,694.9mil

Address **101 Ash St.**
San Diego, CA 92112
Tel **619-696-2000**
Fax **619-696-1814**
Exchange **NYSE**
Ticker **SDO**
President & CEO **Thomas A. Page**
Chairman **Thomas A. Page**

Sara Lee

Industry: **Other Food**

Sara Lee produces food products and consumer goods. It sells Sara Lee frozen baked goods, Mr. Turkey luncheon meats, Hillshire Farms smoked sausage, Jimmy Dean sausages, and Ball Park hot dogs. Its nonfood operations, which account for slightly more than half of sales, include Hanes hosiery and clothing, Champion activewear, L'eggs hosiery, Kiwi leather-care products, and Coach leather goods. Sara Lee markets these products in the U.S. and abroad, with international sales accounting for about 35% of the total. The company operates manufacturing facilities worldwide.

$ mil	06/92	06/93	06/94	% Change				
Sales	**13,243.0**	**14,580.0**	**15,536.0**	**6.6**	P/E Ratio	**71.9**	Price (9/30/95)	**29.75**
Net Income	**761.0**	**704.0**	**199.0**	**-71.7**	P/B Ratio	**3.9**	52 Wk Hi-Low	**30.38-22.38**
Book Value	**3,733.0**	**3,908.0**	**3,657.0**	**-6.4**	Yield %	**2.1**	Market Cap	**US$14,269mil**

Address **Three First National Plz.** **Chicago, IL 60602**
Tel **312-726-2600** Fax **312-726-3712**
Exchange **NYSE** Ticker **SLE**
Chief Executive **John H. Bryan** Chairman **John H. Bryan**

SBC Communications

Industry: **Regional Telephone Systems**

SBC Communications, a regional Bell holding company, provides telecommunication and information services. Southwestern Bell Telephone, a subsidiary, accounts for most of the company's revenues and offers local-exchange and long-distance telephone service to 13.2 million customers in Arkansas, Kansas, Missouri, Oklahoma, and Texas. Other subsidiaries offer cellular-telephone and paging services, publish phone books, and have ownership interests in telephone-directory, cable-television, and telecommunication businesses in Australia, Israel, Mexico, and the U.K.

$ mil	12/92	12/93	12/94	% Change				
Sales	**10,015.4**	**10,690.3**	**11,618.5**	**8.7**	P/E Ratio	**20.1**	Price (9/30/95)	**55.00**
Net Income	**1,301.7**	**-845.2**	**1,648.7**	**-295.1**	P/B Ratio	**4.0**	52 Wk Hi-Low	**55.00-39.75**
Book Value	**9,304.3**	**7,608.6**	**8,355.6**	**9.8**	Yield %	**2.9**	Market Cap	**US$33,516mil**

Address **175 E. Houston** **San Antonio, TX 78299**
Tel **210-821-4105** Fax **210-351-2071**
Exchange **NYSE** Ticker **SBC**
Chief Executive **Edward E. Whitacre, Jr.** Chairman **Edward E. Whitacre, Jr.**

Schering-Plough

Industry: **Pharmaceuticals**

Schering-Plough makes pharmaceutical and health-care products, including prescription and over-the-counter drugs, and vision-care, animal-health, and foot-care products. The company's product lines include Drixoral cold and decongestant medications, Gyne-Lotrimin feminine health-care products, Durasoft contact lenses, and Dr. Scholl's foot-care products. Its respiratory, antibiotic, and dermatological prescription medications are sold to managed-health-care organizations and hospitals, wholesale and retail pharmaceutical distributors, and pharmacists and physicians.

$ mil	12/92	12/93	12/94	% Change				
Sales	**4,055.7**	**4,341.3**	**4,657.1**	**7.3**	P/E Ratio	**21.4**	Price (9/30/95)	**51.50**
Net Income	**720.4**	**730.8**	**922.0**	**26.2**	P/B Ratio	**12.2**	52 Wk Hi-Low	**52.50-34.94**
Book Value	**1,596.9**	**1,581.9**	**1,574.4**	**-0.5**	Yield %	**1.9**	Market Cap	**US$19,162mil**

Address **1 Giralda Farms** **Madison, NJ 07940-1000**
Tel **201-822-7000** Fax **201-822-7048**
Exchange **NYSE** Ticker **SGP**
President **Richard J. Kogan** Chairman & CEO **Robert P. Luciano**

Schlumberger

Industry: **Oilfield Equipment & Services - Other**

Schlumberger provides oil companies with well maintenance and analytical/troubleshooting services and products. Its products include MAXIS mobile-computer laboratories, subsurface sensors for use in wells, and coiled tubing. Its maintenance services include mainly oil-platform upgrades and oil-derrick refits to extend oil-field viability. The company also develops remote meter-reading technology for utilities and semiconductor-testing devices. Roughly two thirds of sales come from outside the U.S.

$ mil	12/92	12/93	12/94	% Change				
Sales	**6,331.5**	**6,705.5**	**6,696.8**	**-0.1**	P/E Ratio	**29.5**	Price (9/30/95)	**65.25**
Net Income	**661.6**	**334.8**	**536.1**	**60.1**	P/B Ratio	**3.4**	52 Wk Hi-Low	**69.50-50.13**
Book Value	**4,230.8**	**4,406.3**	**4,583.0**	**4.0**	Yield %	**1.8**	Market Cap	**US$15,783mil**

Address **277 Park Ave.** **New York, NY 10172**
Tel **212-350-9400** Fax **212-350-9564**
Exchange **NYSE** Ticker **SLB**
Chief Executive **Euan Baird** Chairman **Euan Baird**

Charles Schwab

Industry: **Securities Brokers**

Charles Schwab is a holding company that offers brokerage and related investment services. Its main subsidiary, Charles Schwab & Company, serves 44% of the discount-brokerage market in terms of commission revenue. Its Mayer & Schweitzer subsidiary offers trade-execution services to institutional clients and broker-dealers, and the company's Charles Schwab Investment Management division serves as investment advisor for its mutual funds. Through its MutualFund OneSource service, customers trade more than 200 mutual funds without brokerage fees.

$ mil	12/92	12/93	12/94	% Change				
Sales	**749.5**	**965.0**	**1,064.6**	**10.3**	P/E Ratio	**36.4**	Price (9/30/95)	**28.00**
Net Income	**81.2**	**117.7**	**135.3**	**15.0**	P/B Ratio	**10.2**	52 Wk Hi-Low	**28.88-9.42**
Book Value	**258.8**	**379.2**	**467.0**	**23.2**	Yield %	**0.3**	Market Cap	**US$4,875.4mil**

Address **101 Montgomery St.** **San Francisco, CA 94104**
Tel **415-627-7000** Fax **415-627-8538**
Exchange **NYSE** Ticker **SCH**
President **David S. Pottruck** Chairman & CEO **Charles R. Schwab**

Scientific-Atlanta

Industry: **Communications Technology**

Scientific-Atlanta designs electronic signal-generating and -receiving equipment. The company's communication products include earth-station satellite antennas, receivers, transmitters, and cable-television-distribution amplifiers. Other products include signal-measurement and -monitoring equipment used by electronic manufacturers, telecommunication-network operators, and military customers. Scientific-Atlanta also makes spectrum analyzers and other testing devices for telecommunication equipment. The company operates manufacturing facilities in the U.S. and Canada.

$ mil	06/93	06/94	06/95	% Change				
Sales	**730.6**	**811.6**	**1,146.5**	**41.3**	P/E Ratio	**20.3**	Price (9/30/95)	**16.88**
Net Income	**20.0**	**35.0**	**63.5**	**81.5**	P/B Ratio	**2.7**	52 Wk Hi-Low	**24.88-16.88**
Book Value	**352.9**	**395.6**	**474.2**	**19.9**	Yield %	**0.4**	Market Cap	**US$1,294.4mil**

Address **One Technology Pkwy. S.**
Norcross, GA 30092-2967
Tel **770-903-5000**
Fax **770-903-4617**
Exchange **NYSE**
Ticker **SFA**
President & CEO **James F. McDonald**
Chairman **James V. Napier**

Scott Paper

Industry: **Household Products (Non-Durable)**

Scott Paper manufactures consumer and commercial products, most of which are paper goods. The company's consumer products include Cottonelle and Scott bathroom tissue, Job Squad and Viva paper towels, Scotties facial tissues, and Baby Fresh baby wipes. Its commercial products include institutional bathroom and facial tissue, paper towels, napkins, paper placemats, toilet-seat covers, janitorial chemicals, and related dispensers. Scott Paper markets its products in the United States and abroad. In 1995, the company agreed to be acquired by Kimberly-Clark.

$ mil	12/92	12/93	12/94	% Change				
Sales	**4,886.2**	**4,748.9**	**3,581.1**	**-24.6**	P/E Ratio	**34.5**	Price (9/30/95)	**48.50**
Net Income	**167.2**	**-277.0**	**209.8**	**-175.7**	P/B Ratio	**4.2**	52 Wk Hi-Low	**51.13-29.94**
Book Value	**2,017.8**	**1,568.6**	**1,752.4**	**11.7**	Yield %	**0.8**	Market Cap	**US$7,344.5mil**

Address **Scott Plz.**
Philadelphia, PA 19113
Tel **610-522-5000**
Fax **610-522-5665**
Exchange **NYSE**
Ticker **SPP**
Chief Executive **Albert J. Dunlap**
Chairman **Albert J. Dunlap**

Seagate Technology

Industry: **Computers**

Seagate Technology designs rigid magnetic-disk drives and components for computer systems. Its products include heads, discs, printed-circuit boards, motors, substrates, and custom semiconductors, in addition to approximately 100 models of disk drives used in computer equipment, from personal digital assistants to supercomputers. Seagate also develops data-management software products. Its products are marketed to original-equipment manufacturers, systems integrators, and distributors worldwide. The company has manufacturing plants in the United States and abroad.

$ mil	06/93	06/94	06/95	% Change				
Sales	**3,043.6**	**3,500.1**	**4,539.6**	**29.7**	P/E Ratio	**12.0**	Price (9/30/95)	**42.13**
Net Income	**195.4**	**225.1**	**260.1**	**15.5**	P/B Ratio	**2.0**	52 Wk Hi-Low	**48.63-21.88**
Book Value	**1,045.2**	**1,328.4**	**1,541.8**	**16.1**	Yield %	**0.0**	Market Cap	**US$3,032.6mil**

Address **920 Disc Dr.**
Scotts Valley, CA 95066
Tel **408-438-6550**
Fax **408-438-0558**
Exchange **NYSE**
Ticker **SEG**
President & CEO **Alan F. Shugart**
Chairman **Alan F. Shugart**

Sears Roebuck & Co.

Industry: **Retailers - Broadline**

Sears, Roebuck conducts retail, insurance, and shopping-center-management operations. The Sears Merchandise Group subsidiary sells general merchandise and provides services through facilities in the U.S., Canada, and Mexico. This subsidiary includes 800 Sears department stores, 633 Western Auto supply stores, 72 Sears Homelife furniture stores, 80 Sears Paint and Hardware stores, and various smaller stores. The Allstate Insurance Group subsidiary provides property-liability insurance and life insurance. The Homart Development subsidiary owns 13 shopping centers.

$ mil	12/92	12/93	12/94	% Change				
Revenues	**52,344.6**	**50,837.5**	**54,559.0**	**7.3**	P/E Ratio	**10.1**	Price (9/30/95)	**36.88**
Net Income	**-3,932.3**	**2,374.4**	**1,454.0**	**-38.8**	P/B Ratio	**1.2**	52 Wk Hi-Low	**37.13-21.80**
Book Value	**10,773.2**	**11,664.1**	**10,801.0**	**-7.4**	Yield %	**4.3**	Market Cap	**US$14,362mil**

Address **Sears Tower**
Chicago, IL 60684
Tel **312-875-2500**
Fax **312-906-0132**
Exchange **NYSE**
Ticker **S**
Chief Executive **Edward A. Brennan**
Chairman **Edward A. Brennan**

Security Capital Pacific Trust

Industry: **Real-Estate Investment**

Security Capital Pacific Trust acquires, develops, and operates income-producing real estate properties in the southwestern United States. As of March 1995, the company owned, operated, or developed 47,120 multifamily units. Its multifamily properties are primarily garden-style, two-story dwellings that range in size from 57 units to 896 units. Resident leases are generally for six-month to twelve-month terms. Security Capital Pacific Trust owns 13 properties that contain corporate efficiency units to be rented for terms shorter than six months.

$ mil	12/92 R	12/93 R	12/94	% Change				
Sales	**32.8**	**78.4**	**186.1**	**137.3**	P/E Ratio	**28.8**	Price (9/30/95)	**19.00**
Net Income	**9.0**	**25.5**	**46.7**	**83.3**	P/B Ratio	**1.1**	52 Wk Hi-Low	**19.25-16.63**
Book Value	**248.1**	**755.0**	**840.6**	**11.3**	Yield %	**5.3**	Market Cap	**US$1,372.0mil**

Address **7777 Market Center Ave.**
El Paso, TX 79912
Tel **915-877-3900**
Fax **N/A**
Exchange **NYSE**
Ticker **PTR**
Chief Executive **C. Ronald Blankenship**
Chairman **C. Ronald Blankenship**

R=Restated.

Sensormatic Electronics

Industry: **General Industrial & Commercial Services**

Sensormatic Electronics is a fully integrated supplier of electronic security systems to retail and nonretail markets worldwide. The company manufactures, installs, and services electronic article-surveillance and electronic asset-protection systems, including reusable tags and disposable labels used with such systems, closed-circuit-television systems, exception monitoring systems, and access-control systems. These systems are principally used to deter shoplifting or other theft in retail stores and nonretail environments such as commercial and industrial facilities.

$ mil	05/92	06/93 *	06/94	% Change				
Sales	309.9	487.3	656.0	34.6	P/E Ratio	19.8	Price (9/30/95)	23.00
Net Income	31.5	54.1	72.1	33.3	P/B Ratio	2.1	52 Wk Hi-Low	36.38-21.00
Book Value	255.7	489.8	727.7	48.6	Yield %	0.9	Market Cap	US$1,674.4mil

Address **500 N.W. 12th Ave.**
Deerfield Beach, FL 33442
Tel **305-420-2000**
Fax **305-420-2017**
Exchange **NYSE**
Ticker **SRM**
President & CEO **Ronald G. Assaf**
Chairman **Ronald G. Assaf**

*Irregular period due to fiscal year change.

Service Corporation

Industry: **Household Services**

Service Corporation International operates funeral homes and cemeteries. The company also provides capital financing to independent funeral-home and cemetery operators. At the end of fiscal 1994, the company operated 1,471 funeral homes, 220 cemeteries, and 102 crematoriums in the United States, Canada, Australia, and the United Kingdom, as well as other funeral- and cemetery-related businesses, including providing mausoleum casket spaces. The funeral homes provide all professional services relating to funerals. Provident Services is the company's finance subsidiary.

$ mil	12/92	12/93	12/94	% Change				
Sales	772.5	899.2	1,117.2	24.2	P/E Ratio	25.9	Price (9/30/95)	39.13
Net Income	86.5	101.1	131.1	29.6	P/B Ratio	3.1	52 Wk Hi-Low	39.38-24.63
Book Value	683.1	884.5	1,196.6	35.3	Yield %	1.1	Market Cap	US$3,769.2mil

Address **1929 Allen Pkwy.**
Houston, TX 77019
Tel **713-522-5141**
Fax **713-525-5267**
Exchange **NYSE**
Ticker **SRV**
President & COO **L. William Heiligbrodt**
Chairman & CEO **Robert L. Waltrip**

ServiceMaster

Industry: **General Industrial & Commercial Services**

ServiceMaster provides management, consumer, and health services. Management and consumer services are its main business groups. The management division includes custodial and similar services; the consumer division includes services such as pest control. The company provides supportive management services to health-care, educational, and commercial facilities. It provides consumer services to homes and commercial facilities through Terminix International, TruGreen-ChemLawn, American Home Shield, and Service Master Residential/Commercial Services.

$ mil	12/92	12/93	12/94	% Change				
Sales	2,488.9	2,758.9	2,985.2	8.2	P/E Ratio	15.5	Price (9/30/95)	28.00
Net Income	122.1	145.9	139.9	-4.1	P/B Ratio	6.9	52 Wk Hi-Low	28.75-21.88
Book Value	209.7	289.2	307.3	6.3	Yield %	3.3	Market Cap	US$2,193.1mil

Address **One ServiceMaster Way**
Downers Grove, IL 60515
Tel **708-271-1300**
Fax **708-271-2710**
Exchange **NYSE**
Ticker **SVM**
President & CEO **Carlos H. Cantu**
Chairman **C. William Pollard**

Shaw Industries

Industry: **Other Home Furnishings**

Shaw Industries manufactures nylon carpeting. Its product line includes approximately 1,050 styles of nylon carpet for residential and commercial use. Shaw markets its carpeting to retailers, distributors, and commercial users under the Philadelphia, Cabin Crafts, Shaw Commercial Carpets, Stratton, Shawmark, and Evans Black trademarks, among others, in the United States and internationally. Sales in the U.S. account for approximately 98% of the total. The company maintains carpet warehouses, customer-service facilities, and redistribution centers across the U.S.

$ mil	06/93	06/94	12/94 *	% Change				
Sales	2,320.8	2,630.0	2,788.5	6.0	P/E Ratio	16.6	Price (9/30/95)	14.75
Net Income	100.6	129.2	127.0	-1.7	P/B Ratio	2.8	52 Wk Hi-Low	17.13-12.50
Book Value	670.0	710.1	713.0	0.4	Yield %	1.5	Market Cap	US$2,003.4mil

Address **616 E. Walnut Ave.**
Dalton, GA 30720
Tel **706-278-3812**
Fax **706-226-6654**
Exchange **NYSE**
Ticker **SHX**
President & CEO **Robert E. Shaw**
Chairman **J.C. Shaw**

*Irregular period due to fiscal year change.

Shawmut National

Industry: **Banks - Eastern U.S.**

Shawmut National is a bank holding company that operates in Connecticut, New Hampshire, Massachusetts, and Rhode Island. Its bank subsidiaries offer corporate, commercial, and individual banking and trust services through more than 330 branches. The company's Shawmut Mortgage division finances home mortgages through its 10 loan-origination offices. Shawmut National also owns the Shawmut family of mutual funds. Consumer loans account for approximately 48% of the bank's total loan portfolio. Shawmut National has agreed to acquire Fleet Financial Group in 1995.

$ mil	12/92	12/93	12/94	% Change				
Revenues	2,023.9	1,931.4	2,316.4	19.9	P/E Ratio	18.0	Price (9/30/95)	33.63
Net Income	75.2	290.8	237.4	-18.4	P/B Ratio	1.8	52 Wk Hi-Low	34.50-16.38
Book Value	1,482.4	1,803.3	2,197.2	21.8	Yield %	2.4	Market Cap	US$4,328.9mil

Address **777 Main St.**
Hartford, CT 06115
Tel **203-986-2000**
Fax **203-986-7707**
Exchange **NYSE**
Ticker **SNC**
President & COO **Gunnar S. Overstrom**
Chairman & CEO **Joel B. Alvord**

Sherwin-Williams

Industry: **Building Materials**

Sherwin-Williams manufactures, distributes, and sells coatings and related products. The company's paint stores distribute Sherwin-Williams-branded architectural coatings, industrial-maintenance products, and related items. Paint products are marketed under the Kids Room, Renaissance, Dutch Boy, as well as the Sherwin-Williams names. The Consumer Brands division developed Tint-a-Color automated tinting equipment, and Sense-a-Color spectral color analyzer. The Automotive Division develops motor-vehicle finish which is marketed through 139 company-operated branches.

$ mil	12/92	12/93	12/94	% Change				
Sales	**2,747.8**	**2,949.3**	**3,100.1**	**5.1**	P/E Ratio	**16.3**	Price (9/30/95)	**35.00**
Net Income	**62.9**	**165.2**	**186.6**	**12.9**	P/B Ratio	**2.8**	52 Wk Hi-Low	**38.00-30.25**
Book Value	**905.8**	**1,033.2**	**1,053.3**	**1.9**	Yield %	**1.6**	Market Cap	**US$2,984.3mil**

Address **101 Prospect Ave. N.W.**, **Cleveland, OH 44115**
Tel **216-566-2000** Fax **216-566-3266**
Exchange **NYSE** Ticker **SHW**
President & COO **Thomas A. Commes**
Chairman & CEO **John G. Breen**

Shoney's

Industry: **Restaurants**

Shoney's operates 1,878 restaurants in the U. S. and Canada. The restaurants include Shoney's, Captain D's, Lee's Famous Recipe, Pargo's, BarbWire's, and Fifth Quarter. Mike Rose Foods, a subsidiary, is a manufacturer of salad dressings and other condiments. The 922 Shoney's restaurants are full-service establishments located in 34 states. Captain D's are 643 quick-service restaurants in 24 states. The 285 Lee's Famous restaurants operate in 17 states and Canada. The 15 Pargo's, 10 Fifth Quarter, and three BarbWire's restaurants are in seven states.

$ mil	10/92	10/93	10/94	% Change				
Sales	**1,030.2**	**1,107.4**	**1,126.5**	**1.7**	P/E Ratio	**6.9**	Price (9/30/95)	**11.00**
Net Income	**-26.6**	**58.0**	**66.0**	**13.8**	P/B Ratio	**NMF**	52 Wk Hi-Low	**15.38-9.38**
Book Value	**-290.5**	**-210.0**	**-136.8**	**-34.9**	Yield %	**0.0**	Market Cap	**US$456.1mil**

Address **1727 Elm Hill Pike**, **Nashville, TN 37210**
Tel **615-391-5201** Fax **615-391-9424**
Exchange **NYSE** Ticker **SHN**
President **Charles E. Porter**
Chairman & CEO **Taylor H. Henry**

Sigma-Aldrich

Industry: **Specialty Chemicals**

Sigma-Aldrich manufactures chemical and metal products and their related components. The company's chemical-product line, including biochemicals, radiolabeled chemicals, diagnostic reagents, and related items, are sold to clinical- and university research-laboratory, health-care, and manufacturing customers. It produces metal components, including struts, cable trays, pipe supports, and supports, for telecommunication and cabling systems. Sigma-Aldrich's Supelco subsidiary manufactures chromatography products, and its Circle AW Products produces electrical goods.

$ mil	12/92	12/93	12/94	% Change				
Sales	**654.4**	**739.4**	**851.2**	**15.1**	P/E Ratio	**21.9**	Price (9/30/95)	**48.50**
Net Income	**95.5**	**96.3**	**110.3**	**14.6**	P/B Ratio	**3.5**	52 Wk Hi-Low	**51.25-31.00**
Book Value	**511.8**	**591.1**	**699.5**	**18.3**	Yield %	**0.7**	Market Cap	**US$2,417.8mil**

Address **3050 Spruce St.**, **St. Louis, MO 63103**
Tel **314-771-5765** Fax **314-534-2674**
Exchange **NASDA** Ticker **SIAL**
President & COO **David R. Harvey**
Chairman & CEO **Tom Cori**

Signet Banking

Industry: **Banks - Southern U.S.**

Signet Banking is a bank holding company with banking, insurance, and related operations in Virginia, Maryland, and Washington, D.C. Its Signet Bank subsidiary manages more than 240 branches in the United States and offers international banking through its Bahamas and Cayman Islands offices. Signet Bank's services include consumer credit cards, student loans, trusts, brokerage, mortgage lending, and insurance. The company's capital-markets division trades U.S. and foreign securities, manages individual portfolios, and provides venture-capital funding for new businesses.

$ mil	12/92	12/93	12/94	% Change				
Revenues	**1,048.2**	**1,164.8**	**1,371.6**	**17.8**	P/E Ratio	**10.1**	Price (9/30/95)	**26.25**
Net Income	**109.2**	**174.4**	**149.8**	**-14.1**	P/B Ratio	**1.4**	52 Wk Hi-Low	**27.88-13.58**
Book Value	**826.6**	**964.7**	**1,111.5**	**15.2**	Yield %	**3.8**	Market Cap	**US$1,540.4mil**

Address **7 N. 8th St.**, **Richmond, VA 23219**
Tel **804-747-2000** Fax **804-771-7599**
Exchange **NYSE** Ticker **SBK**
President & COO **Malcolm S. McDonald**
Chairman & CEO **Robert M. Freeman**

Silicon Graphics

Industry: **Computers**

Silicon Graphics designs, manufactures, and supports work-station and server systems, using three-dimensional graphics, digital-media and multiprocessing technologies. The work-station products are available in desktop and deskside configurations, and are used primarily to simulate, analyze, and display 3-D graphics. Customers include large manufacturing companies, government contractors, consumer-product companies, and research laboratories. The company's MIPS Technologies subsidiary develops computer architecture and microprocessor design.

$ mil	06/92	06/93	06/94	% Change				
Sales	**866.6**	**1,091.2**	**1,481.6**	**35.8**	P/E Ratio	**34.0**	Price (9/30/95)	**34.38**
Net Income	**-118.4**	**95.2**	**140.7**	**47.8**	P/B Ratio	**5.2**	52 Wk Hi-Low	**44.88-24.88**
Book Value	**479.5**	**633.7**	**921.3**	**45.4**	Yield %	**0.0**	Market Cap	**US$5,451.0mil**

Address **2011 N. Shoreline Blvd.**, **Mountain View, CA 94043**
Tel **415-390-2607** Fax **415-390-6220**
Exchange **NYSE** Ticker **SGI**
President & COO **Thomas Jermoluk**
Chairman & CEO **Edward R. McCracken**

SLMA

Industry: **Financial Services - Diversified**

Student Loan Marketing Association (SLMA) is an intermediary in the U.S. education-credit market. The company was chartered by Congress to provide liquidity for originators of student loans made under federally sponsored student-loan programs and to support educational institutions' credit needs. The company purchases and services insured student loans and makes advance loans to certain financial and educational institutions and public agencies that offer education-related loans. SLMA also finances academic physical-plant and equipment facilities through loans and bonds.

$ mil	12/92	12/93	12/94	% Change				
Revenues	**2,614.9**	**2,417.5**	**2,851.6**	**18.0**	P/E Ratio	**11.0**	Price (9/30/95)	**54.00**
Net Income	**393.9**	**430.1**	**402.8**	**-6.3**	P/B Ratio	**2.7**	52 Wk Hi-Low	**55.38-31.38**
Book Value	**1,220.1**	**1,280.1**	**1,471.2**	**14.9**	Yield %	**2.6**	Market Cap	**US$3,936.6mil**

Address **1050 Thomas Jefferson St. N.W.**
Washington, DC 20007
Tel **202-333-8000**
Fax **202-337-1207**
Exchange **NYSE**
Ticker **SLM**
President & CEO **Lawrence A. Hough**
Chairman **William Arceneaux**

Snap-On Tools

Industry: **Other Auto Parts**

Snap-On manufactures and distributes 14,000 hand tools, power tools, tool-storage products, and diagnostic and shop equipment for use by mechanics and other professional users. Subsidiaries include Sun Electric, which manufactures and distributes high-end diagnostic test and service shop equipment; J.H. Williams, a manufacturer of industrial quality hand tools; and A.T.I. Tools, a producer of tools and equipment for aerospace and industrial applications. The company conducts operations in the U.S., Canada, Mexico, Brazil, Taiwan, Japan, Australia, and Europe.

$ mil	12/92	12/93	12/94	% Change				
Sales	**983.8**	**1,132.0**	**1,194.3**	**5.5**	P/E Ratio	**16.5**	Price (9/30/95)	**38.00**
Net Income	**66.0**	**85.8**	**98.3**	**14.6**	P/B Ratio	**2.1**	52 Wk Hi-Low	**41.88-30.75**
Book Value	**664.7**	**701.7**	**766.4**	**9.2**	Yield %	**2.8**	Market Cap	**US$1,532.4mil**

Address **2801 - 80th St.**
Kenosha, WI 53141
Tel **414-656-5200**
Fax **414-656-5577**
Exchange **NYSE**
Ticker **SNA**
President & CEO **Robert A. Cornog**
Chairman **Robert A. Cornog**

Solectron

Industry: **Electrical Components & Equipment**

Solectron provides customized manufacturing services. These include engineering, materials management, printed-circuit-board assembly, flexible-circuit assembly, systems integration, software manufacturing, testing, packaging, and product remanufacturing. Solectron markets its expertise in these areas to original-equipment manufacturers in the electronics industry. The company operates manufacturing facilities in California, North Carolina, Washington, France, Scotland, and Malaysia. Operations in the United States account for approximately 65% of sales.

$ mil	08/92	08/93	08/94	% Change				
Sales	**406.9**	**836.3**	**1,456.8**	**74.2**	P/E Ratio	**29.9**	Price (9/30/95)	**39.50**
Net Income	**14.5**	**30.6**	**55.6**	**81.5**	P/B Ratio	**4.9**	52 Wk Hi-Low	**40.13-22.50**
Book Value	**104.3**	**261.0**	**330.8**	**26.7**	Yield %	**0.0**	Market Cap	**US$1,650.7mil**

Address **777 Gibralter Dr.**
Milpitas, CA 95035
Tel **408-957-8500**
Fax **408-956-6075**
Exchange **NYSE**
Ticker **SLR**
President & CEO **Koichi Nishimura**
Chairman **Charles A. Dickinson**

Sonat

Industry: **Pipelines**

Sonat, an energy holding company, operates natural-gas and oil businesses. Through subsidiaries, including Citrus and Southern Natural Gas, the company purchases, transports, and sells natural gas, primarily in the southern United States. Other company subsidiaries operate 48 onshore oil and natural-gas wells in the U.S., and 23 offshore rigs, primarily in the Gulf of Mexico, the North Sea, and the Middle East. Business operations in the U.S. account for about 95% of revenues. The company's exploration and production business provides about 37% of operating income.

$ mil	12/92	12/93	12/94	% Change				
Sales	**1,484.4**	**1,741.1**	**1,773.9**	**1.9**	P/E Ratio	**19.8**	Price (9/30/95)	**32.00**
Net Income	**212.4**	**261.2**	**141.4**	**-45.9**	P/B Ratio	**2.0**	52 Wk Hi-Low	**33.00-26.38**
Book Value	**1,172.3**	**1,363.2**	**1,391.9**	**2.1**	Yield %	**3.4**	Market Cap	**US$2,764.1mil**

Address **AmSouth-Sonat Tower**
Birmingham, AL 35203
Tel **205-325-3800**
Fax **205-325-7490**
Exchange **NYSE**
Ticker **SNT**
President & CEO **Ronald L. Kuehn**
Chairman **Ronald L. Kuehn**

Sonoco Products

Industry: **Containers & Packaging**

Sonoco Products manufactures packaging products for the food, textile, electronics, and pharmaceutical industries. The company's converted-products division makes fiber and plastic tubes, cores, cones, and drums; composite canisters; caulking cartridges; and pressure-sensitive labels. Its paper division makes paperboard, largely for the company's packaging-manufacturing operations. The company also makes high-density plastic films used in agricultural applications, plastic bags used in retail stores, and metal and wood spools used by the wire and cable industry.

$ mil	12/92	12/93	12/94	% Change				
Sales	**1,838.0**	**1,947.2**	**2,300.1**	**18.1**	P/E Ratio	**19.8**	Price (9/30/95)	**27.75**
Net Income	**43.4**	**118.8**	**129.8**	**9.2**	P/B Ratio	**2.9**	52 Wk Hi-Low	**28.38-19.05**
Book Value	**561.9**	**788.4**	**832.2**	**5.6**	Yield %	**2.0**	Market Cap	**US$2,530.9mil**

Address **N. Second St.**
Hartsville, SC 29550
Tel **803-383-7000**
Fax **803-339-6078**
Exchange **NASDA**
Ticker **SONO**
Chief Executive **Charles W. Coker**
Chairman **Charles W. Coker**

Industry: **Electrical Utilities - Southern U.S.**

Southern

Southern generates and distributes electricity and provides related services. The company owns five electric utilities in Alabama, Georgia, Florida, and Mississippi. It owns and operates 33 hydroelectric, 31 fossil-fuel, and three nuclear-power stations. About 75% of the company's electricity is generated at coal-fired stations. Residential customers account for 25% of electricity revenues. Its subsidiaries provide consulting services to consumers and other utility companies. Southern agreed to acquire South Western Electricity, a British utility company, in 1995.

$ mil	12/92	12/93	12/94	% Change				
Sales	8,073.0	8,489.0	8,297.3	-2.3	P/E Ratio	15.5	Price (9/30/95)	23.63
Net Income	953.0	1,002.0	988.8	-1.3	P/B Ratio	1.9	52 Wk Hi-Low	23.63-18.38
Book Value	7,234.0	7,684.0	8,186.0	6.5	Yield %	5.0	Market Cap	US$15,729mil

Address **64 Perimeter Ctr. E.**
Atlanta, GA 30346
Tel **404-393-0650**
Fax **404-668-2674**
Exchange **NYSE**
Ticker **SO**
President & CEO **A. William Dahlberg**
Chairman **A. William Dahlberg**

Industry: **Banks - Southern U.S.**

SouthTrust

SouthTrust is a bank holding company with 40 banks and several bank-related affiliates in the southeastern United States. The banks, which include SouthTrust Bank of Alabama, operate 420 offices in a seven-state area. SouthTrust's other subsidiaries offer investment management, mortgages, insurance, discount-brokerage, leasing, and estate and trust services. Most of the company's subsidiary banks offer VISA and MasterCard credit cards. Commercial banking is SouthTrust's predominant business, and its subsidiary banks contribute most of the company's revenues and assets.

$ mil	12/92	12/93	12/94	% Change				
Revenues	964.8	1,102.3	1,293.4	17.3	P/E Ratio	11.7	Price (9/30/95)	25.13
Net Income	114.2	150.5	173.0	15.0	P/B Ratio	1.8	52 Wk Hi-Low	27.13-17.13
Book Value	860.4	1,051.8	1,135.3	7.9	Yield %	2.7	Market Cap	US$2,097.0mil

Address **420 N. 20th St.**
Birmingham, AL 35203
Tel **205-254-5509**
Fax **205-254-5404**
Exchange **NASDA**
Ticker **SOTR**
President & COO **Roy W. Gilbert, Jr.**
Chairman & CEO **Wallace D. Malone, Jr.**

Industry: **Airlines**

Southwest Airlines

Southwest Airlines is a commercial airline that provides single-class passenger and freight transportation to 45 airports in 44 cities in the midwestern, southwestern, and western United States. The airline specializes in short-haul routes, and targets business commuters. The company's most-traveled routes are intrastate flights in California and Texas. Its fleet consists of about 200 Boeing 737s. Its Morris Air subsidiary provides chartered-travel services. Passenger transportation generates almost all revenues, accounting for more than 96% of the total.

$ mil	12/92	12/93	12/94	% Change				
Sales	1,685.2	2,296.7	2,591.9	12.9	P/E Ratio	20.7	Price (9/30/95)	25.25
Net Income	103.6	169.5	179.3	5.8	P/B Ratio	2.9	52 Wk Hi-Low	29.75-15.75
Book Value	854.3	1,054.0	1,238.7	17.5	Yield %	0.2	Market Cap	US$3,625.4mil

Address **2702 Love Field Dr.**
Dallas, TX 75235
Tel **214-904-4000**
Fax **214-904-5015**
Exchange **NYSE**
Ticker **LUV**
President & CEO **Herbert D. Kelleher**
Chairman **Herbert D. Kelleher**

Industry: **Long Distance Telephone Systems**

Sprint

Sprint provides telecommunication and information services. An independent telecommunication company, it provides local-exchange and long-distance telephone service in the United States, with approximately eight million long-distance customers. Its local operating companies provide telecommunication services to more than six million customers and publish 270 directories in 19 states. Through its Sprint Cellular subsidiary, the company also provides cellular-telephone, paging, calling-card, and other wireless-communication services to approximately 665,000 customers.

$ mil	12/92	12/93	12/94	% Change				
Sales	9,230.4	11,367.8	12,661.8	11.4	P/E Ratio	13.7	Price (9/30/95)	35.00
Net Income	457.1	54.9	890.7	NMF	P/B Ratio	2.7	52 Wk Hi-Low	39.00-26.50
Book Value	2,816.8	3,918.3	4,561.9	16.4	Yield %	2.9	Market Cap	US$12,202mil

Address **2330 Shawnee Mission Pkwy.**
Westwood, KS 66205
Tel **913-624-3000**
Fax **913-624-3088**
Exchange **NYSE**
Ticker **FON**
Chief Executive **William T. Esrey**
Chairman **William T. Esrey**

Industry: **Advanced Medical Technology**

St. Jude Medical

St. Jude Medical manufactures cardiovascular medical devices, including the world's most widely used replacement heart valve. The company's products include tissue heart valves, intra-aortic balloon-pump systems and catheters, centrifugal-pump systems, and other products related to cardiovascular surgery. St. Jude Medical markets these products through a direct-sales force and representatives to more than 1,500 open-heart-surgery centers worldwide. Business within the United States and Canada accounts for approximately 70% of the company's total net sales.

$ mil	12/92	12/93	12/94	% Change				
Sales	239.5	252.6	359.6	42.4	P/E Ratio	37.4	Price (9/30/95)	63.25
Net Income	101.7	109.6	79.2	-27.7	P/B Ratio	5.3	52 Wk Hi-Low	63.25-34.00
Book Value	429.0	484.2	552.2	14.0	Yield %	0.5	Market Cap	US$2,949.5mil

Address **One Lillehei Plz.**
St. Paul, MN 55117
Tel **612-483-2000**
Fax **612-490-4333**
Exchange **NASDA**
Ticker **STJM**
President & CEO **Ronald A. Matricaria**
Chairman **Ronald A. Matricaria**

St. Paul

Industry: **Insurance - Property & Casualty**

St. Paul is a financial-services firm that provides insurance underwriting, brokerage services, and investment products. It underwrites medical-service, business, workers' compensation, and property- and professional-liability insurance; fidelity bonds; and directors' and officers' liability policies for depository institutions. St. Paul also owns an insurance-brokerage company and John Nuveen, an investment-banking and asset-management organization that specializes in municipal financing. Insurance underwriting makes up approximately 88% of the company's revenues.

$ mil	12/92	12/93	12/94	% Change				
Revenues	4,498.7	4,460.2	4,701.3	5.4	P/E Ratio	11.4	Price (9/30/95)	58.38
Net Income	-156.0	427.6	442.8	3.6	P/B Ratio	1.8	52 Wk Hi-Low	58.38-39.50
Book Value	2,201.9	3,003.8	2,737.5	-8.9	Yield %	2.6	Market Cap	US$4,935.0mil

Address	**385 Washington St.**	Tel	**612-221-7911**	Exchange	**NYSE**	President & CEO	**Douglas W. Leatherdale**
	St. Paul, MN 55102	Fax	**612-221-7318**	Ticker	**SPC**	Chairman	**Douglas W. Leatherdale**

Standard-Pacific

Industry: **Home Construction**

Standard Pacific builds single-family housing, provides related services, and manufactures office furniture. The company builds midprice houses in California and Texas, mostly in California, at an average selling price of approximately $296,000. It arranges financing for these houses through its savings and loan subsidiary, Standard Pacific Savings. Another subsidiary, Panel Concepts, manufactures and markets office furniture throughout the U.S. Standard Pacific's residential-building business accounts for more than 89% of the company's total revenues.

$ mil	12/92	12/93	12/94	% Change				
Sales	304.7	293.8	420.5	43.1	P/E Ratio	36.8	Price (9/30/95)	7.00
Net Income	4.5	2.7	5.9	118.1	P/B Ratio	0.7	52 Wk Hi-Low	8.13-5.13
Book Value	291.2	290.4	291.1	0.3	Yield %	1.7	Market Cap	US$214.4mil

Address	**1565 W. MacArthur Blvd.**	Tel	**714-668-4300**	Exchange	**NYSE**	President	**Ronald R. Foell**
	Costa Mesa, CA 92626	Fax	**714-546-2013**	Ticker	**SPF**	Chairman & CEO	**Arthur E. Svendsen**

Stanley Works

Industry: **Industrial - Diversified**

Stanley Works produces tools and hardware for home-improvement, consumer, industrial, and professional use. Its tools division consists of consumer, industrial, and engineered tools. Consumer tools include hand tools such as hammers and saws. Industrial tools include products, such as air tools and tool boxes, under the Stanley-Proto and Mac brand names. Engineered tools include air tools and Stanley-Bostitch fasteners. Hardware consists of products such as hinges; specialty hardware consists of residential door systems, power-operated doors, and other related items.

$ mil	12/92	12/93	12/94	% Change				
Sales	2,217.7	2,273.1	2,510.9	10.5	P/E Ratio	15.5	Price (9/30/95)	43.38
Net Income	98.1	84.1	125.3	49.0	P/B Ratio	2.6	52 Wk Hi-Low	45.75-35.38
Book Value	696.3	680.9	744.2	9.3	Yield %	3.2	Market Cap	US$1,924.1mil

Address	**1000 Stanley Dr.**	Tel	**203-225-5111**	Exchange	**NYSE**	President & COO	**R. Alan Hunter**
	New Britain, CT 06053	Fax	**203-827-3895**	Ticker	**SWK**	Chairman & CEO	**Richard H. Ayers**

Star Banc

Industry: **Banks - Central U.S.**

Star Banc, a holding company with banks in Ohio, Kentucky, and Indiana, also provides insurance and consumer-finance services. Its three banks offers commercial-banking and trust services through more than 200 branches, providing consumer, commercial, and trust financial products and investment services. The company also owns and manages the Star mutual fund family, and markets other mutual funds and annuities. Star Banc's Miami Valley Insurance subsidiary issues credit, life, accident, and health insurance, and its Star Banc Finance subsidiary originates consumer loans.

$ mil	12/92	12/93	12/94	% Change				
Revenues	641.9	631.1	686.7	8.8	P/E Ratio	13.8	Price (9/30/95)	53.50
Net Income	76.1	100.3	116.6	16.3	P/B Ratio	2.2	52 Wk Hi-Low	53.88-33.88
Book Value	602.3	675.8	718.2	6.3	Yield %	2.6	Market Cap	US$1,596.5mil

Address	**425 Walnut St.**	Tel	**513-632-4000**	Exchange	**NYSE**	President & CEO	**Jerry A. Grundhofer**
	Cincinnati, OH 45202	Fax	**513-632-5511**	Ticker	**STB**	Chairman	**Jerry A. Grundhofer**

State Street Boston

Industry: **Banks - Eastern U.S.**

State Street Boston is a bank holding company. Its State Street Bank and Trust subsidiary provides commercial-banking services and manages financial assets. It offers custodian, accounting, and investment-management services to corporations, individuals, governmental units, and nonprofit organizations. State Street Boston owns and manages the Seven Seas family of mutual funds. It is also the leading mutual-fund custodian in the U.S, servicing approximately 36% of all registered mutual funds. In addition, the company creates investment vehicles for institutions.

$ mil	12/92	12/93	12/94	% Change				
Revenues	1,417.3	1,532.3	1,885.8	23.1	P/E Ratio	14.8	Price (9/30/95)	40.00
Net Income	160.4	179.8	207.4	15.4	P/B Ratio	2.5	52 Wk Hi-Low	41.13-28.38
Book Value	953.1	1,105.0	1,231.3	11.4	Yield %	1.5	Market Cap	US$3,306.4mil

Address	**225 Franklin St.**	Tel	**617-786-3000**	Exchange	**NASDA**	Chief Executive	**Marshall N. Carter**
	Boston, MA 02110	Fax	**617-654-4006**	Ticker	**STBK**	Chairman	**Marshall N. Carter**

Industry: **Containers & Packaging**

Stone Container

Stone Container manufactures forest products for sale to commercial customers in the United States and abroad. The company's principal products are paperboard and paper packaging, including containerboard and corrugated containers, kraft-paper bags, and folding cartons, which it sells primarily to food, beverage, and tobacco producers and retailers. It also manufactures newsprint, publishing and computer papers, market pulp, dimensional lumber, plywood, and veneer. Stone operates about 200 production facilities and 335,000 acres of timberland.

$ mil	12/92	12/93	12/94	% Change				
Sales	**5,520.7**	**5,059.6**	**5,748.7**	**13.6**	P/E Ratio	**NMF**	Price (9/30/95)	**19.00**
Net Income	**-170.5**	**-358.7**	**-208.6**	**-41.8**	P/B Ratio	**2.7**	52 Wk Hi-Low	**24.38-15.00**
Book Value	**1,203.8**	**607.1**	**648.1**	**6.8**	Yield %	**0.0**	Market Cap	**US$1,819.2mil**

Address **150 N. Michigan Ave.**
Chicago, IL 60601
Tel **312-346-6600**
Fax **312-580-4919**
Exchange **NYSE**
Ticker **STO**
President & CEO **Roger W. Stone**
Chairman **Roger W. Stone**

Industry: **Heavy Construction**

Stone & Webster

Stone & Webster provides engineering, construction, and consulting services for petrochemical, refining, power, and other projects. The company also owns and operates cold-storage warehousing facilities in Georgia. Stone & Webster owns natural-gas- and oil-production facilities in Texas, Louisiana, and Canada; explores for natural gas and oil in the U.S. and Canada; owns compressor stations; and owns and operates natural-gas gathering and transporting systems. The company has mineral interests and is developing a corporate office and business center in Tampa, Florida.

$ mil	12/92	12/93	12/94	% Change				
Sales	**265.8**	**262.1**	**818.2**	**212.2**	P/E Ratio	**NMF**	Price (9/30/95)	**37.75**
Net Income	**12.8**	**2.0**	**-7.8**	**-490.5**	P/B Ratio	**1.5**	52 Wk Hi-Low	**39.25-27.63**
Book Value	**403.1**	**425.4**	**375.3**	**-11.8**	Yield %	**1.6**	Market Cap	**US$544.2mil**

Address **250 W. 34th St.**
New York, NY 10119
Tel **212-290-7500**
Fax **212-290-7507**
Exchange **NYSE**
Ticker **SW**
President & CEO **Bruce C. Coles**
Chairman **William F. Allen, Jr.**

Industry: **Computers**

Storage Technology

Storage Technology manufactures information-storage and -retrieval subsystems. These subsystems are designed to operate with high-performance and midrange computer systems, as well as computer networks. The company has three product lines: serial-access storage subsystems, random-access storage subsystems, and midrange computer products. It markets its products to end users, value-added resellers, and original-equipment manufacturers of computer systems in North America, Europe, Asia, Australia, and South America; sales in the U.S. account for 61% of revenues.

$ mil	12/92	12/93	12/94	% Change				
Sales	**1,521.5**	**1,404.8**	**1,625.0**	**15.7**	P/E Ratio	**37.1**	Price (9/30/95)	**24.50**
Net Income	**15.5**	**-77.8**	**41.4**	**-153.2**	P/B Ratio	**1.0**	52 Wk Hi-Low	**32.63-18.00**
Book Value	**918.5**	**1,017.3**	**1,074.6**	**5.6**	Yield %	**0.0**	Market Cap	**US$1,286.8mil**

Address **2270 S. 88th St.**
Louisville, CO 80028
Tel **303-673-5151**
Fax **303-673-8876**
Exchange **NYSE**
Ticker **STK**
President & CEO **Ryal R. Poppa**
Chairman **Ryal R. Poppa**

Industry: **Footwear**

Stride Rite

Stride Rite sells children's footwear, including dress and recreational shoes, boots, and sneakers under the Stride Rite trademark. The company also markets sneakers and casual footwear for adults and children under the Keds and PRO-Keds trademarks; casual footwear for women under the Grasshoppers label; and outdoor recreational and dress footwear under the Sperry Top-Sider trademark. The company operates 136 Stride Rite Bootery stores, 103 leased children's shoe departments in department stores, one retail store for Keds products and 11 manufacturers' outlet stores.

$ mil	11/92	11/93	11/94	% Change				
Sales	**585.9**	**582.9**	**523.9**	**-10.1**	P/E Ratio	**28.4**	Price (9/30/95)	**11.38**
Net Income	**61.5**	**58.3**	**19.8**	**-66.0**	P/B Ratio	**1.9**	52 Wk Hi-Low	**15.13-10.00**
Book Value	**271.5**	**302.5**	**292.5**	**-3.3**	Yield %	**3.3**	Market Cap	**US$563.5mil**

Address **Five Cambridge Ctr.**
Cambridge, MA 02142
Tel **617-491-8800**
Fax **617-864-1372**
Exchange **NYSE**
Ticker **SRR**
President & CEO **Robert C. Siegel**
Chairman **Robert C. Siegel**

Industry: **Advanced Medical Technology**

Stryker

Stryker manufactures specialty surgical and medical products. The company's products include endoscopic systems such as medical video cameras, light sources, and manual instruments; orthopedic and spinal implants; powered surgical instruments; and patient-handling equipment. The firm markets its products to physicians and hospitals worldwide. It also operates about 135 physical-therapy centers. Business operations in the United States account for approximately 76% of net sales. Stryker operates manufacturing facilities in the U.S., France, and the Netherlands.

$ mil	12/92	12/93	12/94	% Change				
Sales	**477.1**	**557.3**	**681.9**	**22.4**	P/E Ratio	**31.1**	Price (9/30/95)	**46.63**
Net Income	**47.7**	**60.2**	**72.4**	**20.3**	P/B Ratio	**6.3**	52 Wk Hi-Low	**48.00-33.13**
Book Value	**232.3**	**288.4**	**358.3**	**24.2**	Yield %	**0.2**	Market Cap	**US$2,258.6mil**

Address **2725 Fairfield Rd.**
Kalamazoo, MI 49002
Tel **616-385-2600**
Fax **616-385-1062**
Exchange **NASDA**
Ticker **STRY**
President & CEO **John W. Brown**
Chairman **John W. Brown**

Sun Company

Industry: **Oil - Integrated Majors**

Sun is a major integrated petroleum company. It owns, on average, a 15% interest in about 3,400 wells, primarily in Canada, and holds net reserves of 78 million barrels of oil and 689 billion cubic feet of natural gas. The company owns refineries, where it produces motor fuels, lubricants, and asphalt. It supplies 4,615 Sunoco and APlus service stations, 663 of which are company-owned or -leased. Radnor, a subsidiary, develops commercial real estate, which it holds as investments, and residential real estate, which it offers for sale, all in the eastern U.S.

$ mil	12/92	12/93	12/94	% Change				
Sales	**10,445.0**	**9,180.0**	**9,818.0**	**6.9**	P/E Ratio	**30.7**	Price (9/30/95)	**25.75**
Net Income	**-559.0**	**288.0**	**90.0**	**-68.8**	P/B Ratio	**1.5**	52 Wk Hi-Low	**32.88-25.75**
Book Value	**1,896.0**	**1,984.0**	**1,863.0**	**-6.1**	Yield %	**7.0**	Market Cap	**US$1,945.2mil**

Address **10 Penn Ctr., 1801 Market St.**
Philadelphia, PA 19103
Tel **215-977-3000**
Fax **215-977-3409**
Exchange **NYSE**
Ticker **SUN**
President & CEO **Robert H. Campbell**
Chairman **Robert H. Campbell**

Sun Microsystems

Industry: **Computers**

Sun Microsystems manufactures computer equipment and software. It markets its products under a number of brand names, including SparcStation, Solaris, SunReady, DeskSet OnLine, Wabi, NEWSprint, Sunergy, Pro Works, and Catalyst. The company supplies network servers, work stations, peripheral equipment, operating software, accessories, and spare parts in the United States and internationally through direct-sales representatives, company-operated sales and service offices, and independent distributors. Sun Microsystems' primary customers are business and technical users.

$ mil	06/93	06/94	06/95	% Change				
Sales	**4,308.6**	**4,689.9**	**5,901.9**	**25.8**	P/E Ratio	**17.5**	Price (9/30/95)	**63.00**
Net Income	**156.7**	**195.8**	**355.8**	**81.7**	P/B Ratio	**2.9**	52 Wk Hi-Low	**64.06-27.56**
Book Value	**1,642.8**	**1,628.3**	**2,122.6**	**30.4**	Yield %	**0.0**	Market Cap	**US$6,021.9mil**

Address **2550 Garcia Ave.**
Mountain View, CA 94043
Tel **415-960-1300**
Fax **415-336-0646**
Exchange **NASDA**
Ticker **SUNW**
President & CEO **Scott G. McNealy**
Chairman **Scott G. McNealy**

SunAmerica

Industry: **Insurance - Life & Health**

SunAmerica provides insurance, investment, and trust services to individuals and institutions. Its Sun Life of America and First SunAmerica subsidiaries offer fixed and variable annuities, as well as guaranteed investment contracts. In addition, the company's SunAmerica Asset Management subsidiary manages mutual funds, pension and profit-sharing plans, and individual and corporate trust accounts. SunAmerica owns two broker/dealers that provide brokerage services. It also owns a subsidiary that administers Keogh, 401(k), individual retirement, and pension-plan accounts.

$ mil	09/92 R	09/93	09/94	% Change				
Revenues	**875.8**	**888.7**	**908.9**	**2.3**	P/E Ratio	**22.7**	Price (9/30/95)	**62.88**
Net Income	**76.8**	**127.0**	**131.8**	**3.8**	P/B Ratio	**2.3**	52 Wk Hi-Low	**62.88-42.75**
Book Value	**730.1**	**1,110.0**	**961.1**	**-13.4**	Yield %	**0.6**	Market Cap	**US$2,277.6mil**

Address **1 SunAmerica Ctr., Century City**
Los Angeles, CA 90067
Tel **310-772-6000**
Fax **N/A**
Exchange **NYSE**
Ticker **SAI**
President & CEO **Eli Broad**
Chairman **Eli Broad**

R=Restated.

Sunbeam-Oster

Industry: **Other Home Furnishings**

Sunbeam manufactures consumer products. The company makes a variety of outdoor, household, and specialty products. Its outdoor barbecue grills, aluminum lawn and patio furniture, and accessories are sold primarily under the Sunbeam brand name. The company's household products range from warming blankets, bath scales, and blood-pressure monitors to hair-care products and small kitchen appliances. Sunbeam also produces hair clippers and trimmers, pet-grooming accessories, and a line of clocks, timers, and thermometers. The company markets its products worldwide.

$ mil	01/93	02/94 *	01/95 *	% Change				
Sales	**967.2**	**1,065.9**	**1,198.4**	**12.4**	P/E Ratio	**11.4**	Price (9/30/95)	**14.88**
Net Income	**48.3**	**88.8**	**107.0**	**20.5**	P/B Ratio	**2.2**	52 Wk Hi-Low	**23.50-13.38**
Book Value	**524.0**	**437.3**	**554.6**	**26.8**	Yield %	**0.3**	Market Cap	**US$1,209.4mil**

Address **200 E. Las Olas Blvd.**
Fort Lauderdale, FL 33301
Tel **305-767-2100**
Fax **N/A**
Exchange **NYSE**
Ticker **SOC**
Chief Executive **Roger W. Schipke**
Chairman **Roger W. Schipke**

*Irregular period due to fiscal year change.

Sundstrand

Industry: **Aerospace & Defense**

Sundstrand produces aerospace and industrial equipment. Its aerospace products include power-generating systems, flight-control components, turbine engines, space power systems, and flight-data and cockpit-voice recorders. The company's industrial products include pumps, compressors, and scientific instruments. The company markets these products to government agencies, aircraft manufacturers, and users in the construction, mining, agribusiness, transportation, and chemical industries in the United States and overseas. Business abroad accounts for 36% of the company's sales.

$ mil	12/92	12/93	12/94	% Change				
Sales	**1,672.7**	**1,383.1**	**1,372.7**	**-0.8**	P/E Ratio	**22.2**	Price (9/30/95)	**64.75**
Net Income	**-121.7**	**140.7**	**95.6**	**-32.1**	P/B Ratio	**4.1**	52 Wk Hi-Low	**69.88-41.75**
Book Value	**530.0**	**512.2**	**493.8**	**-3.6**	Yield %	**1.9**	Market Cap	**US$2,027.9mil**

Address **4949 Harrison Ave.**
Rockford, IL 61125
Tel **815-226-6000**
Fax **815-226-2699**
Exchange **NYSE**
Ticker **SNS**
Chief Executive **Don R. O'Hare**
Chairman **Don R. O'Hare**

SunTrust Banks

Industry: **Banks - Southern U.S.**

SunTrust Banks is a banking and financial-services holding company that operates in the southeastern U.S. The company has four principal subsidiaries: SunBanks (15 bank divisions), Trust Company of Georgia (10), and Third National (7). The subsidiaries operate 658 branches in Alabama, Florida, Georgia, Tennessee, and offer deposit and credit services, trust and investment management, investment banking, corporate-finance services, mortgage banking, discount brokerage, and credit-related insurance services. It also owns the STI Classic mutual-fund family.

$ mil	12/92	12/93	12/94	% Change				
Revenues	**3,110.3**	**3,088.8**	**3,255.0**	**5.4**	P/E Ratio	**15.1**	Price (9/30/95)	**66.13**
Net Income	**413.3**	**473.7**	**522.7**	**10.4**	P/B Ratio	**2.2**	52 Wk Hi-Low	**67.50-46.50**
Book Value	**2,703.5**	**3,609.6**	**3,453.3**	**-4.3**	Yield %	**2.0**	Market Cap	**US$7,552.5mil**

Address **25 Park Pl. N.E.**
Atlanta, GA 30303
Tel **404-588-7711**
Fax **404-581-1664**
Exchange **NYSE**
Ticker **STI**
President **L. Phillip Humann**
Chairman & CEO **James B. Williams**

SuperValu

Industry: **Food Retailers & Wholesalers**

Supervalu is a food wholesaler and retailer. The company sells food and nonfood products at wholesale to approximately 4,600 stores in 48 states. The company also operates about 300 retail-food supermarkets, discount-food warehouses, combination wholesale and retail stores, limited-assortment and other stores, mainly under the Cub Foods, Shop 'n Save, Save-A-Lot, Scott's, Laneco, Hornbacher's, Twin Valu, Max Club, Sweet Life Foods, and Ultra IGA names. It also has a 46% interest in ShopKo which operates more than 100 department stores in 15 states.

$ mil	02/93	02/94	02/95	% Change				
Sales	**12,568.0**	**15,936.9**	**16,563.8**	**3.9**	P/E Ratio	**48.2**	Price (9/30/95)	**29.38**
Net Income	**164.5**	**185.3**	**43.3**	**-76.6**	P/B Ratio	**1.7**	52 Wk Hi-Low	**31.00-22.13**
Book Value	**1,134.8**	**1,275.5**	**1,193.2**	**-6.5**	Yield %	**3.2**	Market Cap	**US$2,004.1mil**

Address **11840 Valley View Rd.**
Eden Prairie, MN 55344
Tel **612-828-4000**
Fax **612-828-8998**
Exchange **NYSE**
Ticker **SVU**
President & CEO **Michael W. Wright**
Chairman **Michael W. Wright**

Sybase

Industry: **Software**

Sybase develops and supports client/server-based software products and services for on-line, enterprise-wide applications. The company's client/server products consist of relational database-management system-servers, interoperability-software-application development tools, and system-management products. These products include the SQL Server database engine, Secure SQL Server, and Replication Server, among other system management tools. Primary-market segments are financial services, manufacturing, telecommunications, defense, and government agencies.

$ mil	12/92	12/93	12/94	% Change				
Sales	**264.6**	**426.7**	**693.8**	**62.6**	P/E Ratio	**23.3**	Price (9/30/95)	**32.13**
Net Income	**23.7**	**44.1**	**75.2**	**70.5**	P/B Ratio	**4.9**	52 Wk Hi-Low	**54.50-20.13**
Book Value	**118.3**	**190.6**	**337.2**	**76.9**	Yield %	**0.0**	Market Cap	**US$2,281.1mil**

Address **6475 Christie Ave.**
Emeryville, CA 94608
Tel **510-922-3500**
Fax **510-658-9441**
Exchange **NASDA**
Ticker **SYBS**
President & CEO **Mark B. Hoffman**
Chairman **Mark B. Hoffman**

Symbol Technologies

Industry: **Industrial Technology**

Symbol Technologies manufactures and services portable bar-code-scanning products and data-collection systems. The company makes several types bar-code-scanning equipment that can scan bar codes from distances of up to 50 feet. Symbol Technologies also makes data-collection systems that collect data at remote sites and transmit information between locations. The data-collection systems can be connected to printers, bar-code readers, and other communications devices. The company also provides support services. Foreign sales account for about 36% of the company's total sales.

$ mil	12/92	12/93	12/94	% Change				
Sales	**344.9**	**360.0**	**465.3**	**29.3**	P/E Ratio	**24.7**	Price (9/30/95)	**33.13**
Net Income	**-16.3**	**12.5**	**35.0**	**181.0**	P/B Ratio	**2.7**	52 Wk Hi-Low	**40.38-24.63**
Book Value	**245.0**	**258.8**	**316.2**	**22.2**	Yield %	**0.0**	Market Cap	**US$861.2mil**

Address **116 Wilbur Pl.**
Bohemia, NY 11716
Tel **516-563-2400**
Fax **N/A**
Exchange **NYSE**
Ticker **SBL**
President **Jan H. Lindelow**
Chairman & CEO **Jerome Swartz**

Synovus Financial

Industry: **Banks - Southern U.S.**

Synovus Financial is a financial-services holding company. It operates 33 commercial-bank subsidiaries in Georgia, Florida, and Alabama. The company's banks offer consumer, business, and mortgage loans; individual retirement and Keogh accounts; automated-teller services; and checking, savings, and money-market accounts. The company owns an 81% stake in TSYS, which provides data-processing services for bankcard and private-label cards, including card production, international and domestic electronic clearing, cardholder-statement preparation, and customer service.

$ mil	12/92	12/93	12/94	% Change				
Revenues	**595.1**	**615.4**	**693.4**	**12.7**	P/E Ratio	**20.3**	Price (9/30/95)	**26.13**
Net Income	**61.2**	**71.1**	**86.5**	**21.6**	P/B Ratio	**3.5**	52 Wk Hi-Low	**27.13-19.38**
Book Value	**416.0**	**476.3**	**508.1**	**6.7**	Yield %	**1.7**	Market Cap	**US$2,004.6mil**

Address **One Arsenal Pl., 901 Front Ave.**
Columbus, GA 31901
Tel **706-649-2387**
Fax **N/A**
Exchange **NYSE**
Ticker **SNV**
President **Stephen L. Burts, Jr.**
Chairman & CEO **James H. Blanchard**

Sysco

Industry: **Restaurants**

Sysco distributes food and related products to the food-service industry. The company's traditional food-service customers include restaurants, hospitals, schools, hotels, and industrial caterers. Chain-restaurant customers include regional pizza and French-style bakery operations, and national hamburger chain operations. The company's SYGMA Network subsidiary specializes in customized service to chain restaurants. Restaurants account for roughly 60% of the company's total sales. The company distributes both nationally branded merchandise, as well as private brands.

$ mil	06/92	06/93	06/94	% Change				
Sales	**8,892.8**	**10,021.5**	**10,942.5**	**9.2**	P/E Ratio	**23.0**	Price (9/30/95)	**27.25**
Net Income	**172.2**	**201.8**	**216.6**	**7.3**	P/B Ratio	**4.0**	52 Wk Hi-Low	**31.25-23.63**
Book Value	**1,056.8**	**1,137.2**	**1,240.9**	**9.1**	Yield %	**1.2**	Market Cap	**US$4,969.1mil**

Address **1390 Enclave Pkwy.**
Houston, TX 77077
Tel **713-584-1390**
Fax **713-584-2524**
Exchange **NYSE**
Ticker **SYY**
President & COO **Bill M. Lindig**
Chairman & CEO **John F. Woodhouse**

Tambrands

Industry: **Cosmetics & Personal Care**

Tambrands manufactures feminine-hygiene products. It is the leading producer of tampons in the world, marketing its products in more than 150 countries. The company's primary product, Tampax tampons, has approximately a 50% share of the U.S. tampon market. Tambrands produces other feminine-hygiene items, including Tampax Compak, Tampax Satin Touch, and Tampax Tampets. The company operates approximately 10 manufacturing facilities in North America, Europe, Russia, and South Africa. Tambrands also holds an 80% interest in a joint venture in China.

$ mil	12/92	12/93	12/94	% Change				
Sales	**684.1**	**611.5**	**644.5**	**5.4**	P/E Ratio	**6.8**	Price (9/30/95)	**16.50**
Net Income	**121.4**	**63.5**	**89.7**	**41.3**	P/B Ratio	**7.4**	52 Wk Hi-Low	**21.38-16.00**
Book Value	**168.2**	**115.0**	**82.0**	**-28.7**	Yield %	**10.3**	Market Cap	**US$2,041.9mil**

Address **777 Westchester Ave.**
White Plains, NY 10604
Tel **914-696-6000**
Fax **914-696-6161**
Exchange **NYSE**
Ticker **TMB**
President & CEO **Edward T. Fogarty**
Chairman **Howard B. Wentz, Jr.**

Tandem Computers

Industry: **Computers**

Tandem Computers designs computer hardware and software systems and networks. Its principal products are on-line transaction-processing systems and related accessories. The company markets its products and services to customers in the banking, communication, service, retail-sales, and manufacturing industries in the United States and internationally. Many of the world's stock exchanges, more than 400 retailers, and the majority of automated-teller machines are connected to Tandem's systems.

$ mil	09/92	09/93	09/94	% Change				
Sales	**2,036.9**	**2,031.0**	**2,108.0**	**3.8**	P/E Ratio	**8.2**	Price (9/30/95)	**12.25**
Net Income	**-41.2**	**-517.7**	**170.2**	**-132.9**	P/B Ratio	**1.5**	52 Wk Hi-Low	**19.75-12.00**
Book Value	**1,236.9**	**736.8**	**938.8**	**27.4**	Yield %	**0.0**	Market Cap	**US$1,424.5mil**

Address **19333 Vallco Parkway**
Cupertino, CA 95014
Tel **408-285-6000**
Fax **408-285-4545**
Exchange **NYSE**
Ticker **TDM**
President & CEO **James G. Treybig**
Chairman **Thomas J. Perkins**

Tandy

Industry: **Other Specialty Retailers**

Tandy is a retailer of consumer electronics. The company's retail operations include the Radio Shack, McDuff, The Edge in Electronics, Computer City, and Incredible Universe store chains. As of the end of 1994, Radio Shack had 4,600 company-owned stores throughout the United States. These stores carry electronic parts and accessories, personal computers, and other products. The company also owns 375 McDuff, and The Edge in Electronics stores, as well as 69 Computer City outlets and nine Incredible Universe electronics stores.

$ mil	06/92	12/93 *	12/94	% Change				
Revenues	**4,680.2**	**4,102.6**	**4,943.7**	**20.5**	P/E Ratio	**20.9**	Price (9/30/95)	**60.75**
Net Income	**183.8**	**96.8**	**224.3**	**131.7**	P/B Ratio	**1.9**	52 Wk Hi-Low	**63.88-41.00**
Book Value	**1,930.7**	**1,950.8**	**1,850.2**	**-5.2**	Yield %	**1.0**	Market Cap	**US$3,960.7mil**

Address **1800 One Tandy Ctr.**
Fort Worth, TX 76102
Tel **817-390-3700**
Fax **817-390-2774**
Exchange **NYSE**
Ticker **TAN**
President & CEO **John V. Roach**
Chairman **John V. Roach**

*Irregular period due to fiscal year change.

Tecumseh Products

Industry: **Electrical Components & Equipment**

Tecumseh Products manufactures refrigeration equipment, lawn-machinery components, and service-industry machinery. The company's principal product lines include compressors for refrigerators, freezers, and air-conditioning units; gasoline engines, transmissions, transaxles, and differentials for lawn equipment and recreational vehicles; and pumps for industrial, commercial, marine, and agricultural applications. In addition, its Little Giant Pump subsidiary makes small submersible pumps. Approximately 30% of the company's revenues are derived from overseas markets.

$ mil	12/92	12/93	12/94	% Change				
Sales	**1,258.5**	**1,314.2**	**1,533.4**	**16.7**	P/E Ratio	**8.4**	Price (9/30/95)	**46.25**
Net Income	**-42.7**	**81.4**	**120.3**	**47.8**	P/B Ratio	**1.3**	52 Wk Hi-Low	**51.00-39.50**
Book Value	**639.8**	**686.8**	**785.5**	**14.4**	Yield %	**2.9**	Market Cap	**US$1,012.0mil**

Address **100 E. Patterson St.**
Tecumseh, MI 49286
Tel **517-423-8411**
Fax **517-423-8526**
Exchange **NASDA**
Ticker **TECU**
President & CEO **Todd W. Herrick**
Chairman **Kenneth G. Herrick**

Tektronix

Industry: **Diversified Technology**

Tektronix manufactures electronic equipment used in testing and measurement, computer graphics, and television systems. The company's products range from digital and analog oscilloscopes to television-waveform monitors. Its test and measurement products generate approximately 54% of sales. Tektronix's subsidiaries include the Grass Valley Group, which produces studio-production equipment and transmission systems, and Dubner Computer Systems, which manufactures television-production equipment. Tektronix markets its products in the United States and internationally.

$ mil	05/93	05/94	05/95	% Change				
Sales	**1,302.4**	**1,318.0**	**1,471.8**	**11.7**	P/E Ratio	**22.4**	Price (9/30/95)	**59.00**
Net Income	**-55.1**	**60.7**	**81.3**	**33.9**	P/B Ratio	**3.1**	52 Wk Hi-Low	**59.00-31.75**
Book Value	**434.9**	**469.5**	**602.7**	**28.4**	Yield %	**1.0**	Market Cap	**US$1,969.5mil**

Address **26600 S.W. Parkway Ave.**
Wilsonville, OR 97070
Tel **503-627-7111**
Fax **503-627-5502**
Exchange **NYSE**
Ticker **TEK**
President & CEO **Jerome J. Meyer**
Chairman **Jerome J. Meyer**

Tele-Communications

Industry: **Broadcasting**

Tele-Communications (TCI) operates the nation's largest cable-television system and provides cable-programming services. The company serves approximately 8.5 million cable-television subscribers. It has ownership interests in Discovery Channel cable service and Turner Broadcasting, among others. TCI has entered into a joint venture with Time Warner Entertainment and Sega of America to form the Sega Channel, which would deliver video games to subscribers. The company also owns subsidiaries that operate cable-television systems in Europe and Asia.

$ mil	12/92	12/93	12/94	% Change				
Sales	**3,574.0**	**4,153.0**	**4,936.0**	**18.9**	P/E Ratio	**NMF**	Price (9/30/95)	**17.50**
Net Income	**-34.0**	**-7.0**	**55.0**	**-885.7**	P/B Ratio	**3.4**	52 Wk Hi-Low	**20.00-12.79**
Book Value	**1,596.0**	**2,130.0**	**2,971.0**	**39.5**	Yield %	**0.0**	Market Cap	**US$11,424mil**

Address **5619 DTC Pkwy.**
Englewood, CO 80111-3000
Tel **303-267-5500**
Fax **303-779-1228**
Exchange **NASDA**
Ticker **TCOM**
President & CEO **John C. Malone**
Chairman **Robert Magness**

Teledyne

Industry: **Conglomerates**

Teledyne is a diversified manufacturer of goods for the aviation, specialty-metals, and consumer markets. The company produces radar and other internal systems and aircraft components for military helicopters, missiles, and rocket systems. Its specialty-metals goods are used in aerospace applications, and its industrial products include engines and machine tools. Teledyne also makes Water-Pik brand oral-hygiene and shower products and components for automotive air-bag safety devices. The company markets its products in the United States and internationally.

$ mil	12/92	12/93	12/94	% Change				
Sales	**2,887.6**	**2,491.7**	**2,391.2**	**-4.0**	P/E Ratio	**NMF**	Price (9/30/95)	**27.13**
Net Income	**33.2**	**-116.5**	**-8.4**	**-92.8**	P/B Ratio	**5.5**	52 Wk Hi-Low	**27.25-15.75**
Book Value	**441.1**	**280.5**	**273.0**	**-2.7**	Yield %	**0.0**	Market Cap	**US$1,510.5mil**

Address **2049 Century Park E.**
Los Angeles, CA 90067
Tel **310-277-3311**
Fax **310-551-4369**
Exchange **NYSE**
Ticker **TDY**
President & COO **Donald B. Rice**
Chairman & CEO **William P. Rutledge**

Temple-Inland

Industry: **Containers & Packaging**

Temple-Inland manufactures paper, packaging, and building products, and provides banking and financial services. The company produces containerboard and corrugated boxes; bleached paperboard for plates, cups, file folders, and greeting cards; and lumber, plywood, gypsum wallboard, and fiberboard. Its Guaranty Federal Bank subsidiary has 123 branches in Texas; another subsidiary, Temple-Inland Mortgage, processes mortgages. Temple-Inland's financial services account for approximately 21% of revenues, and the manufacture of forestry products generates the balance.

$ mil	12/92	12/93	12/94	% Change				
Sales	**2,075.4**	**2,100.7**	**2,306.0**	**9.8**	P/E Ratio	**22.7**	Price (9/30/95)	**53.25**
Net Income	**146.9**	**117.4**	**131.4**	**11.9**	P/B Ratio	**1.7**	52 Wk Hi-Low	**56.13-41.50**
Book Value	**1,632.6**	**1,700.2**	**1,783.0**	**4.9**	Yield %	**1.9**	Market Cap	**US$2,986.6mil**

Address **303 S. Temple Dr.**
Diboll, TX 75941
Tel **409-829-1313**
Fax **409-829-3333**
Exchange **NYSE**
Ticker **TIN**
Chief Executive **Clifford J. Grum**
Chairman **Clifford J. Grum**

Tenet Healthcare

Industry: **Health Care Providers**

Tenet Healthcare operates health-care facilities. The company wholly or partially owns 72 general hospitals, with more than 15,400 beds. Most of its hospitals are in the southern United States and California. The company also owns seven long-term care facilities, five physical rehabilitation hospitals, five psychiatric facilities, and ancillary facilities that are connected with its general hospitals. Medical Ambulatory Care, a subsidiary, operates 36 kidney-dialysis centers. The company also owns 42% of Westminster Health Care Holdings in the United Kingdom.

$ mil	05/93	05/94	05/95	% Change				
Sales	**3,762.0**	**2,967.0**	**3,318.0**	**11.8**	P/E Ratio	**18.7**	Price (9/30/95)	**17.38**
Net Income	**160.0**	**-425.0**	**165.0**	**-138.8**	P/B Ratio	**1.7**	52 Wk Hi-Low	**18.00-12.63**
Book Value	**1,752.0**	**1,320.0**	**1,986.0**	**50.5**	Yield %	**0.0**	Market Cap	**US$3,475.0mil**

Address **2700 Colorado Ave.**
Santa Monica, CA 90404
Tel **310-998-8000**
Fax **310-998-8329**
Exchange **NYSE**
Ticker **NME**
President **Michael H. Focht, Sr.**
Chairman & CEO **Jeffrey C. Barbakow**

Tenneco

Industry: **Industrial - Diversified**

Tenneco transports natural gas and manufactures chemicals and industrial, agricultural and automotive products. Its Tenneco Gas subsidiary maintains a 16,300-mile natural-gas transmission system. Tenneco makes automotive exhaust-system parts, brake products, farm and construction machinery. The company also builds ships. Tenneco's natural-gas transmission business generates about 20% of revenues, and sales of farm and construction equipment account for 32%. The company purchased Mobil's plastic division, whose products include Hefty plastic bags, in 1995.

$ mil	12/92	12/93	12/94	% Change				
Sales	**13,139.0**	**13,255.0**	**12,174.0**	**-8.2**	P/E Ratio	**21.0**	Price (9/30/95)	**46.25**
Net Income	**-1,323.0**	**426.0**	**408.0**	**-4.2**	P/B Ratio	**2.8**	52 Wk Hi-Low	**50.00-37.38**
Book Value	**1,521.0**	**2,764.0**	**3,047.0**	**10.2**	Yield %	**3.5**	Market Cap	**US$8,362.6mil**

Address **1010 Milam, Houston, TX 77002** | Tel **713-757-2131** | Fax **713-757-1639** | Exchange **NYSE** | Ticker **TGT** | President & CEO **Dana G. Mead** | Chairman **Dana G. Mead**

Texaco

Industry: **Oil - Integrated Majors**

Texaco is a petroleum exploration and production company. The company owns an average 41% interest in about 59,000 oil and natural-gas wells and holds net reserves of approximately six trillion cubic feet of natural gas and 2.5 billion barrels of oil. The company has ownership interest in more than 32,000 miles of pipeline for the transportation of its petroleum products. It markets its products through Texaco and Star Mart retail outlets worldwide. In addition, the company owns half of Caltex, a petroleum refinery and retail business, in a joint venture with Chevron.

$ mil	12/92	12/93	12/94	% Change				
Sales	**36,812.0**	**33,245.0**	**32,540.0**	**-2.1**	P/E Ratio	**20.4**	Price (9/30/95)	**64.63**
Net Income	**712.0**	**1,068.0**	**910.0**	**-14.8**	P/B Ratio	**1.7**	52 Wk Hi-Low	**69.13-59.63**
Book Value	**9,973.0**	**10,279.0**	**9,749.0**	**-5.2**	Yield %	**5.0**	Market Cap	**US$16,785mil**

Address **2000 Westchester Ave., White Plains, NY 10650** | Tel **914-253-4000** | Fax **914-253-7246** | Exchange **NYSE** | Ticker **TX** | Chief Executive **Alfred C. DeCrane, Jr.** | Chairman **Alfred C. DeCrane, Jr.**

Texas Instruments

Industry: **Diversified Technology**

Texas Instruments (TI) manufactures computers and electronic equipment. It produces semiconductors, defense-electronics systems for missiles and radar, application-software-development tools, computers and peripheral products, electrical controls, and consumer-electronic products, such as calculators. TI markets its products to original-equipment manufacturers, governmental agencies, and retailers worldwide. Contracts with the U.S. government account for approximately 10% of the company's net revenues. TI operates manufacturing facilities in 10 countries.

$ mil	12/92	12/93	12/94	% Change				
Sales	**7,440.0**	**8,523.0**	**10,315.0**	**21.0**	P/E Ratio	**22.0**	Price (9/30/95)	**79.88**
Net Income	**247.0**	**472.0**	**691.0**	**46.4**	P/B Ratio	**4.9**	52 Wk Hi-Low	**82.38-31.94**
Book Value	**1,947.0**	**2,315.0**	**3,039.0**	**31.3**	Yield %	**0.6**	Market Cap	**US$15,009mil**

Address **13500 N. Central Expressway, Dallas, TX 75265** | Tel **214-995-3773** | Fax **214-995-4360** | Exchange **NYSE** | Ticker **TXN** | President & CEO **Jerry R. Junkins** | Chairman **Jerry R. Junkins**

Texas Utilities

Industry: **Electrical Utilities - Southern U.S.**

Texas Utilities is a holding company. Its principal subsidiary is Texas Utilities Electric, which serves more than two million customers in Texas. Residential customers account for about 36% of energy sales; commercial and industrial users 53%. The company operates 23 fossil-fuel generating stations, the source for roughly 80% of its power; and one nuclear-power station that produces another 11%. The remainder is purchased from third parties. Texas Utilities' other subsidiaries provide support services for the utility, including the production and storage of natural gas.

$ mil	12/92	12/93	12/94	% Change				
Sales	**4,907.9**	**5,434.5**	**5,663.5**	**4.2**	P/E Ratio	**14.5**	Price (9/30/95)	**34.88**
Net Income	**700.1**	**368.7**	**542.8**	**47.2**	P/B Ratio	**1.2**	52 Wk Hi-Low	**36.13-30.50**
Book Value	**6,590.5**	**6,571.0**	**6,490.1**	**-1.2**	Yield %	**8.8**	Market Cap	**US$7,876.2mil**

Address **Energy Plz., 1601 Bryan St., Dallas, TX 75201** | Tel **214-812-4600** | Fax **214-812-3040** | Exchange **NYSE** | Ticker **TXU** | President **Erle Nye** | Chairman & CEO **J.S. Farrington**

Textron

Industry: **Conglomerates**

Textron provides aerospace technology, commercial products, and financial services. The company's Bell Helicopter subsidiary manufactures commercial and military helicopters, business jets, and aircraft engines and control systems. Textron produces automotive components, fasteners, and powered equipment. Its financial services include consumer loans, commercial finance, and disability insurance. The company markets its products and services in the United States and internationally. Contracts with the U.S. Government account for approximately 17% of the company's revenues.

$ mil	12/92	12/93	12/94	% Change				
Sales	**5,616.7**	**6,271.3**	**6,678.0**	**6.5**	P/E Ratio	**14.2**	Price (9/30/95)	**68.25**
Net Income	**-355.4**	**379.1**	**433.0**	**14.2**	P/B Ratio	**2.0**	52 Wk Hi-Low	**69.63-46.50**
Book Value	**2,487.8**	**2,780.2**	**2,882.0**	**3.7**	Yield %	**2.1**	Market Cap	**US$5,807.2mil**

Address **40 Westminster St., Providence, RI 02903** | Tel **401-421-2800** | Fax **401-421-2878** | Exchange **NYSE** | Ticker **TXT** | President **Lewis B. Campbell** | Chairman & CEO **James F. Hardymon**

Thomas & Betts

Industry: **Electrical Components & Equipment**

Thomas & Betts manufactures electrical and electronic components, connectors, and systems. The company's products include electrical grounding systems, electricians' supplies, utility poles, lighting products, fiberoptic and printed-circuit-board connectors, and ceramic-chip capacitors. It markets these products under the Perfect-Line, Sta-Kon, Nevada Western, Reznor, and Hazlux brand names, among others, to users in the industrial- and commercial-construction, telecommunication, automotive, electronics, and computer industries worldwide.

$ mil	12/92	12/93	12/94	% Change				
Sales	**1,051.1**	**1,075.9**	**1,076.2**	**0.0**	P/E Ratio	**18.4**	Price (9/30/95)	**64.63**
Net Income	**50.9**	**56.5**	**67.8**	**20.0**	P/B Ratio	**2.3**	52 Wk Hi-Low	**71.25-62.63**
Book Value	**463.1**	**480.8**	**553.0**	**15.0**	Yield %	**3.5**	Market Cap	**US$1,271.1mil**

Address **1555 Lynnfield Rd.**
Memphis, TN 38119
Tel **901-682-7766**
Fax **901-680-5435**
Exchange **NYSE**
Ticker **TNB**
President & COO **Clyde R. Moore**
Chairman & CEO **T. Kevin Dunnigan**

3Com

Industry: **Computers**

3Com is an independent global data-networking company, which concentrates on multivendor interoperability. Its networking solutions include router, hubs, remote-access servers, switches, and adapters for Ethernet, Token Ring, and fiber distributed-data-interface networks. The company's products and systems are distributed and serviced in the United States and internationally through 3Com and its partners, mainly systems integrators, value-added resellers, national resellers and dealers, and distributors. In 1995, the company agreed to acquire Chipcom.

$ mil	05/93	05/94	05/95	% Change				
Sales	**617.2**	**827.0**	**1,295.3**	**56.6**	P/E Ratio	**52.6**	Price (9/30/95)	**45.50**
Net Income	**38.6**	**-28.7**	**125.7**	**-538.1**	P/B Ratio	**13.5**	52 Wk Hi-Low	**48.13-22.88**
Book Value	**258.3**	**280.8**	**464.9**	**65.6**	Yield %	**0.0**	Market Cap	**US$6,300.0mil**

Address **5400 Bayfront Plz.**
Santa Clara, CA 95052-8145
Tel **408-764-5000**
Fax **408-764-5001**
Exchange **NASDA**
Ticker **COMS**
President & CEO **Eric A. Benhamou**
Chairman **Eric A. Benhamou**

3M

Industry: **Diversified Technology**

Minnesota Mining and Manufacturing (3M) manufactures adhesive, coating, imaging, electronic, and health-care products. The company's industrial and consumer division develops adhesive tapes, sealants, and lubricants; sandpaper and other abrasives; and automotive gaskets and moldings. Its information, imaging, and electronic sector produces Scotch audio and video tapes; packaging and insulation materials; and printing supplies. Its life-sciences division manufactures personal-safety equipment, pharmaceuticals, transdermal drug-delivery systems, and medical equipment.

$ mil	12/92	12/93	12/94	% Change				
Sales	**13,883.0**	**14,020.0**	**15,079.0**	**7.6**	P/E Ratio	**18.1**	Price (9/30/95)	**56.50**
Net Income	**1,233.0**	**1,263.0**	**1,322.0**	**4.7**	P/B Ratio	**3.5**	52 Wk Hi-Low	**61.75-50.63**
Book Value	**6,599.0**	**6,512.0**	**6,734.0**	**3.4**	Yield %	**3.1**	Market Cap	**US$23,742mil**

Address **3M Ctr.**
St. Paul, MN 55144-1000
Tel **612-733-1110**
Fax **612-733-9973**
Exchange **NYSE**
Ticker **MMM**
Chief Executive **L.D. DeSimone**
Chairman **L.D. DeSimone**

Tidewater

Industry: **Marine Transportation**

Tidewater provides support services and equipment to energy industries. Its Tidewater Marine division provides support services to the international offshore petroleum industry. Roughly 35% of the company's marine vessels operate in the U.S. Gulf of Mexico. The company's Tidewater Compression division principally provides natural gas and air-compression equipment and services, primarily to the oil and gas and petrochemical industries in the United States. Its Quality Shipyards subsidiary operates two shipyards in Louisiana that build, repair, modify, and dry-dock vessels.

$ mil	03/93	03/94	03/95	% Change				
Sales	**475.5**	**522.1**	**538.8**	**3.2**	P/E Ratio	**35.2**	Price (9/30/95)	**28.13**
Net Income	**24.3**	**24.2**	**42.6**	**76.2**	P/B Ratio	**2.6**	52 Wk Hi-Low	**29.38-16.75**
Book Value	**547.7**	**557.0**	**580.2**	**4.2**	Yield %	**1.4**	Market Cap	**US$1,498.2mil**

Address **Tidewater Pl., 1440 Canal St.**
New Orleans, LA 70112
Tel **504-568-1010**
Fax **504-566-4582**
Exchange **NYSE**
Ticker **TDW**
President **William C. O'Malley**
Chairman **William C. O'Malley**

Time Warner

Industry: **Entertainment**

Time Warner is a media and entertainment conglomerate. Its publishing operations include large-circulation magazines such as Time, Life, and Sports Illustrated, and book publishing. Time Warner produces and licenses compact discs, cassette tapes, and music videos. Its entertainment division also produces and distributes motion pictures, television shows, and video recordings, and owns the HBO and Cinemax cable-television networks. The company markets its publications and programs in the U.S. and overseas. Time Warner agreed to acquire Turner Broadcasting System in 1995.

$ mil	12/92	12/93	12/94	% Change				
Sales	**13,070.0**	**6,581.0**	**7,396.0**	**12.4**	P/E Ratio	**NMF**	Price (9/30/95)	**39.75**
Net Income	**86.0**	**-221.0**	**-91.0**	**-58.8**	P/B Ratio	**13.1**	52 Wk Hi-Low	**45.38-32.25**
Book Value	**8,167.0**	**1,370.0**	**1,148.0**	**-16.2**	Yield %	**0.9**	Market Cap	**US$15,350mil**

Address **75 Rockefeller Plz.**
New York, NY 10019
Tel **212-484-8000**
Fax **212-484-8734**
Exchange **NYSE**
Ticker **TWX**
President **Richard D. Parsons**
Chairman & CEO **Gerald M. Levin**

Times Mirror

Industry: **Publishing**

Times Mirror publishes newspapers, magazines, and other materials and operates cable-television companies. The company's newspapers include The Los Angeles Times, The New York Newsday, and The Baltimore Sun, and have a combined daily circulation of about 2.5 million readers. Its other publishing operations include professional books, journals, and other materials for the legal, health-care, scientific, and aviation fields. Its magazines include Field & Stream, Popular Science, and Outdoor Life, which have a combined monthly circulation of more than 8 million readers.

$ mil	12/92	12/93	12/94	% Change				
Sales	**3,702.0**	**3,714.2**	**3,357.5**	**-9.6**	P/E Ratio	**21.3**	Price (9/30/95)	**28.75**
Net Income	**-66.6**	**317.2**	**173.1**	**-45.4**	P/B Ratio	**1.9**	52 Wk Hi-Low	**32.63-17.25**
Book Value	**1,700.6**	**1,899.3**	**1,957.0**	**3.0**	Yield %	**3.8**	Market Cap	**US$3,228.9mil**

Address **Times Mirror Sq.**
Los Angeles, CA 90053
Tel **213-237-3700**
Fax **212-237-5493**
Exchange **NYSE**
Ticker **TMC**
President & CEO **Robert F. Erburu**
Chairman **Robert F. Erburu**

Timken

Industry: **Other Auto Parts**

Timken manufactures roller bearings and specialty-steel products. The company provides bearings, including antifriction, super-precision-ball, jet-engine, tapered-roller, and custom-designed bearings, for use in automobiles, aircraft, missile-guidance systems, trucks, computer peripherals, medical instruments, and railroad, agricultural, and industrial equipment. In addition, Timken produces vacuum-processed, intermediate- and low-grade, and tool-steel alloys primarily as material for its bearing-manufacturing operations and for sale to other bearing manufacturers.

$ mil	12/92	12/93	12/94	% Change				
Sales	**1,642.3**	**1,708.8**	**1,930.4**	**13.0**	P/E Ratio	**19.3**	Price (9/30/95)	**42.63**
Net Income	**4.5**	**-271.9**	**68.5**	**-125.2**	P/B Ratio	**1.8**	52 Wk Hi-Low	**48.00-31.63**
Book Value	**985.1**	**685.3**	**732.9**	**6.9**	Yield %	**2.3**	Market Cap	**US$1,326.0mil**

Address **1835 Dueber Ave. S.W.**
Canton, OH 44706
Tel **216-438-3000**
Fax **216-438-3452**
Exchange **NYSE**
Ticker **TKR**
President & CEO **Joseph F. Toot, Jr.**
Chairman **W.R. Timken, Jr.**

TJ International

Industry: **Building Materials**

TJ International manufactures engineered-lumber building products, which substitute for traditional sawn structural lumber obtained from old growth trees. Its products include roof and floor joists and beams, columns and posts, and headers. The company also manufactures and markets a broad line of wood and vinyl windows and patio doors. TJ International sells its building products to lumberyards throughout North America. The company has also developed TJXpert, a software program that converts blueprints into a framing plan that incorporates the company's engineered lumber.

$ mil	01/93	12/93	12/94	% Change				
Sales	**400.5**	**551.2**	**618.9**	**12.3**	P/E Ratio	**41.3**	Price (9/30/95)	**19.00**
Net Income	**7.3**	**12.5**	**8.8**	**-29.6**	P/B Ratio	**1.3**	52 Wk Hi-Low	**21.25-15.88**
Book Value	**128.9**	**233.4**	**240.6**	**3.1**	Yield %	**1.2**	Market Cap	**US$321.7mil**

Address **200 E. Mallard Dr.**
Boise, ID 83706
Tel **208-364-3300**
Fax **N/A**
Exchange **NASDA**
Ticker **TJCO**
President & CEO **Thomas H. Denig**
Chairman **Harold E. Thomas**

TJX Companies

Industry: **Apparel Retailers**

TJX is the largest off-price specialty apparel retailer in North America based on sales. The company operates 551 T. J. Maxx stores and 490 Hit or Miss stores in the U.S., as well as 37 Winners Apparel Ltd. stores in Canada, and the proposed T. J. Maxx stores in the U.K. The company also operates the Chadwick's of Boston mail-order catalog of women's apparel. T. J. Maxx stores sell brand-name apparel and accessories, and are located in suburban shopping centers. Hit or Miss sells current-season brand-name women's apparel. Winners is an off-price family-apparel retailer.

$ mil	01/93	01/94	01/95	% Change				
Revenues	**3,261.2**	**3,626.6**	**3,842.8**	**6.0**	P/E Ratio	**11.5**	Price (9/30/95)	**11.88**
Net Income	**102.8**	**124.4**	**82.6**	**-33.6**	P/B Ratio	**1.4**	52 Wk Hi-Low	**21.00-11.50**
Book Value	**505.2**	**590.9**	**607.0**	**2.7**	Yield %	**4.7**	Market Cap	**US$859.8mil**

Address **770 Cochituate Rd.**
Framingham, MA 01701
Tel **508-390-1000**
Fax **508-390-2091**
Exchange **NYSE**
Ticker **TJX**
President & CEO **Bernard Cammarata**
Chairman **Sumner L. Feldberg**

TNT Freightways

Industry: **Trucking**

TNT Freightways is a holding company for six regional trucking companies and three logistics companies. The regional trucking companies specialize in time-sensitive less-than-truckload (less than 10,000 pound) shipments. These subsidiaries include Holland, which operates in the midwest United States; Red Star, which operates in the East Coast; Bestway, which operates in the Southwest and West Coast; Reddaway, which operates in the West Coast; Dugan, which serves the central U.S.; and United, which serves the Rocky Mountain and Pacific Northwest regions.

$ mil	12/92	12/93	12/94	% Change				
Sales	**800.0**	**898.9**	**1,016.5**	**13.1**	P/E Ratio	**13.0**	Price (9/30/95)	**18.88**
Net Income	**6.9**	**27.4**	**32.1**	**17.3**	P/B Ratio	**2.0**	52 Wk Hi-Low	**28.00-17.88**
Book Value	**229.8**	**180.5**	**208.1**	**15.3**	Yield %	**2.0**	Market Cap	**US$414.9mil**

Address **9700 Higgins Rd., Ste. 570**
Rosemont, IL 60018
Tel **708-696-0200**
Fax **708-696-2080**
Exchange **NASDA**
Ticker **TNTF**
President & CEO **John C. Carruth**
Chairman **Morley Koffman**

Torchmark

Industry: **Insurance - Life & Health**

Torchmark is an insurance and financial-services holding company. It operates six insurance subsidiaries that offer life, health, and property and casualty insurance throughout the United States. Torchmark also sells senior-life and health-care insurance, including Medicare Supplement and long-term-care coverage. Other subsidiaries include Waddell & Reed, which provides investment-management services and administers the United and Waddell groups of mutual funds, and Torch Energy, which operates oil and gas wells, and provides oil- and gas-production-management services.

$ mil	12/92	12/93	12/94	% Change				
Revenues	**2,045.8**	**2,176.8**	**1,922.6**	**-11.7**	P/E Ratio	**11.3**	Price (9/30/95)	**42.13**
Net Income	**265.5**	**298.0**	**268.9**	**-9.8**	P/B Ratio	**2.4**	52 Wk Hi-Low	**43.88-32.63**
Book Value	**1,115.7**	**1,417.3**	**1,242.6**	**-12.3**	Yield %	**2.7**	Market Cap	**US$3,015.3mil**

Address **2001 Third Ave. S.**
Birmingham, AL 35233
Tel **205-325-4200**
Fax **205-325-4157**
Exchange **NYSE**
Ticker **TMK**
Chief Executive **Ronald K. Richey**
Chairman **Ronald K. Richey**

Toys 'R' Us

Industry: **Other Specialty Retailers**

Toys 'R' Us operates more than 1,100 children's specialty-retail stores. These stores consist of 618 U.S. and 299 international toy stores under the name Toys 'R' Us and 206 children's clothing stores under the name Kids 'R' Us, as of April, 1995. Toys 'R' Us stores sell children's and adult toys, games, bicycles and other wheel goods, sporting goods, electronic and video games, infant's and children's clothing, and similar items. Most Toys 'R' Us stores are approximately 46,000 square feet and are freestanding units. Kids 'R' Us feature brand-name children's clothing.

$ mil	01/93	01/94	01/95	% Change				
Revenues	**7,169.3**	**7,946.1**	**8,745.6**	**10.1**	P/E Ratio	**14.6**	Price (9/30/95)	**27.00**
Net Income	**437.5**	**483.0**	**531.8**	**10.1**	P/B Ratio	**2.2**	52 Wk Hi-Low	**38.88-23.75**
Book Value	**2,889.0**	**3,148.3**	**3,428.9**	**8.9**	Yield %	**0.0**	Market Cap	**US$7,461.6mil**

Address **461 From Rd.**
Paramus, NJ 07652
Tel **201-262-7800**
Fax **201-262-7606**
Exchange **NYSE**
Ticker **TOY**
Chief Executive **Michael Goldstein**
Chairman **Charles Lazarus**

Transamerica

Industry: **Insurance - Full Line**

Transamerica is one of the world's largest providers of financial and insurance services. With more than 1,000 offices worldwide, its Transamerica Finance Group provides consumer and commercial lending, leasing, and real-estate services. The company offers life insurance, annuities, and asset-management services through its Transamerica Life subsidiary, with nearly 30,000 active brokers nationwide. It also rents cargo containers to commercial customers worldwide. Approximately 61% of the company's revenues are derived from its insurance operations.

$ mil	12/92	12/93	12/94	% Change				
Revenues	**4,987.8**	**4,833.0**	**5,354.5**	**10.8**	P/E Ratio	**4.3**	Price (9/30/95)	**23.38**
Net Income	**243.2**	**377.4**	**427.2**	**13.2**	P/B Ratio	**0.6**	52 Wk Hi-Low	**25.63-16.88**
Book Value	**3,300.1**	**3,363.5**	**2,735.8**	**-18.7**	Yield %	**8.6**	Market Cap	**US$1,806.5mil**

Address **600 Montgomery St.**
San Francisco, CA 94111
Tel **415-983-4000**
Fax **415-983-4300**
Exchange **NYSE**
Ticker **TA**
President & CEO **Frank C. Herringer**
Chairman **James R. Harvey**

Travelers

Industry: **Financial Services - Diversified**

Travelers Group provides insurance, managed health care, and investment services. Through affiliated companies, it offers commercial property and casualty, workers' compensation, life, and disability insurance. The company offers managed health-care programs, annuities, pension and investment-management services, loans, individual retirement accounts, and Keogh plans. A joint venture between the company and Met Life operates a health-maintenance organization. Travelers Group also provides investment-banking and asset-management services through its Smith Barney subsidiary.

$ mil	12/92	12/93	12/94	% Change				
Revenues	**9,675.0**	**6,797.0**	**18,464.7**	**171.7**	P/E Ratio	**13.8**	Price (9/30/95)	**53.13**
Net Income	**-658.0**	**916.0**	**1,326.0**	**44.8**	P/B Ratio	**1.9**	52 Wk Hi-Low	**53.13-31.00**
Book Value	**5,054.0**	**9,436.0**	**8,778.0**	**-7.0**	Yield %	**1.1**	Market Cap	**US$16,952mil**

Address **388 Greenwich St.**
New York, NY 10013
Tel **212-891-8900**
Fax **212-891-8915**
Exchange **NYSE**
Ticker **TRV**
President COO **James Dimon**
Chairman & CEO **Sanford I. Weill**

Tribune

Industry: **Publishing**

Tribune is an information and entertainment-services company. It publishes six daily newspapers, including The Chicago Tribune, The Fort Lauderdale Sun-Sentinel, and The Orlando Sentinel. The company also operates eight independent television stations and six radio stations. It produces and syndicates television and radio programming. Tribune also owns the Chicago Cubs baseball team and its stadium, Wrigley Field. Tribune's publishing businesses generate approximately 60% of its operating revenues; its broadcasting and baseball businesses account for the balance.

$ mil	12/92	12/93	12/94	% Change				
Sales	**2,108.6**	**1,952.5**	**2,154.9**	**10.4**	P/E Ratio	**20.0**	Price (9/30/95)	**66.38**
Net Income	**119.8**	**188.6**	**242.0**	**28.3**	P/B Ratio	**3.3**	52 Wk Hi-Low	**68.25-49.63**
Book Value	**911.9**	**1,095.6**	**1,333.0**	**21.7**	Yield %	**1.6**	Market Cap	**US$4,321.1mil**

Address **435 N. Michigan Ave.**
Chicago, IL 60611
Tel **312-222-9100**
Fax **312-222-0449**
Exchange **NYSE**
Ticker **TRB**
President & COO **John W. Madigan**
Chairman & CEO **Charles T. Brumback**

Trinity Industries

Industry: **Land Transportation**

Trinity Industries manufactures railroad, marine, and structural products. It makes freight and tank rail cars, crew and commercial boats, military marine vessels, and barges, as well as large transportation and storage containers. Trinity's structural beams and girders are used in bridge and highway construction. The company also owns Stearns Airport Equipment, which provides passenger-boarding bridges and baggage-handling systems. Its Trinity Industries Leasing subsidiary leases railcars to railroad companies. Trinity operates manufacturing facilities in 18 states.

$ mil	03/92	03/94 *	03/95	% Change				
Sales	**1,192.3**	**1,784.9**	**2,314.9**	**29.7**	P/E Ratio	**14.1**	Price (9/30/95)	**31.00**
Net Income	**22.1**	**76.2**	**89.1**	**16.9**	P/B Ratio	**1.9**	52 Wk Hi-Low	**40.25-30.50**
Book Value	**345.6**	**570.5**	**641.2**	**12.4**	Yield %	**2.2**	Market Cap	**US$1,287.9mil**

Address **2525 Stemmons Fwy.**
Dallas, TX 75207-2401
Tel **214-689-0592**
Fax **214-689-0501**
Exchange **NYSE**
Ticker **TRN**
President & CEO **W. Ray Wallace**
Chairman **W. Ray Wallace**

*Irregular period due to fiscal year change.

Trinova

Industry: **Industrial - Diversified**

Trinova manufactures engineered components and systems. It markets these products through its operating subsidiaries, Aeroquip and Vickers, to users in the industrial, aerospace, defense, transportation, and automotive industries in the United States and internationally. Aeroquip's main products include hoses, fittings, air-conditioning and power-steering systems, and engine parts. Vickers produces hydraulic-, pneumatic-, and electronic-control systems, as well as pumps, generators, and motors. Business operations in markets outside of the U.S. account for 35% of sales.

$ mil	12/92	12/93	12/94	% Change				
Sales	**1,695.5**	**1,643.8**	**1,794.7**	**9.2**	P/E Ratio	**14.9**	Price (9/30/95)	**33.75**
Net Income	**14.4**	**-59.7**	**65.9**	**-210.3**	P/B Ratio	**3.0**	52 Wk Hi-Low	**38.75-23.63**
Book Value	**352.9**	**253.2**	**320.0**	**26.4**	Yield %	**2.0**	Market Cap	**US$972.4mil**

Address **3000 Strayer**
Maumee, OH 43537
Tel **419-867-2200**
Fax **419-867-2395**
Exchange **NYSE**
Ticker **TNV**
President & CEO **Darryl F. Allen**
Chairman **Darryl F. Allen**

True North Communications

Industry: **Advertising**

True North Communications provides advertising, direct-marketing, and other sponsor services, primarily through its Foote Cone & Belding (FCB) subsidiary. The company's activities are conducted through 190 offices in 57 countries, including the combined Publicis-FCB group in Europe. Clients include Kimberly-Clark, Campbell Soup, Levi Strauss, Farmers Insurance, Taco Bell, Coors Brewing, Citibank, and others. The company creates advertising for clients and places it in print and electronic media. Offices are located in the United States, Canada, Latin America and Asia.

$ mil	12/92	12/93	12/94	% Change				
Sales	**353.3**	**342.0**	**403.7**	**18.0**	P/E Ratio	**14.9**	Price (9/30/95)	**20.00**
Net Income	**21.7**	**25.7**	**30.3**	**17.9**	P/B Ratio	**2.2**	52 Wk Hi-Low	**23.25-15.75**
Book Value	**183.3**	**200.0**	**207.8**	**3.9**	Yield %	**3.0**	Market Cap	**US$463.9mil**

Address **101 E. Erie St.**
Chicago, IL 60611
Tel **312-751-7227**
Fax **312-751-3501**
Exchange **NYSE**
Ticker **TNO**
Chief Executive **Bruce Mason**
Chairman **Bruce Mason**

TRW

Industry: **Diversified Technology**

TRW provides technology-based automotive, aerospace, and defense products and information services. The company manufactures automotive systems such as occupant restraints, steering systems, and engine components, and produces electronic components and systems for spacecraft and defense applications. TRW's information services include an on-line consumer-credit-report service. The company markets its products and services to governmental agencies and users in the automotive, defense, banking, finance, and other industries. International sales account for 30% of the total.

$ mil	12/92	12/93	12/94	% Change				
Sales	**8,311.0**	**7,948.0**	**9,087.0**	**14.3**	P/E Ratio	**14.7**	Price (9/30/95)	**74.38**
Net Income	**-156.0**	**195.0**	**333.0**	**70.8**	P/B Ratio	**2.6**	52 Wk Hi-Low	**82.00-61.75**
Book Value	**1,416.0**	**1,534.0**	**1,822.0**	**18.8**	Yield %	**2.6**	Market Cap	**US$4,840.7mil**

Address **1900 Richmond Rd.**
Cleveland, OH 44124
Tel **216-291-7000**
Fax **216-291-7758**
Exchange **NYSE**
Ticker **TRW**
President & COO **Peter S. Hellman**
Chairman & CEO **Joseph T. Gorman**

Tyco International

Industry: **Industrial - Diversified**

Tyco International produces fire-protection systems, health-care products, flow-control products, electrical and electronic components, and packaging materials. Its products include fire-detection and automatic-sprinkler systems; valves, pipes, and tubing; underwater fiberoptic cables and printed circuit boards; and woven vinyl and polyethylene films. The company's health-care products include catheters, medical pumps, elastic stockings, and Curity- and Curad-brand bandages. Tyco International's sales outside North America account for approximately 30% of its total.

$ mil	06/93	06/94	06/95	% Change				
Sales	**3,114.5**	**3,262.8**	**4,534.7**	**39.0**	P/E Ratio	**22.3**	Price (9/30/95)	**63.00**
Net Income	**1.3**	**124.6**	**214.0**	**71.7**	P/B Ratio	**2.9**	52 Wk Hi-Low	**63.00-43.88**
Book Value	**919.7**	**1,079.1**	**1,634.7**	**51.5**	Yield %	**0.6**	Market Cap	**US$4,809.4mil**

Address **One Tyco Park**
Exeter, NH 03833
Tel **603-778-9700**
Fax **603-778-7330**
Exchange **NYSE**
Ticker **TYC**
President & CEO **L. Dennis Kozlowski**
Chairman **L. Dennis Kozlowski**

Tyson Foods

Industry: **Other Food**

Tyson Foods produces a variety of food products, including value-enhanced poultry, fresh and frozen poultry, value-enhanced beef and pork products, and flour and corn tortillas and other Mexican-food products. Additionally, the company has live swine, animal feed, and pet-food operations. The company's products are sold to grocery chains, grocery wholesalers, and warehouse stores, military commissaries, convenience stores, hospitals, and other vendors. Product names include Tyson, Holly Farms, Weaver, Tastybird, Ocean Master, Crab Delights, and others.

	$ mil 09/92	09/93	09/94	% Change				
Sales	**4,168.8**	**4,707.4**	**5,110.3**	**8.6**	P/E Ratio	**NMF**	Price (9/30/95)	**26.88**
Net Income	**160.5**	**180.3**	**-2.1**	**-101.2**	P/B Ratio	**3.0**	52 Wk Hi-Low	**27.25-20.75**
Book Value	**980.2**	**1,360.7**	**1,289.4**	**-5.2**	Yield %	**0.3**	Market Cap	**US$3,889.4mil**

Address	**2210 W. Oaklawn Dr.**	Tel	**501-290-4000**	Exchange	**NASDA**	President & CEO	**Leland Tollett**
	Springdale, AR 72762	Fax	**501-290-4061**	Ticker	**TYSNA**	Chairman	**Don Tyson**

UAL

Industry: **Airlines**

UAL is a holding company that has United Airlines as its principal subsidiary. United Airlines provides passenger and cargo transportation to 152 airports in 29 countries from hubs in Chicago, Denver, San Francisco, Washington, DC, London, and Tokyo. It also offers commuter service under the name United Express through partnerships with several regional carriers. Operations outside the United States account for approximately 40% of revenues. Mileage Plus, a subsidiary, administers frequent-flyer-bonus programs for United. The company indirectly owns Air Wis Services.

	$ mil 12/92	12/93	12/94	% Change				
Sales	**12,889.7**	**14,511.0**	**13,950.0**	**-3.9**	P/E Ratio	**NMF**	Price (9/30/95)	**170.88**
Net Income	**-956.8**	**-50.0**	**51.0**	**-202.0**	P/B Ratio	**NMF**	52 Wk Hi-Low	**172.00-83.63**
Book Value	**705.6**	**1,203.0**	**-316.0**	**-126.3**	Yield %	**0.0**	Market Cap	**US$2,117.0mil**

Address	**1200 E. Algonquin Rd.**	Tel	**708-952-4000**	Exchange	**NYSE**	President	**John A. Edwardson**
	Elk Grove, IL 60007	Fax	**708-952-4081**	Ticker	**UAL**	Chairman & CEO	**Gerald Greenwald**

UJB Financial

Industry: **Banks - Eastern U.S.**

UJB Financial is a bank holding company with two bank and nine nonbank subsidiaries. It operates 197 banking branches in New Jersey and 73 in Pennsylvania. The company's principal subsidiary is United Jersey Bank, which engaged in consumer and commercial banking. UJB Financial's nonbank subsidiaries are involved in such businesses as discount brokerage, mortgage banking, venture-capital investment, equipment leasing, commercial-finance lending, credit life reinsurance, and data processing. UJB Financial ageed to acquire Summit Bancorp in 1995.

	$ mil 12/92	12/93	12/94	% Change				
Revenues	**1,129.6**	**1,062.5**	**1,138.3**	**7.1**	P/E Ratio	**13.6**	Price (9/30/95)	**32.00**
Net Income	**53.8**	**78.1**	**130.2**	**66.6**	P/B Ratio	**1.6**	52 Wk Hi-Low	**36.50-23.13**
Book Value	**920.3**	**976.1**	**1,104.3**	**13.1**	Yield %	**2.9**	Market Cap	**US$1,839.2mil**

Address	**301 Carnegie Ctr.**	Tel	**609-987-3200**	Exchange	**NYSE**	President	**Robert E. Wilkes**
	Princeton, NJ 08543	Fax	**609-987-3535**	Ticker	**UJB**	Chairman & CEO	**T. Joseph Semrod**

Unicom

Industry: **Electrical Utilities - Eastern U.S.**

Unicom is a public electric utility. It delivers electricity to about 3.3 million retail and wholesale customers in an area that covers one fifth of Illinois and includes Chicago, which provides the company with one third of its revenues. Residential customers account for approximately 37% of electric operating revenues; commercial and industrial users make up roughly another 54%. The company generates about 75% of its electricity at nuclear-power plants and 23% at coal-fired stations. Most of the Unicom's revenue is derived from its Commonwealth Edison subsidiary.

	$ mil 12/92	12/93	12/94	% Change				
Sales	**6,044.7**	**6,547.2**	**6,293.4**	**-3.9**	P/E Ratio	**18.2**	Price (9/30/95)	**30.25**
Net Income	**514.0**	**112.4**	**354.9**	**215.8**	P/B Ratio	**1.2**	52 Wk Hi-Low	**30.25-20.75**
Book Value	**6,462.8**	**6,173.3**	**5,448.0**	**-11.7**	Yield %	**5.3**	Market Cap	**US$6,491.5mil**

Address	**1 First Nat'l Plz., 10 S. Dearborn**	Tel	**312-394-7399**	Exchange	**NYSE**	President	**Samuel K. Skinner**
	Chicago, IL 60690	Fax	**312-394-3110**	Ticker	**UCM**	Chairman & CEO	**James J. O'Connor**

Unifi

Industry: **Clothing & Fabrics**

Unifi engages in the processing of natural and synthetic yarns. Its products include textured synthetic-filament polyester and nylon, and spun-cotton and cotton-blend fibers, sold under the Unifi, Trifi, Mactex, and Bi-Dye trademarks. Unifi markets these yarns to knitters and weavers who produce fabrics for apparel, hosiery, home furnishings, auto upholstery, activewear, and underwear worldwide. Business operations outside the U.S. account for approximately 15% of sales. Unifi operates manufacturing facilities in North Carolina, Virginia, and Ireland.

	$ mil 06/93	06/94	06/95	% Change				
Sales	**1,332.2**	**1,384.8**	**1,554.6**	**12.3**	P/E Ratio	**14.7**	Price (9/30/95)	**24.50**
Net Income	**128.1**	**76.5**	**116.2**	**51.9**	P/B Ratio	**2.7**	52 Wk Hi-Low	**28.75-23.00**
Book Value	**529.2**	**588.5**	**603.5**	**2.5**	Yield %	**1.6**	Market Cap	**US$1,669.4mil**

Address	**7201 W. Friendly Ave.**	Tel	**910-294-4410**	Exchange	**NYSE**	President & CEO	**William T. Kretzer**
	Greensboro, NC 27419	Fax	**910-316-5422**	Ticker	**UFI**	Chairman	**G. Allen Mebane**

Union Camp

Industry: **Paper Products**

Union Camp manufactures forest products and chemicals. The company's paper and paperboard division makes kraft paper and paperboard, which are used in its own conversion operations and those of outside companies, and printing papers. Its packaging-products division produces grocery bags, multiwall paper bags used to package heavy products such as cement, and paperboard and corrugated containers. The company's wood products include dimensional lumber, plywood, and particleboard. Its chemical products, such as tall oil and turpentine, are by-products of its pulp mills.

$ mil	12/92	12/93	12/94	% Change				
Sales	**3,064.4**	**3,120.4**	**3,395.8**	**8.8**	P/E Ratio	**35.6**	Price (9/30/95)	**57.63**
Net Income	**76.2**	**50.0**	**113.5**	**127.0**	P/B Ratio	**2.2**	52 Wk Hi-Low	**60.63-44.50**
Book Value	**1,881.9**	**1,815.8**	**1,836.3**	**1.1**	Yield %	**2.7**	Market Cap	**US$4,042.0mil**

Address **1600 Valley Rd.**
Wayne, NJ 07470
Tel **201-628-2000**
Fax **201-628-2218**
Exchange **NYSE**
Ticker **UCC**
President & COO **Jerry H. Ballengee**
Chairman & CEO **W. Craig McClelland**

Union Carbide

Industry: **Commodity Chemicals**

Union Carbide manufactures chemicals and plastics. The company produces certain commodity chemicals, principally polyethylene and ethylene glycol. Polyethylene is the world's most widely used plastic and ethylene glycol is used for antifreeze. The company also makes and buys materials to produce acrylates, acetic esters, and alcohols. Markets include paints, coatings, packaging and consumer plastic products, wire and cable, oil and gas. Trademarks include Union Carbide, Ucar, and Unipol. The company has approximately 50 plants, factories, and laboratories worldwide.

$ mil	12/92	12/93	12/94	% Change				
Sales	**4,872.0**	**4,640.0**	**4,865.0**	**4.8**	P/E Ratio	**16.3**	Price (9/30/95)	**39.75**
Net Income	**-175.0**	**68.0**	**389.0**	**472.1**	P/B Ratio	**4.0**	52 Wk Hi-Low	**42.13-25.50**
Book Value	**1,238.0**	**1,428.0**	**1,553.0**	**8.8**	Yield %	**1.9**	Market Cap	**US$5,456.1mil**

Address **39 Old Ridgebury Rd.**
Danbury, CT 06817
Tel **203-794-2000**
Fax **203-794-4336**
Exchange **NYSE**
Ticker **UK**
President **William H. Joyce**
Chairman & CEO **Robert D. Kennedy**

Union Electric

Industry: **Electrical Utilities - Central U.S.**

Union Electric provides electricity and natural-gas service to an area of 24,500 square miles in Missouri and Illinois. About 95% of the company's revenues are derived from the sale of electricity to its more than one million customers. Residential customers account for roughly 42% of electric revenues. Union Electric generates about 65% of its electricity from fossil fuels, and 25% at nuclear-power stations. The remainder is either generated at the company's hydroelectric-generation plants or purchased from third parties. In 1995, the company agreed to merge with Cipsco.

$ mil	12/92	12/93	12/94	% Change				
Sales	**2,015.1**	**2,066.0**	**2,056.1**	**-0.5**	P/E Ratio	**12.4**	Price (9/30/95)	**37.38**
Net Income	**302.7**	**297.2**	**320.8**	**7.9**	P/B Ratio	**1.5**	52 Wk Hi-Low	**38.13-34.75**
Book Value	**2,382.5**	**2,425.4**	**2,488.2**	**2.6**	Yield %	**6.4**	Market Cap	**US$3,816.9mil**

Address **1901 Chouteau Ave.**
St. Louis, MO 63103
Tel **314-621-3222**
Fax **314-554-3268**
Exchange **NYSE**
Ticker **UEP**
President & CEO **Charles W. Mueller**
Chairman --

Union Pacific

Industry: **Railroads**

Union Pacific primarily operates railroads in the United States and Canada. Its Union Pacific Railroad subsidiary owns about 17,500 miles of track, making it the third-largest rail system in the United States. Union Pacific Railroad contributes roughly 66% of the company's revenues. The company also has operations in petroleum production, mining, trucking, and hazardous-waste management. Its other subsidiaries include Missouri Pacific Railroad, Union Pacific Resources, and Overnite Transportation. The company agreed to acquire Southern Pacific Rail in 1995.

$ mil	12/92	12/93	12/94	% Change				
Sales	**7,294.0**	**7,561.0**	**7,798.0**	**3.1**	P/E Ratio	**24.9**	Price (9/30/95)	**66.25**
Net Income	**728.0**	**530.0**	**546.0**	**3.0**	P/B Ratio	**2.7**	52 Wk Hi-Low	**69.38-44.63**
Book Value	**4,639.0**	**4,885.0**	**5,131.0**	**5.0**	Yield %	**2.5**	Market Cap	**US$13,605mil**

Address **Martin Tower, 8th & Eaton Aves.**
Bethlehem, PA 18018
Tel **610-861-3200**
Fax **610-861-3157**
Exchange **NYSE**
Ticker **UNP**
President **Richard K. Davidson**
Chairman & CEO **Drew Lewis**

Union Texas Petroleum

Industry: **Oil - Secondary**

Union Texas Petroleum Holdings operates oil and natural-gas wells and related businesses. The company owns an average 11% interest in about 420 wells and holds net reserves of approximately 97 million barrels of oil and 1.4 trillion cubic feet of natural gas. Although its production activities are concentrated in Indonesia, Pakistan, and the North Sea, the company explores worldwide. It owns a 190-mile ethane-gathering pipeline that supplies the 42%-owned Geismar ethylene plant in Louisiana, the production from which is sold to manufacturers of various consumer goods.

$ mil	12/92	12/93	12/94	% Change				
Sales	**669.5**	**681.9**	**747.9**	**9.7**	P/E Ratio	**24.0**	Price (9/30/95)	**18.25**
Net Income	**13.6**	**26.9**	**66.7**	**148.1**	P/B Ratio	**4.6**	52 Wk Hi-Low	**23.88-18.13**
Book Value	**269.2**	**281.2**	**349.5**	**24.3**	Yield %	**1.1**	Market Cap	**US$1,601.6mil**

Address **1330 Post Oak Blvd.**
Houston, TX 77056
Tel **713-623-6544**
Fax **713-968-2771**
Exchange **NYSE**
Ticker **UTH**
Chief Executive **A. Clark Johnson**
Chairman **A. Clark Johnson**

Unisys

Industry: **Computers**

Unisys produces information systems and software and provides related services. The company provides network servers, peripherals, work stations, software, and systems-integration and equipment-maintenance services; it also provides custom products and services such as specialized information-processing systems marketed to government defense agencies. Unisys primarily focuses on customers with transaction-intensive businesses, such as banks and airlines. Sales to defense agencies of the U.S., Canada, and other allied governments account for 16% of its sales.

$ mil	12/92	12/93	12/94	% Change				
Sales	8,421.9	7,742.5	7,399.7	-4.4	P/E Ratio	NMF	Price (9/30/95)	7.88
Net Income	361.2	565.4	100.5	-82.2	P/B Ratio	0.5	52 Wk Hi-Low	11.50-7.75
Book Value	2,244.1	2,695.5	2,604.5	-3.4	Yield %	0.0	Market Cap	US$1,349.4mil

Address **Township Line & Union Meeting, Blue Bell, PA 19424**
Tel **215-986-4011** Fax **215-986-3170**
Exchange **NYSE** Ticker **UIS**
Chief Executive **James A. Unruh**
Chairman **James A. Unruh**

United Technologies

Industry: **Diversified Technology**

United Technologies manufactures aerospace, building, and automotive products. Its subsidiaries, Pratt & Whitney, Sikorsky, and Hamilton Standard manufacture helicopters, aircraft engines and parts, flight-control and radar systems, and rocket boosters. Its other products include Carrier heating and air-conditioning equipment, Otis elevators, and automotive parts. The company markets its products to government agencies, commercial and industrial users, and individuals in the United States and internationally. International operations account for about 48% of revenues.

$ mil	12/92	12/93	12/94	% Change				
Sales	21,641.0	20,736.0	20,801.0	0.3	P/E Ratio	20.1	Price (9/30/95)	88.38
Net Income	-287.0	487.0	585.0	20.1	P/B Ratio	2.7	52 Wk Hi-Low	88.38-55.38
Book Value	3,521.0	3,774.0	4,091.0	8.4	Yield %	2.1	Market Cap	US$10,891mil

Address **United Technologies Bldg., Hartford, CT 06101**
Tel **203-728-7000** Fax **203-728-6463**
Exchange **NYSE** Ticker **UTX**
President & CEO **George David**
Chairman **Robert F. Daniell**

United Water Resources

Industry: **Water Utilities**

United Water Resources provides water-utility and related services. Hackensack Water Company, Spring Valley Water, and Mid-Atlantic Utilities, its operating subsidiaries, treat and distribute water to more than 250,000 customers in New York and New Jersey. The company also provides laboratory-testing, meter-reading, and consulting services to other water-utility companies. Residential customers account for about 62% of utility revenues; commercial and industrial users provides another 34% of the total. Revenues generated from public fire protection make up the balance.

$ mil	12/92	12/93	12/94	% Change				
Sales	164.9	200.4	293.0	46.2	P/E Ratio	12.6	Price (9/30/95)	12.75
Net Income	15.8	20.0	31.3	56.5	P/B Ratio	0.9	52 Wk Hi-Low	14.00-12.38
Book Value	179.5	202.1	424.3	109.9	Yield %	7.2	Market Cap	US$409.4mil

Address **200 Old Hook Rd., Harrington Park, NJ 07640**
Tel **201-784-9434** Fax **201-767-2892**
Exchange **NYSE** Ticker **UWR**
President & CEO **Donald L. Correll**
Chairman **Donald L. Correll**

Unitrin

Industry: **Insurance - Full Line**

Unitrin is an insurance and financial-services company. Its United Insurance Company of America and Trinity Universal Insurance subsidiaries underwrite life, health, and property and casualty insurance. A significant part of Unitrin's property and casualty insurance policies are sold in the South, the Midwest, California, and Texas. Its Fireside Thrift subsidiary offers automobile and personal loans and investment instruments, including certificates of deposit, money-market accounts, and individual retirement accounts.

$ mil	12/92	12/93	12/94	% Change				
Revenues	1,362.6	1,363.2	1,365.5	0.2	P/E Ratio	15.9	Price (9/30/95)	47.00
Net Income	123.4	95.0	148.4	56.2	P/B Ratio	1.3	52 Wk Hi-Low	50.38-41.50
Book Value	1,953.5	2,098.5	1,765.1	-15.9	Yield %	3.2	Market Cap	US$1,872.5mil

Address **1 E. Wacker Dr., Chicago, IL 60601**
Tel **312-661-4600** Fax **312-661-4690**
Exchange **NASDA** Ticker **UNIT**
President & CEO **Richard C. Vie**
Chairman **Jerrold V. Jerome**

Universal

Industry: **Tobacco**

Universal is a company with operations in tobacco, lumber and building products, and agricultural products. The company is the world's largest independent tobacco merchant, providing buying, processing, packing, storing, and financing services for manufacturers of tobacco products worldwide. Universal Leaf Tobacco is the company's tobacco-leaf dealer. Lumber and building products operations involve distribution to the construction trade in Europe. Other operations include the buying, selling, and processing of sunflower seeds and the trading of other products.

$ mil	06/92	06/93	06/94	% Change				
Sales	2,989.0	3,047.2	2,975.1	-2.4	P/E Ratio	85.6	Price (9/30/95)	22.50
Net Income	70.7	80.2	9.2	-88.5	P/B Ratio	2.1	52 Wk Hi-Low	24.75-19.13
Book Value	301.7	417.9	377.5	-9.7	Yield %	4.2	Market Cap	US$788.1mil

Address **1501 Hamilton St., Richmond, VA 23230**
Tel **804-359-9311** Fax **804-254-3584**
Exchange **NYSE** Ticker **UVV**
President & COO **Allen B. King**
Chairman & CEO **Henry H. Harrell**

Unocal

Industry: **Oil - Integrated Majors**

Unocal is a major integrated petroleum company. It owns, on average, a 62% interest in 9,800 petroleum wells, primarily in Alaska, California, Louisiana, and Texas, and holds net reserves of 697 million barrels of oil and 6.9 trillion cubic feet of natural gas. The company owns three refineries and a 50% interest in a refinery in Chicago, and sells gasoline and other refined products under the Unocal 76 name at 1,600 service stations in the midwestern and western U.S. It also operates a fertilizer plant in Alaska; its products are sold in the western U.S. and abroad.

$ mil	12/92	12/93	12/94	% Change				
Sales	**9,887.0**	**8,077.0**	**7,797.0**	**-3.5**	P/E Ratio	**NMF**	Price (9/30/95)	**28.50**
Net Income	**220.0**	**213.0**	**-153.0**	**-171.8**	P/B Ratio	**2.5**	52 Wk Hi-Low	**30.13-25.50**
Book Value	**3,131.0**	**3,129.0**	**2,815.0**	**-10.0**	Yield %	**2.8**	Market Cap	**US$7,020.0mil**

Address **1201 W. Fifth St.**
Los Angeles, CA 90017
Tel **213-977-7600**
Fax **213-977-5158**
Exchange **NYSE**
Ticker **UCL**
Chief Executive **Roger C. Beach**
Chairman **Richard J. Stegemeier**

UNUM

Industry: **Insurance - Life & Health**

UNUM is an insurance holding company with operations throughout the United States, the United Kingdom, and the Pacific Rim. The company provides individual and group insurance, including life, disability, health, and dental coverage. It also offers annuities and long-term-care insurance, which are marketed through an independent-broker network of 33 offices in the United States and Canada. UNUM's investment portfolio includes mortgage loans and real-estate investments of various use. The employee-benefits segment accounts for approximately 47% of the company's revenues.

$ mil	12/92	12/93	12/94	% Change				
Revenues	**2,641.2**	**3,397.0**	**3,623.7**	**6.7**	P/E Ratio	**25.2**	Price (9/30/95)	**52.75**
Net Income	**248.8**	**299.9**	**154.7**	**-48.4**	P/B Ratio	**2.0**	52 Wk Hi-Low	**53.88-36.25**
Book Value	**1,686.5**	**2,102.7**	**1,915.4**	**-8.9**	Yield %	**1.7**	Market Cap	**US$3,828.8mil**

Address **2211 Congress St.**
Portland, ME 04122
Tel **207-770-2211**
Fax **207-770-6933**
Exchange **NYSE**
Ticker **UNM**
Chief Executive **James F. Orr III**
Chairman **James F. Orr III**

Upjohn

Industry: **Pharmaceuticals**

Upjohn makes pharmaceutical and agricultural products. Its brand-name pharmaceuticals include Halcion, Rogaine, and Xanax prescription drugs, and Motrin IB, Cortaid, Dramamine, and Kaopectate nonprescription products. Upjohn has submitted Rogaine, a topical hair-loss treatment, for FDA approval. The company's Oxford Veterinary Laboratories subsidiary produces animal vaccines and its Aristogenes division breeds vegetables. Upjohn markets both its pharmaceutical and agricultural products in the United States and overseas. In 1995, the company agreed to merge with Pharmacia.

$ mil	12/92	12/93	12/94	% Change				
Sales	**3,638.9**	**3,611.2**	**3,275.0**	**-9.3**	P/E Ratio	**16.2**	Price (9/30/95)	**44.63**
Net Income	**324.3**	**392.4**	**490.8**	**25.1**	P/B Ratio	**3.2**	52 Wk Hi-Low	**45.50-30.00**
Book Value	**2,015.5**	**2,085.7**	**2,382.6**	**14.2**	Yield %	**3.3**	Market Cap	**US$7,639.7mil**

Address **7000 Portage Rd.**
Kalamazoo, MI 49001
Tel **616-323-4000**
Fax **616-323-7034**
Exchange **NYSE**
Ticker **UPJ**
President & COO **Ley S. Smith**
Chairman & CEO **John L. Zabriskie**

U.S. Bancorp

Industry: **Banks - Western U.S.**

U.S. Bancorp is a bank holding company that provides corporate- and individual-banking services through 430 branches in the Pacific Northwest and Far West states. The company's primary subsidiaries include U.S. Bank of Oregon, the largest bank in Oregon by deposits, and the U.S. Bank of Washington, the third-largest bank in Washington by deposits. U.S. Bancorp's subsidiaries also provide lease-financing, discount-brokerage, and insurance services. U.S. Bancorp has agreed to merge with West One Bancorp, a bank holding company that operates in Idaho.

$ mil	12/92	12/93	12/94	% Change				
Revenues	**1,935.0**	**1,965.5**	**1,936.2**	**-1.5**	P/E Ratio	**20.2**	Price (9/30/95)	**28.25**
Net Income	**148.2**	**257.9**	**151.5**	**-41.3**	P/B Ratio	**1.6**	52 Wk Hi-Low	**29.44-22.25**
Book Value	**1,631.3**	**1,818.2**	**1,777.3**	**-2.2**	Yield %	**3.3**	Market Cap	**US$2,774.2mil**

Address **111 S.W. Fifth Ave.**
Portland, OR 97204
Tel **503-275-6111**
Fax **503-275-4005**
Exchange **NASDA**
Ticker **USBC**
President & CEO **Gerry B. Cameron**
Chairman **Gerry B. Cameron**

U.S. Healthcare

Industry: **Health Care Providers**

U.S. Healthcare provides comprehensive managed-health-care services through health maintenance organizations (HMOs) in the mid-Atlantic, greater New York, and New England regions. The company markets its HMOs to employer groups, and provides services through networks of health-care providers, including selected independent primary-care physicians. Other services include dental and vision plans. The company's HMOs serve roughly 1.7 million members. Most of the company's members are in fully insured HMO plans and the other members are in employer-funded HMO plans.

$ mil	12/92	12/93	12/94	% Change				
Sales	**2,189.2**	**2,645.2**	**2,974.5**	**12.4**	P/E Ratio	**14.6**	Price (9/30/95)	**35.38**
Net Income	**200.0**	**299.7**	**391.1**	**30.5**	P/B Ratio	**6.3**	52 Wk Hi-Low	**47.94-26.75**
Book Value	**505.1**	**769.7**	**905.7**	**17.7**	Yield %	**2.0**	Market Cap	**US$5,444.8mil**

Address **980 Jolly Rd.**
Blue Bell, PA 19422
Tel **215-628-4800**
Fax **215-283-6580**
Exchange **NASDA**
Ticker **USHC**
Chief Executive **Leonard Abramson**
Chairman **Leonard Abramson**

U.S. WEST

Industry: **Regional Telephone Systems**

U.S. WEST provides telecommunication and information services. This regional Bell company provides local telephone services to 25 million customers in 14 western states. It also offers cellular communications, directory publishing, marketing and entertainment, and other services. About 80% of revenues come from providing wireline-telephone services, and cellular and paging services account for most of the remainder. It also generates revenue by publishing residential and business telephone directories. The company is planning to provide video services.

$ mil	12/92	12/93	12/94	% Change				
Sales	10,281.1	10,293.6	10,953.0	6.4	P/E Ratio	15.0	Price (9/30/95)	47.13
Net Income	-614.0	-2,805.8	1,426.0	-150.8	P/B Ratio	3.0	52 Wk Hi-Low	47.88-34.88
Book Value	8,267.9	5,861.2	7,433.0	26.8	Yield %	4.5	Market Cap	US$22,187mil

Address **7800 E. Orchard Rd.**
Englewood, CO 80155
Tel **303-793-6500**
Fax **303-793-6654**
Exchange **NYSE**
Ticker **USW**
President & CEO **Richard D. McCormick**
Chairman **Richard D. McCormick**

USAir Group

Industry: **Airlines**

USAir Group operates passenger air-transportation. The company provides passenger service through the USAir, Pennsylvania Commuter, Henson Aviation, and Jetstream International airlines. The company provides services through 119 airports to 152 cities in the United States, Canada, the Bahamas, Bermuda, the Cayman Islands, Germany, France, and the Virgin Islands. Its nonairline subsidiaries provide services that include aircraft remarketing, airplane spare-parts sales, and fuel services. British Airways owns approximately 22% of the voting interest in USAir.

$ mil	12/92	12/93	12/94	% Change				
Sales	6,686.4	7,083.2	6,997.2	-1.2	P/E Ratio	NMF	Price (9/30/95)	11.50
Net Income	-1,228.9	-393.1	-684.9	74.2	P/B Ratio	NMF	52 Wk Hi-Low	13.88-4.00
Book Value	402.1	546.4	-138.2	-125.3	Yield %	0.0	Market Cap	US$715.4mil

Address **2345 Crystal Dr.**
Arlington, VA 22227
Tel **703-418-5306**
Fax **703-418-5307**
Exchange **NYSE**
Ticker **U**
President & COO **Frank L. Salizzoni**
Chairman & CEO **Seth E. Schofield**

USF&G

Industry: **Insurance - Property & Casualty**

USF&G is a holding company for insurance and investment-management subsidiaries. Its primary subsidiary, United States Fidelity and Guaranty, underwrites marine, auto, workers' compensation, and property and casualty insurance policies. Life-insurance products are underwritten by its Fidelity and Guaranty Life Insurance subsidiary. The company underwrites most of its insurance policies in the northeastern United States. Its noninsurance services include management consulting and asset management.

$ mil	12/92	12/93	12/94	% Change				
Revenues	3,660.0	3,249.0	3,221.0	-0.9	P/E Ratio	9.1	Price (9/30/95)	19.38
Net Income	28.0	165.0	232.0	40.6	P/B Ratio	1.4	52 Wk Hi-Low	19.38-12.88
Book Value	1,270.0	1,511.0	1,369.0	-9.4	Yield %	1.0	Market Cap	US$2,163.2mil

Address **100 Light St.**
Baltimore, MD 21202
Tel **410-547-3000**
Fax **410-625-2829**
Exchange **NYSE**
Ticker **FG**
President & CEO **Norman P. Blake, Jr.**
Chairman **Norman P. Blake, Jr.**

USG

Industry: **Building Materials**

USG manufactures building products, most of which are constructed from gypsum. United States Gypsum, the company's primary subsidiary, manufactures gypsum wallboard, plaster, and joint compound under the Durock and Sheetrock names. Other subsidiaries include USG Interiors, which makes acoustical ceiling tile, access wall and floor systems, and mineral-wool insulation; and L&W Supply, which operates about 125 distribution centers worldwide for USG products. Product names include Acoustone and Auratone ceiling tile and DX, Fineline, Centricitee, and Donn ceiling grids.

$ mil	12/92	12/93	12/94	% Change				
Sales	1,777.0	1,916.0	2,290.0	19.5	P/E Ratio	NMF	Price (9/30/95)	28.00
Net Income	-191.0	1,305.0	-92.0	-107.0	P/B Ratio	NMF	52 Wk Hi-Low	29.13-20.88
Book Value	-1,880.0	-134.0	-8.0	-94.0	Yield %	0.0	Market Cap	US$1,262.6mil

Address **125 S. Franklin St.**
Chicago, IL 60606
Tel **312-606-4000**
Fax **N/A**
Exchange **NYSE**
Ticker **USG**
President & COO **William C. Foote**
Chairman & CEO **Eugene B. Connolly**

USLife

Industry: **Insurance - Life & Health**

USLife is an insurance and financial-services holding firm. Its six life-insurance subsidiaries are licensed in all 50 states and offer life-and credit-insurance policies and annuity products for individuals, and group life, accident, and health insurance. Other USLife segments provide investment-advisory, broker-dealer, real-estate, and data-processing services for the life-insurance subsidiaries. The company's group-life policies are sold primarily to small groups and associations. Several subsidiaries also offer products designed for pension and profit-sharing plans.

$ mil	12/92	12/93	12/94	% Change				
Revenues	1,529.5	1,600.0	1,651.2	3.2	P/E Ratio	14.0	Price (9/30/95)	29.25
Net Income	31.6	97.2	96.2	-1.0	P/B Ratio	1.1	52 Wk Hi-Low	30.75-20.67
Book Value	890.4	966.0	877.9	-9.1	Yield %	2.2	Market Cap	US$1,005.6mil

Address **125 Maiden Ln.**
New York, NY 10038
Tel **212-709-6000**
Fax **212-709-6543**
Exchange **NYSE**
Ticker **USH**
President & CEO **William A. Simpson**
Chairman **Gordon E. Crosby, Jr.**

UST

Industry: **Tobacco**

UST manufactures smokeless-tobacco products and wine. The company's tobacco products are sold under brand names such as Copenhagen, Skoal, and Red Seal. UST owns vineyards and produces wines in Washington State under the Columbia Crest, Chateau Ste. Michelle, and Domaine Ste. Michelle names, and in California under the Conn Creek and Villa Mt. Eden names. Its Cabin Fever Entertainment subsidiary provides video and television programming. Smokeless-tobacco products generate 85% of the company's net sales.

$ mil	12/92	12/93	12/94	% Change				
Sales	**1,044.4**	**1,110.4**	**1,223.0**	**10.1**	P/E Ratio	**15.3**	Price (9/30/95)	**28.63**
Net Income	**312.6**	**349.0**	**387.5**	**11.0**	P/B Ratio	**15.5**	52 Wk Hi-Low	**32.50-26.25**
Book Value	**516.6**	**463.0**	**361.7**	**-21.9**	Yield %	**3.9**	Market Cap	**US$5,589.0mil**

Address **100 W. Putnam Ave.**
Greenwich, CT 06830
Tel **203-661-1100**
Fax **203-622-3561**
Exchange **NYSE**
Ticker **UST**
President & CEO **Vincent A. Gierer, Jr.**
Chairman **Vincent A. Gierer, Jr.**

USX-Marathon

Industry: **Oil - Integrated Majors**

USX-Marathon Group handles most of the petroleum operations of USX. The company owns, on average, a 37% interest in about 20,000 wells worldwide and holds net reserves of approximately 795 million barrels of oil and 3.8 trillion cubic feet of natural gas. It operates refineries and supplies gasoline and other refined products to 2,300 Marathon service stations, primarily in the Midwest. The company also provides natural-gas-utility service in Pennsylvania and West Virginia, and operates crude-oil and refined-product pipelines in the central United States.

$ mil	12/92	12/93	12/94	% Change				
Sales	**12,782.0**	**11,962.0**	**12,757.0**	**6.6**	P/E Ratio	**18.0**	Price (9/30/95)	**19.75**
Net Income	**-222.0**	**-29.0**	**321.0**	**NMF**	P/B Ratio	**1.8**	52 Wk Hi-Low	**21.38-15.88**
Book Value	**3,335.0**	**3,110.0**	**3,241.0**	**4.2**	Yield %	**3.4**	Market Cap	**US$5,671.4mil**

Address **600 Grant St.**
Pittsburgh, PA 15219
Tel **412-433-1121**
Fax **412-433-2015**
Exchange **NYSE**
Ticker **MRO**
President **Victor G. Beghini**
Chairman & CEO **Charles A. Corry**

USX-U.S. Steel

Industry: **Steel**

USX-U.S. Steel produces oil and gas, and gathers, processes, and transports natural gas. The company also produces steel products. The U.S. Steel Group, a unit of the company, is engaged in the production and sale of steel-mill products, coke, and taconite pellets. The Group also manages mineral resources, engineering and consulting services, and technology licensing. Other businesses that are part of the group include real-estate development and management, leasing and financing activities. The group also has a majority interest in a titanium metal-products company.

$ mil	12/92	12/93	12/94	% Change				
Sales	**4,947.0**	**5,612.0**	**6,066.0**	**8.1**	P/E Ratio	**13.2**	Price (9/30/95)	**31.00**
Net Income	**-1,606.0**	**-238.0**	**201.0**	**-184.5**	P/B Ratio	**2.5**	52 Wk Hi-Low	**42.63-29.38**
Book Value	**247.0**	**617.0**	**945.0**	**53.2**	Yield %	**3.2**	Market Cap	**US$2,534.2mil**

Address **600 Grant St.**
Pittsburgh, PA 15219
Tel **412-433-1121**
Fax **412-433-2015**
Exchange **NYSE**
Ticker **X**
President **Paul J. Wilhelm**
Chairman & CEO **Charles A. Corry**

Valspar

Industry: **Building Materials**

Valspar manufactures paint and coatings used in consumer, packaging, industrial, and specialty applications. Its products include latex and oil-based paints, stains, varnishes, clear polyurethanes, marine paints, coatings for food and beverage packaging, floor coatings, and protective coatings for wood, metal, and plastics. The company's consumer paints and coatings are sold under the Colony, Valspar, Enterprise, Magicolor, McCloskey, BPS, and Masury brand names, as well as under private labels. Valspar markets these products to individuals and industrial users worldwide.

$ mil	10/92	10/93	10/94	% Change				
Sales	**683.5**	**693.7**	**786.8**	**13.4**	P/E Ratio	**18.4**	Price (9/30/95)	**38.25**
Net Income	**34.4**	**40.2**	**45.5**	**13.1**	P/B Ratio	**4.7**	52 Wk Hi-Low	**41.50-33.50**
Book Value	**169.4**	**196.5**	**174.1**	**-11.4**	Yield %	**1.4**	Market Cap	**US$840.2mil**

Address **1101 Third St. S.**
Minneapolis, MN 55415
Tel **612-332-7371**
Fax **612-375-7723**
Exchange **NYSE**
Ticker **VAL**
President **Richard M. Rompala**
Chairman **C. Angus Wurtele**

Vanguard Cellular

Industry: **Mobile Communication Systems**

Vanguard Cellular Systems provides nonwireline cellular-telephone service in the eastern United States. It also sells and rents cellular-telephone equipment and related accessories. Under the Cellular One service mark, the company provides service to approximately 245,000 subscribers, concentrated mostly in the areas of Pennsylvania, Florida, the Carolinas, New England, and West Virginia. In addition, Vanguard Cellular Systems has ownership interest in Geotek, a company developing a specialized mobile-radio wireless-communication network based on new technology.

$ mil	12/92	12/93	12/94	% Change				
Sales	**89.6**	**124.0**	**168.0**	**35.5**	P/E Ratio	**NMF**	Price (9/30/95)	**25.63**
Net Income	**-26.7**	**-19.0**	**-22.3**	**17.6**	P/B Ratio	**NMF**	52 Wk Hi-Low	**29.13-22.00**
Book Value	**30.3**	**21.9**	**39.2**	**79.0**	Yield %	**0.0**	Market Cap	**US$1,055.5mil**

Address **2002 Pisgah Church Rd.**
Greensboro, NC 27455
Tel **910-282-3690**
Fax **910-545-2500**
Exchange **NASDA**
Ticker **VCELA**
President & CEO **Haynes G. Griffin**
Chairman **Stuart S. Richardson**

Varian Associates

Industry: **Diversified Technology**

Varian Associates manufactures electronic systems and components. The company produces radiation equipment for cancer therapy and industrial inspections, and wafer-fabrication equipment for the semiconductor industry. Other product lines include analytical instruments, electron tubes, vacuum equipment, and leak detectors sold for use in industry and research. The company markets these products to users in the fields of communication, health-care, industrial production, scientific and industrial research, defense, and environmental monitoring in the U.S. and abroad.

$ mil	09/92	09/93	09/94	% Change				
Sales	**1,288.0**	**1,311.0**	**1,552.5**	**18.4**	P/E Ratio	**23.9**	Price (9/30/95)	**53.00**
Net Income	**38.7**	**45.8**	**79.4**	**73.3**	P/B Ratio	**4.0**	52 Wk Hi-Low	**57.25-31.13**
Book Value	**428.0**	**421.8**	**449.5**	**6.6**	Yield %	**0.4**	Market Cap	**US$1,794.5mil**

Address **3050 Hansen Way, Palo Alto, CA 94304-1000**
Tel **415-493-4000** Fax **415-493-0307**
Exchange **NYSE** Ticker **VAR**
Chief Executive **J. Tracy O'Rourke**
Chairman **J. Tracy O'Rourke**

Varity

Industry: **Other Auto Parts**

Varity manufactures automotive components, agricultural equipment, diesel engines, hydraulic products, and replacement parts. Varity's product line includes antilock braking devices, electromechanical sensors, door-lock components, and multicylinder water-cooled diesel engines. The company markets its products under the Kelsey-Hayes and Perkins trademarks. It also produces low-emission diesel engines in the United Kingdom in a joint venture with Japan's Ishikawajima-Shibaura Machinery. Varity operates facilities in the United States, Canada, Europe, and Singapore.

$ mil	01/93	01/94	01/95	% Change				
Sales	**3,374.5**	**2,725.8**	**2,267.8**	**-16.8**	P/E Ratio	**13.7**	Price (9/30/95)	**44.50**
Net Income	**27.0**	**-71.5**	**144.7**	**-302.4**	P/B Ratio	**2.4**	52 Wk Hi-Low	**50.25-33.63**
Book Value	**548.5**	**630.7**	**783.7**	**24.3**	Yield %	**0.0**	Market Cap	**US$1,815.5mil**

Address **672 Delaware Ave., Buffalo, NY 14209-2202**
Tel **716-888-8000** Fax **716-888-8065**
Exchange **NYSE** Ticker **VAT**
Chief Operating **J.A. Gilroy**
Chairman & CEO **Victor Rice**

VF Corporation

Industry: **Clothing & Fabrics**

VF Corporation manufactures clothing, specializing in jeanswear, casualwear, and lingerie. The company makes jeans and casual shirts and pants, which account for about half of company sales, under the names Lee, Rustler, Wrangler, and Marithe & Francois Girbaud. Its other products include Jantzen swimwear and sportswear; JanSport daypacks and backpacking gear; and Vanity Fair, and Vassarette intimate apparel. VF also makes Red Kap and Big Ben work clothes, sold primarily to commercial-clothing companies, and Healthtex infant and children's clothing.

$ mil	12/92	12/93	12/94	% Change				
Sales	**3,824.4**	**4,320.4**	**4,971.7**	**15.1**	P/E Ratio	**12.1**	Price (9/30/95)	**51.00**
Net Income	**237.0**	**246.4**	**274.5**	**11.4**	P/B Ratio	**1.9**	52 Wk Hi-Low	**57.00-44.38**
Book Value	**1,165.5**	**1,563.0**	**1,753.7**	**12.2**	Yield %	**2.5**	Market Cap	**US$3,255.9mil**

Address **1047 N. Park Rd., Wyomissing, PA 19610**
Tel **610-378-1151** Fax **610-375-9371**
Exchange **NYSE** Ticker **VFC**
President & COO **Mackey J. McDonald**
Chairman & CEO **Lawrence R. Pugh**

Vons Companies

Industry: **Food Retailers & Wholesalers**

Vons Companies is the largest supermarket chain in Southern California based on sales. As of January 1, 1995, the company operated 334 supermarkets and food and drug retail stores under the names Vons, Vons Food and Drug, Pavillions, Tianguis, and EXPO. The largest sales territory is Los Angeles, which has 126 stores. The company also operates a fluid-milk-processing facility, an ice-cream plant, and distribution facilities for meat, groceries, produce, and general merchandise. The company has a private label and sells products under the trade name Club Pack.

$ mil	12/92	12/93	12/94	% Change				
Sales	**5,595.5**	**5,074.5**	**4,996.6**	**-1.5**	P/E Ratio	**38.9**	Price (9/30/95)	**23.75**
Net Income	**53.8**	**31.6**	**26.6**	**-15.8**	P/B Ratio	**1.9**	52 Wk Hi-Low	**23.88-16.25**
Book Value	**493.2**	**524.9**	**552.4**	**5.2**	Yield %	**0.0**	Market Cap	**US$1,033.1mil**

Address **618 Michillinda Ave., Arcadia, CA 91007**
Tel **818-821-7000** Fax **818-821-7933**
Exchange **NYSE** Ticker **VON**
Chief Executive **Lawrence A. Del Santo**
Chairman **Roger E. Strangeland**

Vornado Realty Trust SBI

Industry: **Real-Estate Investment**

Vornado Realty Trust is a real estate investment trust that owns, leases, and manages retail and industrial properties located in the Mid-Atlantic and Northeast regions of the United States. As of December 31, 1994, the company owned 56 shopping centers in seven states containing 9.5 million square feet. The company's shopping centers accounted for 91% of its revenues during that year. The occupancy rate of the company's shopping-center properties was at 94% during fiscal 1994. The company also owns eight industrial properties and one office building in New Jersey.

$ mil	12/92 R	12/93 R	12/94	% Change				
Sales	**82.0**	**88.8**	**94.0**	**5.9**	P/E Ratio	**19.8**	Price (9/30/95)	**37.50**
Net Income	**1.2**	**28.0**	**41.2**	**47.3**	P/B Ratio	**7.0**	52 Wk Hi-Low	**38.88-32.63**
Book Value	**-3.2**	**115.7**	**116.7**	**0.9**	Yield %	**5.3**	Market Cap	**US$909.0mil**

Address **Park 80 West, Plaza II, Saddle Brook, NJ 07663**
Tel **201-587-1000** Fax **N/A**
Exchange **NYSE** Ticker **VNO**
Chief Executive **Steven Roth**
Chairman **Steven Roth**

R=Restated.

Vulcan Materials

Industry: **Building Materials**

Vulcan Materials operates quarries and manufactures chemicals and construction materials. The company operates 127 limestone and granite quarries and 12 sand and gravel quarries in the midwestern and southeastern U.S., the production from which it uses to make construction aggregates, ready-mix concrete, and asphalt paving materials. It supplies chemicals, primarily chlorine, muriatic acid, caustic soda and potash, and chlorinated hydrocarbons produced at plants in Kansas, Louisiana, and Wisconsin, to the energy, pharmaceutical, chemical, and water-treatment industries.

$ mil	12/92	12/93	12/94	% Change				
Sales	**1,078.0**	**1,133.5**	**1,253.4**	**10.6**	P/E Ratio	**19.9**	Price (9/30/95)	**53.00**
Net Income	**94.0**	**88.2**	**98.0**	**11.1**	P/B Ratio	**2.6**	52 Wk Hi-Low	**60.00-46.75**
Book Value	**700.1**	**703.0**	**731.6**	**4.1**	Yield %	**2.5**	Market Cap	**US$1,901.6mil**

Address **One Metroplex Dr.**
Birmingham, AL 35209
Tel **205-877-3000**
Fax **205-877-3094**
Exchange **NYSE**
Ticker **VMC**
Chief Executive **Herbert A. Sklenar**
Chairman **Herbert A. Sklenar**

Wachovia

Industry: **Banks - Southern U.S.**

Wachovia is the holding company for four banking subsidiaries that operate 493 branches in North Carolina, South Carolina, and Georgia. Its banks provide personal-, commercial-, trust-, and institutional-banking services. The company also underwrites and sells municipal securities and provides discount-brokerage services. Mortgage-banking operations are conducted through the company's Wachovia Mortgage Company subsidiary, with 18 residential-loan offices in the southern United States. Another division acts as a reinsurer of credit life, accident, and health insurance.

$ mil	12/92	12/93	12/94	% Change				
Revenues	**2,757.3**	**2,723.0**	**2,966.7**	**8.9**	P/E Ratio	**13.8**	Price (9/30/95)	**43.13**
Net Income	**433.2**	**492.1**	**539.1**	**9.6**	P/B Ratio	**2.2**	52 Wk Hi-Low	**44.63-31.63**
Book Value	**2,774.8**	**3,017.9**	**3,286.5**	**8.9**	Yield %	**2.9**	Market Cap	**US$7,383.3mil**

Address **301 N. Main St.**
Winston-Salem, NC 27150
Tel **910-770-5000**
Fax **910-770-5931**
Exchange **NYSE**
Ticker **WB**
President & CEO **L.M. Baker, Jr.**
Chairman **John G. Medlin, Jr.**

Walgreen

Industry: **Drug-based Retailers**

Walgreen operates more than 1,900 retail drugstores in 30 states across the U.S., with a large concentration in the Midwest and Florida. The company's drugstores sell prescription and nonprescription drugs, and also carry cosmetics and toiletries, liquor and other beverages, food, tobacco, and general merchandise. Prescription drugs, which approximate 41% of sales, are the stores' largest source of revenue. Virtually all of the company's stores are part of a satellite-linkage system. Walgreens Healthcare Plus is the company's pharmacy mail-service subsidiary.

$ mil	08/92	08/93	08/94	% Change				
Revenues	**7,475.0**	**8,294.8**	**9,235.0**	**11.3**	P/E Ratio	**24.6**	Price (9/30/95)	**28.00**
Net Income	**220.6**	**221.7**	**281.9**	**27.2**	P/B Ratio	**4.4**	52 Wk Hi-Low	**28.25-18.50**
Book Value	**1,233.3**	**1,378.8**	**1,573.6**	**14.1**	Yield %	**1.2**	Market Cap	**US$6,892.0mil**

Address **200 Wilmot Rd.**
Deerfield, IL 60015
Tel **708-940-2500**
Fax **708-940-2896**
Exchange **NYSE**
Ticker **WAG**
President **L. Daniel Jorndt**
Chairman **Charles R. Walgreen III**

Wal-Mart Stores

Industry: **Retailers - Broadline**

Wal-Mart Stores is the largest retail company in the U.S. based on sales. The company operates Wal-Mart department stores, Sam's Clubs, and Wal-Mart Supercenters (combination supermarket and discount department stores). As of January 31, 1995, the company operated 1,990 Wal-Mart stores, 425 Sam's Clubs, and 143 Wal-Mart Supercenters. Most of the stores' sales are in nationally advertised merchandise. In addition, Wal-Mart Stores markets merchandise under the names Sam's American Choice, Popular Mechanics, and Better Homes & Gardens.

$ mil	01/93	01/94	01/95	% Change				
Revenues	**55,483.8**	**67,344.6**	**82,494.0**	**22.5**	P/E Ratio	**21.3**	Price (9/30/95)	**24.88**
Net Income	**1,994.8**	**2,333.3**	**2,681.0**	**14.9**	P/B Ratio	**4.5**	52 Wk Hi-Low	**27.50-20.75**
Book Value	**8,759.2**	**10,752.4**	**12,726.0**	**18.4**	Yield %	**0.7**	Market Cap	**US$57,146mil**

Address **702 S.W. 8th St.**
Bentonville, AR 72716
Tel **501-273-4000**
Fax **501-273-2461**
Exchange **NYSE**
Ticker **WMT**
President & CEO **David D. Glass**
Chairman **S. Robson Walton**

Walt Disney

Industry: **Other Recreational Products & Services**

Walt Disney operates theme parks and distributes motion pictures. It operates Walt Disney World resort in Florida and Disneyland theme park and Disneyland Hotel in California; earns royalties from the Tokyo Disneyland theme park; and holds a 39% equity interest in Disneyland Paris, formerly known as Euro Disney. Walt Disney Pictures and Television produces motion pictures that are distributed under the names Walt Disney Pictures, Touchstone Pictures, and Hollywood Pictures, and is a distributor for Miramax Film. In 1995, the company agreed to acquire Capital Cities/ABC.

$ mil	09/92	09/93	09/94	% Change				
Sales	**7,504.0**	**8,529.2**	**10,055.1**	**17.9**	P/E Ratio	**28.1**	Price (9/30/95)	**57.38**
Net Income	**816.7**	**299.8**	**1,110.4**	**270.4**	P/B Ratio	**5.5**	52 Wk Hi-Low	**61.50-37.88**
Book Value	**4,704.6**	**5,030.5**	**5,508.3**	**9.5**	Yield %	**0.5**	Market Cap	**US$29,994mil**

Address **500 S. Buena Vista St.**
Burbank, CA 91521
Tel **818-560-1000**
Fax **818-560-1930**
Exchange **NYSE**
Ticker **DIS**
President **Michael Ovitz**
Chairman & CEO **Michael D. Eisner**

Warner-Lambert

Industry: **Pharmaceuticals**

Warner-Lambert is a diversified manufacturer of pharmaceutical, consumer, and confectionery products. The company's Parke-Davis and Goedecke pharmaceuticals include therapeutic drugs, vaccines, oral contraceptives, and the Nicotrol transdermal nicotine patch. Warner-Lambert's consumer products include Tetra aquarium products, Schick razors, Rolaids antacids, and Listerine mouthwash. Its confectionary-product line includes Certs breath mints and Sugar Babies candy. The company's international sales excluding exports account for approximately 54% of its revenues.

$ mil	12/92	12/93	12/94	% Change				
Sales	**5,597.6**	**5,793.7**	**6,416.8**	**10.8**	P/E Ratio	**18.4**	Price (9/30/95)	**95.25**
Net Income	**643.7**	**331.0**	**694.0**	**109.7**	P/B Ratio	**7.1**	52 Wk Hi-Low	**97.38-73.38**
Book Value	**1,528.5**	**1,389.6**	**1,816.4**	**30.7**	Yield %	**2.6**	Market Cap	**US$12,842mil**

Address **201 Tabor Rd.**
Morris Plains, NJ 07950
Tel **201-540-2000**
Fax **201-540-3761**
Exchange **NYSE**
Ticker **WLA**
President **Lodewijk J.R. de Vink**
Chairman & CEO **Melvin R. Goodes**

Washington Federal

Industry: **Savings & Loans (U.S. Only)**

Washington Federal is a savings and loan association that operates 82 branches in Washington, Idaho, Oregon, Arizona, and Utah. Through several subsidiaries, Washington Federal also provides insurance-brokerage services and develops real estate. The association uses its deposits to originate loans secured primarily by first-mortgage liens on residential and commercial real estate. It also offers savings, checking, and money-market accounts. Single-family mortgage loans account for approximately 70% of the company's total loan portfolio.

$ mil	09/92	09/93	09/94	% Change				
Revenues	**276.7**	**288.9**	**295.9**	**2.4**	P/E Ratio	**10.2**	Price (9/30/95)	**23.75**
Net Income	**81.9**	**91.2**	**92.8**	**1.8**	P/B Ratio	**1.7**	52 Wk Hi-Low	**24.13-16.75**
Book Value	**424.1**	**486.2**	**546.8**	**12.5**	Yield %	**3.5**	Market Cap	**US$929.7mil**

Address **425 Pike St.**
Seattle, WA 98101
Tel **206-624-7930**
Fax **206-624-2334**
Exchange **NASDA**
Ticker **WFSL**
President & CEO **Guy C. Pinkerton**
Chairman **Guy C. Pinkerton**

Washington Mutual Savings Bank

Industry: **Savings & Loans (U.S. Only)**

Washington Mutual is the largest consumer bank in the Pacific Northwest. The bank operates 232 financial and 22 home-loan centers in Washington, Oregon, and Idaho. The company principally engages in such savings-bank activities as receiving deposits and making consumer and limited types of commercial-real-estate loans. It owns several nonbank subsidiaries, including a securities broker/dealer, an insurance company, and a travel agency. The company's Composite Research & Management subsidiary offers investment-advisory services and manages a family of eight mutual funds.

$ mil	12/92	12/93	12/94	% Change				
Revenues	**780.1**	**1,179.8**	**1,315.7**	**11.5**	P/E Ratio	**10.4**	Price (9/30/95)	**26.50**
Net Income	**95.4**	**179.7**	**172.3**	**-4.1**	P/B Ratio	**1.3**	52 Wk Hi-Low	**26.50-16.00**
Book Value	**882.6**	**1,195.7**	**1,304.6**	**9.1**	Yield %	**2.6**	Market Cap	**US$1,712.4mil**

Address **1201 Third Ave.**
Seattle, WA 98101
Tel **206-461-2000**
Fax **206-554-7208**
Exchange **NASDA**
Ticker **WAMU**
President & CEO **Kerry Killinger**
Chairman **Kerry Killinger**

Washington Post

Industry: **Publishing**

Washington Post publishes newspapers, and operates broadcast- and cable-television companies. The company publishes The Washington Post, which has a daily circulation of about 822,000 and a Sunday circulation of 1.2 million; Newsweek magazine, which has a circulation of three million; and 14 weekly community newspapers in Maryland with an aggregate circulation of 238,000. It operates NBC affiliates in Detroit and Houston, ABC affiliates in Miami and San Antonio, and CBS affiliates in Connecticut and Florida. It also provides cable-television service to 500,000 subscribers.

$ mil	12/92	12/93	12/94	% Change				
Sales	**1,450.9**	**1,498.2**	**1,614.0**	**7.7**	P/E Ratio	**21.2**	Price (9/30/95)	**311.00**
Net Income	**127.8**	**165.4**	**169.7**	**2.6**	P/B Ratio	**3.1**	52 Wk Hi-Low	**315.00-234.25**
Book Value	**993.0**	**1,087.4**	**1,126.9**	**3.6**	Yield %	**1.4**	Market Cap	**US$3,421.9mil**

Address **1150 15th St. N.W.**
Washington, DC 20071
Tel **202-334-6000**
Fax **202-334-4536**
Exchange **NYSE**
Ticker **WPO**
President & COO **Alan G. Spoon**
Chairman & CEO **Donald E. Graham**

Weingarten Realty

Industry: **Real-Estate Investment**

Weingarten Realty Investors is engaged in the acquisition and development of anchored shopping centers, ranging from 100,000 to 400,000 square feet. The company owns 150 income-producing properties in eight states, primarily in the Southwest. Included in its portfolio are 141 shopping centers, 16 industrial complexes, three multifamily apartment projects, and one office building. The properties total 16.3 million square feet of building area and are situated on 71.2 million square feet of land. The company also owns interests in 8.3 million square feet of undeveloped land.

$ mil	12/92	12/93	12/94	% Change				
Sales	**90.0**	**103.3**	**120.8**	**16.9**	P/E Ratio	**21.2**	Price (9/30/95)	**35.38**
Net Income	**20.1**	**36.2**	**43.8**	**21.0**	P/B Ratio	**2.2**	52 Wk Hi-Low	**38.13-32.88**
Book Value	**205.4**	**427.1**	**423.4**	**-0.9**	Yield %	**6.4**	Market Cap	**US$938.5mil**

Address **2600 Citadel Plaza Dr.**
Houston, TX 77292
Tel **713-866-6000**
Fax **713-866-6049**
Exchange **NYSE**
Ticker **WRI**
President & COO **Martin Debrovner**
Chairman & CEO **Stanford Alexander**

Wells Fargo & Co.

Industry: **Banks - Western U.S.**

Wells Fargo & Company is a banking and investment-management holding company. Its Wells Fargo Bank subsidiary operates more than 600 branches and 1,900 automated-teller machines in California. The bank offers personal trust, corporate pension-planning, and online-banking services, as well as credit cards. Wells Fargo Bank also originates real-estate, business, and consumer loans. Real-estate loans account for approximately 50% of the bank's total loan portfolio. The company also owns three mutual-fund families: Overland Express, Stagecoach, and WellsFunds.

$ mil	12/92	12/93	12/94	% Change				
Revenues	**5,204.0**	**4,854.0**	**4,965.0**	**2.3**	P/E Ratio	**12.6**	Price (9/30/95)	**185.63**
Net Income	**283.0**	**612.0**	**841.0**	**37.4**	P/B Ratio	**2.4**	52 Wk Hi-Low	**189.00-141.00**
Book Value	**3,809.0**	**4,315.0**	**3,911.0**	**-9.4**	Yield %	**2.2**	Market Cap	**US$8,958.1mil**

Address **420 Montgomery St.**, **San Francisco, CA 94163**
Tel **415-477-1000** Fax **415-362-6958**
Exchange **NYSE** Ticker **WFC**
President & COO **William F. Zuendt**
Chairman & CEO **Paul Hazen**

Wendy's

Industry: **Restaurants**

Wendy's International operates and franchises quick-serving restaurants. Each restaurant offers a standard menu featuring hamburgers and chicken sandwiches prepared to order, and a hot- and cold-food buffet. Customers spend an average of four dollars at each visit. More than 4,400 Wendy's restaurants operate in the United States and 28 operate in other countries. Of these restaurants, more than 1,200 are operated by the company, and about 3,100 are operated by the company's franchise owners. The restaurants are freestanding and located in urban or suburban areas.

$ mil	12/92	12/93	12/94	% Change				
Sales	**1,238.5**	**1,320.1**	**1,397.9**	**5.9**	P/E Ratio	**22.7**	Price (9/30/95)	**21.13**
Net Income	**64.7**	**79.3**	**97.2**	**22.5**	P/B Ratio	**3.2**	52 Wk Hi-Low	**22.63-13.75**
Book Value	**528.7**	**600.8**	**681.5**	**13.4**	Yield %	**1.1**	Market Cap	**US$2,161.0mil**

Address **4288 W. Dublin-Granville Rd.**, **Dublin, OH 43017**
Tel **614-764-3100** Fax **614-764-3459**
Exchange **NYSE** Ticker **WEN**
President & CEO **Gordon F. Teter**
Chairman **James W. Near**

Werner Enterprises

Industry: **Trucking**

Werner Enterprises provides over-the-road transportation services. It is an irregular-route truckload carrier of such commodities as retail merchandise, nonperishable foodstuffs, beverages, paper products, lumber, building materials, and other cargoes throughout the 48 continental states and portions of Canada. It also provides trailer services in Mexico. Werner provides nationwide long-haul as well as regional short-haul, temperature-controlled freight, and dry van-transportation services using a fleet of more than 4,000 trucks and 10,300 trailers.

$ mil	02/93	02/94	12/94 *	% Change				
Sales	**366.3**	**432.7**	**516.0**	**19.3**	P/E Ratio	**14.3**	Price (9/30/95)	**20.75**
Net Income	**23.9**	**31.3**	**36.7**	**17.1**	P/B Ratio	**1.9**	52 Wk Hi-Low	**25.25-18.00**
Book Value	**165.9**	**249.3**	**276.4**	**10.9**	Yield %	**0.5**	Market Cap	**US$522.0mil**

Address **Interstate 80 & Highway 50**, **Omaha, NE 68137**
Tel **402-895-6640** Fax **N/A**
Exchange **NYSE** Ticker **WERN**
President **Gary L. Werner**
Chairman & CEO **Clarence L. Werner**

*Irregular period due to fiscal year change.

West One Bancorp

Industry: **Banks - Western U.S.**

West One Bancorp is a bank holding company with more than 200 offices and retail branches in Idaho, Oregon, Washington, and Utah. The company's principal subsidiary is West One Bank, Idaho, which offers a full range of commercial and personal banking and trust services. Its corporate-banking department provides customized credit products to middle-market and large corporate borrowers. The company's other subsidiaries are engaged in domestic commercial banking, investment and fund management, trust operations, corporate services, mortgage banking, and credit life insurance.

$ mil	12/92	12/93	12/94	% Change				
Revenues	**517.2**	**599.8**	**676.4**	**12.8**	P/E Ratio	**13.9**	Price (9/30/95)	**40.13**
Net Income	**63.4**	**83.2**	**103.2**	**24.0**	P/B Ratio	**2.1**	52 Wk Hi-Low	**42.00-24.69**
Book Value	**489.8**	**623.6**	**715.8**	**14.8**	Yield %	**1.8**	Market Cap	**US$1,449.4mil**

Address **101 S. Capitol Blvd.**, **Boise, ID 83702**
Tel **208-383-7000** Fax **208-383-3864**
Exchange **NASDA** Ticker **WEST**
President **D. Michael Jones**
Chairman & CEO **Daniel R. Nelson**

Western Atlas

Industry: **Oilfield Equipment & Services - Other**

Western Atlas provides oil-field-information services and sells industrial-automation products. The company's oil-field-information division provides land and marine seismic-survey, well-logging, and reservoir-description services, as well as data interpretation, software development, and the manufacture of specialized oil-field-services equipment. Its industrial-automation business designs integrated manufacturing, automated data-collection, and material-handling and -management systems for use in automotive, manufacturing, package-handling, and retail applications.

$ mil	07/93	12/93 *	12/94	% Change				
Sales	**2,006.0**	**856.1**	**2,165.7**	**153.0**	P/E Ratio	**29.6**	Price (9/30/95)	**47.38**
Net Income	**72.8**	**-183.3**	**77.7**	**-142.4**	P/B Ratio	**2.0**	52 Wk Hi-Low	**51.50-35.75**
Book Value	**1,087.4**	**957.9**	**1,248.3**	**30.3**	Yield %	**0.0**	Market Cap	**US$2,515.4mil**

Address **360 N. Crescent Dr.**, **Beverly Hills, CA 90210**
Tel **310-888-2500** Fax **310-888-2848**
Exchange **NYSE** Ticker **WAI**
Chief Executive **Alton J. Brann**
Chairman **Alton J. Brann**

*Irregular period due to fiscal year change.

Western Resources

Industry: **Electrical Utilities - Central U.S.**

Western Resources is a public utility providing electric and natural-gas service. The company generates about 80% of its electric power using fossil fuels, primarily low-sulfur coal; it produces the remainder at the nuclear-powered Wolf Creek Generating Station. Western's subsidiary, Kansas Gas & Electric, provides electric service in Kansas and natural-gas service in Kansas, Missouri, and Oklahoma. Residential customers account for about 35% of electric and 66% of natural-gas revenues; commercial and industrial users make up 52% and 27% of these figures, respectively.

$ mil	12/92	12/93	12/94	% Change				
Sales	**1,556.2**	**1,909.4**	**1,617.9**	**-15.3**	P/E Ratio	**11.6**	Price (9/30/95)	**32.63**
Net Income	**127.9**	**177.4**	**187.4**	**5.6**	P/B Ratio	**1.2**	52 Wk Hi-Low	**33.00-27.38**
Book Value	**1,424.7**	**1,597.0**	**1,649.3**	**3.3**	Yield %	**6.1**	Market Cap	**US$2,019.1mil**

Address **818 Kansas Ave.** **Topeka, KS 66612**
Tel **913-575-6300** Fax **913-575-6399**
Exchange **NYSE** Ticker **WR**
President & CEO **John E. Hayes, Jr.**
Chairman **John E. Hayes, Jr.**

Westinghouse

Industry: **Electrical Components & Equipment**

Westinghouse Electric provides technological products and related services. It develops fossil-fuel and nuclear-power systems and plants; electronic-warfare systems; and refrigeration and heating systems and related products for trailers, trucks, rail cars, and marine containers. The company also controls broadcasting businesses, including 16 radio and five television stations. The company markets its products and services to users in governmental, industrial, and commercial markets worldwide. In 1995, Westinghouse Electric agreed to acquire CBS.

$ mil	12/92	12/93	12/94	% Change				
Sales	**8,447.0**	**8,875.0**	**8,848.0**	**-0.3**	P/E Ratio	**NMF**	Price (9/30/95)	**15.00**
Net Income	**-1,291.0**	**-326.0**	**77.0**	**-123.6**	P/B Ratio	**3.0**	52 Wk Hi-Low	**16.00-12.00**
Book Value	**2,344.0**	**1,045.0**	**1,792.0**	**71.5**	Yield %	**1.3**	Market Cap	**US$5,881.1mil**

Address **11 Stanwix St.** **Pittsburgh, PA 15222**
Tel **412-244-2000** Fax **412-642-3404**
Exchange **NYSE** Ticker **WX**
President **Gary M. Clark**
Chairman **Michael H. Jordan**

Westvaco

Industry: **Paper Products**

Westvaco manufactures paper products and specialty chemicals. It owns about 1.5 million acres of timberland in the United States and Brazil, and operates paper-production facilities in those countries. Its principal paper products include corrugated boxes, envelopes, and printing papers. Westvaco's chemical plants are located in the southern U.S. and produce activated-carbon products, printing-ink resins, and tall-oil derivatives. Westvaco markets its products through a direct-sales force worldwide. International sales account for approximately 19% of the total.

$ mil	10/92	10/93	10/94	% Change				
Sales	**2,335.6**	**2,344.6**	**2,607.5**	**11.2**	P/E Ratio	**29.4**	Price (9/30/95)	**45.63**
Net Income	**135.9**	**104.3**	**103.6**	**-0.7**	P/B Ratio	**1.6**	52 Wk Hi-Low	**47.38-32.88**
Book Value	**1,777.1**	**1,824.0**	**1,862.0**	**2.1**	Yield %	**2.4**	Market Cap	**US$3,079.1mil**

Address **Westvaco Bldg., 299 Park Ave.** **New York, NY 10171**
Tel **212-688-5000** Fax **212-318-5045**
Exchange **NYSE** Ticker **W**
President & CEO **John A. Luke, Jr.**
Chairman **David L. Luke III**

Weyerhaeuser

Industry: **Forest Products**

Weyerhaeuser is a diversified forest-products company that also has real-estate operations. The company owns approximately 5.6 million acres of forestland in the northwestern and southern U.S and holds licenses for about 17.8 million acres in Canada. It makes building products, primarily lumber, plywood, and strand board, at more than 50 facilities, and paper goods, primarily packaging, containerboard, and pulp, at 85 others. Weyerhaeuser Real Estate, a subsidiary, builds houses and apartments, develops commercial and residential lots, and provides mortgage financing.

$ mil	12/92	12/93	12/94	% Change				
Sales	**9,218.7**	**9,544.8**	**10,398.3**	**8.9**	P/E Ratio	**16.0**	Price (9/30/95)	**45.63**
Net Income	**372.0**	**579.3**	**588.7**	**1.6**	P/B Ratio	**2.2**	52 Wk Hi-Low	**50.13-35.88**
Book Value	**3,646.0**	**3,966.1**	**4,290.0**	**8.2**	Yield %	**2.6**	Market Cap	**US$9,274.8mil**

Address **33663 Weyerhaeuser Way** **Tacoma, WA 98477**
Tel **206-924-2345** Fax **206-924-3543**
Exchange **NYSE** Ticker **WY**
President & CEO **John W. Creighton, Jr.**
Chairman **G.H. Weyerhaeuser**

Whirlpool

Industry: **Other Home Furnishings**

Whirlpool manufactures major home and commercial-use appliances. It markets these appliances under the Whirlpool, KitchenAid, Roper, and Ignis brand names in North America, Europe, Latin America, and Asia. The company supplies Sears with refrigerators, dishwashers, ranges, and other products sold under the Kenmore and Sears trade names. In addition, Whirlpool is the principal supplier of home-laundry appliances to that retailer. The company also finances retailers' inventories and consumer purchases of its products through its Whirlpool Financial subsidiary.

$ mil	12/92	12/93	12/94	% Change				
Sales	**7,097.0**	**7,368.0**	**7,949.0**	**7.9**	P/E Ratio	**27.5**	Price (9/30/95)	**57.75**
Net Income	**205.0**	**51.0**	**158.0**	**209.8**	P/B Ratio	**2.5**	52 Wk Hi-Low	**60.63-45.38**
Book Value	**1,600.0**	**1,648.0**	**1,723.0**	**4.6**	Yield %	**2.1**	Market Cap	**US$4,265.4mil**

Address **2000 M-63 N.** **Benton Harbor, MI 49022**
Tel **616-923-5000** Fax **616-923-3568**
Exchange **NYSE** Ticker **WHR**
President & COO **William D. Marohn**
Chairman & CEO **David R. Whitwam**

Whitman

Industry: **Soft Drinks**

Whitman is a diversified consumer-products and -services company. Its Pepsi-Cola General Bottlers subsidiary manufactures soft drinks, primarily from syrups and concentrates purchased from PepsiCo, and distributes them in 12 midwestern and southeastern states. Midas International, another subsidiary, operates approximately 2,600 franchised Midas automotive muffler-, brake-, and steering-service shops, primarily in the United States, Canada, and Europe. Hussman, another subsidiary, makes refrigerated displays for food stores in North America and the United Kingdom.

$ mil	12/92	12/93	12/94	% Change				
Sales	**2,388.0**	**2,529.7**	**2,658.8**	**5.1**	P/E Ratio	**21.3**	Price (9/30/95)	**20.63**
Net Income	**59.8**	**78.2**	**103.2**	**32.0**	P/B Ratio	**3.9**	52 Wk Hi-Low	**21.25-15.75**
Book Value	**478.5**	**517.0**	**552.6**	**6.9**	Yield %	**1.6**	Market Cap	**US$2,162.3mil**

Address **3501 Algonquin Rd., Rolling Meadows, IL 60008**
Tel **708-818-5000**
Fax **708-818-5045**
Exchange **NYSE**
Ticker **WH**
Chief Executive **Bruce S. Chelberg**
Chairman **Bruce S. Chelberg**

Willamette Industries

Industry: **Forest Products**

Willamette Industries is a forest-products manufacturing company. The company's plants and mills produce containerboard, bag paper, fine paper, bleached hardwood market pulp, specialty printing papers, corrugated containers, business forms, cut sheet paper, inks, lumber, plywood, particle board, fiberboard, and value-added wood products. Willamette's paper products account for approximately 63% of revenues; its building materials constitute the balance. The company owns or controls cutting rights to about 1.2 million acres of timber in the southern and southeastern U.S.

$ mil	12/92	12/93	12/94	% Change				
Sales	**2,372.4**	**2,622.2**	**3,007.9**	**14.7**	P/E Ratio	**20.7**	Price (9/30/95)	**66.75**
Net Income	**81.6**	**137.0**	**177.6**	**29.6**	P/B Ratio	**2.6**	52 Wk Hi-Low	**72.38-41.00**
Book Value	**1,164.8**	**1,257.9**	**1,387.9**	**10.3**	Yield %	**1.4**	Market Cap	**US$3,682.9mil**

Address **3800 First Interstate Tower, Portland, OR 97201**
Tel **503-227-5581**
Fax **503-273-5608**
Exchange **NASDA**
Ticker **WMTT**
President & COO **Steven R. Rogel**
Chairman & CEO **William Swindells**

Williams Companies

Industry: **Pipelines**

Williams Companies produces and transports natural gas and petroleum products, and provides telephone service. The company's energy division owns natural-gas-producing properties in the San Juan Basin. It operates natural-gas and petroleum-products pipelines in the western United States and Louisiana that primarily serve industrial customers. Its WilTel subsidiary is a long-distance carrier that provides telecommunication services nationwide. Williams' telecommunication business provides approximately 40% of revenues; the balance is generated by energy-related activities.

$ mil	12/92	12/93	12/94	% Change				
Sales	**2,448.1**	**2,438.2**	**1,751.1**	**-28.2**	P/E Ratio	**16.8**	Price (9/30/95)	**39.00**
Net Income	**138.2**	**231.8**	**246.7**	**6.4**	P/B Ratio	**2.4**	52 Wk Hi-Low	**39.13-24.00**
Book Value	**1,518.3**	**1,724.0**	**1,505.5**	**-12.7**	Yield %	**2.2**	Market Cap	**US$3,979.3mil**

Address **One Williams Ctr., Tulsa, OK 74172**
Tel **918-588-2000**
Fax **918-588-2296**
Exchange **NYSE**
Ticker **WMB**
President & CEO **Keith E. Bailey**
Chairman **Keith E. Bailey**

Wilmington Trust

Industry: **Banks - Eastern U.S.**

Wilmington Trust Company is the holding company for Wilmington Trust, which operates 65 branches in Delaware, Florida, Maryland, and Pennsylvania. The bank provides commercial-banking and lending services, and offers automated-teller-machine services, as well as credit and debit cards. Wilmington Trust's subsidiaries provide brokerage of life, casualty, and property insurance; credit life reinsurance; and travel-agency services. The company also owns and manages the Rodney Square family of mutual funds, for which Wilmington Trust serves as the distributor.

$ mil	12/92	12/93	12/94	% Change				
Revenues	**425.8**	**404.6**	**421.0**	**4.1**	P/E Ratio	**12.4**	Price (9/30/95)	**29.50**
Net Income	**64.0**	**82.8**	**85.2**	**2.9**	P/B Ratio	**2.5**	52 Wk Hi-Low	**31.50-22.25**
Book Value	**377.2**	**395.2**	**418.2**	**5.8**	Yield %	**3.6**	Market Cap	**US$1,041.6mil**

Address **Rodney Sq. N., 1100 N. Market St., Wilmington, DE 19890**
Tel **302-651-1000**
Fax **302-651-8454**
Exchange **NASDA**
Ticker **WILM**
President & CEO **Leonard W. Quill**
Chairman **Leonard W. Quill**

Winn-Dixie Stores

Industry: **Food Retailers & Wholesalers**

Winn-Dixie Stores is a food retailer. The company operates a chain of retail self-service food stores that sell dry groceries, meat, dairy, seafood, fresh produce, deli and bakery items, pharmaceuticals, hardware, cigarettes, and general-merchandise items. The stores offer nationally advertised and private-label brands, as well as unbranded merchandise. The company has more than 1,170 stores in 13 southeastern and southwestern states, and 14 food retail stores in the Bahamas. Stores operate under the names Winn-Dixie, Marketplace, Buddies, and The City Meat Markets.

$ mil	06/93	06/94	06/95	% Change				
Sales	**10,831.5**	**11,082.2**	**11,787.8**	**6.4**	P/E Ratio	**19.2**	Price (9/30/95)	**59.63**
Net Income	**236.4**	**216.1**	**232.2**	**7.4**	P/B Ratio	**3.6**	52 Wk Hi-Low	**61.50-49.88**
Book Value	**985.0**	**1,057.5**	**1,241.2**	**17.4**	Yield %	**2.6**	Market Cap	**US$4,504.1mil**

Address **5050 Edgewood Ct., Jacksonville, FL 32254**
Tel **904-783-5000**
Fax **904-783-5637**
Exchange **NYSE**
Ticker **WIN**
President **James Kufeldt**
Chairman & CEO **A. Dano Davis**

Wisconsin Energy

Industry: **Electrical Utilities - Central U.S.**

Wisconsin Energy is a utility holding company providing electrical power and natural-gas service. Wisconsin Electric Power supplies electricity to about 2.2 million customers in southeastern, east-central, and northern Wisconsin and in the Upper Peninsula of Michigan. Wisconsin Natural Gas provides natural-gas service to about 1.1 million customers, primarily within the same area. Residential customers account for roughly 26% of electricity sales and 57% of natural-gas sales. Commercial and industrial users account for 63% of electricity sales and 37% of natural gas sales.

$ mil	12/92	12/93	12/94	% Change				
Sales	1,551.8	1,643.7	1,742.2	6.0	P/E Ratio	16.9	Price (9/30/95)	28.25
Net Income	169.7	188.5	180.9	-4.0	P/B Ratio	1.7	52 Wk Hi-Low	28.75-24.63
Book Value	1,543.5	1,650.8	1,774.6	7.5	Yield %	5.0	Market Cap	US$3,105.7mil

Address **231 W. Michigan St.** **Milwaukee, WI 53201**
Tel **414-221-2100** Fax **414-221-3586**
Exchange **NYSE** Ticker **WEC**
President & CEO **Richard A. Abdoo** Chairman **Richard A. Abdoo**

WMX Technologies

Industry: **Pollution Control, Waste Management**

WMX Technologies provides waste-management services, including the collection and disposal of solid waste, recyclable-materials processing, leasing of portable sanitation facilities, hazardous-waste treatment, environmental engineering, and street cleaning. Chemical Waste Management, a 79%-owned subsidiary, treats and disposes of chemical waste. The company markets these services to residential, municipal, commercial, and industrial customers in the U.S. and internationally. Business operations outside the U.S. account for approximately 15% of consolidated revenues.

$ mil	12/92	12/93	12/94	% Change				
Sales	8,661.0	9,135.6	10,097.3	10.5	P/E Ratio	17.6	Price (9/30/95)	28.50
Net Income	850.0	452.8	784.4	73.2	P/B Ratio	3.0	52 Wk Hi-Low	32.50-24.88
Book Value	4,319.6	4,159.5	4,541.0	9.2	Yield %	2.1	Market Cap	US$13,814mil

Address **3003 Butterfield Rd.** **Oak Brook, IL 60521**
Tel **708-572-8800** Fax **708-572-3094**
Exchange **NYSE** Ticker **WMX**
President & COO **Phillip B. Rooney** Chairman & CEO **Dean L. Buntrock**

Woolworth

Industry: **Retailers - Broadline**

Woolworth operates a multinational retailing business. The company sells merchandise through approximately 8,600 stores and leased departments in the U.S., Canada, Belgium, England, the Netherlands, France, Germany, Italy, Luxembourg, Spain, Mexico, Hong Kong, and Australia. In addition to Woolworth, store names include Foot Locker, Champs Sports, Northern Reflections, The Bargain! Shop, Kinney, and others. Departments within some stores are operated by licensees who pay a fee for use of the space. The company also operates as a franchisee in some Burger King Restaurants.

$ mil	01/93	01/94	01/95	% Change				
Revenues	9,962.0	9,626.0	8,293.0	-13.8	P/E Ratio	43.8	Price (9/30/95)	15.75
Net Income	280.0	-495.0	47.0	-109.5	P/B Ratio	1.5	52 Wk Hi-Low	19.25-13.00
Book Value	2,059.0	1,349.0	1,358.0	0.7	Yield %	4.7	Market Cap	US$2,087.1mil

Address **233 Broadway** **New York, NY 10279**
Tel **212-553-2000** Fax **212-553-2495**
Exchange **NYSE** Ticker **Z**
Chief Executive **Roger N. Farah** Chairman **Roger N. Farah**

Worthington Industries

Industry: **Steel**

Worthington Industries processes steel products, as well as custom and cast products. The company's processed-steel-products segment processes flat-rolled steel to close tolerances to industrial customers who require steel of precise thickness, length, width, shape, surface finish, and temper for product fabrication. The custom-products division produces injection-molded plastic and precision-metal parts for manufacturers of automobiles and appliances across North America. The cast-products division produces cast-steel products for the railcar and transit markets.

$ mil	05/93	05/94	05/95	% Change				
Sales	1,115.7	1,285.1	1,483.6	15.4	P/E Ratio	14.2	Price (9/30/95)	18.38
Net Income	66.2	84.9	116.7	37.5	P/B Ratio	2.8	52 Wk Hi-Low	23.25-18.13
Book Value	433.1	503.9	590.3	17.1	Yield %	2.2	Market Cap	US$1,669.2mil

Address **1205 Dearborn Dr.** **Columbus, OH 43085**
Tel **614-438-3210** Fax **614-438-3136**
Exchange **NASDA** Ticker **WTHG**
Chief Executive **John P. McConnell** Chairman **John H. McConnell**

Wm. Wrigley Jr.

Industry: **Other Food**

Wm. Wrigley Jr. manufactures chewing gum sold in approximately 120 countries and holds a 49% market share in the United States. The company's primary brand names include Wrigley's Spearmint, Doublemint, Juicy Fruit, Big Red, Freedent, and Extra chewing gum. Amurol, a subsidiary, makes chewing gum under the Big League Chew and Hubba Bubba brands, and individually wrapped hard roll candies under the Reed's name. Wrigley operates 13 gum factories and three raw-material-processing plants, and owns the Wrigley Building in Chicago.

$ mil	12/92	12/93	12/94	% Change				
Sales	1,286.9	1,428.5	1,596.6	11.8	P/E Ratio	25.5	Price (9/30/95)	50.50
Net Income	141.3	174.9	230.5	31.8	P/B Ratio	8.5	52 Wk Hi-Low	50.50-39.63
Book Value	498.9	575.2	688.5	19.7	Yield %	1.8	Market Cap	US$5,865.4mil

Address **410 N. Michigan Ave.** **Chicago, IL 60611**
Tel **312-644-2121** Fax **312-644-2135**
Exchange **NYSE** Ticker **WWY**
President & CEO **William Wrigley** Chairman **--**

Xerox

Industry: **Office Equipment**

Xerox produces document-processing machines. It manufactures products for black-and-white copying, digital publishing, electronic printing, and color printing and copying. The company's product line includes photocopiers, duplicators, digital-publishing equipment, ink-jet printers, laser printers, electrostatic printers, facsimile products, computer software, and related supplies, which are marketed more than 130 countries. Sales overseas account for about half of revenues. Xerox also arranges financing for the purchase of its equipment through its Xerox Credit subsidiary.

$ mil	12/92	12/93	12/94	% Change				
Sales	18,261.0	17,410.0	17,837.0	2.5	P/E Ratio	20.0	Price (9/30/95)	134.38
Net Income	-1,020.0	-126.0	794.0	-730.2	P/B Ratio	2.8	52 Wk Hi-Low	134.38-91.00
Book Value	4,947.0	5,038.0	5,009.0	-0.6	Yield %	2.2	Market Cap	US$14,450mil

Address **800 Long Ridge Rd.**
Stamford, CT 06904
Tel **203-968-3000**
Fax **203-968-4312**
Exchange **NYSE**
Ticker **XRX**
Chief Executive **Paul A. Allaire**
Chairman **Paul A. Allaire**

Xtra

Industry: **General Industrial & Commercial Services**

Xtra leases transportation equipment to customers in the general freight-transportation market. Its fleet includes roughly 183,000 over-the-road, mobile-storage, intermodal trailers, and containers. The company leases equipment to private fleet owners, common and contract carriers, and rail-service companies in North America. The lease of intermodal equipment accounts for approximately 56% of the company's total revenues. Xtra maintains 92 storage and distribution facilities throughout the United States.

$ mil	09/92	09/93	09/94	% Change				
Sales	202.6	329.2	355.3	7.9	P/E Ratio	13.1	Price (9/30/95)	44.38
Net Income	27.0	37.8	57.6	52.3	P/B Ratio	2.3	52 Wk Hi-Low	51.88-40.50
Book Value	190.7	280.3	330.5	17.9	Yield %	1.2	Market Cap	US$743.9mil

Address **60 State St.**
Boston, MA 02109
Tel **617-367-5000**
Fax **617-227-3173**
Exchange **NYSE**
Ticker **XTR**
President & CEO **Lewis Rubin**
Chairman **Robert B. Goergen**

Yellow

Industry: **Trucking**

Yellow provides freight-transportation services to the less-than-truckload-shipment market. Its largest subsidiary, Yellow Freight System, consolidates, transports, and redistributes general-commodities freight for more than 300,000 customers; it contributed 77% of the company's total revenues. Other subsidiaries include the carriers Saia, CSI/Reeves, Preston Trucking, and WestEx as well as subsidiaries providing logistics-management and information-technology services. The company operates 50,000 tractors and trailers.

$ mil	12/92	12/93	12/94	% Change				
Sales	2,262.7	2,856.5	2,867.5	0.4	P/E Ratio	NMF	Price (9/30/95)	13.75
Net Income	29.5	18.8	-7.9	-142.1	P/B Ratio	0.8	52 Wk Hi-Low	23.88-13.75
Book Value	485.5	486.5	460.8	-5.3	Yield %	6.8	Market Cap	US$386.5mil

Address **10777 Barkley**
Overland Park, KS 66207
Tel **913-967-4300**
Fax **913-967-4404**
Exchange **NASDA**
Ticker **YELL**
President & CEO **George E. Powell III**
Chairman **George E. Powell, Jr.**

York International

Industry: **Electrical Components & Equipment**

York International manufactures heating, ventilating, air-conditioning, and refrigeration products. The company's products include residential and commercial air-conditioning and furnace units, as well as industrial refrigeration and gas-compression equipment designed for the food, beverage, chemical, and petrochemical industries. York International markets its products under the York, Luxaire, Fraser-Johnston, Moncrief, Homeair, Bristol, Tempmaster, Miller-Picking, Frick, and Frigid Coil brand names through more than 700 sales facilities in more than 120 countries.

$ mil	12/92	12/93	12/94	% Change				
Sales	1,939.4	2,031.9	2,421.9	19.2	P/E Ratio	17.6	Price (9/30/95)	42.13
Net Income	50.9	5.2	89.8	NMF	P/B Ratio	3.0	52 Wk Hi-Low	48.00-34.88
Book Value	455.3	457.0	526.9	15.3	Yield %	0.4	Market Cap	US$1,765.8mil

Address **631 S. Richland Ave.**
York, PA 17403
Tel **717-771-7890**
Fax **717-771-7440**
Exchange **NYSE**
Ticker **YRK**
President & CEO **Robert N. Pokelwaldt**
Chairman **Robert N. Pokelwaldt**

Zeigler Coal Holding

Industry: **Coal**

Zeigler Coal Holding operates coal mines in Illinois, Indiana, Kentucky, Ohio, West Virginia, and Wyoming. Its 13 underground and surface coal mines contain reserves of approximately 1.4 billion tons of coal. Zeigler Coal Holding markets its coal mainly to electric utilities, which account for about 90% of the company's total sales. It also operates import and export terminals in Virginia and South Carolina and owns a clean-coal-technology demonstration plant in Wyoming. The company's Franklin Coal Sales subsidiary provides marketing and brokerage services to the company.

$ mil	12/92 R	12/93	12/94	% Change				
Sales	503.0	873.0	870.9	-0.2	P/E Ratio	11.6	Price (9/30/95)	11.75
Net Income	74.4	-146.2	25.1	-117.2	P/B Ratio	3.4	52 Wk Hi-Low	13.25-10.00
Book Value	152.2	6.1	98.4	NMF	Yield %	0.4	Market Cap	US$333.2mil

Address **50 Jerome Ln.**
Fairview Heights, IL 62208
Tel **618-394-2400**
Fax **N/A**
Exchange **NYSE**
Ticker **ZEI**
President & CEO **Chand B. Vyas**
Chairman **Michael K. Reilly**

R=Restated.

Industry: **Other Home Furnishings**

Zenith Electronics

Zenith Electronics develops video products that are sold through retail dealers and wholesale distributors in the United States and abroad. Its consumer products include color televisions, videocassette recorders, and related parts and accessories. The company also produces video monitors, color picture tubes, cable- and subscription-television components, power supplies, lighting products, and electronic-security equipment. The company operates manufacturing and warehousing facilities in the U.S. and Mexico. LG Group plans to acquire a 58% stake in the company.

$ mil	12/92	12/93	12/94	% Change				
Sales	**1,243.5**	**1,228.2**	**1,469.0**	**19.6**	P/E Ratio	**NMF**	Price (9/30/95)	**8.63**
Net Income	**-105.9**	**-97.0**	**-14.2**	**-85.4**	P/B Ratio	**1.7**	52 Wk Hi-Low	**14.00-7.00**
Book Value	**210.1**	**152.4**	**228.3**	**49.8**	Yield %	**0.0**	Market Cap	**US$404.5mil**

Address **1000 Milwaukee Ave.**
Glenview, IL 60025
Tel **708-391-7000**
Fax **708-391-7253**
Exchange **NYSE**
Ticker **ZE**
President & COO **Albin F. Moschner**
Chairman & CEO **Jerry K. Pearlman**

Industry: **Banks - Western U.S.**

Zions Bancorporation

Zions Bancorporation is a bank holding company. The company subsidiaries provide banking and related services in Utah, Nevada, and Arizona. Its Zions First National Bank subsidiary is a registered dealer in and underwriter of general obligation debt and manages 86 branches in Utah and one office in the Cayman Islands. The company's Nevada State Bank subsidiary operates 21 branches and its National Bank of Arizona subsidiary manages 10 branches. Zions Bancorporation's divisions also offer mortgage-banking services and sell credit and other lines of insurance.

$ mil	12/92	12/93	12/94	% Change				
Revenues	**320.1**	**345.9**	**427.5**	**23.6**	P/E Ratio	**14.0**	Price (9/30/95)	**61.25**
Net Income	**43.4**	**53.0**	**63.8**	**20.4**	P/B Ratio	**2.4**	52 Wk Hi-Low	**61.50-33.50**
Book Value	**242.5**	**290.4**	**365.8**	**26.0**	Yield %	**1.9**	Market Cap	**US$889.5mil**

Address **1380 Kennecott Bldg.**
Salt Lake City, UT 84133
Tel **801-524-4787**
Fax **801-524-2129**
Exchange **NASDA**
Ticker **ZION**
President & CEO **Harris H. Simmons**
Chairman **Roy W. Simmons**

Industry: **Heavy Construction**

Zurn Industries

Zurn Industries makes power plants, mechanical devices, and golf equipment. The company's power-systems segment primarily builds power plants that use energy sources such as wood, used tires, and the heat from industrial exhaust. Its water-control segment manufactures plumbing products under the Zurn and Wilkins names, municipal water-treatment facilities, and fire-control sprinklers. Its golf-products segment makes Lynx golf equipment. Zurn Industries also produces mechanical devices such as clutches and couplings used in the petrochemical, mining, and paper industries.

$ mil	03/93	03/94	03/95	% Change				
Sales	**669.8**	**785.7**	**463.2**	**-41.0**	P/E Ratio	**33.4**	Price (9/30/95)	**25.38**
Net Income	**27.5**	**-13.9**	**9.3**	**-167.1**	P/B Ratio	**1.4**	52 Wk Hi-Low	**26.00-17.00**
Book Value	**249.1**	**221.6**	**218.9**	**-1.2**	Yield %	**3.5**	Market Cap	**US$313.2mil**

Address **One Zurn Pl.**
Erie, PA 16514-2000
Tel **814-452-2111**
Fax **N/A**
Exchange **NYSE**
Ticker **ZRN**
President **William A. Freeman**
Chairman & CEO **Robert R. Womack**

Alphabetical Index

Alphabetical Index

Alphabetical Index

Alphabetical Index

Alphabetical Index

Alphabetical Index

Alphabetical Index

Alphabetical Index

Alphabetical Index

Alphabetical Index

Alphabetical Index

Alphabetical Index

Alphabetical Index

Alphabetical Index

Industry Index

Dow Jones World Stock Index

Basic Materials

Chemicals - All

Commodity Chemicals

Specialty Chemicals

Industry Index

Industry Index

Industry Index

Industry Index

Industry Index

Industry Index

Banks - Central U.S.

Banks - Eastern U.S.

Banks - Southern U.S.

Industry Index

Insurance - Life & Health

Insurance - Property & Casualty

Real-Estate Investment

Industry Index

Containers & Packaging

Electrical Components & Equipment

Industry Index

Industry Index

Industry Index

Industry Index

Indepent

Overseas Trading

Plantations

Market Sector Codes and Definitions

Basic Materials **M/BSC**

Producers of raw materials, who may also make finished or semi-finished products from raw materials. Includes:

Chemicals (All)	I/CHM
Commodity Chemical	I/CHC
Specialty Chemical	I/CHS
Forest Products	I/FOR
Mining, Diversified	I/MNG
Non-Ferrous Metals (All)	I/NFR
Non-Ferrous Metals - Aluminum	I/ALU
Non-Ferrous Metals - Other	I/ONF
Paper Products	I/PAP
Precious Metals	I/PCS
Steel	I/STL

Consumer, Cyclical **M/CYC**

Providers of nonessential goods and services to the retail market, whose profits are strongly affected by changes in consumer spending. Includes:

Advertising	I/ADV
Airlines	I/AIR
Automobile Manufacturers	I/AUT
Automobile Parts & Equipment	I/AUP
Tires & Rubber	I/TIR
Other Auto Parts	I/OTA
Entertainment & Leisure (All)	I/ENT
Casinos	I/CNO
Recreational Products & Services (All)	I/REC
Entertainment	I/MOV
Toys	I/TMF
Other Recreational Products & Services	I/REQ
Restaurants	I/RES
Home Construction	I/HOM
Home Furnishings & Appliances	I/HMF
Consumer Electronics	I/CSE
Other Home Furnishings	I/OMF
Lodging	I/LOD
Media (All)	I/MED
Media, Broadcasting	I/BRD
Media, Publishing	I/PUB
Retailers - Broadline	I/RTB
Retailers - Specialty (All)	I/RTS
Retailers - Specialty Apparel	I/SAP
Retailers - Specialty Other	I/OTS
Retailers - Specialty Drug-Based	I/RTD
Textiles & Apparel (All)	I/TEX
Clothing & Fabrics	I/CLO
Footwear	I/FOT

Consumer, Non-Cyclical **M/NCY**

Providers of basic goods and services to the retail market, whose profits are not strongly affected by changes in consumer spending. Includes:

Beverages (All)	I/BVG
Beverages - Distillers & Brewers	I/DST
Beverages - Soft Drinks	I/SFT
Consumer & Household Products & Services (All)	I/HOU
Consumer Services	I/CSV
Household Products (All)	I/HPR
Household Products, Non-Durable	I/HPN
Housewares, Durables	I/HPD
Cosmetics/Personal Care	I/COS
Food	I/FOD
Fishing	I/FPR
Other Food	I/OFD
Food Retailers & Wholesalers	I/FDR
Health Care Providers	I/HEA
Medical Supplies	I/MDS
Pharmaceuticals	I/DRG
Tobacco	I/TOB

Energy **M/ENE**

Liquid, solid or gaseous fossil fuel providers and the companies that service them. Includes:

Coal	I/COA
Oilfield Equipment & Services (All)	I/OIE
Oilfield Equipment & Services - Oil Drilling	I/DRL
Oilfield Equipment & Services - Other	I/EQS
Oil - Integrated Majors	I/OIL
Oil - Secondary	I/OIS
Pipelines	I/PIP

Financial **M/FIN**

Companies whose primary source of profits is the return on financial assets. Includes:

Banks (All)	I/BNK
Banks - Major International	I/BAN
Banks - Regional	I/BAR
Banks - Eastern U.S.	I/BAE
Banks - Central U.S.	I/BAC
Banks - Southern U.S.	I/BAS
Banks - Western U.S.	I/BAW
Financial Services - Diversified	I/FIS
Insurance (All)	I/INS
Insurance - Full Line	I/INF
Insurance - Life	I/INL
Insurance - Property & Casualty	I/INP
Real Estate Investment	I/REA
Savings & Loans (U.S. Only)	I/SAL
Securities Brokers	I/SCR

Independent **M/MCG**
Very large companies whose activities cut across industries and cannot be classified in any one economic sector. Includes:

Conglomerates	I/CGL
Overseas Trading	I/OVS
Plantations	I/PLN

Industrial **M/IDU**
Capital goods manufacturers and companies that provide industrial services. Includes:

Air Freight & Couriers	I/AIF
Building Materials	I/BLD
Containers & Packaging	I/CTR
Electrical Components & Equipment	I/ELQ
Factory Equipment	I/FAC
Heavy Construction	I/CON
Heavy Machinery	I/MAC
Industrial & Commercial Services (All)	I/SVC
Other Industrial & Commercial Services	I/ICS
Pollution Control / Waste Management	I/POL
Industrial - Diversified	I/IDD
Marine Transportation	I/MAR
Railroads	I/RAI
Transportation Equipment (All)	I/TRQ
Land Transportation	I/LDT
Shipbuilding	I/SHP
Trucking	I/TRK

Technology **M/TEC**
Industries experiencing rapid product changes due primarily to scientific advances. Includes:

Aerospace & Defense	I/ARO
Communications Technology	I/CMT
Communications Technology w/o AT&T (U.S. Only)	I/CMN
Computers	I/CPR
Computers w/o IBM (U.S. Only)	I/CPN
Diversified Technology	I/DTC
Industrial Technology	I/ITC
Medical & Biological Technology (All)	I/MTC
Advanced Technology Medical Devices	I/MDV
Biotechnology	I/BTC
Office Equipment	I/OFF
Semiconductors	I/SEM
Software	I/SOF

Utilities **M/UTI**
Electrical, water, natural gas and telephone utilities. Includes:

Electrical Utilities (All)	I/ELC
Electrical Utilities, Eastern U.S.	I/UEE
Electrical Utilities, Central U.S.	I/UEC
Electrical Utilities, Southern U.S.	I/UES
Electrical Utilities, Western U.S.	I/UEW
Gas Utilities	I/GAS
Telephone Systems - All	I/TLS
Regional Telephone Systems (U.S. Only)	I/RTL
Long Distance Telephone Systems (U.S. Only)	I/LDS
Mobile Communications Systems (U.S. Only)	I/CTS
Water Utilities	I/WAT

Industry Group Codes and Definitions

Basic Materials M/BSC

Producers of raw materials, who may also make finished or semi-finished products from raw materials.

I/CHM Chemicals - All
Umbrella group for Commodity (I/CHC) and Specialty (I/CHS) Chemicals. Any company whose business is primarily the production of chemicals, either for other industries or for end users. Producers of plastics and chemical fertilizers are included. Producers of certain specialty chemicals, such as flavors and fragrances, may be placed within the industry that specifically uses the products.

I/CHC Commodity Chemicals
Producers of simple chemical products, including petrochemical feedstocks that are used to formulate more complex chemicals. Also includes plastics.

I/CHS Specialty Chemicals
Producers of finished chemicals either for other industries or for end users.

I/FOR Forest Products
Producers of wood and lumber products for the building industry (like plywood, wooden beams, etc.).

I/MNG Mining, Diversified
Companies that mine minerals and metal ores, but do not necessarily process the resources into finished products. Gold and coal mining are specifically excluded from this category. Gold is listed under Precious Metals (I/PCS); coal under I/COA.

I/NFR Non-Ferrous Metals - All
Umbrella group for Aluminum (I/ALU) and Other Non-Ferrous metals (I/ONF), Non-ferrous metals including copper, zinc and nickel.

I/ALU Aluminum
Companies that mine or process bauxite and make semi-finished or finished aluminum products. Aluminum building products, such as siding, are included under Building Materials (I/BLD).

I/ONF Non-Ferrous Metals - Other
Producers of other non-iron metals, such as copper. Precious metals are in their own group (I/PCS).

I/PAP Paper Products
Manufacturers of paper products, both raw and finished. Includes writing paper, envelopes, cardboard and pulp. Paper items like cups, napkins and diapers are included under Non-Durable Household Products (I/HPN).

I/PCS Precious Metals
Producers of gold, silver and other precious metals as well as precious stones, such as diamonds.

I/STL Steel
Steel and iron manufacturers. Includes pipes, tubes, wire, rolls and bars made from these metals.

Consumer, Cyclical M/CYC

Providers of nonessential goods and services to the retail market, whose profits are strongly affected by changes in consumer spending.

I/ADV Advertising
Companies providing advertising, public relations and/or marketing services.

I/AIR Airlines
Companies providing primarily passenger air transport.

I/AUT Automobile Manufacturers
Makers of passenger vehicles, including cars and light trucks. Heavy trucks are listed under Land Transportation Equipment (I/LDT); recreational vehicles under Other Recreational Products and Services (I/REQ).

I/AUP Automobile Parts & Equipment
Tire makers and rubber producers. Manufacturers of new and replacement parts for automobiles and trucks. Also, companies that produce accessories for the automobile industry.

I/OTA Other Auto Parts
Manufacturers of new and replacement parts for automobiles and trucks. Also, companies that produce accessories for the automobile industry.

I/TIR Tires & Rubber
Tire makers and rubber producers.

I/ENT Entertainment & Leisure - All
Umbrella group for Casinos (I/CNO), Recreational Products and Services (I/REC), Restaurants (I/RES), Entertainment (I/MOV), Toy Manufacturers (I/TMF) and Other Recreational Products & Services (I/REQ).

I/CNO Casinos
Casino operators and hotels with gaming rooms. Does not include lottery machines and race tracks, which are listed under Other Recreational Products & Services (I/REQ).

I/REC Recreational Products & Services - All
Umbrella group for Entertainment (I/MOV), Toys (I/TMF) and Other Recreational Products & Services (I/REQ). Companies that provide leisure-time services or products.

I/MOV Entertainment
Companies engaged in the development, production or distribution of movies, television shows and pre-recorded

music. These companies produce and sell entertainment. The television industry is included under Media (I/MED).

I/TOY Toys
Makers of toys and video/computer games.

I/REQ Recreational Products & Services - Other
Companies that provide leisure-time services such as movie theaters, amusement parks, camera makers, golf courses, cruise ships and products such as records, CDs and blank VCR tapes. Resorts are included in Lodging (I/LOD).

I/RES Restaurants
Corporations that own and operate restaurants, bars, fast-food facilities or provide large-scale food catering services.

I/HOM Home Construction
Residential home builders, mainly specializing in one-to-four family units. Also includes makers of mobile and prefabricated homes that are intended for use in one place.

I/HMF Home Furnishings & Appliances
Makers of large home appliances, home furniture and carpeting. Includes stereos, VCRs, refrigerators, microwaves, power tools, sewing machines, regular and high-definition televisions (HDTVs).

I/CSE Consumer Electronics
Makers of consumer electronics products, such as televisions, video recorders and stereo equipment.

I/OMF Other Home Furnishings
Makers of home furnishings and carpeting excluding consumer electronics products.

I/LOD Lodging
Operators of hotels, motels, lodges, resorts and campgrounds.

I/MED Media - All
Umbrella group for Publishing (I/PUB) and Broadcasting (I/BRD). Publishers of newspapers, magazines and books, television and radio broadcasters, and cable TV companies. Also includes greeting cards and collectible cards (i.e. baseball).

I/BRD Broadcasting
Television, radio and cable broadcasters and operators.

I/PUB Publishing
Newspapers, books, magazine publishers and information-service companies that produce original material. Electronic publishers that redistribute news are included under General Services (I/ICS).

I/RTB Retailers - Broadline
Retail stores that offer a wide spectrum of products, including both soft goods and hard goods. Includes department stores.

I/RTS Retailers - Specialty - All
Umbrella group for Apparel (I/SAP), Drug (I/RTD). and Other Specialty Retailers (I/RTS). All retailers that specialize in one or a few lines rather than a wide range of products.

I/SAP Retailers - Specialty Apparel
Retailers specializing mainly in clothing and accessories.

I/OTS Retailers - Other Specialty
Retailers whose marketing strategy focuses on a limited product line, such as jewelry, automotive parts or close-outs.

I/RTD Drug Retailers & Wholesalers
Operators of pharmacies or drug stores. Wholesalers catering strictly to these retailers are included in the category.

I/TEX Textiles & Apparel - All
Umbrella group for Footwear (I/FOT) and Clothing and Fabrics (I/CLO). Makers of textiles, jewelry, finished clothing and leather goods, including shoes and handbags.

I/CLO Clothing & Fabrics
Manufacturers of apparel, jewelry, fabrics and leather goods, excluding footwear. Luggage included under Housewares (I/HPD).

I/FOT Footwear
Makers of shoes, boots and other footwear.

Consumer, Non-Cyclical M/NCY

Providers of basic goods and services to the retail market, whose profits are not strongly affected by changes in consumer spending.

I/BVG Beverages - All
Umbrella group for Distillers & Brewers (I/DST) and Soft Drinks (I/SFT).

I/DST Distillers & Brewers
Makers of alcoholic beverages. Also covers public houses in the United Kingdom. Bars are listed under Restaurants (I/RES).

I/SFT Soft Drinks
Makers of non-alcoholic beverages, excluding milk and fruit juices, which are included in Food (I/FOD). Bottled water included here.

I/HOU Consumer & Household Products & Services - All
Umbrella group for the Consumer & Household Products and Services Industries.

I/CSV Consumer Services - Only
Providers of consumer services such as lawn maintenance, tax preparation, day care, bus lines, language and training schools and funeral services.

I/HPR Household Products - Only
Umbrella group for Non-Durable Household Products (I/HPN) and Housewares (I/HPD). Covers soaps, utensils, kitchen and bathroom accessories and paper goods.

I/HPN Household Products (Non-Durable)
Producers of non-durable household products such as soaps, detergents, batteries and paper goods including napkins, toilet tissue, paper plates and diapers.

I/HPD Housewares (Durable)
Producers of durable household products such as utensils, non-electric appliances and luggage.

I/COS Cosmetics & Personal Care
Makers of cosmetics, perfumes and personal-care and hygiene products such as deodorant, contraceptives and feminine hygiene products.

I/FOD Food
Food manufacturers and processors including farming, fisheries and meat-packers. Milk and fruit juices are products in this industry. Bottled water is listed under Soft Drinks (I/SFT).

I/FPR Fishing
Fishing companies. This also includes producers of fish products.

I/OFD Other Food
Food manufacturers and processors, excluding fish products.

I/FDR Food Retailers & Wholesalers
Operators of supermarkets, food-oriented convenience stores and other food retailers.

I/HEA Health Care Providers
Operators of hospitals, nursing and convalescent homes, long-term care facilities, in-home health services.

I/MDS Medical Supplies
Manufacturers of medical supplies used mainly by health-care providers and not generally available at retail. Includes contact lenses, animal drugs and chemicals used to make drugs.

I/DRG Pharmaceuticals
Makers of prescription drugs and over-the-counter products, such as aspirin, cold remedies and other remedies.

I/TOB Tobacco
Tobacco products manufacturers.

Energy M/ENE

Liquid, solid or gaseous fossil fuel providers and the companies that service them.

I/COA Coal
Coal producers and coal mining. Excludes coal-fired electric plants, which are in Electrical Utilities (I/ELC).

I/OIE Oilfield Equipment & Services - All
Umbrella group for Oil Drilling (I/DRL) and Other Oilfield Equipment & Services (I/EQS).

I/DRL Oil Drilling
Corporations whose major line of business is drilling and exploration for oil, typically under contract for others.

I/EQS Oilfield Equipment & Services - Other
Suppliers of equipment and services for oilfield or platform users.

I/OIL Oil - Integrated Majors
Large oil producers whose activities include drilling and refining. Normally, companies in this category conduct substantial amounts of international business.

I/OIS Oil - Secondary
Smaller oil companies, whose operations are restricted in geography or to certain activities, such as the manufacture of motor oil. Companies in this category usually do the bulk of their business domestically. Also includes gasoline and natural gas.

I/PIP Pipelines
Operators of pipelines carrying oil, gas or other forms of fuel. Companies that derive the majority of their revenues from direct consumer sales are classified under Gas Utilities (I/GAS).

Financial M/FIN

Companies whose primary source of profits is the return on financial assets.

I/BNK Banks - All
Umbrella group covering the global banking industry. All major and regional banks get this code. Excludes investment banking, which is covered under Securities Industry (I/SCR).

I/BAN Banks - Major International
Banks with a major presence in more than one country, such as Citicorp and Swiss Bank; money-center banks.

I/BAR Banks - Regional
Umbrella group for the regional banks. Banks that offer services statewide or cover a particular region. For U.S.

regional banks only, group composed of four geographic regions.

I/BAC Banks - Central U.S.
Banks in Illinois, Indiana, Iowa, Kansas, Michigan, Minnesota, Missouri, Nebraska, North Dakota, Ohio, Oklahoma, South Dakota and Wisconsin.

I/BAE Banks - Eastern U.S.
Banks in Connecticut, District of Columbia, Delaware, Maryland, Maine, Massachusetts, New Hampshire, New Jersey, New York, Pennsylvania, Rhode Island, Vermont and West Virginia.

I/BAS Banks - Southern U.S.
Banks in Alabama, Arkansas, Canal Zone, Florida, Georgia, Kentucky, Louisiana, Mississippi, North Carolina, Puerto Rico, South Carolina, Tennessee, Texas, Virginia and Virgin Islands.

I/BAW Banks - Western U.S.
Banks in Alaska, Arizona, California, Colorado, Guam, Hawaii, Idaho, Montana, Nevada, New Mexico, Oregon, Utah, Washington and Wyoming.

I/FIS Financial Services - Diversified
Companies involved in two or more industries in the financial market sector or whose products are used in many diverse industries. Includes Fannie Mae, American Express and mutual fund companies.

I/INS Insurance - All
Umbrella group for Full Line (I/INF), Life and Health (I/INL), and Property and Casualty Insurance (I/INP).

I/INF Insurance - Full Line
Companies that offer a full line of insurance, including life, health, property and casualty.

I/INL Insurance - Life
Life and health insurers.

I/INP Insurance - Property & Casualty
Property and casualty insurers. Includes auto insurance and re-insurance companies.

I/REA Real Estate Investment
Companies that invest directly or indirectly in real estate, either through development, management or outright ownership. Also includes Real Estate Investment Trusts (REITs).

I/SAL Savings & Loans (U.S. Only)
S&Ls, savings banks, thrifts and building associations.

I/SCR Securities Brokers
Securities brokers and dealers, including investment banks and merchant banks.

Independent M/MCG

Very large companies whose activities cut across industries and cannot be classified in any one economic sector.

I/CGL Conglomerates
Very large companies whose activities cut across market sectors and cannot be classified under any single industry or sector.

I/OVS Overseas Trading
Large, diversified companies engaged in large-scale export trade.

I/PLN Plantations
Large agricultural companies, typically located in the tropics.

Industrial M/IDU

Capital goods manufacturers and companies that provide industrial services.

I/AIF Air Freight & Couriers
Operators of courier services for commercial and consumer users. Includes all types of couriers except Marine Transportation, which is I/MAR.

I/BLD Building Materials
Makers of basic building materials, such as concrete, wallboard, flooring, tile, lighting, bathroom and kitchen fixtures and home water heaters. Includes paint if it is an end product; if just the pigment, included under Specialty Chemicals (I/CHS). Excludes lumber, which is in Forest Products (I/FOR).

I/CTR Containers & Packaging
Makers of bags, cans, boxes, jars, drums and glass used for packaging. Manufacturers of small specialty packaging machines are included here. Makers of large packaging equipment are in Factory Equipment (I/FAC).

I/ELQ Electrical Components & Equipment
Makers of electrical parts used in the fabrication of finished products. Includes ceramics and transistors. Also includes finished products such as large-scale heating, ventilation, air conditioning and lighting units. Semiconductors and superconductivity included under Semiconductors (I/SEM).

I/FAC Factory Equipment
Manufacturers of large machinery designed specifically for the production of products for factories including turbines and machines used on assembly lines. Robotics are included in Industrial Technology (I/ITC).

I/CON Heavy Construction
Companies engaged in the construction of infrastructures, industrial and commercial buildings and large multi-family residential buildings.

I/MAC Heavy Machinery
Makers of large machinery not intended for fixed factory use. Machinery in this category normally can be moved to temporary work sites. Includes farm and construction vehicles such as tractors and bulldozers.

I/SVC Industrial & Commercial Services - All
Umbrella group for General Services (I/ICS) and Pollution & Waste Control (I/POL).

I/ICS Other Industrial and Commercial Services
Companies that provide services to other commercial enterprises, such as commercial cleaning, travel agencies, educational services for business, leasing, temporary service agencies, security agencies, credit services, printing, and management, engineering and other types of consultants. Electronic information providers that do not generate their own information are included here; those that generate their own information are included under Media (I/MED).

I/POL Pollution Control / Waste Management
Providers of pollution-control services and products.

I/IDD Industrial - Diversified
Companies that are involved in two or more industries in the Industrial Market Sector and whose products are used in many different industries. A maker of pumps is an example.

I/MAR Marine Transportation
Corporations that provide on-water transportation commercial and consumer markets. Ports and marine terminals included under General Services (I/ICS). Cruise lines are excluded from this category and are in Other Recreational Products & Services (I/REQ).

I/RAI Railroads
Providers of railway transportation and railway lines. Not for rail-car manufacturing, which is included in Land Transportation Equipment (I/LDT).

I/TRQ Transportation Equipment - All
Umbrella group for Land Transportation Equipment (I/LDT) and Trucking (I/TRK).

I/LDT Land Transportation Equipment
Manufacturers of rail cars, buses and commercial land vehicles, including heavy trucks and truck parts.

I/SHP Shipbuilding
Companies that build ships and other forms of water transportation. Includes ship parts. Does not include small pleasure craft, which are in Other Recreational Products & Services (I/REQ).

I/TRK Trucking
Companies that provide commercial trucking. Truck makers included under Land Transportation Equipment (I/LDT).

Technology M/TEC

Industries experiencing rapid product changes due primarily to scientific advances.

I/ARO Aerospace & Defense
Makers of air transportation vehicles, major weapons, defense equipment and systems, and radar.

I/CMT Communications Technology
Makers of high-technology products for communications, including satellites, PBX systems, switching devices, local and wide area networks (LANs and WANs), computer network equipment and connectivity devices for computers.

I/CPR Computers
Manufacturers of computers, computer hardware and computer sub-systems, such as mass storage drives. Also includes makers of automatic teller machines (ATMs). Data processing included under General Services (I/ICS).

I/DTC Diversified Technology
High-tech companies that are involved in two or more industries in the technology market sector, or whose products are used in many different industries.

I/ITC Industrial Technology
Companies whose technology and high-tech products are primarily directed toward industrial production and/or quality control. These include makers of instruments and gauges, lasers, robotics, bar scanners and other high-tech factory equipment.

I/MTC Medical & Biological Technology - All
Umbrella group encompassing Biotechnology (I/BTC) and Advanced Technology Medical Devices (I/MDV). Corporations engaged in genetic research and/or the marketing and development of recombinant DNA products. Includes makers of prosthetics, including pacemakers and breast implants. Also includes medical research.

I/MDV Advanced Technology Medical Devices
Manufacturers of advanced technology medical equipment such as prosthetics, pacemakers and advanced imaging devices. The products are used primarily by health-care providers and not generally available at the retail level.

I/BTC Biotechnology
Companies engaged in genetic research and/or the marketing and development of recombinant DNA products.

I/OFF Office Equipment
Makers of office equipment, such as duplicating machines, non-computer graphics products, word processors, cash registers, typewriters and fax machines.

I/SEM Seminconductors
Producers of semiconductors and other integrated chips, including circuit boards. Includes any other products related to the semiconductor industry.

I/SOF Software
Publishers of software for all sizes of computers.

Utilities M/UTI

Electrical, water, natural gas and telephone utilities.

I/ELC Electrical Utilities - All
Umbrella code for regional Electric Utilities. Includes fusion, fission and nuclear power. Cogeneration is included under Industrial Diversified (I/IDD).

I/UEC Electrical Utilities - Central U.S.
Providers of electricity in Illinois, Indiana, Iowa, Kansas, Michigan, Minnesota, Missouri, Nebraska, North Dakota, Ohio, Oklahoma, South Dakota and Wisconsin.

I/UEE Electrical Utilities - Eastern U.S.
Providers of electricity in Connecticut, District of Columbia, Delaware, Maryland, Maine, Massachussets, New Hampshire, New Jersey, New York, Pennsylvania, Rhode Island, Vermont and West Virginia.

I/UES Electrical Utilities - Southern U.S.
Providers of electricity in Alabama, Arkansas, Canal Zone, Florida, Georgia, Kentucky, Louisiana, Mississippi, North Carolina, Puerto Rico, South Carolina, Tennessee, Texas, Virginia and Virgin Islands.

I/UEW Electrical Utilities - Western U.S.
Providers of electricity in Alaska, Arizona, California, Colorado, Guam, Hawaii, Idaho, Montana, Nevada, New Mexico, Oregon, Utah, Washington and Wyoming.

I/GAS Gas Utilities
Gas utilities and services provided for the utilities. Does not include natural gas as a commodity, which is included in the Oil groups (I/OIL or I/OIS).

I/TLS Telephone Systems - All
Umbrella group for Regional (I/RTL), Long Distance (I/LDS) and Mobile Telephone Systems (I/CTS), including regulated cellular systems.

I/LDS Long-Distance Telephone Systems
Providers of long-distance telephone service.

I/CTS Mobile Communications Systems
Providers of mobile telephone service, including cellular telephone systems.

I/RTL Regional Telephone Systems
Providers of local telephone service.

I/WAT Water Utilities
Investor-owned water utilities.